WEBSTER'S
CONCISE
AMERICAN
FAMILY
DICTIONARY

RANDOM HOUSE
NEW YORK

Webster's Concise American Family Dictionary

Copyright © 1999 by Random House, Inc.

This dictionary is based on the *Webster's American Family Dictionary*, copyright © 1997, by Random House, Inc.

The *Random House Dictionary Database*™, is a trademark of Random House, Inc.

This book is available for special purchases in bulk by organizations and institutions, not for resale, at special discounts. Please direct your sales inquiries to Random House Premium Sales, fax 212-572-4961.

Please address inquiries about electronic licensing of this division's products, for use on a network on in software or on CD-ROM, to the Subsidiary Rights Department, Random House Reference, fax 212-940-7352.

Library of Congress Cataloging-in-Publication Data for 1999 version:
Webster's concise American family dictionary.—1st Random House ed.
    p.   cm.
    ISBN 0-375-40507-0
    1. English language—Dictionaries. I. Title: Concise American family dictionary
    PE1628.W55113 1999
    423--dc21   98-48027
                                         CIP

Visit the Random House Reference Web site at: www.randomwords.com

Typeset and printed in the United States of America.

10 9 8 7 6 5 4 3 2 1

ISBN: 0-375-72003-0

New York   Toronto   London   Sydney   Auckland

CONTENTS

STAFF

Project Editor: Georgia S. Maas
Copyeditor: Trudy Nelson
Support Staff: Bruna Darini, Jessica Erace, Joan Ginsberg,
Erika Illyes, Michael Lewis
Editorial Production Services: Jennifer Dowling, Seaside Press
Production Editor: Joseph W. Sora
Database Associate: Diane M. João
Database Manager: Constance A. Baboukis
Managing Editor: Andrew Ambraziejus
Production Director: Patricia W. Ehresmann
Editorial Director: Wendalyn Nichols
Associate Publisher: Page Edmunds
Publisher: Charles M. Levine

PREFACE

This modern, authoritative dictionary, based on *Webster's American Family Dictionary*, provides more comprehensive coverage of American language and culture than other dictionaries in a compact, easily accessible form. The editors' goal in creating this dictionary has been to provide families with a reliable, affordable dictionary that covers a comprehensive selection of historical and cultural references as well as basic vocabulary. Deliberately excluded from this dictionary are words and meanings which, although common in speech, are offensive to many people.

Here you will find clear, concise definitions—not only of basic vocabulary words, but of new words entering the language—plus scientific and computer terms, hundreds of geographical and biographical entries, names of people and places in the Bible, and terms relating to United States and world history and to the world's major religions. Popular proverbs and sayings that are a part of our culture are also included in the A to Z section of the dictionary to make them easy to find.

Throughout the dictionary are more than 150 drawings, including maps illustrating entries ranging from Canaan to the Louisiana Purchase and from the Roman Empire to the Oregon Trail. In the back of the dictionary are useful charts, maps, and tables, including U.S. presidents, the chemical elements, books of the Bible, and geologic time divisions. Here too you will find the full text of the Declaration of Independence and the Gettysburg Address, as well as a summary of the Amendments to the U.S. Constitution.

Users are encouraged to study the "Guide to the Dictionary" on page vii. A Sample Page that points out the various features of the dictionary precedes the Guide.

SAMPLE PAGE

aard•vark (ärd'värk'), *n.* a large burrowing African
  mammal that feeds on ants and termites. [< Afrik
  < D, = *aarde* earth + *varken* pig]

ab•a•cus (ab'ə kəs), *n., pl.* **-a•cus•es, -a•ci** (-ə sī',
  -kī'). a device for making arithmetic calculations,
  consisting of a frame set with rods on which beads
  are moved.

— main entry

— etymology

— pronunciation

abacus

— illustration and caption

— syllable dots

A•bed•ne•go (ə bed'ni gō'), *n.* a companion of
  Daniel. Compare SHADRACH. Dan. 3:12–30.

— cross reference to another entry

ache (āk), *v.,* **ached, ach•ing.** *n.* —*v.i.* **1.** to have a
  continuous dull pain. **2.** to yearn; long. —*n.* **3.** a
  continuous dull pain. —**ach'y,** *adj.,* -i•er, -i•est.

— verb inflected forms

— adjective inflected forms

a•cous'tics, *n.* **1.** (*used with a sing. v.*) the branch
  of physics that deals with sound. **2.** (*used with a pl.
  v.*) the qualities of a room, auditorium, etc., that determine the audibility of sounds in it.

— grammatical information

A.D. or **AD,** in the year of the Lord (used with
  dates): *Charlemagne was born in* A.D. *742.* [< L
  annō Dominī] —**Usage.** A.D. is usu. placed before
  a date: *The Roman conquest of Britain began in* A.D.
  43. The abbreviation B.C. is always placed after a
  date.

— usage note

add (ad), *v.t.* **1.** to unite or join so as to increase in
  number, quantity, size, or importance. **2.** to find the
  sum of. —*v.i.* **3.** to perform arithmetic addition. **4.**
  add up, to seem reasonable. **5. ~ up to,** to amount
  to; signify.

— phrasal verbs

ADD, attention deficit disorder.

— abbreviation

ad•min/is•tra'tion, *n.* **1.** management, as of a
  government or business. **2.** (*often cap.*) the executive
  branch of a government. **3.** *Law.* the management of
  an estate. **4.** the act of administering.

— capitalization style

— subject label

age (āj), *n., v.,* **aged, ag•ing** or **age•ing.** —*n.* **1.** the
  length of time during which a being or thing has ex-
  isted. **2.** a period of human life. **3.** old age. **4.** (*often
  cap.*) a historical or geological period. **5.** Usu., **ages.**
  a long time. —*v.i., v.t.* **6.** to grow or cause to grow
  old. **7.** to mature, as wine. —***Idiom.* 8. of age,**
  having reached adulthood, esp. as specified by law.

— summary of parts of speech

— idiom

-age, a suffix meaning: action or process (*coverage*);
  result of (*wreckage*); residence of (*parsonage*).

— suffix

a•gree'ment, *n.* **1.** the state of being in accord. **2.**
  a. an arrangement accepted by all parties. **b.** a document setting forth such an arrangement.

— lettered subdefinitions

al•low (ə lou'), *v.t.* **1.** to permit. **2.** to let have. **3.** to
  acknowledge; concede: *I had to allow that he was
  right.* —*v.i.* **4.** to permit as a possibility; admit. **5.** to
  make provision: *to allow for breakage.*

— example sentences or phrases

al'pha rhythm', *n.* a pattern of slow brain waves
  (**al'pha waves'**) in normal persons at rest with
  closed eyes.

— hidden entry

a•men•i•ty (ə men'i tē, ə mē'ni-), *n., pl.* **-ties. 1.**
  an agreeable act or manner; courtesy or civility: *social amenities.* **2.** a feature that provides comfort,
  convenience, or pleasure.

— variant pronunciation

Am•er•ind (am'ə rind), *n.* AMERICAN INDIAN. Also
  called **Am'er•in'di•an** (-rin'dē ən).

— variant form

an•eu•rysm or **-rism** (an'yə riz'əm), *n.* a permanent cardiac or arterial dilatation usu. caused by
  weakening of the vessel wall.

— variant spelling

An•go•ra (ang gôr'ə), *n., pl.* **-ras. 1.** a cat, goat, or
  rabbit with long, silky hair. **2.** (*often l.c.*) a yarn
  made from the hair of the Angora goat or rabbit.

— lowercase style

an•ti•pas•to (an'ti pä'stō, än'tē-), *n., pl.* **-pas•tos,
  -pas•ti** (-pä'stē). an appetizer course in an Italian
  meal.

— variant plural

ap•par•el (ə par'əl), *n., v.,* **-eled, -el•ing** or (*esp.
  Brit.*) **-elled, -el•ling.** —*n.* **1.** clothing, esp. outerwear; garments. —*v.t.* **2.** to dress; clothe.

— variant inflected forms

vi

GUIDE TO THE DICTIONARY

ENTRIES: WHERE AND HOW TO FIND THEM

MAIN ENTRIES AND THEIR VARIANTS

All **main entries,** whether they are single words, phrases, abbreviations, proper names, prefixes, or suffixes, are shown in one vocabulary listing in strict letter-by-letter alphabetical order. They appear in **large boldface type,** even with the left margin of the column.

Alternate forms are common alternatives to the entry term, having only minor spelling differences or a difference in suffix. They follow the main entry, in the same **large boldface type,** and are introduced by "or" or "also."
Examples: **medieval; elegiac**

Variants that are more substantially different in form are shown for some nouns. They appear in **smaller boldface type,** introduced by the words "Also called."
Example: **goose flesh**
Any variants that do not apply to the entire entry are shown either at the portion of the entry to which they apply or at the end of the entry, with numbers indicating the definitions for which they are appropriate alternatives.
Example: **ammonia** (def. 2)

HOMOGRAPHS

Homographs are identically spelled terms that differ in derivation. They are given separate main entries, each marked with a small superscript number.
Example: **cuff**[1], **cuff**[2]

GUIDE WORDS

Guide words, which are shown at the top left of even-numbered pages and the top right of odd-numbered ones, give the range of main entries covered on that page.

RUN-ONS

Run-ons are words closely related to the main entry, but having a different grammatical function. Preceded by a lightface dash, these words appear at the end of an individual entry.
Run-ons are typically formed by adding a suffix. Although a run-on is not explicitly defined, its meaning can be understood by combining the senses of its root word and suffix, taking into account the part of speech. Thus the adverb **elaborately,** run-on to the adjective **elaborate,** is understood to mean "in an elaborate manner."
Some run-ons are formed in other ways, for example by deleting or changing a suffix.

LIST WORDS

List words are grouped by the prefix they share, and are understood by adding the sense of that prefix to the meaning of the root. Thus **anti- + war** means "against war." All such lists start at the bottom of the page containing the entry for the prefix, or on the following page.

HIDDEN ENTRIES

Hidden entries are parenthesized boldface terms shown in the context of a definition, where the sense of the hidden entry is made clear. Example: **intestine**

PHRASAL VERBS

Phrasal verbs, like **back off, clear up,** and **stand by** follow all other verb senses in an entry. In any entry showing two or more such phrases, the first is spelled out completely, while those that follow show a swung dash (~) replacing the entry verb in the phrase.

IDIOMS

Idioms, like **make one's mark,** are expressions whose meanings cannot be predicted from the usual meanings of their components. Idioms appear in a labeled group as the final definitions in an entry.

ENTRIES: HOW THEY ARE SHOWN

SYLLABIFICATION

All single-word entries of more than one syllable are **syllabified.** That is, they are divided into syllables by boldface centered dots. These dots indicate possible hyphenation points, places where a word may break at the end of a line in printed or typed text.

STRESS

Primary and secondary stress marks replace centered dots at some syllable breaks. These marks serve as an aid to pronunciation by indicating the relative differences in emphasis between syllables. A primary stress mark (ʹ) follows the syllable with greatest emphasis and a secondary stress mark (ʹ) follows one with lesser emphasis.

Entries consisting of two or more words are not fully syllabified, but are shown with a pattern of stress that reveals the relationship of each word to the others.

Example: **physical therapy**

PRONUNCIATION

Pronunciations are shown in parentheses immediately following the entry form, using a system of diacritical marks over vowels. Use the "Pronunciation Key" in this book.

Many entries show full pronunciations. Entries that are not pronounced fully are similar in pronunciation to nearby related entries or have component parts pronounced elsewhere in the dictionary. In these cases, the word is syllabified and stressed, with either no pronunciation or with a pronunciation for only that portion of the word that changes significantly.

MAJOR PARTS OF THE ENTRY

PARTS OF SPEECH

Italicized **part-of-speech** labels, usually abbreviated, are given for main entries, run-ons, and list words to show their grammatical function in a sentence. Thus a main entry that is commonly used as a noun would receive the label *n.* (Trademarks, however, defined as such, are capitalized and labeled *Trademark.*)

Example: **minʹeral waʹter,** *n.*

If a main entry has more than one grammatical function, a part-of-speech label precedes each group of definitions given for that part of speech. Such an entry also includes a summary of all its parts of speech with inflected forms if appropriate.

Example: **netʹtle,** *n., v.* **-tled, -tling.**—*n.* **1.** a plant with stinging hairs.—*v.t.* **2.** to irritate or annoy.

INFLECTED FORMS

Inflected forms are, typically, plurals of nouns, past tenses and participles of verbs, and comparatives and superlatives of adjectives and adverbs.

Such forms regarded as "regular" are not shown in the dictionary for the following:

1. nouns whose plural is formed by the simple addition of *-s* or *-es,* as *dogs* or *classes.* Nor are plurals shown for "mass nouns," nouns that would not be pluralized.

2. verbs whose past tense and past participle is formed by the addition of *-ed* and whose present participle is formed by the addition of *-ing,* with no alteration of the spelling (as in *talk, talked, talking*).

This dictionary does show inflected forms for:
1. **nouns** that form their plurals irregularly.
2. **nouns** ending in a vowel, where even if the plural is regular, some confusion about its form might exist.
3. **nouns** whose plurals require pronunciation.
4. **verbs** with irregular inflections.
5. **adjectives** and **adverbs** that form the comparative and superlative with an internal change in form or by adding -er and -est. The comparative and superlative are not shown for adjectives and adverbs that, by definition, cannot be compared or for those forming their inflections with more and most.

Inflected forms for verbs are shown in the following order: past tense, past participle (where this differs from the past tense), and present participle.

DEFINITIONS

Definitions within an entry are individually numbered in a single sequence, regardless of their groupings according to part of speech. In general, the most common part of speech is listed first, as is the most frequent meaning within the part-of-speech group.

Closely related definitions may be grouped together and sequentially marked with boldface letters under the same boldface definition number.

Plural forms of singular main entries are spelled out, while a change in typeface from roman to italics, or a change in capitalization, is shown by means of an italicized label. Examples: **card**¹ (def. 3); **democrat** (def. 2)

USAGE AND OTHER LABELS

Entries that are limited to a particular region, time, subject, or level of usage are marked with appropriate labels, as Brit., Archaic, Law, Slang, and Informal.

CROSS REFERENCES

Definitions that serve as **cross references** to another part of the alphabet, where the entry with the full definition is shown, are displayed in small capital letters. Examples: CRAPE; BURMA

Variants of main entries are given their own alphabetical main entries when they would otherwise be difficult to find.

ETYMOLOGIES

Etymologies, or word histories, appear in square brackets after the definitions. All symbols and abbreviations used in the etymologies are explained in the Abbreviations Key.

A word displayed in small capital letters is a cross reference to another entry where further information can be found.

A language label is shown without an accompanying italicized form when there is no significant difference in form or meaning between the word in the given language and the preceding word in the etymology, or the main-entry word itself.

USAGE

Usage notes, preceded by the label—**Usage,** appear at the end of selected entries throughout the dictionary. These notes discuss many of the problems and controversies that arise in matters of grammar and usage. They reflect the opinions of educated users of English.

SELECTED KEY TERMS—TOPICAL INDEX

Proverbs and Sayings

After the feast comes the reckoning.
All that glitters is not gold.
The apple doesn't fall far from the tree.
As you sow, so shall you reap.
Better to light one little candle than to curse the darkness.
Beware of Greeks bearing gifts.
Don't kill the goose that laid the golden eggs.
Don't put all your eggs in one basket.
Early to bed and early to rise makes a man healthy, wealthy, and wise.
For want of a nail the kingdom was lost.
From the sublime to the ridiculous is but a step.
The game is not worth the candle.
Give me liberty, or give me death!
Good fences make good neighbors.
A good name is better than precious ointment.
Government of the people, by the people, and for the people.
He who pays the piper calls the tune.
If you can't stand the heat, get out of the kitchen.
Judge not, that ye be not judged.
Justice is blind.
The lion shall lie down with the lamb.

Man proposes, God disposes.
A merry heart makes a cheerful countenance.
No man is an island.
Oil and water don't mix.
One swallow does not make a summer.
The pen is mightier than the sword.
A plague on both your houses.
Practice what you preach.
Praise the Lord and pass the ammunition.
The proof of the pudding is in the eating.
A prophet is not without honor, save in his own country.
A rolling stone gathers no moss.
Speak softly and carry a big stick.
Still waters run deep.
Strain at a gnat and swallow a camel.
There is nothing new under the sun.
They that sow the wind shall reap the whirlwind.
Those who cannot remember the past are condemned to repeat it.
To everything there is a season, and a time to every purpose under the heaven.
United we stand, divided we fall.
Vanity of vanities, all is vanity.
Variety is the spice of life.
Where there is no vision, the people perish.
You can catch more flies with honey than with vinegar.

ABBREVIATIONS

<	descended from, borrowed from	fig.	figurative	n.pl.	plural noun
< <	descended from, borrowed from though intermediate stages not shown	fl.	flourished	Num.	Numbers
		fol.	followed	obj.	objective
		Fr.	French	Obs., obs.	obsolete
		ft.	foot, feet	OE	Old English
		fut.	future	OF	Old French
=	equivalent to	G	German	OHG	Old High German
ab.	about	Gal.	Galatians	ON	Old Norse
Abbr., abbr.	abbreviation	Gen.	Genesis	orig.	originally
abl.	ablative	gen.	genitive	pass.	passive
acc.	accusative	Geol.	Geology	past part.	past participle
adj.	adjective	Geom.	Geometry	perh.	perhaps
adv.	adverb	Gk, Gk.	Greek	Pers, Pers.	Persian
AF	Anglo-French	Gmc	Germanic	pers.	person
Afr.	African	Gram.	Grammar	Pg	Portuguese
AmerSp	American Spanish	Heb, Heb.	Hebrew(s)	pl.	plural
Ar	Arabic	Hos.	Hosea	Pop.	population
Aram	Aramaic	in.	inch(es)	poss.	possessive
at. no.	atomic number	indic.	indicative	pp.	past participle
at. wt.	atomic weight	inf.	infinitive	prec.	preceded
b.	blend	interj.	interjection	prep.	preposition
b.	born	Ir	Irish	pres.	present, present tense
bef.	before	irreg.	irregular		
Biol.	Biology	Is.	Isaiah	pres. part.	present participle
Bot.	Botany	It, It.	Italian	prob.	probably
Brit.	British	Japn, Japn.	Japanese	Pron., pron.	pronunciation, pronounced
c	circa	Jer.	Jeremiah		
CanF	Canadian French	Judg.	Judges	pron.	pronoun
Cap.	capital (city)	km	kilometer(s)	Prov.	Proverbs
cap.	capital	L	Latin	prp.	present participle
caps.	capitals	Lam.	Lamentations	Ps.	Psalms
cent.	century	l.c.	lowercase	pt.	preterit (past tense)
Cf., cf.	compare	Lev.	Leviticus		
chem.	Chemistry	LG	Low German	ptp.	past participle
Chron.	Chronicles	lit.	literally	Rev.	Revelations
cm	centimeter(s)	LL	Late Latin	Rom.	Romans
Col.	Colossians	m	meter(s)	Russ	Russian
compar.	comparative	masc.	masculine	S	south, southern
conj.	conjunction	Matt.	Matthew	s.	stem
contr.	contraction	MD	Middle Dutch	Sam.	Samuel
Cor.	Corinthians	ME	Middle English	Scand	Scandinavian
D	Dutch	Med.	Medicine	Scot.	Scottish
d.	died	MexSp	Mexican Spanish	sing.	singular
Dan.	Daniel	MF	Middle French	Skt, Skt.	Sanskrit
dat.	dative	MHG	Middle High German	Sp, Sp.	Spanish
def.	definition	mi.	mile(s)	sp.	spelling, spelled
defs.	definitions	Mil.	Military	sp.gr.	specific gravity
der.	derivative	ML	Medieval Latin	sq.	square
Deut.	Deuteronomy	MLG	Middle Low German	subj.	subjunctive
Dial., dial.	dialect, dialectal			superl.	superlative
dim.	diminutive	mm	millimeter(s)	Sw, Sw.	Swedish
Du.	Dutch	mod.	modern	syll.	syllable
E	east, eastern	ModGk	Modern Greek	Thes.	Thessalonians
E	English	ModHeb	Modern Hebrew	Tim.	Timothy
Eccl.	Ecclesiastes	Naut.	Nautical	Usu., usu.	usually
Eng.	England, English	N	north, northern	v.	verb
esp.	especially	n.	noun	var.	variant
etym.	etymology	Neh.	Nehemiah	v.i.	intransitive
Ex.	Exodus	neut.	neuter	VL	Vulgar Latin
Ezek.	Ezekiel	NL	New Latin	v.t.	transitive verb
F	French	nom.	nominative	W	west, western
fem.	feminine	Norw, Norw.	Norwegian	yd.	yard(s)

PRONUNCIATION KEY

STRESS

Pronunciations are marked for stress to reveal the relative differences in emphasis between syllables. In words of two or more syllables, a primary stress mark (′), as in *mother* (**muth′ər**), follows the syllable having greatest stress. A secondary stress mark (′), as in *grandmother* (**grand′muth′ər**), follows a syllable having slightly less stress than primary but more stress than an unmarked syllable.

ENGLISH SOUNDS

a	act, bat, marry	oi	oil, joint, joy
ā	age, paid, say	ŏŏ	oomph, book, tour
â(r)	air, dare, Mary	ōō	ooze, fool, too
ä	ah, part, balm	ou	out, loud, cow
b	back, cabin, cab	p	pot, supper, stop
ch	beach, child	r	read, hurry, near
d	do, madder, bed	s	see, passing, miss
e	edge, set, merry	sh	shoe, fashion, push
ē	equal, bee, pretty	t	ten, matter, bit
ēr	ear, mere	th	thin, ether, path
f	fit, differ, puff	th	that, either, smooth
g	give, trigger, beg	u	up, sun
h	hit, behave	ûr	urge, burn, cur
hw	which, nowhere	v	voice, river, live
i	if, big, mirror	w	witch, away
ī	ice, bite, deny	y	yes, onion
j	just, tragic, fudge	z	zoo, lazy, those
k	keep, token, make	zh	treasure, mirage
l	low, mellow, bottle (bot′l)	ə	used in unaccented syllables to indicate the sound of the reduced vowel in alone, system, easily, gallop, circus
m	my, summer, him		
n	now, sinner, button (but′n)		
ng	sing, Washington	ᵊ	used between i and r and between ou and r to show triphthongal quality, as in fire (fīᵊr), hour (ouᵊr)
o	ox, bomb, wasp		
ō	over, boat, no		
ô	order, ball, raw		

NON-ENGLISH SOUNDS

A	as in French **ami** (A mē′)		Spanish and a sound in French and German similar to KH but pronounced with voice]
KH	as in Scottish **loch** (lôKH)		
N	as in French **bon** (bôN) [used to indicate that the preceding vowel is nasalized]	Y	as in French **tu** (tY)
Œ	as in French **feu** (fŒ)	ᵊ	as in French **bastogne** (ba stôn′yᵊ)
R	[a symbol for any non-english r sound, including a trill or flap in Italian and		

xiv

A

A, a (ā), *n., pl.* **As** or **A's, as** or **a's.** the first letter of the English alphabet, a vowel.

a[1] (ə; *when stressed* ā), *indefinite article.* **1.** any one (used before a singular noun): *a new car.* **2.** one: *a dozen eggs.* **3.** the same: *two at a time.* **4.** any single: *not a one.* —**Usage.** In spoken and written English, A is used before words beginning with a consonant sound, including the sounds (y) or (w): *a book; a union; a one-room apartment.* AN is used before words beginning with a vowel sound (including a silent *h*): *an apple; an hour.* The use of AN before a pronounced *h* is usu. considered old-fashioned: *an historian; an hero.*

a[2] (ə; *when stressed* ā), *prep.* per: *fifty cents a ride.* —**Usage.** See PER.

A, **1.** ampere. **2.** angstrom. **3.** answer.

A, *Symbol.* **1.** the first in order or in a series. **2.** a grade or mark indicating excellence or superiority. **3.** a major blood group.

a-[1], a prefix meaning: on (*afoot*); in (*abed*); to (*ashore*); at (*aside*).

a-[2], a prefix meaning: of (*akin*); from (*anew*).

a-[3], a prefix meaning: not (*atypical*); without (*amorality*).

A., **1.** America. **2.** American. **3.** April.

a., **1.** about. **2.** acre. **3.** adjective. **4.** alto. **5.** answer.

A-1 or **A 1** (ā′wun′), *adj.* A ONE.

AA, **1.** administrative assistant. **2.** Alcoholics Anonymous. **3.** antiaircraft.

A.A., Associate of Arts.

AAA, **1.** American Automobile Association. **2.** antiaircraft artillery.

aard•vark (ärd′värk′), *n.* a large burrowing African mammal that feeds on ants and termites. [< Afrik < D, = *aarde* earth + *varken* pig]

Aar•on (âr′ən, ar′-), *n.* **1.** the older brother of Moses. Ex. 28; 40:13–16. **2.** **Henry Louis** ("Hank"), born 1934, U.S. baseball player.

AARP, American Association of Retired Persons.

AB, Alberta.

AB, *Symbol.* a major blood group.

ab., about.

A.B., **1.** able-bodied seaman. **2.** Bachelor of Arts. [< L *Artium Baccalaureus*]

a.b., *Baseball.* (times) at bat.

A.B.A., American Bar Association.

a•back (ə bak′), *adv.* **1.** toward the back. —**Idiom.** **2.** **taken aback,** surprised; startled; disconcerted.

ab•a•cus (ab′ə kəs), *n., pl.* **-cus•es, -a•ci** (-ə sī′, -kī′). a device for making arithmetic calculations, consisting of a frame set with rods on which beads are moved.

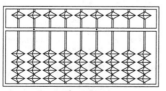

abacus

A•bad•don (ə bad′n), *n.* **1.** APOLLYON. **2.** a place of destruction; the depths of hell.

a•baft (ə baft′, ə bäft′), *Naut.* —*prep.* **1.** to the rear of. —*adv.* **2.** aft.

ab•a•lo•ne (ab′ə lō′nē), *n.* an edible mollusk with a flat, oval shell that is a source of mother-of-pearl.

a•ban•don[1] (ə ban′dən), *v.t.* **1.** to leave; desert: *to abandon a sinking ship.* **2.** to give up; discontinue: *to abandon a project.* —**a•ban′don•ment,** *n.*

a•ban•don[2] (ə ban′dən), *n.* a complete surrender to natural impulses; freedom from constraint.

a•ban′doned, *adj.* lacking in moral restraint; shameless or wicked. —**a•ban′doned•ly,** *adv.*

a•base (ə bās′), *v.t.* **a•based, a•bas•ing.** to humble or degrade. —**a•base′ment,** *n.*

a•bash (ə bash′), *v.t.* to embarrass; disconcert. —**a•bash′ed•ly,** *adv.* —**a•bash′ment,** *n.*

a•bate (ə bāt′), *v.,* **a•bat•ed, a•bat•ing.** —*v.t.* **1.** to reduce in amount, degree, or intensity. **2.** *Law.* to stop or suppress (an action, nuisance, etc.). —*v.i.* **3.** to diminish in amount, degree, or intensity. —**a•bate′ment,** *n.*

ab•at•toir (ab′ə twär′, ab′ə twär′), *n.* a slaughterhouse.

Ab•ba (ab′ə), *n.* (*sometimes l.c.*) (in the New Testament) a term for father, used by Jesus in addressing God and then taken up by the early Christians. Mark 14:36; Rom. 8:15; Gal. 4:6. [< Aram *abbā* father]

ab•ba•cy (ab′ə sē), *n., pl.* **-cies.** the position or term of office of an abbot.

ab•bé (a bā′, ab′ā), *n.* a title of respect for a French ecclesiastic or clergyman.

ab•bess (ab′is), *n.* the superior of a convent of nuns.

ab•bey (ab′ē), *n., pl.* **-beys. 1.** a monastery or convent. **2.** the church of an abbey.

ab•bot (ab′ət), *n.* the superior of a monastery. [< L < Gk < Aram *abbā* father]

abbr. or **abbrev.,** abbreviation.

ab•bre•vi•ate (ə brē′vē āt′), *v.t.,* **-at•ed, -at•ing. 1.** to shorten (a word or phrase) by omitting letters. **2.** to make briefer.

ab•bre•vi•a′tion, *n.* **1.** a shortened form of a word or phrase used to represent the whole, as *Dr.* for *Doctor.* **2.** an act or result of abbreviating.

ABCs or **ABC's,** *n.* (*used with a pl. v.*) **1.** the alphabet. **2.** the basic facts, principles, or skills of a subject.

ab•di•cate (ab′di kāt′), *v.t., v.i.,* **-cat•ed, -cat•ing.** to give up or relinquish (a throne, right, or power), esp. in a formal way. —**ab′di•ca′tion,** *n.*

ab•do•men (ab′də mən, ab dō′-), *n.* **1.** the part of the body between the thorax and the pelvis; belly. **2.** the posterior segment of the body of an arthropod. —**ab•dom′i•nal** (-dom′ə nl), *adj.*

ab•duct (ab dukt′), *v.t.* to carry off (a person) by force, esp. to kidnap. —**ab•duc′tion,** *n.* —**ab•duc′-tor,** *n.*

a•beam (ə bēm′), *adv.* at right angles to a ship's keel.

a•bed (ə bed′), *adv.* in bed.

A•bed•ne•go (ə bed′ni gō′), *n.* a companion of Daniel. Compare SHADRACH. Dan. 3:12–30.

A•bel (ā′bəl), *n.* the second son of Adam and Eve, slain by his brother, Cain. Gen. 4.

ab•er•ra•tion (ab′ə rā′shən), *n.* **1.** deviation from what is usual, normal, or right. **2.** mental unsoundness or disorder. **3.** a disturbance of the rays of a light such that they can no longer be brought to a sharp focus or form a clear image. —**ab•er•rant** (ə ber′ənt, ab′ər-), *adj.* —**ab′er•ra′tion•al,** *adj.*

a•bet (ə bet′), *v.t.,* **a•bet•ted, a•bet•ting.** to encourage or support, esp. in wrongdoing. —**a•bet′tor, a•bet′ter,** *n.*

a•bey•ance (ə bā′əns), *n.* temporary inactivity, cessation, or suspension: *to hold a question in abeyance.*

ab•hor (ab hôr′), *v.t.,* **-horred, -hor•ring.** to regard with repugnance or aversion; detest. —**ab•hor′rence,** *n.* —**ab•hor′rer,** *n.*

ab·hor′rent (-hôr′ənt, -hor′-), *adj.* causing repugnance or aversion; detestable. —**ab·hor′rent·ly,** *adv.*

a·bide (ə bīd′), *v.,* **a·bode** or **a·bid·ed, a·bid·ing.** —*v.i.* **1.** to remain; stay. **2.** to dwell; reside. —*v.t.* **3.** to put up with; tolerate. **4. abide by, a.** to comply with; submit to. **b.** to remain faithful to; keep. —**a·bid′ance,** *n.*

a·bid′ing, *adj.* enduring; steadfast. —**a·bid′ing·ly,** *adv.*

Ab·i·djan (ab′i jän′), *n.* the commercial capital of the Ivory Coast. 1,850,000.

Ab·i·gail (ab′i gāl′), *n.* a wife of David. I Sam. 25.

Ab·i·lene (ab′ə lēn′), *n.* a city in central Texas. 106,654.

a·bil·i·ty (ə bil′i tē), *n., pl.* **-ties. 1.** power or capacity to do or act. **2.** a talent, skill, or aptitude.

ab·ject (ab′jekt, ab jekt′), *adj.* **1.** miserable or wretched. **2.** contemptible; despicable. —**ab·jec′tion,** *n.* —**ab·ject′ly,** *adv.*

ab·jure (ab jŏŏr′, -jûr′), *v.t.,* **-jured, -jur·ing. 1.** to repudiate or retract; recant. **2.** to renounce under oath. **3.** to refrain from. —**ab′ju·ra′tion** (-jə rā′shən), *n.* —**ab·jur′a·to′ry,** *adj.* **ab·jur′er,** *n.*

ab·late (a blāt′), *v.,* **-lat·ed, -lat·ing.** —*v.t.* **1.** to remove by surgery, melting, erosion, etc. —*v.i.* **2.** to become ablated. —**a·bla′tion,** *n.*

ab·la·tive (ab′lə tiv), *adj.* **1.** designating a grammatical case that marks the starting point of an action and, in Latin, indicates manner, instrument, or agent. —*n.* **2.** the ablative case.

a·blaze (ə blāz′), *adj.* **1.** on fire. **2.** gleaming. **3.** excited; ardent.

a·ble (ā′bəl), *adj.,* **a·bler, a·blest. 1.** having the necessary power, skill, or resources. **2.** having or showing intelligence, skill, or talent. —**a′bly,** *adv.*

-able, a suffix meaning: able to be (*readable*); tending to (*changeable*); worthy of (*lovable*).

a′ble-bod′ied, *adj.* physically fit.

a′ble·ism, *n.* discrimination against disabled people.

a′ble sea′man, *n.* a skilled or experienced seaman. Also called **a′ble-bod′ied sea′man.**

a·bloom (ə blōōm′), *adj.* in bloom.

ab·lu·tion (ə blōō′shən), *n.* a cleansing of the body, esp. as a religious ritual.

-ably, a suffix meaning in an -*able* manner (*enjoyably*).

ABM, antiballistic missile.

ab·ne·gate (ab′ni gāt′), *v.t.,* **-gat·ed, -gat·ing.** to deny (rights, comforts, etc.) to oneself; renounce. —**ab′ne·ga′tion,** *n.*

ab·nor·mal (ab nôr′məl), *adj.* not normal, average, typical, or usual. —**ab′nor·mal′i·ty,** *n., pl.* **-ties.** —**ab·nor′mal·ly,** *adv.*

a·board (ə bôrd′), *adv., prep.* **1.** on, in, or into (a ship, train, airplane, etc.). **2.** alongside.

a·bode¹ (ə bōd′), *n.* **1.** a residence; home. **2.** a stay; sojourn.

a·bode² (ə bōd′), *v.* a pt. and past part. of ABIDE.

a·bol·ish (ə bol′ish), *v.t.* to do away with; put an end to.

ab·o·li·tion (ab′ə lish′ən), *n.* **1.** the act of abolishing or state of being abolished. **2.** (*sometimes cap.*) the legal termination of slavery in the U.S. —**ab′o·li′tion·ism,** *n.* —**ab′o·li′tion·ist,** *n., adj.*

A-bomb (ā′bom′), *n.* ATOMIC BOMB.

a·bom·i·na·ble (ə bom′ə nə bəl), *adj.* **1.** repugnantly hateful; detestable. **2.** very bad or unpleasant. —**a·bom′i·na·bly,** *adv.*

a·bom·i·nate (-nāt′), *v.t.,* **-nat·ed, -nat·ing. 1.** to loathe intensely. **2.** to dislike strongly. —**a·bom′i·na′tion,** *n.*

ab·o·rig·i·nal (ab′ə rij′ə nl), *adj.* **1.** of aborigines. **2.** native; indigenous. **3.** (*usu. cap.*) of the Aborigines of Australia. —*n.* **4.** ABORIGINE.

ab′o·rig′i·ne (-nē), *n., pl.* **-nes. 1.** one of the original or earliest known inhabitants of a country or region. **2.** (*usu. cap.*) a member of any of the peoples

who are the aboriginal inhabitants of Australia. [< L *ab origine* from the origin]

a·born·ing (ə bôr′ning), *adv., adj.* in birth; coming into being: *The scheme died aborning. A new era is aborning.*

a·bort (ə bôrt′), *v.i., v.t.* **1.** to undergo or cause to undergo abortion. **2.** to terminate (a missile flight, a mission, or a procedure) before completion. —*n.* **3.** the termination of a missile flight, a mission, or a procedure before completion. —**a·bor′tive,** *adj.* —**a·bor′tive·ly,** *adv.*

a·bor′tion (ə bôr′shən), *n.* **1.** the removal of an embryo or fetus from the uterus in order to end a pregnancy. **2.** something that fails to develop, progress, or mature. —**a·bor′tion·ist,** *n.*

a·bound (ə bound′), *v.i.* **1.** to occur or exist in great quantities or numbers. **2.** to be well supplied (usu. fol. by *in*). **3.** to be filled; teem (usu. fol. by *with*).

a·bout (ə bout′), *prep.* **1.** in regard to; concerning. **2.** in connection or association with. **3.** close to; near. **4.** on every side of. **5.** on the verge of. —*adv.* **6.** approximately. **7.** nearly; almost. **8.** not far off; nearby. **9.** on every side. **10.** in the opposite direction. —*adj.* **11.** moving around; astir.

a·bout-face (*n.* ə bout′fās′, -fās′; *v.* ə bout′fās′), *n., v.,* **-faced, -fac·ing.** —*n.* **1.** a complete reversal in position, direction, principle, or attitude. —*v.i.* **2.** to perform an about-face.

a·bove (ə buv′), *adv.* **1.** in or to a higher place. **2.** overhead, upstairs, or in the sky. **3.** higher in rank, authority, or power. **4.** before or earlier, esp. in a text. —*prep.* **5.** in or to a higher place than; over. **6.** greater in quantity or number than. **7.** superior in rank or standing to. **8.** of too fine a character for. —*adj.* **9.** said, mentioned, or written above. —*n.* **10.** something that is above. —*Idiom.* **11. above all,** most importantly; principally.

a·bove′board′, *adv., adj.* without tricks, concealment, or disguise.

ab·ra·ca·dab·ra (ab′rə kə dab′rə), *n.* **1.** a mystical word once used as a magical means of warding off misfortune. **2.** meaningless talk; gibberish.

a·brade (ə brād′), *v.t., v.i.,* **a·brad·ed, a·brad·ing. 1.** to wear off or down by rubbing. **2.** to scrape or rub off. —**a·bra′sion** (ə brā′zhən), *n.*

A·bra·ham (ā′brə ham′, -həm), *n.* the first Biblical patriarch, the traditional founder of the Hebrew nation: considered an ancestor of the Arab peoples through his son Ishmael. Gen. 11:26–25:10.

A′braham's bos′om, *n.* heaven. Luke 16:22.

a·bra·sive (ə brā′siv, -ziv), *adj.* **1.** causing abrasion. **2.** tending to annoy. —*n.* **3.** a material, as sandpaper, used for grinding, polishing, or smoothing. —**a·bra′sive·ly,** *adv.* —**a·bra′sive·ness,** *n.*

a·breast (ə brest′), *adv., adj.* **1.** side by side. **2.** informed; aware.

a·bridge (ə brij′), *v.t.,* **a·bridged, a·bridg·ing. 1.** to shorten while retaining the substance. **2.** to diminish or curtail. [< ML *abbreviāre* to shorten] —**a·bridg′ment, a·bridge′ment,** *n.*

a·broad (ə brôd′), *adv.* **1.** in or to a foreign country. **2.** out of doors. **3.** in general circulation. **4.** over a large area; far and wide.

ab·ro·gate (ab′rə gāt′), *v.t.,* **-gat·ed, -gat·ing.** to abolish formally or officially; annul. —**ab′ro·ga′tion,** *n.* —**ab′ro·ga′tor,** *n.*

ab·rupt (ə brupt′), *adj.* **1.** sudden or unexpected. **2.** curt or brusque, as in speech. **3.** lacking in continuity or smoothness. **4.** steep; precipitous. —**ab·rupt′ly,** *adv.* —**ab·rupt′ness,** *n.*

abs (abz), *n.pl. Informal.* abdominal muscles.

ABS, antilock braking system.

Ab·sa·lom (ab′sə ləm), *n.* the third son of David. II Sam. 13–18.

ab·scess (ab′ses), *n.* a localized accumulation of pus in body tissues. —**ab′scessed,** *adj.*

ab·scis·sa (ab sis′ə), *n., pl.* **-scis·sas, -scis·sae** (-sis′ē). (in plane Cartesian coordinates) the x-coordinate of a point: its distance from the y-axis measured parallel to the x-axis.

ab·scis·sion (ab sizh′ən), *n.* **1.** the act of cutting off. **2.** the normal separation of flowers, fruit, and leaves from plants.

ab•scond (ab skond'), *v.i.* to depart suddenly and secretly, esp. to avoid capture and legal prosecution. —**ab•scond'er,** *n.*

ab•sence (ab'səns), *n.* **1.** the state of being away. **2.** a period of being away. **3.** lack; deficiency.

ab•sent (*adj., prep.* ab'sənt; *v.* ab sent', ab'sənt), *adj.* **1.** not present at a given time; away. **2.** not in existence; lacking. **3.** not attentive; preoccupied. —*v.t.* **4.** to take or keep (oneself) away. —*prep.* **5.** in the absence of; without. —**ab'sent•ly,** *adv.*

ab'sen•tee' (-tē'), *n., pl.* -**tees.** a person who is absent, esp. from work or school. —**ab'sen•tee'ism,** *n.*

ab'sentee bal'lot, *n.* a ballot mailed by a voter who cannot come to the polls.

ab'sent-mind'ed, *adj.* preoccupied so as to be unaware or forgetful of other matters. —**ab'sent-mind'ed•ly,** *adv.* —**ab'sent-mind'ed•ness,** *n.*

ab•so•lute (ab'sə lōōt'), *adj.* **1.** being fully as indicated; complete or perfect. **2.** free from restriction, limitation, or exception. **3.** outright; unqualified. **4.** not limited by laws or a constitution. **5.** not comparative or relative. **6.** positive; certain. **7.** not mixed; pure. **8.** relatively independent syntactically in relation to other elements in a sentence. **9.** *Physics.* pertaining to a system of units based on some primary units, esp. of length, mass, and time. —**ab'so•lute'ly,** *adv.*

ab'solute pitch', *n.* **1.** the exact pitch of a tone in terms of vibrations per second. **2.** the ability to sing or recognize the pitch of a tone.

ab'solute val'ue, *n.* the magnitude of a real number or quantity irrespective of sign.

ab'solute ze'ro, *n.* the temperature of −273.16°C (−459.69°F), the hypothetical point at which all molecular activity ceases.

ab'so•lu'tion, *n.* **1.** the act of absolving. **2.** a remission of sin as effected by a priest in the sacrament of penance.

ab'so•lut•ism, *n.* the principle or the exercise of unrestricted power in or by government. —**ab'so•lut'ist,** *n., adj.*

ab•solve (ab zolv', -solv'), *v.t.,* -**solved, -solv•ing.** **1.** to free from guilt or blame. **2.** to release from a duty, obligation, or responsibility. **3.** to grant remission of sins to. —**ab•solv'a•ble,** *adj.*

ab•sorb (ab sôrb', -zôrb'), *v.t.* **1.** to take up or drink in (a liquid); soak up. **2.** to take in and assimilate; incorporate. **3.** to occupy or fill fully; engross. **4.** to take in without echo, recoil, or reflection: *to absorb sound.* —**ab•sorb'ing,** *adj.*

ab•sorb'ent, *adj.* **1.** capable of absorbing. —*n.* **2.** a substance that absorbs. —**ab•sorb'en•cy,** *n.*

ab•sorp'tion (-sôrp'shən, -zôrp'-), *n.* **1.** the process of absorbing or being absorbed. **2.** mental preoccupation; engrossment. —**ab•sorp'tive,** *adj.*

ab•stain (ab stān'), *v.i.* to refrain voluntarily. —**ab•stain'er,** *n.* —**ab•sten'tion** (-sten'shən), *n.*

ab•ste•mi•ous (ab stē'mē əs), *adj.* sparing or moderate, esp. in eating and drinking; temperate.

ab•sti•nence (ab'stə nəns), *n.* **1.** forbearance from indulgence of an appetite. **2.** avoidance of alcoholic liquors or of certain foods. —**ab'sti•nent,** *adj.*

ab•stract (*adj.* ab strakt', ab'strakt; *n.* ab'strakt; *v.* ab strakt' *for 7, 8,* ab'strakt *for 9*), *adj.* **1.** thought of apart from concrete realities or specific objects. **2.** expressing a quality apart from any specific object or instance. **3.** not applied or practical; theoretical. **4.** (in art) emphasizing line, color, and nonrepresentational form. —*n.* **5.** a summary, as of an article. **6.** something abstract, as an idea or term. —*v.t.* **7.** to take away; remove. **8.** to draw away the attention of. **9.** to summarize. —**ab•stract'ly,** *adv.* —**ab'stract•ness,** *n.*

ab•stract'ed, *adj.* lost in thought; preoccupied.

ab'stract expres'sionism, *n.* (*sometimes caps.*) experimental, nonrepresentational painting marked by technical freedom and spontaneous expression. —**ab'stract expres'sionist,** *n.*

ab•strac'tion, *n.* **1.** an abstract idea or term. **2.** the

act or process of abstracting. **3.** absent-mindedness; inattention. **4.** an abstract work of art.

ab•struse (ab strōōs'), *adj.* hard to understand; recondite. —**ab•struse'ly,** *adv.* —**ab•struse'ness,** *n.*

ab•surd (ab sûrd', -zûrd'), *adj.* contrary to all reason or common sense; laughably foolish. —**ab•surd'i•ty,** *n., pl.* -**ties.** —**ab•surd'ly,** *adv.* —**ab•surd'ness,** *n.*

A•bu Dha•bi (ä'bōō dä'bē), *n.* a sheikdom in the N United Arab Emirates. 670,125.

A•bu•ja (ə bōō'jə), *n.* the capital of Nigeria. 378,671.

a•bun•dant (ə bun'dənt), *adj.* **1.** present in great quantity. **2.** well supplied; rich. —**a•bun'dance,** *n.* —**a•bun'dant•ly,** *adv.*

a•buse (*v.* ə byōōz'; *n.* ə byōōs'), *v.,* **a•bused, a•bus•ing,** *n.* —*v.t.* **1.** to use wrongly or improperly; misuse. **2.** to treat in a harmful way. **3.** to insult; revile. —*n.* **4.** wrong, improper, or harmful use; misuse. **5.** harshly or coarsely insulting language. **6.** bad treatment; maltreatment. —**a•bu'sive** (-siv), *adj.* —**a•bu'sive•ly,** *adv.* —**a•bu'sive•ness,** *n.*

a•but (ə but'), *v.,* **a•but•ted, a•but•ting.** —*v.i.* **1.** to touch or join at the border. —*v.t.* **2.** to border on.

a•but'ment, *n.* a mass, as of masonry, supporting and receiving the thrust of an arch or vault.

a•buzz (ə buz'), *adj.* full of or alive with activity or talk.

a•bys•mal (ə biz'məl), *adj.* **1.** of or like an abyss; immeasurably deep. **2.** extremely bad; dreadful. —**a•bys'mal•ly,** *adv.*

a•byss (ə bis'), *n.* **1.** an immeasurably deep, vast chasm. **2.** something profound or infinite. **3. a.** the primal chaos before Creation. **b.** hell.

Ab•ys•sin•i•a (ab'ə sin'ē ə), *n.* ancient name of ETHIOPIA.

AC, **1.** air conditioning. **2.** Also, **ac, a.c., A.C.** alternating current.

Ac, *Chem. Symbol.* actinium.

a/c, account.

a•ca•cia (ə kā'shə), *n., pl.* -**cias.** **1.** a small tree or shrub with clusters of small yellow flowers. **2.** the locust tree.

ac•a•dem•ic (ak'ə dem'ik), *adj.* **1.** of a school or college. **2.** pertaining to areas of study that are not vocational or applied. **3.** not practical or directly useful; theoretical. —**ac'a•dem'i•cal•ly,** *adv.*

ac•a•de•mi•cian (ak'ə də mish'ən, ə kad'ə-), *n.* a member of an association for the advancement of arts, sciences, or letters.

a•cad•e•my (ə kad'ə mē), *n., pl.* -**mies.** **1.** a secondary school, esp. a private one. **2.** a school or college for special instruction or training. **3.** an association for the advancement of arts, sciences, or letters. [< L < Gk *akadémeia* name of the garden where Plato taught]

a•can•thus (ə kan'thəs), *n., pl.* -**thus•es, -thi** (-thī). **1.** a plant of the Mediterranean region, having spiny or toothed leaves. **2.** an architectural ornament resembling the leaves of the acanthus.

a cap•pel•la (ä' kə pel'ə), *adv., adj.* without instrumental accompaniment.

A•ca•pul•co (ak'ə pōōl'kō, ä'kə-), *n.* a seaport and resort in SW Mexico. 456,700.

ac•cede (ak sēd'), *v.i.,* -**ced•ed, -ced•ing.** **1.** to give one's consent; agree. **2.** to assume an office, title, or dignity.

ac•cel•er•ate (ak sel'ə rāt'), *v.,* -**at•ed, -at•ing.** —*v.t.* **1.** to increase the speed of. **2.** to hasten the occurrence of. —*v.i.* **3.** to move or go faster. —**ac•cel'er•a'tion,** *n.*

ac•cel'er•a'tor, *n.* **1.** a foot pedal used to control the speed of a motor vehicle. **2.** a device, as a cyclotron, that produces high-energy particles.

ac•cent (*n.* ak'sent; *v. also* ak sent'), *n.* **1.** prominence of a syllable in terms of differential loudness or pitch. **2.** degree of prominence of a syllable within a word or of a word within a phrase. **3.** a mark indicating stress or vowel quality. **4.** a distinctive mode of pronunciation. **5.** greater emphasis on one musical tone than on surrounding tones. —*v.t.* **6.** to pronounce with prominence. **7.** to give emphasis to.

ac•cen•tu•ate (ak sen′chōō āt′), *v.t.*, **-at•ed, -at•ing. 1.** to give emphasis to. **2.** to pronounce with an accent. —**ac•cen′tu•a′tion,** *n.*

ac•cept (ak sept′), *v.t.* **1.** to receive willingly or with approval. **2.** to answer affirmatively to. **3.** to undertake the duties, responsibilities, or honors of. **4.** to admit formally, as to a club. **5.** to regard as true. **6.** to agree to pay, as a draft.

ac•cept′a•ble, *adj.* **1.** capable or worthy of being accepted. **2.** barely adequate or satisfactory. —**ac•cept′a•bil′i•ty,** *n.* —**ac•cept′a•bly,** *adv.*

ac•cept′ance, *n.* **1.** the act of accepting or state of being accepted or acceptable. **2.** a pledge to pay an order, draft, or bill of exchange.

ac′cep•ta′tion (-tā′shən), *n.* the usual or accepted meaning of a word.

ac•cept′ed, *adj.* generally approved.

ac•cess (ak′ses), *n.* **1.** the ability or right to enter, approach, or use. **2.** a way or means of approach. **3.** a sudden outburst, as of rage. —*v.t.* **4.** to gain access to. **5.** to locate (data) for transfer from one part of a computer system to another.

ac•ces′si•ble, *adj.* easy to approach, enter, use, or obtain. —**ac•ces′si•bil′i•ty,** *n.* —**ac•ces′si•bly,** *adv.*

ac•ces′sion (-sesh′ən), *n.* **1.** the act of acceding to an office, title, or dignity. **2.** an increase by addition. **3.** something added.

ac•ces′so•ry (-ses′ə rē), *n.*, *pl.* **-ries,** *adj.* —*n.* **1.** a supplementary part or object. **2.** *Law.* one who, although absent, assists another in committing a felony. —*adj.* **3.** supplementary; subsidiary. **4.** *Law.* giving aid as an accessory.

ac•ci•dent (ak′si dənt), *n.* **1.** an unintentional and unfortunate happening. **2.** something that happens unexpectedly. **3.** chance; fortune. —**ac′ci•den′tal** (-den′tl), *adj.* —**ac′ci•den′tal•ly,** *adv.*

ac•claim (ə klām′), *v.t.* **1.** to greet or salute with loud approval. —*n.* **2.** loud approval.

ac•cla•ma•tion (ak′lə mā′shən), *n.* **1.** a loud demonstration of welcome or approval. —*Idiom.* **2. by acclamation,** by a majority voice vote or applause.

ac•cli•mate (ak′lə māt′, ə klī′mit), *v.t.*, *v.i.*, **-mat•ed, -mat•ing.** to accustom or become accustomed to a new climate or environment. —**ac′cli•ma′tion,** *n.*

ac•cli•ma•tize (ə klī′mə tīz′), *v.t.*, *v.i.*, **-tized, -tiz•ing.** to acclimate. —**ac•cli′ma•ti•za′tion,** *n.*

ac•cliv•i•ty (ə kliv′i tē), *n.*, *pl.* **-ties.** an upward slope.

ac•co•lade (ak′ə lād′, -läd′), *n.* an award, honor, or laudatory notice.

ac•com•mo•date (ə kom′ə dāt′), *v.t.*, **-dat•ed, -dat•ing. 1.** to do a favor for. **2.** to provide with something needed or wanted. **3.** to provide with lodging. **4.** to have or make room for. **5.** to adapt or adjust.

ac•com′mo•dat′ing, *adj.* eager to help or please.

ac•com′mo•da′tion, *n.* **1.** the act of accommodating or state of being accommodated. **2.** adjustment or reconciliation. **3.** something that supplies a need or want. **4.** Usu.,**-tions. a.** lodging. **b.** space, as a seat or berth, on a public conveyance.

ac•com•pa•ni•ment (ə kum′pə ni mənt, ə kump′ni-), *n.* **1.** something added, as for ornament. **2.** a musical part supporting the principal part.

ac•com•pa•ny, *v.t.*, **-nied, -ny•ing. 1.** to go, exist, or occur with. **2.** to perform an accompaniment to or for. —**ac•com′pa•nist,** *n.*

ac•com•plice (ə kom′plis), *n.* a person who helps another in a crime.

ac•com•plish (ə kom′plish), *v.t.* to bring to a successful conclusion.

ac•com′plished, *adj.* **1.** successfully completed. **2.** skilled; expert.

ac•com′plish•ment, *n.* **1.** the act of accomplishing. **2.** something accomplished; achievement. **3.** a social grace or skill.

ac•cord (ə kôrd′), *v.i.* **1.** to agree. —*v.t.* **2.** to make agree or correspond. **3.** to grant; bestow. —*n.* **4.**

agreement; harmony. —*Idiom.* **5. of one′s own accord,** voluntarily.

ac•cord′ance, *n.* **1.** agreement; conformity. **2.** the act of granting. —**ac•cord′ant,** *adj.*

ac•cord′ing•ly, *adv.* **1.** in accordance. **2.** therefore.

accord′ing to′, *prep.* **1.** in accord with. **2.** as stated by.

ac•cor•di•on (ə kôr′dē ən), *n.* **1.** a portable musical instrument with a keyboard and a bellows for forcing air through reeds. —*adj.* **2.** having folds like the bellows of an accordion: *accordion pleats.*

ac•cost (ə kôst′, ə kost′), *v.t.* to approach, esp. with a greeting, question, or remark.

ac•count (ə kount′), *n.* **1.** a report of events or situations. **2.** an explanatory statement. **3.** reason or basis. **4.** importance or worth. **5.** an amount of money deposited with a bank. **6.** a statement of financial transactions. **7.** a business relation in which credit is used. —*v.i.* **8.** to give an explanation. —*v.t.* **9.** to consider as; regard. —*Idiom.* **10. on account,** as partial payment. **11. on account of,** because of. **12. on no account,** absolutely not. **13. take into account,** to take into consideration.

ac•count′a•ble, *adj.* **1.** responsible; answerable. **2.** explicable. —**ac•count′a•bil′i•ty,** *n.*

ac•count′ant, *n.* a person whose profession is accounting.

ac•count′ing, *n.* the organizing, maintaining, and auditing of financial records.

ac•cou•ter or **-tre** (ə kōō′tər), *v.t.* to equip or outfit.

ac•cou′ter•ments or **-tre•ments** (-trə mənts, -tər-), *n.pl.* personal clothing or equipment, esp. of a soldier.

Ac•cra (ak′rə, ə krä′), *n.* the capital of Ghana. 867,459.

ac•cred•it (ə kred′it), *v.t.* **1.** to certify as meeting official requirements. **2.** to provide with credentials. **3.** to attribute; credit. —**ac•cred′i•ta′tion,** *n.*

ac•cre•tion (ə krē′shən), *n.* **1.** an increase by growth or addition. **2.** an added part; addition. **3.** the growing together of parts into a whole.

ac•crue (ə krōō′), *v.i.*, **-crued, -cru•ing. 1.** to result from natural growth. **2.** to be added as a periodic gain, as interest on money. —**ac•cru′al,** *n.*

acct., account.

ac•cul•tur•a•tion (ə kul′chə rā′shən), *n.* adoption of the cultural traits or patterns of another group, esp. a dominant one.

ac•cu•mu•late (ə kyōō′myə lāt′), *v.t.*, *v.i.*, **-lat•ed, -lat•ing.** to gather or collect, esp. by degrees; amass or mount up. —**ac•cu′mu•la′tion,** *n.*

ac•cu•rate (ak′yər it), *adj.* **1.** free from error. **2.** carefully precise. —**ac′cu•ra•cy, ac′cu•rate•ness,** *n.* —**ac′cu•rate•ly,** *adv.*

ac•curs•ed (ə kûr′sid, ə kûrst′) also **ac•curst** (ə kûrst′), *adj.* **1.** under a curse. **2.** damnable. —**ac•curs′ed•ness,** *n.*

ac•cu•sa•tion (ak′yōō zā′shən), *n.* **1.** a charge of guilt or blame. **2.** the act of accusing. —**ac•cu•sa•to•ry** (ə kyōō′zə tôr′ē), *adj.*

ac•cu•sa•tive (ə kyōō′zə tiv), *adj.* **1.** designating a grammatical case that indicates the object of a verb or preposition. —*n.* **2.** the accusative case.

ac•cuse (ə kyōōz′), *v.t.*, **-cused, -cus•ing. 1.** to charge with a fault, offense, or crime. **2.** to blame. —**ac•cus′er,** *n.*

ac•cus•tom (ə kus′təm), *v.t.* to familiarize by custom or use; habituate.

ac•cus′tomed, *adj.* customary; habitual.

AC/DC (ā′sē dē′sē), alternating current or direct current.

ace (ās), *n.*, *v.*, **aced, ac•ing.** —*n.* **1.** a playing card with one spot. **2.** a point, as in tennis, made on a serve that an opponent fails to touch. **3.** a fighter pilot who downs a number of enemy planes. **4.** an expert. —*v.t.* **5.** to score an ace against (an opponent). **6.** *Slang.* to defeat (usu. fol. by *out*). **7.** *Slang.* to receive a grade of A in or on.

A•cel•da•ma (ə sel′də mə, ə kel′-), *n.* the place

near Jerusalem purchased with the bribe Judas took for betraying Jesus. Acts 1:18, 19.

ac•er•bate (as′ər bāt′), *v.t.*, **-bat•ed, -bat•ing. 1.** to make sour or bitter. **2.** to exasperate or embitter.

a•cer•bic (ə sûr′bik), *adj.* **1.** sour or bitter in taste. **2.** sharp or bitter, as in expression. —**a•cer′bi•ty,** *n.*

a•ce•ta•min•o•phen (ə sē′tə min′ə fən), *n.* a crystalline substance used to reduce pain or fever.

ac•e•tate (as′i tāt′), *n.* **1.** a salt or ester of acetic acid. **2.** a synthetic material derived from the acetic ester of cellulose.

a•ce•tic (ə sē′tik), *adj.* of or producing vinegar or acetic acid.

ace′tic ac′id, *n.* a pungent liquid, the essential constituent of vinegar.

ac•e•tone (as′i tōn′), *n.* a volatile, flammable liquid used as a solvent.

a•cet•y•lene (ə set′l ēn′), *n.* a colorless gas used for lighting and in welding.

a•ce′tyl•sal•i•cyl′ic ac′id (ə sēt′l sal′ə sil′ik), *n.* ASPIRIN (def. 1).

ache (āk), *v.,* **ached, ach•ing,** *n.* —*v.i.* **1.** to have a continuous dull pain. **2.** to yearn; long. —*n.* **3.** a continuous dull pain. —**ach′y,** *adj.,* **-i•er, -i•est.**

a•chene (ā kēn′, ə kēn′), *n.* a small, dry, one-seeded fruit.

a•chieve (ə chēv′), *v.t.,* **a•chieved, a•chiev•ing. 1.** to bring to a successful end. **2.** to get by hard work or effort. —**a•chieve′ment,** *n.* —**a•chiev′er,** *n.*

A•chil•les (ə kil′ēz), *n.* the greatest Greek warrior in the Trojan War and hero of the *Iliad*, killed by Paris.

Achil′les (or **Achil′les′**) **heel′,** *n.* a weak or vulnerable spot.

Achil′les ten′don, *n.* the tendon joining the calf muscles to the heel bone.

ach•ro•mat•ic (ak′rə mat′ik), *adj.* **1.** free from color. **2.** able to emit, transmit, or receive light without separating it into colors.

ac•id (as′id), *n.* **1.** a compound usu. having a sour taste and capable of neutralizing alkalis and turning blue litmus paper red. **2.** a substance with a sour taste. —*adj.* **3.** of an acid. **4.** sour to the taste. **5.** sharp, biting, or ill-natured; caustic. —**a•cid•ic** (ə-sid′ik), *adj.* —**a•cid′i•ty,** *n.*

a•cid•i•fy (ə sid′ə fī′), *v.t., v.i.,* **-fied, -fy•ing. 1.** to convert into an acid. **2.** to make or become sour.

ac•i•do•sis (as′i dō′sis), *n.* a blood condition in which the bicarbonate concentration is below normal.

ac′id rain′, *n.* rain containing acid-forming chemicals, resulting from the release into the atmosphere of industrial pollutants.

ac′id test′, *n.* a severe, conclusive test.

a•cid•u•lous (ə sij′ə ləs), *adj.* **1.** slightly sour. **2.** sharp; caustic.

-acious, a suffix meaning tending to or abounding in (*tenacious*).

-acity, a suffix meaning tendency toward or abundance in (*tenacity*).

ac•knowl•edge (ak nol′ij), *v.t.,* **-edged, -edg•ing. 1.** to admit to be real or true. **2.** to show recognition or realization of. **3.** to recognize the authority or claims of. **4.** to express appreciation for. **5.** to make known the receipt of. —**ac•knowl′edg•ment, ac•knowl′edge•ment,** *n.*

ACLU, American Civil Liberties Union.

ac•me (ak′mē), *n., pl.* **-mes.** the highest point or stage; peak.

ac•ne (ak′nē), *n.* a disorder of the sebaceous glands characterized by pimples, esp. on the face.

ac•o•lyte (ak′ə līt′), *n.* **1.** an altar attendant in public worship; altar boy. **2.** an attendant or assistant.

ac•o•nite (ak′ə nīt′), *n.* a plant with irregular flowers usu. in loose clusters, including species with poisonous and medicinal properties.

a•corn (ā′kôrn, ā′kərn), *n.* the typically ovoid fruit or nut of an oak.

a′corn squash′, *n.* an acorn-shaped variety of winter squash with dark green ridged skin.

a•cous•tic (ə kōō′stik) also **-ti•cal,** *adj.* **1.** pertain-

ing to hearing, sound, or the science of sound. **2.** designed for controlling sound: *acoustic tile.* **3.** sounded without electric or electronic enhancement: *an acoustic guitar.* —**a•cous′ti•cal•ly,** *adv.*

a•cous′tics, *n.* **1.** (*used with a sing. v.*) the branch of physics that deals with sound. **2.** (*used with a pl. v.*) the qualities of a room, auditorium, etc., that determine the audibility of sounds in it.

ac•quaint (ə kwānt′), *v.t.* **1.** to make familiar or aware. **2.** to provide with knowledge; inform.

ac•quaint′ance, *n.* **1.** a person whom one knows casually. **2.** personal knowledge. —**ac•quaint′ance•ship′,** *n.*

ac•qui•esce (ak′wē es′), *v.i.,* **-esced, -esc•ing.** to comply silently or without protest. —**ac′qui•es′cence,** *n.* —**ac′qui•es′cent,** *adj.*

ac•quire (ə kwīʳr′), *v.t.,* **-quired, -quir•ing. 1.** to get possession of. **2.** to gain through one's efforts. —**ac•quir′a•ble,** *adj.* —**ac•quire′ment,** *n.*

ac•qui•si•tion (ak′wə zish′ən), *n.* **1.** the act of acquiring. **2.** something acquired.

ac•quis•i•tive (ə kwiz′i tiv), *adj.* tending or seeking to acquire, often greedily. —**ac•quis′i•tive•ness,** *n.*

ac•quit (ə kwit′), *v.t.,* **-quit•ted, -quit•ting. 1.** to declare not guilty of a crime or offense. **2.** to conduct (oneself); behave. **3.** to release from an obligation. —**ac•quit′tal,** *n.*

a•cre (ā′kər), *n.* a unit of land measure equal to 43,560 square feet.

a′cre•age (-ij), *n.* extent or area in acres; acres collectively.

ac•rid (ak′rid), *adj.* **1.** harshly or bitterly pungent in taste or smell. **2.** sharply stinging or bitter; caustic: *acrid remarks.* —**a•crid•i•ty** (ə krid′i tē), **ac′rid•ness,** *n.* —**ac′rid•ly,** *adv.*

ac•ri•mo•ny (ak′rə mō′nē), *n.* sharpness, harshness, or bitterness of nature, speech, or disposition. —**ac′ri•mo′ni•ous,** *adj.*

ac•ro•bat (ak′rə bat′), *n.* a performer of gymnastic feats requiring agility, balance, and coordination. —**ac′ro•bat′ic,** *adj.*

ac′ro•bat′ics, *n.* (*used with a pl. v.*) **1.** the feats of an acrobat. **2.** any feats requiring great agility: *verbal acrobatics.*

ac•ro•nym (ak′rə nim), *n.* a word, as *laser,* formed from the initial letters or groups of letters of words in a name or phrase.

ac•ro•pho•bi•a (ak′rə fō′bē ə), *n.* a pathological fear of heights.

a•crop•o•lis (ə krop′ə lis), *n.* **1.** the citadel or high fortified area of an ancient Greek city. **2. the Acropolis,** the citadel of Athens.

a•cross (ə krôs′, ə kros′), *prep.* **1.** from one side to the other of. **2.** on or to the other side of. **3.** into contact with, usu. by accident. **4.** transversely over; crosswise of. —*adv.* **5.** from one side to another. **6.** on the other side. **7.** crosswise; transversely.

across′-the-board′, *adj.* **1.** applying to all members or categories. **2.** (of a bet, esp. in a horse race) covering win, place, and show.

a•cros•tic (ə krô′stik, ə kros′tik), *n.* a series of written lines or verses in which the first, last, or other particular letters form a word or phrase.

a•cryl•ic (ə kril′ik), *n.* **1.** a paint with an acrylic resin as the vehicle. **2.** any of a group of synthetic textile fibers, as Orlon. **3.** ACRYLIC RESIN.

acryl′ic res′in, *n.* any of a group of thermoplastic resins used to make paints, plastics, etc.

act (akt), *n.* **1.** something done; deed. **2.** the process of doing. **3.** a law, decree, edict, or statute. **4.** one of the main divisions of a play or opera. **5.** a short performance in a variety show. **6.** a display of insincere behavior. —*v.i.* **7.** to do something; carry out an action. **8.** to carry out a particular function; serve. **9.** to produce an effect. **10.** to conduct oneself; behave. **11.** to pretend or feign. **12.** to perform as an actor. —*v.t.* **13.** to perform (a dramatic role) on a stage. **14. act up, a.** to malfunction. **b.** to behave willfully.

ACTH, a pituitary hormone that stimulates the production of steroids in the adrenal cortex. [*a*(dreno)*c*(ortico)*t*(ropic) *h*(ormone)]

act·ing, *adj.* **1.** serving temporarily, esp. as a substitute during another's absence. —*n.* **2.** the art, profession, or activity of an actor.

ac·ti·nide se'ries (ak'tə nīd'), *n.* the series of radioactive elements whose atomic numbers range from 89 (actinium) through 103 (lawrencium).

ac·tin·i·um (ak tin'ē əm), *n.* a radioactive, silver-white metallic element. *Symbol:* Ac; *at. no.:* 89; *at. wt.:* 227.

ac·tion (ak'shən), *n.* **1.** the process of acting or the state of being active. **2.** an act or deed. **3. actions,** behavior; conduct. **4.** energetic activity. **5.** effect or influence. **6.** the mechanism by which something, as a gun, is operated. **7.** military combat. **8.** an event or series of events that form a literary or dramatic plot. **9.** a legal proceeding. —*Proverb.* **10. Actions speak louder than words,** deeds are more important than what is said. —**ac'tion·less,** *adj.*

ac'tion·a·ble, *adj.* furnishing grounds for a lawsuit.

ac·ti·vate (ak'tə vāt'), *v.t.,* **-vat·ed, -vat·ing. 1.** to make active. **2.** *Physics.* to induce radioactivity in. **3.** to aerate (sewage) in order to accelerate decomposition. **4.** to place (a military unit) on an active status. —ac'ti·va'tion, *n.*

ac'tivated car'bon, *n.* a form of carbon having very fine pores, used chiefly for adsorbing gases or solutes. Also called **ac'tivated char'coal.**

ac·tive (ak'tiv), *adj.* **1.** engaged in action or activity. **2.** being in existence, progress, or motion. **3.** giving rise to action or change. **4.** agile; nimble. **5.** characterized by current activity, participation, or use. **6.** noting the voice of a verb having a subject that performs the action. —*n.* **7.** the active voice. —**ac'tive·ly,** *adv.*

ac'tiv·ism, *n.* the doctrine or practice of vigorous action to achieve political or social goals. —**ac'tiv·ist,** *n., adj.*

ac·tiv'i·ty (-i tē), *n., pl.* **-ties. 1.** the state or quality of being active. **2.** energetic action; animation. **3.** a specific deed, action, occupation, or sphere of action.

ac·tor (ak'tər), *n.* a person who acts in stage plays or motion pictures.

ac'tress (-tris), *n.* a woman who acts in stage plays or motion pictures.

Acts' of the Apos'tles, *n.* a book of the New Testament. Also called **Acts.**

ac·tu·al (ak'chōō əl), *adj.* **1.** existing in fact or reality. **2.** existing at the present time. —**ac'tu·al'i·ty,** *n., pl.* **-ties.** —**ac'tu·al·ly,** *adv.*

ac'tu·al·ize', *v.t.,* **-ized, -iz·ing.** to make actual or real; turn into action or fact. —**ac'tu·al·i·za'tion,** *n.*

ac·tu·ar·y (ak'chōō er'ē), *n., pl.* **-ar·ies.** a person who computes insurance premium rates, risks, etc. —**ac'tu·ar'i·al,** *adj.*

ac'tu·ate' (-āt'), *v.t.,* **-at·ed, -at·ing. 1.** to incite to action. **2.** to put into action. —**ac'tu·a'tion,** *n.* —**ac'tu·a'tor,** *n.*

a·cu·i·ty (ə kyōō'i tē), *n.* sharpness of perception.

a·cu·men (ə kyōō'mən), *n.* keen insight; shrewdness.

ac·u·punc·ture (ak'yōō pungk'chər), *n.* a Chinese medical practice that treats illness or relieves pain by the insertion of needles at specified sites of the body. —ac'u·punc'tur·ist, *n.*

a·cute (ə kyōōt'), *adj.* **1.** sharp or severe: *acute pain.* **2.** extremely serious; critical. **3.** (of disease) brief and severe. **4.** penetrating in insight or perception. **5.** extremely sensitive: *acute eyesight.* **6.** (of an angle) less than 90°. —**a·cute'ly,** *adv.* —**a·cute'ness,** *n.*

acute' ac'cent, *n.* a mark (´) used to indicate vowel quality or word stress.

ad (ad), *n.* an advertisement.

A.D. or **AD,** in the year of the Lord (used with dates): *Charlemagne was born in* A.D. 742. [< L *annō Dominī*] —**Usage.** A.D. is usu. placed before a date: *The Roman conquest of Britain began in* A.D. *43.* The abbreviation B.C. is always placed after a date.

ad·age (ad'ij), *n.* a traditional saying; proverb.

a·da·gio (ə dä'jō, -zhē ō'), *adv., adj., n., pl.* **-gios.**

—*adv.* **1.** *Music.* slowly. —*adj.* **2.** *Music.* slow. —*n.* **3.** *Music.* an adagio movement. **4.** a technically demanding ballet duet or trio. [< It, for *ad agio* at ease]

Ad·am (ad'əm), *n.* the first man, husband of Eve. Gen. 2:7; 5:1-5.

ad·a·mant (ad'ə mənt), *adj.* **1.** utterly unyielding; inflexible. —*n.* **2.** a legendary stone of impenetrable hardness. —**ad'a·mant·ly,** *adv.*

Ad·ams (ad'əmz), *n.* **1. Abigail (Smith),** 1744–1818, U.S. social and political figure (wife of John Adams). **2. John,** 1735–1826, 2nd president of the U.S. 1797–1801: a leader in the American Revolution. **3. John Quincy,** 1767–1848, 6th president of the U.S. 1825–29 (son of John Adams). **4. Samuel,** 1722–1803, a leader in the American Revolution.

Ad'am's ap'ple, *n.* a projection of the thyroid cartilage at the front of the neck.

a·dapt (ə dapt'), *v.t., v.i.* to adjust or become adjusted to new requirements or conditions. —**a·dapt'a·ble,** *adj.* —**a·dapt'a·bil'i·ty,** *n.* —**ad·ap·ta·tion** (ad'əp tā'shən), *n.*

a·dapt'er or **a·dap'tor,** *n.* **1.** a connector for joining parts of different sizes or designs. **2.** an accessory to convert a machine, tool, or part to a new use.

add (ad), *v.t.* **1.** to unite or join so as to increase in number, quantity, size, or importance. **2.** to find the sum of. **3.** to say or write further. —*v.i.* **4.** to perform arithmetic addition. **5.** to be or serve as an addition. **6. add up,** to seem reasonable. **7. ~ up to,** to amount to; signify.

ADD, attention deficit disorder.

Ad·dams (ad'əmz), *n.* **Jane,** 1860–1935, U.S. social worker.

ad·dend (ad'end, ə dend'), *n.* a number to be added to another.

ad·den'dum (-dəm), *n., pl.* **-da** (-də). **1.** an addition. **2.** an appendix to a book.

ad·der (ad'ər), *n.* **1.** the common European viper. **2.** a snake resembling the viper.

ad·dict (*v.* ə dikt'; *n.* ad'ikt), *v.t.* **1.** to cause to become physiologically dependent on a drug. **2.** to abandon (oneself) to something compulsively or obsessively. —*n.* **3.** one who is addicted, esp. to a drug. —**ad·dic'tion,** *n.* —**ad·dic'tive,** *adj.*

Ad·dis A·ba·ba (ad'is ab'ə bə), *n.* the capital of Ethiopia. 1,412,575.

ad·di·tion (ə dish'ən), *n.* **1.** the act or process of adding. **2.** the process of uniting numbers to find their sum. **3.** something added. —*Idiom.* **4. in addition,** besides; also. **5. in addition to,** as well as; besides. —**ad·di'tion·al,** *adj.* —**ad·di'tion·al·ly,** *adv.*

ad·di·tive (ad'i tiv), *n.* **1.** a substance added to another to alter or improve its quality. —*adj.* **2.** characterized or produced by addition.

ad·dle (ad'l), *v.t., v.i.,* **-dled, -dling.** to make or become confused.

add'-on', *n.* **1.** a device or unit added to equipment or a building. **2.** anything added on, as a charge, tax, or provision.

ad·dress (*n.* ə dres', ad'res; *v.* ə dres'), *n.* **1.** the place where a person or organization is located. **2.** the location and name of the intended recipient indicated on a piece of mail. **3.** a formal speech. **4.** skillful management. **5.** a code that designates the location of information stored in computer memory. —*v.t.* **6.** to direct a speech or statement to. **7.** to use a specified form or title in speaking or writing to. **8.** to put the directions for delivery on. **9.** to direct the energy or efforts of (oneself).

ad·dress·ee (ad're sē', ə dre-), *n., pl.* **-ees.** one to whom mail is addressed.

ad·duce (ə dōōs', ə dyōōs'), *v.t.,* **-duced, -duc·ing.** to bring forward, as in evidence.

Ad·e·laide (ad'l ād'), *n.* a city in S Australia. 993,100.

A·den (äd'n, ād'n), *n.* **1.** the economic capital of the Republic of Yemen. 318,000. **2. Gulf of,** an arm of the Arabian Sea, S of Arabia.

ad•e•nine (ad'n in, -ēn', -īn'), *n.* a purine base that is a fundamental component of DNA and RNA.
ad•e•noids (ad'n oidz'), *n.pl.* growths of lymphoid tissue in the upper throat. —**ad'e•noi'dal,** *adj.*
a•dept (*adj.* ə dept'; *n.* ad'ept, ə dept'), *adj.* **1.** very skilled; expert. —*n.* **ad•ept 2.** a skilled person; expert. —**a•dept'ly,** *adv.* —**a•dept'ness,** *n.*
ad•e•quate (ad'i kwit), *adj.* **1.** fully sufficient for a requirement or purpose. **2.** barely sufficient or suitable. —**ad'e•qua•cy** (-kwə sē), *n.* —**ad'e•quate•ly,** *adv.*
ADHD, attention deficit hyperactivity disorder.
ad•here (ad hēr'), *v.i.,* **-hered, -her•ing. 1.** to stick fast; cling. **2.** to hold closely or firmly. **3.** to be devoted in support or allegiance. —**ad•her'ence,** *n.* —**ad•her'ent,** *n., adj.*
ad•he•sion (ad hē'zhən), *n.* **1.** the act or state of adhering. **2.** the abnormal union of adjacent bodily tissues.
ad•he'sive (-siv, -ziv), *adj.* **1.** coated with a sticky substance. **2.** tending to adhere; sticky. —*n.* **3.** an adhesive substance or material.
adhe'sive tape', *n.* tape coated with an adhesive substance, as for holding a bandage in place.
ad hoc (ad hok', hōk'), *adj., adv.* for a particular purpose or end: *an ad hoc committee.*
a•dieu (ə dōō', ə dyōō'), *interj., n., pl.* **a•dieus, a•dieux** (ə dōōz', ə dyōōz'). good-bye. [< MF, = *a* (< L *ad* to) + *dieu* (< L *deus* god)]
ad in•fi•ni•tum (ad in'fə nī'təm), *adv.* without limit; endlessly.
ad•i•os (ad'ē ōs', ä'dē-), *interj.* good-bye. [< Sp]
ad•i•pose (ad'ə pōs'), *adj.* consisting of, resembling, or pertaining to fat; fatty.
Ad'i•ron'dack Moun'tains (ad'ə ron'dak, ad'-), *n.pl.* a mountain range in NE New York. Also called **Ad'i•ron'dacks.**
adj., 1. adjective. **2.** adjustment. **3.** adjutant.
ad•ja•cent (ə jā'sənt), *adj.* lying near or contiguous; nearby or adjoining. —**ad•ja'cen•cy,** *n.* —**ad•ja'cent•ly,** *adv.*
ad•jec•tive (aj'ik tiv), *n.* a word functioning as a modifier of a noun. —**ad'jec•ti'val** (-tī'vəl), *adj.* —**ad'jec•ti'val•ly,** *adv.*
ad•join (ə join'), *v.t.* **1.** to be close or next to. —*v.i.* **2.** to be close or in contact. —**ad•join'ing,** *adj.*
ad•journ (ə jûrn'), *v.t.* **1.** to suspend to a future time, another place, or indefinitely. —*v.i.* **2.** to postpone, suspend, or transfer a proceeding. **3.** to go to another place. —**ad•journ'ment,** *n.*
ad•judge (ə juj'), *v.t.,* **-judged, -judg•ing. 1.** to award judicially. **2.** to decide by judicial procedure. **3.** to deem; consider.
ad•ju•di•cate (ə jōō'di kat'), *v.t.,* **-cat•ed, -cat•ing.** to settle or determine (an issue or dispute) judicially. —**ad•ju'di•ca'tion,** *n.* —**ad•ju'di•ca'tive** (-kā'tiv, -kə tiv), *adj.* —**ad•ju'di•ca'tor,** *n.*
ad•junct (aj'ungkt), *n.* something added to another but not essential to it.
ad•jure (ə jōōr'), *v.t.,* **-jured, -jur•ing. 1.** to charge or command solemnly. **2.** to entreat earnestly. —**ad•ju•ra•tion** (aj'ōō rā'shən), *n.*
ad•just (ə just'), *v.t.* **1.** to change so as to fit, correspond, or conform. **2.** to put in working order or in a proper state. **3.** to settle satisfactorily. **4.** to determine the amount to be paid in settlement of (an insurance claim). —*v.i.* **5.** to adapt oneself. —**ad•just'a•ble,** *adj.* —**ad•just'er,** **ad•jus'tor,** *n.* —**ad•just'ment,** *n.*
ad•ju•tant (aj'ə tənt), *n.* a military staff officer who assists a commanding officer. **2.** an assistant.
ad lib (ad lib', ad'), *n.* **1.** something improvised in speech, music, etc. —*adv.* **2.** at one's pleasure; without restriction. **3.** as needed; freely.
ad-lib (ad lib', ad'-), *v.,* **-libbed, -lib•bing,** *adj.* —*v.t., v.i.* **1.** to improvise (words, music, etc.). —*adj.* **2.** impromptu; extemporaneous.
Adm. or **ADM, 1.** admiral. **2.** admiralty.
adm., 1. administration. **2.** administrative. **3.** administrator.

ad•man (ad'man', -mən), *n., pl.* **-men.** a person whose profession is writing, designing, or selling advertisements.
ad•min•is•ter (ad min'ə stər), *v.t.* **1.** to direct or manage. **2.** to give out, esp. formally; dispense. **3.** to give remedially. **4.** to tender (an oath). **5.** *Law.* to manage or dispose of (an estate).
ad•min'is•trate' (-strāt'), *v.t.,* **-trat•ed, -trat•ing.** to administer.
ad•min'is•tra'tion, *n.* **1.** management, as of a government or business. **2.** (*often cap.*) the executive branch of a government. **3.** the period during which an administrator or body of administrators serves. **4.** *Law.* the management of an estate. **5.** the act of administering. —**ad•min'is•tra'tive,** *adj.*
ad•min'is•tra'tor, *n.* **1.** a person who administers. **2.** *Law.* a person appointed to administer an estate.
ad•mi•ra•ble (ad'mər ə bəl), *adj.* worthy of admiration. —**ad'mi•ra•bly,** *adv.*
ad•mi•ral (ad'mər əl), *n.* **1.** the commander in chief of a fleet. **2.** a naval officer of the second-highest rank.
ad'mi•ral•ty, *n., pl.* **-ties. 1.** the department of state having charge of naval affairs, as in Great Britain. **2.** a court dealing with maritime questions.
ad•mire (ad mīr'), *v.t.,* **-mired, -mir•ing. 1.** to regard with pleasure, approval, and often wonder. **2.** to regard highly; respect. —**ad'mi•ra'tion** (-mə rā'shən), *n.* —**ad•mir'er,** *n.* —**ad•mir'ing•ly,** *adv.*
ad•mis•si•ble (ad mis'ə bəl), *adj.* capable of being admitted or allowed. —**ad•mis'si•bil'i•ty,** *n.*
ad•mis'sion, *n.* **1.** the act of admitting. **2.** right or permission to enter. **3.** the price paid for entrance. **4.** confession of a charge, error, or crime.
Admis'sion Day', *n.* any of several legal holidays set aside in various U.S. states to mark their admission into the Union.
ad•mit' (-mit'), *v.,* **-mit•ted, -mit•ting.** —*v.t.* **1.** to allow to enter. **2.** to permit to exercise a particular function. **3.** to concede as valid. **4.** to acknowledge; confess. **5.** to have capacity for. —*v.i.* **6.** to offer opportunity; allow: *It admits of no other interpretation.* —**ad•mit'tance,** *n.* —**ad•mit'ted•ly,** *adv.*
ad•mix (ad miks'), *v.t., v.i.* to add to or mingle with something else. —**ad•mix'ture** (-chər), *n.*
ad•mon•ish (ad mon'ish), *v.t.* **1.** to caution or advise against something. **2.** to reprove, esp. in a mild manner. —**ad•mo•ni•tion** (ad'mə nish'ən), *n.* —**ad•mon'i•to'ry** (-mon'i tôr'ē), *adj.*
ad nau•se•am (ad nô'zē əm), *adv.* to a sickening or disgusting degree.
a•do (ə dōō'), *n.* **1.** bustling activity; fuss.
a•do•be (ə dō'bē), *n., pl.* **-bes. 1.** sun-dried brick made of clay and straw. **2.** a silt or clay used to make bricks. **3.** a building constructed of adobe. [< Sp < Ar *al-tub* the brick]
ad•o•les•cence (ad'l es'əns), *n.* the transitional period between puberty and adulthood; youth. —**ad'o•les'cent,** *n., adj.*
A•do•ni•Be•zek (ə dō'nī bē'zek), *n.* a king in Judah who was captured by the Hebrews. Judg. 1:5–6.
A•don•is (ə don'is, ə dō'nis), *n.* **1.** a youth of Greek myth who was loved by Aphrodite. **2.** a very handsome young man.
a•dopt (ə dopt'), *v.t.* **1.** to take and use as one's own. **2.** to become the legal parent of (the child of another). **3.** to vote to accept. —**a•dopt'a•ble,** *adj.* —**a•dop'tion,** *n.* —**a•dop'tive,** *adj.*
a•dor•a•ble (ə dôr'ə bəl), *adj.* **1.** very charming. **2.** worthy of being adored. —**a•dor'a•bly,** *adv.*
a•dore' *v.t.,* **a•dored, a•dor•ing. 1.** to regard with the utmost love and respect. **2.** to worship. **3.** to like or admire very much. —**ad•o•ra•tion** (ad'ə rā'shən), *n.* —**a•dor'er,** *n.* —**a•dor'ing•ly,** *adv.*
a•dorn (ə dôrn'), *v.t.* **1.** to decorate with or as if with ornaments. **2.** to enhance. —**a•dorn'ment,** *n.*
ad•re•nal (ə drēn'l), *adj.* **1.** of or produced by the adrenal glands. **2.** situated near or on the kidneys.
adre'nal gland', *n.* one of a pair of ductless glands located above the kidneys.
a•dren•a•line (ə dren'l in), *n.* EPINEPHRINE.

A′dri•at′ic Sea′ (ā′drē at′ik, ā′drē-), *n.* an arm of the Mediterranean Sea between Italy and the Balkan Peninsula.

a•drift (ə drift′), *adj.*, *adv.* **1.** floating without anchor or mooring. **2.** without aim or direction.

a•droit (ə droit′), *adj.* **1.** manually dexterous. **2.** cleverly skillful or resourceful. —**a•droit′ly**, *adv.* —**a•droit′ness**, *n.*

ad•sorb (ad sôrb′, -zôrb′), *v.t.* to hold (a gas, liquid, or dissolved substance) on a surface in a condensed layer. —**ad•sorb′ent**, *adj.*, *n.* —**ad•sorp′tion** (-sôrp′shən, -zôrp′-), *n.* —**ad•sorp′tive**, *adj.*

ad•u•late (aj′ə lāt′), *v.t.* to flatter or admire excessively. —**ad′u•la′tion**, *n.* —**ad′u•la•to′ry** (-lə tôr′ē), *adj.*

a•dult (ə dult′, ad′ult), *adj.* **1.** having attained maturity. **2.** of, befitting, or intended for adults. —*n.* **3.** a person who has attained maturity or legal age. **4.** a full-grown animal or plant. —**a•dult′hood**, *n.*

a•dul•ter•ant (ə dul′tər ənt), *n.* **1.** a substance that adulterates. —*adj.* **2.** adulterating.

a•dul′ter•ate′, *v.t.*, -at•ed, -at•ing. to make impure by adding inferior, alien, or less desirable materials or elements. —**a•dul′ter•a′tion**, *n.*

a•dul•ter•y (ə dul′tə rē), *n.*, *pl.* -ter•ies. voluntary sexual intercourse between a married person and someone other than the spouse. —**a•dul′ter•er**, *n.* —**a•dul′ter•ess**, *n.* —**a•dul′ter•ous**, *adj.*

ad•um•brate (a dum′brāt, ad′əm brāt′), *v.t.*, -brat•ed, -brat•ing. **1.** to outline sketchily. **2.** to foreshadow; prefigure. **3.** to darken or conceal partially. —**ad′um•bra′tion**, *n.*

adv., **1.** advance. **2.** adverb. **3.** adverbial. **4.** advertisement.

ad va•lo•rem (ad və lôr′əm), *adj.* fixed at a percentage of the value: *an ad valorem tax.*

ad•vance (ad vans′, -väns′), *v.*, -vanced, -vanc•ing, *n.*, *adj.* —*v.t.* **1.** to move, send, or bring forward. **2.** to present for consideration; propose. **3.** to further the development, progress, or prospects of. **4.** to raise in rank; promote. **5.** to raise in rate or amount; increase. **6.** to supply (money or goods) on credit. —*v.i.* **7.** to go forward; proceed. **8.** to make progress; improve. **9.** to rise, as in importance or status. —*n.* **10.** a forward movement. **11.** progress; improvement. **12.** a promotion. **13.** Usu., -vances. attempts made to form an acquaintanceship, reach an agreement, or gain favor. **14.** a rise in price or value. **15.** something, as money, furnished on credit. —*adj.* **16.** going or placed before. **17.** made, given, or issued ahead of time. —**Idiom.** **18. in advance**, beforehand. —**ad•vance′ment**, *n.*

ad•vanced′, *adj.* **1.** beyond the beginning, elementary, or intermediate. **2.** far along in progress, development, or time.

advance′ man′, *n.* a person who makes advance arrangements for an event, esp. the appearance of a politician.

ad•van•tage (ad van′tij, -vän′-), *n.* **1.** a circumstance favorable to success. **2.** benefit; gain. **3.** a position of superiority. **4.** the first point in tennis scored after deuce. —**Idiom.** **5. take advantage of**, **a.** to make good use of. **b.** to impose upon, esp. by exploiting a weakness. —**ad′van•ta′geous** (-vən tā′jəs), *adj.* —**ad′van•ta′geous•ly**, *adv.*

ad•vent (ad′vent), *n.* **1.** an arrival; a coming. **2. a.** (*usu. cap.*) the coming of Christ. **b.** (*cap.*) the period beginning four Sundays before Christmas.

ad•ven•ti•tious (ad′vən tish′əs), *adj.* **1.** not inherent; extrinsic. **2.** appearing in an abnormal place, as a root on a stem. —**ad′ven•ti′tious•ly**, *adv.*

ad•ven•ture (ad ven′chər), *n.*, *v.*, -tured, -tur•ing. —*n.* **1.** an exciting and unusual experience. **2.** an uncertain and usu. risky undertaking. **3.** a commercial or financial venture. —*v.t.*, *v.i.* **4.** to risk or hazard. —**ad•ven′tur•ous**, **ad•ven′ture•some**, *adj.* —**ad•ven′tur•ous•ly**, *adv.*

ad•ven′tur•er, *n.* **1.** a person who has or seeks out adventures. **2.** SOLDIER OF FORTUNE. **3.** a person who unscrupulously seeks wealth or social position.

ad•verb (ad′vûrb), *n.* a word that modifies a verb, an adjective, or another adverb. —**ad•ver′bi•al**, *adj.*

ad•ver•sar•y (ad′vər ser′ē), *n.*, *pl.* -sar•ies. an opponent; enemy. —**ad′ver•sar′i•al**, *adj.*

ad•verse (ad vûrs′, ad′vûrs), *adj.* **1.** unfavorable or antagonistic. **2.** opposed to one's interests. —**ad•verse′ly**, *adv.*

ad•ver′si•ty (-vûr′si tē), *n.*, *pl.* -ties for 2. **1.** adverse fortune; misfortune. **2.** an adverse event or circumstance.

ad•vert (ad vûrt′), *v.i.* to turn or call the attention; refer.

ad•ver•tise (ad′vər tīz′), *v.*, -tised, -tis•ing. —*v.t.* **1.** to describe or announce (a product or service) publicly, esp. in order to promote sales. **2.** to call public attention to. —*v.i.* **3.** to seek something or offer goods or services through advertisements. —**ad′ver•tis′er**, *n.* —**ad′ver•tis′ing**, *n.*

ad•ver•tise•ment (ad′vər tīz′mənt, ad vûr′tismənt, -tiz-), *n.* a public announcement intended to advertise something.

ad′ver•to′ri•al (-tôr′ē əl), *n.* a printed advertisement that promotes a product while appearing to be an editorial or provide information.

ad•vice (ad vīs′), *n.* **1.** an opinion offered as a guide to action. **2.** a communication containing information.

advice′ and consent′, *n.* a phrase in the U.S. Constitution (Article II, Section 2) granting the U.S. Senate the power to approve or reject appointments and treaties made by a president.

ad•vis•a•ble (ad vī′zə bəl), *adj.* wise, as a course of action; prudent. —**ad•vis′a•bil′i•ty**, *n.*

ad•vise (ad vīz′), *v.t.*, -vised, -vis•ing. **1.** to give advice to. **2.** to recommend as desirable or prudent. **3.** to give information or notice to. —**ad•vis′er**, **ad•vi′sor**, *n.*

ad•vis′ed•ly, *adv.* after careful consideration; deliberately.

ad•vise′ment (-mənt), *n.* careful consideration: *The petition was taken under advisement.*

ad•vi′so•ry, *adj.*, *n.*, *pl.* -ries. —*adj.* **1.** giving advice. **2.** having the power or duty to advise. —*n.* **3.** a report on existing or predicted conditions, often with advice for dealing with them.

ad•vo•cate (*v.* ad′və kāt′; *n.* -kit, -kāt′), *v.*, -cat•ed, -cat•ing, *n.* —*v.t.* **1.** to support or urge by argument, esp. publicly. —*n.* **2.** a person who speaks or writes in support of a cause. **3.** a person who pleads for or in behalf of another. [< L *advocātus* legal counselor] —**ad′vo•ca•cy** (-kə sē), *n.*

advt., advertisement.

adz or **adze** (adz), *n.* an axlike tool with a curved head used esp. for dressing timbers.

Ae•ge′an Sea′ (i jē′ən), *n.* an arm of the Mediterranean Sea between Greece and Turkey.

ae•gis (ē′jis), *n.* **1.** sponsorship; auspices. **2.** protection; support.

Ae•ne•as (i nē′əs), *n.* a Trojan hero, the legendary ancestor of the Romans.

Ae•ne•id (i nē′id), a Latin epic poem by Virgil, recounting the adventures of Aeneas after the fall of Troy.

Ae•non (ē′non), *n.* a spring in Palestine where John the Baptist was baptizing during the ministry of Jesus in Judea. John 3:23.

ae•on (ē′ən, ē′on), *n.* EON.

aer•ate (âr′āt, ā′ə rāt′), *v.t.*, -at•ed, -at•ing. **1.** to expose to or supply with air. **2.** to charge or treat with air or a gas, esp. with carbon dioxide. —**aer•a′tion**, *n.* —**aer′a•tor**, *n.*

aer•i•al (âr′ē əl), *adj.* **1.** of, in, produced by, or done in the air. **2.** inhabiting or frequenting the air. **3.** growing in the air, as the adventitious roots of some trees. **4.** of aircraft. —*n.* **5.** a radio or television antenna. —**aer′i•al•ly**, *adv.*

aer′i•al•ist, *n.* a trapeze artist.

aer•ie (âr′ē, ēr′ē), *n.*, *pl.* -ies. the lofty nest of an eagle or other bird of prey.

aero- or **aer-,** a combining form meaning air or aircraft (aerodynamics).

aer•o•bat•ics (âr′ə bat′iks), n. (used with a pl. v.) stunts performed in flight by an aircraft.

aer•o•bic (â rō′bik), adj. 1. (of an organism or tissue) requiring oxygen to sustain life. 2. of aerobics.

aer•o′bics, n. (used with a sing. or pl. v.) exercises, as jogging, designed esp. to stimulate and strengthen the heart.

aer•o•dy•nam•ics (âr′ō dī nam′iks), n. the study of the motion of gases and of the effects of such motion on bodies in the gas. —aer′o•dy•nam′ic, adj. —aer′o•dy•nam′i•cal•ly, adv.

aer•o•nau•tics (âr′ə nô′tiks, -not′iks), n. the science or art of flight. —aer′o•nau′ti•cal, adj.

aer•o•plane (âr′ə plān′), n. Brit. AIRPLANE.

aer•o•sol (âr′ə sôl′, -sol′), n. 1. a system of colloidal particles dispersed in a gas. 2. a liquid substance sealed under pressure and released as a spray or foam.

aer•o•space (âr′ō spās′), n. 1. the atmosphere and the space beyond. —adj. 2. pertaining to missiles, spacecraft, etc., designed for use in aerospace.

Aes•chy•lus (es′kə ləs), n. 525–456 B.C., Greek poet and dramatist.

Ae•sop (ē′səp, ē′sop), n. c620–c560 B.C., Greek writer of fables.

aes•thete (es′thēt), n. a person who has or affects refined sensitivity toward the beauties of art or nature.

aes•thet′ic (-thet′ik), adj. 1. pertaining to a sense of beauty or to aesthetics. 2. having a sense or love of beauty. —aes•thet′i•cal•ly, adv.

aes•thet′ics, n. the branch of philosophy dealing with beauty in nature and art.

AF, 1. Air Force. **2.** Anglo-French.

A.F. or **a.f.,** audio frequency.

a•far (ə fär′), adv. from, at, or to a distance.

af•fa•ble (af′ə bəl), adj. warm and friendly; pleasant. —af′fa•bil′i•ty, n. —af′fa•bly, adv.

af•fair (ə fâr′), n. 1. something requiring action. 2. affairs, matters of commercial or public interest. 3. a private or personal concern. 4. an amorous relationship. 5. a notorious incident. 6. a social gathering.

af•fect[1] (ə fekt′), v.t. 1. to produce an effect on. 2. to impress the mind or move the feelings of. —Usage. AFFECT and EFFECT are sometimes confused in writing. The verb AFFECT means "to act on" or "to move": His speech affected the crowd so deeply that many wept. The verb EFFECT means "to bring about, accomplish": The new regime effected radical changes.

af•fect[2] (ə fekt′), v.t. 1. to pretend or feign. 2. to assume pretentiously or for effect. 3. to use or adopt by preference.

af•fec•ta•tion (af′ek tā′shən), n. artificiality of manner, attitude, behavior, or appearance; pretension.

af•fect•ed (ə fek′tid), adj. 1. characterized by affectation or pretension. 2. assumed artificially; feigned.

af•fect′ing, adj. moving the emotions. —af•fect′-ing•ly, adv.

af•fec•tion (ə fek′shən), n. fond devotion; love. —af•fec′tion•ate (-shə nit), adj. —af•fec′tion•ate•ly, adv.

af•fer•ent (af′ər ənt), adj. leading toward a central organ or part, as a nerve.

af•fi•ance (ə fī′əns), v.t., -anced, -anc•ing. to betroth.

af•fi•da•vit (af′i dā′vit), n. a written declaration made under oath before an authorized official. [< ML: (he) has declared on oath]

af•fil•i•ate (v. ə fil′ē āt′; n. -it, -āt′), v., -at•ed, -at•ing, n. —v.t. 1. to bring into close association or connection. —v.i. 2. to associate oneself; be united. —n. 3. an affiliated person or organization. —af•fil′i•a′tion, n.

af•fin•i•ty (ə fin′i tē), n., pl. -ties. 1. a natural liking or attraction. 2. relationship, esp. by marriage; kinship.

affin′ity group′, n. a group of persons affiliated with the same organization, college, etc., often receiving certain discounts or other privileges.

af•firm (ə fûrm′), v.t. 1. to assert positively; declare. 2. to confirm or ratify. —v.i. 3. to state something solemnly but without oath. —af•fir•ma•tion (af′ər mā′shən), n.

af•firm•a•tive (ə fûr′mə tiv), adj. 1. affirming that something is true, valid, or a fact. 2. expressing agreement or consent. —n. 3. something, as a reply, that indicates assent. 4. the side, as in a debate, that defends a proposition. —af•firm′a•tive•ly, adv.

affirm′ative ac′tion, n. a policy to increase opportunities for women and minorities, esp. in education and employment.

af•fix (v. ə fiks′; n. af′iks), v.t. 1. to fasten, join, or attach. 2. to add on; append. —n. 3. something affixed. 4. a prefix or suffix.

af•fla•tus (ə flā′təs), n. inspiration.

af•flict (ə flikt′), v.t. to distress with mental or bodily pain. —af•flic′tion, n.

af•flu•ent (af′lōō ənt), adj. 1. wealthy; rich. 2. abundant; copious. —af′flu•ence, n. —af′flu•ent•ly, adv.

af′fluent soci′ety, n. a prosperous society whose wealth is not shared by all. [from title of a book (1958) by J.K. Galbraith]

af•ford (ə fôrd′), v.t. 1. to be able to do or bear without serious consequence. 2. to be able to meet the expense of. 3. to furnish; supply. —af•ford′a•ble, adj.

af•for•est (ə fôr′ist, ə for′-), v.t. to convert into forest. —af•for′est•a′tion, n.

af•fray (ə frā′), n. a public fight; noisy brawl.

af•front (ə frunt′), n. 1. a deliberate insult. —v.t. 2. to insult deliberately.

Af•ghan (af′gan, -gən), n. 1. a native or inhabitant of Afghanistan. 2. (l.c.) a soft knitted or crocheted blanket. 3. Also called Af′ghan hound′. a hound with a long head and long, silky fur.

Af•ghan•i•stan (af gan′ə stan′), n. a republic in SW Asia, E of Iran. 12,700,000.

a•fi•cio•na•do (ə fish′yə nä′dō, ə fish′ə-), n., pl. -dos. an ardent devotee; fan.

a•field (ə fēld′), adv. 1. away from home. 2. off the subject or mark. 3. in or to the field.

a•fire (ə fīʳr′), adj. on fire.

a•flame (ə flām′), adj. on fire; ablaze.

AFL-CIO, American Federation of Labor and Congress of Industrial Organizations.

a•float (ə flōt′), adv., adj. 1. floating on the water. 2. on board a ship; at sea. 3. covered with water; flooded.

a•flut•ter (ə flut′ər), adj. 1. agitated or excited. 2. fluttering.

a•foot (ə fŏŏt′), adv., adj. 1. on foot. 2. in progress; astir.

a•fore•men•tioned (ə fôr′men′shənd), adj. mentioned previously.

a•fore′said′, adj. said previously.

a•fore′thought′, adj. thought of previously; premeditated: with malice aforethought.

a•foul (ə foul′), adv., adj. 1. in a state of collision or entanglement. —Idiom. 2. run or fall afoul of, to come into conflict with.

a•fraid (ə frād′), adj. 1. feeling fear; apprehensive. 2. feeling regret. 3. feeling reluctance; disinclined.

a•fresh (ə fresh′), adv. once more; anew.

Af•ri•ca (af′ri kə), n. a continent S of Europe and between the Atlantic and Indian oceans.

Af′ri•can, adj. 1. of Africa. —n. 2. a native or inhabitant of Africa, esp. black Africa. 3. a person of African ancestry, esp. a black.

Af′ri•can-A•mer′i•can, n. 1. a black American of African descent. —adj. 2. of African-Americans.

Af′rican vi′olet, n. a tropical African plant with hairy leaves and purple, pink, or white flowers.

Af•ri•kaans (af′ri käns′, -känz′), n. an official language of South Africa, developed from 17th-century Dutch.

Af•ro (af′rō), *adj., n., pl.* **-ros.** —*adj.* **1.** of African-Americans or their traditions, culture, etc. —*n.* **2.** a full, bushy hairstyle.

Af′ro-A•mer′i•can, *n., adj.* AFRICAN-AMERICAN.

aft (aft, äft), *adv.* **1.** at, close to, or toward the stern of a ship or tail of an aircraft. —*adj.* **2.** situated toward or at the stern or tail.

af•ter (af′tər, äf′-), *prep.* **1.** behind in place or position. **2.** later in time than. **3.** below in rank or estimation. **4.** in imitation of: *fashioned after Raphael.* **5.** in pursuit or search of: *I'm after a better job.* **6.** concerning; about: *They asked after you.* —*adv.* **7.** behind. **8.** afterward. —*adj.* **9.** later: *in after years.* **10.** located close to the rear, esp. to the stern or tail. —*conj.* **11.** subsequent to the time that: *after the boys left.*

af′ter•birth′, *n.* the placenta and fetal membranes expelled from the uterus after childbirth.

af′ter•burn′er, *n.* a device for burning exhaust gases, as from a jet or internal-combustion engine.

af′ter•care′, *n.* the care and treatment of a convalescent patient.

af′ter•ef•fect′, *n.* a delayed or secondary effect.

af′ter•glow′, *n.* **1.** the glow frequently seen in the sky after sunset. **2.** the pleasant remembrance of a past experience.

af′ter•im′age, *n.* a visual image that persists after the stimulus is no longer operative.

af′ter•life′, *n.* life after death.

af′ter•math′ (-math′), *n.* **1.** a result, esp. a calamitous one; consequence. **2.** a new growth of a crop, esp. grass.

af′ter•noon′, *n.* the time from noon until evening.

af′ter•taste′, *n.* a taste lingering in the mouth.

af′ter•thought′, *n.* **1.** a later thought. **2.** something, as a part, added later.

af′ter•ward (-wərd) also **-wards,** *adv.* at a later time; subsequently.

Ag, *Chem. Symbol.* silver. [< L *argentum*]

a•gain (ə gen′), *adv.* **1.** once more; another time. **2.** moreover; besides. **3.** on the other hand. —*Idiom.* **4.** again and again, repeatedly; often. **5.** as much again, twice as much.

a•gainst (ə genst′), *prep.* **1.** in opposition to; contrary to. **2.** in resistance to, defense from, or preparation for: *protection against mosquitoes.* **3.** in an opposite direction to. **4.** in or into contact with; upon. **5.** in competition with.

Ag•a•mem•non (ag′ə mem′non, -nən), *n.* a legendary king who led the Greeks in the Trojan War.

a•gape¹ (ə gāp′), *adv., adj.* with the mouth wide open, as in wonder.

a•ga•pe² (ä gä′pā, ä′gə pā′, ag′ə-), *n., pl.* **-pae** (-pī, -pī′, -pē′). **1.** nonerotic love, as of God for humankind or of humankind for God or for one another. **2.** LOVE FEAST (defs. 1, 2).

a•gar (ä′gär, ag′ər), *n.* a gel prepared from red algae, used as a culture medium and as a food thickener and stabilizer. Also, **a′gar-a′gar.**

ag•ate (ag′it), *n.* **1.** a variegated chalcedony with colored bands. **2.** a playing marble of agate or glass.

a•ga•ve (ə gä′vē), *n.* a desert plant with thick leaves.

age (āj), *n., v.,* **aged, ag•ing** or **age•ing.** —*n.* **1.** the length of time during which a being or thing has existed. **2.** a period of human life. **3.** the time of life at which a person becomes qualified or disqualified for something. **4.** old age. **5.** (*often cap.*) a historical or geological period. **6.** Usu., **ages.** a long time. —*v.i., v.t.* **7.** to grow or cause to grow old. **8.** to mature, as wine. —*Idiom.* **9. of age,** having reached adulthood, esp. as specified by law.

-age, a suffix meaning: action or process (*coverage*); result of (*wreckage*); residence of (*parsonage*); aggregate (*coinage*); charge (*postage*).

a•ged (ā′jid *for 1, 3;* ājd *for 1, 2*), *adj.* **1.** of advanced age; old. **2.** of the age of. —*n.* **3. the aged,** (*used with a pl. v.*) old people collectively.

age′ism, *n.* discrimination against older persons. —**age′ist,** *adj., n.*

age′less (-lis), *adj.* **1.** not appearing to age. **2.** lasting forever.

a•gen•cy (ā′jən sē), *n., pl.* **-cies. 1.** an organization, company, or bureau representing or doing business for another. **2.** a government bureau. **3.** the duty, function, or office of an agent. **4.** a means of accomplishing something; instrumentality.

a•gen•da (ə jen′də), *n., pl.* **-das.** a list of things to be done.

a•gent (ā′jənt), *n.* **1.** a person or business authorized to act for another. **2.** one that acts. **3.** a means; instrument. **4.** an official or representative of a government agency.

A′gent Or′ange, *n.* a powerful herbicide and defoliant, used during the Vietnam War.

Age′ of Rea′son, *n.* the 17th and 18th centuries in France, England, etc.

age′-old′, *adj.* ancient.

Ag•ga•dah (ə gä′də) also **Haggadah,** *n.* (*often l.c.*) the nonlegal or narrative material in the Talmud and other rabbinical literature. [< Heb *haggādhāh,* der. of *higgīdh* to narrate] —**Ag•gad•ic, ag•gad•ic** (ə gad′ik, ə gä′dik), *adj.*

ag•glom•er•ate (*v.* ə glom′ə rāt′; *n.* -ər it, -ə rāt′), *v.,* -at•ed, -at•ing, *n.* —*v.t., v.i.* **1.** to gather into a cluster or mass. —*n.* **2.** a mass of things clustered together. **3.** rock composed of volcanic fragments. —**ag•glom′er•a′tion,** *n.*

ag•glu•ti•nate (ə glōōt′n āt′), *v.t.,* -nat•ed, -nat•ing. **1.** to cause to adhere. **2.** to cause (bacteria or cells) to clump. —**ag•glu′ti•na′tion,** *n.*

ag•gran•dize (ə gran′dīz, ag′rən dīz′), *v.t.,* -dized, -diz•ing. to make great or greater, as in power. —**ag•gran′dize•ment** (-diz mənt), *n.*

ag•gra•vate (ag′rə vāt′), *v.t.,* -vat•ed, -vat•ing. **1.** to make worse or more severe; intensify. **2.** to annoy; irritate. —**ag′gra•va′tion,** *n.* —**Usage.** The sense "to annoy" is sometimes objected to, and is used somewhat less frequently than the sense "to make worse" in formal speech and writing. Both senses, however, have been standard since the early 17th century.

ag′gra•vat′ed, *adj. Law.* characterized by a feature that makes a crime more serious: *aggravated assault.*

ag•gre•gate (*adj., n.* ag′ri git, -gāt′; *v.* -gāt′), *adj., n., v.,* -gat•ed, -gat•ing. —*adj.* **1.** formed by the collection of particulars into a whole. —*n.* **2.** a sum, mass, or assemblage. —*v.t., v.i.* **3.** to collect into one sum, mass, or body. —**ag′gre•ga′tion,** *n.*

ag•gres•sion (ə gresh′ən), *n.* **1.** an unprovoked attack. **2.** offensive action in general. **3.** hostile behavior. —**ag•gres′sor,** *n.*

ag•gres•sive (ə gres′iv), *adj.* **1.** characterized by or tending toward aggression. **2.** vigorously energetic, esp. in the use of initiative. **3.** using daring or forceful methods: *aggressive treatment of infection.* —**ag•gres′sive•ly,** *adv.* —**ag•gres′sive•ness,** *n.*

ag•grieve (ə grēv′), *v.t.,* -grieved, -griev•ing. **1.** to wrong grievously. **2.** to afflict with pain or distress. —**ag•grieve′ment,** *n.*

a•ghast (ə gast′, ə gäst′), *adj.* struck with shock, amazement, or horror.

ag•ile (aj′əl, -īl), *adj.* quick and well-coordinated; nimble. —**ag′ile•ly,** *adv.* —**a•gil•i•ty** (ə jil′i tē), *n.*

Ag•in•court (aj′in kôrt′, -kōrt′, azh′in kŏōr′), *n.* a village in N France: victory of the English over the French 1415.

ag•i•ta (aj′i tə), *n.* **1.** heartburn; indigestion. **2.** agitation; anxiety.

ag•i•tate (aj′i tāt′), *v.,* -tat•ed, -tat•ing. —*v.t.* **1.** to shake or move briskly. **2.** to disturb emotionally; perturb. —*v.i.* **3.** to arouse or try to arouse public interest. —**ag′i•ta′tion,** *n.* —**ag′i•ta′tor,** *n.*

a•gleam (ə glēm′), *adj.* gleaming.

a•glit•ter (ə glit′ər), *adj.* glittering.

a•glow (ə glō), *adj.* glowing.

ag•nos•tic (ag nos′tik), *n.* **1.** a person who holds that the existence of the ultimate cause, as God, is unknown and unknowable. —*adj.* **2.** of agnostics. —**ag•nos′ti•cism** (-tə siz′əm), *n.*

Ag•nus De•i (ag′nəs dē′ī, de′ē; ä′nyŏŏs de′ē), *n.* **1.**

a figure of a lamb as emblematic of Christ. **2.** a prayer addressed to Christ preceding the communion in the Mass. [< L: lamb of God]

a•go (ə gō′), *adj.* **1.** gone by; past. —*adv.* **2.** in the past.

a•gog (ə gog′), *adj.* highly excited, as in anticipation.

ag•o•nize (ag′ə nīz′), *v.i., v.t.,* **-nized, -niz•ing.** to suffer or cause to suffer extreme pain or anguish. —**ag′o•niz′ing•ly,** *adv.*

ag′o•ny (-nē), *n., pl.* **-nies. 1.** extreme mental or physical suffering. **2.** the struggle preceding death.

ag•o•ra•pho•bi•a (ag′ər ə fō′bē ə), *n.* abnormal fear of being in open areas. —**ag′o•ra•pho′bic,** *adj., n.*

a•grar•i•an (ə grâr′ē ən), *adj.* **1.** of land or land tenure. **2.** of farmers or agricultural interests. —*n.* **3.** one who favors the equal division of landed property. —**a•grar′i•an•ism,** *n.*

a•gree (ə grē′), *v.,* **a•greed, a•gree•ing.** —*v.i.* **1.** to be in accord in opinion or feeling. **2.** to give consent; assent. **3.** to arrive at a settlement or understanding. **4.** to be consistent; correspond. **5.** to be suitable or beneficial: *The climate did not agree with him.* **6.** to correspond in case, number, gender, or person. —*v.t.* **7.** to concede; grant: *I agree that he is the ablest of us.*

a•gree′a•ble, *adj.* **1.** to one's liking; pleasing. **2.** willing or ready to agree. **3.** suitable; conformable. —**a•gree′a•bly,** *adv.*

a•gree′ment, n. 1. the state of being in accord; harmony. **2. a.** an arrangement accepted by all parties. **b.** a document setting forth such an arrangement.

ag•ri•busi•ness (ag′rə biz′nis), *n.* the businesses collectively associated with the production, processing, and distribution of agricultural products.

ag′ri•cul′ture, *n.* the science, art, or occupation of cultivating land and raising crops and livestock; farming. —**ag′ri•cul′tur•al,** *adj.* —**ag′ri•cul′tur•al•ly,** *adv.*

a•gron•o•my (ə gron′ə mē), *n.* the science of farm management and the production of field crops. —**ag•ro•nom•ic** (ag′rə nom′ik), *adj.* —**a•gron′o•mist,** *n.*

a•ground (ə ground′), *adv., adj.* on or onto the ground beneath a body of water.

a•gue (ā′gyoō), *n.* chills, fever, and sweating, esp. when associated with malaria.

ah (ä), *interj.* an exclamation of pain, surprise, joy, etc.

a•ha (ä hä′, ə hä′), *interj.* an exclamation of triumph, mockery, surprise, etc.

A•hab (ā′hab), *n.* **1.** a king of Israel and husband of Jezebel, reigned 874?–853? B.C. I Kings 16–22. **2.** captain of the ship *Pequod* in Herman Melville's *Moby Dick.*

A•has•u•e•rus (ə haz′yoō ēr′əs, ə has′-), *n.* a king of ancient Persia, usu. identified as Xerxes I.

a•head (ə hed′), *adv.* **1.** in, at, or to the front. **2.** forward; onward. **3.** into or for the future. **4.** onward toward success: *to get ahead in the world.* —*Idiom.* **5.** ahead of, before or further than.

a•hem (*pronounced as if clearing the throat; spelling pron.* ə hem′, hem), *interj.* a sound used to attract attention, express doubt, etc.

A•him•e•lech (ə him′ə lek′), *n.* a priest who was killed by Saul. I Sam. 21:1–9; 22:9–23.

A•hith•o•phel (ə hith′ə fel′), *n.* an adviser to David who later turned against him by joining the rebellion of Absalom. II Sam. 15–17.

-aholic, a combining form extracted from ALCOHOLIC, meaning one who is addicted to or obsessed with an object or activity (*workaholic*).

a•hoy (ə hoi′), *interj.* a call used at sea to hail a ship.

A•hu•na Var•ya (ä′hoō nä vär′yä), *n. Zoroastrianism.* the best-known and most frequently recited prayer. Also called **A•hun•var** (ä′hoōn vär′).

aid (ād), *v.t., v.i.* **1.** to help; assist. —*n.* **2.** help; assistance. **3.** a helper; assistant. —**Usage.** Although the nouns AID and AIDE both have among their mean-

ings "an assistant," the spelling AIDE is increasingly used in this sense: *the Senator's aide.*

aide (ād), *n.* **1.** an assistant. **2.** AIDE-DE-CAMP. —**Usage.** See AID.

aide-de-camp (ād′də kamp′), *n., pl.* **aides-de-camp** (ādz′-). a military officer acting as a confidential assistant to a superior.

AIDS (ādz), *n.* a disease of the immune system characterized by increased susceptibility to opportunistic infections, certain cancers, etc. [*a(cquired) i(mmune) d(eficiency) s(yndrome)*]

ai•grette (ā′gret, ā gret′), *n.* a plume of feathers, esp. from a heron, worn as a head ornament.

Ai•ja•lon (ā′jə lon′), *n.* an ancient city west of Jerusalem: one of the cities of refuge. Josh. 19:42; I Sam. 14:31.

ail (āl), *v.t.* **1.** to cause pain or trouble to. —*v.i.* **2.** to be ill.

ai•ler•on (ā′lə ron′), *n.* a movable surface on an aircraft wing, used to control roll.

ail′ment, *n.* a physical disorder, esp. a minor one.

aim (ām), *v.t.* **1.** to direct (a gun, punch, remark, etc.) so as to hit. —*v.i.* **2.** to direct a gun, punch, etc. **3.** to direct one's efforts: *I aim at perfection.* —*n.* **4.** the act of aiming. **5.** the direction in which something is aimed. **6.** something intended; purpose. —*Idiom.* **7. take aim,** to aim a weapon.

aim′less, *adj.* being without purpose. —**aim′less•ly,** *adv.* —**aim′less•ness,** *n.*

ain't (ānt), **1.** *Nonstandard except in some dialects.* am not; are not; is not. **2.** *Nonstandard.* have not; has not. —**Usage.** AIN'T is more common in uneducated speech, though it occurs with some frequency in the informal speech of the educated. AIN'T also occurs in some humorous or set phrases: *Ain't it the truth!*

air (âr), *n.* **1.** the mixture of nitrogen, oxygen, and minute amounts of other gases that surrounds the earth. **2.** a light breeze. **3.** general character or appearance; aura. **4. airs,** affected manners. **5.** a tune; melody. **6.** aircraft as a means of transportation. **7.** the medium through which radio waves are transmitted. **8.** *Informal.* air conditioning. —*v.t.* **9.** to expose to the air; ventilate. **10.** to bring to public notice; publicize. **11.** to broadcast or televise. —*Idiom.* **12. in the air,** in circulation; current. **13. off the air,** not broadcasting. **14. on the air,** broadcasting. **15. up in the air,** not decided; unsettled. —*Saying.* **16. Don't air your dirty linen in public,** don't talk about private matters.

air′ bag′, *n.* a bag that inflates automatically on impact to cushion automobile passengers.

air′ base′, *n.* an operations center for units of an air force.

air′borne′, *adj.* **1.** carried by the air. **2.** in flight.

air′ brake′, *n.* a brake operated by compressed air.

air′brush′, *n.* **1.** an atomizer for spraying paint. —*v.t.* **2.** to paint using an airbrush.

air′-condi′tion, *v.t.* to furnish with air conditioning. —**air′ condi′tioner,** *n.*

air′ condi′tioning, *n.* a system for reducing the temperature and humidity of air.

air′-cool′, *v.t.* to cool with circulating air.

air′craft′, *n., pl.* **-craft.** a machine, as an airplane, glider, or helicopter, supported for flight in the air.

air′craft car′rier, *n.* a warship with a deck for the taking off and landing of aircraft.

air′drop′, *v.,* **-dropped, -drop•ping,** *n.* —*v.t.* **1.** to drop (persons or cargo) by parachute from an aircraft in flight. —*n.* **2.** the act or process of airdropping.

Aire•dale (âr′dāl′), *n.* a large terrier with a wiry black-and-tan coat.

air′field′, *n.* a level area on which airplanes take off and land.

air′flow′, *n.* the air flowing past or through a moving body.

air′foil′, *n.* a surface, as a wing, designed to aid in lifting or controlling an aircraft.

air′ force′, *n.* the military unit of a nation charged with carrying out air operations.

air′ gun′, *n.* a gun operated by compressed air.

air′ lane′, *n.* a route regularly used by airplanes; airway.

air′lift′, *n.* **1.** a system for transporting persons or cargo by aircraft, esp. in an emergency. —*v.t.* **2.** to transport by airlift.

air′line′, *n.* a system or company furnishing air transport, usu. scheduled.

air′lin′er, *n.* a passenger aircraft operated by an airline.

air′ lock′, *n.* an airtight chamber permitting passage between spaces of different pressure.

air′mail′ or **air′ mail′,** *n.* **1.** the system of sending mail by airplane. **2.** mail sent by airmail. —*v.t.* **3.** to send by airmail.

air′man, *n., pl.* **-men. 1.** an aviator. **2.** *U.S. Air Force.* an enlisted person of one of the three lowest ranks (**air′man ba′sic, airman, air′man first′ class′).**

air′ mass′, *n.* a body of air covering a wide area and exhibiting approximately uniform properties throughout.

air′plane′, *n.* a heavier-than-air aircraft kept aloft by the upward thrust exerted by the passing air on its fixed wings and driven by propellers or jet propulsion.

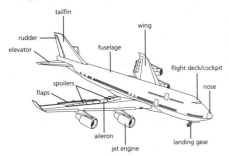

airplane

air′ pock′et, *n.* a nearly vertical air current that can cause an aircraft to lose altitude suddenly.

air′port′, *n.* a facility for the landing, takeoff, and repair of aircraft, esp. one used for transporting passengers and cargo.

air′ pres′sure, *n.* the pressure exerted by compressed air or by the atmosphere.

air′ raid′, *n.* a raid by enemy aircraft.

air′ ri′fle, *n.* an air gun with rifled bore.

air′ship′, *n.* a self-propelled, lighter-than-air aircraft; dirigible.

air′space′, *n.* the space above a nation over which the nation has jurisdiction.

air′strip′, *n.* a strip of land serving as a runway.

air′tight′, *adj.* **1.** preventing the entrance or escape of air or gas. **2.** having no weak points: *an airtight contract.*

air′-to-air′, *adj.* operating between airborne objects, esp. aircraft.

air′-to-sur′face, *adj.* operating or directed from a flying aircraft to the ground: *air-to-surface missiles.*

air′waves′, *n.pl.* the medium of radio and television broadcasting.

air′way′, *n.* **1.** AIR LANE. **2.** AIRLINE.

air′wor′thy, *adj.,* -thi•er, -thi•est. (of an aircraft) safe or fit to fly.

air′y, *adj.,* -i•er, -i•est. **1.** open to the air; breezy. **2.** of or like air. **3.** light and thin; delicate. **4.** insubstantial; unreal. **5.** high in the air; lofty. —**air′i•ly,** *adv.* —**air′i•ness,** *n.*

aisle (īl), *n.* a passage between or along sections of seats or shelves, as in a theater or department store.

a•jar (ə jär′), *adj., adv.* partly open.

AK, Alaska.

a.k.a., also known as.

A•khe•na•ton or **A•khe•na•ten** (äk nät′n, ä′kə-), also **Akh•na•ton** (äk nät′n), *n.* (*Amenhotep IV*) died 1357? B.C., king of Egypt 1375?-1357?: reformer of ancient Egyptian religion.

Ak•hi•sar (äk′hi sär′), *n.* a town in W Turkey, NE of Izmir. 61,491. Ancient, **Thyatira.**

a•kim•bo (ə kim′bō), *adj., adv.* with hand on hip and elbow bent outward.

a•kin (ə kin′), *adj.* **1.** related by blood. **2.** allied by nature or inclination.

Ak•mo•la (ak mō′lə), *n.* the capital of Kazakhstan. 276,000.

Ak•ron (ak′rən), *n.* a city in NE Ohio. 221,886.

-al¹, an adjective suffix meaning: of or pertaining to (*tribal*); characterized by (*typical*).

-al², a noun suffix meaning act or process (*refusal*).

AL, 1. Alabama. **2.** Anglo-Latin.

Al, *Chem. Symbol.* aluminum.

à la or **a la** (ä′ lä, ä′ lə), *prep.* in the manner or style of.

Ala., Alabama.

Al•a•bam•a (al′ə bam′ə), *n.* a state in the SE United States. 4,273,084. *Cap.:* Montgomery. *Abbr.:* AL, Ala. —**Al′a•bam′i•an, Al′a•bam′an,** *adj., n.*

al•a•bas•ter (al′ə bas′tər, -bä′stər), *n.* a finely granular variety of gypsum, often white and translucent, used for ornamental objects or work.

à la carte or **a la carte** (ä′ lə kärt′), *adv., adj.* with a separate price for each item on the menu.

a•lac•ri•ty (ə lak′ri tē), *n.* **1.** cheerful readiness. **2.** liveliness; briskness.

à′ la king′ (ä′ lə), *adj.* served in a cream sauce containing mushrooms, pimento, and green pepper.

Al•a•mo (al′ə mō′), *n.* a Franciscan mission in San Antonio, Tex., taken by Mexicans in 1836 during the Texan war for independence.

à′ la mode′ or **a′ la mode′,** *adj.* **1.** stylish; fashionable. **2.** served with ice cream. [< F]

a•larm (ə lärm′), *n.* **1.** sudden fear caused by danger. **2.** a warning of approaching danger. **3.** a device that gives a warning signal. **4.** a call to arms. —*v.t.* **5.** to make fearful; frighten. **6.** to warn of danger. —**a•larm′ing•ly,** *adv.*

a•larm′ist, *n.* a person who tends to alarm others, esp. without sufficient reason.

a•las (ə las′, ə läs′), *interj.* an exclamation of sorrow, pity, etc.

Alas., Alaska.

A•las•ka (ə las′kə), *n.* a state of the United States in NW North America. 607,007. *Cap.:* Juneau. *Abbr.:* AK, Alas. —**A•las′kan,** *adj., n.*

Alas′ka Pur′chase, *n.* purchase of the territory of Alaska by the U.S. from Russia in 1867 for $7,200,000. Compare SEWARD'S FOLLY.

alb (alb), *n.* a long-sleeved linen vestment worn by priests.

al•ba•core (al′bə kôr′), *n., pl.* **-cores, -core.** a long-finned tuna.

Al•ba•ni•a (al bā′nē ə), *n.* a republic in S Europe, NW of Greece. 3,293,252. —**Al•ba′ni•an,** *adj., n.*

Al•ba•ny (ôl′bə nē), *n.* the capital of New York. 104,828.

al•ba•tross (al′bə trôs′, -tros′), *n., pl.* **-tross•es** or, for 1, **-tross. 1.** a large, web-footed bird of S and tropical oceanic waters. **2.** a burden.

al•be•it (ôl bē′it), *conj.* even if; although.

Al•ber•ta (al bûr′tə), *n.* a province in W Canada. 2,365,825. *Cap.:* Edmonton. *Abbr.:* AB, Alta. —**Al•ber′tan,** *adj., n.*

Al•bi•gen•ses (al′bi jen′sēz), *n.pl.* members of an ascetic Christian sect that arose in Albi in the 11th century. —**Al′bi•gen′si•an** (-sē ən, -shən), *adj., n.* —**Al′bi•gen′si•an•ism,** *n.*

al•bi•no (al bī′nō), *n., pl.* **-nos.** a person, animal, or plant deficient in pigmentation, esp. a person with pale skin, white hair, and pinkish eyes. —**al′bi•nism,** *n.*

al•bum (al′bəm), *n.* **1.** a book with blank pages for displaying a collection, as of photographs. **2.** a phonograph record or set of records containing musical selections or a complete musical work.

al•bu•men (al byōō′mən), n. 1. the white of an egg. 2. ALBUMIN.

al•bu′min (-mən), n. any of a class of water-soluble proteins found in egg white, milk, blood, and animal and vegetable tissue.

Al•bu•quer•que (al′bə kûr′kē), n. a city in central New Mexico. 411,994.

al•che•my (al′kə mē), n. chemistry of the Middle Ages, concerned chiefly with attempts to turn base metals into gold. —**al′che•mist,** n.

al•co•hol (al′kə hôl′, -hol′), n. 1. a colorless, volatile, flammable liquid produced by yeast fermentation of carbohydrates or synthetically: used chiefly as a solvent and in beverages and medicines. 2. an intoxicating liquor containing alcohol. [< NL < ML < Ar al-kuḥl the powdered antimony]

al′co•hol′ic, adj. 1. of, containing, or caused by alcohol. 2. suffering from alcoholism. —n. 3. a person suffering from alcoholism.

al′co•hol•ism, n. a chronic disorder characterized by dependence on and excessive use of alcoholic beverages.

Al•cott (ôl′kət, -kot), n. 1. (Amos) Bronson, 1799–1888, U.S. educator and philosopher. 2. Louisa May, 1832–88, U.S. author.

al•cove (al′kōv), n. 1. a recess opening out of a room. 2. a recessed space in a wall, as for a bed.

al•der (ôl′dər), n. a shrub or tree of the birch family that grows in moist places in colder regions.

al′der•man, n., pl. -men. a member of a municipal legislative body.

Al•drin (ôl′drin), n. Edwin Eugene, Jr. ("Buzz"), born 1930, U.S. astronaut: second person to walk on the moon, 1969.

ale (āl), n. a malt beverage like but more bitter than beer.

a•le•a•to•ry (ā′lē ə tôr′ē, al′ē-), adj. 1. Law. depending on an uncertain event. 2. dependent on luck or chance.

a•lem•bic (ə lem′bik), n. a vessel formerly used in distilling.

a•lert (ə lûrt′), adj. 1. fully aware and attentive; observant. 2. quick to understand or respond; perceptive. 3. watchful; vigilant. —n. 4. a warning or alarm of danger. 5. the period during which an alert is in effect. —v.t. 6. to warn, as to prepare for an attack. —**Idiom.** 7. on the alert, vigilant. —**a•lert′ly,** adv. —**a•lert′ness,** n.

A•leu′tian Is′lands (ə lōō′shən), n.pl. an archipelago extending SW from Alaska. —**A•leu′tian,** adj., n.

ale′wife′, n., pl. -wives. a North American fish similar to a shad.

Al•ex•an′der the Great′ (al′ig zan′dər, -zän′-), n. 356–323 B.C., king of Macedonia 336–323: conqueror of Greece and Persia.

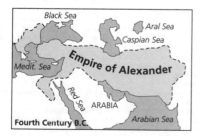

Al′ex•an′dri•a (-drē ə), n. 1. a seaport in N Egypt. 2,893,000. 2. a city in NE Virginia. 112,879.

Al′ex•an′dri•an, adj. 1. of Alexandria, Egypt. 2. of Alexander the Great or the period of his rule.

al•fal•fa (al fal′fə), n., pl. -fas. a plant of the legume family that is widely cultivated for forage.

Al′fred the Great′ (al′frid, -fred), n. A.D. 849–899, king of the West Saxons 871–899.

al•fres•co or **al fres•co** (al fres′kō), adv., adj. in the open air.

al•gae (al′jē), n.pl., sing. -ga (-gə). any of numerous one-celled or colonial organisms that contain chlorophyll and usu. flourish in aquatic environments. —**al′gal,** adj.

al•ge•bra (al′jə brə), n. a branch of mathematics that utilizes symbols, as letters, to represent specific numbers, values, or vectors. [< ML < Ar al-jabr restoration] —**al′ge•bra′ic** (-brā′ik), adj. —**al′ge•bra′i•cal•ly,** adv.

Al•ge•ri•a (al jēr′ē ə), n. a republic in NW Africa. 29,830,370. —**Al•ger′i•an,** adj., n.

Al•giers′ (-jērz′), n. the capital of Algeria. 1,839,000.

ALGOL (al′gol, -gôl), n. a computer language in which information is expressed in algebraic notation. [algo(rithmic) l(anguage)]

Al•gon•qui•an (al gong′kē ən, -kwē ən) also -**ki•an** (-kē ən), n. 1. a widespread family of North American Indian languages. 2. a member of an Algonquian-speaking people.

al•go•rithm (al′gə rith′əm), n. 1. a set of rules for solving a problem in a finite number of steps, as for finding the greatest common divisor. 2. a sequence of steps designed for programming a computer to solve a specific problem. —**al′go•rith′mic,** adj.

A•li (ä′lē, ä lē′ for 1; ä lē′ for 2), n. 1. ('Alī ibn-abu-Talib), A.D. c600-61, fourth caliph of Islam 656-661 (cousin and son-in-law of Muhammad): considered the first caliph by Shi'ites. 2. Muhammad (Cassius Marcellus Clay, Jr.), born 1942, U.S. boxer.

a•li•as (ā′lē əs), n., pl. -as•es, adv. —n. 1. an assumed name. —adv. 2. otherwise called.

al•i•bi (al′ə bī′), n., pl. -bis, v., -bied (-bīd′), -bi•ing. —n. 1. the defense by an accused person of having been elsewhere when an offense was committed. 2. an excuse. —v.i. 3. to give an excuse.

al•ien (āl′yən, ā′lē ən), n. 1. a foreign-born resident who has not been naturalized. 2. a creature from outer space. —adj. 3. not naturalized. 4. foreign; strange. 5. opposed; hostile: ideas alien to modern thinking.

al′ien•a•ble, adj. capable of being sold or transferred. —**al′ien•a•bil′i•ty,** n.

al′ien•ate′ (-nāt′), v.t., -at•ed, -at•ing. 1. to cause to be indifferent or hostile. 2. to transfer (title, property, etc.) to another. —**al′ien•a′tion,** n.

al′ien•ist, n. a psychiatrist, esp. one acting as an expert witness.

a•light¹ (ə līt′), v.i., a•light•ed or a•lit, a•light•ing. 1. to dismount, as from a horse, or descend, as from a vehicle. 2. to settle after descending.

a•light² (ə līt′), adv., adj. 1. lighted up. 2. burning.

a•lign (ə līn′), v.t. 1. to arrange in a straight line. 2. to adjust for coordinated functioning, as the wheels of a car. 3. to ally (oneself) with a particular group, cause, etc. —v.i. 4. to be in or fall into line. —**a•lign′ment,** n.

a•like (ə līk′), adv. 1. in the same manner. 2. to the same degree. —adj. 3. similar or comparable.

al•i•ment (al′ə mənt), n. something that nourishes; food.

al′i•men′ta•ry (-men′tə rē), adj. of, pertaining to, or providing nourishment.

alimen′tary canal′, n. a tubular passage functioning in the digestion of food and extending from the mouth to the anus.

al•i•mo•ny (al′ə mō′nē), n. an allowance paid to a spouse or former spouse for maintenance following a divorce or legal separation.

a•lit (ə lit′), v. a pt. and pp. of ALIGHT¹.

a•live (ə līv′), adj. 1. having life; living. 2. in existence or operation; active. 3. full of energy and spirit; lively. —**Idiom.** 4. alive to, alert or sensitive to. 5. alive with, filled with.

a•li•yah (ä′lē ä′), n., pl. a•li•yahs, a•li•yot 1. the immigration of Jews to Israel. 2. the honor of being called to the reading table in a synagogue to recite the blessings over the Torah.

al•ka•li (al′kə lī′), *n., pl.* **-lis, -lies. 1.** any of various bases that neutralize acids to form salts and turn red litmus paper blue. **2.** a mixture of soluble salts present in arid soils and detrimental to farming. —**al′ka•line′** (-lin′), *adj.* —**al′ka•lin′i•ty** (-lin′i tē), *n.*

al′ka•loid′, *n.* any of various bitter-tasting nitrogen-containing compounds common in plants and including caffeine, nicotine, and quinine.

al•kyd (al′kid), *n.* a sticky resin used in adhesives and paints.

all (ôl), *adj.* **1.** the whole of: *all the cake.* **2.** the whole number of: *all students.* **3.** the greatest possible: *with all speed.* **4.** any whatever: *beyond all doubt.* **5.** nothing but: *The coat is all wool.* —*pron.* **6.** the whole number, quantity, or amount: *Did you eat all of the peanuts?* **7.** everything: *Is that all you've got to say?* —*n.* **8.** one's whole interest, energy, or property: *Give it your all.* —*adv.* **9.** wholly; completely: *all alone.* **10.** each; apiece: *The score was one all.* —*Idiom.* **11. all but,** very nearly; almost. **12. all in all,** everything considered. **13. at all, a.** in the slightest degree. **b.** for any reason. **c.** in any way.

Al•lah (al′ə, ä′lə), *n. Islam.* the Supreme Being; God.

all′-Amer′ican, *adj.* **1.** selected as the best in the U.S., as in a sport. **2.** typically American. —*n.* **3.** an all-American player or team.

all′-around′, *adj.* **1.** able to do many things; versatile. **2.** comprehensive.

al•lay (ə lā′), *v.t.* **1.** to put (fear, doubt, etc.) to rest; calm. **2.** to lessen or relieve; alleviate.

al•le•ga•tion (al′i gā′shən), *n.* **1.** an assertion made in a legal proceeding that must be proved. **2.** an assertion made without proof.

al•lege (ə lej′), *v.t.,* **-leged, -leg•ing. 1.** to assert without proof. **2.** to offer as a reason or excuse. —**al•leged** (ə lejd′, ə lej′id), *adj.* —**al•leg′ed•ly,** *adv.*

Al•le•ghe•ny (al′i gā′nē), *n.* a river flowing NW from Pennsylvania into SW New York and then S through W Pennsylvania, joining the Monongahela at Pittsburgh to form the Ohio River. 325 mi. (525 km) long. —**Al′le•ghe′ni•an, Al′le•gha′ni•an,** *adj.*

Al′le•ghe′ny Moun′tains (al′i gā′nē, al′-), *n.pl.* a mountain range in Pennsylvania, Maryland, West Virginia, and Virginia. Also called **Al′le•ghe′nies.**

al•le•giance (ə lē′jəns), *n.* loyalty to a government, sovereign, person, group, or cause.

al•le•go•ry (al′ə gôr′ē), *n., pl.* **-ries.** a narrative in which the actions of characters represent abstract ideas or moral principles. —**al′le•gor′i•cal** (-gôr′i-kəl, -gor′-), *adj.* —**al′le•gor′ist,** *n.*

al•le•gret•to (al′i gret′ō), *adj., adv. Music.* light and moderately fast.

al•le•gro (ə lā′grō, ə leg′rō), *adj., adv. Music.* brisk and rapid in tempo.

al•lele (ə lēl′), *n.* one of two or more alternative forms of a gene occupying the same position on matching chromosomes. —**al•lel′ic,** *adj.*

al•le•lu•ia (al′ə lōō′yə), *interj.* HALLELUJAH.

Al•len (al′ən), *n.* Ethan, 1738–89, American soldier in the Revolutionary War: leader of the "Green Mountain Boys" of Vermont.

al•ler•gen (al′ər jən, -jen′), *n.* a substance that induces an allergic reaction. —**al′ler•gen′ic,** *adj.*

al′ler•gist (-jist), *n.* a physician specializing in the treatment of allergies.

al′ler•gy (-jē), *n., pl.* **-gies. 1.** an overreaction of the immune system to an ordinarily harmless substance, resulting in symptoms such as skin rash or sneezing. **2.** *Informal.* an aversion. —**al•ler•gic** (ə lûr′jik), *adj.*

al•le•vi•ate (ə lē′vē āt′), *v.t.,* **-at•ed, -at•ing.** to make easier to endure; ease. —**al•le′vi•a′tion,** *n.*

al•ley (al′ē), *n., pl.* **-leys. 1.** a narrow street or passage behind or between buildings. **2.** a bowling alley. —*Idiom.* **3. up one's alley,** compatible with one's interests or abilities.

al′ley cat′, *n.* a domestic cat, esp. of unknown parentage.

All•hal•lows (ôl′hal′ōz), *n.* ALL SAINTS' DAY.

al•li•ance (ə lī′əns), *n.* **1.** a formal agreement, esp. between two or more nations, to cooperate for specific purposes. **2.** the persons or entities in an alliance. **3.** close relationship, as that created by marriage.

Alli′ance for Prog′ress, *n.* a program of foreign policy toward Latin America under the administration of John F. Kennedy.

al•lied (ə līd′, al′īd), *adj.* **1.** joined by treaty or common cause. **2.** related; kindred.

al•li•ga•tor (al′i gā′tər), *n.* a large reptile with a shorter and broader snout than the crocodile. [< Sp *el lagarto* the lizard < L *lacertus* lizard]

al′ligator pear′, *n.* the fruit of the avocado.

al•lit•er•a•tion (ə lit′ə rā′shən), *n.* repetition of the same sound at the beginning of two or more stressed syllables. —**al•lit′er•a′tive,** *adj.*

All′ men′ are creat′ed e′qual, a statement by Thomas Jefferson in the *Declaration of Independence* (1776) holding that human beings possess fundamental, equal rights from the start.

al•lo•cate (al′ə kāt′), *v.t.,* **-cat•ed, -cat•ing.** to set apart for a particular purpose. —**al′lo•ca′tion,** *n.*

al•lot (ə lot′), *v.t.,* **-lot•ted, -lot•ting. 1.** to set apart or distribute as a portion. **2.** to allocate. —**al•lot′-ment,** *n.*

all′-out′, *adj.* using all one's resources.

all′ov′er, *adj.* extending over the entire surface.

al•low (ə lou′), *v.t.* **1.** to permit. **2.** to let have. **3.** to acknowledge; concede: *I had to allow that he was right.* **4.** to set apart; allocate. —*v.i.* **5.** to permit as a possibility; admit. **6.** to make provision: *to allow for breakage.* —**al•low′a•ble,** *adj.*

al•low′ance (-əns), *n.* **1.** an amount or share allotted. **2.** a sum of money allotted on a regular basis or for a particular purpose. **3.** a reduction in price, as for damage. —*Idiom.* **4. make allowance(s) for,** to excuse.

al•loy (*n.* al′oi, ə loi′; *v.* ə loi′), *n.* **1.** a substance composed of two or more metals intimately mixed, as by fusion. **2.** something added that reduces quality or purity. —*v.t.* **3.** to mix so as to form an alloy.

all′ right′, *adv.* **1.** very well; yes. **2.** satisfactorily. **3.** without fail; certainly. —*adj.* **4.** safe; sound. **5.** acceptable; passable. **6.** reliable; good. —**Usage.** See ALRIGHT.

all′-round′, *adj.* ALL-AROUND.

All′ Saints′' Day′, *n.* a church festival celebrated Nov. 1 in honor of all the saints; Allhallows.

all′ sorts′ and condi′tions of men′, *n.pl.* everyone: a phrase in the *Book of Common Prayer.*

all′spice′, *n.* a spice made from the berries of an aromatic tropical American tree of the myrtle family.

all′-star′, *adj.* **1.** consisting entirely of star performers. —*n.* **2.** a player on an all-star team.

all′-time′, *adj.* never equaled or surpassed.

al•lude (ə lōōd′), *v.i.,* **-lud•ed, -lud•ing.** to refer casually or indirectly.

al•lure (ə lŏŏr′), *v.,* **-lured, -lur•ing,** *n.* —*v.t., v.i.* **1.** to tempt with something desirable. —*n.* **2.** the capacity to allure; fascination or charm. —**al•lure′ment,** *n.* —**al•lur′ing,** *adj.*

al•lu•sion (ə lōō′zhən), *n.* **1.** a casual or indirect reference to something. **2.** the act of alluding. —**al•lu′sive** (-siv), *adj.* —**al•lu′sive•ly,** *adv.* —**al•lu′sive•ness,** *n.*

al•lu•vi•um (ə lōō′vē əm), *n., pl.* **-vi•ums, -vi•a** (-vē ə). sedimentary matter, as sand or mud, deposited by flowing water. —**al•lu′vi•al,** *adj.*

al•ly (*n.* al′ī, ə lī′; *v.* ə lī′), *n., pl.* **-lies,** *v.,* **-lied, -ly•ing.** —*n.* **1.** a nation, group, or person united with another for a common purpose. —*v.t., v.i.* **2.** to unite or become united formally, as by treaty, league, or marriage.

al•ma ma•ter (äl′mə mä′tər; al′mə mā′tər), *n.* a school, college, or university at which one has studied.

al•ma•nac (ôl′mə nak′), *n.* a publication containing

statistical information, astronomical or meteorological data, and other useful facts.

al•might•y (ôl mīt′ē), *adj.* **1.** having unlimited power; omnipotent. **2.** having very great power. —*n.* **3. the Almighty,** God.

almight′y dol′lar, *n.* undue importance given to money.

al•mond (ä′mənd, am′ənd), *n.* **1.** the nutlike kernel of the fruit of a tree of the rose family. **2.** the tree itself.

al•most (ôl′mōst, ôl mōst′), *adv.* very nearly; all but.

alms (ämz), *n.* (*used with a sing. or pl. v.*) something, as money or food, given to the poor or needy.

al•oe (al′ō), *n., pl.* **-oes.** a chiefly African shrub of the lily family.

a•loft (ə lôft′, ə loft′), *adv.* **1.** high up in the air. **2.** on, to, or in the upper rigging of a ship.

a•lo•ha (ə lō′ə, ä lō′hä), *n., pl.* **-has,** *interj.* **1.** hello. **2.** farewell. [< Hawaiian: lit., love]

a•lone (ə lōn′), *adj., adv.* **1.** apart from others. **2.** without another person. **3.** only. **4.** without equal. —*Idiom.* **5. let alone, a.** to refrain from bothering or interfering with. **b.** not to mention.

a•long (ə lông′, ə long′), *prep.* **1.** over the length or direction of. **2.** in the course of. —*adv.* **3.** parallel in the same direction. **4.** so as to progress; onward. **5.** in company; together. **6.** as a companion. **7.** from one person or place to another. **8.** as an accompanying item. —*Idiom.* **9. all along,** from the start. **10. be along,** *Informal.* to arrive at a place.

a•long′shore′, *adv., adj.* by or along the shore.

a•long′side′, *adv.* **1.** along or at the side. —*prep.* **2.** by the side of. **3. alongside of,** beside; alongside.

a•loof (ə lōōf′), *adj.* **1.** reserved or reticent in feeling or manner. —*adv.* **2.** at a distance in feeling or manner. —**a•loof′ness,** *n.*

a•loud (ə loud′), *adv.* **1.** with the normal speaking voice; vocally. **2.** loudly.

al•pac•a (al pak′ə), *n., pl.* **-as. 1.** a domesticated South American hoofed mammal related to the llama and having long, soft, silky fleece. **2. a.** the fleece of the alpaca. **b.** a yarn or fabric made of it.

al•pha (al′fə), *n., pl.* **-phas.** the first letter of the Greek alphabet (A, α).

al′pha and ome′ga, *n.* **1.** the beginning and the end. Rev. 1:8. **2.** the basic elements: *the alpha and omega of law.* **3.** (*cap.*) God. Rev. 1:8. **4.** (*cap.*) Jesus. Rev. 21:6; 22:13.

al•pha•bet (al′fə bet′, -bit), *n.* the letters of a language, esp. in their customary order. [< LL < Gk *alphábētos* = *alpha* + *bēta* first two letters of the Greek alphabet] —**al′pha•bet′i•cal,** **al′pha•bet′ic,** *adj.* —**al′pha•bet′i•cal•ly,** *adv.*

al′pha•bet•ize′ (-bi tīz′), *v.t.,* **-ized, -iz•ing.** to put in alphabetical order. —**al′pha•bet′i•za′tion** (-bet′ə-zā′shən), *n.* —**al′pha•bet•iz′er,** *n.*

al′pha•nu•mer′ic also **-mer′i•cal,** *adj.* utilizing both letters and numbers. —**al′pha•nu•mer′i•cal•ly,** *adv.*

al′pha par′ticle, *n.* a positively charged particle consisting of two protons and two neutrons, emitted in radioactive decay or nuclear fission.

al′pha ray′, *n.* a stream of alpha particles.

al′pha rhythm′, *n.* a pattern of slow brain waves (**al′pha waves′**) in normal persons at rest with closed eyes.

al•pine (al′pīn, -pin), *adj.* **1.** of or like a lofty mountain. **2.** (*cap.*) of the Alps. **3.** native to the heights above the timberline.

Alps (alps), *n.pl.* a mountain range in S Europe.

al•read•y (ôl red′ē), *adv.* **1.** prior to a specified time; previously. **2.** so soon; so early. —**Usage.** AL-READY is sometimes confused with ALL READY. ALREADY means "previously": *The plane had already left the airport.* ALL READY means "completely prepared or ready": *The troops were all ready to attack.*

al•right (ôl rīt′), *adv., adj.* ALL RIGHT. —**Usage.** The form ALRIGHT as a one-word spelling of the phrase ALL RIGHT probably arose by analogy with such words as *already* and *altogether.* Although AL-

RIGHT is a common spelling in informal writing, it is usu. considered unacceptable in standard English.

Al•sace (al sas′, -säs′), *n.* a historic region of NE France.

Al Si•rat (al si rät′), *n. Islam.* **1.** the correct path of religion. **2.** the bridge to paradise. [< Ar, = *al* the + *şirāṭ* road < L (*via*) *strāta* paved (way)]

al•so (ôl′sō), *adv.* in addition; besides.

al′so-ran′, *n.* a person who is defeated, as in a contest or an election.

alt., 1. alteration. **2.** alternate. **3.** altitude. **4.** alto.

Alta., Alberta.

al•tar (ôl′tər), *n.* a mound or platform at which religious rites are performed or on which sacrifices are offered.

al′tar boy′, *n.* ACOLYTE (def. 1).

al•ter (ôl′tər), *v.t.* **1.** to make different, as in size or style. **2.** to castrate or spay. —*v.i.* **3.** to become different. —**al′ter•a′tion,** *n.*

al•ter•ca•tion (ôl′tər kā′shən), *n.* a heated or angry dispute.

al′ter e′go, *n.* **1.** an intimate friend. **2.** a second self.

al•ter•nate (*v.* ôl′tər nāt′; *adj., n.* -nit), *v.,* **-nat•ed, -nat•ing,** *adj., n.* —*v.i., v.t.* **1.** to happen or bring about by turns. **2.** to shift or cause to shift back and forth, as between states or actions. —*adj.* **3.** occurring by turns. **4.** being every second one of a series. —*n.* **5.** a substitute. —**al′ter•nate•ly,** *adv.* —**al′ter•na′tion,** *n.*

al′ternating cur′rent, *n.* an electric current that reverses direction at regular intervals.

al•ter′na•tive (-tûr′nə tiv), *n.* **1.** a choice limited to one of two or more possibilities. **2.** one of the possibilities that can be chosen. —*adj.* **3.** affording a choice. **4.** nontraditional or unconventional, as in ideas or methods. —**al•ter′na•tive•ly,** *adv.*

alter′native med′icine, *n.* health care and treatment practices, including traditional Chinese medicine, chiropractic, folk medicine, and naturopathy, that minimize or avoid the use of surgery and drugs.

al′ter•na′tor (-tər nā′tər), *n.* a generator of alternating current.

al•though (ôl t͟hō′), *conj.* in spite of the fact that; though. —**Usage.** See THOUGH.

al•tim•e•ter (al tim′i tər, al′tə mē′tər), *n.* a device used to measure altitude.

al•ti•tude (al′ti tōōd′, -tyōōd′), *n.* **1.** the height of a thing above a given reference plane, esp. above sea level. **2.** the angular distance of a heavenly body above the horizon. **3.** the perpendicular distance from the vertex of a geometric figure to the side opposite the vertex. —**al′ti•tu′di•nal,** *adj.*

al•to (al′tō), *n., pl.* **-tos. 1.** CONTRALTO. **2.** COUNTERTENOR.

al•to•geth•er (ôl′tə get͟h′ər, ôl′tə get͟h′ər), *adv.* **1.** wholly; entirely. **2.** with everything included. **3.** with everything considered; on the whole. —**Usage.** The forms ALTOGETHER and ALL TOGETHER are distinct in meaning. The adverb ALTOGETHER means "wholly, entirely": *an altogether confused report.* The phrase ALL TOGETHER means "in a group": *The children were all together in the kitchen.*

al•tru•ism (al′trōō iz′əm), *n.* unselfish concern for the welfare of others. —**al′tru•ist,** *n.* —**al′tru•is′tic,** *adj.* —**al′tru•is′ti•cal•ly,** *adv.*

al•um (al′əm), *n.* a crystalline double sulfate of aluminum and potassium, used as an astringent and styptic.

al•u•min•i•um (al′yə min′ē əm), *n. Chiefly Brit.* ALUMINUM.

a•lu•mi•num (ə lōō′mə nəm), *n.* a silver-white metallic element, light in weight, ductile, and malleable, used in alloys. *Symbol:* Al; *at. wt.:* 26.98; *at. no.:* 13.

a•lum•na (ə lum′nə), *n., pl.* **-nae** (-nē, -nī). a female graduate or former student of a school, college, or university.

a•lum′nus (-nəs), *n., pl.* **-ni** (-nī, -nē). a graduate or former student of a school, college, or university.

al•ways (ôl′wāz, -wēz), *adv.* **1.** on every occasion;

every time. **2.** all the time; continuously. **3.** forever. **4.** in any event; if necessary.

Alz'hei•mer's disease' (älts'hī mərz, ôlts'-), *n.* a disease marked by progressive memory loss and mental deterioration associated with brain damage. [after A. *Alzheimer* (1864–1915), German neurologist]

am (am; *unstressed* əm, m), *v.* 1st pers. sing. pres. indic. of BE.

AM, 1. amplitude modulation: a method of impressing a signal on a radio carrier wave by varying its amplitude. **2.** a system of broadcasting using AM.

Am, *Chem. Symbol.* americium.

Am., 1. America. **2.** American.

A.M., Master of Arts. [< L *Artium Magister*]

a.m. or **A.M., 1.** before noon. **2.** the period from midnight to noon. [< L *ante merīdiem*]

A.M.A., American Medical Association.

Am•a•lek (am'ə lek'), *n.* **1.** the son of Eliphaz and grandson of Esau. Gen. 36:12; I Chron. 1:36. **2.** a nomadic tribe or nation descended from Amalek and hostile to Israel. Num. 24:20.

a•mal•gam (ə mal'gəm), *n.* **1.** an alloy of mercury with another metal, used as a dental filling. **2.** a mixture or combination.

a•mal'ga•mate' (-gə māt'), *v.t., v.i.,* **-mat•ed, -mat•ing.** to mix, merge, or unite. **—a•mal'ga•ma'tion,** *n.*

am•an•u•en•sis (ə man'yōō en'sis), *n., pl.* **-ses** (-sēz). a secretary.

am•a•ranth (am'ə ranth'), *n.* **1.** any of various erect plants, some of which are cultivated for their showy flower clusters. **2.** an imaginary flower that never dies.

Am•a•ril•lo (am'ə ril'ō), *n.* a city in NW Texas. 165,036.

am•a•ryl•lis (am'ə ril'is), *n.* a bulbous plant with large red or pink flowers resembling lilies.

a•mass (ə mas'), *v.t.* to collect; accumulate.

am•a•teur (am'ə chōōr', -chər, -tər), *n.* **1.** a person who engages in an activity for pleasure rather than financial benefit. **2.** a person who lacks experience or skill. *—adj.* **3.** of, being, or engaged in by an amateur. **—am'a•teur'ish,** *adj.* **—am'a•teur•ism,** *n.*

am•a•to•ry (am'ə tôr'ē), *adj.* pertaining to or expressive of love.

a•maze (ə māz'), *v.t.,* **a•mazed, a•maz•ing** to overwhelm with surprise or wonder; astonish. **—a•maze'ment,** *n.* **—a•maz'ing,** *adj.* **—a•maz'ing•ly,** *adv.*

Am•a•zon (am'ə zon', -zən), *n.* **1.** a river in N South America. 3900 mi. (6280 km) long. **2.** (in ancient Greek legends) a member of a nation of female warriors. **3.** (*often l.c.*) a tall, powerful woman. **—Am'a•zo'ni•an** (-zō'nē ən), *adj.*

am•bas•sa•dor (am bas'ə dər, -dôr'), *n.* a diplomatic official of the highest rank, sent by one sovereign or state to another. **—am•bas'sa•do'ri•al,** *adj.* **—am•bas'sa•dor•ship',** *n.*

am•ber (am'bər), *n.* **1.** a yellow, red, or brown translucent fossil resin of coniferous trees that is used for jewelry. **2.** the yellowish brown color of amber.

am•ber•gris (am'bər grēs', -gris), *n.* an ash-colored secretion of the sperm whale intestine, used in perfumery.

ambi-, a prefix meaning both (*ambiguous*).

am•bi•ance or **-ence** (am'bē əns), *n.* the special atmosphere of a place, situation, or environment.

am•bi•dex•trous (am'bi dek'strəs), *adj.* able to use both hands equally well. **—am'bi•dex•ter'i•ty,** *n.* **—am'bi•dex'trous•ly,** *adv.*

am•bi•ent (am'bē ənt), *adj.* surrounding; encompassing.

am•bi•gu•i•ty (am'bi gyōō'i tē), *n., pl.* **-ties. 1.** doubtfulness or uncertainty. **2.** the condition or quality of being ambiguous. **3.** an ambiguous word or expression.

am•big'u•ous (-big'yōō əs), *adj.* **1.** having several

possible meanings or interpretations. **2.** doubtful or uncertain. **—am•big'u•ous•ly,** *adv.*

am•bi•tion (am bish'ən), *n.* **1.** an earnest desire for achievement, distinction, wealth, or power. **2.** the object of ambition.

am•bi'tious, *adj.* **1.** having or marked by ambition. **2.** requiring exceptional effort. **—am•bi'tious•ly,** *adv.*

am•biv•a•lence (am biv'ə ləns), *n.* coexistence of conflicting thoughts or feelings. **—am•biv'a•lent,** *adj.* **—am•biv'a•lent•ly,** *adv.*

am•ble (am'bəl), *v.,* **-bled, -bling,** *n.* **—v.i. 1.** to go at a slow, easy pace. **—n. 2.** a slow, easy pace. **—am'bler,** *n.*

am•bro•sia (am brō'zhə), *n.* **1.** the food of the ancient Greek and Roman gods. **2.** something that has a delicious taste or smell. **—am•bro'sial,** *adj.*

am•bu•lance (am'byə ləns), *n.* a vehicle equipped for carrying sick or injured people.

am'bu•late' (-lāt'), *v.i.,* **-lat•ed, -lat•ing.** to walk or move about. **—am'bu•lant** (-lənt), *adj.* **—am'bu•la'tion,** *n.* **—am'bu•la'tor,** *n.*

am'bu•la•to'ry (-lə tôr'ē), *adj., n., pl.* **-ries. —adj. 1.** of or capable of walking. **2.** moving about. **—n. 3.** the covered walk of a cloister.

am•bus•cade (am'bə skād'), *n., v.t., v.i.,* **-cad•ed, -cad•ing.** AMBUSH. **—am'bus•cad'er,** *n.*

am•bush (am'bŏŏsh), *n.* **1.** an act or instance of lying concealed so as to attack by surprise. **2.** the concealed position itself. **—v.t., v.i. 3.** to attack from or lie in ambush. **—am'bush•er,** *n.*

a•me•ba (ə mē'bə), *n., pl.* **-bas, -bae** (-bē). **1.** a one-celled protozoan with a mass of cytoplasm that changes in shape as the organism moves and engulfs food. **2.** a protozoan of the genus *Amoeba,* inhabiting bottom vegetation of freshwater ponds and streams: used widely in laboratory studies. **—a•me'bic,** *adj.* **—a•me'boid,** *adj.*

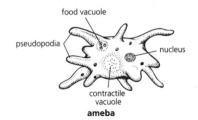

ameba

a•mel•io•rate (ə mēl'yə rāt'), *v.t., v.i.,* **-rat•ed, -rat•ing.** to make or become better; improve. **—a•mel'io•ra'tion,** *n.* **—a•mel'io•ra'tive,** *adj.*

a•men (ā'men', ä'men'), *interj.* so be it (used after a formal statement, esp. a prayer, to express solemn ratification or agreement). [< LL < Heb *āmēn*]

a•me•na•ble (ə mē'nə bəl, ə men'ə-), *adj.* **1.** ready or willing to agree or yield. **2.** liable to be called to account; answerable. **—a•me'na•bil'i•ty,** *n.* **—a•me'na•bly,** *adv.*

a•mend (ə mend'), *v.t.* **1.** to modify or rephrase (a bill, law, etc.) by formal procedure. **2.** to improve. **3.** to remove faults in; correct. **—a•mend'a•ble,** *adj.*

a•mend'ment, *n.* **1.** the act of amending or state of being amended. **2.** an alteration of or addition to a bill, law, etc.

a•mends', *n.* (*used with a sing. or pl. v.*) reparation for loss, damage, or injury.

a•men•i•ty (ə men'i tē, ə mē'ni-), *n., pl.* **-ties. 1.** an agreeable act or manner; courtesy or civility: *social amenities.* **2.** a feature that provides comfort, convenience, or pleasure.

Amer., 1. America. **2.** American.

Am•er•a•sian (am'ə rā'zhən), *n.* a person of mixed American and Asian descent.

A•mer•i•ca (ə mer'i kə), *n.* **1.** UNITED STATES. **2.** NORTH AMERICA. **3.** SOUTH AMERICA. **4.** Also called **the Americas.** North and South America considered together. —*Saying.* **5. Never sell America short,** have faith in the American future.

A•mer′i•can, *adj.* **1.** of the United States or its inhabitants. **2.** of North or South America. —*n.* **3.** a citizen of the United States. **4.** a native or inhabitant of the Western Hemisphere.

A•mer′i•ca′na (-kan′ə, -kä′nə), *n.pl.* books, papers, etc., relating to America, esp. to its history and culture.

Amer′ican Antislav′ery Soci′ety, *n.* a society, founded in 1833 and led by William Lloyd Garrison, to abolish slavery.

Amer′ican In′dian, *n.* a member of any of the indigenous peoples of North and South America.

A•mer′i•can•ism, *n.* a custom, trait, or language feature peculiar to the United States or its citizens.

A•mer′i•can•ize′, *v.t., v.i.,* **-ized, -iz•ing.** to make or become American in character. —**A•mer′i•can•i•za′tion,** *n.*

Amer′ican plan′, *n.* a system of paying a fixed hotel rate that covers room, service, and meals.

Amer′ican Revised′ Ver′sion, *n.* a revision of the Bible, published in the U.S. in 1901.

Amer′ican Revolu′tion, *n.* the war (1775–83) by which the American colonies won independence from Great Britain.

TIMETABLE OF EVENTS OF THE AMERICAN REVOLUTION

1763	October	Proclamation Line
1764	March–April	Revenue Act of 1764 (Sugar Act)
		Currency Act
1765	March	Stamp Act
1766	March	Parliament repeals the Stamp Act
		and passes the Declaratory Act
		on the same day (March 18)
1767	June	Townshend Acts
1770	March	Boston Massacre
1773	December	Boston Tea Party
1774	March–May	Parliament passes the Coercive
		(Intolerable) Acts
	September	First Continental Congress
		convenes
1775	April	Battles of Lexington and Concord
	May	Second Continental Congress
		convenes
	June	Battle of Bunker Hill
	December	Battle of Great Bridge
		Parliament passes the American
		Prohibitory Act
1776	July	Second Continental Congress
		adopts the Declaration
		of Independence

Amer′ican Samo′a, *n.* the islands of Samoa belonging to the U.S. 61,819.

Amer′ican Sign′ Lan′guage, *n.* a visual-gesture language used by deaf people in the U.S. and English-speaking parts of Canada.

am•er•i•ci•um (am′ə rish′ē əm), *n.* a radioactive element produced by helium bombardment of uranium and plutonium. *Symbol:* Am; *at. no.:* 95.

Am•er•ind (am′ə rind), *n.* = AMERICAN INDIAN. Also called **Am′er•in′di•an** (-rin′dē ən).

am•e•thyst (am′ə thist), *n.* a purple or violet quartz used as a gem.

a•mi•a•ble (ā′mē ə bəl), *adj.* having or showing agreeable personal qualities; pleasant and friendly. —**a′mi•a•bil′i•ty,** *n.* —**a′mi•a•bly,** *adv.*

am•i•ca•ble (am′i kə bəl), *adj.* friendly; peaceable. —**am′i•ca•bil′i•ty,** *n.* —**am′i•ca•bly,** *adv.*

a•mid (ə mid′) also **a•midst** (ə midst′), *prep.* in the middle of; among.

am•ide (am′īd, -id), *n.* an organic compound formed from ammonia.

a•mid′ships′ or **-ship′,** *adv.* in or toward the middle part of a ship or aircraft.

a•mi•go (ə mē′gō, ä mē′-), *n., pl* **-gos.** a male friend.

a•mil•len•ni•al•ism (ā′mi len′ē ə liz′əm), *n.* the

belief that the spiritual rule of Christ in heaven is the millennium. Also called **nonmillennialism.**

a•mi′no ac′id (ə mē′nō, am′ə nō), *n.* any of a class of organic compounds that are the building blocks from which proteins are constructed.

A•mish (ä′mish, am′ish), *adj.* **1.** of or pertaining to a strict sect of Mennonites that oppose ritualism and wear unadorned clothing. —*n.* **2.** (*used with a pl. v.*) the Amish Mennonites. [< G *amisch,* after Jakob *Ammann,* Swiss Mennonite bishop of the 17th cent.]

a•miss (ə mis′), *adv.* **1.** out of the right or proper course or order. —*adj.* **2.** wrong or improper.

am•i•ty (am′i tē), *n.* peaceful relations, as between nations; friendship.

Am•man (ä män′), *n.* the capital of Jordan. 777,500.

am•me•ter (am′mē′tər), *n.* an instrument for measuring current in amperes.

am•mo (am′ō), *n. Informal.* ammunition.

am•mo•nia (ə mōn′yə), *n., pl.* **-nias. 1.** a colorless, pungent gaseous compound used in the manufacture of chemicals and reagents. **2.** Also called **ammo′nia wa′ter.** ammonia dissolved in water.

am•mu•ni•tion (am′yə nish′ən), *n.* **1.** projectiles, esp. bullets or shells, fired by guns. **2.** a means of offense or defense.

am•ne•sia (am nē′zhə), *n.* complete or partial loss of memory. —**am•ne′si•ac′** (-zhē ak′, -zē-), **am•ne′sic** (-sik, -zik), *adj., n.*

am•nes•ty (am′nə stē), *n., pl.* **-ties,** *v.,* **-tied, -ty•ing.** —*n.* **1.** a general pardon for offenses against a government. —*v.t.* **2.** to grant amnesty to.

am•ni•o (am′nē ō′), *n., pl.* **-ni•os.** *Informal.* amniocentesis.

am′ni•o•cen•te′sis (-sen tē′sis), *n., pl.* **-ses** (-sēz) the surgical procedure of withdrawing a sample of fluid from the uterus of a pregnant woman for genetic diagnosis of the fetus.

Am•non (am′non), *n.* the oldest son of David. II Sam. 3:2; I Chron. 3:1.

a•moe•ba (ə mē′bə), *n., pl.* **-bas, -bae** (-bē). AMEBA.

a•mok (ə muk′, ə mok′), *adj., adv.* AMUCK.

a•mong (ə mung′), *prep.* **1.** in, into, or through the midst of. **2.** with a share for each of. **3.** in the class or group of. **4.** by the joint or reciprocal action of. —**Usage.** Traditionally, AMONG expresses relationship when more than two are involved: *The winnings were divided among the six men.* BETWEEN is used when only two persons or things are involved: *to decide between tea and coffee.* This distinction is not very widely maintained in the case of BETWEEN, which is often used when more than two are involved.

a•mongst (ə mungst′), *prep.* AMONG.

a•mor•al (ā môr′əl, ā mor′-), *adj.* **1.** neither moral nor immoral. **2.** lacking or indifferent to moral principles. —**a•mo•ral•i•ty** (ā′mə ral′i tē), *n.* —**a•mor′al•ly,** *adv.*

am•o•rous (am′ər əs), *adj.* **1.** inclined to love, esp. sexual love. **2.** being in love; enamored. **3.** expressing or pertaining to love. —**am′o•rous•ly,** *adv.* —**am′o•rous•ness,** *n.*

a•mor•phous (ə môr′fəs), *adj.* **1.** lacking definite form. **2.** of no particular kind or character; indeterminate. **3.** not crystalline. —**a•mor′phous•ly,** *adv.* —**a•mor′phous•ness,** *n.*

am•or•tize (am′ər tīz′, ə môr′tīz), *v.t.,* **-tized, -tiz•ing.** to liquidate or extinguish (a debt or other liability), esp. by periodic payments. —**am′or•ti•za′tion,** *n.*

A•mos (ā′məs), *n.* **1.** a Minor Prophet of the 8th century B.C. **2.** a book of the Bible bearing his name.

a•mount (ə mount′), *n.* **1.** the total of two or more quantities or sums. **2.** quantity; measure. —*v.i.* **3.** to yield a sum or total; add up. **4.** to be equal in value, effect, or extent. —**Usage.** Traditionally, AMOUNT is used with mass or uncountable nouns (*the amount of paperwork; the amount of energy*) and NUMBER is used with countable nouns (*a number of songs; a number of days*). However, AMOUNT is occasionally used with countable nouns, esp. when the noun can be considered as a unit or group (the amount of people present; the amount of weapons).

a•mour (ə mŏŏr/), n. a love affair, esp. an illicit one.

a•mour-pro•pre (A mŏŏr prô/pRə), n. French. self-esteem.

amp., 1. amperage. 2. ampere.

am•per•age (am/pər ij, am pēr/-), n. the strength of an electric current measured in amperes.

am•pere (am/pēr), n. a unit of electric current equal to the steady current produced by one volt acting through a resistance of one ohm.

am•per•sand (am/pər sand/), n. a symbol (& or ·) for and. [contr. of and per se and lit., (the symbol) & by itself (stands for) and]

am•phet•a•mine (am fet/ə mēn/, -min), n. a drug that stimulates the central nervous system: used chiefly to counteract depression.

am•phib•i•an (am fib/ē ən), n. 1. an amphibious cold-blooded vertebrate, as a frog. 2. an amphibious airplane or military vehicle. —adj. 3. AMPHIBIOUS.

am•phib•i•ous (am fib/ē əs), adj. 1. capable of living or operating on land and in water. 2. pertaining to military operations by both land and naval forces. —am•phib/i•ous•ly, adv.

Am•phip•o•lis (am fip/ə lis), n. a city of Macedonia through which the Apostle Paul passed. Acts 17:1.

am•phi•the•a•ter (am/fə thē/ə tər, -thē²/-), n. an oval or round building or room with tiers of seats around a central open area. Often, **am/phi•the/a•tre.**

am•ple (am/pəl), adj., -pler, -plest. 1. fully sufficient for a purpose or need. 2. large; roomy. —am/•ply, adv.

am•pli•fi•er (am/plə fī/ər), n. an electronic component or circuit for amplifying power, current, or voltage.

am•pli•fy/, v., -fied, -fy•ing. —v.t. 1. to make larger, greater, or stronger. 2. to expand or clarify by expanding. 3. to increase the amplitude of. —v.i. 4. to discourse at length. —am/pli•fi•ca/tion, n.

am/pli•tude/ (-tōŏd/, -tyōŏd/), n. 1. ample breadth or width; largeness. 2. large measure or quantity. 3. range, scope, or capacity, as of intellect. 4. the absolute value of the maximum displacement during an oscillation. 5. the maximum deviation of an alternating current from its average value.

am/plitude modula/tion, n. See AM.

am•pule or **-pul** or **-poule** (am/pyōōl, -pōōl), n. a sealed glass or plastic bulb containing a solution for a hypodermic injection.

am•pu•tate (am/pyŏŏ tāt/), v.t., -tat•ed, -tat•ing. to cut off (a limb or digit of the body), as by surgery. —am/pu•ta/tion, n.

am/pu•tee/, n., pl. -tees. a person who has lost a limb or digit by amputation.

Am•ram (am/ram), n. the father of Aaron, Moses and Miriam. Ex. 6:20.

Am•ster•dam (am/stər dam/), n. the official capital of the Netherlands. 712,294.

amt., amount.

a•muck (ə muk/), adj. 1. being in a murderous frenzy. —adv., **Idiom.** 2. **run** or **go amuck, a.** to rush about in a murderous frenzy. **b.** to be out of control. [< Malay]

am•u•let (am/yə lit), n. a charm worn to ward off evil.

A•mund•sen (ä/mənd sən, ä mən-), n. **Ro•ald** (rō-/äl), 1872–1928, Norwegian explorer: discovered the South Pole in 1911.

a•muse (ə myōōz/), v.t., a•mused, a•mus•ing. 1. to occupy pleasantly; divert. 2. to cause to laugh. —a•muse/ment, n.

amuse/ment park/, n. a park equipped with recreational devices such as a Ferris wheel or roller coaster.

am•yl•ase (am/ə lās/, -lāz/), n. any of several digestive enzymes that break down starches.

an¹ (ən; when stressed an), indefinite article. the

form of A¹ before an initial vowel sound (an arch; an honor). —Usage. See A¹.

an² (ən; when stressed an), prep. the form of A² before an initial vowel sound: 55 miles an hour.

-an¹, an adjective suffix meaning of, belonging to, or resembling (American).

-an², a noun suffix meaning: one belonging to or residing in (Hawaiian); one skilled in (artisan).

a•nach•ro•nism (ə nak/rə niz/əm), n. 1. an error in which a person, object, or event is assigned an incorrect date or period. 2. a thing or person that belongs to another, esp. an earlier, time. —a•nach/ro•nis/tic, adj.

an•a•con•da (an/ə kon/də), n., pl. -das. a South American boa that often grows to more than 25 ft. (7.6 m).

an•aer•o•bic (an/ə rō/bik, an/â-), adj. (of an organism or tissue) living in the absence of air or free oxygen.

an•aes•the•sia (an/əs thē/zhə), n. ANESTHESIA.

an•a•gram (an/ə gram/), n. a word or phrase formed from another by rearranging its letters.

An•a•heim (an/ə hīm/), n. a city in SW California. 282,133.

a•nal (ān/l), adj. of or near the anus. —a/nal•ly, adv.

an•al•ge•si•a (an/l jē/zē ə), n. absence of sense of pain; insensibility to pain. —an/al•ge/sic (-zik), adj., n.

an•a•log (an/l ôg/, -og/), n. 1. ANALOGUE. —adj. 2. of a mechanism that represents data by measurement of a continuous physical variable. 3. using hands on a dial to show the time: an analog watch.

an/alog comput/er, n. a computer that represents data by measurable quantities, as voltages, rather than by numbers.

a•nal•o•gous (ə nal/ə gəs), adj. 1. having or showing an analogy; similar or comparable. 2. Biol. corresponding in function but of different origin and evolution. —a•nal/o•gous•ly, adv.

an•a•logue (an/l ôg/, -og/), n. 1. something analogous to something else. 2. Biol. an analogous organ.

a•nal•o•gy (ə nal/ə jē), n., pl. -gies. 1. a similarity between like features of unlike things on which a comparison may be based. 2. a form of reasoning in which one thing is inferred to be similar to another thing in a certain respect on the basis of known similarities in other respects. —an•a•log•i•cal (an/l oj/i-kəl), adj.

a•nal/y•sand/ (-sand/), n. a person undergoing psychoanalysis.

a•nal/y•sis (-sis), n., pl. -ses (-sēz/). 1. separation of a material or abstract entity into its constituent elements, esp. as a method of studying its nature or determining its essential features. 2. a presentation, usu. in writing, of the results of analysis. 3. PSYCHOANALYSIS. —an•a•lyt•ic (an/l it/ik), an/a•lyt/i•cal, adj. —an/a•lyt/i•cal•ly, adv.

an•a•lyst (an/l ist), n. 1. one who analyzes. 2. a psychoanalyst.

an/a•lyze/ (-līz/), v.t., -lyzed, -lyz•ing. 1. to subject to analysis. 2. to examine critically. 3. to psychoanalyze. —an/a•lyz/a•ble, adj. —an/a•lyz/er, n.

An•a•ni•as (an/ə nī/əs), n. 1. a man who was struck dead for lying. Acts 5:1–5. 2. a liar.

an•a•pest (an/ə pest/), n. a metrical foot of two unstressed syllables followed by a stressed syllable.

an•ar•chism (an/ər kiz/əm), n. 1. a doctrine urging the abolition of government as the indispensable condition for full liberty. 2. political disorder or violence. —an/ar•chist, n. —an/ar•chis/tic, adj.

an/ar•chy (-kē), n. 1. a state of society without government or law. 2. confusion; disorder. —an•ar/chic (-är/kik), an•ar/chi•cal, adj. —an•ar/chi•cal•ly, adv.

a•nath•e•ma (ə nath/ə mə), n., pl. -mas. 1. a person or thing detested or loathed. 2. a person or thing condemned to damnation. 3. a formal ecclesiastical curse of excommunication.

a•nath/e•ma•tize/ (-tīz/), v.t., -tized, -tiz•ing. to pronounce an anathema against.

An•a•thoth (an'ə thoth'), *n.* the birthplace of the prophet Jeremiah. Jer. 1:1, 29:27, 32:7–9.

a•nat•o•mize (ə nat'ə mīz'), *v.t.* -mized, -miz•ing. **1.** to dissect. **2.** to examine in great detail. —**a•nat'-o•mist,** *n.*

a•nat'o•my, *n.*, *pl.* -mies. **1.** the science dealing with the structure of animals and plants. **2.** the structure of an animal or plant. **3.** a minute examination; analysis. —**an•a•tom•i•cal** (an'ə tom'i kəl), **an'a•tom'ic,** *adj.*

-ance, a suffix meaning: action (*appearance*); state or quality (*brilliance*); thing or object (*contrivance*).

an•ces•tor (an'ses tər), *n.* **1.** a person from whom one is descended; forebear. **2.** the form or stock from which an organism has descended. **3.** something serving as a prototype or forerunner. —**an•ces'tral,** *adj.*

an'ces•try, *n.*, *pl.* -tries. **1.** ancestral descent; lineage. **2.** a series of ancestors.

an•chor (ang'kər), *n.* **1.** a heavy device thrown overboard to restrict the motion of a ship. **2.** something that gives support or stability. **3.** a broadcaster, as on a news program, who coordinates the reports of other broadcasters. **4.** a TV program that attracts many viewers who are likely to stay tuned to the network for the programs that follow. **5.** a well-known store that attracts customers to the shopping center in which it is located. —*v.t.* **6.** to hold fast by or as if by an anchor. **7.** to serve as a radio or television anchor for. —*v.i.* **8.** to lie at anchor. —*Idiom.* **9. at anchor,** kept in place by an anchor.

an'chor•age (-ij), *n.* **1.** a place for anchoring ships. **2.** a charge for occupying an anchorage.

An'chor•age, *n.* a seaport in S Alaska. 253,649.

an•cho•rite (ang'kə rīt'), *n.* a person living in religious seclusion; hermit.

an'chor•man' or **-wom'an** or **-per'son,** *n.*, *pl.* -men or -wom•en or -per•sons. a person who anchors a program of news, sports, etc.; anchor.

an•cho•vy (an'chō vē, -chə-), *n.*, *pl.* -vies. a small herringlike fish that is used in cooking.

an•cien ré•gime (äN syaN RĀ zhēm'), *n. French.* **1.** the political and social system of France before the revolution of 1789. **2.** any former political and social system.

an•cient (ān'shənt), *adj.* **1.** of or belonging to times long past, esp. before the end of the Western Roman Empire. **2.** very old; aged. —*n.* **3.** a person who lived in ancient times, esp. a Greek or a Roman. **4.** a very old person. —**an'cient•ness,** *n.*

an'cient•ly, *adv.* in ancient times; of old.

An'cient of Days', *n.* God. Dan. 7:9, 13, 22.

an•cil•lar•y (an'sə ler'ē), *adj.* **1.** subordinate. **2.** auxiliary.

-ancy, a suffix meaning state or quality (*brilliancy*).

and (and; *unstressed* ənd, ən, n), *conj.* **1.** as well as; in addition to. **2.** added to; plus. **3.** then. **4.** at the same time. **5.** *Informal.* to: *Try and* do it.

an•dan•te (än dän'tā), *adj.*, *adv. Music.* moderately slow.

An•der•sen (an'dər sən), *n.* **Hans Christian,** 1805–75, Danish author of fairy tales.

An•der•son (an'dər sən), *n.* **1. Marian,** 1902–93, U.S. contralto. **2. Maxwell,** 1888–1959, U.S. dramatist.

An•der•son•ville (an'dər sən vil'), *n.* a village in SW Georgia: site of a Confederate military prison. 267.

An•des (an'dēz), *n.pl.* a mountain range in W South America. —**An'de•an,** *adj.*

and•i•ron (and'ī'ərn), *n.* one of a pair of metal supports for logs in a fireplace.

and/or, *conj.* (used to imply that either or both of the things mentioned may be involved): *accident and/or health insurance.*

An•dor•ra (an dôr'ə, -dor'ə), *n.* a republic in the E Pyrenees. 74,839.

An•drew (an'drōō), *n.* one of the 12 apostles of Jesus. Mark 3:18; John 1:40–42.

An•drews (an'drōōz), *n.* **Julie,** born 1934, English singer and actress.

an•dro•gen (an'drə jən, -jen'), *n.* a substance, as testosterone, that promotes male characteristics.

an•drog•y•nous (an droj'ə nəs), *adj.* having both masculine and feminine characteristics. —**an•drog'y•ny,** *n.*

an•droid (an'droid), *n.* an automaton in the form of a human being.

an•ec•dote (an'ik dōt'), *n.* a short account of an interesting, often biographical incident. —**an'ec•do'tal,** *adj.* —**an'ec•dot'ist,** *n.*

a•ne•mi•a (ə nē'mē ə), *n.* a reduction in the hemoglobin of red blood cells with consequent deficiency of oxygen, leading to weakness and pallor. —**a•ne'mic,** *adj.*

an•e•mom•e•ter (an'ə mom'i tər), *n.* an instrument for measuring the speed of wind.

a•nem•o•ne (ə nem'ə nē'), *n.*, *pl.* -nes. **1.** a plant of the buttercup family, with petallike sepals in a variety of colors. **2.** SEA ANEMONE.

a•nent (ə nent'), *prep.* in regard to; concerning.

an'er•oid barom'eter (an'ə roid'), *n.* a barometer consisting of a chamber with an elastic cover that is compressed by the outside air.

an•es•the•sia (an'əs thē'zhə), *n.* general or localized insensibility to pain or other sensation. —**an•es•the•tist** (ə nes'thi tist), *n.*

an'es•the'si•ol•o•gy (-zē ol'ə jē), *n.* the science of administering anesthetics. —**an'es•the'si•ol•o•gist,** *n.*

an'es•thet'ic (-thet'ik), *n.* **1.** a substance, as ether, that produces anesthesia. —*adj.* **2.** pertaining to or causing anesthesia.

an•es•the•tize (ə nes'thi tīz'), *v.t.* -tized, -tiz•ing. to induce anesthesia in.

an•eu•rysm or **-rism** (an'yə riz'əm), *n.* a permanent cardiac or arterial dilatation usu. caused by weakening of the vessel wall.

a•new (ə nōō', ə nyōō'), *adv.* **1.** once more. **2.** in a new form or manner.

an•gel (ān'jəl), *n.* **1.** a celestial attendant of God. **2.** a conventional representation of an angel, in human form, with wings. **3.** a messenger, esp. of God. **4.** a very kind person. **5.** *Informal.* a financial backer, as of a play. —*Idiom.* **6. on the side of the angels,** holding a morally correct viewpoint. —*Saying.* **7. to entertain an angel unaware,** to offer hospitality to a stranger who may be of great merit. Heb. 13:1. [OE *engel* < LL *angelus* < Gk *ángelos* messenger, trans. of Heb *malakh*] —**an•gel•ic** (an jel'ik), **an•gel'i•cal,** *adj.*

an'gel•fish', *n.*, *pl.* -fish, -fish•es. a brightly colored South American freshwater fish.

an'gel food' cake', *n.* a light, white cake made with stiffly beaten egg whites.

angel'ic hymn', *n. Gloria in excelsis deo,* sung by the angels who appeared to the shepherds at Bethlehem. Luke 2:14.

An•ge•lus (an'jə ləs), *n.* (*often l.c.*) a devotion in honor of the Annunciation and the Incarnation. [< LL, from the first word of the service: *Angelus* (*dominī nūntiāvit Mariae*). See ANGEL]

an•ger (ang'gər), *n.* **1.** a strong feeling of displeasure and belligerence. —*v.t.*, *v.i.* **2.** to make or become angry.

an•gi•na pec•to•ris (an jī'nə pek'tə ris), *n.* a sensation of crushing pressure in the chest, caused by inadequate blood flow to the heart muscle. Also called **an•gi'na.**

an•gi•o•plas•ty (an'jē ə plas'tē), *n.*, *pl.* -ties. the surgical repair of a blood vessel, as by inserting a balloon-tipped catheter to unclog it.

an•gi•o•sperm (an'jē ə spûrm'), *n.* a plant whose seeds are enclosed in a fruit, grain, pod, or capsule.

an•gle¹ (ang'gəl), *n.*, *v.*, -gled, -gling. —*n.* **1. a.** the space within two lines diverging from a common point. **b.** a figure so formed. **c.** the amount of rotation needed to bring one line into coincidence with another. **2.** a projecting corner. **3.** a point of view; standpoint. **4.** *Informal.* a secret motive or plan.

—*v.t.*, *v.i.* **5.** to move or bend at an angle. **6.** to hit or direct at an angle. **7.** to write from a particular or biased viewpoint.

an•gle² (ang′gəl), *v.i.*, **-gled, -gling. 1.** to fish with hook and line. **2.** to attempt to get something by sly or artful means. **—an′gler,** *n.*

An′gle, *n.* a member of a Germanic people who migrated to England in the 5th century A.D.

an′gle i′ron, *n.* a piece of structural iron or steel having a cross section in the form of an **L**.

an′gle•worm′, *n.* an earthworm, esp. as used for bait.

An•gli•can (ang′gli kən), *adj.* **1.** of the Church of England. **2.** of England or its inhabitants. **—***n.* **3.** a member of the Church of England. **—An′gli•can•ism,** *n.*

An′gli•cism (-siz′əm), *n.* an English word, idiom, etc., occurring in another language.

An′gli•cize′ (-sīz′), *v.t.*, *v.i.*, **-cized, -ciz•ing.** to make or become English in form or character. **—An′-gli•ci•za′tion,** *n.*

An•glo (ang′glō), *n.*, *pl.* **-glos.** a white American of non-Hispanic descent.

Anglo-, a combining form meaning English (*Anglo-phile*).

An•glo-French (ang′glō french′), *n.* the French language used in England from the Norman Conquest to the end of the Middle Ages.

An•glo•phile (ang′glə fīl′), *n.* a person who admires England and English customs.

An•glo-Sax•on (ang′glō sak′sən), *n.* **1.** a member of any of the Germanic peoples who invaded and occupied England in the 5th and 6th centuries A.D. **2.** OLD ENGLISH. **3.** a person of English ancestry. **—***adj.* **4.** of the Anglo-Saxons.

An•go•la (ang gō′lə), *n.* a republic in SW Africa. 10,623,994. **—An•go′lan,** *adj.*, *n.*

An•go•ra (ang gôr′ə), *n.*, *pl.* **-ras. 1.** a cat, goat, or rabbit with long, silky hair. **2.** (*often l.c.*) a yarn or fabric made from the hair of the Angora goat or rabbit.

an•gry (ang′grē), *adj.*, **-gri•er, -gri•est. 1.** feeling or showing anger. **2.** inflamed, as a sore. **3.** exhibiting characteristics associated with anger or danger: *an angry sea.* **—an′gri•ly,** *adv.* **—an′gri•ness,** *n.*

angst (ängkst), *n.* a feeling of dread, anxiety, or anguish.

ang•strom (ang′strəm), *n.* (*often cap.*) a unit of length equal to one ten millionth of a millimeter, primarily used to express electromagnetic wavelengths.

an•guish (ang′gwish), *n.* **1.** acute suffering or pain. **—***v.i.*, *v.t.* **2.** to suffer or cause to suffer anguish. **—an′guished,** *adj.*

an•gu•lar (ang′gyə lər), *adj.* **1.** having, consisting of, or forming an angle. **2.** measured by an angle. **3.** bony, lean, or gaunt. **4.** moving awkwardly; stiff. **—an′gu•lar′i•ty,** *n.*

an•hy•dride (an hī′drīd, -drid), *n.* a compound from which water has been abstracted.

an•hy′drous (-drəs), *adj.* (of a chemical compound) with all water removed.

an•i•line (an′l in, -īn′), *n.* a colorless, oily liquid used chiefly in the synthesis of dyes and drugs.

an•i•mad•vert (an′ə mad vûrt′), *v.i.* to comment unfavorably or critically. **—an′i•mad•ver′sion,** *n.*

an•i•mal (an′ə məl), *n.* **1.** a multicellular organism that can move voluntarily and can actively acquire food and digest it internally. **2.** an animal other than a human being. **3.** a brutish or beastlike person. **—***adj.* **4.** of or derived from animals. **5.** pertaining to the physical rather than the spiritual or intellectual nature of human beings.

an•i•mal•cule (an′ə mal′kyōōl), *n.* a minute or microscopic animal.

an′i•mate′ (*v.* -māt′; *adj.* -mit), *v.*, **-mat•ed, -mat•ing,** *adj.* **—***v.t.* **1.** to give life to. **2.** to give zest to. **3.** to move or stir to action. **4.** to prepare or produce as an animated cartoon. **—***adj.* **5.** possessing life; alive. **6.** of or relating to animal life. **—an′i•mat′ed,** *adj.* **—an′i•ma′tion,** *n.* **—an′i•ma′tor,** *n.*

an′imated cartoon′, *n.* a motion picture consisting of a sequence of drawings that seem to move.

an•i•mism (an′ə miz′əm), *n.* the belief that natural objects and phenomena possess souls. **—an′i•mist,** *n.*, *adj.* **—an′i•mis′tic,** *adj.*

an•i•mos•i•ty (an′ə mos′i tē), *n.*, *pl.* **-ties.** a feeling of ill will; hostility.

an′i•mus (-məs), *n.* strong dislike; animosity.

an•i•on (an′ī′ən), *n.* a negatively charged ion, esp. one that is attracted to the anode in electrolysis. **—an′i•on′ic** (-on′ik), *adj.*

an•ise (an′is), *n.* **1.** a Mediterranean plant of the parsley family that yields aniseed. **2.** ANISEED.

an′i•seed′ (-ə sēd′), *n.* the aromatic seed of the anise, used in medicine and in cooking.

An•ka•ra (ang′kər ə), *n.* the capital of Turkey. 2,251,533.

ankh (angk), *n.* a cross with a loop as its top, used esp. in ancient Egypt as a symbol of life.

ankh

an•kle (ang′kəl), *n.* **1.** the joint between the foot and leg. **2.** the slender part of the leg above the foot.

an′kle•bone′, *n.* the uppermost of the tarsal bones.

an′klet (-klit), *n.* **1.** a sock that reaches just above the ankle. **2.** an ornament worn around the ankle.

An•na (an′ə), *n.* a woman with prophetic gifts who greeted Jesus as the Messiah. Luke 2:36–38.

an•nals (an′lz), *n.pl.* **1.** a record of events, esp. a yearly record, in chronological order. **2.** historical records; chronicles.

An•nap•o•lis (ə nap′ə lis), *n.* the capital of Maryland, in the central part, on Chesapeake Bay: U.S. Naval Academy. 33,360.

An•na•pur•na (an′ə pûr′nə), *n.* a mountain in N Nepal. 26,503 ft. (8078 m).

Ann Ar•bor (an är′bər), *n.* a city in SE Michigan. 108,817.

an•neal (ə nēl′), *v.t.* **1.** to free (glass, metal, etc.) from internal stress by heating and gradually cooling. **2.** to toughen or temper.

an•ne•lid (an′l id), *n.* a segmented worm, as an earthworm.

an•nex (*v.* ə neks′, an′eks; *n.* an′eks), *v.t.* **1.** to attach or append, esp. to something larger. **2.** to incorporate (territory) into the domain of a state. **—***n.* **3.** something annexed. **4.** a subsidiary building or an addition to a building. **—an′nex•a′tion,** *n.*

an•ni•hi•late (ə nī′ə lāt′), *v.t.*, **-lat•ed, -lat•ing.** to reduce to utter ruin or nonexistence; destroy utterly. **—an•ni′hi•la′tion,** *n.* **—an•ni′hi•la′tor,** *n.*

an•ni•ver•sa•ry (an′ə vûr′sə rē), *n.*, *pl.* **-ries. 1.** the yearly recurrence of the date of a past event. **2.** the celebration or commemoration of an anniversary.

an•no•tate (an′ə tāt′), *v.t.*, **-tat•ed, -tat•ing.** to supply (a text) with critical or explanatory notes. **—an′no•ta′tion,** *n.* **—an′no•ta′tive,** *adj.* **—an′no•ta′tor,** *n.*

an•nounce (ə nouns′), *v.*, **-nounced, -nounc•ing.** **—***v.t.* **1.** to make known publicly. **2.** to state the approach or arrival of. **—***v.i.* **3.** to serve as an announcer, esp. of a broadcast. **4.** to declare one's candidacy, as for a political office. **—an•nounce′ment,** *n.*

an•nounc′er, *n.* a person who announces, esp. one who introduces programs on radio or television.

an•noy (ə noi′), *v.t.* to disturb or bother, esp. persistently; irritate. **—an•noy′ance,** *n.* **—an•noy′ing,** *adj.* **—an•noy′ing•ly,** *adv.*

an•nu•al (an′yōō əl), *adj.* **1.** pertaining to a year. **2.** occurring or recurring once a year. **3.** (of a plant) living only one growing season. **4.** performed during a year. —*n.* **5.** an annual plant. **6.** a publication issued once a year. —**an′nu•al•ly,** *adv.*

an′nual ring′, *n.* a yearly formation of new wood in woody plants, observable as a ring on the cross section of a tree trunk.

an•nu•i•tant (ə nŏō′i tnt, ə nyŏō′-), *n.* a person who receives an annuity.

an•nu′i•ty, *n., pl.* **-ties. 1.** an amount of money payable at stated intervals, usu. annually. **2.** the right to receive an annuity.

an•nul (ə nul′), *v.t.,* **-nulled, -nul•ling. 1.** to declare void or null; invalidate. **2.** to reduce to nothing; obliterate. —**an•nul′ment,** *n.*

an•nu•lar (an′yə lər), *adj.* having the form of a ring. —**an′nu•lar/i•ty,** *n.*

An•nun•ci•a•tion (ə nun′sē ā′shən), *n.* **1. a.** the angel Gabriel's announcement to the Virgin Mary of her conception of Christ. **b.** the church festival, March 25, in memory of this. **2.** (*l.c.*) an act or instance of announcing.

an•ode (an′ōd), *n.* **1.** the electrode by which current enters an electrolytic cell. **2.** the negative terminal of a battery. **3.** the positive electrode of an electron tube.

an•o•dyne (an′ə dīn′), *n.* something that relieves pain or distress.

a•noint (ə noint′), *v.t.* **1.** to apply oil to by rubbing or sprinkling. **2.** to consecrate by applying oil. —**a•noint′er,** *n.* —**a•noint′ment,** *n.*

a•nom•a•ly (ə nom′ə lē), *n., pl.* **-lies. 1.** a deviation from the common type, rule, arrangement, or form. **2.** someone or something abnormal, unusual, or irregular. —**a•nom′a•lous,** *adj.*

a•non (ə non′), *adv.* **1.** soon. **2.** at another time.

anon., *n.* **1.** anonymous. **2.** anonymously.

a•non•y•mous (ə non′ə məs), *adj.* **1.** of unknown or unacknowledged origin. **2.** not named or identified. **3.** lacking individuality or distinction. —**an•o•nym•i•ty** (an′ə nim′i tē), *n.* —**a•non′y•mous•ly,** *adv.*

a•noph•e•les (ə nof′ə lēz′), *n., pl.* **-les.** a mosquito that is a vector of the parasite causing malaria in humans.

an•o•rex•i•a (an′ə rek′sē ə), *n.* **1.** loss of appetite. **2.** Also called **anorex′ia ner•vo′sa** (nûr vō′sə). an eating disorder marked by excessive dieting and often emaciation. —**an′o•rex′ic, an′o•rec′tic,** *adj., n.*

an•oth•er (ə nuth′ər), *adj.* **1.** being one more of the same; additional. **2.** of a different kind; distinct. —*pron.* **3.** an additional one. **4.** a different one. **5.** a person other than oneself or the one specified.

an•swer (an′sər, än′-), *n.* **1.** a spoken or written reply or response to a question, request, letter, etc. **2.** a correct response to a question. **3.** an equivalent or approximation; counterpart: *the French answer to the Beatles.* **4.** an action serving as a reply or response: *His answer was a stern look.* **5.** a solution to a problem, esp. in mathematics. **6.** a reply to a charge or accusation. **7.** the defendant's reply to the plaintiff's charge. —*v.i.* **8.** to speak or write in response; make answer; reply. **9.** to respond by an act or motion: *He answered with a quick shake of his head.* **10.** to act or suffer in consequence (usu. fol. by *for*). **11.** to be or declare oneself responsible or accountable (usu. fol. by *for*): *I will answer for his safety.* **12.** to be satisfactory or serve (usu. fol. by *for*). **13.** to conform; correspond (usu. fol. by *to*): *She answered to the description.* —*v.t.* **14.** to speak or write in response to; reply to. **15.** to act or move in response to: *Answer the doorbell.* **16.** to solve or present a solution of. **17.** to serve or fulfill: *This will answer the purpose.* **18.** to discharge (a responsibility, claim, debt, etc.). **19.** to conform or correspond to: *This dog answers your description.* **20.** to reply or respond favorably to: *to answer a request.* **21.** to atone for; make amends for. **22. answer back,** to reply impertinently. —*Proverb.* **23. A soft answer turneth away wrath,** gentle words deflect animosity. Prov. 15:1.

an′swering machine′, *n.* a device that answers

telephone calls with a recorded message and records messages from callers.

ant (ant), *n.* any of numerous small insects, usu. wingless, that live in highly organized colonies.

ant-, var. of ANTI-.

-ant, a suffix meaning: one that performs or promotes (*pollutant*); performing, promoting, or being (*pleasant*).

ant•ac•id (ant as′id), *adj.* **1.** neutralizing or counteracting acidity. —*n.* **2.** an antacid agent.

an•tag•o•nism (an tag′ə niz′əm), *n.* **1.** active hostility or opposition. **2.** an opposing force, principle, or tendency. —**an•tag′o•nis′tic,** *adj.*

an•tag′o•nist, *n.* **1.** an opponent; adversary. **2.** (in drama or literature) the opponent of the hero or protagonist.

an•tag′o•nize′, *v.t.,* **-nized, -niz•ing.** to cause to become hostile.

An•ta•na•na•ri•vo (an′tə nan′ə rē′vō), *n.* the capital of Madagascar. 703,000.

ant•arc•tic (ant ärk′tik, -är′tik), *adj.* **1.** of, at, or near the South Pole. —*n.* **2. the Antarctic,** the Antarctic Ocean and Antarctica.

Ant•arc′ti•ca (-ti kə), *n.* the continent surrounding the South Pole.

Antarc′tic Cir′cle, *n.* an imaginary line drawn parallel to the equator, at 23°28′ N of the South Pole.

Antarc′tic O′cean, *n.* the waters surrounding Antarctica.

ant′ bear′, *n.* AARDVARK.

an•te (an′tē), *n., pl.* **-tes,** *v.,* **-ted** or **-teed, -te•ing.** —*n.* **1.** (in poker) a stake put into the pot by each player before the deal. **2.** the price or cost of something. —*v.t., v.i.* **3.** (in poker) to put (one's ante) into the pot. **4.** to produce or pay (one's share).

ante-, a prefix meaning: happening before (*antediluvian*); in front of (*anteroom*).

ant′eat′er, *n.* any of several tropical New World mammals having a long snout and feeding on ants and termites.

an•te•bel•lum (an′tē bel′əm), *adj.* existing before a war, esp. the American Civil War.

an•te•ced•ent (an′tə sēd′nt), *adj.* **1.** preceding; prior. —*n.* **2.** a preceding circumstance or event. **3. antecedents,** ancestors. **4.** a word, phrase, or clause referred to by a pronoun. —**an′te•ced′ence,** *n.*

an′te•cham′ber (an′tē-), *n.* a room that serves as a waiting room and entrance to a larger room.

an•te•date (an′ti dāt′), *v.t.,* **-dat•ed, -dat•ing. 1.** to be of earlier date than. **2.** PREDATE (def. 1).

an•te•di•lu•vi•an (an′tē di lōō′vē ən), *adj.* **1.** of the period before the Biblical Flood. **2.** out of date; antiquated.

an•te•lope (an′tl ōp′), *n., pl.* **-lopes, -lope. 1.** any of several ruminants, chiefly of Africa and Asia, having permanent unbranched horns. **2.** PRONGHORN.

an′te me•rid′i•em (an′tē mə rid′ē əm), *adj.* See A.M.

an•ten•na (an ten′ə), *n., pl.* **-ten•nas** for 1, **-ten•nae** (-ten′ē) for 2. **1.** a conductor by which electromagnetic waves are sent out or received; aerial. **2.** one of the movable, sensory appendages occurring in pairs on the heads of insects and most other arthropods.

an•te•ri•or (an tēr′ē ər), *adj.* **1.** situated before or in front. **2.** preceding in time; earlier.

an•te•room (an′tē rōōm′, -rōōm′), *n.* ANTECHAMBER.

an•them (an′thəm), *n.* **1.** a hymn of praise, devotion, or patriotism. **2.** a piece of sacred vocal music.

an•ther (an′thər), *n.* the pollen-bearing part of a stamen.

ant•hill (ant′hil′), *n.* a mound formed by ants in constructing their nest.

an•thol•o•gy (an thol′ə jē), *n., pl.* **-gies.** a collection of selected writings. —**an•thol′o•gist,** *n.* —**an•thol′o•gize′,** *v.i., v.t.,* **-gized, -giz•ing.**

An•tho•ny (an′tə nē, -thə- *for* ; an′thə nē *for* 0), *n.* **Susan Brownell,** 1820–1906, U.S. reformer and suffragist.

an•thra•cite (an′thrə sīt′), *n.* a hard coal that

burns with little smoke. —**an′thra•cit′ic** (-sit′ik), *adj.*

an•thrax (an′thraks), *n.* an infectious bacterial disease of cattle, sheep, and other mammals that can be transmitted to humans.

an•thro•po•cen•tric (an′thrə pō sen′trik), *adj.* viewing and interpreting everything in terms of human experience and values.

an•thro•poid (an′thrə poid′), *adj.* **1.** resembling a human. —*n.* **2.** ANTHROPOID APE.

an′thropoid ape′, *n.* an ape resembling a human, as a gorilla or chimpanzee.

an′thro•pol′o•gy (-pol′ə jē), *n.* the science that deals with the origins, development, characteristics, and customs of humankind. —**an′thro•po•log′i•cal** (-pə loj′i kəl), *adj.* —**an′thro•pol′o•gist,** *n.*

an′thro•po•mor′phic (-pə môr′fik), *adj.* ascribing human form or attributes to a nonhuman thing or being. —**an′thro•po•mor′phism,** *n.*

an•ti (an′tī, an′tē), *n., pl.* **-tis.** a person who is opposed, as to a policy.

anti-, a prefix meaning: against or opposed to (*antislavery*); preventing or counteracting (*anticoagulant*); opposite or contrary to (*antihero*); rivaling (*Antichrist*).

an′ti•bal•lis′tic mis′sile (an′tē bə lis′tik, an′tī-), *n.* a missile designed to intercept and destroy a ballistic missile.

an•ti•bi•ot•ic (an′ti bī ot′ik), *n.* a substance, as penicillin, produced by a microorganism, capable of inhibiting or destroying other microorganisms, and used to treat infectious diseases.

an′ti•bod′y, *n., pl.* **-bod•ies.** a protein produced by the body that combines with a foreign antigen, as of a virus or bacterium, and disables it.

an•tic (an′tik), *n.* **1.** a playful prank. **2.** a ludicrous gesture or act. —*adj.* **3.** ludicrous; funny.

An′ti•christ′, *n.* **1.** a personage or power expected to corrupt the world but be conquered by Christ's Second Coming. **2.** (*often l.c.*) any opponent of or disbeliever in Christ. **3.** a false Christ.

an•tic•i•pate (an tis′ə pāt′), *v.t.,* **-pat•ed, -pat•ing. 1.** to realize beforehand; foresee. **2.** to look forward to, esp. with pleasure. **3.** to prevent or thwart by acting in advance; forestall. —**an•tic′i•pa′tion,** *n.* —**an•tic′i•pa•to′ry** (-pə tôr′ē), *adj.*

an•ti•cli•max (an′tē klī′maks, an′tī-), *n.* **1.** an event, conclusion, or statement that is far less important or powerful than expected. **2.** a disappointing or inglorious descent. —**an′ti•cli•mac′tic,** *adj.*

an•ti•cline (an′ti klīn′), *n.* an arched fold of rock whose layers slope downward.

an•ti•co•ag•u•lant (an′tē kō ag′yə lənt, an′tī-), *n.* a substance that prevents coagulation of blood.

an′ti•cy′clone, *n.* a circulation of winds around a central region of high atmospheric pressure. —**an′ti•cy•clon′ic** (-sī klon′ik), *adj.*

an′ti•de•pres′sant, *n.* a drug used to relieve mental depression.

an•ti•dote (an′ti dōt′), *n.* **1.** a remedy for counteracting the effects of a poison. **2.** something that counteracts injurious or unwanted effects.

An•tie•tam (an tē′təm), *n.* a creek flowing from S Pennsylvania through NW Maryland into the Potomac: Civil War battle fought near here at Sharpsburg, Md., in 1862.

an•ti•freeze (an′ti frēz′, an′tē-), *n.* a liquid used in the radiator of an internal-combustion engine to lower the freezing point of the cooling medium.

an•ti•gen (an′ti jən, -jen′), *n.* a substance that stimulates the production of antibodies. —**an′ti•gen′ic,** *adj.* —**an′ti•ge•nic′i•ty** (-jə nis′i tē), *n.*

an•ti•ges•ta′tion•al drug′ (an′tē jes tā′shə nl, an′tī-), *n.* a drug that averts a pregnancy by preventing the fertilized egg from attaching to the uterine wall.

An•ti′gua and Bar•bu′da (an tē′gə, -gwə; bär-bōō′də), *n.* an island state in the E West Indies, comprising three islands. 81,500.

an•ti•he•ro (an′tē hēr′ō, an′tī-), *n., pl.* **-roes.** a protagonist who lacks the ennobling qualities of a hero.

an′ti•his′ta•mine′, *n.* any of various drugs that block the action of histamines and are used esp. for treating allergies.

an′ti•knock′, *adj.* of or being a substance added to the fuel of an internal-combustion engine to minimize knock.

An•til•les (an til′ēz), *n.pl.* a chain of islands in the West Indies, including Cuba, Hispaniola, Jamaica, and Puerto Rico **(Greater Antilles),** and a group of smaller islands to the SE **(Lesser Antilles).** —**An•til′le•an,** *adj., n.*

an′ti•lock brake′ (an′tē lok′, an′tī-), *n.* a brake equipped with a computer-controlled device that prevents the wheel from locking.

an•ti•log•a•rithm (an′ti lô′gə riŧh′əm, -log′ə-), *n.* the number of which a given number is the logarithm.

an•ti•mat•ter (an′tē mat′ər, an′tī-), *n.* matter composed only of antiparticles.

an•ti•mo•ny (an′tə mō′nē), *n.* a brittle, lustrous, white metallic element used chiefly in alloys. *Symbol:* Sb; *at. no.:* 51; *at. wt.:* 121.75.

an•ti•ox•i•dant (an′tē ok′si dənt, an′tī-), *n.* **1.** a substance that inhibits oxidation. **2.** an enzyme or other organic substance capable of counteracting the damaging effects of oxidation in animal tissues.

an•ti•par•ti•cle (an′tē pär′ti kəl, an′tī-), *n.* a particle whose properties are identical in magnitude to those of a specific elementary particle but are of opposite sign.

an•ti•pas•to (an′ti pä′stō, än′tē-), *n., pl.* **-pas•tos, -pas•ti** (-pä′stē). an appetizer course in an Italian meal.

an•tip•a•thy (an tip′ə thē), *n., pl.* **-thies. 1.** a natural repugnance; aversion. **2.** an object of antipathy.

an•ti•per•son•nel (an′tē pûr′sə nel′, an′tī-), *adj.* designed to destroy enemy troops rather than vehicles or matériel.

an•ti•per•spi•rant (an′ti pûr′spər ənt), *n.* an astringent preparation for reducing perspiration.

an•ti•phon (an′tə fon′), *n.* a verse, prayer, or song sung in response. —**an•tiph′o•nal** (-tif′ə nl), *adj.*

an•tip•o•des (an tip′ə dēz′), *n.pl.* places diametrically opposite each other on the globe. —**an•tip′o•dal,** *adj.*

an•ti•pope (an′ti pōp′), *n.* a person who claims to be pope in opposition to the one canonically chosen.

an•ti•quar•i•an (an′ti kwâr′ē ən), *adj.* **1.** of antiquaries or antiquities. —*n.* **2.** an antiquary. —**an′ti•quar′i•an•ism,** *n.*

an′ti•quar′y (-kwer′ē), *n., pl.* **-quar•ies.** an expert on or collector of antiquities.

an′ti•quate′ (-kwāt′), *v.t.,* **-quat•ed, -quat•ing.** to make obsolete or old-fashioned.

an•tique (an tēk′), *adj., n., v.,* **-tiqued, -ti•quing.** —*adj.* **1.** of, belonging to, or dating from a period long ago. **2.** in the tradition or style of an earlier period. **3.** old-fashioned; antiquated. —*n.* **4.** a piece of furniture, work of art, etc., produced in a former period. —*v.t.* **5.** to finish or treat so as to give an antique appearance. —*v.i.* **6.** to shop for antiques.

an•tiq′ui•ty (-tik′wi tē), *n., pl.* **-ties. 1.** the quality of being ancient. **2.** ancient times. **3. antiquities,** things, as relics, remaining from ancient times.

an•ti-Sem•ite (an′tē sem′īt, an′tī-), *n.* a person hostile toward Jews. —**an′ti-Se•mit′ic,** *adj.* —**an′ti-Sem′i•tism,** *n.*

an•ti•sep•sis (an′tə sep′sis), *n.* destruction of the microorganisms that cause infection or decay.

an′ti•sep′tic (-tik), *adj.* **1.** pertaining to or effecting antisepsis. **2.** exceptionally clean. —*n.* **3.** an antiseptic agent. —**an′ti•sep′ti•cal•ly,** *adv.*

an′ti•se′rum, *n., pl.* **-se•rums, -se•ra** (-sēr′ə). a serum that contains antibodies.

an•ti•so•cial (an′tē sō′shəl, an′tī-), *adj.* **1.** unwilling to associate in a normal or friendly way with others. **2.** detrimental to society. —**an′ti•so′cial•ly,** *adv.*

an•tith•e•sis (an tith′ə sis), *n., pl.* **-ses** (-sēz′). **1.**

opposition; contrast. **2.** the direct opposite. —**an′ti•thet′i•cal** (-tə thet′i kəl), **an′ti•thet′ic,** adj. —**an′ti•thet′i•cal•ly,** adv.

an•ti•tox•in (an′ti tok′sin), n. **1.** a substance formed in the body that counteracts a specific toxin. **2.** the antibody formed in immunization with a given toxin.

an•ti•trust (an′tē trust′, an′tī-), adj. opposing or intended to restrain trusts or monopolies.

ant•ler (ant′lər), n. one of the solid horns, usu. branched, of an animal of the deer family.

ant′ li′on, n. an insect whose larva digs a pit to trap ants or other insects.

An•to•ny (an′tə nē), n. **Mark,** 83?–30 B.C., Roman general.

an•to•nym (an′tə nim), n. a word opposite in meaning to another.

Ant•werp (an′twərp), n. a seaport in N Belgium. 476,044.

a•nus (ā′nəs), n., pl. **a•nus•es.** the excretory opening at the lower end of the alimentary canal.

an•vil (an′vil), n. a heavy iron block on which heated metals are hammered into desired shapes.

anx•i•e•ty (ang zī′i tē), n., pl. **-ties. 1.** mental uneasiness caused by fear, as of danger. **2.** a state of apprehension and psychic tension occurring in some forms of mental disorder.

anx•ious (angk′shəs, ang′-), adj. **1.** uneasy in the mind; worried. **2.** earnestly desirous; eager. —**anx′ious•ly,** adv. —**anx′ious•ness,** n. —**Usage.** ANXIOUS has had the meaning "earnestly desirous, eager" since the mid-18th century: We are anxious to see our new grandson. Although some insist that ANXIOUS must always convey a sense of distress or worry, the sense "eager" is fully standard.

an•y (en′ē), adj. **1.** one or more without specification: Pick out any six you like. **2.** whatever it may be: at any price. **3.** some: Do you have any butter? **4.** every; all: Any schoolchild would know that. —pron. **5.** anybody; anyone. **6.** an unspecified quantity or number. —adv. **7.** to whatever degree or extent; at all.

an′y•bod′y (-bod′ē, -bud′ē), pron. any person.

an′y•how′, adv. **1.** in any way whatever. **2.** in any case; at all events.

an′y•more′, adv. **1.** any longer. **2.** at the present time; nowadays.

an′y•one′, pron. any person at all; anybody.

an′y•place′, adv. ANYWHERE.

an′y•thing′, pron. **1.** any thing whatever. —adv. **2.** in any way; at all. —**Idiom. 3. anything but,** in no degree or respect.

an′y•time′, adv. at any time; whenever.

an′y•way′, adv. in any case; anyhow.

an′y•where′, adv. **1.** in, at, or to any place. **2.** to any extent or degree. —**Idiom. 3. get anywhere,** to achieve success.

A/O or **a/o,** account of.

A-OK or **A-O•kay** (ā′ō kā′), adj., adv. Informal. OK; perfect.

A one or **A-1** or **A 1** (ā′ wun′), adj. first-class; excellent.

a•or•ta (ā ôr′tə), n., pl. **-tas, -tae** (-tē). the main artery of the mammalian circulatory system, conveying blood from the heart. —**a•or′tic,** adj.

AP, Associated Press.

A/P or **a/p, 1.** account paid. **2.** accounts payable.

a•pace (ə pās′), adv. with speed; quickly.

A•pach•e (ə pach′ē), n., pl. **A•pach•e, A•pach•es.** a member of a group of American Indian peoples of the U.S. Southwest.

a•part (ə pärt′), adv. **1.** into pieces or parts. **2.** separately in place, time, or motion. **3.** to or at one side; aside. —adj. **4.** having unique characteristics. —**Idiom. 5. apart from,** besides.

a•part′heid (-hāt, -hīt), n. a former rigid policy of segregation of the nonwhite population in the Republic of South Africa.

a•part′ment (-mənt), n. a room or group of rooms used as a dwelling.

apart′ment house′, n. a building containing a number of apartments.

ap•a•thy (ap′ə thē), n., pl. **-thies. 1.** absence of emotion. **2.** lack of interest or concern. —**ap′a•thet′ic** (-thet′ik), adj.

APB, pl. **APBs, APB′s.** all-points bulletin.

ape (āp), n., v., **aped, ap•ing.** —n. **1.** a tailless anthropoid primate with long arms and a broad chest. **2.** a monkey. **3.** an imitator; mimic. **4.** a clumsy or coarse person. —v.t. **5.** to imitate; mimic. —**ape′like′,** adj.

Ap•en•nines (ap′ə nīnz′), n.pl. a mountain range in central Italy.

a•pé•ri•tif (ə per′i tēf′), n. an alcoholic drink taken to stimulate the appetite before a meal.

ap•er•ture (ap′ər chər), n. an opening, as a hole, slit, or gap.

a•pex (ā′peks), n., pl. **a•pex•es, a•pi•ces** (ā′pə sēz′, ap′ə-). **1.** the highest point; peak. **2.** the tip or point.

a•pha•sia (ə fā′zhə), n. loss of the ability to speak or to understand language. —**a•pha′sic** (-zik), adj., n.

a•phe•li•on (ə fē′lē ən, ap hē′-), n., pl. **a•phe•li•a** (-lē ə). the point farthest from the sun in the orbit of a planet or a comet. —**a•phe′li•an,** adj.

a•phid (ā′fid, af′id), n. a tiny, soft-bodied insect that sucks sap from plants.

aph•o•rism (af′ə riz′əm), n. a terse saying embodying a general truth. —**aph′o•ris′tic,** adj. —**aph′o•ris′ti•cal•ly,** adv.

aph•ro•dis•i•ac (af′rə dē′ze ak′, -diz′ē ak′), adj. **1.** arousing sexual desire. —n. **2.** an aphrodisiac drug, food, etc.

Aph•ro•di•te (af′rə dī′tē), n. the ancient Greek goddess of love and beauty.

a•pi•ar•y (ā′pē er′ē), n., pl. **-ar•ies.** a place in which bees are kept. —**a′pi•a•rist** (-ə rist), n.

a•pi•cal (ā′pi kəl, ap′i-), adj. of, at, or forming an apex. —**a′pi•cal•ly,** adv.

a•piece (ə pēs′), adv. for each one; each.

a•plen•ty (ə plen′tē), adj., adv. in generous amounts.

a•plomb (ə plom′, ə plum′), n. self-possession; poise.

APO or **A.P.O.,** Army & Air Force Post Office.

a•poc•a•lypse (ə pok′ə lips), n. **1.** (cap.) REVELATION (def. 4). **2.** a prophetic revelation, esp. of a cataclysm in which good triumphs over evil. —**a•poc′a•lyp′tic** (-lip′tik), adj.

a•poc•ry•pha (ə pok′rə fə), n. (used with a sing. or pl. v.) **1.** (cap.) a group of books not found in Jewish or Protestant versions of the Old Testament but included in the Septuagint and the Vulgate. **2.** writings of doubtful authorship or authenticity.

---

an′ti•a•bor′tion, adj.
an′ti•air′craft, adj., n.
an′ti•bac•te′ri•al, adj.
an′ti•can′cer, adj.
an′ti•co•ag′u•lat′ing, adj.
an′ti•com′mu•nist, n., adj.
an′ti•dem′o•crat′ic, adj.
an′ti•fas′cist, n., adj.
an′ti•fun′gal, adj.
an′ti-in′tel•lec′tu•al, adj., n.

an′ti•la′bor, adj.
an′ti•lib′er•al, adj.
an′ti•ma•lar′i•al, adj.
an′ti•mi•cro′bi•al, adj.
an′ti•mil′i•ta•rism, n.
an′ti•mil′i•ta•ris′tic, adj.
an′ti•mon′ar•chist, n., adj.
an′ti•mo•nop′o•lis′tic, adj.
an′ti•na′tion•al•ist, n., adj.
an′ti•noise′, adj.
an′ti•pol•lu′tion, adj.
an′ti•pov′er•ty, adj.

an′ti•rad′i•cal, adj., n.
an′ti•ra′tion•al, adj.
an′ti•re•li′gious, adj.
an′ti•rev′o•lu′tion•ar′y, adj.
an′ti•slav′er•y, adj., n.
an′ti•spas•mod′ic, adj., n.
an′ti•sub′ma•rine′, adj.
an′ti•tank′, adj.
an′ti•un′ion, adj.
an′ti•vi′ral, adj.
an′ti•viv′i•sec′tion•ist, n., adj.
an′ti•war′, adj.

a·poc'ry·phal, *adj.* **1.** (*cap.*) of the Apocrypha. **2.** of doubtful authorship or authenticity.

ap·o·gee (ap'ə jē'), *n., pl.* **-gees. 1.** the point farthest from the earth in the orbit of the moon or a satellite. **2.** the highest point; climax.

a·po·lit·i·cal (ā'pə lit'i kəl), *adj.* not involved or interested in politics.

A·pol·lo (ə pol'ō), *n., pl.* **-los. 1.** the ancient Greek and Roman god of light, healing, music, poetry, and prophecy. **2.** a very handsome young man.

Apol'lo pro'gram, *n.* a U.S. program of space exploration, beginning in 1961, to make a landing on the moon.

A·pol·lyon (ə pol'yən), *n.* the angel of the bottomless pit. Rev. 9:11. [< Gk *apollýōn*, der. of *apollýnai* to utterly destroy]

a·pol·o·get·ic (ə pol'ə jet'ik), *adj.* containing or expressing an apology. —**a·pol·o·get'i·cal·ly,** *adv.*

ap·o·lo·gi·a (ap'ə lō'jē ə), *n., pl.* **-gi·as.** a defense, as of one's actions.

a·pol·o·gist (ə pol'ə jist), *n.* a person who defends an idea, faith, cause, or institution.

a·pol'o·gize', *v.i.,* **-gized, -giz·ing.** to make an apology.

a·pol'o·gy, *n., pl.* **-gies. 1.** an expression of regret, as for having been rude. **2.** a defense, as of a cause.

ap·o·plex·y (ap'ə plek'sē), *n.* STROKE¹ (def. 3). —**ap·o·plec'tic,** *adj.*

a·pos·ta·sy (ə pos'tə sē), *n., pl.* **-sies.** renunciation or abandonment of a previous loyalty, as to one's religious faith.

a·pos'tate (-tāt, -tit), *n.* a person who commits apostasy. —**a·pos'ta·tize'** (-tə tīz'), *v.i.,* **-tized, -tiz·ing.**

a pos·te·ri·o·ri (ā' po stēr'ē ôr'ī, -ôr'ē), *adj.* **1.** from particular instances to a general principle. **2.** based on observation or experiment. [< L: lit., from the one behind]

a·pos·tle (ə pos'əl), *n.* **1.** (*sometimes cap.*) one of Christ's original 12 disciples. **2.** a pioneer of a reform movement.

Apos'tles' Creed', *n.* a creed dating from about A.D. 500, traditionally ascribed to Christ's apostles.

ap·os·tol·ic (ap'ə stol'ik), *adj.* **1.** of an apostle. **2.** of the pope; papal.

a·pos·tro·phe¹ (ə pos'trə fē), *n.* the sign (') used to indicate the omission of one or more letters from a word, the possessive case, or plurals of abbreviations and symbols.

a·pos·tro·phe² (ə pos'trə fē), *n.* a rhetorical digression to address someone not present or a personified object or idea.

a·poth·e·car·y (ə poth'ə ker'ē), *n., pl.* **-car·ies.** a druggist; pharmacist.

ap·o·thegm (ap'ə them'), *n.* a short, pithy saying.

a·poth·e·o·sis (ə poth'ē ō'sis, ap'ə thē'ə sis), *n., pl.* **-ses** (-sēz, -sēz'). **1.** elevation to the rank of a god. **2.** the ideal example; epitome.

app (ap), *n.* Computers (*informal*). an application program; application software.

Ap·pa·la·chi·a (ap'ə lā'chē ə, -lach'ē ə), *n.* a region in the E United States, in the area of the S Appalachian Mountains, extending from NE Alabama to SW Pennsylvania. Also called **Ap'pa·la'chi·an,** *adj., n.*

Appala'chian Moun'tains, *n.pl.* a mountain range in E North America, extending from S Quebec to N Alabama. Also called **Ap'pa·la'chi·ans.**

ap·pall (ə pôl'), *v.t.* to fill with consternation; dismay. —**ap·pall'ing,** *adj.*

Ap·pa·loo·sa (ap'ə lōō'sə), *n., pl.* **-sas.** a Western riding horse with a mottled coat and vertically striped hoofs.

ap·pa·rat·us (ap'ə rat'əs, -rā'təs), *n., pl.* **-tus, -tus·es. 1.** a combination of instruments or materials having a particular function. **2.** a complex mechanism for a particular purpose. **3.** the means by which a system functions.

ap·par·el (ə par'əl), *n., v.,* **-eled, -el·ing** or (*esp. Brit.*) **-elled, -el·ling.** —*n.* **1.** clothing, esp. outerwear; garments. —*v.t.* **2.** to dress; clothe.

ap·par·ent (ə par'ənt, ə pâr'-), *adj.* **1.** readily seen; open to view. **2.** easily understood; obvious. **3.** according to appearances; ostensible. —**ap·par'ent·ly,** *adv.*

ap·pa·ri·tion (ap'ə rish'ən), *n.* **1.** a ghost. **2.** something making a strange or incongruous appearance.

ap·peal (ə pēl'), *n.* **1.** an earnest plea; entreaty. **2.** a request to an authority, as for help or a decision. **3.** an application for review by a higher court. **4.** the power or ability to attract. —*v.i.* **5.** to make an earnest plea. **6.** to apply for review of a case to a higher court. **7.** to exert an attraction. —*v.t.* **8.** to apply for review of (a case) to a higher court. —**ap·peal'ing,** *adj.*

ap·pear (ə pēr'), *v.i.* **1.** to come into sight. **2.** to have the appearance of being. **3.** to be or become obvious. **4.** to come before the public. **5.** to come before a court.

ap·pear'ance (-əns), *n.* **1.** the act or process of appearing. **2.** outward look; aspect. **3.** outward show; semblance. —**Idiom. 4. put in an appearance,** to attend a gathering, esp. for a short time.

ap·pease (ə pēz'), *v.t.,* **-peased, -peas·ing. 1.** to bring to a state of calm; pacify. **2.** to satisfy; relieve. **3.** to yield to the demands of, esp. at the expense of one's principles. —**ap·pease'ment,** *n.* —**ap·peas'er,** *n.*

ap·pel·lant (ə pel'ənt), *n.* a person who appeals, as to a higher court.

ap·pel'late (-it), *adj.* **1.** of appeals. **2.** (of a court) having the authority to review and decide appeals.

ap·pel·la·tion (ap'ə lā'shən), *n.* a name, title, or designation.

ap·pend (ə pend'), *v.t.* **1.** to add as a supplement. **2.** to affix.

ap·pend·age (ə pen'dij), *n.* **1.** a subsidiary part, as a limb, that diverges from a central or principal structure. **2.** something appended.

ap·pen·dec·to·my (ap'ən dek'tə mē), *n., pl.* **-mies.** surgical removal of the appendix.

ap·pen·di·ci·tis (ə pen'də sī'tis), *n.* inflammation of the appendix.

ap·pen·dix (ə pen'diks), *n., pl.* **-dix·es, -di·ces** (-də sēz'). **1.** supplementary material at the end of a text. **2.** a tube, closed at the end, extending from the cecum of the large intestine. —**Usage.** The plural APPENDICES is sometimes used, esp. in scholarly writing, for definition **1.**

ap·per·tain (ap'ər tān'), *v.i.* to belong as a rightful attribute or part; pertain.

ap·pe·tite (ap'i tīt'), *n.* **1.** a desire for food. **2.** a desire to satisfy a need or craving.

ap'pe·tiz'er (-tī'zər), *n.* a portion of food or drink served before a meal to stimulate the appetite.

ap'pe·tiz'ing, *adj.* appealing to the appetite. —**ap'pe·tiz'ing·ly,** *adv.*

Ap'pi·an Way' (ap'ē ən), *n.* an ancient Roman highway extending from Rome to Brundisium (now Brindisi): begun 312 B.C. by Appius Claudius Caecus. ab. 350 mi. (565 km) long.

ap·plaud (ə plôd'), *v.i., v.t.* **1.** to clap the hands in approval or appreciation (of). **2.** to praise. —**ap·plaud'er,** *n.*

ap·plause (ə plôz'), *n.* **1.** hand clapping as an expression of approval or appreciation. **2.** approval; praise.

ap·ple (ap'əl), *n.* **1.** the rounded, edible, usu. red fruit of a tree of the rose family. **2.** a tree that bears apples. —**Proverb. 3.** The apple doesn't fall far from the tree, children resemble their parents.

ap'ple·sauce', *n.* apples stewed to a pulp.

Ap·ple·seed (ap'əl sēd'), *n.* **Johnny** (*John Chapman*), 1774–1845, American pioneer and orchardist.

app·let (ap'lit), *n.* Computers. a small application program that can be called up for use while working in another application.

ap·pli·ance (ə plī'əns), *n.* a device used esp. in the home to carry out a specific function, as toasting bread.

ap·pli·ca·ble (ap'li kə bəl, ə plik'ə-), *adj.* capable

of being applied; relevant. —ap′pli•ca•bil′i•ty, n. —ap′pli•ca•bly, adv.

ap′pli•cant (-kant), n. a person who applies.

ap′pli•ca′tion (-kā′shən), n. 1. the act of applying. 2. the use to which something is put. 3. appropriateness; relevance. 4. a petition; request. 5. a form to be filled out by an applicant. 6. persistent attention. 7. a salve or ointment. 8. a. a specific kind of task, as database management, that can be done using an application program. b. APPLICATION PROGRAM.

applica′tion pro′gram, n. a computer program used for a specific kind of task, as word processing.

ap′pli•ca′tor, n. a device for applying a substance, as medication.

ap•plied (ə plīd′), adj. having or put to a practical purpose or use: applied mathematics.

ap•pli•qué (ap′li kā′), n., v., -quéd, -qué•ing. —n. 1. a cutout design of one material applied to another. —v.t. 2. to decorate with appliqué.

ap•ply (ə plī′), v., -plied, -ply•ing. —v.t. 1. to make use of. 2. to assign to a specific purpose. 3. to employ diligently. 4. to bring into contact; lay or spread on. —v.i. 5. to be pertinent or suitable. 6. to make an application or request. —ap•pli′er, n.

ap•point (ə point′), v.t. 1. to name or assign officially. 2. to fix; set. 3. to equip; furnish.

ap•point•ee (ə poin tē′), n., pl. -ees. a person who is appointed.

ap•poin′tive, adj. pertaining to or filled by appointment.

ap•point′ment, n. 1. an agreement to meet; engagement. 2. the act of appointing. 3. an office or position to which a person is appointed. 4. Usu., -ments. equipment or furnishings.

Ap•po•mat•tox (ap′ə mat′əks), n. a town in central Virginia where Lee surrendered to Grant on April 9, 1865, ending the Civil War.

ap•por•tion (ə pôr′shən), v.t. to distribute or allocate proportionally. —ap•por′tion•ment, n.

ap•pose (ə pōz′), v.t., -posed, -pos•ing. to place side by side.

ap•po•site (ap′ə zit, ə poz′it), adj. suitable; apt. —ap′po•site•ly, adv. —ap′po•site•ness, n.

ap′po•si′tion (-zish′ən), n. a grammatical relation between two usu. consecutive expressions, the second one identifying or supplementing the first, as in Washington, our first president, was born in Virginia. —ap•pos•i•tive (ə poz′i tiv), adj., n.

ap•praise (ə prāz′), v.t., -praised, -prais•ing. 1. to determine the value of. 2. to estimate the quality or importance of. —ap•prais′al, n. —ap•prais′er, n.

ap•pre•ci•a•ble (ə prē′shē ə bəl, -shə bəl), adj. sufficient to be readily perceived or estimated. —ap•pre′ci•a•bly, adv.

ap•pre′ci•ate′ (-shē āt′), v., -at•ed, -at•ing. —v.t. 1. to be thankful for. 2. to value or regard highly. 3. to be fully conscious of. —v.i. 4. to increase in value. —ap•pre′ci•a•to′ry (-ə tôr′ē), adj.

ap•pre′ci•a′tion, n. 1. gratitude. 2. recognition, esp. of aesthetic quality. 3. increase in value, as of property.

ap•pre′cia•tive (-shə tiv, -shē ə-), adj. feeling or showing appreciation. —ap•pre′cia•tive•ly, adv.

ap•pre•hend (ap′ri hend′), v.t. 1. to take into custody; arrest. 2. to grasp the meaning of; understand. 3. to anticipate with anxiety or fear.

ap′pre•hen′sion (-hen′shən), n. 1. anxiety or fear, esp. of future trouble. 2. the faculty or act of understanding. 3. the act of arresting; seizure.

ap′pre•hen′sive (-siv), adj. anxious or fearful, esp. about something that might happen. —ap′pre•hen′sive•ly, adv. —ap′pre•hen′sive•ness, n.

ap•pren•tice (ə pren′tis), n., v., -ticed, -tic•ing. —n. 1. a person who works for another in order to learn a trade. 2. a learner; novice. —v.t., v.i. 3. to place as or serve as an apprentice. —ap•pren′tice•ship′, n.

ap•prise (ə prīz′), v.t., -prised, -pris•ing. to give notice to; inform.

ap•proach (ə prōch′), v.t. 1. to come nearer to. 2. to come within range, as for comparison. 3. to begin

work on; set about. —v.i. 4. to come nearer. —n. 5. an act or instance of approaching. 6. a means of access. 7. the method used or steps taken in setting about a task. —ap•proach′a•ble, adj.

ap•pro•ba•tion (ap′rə bā′shən), n. approval.

ap•pro•pri•ate (adj. ə prō′prē it; v. -āt′), adj., v., -at•ed, -at•ing. —adj. 1. particularly suitable; fitting. —v.t. 2. to set apart for a specific purpose or use. 3. to take possession of, esp. without permission. —ap• pro′pri•ate•ly, adv. —ap•pro′pri•ate•ness, n. —ap•pro′pri•a′tor, n.

ap•pro′pri•a′tion (-ā′shən), n. 1. the act of appropriating. 2. money officially authorized to be paid from a public treasury.

ap•prov•al (ə prōō′vəl), n. 1. the act of approving. 2. permission; consent. —Idiom. 3. on approval, subject to being rejected if not satisfactory.

ap•prove′, v., -proved, -prov•ing. —v.t. 1. to speak or think favorably of. 2. to confirm or sanction formally; ratify. —v.i. 3. to have a favorable view. —ap•prov′ing•ly, adv.

ap•prox•i•mate (adj. ə prok′sə mit; v. -māt′), adj., v., -mat•ed, -mat•ing. —adj. 1. nearly exact but not perfectly accurate. —v.t. 2. to come near to in quantity, quality, or condition. —ap•prox′i•mate•ly, adv. —ap•prox′i•ma′tion, n.

ap•pur•te•nance (ə pûr′tn əns), n. 1. something subordinate to another. 2. a legal right belonging to and passing with a principal property. 3. appurtenances, accessories. —ap•pur′te•nant, adj.

Apr or Apr., April.

ap•ri•cot (ap′ri kot′, ā′pri-), n. 1. the downy, yellowish orange, peachlike fruit of a tree of the rose family. 2. the tree itself.

A•pril (ā′prəl), n. the fourth month of the year, containing 30 days.

a pri•o•ri (ä′ prē ôr′ī, -ôr′ē), adj. 1. from a general law to a particular instance. 2. existing in the mind independent of experience. [< L]

a•pron (ā′prən), n. 1. a garment covering the front of the body and worn to protect the clothing. 2. a paved area where airplanes are parked. 3. the part of a stage floor in front of the curtain line.

ap•ro•pos (ap′rə pō′), adv. 1. by the way; incidentally. —adj. 2. being appropriate and timely. —Idiom. 3. apropos of, with reference to.

apse (aps), n. a usu. vaulted recess in a building, esp. at the end of a church.

apt (apt), adj. 1. having a tendency; likely. 2. being quick to learn; bright. 3. suited to a purpose or occasion. —apt′ly, adv. —apt′ness, n.

apt., apartment.

ap•ti•tude (ap′ti tōōd′, -tyōōd′), n. 1. innate ability; talent. 2. readiness or quickness in learning. 3. suitability; fitness.

aq•ua (ak′wə, ä′kwə), n., pl. aq•uae (ak′wē, ä′kwē), aq•uas. 1. a. water. b. a solution, esp. in water. 2. a light greenish blue.

aq′ua•cul′ture, n. the cultivation of aquatic animals or plants.

aq′ua•ma•rine′, n. 1. a transparent light blue or greenish blue gem. 2. a light blue-green or greenish blue.

aq′ua•naut′ (-nôt′, -not′), n. a scuba diver who works for an extended period of time in and around a submerged structure.

aq′ua•plane′, n., v., -planed, -plan•ing. —n. 1. a board on which a person stands while it is towed by a motorboat. —v.i. 2. to ride an aquaplane.

a•quar•i•um (ə kwâr′ē əm), n., pl. -i•ums, -i•a (-ē ə). 1. a glass-sided container in which aquatic animals or plants are kept. 2. a place in which aquatic animals or plants are kept for exhibit.

A•quar′i•us (-əs), n. the 11th sign of the zodiac. [< L: water carrier]

a•quat•ic (ə kwat′ik, ə kwot′-), adj. 1. living or growing in water. 2. taking place or practiced on or in water. —n. 3. aquatics, aquatic sports. —a•quat′i•cal•ly, adv.

aq•ue•duct (ak′wi dukt′), n. 1. a conduit or channel for conducting water from a distance. 2. a bridgelike structure that carries an aqueduct across a valley or over a river.

a•que•ous (ā′kwē əs, ak′wē-), *adj.* of, like, or containing water; watery.

a′queous hu′mor, *n.* the watery fluid between the cornea and the lens of the eye.

aq•ui•fer (ak′wə fər), *n.* a geological formation of permeable rock, gravel, or sand containing or conducting groundwater.

Aq•ui•la (ak′wə lə), *n.* leader in the early Christian church. Acts 18:2.

aq•ui•line (ak′wə līn′, -lin), *adj.* **1.** of or resembling an eagle. **2.** curved like an eagle's beak.

A•qui•nas (ə kwī′nəs), *n.* **Saint Thomas,** 1225?–74, Italian theologian and philosopher.

AR, Arkansas.

Ar, *Chem. Symbol.* argon.

A/R, accounts receivable.

Ar•ab (ar′əb), *n.* **1.** a member of an Arabic-speaking people. **2.** a member of a Semitic people inhabiting Arabia, SW Asia, and N Africa.

ar•a•besque (ar′ə besk′), *n.* an ornament in which flowers, foliage, etc., are represented in an interlaced pattern.

A•ra•bi•a (ə rā′bē ə), *n.* a peninsula in SW Asia. Also called **Ara′bian Penin′sula.** —**A•ra′bi•an,** *adj., n.*

Ara′bian horse′, *n.* any of a breed of horses raised orig. in Arabia and noted for their grace and speed.

Ar•a•bic (ar′ə bik), *n.* **1.** a Semitic language spoken over much of N Africa, the Sahara, and SW Asia. —*adj.* **2.** of Arabic, the Arabs, or Arabia.

Ar′abic nu′meral, *n.* any of the numerical symbols 0, 1, 2, 3, 4, 5, 6, 7, 8, and 9.

ar•a•ble (ar′ə bəl), *adj.* capable of producing crops by being plowed or tilled. —**ar′a•bil′i•ty,** *n.*

a•rach•nid (ə rak′nid), *n.* any of numerous arthropods, including spiders and scorpions, characterized by a body with eight appendages.

Ar•a•fat (ar′ə fat′, är′ə fät′), *n.* **Ya•sir** (yä′sər, -sir, yas′ər), born 1929, Palestinian leader: head of the Palestine Liberation Organization.

ʿA•ra•fat (är′ə fat′, ar′ə fat′), *n.* a hill 15 mi. (24 km) southeast of Mecca, in Saudi Arabia.

A•ram (ā′ram, âr′əm), *n.* Biblical name of ancient Syria.

Ar•a•ma•ic (ar′ə mā′ik), *n.* a Semitic language that was supplanted by Arabic.

Ar•a•rat (ar′ə rat′), *n.* a mountain in E Turkey: traditionally considered the landing place of Noah's Ark. 16,945 ft. (5165 m).

ar•bi•ter (är′bi tər), *n.* a person empowered to decide matters at issue; judge.

ar′bi•trage′ (-träzh′), *n.* the simultaneous purchase and sale of the same security in different markets to profit from price differences. —**ar′bi•trag′er, ar′bi•tra•geur′** (-trä zhûr′), *n.*

ar•bit•ra•ment (är bi′trə mənt), *n.* **1.** the act of arbitrating. **2.** the decision of an arbiter.

ar′bi•trar′y (-trer′ē), *adj.* **1.** subject to individual will or judgment without restriction. **2.** dictatorial; despotic. **3.** capricious; unreasonable. —**ar′bi•trar′i•ly,** *adv.* —**ar′bi•trar′i•ness,** *n.*

ar′bi•trate′ (-trāt′), *v.,* -**trat•ed, -trat•ing.** —*v.t.* **1.** to decide as arbitrator. **2.** to submit to or settle by arbitration. —*v.i.* **3.** to act as arbitrator. —**ar′bi•tra′tion,** *n.*

ar′bi•tra′tor, *n.* a person empowered to decide a dispute or settle differences.

ar•bor (är′bər), *n.* **1.** a leafy, shady recess. **2.** a latticework bower intertwined with vines.

ar•bo′re•al (-bôr′ē əl), *adj.* **1.** of or like trees. **2.** living in trees.

ar•bo•re•tum (är′bə rē′təm), *n., pl.* -**tums, -ta** (-tə). a parklike area where trees or shrubs are grown for study or display.

ar•bor•vi•tae (är′bər vī′tē), *n.* any of several evergreen trees of the cypress family, with scaly bark and scalelike leaves.

ar•bu•tus (är byōō′təs), *n., pl.* -**tus•es. 1.** an ever-

green tree or shrub with scarlet berries. **2.** a creeping plant with fragrant white or pink flower clusters.

arc (ärk), *n., v.,* **arced** or **arcked, arc•ing** or **arck•ing.** —*n.* **1.** an unbroken part of a curved line. **2.** a luminous bridge formed in a gap between two electrodes. **3.** something curved like an arc. —*v.i.* **4.** to form or move in an arc.

ar•cade (är kād′), *n.* **1.** a series of arches supported on columns. **2.** a covered passageway, usu. with shops on each side. **3.** an establishment with coin-operated games.

ar•cane (är kān′), *adj.* known or understood only by those with special knowledge; secret.

arch¹ (ärch), *n.* **1.** a curved construction spanning an opening and supporting weight. **2.** an archway. **3.** something resembling an arch. —*v.i., v.t.* **4.** to form or form into an arch.

arch² (ärch), *adj.* coyly roguish or mischievous. —**arch′ly,** *adv.* —**arch′ness,** *n.*

arch-, a combining form meaning: principal (*archenemy*); extreme or ultimate (*archfiend*).

-arch, a combining form meaning ruler (*monarch*).

arch., **1.** archaic. **2.** archipelago. **3.** architect; architecture.

ar•chae•ol•o•gy or **ar•che•ol•o•gy** (är′kē ol′ə jē), *n.* the scientific study of past peoples and cultures by analysis of physical remains, as artifacts. —**ar′chae•o•log′i•cal** (-ə loj′i kəl), *adj.* —**ar′chae•ol′o•gist,** *n.*

ar•cha•ic (är kā′ik), *adj.* **1.** marked by the characteristics of an earlier period; antiquated. **2.** (of a linguistic form) commonly used in an earlier time but rare in present-day usage. —**ar•cha′i•cal•ly,** *adv.*

ar•cha•ism (är′kē iz′əm, -kā-), *n.* an archaic verbal usage.

arch•an•gel (ärk′ān′jəl), *n.* a chief or principal angel.

arch•bish•op (ärch′bish′əp), *n.* a bishop of the highest rank.

arch′bish′op of Can′terbury, *n.* the head of the Anglican Communion.

arch•bish•op•ric (-rik), *n.* the see, diocese, or office of an archbishop.

arch′dea′con, *n.* an ecclesiastic who ranks next below a bishop.

arch′di•o•cese′, *n.* the diocese of an archbishop. —**arch′di•oc′e•san** (-os′ə sən), *adj.*

arch′duke′, *n.* a prince of the former ruling house of Austria.

Ar•che•la•us (är′ki lā′əs), *n.* the oldest son of Herod the Great. Matt. 2:22.

arch′en′e•my, *n., pl.* -**mies.** a chief enemy.

arch•er (är′chər), *n.* a person who shoots with a bow and arrow.

ar′cher•y, *n.* the art, practice, or skill of shooting with a bow and arrow.

ar•che•type (är′ki tīp′), *n.* an original pattern or model from which all things of the same kind are copied or on which they are based; prototype. —**ar′che•typ′al** (-tī′pəl), **ar′che•typ′i•cal** (-tip′i kəl), *adj.*

arch′fiend′ (ärch′fēnd′), *n.* **SATAN.**

Ar•chi•me•des (är′kə mē′dēz), *n.* 287?–212 B.C., Greek mathematician. —**Ar′chi•me′de•an** (-mē′dē ən, -mi dē′ən), *adj.*

ar•chi•pel•a•go (är′kə pel′ə gō′), *n., pl.* -**gos, -goes. 1.** a group of islands. **2.** a large body of water with many islands.

ar•chi•tect (är′ki tekt′), *n.* **1.** a person who engages in the profession of architecture. **2.** planner or designer.

ar′chi•tec•ton′ics (-tek ton′iks), *n.* the science of planning and constructing buildings.

ar′chi•tec′ture (-tek′chər), *n.* **1.** the profession of designing buildings, communities, etc. **2.** the character or style of building. **3.** the design or structure of something. —**ar′chi•tec′tur•al,** *adj.* —**ar′chi•tec′tur•al•ly,** *adv.*

ar•chive (är′kīv), *n.* **1.** Often, **-chives.** a place where materials of public or historic importance are preserved. **2.** Usu., **-chives.** the materials preserved in an archive. —ar•chi′val, adj. —ar′chi•vist (-kə-vist), n.

arch•way (ärch′wā′), n. 1. an entrance or passage under an arch. 2. an arch over a passage.

-archy, a combining form meaning rule or government (monarchy).

arc•tic (ärk′tik, är′tik), adj. 1. (often cap.) of, at, or near the North Pole. 2. extremely cold; frigid. —n. 3. (often cap.) the region lying north of the Arctic Circle. [≪ Gk arktikós northern, lit., of the Bear (constellation)]

Arc′tic Cir′cle, n. an imaginary line drawn parallel to the equator, at 23°28′ S of the North Pole.

Arc′tic O′cean, n. an ocean surrounding the North Pole.

-ard, a suffix meaning a person who does something regularly or excessively (drunkard).

Ar•dennes (är den′; Fr. AR den′), n. Forest of, a wooded plateau region in W Europe, in NE France, SE Belgium, and Luxembourg: World War I battle 1914; World War II battle 1944–45.

ar•dent (är′dnt), adj. 1. characterized by intense feeling; fervent. 2. fiercely bright. 3. fiery; hot. —ar′dent•ly, adv.

ar•dor (är′dər), n. 1. great intensity of feeling; fervor. 2. intense heat. Also, esp. Brit., ar′dour.

ar•du•ous (är′jōō əs; esp. Brit. -dyōō-), adj. requiring or marked by great exertion; laborious. —ar′du•ous•ly, adv. —ar′du•ous•ness, n.

are¹ (är; unstressed ər), v. pres. indic. pl. and 2nd pers. sing. of BE.

are² (âr, är), n. a surface measure equal to 100 square meters.

ar•e•a (âr′ē ə), n., pl. ar•e•as. 1. an extent of space or surface. 2. a geographical region. 3. extent; scope. 4. field; sphere. 5. the quantitative measure of a plane or curved surface. —ar′e•al, adj.

ar′ea code′, n. a three-digit code that identifies one of the telephone areas into which the U.S. and certain other countries are divided.

a•re•na (ə rē′nə), n., pl. -nas. 1. a space or building used for sports or other entertainments. 2. a field of competition or activity.

are′na the′ater, n. a theater with seats arranged around a central stage.

aren't (ärnt, är′ənt), contraction of are not.

Ar•es (âr′ēz), n. the ancient Greek god of war.

ar•gent (är′jənt), n. 1. the heraldic color silver. 2. Archaic. the metal silver.

Ar•gen•ti•na (är′jən tē′nə), n. a republic in S South America. 35,797,536. —Ar′gen•tine′ (-tēn′, -tīn′), Ar′gen•tin′e•an (-tin′ē ən), n., adj.

ar•gon (är′gon), n. a chemically inactive gaseous element that is used for filling light bulbs and vacuum tubes. Symbol: Ar; at. no.: 18; at. wt.: 39.948.

ar•go•sy (är′gə sē), n., pl. -sies. 1. a large merchant ship. 2. a fleet of such ships.

ar•got (är′gō, -gət), n. a specialized vocabulary peculiar to a particular group of people.

ar•gue (är′gyōō), v., -gued, -gu•ing. —v.i. 1. to present reasons for or against a thing. 2. to contend orally; dispute. —v.t. 3. to present reasons for or against. 4. to persuade or compel by reasoning. —ar′gu•a•ble, adj. —ar′gu•a•bly, adv.

ar•gu•ment (är′gyə mənt), n. 1. an oral disagreement; quarrel. 2. a discussion involving differing points of view; debate. 3. a statement or fact for or against a point. 4. discourse intended to persuade.

ar′gu•men•ta′tion (-men tā′shən), n. the process of developing or presenting an argument; reasoning.

ar′gu•men′ta•tive (-tə tiv), adj. given to argument; disputatious.

ar•gyle (är′gīl), n. (often cap.) a diamond-shaped knitting pattern of two or more colors.

a•ri•a (är′ē ə), n., pl. a•ri•as. an elaborate vocal solo with accompaniment, as in an opera.

-arian, a suffix meaning: one whose work is connected with (librarian); one who supports, advocates, or practices (vegetarian).

ar•id (ar′id), adj. 1. barren or unproductive due to lack of moisture. 2. lacking vitality or imagination. —a•rid•i•ty (ə rid′i tē), n.

A•ri•el (âr′ē el′), n. Jerusalem. Isa. 29:1–2, 7.

Ar•ies (âr′ēz), n. the first sign of the zodiac. [< L: ram]

a•right (ə rīt′), adv. to rights; correctly.

Ar•i•ma•thae•a or Ar•i•ma•the•a (ar′ə mə thē′-ə), n. a town in ancient Palestine. Matt. 27:57. —Ar′i•ma•thae′an, adj.

a•rise (ə rīz′), v.i., a•rose, a•ris•en (ə riz′ən), a•ris•ing. 1. to get up, as from a sitting position. 2. to move upward; ascend. 3. to come into being; spring up.

ar•is•toc•ra•cy (ar′ə stok′rə sē), n., pl. -cies. 1. the hereditary nobility. 2. government by an aristocracy, elite, or privileged upper class. 3. a class or group regarded as superior.

a•ris•to•crat (ə ris′tə krat′), n. a member of the aristocracy. —a•ris′to•crat′ic, adj. —a•ris′to•crat′i•cal•ly, adv.

Ar•is•toph•a•nes (ar′ə stof′ə nēz′), n. 448?–385? B.C., Athenian comic dramatist.

Ar•is•tot•le (ar′ə stot′l), n. 384–322 B.C., Greek philosopher: pupil of Plato; tutor of Alexander the Great.

a•rith•me•tic (n. ə rith′mə tik; adj. ar′ith met′ik), n. 1. the method or process of computation with figures. —adj. ar•ith•met•ic 2. Also, ar′ith•met′i•cal. of arithmetic. —ar′ith•met′i•cal•ly, adv.

ar′ithmet′ic mean′, n. the mean obtained by adding several quantities together and dividing the sum by the number of quantities.

Ariz., Arizona.

Ar•i•zo•na (ar′ə zō′nə), n. a state in the SW United States. 4,428,068. Cap.: Phoenix. Abbr.: AZ, Ariz. —Ar′i•zo′nan, Ar′i•zo′ni•an, adj., n.

ark (ärk), n. 1. the boat built by Noah for safety during the Biblical Flood. Gen. 6–9. 2. a chest containing tablets inscribed with the Ten Commandments, kept in the Biblical Tabernacle. 3. a cabinet in a synagogue for the Torah scrolls.

Ark., Arkansas.

Ar•kan•sas (är′kən sô′), n. 1. a state in the S central United States. 2,509,793. Cap.: Little Rock. Abbr.: AR, Ark. 2. a river flowing E and SE from central Colorado into the Mississippi in SE Arkansas. 1450 mi. (2335 km) long. —Ar•kan′san (-kan′zən), n., adj.

ark′ of the cov′enant, n. ARK (def. 2).

Ar•ling•ton (är′ling tən), n. 1. a county in NE Virginia, opposite Washington, D.C.: site of national cemetery (Ar′lington Na′tional Cem′etery). 174,603. 2. a city in N Texas. 286,922.

arm¹ (ärm), n. 1. an upper limb of the human body. 2. an armlike part or attachment. 3. a combat branch of a military service. 4. power; authority: the long arm of the law. —Idiom. 5. at arm's length, at a distance.

arm² (ärm), n. 1. Usu., arms. weapons, esp. firearms. 2. arms, heraldic devices, as of a family. —v.i. 3. to make ready for war. —v.t. 4. to equip with weapons. —Idiom. 5. up in arms, provoked; indignant. —armed, adj.

Ar•ma•da (är mä′də, -mā′-), n., adj. -das. 1. Also called Spanish Armada. the fleet sent against England by Philip II of Spain in 1588, defeated by the English navy. 2. (l.c.) a fleet of warships. 3. (l.c.) a large group of vehicles, airplanes, etc.

ar•ma•dil•lo (är′mə dil′ō), n., pl. -los. a burrowing mammal covered with jointed plates of bone and horn.

Ar•ma•ged•don (är′mə ged′n), n. 1. the place where the final battle between good and evil will be fought. Rev. 16:16. 2. a final, destructive battle.

ar•ma•ment (är′mə mənt), n. 1. military weapons and equipment. 2. Usu., -ments. military strength collectively. 3. the process of arming for war.

ar•ma•ture (är′mə chər), n. 1. a protective covering of an animal or plant. 2. a. the part of a generator, including the main current-carrying winding, in which the electromotive force is induced. b. the moving part in an electromagnetic device, as a buzzer.

arm'chair', *n.* a chair with supports for the arms.

armed' forc'es, *n.pl.* military, naval, and air forces.

Ar•me•ni•a (är mē'nē ə), *n.* a republic in W Asia, W of Azerbaijan: formerly a part of the USSR. 3,465,611. —Ar•me'ni•an, *adj., n.*

Arme'nian mas'sacres, *n.pl.* a series of massacres of Armenian Christians by Turkish government forces between 1895 and 1915.

arm'ful', *n., pl.* -fuls. the amount an arm can hold.

arm'hole', *n.* an opening for the arm in a garment.

ar•mi•stice (är'mə stis), *n.* a temporary suspension of hostilities by agreement of the warring parties; truce.

Ar'mistice Day', *n.* former name of VETERANS DAY.

arm'let (-lit), *n.* an ornamental band worn high on the arm.

ar•mor (är'mər), *n.* 1. any covering that serves as a protection or defense, as against weapons. 2. the armored divisions of an army. —*v.t.* 3. to cover or equip with armor. Also, *esp. Brit.,* **ar'mour**. —ar'mored, *adj.*

ar'mor•er, *n.* 1. a maker of arms or armor. 2. a person who manufactures or services firearms.

ar•mo•ri•al (är môr'ē əl), *adj.* of or bearing a coat of arms.

ar'mor•y (-mə rē), *n., pl.* -mor•ies. 1. a storage place for weapons. 2. a National Guard headquarters and drill center. 3. a place where arms and armor are made.

arm'pit', *n.* the hollow under the arm at the shoulder.

arm'rest', *n.* an often padded support for the forearm.

Arm•strong (ärm'strông'), *n.* 1. (Daniel) Louis ("Satchmo"), 1900–71, U.S. jazz trumpeter. 2. Neil A., born 1930, U.S. astronaut: first person to walk on the moon, July 20, 1969.

ar•my (är'mē), *n., pl.* -mies. 1. the military forces of a nation trained to fight on land. 2. a body of persons trained and armed for war. 3. a large or organized group. —*Proverb.* 4. An army marches on its stomach, an army must be well-nourished.

Ar'my of the Poto'mac, *n.* 1. Union forces that guarded Washington, D.C., against a Confederate invasion across the Potomac and fought battles in the eastern sector during the Civil War. 2. Confederate forces from the Alexandria, Potomac, and Shenandoah districts from mid-1861 to mid-1862: later known as Army of Northern Virginia.

Ar•nold (är'nld), *n.* Benedict, 1741–1801, American general in the Revolutionary War who became a traitor.

a•ro•ma (ə rō'mə), *n., pl.* -mas. a distinctive, usu. agreeable odor; fragrance. —ar•o•mat•ic (ar'ə mat'ik), *adj.*

a•ro'ma•ther'a•py, *n.* 1. the use of fragrances to affect or alter a person's mood or behavior. 2. treatment of facial skin by the application of fragrant floral and herbal substances.

a•rose (ə rōz'), *v.* pt. of ARISE.

a•round (ə round'), *adv.* 1. in a circle or ring. 2. on all sides. 3. in all directions. 4. in circumference. 5. in or to another or opposite direction. 6. in the vicinity; nearby. —*prep.* 7. on all sides of; encircling. 8. on the edge or border of. 9. in all or various directions from. 10. in the vicinity of; near. 11. here and there in. 12. on or to the other side of.

a•rouse (ə rouz'), *v.t.,* a•roused, a•rous•ing. 1. to stir up; excite. 2. to awaken from sleep. —a•rous'al, *n.*

ar•peg•gi•o (är pej'ē ō', -pej'ō), *n., pl.* -gi•os. the sounding of the notes of a chord in rapid succession instead of simultaneously.

ar•raign (ə rān'), *v.t.* 1. to bring before a court to answer an indictment. 2. to accuse or charge. —ar•raign'ment, *n.*

ar•range (ə rānj'), *v.,* -ranged, -rang•ing. —*v.t.* 1. to place in proper, desired, or convenient order. 2. to

come to an agreement regarding. 3. to adapt (a musical work) for particular instrumentation. —*v.i.* 4. to make plans or preparations. 5. to come to an agreement. —ar•range'ment, *n.* —ar•rang'er, *n.*

ar•rant (ar'ənt), *adj.* downright; unmitigated.

ar•ras (ar'əs), *n.* 1. a tapestry. 2. a wall hanging, esp. a tapestry.

ar•ray (ə rā'), *v.t.* 1. to place in order; marshal. 2. to clothe, esp. in finery. —*n.* 3. order, as of troops drawn up for battle. 4. a large and impressive group. 5. fine attire.

ar•rear (ə rēr'), *n.* 1. Usu., arrears. the state of being late in repaying a debt. 2. Often, arrears. an unpaid debt.

ar•rest (ə rest'), *v.t.* 1. to seize (a person) by legal authority. 2. to catch and hold; engage: *A noise arrested our attention.* 3. to check the course of; stop. —*n.* 4. the taking of a person into legal custody. 5. the act of stopping or state of being stopped.

ar•rest'ing, *adj.* attracting or capable of attracting attention or interest.

ar•rhyth•mi•a (ə riᵗh'mē ə), *n.* a disturbance in the rhythm of the heartbeat. —ar•rhyth'mic, ar•rhyth'mi•cal, *adj.*

ar•ri•val (ə rī'vəl), *n.* 1. the act of arriving. 2. a person or thing that arrives.

ar•rive (ə rīv'), *v.i.,* -rived, -riv•ing. 1. to reach one's destination. 2. to come: *The moment has arrived.* 3. to attain a position of success. 4. arrive at, to reach in a process or course.

ar•ro•gant (ar'ə gənt), *adj.* characterized by or proceeding from overbearing superiority or self-importance. —ar'ro•gance, *n.* —ar'ro•gant•ly, *adv.*

ar'ro•gate' (-gāt'), *v.t.,* -gat•ed, -gat•ing. to claim or appropriate without right. —ar'ro•ga'tion, *n.*

ar•row (ar'ō), *n.* 1. a slender feathered and pointed shaft shot from a bow. 2. a figure with a wedge-shaped end used to indicate direction.

ar'row•head', *n.* the pointed tip of an arrow.

ar'row•root', *n.* 1. a tropical American plant whose fleshy tubers yield an edible starch. 2. the starch of the arrowroot.

ar•roy•o (ə roi'ō), *n., pl.* -os. (chiefly in the southwestern U.S.) a watercourse or gulch that is usu. dry except after heavy rains.

ar•se•nal (är'sə nl), *n.* 1. a military establishment for producing and storing weapons. 2. a supply; collection.

ar'senal of democ'racy, *n.* the role of the United States in supplying arms to nations fighting the Axis powers during World War II.

ar•se•nic (är'sə nik), *n.* a grayish white element having a metallic luster and forming poisonous compounds. *Symbol:* As; *at. wt.* 74.92; *at. no.:* 33.

ar•son (är'sən), *n.* the malicious burning of property. —ar'son•ist, *n.*

art¹ (ärt), *n.* 1. the production, expression, or realm of what is beautiful. 2. objects subject to aesthetic criteria, as paintings. 3. a field or category of art. 4. illustrative or decorative material. 5. skill in conducting a human activity. 6. a branch of learning, esp. one of the humanities. 7. skilled workmanship or execution.

art² (ärt), *v.* Archaic. 2nd pers. sing. pres. indic. of BE.

-art, var. of -ARD: *braggart.*

art' dec'o (dek'ō), *n.* (*often caps.*) a style of decorative art developed in the 1920s and marked chiefly by geometric motifs.

Ar•te•mis (är'tə mis), *n.* an ancient Greek goddess characterized as a virgin hunter and associated with the moon.

ar•te•ri•ole (är tēr'ē ōl'), *n.* any of the smallest branches of an artery.

ar•te•ri•o•scle•ro•sis (är tēr'ē ō sklə rō'sis), *n.* abnormal thickening and loss of elasticity in the arterial walls.

ar•ter•y (är'tə rē), *n., pl.* -ter•ies. 1. a blood vessel that conveys blood away from the heart. 2. a main channel or highway. —ar•te'ri•al (-tēr'ē əl), *adj.*

ar•te′sian well′ (är tē′zhən), *n.* a well in which water rises under pressure from a permeable stratum overlaid by impermeable rock.

art′ful, *adj.* **1.** slyly crafty; cunning. **2.** skillful or clever; ingenious. —**art′ful•ly,** *adv.* —**art′ful•ness,** *n.*

ar•thri•tis (är thrī′tis), *n.* inflammation of one or more joints. —**ar•thrit′ic** (-thrit′ik), *adj., n.*

ar•thro•pod (är′thrə pod′), *n.* any of a group of invertebrates with a segmented body and jointed limbs, including insects, spiders, and crustaceans.

Ar•thur (är′thər), *n.* **1. Chester Alan,** 1830–86, 21st president of the U.S. 1881–85. **2.** a legendary king of Britain, whose life was based on the exploits of one or more historical figures of the 6th century A.D.

Ar•thu•ri•an (är thŏŏr′ē ən), *adj.* of King Arthur and associated legendary figures.

ar•ti•choke (är′ti chōk′), *n.* **1.** a thistlelike plant with an edible flower head. **2.** the flower head.

ar•ti•cle (är′ti kəl), *n.* **1.** a factual piece of writing, usu. on a single topic, appearing in a publication. **2.** an individual item. **3.** a word, as *a, an,* or *the,* that is linked to a noun and identifies the noun as a noun. **4.** a separate clause or section in a document, as a statute.

Ar′ticles of Confedera′tion, *n.pl.* the first constitution of the 13 American states, adopted in 1781.

ar•tic•u•late (*adj.* är tik′yə lit; *v.* -lāt′), *adj., v.,* **-lat•ed, -lat•ing.** —*adj.* **1.** uttered clearly. **2.** capable of speech. **3.** capable of, expressed with, or marked by clarity and effectiveness of language. **4.** having joints or segments. —*v.t.* **5.** to pronounce clearly and distinctly. **6.** to give clarity or coherence to. **7.** to unite by joints. —*v.i.* **8.** to speak clearly. **9.** to form a joint. —**ar•tic′u•late•ly,** *adv.* —**ar•tic′u•la′tion,** *n.*

ar•ti•fact (är′tə fakt′), *n.* an object made by human beings, esp. one belonging to an earlier time or cultural stage.

ar•ti•fice (är′tə fis), *n.* **1.** a clever trick; stratagem. **2.** trickery; guile. **3.** cleverness; ingenuity.

ar•tif′i•cer (-tif′ə sər), *n.* **1.** an inventor. **2.** a skillful worker; craftsperson.

ar′tifi′cial (-tə fish′əl), *adj.* **1.** produced by humans and not by nature. **2.** not real; simulated. **3.** not natural; forced or affected. —**ar′ti•fi′ci•al′i•ty** (-fish′ē al′i tē), *n.* —**ar′tifi′cial•ly,** *adv.*

artifi′cial intel′ligence, *n.* the ability of a specially programmed computer, robot, or other mechanical device to perform functions analogous to learning and decision making.

ar′tifi′cial life′, *n.* the simulation of any aspect of life, as through computers, robotics, or biochemistry.

artifi′cial respira′tion, *n.* the stimulation of natural respiratory functions in a person whose breathing has failed by forcing air into and out of the lungs.

ar•til•ler•y (är til′ə rē), *n.* **1.** mounted projectile-firing guns or missile launchers. **2.** the branch of an army using artillery. —**ar•til′ler•y•man,** *n., pl.* **-men.**

ar•ti•san (är′tə zən), *n.* a person skilled in an applied art.

art•ist (är′tist), *n.* **1.** a person who practices one of the fine arts, esp. painting or sculpture. **2.** a person proficient in a performing art, as a musician.

ar•tiste (är tēst′), *n.* a public performer.

ar•tis′tic (-tis′tik), *adj.* **1.** of or characteristic of art or artists. **2.** showing skill in execution. —**ar•tis′ti•cal•ly,** *adv.*

art′ist•ry, *n.* artistic workmanship, quality, or ability.

art′less, *adj.* **1.** free from deceit or cunning; ingenuous. **2.** not artificial; natural. **3.** lacking art, knowledge, or skill. —**art′less•ly,** *adv.* —**art′less•ness,** *n.*

art nou•veau (ärt′ nŏŏ vō′, är′), *n.* (*often caps.*) a style of decorative art current in the late 19th and early 20th centuries, characterized chiefly by curvilinear motifs.

art′work′, *n.* **1.** the production of artistic or craft objects. **2.** an object or objects so produced.

art′y, *adj.,* **-i•er, -i•est.** *Informal.* pretentiously artistic. —**art′i•ness,** *n.*

A•ru•ba (ə rōō′bə), *n.* a self-governing Dutch island in the S Caribbean. 62,500.

ar′um (âr′əm), *n.* a plant bearing numerous flowers on a fleshy spike sheathed by a large spathe.

-ary, a suffix meaning pertaining to or connected with (*elementary*).

Ar•y•an (âr′ē ən, -yən, ar′-), *n.* **1.** a member or descendant of the prehistoric people who spoke Indo-European. **2.** (in Nazi doctrine) a non-Jewish Caucasian, esp. of Nordic stock.

as (az; *unstressed* əz), *adv.* **1.** to the same degree or extent; equally. **2.** for example. **3.** thought to be: *the square as distinct from the rectangle.* —*conj.* **4.** to the same degree or extent that: *to run quick as a rabbit.* **5.** in the same manner that. **6.** while; when. **7.** since; because. **8.** though: *Strange as it seems, it is so.* **9.** that the result is. —*pron.* **10.** that, who, or which. **11.** a fact that. —*prep.* **12.** in the role or function of. —**Idiom.** **13. as for** or **to,** with respect to; about. **14. as if** or **though,** as it would be if. **15. as is,** just the way it exists or appears. **16. as it were,** so to speak. **17. as of,** beginning on; from. —**Usage.** See LIKE¹.

As, *Chem. Symbol.* arsenic.

As•a•hel (as′ə hel′), *n.* the half-brother of David. II Sam. 2:18–23.

ASAP (ā′sap), *adv.* without delay; promptly.

A.S.A.P. or **a.s.a.p.,** as soon as possible.

A•saph (ā′saf), *n.* a famous musician during the time of David. I Chron. 16:5.

A•sa•rah Be•te•vet (or **Be•te•bet**) (*Seph. Heb.* ä-sä Rä′ bə te′vet; *Ashk. Heb.* ä sô′Rə bə tā′väs), *n.* a Jewish fast day commemorating the beginning of the siege of Jerusalem in 586 B.C.

as•bes•tos (as bes′təs, az-), *n.* a fibrous mineral formerly used for making fireproof articles and in building insulation.

As•bur•y (az′bə rē), *n.* **Francis,** 1745–1816, English missionary: first bishop of the Methodist Church in America.

as•cend (ə send′), *v.i.* **1.** to move upward; rise. —*v.t.* **2.** to succeed to: *The prince ascended the throne.*

as•cend′an•cy or **-en•cy,** *n.* the state of being in the ascendant.

as•cend′ant or **-ent,** *n.* **1.** a position of dominance. —*adj.* **2.** ascending; rising. **3.** superior; dominant.

as•cen•sion (ə sen′shən), *n.* **1.** the act of ascending. **2. the Ascension,** the bodily ascending of Christ to heaven. **3.** (*cap.*) ASCENSION DAY.

Ascen′sion Day′, *n.* the 40th day after Easter, commemorating the Ascension of Christ.

as•cent (ə sent′), *n.* **1.** the act of ascending. **2.** an upward slope; acclivity.

as•cer•tain (as′ər tān′), *v.t.* to find out definitely. —**as′cer•tain′a•ble,** *adj.* —**as′cer•tain′ment,** *n.*

as•cet•ic (ə set′ik), *n.* **1.** a person who practices self-denial, esp. for religious reasons. —*adj.* **2.** rigorously abstinent; austere. —**as•cet′i•cism,** *n.*

ASCII (as′kē), *n.* a standardized code in which characters are represented for computer storage and transmission by the numbers 0 through 127. [*A*(*merican*) *S*(*tandard*) *C*(*ode for*) *I*(*nformation*) *I*(*nterchange*)]

a•scor′bic ac′id (ə skôr′bik), *n.* a water-soluble vitamin occurring in citrus fruits, green vegetables, etc., essential for normal metabolism.

as•cot (as′kət, -kot), *n.* a tie or scarf with broad ends looped to lie flat one upon the other.

as•cribe (ə skrīb′), *v.t.,* **-cribed, -crib•ing.** to credit to a cause or source; attribute. —**as•scrib′a•ble,** *adj.* —**a•scrip•tion** (ə skrip′shən), *n.*

a•sep•tic (ə sep′tik, ā sep′-), *adj.* free from the living germs of disease.

a•sex•u•al (ā sek′shŏŏ əl), *adj.* **1.** having no sex or sexual organs. **2.** independent of sexual processes, esp. not involving the union of male and female germ cells. —**a•sex′u•al′i•ty,** *n.* —**a•sex′u•al•ly,** *adv.*

ash¹ (ash), *n.* **1.** the powdery residue of matter that remains after burning. **2.** finely pulverized lava thrown out by a volcano during eruption. **3. ashes,** mortal remains, esp. after cremation.

ash² (ash), *n.* any of various trees of the olive family with tough, straight-grained wood.

a•shamed (ə shāmd′), *adj.* **1.** feeling shame; embarrassed. **2.** unwilling because of fear of shame, ridicule, or disapproval. —**a•sham′ed•ly,** *adv.*

ash•en (ash′ən), *adj.* **1.** ash-colored; gray. **2.** extremely pale; pallid.

Ash•er (ash′ər), *n.* **1.** a son of Jacob and Zilpah. Gen. 30:12–13. **2.** one of the 12 tribes of Israel.

Ash•ke•naz•i (äsh′kə nä′zē), *n., pl.* -**naz•im** (-nä′-zim). a Jew of central or E European origin. Compare SEPHARDI. —**Ash′ke•naz′ic,** *adj.*

Ash•kha•bad (äsh′kə bäd′), *n.* the capital of Turkmenistan. 398,000.

a•shore (ə shôr′), *adv.* to or onto the shore.

ash•ram (äsh′rəm), *n.* **1.** a secluded place for retreat or instruction in Hinduism. **2.** the community living there.

ash′tray′, *n.* a receptacle for tobacco ashes.

Ash′ Wednes′day, *n.* the first day of Lent.

ash′y, *adj.,* -**i•er,** -**i•est.** ashen.

A•sia (ā′zhə), *n.* a continent bounded by Europe and the Arctic, Pacific, and Indian oceans.

A′sia Mi′nor, *n.* a peninsula in W Asia between the Black and Mediterranean seas.

A′sian, *adj.* **1.** of Asia or its inhabitants. —*n.* **2.** a native or inhabitant of Asia.

a•side (ə sīd′), *adv.* **1.** on, to, or toward one side. **2.** away, as from one's thoughts. **3.** in reserve: *to lay money aside.* —*n.* **4.** something spoken by an actor to the audience and supposedly not heard by others on stage. —*Idiom.* **5.** aside from, **a.** apart from; besides. **b.** except for.

As•i•mov (az′ə môf′, -mof′), *n.* **Isaac,** 1920–92, U.S. science and science-fiction writer, born in Russia.

as•i•nine (as′ə nīn′), *adj.* silly; stupid. —**as′i•nine′ly,** *adv.* —**as′i•nin′i•ty** (-nin′i tē), *n.*

ask (ask, äsk), *v.t.* **1.** to put a question to. **2.** to request information about. **3.** to put into words; utter. **4.** to request or request of. **5.** to set a price of. **6.** to invite. —*v.i.* **7.** to make inquiry; inquire. **8.** to make a request or petition. —*Proverb.* **9. Ask, and it shall be given you; seek, and you shall find; knock, and it shall be opened unto you,** know that what you seek will be given to you. Matt. 7:7. —**ask′er,** *n.*

a•skance (ə skans′), *adv.* **1.** with a side glance. **2.** with suspicion; skeptically.

a•skew (ə skyŏo′), *adv.* **1.** to one side; awry. —*adj.* **2.** crooked; awry.

ask′ing price′, *n.* the price at which something is offered by a seller.

a•slant (ə slant′, ə slänt′), *adv.* **1.** at a slant. —*adj.* **2.** slanting. —*prep.* **3.** slantingly across.

a•sleep (ə slēp′), *adv.* **1.** in or into a state of sleep. —*adj.* **2.** sleeping. **3.** dormant; inactive. **4.** numb. **5.** dead.

As•ma•ra (äs mär′ə), *n.* the capital of Eritrea. 276,355.

a•so•cial (ā sō′shəl), *adj.* **1.** not sociable or gregarious; antisocial. **2.** selfish.

asp (asp), *n.* any of several venomous Eurasian snakes.

as•par•a•gus (ə spar′ə gəs), *n.* **1.** a plant of the lily family cultivated for its edible shoots. **2.** these shoots.

as•par•tame (ə spär′tām, as′pər tām′), *n.* a white crystalline powder used as a low-calorie sugar substitute.

as•pect (as′pekt), *n.* **1.** appearance to the eye or mind; look. **2.** a way in which something may be regarded. **3.** a phase, as of a problem. **4.** a side or surface facing a given direction.

as•pen (as′pən), *n.* any of various poplars having leaves that tremble in the slightest breeze.

as•per•i•ty (ə sper′i tē), *n.* **1.** harshness or sharpness of temper or manner. **2.** roughness, as of surface.

as•per•sion (ə spûr′zhən, -shən), *n.* **1.** a damaging

or slandering remark. **2.** the act of slandering; defamation.

as•phalt (as′fôlt), *n.* **1.** a mixture of dark-colored, bituminous substances with gravel or crushed rock, used esp. for paving. —*v.t.* **2.** to cover or pave with asphalt.

as•pho•del (as′fə del′), *n.* any of various plants of the lily family, having white, pink, or yellow flowers.

as•phyx•i•a (as fik′sē ə), *n.* lack of oxygen and excess of carbon dioxide in the blood, as from suffocation, that causes unconsciousness or death.

as•phyx′i•ate′, *v.,* -**at•ed,** -**at•ing.** —*v.t.* **1.** to produce asphyxia in. —*v.i.* **2.** to become asphyxiated. —**as•phyx′i•a′tion,** *n.*

as•pic (as′pik), *n.* a savory jelly made from meat or fish stock or vegetable juice.

as•pir•ant (as′pər ənt, ə spīr′-), *n.* a person who aspires.

as•pi•rate (*v.* as′pə rāt′; *n., adj.,* -pər it), *v.,* -**rat•ed,** -**rat•ing,** *n.* —*v.t.* **1. a.** to articulate (a speech sound) so as to produce an audible puff of breath. **b.** to articulate (the beginning of a word) with an *h*-sound. **2.** to remove (a fluid) from a body cavity by aspiration. —*n.* **3.** an aspirated speech sound. —**as′pi•ra′tor,** *n.*

as′pi•ra′tion, *n.* **1.** a strong desire, longing, or hope. **2.** a goal or objective desired. **3.** the articulation of an aspirate in speech. **4.** the removal of a fluid from a body cavity with a suction syringe.

as•pire (ə spīr′), *v.i.,* -**pired,** -**pir•ing.** to long, aim, or seek ambitiously, esp. for something great or of high value.

as•pi•rin (as′pər in, -prin), *n., pl.* -**rin, -rins. 1.** a white, crystalline derivative of salicylic acid used to relieve pain and fever. **2.** a tablet of aspirin.

ass (as), *n.* **1.** a long-eared domesticated mammal related to the horse. **2.** a stupid, foolish, or stubborn person.

as•sail (ə sāl′), *v.t.* **1.** to attack vigorously or violently. **2.** to attack verbally. —**as•sail′a•ble,** *adj.* —**as•sail′ant,** *n.*

as•sas•sin (ə sas′in), *n.* a murderer, esp. one who kills a politically prominent person. [< ML *assassīnī* (pl.) < Ar *hashshāshīn* lit., eaters of hashish]

as•sas′si•nate′ (-nāt′), *v.t.,* -**nat•ed,** -**nat•ing.** to murder (a politically prominent person). —**as•sas′si•na′tion,** *n.*

as•sault (ə sôlt′), *n.* **1.** a sudden violent attack. **2.** an unlawful threat or attempt to do bodily harm. **3.** RAPE¹ (def. 1). —*v.t.* **4.** to make an assault upon.

as•say (*v.* ə sā′; *n.* as′ā, ə sā′), *v.t.* **1.** to examine or analyze. **2.** to analyze (an ore, alloy, etc.) to determine the presence of metal, as gold. **3.** to analyze (a drug) to determine potency or composition. —*n.* **4.** an analysis of the composition, characteristics, or strength of a substance. —**as•say′er,** *n.*

as•sem•blage (ə sem′blij; *for 3 also Fr.* A sän-blAzh′), *n.* **1.** a group of persons or things; assembly. **2.** the act of assembling. **3.** a sculpture made up of a group of unrelated objects.

as•sem•ble (ə sem′bəl), *v.,* -**bled,** -**bling.** —*v.t.* **1.** to bring together into one place, body, or whole. **2.** to put together the parts of. —*v.i.* **3.** to come together.

as•sem′bly, *n., pl.* -**blies. 1.** a group of persons gathered together. **2.** (*usu. cap.*) a legislative body, esp. the lower house of a legislature. **3.** a bugle call summoning troops to fall into ranks. **4.** the putting together of parts, as of complex machinery.

assem′bly dis′trict, *n.* one of the districts into which a state is divided, each district electing one member to the lower house of the state legislature. Compare CONGRESSIONAL DISTRICT, SENATORIAL DISTRICT.

assem′bly lan′guage, *n.* a computer language most of whose expressions are symbolic equivalents of the machine-language instructions of a particular computer.

assem′bly line′, *n.* an arrangement of machines, tools, and workers in which a product is assembled in a sequence as it is moved along a direct route.

as•sem′bly•man or **-wom′an,** *n., pl.* **-men** or **-wom•en.** a member of a legislative assembly.

as•sent (ə sent′), *v.i.* **1.** to agree or concur; acquiesce. —*n.* **2.** agreement or concurrence; acquiescence.

as•sert (ə sûrt′), *v.t.* **1.** to state positively; declare. **2.** to maintain or defend (claims, rights, etc.). —*Idiom.* **3.** assert oneself, to claim one's rights or declare one's views insistently.

as•ser′tion, *n.* a positive statement; declaration.

as•ser′tive, *adj.* confidently aggressive or self-assured. —**as•ser′tive•ly,** *adv.* —**as•ser′tive•ness,** *n.*

as•sess (ə ses′), *v.t.* **1.** to estimate the value of (property) for tax purposes. **2.** to determine the amount of (damages, a fine, etc.). **3.** to impose a tax or other charge on. **4.** to judge the value or character of; evaluate. —**as•sess′ment,** *n.* —**as•ses′sor,** *n.*

as•set (as′et), *n.* **1.** a useful and desirable thing or quality. **2.** a single item of ownership having exchange value. **3.** assets, **a.** the total resources of a person or business, as cash or real estate. **b.** property available for the payment of debts.

as•sev•er•ate (ə sev′ə rāt′), *v.t.,* **-at•ed, -at•ing.** to declare earnestly or solemnly. —**as•sev′er•a′tion,** *n.*

as•sid•u•ous (ə sij′ŏo əs), *adj.* **1.** constant; unremitting. **2.** working diligently at a task; industrious. —**as•si•du•i•ty** (as′i dŏo′i tē, -dyŏo′-), **as•sid′u•ous•ness,** *n.* —**as•sid′u•ous•ly,** *adv.*

as•sign (ə sīn′), *v.t.* **1.** to allocate; allot. **2.** to give out as a task. **3.** to appoint, as to a post or duty. **4.** to name; specify. **5.** to ascribe; attribute. **6.** *Law.* to transfer (property, rights, etc.). —**as•sign′a•ble,** *adj.* —**as•sign′er;** *Chiefly Law,* **as•sign•or** (ə sī nôr′), *n.* —**as•sign′ment,** *n.*

as•sig•na•tion (as′ig nā′shən), *n.* an appointment for a meeting, esp. a secret rendezvous or tryst.

as•sim•i•late (ə sim′ə lāt′), *v.,* **-lat•ed, -lat•ing.** —*v.t.* **1.** to take in and incorporate as one's own. **2.** to bring into conformity with the customs and traditions of a dominant culture. **3.** to absorb (food) and incorporate it into the body. —*v.i.* **4.** to be or become assimilated. —**as•sim•i•la′tion,** *n.*

as•sist (ə sist′), *v.t., v.i.* **1.** to aid; help. —*n.* **2.** a play helping a teammate to score or put out an opponent. **3.** a helpful act. —**as•sis′tance,** *n.*

as•sis′tant, *n.* **1.** a person who assists; helper. —*adj.* **2.** assisting; helpful. **3.** subordinate.

assist′ed su′icide, *n.* suicide aided by a person, esp. a physician, who organizes the logistics of the suicide, as by providing the necessary quantities of a poison.

as•size (ə sīz′), *n.* **1.** Usu., **assizes.** (in England) trial sessions held periodically by a high court. **2.** a judicial inquiry.

assn. or **Assn.,** association.

assoc., 1. associate. **2.** associated. **3.** association.

as•so•ci•ate (*v.* ə sō′shē āt′, -sē-; *n., adj.,* -it, -āt′), *v.,* **-at•ed, -at•ing,** *n., adj.* —*v.t.* **1.** to connect in thought, feeling, or memory. **2.** to commit (oneself) as a companion, partner, or colleague. **3.** to unite; combine. —*v.i.* **4.** to join together as partners, companions, or colleagues. —*n.* **5.** a partner or colleague. **6.** a companion; comrade. —*adj.* **7.** connected or joined, esp. as a companion or colleague. **8.** having subordinate status.

as•so′ci•a′tion (-sē ā′shən, -shē-), *n.* **1.** an organization of people with a common purpose. **2.** the act of associating or state of being associated.

asso′cia′tion foot′ball, *n. Brit.* SOCCER.

as•so′ci•a•tive (-sō′shē ā′tiv, -sē-, -shə tiv), *adj.* **1.** of or resulting from association. **2.** *Math.* giving an equivalent expression when elements are grouped without change of order.

as•so•nance (as′ə nəns), *n.* **1.** similarity of sounds in words or syllables. **2.** rhyme in which the same vowel sounds are used with different consonants. —**as′so•nant,** *adj.*

as•sort (ə sôrt′), *v.t.* to distribute or arrange according to kind or class; classify.

as•sort′ed, *adj.* consisting of various kinds; miscellaneous.

as•sort′ment, *n.* **1.** the act of assorting. **2.** a mixed collection.

asst., assistant.

as•suage (ə swāj′, ə swäzh′), *v.t.,* **-suaged, -suag•ing. 1.** to make less severe; ease. **2.** to appease; satisfy.

as•sume (ə sŏom′), *v.t.,* **-sumed, -sum•ing. 1.** to take for granted without proof; suppose. **2.** to take upon oneself. **3.** to take over the duties or responsibilities of. **4.** to pretend to have or be; feign.

as•sump•tion (ə sump′shən), *n.* **1.** something taken for granted; a supposition. **2.** the act of assuming. **3. a.** (*cap.*) the bodily taking up into heaven of the Virgin Mary. **b.** a feast commemorating this, celebrated on August 15. —**as•sump′tive,** *adj.*

as•sur•ance (ə shŏor′əns, -shûr′-), *n.* **1.** a positive declaration intended to give confidence. **2.** a promise or pledge. **3.** freedom from doubt; certainty. **4.** self-confidence. **5.** the doctrine that believing Christians are assured of being saved. Col. 2:2. **6.** *Chiefly Brit.* INSURANCE.

as•sure (ə shŏor′, ə shûr′), *v.t.,* **-sured, -sur•ing. 1.** to declare positively or confidently to. **2.** to make (a future event) sure; guarantee. **3.** to give confidence to; reassure. **4.** *Chiefly Brit.* to insure against loss. —**as•sur′er, as•su′ror,** *n.*

as•sured′, *adj.* **1.** guaranteed; sure. **2.** self-confident. —*n.* **3.** the beneficiary of an insurance policy. —**as•sur′ed•ly,** *adv.*

As•syr•i•a (ə sēr′ē ə), *n.* an ancient empire of SW Asia: greatest extent from c750 to 612 B.C. —**As•syr′i•an,** *adj., n.*

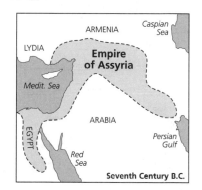

A•staire (ə stâr′), *n.* **Fred** (*Frederick Austerlitz*), 1899–1987, U.S. dancer.

as•ta•tine (as′tə tēn′, -tin), *n.* a rare element of the halogen family. *Symbol:* At; *at. no.:* 85.

as•ter (as′tər), *n.* any of various plants with white, pink, or blue rays around a yellow disk. [< L < Gk *astēr* star]

as•ter•isk (as′tə risk), *n.* a starlike symbol (*) used in writing and printing as a reference mark or to indicate an omission.

a•stern (ə stûrn′), *adv.* **1.** behind a ship or aircraft. **2.** in a backward direction.

as•ter•oid (as′tə roid′), *n.* any of the thousands of typically small, solid bodies that revolve about the sun in orbits mostly between Mars and Jupiter.

asth•ma (az′mə), *n.* an often allergic respiratory disorder characterized by wheezing and difficulty in breathing. —**asth•mat′ic** (-mat′ik), *adj., n.*

a•stig•ma•tism (ə stig′mə tiz′əm), *n.* a defect of the eye or of a lens in which rays of light do not converge on a single focal point. —**as•tig•mat•ic** (as′tig mat′ik), *adj.*

a•stir (ə stûr′), *adj.* **1.** moving or stirring. **2.** out of bed.

as•ton•ish (ə ston′ish), *v.t.* to fill with sudden surprise or wonder; amaze. —as•ton′ish•ing, adj. —as•ton′ish•ing•ly, adv. —as•ton′ish•ment, n.

As•tor (as′tər), n. **1.** John Jacob, 1763–1848, U.S. capitalist and fur merchant. **2.** Nancy (Langhorne), Viscountess, 1879–1964, first woman member of Parliament in England.

as•tound (ə stound′), v.t. to overwhelm with amazement. —as•tound′ing, adj. —as•tound′ing•ly, adv.

a•strad•dle (ə strad′l), adv., prep. ASTRIDE.

as•tra•khan (as′trə kən, -kan′), n. the lustrous, tightly curled wool of young lambs from Astrakhan, a city in the Russian Federation.

as•tral (as′trəl), adj. of, from, or like the stars.

a•stray (ə strā′), adv., adj. **1.** off the correct path or route. **2.** in or into error.

a•stride (ə strīd′), adv. **1.** with a leg on either side. **2.** with legs apart. —prep. **3.** with a leg on each side of. **4.** on both sides of.

as•trin•gent (ə strin′jənt), adj. **1.** causing constriction of soft tissue. **2.** harshly biting; caustic. —n. **3.** an astringent substance. —as•trin′gen•cy, n.

astro-, a combining form meaning pertaining to stars or to outer space (astrophysics).

as•tro•labe (as′trə lāb′), n. an ancient astronomical instrument used to determine the position of the sun or stars.

as•trol•o•gy (ə strol′ə jē), n. the study that assumes and attempts to interpret the influence of the heavenly bodies on human affairs. —as•trol′o•ger, n. —as•tro•log•i•cal (as′trə loj′i kəl), adj.

as•tro•naut (as′trə nôt′, -not′), n. a person engaged in or trained for spaceflight.

as′tro•nau′tics, n. the science and technology of spaceflight, including interplanetary and interstellar flight. —as′tro•nau′tic, as′tro•nau′ti•cal, adj.

as•tro•nom•i•cal (as′trə nom′i kəl) also **-nom′ic**, adj. **1.** of astronomy. **2.** extremely large; enormous. —as′tro•nom′i•cal•ly, adv.

astronom′ical u′nit, n. a unit of length equal to the mean distance of the earth from the sun: approximately 93 million miles (150 million km).

as•tron•o•my (ə stron′ə mē), n. the science that deals with the material universe beyond the earth's atmosphere. —as•tron′o•mer, n.

as•tro•phys•ics (as′trō fiz′iks), n. the branch of astronomy that deals with the physical properties of celestial bodies. —as′tro•phys′i•cist (-ə sist), n.

as•tute (ə stoot′, ə styoot′), adj. **1.** keenly perceptive or discerning. **2.** shrewd; crafty. —as•tute′ly, adv. —as•tute′ness, n.

A•sun•ción (ä′soon syôn′), n. the capital of Paraguay. 457,210.

a•sun•der (ə sun′dər), adv., adj. **1.** in or into separate parts. **2.** widely separated; apart.

a•sy•lum (ə sī′ləm), n. **1.** (esp. formerly) an institution for the care of ill or needy persons. **2.** a place of refuge; sanctuary. **3.** protection granted by a government to political refugees.

a•sym•met•ric (ā′sə me′trik, as′ə-) also **-met′ri•cal**, adj. not symmetrical; lacking symmetry. —a•sym•me•try (ā sim′i trē), n.

at (at; unstressed ət, it), prep. **1.** (used to indicate a point or place in space): stood at the door. **2.** (used to indicate a location or position, as in time): at age 65. **3.** (used to indicate amount, degree, or rate): at great speed. **4.** (used to indicate a direction or objective): Look at that. **5.** (used to indicate involvement): at play. **6.** (used to indicate a condition): at ease. **7.** (used to indicate a cause): annoyed at their carelessness. **8.** (used to indicate relative value): at cost.

At, Chem. Symbol. astatine.

at•a•vism (at′ə viz′əm), n. the reappearance in an individual of characteristics of a remote ancestor that have been absent in intervening generations. —at′a•vist, n. —at′a•vis′tic, adj.

ate (āt; Brit. et), v. pt. of EAT.

-ate¹, a suffix meaning: of, having, or resembling (compassionate); to become or cause to become (agitate); to produce (ulcerate); to treat with (aerate).

-ate², a suffix meaning a salt of an acid (sulfate).

-ate³, a suffix meaning office, rule, or function (consulate).

at•el•ier (at′l yā′), n. a workshop or studio, esp. of an artist.

Ath•a•bas•kan or **-bas•can** (ath′ə bas′kən) also **-pas′kan** (-pas′-), n. **1.** a family of North American Indian languages. **2.** a member of an Athabaskan-speaking people.

Ath•a•li•ah (ath′ə lī′ə), n. a daughter of Ahab and Jezebel and usurper of the throne of Judah, reigned 842–837 B.C. II Kings 11:1–3.

a•the•ism (ā′thē iz′əm), n. the doctrine or belief that there is no God. —a′the•ist, n. —a′the•is′tic, adj.

A•the•na (ə thē′nə), n. the ancient Greek goddess of wisdom, the arts, and warfare.

Ath•ens (ath′inz), n. the capital of Greece. 885,136. —A•the•ni•an (ə thē′nē ən), adj., n.

ath•er•o•scle•ro•sis (ath′ə rō sklə rō′sis), n. arteriosclerosis in which fatty substances form a deposit on the lining of arterial walls.

a•thirst (ə thûrst′), adj. keenly desirous, eager.

ath•lete (ath′lēt), n. a person trained or gifted in exercises or contests involving physical agility, stamina, or strength.

ath′lete's foot′, n. ringworm of the feet.

ath•let•ic (ath let′ik), adj. **1.** physically strong; sturdy. **2.** of or involving athletes or athletics. —ath•let′i•cal•ly, adv.

ath•let′ics, n. (usu. used with a pl. v.) exercises, sports, or contests in which athletes participate.

-athon, a combining form extracted from MARATHON, used in coinages meaning an event drawn out to unusual length (walkathon).

a•thwart (ə thwôrt′), adv. **1.** from side to side; crosswise. —prep. **2.** from side to side of; across. **3.** in opposition to; against.

a•tilt (ə tilt′), adj., adv. at a tilt; tilted.

-ation, a suffix meaning: act or process of (consolation); condition of (deprivation); result of (combination).

-ative, a suffix meaning: of or relating to (qualitative); tending or serving to (talkative).

At•lan•ta (at lan′tə), n. the capital of Georgia. 396,052.

Atlan′tic Char′ter, n. the joint declaration of President Roosevelt and Prime Minister Churchill (August 14, 1941), setting forth the peace aims of their governments for the period following World War II.

Atlan′tic Commu′nity, n. the member countries of NATO.

At•lan′tic O′cean (at lan′tik), n. an ocean bounded by the Americas in the west and by Europe and Africa in the east. Also called **the Atlan′tic.**

at•las (at′ləs), n. a bound collection of maps.

At•las (at′ləs), n., pl. **At•las•es. 1.** a Titan condemned by Zeus to support the sky on his shoulders. **2.** a liquid-propellant booster rocket used to launch satellites into orbit around the earth and send probes to the moon and planets.

ATM, an electronic machine that provides banking services when activated by insertion of a plastic card. [a(utomated)-t(eller) m(achine)]

at•mos•phere (at′məs fēr′), n. **1.** the gaseous envelope surrounding a heavenly body, esp. the earth; air. **2.** a conventional unit of pressure, the normal pressure of the air at sea level, about 14.7 pounds per square inch. **3.** a pervading environment or influence. **4.** a dominant mood or tone, as of a work of art. —at′mos•pher′ic (-fer′ik), adj. —at′mos•pher′i•cal•ly, adv.

at. no., atomic number.

at•oll (at′ôl, -ol, -ōl), n. a ring-shaped coral reef enclosing a lagoon.

at•om (at′əm), n. **1.** the smallest component of an element having the properties of that element, consisting of a nucleus of neutrons and protons surrounded by electrons. **2.** something extremely small; speck.

a•tom•ic (ə tom′ik), *adj.* **1.** of or using atoms, atomic energy, or atomic bombs. **2.** existing as free, uncombined atoms. **3.** extremely minute. —**a•tom′i•cal•ly,** *adv.*

atom′ic (or **at′om**) **bomb′,** *n.* a bomb whose explosive force comes from a chain reaction based on nuclear fission.

atom′ic en′ergy, *n.* energy released by reactions in atomic nuclei; nuclear energy.

atom′ic num′ber, *n.* the number of protons in the atomic nucleus of an element.

atom′ic weight′, *n.* the average weight of an atom of an element based on ¹/₁₂ the weight of the carbon-12 atom.

at•om•iz•er (at′ə mī′zər), *n.* an apparatus for reducing liquids to a fine spray, as for cosmetic application.

a•ton•al (ā tōn′l), *adj. Music.* lacking tonality. —a′to•nal′i•ty, *n.*

a•tone (ə tōn′), *v.i.,* **a•toned, a•ton•ing.** to make amends, as for an offense or sin.

a•tone′ment, *n.* **1.** amends for a wrong or injury. **2.** (*sometimes cap.*) the reconciliation of God and humankind through Christ's death.

a•top (ə top′), *adj., adv.* **1.** on or at the top. —*prep.* **2.** on the top of.

ATP, adenosine triphosphate: a compound that is the primary source of energy in all living cells.

a•tri•um (ā′trē əm), *n., pl.* **a•tri•a** (ā′trē ə), **a•tri•ums. 1. a.** an often skylighted court in a public building, as a hotel. **b.** the main or central room of an ancient Roman house. **2.** either of the two upper chambers of the heart that receive blood from the veins. —a′tri•al, *adj.*

a•tro•cious (ə trō′shəs), *adj.* **1.** extremely wicked, cruel, or brutal. **2.** shockingly bad; abominable. —a•tro′cious•ly, *adv.* —a•tro′cious•ness, *n.*

a•troc•i•ty (ə tros′i tē), *n., pl.* **-ties.** an atrocious act, thing, or circumstance.

at•ro•phy (a′trə fē), *n., v.,* **-phied, -phy•ing.** —*n.* **1.** a wasting away of the body or of a bodily organ or part. —*v.t., v.i.* **2.** to affect with or undergo atrophy.

at•ro•pine (a′trə pēn′, -pin), *n.* a poisonous alkaloid obtained from belladonna and used esp. to dilate the pupil of the eye.

at•tach (ə tach′), *v.t.* **1.** to fasten or join; connect. **2.** to assign or attribute. **3.** to bind by emotional ties, as of affection. **4.** to take (property) by legal authority. —*v.i.* **5.** to become attached. —at•tach′a•ble, *adj.*

at•ta•ché (at′ə shā′), *n., pl.* **-chés.** a diplomatic official or military officer assigned to an embassy, esp. in a technical capacity.

attaché′ case′, *n.* a flat, usu. rigid briefcase.

at•tach•ment (ə tach′mənt), *n.* **1.** the act of attaching or state of being attached. **2.** an emotional tie, as of affection. **3.** a fastening or tie. **4.** an additional or supplementary device. **5.** seizure of property by legal authority.

at•tack (ə tak′), *v.t.* **1.** to set upon in a forceful, violent, hostile, or aggressive way. **2.** to abuse verbally. **3.** to go to work on vigorously. —*v.i.* **4.** to make an attack. —*n.* **5.** the act of attacking. **6.** an onset of disease or illness. —at•tack′er, *n.*

at•tain (ə tān′), *v.t.* **1.** to achieve or accomplish, esp. by effort. —*v.i.* **2.** to arrive at or succeed in reaching or obtaining something. —at•tain′a•ble, *adj.* —at•tain′a•bil′i•ty, *n.* —at•tain′ment, *n.*

at•tain′der (-dər), *n.* the loss of all civil rights upon being sentenced to death or outlawry for treason or a felony.

at•tar (at′ər), *n.* a perfume or essential oil obtained from flowers.

at•tempt (ə tempt′), *v.t.* **1.** to make an effort at; try. —*n.* **2.** an effort made to accomplish something. **3.** an attack or assault.

at•tend (ə tend′), *v.t.* **1.** to be present at. **2.** to go with; accompany. **3.** to take care of; minister to. **4.** to wait upon; serve. —*v.i.* **5.** to take care or charge.

6. to apply oneself. **7.** to pay attention. **8.** to be present.

at•tend′ance, *n.* **1.** the act of attending. **2.** the persons or number of persons attending.

at•tend′ant, *n.* **1.** a person who attends another, as to perform a service. —*adj.* **2.** being present or in attendance; accompanying.

at•ten′tion (-shən), *n.* **1.** the act or faculty of concentrating the mind on a single object, thought, or event. **2.** observant care or consideration. **3.** civility or courtesy. **4.** a military position with eyes to the front, arms to the sides, and heels together. —at•ten′tive, *adj.* —at•ten′tive•ly, *adv.* —at•ten′tive•ness, *n.*

atten′tion def′icit disor′der, *n.* a developmental disorder of children characterized by inattention and passivity.

atten′tion def′icit hyperactiv′ity disor′der, *n.* a condition, usu. in children, characterized by inattention, hyperactivity, and impulsiveness.

at•ten′u•ate′ (-yoo̅ āt′), *v.,* **-at•ed, -at•ing.** —*v.t.* **1.** to reduce in force, intensity, effect, or strength; weaken. **2.** to make slender or fine. —*v.i.* **3.** to become attenuated. —at•ten′u•a′tion, *n.*

at•test (ə test′), *v.t.* **1.** to affirm as correct, accurate, or genuine, esp. in writing. **2.** to give proof or evidence of; manifest. —*v.i.* **3.** to testify or bear witness. —at•tes•ta•tion (at′es tā′shən), *n.*

at•tic (at′ik), *n.* the part of a building, esp. of a house, directly under the roof.

At•ti•la (at′l ə, ə til′ə), *n.* A.D. 406?–453, king of the Huns.

at•tire (ə tīr′), *v.,* **-tired, -tir•ing,** *n.* —*v.t.* **1.** to dress or array. —*n.* **2.** clothes or apparel.

at•ti•tude (at′i too̅d′, -tyoo̅d′), *n.* **1.** manner, disposition, or feeling with regard to a person or thing. **2.** position or posture of the body. **3.** the inclination of the three principal axes of an aircraft relative to a reference point, as the ground. **4.** *Slang.* a testy, uncooperative disposition. —at′ti•tu′di•nal, *adj.*

at′ti•tu′di•nize′ (-too̅d′n īz′, -tyoo̅d′-), *v.i.,* **-nized, -niz•ing.** to assume an attitude for effect.

attn., attention.

at•tor•ney (ə tûr′nē), *n., pl.* **-neys.** a person legally authorized to act for another, esp. a lawyer. [< AF *attourne* lit., (one who is) turned to]

attor′ney-at-law′, *n., pl.* **attorneys-at-law.** a lawyer.

attor′ney gen′eral, *n., pl.* **attorneys general, attorney generals.** the chief law officer of a country or state and head of its legal department.

at•tract (ə trakt′), *v.t.* **1.** to draw or pull by a physical force. **2.** to draw by appealing to the emotions or senses or by stimulating interest. —*v.i.* **3.** to possess attraction. —at•tract′a•ble, *adj.*

at•tract′ant, *n.* a substance that attracts.

at•trac′tion, *n.* **1.** the act, power, or property of attracting. **2.** an attractive quality or feature. **3.** a person or thing that attracts or entices. **4.** an electric or magnetic force that tends to draw oppositely charged bodies together.

at•trac′tive (-tiv), *adj.* **1.** providing pleasure; charming. **2.** arousing interest. **3.** having the power to attract. —at•trac′tive•ly, *adv.* —at•trac′tive•ness, *n.*

attrib., **1.** attribute. **2.** attributive. **3.** attributing.

at•trib•ute (*v.* ə trib′yoot; *n.* a′trə byoot′), *v.,* **-ut•ed, -ut•ing,** *n.* —*v.t.* **1.** to regard as caused by, created by, or belonging to a specified person or thing. —*n.* **at•tri•bute 2.** a quality, characteristic, or property of a person or thing. —at•trib′ut•a•ble, *adj.* —at•tri•bu′tion, *n.*

at•trib′u•tive (-trib′yə tiv), *adj.* **1.** of or having the character of an attribute. **2.** being an adjective or a noun that is adjacent to the noun it modifies. —*n.* **3.** an attributive word, esp. an adjective. —at•trib′u•tive•ly, *adv.*

at•tri•tion (ə trish′ən), *n.* **1.** a reduction in a work force without firing of personnel, as when workers retire and are not replaced. **2.** a wearing down or away by or as if by friction. —at•tri′tion•al, *adj.*

at•tune (ə tōōn′, ə tyōōn′), *v.t.*, **-tuned, -tun•ing.** to bring into accord, harmony, or sympathetic relationship.

atty., attorney.

ATV, a small motor vehicle with treads, wheels, or both, capable of going over any nonroad surface including water. [*a(ll)-t(errain) v(ehicle)*]

a•twit•ter (ə twit′ər), *adj.* excited or nervous.

at. wt., atomic weight.

a•typ•i•cal (ā tip′i kəl), *adj.* not typical; irregular. —**a•typ′i•cal•ly,** *adv.*

Au, *Chem. Symbol.* gold. [< L *aurum*]

au•burn (ô′bərn), *n.* **1.** a reddish brown color. —*adj.* **2.** of the color auburn.

Auck•land (ôk′lənd), *n.* a seaport in N New Zealand. 841,700.

auc•tion (ôk′shən), *n.* **1.** a public sale at which property or goods are sold to the highest bidder. —*v.t.* **2.** to sell at auction. —**auc′tion•eer′,** *n.*

auc•to•ri•al (ôk tôr′ē əl, ouk′-), *adj.* of or pertaining to an author.

au•da•cious (ô dā′shəs), *adj.* **1.** bold; daring. **2.** insolent; brazen. —**au•da′cious•ly,** —**au•dac• i•ty** (ô das′i tē), *n.*

au•di•ble (ô′də bəl), *adj.* capable of being heard. —**au′di•bil′i•ty,** *n.* —**au′di•bly,** *adv.*

au•di•ence (ô′dē əns), *n.* **1.** a group of spectators or listeners. **2.** the persons reached by a book, broadcast, film, etc.; public. **3.** an opportunity to be heard. **4.** a formal interview, as with a sovereign.

au•di•o (ô′dē ō′), *adj.* **1.** of or used in the transmission, reception, or reproduction of sound. **2.** of frequencies in the audible range. —*n.* **3.** the audio elements of television or films. **4.** the transmission, reception, or reproduction of sound.

au′dio book′ or **au′di•o•book′,** *n.* a recording of an oral reading of a book, often in abridged form.

au′di•ol′o•gy (-ol′ə jē), *n.* the study and treatment of hearing disorders. —**au′di•o•log′i•cal** (-ə loj′i-kəl), *adj.* —**au′di•ol′o•gist,** *n.*

au′di•om′e•ter (-om′i tar), *n.* an instrument for gauging and recording acuity of hearing.

au′di•o•phile′ (-fīl′), *n.* a person who is esp. interested in high-fidelity sound reproduction.

au′di•o•tape′ (ô′dē ō-), *n.* magnetic tape on which sound is recorded.

au′di•o•vis′u•al, *adj.* of, involving, or directed at both hearing and sight.

au•dit (ô′dit), *n.* **1.** an official examination and verification of financial accounts and records. —*v.t.* **2.** to make an audit of. **3.** to attend (a course) as an auditor.

au•di•tion (ô dish′ən), *n.* **1.** a trial hearing or viewing, esp. of a performer seeking employment. —*v.t., v.i.* **2.** to give an audition (to).

au•di•tor (ô′di tər), *n.* **1.** a person authorized to audit financial accounts. **2.** one who attends an academic course to listen but not receive credit. **3.** a hearer; listener.

au′di•to′ri•um (-tôr′ē əm), *n.* **1.** a room set apart for an audience, as in a school. **2.** a building or hall for public gatherings.

au′di•to′ry, *adj.* of hearing, the sense of hearing, or the organs of hearing.

Au•du•bon (ô′də bon′, -bən), *n.* **John James,** 1785–1851, U.S. naturalist who painted and wrote about the birds of North America.

auf Wie•der•seh•en (ouf vē′dər zā′ən), *interj.* German. good-bye; until we see each other again.

Aug or **Aug.,** August.

au•ger (ô′gər), *n.* a tool for boring holes.

aught¹ (ôt), *n.* anything whatever: *for aught I know.*

aught² (ôt), *n.* a cipher (0); zero.

aug•ment (ôg ment′), *v.t., v.i.,* to make or become larger; enlarge. —**aug′men•ta′tion,** *n.*

au gra•tin (ō grat′n, ō grät′n), *adj.* topped with buttered breadcrumbs or grated cheese and browned. [< F]

Augs′burg Confes′sion, *n.* the statement of beliefs and doctrines of the Lutherans.

au•gur (ô′gər), *n.* **1.** a soothsayer; prophet. —*v.t.* **2.** to predict, as from omens. **3.** to serve as an omen of; foreshadow. —*v.i.* **4.** to be a sign; bode.

au•gu•ry (ô′gyə rē), *n., pl.* **-ries. 1.** the art or practice of auguring. **2.** an omen, token, or indication.

au•gust (ô gust′), *adj.* inspiring reverence or admiration; majestic. —**au•gust′ly,** *adv.* —**au•gust′ness,** *n.*

Au•gust (ô′gəst), *n.* the eighth month of the year, containing 31 days.

Au•gus•ta (ô gus′tə, ə gus′-), *n.* the capital of Maine. 21,819.

Au•gus•tine (ô′gə stēn′, ə gus′tin), *n.* **Saint,** A.D. 354–430, early Christian Church father. —**Au′gus• tin′i•an** (-stin′ē ən), *adj., n.*

Au•gus•tus (ə gus′təs), *n.* 63 B.C.–A.D. 14, first Roman emperor 27 B.C.–A.D. 14. —**Au•gus′tan,** *adj.*

au jus (ō zhōōs′; *Fr.* ō zhʏ′), *adj.* (of meat) served in the natural juices.

auk (ôk), *n.* a diving bird of northern seas, with webbed feet and small wings.

auld lang syne (ôld′ lang zīn′), *n.* fondly remembered times.

aunt (ant, änt), *n.* **1.** the sister of one's father or mother. **2.** the wife of one's uncle.

au pair (ō pâr′), *n.* a person, usu. a young foreign visitor, who performs household tasks in exchange for room and board.

au•ra (ôr′ə), *n., pl.* **-ras. 1.** a distinctive and pervasive quality surrounding a person or thing. **2.** a light or radiance claimed to emanate from the body.

au•ral (ôr′əl), *adj.* of the ear or the sense of hearing. —**au′ral•ly,** *adv.*

au•re•ole (ôr′ē ōl′), *n.* a halo.

au re•voir (ō Rə vwAR′; *Eng.* ō′ rə vwär′), *interj.* French. good-bye; until we see each other again.

au•ri•cle (ôr′i kəl), *n.* **1.** the outer ear. **2.** (loosely) the atrium of the heart.

au•ric•u•lar (ô rik′yə lər), *adj.* **1.** aural. **2.** of an auricle.

Au•ro•ra (ə rôr′ə), *n., pl.* **-ras** for 2. **1.** the Roman goddess of the dawn. **2.** (*l.c.*) a display of bands of light sporadically seen in night skies of both hemispheres. **3.** a city in central Colorado. 250,717.

auro′ra aus•tra′lis (ô strā′lis), *n.* the aurora of the S Hemisphere.

auro′ra bo•re•al′is (bôr′ē al′is, -ā′lis), *n.* the aurora of the N Hemisphere.

Ausch•witz (oush′vits), *n.* a town in SW Poland: site of Nazi death camp during World War II. 39,600.

aus•cul•ta•tion (ô′skəl tā′shən), *n.* the act of listening to sounds within the body as a method of diagnosis. —**aus′cul•tate′,** *v.t., v.i.,* **-tat•ed, -tat•ing.**

aus•pice (ô′spis), *n., pl.* **aus•pic•es** (ô′spə siz). **1.** Usu., **-pices.** patronage; sponsorship. **2.** Often, **-pices.** a sign, esp. a favorable one; portent.

aus•pi′cious, *adj.* **1.** promising success; favorable. **2.** favored by fortune; fortunate. —**aus•pi′cious•ly,** *adv.* —**aus•pi′cious•ness,** *n.*

Aus•sie (ô′sē), *n. Informal.* an Australian.

Aus•ten (ô′stən), *n.* **Jane,** 1775–1817, English novelist.

aus•tere (ô stēr′), *adj.* **1.** severe, as in manner; forbidding. **2.** severely moral; ascetic. **3.** without ornament or adornment. —**aus•tere′ly,** *adv.* —**aus•ter′i• ty** (ô ster′-), *n.*

Aus•tin (ô′stən), *n.* the capital of Texas. 514,013.

aus•tral (ô′strəl), *adj.* southern.

Aus•tral•ia (ô strāl′yə), *n.* **1.** a continent SE of Asia, between the Indian and Pacific oceans. **2.** a nation consisting of this continent and the island of Tasmania. 16,250,000. —**Aus•tral′ian,** *adj., n.*

Aus•tri•a (ô′strē ə), *n.* a republic in central Europe. 8,054,078. —**Aus′tri•an,** *adj., n.*

aut-, var. of AUTO-.

au•then•tic (ô then′tik), *adj.* **1.** not false or copied; genuine; real. **2.** entitled to acceptance or belief because of agreement with known facts or experience; trustworthy. —**au•then′ti•cal•ly,** *adv.* —**au′then• tic′i•ty** (-tis′i tē), *n.*

au•then′ti•cate′, *v.t.*, **-cat•ed, -cat•ing.** to establish as genuine. —**au•then′ti•ca′tion,** *n.*

au•thor (ô′thər), *n.* **1.** the composer of a literary work; writer. **2.** one who creates or originates something. **3.** the writer of a software program. —*v.t.* **4.** to be the author of.

au•thor•i•tar•i•an (ə thôr′i târ′ē ən, ə thor′-), *adj.* **1.** favoring or requiring complete obedience to authority. **2.** of or being a government in which authority is centered in a person or group not accountable to the people. —*n.* **3.** one who favors or acts according to authoritarian principles. —**au•thor′i•tar′i•an•ism,** *n.*

au•thor′i•ta′tive (-tā′tiv), *adj.* **1.** having the sanction or weight of authority. **2.** supported by evidence and accepted by most authorities. —**au•thor′i•ta′tive•ly,** *adv.* —**au•thor′i•ta′tive•ness,** *n.*

au•thor′i•ty, *n., pl.* **-ties. 1.** the power to control, command, or determine. **2.** a power or right delegated or given. **3.** a person or body of persons in whom authority is vested. **4.** Usu., **-ties.** government. **5. a.** an accepted source of information, advice, or substantiation. **b.** a quotation or citation from such a source. **6.** an expert on a subject. **7.** persuasive force; conviction.

au•thor•ize (ô′thə rīz′), *v.t.,* **-ized, -iz•ing. 1.** to give authority or official power to. **2.** to give approval for; sanction. **3.** to justify. —**au′thor•i•za′tion,** *n.*

Au′thorized Ver′sion, *n.* KING JAMES VERSION.

au′thor•ship′, *n.* **1.** origin of a piece of writing. **2.** the occupation of writing.

au•tism (ô′tiz əm), *n.* a developmental disorder characterized by extreme self-absorption, and detachment from reality. —**au•tis′tic,** *adj.*

au•to (ô′tō), *n., pl.* **-tos.** an automobile.

auto-, a combining form meaning self or same (*autograph*).

au•to•bi•og•ra•phy (ô′tə bī og′rə fē, -bē-), *n., pl.* **-phies.** a history of a person's life written by that person. —**au′to•bi•o•graph′i•cal** (-ə graf′i kəl), *adj.*

au•toc•ra•cy (ô tok′rə sē), *n., pl.* **-cies.** government in which one person has unlimited authority.

au′to•crat (ô′tə krat′), *n.* **1.** a ruler with unlimited power. **2.** an authoritarian or domineering person. —**au′to•crat′ic,** *adj.* —**au′to•crat′i•cal•ly,** *adv.*

au•to•di•dact (ô′tō dī′dakt), *n.* a self-taught person.

au•to•graph (ô′tə graf′, -gräf′), *n.* **1.** a person's signature. **2.** something, esp. a manuscript, written in a person's own hand. —*v.t.* **3.** to write one's signature on or in.

au•to•im•mune (ô′tō i myōōn′), *adj.* of or pertaining to the immune response of an organism against any of its own components.

au•to•mate (ô′tə māt′), *v.t., v.i.,* **-mat•ed, -mat•ing.** to operate by or undergo automation.

au′to•mat′ic (-mat′ik), *adj.* **1.** capable of operating independently of human intervention. **2.** involuntary; reflex. **3.** done unconsciously or from force of habit; mechanical. **4.** (of a firearm) capable of continuous operation. —*n.* **5.** an automatic machine or device, esp. a pistol. —**au′to•mat′i•cal•ly,** *adv.*

au′tomat′ic pi′lot, *n.* an electronic control system, as on an aircraft, that automatically maintains a preset heading and attitude.

au′to•ma′tion (-mā′shən), *n.* the technique or system of operating or controlling a mechanical process by automatic means, as by electronic devices.

au•tom•a•tism (ô tom′ə tiz′əm), *n.* the quality or condition of being automatic. —**au•tom′a•ti•za′tion,** *n.* —**au•tom′a•tize′, -tized, -tiz•ing.**

au•tom′a•ton′ (-ton′, -tn) *n., pl.* **-tons, -ta** (-tə). **1.** a robot. **2.** a person who acts in a mechanical manner.

au•to•mo•bile (ô′tə mə bēl′), *n.* a passenger vehicle typically having four wheels and an internal-combustion engine.

au′to•mo′tive (-mō′tiv), *adj.* **1.** of motor vehicles, esp. automobiles. **2.** propelled by a self-contained motor or engine.

au′to•nom′ic nerv′ous sys′tem (ô′tə nom′ik, ô′tə-), *n.* the system of nerves and ganglia that controls involuntary functions and consists of sympathetic and parasympathetic portions.

au•ton•o•mous (ô ton′ə məs), *adj.* **1.** self-governing. **2.** existing or functioning independently. —**au•ton′o•mous•ly,** *adv.* —**au•ton′o•my,** *n.*

au•top•sy (ô′top sē), *n., pl.* **-sies,** *v.,* **-sied, -sy•ing.** —*n.* **1.** examination of a body after death, as for determination of the cause of death. —*v.t.* **2.** to perform an autopsy on.

au•tumn (ô′təm), *n.* the season between summer and winter; fall. —**au•tum•nal** (ô tum′nl), *adj.*

aux•il•ia•ry (ôg zil′yə rē, -zil′ə-), *adj., n., pl.* **-ries.** —*adj.* **1.** additional; supplementary. **2.** used as a reserve in case of need. **3.** subsidiary; secondary. —*n.* **4.** an auxiliary person, thing, or group. **5.** AUXILIARY VERB.

auxil′iary verb′, *n.* a verb, as *be* or *have,* used with a main verb to express distinctions of tense, voice, etc.

aux•in (ôk′sin), *n.* a substance that regulates or modifies the growth of plants.

a•vail (ə vāl′), *v.t., v.i.* **1.** to be of use, advantage, or value (to). —*n.* **2.** use or advantage. —*Idiom.* **3. avail oneself of,** to make use of.

a•vail′a•ble, *adj.* **1.** ready for use; at hand. **2.** readily obtainable; accessible. —**a•vail′a•bil′i•ty,** *n.*

av•a•lanche (av′ə lanch′, -länch′), *n.* **1.** a large mass of snow, ice, etc., sliding down a mountain slope. **2.** an overwhelming quantity.

a•vant-garde (ə vänt′gärd′, av′änt-), *n.* **1.** the advance group in a field, esp. in the arts, whose works are unorthodox and experimental. —*adj.* **2.** characteristic of or belonging to the avant-garde.

av•a•rice (av′ər is), *n.* insatiable greed for riches. —**av′a•ri′cious** (-ə rish′əs), *adj.* —**av′a•ri′cious•ly,** *adv.*

a•vast (ə vast′, ə väst′), *interj. Naut.* stop! cease!

av•a•tar (av′ə tär′), *n.* an incarnation of a Hindu god.

a•vaunt (ə vônt′, ə vänt′), *interj. Archaic.* go away!

avdp., avoirdupois.

ave., avenue.

A•ve Ma•ri•a (ä′vä mə rē′ə), *n.* a prayer based on the salutation of the angel Gabriel to the Virgin Mary. Also called **Hail Mary.**

a•venge (ə venj′), *v.t.,* **a•venged, a•veng•ing. 1.** to take vengeance or exact satisfaction for. **2.** to take vengeance on behalf of. —**a•veng′er,** *n.*

aveng′er of blood′, *n.* one who was entitled to take vengeance on a person who had slain one of his family. Josh. 20:5.

av•e•nue (av′ə nyōō′, -nōō′), *n.* **1.** a wide street or main thoroughfare. **2.** a means of access or attainment.

a•ver (ə vûr′), *v.t.,* **a•verred, a•ver•ring.** to assert with confidence; declare.

av•er•age (av′ər ij, av′rij), *n., adj., v.,* **-aged, -ag•ing.** —*n.* **1.** an arithmetic mean. **2.** a typical or usual amount, rate, or level. —*adj.* **3.** of or forming an average. **4.** not unusual; common. —*v.t.* **5.** to find an average value for. **6.** (of a variable quantity) to have as an arithmetic mean. **7.** to do, be, or have typically. —*v.i.* **8.** to have or be at an average. —*Idiom.* **9. on the average,** usually; typically.

a•verse (ə vûrs′), *adj.* having a strong feeling of antipathy or repugnance.

a•ver•sion (ə vûr′zhən), *n.* **1.** a feeling of repugnance for something and a desire to avoid it. **2.** a cause or object of aversion.

a•vert (ə vûrt′), *v.t.* **1.** to turn away or aside. **2.** to ward off; prevent.

avg., average.

a•vi•an (ā′vē ən), *adj.* of birds.

a′vi•ar′y (-er′ē), *n., pl.* **-ar•ies.** a place, as a large cage, in which birds are kept. —**a′vi•a•rist** (-ər ist), *n.*

a•vi•a•tion (ā′vē ā′shən), *n.* the design, development, production, operation, or use of aircraft. [< F, = L *avi(s)* bird + *-ation*]

a·vi·a·tor, *n.* an airplane pilot.

av·id (av'id), *adj.* **1.** enthusiastic; keen. **2.** keenly desirous; eager. —**a·vid·i·ty** (ə vid'i tē), *n.* —**av'id·ly**, *adv.*

A·vi·gnon (A vē nyôn'), *n.* a city in SE France: papal residence 1309–77. 93,024.

a·vi·on·ics (ā'vē on'iks), *n.* the science and technology of electrical and electronic devices in aviation.

a·vi·ta·min·o·sis (ā vī'tə mə nō'sis), *n.* a disease caused by a deficiency of vitamins.

av·o·ca·do (av'ə kä'dō, ä'və-), *n., pl.* **-dos. 1.** a pear-shaped fruit with soft, light green pulp. **2.** the tropical American tree that bears avocados.

av·o·ca·tion (av'ə kā'shən), *n.* something done in addition to a principal occupation, esp. for pleasure; hobby. —**av'o·ca'tion·al**, *adj.*

a·void (ə void'), *v.t.* **1.** to keep clear of; shun. **2.** to prevent from happening. —**a·void'a·ble**, *adj.* —**a·void'a·bly**, *adv.* —**a·void'ance**, *n.*

av·oir·du·pois (av'ər də poiz'), *n.* **1.** AVOIRDUPOIS WEIGHT. **2.** *Informal.* bodily weight, esp. excess heaviness.

avoirdupois' weight', *n.* the system of weights based on a pound of 16 ounces, used in Great Britain and the U.S.

a·vouch (ə vouch'), *v.t.* **1.** to declare or assert with positiveness. **2.** to vouch for; guarantee.

a·vow (ə vou'), *v.t.* to declare frankly or openly. —**a·vow'al**, *n.* —**a·vowed'**, *adj.* —**a·vow'ed·ly**, *adv.*

a·vun·cu·lar (ə vung'kyə lər), *adj.* of or characteristic of an uncle.

a·wait (ə wāt'), *v.t.* **1.** to wait for; expect. **2.** to be in store for. —*v.i.* **3.** to wait.

a·wake (ə wāk'), *v.,* **a·woke** or **a·waked, a·woke** or **a·waked** or **a·wo·ken, a·wak·ing**, *adj.* —*v.t., v.i.* **1.** to rouse or emerge from sleep. **2.** to make or become active or alert. —*adj.* **3.** not sleeping. **4.** vigilant; alert.

a·wak'en, *v.t., v.i.,* to awake; waken. —**a·wak'en·ing**, *adj., n.*

a·ward (ə wôrd'), *v.t.* **1.** to give as due or merited. **2.** to assign by judicial decree. —*n.* **3.** something awarded. **4.** a decision, as of an arbitrator.

a·ware (ə wâr'), *adj.* **1.** having knowledge or realization; conscious. **2.** informed. —**a·ware'ness**, *n.*

a·wash (ə wosh', ə wôsh'), *adj., adv.* **1.** washed by waves or water. **2.** covered with water. **3.** covered, filled, or crowded.

a·way (ə wā'), *adv.* **1.** from this or that place. **2.** to another place or in another direction. **3.** to or at a distance; far. **4.** out of one's possession or use: *to give money away.* **5.** out of existence or notice: *to fade away.* **6.** incessantly or relentlessly. **7.** without hesitation: *Fire away.* —*adj.* **8.** absent. **9.** distant in place or time.

awe (ô), *n., v.,* **awed, aw·ing.** —*n.* **1.** a feeling of reverence, fear, and wonder. —*v.t.* **2.** to inspire or fill with awe.

a·weigh (ə wā'), *adj.* (of an anchor) just free of the bottom.

awe·some (ô'səm), *adj.* **1.** inspiring or characterized by awe. **2.** *Slang.* very impressive. —**awe'some·ly**, *adv.* —**awe'some·ness**, *n.*

awe'struck' or **-strick'en,** *adj.* filled with awe.

aw·ful (ô'fəl), *adj.* **1.** extremely bad or unpleasant. **2.** inspiring fear. **3.** inspiring awe. **4.** *Informal.* very great. —*adv.* **5.** *Informal.* very; extremely. —**aw'ful·ly**, *adv.* —**aw'ful·ness**, *n.*

a·while (ə hwīl', ə wīl'), *adv.* for a short time. —**Usage.** The adverb AWHILE is always spelled as one word: *We rested awhile.* The noun phrase A WHILE is used when a preposition is expressed: *We rested for a while.*

a·whirl (ə hwûrl', ə wûrl'), *adj.* rotating rapidly; spinning.

awk·ward (ôk'wərd), *adj.* **1.** lacking skill or dexterity; clumsy. **2.** lacking grace or ease. **3.** hard to use or handle; unwieldy. **4.** hard to deal with; difficult. **5.** embarrassing or inconvenient. —**awk'ward·ly**, *adv.* —**awk'ward·ness**, *n.*

awl (ôl), *n.* a pointed instrument for piercing holes, as in leather.

awn (ôn), *n.* any of the bristles on a spike of a grass plant.

awn·ing (ô'ning), *n.* a rooflike shelter, as of canvas, that provides protection from the sun or rain.

a·woke (ə wōk'), *v.* a pt. and pp. of AWAKE.

a·wo'ken, *v.* a pp. of AWAKE.

AWOL (*pronounced as initials or* ā'wôl, ā'wol), *adj., adv.* **1.** absent without leave. —*n.* **2.** a person, esp. a soldier, who is absent without leave.

a·wry (ə rī'), *adv., adj.* **1.** askew. **2.** amiss; wrong.

ax or **axe** (aks), *n., v.,* **axed, ax·ing.** —*n.* **1.** a chopping tool with a blade on a handle. —*v.t.* **2.** to chop or split with an ax. **3.** to dismiss or remove, esp. brutally or summarily. —*Idiom.* **4.** **have an ax to grind,** to have a particular personal or selfish motive.

ax·i·al (ak'sē əl), *adj.* **1.** of or forming an axis. **2.** situated in or on an axis. —**ax'i·al·ly**, *adv.*

ax·i·om (ak'sē əm), *n.* **1.** a self-evident truth that requires no proof. **2.** a proposition assumed without proof for the sake of studying its consequences. —**ax'i·o·mat'ic**, *adj.* —**ax'i·o·mat'i·cal·ly**, *adv.*

ax·is (ak'sis), *n., pl.* **ax·es** (ak'sēz). **1.** the line about which a rotating body turns. **2. a.** a central line that bisects a body or figure and in relation to which symmetry is determined. **b.** a line used as a reference for determining the position of a point or series of points. **3.** the main support of a plant or inflorescence.

ax·le (ak'səl), *n.* a spindle or shaft on which a wheel or pair of wheels rotates.

ax'le·tree', *n.* a fixed bar with a spindle at each end upon which a wheel rotates.

ax·on (ak'son), *n.* the appendage of a neuron that transmits impulses away from the cell body.

a·ya·tol·lah (ä'yə tō'lə), *n.* a title for a Shi'ite cleric with advanced knowledge of Islamic law. [< Pers < Ar *āyat allāh* sign of God]

aye¹ or **ay** (ī), *adv., n., pl.* **ayes.** —*adv.* **1.** yes. —*n.* **2.** an affirmative vote or voter.

aye² or **ay** (ā), *adv. Archaic.* ever or always.

AZ, Arizona.

a·zal·ea (ə zāl'yə), *n., pl.* **-eas.** a shrub of the heath family, with variously colored flowers.

a·zan (ä zän'), *n.* (in Islamic countries) the call to prayer proclaimed five times a day.

A·za·zel (ə zā'zəl, az'ə zel'), *n.* **1.** the demon or place in the wilderness to which the scapegoat is released in an atonement ritual. Lev. 16:8, 10, 26. **2.** the scapegoat itself.

Az·er·bai·jan (az'ər bī jän'), *n.* a republic in W Asia, N of Iran: formerly a part of the USSR. 7,735,918.

az·i·muth (az'ə məth), *n.* **1.** the arc of the horizon measured clockwise from the south point, in astronomy, or from the north point, in navigation. **2.** (in surveying) the angle of horizontal deviation.

A·zores (ā'zôrz), *n.pl.* a group of Portuguese islands in the N Atlantic, W of Portugal. 253,500.

AZT, *Trademark.* an antiviral drug used in the treatment of AIDS.

Az·tec (az'tek), *n.* a member of an American Indian people whose empire in Mexico was conquered by Spaniards in 1521. —**Az'tec·an**, *adj.*

az·ure (azh'ər), *n.* **1.** the blue of a clear or unclouded sky. —*adj.* **2.** of or having the color azure.

B

B, b (bē), *n., pl.* **Bs** or **B's, bs** or **b's.** the second letter of the English alphabet, a consonant.

B, *Symbol.* **1.** the second in order or in a series. **2.** a grade or mark indicating good but not excellent quality. **3.** a major blood group. **4.** *Chem.* boron. **5.** a designation for a low-budget motion picture.

b., **1.** bachelor. **2.** bass. **3.** born.

Ba, *Chem. Symbol.* barium.

B.A., Bachelor of Arts.

baa (ba, bä), *n.* **1.** a sheep's bleat. —*v.i.* **2.** to bleat.

Ba•al (bā′əl, bāl), *n., pl.* **Ba•al•im** (bā′ə lim, bā′- lim). **1.** any of numerous ancient Semitic fertility gods. **2.** (*sometimes l.c.*) a false god.

Bab•bage (bab′ij), *n.* **Charles,** 1792–1871, English mathematician: invented the precursor of the modern computer.

bab•ble (bab′əl), *v.,* **-bled, -bling,** *n.* —*v.i.* **1.** to utter sounds or words indistinctly. **2.** to talk irrationally or excessively. **3.** to make a murmuring sound. —*v.t.* **4.** to utter in a foolish or meaningless fashion. **5.** to reveal thoughtlessly. —*n.* **6.** the act or sound of babbling. —**bab′bler,** *n.*

babe (bāb), *n.* **1.** an infant; baby. **2.** a naive person.

Ba•bel (bā′bəl, bab′əl), *n.* **1.** a city where construction of a tower to heaven was abandoned when God caused a confusion of languages. Gen. 11:4–9. **2.** (*usu. l.c.*) **a.** a confused mixture of sounds or voices. **b.** a scene of confusion.

ba•boon (ba bōōn′, bə-), *n.* a large monkey of Africa and Arabia with a doglike muzzle.

ba•bush•ka (bə bŏŏsh′kə), *n., pl.* **-kas.** a woman's head scarf tied under the chin.

ba•by (bā′bē), *n., pl.* **-bies,** *adj., v.,* **-bied, -by•ing.** —*n.* **1.** an infant or very young child. **2.** the youngest member of a family or group. **3.** a childish person. **4.** *Informal.* something that elicits one's special attention or pride. —*adj.* **5.** of, for, or like a baby. **6.** smaller than the usual. —*v.t.* **7.** to pamper. —**ba′by• hood′,** *n.* —**ba′by•ish,** *adj.*

ba′by boom′, *n.* a period of increase in the birthrate, as that following World War II. —**ba′by boom′er,** *n.*

ba′by car′riage, *n.* a conveyance for pushing a baby about, resembling a basket set on four wheels.

ba′by grand′, *n.* the smallest form of grand piano.

Bab•y•lon (bab′ə lən, -lon′), *n.* the capital of Babylonia, on the Euphrates River, noted for luxury and wickedness.

Bab•y•lo•ni•a (-lō′nē ə), *n.* an ancient empire in S Mesopotamia. —**Bab′y•lo′ni•an,** *adj., n.*

Babylo′nian captiv′ity, *n.* **1.** the period of the exile of the Jews in Babylonia, 597–538 B.C. **2.** the exile of the popes at Avignon, 1309–77.

ba′by's-breath′, *n.* a tall plant with numerous small white or pink flowers.

ba′by-sit′, *v.,* **-sat, -sit•ting.** —*v.i.* **1.** to take charge of a child while the parents are temporarily away. —*v.t.* **2.** to baby-sit for (a child). —**ba′by-sit′ter,** *n.*

bac•ca•lau•re•ate (bak′ə lôr′ē it, -lor′-), *n.* **1.** BACHELOR'S DEGREE. **2.** a religious service held for a graduating class.

bac•cha•nal (bak′ə nal′), *n.* **1.** a worshiper of Bacchus. **2.** an occasion of drunken revelry. —**bac′cha• na′li•an** (-nā′lē ən, -nāl′yən), *adj., n.*

Bac•chus (bak′əs), *n.* DIONYSUS. —**Bac′chic,** *adj.*

Bach (bäĸн), *n.* **1.** Johann Sebastian, 1685–1750, German organist and composer. **2.** his sons, Carl Philipp Emanuel, 1714–88, and Johann Christian, 1735–82, German organists and composers.

bach•e•lor (bach′ə lər), *n.* **1.** an unmarried man. **2.** a person with a bachelor's degree. [< OF < VL *baccalār(is)* farmhand] —**bach′e•lor•hood′,** *n.*

bach′elor's-but′ton, *n.* any of various plants with round flower heads, esp. the cornflower.

bach′elor's degree′, *n.* a degree awarded by a college or university to a person who has completed undergraduate studies.

ba•cil•lus (bə sil′əs), *n., pl.* **-cil•li** (-sil′ī). any of several rod-shaped bacteria that produce spores. —**bac•il•lar•y** (bas′ə ler′ē), *adj.*

back¹ (bak), *n.* **1.** the rear part of the human body, from the neck to the end of the spine. **2.** the corresponding part of an animal's body. **3.** the part that forms the rear or reverse of any object or structure. **4.** the backbone. **5.** a football player stationed in the backfield. —*v.t.* **6.** to support, as with authority or money: *to back a candidate.* **7.** to bet on. **8.** to cause to move backward. —*v.i.* **9.** to go or move backward. **10.** **back down,** to abandon an argument or position. **11.** ~ **off,** to move back from something; retreat. **12.** ~ **out,** to fail to keep an engagement or promise. **13.** ~ **up, a.** to move backward. **b.** to support. **c.** to accumulate or become clogged due to a stoppage. **d.** to copy (a computer file or program) as a precaution against failure. —*adj.* **14.** situated at or in the rear. **15.** pertaining to the past. **16.** in arrears: *back pay.* **17.** moving backward. —*Idiom.* **18.** **behind one's back,** without one's knowledge, esp. treacherously or secretly. **19.** **(in) back of,** at the rear of; behind. —**Usage.** The phrases IN BACK OF and BACK OF, meaning "behind," although objected to by some, are fully established as standard in American English: *The car was parked (in) back of the house.*

back² (bak), *adv.* **1.** at, to, or toward the rear. **2.** in or toward the past. **3.** at or toward the original starting place or condition. **4.** in direct payment or return: *to answer back.* **5.** in a state of restraint or retention. —*Idiom.* **6.** **back and forth,** backward and forward. **7.** **go back on,** to fail to keep: *to go back on a promise.*

back′ache′, *n.* a pain or ache in the back.

back′bite′, *v.t., v.i.,* **-bit, -bit•ten** or **-bit, -bit•ing.** to slander (an absent person). —**back′bit′er,** *n.*

back′board′, *n.* **1.** a board placed at or forming the back of anything. **2.** *Basketball.* the vertical board to which the basket is attached.

back′bone′, *n.* **1.** the spinal column; spine. **2.** strength of character. **3.** a major support.

back′break′ing, *adj.* demanding great effort, endurance, etc.

back′ burn′er, *n.* a condition of low priority or temporary deferment: *an issue put on the back burner until after the election.*

back′drop′, *n.* **1.** the rear curtain of a stage setting. **2.** the background of an event; setting.

back′er, *n.* a person who supports a cause, enterprise, etc.

back′field′, *n.* the football players stationed behind the line.

back′fire′, *v.,* **-fired, -fir•ing,** *n.* —*v.i.* **1.** (of an internal-combustion engine) to have a premature explosion in the intake manifold. **2.** to bring a result opposite to that planned or expected. —*n.* **3.** a premature, explosive ignition of fuel in an engine.

back′gam′mon (-gam′ən), *n.* a game for two persons in which pieces are moved around a board in accordance with throws of the dice.

back′ground′, *n.* **1.** the parts, as of a scene, situated in the rear. **2.** one's origin, education, experience, etc. **3.** the antecedents or causes of an event or condition. —*adj.* **4.** of or serving as a background: *background noise.*

back′ground′er, *n.* any official briefing or report that provides background information.

back′hand′, *n.* **1.** (in tennis, squash, etc.) a stroke made with the back of the hand facing the direction of movement. **2.** handwriting that slopes toward the left. —*adj.* **3.** backhanded. —*adv.* **4.** in a backhanded way. —*v.t.* **5.** to hit with a backhand.

back′hand′ed, *adj.* **1.** performed with the back of the hand turned forward. **2.** sloping in a downward direction from left to right. **3.** oblique or ambiguous in meaning.

back′ing, *n.* **1.** aid or support of any kind. **2.** supporters collectively. **3.** something that forms a back, esp. for support or protection.

back′lash′, *n.* **1.** a sudden, forceful backward movement; recoil. **2.** a strong negative reaction, as to social change.

back′log′, *n., v.,* **-logged, -log•ging.** —*n.* **1.** an accumulation, as of unfinished tasks. —*v.i.* **2.** to accumulate in a backlog.

back′ or′der, *n.* an order that will be filled as soon as the merchandise is back in stock. —**back′-or′der,** *v.t., v.i.*

back′pack′, *n.* **1.** a pack of supplies carried on one's back, sometimes supported on a frame. —*v.i.* **2.** to hike with a backpack. —*v.t.* **3.** to carry in a backpack. —**back′pack′er,** *n.*

back′-ped′al, *v.i.,* **-aled, -al•ing** or (*esp. Brit.*) **-alled, -al•ling. 1.** to retard the motion of a bicycle by pressing backward on the pedal. **2.** to retreat from or reverse one's previous stand.

back′rest′, *n.* a support against which to rest one's back.

back′seat driv′er, *n.* **1.** an automobile passenger who offers the driver unsolicited advice. **2.** any meddlesome person who offers unsolicited advice.

back′side′, *n.* the rump; buttocks.

back′slap′ping, *n.* an effusive display of friendliness. —**back′slap′per,** *n.*

back′slide′, *v.i.,* **-slid, -slid** or **-slid•den, -slid•ing.** to relapse into bad habits or sinful behavior. —**back′slid′er,** *n.*

back′space′, *v.i.,* **-spaced, -spac•ing.** to move the typing element of a typewriter or the cursor on a computer display one space backward.

back′spin′, *n.* reverse rotation of a ball causing it to bounce or roll backward.

back′stage′, *adv.* **1.** behind the proscenium in a theater, esp. in the wings or dressing rooms. —*adj.* **2.** located or occurring backstage. **3.** pertaining to secret activities. **4.** pertaining to the private lives of entertainers.

back′stairs′ or **-stair′,** *adj.* secret, underhanded, or scandalous.

back′stop′, *n.* **1.** a wall, screen, etc., preventing a ball from going beyond the normal playing area. **2.** a safeguard or reinforcement.

back′stretch′, *n.* the straight part of a racetrack opposite the homestretch.

back′stroke′, *n.* a swimming stroke performed in a supine position.

back′ talk′, *n.* an impudent response.

back′-to-back′, *adj.* following one after the other; consecutive.

back′track′, *v.i.* **1.** to return over the same course or route. **2.** to withdraw from an undertaking, position, etc.

back′up′, *n.* **1.** a person or thing that supports or reinforces another. **2.** an accumulation due to a stoppage. **3.** an alternate kept in reserve. **4.** a copy of a computer file or program kept in case the original is damaged or lost.

back′ward (-wərd), *adv.* Also, **back′wards. 1.** toward the rear. **2.** with the back foremost. **3.** in the reverse of the usual way. **4.** toward the past. —*adj.* **5.** directed toward the back or past. **6.** reversed or returning. **7.** behind in progress or development. **8.** bashful or hesitant. —*Idiom.* **9. bend over backward,** to exert oneself to the utmost. —**back′ward•ness,** *n.*

back′wash′, *n.* water thrown backward by the motion of oars, propellers, etc.

back′wa′ter, *n.* **1.** water held or forced back, as by a dam or flood. **2.** a place or state of stagnant backwardness.

back′woods′, *n.* **1.** (*often used with a sing. v.*) wooded or sparsely settled districts. **2.** any remote or isolated area. —*adj.* **3.** of or like the backwoods.

back′yard′, *n.* the yard behind a house.

ba•con (bā′kən), *n.* **1.** the back and sides of a hog, salted and dried or smoked. —*Idiom.* **2. bring home the bacon, a.** to earn a living. **b.** to succeed.

Ba′con, *n.* **1. Francis,** 1561–1626, English essayist and philosopher. **2. Francis,** 1910–92, English painter, born in Ireland. **3. Nathaniel,** 1647–76, American colonist, born in England: leader of a rebellion in Virginia 1676.

bac•te•ri•a (bak tēr′ē ə), *n.pl., sing.* **-um** (-əm). any of numerous groups of one-celled organisms, various species of which are involved in infectious diseases, fermentation, etc. —**bac•te′ri•al,** *adj.*

bac•te′ri•cide′ (-ə sīd′), *n.* any substance capable of killing bacteria. —**bac•te′ri•cid′al,** *adj.*

bac•te′ri•ol′o•gy (-ē ol′ə jē), *n.* the science that deals with bacteria. —**bac•te′ri•o•log′i•cal** (-ə loj′i-kəl), *adj.* —**bac•te′ri•ol′o•gist,** *n.*

bad (bad), *adj.,* **worse, worst,** *n., adv.* —*adj.* **1.** not good in any manner or degree. **2.** wicked. **3.** disobedient or naughty. **4.** of inferior quality. **5.** inaccurate or faulty. **6.** suffering from ill health. **7.** spoiled or rotten. **8.** harmful or detrimental. **9.** disagreeable; unpleasant. **10.** severe. **11.** regretful or upset. **12.** unfortunate or unfavorable. **13.** (of a debt) uncollectible. —*n.* **14.** something bad. —*adv.* **15.** *Informal.* badly. —*Idiom.* **16. not bad,** somewhat good. **17. too bad,** unfortunate or disappointing. —**bad′ness,** *n.* —**Usage.** The adjective BAD is the usual form to follow such verbs as *sound, smell, look, taste,* etc.: *The water tasted bad. The locker room smells bad.* After the verb *feel,* the adjective BADLY in reference to physical or emotional states is also used and is standard, although BAD is more common in formal writing. BAD as an adverb appears mainly in informal contexts. See also BADLY.

bad′ blood′, *n.* unfriendly relations; enmity.

bade (bad), *v.* a pt. of BID.

badge (baj), *n.* **1.** an emblem worn as a sign of membership, authority, etc. **2.** any distinctive mark.

badg•er (baj′ər), *n.* **1.** a burrowing, carnivorous mammal of North America, Europe, and Asia. **2.** its fur. —*v.t.* **3.** to harass persistently; nag.

bad′ hair′ day′, *n.* a disagreeable or unpleasant day, esp. when one feels unattractive.

bad•i•nage (bad′n äzh′), *n.* light, playful banter.

bad′lands′, *n.pl.* a barren area in which soft rock strata are eroded into varied, fantastic forms.

bad′ly, *adv.,* **worse, worst,** *adj.* —*adv.* **1.** in a bad way or manner. **2.** greatly or very much. —*adj.* **3.** in ill health; sick. **4.** sorry; regretful. —**Usage.** In the sense "very much," BADLY is fully standard: *He needs help badly.* See also BAD.

bad•min•ton (bad′min tn), *n.* a game played on a rectangular court with light rackets used to volley a shuttlecock over a net.

bad′-mouth′ or **bad′mouth′** (-mouth′, -mouth′), *v.t.* to criticize, often disloyally.

baf•fle (baf′əl), *v.,* **-fled, -fling,** *n.* —*v.t.* **1.** to bewilder or perplex. **2.** to frustrate or thwart. —*n.* **3.** an artificial obstruction for checking or deflecting the flow of sounds, light, gases, etc. —**baf′fle•ment,** *n.* —**baf′fler,** *n.* —**baf′fling,** *adj.*

bag (bag), *n., v.,* **bagged, bag•ging.** —*n.* **1.** a pliant container capable of being closed at the mouth. **2.** a piece of luggage. **3.** a purse. **4.** something hanging in a loose, pouchlike manner. **5.** BASE¹ (def. 4b). **6.** a hunter's total amount of game taken. **7.** *Slang.* a person's avocation or hobby. —*v.i.* **8.** to hang loosely. **9.** to swell or bulge. —*v.t.* **10.** to put into a bag. **11.** to kill or catch. **12.** to cause to swell. —*Idiom.* **13. in the bag,** *Informal.* virtually certain.

bag•a•telle (bag′ə tel′), *n.* a trifle.

ba•gel (bā′gəl), *n.* a doughnut-shaped roll of dough that is simmered in water and baked.

bag•gage (bag′ij), *n.* trunks, suitcases, etc., used in traveling.

bag′gy, *adj.,* **-gi•er, -gi•est.** hanging loosely; bulging. —**bag′gi•ly,** *adv.* —**bag′gi•ness,** *n.*

Bagh•dad or **Bag•dad** (bag′dad), *n.* the capital of Iraq. 4,648,609.

bag′pipe′, *n.* Often, **-pipes.** a reed instrument consisting of pipes protruding from a bag into which air is blown. —**bag′pip′er,** *n.*

bagpipe

ba•guette (ba get′), *n.* **1.** a gem having a rectangular cut. **2.** a long, narrow loaf of French bread.

Ba•ha•′i (bə hä′ē, -hē′), *n.; pl.* **-ha•′is,** *adj.* —*n.* **1.** a religion founded in Iran and teaching the essential worth of all races and religions and equality of the sexes. **2.** an adherent of Baha′i. —*adj.* **3.** pertaining to Baha′i or Baha′is. Also, **Ba•ha′i.** —**Ba•ha′′ism,** *n.* —**Ba•ha′′ist,** *adj.*

Ba•ha•mas (bə hä′məz), *n.* a country comprising a group of islands **(Baha′ma Is′lands)** in the W Atlantic Ocean, SE of Florida. 262,034. —**Ba•ha′mi•an** (-hä′-, -hä′-), *n., adj.*

Bah•rain or **-rein** (bä rān′, -rīn′, bə-), *n.* a sheikdom in the Persian Gulf, consisting of a group of islands. 603,318. —**Bah•rain′i,** *n., pl.* **-is,** *adj.*

bail¹ (bāl), *n.* **1.** money given as surety that a person released from legal custody will return at an appointed time. **2.** the state of release upon being bailed. **3.** one who provides bail. —*v.t.* **4.** to obtain the release of (an arrested person) by providing bail. **5.** to assist in escaping a predicament (usu. fol. by *out*).

bail² (bāl), *n.* the semicircular handle of a kettle or pail.

bail³ (bāl), *v.t., v.i.* **1.** to dip (water) out of a boat, as with a bucket. **2. bail out,** to parachute from an airplane. —*n.* **3.** a container used for bailing.

bail•iff (bā′lif), *n.* **1.** an officer, similar to a sheriff, employed to keep order in the court, make arrests, etc. **2.** (in Britain) **a.** the chief magistrate in a town. **b.** an overseer of a landed estate.

bail•i•wick (bā′lə wik′), *n.* **1.** the district of a bailiff. **2.** a person's area of skill, knowledge, authority, etc.

bails•man (bālz′mən), *n., pl.* **-men.** one who provides bail.

bait (bāt), *n.* **1.** food or some substitute, used as a lure in fishing or trapping. **2.** anything that lures; enticement. —*v.t.* **3.** to prepare (a hook or trap) with bait. **4.** to lure, as with bait. **5.** to set dogs upon (an animal) for sport. **6.** to torment, esp. with malicious remarks.

baize (bāz), *n.* a soft feltlike fabric, commonly used for the tops of game tables.

Ba′ja Califor′nia (bä′hä), *n.* a peninsula in NW Mexico between the Gulf of California and the Pacific.

bake (bāk), *v.,* **baked, bak•ing.** —*v.t.* **1.** to cook by dry heat, as in an oven. **2.** to harden by heat, as pottery. —*v.t.* **3.** to prepare food by baking it. **4.** to become baked.

bak′er, *n.* a person who bakes, esp. one who makes and sells bread, cake, etc.

bak′er's doz′en, *n.* a dozen plus one; 13.

bak′er•y, *n., pl.* **-er•ies.** a place where baked goods are made or sold. Also called **bake′shop′.**

bak′ing pow′der, *n.* a leavening agent used in

baking, consisting of sodium bicarbonate, an acid substance, and a starch.

bak′ing so′da, *n.* SODIUM BICARBONATE.

Ba•ku (bu kōō′), *n.* the capital of Azerbaijan. 1,757,000.

bal•a•lai•ka (bal′ə lī′kə), *n., pl.* **-kas.** a Russian stringed instrument with a triangular body and a guitarlike neck.

bal•ance (bal′əns), *n., v.,* **-anced, -anc•ing.** —*n.* **1.** a state of equilibrium. **2.** something used to produce equilibrium. **3.** steadiness of the body or emotions. **4.** an instrument for determining weight, usu. one having pans suspended from both ends of a bar. **5.** the remainder or rest. **6. a.** equality between the total debits and total credits of an account. **b.** the difference between these totals. —*v.t.* **7.** to bring to or hold in equilibrium. **8.** to be equal or proportionate to. **9.** to add up the two sides of (an account) and determine the difference. **10.** to weigh in a balance. **11.** to estimate the relative weight or importance of. **12.** to counteract or offset. —*v.i.* **13.** to be in equilibrium. **14.** to be equal. **15.** to be in a state wherein debits equal credits. —*Idiom.* **16. in the balance,** with the outcome in doubt.

bal′ance beam′, *n.* a horizontal wooden rail on upright posts, used by gymnasts for balancing feats.

bal′ance sheet′, *n.* a statement of the financial position of a business on a specified date.

bal•co•ny (bal′kə nē), *n., pl.* **-nies. 1.** a railed platform projecting from the wall of a building. **2.** a gallery in a theater.

bald (bôld), *adj.* **1.** having little or no hair on the scalp. **2.** destitute of some natural growth or covering. **3.** plain or undisguised: *a bald lie.* **4.** having white fur or feathers on the head. —*v.i.* **5.** to become bald. —**bald′ness,** *n.*

bald′ ea′gle, *n.* a large eagle of the U.S. and Canada, having white plumage on the head and tail.

bald eagle

bal•der•dash (bôl′dər dash′), *n.* nonsense.

bale (bāl), *n., v.,* **baled, bal•ing.** —*n.* **1.** a large bundle, esp. one compressed and secured by wires, cords, or the like. —*v.t.* **2.** to make into bales. —**bal′er,** *n.*

ba•leen (bə lēn′), *n.* WHALEBONE (def. 1).

bale′ful, *adj.* menacing or malign; threatening evil. —**bale′ful•ly,** *adv.*

Ba•li (bä′lē, bal′ē), *n.* an island in Indonesia, E of Java. —**Ba′li•nese′** (-ə nēz′, -nēs′), *adj., n., pl.* **-nese.**

balk (bôk), *v.i.* **1.** to refuse curtly and firmly (usu. fol. by *at*). **2.** to stop short and refuse to go on. —*v.t.* **3.** to hinder or thwart. —*n.* **4.** an illegal motion made by a baseball pitcher, allowing runners to advance to the next base. **5.** a check or hindrance. —**balk′er,** *n.*

Bal•kan (bôl′kən), *adj.* **1.** of the Balkan Peninsula or its inhabitants. —*n.* **2. the Balkans.** Also called **the Bal′kan States′.** the countries in the Balkan Peninsula: Yugoslavia, Bosnia and Herzegovina, Croatia, Macedonia, Slovenia, Romania, Bulgaria, Albania, Greece, and the European part of Turkey.

Bal′kan Penin′sula, *n.* a peninsula in S Europe, S of the Danube River and bordered by the Adriatic, Ionian, Aegean, and Black seas.

balk′y, *adj.,* **-i•er, -i•est.** given to balking; stubborn.

ball¹ (bôl), *n.* **1.** a spherical or approximately spherical body. **2.** a round or roundish body for use in games. **3.** a game played with a ball, esp. baseball. **4.** a pitched ball in baseball that is not swung at by the batter and is not a strike. **5.** a spherical projectile for a weapon. **6.** a part of the body that is rounded or protuberant. —*v.t., v.i.* **7.** to form into a ball. **8. ball up,** to make into a mess; confuse. —*Idiom.* **9. on the ball, a.** alert or watchful. **b.** efficient; competent. —*Saying.* **10. The ball is in one's court,** it is one's turn to take action. —**ball′er,** *n.*

ball² (bôl), *n.* **1.** a large formal party featuring social dancing. **2.** *Informal.* a very good time.

bal•lad (bal′əd), *n.* **1.** a simple narrative poem, esp. of folk origin, adapted for singing. **2.** a simple song. **3.** a slow, romantic popular song. —**bal′lad•eer′,** *n.* —**bal′lad•ry,** *n.*

bal•last (bal′əst), *n.* **1.** any heavy material carried on a ship or vehicle to provide stability. **2.** gravel or broken stone placed under the ties of a railroad. —*v.t.* **3.** to furnish with ballast.

ball′ bear′ing, *n.* **1.** a bearing consisting of hard balls running in a ring-shaped groove on which a shaft turns. **2.** any of the balls so used.

bal•le•ri•na (bal′ə rē′nə), *n., pl.* **-nas.** a female ballet dancer.

bal•let (ba lā′), *n.* **1.** a dance form characterized by graceful movements and conventionalized steps and gestures. **2.** a theatrical performance of such dancing and its accompanying music. **3.** a company of ballet dancers. —**bal•let′ic** (-let′ik), *adj.*

ballis′tic mis′sile, *n.* a missile that travels to its target unpowered and unguided after being launched.

bal•lis•tics (bə lis′tiks), *n.* the science or study of the motion of projectiles. —**bal•lis′tic,** *adj.*

bal•loon (bə lōōn′), *n.* **1.** an inflatable rubber bag used as a toy. **2.** a fabric bag filled with heated air or a gas lighter than air, designed to rise and float and often having a gondola for passengers or instruments. —*v.i.* **3.** to ride in a balloon. **4.** to puff out. **5.** to increase rapidly. —*v.t.* **6.** to inflate or distend. —*adj.* **7.** puffed out like a balloon. —**bal•loon′ist,** *n.*

bal•lot (bal′ət), *n.* **1.** a sheet of paper or the like on which a vote is registered. **2.** the method or act of voting. **3.** the right to vote. **4.** the whole number of votes recorded. —*v.i.* **5.** to vote by ballot. —**bal′-lot•er,** *n.*

bal′lot box′, *n.* **1.** a receptacle for voters' ballots. **2.** a system or instance of voting by ballot. —*Idiom.* **3. stuff the ballot box,** to commit electoral fraud.

ball′park′, *n.* **1.** a stadium where ball games, esp. baseball, are played. —*adj.* **2.** being an approximation.

ball′point′, *n.* a pen in which the point is a fine ball bearing that rotates against a supply of ink in a cartridge. Also called **ball′point pen′.**

ball′room′, *n.* a large room for dancing.

bal•ly•hoo (bal′ē hōō′), *n., pl.* **-hoos,** *v.,* **-hooed, -hoo•ing.** —*n.* **1.** a clamorous attempt to win customers or advance a cause. —*v.t., v.i.* **2.** to promote with ballyhoo.

balm (bäm), *n.* **1.** a fragrant gum resin or ointment used in perfumery or medicine. **2.** any of various aromatic plants. **3.** anything that heals or soothes pain. [< OF *basme* < L *balsamum* balsam]

balm′ in Gil′ead, *n.* a remedy or consolation. Jer. 8:22; 46:11.

balm′y, *adj.,* **-i•er, -i•est. 1.** mild and refreshing; soothing. **2.** *Informal.* crazy; foolish. —**balm′i•ness,** *n.*

ba•lo•ney (bə lō′nē), *n.* **1.** *Slang.* foolishness; nonsense. **2.** BOLOGNA.

bal•sa (bôl′sə, bäl′-), *n., pl.* **-sas. 1.** a tropical American tree yielding a very light wood. **2.** the wood.

bal•sam (bôl′səm), *n.* **1.** a fragrant resin exuded from certain trees. **2.** any of various trees yielding a balsam. **3.** any aromatic ointment for ceremonial or medicinal use.

Bal•tha•zar (bôl thaz′ər, bal-, bôl′thə zär′, bal′-), *n.* one of the three Magi.

Bal•tic (bôl′tik), *adj.* of the Baltic Sea or the countries on its coast.

Bal′tic Sea′, *n.* a sea in N Europe, N of Poland.

Bal•ti•more (bôl′tə môr′), *n.* a seaport in N Maryland. 702,979.

bal•us•ter (bal′ə stər), *n.* any of a number of closely spaced supports for a railing.

bal′us•trade′ (-strād′), *n.* a railing with its supporting balusters.

Bal•zac (bôl′zak, bal zak′), *n.* **Honoré de,** 1799–1850, French novelist.

bam•boo (bam bōō′), *n., pl.* **-boos.** a tall, treelike tropical grass with woody, hollow stems, used for making furniture, poles, etc.

bam•boo•zle (bam bōō′zəl), *v.t.,* **-zled, -zling.** to deceive by trickery; hoodwink.

ban (ban), *v.,* **banned, ban•ning,** *n.* —*v.t.* **1.** to prohibit, esp. by official authority. —*n.* **2.** the act of prohibiting by law. **3.** an informal denunciation, as by public opinion. **4.** a formal ecclesiastical condemnation.

ba•nal (bə nal′, -näl′, bān′l), *adj.* hackneyed; trite. —**ba•nal′i•ty,** *n., pl.* **-ties.** —**ba•nal′ly,** *adv.*

ba•nan•a (bə nan′ə), *n., pl.* **-nan•as. 1.** a tropical plant, certain species of which are cultivated for their nutritious fruit. **2.** the fruit, having a yellow or reddish rind. [< Sp < Pg < a West African language]

band¹ (band), *n.* **1.** a company of persons, animals, or things acting together. **2.** a group of musicians, usu. using brass, woodwind, and percussion instruments. —*v.t., v.i.* **3.** to unite in a group or company.

band² (band), *n.* **1.** a thin strip of material, as for binding or trimming. **2.** a stripe, as of color. **3.** a segment of a phonograph record on which sound is recorded. **4.** a specific range of frequencies, as in radio. —*v.t.* **5.** to mark or furnish with a band.

band•age (ban′dij), *n., v.,* **-aged, -ag•ing.** —*n.* **1.** a strip of material used to bind up a wound, sprain, etc. —*v.t.* **2.** to bind or cover with a bandage.

Band′-Aid′, **1.** *Trademark.* an adhesive bandage with a gauze pad in the center, used for minor abrasions and cuts. —*n.* **2.** (*often l.c.*) a makeshift aid or solution.

ban•dan•na or **-dan•a** (ban dan′ə), *n., pl.* **-dan•nas** or **-dan•as.** a large, usu. figured handkerchief often worn as a head scarf.

ban•dit (ban′dit), *n.* a robber, esp. a member of a marauding band. —**ban′dit•ry,** *n.*

ban•do•lier or **-leer** (ban′dl ēr′), *n.* a belt with loops or pockets for cartridges, worn over the shoulder by soldiers.

band′stand′, *n.* a platform for a band or orchestra.

band′wag′on, *n.* **1.** a large, ornate wagon for carrying a musical band, as in a circus parade. —*Idiom.* **2. climb** or **jump on the bandwagon,** to join a cause, movement, etc., that appears to have popular support.

ban•dy (ban′dē), *v.,* **-died, -dy•ing,** *adj.* —*v.t.* **1.** to trade or exchange. **2.** to throw or strike to and fro. **3.** to circulate freely. —*adj.* **4.** (of legs) curved outward; bowed.

ban′dy-leg′ged (-leg′id, -legd′), *adj.* bowlegged.

bane (bān), *n.* **1.** a person or thing that ruins or spoils: *Gambling was the bane of his existence.* **2.** a deadly poison (often used in combination, as in the name of poisonous plants). —**bane′ful,** *adj.*

bang¹ (bang), *n.* **1.** a loud, sudden, explosive noise. **2.** a resounding blow. **3.** *Informal.* thrill; excitement. —*v.t.* **4.** to strike or beat resoundingly; pound. —*v.i.* **5.** to strike violently or noisily. **6.** to make a loud, explosive noise. **7. bang up,** to damage. —*adv.* **8.** abruptly or violently. **9.** directly; precisely.

bang² (bang), *n.* Often, **bangs.** a fringe of hair cut to fall over the forehead.

Bang•kok (bang′kok, bang kok′), *n.* the capital of Thailand. 5,609,352.

Ban•gla•desh (bäng′glə desh′, bang′-), *n.* a republic in S Asia, N of the Bay of Bengal. 104,100,000. —**Ban′gla•desh′i,** *n., pl.* **-is,** *adj.*

ban•gle (bang′gəl), *n.* a rigid bracelet.

Ban•gui (*Fr.* bäɴ gēʹ), *n.* the capital of the Central African Republic. 596,776.

bang′-up′, *adj. Informal.* excellent; extraordinary.

ban•ish (banʹish), *v.t.* **1.** to condemn to exile. **2.** to send, drive, or put away. —**ban′ish•ment,** *n.*

ban•is•ter (banʹə stər), *n.* **1.** a handrail and its supporting posts, esp. on a staircase. **2.** a handrail, esp. on a staircase.

ban•jo (banʹjō), *n., pl.* **-jos, -joes.** a stringed musical instrument having a circular body covered in front with stretched parchment. —**ban′jo•ist,** *n.*

Ban•jul (bänʹjŏŏl), *n.* the capital of the Gambia. 44,188.

bank¹ (bangk), *n.* **1.** a long pile or heap. **2.** a slope; incline. **3.** the slope bordering a river, lake, etc. **4.** a broad elevation of the sea floor. **5.** the inclination of the bed of a banked road or track. **6.** the lateral inclination of an aircraft during a turn. —*v.t.* **7.** to border with or like a bank. **8.** to form into a heap. **9.** to build (a road or track) with an upward slope at a curve. **10.** to incline (an airplane) laterally. **11.** to cover (a fire) with ashes or fuel to make it burn slowly.

bank² (bangk), *n.* **1.** an institution for receiving, lending, and safeguarding money. **2.** a storage place for reserves: *a blood bank.* —*v.i., v.t.* **3.** to deposit in a bank. **4. bank on,** to depend on. —**bank′a•ble,** *adj.*

bank³ (bangk), *n.* **1.** an arrangement of objects in a line or in tiers. —*v.t.* **2.** to arrange in a bank.

bank′book′, *n.* a book held by a depositor in which a bank records deposits and withdrawals.

bank′er, *n.* a person employed by a bank, esp. as an executive.

bank′ing, *n.* the business carried on by or with a bank.

bank′note′, *n.* a promissory note issued by an authorized bank and circulating as money.

bank′roll′, *n.* **1.** money in one's possession. —*v.t.* **2.** to finance.

bank′rupt (-rupt), *n.* **1.** a person who is adjudged insolvent by a court and whose property is divided among creditors. **2.** a person lacking in a particular thing or quality. —*adj.* **3.** subject to legal process because of insolvency. **4.** lacking something. —*v.t.* **5.** to make bankrupt. —**bank′rupt•cy** (-rəpt sē, -rəp-), *n., pl.* **-cies.**

ban•ner (banʹər), *n.* **1.** a flag or an ensign bearing some device, motto, or slogan. **2.** a headline extending across a newspaper page. —*adj.* **3.** leading or foremost.

banns (banz), *n.* (*used with a pl. v.*) notice of an intended marriage, given in a parish church.

ban•quet (bangʹkwit), *n.* **1.** a lavish meal. **2.** a ceremonious public dinner. —*v.t.* **3.** to entertain with a banquet. —**ban′quet•er,** *n.*

ban•quette (bang ketʹ), *n.* **1.** a long upholstered bench, esp. one along a wall. **2.** a platform along the inside of a parapet for gunners.

ban•shee (banʹshē), *n., pl.* **-shees.** (in Irish folklore) a female spirit whose wailing is a sign that a loved one is about to die. [< Ir *bean sídhe* lit., woman of a fairy mound]

ban•tam (banʹtəm), *n.* **1.** a chicken of very small size. **2.** a small and quarrelsome person. —*adj.* **3.** diminutive; tiny.

ban′tam•weight′, *n.* a boxer weighing up to 118 pounds (53 kg).

ban•ter (banʹtər), *n.* **1.** an exchange of light, playful remarks. —*v.i.* **2.** to use banter.

Ban•tu (banʹtŏŏ), *n., pl.* **-tu, -tus. 1.** a family of languages spoken in central and S Africa. **2.** a member of a Bantu-speaking people.

ban•yan (banʹyən), *n.* an East Indian fig tree whose branches send roots to the ground that become new trunks.

ba•o•bab (bāʹō bab′, bäʹō-), *n.* a large tropical African tree with an extremely thick trunk and a gourdlike fruit.

bap•tism (bapʹtiz əm), *n.* **1.** a ceremonial immersion in water, or application of water, as an initiatory sacrament of the Christian church. **2.** any ceremony of initiation. —**bap•tis′mal,** *adj.*

Bap′tist (-tist), *n.* a member of a Protestant denomination that baptizes believers by immersion.

bap′tis•ter•y or **-tis•try** (-tə strē), *n., pl.* **-ter•ies** or **-tries.** a building or a part of a church in which baptism is administered.

bap•tize (bap tīz′, bapʹtīz), *v.t.,* **-tized, -tiz•ing. 1.** to administer baptism to. **2.** to give a name to at baptism. **3.** to initiate by purifying. —**bap•tiz′er,** *n.*

bar (bär), *n., v.,* **barred, bar•ring,** *prep.* —*n.* **1.** a relatively long piece of metal or wood, used as a guard or obstruction or for a mechanical purpose. **2.** an oblong piece of any solid material: *a bar of soap.* **3.** a long ridge of sand or other material near the surface of a body of water, often obstructing navigation. **4.** any obstacle or barrier. **5.** a counter or place where beverages, esp. liquors, or light foods are served. **6. a.** the legal profession. **b.** a railing in a courtroom separating the public from the judges, jury, attorneys, etc. **7.** a band or stripe. **8. a.** the line marking the division between two measures of music. **b.** the unit of music between two bar lines; measure. —*v.t.* **9.** to equip or fasten with a bar. **10.** to block by or as if by bars. **11.** to exclude. **12.** to mark with bars. —*prep.* **13.** except; but: *bar none.* —*Idiom.* **14. behind bars,** in jail.

Bar•ab•bas (bə rabʹəs), *n.* the criminal pardoned instead of Jesus to appease the mob. Mark 15:6–11, John 18:40.

Bar•ak (bârʹək, bāʹrak), *n.* a commander who, with Deborah, destroyed the Canaanite army. Judg. 4.

barb (bärb), *n.* **1.** a point projecting backward from a main point, as of a fishhook or arrowhead. **2.** an unpleasant or carping remark. —*v.t.* **3.** to furnish with a barb. —**barbed,** *adj.*

Bar•ba•dos (bär bāʹdōz, -dōs), *n.* a country on an island in the E West Indies. 257,731. —**Bar•ba′-di•an,** *adj., n.*

bar•bar•i•an (bär bârʹē ən), *n.* **1.** a person regarded as savage, primitive, or uncivilized. **2.** a person without culture or education. —*adj.* **3.** uncivilized; crude; savage. —**bar•bar′i•an•ism,** *n.*

bar•bar′ic (-barʹik), *adj.* **1.** uncivilized; primitive. **2.** of or characteristic of barbarians.

bar′ba•rism (-bə rizʹəm), *n.* **1.** a primitive or uncivilized condition. **2.** a barbarous act. **3.** a word or construction felt to be nonstandard.

bar•bar′i•ty (-barʹi tē), *n., pl.* **-ties. 1.** brutality; cruelty. **2.** an act of cruelty. **3.** crudity of style, expression, etc.

bar′ba•rous (-bər əs), *adj.* **1.** uncivilized; wild; savage. **2.** savagely cruel or harsh. **3.** not conforming to accepted usage, as language. —**bar•ba•rous•ly,** *adv.*

bar•be•cue or **-que** (bärʹbi kyōō′), *n., v.,* **-cued** or **-qued, -cu•ing** or **-qu•ing.** —*n.* **1.** meat or poultry roasted over an open fire. **2.** an outdoor meal at which foods are so cooked. —*v.t.* **3.** to roast over an open fire. **4.** to cook in a piquant sauce of tomatoes, vinegar, and sugar. [< Sp *barbacoa* < Taino (West Indian language): raised frame of sticks] —**bar′be•cu′er,** *n.*

barbed′ wire′, *n.* strands of wire twisted together with barbs at short intervals, used for fencing.

bar•bel (bärʹbəl), *n.* a slender, external process on the head of certain fishes.

bar′bell′, *n.* a bar with replaceable weights attached to the ends, used in weightlifting.

bar•ber (bärʹbər), *n.* **1.** a person whose occupation is to cut hair, shave beards, etc. —*v.t.* **2.** to cut the hair or beard of. —*v.i.* **3.** to work as a barber.

bar•ber•ry (bärʹberʹē, -bə rē), *n., pl.* **-ries. 1.** a shrub with yellow flowers. **2.** the red fruit of this shrub.

bar•bi•tu•rate (bär bichʹər it, bärʹbi tŏŏr′it, -tyŏŏr′-), *n.* any of a group of derivatives of a crystalline powder **(bar′bitur′ic ac′id)**, used as sedatives and hypnotics.

Bar•ce•lo•na (bärʹsə lōʹnə), *n.* a seaport in NE Spain. 2,000,000.

bar′ chart′, *n.* BAR GRAPH.

bar′ code′, *n.* a series of contiguous lines coded by width and applied to a consumer item for identification by a computerized scanner.

bar code

bard (bärd), *n.* **1.** an ancient Celtic poet. **2.** any poet. —**bard′ic,** *adj.*

Bard′ of A′von, *n.* William Shakespeare: so called from his birthplace, Stratford-on-Avon.

bare (bâr), *adj.,* **bar•er, bar•est,** *v.,* **bared, bar•ing.** —*adj.* **1.** without covering or clothing; naked. **2.** without the usual furnishings. **3.** unadorned; plain. **4.** scarcely sufficient: *bare necessities.* —*v.t.* **5.** to reveal or divulge. —**bare′ness,** *n.*

bare′back′ or **-backed′,** *adv., adj.* without a saddle.

bare′faced′, *adj.* **1.** with the face uncovered. **2.** without concealment; boldly open.

bare′foot′ or **-foot′ed,** *adj., adv.* with the feet bare.

bare′hand′ed, *adj., adv.* **1.** with hands uncovered. **2.** without the necessary tools or weapons.

bare′ly, *adv.* **1.** scarcely; no more than. **2.** without disguise or concealment. **3.** scantily; meagerly. —**Usage.** See HARDLY.

bar•gain (bär′gən), *n.* **1.** an advantageous purchase acquired at less than the usual cost. **2.** an agreement between parties settling the terms of a transaction. **3.** something acquired by bargaining. —*v.i.* **4.** to discuss the terms of a bargain; negotiate. **5.** to conclude a bargain. **6. bargain for** or **on,** to expect; anticipate. —**bar′gain•er,** *n.*

barge (bärj), *n., v.,* **barged, barg•ing.** —*n.* **1.** a flat-bottomed vessel, pushed or towed in transporting freight. **2.** a large boat used in pageants or state ceremonies. —*v.i.* **3.** to move aggressively and clumsily. **4.** to intrude rudely: *They barged into the room.* —*v.t.* **5.** to transport by barge.

bar′ graph′, *n.* a graph using parallel bars of varying lengths, as to illustrate comparative quantities, costs, etc.

bar•i•tone (bar′i tōn′), *n.* **1.** a male voice or voice part between tenor and bass. **2.** a singer with such a voice.

bar•i•um (bâr′ē əm, bar′-), *n.* an active metallic element occurring in combination. *Symbol:* Ba; *at. wt.:* 137.34; *at. no.:* 56.

Bar-Je•sus (bär′jē′zəs), *n.* a false prophet who opposed the apostles Paul and Barnabas. Acts 13:6–12. Also called **Elymas.**

Bar-Jo•nah (bär′jō′nə), *n.* "son of Jonah," the family name of the apostle Simon Peter. Matt. 16:17; John 1:42; 21:15–17.

bark¹ (bärk), *n.* **1.** the abrupt, explosive cry of a dog or other animal. **2.** a short, explosive sound. —*v.i.* **3.** to utter or produce a bark. **4.** to speak sharply or gruffly. —*v.t.* **5.** to utter gruffly. —*Idiom.* **6. bark up the wrong tree,** to misdirect one's thoughts or efforts.

bark² (bärk), *n.* **1.** the external covering of the woody stems, branches, and roots of plants. —*v.t.* **2.** to scrape the skin of. **3.** to strip the bark from.

bark′er, *n.* a person who stands at the entrance to a show, as in a carnival, calling out its attractions to passersby.

bar•ley (bär′lē), *n.* **1.** a cereal plant. **2.** the grain of this plant, used as food and in making beer and whiskey.

bar mitz•vah (bär mits′və), *n., v.,* **-vahed, -vahing.** —*n.* (*often caps.*) **1.** a ceremony for admitting a boy of 13 as an adult member of the Jewish community. **2.** the boy participating in this ceremony. —*v.t.* **3.** to administer this ceremony to.

barn (bärn), *n.* **1.** a building for storing hay, grain,

etc., and often for housing livestock. —*Saying.* **2. lock the barn door after the horse has fled,** to take action after a loss has occurred. —**barn′like′,** *adj.*

Bar•na•bas (bär′nə bəs), *n.* surname of the Cyprian Levite Joseph, a companion of Paul. Acts 4:36, 37.

bar•na•cle (bär′nə kəl), *n.* a marine crustacean that attaches itself to ship bottoms and floating timber. —**bar′na•cled,** *adj.*

barn′storm′, *v.i., v.t.* to tour (rural areas) giving political speeches, theatrical performances, etc. —**barn′storm′er,** *n.*

Bar•num (bär′nəm), *n.* P(hineas) T(aylor), 1810–91, U.S. showman and circus impresario.

barn′yard′, *n.* a yard next to or surrounding a barn.

ba•rom•e•ter (bə rom′i tər), *n.* **1.** an instrument that measures atmospheric pressure. **2.** anything that indicates changes. —**bar•o•met•ric** (bar′ə me′trik), *adj.* —**bar′o•met′ri•cal•ly,** *adv.*

bar•on (bar′ən), *n.* **1.** a member of the lowest grade of nobility. **2.** a powerful, wealthy man in some industry or activity. —**ba•ro•ni•al** (bə rō′nē əl), *adj.*

bar′on•age (-ə nij), *n.* the entire British peerage.

bar′on•ess (-ə nis), *n.* **1.** the wife of a baron. **2.** a woman holding a baronial title.

bar′on•et (-ə nit, -net′), *n.* a member of a British hereditary order of honor, ranking below the barons. —**bar′on•et•cy,** *n., pl.* **-cies.**

ba•roque (bə rōk′), *adj.* (*often cap.*) **1.** of a style of architecture and art of the 17th to mid-18th century, characterized by elaborate and grotesque forms and ornamentation. **2.** of the musical period following the Renaissance, extending roughly from 1600 to 1750.

bar•racks (bar′əks), *n.* (*used with a sing. or pl. v.*) a building or group of buildings for lodging soldiers.

bar•ra•cu•da (bar′ə kōō′də), *n., pl.* **-das, -da.** any of several elongated, predaceous marine fishes.

bar•rage (bə räzh′), *n., v.,* **-raged, -rag•ing.** —*n.* **1.** a heavy barrier of artillery fire. **2.** an overwhelming quantity. —*v.t.* **3.** to subject to a barrage.

barre (bär), *n.* a handrail placed along a wall at hip height, used by a ballet dancer to maintain balance during practice.

bar•rel (bar′əl), *n., v.,* **-reled, -rel•ing** or (*esp. Brit.*) **-relled, -rel•ling.** —*n.* **1.** a cylindrical wooden container with slightly bulging sides and flat ends. **2.** the standard capacity of a barrel, 31.5 gallons of liquid. **3.** any large quantity. **4.** the tubelike part of a gun. —*v.i.* **5.** to travel or drive very fast.

bar′rel or′gan, *n.* a musical instrument that plays tunes by means of pins inserted into a revolving barrel.

bar•ren (bar′ən), *adj.* **1.** not producing offspring; sterile. **2.** unproductive; unfruitful. **3.** without capacity to interest or attract. **4.** bereft; lacking: *barren of compassion.* —*n.* **5.** Usu., **-rens.** level or slightly rolling land, usu. infertile. —**bar′ren•ness,** *n.*

bar•rette (bə ret′), *n.* a clasp for holding a woman's hair in place.

bar•ri•cade (bar′i kād′, bar′i kād′), *n., v.,* **-cad•ed, -cad•ing.** —*n.* **1.** a hastily constructed defensive barrier. **2.** any barrier. —*v.t.* **3.** to obstruct or shut in with a barricade.

bar•ri•er (bar′ē ər), *n.* **1.** anything that bars passage, as a fence. **2.** anything that obstructs or limits.

bar•ring (bär′ing), *prep.* excepting; except for.

bar•ris•ter (bar′ə stər), *n.* (in England) a lawyer who has the privilege of pleading in the higher courts.

bar′room′ (bär′-), *n.* an establishment with a bar for serving alcoholic drinks.

bar•row¹ (bar′ō), *n.* a handbarrow or wheelbarrow.

bar•row² (bar′ō), *n.* an artificial mound, esp. over a grave.

Bar•ry•more (bar′ə môr′, -mōr′), *n.* **1.** Maurice (*Herbert Blythe*), 1847–1905, U.S. actor. **2.** his children: **Ethel,** 1879–1959, **John,** 1882–1942, and **Lionel,** 1878–1954, U.S. actors.

Bar•sab•bas (bär sab′əs, -sä′bəs), *n.* **1. Joseph the Just,** a candidate to replace Judas Iscariot as an apostle. Acts 1:23–26. **2. Judas,** a prophet who accompanied Paul, Barnabas, and Silas to Antioch in Syria. Acts 15:22, 27.

bar′tend′er, *n.* a person who mixes and serves alcoholic drinks at a bar.

bar•ter (bär′tər), *v.i.* **1.** to trade by exchange of commodities rather than by use of money. —*v.t.* **2.** to exchange in trade. —*n.* **3.** the act of bartering. **4.** items or an item for bartering. —**bar′ter•er,** *n.*

Bar•thol•di (bär thol′dē, -tol′-), *n.* **Frédéric Auguste,** 1834–1904, French sculptor: designed Statue of Liberty.

Bar•thol•o•mew (bär thol′ə myōō′), *n.* one of the 12 apostles: sometimes called Nathanael. Mark 3:18.

Bar•tók (bär′tok, -tôk), *n.* **Béla,** 1881–1945, Hungarian composer.

Bar•ton (bär′tn), *n.* **Clara,** 1821–1912, U.S. philanthropist who organized the American Red Cross in 1881.

Bar•uch (bâr′ək *for 1;* bə rōōk′ *for 2*), *n.* **1.** the amanuensis and friend of Jeremiah and nominal author of the book of Baruch in the Apocrypha. Jer. 32:12. **2. Bernard M(annes),** 1870–1965, U.S. financier.

bar•y•on (bar′ē on′), *n.* any of a group of strongly interacting elementary particles.

Ba•rysh•ni•kov (bə rish′ni kôf′, -kof′), *n.* **Mikhail,** born 1948, Russian ballet dancer, born in Latvia; in the U.S. since 1974.

ba•sal (bā′səl, -zəl), *adj.* **1.** of, at, or forming the base. **2.** fundamental; basic. —**ba′sal•ly,** *adv.*

ba′sal metab′olism, *n.* the minimal amount of energy necessary to maintain vital body functions while fasting and at total rest.

ba•salt (bə sôlt′, bā′sôlt), *n.* the dark, dense, igneous rock of a lava flow. —**ba•sal′tic,** *adj.*

base¹ (bās), *n., adj., v.,* **based, bas•ing.** —*n.* **1.** a bottom support; the part on which a thing rests. **2.** a fundamental principle; basis. **3.** the principal element or ingredient. **4. a.** each of the four corners of a baseball diamond. **b.** a canvas sack marking first, second, or third base. **5.** a military headquarters or supply installation. **6. a.** the lower side or surface of a geometric figure. **b.** the number that serves as a starting point for a numerical system. **7.** a chemical compound that reacts with an acid to form a salt. **8.** the part of a complex word to which affixes may be added. —*adj.* **9.** serving as or forming a base. —*v.t.* **10.** to form a base for. **11.** to establish, as a conclusion. —*Idiom.* **12. off base, a.** (in baseball) not touching a base. **b.** badly mistaken.

base² (bās), *adj.,* **bas•er, bas•est. 1.** morally low; meanspirited. **2.** of little or no value. **3.** debased or counterfeit. —**base′ly,** *adv.* —**base′ness,** *n.*

base′ball′, *n.* **1.** a game involving the batting of a ball, played by two teams on a diamond formed by four bases. **2.** the ball used in this game.

base′board′, *n.* a board or molding forming the foot of an interior wall.

base′ hit′, *n. Baseball.* a fair ball enabling the batter to reach base safely without an error in the field or with no runner forced out.

base′less, *adj.* having no base or foundation; groundless.

base′line′ or **base′ line′,** *n.* **1.** the area on a baseball diamond within which a runner must keep when running between bases. **2.** the line at each end of a tennis court. **3.** a basic standard or level; guideline.

base′ment, *n.* a story of a building, partly or wholly underground.

base′ on balls′, *n., pl.* **bases on balls.** *Baseball.* the awarding of first base to a batter to whom four balls have been pitched.

base′ pay′, *n.* pay received for a given work period, not including overtime, bonuses, etc.

bash (bash), *v.t.* **1.** to strike with a crushing blow. **2. a.** to assault physically. **b.** to abuse verbally. —*n.* **3.** a crushing blow. **4.** a lively social event.

Ba•shan (bā′shən), *n.* a region in ancient Palestine, E of the Jordan River. Ps. 22:12; Isa. 2:15; Jer. 50:19.

bash′ful, *adj.* easily embarrassed; shy. —**bash′ful•ly,** *adv.* —**bash′ful•ness,** *n.*

bash′ing, *n.* **1.** the act of assaulting or abusing. **2.** (used in combination) **a.** physical assaults against members of a specified group: *gay-bashing.* **b.** verbal abuse of a group or a nation: *feminist-bashing.*

ba•sic (bā′sik), *adj.* **1.** of or forming a base or basis; fundamental. **2. a.** pertaining to a chemical base. **b.** alkaline. —*n.* **3.** Often, **-sics.** an essential ingredient, principle, procedure, etc. —**ba/si•cal•ly,** *adv.*

BASIC (bā′sik), *n.* a high-level computer programming language that uses English words, punctuation marks, and algebraic notation.

bas•il (baz′əl, bā′zəl), *n.* an aromatic herb whose leaves are used in cooking.

ba•sil•i•ca (bə sil′i kə), *n., pl.* **-cas. 1.** an early Christian church having a nave, aisles, and vaulted apses. **2.** one of the seven main churches of Rome, or another Roman Catholic church accorded the same religious privileges. [< L < Gk *basilikḗ (oikía)* royal (house)]

ba•sin (bā′sən), *n.* **1.** a shallow, circular container, used chiefly to hold water. **2.** the quantity held by a basin. **3.** a sheltered area along a shore. **4. a.** a depression in the earth's surface. **b.** an area drained by a river.

ba•sis (bā′sis), *n., pl.* **-ses** (-sēz). **1.** a bottom or base; foundation. **2.** a fundamental principle. **3.** the principal constituent.

bask (bask, bäsk), *v.i.* **1.** to lie in pleasant warmth. **2.** to take great pleasure: *to bask in royal favor.*

bas•ket (bas′kit, bä′skit), *n.* **1.** a container made of twigs, straw, etc., woven together. **2.** the amount contained in a basket. **3.** the goal on a basketball court, an open net suspended from a metal hoop.

bas′ket•ball′, *n.* **1.** a game played by two teams who score points by tossing a ball through a goal on the opponent's side of the court. **2.** the ball used in this game.

bas′ket weave′, *n.* a textile weave with a checkered, basketlike pattern.

bas mitz•vah (bäs mits′və), *n.* (*often caps.*) BAT MITZVAH.

Basque (bask), *n.* **1.** a member of a people living in the W Pyrenees. **2.** the language of the Basques.

Bas•ra (bäs′rə), *n.* a port in SE Iraq. 616,700.

bas-re•lief (bä′ri lēf′), *n.* relief sculpture in which the figures project slightly from the background.

bass¹ (bās), *adj.* **1.** of the lowest pitch or range. **2.** of the lowest part in harmonic music. —*n.* **3.** the bass part. **4.** a bass voice, singer, or instrument. **5.** DOUBLE BASS.

bass² (bas), *n., pl.* **bass•es, bass.** any of numerous edible, spiny-finned, freshwater or marine fishes.

bas′set hound′ (bas′it), *n.* one of a breed of short-legged hounds with a long body and long, drooping ears.

bas•si•net (bas′ə net′), *n.* a basket with a hood over one end, for use as a baby's cradle.

bas•so (bas′ō, bä′sō), *n., pl.* **-sos, -si** (-sē). a bass singer, esp. in opera.

bas•soon (ba sōōn′, bə-), *n.* a large woodwind instrument of low range, having a double-reed mouthpiece. —**bas•soon′ist,** *n.*

bast (bast), *n.* a strong, woody fiber used in the manufacture of woven goods and cordage.

bas•tard (bas′tərd), *n.* **1.** an illegitimate child. **2.** a mean, despicable person. —*adj.* **3.** illegitimate in birth. **4.** made or done in imitation; spurious; false. —**bas′tard•ly,** *adj.*

bas′tard•ize′, *v.t.,* **-ized, iz•ing. 1.** to lower the worth or condition of; debase. **2.** to declare or prove to be a bastard. —**bas′tard•i•za′tion,** *n.*

baste¹ (bāst), *v.t.,* **bast•ed, bast•ing.** to sew with long, loose, temporary stitches.

baste² (bāst), *v.t.,* **bast•ed, bast•ing.** to moisten (meat or other food) with drippings, butter, etc., while cooking.

baste³ (bāst), *v.t.,* **bast•ed, bast•ing. 1.** to beat with a stick. **2.** to denounce or scold vigorously.

bas•tille or **bas•tile** (ba stēl′), n. 1. (cap.) a fortress in Paris, used as a prison, captured by revolutionaries on July 14, 1789. 2. any prison.

Bastille′ Day′, n. July 14, a French national holiday commemorating the fall of the Bastille in 1789.

bas•tion (bas′chən), n. 1. a projecting portion of a fortification. 2. a fortified place. 3. anything seen as preserving or protecting some quality, condition, etc. —**bas′tioned,** adj.

bat¹ (bat), n., v., **bat•ted, bat•ting.** —n. 1. the wooden club used in certain games, as baseball and cricket, to strike the ball. 2. a heavy stick or club. 3. a blow, as with a bat. —v.t. 4. to hit with or as if with a bat. —v.i. 5. to take one's turn as a batter.

bat² (bat), n. a nocturnal flying mammal with large wings made of membranes.

bat³ (bat), v.t., **bat•ted, bat•ting.** 1. to blink; wink; flutter. —**Idiom.** 2. **not bat an eye,** to show no surprise or other emotion.

batch (bach), n. 1. a quantity or number coming at one time or taken together; group; lot. 2. the quantity of bread, dough, etc., made at one baking. 3. a group of jobs, data, programs, or commands treated as a unit for computer processing.

bate (bāt), v.t., **bat•ed, bat•ing.** 1. to lessen or diminish; abate. —**Idiom.** 2. **with bated breath,** in a state of suspenseful anticipation.

Bates (bāts), n. **Katharine Lee,** 1859–1929, U.S. teacher and hymn writer, author of America the Beautiful.

bath (bath, bäth), n., pl. **baths** (bathz, bäthz, baths, bäths). 1. a washing or immersing of the body in water, steam, etc. 2. a quantity of water or other liquid used for this purpose. 3. BATHTUB. 4. BATHROOM. 5. BATHHOUSE (def. 2). 6. Usu. **baths.** a spa. 7. a preparation, as an acid solution, in which something is immersed.

bathe (bāth), v., **bathed, bath•ing.** —v.t. 1. to immerse in water or other liquid, as for cleansing or refreshment. 2. to give a bath to. 3. to apply water or other liquid to. 4. to wash over or against, as by the action of the sea. 5. to cover or surround: sunlight bathing the room. 6. to take a bath. 7. to swim for pleasure. —**bath′er,** n.

bath′house′, n. 1. a structure, as at the seaside, containing dressing rooms for bathers. 2. a building having bathing facilities.

bath′ing suit′, n. a garment worn for swimming.

ba•thos (bā′thos, -thōs), n. 1. a ludicrous descent from the lofty to the commonplace. 2. insincere pathos; sentimentality. 3. triteness or triviality. —**ba•thet•ic** (bə thet′ik), adj.

bath′robe′, n. a loose, coatlike garment worn before and after a bath and over sleepwear.

bath′room′, n. a room with a bathtub or shower and usu. a sink and toilet.

Bath•she•ba (bath shē′bə, bath′shə-), n. the wife of Uriah the Hittite and afterward of David: mother of Solomon. II Sam. 11, 12.

bath′tub′, n. a tub to bathe in.

ba•tik (bə tēk′), n. 1. a technique of dyeing fabric using wax to cover those parts not to be dyed. 2. a fabric so decorated.

ba•tiste (bə tēst′, ba-), n. a fine, often sheer fabric made of any of various fibers.

bat mitzvah (bät mits′və), n. (often caps.) 1. a ceremony for admitting a girl of 12 or 13 as an adult member of the Jewish community. 2. the girl participating in this ceremony.

ba•ton (bə ton′, ba-), n. 1. a wand with which a conductor directs an orchestra or band. 2. a metal rod twirled by a drum major or majorette. 3. a staff serving as a mark of office or authority.

Bat•on Rouge (bat′n roozh′), n. the capital of Louisiana. 227,482.

bat•tal•ion (bə tal′yən), n. 1. a military unit comprising a headquarters and two or more companies. 2. an army in battle array. [< MF bataillon < It battaglione large body of troops]

bat•ten (bat′n), n. 1. a strip of wood used for vari-

ous building purposes, as to cover joints between boards. —v.t. 2. to furnish or bolster with battens.

bat•ter¹ (bat′ər), v.t. 1. to beat or pound repeatedly. 2. to subject (a person, esp. a wife or child) to repeated beating or other abuse. 3. to damage by beating or rough usage. —v.i. 4. to pound steadily.

bat•ter² (bat′ər), n. a mixture typically of flour, milk or water, and eggs, used to make cakes, pancakes, etc.

bat•ter³ (bat′ər), n. a player whose turn it is to bat, as in baseball or cricket.

bat′tering ram′, n. a device with a heavy horizontal beam for battering down walls, gates, etc.

bat•ter•y (bat′ə rē), n., pl. **-ter•ies.** 1. a cell or combination of cells for producing electric energy. 2. two or more pieces of artillery used for combined action. 3. a group of guns on a warship. 4. any group or series of similar or related things: a battery of tests. 5. Law. an unlawful attack upon another person, esp. by beating. 6. a baseball pitcher and catcher considered as a unit.

bat′ting, n. cotton, wool, or other fibers matted into sheets.

bat•tle (bat′l), n., v., **-tled, -tling.** —n. 1. a hostile military encounter. 2. any fight, conflict, or struggle. —v.t., v.i. 3. to fight. —**bat′tler,** n.

bat′tle-ax′ (or **-axe′**), n., pl. **-ax•es.** a large ax formerly used as a weapon of war.

bat′tle•field′, n. the field or ground on which a battle is fought.

bat′tle•ment, n. Often, **-ments.** a parapet of a fortification, with open spaces for shooting. —**bat′tle•ment′ed,** adj.

bat′tle•ship′, n. any of a class of warships with the heaviest armor and most powerful guns.

bat•ty (bat′ē), adj., **-ti•er, -ti•est.** Slang. crazy or eccentric.

bau•ble (bô′bəl), n. a cheap, showy trinket.

baux•ite (bôk′sīt, bō′zīt), n. a claylike rock that is the principal ore of aluminum.

Ba•var•i•a (bə vâr′ē ə), n. a state in SE Germany. —**Ba•var′i•an,** adj., n.

bawd•y (bô′dē), adj., **-i•er, -i•est.** indecent; lewd; obscene. —**bawd′i•ly,** adv. —**bawd′i•ness,** n.

bawl (bôl), v.i. 1. to cry or wail lustily. —v.t. 2. to shout out. 3. **bawl out,** Informal. to scold vigorously. —n. 4. a loud shout. 5. a loud weeping. —**bawl′er,** n.

bay¹ (bā), n. a body of water forming an indentation of the shoreline.

bay² (bā), n. 1. a recess in a wall, usu. containing a window. 2. a compartment, as in an aircraft or ship, set off by walls or bulkheads.

bay³ (bā), n. 1. a deep, prolonged howl, as of a hound. 2. the situation of a cornered animal or fugitive forced to face and resist pursuers: a stag at bay. —v.i. 3. to howl.

bay⁴ (bā), n. LAUREL (def. 1).

bay⁵ (bā), n. 1. a reddish brown horse or other animal. 2. a reddish brown. —adj. 3. reddish brown.

bay′ber′ry, n., pl. **-ries.** 1. an aromatic shrub bearing a waxy berry. 2. the berry.

bay′ leaf′, n. the dried leaf of the laurel, used in cooking.

bay•o•net (bā′ə net′, bā′ə nit), n., v., **-net•ed** or **-net•ted, -net•ing** or **-net•ting.** —n. 1. a daggerlike weapon attached to the muzzle of a gun for hand-to-hand combat. —v.t. 2. to stab with a bayonet. [< F baïonnette, after Bayonne, France, where first made or used]

bay•ou (bī′oo), n., pl. **-ous.** (in the southern U.S.) a marshy inlet or outlet of a lake, river, etc., usu. sluggish or stagnant.

bay′ win′dow, n. 1. a large window projecting from an outside wall and forming an alcove of a room. 2. Informal. a protruding belly.

ba•zaar (bə zär′), n. 1. a shopping quarter, esp. in the Middle East. 2. a sale of miscellaneous articles to benefit a charity.

ba•zoo•ka (bə zoo′kə), n., pl. **-kas.** a tube-shaped,

portable weapon that fires an armor-penetrating missile.

BB (bē′bē′), *n.* a size of shot, 0.18 in. (0.46 cm) in diameter, fired from an air rifle (**BB gun**).

BBS, bulletin board system.

B.C. or **BC, 1.** before Christ (used with dates): *Cleopatra was born in 69* B.C. **2.** British Columbia. —**Usage.** See A.D.

B.C.E., before the Common (or Christian) Era (used with dates).

B′ cell′, *n.* a type of lymphocyte that produces antibody.

be (bē; *unstressed* bē, bi), *v.* and *auxiliary v., pres. sing. 1st pers.* **am,** *2nd* **are,** *3rd* **is,** *pres. pl.* **are;** *past sing. 1st pers.* **was,** *2nd* **were,** *3rd* **was,** *past pl.* **were;** *pres. subj.* **be;** *past subj. sing. 1st, 2nd, and 3rd pers.* **were;** *past subj. pl.* **were;** *past part.* **been;** *pres. part.* **be•ing.** —*v.i.* **1.** to exist or live. **2.** to occur. **3.** to occupy a position. **4.** to continue as before. **5.** (used to connect the subject with its predicate adjective or nominative): *He is tall.* **6.** (used to introduce or form interrogative or imperative sentences): *Is that right? Be quiet!* —*auxiliary verb.* **7.** (used with the present participle of another verb to form progressive tenses): *I am waiting.* **8.** (used with the infinitive or participle of another verb to indicate a command, arrangements, or future action): *He is to see me today.* **9.** (used with the past participle of another verb to form the passive voice): *The date was fixed.* **10.** (used in archaic constructions with some intransitive verbs to form perfect tenses): *He is come.*

Be, *Chem. Symbol.* beryllium.

be-, a prefix meaning: about or around (*besiege*); all over (*bedaub*); to provide with (*bejewel*); at or regarding (*bewail*); to make (*befriend*).

beach (bēch), *n.* **1.** an expanse of sand or pebbles along a shore. —*v.t.* **2.** to haul or run onto a beach.

beach′comb′er, *n.* **1.** a person who lives by gathering salable jetsam or refuse from beaches. **2.** a vagrant who lives on the seashore.

beach′head′, *n.* the area that is the first objective of a military force landing on an enemy shore.

bea•con (bē′kən), *n.* **1.** a guiding or warning signal, as a light or fire. **2.** a tower or hill used for such purposes. **3.** a radio transmitter that sends out a signal as a navigational aid for ships and aircraft.

bead (bēd), *n.* **1.** a small, usu. round object of glass, wood, etc., pierced for stringing. **2. beads, a.** a necklace of beads. **b.** a rosary. **3.** any small globular body: *beads of sweat.* **4.** the front sight of a gun. **5.** a reinforced area of a rubber tire. —*v.t.* **6.** to ornament with beads. —*v.i.* **7.** to form in beads. —*Idiom.* **8. count** or **say one's beads,** to pray using rosary beads. **9. draw a bead on,** to take careful aim at.

bea•dle (bēd′l), *n.* a parish officer who performs various duties, as keeping order during the service.

bea•gle (bē′gəl), *n.* a small hound with drooping ears.

beak (bēk), *n.* **1.** the bill of a bird. **2.** any horny or stiff projecting mouthpart of an animal, fish, or insect. —**beaked** (bēkt, bē′kid), *adj.*

beak′er, *n.* **1.** a large drinking cup with a wide mouth. **2.** a cuplike container with a pouring lip, used in a laboratory.

beam (bēm), *n.* **1.** a long piece of metal or wood, used as a rigid part of a structure or machine. **2.** the extreme width of a ship. **3.** the crossbar of a balance from which the scales are suspended. **4.** a ray of light or other radiation. **5.** a group of nearly parallel rays. **6.** a radio signal used to guide pilots. **7.** a radiant smile. —*v.t.* **8.** to emit in or as if in beams. **9.** to transmit (a radio or television signal) in a particular direction. —*v.i.* **10.** to emit beams, as of light. **11.** to smile radiantly.

bean (bēn), *n.* **1.** the edible seed or pod of various plants of the legume family. **2.** a plant producing beans. **3.** any other beanlike seed or plant, as the coffee bean. **4.** *Slang.* a person's head. —*v.t.* **5.** *Slang.* to hit on the head, esp. with a baseball. —*Idiom.* **6. spill the beans,** *Informal.* to disclose a secret.

bean′ count′er, *n. Informal.* a person who makes judgments chiefly on the basis of numerical calculations.

bear¹ (bâr), *v.,* **bore, borne** or **born, bear•ing.** —*v.t.* **1.** to hold up or support. **2.** to give birth to. **3.** to produce by natural growth. **4.** to sustain or be capable of. **5.** to conduct (oneself, one's body, etc.). **6.** to suffer; endure. **7.** to warrant: *It doesn't bear repeating.* **8.** to carry; bring. **9.** to give: *to bear testimony.* **10.** to exhibit; show: *to bear a resemblance.* —*v.i.* **11.** to tend in a direction; go: *to bear left.* **12.** to be situated. **13.** to bring forth young or fruit. **14. bear down, a.** to press down. **b.** to strive harder. **15. ~ down on, a.** to press down on. **b.** to move toward rapidly. **16. ~ on,** to be relevant to. **17. ~ out,** to confirm. **18. ~ up,** to endure. **19. ~ with,** to be patient with. —*Idiom.* **20. bear the burden and the heat of the day,** to endure hardship and adversity. Matt. 20:12. —**bear′a•ble,** *adj.* —**bear′er,** *n.* —**Usage.** The past participle of BEAR is BORN only in senses referring, literally or figuratively, to birth, and it only occurs in the passive: *I was born in Ohio. A strange desire was born of the experience.* In other senses, and in the sense "to give birth to" focusing on the mother, the spelling BORNE is used: *Judges have always borne a burden of responsibility. She had borne a son the previous year.*

bear² (bâr), *n., pl.* **bears, bear,** *adj.* —*n.* **1.** a large, stocky, omnivorous mammal with thick, coarse fur. **2.** a gruff, clumsy, or rude person. **3.** a person who believes that stock prices will decline. **4.** (*cap.*) either of two constellations, Ursa Major or Ursa Minor. —*adj.* **5.** marked by declining prices, esp. of stocks.

beard (bērd), *n.* **1.** hair growing on the lower part of a man's face. **2.** a similar growth on the chin of some animals. **3.** an awn, as on wheat. —*v.t.* **4.** to oppose boldly. **5.** to supply with a beard.

bear′ hug′, *n.* a forcefully tight embrace.

bear′ing, *n.* **1.** the manner in which one conducts or carries oneself. **2.** the act, capability, or period of bringing forth. **3.** reference or relation. **4.** the support and guide for a rotating or sliding shaft, pivot, or wheel. **5.** Often, **-ings.** direction or relative position.

bear′ish, *adj.* **1.** like a bear; rough, burly, or clumsy. **2.** (of the stock market) marked by falling prices. —**bear′ish•ly,** *adv.* —**bear′ish•ness,** *n.*

beast (bēst), *n.* **1.** any nonhuman animal. **2.** a cruel, coarse person.

beast′ly, *adj.,* **-li•er, -li•est. 1.** of or like a beast; bestial. **2.** nasty; disagreeable. —**beast′li•ness,** *n.*

beast′ of bur′den, *n.* an animal used for carrying heavy loads, as a donkey.

beat (bēt), *v.,* **beat, beat•en** or **beat, beat•ing,** *n., adj.* —*v.t.* **1.** to strike forcefully and repeatedly. **2.** to thrash or flog in punishment (often fol. by *up*). **3.** to dash against. **4.** to flutter or flap (wings). **5.** to sound, as on a drum: *to beat a tattoo.* **6.** to stir vigorously. **7.** to make (a path) by repeated treading. **8.** to mark (time) with the hand or a metronome. **9.** to scour (the forest, grass, or brush) to rouse game. **10.** to overcome; defeat. **11.** to be superior to. **12.** *Informal.* to baffle. **13.** *Slang.* to escape or avoid (blame or punishment). —*v.i.* **14.** to strike repeatedly; pound. **15.** to throb. **16. beat down,** to subdue. **17. ~ off,** to ward off; repulse. —*n.* **18.** a stroke or blow. **19.** a throb or pulsation. **20.** one's regular path or habitual round. **21.** the marking of the metrical divisions of music. **22.** the accent stress in a rhythmical unit of poetry. **23.** (*often cap.*) BEATNIK. —*adj.* **24.** *Informal.* exhausted; worn out. **25.** (*often cap.*) of or characteristic of beatniks. —*Idiom.* **26. beat it,** *Informal.* to go away. —*Saying.* **27. beat swords into plowshares,** to turn from war to peace. Isa. 2:4. —**beat′a•ble,** *adj.* —**beat′er,** *n.*

be•a•tif•ic (bē′ə tif′ik), *adj.* **1.** bestowing bliss. **2.** blissful; saintly. —**be′a•tif′i•cal•ly,** *adv.*

be•at•i•fy (at′ə fī′), *v.t.,* **-fied, -fy•ing. 1.** to make blissfully happy. **2.** (in the Roman Catholic Church) to declare (a deceased person) to be among the blessed in heaven. —**be•at′i•fi•ca′tion,** *n.*

be•at/i•tude/ (-tōōd′, -tyōōd′), n. 1. supreme blessedness or happiness. 2. (often cap.) any of the declarations of blessedness pronounced by Jesus in the Sermon on the Mount.

Bea•tles (bēt′lz), n.pl. **the,** British rock group (1962–70) including **George Harrison** (born 1943), **John (Winston) Len•non** (len′ən) (1940–80), **Paul (James) Mc•Cart•ney** (mə kärt′nē) (born 1942), and **Ringo Starr** (Richard Starkey) (born 1940).

beat/nik (-nik), n. a disillusioned young person, esp. of the 1950s, rejecting conventional behavior, dress, etc.

beat/-up/, adj. Informal. dilapidated; broken-down.

beau (bō), n., pl. **beaus, beaux** (bōz). a girl's or woman's sweetheart.

Beau•mont (bō′mont), n. a city in SE Texas. 115,022.

beau•te•ous (byōō′tē əs), adj. beautiful. —**beau/te•ous•ly,** adv.

beau•ti/cian (-tish′ən), n. a person who works in a beauty parlor.

beau/ti•ful (-tə fəl), adj. 1. having beauty; aesthetically pleasing. 2. wonderful; remarkable. —**beau/ti•ful•ly,** adv.

beau/ti•fy (-fī′), v.t., v.i., -fied, -fy•ing. to make or become beautiful. —**beau/ti•fi•ca/tion,** n. —**beau/ti•fi/er,** n.

beau/ty, n., pl. -ties. 1. the quality in a person or thing that gives intense aesthetic pleasure. 2. a beautiful person or thing. —**Proverb.** 3. **Beauty is in the eye of the beholder,** beauty depends on who perceives it. 4. **Beauty is only skin-deep,** inner beauty is more important than outer.

beau/ty par/lor, n. an establishment where women go for haircuts, manicures, etc. Also called **beau/ty shop/.**

bea•ver (bē′vər), n., pl. -vers, -ver. 1. a large amphibious rodent with sharp incisors, webbed hind feet, and a flattened tail. 2. its fur.

be•calm (bi käm′), v.t. 1. to deprive (a sailing ship) of the wind necessary to move it. 2. to make calm.

be•cause (bi kôz′, -koz′, -kuz′), conj. 1. for the reason that. —**Idiom.** 2. **because of,** by reason of; due to. —**Usage.** See REASON.

beck (bek), n. 1. a beckoning gesture. —**Idiom.** 2. **at someone's beck and call,** subject to someone's every wish.

Beck•et (bek′it), n. **Saint Thomas à,** 1118?–70, archbishop of Canterbury.

Beck•ett (bek′it), n. **Samuel,** 1906–89, Irish playwright and novelist.

beck/on (-ən), v.t., v.i. 1. to signal or summon by a gesture of the head or hand. 2. to lure; entice.

be•cloud (bi kloud′), v.t. 1. to darken or obscure with clouds. 2. to make confused.

be•come (bi kum′), v., -came, -come, -com•ing. —v.i. 1. to come, change, or grow to be. —v.t. 2. to befit; suit. —**Idiom.** 3. **become of,** to happen to.

be•com/ing, adj. 1. pleasing or attractive. 2. suitable; proper.

bed (bed), n., v., **bed•ded, bed•ding.** —n. 1. a piece of furniture upon which a person sleeps. 2. an area of ground in which plants are grown. 3. the bottom of a lake, river, etc. 4. a foundation or base. 5. a layer of rock; stratum. —v.t. 6. to provide with a bed. 7. to put to bed. 8. to plant in a bed. 9. to place in layers. 10. to embed. —v.i. 11. to have sleeping accommodations. 12. to form layers.

be•daub (bi dôb′), v.t. to besmear; soil.

be•daz•zle (bi daz′əl), v.t., -zled, -zling. to dazzle so as to blind or confuse. —**be•daz/zle•ment,** n.

bed/bug/, n. a flat, wingless, bloodsucking bug that infests houses and esp. beds.

bed/clothes/, n.pl. coverings for a bed, as sheets and blankets.

bed/ding, n. BEDCLOTHES.

Bede (bēd) also **Baeda,** n. **Saint** ("the Venerable Bede"), A.D. 673?–735, English monk, historian, and theologian.

be•deck (bi dek′), v.t. to adorn, esp. in a showy manner.

be•dev•il (bi dev′əl), v.t., -iled, -il•ing or (esp. Brit.) -illed, -il•ling. 1. to torment maliciously. 2. to confuse; confound. —**be•dev/il•ment,** n.

bed/fel/low, n. 1. a person who shares one's bed. 2. an associate or collaborator.

be•di•zen (bi dī′zən, -diz′ən), v.t. to dress or adorn gaudily.

bed•lam (bed′ləm), n. a scene or state of wild uproar and confusion.

bed/ of ros/es, n. a situation of luxurious ease.

Bed•ou•in or **-u•in** (bed′ōō in), n., pl. -in, -ins. a traditionally tent-dwelling Arab of the deserts of SW Asia and N Africa.

bed/pan/, n. a shallow pan used as a toilet by persons confined to bed.

be•drag•gle (bi drag′əl), v.t., -gled, -gling. to make limp and soiled, as with rain or dirt.

bed/rid/den, adj. confined to bed.

bed/rock/, n. 1. unbroken solid rock, overlaid by soil. 2. any firm foundation or basis.

bed/roll/, n. bedding rolled for portability, used esp. out-of-doors.

bed/room/, n. a room used for sleeping.

bed/side/, n. 1. the side of a bed, esp. as the place of one attending the sick. —adj. 2. at or for a bedside.

bed/sore/, n. a skin ulcer on the body of a bedridden person, caused by immobility and prolonged pressure.

bed/spread/, n. a decorative outer covering for a bed.

bed/stead/ (-sted′, -stid), n. the framework of a bed supporting the springs and mattress.

bed/time/, n. the time a person usually goes to bed.

bee (bē), n. 1. any of a large group of four-winged hairy insects, some species of which produce honey. 2. a social gathering to work together or to compete: a quilting bee.

beech (bēch), n. 1. a tree having a smooth, gray bark and bearing small, edible, triangular nuts. 2. its wood.

Bee•cher (bē′chər), n. **Henry Ward,** 1813–87, U.S. preacher and writer.

beech/nut/, n. the nut of the beech.

beef (bēf), n., pl. **beeves** (bēvz) for 1; **beefs** for 4, v. —n. 1. an adult cow, steer, or bull raised for its meat. 2. its meat. 3. Informal. muscular strength. 4. Slang. a complaint. —v.i. 5. Slang. to complain. 6. **beef up,** to strengthen; reinforce.

beef/steak/, n. a cut of beef for broiling, frying, etc.

beef/y, adj., -i•er, -i•est. brawny; thickset.

bee/hive/, n. 1. a dwelling place for bees. 2. a crowded, busy place.

bee/keep/er, n. a person who raises honeybees. —**bee/keep/ing,** n.

bee/line/, n. a direct course or route.

Be•el•ze•bub (bē el′zə bub′, bēl′zə-), n. the chief devil; Satan. Mark 3:22–26; Matt. 12:26–27; Luke 11:15–19.

been (bin), v. pp. of BE.

beep (bēp), n. 1. a short, usu. high-pitched tone produced by an automobile horn, electronic device, etc. —v.i., v.t. 2. to make or cause to make such a sound.

beep/er, n. a pocket-size electronic device whose signal notifies the person carrying it of a telephone message.

beer (bēr), n. 1. an alcoholic, fermented beverage made from malt and hops. 2. any of various beverages made from plants, as root beer.

Beer•she•ba (bēr shē′bə, bēr′shə-), n. a city in Israel: the southernmost city of ancient Palestine. 114,600.

bees/wax/, n. WAX¹ (def. 1).

beet (bēt), n. 1. a plant with a fleshy red or white root. 2. its edible root.

Bee•tho•ven (bā′tō vən), *n.* **Ludwig van,** 1770–1827, German composer.

bee•tle[1] (bēt′l), *n.* an insect with hard, horny forewings that cover and protect the membranous flight wings.

bee•tle[2] (bēt′l), *adj., v.,* **-tled, -tling.** —*adj.* **1.** projecting; overhanging. —*v.i.* **2.** to project or overhang.

bee′tle-browed′, *adj.* **1.** having heavy projecting eyebrows. **2.** scowling or sullen.

be•fall (bi fôl′), *v.t., v.i.,* **-fell, -fall•en, -fall•ing.** to happen (to), esp. by chance or fate.

be•fit (bi fit′), *v.t.,* **-fit•ted, -fit•ting.** to be appropriate for; suit; fit.

be•fog (bi fog′, -fôg′), *v.t.,* **-fogged, -fog•ging. 1.** to envelop in fog. **2.** to make unclear or confused.

be•fore (bi fôr′), *prep.* **1.** previous to; earlier than. **2.** in front or ahead of. **3.** awaiting. **4.** in preference to. **5.** in precedence of, as in order or rank. **6.** in the presence or sight of. **7.** under the consideration or jurisdiction of: *summoned before a magistrate.* —*adv.* **8.** previously. **9.** earlier or sooner. **10.** in front; in advance. —*conj.* **11.** previous to the time when: *See me before you go.* **12.** rather than: *I will die before I submit.*

be•fore′hand′, *adv., adj.* in advance; ahead of time.

be•foul (bi foul′), *v.t.* to make filthy; defile.

be•friend (bi frend′), *v.t.* to act as a friend to.

be•fud•dle (bi fud′l), *v.t.,* **-dled, -dling.** to confuse thoroughly. —**be•fud′dle•ment,** *n.*

beg (beg), *v.t., v.i.,* **begged, beg•ging. 1.** to ask for (alms or charity). **2.** to ask humbly or earnestly. **3. beg off,** to request release from an obligation. —*Idiom.* **4. beg the question, a.** to assume the truth of the point in question. **b.** to evade the issue. **c.** to raise the question. **5. go begging,** to remain unused or unwanted.

be•gan (bi gan′), *v.* pt. of BEGIN.

be•get (bi get′), *v.t.,* **be•got, be•got•ten** or **be•got, be•get•ting. 1.** to be the father of. **2.** to cause; produce as an effect. —**be•get′ter,** *n.*

beg•gar (beg′ər), *n.* **1.** a person who lives by begging. **2.** a penniless person. —*v.t.* **3.** to impoverish. **4.** to cause to seem inadequate: *The place beggars description.* —*Proverb.* **5. Beggars can't be choosers,** one should not be fussy when in need. —**beg′gar•hood′,** *n.*

beg′gar•ly (-lē), *adj.* **1.** like or befitting a beggar. **2.** meanly inadequate. —**beg′gar•li•ness,** *n.*

be•gin (bi gin′), *v.i., v.t.,* **be•gan, be•gun, be•gin•ning. 1.** to perform the first or earliest part of (something). **2.** to come or bring into existence. —**be•gin′ner,** *n.*

be•gin′ning, *n.* **1.** the act of starting. **2.** the time or place at which anything starts. **3.** origin; source.

be•gone (bi gôn′, -gon′), *v.i.* to go away; depart (usu. used in the imperative).

be•go•nia (bi gōn′yə), *n., pl.* **-nias.** a tropical plant cultivated for its ornamental leaves and flowers.

be•grime (bi grīm′), *v.t.,* **-grimed, -grim•ing.** to make grimy.

be•grudge (bi gruj′), *v.t.,* **-grudged, -grudg•ing. 1.** to envy the pleasure or good fortune of. **2.** to be reluctant to give or allow. —**be•grudg′ing•ly,** *adv.*

be•guile (bi gīl′), *v.t.,* **-guiled, -guil•ing. 1.** to influence by guile; delude. **2.** to charm or divert. **3.** to pass (time) pleasantly. —**be•guile′ment,** *n.* —**be•guil′er,** *n.* —**be•guil′ing•ly,** *adv.*

be•gun (bi gun′), *v.* pp. of BEGIN.

be•half (bi haf′, -häf′), *n.* **1.** interest; support. —*Idiom.* **2. in** or **on behalf of,** as a representative of.

be•have (bi hāv′), *v.,* **-haved, -hav•ing.** —*v.i.* **1.** to act or react in a particular way. **2.** to act properly. —*v.t.* **3.** to conduct (oneself) in a proper manner.

be•hav′ior (-yər), *n.* **1.** one's manner of behaving or acting. **2.** the action or reaction of a material, machine, etc., under given circumstances. Also, *esp. Brit.,* **be•hav′iour.** —**be•hav′ior•al,** *adj.*

behav′ioral sci′ence, *n.* a science, as psychology or sociology, that is concerned with the behavior of living organisms. —**behav′ioral sci′entist,** *n.*

be•hav′ior•ism, *n.* the doctrine that regards objective behavior as the only proper subject for psychological study. —**be•hav′ior•ist,** *n.*

be•head (bi hed′), *v.t.* to cut off the head of.

be•held (bi held′), *v.* pt. and pp. of BEHOLD.

be•he•moth (bi hē′məth), *n.* **1.** an animal, perhaps the hippopotamus, mentioned in Job 40:15–24. **2.** any creature or thing of monstrous size or power.

be•hest (bi hest′), *n.* **1.** a command; directive. **2.** an earnest request.

be•hind (bi hīnd′), *prep.* **1.** at or toward the rear of. **2.** later than; after. **3.** in the state of making less progress than. **4.** beyond. **5.** promoting or supporting. **6.** hidden or unrevealed by: *Malice lay behind her smile.* —*adv.* **7.** at or toward the rear. **8.** in a place or stage already passed. **9.** in arrears. **10.** slow; late. —*n.* **11.** *Informal.* the buttocks. —*Proverb.* **12. Behind every great man is a great woman,** a man's success is often dependent on a woman's help.

be•hold (bi hōld′), *v.,* **-held, -hold•ing,** *interj.* —*v.t.* **1.** to look at; see. —*interj.* **2.** look! see! —**be•hold′er,** *n.*

be•hold′en, *adj.* obligated; indebted.

be•hoove (bi hōōv′), *v.t.,* **-hooved, -hoov•ing.** to be necessary or proper for: *It behooves us to reconsider.*

beige (bāzh), *n.* **1.** a light grayish brown. —*adj.* **2.** of the color beige.

Bei•jing (bā′jing′) also **Peking,** *n.* the capital of the People's Republic of China. 5,860,000.

be•ing (bē′ing), *n.* **1.** the fact of existing; existence. **2.** essential substance or nature. **3.** a living person or thing.

Bei•rut (bā rōōt′), *n.* the capital of Lebanon. 702,000.

be•jew•el (bi jōō′əl), *v.t.,* **-eled, -el•ing** or (*esp. Brit.*) **-elled, -el•ling.** to adorn with or as if with jewels.

be•kah or **be•ka** (bā′kə, -kä), *n.* a unit of weight in the Bible; half a shekel. Ex. 38:26.

be•la•bor (bi lā′bər), *v.t.* **1.** to explain, worry about, or work at unduly. **2.** to assail, as with ridicule. **3.** to beat; pummel.

Be•la•rus (byel′ə rōōs′, bel′-), *n.* a republic in E Europe, N of Ukraine: formerly a part of the USSR. 10,203,683.

be•lat•ed (bi lā′tid), *adj.* late or delayed. —**be•lat′ed•ly,** *adv.*

be•lay (bi lā′), *v.t., v.i.* **1.** to fasten (a rope) by winding around a pin or short rod. **2.** to stop (used chiefly in the imperative).

bel can•to (bel′ kan′tō, -kän′-), *n.* a smooth cantabile style of operatic singing. [< lit., fine singing]

belch (belch), *v.i., v.t.* **1.** to expel (gas) noisily from the stomach through the mouth. **2.** to gush forth: *Smoke belched from the chimney.* —*n.* **3.** an act or instance of belching.

be•lea•guer (bi lē′gər), *v.t.* **1.** to surround with military forces. **2.** to beset, as with difficulties.

Bel•fast (bel′fast, -fäst, bel fast′, -fäst′), *n.* the capital of Northern Ireland. 374,300.

bel•fry (bel′frē), *n., pl.* **-fries. 1.** a bell tower. **2.** the part of a steeple in which a bell is hung.

Belg., Belgium.

Bel•gium (bel′jəm), *n.* a kingdom in W Europe. 9,813,152. —**Bel′gian,** *n., adj.*

Bel•grade (bel′grād, -gräd), *n.* the capital of Yugoslavia. 1,470,073.

be•lie (bi lī′), *v.t.,* **-lied, -ly•ing. 1.** to show to be false; contradict. **2.** to misrepresent. **3.** to be false to or disappoint: *to belie one's faith.*

be•lief (bi lēf′), *n.* **1.** something believed; opinion; conviction. **2.** confidence; faith; trust. **3.** a religious creed or faith.

be•lieve (bi lēv′), *v.,* **-lieved, -liev•ing.** —*v.i.* **1.** to accept the truth, existence, reliability, or value of something. —*v.t.* **2.** to accept as true or real. **3.** to have confidence in the assertions of (a person). **4.** to suppose; think. —**be•liev′a•ble,** *adj.* —**be•liev′er,** *n.*

be•lit•tle (bi lit′l), *v.t.,* **-tled, -tling.** to regard or portray as less impressive or important; disparage. —**be•lit′tle•ment,** *n.*

Be•lize (bə lēz′), *n.* a country in N Central America. 224,663. —**Be•li′ze•an** (-zē ən), *adj., n.*

bell (bel), *n.* **1.** a hollow, cup-shaped metal instrument that rings when struck. **2.** the sound of a bell. **3.** something having the form of a bell. **4.** any of the half-hour units of nautical time rung on the bell of a ship. —*v.t.* **5.** to put a bell on. —*v.i.* **6.** to have the form of a bell.

Bell, *n.* **Alexander Graham,** 1847–1922, U.S. scientist, born in Scotland: inventor of the telephone.

bel•la•don•na (bel′ə don′ə), *n., pl.* **-nas. 1.** a poisonous plant with purplish red flowers and black berries. **2.** ATROPINE.

bell′-bot′tom, *adj.* **1.** (of trousers) wide and flaring at the bottoms of the legs. —*n.* **2. -bottoms,** (*used with a pl. v.*) bell-bottom trousers.

bell′boy′, *n.* BELLHOP.

belle (bel), *n.* a woman or girl admired for her beauty and charm.

belle é•poque (bel′ ā pôk′), *n.* the period of peace and cultural productivity in W Europe before the outbreak of World War I.

belles-let•tres (*Fr.* bel le′tʀ³), *n.* literature that is polished and elegant and often inconsequential in content. —**bel•let′rist** (-trist), *n.* —**bel′let•ris′tic** (-li tris′tik), *adj.*

bell′hop′, *n.* a person employed, esp. by a hotel, to carry luggage and run errands.

bel•li•cose (bel′i kōs′), *adj.* inclined or eager to fight or quarrel. —**bel′li•cos′i•ty** (-kos′i tē), *n.*

bel•lig•er•ent (bə lij′ər ənt), *adj.* **1.** engaged in warfare. **2.** aggressively hostile. —*n.* **3.** a state or nation at war. **4.** a belligerent person. —**bel•lig′er•ence, be•lig′er•en•cy,** *n.* —**bel•lig′er•ent•ly,** *adv.*

bell′ jar′, *n.* a bell-shaped glass cover, used esp. in laboratories to contain gases or a vacuum.

bel•low (bel′ō), *v.i.* **1.** to emit the loud hollow cry typical of a bull. **2.** to roar; bawl. —*v.t.* **3.** to utter in a loud deep voice. —*n.* **4.** a bellowing sound.

Bel′low, *n.* **Saul,** born 1915, U.S. novelist, born in Canada.

bel•lows (bel′ōz, -əz), *n.* (*used with a sing. or pl. v.*) **1.** a device for producing a strong current of air, consisting of a chamber that can be expanded and contracted. **2.** something resembling a bellows.

bell•weth•er (bel′weth′ər), *n.* **1.** one that leads or marks a trend. **2.** a sheep wearing a bell and leading a flock.

bel•ly (bel′ē), *n., pl.* **-lies,** *v.,* **-lied, -ly•ing.** —*n.* **1.** the abdomen or underpart of an animal. **2.** the stomach with its adjuncts. **3.** the deep interior of something: *a ship's belly.* —*v.t., v.i.* **4.** to swell out.

bel′ly•ache′, *n., v.,* **-ached, -ach•ing.** —*n.* **1.** a pain in the abdomen. —*v.i.* **2.** *Informal.* to complain.

bel′ly•but′ton or **bel′ly but′ton,** *n. Informal.* NAVEL.

bel′ly dance′, *n.* a solo dance performed by a woman, emphasizing sinuous movements of the hips and belly. —**bel′ly danc′er,** *n.* —**bel′ly danc′ing,** *n.*

bel′ly•ful′, *n., pl.* **-fuls.** an intolerable amount.

bel′ly laugh′, *n.* a loud hearty laugh.

be•long (bi lông′, -long′), *v.i.* **1.** to be properly placed. **2.** to be appropriate or suitable. **3. belong to, a.** to be the property of. **b.** to be a part or adjunct of: *That cover belongs to this jar.* **c.** to be a member of.

be•long′ings, *n.pl.* possessions; personal effects.

Be′lo•rus′sia or **Bye′lo•rus′sia** (byel′ə-, bel′-), *n.* BELARUS. —**Be′lo•rus′sian,** *adj., n.*

be•lov•ed (bi luv′id, -luvd′), *adj.* **1.** greatly loved. —*n.* **2.** a person who is beloved.

Belov′ed Disci′ple, *n.* the apostle John. John 13:23; 19:26; 20:2.

Belov′ed Physi′cian, *n.* the apostle Luke. Col. 4:14.

be•low (bi lō′), *adv.* **1.** in or toward a lower place. **2.** on, in, or toward a lower deck or floor. **3.** on earth. **4.** in hell. **5.** at a later point in a text. **6.** in a lower rank or grade. —*prep.* **7.** lower down than. **8.** too undignified to be worthy of.

Bel•shaz•zar (bel shaz′ər), *n.* the last king of Babylon. Dan. 5.

belt (belt), *n.* **1.** a band of flexible material, as leather, for encircling the waist. **2.** any encircling band or strip. **3.** an extended region having distinctive characteristics. **4.** an endless band passing about pulleys, used to transmit motion or convey objects. **5.** *Slang.* **a.** a hard blow. **b.** a swallow of liquor. —*v.t.* **6.** to gird or furnish with a belt. **7.** to sing loudly. **8.** *Slang.* to hit; strike. —*Idiom.* **9. below the belt,** unfair or unfairly.

belt′ bag′, *n.* FANNY PACK.

belt′way′, *n.* a highway around the perimeter of an urban area.

be•ma (bē′mə), *n., pl.* **-ma•ta** (-mə tə), **-mas. 1.** the enclosed space around the altar in an Eastern church. **2.** Also, **bimah.** a platform in a synagogue for the table used when reading from the Torah.

be•moan (bi mōn′), *v.t.* to express distress or grief over.

be•muse (bi myōoz′), *v.t.,* **-mused, -mus•ing. 1.** to bewilder; confuse. **2.** to cause to become lost in thought. —**be•muse′ment,** *n.*

bench (bench), *n.* **1.** a long, hard seat for several people. **2.** a seat occupied by a judge. **3. a.** the office or dignity of a judge. **b.** judges collectively. **4.** the seat on which the players of a team sit while not playing in a game. **5.** WORKBENCH. —*v.t.* **6.** to seat on a bench. **7.** to remove (a player) from a game.

bench′mark′ or **bench′ mark′,** *n.* a standard or reference by which others can be measured or judged.

bench′ press′, *n.* a weightlifting exercise in which a barbell is raised above the chest while the lifter lies on a bench. —**bench′-press′,** *v.t., v.i.*

bench′ war′rant, *n.* a warrant issued by a judge for the apprehension of an offender.

bend (bend), *v.,* **bent, bend•ing,** *n.* —*v.t.* **1.** to force from a straight form into a curved or angular one. **2.** to guide in a particular direction. **3.** to cause to submit. —*v.i.* **4.** to become curved or bent. **5.** to assume a bent posture; stoop. **6.** to turn or incline in a particular direction. **7.** to yield; submit. —*n.* **8.** the act of bending. **9.** something bent. —**bend′a•ble,** *adj.*

be•neath (bi nēth′, -nēth′), *adv.* **1.** in or to a lower position; below. **2.** underneath. —*prep.* **3.** below; under. **4.** below the level or dignity of: *behavior beneath contempt.*

Ben•e•dict (ben′i dikt), *n.* **1. Ruth (Fulton),** 1887–1948, U.S. anthropologist. **2. Saint,** A.D. 480?–543?, Italian monk: founded Benedictine order.

Ben•e•dic•tine (ben′i dik′tin, -tēn, -tīn), *n.* **1. a.** a member of an order of monks founded at Monte Cassino by St. Benedict about A.D. 530. **b.** a member of any congregation of nuns following the rule of St. Benedict. —*adj.* **2.** of or pertaining to St. Benedict or the Benedictines.

ben•e•dic•tion (ben′i dik′shən), *n.* the invocation of a blessing, esp. the short blessing at the close of a religious service.

ben′e•fac′tion (-fak′shən), *n.* a charitable donation or act.

ben′e•fac′tor, *n.* **1.** a kindly helper. **2.** a person who makes a bequest or endowment, as to an institution.

ben′e•fac′tress (-tris), *n.* a woman who gives help or makes a bequest or endowment.

ben′e•fice (-fis), *n.* a post granted to an ecclesiastic that guarantees a fixed amount of income.

be•nef•i•cence (bə nef′ə səns), *n.* **1.** the quality or state of being beneficent. **2.** BENEFACTION.

be•nef′i•cent, *adj.* doing good or causing good to be done; charitable. —**be•nef′i•cent•ly,** *adv.*

ben•e•fi•cial (ben'ə fish'əl), *adj.* conferring benefit; advantageous. —**ben'e•fi'cial•ly,** *adv.*

ben'e•fi'ci•ar'y (-fish'ē er'ē, -fish'ə rē), *n., pl.* **-ar•ies. 1.** one that receives benefits. **2.** a recipient of funds or other property under a will, trust, etc.

ben'e•fit (-fit), *n.* **1.** something that is advantageous or good. **2.** a payment made by an insurance company, public agency, etc. **3.** a social event or a performance to raise money for a cause. —*v.t.* **4.** to be advantageous to. —*v.i.* **5.** to derive benefit.

ben'efit of cler'gy, *n.* **1.** the rites or sanctions of a church. **2.** the medieval privilege of clerics to be tried by ecclesiastic rather than secular courts.

Be•nét (bi nā'), *n., pl.* **Stephen Vincent,** 1898–1943, U.S. poet. **2.** his brother **William Rose,** 1886–1950, U.S. poet and critic.

be•nev•o•lent (bi nev'ə lənt), *adj.* **1.** characterized by goodwill. **2.** desiring to help others; charitable. **3.** established for good works. —**be•nev'o•lence,** *n.* —**be•nev'o•lent•ly,** *adv.*

Ben•gal (ben gôl', -gäl'), *n.* **Bay of,** a part of the Indian Ocean between India and Myanmar.

Ben-Gu•rion (ben gōōr'ē ən; *Seph. Heb.* ben'gōō-RYôn'), *n.* **David,** 1886–1973, prime minister of Israel 1948–53, 1955–63.

be•night•ed (bi nī'tid), *adj.* **1.** ignorant. **2.** overtaken by darkness or night.

be•nign (bi nīn'), *adj.* **1.** having a kindly disposition. **2.** favorable; propitious. **3.** not malignant. —**be•nign'ly,** *adv.*

be•nig'nant (-nig'nənt), *adj.* **1.** benign; gracious. **2.** beneficial.

Be•nin (be nēn'), *n.* a republic in W Africa. 4,440,000. Formerly, **Dahomey.** —**Be•ni'nese,** *adj., n., pl.* **-nese.**

Ben•ja•min (ben'jə mən), *n.* **1.** the youngest son of Jacob and Rachel, and the brother of Joseph. Gen. 35:18. **2.** one of the 12 tribes of Israel.

bent (bent), *adj.* **1.** curved; crooked. **2.** determined; resolved. —*n.* **3.** a predilection; talent.

be•numb (bi num'), *v.t.* **1.** to make numb. **2.** to make inactive; stupefy.

ben•zene (ben'zēn, ben zēn'), *n.* a colorless, flammable liquid obtained chiefly from coal tar: used in chemicals and dyes and as a solvent.

be•queath (bi kwēth', -kwēth'), *v.t.* **1.** to dispose of (property or money) in a will. **2.** to hand down.

be•quest (bi kwest'), *n.* **1.** the act of bequeathing. **2.** something bequeathed.

be•rate (bi rāt'), *v.t.,* **-rat•ed, -rat•ing.** to scold; rebuke.

Ber•ber (bûr'bər), *n.* **1.** a member of any of a group of peoples of North Africa. **2.** the group of languages spoken by these peoples.

Be•re•a (bēr'ē ə), *n.* a city in Macedonia where the Apostle Paul preached. Acts 17:10.

be•reave (bi rēv'), *v.t.,* **-reaved** or **-reft, -reav•ing. 1.** to deprive and make desolate, esp. by death. **2.** to deprive ruthlessly or by force. —**be•reave'ment,** *n.* —**be•reft'** (-reft'), *adj.*

be•ret (bə rā'), *n.* a soft, visorless cap.

ber•i•ber•i (ber'ē ber'ē), *n.* a disease caused by lack of vitamin B₁, leading to paralysis and emaciation.

Ber'ing Sea' (bēr'ing, bâr'-), *n.* a part of the N Pacific between Alaska and Siberia.

Ber'ing Strait', *n.* a strait connecting the Bering Sea and the Arctic Ocean.

Berke•ley (bûrk'lē), *n.* a city in W California. 103,660.

ber•ke•li•um (bər kē'lē əm), *n.* a synthetic radioactive element. *Symbol:* Bk; *at. no.:* 97.

Ber•lin (bər lin'), *n.* **1. Irving,** 1888–1989, U.S. songwriter. **2.** the capital of Germany. 3,121,000. Formerly divided into a western zone **(West Berlin)** and an eastern zone **(East Berlin).**

Ber'lin Air'lift, *n.* the air shipment of necessities to West Berlin from 1948 through 1949.

Ber'lin Wall', *n.* a guarded concrete wall 28 mi.

(45 km) long, erected across Berlin by East Germany in 1961, dismantled in 1989.

Ber•mu•da (bər myōō'də), *n.* a group of British islands in the W Atlantic. 62,569. —**Ber•mu'dan, Ber•mu'di•an,** *adj., n.*

Bern or **Berne** (bûrn, bârn), *n.* the capital of Switzerland. 136,300.

Bern•hardt (bûrn'härt), *n.* **Sarah,** 1845–1923, French actress.

Ber•ni•ce (bûr nī'sē), *n.* the oldest daughter of Herod Agrippa. Acts 25:13.

Bern•stein (bûrn'stīn, -stēn), *n.* **Leonard,** 1918–90, U.S. conductor and composer.

ber•ry (ber'ē), *n., pl.* **-ries,** *v.,* **-ried, -ry•ing.** —*n.* **1.** any small, usu. stoneless, juicy fruit, as the strawberry. **2.** a dry seed or kernel, as of wheat. —*v.i.* **3.** to gather or produce berries. —**ber'ry•like',** *adj.*

ber•serk (bər sûrk', -zûrk'), *adj.* violently or destructively frenzied. [< ON *berserkr* frenzied warrior = *ber-* bear + *serkr* shirt]

berth (bûrth), *n.* **1.** a shelflike sleeping space, as on a ship or train. **2.** a space allotted for a ship to dock or lie at anchor. **3.** a job; position. —*v.t.* **4.** to slip into a berth. —*v.i.* **5.** to come into a berth. —*Idiom.* **6. give a wide berth to,** to keep a careful distance from.

ber•yl (ber'əl), *n.* a mineral, varieties of which are valued as gems: the chief ore of beryllium.

be•ryl•li•um (bə ril'ē əm), *n.* a hard, light metallic element used chiefly in copper alloys to reduce fatigue. *Symbol:* Be; *at. wt.:* 9.0122; *at. no.:* 4.

be•seech (bi sēch'), *v.t., v.i.,* **-sought** or **-seeched, -seech•ing.** to beg or ask eagerly (for). —**be•seech'er,** *n.* —**be•seech'ing•ly,** *adv.*

be•set (bi set'), *v.t.,* **-set, -set•ting. 1.** to attack on all sides; harass. **2.** to surround.

be•side (bi sīd'), *prep.* **1.** by or at the side of; near. **2.** compared with. **3.** apart from: *beside the point.* **4.** BESIDES (defs. 4, 5). —*Idiom.* **5. beside oneself,** frantic; distraught. —**Usage.** For the prepositional meanings "in addition to" and "except," BESIDES is preferred, esp. in edited writing.

be•sides' (bi sīdz'), *adv.* **1.** moreover; furthermore. **2.** in addition. **3.** otherwise; else. —*prep.* **4.** in addition to. **5.** other than; except: *no one here besides me.* —**Usage.** See BESIDE.

be•siege (bi sēj'), *v.t.,* **-sieged, -sieg•ing. 1.** to lay siege to. **2.** to crowd around. **3.** to importune, as with requests. —**be•sieg'er,** *n.*

be•smear (bi smēr'), *v.t.* to smear.

be•smirch (bi smûrch'), *v.t.* to soil; sully.

be•som (bē'zəm), *n.* a broom, esp. one of twigs.

be•sot (bi sot'), *v.t.,* **-sot•ted, -sot•ting. 1.** to stupefy with drink. **2.** to make stupid or foolish, esp. with infatuation.

be•sought (bi sôt'), *v.* a pt. and pp. of BESEECH.

be•spat•ter (bi spat'ər), *v.t.* to spatter.

be•speak (bi spēk'), *v.t.,* **-spoke, -spo•ken** or **-spoke, -speak•ing. 1.** to reserve beforehand. **2.** to show; indicate.

best (best), *adj., superl. of* **good** *with* **better** *as compar.* **1.** of the highest quality or standing. **2.** most advantageous or suitable. **3.** *the best part of a day.* —*adv., superl. of* **well** *with* **better** *as compar.* **4.** most excellently. **5.** in or to the highest degree. —*n.* **6.** someone or something that is best. **7.** salutations: *Give them my best.* —*v.t.* **8.** to get the better of; beat or surpass. —*Idiom.* **9. at best,** even under the most favorable circumstances. **10. get the best of, a.** to gain the advantage over. **b.** to defeat; subdue. **11. make the best of,** to cope with; accept.

bes•tial (bes'chəl, bēs'-), *adj.* **1.** of or having the form of a beast. **2.** brutal or inhuman. —**bes'ti•al'i•ty** (-chē al'i tē), *n.* —**bes'ti•al•ly,** *adv.*

bes'ti•ar'y (-chē er'ē), *n., pl.* **-ar•ies.** a collection of moralizing tales about real and mythical animals.

be•stir (bi stûr'), *v.t.,* **-stirred, -stir•ring.** to rouse to action.

best' man', *n.* the chief attendant of the bridegroom at a wedding.

be•stow (bi stō′), *v.t.* to present as a gift; confer. —**be•stow′al,** *n.*

be•stride (bi strīd′), *v.t.,* **-strode** or **-strid, -strid•den** or **-strid, -strid•ing.** **1.** to get or be astride of. **2.** to step over with long strides.

best′sell′er, *n.* a product, as a book, that among those of its class sells very well at a given time. —**best′-sell′ing,** *adj.*

bet (bet), *v.,* **bet** or **bet•ted, bet•ting,** *n.* —*v.t.* **1.** to pledge (money, etc.) as a forfeit if one's forecast of a future event is wrong. **2.** to maintain as in a bet. —*v.i.* **3.** to make a bet. —*n.* **4.** a pledge made in betting. **5.** a thing pledged. **6.** something bet on. **7.** a person or thing considered a good choice. —*Idiom.* **8. bet one's boots,** to be sure of something.

be•ta (bā′tə; *esp. Brit.* bē′-), *n., pl.* **-tas.** the second letter of the Greek alphabet (B, β).

be′ta block′er, *n.* a drug used to reduce the heart rate or force in the treatment of angina, arrhythmias, or hypertension.

be′ta car′otene, *n.* the most abundant of various isomers of carotene, found in dark yellow or green fruits and vegetables.

be•take (bi tāk′), *v.t.,* **-took, -tak•en, -tak•ing.** to cause (oneself) to go.

be′ta par′ticle, *n.* an electron or positron emitted from an atomic nucleus during radioactive decay.

be′ta ray′, *n.* a stream of beta particles.

be′ta rhythm′, *n.* a pattern of high-frequency brain waves (**be′ta waves′**) observed in normal persons upon sensory stimulation or when they are engaging in purposeful mental activity.

be′ta test′, *n.* a test of new or updated computer software or hardware conducted at select user sites just prior to release of the product. —**be′ta-test′,** *v.t., v.i.*

be•tel (bēt′l), *n.* an East Indian pepper plant.

be′tel nut′, *n.* the seed of a palm, chewed in many tropical regions together with slaked lime and betel leaves as a stimulant.

bête noire (bāt′ nwär′, bet′), *n., pl.* **bêtes noires** (bāt′ nwärz′, bet′). a person or thing disliked or dreaded. [< F]

Beth•a•ny (beth′ə nē), *n.* a village in W Jordan, at the foot of the Mount of Olives; home of Lazarus; site of Jesus' ascension into heaven. Mark 11:1; Matt. 21:17; 16:6; John 12:1; Luke 24:50–51.

Beth•el (beth′əl, -el, beth′el′), *n.* a village in W Jordan, near Jerusalem; dream of Jacob. Gen. 28:19.

Be•thes•da (bə thez′də), *n.* a pool in Biblical Jerusalem believed to have healing powers. John 5:2–4.

be•think (bi thingk′), *v.t.,* **-thought, -think•ing.** to cause (oneself) to consider or recollect.

Beth•le•hem (beth′li hem′, -lē əm), *n.* a town in the West Bank, near Jerusalem: birthplace of Jesus and David. 16,313

Beth Mid•rash (*Seph.* bet′ mē dräsh′), *n. Hebrew.* a place where Jews gather to study religious writings.

Beth′ Pe′or (pē′ôr), *n.* the place where Moses delivered his final exhortation to the Israelites and where he was later buried. Deut. 4:44–46; 34:1–6.

Beth•sa•i•da (beth sā′i də), *n.* an ancient town in N Israel, near the N shore of the Sea of Galilee.

Beth′ She′mesh (shē′mesh), *n.* **1.** sometimes assumed to be the birthplace of Samson. Judg. 13–16. **2.** the place where men died after looking into the ark of the covenant. I Sam. 6:19–21.

be•tide (bi tīd′), *v.t., v.i.,* **-tid•ed, -tid•ing.** to happen (to).

be•times (bi tīmz′), *adv.* early; in good time.

be•to•ken (bi tō′kən), *v.t.* **1.** to give evidence of; indicate. **2.** to portend.

be•tray (bi trā′), *v.t.* **1.** to deliver or expose to an enemy by treachery. **2.** to be unfaithful or disloyal to. **3.** to reveal (something meant to be hidden). **4.** to seduce and desert. —**be•tray′al,** *n.* —**be•tray′er,** *n.*

be•troth (bi trōᵺ′, -trôth′), *v.t.* to promise to give in marriage. —**be•troth′al,** *n.*

be•trothed′, *adj.* **1.** engaged to be married. —*n.* **2.** the person to whom one is betrothed.

bet•ter (bet′ər), *adj., compar. of* **good** *with* **best** *as superl.* **1.** of superior quality or excellence. **2.** of superior suitability; preferable. **3.** larger; greater. **4.** improved in health. —*adv., compar. of* **well** *with* **best** *as superl.* **5.** in a more excellent manner. **6.** more completely. **7.** more: *lives better than a mile away.* —*v.t.* **8.** to make better; improve. **9.** to surpass or exceed. —*n.* **10.** something that is preferable. **11.** Usu., **-ters.** those superior to oneself. —*Idiom.* **12. get the better of,** to prevail against. —*Saying.* **13. better safe than sorry,** precautions should be taken to avoid misfortune.

bet′ter•ment, *n.* the act of bettering; improvement.

bet′tor or **bet′ter,** *n.* one who bets.

be•tween (bi twēn′), *prep.* **1.** in the space separating. **2.** intermediate to in time, quantity, or degree. **3.** linking; connecting. **4.** by the common participation of: *Between us, we can finish the job.* **5.** distinguishing one from the other in comparison. **6.** existing confidentially for: *We'll keep this between ourselves.* —*adv.* **7.** in the intervening space or time. —**Usage.** BETWEEN YOU AND I, though occasionally heard in the speech of educated persons, is not the commonly accepted form. Since the pronouns are objects of the preposition BETWEEN, the usual form is *between you and me.* See also AMONG.

be•twixt′ (-twikst′), *prep., adv.* **1.** between. —*Idiom.* **2. betwixt and between,** in the middle.

Beu•lah (byōō′lə), *n.* the land of Israel. Isa. 62:4. [< Heb *bə′ūlāh* lit., married woman]

bev•el (bev′al), *n., v.,* **-eled, -el•ing** or (*esp. Brit.*) **-elled, -el•ling.** —*n.* **1.** the inclination or angle that one line or surface makes with another when not at right angles. **2.** an adjustable tool for laying out or measuring angles. —*v.t.* **3.** to cut at a bevel. —*v.i.* **4.** to slant; incline.

bev′el gear′, *n.* a gear meshing with a similar gear set at right angles.

bev•er•age (bev′ər ij), *n.* any drinkable liquid, esp. other than water. [< AF, = *bevre* to drink (< L *bibere*) + *-age*]

Bev′erly Hills′ (bev′ər lē), *n.* a city in SW California, surrounded by the city of Los Angeles. 32,367.

bev•y (bev′ē), *n., pl.* **-bev•ies. 1.** a group of birds, esp. quail. **2.** a large group or collection.

be•wail (bi wāl′), *v.t.* to express deep sorrow for; lament.

be•ware (bi wâr′), *v.t., v.i.* **1.** to be wary, cautious, or careful (of). —*Saying.* **2. Beware of Greeks bearing gifts,** be cautious in accepting gifts from enemies. Virgil, *The Aeneid,* Book II.

be•wigged (bi wigd′), *adj.* wearing a wig.

be•wil•der (bi wil′dər), *v.t.* to confuse or puzzle completely. —**be•wil′der•ment,** *n.*

be•witch (bi wich′), *v.t.* **1.** to affect by witchcraft or magic. **2.** to charm; fascinate. —**be•witch′ing•ly,** *adv.* —**be•witch′ment,** *n.*

bey (bā), *n., pl.* **beys.** (formerly) a title of respect for Turkish dignitaries.

be•yond (bē ond′), *prep.* **1.** on, at, or to the farther side of. **2.** more distant than. **3.** outside the limits or reach of. —*adv.* **4.** farther on or away. **5. the beyond, a.** that which is at a great distance. **b.** Also, **the great beyond.** life after death.

bez•el (bez′əl), *n.* **1.** the diagonal face at the end of the blade of a chisel or the like. **2.** the part of a cut gem above the setting. **3.** a grooved rim holding a gem or watch crystal in its setting.

bf or **b.f.,** boldface.

Bho•pal (bō päl′), *n.* a city in central India. 672,000.

Bhu•tan (bōō tän′), *n.* a kingdom in the Himalayas, NE of India. 1,865,191. —**Bhu•tan•ese** (bōōt′n ēz′, -ēs′), *n., pl.* **-ese,** *adj.*

Bi, *Chem. Symbol.* bismuth.

bi-, a combining form meaning: twice (*biannual*); two (*bilateral*). —**Usage.** Most words referring to periods of time and prefixed by BI- can be ambiguous. Since BI- can be taken to mean either "twice each" or "every two," a word like *biweekly* can be understood as "twice each week" or "every two weeks." Confusion is often avoided by using the prefix SEMI- meaning "twice each" or by using the appropriate phrases: *twice a week; every two months.*

bi•an•nu•al (bī an′yōō əl), *adj.* occurring twice a year; semiannual. —**bi•an′nu•al•ly,** *adv.*

bi•as (bī′əs), *n., adv., v.,* **bi•ased, bi•as•ing** or (*esp.* Brit.) **bi•assed, bi•as•sing.** —*n.* **1.** a diagonal line running across a woven fabric. **2.** a particular tendency or inclination; prejudice. —*adv.* **3.** in a diagonal manner. —*v.t.* **4.** to cause partiality in; prejudice.

bi•ath•lon (bī ath′lon) *n.* **1.** an athletic contest combining cross-country skiing with rifle shooting. **2.** an athletic contest comprising any two consecutive events.

bib (bib), *n.* **1.** a shield of cloth, paper, etc., tied under the chin to protect the clothing during a meal. **2.** the upper front part of an apron, overalls, or the like.

Bib., **1.** Bible. **2.** biblical.

Bi•ble (bī′bəl), *n.* **1.** the sacred writings of the Christian religion, comprising the Old and New Testaments. **2.** the sacred writings of the Jewish religion; Old Testament. **3.** (*l.c.*) a reference work esteemed for its usefulness and authority. [< OF < ML < Gk *biblíon* book, papyrus roll, der. of *býblos* papyrus, after *Býblos,* Phoenician port known for export of papyrus] —**Bib•li•cal, bib•li•cal** (bib′li kəl), *adj.*

biblio-, a combining form meaning book (*bibliophile*).

bib•li•og•ra•phy (bib′lē og′rə fē), *n., pl.* **-phies.** a list of writings compiled upon some common principle, as authorship or subject. —**bib′li•og′ra•pher,** *n.* —**bib′li•o•graph′i•cal,** *adj.*

bib•li•o•phile′ (-ə fīl′), *n.* one who loves or collects books.

bib•u•lous (bib′yə ləs), *adj.* fond of or addicted to drink.

bi•cam•er•al (bī kam′ər əl), *adj.* having two branches, as a legislative body.

bi•car′bo•nate of so′da (bī kär′bə nit, -nāt′), *n.* SODIUM BICARBONATE.

bi•cen•ten′ni•al, *adj.* **1.** lasting 200 years. **2.** occurring every 200 years. —*n.* **3.** a 200th anniversary.

bi•ceph•a•lous (bī sef′ə ləs), *adj.* having two heads.

bi•ceps (-seps), *n., pl.* **-ceps, -ceps•es** (-sep siz). a muscle with two points of origin, as the muscle at the front of the upper arm.

bick•er (bik′ər), *v.i.* **1.** to engage in peevish argument. —*n.* **2.** a peevish quarrel. —**bick′er•er,** *n.*

bi•con′cave, *adj.* concave on both sides.

bi•con′vex, *adj.* convex on both sides.

bi•cus′pid, *adj.* **1.** having two cusps or points, as certain teeth. —*n.* **2.** PREMOLAR (def. 1).

bi•cy•cle (bī′si kəl), *n., v.,* **-cled, -cling.** —*n.* **1.** a vehicle with two wheels in tandem, propelled by pedals and having handlebars for steering. —*v.i.* **2.** to ride a bicycle. —**bi′cy•clist,** *n.*

bid (bid), *v.,* **bade** or **bid, bid•den** or **bid, bid•ding,** *n.* —*v.t.* **1.** to command; order. **2.** to say as a greeting or wish. **3.** to offer (a sum) as the price one will charge or pay. **4.** to enter a bid of (a given quantity or suit at cards). —*v.i.* **5.** to make a bid. —*n.* **6.** the act of bidding. **7.** (in card games) **a.** an offer to make a specified number of points or tricks. **b.** the amount bid. **c.** a turn to bid. **8.** an invitation. **9.** an attempt to attain some goal or purpose. —**bid′der,** *n.*

bid•dy[1] (bid′ē), *n., pl.* **-dies.** HEN.

bid•dy[2] (bid′ē), *n., pl.* **-dies.** a fussy old woman.

bide (bīd), *v.i.,* **bid•ed** or **bode, bid•ed, bid•ing.** **1.** to wait; remain. —*Idiom.* **2.** bide one's time, to wait for a favorable opportunity.

bi•det (bē dā′, bi det′), *n.* a low, basinlike bathroom fixture used for bathing the genital and perineal areas.

bi•en•ni•al (bī en′ē əl), *adj.* **1.** happening every two years. **2.** lasting for two years. **3.** (of a plant) living for two years, blooming and forming seeds in the second year. —*n.* **4.** an event occurring once in two years. **5.** a biennial plant.

bier (bēr), *n.* a frame on which a corpse or coffin is laid before burial.

bi•fo•cal (bī fō′kəl, bī′fō′-), *adj.* **1.** (of an eyeglass lens) having two portions, one for near and one for far vision. —*n.* **2.** **-cals,** eyeglasses with bifocal lenses.

bi•fur•cate (bī′fər kāt′), *v.t., v.i.,* **-cat•ed, -cat•ing.** to divide or fork into two branches. —**bi′fur•cate′** (-kāt′, -kit), *adj.* —**bi′fur•ca′tion,** *n.*

big (big), *adj.,* **big•ger, big•gest,** *adv.* —*adj.* **1.** large in size, amount, etc. **2.** of major importance. **3.** grown-up; mature. **4.** magnanimous: *a big heart.* **5.** boastful. **6.** loud: *a big voice.* **7.** pregnant. —*adv.* **8.** boastfully. **9.** successfully. —**big′ness,** *n.* —*Proverb.* **10. The bigger they are, the harder they fall,** failure is more conspicuous in the powerful.

big•a•my (big′ə mē), *n.* the act of marrying one person while still being legally married to another. —**big′a•mist,** *n.* —**big′a•mous,** *adj.*

big′ bang′ the′ory, *n.* a theory that the universe began with an explosion of a dense mass of matter and is still expanding.

Big′ Dip′per, *n.* See under DIPPER (def. 2a).

Big′ Five′, *n.* **1.** the United States, Great Britain, France, Italy, and Japan during World War I and at the Paris Peace Conference in 1919. **2.** (after World War II) the United States, Great Britain, the Soviet Union, China, and France.

big′ gov′ernment, *n.* large, inefficient government.

big′heart′ed, *adj.* generous; kind.

big′horn′, *n., pl.* **-horns, -horn.** a wild sheep of the Rocky Mountains with large, curving horns.

bighorn

bight (bīt), *n.* **1.** a loop or slack part in a rope. **2.** a curve in the shore of a sea or river. **3.** a bay or gulf.

big′mouth′, *n.* a loud, talkative, and usu. indiscreet or boastful person.

big•ot (big′ət), *n.* a person who is extremely intolerant of another's creed, belief, or opinion. —**big′ot•ed,** *adj.* —**big′ot•ry,** *n.*

big′ shot′, *n. Informal.* an important or influential person.

big′ tent′, *n. Informal.* a political party that welcomes a wide range of opinions.

bike (bīk), *n., v.,* **biked, bik•ing.** —*n.* **1.** a bicycle, motorbike, or motorcycle. —*v.i.* **2.** to ride a bike. —**bik′er,** *n.*

bi•ki•ni (bi kē′nē), *n., pl.* **-nis.** **1.** a very brief two-piece bathing suit for women. **2.** a very brief bathing suit for men. **3.** underwear briefs fitted low on the hip.

bi•lat•er•al (bī lat′ər əl), *adj.* **1.** having two sides. **2.** of or involving two or both sides, factions, or the like. —**bi•lat′er•al•ly,** *adv.*

bile (bīl), *n.* **1.** a bitter yellow or greenish liquid, secreted by the liver, that aids in digestion of fats. **2.** ill temper.

bilge (bilj), *n.* **1.** the lowest interior part of a ship's hull. **2.** Also called **bilge′ wa′ter.** seepage accumulated in bilges. **3.** *Slang.* foolish or worthless talk or ideas.

Bil•hah (bil′hə), *n.* the mother of Dan and Naphtali. Gen. 30:1–8.

bi•lin•gual (bī ling′gwəl), *adj.* **1.** able to speak two languages. **2.** expressed in, involving, or using two languages. —**bi•lin′gual•ism,** *n.*

bil•ious (bil′yəs), *adj.* **1.** pertaining to bile. **2.** suffering from or attended by trouble with the liver. **3.** peevish; irritable. —**bil′ious•ness,** *n.*

bilk (bilk), *v.t.* to defraud; cheat. —**bilk′er,** *n.*

bill¹ (bil), *n.* **1.** a statement of money owed for goods or services supplied. **2.** a piece of paper money. **3.** a draft of a statute presented to a legislature. **4.** a public notice or advertisement. **5.** any written statement of particulars. **6.** a written statement, usu. of complaint, presented to a court. **7.** entertainment scheduled for presentation; program. —*v.t.* **8.** to send a bill. **9.** to enter (charges) in a bill. **10.** to advertise by bill or public notice. —*Idiom.* **11. fill the bill,** to fulfill a particular purpose or need.

bill² (bil), *n.* **1.** the parts of a bird's jaws that are covered with a horny or leathery sheath; beak. —*v.i.* **2.** to join bills, as doves. —*Idiom.* **3. bill and coo,** to kiss or fondle and whisper endearments.

bill′board′, *n.* a flat board, usu. outdoors, on which large advertisements are posted.

bil•let (bil′it), *n.* **1.** lodging for a soldier in a nonmilitary building. **2.** an official order directing the addressee to provide such lodging. **3.** a job; position; appointment. —*v.t.* **4.** to provide lodging for; quarter.

bil•let-doux (bil′ā dōō′), *n., pl.* **bil•lets-doux** (bil′ā-dōōz′, -dōō′). a love letter. [< F]

bill′fold′, *n.* WALLET.

bil•liards (bil′yərdz), *n.* a game played with hard balls that are driven with a cue on a cloth-covered table. —**bill′liard,** *adj.*

bill′ing, *n.* **1.** the relative prominence given to a performer or act on a marquee or playbill. **2.** advertising; publicity.

bil•lings•gate (bil′ingz gāt′), *n.* coarse or vulgar abusive language. [after the kind of speech considered customary at *Billingsgate*, a London fish market]

bil•lion (bil′yən), *n., pl.* **-lions, -lion.** a cardinal number represented in the U.S. by 1 followed by 9 zeros, and in Great Britain by 1 followed by 12 zeros. —**bil′lionth,** *adj., n.*

bil′lion•aire′ (-âr′), *n.* a person with assets worth a billion or more dollars, pounds, etc.

bill′ of exchange′, *n.* a written order to pay a specified sum of money to the person indicated.

bill′ of fare′, *n.* a menu.

bill′ of lad′ing, *n.* a receipt given by a carrier for goods accepted for transportation.

Bill′ of Rights′, *n.* **1.** a formal statement of the rights of the people of the United States, incorporated in the Constitution as Amendments 1–10, and in all state constitutions. **2.** (*l.c.*) a statement of the fundamental rights of any group of people. **3.** an English statute of 1689 confirming the rights and liberties of the people.

bill′ of sale′, *n.* a document transferring title in personal property from seller to buyer.

bil•low (bil′ō), *n.* **1.** a great wave or surge of the sea. **2.** any surging mass: *billows of smoke.* —*v.i.* **3.** to rise, roll, or swell in billows. —**bil′low•y,** *adj.*

bil•ly (bil′ē), *n., pl.* **-lies.** a heavy wooden stick used as a weapon, esp. by the police. Also called **bil′ly club′.**

bil′ly goat′, *n.* a male goat.

bi•month•ly (bī munth′lē), *adj., n., pl.* **-lies.** —*adj.* **1.** occurring every two months. **2.** occurring twice a month; semimonthly. —*n.* **3.** a bimonthly publication. —*Usage.* See BI-.

bin (bin), *n.* a box or enclosed place for storing grain, coal, etc.

bi•na•ry (bī′nə rē), *adj., n., pl.* **-ries.** —*adj.* **1.** consisting of, indicating, or involving two. **2.** of or being a system of numerical notation to the base 2, in which each place of a number, expressed as 0 or 1, corresponds to a power of 2. **3.** of or involving a choice between two alternatives. —*n.* **4.** a whole composed of two.

bind (bīnd), *v.,* **bound, bind•ing,** *n.* —*v.t.* **1.** to fasten or encircle with a band, cord, etc. **2.** to bandage (often fol. by *up*). **3.** to fix in place by girding. **4.** to cause to cohere. **5.** to constrain or obligate, as by oath or law. **6.** to secure (a book) within a cover. **7.** to cover the edge of, as for protection or ornament. **8.** (of clothing) to chafe or restrict (the wearer). **9.** to constipate. —*v.i.* **10.** to cohere. **11.** to be obligatory. —*n.* **12.** something that binds. **13.** a difficult situation or predicament. —**bind′er,** *n.*

bind•er•y (bīn′də rē), *n., pl.* **-er•ies.** a place where books are bound.

bind′ing, *n.* **1.** anything that binds. **2.** the covering within which the leaves of a book are bound. —*adj.* **3.** having power to bind; obligatory.

binge (binj), *n., v.,* **binged, bing•ing.** —*n.* **1.** a bout of excessive indulgence, as in eating or drinking. —*v.i.* **2.** to go on a binge.

bin•go (bing′gō), *n.* a game of chance similar to lotto, usu. played by a large number of persons in competition for prizes.

bin•na•cle (bin′ə kəl), *n.* a stand or housing for a nautical compass.

bin•oc•u•lar (bə nok′yə lər, bī-), *n.* **1.** Usu., **-lars.** an optical instrument for use with both eyes, consisting of two small telescopes fitted together side by side. —*adj.* **2.** involving both eyes. [< L *bin-* double + *oculus* eye]

bi•no•mi•al (bī nō′mē əl), *n.* **1.** an algebraic expression that is a sum or difference of two terms, as $3x + 2y$ or $x^2 − 4x.$ **2.** a taxonomic name consisting of a generic and a specific term, used to designate species. —*adj.* **3.** pertaining to a term that has two parts.

bio-, a combining form meaning life or living organisms (*biodegradable*).

bi•o•chem•is•try (bī′ō kem′ə strē), *n.* the study of the chemical substances and processes of living matter. —**bi′o•chem′i•cal,** *adj.* —**bi′o•chem′ist,** *n.*

bi′o•de•grad′a•ble, *adj.* capable of decaying through the action of living organisms: *biodegradable paper.* —**bi′o•de•grad′a•bil′i•ty,** *n.*

bi′o•di•ver′si•ty, *n.* diversity of plant and animal species in an environment.

bi′o•eth′ics, *n.* a field concerned with the ethical implications of certain medical procedures, as genetic engineering.

bi′o•feed′back′, *n.* a method of learning to modify a particular body function, as blood pressure, by monitoring it with the aid of an electronic device.

bi•og•ra•phy (bī og′rə fē), *n., pl.* **-phies.** a written account of another person's life. —**bi•og′ra•pher,** *n.* —**bi′o•graph′i•cal** (-ə graf′i kəl), *adj.*

biol., **1.** biological. **2.** biologist. **3.** biology.

biolog′ical clock′, *n.* **1.** an innate mechanism of the body that regulates its rhythmic and periodic cycles. **2.** such a mechanism perceived as marking the passage of one's ability to bear children.

biolog′ical war′fare, *n.* the wartime use of pathogenic organisms or toxins to destroy resources or human lives.

bi•ol•o•gy (bī ol′ə jē), *n.* **1.** the scientific study of life or living matter in all its forms and processes. **2.** the biological phenomena characteristic of an organism. —**bi′o•log′i•cal** (-ə loj′i kəl), *adj.* —**bi′o•log′i•cal•ly,** *adv.* —**bi•ol′o•gist,** *n.*

bi•on•ic (bī on′ik), *adj.* **1.** having normal functions enhanced by electronic devices and mechanical parts. **2.** of bionics.

bi•on′ics, *n.* the design of electronic devices and mechanical parts that perform tasks after the manner of humans and animals.

bi′o•phys′ics (bī′ō-), *n.* the branch of biology that applies the methods of physics to the study of biological processes. —**bi′o•phys′i•cist,** *n.*

bi•o•pic (bī′ō pik′), *n.* a biographical motion picture.

bi•op•sy (bī′op sē), *n., pl.* **-sies.** the removal for diagnostic study of a piece of tissue from a living body.

bi′o•rhythm (bī′ō-), *n.* an innate periodicity in an

organism's physiological processes, as sleep and wake cycles.

bi′o•sphere′ (bī′ə-), *n.* the part of the earth's crust, waters, and atmosphere that supports life.

bi′o•tech•nol′o•gy (bī′ō-), *n.* the use of living organisms in the manufacture of drugs or other products or for environmental management.

bi•o•tin (bī′ə tin), *n.* a crystalline, water-soluble vitamin of the vitamin B complex, present in all living cells.

bi•par•ti•san (bī pär′tə zən), *adj.* representing, characterized by, or including members from two parties or factions. —**bi•par′ti•san•ship′,** *n.*

bi•par′tite (-pär′tīt), *adj.* **1.** divided into or consisting of two parts. **2.** shared by two; joint.

bi′ped (-ped), *n.* a two-footed animal.

bi′plane′, *n.* an airplane with two sets of wings, one above the other.

bi•po′lar, *adj.* **1.** having two poles, as the earth. **2.** pertaining to or found at both polar regions. —**bi′po•lar′i•ty,** *n.*

bipo′lar disor′der, *n.* manic-depressive illness.

bi•ra′cial, *adj.* representing or combining members of two races.

birch (bûrch), *n.* **1.** a tree with a smooth, laminated outer bark and close-grained wood. **2.** the wood itself. **3.** a bundle of birch twigs used for whipping.

bird (bûrd), *n.* **1.** a warm-blooded, egg-laying vertebrate having feathers and forelimbs modified into wings. —***Idiom.* 2. for the birds,** *Informal.* worthless. —***Proverb.* 3. A bird in the hand is worth two in the bush,** it's better to possess something in fact now than to count on possessing something better in the future. **4. Birds of a feather flock together,** those with similar concerns tend to congregate.

bird′ie, *n.* a score of one stroke under par on a golf hole.

bird′ of par′adise, *n.* any of various songbirds of the New Guinea region, the males of which have elegant plumes.

bird's′-eye′, *adj.* **1.** seen from above; panoramic: *a bird's-eye view of the city.* **2.** superficial; general. **3.** having markings resembling birds' eyes: *bird's-eye tweed.*

bi•ret•ta (bə ret′ə), *n.,* pl. **-tas.** a stiff square cap with three or four upright projecting pieces, worn by ecclesiastics.

Bir•ming•ham (bûr′ming əm *for 1;* -ham′ *for 2*), *n.* **1.** a city in central England. 1,084,600. **2.** a city in central Alabama. 264,527.

birth (bûrth), *n.* **1.** an act or instance of being born. **2.** the act of bringing forth offspring. **3.** lineage; descent. **4.** any coming into existence. —***Idiom.* 5. give birth to, a.** to bear (a child). **b.** to originate.

birth′ control′, *n.* regulation of the number of children born through control or prevention of conception.

birth′day′, *n.* the anniversary of a birth.

birth′mark′, *n.* a minor disfigurement or blemish on a person's skin at birth.

birth′place′, *n.* place of birth or origin.

birth′rate′, *n.* the number of births in a place in a given time, usu. expressed as a quantity per 1000 of population.

birth′right′, *n.* any right or privilege to which a person is entitled by birth.

birth′stone′, *n.* a gem traditionally associated with the month of one's birth.

bis•cuit (bis′kit), *n.* **1.** a small, soft, raised bread, usu. leavened with baking powder or soda. **2.** *Chiefly Brit.* a cracker or cookie. [< MF *biscuit* seamen's bread, lit., twice cooked]

bi•sect (bī sekt′), *v.t.* **1.** to cut or divide into two equal parts. **2.** to intersect or cross. —*v.i.* **3.** to split into two, as a road; fork. —**bi•sec′tor,** *n.*

bi•sex′u•al, *adj.* **1.** of both sexes. **2.** sexually responsive to both sexes. —*n.* **3.** a person who is bisexual. —**bi′sex•u•al′i•ty,** *n.*

Bish•kek (bish kek′), *n.* the capital of Kyrgyzstan. 616,000.

Bish•op (bish′əp), *n.* **Elizabeth,** 1911–79, U.S. poet.

bish′op•ric (-rik), *n.* the see, diocese, or office of a bishop.

Bis•marck (biz′märk), *n.* **1. Otto von,** 1815–98, German statesman. **2.** the capital of North Dakota. 44,485.

bis•muth (biz′məth), *n.* a brittle, grayish white metallic element used in the manufacture of fusible alloys and in medicine. *Symbol:* Bi; *at. wt.:* 208.980; *at. no.:* 83.

bi•son (bī′sən), *n.,* pl. **-son.** a North American buffalo, having a large head and high, humped shoulders.

bisque (bisk), *n.* a thick cream soup, esp. of puréed shellfish or vegetables.

Bis•sau (bi sou′), *n.* the capital of Guinea-Bissau. 109,214.

bis•tro (bis′trō, bē′strō), *n.* a small, modest, European-style restaurant or café.

bit¹ (bit), *n.* **1.** the mouthpiece of a bridle. **2.** a removable drilling or boring tool for use in a brace, drill press, etc.

bit² (bit), *n.* **1.** a small piece or quantity of something. **2.** a short time. **3.** a stereotypic set of behaviors, attitudes, or actions associated with a particular role, situation, etc.: *the whole Wall Street bit.* **4.** a very small role, as in a movie. **5.** *Informal.* an amount equal to 12½ cents: *two bits.* —***Idiom.* 6. a bit,** somewhat: *a bit sleepy.* **7. bit by bit,** gradually. **8. do one's bit,** to contribute one's share to an effort.

bit³ (bit), *n.* a single, basic unit of computer information, valued at either 0 or 1 to indicate the choice made between two alternatives. [*b(inary)* + *(dig)it*]

bitch (bich), *n.* **1.** a female dog. **2.** a female of canines generally.

bite (bīt), *v.,* **bit, bit•ten** or **bit, bit•ing,** *n.* —*v.t.* **1.** to cut, wound, or tear with the teeth. **2.** to grip with the teeth. **3.** to sting, as an insect. **4.** to cause to sting or smart. **5.** to corrode. —*v.i.* **6.** to attack with the jaws, bill, sting, etc. **7.** (of fish) to take bait. **8.** to accept a deceptive offer or suggestion. **9.** to take a firm hold. —*n.* **10.** the act of biting. **11.** a wound made by biting. **12.** a cutting, stinging, or nipping effect. **13.** a small meal. **14.** a morsel of food. **15.** an exacted portion: *the tax bite.*

bit′ing, *adj.* **1.** nipping; keen. **2.** cutting; sarcastic.

bit•ter (bit′ər), *adj.,* **-ter•er, -ter•est. 1.** having a harsh, acrid taste. **2.** hard to bear; grievous. **3.** causing sharp pain: *a bitter chill.* **4.** characterized by intense hostility or resentment. **5.** experienced at great cost: *a bitter lesson.* —***Idiom.* 6. take the bitter with the sweet,** to accept unpleasant as well as pleasant things. —**bit′ter•ly,** *adv.* —**bit′ter•ness,** *n.*

bit•tern (bit′ərn), *n.* any of several wading birds of the heron family that inhabit reedy marshes.

bit′ters, *n.* (*used with a pl. v.*) a usu. alcoholic liquor flavored with bitter herbs and used in mixed drinks or as a tonic.

bit′ter•sweet′, *adj.* **1.** both bitter and sweet to the taste. **2.** both pleasant and painful. —*n.* **3.** a climbing or trailing plant with scarlet berries. **4.** a climbing plant bearing orange capsules opening to expose red-coated seeds.

bi•tu•men (bī tōō′mən, -tyōō′-), *n.* any of various natural substances, as asphalt, consisting mainly of hydrocarbons. —**bi•tu′mi•nous,** *adj.*

bitu′minous coal′, *n.* a coal rich in volatile hydrocarbons and burning with a yellow, smoky flame.

bi•va•lent (bī vā′lənt, biv′ə-), *adj.* having a valence of two.

bi′valve′, *n.* a mollusk, as the oyster or clam, having two shells hinged together.

biv•ou•ac (biv′ōō ak′), *n.,* *v.,* **-acked, -ack•ing.** —*n.* **1.** a military encampment made with tents or improvised shelters. —*v.i.* **2.** to assemble in a bivouac.

bi•week′ly (bī-), *adj.* **1.** occurring every two weeks.

2. occurring twice a week; semiweekly. —**Usage.** See BI-.

bi•zarre (bi zär′), *adj.* markedly unusual; strange; odd. —**bi•zarre′ly,** *adv.*

Bi•zet (bē zā′), *n.* **Georges,** 1838–75, French composer.

Bk, *Chem. Symbol.* berkelium.

bk., **1.** bank. **2.** book.

bl., **1.** bale. **2.** barrel. **3.** black. **4.** blue.

b/l or **B/L,** bill of lading.

blab (blab), *v.,* **blabbed, blab•bing.** —*v.t.* **1.** to reveal indiscreetly and thoughtlessly. —*v.i.* **2.** to chatter indiscreetly or thoughtlessly.

black (blak), *adj.,* **-er, -est,** *n., v.* —*adj.* **1.** lacking hue and brightness; opposite to white. **2.** enveloped in darkness. **3.** (*sometimes cap.*) **a.** of or belonging to any of the dark-skinned peoples of Africa, Oceania, and Australia. **b.** AFRICAN-AMERICAN (def. 2). **4.** soiled or stained. **5.** gloomy; dismal. **6.** sullen or hostile. **7.** evil or wicked. —*n.* **8.** the color opposite to white, absorbing all wavelengths of light. **9.** (*sometimes cap.*) **a.** a member of any of various dark-skinned peoples of Africa, Oceania, and Australia. **b.** AFRICAN-AMERICAN (def. 1). **10.** black clothing, esp. as a sign of mourning. —*v.t., v.i.* **11.** to make or become black. **12. black out,** to lose consciousness. **13. in the black,** operating at a profit. —**black′ness,** *n.* —**Usage.** BLACK, COLORED, and NEGRO have all been used to describe or name the dark-skinned African peoples or their descendants. COLORED, now somewhat old-fashioned, is often offensive. In the 1950s BLACK began to replace NEGRO and is still widely used and accepted. AFRICAN-AMERICAN, urged by leaders in the American black community, is now widely used in both print and speech.

black′-and-blue′, *adj.* discolored, as by bruising.

black′ball′, *v.t.* **1.** to vote against. **2.** to ostracize. —*n.* **3.** a negative vote.

black′ belt′, *n.* **1.** a black sash worn by a participant in a martial art to indicate the highest level of expertise. **2.** a person at this level.

black′ber′ry, *n., pl.* **-ries. 1.** the black or dark purple fruit of certain brambles. **2.** a plant bearing blackberries.

black′bird′, *n.* any of several American birds with black or mostly black plumage.

black′board′, *n.* a sheet of smooth, hard material, esp. dark slate, used for writing on with chalk.

Black′ Death′, *n.* an outbreak of bubonic plague that spread over Europe and Asia in the 14th century and killed an estimated quarter of the population.

black′en, *v.t.* **1.** to make black; darken. **2.** to defame; slander. —*v.i.* **3.** to grow black. —**black′en•er,** *n.*

Black′ (or **black′**) **Eng′lish,** *n.* a dialect of American English spoken by some members of black communities in North America.

black′ eye′, *n.* discoloration of the skin around the eye, resulting from a blow, bruise, etc.

black′-eyed′ Su′san, *n.* a plant having yellow, daisylike flowers with a dark center disk.

black•guard (blag′ärd, -ard), *n.* a contemptible person; scoundrel.

Black′ Hawk′ War′, *n.* a war fought in northern Illinois and present-day southern Wisconsin, 1831–32, in which U.S. regulars and militia with Indian allies defeated the Sauk and Fox Indians, led by Chief Black Hawk.

black′head′, *n.* a small, black-tipped fatty mass in a skin follicle, esp. of the face.

black′ hole′, *n.* a theoretical object in space, perhaps a collapsed star, whose gravitational field is so intense that no light can escape.

black′ light′, *n.* invisible infrared or ultraviolet light.

black′list′, *n.* **1.** a list of persons who are under suspicion, disfavor, or censure. —*v.t.* **2.** to put on a blacklist.

black′ mag′ic, *n.* sorcery.

black′mail′, *n.* **1.** a payment extorted by intimidation, as by threats of injurious revelations. —*v.t.* **2.**

to subject to blackmail. [*black* + *mail* rent, tribute (now dial.) < ON] —**black′mail′er,** *n.*

black′ mar′ket, *n.* the illicit buying and selling of goods in violation of price controls, rationing, etc.

black′out′, *n.* **1.** the extinguishing or concealment of lights, as from a power failure or as a precaution against air raids. **2.** a temporary loss of consciousness. **3.** a stoppage or suppression: *a news blackout.*

black′ pow′er, *n.* (*often caps.*) the political and economic power of black Americans, esp. as used for achieving racial equality.

Black′ Sea′, *n.* a sea between SE Europe and Asia.

black′ sheep′, *n.* a person who causes shame or embarrassment to his or her family.

black′smith′, *n.* **1.** a person who makes horseshoes and shoes horses. **2.** a person who forges objects of iron.

black′thorn′, *n.* a thorny shrub with white flowers and small plumlike fruits.

black′top′, *n., v.,* **-topped, -top•ping.** —*n.* **1.** a bituminous paving substance, as asphalt. —*v.t.* **2.** to pave with blacktop.

black′ wid′ow, *n.* a venomous black spider of warm regions, including the U.S.

blad•der (blad′ar), *n.* **1.** a saclike organ serving as a receptacle for liquids or gases, esp. urine. **2.** an inflatable object resembling a bladder.

blade (blād), *n.* **1.** the flat cutting part of an implement, as a knife. **2.** SWORD. **3. a.** the leaf of a plant, esp. grass. **b.** the broad part of a leaf. **4.** the metal part of an ice skate in contact with the ice. **5.** a thin, flat part of something, as of an oar. **6.** a dashing young man.

blad′ing, *n.* the act of skating on in-line skates.

blame (blām), *v.,* **blamed, blam•ing,** *n.* —*v.t.* **1.** to hold responsible. **2.** to find fault with; censure. **3.** to place the responsibility for (a fault, error, etc.). —*n.* **4.** censure; reproof. **5.** responsibility for anything deserving of censure. —**blam′a•ble, blame′a•ble,** *adj.* —**blame′less,** *adj.* —**blame′less•ly,** *adv.*

blame′wor′thy, *adj.* deserving blame; blamable.

blanch (blanch, blänch), *v.t.* **1.** to whiten; bleach. **2.** to boil (food) briefly, as to facilitate removal of skins. **3.** to make pale, as with fear. —*v.i.* **4.** to turn pale.

bland (bland), *adj.,* **-er, -est. 1.** pleasantly gentle or agreeable. **2.** not highly flavored. **3.** insipid; dull. —**bland′ly,** *adv.* —**bland′ness,** *n.*

blan•dish (blan′dish), *v.t, v.i.* to coax by gentle flattery; cajole. —**blan′dish•er,** *n.* —**blan′dish•ment,** *n.*

blank (blangk), *adj.,* **-er, -est,** *n., v.* —*adj.* **1.** not written or printed on. **2.** not filled in. **3.** unrelieved by ornament. **4.** void of interest. **5.** expressionless. **6.** complete; utter. —*n.* **7.** a place or space where something is lacking. **8.** a printed form containing such spaces. **9.** a cartridge containing powder only, without a bullet. —*v.t.* **10.** to keep (an opponent) from scoring in a game. **11. blank out,** to cross out or delete. —**blank′ly,** *adv.* —**blank′ness,** *n.*

blank′ check′, *n.* **1.** a check bearing a signature but no stated amount. **2.** unrestricted authority.

blan•ket (blang′kit), *n.* **1.** a large piece of soft fabric used esp. as a bed covering for warmth. **2.** any extended covering: *a blanket of snow.* —*v.t.* **3.** to cover with a blanket. **4.** to interrupt; obstruct. —*adj.* **5.** covering a large group of things, conditions, etc.

blank′ verse′, *n.* unrhymed verse written in iambic pentameter.

blare (blâr), *v.,* **blared, blar•ing,** *n.* —*v.i., v.t.* **1.** to sound or exclaim loudly. —*n.* **2.** a loud, raucous noise.

blar•ney (blär′nē), *n.* flattery; cajolery.

bla•sé (blä zā′), *adj.* indifferent or bored, as from an excess of worldly pleasures.

blas•pheme (blas fēm′), *v.,* **-phemed, -phem•ing.** —*v.t.* **1.** to speak irreverently of (God or sacred things). **2.** to speak evil of; slander. —*v.i.* **3.** to speak blasphemy.

blas′phe•my (-fa mē), *n., pl.* **-mies.** impious utterance or action concerning God or sacred things. —**blas′phe•mous,** *adj.*

blast (blast, bläst), *n.* **1.** a violent gust of wind. **2.** the blowing of a trumpet, whistle, etc. **3.** a loud, sudden sound. **4.** a vigorous criticism. **5.** an explosion. **6.** a blight. —*v.t.* **7.** to make a loud noise on; blow. **8.** to blight or wither. **9.** to shatter by or as if by an explosion. **10.** to criticize vigorously. —*v.i.* **11.** to produce a loud, blaring sound. **12.** to detonate explosives. **13. blast off,** (of a self-propelled rocket) to leave a launch pad. —*Idiom.* **14. (at) full blast,** at or with full volume or speed.

blast/ fur/nace, *n.* a furnace into which air is forced to increase the rate of combustion.

blast/off/, *n.* the launching of a rocket, guided missile, or spacecraft.

bla·tant (blāt/nt), *adj.* **1.** brazenly obvious: *a blatant error.* **2.** offensively noisy or loud. —**bla/tan·cy,** *n.* —**bla/tant·ly,** *adv.*

blath·er (blath/ər), *n.* **1.** foolish, voluble talk. —*v.i.* **2.** to talk foolishly.

blaze[1] (blāz), *n., v.,* **blazed, blaz·ing.** —*n.* **1.** a bright fire. **2.** a bright, hot glow. **3.** a vivid display. **4.** a sudden, intense outburst, as of fury. —*v.i.* **5.** to burn brightly. **6.** to shine like flame. **7.** to burst out suddenly or intensely.

blaze[2] (blāz), *n., v.,* **blazed, blaz·ing.** —*n.* **1.** a mark made on a tree to indicate a trail or boundary. **2.** a white area on the face of a horse, cow, etc. —*v.t.* **3.** to mark with blazes.

blaze[3] (blāz), *v.t.,* **blazed, blaz·ing.** to make known; proclaim.

blaz/er, *n.* a sports jacket usu. with metal buttons.

bla·zon (blā/zən), *v.t.* **1.** to proclaim. **2.** to adorn or embellish. —*n.* **3.** COAT OF ARMS. **4.** conspicuous display.

bldg., building.

bleach (blēch), *v.t., v.i.* **1.** to make or become whiter or lighter in color. —*n.* **2.** a bleaching agent.

bleach/er, *n.* Usu. **-ers.** a typically roofless section of tiered seating, esp. at an athletic stadium.

bleak (blēk), *adj.* **-er, -est. 1.** bare, desolate, and windswept. **2.** cold and raw. **3.** without hope or encouragement. —**bleak/ly,** *adv.* —**bleak/ness,** *n.*

blear·y (blēr/ē), *adj.,* **-i·er, -i·est. 1.** (of the eyes or sight) blurred or dimmed. **2.** indistinct; unclear. —**blear/i·ness,** *n.*

bleat (blēt), *n.* **1.** the cry of a sheep or goat, or a similar sound. —*v.i.* **2.** to utter a bleat.

bleed (blēd), *v.,* **bled** (bled), **bleed·ing.** —*v.i.* **1.** to lose blood. **2.** to exude sap, resin, etc. **3.** to run, as a dye. **4.** to feel pity, sorrow, or anguish. —*v.t.* **5.** to cause to lose blood. **6.** to drain sap, water, etc., from. **7.** to extort money from.

bleed/er, *n.* a hemophiliac.

bleed/ing heart/, *n.* a garden plant with rose or red heart-shaped flowers.

blem·ish (blem/ish), *v.t.* **1.** to destroy or diminish the perfection of. —*n.* **2.** a defect or flaw.

blench[1] (blench), *v.i.* to shrink; flinch; quail.

blench[2] (blench), *v.t., v.i.* to whiten; blanch.

blend (blend), *v.t.* **1.** to mix smoothly and inseparably. **2.** to prepare by mixing varieties: *to blend tobacco.* —*v.i.* **3.** to mix or mingle. **4.** to fit or relate harmoniously. **5.** to have no perceptible separation: *Sea and sky seemed to blend.* —*n.* **6.** something produced by blending.

blend/er, *n.* **1.** a person or thing that blends. **2.** an electrical appliance that chops, liquefies, or mixes foods.

bless (bles), *v.t.,* **blessed** or **blest, bless·ing. 1.** to make or pronounce holy. **2.** to request divine favor for. **3.** to bestow some benefit upon. **4.** to extol as holy. **5.** to make the sign of the cross over.

bless·ed (bles/id; *esp. for 2* blest), *adj.* **1.** sacred; holy. **2.** favored or fortunate. **3.** beatified. —**bless/ed·ly,** *adv.* —**bless/ed·ness,** *n.*

Bless/ed Sac/rament, *n.* the consecrated Host.

bless/ing, *n.* **1.** the act or words of a person who blesses. **2.** a special favor, mercy, or benefit: *the blessings of liberty.* **3.** a gift bestowed by God. **4.** the invoking of God's favor upon a person. **5.** grace said before a meal. **6.** approval. —*Idiom.* **7. blessing in**

disguise, a misfortune that has brought some benefit.

blew (bloō), *v.* pt. of BLOW[2].

blight (blīt), *n.* **1.** any of various diseases that wither or destroy plants. **2.** any cause of impairment or frustration. —*v.t.* **3.** to cause to wither. **4.** to destroy; ruin.

blimp (blimp), *n.* a small, nonrigid airship or dirigible.

blind (blīnd), *adj.,* **-er, -est,** *v., n.* —*adj.* **1.** unable to see. **2.** not characterized by control: *blind chance.* **3.** not based on reason or intelligent judgment: *blind faith.* **4.** hidden from immediate view: *a blind corner.* **5.** having no outlets: *a blind passage.* **6.** done by instruments alone: *blind flying.* **7.** of or for blind persons. —*v.t.* **8.** to make sightless. **9.** to deprive of reason or judgment. **10.** to outshine; eclipse. —*n.* **11.** something that obstructs vision. **12.** a window covering. **13.** a structure in which hunters conceal themselves. **14.** a decoy or subterfuge. —*Proverb.* **15. If the blind lead the blind, both shall fall into the ditch,** leadership is disastrous if it is ignorant. Matt. 15:14. **16. There are none so blind as those who will not see,** those who remain willfully ignorant are the blindest of all. —**blind/er,** *n.* —**blind/ly,** *adv.* —**blind/ness,** *n.*

blind/ date/, *n.* a prearranged date between two people who have not met.

blind/fold, *v.t.* **1.** to cover the eyes of, as with a cloth. —*n.* **2.** a cloth or bandage for covering the eyes. —*adj.* **3.** done with the eyes covered. **4.** rash; unthinking.

blind/ side/, *n.* **1.** the part of one's field of vision where one cannot see approaching objects. **2.** the side opposite that toward which a person is looking.

blind·side (blīnd/sīd/), *v.t.,* **-sid·ed, -sid·ing. 1.** to attack from the blind side. **2.** to attack where a person is vulnerable.

blind/ spot/, *n.* **1.** a small area of the retina that is insensitive to light. **2.** a subject about which one is uninformed or prejudiced.

blink (blingk), *v.i.* **1.** to open and close the eye, esp. involuntarily. **2.** to flash; twinkle. —*v.t.* **3.** to cause (the eyes or something else) to blink. **4. blink at,** to ignore. —*n.* **5.** the act of blinking. **6.** a gleam; glimmer. —*Idiom.* **7. on the blink,** not working properly.

blink/er, *n.* a device for flashing light signals.

blintz (blints), *n.* a thin pancake folded around a filling, as of cheese or fruit.

blip (blip), *n.* a spot of light on a radar screen indicating the position of an object.

bliss (blis), *n.* **1.** supreme happiness. **2.** heaven; paradise. —**bliss/ful,** *adj.* —**bliss/ful·ly,** *adv.* —**bliss/ful·ness,** *n.*

blis·ter (blis/tər), *n.* **1.** a thin swelling on the skin containing watery matter, as from a burn. **2.** any similar swelling. —*v.t.* **3.** to raise a blister on. **4.** to rebuke severely. —*v.i.* **5.** to become blistered.

blithe (blīth, blīth), *adj.,* **blith·er, blith·est. 1.** lighthearted; cheerful. **2.** carefree; heedless. —**blithe/ly,** *adv.* —**blithe/some,** *adj.*

blitz (blits), *n.* **1.** a sudden and overwhelming military attack, esp. an aerial bombing. **2.** any swift, vigorous attack or barrage. —*v.t.* **3.** to attack with a blitz. [shortening of *blitzkrieg,* < G, = *Blitz* lightning + *Krieg* war]

bliz·zard (bliz/ərd), *n.* a heavy and windy snowstorm.

bloat (blōt), *v.t.* **1.** to expand or distend, as with air or water. —*v.i.* **2.** to become swollen.

blob (blob), *n.* **1.** a small lump or drop of a glutinous substance. **2.** a shapeless mass.

bloc (blok), *n.* a group, as of nations or legislators, united to further common interests.

block (blok), *n.* **1.** a solid mass of wood, stone, etc., usu. with one or more flat faces. **2.** a piece of wood used in making woodcuts or wood engravings. **3.** a platform for an auctioneer. **4.** a frame enclosing one or more pulleys. **5.** an obstacle or hindrance. **6.** an obstruction in a physiological or mental process. **7.** a quantity or section taken as a unit: *a block of theater tickets.* **8.** a section of a city enclosed by intersecting streets, or the length of one side of such a section. —*v.t.* **9.** to obstruct or hinder. **10.** to mount or shape on a block. **11. block out,** to sketch or outline roughly. —**block′age,** *n.* —**block′er,** *n.*

block•ade (blo kād′), *n.,* *v.,* -**ad•ed,** -**ad•ing.** —*n.* **1.** the closing off of a port, city, etc., by ships or troops to prevent entrance or exit. **2.** any obstruction of passage. —*v.t.* **3.** to subject to a blockade.

block′ and tack′le, *n.* the ropes and blocks used in a hoisting tackle.

block′bust′er, *n.* a highly successful motion picture, novel, etc.

block′bust′ing, *n.* the practice of inducing homeowners to sell at a low price by exploiting fears that minority groups will move into the neighborhood.

block′head′, *n.* a stupid person.

block′house′, *n.* **1.** a defensive military structure used for observation and directing gunfire. **2.** a concrete structure for protecting personnel during rocket launchings.

blond (blond), *adj.,* -**er,** -**est,** *n.* —*adj.* **1.** having light-colored hair and skin. **2.** light-colored: *blond curls; blond wood.* —*n.* **3.** a blond person. —**blond′-ness,** *n.*

blonde (blond), *adj.* **1.** (of a female) blonde. —*n.* **2.** a blond woman or girl.

blood (blud), *n.* **1.** the red fluid that circulates in the vascular system of vertebrates. **2.** the vital principle; life. **3.** a person or group regarded as a source of vitality: *The company needs new blood.* **4.** bloodshed; slaughter. **5.** the sap of plants. **6.** temperament. **7.** descent from a common ancestor. —*Idiom.* **8. in cold blood,** with merciless lack of feeling. —*Proverb.* **9. Blood is thicker than water,** family ties are stronger than any others. —*Saying.* **10. I have nothing to offer but blood, toil, tears, and sweat,** patriots should be willing to sacrifice their time, efforts, and even their lives for their country: from a speech by Winston Churchill, May 13, 1940

blood′ bank′, *n.* a place where blood or plasma is collected, stored, and distributed.

blood′bath′, *n.* a ruthless slaughter; massacre.

blood′ count′, *n.* the number of red and white blood cells in a specific volume of blood.

blood′cur′dling, *adj.* arousing terror; horrifying.

blood′ed, *adj.* **1.** having blood of a specified kind: *warm-blooded.* **2.** purebred.

blood′ group′, *n.* any of the classes into which human blood can be divided, based on the presence or absence of specific antigens on red blood cells. Also called **blood′ type′.**

blood′hound′, *n.* a large hound with an acute sense of smell, used in tracking humans.

blood′mo•bile′ (-mə bēl′), *n.* a small truck with medical equipment for receiving blood donations.

blood′ poi′soning, *n.* invasion of the blood by toxic matter or microorganisms, characterized by chills, fever, and prostration.

blood′ pres′sure, *n.* the pressure of the blood against the inner walls of the blood vessels.

blood′ rela′tion (or **rel′ative**), *n.* a person related by birth.

blood′shed′, *n.* destruction of life, as in war.

blood′shot′, *adj.* (of the eyes) red because of dilated blood vessels.

blood′stream′, *n.* the blood flowing through the circulatory system.

blood′suck′er, *n.* any animal that sucks blood, esp. a leech.

blood′thirst′y, *adj.* **1.** eager to shed blood; murderous. **2.** indicating a desire for violence. —**blood′-thirst′i•ness,** *n.*

blood′ ves′sel, *n.* an artery, vein, or capillary.

blood′y, *adj.,* -**i•er,** -**i•est,** *v.,* -**ied,** -**y•ing.** —*adj.* **1.** stained with blood or bleeding. **2.** characterized by bloodshed. **3.** bloodthirsty. —*v.t.* **4.** to stain with blood. **5.** to cause to bleed. —**blood′i•ness,** *n.*

bloom (bloom), *n.* **1.** the flower of a plant. **2.**

flowers collectively. **3.** the state of flowering. **4.** the time of greatest beauty, vigor, or freshness. **5.** a glowing indicative of health or youth. **6.** a whitish, powdery coating on certain fruits and leaves. —*v.i.* **7.** to produce blossoms. **8.** to flourish. **9.** to be in a state of beauty and vigor. —**bloom′er,** *n.*

bloo•mers (bloo′mərz), *n.* (*used with a pl. v.*) loose trousers gathered at the knee, formerly worn by women for sports or as an undergarment. [after A. *Bloomer* (1818–1894), U.S. social reformer and advocate of the costume]

bloom′ing, *adj.* **1.** in bloom. **2.** flourishing.

bloop•er (bloo′pər), *n.* **1.** an embarrassing mistake, as something said on television. **2.** *Baseball.* a fly ball that carries just beyond the infield.

blos•som (blos′əm), *n.* **1.** the flower of a plant. **2.** the state of flowering. —*v.i.* **3.** to produce blossoms. **4.** to develop successfully; flourish. —**blos′som•y,** *adj.*

blot (blot), *n.,* *v.,* **blot•ted, blot•ting.** —*n.* **1.** a spot or stain, esp. of ink on paper. **2.** a blemish on a person's reputation. —*v.t.* **3.** to spot or stain. **4.** to dry or remove with absorbent paper or the like. —*v.i.* **5.** to make a blot. **6.** to become blotted. **7. blot out,** to destroy completely; obliterate.

blotch (bloch), *n.* **1.** a large, irregular spot or blot. **2.** a skin blemish. —*v.t.* **3.** to mark with blotches. —**blotch•y,** *adj.,* -**i•er,** -**i•est.**

blot′ter, *n.* **1.** a piece of blotting paper. **2.** a book in which events are recorded as they occur: *a police blotter.*

blot′ting pa′per, *n.* a soft, absorbent paper, used esp. to dry ink.

blouse (blous, blouz), *n.,* *v.,* **bloused, blous•ing.** —*n.* **1.** a garment for women and children, covering the body from the neck to the waistline. **2.** a single-breasted military jacket. —*v.i.* **3.** to puff out in a drooping fullness.

blow¹ (blō), *n.* **1.** a sudden, hard stroke with a hand, fist, or weapon. **2.** a sudden shock, calamity, etc. **3.** a sudden attack. —*Idiom.* **4. come to blows,** to begin to fight.

blow² (blō), *v.,* **blew, blown, blow•ing,** *n.* —*v.i.* **1.** (of the wind or air) to be in motion. **2.** to move along, carried by or as if by the wind. **3.** to produce a current of air, as with the mouth. **4.** to give out sound by blowing or being blown. **5.** (of horses) to pant. **6.** to brag. **7.** (of a whale) to spout. **8.** (of a fuse, tire, etc.) to stop functioning or be destroyed. —*v.t.* **9.** to drive by means of a current of air. **10.** to clear by forcing air through. **11.** to shape (glass, smoke, etc.) with a current of air. **12.** to cause to sound by blowing: *to blow a horn.* **13.** to cause to explode. **14.** to melt (a fuse). **15.** *Informal.* to squander (money). **16.** *Informal.* to bungle. **17. blow over,** to pass away; subside. **18. ~ up, a.** to explode. **b.** to lose one's temper. —*n.* **19.** a blast of air or wind. **20.** a violent windstorm. **21.** the act of blowing. —*Idiom.* **22. blow off steam,** to release tension, as by loud talking. —**blow′er,** *n.*

blow′-by-′blow′, *adj.* precisely detailed: *a blow-by-blow account.*

blow′-dry′, *v.t.,* -**dried,** -**dry•ing.** to dry or style (hair) with warm air from a hand-held electrical appliance (**blow′ dry′er**).

blow′ fly′ or **blow′fly′,** *n.* a fly that deposits its eggs on carrion, excrement, etc.

blow′gun′, *n.* a pipe through which missiles are blown by the breath.

blow′out′, *n.* **1.** a sudden bursting of an automobile tire. **2.** a lavish party or entertainment.

blow′torch′, *n.* a small apparatus that gives an extremely hot gasoline flame.

blow′up′, *n.* **1.** an explosion. **2.** a violent outburst of temper. **3.** an enlargement of a photograph.

blow′y, *adj.,* -**i•er,** -**i•est.** windy.

blowz•y or **blows•y** (blou′zē), *adj.,* -**i•er,** -**i•est.** disheveled or unkempt.

B.L.S., Bachelor of Library Science.

BLT, *n.,* *pl.* **BLTs, BLT's.** a bacon, lettuce, and tomato sandwich.

blub•ber (blub′ər), *n*. **1.** the fat of whales or other large marine mammals. **2.** a noisy weeping. —*v.i.* **3.** to weep noisily. —**blub′ber•y,** *adj.*

bludg•eon (bluj′ən), *n*. **1.** a short, heavy club with one end heavier than the other. —*v.t.* **2.** to strike with a bludgeon. **3.** to coerce; bully.

blue (bloō), *n., adj.,* **blu•er, blu•est,** *v.,* **blued, blu•ing** or **blue•ing.** —*n*. **1.** the pure color of a clear sky. **2.** something having a blue color. **3.** (*often cap.*) a member of the Union army in the American Civil War, or the army itself. Compare GRAY (def. 7). **4. the blue, a.** the sky. **b.** the sea. —*adj.* **5.** of the color blue. **6.** (of the skin) discolored. **7.** depressed or melancholy. **8.** puritanical. **9.** indecent; suggestive. —*v.t., v.i.* **10.** to make or become blue. —*Idiom.* **11. out of the blue,** suddenly and unexpectedly.

blue′ ba′by, *n*. an infant born with bluish skin resulting from a congenital heart or lung defect.

blue′bell′, *n*. any of numerous plants with blue, bell-shaped flowers.

blue′ber′ry, *n., pl.* **-ries. 1.** the edible, usu. bluish berry of various shrubs. **2.** any of these shrubs.

blue′bird′, *n*. any of several North American songbirds, the male of which is predominantly blue.

blue′ blood′, *n*. an aristocrat or noble. —**blue′-blood′ed,** *adj.*

blue′ cheese′, *n*. any of various strong-flavored cheeses streaked with bluish mold.

blue′ chip′, *n*. a common stock issued by a company with a reputation for financial strength and regular dividend payments. —**blue′-chip′,** *adj.*

blue′-col′lar, *adj.* of or designating factory workers or other manual laborers.

blue′gill′, *n*. a bluish freshwater sunfish.

blue′grass′, *n*. **1.** a grass with tufts of bluish green blades. **2.** country music, played on stringed instruments.

blue′ jay′, *n*. a common crested jay with a bright blue back and gray breast.

blue′ jeans′, *n*. (*used with a pl. v.*) trousers of blue denim.

blue′ law′, *n*. any puritanical law that forbids certain practices, as doing business, on Sunday.

blue′nose′, *n*. a puritanical person.

blue′-pen′cil, *v.t.,* **-ciled** or **-cilled, -cil•ing** or **-cil•ling.** to edit.

blue′point′, *n*. an edible Atlantic oyster, esp. one from off Blue Point, Long Island.

blue′print′, *n*. **1.** a photographic print, esp. of architectural drawings, using white lines on a blue background. **2.** a detailed plan of action. —*v.t.* **3.** to make a blueprint of.

blue′ rib′bon, *n*. the highest award or distinction, as first prize in a contest.

blues, *n*. **1. the blues,** (*used with a pl. v.*) depressed spirits; melancholy. **2.** (*used with a sing. v.*) a genre of jazz and popular music comprising songs of woe and yearning.

blue′stock′ing, *n*. a woman with considerable intellectual ability or interests.

blu•et (bloō′it), *n*. any of various plants with blue flowers.

bluff¹ (bluf), *adj.,* **-er, -est,** *n*. —*adj.* **1.** good-naturedly blunt or frank. **2.** presenting a nearly perpendicular front. —*n*. **3.** a cliff or hill with a broad, steep face.

bluff² (bluf), *v.t., v.i.* **1.** to mislead (someone) by feigning confidence. —*n*. **2.** the act of bluffing. **3.** a person who bluffs. —**bluff′er,** *n.*

blu′ing or **blue′ing,** *n*. a substance used to whiten clothes or give them a bluish tinge.

blu′ish or **blue′ish,** *adj.* slightly blue.

blun•der (blun′dər), *n*. **1.** a gross or stupid mistake. —*v.i.* **2.** to move or act clumsily or stupidly. **3.** to make a mistake, esp. through stupidity. —*v.t.* **4.** to bungle; botch. —**blun′der•er,** *n.*

blun′der•buss′ (-bus′), *n*. **1.** a short musket formerly used to scatter shot at close range. **2.** an insensitive, blundering person.

blunt (blunt), *adj.,* **-er, -est,** *v.* —*adj.* **1.** having a dull edge or point. **2.** abrupt in manner. **3.** slow in perception. —*v.t., v.i.* **4.** to make or become blunt. —**blunt′ly,** *adv.* —**blunt′ness,** *n.*

blur (blûr), *v.,* **blurred, blur•ring,** *n*. —*v.t., v.i.* **1.** to make or become indistinct. **2.** to blot or smear. **3.** to make or become dull. —*n*. **4.** a smudge that obscures. **5.** a blurred condition or thing. —**blur′ry,** *adj.,* **-ri•er, -ri•est.**

blurb (blûrb), *n*. a brief advertisement, as on a book jacket.

blurt (blûrt), *v.t.* to utter impulsively or inadvertently (usu. fol. by *out*).

blush (blush), *v.i.* **1.** to redden, as from embarrassment. **2.** to feel shame or embarrassment. —*n*. **3.** a reddening, as of the face. **4.** a rosy tinge. —*Idiom.* **5. at first blush,** at first glance.

blush′er, *n*. **1.** a person who blushes. **2.** a cosmetic used to color the cheeks.

blus•ter (blus′tər), *v.i.* **1.** to roar and be tumultuous, as wind. **2.** to be noisy or swaggering. —*n*. **3.** boisterous noise and violence. **4.** noisy, empty threats or protests. —**blus′ter•er,** *n*. —**blus′ter•y,** *adj.*

blvd., boulevard.

BM, bowel movement.

B.O., *Informal.* body odor.

bo•a (bō′ə), *n*. **1.** a nonvenomous, chiefly tropical snake, as the boa constrictor. **2.** a scarf or stole, usu. of feathers or fur.

bo′a constric′tor, *n*. a large snake of tropical America able to suffocate prey by coiling around it.

Bo•a•ner•ges (bō′ə nûr′jēz), *n*. a surname given by Jesus to James and John. Mark 3:17.

boar (bôr), *n*. **1.** the uncastrated male swine. **2.** a wild Old World swine.

board (bôrd), *n*. **1.** a rectangular piece of sawed wood. **2.** a flat piece of wood or other stiff material for a specific purpose: *a cutting board.* **3.** a group of persons who direct some activity: *a board of directors.* **4.** daily meals, esp. as provided for pay: *room and board.* **5.** the side of a ship. **6. a.** a piece of fiberglass or other material upon which an array of computer chips is mounted. **b.** CIRCUIT BOARD. —*v.t.* **7.** to cover or close with boards (often fol. by *up*). **8.** to furnish with meals, or meals and lodging, esp. for pay. **9.** to get on (a ship, train, etc.). —*v.i.* **10.** to take one's meals at a fixed price. —*Idiom.* **11. on board,** on or in a ship, plane, etc. —**board′er,** *n.*

board′ing•house′, *n*. a house at which meals and lodging may be obtained for payment.

board′walk′, *n*. a promenade of wooden boards, usu. along a beach.

boast (bōst), *v.i.* **1.** to speak with excessive pride; brag. —*v.t.* **2.** to speak of with excessive pride. **3.** to be proud in the possession of: *The town boasts two new schools.* —*n*. **4.** a thing boasted of. **5.** exaggerated speech; bragging. —**boast′er,** *n*. —**boast′ful,** *adj.* —**boast′ful•ly,** *adv.*

boat (bōt), *n*. **1.** a vessel for transport by water. **2.** a boat-shaped serving dish. —*v.i.* **3.** to go in a boat. —*Idiom.* **4. in the same boat,** in similar difficult circumstances. —**boat′ing,** *n.*

boat′er, *n*. **1.** a person who boats. **2.** a stiff straw hat with a flat-topped crown.

boat′ shoe′, *n*. a moccasin-like shoe with a rubber sole that provides a firm hold on the deck of a boat.

boat•swain (bō′sən), *n*. an officer on a ship in charge of rigging, anchors, etc.

Bo•az (bō′az), *n*. husband of Ruth. Ruth 2–4.

bob¹ (bob), *n., v.,* **bobbed, bob•bing.** —*n*. **1.** a short, jerky motion. —*v.t., v.i.* **2.** to move quickly down and up. **3. bob up,** to appear unexpectedly.

bob² (bob), *n., v.,* **bobbed, bob•bing.** —*n*. **1.** a short, caplike haircut. **2.** a dangling object, as the weight on a pendulum. **3.** a float for a fishing line. —*v.t.* **4.** to cut short.

bob•bin (bob′in), *n*. a reel or spool on which thread is wound.

bob•ble (bob′əl), *n., v.,* **-bled, -bling.** —*n*. **1.** a momentary fumbling of a baseball. —*v.t.* **2.** to fumble (a baseball) momentarily.

bob•by (bob′ē), *n.*, *pl.* **-bies.** *Brit.* POLICEMAN. [generic use of *Bobby*, for Sir *Robert* Peel, who set up the Metropolitan Police system of London in 1828]

bob′by pin′, *n.* a flat, springlike metal hairpin.

bob′by•socks′ or **-sox′,** *n.pl.* ankle-length socks worn by girls.

bob′by•sox′er (-sok′sər), *n.* an adolescent girl, esp. of the 1940s.

bob′cat′, *n.*, *pl.* **-cats, -cat.** a North American lynx having a brownish coat with black spots.

bob′sled′, *n.*, *v.,* **-sled•ded, -sled•ding.** —*n.* **1.** a long sled having two pairs of runners, a brake, and a steering mechanism. —*v.i.* **2.** to ride on a bobsled. —**bob′sled′der,** *n.*

bob′tail′, *n.* **1.** a short tail. **2.** an animal with such a tail.

bob′white′, *n.* any of several small New World quails.

Boc•cac•ci•o (bə kä′chō, -chē ō′), *n.* **Giovanni,** 1313–75, Italian writer.

boc•cie or **boc•ci** or **boc•ce** (boch′ē), *n.* a variety of lawn bowling.

bode[1] (bōd), *v.t.,* *v.i.,* **bod•ed, bod•ing.** to portend.

bode[2] (bōd), *v.* a pt. of BIDE.

bod•ice (bod′is), *n.* the part of a dress covering the body above the waist.

bod•i•ly (bod′l ē), *adj.* **1.** of the body. —*adv.* **2.** as a physical entity. **3.** in person.

bod•kin (bod′kin), *n.* **1.** a small, pointed instrument for making holes in cloth or leather. **2.** a blunt needle for drawing tape or cord through a loop or hem.

bod•y (bod′ē), *n.*, *pl.* **-bod•ies. 1. a.** the physical structure and substance of an animal or plant. **b.** the trunk or torso. **c.** a corpse. **2.** the main or central mass of a thing. **3.** a separate physical mass. **4.** *Informal.* a person. **5.** a collective group: *the student body.* **6.** substance; consistency.

bod′y•guard′, *n.* a person employed to guard an individual from bodily harm.

bod′y lan′guage, *n.* nonverbal communication through gestures, facial expressions, etc.

bod′y pierc′ing, *n.* the piercing of a part of the body, as the navel, in order to insert an ornamental ring or stud.

bod′y pol′itic, *n.* a people forming a political body under a government.

bod′y stock′ing, *n.* a close-fitting garment covering the feet, legs, and trunk.

Boer (bôr, bōōr), *n.* a white South African who speaks Afrikaans.

Boer′ War′, *n.* a war in which Great Britain fought against the Transvaal and Orange Free State, 1899–1902.

bog (bog, bôg), *n.*, *v.,* **bogged, bog•ging.** —*n.* **1.** wet, spongy ground. —*v.t.,* *v.i.* **2.** to sink in or as if in a bog. —**bog′gy,** *adj.,* **-gi•er, -gi•est.**

bo•gey (bō′gē; *for 2 also* bōō′gē, bōō′gē), *n.*, *pl.* **-geys. 1.** a golf score of one stroke over par on a hole. **2.** BOGY.

bog•gle (bog′əl), *v.,* **-gled, -gling.** —*v.t.* **1.** to overwhelm or bewilder, as with complexity. —*v.i.* **2.** to be overwhelmed or bewildered. **3.** to hesitate or waver. **4.** to start with fright.

Bo•go•tá (bō′gə tä′), *n.* the capital of Colombia. 3,982,941.

bo•gus (bō′gəs), *adj.* not genuine; counterfeit.

bo•gy or **-gie** (bō′gē, bōōg′ē, bōō′gē), *n.*, *pl.* **-gies. 1.** a hobgoblin. **2.** anything that haunts, frightens, or harasses.

Bo•he•mi•a (bō hē′mē ə), *n.* a region in the W part of the Czech Republic: formerly a kingdom.

Bo•he′mi•an, *n.* **1.** a native of Bohemia. **2.** (*usu. l.c.*) a person who lives an unconventional life, as a writer or artist. —*adj.* **3.** of Bohemia or its inhabitants. **4.** (*usu. l.c.*) of or characteristic of a bohemian.

boil[1] (boil), *v.i.* **1.** to change from a liquid to a gaseous state, as a result of heat, producing bubbles of gas. **2.** to reach the boiling point. **3.** to be in an agi-

tated state. **4.** to be deeply angry. **5.** to undergo cooking in boiling water. —*v.t.* **6.** to cause to boil. **7.** to cook in boiling water. **8. boil down, a.** to reduce by boiling. **b.** to shorten; abridge. —*n.* **9.** the act or state of boiling.

boil[2] (boil), *n.* an inflammation of the skin with a pus-filled core.

boil′er, *n.* **1.** a closed vessel in which water is heated to make steam. **2.** a tank in which water is heated and stored.

boil′ing point′, *n.* **1.** the temperature at which a liquid boils, equal to 212°F (100°C) for water at sea level. **2.** the point beyond which one becomes visibly angry.

Boi•se (boi′zē; *esp. locally* -sē), *n.* the capital of Idaho. 145,987.

bois•ter•ous (boi′stər əs), *adj.* **1.** rough and noisy. **2.** turbulent and stormy. —**bois′ter•ous•ly,** *adv.* —**bois′ter•ous•ness,** *n.*

bo•la (bō′lə), *n.*, *pl.* **-las.** a cord with a heavy ball secured to each end, hurled at cattle to entangle the legs.

bold (bōld), *adj.,* **-er, -est. 1.** courageous and daring. **2.** scorning or ignoring the rules of propriety. **3.** flashy; showy: *a bold pattern.* **4.** steep; abrupt. —**bold′ly,** *adv.* —**bold′ness,** *n.*

bold′face′, *n.* type or print that has thick, heavy lines. —**bold′faced′,** *adj.*

bole (bōl), *n.* the stem or trunk of a tree.

bo•le•ro (bə lâr′ō, bō-), *n.*, *pl.* **-ros. 1.** a lively Spanish dance in triple meter. **2.** the music for this dance. **3.** a waist-length jacket, worn open in front.

bol•i•var (bol′ə vər, bə lē′vär), *n.* the basic monetary unit of Venezuela.

Bol′í•var, *n.* **Simón,** 1783–1830, South American statesman and revolutionary leader.

Bo•liv•i•a (bə liv′ē ə), *n.* a republic in W South America. 7,669,868. —**Bo•liv′i•an,** *adj.,* *n.*

boll (bōl), *n.* a rounded seed pod of a plant, esp. of flax or cotton.

boll′ wee′vil, *n.* a snout beetle that attacks the bolls of cotton.

bo•lo•gna (bə lō′nē), *n.* a cooked and smoked sausage usu. made of beef and pork. [after *Bologna*, Italy, where first made]

Bol•she•vik (bōl′shə vik, -vēk′, bol′-), *n.*, *pl.* **-viks, -vik•i** (-vik′ē, -vē′kē). **1.** a member of the group of radical Russian Marxists who seized control of the government in 1917. **2.** a member of any Communist Party. —**Bol′she•vism** (-viz′əm), *n.* —**Bol′she•vist,** *n.,* *adj.*

bol•ster (bōl′stər), *n.* **1.** a long, often cylindrical cushion for a bed, sofa, etc. —*v.t.* **2.** to support with or as if with a bolster.

bolt[1] (bōlt), *n.* **1.** a strong fastening rod, usu. threaded to receive a nut. **2.** a movable bar used to lock a door. **3.** the part of a lock that is manipulated by the action of the key. **4.** a sudden dash. **5.** a roll of woven goods. **6.** a short, heavy arrow for a crossbow. **7.** a thunderbolt. —*v.t.* **8.** to fasten with or as if with a bolt. **9.** to break with: *to bolt a political party.* **10.** to say impulsively. **11.** to swallow (food) hurriedly. —*v.i.* **12.** to make a sudden flight or escape. **13.** to break away, as from one's party. —*Idiom.* **14. bolt upright,** stiffly or rigidly erect. —**bolt′er,** *n.*

bolt[2] (bōlt), *v.t.* to sift.

bo•lus (bō′ləs), *n.*, *pl.* **-lus•es. 1.** a round medicinal material, larger than an ordinary pill. **2.** a soft, roundish lump, esp. of chewed food.

bomb (bom), *n.* **1.** a case filled with a bursting charge and exploded by a detonating device or by impact. **2.** an aerosol can and its contents. **3.** *Slang.* an absolute failure. —*v.t.* **4.** to attack with bombs. —*v.i.* **5.** *Slang.* to fail decisively.

bom•bard (bom bärd′), *v.t.* **1.** to attack with artillery fire. **2.** to assail vigorously. **3.** to direct highenergy particles or radiation against. —**bom•bard′ment,** *n.*

bom′bar•dier′ (-bər dēr′, -bə-), *n.* the member of a bomber crew who releases the bombs.

bom•bast (bom′bast), *n.* pompous oratory or pretentious writing. —**bom•bas′tic,** *adj.* —**bom•bas′ti•cal•ly,** *adv.*

Bom•bay (bom bā′), *n.* a seaport in W India. 8,227,000.

bomb•er (bom′ər), *n.* **1.** an airplane equipped to drop bombs. **2.** a person who drops or sets bombs.

bomb′shell′, *n.* **1.** a bomb. **2.** something or someone having a sensational effect.

bo•na fide (bō′nə fīd′ fī′dē), *adj.* **1.** in good faith; without deception or fraud. **2.** genuine; real.

bo•nan•za (bə nan′zə), *n. pl.* **-zas. 1.** a rich mass of ore. **2.** a source of great and sudden wealth.

Bo•na•parte (bō′nə pärt′), *n.* **Napoléon, NAPOLEON I.**

bon•bon (bon′bon′), *n.* a small piece of candy, usu. chocolate-coated.

bond (bond), *n.* **1.** something that binds, fastens, or confines. **2.** something that binds a person to a certain line of behavior: *the bond of matrimony.* **3.** something, as an agreement, that unites individuals or peoples. **4.** any written obligation under seal. **5.** the state of dutiable goods stored without payment of duties. **6.** an interest-bearing certificate of debt due to be paid by a government or corporation to an individual holder. **7. a.** a surety agreement. **b.** the money deposited as surety. **8.** a substance that causes particles to adhere. **9.** the attraction between atoms in a molecule. **10.** BOND PAPER. —*v.t.* **11.** to put on or under bond. **12.** to connect or bind.

bond•age (bon′dij), *n.* slavery or involuntary servitude.

bond′hold′er, *n.* a holder of a bond issued by a government or corporation.

bond′man or **-wom′an,** *n., pl.* **-men** or **-wom•en. 1.** a slave or serf. **2.** a person bound to service without wages.

bond′ pa′per, *n.* a superior variety of paper usu. with high cotton fiber content.

bonds′man, *n., pl.* **-men. 1.** a person who by means of a bond becomes surety for another. **2.** BONDSMAN.

bone (bōn), *n., v.,* **boned, bon•ing.** —*n.* **1. a.** one of the structures composing the skeleton of a vertebrate. **b.** the hard connective tissue forming these structures. **2.** any of various similarly hard or structural animal substances, as whalebone. **3.** something resembling such a substance. —*v.t.* **4.** to remove the bones from. **5. bone up,** *Informal.* to study intensely; cram. —*Idiom.* **6. have a bone to pick with,** to have cause for reproaching. **7. make no bones about,** to act or speak openly about.

bone′ chi′na, *n.* a fine, naturally white china.

bone′-dry′, *adj.* very dry.

bone′head′, *n. Slang.* a foolish or stupid person.

bone′ meal′, *n.* bones ground to a coarse powder, used as fertilizer or feed.

bon′er, *n. Slang.* a stupid mistake.

bon′fire′, *n.* a large fire built in the open air.

bong (bong, bông), *n.* **1.** a dull, resonant sound, as of a bell. —*v.i.* **2.** to produce this sound.

bon•go (bong′gō, bông′-), *n., pl.* **-gos, -goes.** one of a pair of tuned drums, played by beating with the fingers.

Bon•hoef•fer (bon′hoe′fər, -hō′-), *n.* **Dietrich,** 1906–45, German Lutheran theologian killed by the Nazis.

bo•ni•to (bə nē′tō), *n., pl.* **-tos, -to.** any of several mackerellike fishes.

bon•jour (bôn zhōōR′), *interj. French.* good day; hello.

bon•kers (bong′kərz), *adj. Slang.* crazy.

bon mot (bôn mō′), *n., pl.* **bons mots** (bôn mōz′). a witty comment.

Bonn (bon, bôn), *n.* a city in W Germany: seat of the government. 291,400.

bon•net (bon′it), *n.* a hat, tied under the chin, worn formerly by women but now mostly by children.

bon•ny (bon′ē), *adj.,* **-ni•er, -ni•est.** *Chiefly Brit.* **1.** handsome or pretty. **2.** pleasing.

bo•no•bo (bə nō′bō), *n., pl.* **-bos.** a small chimpanzee primarily of rain forests in the Democratic Republic of the Congo.

bon•sai (bon sī′, bôn-), *n., pl.* **-sai.** a tree or shrub that has been dwarfed, as by pruning.

bo•nus (bō′nəs), *n., pl.* **-nus•es.** something given or paid over and above what is due.

bon vi•vant (*Fr.* bôn vē vän′), *n., pl.* **bons vi•vants** (*Fr.* bôn vē vän′). a person who lives luxuriously and enjoys good food and drink. [< F]

bon vo•yage (*Fr.* bôn vwa yazh′), *interj.* (used to wish someone a pleasant trip.)

bon•y (bō′nē), *adj.,* **-i•er, -i•est. 1.** of or like bone. **2.** full of bones. **3.** skinny; gaunt.

boo (bōō), *n., pl.* **boos,** *v.,* **booed, boo•ing.** —*n.* **1.** a sound made to express contempt or disapproval. —*v.i., v.t.* **2.** to cry "boo" (at).

boob′ tube′ (bōōb), *n. Slang.* **1.** television. **2.** a television set.

boo•by (bōō′bē), *n., pl.* **-bies.** a stupid person. Also, **boob.**

boo′by prize′, *n.* a prize given to the worst player in a contest.

boo′by trap′, *n.* any hidden trap set for an unsuspecting person.

boo•dle (bōōd′l), *n.* **1.** a bribe or other illicit payment. **2.** stolen goods; loot.

Boog′ie Board′, *Trademark.* a small, flexible plastic surfboard.

book (bōōk), *n.* **1.** a long printed work, on sheets of paper bound together within covers. **2.** a division of a literary work. **3. the Book,** the Bible. **4.** a libretto. **5. books,** financial records. **6.** a bound packet of tickets, checks, stamps, etc. —*v.t.* **7.** to enter in a book or list. **8.** to engage (rooms, transportation, or entertainment) beforehand. **9.** to enter a charge against (an arrested person) in a police register. —*Proverb.* **10. Don't judge a book by its cover,** don't be misled by appearances.

book′case′, *n.* a set of shelves for books.

book′end′, *n.* a support at each end of a row of books to hold them upright.

book′ie, *n.* BOOKMAKER.

book′ing, *n.* an engagement of a professional entertainer.

book′ish, *adj.* **1.** fond of reading; studious. **2.** stilted; pedantic.

book′keep′ing, *n.* the system or occupation of keeping detailed records of business transactions. —**book′keep′er,** *n.*

book′let (-lit), *n.* a little book; pamphlet.

book′mak′er, *n.* a person who makes a business of accepting bets, esp. on horse races. —**book′mak′ing,** *n., adj.*

book′mark′, *n.* something placed between the pages of a book to mark a place.

book′mo•bile′ (-mə bēl′), *n.* a motor vehicle designed to serve as a traveling library.

Book′ of Com′mon Prayer′, *n.* the service book of the Church of England, first composed in 1549.

Book′ of Mor′mon, *n.* a sacred book of the Church of Jesus Christ of Latter-day Saints, believed by church members to be an abridgment by a prophet (**Mormon**) of a record of ancient peoples in America, discovered and translated (1827–30) by Joseph Smith.

book′shelf′, *n., pl.* **-shelves.** a shelf for holding books.

book′store′, *n.* a store where books are sold.

book′worm′, *n.* **1.** a person who spends much time reading. **2.** any of various insects that feed on books.

boom[1] (bōōm), *v.i., v.t.* **1.** to make or cause to make a deep, resonant sound. **2.** to flourish or cause to flourish vigorously. —*n.* **3.** a deep, resonant sound. **4.** a rapid increase in sales, worth, etc. **5.** a period of rapid economic growth.

boom[2] (bōōm), *n.* **1.** a spar projecting from a ship's mast and used to extend sails. **2.** a chain, cable, etc., used to obstruct navigation. **3.** a beam projecting from the mast of a derrick for supporting objects to be lifted. **4.** a beam on a mobile crane for holding a microphone.

boom′ box′ or **boom′box′**, *n.* a large portable radio and CD or cassette player.

boo•mer•ang (boo′mə rang′), *n.* **1.** a curved piece of wood that can be thrown so as to return to the thrower. **2.** a scheme, argument, etc., that injures the originator. —*v.i.* **3.** to act as a boomerang.

boon[1] (boon), *n.* a blessing; benefit.

boon[2] (boon), *adj.* jovial; convivial: *boon companions.*

boon′docks′, *n.* the, (*used with a pl. v.*) **1.** a backwoods or marsh. **2.** a remote rural area.

boon′dog′gle (-dog′əl, -dô′gəl), *n., v.,* **-gled, ing.** —*n.* **1.** futile value done merely to keep or look busy. —*v.i.* **2.** to do such work. —**boon′dog′gler,** *n.*

Boone (boon), *n.* **1. Daniel,** 1734–1820, American pioneer, esp. in Kentucky. **2. Pat,** born 1934, U.S. singer.

boor (boor), *n.* a rude, unmannerly person. —**boor′ish,** *adj.* —**boor′ish•ly,** *adv.*

boost (boost), *v.t.* **1.** to lift by pushing from below. **2.** to aid by speaking well of; promote. **3.** to increase; raise. —*n.* **4.** an upward shove or lift. **5.** an increase. **6.** an act or remark that helps one's progress, morale, etc.

boost′er, *n.* **1.** an enthusiastic supporter. **2.** a rocket used as the principal source of thrust in takeoff. **3.** Also called **boost′er shot′.** a dose of an immunizing substance given to maintain the effect of a previous one.

boot[1] (boot), *n.* **1.** a covering of leather, rubber, etc., for the foot and part of the leg. **2.** any sheathlike protective covering. **3.** a U.S. Navy or Marine Corps recruit. **4.** a kick. **5. the boot,** *Slang.* a dismissal. —*v.t.* **6.** to kick. **7.** to put boots on. **8.** to start (a computer) by loading the operating system. **9.** *Slang.* to dismiss.

boot[2] (boot), *n.* **1.** *Archaic.* something given into the bargain. —*Idiom.* **2. to boot,** in addition; besides.

boot′black′, *n.* a person who shines shoes and boots for a living.

boot•ee or **boot•ie** (boo tē′, boo′tē), *n., pl.* **-ees** or **-ies.** a baby's socklike shoe, usu. knitted or crocheted.

Booth (booth; *Brit.* booth), *n.* **1. John Wilkes,** 1838–65, U.S. actor: assassin of Abraham Lincoln. **2. William** ("*General Booth*"), 1829–1912, English religious leader: founder of the Salvation Army 1865.

boot′leg′, *n., v.,* **-legged, -leg•ging,** *adj.* —*n.* **1.** something, esp. liquor, that is unlawfully made, sold, or transported. —*v.t., v.i.* **2.** to deal in (liquor or other goods) unlawfully. —*adj.* **3.** made, sold, or transported unlawfully. —**boot′leg′ger,** *n.*

boot′less, *adj.* unavailing; useless.

boo•ty (boo′tē), *n., pl.* **-ties. 1.** plunder taken in war. **2.** something seized by violence and robbery.

bop[1] (bop), *n., v.,* **bopped, bop•ping.** —*n.* **1.** jazz marked by dissonant harmony, eccentric rhythms, and melodic intricacy. —*v.i.* **2.** *Slang.* to move, go, or proceed.

bop[2] (bop), *v.,* **bopped, bop•ping,** *n. Slang.* —*v.t.* **1.** to hit. —*n.* **2.** a blow.

bo•rax (bôr′aks), *n.* a white crystalline substance used as a cleansing agent, in glassmaking, etc.

Bor•deaux (bôr dō′), *n., pl.* **-deaux** (-dōz′). any of various wines produced in the region surrounding Bordeaux, a seaport in SW France.

bor•der (bôr′dər), *n.* **1.** the edge of a surface or area that forms its outer boundary. **2.** the line that separates one country, state, etc., from another. **3.** an ornamental design around an edge. —*v.t.* **4.** to make a border around. **5.** to form a border to. **6.** to adjoin. **7. border on,** to verge on; approach.

bor′der•line′, *n.* **1.** a boundary. —*adj.* **2.** on or near a border. **3.** indefinite or indeterminate.

Bor′der State′, *n.* (*sometimes l.c.*) any of the Slave States bordering on the North before the Civil War.

bore[1] (bôr), *v.,* **bored, bor•ing,** *n.* —*v.t.* **1.** to pierce

(a solid substance), as with a drill. **2.** to make (a hole or passage) by drilling or digging. —*v.i.* **3.** to make a hole, as with a drill. —*n.* **4.** a hole made or enlarged by boring. **5.** the inside diameter of a hole or cylinder, as a gun barrel.

bore[2] (bôr), *v.,* **bored, bor•ing,** *n.* —*v.t.* **1.** to weary by dullness. —*n.* **2.** a dull, tiresome person or thing. —**bore′dom,** *n.*

bore[3] (bôr), *v.* pt. of BEAR[1].

bo′ric ac′id (bôr′ik), *n.* a white, crystalline acid, used as an antiseptic.

bor′ing (-ing), *adj.* tedious; tiresome.

born (bôrn), *adj.* **1.** brought forth by birth. **2.** possessing from birth the quality stated: *a born musician.* —*v.* **3.** a pp. of BEAR[1]. —**Usage.** See BEAR[1].

born′-again′, *adj.* **1.** committed or recommitted to faith through an intensely religious experience: *a born-again Christian.* **2.** reactivated or revitalized: *a born-again conservative.*

borne (bôrn), *v.* a pp. of BEAR[1]. —**Usage.** See BEAR[1].

Bor•ne•o (bôr′nē ō′), *n.* an island in the Malay Archipelago. —**Bor′ne•an,** *adj., n.*

bo•ron (bôr′on), *n.* a nonmetallic element used in alloys and nuclear reactors. *Symbol:* B; *at. wt.:* 10. 811; *at. no.:* 5.

bor•ough (bûr′ō, bur′ō), *n.* **1.** an incorporated municipality smaller than a city. **2.** one of the five administrative divisions of New York City.

bor•row (bor′ō, bôr′ō), *v.t., v.i.* **1.** to obtain (something) with the promise to return it. **2.** to appropriate (an idea, etc.) from another source. —**bor′row•er,** *n.*

borscht (bôrsht), *n.* a beet soup, usu. served with sour cream.

bor•zoi (bôr′zoi), *n., pl.* **-zois.** a tall, slender dog with long, silky hair and a narrow head.

Bos•ni•a (boz′nē ə), *n.* a region in the N part of Bosnia and Herzegovina. —**Bos′ni•an,** *adj., n.*

Bos•nia and Her•ze•go•vi•na (boz′nē ə; hûr′tsə-gō vē′nə), a republic in SE Europe: formerly part of Yugoslavia. 2,607,734.

bos•om (booz′əm, boo′zəm), *n.* **1.** the breast of a human being. **2.** the breast conceived of as the center of feelings. **3.** a state of enclosing intimacy: *the bosom of the family.* —*adj.* **4.** intimate or confidential.

bos′om•y, *adj.* having large breasts.

boss[1] (bôs, bos), *n.* **1.** a person who employs or supervises workers. **2.** a politician who controls the party organization. **3.** a person who is in charge. —*v.t.* **4.** to direct; control. **5.** to order about. —*adj.* **6.** *Slang.* first-rate. [< D *baas* master] —**boss′y,** *adj.,* **-i•er, -i•est.** —**boss′i•ness,** *n.*

boss[2] (bôs, bos), *n.* **1.** an ornamental protuberance of metal, ivory, etc. —*v.t.* **2.** to ornament with bosses. [< AF *boce* lump]

boss′ism, *n.* control by bosses, esp. political bosses.

Bos•ton (bô′stən, bos′tən), *n.* the capital of Massachusetts. 574,725. —**Bos•to′ni•an** (-stō′nē ən), *adj., n.*

Bos′ton Tea′ Par′ty, *n.* a raid on British tea ships in Boston Harbor (Dec. 16, 1773) in which colonists, disguised as Indians, threw the tea overboard as a protest against British taxes.

Bos′ton ter′rier, *n.* a small, shorthaired dog having a brindled or black coat with white markings.

bo•sun (bō′sən), *n.* BOATSWAIN.

Bos•well (boz′wel′, -wəl), *n.* **James,** 1740–95, Scottish author: biographer of Samuel Johnson.

Bos′worth Field′ (boz′wərth), *n.* a battlefield in central England where Richard III was defeated by the future Henry VII in 1485.

bot•a•ny (bot′n ē), *n.* the science that deals with plant life. —**bo•tan•i•cal** (bə tan′i kəl), **bo•tan′ic,** *adj.* —**bot′a•nist,** *n.*

botch (boch), *v.t.* **1.** to bungle. **2.** to patch clumsily. —*n.* **3.** a poor piece of work. —**botch′er,** *n.*

both (bōth), *adj., pron.* **1.** one and the other; the two: *I met both sisters. Both of them were ill.* —*conj.* **2.** (used before words or phrases joined by *and* to indicate that each of the joined elements is included): *I am both ready and willing.*

both•er (both′ər), *v.t., v.i.* **1.** to annoy (someone). **2.** to trouble or inconvenience (oneself). —*n.* **3.** something or someone troublesome or annoying. —**both′er•some,** *adj.*

Bot•swa•na (bot swä′nə), *n.* a republic in S Africa. 1,500,765.

Bot•ti•cel•li (bot′i chel′ē), *n.* **Sandro** (*Alessandro di Mariano dei Filipepi*), 1444?–1510, Italian painter.

bot•tle (bot′l), *n., v.,* **-tled, -tling.** —*n.* **1.** a glass or plastic container for liquids, having a neck and mouth. **2.** the contents of such a container. —*v.t.* **3.** to put into or seal in a bottle. **4. bottle up,** to repress or restrain. —**bot′tler,** *n.*

bot′tle•neck′, *n.* **1.** a narrow entrance or passageway. **2.** a place or stage at which progress is impeded.

bot•tom (bot′əm), *n.* **1.** the lowest part of anything. **2.** the under or lower side. **3.** the ground under any body of water. **4.** the seat of a chair. **5.** *Informal.* the buttocks. **6.** the cause; origin. —*v.i.* **7. bottom out,** to reach the lowest state or level. —*adj.* **8.** lowest: *bottom prices.* **9.** fundamental. —*Idiom.* **10. at bottom,** fundamentally. —**bot′tom•less,** *adj.*

bot′tom line′, *n.* **1.** the last line of a financial statement, showing net profit or loss. **2.** the ultimate result or consideration.

bot•u•lism (boch′ə liz′əm), *n.* a sometimes fatal disease of the nervous system caused by a toxin in spoiled foods.

bou•doir (bōō′dwär, -dwôr), *n.* a woman's bedroom or private sitting room. [< F: lit., a sulking place]

bouf•fant (bōō fänt′), *adj.* puffed out; full: *a bouffant hairdo.*

bou•gain•vil•le•a (bōō′gən vil′ē ə, -vil′yə), *n., pl.* **-le•as.** a climbing shrub having small flowers with showy, variously colored bracts.

bough (bou), *n.* a large branch of a tree.

bought (bôt), *v.* pt. and pp. of BUY.

bouil•la•baisse (bōō′yə bäs′, bōōl′-), *n.* a stew containing several kinds of fish.

bouil•lon (bōōl′yon, -yən, bōō′-), *n.* a clear broth.

boul•der (bōl′dər), *n.* a large and rounded or worn rock.

boul•e•vard (bōōl′ə värd′), *n.* a broad avenue, often lined with trees.

bounce (bouns), *v.,* **bounced, bounc•ing,** *n.* —*v.i.* **1.** to strike a surface and rebound. **2.** to move in a lively, energetic manner. **3.** (of a check) to be refused due to insufficient funds in the account. —*v.t.* **4.** to cause to bounce. **5.** *Slang.* to expel or dismiss summarily or forcibly. —*n.* **6.** a bound or rebound. **7.** a sudden spring or leap. **8.** ability to rebound; resilience. **9.** vitality; energy. **10. the bounce,** *Slang.* a dismissal. —**bounc•y,** *adj.,* **-i•er, -i•est.**

bounc′er, *n.* a person employed at a bar, nightclub, etc., to eject disorderly persons.

bounc′ing, *adj.* stout, strong, or vigorous.

bound¹ (bound), *v.* **1.** pt. and pp. of BIND. —*adj.* **2.** tied; in bonds. **3.** made fast as if by a bond. **4.** secured within a cover, as a book. **5.** under obligation. **6.** destined or certain: *It is bound to happen.* **7.** determined or resolved.

bound² (bound), *v.i.* **1.** to move by leaps. **2.** to rebound; bounce. —*n.* **3.** a jump. **4.** a bounce.

bound³ (bound), *n.* **1.** Usu., **bounds.** limit or boundary: *within the bounds of reason.* **2. bounds,** territories on or near a boundary. —*v.t.* **3.** to limit. **4.** to form the boundary or limit of. **5.** to name the boundaries of. —*Idiom.* **6. out of bounds, a.** beyond prescribed limits. **b.** prohibited. —**bound′less,** *adj.* —**bound′less•ly,** *adv.*

bound⁴ (bound), *adj.* going or intending to go: *bound for Denver.*

bound•a•ry (boun′də rē, -drē), *n., pl.* **-ries.** something that indicates bounds or limits.

bound′en, *adj.* obligatory; compulsory: *one's bounden duty.*

bound′er, *n.* an obtrusive, ill-bred person.

boun•te•ous (boun′tē əs), *adj.* **1.** giving generously. **2.** plentiful; abundant. —**boun′te•ous•ly,** *adv.* —**boun′te•ous•ness,** *n.*

boun′ti•ful, *adj.* BOUNTEOUS. —**boun′ti•ful•ly,** *adv.* —**boun′ti•ful•ness,** *n.*

boun′ty, *n., pl.* **-ties. 1.** a premium or reward. **2.** a generous gift. **3.** generosity.

bou•quet (bō kā′, bōō- *for 1;* bōō kā′ *for 2*), *n.* **1.** a bunch of flowers. **2.** a characteristic aroma, esp. of a wine.

Bour•bon (bōōr′bən, bôor bôn′ *for 1;* bûr′bən *for 2*), *n.* **1.** a member of a French royal family that ruled in France 1589–1792, 1814–1848. Branches of the family have ruled in Spain, Sicily, and Naples. **2.** (*l.c.*) Also called **bour′bon whis′key.** a whiskey distilled from a mash having 51 percent or more corn.

bour•geois (bōōr zhwä′), *n., pl.* **-geois,** *adj.* —*n.* **1.** a member of the bourgeoisie or middle class. —*adj.* **2.** of or characteristic of the middle class. **3.** overly concerned with respectability or success.

bour′geoi•sie′ (-zē′), *n.* **1.** the middle class. **2.** (in Marxist theory) the capitalist class in conflict with the proletariat.

bout (bout), *n.* **1.** a contest, as of boxing. **2.** a period; spell.

bou•tique (bōō tēk′), *n.* a small shop that sells fashionable items.

bou•ton•niere (bōōt′n ēr′, bōō′tən yâr′), *n.* a flower or small bouquet worn on a lapel.

bo•vine (bō′vīn, -vēn), *adj.* **1.** of or resembling an ox or cow. **2.** stolid; dull. —*n.* **3.** a bovine animal.

bo′vine spon′gi•form encephalop′athy, (spun′jə fôrm′), *n.* a fatal dementia of cattle, thought to be caused by an abnormal, infectious form of cellular protein. Also called **mad cow disease.**

bow¹ (bou), *v.i.* **1.** to bend the body or head, as in reverence or salutation. **2.** to yield; submit. —*v.t.* **3.** to bend (the body or head). **4.** to subdue; crush. —*n.* **5.** an inclination of the body or head in reverence, salutation, etc. —*Idiom.* **6. take a bow,** to stand up to receive applause, etc.

bow² (bō), *n.* **1.** a flexible strip of wood, bent by a string stretched between its ends, for shooting arrows. **2.** a bend or curve. **3.** a readily loosened knot having two projecting loops. **4.** a flexible rod strung with horsehairs used for playing an instrument of the violin family. —*adj.* **5.** curved: *bow legs.* —*v.t., v.i.* **6.** to bend; curve. **7.** to play (a stringed instrument) with a bow.

bow³ (bou), *n.* the forward end of a ship or boat.

bowd•ler•ize (bōd′lə rīz′, boud′-), *v.t.,* **-ized, -iz•ing.** to expurgate (a play, novel, or other written work) in a prudish manner. [after T. *Bowdler* (1754–1825), English editor of an expurgated edition of Shakespeare] —**bowd′ler•i•za′tion,** *n.*

bow•el (bou′əl, boul), *n.* **1.** Usu., **-els.** the intestine. **2. bowels,** the interior parts: *the bowels of the earth.* —*Idiom.* **3. move one's bowels,** to defecate.

bow•er (bou′ər), *n.* a leafy shelter; arbor.

bow′ie knife′ (bō′ē, bōō′ē), *n.* a heavy knife having a long, single-edged blade. [after J. *Bowie* (1799–1836), U.S. pioneer, for whom the knife was designed]

bowl¹ (bōl), *n.* **1.** a deep, round dish. **2.** the contents of a bowl. **3.** a rounded, hollow part. **4.** an amphitheater; stadium.

bowl² (bōl), *n.* **1.** a ball used in lawn bowling. **2. bowls,** LAWN BOWLING. **3.** a delivery of the ball in bowling. —*v.i.* **4.** to play at bowling. **5.** to move along smoothly and rapidly. —*v.t.* **6.** to roll (a ball) in bowling. **7. bowl over,** to surprise greatly. —**bowl′er,** *n.*

bow′leg′ (bō′-), *n.* outward curvature of the legs. —**bow′leg′ged,** *adj.*

bowl′ing, *n.* any of several games in which players roll balls along a grassy lane (**bowl′ing green′**) or a wooden lane (**bowl′ing al′ley**) at a mark or a group of pins.

bow•sprit (bou′sprit, bō′-), *n.* a spar projecting from the upper end of the bow of a sailing ship.

bow′ tie′ (bō), *n.* a small necktie tied in a bow.

box[1] (boks), *n.* **1.** a container or case, usu. having a lid. **2.** the quantity contained in a box. **3.** a compartment for a small group of people, as in a theater. **4.** a small enclosure in a courtroom. **5.** a small shelter: *a sentry's box.* **6.** any of the spaces on a baseball diamond marking the positions of the pitcher, batter, etc. —*v.t.* **7.** to put into a box. **8.** to enclose or confine (often fol. by *in* or *up*).

box[2] (boks), *n.* **1.** a blow with the hand or fist. —*v.t.* **2.** to strike with the fist. **3.** to fight against (someone) in a boxing match. —*v.i.* **4.** to participate in a boxing match.

box[3] (boks), *n.* an evergreen shrub used for ornamental borders and hedges.

box′car′, *n.* a completely enclosed railroad freight car.

box′er, *n.* **1.** a person who fights as a sport, usu. with gloved fists. **2.** a stocky, shorthaired dog with a square muzzle.

box′ing, *n.* the act, technique, or profession of fighting with the fists.

box′ of′fice, *n.* an office, as in a theater, at which tickets are sold.

boy (boi), *n.* **1.** a male child. **2.** man, esp. when referred to familiarly. —*interj.* **3.** an exclamation of wonder, displeasure, etc. —**boy′hood,** *n.* —**boy′ish,** *adj.* —**boy′ish•ly,** *adv.* —**boy′ish•ness,** *n.*

boy•cott (boi′kot), *v.t.* **1.** to abstain from dealing with or buying, as a means of protest or coercion. —*n.* **2.** the act of boycotting. [after C. C. *Boycott* (1832–97), English estate manager, first victim]

boy′friend′, *n.* **1.** a favored male companion, sweetheart, or lover. **2.** a male friend.

boy′ scout′, *n.* (*sometimes caps.*) a member of an organization of boys (**Boy′ Scouts′**) that emphasizes self-reliance and service to others.

boy•sen•ber•ry (boi′zən ber′ē, -sən-), *n., pl.* **-ries.** a blackberrylike fruit with a flavor similar to that of raspberries.

bps or **BPS,** *Computers.* bits per second.

Br, *Chem. Symbol.* bromine.

bra (brä), *n.* BRASSIERE. —**bra′less,** *adj.*

brace (brās), *n., v.,* **braced, brac•ing.** —*n.* **1.** something that holds parts together or in place. **2.** anything that imparts rigidity or steadiness. **3.** a device for holding and turning a bit. **4.** Usu., **braces.** an oral appliance for straightening irregularly arranged teeth. **5.** an orthopedic appliance for supporting a weak joint or joints. **6. braces,** *Chiefly Brit.* SUSPENDERS. **7.** a pair; couple. **8.** one of two characters, { or }, used to enclose words or lines to be considered together. —*v.t.* **9.** to fasten or strengthen with a brace. **10.** to steady (oneself), as against a shock. **11.** to stimulate or invigorate.

brace•let (brās′lit), *n.* an ornamental band for the wrist or arm.

brack•en (brak′ən), *n.* **1.** a large, coarse fern. **2.** a cluster or thicket of such ferns.

brack•et (brak′it), *n.* **1.** a supporting piece projecting from a wall or the like. **2.** a shelf so supported. **3.** one of two marks, [or], used to enclose written or printed material. **4.** a class or grouping: *the low-income bracket.* —*v.t.* **5.** to furnish with brackets. **6.** to place within brackets. **7.** to associate or class together.

brack•ish (brak′ish), *adj.* **1.** salty or briny. **2.** distasteful; unpleasant. —**brack′ish•ness,** *n.*

bract (brakt), *n.* a specialized leaflike plant part at the base of a flower or inflorescence.

brad (brad), *n.* a slender wire nail with a small, deep head.

brag (brag), *v.,* **bragged, brag•ging,** *n.* —*v.i., v.t.* **1.** to boast. —*n.* **2.** a boast or vaunt. **3.** one who boasts. —**brag′ger,** *n.*

brag•ga•do•ci•o (brag′ə dō′shē ō′), *n., pl.* **-ci•os. 1.** empty boasting. **2.** a braggart.

brag′gart (-ərt), *n.* one who brags a great deal.

Brah•ma (brä′mə), *n.* "the Creator," the chief member of the Hindu trinity, along with Vishnu and Shiva.

Brah•man (brä′mən), *n.* **1.** a member of the high-

est, or priestly, class among the Hindus. **2.** a breed of cattle developed from Indian stock. —**Brah′man•ism,** *n.*

Brah•min (brä′min), *n.* **1.** (esp. in New England) a person from an old, upper–class family. **2.** BRAHMAN (def. 1).

Brahms (brämz), *n.* **Jo•han•nes** (yō hä′nəs), 1833–97, German composer.

braid (brād), *v.t.* **1.** to weave together three or more strands of. **2.** to trim with braid, as a garment. —*n.* **3.** a braided length or plait, esp. of hair. **4.** a plaited band of material, used as trimming.

Braille (brāl), *n.* (*often l.c.*) a system of writing for the blind, using combinations of raised dots. [after L. *Braille* (1809–52), French deviser of system]

brain (brān), *n.* **1.** the part of the central nervous system enclosed in the cranium of vertebrates, serving to control mental and physical actions. **2.** Sometimes, **brains.** intelligence. —*v.t.* **3.** to smash the skull of. —**brain′less,** *adj.*

brain′child′, *n.* a product of one's creative work or thought.

brain′ death′, *n.* complete cessation of brain function: sometimes used as a legal definition of death. —**brain′-dead′,** *adj.*

brain′ drain′, *n.* a loss of trained professional personnel to another company, nation, etc.

brain′storm′, *n.* a sudden inspiration or idea.

brain′storm′ing, *n.* a group problem-solving technique characterized by unrestrained, spontaneous discussion.

brain′teas′er, *n.* a puzzle or problem whose solution requires great ingenuity.

brain′wash′, *v.t.* to subject to brainwashing.

brain′wash′ing, *n.* a method for changing attitudes or beliefs, esp. through torture or psychological-stress techniques.

brain′ wave′, *n.* Usu., **brain waves.** electrical impulses given off by brain tissue.

brain′y, *adj.,* **-i•er, -i•est.** *Informal.* intelligent; intellectual. —**brain′i•ness,** *n.*

braise (brāz), *v.t.,* **braised, brais•ing.** to cook in fat and then simmer in a small amount of liquid.

brake (brāk), *n., v.,* **braked, brak•ing.** —*n.* **1.** a device for slowing or stopping a vehicle or mechanism. —*v.t., v.i.* **2.** to slow or stop by or as if by a brake.

brake′man, *n., pl.* **-men.** a railroad worker who assists the conductor in the operation of a train.

bram•ble (bram′bəl), *n.* a prickly shrub of the rose family, as the blackberry. —**bram′bly,** *adj.,* **-bli•er, -bli•est.**

Bramp•ton (bramp′tən), *n.* a city in SE Ontario, in S Canada. 188,498.

bran (bran), *n.* the partly ground husk of wheat or other grain, separated from the flour by sifting.

branch (branch, bränch), *n.* **1.** a division of the stem or axis of a tree or shrub. **2.** any section or subdivision of a body or system. **3.** a local operating division of an organization. **4.** a division of a family. **5.** a tributary stream. —*v.i.* **6.** to spread in branches. **7.** to diverge: *The road branches off to the left.* **8. branch out,** to expand or extend, as business activities. —**branched,** *adj.* —**branch′like′,** *adj.*

brand (brand), *n.* **1.** kind, grade, or make: *the best brand of coffee.* **2.** a mark made by burning or other means, to indicate kind, ownership, etc. **3.** a stigma. **4.** an iron for branding. **5.** a burning or partly burned piece of wood. —*v.t.* **6.** to mark with a brand. **7.** to stigmatize. —**brand′er,** *n.*

Bran•deis (bran′dīs), *n.* **Louis Dembitz,** 1856–1941, associate justice of the U.S. Supreme Court 1916–39.

bran•dish (bran′dish), *v.t.* to shake or wave threateningly, as a weapon. —**bran′dish•er,** *n.*

brand′-new′ (bran′-, brand′-), *adj.* entirely new.

bran•dy (bran′dē), *n., pl.* **-dies,** *v.,* **-died, -dy•ing.** —*n.* **1.** a spirit distilled from wine or fermented fruit juice. —*v.t.* **2.** to flavor or preserve with brandy. [short for *brandywine* < D *brandewijn* burnt (i.e., distilled) wine]

brash (brash), *adj.*, **-er, -est. 1.** impudent; tactless. **2.** rash; impetuous. —**brash′ly,** *adv.* —**brash′ness,** *n.*

Bra•síl•ia (brə zil′yə), *n.* the capital of Brazil, on the central plateau. 411,505.

brass (bras, bräs), *n.* **1.** a metal alloy consisting mainly of copper and zinc. **2.** Often, **brasses.** the brass instruments of a band or orchestra. **3.** high-ranking officials, esp. military officers. **4.** impudence; effrontery. —*adj.* **5.** made of brass. —*Idiom.* **6. get down to brass tacks,** to concentrate on essential matters. —**brass′y,** *adj.*, **-i•er, -i•est.**

bras•siere (bra zēr′), *n.* a woman's undergarment for supporting the breasts.

brass′ tacks′, *n.pl.* the most fundamental considerations; essentials.

brat (brat), *n.* a spoiled or impolite child. —**brat′ty,** *adj.*, **-ti•er, -ti•est.**

Bra•ti•sla•va (brat′ə slä′və, brä′tə-), *n.* the capital of Slovakia. 440,421.

brat•wurst (brat′wûrst, -vōorst′, brät′-), *n.* a sausage made of pork, spices, and herbs.

bra•va•do (bra vä′dō), *n.*, *pl.* **-does, -dos.** an ostentatious display of courage.

brave (brāv), *adj.*, **brav•er, brav•est,** *n.*, *v.*, **braved, brav•ing.** —*adj.* **1.** possessing or exhibiting courage. **2.** making a fine appearance. —*n.* **3.** a warrior, esp. among North American Indians. —*v.t.* **4.** to meet or face courageously. **5.** to defy; challenge. —**brave′ly,** *adv.*

brav′er•y, *n.* brave spirit or conduct.

bra•vo (brä′vō, brä vō′), *interj.*, *n.*, *pl.* **-vos.** —*interj.* **1.** well done! good! —*n.* **2.** a shout of "bravo!"

bra•vu•ra (bra vyŏŏr′ə, -vŏŏr′ə, brä-), *n.*, *pl.* **-ras. 1.** a florid musical passage or piece. **2.** a daring or brilliant performance.

brawl (brôl), *n.* **1.** a noisy fight or quarrel. —*v.i.* **2.** to quarrel angrily and noisily. —**brawl′er,** *n.*

brawn (brôn), *n.* **1.** well-developed muscles. **2.** muscular strength. —**brawn′y,** *adj.*, **-i•er, -i•est.** —**brawn′i•ness,** *n.*

bray (brā), *n.* **1.** a harsh cry, as of a donkey. —*v.i.* **2.** to utter a bray.

braze (brāz), *v.t.*, **brazed, braz•ing.** to unite (metal objects) by soldering at very high temperatures. —**braz′er,** *n.*

bra•zen (brā′zən), *adj.* **1.** shameless or impudent. **2.** made of brass. **3.** like brass, as in sound, color, or strength. —**bra′zen•ly,** *adv.*

bra•zier¹ (brā′zhər), *n.* a metal receptacle for holding live coals.

bra•zier² (brā′zhər), *n.* one who makes articles of brass.

Bra•zil (brə zil′), *n.* a federal republic in South America. 164,511,366. —**Bra•zil′ian,** *adj.*, *n.*

Brazil′ nut′, *n.* the three-sided, edible seed of a South American tree.

Braz•za•ville (braz′ə vil′, brä′zə-), *n.* the capital of the People's Republic of the Congo. 585,812.

breach (brēch), *n.* **1.** an infraction or violation, as of a law. **2.** a gap made in a wall, fortification, etc. **3.** a severance of friendly relations. —*v.t.* **4.** to make a breach in.

bread (bred), *n.* **1.** a baked food made of a dough containing flour or meal and usu. a leavening agent. **2.** livelihood. —*v.t.* **3.** to coat with breadcrumbs. —*Idiom.* **4. break bread,** to eat a meal. —*Proverb.* **5. Cast thy bread upon the waters,** worthy actions will ultimately benefit you. Eccl. 11:1. **6. Man does not live by bread alone,** human beings have spiritual as well as physical needs. Deut. 8:3.

bread′crumb′, *n.* a crumb of bread, either dried or soft.

bread′fruit′, *n.* **1.** the large, round fruit of a tropical tree, eaten baked or roasted. **2.** the tree itself.

Bread′ of Life′, *n.* Jesus Christ. John 6:35, 48.

breadth (bredth, bretth), *n.* **1.** the measure of the side-to-side dimension; width. **2.** freedom from narrowness, as of viewpoint. **3.** extent; scope.

bread′win′ner, *n.* a person who earns a livelihood to support dependents.

break (brāk), *v.*, **broke, bro•ken, break•ing,** *n.* —*v.t.* **1.** to split into pieces; smash. **2.** to make useless by or as if by smashing. **3.** to crack or fracture. **4.** to violate (a law, promise, etc.). **5.** to rupture the surface of: *to break the skin.* **6.** to disrupt the regularity, uniformity, or continuity of. **7.** to end. **8.** to solve or decipher. **9.** to escape from. **10.** to better (a score or record). **11.** to disclose or reveal, as news. **12.** to bankrupt. **13.** to wear down the spirit or resistance of. **14.** to reduce in rank. **15.** to weaken the force of: *to break a fall.* **16.** to train to obedience. **17.** to train away from a habit. —*v.i.* **18.** to split into parts or fragments. **19.** to become useless or inoperative. **20.** to become disassociated: *to break with the past.* **21.** to move suddenly. **22.** to interrupt an activity. **23.** to appear or begin suddenly: *the storm broke.* **24.** (of the heart) to be overwhelmed with sorrow. **25.** (of the voice) to change tone abruptly. **26. break down, a.** to cease to function. **b.** to have a physical or mental collapse. **27. ~ in, a.** to enter property by force. **b.** to train or initiate. **c.** to begin to use. **d.** to interrupt. **28. ~ off,** to stop suddenly. **29. ~ out, a.** to begin abruptly. **b.** to manifest a skin eruption. **c.** to escape. **30. ~ up, a.** to separate; scatter. **b.** to end a personal relationship. **c.** to laugh or make laugh. —*n.* **31.** a crack or opening made by breaking. **32.** the act of breaking. **33.** an interruption of continuity. **34.** a brief rest, as from work. **35.** a beginning: *the break of day.* **36.** an abrupt change. **37.** a sudden dash; escape. **38.** a stroke of luck. —**break′a•ble,** *adj.*

break•age (brā′kij), *n.* **1.** the act of breaking or state of being broken. **2.** things broken. **3.** an allowance for articles broken.

break′down′, *n.* **1.** a breaking down. **2.** a mental or physical collapse. **3.** a classification; analysis.

break′er, *n.* **1.** one that breaks. **2.** a wave that breaks into foam.

break•fast (brek′fəst), *n.* **1.** the first meal of the day. —*v.i.* **2.** to eat breakfast.

break′front′, *n.* a cabinet having a central section extending forward.

break′-in′, *n.* an illegal forcible entry into a home, office, etc.

break′neck′, *adj.* reckless or dangerous, esp. because of excessive speed.

break′through′, *n.* **1.** a significant advance, as in scientific knowledge. **2.** an act of surmounting an obstruction or restriction.

break′up′, *n.* **1.** a dispersal or disintegration **2.** the ending of a personal relationship.

break′wa′ter, *n.* a barrier that breaks the force of waves, as before a harbor.

breast (brest), *n.* **1.** either of the pair of mammary glands on the chest of primates, esp. of the postpubertal female. **2.** the upper, front part of the body; chest. **3.** the bosom conceived of as the center of emotion. —*v.t.* **4.** to meet or oppose boldly.

breast′bone′, *n.* STERNUM.

breast′-feed′, *v.t.*, **-fed, -feed•ing.** to nurse (a baby) at the breast.

breast′plate′, *n.* a piece of plate armor for the front of the torso.

breast′stroke′, *n.* a swimming stroke in which the arms move forward, outward, and rearward while the legs kick outward.

breast′work′, *n.* a hastily erected fortification, usu. breast high.

breath (breth), *n.* **1.** the air inhaled and exhaled in respiration. **2.** respiration. **3.** life; vitality. **4.** the ability to breathe easily. **5.** a single inhalation. **6.** a slight suggestion. **7.** a light current of air. —*Idiom.* **8. out of breath,** gasping for breath. **9. under one's breath,** in a whisper. —**breath′less,** *adj.* —**breath′less•ly,** *adv.*

breathe (brēth), *v.i.*, *v.t.*, **breathed, breath•ing. 1.** to inhale and exhale (air) in respiration. **2.** to pause, as to rest. **3.** to live; exist. **4.** to whisper. —**breath′a•ble,** *adj.*

breath·er (brē'thər), n. 1. a pause, as for breath. 2. a person who breathes.

breath'tak'ing (breth'-), adj. astonishingly beautiful, remarkable, exciting, etc. —breath'tak'ing·ly, adv.

breath·y (breth'ē), adj., -i·er, -i·est. (of the voice) characterized by audible emission of breath.

Brecht (brekt, breкHt), n. **Bertolt**, 1898–1956, German dramatist and poet.

bred (bred), v. pt. and pp. of BREED.

breech (brēch), n. 1. the rear part of the bore of a gun. 2. the buttocks.

breech·es (brich'iz), n. (used with a pl. v.) 1. knee-length trousers for men. 2. Informal. TROUSERS.

breed (brēd), v., **bred, breed·ing**, n. —v.t. 1. to produce (offspring). 2. to give rise to; engender. 3. to bring up; rear. 4. to raise (cattle, etc.) —v.i. 5. to produce offspring. 6. to be produced. —n. 7. a stock; strain. 8. sort; kind; group. —breed'er, n.

breed'ing, n. 1. the producing of offspring. 2. the improvement of livestock or plants by selection. 3. training; nurture. 4. good manners.

breeze (brēz), n., v., **breezed, breez·ing**. —n. 1. a light wind. 2. an easy task. —v.i. 3. to proceed quickly and easily. —breez'y, adj., -i·er, -i·est. —breez'i·ly, adv. —breez'i·ness, n.

breeze'way', n. an open-sided roofed passageway for connecting two buildings.

Brem·en (brem'ən, brā'mən), n. a port in NW Germany. 522,000.

breth·ren (breth'rin), n.pl. 1. fellow members. 2. Archaic. brothers.

Bret'ton Woods' Con'ference (bret'n), n. an international conference called at Bretton Woods, N.H., in July 1944 to deal with international monetary and financial problems.

Breu·ghel or **Breu·gel** or **Brue·ghel** (broi'gəl, brōō'-, brœ'-), n. 1. **Pieter the Elder**, c1525–69, Flemish painter. 2. his sons, **Jan**, 1568–1625, and **Pieter the Younger**, 1564–1637?, Flemish painters.

bre·vet (brə vet', brev'it), n., v., -vet·ted or vet·ed, -vet·ting or -vet·ing. —n. 1. a commission promoting a military officer to a higher rank without increase of pay. —v.t. 2. to promote by brevet.

bre·vi·ar·y (brē'vē er'ē, brev'ē-), n., pl. -ar·ies. a book containing the divine office of the Roman Catholic Church.

brev·i·ty (brev'i tē), n. shortness of duration.

brew (brōō), v.t. 1. to make (beer, ale, etc.) by steeping, boiling, and fermenting malt and hops. 2. to prepare (tea or coffee) by boiling, steeping, etc. 3. to contrive or bring about. —v.i. 4. to make beer or ale. 5. to form: Trouble was brewing. —n. 6. a brewed beverage. —brew'er, n.

brew·er·y, n., pl. -er·ies. a place for brewing beer or other malt liquors.

brew'pub', n. a bar serving beer brewed at a microbrewery on the premises.

Brey·er (brī'ər), n. **Stephen G(erald)**, born 1938, associate justice of the U.S. Supreme Court since 1994.

bri·ar (brī'ər), n. 1. BRIER¹. 2. BRIER².

bribe (brīb), n., v., **bribed, brib·ing**. —n. 1. anything given to persuade or induce, esp an illicit payment. —v.t. 2. to give or promise a bribe to. —brib'er, n. —brib'er·y, n.

bric-a-brac (brik'ə brak'), n. (used with a sing. or pl. v.) small articles collected for their decorative or other interest; knickknacks.

brick (brik), n. 1. a block of clay hardened by heat and used for building, paving, etc. —v.t. 2. to pave or build with brick.

brick'bat', n. 1. a piece of broken brick used as a missile. 2. a caustic criticism.

brick'lay'ing, n. the act or occupation of laying bricks in construction. —brick'lay'er, n.

brid·al (brīd'l), adj. of or for a bride or a wedding.

bride (brīd), n. a newly married woman or one about to be married.

bride'groom', n. a newly married man or one about to be married.

brides'maid', n. a woman who attends the bride at a wedding ceremony.

bridge¹ (brij), n., v., **bridged, bridg·ing**, adj. —n. 1. a structure spanning and providing passage over a river, road, etc. 2. a connection or transition between two adjacent elements, conditions, etc. 3. a raised platform from which a ship is navigated. 4. the ridge of the nose. 5. an artificial replacement for a missing tooth or teeth. —v.t. 6. to make a bridge or passage over. —adj. 7. (esp. of clothing) less expensive than a manufacturer's most expensive products. —bridge'a·ble, adj.

bridge² (brij), n. a card game in which one partnership plays to fulfill a certain declaration against an opposing partnership.

bridge'head', n. a position secured in enemy territory that can be used as a foothold for further advancement.

Bridge'port', n. a seaport in SW Connecticut. 141,686.

bridge'work', n. a dental bridge or bridges.

bri·dle (brīd'l), n., v., -dled, -dling. —n. 1. the head harness of a horse, including bit and reins. 2. a restraint; curb. —v.t. 3. to put a bridle on. 4. to restrain; curb. —v.i. 5. to show resentment.

bri'dle path', n. a wide path for riding horses.

brief (brēf), adj., -er, -est, n., v. —adj. 1. lasting a short time. 2. concise. —n. 3. a memorandum of points of fact or of law for use in conducting a case. 4. a summary or synopsis. 5. **briefs**, close-fitting legless underpants. —v.t. 6. to make a summary of. 7. to instruct by a brief. —brief'ing, n. —brief'ly, adv.

brief'case', n. a flat rectangular case for carrying books, papers, etc.

bri·er¹ (brī'ər), n. a prickly plant or shrub.

bri·er² (brī'ər), n. a white heath, the woody root of which is used for making tobacco pipes.

brig (brig), n. 1. a two-masted sailing vessel square-rigged on both masts. 2. a military prison.

bri·gade (bri gād'), n. 1. a military unit consisting of a headquarters and two or more regiments, squadrons, etc. 2. a group organized for a particular purpose.

brig'a·dier gen'eral (brig'ə dēr'), n., pl. **brig·a·dier generals**. an army officer of the rank between colonel and major general.

brig·and (brig'ənd), n. a bandit, esp. one of a roving band. —brig'and·age, n.

brig·an·tine (brig'ən tēn', -tīn'), n. a two-masted sailing vessel, square-rigged and having a fore-and-aft mainsail.

bright (brīt), adj., -er, -est. 1. radiating much light. 2. vivid or brilliant. 3. quick-witted or intelligent. 4. cheerful or lively. 5. favorable or auspicious. 6. illustrious or glorious. —bright'ly, adv. —bright'ness, n.

bright'en, v.i., v.t. to become or make bright or brighter. —bright'en·er, n.

bril·liant (bril'yənt), adj. 1. shining brightly. 2. distinguished; outstanding. 3. having great intelligence, talent, etc. —bril'liance, bril'lian·cy, n. —bril'liant·ly, adv.

bril·lian·tine (bril'yən tēn'), n. an oily preparation used to make the hair lustrous.

brim (brim), n., v., **brimmed, brim·ming**. —n. 1. the upper edge of anything hollow. 2. a projecting edge, as of a hat. —v.i., v.t. 3. to be full or fill to the brim. —brim'less, adj.

brim'ful', adj. full to the brim.

brim'stone', n. (not in technical use) SULFUR.

Brin·di·si (brin'də zē', brēn'-), n. a port on the Adriatic Sea in SE Italy. 87,420.

brin·dle (brin'dl), n. 1. a brindled coloring. —adj. 2. BRINDLED.

brin'dled, adj. gray or tawny with darker streaks or spots.

brine (brīn), n. 1. water saturated with salt. 2. the sea or ocean. —brin'y, adj., -i·er, -i·est. —brin'i·ness, n.

bring (bring), v.t., **brought, bring·ing**. 1. to cause (someone or something) to come with, to, or toward the speaker. **2.** to cause to occur or exist. **3.** to persuade or compel. **4.** to sell for. **5. bring about,** to accomplish; cause. **6. ~ forth,** to produce. **7. ~ off,** to accomplish. **8. ~ out, a.** to reveal. **b.** to publish. **9. ~ up, a.** to rear. **b.** to mention for consideration. **c.** to vomit. **d.** to stop quickly or abruptly. —**bring′er,** *n.*

brink (bringk), *n.* **1.** the edge of a steep place or of land bordering water. **2.** any extreme edge.

brink′man•ship′ or **brinks′man•ship′,** *n.* the technique of maneuvering a dangerous situation to the limits of safety.

bri•oche (brē ōsh′), *n.* a light, rich, sweet roll of yeast-leavened dough.

bri•quette or **-quet** (bri ket′), *n.* a small block of compressed coal dust or charcoal used for fuel.

Bris•bane (briz′bān, -bən), *n.* a seaport in E Australia. 1,171,300.

brisk (brisk), *adj.,* **-er, -est. 1.** quick and active; lively. **2.** sharp and stimulating. —**brisk′ly,** *adv.* —**brisk′ness,** *n.*

bris•ket (bris′kit), *n.* **1.** the breast of an animal. **2.** a cut of meat from the brisket.

bris•tle (bris′əl), *n., v.,* **-tled, -tling.** —*n.* **1.** a short, stiff hair of certain animals, esp. hogs. **2.** anything resembling these hairs. —*v.i.* **3.** to stand or rise stiffly. **4.** to become rigid with anger. **5.** to be thickly filled. —**bris′tly,** *adj.,* **-tli•er, -tli•est.**

bris′tle•cone′ pine′, *n.* a small pine of the high S Rocky Mountains.

Bris•tol (bris′tl), *n.* a seaport in SW England. 420,100.

Brit., 1. Britain. **2.** British.

Brit•ain (brit′n), *n.* GREAT BRITAIN.

britch•es (brich′iz), *n.* (*used with a pl. v.*) BREECHES.

Brit•i•cism (brit′ə siz′əm), *n.* a word or phrase characteristic of English as spoken in Great Britain.

Brit•ish (brit′ish), *adj.* **1.** of Great Britain or its inhabitants. —*n.* **2.** (*used with a pl. v.*) the people of Great Britain.

Brit′ish Colum′bia, *n.* a province in W Canada. 2,883,367. *Cap.:* Victoria. *Abbr.:* BC, B.C. —**Brit′ish Colum′bian,** *n., adj.*

Brit′ish Com′monwealth of Na′tions, *n.* former name of the COMMONWEALTH OF NATIONS. Also called **Brit′ish Com′monwealth.**

Brit′ish Isles′, *n.pl.* Great Britain, Ireland, and adjacent islands.

Brit′ish ther′mal u′nit, *n.* the amount of heat required to raise the temperature of 1 lb. (0.4 kg) of water 1°F. *Abbr.:* Btu, BTU

Brit•on (brit′n), *n.* **1.** a native or inhabitant of Great Britain, esp. of England. **2.** a member of a Celtic-speaking people inhabiting ancient Britain.

brit•tle (brit′l), *adj.,* **-tler, -tlest.** having hardness and rigidity but breaking readily. —**brit′tle•ness,** *n.*

broach (brōch), *n.* **1.** a tapered tool for shaping and enlarging holes. —*v.t.* **2.** to mention for the first time. **3.** to tap or pierce. —**broach′er,** *n.*

broad (brôd), *adj.,* **-er, -est. 1.** of great breadth. **2.** of great extent. **3.** open; full: *in broad daylight.* **4.** of extensive range or scope. **5.** liberal; tolerant. **6.** not detailed; general: *a broad outline.* **7.** plain or clear: *a broad hint.* —**broad′ly,** *adv.* —**broad′ness,** *n.*

broad′cast′, *v.,* **-cast** or **-cast•ed, -cast•ing,** *n., adv.* —*v.t., v.i.* **1.** to transmit (programs) by radio or television. **2.** to scatter or spread widely. —*n.* **3.** something broadcast. **4.** a radio or television program. —*adv.* **5.** over a wide area. —**broad′cast′er,** *n.*

broad′cloth′, *n.* a closely woven fabric of cotton, rayon, or silk, having a soft finish.

broad′en, *v.i., v.t.* to widen.

broad′ jump′, *n.* LONG JUMP.

broad′loom′, *n.* any carpet woven on a wide loom.

broad′-mind′ed, *adj.* free from prejudice or narrowness; tolerant. —**broad′-mind′ed•ness,** *n.*

broad′side′, *n.* **1.** the side of a ship above the water line. **2.** a simultaneous discharge of all guns on

one side of a warship. **3.** a concerted verbal attack. —*adv.* **4.** directly in the side: *The truck hit the fence broadside.* **5.** at random.

broad′-spec′trum, *adj.* (of an antibiotic) effective against a wide range of organisms.

broad′sword′, *n.* a sword having a straight, broad, flat blade.

Broad′way′, *n.* **1.** an avenue in New York City noted for its theaters. **2.** the commercial theater in the U.S.

bro•cade (brō kād′), *n., v.,* **-cad•ed, -cad•ing.** —*n.* **1.** fabric woven with a raised design. —*v.t.* **2.** to weave with a raised design.

broc•co•li (brok′ə lē), *n., pl.* **-lis.** a plant resembling the cauliflower, eaten as a vegetable.

bro•chette (brō shet′), *n.* a skewer.

bro•chure (brō shŏor′), *n.* a pamphlet or leaflet.

bro•gan (brō′gən), *n.* a sturdy, ankle-high work shoe.

brogue¹ (brōg), *n.* an Irish accent in the pronunciation of English.

brogue² (brōg), *n.* a durable, low-heeled shoe.

broil (broil), *v.t., v.i.* **1.** to cook by direct heat. —*n.* **2.** something broiled.

broil′er, *n.* **1.** a compartment in a stove in which food is broiled. **2.** a young chicken suitable for broiling.

broke (brōk), *v.* **1.** pt. of BREAK. —*adj.* **2.** without money. **3.** bankrupt.

bro•ken (brō′kən), *v.* **1.** pp. of BREAK. —*adj.* **2.** fragmented or fractured. **3.** not functioning properly. **4.** infringed or violated. **5.** interrupted or disconnected. **6.** tamed; subdued. **7.** imperfectly spoken: *broken English.* **8.** disunited or divided: *broken families.* **9.** overwhelmed with sorrow. **10.** ruined; bankrupt. —**bro′ken•ly,** *adv.* —**bro′ken•ness,** *n.*

bro′ken•heart′ed, *adj.* suffering from great sorrow or disappointment.

bro′ker, *n.* **1.** an agent who buys or sells for others on commission. **2.** a mediator who negotiates agreements or contracts.

bro′ker•age (-ij), *n.* **1.** the business of a broker. **2.** the commission charged by a broker.

bro•mide (brō′mīd *or, for 1,* -mid), *n.* **1.** a compound containing bromine. **2.** potassium bromide, formerly used as a sedative. **3.** a trite saying. —**bro•mid′ic** (-mid′ik), *adj.*

bro•mine (brō′mēn, -min), *n.* a reddish, toxic liquid element used in antiknock compounds, pharmaceuticals, etc. *Symbol:* Br; *at. wt.:* 79.909; *at. no.:* 35.

bron•chi•al (brong′kē əl), *adj.* pertaining to the bronchi.

bron•chi′tis (-kī′tis), *n.* inflammation of the membrane lining of the bronchial tubes.

bron′chus (-kəs), *n., pl.* **-chi** (-kē, -kī). either of the two branches of the trachea.

bron•co (brong′kō), *n., pl.* **-cos.** a wild or untamed range pony or mustang of the western U.S.

bron′co•bust′er, *n.* a person who breaks broncos to the saddle.

Bron•të (bron′tē), *n.* **1.** Anne (*"Acton Bell"*), 1820–49, English novelist. **2.** her sister **Charlotte** (*"Currer Bell"*), 1816–55, English novelist. **3.** her sister **Emily Jane** (*"Ellis Bell"*), 1818–48, English novelist.

brontosaur

bron•to•saur (bron′tə sôr′) or **bron′to•sau′rus** (-sôr′əs), *n., pl.* **-saurs** or **-sau•rus•es, -sau•ri** (-sôr′ī). a huge herbivorous dinosaur. [< NL, = Gk *brontē* thunder + *saûros* lizard]

Bronx (brongks), *n.* **the,** a borough of New York City. 1,203,789.

bronze (bronz), *n.*, *v.*, **bronzed, bronz•ing,** *adj.* —*n.* **1.** an alloy of copper and tin. **2.** a metallic brownish color. —*v.t.* **3.** to give the appearance of bronze to. —*adj.* **4.** made of or coated with bronze.

Bronze′ Age′, *n.* a period in the history of humankind, following the Stone Age and preceding the Iron Age, during which bronze weapons and implements were used: representative cultures are the Minoan and Mycenaean.

bronze′ med′al, *n.* a medal, traditionally of bronze, awarded to the third-place winner in a competition. —**bronze′ med′alist,** *n.*

brooch (brōch), *n.* an ornamental clasp or pin.

brood (brōōd), *n.* **1.** a number of young hatched at one time. **2.** all the children in a family. —*v.i.* **3.** to sit upon eggs to be hatched. **4.** to dwell on a subject morbidly. —*adj.* **5.** kept for breeding.

brood′er, *n.* **1.** a heated structure for the rearing of young chickens. **2.** a person who broods.

brood′mare′, *n.* a mare used for breeding.

brook[1] (brŏŏk), *n.* a small natural stream of fresh water.

brook[2] (brŏŏk), *v.t.* to bear; tolerate.

Brook′ Farm′, *n.* a farm in West Roxbury, Mass.: experimental cooperative community 1841–47.

Brook•lyn (brŏŏk′lin), *n.* a borough of New York City, on Long Island. 2,300,664.

broom (brŏŏm, brŏŏm), *n.* **1.** a long-handled implement for sweeping, with a brush of straw or similar material. **2.** a flowering shrub of the legume family. —*Saying.* **3. A new broom sweeps clean,** a new manager makes significant changes.

broom′stick′, *n.* the long slender handle of a broom.

bros. or **Bros.,** brothers.

broth (brôth, broth), *n.* a thin soup made by boiling meat, vegetables, or fish in water.

broth•el (broth′əl, brô′thəl), *n.* a house of prostitution.

broth•er (bruth′ər), *n.* **1.** a male sibling. **2.** a male numbered in the same kinship group, nationality, etc., as another. **3.** (*often cap.*) a man who devotes himself to the duties of a religious order without taking holy orders. —**broth′er•ly,** *adj.*

broth′er•hood′, *n.* **1.** the condition or quality of being a brother or brothers. **2.** fellowship. **3.** all those engaged in a particular trade.

broth′er-in-law′, *n.*, *pl.* **broth•ers-in-law. 1.** the brother of one's spouse. **2.** the husband of one's sister. **3.** the husband of one's spouse's sister.

brought (brôt), *v.* pt. and pp. of BRING.

brou•ha•ha (brōō′hä hä′), *n.*, *pl.* **-has.** an uproar.

brow (brou), *n.* **1.** the ridge over the eye. **2.** an eyebrow. **3.** the forehead. **4.** the edge of a steep place.

brow′beat′, *v.t.*, **-beat, -beat•en, -beat•ing.** to intimidate by overbearing looks or words.

brown (broun), *n.*, *adj.*, **-er, -est,** *v.* —*n.* **1.** a dark color with a yellowish or reddish hue. —*adj.* **2.** of the color brown. **3.** sunburned or tanned. —*v.t.*, *v.i.* **4.** to make or become brown. **5.** to fry, roast, etc., to a brown color. —**brown′ish,** *adj.*

Brown (broun), *n.* **John** (*"Old Brown of Osawatomie"*), 1800–59, U.S. abolitionist: leader of the attack at Harpers Ferry.

brown′-bag′, *v.t.*, **-bagged, -bag•ging.** to bring (one's lunch) to work or school, usu. in a small brown paper bag. —**brown′-bag′ger,** *n.*

Brown′ Bomb′er, *n.* nickname of Joe Louis.

brown•ie (brou′nē), *n.* **1.** an elf who secretly helps with chores. **2.** a bar of flat, chewy chocolate cake. **3.** (*cap.*) a Girl Scout between the ages of 6 and 8.

Brown•ing (brou′ning), *n.* **1. Elizabeth Barrett,** 1806–61, English poet. **2.** her husband, **Robert,** 1812–89, English poet.

brown′out′, *n.* a curtailment of electric power to prevent a blackout.

brown′ rice′, *n.* unpolished rice.

brown′stone′, *n.* **1.** a reddish brown sandstone,

used for building. **2.** a row house fronted with this stone.

brown′ stud′y, *n.* deep, serious thought.

brown′ sug′ar, *n.* sugar that retains some molasses.

Browns′ville′, *n.* a seaport in S Texas. 112,904.

Brown v. Board of Education, *n.* a 1954 decision of the U.S. Supreme Court ruling that segregated schools are unequal and therefore violate the Fourteenth Amendment.

browse (brouz), *v.*, **browsed, brows•ing,** *n.* —*v.t.*, *v.i.* **1.** to eat or nibble at (foliage, berries, etc.). **2.** to look through casually. —*n.* **3.** tender shoots or twigs as food for cattle.

brows′er, *n.* **1.** a person or thing that browses. **2.** *Computers.* an application program that allows the user to examine encoded documents in a form suitable for display, esp. such a program for use on the World Wide Web.

bru•in (brōō′in), *n.* a bear.

bruise (brōōz), *v.*, **bruised, bruis•ing,** *n.* —*v.t.* **1.** to injure and discolor without breaking the skin. **2.** to hurt slightly, as with an insult. **3.** to crush (drugs or food) by pounding. —*v.i.* **4.** to bruise body tissue. **5.** to become bruised emotionally. —*n.* **6.** an injury due to bruising.

bruis′er, *n. Informal.* a strong, tough man.

bruit (brōōt), *v.t.* to voice abroad; rumor.

brunch (brunch), *n.* a meal that serves as both breakfast and lunch.

Bru•nei (brōō nī′, -nā′), *n.* a sultanate on the NW coast of Borneo. 307,616. —**Bru•nei′an,** *adj.*, *n.*

bru•nette (brōō net′), *adj.* **1.** (of a female) having dark hair and, often, dark eyes and complexion. —*n.* **2.** a girl or woman with such coloration.

brunt (brunt), *n.* the main force or impact, as of an attack or blow.

brush[1] (brush), *n.* **1.** an implement consisting of bristles and a handle, used for painting, grooming, etc. **2.** the bushy tail of an animal, esp. a fox. **3.** a light, stroking touch. **4.** a close encounter. —*v.t.* **5.** to sweep, paint, etc., with a brush. **6.** to touch lightly in passing. **7.** to remove by brushing. —*v.i.* **8.** to skim with a slight contact. **9. brush off,** to rebuff. **10.** ~ **up on,** to review (studies, a skill, etc.).

brush[2] (brush), *n.* **1.** a dense growth of bushes, shrubs, etc. **2.** BRUSHWOOD.

brush′-off′, *n.* an abrupt rebuff.

brush′wood′, *n.* branches broken from trees.

brusque or **brusk** (brusk), *adj.* abrupt in manner or speech. —**brusque′ly,** *adv.* —**brusque′ness,** *n.*

Brus•sels (brus′əlz), *n.* the capital of Belgium. 1,050,787 (with suburbs).

Brus′sels sprouts′ (or **sprout′**), *n.* a plant with small, cabbagelike, edible heads along the stalk.

bru•tal (brōōt′l), *adj.* **1.** savage; cruel. **2.** harsh; severe. —**bru•tal′i•ty,** *n.*, *pl.* **-ties.** —**bru′tal•ly,** *adv.*

bru′tal•ize′, *v.t.*, **-ized, -iz•ing. 1.** to make brutal. **2.** to treat with brutality. —**bru′tal•i•za′tion,** *n.*

brute (brōōt), *n.* **1.** an animal; beast. **2.** an insensitive or crude person. —*adj.* **3.** animallike. **4.** irrational. **5.** savage; cruel. —**brut′ish,** *adj.* —**brut′ish•ly,** *adv.*

Bry•an (brī′ən), *n.* **William Jennings,** 1860–1925, U.S. political leader.

B.S., Bachelor of Science.

Btu or **BTU,** British thermal unit.

bub•ba (bub′ə), *n.*, *pl.* **-bas. 1.** *Chiefly Southern U.S.* brother. **2.** *Slang.* an uneducated, conservative Southern white male.

bub•ble (bub′əl), *n.*, *v.*, **-bled, -bling.** —*n.* **1.** a spherical body of gas in a liquid. **2.** a globule of gas in a thin liquid envelope. **3.** anything that lacks firmness, substance, or permanence. **4.** a transparent dome. —*v.i.* **5.** to form or produce bubbles. **6.** to flow with a gurgling noise. —**bub′bly,** *adj.*, **-bli•er, -bli•est.**

bub′ble•gum′, *n.* a chewing gum that can be blown into large bubbles.

Bu•ber (bōō′bər), *n.* **Martin,** 1878–1965, Jewish philosopher, theologian, and scholar: born in Austria.

bu•bo (bōō′bō, byōō′-), *n.*, *pl.* **-boes.** an inflammatory swelling of a lymph node.

bu•bon′ic plague′ (bōō bon′ik, byōō-), *n.* a severe infection characterized by buboes at the armpits and groin. Compare BLACK DEATH.

buc•ca•neer (buk′ə nēr′), *n.* a pirate. [< F *boucanier* lit., barbecuer]

Bu•chan•an (byōō kan′ən, bə-), *n.* **James,** 1791–1868, 15th president of the U.S. 1857–61.

Bu•cha•rest (bōō′kə rest′), *n.* the capital of Romania. 1,975,808.

buck¹ (buk), *n.* **1.** the male of the deer, antelope, etc. **2.** BUCKSKIN. **3.** an impetuous man or youth.

buck² (buk), *v.i.* **1.** to leap with arched back so as to dislodge a rider. **2.** to resist or oppose something obstinately. —*v.t.* **3.** to throw (a rider) by bucking. **4.** to resist or oppose obstinately. —**buck′er,** *n.*

buck³ (buk), *n.* **1.** a sawhorse. **2.** a leather-covered block used in gymnastics for vaulting.

buck⁴ (buk), *n.* **1.** ultimate responsibility. —*Idiom.* **2. pass the buck,** to shift responsibility or blame to another person.

buck⁵ (buk), *n. Slang.* a dollar.

buck′board′, *n.* a carriage in which a long board is used in place of body and springs.

buck•et (buk′it), *n.* **1.** a deep, cylindrical container with a semicircular handle. **2.** a scoop, as on a steam shovel. **3.** the amount a bucket can hold. —*Idiom.* **4. drop in the bucket,** a small, inadequate amount. **5. kick the bucket,** *Slang.* to die.

buck′et seat′, *n.* an individual seat with a contoured back, as in some automobiles.

buck′eye′, *n.* **1.** any of various trees of the horse chestnut family. **2.** the brown nut of any of these trees.

buck•le (buk′əl), *n.*, *v.*, **-led, -ling.** —*n.* **1.** a clasp used for fastening two loose ends, as of a belt. **2.** a bend, bulge, or warp, as in a board. —*v.t.*, *v.i.* **3.** to fasten with a buckle. **4.** to bend or warp. **5. buckle down,** to set to work with determination.

buck′ler, *n.* a round shield held by a grip.

buck•ram (buk′rəm), *n.* a stiff cotton fabric for interlinings, book bindings, etc.

buck′saw′, *n.* a two-handed saw having a blade set across an upright frame.

buck′shot′, *n.* a large size of lead shot used for hunting game.

buck′skin′, *n.* **1.** a strong, soft leather, orig. made from deerskins, now usu. from sheepskins. **2. -skins,** clothes or shoes made of buckskin.

buck′tooth′, *n.*, *pl.* **-teeth.** a projecting front tooth. —**buck′toothed′,** *adj.*

buck′wheat′, *n.* **1.** any of several plants cultivated for their edible triangular seeds. **2.** the seeds of this plant, made into flour or a cereal.

bu•col•ic (byōō kol′ik), *adj.* **1.** of shepherds; pastoral. **2.** of or suggesting an idyllic rural life. —**bu•col′i•cal•ly,** *adv.*

bud (bud), *n.*, *v.*, **bud•ded, bud•ding.** —*n.* **1.** any of the small terminal bulges on a plant stem, from which leaves or flowers develop. **2.** an undeveloped person or thing. —*v.i.* **3.** to put forth buds. **4.** to begin to develop. —*Idiom.* **5. in the bud,** in an undeveloped, early stage. —**bud′der,** *n.*

Bu•da•pest (bōō′də pest′), *n.* the capital of Hungary. 2,104,000.

Bud•dha (bōō′də, bŏŏd′ə), *n.*, *pl.* **-dhas. 1.** Also called **Gautama.** (*Prince Siddhāttha* or *Siddhartha*) 566?–c480 B.C., Indian religious leader: founder of Buddhism. **2.** a representation of Buddha.

Bud•dhism (bōō′diz əm, bŏŏd′iz-), *n.* an Asian religion holding that the extinction of desire culminates in the attainment of Nirvana. —**Bud′dhist,** *n.*, *adj.*

bud•dy (bud′ē), *n.*, *pl.* **-dies.** *Informal.* a friend; comrade.

budge (buj), *v.t.*, *v.i.*, **budged, budg•ing. 1.** to move slightly: *The car wouldn't budge.* **2.** to yield or cause to yield.

budg•er•i•gar (buj′ər i gär′), *n.* an Australian parakeet bred as a pet in a variety of colors.

budg•et (buj′it), *n.* **1.** an estimate of expected income and expenses. **2.** a plan of operations based on such an estimate. **3.** a limited stock or supply. —*v.t.* **4.** to allot (funds, time, etc.). —**budg′et•ar′y** (-i ter′ē), *adj.*

budg•ie (buj′ē), *n.* BUDGERIGAR.

Bue′na Vis′ta (bwā′nə vis′tə, vēs′-), *n.* a village in NE Mexico: site of U.S. victory in battle (1847) during the Mexican War.

Bue•nos Ai•res (bwā′nəs ī′r′iz, bō′nəs), *n.* the capital of Argentina. 9,927,404.

buff (buf), *n.* **1.** a soft, thick, light yellow leather. **2.** a brownish yellow color. **3.** a devotee of some activity or subject. **4.** *Informal.* the bare skin: *in the buff.* —*adj.* **5.** of the color buff. **6.** made of buff. **7.** *Slang.* physically attractive; muscular. —*v.t.* **8.** to clean or polish with a buffer.

buf•fa•lo (buf′ə lō′), *n.*, *pl.* **-loes, -los, -lo,** *v.*, **-loed, -lo•ing.** —*n.* **1.** any of several large wild oxen, as the bison or water buffalo. —*v.t.* *Informal.* **2.** to puzzle or baffle. **3.** to intimidate. [< Pg < LL *būfalus* « Gk *boúbalos*]

Buf′fa•lo′, *n.* a port in W New York. 312,965.

buf′falo wing′, *n.* a deep-fried chicken wing served in a spicy sauce and usu. with celery and blue cheese.

buff′er¹, *n.* **1.** anything used for absorbing shock, as during a collision. **2.** a temporary storage area that holds data until the computer is ready to process it. **3.** any substance capable of neutralizing both acids and bases in a solution.

buff′er², *n.* a leather-covered stick, block, or wheel used for polishing or buffing.

buf•fet¹ (buf′it), *n.* **1.** a blow or violent shock. —*v.t.* **2.** to strike, as with the fist. **3.** to strike against or push repeatedly: *The wind buffeted the house.*

buf•fet² (bə fā′, bŏŏ-), *n.* **1.** a cabinet for holding china, linen, etc. **2.** a meal laid out so that guests may serve themselves. **3.** a counter for food or refreshments.

buf•foon (bə fōōn′), *n.* a person who amuses others by jokes, pranks, etc. —**buf•foon′er•y,** *n.* —**buf•foon′ish,** *adj.*

bug (bug), *n.*, *v.*, **bugged, bug•ging.** —*n.* **1.** any of a group of insects with sucking mouthparts. **2.** (loosely) any insect. **3.** *Informal.* any microorganism, esp. a virus. **4.** a defect, as in computer software. **5.** a hidden electronic eavesdropping device. —*v.t.* **6.** to install a secret listening device in or on. **7.** *Informal.* to annoy or pester.

bug•a•boo (bug′ə bōō′), *n.*, *pl.* **-boos.** BUGBEAR.

bug′bear′, *n.* any source, real or imaginary, of fright or fear.

bug′-eyed′, *adj.* with bulging eyes.

buddha

bug•gy (bug′ē), *n.*, *pl.* **-gies. 1.** a light, horse-drawn carriage with a single seat. **2.** BABY CARRIAGE.

bu•gle (byōō′gəl), *n.*, *v.*, **-gled, -gling.** —*n.* **1.** a brass wind instrument like a cornet but usu. without valves. —*v.i.* **2.** to sound a bugle. —**bu′gler,** *n.*

build (bild), *v.*, **built, build•ing,** *n.* —*v.t.* **1.** to construct by joining parts or materials. **2.** to establish or base. **3.** to form or create. —*v.i.* **4.** to engage in building. **5.** to increase in intensity, tempo, etc. **6.** build up, **a.** to develop or increase. **b.** to praise or promote. —*n.* **7.** physique: *a strong build.* —**build′er,** *n.*

build′ing, *n.* **1.** any relatively permanent structure with a roof and walls. **2.** the act or business of constructing houses or other buildings.

build′up′ or **build′-up′,** *n.* **1.** an increase in number, strength, etc. **2.** extravagant praise or publicity.

built′-in′, *adj.* **1.** built as part of a larger construction: *built-in bookcases.* **2.** inherent.

built′-up′, *adj.* **1.** built or enlarged by adding something. **2.** filled in with buildings.

Bu•jum•bu•ra (boo′joom boor′ə), *n.* the capital of Burundi. 272,600.

bulb (bulb), *n.* **1. a.** a swollen, underground stem with fleshy leaves, as in the onion or daffodil. **b.** a plant growing from such a stem. **2.** any round, enlarged part. **3.** an incandescent lamp or its glass housing. —**bul′bous,** *adj.*

Bul•gar•i•a (bul gâr′ē ə, bŏŏl-), *n.* a republic in SE Europe. 8,652,745. —**Bul•gar′i•an,** *n., adj.*

Bulge (bulj), *n.* **Battle of the,** the final major German counteroffensive in World War II, in the Ardennes Forest in Belgium and Luxembourg: begun in 1944 and repulsed by the Allies in January, 1945; so called from the "bulge" in the German lines caused by the territories they seized.

bu•lim•i•a (byoo lim′ē ə, -lē′mē ə, boo-), *n.* an eating disorder marked by excessive eating binges followed by self-induced vomiting. —**bu•lim′ic,** *adj., n.*

bulk (bulk), *n.* **1.** magnitude in three dimensions, esp. when great. **2.** the main mass or body. —*adj.* **3.** being or involving material in bulk. —*v.i.* **4.** to increase in size or importance. —**bulk′y,** *adj.,* **-i•er, -i•est.**

bulk′head′, *n.* **1.** a wall-like construction inside a ship for forming watertight compartments. **2.** a retaining structure for shore protection. **3.** a boxlike structure covering a stairwell.

bull¹ (bŏŏl), *n.* **1.** the male of a bovine animal or of certain other large animals, as the elephant and moose. **2.** a speculator who believes that stock prices will increase. —*adj.* **3.** male. **4.** marked by rising prices, esp. of stocks: *a bull market.* —**Idiom. 5.** bull in a china shop, an extremely awkward or clumsy person. **6. take the bull by the horns,** to attack a difficult or risky problem fearlessly.

bull² (bŏŏl), *n.* a formal papal document.

bull³ (bŏŏl), *n.* exaggerations; lies; nonsense.

bull′dog′, *n.* **1.** a shorthaired, muscular dog with prominent, undershot jaws. **2.** a stubbornly persistent person. —*adj.* **3.** like a bulldog; stubborn.

bull′doze′, *v.t.,* **-dozed, -doz•ing. 1.** to clear or level with a bulldozer. **2.** to coerce or intimidate.

bull′doz′er, *n.* a large, powerful tractor having a vertical blade at the front end for moving earth, rocks, etc.

bul•let (bŏŏl′it), *n.* a small metal projectile for firing from small arms.

bul•le•tin (bŏŏl′i tn, -tin), *n.* **1.** a brief public statement, as of late news. **2.** a periodical publication issued by an organization.

bul′letin board′, *n.* a board for the posting of bulletins, notices, etc.

bul′letin board′ sys′tem, *n.* a facility for relaying electronic messages, software, etc., by modem.

bul′let•proof′, *adj.* **1.** capable of resisting the impact of a bullet. —*v.t.* **2.** to make bulletproof.

bull′fight′, *n.* a traditional spectacle, as in Spain and Mexico, in which a bull is fought and killed by a matador. —**bull′fight′er,** *n.* —**bull′fight′ing,** *n.*

bull′finch′, *n.* a Eurasian finch, the male of which has a rosy breast.

bull′frog′, *n.* a large North American frog with a deep voice.

bull′head′ed, *adj.* stubborn.

bull′horn′, *n.* a high-powered, electrical megaphone.

bul•lion (bŏŏl′yən), *n.* gold or silver in bars or ingots.

bull′ish, *adj.* **1.** like a bull; stubborn. **2.** (of the stock market) marked by rising prices. **3.** optimistic.

Bull′ Moose′, *n.* a member of the Progressive Party under the leadership of Theodore Roosevelt. Also called **Bull′ Moos′er** (moo′sər).

bul•lock (bŏŏl′ək), *n.* a castrated bull; steer.

bull′pen′, *n.* **1.** a place where relief pitchers warm up during a baseball game. **2.** *Informal.* a cell for the temporary detention of prisoners.

Bull′ Run′, *n.* a creek in NE Virginia, near Washington, D.C.: the first battle of the American Civil War **(Battle of Bull Run)** was fought near there in 1861, and a second battle in 1862. Also called **Manassas.**

bull′ ses′sion, *n.* an informal, spontaneous group discussion.

bull's′-eye′, *n., pl.* **-eyes. 1.** the circular spot at the center of a target. **2.** a shot that hits this.

bul•ly (bŏŏl′ē), *n., pl.* **-lies,** *v.,* **-lied, -ly•ing.** —*n.* **1.** person who habitually intimidates weaker people. —*v.t.* **2.** to intimidate. —*v.i.* **3.** to be loudly arrogant.

bul•rush (bŏŏl′rush′), *n.* any of various rushes of the sedge family and the cattail family.

bul•wark (bŏŏl′wərk, -wôrk), *n.* **1.** a defense wall; rampart. **2.** a protection or defense. **3.** Usu., **-warks.** a wall enclosing the perimeter of a ship's deck.

bum (bum), *n., v.,* **bummed, bum•ming,** *adj.* —*n.* **1.** a loafer; idler. **2.** a tramp, hobo, or derelict. **3.** *Informal.* an enthusiast: *a ski bum.* —*v.t.* **4.** *Informal.* to borrow without expectation of returning. —*v.i.* **5.** to live as a bum. —*adj. Slang.* **6.** of poor quality. **7.** false or misleading: *a bum rap.* **8.** lame.

bum•ble (bum′bəl), *v.,* **-bled, -bling.** —*v.i.* **1.** to blunder. **2.** to stumble. —*v.t.* **3.** to bungle or botch. —**bum′bler,** *n.*

bum′ble•bee′ or **bum′ble bee′,** *n.* any of several large, hairy social bees.

bum•mer (bum′ər), *n. Slang.* any unpleasant experience.

bump (bump), *v.t., v.i.* **1.** to strike or collide (with). **2.** to bounce along with jolts. **3. bump into,** to meet by chance. **4.** ~ **off,** *Slang.* to murder. —*n.* **5.** a collision; blow. **6.** a swelling from a blow. **7.** a small area higher than the surrounding surface. —**bump′y,** *adj.,* **-i•er, -i•est.**

bump′er, *n.* **1.** a metal guard for protecting the front or rear of an automobile, truck, etc. —*adj.* **2.** unusually abundant: *a bumper crop.*

bump′er stick′er, *n.* a gummed paper strip bearing a printed slogan or witty saying, for sticking on an automobile bumper.

bump•kin (bump′kin), *n.* an awkward, simple rustic; yokel.

bump′tious (-shəs), *adj.* offensively self-assertive.

bums′ rush′, *n. Slang.* **1.** forcible and swift ejection from a place. **2.** any rude or abrupt dismissal.

bun (bun), *n.* **1.** a bread roll, either plain or slightly sweetened. **2.** hair gathered into a round coil.

bunch (bunch), *n.* **1.** a connected group; cluster: *a bunch of grapes.* **2.** a group of people or things. —*v.t., v.i.* **3.** to gather into a bunch.

bun•dle (bun′dl), *n., v.,* **-dled, -dling.** —*n.* **1.** a quantity of material gathered or bound together. **2.** a package. **3.** a group of things; bunch. **4.** *Slang.* a great deal of money. —*v.t.* **5.** to tie or wrap in a bundle. **6.** to send away hurriedly. **7. bundle up,** to dress warmly.

bung (bung), *n.* a stopper for a bunghole.

bun•ga•low (bung′gə lō′), *n.* a small house, usu. one-storied.

bun′gee cord′ (bun′jē), *n.* an elasticized cord, typically with a hook at each end, used chiefly as a fastener. Also called **bun′gee.**

bun′gee jump′ing, *n.* the sport of jumping off a high structure to which one is attached by bungee cords, so that the body springs back just before impact.

bung'hole', n. a hole in a cask through which it is filled.

bun•gle (bung'gəl), v., **-gled, -gling,** n. —v.t., v.i. **1.** to do or work clumsily or inadequately. —n. **2.** something bungled. —**bun'gler,** n.

bun•ion (bun'yən), n. an inflammation of the bursa of the big toe.

bunk¹ (bungk), n. **1.** a built-in platform bed, as on a ship. **2.** BUNKHOUSE. —v.i. **3.** to occupy a bunk. —v.t. **4.** to provide with a place to sleep.

bunk² (bungk), n. Informal. BUNKUM.

bun•ker (bung'kər), n. **1.** a large bin or receptacle. **2.** a partially underground bomb shelter or fortification. **3.** Golf. any obstacle constituting a hazard. —adj. **4.** characterized by or given to extreme measures to avoid defeat: a bunker mentality.

Bun'ker Hill', n. a hill in Charlestown, Mass., near Boston: the first major battle of the Revolutionary War **(Battle of Bunker Hill)** was fought on adjoining Breed's Hill on June 17, 1775.

bunk'house', n. a rough building housing ranch hands, campers, etc.

bun•kum (bung'kəm), n. insincere or empty talk. [after a pointless speech in Congress by F. Walker, who explained that he was expected to make a speech by his constituents in Buncombe, county in North Carolina]

bun•ny (bun'ē), n., pl. **-nies.** a rabbit, esp. a young one.

Bun'sen burn'er (bun'sən), n. a gas burner commonly used in chemical laboratories. [after R. W. Bunsen (1811–99), German chemist]

bunt (bunt), v.t., v.i. **1.** to push (something) with the horns or head. **2.** to tap (a pitched baseball) close to home plate. —n. **3.** a push with the head or horns. **4.** a bunted baseball. —**bunt'er,** n.

bun•ting¹ (bun'ting), n. **1.** a coarse, open fabric for flags, etc. **2.** flags collectively.

bun•ting² (bun'ting), n. a small, seed-eating songbird.

bun•ting³ (bun'ting), n. a hooded sleeping garment for infants.

Bun•yan (bun'yən), n **1. John,** 1628–88, English preacher: author of The Pilgrim's Progress. **2. Paul.** PAUL BUNYAN.

bu•oy (bōō'ē, boi), n., pl. **-oys,** v. —n. **1.** an anchored float used as a marker or mooring. **2.** a ringlike life preserver. —v.t. **3.** to keep afloat. **4.** to mark with buoys. **5.** to sustain or encourage.

buoy•an•cy (boi'ən sē, bōō'yən-), n. **1.** the power to float in a fluid. **2.** the upward pressure exerted by the fluid in which a body is immersed. **3.** cheerfulness. —**buoy'ant,** adj. —**buoy'ant•ly,** adv.

bur (bûr), n. **1.** a rough prickly case around the seeds of certain plants. **2.** any bur-bearing plant. **3.** BURR¹ (defs. 1, 2).

Bur•bank (bûr'bangk'), n. **Luther,** 1849–1926, U.S. horticulturist and plant breeder.

bur•den¹ (bûr'dn), n. **1.** that which is carried; load. **2.** that which is borne with difficulty; onus. —v.t. **3.** to load heavily. **4.** to load oppressively; trouble. —**bur'den•some,** adj.

bur•den² (bûr'dn), n. **1.** a repeated main point or idea. **2.** a musical refrain; chorus.

bur•dock (bûr'dok), n. a coarse broad-leaved weed bearing prickly heads of burs.

bu•reau (byōōr'ō), n., pl. **bu•reaus, bu•reaux** (byōōr'ōz). **1.** a chest of drawers. **2.** a government department or administrative unit. **3.** a business of-fice or agency.

bu•reauc•ra•cy (byōō rok'rə sē), n., pl. **-cies. 1.** government by a rigid hierarchy of administrators and officials. **2.** a body of officials and administrators. **3.** administration characterized by excessive red tape and routine. —**bu'reau•crat** (byōōr'ə krat'), n. —**bu'reau•crat'ic,** adj. —**bu'reau•crat'i•cal•ly,** adv.

bu•reauc'ra•tize' (-tīz'), v.t., v.i., **-tized, -tiz•ing.** to make or become bureaucratic. —**bu•reauc'ra•ti•za'tion,** n.

bu•rette (byōō ret'), n. a glass tube used in a laboratory to measure liquids.

burg (bûrg), n. Informal. a small, quiet city or town.

bur•geon (bûr'jən), v.i. **1.** to grow or develop quickly. **2.** to begin to grow, as a bud.

burg•er (bûr'gər), n. a hamburger.

bur•gess (bûr'jis), n. a representative in the House of Burgesses.

burgh (bûr'ō, bûr'ō, bûr'ə, bur'ə), n. (in Scotland) an incorporated town.

burgh•er (bûr'gər), n. an inhabitant of a town, esp. a member of the middle class.

bur•glar (bûr'glər), n. a person who commits burglary.

bur'glar•ize', v.t., v.i., **-ized, -iz•ing.** to commit burglary (in).

bur'gla•ry, n., pl. **-ries.** the felony of breaking into and entering a building with intent to steal.

bur'gle (-gəl), v.t., v.i., **-gled, -gling.** Informal. to burglarize.

bur•go•mas'ter (bûr'gə-), n. the chief magistrate of a town of Holland, Flanders, Germany, or Austria.

bur•goo (bûr'gōō, bûr gōō'), n., pl. **-goos** for 2b. **1.** a thick oatmeal gruel. **2.** Chiefly Kentucky and Tennessee. a thick, highly seasoned stew, made of chicken or small game and corn, tomatoes, and onions.

Bur•goyne (bər goin'), n. **John,** 1722–92, British general: surrendered at Saratoga in the American Revolution.

Bur•gun•dy (bûr'gən dē), n., pl. **-dies.** (often l.c.) any of the red or white wines orig. produced in Burgundy, a region in central France.

bur•i•al (ber'ē əl), n. the act or ceremony of burying.

Bur•ki•na Fa•so (bər kē'nə fä'sō), n. a republic in W Africa. 10,891,159. Formerly, **Upper Volta.**

burl (bûrl), n. **1.** a small knot or lump in cloth. **2.** a dome-shaped growth on the trunk of a tree, sliced to make veneer. —**burled,** adj.

bur•lap (bûr'lap), n. a coarse fabric of jute or hemp.

bur•lesque (bər lesk'), n., v., **-lesqued, -lesqu•ing.** —n. **1.** a parody or caricature. **2.** a stage show featuring bawdy comedy and striptease acts. —v.t., v.i. **3.** to mock by burlesque.

bur•ly (bûr'lē), adj., **-li•er, -li•est.** large in bodily size; sturdy. —**bur'li•ness,** n.

Bur•ma (bûr'mə), n. former name of MYANMAR. —**Bur•mese'** (-mēz', -mēs'), n., pl., **-mese,** adj.

burn (bûrn), v., **burned** or **burnt, burn•ing,** n. —v.i. **1.** to be on fire. **2.** to give off light. **3.** to be hot. **4.** to be injured, damaged, or destroyed by fire, heat, or acid. **5.** to feel strong emotion. —v.t. **6.** to cause to be consumed by fire. **7.** to use as fuel. **8.** to sunburn. **9.** to injure, damage, or destroy with or as if with fire. **10.** to produce with fire: to burn a hole. **11.** to cause a stinging sensation in. **12. burn down,** to burn to the ground. **13. ~ out,** to exhaust or become exhausted through overwork and stress. **14. ~ up,** Informal. to make or become angry. —n. **15.** an injury caused by burning. **16.** the process or result of burning. —**burn'a•ble,** adj.

Burne-Jones (bûrn'jōnz'), n. **Sir Edward Coley,** 1833–98, English painter and designer.

burn'er, n. the part of a gas or electric fixture or appliance from which flame or heat issues.

Bur•nett (bər net'), n. **Frances Hodgson,** 1849–1924, U.S. novelist, born in England.

burn'ing bush', n. **1.** a desert bush that burned but was not consumed, and from which an angel of God appeared to Moses. Ex. 3:2-4. **2.** a shrubby plant having foliage that turns red in autumn. **3.** any of various plants that have bright red foliage in autumn.

bur•nish (bûr'nish), v.t., v. **1.** to polish (a surface) by friction. —n. **2.** brightness; luster. —**bur'nish•er,** n.

bur•noose (bər nōōs'), n. a hooded mantle or cloak worn by Arabs.

burn'out', n. **1.** the termination of effective combustion in a rocket engine, due to exhaustion of propellant. **2.** fatigue and frustration resulting from prolonged stress and overwork.

Burns (bûrnz), *n.* **Robert,** 1759–96, Scottish poet.

burnt (bûrnt), *v.* a pt. and pp. of BURN.

burp (bûrp), *Informal.* —*n.* **1.** a belch. —*v.i.* **2.** to belch. —*v.t.* **3.** to cause (a baby) to belch.

Burr (bûr), *n.* **Aaron,** 1756–1836, vice president of the U.S. 1801–05.

bur•ro (bûr′ō, bŏŏr′ō, bur′ō), *n., pl.* **-ros.** a donkey.

Bur•roughs (bûr′ōz, bur′-), *n.* **1. Edgar Rice,** 1875–1950, U.S. novelist. **2. John,** 1837–1921, U.S. naturalist and essayist. **3. William Seward,** 1855–98, U.S. inventor of the adding machine.

bur•row (bûr′ō, bur′ō), *n.* **1.** a hole dug in the ground by an animal. **2.** a place of retreat. —*v.i.* **3.** to dig a burrow. **4.** to lodge or hide in a burrow. **5.** to proceed by or as if by digging. —*v.t.* **6.** to dig a burrow into. **7.** to make by burrowing. —**bur′-row•er,** *n.*

bur•sa (bûr′sə), *n., pl.* **-sae** (-sē), **-sas.** a sac containing lubricating fluid, as between a tendon and a bone.

bur•sar (bûr′sər, -sär), *n.* a treasurer, esp. of a college.

bur•si•tis (bər sī′tis), *n.* inflammation of a bursa.

burst (bûrst), *v.,* **burst, burst•ing,** *n.* —*v.i.* **1.** to break apart with sudden violence. **2.** to issue forth suddenly. **3.** to give sudden expression to emotion. **4.** to be extremely full. **5.** to appear suddenly. —*v.t.* **6.** to cause to burst. —*n.* **7.** an act or instance of bursting. **8.** a sudden display of intense activity. **9.** a sudden expression of emotion. **10.** a rapid sequence of shots.

Bu•run•di (bŏŏ rŏŏn′dē), *n.* a republic in central Africa. 6,052,614. —**Bu•run′di•an,** *adj., n.*

bur•y (ber′ē), *v.t.,* **-ied, -y•ing. 1.** to put in the ground and cover with earth. **2.** to put (a corpse) in the ground or a vault. **3.** to plunge in deeply. **4.** to conceal from sight. **5.** to involve (oneself) deeply.

Bur•y St. Ed•munds (ber′ē sānt ed′məndz, -sənt-), *n.* a city in W Suffolk, in E England: medieval shrine. 25,629.

bus¹ (bus), *n., pl.* **bus•es, bus•ses,** *v.,* **bused** or **bussed, bus•ing** or **bus•sing.** —*n.* **1.** a large motor vehicle for many passengers. **2.** a circuit that connects the CPU with other devices in a computer. —*v.t.* **3.** to transport by bus. —*v.i.* **4.** to travel by bus. [short for *omnibus*]

bus² (bus), *v.i., v.t.,* **bused** or **bussed, bus•ing** or **bus•sing.** to work as a busboy.

bus′boy′, *n.* a waiter's helper in a restaurant.

bus•by (buz′bē), *n., pl.* **-bies.** a tall military hat of fur or feathers.

bush (bŏŏsh), *n.* **1.** a low plant with many branches. **2.** something resembling this, as a shaggy head of hair. **3.** a large uncleared area. —*v.i.* **4.** to spread like a bush. —*Idiom.* **5. beat around the bush,** to avoid talking about a subject directly. —**bush′y,** *adj.,* **-i•er, -i•est.**

Bush, *n.* **George (Herbert Walker),** born 1924, 41st president of the U.S. 1989–93.

bushed, *adj. Informal.* exhausted; tired out.

bush•el (bŏŏsh′əl), *n.* **1.** a unit of dry measure equal to 4 pecks, 2150.42 cubic inches, or 35.24 liters. **2.** a large, unspecified amount.

bush′ing, *n.* a lining intended to protect moving machine parts or electrical conductors from abrasion.

bush′ league′, *n.* a secondary baseball league. —**bush′-league′,** *adj.* —**bush′ lea′guer,** *n.*

bush′man, *n., pl.* **-men.** a dweller in the Australian bush.

bush′mas′ter, *n.* a large tropical American pit viper.

busi•ness (biz′nis), *n.* **1.** an occupation, profession, or trade. **2.** a profit-seeking enterprise or concern. **3.** trade or patronage. **4.** a person's principal concern. **5.** affair; matter. —*adj.* **6.** of or suitable for business. —*Idiom.* **7. mean business,** to be in earnest.

busi′ness col′lege, *n.* a school for training students in business skills.

busi′ness•like′, *adj.* showing attributes prized in business, as practicality and efficiency.

busi′ness•man′ or **-wo′man** or **-per′son,** *n., pl.* **-men** or **-wo•men** or **-per•sons.** a person engaged in business or commerce, esp. an executive.

bus•ing or **bus•sing** (bus′ing), *n.* the transporting of students by bus to schools outside their neighborhoods, esp. to achieve racial balance.

bus•kin (bus′kin), *n.* **1.** a high, thick-soled shoe worn by ancient Greek and Roman tragedians. **2.** tragic drama.

bus′man′s hol′iday, *n.* a vacation spent in an activity closely resembling one's work.

buss (bus), *v.t., v.i., n.* KISS.

bust¹ (bust), *n.* **1.** a representation of the head and shoulders of a human subject. **2.** a woman's bosom.

bust² (bust), *Informal.* —*v.i.* **1.** to burst. **2.** to go bankrupt. —*v.t.* **3.** to burst or break. **4.** to ruin financially. **5.** to demote. **6.** to tame: *to bust a bronco.* **7.** to arrest. **8.** to hit. —*n.* **9.** a failure. **10.** a hit; punch. **11.** an economic depression. **12.** an arrest.

bus•tle¹ (bus′əl), *v.,* **-tled, -tling,** *n.* —*v.i.* **1.** to move or act with great energy. —*n.* **2.** energetic activity. —**bus′tler,** *n.*

bus•tle² (bus′əl), *n.* a pad formerly worn to expand the back of a woman's skirt.

bus•y (biz′ē), *adj.,* **-i•er, -i•est,** *v.,* **-ied, -y•ing.** —*adj.* **1.** actively engaged in work. **2.** not at leisure. **3.** full of activity. **4.** (of a telephone line) in use. **5.** cluttered with fussy details. —*v.t.* **6.** to make or keep busy. —**bus′i•ly,** *adv.* —**bus′y•ness,** *n.*

bus′y•bod′y, *n., pl.,* **-bod•ies.** a person who meddles in the affairs of others.

but (but; *unstressed* bət), *conj.* **1.** on the contrary: *He went, but I did not.* **2.** and yet; nevertheless: *strange but true.* **3.** except; save: *did nothing but complain.* **4.** without the circumstance that: *It never rains but it pours.* **5.** otherwise than: *There is no hope but by prayer.* **6.** that: *I don't doubt but you'll do it.* **7.** that ... not: *No leaders ever existed but they were optimists.* —*prep.* **8.** other than; except: *nothing but trouble.* —*adv.* **9.** only; just: *There is but one answer.* —*Idiom.* **10.** but for, were it not for.

bu•tane (byŏŏ′tān), *n.* a colorless, flammable gas, used as fuel.

butch (bŏŏch), *adj. Slang.* **1.** (of a woman) having traits usu. associated with males. **2.** (of a male) exaggerated masculine.

butch•er (bŏŏch′ər), *n.* **1.** a dealer in meat. **2.** a person who slaughters or dresses animals for food. **3.** a brutal murderer. —*v.t.* **4.** to slaughter or dress (animals) for market. **5.** to kill brutally. **6.** to bungle; botch. —**butch′er•y,** *n., pl.* **-er•ies.**

but•ler (but′lər), *n.* the chief male servant of a household.

butt¹ (but), *n.* **1.** the thicker or larger end of anything: *a rifle butt.* **2.** an unused end or remnant. **3.** *Slang.* the buttocks.

butt² (but), *n.* **1.** an object of ridicule. **2.** a target. —*v.t., v.i.* **3.** to set end to end.

butt³ (but), *v.t., v.i.* **1.** to strike or push with the head or horns. **2. butt in,** to intrude or meddle. —*n.* **3.** a push or blow with the head or horns.

butt⁴ (but), *n.* a large cask for wine, beer, or ale.

butte (byŏŏt), *n.* an isolated hill rising abruptly above the surrounding land.

but•ter (but′ər), *n.* **1.** a fatty solid that separates from milk or cream when it is churned. **2.** any substance of butterlike consistency. —*v.t.* **3.** to put butter on or in. **4. butter up,** to flatter. —**but′ter•y,** *adj.*

but′ter•cup′, *n.* a plant with glossy yellow flowers.

but′ter•fat′, *n.* the fatty portion of milk, from which butter is made.

but′ter•fin′gers, *n., pl.* **-gers.** a person who drops things; a clumsy person.

but′ter•fly′, *n., pl.* **-flies.** any of numerous insects with a slender body and broad, often conspicuously marked wings.

but′ter•milk′, *n.* the sour liquid remaining after butter has been separated from milk.

but′ter•nut′, *n.* **1.** the edible oily nut of an American tree of the walnut family. **2.** the tree itself.

but′ter•scotch′, *n.* a flavoring or a hard, brittle taffy made with butter, brown sugar, etc.

but•tock (but′ək), *n.* **1.** either of the two fleshy protuberances forming the human rump. **2. buttocks,** the human rump.

but•ton (but′n), *n.* **1.** a small disk or knob used as a fastener, as on clothing. **2.** anything resembling a button. —*v.t., v.i.* **3.** to fasten or be fastened with a button or buttons.

but′ton-down′, *adj.* **1.** (of a collar) having buttonholes with which it can be buttoned to the garment. **2.** conventional; unimaginative.

but′ton•hole′, *n., v.,* **-holed, -hol•ing.** —*n.* **1.** the slit through which a button is passed. —*v.t.* **2.** to accost and detain in conversation.

but•tress (bu′tris), *n.* **1.** a projecting support built into or against a wall. **2.** any prop or support. —*v.t.* **3.** to support or prop up.

buttress

bux•om (buk′səm), *adj.* (of a woman) full-bosomed.

Bux•te•hu•de (boͦok′stə hoͦo′də), *n.* **Dietrich,** 1637–1707, Danish organist and composer, in Germany after 1668.

buy (bī), *v.,* **bought, buy•ing,** *n.* —*v.t.* **1.** to acquire by paying money; purchase. **2.** to acquire by exchange or concession. **3.** to bribe. **4.** *Informal.* to accept or believe. —*v.i.* **5.** to be or become a purchaser. **6. buy off,** to bribe. **7. ~ out,** to purchase all the business shares belonging to. **8. ~ up,** to buy as much as one can of. —*n.* **9.** something bought. **10.** a bargain.

buy′back′, *n.* a repurchase by a company of its own stock.

buy′er, *n.* **1.** a person who buys. **2.** a purchasing agent, as for a department store.

buy′out′, *n.* the purchase of all or a controlling percentage of the shares in a company.

buzz (buz), *n.* **1.** a low, humming sound, as of bees. **2.** *Informal.* a phone call. —*v.i.* **3.** to make a low, humming sound. **4.** to be filled with such a sound, as a room. **5.** to whisper; gossip. —*v.t.* **6.** to signal with a buzzer. **7.** *Informal.* to telephone. **8.** to fly a plane low over.

buz•zard (buz′ərd), *n.* **1.** any of several broad-winged Old World hawks. **2.** any of several New World vultures, esp. the turkey vulture.

buzz′er, *n.* a signaling apparatus that produces a buzzing sound.

buzz′ saw′, *n.* a power-operated circular saw.

buzz′word′, *n.* a word or phrase that has come into vogue in a particular profession.

bx., pl. bxs. box.

by (bī), *prep.* **1.** near or next to: *a home by a lake.* **2.** by way of; via: *She came by air.* **3.** beyond; past: *We drove by the church.* **4.** during: *by day.* **5.** not later than: *I'll be done by noon.* **6.** to the extent or amount of: *taller by three inches.* **7.** according to: *by law.* **8.** through the agency of: *issued by the government.* **9.** from the hand or mind of: *a poem by Keats.* **10.** on behalf of: *to do well by one's children.* **11.** after; next after: *piece by piece.* **12.** the number of times specified by a multiplier or divisor: *Multiply 18 by 57.* **13.** with another dimension of: *10 by 12 feet.* **14.** in terms or amounts of: *sold by the bushel.* **15.** to, into, or at: *Come by my office.* —*adv.* **16.** at hand; near: *The school is close by.* **17.** past: *The car drove by.* **18.** aside; away: *to put money by.* **19.** past; over: *in times gone by.* —*Idiom.* **20. by and by,** before long. **21. by and large,** in general.

by-, a combining form of BY: *by-product; bystander.*

by′-and-by′, *n.* the future.

bye (bī), *n.* (in a tournament) the status of a player not paired with a competitor in an early round and thus advanced to the next round.

bye′-bye′, *interj.* GOOD-BYE.

by′-elec′tion, *n.* a special election held between general elections to fill a vacancy.

Bye′lo•rus′sia or **Be′lo•rus′sia** (byel′ə-, bel′-), *n.* BELARUS. —**Bye′lo•rus′sian,** *adj., n.*

by′gone′, *adj.* **1.** former; past. —*n.* **2.** something in the past. —*Idiom.* **3. let bygones be bygones,** to forget past disagreements.

by′law′, *n.* a rule governing the internal affairs of a corporation or society.

by′line′, *n.* a line in a newspaper or magazine article giving the author's name.

by′pass′, *n.* **1.** a road enabling motorists to avoid a city or to drive around an obstruction. **2.** a surgical procedure in which a diseased or obstructed organ is circumvented. —*v.t.* **3.** to avoid by following a bypass. **4.** to neglect to consult.

by′-path′, *n.* a secondary path; byway.

by′play′, *n.* action or speech carried on aside from the main action.

by′-prod′uct, *n.* **1.** a secondary or incidental product, as in a manufacturing process. **2.** the result of another action.

Byrd (bûrd), *n.* **1. Richard Evelyn,** 1888–1957, rear admiral in the U.S. Navy: polar explorer. **2. William,** c1540–1623, English composer.

by′-road′, *n.* a side road.

By•ron (bī′rən), *n.* **George Gordon, Lord** (*6th Baron Byron*), 1788–1824, English poet.

by′stand′er, *n.* a person present but not involved.

byte (bīt), *n.* a group of adjacent bits, usu. eight, processed by a computer as a unit. [perh. alteration (influenced by BIT³) of BITE]

by′way′, *n.* a little-used road.

by′word′, *n.* **1.** a proverb. **2.** a person regarded as the embodiment of some quality. **3.** an object of scorn.

Byz•an•tine (biz′ən tēn′, -tīn′), *adj.* **1.** of the Byzantine Empire or its ornate style of architecture. **2.** (*sometimes l.c.*) **a.** very complex or intricate. **b.** characterized by intrigue.

Byz′antine Em′pire, *n.* an empire, A.D. 476-1453, in SE Europe and SW Asia.

C

C, c (sē), *n., pl.* **Cs** or **C's, cs** or **c's.** the third letter of the English alphabet, a consonant.

C, *Symbol.* **1.** the third in order or in a series. **2.** a grade or mark indicating fair or average quality. **3.** the Roman numeral for 100. **4.** Celsius. **5.** Centigrade. **6.** *Chem.* carbon.

c, 1. circa. **2.** curie. **3.** cycle.

C., 1. Calorie. **2.** Catholic. **3.** College.

c., 1. calorie. **2.** carat. **3.** *Baseball.* catcher. **4.** cent. **5.** centimeter. **6.** century. **7.** chapter. **8.** circa. **9.** cognate. **10.** copyright. **11.** cubic. **12.** cycle.

CA, California.

Ca, *Chem. Symbol.* calcium.

ca or **ca.,** circa.

cab (kab), *n.* **1.** a taxicab. **2.** a horse-drawn vehicle for public hire. **3.** the enclosed part of a locomotive, truck, etc., where the operator sits.

ca•bal (kə bal'), *n.* **1.** a small group of secret plotters, as against a government. **2.** secret plots and schemes.

cab•a•la (kab'ə lə, kə bä'-), *n.* an esoteric philosophy developed by medieval rabbis, based on a mystical interpretation of the Scriptures.

ca•bal•le•ro (kab'əl yâr'ō, -ə lâr'ō), *n., pl.* **-ros. 1.** a Spanish gentleman. **2.** *Southwestern U.S.* **a.** a horseman. **b.** a woman's escort.

ca•ban•a (kə ban'ə, -ban'yə), *n., pl.* **-ban•as.** a small structure for use as a bathhouse at a beach or swimming pool.

cab•a•ret (kab'ə rā'), *n.* a restaurant providing musical entertainment.

cab•bage (kab'ij), *n.* a vegetable with leaves formed into a compact head. [< OF « L *caput* head]

cab'by or **cab'bie,** *n., pl.* **-bies.** *Informal.* a person who drives a cab.

cab•in (kab'in), *n.* **1.** a small house or cottage of simple design and construction. **2.** the enclosed space for the passengers, pilot, or cargo in an air or space vehicle. **3.** an apartment or room in a ship.

cab•i•net (kab'ə nit), *n.* **1.** a piece of furniture with shelves, drawers, etc., for holding or displaying items. **2.** a wall cupboard. **3.** the case enclosing a radio, television, etc. **4.** (*often cap.*) a council advising a sovereign or a chief executive.

cab'i•net•mak'er, *n.* a person who makes fine wooden furniture. —**cab'i•net•mak'ing,** *n.*

cab'i•net•work', *n.* fine wooden furniture.

cab'in fe'ver, *n.* mounting boredom and restlessness resulting from a prolonged stay in a remote or confined place.

ca•ble (kā'bəl), *n., v.,* **-bled, -bling.** —*n.* **1.** a heavy, strong rope of fiber or metal wire. **2.** an insulated electrical conductor, often in strands. **3.** CABLEGRAM. **4.** CABLE TELEVISION. —*v.t.* **5.** to send (a message) by cable. **6.** to send a cablegram to. **7.** to fasten with a cable. —*v.i.* **8.** to send a message by cable.

ca'ble car', *n.* a vehicle used on a cable railway or tramway.

ca'ble•cast', *n., v.,* **-cast** or **-cast•ed, -cast•ing.** —*n.* **1.** a broadcast via cable television. —*v.t., v.i.* **2.** to broadcast via cable television.

ca'ble•gram', *n.* a telegram sent by underwater cable.

ca'ble tel'evision, *n.* a system of televising programs to private subscribers by means of coaxial cable.

cab•o•chon (kab'ə shon'), *n.* a gemstone cut so as to have a domed surface.

ca•boo•dle (kə bood'l), *n. Informal.* the lot, pack, or crowd: *the whole caboodle.*

ca•boose (kə boos'), *n.* a car for the crew at the rear of a freight train.

Cab•ot (kab'ət), *n.* **1. John** (*Giovanni Caboto*),

c1450–98?, Italian navigator for England: discoverer of North American mainland 1497. **2.** his son, **Sebastian,** 1474?–1557, English navigator and explorer.

Ca•bri•ni (kə brē'nē), *n.* **Saint Frances Xavier** ("*Mother Cabrini*"),1850–1917, U.S. nun, born in Italy; founder of the Missionary Sisters of the Sacred Heart of Jesus.

ca•ca•o (kə kä'ō, -kā'ō), *n., pl.* **-ca•os. 1.** a small tropical American evergreen tree. **2.** the seeds of this tree, the source of cocoa and chocolate.

cache (kash), *n., v.,* **cached, cach•ing.** —*n.* **1.** a hiding place for food, treasures, etc. **2.** anything hidden in a cache. —*v.t.* **3.** to hide in a cache.

cache'pot' (-pot', -pō'), *n.* an ornamental container for holding a flowerpot.

ca•chet (ka shā'), *n.* **1.** an official seal, as on a document. **2.** an official sign of approval. **3.** superior status; prestige. **4.** a design, slogan, etc., printed on an envelope for philatelic purposes.

cack•le (kak'əl), *v.,* **-led, -ling,** *n.* —*v.i.* **1.** to utter a shrill, broken cry, as of a hen. **2.** to laugh in a shrill, broken manner. —*n.* **3.** the act or sound of cackling. —**cack'ler,** *n.*

ca•coph•o•ny (kə kof'ə nē), *n., pl.* **-nies.** harsh, discordant sound. —**ca•coph'o•nous,** *adj.*

cac•tus (kak'təs), *n., pl.* **-ti** (-tī), **-tus•es, -tus.** a desert plant with succulent, leafless stems usu. bearing spines.

cad (kad), *n.* a man who behaves dishonorably toward women. —**cad'dish,** *adj.* —**cad'dish•ness,** *n.*

ca•dav•er (kə dav'ər), *n.* a corpse, as for dissection.

ca•dav'er•ous, *adj.* like a corpse; pale.

CAD/CAM (kad'kam'), *n.* computer-aided design and computer-aided manufacturing.

cad•die (kad'ē), *n., v.,* **-died, -dy•ing.** —*n.* **1.** a person hired to carry a golfer's clubs. —*v.i.* **2.** to work as a caddie.

cad•dy (kad'ē), *n., pl.* **-dies.** a small storage container, esp. for tea.

-cade, a combining form meaning procession (*motorcade*).

ca•dence (kād'ns), *n.* **1.** rhythmic flow, as of sounds or words. **2.** the beat or measure of any rhythmic movement. **3.** modulation of the voice in speaking. —**ca'denced,** *adj.*

ca•den•za (kə den'zə), *n., pl.* **-zas.** an elaborate solo passage, as near the end of an aria.

ca•det (kə det'), *n.* a student at a military or naval academy.

cadge (kaj), *v.t., v.i.,* **cadged, cadg•ing.** to obtain (something) by begging or by sponging on another.

cad•mi•um (kad'mē əm), *n.* a white, ductile metallic element, used in plating and in making alloys. *Symbol:* Cd; *at. wt.:* 112.41; *at. no.:* 48.

ca•dre (kad'rē, kä'drā), *n.* a core group of trained workers around which an expanded organization can be built.

caduceus

ca•du•ce•us (kə doo'sē əs, -dyoo'-), *n., pl.* **-ce•i** (-sē ī'). a winged staff with two entwined snakes, used as a symbol of the medical profession.

Cae•sar (sē'zər), *n.* **1. Gaius Julius,** c100–44 B.C.,

Roman general, statesman, and historian. **2.** a title of the Roman emperors after Augustus. **3.** any emperor. **4.** any temporal ruler; civil authority. Matt. 22:21.

Cae•sar•e•an (si zârʹē ən), n. (sometimes l.c.) CESAREAN.

cae•su•ra (si zhŏŏrʹə, -zōŏrʹə), n., pl. **-su•ras, -su•rae** (-zhŏŏrʹē, -zōŏrʹē). a pause near the middle of a line of verse.

ca•fé (ka fāʹ, kə-), n., pl. **-fés. 1.** a restaurant, usu. small and unpretentious. **2.** a barroom or nightclub. [< F: lit., coffee]

ca•fé au lait (kafʹā ō lāʹ), n. hot coffee served with an equal amount of hot or scalded milk. [F: lit., coffee with milk]

caf•e•te•ri•a (kafʹi tērʹē ə), n., pl. **-ri•as.** a restaurant in which patrons select food at a counter and carry it to tables.

caf•feine (ka fēnʹ), n. a bitter alkaloid, usu. derived from coffee or tea, used as a stimulant.

caf•fè lat•te (kafʹā läʹtā), n. Italian. LATTE.

caf•tan (kafʹtan, kaf tanʹ), n. a long coatlike garment with wide sleeves, worn in the Middle East.

cage (kāj), n., v., **caged, cag•ing. —n. 1.** an enclosure with wires, bars, etc., for confining birds or animals. **2.** a similar enclosure, as for a cashier. —v.t. **3.** to put or confine in or as if in a cage.

Cage (kāj), n. **John,** 1912–92, U.S. composer.

cag′ey or **cag′y,** adj., **-i•er, -i•est.** cautious; shrewd. —**cag′i•ly,** adv. —**cag′i•ness,** n.

Caho′kia Mounds′, n.pl. a group of large prehistoric Indian earthworks in SW Illinois, consisting of flat mounds that supported temples and other structures of mud and thatch.

ca•hoot (kə hōōtʹ), n. Informal. —**Idiom. ın cahoots,** in partnership or conspiracy; in league.

Cai•a•phas (kāʹə fəs, kīʹ-), n. a high priest of the Jews who presided over the assembly that condemned Jesus to death. Matt. 26.

Cain (kān), n. **1.** the first son of Adam and Eve, who murdered his brother Abel. Gen. 4. —**Idiom. 2. raise Cain,** Slang. to cause a disturbance.

cairn (kârn), n. a heap of stones set up as a landmark, monument, etc.

cairn′ ter′rier, n. one of a Scottish breed of small, short-legged terriers with a broad head and a rough coat.

Cai•ro (kīʹrō), n. the capital of Egypt. 6,325,000.

cais•son (kāʹson, -sən), n. **1.** a pressurized, watertight chamber for use in underwater construction. **2.** a two-wheeled wagon, used for carrying ammunition.

ca•jole (kə jōlʹ), v.t., v.i., **-joled, -jol•ing.** to persuade by flattery or promises. —**ca•jol′er,** n. —**ca•jol′er•y,** n.

Ca•jun (kāʹjən), n. **1.** a native of Louisiana descended from French immigrants from E Canada. **2.** the form of French spoken by the Cajuns.

cake (kāk), n., v., **caked, cak•ing. —n. 1.** a sweet, baked, breadlike food. **2.** a thin baked or fried mass of batter or minced food. **3.** a shaped, hard mass: a cake of soap. —v.t., v.i. **4.** to form into a crust or compact mass. —**Idiom. 5. piece of cake,** something that can be done easily. **6. take the cake,** to win the hypothetical prize.

Cal., California.

cal., **1.** caliber. **2.** calorie.

cal•a•bash (kalʹə bashʹ), n. **1.** the large, gourdlike fruit of a tropical American tree. **2.** a container or utensil made from its shell.

cal•a•boose (kalʹə bōōsʹ), n. Slang. a jail.

cal•a•mine (kalʹə mīnʹ), n. a pink powder consisting of zinc and iron oxides, used in skin lotions.

ca•lam•i•ty (kə lamʹi tē), n., pl. **-ties. 1.** a great misfortune. **2.** grievous affliction; misery. —**ca•lam′i•tous,** adj.

Calam′ity Jane′, n. (Martha Jane Canary Burke) 1852?–1903, U.S. frontier markswoman.

cal•car•e•ous (kal kârʹē əs), adj. of, containing, or like calcium carbonate; chalky.

cal•ci•fy (kalʹsə fīʹ), v.t., v.i., **-fied, -fy•ing.** to

harden by the deposit of calcium salts. —**cal′ci•fi•ca′tion,** n.

cal′ci•mine′ (-mīnʹ), n., v., **-mined, -min•ing.** —n. **1.** a white or tinted wash for walls, ceilings, etc. —v.t. **2.** to wash or cover with calcimine.

cal•cine (kalʹsīn), v.t., v.i., **-cined, -cin•ing.** to convert into an ashlike powder by heating.

cal•cite (kalʹsīt), n. a common mineral, calcium carbonate, a major constituent of limestone, marble, and chalk.

cal•ci•um (kalʹsē əm), n. a silver-white metal, occurring in combination in chalk, limestone, etc., and also found in bones and shells. Symbol: Ca; at. wt.: 40.08; at. no.: 20.

cal′cium car′bonate, n. a white powder occurring as calcite, chalk, etc., used in dentifrices, polishes, etc.

cal′cium fluor′ide, n. a white, crystalline compound, CaF_2, used as a decay preventive in dentifrices.

cal•cu•late (kalʹkyə lātʹ), v., **-lat•ed, -lat•ing.** —v.t. **1.** to determine by using mathematics; compute. **2.** to determine by reasoning; estimate. **3.** to make fit for a purpose: The remarks were calculated to inspire confidence. —v.i. **4.** to make a calculation. **5.** to count or rely. —**cal′cu•la•ble,** adj.

cal′cu•lat′ed, adj. carefully thought out or planned.

cal′cu•lat′ing, adj. **1.** shrewd. **2.** selfishly scheming.

cal′cu•la′tion, n. **1.** the act or process of calculating. **2.** the result of calculating. **3.** careful planning.

cal′cu•la′tor, n. **1.** an electronic or mechanical device that performs calculations. **2.** a person who calculates.

cal′cu•lus, n., pl. **-li** (-līʹ), **-lus•es. 1.** a method of calculation by a special system of algebraic notations. **2.** a stone formed in the gallbladder, kidney, etc. [< L: pebble, small stone (used in calculating)]

Cal•cut′ta (kal kutʹə), n. a seaport in E India. 9,166,000.

Cal•der (kôlʹdər), n. **Alexander,** 1898–1976, U.S. sculptor; originator of mobiles.

Ca•leb (kāʹləb), n. a Hebrew leader, sent as a spy into the land of Canaan. Num. 13:6.

cal•en•dar (kalʹən dər), n. **1.** a table with the days of each month and week in a year. **2.** a system of reckoning the beginning, length, and divisions of the year. **3.** a schedule of appointments, cases to be tried in court, etc. —v.t. **4.** to enter in a calendar.

cal•en•der (kalʹən dər), n. **1.** a machine in which cloth or paper is smoothed or glazed by pressing between rotating cylinders. —v.t. **2.** to press in a calender.

calf[1] (kaf, käf), n., pl. **calves. 1.** the young of the domestic cow or other bovine animal. **2.** the young of certain other mammals, as the elephant or whale. **3.** calfskin leather.

calf[2] (kaf, käf), n., pl. **calves.** the fleshy back part of the human leg below the knee.

calf′skin′, n. **1.** the skin of a calf. **2.** leather made from this skin.

Cal•ga•ry (kalʹgə rē), n. a city in S Alberta, in SW Canada. 636,104.

Ca•li (käʹlē), n. a city in SW Colombia. 1,350,565.

cal•i•ber (kalʹə bər), n. **1.** the diameter of a circular section, esp. the inside of a tube. **2.** the diameter of the bore of a gun. **3.** degree of competence. Also, esp. Brit., **cal′i•bre.**

cal′i•brate′ (-brātʹ), v.t., **-brat•ed, -brat•ing. 1.** to mark (a thermometer or other instrument) with indexes of degree or quantity. **2.** to determine the correct range for (a gun, mortar, etc.). —**cal′i•bra′tion,** n. —**cal′i•bra′tor,** n.

cal•i•co (kalʹi kōʹ), n., pl. **-coes, -cos,** adj. —n. **1.** a plain-woven cotton cloth printed with a figured pattern. —adj. **2.** mottled or variegated in color: a calico cat.

Calif., California.

Cal•i•for•nia (kalʹə fôrnʹyə, -fôrʹnē ə), n. **1.** a state in the W United States, on the Pacific coast.

31,878,234. *Cap.*: Sacramento. *Abbr.*: CA, Cal., Calif.
2. Gulf of, an arm of the Pacific Ocean, between W Mexico and Baja California. —**Cal′i•for′nian,** *adj., n.*
cal•i•for′ni•um (-fôr′nē əm), *n.* a synthetic, radioactive metallic element. *Symbol*: Cf; *at. no.*: 98.
Ca•lig•u•la (kə lig′yə lə), *n.* A.D. 12–41, emperor of Rome 37–41.
cal•i•per (kal′ə pər), *n.* **1.** Usu., **-pers.** an instrument for measuring thicknesses and diameters, consisting usu. of a pair of adjustable pivoted legs. —*v.t., v.i.* **2.** to measure with calipers.
ca•liph (kā′lif, kal′if), *n.* a former title for a religious and civil ruler of the Islamic world. —**cal•iph•ate** (kal′ə fāt′, -fit), *n.*
cal•is•then•ics (kal′əs then′iks), *n.* (*used with a sing. or pl. v.*) gymnastic exercises for health. —**cal′is•then′ic,** *adj.*
calk (kôk), *v.t. n.* CAULK.
call (kôl), *v.t.* **1.** to cry out in a loud voice. **2.** to summon. **3.** to telephone. **4.** to waken. **5.** to convene: *to call a meeting.* **6.** to name (someone) as. **7.** to designate as something specified: *She called me a liar.* **8.** to demand payment of (a loan). —*v.i.* **9.** to speak loudly. **10.** to make a short visit. **11.** to telephone. **12.** (of a bird or animal) to utter its characteristic cry. **13. call for, a.** to come to get. **b.** to demand. **14. ~ off,** to cancel (something planned). **15. ~ up, a.** to remember. **b.** to telephone. **c.** to summon for action, esp. military service. —*n.* **16.** a cry or shout. **17.** the vocal sound of a bird or other animal. **18.** the act of telephoning. **19.** a short visit. **20.** a summons or invitation. **21.** fascination or appeal: *the call of the sea.* **22.** a need or occasion: *no call for panic.* **23.** a demand or claim: *a call on one's time.* —**call′er,** *n.*
cal•la (kal′ə), *n., pl.* **-las.** a plant with arrow-shaped leaves and a large white spathe enclosing a yellow spike. Also called **cal′la lil′y.**
caller ID, *n.* a telephone service that allows a subscriber to identify a caller before answering by displaying the caller's telephone number on a small screen.
cal•lig•ra•phy (kə lig′rə fē), *n.* fancy penmanship or the art of writing beautifully. —**cal•lig′ra•pher,** *n.*
call′ing, *n.* **1.** a vocation or profession. **2.** a strong impulse or inclination.
call′ing card′, *n.* **1.** a small card with a person's name and often address presented on a social visit. **2.** Also called **phone card.** a prepaid card or charge card that can be used at a public telephone instead of coins.
cal•li•o•pe (kə lī′ə pē, kal′ē ōp′), *n.* a musical instrument consisting of a set of harsh-sounding steam whistles.
cal•lous (kal′əs), *adj.* **1.** thickened and hardened, as skin. **2.** insensitive; unsympathetic. —**cal′lous•ness,** *n.*
cal•low (kal′ō), *adj.* immature or inexperienced. —**cal′low•ness,** *n.*
call′-up′, *n.* an order to report for active military service.
cal•lus (kal′əs), *n., pl.* **-lus•es. 1.** a hardened or thickened part of the skin. —*v.i., v.t.* **2.** to form a callus (on).
call′ wait′ing, *n.* a telephone service whereby a person engaged in a phone call is notified by a tone that a second call is being made to the same number.
calm (käm), *adj.,* **-er, -est,** *n., v.* —*adj.* **1.** without rough motion. **2.** not windy. **3.** tranquil; serene. —*n.* **4.** freedom from motion or disturbance. **5.** absence of wind. **6.** serenity; tranquillity. —*v.t., v.i.* **7.** to make or become calm. —**calm′ly,** *adv.* —**calm′ness,** *n.*
ca•lor•ic (kə lôr′ik, -lor′-), *adj.* **1.** of calories. **2.** of heat.
cal•o•rie (kal′ə rē), *n.* **1.** the amount of heat necessary to raise the temperature of one gram of water by 1°C **(small calorie),** or of one kilogram of water by 1°C **(large calorie). 2.** a unit equal to the large calorie, used to express the heat output of an organism and the energy value of food.

cal′o•rif′ic (-rif′ik), *adj.* pertaining to conversion into heat.
cal•u•met (kal′yə met′), *n.* a ceremonial pipe used by North American Indians.
ca•lum•ni•ate (kə lum′nē āt′), *v.t.,* **-at•ed, -at•ing.** to make false and malicious statements about; slander. —**ca•lum′ni•a′tion,** *n.* —**ca•lum′ni•a′tor,** *n.*
cal•um•ny (kal′əm nē), *n., pl.* **-nies.** a false and malicious statement; slander. —**ca•lum′ni•ous** (kə-lum′nē əs), *adj.*
Cal•va•ry (kal′və rē), *n., pl.* **-ries. 1.** the place where Jesus was crucified, near Jerusalem. Luke 23:33, Matt. 27:33. **2.** (*often l.c.*) a representation of the Crucifixion. **3.** (*l.c.*) an experience of extreme suffering. [< LL *Calvāria*; L: skull, trans. of Gk *kraníon,* itself a trans. of the Aramaic name; see GOLGO-THA]
calve (kav, käv), *v.i., v.t.,* **calved, calv•ing.** to give birth to (a calf).
calves, *n.* pl. of CALF.
Cal•vin (kal′vin), *n.* **John** (*Jean Chauvin* or *Caulvin*), 1509–64, French theologian and reformer in Switzerland: leader in the Protestant Reformation.
Cal•vin•ism (kal′və niz′əm), *n.* **1.** the doctrines and teachings of John Calvin or his followers, emphasizing predestination, supreme authority of the Scriptures, and irresistibility of grace. **2.** adherence to these doctrines. —**Cal′vin•ist,** *n., adj.* —**Cal′vin•is′-tic,** *adj.*
ca•lyp•so (kə lip′sō), *n., pl.* **-sos.** a musical style of West Indian origin, influenced by jazz.
ca•lyx (kā′liks, kal′iks), *n., pl.* **ca•lyx•es, cal•y•ces** (kal′ə sēz′, kā′lə-). the outermost group of floral parts; the sepals collectively.
cam (kam), *n.* an irregularly shaped disk or cylinder that gives a rocking motion to any contiguous part.
ca•ma•ra•de•rie (kä′mə rä′də rē, kam′ə-), *n.* comradeship; good-fellowship.
cam•ber (kam′bər), *v.t., v.i.* **1.** to arch slightly; curve upward in the middle. —*n.* **2.** a slight arching, upward curve, or convexity.
cam•bi•um (kam′bē əm), *n., pl.* **-bi•ums, -bi•a** (-bē ə). a layer of tissue between the inner bark and wood that produces new bark and wood cells, forming the annual ring in trees. —**cam′bi•al,** *adj.*
Cam•bo•di•a (kam bō′dē ə), *n.* a republic in SE Asia. 11,163,861. Formerly, **Kampuchea.** —**Cam•bo′di•an,** *adj., n.*
Cam•bri•an (kam′brē ən), *adj.* noting or pertaining to the earliest period of the Paleozoic Era.
cam•bric (kām′brik), *n.* a thin cotton or linen fabric.
Cam•bridge (kām′brij), *n.* **1.** a city in E England. 98,400. **2.** a city in E Massachusetts. 90,290.
cam•cord•er (kam′kôr′dər), *n.* a hand-held television camera with an incorporated VCR.
came (kām), *v.* pt. of COME.
cam•el (kam′əl), *n.* **1.** either of two large, humped ruminants of the Old World. —*Proverb.* **2. It is easier for a camel to go (or pass) through the eye of a needle than it is for a rich man to enter the kingdom of Heaven,** the rich will not have treasure in heaven unless they share their wealth with the poor. Matt. 19:24. [< L *camēlus* < Gk *kámēlos* < Semitic; cf. Heb *gāmāl*]
ca•mel•lia (kə mēl′yə, -mē′lē ə), *n., pl.* **-lias.** a shrub with glossy evergreen leaves and roselike flowers. [after G. J. *Camellus* (1661–1706), Jesuit missionary who brought it to Europe]
Cam•e•lot (kam′ə lot′), *n.* **1.** the legendary site of King Arthur's palace and court, possibly near Exeter, England. **2.** any idyllic place or period. **3.** the ambience of Washington, D.C., during the administration of President John F. Kennedy, 1961–63. **4.** (*italics*) a musical (1960) with lyrics by Alan Jay Lerner and music by Frederick Loewe. —**Cam′e•lot′i•an,** *adj.*
Cam•em•bert (kam′əm bâr′), *n.* a soft, creamy cheese. [after *Camembert,* village in France]
cam•e•o (kam′ē ō′), *n., pl.* **cam•e•os. 1.** a jewel with a head in profile carved or set in relief. **2.** an ef-

fective literary sketch or small dramatic scene. **3.** a small but notable part in a film or play.

cam•er•a (kam′ər ə), *n., pl.* **-er•as. 1.** a photographic device with an aperture that opens to admit light: focused by a lens, the light forms an image on a light-sensitive film or plate. **2.** the device in which a picture to be televised is formed before it is changed into electric impulses. —*Idiom.* **3. in camera,** privately.

cam′er•a•man′, *n., pl.* **-men.** a person who operates a motion-picture or television camera.

Cam•e•roon (kam′ə rōōn′), *n.* a republic in W equatorial Africa. 14,677,510. —**Cam′e•roon′i•an,** *adj., n.*

cam•i•sole (kam′ə sōl′), *n.* a short garment worn underneath a sheer bodice.

cam•o•mile (kam′ə mīl′, -mēl′), *n.* CHAMOMILE.

cam•ou•flage (kam′ə fläzh′), *n., v.,* **-flaged, -flag•ing.** —*n.* **1.** the disguising of elements of a military installation to conceal it from the enemy. **2.** a disguise or deception. —*v.t.* **3.** to disguise or deceive by means of camouflage. —**cam′ou•flag′er,** *n.*

camp¹ (kamp), *n.* **1. a.** a place where a group of persons is lodged in tents or other temporary shelters. **b.** such shelters collectively. **c.** the persons so sheltered. **2.** a group of people favoring the same ideals, doctrines, etc. **3.** a recreation area in the country, esp. one for children. —*v.i.* **4.** to establish a camp. **5.** to live in or as if in a camp: *They camped out by the stream.*

camp² (kamp), *n.* **1.** something that provides amusement by virtue of its being contrived, overdone, or tasteless. —*adj.* **2.** campy.

cam•paign (kam pān′), *n.* **1.** a series of military operations for a specific objective. **2.** a systematic course of aggressive activities: *a sales campaign; a campaign for mayor.* —*v.i.* **3.** to conduct a campaign. —**cam•paign′er,** *n.*

cam•pa•ni•le (kam′pə nē′lē, -nēl′), *n., pl.* **-ni•les, -ni•li** (-nē′lē). a bell tower.

Camp•bell (kam′bəl, kam′əl), *n.* **Joseph,** 1904–87, U.S. mythologist.

Camp′ Da′vid (dā′vid), *n.* U.S. presidential retreat in the Catoctin Mountains, Md.

camp′er, *n.* **1.** a person who lives or stays in a camp. **2.** a trucklike vehicle suitable for recreational camping.

camp′fire′, *n.* **1.** an outdoor fire for warmth or cooking. **2.** a reunion of soldiers, scouts, etc.

cam•phor (kam′fər), *n.* a white, pleasant-smelling substance used chiefly as a moth repellent.

camp′ meet′ing, *n.* a religious gathering held outdoors.

camp′site′, *n.* a place for camping.

cam•pus (kam′pəs), *n., pl.* **-pus•es.** the grounds, often including the buildings, of a college or other school.

camp′y, *adj.,* **-i•er, -i•est.** characterized by camp: *a campy spoof of romantic operetta.*

cam′shaft′, *n.* an engine shaft fitted with cams.

Ca•mus (kA my′; *Eng.* ka mōō′), *n.* **Albert,** 1913–60, French writer.

can¹ (kan; *unstressed* kən), *auxiliary v., pres.* **can,** *past* **could. 1.** to be able to: *She can solve the problem.* **2.** to know how to: *I can play chess.* **3.** to have the power to: *a dictator who can impose harsh laws.* **4.** to have the right to: *He can say whatever he wishes.* **5.** may; have permission to: *Can I speak to you?* **6.** to be likely to: *A coin can land on either side.* —**Usage.** The verbs CAN and MAY are often interchangeable in the sense of possibility: *A power failure can* (or *may*) *occur at any time.* Despite a traditional argument that only MAY conveys permission, both words are regularly used in this sense: *Can* (or *May*) *I borrow your car?*

can² (kan), *n., v.,* **canned, can•ning.** —*n.* **1.** a sealed metal container for food, beverages, etc. **2.** a receptacle for garbage, ashes, etc. —*v.t.* **3.** to preserve by sealing in a can, jar, etc. **4.** *Slang.* to dismiss; fire.

Can., 1. Canada. **2.** Canadian.

Ca•na (kā′nə), *n.* an ancient town in N Israel, in Galilee: scene of Jesus' first miracle. John 2:1, 11.

Ca•naan (kā′nən), *n.* **1.** the ancient region lying between the Jordan, the Dead Sea, and the Mediterranean. Gen. 12:5–10. **2.** Biblical name of PALESTINE (def. 1).

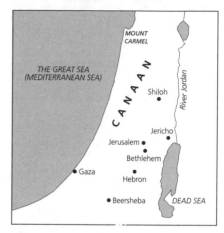

Can•a•da (kan′ə də), *n.* a nation in N North America. 29,123,194. *Cap.:* Ottawa. —**Ca•na•di•an** (kə nā′dē ən), *adj., n.*

Cana′dian ba′con, *n.* bacon from the pork loin.

Ca•na′di•an•ism, *n.* a custom, trait, or English usage originating in or distinctive to Canada.

ca•nal (kə nal′), *n.* **1.** an artificial waterway for navigation, irrigation, etc. **2.** a tubular passage for food, air, etc., in an animal or plant.

Canal′ Zone′, *n.* a zone in central Panama, on both sides of the Panama Canal.

can•a•pé (kan′ə pē, -pā′), *n., pl.* **-pés.** a cracker or piece of bread topped with savory food.

ca•nard (kə närd′, -när′), *n.* a false story or report, usu. derogatory.

ca•nar•y (kə nâr′ē), *n., pl.* **-nar•ies. 1.** a yellow finch of the Canary Islands, bred as a cage bird. **2.** a light yellow.

Canar′y Is′lands, *n.pl.* a group of Spanish islands in the Atlantic, near the NW coast of Africa. 1,614,882.

ca•nas•ta (kə nas′tə), *n.* a variety of rummy played with two decks of cards.

Ca•nav•er•al (kə nav′ər əl), *n.* **Cape,** a cape on the E coast of Florida: site of John F. Kennedy Space Center. Formerly (1963–73), **Cape Kennedy.**

Can•ber•ra (kan′ber ə, -bər ə), *n.* the capital of Australia. 285,800.

can′can′, *n.* a lively exhibition dance marked by high kicking.

can•cel (kan′səl), *v.t.,* **-celed, -cel•ing** or (*esp. Brit.*) **-celled, -cel•ling. 1.** to make void. **2.** to call off. **3.** to mark (a postage stamp, ticket, etc.) so as to render invalid for reuse. **4.** to compensate for; neutralize. **5. a.** to eliminate (a common factor) from a denominator and numerator. **b.** to eliminate (equivalent terms) on opposite sides of an equation. **6.** to cross out with lines. —**can′cel•la′tion,** *n.*

can•cer (kan′sər), *n.* **1.** a malignant growth or tumor that tends to spread. **2.** any evil that spreads destructively. **3.** (*cap.*) the fourth sign of the zodiac. [< L: crab] —**can′cer•ous,** *adj.*

Can•cún (kan kōōn′, käng-), *n.* an island off the Yucatán Peninsula, in SE Mexico: resort.

can•de•la•bra (kan′dl ä′brə), *n., pl.* **-bras** for 2. **1.** a pl. of CANDELABRUM. **2.** a candelabrum.

can′de•la′brum (-brəm), *n., pl.* **-bra** (-brə),

-**brums.** a branched holder for more than one candle.

can•did (kan'did), *adj.* **1.** frank; outspoken. **2.** informal; unposed: *a candid photo.* —**can'did•ly,** *adv.* —**can'did•ness,** *n.*

can•di•date (kan'di dāt', -dit), *n.* a person who seeks or is nominated for an office, honor, etc. [< L *candidātus* clothed in white (in reference to the white togas worn by those seeking office)] —**can'di•da•cy** (-də sē), *n., pl.* -**cies.**

can'died, *adj.* **1.** cooked in sugar or syrup. **2.** flattering: *candied words.*

can•dle (kan'dl), *n., v.,* -**dled, -dling.** —*n.* **1.** a long, slender piece of tallow or wax with an embedded wick, burned to give light. —*v.t.* **2.** to examine (eggs) for freshness by holding up to a light. —**can'dler,** *n.*

can'dle•stick', *n.* a device with a socket or a spike for holding a candle.

can•dor (kan'dər), *n.* **1.** the state or quality of being candid. **2.** freedom from bias. Also, *esp. Brit.,* **can'dour.**

can•dy (kan'dē), *n., pl.* -**dies,** *v.,* -**died, -dy•ing.** —*n.* **1.** a confection made of sugar or syrup, combined with flavoring, fruit, etc. —*v.t.* **2.** to cook in sugar or syrup, as yams. **3.** to preserve by cooking in heavy syrup, as fruit. **4.** to reduce (sugar, syrup, etc.) to a crystalline form. [ME *sugre candi* candied sugar < MF < Ar *qandī* ≪ Skt *khaṇḍakaḥ* sugar candy]

cane (kān), *n., v.,* **caned, can•ing.** —*n.* **1.** a short stick used as a support in walking. **2.** a long, jointed woody stem, as that of bamboo. **3.** a plant having such a stem. **4.** split rattan. **5.** a rod used for flogging. —*v.t.* **6.** to flog with a cane. **7.** to make with cane: *to cane chairs.* —**can'er,** *n.*

cane'brake', *n.* a thicket of canes.

ca•nine (kā'nīn), *adj.* **1.** of or like a dog. **2.** of the four pointed teeth next to the incisors. —*n.* **3.** a dog or member of the dog family. **4.** one of the four pointed teeth of the jaws.

can•is•ter (kan'ə stər), *n.* a small box or can for holding tea, sugar, etc.

can•ker (kang'kər), *n.* a gangrenous or ulcerous sore, esp. in the mouth. Also called **can'ker sore'.** —**can'ker•ous,** *adj.*

can•na•bis (kan'ə bis), *n.* **1.** the hemp plant. **2.** the flowering tops of this plant.

canned, *adj.* **1.** preserved in a can or jar. **2.** recorded or prerecorded: *canned laughter.*

can'ner•y, *n., pl.* -**ner•ies.** a factory where foodstuffs are canned.

can•ni•bal (kan'ə bəl), *n.* **1.** a person who eats human flesh. **2.** an animal that eats its own kind. —*adj.* **3.** of or like cannibals. —**can'ni•bal•ism,** *n.* —**can'ni•bal•is'tic,** *adj.*

can'ni•bal•ize', *v.t., v.i.,* -**ized, -iz•ing.** to take from one thing, as a part from a machine, for use on or in another.

can•non (kan'ən), *n., pl.* -**nons, -non.** a mounted gun for firing heavy projectiles.

can'non•ade' (-ə nād'), *n., v.,* -**ad•ed, -ad•ing.** —*n.* **1.** a continued discharge of cannon. —*v.t., v.i.* **2.** to attack with or discharge cannon.

can•not (kan'ot, ka not', kə-), *v.* **1.** a form of *can not.* —**Idiom. 2. cannot but,** to have no choice but to. —**Usage.** CANNOT is sometimes spelled CAN NOT, but the one-word spelling is by far the more common. Its contraction, *can't,* is found chiefly in speech and informal writing.

can•ny (kan'ē), *adj.,* -**ni•er, -ni•est. 1.** careful; prudent. **2.** astute; shrewd. —**can'ni•ly,** *adv.* —**can'ni•ness,** *n.*

ca•noe (kə nōō'), *n., v.,* -**noed, -noe•ing.** —*n.* **1.** a slender, open boat propelled by paddles. —*v.i.* **2.** to paddle or go in a canoe. —**ca•noe'ist,** *n.*

can•on' (kan'ən), *n.* **1.** a rule or law enacted by a church council. **2.** the body of ecclesiastical law. **3.** a principle or rule. **4.** the books of the Bible officially recognized by any Christian church. **5.** the works of an author accepted as authentic.

can•on² (kan'ən), *n.* a member of the clergy who serves in a cathedral.

ca•non•i•cal (kə non'i kəl), *adj.* **1.** pertaining or conforming to a canon. **2.** authorized; accepted.

can'on•ize', *v.t.,* -**ized, -iz•ing. 1.** to declare officially as a saint. **2.** to glorify or exalt. —**can'on•i•za'tion,** *n.*

can'on law', *n.* the body of codified ecclesiastical law, esp. of the Roman Catholic or Anglican Church.

can•o•py (kan'ə pē), *n., pl.* -**pies,** *v.,* -**pied, -py•ing.** —*n.* **1.** a covering suspended above a bed, throne, etc. **2.** an awning stretching from a doorway to a curb. **3.** a rooflike projection or covering. —*v.t.* **4.** to cover with a canopy.

cant' (kant), *n.* **1.** insincere statements, esp. pious platitudes. **2.** the private language of the underworld. **3.** the vocabulary of a particular class, profession, etc. —*v.i.* **4.** to talk piously or hypocritically.

cant² (kant), *n.* **1.** a salient angle. **2.** a slanting or tilted position. **3.** an oblique line or surface. —*v.t., v.i.* **4.** to tilt or tip.

can't (kant, känt), contraction of *cannot.* —**Usage.** See CANNOT.

can•ta•bi•le (kän tä'bi lā', -bē-), *Music. adj., adv.* songlike and flowing in style.

can•ta•loupe or **-loup** (kan'tl ōp'), *n.* a muskmelon having a rough rind and pale-orange edible flesh.

can•tan•ker•ous (kan tang'kər əs), *adj.* quarrelsome; irritable. —**can•tan'ker•ous•ly,** *adv.* —**can•tan'ker•ous•ness,** *n.*

can•ta•ta (kən tä'tə), *n. pl.* -**tas.** a choral composition resembling a short oratorio.

can•teen (kan tēn'), *n.* **1.** a small container for carrying water. **2.** a cafeteria or snack bar, as at a military base. **3.** a place where free entertainment is provided for military personnel. [< F *cantine* < It *cantina* cellar]

can•ter (kan'tər), *n.* **1.** an easy gallop. —*v.i., v.t.* **2.** to move or cause to move at a canter.

Can•ter•bur•y (kan'tər ber'ē, -bə rē; *esp. Brit.* -brē), *n.* a city in E Kent, in SE England: early ecclesiastical center of England. 129,500. —**Can'ter•bu'ri•an** (-byōōr'ē ən), *adj.*

can•ti•cle (kan'ti kəl), *n.* a hymn or chant, chiefly from the Bible, used in church services.

Can'ticle of Can'ticles, *n.* SONG OF SOLOMON, The.

can•ti•le•ver (kan'tl ē'vər, -ev'ər), *n.* **1.** any rigid structural member projecting from a vertical support, used as a structural element of a bridge, dam, etc. —*v.t.* **2.** to construct with a cantilever.

can•to (kan'tō), *n., pl.* -**tos.** one of the main divisions of a long poem.

can•ton (kan'tn, kan ton'), *n.* a small territorial district, esp. one of the states of Switzerland.

Can•ton (kan ton', kan'ton), *n.* GUANGZHOU.

Can'ton•ese' (-tn ēz', -ēs'), *n., adj.* -**ese,** *adj.* —*n.* **1.** a Chinese dialect spoken in Guangzhou, Hong Kong, and Macao. **2.** a native of Guangzhou. —*adj.* **3.** of Guangzhou, its inhabitants, or their dialect.

can•ton•ment (kan ton'mənt, -tōn'-), *n.* **1.** a camp for training military personnel. **2.** military quarters.

can•tor (kan'tər), *n.* a synagogue official who sings certain prayers designed as solos. —**can•to'ri•al** (-tôr'ē əl), *adj.*

can•vas (kan'vəs), *n.* **1.** a closely woven, heavy cloth used for tents; sails, etc. **2.** a painting on canvas. **3.** tents or sails collectively.

can'vas•back', *n., pl.* -**backs, -back.** a North American duck with a whitish back.

can•vass (kan'vəs), *v.t., v.i.* **1.** to solicit votes, opinions, sales, etc., from (a district or group of people). —*n.* **2.** a soliciting of votes, opinions, etc. —**can'vass•er,** *n.*

can•yon (kan'yən), *n.* a deep valley with steep sides. [< MexSp < Sp *cañón* a long tube, a hollow]

cap (kap), *n., v.,* **capped, cap•ping.** —*n.* **1.** a close-fitting covering for the head, sometimes having a visor. **2.** anything resembling a cap in shape or use: *a bottle cap.* **3.** a maximum limit. **4.** a noise-making device for toy pistols. —*v.t.* **5.** to put a cap on. **6.** to outdo.

CAP, computer-aided publishing.

cap., **1.** capital. **2.** capital letter.

ca•pa•ble (kā′pə bəl), *adj.* **1.** having ability; competent. **2.** capable of, **a.** having the ability for. **b.** predisposed to: *capable of murder.* —**ca′pa•bil′i•ty,** *n.,* *pl.* **-ties.** —**ca′pa•bly,** *adv.*

ca•pa•cious (kə pā′shəs), *adj.* spacious or roomy. —**ca•pa′cious•ly,** *adv.* —**ca•pa′cious•ness,** *n.*

ca•pac•i•tor (kə pas′i tər), *n.* a device for accumulating and holding a charge of electricity.

ca•pac′i•ty, *n.,* *pl.* **-ties.** **1.** the ability to receive or contain. **2.** cubic contents or volume. **3.** mental ability. **4.** the ability to do something. **5.** a position; function: *to serve in an advisory capacity.*

ca•par•i•son (kə par′ə sən), *n.* **1.** a decorative covering for a horse. —*v.t.* **2.** to cover with a caparison.

cape¹ (kāp), *n.* a sleeveless garment fastened at the neck and falling loosely from the shoulders. —**caped,** *adj.*

cape² (kāp), *n.* a piece of land jutting into a large body of water.

Cape′ Cod′, *n.* **1.** a sandy peninsula in SE Massachusetts: resorts. **2.** a rectangular one- or one-and-a-half-story wooden cottage with a gable roof.

Cape′ Horn′, *n.* a headland on a small island at the S extremity of South America: belongs to Chile.

Cape′ of Good′ Hope′, *n.* a cape in S Africa, in the SW Republic of South Africa.

ca•per¹ (kā′pər), *v.i.* **1.** to leap about in a sprightly manner. —*n.* **2.** a playful leap. **3.** a prank.

ca•per² (kā′pər), *n.* a shrub of Mediterranean regions whose flower bud is pickled and used for seasoning.

Ca•per•na•um (kə pûr′nā əm, -nē-), *n.* an ancient site in N Israel, on the Sea of Galilee.

cape′skin′, *n.* a light, pliable leather made from lambskin or sheepskin.

Cape′ Town′, *n.* the legislative capital of South Africa. 789,580.

Cape′ Verde′ (vûrd), *n.* a republic consisting of a group of islands in the Atlantic, W of Senegal in W Africa. 393,843.

cap•il•lar•i•ty (kap′ə lar′i tē), *n.* a manifestation of surface tension by which the portion of the surface of a liquid coming in contact with a solid is elevated or depressed.

cap′il•lar′y (-ler′ē), *n.,* *pl.* **-lar•ies,** *adj.* —*n.* **1.** one of the minute blood vessels that connect the arteries and veins. **2.** a tube with a small bore. —*adj.* **3.** pertaining to capillaries or capillarity. **4.** like hair.

cap•i•tal¹ (kap′i tl), *n.* **1.** a city that is the seat of government of a country, state, etc. **2.** CAPITAL LETTER. **3.** the wealth, as in money or property, owned or used in business. —*adj.* **4.** pertaining to financial capital. **5.** principal; primary. **6.** of or being the seat of government. **7.** excellent or first-rate. **8.** punishable by death. [< AF < L *capitālis* of the head]

cap•i•tal² (kap′i tl), *n.* the distinctively treated upper end of an architectural column. [≪ LL *capitellum* little head]

cap′ital gain′, *n.* profit from the sale of assets, as bonds or real estate.

cap′ital goods′, *n.pl.* machines and tools used in the production of other goods.

cap′i•tal•ism, *n.* an economic system in which the means of production and distribution are privately owned.

cap′i•tal•ist, *n.* **1.** a person who invests capital in business. **2.** an advocate of capitalism. **3.** a wealthy person. —**cap′i•tal•is′tic,** *adj.*

cap′i•tal•ize′, *v.t.,* **-ized, -iz•ing. 1.** to write in capital letters or with an initial capital. **2.** to convert into or use as capital. **3.** to supply with capital. **4. capitalize on,** to take advantage of. —**cap′i•tal•i•za′tion,** *n.*

cap′ital let′ter, *n.* a letter of the alphabet that differs from its corresponding lowercase letter in form and height.

cap′i•tal•ly, *adv.* excellently.

cap′ital pun′ishment, *n.* punishment by death for a crime.

cap•i•ta•tion (kap′i tā′shən), *n.* **1.** a poll tax. **2.** a fee or payment of a uniform amount for each person. —**cap′i•ta′tive,** *adj.*

Cap•i•tol (kap′i tl), *n.* **1.** the building in Washington, D.C., in which the U.S. Congress meets. **2.** (*often l.c.*) a building occupied by a state legislature.

Cap′itol Hill′, *n.* **1.** the small hill in Washington, D.C., on which the Capitol stands. **2.** the U.S. Congress.

ca•pit•u•late (kə pich′ə lāt′), *v.i.,* **-lat•ed, -lat•ing. 1.** to surrender on stipulated terms. **2.** to give up resistance. —**ca•pit′u•la′tion,** *n.*

cap•let (kap′lit), *n.* an oval-shaped pharmaceutical tablet that is coated to facilitate swallowing.

ca•pon (kā′pon, -pən), *n.* a cockerel castrated to improve its flesh for use as food.

cap•puc•ci•no (kap′ə chē′nō, kä′pə-), *n.,* *pl.* **-nos.** espresso coffee mixed with foaming steamed milk and sprinkled with cinnamon.

ca•price (kə prēs′), *n.* **1.** a sudden, unpredictable change. **2.** a tendency to change one's mind without motive. —**ca•pri′cious** (-prish′əs), *adj.* —**ca•pri′cious•ly,** *adv.* —**ca•pri′cious•ness,** *n.*

Cap•ri•corn (kap′ri kôrn′), *n.* the tenth sign of the zodiac. [< L: goat]

cap•size (kap′sīz, kap sīz′), *v.i.,* *v.t.,* **-sized, -siz•ing.** to turn bottom up; overturn.

cap•stan (kap′stən, -stan), *n.* a windlass rotated in a horizontal plane, for winding in ropes, cables, etc.

cap′stone′, *n.* a finishing stone of a structure.

cap•sule (kap′səl, -sōōl, -syōōl), *n.,* *v.,* **-suled, -sul•ing,** *adj.* —*n.* **1.** a gelatinous case enclosing a dose of medicine. **2.** a dry fruit composed of two or more carpels. **3.** a pressurized cabin in a spacecraft. **4.** a concise report. —*v.t.* **5.** to enclose in a capsule. **6.** to summarize. —*adj.* **7.** short and concise. —**cap′su•lar,** *adj.*

capt., captain.

cap•tain (kap′tən, -tin), *n.* **1.** a person in authority over others. **2.** an army officer ranking above a first lieutenant. **3.** a naval officer ranking above a commander. **4.** the commander of a merchant vessel. **5.** the pilot of an airplane. **6.** the field leader of a sports team. —*v.t.* **7.** to command as a captain. —**cap′-tain•cy,** *n.*

cap•tion (kap′shən), *n.* **1.** an explanation for a picture or illustration. **2.** a motion-picture or television subtitle. —*v.t.* **3.** to supply a caption for.

cap•tious (kap′shəs), *adj.* **1.** faultfinding. **2.** designed to ensnare or perplex. —**cap′tious•ly,** *adv.* —**cap′tious•ness,** *n.*

cap•ti•vate (kap′tə vāt′), *v.t.,* **-vat•ed, -vat•ing.** to attract intensely; enchant. —**cap′ti•va′tion,** *n.*

cap•tive (-tiv), *n.* **1.** a prisoner. —*adj.* **2.** unable to avoid listening to something: *a captive audience.* —**cap•tiv′i•ty,** *n.,* *pl.* **-ties.**

cap′tor (-tər), *n.* a person who has captured a person or thing.

cap′ture (-chər), *v.,* **-tured, -tur•ing,** *n.* —*v.t.* **1.** to take by force or stratagem; seize. **2.** to record in lasting form: *a movie that captures Berlin in the 1930s.* **3. a.** to enter (data) into a computer for processing or storage. **b.** to record (data) in preparation for such entry. —*n.* **4.** the act of capturing.

car (kär), *n.* **1.** an automobile. **2.** a vehicle running on rails, as a streetcar. **3.** the part of a conveyance, as an elevator, that carries the passengers or freight. **4.** any wheeled vehicle. [< AF < L *carra* < Celtic]

Ca•ra•cas (kə rä′kəs), *n.* the capital of Venezuela. 1,044,851.

car•a•cul (kar′ə kəl), *n.* KARAKUL.

ca•rafe (kə raf′, -räf′), *n.* a bottle for holding wine, coffee, or other beverages.

ca•ram•bo•la (kar′əm bō′lə), *n.,* *pl.* **-las. 1.** a SE Asian tree bearing deeply ridged, yellow-brown fruit. **2.** Also called **star fruit.** the fruit itself.

car•a•mel (kar′ə məl, -mel′, kär′məl), *n.* **1.** burnt sugar, used for coloring and flavoring food. **2.** a chewy candy made from sugar, butter, milk, etc.

car′a•mel•ize′, v.t., v.i., -ized, -iz•ing. to convert or be converted into caramel. —car′a•mel•i•za′tion, n.

car•a•pace (kar′ə pās′), n. a hard shell covering the back of an animal, as of a turtle.

car•at (kar′ət), n. 1. a unit of weight in gemstones, 200 milligrams. 2. KARAT.

car•a•van (kar′ə van′), n. 1. a group traveling together for safety, as through a desert. 2. a large van. [< It carovana < Pers kārwān]

car′a•van′sa•ry (-sə rē), n., pl. -ries. (in the Near East) an inn for caravans.

car•a•vel (kar′ə vel′), n. a small Spanish or Portuguese sailing ship of the Middle Ages and later.

car•a•way (kar′ə wā′), n. 1. a plant of the parsley family. 2. the aromatic, seedlike fruit of this plant used in cooking.

car•bide (kär′bīd, -bid), n. a compound of carbon with another element or group.

car•bine (kär′bēn, -bīn), n. a light, gas-operated semiautomatic rifle.

carbo-, a combining form meaning carbon (carbohydrate).

car•bo•hy•drate (kär′bō hī′drāt, -bə-), n. any of a class of organic compounds composed of carbon, hydrogen, and oxygen, including starches and sugars.

car•bol′ic ac′id (kär bol′ik), n. PHENOL.

car•bon (kär′bən), n. 1. a nonmetallic element found combined with other elements in all organic matter and in a pure state as diamond and graphite. Symbol: C; at. wt.: 12.011; at. no.: 6. 2. Also called **car′bon cop′y.** a duplicate made with carbon paper. 3. a sheet of carbon paper.

carbon 14, n. RADIOCARBON.

car′bon•ate′ (n. -bə nāt′, -nit; v. -nāt′), n., v., -at•ed, -at•ing. —n. 1. a salt or ester of carbonic acid. —v.t. 2. to charge with carbon dioxide. —car′bon•a′tion, n.

car′bon black′, n. a finely divided form of carbon, used in pigments, rubbers, etc.

car′bon-date′, v.t., -dat•ed, -dat•ing. to estimate the age of (organic materials) by measurement of their radiocarbon content. —car′bon dat′ing, n.

car′bon diox′ide, n. an incombustible gas present in the atmosphere and formed during respiration.

car•bon′ic ac′id (kär bon′ik), n. the acid formed when carbon dioxide dissolves in water.

Car•bon•if•er•ous (kär′bə nif′ər əs), adj. 1. noting or pertaining to a period of the Paleozoic Era, from 345 million to 280 million years ago. 2. (l.c.) containing or producing carbon or coal.

car′bon monox′ide, n. a colorless, odorless, poisonous gas produced when carbon burns with insufficient air.

car′bon pa′per, n. paper faced with a preparation of carbon or the like, used to make copies of typed or written material.

car′bon tet•ra•chlo′ride (te′trə klôr′īd), n. a vaporous, toxic liquid, used as a fire extinguisher, cleaning fluid, etc.

Car•bo•run•dum (kär′bə run′dəm), Trademark. an abrasive of carbon, silicon, and other materials.

car•boy (kär′boi′), n. a large glass bottle encased in a basket or box, used esp. for holding corrosive liquids.

car•bun•cle (kär′bung kəl), n. a skin inflammation of deep interconnected boils. —car•bun′cu•lar (-kyə lər), adj.

car•bu•re•tor (kär′bə rā′tər, -byə-), n. a device for mixing vaporized fuel with air to produce an explosive mixture, as for an internal-combustion engine.

car•cass (kär′kəs), n. 1. the dead body of an animal. 2. a framework or shell.

car•cin•o•gen (kär sin′ə jən), n. any substance that tends to produce a cancer. —car′cin•o•gen′ic, adj. —car′ci•no•ge•nic′i•ty (-jə nis′i tē), n.

car′ci•no′ma (-sə nō′mə), n., pl. -mas, -ma•ta (-mə tə). a malignant tumor composed of epithelial tissue.

car′ coat′, n. a hip-length overcoat or jacket.

card¹ (kärd), n. 1. a piece of stiff paper, thin paste-

board, or plastic for various uses, as to record information. 2. one of a set of thin pieces of cardboard used in playing various games. 3. **cards,** a game played with such a set. 4. a folded piece of thin cardboard printed with a message of holiday greeting, congratulations, etc. 5. POSTCARD. 6. BOARD (def. 6a). 7. an amusing or witty person. —**Idiom. 8. put** or **lay one's cards on the table,** to be completely straightforward.

card² (kärd), n. 1. a machine for combing fibers of cotton, flax, wool, etc. —v.t. 2. to dress (wool or the like) with a card. —card′er, n.

card′board′, n. a thin, stiff pasteboard, used for signs, boxes, etc.

car•di•ac (kär′dē ak′), adj. of or near the heart.

car′diac arrest′, n. the abrupt cessation of heartbeat.

car•di•gan (kär′di gən), n. a sweater or jacket that opens down the front. [after the Earl of Cardigan (1797–1868), British hero in Crimean War]

car•di•nal (kär′dn l), adj. 1. of prime importance. 2. deep red. —n. 3. a high ecclesiastic appointed by the pope and standing next in rank. 4. a bright red North American songbird. 5. a deep, rich red color. —car′di•nal•ly, adv.

car′dinal num′ber, n. any of the numbers that express amount, as one, two, three.

cardio-, a combining form meaning heart (cardiogram).

car•di•o•gram (kär′dē ə gram′), n. ELECTROCARDIOGRAM.

car′di•o•graph′, n. ELECTROCARDIOGRAPH.

car′di•ol′o•gy (-ol′ə jē), n. the study of the heart and its functions. —car′di•o•log′i•cal (-ə loj′i kəl), adj. —car′di•ol′o•gist, n.

car′di•o•pul′mo•nar′y, adj. of the heart and lungs.

car′di•o•vas′cu•lar, adj. of the heart and blood vessels.

card′sharp′, n. a person who cheats at card games. Also called **card′ shark′.**

CARE or **Care** (kâr), n. a private organization for the collection of funds, goods, etc., for distribution to the needy in foreign countries. [C(ooperative for) A(merican) R(elief) E(verywhere)]

ca•reen (kə rēn′), v.i., v.t. to lean or cause to lean over to one side.

ca•reer (kə rēr′), n. 1. an occupation followed as one's lifework. 2. a person's general course of action through life. 3. a swift course. —v.i. 4. to go at full speed.

care′free′, adj. without worry.

care′ful, adj. 1. cautious in one's action. 2. done with accuracy or caution. —care′ful•ly, adv.

care′giv′er, n. a person who cares for a child or for someone who is sick or disabled.

care′less (-lis), adj. 1. not paying enough attention to what one does. 2. not exact or accurate. 3. heedless; unconsidered. 4. unconcerned. —care′less•ly, adv. —care′less•ness, n.

ca•ress (kə res′), n. 1. a light stroking gesture expressing affection. —v.t. 2. to stroke lightly and affectionately.

car•et (kar′it), n. a mark (^) made in written or printed matter to indicate where something is to be inserted. [< L: (there) is lacking]

care′tak′er, n. 1. a person in charge of maintaining a building, estate, etc. 2. a person or group that temporarily performs the duties of an office. 3. a person who takes care of another.

care′worn′, adj. showing signs of care or worry.

car′fare′, n. the cost of a ride on a subway, bus, etc.

car•go (kär′gō), n., pl. -goes, -gos. the load of goods carried by a ship, plane, etc.; freight.

Car•ib•be•an (kar′ə bē′ən, kə rib′ē-), n. 1. Also called **Car′ibbe′an Sea′.** a part of the Atlantic Ocean bounded by Central America, the West Indies, and South America. —adj. 2. of the Caribbean Sea and its islands.

car•i•bou (kar′ə bōō′), *n., pl.* **-bous, -bou.** the reindeer of North America. [< CanF < Algonquian *γalipu* shoveler, referring to its habit of scraping aside snow to find food]

car•i•ca•ture (kar′i kə chər), *n., v.,* **-tured, -tur•ing. —***n.* **1.** a ludicrously exaggerated depiction of a person or thing. **2.** an imitation so inferior as to be ludicrous. **—***v.t.* **3.** to make a caricature of. **—car′i•ca•tur•ist,** *n.*

car•ies (kâr′ēz), *n., pl.* **-ies.** decay, as of bone or teeth.

car•il•lon (kar′ə lon′, -lən), *n.* a set of stationary bells in a tower, sounded by manual or pedal action or by machinery.

car•jack•ing (kär′jak′ing), *n.* the forcible stealing of a vehicle from a motorist. **—car′jack′er,** *n.*

Car•mi•chael (kär′mī kəl), *n.* **1. Hoagland Howard,** ("*Hoagy*"), 1899–1981, U.S. songwriter and musician. **2. Stokely,** born 1941, U.S. civil-rights leader, born in Trinidad.

car•mine (kär′min, -mīn), *n.* a crimson or purplish red color.

car•nage (kär′nij), *n.* the slaughter of many people, as in battle.

car′nal (-nl), *adj.* **1.** of the flesh or body; sensual. **2.** not spiritual; worldly. **—car•nal′i•ty,** *n.* **—car′nal•ly,** *adv.*

car•na•tion (kär nā′shən), *n.* a cultivated plant with fragrant flowers in a variety of colors.

Car•ne•gie (kär′ni gē *or, for 1,* kär nā′gē, -neg′ē), *n.* **1. Andrew,** 1835–1919, U.S. steel manufacturer and philanthropist, born in Scotland. **2. Dale,** 1888–1955, U.S. author and teacher of self-improvement techniques.

car•nel•ian (kär nēl′yən), *n.* a reddish variety of chalcedony used in jewelry.

car•ni•val (kär′nə vəl), *n.* **1.** a traveling amusement show with sideshows and rides. **2.** a festival. **3.** the period of merrymaking immediately before Lent. [< It *carnevale,* OIt *carnelevare* taking meat away]

car•ni•vore (kär′nə vôr′), *n.* **1.** an animal that eats flesh. **2.** a plant that eats insects.

car•niv′o•rous (-niv′ər əs), *adj.* **1.** flesh-eating. **2.** of the carnivores. **—car•niv′o•rous•ness,** *n.*

car•ol (kar′əl), *n., v.,* **-oled, -ol•ing** or (*esp. Brit.*) **-olled, -ol•ling. —***n.* **1.** a song of joy or praise. **2.** a Christmas song. **—***v.i., v.t.* **3.** to sing joyously. **—car′ol•er, car′ol•ler,** *n.*

car•om (kar′əm), *n.* **1.** a shot in billiards in which the cue ball hits two balls in succession. **2.** any hit and rebound. **—***v.i.* **3.** to make a carom. **4.** to hit and rebound.

car•o•tene (kar′ə tēn′), *n.* any of three yellow or orange pigments found in many plants, esp. carrots, and transformed into vitamin A in the liver.

ca•rot•id (kə rot′id), *n.* **1.** either of two large arteries, one on each side of the neck, that carry blood to the head. **—***adj.* **2.** pertaining to a carotid artery.

ca•rous•al (kə rou′zəl), *n.* a noisy or drunken gathering; revel.

ca•rouse (kə rouz′), *v.,* **-roused, -rous•ing,** *n.* **—***v.i.* **1.** to engage in a drunken revel. **—***n.* **2.** CAROUSAL. **—ca•rous′er,** *n.*

car•ou•sel (kar′ə sel′), *n.* **1.** MERRY-GO-ROUND (def. 1). **2.** a revolving conveyor on which items are placed: *a baggage carousel.*

carp¹ (kärp), *v.i.* to find fault unreasonably; cavil. **—carp′er,** *n.*

carp² (kärp), *n., pl.* **carps, carp.** a large freshwater food fish.

car•pal (kär′pəl), *adj.* **1.** pertaining to the carpus. **—***n.* **2.** a wrist bone.

car•pel (kär′pəl), *n.* a simple pistil or a single member of a compound pistil.

car•pen•ter (kär′pən tər), *n.* a person who builds or repairs wooden structures. **—car′pen•try,** *n.*

car•pet (kär′pit), *n.* **1.** a heavy woven fabric for covering floors. **2.** any covering resembling a carpet. **—***v.t.* **3.** to cover with a carpet. **—Idiom. 4. on the carpet,** reprimanded.

car′pet•bag′, *n., v.,* **-bagged, -bag•ging. —***n.* **1.** a bag for traveling, esp. one made of carpeting. **—***v.i.* **2.** to act as a carpetbagger.

car′pet•bag′ger, *n.* a Northerner who went to the South after the Civil War to profit from the unsettled conditions there.

car′pool′, *n.* an arrangement among automobile owners by which each in turn drives the others to and from a designated place.

car′port′, *n.* a roof projecting from the side of a building for sheltering an automobile.

car•pus (kär′pəs), *n., pl.* **-pi** (-pī). **1.** the wrist. **2.** the wrist bones collectively.

car•rel or **-rell** (kar′əl), *n.* a cubicle or desk partitioned off for private study in a library.

car•riage (kar′ij), *n.* **1.** a horse-drawn vehicle for conveying persons. **2.** BABY CARRIAGE. **3.** a movable part, as of a machine, designed for carrying something: *a wide carriage on a dot-matrix printer.* **4.** bearing of the head and body.

car′ri•er (-ē ər), *n.* **1.** a person or thing that carries. **2.** a company that transports passengers or goods. **3.** AIRCRAFT CARRIER. **4.** an individual who transmits a disease to others.

car′rier pig′eon, *n.* a homing pigeon.

car•ri•on (kar′ē ən), *n.* dead and putrefying flesh.

Car•roll (kar′əl), *n.* **Lewis,** pen name of Charles Lutwidge DODGSON.

car•rot (kar′ət), *n.* **1.** a plant widely cultivated for its edible orange root. **2.** this root. **3.** something offered as an incentive.

car•ry (kar′ē), *v.,* **-ried, -ry•ing,** *n., pl.* **-ries. —***v.t.* **1.** to move while supporting or holding; transport. **2.** to wear, hold, or have around one. **3.** to serve as a medium for the transmission of. **4.** to transfer to a subsequent time, page, or column. **5.** to bear the weight or burden of. **6.** to hold (the body or head) in a certain manner. **7.** to bear (oneself) in a specified manner. **8.** to secure the passage of (a motion or bill). **9.** to gain a majority of votes in (a district). **10.** to have as a consequence: *Violation carries a stiff penalty.* **11.** to keep in stock. **—***v.i.* **12.** to act as a bearer or conductor. **13.** to be transmitted or sustained. **14. ~ away,** to stir strong emotions in. **15. ~ on, a.** to manage. **b.** to persevere. **c.** to be disruptive. **16. ~ out, a.** to execute. **b.** to accomplish; complete. **17. ~ over,** to postpone. **—***n.* **18.** range, as of a gun. **19.** a portage.

car′rying charge′, *n.* a charge for maintaining an account, as an installment payment.

car′ry-on′, *adj.* **1.** small enough to be carried by a passenger onto an airplane. **—***n.* **2.** a piece of carry-on luggage.

car′ry•o′ver, *n.* something postponed to a later time.

car′ seat′, *n.* a removable seat used to hold a small child safely in an automobile.

car′sick′, *adj.* ill with motion sickness during automobile travel.

Car•son (kär′sən), *n.* **1. Christopher** ("*Kit*"), 1809–68, U.S. frontiersman and scout. **2. Rachel Louise,** 1907–1964, U.S. marine biologist and author.

Car′son Cit′y (kär′sən), *n.* the capital of Nevada. 36,650.

cart (kärt), *n.* **1.** a two-wheeled vehicle drawn by a horse, ox, etc. **2.** any small vehicle pulled by hand. **—***v.t.* **3.** to haul, as in a cart or truck. **—cart′er,** *n.*

cart•age (kär′tij), *n.* the act or cost of carting.

carte blanche (kärt′ blänch′, blänsh′), *n.* full discretionary power. [< F: lit., blank document]

car•tel (kär tel′), *n.* an international syndicate formed to control prices and output in some field of business.

Car•ter (kär′tər), *n.* **James Earl, Jr.** (*Jimmy*), born 1924, 39th president of the U.S. 1977–81.

Car•te′sian coor′dinates (kär te′zhən), *n.pl.* a system of coordinates for locating a point on a plane by its distance from each of two intersecting lines.

Car•tier (kär′tē ā′, kär tyä′), *n.* **Jacques,** 1491–1557, French navigator: discovered the St. Lawrence River.

car·ti·lage (kär′tl ij), *n.* a firm, elastic type of connective tissue. —**car′ti·lag′i·nous** (-tl aj′ə nəs), *adj.*

car·tog·ra·phy (kär tog′rə fē), *n.* the production of maps. —**car·tog′ra·pher,** *n.* —**car′to·graph′ic** (-tə graf′ik), *adj.*

car·ton (kär′tn), *n.* a large cardboard or plastic box.

car·toon (kär tōōn′), *n.* **1.** a drawing caricaturing some action or subject. **2.** COMIC STRIP. **3.** ANIMATED CARTOON. —*v.t., v.i.* **4.** to draw a cartoon (of). —**car·toon′ist,** *n.*

car·tridge (kär′trij), *n.* **1.** a cylindrical case for holding a charge of powder and usu. a bullet for a firearm. **2.** a compact container, as for magnetic tape or a roll of film.

cart′wheel′, *n.* **1.** a handspring done to the side. —*v.i.* **2.** to roll forward end over end.

Ca·ru·so (kə rōō′sō), *n.* **Enrico,** 1873–1921, Italian tenor.

carve (kärv), *v.,* **carved, carv·ing.** —*v.t.* **1.** to cut so as to form something. **2.** to form by or as if by cutting: *to carve a statue out of stone.* **3.** to cut into slices, as meat. **4.** to decorate with designs cut on the surface. —*v.i.* **5.** to form designs by carving. **6.** to carve meat. —**carv′er,** *n.* —**carv′ing,** *n.*

Car·ver (kär′vər), *n.* **1. George Washington,** 1864?–1943, U.S. botanist and chemist. **2. John,** 1575?–1621, Pilgrim leader: first governor of Plymouth Colony 1620–21. **3. Raymond,** 1938–88, U.S. short-story writer and poet.

car′ wash′, *n.* a place having special equipment for washing automobiles.

car·y·at·id (kar′ē at′id), *n., pl.* **-ids, -i·des** (-i dēz′). a sculptured female figure used as a column.

caryatids

ca·sa·ba (kə sä′bə), *n., pl.* **-bas.** a winter melon with a yellow rind and sweet, juicy edible flesh. [after *Kassaba* (now Turgutlu), Turkey, which exported it]

Cas·a·blan·ca (kas′ə blang′kə, kä′sə bläng′kə), *n.* a seaport in NW Morocco. 2,139,204.

Cas·a·no·va (kaz′ə nō′və, kas′-), *n., pl.* **-vas** for 2. **1. Giovanni,** 1725–98, Italian adventurer and writer. **2.** a man known for his amorous adventures.

cas·cade (kas kād′), *n., v.,* **-cad·ed, -cad·ing.** —*n.* **1.** a waterfall descending over a steep, rocky surface. **2.** anything flowing or falling in abundance; torrent. —*v.i., v.t.* **3.** to fall or cause to fall in a cascade.

cas·car·a (kas kâr′ə), *n., pl.* **-car·as.** a buckthorn of the northwestern U.S.

case¹ (kās), *n.* **1.** a specific instance or example. **2.** the actual state of things: *That is not the case.* **3.** a patient or client. **4.** a specific matter requiring discussion, decision, or investigation. **5.** a statement of facts in support of an argument. **6.** a suit or action at law. **7.** a category in the inflection of nouns or pronouns, noting their syntactic relation to other words. —*Idiom.* **8. in any case,** anyhow. **9. in case of,** in the event of.

case² (kās), *n., v.,* **cased, cas·ing.** —*n.* **1.** a container for enclosing something. **2.** an outer covering. **3.** a box with its contents. **4.** a surrounding frame, as of a door. —*v.t.* **5.** to put in a case. **6.** *Slang.* to examine (a house, bank, etc.), esp. in planning a crime.

case′hard′en, *v.t.* to harden the surface of (an iron-based alloy).

ca·sein (kā′sēn, -sē in), *n.* a protein precipitated from milk, forming the basis of cheese and certain plastics.

case′load′, *n.* the number of cases handled by a court, social worker, etc.

case′ment, *n.* a window sash opening on side hinges.

case′work′, *n.* social work involving direct contact between the social worker and the client. —**case′work′er,** *n.*

cash (kash), *n.* **1.** money in the form of coins or banknotes. **2.** money or an equivalent paid at the time of purchase. —*v.t.* **3.** to give or obtain cash for (a check, money order, etc.). **4. cash in,** to turn in and get cash for.

cash·ew (kash′ōō, kə shōō′), *n.* the small, kidney-shaped, edible nut of a tropical American tree.

cash·ier¹ (ka shēr′), *n.* **1.** an employee, as in a market, who collects payment for purchases. **2.** an exec utive who superintends the financial transactions of a company.

cash·ier² (ka shēr′), *v.t.* to dismiss from a position of trust, esp. with disgrace.

cashier′s′ check′, *n.* a check drawn by a bank on its own funds and signed by its cashier.

cash′ machine′, *n.* AUTOMATED-TELLER MACHINE.

cash·mere (kazh′mēr, kash′-), *n.* **1.** a fine, downy wool from goats of Kashmir and Tibet. **2.** a fabric made from this wool.

cash′ reg′ister, *n.* a business machine that records and totals receipts and has a money drawer.

cas′ing, *n.* **1.** a case or covering. **2.** a framework, as around a door. **3.** the outer covering of an automobile tire. **4.** the skin of a sausage or salami.

ca·si·no (kə sē′nō), *n., pl.* **-nos. 1.** a place for gambling. **2.** a card game for two, three, or four players.

cask (kask, käsk), *n.* **1.** a container resembling a barrel but larger and stronger. **2.** the quantity such a container holds.

cas·ket (kas′kit, kä′skit), *n.* **1.** a coffin. **2.** a small chest or box, as for jewels.

Cas·par (kas′pər), *n.* one of the three Magi.

Cas′pi·an Sea′ (kas′pē ən), *n.* a salt lake between SE Europe and Asia.

Cas·san·dra (kə san′drə), *n., pl.* **-dras. 1.** (in Greek myth) a daughter of King Priam of Troy, endowed with prophetic powers, but fated never to be believed. **2.** a person who prophesies doom or disaster.

Cas·satt (kə sat′), *n.* **Mary,** 1845–1926, U.S. painter.

cas·sa·va (kə sä′və), *n., pl.* **-vas. 1.** a tropical American plant with tuberous roots. **2.** a starch from the roots, the source of tapioca.

cas·se·role (kas′ə rōl′), *n.* **1.** a baking and serving dish of glass, pottery, etc. **2.** food baked in such a dish.

cas·sette (kə set′, ka-), *n.* a case in which audiotape or videotape runs between two reels.

cas·sia (kash′ə, kas′ē ə), *n., pl.* **-sias. 1.** an ornamental tropical tree having long pods. **2.** the pulp of these pods, used medicinally and as a flavoring.

cas·sock (kas′ək), *n.* a long, close-fitting garment worn by clerics.

cast (kast, käst), *v.,* **cast, cast·ing,** *n.* —*v.t.* **1.** to throw or hurl. **2.** to direct (the eye, a glance, etc.). **3.** to send forth: *to cast light.* **4.** to shed or drop: *The snake casts its skin.* **5.** to deposit (a ballot or vote). **6.** to select (performers) for (a play or role). **7.** to form (an object) by pouring into a mold. —*v.i.* **8.** to throw. **9. ~ about,** to seek. **10. ~ away** or **aside,** to reject; discard. **11. ~ off, a.** to discard. **b.** to let loose, as a ship from a mooring. —*n.* **12.** the act of throwing. **13.** a throw of dice. **14.** the performers in a play, motion picture, etc. **15.** something made in a mold. **16.** a rigid surgical dressing, as for a broken limb. **17.** sort; kind. **18.** a hue; shade.

cas·ta·net (kas′tə net′), *n.* a handheld percussion instrument consisting of two wooden shells clicked together, esp. to accompany dancing.

cast′a•way′, *n.* **1.** a shipwrecked person. **2.** anything thrown away. —*adj.* **3.** shipwrecked. **4.** thrown away.

caste (kast, käst), *n.* **1.** any of the hereditary social divisions of traditional Hindu society. **2.** any rigid system of social distinctions. **3.** social position: *to lose caste.*

cast′er, *n.* **1.** a small wheel on a swivel, set under a piece of furniture to facilitate moving it. **2.** a bottle or cruet for holding a condiment.

cas•ti•gate (kas′ti gāt′), *v.t.*, **-gat•ed, -gat•ing.** to criticize severely. —**cas′ti•ga′tion**, *n.* —**cas′ti•ga′tor**, *n.*

cast′ing, *n.* **1.** something cast in a mold. **2.** the process of choosing performers, as for a play.

cast′ i′ron, *n.* a hard, brittle alloy of carbon and other elements. —**cast′-i′ron**, *adj.*

cas•tle (kas′əl, kä′səl), *n.* **1.** a fortified residence, as of a noble in feudal times. **2.** a strongly fortified stronghold. **3.** *Chess.* the rook. [< L *castellum* fortress]

cast′off′, *adj.* **1.** discarded. —*n.* **2.** one that has been discarded.

Cas′tor and Pol′lux, *n.pl.* (in Greek myth) twin brothers of Helen of Troy, famous for their fraternal affection and regarded as the protectors of persons at sea.

cas′tor oil′, *n.* a colorless or pale oil from the bean of a tropical plant, used as a lubricant and cathartic.

cas•trate (kas′trāt), *v.t.*, **-trat•ed, -trat•ing.** to remove the testes of; emasculate. —**cas•tra′tion**, *n.*

cas•u•al (kazh′ōō əl), *adj.* **1.** happening by chance. **2.** offhand or cursory. **3.** indifferent; apathetic. **4.** appropriate for informal occasions. **5.** irregular; occasional. —**cas′u•al•ly**, *adv.* —**cas′u•al•ness**, *n.*

cas′u•al•ty, *n., pl.* **-ties. 1.** a member of the armed forces lost through death, wounds, etc. **2.** one who is injured or killed in an accident. **3.** a serious accident.

cas•u•ist (kazh′ōō ist), *n.* an oversubtle or disingenuous reasoner. —**cas′u•is′tic**, *adj.* —**cas′u•ist•ry**, *n.*

cat (kat), *n.* **1.** a small domesticated carnivore popular as a pet. **2.** any related carnivore, as the lion, tiger, or leopard. **3.** a spiteful woman. —*Idiom.* **4. let the cat out of the bag,** to divulge a secret. —*Proverb.* **5. When the cat's away, the mice will play,** people will take advantage of an overseer's absence.

cat•a•clysm (kat′ə kliz′əm), *n.* any violent upheaval. —**cat′a•clys′mic**, *adj.*

cat•a•comb (kat′ə kōm′), *n.* **1.** Usu., **catacombs.** an underground cemetery, esp. one consisting of tunnels and rooms with recesses dug out for coffins and tombs. **2. the Catacombs,** the subterranean burial chambers of the early Christians in and near Rome, Italy. **3.** an underground passageway, esp. one full of twists and turns.

cat′a•falque′ (-fôk′, -fôlk′, -falk′), *n.* a raised structure on which a corpse lies in state.

cat•a•lep•sy (kat′l ep′sē), *n.* a seizure characterized by postural rigidity and mental stupor. —**cat′a•lep′tic**, *adj., n.*

cat•a•log (kat′l ôg′, -og′), *n.* **1.** a systematic list, as of items for sale or courses at a university, often including descriptive material. **2.** a book or pamphlet that contains such a list. **3.** a list of the contents of a library. —*v.t., v.i.* **4.** to make a catalog (of). —**cat′a•log′er**, *n.* CATALOG.

cat•a•logue (kat′l ôg′, -og′), *n., v.t., v.i.*, **-logued, -logu•ing.** CATALOG. —**cat′a•logu′er**, *n.*

ca•tal•pa (kə tal′pə), *n., pl.* **-pas.** a tree with white flower clusters and long, beanlike seed pods.

ca•tal•y•sis (kə tal′ə sis), *n., pl.* **-ses** (-sēz′). the causing or accelerating of a chemical change by the addition of a catalyst. —**cat•a•lyt•ic** (kat′l it′ik), *adj., n.*

cat•a•lyst (kat′l ist), *n.* **1.** a substance that causes or speeds a chemical reaction without itself being affected. **2.** anything that precipitates an event.

catalyt′ic convert′er, *n.* an automotive device that makes some pollutants in the exhaust gases harmless.

cat′a•lyze′, *v.t.*, **-lyzed, -lyz•ing.** to act upon by catalysis. —**cat′a•lyz′er**, *n.*

cat•a•ma•ran (kat′ə mə ran′), *n.* **1.** a sailboat whose frame is set on two parallel hulls. **2.** a raft formed of logs lashed together.

cat•a•mount (kat′ə mount′), *n.* a wild cat, esp. the cougar or the lynx.

cat•a•pult (kat′ə pult′, -pōōlt′), *n.* **1.** an ancient military engine for hurling stones, arrows, etc. **2.** a device for launching an airplane from the deck of a ship. —*v.t., v.i.* **3.** to hurl or be hurled from or as if from a catapult.

cat•a•ract (kat′ə rakt′), *n.* **1.** a large waterfall. **2. a.** an abnormality of the eye characterized by opacity of the lens. **b.** the opaque area.

ca•tarrh (kə tär′), *n.* inflammation of a mucous membrane, esp. of the respiratory tract.

ca•tas•tro•phe (kə tas′trə fē), *n., pl.* **-phes. 1.** a sudden and widespread disaster. **2.** a fiasco. —**cat•a•stroph•ic** (kat′ə strof′ik), *adj.*

cat•a•to•ni•a (kat′ə tō′nē ə), *n.* a psychotic syndrome, esp. in schizophrenia, characterized by muscular rigidity and mental stupor. —**cat′a•ton′ic** (-ton′ik), *adj., n.*

cat′bird′, *n.* a North American songbird with catlike vocalizations.

cat′boat′, *n.* a boat having a single sail and mast set well forward.

cat′ bur′glar, *n.* a burglar who breaks into buildings by climbing through upstairs windows, across roofs, etc.

cat′call′, *n.* **1.** a shrill sound or raucous shout expressing disapproval. —*v.t., v.i.* **2.** to sound catcalls (at).

catch (kach), *v.*, **caught, catch•ing**, *n.* —*v.t.* **1.** to seize or capture. **2.** to trap or ensnare. **3.** to take and hold: *to catch a ball.* **4.** to surprise in some action. **5.** to receive or contract: *to catch a cold.* **6.** to be in time to get aboard (a train, boat, etc.). **7.** to entangle. **8.** to attract: *to catch our attention.* **9.** to see or hear. **10.** to comprehend. —*v.i.* **11.** to become gripped or entangled. **12.** to take hold. **13. ~ at,** to grasp at eagerly. **14. ~ on, a.** to become popular. **b.** to understand. **15. ~ up, a.** to overtake something moving. **b.** to do enough so that one is no longer behind. —*n.* **16.** the act of catching. **17.** anything that catches, as a door latch. **18.** any tricky or concealed drawback. **19.** a momentary break in the voice. **20.** something caught, as a quantity of fish. **21.** one that is worth getting. **22.** a fragment: *catches of a song.*

catch′all′, *n.* a receptacle for odds and ends.

catch′er, *n.* the baseball player behind home plate who catches pitches not hit by the batter.

catch′ing, *adj.* **1.** contagious. **2.** attractive.

catch′ment, *n.* **1.** something for catching water. **2.** the water so caught. **3.** the act of catching water.

Catch-22 (kach′twen′tē tōō′), *n., pl.* **Catch-22s, Catch-22′s.** a frustrating situation in which one is trapped by contradictory regulations or conditions. [from a military regulation in J. Heller's novel of the same name (1961)]

catch′word′, *n.* a word or phrase repeated so often that it becomes a slogan.

catch′y, *adj.*, **-i•er, -i•est. 1.** pleasing and easily remembered. **2.** likely to attract attention. **3.** tricky; deceptive.

cat•e•chism (kat′i kiz′əm), *n.* a summary of the principles of a Christian religion, in the form of questions and answers. —**cat′e•chist**, *n.* —**cat′e•chize′** (-kīz′), *v.t.*, **-chized, -chiz•ing.**

cat•e•gor•i•cal (kat′i gôr′i kəl, -gor′-), *adj.* **1.** unconditional; absolute. **2.** belonging to a category. —**cat′e•gor′i•cal•ly**, *adv.*

cat′e•go•rize′ (-gə rīz′), *v.t.*, **-rized, -riz•ing.** to arrange in categories; classify. —**cat′e•go•ri•za′tion**, *n.*

cat′e•go′ry (-gôr′ē), *n., pl.* **-ries.** any division in a system of classification.

ca•ter (kā′tər), *v.i.* **1.** to provide food and service. **2.** to provide what is desired: *to cater to popular demand.* —*v.t.* **3.** to provide food and service for: *to cater a reception.* —**ca′ter•er**, *n.*

cat′er-cor′nered (kat′i-, kat′ē-, kat′ər-), *adj.* **1.** diagonal. —*adv.* **2.** diagonally.

cat•er•pil•lar (kat′ə pil′ər, kat′ər-), *n.* the larva of a butterfly or a moth, resembling a worm.

cat•er•waul (kat′ər wôl′), *v.i.* **1.** to utter long wailing cries, as cats in rutting time. —*n.* **2.** such a cry.

cat′fish′, *n., pl.* -fish, -fish•es. a scaleless fish with barbels around the mouth that resemble a cat's whiskers.

catfish

cat′gut′, *n.* a strong cord made from dried intestines, as of sheep.

ca•thar•sis (kə thär′sis), *n., pl.* -ses (-sēz). **1.** the purging of the emotions, esp. through a work of art. **2.** purgation of the bowels. [< NL < Gk *katharsis* a cleansing, der. of *katharos* pure]

ca•thar•tic (kə thär′tik), *adj.* **1.** pertaining to catharsis. **2.** purgative. —*n.* **3.** a purgative. [1605–15; < LL *catharticus* < Gk *kathartikós* fit for cleansing]

ca•the•dral (kə thē′drəl), *n.* **1.** the principal church of a diocese, containing the bishop's throne. **2.** (in nonepiscopal denominations) any of various important churches.

Cath•er (kath′ər), *n.* **Willa (Sibert),** 1876–1947, U.S. novelist.

Cath•er•ine (kath′ər in, kath′rin), *n.* **Catherine II,** ("Catherine the Great") 1729–96, empress of Russia 1762–96.

cath•e•ter (kath′i tər), *n.* a thin tube inserted into a bodily passage, as to allow fluids to pass into or out of it. —**cath′e•ter•ize′**, *v.t.*, -ized, -iz•ing.

cath•ode (kath′ōd), *n.* **1.** the negative electrode of an electrolytic cell. **2.** the positive terminal of a battery. **3.** the negative electrode of an electron tube. —**ca•thod′ic** (ka thod′ik), *adj.*

cath′ode ray′, *n.* a narrow beam of electrons emanating from a cathode.

cath′ode-ray′ tube′, *n.* a vacuum tube generating a beam of electrons directed at a screen, used to display images on a television receiver or computer monitor.

cath•o•lic (kath′ə lik, kath′lik), *adj.* **1.** universal in extent. **2.** broad-minded. —**cath′o•lic′i•ty** (-lis′i tē), *n.*

Cath′o•lic, *adj.* **1.** of the Roman Catholic Church. —*n.* **2.** a member of the Roman Catholic Church. —**Ca•thol•i•cism** (kə thol′ə siz′əm), *n.*

cat•i•on (kat′ī′ən, -on), *n.* a positively charged ion attracted to the cathode in electrolysis.

cat′kin (kat′kin), *n.* a spike of flowers with scaly bracts and no petals, as on the willow.

cat′nap′, *n., v.*, -napped, -nap•ping. —*n.* **1.** a short, light nap. —*v.i.* **2.** to sleep briefly; doze.

cat′nip′, *n.* a plant of the mint family, having aromatic leaves that are a cat attractant.

cat′-o′-nine′-tails′ (kat′ə nīn′-), *n., pl.* -tails. a whip having nine knotted cords fastened to a handle.

CAT′ scan′ (kat), *n.* **1.** an examination employing beams of x-rays in two planes at various angles to produce computerized cross-sectional images of the body. **2.** an image so produced. [C(OMPUTERIZED) A(X-IAL) T(OMOGRAPHY)] —**CAT′ scan′ner,** *n.*

cat′s′ cra′dle, *n.* a game in which two players alternately stretch a looped string over their fingers so as to produce different designs.

Cats′kill Moun′tains (kat′skil), *n.pl.* a range of mountains in E New York. Also called **Cats′kills.**

cat′s′-paw′, *n.* a person used by another as a dupe.

cat•sup (kat′səp, kech′əp, kach′-), *n.* KETCHUP.

cat′tail′, *n.* a tall, reedlike marsh plant with cylindrical clusters of minute brown flowers.

cat•tle (kat′l), *n. (used with a pl. v.)* bovine animals, as cows and steers. —**cat′tle•man,** *n., pl.* -men.

cat′ty, *adj.*, -ti•er, -ti•est. **1.** slyly malicious. **2.** like a cat. —**cat′ti•ly,** *adv.* —**cat′ti•ness,** *n.*

cat′ty-cor′nered, *adj., adv.* CATER-CORNERED.

Ca•tul•lus (kə tul′əs), *n.* **Gaius Valerius,** 84?–54? B.C., Roman poet.

CATV, community antenna television: a cable television service for areas where reception is poor.

cat′walk′, *n.* a narrow walkway high above the surrounding area.

Cau•ca•sian (kô kā′zhən), *adj.* **1.** of or designating one of the traditional racial divisions of humankind, marked by minimum skin pigmentation. **2.** of the Caucasus. —*n.* **3.** a person belonging to the Caucasian race. **4.** a native of the Caucasus.

Cau′ca•soid′ (-kə soid′), *adj., n.* CAUCASIAN (defs. 1, 3).

Cau′ca•sus (-səs), *n.* **the, 1.** Also, **Cau•ca′sia** (-kā′-zhə, -shə). a region between the Black and Caspian seas. **2.** a mountain range in this region.

cau•cus (kô′kəs), *n., pl.* -cus•es, *v.* —*n.* **1.** a meeting of the members of a political party to nominate candidates, determine policy, etc. —*v.i.* **2.** to hold a caucus.

cau•dal (kôd′l), *adj.* of, at, or near the tail end of the body. —**cau′dal•ly,** *adv.*

caught (kôt), *v.* pt. and pp. of CATCH.

caul•dron (kôl′drən), *n.* a large kettle.

cau•li•flow•er (kô′lə flou′ər, kol′ē-), *n.* **1.** a cultivated plant whose inflorescence forms a compact, whitish head. **2.** this head, used as a vegetable.

caulk (kôk), *v.t.* **1.** to fill (seams) of (a window, ship's hull, etc.) to make watertight or airtight. —*n.* **2.** a material used to caulk. —**caulk′er,** *n.*

caus•al (kô′zəl), *adj.* **1.** of, constituting, or implying a cause. **2.** expressing a cause, as the conjunction *because.* —**caus•al′i•ty,** *n., pl.* -ties. —**caus′al•ly,** *adv.*

cau•sa′tion (-zā′shən), *n.* **1.** the act of causing. **2.** the relation of cause to effect. **3.** anything that produces an effect.

cause (kôz), *n., v.*, caused, caus•ing. —*n.* **1.** that produces a result. **2.** a reason or motive. **3.** a ground of legal action. **4.** an ideal or goal to which a person is dedicated. —*v.t.* **5.** to be the cause of. —**caus′a•tive,** *adj.* —**cause′less,** *adj.* —**caus′er,** *n.*

cause cé•lè•bre (kôz′ sə leb′; *Fr.* kōz sā leb′R⁹), *n., pl.* **causes cé•lè•bres** (kôz′ sə leb′; *Fr.* kōz sā leb′-R⁹). a controversy that attracts great public attention. [< F]

cau•se•rie (kō′zə rē′), *n.* **1.** a chat. **2.** a short, informal essay.

cause′way′, *n.* a raised road, as over wet ground.

caus•tic (kô′stik), *adj.* **1.** capable of burning or corroding living tissue. **2.** severely critical or sarcastic. —*n.* **3.** a caustic substance. —**caus′ti•cal•ly,** *adv.* —**caus•tic′i•ty** (-stis′i tē), *n.*

cau•ter•ize (kô′tə rīz′), *v.t.*, -ized, -iz•ing. to burn with a hot iron, a caustic, etc., esp. for curative purposes. —**cau′ter•i•za′tion,** *n.*

cau•tion (kô′shən), *n.* **1.** alertness and prudence in a hazardous situation. **2.** a warning. —*v.t., v.i.* **3.** to warn. —*Idiom.* **4. throw caution to the wind,** to abandon all consideration of risks. —**cau′tion•ar′y,** *adj.* —**cau′tious,** *adj.* —**cau′tious•ly,** *adv.* —**cau′tious•ness,** *n.*

cav•al•cade (kav′əl kād′, kav′əl kād′), *n.* a procession, as of automobiles.

cav•a•lier (kav′ə lēr′), *n.* **1.** an armed horseman; knight. **2.** a courtly gentleman. **3.** (*cap.*) an adherent of King Charles I of England in his dispute with Parliament. —*adj.* **4.** haughty; disdainful. **5.** casual; lighthearted. [< MF: horseman ≪ LL *caballārius* groom] —**cav′a•lier′ly,** *adv.*

cav•al•ry (kav′əl rē), *n., pl.* -ries. **1.** troops that serve on horseback. **2.** troops that ride in armored motor vehicles. —**cav′al•ry•man,** *n., pl.* -men.

cave (kāv), *n., v.*, caved, cav•ing. —*n.* **1.** a hollow in the earth, esp. one opening into a hill or mountain. —*v.i., v.t.* **2. cave in, a.** to collapse or cause to collapse. **b.** to yield; surrender.

ca•ve•at (kav′ē ät′, kä′vē-, kā′-), *n.* a warning or caution.

ca′veat emp′tor (emp′tôr), let the buyer beware. [< L]

cave′-in′, *n.* **1.** a collapse, as of anything hollow. **2.** a site of such a collapse.

cave′ man′, *n.* **1.** a cave dweller, esp. of the Stone Age. **2.** a rough, brutal man.

cav•ern (kav′ərn), *n.* a large cave that is mostly underground. —**cav′ern•ous,** *adj.*

cav•i•ar (kav′ē är′), *n.* the roe of sturgeon, salmon, etc.

cav•il (kav′əl), *v.,* **-iled, -il•ing** or (*esp. Brit.*) **-illed, -il•ling,** *n.* —*v.i.* **1.** to raise trivial objections. —*n.* **2.** a trivial and annoying objection. —**cav′il•er;** *esp. Brit.,* **cav′il•ler,** *n.*

cav•i•ty (kav′i tē), *n., pl.* **-ties. 1.** any hollow place. **2.** a hollow in a tooth, produced by decay.

ca•vort (kə vôrt′), *v.i.* **1.** to caper about. **2.** to make merry.

caw (kô), *n.* **1.** the harsh call of a crow. —*v.i.* **2.** to utter this cry.

Cax•ton (kak′stən), *n.* **William,** 1422?–91, English printer: established first printing press in England 1476.

cay•enne (kī en′, kā-), *n.* a hot condiment composed of the ground pods and seeds of a pepper plant.

Cay•enne′, *n.* the capital of French Guiana. 38,135.

Cay′man Is′lands (kā′mən′, -mən), *n.pl.* three islands in the West Indies, NW of Jamaica.

cay•use (kī yōōs′, kī′ōōs), *n. Western U.S.* a horse, esp. an Indian pony.

CB, citizens band: a band of radio frequencies used for short-distance private communications.

Cb, *Chem. Symbol.* columbium.

cc, 1. carbon copy. **2.** cubic centimeter.

CCU, coronary-care unit.

CD, 1. certificate of deposit. **2.** Civil Defense. **3.** compact disc.

Cd, *Chem. Symbol.* cadmium.

CDC, Centers for Disease Control.

CD player, *n.* a device for playing compact discs.

CD-ROM (sē′dē′rom′), *n.* a compact disc on which a large amount of digitized read-only data can be stored.

Ce, *Chem. Symbol.* cerium.

cease (sēs), *v.,* **ceased, ceas•ing,** *n.* —*v.i., v.t.* **1.** to stop; discontinue. —*n.* **2.** cessation.

cease′-fire′, *n.* a temporary cessation of hostilities.

cease′less, *adj.* without stop; unending. —**cease′less•ly,** *adv.*

ce•cum (sē′kəm), *n., pl.* **-ca** (-kə). an anatomical cul-de-sac in which the large intestine begins. —**ce′cal,** *adj.*

ce•dar (sē′dər), *n.* **1.** any of several coniferous trees. **2.** the wood of these trees.

cede (sēd), *v.t.,* **ced•ed, ced•ing. 1.** to surrender formally. **2.** to grant or transfer, as by a will.

ce•dil•la (si dil′ə), *n.* a mark (,) placed under a letter to indicate its pronunciation, as under *c* in French to indicate that it is pronounced (s).

ceil•ing (sē′ling), *n.* **1.** the overhead interior surface of a room. **2.** an upper limit: *a price ceiling.* **3.** the height above ground level of clouds covering more than half the sky.

cel•e•brant (sel′ə brənt), *n.* **1.** a participant in any celebration. **2.** the officiating priest in the celebration of the Eucharist.

cel•e•brate (sel′ə brāt′), *v.,* **-brat•ed, -brat•ing.** —*v.t.* **1.** to observe or commemorate with festivities. **2.** to perform with appropriate rites. —*v.i.* **3.** to have a good time. —**cel′e•bra′tion,** *n.* —**cel′e•bra′tor,** *n.*

cel′e•brat′ed, *adj.* renowned; well-known.

ce•leb•ri•ty (sə leb′ri tē), *n., pl.* **-ties. 1.** a famous person. **2.** fame.

ce•ler•i•ty (sə ler′i tē), *n.* swiftness; speed.

cel•er•y (sel′ə rē, sel′rē), *n.* a plant with stiff, edible leafstalks.

ce•les•ta (sə les′tə), *n., pl.* **-tas.** a keyboard instrument consisting of graduated steel plates struck with hammers.

ce•les•tial (sə les′chəl), *adj.* **1.** of the sky. **2.** heavenly; divine. —**ce•les′tial•ly,** *adv.*

Celes′tial Cit′y, *n.* NEW JERUSALEM.

cel•i•ba•cy (sel′ə bə sē), *n.* **1.** abstention from sexual relations. **2.** the state of being unmarried. —**cel′i•bate** (-bit, -bāt′), *n., adj.*

cell (sel), *n.* **1.** a small room, as in a prison. **2.** a small compartment forming part of a whole. **3.** a plant or animal structure containing nuclear material; the basic unit of all organisms. **4.** a small unit of an organization. **5.** a device that converts chemical energy into electricity. **6.** a device for producing electrolysis, consisting of the electrolyte, its container, and the electrodes. —**celled,** *adj.*

cel•lar (sel′ər), *n.* an underground room or rooms, usu. beneath a building.

Cel•li•ni (chə lē′nē), *n.* **Benvenuto,** 1500–71, Italian metalsmith and sculptor.

cel•lo (chel′ō), *n., pl.* **-los.** the second largest member of the violin family. —**cel′list,** *n.*

cel•lo•phane (sel′ə fān′), *n.* a transparent, paperlike product of viscose, used for wrapping.

cel•lu•lar (sel′yə lər), *adj.* of or consisting of cells.

cel′lular phone′, *n.* a mobile telephone using a system of radio transmitters and computers for switching calls. Also called **cell′ phone′.**

cel•lu•lite (sel′yə līt′, -lēt′), *n.* (not used scientifically) lumpy fat deposits, esp. in the thighs and buttocks.

cel•lu•loid (sel′yə loid′), *n.* a tough, flammable thermoplastic consisting of nitrocellulose and camphor.

cel•lu•lose (sel′yə lōs′), *n.* the chief constituent of the cell walls of plants, used to make paper, textiles, etc.

cel′lulose ac′etate, *n.* any of a group of acetic esters of cellulose, used to make textiles, photographic films, etc.

Cel•si•us (sel′sē əs), *adj.* of or noting a temperature scale in which 0° represents the freezing point of water and 100° the boiling point; Centigrade. [after A. *Celsius* (1701–44), Swedish astronomer who devised the scale]

Celt (kelt, selt), *n.* **1.** a member of any of a group of Indo-European peoples inhabiting the British Isles and areas of W and central Europe in antiquity. **2.** a speaker of a Celtic language.

Celt′ic, *n.* **1.** a branch of the Indo-European language family, including Irish and Welsh. —*adj.* **2.** of the Celts or their languages.

ce•ment (si ment′), *n.* **1.** a mixture of clay and limestone, mixed with water, sand, and gravel to form concrete. **2.** any sticky substance that makes things adhere. —*v.t.* **3.** to unite by or as if by cement. **4.** to cover with cement. —*v.i.* **5.** to become cemented.

cem•e•ter•y (sem′i ter′ē), *n., pl.* **-ter•ies.** a burial ground for the dead.

Cen•chre•a (sen′krē ə), *n.* a town in Greece from which the Apostle Paul sailed on his second missionary journey. Acts 18:18.

ce•no•bite (sē′nə bīt′, sen′ə-), *n.* a member of a religious order living in a convent or monastery. —**ce′no•bit′ic** (-bit′ik), *adj.*

cen•o•taph (sen′ə taf′, -täf′), *n.* a monument commemorating a dead person whose body is buried elsewhere.

Ce•no•zo•ic (sē′nə zō′ik, sen′ə-), *adj.* noting or pertaining to the present era, beginning 65 million years ago and characterized by the ascendancy of mammals.

cen•ser (sen′sər), *n.* a container in which incense is burned.

cen•sor (sen′sər), *n.* **1.** an official who examines books, films, etc., to suppress anything objectionable. —*v.t.* **2.** to act upon as a censor. —**cen′sor•ship′,** *n.*

cen•so'ri•ous (-sôr'ē əs), *adj.* severely critical. —**cen•so'ri•ous•ly,** *adv.*

cen'sure (-shər), *n., v.,* **-sured, -sur•ing.** —*n.* 1. strong disapproval. —*v.t., v.i.* 2. to criticize harshly. —**cen'sur•a•ble,** *adj.*

cen•sus (sen'səs), *n., pl.* **-sus•es.** an official enumeration of the population, with details as to age, sex, occupation, etc.

cent (sent), *n.* a coin and monetary unit of the U.S., equal to $^1/_{100}$ of a dollar. [< L *centēsimus* hundredth]

cent., century.

cen•taur (sen'tôr), *n.* a race of creatures in Greek myth having the head and upper torso of a man and the body of a horse.

cen•ta•vo (sen tä'vō), *n., pl.* **-vos.** a monetary unit of various Latin American nations, equal to $^1/_{100}$ of the basic currency.

cen•te•nar•i•an (sen'tn âr'ē ən), *n.* a person who has reached the age of 100.

cen•ten•ar•y (sen ten'ə rē, sen'tn er'ē), *adj., n., pl.* **-ar•ies.** —*adj.* 1. of a centennial. 2. of a century. —*n.* 3. a centennial. 4. a century.

cen•ten'ni•al (-ten'ē əl), *adj.* 1. of a 100th anniversary. 2. lasting 100 years. —*n.* 3. a 100th anniversary or its celebration.

cen•ter (sen'tər), *n.* 1. the point within a circle equally distant from all points of the circumference. 2. a pivot or axis. 3. the middle of something. 4. the source of an influence, action, or force. 5. a focus of interest or concern. 6. a principal point, place, or object: *a shipping center.* 7. (*usu. cap.*) a group holding political views intermediate between those of the Right and Left. 8. a player who plays primarily in the center. —*v.t.* 9. to place in a center. 10. to focus. —*v.i.* 11. to be at or come to a center.

cen'ter•board', *n.* a pivoted keel on a sailboat that can be retracted.

cen'ter•fold', *n.* a pair of facing pages, or a large page that folds out, at the center of a magazine.

cen'ter of grav'ity, *n.* the center of mass with reference to gravity as the external force.

cen'ter•piece', *n.* an ornamental object placed on the center of a dining table.

Cen'ters for Disease' Control', *n.* an agency of the U.S. Public Health Service charged with the investigation and control of contagious disease in the nation. *Abbr.:* CDC

centi-, a combining form meaning hundredth or hundred (*centimeter*).

Cen•ti•grade (sen'ti grād'), *adj.* CELSIUS.

cen'ti•gram', *n.* $^1/_{100}$ of a gram.

cen•time (sän'tēm, sän tēm'), *n., pl.* **-times** (-tēmz, -tēm'). a monetary unit of various nations, including France, Belgium, and Switzerland, equal to $^1/_{100}$ of the basic currency.

cen'ti•me'ter (sen'tə-), *n.* $^1/_{100}$ of a meter, equivalent to 0.3937 inch.

cen'ti•pede' (-pēd'), *n.* a segmented arthropod with a pair of legs on each segment.

cen•tral (sen'trəl), *adj.* 1. of or forming the center. 2. in, at, or near the center. 3. constituting something from which other things proceed or upon which they depend: *a central office.* 4. principal; dominant. —**cen'tral•ly,** *adv.*

Cen'tral Af'rican Repub'lic, *n.* a republic in central Africa. 3,342,051.

Cen'tral Amer'ica, *n.* continental North America S of Mexico. —**Cen'tral Amer'ican,** *n., adj.*

cen'tral cit'y, *n.* a densely populated city that is the core of a metropolitan area.

Cen'tral Intel'ligence A'gency, *n.* See CIA.

cen'tral•ize, *v.,* **-ized, -iz•ing.** —*v.t.* 1. to gather about a center. 2. to bring under one control. —*v.i.* 3. to form a center. —**cen'tral•i•za'tion,** *n.*

cen'tral nerv'ous sys'tem, *n.* the part of the nervous system comprising the brain and spinal cord.

cen•tre (sen'tər), *n., v.,* **-tred, -tring.** *Chiefly Brit.* CENTER.

cen•trif'u•gal (-trif'yə gəl, -ə gəl), *adj.* 1. directed outward from the center. 2. operated by centrifugal force.

centrif'ugal force', *n.* the force experienced by a body moving in a curved path that appears to propel the body outward.

cen'tri•fuge' (-fyŏōj'), *n.* an apparatus that rotates at high speed and separates substances of different densities.

cen•trip'e•tal (-trip'i tl), *adj.* directed toward the center.

centrip'etal force', *n.* the force acting on a body moving in a curved path that constrains the body to the path.

cen•trist (sen'trist), *n.* (*sometimes cap.*) a person with moderate political views.

cen•tu•ri•on (sen tŏōr'ē ən, -tyŏōr'-), *n.* (in the ancient Roman army) the commander of a 100-man unit.

cen•tu•ry (sen'chə rē), *n., pl.* **-ries.** 1. a period of 100 years. 2. one of the successive periods of 100 years reckoned forward or backward from A.D. 1.

CEO, chief executive officer.

ce•phal•ic (sə fal'ik), *adj.* 1. of the head. 2. situated or directed toward the head.

Ce•phas (sē'fəs), *n.* the name Jesus gave to Simon Peter. John 1:42.

ce•ram•ic (sə ram'ik), *adj.* 1. of products made from clay and similar materials, as pottery and brick. —*n.* 2. ceramic material.

ce•ram'ics, *n.* 1. (*used with a sing. v.*) the art of making objects of clay and similar materials treated by firing. 2. (*used with a pl. v.*) articles of earthenware, porcelain, etc. —**ce•ram•ist** (sə ram'ist, ser'ə-mist), **ce•ram'i•cist** (-ram'ə sist), *n.*

ce•re•al (sēr'ē əl), *n.* 1. any plant of the grass family, as wheat or rye, yielding an edible grain. 2. the grain itself. 3. some edible preparation of it.

cer•e•bel•lum (ser'ə bel'əm), *n., pl.* **-bel•lums, -bel•la** (-bel'ə). the portion of the brain that coordinates movement and balance. —**cer'e•bel'lar,** *adj.*

ce•re•bral (sə rē'brəl, ser'ə-), *adj.* 1. of the cerebrum or brain. 2. characterized by the use of the intellect.

cere'bral cor'tex, *n.* the outer layer of the cerebrum associated with the higher brain functions, as learning.

cere'bral pal'sy, *n.* a condition marked by difficulty in coordinating voluntary movement, owing to brain damage.

cer•e•brate (ser'ə brāt'), *v.i.,* **-brat•ed, -brat•ing.** to think. —**cer'e•bra'tion,** *n.*

ce•re•brum (sə rē'brəm, ser'ə-), *n., pl.* **-brums, -bra** (-brə). the forward and upper part of the brain, involved with voluntary movement and conscious processes.

cer•e•mo•ni•al (ser'ə mō'nē əl), *adj.* 1. of or characterized by ceremony. —*n.* 2. a ceremonial act or system of rites. —**cer'e•mo'ni•al•ly,** *adv.*

cer'e•mo'ni•ous, *adj.* 1. carefully observant of ceremony. 2. elaborately formal. —**cer'e•mo'ni•ous•ly,** *adv.*

cer'e•mo'ny, *n., pl.* **-nies.** 1. the formalities observed on some solemn occasion. 2. a solemn rite. 3. any meaningless formal act. 4. strict adherence to conventional forms. —*Idiom.* 5. **stand on ceremony,** to behave in a formal manner.

ce•rise (sə rēs', -rēz'), *adj., n.* moderate to deep red.

ce•ri•um (sēr'ē əm), *n.* a steel-gray, ductile metallic element. *Symbol:* Ce; *at. wt.:* 140.12; *at. no.:* 58.

cer•met (sûr'met), *n.* a durable alloy of a metal and a ceramic substance.

cer•tain (sûr'tn), *adj.* 1. free from doubt or reservation. 2. quite sure. 3. inevitable. 4. established as true. 5. fixed; agreed upon. 6. definite but not specified: *certain persons.* 7. trustworthy. 8. some though not much: *a certain reluctance.* —*Idiom.* 9. **for certain,** without a doubt. —**cer'tain•ly,** *adv.*

cer'tain•ty, *n., pl.* **-ties.** 1. the state of being certain. 2. something certain.

cer•tif•i•cate (sər tif′i kit), *n.* a document providing evidence of status or qualifications.

certif′icate of depos′it, *n.* a bank receipt for money deposited, indicating the interest to be paid for a specified period.

cer′tified pub′lic account′ant, *n.* a person certified by a state as having fulfilled the legal requirements to be a public accountant.

cer•ti•fy (sûr′tə fī′), *v.t.,* **-fied, -fy•ing. 1.** to attest as certain. **2.** to guarantee; endorse. **3.** to guarantee (a check) as to sufficiency of funds to cover payment. **4.** to license. —**cer′ti•fi•a•ble,** *adj.* —**cer′ti•fi•ca′tion,** *n.*

cer′ti•tude′ (-tōōd′, -tyōōd′), *n.* freedom from doubt.

ce•ru•le•an (sə rōō′lē ən), *adj., n.* deep blue; azure.

Cer•van•tes (sər van′tēz, -vän′tās), *n.* **Miguel de,** (*Miguel de Cervantes Saavedra*), 1547–1616, Spanish novelist.

cer•vix (sûr′viks), *n., pl.* **cer•vix•es, cer•vi•ces** (sûr′və sēz′, sər vī′sēz). a necklike part, esp. the constricted lower end of the uterus. —**cer′vi•cal** (-vi-kəl), *adj.*

Ce•sar•e•an (si zâr′ē ən), *n.* (*sometimes l.c.*) the delivery of a baby by incision through the walls of the abdomen and uterus. Also called **Cesar′ean sec′-tion.**

ce•si•um (sē′zē əm), *n.* a soft metallic element used chiefly in photoelectric cells. *Symbol:* Cs; *at. wt.:* 132.905; *at. no.:* 55.

ces•sa•tion (se sā′shən), *n.* a temporary or complete stopping.

ces•sion (sesh′ən), *n.* **1.** the act of ceding, as by treaty. **2.** something ceded, as territory.

cess•pool (ses′pōōl′), *n.* **1.** a reservoir for receiving the sewage from a house. **2.** a place of filth or immorality.

ce•ta•cean (si tā′shən), *adj.* **1.** belonging to an order of aquatic, chiefly marine mammals, including the whales and dolphins. —*n.* **2.** a cetacean mammal.

Cey•lon (si lon′, sā-), *n.* former name of SRI LANKA. —**Cey•lon•ese** (sē′lə nēz′, -nēs′, sā′-), *adj., n., pl.* **-ese.**

Cé•zanne (sā zan′, -zän′), *n.* **Paul,** 1839–1906, French painter.

Cf, *Chem. Symbol.* californium.

cf., compare. [< L *confer*]

cg., centigram.

ch. or **Ch., 1.** chapter. **2.** church.

Cha•blis (sha blē′), *n.* a dry, white Burgundy wine, orig. produced in Chablis, France.

cha-cha (chä′chä′), *n.* a rhythmic Latin American ballroom dance.

Chad (chad), *n.* a republic in N central Africa. 7,166,023. —**Chad′i•an,** *n., adj.*

chad•or (chud′ər), *n.* the traditional garment of Muslim and Hindu women.

chafe (chāf), *v.,* **chafed, chaf•ing.** —*v.t.* **1.** to wear away or make sore by rubbing. **2.** to irritate; annoy. **3.** to warm by rubbing. —*v.i.* **4.** to rub. **5.** to become annoyed.

chaff¹ (chaf, chäf), *n.* **1.** the husks of grains separated during threshing. **2.** worthless matter.

chaff² (chaf, chäf), *v.t., v.i.* **1.** to tease; banter. —*n.* **2.** good-natured teasing.

chaf′ing dish′ (chā′fing), *n.* a metal pan mounted atop a heating device for cooking or warming food at the table.

Cha•gall (shə gäl′), *n.* **Marc,** 1887–1985, Russian painter in France.

cha•grin (shə grin′), *n., v.,* **-grined** or **-grinned, -grin•ing** or **-grin•ning.** —*n.* **1.** a feeling of vexation marked by disappointment or humiliation. —*v.t.* **2.** to cause to feel chagrin.

chain (chān), *n.* **1.** a series of metal rings passing through one another. **2. chains, a.** shackles or fetters. **b.** bondage; servitude. **3.** a series of things following in succession: *a chain of events.* **4.** a range of mountains. **5.** a number of stores or other estab-

lishments under one ownership. **6.** a distance-measuring device used by surveyors. —*v.t.* **7.** to fasten with a chain. **8.** to confine or restrain.

chain′ gang′, *n.* a group of convicts chained together, esp. when working outside.

chain′ let′ter, *n.* a letter sent to a number of people each of whom is asked to make and mail copies to others who are to do likewise.

chain′ reac′tion, *n.* **1.** a nuclear or chemical reaction in which the reaction products in turn trigger additional reactions. **2.** a series of events in which each event is the result of the preceding one.

chain′ saw′, *n.* a portable power saw having teeth set on an endless chain. —**chain′-saw′,** *v.t., v.i.*

chair (châr), *n.* **1.** a seat for one person with a rest for the back. **2.** a position of authority. **3.** a chairman or chairwoman. —*v.t.* **4.** to seat in a chair. **5.** to preside over as chairman or chairwoman.

chair′lift′, *n.* a series of chairs suspended from a motor-driven endless cable, for conveying skiers up a slope.

chair′man or **-wom′an** or **-per′son,** *n., pl.* **-men** or **-wom•en** or **-per•sons.** the presiding officer of a meeting, committee, etc., or the head of a board or department. —**chair′man•ship′,** *n.*

chaise (shāz), *n.* a light, open carriage, usu. with a hood.

chaise′ longue′ (lông′) *n., pl.* **chaise longues, chaises longues** (shāz′ lông′). a chair with a seat long enough to form a complete leg rest.

chal•ced•o•ny (kal sed′n ē, kal′si dō′nē), *n., pl.* **-nies.** a translucent variety of quartz, often milky or grayish.

Chal•de•an (kal dē′ən), *n.* **1.** a Semitic people of Chaldea who seized Babylon from the Assyrians in the 7th century B.C., **2.** soothsayer. Dan. 1:4; 2:2. —*adj.* **3.** of or pertaining to Chaldea or the Chaldeans.

cha•let (sha lā′, shal′ā), *n.* **1.** a wooden Alpine house with wide eaves and decorative carving. **2.** any dwelling built in this style.

chal•ice (chal′is), *n.* **1.** a cup for the wine of the Eucharist. **2.** a goblet.

chalk (chôk), *n.* **1.** a soft, white, powdery limestone. **2.** a piece of chalk or chalklike substance for writing on a blackboard. —*v.t.* **3.** to mark or rub with chalk. **4. chalk up,** to score or earn.

chalk′board′, *n.* a blackboard.

chal•lenge (chal′inj), *n., v.,* **-lenged, -leng•ing.** —*n.* **1.** a summons to engage in a contest or duel. **2.** a demand to explain, justify, etc. **3.** a stimulating or demanding situation, undertaking, etc. **4.** the demand of a sentry for identification. **5.** a formal objection to the qualifications of a juror. —*v.t.* **6.** to subject to a challenge. —*v.i.* **7.** to issue a challenge. —**chal′leng•er,** *n.*

chal′lenged, *adj.* (used as a euphemism) disabled or deficient: *physically challenged; ethically challenged.*

chal•lis (shal′ē), *n.* a soft plain-weave fabric in wool, cotton, or rayon.

cham•ber (chām′bər), *n.* **1.** a room, esp. a bedroom. **2. a.** a legislative, judicial, or deliberative body. **b.** a room housing such a body. **3. chambers,** a place where a judge hears matters not requiring action in open court. **4.** an enclosed space: *a chamber of the heart.* **5.** a receptacle for cartridges in a firearm. —**cham′bered,** *adj.*

cham′ber•lain (-lin), *n.* **1.** an official who manages the living quarters of a sovereign or noble. **2.** a high official of a royal court.

cham′ber•maid′, *n.* a maid who cleans bedrooms, as in a hotel.

cham′ber mu′sic, *n.* music for performance by a small ensemble in a room or a small concert hall.

cham′ber of com′merce, *n.* an association for promoting the commercial interests of an area.

cham′ber pot′, *n.* a portable container formerly used as a bedroom toilet.

cham•bray (sham′brā), *n.* a fine cloth of cotton, silk, or linen, with a colored warp and white weft.

cha•me•le•on (kə mē′lē ən, -mēl′yən), *n.* any of

various lizards having the ability to change color. [< MF < L < Gk *chamailéōn* lit., dwarf lion]

cham·ois (sham′ē; *for 1 also* sham wä′), *n., pl.* **-ois, -oix** (-ēz; *for 1 also* -wä′) **1.** an agile goat antelope of high mountains of Europe. **2.** a soft, pliable leather from any of various animal skins dressed with oil.

chamois

cham·o·mile (kam′ɔ mīl′, -mēl′), *n.* a plant with scented foliage and daisylike flowers used medicinally and as a tea.

champ¹ (champ, chomp), *v.t., v.i.* to chew vigorously or noisily.

champ² (champ), *n. Informal.* a champion.

cham·pagne (sham pān′), *n.* a sparkling white wine, esp. one from the region of Champagne in France.

cham·pi·on (cham′pē ən), *n.* **1.** one who has placed first among all competitors. **2.** one who fights for or defends a person or cause. —*v.t.* **3.** to defend; support. —*adj.* **4.** first among all competitors.

Cham·plain (sham plān′), *n.* **1. Samuel de,** 1567–1635, French explorer: founder of Quebec; first colonial governor 1633–35. **2. Lake,** a lake between New York and Vermont. 125 mi. (200 km) long; ab. 600 sq. mi. (1550 sq. km).

chance (chans, chäns), *n., v.,* **chanced, chanc·ing,** *adj.* —*n.* **1.** the unpredictable element of an occurrence. **2.** luck: *a game of chance.* **3.** a possibility or probability. **4.** an opportunity. **5.** a risk or hazard. **6.** a ticket in a lottery. —*v.i.* **7.** to happen by chance. —*v.t.* **8.** to risk. **9. chance on** or **upon,** to meet accidentally. —*adj.* **10.** accidental. —*Idiom.* **11. by chance,** accidentally. **12. on the (off) chance,** counting on the (slight) possibility.

chan·cel (chan′səl, chän′-), *n.* the space around the altar of a church for the clergy and choir.

chan′cel·ler·y (-sə lə rē, -slə rē, -səl rē), *n., pl.,* **-ler·ies. 1.** the position or department of a chancellor. **2.** a building occupied by a chancellor's department.

chan′cel·lor (-sə lər, -slər), *n.* **1.** the chief minister of state in some parliamentary governments. **2.** the chief administrative officer in some American universities. —**chan′cel·lor·ship′,** *n.*

chan′cer·y (-sə rē), *n., pl.* **-cer·ies. 1.** CHANCELLERY (def. 1). **2.** an office of public records. **3.** a court of equity. **4.** the administrative office of a diocese.

chan·cre (shang′kər), *n.* the initial lesion of syphilis and certain other infectious diseases.

chanc·y (chan′sē, chän′sē), *adj.,* **-i·er, -i·est.** risky; uncertain.

chan·de·lier (shan′dl ēr′), *n.* a decorative light fixture suspended from a ceiling.

chan·dler (chand′lər, chänd′-), *n.* **1.** a person who makes or sells candles or soap. **2.** a dealer in supplies, esp. for ships.

change (chānj), *v.,* **changed, chang·ing.** —*v.t.* **1.** to make different. **2.** to exchange: *to change places.* **3.** to give or get foreign money in exchange for. **4.** to remove and replace the coverings or garments of: *to change a baby.* —*v.i.* **5.** to become different. **6.** to make an exchange. **7.** to transfer between conveyances. **8.** to put on different clothes. **9. change off,** to take turns. —*n.* **10.** the act or result of changing. **11.** a variation or deviation. **12.** the substitution of one thing for another. **13.** a fresh set of clothes. **14.**

variety or novelty. **15.** the money returned when the sum offered in payment is larger than the sum due. —**change′a·ble,** *adj.*

change′ling (-ling), *n.* an infant exchanged by stealth for another child.

change′ of life′, *n.* MENOPAUSE.

change′o′ver, *n.* a conversion from one condition or system to another.

Chang Jiang (chäng′ jyäng′), *n.* a river flowing through central China to the East China Sea. ab. 3200 mi. (5150 km) long. Also called **Yangtze.**

chan·nel (chan′l), *n., v.,* **-neled, -nel·ing** or (*esp. Brit.*) **-nelled, -nel·ling.** —*n.* **1.** the bed or deeper part of a river or other waterway. **2.** a wide strait, as between a continent and an island. **3.** a groove or furrow. **4.** a route through which anything passes. **5. channels,** the official course of communication. **6.** a frequency band used by a radio or television station. **7.** a tubular passage for liquids or fluids. —*v.t.* **8.** to convey through a channel. **9.** to direct: *to channel one's interests.*

Chan′nel Is′lands, *n.pl.* a British island group in the English Channel.

chan′nel·ize′, *v.t.,* **-ized, -iz·ing.** to channel. —**chan′nel·i·za′tion,** *n.*

chan′nel-surf′, *v.i.* to change from one television channel to another with great or unusual frequency, esp. with a remote control. —**chan′nel surf′er,** *n.*

chan·son (Fr. shän sôN′), *n., pl.* **-sons** (Fr. -sôN′). a song.

chant (chant, chänt), *n.* **1.** a simple melody, esp. the monodic intonation of plainsong. **2.** a psalm or canticle for chanting. **3.** a phrase or slogan repeated rhythmically, as by a crowd. —*v.t., v.i.* **4.** to sing or utter in a chant. —**chant′er,** *n.*

chan·teuse (shän tœz′, -tōōz′), *n., pl.* **-teuses** (-tœz′, -tōō′ziz). a female singer in a nightclub.

chant·ey or **chant·y** (shan′tē, chan′-), *n., pl.* **-eys** or **-ies.** a sailors' song, esp. one sung in rhythm to work.

chan·ti·cleer (chan′ti klēr′), *n.* a rooster.

Cha·nu·kah (KHä′nə kə, hä′-), *n.* HANUKKAH.

cha·os (kā′os), *n.* utter confusion or disorder. —**cha·ot′ic** (-ot′ik), *adj.*

chap¹ (chap), *v.,* **chapped, chap·ping,** *n.* —*v.t.* **1.** to crack and redden (the skin). —*v.i.* **2.** to become chapped. —*n.* **3.** a fissure or crack in the skin.

chap² (chap), *n. Informal.* a fellow; guy.

chap., chapter.

chap·ar·ral (shap′ə ral′, chap′-), *n.* a dense growth of shrubs.

cha·peau (sha pō′), *n., pl.* **-peaux** (-pōz′, -pō′), **-peaus.** a hat.

chap·el (chap′əl), *n.* **1.** a private or subordinate place of worship, as in a hospital. **2.** a separate part of a church, used for special services.

chap·er·on or **-one** (shap′ə rōn′), *n., v.,* **-oned, -on·ing.** —*n.* **1.** a person, usu. an older woman, who, for propriety, accompanies young unmarried couples. —*v.t., v.i.* **2.** to act as chaperon (for). —**chap′er·on′age** (-rō′nij), *n.*

chap·lain (chap′lin), *n.* an ecclesiastic associated with a chapel, military unit, etc. —**chap′lain·cy,** *n.*

chap·let (chap′lit), *n.* **1.** a wreath for the head. **2.** a string of beads, one-third of the length of a rosary.

Chap·lin (chap′lin), *n.* **Sir Charles Spencer** (*Charlie*), 1889–1977, English actor and director.

chaps (chaps, shaps), *n.* (*used with a pl. v.*) leather leggings worn over work pants, typically by cowboys and cowgirls.

chap·ter (chap′tər), *n.* **1.** a main division of a book, treatise, etc. **2.** a branch of a society, fraternity, etc. **3.** an assembly of the canons of a church.

chap′ter and verse′, *n.* **1.** any specific chapter and verse of the Bible. **2.** full, cited authority.

char (chär), *v.t., v.i.,* **charred, char·ring. 1.** to reduce to charcoal. **2.** to burn slightly.

char·ac·ter (kar′ik tər), *n.* **1.** the aggregate of features and traits that form the individual nature of a person or thing. **2.** a trait or characteristic. **3.**

moral quality or integrity. **4.** reputation. **5.** an eccentric or unusual person. **6.** a person represented in a drama, story, etc. **7.** a symbol used in a system of writing.

char′ac•ter•is′tic (-tə ris′tik), *adj.* **1.** distinctive; typical. —*n.* **2.** a distinguishing feature or quality. —**char′ac•ter•is′ti•cal•ly,** *adv.*

char′ac•ter•ize′, *v.t.,* **-ized, -iz•ing. 1.** to be a characteristic of. **2.** to describe the character of. —**char′ac•ter•i•za′tion,** *n.*

cha•rade (shə rād′), *n.* **1. charades,** a game in which a player pantomimes a word or phrase, often syllable by syllable, for others to guess. **2.** a blatant pretense or deception.

char′broil′, *v.t.* to broil over a charcoal fire.

char′coal′, *n.* a black, carbon-containing material obtained by heating an organic substance, as wood, in the absence of air.

chard (chärd), *n.* a variety of beet with leafstalks that are used as a vegetable.

charge (chärj), *v.,* **charged, charg•ing,** *n.* —*v.t.* **1.** to ask as a price. **2.** to defer payment for (a purchase) until a bill is rendered. **3.** to hold liable for payment. **4.** to attack by rushing violently against. **5.** to accuse. **6.** to lay a command or injunction upon. **7.** to fill or load, as with bullets. **8.** to supply with a quantity of electrical energy. **9.** to suffuse, as with emotion. —*v.i.* **10.** to attack or rush violently. **11.** to require payment. —*n.* **12.** an expense or cost. **13.** an impetuous attack, as of soldiers. **14.** a duty or responsibility. **15.** care, custody, or superintendence. **16.** someone or something committed to one's care. **17.** a command or injunction. **18.** an accusation or indictment. **19.** the quantity that an apparatus is fitted to hold at one time: *a charge of coal for a furnace.* **20.** the quantity of electricity in a substance. —*Idiom.* **21. in charge,** in command; having the care or supervision. —**charge′a•ble,** *adj.*

charge′ account′, *n.* an account that permits a customer to buy goods and be billed at a later date.

charge′ card′, *n.* CREDIT CARD.

charg′er, *n.* **1.** a person or thing that charges. **2.** a horse ridden in battle.

char•i•ot (char′ē ət), *n.* a light, horse-drawn, two-wheeled vehicle of the ancient world, used in warfare, races, etc. —**char′i•ot•eer′** (-ə tēr′), *n.*

cha•ris•ma (kə riz′mə), *n.* a personal magnetism that enables an individual to attract or influence people.

char•is•mat•ic (kar′iz mat′ik), *adj.* **1.** of or having charisma. **2.** characterizing Christians who seek an ecstatic religious experience, sometimes including speaking in tongues. —*n.* **3.** a Christian who emphasizes such a religious experience.

char•i•ta•ble (char′i tə bəl), *adj.* **1.** generous to the needy. **2.** kindly or lenient. **3.** concerned with charity. —**char′i•ta•ble•ness,** *n.* —**char′i•ta•bly,** *adv.*

char′i•ty, *n., pl.* **-ties. 1.** generosity toward the needy. **2.** a charitable act or work. **3.** a charitable fund or institution. **4.** leniency in judging others. **5.** Christian love; agape: one of the three Christian virtues. —*Proverb.* **6.** Charity begins at home, love should first apply to the ones nearest us.

char•la•tan (shär′lə tn), *n.* a quack; fraud.

Char•le•magne (shär′lə mān′), *n.* ("*Charles the Great*") A.D. 742–814, king of the Franks 768–814; as Charles I, first emperor of the Holy Roman Empire 800–814.

Charles (chärlz), *n.* **1.** (*Prince of Edinburgh and of Wales*) born 1948, heir apparent to the throne of Great Britain (son of Elizabeth II). **2. Ray** (*Ray Charles Robinson*), born 1930, U.S. blues singer and pianist. **3.** a river in E Massachusetts, flowing between Boston and Cambridge into the Atlantic. 47 mi. (75 km) long.

Charles•ton¹ (chärlz′tən, chärl′stən), *n.* **1.** a seaport in SE South Carolina. 81,030. **2.** the capital of West Virginia. 55,730.

Charles•ton² (chärlz′tən, chärl′stən), *n.* **1.** a vigorous, rhythmic ballroom dance popular in the 1920s. —*v.i.* **2.** to dance the Charleston.

char′ley horse′ (chär′lē) *n.* a cramp or a sore muscle, esp. in the leg.

Char•lotte (shär′lət), *n.* a city in S North Carolina. 437,797.

Char′lotte•town′, *n.* the capital of Prince Edward Island, in SE Canada. 15,776.

charm (chärm), *n.* **1.** a power of pleasing or attracting, as through personality. **2.** a trinket on a bracelet or necklace. **3.** an amulet. **4.** a formula or action credited with magical power. —*v.t., v.i.* **5.** to delight or please by attractiveness. **6.** to act (upon) with a magical force. —**charm′er,** *n.* —**charm′ing,** *adj.* —**charm′ing•ly,** *adv.*

char′nel house′ (chär′nl), *n.* a place where the bodies of the dead are deposited.

Char•on (kâr′ən, kar′-), *n.* a ferryman of Greek myth who conveyed the souls of the dead across the Styx.

chart (chärt), *n.* **1.** a sheet giving information in tabular or diagrammatic form. **2.** a graph. **3.** a map, esp. a marine map. —*v.t.* **4.** to make a chart of. **5.** to plan.

char•ter (chär′tər), *n.* **1.** a governmental document outlining the conditions under which a business, city, or other corporate body is organized. **2.** a document defining the formal organization of a corporate body; constitution. **3.** an authorization from a central organization to establish a new branch, chapter, etc. **4.** a temporary lease of a ship or aircraft. —*v.t.* **5.** to establish by charter. **6.** to hire for exclusive use.

char′ter col′ony, *n.* (in colonial America) a colony, as Rhode Island or Connecticut, governed under a charter from the British crown and allowed much autonomy.

char′ter mem′ber, *n.* an original member of an organization.

char•treuse (shär trōōz′, -trōōs′), *n.* a clear, yellowish green.

char′wom′an (chär′-), *n., pl.* **-wom•en.** a woman hired to do general cleaning.

char•y (châr′ē), *adj.,* **-i•er, -i•est. 1.** careful; wary. **2.** sparing; frugal. —**char′i•ly,** *adv.* —**char′i•ness,** *n.*

chase¹ (chās), *v.,* **chased, chas•ing,** *n.* —*v.t.* **1.** to pursue in order to seize. **2.** to hunt. **3.** to devote attention to with the hope of attracting. **4.** to expel forcibly: *to chase the cat out of the room.* —*v.i.* **5.** to follow in pursuit. **6.** to rush; hasten. —*n.* **7.** the act of chasing. **8.** an object of pursuit. —*Idiom.* **9. give chase,** to pursue.

chase² (chās), *v.t.,* **chased, chas•ing.** to ornament (metal) by engraving or embossing.

chas′er, *n.* **1.** one that chases. **2.** a mild beverage taken after a drink of liquor.

chasm (kaz′əm), *n.* **1.** a deep cleft in the earth's surface; gorge. **2.** any gap or break.

chas•sis (chas′ē, shas′ē), *n., pl.* **chas•sis** (chas′ēz, shas′-). **1.** the frame, wheels, and machinery of a motor vehicle. **2.** a frame for mounting the circuit components of a radio or television set.

chaste (chāst), *adj.,* **chast•er, chast•est. 1.** refraining from unsanctioned sexual activity. **2.** celibate. **3.** decent and modest. **4.** simple; unadorned. —**chaste′ly,** *adv.*

chas•ten (chā′sən), *v.t.* **1.** to inflict punishment upon to humble or improve. **2.** to restrain; subdue.

chas•tise (chas tīz′, chas′tīz), *v.t.,* **-tised, -tis•ing. 1.** to discipline, esp. by corporal punishment. **2.** to criticize severely. —**chas′tise•ment** (chas′tiz-, chas-tīz′-), *n.* —**chas•tis′er,** *n.*

chas′ti•ty (-ti tē), *n.* the state or quality of being chaste.

chas•u•ble (chaz′yə bəl, -ə bəl, chas′-), *n.* a sleeveless outer vestment worn by the celebrant at mass.

chat (chat), *v.,* **chat•ted, chat•ting,** *n.* —*v.i.* **1.** to converse informally. —*n.* **2.** an informal conversation.

châ•teau (sha tō′), *n., pl.* **-teaus** (-tōz′), **-teaux** (-tōz′, -tō′). **1.** a castle in France. **2.** a large country house or estate, esp. in France.

chat•e•laine (shat′l ān′), *n.* **1.** the mistress of a castle. **2.** a hooklike clasp with chains for suspending small objects, as sewing implements.

chat′ room′, *n.* a branch of a computer system in which participants can engage in live discussions with one another.

Chat•ta•noo•ga (chat′ə noō′gə), *n.* a city in SE Tennessee. 152,259.

chat•tel (chat′l), *n.* a movable article of personal property.

chat•ter (chat′ər), *v.i.* **1.** to talk rapidly, continuously, and pointlessly. **2.** to utter rapid, speechlike sounds, as a monkey. **3.** to make a rapid clicking noise by striking together: *teeth chattering from the cold.* —*n.* **4.** rapid, pointless talk. **5.** the act or sound of chattering. —**chat′ter•er,** *n.*

chat′ter•box′, *n.* an excessively talkative person.

chat′ty, *adj.,* -ti•er, -ti•est. **1.** characterized by a friendly, informal style. **2.** given to chatting. —**chat′-ti•ness,** *n.*

Chau•cer (chô′sər), *n.* **Geoffrey,** 1340?–1400, English poet. —**Chau•ce′ri•an** (-sēr′ē ən), *adj., n.*

chauf•feur (shō′fər, shō fûr′), *n.* **1.** a person employed to drive a private automobile. —*v.t., v.i.* **2.** to serve as a chauffeur (for); drive.

chau•vin•ism (shō′və niz′əm), *n.* **1.** zealous and aggressive patriotism. **2.** biased devotion to any group, attitude, or cause. —**chau′vin•ist,** *n.* —**chau′-vin•is′tic,** *adj.*

cheap (chēp), *adj.,* -er, -est, *adv.* —*adj.* **1.** inexpensive. **2.** shoddy or inferior. **3.** costing little labor or trouble: *Talk is cheap.* **4.** mean or contemptible. **5.** of little value: *Life was cheap.* **6.** stingy; miserly. —*adv.* **7.** at a low price. —**cheap′ly,** *adv.* —**cheap′-ness,** *n.*

cheap′en, *v.t., v.i.* to make or become cheap.

cheap′ shot′, *n.* any mean or unsportsmanlike remark or action.

cheap′skate′, *n. Informal.* a stingy person.

cheat (chēt), *v.t.* **1.** to defraud; swindle. **2.** to elude; escape: *to cheat death.* —*v.i.* **3.** to practice fraud or deceit. **4.** to violate rules or agreements. **5.** to be sexually unfaithful. —*n.* **6.** a person who cheats. **7.** a fraud or swindle. —**cheat′er,** *n.*

check (chek), *v.t.* **1.** to stop the motion of suddenly. **2.** to restrain; control. **3.** to verify the correctness of. **4.** to inquire into, search through, etc. **5.** to inspect the performance, safety, etc., of. **6.** to mark so as to indicate choice, correctness, etc. **7.** to leave in temporary custody: *Check your coats at the door.* **8.** to surrender (baggage) for conveyance. **9.** (in chess) to place (an opponent's king) under direct attack. —*v.i.* **10.** to correspond accurately. **11.** to make an inquiry or investigation. **12. check in,** to register or report one's arrival, as at a hotel or airport. **13. ~ out, a.** to leave a hotel, hospital, etc., officially. **b.** to verify or become verified. —*n.* **14.** a written order directing a bank to pay money. **15.** a bill at a restaurant. **16.** a ticket showing ownership. **17.** an inquiry or examination. **18.** a mark (✓) to indicate approval, verification, etc. **19.** a sudden stoppage. **20.** a means of stopping or restraining. **21.** a test or inspection. **22.** a pattern formed of squares. **23.** (in chess) the exposure of the king to direct attack. —*Idiom.* **24.** in **check,** under restraint.

check′book′, *n.* a book containing blank checks to be drawn against an account.

checked, *adj.* having a pattern of squares.

check′er¹, *n.* **1.** a small, usu. red or black disk used in playing checkers. **2. checkers,** a game played by two persons, each with 12 playing pieces, on a checkerboard.

check′er², *n.* **1.** one that checks. **2.** a cashier, as in a supermarket. **3.** a checkroom employee.

check′er•board′, *n.* a board marked into 64 squares of two alternating colors, used in checkers or chess.

check′ered, *adj.* **1.** marked by numerous changes: *a checkered career.* **2.** marked by dubious episodes: *a checkered past.* **3.** marked with squares.

Check′ers Speech′, *n.* a television address given by Richard Nixon in the 1952 presidential campaign, in which he sentimentally and successfully defended himself against charges of bribery. [so called from Nixon's reference to his dog named Checkers]

check′ing account′, *n.* a bank deposit against which checks can be drawn.

check′list′, *n.* a list of items for comparison, verification, or other checking purposes.

check′mate′ (-māt′), *n., v.,* -mat•ed, -mat•ing. —*n.* **1. a.** (in chess) the maneuvering of the opponent's king into a check from which it cannot escape, thus winning the game. **b.** this position. **2.** a thwarting or defeat. —*v.t.* **3.** to put in checkmate. **4.** to defeat.

check′off′, *n.* the withholding of union dues by employers.

check′out′, *n.* **1.** the act of vacating and paying for one's hotel room. **2.** the time by which a hotel room must be vacated. **3.** a counter where customers pay for purchases.

check′point′, *n.* a place, as at a border, where travelers are stopped for inspection.

check′room′, *n.* a room where coats, parcels, etc., may be checked.

checks′ and bal′ances, *n.pl.* limits imposed by the U.S. Constitution on all branches (executive, judicial, and legislative) of the government by vesting in each branch the right to amend or void those acts of another branch that fall within its purview.

check′up′, *n.* a comprehensive physical examination.

ched•dar (ched′ər), *n.* a hard, smooth cheese that varies in flavor from mild to sharp as it ages.

Ched•or•la•o•mer (ked′ər lā ō′mər), *n.* a king of Elam who did battle against Sodom and Gomorrah. Gen. 14:1–24.

cheek (chēk), *n.* **1.** either side of the face below the eye and above the jaw. **2.** impudence or effrontery.

cheek′bone′, *n.* the bony arch below the eye.

cheek′y, *adj.,* -i•er, -i•est. impudent; insolent. —**cheek′i•ly,** *adv.* —**cheek′i•ness,** *n.*

cheep (chēp), *v.i., v.t.* **1.** to chirp. —*n.* **2.** a chirp.

cheer (chēr), *n.* **1.** a shout of encouragement, approval, etc. **2.** a state of feeling or spirits: *Be of good cheer.* **3.** gladness; gaiety. —*interj.* **4. cheers,** to your health (used as a toast). —*v.t.* **5.** to encourage or salute with cheers. **6.** to raise the spirits of: *The good news cheered her up.* —*v.i.* **7.** to utter cheers. **8.** to become cheerful: *cheered up when she heard the news.*

cheer′ful, *adj.* **1.** full of cheer. **2.** pleasant and bright. **3.** wholehearted; ungrudging: *a cheerful giver.* —**cheer′ful•ly,** *adv.* —**cheer′ful•ness,** *n.*

cheer′lead′er, *n.* a person who leads spectators in organized cheering at an athletic event.

cheer′less, *adj.* not cheerful; gloomy: *cheerless surroundings.* —**cheer′less•ly,** *adv.* —**cheer′less•ness,** *n.*

cheer′y, *adj.,* -i•er, -i•est. **1.** cheerful. **2.** promoting cheer. —**cheer′i•ly,** *adv.* —**cheer′i•ness,** *n.*

cheese (chēz), *n.* a food prepared from the curds of milk separated from the whey, often pressed and allowed to ripen. [< L *cāseus*]

cheese′burg′er, *n.* a hamburger topped with melted cheese.

cheese′cake′, *n.* a firm, custardlike cake made with sweetened cream cheese or cottage cheese.

cheese′cloth′, *n.* a lightweight cotton gauze of loose weave.

chees′y, *adj.,* -i•er, -i•est. **1.** of or like cheese. **2.** *Slang.* inferior or cheap; shoddy.

chee•tah (chē′tə), *n.* a swift, long-legged, black-spotted cat of SW Asia and Africa.

Chee•ver (chē′vər), *n.* **John,** 1912–82, U.S. novelist and short-story writer.

chef (shef), *n.* a cook, esp. the chief cook in a restaurant.

Che•khov (chek′ôf, -of), *n.* **Anton,** 1860–1904, Russian writer. —**Che•kho•vi•an** (che kō′vē ən), *adj.*

chem., **1.** chemical. **2.** chemist. **3.** chemistry.

chem•i•cal (kem′i kəl), *n.* **1.** a substance produced by or used in chemistry. —*adj.* **2.** of, used in, produced by, or concerned with chemistry or chemicals. —**chem/i•cal•ly,** *adv.*

chem/ical engineer/ing, *n.* the science of applying chemistry to industrial processes. —**chem/ical engineer/,** *n.*

chem/ical war/fare, *n.* warfare with asphyxiating, poisonous, or corrosive gases, oil flames, etc.

che•mise (shə mēz/), *n.* **1.** a woman's loose-fitting, shirtlike undergarment. **2.** a dress with an unfitted waist.

chem•ist (kem/ist), *n.* **1.** a specialist in chemistry. **2.** *Chiefly Brit.* DRUGGIST.

chem/is•try (-ə strē), *n.* **1.** the science that studies the composition, properties, and activity of substances and various elementary forms of matter. **2.** rapport.

che•mo (kē/mō), *n. Informal.* chemotherapy.

che•mo•ther•a•py (kē/mō ther/ə pē), *n.* the treatment of disease by means of chemicals. —**che/mo•ther/a•peu/tic** (-pyōō/tik), *adj.*

chem•ur•gy (kem/ûr jē, kə mûr/-), *n.* chemistry concerned with the industrial use of organic substances. —**chem•ur/gic,** *adj.*

che•nille (shə nēl/), *n.* **1.** a yarn with a high velvety pile. **2.** a fabric made with such yarn.

cheque (chek), *n. Brit.* CHECK (def. 14).

cher•ish (cher/ish), *v.t.* **1.** to regard or treat as dear. **2.** to cling fondly to: *to cherish a memory.*

Cher•no•byl (chûr nō/bəl, cher-), *n.* a city in N Ukraine 80 mi. NW of Kiev: nuclear-plant accident 1986.

Cher•o•kee (cher/ə kē/), *n., pl.* **-kee, -kees.** a member of an American Indian people of the Carolinas and Tennessee, living today in Oklahoma and North Carolina.

che•root (shə rōōt/), *n.* a cigar having open, untapered ends.

cher•ry (cher/ē), *n., pl.* **-ries. 1.** a pulpy, globular fruit containing one smooth pit. **2.** the tree bearing such a fruit. **3.** the wood of this tree. **4.** a bright red. —*Saying.* **5. Life is just a bowl of cherries,** life is pleasant and enjoyable (song with words by Lew Brown and music by Ray Henderson, 1931).

cher/ry•stone/, *n.* the quahog clam when larger than a littleneck.

chert (chûrt), *n.* a compact rock consisting of fine-grained quartz.

cher•ub (cher/əb), *n., pl.* **cher•ubs** for 3; **cher•u•bim** (cher/ə bim, -yōō bim) for 1, 2. **1.** a celestial being. Gen. 3:24; Ezek. 1, 10. **2.** a member of the second order of angels, often represented as a winged child. **3.** a child with a sweet, chubby, innocent face. —**che•ru•bic** (chə rōō/bik), *adj.*

cher•vil (chûr/vil), *n.* an herb of the parsley family, with leaves used to flavor soups, salads, etc.

Ches•a•peake (ches/ə pēk/), *n.* a city in SE Virginia. 180,577.

Ches/apeake Bay/, *n.* an inlet of the Atlantic, in Maryland and Virginia.

chess (ches), *n.* a game played on a chessboard by two people, each with 16 pieces.

chess/board/, *n.* a checkerboard used for playing chess.

chess/man/ (-man/, -mən), *n., pl.* **-men.** any piece used in chess.

chest (chest), *n.* **1.** the portion of the body enclosed by ribs. **2.** a large, heavy box with a lid. **3.** a set of drawers in a frame, as for holding clothes. **4.** a small cabinet, esp. one hung on a wall, for storage of toiletries and medicines.

ches•ter•field (ches/tər fēld/), *n.* **1.** a single- or double-breasted coat with a velvet collar. **2.** a large overstuffed sofa with high arms.

chest/nut/, *n.* **1.** any of several trees of the beech family, bearing edible nuts. **2.** the nut of these trees. **3.** the wood of these trees. **4.** reddish brown. **5.** a stale joke, anecdote, etc.

chev•i•ot (shev/ē ət), *n.* a woolen fabric in a coarse twill weave, used for coats, suits, etc.

chev•ron (shev/rən), *n.* a badge of V-shaped stripes on the sleeve of a uniform, indicating rank, length of service, etc.

chew (chōō), *v.t., v.i.* **1.** to crush or grind with the teeth. **2. chew out,** *Slang.* to scold harshly. —*n.* **3.** an act or instance of chewing. **4.** something chewed or intended for chewing. —*Idiom.* **5. chew the fat** or **rag,** *Informal.* to have a chat. —**chew/er,** *n.*

chew/ing gum/, *n.* a flavored preparation for chewing, usu. made of chicle.

chew/y, *adj.,* **-i•er, -i•est.** (of food) not easily chewed. —**chew/i•ness,** *n.*

Chey•enne (shī en/, -an/), *n., pl.* **-enne, -ennes. 1.** a member of an American Indian people of the western plains, living today in Montana and Oklahoma. **2.** the capital of Wyoming. 54,010.

chg. or **chge., 1.** change. **2.** charge.

chi (kī), *n., pl.* **chis.** the 22nd letter of the Greek alphabet (X, χ).

Chi•an•ti (kē än/tē, -an/-), *n.* a dry red wine of Italy.

chi•a•ro•scu•ro (kē är/ə skyōōr/ō, -skōōr/ō), *n., pl.* **-ros.** the distribution of light and shade in a picture.

chic (shēk), *adj.,* **-er, -est,** *n.* —*adj.* **1.** fashionable; stylish. —*n.* **2.** style and elegance, esp. in dress.

Chi•ca•go (shi kä/gō, -kô/-), *n.* a city in NE Illinois. 2,731,743. —**Chi•ca/go•an,** *n.*

Chica/go Fire/, *n.* a three-day fire in Chicago, Ill., in 1871 that largely destroyed the city and took several hundred lives.

Chi•ca•na (chi kä/nə, -kan/ə), *n., pl.* **-nas.** a Mexican-American girl or woman.

chi•can•er•y (shi kä/nə rē, chi-), *n., pl.* **-er•ies. 1.** trickery or deception. **2.** a trick.

Chi•ca•no (chi kä/nō, -kan/ō), *n., pl.* **-nos.** a Mexican-American.

chi•chi (shē/shē/), *adj.* pretentiously elegant or trendy.

chick (chik), *n.* a young chicken or other bird.

chick•a•dee (chik/ə dē/), *n., pl.* **-dees.** a North American bird of the titmouse family, with a dark-colored throat and cap.

Chick•a•saw (chik/ə sô/), *n., pl.* **-saw, -saws.** a member of an American Indian people of Mississippi, later removed to Oklahoma.

chick•en (chik/ən), *n.* **1.** the common domestic fowl. **2.** the young of this bird. **3.** the flesh of the chicken, used as food. **4.** *Slang.* a coward. —*adj.* **5.** *Slang.* cowardly. —*v.* **6. chicken out,** *Slang.* to withdraw because of cowardice. —*Proverb.* **7. Chickens come home to roost,** one must eventually pay for one's errors. —*Saying.* **8. A chicken in every pot,** general prosperity: popularized in the 1928 U.S. presidential campaign.

chick/en feed/, *n. Slang.* an insignificant sum of money.

chick/en-heart/ed, *adj.* fearful; cowardly.

chick/en-pox/, *n.* a viral disease, commonly of children, characterized by fever and the eruption of blisters.

chick/en wire/, *n.* a light wire netting having a large hexagonal mesh.

chick/pea/, *n.* **1.** a plant of the legume family, bearing edible, pealike seeds. **2.** its seed.

chick/weed/, *n.* a common weed whose leaves and seeds are relished by birds.

chic•le (chik/əl), *n.* a gumlike substance from certain tropical American trees, used in chewing gum.

chic•o•ry (chik/ə rē), *n., pl.* **-ries. 1.** a plant with toothed oblong leaves used for salad. **2.** the root of this plant, used in or as a substitute for coffee.

chide (chīd), *v.t., v.i.,* **chid•ed** or **chid** (chid), **chid•ed** or **chid** or **chid•den** (chid/n), **chid•ing.** to scold or reproach.

chief (chēf), *n.* **1.** a head or leader. —*adj.* **2.** most important; principal. —**chief/ly,** *adv.*

Chief/ Exec/utive, *n.* **1.** the president of the United States. **2.** (*l.c.*) the governor of a U.S. state. **3.** (*l.c.*) the head of a government.

chief/ jus/tice, *n.* **1.** the presiding judge of a court having several members. **2.** (*caps.*) Official title, **Chief′ Jus′tice of the Unit′ed States′.** the presiding judge of the U.S. Supreme Court.

chief′ of state′, *n.* the titular head of a nation, as a president or king.

chief′tain (-tan), *n.* the chief of a clan or a tribe.

chif•fon (shi fon′, shif′on), *n.* **1.** a sheer fabric of silk, nylon, or rayon. —*adj.* **2.** made of chiffon. **3.** having a light, fluffy texture, as from beaten egg whites.

chig•ger (chig′ər), *n.* the bloodsucking larva of a mite parasitic on humans and other mammals.

chi•gnon (shēn′yon), *n.* a large knot of hair worn at the nape of the neck.

Chi•hua•hua (chi wä′wä, -wə), *n., pl.* -huas for 2. **1.** a city in N Mexico. 406,830. **2.** one of a Mexican breed of very small dogs with large erect ears.

chil•blain (chil′blān), *n.* an inflammation of the hands and feet caused by exposure to cold.

child (chīld), *n., pl.* **chil•dren. 1.** a boy or girl. **2.** a son or daughter. **3.** an infant. —*Idiom.* **4. with child,** pregnant. —**child′hood,** *n.* —**child′ish,** *adj.* —**child′ish•ly,** *adv.* —**child′ish•ness,** *n.* —**child′less,** *adj.* —**child′like′,** *adj.* —*Proverb.* **5. The child is father of the man,** adult characteristics are determined in childhood.

child′bear′ing, *n.* the act of producing or bringing forth children.

child′birth′, *n.* an act or instance of bringing forth a child.

chil•dren (chil′drən), *n.* pl. of CHILD.

chil′dren of Is′rael, *n.pl.* the Hebrews; Jews.

child′s′ play′, *n.* something easily done.

Chil•e (chil′ē), *n.* a republic in SW South America. 14,508,168. —**Chil′e•an,** *adj., n.*

chil•i or **chil•e** (chil′ē), *n., pl.* -ies or -es. **1.** the pungent pod of a red pepper, used in cooking. **2.** CHILI CON CARNE.

chil′i con car′ne (kon kär′nē), *n.* a highly seasoned dish of beef, chilies, and often tomatoes and beans.

chil′i sauce′, *n.* a sauce of tomatoes cooked with chili peppers and spices.

chill (chil), *n.* **1.** a moderate but penetrating coldness. **2.** a sensation of cold, usu. with shivering. **3.** a depressing influence or feeling. —*adj.* **4.** moderately cold. —*v.i., v.t.* **5.** to become or make cold. —**chill′ness,** *n.*

chill′er, *n.* a frightening story or film.

chill′y, *adj.,* -i•er, -i•est. **1.** mildly cold. **2.** without warmth of feeling. —**chill′i•ness,** *n.*

chime (chīm), *n., v.,* chimed, chim•ing. —*n.* **1.** Often, **chimes. a.** a set of bells producing musical tones when struck. **b.** the musical tones thus produced. **2.** harmonious sound in general. —*v.i.* **3.** to sound chimes. **4.** to harmonize; agree. —*v.t.* **5.** to announce by chiming: *Bells chimed the hour.* **6. chime in, a.** to interrupt a conversation. **b.** to harmonize. —**chim′er,** *n.*

chi•me•ra (ki mēr′ə, kī-), *n., pl.* -ras for 2. **1.** (*cap.*) a monster of classical myth, with a lion's head, goat's body, and serpent's tail. **2.** a fancy or dream; an imagining.

chi•mer′i•cal (-mer′i kəl, -mēr′-), *adj.* **1.** unreal; imaginary. **2.** wildly fanciful.

chim•ney (chim′nē), *n., pl.* -neys. **1.** a structure containing a flue by which the smoke, gases, etc., of a fire or furnace are carried off. **2.** a glass tube surrounding the flame of a lamp.

chimp (chimp), *n.* a chimpanzee.

chim•pan•zee (chim′pan zē′, chim pan′zē), *n., pl.* -zees. a large anthropoid ape of equatorial Africa.

chin (chin), *n., v.,* chinned, chin•ning. —*n.* **1.** the lower extremity of the face, below the mouth. —*v.t.* **2.** to grasp an overhead bar and pull (oneself) up until the chin is level with the bar. —*Idiom.* **3. keep one's chin up,** to maintain one's courage and optimism during a period of adversity. **4. take it on the chin,** *Informal.* **a.** to be defeated thoroughly. **b.** to endure punishment stoically.

Chin. or **Chin, 1.** China. **2.** Chinese.

chi•na (chī′nə), *n.* **1.** porcelain or a similar translucent ceramic material. **2.** porcelain or ceramic tableware.

Chi′na, *n.* **1. People's Republic of,** a country in E Asia. 1,221,591,778. **2. Republic of,** TAIWAN.

chin•chil•la (chin chil′ə), *n., pl.* -las. **1.** a small South American rodent raised for its silvery gray fur. **2.** this fur. **3.** a woolen coat fabric with a curly nap.

Chi•nese (chī nēz′, -nēs′), *n., pl.* -nese, *adj.* —*n.* **1.** a native or descendant of a native of China. **2.** a language or language family of China, comprising a wide variety of speech forms. —*adj.* **3.** of China, its people, or their language.

Chi′nese check′ers, *n.* a board game in which marbles set in holes are moved to the opposite side of the board.

Chi′nese lan′tern, *n.* a collapsible lantern of thin colored paper.

chink¹ (chingk), *n.* **1.** a crack, as in a wall. —*v.t.* **2.** to fill up chinks in.

chink² (chingk), *v.i., v.t.* **1.** to make or cause to make a short, sharp, ringing sound. —*n.* **2.** a chinking sound.

chi•no (chē′nō), *n., pl.* -nos. **1.** a twilled cotton cloth used for uniforms, sportswear, etc. **2.** Usu., **-nos.** trousers of this cloth.

Chi•nook (shi nŏŏk′, -nōōk′, chi-), *n., pl.* -nook, -nooks. **1.** a member of an American Indian people orig. inhabiting Oregon. **2.** (*l.c.*) a warm, dry wind that blows at intervals down the E slopes of the Rocky Mountains.

chintz (chints), *n.* a cotton fabric, usu. glazed and printed in bright patterns.

chintz′y, *adj.,* -i•er, -i•est. **1.** like chintz. **2.** cheap or gaudy.

chip (chip), *n., v.,* chipped, chip•ping. —*n.* **1.** a small piece, as of wood, separated by chopping or breaking. **2.** a small piece of food: *chocolate chips.* **3.** a flaw made by the breaking off of a small piece. **4.** a small disk used in gambling games as a counter. **5.** a tiny slice of semiconducting material on which a transistor or an integrated circuit is formed. —*v.t.* **6.** to break a fragment from. —*v.i.* **7.** to break off in small pieces. **8. chip in,** to contribute money, time, etc. —*Idiom.* **9. chip off the old block,** a person who strongly resembles one parent in appearance or behavior. **10. chip on one's shoulder,** a readiness to quarrel. **11. let the chips fall where they may,** to take action and disregard the consequences. **12. when the chips are down,** when the need for support is greatest.

chip•munk (chip′mungk), *n.* a small, striped North American or Asian ground squirrel.

chipmunk

chipped′ beef′, *n.* shavings of dried, smoked beef, often served in a cream sauce.

chip•per (chip′ər), *adj.* being in sprightly good humor and health.

Chip•pe•wa (chip′ə wä′, -wā′, -wə), *n., pl.* -wa, -was. OJIBWA.

chi•rog•ra•phy (kī rog′rə fē), *n.* handwriting; penmanship.

chi•rop•o•dy (ki rop′ə dē, kī-; *often* shə-), *n.* PODIATRY. —**chi•rop′o•dist,** *n.*

chi•ro•prac•tic (kī′rə prak′tik), *n.* a therapeutic system based upon adjusting the segments of the spinal column. —**chi′ro•prac′tor,** *n.*

chirp (chûrp), *n.* **1.** the short, sharp sound made by small birds. **2.** any similar sound. —*v.i., v.t.* **3.** to make or express with such a sound.

chir•rup (chēr′əp, chûr′-), *v.i., v.t.* **1.** to chirp. —*n.* **2.** the sound of chirruping.

chis•el (chiz′əl), *n., v.,* **-eled, -el•ing** or (*esp. Brit.*) **-elled, -el•ling.** —*n.* **1.** a wedgelike, sharp-edged tool for cutting or shaping wood, stone, etc. —*v.t., v.i.* **2.** to cut or work with a chisel. **3.** *Slang.* **a.** to cheat or swindle (someone). **b.** to get by trickery. —**chis′el•er;** *esp. Brit.,* **chis′el•ler,** *n.*

Chis•holm (chiz′əm), *n.* **Shirley (Anita St. Hill),** born 1924, U.S. politician: congresswoman 1969–83; first black woman elected to the House of Representatives.

chit (chit), *n.* a signed note for money owed for food, drink, etc.

chit•chat (chit′chat′), *n.* light conversation; casual talk.

chi•tin (kī′tin), *n.* a horny substance that is a principal constituent of the outer covering of insects, crustaceans, and arachnids. —**chi′tin•ous,** *adj.*

chit•ter•lings or **chit•lings** or **chit•lins** (chit′linz, -lingz), *n.* (*used with a sing. or pl. v.*) the small intestine of swine, esp. when prepared as food.

chiv•al•rous (shiv′əl rəs), *adj.* **1.** of chivalry. **2.** having the qualities of a knight, as courage, courtesy, and loyalty. **3.** courteous to women; gallant. —**chiv′al•rous•ly,** *adv.* —**chiv′al•rous•ness,** *n.*

chiv′al•ry, *n.* **1.** the qualities expected of a knight, including courage, generosity, and courtesy. **2.** the institution of medieval knighthood.

chive (chīv), *n.* a plant related to the onion, having slender leaves used as a flavoring.

chlo•ral (klôr′əl), *n.* a white crystalline solid used as a hypnotic. Also called **chlo′ral hy′drate.**

chlo•ride (klôr′īd, -id), *n.* a salt of hydrochloric acid consisting of two elements, one of which is chlorine.

chlo•ri•nate (klôr′ə nāt′), *v.t.,* **-nat•ed, -nat•ing.** to combine or treat with chlorine, esp. for disinfecting. —**chlo′ri•na′tion,** *n.*

chlo•rine (klôr′ēn, -in), *n.* a greenish yellow, poisonous, gaseous element, used to purify water and to make bleaching powder and various chemicals. *Symbol:* Cl; *at. wt.:* 35.453; *at. no.:* 17.

chlo•ro•form (klôr′ə fôrm′), *n.* **1.** a colorless volatile liquid used as a solvent and formerly as an anesthetic. —*v.t.* **2.** to administer chloroform to.

chlo′ro•phyll (-fil), *n.* the green pigment of plant leaves, essential to photosynthesis.

chock (chok), *n.* **1.** a wedge for filling in a space, holding an object steady, etc. —*v.t.* **2.** to furnish with chocks. —*adv.* **3.** as tight as possible.

chock′-full′ (chok′-, chuk′-), *adj.* full to the limit; crammed.

choc•o•late (chô′kə lit, chok′ə-, chôk′lit, chok′-), *n.* **1.** a preparation of the seeds of cacao, often sweetened and flavored. **2.** a candy or beverage made from such a preparation. **3.** a dark brown color. —*adj.* **4.** made or flavored with chocolate. **5.** having the color of chocolate. —**choc′o•lat•y, choc′-o•lat•ey,** *adj.*

Choc•taw (chok′tô), *n., pl.* **-taw, -taws.** a member of an American Indian people of Mississippi, later removed to Oklahoma.

choice (chois), *n., adj.,* **choic•er, choic•est.** —*n.* **1.** the act of choosing. **2.** the right or opportunity to choose. **3.** the person or thing chosen. **4.** an alternative. **5.** a variety from which to choose. **6.** the best part. —*adj.* **7.** excellent; superior. **8.** carefully selected.

choir (kwīr), *n.* **1.** a group of singers, as in a church. **2.** the part of a church occupied by a choir. **3.** (in medieval angelology) one of the orders of angels. [< OF *cuer* < L *chōrus* chorus]

choke (chōk), *v.,* **choked, chok•ing,** *n.* —*v.t.* **1.** to stop the breath of by obstructing the windpipe. **2.** to obstruct; clog. **3.** to suppress or hinder. **4.** to enrich the fuel mixture of (an internal-combustion engine) by diminishing the air supply to the carburetor. —*v.i.* **5.** to become suffocated. **6.** to become obstructed. **7. choke up,** to become speechless, as

from emotion. —*n.* **8.** the act or sound of choking. **9.** a device in an automotive engine that controls the flow of air.

chok′er, *n.* a necklace that fits snugly around the neck.

chol•er (kol′ər), *n.* irascibility; anger.

chol•er•a (kol′ər ə), *n.* a severe, contagious infection of the small intestine, commonly transmitted through contaminated drinking water.

chol•er•ic (kol′ər ik, kə ler′ik), *adj.* extremely irritable or easily angered.

cho•les•ter•ol (kə les′tə rōl′, -rôl′), *n.* a fatty, crystalline substance abundant in animal fats, meat, and eggs.

chomp (chomp), *v.t., v.i.* CHAMP¹.

Chong•qing (chông′ching′) also **Chungking,** *n.* a city in S central China. 2,780,000.

choose (chōōz), *v.,* **chose, cho•sen, choos•ing.** —*v.t.* **1.** to pick by preference; select. **2.** to decide or desire. —*v.i.* **3.** to make a choice. —**choos′er,** *n.*

choos′y, *adj.,* **-i•er, -i•est.** hard to please; particular. —**choos′i•ness,** *n.*

chop¹ (chop), *v.,* **chopped, chop•ping,** *n.* —*v.t.* **1.** to cut with quick, heavy blows. **2.** to cut into small pieces. —*v.i.* **3.** to make quick, heavy strokes, as with an ax. —*n.* **4.** an act or instance of chopping. **5.** a short downward blow or stroke. **6.** a cut of lamb, pork, veal, etc. **7.** a short, irregular motion of waves.

chop² (chop), *n.* Usu., **chops. 1.** the jaw. **2.** the lower part of the cheek; the flesh over the lower jaw.

chop′house′, *n.* a restaurant specializing in chops and steaks.

Cho•pin (shō′pan; *Fr.* shō paN′), *n.* **Frédéric,** 1810–49, Polish composer in France after 1831.

chop′per, *n.* **1.** one that chops. **2.** *Informal.* a helicopter.

chop′py, *adj.,* **-pi•er, -pi•est. 1.** (of the sea, a lake, etc.) forming short, broken waves. **2.** uneven in style or quality. —**chop′pi•ly,** *adv.* —**chop′pi•ness,** *n.*

chop′stick′, *n.* one of a pair of tapered sticks used as an eating utensil in some Asian countries.

chop′ su′ey (sōō′ē), *n.* a Chinese-style dish of meat, bean sprouts, etc., served with rice.

cho•ral (kôr′əl), *adj.* of a chorus or a choir. —**cho′ral•ly,** *adv.*

cho•rale (kə ral′, -räl′), *n.* **1.** a hymn, esp. one with strong harmonization. **2.** a group of singers specializing in church music.

chord¹ (kôrd), *n.* **1.** a feeling or emotion. **2.** the line segment between two points on a given curve.

chord² (kôrd), *n.* a combination of three or more musical tones sounded simultaneously. —**chord′al,** *adj.*

chor•date (kôr′dāt), *adj.* **1.** comprising the true vertebrates and those animals having a notochord. —*n.* **2.** a chordate animal.

chore (chôr), *n.* **1.** a small or routine task. **2.** a hard or unpleasant task.

cho•re•a (kə rē′ə, kô-), *n.* any of several diseases of the nervous system characterized by jerky, involuntary movements.

cho•re•o•graph (kôr′ē ə graf′, -gräf′), *v.t., v.i.* to provide the choreography for (a ballet, etc.).

cho′re•og′ra•phy (-og′rə fē), *n.* **1.** the art of composing ballets and other dances. **2.** the movements, steps, and patterns composed for a dance, show, piece of music, etc. —**cho′re•og′ra•pher,** *n.* —**cho′-re•o•graph′ic** (-ə graf′ik), *adj.*

chor•is•ter (kôr′ə stər, kor′-), *n.* a singer in a choir.

cho•roid (kôr′oid), *n.* a pigmented, highly vascular layer of the eye.

chor•tle (chôr′tl), *v.,* **-tled, -tling,** *n.* —*v.i.* **1.** to chuckle gleefully. —*n.* **2.** a gleeful chuckle. [b. of *chuckle* and *snort*; coined by Lewis Carroll in *Through the Looking-Glass* (1871)] —**chor′tler,** *n.*

cho•rus (kôr′əs), *n., pl.* **-rus•es,** *v.* —*n.* **1. a.** a group of persons singing in unison. **b.** a piece of music for singing in unison. **2.** a part of a song that recurs at intervals; refrain. **3.** a simultaneous utterance by many people, birds, etc. **4.** the sounds so uttered:

a chorus of jeers. —*v.t., v.i.* **5.** to sing or speak simultaneously. —**Idiom. 6. in chorus,** in unison.

chose (chōz), *v.* pt. of CHOOSE.

cho′sen, *v.* **1.** pp. of CHOOSE. —*adj.* **2.** selected; preferred. **3. the chosen,** ELECT (def. 9).

cho′sen peo′ple, *n.pl. (often caps.)* the Israelites. Ex. 19.

chow¹ (chou), *n. Slang.* food.

chow² (chou), *n. (often cap.)* CHOW CHOW.

chow′ chow′, *n. (often caps.)* one of a Chinese breed of medium-sized dogs with a stocky body and a large head.

chow•der (chou′dər), *n.* a thick soup of clams, fish, or vegetables, usu. with potatoes and milk.

chow′ mein′ (mān), *n.* a Chinese-style dish of vegetables, chicken, etc., served with fried noodles.

chrism (kriz′əm), *n.* a consecrated oil used in various rites, as in baptism.

chris•om (kriz′əm), *n.* **1.** CHRISM. **2.** a white cloth or robe put on a person at baptism to signify innocence.

Christ (krīst), *n.* Jesus of Nazareth, held by Christians to be the Messiah prophesied in the Old Testament. [< L *Chrīstus* < Gk *Chrīstós* lit., anointed]

chris•ten (kris′ən), *v.t.* **1.** to receive into the Christian church by baptism; baptize. **2.** to give a name to, esp. at baptism.

Chris•ten•dom (kris′ən dəm), *n.* **1.** Christians collectively. **2.** the Christian world.

chris•ten•ing (kris′ə ning, kris′ning), *n.* **1.** the ceremony of baptism, esp. as accompanied by the giving of a name to a child. **2.** a ceremony in which a new ship is named. **3.** an act of naming something new.

Chris•tian (kris′chən), *adj.* **1.** of Jesus Christ or His teachings. **2.** of or adhering to the religion based on the teachings of Jesus Christ. **3.** of Christians. —*n.* **4.** an adherent of Christianity.

Chris′tian E′ra, *n.* the period since the assumed year of Jesus' birth.

Chris′ti•an′i•ty (-chē an′i tē), *n.* **1.** the Christian religion. **2.** the state of being a Christian. **3.** CHRISTENDOM.

Chris′tian•ize′ (-chə nīz′), *v.t.,* **-ized, -iz•ing. 1.** to make Christian. **2.** to imbue with Christian principles.

Chris′tian name′, *n.* the name given at baptism, as distinguished from the family name.

Chris′tian Sci′ence, *n.* a religion that is based on the Scriptures and emphasizes spiritual healing. —**Chris′tian Sci′entist,** *n.*

Chris′tian vir′tues, *n.pl.* faith, hope, and charity. I Cor. 13:13.

Chris•tie (kris′tē), *n.* **Agatha,** 1891–1976, English mystery writer.

Christ•mas (kris′məs), *n.* an annual Christian festival commemorating Jesus' birth, celebrated on December 25.

chro•mat•ic (krō mat′ik, krə-), *adj.* **1.** pertaining to color. **2.** progressing by semitones. —**chro•mat′i•cal•ly,** *adv.*

chrome (krōm), *n., v.,* **chromed, chrom•ing.** —*n.* **1.** (not in technical use) CHROMIUM. **2.** chromium-plated trim, as on an automobile. —*v.t.* **3.** to plate with chromium.

chro•mi•um (krō′mē əm), *n.* a lustrous metallic element used in alloy steels for hardness. *Symbol:* Cr; *at. wt.:* 51.996; *at. no.:* 24.

chro•mo•some (krō′mə sōm′), *n.* one of a set of threadlike structures that are composed of DNA and a protein and that carry the genes. —**chro′mo•so′mal,** *adj.*

chron•ic (kron′ik), *adj.* **1.** habitual or longstanding: *a chronic liar.* **2.** continuing a long time or recurring frequently, as a disease. —**chron′i•cal•ly,** *adv.*

chron′ic fatigue′ syn′drome, *n.* a viral disease of the immune system, usu. characterized by debilitating fatigue and flulike symptoms.

chron•i•cle (kron′i kəl), *n., v.,* **-cled, -cling.** —*n.* **1.** a chronological record of events. —*v.t.* **2.** to record in a chronicle. —**chron′i•cler,** *n.*

Chron•i•cles (kron′i kəlz), *n. (used with a sing. v.)* either of two books of the Old Testament, I Chronicles or II Chronicles.

chrono-, a combining form meaning time (*chronometer*).

chro•nol•o•gy (krə nol′ə jē), *n., pl.* **-gies. 1.** an arrangement according to the order in which things occur. **2.** a table or list so arranged. **3.** the science of arranging time in periods and ascertaining the dates of past events. —**chron•o•log•i•cal** (kron′l oj′i kəl), *adj.* —**chron′o•log′i•cal•ly,** *adv.*

chro•nom•e•ter (krə nom′i tər), *n.* a timepiece designed for the highest accuracy.

chrys•a•lis (kris′ə lis), *n., pl.* **chrys•a•lis•es, chry•sal•i•des** (kri sal′i dēz′). the hard-shelled pupa of a moth or butterfly.

chry•san•the•mum (kri san′thə məm), *n.* **1.** any of many cultivated varieties of plants with showy flowers. **2.** the flower.

chub•by (chub′ē), *adj.,* **-bi•er, -bi•est.** round and plump. —**chub′bi•ness,** *n.*

chuck¹ (chuk), *v.t.* **1.** to toss; throw. **2.** to throw away. **3.** to resign from. **4.** to pat lightly, as under the chin. —*n.* **5.** a light pat. **6.** a toss; pitch.

chuck² (chuk), *n.* **1.** the cut of beef between the neck and the shoulder blade. **2.** a device for clamping work in a lathe or other machine tool.

chuck•le (chuk′əl), *v.,* **-led, -ling,** *n.* —*v.i.* **1.** to laugh softly. —*n.* **2.** a softly moderated laugh.

chuck′ wag′on, *n.* a wagon carrying cooking facilities and food for people working outdoors, as at a ranch.

chug¹ (chug), *n., v.,* **chugged, chug•ging.** —*n.* **1.** a short, dull, explosive sound: *the chug of an engine.* —*v.i.* **2.** to make or move while making this sound.

chug² (chug), *v.t., v.i.,* **chugged, chug•ging.** to drink (a container of beverage) in one continuous draught.

chuk′ka boot′ (chuk′ə), *n.* an ankle-high shoe laced through two pairs of eyelets.

Chu•la Vis•ta (chōo′lə vis′tə), *n.* a city in SW California. 149,255.

chum (chum), *n., v.,* **chummed, chum•ming.** —*n.* **1.** a close friend. —*v.i.* **2.** to associate closely. —**chum′my,** *adj.,* **-mi•er, -mi•est.**

chump (chump), *n. Informal.* a foolish or gullible person.

chump′ change′, *n. Slang.* a small or insignificant amount of money.

Chung•king (chŏŏng′king′), *n.* CHONGQING.

chunk (chungk), *n.* **1.** a thick mass or lump of anything. **2.** a substantial amount.

chunk′y, *adj.,* **-i•er, -i•est. 1.** thick or stout; stocky. **2.** full of chunks. —**chunk′i•ness,** *n.*

church (chûrch), *n.* **1.** a building that is used for public Christian worship. **2.** a religious service. **3.** *(sometimes cap.)* **a.** the body of Christian believers. **b.** a Christian denomination. **4.** religious authority as distinguished from the state. —*v.t.* **5.** to perform a church service of thanksgiving for (a woman after childbirth). [< Gk *kȳri(a)kón (dôma)* the Lord's (house)]

church′go′er, *n.* a person who goes to church regularly.

Church•ill (chûr′chil, -chəl), *n.* **Sir Winston (Leonard Spencer),** 1874–1965, British prime minister 1940–45, 1951–55.

church′man or **-wom′an,** *n., pl.* **-men** or **-women. 1.** a member of the clergy. **2.** a church member.

Church′ of Christ′, Sci′entist, *n.* the official name of the Christian Science Church.

Church′ of Eng′land, *n.* the established church in England, Catholic in faith and order, but independent of the papacy.

Church′ of Je′sus Christ′ of Lat′ter-day Saints′, *n.* a denomination founded in the U.S. in 1830 by Joseph Smith.

church′ward′en, *n.* a lay officer in the Anglican or Episcopal Church with certain secular responsibilities.

church′yard′, *n.* the yard or ground adjoining a church, often used as a graveyard.

churl (chûrl), *n.* **1.** a rude or surly person. **2.** a peasant; rustic. —**churl′ish,** *adj.* —**churl′ish•ness,** *n.*

churn (chûrn), *n.* **1.** a container in which cream or milk is agitated to make butter. —*v.t.* **2.** to agitate (cream or milk) in a churn. **3.** to make (butter) in a churn. **4.** to shake or agitate. **5.** (of a stockbroker) to trade (a customer's securities) excessively. —*v.i.* **6.** to operate a churn. **7.** to move or shake in agitation. **8. churn out,** to produce mechanically and in abundance. —**churn′er,** *n.*

chute[1] (shōōt), *n.* an inclined trough or shaft for conveying water, grain, etc., to a lower level.

chute[2] (shōōt), *n.* a parachute.

chut•ney (chut′nē), *n.* a sweet and sour relish of Indian origin.

chutz•pa or **-pah** (кнŏŏt′spə, hŏŏt′-), *n. Slang.* nerve; gall. [< Yiddish *chutspe* < Heb *ḥuṣpā*]

CIA, Central Intelligence Agency: *a federal agency that coordinates U.S. intelligence activities.*

ciao (chou), *interj.* an expression of greeting or farewell. [< It]

ci•ca•da (si kā′də, -kä′-), *n., pl.* **-das, -dae** (-dē). a large insect, the male of which produces a shrill sound.

cic•a•trix (sik′ə triks), *n., pl.* **cic•a•tri•ces** (sik′ə trī′-sēz). new tissue that forms over a wound and later contracts into a scar.

Cic•e•ro (sis′ə rō′), *n.* **Marcus Tullius,** (*"Tully"*), 106–43 B.C., Roman statesman, orator, and writer.

-cide, a combining form meaning: a killer (*pesticide*); the act of killing (*homicide*).

ci•der (sī′dər), *n.* the juice pressed from apples, used for drinking or for making vinegar.

ci•gar (si gär′), *n.* a roll of cured tobacco wrapped in a tobacco leaf for smoking.

cig•a•rette (sig′ə ret′), *n.* a short roll of finely cut tobacco wrapped in paper for smoking.

cig′a•ril′lo (-ril′ō), *n., pl.* **-los.** a small, thin cigar.

cil•i•a (sil′ē ə), *n.pl., sing.* **-i•um** (-ē əm). the short, hairlike, rhythmically beating organelles on the surface of certain cells.

cinch (sinch), *n.* **1.** a strong girth for securing a pack or saddle. **2.** *Informal.* something sure or easy. —*v.t.* **3.** to gird or bind firmly. **4.** *Informal.* to make sure of.

cin•cho•na (sing kō′nə, sin-), *n., pl.* **-nas. 1.** any of several trees or shrubs native to the Andes whose bark yields quinine. **2.** this bark.

Cin•cin•nat•i (sin′sə nat′ē), *n.* a city in SW Ohio. 358,170.

cinc•ture (singk′chər), *n.* a belt or girdle.

cin•der (sin′dər), *n.* **1.** a partially burned piece of coal, wood, etc. **2. cinders,** any residue of combustion; ashes.

cin•e•ma (sin′ə mə), *n., pl.* **-mas. 1. the cinema,** motion pictures, as an art or industry. **2.** a motion-picture theater. —**cin′e•mat′ic** (-mat′ik), *adj.* —**cin′-e•mat′i•cal•ly,** *adv.*

cin′e•ma•tog′ra•phy (-tog′rə fē), *n.* the art or technique of motion-picture photography. —**cin′e•ma•tog′ra•pher,** *n.* —**cin′e•mat′o•graph′ic** (-mat′-ə graf′ik), *adj.*

cin•na•bar (sin′ə bär′), *n.* a red mineral that is the principal ore of mercury.

cin•na•mon (sin′ə mən), *n.* the aromatic inner bark of an East Indian tree, used as a spice.

ci•pher (sī′fər), *n.* **1.** ZERO (def. 1). **2.** a nonentity. **3.** a secret method of writing, as by code. **4.** the key to a secret method of writing. —*v.i.* **5.** to use numerals arithmetically.

cir•ca (sûr′kə), *prep.* about: used before approximate dates.

cir•ca•di•an (sûr kā′dē ən), *adj.* of rhythmic cycles recurring at regular approximately 24-hour intervals.

cir•cle (sûr′kəl), *n., v.,* **-cled, -cling.** —*n.* **1.** a closed plane curve consisting of all points at a given distance from the center. **2.** the portion of a plane bounded by such a curve. **3.** any circular object, for-

mation, etc.: *a circle of dancers.* **4.** a realm or sphere: *a circle of influence.* **5.** a series forming a connected whole; cycle. **6.** a number of persons bound by a common tie. —*v.t.* **7.** to enclose in a circle. **8.** to rotate or revolve around. —*v.i.* **9.** to move in a circle. —**cir′cler,** *n.*

cir′clet (-klit), *n.* **1.** a small circle. **2.** a ring-shaped ornament.

cir′cuit (-kit), *n.* **1.** the act of moving around. **2.** a circular journey. **3.** a periodic journey from place to place, as by judges, ministers, etc. **4.** the line bounding any area or object. **5.** the complete path of an electric current, including the generating apparatus, etc. **6.** a chain of theaters, nightclubs, etc. —*v.t.* **7.** to make the circuit of. —*v.i.* **8.** to go in a circuit.

cir′cuit board′, *n.* a sheet of fiberglass or other material on which electronic components are installed.

cir′cuit break′er, *n.* a device for interrupting an electric circuit to prevent excessive current.

cir′cuit court′, *n.* a court holding sessions at various intervals in different sections of a judicial district.

cir•cu•i•tous (sər kyōō′i təs), *adj.* roundabout; not direct. —**cir•cu′i•tous•ly,** *adv.* —**cir•cu′i•tous•ness,** **cir•cu′i•ty,** *n.*

cir′cuit•ry, *n.* the components of an electric circuit.

cir′cu•lar (-kyə lər), *adj.* **1.** having the form of a circle; round. **2.** moving in or forming a circle. **3.** circuitous; indirect. —*n.* **4.** a letter or advertisement for general circulation. —**cir′cu•lar′i•ty,** *n.*

cir′cu•late′ (-lāt′), *v.,* **-lat•ed, -lat•ing.** —*v.i.* **1.** to move in a circle or circuit. **2.** to pass from place to place, from person to person, etc. —*v.t.* **3.** to disseminate; distribute. —**cir′cu•la•to′ry** (-lə tôr′ē), *adj.*

cir′cu•la′tion, *n.* **1.** an act or instance of circulating. **2.** the continuous movement of blood through the heart and blood vessels. **3.** the distribution of copies of a periodical among readers.

cir′culatory sys′tem, *n.* the system of organs and tissues involved in circulating blood and lymph through the body.

circum-, a prefix meaning around or about (*circumnavigate*).

cir•cum•cise (sûr′kəm sīz′), *v.t.,* **-cised, -cis•ing.** to remove the prepuce of (a male), esp. as a religious rite. —**cir•cum•ci′sion** (-sizh′ən), *n.*

cir•cum•fer•ence (sər kum′fər əns), *n.* **1.** the outer boundary of a circular area. **2.** the length of such a boundary.

cir′cum•flex (sûr′kəm fleks′), *n.* a mark (^, % ˜, or ¯) placed over a vowel to indicate length, nasalization, etc.

cir′cum•lo•cu′tion (-lō kyōō′shən), *n.* a roundabout or indirect way of speaking.

cir′cum•nav′i•gate′, *v.t.,* **-gat•ed, -gat•ing.** to sail or fly completely around. —**cir′cum•nav′i•ga′tion,** *n.*

cir′cum•scribe′ (-skrīb′), *v.t.,* **-scribed, -scrib•ing. 1.** to draw or trace a line around; encircle. **2.** to enclose within bounds; restrict. —**cir′cum•scrip′tion** (-skrip′shən), *n.*

cir′cum•spect′ (-spekt′), *adj.* cautious; prudent. —**cir′cum•spec′tion,** *n.*

cir′cum•stance′ (-stans′), *n.* **1.** a condition or attribute that accompanies or determines a fact or event. **2.** Usu., **circumstances.** the existing conditions or state of affairs. **3. circumstances,** the condition of a person with respect to material welfare: *a family in reduced circumstances.* **4.** an incident or occurrence. **5.** ceremonious display: *pomp and circumstance.* —**Idiom. 6. under no circumstances,** never.

cir′cum•stan′tial (-stan′shəl), *adj.* **1.** of or derived from circumstances. **2.** incidental. **3.** detailed; particular. —**cir′cum•stan′tial•ly,** *adv.*

cir′cumstan′tial ev′idence, *n.* proof of facts offered as evidence from which other facts are to be inferred.

cir′cum•vent′ (-vent′), *v.t.* to avoid by artfulness; elude. —**cir′cum•ven′tion,** *n.*

cir•cus (sûr′kəs), *n., pl.* **-cus•es. 1.** an entertainment featuring performing animals, clowns, acrobats, etc. **2.** (in ancient Rome) an amphitheater for chariot races, public games, etc. **3.** a display of rowdy sport or wild activity.

cir•rho•sis (si rō′sis), *n.* a chronic disease of the liver in which fibrous tissue replaces normal tissue.

cir•rus (sir′əs), *n., pl.* **cir•ri** (sir′ī). a high-altitude cloud composed of ice crystals and characterized by thin white bands.

C.I.S., Commonwealth of Independent States.

cis•tern (sis′tərn), *n.* a reservoir or tank for storing water.

cit•a•del (sit′ə dl, -ə del′), *n.* a fortress for defending a city.

cite (sīt), *v.t.,* **cit•ed, cit•ing. 1.** to quote (a book, author, etc.), esp. as an authority. **2.** to mention in support or proof. **3.** to summon to appear in court. **4.** to commend, as for outstanding service. —**ci•ta′tion,** *n.*

Cit′ies of Ref′uge, *n.pl.* six cities, three on each side of the Jordan River, reserved under Mosaic law to be a refuge for persons who committed accidental homicide. Josh. 20:2–9.

Cit′ies of the Plain′, *n.pl.* Sodom and Gomorrah. Gen. 14:2.

cit•i•fied (sit′i fīd′), *adj.* having city habits, fashions, etc.

cit•i•zen (sit′ə zən, -sən), *n.* a native or naturalized member of a state or nation who owes allegiance to its government and is entitled to its protection. —**cit′i•zen•ship′,** *n.*

cit′i•zen•ry, *n., pl.* **-ries.** citizens collectively.

cit′ric ac′id (si′trik), *n.* a white powder occurring in citrus fruits, used chiefly in flavorings.

cit•ron (si′trən), *n.* **1.** a pale yellow fruit resembling the lemon but larger. **2.** the candied rind of this fruit.

cit•ron•el•la (si′trə nel′ə), *n.* **1.** a fragrant, S Asian grass. **2.** a pungent oil distilled from this grass, used in perfumes and insect repellents.

cit•rus (si′trəs), *n., pl.* **-rus•es,** *adj.* —*n.* **1.** any tree or shrub of the genus that includes the lemon, lime, orange, etc. **2.** the fruit of any of these trees or shrubs. —*adj.* **3.** Also, **cit′rous.** of such trees or shrubs.

cit•y (sit′ē), *n., pl.* **-cit•ies. 1.** a large or important town. **2.** an incorporated municipality, usu. governed by a mayor and council. **3.** the inhabitants of a city collectively. [< AF, OF *cite(t)* < L *cīvitātem,* acc. of *cīvitās* citizenry]

cit′y hall′, *n.* the administration building of a city government.

Cit′y of Broth′erly Love′, *n.* Philadelphia, Pa. (used as a nickname).

Cit′y of God′, *n.* the New Jerusalem; heaven.

Cit′y of the Lord′, *n.* Jerusalem. Also called **Cit′y of the Lord′ of Hosts′.**

cit′y on a hill′, *n.* an ideal of civic virtue. Matt. 5:14.

civ•et (siv′it), *n.* **1.** a catlike carnivore of the Orient or Africa. **2.** a musky secretion of civets, used in perfumery.

civ•ic (siv′ik), *adj.* of a city, citizenship, or citizens.

civ′ics, *n.* the study of civic affairs and the privileges and obligations of citizens.

civ′il (-əl), *adj.* **1.** of citizens. **2.** of the ordinary life of citizens, as distinguished from military and ecclesiastical life. **3.** civilized. **4.** polite. —**civ′il•ly,** *adv.*

civ′il disobe′dience, *n.* the refusal to obey certain governmental laws or demands in order to influence legislation or policy, characterized by such nonviolent methods as nonpayment of taxes and boycotting.

civ′il engineer′ing, *n.* the design, construction, and maintenance of public works, as roads and bridges. —**civ′il engineer′,** *n.*

ci•vil•ian (si vil′yən), *n.* **1.** a person not on active duty with a military, police, or firefighting organization. —*adj.* **2.** of civilians.

civil′ian review′, *n.* a group appointed to hear complaints made against the police.

ci•vil′i•ty (-i tē), *n., pl.* **-ties. 1.** courtesy; politeness. **2.** a polite action.

civ•i•li•za•tion (siv′ə lə zā′shən), *n.* **1.** an advanced state of human society, in which a high level of culture, science, and government has been reached. **2.** those people or nations that have reached such a state. **3.** the type of culture of a specific place, time, or group.

civ′i•lize′, *v.t.,* **-lized, -liz•ing.** to bring out of a savage, uneducated state; enlighten or refine. —**civ′i•lized′,** *adj.*

civ′il law′, *n.* the body of laws regulating private, as distinct from criminal, actions.

civ′il lib′erty, *n.* **1.** Often, **civil liberties.** a fundamental right, as freedom of speech, guaranteed to an individual by the laws of a country. **2.** the liberty of an individual to exercise such a right without unwarranted government interference. —**civ′il libertar′ian,** *n.*

civ′il rights′, *n.pl.* (*often caps.*) rights to personal liberty, esp. as established by the 13th and 14th Amendments to the U.S. Constitution and certain Congressional acts. —**civ′il-rights′,** *adj.*

civ′il serv′ant, *n.* a civil-service employee.

civ′il serv′ice, *n.* those branches of public service concerned with governmental administrative functions outside the armed services.

civ′il war′, *n.* **1.** a war between factions in the same country. **2.** (*caps.*) the war in the U.S. between the North and South, 1861–65.

civ•vies (siv′ēz), *n.pl. Informal.* civilian clothes.

ck., check.

Cl, *Chem. Symbol.* chlorine.

clack (klak), *v.i., v.t.* **1.** to make or cause to make a quick, sharp sound. —*n.* **2.** a clacking sound.

clad (klad), *v.* **1.** a pt. and pp. of CLOTHE. —*adj.* (usu. used in combination) **2.** dressed: *ill-clad vagrants.* **3.** bonded with a protective metallic coat: *copper-clad cookware.*

claim (klām), *v.t.* **1.** to demand as a right. **2.** to assert as a fact. **3.** to require as due or fitting. —*n.* **4.** a demand for something as due. **5.** an assertion of something as a fact. **6.** a right to claim or demand. **7.** something that is claimed. —**claim′a•ble,** *adj.* —**claim′ant, claim′er,** *n.*

clair•voy•ance (klâr voi′əns), *n.* the paranormal power of perceiving objects or actions beyond the range of the senses. —**clair•voy′ant,** *adj.*

clam (klam), *n., v.* **1.** any of various usu. edible bivalve mollusks. —*v.i.* **2.** to dig for clams. **3. clam up,** *Informal.* to refuse to talk.

clam′bake′, *n.* a seaside picnic at which clams and other seafood are baked.

clam•ber (klam′bər, klam′ər), *v.t., v.i.* to climb with difficulty, using both feet and hands.

clam•my (klam′ē), *adj.,* **-mi•er, -mi•est.** cold and damp. —**clam′mi•ness,** *n.*

clam•or (klam′ər), *n.* **1.** a loud uproar, as from a crowd of people. **2.** a vehement expression of desire or dissatisfaction. —*v.i.* **3.** to make a clamor. —**clam′or•ous,** *adj.*

clamp (klamp), *n.* **1.** a device for holding or fastening objects together. —*v.t.* **2.** to fasten with a clamp. **3. clamp down,** to impose more strict control.

clan (klan), *n.* **1.** a group of families, as among the Scottish Highlanders, whose heads claim descent from a common ancestor. **2.** a group of people of common descent. —**clan′nish,** *adj.* —**clan′nish•ness,** *n.*

clan•des•tine (klan des′tin), *adj.* stealthy or surreptitious. —**clan•des′tine•ly,** *adv.*

clang (klang), *v.i., v.t.* **1.** to make or cause to make a loud, resonant sound, as that produced by a large bell. —*n.* **2.** a clanging sound.

clang•or (klang′ər, klang′gər), *n.* a loud, resonant sound. —**clang′or•ous,** *adj.*

clank (klangk), *n.* **1.** a sharp, hard, nonresonant sound. —*v.i., v.t.* **2.** to make or cause to make such a sound.

clap (klap), *v.,* **clapped, clap•ping,** *n.* —*v.t.* **1.** to strike (one's hands) together, as in applauding. **2.** to strike with a light slap, as in greeting. **3.** to strike with an abrupt, sharp sound. **4.** to put or place quickly or forcefully. —*v.i.* **5.** to applaud. **6.** to make an abrupt, sharp sound. —*n.* **7.** the act or sound of clapping. **8.** a resounding slap. **9.** a loud and explosive noise.

clap•board (klab′ərd, klap′bôrd′), *n.* **1.** a thin board, thicker along one edge than the other, used in covering the outer walls of buildings. —*v.t.* **2.** to cover with clapboards.

clap•per (klap′ər), *n.* **1.** a person who applauds. **2.** the tongue of a bell.

clap′trap′, *n.* pretentious and insincere language intended to win applause.

claque (klak), *n.* a group of persons hired to applaud an act or performer.

clar•et (klar′it), *n.* a dry red table wine.

clar•i•fy (klar′ə fī′), *v.t., v.i.,* **-fied, -fy•ing.** to make or become clear or intelligible. —**clar′i•fi•ca′- tion,** *n.*

clar•i•net (klar′ə net′), *n.* a single-reed woodwind instrument in the form of a cylindrical tube. —**clar′i• net′ist,** **clar′i•net′tist,** *n.*

clar′i•on (-ē ən), *adj.* clear and shrill: *the trumpet's clarion call.*

clar′i•ty (-i tē), *n.* the state or quality of being clear.

Clark (klärk), *n.* **William,** 1770–1838, U.S. explorer: on expedition with Meriwether Lewis.

clash (klash), *v.i.* **1.** to collide with a loud, harsh noise. **2.** to conflict; disagree. —*v.t.* **3.** to strike with a loud, harsh noise. —*n.* **4.** a loud, harsh noise. **5.** a conflict, esp. of views or interests. **6.** a battle or fight.

clasp (klasp, kläsp), *n.* **1.** a device for fastening things or parts together. **2.** a firm grasp or grip. **3.** a tight embrace. —*v.t.* **4.** to fasten with a clasp. **5.** to grasp with the hand. **6.** to hold in a tight embrace.

class (klas, kläs), *n.* **1.** a number of persons or things regarded as belonging together because of common attributes or traits. **2. a.** a group of students studying together with a teacher. **b.** a meeting of such a group. **3.** a group of students graduated in the same year. **4.** a social stratum whose members share the same social position. **5.** any division of persons or things according to rank or grade. **6.** *Informal.* elegance, as in dress and behavior. **7.** any of several grades of passenger accommodations. —*v.t.* **8.** to classify. —**class′less,** *adj.*

class′ ac′tion, *n.* a legal proceeding brought by one or more persons representing the interests of a larger group.

clas•sic (klas′ik), *adj.* **1.** of the highest class or rank. **2.** serving as a standard or model. **3.** CLASSICAL (defs. 1, 2). **4.** of enduring interest, quality, or style. **5.** traditional or typical: *a classic comedy routine.* —*n.* **6.** an author or a literary work of the first rank. **7. the classics,** the literature of ancient Greece and Rome. **8.** a typical or traditional event.

clas•si•cal, *adj.* **1.** of or characteristic of ancient Greece and Rome. **2.** conforming to ancient Greek and Roman models in literature or art. **3.** of or being music of the European tradition marked by sophistication of structural elements. **4.** versed in the ancient classics: *a classical scholar.* **5.** accepted as standard and authoritative: *classical physics.* —**clas′si•cal•ly,** *adv.*

clas′si•cism (-siz′əm), *n.* **1.** the principles of ancient Greek and Roman literature and art. **2.** adherence to such principles. **3.** classical scholarship or learning. —**clas′si•cist,** *n.*

clas′sified ad′, *n.* a brief printed advertisement offering or requesting a job, house, etc. —**clas′sified ad′vertising,** *n.*

clas•si•fy (klas′ə fī′), *v.t.,* **-fied, -fy•ing.** **1.** to arrange or organize in classes. **2.** to limit the availability of (information, a document, etc.) to authorized persons. —**clas′si•fi′a•ble,** *adj.* —**clas′si•fi•ca′tion,** *n.*

clas•sis (klas′is), *n., pl.* **clas•ses** (klas′ēz). (in certain Reformed churches) **1.** the organization that

governs a group of local churches. **2.** the group of churches so governed.

class′mate′, *n.* a member of the same class at a school or college.

class′room′, *n.* a room in a school in which classes are held.

class′y, *adj.,* **-i•er, -i•est.** *Informal.* stylish; elegant. —**class′i•ness,** *n.*

clat•ter (klat′ər), *v.i., v.t.* **1.** to make or cause to make a loud, rattling sound. —*n.* **2.** a clattering sound. **3.** a noisy disturbance; din.

clause (klôz), *n.* **1.** a syntactic construction containing a subject and predicate. **2.** a distinct article or provision in a document. —**claus′al,** *adj.*

claus•tro•pho•bi•a (klô′strə fō′bē ə), *n.* an abnormal fear of being in enclosed or narrow places. —**claus′tro•pho′bic,** *adj.*

clav•i•chord (klav′i kôrd′), *n.* an early keyboard instrument whose strings are struck by metal blades.

clav•i•cle (klav′i kəl), *n.* either of two slender bones that connect the sternum and the scapula.

cla•vier (klə vēr′, klav′ē ər, klā′vē-), *n.* **1.** the keyboard of a musical instrument. **2.** a keyboard instrument with strings, as a harpsichord.

claw (klô), *n.* **1.** a sharp, curved nail on the foot of an animal. **2.** a pincerlike appendage of a lobster, crab, etc. —*v.t.* **3.** to tear, scratch, etc., with or as if with claws.

Clay (klā), *n.* **1. Cassius Marcellus, Jr.,** original name of Muhammad ALI. **2. Henry,** 1777–1852, U.S. statesman and orator.

Clay′ton Antitrust′ Act′, *n.* an act of Congress in 1914 supplementing the Sherman Antitrust Act and establishing the FTC.

clean (klēn), *adj.* and *adv.,* **-er, -est,** *v.* —*adj.* **1.** free from dirt or stains. **2.** free from foreign matter or pollutants. **3.** free from irregularity: *a clean cut.* **4.** trim: *the clean lines of a ship.* **5.** complete: *a clean break with tradition.* **6.** morally pure. **7.** fair: *a clean fight.* **8.** made without difficulty or interference: *a clean getaway.* **9.** habitually clean or neat. **10.** empty; bare: *a clean sheet of paper.* —*adv.* **11.** in a clean manner. **12.** wholly; completely. —*v.t., v.i.* **13.** to make or become clean. **14. clean up, a.** to tidy up. **b.** to finish. **c.** to make a large profit. —**Idiom. 15. come clean,** *Slang.* to admit one's guilt. —**clean′a•ble,** *adj.* —**clean′ness,** *n.*

clean′-cut′, *adj.* **1.** having a distinct, regular shape. **2.** clearly outlined. **3.** neat and wholesome.

clean′er, *n.* **1.** one that cleans. **2.** Usu., **-ers.** a dry-cleaning establishment.

clean•li•ness (klen′lē nis), *n.* **1.** the quality or state of being cleanly. —**Proverb. 2. Cleanliness is next to godliness,** only religious devotion is more important than being personally and habitually neat.

clean•ly (*adj.* klen′lē; *adv.* klēn′-), *adj.,* **-li•er, -li• est,** *adv.* —*adj.* **1.** habitually clean or neat. —*adv.* **2.** in a clean manner.

clean′ room′, *n.* a room in which contaminants in the air are reduced to create a nearly sterile environment for biological or manufacturing procedures.

cleanse (klenz), *v.t.,* **cleansed, cleans•ing.** to clean or purify. —**cleans′er,** *n.*

clean′up′, *n.* the act or process of cleaning up.

clear (klēr), *adj.* and *adv.,* **-er, -est,** *v.* —*adj.* **1.** free from darkness or cloudiness. **2.** transparent: *clear water.* **3.** easily seen; sharply defined. **4.** easily heard. **5.** easily understood. **6.** evident; plain. **7.** free from confusion. **8.** free from blame or guilt: *a clear conscience.* **9.** free from obstructions. **10.** free from entanglement or contact. **11.** without limitation or qualification. **12.** free from debt. **13.** net: *a clear profit of $1000.* —*adv.* **14.** in a clear manner. **15.** entirely; completely. —*v.t.* **16.** to remove (people or things) from (a place or surface): *Please clear the table.* **17.** to make clear or transparent. **18.** to make free of confusion or doubt. **19.** to make understandable. **20.** to make (a path) by removing obstructions. **21.** to relieve (the throat) of phlegm. **22.** to free from suspicion or accusation. **23.** to pass by or over without contact or entanglement: *The ship cleared the* *reef.* **24.** to pass (commercial paper) through a clearinghouse. **25.** to gain as profit. **26.** to receive authorization for. **27.** to authorize. —*v.i.* **28.** to become clear. **29. clear away,** to leave. **30.** ~ **out, a.** to remove the contents of. **b.** to go away, esp. quickly. **31.** ~ **up,** to make clear; explain. —**clear′ly,** *adv.* —**clear′ness,** *n.*

clear′ance, *n.* **1.** the act of clearing. **2.** the distance between two objects; an amount of clear space. **3.** a formal authorization permitting access to classified material.

clear′-cut′, *adj.* **1.** having clearly defined outlines. **2.** completely evident; definite.

clear′ing, *n.* a tract of land, as in a forest, that contains no trees or bushes.

clear′ing•house′, *n.* an institution where mutual claims and accounts are settled, as between banks.

cleat (klēt), *n.* a piece of wood, metal, etc., fastened to a surface to serve as a support or to give a foothold.

cleav•age (klē′vij), *n.* **1.** the act of splitting or state of being cleft. **2.** a split or division.

cleave¹ (klēv), *v.i.,* **cleaved, cleav•ing. 1.** to adhere closely; cling (usu. fol. by *to*). **2.** to remain faithful: *to cleave to one's principles.*

cleave² (klēv), *v.t., v.i.,* **cleft** or **cleaved** or **clove, cleft** or **cleaved** or **clo•ven, cleav•ing.** to split or divide by or as if by a cutting blow.

cleav′er, *n.* a heavy knife or long-bladed hatchet, esp. one used by butchers.

clef (klef), *n.* a sign at the beginning of a musical staff to show the pitch of the notes.

cleft¹ (kleft), *n.* a space or opening made by cleavage; a split.

cleft² (kleft), *v.* **1.** a pt. and pp. of CLEAVE². —*adj.* **2.** split; divided.

cleft′ lip′, *n.* a congenital defect in which there is a vertical fissure in the upper lip.

cleft′ pal′ate, *n.* a congenital defect of the palate in which a longitudinal fissure exists in the roof of the mouth.

clem•a•tis (klem′ə tis, kli mat′is), *n.* a vine of the buttercup family having showy flowers.

Clem•ens (klem′ənz), *n.* **Samuel Langhorne,** ("*Mark Twain*"), 1835–1910, U.S. author and humorist.

clem•ent (klem′ənt), *adj.* **1.** lenient; compassionate. **2.** (of the weather) mild or temperate. —**clem′en•cy,** *n., pl.* -**cies.** —**clem′ent•ly,** *adv.*

Clem′ent of Alexan′dria, *n.* (*Titus Flavius Clemens*) A.D. c150–c215, Greek Christian theologian and writer.

clench (klench), *v.t.* **1.** to close (the hands, teeth, etc.) tightly. **2.** to grasp firmly. —*n.* **3.** a tight hold; grip.

Cle•o•pas (klē′ə pas′), *n.* one of two disciples who met the resurrected Jesus on the road to Emmaus. Luke 24:13–35.

Cle•o•pa•tra (klē′ə pa′trə, -pä′-, -pā′-), *n.* 69–30 B.C., queen of Egypt 51–49, 48–30.

clere•sto•ry (klēr′stôr′ē), *n., pl.* -**ries.** a portion of an interior rising above adjacent rooftops and having windows.

cler•gy (klûr′jē), *n., pl.* -**gies.** the body of ordained persons in a religion.

cler′gy•man or -**wom′an,** *n., pl.* -**men** or -**wom• en.** a member of the clergy.

cler•ic (kler′ik), *n.* a member of the clergy.

cler′i•cal, *adj.* **1.** of or pertaining to an office clerk. **2.** of or characteristic of the clergy or a cleric.

cler′i•cal•ism, *n.* power or influence of the clergy in government, politics, etc.

clerk (klûrk), *n.* **1.** a person employed to perform general office tasks. **2.** a salesclerk. **3.** a person who keeps the records of a court, legislature, etc. —*v.i.* **4.** to serve as a clerk. —**clerk′ship,** *n.*

Cleve•land (klēv′lənd), *n.* **1. (Stephen) Grover,** 1837–1908, 22nd and 24th president of the U.S. 1885–89, 1893–97. **2.** a port in NE Ohio. 492,901.

clev•er (klev′ər), *adj.,* -**er•er, -er•est. 1.** mentally

bright. **2.** superficially skillful or witty; facile. **3.** ingenious. —**clev′er•ly,** *adv.* —**clev′er•ness,** *n.*

clev•is (klev′is), *n.* a U-shaped yoke at the end of a chain or rod, between the ends of which a lever, hook, etc., can be pinned or bolted.

clew (klōō), *n.* **1.** either lower corner of a square sail. **2.** a ball or skein of thread, yarn, etc.

cli•ché (klē shā′, kli-), *n., pl.* -**chés.** a trite, stereotyped expression. —**cli•chéd′,** *adj.*

click (klik), *n.* **1.** a slight, sharp sound: *the click of a latch.* —*v.i.* **2.** to make a click or series of clicks. **3.** *Informal.* **a.** to succeed. **b.** to function well together. **4.** *Computers.* to depress and release a mouse button rapidly, as to select an icon. —*v.t.* **5.** to cause to click.

cli•ent (klī′ənt), *n.* **1.** a person who uses the professional services of a lawyer, accountant, etc. **2.** a person receiving the benefits or services of a social or government agency. **3.** a customer.

cli•en•tele′ (-ən tel′), *n.* a body of clients and customers.

cliff (klif), *n.* a high, steep rock face; precipice.

cliff′ dwell′er, *n.* (*usu. caps.*) a member of a prehistoric people of the southwestern U.S. who were ancestors of the Pueblo Indians and built shelters in caves or on the ledges of cliffs.

cliff′-hang′er or **cliff′hang′er,** *n.* **1.** a melodramatic adventure serial in which each installment ends in suspense. **2.** a suspenseful situation or contest.

cli•mac•ter•ic (klī mak′tər ik, klī′mak ter′ik), *n.* **1.** a period of decreasing reproductive capacity, culminating, in women, in the menopause. **2.** any critical period.

cli•mate (klī′mit), *n.* **1.** the prevailing weather conditions of a region. **2.** a region characterized by a given climate. **3.** a prevailing attitude, atmosphere, or condition. —**cli•mat′ic** (-mat′ik), *adj.*

cli•ma•tol•o•gy (klī′mə tol′ə jē), *n.* the science that deals with climatic conditions. —**cli′ma•tol′o• gist,** *n.*

cli•max (klī′maks), *n.* **1.** the highest or most intense point in the development of something. **2.** a decisive moment in the plot of a dramatic or literary work. **3.** an orgasm. —*v.t., v.i.* **4.** to bring to or reach a climax. —**cli•mac′tic,** *adj.*

climb (klīm), *v.i.* **1.** to move upward or toward the top of something. **2.** to slope upward. **3.** to ascend by twining, as a plant. **4.** to move by using the hands and feet. —*v.t.* **5.** to ascend or get to the top of, esp. by the use of the hands and feet. —*n.* **6.** an act or instance of climbing. **7.** a place to be climbed. —**climb′a•ble,** *adj.* —**climb′er,** *n.*

clime (klīm), *n.* CLIMATE.

clinch (klinch), *v.t.* **1.** to settle (a matter) decisively. **2.** to secure (a nail, screw, etc.) in position by beating down the protruding point. —*v.i.* **3.** to engage in a clinch in boxing. **4.** *Slang.* to embrace passionately. —*n.* **5.** the act of clinching. **6.** an act or instance of a boxer holding an opponent about the arms to prevent punching. **7.** *Slang.* a passionate embrace.

clinch′er, *n.* **1.** one that clinches. **2.** a decisive fact, argument, etc.

cling (kling), *v.i.,* **clung, cling•ing. 1.** to adhere closely. **2.** to hold tight, as by embracing. **3.** to remain attached, as to an idea. —**cling′er,** *n.*

clin•ic (klin′ik), *n.* **1.** a place for the medical treatment of outpatients. **2.** a place where physicians, dentists, etc., practice together. **3.** a group convening for instruction or remedial work: *a reading clinic.* **4.** the instruction of medical students by treating patients in their presence. [≪ L *clīnicus* < Gk *klīnikós* pertaining to a sickbed]

clin′i•cal, *adj.* **1.** pertaining to a clinic. **2.** concerned with actual treatment of patients rather than experimentation or theory. **3.** dispassionately analytic. —**clin′i•cal•ly,** *adv.*

cli•ni•cian (kli nish′ən), *n.* a physician, psychologist, etc., who is involved in the treatment of patients.

clink¹ (klingk), *v.i., v.t.* **1.** to make or cause to make a light, sharp, ringing sound. —*n.* **2.** a clinking sound.

clink² (klingk), *n. Slang.* a jail.

clink′er¹, *n.* **1.** a mass of incombustible matter fused together, as in the burning of coal. **2.** a hard Dutch brick.

clink′er², *n. Slang.* a mistake or error.

Clin•ton (klin′tn), *n.* **1. De Witt** 1769–1828, U.S. statesman. **2. George,** 1739–1812, vice president of the U.S. 1805–12. **3. William Jefferson** (*Bill*), born 1946, 42nd president of the U.S. since 1993.

cli•o•met•rics (klē′ō me′triks, klī′ō-), *n.* the study of historical data by the use of statistical techniques. —**cli′o•met′ric,** *adj.* —**cli′o•met′ri•cal•ly,** *adv.* —**cli′o•me•tri′cian** (-mi trish′ən), *n.*

clip¹ (klip), *v.,* **clipped, clip•ping.** —*v.t.* **1.** to cut, cut off, or trim, as with shears. **2.** to cut the hair or fleece of; shear. **3.** to cut short. **4.** *Informal.* to hit with a quick, sharp blow. **5.** *Slang.* to swindle. —*v.i.* **6.** to clip something. **7.** to move swiftly. —*n.* **8.** the act of clipping. **9.** anything clipped off. **10.** *Informal.* a quick, sharp blow. **11.** rate; pace: *at a rapid clip.*

clip² (klip), *n.,* *v.,* **clipped, clip•ping.** —*n.* **1.** a device that grips and holds tightly. —*v.t.,* *v.i.* **2.** to fasten with or as if with a clip.

clip′board′, *n.* a writing board with a clip at the top for holding papers.

clip′ joint′, *n. Slang.* a business, esp. a place of entertainment, that overcharges customers.

clipped′ form′, *n.* a shortened form of a word, as *deli* for *delicatessen.*

clip′per, *n.* **1.** Often, **-pers.** a cutting tool, esp. shears. **2.** a swift sailing ship, esp. a three-masted one.

clip′ping, *n.* an item clipped from a newspaper or magazine.

clique (klēk, klik), *n.* a small, exclusive group of people. —**cli′quish,** *adj.* —**cli′quish•ly,** *adv.* —**cli′quish•ness,** *n.*

clit•o•ris (klit′ər is), *n.,* *pl.* **clit•o•ris•es, cli•to•ri•des** (kli tôr′i dēz′). the erectile organ of the vulva. —**clit′o•ral,** *adj.*

Clive (klīv), *n.* **Robert** (*Baron Clive of Plassey*), 1725–74, British general and statesman in India.

cloak (klōk), *n.* **1.** a loose outer garment, as a cape or coat. **2.** a disguise; pretense. —*v.t.* **3.** to cover with a cloak. **4.** to hide; conceal.

cloak′-and-dag′ger, *adj.* pertaining to espionage or intrigue.

clob•ber (klob′ər), *v.t. Informal.* **1.** to batter severely. **2.** to defeat decisively.

cloche (klōsh, klôsh), *n.* a woman's close-fitting, bell-shaped hat.

clock¹ (klok), *n.* **1.** an instrument, normally larger than a watch, for measuring and recording time. —*v.t.* **2.** to time with a stopwatch.

clock² (klok), *n.* an embroidered or woven design on the side of a sock or stocking.

clock′wise′, *adv.* **1.** in the direction of the rotation of the hands of a clock. —*adj.* **2.** directed clockwise.

clock′work′, *n.* **1.** the mechanism of a clock. —*Idiom.* **2.** like clockwork, with perfect regularity.

clod (klod), *n.* **1.** a lump, esp. of earth or clay. **2.** a stupid person. —**clod′dish,** *adj.*

clod′hop′per, *n.* **1.** a clumsy boor. **2. clodhoppers,** heavy shoes.

clog (klog, klôg), *v.,* **clogged, clog•ging,** *n.* —*v.t.* **1.** to hinder or obstruct. —*v.i.* **2.** to become clogged. —*n.* **3.** anything that impedes movement. **4.** a shoe with a thick sole of wood, cork, etc.

cloi•son•né (kloi′zə nā′), *n.* enamelwork in which colored areas are separated by thin metal bands.

clois•ter (kloi′stər), *n.* **1.** a covered walk having an open arcade and opening onto a courtyard. **2.** a place of religious seclusion, as a monastery or convent. —*v.t.* **3.** to confine, as in a cloister.

clone (klōn), *n.,* *v.,* **cloned, clon•ing.** —*n.* **1. a.** an organism that is genetically identical to the individual from which it was asexually derived. **b.** a group of such organisms. **2.** a person or thing that closely re-

sembles another in appearance, function, etc. —*v.i.,* *v.t.* **3.** to grow or cause to grow as a clone.

clop (klop), *n.,* *v.,* **clopped, clop•ping.** —*n.* **1.** a sound made by or as if by a horse's hoof. —*v.i.* **2.** to make or move with such a sound.

close (*v.,* *n.* klōz; *adj.,* *adv.* klōs), *v.,* **closed, clos•ing,** *adj.,* **clos•er, clos•est,** *adv.,* *n.* —*v.t.* **1.** to block or bar an opening in or passage through; shut. **2.** to stop or obstruct (a gap, aperture, etc.). **3.** to bring together; join: *Close up ranks!* **4.** to bring to an end. —*v.i.* **5.** to become closed. **6.** to unite. **7.** to come to an end. **8.** to reach an agreement. **9. close down,** to terminate the operation of. **10. ~ in on,** to approach stealthily, as to capture. **11. ~ out, a.** to reduce the price of (merchandise) for quick sale. **b.** to liquidate. —*adj.* **12.** compact; dense. **13.** being in or having proximity in space or time. **14.** similar in degree, action, etc.: *Dark pink is close to red.* **15.** near in kind or relationship: *a close relative.* **16.** intimate; dear. **17.** left flush with the surface or very short. **18.** strict; minute: *close investigation.* **19.** not deviating from a model. **20.** nearly even or equal: *a close contest.* **21.** without opening. **22.** confined; narrow. **23.** stuffy. **24.** secretive; reticent. **25.** parsimonious; stingy. **26.** scarce, as money. —*adv.* **27.** in a close manner. **28.** near; close by. —*n.* **29.** the act of closing. **30.** the end or conclusion. —**close′ly** (klōs′-), *adv.* —**close′ness** (klōs′-), *n.*

close′ call′ (klōs), *n.* a narrow escape from danger.

closed′-cap′tioned, *adj.* (of a television program) broadcast with captions visible only with the use of a decoding device.

closed′-cir′cuit tel′evision, *n.* a system of televising by cable to designated viewing sets.

closed′ shop′, *n.* a business establishment in which union membership is a condition of employment.

close′fist′ed (klōs′-), *adj.* stingy; miserly.

close′-fit′ting, *adj.* (of a garment) fitting snugly to the body.

close′-knit′, *adj.* tightly united or connected.

close′mouthed′, *adj.* reticent; uncommunicative.

close′out′ (klōz′-), *n.* a sale on merchandise at greatly reduced prices.

clos•et (kloz′it), *n.* **1.** a small room or cabinet for storing clothing, utensils, etc. —*v.t.* **2.** to shut up in a private room for a conference, interview, etc.

close′up′ (klōs′-), *n.* **1.** a photograph taken at close range. **2.** an intimate view of anything.

clo•sure (klō′zhər), *n.* **1.** the act of closing or state of being closed. **2.** a conclusion or end. **3.** something that closes. **4.** CLOTURE.

cloister

clot (klot), *n.,* *v.,* **clot•ted, clot•ting.** —*n.* **1.** a semisolid mass, as of coagulated blood. —*v.i.,* *v.t.* **2.** to form into clots.

cloth (klôth, kloth), *n.,* *pl.* **cloths** (klôthz, klothz, klŏths, kloths), *adj.* —*n.* **1.** a fabric made by weaving, felting, or knitting and used for garments, upholstery, etc. **2.** a piece of such a fabric for a particular purpose: *an altar cloth.* **3. the cloth,** the clergy. —*adj.* **4.** made of cloth.

clothe (klōṯẖ), *v.t.,* **clothed** or **clad, cloth•ing. 1.** to provide with clothing. **2.** to cover.

clothes (klōz, klōṯẖz), *n.pl.* garments for the body.

clothes•line (klōz′līn′, klōṯẖz′-), *n.* a strong cord on which clean laundry is hung to dry, usu. outdoors.

clothes′pin′, *n.* a device for fastening articles to a clothesline.

cloth•ier (klōṯẖ′yər, -ē ər), *n.* a retailer of clothing.

cloth′ing, *n.* **1.** garments collectively. **2.** a covering.

clo•ture (klō′chər), *n.* a closing of legislative debate in order to bring the question to a vote.

cloud (kloud), *n.* **1.** a visible collection of particles of water or ice suspended in the air. **2.** any similar mass, esp. of smoke or dust. **3.** anything that causes gloom, trouble, etc. **4.** a great number of insects, birds, etc., flying together. —*v.t.* **5.** to cover with clouds. **6.** to make gloomy. **7.** to make obscure. **8.** to place under suspicion, disgrace, etc. —*v.i.* **9.** to grow cloudy. —*Idiom.* **10. have one's head in the clouds, a.** to be lost in reverie. **b.** to be impractical. **11. under a cloud,** in disgrace; under suspicion. —*Proverb.* **12. Every cloud has a silver lining,** even misfortune may contain something beneficial. —**cloud′less,** *adj.* —**cloud′y,** *adj.,* **-i•er, -i•est.**

cloud′burst′, *n.* a sudden and very heavy rainfall.

cloud′ nine′, *n. Informal.* a state of perfect happiness.

clout (klout), *n.* **1.** a blow, esp. with the hand. **2.** *Informal.* the ability to influence decisions, esp. those made by public figures. —*v.t.* **3.** to hit or cuff.

clove[1] (klōv), *n.* the dried flower bud of a tropical tree, used whole or ground as a spice.

clove[2] (klōv), *n.* a small section of a bulb, as of garlic.

clove[3] (klōv), *v.* a pt. of CLEAVE[2].

clo′ven (klō′vən), *v.* **1.** a pp. of CLEAVE[2]. —*adj.* **2.** cleft; split.

clo•ver (klō′vər), *n.* any of various plants with leaves of three leaflets and dense flower heads.

clo′ver•leaf′, *n., pl.* **-leafs, -leaves.** a road arrangement for permitting traffic movement between two intersecting high-speed highways.

clown (kloun), *n.* **1.** a comic performer, esp. in a circus, who entertains by pantomime, tumbling, etc. **2.** a prankster. **3.** a boor or fool. —*v.i.* **4.** to act like a clown. [perh. akin to ON *klunni* boor] —**clown′ish,** *adj.* —**clown′ish•ly,** *adv.* —**clown′ish•ness,** *n.*

cloy (kloi), *v.t., v.i.* to weary by excess, as of sweetness.

club (klub), *n., v.,* **clubbed, club•bing.** —*n.* **1.** a heavy stick, suitable for use as a weapon. **2.** a stick used in various games, as golf. **3. a.** a group of people organized for a social, literary, or other purpose. **b.** its meeting place. **4.** any of a suit of playing cards bearing black trefoil-shaped figures. —*v.t., v.i.* **5.** to beat with or as if with a club. **6.** to unite; join together.

club′foot′, *n., pl.* **-feet.** a congenitally deformed foot. —**club′foot′ed,** *adj.*

club′house′, *n.* **1.** a building occupied by a club. **2.** the dressing room of an athletic team.

club′ sand′wich, *n.* a sandwich having three slices of bread interlaid with meat, lettuce, tomato, and mayonnaise.

club′ so′da, *n.* SODA WATER.

cluck (kluk), *v.i.* **1.** to utter the cry of a hen brooding or calling her chicks. —*n.* **2.** a clucking sound.

clue (klōō), *n., v.,* **clued, clu•ing.** —*n.* **1.** a guide in the solution of a problem, mystery, etc. —*v.t.* **2.** to direct by a clue.

clump (klump), *n.* **1.** a cluster, esp. of trees or other plants. **2.** a lump or mass. **3.** a heavy, thumping step, sound, etc. —*v.i.* **4.** to walk heavily and clumsily. **5.** to gather or be gathered into clumps. —**clump′y,** *adj.*

clum•sy (klum′zē), *adj.,* **-si•er, -si•est. 1.** awkward in movement or action. **2.** awkwardly done: *a clumsy apology.* —**clum′si•ly,** *adv.* —**clum′si•ness,** *n.*

clung (klung), *v.* pt. and pp. of CLING.

clunk•er (klung′kər), *n. Informal.* an old, worn-out machine, esp. a car.

clunk′y, *adj.,* **-i•er, -i•est.** *Informal.* clumsy or unwieldy.

clus•ter (klus′tər), *n.* **1.** a group of persons or things close together. —*v.t., v.i.* **2.** to gather into or form a cluster.

clus′ter head′ache, *n.* a recurrent headache characterized by attacks of intense pain on one side of the head.

clutch[1] (kluch), *v.t.* **1.** to seize or grasp with or as if with the hands or claws. —*v.i.* **2.** to try to seize or grasp. —*n.* **3.** power or control: *fell into the clutches of the enemy.* **4.** a tight grip. **5.** a mechanism for engaging or disengaging a shaft that drives a mechanism or is driven by another part. **6.** a critical moment.

clutch[2] (kluch), *n.* **1.** a hatch of eggs. **2.** a brood of chickens. **3.** a number of similar things or individuals.

clut•ter (klut′ər), *v.t.* **1.** to fill or litter with things in a disorderly manner. —*n.* **2.** a disorderly heap or assemblage; litter. **3.** echoes on a radar screen that do not come from the target.

Clydes•dale (klīdz′dāl′), *n.* any of a Scottish breed of strong, high-stepping draft horses. [after *Clydesdale,* the valley of the Clyde]

Cm, *Chem. Symbol.* curium.

cm or **cm.,** centimeter.

cni•dar•i•an (nī dâr′ē ən), *n.* any of a phylum of invertebrates with a saclike digestive cavity, including the hydras, jellyfishes, sea anemones, and corals.

CO, 1. Colorado. **2.** Commanding Officer.

Co, *Chem. Symbol.* cobalt.

co-, a prefix meaning: together (*cooperate*); joint or jointly (*coauthor*); equally (*coextensive*).

Co. or **co., 1.** Company. **2.** County.

c/o, care of.

coach (kōch), *n.* **1.** a large, horse-drawn, four-wheeled carriage. **2.** a public motorbus. **3.** the least expensive class of airline accommodations. **4.** a person who trains an athlete or team. **5.** a private tutor. —*v.t.* **6.** to instruct as a coach. —*v.i.* **7.** to work as a coach.

coach′-and-four′, *n.* a coach together with the four horses by which it is drawn.

coach′man, *n., pl.* **-men.** a person employed to drive a coach.

co•ad•ju•tor (kō aj′ə tər, kō′ə jōō′tər), *n.* **1.** an assistant. **2.** a bishop who assists another bishop and has the right of succession.

co•ag•u•late (kō ag′yə lāt′), *v.i., v.t.,* **-lat•ed, -lat•ing.** to change from a fluid into a thickened mass. —**co•ag′u•lant** (-lənt), *n.* —**co•ag′u•la′tion,** *n.* —**co•ag′u•la′tor,** *n.*

coal (kōl), *n.* **1.** a black combustible mineral used as a fuel. **2.** an ember. —*Idiom.* **3. rake** or **haul over the coals,** to reprimand severely.

co•a•lesce (kō′ə les′), *v.i.,* **-lesced, -lesc•ing.** to grow together or unite into one body. —**co′a•les′cence,** *n.* —**co′a•les′cent,** *adj.*

coal′ gas′, *n.* **1.** a gas used for illuminating and heating, produced by distilling bituminous coal. **2.** the gas formed by burning coal.

co/a•li′tion (-lish′ən), *n.* an alliance, esp. a temporary one between factions, parties, etc.

coal′ tar′, *n.* a viscid black liquid obtained by distillation of coal, used in making dyes, drugs, etc.

coarse (kôrs), *adj.,* **coars•er, coars•est. 1.** composed of relatively large parts or particles. **2.** lacking in fineness of texture, structure, etc. **3.** harsh; grating. **4.** lacking refinement; crude. —**coarse′ly,** *adv.* —**coarse′ness,** *n.*

coars′en, *v.t., v.i.* to make or become coarse.

coast (kōst), *n.* **1.** the land next to the sea. **2.** a slide down a hill, as on a sled. —*v.i.* **3.** to descend a hill on acquired momentum. **4.** to progress or move with little or no effort. **—coast′al,** *adj.*

coast′er, *n.* **1.** one that coasts. **2.** a small dish or mat for placing under a glass.

coast′er brake′, *n.* a bicycle brake operated by back pressure on the pedals.

Coast′ Guard′, *n.* a U.S. military service charged with enforcing maritime laws, saving lives and property at sea, etc.

coast′line′, *n.* the contour of a coast.

coat (kōt), *n.* **1.** an outer garment covering at least the upper part of the body. **2.** a natural covering, as hair, fur, or bark. **3.** a layer of anything that covers a surface: *a coat of paint.* **—***v.t.* **4.** to cover or provide with a coat. **—***Idiom.* **5. cut one's coat according to one's cloth,** to adapt to existing conditions.

coat′ of arms′, *n.* a full display of the armorial insignia of a person, family, or corporation, usu. on a shield.

coat′ of man′y col′ors, *n.* the coat that Jacob made for his son Joseph. Gen. 37:3–33.

coat′tail′, *n.* **1.** the back of the skirt on a man's coat or jacket. **—***Idiom.* **2. on someone's coattails,** aided by association with another person.

co•au•thor (kō ô′thər, kō′ô′-), *n.* **1.** one of two or more joint authors. **—***v.t.* **2.** to be a coauthor of.

coax (kōks), *v.t., v.i.* to attempt to influence (a person) by gentle persuasion, flattery, etc. **—coax′er,** *n.* **—coax′ing•ly,** *adv.*

co•ax•i•al (kō ak′sē əl), *adj.* having a common axis or axes.

coax′ial ca′ble, *n.* a cable consisting of an insulated tube through which an insulated conductor runs, used for transmitting high-frequency television or other signals.

cob (kob), *n.* **1.** CORNCOB. **2.** a short-legged, thick-set horse.

co•balt (kō′bôlt), *n.* a hard, ductile element occurring in compounds that provide blue coloring substances. *Symbol:* Co; *at. wt.:* 58.933; *at. no.:* 27.

cob•ble (kob′əl), *v.t.,* **-bled, -bling. 1.** to mend (shoes, boots, etc.). **2.** to put together clumsily.

cob′bler, *n.* **1.** a person who mends shoes. **2.** a deep dish fruit pie with a thick biscuit crust.

cob′ble•stone′, *n.* a naturally rounded stone formerly used in paving.

COBOL (kō′bôl), *n.* a high-level computer language for writing programs to process large files of data. [*co(mmon) b(usiness)-o(riented) l(anguage)*]

co•bra (kō′brə), *n., pl.* **-bras.** a venomous Old World snake able to flatten the neck into a hood.

cob′web′, *n.* **1.** a web spun by a spider. **2.** anything finespun, flimsy, or insubstantial.

co•caine (kō kān′, kō′kān), *n.* a white alkaloid obtained from the leaves of a South American shrub, used as a local anesthetic and illegally as a stimulant.

coc•cus (kok′əs), *n., pl.* **-ci** (-sī, -sē). a spherical bacterium.

coc•cyx (kok′siks), *n., pl.* **coc•cy•ges** (kok sī′jēz, kok′si jēz′). a triangular bone at the lower end of the spinal column; tailbone. **—coc•cyg′e•al** (-sij′ē-əl), *adj.*

coch•le•a (kok′lē ə), *n., pl.* **-le•ae** (-lē ē′, -lē ī′), **-le•as.** the spiral-shaped part of the inner ear in mammals. **—coch′le•ar,** *adj.*

cock¹ (kok), *n.* **1.** a rooster or other male bird. **2.** a hand-operated valve or faucet. **3. a.** the hammer of a firearm. **b.** its position preparatory to firing. **—***v.t.* **4.** to draw back the hammer of (a firearm).

cock² (kok), *v.t.* **1.** to turn up or to one side, often in a jaunty manner. **—***n.* **2.** the act of turning up or to one side.

cock³ (kok), *n.* a conical pile of hay, dung, etc.

cock•ade (ko kād′), *n.* a rosette or the like, worn on the hat as an indication of rank.

cock•a•ma•mie (kok′ə mā′mē), *adj. Slang.* ridiculous; nonsensical.

cock′-and-bull′ sto′ry, *n.* an absurd, improbable story presented as the truth.

cockatoo

cock•a•too (kok′ə tōō′, kok′ə tōō′), *n., pl.* **-toos.** a crested parrot of the Australian region.

cock•a•trice (kok′ə tris), *n.* a legendary monster, part serpent and part fowl, that could kill with a glance.

cock′crow′, *n.* daybreak; dawn.

cocked′ hat′, *n.* a man's hat with a wide, stiff brim turned up so as to appear three-cornered.

cock•er•el (kok′ər əl), *n.* a young domestic cock.

cock′er span′iel, *n.* a small spaniel with long drooping ears and a soft flat or wavy coat.

cock′eyed′, *adj.* **1.** cross-eyed. **2.** *Slang.* **a.** tilted to one side. **b.** foolish; absurd.

cock′fight′, *n.* a fight between gamecocks, usu. fitted with spurs. **—cock′fight′ing,** *n.*

cock•le¹ (kok′əl), *n.* **1.** a bivalve mollusk with heart-shaped valves. **—***Idiom.* **2. cockles of one's heart,** the place of one's deepest feelings.

cock•le² (kok′əl), *n.* any of various weeds of grain fields.

cock•ney (kok′nē), *n., pl.* **-neys.** (*sometimes cap.*) **1.** a native of the East End district of London, England. **2.** the dialect of this population.

cock′pit′, *n.* **1.** an enclosed space in an airplane containing the flying controls, instrument panel, and seats for the pilot and copilot. **2.** a pit or enclosed place for cockfights.

cock′roach′, *n.* an insect characterized by a flattened body, rapid movements, and nocturnal habits: a common household pest.

cocks′comb′, *n.* **1.** the comb of a rooster. **2.** a garden plant with flowers resembling a rooster's comb.

cock•sure (kok′shŏŏr′, -shûr′), *adj.* overconfident.

cock′tail′, *n.* **1.** a chilled, mixed drink of liquor and juice or other flavorings. **2.** an appetizer: *shrimp cocktail.*

cock′y, *adj.,* **-i•er, -i•est.** saucy and arrogant; conceited. **—cock′i•ly,** *adv.* **—cock′i•ness,** *n.*

co•co (kō′kō), *n., pl.* **-cos.** **1.** COCONUT PALM. **2.** COCONUT.

co•coa (kō′kō), *n.* **1.** a powder made from roasted cacao seeds. **2.** a beverage made by mixing cocoa powder with hot milk or water and sugar. **3.** yellowish or reddish brown.

co′coa but′ter, *n.* a fatty substance obtained from cacao seeds.

co•co•nut (kō′kə nut′, -nət), *n.* the large, hardshelled seed of the coconut palm, containing a white edible meat and a milky liquid.

co′conut palm′, *n.* a tropical palm tree bearing coconuts.

co•coon (kə kōōn′), *n.* the silky envelope spun by the larvae of many insects, as silkworms, serving as a covering while they are in the pupal stage.

cod (kod), *n., pl.* **cods, cod.** a food fish of cool, N Atlantic waters.

Cod (kod), *n.* Cape, CAPE COD.

C.O.D. or **c.o.d.,** cash, or collect, on delivery.

co•da (kō′də), *n., pl.* **-das.** a concluding passage of a musical movement following the last formal section.

cod•dle (kod′l), *v.t.,* **-dled, -dling. 1.** to pamper. **2.** to cook (eggs, fruit, etc.) in water just below the boiling point. **—cod′dler,** *n.*

code (kōd), *n., v.,* **cod•ed, cod•ing.** **—***n.* **1.** a system of signals for communication by telegraph. **2.** a system used for brevity or secrecy of written communication. **3.** a systematically arranged collection of existing laws. **4.** the symbolic arrangement of statements or instructions in a computer program or the set of instructions in such a program. **5.** any system of rules and regulations: *a code of behavior.* —*v.t.* **6.** to put into code.

co•deine (kō′dēn), *n.* an alkaloid obtained from opium, used chiefly as an analgesic and cough suppressant.

co•de•pend•ent (kō′di pen′dənt), *adj.* **1.** pertaining to a relationship in which one person is physically or psychologically addicted, as to alcohol or gambling, and the other person is psychologically dependent on the first in an unhealthy way. —*n.* **2.** one who is in a codependent relationship.

co•dex (kō′deks), *n.*, *pl.* **co•di•ces** (kō′də sēz′, kod′ə-). a manuscript volume, usu. of an ancient classic or the Scriptures.

cod′fish′, *n.*, *pl.* **-fish, -fish•es.** COD.

codg•er (koj′ər), *n.* an eccentric man, esp. one who is old.

cod•i•cil (kod′ə səl), *n.* a supplement to a will, containing an addition, modification, etc.

cod•i•fy (kod′ə fī′, kō′də-), *v.t.*, **-fied, -fy•ing. 1.** to reduce (laws, rules, etc.) to a code. **2.** to make a systematic arrangement of. —**cod′i•fi•ca′tion,** *n.*

Co•dy (kō′dē), *n.* **William Frederick** (*"Buffalo Bill"*), 1846–1917, U.S. Army scout and showman.

co•ed (kō′ed′, -ed′), *adj.* **1.** serving both men and women; coeducational. **2.** of a coed. —*n.* **3.** a female student in a coeducational institution.

co′ed•u•ca′tion, *n.* the education of both sexes in the same classes. —**co′ed•u•ca′tion•al,** *adj.*

co•ef•fi•cient (kō′ə fish′ənt), *n.* **1.** a number or quantity multiplying another quantity, as *3* in the expression *3x.* **2.** *Physics.* a constant that is a measure of a property of a substance, body, or process: *coefficient of friction.*

coe•len•ter•ate (si len′tə rāt′, -tər it), *n.* any of the invertebrates formerly included in the phylum Coelenterata, comprising the cnidarians and comb jellies.

co•e•qual (kō ē′kwəl), *adj.* **1.** equal with another or each other. —*n.* **2.** a coequal person or thing. —**co•e′qual•ly,** *adv.*

co•erce (kō ûrs′), *v.t.*, **-erced, -erc•ing. 1.** to compel or bring about by force or intimidation. **2.** to dominate or control. —**co•er′cion** (-ûr′shən), *n.* —**co•er′cive** (-siv), *adj.*

co•e•val (kō ē′vəl), *adj.* **1.** of the same age, time, or duration. —*n.* **2.** a contemporary. —**co•e′val•ly,** *adv.*

co•ex•ist (kō′ig zist′), *v.i.* **1.** to exist simultaneously. **2.** (esp. of nations) to exist together peacefully. —**co′ex•ist′ence,** *n.* —**co′ex•ist′ent,** *adj.*

co•ex•ten•sive (kō′ik sten′siv), *adj.* equal or coincident in space, time, or scope. —**co′ex•ten′sive•ly,** *adv.*

cof•fee (kô′fē, kof′ē), *n.* **1.** a beverage made from the roasted, ground seeds **(cof′fee beans′)** of certain coffee trees. **2.** the seeds themselves. **3.** a tropical tree that yields coffee beans. **4.** medium to dark brown.

cof′fee break′, *n.* a break from work for coffee, a snack, etc.

cof′fee•cake′, *n.* a cake or sweetened bread, often made with nuts, raisins, and cinnamon.

cof′fee•house′, *n.* an establishment that serves coffee and other refreshments.

cof′fee•pot′, *n.* a container in which coffee is made or served.

cof′fee shop′, *n.* a restaurant where light refreshments or meals are served.

cof′fee ta′ble, *n.* a low table, usu. in front of a sofa, for holding glasses, magazines, etc.

cof•fer (kô′fər, kof′ər), *n.* **1.** a box or chest, esp. one for valuables. **2. coffers,** a treasury, as of an organization.

cof•fin (kô′fin, kof′in), *n.* the box in which a corpse is buried.

cog (kog, kôg), *n.* **1.** a gear tooth. **2.** a person who plays a minor part in an organization.

co•gent (kō′jənt), *adj.* convincing; believable. —**co′gen•cy,** *n.* —**co′gent•ly,** *adv.*

cog•i•tate (koj′i tāt′), *v.i.*, *v.t.*, **-tat•ed, -tat•ing.** to think hard (about); ponder. —**cog′i•ta′tion,** *n.* —**cog′i•ta′tive,** *adj.* —**cog′i•ta′tor,** *n.*

co•gnac (kōn′yak, kon′-, kôn′-), *n.* **1.** (*often cap.*) the brandy produced near the French town of Cognac. **2.** (loosely) any good brandy.

cog•nate (kog′nāt), *adj.* **1.** related by birth. **2.** descended from the same language or form. **3.** similar in nature. —*n.* **4.** a cognate person or thing. **5.** a cognate word.

cog•ni′tion (-nish′ən), *n.* **1.** the act or process of knowing. **2.** something known or perceived.

cog•ni•za•ble (kog′nə zə bəl, kon′ə-), *adj.* **1.** capable of being perceived or known. **2.** being within the jurisdiction of a court.

cog′ni•zance, *n.* **1.** awareness or realization. **2.** judicial notice as taken by a court in dealing with a cause. —**cog′ni•zant,** *adj.*

cog•no•men (kog nō′mən), *n.*, *pl.* **-no•mens, -nom•i•na** (-nom′ə nə). **1.** any name, esp. a nickname or epithet. **2.** a surname.

co•gno•scen•ti (kon′yə shen′tē, kog′nə-), *n.pl.*, *sing.* **-te** (-tā, -tē). those who have superior knowledge of a particular field, as in the arts.

cog′wheel′, *n.* a wheel having teeth or cogs that engage with those of another wheel or part.

co•hab•it (kō hab′it), *v.i.* to live together as husband and wife without being legally married. —**co•hab′it•ant,** *n.* —**co•hab′i•ta′tion,** *n.*

co•heir (kō âr′), *n.* a joint heir.

co•here (kō hēr′), *v.i.*, **-hered, -her•ing. 1.** to stick together. **2.** to be logically connected.

co•her′ent (-hēr′ənt, -her′-), *adj.* **1.** logically connected; consistent. **2.** cohering; sticking together. —**co•her′ence,** *n.* —**co•her′ent•ly,** *adv.*

co•he′sion (-hē′zhən), *n.* **1.** the act or state of cohering. **2.** the molecular force between particles within a body or substance that acts to unite them. —**co•he′sive** (-siv), *adj.* —**co•he′sive•ly,** *adv.* —**co•he′sive•ness,** *n.*

co•hort (kō′hôrt), *n.* **1.** a companion or associate. **2.** a group, esp. of warriors or soldiers.

coif[1] (koif), *n.* a hood-shaped cap, esp. as worn beneath a veil by nuns.

coif[2] (kwäf, koif), *n.* COIFFURE.

coif•fure (kwä fyŏŏr′), *n.* a style of arranging the hair.

coil (koil), *v.t.*, *v.i.* **1.** to wind into rings one above or around the other. —*n.* **2.** a series of spirals or rings into which something is wound: *a coil of rope.* **3.** a single such ring. **4.** an electrical conductor, as a copper wire, wound up in a spiral or other form.

coin (koin), *n.* **1.** a piece of metal issued by a government as money. **2.** a number of such pieces. —*v.t.* **3.** to make (coins) by stamping metal. **4.** to create or invent (a word or phrase). —**coin′age** (koi′nij), *n.*

co•in•cide (kō′in sīd′), *v.i.*, **-cid•ed, -cid•ing. 1.** to occupy the same location or time period. **2.** to correspond exactly.

co•in′ci•dence (-si dəns), *n.* **1.** a striking occurrence by mere chance of two or more events at one time. **2.** the fact of coinciding. —**co•in′ci•den′tal** (-den′tl), *adj.* —**co•in′ci•den′tal•ly,** *adv.*

co•i•tus (kō′i təs), *n.* sexual intercourse, esp. between a man and a woman. —**co′i•tal,** *adj.*

coke (kōk), *n.* the solid product obtained by destructive distillation of coal, used as a fuel.

col-, var. of COM- before *l.*

Col., **1.** Colonel. **2.** Colorado.

co•la[1] (kō′lə), *n.*, *pl.* **-las.** a carbonated soft drink containing an extract made from kola nuts.

co•la[2] (kō′lə), *n.* a pl. of COLON[2].

COLA (kō′lə), *n.* an adjustment in wages or social-security payments to offset fluctuations in the cost of living. [*C(ost) O(f) L(iving) A(djustment)*]

col·an·der (kul/ən dər, kol/-), *n.* a container with a perforated bottom and sides, for draining foods.

cold (kōld), *adj.,* **-er, -est,** *n., adv.* —*adj.* **1.** having a low or lower than normal temperature. **2.** feeling a lack of warmth. **3.** lacking in passion, enthusiasm, etc. **4.** not affectionate or friendly. **5.** lacking sensual desire. **6.** unconscious, as from a blow. **7.** lifeless; dead. —*n.* **8.** the absence of heat. **9.** cold weather. **10.** a respiratory viral infection characterized by sneezing, sore throat, etc. —*adv.* **11.** thoroughly: *He knew his speech cold.* **12.** without preparation. —*Idiom.* **13.** **catch cold,** to become infected with a cold. **14.** **(out) in the cold,** neglected. —**cold/ly,** *adv.* —**cold/ness,** *n.*

cold/-blood/ed, *adj.* **1.** designating animals, as fishes and reptiles, whose blood temperature varies with that of the surrounding medium. **2.** without emotion or feeling.

cold/ call/, *n.* a visit or telephone call to a prospective customer without an appointment or a previous introduction.

cold/ cuts/, *n.pl.* various meats and sometimes cheeses, sliced and served cold.

cold/ feet/, *n. Informal.* a lack of confidence or courage.

cold/ front/, *n.* the zone separating two air masses, with the cooler replacing the warmer one.

cold/ shoul/der, *n.* a deliberate show of indifference.

cold/ sore/, *n.* a cluster of blisters appearing in or around the mouth in herpes simplex.

cold/ tur/key, *Informal.* —*n.* **1.** abrupt and complete withdrawal from the use of a narcotic drug or nicotine. —*adv.* **2.** without preparation; impromptu.

cold/ war/, *n.* **1.** intense political, military, and ideological rivalry between nations just short of armed conflict. **2.** (*caps.*) such rivalry after World War II between the Soviet Union and the U.S., and their respective allies. **3.** rivalry and tension between people or factions. —**cold/ war/rior,** *n.*

Cole·ridge (kōl/rij, kō/lə-), *n.* **Samuel Taylor,** 1772–1834, English poet, critic, and philosopher.

cole·slaw (kōl/slô/), *n.* a salad of finely chopped raw cabbage. [< D *koolsla* = *kool* cabbage + *sla* salad]

co·le·us (kō/lē əs), *n., pl.* **-us·es.** a plant cultivated for its colorful leaves.

col·ic (kol/ik), *n.* **1.** acute pain in the abdomen or bowels. **2.** a condition of unknown cause in young infants characterized by prolonged crying. —**col/·ick·y,** *adj.*

col·i·se·um (kol/i sē/əm), *n.* a large building for sporting events, exhibitions, etc.

co·li·tis (kə lī/tis, kō-), *n.* inflammation of the colon.

coll., **1.** collect. **2.** college.

col·lab·o·rate (kə lab/ə rāt/), *v.i.,* **-rat·ed, -rat·ing.** **1.** to work with another, as on a literary work. **2.** to cooperate with an enemy nation. —**col·lab/o·ra/tion,** *n.* —**col·lab/o·ra/tive,** *adj.* —**col·lab/o·ra/tor,** *n.*

col·lage (kə läzh/), *n.* a work of art made by pasting various materials on a surface.

col·lapse (kə laps/), *v.,* **-lapsed, -laps·ing,** *n.* —*v.i.* **1.** to fall or cave in. **2.** to fold up, as for storage. **3.** to break down; fail utterly. **4.** to fall unconscious, as from exhaustion. —*v.t.* **5.** to cause to collapse. —*n.* **6.** a falling in, down, or together. **7.** a breakdown. —**col·laps/i·ble,** *adj.*

col·lar (kol/ər), *n.* **1.** the part of a shirt, coat, etc., around the neck. **2.** anything worn around the neck. **3.** a band or a chain fastened around the neck of an animal as a means of restraint or identification. —*v.t.* **4.** to put a collar on. **5.** to seize or detain. —**col/lar·less,** *adj.*

col/lar·bone/, *n.* CLAVICLE.

col·lard (kol/ərd), *n.* a variety of kale grown in the southern U.S.

col·late (kə lāt/, kō/lāt, kol/āt), *v.t.,* **-lat·ed, -lat·ing.** **1.** to gather or arrange (pages) in their proper sequence. **2.** to compare (texts, statements, etc.) critically.

col·lat·er·al (kə lat/ər əl), *n.* **1.** security pledged for the payment of a loan. —*adj.* **2.** accompanying; auxiliary. **3.** additional: *collateral evidence.* **4.** secured by collateral. **5.** secondary or incidental. **6.** (of a relative) descended from the same stock, but in a different line. **7.** situated or running side by side; parallel.

col·la·tion (kə lā/shən, kō-, ko-), *n.* **1.** the act of collating. **2.** a light meal.

col·league (kol/ēg), *n.* a fellow worker or fellow member of a profession.

col·lect¹ (kə lekt/), *v.t.* **1.** to gather together. **2.** to gather as a hobby: *to collect stamps.* **3.** to demand and receive payment of. **4.** to regain control of (oneself). —*v.i.* **5.** to assemble or accumulate. —*adj., adv.* **6.** requiring payment by the recipient: *a collect phone call.* —**col·lect/i·ble, col·lect/a·ble,** *adj.* —**col·lec/tion,** *n.* —**col·lec/tor,** *n.*

col·lect² (kol/ekt), *n.* any of certain brief prayers used in Western churches.

col·lect/ed, *adj.* **1.** having control of one's emotions. **2.** brought together.

col·lec/tive, *adj.* **1.** formed by collection. **2.** combined: *collective assets.* **3.** characteristic of a group: *collective wishes.* —*n.* **4.** COLLECTIVE NOUN. **5.** a collective body or organization, as a farm. —**col·lec/tive·ly,** *adv.*

collec/tive bar/gaining, *n.* negotiation between a union and employer for determining wages, working conditions, etc.

collec/tive noun/, *n.* a noun, as *herd* or *clergy,* that is singular in form but denotes a group.

col·lec/tiv·ism, *n.* the socialist principle of state control of all means of production. —**col·lec/tiv·ist,** *n., adj.* —**col·lec/ti·vize/,** *v.t.,* **-vized, -viz·ing.** —**col·lec/ti·vi·za/tion,** *n.*

col·leen (kol/ēn, ko lēn/), *n.* an Irish girl.

col·lege (kol/ij), *n.* **1.** a degree-granting institution of higher learning. **2.** a constituent unit of a university. **3.** an institution for specialized instruction: *a barber college.* **4.** an organized association of persons with certain powers and rights: *the electoral college.*

Col/lege of Car/dinals, *n.* a body comprising all of the cardinals of the Roman Catholic Church.

col·le·gial (kə lē/jəl, -jē əl; *for 2 also* -gē əl), *adj.* **1.** collegiate. **2.** (of colleagues) sharing responsibility in a group endeavor.

col·le/gi·al/i·ty, *n.* cooperative interaction among colleagues.

col·le/gian, *n.* a college student.

col·le/giate (-jit, -jē it), *adj.* **1.** of a college. **2.** of or for college students.

colle/giate church/, *n.* **1.** a church that has a chapter of canons but no bishop's see. **2.** (in the U.S.) a church or group of churches governed by a consistory or session. **3.** (in Scotland) a church having two or more pastors.

col·lide (kə līd/), *v.i.,* **-lid·ed, -lid·ing.** **1.** to strike one another with forceful impact; crash. **2.** to clash; conflict. —**col·li/sion** (-lizh/ən), *n.*

col·lie (kol/ē), *n.* a large dog with a long, narrow head, raised orig. for herding sheep.

col·lier (kol/yər), *n.* **1.** a ship for carrying coal. **2.** a coal miner.

col/lier·y, *n., pl.* **-lier·ies.** a coal mine.

col·lo·cate (kol/ə kāt/), *v.t.,* **-cat·ed, -cat·ing.** to arrange in proper order, esp. to place side by side. —**col/lo·ca/tion,** *n.*

col·loid (kol/oid), *n.* a substance made up of minuscule particles dispersed in a continuous gaseous, liquid, or solid medium. —**col·loi·dal** (kə loid/l), *adj.*

colloq., **1.** colloquial. **2.** colloquium.

col·lo·qui·al (kə lō/kwē əl), *adj.* characteristic of ordinary or familiar conversation or writing rather than formal speech or writing. —**col·lo/qui·al·ism,** *n.* —**col·lo/qui·al·ly,** *adv.*

col·lo/qui·um (-kwē əm), *n., pl.* **-qui·ums, -qui·a** (-kwē ə). a conference at which experts discuss a specific topic.

col•lo•quy (kol′ə kwē), *n.*, *pl.* **-quies. 1.** a dialogue. **2.** a conference.

col•lu•sion (kə lōō′zhən), *n.* a conspiracy for fraudulent purposes. —**col•lude′** (-lōōd′), *v.i.*, **-lud•ed, -lud•ing.** —**col•lu′sive** (-siv), *adj.*

Colo., Colorado.

co•logne (kə lōn′), *n.* a mildly perfumed toilet water.

Co•logne′, *n.* a city in W Germany. 914,300.

Co•lom•bi•a (kə lum′bē ə), *n.* a republic in NW South America. 37,418,290 —**Co•lom′bi•an,** *adj., n.*

Co•lom•bo (kə lum′bō), *n.* the capital of Sri Lanka. 587,647.

co•lon[1] (kō′lən), *n.*, *pl.* **-lons.** a punctuation mark (:) used in a sentence to indicate that what follows is an elaboration, summation, etc.

co•lon[2] (kō′lən), *n.*, *pl.* **-lons, -la** (-lə). the part of the large intestine extending from the cecum to the rectum.

colo•nel (kûr′nl), *n.* a commissioned military officer ranking above lieutenant colonel. —**colo′nel•cy,** *n.*, *pl.* **-cies.**

co•lo•ni•al (kə lō′nē əl), *adj.* **1.** of a colony or colonies. **2.** (*often cap.*) pertaining to the 13 British colonies that became the United States of America, or to their historical period. —*n.* **3.** an inhabitant of a colony. —**co•lo′ni•al•ly,** *adv.*

co•lo′ni•al•ism, *n.* the policy by which a nation seeks to extend its authority over other territories. —**co•lo′ni•al•ist,** *n., adj.*

col•o•nist (kol′ə nist), *n.* **1.** an inhabitant of a colony. **2.** a member of a colonizing expedition.

col′o•nize′, *v.t., v.i.*, **-nized, -niz•ing.** to establish a colony (in). —**col′o•ni•za′tion,** *n.* —**col′o•niz′er,** *n.*

col•on•nade (kol′ə nād′), *n.* a series of columns usu. supporting one side of a roof. —**col′on•nad′ed,** *adj.*

co•lon•os•co•py (kō′lə nos′kə pē), *n.*, *pl.* **-pies.** an examination of the colon by means of a flexible fiberoptic instrument passed through the rectum.

col•o•ny, *n.*, *pl.* **-nies. 1.** a group of people who form a settlement in a new land that is subject to the parent nation. **2.** the region so settled. **3.** any territory separated from but subject to a ruling power. **4.** a group of people with the same nationality, interests, etc., living in a particular locality: *a colony of artists.* **5.** a group of like organisms living or growing in close association.

col•o•phon (kol′ə fon′, -fən), *n.* a publisher's or printer's distinctive emblem.

col•or (kul′ər), *n.* **1.** the quality of an object or substance with respect to light reflected by it. **2.** the natural hue of the skin. **3.** a vivid or distinctive quality. **4.** a pigment; dye. **5. colors, a.** a badge, ribbon, or uniform worn to signify allegiance, membership, etc. **b.** attitude; personality: *showed his true colors.* **c.** a flag or ensign. **6.** outward appearance: *a lie with the color of truth.* —*v.t.* **7.** to give or apply color to. **8.** to cause to appear different from the reality. **9.** to give a special character to: *The author's feelings color his writing.* —*v.i.* **10.** to take on or change color. **11.** to flush; blush.

Col•o•rad•o (kol′ə rad′ō, -rä′dō), *n.* **1.** a state in the W United States. 3,294,394. *Cap.:* Denver. *Abbr.:* CO, Col., Colo. **2.** a river flowing from N Colorado to the Gulf of California. —**Col′o•rad′an,** *adj., n.*

Col′orad′o Springs′, *n.* a city in central Colorado; U.S. Air Force Academy. 316,480.

col′or•ant (-ənt), *n.* a pigment; dye.

col′or•a′tion, *n.* arrangement or use of colors; coloring.

col•o•ra•tu•ra (kul′ər ə tŏŏr′ə, -tyŏŏr′ə, kol′-), *n.*, *pl.* **-ras. 1.** runs, trills, and other florid decorations in vocal music. **2.** a soprano specializing in such music.

col′or-blind′, *adj.* **1.** unable to distinguish one or more chromatic colors. **2.** showing or characterized by freedom from racial bias. —**col′or blind′ness,** *n.*

col′ored, *adj.* **1.** having color. **2.** influenced or biased.

col′or•fast′, *adj.* maintaining color without fading or running.

col′or•ful, *adj.* **1.** abounding in color. **2.** having vivid, striking elements. —**col′or•ful•ly,** *adv.* —**col′or•ful•ness,** *n.*

col′or•ing, *n.* **1.** the act or method of applying color. **2.** appearance as to color. **3.** a substance used to color something. **4.** aspect or tone.

col′or•ize′, *v.t.*, **-ized, -iz•ing.** to enhance with color, esp. by computer: *to colorize black-and-white movies.* —**col′or•i•za′tion,** *n.*

col′or•less, *adj.* **1.** without color. **2.** drab; lackluster. —**col′or•less•ness,** *n.*

Co•los•sae (kə los′ē), *n.* an ancient city in SW Phrygia.

co•los•sal (kə los′əl), *adj.* gigantic; huge. —**co•los′sal•ly,** *adv.*

Co•los•sians (kə losh′ənz), *n.* a book of the New Testament written by Paul to the church at Colossae.

co•los′sus (-los′əs), *n.*, *pl.* **-los•si** (-los′ī), **-los•sus•es. 1.** a gigantic statue. **2.** anything gigantic or very powerful.

co•los•to•my (kə los′tə mē), *n.*, *pl.* **-mies.** the surgical construction of an artificial opening from the colon to the outside of the body.

co•los•trum (kə los′trəm), *n.* a fluid secreted by the mammary glands during the first few days of lactation.

col•our (kul′ər), *n., v.t., v.i. Chiefly Brit.* COLOR.

Colt (kōlt), *n.* **Samuel,** 1814–62, U.S. inventor of the Colt revolver.

Co•lum•bi•a (kə lum′bē ə), *n.* **1.** a river in SW Canada and the NW United States. 1214 mi. (1955 km) long. **2.** the capital of South Carolina. 104,101. **3.** the United States of America.

col•um•bine (kol′əm bīn′), *n.* a plant of the buttercup family, having showy flowers with white to blue sepals.

Co•lum•bus (kə lum′bəs), *n.* **1. Christopher** (Sp. *Cristóbal Colón;* It. *Cristoforo Colombo*), 1446?–1506, Italian navigator in Spanish service: traditionally considered the discoverer of America 1492. **2.** the capital of Ohio, in the central part. 635,913. **3.** a city in W Georgia. 186,470.

col•umn (kol′əm), *n.* **1.** a decorative pillar with a capital and usu. a base. **2.** any columnlike object, mass, or formation: *a column of smoke.* **3.** a vertical row or list. **4.** a vertical arrangement on a page of horizontal lines of type. **5.** a feature article that appears regularly in a newspaper or magazine. **6.** a long, narrow file of troops. —**co•lum•nar** (kə lum′nər), *adj.* —**col′umned,** *adj.*

col′um•nist (-əm nist, -ə mist), *n.* a person who writes a newspaper or magazine column.

com-, a prefix meaning: with or together (*commingle*); completely (*commit*).

Com., 1. Commission. **2.** Commissioner. **3.** Committee.

co•ma (kō′mə), *n.*, *pl.* **-mas.** a state of prolonged unconsciousness from which it is impossible to rouse a person.

Co•man•che (kə man′chē, kō-), *n.*, *pl.* **-che, -ches.** a member of an American Indian people of the S Great Plains, living today in Oklahoma.

com•a•tose (kom′ə tōs′, kō′mə-), *adj.* **1.** affected with or characterized by coma. **2.** lacking vitality or alertness.

comb (kōm), *n.* **1.** a toothed strip of plastic, metal, etc., used to untangle or arrange the hair. **2.** the fleshy outgrowth on the head of certain roosters. **3.** a honeycomb. **4.** a machine for separating long cotton or wool fibers from short ones. —*v.t.* **5.** to arrange (the hair) with a comb. **6.** to search everywhere in: *to comb the files.* **7.** to separate (textile fibers) with a comb.

com•bat (*v.* kəm bat′, kom′bat; *n.* kom′bat), *v.*, **-bat•ed, -bat•ing** *or* (*esp. Brit.*) **-bat•ted, -bat•ting,** *n.* —*v.t., v.i.* **1.** to fight (against). —*n.* **2.** active fighting with enemy forces. **3.** any struggle or controversy. —**com•bat•ant** (kəm bat′nt, kom′bə tənt), *n.* —**com•bat′ive,** *adj.*

com′bat fatigue′, *n.* a mental disorder characterized by anxiety, nightmares, etc., occurring among soldiers in active and usu. prolonged combat.

comb′er, *n.* **1.** one that combs. **2.** a long, curling wave.

com•bi•na•tion (kom′bə nā′shən), *n.* **1.** the act of combining or state of being combined. **2.** something formed by combining. **3.** an alliance of persons, parties, etc. **4.** the series of numbers dialed to open a special lock without a key.

com•bine (*v.* kəm bīn′; *n.* kom′bīn), *v.,* **-bined, -bin•ing,** *n.* —*v.t., v.i.* **1.** to join into a close union or whole; unite. —*n.* **2.** a combination of persons or groups to further their interests, as a syndicate or cartel. **3.** a harvesting machine for cutting and threshing grain in the field. —**com•bin′er,** *n.*

comb′ings, *n.pl.* hairs removed with a comb or brush.

combin′ing form′, *n.* a linguistic form that occurs only in compound words, joining with either an independent word (*mini-* + *skirt*) or another combining form (*photo-* + *-graphy*).

comb′ jel′ly, *n.* any of a phylum of marine invertebrates having an oval, transparent body propelled by eight comblike appendages.

com•bo (kom′bō), *n., pl.* **-bos.** *Informal.* **1.** a small jazz or dance band. **2.** a combination.

com•bus•ti•ble (kəm bus′tə bəl), *adj.* capable of catching fire and burning. —**com•bus′ti•bil′i•ty,** *n.*

com•bus′tion (-chən), *n.* **1.** the act or process of burning. **2.** rapid oxidation accompanied by heat and usu. light. —**com•bus′tive,** *adj.*

come (kum), *v.i.,* **came, come, com•ing. 1.** to move toward someone or something. **2.** to arrive: *The train is coming.* **3.** to move into view. **4.** to extend; reach: *The dress comes to her knees.* **5.** to occur; happen. **6.** to be available: *Toothpaste comes in a tube.* **7.** to issue; be derived. **8.** to result: *This comes of carelessness.* **9.** to enter into a specified state: *to come into popular use.* **10.** to do or manage. **11. come about,** to happen. **12. ~ across** or **upon,** to encounter, esp. by chance. **13. ~ along, a.** to accompany someone. **b.** to proceed. **c.** to appear. **14. ~ around** or **round, a.** to revive. **b.** to change one's opinion or decision. **15. ~ by,** to obtain; acquire. **16. ~ down with,** to become afflicted with (an illness). **17. ~ into, a.** to acquire. **b.** to inherit. **18. ~ off, a.** to happen. **b.** to acquit oneself. **c.** to be effective. **19. ~ out, a.** to be revealed or published. **b.** to make a debut. **c.** to end. **20. ~ through, a.** to endure successfully. **b.** to fulfill demands. **21. ~ to, a.** to recover consciousness. **b.** to total. **22. ~ up,** to be referred to. **23. ~ up with,** to produce; supply.

come′back′, *n.* **1.** a return to a former higher status, prosperity, etc. **2.** a clever retort.

co•me•di•an (kə mē′dē ən), *n.* **1.** a professional entertainer who amuses an audience, as by telling jokes. **2.** an actor in comedy.

co•me′di•enne′ (-en′), *n.* a woman who is a comic entertainer or actress.

come′down′, *n.* a descent from dignity, importance, or wealth.

com•e•dy (kom′i dē), *n., pl.* **-dies. 1.** a humorous play, movie, etc., with a cheerful ending. **2.** any comic incident or incidents. —**co•me•dic** (kə mē′dik), *adj.*

come′ly (kum′lē), *adj.,* **-li•er, -li•est.** attractive; good-looking. —**come′li•ness,** *n.*

come′-on′, *n.* an inducement or lure.

com•er (kum′ər), *n.* a person or thing that is very promising.

co•mes•ti•ble (kə mes′tə bəl), *adj.* **1.** edible. —*n.* **2.** Usu., **-bles.** food.

com•et (kom′it), *n.* a celestial body, consisting of a central solid mass and a tail of dust and gas, that orbits the sun along a highly eccentric course.

come′up′pance (-up′əns), *n.* deserved punishment.

com•fit (kum′fit, kom′-), *n.* a candy containing a nut or piece of fruit.

com•fort (kum′fərt), *v.t.* **1.** to soothe or console.

—*n.* **2.** consolation; solace. **3.** a person or thing that consoles. **4.** a state of ease and satisfaction of bodily wants.

com•fort•a•ble (kumf′tə bəl, kum′fər tə-), *adj.* **1.** affording physical comfort or ease. **2.** contented and at ease. **3.** adequate or sufficient. —**com′fort•a•bly,** *adv.*

com•fort•er (kum′fər tər), *n.* **1.** one that comforts. **2.** a thick quilted bedcover. **3. the Comforter,** the Holy Spirit. John 14:16, 26; 16:7.

com′fort sta′tion, *n.* a public lavatory or restroom.

com•fy (kum′fē), *adj.,* **-fi•er, -fi•est.** *Informal.* comfortable.

com•ic (kom′ik), *adj.* **1.** pertaining to comedy. **2.** humorous; funny. —*n.* **3.** a comedian. **4. comics,** comic strips. —**com′i•cal,** *adj.* —**com′i•cal•ly,** *adv.*

com′ic book′, *n.* a magazine of comic strips.

com′ic strip′, *n.* a sequence of drawings relating a comic incident, an adventure, etc., often serialized in daily newspapers.

com•ing (kum′ing), *n.* **1.** approach; arrival. —*adj.* **2.** impending; approaching. **3.** promising future fame or success.

com•i•ty (kom′i tē), *n., pl.* **-ties.** mutual courtesy.

comm., **1.** commission. **2.** committee.

com•ma (kom′ə), *n., pl.* **-mas.** a punctuation mark (,) used to indicate a division in a sentence.

com•mand (kə mand′, -mänd′), *v.t.* **1.** to direct with authority; order. **2.** to demand. **3.** to deserve and receive (respect, attention, etc.). **4.** to dominate by reason of location. **5.** to be master of. —*v.i.* **6.** to have authority. —*n.* **7.** the act of commanding or ordering. **8.** an order given by one in authority. **9.** the possession of controlling authority. **10.** expertise; mastery. **11.** a signal, as a keystroke, instructing a computer to perform a specific task.

com•man•dant (kom′ən dant′, -dänt′), *n.* a commanding officer.

com′man•deer′ (-dēr′), *v.t.* to seize (private property) for military or other public use.

com•mand•er (kə man′dər, -män′-), *n.* **1.** a person who commands. **2.** an officer in the U.S. Navy or Coast Guard ranking below a captain and above a lieutenant commander.

command′er in chief′, *n., pl.* **commanders in chief.** the supreme commander of the armed forces of a nation.

com•mand′ment, *n.* **1.** a command or mandate. **2.** (*sometimes cap.*) *Bible.* any of the Ten Commandments.

com•man•do (kə man′dō, -män′-), *n., pl.* **-dos, -does. 1.** a member of a specially trained military unit used for surprise destructive raids. **2.** a member of an assault team trained to operate against terrorist attacks.

com•mem•o•rate (kə mem′ə rāt′), *v.t.,* **-rat•ed, -rat•ing. 1.** to serve as a memorial of. **2.** to honor the memory of by some observance. —**com•mem′o•ra′tion,** *n.* —**com•mem′o•ra′tive,** *adj.*

com•mence (kə mens′), *v.i., v.t.,* **-menced, -menc•ing.** to begin; start.

com•mence′ment, *n.* **1.** a beginning. **2.** the ceremony of conferring degrees or diplomas at a school.

com•mend (kə mend′), *v.t.* **1.** to mention as worthy of confidence, attention, etc. **2.** to entrust. **3.** to cite with special praise. —**com•mend′a•ble,** *adj.* —**com•mend′a•bly,** *adv.* —**com•men•da•tion** (kom′ən dā′shən), *n.* —**com•mend′a•to′ry** (-mend′də tôr′ē), *adj.*

com•men•su•ra•ble (kə men′sər ə bəl, -shər ə-), *adj.* **1.** having the same measure or divisor. **2.** proportionate; commensurate. —**com•men′su•ra•bly,** *adv.*

com•men•su•rate (-it), *adj.* **1.** having the same measure. **2.** corresponding in amount, magnitude, or degree. —**com•men′su•rate•ly,** *adv.*

com•ment (kom′ent), *n.* **1.** a remark; observation. **2.** gossip; talk. **3.** a criticism or interpretation: *The play is a comment on modern society.* **4.** an annotation to a text. —*v.i., v.t.* **5.** to make a comment or comments (on).

com•men•tar′y (-ən ter′ē), n., pl. **-tar•ies. 1.** a series of comments. **2.** an explanatory essay or treatise. **3.** anything serving to illustrate or exemplify.

com•men•ta′tor (-tā′tər), n. a person who discusses news or other topics on television or radio.

com•merce (kom′ərs), n. an interchange of goods between different countries or between areas of the same country; trade.

com•mer•cial (kə mûr′shəl), adj. **1.** pertaining to commerce. **2.** produced, marketed, etc., for profit. —n. **3.** a paid advertisement on radio or television. —**com•mer′cial•ly,** adv.

com•mer′cial•ism, n. the principles, practices, and spirit of commerce.

com•mer′cial•ize′, v.t., **-ized, -iz•ing.** to make commercial in character, methods, etc. —**com•mer′cial•i•za′tion,** n.

com•min•gle (kə ming′gəl), v.t., v.i., **-gled, -gling.** to mix or mingle together. —**com•min′gler,** n.

com•mis•er•ate (kə miz′ə rāt′), v., **-at•ed, -at•ing.** —v.t. **1.** to feel or express sorrow or sympathy for. —v.i. **2.** to sympathize (usu. fol. by with). —**com•mis′er•a′tion,** n. —**com•mis′er•a′tive,** adj.

com•mis•sar (kom′ə sär′), n. the head of a commissariat: called minister after 1946.

com′mis•sar′i•at (-sâr′ē ət), n. a major governmental division in the U.S.S.R.: called ministry after 1946.

com′mis•sar′y (-ser′ē), n., pl. **-sar•ies. 1.** a store selling food and supplies, esp. in a military post. **2.** a dining room or cafeteria, esp. in a motion-picture studio.

com•mis•sion (kə mish′ən), n. **1.** the act of committing. **2.** an authoritative order. **3.** authority granted for a particular action or function. **4.** a document conferring authority, esp. one issued to military officers. **5.** the rank of a military officer. **6.** a group of persons authoritatively charged with particular functions. **7.** a sum or percentage allowed to agents, sales representatives, etc., for their services. —v.t. **8.** to give a commission to. **9.** to authorize. **10.** to order (a ship) to active duty. —**Idiom. 11. in** (or **out of**) **commission,** in (or not in) operating order.

commis′sioned of′ficer, n. a military officer holding rank by commission.

com•mis′sion•er, n. **1.** a member of a commission. **2.** a government official in charge of a department. **3.** an official chosen by an athletic association to exercise broad authority.

com•mit (kə mit′), v.t., **-mit•ted, -mit•ting. 1.** to give in trust or charge. **2.** to bind or obligate, as by pledge. **3.** to do; perform; perpetrate. **4.** to consign, as to a mental institution. —**com•mit′ment,** n. —**com•mit′tal,** n.

com•mit•tee (kə mit′ē), n. a group of persons chosen to investigate or act on a matter. —**com•mit′tee•man,** n., pl. **-men.** —**com•mit′tee•wom′an,** n., pl. **-wom•en.**

com•mode (kə mōd′), n. **1.** a low, highly ornamented chest of drawers. **2.** a stand containing a chamber pot or washbasin. **3.** TOILET (def. 1).

com•mo•di•ous (kə mō′dē əs), adj. spacious; roomy.

com•mod•i•ty (kə mod′i tē), n., pl. **-ties. 1.** an article of trade or commerce. **2.** something of use, advantage, or value. **3.** any unprocessed good, as a grain or a precious metal.

com•mo•dore (kom′ə dôr′), n. (formerly) a commissioned officer in the U.S. Navy or Coast Guard ranking above a captain.

com•mon (kom′ən), adj., **-er, -est,** n. —adj. **1.** belonging to or shared by all in question. **2.** belonging equally to an entire community, nation, or culture: a common language. **3.** widespread; general. **4.** usual; familiar. **5.** of mediocre or inferior quality. **6.** coarse; vulgar. **7.** noting a noun, as woman or pen, that is not the name of any particular person or thing. —n. **8.** Often, **commons.** land owned or used by the residents of a community. **9. commons,** the common people. **10. commons,** (used with a sing. v.) a large

dining room at a college. —**Idiom. 11. in common,** shared equally. —**com′mon•ly,** adv.

com′mon•al•ty (-ə nl tē), n., pl. **-ties.** the ordinary or common people.

com′mon car′rier, n. (in federal regulatory and other legal usage) a carrier offering its services at published rates for interstate transportation.

com′mon denom′inator, n. **1.** a number that is a multiple of all the denominators of a set of fractions. **2.** a shared characteristic, belief, etc.

com′mon divi′sor, n. a number that is an exact divisor of two or more given numbers.

com′mon•er, n. a member of the commonalty; a person without a title of nobility.

com′mon law′, n. the system of law originating in England, based on custom or court decision rather than civil or ecclesiastical law.

com′mon-law′ mar′riage, n. a marriage without a civil or ecclesiastical ceremony.

Com′mon Mar′ket, n. **1.** EUROPEAN ECONOMIC COMMUNITY. **2.** (often l.c.) any economic association of nations.

com′mon mul′tiple, n. a number that is a multiple of all the numbers of a given set.

com′mon•place′, adj. **1.** ordinary. **2.** dull or platitudinous. —n. **3.** a trite or uninteresting saying. **4.** anything common or ordinary.

com′mon sense′, n. sound practical judgment that is independent of specialized knowledge or training. —**com′mon•sense′,** adj. —**com′mon•sen′si•cal,** adj.

Com′mon Sense′, a pamphlet (1776) by Thomas Paine in which he asserts that the American colonies should be independent.

com′mon stock′, n. the ordinary stock of a corporation, yielding to preferred stock in dividends.

com′mon•weal′, n. the common welfare; public good.

com′mon•wealth′, n. **1.** the people of a nation or state; the body politic. **2.** a republican or democratic state. **3.** (cap.) a federation of states: the Commonwealth of Australia.

Com′monwealth of In′dependent States′, n. an alliance of former Soviet republics formed in December 1991, including: Armenia, Azerbaijan, Belarus, Kazakhstan, Kyrgyzstan, Moldova, Russian Federation, Tajikistan, Turkmenistan, Ukraine, and Uzbekistan. Abbr: C.I.S.

Com′monwealth of Na′tions, n. a voluntary association of independent nations and their dependencies linked by historical ties as parts of the former British Empire and cooperating on matters of mutual concern. Formerly, **British Commonwealth of Nations.**

com•mo′tion (kə mō′shən), n. **1.** tumultuous activity; agitation. **2.** disturbance or upheaval.

com•mu•nal (kə myōōn′l, kom′yə nl), adj. **1.** shared by everyone in a group. **2.** of, by, or belonging to a community. **3.** pertaining to a commune. —**com•mu′nal•ly,** adv.

com•mune¹ (kə myōōn′), v.i., **-muned, -mun•ing.** to talk together intimately.

com•mune² (kom′yōōn), n. **1.** a small group of persons living together and sharing possessions, work, income, etc. **2.** the smallest administrative division in France, Italy, etc.

com•mu•ni•ca•ble (kə myōō′ni kə bəl), adj. capable of being communicated or transmitted: a communicable disease. —**com•mu′ni•ca•bil′i•ty,** n.

com•mu′ni•cant (-kənt), n. a church member entitled to receive the Eucharist.

com•mu′ni•cate′, v., **-cat•ed, -cat•ing.** —v.t. **1.** to make known. **2.** to give to another; transmit. —v.i. **3.** to give or interchange thoughts, information, etc. **4.** to be connected, as rooms. —**com•mu′ni•ca′tor,** n.

com•mu′ni•ca′tion, n. **1.** the act of communicating. **2.** something communicated. **3. communications,** a means of sending messages, orders, etc., as telephone or telegraph. —**com•mu′ni•ca′tive,** adj.

com•mun•ion (kə myōōn′yən), n. **1.** (often cap.)

HOLY COMMUNION. **2.** a religious denomination. **3.** interchange of thoughts or emotions.

com•mun/ion of saints/, *n.* the spiritual fellowship existing among all faithful Christians, both living and dead: a phrase from the Nicene Creed.

com•mu•ni•qué (kə myo͞o/ni kā/), *n.*, *pl.* **-qués.** an official bulletin.

com•mu•nism (kom/yə niz/əm), *n.* **1.** a system of social organization based on the holding of all property in common. **2.** (*often cap.*) a political doctrine based on Marxism, seeking the creation of a classless society. **3.** (*often cap.*) a system of social organization in which all economic and social activity is controlled by a totalitarian state. [< F < L *commūnis* common + -ISM] —**com/mu•nist,** *n., adj.* —**com/mu•nis/tic,** *adj.*

com•mu•ni•ty (kə myo͞o/ni tē), *n., pl.* **-ties. 1. a.** a group of people who reside in a specific locality and share government. **b.** such a locality. **2.** a group sharing common interests: *the business community.* **3.** joint possession or ownership. **4.** similar character; agreement: *community of interests.*

commu/nity col/lege, *n.* a junior college supported in part by local government funds.

com•mu•ta•tive (kə myo͞o/tə tiv, kom/yə tā/tiv), *adj.* **1.** pertaining to exchange. **2.** (of a mathematical operation) having the property that one term operating on a second is equal to the second operating on the first, as *a × b = b × a.*

com•mu•ta•tor (kom/yə tā/tər), *n.* a device for reversing the direction of an electric current.

com•mute (kə myo͞ot/), *v.*, **-mut•ed, -mut•ing,** *n.* —*v.t.* **1.** to change (a prison sentence or other penalty) to a less severe form. **2.** to exchange for something else. —*v.i.* **3.** to travel regularly over some distance, as between a suburb and a city. —*n.* **4.** a trip made by commuting. —**com•mu•ta•tion** (kom/yə tā/shən), *n.* —**com•mut/er,** *n.*

Com•o•ros (kom/ə rōz/), *n.* a republic in the Indian Ocean comprising three islands. 589,797.

comp., *1.* comparative. *2.* compound.

com•pact[1] (*adj.* kəm pakt/, kom-, kom/pakt; *v.* kəm pakt/; *n.* kom/pakt), *adj.* **1.** joined or packed closely together. **2.** small in size. **3.** pithy; terse. —*v.t.* **4.** to join or pack closely together. **5.** to form by close union. —*n.* **6.** a small case containing a mirror and face powder. **7.** a small automobile. —**com•pact/ly,** *adv.* —**com•pact/ness,** *n.*

com•pact[2] (kom/pakt), *n.* a formal agreement between two or more parties, states, etc.

com/pact disc/, *n.* an optical disc on which music, data, or images are digitally recorded for playback.

com•pac•tor (kəm pak/tər, kom/pak-), *n.* an appliance that compresses trash into small bundles.

com•pan•ion (kəm pan/yən), *n.* **1.** a person who frequently associates with another. **2.** a person in an intimate relationship with another. **3.** a person employed to accompany, assist, or live with another. **4.** a mate or match for something. —**com•pan/ion•a•ble,** *adj.* —**com•pan/ion•ship/,** *n.*

com•pan/ion•way/, *n.* a stair or ladder within the hull of a ship.

com•pa•ny (kum/pə nē), *n., pl.* **-nies. 1.** a group of people. **2.** a guest or guests. **3.** companionship. **4.** a number of persons united for joint action, esp. for business. **5.** a basic unit of troops. —*Idiom.* **6. keep company,** to associate with, as in courtship. **7. part company,** to cease association.

com•pa•ra•ble (kom/pər ə bəl *or, sometimes,* kəm-pâr/-), *adj.* **1.** capable of being compared. **2.** worthy of comparison. —**com/pa•ra•bil/i•ty,** *n.* —**com/pa•ra•bly,** *adv.*

com•par•a•tive (kəm par/ə tiv), *adj.* **1.** pertaining to comparison. **2.** relative: *to live in comparative luxury.* **3.** designating the intermediate degree of comparison of adjectives and adverbs, as *smaller,* and *more carefully.* —*n.* **4.** the comparative degree. —**com•par/a•tive•ly,** *adv.*

com•pare (kəm pâr/), *v.*, **-pared, -par•ing,** *n.* —*v.t.* **1.** to examine for similarities and differences. **2.** to liken. **3.** to form the degrees of comparison of (an

adjective or adverb). —*v.i.* **4.** to be worthy of comparison. **5.** to make comparisons. —*n.* **6.** comparison: *a beauty beyond compare.* —**com•par/er,** *n.* —**Usage.** The traditional rule states that COMPARE should be followed by *to* only when it points out likeness between unlike persons or things: *She compared his handwriting to a knotted string.* It should be followed by *with* when it examines two entities of the same general class: *She compared his handwriting with mine.*

com•par•i•son (-par/ə sən), *n.* **1.** the act of comparing or state of being compared. **2.** a likening; comparative estimate. **3.** the modification of an adjective or adverb to indicate degrees of quality, quantity, or intensity, as in *mild, milder, mildest.* —*Saying.* **4. Comparisons are odious,** one should judge people or things on their own merits.

com•part•ment (kəm pärt/mənt), *n.* **1.** a space that is partitioned off. **2.** a separate room, section, etc. —**com•part•men/tal** (-men/tl), *adj.* —**com•part•men/tal•ize/,** *v.t.,* **-ized, -iz•ing.** —**com•part•men/tal•i•za/tion,** *n.*

com•pass (kum/pəs), *n.* **1.** an instrument for determining directions, as by a magnetized needle that points north. **2.** an instrument with two hinged, movable legs for drawing circles, measuring distances, etc. **3.** the enclosing limits of an area. **4.** extent; range. **5.** due or proper limits. —*v.t.* **6.** to go or move around. **7.** to surround; encircle. **8.** to attain or achieve. **9.** to contrive; plot.

com•pas•sion (kəm pash/ən), *n.* a feeling of sympathy for another's misfortune. —**com•pas/sion•ate** (-ə nit), *adj.* —**com•pas/sion•ate•ly,** *adv.*

com•pat•i•ble (kəm pat/ə bəl), *adj.* **1.** capable of existing together in harmony. **2. a.** (of software) able to run on a specified computer. **b.** (of hardware) able to work with a specified device. —**com•pat/i•bil/i•ty,** *n.* —**com•pat/i•bly,** *adv.*

com•pa•tri•ot (kəm pā/trē ət; *esp. Brit.* -pa/-), *n.* a fellow countryman or countrywoman.

com•peer (kəm pēr/, kom/pēr), *n.* **1.** a peer; colleague. **2.** a friend; comrade.

com•pel (kəm pel/), *v.t.,* **-pelled, -pel•ling.** to force or secure by force.

com•pen•di•um (kəm pen/dē əm), *n., pl.* **-di•ums, -di•a** (-dē ə). a summary or abridgment.

com•pen•sate (kom/pən sāt/), *v.*, **-sat•ed, -sat•ing.** —*v.t.* **1.** to recompense; pay. **2.** to counterbalance; offset. —*v.i.* **3.** to make amends. —**com/pen•sa/tion,** *n.* —**com•pen•sa•to•ry** (kəm pen/sə tôr/ē), *adj.*

com•pete (kəm pēt/), *v.i.,* **-pet•ed, -pet•ing.** to strive to outdo another; vie.

com•pe•tence (kom/pi təns) also **-ten•cy,** *n., pl.* **-tenc•es** also **-ten•cies. 1.** the state of being competent. **2.** an income sufficient for the modest comforts of life.

com/pe•tent, *adj.* **1.** having suitable skill, experience, etc., for some purpose. **2.** adequate but not exceptional. **3.** legally qualified as to age, soundness of mind, etc. —**com/pe•tent•ly,** *adv.*

com•pe•ti•tion (kom/pi tish/ən), *n.* **1.** the act of competing. **2.** a contest for some prize, honor, etc. —**com•pet•i•tive** (kəm pet/i tiv), *adj.*

com•pet•i•tor (kəm pet/i tər), *n.* a person, team, etc., that competes; rival.

com•pile (kəm pīl/), *v.t.,* **-piled, -pil•ing. 1.** to put together (documents, data, etc.) in one book or work. **2.** to make of materials from various sources: *to compile an anthology of plays.* **3.** to gather together; amass. —**com•pi•la•tion** (kom/pə lā/shən), *n.* —**com•pil/er,** *n.*

com•pla•cen•cy (kəm plā/sən sē) also **-cence** (-səns), *n., pl.* **-cenc•ies** also **-cenc•es.** a feeling of quiet pleasure or security, often while unaware of unpleasant possibilities. —**com•pla/cent,** *adj.* —**com•pla/cent•ly,** *adv.*

com•plain (kəm plān/), *v.i.* **1.** to express dissatisfaction, pain, etc. **2.** to make a formal accusation. —**com•plain/er,** *n.*

com·plain′ant, *n.* a person or group that makes a complaint, as in a legal action.

com·plaint′, *n.* **1.** an expression of discontent, pain, etc. **2.** a cause of discontent, pain, etc. **3.** an ailment; malady. **4.** (in a civil action) a formal accusation.

com·plai·sant (kəm plā′sənt, -zənt), *adj.* inclined or disposed to please. —**com·plai′sance,** *n.* —**com·plai′sant·ly,** *adv.*

com·plect′ed (kəm plek′tid), *adj.* complexioned.

com·ple·ment (*n.* kom′plə mənt; *v.* -ment′), *n.* **1.** something that completes or perfects. **2.** the amount that completes anything: *a full complement of workers.* **3.** any word or words used to complete a grammatical construction, esp. in the predicate. **4.** the quantity by which an angle or an arc falls short of 90°. —*v.t.* **5.** to form a complement to. —**com′ple·men′ta·ry,** *adj.*

com·plete (kəm plēt′), *adj., v.,* **-plet·ed, -plet·ing.** —*adj.* **1.** whole; entire. **2.** finished; concluded. **3.** thorough; unqualified. —*v.t.* **4.** to make whole. **5.** to bring to an end. —**com·plete′ly,** *adv.* —**com·plete′ness,** *n.* —**com·ple′tion,** *n.* —**Usage.** Occasionally there are objections to modifying COMPLETE with qualifiers such as *almost, more, nearly,* etc., because they suggest that COMPLETE is relative rather than absolute. However, such uses are fully standard in all varieties of speech and writing.

com·plex (*adj.* kəm pleks′, kom′pleks; *n.* kom′pleks), *adj.* **1.** composed of interconnected parts. **2.** complicated or involved. —*n.* **3.** an intricate assemblage of related parts, units, etc. **4.** a cluster of interrelated, emotion-charged ideas and impulses that influences behavior. —**com·plex′i·ty,** *n., pl.* **-ties.**

com′plex frac′tion, *n.* a fraction in which the numerator, denominator, or both contain a fraction.

com·plex·ion (kəm plek′shən), *n.* **1.** the color, texture, etc., of the skin, esp. of the face. **2.** aspect; character.

com·plex′ioned, *adj.* having a specified complexion: *light-complexioned.*

com′plex sen′tence, *n.* a sentence containing one or more dependent clauses in addition to the main clause.

com·pli·ance (kəm plī′əns), *n.* **1.** the act of conforming or acquiescing. **2.** a tendency to yield readily to others. —**com·pli′ant,** *adj.*

com·pli·cate (kom′pli kāt′), *v.t.,* **-cat·ed, -cat·ing.** to make complex or difficult. —**com′pli·ca′tion,** *n.*

com′pli·cat′ed, *adj.* **1.** composed of elaborately interconnected parts. **2.** difficult to analyze, understand, or explain.

com·plic·i·ty (kəm plis′i tē), *n., pl.* **-ties.** partnership or involvement in wrongdoing.

com·pli·ment (*n.* kom′plə mənt; *v.* -ment′), *n.* **1.** an expression of praise or admiration. **2.** a formal act of respect or regard. —*v.t.* **3.** to pay a compliment to.

com′pli·men′ta·ry, *adj.* **1.** of, conveying, or expressing a compliment. **2.** given free as a gift or courtesy.

com·ply (kəm plī′), *v.i.,* **-plied, -ply·ing.** to act in accordance with requests, requirements, etc.

com·po·nent (kəm pō′nənt, kom-), *n.* **1.** a constituent part; element. **2.** a part of a mechanical or electrical system. —*adj.* **3.** being or serving as an element in something larger.

com·port (kəm pôrt′), *v.t.* **1.** to bear or conduct (oneself); behave. —*v.i.* **2.** to be in agreement. —**com·port′ment,** *n.*

com·pose (kəm pōz′), *v.,* **-posed, -pos·ing.** —*v.t.* **1.** to make up; constitute. **2.** to make by combining things, parts, etc. **3.** to create (a musical or literary work). **4.** to calm; settle. **5.** to set (type). **6.** to set type for (an article, book, etc.). —*v.i.* **7.** to create a musical or literary work. —**com·pos′er,** *n.*

com·posed′, *adj.* calm or tranquil.

com·pos·ite (kəm poz′it), *adj.* **1.** made up of separate elements. **2.** belonging to a family of plants, as the daisy, in which the florets are borne in a close head. —*n.* **3.** something composite. **4.** a composite plant. —**com·pos′ite·ly,** *adv.*

com·po·si·tion (kom′pə zish′ən), *n.* **1.** the combination of parts to form a whole. **2.** makeup; constitution. **3.** the act of composing. **4.** something composed, as a piece of music or a short essay.

com·pos′i·tor, *n.* a person who sets the type for printing.

com·post (kom′pōst), *n.* a mixture of decaying organic matter, used for fertilizing soil.

com·po·sure (kəm pō′zhər), *n.* a self-controlled manner; calmness.

com·pote (kom′pōt), *n.* **1.** fruit stewed in a syrup. **2.** a stemmed dish for nuts, candy, etc.

com·pound¹ (*adj.* kom′pound, kom pound′; *n.* kom′pound; *v.* kəm pound′, kom′pound), *adj.* **1.** composed of two or more parts or ingredients. —*n.* **2.** something formed by combining parts, elements, etc. **3.** a substance composed of two or more elements whose chemical composition is constant. **4.** a word composed of two or more parts that are also words. —*v.t.* **5.** to combine. **6.** to make by combining parts, elements, etc. **7.** to add to, esp. so as to worsen. **8.** to agree, for a consideration, not to prosecute (a crime or felony). **9.** to pay (interest) on the accrued interest as well as the principal. —**com·pound′a·ble,** *adj.*

com·pound² (kom′pound), *n.* an enclosure containing residences or other buildings.

com′pound eye′, *n.* an eye, typical of insects, composed of many individual light-sensitive units.

com′pound frac′ture, *n.* a fracture in which the broken bone perforates the skin.

com′pound in′terest, *n.* interest paid on both the principal and the accrued interest.

com′pound sen′tence, *n.* a sentence containing two or more coordinate independent clauses, but no dependent clause.

com·pre·hend (kom′pri hend′), *v.t.* **1.** to understand. **2.** to include; comprise. —**com′pre·hen′si·ble** (-hen′sə bəl), *adj.* —**com′pre·hen′si·bly,** *adv.* —**com′pre·hen′sion** (-shən), *n.*

com′pre·hen′sive (-hen′siv), *adj.* wide in scope or content. —**com′pre·hen′sive·ness,** *n.*

com·press (*v.* kəm pres′; *n.* kom′pres), *v.t.* **1.** to press together and force into less space. **2.** to condense or shorten. —*n.* **3.** a pad held on the body to supply moisture or medication. —**com·pressed′,** *adj.* —**com·pres′sion,** *n.*

com·pres′sor, *n.* a machine for increasing the pressure of gases.

com·prise (kəm prīz′), *v.t.,* **-prised, -pris·ing. 1.** to include or contain. **2.** to consist of. **3.** to form or constitute.

com·pro·mise (kom′prə mīz′), *n., v.,* **-mised, -mis·ing.** —*n.* **1.** a settlement of differences by mutual concessions. **2.** something intermediate between different things. —*v.t.* **3.** to settle by compromise. **4.** to make vulnerable to danger, scandal, etc. —*v.i.* **5.** to make a compromise.

comp′ time′, *n.* time off from work, granted to an employee in lieu of overtime pay. [*comp(ensatory) time*]

comp·trol·ler (kən trō′lər), *n.* CONTROLLER (def. 1).

com·pul·sion (kəm pul′shən), *n.* **1.** the act of compelling or state of being compelled. **2.** a strong, irresistible impulse. —**com·pul′sive** (-siv), *adj.* —**com·pul′sive·ly,** *adv.* —**com·pul′sive·ness,** *n.*

com·pul·so·ry (-sə rē), *adj.* **1.** required; mandatory. **2.** compelling; constraining.

com·punc·tion (kəm pungk′shən), *n.* uneasiness arising from guilt.

com·pute (kəm pyōōt′), *v.,* **-put·ed, -put·ing.** —*v.t.* **1.** to determine by arithmetical calculation. —*v.i.* **2.** to reckon; calculate. **3.** to use a computer or calculator. —**com·pu·ta·tion** (kom′pyōō tā′shən), *n.*

com·put′er, *n.* **1.** a programmable electronic device that performs prescribed operations on data at high speed. **2.** one that computes.

com·put′er·ize′, *v.t.,* **-ized, -iz·ing. 1.** to control, process, or store by means of a computer. **2.** to automate by computers: *to computerize a business.* —**com·put′er·i·za′tion,** *n.*

comput′erized ax′ial tomog′raphy, *n.* the process of producing a CAT scan.

comput′er vi′rus, *n.* VIRUS (def. 4).

com•rade (kom′rad, -rid), *n.* **1.** a companion or friend. **2.** a fellow member of a fraternal group, political party, etc. —**com′rade•ship′,** *n.*

Com′stock Lode′, *n.* the most valuable deposit of silver ore ever recorded, discovered in 1859 by Henry T. P. Comstock near Virginia City, Nev. Also called **Com′stock Sil′ver Lode′.**

con¹ (kon), *adv.* **1.** against. —*n.* **2.** the argument or vote against something.

con² (kon), *adj., v.,* **conned, con•ning.** —*adj.* **1.** involving abuse of confidence. —*v.t.* **2.** to swindle. **3.** to persuade by deception.

con³ (kon), *n. Informal.* a convict.

con-, var. of COM-.

con•cat•e•nate (kon kat′n āt′, kən-), *v.t.,* **-nat•ed, -nat•ing.** to link together, as in a chain. —**con•cat′e• na′tion,** *n.*

con•cave (kon kāv′, kon′kāv), *adj.* curved inward like the inside of a circle.

con•ceal (kən sēl′), *v.t.* **1.** to hide. **2.** to keep secret. —**con•ceal′er,** *n.* —**con•ceal′ment,** *n.*

con•cede (kən sēd′), *v.,* **-ced•ed, -ced•ing.** —*v.t.* **1.** to acknowledge as true, just, or proper. **2.** to grant as a right or privilege. —*v.i.* **3.** to make a concession.

con•ceit (kən sēt′), *n.* **1.** an excessively favorable opinion of one's own ability, importance, etc. **2.** a whim; fanciful notion. —**con•ceit′ed,** *adj.*

con•ceive (kən sēv′), *v.,* **-ceived, -ceiv•ing.** —*v.t.* **1.** to form (a notion, purpose, etc.). **2.** to imagine. **3.** to become pregnant with. —*v.i.* **4.** to form an idea; think. **5.** to become pregnant. —**con•ceiv′a•ble,** *adj.* —**con•ceiv′a•bly,** *adv.*

con•cen•trate (kon′sən trāt′), *v.,* **-trat•ed, -trat• ing,** *n.* —*v.t.* **1.** to direct toward one point; focus. **2.** to put or bring into a single place, group, etc. **3.** to make denser, stronger, or purer. —*v.i.* **4.** to bring all efforts, faculties, etc., to bear on one objective. —*n.* **5.** a concentrated product. —**con′cen•tra′tion,** *n.*

concentra′tion camp′, *n.* a guarded compound for the confinement of political prisoners, minorities, etc.

con•cen•tric (kən sen′trik), *adj.* (esp. of circles or spheres) having a common center. —**con•cen′tri• cal•ly,** *adv.*

con•cept (kon′sept), *n.* a general notion or idea. —**con•cep•tu•al** (kən sep′chōō əl), *adj.* —**con•cep′- tu•al•ly,** *adv.*

con•cep•tion (kən sep′shən), *n.* **1.** the act of conceiving or state of being conceived. **2.** the formation of a zygote from the union of sperm and egg; fertilization. **3.** a concept. **4.** origination; beginning.

con•cep′tu•al•ize′ (-chōō ə līz′), *v.,* **-ized, -iz•ing.** —*v.t.* **1.** to form a concept of. —*v.i.* **2.** to think in concepts. —**con•cep′tu•al•i•za′tion,** *n.*

con•cern (kən sûrn′), *v.t.* **1.** to affect; involve. **2.** to relate to. **3.** to trouble; disturb. —*n.* **4.** something that relates to a person. **5.** a matter that engages one's attention or affects one's welfare. **6.** solicitude or anxiety. **7.** a commercial company.

con•cerned′, *adj.* **1.** interested or affected. **2.** troubled or anxious.

con•cern′ing, *prep.* relating to; regarding; about.

con•cert (kon′sûrt, -sərt), *n.* **1.** a public performance of music. **2.** accord or harmony. —**Idiom. 3. in concert,** jointly.

con•cert•ed (kən sûr′tid), *adj.* **1.** planned together. **2.** performed together or in cooperation. —**con•cert′- ed•ly,** *adv.*

con•cer•ti•na (kon′sər tē′nə), *n., pl.* **-nas.** a small musical instrument resembling an accordion.

con′cert•ize′, *v.i.,* **-ized, -iz•ing.** to give concerts professionally, esp. on tour.

con′cert•mas′ter, *n.* the principal first violinist in a symphony orchestra, often serving as assistant to the conductor.

con•cer•to (kən cher′tō), *n., pl.* **-tos, -ti** (-tē). a

musical composition for one or more principal instruments and orchestra.

con•ces•sion (kən sesh′ən), *n.* **1.** the act of conceding or yielding. **2.** the thing or point yielded. **3.** something conceded by a government or a controlling authority, as a grant of land or a franchise. —**con•ces′sion•al,** *adj.*

con•ces′sion•aire′ (-ə nâr′), *n.* the holder of a concession.

conch (kongk, konch), *n., pl.* **conchs** (kongks), **con• ches** (kon′chiz). **1.** a marine gastropod mollusk with a spiral shell. **2.** the shell of a conch. [< L < Gk *kónchē* shell]

conch

con•cierge (kon′sē ârzh′; *Fr.* kôn syɛʀzh′), *n., pl.* **-cierges** (-sē âr′zhiz; *Fr.* -syɛʀzh′). a member of a hotel or apartment-house staff in charge of various services for guests or tenants.

con•cil•i•ate (kən sil′ē āt′), *v.,* **-at•ed, -at•ing.** —*v.t.* **1.** win over; placate. **2.** to win or gain (goodwill, regard, or favor). —**con•cil′i•a′tion,** *n.* —**con• cil′i•a′tor,** *n.* —**con•cil′i•a•to′ry** (-ə tôr′ē), *adj.*

con•cise (kən sīs′), *adj.* expressing much in few words. —**con•cise′ly,** *adv.* —**con•cise′ness,** *n.*

con•clave (kon′klāv, kong′-), *n.* **1.** a private or secret meeting, esp. of cardinals to elect a pope. **2.** an assembly or gathering, esp. one with special authority.

con•clude (kən klōōd′), *v.,* **-clud•ed, -clud•ing.** —*v.t.* **1.** to bring to an end. **2.** to bring to a settlement. **3.** to deduce; infer. **4.** to determine or resolve. —*v.i.* **5.** to come to an end.

con•clu•sion (-klōō′zhən), *n.* **1.** the end or close. **2.** a result or outcome. **3.** a deduction or inference. **4.** a final decision.

con•clu′sive (-siv), *adj.* serving to settle or decide a question; decisive. —**con•clu′sive•ly,** *adv.* —**con• clu′sive•ness,** *n.*

con•coct (kon kokt′, kən-), *v.t.* **1.** to prepare by combining ingredients. **2.** to devise; contrive. —**con• coc′tion,** *n.*

con•com•i•tant (kon kom′i tənt, kən-), *adj.* **1.** accompanying; concurrent. —*n.* **2.** a concomitant quality or thing. —**con•com′i•tant•ly,** *adv.*

con•cord (kon′kôrd, kong′-), *n.* **1.** agreement; harmony. **2.** peace; amity.

Con•cord (kong′kərd, -kôrd, kon′-), *n.* **1.** the capital of New Hampshire. 30,400. **2.** a town in E Massachusetts: second battle of the Revolution April 19, 1775. 16,293. **3.** Also called **Con′cord grape′.** a large, dark-blue grape used in making jelly, juice, and wine.

con•cord•ance (kon kôr′dns, kən-), *n.* **1.** concord; harmony. **2.** an alphabetical index of the words of a book, as of the Bible, with a reference to the passage in which each occurs.

con•cord′ant, *adj.* agreeing; harmonious.

con•cor•dat (kon kôr′dat), *n.* **1.** an official agreement. **2.** an agreement between the pope and a secular government regarding the regulation of church matters.

con•course (kon′kôrs, kong′-), *n.* **1.** an assemblage; gathering. **2.** a broad thoroughfare. **3.** a large open space for crowds, as in a railroad station.

con•crete (kon′krēt, kong′-, kon krēt′, kong-), *adj., n., v.,* **-cret•ed, -cret•ing.** —*adj.* **1.** constituting an actual thing or instance; real; perceptible. **2.** particular as opposed to general. **3.** made of concrete. —*n.* **4.** a stonelike building material made by mixing cement with sand or gravel. —*v.t., v.i.* **5.** to treat with concrete. **6.** to make or become solid; harden. **—con•crete′ly**, *adv.* **—con•crete′ness**, *n.*

con•cre′tion (-krē′shən), *n.* **1.** coalescence; solidification. **2.** a solid mass formed by coalescence.

con•cu•bine (kong′kyə bīn′, kon′-), *n.* **1.** a woman who cohabits with a man to whom she is not married, esp. a woman regarded as subservient. **2.** (among polygamous peoples) a secondary wife, usu. of inferior rank.

con•cu•pis•cence (kon kyōō′pi səns, kong-), *n.* sexual desire; lust. **—con•cu′pis•cent**, *adj.*

con•cur (kən kûr′), *v.i.*, **-curred, -cur•ring. 1.** to agree. **2.** to work together. **3.** to occur at the same time. **—con•cur′rence**, *n.*

con•cur′rent (-kûr′ənt, -kur′-), *adj.* **1.** occurring simultaneously. **2.** acting in conjunction. **3.** having equal authority or jurisdiction. **—con•cur′rent•ly**, *adv.*

con•cus•sion (kən kush′ən), *n.* **1.** an injury to the brain from a blow, fall, etc. **2.** a shock caused by the impact of a collision, blow, etc. **—con•cus′sive**, *adj.*

con•demn (kən dem′), *v t* **1.** to express strong disapproval of. **2.** to sentence to severe punishment. **3.** to pronounce guilty. **4.** to force into a specified, usu. unhappy state: *Lack of education condemned him to a life of poverty.* **5.** to pronounce to be unfit for use or service: *to condemn an old building.* **6.** to take over (land) for a public purpose. **—con′dem•na′tion**, *n.* **—con•dem•na•to•ry** (-nə tôr′ē), *adj.*

con•dense (kən dens′), *v.*, **-densed, -dens•ing. —v.t. 1.** to make more dense or compact. **2.** to shorten; abridge. **3.** to reduce to another and denser form, as a vapor to a liquid. **—v.i. 4.** to become condensed. **—con•den•sa•tion** (kon′den sā′shən, -dən-), *n.*

condensed′ milk′, *n.* whole milk reduced by evaporation to a thick consistency, with sugar added.

con•dens′er, *n.* **1.** one that condenses. **2.** an apparatus for reducing gases or vapors to liquid or solid form. **3.** a lens that concentrates light in a specified direction.

con•de•scend (kon′də send′), *v.i.* **1.** to behave as if one is descending from a superior position. **2.** to stoop or deign to do something: *He would not condescend to misrepresent the facts.* **—con′de•scend′ing•ly**, *adv.* **—con′de•scen′sion** (-sen′shən), *n.*

con•dign (kən dīn′), *adj.* well-deserved: *condign punishment.*

con•di•ment (kon′də mənt), *n.* something used to flavor food, as ketchup, mustard, or a spice.

con•di•tion (kən dish′ən), *n.* **1.** a particular state or situation of a person or thing. **2.** state of health. **3.** social position. **4.** a modifying circumstance: *It can happen only under certain conditions.* **5.** a prerequisite. **6.** Usu., **conditions.** existing circumstances: *poor living conditions.* **7.** a bodily disorder. **—v.t. 8.** to put in a fit state. **9.** to accustom. **10.** to impose a condition on. **11.** to make (something) a condition. **—con•di′tion•er**, *n.*

con•di′tion•al, *adj.* **1.** imposing, containing, or depending on a condition. **2.** involving or expressing a condition, as the first clause in the sentence *If it rains, we won't go.* **—con•di′tion•al•ly**, *adv.*

con•di′tioned, *adj.* **1.** subject to conditions. **2.** characterized by a consistent pattern of behavior. **3.** acquired or learned: *conditioned behavior patterns.*

con•do (kon′dō), *n., pl.* **-dos.** CONDOMINIUM (def. 1).

con•dole (kən dōl′), *v.i.*, **-doled, -dol•ing.** to express sympathy with a person suffering sorrow, misfortune, or grief: *to condole with a friend whose father has died.* **—con•do′lence**, *n.*

con•dom (kon′dəm, kun′-), *n.* a thin rubber sheath worn over the penis during intercourse to prevent conception or infection.

con•do•min•i•um (kon′də min′ē əm), *n.* **1. a.** an apartment house or office building, the units of which are individually owned. **b.** a unit in such a building. **2. a.** joint sovereignty over a territory by several states. **b.** the territory itself.

con•done (kən dōn′), *v.t.*, **-doned, -don•ing.** to disregard (something illegal, objectionable, etc.). **—con•don′a•ble**, *adj.*

con•dor (kon′dər, -dôr), *n.* either of two New World vultures: the largest flying birds in the Western Hemisphere.

con•duce (kən dōōs′, -dyōōs′), *v.i.*, **-duced, -duc•ing.** to lead or contribute to a result. **—con•du′cive**, *adj.*

con•duct (*n.* kon′dukt; *v.* kən dukt′), *n.* **1.** personal behavior; deportment. **2.** direction or management. **—v.t. 3.** to behave (oneself). **4.** to manage or carry on. **5.** to direct, as an orchestra. **6.** to lead or guide. **7.** to serve as a medium for (heat, electricity, etc.). **—v.i. 8.** to act as conductor. **—con•duc′tion**, *n.* **—con•duc′tive**, *adj.* **—con′duc•tiv′i•ty**, *n.*

con•duct′ance, *n.* the ability of a conductor to transmit electricity.

con•duc′tor, *n.* **1.** the person in charge of a train. **2.** a person who directs an orchestra or chorus. **3.** a substance or device that conducts heat, electricity, etc.

con•duit (kon′dwit, -dōō it, -dyōō -), *n.* **1.** a channel for conveying fluids. **2.** a structure containing ducts for electrical conductors or cables.

cone (kōn), *n.* **1. a** solid with a circular base and a plane curve tapering uniformly to a vertex. **2.** anything shaped like a cone. **3.** the cone-shaped multiple fruit of the pine, fir, etc. **4.** one of the cone-shaped cells in the retina of the eye.

Con′es•to′ga wag′on (kon′ə stō′gə, kon′-), *n.* a large, broad-wheeled covered wagon, used to transport freight across North America during the early westward migration. Also called **Con′es•to′ga.**

con•fab (kon′fab), *n.* a conversation; discussion.

con•fab′u•late′ (-yə lāt′), *v.i.*, **-lat•ed, -lat•ing.** to converse informally. **—con•fab′u•la′tion**, *n.*

con•fec•tion (kən fek′shən), *n.* a sweet preparation, as a candy or preserve.

con•fec′tion•er, *n.* a person who makes or sells candies or other confections.

con•fec′tion•er•y (-ner′ē), *n., pl.* **-er•ies. 1.** confections collectively. **2.** a confectioner's shop.

con•fed•er•a•cy (kən fed′ər ə sē), *n., pl.* **-cies. 1.** an alliance. **2. the Confederacy,** the group of 11 Southern states that seceded from the U.S. in 1860-61.

con•fed•er•ate (*adj., n.* kən fed′ər it; *v.* -ə rāt′), *adj., n., v.*, **-at•ed, -at•ing. —adj. 1.** united in an alliance. **2.** (*cap.*) of the Confederacy. **—n. 3.** an ally. **4.** an accomplice. **5.** (*cap.*) a supporter of the Confederacy. **—v.t., v.i. 6.** to unite in an alliance.

con•fed′er•a′tion, *n.* **1.** the act of confederating or state of being confederated. **2.** a league or alliance.

con•fer (kən fûr′), *v.*, **-ferred, -fer•ring. —v.i. 1.** to consult or discuss something together. **—v.t. 2.** to bestow upon as a gift, honor, etc. **—con•fer•ee** (con′fə rē′), *n., pl.* **-ees. —con•fer′ral, con•fer′ment**, *n.* **—con•fer′rer**, *n.*

con•fer•ence (kon′fər əns), *n.* **1.** a meeting for discussion. **2.** an association of athletic teams, schools, or churches.

con•fess (kən fes′), *v.t., v.i.* **1.** to acknowledge or reveal (a fault, crime, etc.). **2.** to declare (one's sins) to a priest. **3.** (of a priest) to hear the confession of (a person).

con•fess′ed•ly (-id lē), *adv.* by confession; admittedly.

con•fes′sion (-fesh′ən), *n.* **1.** acknowledgment; admission. **2.** acknowledgment of sin to a priest to obtain absolution. **3.** something confessed. **4.** an organized religious group sharing the same beliefs.

con•fes′sion•al, *adj.* **1.** characteristic of confession. **—n. 2.** a place set apart for the hearing of confessions by a priest.

Con•fes•sions (kən fesh′ənz), an autobiography (A.D. 400) by St. Augustine.

con•fes′sor, *n.* **1.** a person who confesses. **2.** a priest authorized to hear confessions.

con•fet•ti (kən fet′ē), *n.* small bits of paper thrown at festive events.

con•fi•dant (kon′fi dant′, -dänt′) or **con′fi•dante′**, *n.* a person to whom secrets are confided.

con•fide (kən fīd′), v., **-fid•ed, -fid•ing.** —v.i. **1.** to impart secrets trustfully. —v.t. **2.** to tell in assurance of secrecy. **3.** to entrust. —**con•fid′er,** n.

con•fi•dence (kon′fi dəns), n. **1.** full trust; reliance. **2.** self-confidence; self-reliance. **3.** certitude; assurance. **4.** a confidential communication.

con′fidence game′, n. a swindle in which the swindler, after gaining the victim's confidence, robs the victim by cheating.

con′fi•dent, adj. **1.** certain; sure. **2.** sure of oneself. —**con′fi•dent•ly,** adv.

con′fi•den′tial (-den′shəl), adj. **1.** secret. **2.** indicating confidence or intimacy. **3.** entrusted with private affairs: a confidential secretary. —**con′fi•den′ti•al′i•ty,** n. —**con′fi•den′tial•ly,** adv.

con•fig•u•ra•tion (kən fig′yə rā′shən), n. **1.** the arrangement of the parts of a thing. **2.** external form. **3. a.** a computer plus the equipment connected to it. **b.** the act of configuring a computer system.

con•fig•ure (kən fig′yər), v.t., **-ured, -ur•ing.** to put together or arrange the parts of in a specific way or for a specific purpose.

con•fine (v. kən fīn′; n. kon′fīn), v., **-fined, -fin•ing,** n. —v.t. **1.** to enclose or keep within bounds. **2.** to shut up, as in prison. —n. **3.** Usu., **-fines.** a boundary or bound. —**con•fine′ment,** n.

con•firm (kən fûrm′), v.t. **1.** to establish the truth, accuracy, etc., of; verify. **2.** to sanction; ratify. **3.** to make firm. **4.** to administer the rite of confirmation to.

con•fir•ma•tion (kon′fər mā′shən), n. **1.** the act of confirming or state of being confirmed. **2.** something that confirms; corroboration. **3.** a ceremony of admission to full membership in a religious community.

confirma′tion hear′ing, n. a proceeding to examine a nominee's fitness for public office.

con•firmed′, adj. **1.** made certain as to truth, accuracy, etc. **2.** habitual; inveterate: a confirmed bachelor.

con•fis•cate (kon′fə skāt′), v.t., **-cat•ed, -cat•ing. 1.** to seize, by way of penalty, for public use. **2.** to seize by or as if by authority. —**con′fis•ca′tion,** n. —**con′fis•ca′tor,** n.

con•fla•gra•tion (kon′flə grā′shən), n. a large and destructive fire.

con•flate (kən flāt′), v.t., **-flat•ed, -flat•ing.** to fuse into one entity. —**con•fla′tion,** n.

con•flict (v. kən flikt′; n. kon′flikt), v.i. **1.** to clash; disagree. —n. **2.** a battle or struggle. **3.** antagonism or opposition. **4.** incompatibility or interference. **5.** a mental struggle. —**con•flic′tive,** adj.

con′flict of in′terest, n. the circumstance of a public officeholder, corporate officer, etc., whose personal interests might benefit from his or her official actions.

con•flu•ence (kon′floo əns), n. **1.** a flowing together of streams, rivers, etc. **2.** their place of junction. **3.** a crowd or throng. —**con′flu•ent,** adj.

con•form (kən fôrm′), v.i. **1.** to act in accordance; comply. **2.** to act in accord with the prevailing standards, attitudes, etc., of a group. **3.** to be or become similar in form or character. —v.t. **4.** to make similar in form or character. **5.** to bring into agreement. —**con•form′er,** n. —**con•form′ism,** n. —**con•form′ist,** n., adj.

con•for•ma•tion (kon′fôr mā′shən), n. **1.** structure or form, as of a physical entity. **2.** symmetrical arrangement of parts.

con•form•i•ty (kən fôr′mi tē), n., pl. **-ties. 1.** action in accord with prevailing social standards, attitudes, etc. **2.** correspondence in form or character.

con•found (kon found′, kən-; for 3 usu. kon′-found′), v.t. **1.** to perplex or amaze. **2.** to throw into confusion. **3.** to damn (used in mild oaths). Confound it! —**con•found′ed,** adj. —**con•found′er,** n.

con•fra•ter•ni•ty (kon′frə tûr′ni tē), n., pl. **-ties. 1.** a religious brotherhood of laymen. **2.** a fraternal society.

con•frere (kon′frâr), n. a fellow member, as of a profession.

con•front (kən frunt′), v.t. **1.** to face in hostility. **2.**

to present for acknowledgment, contradiction, etc. **3.** to stand or come in front of. —**con•fron•ta•tion** (kon′frən tā′shən), n. —**con′fron•ta′tion•al,** adj.

Con•fu•cian•ism (kən fyoo′shə niz′əm), n. the system of ethics, education, and statesmanship taught by Confucius.

Con•fu•cius (kən fyoo′shəs), n. 551?–478? B.C., Chinese philosopher and teacher. Chinese, **K′ung Fu-tzu.** —**Con•fu′cian,** adj., n.

con•fuse (kən fyooz′), v.t., **-fused, -fus•ing. 1.** to perplex or bewilder. **2.** to make unclear or indistinct. **3.** to fail to distinguish between. —**con•fus′ed•ly,** adv. —**con•fus′ing•ly,** adv.

con•fu′sion, n. **1.** disorder. **2.** lack of clearness. **3.** bewilderment.

con•fute′ (-fyoot′), v.t., **-fut•ed, -fut•ing. 1.** to prove to be false, invalid, or defective; disprove. **2.** to prove (a person) to be wrong by argument or proof. —**con•fu•ta•tion** (kon′fyoo tā′shən), n.

Cong., 1. Congregational. **2.** Congress. **3.** Congressional.

con•ga (kong′gə), n., pl. **-gas. 1.** a Cuban ballroom dance. **2.** an Afro-Cuban drum played with the hands.

con•geal (kən jēl′), v.t., v.i. **1.** to change from a fluid to a solid state, as by cooling. **2.** to coagulate. —**con•geal′ment,** n.

con•gen•ial (kən jēn′yəl), adj. **1.** agreeable or suitable in nature. **2.** suited in tastes, temperament, etc. —**con•ge′ni•al′i•ty** (-jē′nē al′i tē), n. —**con•gen′ial•ly,** adv.

con•gen•i•tal (kən jen′i tl), adj. present or existing at the time of birth: a congenital abnormality. —**con•gen′i•tal•ly,** adv.

con•ger (kong′gər), n. a large, edible marine eel.

con•ge•ries (kon jēr′ēz, kon′jə rēz), n. (used with a sing. or pl. v.) a collection of items; heap.

con•gest (kən jest′), v.t. **1.** to fill to excess; overcrowd or overburden; clog. **2.** to cause an unnatural accumulation of blood or other fluid in (a body part or blood vessel): The cold congested her sinuses. —**con•ges′tion,** n. —**con•ges′tive,** adj.

con•glom•er•ate (n., adj. kən glom′ər it, kəng-; v. -ə rāt′), n., adj., v., **-at•ed, -at•ing.** —n. **1.** anything composed of heterogeneous elements. **2.** a corporation consisting of a number of subsidiary companies in unrelated industries. **3.** a rock consisting of pebbles or the like cemented together. —adj. **4.** consisting of heterogeneous elements. **5.** clustered. **6.** of a corporate conglomerate. —v.t., v.i. **7.** to collect or cluster together. —**con•glom′er•a′tion,** n.

Con•go (kong′gō), n. **1. People's Republic of the,** a republic in central Africa, W of the Democratic Republic of the Congo. 2,583,198. **2. Democratic Republic of the,** a republic in central Africa. 32,560,000. Formerly, **Zaire. 3.** Also called **Zaire.** a river in central Africa, flowing to the Atlantic. ab. 3000 mi. (4800 km) long. —**Con′go•lese′** (-gə lēz′, -lēs′), adj., n., pl. **-lese.**

con•grat•u•late (kən grach′ə lāt′), v.t., **-lat•ed, -lat•ing. 1.** to express pleasure to (a person), as on a happy occasion. **2.** to feel satisfaction or pride in (oneself) for an accomplishment or good fortune: She congratulated herself on her narrow escape. —**con•grat′u•la•to′ry** (-lə tôr′ē), adj.

con•grat′u•la′tion, n. **1.** the act of congratulating. **2. congratulations,** an expression of pleasure in the success or good fortune of another.

con•gre•gate (kong′gri gāt′), v.i., v.t., **-gat•ed, -gat•ing.** to come or bring together in a crowd; assemble. —**con′gre•gant** (-gənt), n.

con′gre•ga′tion, n. **1.** an assembly of people for religious worship. **2.** a gathering; an assemblage.

con′gre•ga′tion•al, adj. **1.** of a congregation. **2.** (cap.) pertaining to a form of Protestant church government in which each local church is self-governing.

con′gre•ga′tion•al•ism (kong′gri gā′shə nl iz′əm), n. **1.** a form of church government in which each local group is self-governing. **2.** (cap.) the system of government and doctrine of Congregational churches. —**con′gre•ga′tion•al•ist,** n., adj.

con•gress (kong′gris), *n.* **1.** (*cap.*) the legislature of the U.S., consisting of the Senate and the House of Representatives. **2.** the legislature of a nation. **3.** a formal meeting or conference. —**con•gres•sion•al** (kən gresh′ə nl, kang-), *adj.*

Congres′sional dis′trict, *n.* one of a fixed number of districts into which a state is divided, each district electing one member to the national House of Representatives. Compare ASSEMBLY DISTRICT, SENATORIAL DISTRICT.

con′gress•man or **-wom′an** or **-per′son,** *n., pl.* **-men** or **-wom•en** or **-per•sons.** (*often cap.*) a member of a congress, esp. of the U.S. House of Representatives.

con•gru•ent (kong′grōo ənt, kən grōō′-), *adj.* **1.** agreeing or corresponding. **2.** (of geometric figures) coinciding at all points when superimposed. —**con′gru•ence,** *n.*

con•gru•i•ty (kən grōō′i tē, kon-), *n., pl.* **-ties. 1.** agreement; harmony. **2.** the quality of being geometrically congruent. —**con•gru•ous** (kong′grōo əs), *adj.*

con•ic (kon′ik) also **-i•cal,** *adj.* having the form of, resembling, or pertaining to a cone. —**con′i•cal•ly,** *adv.*

co•ni•fer (kō′nə fər, kon′ə-), *n.* an evergreen tree or shrub that bears both seeds and pollen on dry scales arranged as a cone. —**co•nif•er•ous** (kō nif′ər əs, kə-), *adj.*

conj., 1. conjugation. **2.** conjunction. **3.** conjunctive.

con•jec•ture (kən jek′chər), *n., v.,* **-tured, -tur•ing.** —*n.* **1.** the formation of an opinion without sufficient evidence. **2.** an opinion so formed. —*v.t., v.i.* **3.** to conclude from insufficient evidence. —**con•jec′tur•al,** *adj.*

con•join (kən join′), *v.t., v.i.* to join together. —**con•join′er,** *n.* —**con•joint′** (-joint′), *adj.* —**con•joint′ly,** *adv.*

con•ju•gal (kon′jə gəl), *adj.* of marriage or the relation of husband and wife.

con•ju•gate (*v.* kon′jə gāt′; *adj.* kon′jə git, -gāt′), *v.,* **-gat•ed, -gat•ing,** *adj.* —*v.t.* **1.** to give the inflected forms of (a verb) in a fixed order. **2.** to join together, esp. in marriage. —*adj.* **3.** joined together, esp. in a pair. **4.** (of words) having a common derivation. —**con′ju•ga′tion,** *n.*

con•junct (kən jungkt′), *adj.* conjoined; united.

con•junc′tion, *n.* **1.** a word functioning as connector between words, phrases, clauses, or sentences, as *but* and *unless.* **2.** union; association. **3.** a combination of events or circumstances. —**con•junc′tive,** *adj.*

con•junc•ti•va (kon′jungk tī′və), *n., pl.* **-vas, -vae** (-vē). the mucous membrane that covers the exposed portion of the eyeball and the inner surface of the eyelid.

con•junc•ti•vi•tis (kən jungk′tə vī′tis), *n.* inflammation of the conjunctiva.

con•junc•ture (kən jungk′chər), *n.* **1.** a combination of circumstances. **2.** a critical state of affairs; crisis.

con•jure (kon′jər, kun′-), *v.,* **-jured, -jur•ing.** —*v.t.* **1.** to summon by or as if by invocation or spell. **2.** to produce by or as if by magic. **3.** to bring to mind. —*v.i.* **4.** to summon a devil or spirit by invocation or spell. **5.** to practice magic. —**con′jur•a′tion,** *n.* —**con′jur•er, con′ju•ror,** *n.*

conk¹ (kongk, kôngk), *Slang.* —*v.t.* **1.** to strike on the head. —*n.* **2.** a blow on the head.

conk² (kongk, kôngk), *v. Slang.* **conk out, 1.** to break down, as an engine. **2.** to go to sleep.

Conn., Connecticut.

con•nect (kə nekt′), *v.t., v.i.* **1.** to join or link together. **2.** to associate mentally. —**con•nect′ed,** *adj.* —**con•nec′tor, con•nect′er,** *n.*

Con•nect•i•cut (kə net′i kət), *n.* a state in the NE United States. 3,295,669. *Cap.:* Hartford. *Abbr.:* CT, Conn., Ct.

con•nec′tion, *n.* **1.** a connecting or being connected. **2.** anything that connects. **3.** association; relationship. **4.** Usu. **-tions.** influential or powerful as-

sociates. **5.** a transfer by a passenger from one conveyance to another. **6.** a relative, esp. by marriage.

con•nec′tive (-tiv), *adj.* **1.** serving to connect. —*n.* **2.** something that connects. **3.** a connecting word, as a conjunction.

con•nip•tion (kə nip′shən), *n. Informal.* a fit of hysterical excitement or anger; tantrum.

con•nive (kə nīv′), *v.i.,* **-nived, -niv•ing. 1.** to cooperate secretly; conspire. **2.** to aid wrongdoing by forbearing to act or speak. [< L *co(n)nīvēre* to wink, turn a blind eye to] —**con•niv′ance,** *n.* —**con•niv′er,** *n.*

con•nois•seur (kon′ə sûr′, -sōor′), *n.* **1.** an expert judge in an art or in matters of taste. **2.** a discerning judge of the best in any field.

con•no•ta•tion (kon′ə tā′shən), *n.* the associated or secondary meaning of a word or expression. —**con′no•ta•tive** (kon′ə tā′tiv, kə nō′tə-), *adj.*

con•note (kə nōt′), *v.t.,* **-not•ed, -not•ing. 1.** to suggest (certain meanings, ideas, etc.) in addition to the explicit meaning. **2.** to involve as an accompaniment: *Injury connotes pain.*

con•nu•bi•al (kə nōō′bē əl, -nyōō′-), *adj.* of marriage; conjugal.

con•quer (kong′kər), *v.t.* **1.** to win in war. **2.** to overcome by force. **3.** to win by effort, personal appeal, etc. **4.** to surmount. —*v.i.* **5.** to be victorious. —**con′quer•a•ble,** *adj.* —**con′quer•or,** *n.*

con•quest (kon′kwest, kong′-), *n.* **1.** the act of conquering. **2.** the winning of favor or affection. **3.** anything acquired by conquering.

con•quis•ta•dor (kong kwis′tə dôr′, -kēs′-), *n., pl.* **-quis•ta•dors, -quis•ta•do•res** (-kēs′tə dôr′ēz, -āz). one of the 16th-century Spanish conquerors of the Americas.

Con•rad (kon′rad), *n.* **Joseph** (*Teodor Jozef Konrad Korzeniowski*), 1857–1924, English novelist, born in Poland.

con•san•guin•e•ous (kon′sang gwin′ē əs), *adj.* having the same ancestry. —**con′san•guin′i•ty,** *n.*

con•science (kon′shəns), *n.* the sense of what is right or wrong in one's conduct or motives. —**con′science•less,** *adj.*

con•sci•en•tious (kon′shē en′shəs), *adj.* **1.** meticulous; careful. **2.** governed by or done according to conscience. —**con′sci•en′tious•ly,** *adv.* —**con′sci•en′tious•ness,** *n.*

conscien′tious objec′tor, *n.* a person who refuses to serve in the armed forces for moral or religious reasons.

con•scious (kon′shəs), *adj.* **1.** aware of one's own existence, sensations, etc. **2.** having the mental faculties fully active. **3.** known to oneself. **4.** intentional: *a conscious effort.* —**con′scious•ly,** *adv.* —**con′scious•ness,** *n.*

con•script (*v.* kən skript′; *n.* kon′skript), *v.t.* **1.** to draft for military service. —*n.* **2.** a drafted recruit. —**con•scrip′tion,** *n.*

con•se•crate (kon′si krāt′), *v.t.,* **-crat•ed, -crat•ing. 1.** to make sacred. **2.** to dedicate to some purpose. **3.** to ordain to a sacred office.

con•se•cra•tion (kon′si krā′shən), *n.* **1.** dedication to the service of a deity. **2.** the act of consecrating the Eucharistic elements of bread and wine. **3.** ordination to a sacred office.

con•sec•u•tive (kən sek′yə tiv), *adj.* following in uninterrupted order; successive. —**con•sec′u•tive•ly,** *adv.*

con•sen•sus (kən sen′səs), *n., pl.* **-sus•es. 1.** solidarity of opinion. **2.** general agreement or harmony. —**Usage.** The phrases *consensus of opinion* and *general consensus* are generally avoided as being redundant.

con•sent (kən sent′), *v.i.* **1.** to agree to or comply with what is done or proposed by another. —*n.* **2.** agreement; compliance.

con•se•quence (kon′si kwens′, -kwəns), *n.* **1.** the result of an earlier occurrence. **2.** importance or significance.

con′se•quent′, *adj.* following as an effect or result. —**con′se•quent•ly,** *adv.*

con′se•quen′tial (-kwen′shəl), *adj.* **1.** consequent. **2.** important.

con•ser•va•tion (kon′sər vā′shən), *n.* **1.** the act of conserving. **2.** the preservation and protection of natural resources. —**con′ser•va′tion•ism,** *n.* —**con′ser•va′tion•ist,** *n.*

con•serv•a•tive (kən sûr′və tiv), *adj.* **1.** disposed to preserve existing conditions, institutions, etc., and to limit change. **2.** cautiously moderate. **3.** traditional in style or manner. —*n.* **4.** a conservative person. —**con•serv′a•tism,** *n.* —**con•serv′a•tive•ly,** *adv.*

con•serv•a•tor (kən sûr′və tər, kon′sər vā′-), *n.* **1.** a person who maintains the condition of objects, as in a museum. **2.** *Law.* a guardian or custodian.

con•serv′a•to′ry (-tôr′ē), *n., pl.* **-ries. 1.** a school of music. **2.** a greenhouse.

con•serve (*v.* kən sûrv′; *n.* kon′sûrv, kən sûrv′), *v.,* **-served, -serv•ing,** *n.* —*v.t.* **1.** to prevent injury, decay, waste, or loss of. **2.** to preserve (fruit). —*n.* **3.** a jam made from a mixture of fruits.

con•sid•er (kən sid′ər), *v.t.* **1.** to think carefully about. **2.** to think, believe, or suppose. **3.** to bear in mind. **4.** to show consideration for.

con•sid′er•a•ble, *adj.* **1.** large or great. **2.** worthy of consideration; important. —**con•sid′er•a•bly,** *adv.*

con•sid′er•ate (-it), *adj.* showing kindly regard for the feelings of others. —**con•sid′er•ate•ly,** *adv.*

con•sid′er•a′tion (-ə rā′shən), *n.* **1.** careful thought or attention. **2.** something kept in mind in making a decision. **3.** thoughtful or sympathetic regard. **4.** a recompense or payment. —*Idiom.* **5. take into consideration,** to take into account.

con•sid′er•ing, *prep.* **1.** in view of. —*conj.* **2.** taking into consideration that.

con•sign (kən sīn′), *v.t.* **1.** to hand over or deliver. **2.** to entrust. **3.** to relegate. **4.** to ship (goods), esp. for sale. —**con•sign•ee′,** *n., pl.* **-ees.** —**con•sign′or, con•sign′er,** *n.*

con•sign′ment, *n.* **1.** the act of consigning. **2.** property sent to an agent. —*Idiom.* **3. on consignment,** (of goods) sent to an agent for sale, with payment due after a sale is made.

con•sist (kən sist′), *v.i.* **1.** to be made up or composed: *Bread consists largely of flour.* **2.** to be inherent; exist or lie: *Our strength consists in unity.*

con•sist′en•cy (-sis′tən sē), *n., pl.* **-cies. 1.** degree of density or firmness. **2.** steadfast adherence to the same principles, course, etc. **3.** agreement among parts. —**con•sist′ent,** *adj.* —**con•sist′ent•ly,** *adv.*

con•sis•to•ry (kən sis′tə rē), *n., pl.* **-ries. 1.** an ecclesiastical council. **2.** a meeting of such a body.

con•sole¹ (kən sōl′), *v.t.,* **-soled, -sol•ing.** to give solace or comfort to. —**con•so•la•tion** (kon′sə lā′shən), *n.* —**con•sol′ing•ly,** *adv.*

con•sole² (kon′sōl), *n.* **1.** a television, phonograph, or radio cabinet that stands on the floor. **2.** a desklike structure containing the keyboards, pedals, etc., of an organ. **3.** the control unit of a computer or of a mechanical, electrical, or electronic system. **4.** a storage tray between automobile bucket seats.

con•sol•i•date (kən sol′i dāt′), *v.t., v.i.,* **-dat•ed, -dat•ing. 1.** to unite or combine into a single whole. **2.** to make or become firm or secure. —**con•sol′i•da′tion,** *n.* —**con•sol′i•da′tor,** *n.*

con•som•mé (kon′sə mā′, kon′sə mā′), *n., pl.* **-més.** a clear soup made from rich stock.

con•so•nance (kon′sə nəns), *n.* **1.** accord or agreement. **2.** the repetition of consonants as a rhyming device.

con′so•nant, *n.* **1.** a speech sound produced by obstructing the flow of air from the lungs. **2.** a letter representing such a sound. —*adj.* **3.** in accord: *behavior consonant with his character.* —**con′so•nan′tal** (-nan′tl), *adj.* —**con′so•nant•ly,** *adv.*

con•sort (*n.* kon′sôrt, *v.* kən sôrt′), *n.* **1.** a spouse, esp. of a reigning monarch. —*v.i., v.t.* **2.** to associate.

con•sor•ti•um (kən sôr′shē əm, -tē-), *n., pl.* **-ti•a**

(-shē ə, -tē ə). a combination, as of corporations, for carrying out a business venture.

con•spec•tus (kən spek′təs), *n., pl.* **-tus•es. 1.** a general survey. **2.** a digest or summary.

con•spic•u•ous (kən spik′yōō əs), *adj.* **1.** easily seen or noticed. **2.** attracting special attention. —**con•spic′u•ous•ly,** *adv.* —**con•spic′u•ous•ness,** *n.*

con•spir•a•cy (kən spir′ə sē), *n., pl.* **-cies. 1.** the act of conspiring. **2.** a group plan to commit an unlawful or evil act. **3.** the persons involved in such a plan. —**con•spir′a•tor,** *n.* —**con•spir′a•to′ri•al** (-tôr′ē əl), *adj.*

con•spire (kən spīᵊr′), *v.i.,* **-spired, -spir•ing. 1.** to agree together, esp. secretly, to do something wrong, evil, or illegal. **2.** to act or work together toward the same goal.

con•sta•ble (kon′stə bəl), *n.* **1.** a small-town peace officer. **2.** *Chiefly Brit.* a police officer.

Con•sta•ble (kun′stə bəl, kon′-), *n.* **John,** 1776–1837, English painter.

con•stab•u•lar•y (kən stab′yə ler′ē), *n., pl.* **-lar•ies. 1.** the body of constables of a district. **2.** a body of peace officers organized on a military basis.

con•stant (kon′stənt), *adj.* **1.** not changing; invariable. **2.** continuing without pause. **3.** regularly recurrent. **4.** steadfast; faithful. —*n.* **5.** something that does not change or vary. —**con′stan•cy,** *n.* —**con′stant•ly,** *adv.*

Con•stan•tine (kon′stən tēn′, -tīn′), *n.* **Constantine I,** (*Flavius Valerius Constantinus*) (*"the Great"*) A.D. 288?–337, Roman emperor 324–337: legally sanctioned Christian worship.

Con•stan•ti•no•ple (kon′stan tn ō′pəl), *n.* former name of ISTANBUL.

con•stel•la•tion (kon′stə lā′shən), *n.* **1.** any of various groups of stars that have been named, as Ursa Major or Orion. **2.** a group of related ideas, qualities, etc.

con•ster•na•tion (kon′stər nā′shən), *n.* a sudden, alarming amazement or dread.

con•sti•pate (kon′stə pāt′), *v.t.,* **-pat•ed, -pat•ing.** to cause constipation in.

con′sti•pa′tion, *n.* a bowel condition in which evacuation is difficult and infrequent.

con•stit•u•en•cy (kən stich′ōō ən sē), *n., pl.* **-cies. 1.** the voters in an electoral district. **2.** the district itself.

con•stit′u•ent (-ənt), *adj.* **1.** serving to make up a thing; component. **2.** having power to frame or alter a political constitution. —*n.* **3.** a component. **4.** a voter in an electoral district.

con•sti•tute (kon′sti tōōt′, -tyōōt′), *v.t.,* **-tut•ed, -tut•ing. 1.** to compose; form. **2.** to appoint. **3.** to establish, as a law. **4.** to give legal form to. —**con′sti•tut′ive,** *adj.*

con′sti•tu′tion, *n.* **1.** makeup; composition. **2.** the physical character of the body: *a strong constitution.* **3. a.** the system of fundamental principles according to which a nation, corporation, etc., is governed. **b.** the document embodying these principles.

con′sti•tu′tion•al, *adj.* **1.** of the constitution of a state, organization, etc. **2.** inherent in the makeup of a person's body or mind. —*n.* **3.** a walk taken for one's health. —**con′sti•tu′tion•al′i•ty,** *n.* —**con′sti•tu′tion•al•ly,** *adv.*

con•strain (kən strān′), *v.t.* **1.** to compel. **2.** to confine. **3.** to repress or restrain. —**con•strained′,** *adj.*

con•straint′, *n.* **1.** confinement or restriction. **2.** unnatural restraint in manner.

con•strict (kən strikt′), *v.t.* to make narrow, as by squeezing. —**con•stric′tion,** *n.* —**con•stric′tive,** *adj.*

con•stric′tor, *n.* a snake that suffocates its prey by squeezing.

con•struct (*v.* kən strukt′; *n.* kon′strukt), *v.t.* **1.** to build by putting together parts. —*n.* **2.** something constructed. —**con•struc′tor,** *n.*

con•struc•tion (kən struk′shən), *n.* **1.** the act of constructing. **2.** a structure. **3.** the arrangement of two or more words in a grammatical unit. **4.** an explanation or interpretation.

con·struc′tion·ist, *n.* a person who interprets laws in a specified manner: *a strict constructionist.*

con·struc′tive (-tiv), *adj.* **1.** helping to improve. **2.** pertaining to construction. —**con·struc′tive·ly,** *adv.*

con·strue (kən strōō′), *v.t.,* **-strued, -stru·ing. 1.** to explain or interpret. **2.** to analyze the grammatical structure of, esp. combined with translating.

con·sul (kon′səl), *n.* **1.** an official appointed by a government to look after its commercial interests and the welfare of its citizens in another country. **2.** either of the two chief magistrates of the ancient Roman republic. —**con′su·lar,** *adj.*

con·su·late (kon′sə lit), *n.* **1.** the premises officially occupied by a consul. **2.** the position or authority of a consul.

con·sult (kən sult′), *v.t.* **1.** to seek guidance or information from. **2.** to have regard for in making plans; consider. —*v.i.* **3.** to take counsel; confer: *to consult with a doctor.* —**con·sult′ant,** *n.* —**con·sul·ta·tion** (kon′səl tā′shən), *n.* —**con·sul·ta·tive** (kən-sul′tə tiv, kon′səl tā′tiv), *adj.*

con·sume (kən sōōm′), *v.t.,* **-sumed, -sum·ing. 1.** to expend by use; use up. **2.** to eat or drink up; devour. **3.** to destroy, as by burning. **4.** to spend (money, time, etc.) wastefully. **5.** to absorb; engross: *consumed with curiosity.* —**con·sum′a·ble,** *adj.*

con·sum′er, *n.* **1.** a person or thing that consumes. **2.** a person who uses a commodity or service.

con·sum′er·ism, *n.* a movement for the protection of the consumer against defective products, misleading advertising, etc.

con·sum·mate (*v.* kon′sə māt′; *adj.* kən sum′it, kon′sə mit), *v.,* **-mat·ed, -mat·ing,** *adj.* —*v.t.* **1.** to bring to completion or fulfillment. **2.** to complete (a marriage) by sexual intercourse. —*adj.* **3.** perfect; superb. —**con·sum′mate·ly,** *adv.* —**con′sum·ma′-tion,** *n.*

con·sump·tion (kən sump′shən), *n.* **1.** the act of consuming. **2.** the amount consumed. **3.** the using up of goods and services. **4.** progressive wasting of the body, esp. from tuberculosis. —**con·sump′tive,** *adj.*

cont., continued.

con·tact (kon′takt), *n.* **1.** a touching or meeting. **2.** immediate proximity or association. **3.** the state of being in communication. **4.** a person through whom one can gain information, favors, etc. **5.** CONTACT LENS. —*v.t.* **6.** to put into contact. **7.** to communicate with. —*v.i.* **8.** to enter into contact.

con′tact lens′, *n.* a small plastic disk placed over the cornea to correct vision defects.

con·ta·gion (kən tā′jən), *n.* **1.** the communication of disease by contact. **2.** a disease so communicated. **3.** the transmission of an idea, emotion, etc.

con·ta′gious, *adj.* **1.** transmitted by contact, as a disease. **2.** carrying a contagious disease. **3.** spreading from person to person: *contagious fear.* —**con·ta′gious·ly,** *adv.* —**con·ta′gious·ness,** *n.*

con·tain (kən tān′), *v.t.* **1.** to hold within its volume or area. **2.** to have capacity for. **3.** to prevent or limit the advance, spread, or influence of. —**con·tain′a·ble,** *adj.* —**con·tain′ment,** *n.*

con·tain′er, *n.* anything that can contain something, as a box or can.

con·tain′er·ize′, *v.t.,* **-ized, -iz·ing.** to package in containers. —**con·tain′er·i·za′tion,** *n.*

con·tam·i·nate (kən tam′ə nāt′), *v.t.,* **-nat·ed, -nat·ing.** to pollute; taint. —**con·tam′i·nant** (-nənt), *n.* —**con·tam′i·na′tion,** *n.*

contd., continued.

con·temn (kən tem′), *v.t.* to treat or regard with contempt.

con·tem·plate (kon′təm plāt′, -tem-), *v.,* **-plat·ed, -plat·ing.** —*v.t.* **1.** to observe thoughtfully. **2.** to consider thoroughly. **3.** to intend. —*v.i.* **4.** to consider deliberately. —**con′tem·pla′tion,** *n.*

con·tem·pla·tive (kən tem′plə tiv, kon′təm plā′-, -tem-), *adj.* **1.** characterized by contemplation. **2.** a person devoted to contemplation, as a monk. —**con·tem′pla·tive·ly,** *adv.*

con·tem·po·ra·ne·ous (kən tem′pə rā′nē əs), *adj.* occurring during the same period of time.

con·tem′po·rar′y (-rer′ē), *adj., n., pl.* **-rar·ies.** —*adj.* **1.** existing, occurring, or living at the same time. **2.** of the present time. **3.** of about the same age or date. —*n.* **4.** a person or thing belonging to the same time period as another. **5.** a person of the same age as another.

con·tempt (kən tempt′), *n.* **1.** a feeling of disdain for anything considered mean or worthless. **2.** the state of being despised. **3.** open disrespect for the rules of a court or legislative body.

con·tempt·i·ble (kən temp′tə bəl), *adj.* deserving of or held in contempt. —**con·tempt′i·bly,** *adv.*

con·temp′tu·ous (-chōō əs), *adj.* showing or expressing contempt. —**con·temp′tu·ous·ly,** *adv.*

con·tend (kən tend′), *v.i.* **1.** to struggle; compete. **2.** to dispute; argue. —*v.t.* **3.** to assert earnestly. —**con·tend′er,** *n.*

con·tent¹ (kon′tent), *n.* **1.** Usu., **-tents. a.** something that is contained. **b.** the subjects covered in a book, document, etc. **2.** significance or meaning. **3.** the amount contained.

con·tent² (kən tent′), *adj.* **1.** satisfied with what one has. —*v.t.* **2.** to make content. —*n.* **3.** satisfaction; contentment. —**con·tent′ly,** *adv.*

con·tent′ed, *adj.* satisfied; content. —**con·tent′-ed·ly,** *adv.* —**con·tent′ed·ness,** *n.*

con·ten′tion (-shən), *n.* **1.** strife; conflict. **2.** dispute; controversy. **3.** a point contended for in controversy. —**con·ten′tious,** *adj.*

con·tent′ment, *n.* the state of being contented; satisfaction.

con·ter·mi·nous (kən tûr′mə nəs), *adj.* **1.** having a common boundary; contiguous. **2.** enclosed within the same boundaries. —**con·ter′mi·nous·ly,** *adv.*

con·test (*n.* kon′test; *v.* kən test′), *n.* **1.** a competition, as for a prize. **2.** a struggle. **3.** a dispute. —*v.t.* **4.** to fight for, as in battle. **5.** to dispute; challenge. —**con·test′a·ble,** *adj.*

con·test·ant (kən tes′tənt), *n.* one who takes part in a contest or competition.

con·text (kon′tekst), *n.* **1.** the parts before and after a statement that can influence its meaning. **2.** the circumstances that surround a particular event, situation, etc. —**con·tex·tu·al** (kən teks′chōō əl), *adj.*

con·tig·u·ous (kən tig′yōō əs), *adj.* **1.** touching; in contact. **2.** near. —**con·ti·gu·i·ty** (kon′ti gyōō′i tē), *n.*

con·ti·nence (kon′tn əns), *n.* **1.** self-restraint or abstinence, esp. in regard to sexual activity. **2.** the ability to voluntarily control urinary and fecal discharge.

con′ti·nent, *n.* **1.** one of the seven main landmasses of the globe. **2. the Continent,** the mainland of Europe, as distinguished from the British Isles. —*adj.* **3.** characterized by self-restraint, esp. in sexual activity. **4.** able to control urinary and fecal discharge.

con·ti·nen·tal (-en′tl), *adj.* **1.** of or like a continent. **2.** (*usu. cap.*) European. **3.** (*cap.*) of the 13 American colonies during the American Revolution.

Con′tinen′tal Ar′my, *n.* the Revolutionary War Army, authorized by the Continental Congress in 1775 and led by George Washington.

Con′tinen′tal Con′gress, *n.* either of two American legislative congresses during and after the American Revolution. The first met in 1774 to petition the British government for a redress of grievances. The second existed from 1775 to 1789 and adopted the Declaration of Independence and the Articles of Confederation.

continen′tal divide′, *n.* **1.** a divide separating river systems that flow to opposite sides of a continent. **2.** (*caps.*) Also called **Great Divide.** the watershed in North America formed by the Rocky Mountains, separating streams flowing west from those flowing east.

con′tinen′tal drift′, *n.* the lateral movement of continents resulting from the motion of crustal plates.

con'tinen'tal shelf', n. the part of a continent submerged in relatively shallow sea.

con•tin•gen•cy (kən tin'jən sē), n., pl. -cies. 1. dependence on chance. 2. a chance event.

con•tin'gent, adj. 1. dependent on something not yet certain. 2. possible. 3. fortuitous; accidental. —n. 4. a quota of troops. 5. one of the groups composing an assemblage.

con•tin•u•al (kən tin'yōō əl), adj. 1. often repeated; very frequent. 2. continuous in time. —con•tin'u•al•ly, adv. —Usage. Although the words are normally used interchangeably in all kinds of speech and writing, commentators generally advise that CONTINUAL be used only to mean "intermittent" and CONTINUOUS only to mean "uninterrupted." To avoid confusion, one could use intermittent and uninterrupted instead.

con•tin'u•ance, n. 1. the act of continuing. 2. duration or prolongation. 3. a postponement of a legal proceeding.

con•tin•u•a'tion (-ā'shən), n. 1. the act of continuing or state of being continued. 2. extension to a further point. 3. a supplement; sequel.

con•tin'ue, v., -ued, -u•ing. —v.i. 1. to go on without interruption. 2. to resume. 3. to last or endure. 4. to remain in a particular state, capacity, or place. —v.t. 5. to go on with. 6. to carry on from the point of interruption. 7. to extend; prolong. 8. to retain, as in a position. 9. to postpone, as a legal proceeding.

con•ti•nu•i•ty (kon'tn ōō'i tē, -tn yōō'-), n., pl. -ties. 1. the state of being continuous. 2. a continuous whole. 3. a motion-picture scenario.

con•tin•u•ous (kən tin'yōō əs), adj. uninterrupted; going on without stop. —con•tin'u•ous•ly, adv. —Usage. See CONTINUAL.

con•tin'u•um (-yōō əm), n., pl. -u•a (-yōō ə). a continuous extent, series, or whole.

con•tort (kən tôrt'), v.t., v.i. to twist or become twisted out of shape. —con•tort'ed, adj. —con•tor'tion, n.

con•tor'tion•ist, n. a person who performs gymnastic feats involving contorted postures.

con•tour (kon'tŏŏr), n. 1. the outline of a figure or body. —v.t. 2. to shape to fit a certain form. —adj. 3. shaped to fit a particular form.

contra-, a prefix meaning against, opposite, or opposing (contradistinction).

con•tra•band (kon'trə band'), n. 1. anything prohibited by law from being imported or exported. 2. goods imported or exported illegally.

con'tra•cep'tion (-sep'shən), n. the deliberate prevention of conception or impregnation. —con'tra•cep'tive, adj., n.

con•tract (n., v. 6, 8 kon'trakt; v. kən trakt'), n. 1. an agreement, esp. one enforceable by law. —v.t. 2. to draw the parts of together: to contract a muscle. 3. to shorten (a word, phrase, etc.) by omitting some elements. 4. to get, as by exposure to contagion. 5. to incur, as a debt. 6. to assign (a job, project, etc.) by contract. —v.i. 7. to become smaller; shrink. 8. to enter into a contract. —con•trac'tu•al, adj.

con•trac•tile (kən trak'tl, -til), adj. capable of contracting or causing contraction.

con•trac'tion (-shən), n. 1. the act of contracting or state of being contracted. 2. a shortened form of a word or phrase, as isn't for is not. 3. the shortening of a muscle, esp. of a uterine muscle during childbirth.

con•trac•tor (kon'trak tər, kən trak'tər), n. one who contracts to furnish supplies or perform work, esp. in construction.

con•tra•dict (kon'trə dikt'), v.t. 1. to assert the contrary of. 2. to imply a denial of: His lifestyle contradicts his principles. —v.i. 3. to utter a contrary statement. —con'tra•dic'tion, n. —con'tra•dic'to•ry (-dik'tə rē), adj.

con'tra•dis•tinc'tion, n. distinction by contrast.

con•trail (kon'trāl'), n. a visible condensation of water droplets or ice crystals in the wake of an aircraft, rocket, or missile. [con(densation) + trail]

con'tra•in'di•cate', v.t., -cat•ed, -cat•ing. to make (a procedure or treatment) inadvisable. —con'tra•in'di•ca'tion, n.

con•tral•to (kən tral'tō), n., pl. -tos. 1. the lowest female voice, intermediate between soprano and tenor. 2. a singer with such a voice.

con•trap•tion (kən trap'shən), n. a contrivance; gadget.

con'tra•pun'tal (-pun'tl), adj. composed of two or more independent melodies sounded together.

con•trar•i•wise (kon'trer ē wīz'), adv. 1. in the opposite way. 2. on the contrary.

con•trar•y (kon'trer ē; for 3 also kən trâr'ē), adj., n., pl. -trar•ies, adv. —adj. 1. opposite in character, direction, etc. 2. unfavorable or adverse. 3. stubbornly opposed or willful. —n. 4. something that is opposite. —adv. 5. oppositely; counter. —Idiom. 6. on the contrary, in opposition to what has been stated. 7. to the contrary, to the opposite effect. —con'trar•i•ly (kon'trer ə lē, kən trâr'-), adv. —con'trar•i•ness, n.

con•trast (v. kən trast', kon'trast; n. kon'trast), v.t. 1. to compare in order to show differences. —v.i. 2. to exhibit unlikeness on comparison. —n. 3. the act of contrasting or state of being contrasted. 4. a striking exhibition of unlikeness. 5. a person or thing that is strikingly unlike in comparison.

con'tra•vene' (-vēn'), v.t., -vened, -ven•ing. 1. to deny or oppose. 2. to go or act against; violate. —con'tra•ven'tion (-ven'shən), n.

con•tre•temps (kon'trə tän'; Fr. kôNTRə tän'), n., pl. -temps (-tänz'; Fr. -tän'). an inopportune or embarrassing occurrence.

con•trib•ute (kən trib'yōōt), v.t., v.i., -ut•ed, -ut•ing. 1. to give (money, assistance, etc.) together with others. 2. to furnish (an article, drawing, etc.) for publication. —Idiom. 3. contribute to, to be a factor in. —con•tri•bu•tion (kon'trə byōō'shən), n. —con•trib'u•tor, n. —con•trib'u•to/ry (-tôr'ē), adj.

con•trite (kən trīt'), adj. caused by or showing sincere remorse. —con•trite'ly, adv. —con•trite'ness, n. —con•tri'tion (-trish'ən), n.

con•trive (kən trīv'), v.t., -trived, -triv•ing. 1. to plan with ingenuity. 2. to bring about by a scheme. —con•triv'ance, n. —con•triv'er, n.

con•trol (kən trōl'), v., -trolled, -trol•ling, n. —v.t. 1. to exercise restraint or direction over. 2. to hold in check. 3. to test (a scientific experiment) by a standard of comparison. —n. 4. the act or power of controlling. 5. a check or restraint. 6. a device for operating a machine. —con•trol'la•ble, adj.

control' freak', n. a person having a strong need to control his or her surroundings.

controlled' sub'stance, n. a drug whose possesion and use are restricted by law.

con•trol'ler, n. 1. a government or corporate officer who superintends finances. 2. a person or device that regulates.

con•tro•ver•sy (kon'trə vûr'sē), n., pl. -sies. 1. a usu. prolonged public dispute. 2. an argument. —con'tro•ver'sial, adj.

con•tro•vert (kon'trə vûrt', kon'trə vûrt'), v.t. 1. to dispute; deny. 2. to argue about; debate. —con'tro•vert'i•ble, adj.

con•tu•ma•cious (kon'tŏŏ mā'shəs, -tyŏŏ-), adj. stubbornly disobedient. —con'tu•ma'cious•ly, adv. —con'tu•ma•cy (-mə sē), n., pl. -cies.

con•tu•me•ly (kon'tŏŏ mə lē, -tyŏŏ-; kən tŏŏ'mə lē, -tyŏŏ'-), n., pl. -lies. an insulting display of contempt. —con'tu•me'li•ous (-mē'lē əs), adj.

con•tu•sion (kən tŏŏ'zhən, -tyŏŏ'-), n. a bruise. —con•tuse' (-tŏŏz', -tyŏŏz'), v.t., -tused, -tus•ing.

co•nun•drum (kə nun'drəm), n. 1. a riddle whose answer involves a pun. 2. anything that puzzles.

con•ur•ba•tion (kon'ər bā'shən), n. a large, continuous group of cities or towns that retain their separate identities.

con•va•lesce (kon'və les'), v.i., -lesced, -lesc•ing. to recover health after illness. —con'va•les'cence, n. —con'va•les'cent, adj., n.

con•vec•tion (kən vek'shən), n. the transfer of

heat by the movement of the heated parts of a liquid or gas.

con·vene (kən vēn′), v.i., v.t., -vened, -ven·ing. to assemble or cause to assemble, esp. for a meeting.

con·ven·ience (kən vēn′yəns), n. 1. the quality of being convenient. 2. anything that saves work or adds to one's comfort. 3. a convenient situation or time: at your convenience. 4. comfort or ease.

con·ven′ient, adj. 1. suitable to the needs or purpose. 2. at hand; accessible. —con·ven′ient·ly, adv.

con·vent (kon′vent, -vənt), n. 1. a community, esp. of nuns, devoted to religious life. 2. the building occupied by such a community.

con·ven·ti·cle (kən ven′ti kəl), n. a secret or unauthorized meeting, esp. for religious worship.

con·ven·tion (kən ven′shən), n. 1. an assembly, as of delegates, to act on matters of common concern. 2. an agreement; compact. 3. an accepted usage, standard, or custom.

con·ven′tion·al, adj. 1. conforming to accepted standards. 2. established by accepted usage. 3. ordinary. 4. nonnuclear: conventional weapons. 5. of a convention. —con·ven′tion·al′i·ty, n., pl. -ties. —con·ven′tion·al·ize′, v.t., -ized, -iz·ing. —con·ven′tion·al·ly, adv.

con·verge (kən vûrj′), v.i, -verged, -verg·ing. to tend to meet in a point or line. —con·ver′gence, n. —con·ver′gent, adj.

con·ver·sant (kən vûr′sənt, kon′vər-), adj. familiar by use or study.

con·ver·sa·tion (kon′vər sā′shən), n. 1. informal oral communication between people. 2. an instance of this. —con′ver·sa′tion·al, adj. —con′ver·sa′tion·al·ist, n. —con′ver·sa′tion·al·ly, adv.

conversa′tion piece′, n. any object that arouses comment because of some striking quality.

con·verse[1] (v. kən vûrs′; n. kon′vûrs), v., -versed, -vers·ing, n. —v.i. 1. to talk informally with another. —n. 2. conversation.

con·verse[2] (adj. kən vûrs′, kon′vûrs; n. kon′vûrs), adj. 1. opposite or contrary in direction, action, etc. —n. 2. something opposite or contrary. —con·verse′ly, adv.

con·vert (v. kən vûrt′; n. kon′vûrt), v.t. 1. to change into a different form. 2. to cause to adopt a different religion, political doctrine, etc. 3. to obtain an equivalent value for in an exchange or calculation, as money or units of measurement. 4. to assume unlawful rights of ownership of (personal property). —v.i. 5. to become converted. —n. 6. a person converted, as to a religion. —con·ver′sion (-vûr′zhən), n. —con·vert′er, n.

con·vert′i·ble, adj. 1. capable of being converted. —n. 2. an automobile or boat with a folding top. 3. a sofa that folds out for use as a bed.

con·vex (kon veks′, kən-), adj. curved or rounded outward like the outside of a circle. —con·vex′i·ty, n.

con·vey (kən vā′), v.t. 1. to take from one place to another. 2. to communicate; impart. —con·vey′a·ble, adj. —con·vey′or, con·vey′er, n.

con·vey′ance, n. 1. the act of conveying. 2. a means of transporting, esp. a vehicle.

convey′or belt′, n. an endless belt or chain for carrying objects short distances.

con·vict (v. kən vikt′; n. kon′vikt), v.t. 1. to prove guilty of an offense, esp. after a legal trial. —n. 2. a person serving a prison sentence.

con·vic′tion, n. 1. a firm belief. 2. the act of convicting or state of being convicted.

con·vince (kən vins′), v.t., -vinced, -vinc·ing. to persuade by argument and evidence. —con·vinc′ing, adj. —con·vinc′ing·ly, adv. ——Usage. Some commentators claim that CONVINCE may never be followed by to, as in We convinced him to enter the contest. However, this use is and always has been standard in all varieties of speech and writing.

con·viv·i·al (kən viv′ē əl), adj. 1. friendly; agreeable. 2. fond of feasting, drinking, and merry company. 3. festive. —con·viv′i·al′i·ty, n.

con·vo·ca·tion (kon′və kā′shən), n. 1. the act of convoking. 2. an assembly.

con·voke (kən vōk′), v.t., -voked, -vok·ing. to summon to meet or assemble.

con·vo·lut·ed (kon′və lōō′tid), adj. 1. twisted; coiled. 2. complicated; intricately involved.

con′vo·lu′tion, n. 1. a coiled condition. 2. a coiling together.

con·voy (kon′voi; v. also kən voi′), n. 1. a ship accompanied by a protecting escort. 2. a group of vehicles traveling together. 3. the act of escorting. —v.t. 4. to escort, usu. for protection.

con·vulse (kən vuls′), v.t., -vulsed, -vuls·ing. 1. to shake violently. 2. to cause to shake violently with laughter, pain, etc.

con·vul′sion, n. 1. a series of violent, involuntary muscular contractions. 2. a violent disturbance. 3. an outburst of laughter. —con·vul′sive, adj. —con·vul′sive·ly, adv.

coo (kōō), v.i. 1. to utter or imitate the murmur of doves. 2. to murmur fondly or amorously. —n. 3. a cooing sound.

cook (kŏŏk), v.t. 1. to prepare (food) by the use of heat. —v.i. 2. to prepare food by the use of heat. 3. (of food) to undergo cooking. 4. cook up, Informal. to concoct or contrive. —n. 5. a person who cooks. ——Proverb. 6. Too many cooks spoil the broth, having too many people work on a project results in confusion and inattention. —cook′er, n.

Cook (kŏŏk), n. Captain James, 1728–79, English explorer.

cook′book′, n. a book containing recipes and instructions for cooking.

cook′er·y, n. the art of cooking.

cook′ie, n. 1. a small, flat, sweet cake. ——Idiom. 2. the way the cookie crumbles, the way things happen.

cook′out′, n. an outdoor gathering at which food is cooked and consumed.

cool (kōōl), adj., -er, -est, n., v. —adj. 1. moderately cold. 2. permitting relief from heat: a cool dress. 3. not excited; calm. 4. lacking in cordiality. 5. calmly audacious. 6. unresponsive; indifferent. 7. Slang. a. great; excellent. b. highly skilled. c. socially adept. —n. 8. a cool part, place, or time: the cool of the evening. 9. calmness; composure. —v.i., v.t 10. to become or make cool. —cool′ly, adv. —cool′ness, n.

cool′ant, n. a substance used to reduce the temperature of a system.

cool′er, n. 1. a container for keeping something cool. 2. a tall, iced drink. 3. Slang. JAIL.

Cool·idge (kōō′lij), n. Calvin, 1872–1933, 30th president of the U.S. 1923–29.

coo·lie (kōō′lē), n. an unskilled laborer hired at low wages, esp. formerly in the Far East.

coon (kōōn), n. a raccoon.

coon′skin′, n. 1. the pelt of a raccoon. 2. an article of clothing made of coonskin, esp. a hat with a tail.

co-op (kō′op), n. a cooperative enterprise, building, or apartment.

coop (kōōp, kŏŏp), n. 1. an enclosure or pen, as for poultry. —v.t. 2. to place in or as if in a coop.

coop·er (kōō′pər, kŏŏp′ər), n. one who makes or repairs casks, barrels, etc. —coop′er·age (-ij), n.

Coo·per (kōō′pər, kŏŏp′ər), n. 1. James Fenimore, 1789–1851, U.S. novelist. 2. Peter, 1791–1833, U.S. inventor and philanthropist.

co·op·er·ate (kō op′ə rāt′), v.i., -at·ed, -at·ing. to work or act together for a common purpose or benefit. —co·op′er·a′tion, n. —co·op′er·a′tor, n.

co·op′er·a·tive (-ər ə tiv, -ə rā′tiv), adj. 1. cooperating or willing to cooperate. —n. 2. an enterprise providing goods or services, owned and operated by its members. 3. a. a building owned and managed by a corporation in which shares are sold, entitling shareholders to occupy individual units. b. an apartment in such a building. —co·op′er·a·tive·ly, adv.

co-opt (kō opt′), v.t. 1. to choose as a fellow member. 2. to win over into a larger group.

co·or·di·nate (adj., n. kō ôr′dn it, -dn āt′; v. -āt′), adj., n., v., -nat·ed, -nat·ing. —adj. 1. of the same order, rank, or degree. 2. of or involving coordination or coordinates. —*n.* **3.** a coordinate person or thing. —*v.t.* **4.** to place in the same order or rank. **5.** to place in proper order or relation. —**co•or′di•na′-tor,** *n.*

coor′dinating conjunc′tion, *n.* a conjunction connecting grammatical elements of equal rank, as *and* in *Sue and Joe.*

co•or′di•na′tion, *n.* **1.** the act of coordinating or state of being coordinated. **2.** harmonious combination or interaction.

coot (kōt), *n.* **1.** any of various swimming or diving birds. **2.** *Informal.* a foolish or crotchety person.

cop¹ (kop), *v.t.,* **copped, cop•ping.** *Slang.* **1.** to steal; filch. **2. cop out, a.** to renege. **b.** to give up or back out.

cop² (kop), *n. Informal.* a police officer.

co•pay (kō′pā′), *n.* a fixed amount required by a health insurer to be paid by the patient to the health-care provider. Also called **co•pay•ment** (kō′pā′-mənt).

cope¹ (kōp), *v.i.,* **coped, cop•ing. 1.** to struggle, esp. successfully. **2.** to deal with responsibilities or problems.

cope

cope² (kōp), *n.* **1.** a long mantle worn by an ecclesiastic, esp. in processions. **2.** any cloaklike covering.

Co•pen•ha•gen (kō′pən hā′gən, -hä′-, kō′pən hā′-, -hä′-), *n.* the capital of Denmark. 802,391.

Co•per•ni•cus (kō pûr′ni kəs, kə-), *n.* **Nicolaus,** 1473–1543, Polish astronomer. —**Co•per′ni•can,** *adj.*

cop•i•er (kop′ē ər), *n.* **1.** one that copies. **2.** an office machine for making instant copies of printed material.

co•pi•lot (kō′pī′lət), *n.* a pilot who is second in command of an aircraft.

cop•ing (kō′ping), *n.* the top covering of an exterior masonry wall.

co•pi•ous (kō′pē əs), *adj.* abundant; plentiful. —**co′pi•ous•ly,** *adv.* —**co′pi•ous•ness,** *n.*

Cop•land (kōp′lənd), *n.* **Aaron,** 1900–90, U.S. composer.

cop′-out′, *n.* an act or instance of copping out.

cop•per (kop′ər), *n.* **1.** a metallic element having a reddish brown color: used as an electrical conductor and in the manufacture of alloys. *Symbol:* Cu; *at. wt.:* 63.54; *at. no.:* 29. **2.** a reddish brown. **3.** a copper or bronze coin. [< L *cuprum*] —**cop′per•y,** *adj.*

cop′per•head′, *n.* a North American pit viper with a copper-colored head.

cop•ra (kop′rə, kō′prə), *n.* the dried, oil-bearing meat of the coconut.

copse (kops) also **cop•pice** (kop′is), *n.* a thicket of small trees or bushes.

cop•ter (kop′tər), *n.* a helicopter.

Cop′tic Church′, *n.* the Christian church in Egypt.

cop•u•la (kop′yə lə), *n., pl.* **-las, -lae** (-lē′). a verb, as *be* or *seem,* that links a subject and predicate. —**cop′u•la′tive** (-lā′tiv, -lə tiv), *adj.*

cop•u•late (kop′yə lāt′), *v.i.,* **-lat•ed, -lat•ing.** to engage in sexual intercourse. —**cop′u•la′tion,** *n.*

cop•y (kop′ē), *n., pl.* **-ies** for 1, 2, *v.,* **-ied, -y•ing.** —*n.* **1.** an imitation, reproduction, or transcript of an

original. **2.** one of the various specimens of the same book, engraving, or the like. **3.** matter to be reproduced in printed form. **4.** the text of a news story, advertisement, etc. —*v.t., v.i.* **5.** to make a copy or copies (of). **6.** to imitate.

cop′y•cat′, *n.* a person or thing that imitates another.

cop′y desk′, *n.* the desk in a newspaper office at which copy is edited and prepared for printing.

cop′y•ed′it, *v.t.* to edit (a text) for publication. —**cop′y•ed′i•tor,** *n.*

cop′y•right′, *n.* **1.** the exclusive right to use a literary, musical, or artistic work, protected by law for a specified period of time. —*v.t.* **2.** to secure a copyright on.

cop′y•writ′er, *n.* a writer of copy, esp. for advertisements.

co•quette (kō ket′), *n.* a woman who flirts insincerely. —**co•quet′tish,** *adj.*

cor-, var. of com- before *r.*

cor•al (kôr′əl, kor′-), *n.* **1.** the hard skeleton secreted by certain marine polyps. **2.** such skeletons collectively, forming reefs, islands, etc. **3.** a yellowish red or pink. —*adj.* **4.** of or like coral.

cor′al snake′, *n.* a venomous snake, with bands of red, yellow, and black.

cor•bel (kôr′bəl), *n.* an architectural bracket projecting from a wall to support a weight.

cord (kôrd), *n.* **1.** a string or thin rope made of several strands twisted or woven together. **2.** a small, flexible, insulated electrical cable. **3.** a ribbed fabric, esp. corduroy. **4.** a rib on the surface of cloth. **5.** a cordlike structure: *the spinal cord.* **6.** a unit of volume used for fuel wood, equal to 128 cubic feet (3.6 cubic meters). —*v.t.* **7.** to fasten with a cord.

cord•age (kôr′dij), *n.* lines, hawsers, etc., esp. on the rigging of a ship.

cor•dial (kôr′jəl), *adj.* **1.** courteous and gracious. —*n.* **2.** a liqueur. —**cor•dial′i•ty** (-jal′i tē, -jē al′-), *n.* —**cor′dial•ly,** *adv.*

cor•dil•le•ra (kôr′dl yâr′ə, -âr′ə), *n., pl.* **-ras.** a chain of mountains.

cord•ite (kôr′dīt), *n.* a smokeless explosive composed of nitroglycerin, cellulose nitrate, and mineral jelly.

cord′less, *adj.* (of an electrical appliance) having a self-contained power supply.

cor•don (kôr′dn), *n.* **1.** a line of police, warships, etc., guarding an area. **2.** a cord or ribbon worn as an ornament. —*v.t.* **3.** to surround with a cordon.

cor•do•van (kôr′də vən), *n.* a soft, smooth leather.

cor•du•roy (kôr′də roi′), *n.* **1.** a cotton-filling pile fabric with lengthwise cords. **2. corduroys,** trousers made of this fabric.

core (kôr), *n., v.,* **cored, cor•ing.** —*n.* **1.** the central part of a fleshy fruit, containing the seeds. **2.** the central or most essential part. —*v.t.* **3.** to remove the core of. —**cor′er,** *n.*

co•re•spond•ent (kō′ri spon′dənt), *n.* a joint defendant, esp. a person charged with adultery in a divorce proceeding.

co•ri•an•der (kôr′ē an′dər), *n.* an herb of the parsley family whose seeds are used as a flavoring.

Cor•inth (kôr′inth, kor′-), *n.* an ancient city in Greece. —**Co•rin′thi•an** (kə rin′thē ən), *adj., n.*

Co•rin•thi•ans (kə rin′thē ənz), *n.* either of two books of the New Testament, I Corinthians or II Corinthians, written by Paul.

cork (kôrk), *n.* **1.** the thick lightweight layer of a Mediterranean oak used for making floats, bottle stoppers, etc. **2.** a piece of cork or the like used as a stopper. —*v.t.* **3.** to stop with or as if with a cork. —**Idiom. 4. blow** or **pop one's cork,** *Informal.* to lose one's temper.

cork′screw′, *n.* **1.** a spiral instrument with a sharp point, used for drawing corks from bottles. —*adj.* **2.** spiral. —*v.t., v.i.* **3.** to move in a spiral course.

corm (kôrm), *n.* a fleshy, bulblike base of a stem, as in a crocus.

crosier

cor•mo•rant (kôr′mər ənt), *n.* a diving seabird with a long neck and a throat pouch for holding fish.

corn[1] (kôrn), *n.* **1. a.** a cereal plant bearing kernels on large ears. **b.** the kernels of this plant, used as food. **c.** the ears of this plant. **2.** *Informal.* old-fashioned, trite, or sentimental material. —*v.t.* **3.** to preserve and season with brine.

corn[2] (kôrn), *n.* a horny growth of tissue formed over a bone, esp. on the toes.

corn′ball′, *Informal.* —*n.* **1.** a person who indulges in clichés. —*adj.* **2.** corny.

corn′ bread′ or **corn′bread′,** *n.* a bread made with cornmeal.

corn′cob′, *n.* the elongated woody core in which the grains of an ear of corn are embedded.

cor•ne•a (kôr′nē ə), *n., pl.* **-ne•as.** the transparent part of the external coat of the eye covering the iris and pupil. —**cor′ne•al,** *adj.*

Cor•nell (kôr nel′), *n.* Ezra, 1809–74, U.S. capitalist and philanthropist.

cor•ner (kôr′nər), *n.* **1.** the meeting place of two converging lines or surfaces. **2.** the angle so formed. **3.** the point where two streets meet. **4.** any narrow or secluded place. **5.** an awkward position from which escape is impossible. **6.** a monopoly on a stock or commodity. **7.** region; quarter. —*adj.* **8.** on, at, or for a corner. —*v.t.* **9.** to place in or drive into a corner. **10.** to gain control of (a stock, commodity, etc.). —*Idiom.* **11. cut corners,** to reduce costs or care in execution.

cor′ner•stone′, *n.* **1.** a stone representing the starting place in the construction of a building, usu. carved with the date. **2.** something that is essential or basic. **3.** (*cap.*) Jesus Christ. Mark 12:10; I Peter 2:6.

cor•net (kôr net′), *n.* a valved wind instrument of the trumpet family.

corn′flow′er, *n.* a European composite plant with blue flower heads.

cor•nice (kôr′nis), *n.* a projecting molded feature surmounting a wall, doorway, or building.

corn′meal′, *n.* meal made from corn.

corn′row′, *n.* a narrow braid of hair plaited tightly against the scalp.

corn′starch′, *n.* a starchy flour made from corn, used for thickening gravies, sauces, etc.

corn′ syr′up, *n.* syrup made from corn.

cor•nu•co•pi•a (kôr′nə kō′pē ə, -nyə-), *n., pl.* **-pi•as. 1.** a horn containing food and drink in endless supply. **2.** an abundant supply. [< LL, = L *cornū* horn + *cōpiae* of plenty]

cornucopia

corn′y, *adj.,* **-i•er, -i•est.** *Informal.* old-fashioned, trite, or sentimental.

co•rol•la (kə rol′ə, -rō′lə), *n., pl.* **-las.** the inner whorl of floral leaves of a flower.

cor•ol•lar•y (kôr′ə ler′ē, kor′-), *n., pl.* **-lar•ies. 1.** *Math.* a proposition that is incidentally proved in proving another proposition. **2.** a natural consequence.

co•ro•na (kə rō′nə), *n., pl.* **-nas, -nae** (-nē). **1.** a circle of light seen around a luminous body, esp. the sun or moon. **2.** an envelope of ionized gas around the sun, visible during a total solar eclipse. —**co•ro′nal,** *adj.*

cor•o•nar•y (kôr′ə ner′ē, kor′-), *adj., n., pl.* **-nar•ies.** —*adj.* **1.** of the heart. **2.** of the arteries that orig-inate in the aorta and supply the heart muscle with blood. —*n.* **3.** a heart attack, esp. a coronary thrombosis.

cor′onary thrombo′sis, *n.* a coronary occlusion in which there is blockage of a coronary arterial branch by a blood clot within the vessel.

cor•o•na•tion (kôr′ə nā′shən, kor′-), *n.* the act of crowning a sovereign.

cor•o•ner (kôr′ə nər, kor′-), *n.* a public officer whose chief function is to investigate any death not clearly resulting from natural causes.

cor•o•net (kôr′ə net′, kor′-), *n.* **1.** a small crown worn by nobles or peers. **2.** a crownlike ornament for the head.

corp. or **Corp.,** corporation.

cor•po•ra (kôr′pər ə), *n.* pl. of CORPUS.

cor•po•ral[1] (kôr′pər əl), *adj.* of the human body; physical: *corporal punishment.*

cor•po•ral[2] (kôr′pər əl), *n.* a noncommissioned officer ranking just below a sergeant.

cor•po•rate (kôr′pər it), *adj.* **1.** of, for, or belonging to a corporation. **2.** united into one.

cor′porate raid′er, *n.* a person who seizes control of a company, as by secretly buying stock.

cor′porate wel′fare, *n.* financial assistance, as tax breaks, given by the government esp. to large companies.

cor′po•ra′tion (-rā′shən), *n.* an association of individuals, created by law and existing as an entity with powers and liabilities independent of those of its members.

cor•po•re•al (kôr pôr′ē əl), *adj.* **1.** of the nature of the physical body. **2.** material; tangible.

corps (kôr, kōr), *n., pl.* **corps** (kôrz). **1. a.** a military organization of officers and enlisted personnel or of officers alone. **b.** a combat unit comprising two or more divisions. **2.** a group of persons associated or acting together.

corpse (kôrps), *n.* a dead body, usu. of a human being.

cor•pu•lence (kôr′pyə ləns), *n.* fatness; portliness. —**cor′pu•lent,** *adj.*

cor•pus (kôr′pəs), *n., pl.* **-po•ra** (-pər ə). **1.** a large or complete collection of writings. **2.** a body, esp. when dead.

Cor•pus Chris•ti[1] (kôr′pəs kris′tē, -tī), *n.* a festival in honor of the Eucharist, celebrated on the Thursday after Trinity Sunday. [< ML: lit., body of Christ]

Cor•pus Chris•ti[2] (kôr′pəs kris′tē), *n.* a seaport in S Texas. 275,419.

cor•pus•cle (kôr′pə səl, -pus əl), *n.* **1.** an unattached cell, esp. a blood or lymph cell. **2.** any minute particle.

cor′pus de•lic′ti (di lik′tī), *n., pl.* **corpora delicti. 1.** the basic element of a crime, as, in murder, the fact that a death has occurred. **2.** the body of a murder victim.

cor•ral (kə ral′), *n., v.,* **-ralled, -ral•ling.** —*n.* **1.** a pen for horses, cattle, etc. —*v.t.* **2.** to confine in or as if in a corral. **3.** *Informal.* to seize; capture.

cor•rect (kə rekt′), *v.t.* **1.** to set make right. **2.** to point out or mark the errors in. **3.** to rebuke or punish. **4.** to counteract the effect of (something hurtful). —*adj.* **5.** true; accurate. **6.** in accordance with an acknowledged standard; proper. —**cor•rect′a•ble,** *adj.* —**cor•rec′tive,** *adj., n.* —**cor•rect′ly,** *adv.* —**cor•rect′ness,** *n.*

cor•rec′tion, *n.* **1.** something substituted for what is wrong or inaccurate. **2.** the act of correcting. **3.** punishment or chastisement. **4.** an adjustment made in order to increase accuracy. —**cor•rec′tion•al,** *adj.*

cor•re•late (kôr′ə lāt′, kor′-), *v.t.,* **-lat•ed, -lat•ing.** to bring into mutual or reciprocal relation. —**cor′re•la′tion,** *n.*

cor•rel•a•tive (kə rel′ə tiv), *adj.* **1.** so related that each implies or complements the other. **2.** *Gram.* complementing one another and used in association, as *either* and *or.* —*n.* **3.** a correlative expression.

cor•re•spond (kôr′ə spond′, kor′-), *v.i.* **1.** to be in agreement or conformity; match. **2.** to be similar or analogous. **3.** to communicate by letters. —**cor′re•spond′ing,** adj.

cor′re•spond′ence, n. **1.** communication by letters. **2.** letters between correspondents. **3.** similarity or analogy. **4.** agreement; conformity.

cor′re•spond′ent, n. **1.** a person who communicates by letters. **2.** a person employed by a newspaper, television network, etc., to report news from a distant place. **3.** a thing that corresponds. —adj. **4.** similar or analogous.

cor•ri•dor (kôr′i dər, -dôr′, kor′-), n. **1.** a hallway. **2.** a narrow tract of land forming an outlet through foreign territory. **3.** a densely populated region with major transportation routes.

cor′ridors of pow′er, n.pl. centers of political and governmental power.

cor•rob•o•rate (kə rob′ə rāt′), v.t., **-rat•ed, -rat•ing.** to make more certain; confirm. —**cor•rob′o•ra′tion,** n. —**cor•rob′o•ra′tive** (-ə rā′tiv, -ər ə tiv), adj. —**cor•rob′o•ra′tor,** n.

cor•rode (kə rōd′), v., **-rod•ed, -rod•ing.** —v.t. **1.** to eat or wear away gradually, esp. by chemical action. —v.i. **2.** to become corroded. —**cor•ro′sion** (-zhən), n. —**cor•ro′sive** (-siv), adj.

cor•ru•gate (kôr′ə gāt′, kor′-), v., **-gat•ed, -gat•ing.** —v.t. **1.** to bend into folds or alternate furrows and ridges. —v.i. **2.** to become corrugated. —**cor′ru•ga′tion,** n.

cor•rupt (kə rupt′), adj. **1.** guilty of dishonest practices, as bribery. **2.** debased in character. —v.t., v.i. **3.** to make or become corrupt. —**cor•rupt′i•ble,** adj. —**cor•rup′tion,** n. —**cor•rupt′ly,** adv.

cor•sage (kôr säzh′), n. a small bouquet worn by a woman, as at the shoulder.

cor•sair (kôr′sâr), n. a pirate or pirate ship, esp. formerly of the Barbary Coast.

cor•set (kôr′sit), n. a close-fitting, stiffened undergarment worn to shape and support the torso.

cor•tege or **-tège** (kôr tezh′, -tāzh′), n. **1.** a procession, esp. a ceremonial one. **2.** a train of attendants; retinue.

cor•tex (kôr′teks), n., pl. **-ti•ces** (-tə sēz′). **1. a.** the outer layer of a body organ or structure. **b.** CEREBRAL CORTEX. **2.** the portion of a plant stem between the epidermis and the vascular tissue. —**cor′ti•cal** (-ti-kəl), adj.

cor•ti•sone (kôr′tə zōn′, -sōn′), n. an adrenal hormone used chiefly in the treatment of autoimmune and inflammatory diseases.

co•run•dum (kə run′dəm), n. a mineral noted for its hardness: transparent varieties, as sapphire and ruby, are used as gems.

cor•us•cate (kôr′ə skat′, kor′-), v.i., **-cat•ed, -cat•ing.** to emit vivid flashes of light; sparkle; scintillate. —**cor′us•ca′tion,** n.

cor•vette (kôr vet′), n. **1.** a sailing warship smaller than a frigate. **2.** a lightly armed ship used esp. as a convoy escort.

co•sign (kō′sīn′, kō sīn′), v.i., v.t. to sign as a cosigner.

co•sig•na•to•ry (kō sig′nə tôr′ē), n., pl. **-ries.** a person who signs a document, as a treaty, jointly with another.

co′sign′er, n. **1.** a cosignatory. **2.** a joint signer of a negotiable instrument, esp. a promissory note.

cos•met•ic (koz met′ik), n. **1.** a preparation for beautifying the skin, hair, etc. —adj. **2.** imparting beauty. **3.** superficial. —**cos•met′i•cal•ly,** adv.

cos•me•tol•o•gy (-mi tol′ə jē), n. the art of applying cosmetics. —**cos′me•tol′o•gist,** n.

cos•mic (koz′mik), adj. **1.** of the cosmos. **2.** vast. —**cos′mi•cal•ly,** adv.

cos′mic ray′, n. a radiation of high penetrating power originating in outer space.

cos•mog•o•ny (-mog′ə nē), n., pl. **-nies.** a theory or story of the origin and development of the universe. —**cos•mog′o•nist,** n.

cos•mol•o•gy (-mol′ə jē), n. the study of the origin and general structure of the universe. —**cos′mo•log′i•cal** (-mə loj′i kəl), adj.

cos′mo•naut′ (-mə nôt′, -not′), n. a Russian or Soviet astronaut.

cos•mo•pol•i•tan (koz′mə pol′i tn), adj. **1.** composed of people or elements from many parts of the world. **2.** worldly; sophisticated. **3.** widely distributed. —n. **4.** a cosmopolitan person. —**cos′mo•pol′i•tan•ism,** n.

cos′mos (-məs, -mōs), n., pl. **-mos, -mos•es** for 2. **1.** the universe regarded as an orderly system. **2.** any complete, orderly system. [< Gk kósmos order, form, arrangement]

Cos•sack (kos′ak, -ək), n. a member of various tribes of warriors living chiefly in S and SW Russia and serving as cavalry under the czars.

cos•set (kos′it), v.t. to pamper; coddle.

cost (kôst, kost), n., v., **cost, cost•ing.** —n. **1.** the price paid to acquire or accomplish anything. **2.** a sacrifice or penalty. —v.t. **3.** to require the payment of. **4.** to result in the loss or injury of. —**Idiom. 5. at all costs,** by any means necessary.

co•star or **co-star** (n. kō′stär′; v. -stär′), n., v., **-starred, -star•ring.** —n. **1.** a performer who shares star billing with another. —v.t., v.i. **2.** to feature or appear as a costar.

Cos•ta Ri•ca (kos′tə rē′kə, kô′stə, kō′-), n. a republic in Central America. 3,534,174. —**Cos′ta Ri′can,** n., adj.

cost′-effec′tive, adj. producing optimum results for the expenditure.

cost′ly, adj., **-li•er, -li•est. 1.** costing much. **2.** resulting in great detriment. —**cost′li•ness,** n.

cost′ of liv′ing, n. the average that a person or family pays for such necessities as food, clothing, and rent.

cos•tume (kos′tōōm, -tyōōm), n., v., **-tumed, -tum•ing.** —n. **1.** the style of dress peculiar to a nation, historical period, etc. **2.** the clothing of another period, place, etc. **3.** an outfit; ensemble. —v.t. **4.** to furnish with a costume. —**cos′tum•er,** n.

cos′tume jew′elry, n. jewelry made of nonprecious metals and often set with imitation stones.

co•sy (kō′zē), adj., **-si•er, -si•est,** n., pl. **-sies.** COZY.

cot[1] (kot), n. a light portable bed, esp. one of canvas on a folding frame.

cot[2] (kot), n. **1.** a small place of shelter. **2.** a protective sheath, as for an injured finger.

cote (kōt), n. a coop or shed for sheep, pigeons, etc.

Côte d'I•voire (Fr. kōt dē vwAR′), n. official name of IVORY COAST.

co•te•rie (kō′tə rē), n., pl. **-ries.** a group of people who associate closely. [< F, MF: an association of tenant farmers]

co•ter•mi•nous (kō tûr′mə nəs), adj. **1.** having the same border or covering the same area. **2.** coextensive in range or scope.

co•til•lion (kə til′yən, kō-), n. **1.** a formal ball, esp. for debutantes. **2.** a formalized dance for a large number of people.

cot•tage (kot′ij), n. **1.** a small house. **2.** a modest vacation house.

cot′tage cheese′, n. a soft, mild-flavored cheese made from skim-milk curds.

cot•ter (kot′ər), n. Scot. a person occupying a cottage and plot of land, paid for in services.

cot′ter pin′, n. a pin having a split end that is spread after being pushed through a hole.

cotton

cot•ton (kot′n), n. **1.** a soft, white substance consisting of the fibers attached to the seeds of certain plants of the mallow family. **2.** the plant itself. **3.** cloth, thread, a garment, etc., of cotton. —v.i. **4.** to take a liking: *He doesn't cotton to strangers.* —**cot′‑ton‑y,** *adj.*

cot′ton gin′, *n.* a machine for separating the fibers of cotton from the seeds.

cot′ton‑mouth′, *n.* a pit viper of southeastern U.S. swamps.

cot′ton‑seed′, *n., pl.* **-seeds, -seed.** the seed of the cotton plant, yielding an oil **(cot′tonseed oil′)** used in cooking, medicine, etc.

cot′ton‑tail′, *n.* a North American rabbit with a fluffy white tail.

cot′ton‑wood′, *n.* an American poplar with cottony tufts on the seeds.

cot‑y‑le‑don (kot′l ēd′n), *n.* the primary leaf of the embryo of seed plants.

couch (kouch), *n.* **1.** a long piece of upholstered furniture for sitting or reclining. —*v.t.* **2.** to express, esp. indirectly.

couch′ pota′to, *n. Informal.* a person whose leisure time is spent watching television.

cou‑gar (kōō′gər), *n., pl.* **-gars, -gar.** a large, tawny wildcat of North and South America.

cough (kôf, kof), *v.i.* **1.** to expel air from the lungs suddenly with a harsh noise. —*v.t.* **2.** to expel by coughing. **3. cough up,** *Informal.* to relinquish, esp. reluctantly. —*n.* **4.** the act or sound of coughing. **5.** an illness characterized by frequent coughing.

cough′ drop′, *n.* a lozenge for relieving a cough, sore throat, etc.

could (kōod; *unstressed* kəd), *auxiliary v.* **1.** pt. of CAN[1]. **2.** (used to express politeness): *Could you open the door, please?* **3.** (used to express doubt): *That could never be true.*

cou‑lomb (kōō lom′, -lōm′), *n.* a unit of electricity equal to the quantity of electric charge transferred in one second by a constant current of one ampere. [after C. A. de *Coulomb* (1736–1806), French physicist]

coun‑cil (koun′səl), *n.* **1.** an assembly of persons convened for deliberation or advice. **2.** a group chosen to act in an advisory, administrative, or legislative capacity. —**Usage.** COUNCIL and COUNSEL are not interchangeable. COUNCIL is only used as a noun, whose most common meaning is "an assembly of persons convened for deliberation or advice." COUNSEL is used as a noun and a verb; the noun means either "advice given to another" or, in legal use, "a legal adviser or advisers."

coun′cil‑man′ or **-wom′an** or **-per′son,** *n., pl.* **-men** or **-wom‑en** or **-per‑sons.** a member of a council, esp. the legislative body of a city.

coun′ci‑lor (-sə lər), *n.* a member of a council.

coun‑sel (koun′səl), *n., pl.* **-sel** for 3, *v.,* **-seled, -sel‑ing** or (*esp. Brit.*) **-selled, -sel‑ling.** —*n.* **1.** advice. **2.** consultation; deliberation. **3.** a lawyer or lawyers. —*v.t.* **4.** to give advice to. **5.** to recommend. —*v.i.* **6.** to give or take advice. —**Usage.** See COUNCIL.

coun′se‑lor (-sə lər), *n.* **1.** an adviser. **2.** a lawyer. Also, *esp. Brit.,* **coun′sel‑lor.**

count[1] (kount), *v.t.* **1.** to check over one by one to determine the total. **2.** to name the numerals up to. **3.** to take into account. **4.** to consider or regard. —*v.i.* **5.** to name numerals in order. **6.** to have a specified numerical value. **7.** to have merit, value, etc. **8. count on** or **upon,** to rely on. —*n.* **9.** the act of counting. **10.** the total. **11.** an accounting. **12.** a separate charge in a legal indictment. —*Proverb.* **13. Don't count your chickens before they hatch,** don't make rash predictions about results.

count[2] (kount), *n.* (in some European countries) a nobleman equivalent in rank to an English earl.

count′down′, *n.* the backward counting from the initiation of a project, as a rocket launching, with firing designated as zero.

coun‑te‑nance (koun′tn əns), *n., v.,* **-nanced, -nanc‑ing.** —*n.* **1.** appearance, esp. facial expression. **2.** the face. **3.** approval. —*v.t.* **4.** to tolerate. **5.** to approve.

count′er[1], *n.* **1.** a table on which goods can be shown, business transacted, food served, etc. **2.** anything used to keep account, esp. a small object used in games. —*Idiom.* **3. over the counter, a.** (of the sale of stock) through a broker's office rather than through the stock exchange. **b.** (of the sale of medicinal drugs) without requiring a prescription. **4. under the counter,** in a clandestine manner, esp. illegally.

coun‑ter[2] (koun′tər), *adv.* **1.** in the reverse direction. **2.** in opposition. —*adj.* **3.** opposite; contrary. —*n.* **4.** something opposite or contrary to something else. —*v.t., v.i.* **5.** to oppose.

counter-, a prefix meaning: against or thwarting (*counterintelligence*); in response to (*counterattack*); opposite (*counterclockwise*); complementary (*counterbalance*).

coun′ter‑act′, *v.t.* to act in opposition or a contrary way to.

coun′ter‑at‑tack′, *n.* **1.** an attack made as an offset or reply to another attack. —*v.t., v.i.* **2.** to make a counterattack (against).

coun‑ter‑bal‑ance (*n.* koun′tər bal′əns; *v.* koun′‑tər bal′əns), *n., v.,* **-anced, -anc‑ing.** —*n.* **1.** a weight balancing another weight. **2.** an equal power or influence acting in opposition. —*v.t., v.i.* **3.** to act as a counterbalance (to).

coun‑ter‑claim (*n.* koun′tər klām′; *v.* koun′tər‑klām′), *n.* **1.** a claim made to offset another claim, esp. in law. —*v.t., v.i.* **2.** to claim in answer to a previous claim.

coun′ter‑clock′wise′, *adj., adv.* in a direction opposite to that of the normal rotation of the hands of a clock.

coun‑ter‑cult′ move′ment (koun′tər kult′), *n.* a group that seeks to reduce the influence of religious cults.

coun′ter‑cul′ture, *n.* the culture of those people who reject the dominant values of society.

coun‑ter‑es′pi‑o‑nage′, *n.* the detection and frustration of enemy espionage.

coun‑ter‑feit (koun′tər fit′), *adj.* **1.** made in imitation with intent to deceive; forged. **2.** pretended; unreal. —*n.* **3.** an imitation intended to be passed off as genuine. —*v.t., v.i.* **4.** to make a counterfeit of (money, stamps, etc.). **5.** to feign. —**coun′ter‑feit′‑er,** *n.*

coun′ter‑in‑sur′gen‑cy, *n., pl.* **-cies.** a program of combating guerrilla warfare and subversion.

coun′ter‑in‑tel′li‑gence, *n.* the activity of thwarting the intelligence-gathering efforts of a foreign power.

coun′ter‑mand′ (-mand′, -mänd′), *v.t.* to revoke or reverse (an order).

coun′ter‑of‑fen′sive, *n.* an attack against an attacking enemy force.

coun′ter‑pane′, *n.* a coverlet for a bed.

coun′ter‑part′, *n.* **1.** a person or thing closely resembling another. **2.** a copy or duplicate.

coun′ter‑point′, *n.* the technique of composing two or more melodies that combine harmoniously.

coun′ter‑poise′, *n., v.,* **-poised, -pois‑ing.** —*n.* **1.** a counterbalance. —*v.t.* **2.** to balance by an opposing weight; counteract by an opposing force.

coun′ter‑pro‑duc′tive, *adj.* thwarting the achievement of an intended goal.

Coun′ter Reforma′tion, *n.* the movement for reform within the Roman Catholic Church that followed the Protestant Reformation of the 16th century.

coun′ter‑rev‑o‑lu′tion, *n.* a revolution against a government recently established by a revolution. —**coun′ter‑rev‑o‑lu′tion‑ar′y,** *n., pl.* **-ar‑ies,** *adj.*

coun′ter‑sign′, *n.* **1.** a secret sign necessary for admission to a guarded area. —*v.t.* **2.** to sign (a document signed by someone else), esp. in authentication. —**coun′ter‑sig′na‑ture,** *n.*

coun′ter‑sink′, *v.t., -sank, -sunk, -sink‑ing.* **1.** to enlarge the upper part of (a hole) to receive the head of a screw or bolt. **2.** to set the head of (a screw or bolt) into such a hole.

coun′ter‑ten′or, *n.* **1.** a tenor who can approximate the vocal range of a female alto. **2.** a voice part for a countertenor.

coun'ter•vail' (-vāl'), *v.t.* to act against with equal power or effect; counteract.

coun'ter•weight', *n.* a counterbalance.

count•ess (koun'tis), *n.* **1.** the wife or widow of a count or earl. **2.** a woman with the rank of count or earl in her own right.

count'less, *adj.* too numerous to count; innumerable.

coun•tri•fied (kun'trə fīd'), *adj.* rustic or rural in appearance, conduct, etc.

coun•try (kun'trē), *n., pl.* -tries, *adj.* —*n.* **1.** a state or nation. **2.** the territory of a nation. **3.** the people of a nation. **4.** the land of one's birth or citizenship. **5.** rural districts. **6.** a territory demarcated by topographical conditions: *mountainous country.* —*adj.* **7.** rural. —*Saying.* **8. our country right or wrong,** patriotism is a paramount virtue.

coun'try club', *n.* a suburban club with facilities for tennis, golf, etc.

coun'try•man or **-wom'an,** *n., pl.* -men or -wom•en. a native or inhabitant of one's own country.

coun'try mu'sic, *n.* music with roots in the folk music of the Southeast and the cowboy music of the West.

coun'try•side', *n.* a rural area.

coun•ty (koun'tē), *n., pl.* -ties. the largest local administrative division in most U.S. states.

coun'ty seat', *n.* **1.** the seat of government of a county. **2.** a building housing these offices; a county courthouse.

coup (kōō), *n., pl.* **coups** (kōōz; *Fr.* kōō). **1.** a successful, unexpected act. **2.** COUP D'ÉTAT.

coup de grâce (kōō' də gräs'), *n., pl.* **coups de grâce** (kōō). **1.** a death blow delivered to end suffering. **2.** any decisive stroke.

coup d'é•tat (kōō' dā tä'), *n., pl.* **coups d'é•tat** (kōō' dā täz', -tä'). a sudden overthrow of a government by force.

coupe (kōōp), *n.* a closed, two-door car.

cou•ple (kup'əl), *n., v.,* -pled, -pling. —*n.* **1.** a combination of two of a kind; pair. **2.** a grouping of two persons, as a husband and wife. —*v.t., v.i.* **3.** to join; connect; unite. —*Idiom.* **4. a couple of,** a few.

cou•plet (kup'lit), *n.* a pair of successive, rhyming lines of verse.

cou'pling, *n.* **1.** the act of a person or thing that couples. **2.** a linking device, as for joining pieces of rolling stock.

cou•pon (kōō'pon, kyōō'-), *n.* **1.** a certificate or ticket entitling the holder to a gift or discount, or for use as an order blank, a contest entry form, etc. **2.** a detachable certificate calling for a periodic interest payment on a bond.

cour•age (kûr'ij, kur'-), *n.* the quality of mind that enables a person to face difficulty, danger, etc., without fear; bravery. —**cou•ra•geous** (kə rā'jəs), *adj.* —cou•ra'geous•ly, *adv.*

cour•i•er (kûr'ē ər, kōōr'-), *n.* a messenger, usu. bearing packages, diplomatic messages, etc.

course (kôrs), *n., v.,* **coursed, cours•ing.** —*n.* **1.** a direction or route taken. **2.** a path, route, or channel. **3.** advance in a particular direction. **4.** a particular manner of proceeding. **5.** a regular or natural order of events: *the course of a disease.* **6.** a systematized series. **7.** a program of instruction, as in a college. **8.** a part of a meal served at one time. —*v.i.* **9.** to run or race. —*Idiom.* **10. in due course,** in the proper or natural order of events. **11. of course,** certainly.

cours•er (kôr'sər), *n.* a swift horse.

court (kôrt), *n.* **1. a.** a place where legal justice is administered. **b.** a judicial tribunal that hears cases. **c.** a session of a judicial assembly. **2.** an open area surrounded by buildings, walls, etc. **3.** a short street. **4.** a quadrangle on which to play tennis, basketball, etc. **5. a.** the residence of a sovereign. **b.** a sovereign's retinue. **c.** a formal assembly held by a sovereign. **6.** devoted attention in order to win favor. —*v.t.* **7.** to try to win the favor of. **8.** to woo. **9.** to act so as to cause: *to court disaster.* —*v.i.* **10.** to woo a person.

cour•te•ous (kûr'tē əs), *adj.* showing good manners; polite. —cour'te•ous•ly, *adv.* —cour'te•ous•ness, *n.*

cour•te•sy (kûr'tə sē), *n., pl.* -sies. **1.** polite behavior. **2.** a courteous act or expression.

court'house', *n.* **1.** a building housing law courts. **2.** a county seat.

cour•ti•er (kôr'tē ər), *n.* an attendant at a royal court.

court'ly, *adj.,* -li•er, -li•est. polite, refined, or elegant. —court'li•ness, *n.*

court'-mar'tial, *n., pl.* **courts-mar•tial, court-mar•tials,** *v.,* -tialed, -tial•ing or (*esp. Brit.*) -tialled, -tial•ling. —*n.* **1.** a military court for trying armed forces personnel charged with infractions of military law. **2.** a trial by such a court. —*v.t.* **3.** to try by court-martial.

court'room', *n.* a room in which a court of law is held.

court'ship', *n.* the wooing of one person by another.

court'yard', *n.* a court open to the sky, esp. one enclosed on all sides.

cous•in (kuz'ən), *n.* the child of an uncle or aunt.

Cous•teau (kōō stō'), *n.* **Jacques Yves** (zhäk ēv), 1910–97, French naval officer, author, and undersea explorer.

cou•tu•ri•er (kōō tŏŏr'ē ər, -ē ā'), *n.* a designer of fashionable, custom-made clothes for women.

cove (kōv), *n.* a small indentation in a shoreline.

cov•en (kuv'ən, kō'vən), *n.* an assembly of witches.

cov•e•nant (kuv'ə nənt), *n.* **1.** a formal agreement. **2.** the conditional promises made to humanity by God, as revealed in Scripture. —*v.i.* **3.** to enter into a covenant. —*v.t.* **4.** to promise by covenant.

Cov•en•try (kuv'ən trē, kov'-), *n.* a city in central England. 337,000.

cov•er (kuv'ər), *v.t.* **1.** to extend over. **2.** to place something over or upon. **3.** to clothe. **4.** to hide from view. **5.** to deal with or provide for: *The rules cover working conditions.* **6.** to offset (an outlay, loss, etc.). **7.** to travel over. **8.** to report (a news event). **9.** to insure against risk or loss. **10.** to shelter; protect. **11.** to aim at, as with a pistol. —*v.i.* **12.** to substitute for someone who is absent. **13.** to provide an alibi. **14. cover up,** to keep secret. —*n.* **15.** something that covers, as the lid of a container. **16.** protection; shelter. **17.** anything that screens from sight: *under cover of darkness.* **18.** an assumed identity, occupation, etc. **19.** COVER CHARGE. —*Idiom.* **20. take cover,** to seek shelter or safety. **21. under cover,** clandestinely; secretly.

cov'er•age (-ij), *n.* **1.** protection against risks specified in an insurance policy. **2.** the reporting of news.

cov'er•all', *n.* Often, -alls. a one-piece work garment worn over other clothing.

cov'er charge', *n.* a fee charged by a restaurant or nightclub for providing entertainment.

cov'er crop', *n.* a crop planted to keep nutrients from leaching or soil from eroding, as during the winter.

Cov•er•dale (kuv'ər dāl'), *n.* **Miles,** 1488–1569, English cleric: translator of the Bible into English 1535.

cov'ered wag'on, *n.* a large wagon with a high canvas top, esp. used by American pioneers.

cov'er•ing, *n.* something laid over or wrapped around a thing.

cov'er•let (-lit), *n.* a bed quilt that does not cover the pillow.

cov'er sto'ry, *n.* a magazine article highlighted by a cover illustration.

co•vert (*adj.* kō'vərt, kuv'ərt; *n.* kuv'ərt, kō'vərt), *adj.* **1.** secret; disguised. —*n.* **2.** a thicket giving shelter to wild animals or game. —co'vert•ly, *adv.*

cov'er-up', *n.* any stratagem or other means of concealing an illegal activity, blunder, etc.

cov•et (kuv'it), *v.t., v.i.* to desire (another's property) wrongfully. —cov'et•ous, *adj.* —cov'et•ous•ly, *adv.* —cov'et•ous•ness, *n.*

cov•ey (kuv′ē), *n.*, *pl.* **-eys.** a small group of game birds, esp. partridges or quail.

cow[1] (kou), *n.* **1.** the mature female of a bovine animal. **2.** the female of various other large animals, as the whale.

cow[2] (kou), *v.t.* to intimidate.

cow•ard (kou′ərd), *n.* **1.** a person who lacks courage. —**cow′ard•ly,** *adj.*, *adv.* —**cow′ard•li•ness,** *n.* —*Proverb.* **2. Cowards die many times before their deaths,** the fear of death is almost as bad as death itself. Shakespeare, *Julius Caesar.*

Cow′ard, *n.* **Noel,** 1899–1973, English author and composer.

cow′ard•ice (-ər dis), *n.* lack of courage.

cow′boy′ or **-girl′,** *n.* a person who herds cattle.

cow•er (kou′ər), *v.i.* to crouch in fear.

cow′hide′, *n.* **1.** the hide of a cow. **2.** the leather made from it.

cowl (koul), *n.* **1.** a hooded garment worn by monks. **2.** the hood itself.

cow′lick′, *n.* a tuft of hair that grows in a direction different from the rest of the hair.

cowl′ing, *n.* a metal housing for an aircraft engine.

co•work•er (kō′wûr′kər, kō wûr′-), *n.* a fellow worker.

cow′poke′, *n.* a cowboy or cowgirl.

cow′pox′, *n.* a mild disease of cattle, caused by a virus formerly used for smallpox vaccinations.

cow′slip′, *n.* an English primrose with fragrant yellow flowers.

cox•comb (koks′kōm′), *n.* a conceited, foolish dandy.

cox•swain (kok′sən, -swān′), *n.* a person who steers a boat or racing shell.

coy (koi), *adj.*, **-er, -est.** artfully shy; coquettish. —**coy′ly,** *adv.* —**coy′ness,** *n.*

coy•o•te (kī ō′tē, kī′ōt), *n.*, *pl.* **-tes, -te.** a carnivorous, wolflike mammal of North America. [< MexSp < Nahuatl *coyotl*]

coz•en (kuz′ən), *v.t.*, *v.i.* to cheat; deceive. —**coz′en•age,** *n.*

Co•zu•mel (kō′zə mel′), *n.* an island off the SE coast of Mexico: resort.

co•zy (kō′zē), *adj.*, **-zi•er, -zi•est,** *n.*, *pl.* **-zies.** —*adj.* **1.** snugly warm and comfortable. —*n.* **2.** a padded covering for a teapot to retain the heat. —**co′zi•ly,** *adv.* —**co′zi•ness,** *n.*

C.P., **1.** command post. **2.** Communist Party.

CPA, certified public accountant.

CPO, chief petty officer.

CPR, cardiopulmonary resuscitation.

CPU, central processing unit: the key component of a computer system.

Cr, *Chem. Symbol.* chromium.

crab[1] (krab), *n.* a crustacean with a wide, flattened body and four pairs of legs.

crab[2] (krab), *n.*, *v.*, **crabbed, crab•bing.** —*n.* **1.** an ill-tempered person. —*v.i.*, *v.t.* **2.** to find fault (with).

crab′ ap′ple, *n.* a small, tart apple.

crab•bed (krab′id), *adj.* **1.** difficult to read, as handwriting. **2.** ill-tempered.

crab′by, *adj.*, **-bi•er, -bi•est.** ill-tempered; grouchy.

crab′ grass′, *n.* a weed grass that roots vigorously.

crab′ louse′, *n.* a crablike louse that infests pubic and other body hair.

crack (krak), *v.i.* **1.** to break without separation of parts. **2.** to make a sudden, sharp sound, as in breaking. **3.** (of the voice) to break abruptly and discordantly. **4.** *Informal.* to break down, esp. under severe pressure. —*v.t.* **5.** to cause to make a sudden, sharp sound. **6.** to cause to break without separation of parts. **7.** to strike forcefully. **8.** to tell: *to crack jokes.* **9.** to solve. **10.** *Informal.* to break into (a safe, vault, etc.). **11. crack down,** to become strict; take severe measures: *to crack down on drug pushers.* **12.** ~ **up,** *Informal.* **a.** to suffer a mental or physical breakdown. **b.** to crash, as in a vehicle. **c.** to laugh unrestrainedly. —*n.* **13.** a break without separation of parts. **14.** a slight opening. **15.** a sudden, sharp noise. **16.** a resounding blow. **17.** a witty or cutting remark. **18.** a break in the tone of the voice. **19.** a chance; try. —*adj.* **20.** first-rate; excellent.

crack′down′, *n.* the stern enforcement of laws.

cracked, *adj.* **1.** broken without separation of parts. **2.** *Informal.* crazy; mad. **3.** broken in tone, as the voice. —*Idiom.* **4. cracked up to be,** *Informal.* reputed to be.

crack′er, *n.* **1.** a thin, crisp biscuit. **2.** a firecracker.

crack′er•jack′, *n.* **1.** a person or thing of excellence. —*adj.* **2.** exceptionally fine.

crack•le (krak′əl), *v.*, **-led, -ling,** *n.* —*v.i.* **1.** to make slight, sharp noises, rapidly repeated. —*n.* **2.** the act or sound of crackling. **3.** a network of fine cracks, as in some glazes. —**crack′ly,** *adj.*

crack′pot′, *Informal.* —*n.* **1.** an eccentric person. —*adj.* **2.** eccentric.

crack′up′, *n.* **1.** a crash; collision. **2.** a breakdown in health, esp. a mental breakdown.

cra•dle (krād′l), *n.*, *v.*, **-dled, -dling.** —*n.* **1.** a small bed for an infant, usu. on rockers. **2.** a support for an object set horizontally, as for the receiver of a telephone. **3.** a place of origin: *Athens is the cradle of democracy.* —*v.t.* **4.** to place or rock in or as if in a cradle. **5.** to nurture during infancy. —*Idiom.* **6. from the cradle to the grave,** from birth to death.

craft (kraft, kräft), *n.*, *pl.* **crafts** or for 5, **craft,** *v.* —*n.* **1.** a trade or occupation requiring manual skill. **2.** skill; dexterity. **3.** cunning; deceit. **4.** the membership of a guild. **5.** a ship or other vessel. **6.** ships, aircraft, etc., collectively. —*v.t.* **7.** to make (an object) with great skill and care.

crafts′man or **-wom′an,** *n.*, *pl.* **-men** or **-wom•en.** a person skilled in a craft; artisan. —**crafts′man•like′,** *adj.* —**crafts′man•ship′,** *n.*

craft′y, *adj.*, **-i•er, -i•est.** cunning; deceitful.

crag (krag), *n.* a steep, rugged rock. —**crag′gy,** *adj.*, **-gi•er, -gi•est.**

cram (kram), *v.*, **crammed, cram•ming.** —*v.t.* **1.** to fill (something) with more than it can easily hold. **2.** to force or stuff. **3.** to overfeed. —*v.i.* **4.** to eat to excess. **5.** to study intensively for an examination at the last minute.

cramp[1] (kramp), *n.* **1.** an involuntary, painful muscle spasm. **2. cramps,** painful abdominal contractions. —*v.t.*, *v.i.* **3.** to affect or be affected with a cramp.

cramp[2] (kramp), *v.t.* to restrict or hamper.

cramped (krampt), *adj.* **1.** spatially confined or limited. **2.** (of handwriting) small and crowded.

cran•ber•ry (kran′ber′ē, -bə rē), *n.*, *pl.* **-ries. 1.** the sour red berry of a trailing plant, used to make a sauce, relish, or juice. **2.** the plant itself.

crane (krān), *n.*, *v.*, **craned, cran•ing.** —*n.* **1.** a large wading bird with long legs, bill, and neck. **2.** a device for lifting and moving heavy weights. —*v.t.*, *v.i.* **3.** to stretch (the neck).

Crane (krān), *n.* **1. (Harold) Hart,** 1899–1932, U.S. poet. **2. Stephen,** 1871–1900, U.S. novelist and short-story writer.

cra•ni•um (krā′nē əm), *n.*, *pl.* **-ni•ums, -ni•a** (-nē ə). **1.** the skull of a vertebrate. **2.** the part of the skull that encloses the brain. —**cra′ni•al,** *adj.*

crank (krangk), *n.* **1.** an arm or lever for imparting motion to a rotating shaft. **2.** *Informal.* an ill-tempered person. **3.** an unbalanced person who is overzealous in advocating a private cause. —*v.t.* **4.** to start or rotate by turning a crank.

crank′case′, *n.* the housing in an internal-combustion engine, enclosing the crankshaft and allied parts.

crank′shaft′, *n.* a shaft having one or more cranks.

crank′y, *adj.*, **-i•er, -i•est. 1.** ill-tempered; grouchy. **2.** eccentric; erratic. —**crank′i•ness,** *n.*

Cran•mer (kran′mər), *n.* **Thomas,** 1489–1556, first Protestant archbishop of Canterbury and primary author of the *Book of Common Prayer* (1549).

cran•ny (kran′ē), *n.*, *pl.* **-nies.** a narrow opening in a wall, rock, etc.

crape (krāp), *n.* CREPE (defs. 1, 2).

craps (kraps), *n.* a gambling game in which two dice are thrown.

crap′shoot′er, *n.* a person who plays craps.

crash (krash), *v.i.* **1.** to make a loud, clattering noise. **2.** to fall or break into pieces noisily. **3.** to strike, go, or collide violently and noisily. **4.** to land in such a way that damage is unavoidable. **5.** to collapse suddenly, as a financial enterprise. **6.** (of a computer) to fail suddenly because of a hardware malfunction or software bug. —*v.t.* **7.** to cause to break into pieces violently and noisily. **8.** to cause (a moving vehicle) to crash. **9.** to enter without invitation or payment. —*n.* **10.** an act or instance of crashing. **11.** a sudden loud noise. **12.** a sudden collapse, as of a business. —*adj.* **13.** characterized by speed and intensive effort: *a crash diet.*

crash′-land′, *v.t., v.i.* to land (an aircraft) in an emergency so that damage is unavoidable. —**crash′-land′ing,** *n.*

crash′ pad′, *n.* *Slang.* a place to sleep or live temporarily.

crass (kras), *adj.,* **-er, -est.** without refinement or sensitivity. —**crass′ly,** *adv.* —**crass′ness,** *n.*

crate (krāt), *n., v.,* **crat•ed, crat•ing.** —*n.* **1.** a slatted wooden box for packing, shipping, etc. —*v.t.* **2.** to pack in a crate.

cra•ter (krā′tər), *n.* **1.** the cup-shaped depression marking the orifice of a volcano. **2.** a similar depression formed by the impact of a meteoroid. **3.** the hole in the ground where a bomb has exploded. [< L < Gk *krátēr* mixing bowl]

cra•vat (krə vat′), *n.* NECKTIE.

crave (krāv), *v.t.,* **craved, crav•ing. 1.** to long for; desire eagerly. **2.** to require; need.

cra•ven (krā′vən), *adj.* **1.** contemptibly timid. —*n.* **2.** a coward. —**cra′ven•ly,** *adv.*

crav′ing, *n.* a great desire; yearning.

craw (krô), *n.* **1.** the crop of a bird or insect. **2.** the stomach of an animal.

craw′fish′, *n., pl.* **-fish, -fish•es.** CRAYFISH.

crawl (krôl), *v.i.* **1.** to move with the body close to the ground or on the hands and knees. **2.** to move slowly or laboriously. **3.** to behave in a cringing manner. **4.** to feel, or feel as if, overrun with crawling things. —*n.* **5.** the act of crawling. **6.** a slow rate of progress. **7.** a swimming stroke in a prone position. —**crawl′er,** *n.*

crawl′space′, *n.* (in a building) an area having a clearance less than human height, for access to plumbing, wiring, etc.

crawl′y, *adj.,* **-i•er, -i•est.** creepy.

cray•fish (krā′fish′), *n., pl.* **-fish, -fish•es.** a freshwater crustacean resembling a small lobster.

cray•on (krā′on, -ən), *n.* **1.** a pointed stick of colored wax, used for drawing or coloring. —*v.t.* **2.** to draw or color with crayons.

craze (krāz), *v.,* **crazed, craz•ing,** —*v.t., v.i.* **1.** to make or become insane. **2.** to make or become minutely cracked, as a ceramic glaze. —*n.* **3.** a fad. **4.** a minute crack or pattern of cracks in the glaze of a ceramic object.

cra•zy (krā′zē), *adj.,* **-zi•er, -zi•est,** *n., pl.* **-zies.** —*adj.* **1.** mentally deranged. **2.** impractical; foolish. **3.** intensely enthusiastic. **4.** infatuated. —*n.* **5.** *Slang.* a crazy person. —*Idiom.* **6. crazy like a fox,** ostensibly insane but in reality shrewd. —**cra′zi•ly,** *adv.* —**cra′zi•ness,** *n.*

Cra′zy Horse′, *n.* (*Tashunca-Uitco*), c1849–77, Lakota Indian leader: defeated General George Custer.

cra′zy quilt′, *n.* **1.** a patchwork quilt made of irregular patches with no pattern. **2.** a conglomeration or hodgepodge; mishmash.

creak (krēk), *v.i.* **1.** to make a sharp, squeaking sound. —*n.* **2.** a creaking sound. —**creak′y,** *adj.,* **-i•er, -i•est.**

cream (krēm), *n.* **1.** the fatty part of milk. **2.** a soft solid preparation applied to the skin for cosmetic or therapeutic purposes. **3.** a food made with cream or having a creamy consistency. **4.** the best part of anything. **5.** a yellowish white. —*v.t.* **6.** to work into a creamy consistency. **7.** to prepare with cream or a

cream sauce. **8.** to add cream to. **9.** *Slang.* to beat up or defeat decisively. —*Idiom.* **10. cream of the crop,** the best or choicest. —*Saying.* **11. Cream rises to the top,** the most accomplished will achieve success. —**cream′y,** *adj.,* **-i•er, -i•est.** —**cream′i•ness,** *n.*

cream′ cheese′, *n.* a spreadable white cheese made of cream or milk and cream.

cream′er, *n.* **1.** a small pitcher for serving cream. **2.** a nondairy product used as a substitute for cream.

cream′er•y, *n., pl.* **-er•ies.** a place where milk and cream are processed or where butter and cheese are produced.

cream′ of tar′tar, *n.* a white powdery substance used esp. in baking powder.

crease (krēs), *n., v.,* **creased, creas•ing.** —*n.* **1.** a ridge produced in anything by folding, striking, etc. **2.** a wrinkle. **3.** a sharp, vertical edge pressed into the front and back of trousers. —*v.t.* **4.** to make a crease in. —*v.i.* **5.** to become creased.

cre•ate (krē āt′), *v.t.,* **-at•ed, -at•ing. 1.** to cause to come into being. **2.** to arrange or bring about.

cre•a′tion, *n.* **1.** the act of creating. **2.** something created. **3. the Creation,** the original bringing into existence of the universe by God. **4.** the universe.

cre•a′tion•ism, *n.* the doctrine that the true story of the creation of the universe is recounted in the Bible. —**cre•a′tion•ist,** *n., adj.*

cre•a′tive (-tiv), *adj.* **1.** having the quality or power of creating. **2.** resulting from originality of thought; imaginative. —**cre•a′tive•ly,** *adv.* —**cre•a′tive•ness,** *n.* —**cre′a•tiv′i•ty,** *n.*

cre•a′tor, *n.* **1.** a person who creates. **2. the Creator,** God.

crea•ture (krē′chər), *n.* **1.** an animal. **2.** a human being.

crèche (kresh, krāsh), *n.* a tableau of the birth of Jesus in the stable at Bethlehem.

cre•dence (krēd′ns), *n.* belief as to the truth of something.

cre•den′tial (kri den′shəl), *n.* Usu., **-tials.** evidence of entitlement to rights, privileges, or the like.

cre•den•za (kri den′zə), *n., pl.* **-zas.** a sideboard, esp. one without legs.

credibil′ity gap′, *n.* **1.** a public distrust of statements made by politicians, corporations, etc. **2.** a perceived discrepancy between statements and behavior.

cred•i•ble (kred′ə bəl), *adj.* **1.** capable of being believed. **2.** effective or reliable. —**cred′i•bil′i•ty,** *n.* —**cred′i•bly,** *adv.*

cred•it (kred′it), *n.* **1.** commendation given for some action, quality, etc. **2.** a source of pride or honor. **3. credits,** the names of all who contributed to a motion picture or television program. **4.** trustworthiness; credibility. **5. a.** permission to pay for goods at a later date. **b.** reputation for paying bills when due. **6.** official acceptance of the work completed by a student in a course. **7.** an entry of payment received on an account. **8.** any sum of money against which a person may draw. —*v.t.* **9.** to believe or trust. **10.** to give credit for or to. —*Idiom.* **11. on credit,** by deferred payment. —*Proverb.* **12. Give credit where credit is due,** acknowledge merit where it is found. Rom. 13:7.

cred′it•a•ble, *adj.* deserving credit or esteem. —**cred′it•a•bly,** *adv.*

cred′it card′, *n.* a card entitling a person to make purchases on credit.

cred′i•tor, *n.* a person or firm to whom money is due.

cred′it un′ion, *n.* a cooperative group that makes loans to its members at low interest rates.

cre•do (krē′dō, krā′-), *n., pl.* **-dos.** a creed.

cred•u•lous (krej′ə ləs), *adj.* willing to believe or trust too readily. —**cre•du•li•ty** (kri dōō′li tē, -dyōō′-), *n.* —**cred′u•lous•ly,** *adv.*

Cree (krē), *n., pl.* **Cree, Crees.** a member of an American Indian people of subarctic Canada.

creed (krēd), *n.* **1.** an authoritative statement of the

chief articles of Christian belief. **2.** an accepted system of religious or other belief. [< L *crēdō* I believe]
creek (krēk, krik), *n.* **1.** a small stream. —*Idiom.* **2. up the creek,** *Slang.* in a difficult situation.
Creek (krēk), *n., pl.* **Creek, Creeks.** a member of a loose confederacy of American Indian peoples that formerly occupied the greater part of Georgia and Alabama.
Creek′ War′, *n.* an uprising in 1813–14 of the Creek Indians against settlers in Alabama.
creel (krēl), *n.* a wickerwork basket, used esp. for carrying fish.
creep (krēp), *v., crept, creep•ing, n.* —*v.i.* **1.** to move slowly with the body close to the ground. **2.** to approach or advance slowly or stealthily. **3.** to grow along the ground, a wall, etc., as a plant. —*n.* **4.** an instance of creeping. **5.** *Slang.* a repellent or obnoxious person. **6. the creeps,** a sensation of anxiety, disgust, etc. —*Idiom.* **7. make one's flesh creep,** to cause one to be frightened or repelled. —**creep′er,** *n.*
creep′y, *adj.,* **-i•er, -i•est.** having or causing a sensation of horror or fear. —**creep′i•ly,** *adv.* —**creep′i•ness,** *n.*
cre•mate (krē′māt), *v.t.,* **-mat•ed, -mat•ing.** to reduce (a dead body) to ashes by fire. —**cre•ma′tion** (kri mā′shən), *n.*
cre•ma•to•ry (krē′mə tôr′ē, krem′ə-), *n., pl.* **-ries.** a funeral establishment or a furnace for cremating.
cren•el•ate or **-el•late** (kren′l āt′), *v.t.,* **-at•ed, -at•ing** or **-lat•ed, -lat•ing.** to furnish with battlements. —**cren′el•a′tion,** *n.*
Cre•ole (krē′ōl), *n.* **1. a.** a member of the French-speaking population of Louisiana that claims descent from the earliest French and Spanish settlers. **b.** a person of mixed black and Creole ancestry. **2.** (*l.c.*) a pidgin that has become the native language of a speech community. —*adj.* **3.** (*usu. l.c.*) made with tomatoes, peppers, onions, and spices.
cre•o•sote (krē′ə sōt′), *n.* an oily liquid distilled from coal and wood tar, used as a wood preservative and an antiseptic.
crepe or **crêpe** (krāp; *for 4 also* krep) *n., pl.* **crepes** or **crêpes** (krāps; *for 4 also* kreps *or* krep). **1.** a lightweight fabric of silk, cotton, etc., with a crinkled surface. **2.** a black piece of crepe, worn as a token of mourning. **3.** Also called **crepe′ pa′per.** a thin, wrinkled paper used for decorating. **4.** a thin, light pancake.
crept (krept), *v.* pt. and pp. of CREEP.
cre•scen•do (kri shen′dō), *n., pl.* **-dos, -di** (-dē). **1.** a gradual increase in loudness. **2.** a musical passage characterized by such an increase.
cres•cent (kres′ənt), *n.* **1.** the figure of the moon in its first or last quarter, resembling a segment of a ring tapering to points at the ends. **2.** any crescent-shaped object.
cress (kres), *n.* a plant, esp. the watercress, having pungent-tasting leaves often used for salad.
crest (krest), *n.* **1.** the highest part of a hill or mountain range. **2.** the highest point or level. **3.** the foamy top of a wave. **4.** a growth on the top of an animal's head, as the comb of a rooster. **5.** a heraldic device. —*v.i.* **6.** to form or rise to a crest. —**crest′ed,** *adj.*
crest′fall′en, *adj.* dejected; discouraged.
Cre•ta•ceous (kri tā′shəs), *adj.* noting or pertaining to a period of the Mesozoic Era, characterized by the extinction of dinosaurs and the advent of flowering plants and modern insects.
Crete (krēt), *n.* a Greek island in the E Mediterranean. —**Cre′tan,** *adj., n.*
cre•tin (krēt′n), *n.* **1.** a person affected with cretinism. **2.** a stupid, obtuse, or boorish person.
cre′tin•ism, *n.* a congenital deficiency of thyroid secretion, resulting in stunted growth, deformity, and mental retardation.
cre•tonne (kri ton′, krē′ton), *n.* a heavy, printed cotton fabric used for drapery and slipcovers.
cre•vasse (krə vas′), *n.* a deep cleft in glacial ice, the earth's surface, etc.
crev•ice (krev′is), *n.* a crack forming an opening.
crew¹ (krōō), *n.* **1.** a group of persons working to-

gether. **2.** the team that rows a racing shell. —**crew′-man,** *n., pl.* **-men.**
crew² (krōō), *v. Chiefly Brit.* a pt. of CROW².
crew′ cut′, *n.* a haircut in which the hair is very closely cropped.
crew•el (krōō′əl), *n.* a worsted yarn for embroidery and edging.
crib (krib), *n., v.,* **cribbed, crib•bing.** —*n.* **1.** a child's bed with enclosed sides. **2.** a manger for fodder. **3.** a bin for storing grain. **4.** *Informal.* an illicit aid used by students while taking exams. —*v.t.* **5.** to plagiarize. **6.** to confine in a crib. —*v.i.* **7.** *Informal.* to use a crib during exams.
crib•bage (krib′ij), *n.* a card game in which points for certain combinations of cards are scored on a small pegboard.
crib′ death′, *n.* SUDDEN INFANT DEATH SYNDROME.
crick (krik), *n.* a sharp, painful spasm of the muscles, as of the neck.
crick•et¹ (krik′it), *n.* a jumping insect, the male of which makes a chirping sound by rubbing the forewings together.
crick•et² (krik′it), *n.* **1.** an outdoor game, popular esp. in England, that is played by two teams using bats, balls, and wickets. **2.** fair play; honorable conduct: *It's not cricket to ask such questions.* —**crick′et•er,** *n.*
cried (krīd), *v.* pt. and pp. of CRY.
cri•er (krī′ər), *n.* **1.** one who cries. **2.** an official who makes public announcements.
crime (krīm), *n.* an action that is legally prohibited.
Cri•me•a (krī mē′ə, kri-), *n.* **the,** a peninsula in SE Ukraine jutting into the Black Sea. —**Cri•me′an,** *adj.*
crim•i•nal (krim′ə nl), *adj.* **1.** guilty of crime. **2.** dealing with crime or its punishment. —*n.* **3.** a person convicted of a crime. —**crim′i•nal′i•ty,** *n.* —**crim′i•nal•ly,** *adv.*
crim′i•nol′o•gy (-nol′ə jē), *n.* the study of crime and criminals. —**crim′i•nol′o•gist,** *n.*
crimp (krimp), *v.t.* **1.** to press into small regular folds. **2.** to curl (hair). —*n.* **3.** the act of crimping. **4.** a crimped condition or form. —*Idiom.* **5. put a crimp in,** to hinder.
crim•son (krim′zən, -sən), *adj.* **1.** deep purplish red. —*n.* **2.** a crimson color. —*v.t., v.i.* **3.** to make or become crimson.
cringe (krinj), *v.i.,* **cringed, cring•ing.** to shrink or crouch, esp. in fear or servility.
crin•kle (kring′kəl), *v.,* **-kled, -kling,** *n.* —*v.t., v.i.* **1.** to wrinkle; ripple. **2.** to rustle. —*n.* **3.** a wrinkle or ripple. —**crin′kly,** *adj.,* **-kli•er, -kli•est.**
crin•o•line (krin′l in), *n.* **1.** a stiff, coarse fabric used as interlining in garments, hats, etc. **2.** a hoop skirt.
crip•ple (krip′əl), *n., v.,* **-pled, -pling.** —*n.* **1.** *Sometimes Offensive.* **a.** a lame or physically disabled person or animal. **b.** a person who is disabled in any way: *a mental cripple.* —*v.t.* **2.** to make a cripple of. **3.** to disable; impair.
cri•sis (krī′sis), *n., pl.* **-ses** (-sēz). **1.** a turning point for better or for worse. **2.** a condition or period of instability, difficulty, etc. **3.** the point in a serious disease at which a decisive change occurs.
crisp (krisp) also **crisp′y,** *adj.,* **-er, -est** also **-i•er, -i•est.** **1.** brittle. **2.** firm and fresh. **3.** decided; clear. **4.** lively; pithy. **5.** bracing; invigorating. **6.** curly. —**crisp′ly,** *adv.* —**crisp′ness,** *n.*
Cris•pus (kris′pəs), *n.* a ruler of the Corinth synagogue who was converted to Christianity. Acts 18:8; I Cor. 1:14.
criss•cross (kris′krôs′, -kros′), *v.t.* **1.** to move back and forth over. **2.** to mark with crossing lines. —*v.i.* **3.** to pass back and forth. —*adj.* **4.** having many crossing lines. —*n.* **5.** a crisscross mark, pattern, etc. —*adv.* **6.** crosswise.
cri•te•ri•on (krī tēr′ē ən), *n., pl.* **-te•ri•a** (-tēr′ē ə) **-te•ri•ons.** a standard of judgment or criticism.
crit•ic (krit′ik), *n.* **1.** a person who judges literary or artistic works. **2.** a person who tends to make harsh judgments.

crit/i·cal, *adj.* **1.** inclined to find fault or judge severely. **2.** requiring skillful judgment. **3.** of critics or criticism. **4.** of the nature of or constituting a crisis. **5.** crucial. —**crit/i·cal·ly**, *adv.*

crit/i·cism (-siz/əm), *n.* **1.** the act of criticizing. **2.** faultfinding or censure. **3.** the art of judging the merits of anything. **4.** a critique.

crit/i·cize/, *v.i., v.t.,* **-cized, -ciz·ing. 1.** to find fault (with). **2.** to evaluate.

cri·tique (kri tēk/), *n., v.,* **-tiqued, -ti·quing.** —*n.* **1.** an article evaluating a literary or other work; review. —*v.t.* **2.** to analyze critically.

crit·ter (krit/ər), *n. Dial.* a creature.

croak (krōk), *v.i.* **1.** to utter a low-pitched, harsh cry, as that of a frog. —*n.* **2.** a croaking sound.

Cro·a·tia (krō ā/shə), *n.* a republic in SE Europe: formerly part of Yugoslavia. 5,026,995. —**Cro/at** (-at, -ät), *n.* —**Cro·a/tian**, *adj., n.*

cro·chet (krō shā/), *n., v.,* **-cheted** (-shād/), **-chet·ing** (-shā/ing). —*n.* **1.** needlework done with a hooked needle for drawing yarn through intertwined loops. —*v.i.* **2.** to do this needlework. —*v.t.* **3.** to form by crochet. —**cro·chet/er**, *n.*

crock (krok), *n.* an earthenware container.

crock·er·y (krok/ə rē), *n.* earthenware.

Crock·ett (krok/it), *n.* **David** (*Davy*), 1786–1836, U.S. frontiersman, politician, and folklore hero.

croc·o·dile (krok/ə dīl/), *n.* a narrow-snouted, large reptile found in tropical waters of both hemispheres.

cro·cus (krō/kəs), *n., pl.* **-cus·es.** a small bulbous plant cultivated for its showy flowers.

crois·sant (*Fr.* кRwä sän/; *Eng.* krə sänt/), *n., pl.* **-sants** (*Fr.* -säN/; *Eng.* -sänts/). a crescent-shaped roll of rich, flaky pastry.

Crom·well (krom/wəl, -wel, krum/-), *n.* **1. Oliver,** 1599–1658, English general and statesman: Lord Protector of England, Scotland, and Ireland 1653–58. **2. Thomas, Earl of Essex,** 1485?–1540, English statesman.

crone (krōn), *n.* a withered, witchlike old woman.

Cron·kite (kron/kīt, krong/-), *n.* **Walter,** born 1916, U.S. newscaster.

cro·ny (krō/nē), *n., pl.* **-nies.** a close friend.

crook (krŏŏk), *n.* **1.** a bent or curved implement; hook. **2.** a dishonest person. **3.** a bend or curve. —*v.t., v.i.* **4.** to bend; curve.

crook·ed (krŏŏk/id *for 1–3;* krŏŏkt *for 4*), *adj.* **1.** not straight; curved. **2.** deformed. **3.** dishonest or illegal. **4.** bent. —**crook/ed·ly**, *adv.* —**crook/ed·ness**, *n.*

crook/neck/, *n.* a squash having a long curved neck.

croon (krōōn), *v.i., v.t.* **1.** to sing or hum in a soft, soothing voice. —*n.* **2.** the act or sound of crooning. —**croon/er**, *n.*

crop (krop), *n., v.,* **cropped, crop·ping.** —*n.* **1.** the cultivated produce of the ground. **2.** the yield of such produce in one season. **3.** the yield of any product in a season. **4.** a group of persons or things. **5.** the handle of a whip. **6.** a short riding whip. **7.** a pouch in the esophagus of many birds, in which food is held for later digestion. **8.** a close cutting of something, as the hair. —*v.t.* **9.** to cut or bite off the top or ends of. **10.** to cut off the ends or a part of: *to crop the ears of a dog.* **11.** to cut short. **12.** to cause to bear a crop. **13. crop up,** to appear unexpectedly.

crop/-dust/ing, *n.* the spraying of insecticides on crops from an airplane. —**crop/ dust/er**, *n.*

crop/per, *n.* **1.** one that crops. **2.** a sharecropper. —*Idiom.* **3. come a cropper,** to fail decisively.

cro·quet (krō kā/), *n.* a lawn game played by knocking wooden balls through metal wickets with mallets.

cro·quette (krō ket/), *n.* a small, deep-fried cake or ball of minced meat, vegetables, etc.

Cros·by (krôz/bē, kroz/-), *n.* **Bing** (*Harry Lillis Crosby*), 1904–77, U.S. singer and actor.

cro·sier (krō/zhər), *n.* a ceremonial staff carried by a bishop or an abbot.

cross (krôs, kros), *n., v., adj.,* **-er, -est.** —*n.* **1.** a fig-

ure consisting of two lines intersecting at right angles. **2.** a structure consisting of an upright and a transverse piece, upon which persons were formerly put to death. **3. the Cross,** the cross upon which Jesus died. **4.** a figure of the Cross as a Christian symbol. **5.** an affliction; misfortune. **6.** a mixing of breeds. **7.** a hybrid; crossbreed. —*v.t.* **8.** to move or extend from one side to the other side of. **9.** to draw a line across. **10.** to intersect. **11.** to place across each other or crosswise: *to cross one's legs.* **12.** to meet and pass. **13.** to crossbreed; hybridize. **14.** to oppose. **15.** to make the sign of the cross upon or over. —*v.i.* **16.** to intersect. **17.** to move or extend from one side or place to another. **18.** to meet and pass. **19.** to crossbreed. **20. cross out** or **off,** to cancel, as by drawing a line through. —*adj.* **21.** angry; ill-humored. **22.** lying crosswise. **23.** contrary; opposite. **24.** crossbred; hybrid. —*Idiom.* **25. cross one's mind,** to occur to one. **26. cross one's path,** to meet. —**cross/ly**, *adv.*

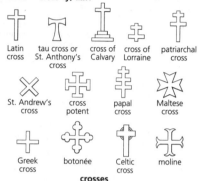

Latin cross — tau cross or St. Anthony's cross — cross of Calvary — cross of Lorraine — patriarchal cross

St. Andrew's cross — cross potent — papal cross — Maltese cross

Greek cross — botonée — Celtic cross — moline

crosses

cross/bar/, *n.* a horizontal bar, line, or stripe.

cross/beam/, *n.* a transverse beam in a structure.

cross/bones/, *n.pl.* two bones placed crosswise, usu. below a skull, to symbolize death.

cross/bow/ (-bō/), *n.* a medieval weapon consisting of a bow fixed transversely on a grooved wooden stock.

cross/breed/, *v.,* **-bred, -breed·ing,** *n.* —*v.t., v.i.* **1.** to hybridize. —*n.* **2.** a hybrid.

cross/-coun/try, *adj.* **1.** proceeding over fields, through woods, etc., rather than on a road, track, or run. **2.** from one end of the country to the other.

cross/-exam/ine, *v.t.,* **-ined, -in·ing.** to examine (a witness called by the opposing side), esp. in order to check or discredit his or her testimony. —**cross/-examina/tion**, *n.*

cross/-eye/, *n.* a condition in which one or both eyes turn inward. —**cross/-eyed/**, *adj.*

cross/ fire/, *n.* **1.** lines of gunfire crossing one another. **2.** a brisk or angry exchange of words or opinions.

cross/hatch/, *v.t.* to shade with two or more intersecting series of parallel lines. —**cross/hatch/ing**, *n.*

cross/ing, *n.* **1.** a place where lines, streets, etc., cross each other. **2.** a place at which a road, river, etc., may be crossed.

cross/ of Cal/vary, *n.* a Latin cross with a representation of steps beneath it.

cross/ of gold/, *n.* the gold standard, referred to in a speech (1896) by William Jennings Bryan.

cross/o/ver, *n.* **1.** a bridge or other structure for crossing a river, highway, etc. **2.** music that crosses over in style, sometimes sharing attributes with several musical styles. **3.** a member of one political party who votes in the primary of another party.

cross/piece/, *n.* a transverse piece.

cross/-pollina/tion, *n.* the transfer of pollen from the flower of one plant to the flower of a genetically different one. —**cross/-pol/linate**, *v.t.,* **-nat·ed, -nat·ing.**

cross′-pur′pose, *n.* **1.** a contrary purpose. **—Idiom. 2. at cross-purposes,** in a way that involves mutual misunderstanding.

cross′ ref′erence, *n.* a reference from one part of a book, index, etc., to another part. **—cross′-refer′,** *v.,* **-ferred, -fer•ring.**

cross′road′, *n.* **1.** a road that crosses another road. **2.** Often, **-roads.** (*used with a sing. or pl. v.*) **a.** a place where roads intersect. **b.** a point at which a decision must be made. **c.** a center of activity.

cross′ sec′tion, *n.* **1.** a section made by a plane cutting something transversely. **2.** a pictorial representation of such a section. **3.** a representative sample of a whole. **—cross′-sec′tional,** *adj.*

cross′town′, *adj.* **1.** extending or traveling across a town. **—***adv.* **2.** across a town.

cross′-train′, *v.t.* to train (a worker, athlete, etc.) to be proficient at different, usu. related, skills or tasks.

cross′walk′, *n.* a lane for pedestrians crossing a street.

cross′wise′, *adv.* across; transversely.

cross′word′ puz′zle, *n.* a puzzle in which words corresponding to numbered clues are fitted into a pattern of horizontal and vertical squares.

crotch (kroch), *n.* **1.** a place where something divides or forks, as the human body between the legs. **2.** the part of trousers, underpants, etc., where the two legs join.

crotch•et (kroch′it), *n.* an odd fancy or whimsical notion.

crotch•et•y (kroch′i tē), *adj.* **1.** eccentric. **2.** grouchy.

crouch (krouch), *v.i.* **1.** to stoop low with the knees bent. **2.** to cringe. **—***n.* **3.** the act of crouching.

croup (kroop), *n.* any condition of the larynx or trachea characterized by a hoarse cough and difficult breathing.

crou•pi•er (kroo′pē ər, -pē ā′), *n.* an attendant who collects and pays the money at a gaming table.

crou•ton (kroo′ton, kroo ton′), *n.* a small cube of toasted bread, used in salads, soups, etc.

crow¹ (krō), *n.* **1.** a large bird with lustrous black plumage. **—Idiom. 2. as the crow flies,** in a straight line. **3. eat crow,** to admit a mistake.

crow² (krō), *v.,* **crowed** or, for 1, (*esp. Brit.*), **crew; crowed; crow•ing;** *n.* **—***v.i.* **1.** to utter the cry of a rooster. **2.** to boast or brag. **3.** to utter a cry of pleasure. **—***n.* **4.** the cry of a rooster. **5.** a cry of pleasure.

crow′bar′, *n.* a flattened steel bar used as a lever.

crowd (kroud), *n.* **1.** a large number of persons or things gathered together. **2.** any group of persons having something in common: *the theater crowd.* **—***v.i.* **3.** to gather in large numbers. **4.** to press forward. **—***v.t.* **5.** to cram. **6.** to push or shove. **—crowd′ed,** *adj.*

crow′foot′, *n., pl.* **-foots.** a plant of the buttercup family, having divided leaves suggestive of a bird's foot.

crown (kroun), *n.* **1.** a headgear worn by a monarch as a symbol of sovereignty. **2.** the power of a sovereign. **3.** (*often cap.*) the sovereign. **4.** a wreath worn on the head as a mark of victory. **5.** an award for an achievement. **6.** the highest part or state of anything. **7. a.** the part of a tooth that is covered by enamel. **b.** an artificial substitute for this. **8.** a former British silver coin, equal to five shillings. **—***v.t.* **9.** to invest with regal power. **10.** to place a crown on. **11.** to honor. **12.** to be at the highest part of. **13.** to bring to a successful conclusion.

crown′ of glo′ry, *n.* heavenly rewards. I Peter 5:4. **2.** a triumph or great achievement.

crown′ prince′, *n.* a male heir apparent to a throne.

crow′s′-foot′, *n., pl.* **-feet.** a tiny wrinkle at the outer corner of the eye.

crow′s′-nest′, *n.* a platform for a lookout high on a ship's mast.

cro•zier (krō′zhər), *n.* CROSIER.

CRT, 1. cathode-ray tube. **2.** a computer monitor that includes a cathode-ray tube.

cru•cial (kroo′shəl), *adj.* of vital or decisive importance. **—cru′cial•ly,** *adv.*

cru•ci•ble (kroo′sə bəl), *n.* **1.** a container used for heating substances to high temperatures. **2.** a severe trial.

cru•ci•fix (kroo′sə fiks), *n.* a cross with the figure of Jesus crucified upon it.

cru′ci•fix′ion (-fik′shən), *n.* **1.** the act of crucifying. **2.** (*cap.*) the death of Jesus upon the Cross.

cru′ci•form′, *adj.* cross-shaped.

cru•ci•fy, *v.t.,* **-fied, -fy•ing. 1.** to put to death by nailing or binding the hands and feet to a cross. **2.** to persecute or torment.

crude (krood), *adj.,* **crud•er, crud•est,** *n.* **—***adj.* **1.** in a raw or unrefined state. **2.** lacking finish, polish, etc.; rough. **3.** lacking culture, refinement, etc.; vulgar. **—***n.* **4.** petroleum before refining. **—crude′ly,** *adv.* **—crude′ness,** *n.* **—crud′i•ty,** *n.*

cru•di•tés (kroo′di tā′), *n.pl.* raw vegetables cut up and served with a dip.

cru•el (kroo′əl), *adj.,* **-er, -est.** willfully causing pain or distress to others. **—cru′el•ly,** *adv.* **—cru′el•ty,** *n., pl.* **-ties.**

cru•et (kroo′it), *n.* a glass bottle to hold vinegar, oil, etc., for the table.

cruise (krooz), *v.,* **cruised, cruis•ing,** *n.* **—***v.i.* **1.** to sail about on a pleasure trip. **2.** to fly, drive, etc., at a constant speed that permits maximum operating efficiency. **3.** to travel or go about slowly, as in search of something. **—***v.t.* **4.** to cruise in. **—***n.* **5.** a pleasure voyage on a ship.

cruise′ mis′sile, *n.* a guided missile designed to fly at low altitudes to avoid radar detection.

cruis′er, *n.* **1.** one that cruises. **2.** a fast warship of medium tonnage. **3.** SQUAD CAR. **4.** a pleasure boat having a cabin for living aboard.

crul•ler (krul′ər), *n.* a twisted oblong doughnut.

crumb (krum), *n.* **1.** a small, broken-off particle of bread, cake, etc. **2.** a fragment of anything; bit. **3.** *Slang.* a contemptible person. **—***v.t.* **4.** (in cooking) to prepare with crumbs. **—crumb′y,** *adj.,* **-i•er, -i•est.**

crum•ble (krum′bəl), *v.,* **-bled, -bling. —***v.i.* **1.** to break into small fragments. **2.** to disintegrate gradually. **—***v.t.* **3.** to break into crumbs. **—crum′bly,** *adj.,* **-bli•er, -bli•est.**

crum•my (krum′ē), *adj.,* **-mi•er, -mi•est.** *Informal.* **1.** run-down; shabby. **2.** cheap; worthless.

crum•pet (krum′pit), *n.* a flat muffin cooked on a griddle.

crum•ple (krum′pəl), *v.,* **-pled, -pling. —***v.t.* **1.** to crush into irregular folds or wrinkles. **—***v.i.* **2.** to contract into wrinkles. **3.** to collapse.

crunch (krunch), *v.t.* **1.** to chew, grind, etc., with a sharp crushing noise. **2.** to manipulate (numbers or data), esp. by computer. **—***v.i.* **3.** to chew with a crushing noise. **—***n.* **4.** an act or sound of crunching. **5.** a shortage or reduction: *the energy crunch.* **6.** a critical situation. **—crunch′y,** *adj.,* **-i•er, -i•est.**

crup•per (krup′ər, kroop′-), *n.* a leather strap fastened to a saddle and looping under the tail of a horse.

cru•sade (kroo sād′), *n., v.,* **-sad•ed, -sad•ing. —***n.* **1.** (*often cap.*) any of the Christian military expeditions of the 11th-13th centuries to recover the Holy Land from the Muslims. **2.** any vigorous movement on behalf of a cause. **—***v.i.* **3.** to go on or engage in a crusade. **—cru•sad′er,** *n.*

crush (krush), *v.t.* **1.** to press with a force that destroys or deforms. **2.** to pound into small particles. **3.** to force out by squeezing. **4.** to suppress utterly. **—***v.i.* **5.** to become crushed. **—***n.* **6.** the act of crushing or state of being crushed. **7.** a great crowd. **8.** *Informal.* a usu. short-lived infatuation. **—crush′er,** *n.*

crust (krust), *n.* **1.** the hard outer surface of bread. **2.** the baked shell of a pie. **3.** any hard external covering. **4.** the outer layer of the earth. **—***v.t., v.i.* **5.** to cover or become crusted with a crust. **—crust′al,** *adj.* **—crust′y,** *adj.,* **-i•er, -i•est.**

crus•ta•cean (kru stā′shən), *n.* any chiefly aquatic

arthropod typically having the body covered with a hard shell, including lobsters, shrimps, etc.

crutch (kruch), *n.* **1.** a support to assist a lame person in walking, usu. with a crosspiece fitting under the armpit. **2.** any support or prop.

crux (kruks), *n.* **1.** the central or pivotal point. **2.** a perplexing difficulty.

cry (krī), *v.,* **cried, cry•ing,** *n., pl.* **cries.** —*v.i.* **1.** to utter sounds of grief or suffering. **2.** to shed tears; weep. **3.** to shout. **4.** (of an animal) to utter a characteristic call. —*v.t.* **5.** to utter loudly. **6.** to announce publicly: *to cry one's wares.* —*n.* **7.** a shout, scream, or wail. **8.** a fit of weeping. **9.** the call of an animal. **10.** an entreaty; appeal. —*Idiom.* **11. a far cry,** altogether different. **12. cry in the wilderness,** a prophet's outcry in the face of ignorance and sin. Isa. 40:3; Matt. 3:3. **13. cry over spilled milk,** to regret what cannot be changed or undone.

cry'ba•by, *n., pl.* **-bies.** a person who complains often.

cry•o•gen•ics (krī'ə jen'iks), *n.* the study of extremely low temperatures. —**cry'o•gen'ic,** *adj.*

cry•o•sur•ger•y (krī'ō sûr'jə rē), *n.* the use of extreme cold to destroy tissue.

crypt (kript), *n.* a subterranean vault, esp. one used as a burial place. [< L < Gk *kryptḗ* hidden place]

cryp•tic (krip'tik), *adj.* **1.** mysterious; puzzling. **2.** secret; occult. —**cryp'ti•cal•ly,** *adv.*

cryp•to•gram (krip'tə gram'), *n.* a message in code or cipher.

cryp•tog•ra•phy (krip tog'rə fē), *n.* the study or use of code and cipher systems. —**cryp•tog'ra•pher,** *n.*

crys•tal (kris'tl), *n.* **1.** a clear, transparent mineral or glass resembling ice. **2.** the transparent form of crystallized quartz. **3.** a solid enclosed by symmetrically arranged plane surfaces, intersecting at definite angles. **4.** a fine-quality, brilliant glass. **5.** glassware, as goblets, made of such glass. **6.** the clear cover over the face of a watch. —*adj.* **7.** composed of crystal. **8.** clear or transparent. —**crys'tal•line** (-in, -īn', -ēn'), *adj.*

crys•tal•lize', *v.i., v.t.,* **-lized, -liz•ing. 1.** to form or cause to form into crystals. **2.** to assume or cause to assume a definite form. —**crys'tal•li•za'tion,** *n.*

Cs, *Chem. Symbol.* cesium.

C'-sec'tion, *n. Informal.* CESAREAN.

CST, Central Standard Time.

CSW or **C.S.W.,** Certified Social Worker.

CT, Connecticut.

Ct., 1. Connecticut. **2.** Count.

ct., 1. carat. **2.** cent. **3.** court.

cten•o•phore (ten'ə fôr', tē'nə-), *n.* COMB JELLY.

CT scan, *n.* CAT SCAN.

Cu, *Chem. Symbol.* copper. [< L *cuprum*]

cu or **cu.,** cubic.

cub (kub), *n.* **1.** the young of certain animals, esp. the bear, wolf, lion, and whale. **2.** a young and inexperienced person.

Cu•ba (kyōō'bə), *n.* an island republic in the Caribbean, S of Florida. 10,999,041. —**Cu'ban,** *adj., n.*

Cu'ban mis'sile cri'sis, *n.* a confrontation in 1962 between the United States and the Soviet Union after the installation of Soviet missile sites in Cuba.

cub•by•hole (kub'ē hōl'), *n.* a small, snug compartment.

cube (kyōōb), *n., v.,* **cubed, cub•ing.** —*n.* **1.** a solid bounded by six equal squares. **2.** a solid or hollow object having or approximating this form: *a sugar cube.* **3.** *Math.* the third power of a quantity, expressed as $a^3 = a \times a \times a$. —*v.t.* **4.** to make into a cube. **5.** to raise (a quantity or number) to the third power.

cube' root', *n.* a quantity of which a given quantity is the cube: *The cube root of 64 is 4.*

cu•bic (kyōō'bik), *adj.* **1.** having three dimensions. **2.** Also, **cu'bi•cal.** having the form of a cube. **3.** pertaining to a unit of linear measure that is multiplied by itself twice to form a unit of measure for volume: *a cubic foot.*

cu'bi•cle, *n.* a small partitioned space or compartment.

cub'ism, *n.* (*sometimes cap.*) a style of painting and sculpture marked by the reduction of natural forms to their geometrical equivalents. —**cub'ist,** *n., adj.*

cu•bit (kyōō'bit), *n.* an ancient linear unit, usu. from 17 to 21 inches (43 to 53 cm).

cub' scout', *n.* (*sometimes caps.*) a member of the junior division (ages 8–10) of the Boy Scouts.

cuck•old (kuk'ōld), *n.* **1.** the husband of an unfaithful wife. —*v.t.* **2.** to make a cuckold of. —**cuck'-old•ry,** *n.*

cuck•oo (kōō'kōō, kŏŏk'ōō), *n., pl.* **-oos. 1.** a slim, stout-billed, long-tailed bird. **2.** *Informal.* a crazy or foolish person. —*adj.* **3.** *Informal.* crazy; foolish.

cu•cum•ber (kyōō'kum bər), *n.* the edible, green-skinned, cylindrical fruit of a plant of the gourd family.

cud (kud), *n.* the coarse food regurgitated by a ruminant from its first stomach for further chewing.

cud•dle (kud'l), *v.,* **-dled, -dling.** *n.* —*v.t.* **1.** to hug tenderly. —*v.i.* **2.** to lie close and snug. —*n.* **3.** a hug. —**cud'dly,** *adj.,* **-dli•er, -dli•est.**

cudg•el (kuj'əl), *n., v.,* **-eled, -el•ing,** or (*esp. Brit.*) **-elled, -el•ling.** —*n.* **1.** a short, thick stick used as a weapon. —*v.t.* **2.** to strike with a cudgel.

cue¹ (kyōō), *n., v.,* **cued, cu•ing.** —*n.* **1.** anything said or done, on or off stage, that is followed by a specific line or action. **2.** anything that elicits action; stimulus. **3.** a hint; intimation. —*v.t.* **4.** to give a cue to.

cue² (kyōō), *n.* a long, tapering rod used to strike the ball in pool, billiards, etc.

cuff¹ (kuf), *n.* **1.** a fold or band at the bottom of a sleeve. **2.** the turned-up fold at the bottom of a trouser leg. —*Idiom.* **3. off the cuff,** *Informal.* impromptu. **4. on the cuff,** *Slang.* on credit.

cuff² (kuf), *v.t.* **1.** to strike with the open hand. —*n.* **2.** a blow or slap.

cuff' link' or **cuff'link',** *n.* one of a pair of linked buttonlike devices for fastening a shirt cuff.

cui•sine (kwi zēn'), *n.* **1.** a style of cooking. **2.** the food prepared, as by a restaurant.

cul-de-sac (kul'də sak', -sak', kōōl'-), *n., pl.* **culs-de-sac** or **cul-de-sacs. 1.** a street closed at one end. **2.** any situation in which further progress is impossible. **3.** a saclike anatomical cavity open at only one end, as the cecum.

cu•li•nar•y (kyōō'lə ner'ē, kul'ə-), *adj.* of cooking or the kitchen.

cull (kul), *v.t.* **1.** to choose; select and gather. **2.** to gather the choice elements from. —*n.* **3.** something picked out and put aside as inferior.

cul•mi•nate (kul'mə nāt'), *v.i.,* **-nat•ed, -nat•ing.** to reach the highest point or climactic stage. —**cul'-mi•na'tion,** *n.*

cu•lottes (kōō lots', kyōō-), *n.* (*used with a pl. v.*) women's trousers cut full to resemble a skirt.

cul•pa•ble (kul'pə bəl), *adj.* deserving blame or censure. —**cul'pa•bil'i•ty,** *n.*

cul•prit (kul'prit), *n.* a person guilty of an offense or fault.

cult (kult), *n.* **1.** a particular system of religious worship. **2.** a group devoted to a person, fad, etc. **3. a.** a religion considered to be false or extremist. **b.** the members of such a religion. —*adj.* **4.** of a cult. **5.** attracting a small group of devotees: *a cult movie.* —**cul'tic,** *adj.* —**cult'ist,** *n.*

cul•ti•vate (kul'tə vāt'), *v.t.,* **-vat•ed, -vat•ing. 1.** to work on (land) in order to raise crops. **2.** to promote the growth of (a plant or crop). **3.** to develop or improve by education or training. **4.** to seek to promote or foster. —**cul'ti•va•ble** (-və bəl), **cul'ti•vat'a•ble,** *adj.* —**cul'ti•va'tion,** *n.* —**cul'ti•va'tor,** *n.*

cul•ture (kul'chər), *n., v.,* **-tured, -tur•ing.** —*n.* **1.** artistic and intellectual pursuits and products. **2.** development or improvement of the mind, morals, etc. **3.** the ways of living built up by a human group and transmitted to succeeding generations. **4.** a particular form or stage of civilization. **5. a.** the cultivation of microorganisms or tissues, as for scientific study. **b.**

the product of such cultivation. **6.** cultivation of the soil. **7.** the raising of plants or animals. —*v.t.* **8.** to cultivate. **9.** to grow (microorganisms, tissues, etc.) in a nutrient medium. —**cul′tur•al,** *adj.* —**cul′tur•al•ly,** *adv.*

cul′ture shock′, *n.* the bewilderment and distress experienced by an individual who is exposed to a new culture.

cul•vert (kul′vərt), *n.* a drain or conduit under a road, sidewalk, etc.

cum., cumulative.

cum•ber (kum′bər), *v.t.* **1.** to hinder; hamper. **2.** to overload; burden.

Cum′berland Gap′, *n.* a pass in the Cumberland Mountains at the junction of the Virginia, Kentucky, and Tennessee boundaries. 1315 ft. (401 m) high.

Cum′berland Moun′tains, *n.pl.* a plateau largely in Kentucky and Tennessee, a part of the Appalachian Mountains: highest point, ab. 4000 ft. (1220 m). Also called **Cum′berland Plateau′.**

cum•ber•some (-səm), *adj.* **1.** burdensome. **2.** unwieldy.

cum•in (kum′ən, koōm′-), *n.* **1.** a small plant bearing aromatic, seedlike fruit used as a spice. **2.** the fruit of this plant.

cum•mer•bund (kum′ər bund′), *n.* a wide sash worn at the waist, esp. with a tuxedo.

cu•mu•la•tive (kyoō′myə lə tiv, -lā′tiv), *adj.* increasing by successive additions. —**cu′mu•la•tive•ly,** *adv.*

cu•mu•lus (kyoō′myə ləs), *n., pl.* **-li** (-lī′). a cloud with dense individual elements in the form of puffs, with flat bases.

cu•ne•i•form (kyoō nē′ə fôrm′), *adj.* **1.** composed of slim triangular elements, as the writing of the ancient Babylonians and others. —*n.* **2.** cuneiform writing.

cun•ning (kun′ing), *n.* **1.** craftiness; guile. **2.** adeptness; dexterity. —*adj.* **3.** showing ingenuity. **4.** crafty; sly. **5.** charmingly cute. —**cun′ning•ly,** *adv.*

cup (kup), *n., v.,* **cupped, cup•ping.** —*n.* **1.** a small, open container for beverages, usu. with a handle. **2.** the quantity in a cup. **3.** a unit of capacity equal to 8 fluid ounces (237 milliliters). **4.** a cuplike object, part, etc. —*v.t.* **5.** to form into a cuplike shape: *to cup one's hands.*

cup•board (kub′ərd), *n.* a closet with shelves for dishes, cups, food, etc.

cup′cake′ (kup′-), *n.* a small cake baked in a cup-shaped mold.

cup′ful, *n., pl.* **-fuls.** the amount a cup can hold.

Cu•pid (kyoō′pid), *n.* the Roman god of carnal love, the son of Venus, commonly represented as a winged, naked infant boy with a bow and arrows.

cu•pid′i•ty, *n.* eager or excessive desire, esp. for wealth.

cu•po•la (kyoō′pə lə), *n., pl.* **-las.** a light structure on a dome or roof.

cupola

cur (kûr), *n.* **1.** a mongrel dog. **2.** a mean, cowardly person.

cu•ra•re (kyoō rär′ē, koō-), *n.* a substance derived from tropical plants, used as an arrow poison.

cu•rate (kyoōr′it), *n.* a cleric assisting a rector or vicar. —**cu′ra•cy** (-ə sē), *n., pl.* **-cies.**

cur•a•tive (kyoōr′ə tiv), *adj.* **1.** serving to cure or heal. —*n.* **2.** a remedy.

cu•ra•tor (kyoō rā′tər, kyoōr′ā-), *n.* one in charge of a museum, art collection, etc. —**cu′ra•to′ri•al** (-ə tôr′ē əl), *adj.*

curb (kûrb), *n.* **1.** an edging, esp. of concrete, for a sidewalk. **2.** a restraint; check. **3.** a bit to which a chain is hooked for control of a horse. —*v.t.* **4.** to control; restrain. **5.** to put a curb on (a horse).

curd (kûrd), *n.* a substance obtained from milk by coagulation and used as food or made into cheese.

cur•dle (kûr′dl), *v.t., v.i.,* **-dled, -dling.** to change into curd; coagulate.

cure (kyoōr), *n., v.,* **cured, cur•ing.** —*n.* **1.** a means of healing; remedy. **2.** a method of remedial treatment. **3.** restoration to health. —*v.t.* **4.** to restore to health. **5.** to relieve or rid of (an illness, bad habit, etc.). **6.** to preserve (meat, fish, etc.), as by smoking or salting. **7.** to process (rubber, tobacco, etc.), as by fermentation or aging. —**cur′a•ble,** *adj.* —**cur′er,** *n.*

cu•ré (kyoō rā′, kyoōr′ā), *n., pl.* **-rés.** (in France) a parish priest.

cure′-all′, *n.* a panacea.

cu•ret•tage (kyoōr′i täzh′, kyoō ret′ij), *n.* the surgical removal of tissue from body cavities, as the uterus.

cur•few (kûr′fyoō), *n.* **1.** an order establishing a time in the evening after which no unauthorized persons may be outdoors. **2.** a parental regulation requiring a child to be home at a stated time.

cu•ri•a (kyoōr′ē ə), *n., pl.* **cu•ri•ae** (kyoōr′ē ē′). (*sometimes cap.*) the body of congregations, offices, etc., that assist the pope in the administration of the Roman Catholic Church.

Cu•rie (kyoōr′ē, kyoō rē′), *n.* **1. Marie,** 1867–1934, Polish physicist and chemist in France: codiscoverer of radium 1898. **2.** her husband, **Pierre,** 1859–1906, French physicist and chemist: codiscoverer of radium.

cu•ri•o (kyoōr′ē ō′), *n., pl.* **-ri•os.** any article, object of art, etc., valued as a curiosity.

cu•ri•os•i•ty (kyoōr′ē os′i tē), *n., pl.* **-ties. 1.** the desire to know about anything. **2.** a rare or novel thing.

cu′ri•ous, *adj.* **1.** eager to know. **2.** prying; meddlesome. **3.** odd or strange. —**cu′ri•ous•ly,** *adv.*

cu•ri•um (kyoōr′ē əm), *n.* a synthetic radioactive element produced from plutonium. *Symbol:* Cm; *at. no.:* 96.

curl (kûrl), *v.t.* **1.** to form into ringlets, as the hair. **2.** to coil. —*v.i.* **3.** to grow in or form ringlets. **4.** to coil or curve. —*n.* **5.** a ringlet of hair. **6.** anything of a spiral or curved shape. —**curl′er,** *n.* —**curl′y,** *adj.,* **-i•er, -i•est.**

cur•lew (kûr′loō), *n.* a large shorebird with a long, slender bill that curves down.

curl•i•cue (kûr′li kyoō′), *n.* an ornamental curl or twist.

curl•ing (kûr′ling), *n.* a game played on ice in which two teams slide large, round stones toward a mark in a circle.

cur•mudg•eon (kər muj′ən), *n.* a bad-tempered, difficult person.

cur•rant (kûr′ənt, kur′-), *n.* **1.** a small seedless raisin. **2.** the small, round, sour berry of certain shrubs of the saxifrage family. **3.** the shrub itself.

cur•ren•cy (kûr′ən sē, kur′-), *n., pl.* **-cies. 1.** any form of money that is in circulation in a country. **2.** general acceptance; prevalence.

cur•rent (kûr′ənt, kur′-), *adj.* **1.** belonging to the time actually passing; present: *the current month.* **2.** generally accepted; prevalent. **3.** widely circulating or circulated. —*n.* **4.** a flowing, as of a river. **5.** a portion of a large body of water or air moving in a certain direction. **6.** the movement or flow of electric charge. **7.** a general tendency. —**cur′rent•ly,** *adv.*

cur•ric•u•lum (kə rik′yə ləm), *n., pl.* **-la** (-lə), **-lums.** the aggregate of courses of study in a school, college, etc. —**cur•ric′u•lar,** *adj.*

Cur•ri•er (kûr′ē ər, kur-), *n.* **Nathaniel,** 1813–88,

U.S. lithographer: with James Merritt Ives produced prints showing American life.

cur•ry¹ (kûr′ē, kur′ē), *n., pl.* **-ries,** *v.,* **-ried, -ry•ing.** —*n.* **1.** a dish of meat, fish, or vegetables flavored with curry powder. **2.** CURRY POWDER. —*v.t.* **3.** to flavor (food) with curry powder.

cur•ry² (kûr′ē, kur′ē), *v.t.,* **-ried, -ry•ing. 1.** to rub and clean (a horse) with a currycomb. **2.** to dress (tanned hides) by soaking, beating, etc. —*Idiom.* **3. curry favor,** to seek to advance oneself through flattery or fawning.

cur′ry•comb′, *n.* **1.** a comb for currying horses. —*v.t.* **2.** to rub or clean with a currycomb.

cur′ry pow′der, *n.* a pungent mixture of ground turmeric, cumin, and other spices.

curse (kûrs), *n., v.,* **cursed** or **curst, curs•ing.** —*n.* **1.** the expression of a wish that misfortune, evil, etc., befall someone. **2.** a profane or obscene word. **3.** an evil or misfortune that has been invoked upon one. —*v.t.* **4.** to invoke evil upon. **5.** to swear at. **6.** to afflict with evil. —*v.i.* **7.** to swear profanely.

curs•ed (kûr′sid, kûrst), *adj.* **1.** under a curse. **2.** hateful; abominable.

Curse′ of Cain′, *n.* God's judgment that Cain should wander homeless. Gen. 4:11–12.

cur•sive (kûr′siv), *adj.* (of handwriting) in flowing strokes with the letters joined together.

cur•sor (kûr′sər), *n.* a movable symbol used to indicate where data may be input on a computer screen.

cur•so•ry (kûr′sə rē), *adj.* hasty and superficial. —**cur′so•ri•ly,** *adv.*

curt (kûrt), *adj.,* **-er, -est.** rudely brief in speech or abrupt in manner. —**curt′ly,** *adv.* —**curt′ness,** *n.*

cur•tail (kər tāl′), *v.t.* to cut short; reduce. —**cur•tail′ment,** *n.*

cur•tain (kûr′tn), *n.* **1.** a hanging piece of fabric used to shut out the light from a window, adorn a room, etc. **2.** a movable drapery that conceals the stage from the audience. —*v.t.* **3.** to provide, conceal, etc., with or as if with a curtain.

curt•sy (kûrt′sē), *n., pl.* **-sies,** *v.,* **-sied, -sy•ing.** —*n.* **1.** a respectful bow made by women, consisting of bending the knees and lowering the body. —*v.i.* **2.** to make a curtsy.

cur•va•ceous (kûr vā′shəs), *adj.* (of a woman) having a well-shaped figure with voluptuous curves.

cur′va•ture (-və chər, -chŏŏr′), *n.* **1.** a curved condition, often abnormal. **2.** the degree of curving of a line or surface.

curve (kûrv), *n., v.,* **curved, curv•ing.** —*n.* **1.** a continuously bending line, without angles. **2.** a curving movement. **3.** any curved form. —*v.i., v.t.* **4.** to bend or move in a curve. —**curv′y,** *adj.,* **-i•er, -i•est.**

cush•ion (kŏŏsh′ən), *n.* **1.** a soft pad or pillow on which to sit, lie, or lean. **2.** anything similar in form or function. **3.** something to absorb shocks. —*v.t.* **4.** to furnish with a cushion. **5.** to lessen or soften the effects of.

cush′y, *adj.,* **-i•er, -i•est.** *Informal.* **1.** easy and profitable: *a cushy job.* **2.** soft and comfortable.

cusp (kusp), *n.* a point or pointed end, as on the crown of a tooth.

cus•pid (kus′pid), *n.* any of the four canine teeth in humans.

cus•pi•dor (kus′pi dôr′), *n.* a large bowl serving as a receptacle for spit, esp. from chewing tobacco.

cus•tard (kus′tərd), *n.* a boiled or baked dish made with eggs, milk, and sugar.

Cus•ter (kus′tər), *n.* **George,** 1839–76, U.S. general.

Cus′ter's Last′ Stand′, *n.* the annihilation of George Armstrong Custer and his military force by Sioux at the Battle of Little Big Horn (June 25, 1876).

cus•to•di•an (ku stō′dē ən), *n.* **1.** a person who has custody; guardian. **2.** the caretaker of a property.

cus•to•dy (kus′tə dē), *n., pl.* **-dies. 1.** guardianship and care. **2.** imprisonment or legal restraint. —**cus•to•di•al** (ku stō′dē əl), *adj.*

cus•tom (kus′təm), *n.* **1.** a habitual practice. **2.** habits or usages collectively; convention. **3. customs,** duties imposed by law on imported or exported

goods. **4.** regular patronage of a shop, restaurant, etc. —*adj.* **5.** made specially for individual customers. **6.** dealing in things so made, or doing work to order.

cus•tom•ar•y (kus′tə mer′ē), *adj.* according to custom; usual; habitual. —**cus′tom•ar′i•ly,** *adv.*

cus′tom-built′, *adj.* built to individual order.

cus′tom•er, *n.* a person who purchases goods or services from another.

cus′tom•house′, *n.* a government building for collecting customs, clearing ships, etc.

cus′tom•ize′, *v.t.,* **-ized, -iz•ing.** to make, alter, or build according to individual specifications. —**cus′tom•i•za′tion,** *n.*

cus′tom-made′, *adj.* made to individual order.

cut (kut), *v.,* **cut, cut•ting,** *adj., n.* —*v.t.* **1.** to penetrate with a sharp-edged instrument. **2.** to divide with a sharp-edged instrument. **3.** to saw down. **4.** to trim by clipping, paring, etc. **5.** to reap; harvest. **6.** to abridge. **7.** to reduce or curtail: *to cut prices.* **8.** to dilute. **9.** *Informal.* to cease. **10.** to grow (a tooth) through the gum. **11.** to make by cutting, as a garment. **12.** to refuse to recognize socially. **13.** to strike sharply. **14.** to absent oneself from: *to cut classes.* **15.** to wound the feelings of. **16.** to divide (a pack of cards) at random. —*v.i.* **17.** to penetrate or divide something, as with a sharp-edged instrument. **18.** to admit of being cut. **19.** to move or cross. **20.** to make a sharp change in direction. **21. ~ back,** to curtail or discontinue. **22. ~ down,** to lessen or curtail. **23. ~ in, a.** to thrust oneself, a vehicle, etc., abruptly between others. **b.** to interrupt. **c.** to interrupt a dancing couple in order to dance with one of them. **24. ~ off, a.** to shut off or stop. **b.** to disinherit. **c.** to sever. **25. ~ out, a.** to delete or excise. **b.** to stop. **26. ~ up, a.** to cut into pieces. **b.** *Informal.* to play pranks. —*adj.* **27.** divided or detached by cutting. **28.** fashioned by cutting. —*n.* **29.** the result of cutting, as an incision. **30.** the act of cutting. **31.** a piece cut off. **32.** a share, esp. of earnings. **33.** a reduction, as in price. **34.** the fashion in which anything is cut. **35.** a passage or course straight across. **36.** an act, speech, etc., that wounds the feelings. **37.** an engraved plate or block used for printing. **38.** a printed picture or illustration **39.** an absence, as from a class. **40.** an individual musical piece on a recording. —*Idiom.* **41. a cut above,** superior to. **42. cut out for,** fitted for; capable of.

cut′-and-dried′, *adj.* lacking in originality or spontaneity; routine.

cu•ta•ne•ous (kyōō tā′nē əs), *adj.* of or affecting the skin.

cut′a•way′, *n.* a man's formal daytime coat cut so as to curve to the tails at the back.

cut′back′, *n.* a reduction in rate, quantity, etc.

cute (kyōōt), *adj.,* **cut•er, cut•est. 1.** attractive or pretty in a dainty way. **2.** clever; shrewd. —**cute′ly,** *adv.* —**cute′ness,** *n.*

cute•sy or **-sie** (-sē), *adj.,* **-si•er, -si•est.** *Informal.* forcedly and consciously cute.

cu•ti•cle (kyōō′ti kəl), *n.* **1.** the hardened skin that surrounds a fingernail or toenail. **2.** the epidermis.

cut•lass (kut′ləs), *n.* a short, heavy, slightly curved sword.

cut•ler•y (kut′lə rē), *n.* cutting instruments collectively, esp. utensils for serving and eating food.

cut•let (kut′lit), *n.* **1.** a slice of meat, esp. of veal, for broiling or frying. **2.** a flat croquette of minced food, as chicken or fish.

cut′off′, *n.* **1.** something that cuts off. **2.** a point serving as the limit beyond which something is no longer effective or possible. **3.** a road that leaves another and provides a shortcut. **4. cutoffs,** shorts made by cutting the legs off a pair of trousers, esp. jeans.

cut′-rate′, *adj.* offered or selling at reduced prices.

cut′ter, *n.* **1.** a person who cuts, as one who cuts fabric for garments. **2.** a single-masted sailing ship.

cut′throat′, *n.* **1.** a murderer. —*adj.* **2.** murderous. **3.** ruthless: *cutthroat competition.*

cut′ting, *n.* **1.** a piece, as a root or stem, cut from a plant and used for propagation. —*adj.* **2.** penetrating by or as if by a cut. **3.** piercing, as a wind. **4.** sarcastic. —**cut′ting•ly,** *adv.*

cut•tle•fish (kut′l fish′), *n., pl.* **-fish, -fish•es.** a marine mollusk having ten arms with suckers and a hard internal shell (**cut′tle•bone′**).

CV, 1. cardiovascular. **2.** curriculum vitae: a résumé.

cwt, hundredweight.

-cy, a suffix meaning: state or condition (*expediency*); rank or office (*magistracy*).

cy•a•nide (sī′ə nīd′, -nid), *n.* a highly poisonous compound containing sodium or potassium.

cyber-, a combining form representing COMPUTER (*cybertalk; cyberart*) and by extension meaning "very modern" (*cyberfashion*).

cy•ber•net•ics (sī′bər net′iks), *n.* the study of organic control and communication systems, and mechanical or electronic systems analogous to them, as robots. —**cy′ber•net′ic,** *adj.*

cy•ber•space (sī′bər spās′), *n.* **1.** the realm of electronic communication. **2.** VIRTUAL REALITY.

cy•cla•men (sī′klə mən), *n.* a plant of the primrose family, having white, purple, or red flowers.

cy•cle (sī′kəl), *n., v.,* **-cled, -cling.** —*n.* **1.** any complete round or recurring series. **2.** a recurring period of time, esp. one in which certain events repeat themselves in the same order and intervals. **3.** a bicycle, motorcycle, etc. **4.** a group of poems, stories, etc., about a central theme or figure. —*v.i.* **5.** to travel by bicycle, motorcycle, etc. **6.** to move in cycles. —**cy•clic** (sī′klik, sik′lik), **cy′cli•cal,** *adj.*

cy′clist, *n.* a person who travels by bicycle, motorcycle, etc.

cyclo-, a combining form meaning circle or cycle (*cyclometer*).

cy•clom•e•ter (sī klom′i tər), *n.* a device for measuring distance by recording the revolutions of a vehicle's wheel.

cy•clone (sī′klōn), *n.* **1.** an atmospheric wind-and-pressure system characterized by low pressure at its center and by circular wind motion. **2.** (not in technical use) a tornado. [< Gk *kyklôn* revolving] —**cy•clon′ic** (-klon′ik), *adj.*

cy•clo•pe•di•a or **-pae•di•a** (sī′klə pē′dē ə), *n., pl.* **-di•as.** an encyclopedia.

Cy•clops (sī′klops), *n., pl.* **Cy•clo•pes** (sī klō′pēz). any of a group of one-eyed giants of Greek myth.

cy•clo•spo•rine (sī′klə spôr′ēn, -in), *n.* a substance that suppresses immune reactions, used for minimizing rejection of organ transplants and for treating certain autoimmune diseases.

cy•clo•tron (sī′klə tron′), *n.* an accelerator in

which particles move in spiral paths in a constant magnetic field.

cyg•net (sig′nit), *n.* a young swan.

cyl•in•der (sil′in dər), *n.* **1.** a surface or solid bounded by two parallel planes and generated by a line tracing a closed curve perpendicular to the planes. **2.** any cylinderlike object or part. **3.** the rotating part of a revolver. —**cy•lin′dri•cal,** *adj.*

cym•bal (sim′bəl), *n.* a percussion instrument consisting of a concave metal plate that produces a sharp, ringing sound when struck. —**cym′bal•ist,** *n.*

cyn•ic (sin′ik), *n.* one who believes that only selfishness motivates human actions. —**cyn′i•cal,** *adj.* —**cyn′i•cal•ly,** *adv.*

cyn′i•cism (-ə siz′əm), *n.* the disposition, character, or belief of a cynic.

cy•no•sure (sī′nə shŏŏr′, sin′ə-), *n.* one that strongly attracts attention.

cy•pher (sī′fər), *n., v.i.* Chiefly Brit. CIPHER.

cy•press (sī′prəs), *n.* **1.** an evergreen tree with dark green, scalelike, overlapping leaves. **2.** its wood.

Cy•prus (sī′prəs), *n.* an island republic in the Mediterranean, S of Turkey. 752,808. —**Cyp•ri•ot** (sip′rē ət), *n., adj.*

cyst (sist), *n.* an abnormal saclike growth of the body in which matter is retained. —**cys′tic,** *adj.*

cys′tic fibro′sis, *n.* a hereditary disease of the exocrine glands characterized by breathing difficulties, infection, and fibrosis.

cy•tol•o•gy (sī tol′ə jē), *n.* the study of the microscopic appearance of cells. —**cy•tol′o•gist,** *n.*

cy•to•plasm (sī′tə plaz′əm), *n.* the cell substance between the cell membrane and the nucleus. —**cy′to•plas′mic,** *adj.*

cy•to•sine (sī′tə sēn′, -zēn′, -sin), *n.* a pyrimidine base that is one of the fundamental components of DNA and RNA.

czar (zär), *n.* **1.** (*often cap.*) the former emperor of Russia. **2.** any person exercising great authority or power. [< Russ *tsar′* ≪ L *Caesar* Caesar]

cza•ri•na (zä rē′nə), *n., pl.* **-nas.** the wife of a czar.

Czech (chek), *n.* **1.** a native or inhabitant of the Czech Republic. **2.** the Slavic language of the Czechs. —*adj.* **3.** of the Czechs, their homeland, or their language.

Czech•o•slo•va•ki•a (chek′ə slə vä′kē ə, -vak′ē ə), *n.* a former republic (1918–92) in central Europe. Compare CZECH REPUBLIC, SLOVAKIA. —**Czech′o•slo′vak** (-slō′vak, -väk), **Czech′o•slo•va′ki•an,** *adj., n.*

Czech′ Repub′lic, *n.* a republic in central Europe: formerly part of Czechoslovakia. 10,318,958.

D

D, d (dē), *n., pl.* **Ds** or **D's, ds** or **d's.** the fourth letter of the English alphabet, a consonant.

'd, 1. contraction of *had, would,* or *did: He'd already left; I'd like that; Where'd you go?* **2.** contraction of *-ed: She OK'd the plan.*

D, Dutch.

D, *Symbol.* **1.** the fourth in order or in a series. **2.** a grade or mark indicating poor quality. **3.** (*sometimes l.c.*) the Roman numeral for 500. **4.** *Chem.* deuterium.

D., 1. December. **2.** Democrat. **3.** Doctor. **4.** dose. **5.** Dutch.

d., 1. date. **2.** deceased. **3.** degree. **4.** delete. **5.** Chiefly Brit. penny; pence. [< L *denārius*] **6.** deputy. **7.** diameter. **8.** dose. **9.** drachma.

D.A. or **DA, 1.** delayed action. **2.** District Attorney. **3.** doesn't answer.

dab (dab), *v.,* **dabbed, dab•bing,** *n.* —*v.t., v.i.* **1.** to pat or tap gently. **2.** to apply by light strokes, as

paint or plaster. —*n.* **3.** a quick or light pat. **4.** a small lump or quantity: *a dab of powder.*

dab•ble (dab′əl), *v.i.,* **-bled, -bling. 1.** to play in or as if in water, esp. with the hands. **2.** to work at anything in a superficial manner: *to dabble in literature.* —**dab′bler,** *n.*

Dac•ca (dak′ə, dä′kə), *n.* DHAKA.

da•cha (dä′chə), *n., pl.* **-chas.** a Russian country house or villa.

Da•chau (dä′KHou), *n.* a city in S Germany, near Munich: site of Nazi concentration camp. 33,950.

dachs•hund (däks′hŏŏnt′, -hŏŏnd′), *n.* one of a German breed of dogs with very short legs and a long body and ears. [< G, = *Dachs* badger + *Hund* dog]

Da•cron (dā′kron, dak′ron), *Trademark.* a brand of polyester fiber.

dac•tyl (dak′til), *n.* a prosodic foot of three syllables, one stressed followed by two unstressed. —**dac• tyl′ic** (-til′ik), *adj.*

dad (dad), *n. Informal.* father.

da•da (dä′dä), *n.* a movement in early 20th-century art and literature whose exponents challenged established canons of art, thought, and morality. —**da′da• ism,** *n.* —**da′da•ist,** *n., adj.*

dad•dy (dad′ē), *n., pl.* -**dies.** *Informal.* father; dad.

dad′dy-long′legs′ or **dad′dy long′legs′,** *n., pl.* -**legs.** a spiderlike arachnid with a compact body and long, slender legs.

da•do (dā′dō), *n., pl.* -**does, -dos. 1.** the part of a pedestal between the base and the cornice or cap. **2.** the lower broad part of an interior wall when distinctively finished with wallpaper, paneling, etc.

dae•mon (dē′mən), *n.* DEMON (def. 1). —**dae•mon• ic** (di mon′ik), *adj.*

daf•fo•dil (daf′ə dil), *n.* a plant having solitary, usu. yellow flowers with a trumpetlike corona.

daffodil

daf•fy (daf′ē), *adj.,* -**fi•er, -fi•est.** *Informal.* silly; crazy. —**daf′fi•ness,** *n.*

daft (daft, däft), *adj.,* -**er, -est. 1.** foolish. **2.** crazy; mad.

dag•ger (dag′ər), *n.* **1.** a short, swordlike weapon with a pointed blade and a handle, used for stabbing. **2.** a printer's mark (†) used esp. for references.

da•guerre•o•type (də gâr′ə tīp′, -gâr′ē ə-), *n.* **1.** an obsolete photographic process in which a picture made on a silver surface is developed by mercury vapor. **2.** a picture made by this process. [after L. J. M. *Daguerre* (1789–1851), French inventor]

dahl•ia (dāl′yə, dāl′-), *n., pl.* -**ias.** a composite plant with tuberous roots and showy flowers. [after Anders *Dahl* (d. 1789), Swedish botanist]

Da•ho•mey (də hō′mē), *n.* former name of BENIN. —**Da•ho′me•an, Da•ho′man,** *adj., n.*

dai•ly (dā′lē), *adj., n., pl.* -**lies,** *adv.* —*adj.* **1.** of, done, occurring, or issued each day or each weekday. **2.** computed by the day: *a daily quota.* —*n.* **3.** a daily newspaper. —*adv.* **4.** every day.

dain•ty (dān′tē), *adj.,* -**ti•er, -ti•est,** *n., pl.* -**ties.** —*adj.* **1.** of delicate beauty or form. **2.** pleasing to the taste. **3.** of delicate taste; particular; fastidious: *a dainty eater.* **4.** overly particular; finicky. —*n.* **5.** a delicacy. —**dain′ti•ly,** *adv.* —**dain′ti•ness,** *n.*

dair•y (dâr′ē), *n., pl.* **dair•ies. 1.** a place where milk and cream are kept and butter and cheese are made. **2.** a farm that produces milk. **3.** a store that sells milk and milk products. **4.** (in the Jewish dietary laws) dairy products.

dair′y•ing, *n.* the business of a dairy.

dair′y•maid′, *n.* a girl or woman employed in a dairy.

dair′y•man or -**wom′an,** *n., pl.* -**men** or -**wom• en.** an owner, manager, or employee of a dairy.

da•is (dā′is), *n.* a raised platform, as for seats of honor.

dai•sy (dā′zē), *n., pl.* -**sies.** a composite plant having flowers with a yellow disk and white rays.

Da•kar (dä kär′), *n.* the capital of Senegal. 1,380,000.

Da•ko•ta (də kō′tə), *n., pl.* -**ta, -tas** for 3. **1.** a former territory in the U.S.: divided into the states of North Dakota and South Dakota 1889. **2. the Dakotas,** North Dakota and South Dakota. **3.** a member of an American Indian people orig. of Minnesota and the N Great Plains. **4.** the Siouan language of the Dakota. —**Da•ko′tan,** *adj., n.*

Da•lai La•ma (dä′lī lä′mə), *n.* **1.** the title for the traditional ruler and chief monk of Tibet. **2.** (*Tenzin Gyatso*), born 1935, Tibetan religious and political leader, in exile since 1959: the Dalai Lama since 1940.

dale (dāl), *n.* a valley, esp. a broad valley.

Da•li (dä′lē), *n.* **Salvador,** 1904–89, Spanish surrealist painter. —**Da/li•esque′,** *adj.*

Dal•las (dal′əs), *n.* a city in NE Texas. 1,006,877.

dal•ly (dal′ē), *v.i.,* -**lied, -ly•ing. 1.** to waste time; loiter; delay. **2.** to act playfully, esp. in a flirtatious way. **3.** to play mockingly; trifle. —**dal′li•ance,** *n.* —**dal′li•er,** *n.*

Dal•ma•tian (dal mā′shən), *n.* a shorthaired dog having a white coat marked with black or brown spots.

dam¹ (dam), *n., v.,* **dammed, dam•ming.** —*n.* **1.** a barrier to obstruct the flow of water, as one built across a stream. —*v.t.* **2.** to furnish with a dam. **3.** to stop up; block up.

dam² (dam), *n.* a female parent of a four-footed domestic animal.

dam•age (dam′ij), *n., v.,* -**aged, -ag•ing.** —*n.* **1.** injury or harm that reduces value, usefulness, etc. **2. damages,** the estimated money equivalent for loss or injury sustained. —*v.t.* **3.** to cause damage to. —**dam′age•a•ble,** *adj.*

Da•mas•cus (də mas′kəs), *n.* the capital of Syria. 1,251,000.

dam•ask (dam′əsk), *n.* **1.** an elaborately patterned, usu. reversible fabric woven on a Jacquard loom. **2.** an ancient type of hard steel with a pattern of wavy lines. **3.** a deep pink color.

dame (dām), *n.* (*cap.*) (in Britain) an official title of honor for a woman, equivalent to that of Sir.

damn (dam), *v.t.* **1.** to declare to be bad, unfit, invalid, or illegal. **2.** to condemn as a failure. **3.** to ruin. **4.** to condemn to hell. —*Idiom.* **5. damn with faint praise,** to praise so moderately as, in effect, to condemn.

dam′na•ble (-nə bəl), *adj.* **1.** worthy of condemnation. **2.** detestable or abominable. —**dam′na•bly,** *adv.*

dam•na′tion, *n.* **1.** a damning or being damned. **2.** a cause or occasion of being damned. **3.** condemnation to hell.

damned (damd), *adj., superl.* **damned•est, damnd• est. 1.** condemned, esp. to eternal punishment. **2.** detestable; loathsome.

damp (damp), *adj.,* -**er, -est,** *n., v.* —*adj.* **1.** slightly wet; moist. **2.** unenthusiastic: *a damp reception.* —*n.* **3.** moisture; humidity. —*v.t.* **4.** to make damp; moisten. **5.** to check or retard; deaden; dampen. **6.** to stifle or suffocate; extinguish: *to damp a furnace.* —**damp′ness,** *n.*

damp′-dry′, *v.i., v.t.,* -**dried, -dry•ing.** to dry partially so that some moisture remains.

damp′en, *v.t.* **1.** to make damp; moisten. **2.** to deaden; depress: *to dampen spirits.*

damp′er, *n.* **1.** one that damps or depresses: *The news put a damper on the party.* **2.** a movable plate for regulating the draft in a stove, furnace, etc. **3.** a device in stringed keyboard instruments to deaden the vibration of the strings.

dam•sel (dam′zəl), *n.* a maiden, orig. one of gentle or noble birth.

dam′sel•fly′, *n., pl.* -**flies.** an insect similar to a dragonfly but having the wings folded back in line with the body when at rest.

dam•son (dam′zən, -sən), *n.* a small, dark blue or purple plum.

Dan (dan), *n.* **1.** a son of Jacob and Bilhah. Gen. 30:6. **2.** one of the 12 tribes of Israel. **3.** the northernmost city of ancient Palestine. —*Idiom.* **4. from Dan to Beersheba,** from one outermost limit to the other. Judg. 20:1.

dance (dans, däns), *v.,* **danced, danc•ing,** *n.* —*v.i.* **1.** to move the feet and body rhythmically, esp. to music. **2.** to leap, skip, etc., as from excitement. **3.** to bob up and down. —*v.t.* **4.** to perform (a dance). **5.** to cause to dance. —*n.* **6.** a pattern of rhythmical bodily motions, usu. to music. **7.** the art of dancing. **8.** a social gathering for dancing. **9.** a piece of music suited to dancing. —**danc′er,** *n.*

D and C, *n.* surgical removal of tissue or an embryo from the uterus by means of scraping.

dan•de•li•on (dan′dl ī′ən), *n.* a weedy composite plant with edible, toothed leaves and golden-yellow flowers. [< MF *dent de lion* tooth of a lion, in allusion to the toothed leaves]

dan•der (dan′dər), *n. Informal.* anger or temper.

dan•dle (dan′dl), *v.t.,* **-dled, -dling.** to move (a child) lightly up and down on one's knee or in one's arms.

dan•druff (dan′drəf), *n.* a seborrheic scurf that forms on the scalp and comes off in scales.

dan•dy (dan′dē), *n., pl.* **-dies,** *adj.,* **-di•er, -di•est.** —*n.* **1.** a man excessively concerned about his clothes and appearance; fop. **2.** something or someone of exceptional quality. —*adj.* **3.** foppish. **4.** fine; first-rate. —**dan′di•fy,** *v.t.,* **-fied, -fy•ing.**

Dane (dān), *n.* a native or inhabitant of Denmark.

dan•ger (dān′jər), *n.* **1.** liability to harm or injury; risk; peril. **2.** an instance or cause of peril; menace.

dan′ger•ous, *adj.* **1.** full of danger or risk; perilous. **2.** able or likely to cause injury. —**dan′ger•ous•ly,** *adv.*

dan•gle (dang′gəl), *v.,* **-gled, -gling.** —*v.i.* **1.** to hang loosely, esp. with a swaying motion. **2.** to follow a person, as if seeking favor or attention. —*v.t.* **3.** to cause to dangle. **4.** to offer as an inducement.

Dan•iel (dan′yəl), *n.* **1.** a Hebrew prophet who escaped from the lions' den. **2.** the book of the Bible bearing his name.

Daniel in the lions' den, an episode in which the prophet Daniel was thrown into a den of lions but suffered no harm because he had prayed to God. Dan. 6.

Dan•ish (dā′nish), *adj.* **1.** of Denmark, the Danes, or their language. —*n.* **2.** the Germanic language of the Danes. **3.** (*sometimes l.c.*) Also called **Dan′ish pas′-try.** a rich, yeast-leavened pastry filled with cheese or fruit.

dank (dangk), *adj.,* **-er, -est.** unpleasantly moist or humid. —**dank′ly,** *adv.* —**dank′ness,** *n.*

dan•seuse (Fr. dän sœz′), *n., pl.* **-seuses** (Fr. -sœz′). a female ballet dancer.

Dan•te (dän′tā, -tē, dan′tē,), *n.* (*Dante Alighieri*), 1265–1321, Italian poet: author of the *Divine Comedy.* —**Dan•te•an** (Dan′tē ən, dan tē′-), *adj., n.* —**Dan•tesque** (dan tesk′), *adj.*

Dan•ube (dan′yōōb), *n.* a river in central and SE Europe, flowing from Germany to the Black Sea. 1725 mi. (2775 km) long.

dap•per (dap′ər), *adj.* **1.** neat, trim, or smart in dress or demeanor. **2.** small and nimble.

dap•ple (dap′əl), *n., adj., v.,* **-pled, -pling.** —*n.* **1.** a spot or mottled marking. **2.** an animal with a mottled skin or coat. —*adj.* **3.** marked with spots. —*v.t., v.i.* **4.** to mark or become marked with dapples.

Dar•da•nelles (där′dn elz′), *n.* (*used with a pl. v.*) the strait between European and Asian Turkey.

dare (dâr), *v.,* **dared, daring,** *n.* —*v.i.* **1.** to have the necessary courage for something. —*v.t.* **2.** to have the boldness to try. **3.** to face courageously. **4.** to challenge (a person) to do something. —*auxiliary v.* **5.** to have the necessary courage to: *How dare you speak to me like that?* —*n.* **6.** an act of daring; challenge. —*Idiom.* **7. I daresay** (or **dare say**), I assume: *I daresay it's too late now.* —**dar′er,** *n.*

dare′dev′il, *n.* **1.** a recklessly daring person. —*adj.* **2.** recklessly daring.

dar′ing, *n.* **1.** adventurous courage. —*adj.* **2.** courageous or fearless. —**dar′ing•ly,** *adv.*

dark (därk), *adj.,* **-er, -est,** *n.* —*adj.* **1.** having little or no light. **2.** admitting or reflecting little light: *dark colors.* **3.** approaching black in hue. **4.** not pale or fair; swarthy. **5.** gloomy; dismal. **6.** evil; wicked. **7.** unenlightened. **8.** hard to understand; obscure. —*n.* **9.** the absence of light. **10.** night; nightfall. —*Idiom.* **11. in the dark,** in ignorance; uninformed. —*Proverb.* **12. It is always darkest just**

before the dawn, relief may come when things seem most hopeless. —**dark′ly,** *adv.*

Dark′ Ag′es, *n.* **1.** the period in European history from about A.D. 476 to about 1000. **2.** (*often l.c.*) a period or stage marked by repressiveness, a lack of advanced knowledge, etc.

dark′en, *v.t., v.i.* **1.** to make or become dark or darker. **2.** to make or become gloomy; sadden. —**dark′en•er,** *n.*

dark′ horse′, *n.* a little-known competitor or candidate that wins unexpectedly.

dark•ness (därk′nis), *n.* **1.** absence or deficiency of light: *the darkness of night.* **2.** wickedness or evil: *the forces of darkness.* **3.** obscurity; concealment. **4.** lack of knowledge or enlightenment. **5.** lack of sight; blindness. —*Idiom.* **6. cast into outer darkness,** to reject and exclude. Matt. 8:12.

dark′room′, *n.* a room in which photographic materials are handled and from which certain rays of light are excluded.

dar•ling (där′ling), *n.* **1.** a person very dear to another. **2.** a favorite: *the darling of café society.* —*adj.* **3.** very dear; cherished. **4.** charming.

darn¹ (därn), *v.t.* **1.** to mend, esp. by interweaving stitches across a hole. —*n.* **2.** a darned place, as in a garment. —**darn′er,** *n.*

darn² (därn), *v.t., interj., n., adj., adv.* DAMN.

Dar•row (dar′ō), *n.* **Clarence (Seward),** 1857–1938, U.S. lawyer.

dart (därt), *n.* **1.** a small, slender missile usu. feathered at one end. **2. darts,** (*used with a sing. v.*) game in which darts are thrown at a target. **3.** a sudden swift movement. **4.** a tapered seam of fabric. —*v.i.* **5.** to move swiftly; dash. —*v.t.* **6.** to thrust or move suddenly or rapidly.

Dar•win (där′win), *n.* **Charles (Robert),** 1809–82, English naturalist. —**Dar•win′i•an,** *adj., n.*

Dar′win•ism, *n.* the Darwinian theory that species originate by descent with variation from parent forms through the natural selection of individuals best adapted for survival. —**Dar′win•ist,** *n., adj.*

dash (dash), *v.t.* **1.** to strike or smash violently, esp. so as to break to pieces. **2.** to throw violently or suddenly. **3.** to splash, often violently. **4.** to apply roughly, as by splashing. **5.** to ruin or frustrate. —*v.i.* **6.** to strike violently. **7.** to rush. **8. dash off, a.** to hurry away; leave. **b.** to write or do hastily. —*n.* **9.** a small quantity added: *a dash of salt.* **10.** a hasty or sudden movement. **11.** a punctuation mark (—) used to note a break, pause, or hesitation. **12.** the splashing of liquid against something. **13.** spirited action. **14.** a short race. **15.** a signal of longer duration than a dot, used in groups of dots, dashes, and spaces to represent letters in Morse code. **16.** a hasty stroke, esp. of a pen. —**dash′er,** *n.*

dash′board′, *n.* a panel with gauges and controls in front of the driver in an automobile.

da•shi•ki (də shē′kē, dä-), *n., pl.* **-kis.** a loose, colorfully patterned pullover garment of African origin.

dash′ing, *adj.* **1.** energetic and spirited. **2.** elegant and gallant. —**dash′ing•ly,** *adv.*

das′tard (das′tərd), *n.* a mean, sneaking coward. —**das′tard•ly,** *adj.*

DAT, digital audiotape.

da•ta (dā′tə, dat′ə), *n.* **1.** pl. of DATUM. **2.** (*used with a pl. v.*) facts, statistics, or items of information. **3.** (*used with a sing. v.*) a collection of facts; information. —*Usage.* DATA is used in English both as a plural noun meaning "facts or pieces of information" (*These data are described fully on page 8*) and as a singular mass noun meaning "information" (*The data has been entered into the computer*). It is almost always treated as a plural in scientific and academic writing.

da′ta bank′ or **da′ta•bank′,** *n.* DATABASE.

da′ta•base′ or **da′ta base′,** *n.* **1.** a collection of data, esp. one in electronic form that can be accessed and manipulated by computer software. **2.** a fund of information on one or more subjects, accessible by computer.

da′ta proc′essing, *n.* the rapid, automated processing of information, esp. by computers. —**da′ta proc′essor,** *n.*

date¹ (dāt), *n., v.,* **dat•ed, dat•ing.** —*n.* **1.** a particular month, day, and year at which some event happened or will happen. **2.** the day of the month. **3.** an inscription on a writing, coin, etc., that shows the time of writing, casting, etc. **4.** the time or period to which any event or thing belongs. **5.** an appointment, esp. a social engagement arranged beforehand. **6.** a person with whom one has such an appointment. **7.** an engagement or booking. —*v.i.* **8.** to have a date. **9.** to belong to a particular period: *This church dates from 1830.* **10.** to go out socially on dates. —*v.t.* **11.** to mark or furnish with a date. **12.** to ascertain the date of. **13.** to show the age of; show to be old-fashioned. **14.** to go out on a date with. —*Idiom.* **15. to date,** up to the present time. —**dat′er,** *n.*

date² (dāt), *n.* the oblong, fleshy fruit of a tropical palm tree.

dat′ed, *adj.* **1.** having or showing a date. **2.** out-of-date; outmoded.

date′line′, *n.* a line at the beginning of a news dispatch, giving the place of origin and usu. the date.

da•tive (dā′tiv), *adj.* **1.** designating a grammatical case that indicates the indirect object of a verb or the object of certain prepositions. —*n.* **2.** the dative case.

da•tum (dā′təm, dat′əm), *n., pl.* **da•ta. 1.** a single piece of information, as a fact or statistic; an item of data. **2.** any proposition from which conclusions may be drawn. —**Usage.** See DATA.

daub (dôb), *v.t., v.i.* **1.** to cover or coat with soft, adhesive matter, as plaster or mud. **2.** to paint unskillfully. —*n.* **3.** something daubed on. **4.** a crude, inartistic painting. —**daub′er,** *n.*

daugh•ter (dô′tər), *n.* **1.** a girl or woman in relation to her parents. **2.** any female descendant.

daugh′ter-in-law′, *n., pl.* **daugh•ters-in-law.** the wife of one's son.

Daugh′ter of Zi′on, *n.* Jerusalem and its inhabitants. Ps. 9:14; Isa. 1:8.

daunt (dônt, dänt), *v.t.* **1.** to overcome with fear; intimidate. **2.** to dishearten. —**daunt′ing•ly,** *adv.*

daunt′less, *adj.* not to be daunted or intimidated; fearless. —**daunt′less•ly,** *adv.* —**daunt′less•ness,** *n.*

dau•phin (dô′fin, dō faN′), *n.* the eldest son of a king of France.

dav•en•port (dav′ən pôrt′), *n.* a large sofa, often one convertible into a bed.

Da•vid (dā′vid *for 1, 2; Fr.* dA vēd′ *for 3*), *n.* **1.** died c970 B.C., the second king of Israel, reigned c1010–c970, successor to Saul. **2. Saint,** A.D. c510–601?, Welsh bishop: patron saint of Wales. **3. Jacques Louis,** 1748–1825, French painter.

da Vin•ci (də vin′chē, dä), *n.* **Leonardo,** LEONARDO DA VINCI.

Da•vis (dā′vis), *n.* **1. Bet•te** (bet′ē), (*Ruth Elizabeth Davis*), 1908-89, U.S. film actress. **2. Jefferson,** 1808–89, president of the Confederate States of America 1861–65. **3. Miles (Dewey, Jr.),** 1926–91, U.S. jazz trumpeter. **4. Sammy, Jr.,** 1925–90, U.S. singer and entertainer.

dav•it (dav′it, dā′vit), *n.* a cranelike device used on a ship for raising and lowering boats, anchors, etc.

daw•dle (dôd′l), *v.i., v.t.,* **-dled, -dling.** to waste (time) by trifling; idle: *We dawdled away the whole morning.* —**daw′dler,** *n.*

dawn (dôn), *n.* **1.** the first appearance of daylight in the morning; daybreak; sunrise. **2.** the beginning of anything; advent. —*v.i.* **3.** to begin to grow light in the morning. **4.** to begin to open or develop. **5.** to begin to be perceived.

day (dā), *n.* **1.** the interval of light between two successive nights. **2.** the period of 24 hours during which the earth makes one rotation on its axis. **3.** the portion of a day allotted to work. **4.** Often, **days.** a particular era: *in olden days.* **5.** a period of existence, power, or influence: *His day will come.* **6.** the contest or battle at hand: *to win the day.* —*Idiom.*

7. call it a day, to stop working for the rest of the day. **8. day in, day out,** every day without fail.

day′bed′, *n.* a couch that can be used as a sofa by day and a bed by night.

day′break′, *n.* the first appearance of daylight in the morning; dawn.

day′ care′, *n.* supervised daytime care for preschool children or the elderly, usu. at a center outside the home. —**day′-care′,** *adj.*

day′dream′, *n.* **1.** a visionary fancy indulged in while awake; reverie. **2.** a fanciful notion or plan. —*v.i.* **3.** to indulge in daydreams. —**day′dream′er,** *n.*

day′ job′, *n.* one's regular job and main source of income, usu. viewed in contrast to a speculative or irregular endeavor.

day′light′, *n.* **1.** the period of light during a day. **2.** public knowledge; openness. **3.** daybreak; dawn. **4. daylights,** wits; sanity: *scared the daylights out of me.*

day′light-sav′ing (or **day′light-sav′ings**) **time′,** *n.* time one hour later than standard time, usu. used in the summer.

Day′ of Atone′ment, *n.* YOM KIPPUR.

Day′ of In′famy, *n.* December 7, 1941, on which Japan attacked Pearl Harbor, bringing the United States into World War II: so referred to by President Franklin D. Roosevelt in his speech to Congress.

Day′ of Judg′ment, *n.* JUDGMENT DAY.

Day′ of the Lord′, *n.* **1.** Also called **Day′ of Yah′-weh.** (in Old Testament eschatology) a day of final judgment. Amos 5:18–21; Ezek. 30. **2.** Also called **Day′ of Christ′, Day of Je′sus Christ′.** the day of the Second Advent. II Peter 3:10; I Cor. 1:14; Phil. 1:10, 2:16.

day′time′, *n.* the time between sunrise and sunset.

day′-to-day′, *adj.* **1.** occurring each day; daily. **2.** routine; normal.

Day•ton (dāt′n), *n.* a city in SW Ohio. 178,540.

Day•to′na Beach′ (dā tō′nə), *n.* a city in NE Florida: seashore resort. 61,921.

daze (dāz), *v.,* **dazed, daz•ing,** *n.* —*v.t.* **1.** to stun with a blow, shock, etc. **2.** to overwhelm; dazzle. —*n* **3.** a dazed condition. —**daz′ed•ly** *adv.*

daz•zle (daz′əl), *v.,* **-zled, -zling,** *n.* —*v.t., v.i.* **1.** to overpower or be overpowered by intense light. **2.** to bewilder or excite admiration by brilliance, splendor, etc. —*n.* **3.** the act of dazzling. —**daz′zler,** *n.*

dB or **db,** decibel.

DBMS, database management system.

DC or **D.C.,** District of Columbia.

D.D., Doctor of Divinity [< L *Divinitatis Doctor*]

D-day or **D-Day** (dē′dā′), *n.* **1.** a day set for beginning something. **2.** June 6, 1944, the day of the invasion of W Europe by Allied forces in World War II.

D.D.S., 1. Doctor of Dental Science. **2.** Doctor of Dental Surgery.

DDT, a toxic compound, formerly widely used as an insecticide.

de-, a prefix meaning: away or off (*deplane*); down or lower (*degrade*); completely (*despoil*); reverse (*deactivate*); remove (*decaffeinate*).

DE, Delaware.

dea•con (dē′kən), *n.* **1.** a member of the clergy ranking just below a priest. **2.** an appointed or elected officer having variously defined duties.

de•ac•ti•vate (dē ak′tə vāt′), *v.t.,* **-vat•ed, -vat•ing. 1.** to make inactive: *to deactivate a chemical.* **2.** to demobilize (a military unit).

dead (ded), *adj.,* **-er, -est,** *n., adv.* —*adj.* **1.** no longer living. **2.** not endowed with life; inanimate. **3.** resembling death; deathlike: *a dead faint.* **4.** bereft of feeling; numb. **5.** extinguished: *a dead cigarette.* **6.** obsolete; no longer in general use. **7.** inoperative: *a dead battery.* **8.** utterly tired; exhausted. **9.** dull or inactive. **10.** complete; absolute: *dead silence.* **11.** exact; precise: *the dead center.* **12.** without bounce: *a dead ball.* —*n.* **13.** the period of greatest darkness, coldness, etc.: *the dead of night.* **14. the dead,** dead persons collectively. —*adv.* **15.** absolutely; completely. **16.** directly; straight.

dead/beat/, *n.* **1.** a person who avoids paying debts. **2.** a sponger.

dead/beat dad/, *n.* a father who neglects his responsibilities as a parent, esp. one who does not pay child support.

dead/bolt/, *n.* a lock bolt that is moved by the turning of a knob or key rather than by spring action.

dead/en, *v.t.* **1.** to make less sensitive, intense, or effective. **2.** to make dull or lifeless. **3.** to soundproof.

dead/ end/, *n.* **1.** a street, corridor, etc., that has no exit. **2.** a position with no hope of progress. —**dead/-end/**, *adj.*

dead/ heat/, *n.* a race in which two or more competitors finish in a tie.

dead/ let/ter, *n.* **1.** a letter that is not deliverable or returnable. **2.** a law that is no longer enforced.

dead/line, *n.* the time by which something must be finished, submitted, accomplished, etc.

dead/lock/, *n.* **1.** a state, as in negotiations, in which progress halts; stalemate. —*v.t., v.i.* **2.** to bring or come to a deadlock.

dead/ly, *adj.*, **-li•er, -li•est,** *adv.* —*adj.* **1.** causing or tending to cause death. **2.** aiming to kill or destroy; implacable: *a deadly enemy.* **3.** like death; deathly. **4.** excruciatingly boring. **5.** excessive; inordinate. **6.** extremely accurate. —*adv.* **7.** extremely; completely. —**dead/li•ness**, *n.*

dead/ly sins/, *n.pl.* pride, covetousness, lust, anger, gluttony, envy, and sloth.

dead/pan/, *adj.* marked by a fixed air of seriousness or detachment; expressionless.

Dead/ Sea/, *n.* a salt lake between Israel and Jordan.

dead/ weight/ or **dead/weight/**, *n.* **1.** the heavy, unrelieved weight of anything inert. **2.** a heavy burden or responsibility.

dead/wood/, *n.* useless or extraneous persons or things.

deaf (def), *adj.,* **-er, -est. 1.** partially or wholly deprived of the sense of hearing. **2.** refusing to heed or be persuaded; unyielding. —**deaf/ness**, *n.*

deaf/en, *v.t.* **1.** to make deaf. **2.** to stun with noise. —**deaf/en•ing**, *adj.*

deal (dēl), *v.,* **dealt, deal•ing**, *n.* —*v.i.* **1.** to be occupied or concerned: *Botany deals with the study of plants.* **2.** to take action with respect to a thing or person. **3.** to conduct oneself. **4.** to trade or do business: *to deal in used cars.* —*v.t.* **5.** to apportion or distribute. **6.** to deliver; administer: *to deal a blow.* —*n.* **7.** a business transaction. **8.** a bargain or arrangement. **9.** a secret or underhand agreement. **10.** *Informal.* treatment received: *a raw deal.* **11.** an indefinite quantity: *a great deal of money.* **12. a.** the distribution of cards to the players in a game. **b.** the turn of a player to deal. —**deal/er**, *n.*

deal/er•ship/, *n.* a franchise to sell a commodity.

deal/ing, *n.* Usu., **-ings.** interactions or transactions with others: *business dealings.*

dean (dēn), *n.* **1. a.** the head of a faculty in a university or college. **b.** an official in a university or college in charge of discipline, counseling, or admissions. **2.** the head of the chapter of a cathedral. **3.** the senior member of a group.

dean/s/ list/, *n.* a list of students of high scholastic standing at a college.

dear (dēr), *adj.,* **-er, -est,** *n., interj.* —*adj.* **1.** beloved; loved. **2.** (used in the salutation of a letter): *Dear Sir or Madam.* **3.** precious; cherished: *our dearest possessions.* **4.** earnest: *no dearer wish.* **5.** expensive. —*n.* **6.** a kind or generous person. **7.** a beloved one. —*interj.* **8.** an exclamation of surprise, distress, etc. —**dear/ly**, *adv.* —**dear/ness**, *n.*

Dear/ John/, *n.* a letter from a woman informing her boyfriend, fiancé, or husband that she is leaving him.

dearth (dûrth), *n.* a scarcity or lack.

death (deth), *n.* **1.** the act of dying or state of being dead. **2.** extinction; destruction. **3.** a cause of death. —*Idiom.* **4. at death's door**, gravely ill. **5. to death**, to an intolerable degree: *bored to death.* —**death/like/**, *adj.*

death/bed/, *n.* **1.** the bed on which a person dies. **2.** the last hours before death.

death/blow/, *n.* **1.** a blow causing death. **2.** anything that ends hope, expectation, or the like.

death/less, *adj.* not subject to death; immortal.

death/ly, *adj.* **1.** causing death; deadly. **2.** resembling death. —*adv.* **3.** in the manner of death: *deathly pale.* **4.** utterly: *deathly afraid.*

death/ row/, *n.* prison cells for inmates awaiting execution.

death/trap/, *n.* an unsafe building, vehicle, etc.

Death/ Val/ley, *n.* an arid basin in E California and S Nevada.

deb (deb), *n.* DEBUTANTE.

de•ba•cle (də bä/kəl, -bak/əl, dā-), *n.* **1.** a disaster or fiasco. **2.** a general rout or dispersal of troops.

de•bar (di bär/), *v.t.,* **-barred, -bar•ring. 1.** to shut out or exclude. **2.** to hinder or prevent; prohibit. —**de•bar/ment**, *n.*

de•bark (di bärk/), *v.i., v.t.* to disembark. —**de•bar•ka•tion** (dē/bär kā/shən), *n.*

de•base (di bās/), *v.t.,* **-based, -bas•ing.** to reduce in quality, value, or dignity. —**de•base/ment**, *n.*

de•bate (di bāt/), *n., v.,* **-bat•ed, -bat•ing.** —*n.* **1.** a discussion involving opposing viewpoints. **2.** a formal contest in which the affirmative and negative sides of a proposition are advocated by opposing speakers. —*v.i., v.t.* **3.** to discuss (a matter or issue) by giving opposing viewpoints. **4.** to participate in a formal debate with (a speaker) or on (an issue). —**de•bat/a•ble**, *adj.* —**de•bat/er**, *n.*

de•bauch (di bôch/), *v.t.* **1.** to corrupt by sensuality, intemperance, etc.; seduce. —*n.* **2.** an orgy. —**de•bauch/er**, *n.* —**de•bauch/er•y**, *n., pl.* **-er•ies.**

de•ben•ture (di ben/chər), *n.* a short-term, negotiable, interest-bearing note representing indebtedness.

de•bil•i•tate (di bil/i tāt/), *v.t.,* **-tat•ed, -tat•ing.** to make weak; enfeeble. —**de•bil/i•ta/tion**, *n.*

de•bil•i•ty (di bil/i tē), *n., pl.* **-ties. 1.** a weakened or enfeebled state. **2.** a handicap or disability.

deb•it (deb/it), *n.* **1.** the record kept of another's indebtedness. **2.** a recorded item of debt. —*v.t.* **3.** to charge (a person or account) with a debt. **4.** to enter as a debt in an account.

deb•o•nair (deb/ə nâr/), *adj.* **1.** suave; worldly. **2.** jaunty; carefree. —**deb/o•nair/ly**, *adv.*

Deb•o•rah (deb/ər ə, deb/rə), *n.* a prophet of Israel. Judg. 4, 5.

de•brief (dē brēf/), *v.t.* **1.** to interrogate (a soldier, astronaut, etc.) to gather information about a completed mission. **2.** to caution against revealing classified information after leaving a position.

de•bris or **dé•bris** (də brē/, dā/brē), *n.* **1.** the remains of anything destroyed or broken. **2.** accumulated loose fragments of rock.

debt (det), *n.* **1.** something that is owed, as money or a favor. **2.** an obligation to pay or render something. **3.** the condition of owing something. —**deb′tor,** *n.*

de•bug (dē bug′), *v.t.,* **-bugged, -bug•ging. 1.** to detect and remove defects or errors from: *to debug a computer program.* **2.** to remove electronic bugs from (a room or building).

de•bunk (di bungk′), *v.t.* to expose as being false or exaggerated.

De•bus•sy (deb′yōō sē′, dā′byōō-), *n.* **Claude,** 1862-1918, French composer.

de•but or **dé•but** (dā byōō′, di-, dā′byōō), *n.* **1.** a first public appearance, as of a performer or new product. **2.** a formal introduction of a young woman into society. —*v.i.* **3.** to make a debut. —*v.t.* **4.** to introduce to the public.

deb•u•tante or **déb•u•tante** (deb′yōō tänt′), *n.* a young woman making a debut into society.

Dec or **Dec.,** December.

deca- or **dec-,** a combining form meaning ten (*decathlon*).

dec•ade (dek′ād), *n.* a period of ten years.

dec•a•dence (dek′ə dəns, di kād′ns), *n.* **1.** the act or process of falling into decay. **2.** moral degeneration. —**dec′a•dent,** *adj., n.*

de•caf (dē′kaf′), *n.* decaffeinated coffee or tea.

de•caf•fein•ate (dē kaf′ə nāt′), *v.t.,* **-at•ed, -at•ing.** to remove caffeine from. —**de•caf′fein•at′ed,** *adj.*

de•cal (dē′kal, di kal′), *n.* a picture or design on specially prepared paper for transfer to wood, metal, glass, etc.

Dec•a•logue or **-log** (dek′ə lôg′, -log′), *n.* (*often l.c.*) TEN COMMANDMENTS.

de•camp (di kamp′), *v.i.* **1.** to pack up and leave a camping ground. **2.** to depart hastily and often secretly. —**de•camp′ment,** *n.*

de•cant (di kant′), *v.t.* to pour liquor gently so as not to disturb the sediment.

de•cant′er, *n.* an ornamental glass bottle for wine, brandy, or the like.

de•cap•i•tate (di kap′i tāt′), *v.t.,* **-tat•ed, -tat•ing.** to cut off the head of. —**de•cap′i•ta′tion,** *n.*

de•cath•lon (di kath′lon), *n.* an athletic contest in which a contestant competes in ten different track-and-field events.

de•cay (di kā′), *v.i.* **1.** to become decomposed; rot. **2.** to decline in health, prosperity, etc.; deteriorate. **3.** (of an atomic nucleus) to undergo radioactive decay. —*v.t.* **4.** to cause to decay. —*n.* **5.** decomposition; rot. **6.** a gradual decline. **7.** a radioactive process in which an atomic nucleus undergoes spontaneous transformation into one or more different nuclei.

de•cease (di sēs′), *n., v.,* **-ceased, -ceas•ing.** —*n.* **1.** death. —*v.i.* **2.** to die.

de•ce•dent (di sēd′nt), *n. Law.* a deceased person.

de•ceit (di sēt′), *n.* **1.** the act or practice of deceiving. **2.** a stratagem intended to deceive. **3.** the quality of being deceitful; duplicity.

de•ceit′ful, *adj.* **1.** given to deceiving. **2.** intended to deceive; misleading. —**de•ceit′ful•ly,** *adv.* —**de•ceit′ful•ness,** *n.*

de•ceive (di sēv′), *v.t., v.i.,* **-ceived, -ceiv•ing.** to mislead by a false appearance or statement; trick. —**de•ceiv′er,** *n.* —**de•ceiv′ing•ly,** *adv.*

de•cel•er•ate (dē sel′ə rāt′), *v.t., v.i.,* **-at•ed, -at•ing.** to slow down. —**de•cel′er•a′tion,** *n.* —**de•cel′er•a′tor,** *n.*

De•cem•ber (di sem′bər), *n.* the 12th month of the year, containing 31 days.

de•cen•cy (dē′sən sē), *n., pl.* **-cies. 1.** the state or quality of being decent. **2.** courtesy; propriety.

de•cen•ni•al (di sen′ē əl), *adj.* **1.** of or for ten years. **2.** occurring every ten years. —*n.* **3.** a decennial anniversary.

de•cent (dē′sənt), *adj.* **1.** conforming to the recognized standard of propriety, as in behavior or speech. **2.** respectable; worthy. **3.** adequate; passable. **4.** kind; obliging. —**de′cent•ly,** *adv.*

de•cen•tral•ize (dē sen′trə līz′), *v.t.,* **-ized, -iz•ing. 1.** to distribute powers or functions of (a central authority) throughout local or regional divisions, branches, etc. **2.** to disperse (something) from an area of concentration. —**de•cen′tral•i•za′tion,** *n.*

de•cep•tion (di sep′shən), *n.* **1.** the act of deceiving or state of being deceived. **2.** a trick; ruse. —**de•cep′tive,** *adj.*

dec•i•bel (des′ə bel′, -bəl), *n.* a unit used to express differences in power, esp. of sounds or voltages.

de•cide (di sīd′), *v.,* **-cid•ed, -cid•ing.** —*v.t.* **1.** to solve or conclude (a dispute) by awarding victory to one side. **2.** to make up one's mind about; resolve. —*v.i.* **3.** to come to a decision. —**de•cid′a•ble,** *adj.*

de•cid•ed, *adj.* **1.** unquestionable; certain. **2.** resolute; determined. —**de•cid′ed•ly,** *adv.*

de•cid•u•ous (di sij′ōō əs), *adj.* **1.** shedding the leaves annually, as certain trees. **2.** falling off at a particular season or stage of growth, as leaves or horns.

dec•i•li•ter (des′ə lē′tər), *n.* a unit of capacity equal to ¹⁄₁₀ of a liter.

dec•i•mal (des′ə məl), *adj.* **1.** pertaining to tenths or to the number 10. **2.** proceeding by tens: *a decimal system.* —*n.* **3.** DECIMAL FRACTION.

dec′imal frac′tion, *n.* a fraction whose denominator is some power of 10, usu. indicated by a dot (**dec′imal point′**) written before the numerator: 0.4 = ⁴⁄₁₀.

dec•i•mate (des′ə māt′), *v.t.,* **-mat•ed, -mat•ing. 1.** to destroy a great number or proportion of. **2.** (esp. in ancient Rome) to select by lot and kill every tenth person of. —**dec′i•ma′tion,** *n.*

de•ci•pher (di sī′fər), *v.t.* **1.** to make out the meaning of (something difficult). **2.** to decode, as something written in cipher. —**de•ci′pher•a•ble,** *adj.*

de•ci•sion (di sizh′ən), *n.* **1.** the act of deciding. **2.** the act of making up one's mind. **3.** something that is decided; resolution. **4.** a judgment, as one pronounced by a court. **5.** firmness; determination. **6.** the final score in any sport or contest.

de•ci′sive (-sī′siv), *adj.* **1.** having the power to decide. **2.** displaying firmness; resolute. **3.** unquestionable; definite; *a decisive lead.* —**de•ci′sive•ly,** *adv.* —**de•ci′sive•ness,** *n.*

deck (dek), *n.* **1.** a floor of a ship. **2.** a porch or other platform suggesting the deck of a ship. **3.** a pack of playing cards. —*v.t.* **4.** to clothe or array in something dressy or festive (often fol. by *out*). **5.** *Informal.* to knock down.

de•claim (di klām′), *v.t., v.i.* to speak or utter loudly and rhetorically. —**de•claim′er,** *n.* —**dec•la•ma•tion** (dek′lə mā′shən), *n.* —**de•clam′a•to′ry** (-klam′ə tôr′ē), *adj.*

de•clar•a•tive (di klar′ə tiv), *adj.* serving to state or explain.

de•clare′ (-klâr′), *v.t.,* **-clared, -clar•ing. 1.** to make known publicly; announce officially. **2.** to state emphatically. **3.** to reveal; indicate. **4.** to make due statement of, as income for taxation. **5.** to bid (a trump suit or no-trump) in bridge. —**dec•la•ra•tion** (dek′lə rā′shən), *n.* —**de•clar′er,** *n.*

de•clas•si•fy (dē klas′ə fī′), *v.t.,* **-fied, -fy•ing.** to remove the security classification from (a document).

de•clen•sion (di klen′shən), *n.* **1.** the inflection of nouns, pronouns, and adjectives. **2.** a bending, sloping, or moving downward. **3.** deterioration; decline.

de•cline (di klīn′), *v.,* **-clined, -clin•ing,** *n.* —*v.t.* **1.** to refuse with courtesy. **2.** to cause to slope or incline downward. **3.** to inflect (a noun, pronoun, or adjective). —*v.i.* **4.** to express courteous refusal. **5.** to deteriorate or weaken. **6.** to fall or drop. **7.** to slope downward. **8.** to draw toward the close, as the day. —*n.* **9.** a downward slope. **10.** a downward movement, as of prices. **11.** a deterioration, as in strength or power. —**dec′li•na′tion** (dek′lə nā′shən), *n.* —**de•clin′er,** *n.*

de•cliv•i•ty (di kliv′i tē), *n., pl.* **-ties.** a downward slope.

de•code (dē kōd′), *v.t.,* **-cod•ed, -cod•ing.** to translate (data or a message) from a code into the original language or form.

dé•col•le•té (dā'kol ə tā', dek'ə lə-), *adj.* **1.** (of a garment) low-necked. **2.** wearing a low-necked garment. [< F]

de•col•o•nize (dē kol'ə nīz'), *v.t.*, **-nized, -niz•ing.** to allow to become self-governing or independent. —**de•col'o•ni•za'tion,** *n.*

de'com•mis'sion, *v.t.* to retire (a ship, airplane, etc.) from active service.

de'com•pose', *v.t., v.i.,* **-posed, -pos•ing. 1.** to separate into constituent parts or elements; disintegrate. **2.** to rot; putrefy. —**de'com•pos'a•ble,** *adj.* —**de'com•po•si'tion** (-kom pə zish'ən), *n.*

de'com•press', *v.t.* to release from air pressure. —**de'com•pres'sion,** *n.*

de•con•ges•tant (dē'kən jes'tənt), *adj.* **1.** relieving mucus congestion of the upper respiratory tract. —*n.* **2.** a decongestant agent.

de'con•struc'tion, *n.* a theory of textual analysis positing that a text has no stable reference and questioning language's ability to represent reality.

de'con•tam'i•nate' (-nāt'), *v.t.,* **-nat•ed, -nat• ing.** to make safe by removing or neutralizing harmful contaminants. —**de'con•tam'i•na'tion,** *n.*

dé•cor or **de•cor** (dā kôr', di-), *n.* style of decoration, as of a room.

dec•o•rate (dek'ə rāt'), *v.t.,* **-rat•ed, -rat•ing. 1.** to furnish or adorn with something ornamental or becoming. **2.** to design the interior of (a room or building). **3.** to confer a medal or honor on. —**dec'o•ra'tive,** *adj.* —**dec'o•ra'tor,** *n.*

dec'o•ra'tion, *n.* **1.** adornment; embellishment. **2.** the act of decorating. **3.** a medal or similar mark of honor.

dec'o•rous, *adj.* showing respect for social customs and manners. —**dec'o•rous•ly,** *adv.*

de•co•rum (di kôr'əm), *n.* **1.** propriety of conduct, manners, or appearance. **2.** Usu., **-rums.** the customs and observances of polite society.

de•cou•page or **dé•cou•page** (dā'kōō päzh'), *n.* the art of decorating something with cutouts of paper, linoleum, or other flat material.

de•coy (*n.* dē'koi, di koi'; *v.* di koi', dē'koi), *n.* **1.** a person who lures another, as into danger or a trap. **2.** anything used as a lure. **3.** an artificial or trained bird or other animal used to entice game into a trap or within gunshot. —*v.t.* **4.** to lure by or as if by a decoy. [< D *de kooi* the cage]

de•crease (*v.* di krēs'; *n.* dē'krēs, di krēs'), *v.,* **-creased, -creas•ing,** *n.* —*v.i., v.t.* **1.** to lessen, as in extent, quantity, or power; diminish. —*n.* **2.** the act or process of decreasing. **3.** the amount by which a thing is lessened.

de•cree (di krē'), *n., v.,* **-creed, -cree•ing.** —*n.* **1.** a formal order usu. having the force of law. **2.** a judicial decision. —*v.t., v.i.* **3.** to ordain or decide by or as if by decree.

de•crep•it (di krep'it), *adj.* **1.** weakened by old age. **2.** worn out by long use. —**de•crep'i•tude',** *n.*

de•cre•scen•do (dē'kri shen'dō, dā'-), *adj., adv. Music.* gradually decreasing in loudness.

de•crim•i•nal•ize (dē krim'ə nl īz'), *v.t.,* **-ized, -iz• ing.** to eliminate criminal penalties for.

de•cry (di krī'), *v.t.,* **-cried, -cry•ing.** to disparage openly; denounce.

ded•i•cate (ded'i kāt'), *v.t.,* **-cat•ed, -cat•ing. 1.** to consecrate to a sacred purpose. **2.** to devote to some purpose or person. **3.** to offer (a book, piece of music, etc.) to someone, as on a prefatory inscription. **4.** to set apart for a specific purpose. —**ded'i•ca'tion,** *n.*

ded'i•cat'ed, *adj.* set apart or designed for a specific use or exclusive application: *a dedicated word processor.*

de•duce (di dōōs', -dyōōs'), *v.t.,* **-duced, -duc•ing. 1.** to derive as a conclusion from something known or assumed; infer. **2.** to trace the course of. —**de• duc'i•ble,** *adj.*

de•duct (di dukt'), *v.t.* to take away from a total. —**de•duct'i•ble,** *adj.*

de•duc'tion, *n.* **1.** the act of deducting; subtraction. **2.** something deducted. **3.** the act or process of deducing. **4.** something deduced. **5. a.** a process of reasoning from the general to the particular. **b.** a conclusion reached by this process. —**de•duc'tive,** *adj.*

deed (dēd), *n.* **1.** something that is done. **2.** an exploit or achievement. **3.** a document executed under seal and delivered to effect a conveyance, esp. of real estate. —*v.t.* **4.** to convey by deed.

dee•jay (dē'jā'), *n.* DISC JOCKEY.

deem (dēm), *v.t.* to hold as an opinion; think.

de-em•pha•size (dē em'fə sīz'), *v.t.,* **-sized, -siz• ing.** to place less emphasis upon; lessen the importance of. —**de-em'pha•sis** (-sis), *n.*

deep (dēp), *adj.* and *adv.,* **-er, -est,** *n.* —*adj.* **1.** extending far down from the top or surface. **2.** extending far in or back from the front. **3.** extending far in width; broad. **4.** having a specified depth: *10 feet deep.* **5.** immersed or involved: *deep in thought.* **6.** difficult to understand. **7.** intense; profound: *deep sorrow.* **8.** dark and vivid: *a deep red.* **9.** low in pitch, as a voice. **10.** mysterious; obscure: *deep, dark secrets.* —*adv.* **11.** to or at a considerable or specified depth. **12.** far on in time: *to look deep into the future.* —*n.* **13.** the deep part of the ocean. **14.** the part of greatest intensity, as of winter. **15. the deep,** *Literary.* the sea or ocean. —**deep'ly,** *adv.* —**deep'ness,** *n.*

deep'en, *v.t., v.i.* to make or become deep or deeper.

deep'-freeze', *v.t.,* **-freezed** or **-froze, -freezed** or **-fro•zen, -freez•ing.** QUICK-FREEZE.

deep'-fry', *v.t.,* **-fried, -fry•ing.** to fry in oil sufficient to cover the food.

deep' pock'ets, *n.pl.* an abundance of money or wealth.

deep'-root'ed, *adj.* firmly implanted or established.

deep'-sea', *adj.* of or associated with the deeper parts of the sea.

deep'-seat'ed, *adj.* firmly implanted or established.

deep' six', *n. Slang.* **1.** burial or discarding at sea. **2.** the abandonment of something. —**deep'-six',** *v.t.*

deep' space', *n.* space beyond the solar system.

deer (dēr), *n., pl.* **deer,** (*occasionally*) **deers.** any of a family of hoofed, ruminant mammals, the males usu. growing and shedding antlers.

Deere (dēr), *n.* **John,** 1804–86, U.S. inventor and manufacturer of farm implements.

de-es•ca•late or **de•es•ca•late** (dē es'kə lāt'), *v.t., v.i.,* **-lat•ed, -lat•ing.** to decrease in intensity, magnitude, etc. —**de-es'ca•la'tion,** *n.*

def (def), *adj. Slang.* excellent.

def., 1. defendant. **2.** definition.

de•face (di fās'), *v.t.,* **-faced, -fac•ing.** to mar the appearance of; disfigure. —**de•face'ment,** *n.*

de fac•to (dē fak'tō, dā), *adv.* **1.** in fact; in reality. —*adj.* **2.** actually existing, esp. without lawful authority: *de facto segregation.*

de•fal•cate (di fal'kāt, -fôl'-), *v.i.,* **-cat•ed, -cat•ing.** to misappropriate money entrusted to one. —**de'fal• ca'tion** (dē'-), *n.*

de•fame (di fām'), *v.t.,* **-famed, -fam•ing.** to attack the good name or reputation of; slander or libel. —**def•a•ma•tion** (def'ə mā'shən), *n.* —**de•fam'a• to'ry** (-fam'ə tôr'ē), *adj.* —**de•fam'er,** *n.*

de•fault (di fôlt'), *n.* **1.** failure to act or appear, esp. in meeting financial or legal obligations. —*v.t.* **2.** to lose by default. —*v.i.* **3.** to fail to fulfill an obligation. —**de•fault'er,** *n.*

de•feat (di fēt'), *v.t.* **1.** to overcome in a contest; vanquish. **2.** to frustrate; thwart. —*n.* **3.** the act of defeating or state of being defeated. —**de•feat'er,** *n.*

de•feat'ism, *n.* the acceptance of defeat too easily; resignation. —**de•feat'ist,** *n., adj.*

def•e•cate (def'i kāt'), *v.i.,* **-cat•ed, -cat•ing.** to void excrement from the bowels through the anus. —**def'e•ca'tion,** *n.*

de•fect (*n.* dē′fekt, di fekt′; *v.* di fekt′), *n.* **1.** a fault or shortcoming; imperfection. **2.** lack of something essential; deficiency. —*v.i.* **3.** to desert a cause, country, etc. —**de•fec′tion,** *n.* —**de•fec′tor,** *n.*

de•fec′tive, *adj.* faulty or imperfect.

de•fend (di fend′), *v.t.* **1.** to guard against attack or injury. **2.** to maintain by argument; uphold. **3.** to contest (a legal charge or claim). **4.** to serve as attorney for (a defendant). **5.** to attempt to retain (a championship title) in competition. —**de•fend′er,** *n.*

de•fend′ant, *n.* one against whom a legal action or suit is brought in a court.

de•fense (di fens′; *esp. for 5,* dē′fens), *n.* **1.** resistance against attack. **2.** something that defends. **3.** the defending of a cause or the like by speech, argument, etc. **4. a.** the defendant's answer to the plaintiff's charge or claim. **b.** a defendant together with counsel. **5. a.** the tactics used to defend oneself or one's goal in a game. **b.** the team defending itself. —**de•fense′less,** *adj.* —**de•fen′si•ble,** *adj.*

defense′ mech′anism, *n.* an unconscious process, as denial, that protects an individual from unacceptable or painful ideas or impulses.

de•fen′sive, *adj.* **1.** serving or done for the purpose of defense. **2.** sensitive to the threat of criticism. —*n.* **3.** a position or attitude of defense.

de•fer[1] (di fûr′), *v.*, **-ferred, -fer•ring.** —*v.t.* **1.** to postpone; delay. **2.** to exempt temporarily from induction into military service. —*v.i.* **3.** to put off action; delay. —**de•fer′ment,** *n.*

de•fer[2] (di fûr′), *v.i.*, **-ferred, -fer•ring.** to yield respectfully in judgment or opinion.

def•er•ence (def′ər əns), *n.* **1.** respectful yielding to the opinion, will, etc., of another. **2.** respectful regard. —**def′er•en′tial,** *adj.*

de•fi•ance (di fī′əns), *n.* **1.** a bold resistance to authority or force. **2.** open disregard; contempt. —**de•fi′ant,** *adj.* —**de•fi′ant•ly,** *adv.*

de•fi•cient (di fish′ənt), *adj.* **1.** lacking some element or characteristic; defective. **2.** insufficient; inadequate. —**de•fi′cien•cy,** *n., pl.* **-cies.**

def•i•cit (def′ə sit), *n.* **1.** the amount by which a sum of money falls short of the required amount. **2.** a loss, as in the operation of a business. **3.** a deficiency or handicap.

def′icit spend′ing, *n.* the practice of spending funds in excess of income, esp. by a government.

de•file[1] (di fīl′), *v.t.*, **-filed, -fil•ing. 1.** to make foul, dirty, or unclean. **2.** to violate the chastity of. **3.** to desecrate. **4.** to sully, as a person's reputation. —**de•file′ment,** *n.* —**de•fil′er,** *n.*

de•file[2] (di fīl′, dē′fīl), *n.* a narrow passage, esp. between mountains.

de•fine (di fīn′), *v.t.*, **-fined, -fin•ing. 1.** to state the meaning of (a word, phrase, etc.). **2.** to explain or identify the qualities of. **3.** to specify. **4.** to make clear the outline or form of. —**de•fin′er,** *n.*

defin′ing, *adj.* decisive; critically important: *Taking a course in architecture was a defining turn in her life.*

defin′ing mo′ment, *n.* a point at which the essential nature or character of a person, group, etc., is revealed or identified.

def•i•nite (def′ə nit), *adj.* **1.** clearly defined or determined; precise. **2.** having fixed limits. **3.** positive; certain. —**def′i•nite•ly,** *adv.* —**def′i•nite•ness,** *n.*

def′inite ar′ticle, *n.* an article, as English *the,* that classes as identified or definite the noun it modifies.

def•i•ni′tion, *n.* **1.** the act of making definite, distinct, or clear. **2.** the formal statement of the meaning of a word, phrase, etc. **3.** the condition of being definite. **4.** sharpness of the image formed by an optical system.

de•fin•i•tive (di fin′i tiv), *adj.* **1.** most reliable or complete: *a definitive edition.* **2.** serving to define or specify definitely. **3.** decisive or conclusive: *a definitive answer.*

de•flate (di flāt′), *v.*, **-flat•ed, -flat•ing.** —*v.t.* **1.** to release the air or gas from. **2.** to reduce in importance or size: *The rebuff deflated his ego.* **3.** to re-

duce (currency, prices, etc.) from an inflated condition. —*v.i.* **4.** to become deflated.

de•fla′tion, *n.* **1.** the act of deflating or state of being deflated. **2.** a fall in the general price level or a contraction of credit and available money.

de•flect (di flekt′), *v.t., v.i.* to bend; turn from a course. —**de•flec′tion,** *n.* —**de•flec′tive,** *adj.* —**de•flec′tor,** *n.*

De•foe (di fō′), *n.* **Daniel,** 1659?–1731, English writer.

de•fog (dē fog′, -fôg′), *v.t.*, **-fogged, -fog•ging.** to remove the fog or moisture from (a car window, mirror, etc.). —**de•fog′ger,** *n.*

de•fo•li•ant (dē fō′lē ənt), *n.* a preparation for defoliating plants.

de•fo′li•ate, *v.t., v.i.*, **-at•ed, -at•ing. 1.** to strip of leaves. **2.** to destroy (an area of jungle, forest, etc.), as to deprive an enemy of concealment. —**de•fo′li•a′tion,** *n.* —**de•fo′li•a′tor,** *n.*

de•for•est (dē fôr′ist, -for′-), *v.t.* to clear of forests or trees. —**de•for′est•a′tion,** *n.*

de•form (di fôrm′), *v.t.* **1.** to mar the natural form or shape of; disfigure. **2.** to mar the beauty of; spoil. —**de•for•ma′tion,** *n.*

de•formed′, *adj.* misshapen or disfigured.

de•form′i•ty, *n., pl.* **-ties. 1.** the quality or state of being deformed. **2.** an abnormally formed part of the body.

de•fraud (di frôd′), *v.t.*, to deprive of a right, money, or property by fraud. —**de•fraud′er,** *n.*

de•fray (di frā′), *v.t.* to pay all or part of: *to defray the costs.* —**de•fray′al,** *n.*

de•frost (di frôst′, -frost′), *v.t.* **1.** to remove the frost or ice from. **2.** to thaw (frozen food). —*v.i.* **3.** to become free of frost. **4.** to thaw. —**de•frost′er,** *n.*

deft (deft), *adj.*, **-er, -est.** skillful; nimble; facile. —**deft′ly,** *adv.* —**deft′ness,** *n.*

de•funct (di fungkt′), *adj.* **1.** no longer in effect or use. **2.** no longer in existence; dead; extinct.

de•fuse (dē fyōoz′), *v.t.*, **-fused, -fus•ing. 1.** to remove the fuse from (a bomb, mine, etc.). **2.** to make less dangerous or tense.

de•fy (di fī′), *v.t.*, **-fied, -fy•ing. 1.** to resist boldly or openly. **2.** to offer effective resistance to. **3.** to challenge (a person) to do something deemed impossible.

De•gas (dā gä′, də-), *n.* **Hilaire Germain Edgar,** 1834–1917, French painter.

de Gaulle (də gōl′, gôl′), *n.* **Charles André Joseph Marie,** 1890–1970, French general: president 1959–69.

de•gen•er•ate (*v.* di jen′ə rāt′; *adj., n.* -ər it), *v.*, **-at•ed, -at•ing,** *adj., n.* —*v.i.* **1.** to decline in physical, mental, or moral qualities; deteriorate. —*adj.* **2.** having declined in physical or moral qualities; deteriorated; degraded. —*n.* **3.** a person who has declined, esp. in morals. **4.** a sexual deviate. —**de•gen′er•a•cy** (-ər ə sē), *n.* —**de•gen′er•a′tion,** *n.* —**de•gen′er•a•tive** (-ər ə tiv, -ə rā′tiv), *adj.*

de•grade (di grād′ *or, for 3,* dē-), *v.*, **-grad•ed, -grad•ing.** —*v.t.* **1.** to lower in dignity or estimation. **2.** to lower in character or quality; debase. **3.** to reduce to a lower rank, degree, etc.

de•gree (di grē′), *n.* **1.** any of a series of steps or stages, as in a process. **2.** a stage in a scale of intensity or amount. **3.** extent, measure, scope, or the like. **4.** an academic title conferred by universities and colleges upon the completion of studies. **5.** a unit of measure for temperature. **6.** *Math.* the 360th part of a complete angle or turn. **7.** the distinctive classification of a crime according to its gravity. **8.** one of the parallel formations of adjectives and adverbs used to express differences in quality, quantity, or intensity. **9.** the sum of the exponents of the variables in an algebraic term. **10.** a tone, step, or note of a musical scale.

de•hu•man•ize (dē hyōo′mə nīz′; *often* -yōo′-), *v.t.*, **-ized, -iz•ing.** to deprive of human qualities; divest of individuality. —**de•hu′man•i•za′tion,** *n.*

de′hu•mid′i•fi′er, *n.* any device for removing

moisture from air. —de'hu•mid'i•fy, v.t., -fied, -fy•ing.

de•hy'drate, v., -drat•ed, -drat•ing. —v.t. 1. to remove water from; dry. —v.i. 2. to lose fluids or water. —de'hy•dra'tion, n. —de•hy'dra•tor, n.

de•hy'dro•gen•ate', v.t., -at•ed, -at•ing. to remove hydrogen from.

de•ice' or de-ice', v.t., -iced, -ic•ing. to free of ice; remove ice from. —de•ic'er, de-ic'er, n.

de•i•fy (dē'ə fī'), v.t., -fied, -fy•ing. 1. to make a god of. 2. to exalt as an object of worship. —de'i•fi•ca'tion, n.

deign (dān), v.t., v.i. to condescend (to do or grant).

de•ism (dē'iz əm), n. belief in the existence of a God on the evidence of reason and nature, with rejection of supernatural revelation. —de'ist, n. —de•is'tic, adj.

de•i•ty (dē'i tē), n., pl. -ties. 1. a god or goddess. 2. divine character or nature; divinity. 3. the Deity, God.

dé•jà vu (dā'zhä vōō'), n. the illusion of having previously experienced something actually being encountered for the first time. [< F: lit., already seen]

de•ject•ed (di jek'tid), adj. depressed in spirits; disheartened. —de•jec'tion, n.

de ju•re (di jŏŏr'ē, dā jŏŏr'ā), adv., adj. by right or according to law.

Del., Delaware.

Del•a•ware (del'ə wâr'), n. 1. a state in the E United States. 668,168. Cap.: Dover. Abbr.: DE, Del. 2. a river flowing from SE New York, along the boundary between Pennsylvania and New Jersey into Delaware Bay. 296 mi. (475 km) long. 3. a member of any of a group of American Indian peoples that formerly occupied the Delaware River valley. —Del'a•war'e•an, n., adj.

de•lay (di lā'), v.t. 1. to put off to a later time; postpone. 2. to impede or retard. —v.i. 3. to put off action; linger. —n. 4. the act of delaying. 5. an instance of being delayed. —de•lay'er, n.

de•lec•ta•ble (di lek'tə bəl), adj. 1. delightful; highly pleasing. 2. delicious.

de•lec•ta•tion (dē'lek tā'shən), n. delight; enjoyment.

del•e•gate (n. del'i git, -gāt'; v. -gāt'), n., v., -gat•ed, -gat•ing. —n. 1. a person designated to act for or represent another or others. 2. a member of the lower house of the legislatures of Virginia, West Virginia, and Maryland. —v.t. 3. to send or appoint as a delegate. 4. to commit (powers, functions, etc.) to another as agent.

del'e•ga'tion, n. 1. a group or body of delegates. 2. the act of delegating or state of being delegated.

de•lete (di lēt'), v.t., -let•ed, -let•ing. to strike out or remove (something written or printed); erase. —de•le'tion, n.

del•e•te•ri•ous (del'i tēr'ē əs), adj. injurious to health; harmful.

delft (delft), n. earthenware having an opaque white glaze with an overglaze decoration, usu. in blue. [after Delft, city in the Netherlands where first produced]

Del•hi (del'ē), n. a city in N India. 6,220,400.

del•i (del'ē), n., pl. -is (-ēz). delicatessen.

de•lib•er•ate (adj. di lib'ər it; v. -ə rāt'), adj., v., -at•ed, -at•ing. —adj. 1. studied or intentional. 2. careful or slow in deciding. 3. slow and even; unhurried. —v.t. 4. to weigh in the mind; consider. —v.i. 5. to consult or confer formally. —de•lib'er•ate•ly, adv.

de•lib'er•a'tion, n. 1. careful consideration. 2. formal discussion. 3. carefulness or slowness.

del•i•ca•cy (del'i kə sē), n., pl. -cies. 1. the quality or state of being delicate. 2. something delightful or pleasing, esp. a choice food.

del'i•cate (-kit), adj. 1. fine in texture, quality, construction, etc. 2. fragile; easily damaged. 3. frail or sickly. 4. fine or precise in action or execution. 5. requiring or showing great care, caution, or tact. 6. keenly sensitive. —del'i•cate•ly, adv. —del'i•cate•ness, n.

del•i•ca•tes•sen (del'i kə tes'ən), n. 1. a store selling prepared foods, as cooked meats, cheese, and salads. 2. the products sold in a delicatessen.

de•li•cious (di lish'əs), adj. 1. highly pleasing to taste or smell. 2. very pleasing; delightful. —de•li'cious•ly, adv. —de•li'cious•ness, n.

de•light (di līt'), n. 1. a high degree of pleasure or enjoyment; joy; rapture. 2. something that gives great pleasure. —v.t. 3. to give delight to. —v.i. 4. to have or take great pleasure. —de•light'ed, adj.

de•light'ful, adj. giving delight; highly pleasing. —de•light'ful•ly, adv.

De•li•lah (di lī'lə), n. Samson's mistress, who betrayed him to the Philistines. Judg. 16.

de•lim•it (di lim'it), v.t. to fix or mark the limits or boundaries of. —de•lim'i•ta'tion, n.

de•lin•e•ate (di lin'ē āt'), v.t., -at•ed, -at•ing. 1. to trace the outline of. 2. to portray or describe in words. —de•lin'e•a'tion, n.

de•lin•quent (di ling'kwənt), adj. 1. failing in or neglectful of a duty or obligation; guilty of a misdeed or offense. 2. past due: a delinquent account. —n. 3. a person who is delinquent, esp. a juvenile delinquent. —de•lin'quen•cy, n., pl. -cies. —de•lin'quent•ly, adv.

del•i•quesce (del'i kwes'), v.i., -quesced, -quesc•ing. to become liquid by absorbing moisture from the air, as certain salts. —del'i•ques'cent, adj.

de•lir•i•ous (di lēr'ē əs), adj. 1. affected with or characteristic of delirium. 2. wild with excitement, enthusiasm, etc. —de•lir'i•ous•ly, adv. —de•lir'i•ous•ness, n.

de•lir•i•um (di lēr'ē əm), n., pl. -i•ums, -i•a (-ē ə) 1. a temporary disturbance of consciousness characterized by restlessness, excitement, and delusions or hallucinations. 2. a state of violent excitement or emotion.

de•liv•er (di liv'ər), v.t. 1. to carry and turn over (letters, goods, etc.) to the intended recipient. 2. to hand over; surrender. 3. to utter or pronounce: to deliver a speech. 4. to strike or throw: to deliver a blow. 5. to set free or liberate. 6. to assist at the birth of. —v.i. 7. to give birth. 8. to do or carry out something. —de•liv'er•er, n.

de•liv'er•ance, n. 1. salvation. 2. liberation or rescue.

de•liv'er•y, n., pl. -er•ies. 1. the delivering of letters, goods, etc. 2. a giving up or handing over; surrender. 3. vocal and bodily behavior while speaking. 4. the act or manner of striking or throwing. 5. childbirth; parturition. 6. something delivered.

dell (del), n. a small, usu. wooded valley.

Del•phi (del'fī), n. an ancient city in central Greece: site of an oracle of Apollo.

del•phin•i•um (del fin'ē əm), n., pl. -i•ums, -i•a (-ē ə). a plant whose tall branching stalks bear colorful spurred flowers.

del•ta (del'tə), n., pl. -tas. 1. the fourth letter of the Greek alphabet (Δ, δ). 2. a nearly flat plain of alluvial, often triangular deposit between diverging branches of the mouth of a river.

del'ta wing', n. a triangular surface that serves as wing and stabilizer of a space vehicle or supersonic aircraft.

de•lude (di lōōd'), v.t., -lud•ed, -lud•ing. to mislead or deceive.

del•uge (del'yōōj), n., v., -uged, -ug•ing. —n. 1. a great flood; inundation. 2. a drenching rain; downpour. 3. anything that overwhelms like a flood. —v.t. 4. to flood; inundate. 5. to overwhelm.

de•lu•sion (di lōō'zhən), n. 1. the act of deluding or state of being deluded. 2. a false belief or opinion, esp. one that is irrational or psychotic. —de•lu'sion•al, de•lu'sive (-siv), adj.

de•luxe (də luks', -lŏŏks'), adj. of special elegance or sumptuousness.

delve (delv), v.i., delved, delv•ing. to investigate or search carefully for information. —delv'er, n.

Dem., 1. Democrat. 2. Democratic.

de•mag•net•ize (dē mag'ni tīz'), v.t., -ized, -iz•

ing. to remove magnetization from. —**de•mag′net•i• za′tion,** *n.* —**de•mag′net•iz′er,** *n.*

dem•a•gogue or **-gog** (dem′ə gog′, -gôg′), *n.* an orator or political leader who gains power by arousing people's emotions and prejudices. —**dem′a• gogu′er•y, dem′a•go′gy** (-gō′jē, -goj′ē), *n.*

de•mand (di mand′, -mänd′), *v.t.* **1.** to ask for with authority; claim as a right. **2.** to ask for peremptorily or urgently. **3.** to call for or require. —*v.i.* **4.** to make a demand; inquire; ask. —*n.* **5.** the act of demanding. **6.** something demanded. **7.** an urgent or pressing requirement. **8. a.** the desire and means to purchase goods. **b.** the amount of goods purchased at a specific price. **9.** the state of being sought for purchase or use: *an article in great demand.* —*Idiom.* **10. on demand,** upon presentation or request for payment.

de•mand′ing, *adj.* making difficult or excessive demands.

demand′-side′, *adj.* pertaining to an economic policy that stimulates consumer demand to increase production and employment. Compare SUPPLY-SIDE. —**demand′-sid′er,** *n.*

de•mar•cate (di mär′kāt, dē′mär kāt′), *v.t.,* **-cat•ed, -cat•ing.** to determine or mark off the boundaries of. —**de′mar•ca′tion,** *n.*

de•mean¹ (di mēn′), *v.t.* to lower in dignity or standing; debase.

de•mean² (di mēn′), *v.t.* to conduct or behave (oneself) in a specified manner.

de•mean′or, *n.* conduct; behavior; deportment. Also, *esp. Brit.,* **de•mean′our.**

de•ment•ed (di men′tid), *adj.* **1.** crazy; insane; mad. **2.** affected with dementia.

de•men′tia (-shə, -shē ə), *n.* severely impaired memory and reasoning ability, associated with damaged brain tissue.

de•mer•it (di mer′it), *n.* a mark against a person for misconduct or deficiency.

de•mesne (di mān′, -mēn′), *n.* **1.** possession of land as one's own. **2.** an estate occupied by and worked exclusively for the owner. **3.** the dominion or territory of a sovereign or state; domain.

De•me•ter (di mē′tər), *n.* the ancient Greek goddess of agriculture.

demi-, a combining form meaning half or lesser (*demigod*).

dem•i•god (dem′ē god′), *n.* **1.** a lesser or minor god. **2.** a deified mortal.

dem•i•john (dem′i jon′), *n.* a large bottle with a short, narrow neck, usu. encased in wickerwork.

de•mil•i•ta•rize (dē mil′i tə rīz′), *v.t.,* **-rized, -riz• ing. 1.** to deprive of military character; place under civil control. **2.** to forbid military use of.

De Mille (də mil′), *n.* **1. Agnes (George),** 1905–93, U.S. choreographer and dancer. **2.** her uncle, **Cecil B(lount),** 1881–1959, U.S. motion-picture producer and director.

de•mise (di mīz′), *n., v.,* **-mised, -mis•ing.** —*n.* **1.** death or decease. **2.** a conveyance or transfer of an estate. —*v.t.* **3.** to transfer (an estate) by bequest or lease.

dem•i•tasse (dem′i tas′, -täs′), *n.* **1.** a small cup for serving black coffee after dinner. **2.** the coffee served.

dem•o (dem′ō), *n., pl.* **dem•os.** a phonograph or tape recording distributed to demonstrate the merits of a new song or performer.

de•mo•bi•lize (dē mō′bə līz′), *v.t.,* **-lized, -liz•ing.** to disband (troops). —**de•mo′bi•li•za′tion,** *n.*

de•moc•ra•cy (di mok′rə sē), *n., pl.* **-cies. 1.** government in which supreme power is exercised directly by the people or by their elected agents. **2.** a state having such government. **3.** a state of society characterized by formal equality of rights and privileges.

dem•o•crat (dem′ə krat′), *n.* **1.** an advocate of democracy. **2.** (*cap.*) a member of the Democratic Party.

dem′o•crat′ic, *adj.* **1.** pertaining to or of the nature

of democracy. **2.** advocating democracy. **3.** (*cap.*) of the Democratic Party. —**dem′o•crat′i•cal•ly,** *adv.*

Dem′ocrat′ic Par′ty, *n.* one of the two major political parties in the U.S., dating from 1828.

de•moc•ra•tize (di mok′rə tīz′), *v.t.,* **-tized, -tiz• ing.** to make democratic. —**de•moc′ra•ti•za′tion,** *n.*

de•mod•u•late (dē moj′ə lāt′), *v.t.,* **-lat•ed, -lat• ing.** to extract the original information-bearing signal from (a modulated carrier wave or signal). —**de• mod′u•la′tion,** *n.* —**de•mod′u•la′tor,** *n.*

dem•o•graph•ics (dem′ə graf′iks), *n.pl.* the statistical data of a human population, as those showing age, income, etc.

de•mog•ra•phy (di mog′rə fē), *n.* the science of vital and social statistics, as of the births, marriages, etc., of human populations. —**de•mog′ra•pher,** *n.* —**dem•o•graph•ic** (dem′ə graf′ik), *adj.*

de•mol•ish (di mol′ish), *v.t.* to destroy or ruin; tear down. —**dem•o•li•tion** (dem′ə lish′ən, dē′mə-), *n.*

de•mon (dē′mən), *n.* **1.** an evil spirit; fiend. **2.** a wicked or cruel person. **3.** one with great energy. —**de•mon•ic** (di mon′ik), *adj.*

de•mon•e•tize (dē mon′i tīz′, -mun′-), *v.t.,* **-tized, -tiz•ing.** to divest (a monetary standard) of value.

de•mo•ni•ac (di mō′nē ak′) also **de•mo•ni•a•cal** (dē′mə nī′ə kəl), *adj.* **1.** of or like a demon. **2.** raging; frantic.

de•mon•stra•ble (di mon′strə bəl), *adj.* capable of being demonstrated or proved. —**de•mon′stra•bly,** *adv.*

dem•on•strate (dem′ən strāt′), *v.,* **-strat•ed, -strat• ing.** —*v.t.* **1.** to describe, explain, or illustrate by examples, experiments, etc. **2.** to make evident by reasoning; prove. **3.** to display openly. **4.** to exhibit the use of (a product). —*v.i.* **5.** to make a public exhibition of group feelings, as by parades or meetings. —**dem′on•stra′tion,** *n.* —**dem′on•stra′tor,** *n.*

de•mon•stra•tive (də mon′strə tiv), *adj.* **1.** given to open expression of one's feelings. **2.** explanatory or illustrative. **3.** serving to prove; conclusive. **4.** singling out the thing referred to: *a demonstrative pronoun.* —*n.* **5.** a demonstrative word, as *this* or *there.*

de•mor•al•ize (di môr′ə līz′, -mor′-), *v.t.,* **-ized, -iz• ing. 1.** to destroy the morale of. **2.** to throw into confusion; bewilder. **3.** to corrupt the morals of. —**de•mor′al•i•za′tion,** *n.*

De•mos•the•nes (di mos′thə nēz′), *n.* 384?–322 B.C., Athenian orator.

de•mote (di mōt′), *v.t.,* **-mot•ed, -mot•ing.** to reduce to a lower grade or rank. —**de•mo′tion,** *n.*

Demp•sey (demp′sē), *n.* **Jack,** 1895–1983, U.S. boxer.

de•mul•cent (di mul′sənt), *adj.* **1.** soothing. —*n.* **2.** a demulcent substance, as an ointment, for use on irritated mucous membrane.

de•mur (di mûr′), *v.i.,* **-murred, -mur•ring.** to make objection, esp. on the grounds of scruples. —**de• mur′ral,** *n.*

de•mure (di myŏŏr′), *adj.,* **-mur•er, -mur•est. 1.** shy and modest. **2.** affectedly or coyly decorous. —**de•mure′ly,** *adv.*

de•mur•rer (di mûr′ər), *n.* **1.** *Law.* a pleading in response to another's complaint asserting that the complaint contains no cause for action. **2.** an objection.

den (den), *n.* **1.** the lair of a wild animal, esp. a predatory mammal. **2.** a room in a home designed to provide a comfortable place for conversation, reading, etc. **3.** a cave used for shelter or concealment. **4.** a squalid abode.

de•na•ture (dē nā′chər), *v.t.,* **-tured, -tur•ing. 1.** to deprive (something) of its natural character. **2.** to render (any of various alcohols) undrinkable.

den•drite (den′drīt), *n.* any branching process of a neuron that conducts impulses toward the cell body.

Deng Xiao•ping (dung′ shou′ping′), *n.* 1904–97, Chinese Communist leader.

de•ni•al (di nī′əl), *n.* **1.** an assertion that an allegation is false. **2.** refusal to believe a doctrine, theory, or the like. **3.** the refusal to satisfy a claim, request, etc. **4.** disavowal or repudiation. **5.** SELF-DENIAL.

de•nier (də nēr′, dən yā′, den′yər), *n.* a unit of weight indicating the fineness of fiber filaments and yarns.

den•i•grate (den′i grāt′), *v.t.,* -grat•ed, -grat•ing. to speak damagingly of; defame or disparage. —**den′•i•gra′tion,** *n.*

den•im (den′əm), *n.* 1. a coarse twill fabric of cotton or other fibers, used esp. for jeans. 2. denims, (*used with a pl. v.*) clothes of denim. [< F: short for *serge de Nîmes* serge of Nîmes (city in France)]

Den•is (den′is; *Fr.* də nē′), *n.* Saint, died A.D. c280, 1st bishop of Paris: patron saint of France.

den•i•zen (den′ə zən), *n.* 1. an inhabitant; resident. 2. a person who frequents a place.

Den•mark (den′märk), *n.* a kingdom in N Europe. 5,268,775.

den′ of thieves′, *n.* a place where one must guard against theft or attack. Matt. 21:13.

de•nom•i•nate (di nom′ə nāt′), *v.t.,* -nat•ed, -nat•ing. to give a name to; denote; designate.

de•nom′i•na′tion, *n.* 1. a particular religious body. 2. one of the grades or degrees in a series of values: *bills of small denomination.* 3. a class or kind of persons or things distinguished by a specific name. —**de•nom′i•na′tion•al,** *adj.*

de•nom′i•na′tor, *n.* 1. the term of a fraction, usu. written under or after the line, that indicates the number of equal parts into which the unit is divided. 2. something held in common.

de•note (di nōt′), *v.t.,* -not•ed, -not•ing. 1. to be a mark or sign of; indicate. 2. to be a name or designation for; mean. —**de•no•ta•tion** (dē′nō tā′shən), *n.* —**de′no•ta′tive,** *adj.*

de•noue•ment or **dé•noue•ment** (dā′nōō män′), *n.* the final resolution of a plot, as of a drama or novel.

de•nounce (di nouns′), *v.t.,* -nounced, -nounc•ing. 1. to condemn or censure openly or publicly. 2. to make a formal accusation against, as to the police. —**de•nounce′ment,** *n.*

dense (dens), *adj.,* dens•er, dens•est. 1. having its parts crowded together; compact. 2. slow-witted; dull. 3. opaque; not clear. 4. difficult to understand. —**dense′ly,** *adv.* —**dense′ness,** *n.*

den′si•ty, *n., pl.* -ties. 1. the state or quality of being dense. 2. stupidity. 3. the average number per unit of area: *population density per square mile.* 4. *Physics.* mass per unit volume. 5. degree of opacity. 6. a measure of how much data can be stored in a given amount of space on a computer disk, tape, etc.

dent (dent), *n.* 1. a small depression in a surface, as from a blow. 2. a slight effect. 3. slight progress: *I haven't made a dent in this pile of work.* —*v.t.* 4. to make a dent in or on. —*v.i.* 5. to become dented.

den•tal (den′tl), *adj.* of or for the teeth or dentistry.

den′tal floss′, *n.* thread used to dislodge food particles from between the teeth.

den′ti•frice (-tə fris), *n.* a preparation for cleaning the teeth.

den′tin (-tn, -tin) also **-tine** (-tēn), *n.* the hard, calcareous tissue that forms the major portion of a tooth.

den′tist (-tist), *n.* a person whose profession is dentistry.

den′tist•ry, *n.* the prevention and treatment of diseases of the teeth, gums, and oral cavity.

den′ture (-chər, -chŏŏr), *n.* an artificial replacement of one or more teeth.

de•nu•cle•ar•ize (dē nōō′klē ə rīz′, -nyōō′- or, *by metathesis,* -kyə lə-), *v.t.,* -ized, -iz•ing. to forbid the construction or deployment of nuclear weapons in.

de•nude (di nōōd′, -nyōōd′), *v.t.,* -nud•ed, -nud•ing. to strip bare.

de•nun•ci•a•tion (di nun′sē ā′shən, -shē-), *n.* an act or instance of denouncing.

Den•ver (den′vər), *n.* the capital of Colorado. 493,559.

de•ny (di nī′), *v.t.,* -nied, -ny•ing. 1. to declare that (a statement) is not true. 2. to refuse to agree to. 3. to withhold the possession, use, or enjoyment of. 4.

---

to refuse to grant a request of. 5. to disavow; repudiate.

de•o•dor•ant (dē ō′dər ənt), *n.* 1. a substance for inhibiting or masking odors. —*adj.* 2. capable of destroying odors.

de•o′dor•ize′, *v.t.,* -ized, -iz•ing. to rid of odor. —**de•o′dor•i•za′tion,** *n.* —**de•o′dor•iz′er,** *n.*

de•ox′y•ri′bo•nu•cle′ic ac′id (dē ok′si rī′bō-nōō klē′ik, -nyōō-, -ok′si rī′-), *n.* See DNA.

de•part (di pärt′), *v.i.* 1. to go away; leave. 2. to diverge or deviate. 3. to die. —*v.t.* 4. to go away from; leave.

de•part•ment (di pärt′mənt), *n.* 1. a distinct part or division, as of a government or business. 2. a sphere of activity or knowledge. —**de•part•men•tal** (di pärt men′tl, dē′pärt-), *adj.*

de•part•men′tal•ize′, *v.t.,* -ized, -iz•ing. to divide into departments. —**de′part•men′tal•i•za′tion,** *n.*

depart′ment store′, *n.* a large retail store organized into departments of merchandise.

de•par•ture (di pär′chər), *n.* 1. an act or instance of departing. 2. divergence or deviation, as from a rule.

de•pend (di pend′), *v.i.* 1. to rely; place trust: *You may depend on our tact.* 2. to be contingent: *Our plans depend on the weather.* 3. to rely for aid or support.

de•pend′a•ble, *adj.* worthy of trust; reliable. —**de•pend′a•bil′i•ty,** *n.*

de•pend′ence, *n.* 1. the state of depending on someone or something for aid or support. 2. reliance; trust. 3. the state of being contingent on something. 4. the state of being physically or psychologically dependent on a drug. Sometimes, **de•pend′ance.**

de•pend′en•cy, *n., pl.* -cies. 1. the state of being dependent. 2. a subject territory that is not a part of the ruling country.

de•pend′ent, *adj.* 1. relying on someone or something for aid, support, etc. 2. contingent. 3. subject to another's rule. 4. *Gram.* used only with other forms; subordinate: *a dependent clause.* —*n.* 5. a person who relies on another for aid, support, etc. Often, *esp. for def. 5,* **de•pend′ant.** —**de•pend′ent•ly,** *adv.*

de•per•son•al•ize (dē pûr′sə nl īz′), *v.t.,* -ized, -iz•ing. to make impersonal.

de•pict (di pikt′), *v.t.* 1. to represent by drawing; portray. 2. to characterize in words; describe. —**de•pic′tion,** *n.*

de•pil•a•to•ry (di pil′ə tôr′ē), *adj., n., pl.* -ries. —*adj.* 1. capable of removing hair. —*n.* 2. a depilatory agent.

de•plane (dē plān′), *v.i.,* -planed, -plan•ing. to disembark from an airplane.

de•plete (di plēt′), *v.t.,* -plet•ed, -plet•ing. to decrease seriously or exhaust the supply of. —**de•ple′tion,** *n.*

de•plor•a•ble (di plôr′ə bəl), *adj.* 1. causing grief or regret. 2. worthy of censure; very bad.

de•plore′, *v.t.,* -plored, -plor•ing. 1. to regret deeply. 2. to disapprove of; censure.

de•ploy (di ploi′), *v.t.* to spread out (troops, weapons, etc.) strategically. —**de•ploy′ment,** *n.*

de•po•lar•ize (dē pō′lə rīz′), *v.t.,* -ized, -iz•ing. to deprive of polarity or polarization, esp. in eliminating a magnetic charge. —**de•po′lar•i•za′tion,** *n.*

de•po•lit•i•cize (dē′pə lit′ə sīz′), *v.t.,* -cized, -ciz•ing. to remove from the arena or influence of politics.

de•po•nent (di pō′nənt), *n.* a person who gives evidence in writing under oath.

de•pop•u•late (dē pop′yə lāt′), *v.t.,* -lat•ed, -lat•ing. to remove or reduce the population of.

de•port (di pôrt′), *v.t.* 1. to expel from a country; banish. 2. to behave (oneself). —**de•por•ta•tion** (dē′pôr tā′shən), *n.*

de•port′ment, *n.* conduct; behavior.

de•pose (di pōz′), *v.t.,* -posed, -pos•ing. 1. to remove from office or position, esp. high office. **2.** to testify under oath.

de•pos•it (di poz′it), *v.t.* **1.** to place in a bank account. **2.** to put or set down. **3.** to throw down or precipitate. **4.** to give as security or in part payment. —*v.i.* **5.** to become deposited. —*n.* **6.** money placed in a bank account. **7.** anything given as security or in part payment. **8.** something precipitated or thrown down, as by a natural process. —**de•pos′i•tor,** *n.*

dep•o•si•tion (dep′ə zish′ən, dē′pə-), *n.* **1.** removal from an office or position. **2.** the act or process of depositing. **3.** something deposited. **4.** written testimony under oath.

de•pos•i•to•ry (di poz′i tôr′ē), *n., pl.* **-ries.** a place where something is deposited for safekeeping.

de•pot (dē′pō; *Mil. or Brit.* dep′ō), *n.* **1.** a railroad or bus station. **2. a.** a warehouse. **b.** a place where military supplies are stored.

de•prave (di prāv′), *v.t.,* **-praved, -prav•ing.** to make morally bad; corrupt. —**de•praved′,** *adj.* —**de•prav′i•ty** (-prav′i tē), *n., pl.* **-ties.**

dep•re•cate (dep′ri kāt′), *v.t.,* **-cat•ed, -cat•ing. 1.** to express earnest disapproval of. **2.** to belittle. —**dep′re•ca′tion,** *n.* —**dep′re•ca•to•ry** (-kə tôr′ē), *adj.*

de•pre•ci•ate (di prē′shē āt′), *v.,* **-at•ed, -at•ing.** —*v.t.* **1.** to lessen the value or price of. **2.** to belittle. —*v.i.* **3.** to decline in value. —**de•pre′ci•a′tion,** *n.*

dep•re•da•tion (dep′ri dā′shən), *n.* the act of preying upon or plundering.

de•press (di pres′), *v.t.* **1.** to make sad; dispirit. **2.** to lower in force or activity; weaken. **3.** to lower in amount or value. —**de•pressed′,** *adj.* —**de•press′ive,** *adj.*

de•pres′sant, *n.* a drug or other agent that reduces irritability or excitement.

de•pres′sion, *n.* **1.** the act of depressing or state of being depressed. **2.** an area lower than the surrounding surface. **3.** sadness or gloom. **4.** emotional dejection and withdrawal greater than that warranted by any objective reason. **5.** a period during which business activity and employment decline severely.

de•prive (di prīv′), *v.t.,* **-prived, -priv•ing. 1.** to divest of something possessed; strip. **2.** to keep from possessing. —**dep•ri•va•tion** (dep′rə vā′shən) *n*

de•pro•gram (dē prō′gram), *v.t.,* **-grammed** or **-gramed, -gram•ming** or **-gram•ing.** to free (a person) from the influence of a cult, sect, etc., by systematic reeducation.

dept., 1. department. **2.** deputy.

depth (depth), *n.* **1.** a dimension taken through an object, usu. downward or inward. **2.** the quality of being deep. **3.** intensity, as of silence. **4.** Often, **depths.** a deep or inner part or place. **5.** Usu., **depths.** a low intellectual or moral condition. —*Idiom.* **6. in depth,** thoroughly.

depth′ charge′, *n.* an explosive device used underwater, esp. against submarines.

dep•u•ta•tion (dep′yə tā′shən), *n.* **1.** the act of appointing a deputy. **2.** the person or body so appointed.

de•pute (də pyo͞ot′), *v.t.,* **-put•ed, -put•ing. 1.** to appoint as one's substitute or agent. **2.** to assign (authority, a function, etc.) to a deputy.

dep•u•tize (dep′yə tīz′), *v.t.,* **-tized, -tiz•ing.** to appoint as deputy.

dep′u•ty, *n., pl.* **-ties. 1.** a person authorized to act as a substitute for another or others. **2.** an assistant to a public official. **3.** a person representing a constituency in certain legislative bodies.

de•rail (dē rāl′), *v.t.* **1.** to cause to run off the rails of a track. **2.** to deflect from a purpose or direction. —*v.i.* **3.** to become derailed. —**de•rail′ment,** *n.*

de•rail•leur (di rā′lər), *n.* a gear-shifting mechanism on a bicycle.

de•range (di rānj′), *v.t.,* **-ranged, -rang•ing. 1.** to disturb the condition, action, or function of. **2.** to make insane. —**de•range′ment,** *n.*

Der•by (dûr′bē; *Brit.* där′-), *n., pl.* **-bies. 1.** any of several annual horse races, esp. the one at Epsom Downs, England, and the Kentucky Derby. **2.** (*l.c.*) a

race or contest, usu. one open to all. **3.** (*l.c.*) a man's stiff felt hat with rounded crown.

de•reg•u•late (dē reg′yə lāt′), *v.t.,* **-lat•ed, -lat•ing.** to remove governing regulations from. —**de•reg′u•la′tion,** *n.*

der•e•lict (der′ə likt), *adj.* **1.** deserted or abandoned. **2.** neglectful of duty; delinquent. —*n.* **3.** a person who has no home or means of support. **4.** a ship abandoned in open water. **5.** any abandoned possession.

der′e•lic′tion, *n.* **1.** deliberate neglect. **2.** the act of abandoning something. **3.** the state of being abandoned.

de•ride (di rīd′), *v.t.,* **-rid•ed, -rid•ing.** to laugh at in scorn or contempt; mock. —**de•ri′sion** (-rish′ən), *n.* —**de•ri′sive** (-rī′siv), *adj.* —**de•ri′sive•ly,** *adv.*

der•i•va•tion (der′ə vā′shən), *n.* **1.** the act of deriving or state of being derived. **2.** source; origin. **3.** the origin and evolution of a word.

de•riv•a•tive (di riv′ə tiv), *adj.* **1.** not original; secondary. —*n.* **2.** something derived. **3.** a word derived from another, as *atomic* from *atom.*

de•rive (di rīv′), *v.,* **-rived, -riv•ing.** —*v.t.* **1.** to receive or obtain from a source. **2.** to trace from a source. **3.** to reach or obtain by reasoning. —*v.i.* **4.** to be derived.

der•ma•ti•tis (dûr′mə tī′tis), *n.* inflammation of the skin.

der′ma•tol′o•gy (-tol′ə jē), *n.* the branch of medicine dealing with the skin and its diseases. —**der′ma•to•log′i•cal** (-tl oj′i kəl), *adj.* —**der′ma•tol′o•gist,** *n.*

der′mis (-mis), *n.* the thick layer of skin beneath the epidermis.

der•o•gate (der′ə gāt′), *v.,* **-gat•ed, -gat•ing.** —*v.i.* **1.** to detract, as from authority or estimation. —*v.t.* **2.** to disparage or belittle. —**der′o•ga′tion,** *n.*

de•rog•a•to•ry (di rog′ə tôr′ē), *adj.* belittling; disparaging.

der•rick (der′ik), *n.* **1.** a boom for lifting heavy cargo. **2.** the towerlike framework over an oil well or the like.

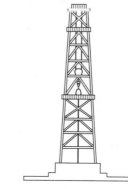

derrick

der•ri•ère (der′ē âr′), *n.* the buttocks.

der•rin•ger (der′in jər), *n.* an early short-barreled pocket pistol. [after H. *Deringer,* 19th-century U.S. gunsmith]

der•vish (dûr′vish), *n.* a member of any of various Muslim ascetic orders, some of which practice ecstatic dancing.

de•sal•i•nate (dē sal′ə nāt′), *v.t.,* **-nat•ed, -nat•ing.** DESALT. —**de•sal′i•na′tion,** *n.*

de•salt (dē sôlt′), *v.t.* to remove the salt from (esp. sea water).

des•cant (*n.* des′kant; *v.* des kant′, dis-), *n.* **1.** a melody or counterpoint accompanying a simple musical theme and usu. written above it. —*v.i.* **2.** to discourse at great length. **3.** to sing.

Des•cartes (dā kärt′), *n.* René, 1596–1650, French philosopher and mathematician.

de•scend (di send′), *v.i.* **1.** to pass from a higher to a lower point or place; move down. **2.** to slope or lead downward. **3.** to be inherited or transmitted. **4.** to attack or approach as if attacking. —*v.t.* **5.** to move downward upon or along.

de•scend′ant, *n.* **1.** a person or animal descended from a specific ancestor. **2.** something deriving from an earlier form.

de•scent′ (-sent′), *n.* **1.** the act or process of descending. **2.** a downward or slope. **3.** derivation from an ancestor; lineage. **4.** any passing from higher to lower. **5.** a sudden attack.

de•scribe (di skrīb′), *v.t.,* **-scribed, -scrib•ing. 1.** to depict in words. **2.** to pronounce or name. **3.** to draw the outline of. —**de•scrib′a•ble,** *adj.*

de•scrip′tion (-skrip′shən), *n.* **1.** a statement or account that describes. **2.** the act or method of describing. **3.** sort; variety. —**de•scrip′tive,** *adj.*

de•scry (di skrī′), *v.t.,* **-scried, -scry•ing. 1.** to see by looking carefully; discern. **2.** to discover; detect.

des•e•crate (des′i krāt′), *v.t.,* **-crat•ed, -crat•ing.** to treat with sacrilege; profane. —**des′e•cra′tion,** *n.*

de•seg•re•gate (dē seg′ri gāt′), *v.t., v.i.* **-gat•ed, -gat•ing.** to eliminate racial segregation in (schools, etc.). —**de•seg′re•ga′tion,** *n.*

de•sen•si•tize (dē sen′si tīz′), *v.t.,* **-tized, -tiz•ing.** to make less sensitive. —**de•sen′si•ti•za′tion,** *n.*

des•ert¹ (dez′ərt), *n.* **1.** an arid, often sandy region capable of supporting only a few life forms. **2.** any lifeless or dull place.

de•sert² (di zûrt′), *v.t., v.i.* **1.** to leave (a person, place, etc.) without intending to return. **2.** (of military personnel) to leave (duty, service, etc.) without permission and with no intention of returning. —**de•sert′er,** *n.* —**de•ser′tion,** *n.*

de•sert³ (di zûrt′), *n.* Often, **-serts.** reward or punishment that is deserved.

des′ert fa′thers, *n.pl.* monks, who lived as hermits in the deserts of Egypt and founded the first Christian monasteries.

de•serve (di zûrv′), *v.t., v.i.* **-served, -serv•ing.** to merit or be worthy of (reward, punishment, aid, etc.). —**de•serv′ed•ly,** *adv.*

des•ha•bille (dez′ə bēl′, -bē′), *n.* DISHABILLE.

des•ic•cate (des′i kāt′), *v.t., v.i.* **-cat•ed, -cat•ing.** to dry thoroughly; dry up. —**des′ic•ca′tion,** *n.*

de•sid•er•a•tum (di sid′ə rā′təm, -rä′-, -zid′-), *n., pl.* **-ta** (-tə). something wanted or needed.

de•sign (di zīn′), *v.t.* **1.** to prepare the preliminary sketches or plans for: *to design a new bridge.* **2.** to plan and fashion skillfully. **3.** to intend for a definite purpose. **4.** to form in the mind. —*v.i.* **5.** to make sketches or plans. **6.** to plan an object, work of art, etc. —*n.* **7.** an outline, sketch, or scheme. **8.** the organization of elements in a work of art or other object. **9.** an ornamental pattern or motif. **10.** a plan or project. **11.** a plot or intrigue. **12.** intention; purpose; end. —**de•sign′er,** *n.*

des•ig•nate (*v.* dez′ig nāt′; *adj.* -nit, -nāt′), *v.,* **-nat•ed, -nat•ing,** *adj.* —*v.t.* **1.** to mark or point out; specify. **2.** to name; entitle. **3.** to select, as for a duty or office. —*adj.* **4.** selected for an office, position, etc., but not yet installed. —**des′ig•na′tion,** *n.*

des′ignated driv′er, *n.* a person who abstains from alcoholic beverages at a gathering in order to be fit to drive companions home safely.

de•sign′ing, *adj.* scheming; crafty.

de•sir•a•ble (di zīᵊr′ə bəl), *adj.* **1.** pleasing; attractive. **2.** arousing desire. **3.** advisable. —**de•sir′a•bil′i•ty,** *n.* —**de•sir′a•bly,** *adv.*

de•sire′, *v.,* **-sired, -sir•ing,** *n.* —*v.t.* **1.** to wish or long for; crave. **2.** to ask for; request. —*n.* **3.** a longing or craving. **4.** an expressed wish; request. **5.** something desired. **6.** sexual urge.

de•sir′ous, *adj.* having or characterized by desire.

de•sist (di zist′, -sist′), *v.i.* to cease, as from an action; stop.

desk (desk), *n.* **1.** an article of furniture having a writing surface. **2.** a specialized section of a large organization: *the copy desk.* —*adj.* **3.** suitable for or done at a desk.

desk′top′, *adj.* designed to be used on a desk or table.

desk′top pub′lishing, *n.* the design and production of publications using a microcomputer.

Des Moines (də moin′), *n.* the capital of Iowa. 193,965.

des•o•late (*adj.* des′ə lit; *v.* -lāt′), *adj., v.,* **-lat•ed, -lat•ing.** —*adj.* **1.** barren or laid waste. **2.** without inhabitants; deserted. **3.** feeling friendless or hopeless; forlorn. **4.** dismal; gloomy. —*v.t.* **5.** to make desolate. —**des′o•late•ly,** *adv.* —**des′o•late•ness,** *n.*

des′o•la′tion, *n.* **1.** the act of making desolate. **2.** a desolate state or place. **3.** loneliness. **4.** sorrow; grief.

De So•to (də sō′tō), *n.* **Hernando** or **Fernando,** c1500–42, Spanish explorer in America.

de•spair (di spâr′), *n.* **1.** loss of hope; hopelessness. **2.** a source of hopelessness. —*v.i.* **3.** to give up hope.

des•patch (di spach′), *v.t., n.* DISPATCH.

des•per•a•do (des′pə rä′dō, -rä′-), *n., pl.* **-does, -dos.** a reckless criminal or outlaw.

des•per•ate (des′pər it), *adj.* **1.** reckless or dangerous because of despair or urgency. **2.** having an urgent need, desire, etc. **3.** leaving little or no hope. **4.** extreme or excessive. —**des′per•ate•ly,** *adv.* —**des′per•a′tion,** *n.*

des•pi•ca•ble (des′pi kə bəl, di spik′ə-), *adj.* deserving to be despised. —**des′pi•ca•bly,** *adv.*

de•spise (di spīz′), *v.t.,* **-spised, -spis•ing. 1.** to regard with contempt; scorn. **2.** to hate.

de•spite (di spīt′), *prep.* in spite of; notwithstanding.

de•spoil (di spoil′), *v.t.* to strip of possessions; rob; plunder. —**de•spoil′ment,** *n.*

de•spond•en•cy (di spon′dən sē), *n.* depression of spirits from loss of courage or hope; dejection. —**de•spond′ent,** *adj.*

des•pot (des′pət, -pot), *n.* **1.** a ruler with absolute power. **2.** any tyrant or oppressor. —**des•pot′ic** (dispot′ik), *adj.* —**des′pot•ism,** *n.*

des•sert (di zûrt′), *n.* a usu. sweet food, as cake or pudding, served as the final course of a meal. [< F, der. of *desservir* to clear the table]

des•ti•na•tion (des′tə nā′shən), *n.* **1.** the place to which a person or thing travels or is sent. **2.** the purpose for which something is destined.

des′tine (-tin), *v.t.,* **-tined, -tin•ing. 1.** to set apart for a particular purpose. **2.** to determine or ordain beforehand.

des′ti•ny, *n., pl.* **-nies. 1.** fate; lot or fortune. **2.** the predetermined course of events.

des•ti•tute (des′ti tōōt′, -tyōōt′), *adj.* **1.** without any means of subsistence. **2.** deprived or lacking: *destitute of feeling.* —**des′ti•tu′tion,** *n.*

de•stroy (di stroi′), *v.t.* **1.** to injure beyond repair; demolish. **2.** to put an end to. **3.** to kill. **4.** to make ineffective or useless.

de•stroy′er, *n.* **1.** a person or thing that destroys. **2.** a fast, small warship.

de•struct (di strukt′), *v.i.* to be destroyed automatically.

de•struc′tion, *n.* **1.** the act of destroying or state of being destroyed. **2.** a cause or means of destroying. —**de•struc′tive,** *adj.* —**de•struc′tive•ly,** *adv.* —**de•struc′tive•ness,** *n.*

des•ue•tude (des′wi tōōd′, -tyōōd′), *n.* the state of being no longer used or practiced.

des•ul•to•ry (des′əl tôr′ē), *adj.* **1.** lacking in consistency or order; disconnected. **2.** digressing; random.

de•tach (di tach′), *v.t.* **1.** to unfasten and separate. **2.** to send (a regiment, ship, etc.) on a special mission. —**de•tach′a•ble,** *adj.*

de•tached′, *adj.* **1.** not attached; separated. **2.** impartial or objective. **3.** not involved; aloof.

de•tach′ment, *n.* **1.** the act of detaching or state of being detached. **2.** aloofness; disinterest. **3.** freedom from partiality. **4.** a body of troops or ships on a special mission.

de•tail (di tāl′, dē′tāl), *n.* **1.** an individual part; particular. **2.** particulars collectively. **3.** attention to a subject in individual parts. **4. a.** an assignment, as of military personnel, for a special task. **b.** the party so selected: *the kitchen detail.* —*v.t.* **5.** to relate with all particulars. **6.** to assign for some particular duty. —*Idiom.* **7. in detail,** item by item.

de•tain (di tān′), *v.t.* **1.** to keep from proceeding; delay. **2.** to keep under restraint. —**de•tain′ment,** *n.*

de•tect (di tekt′), *v.t.* to discover or notice the existence or presence of. —**de•tect′a•ble,** *adj.* —**de•tec′-tion,** *n.* —**de•tec′tor,** *n.*

de•tec′tive, *n.* a police officer or private investigator who investigates crimes, obtains evidence, etc.

dé•tente (dā tänt′, -täNt′), *n.* a relaxing of tension, esp. between nations. [< F]

de•ten•tion (di ten′shən), *n.* **1.** the act of detaining or state of being detained. **2.** maintenance of a person in custody. **3.** the keeping of a student after school hours as a punishment.

de•ter (di tûr′), *v.t.,* **-terred, -ter•ring.** to discourage from acting or proceeding, as through fear. —**de•ter′ment,** *n.*

de•ter•gent (di tûr′jənt), *n.* a synthetic water-soluble cleaning agent that acts like soap.

de•te•ri•o•rate (di tēr′ē ə rāt′), *v.t., v.i.,* **-rat•ed, -rat•ing.** to make or become worse in character, quality, etc. —**de•ter′i•o•ra′tion,** *n.*

de•ter•mi•nant (di tûr′mə nənt), *n.* a determining agent or factor.

de•ter′mi•nate (-nit), *adj.* **1.** having defined limits; definite. **2.** settled; positive.

de•ter′mi•na′tion (-nā′shən), *n.* **1.** the act of coming to a decision. **2.** the decision reached. **3.** firmness of purpose. **4.** the act of ascertaining or fixing something.

de•ter′mine (-min), *v.,* **-mined, -min•ing.** —*v.t.* **1.** to settle or resolve (a dispute, question, etc.) conclusively. **2.** to conclude or ascertain, as after observation. **3.** to fix the position of. **4.** to cause or control. **5.** to decide upon. —*v.i.* **6.** to decide. —**de•ter′mi•na•ble,** *adj.*

de•ter′mined, *adj.* **1.** resolute; unwavering. **2.** decided; settled.

de•ter•rence (di tûr′əns), *n.* the act of deterring, esp. of deterring a nuclear attack by the capability for retaliation.

de•ter′rent, *adj.* **1.** serving to deter. —*n.* **2.** something that deters.

de•test (di test′), *v.t.* to hate; dislike intensely. —**de•test′a•ble,** *adj.* —**de•tes•ta•tion** (dē′te stā′-shən), *n.*

de•throne (dē thrōn′), *v.t.,* **-throned, -thron•ing.** to remove from a throne or position of authority; depose.

det•o•nate (det′n āt′), *v.i., v.t.,* **-nat•ed, -nat•ing.** to explode with sudden violence. —**det′o•na′tion,** *n.* —**det′o•na′tor,** *n.*

de•tour (dē′tŏŏr, di tŏŏr′), *n.* **1.** a roundabout course, esp. one used temporarily when a route is closed. —*v.i., v.t.* **2.** to make or cause to make a detour.

de•tox (*n.* dē′toks; *v.* dē toks′), *n., v.,* **-toxed, -tox•ing.** *Informal.* —*n.* **1.** detoxification. —*v.t.* **2.** to detoxify.

de•tox′i•fy, *v.t.,* **-fied, -fy•ing.** to rid of poison or the effects of alcohol or drug use. —**de•tox′i•fi•ca′tion,** *n.*

de•tract (di trakt′), *v.i.* **1.** to take away a part, as from value or reputation (usu. fol. by *from*). —*v.t.* **2.** to divert. —**de•trac′tion,** *n.* —**de•trac′tor,** *n.*

det•ri•ment (de′trə mənt), *n.* **1.** loss, damage, or disadvantage. **2.** a cause of loss or damage. —**det′ri•men′tal,** *adj.*

de•tri•tus (di trī′təs), *n.* **1.** rock particles worn away from a mass. **2.** any disintegrated material; debris.

De•troit (di troit′), *n.* a city in SE Michigan. 992,038.

deuce (dōōs, dyōōs), *n.* **1.** a card or die with two pips. **2.** a tie score, as in tennis, after which a player must score two successive points to win.

deu•te•ri•um (dōō tēr′ē əm, dyōō-), *n.* an isotope of hydrogen, having twice the mass of ordinary hydrogen. *Symbol:* D; *at. wt.:* 2.01; *at. no.:* 1.

Deu•ter•on•o•my (dōō′tə ron′ə mē, dyōō′-), *n.* the fifth book of the Old Testament.

Deut•sche mark (doi′chə märk′, doich′), *n.* MARK[2].

de•val•ue (dē val′yōō), *v.t.,* **-val•ued, -val•u•ing. 1.** to set a lower exchange value on (a currency). **2.** to reduce the value of. —**de•val′u•a′tion,** *n.*

dev•as•tate (dev′ə stāt′), *v.t.,* **-tat•ed, -tat•ing. 1.** to lay waste; render desolate. **2.** to overwhelm, as with shock. —**dev′as•ta′tion,** *n.*

de•vel•op (di vel′əp), *v.t.* **1.** to bring to a more advanced, effective, or usable state. **2.** to cause to grow or expand. **3.** to bring into being or activity. **4.** to generate or acquire, as by natural processes. **5.** to elaborate in detail. **6.** to treat (an exposed film) with chemicals so as to make the image visible. —*v.i.* **7.** to become more advanced, mature, etc. **8.** to come gradually into existence or operation. **9.** to be disclosed: *The plot develops slowly.* —**de•vel′op•er,** *n.* —**de•vel′op•ment,** *n.* —**de•vel′op•men′tal,** *adj.* —**de•vel′op•men′tal•ly,** *adv.*

de•vel′op•ing, *adj.* (of a nation or area) having relatively low living standards or industrial productivity.

de•vi•ant (dē′vē ənt), *adj.* **1.** deviating from an accepted norm, esp. of behavior. —*n.* **2.** a deviant person or thing. —**de′vi•ance,** *n.*

de′vi•ate (*v.* -āt′; *n.* -it), *v.,* **-at•ed, -at•ing,** *n.* —*v.i.* **1.** to turn aside or differ, as from a course, standard, or topic. —*n.* **2.** a deviant, esp. a person whose sexual behavior departs from the norm. —**de′-vi•a′tion,** *n.*

de•vice (di vīs′), *n.* **1.** a thing made for a particular purpose, esp. a mechanical or electronic contrivance. **2.** a plan, scheme, or procedure. **3.** a design used as a badge, emblem, trademark, etc. —*Idiom.* **4. leave to one's own devices,** to allow to act according to one's inclination.

dev•il (dev′əl), *n., v.,* **-iled, -il•ing** or (*esp. Brit.*) **-illed, -il•ling.** —*n.* **1. a.** (*sometimes cap.*) the supreme spirit of evil; Satan. **b.** a subordinate evil spirit. **2.** a wicked, cruel person. **3.** a clever or mischievous person. **4.** a person: *the lucky devil.* —*v.t.* **5.** to annoy; harass. **6.** to prepare with hot seasonings: *deviled eggs.* —*Idiom.* **7. let the devil take the hindmost,** to leave the least fortunate persons to suffer adverse consequences: *They ran from the pursuing mob and let the devil take the hindmost.* —*Proverb.* **8. The devil can cite scripture for his own purpose,** Satan will distort anything, even a holy text. [< L < Gk *diábolos* Satan, lit., slanderer] —**dev′il•ish,** *adj.* —**dev′il•ish•ly,** *adv.*

dev′il-may-care′, *adj.* reckless; careless.

dev′il•ment, *n.* mischief; deviltry.

dev′il's ad′vocate, *n.* **1.** a person who advocates an opposing view, as for the sake of argument. **2.** an official of the Roman Catholic Church whose duty is to argue against a proposed beatification or canonization.

dev′il's food′ cake′, *n.* a rich, dark chocolate cake.

dev′il•try (-əl trē) also **-il•ry** (-əl rē), *n., pl.* **-tries** also **-ries. 1.** reckless mischief. **2.** diabolic action; wickedness.

de•vi•ous (dē′vē əs), *adj.* **1.** departing from the most direct way; roundabout. **2.** not straightforward or sincere. —**de′vi•ous•ly,** *adv.* —**de′vi•ous•ness,** *n.*

de•vise (di vīz′), *v.,* **-vised, -vis•ing,** *n.* —*v.t.* **1.** to contrive or create: *to devise a method.* **2.** to bequeath (property) by will. —*v.i.* **3.** to form a plan. —*n.* **4.** a bequest of real property.

de•vi•tal•ize (dē vīt′l īz′), *v.t.,* **-ized, -iz•ing.** to deprive of vitality.

de•void (di void′), *adj.* totally lacking; destitute: *devoid of humor.*

de•volve (di volv′), v.t., v.i., -volved, -volv•ing. to pass or be passed on from one to another, as a responsibility.

de•vote (di vōt′), v.t., -vot•ed, -vot•ing. 1. to give up or apply to a particular pursuit, purpose, cause, etc.: to devote one's time to study. 2. to dedicate solemnly; consecrate.

de•vot′ed, adj. zealous in loyalty or affection. —de•vot′ed•ly, adv.

dev•o•tee (dev′ə tē′, -tā′), n., pl. -tees. a person who is greatly devoted to something; enthusiast.

de•vo•tion (di vō′shən), n. 1. earnest attachment to a cause, person, etc. 2. profound dedication, esp. to religion. 3. the act of devoting. 4. Often, -tions. religious observances; special prayers. —de•vo′tion•al, adj.

de•vour (di vour′), v.t. 1. to eat up hungrily. 2. to consume destructively; demolish. 3. to take in greedily with the senses or intellect.

de•vout (di vout′), adj., -er, -est. 1. devoted to divine worship; pious. 2. expressing piety. 3. earnest; fervent. —de•vout′ly, adv.

dew (dōō, dyōō), n. 1. moisture condensed from the atmosphere, esp. at night, and deposited in small drops on a cool surface. 2. something compared to dew, as in purity. —dew′y, adj., -i•er, -i•est.

dew′ber′ry (-ber′ē, -bə rē), n., pl. -ries. 1. the fruit of any of several trailing blackberries. 2. any of these plants.

dew′claw′, n. a functionless claw on some dogs that does not reach the ground in walking.

dew′drop′, n. a drop of dew.

Dew•ey (dōō′ē, dyōō′ē), n. 1. **George,** 1837–1917, U.S. admiral during the Spanish-American War. 2. **John,** 1859–1952, U.S. philosopher and educator. 3. **Mel•vil** (mel′vil), (Melville Louis Kossuth Dewey), 1851–1931, U.S. educator and innovator in library science.

dew′lap′, n. a pendulous fold of skin under the throat, esp. of a bovine animal.

dew′ point′, n. the temperature at which moisture in the air condenses and dew begins to form.

dex•ter•i•ty (dek ster′i tē), n. skill or adroitness in using the hands, body, or mind.

dex′ter•ous (-strəs, -stər əs), adj. 1. possessing dexterity. 2. done with dexterity.

dex•trose (dek′strōs), n. a form of glucose occurring in fruits and in animal tissues.

Dha•ka (dak′ə, dä′kə), n. the capital of Bangladesh. 3,440,147.

dhar•ma (där′mə, dur′-), n. 1. (in Hinduism and Buddhism) a. conformity to religious law, custom, duty, or to one's own character. b. the essential nature of the universe or one's own character. 2. the doctrine or teaching of the Buddha. —dhar′mic, adj.

DHEA, dehydroepiandrosterone: a steroid hormone naturally produced by the adrenal glands and sold in synthetic form as a nutritional supplement.

dho•ti (dō′tē), n., pl. -tis. a loincloth worn by many Hindu men.

di-¹, a combining form meaning two or double (dicotyledon).

di-², var. of DIS-.

di•a•be•tes (dī′ə bē′tis, -tēz), n. any of several disorders characterized by high levels of glucose in the blood and urine. —di′a•bet′ic (-bet′ik), adj., n.

di•a•bol•ic (dī′ə bol′ik) also -i•cal, adj. devilish; fiendish. —di′a•bol/i•cal•ly, adv.

di•a•crit•ic (dī′ə krit′ik), n. 1. Also called diacrit′ical mark′. a mark, as a circumflex, added to a letter to give it a particular phonetic value. —adj. Also, di′a•crit/i•cal. 2. serving to distinguish.

di•a•dem (dī′ə dem′), n. a crown or headband worn as a symbol of royalty.

di•ag•nose (dī′əg nōs′, -nōz′), v., -nosed, -nos•ing. —v.t., v.i. to make a diagnosis (of).

di′ag•no′sis (-nō′sis), n., pl. -ses (-sēz). 1. a. the process of determining by medical examination the nature of a diseased condition. b. the decision reached. 2. an analysis of the cause or nature of any

problem. —di′ag•nos′tic (-nos′tik), adj. —di′ag•nos•ti′cian (-no stish′ən), n.

di•ag•o•nal (dī ag′ə nl), adj. 1. connecting two nonadjacent corners of a polygon or polyhedron: a diagonal line. 2. having an oblique direction. 3. having oblique lines or markings. —n. 4. a diagonal line or plane. —di•ag′o•nal•ly, adv.

di•a•gram (dī′ə gram′), n., v., -gramed or -grammed, -gram•ing or -gram•ming. —n. 1. a drawing, chart, or plan that outlines and explains something. —v.t. 2. to make a diagram of.

di•al (dī′əl, dīl), n., v., -aled, -al•ing or (esp. Brit.) -alled, -al•ling. —n. 1. a marked plate or disk for indicating time, direction, or amount. 2. a knob or plate on a radio or television for tuning in stations. 3. a rotatable disk on a telephone, used in making calls. —v.t. 4. to indicate or measure on or as if on a dial. 5. to make a telephone call to. —v.i. 6. to use a dial. —di′al•er, n.

di•a•lect (dī′ə lekt′), n. a variety of a language used by a group of speakers set off from others geographically or socially. —di′a•lec′tal, adj.

di′a•lec′tic, adj. Also, **di′a•lec′ti•cal.** 1. pertaining to or of the nature of logical argumentation. —n. 2. Often, -tics. the art or practice of debate or conversation by which the truth of a theory or opinion is arrived at logically.

di•a•logue or -log (dī′ə lôg′, -log′), n. 1. conversation between two or more persons. 2. the conversation between characters in a novel, drama, etc. 3. an exchange of ideas or opinions.

di•al•y•sis (dī al′ə sis), n., pl. -ses (-sēz′). 1. the separation of soluble substances from colloids in a solution by diffusion through a membrane. 2. (in kidney disease) this process used to remove waste products from the blood.

di•am•e•ter (dī am′i tər), n. 1. a straight line passing through the center of a circle or sphere and meeting the circumference or surface at each end. 2. the length of such a line. 3. the width of a circular or cylindrical object.

di′a•met′ri•cal (-ə me′tri kəl) also -met′ric, adj. directly opposite: diametrical opinions. —di′a•met′ri•cal•ly, adv.

dia•mond (dī′mənd, dī′ə-), n. 1. an extremely hard form of crystallized carbon. 2. a piece of this substance, valued as a precious gem or used in a cutting tool. 3. an equilateral figure having two acute and two obtuse angles. 4. any of a suit of playing cards bearing diamond-shaped figures. 5. the infield or the entire playing field in baseball. —adj. 6. made of or like diamonds. 7. indicating the 60th or 75th year, as a wedding anniversary.

dia′mond•back′, n. a large venomous rattlesnake with diamond-shaped markings on the back.

di•a•pa•son (dī′ə pā′zən, -sən), n. 1. a rich outpouring of melodious sound. 2. an organ stop extending through the range of the instrument.

dia•per (dī′pər, dī′ə pər), n. 1. a piece of cloth or other absorbent material worn as underpants by a baby not yet toilet-trained. —v.t. 2. to put a diaper on.

di•aph•a•nous (dī af′ə nəs), adj. very sheer and light; nearly transparent.

di•a•phragm (dī′ə fram′), n. 1. the muscular wall separating the chest and abdominal cavities. 2. a disk that vibrates when receiving or producing sound waves, as in a telephone. 3. a contraceptive device that fits over the uterine cervix. 4. a plate used to control the amount of light entering an optical instrument. —di′a•phrag•mat′ic (-frag mat′ik), adj.

di•ar•rhe•a or -rhoe•a (dī′ə rē′ə), n. an intestinal disorder characterized by frequent and fluid bowel movements.

di•a•ry (dī′ə rē), n., pl. -ries. 1. a daily written record of one's experiences and feelings. 2. a book for noting daily appointments. —di′a•rist, n.

Di•as•po•ra (dī as′pər ə), n. 1. the scattering of the Jews to countries outside of Palestine after the Babylonian captivity. 2. (often l.c.) the body of Jews living in countries outside Palestine. 3. (l.c.) any group migration from a region; dispersion. **4.** (*l.c.*) any group that has been dispersed outside its traditional homeland. [< Gk *diasporá* a dispersion]

di•as•to•le (dī as′tl ē′), *n.* the normal rhythmical expansion of the heart during which the chambers are filling with blood. —**di′as•tol′ic** (-ə stol′ik), *adj.*

di•a•tom (dī′ə təm, -tom′), *n.* any of numerous one-celled algae enclosed in a double shell of silica.

di•a•tom•ic (dī′ə tom′ik), *adj.* having two atoms in the molecule.

di•a•ton•ic (dī′ə ton′ik), *adj.* of or noting a major or minor musical scale containing five whole tones and two semitones.

di•a•tribe (dī′ə trīb′), *n.* a bitter, abusive denunciation or criticism.

dib•ble (dib′əl), *n.* a pointed implement for making holes in soil, as for planting seedlings and bulbs.

dice (dīs), *n.pl.*, *sing.* **die,** *v.*, **diced, dic•ing.** —*n.* **1.** small cubes, marked on each side with one to six spots, used in games or gambling. **2.** a game played with dice. —*v.t.* **3.** to cut into small cubes. —*v.i.* **4.** to play at dice.

di•chot•o•my (dī kot′ə mē), *n.*, *pl.* **-mies. 1.** division into halves or pairs. **2.** division into two opposed or contradictory groups. —**di•chot′o•mous,** *adj.*

dick (dik), *n.* Slang. DETECTIVE.

Dick•ens (dik′inz), *n.* **Charles** (*"Boz"*), 1812–70, English novelist. —**Dick•en•si•an** (di ken′zē ən), *adj.*

dick•er (dik′ər), *v.i.* to bargain; haggle.

dick•ey or **dick•y** (dik′ē), *n.*, *pl.* **-eys** or **-ies. 1.** a garment that resembles the front of a shirt and is inserted under a jacket, dress, etc. **2.** a small bird.

Dick•in•son (dik′in sən), *n.* **Emily (Elizabeth),** 1830–86, U.S. poet.

di•cot•y•le•don (dī kot′l ēd′n, dī′kot l-), *n.* a flowering plant having two embryonic seed leaves. —**di•cot′y•le′don•ous,** *adj.*

Dic•ta•phone (dik′tə fōn′), *Trademark.* a brand name for a machine that records and plays back dictated speech.

dic•tate (*v.* dik′tāt, dik tāt′; *n.* dik′tāt), *v.*, **-tat•ed, -tat•ing.** —*v.t.* **1.** to say or read aloud (something) for a person to transcribe or for a machine to record. **2.** to command authoritatively. —*n.* **3.** an authoritative order or command. —**dic•ta′tion,** *n.*

dic′ta•tor, *n.* a ruler or tyrant exercising absolute power. —**dic′ta•to′ri•al** (-tə tôr′ē əl), *adj.* —**dic•ta′tor•ship′,** *n.*

dic•tion (dik′shən), *n.* **1.** style of speaking or writing as dependent upon choice of words. **2.** enunciation or delivery.

dic•tion•ar•y (dik′shə ner′ē), *n.*, *pl.* **-ar•ies. 1.** a book containing a selection of the words of a language, usu. arranged alphabetically, with information about their meanings, pronunciations, etc. **2.** a book giving information on particular subjects or on a particular class of words, usu. arranged alphabetically: *a biographical dictionary.* **3.** a list of words used by a word-processing program to check spellings in text.

dic•tum (dik′təm), *n.*, *pl.* **-ta** (-tə), **-tums. 1.** an authoritative pronouncement. **2.** a saying; maxim.

did (did), *v.* pt. of DO[1].

di•dac•tic (dī dak′tik), *adj.* **1.** intended for instruction. **2.** moralizing or preaching.

did•dle (did′l), *v.t., v.i.,* **-dled, -dling.** *Informal.* **1.** to cheat. **2.** to waste time. —**did′dler,** *n.*

di•do (dī′dō), *n.*, *pl.* **-dos, -does.** a mischievous trick; prank.

Did•y•mus (did′ə məs), *n.* the apostle Thomas. John 11:16; 20:24; 21:2.

die[1] (dī), *v.i.,* **died, dy•ing. 1.** to cease to live. **2.** to cease to exist. **3.** to lose force, strength, or activity. **4.** to cease to function. **5.** to suffer: *I'm dying of boredom!* **6.** to desire keenly: *I'm dying for coffee.* **7. die off,** to die one after another until the number is greatly reduced. **8. ~ out,** to cease to exist. —**Idiom. 9. die hard,** to give way or cease to exist only slowly or after a bitter struggle: *Childhood be-*

liefs die hard. **10. to die for,** stunning; remarkable: *That dress is to die for.*

die[2] (dī), *n.*, *pl.* **dies** for 1, 2; **dice** for 3. **1.** a device for cutting or forming material in a press or a stamping machine. **2.** an engraved stamp for impressing a design upon some softer material, as in coining money. **3.** sing. of DICE.

die′-hard′ or **die′hard′,** *n.* a person who vigorously resists change.

di•e•lec•tric (dī′i lek′trik), *n.* a nonconductor of electricity; insulator.

Dien Bien Phu (dyen′ byen′ fōō′), *n.* a town in NW Vietnam: site of defeat of French forces by Vietminh 1954.

di•er•e•sis (dī er′ə sis), *n.*, *pl.* **-ses** (-sēz′). a sign (¨) placed over the second of two adjacent vowels to indicate that it is to be pronounced separately.

die•sel (dē′zəl, -səl), *n.* a vehicle powered by a diesel engine. [after R. *Diesel* (1858–1913), German automotive engineer]

die′sel en′gine, *n.* an internal-combustion engine in which fuel oil is ignited by heat produced by air compression.

di•et[1] (dī′it), *n.* **1.** food and drink considered in terms of composition and effects on health. **2.** a particular selection of food, as for losing weight. **3.** anything habitually partaken of. —*v.i., v.t.* **4.** to go or put on a diet. —**di′e•tar•y** (-i ter′ē), *adj.* —**di′et•er,** *n.*

di•et[2] (dī′it), *n.* the legislative body of certain countries.

di′etary law′, *n. Judaism.* any of the laws dealing with permitted foods, food preparation and combinations, and the utensils and dishes coming into contact with food. Compare KASHRUTH.

di•e•tet′ic (-i tet′ik), *adj.* **1.** pertaining to diet. **2.** suitable for special diets, as those requiring a restricted caloric intake. —*n.* **3. dietetics,** the science concerned with nutrition and food preparation.

di•e•ti′tian or **-cian** (dī′i tish′ən), *n.* a person who is an expert in nutrition or dietetics.

dif•fer (dif′ər), *v.i.* **1.** to be unlike or dissimilar. **2.** to disagree in opinion.

dif•fer•ence (dif′ər əns, dif′rəns), *n.* **1.** the state, relation, or degree of being different. **2.** an instance of dissimilarity. **3.** a change from a previous state. **4.** a distinguishing characteristic. **5.** a disagreement or dispute. **6.** the amount by which one quantity is greater or less than another.

dif•fer•ent, *adj.* **1.** not alike in character or quality; dissimilar. **2.** not identical; distinct. **3.** various; several. **4.** not ordinary. —**dif′fer•ent•ly,** *adv.* —**Usage.** Although it is frequently claimed that DIFFERENT should be followed only by *from,* not by *than,* in actual usage both alternatives have occurred for at least 300 years and are standard in all varieties of spoken and written American English.

dif′fer•en′tial (-ren′shəl), *adj.* **1.** of, constituting, or exhibiting a difference. —*n.* **2.** an amount of difference, as in rate, cost, or quality, between comparable things. **3.** DIFFERENTIAL GEAR.

dif′feren′tial gear′, *n.* a train of gears designed to permit two or more shafts to revolve at different speeds.

dif′fer•en′ti•ate′ (-shē āt′), *v.,* **-at•ed, -at•ing.** —*v.t.* **1.** to form or mark differently from other such things; distinguish. **2.** to perceive the difference in or between. —*v.i.* **3.** to become unlike or dissimilar; become distinct. **4.** to make a distinction. —**dif′fer•en′ti•a′tion,** *n.* —**dif′fer•en′ti•a′tor,** *n.*

dif•fi•cult (dif′i kult′, -kəlt), *adj.* **1.** requiring special effort or skill; hard. **2.** hard to understand or solve. **3.** hard to deal with or satisfy. **4.** fraught with hardship. —**dif′fi•cult′ly,** *adv.*

dif′fi•cul′ty, *n.*, *pl.* **-ties. 1.** the fact or condition of being difficult. **2.** an embarrassing situation, esp. of financial affairs. **3.** a trouble or struggle. **4.** a disagreement or dispute. **5.** an impediment; obstacle.

dif•fi•dent (dif′i dənt), *adj.* lacking confidence in oneself; timid; shy. —**dif′fi•dence,** *n.*

dif•frac•tion (di frak′shən), *n.* a modulation of

waves, as of sound or light, in response to an obstacle in their path.

dif•fuse (v. di fyo͞oz'; adj. -fyo͞os'), v., **-fused, -fusing,** adj. —v.t., v.i. **1.** to pour out and spread. **2.** to scatter widely or thinly. —adj. **3.** discursive or wordy. **4.** widely spread or scattered. —**dif•fuse'ly** (-fyo͞os'lē), adv. —**dif•fuse'ness,** n. —**dif•fu'sion,** n. —**dif•fu'sive** (-siv), adj.

dig¹ (dig), v., **dug, dig•ging,** n. —v.i. **1.** to break up, turn over, or remove earth, sand, etc. **2.** to make one's way by removing or turning over material. —v.t. **3.** to break up, turn over, or loosen (earth, sand, etc.). **4.** to form or excavate by removing material. **5.** to unearth or obtain by digging. **6.** to find or discover by effort or search. **7. dig in,** a. to maintain one's opinion or position. **b.** Informal. to start eating. —n. **8.** a thrust; poke. **9.** a sarcastic remark. **10.** an archaeological excavation. **11. digs,** Informal. living quarters. —**dig'ger,** n.

dig² (dig), v., **dug, dig•ging.** Slang. —v.t. **1.** to understand. **2.** to take notice of. **3.** to like.

dig•e•ra•ti (dij'ə rä'tē, -ra'-), n.pl. people skilled with or knowledgeable about computers. [dig(ital) + (lit)erati]

di•gest (v. di jest', dī-; n. dī'jest), v.t. **1.** to convert (food) in the alimentary canal into a form that can be assimilated by the body. **2.** to assimilate mentally. **3.** to abridge or summarize. —v.i. **4.** to undergo digestion. —n. **5.** a collection or compendium, esp. when classified or condensed. —**di•gest'i•ble,** adj. —**di•ges'tion,** n. —**di•ges'tive,** adj.

dig•it (dij'it), n. **1.** any of the Arabic numerals of 1 through 9 and 0. **2.** a finger or toe.

dig'it•al (-i tl), adj. **1.** of or resembling a digit or finger. **2.** of or using data in the form of numerical digits. **3.** displaying the time by numerical digits rather than by hands on a dial: *a digital clock.* **4.** readable and manipulable by computer. —**dig'it•al•ly,** adv.

dig'ital au'diotape, n. magnetic tape on which sound is digitally recorded with high fidelity for playback.

dig'ital comput'er, n. a computer that processes information in digital form.

dig•i•tal•is (dij'i tal'is, -tā'lis), n. the dried leaves of the foxglove, used as a heart stimulant.

dig•ni•fied (dig'nə fīd'), adj. characterized by dignity of aspect or manner.

dig'ni•fy', v.t., **-fied, -fy•ing.** to confer honor or dignity upon.

dig'ni•tar'y (-ter'ē), n., pl. **-tar•ies.** a person who holds a high rank or office.

dig'ni•ty, n., pl. **-ties. 1.** bearing, conduct, or manner indicative of self-respect, formality, or gravity. **2.** nobility or elevation of character; worthiness. **3.** elevated rank, office, station, etc.

di•graph (dī'graf, -gräf), n. a pair of letters representing a single speech sound, as *th* in *path*.

di•gress (di gres', dī-), v.i. to wander away from the main topic or argument in speaking or writing. —**di•gres'sion,** n. —**di•gres'sive,** adj.

dike (dīk), n. an embankment for controlling or holding back the waters of the sea or a river.

di•lap•i•dat•ed (di lap'i dā'tid), adj. fallen into partial ruin or decay. —**di•lap'i•da'tion,** n.

di•late (dī lāt'), v., **-lat•ed, -lat•ing.** —v.t. **1.** to make wider or larger. —v.i. **2.** to speak or write at length (often fol. by *on* or *upon*). —**di•la'tion,** n.

dil•a•to•ry (dil'ə tôr'ē), adj. **1.** tending to delay or procrastinate. **2.** intended to cause delay.

di•lem•ma (di lem'ə), n., pl. **-mas. 1.** a situation requiring a choice between equally undesirable alternatives. **2.** any perplexing problem.

dil•et•tante (dil'i tänt', dil'i tänt', -tän'tā, -tan'tē), n., pl. **-tantes, -tan•ti** (-tän'tē). a person who takes up an art, activity, or subject for amusement, esp. in a superficial way; dabbler. —**dil'et•tant'ism,** n.

dil•i•gent (dil'i jənt), adj. **1.** constant and earnest in effort and application. **2.** done painstakingly. —**dil'i•gence,** n. —**dil'i•gent•ly,** adv.

dill (dil), n. a plant of the parsley family, having aromatic seeds and leaves used as a flavoring.

dil•ly (dil'ē), n., pl. **-lies.** Informal. one regarded as remarkable or unusual.

dil•ly•dal•ly (dil'ē dal'ē), v.i., **-lied, -ly•ing.** to waste time, esp. by indecision.

di•lute (di lo͞ot', dī-), v., **-lut•ed, -lut•ing,** adj. —v.t. **1.** to make (a liquid) thinner or weaker by the addition of water or the like. **2.** to reduce the strength of by admixture. —adj. **3.** reduced in strength; weak. —**di•lu'tion,** n.

dim (dim), adj., **dim•mer, dim•mest,** v., **dimmed, dim•ming.** —adj. **1.** not bright; obscure from insufficient light. **2.** indistinct or faint. **3.** not clear to the mind; vague. **4.** dull in luster. **5.** not seeing clearly. **6.** unlikely to occur. **7.** stupid; dim-witted. —v.t., v.i. **8.** to make or become dim or dimmer. —**Idiom. 9. take a dim view of,** to regard with disapproval or skepticism. —**dim'ly,** adv. —**dim'ness,** n.

dim., 1. dimension. **2.** diminish. **3.** diminuendo. **4.** diminutive.

Di•Mag•gi•o (də mä'jē ō', -maj'ē ō'), n. **Joseph Paul** (*Joe*), born 1914, U.S. baseball player.

dime (dīm), n. a coin of the U.S. and Canada worth 10 cents.

di•men•sion (di men'shən, dī-), n. **1.** a property of space; extension in a given direction. **2.** Usu., **-sions. a.** measurement in length, width, and thickness. **b.** scope; extent. —**di•men'sion•al,** adj.

dime' store', n. FIVE-AND-TEN.

di•min•ish (di min'ish), v.t., v.i. to make or become smaller, less, or less important. —**di•min•i•nu•tion** (dim'ə no͞o'shən, -nyo͞o'-), n.

di•min•u•en•do (di min'yo͞o en'dō), adj., adv. Music. gradually reducing in force or loudness.

di•min•u•tive (di min'yə tiv), adj. **1.** much smaller than the average or usual; tiny. **2.** denoting smallness, familiarity, affection, or triviality, as the suffix *-let* in *droplet.* —n. **3.** a diminutive word or element.

dim•i•ty (dim'i tē), n., pl. **-ties.** a thin cotton fabric woven with a stripe or check of heavier yarn.

dim'mer, n. a rheostat or similar device by which the intensity of an electric light may be varied.

dim•ple (dim'pəl), n., v., **-pled, -pling.** —n. **1.** a small natural hollow on the surface of the human body, esp. one formed in the cheek when smiling. —v.t., v.i. **2.** to mark with or show a dimple. —**dim'ply,** adj.

dim'wit', n. Slang. a stupid person. —**dim'wit'ted,** adj.

din (din), n., v., **dinned, din•ning.** —n. **1.** a loud, confused noise. —v.t. **2.** to assail with a din. **3.** to utter with noisy repetition.

Di•nah (dī'nə), n. the daughter of Jacob and Leah. Gen. 30:21.

di•nar (di när'), n. **1.** the basic monetary unit of Algeria, Bahrain, Iraq, Jordan, Kuwait, Libya, Sudan, Tunisia, and Yugoslavia. **2.** a monetary unit of Iran, equal to 1/100 of a rial.

dine (dīn), v., **dined, din•ing,** —v.i. **1.** to have dinner. **2.** to eat any meal. —v.t. **3.** to entertain at or provide with dinner.

din'er, n. **1.** a person who dines. **2.** a railroad dining car. **3.** a restaurant shaped like such a car.

di•nette' (-net'), n. a space or alcove serving as a dining area.

ding (ding), n. a ringing sound, as of a bell.

din•ghy (ding'gē), n., pl. **-ghies.** any small boat, esp. a lifeboat. [< Hindi *diṅgī,* dim. of *ḍiṅgā* boat]

din•gle (ding'gəl), n. a wooded valley; dell.

din•go (ding'gō), n., pl. **-goes.** an Australian wild dog.

ding•us (ding'əs), n., pl. **-us•es.** Informal. a gadget or device, whose name is unknown or forgotten.

din•gy (din'jē), adj., **-gi•er, -gi•est. 1.** of a dark, dull, or dirty color. **2.** shabby; dismal. —**din'gi•ness,** n.

dink•y (ding'kē), adj., **-i•er, -i•est.** Informal. small and unimpressive.

din•ner (din'ər), n. **1.** the main meal of the day. **2.** a formal meal in honor of some person or occasion.

din·ner jack·et, *n.* a tuxedo jacket.

din·ner·ware, *n.* china, glasses, and silver used for table service.

di·no·saur (dī′nə sôr′), *n.* **1.** any of various extinct, prehistoric reptiles, some of which were huge. **2.** something that is unwieldy in size, anachronistically outmoded, or unable to adapt to change. [< NL < Gk *deino-* terrible + *saúros* lizard]

dinosaur

dint (dint), *n.* **1.** force; power: *by dint of hard work.* **2.** a dent.

di·o·cese (dī′ə sis, -sēz′, -sēs′), *n.* a district under the jurisdiction of a bishop. —**di·oc′e·san** (-os′ə-sən), *adj.*

Di·o·cle·tian (dī′ə klē′shən), *n.* (*Gaius Aurelius Valerius Diocletianus*), A.D. 245–316, emperor of Rome 284–305.

di·ode (dī′ōd), *n.* a device, as a two-element electron tube or a semiconductor, through which current can pass in only one direction.

Di·og·e·nes (dī oj′ə nēz′), *n.* 412?–323 B.C., Greek philosopher.

Di·o·ny·sus (dī′ə nī′səs), *n.* an ancient Greek and Roman fertility god, associated esp. with wine and with drama.

di·o·ram·a (dī′ə ram′ə, -rä′mə), *n.*, *pl.* -**ram·as.** a scene in miniature reproduced in three dimensions against a painted background.

di·ox·in (dī ok′sin), *n.* a hydrocarbon that is a toxic by-product of pesticide manufacture.

dip (dip), *v.*, **dipped, dip·ping,** *n.* —*v.t.* **1.** to plunge briefly into a liquid. **2.** to take up by bailing or ladling. **3.** to lower and raise: *to dip a flag in salute.* —*v.i.* **4.** to plunge into a liquid and emerge quickly. **5.** to reach into a container so as to remove something. **6.** to withdraw something in small amounts: *to dip into savings.* **7.** to sink or drop suddenly. **8.** to incline downward. **9.** to look into a subject or book casually or superficially. —*n.* **10.** the act of dipping. **11.** something taken up by dipping. **12.** a substance into which something is dipped. **13.** a creamy mixture of foods for scooping with a cracker, potato chip, etc. **14.** a drop or decline. **15.** a downward slope or course. **16.** a brief swim.

diph·the·ri·a (dif thēr′ē ə, dip-), *n.* an infectious disease marked by high fever and breathing difficulty.

diph·thong (dif′thông, -thong, dip′-), *n.* a gliding speech sound varying continuously in phonetic quality but considered to be a single sound, as *oi* in *boil.*

dip·loid (dip′loid), *adj.* having two similar complements of chromosomes.

di·plo·ma (di plō′mə), *n.*, *pl.* -**mas.** a document given by an educational institution conferring a degree or certifying the successful completion of a course of study.

di·plo·ma·cy (di plō′mə sē), *n.* **1.** the conduct by government officials of negotiations and other relations between nations. **2.** tactful dealing with others.

dip·lo·mat (dip′lə mat′), *n.* **1.** a person appointed by a government to conduct relations with other governments. **2.** a tactful person.

dip′lo·mat′ic, *adj.* **1.** of or engaged in diplomacy. **2.** tactful or suave. —**dip′lo·mat′i·cal·ly,** *adv.*

di·pole (dī′pōl), *n.* an antenna of a transmitter or

receiver consisting of two equal rods extending in opposite directions.

dip′per, *n.* **1.** a cuplike container with a long handle, used for dipping. **2.** (*cap.*) **a.** Also called **Big Dipper.** seven bright stars in Ursa Major resembling a dipper. **b.** Also called **Little Dipper.** a similar constellation in Ursa Minor.

dip·so·ma·ni·a (dip′sə mā′nē ə, -sō-), *n.* an irresistible, typically periodic craving for alcoholic drink. —**dip′so·ma′ni·ac′,** *n.*

dip′stick′, *n.* a rod for measuring the depth of a liquid.

dip·ter·ous (dip′tər əs), *adj.* having two wings, as a fly, or two winglike parts, as certain seeds.

dip·tych (dip′tik), *n.* a pair of pictures on two panels, usu. hinged together.

dire (dīʳr), *adj.*, **dir·er, dir·est. 1.** causing or involving great fear or suffering. **2.** indicating trouble or disaster. **3.** urgent; desperate. —**dire′ly,** *adv.*

di·rect (di rekt′, dī-), *v.t.* **1.** to manage or guide by advice, instruction, etc. **2.** to command or order. **3.** to serve as director of (a play, motion picture, etc.). **4.** to show (a person) the way. **5.** to aim or send toward a place or object: *to direct one's aim.* **6.** to address (words, a speech, etc.) to a person or persons. **7.** to address (a letter, package, etc.). —*v.i.* **8.** to give guidance or orders. **9.** to serve as a director. —*adj.* **10.** proceeding in a straight line. **11.** proceeding in an unbroken line of descent. **12.** without intermediary agents, conditions, etc. **13.** straightforward; frank. **14.** absolute; exact: *the direct opposite.* **15.** consisting of the exact words of a speaker: *a direct quote.* —*adv.* **16.** in a direct manner. —**di·rect′ness,** *n.*

direct′ cur′rent, *n.* an electric current flowing continuously in one direction.

di·rec′tion, *n.* **1.** an act or instance of directing. **2.** the line along which anything lies, faces, moves, etc., with reference to the point or region toward which it is directed. **3.** a tendency or inclination. **4.** Usu., **-tions.** instruction or guidance for making, using, etc. **5.** an order; command. **6.** management; supervision. —**di·rec′tion·al,** *adj.*

di·rec′tive, *adj.* **1.** serving to direct; directing. —*n.* **2.** an authoritative instruction or direction; specific order.

di·rect′ly, *adv.* **1.** in a direct line, way, or manner. **2.** at once; without delay. **3.** from one to another; with nothing between. **4.** exactly; precisely.

direct′ ob′ject, *n.* a word or words representing the person or thing upon which the action of a verb is performed, as *it* in *I saw it.*

di·rec′tor, *n.* **1.** one that directs. **2.** one of a group of persons chosen to govern the affairs of a company. **3.** the person who guides the performers in a play, motion picture, etc. —**di·rec′tor·ship′,** *n.*

di·rec′to·rate (-tər it), *n.* **1.** the office of a director. **2.** a body of directors.

di·rec′to·ry, *n.*, *pl.* -**ries. 1.** an alphabetical listing of the names and addresses of persons in an area, organization, etc. **2. a.** a division in a hierarchical structure that organizes the storage of computer files on a disk. **b.** a listing of such files.

dirge (dûrj), *n.* a song or poem in commemoration of the dead.

dir·i·gi·ble (dir′i jə bəl, di rij′ə-), *n.* AIRSHIP.

dirk (dûrk), *n.* a dagger, esp. of the Scottish Highlands.

dirn·dl (dûrn′dl), *n.* a dress with a close-fitting bodice and full skirt.

dirt (dûrt), *n.* **1.** any foul or filthy substance, as mud or grime. **2.** earth or soil. **3.** moral filth; vileness. **4.** obscene language. **5.** gossip, esp. of a malicious nature.

dirt′-cheap′, *adj.* **1.** very cheap. —*adv.* **2.** very cheaply.

dirt′y, *adj.*, -**i·er,** -**i·est,** *v.*, -**ied,** -**y·ing.** —*adj.* **1.** soiled or soiling with dirt. **2.** vile; contemptible. **3.** obscene; lewd. **4.** undesirable or unpleasant: *dirty work.* **5.** not fair; dishonest. **6.** hostile or resentful: *a* *dirty look.* **7.** (of the weather) stormy. —*v.t., v.i.* **8.** to make or become dirty. —**dirt′i•ness,** *n.*

dis (dis), *v.,* **dissed, dis•sing,** *n. Slang.* —*v.t.* **1.** to show disrespect for. **2.** to disparage. —*n.* **3.** disparagement or criticism.

dis-, a prefix meaning: reversal (*disconnect*); negation or lack (*distrust*); removal or separation (*disbar*).

dis•a•bil•i•ty (dis′ə bil′i tē), *n., pl.* **-ties. 1.** anything that disables or disqualifies, as a physical or mental handicap. **2.** the condition of being disabled.

dis•a′ble (-ā′bəl), *v.t.,* **-bled, -bling. 1.** to make unable or unfit; incapacitate. **2.** to disqualify legally.

dis•a′bled, *adj.* handicapped; incapacitated.

dis•a•buse′ (-byōoz′), *v.t.,* **-bused, -bus•ing.** to free from deception or error.

dis′ad•van′tage, *n.* **1.** an unfavorable circumstance or condition; handicap. **2.** injury to reputation, credit, etc.; loss. —**dis•ad′van•ta′geous,** *adj.*

dis′ad•van′taged, *adj.* lacking economic and social opportunity.

dis′af•fect′, *v.t.* to make discontented or disloyal. —**dis′af•fec′tion,** *n.*

dis′af•fil′i•ate′ (-āt′), *v.t., v.i.,* **-at•ed, -at•ing.** to sever affiliation (with). —**dis′af•fil′i•a′tion,** *n.*

dis′a•gree′, *v.i.* **1.** to fail to agree; differ. **2.** to differ in opinion. **3.** to quarrel. **4.** to cause physical discomfort or ill effect. —**dis′a•gree′ment,** *n.*

dis′a•gree′a•ble, *adj.* **1.** contrary to one's taste or liking; offensive. **2.** unpleasant; surly; grouchy. —**dis′a•gree′a•bly,** *adv.*

dis′al•low′, *v.t.* to refuse to allow; reject.

dis′ap•pear′, *v.i.* **1.** to cease to be seen. **2.** to cease to exist or be known. —**dis′ap•pear′ance,** *n.*

dis′ap•point′, *v.t.* to fail to fulfill the expectations or wishes of. —**dis′ap•point′ment,** *n.*

dis′ap•pro•ba′tion, *n.* disapproval; condemnation.

dis′ap•prove′, *v.,* **-proved, -prov•ing.** —*v.t.* **1.** to censure or condemn in opinion. **2.** to withhold approval from. —*v.i.* **3.** to have an unfavorable opinion (usu. fol. by *of*). —**dis′ap•prov′al,** *n.* —**dis′ap•prov′ing•ly,** *adv.*

dis•arm′, *v.t.* **1.** to deprive of weapons. **2.** to deprive of the means to attack or defend. **3.** to relieve of hostility; win over. —*v.i.* **4.** (of a country) to reduce armaments or armed forces. —**dis•ar′ma•ment,** *n.*

dis′ar•range′, *v.t.,* **-ranged, -rang•ing.** to disturb the arrangement of; unsettle. —**dis′ar•range′ment,** *n.*

dis′ar•ray′, *v.t.* **1.** to throw into disorder. —*n.* **2.** disorder; confusion.

dis′as•sem′ble, *v.t.,* **-bled, -bling.** to take apart.

dis′as•so′ci•ate′ (-āt′), *v.t.,* **-at•ed, -at•ing.** to dissociate.

dis•as′ter (di zas′tər, -zä′stər), *n.* a calamitous event, esp. one occurring suddenly and causing great damage. —**dis•as′trous,** *adj.* —**dis•as′trous•ly,** *adv.*

dis•a•vow′ (dis′ə vou′), *v.t.* to disclaim knowledge of, connection with, or responsibility for; disown. —**dis′a•vow′al,** *n.*

dis•band′, *v.t., v.i.* to break up or dissolve (an organization).

dis•bar′, *v.t.,* **-barred, -bar•ring.** to expel from the legal profession. —**dis•bar′ment,** *n.*

dis′be•lieve′, *v.t., v.i.,* **-lieved, -liev•ing.** to refuse to believe. —**dis′be•lief′,** *n.*

dis•burse (dis bûrs′), *v.t.,* **-bursed, -burs•ing.** to pay out, esp. for expenses. —**dis•burse′ment,** *n.*

disc (disk), *n.* **1.** a phonograph record. **2.** DISK.

dis•card (*v.* di skärd′; *n.* dis′kärd), *v.t.* **1.** to cast aside or dispose of; get rid of. **2.** to throw out (a playing card) from one's hand. —*v.i.* **3.** to discard a playing card. —*n.* **4.** the act of discarding. **5.** a person or thing discarded.

dis•cern (di sûrn′, -zûrn′), *v.t., v.i.* **1.** to perceive by the sight or the intellect. **2.** to distinguish mentally. —**dis•cern′i•ble,** *adj.* —**dis•cern′ment,** *n.*

dis•charge (*v.* dis chärj′; *n.* dis′chärj, dis chärj′), *v.,*

-charged, -charg•ing, *n.* —*v.t.* **1.** to remove the contents of. **2.** to remove or send forth. **3.** to shoot (a firearm or missile). **4.** to pour forth; emit. **5.** to relieve of obligation or responsibility. **6.** to fulfill the requirements of (a duty, function, etc.). **7.** to dismiss from office or employment. **8.** to release or allow to go. **9.** to pay (a debt). **10.** to rid (a battery, capacitor, etc.) of an electric charge. —*v.i.* **11.** to get rid of a burden or load. **12.** to pour forth. **13.** to go off, as a firearm. —*n.* **14.** the act of discharging a ship, load, etc. **15.** the act of shooting a weapon. **16.** an ejection or emission. **17.** fulfillment of an obligation. **18.** a release or dismissal, as from employment. **19.** the removal of an electric charge, as by the conversion of chemical energy to electrical energy.

dis•ci•ple (di sī′pəl), *n.* **1.** any professed follower of Christ in His lifetime, esp. one of the 12 apostles. **2.** a pupil or an adherent of another; follower.

dis•ci•pli•nar•i•an (dis′ə plə när′ē ən), *n.* a person who enforces or advocates strict discipline.

dis′ci•pline (-plin), *n., v.,* **-plined, -plin•ing.** —*n.* **1.** training to act in accordance with rules. **2.** a regimen that develops or improves a skill. **3.** punishment inflicted by way of correction and training. **4.** behavior in accord with rules of conduct. **5.** a branch of instruction or learning. **6.** a system of rules. —*v.t.* **7.** to train by instruction and exercise. **8.** to bring under control. **9.** to punish. —**dis′ci•pli•nar′y,** *adj.*

disc′ jock′ey, *n.* a person who plays and comments on popular recorded music on a radio program.

dis•claim (dis klām′), *v.t.* **1.** to deny or repudiate interest in or connection with; disavow; disown. **2.** to renounce a claim or right to. —**dis•claim′er,** *n.*

dis•close (di sklōz′), *v.t.,* **-closed, -clos•ing.** to make known; reveal. —**dis•clo′sure** (-klō′zhər), *n.*

dis•co (dis′kō), *n., pl.* **-cos. 1.** a discotheque. **2.** a style of popular music for dancing, having a heavy, rhythmic beat.

dis•col•or (dis kul′ər), *v.t., v.i.* to change color; fade; stain. —**dis•col′or•a′tion,** *n.*

dis•com•bob•u•late (dis′kəm bob′yə lāt′), *v.t.,* **-lat•ed, -lat•ing.** to confuse or disconcert. —**dis′•com•bob′u•la′tion,** *n.*

dis•com•fit (dis kum′fit), *v.t.* **1.** to confuse and deject. **2.** to frustrate; thwart. —**dis•com′fi•ture** (-fi•chər), *n.*

dis•com•fort (dis kum′fərt), *n.* **1.** an absence of comfort or ease; mild pain. **2.** anything that is disturbing to comfort. —*v.t.* **3.** to make uncomfortable or uneasy.

dis•com•mode (dis′kə mōd′), *v.t.,* **-mod•ed, -mod•ing.** to cause inconvenience to.

dis′com•pose′, *v.t.,* **-posed, -pos•ing. 1.** to upset the order of. **2.** to disturb the composure of. —**dis′/com•po′sure,** *n.*

dis•con•cert (dis′kən sûrt′), *v.t.* to disturb the self-possession of; perturb.

dis′con•nect′, *v.t.* **1.** to sever or interrupt the connection of or between. **2.** to withdraw into one's private world. —**dis′con•nec′tion,** *n.*

dis′con•nect′ed, *adj.* **1.** separated; broken. **2.** not coherent.

dis•con•so•late (dis kon′sə lit), *adj.* **1.** without consolation or solace. **2.** cheerless or gloomy. —**dis•con′so•late•ly,** *adv.*

dis′con•tent′ (-kən tent′), *adj.* **1.** not content; discontented. —*n.* **2.** Also, **dis′con•tent′ment.** lack of contentment. —*v.t.* **3.** to make discontent.

dis′con•tent′ed, *adj.* dissatisfied; restlessly unhappy.

dis′con•tin′ue, *v.,* **-tin•ued, -tin•u•ing.** —*v.t.* **1.** to put an end to; stop. **2.** to cease using, taking, etc. —*v.i.* **3.** to come to an end; cease. —**dis′con•tin′u•ance, dis′con•tin′u•a′tion,** *n.* —**dis′con•tin′u•ous,** *adj.*

dis′con•ti•nu′i•ty, *n., pl.* **-ties. 1.** lack of continuity; irregularity. **2.** a break or gap.

dis•cord (dis′kôrd), *n.* **1.** lack of concord or harmony. **2.** difference of opinion. **3.** an inharmonious combination of musical sounds. **4.** any confused or harsh noise. —**dis•cord′ant,** *adj.*

dis•co•theque or **-thèque** (dis/kə tek/, dis/kə-tek/), *n.* a nightclub for dancing to live or recorded music.

dis•count (*v.* dis/kount, dis kount/; *n.* dis/kount), *v.t.* **1.** to deduct an amount from (a bill, charge, etc.). **2.** to sell at a reduced price. **3.** to buy, sell, or lend money on (commercial paper) after deducting interest. **4.** to allow for exaggeration in (a statement, opinion, etc.). **5.** to disregard or minimize. —*n.* **6.** an act or instance of discounting. **7.** an amount deducted from the usual or list price. **8.** a deduction of interest in advance upon a loan of money. —**dis/count•er**, *n.*

dis•coun/te•nance, *v.t.,* **-nanced, -nanc•ing. 1.** to disconcert or embarrass regularly. **2.** to show disapproval of.

dis/count house/, *n.* a store that regularly sells merchandise at less than the usual price. Also called **dis/count store/.**

dis•cour•age (di skûr/ij, -skur/-), *v.t.,* **-aged, -ag•ing. 1.** to deprive of courage or confidence; dishearten. **2.** to dissuade. **3.** to obstruct or hinder. —**dis•cour/age•ment**, *n.* —**dis•cour/ag•ing•ly**, *adv.*

dis•course (*n.* dis/kôrs; *v.* dis kôrs/), *n., v.,* **-coursed, -cours•ing.** —*n.* **1.** communication by words; talk; conversation. **2.** a formal discussion of a subject in speech or writing. —*v.i.* **3.** to talk or converse. **4.** to treat a subject formally in speech or writing.

dis•cour/te•ous, *adj.* not courteous; impolite.

dis•cour/te•sy, *n., pl.* **-sies. 1.** lack of courtesy; rudeness. **2.** a discourteous act.

dis•cov•er (di skuv/ər), *v.t.* **1.** to gain sight or knowledge of for the first time. **2.** to notice or realize. —**dis•cov/er•er**, *n.* —**dis•cov/er•y**, *n., pl.* **-er•ies.**

dis•cred/it, *v.t.* **1.** to injure the reputation of; defame. **2.** to show to be unreliable. **3.** to disbelieve. —*n.* **4.** loss or lack of belief or confidence. **5.** disgrace; disrepute. —**dis•cred/it•a•ble**, *adj.*

dis•creet (di skrēt/), *adj.* judicious in one's conduct or speech; prudent. —**dis•creet/ly**, *adv.*

dis•crep•an•cy (di skrep/ən sē), *n., pl.* **-cies. 1.** lack of agreement; difference; inconsistency. **2.** an instance of this. —**dis•crep/ant**, *adj.*

dis•crete (di skrēt/), *adj.* **1.** apart or detached from others; distinct. **2.** consisting of distinct parts.

dis•cre•tion (di skresh/ən), *n.* **1.** the power to decide or act according to one's own judgment. **2.** the quality of being discreet; prudence. —**Proverb. 3. Discretion is the better part of valor,** caution should be the first priority. —**dis•cre/tion•ar•y**, *adj.*

dis•crim•i•nate (di skrim/ə nāt/), *v.i.,* **-nat•ed, -nat•ing. 1.** to make a distinction on the basis of a prejudice; show partiality. **2.** to note a difference; distinguish accurately. —**dis•crim/i•nat/ing**, *adj.* —**dis•crim/i•na/tion**, *n.* —**dis•crim/i•na•tor/y** (-nə-tôr/ē), *adj.*

dis•cur•sive (di skûr/siv), *adj.* passing aimlessly from one subject to another; digressive.

dis•cus (dis/kəs), *n.* a circular disk, usu. wooden with a metal rim, for throwing in athletic competition.

dis•cuss (di skus/), *v.t.* to consider or examine by argument, comment, etc.; debate. —**dis•cus/sion**, *n.*

dis•cus/sant, *n.* a participant in a formal discussion or symposium.

dis•dain (dis dān/, di stān/), *v.t.* **1.** to look upon or treat with contempt; scorn. **2.** to think unworthy of notice, response, etc. —*n.* **3.** contempt; scorn. —**dis•dain/ful**, *adj.*

dis•ease (di zēz/), *n.* a disordered or abnormal condition of an organ or other part of an organism; illness. —**dis•eased/**, *adj.*

dis•em•bark (dis/em bärk/), *v.t., v.i.* to leave or unload a ship or airplane. —**dis/em•bar•ka/tion**, *n.*

dis/em•bod/y, *v.t.,* **-ied, -y•ing.** to divest of a body or bodily existence. —**dis/em•bod/i•ment**, *n.*

dis•em•bow•el (dis/em bou/əl), *v.t.,* **-eled, -el•ing** or (*esp. Brit.*) **-elled, -el•ling.** to remove the bowels or entrails from; eviscerate.

dis/en•chant/, *v.t.* to free from enchantment, illusion, credulity, etc.; disillusion. —**dis/en•chant/-ment**, *n.*

dis/en•cum/ber, *v.t.* to free from a burden or other encumbrance.

dis/en•gage/, *v.,* **-gaged, -gag•ing.** —*v.t.* **1.** to release from attachment or connection. **2.** to free from an engagement, obligation, etc. —*v.i.* **3.** to become disengaged. —**dis/en•gage/ment**, *n.*

dis/en•tan/gle, *v.t., v.i.,* **-gled, -gling.** to free or become free from entanglement. —**dis/en•tan/gle•ment**, *n.* —**dis/en•tan/gler**, *n.*

dis/es•tab/lish, *v.t.* to withdraw exclusive state support from (a church). —**dis/es•tab/lish•ment**, *n.*

dis•es•teem/, *n.* lack of esteem.

dis•fa/vor, *n.* **1.** unfavorable regard; displeasure; dislike. **2.** the state of being regarded unfavorably.

dis•fig/ure, *v.t.,* **-ured, -ur•ing.** to mar the appearance of; deface. —**dis•fig/ure•ment**, *n.*

dis•fran/chise or **dis/en•fran/chise**, *v.t.,* **-chised, -chis•ing.** to deprive of a right or privilege, esp. the right to vote. —**dis•fran/chise•ment**, *n.*

dis•gorge (dis gôrj/), *v.t.,* **-gorged, -gorg•ing. 1.** to throw up; vomit forth. **2.** to discharge or eject forcefully.

dis•grace (dis grās/), *n., v.,* **-graced, -grac•ing.** —*n.* **1.** loss of respect, honor, or esteem. **2.** a person, act, or thing that causes shame or reproach. —*v.t.* **3.** to bring or reflect shame or reproach upon. —**dis•grace/ful**, *adj.* —**dis•grace/ful•ly**, *adv.*

dis•grun•tle (dis grun/tl), *v.t.,* **-tled, -tling.** to put into a state of sulky dissatisfaction.

dis•guise (dis gīz/, di skīz/), *v.,* **-guised, -guis•ing,** *n.* —*v.t.* **1.** to conceal identity or mislead, as with deceptive garb. **2.** to conceal the truth or actual character of; misrepresent. —*n.* **3.** something that disguises identity, character, or quality; a deceptive covering. **4.** the state of being disguised.

dis•gust (dis gust/, di skust/), *v.t.* **1.** to cause loathing or nausea in. **2.** to offend the good taste, moral sense, etc., of. —*n.* **3.** a strong loathing; repugnance. —**dis•gust/ed**, *adj.* —**dis•gust/ing**, *adj.*

dish (dish), *n.* **1.** an open, shallow container used esp. for holding food. **2.** a particular article or preparation of food. **3.** the quantity held by a dish. **4.** something like a dish in form or use. **5.** Also called **dish/ anten/na.** a dish-shaped reflector, used esp. for receiving satellite and microwave signals. —*v.t.* **6.** to put into or serve in a dish. —*Idiom.* **7. dish out,** *Informal.* to deal out; distribute. [< L *discus* dish]

dis•ha•bille (dis/ə bēl/, -bē/), *n.* the state of being carelessly or partially dressed.

dis•har/mo•ny, *n., pl.* **-nies.** lack of harmony; discord. —**dis/har•mo/ni•ous**, *adj.*

dish/cloth/, *n.* a cloth for washing dishes.

dis•heart/en, *v.t.* to depress the hope, courage, or spirits of; discourage.

di•shev•el (di shev/əl), *v.t.,* **-eled, -el•ing** or (*esp. Brit.*) **-elled, -el•ling.** to let down, as hair, or let hang in loose disorder, as clothing. —**di•shev/el•ment**, *n.*

dis•hon/est, *adj.* **1.** not honest; untrustworthy. **2.** disposed to lie or cheat; fraudulent. —**dis•hon/est•ly**, *adv.* —**dis•hon/es•ty**, *n.*

dis•hon/or, *n.* **1.** lack or loss of honor; disgrace. **2.** a cause of shame or disgrace. —*v.t.* **3.** to deprive of honor; disgrace. **4.** to refuse to pay (a check, draft, etc.). —**dis•hon/or•a•ble**, *adj.*

dish/pan/, *n.* a pan in which dishes, pots, etc., are washed.

dish/rag/, *n.* DISHCLOTH.

dish/tow/el, *n.* a towel for drying dishes.

dish/wash/er, *n.* **1.** a person who washes dishes. **2.** a machine for washing dishes.

dis/il•lu/sion, *v.t.* to free from or deprive of illusion, idealism, etc.; disenchant. —**dis/il•lu/sion•ment**, *n.*

dis/in•cline/, *v.t.,* **-clined, -clin•ing.** to make averse or unwilling.

dis′•in•fect′, *v.t.* to cleanse in order to destroy disease germs. —**dis′in•fect′ant,** *n., adj.*

dis′in•gen′u•ous, *adj.* lacking in candor or sincerity; insincere.

dis′in•her′it, *v.t.* to deprive of an inheritance or heritage.

dis•in′te•grate′, *v.i., v.t.,* **-grat•ed, -grat•ing. 1.** to separate into parts; break up. **2.** (of a nucleus) to decay. —**dis•in′te•gra′tion,** *n.*

dis′in•ter′, *v.t.,* **-terred, -ter•ring.** to take out of the place of interment; unearth. —**dis′in•ter′ment,** *n.*

dis•in′ter•est′ed, *adj.* **1.** unbiased by personal interest. **2.** not interested; indifferent. —**Usage.** There is a consensus among critics that DISINTERESTED should only be used to mean "unbiased, impartial"; only UNINTERESTED can be used to mean "not interested." However, DISINTERESTED is often found, in all levels of English, in the meaning "not interested."

dis•joint′, *v.t.* **1.** to take apart at the joints. **2.** to put out of order; make disconnected. —**dis•joint′ed,** *adj.*

disk (disk), *n.* **1.** any thin, flat, circular plate, object, or surface. **2.** DISC (def. 1). **3.** any of several types of media for storing electronic data consisting of thin round plates of plastic or metal. **4.** a roundish, flat anatomical structure or part.

disk′ drive′, *n.* a device in or attached to a computer that enables the user to read data from or store data on a disk.

disk•ette (di sket′), *n.* FLOPPY DISK.

dis•like′, *v.,* **-liked, -lik•ing,** *n.* —*v.t.* **1.** to regard with displeasure or aversion. —*n.* **2.** a feeling of aversion; antipathy.

dis•lo•cate (dis′lō kāt′, dis lō′kāt), *v.t.,* **-cat•ed, -cat•ing. 1.** to put out of place or order; disrupt. **2.** to put out of joint, as a limb. —**dis′lo•ca′tion,** *n.*

dis•lodge′, *v.t.,* **-lodged, -lodg•ing.** to force out of a place or position.

dis•loy′al, *adj.* not loyal; faithless. —**dis•loy′al•ty,** *n., pl.* **-ties.**

dis•mal (diz′məl), *adj.* **1.** causing gloom or dejection; dreary. **2.** very bad; poor. —**dis′mal•ly,** *adv.*

dis•man•tle (dis man′tl), *v.t.,* **-tled, -tling. 1.** to deprive or strip of furniture, equipment, etc. **2.** to take apart. —**dis•man′tle•ment,** *n.*

dis•may (dis mā′), *v.t.* **1.** to break down the courage of completely; daunt. —*n.* **2.** sudden or complete loss of courage; consternation.

dis•mem′ber (dis mem′bər), *v.t.* **1.** to deprive of limbs. **2.** to divide into parts. —**dis•mem′ber•ment,** *n.*

dis•miss (dis mis′), *v.t.* **1.** to direct or allow to leave. **2.** to discharge from office or service. **3.** to put aside from consideration; reject. **4.** to remove from a court's consideration. —**dis•miss′al,** *n.*

dis•mount′, *v.i.* **1.** to alight, as from a horse. —*v.t.* **2.** to throw down, as from a horse. **3.** to take (a mechanism) apart. **4.** to remove (a thing) from its mounting.

Dis•ney (diz′nē), *n.* **Walt(er E.),** 1901–66, U.S. creator and producer of animated cartoons, motion pictures, etc.

dis•o•be•di•ence (dis′ə bē′dē əns), *n.* lack of obedience or refusal to comply. —**dis′o•be′di•ent,** *adj.*

dis′o•bey′, *v.t., v.i.* to neglect or refuse to obey.

dis′o•blige′, *v.t.,* **-bliged, -blig•ing. 1.** to refuse or neglect to oblige. **2.** to give offense to.

dis•or′der, *n.* **1.** lack of order; confusion. **2.** a public disturbance. **3.** a physical or mental disturbance; illness. —*v.t.* **4.** to destroy the order of. **5.** to upset the physical or mental functions of.

dis•or′der•ly, *adj.* **1.** not tidy or neat. **2.** unruly; tumultuous. **3.** disturbing public order and peace. —**dis•or′der•li•ness,** *n.*

dis•or′gan•ize′, *v.t.,* **-ized, -iz•ing.** to destroy the systematic arrangement of; throw into confusion. —**dis•or′gan•i•za′tion,** *n.*

dis•o′ri•ent′, *v.t.* **1.** to cause to lose one's way. **2.** to confuse mentally. —**dis•o′ri•en•ta′tion,** *n.*

dis•own′, *v.t.* to refuse to acknowledge as belonging to oneself; repudiate.

dis•par•age (di spar′ij), *v.t.,* **-aged, -ag•ing. 1.** to speak of or treat slightingly. **2.** to bring reproach or discredit upon. —**dis•par′age•ment,** *n.* —**dis•par′ag•ing,** *adj.*

dis•pa•rate (dis′pər it, di spar′-), *adj.* distinct in kind; dissimilar. —**dis•par′i•ty,** *n., pl.* **-ties.**

dis•pas′sion•ate, *adj.* devoid of personal feeling or bias; impartial; calm. —**dis•pas′sion•ate•ly,** *adv.*

dis•patch (di spach′), *v.t.* **1.** to send off with speed, as a messenger or telegram. **2.** to put to death. **3.** to dispose of (a matter) promptly. —*n.* **4.** the sending off of a messenger, letter, etc. **5.** a putting to death; execution. **6.** speedy action. **7.** a message sent with speed. **8.** a news story transmitted to a newspaper by a reporter. —**dis•patch′er,** *n.*

dis•pel′ (di spel′), *v.t.,* **-pelled, -pel•ling. 1.** to drive off in various directions; disperse. **2.** to cause to vanish.

dis•pen•sa•ble (di spen′sə bəl), *adj.* **1.** capable of being done without; not necessary. **2.** capable of being dispensed or administered.

dis•pen•sa•ry (di spen′sə rē), *n., pl.* **-ries.** a place where medicines and emergency medical treatment are available.

dis•pen•sa•tion (dis′pən sā′shən, -pen-), *n.* **1.** an act or instance of dispensing. **2.** something dispensed. **3.** a system of administration. **4.** an official exemption from a law or obligation. **5.** the divine ordering of the affairs of the world.

dis•pense (di spens′), *v.t.,* **-pensed, -pens•ing. 1.** to deal out; distribute. **2.** to administer. **3.** to make up and distribute (medicine). **4. dispense with, a.** to do without. **b.** to do away with. —**dis•pens′er,** *n.*

dis•perse (di spûrs′), *v.,* **-persed, -pers•ing.** —*v.t.* **1.** to send off in various directions; scatter. **2.** to spread widely; disseminate. **3.** to dispel; cause to vanish. —*v.i.* **4.** to become scattered. —**dis•per′sal,** **dis•per′sion** (-zhən, -shən), *n.*

dis•pir•it (di spir′it), *v.t.* to deprive of spirit or hope; discourage. —**dis•pir′it•ed,** *adj.*

dis•place′, *v.t.,* **-placed, -plac•ing. 1.** to compel (a person) to leave home, country, etc. **2.** to put out of the usual or proper place. **3.** to take the place of; supplant. **4.** to remove from a position or office.

displaced′ per′son, *n.* a person driven or expelled from his or her homeland by war, tyranny, etc.

dis•place′ment, *n.* **1.** the act of displacing. **2.** the state of being displaced. **3.** the linear or angular distance in a given direction between a body or point and a reference position. **4.** the weight or volume of fluid displaced by a floating or submerged body.

dis•play (di splā′), *v.t.* **1.** to show or exhibit; make visible. —*n.* **2.** an act or instance of displaying. **3. a.** a visual representation of the output of an electronic device. **b.** the portion of the device, as a screen, that shows this representation.

dis•please′, *v.t., v.i.,* **-pleased, -pleas•ing.** to cause displeasure; annoy or offend.

dis•pleas′ure, *n.* dissatisfaction, disapproval, or annoyance.

dis•port (di spôrt′), *v.t.* **1.** to divert or amuse (oneself). —*v.i.* **2.** to play; frolic.

dis•pos•al (di spō′zəl), *n.* **1.** arrangement, as of troops. **2.** a getting rid of something. **3.** a transferring, as by gift or sale; bestowal. **4.** power to dispose of a thing; control: *left at my disposal.*

dis•pose′, *v.t.,* **-posed, -pos•ing. 1.** to give a tendency to; incline. **2.** to put in a particular place or order; arrange. **3. dispose of, a.** to settle. **b.** to get rid of. **c.** to give away or sell. —**dis•pos′a•ble,** *adj., n.*

dis•po•si•tion (dis′pə zish′ən), *n.* **1.** one's mental outlook; characteristic attitude. **2.** inclination or tendency. **3.** arrangement or placing. **4.** final settlement of a matter. **5.** bestowal, as by gift or sale. **6.** power to settle or control.

dis′pos•sess′, *v.t.* to put (a person) out of possession, esp. of real property.

dis′pro•por′tion, *n.* lack of proportion. **—dis′pro•por′tion•ate,** *adj.*

dis•prove′, *v.t.,* **-proved, -prov•ing.** to prove to be false. **—dis•prov′a•ble,** *adj.*

dis•pu•ta•tion (dis′pyōō tā′shən), *n.* **1.** the act of disputing or debating. **2.** the formal arguing of an academic thesis.

dis•pu•ta′tious, *adj.* fond of or given to disputation; argumentative.

dis•pute (di spyōōt′), *v.,* **-put•ed, -put•ing,** *n.* **—v.i. 1.** to engage in argument or debate. **2.** to argue vehemently; quarrel. **—v.t. 3.** to argue or debate about. **4.** to argue against. **5.** to quarrel or fight about. **—n. 6.** a controversy or difference of opinion. **7.** a quarrel. **—dis•put′a•ble,** *adj.* **—dis•pu′tant** (-pyōō′nt), *n.,* *adj.*

dis•qual′i•fy′, *v.t.,* **-fied, -fy•ing. 1.** to deprive of qualification or fitness. **2.** to declare ineligible or unqualified. **—dis•qual′i•fi•ca′tion,** *n.*

dis•qui′et, *n.* **1.** lack of calm or peace. **—v.t. 2.** to deprive of calm or peace.

dis•qui•si•tion (dis′kwə zish′ən), *n.* a formal discourse or treatise.

Dis•rae•li (diz rā′lē), *n.* **Benjamin,** (*"Dizzy"*), 1804–81, British prime minister 1868, 1874–80.

dis•re•gard′, *v.t.* **1.** to pay no attention to; ignore. **2.** to treat without due respect or attentiveness. **—n. 3.** lack of attention; neglect. **4.** lack of due respect or regard. **—dis′re•gard′ful,** *adj.*

dis′re•pair′, *n.* the condition of needing repair.

dis•rep′u•ta•ble, *adj.* **1.** having a bad reputation. **2.** shabby or shoddy.

dis′re•pute′, *n.* bad repute; disfavor.

dis′re•spect′, *n.* **1.** lack of respect; rudeness. **—v.t. 2.** to treat with rudeness; insult. **—dis′re•spect′ful,** *adj.*

dis•robe′, *v.t.,* *v.i.,* **-robed, -rob•ing.** to undress.

dis•rupt (dis rupt′), *v.t.* **1.** to cause disorder in. **2.** to disturb or interrupt. **3.** to break apart. **—dis•rup′tion,** *n.* **—dis•rup′tive,** *adj.*

dis′sat•is•fac′tion, *n.* **1.** the state or attitude of not being satisfied. **2.** a particular cause or feeling of displeasure.

dis•sat′is•fy′, *v.t.,* **-fied, -fy•ing.** to fail to satisfy; disappoint. **—dis•sat′is•fied′,** *adj.*

dis•sect (di sekt′, dī-), *v.t.* **1.** to cut apart (an animal body, plant, etc.) to examine the structure. **2.** to examine part by part; analyze. **—dis•sec′tion,** *n.*

dis•sem•ble (di sem′bəl), *v.t.,* *v.i.,* **-bled, -bling.** to conceal by pretense, as one's motives or thoughts. **—dis•sem′blance,** *n.* **—dis•sem′bler,** *n.*

dis•sem•i•nate (di sem′ə nāt′), *v.t.,* **-nat•ed, -nat•ing.** to scatter or spread widely. **—dis•sem′i•na′tion,** *n.*

dis•sen•sion (di sen′shən), *n.* strong disagreement; discord.

dis•sent (di sent′), *v.i.* **1.** to differ in sentiment or opinion (often fol. by *from*). **2.** to reject the doctrines or authority of an established church. **—n. 3.** difference of opinion. **4.** refusal to conform to an established church. **—dis•sent′er,** *n.*

dis•ser•ta•tion (dis′ər tā′shən), *n.* a formal discourse or thesis, esp. one written by a candidate for a doctorate.

dis•serv′ice, *n.* harm or injury.

dis•sev′er (di sev′ər), *v.t.* **1.** to sever. **2.** to divide into parts. **—v.i. 3.** to part; separate.

dis•si•dent (dis′i dənt), *n.* **1.** a person who dissents, esp. from established opinions. **—adj. 2.** dissenting, as in opinion or attitude. **—dis′si•dence,** *n.*

dis•sim′i•lar, *adj.* not similar; unlike. **—dis•sim′i•lar′i•ty,** *n.,* *pl.* **-ties.**

dis•si•mil′i•tude′, *n.* **1.** unlikeness; difference. **2.** a point of difference.

dis•sim•u•late (di sim′yə lāt′), *v.t.,* *v.i.,* **-lat•ed, -lat•ing.** to dissemble. **—dis•sim′u•la′tion,** *n.* **—dis•sim′u•la′tor,** *n.*

dis•si•pate (dis′ə pāt′), *v.,* **-pat•ed, -pat•ing. —v.t. 1.** to scatter; dispel. **2.** to spend or use wastefully or

extravagantly. **—v.i. 3.** to become scattered. **4.** to indulge in dissolute behavior. **—dis′si•pa′tion,** *n.*

dis•so•ci•ate (di sō′shē āt′, -sē-), *v.t.,* *v.i.,* **-at•ed, -at•ing.** to break the association of; disconnect. **—dis•so′ci•a′tion,** *n.*

dis•so•lute (dis′ə lōōt′), *adj.* indifferent to moral restraints; given to improper conduct. **—dis′so•lute′ly,** *adv.* **—dis′so•lute′ness,** *n.*

dis•so•lu′tion, *n.* **1.** the act or process of dissolving into parts or elements. **2.** the resulting state. **3.** the breaking of a bond. **4.** the breaking up of an assembly or organization. **5.** death; decease. **6.** disintegration or termination.

dis•solve (di zolv′), *v.,* **-solved, -solv•ing. —v.t. 1.** to make a solution of, as by mixing with a liquid. **2.** to melt; liquefy. **3.** to break (a tie, union, etc.). **4.** to dismiss or terminate (an assembly or organization). **5.** to separate into parts or elements. **—v.i. 6.** to become dissolved. **7.** to disappear gradually; fade away. **8.** to break down emotionally.

dis•so•nance (dis′ə nəns), *n.* **1.** inharmonious sound; discord. **2.** lack of harmony or agreement. **—dis′so•nant,** *adj.*

dis•suade (di swād′), *v.t.,* **-suad•ed, -suad•ing.** to deter by advice or persuasion. **—dis•sua′sion** (-swā′zhən), *n.* **—dis•sua′sive** (-siv), *adj.*

dis•taff (dis′taf, -täf), *n.* **1.** a staff for holding wool, flax, etc., from which the thread is drawn in spinning. **—adj. 2.** of or pertaining to women.

dis•tal (dis′tl), *adj.* situated away from the point of origin or attachment, as of a limb or bone. **—dis′tal•ly,** *adv.*

dis•tance (dis′təns), *n.,* *v.,* **-tanced, -tanc•ing. —n. 1.** the extent of space between two things, points, etc. **2.** the state or fact of being apart in space or time. **3.** remoteness in any respect. **4.** a distant region. **5.** reserve; coolness. **—v.t. 6.** to leave behind at a distance, as at a race. **7.** to place at a distance.

dis′tant, *adj.* **1.** far off or apart in space or time; remote. **2.** remote or far apart in any respect: *a distant relative.* **3.** reserved or aloof. **4.** arriving from or going to a distance. **—dis′tant•ly,** *adv.*

dis•taste′, *n.* dislike; disinclination. **—dis•taste′ful,** *adj.*

dis•tem′per, *n.* **1.** an infectious viral disease chiefly of young dogs, characterized by fever, convulsions, and vomiting. **2.** a deranged condition of mind or body.

dis•tend (di stend′), *v.t.,* *v.i.* to stretch out or swell. **—dis•ten′tion,** *n.*

dis•till (di stil′), *v.t.,* *v.i.* **1.** to subject to or undergo distillation. **2.** to give forth or fall in drops. **—dis•till′er,** *n.*

dis•til•late (dis′tl it, -āt′, di stil′it), *n.* the product obtained from the condensation of vapors in distillation.

dis′til•la′tion, *n.* **1.** the process of heating, evaporating, and subsequently condensing a liquid. **2.** the purification of a substance or the separation of one substance from another by such a process.

dis•till′er•y, *n.,* *pl.* **-er•ies.** a place for the distilling of liquors.

dis•tinct (di stingkt′), *adj.* **1.** not identical; separate. **2.** different in nature or quality; dissimilar. **3.** clear or plain; unmistakable. **4.** exceptional or notable. **—dis•tinct′ly,** *adv.*

dis•tinc′tion, *n.* **1.** a distinguishing as different. **2.** the recognizing of differences; discrimination. **3.** a distinguishing quality or characteristic. **4.** a special honor. **5.** marked superiority.

dis•tinc′tive, *adj.* **1.** serving to distinguish; characteristic. **2.** having a special quality; notable. **—dis•tinc′tive•ly,** *adv.* **—dis•tinc′tive•ness,** *n.*

dis•tin•guish (di sting′gwish), *v.t.* **1.** to mark off as different. **2.** to recognize as distinct. **3.** to perceive clearly; discern. **4.** to make prominent or eminent. **5.** to divide into classes; classify. **—v.i. 6.** to indicate or show a difference. **—dis•tin′guish•a•ble,** *adj.*

dis•tin′guished, *adj.* **1.** characterized by distinction or excellence. **2.** dignified or elegant.

dis•tort (di stôrt′), *v.t.* **1.** to twist out of shape. **2.**

to give a false meaning to; misrepresent. **3.** to reproduce or amplify (an electronic signal) inaccurately. —**dis•tor′tion,** *n.*

dis•tract (di strakt′), *v.t.* **1.** to divert, as the mind or attention. **2.** to disturb or trouble greatly. —**dis•tract′ed,** *adj.* —**dis•tract′ing,** *adj.* —**dis•trac′tion,** *n.*

dis•trait (di strā′), *adj.* distracted; absent-minded.

dis•traught (di strôt′), *adj.* **1.** bewildered; deeply agitated. **2.** mentally deranged; crazed.

dis•tress (di stres′), *n.* **1.** acute anxiety, pain, or sorrow. **2.** anything that causes anxiety, pain, or sorrow. **3.** a state of extreme necessity, misfortune, or danger. —*v.t.* **4.** to afflict with pain, anxiety, or sorrow; trouble. —**dis•tress′ful,** *adj.*

dis•trib•ute (di strib′yo̅o̅t), *v.t.,* **-ut•ed, -ut•ing. 1.** to divide and give out in shares; allot. **2.** to spread over a space; scatter. **3.** to sell and deliver (merchandise). **4.** to divide into classes. —**dis′tri•bu′tion,** *n.*

dis•trib′u•tor, *n.* **1.** one that distributes. **2.** a firm, esp. a wholesaler, that distributes merchandise. **3.** a device in a multicylinder engine that distributes the igniting voltage to the spark plugs.

dis•trict (dis′trikt), *n.* **1.** a division of territory marked off for administrative or other purposes. **2.** a region or locality.

dis′trict attor′ney, *n.* an attorney for the government within a specified district.

Dis′trict of Colum′bia, *n.* a federal area in the E United States, on the Potomac, coextensive with the federal capital, Washington. 543,213.

dis•trust′, *v.t.* **1.** to regard with suspicion; have no trust in. —*n.* **2.** lack of trust; suspicion. —**dis•trust′ful,** *adj.*

dis•turb (di stûrb′), *v.t.* **1.** to interrupt the quiet, rest, or peace of. **2.** to interfere with; interrupt. **3.** to put out of order; disarrange. **4.** to perplex; trouble. —**dis•turb′ance,** *n.*

dis′u•nite′, *v.t., v.i.,* **-nit•ed, -nit•ing.** to separate into parts. —**dis•u′ni•ty,** *n.*

dis•use (*n.* dis yo̅o̅s′; *v.* -yo̅o̅z′), *n., v.,* **-used, -us•ing.** —*n.* **1.** discontinuance of use or practice. —*v.t.* **2.** to cease to use.

ditch (dich), *n.* **1.** a long, narrow channel in the ground, as for irrigation. —*v.t.* **2.** to dig a ditch in. **3.** to crash-land on water and abandon (an aircraft). **4.** *Slang.* to get rid of.

dith•er (di*th*′ər), *n.* **1.** a trembling; vibration. **2.** flustered excitement or fear. —*v.i.* **3.** to act irresolutely; vacillate.

dit•to (dit′ō), *n., pl.* **-tos. 1.** the aforesaid; the above or the same (used in accounts, lists, etc., to avoid repetition). **2.** DITTO MARK. [< It < L *dictus* said]

dit′to mark′, *n.* Often, **ditto marks.** two small marks (″) used as a sign for *ditto.*

dit•ty (dit′ē), *n., pl.* **-ties.** a short, simple song.

di•u•ret•ic (dī′ə ret′ik), *adj.* **1.** increasing the volume of the urine excreted. —*n.* **2.** a diuretic medicine or agent.

di•ur•nal (dī ûr′nl), *adj.* **1.** occurring each day; daily. **2.** of, belonging to, or active in the daytime. —**di•ur′nal•ly,** *adv.*

div., **1.** dividend. **2.** division. **3.** divorced.

di•va (dē′və, -vä), *n., pl.* **-vas, -ve** (-ve). PRIMA DONNA (def. 1).

di•va•lent (dī vā′lənt), *adj.* having a valence of two or two valences. —**di•va′lence,** *n.*

di•van (di van′, -vän′), *n.* a sofa or couch, usu. without arms or back.

dive (dīv), *v.,* **dived** or **dove, dived, div•ing,** *n.* —*v.i.* **1.** to plunge into water, esp. headfirst. **2.** to submerge, as a submarine. **3.** to plunge, fall, or descend through the air. **4.** to dart or dash. **5.** to plunge into a subject, activity, etc. —*v.t.* **6.** to cause to plunge, submerge, or descend. —*n.* **7.** an act or instance of diving. **8.** a jump or plunge into water, esp. in a prescribed way from a diving board. **9.** the steep descent of an airplane at a speed far exceeding that in level flight. **10.** a sudden decline, as in stock prices. **11.** *Informal.* a disreputable bar or nightclub. —**div′er,** *n.* —**Usage.** Both DIVED and DOVE are

standard as the past tense of DIVE. DOVE is the much newer form, and is therefore often objected to, but it is so common in all varieties of written and spoken English that it must be considered standard.

di•verge (di vûrj′, dī-), *v.i.,* **-verged, -verg•ing. 1.** to move or extend in different directions from a common point; branch off. **2.** to differ in opinion, form, etc. **3.** to deviate, as from a path or plan. —**di•ver′gence,** *n.* —**di•ver′gent,** *adj.*

di•vers (dī′vərz), *adj.* various; sundry.

di•verse (di vûrs′, dī-), *adj.* **1.** of a different kind; unlike. **2.** of various kinds; varied. —**di•verse′ly,** *adv.*

di•ver′si•fy′, *v.,* **-fied, -fy•ing.** —*v.t.* **1.** to make diverse; vary. **2.** to distribute (investments) among different types of securities. —*v.i.* **3.** to become diversified. —**di•ver′si•fi•ca′tion,** *n.*

di•ver•sion (di vûr′zhən dī-), *n.* **1.** the act of diverting or turning aside. **2.** a distraction; pastime. —**di•ver′sion•ar•y** (-zhə ner′ē), *adj.*

di•ver′si•ty, *n., pl.* **-ties. 1.** the state or fact of being diverse; difference or variety. **2.** a point of difference.

di•vert (di vûrt′, dī-), *v.t.* **1.** to turn aside, as from a path or course. **2.** to distract. **3.** to entertain or amuse.

Di•ves (dī′vēz), *n.* **1.** the rich man of the parable in Luke 16:19–31. **2.** any rich man. [< L *dīves* rich, rich man]

di•vest (di vest′, dī-), *v.t.* **1.** to strip of clothing, ornament, etc. **2.** to deprive, esp. of property or rights. **3.** to rid or free.

di•vide (di vīd′), *v.,* **-vid•ed, -vid•ing,** *n.* —*v.t.* **1.** to separate into parts, sections, etc. **2.** to sever or cut off. **3.** to deal out in parts; apportion. **4.** to separate in opinion or feeling. **5.** to classify. **6.** to separate into equal parts by the process of mathematical division. —*v.i.* **7.** to become divided. **8.** to share with others. **9.** to diverge; branch; fork. **10.** to perform mathematical division. —*n.* **11.** a division. **12.** a ridge dividing two adjacent drainage basins. —**di•vid′a•ble,** *adj.* —**di•vid′er,** *n.*

div•i•dend (div′i dend′), *n.* **1.** a number to be divided by a divisor. **2. a.** a sum paid to shareholders out of company earnings. **b.** a single share of such a sum. **3.** a bonus.

div•i•na•tion (div′ə nā′shən), *n.* **1.** the practice of seeking to foretell future events. **2.** intuitive perception.

di•vine (di vīn′), *adj.,* **-vin•er, -vin•est,** *n., v.,* **-vined, -vin•ing.** —*adj.* **1.** of, like, or from God or a god. **2.** devoted to God or a god; sacred. **3.** heavenly; celestial: *the divine kingdom.* **4.** extremely good. **5.** being a god; being God. —*n.* **6.** a theologian. **7.** a cleric. —*v.t.* **8.** to declare by divination; prophesy. **9.** to discover (water, metal, etc.) by means of a divining rod. **10.** to perceive by intuition; conjecture. —*v.i.* **11.** to practice divination. **12.** to conjecture. [< L *dīvīnus*] —**di•vine′ly,** *adv.* —**di•vin′er,** *n.*

divin′ing rod′, *n.* a forked stick supposedly useful in locating underground water or metal deposits.

di•vin′i•ty (-vin′i tē), *n., pl.* **-ties. 1.** the quality of being divine. **2.** a divine being. **3. the Divinity,** God. **4.** theology.

divin′ity school′, *n.* a Protestant seminary.

di•vis•i•ble (di viz′ə bəl), *adj.* capable of being divided, esp. of being evenly divided without a remainder. —**di•vis′i•bil′i•ty,** *n.*

di•vi′sion (-vizh′ən), *n.* **1.** the act of dividing or state of being divided. **2.** the arithmetic operation of finding how many times one number is contained in another. **3.** something that divides or separates. **4.** one of the parts into which a thing is divided. **5.** disagreement; dissension. **6.** a major administrative and tactical unit of the army or navy. —**di•vi′sion•al,** *adj.*

di•vi′sive (-vī′siv), *adj.* creating dissension or discord. —**di•vi′sive•ly,** *adv.* —**di•vi′sive•ness,** *n.*

di•vi′sor (-zər), *n.* a number by which another number, the dividend, is divided.

di•vorce (di vôrs′), *n., v.,* **-vorced, -vorc•ing.** —*n.*
1. legal or formal dissolution of a marriage. **2.** total
separation. —*v.t.* **3.** to separate by divorce. **4.** to free
oneself from (one's spouse) by divorce. **5.** to separate. —*v.i.* **6.** to get a divorce.

di•vor•cée′ or **-cee′** (-vôr sā′, -sē′), *n., pl.* **-cées** or
-cees. a divorced woman.

div•ot (div′ət), *n.* a piece of turf gouged out with a
golf club in making a stroke.

di•vulge (di vulj′, dī-), *v.t.,* **-vulged, -vulg•ing.** to
disclose or reveal (something secret).

div•vy (div′ē), *v.t., v.i.,* **-vied, -vy•ing.** to divide;
distribute (often fol. by *up*).

Dix (diks), *n.* **Dorothea Lynde** (*Dorothy*), 1802–87,
U.S. educator and social reformer.

Dix•ie (dik′sē), *n.* the southern states of the U.S.,
esp. those that were part of the Confederacy.

Dix′ie•land′, *n.* a style of jazz marked by accented
four-four rhythm and improvisation.

diz•zy (diz′ē), *adj.,* **-zi•er, -zi•est. 1.** having a sensation of whirling and a tendency to fall. **2.** bewildered; confused. **3.** causing giddiness or confusion.
4. *Informal.* foolish; silly. —**diz′zi•ly,** *adv.* —**diz′zi•
ness,** *n.*

D.J., 1. Also, **DJ** (dē′jā′). disc jockey. **2.** Doctor of
Law. [< L *Doctor Jūris*]

Dji•bou•ti (ji bōō′tē), *n.* **1.** a republic in E Africa.
434,116. **2.** the capital of this republic. 290,000.

DMZ, demilitarized zone.

DNA, deoxyribonucleic acid: a nucleic acid molecule
that is the main constituent of the chromosome and
that carries the genes along its strands.

Dnie•per or **Dne•pr** (nē′pər; *Russ.* dnyepR), *n.* a
river flowing S from the W Russian Federation to the
Black Sea. 1400 mi. (2250 km) long.

DNR, do not resuscitate: used in hospitals to indicate
a prior decision by the patient or the patient's family
to avoid extraordinary means of prolonging life.

do¹ (dōō; *unstressed* dŏŏ, də), *v.,* **did, done, do•ing,**
n., pl. **dos, do's.** —*v.t.* **1.** to perform (an act, duty,
role, etc.). **2.** to execute (a piece or amount of
work). **3.** to accomplish; finish. **4.** to put forth; exert:
Do your best. **5.** to be the cause of (good, harm,
etc.). **6.** to render, give, or pay: *to do justice.* **7.** to
deal with as the case may require: *to do the wash.* **8.**
to travel; traverse. **9.** to suffice for. **10.** to travel at
the rate of (a specified speed). **11.** to serve (a term
of time) in prison. **12.** to create or bring into being.
13. to study or work at. **14.** to decorate. —*v.i.* **15.** to
act or conduct oneself. **16.** to proceed: *to do wisely.*
17. to get along. **18.** to be in a specified state of
health. **19.** to be enough. **20.** to finish or be finished.
21. to happen; take place. —*auxiliary v.* **22.** (used to
avoid repetition of a verb): *I think as you do.* **23.**
(used in interrogative and negative constructions):
Do you like music? I don't care. **24.** (used to lend
emphasis): *Do visit us!* **25. do away with, a.** to
abolish. **b.** to kill. **26. ~ in, a.** to kill. **b.** to exhaust.
27. ~ out of, *Informal.* to swindle; cheat. **28. ~ up,**
to wrap up, fasten, or tie. **29. ~ with,** to benefit
from; use. **30. ~ without,** to forgo. —*n.* **31.** *Informal.* a hairdo. **32.** a festive gathering; party.
—*Idiom.* **33. do or die,** to make a supreme effort.
34. dos and don'ts, customs, rules, or regulations.
—**do′a•ble,** *adj.*

do² (dō), *n., pl.* **dos.** the musical syllable used for
the first note of an ascending diatonic scale.

Do•ber•man pin•scher (dō′bər mən pin′shər), *n.*
a large, muscular dog with a short, usu. black or
brown coat.

doc (dok), *n. Informal.* doctor.

do•cent (dō′sənt), *n.* a lecturer or guide, esp. in a
museum.

doc•ile (dos′əl), *adj.* readily trained or handled; submissive. —**do•cil•i•ty** (do sil′i tē), *n.*

dock¹ (dok), *n.* **1.** a landing pier or wharf. **2.** a waterway between two piers for receiving a ship while
in port. **3.** such a waterway together with the surrounding piers. **4.** a platform for loading trucks,
freight cars, etc. —*v.t.* **5.** to bring (a ship) into a
dock. **6.** to join (an orbiting space vehicle) with an-

other spacecraft. —*v.i.* **7.** to come into a dock. **8.** (of
two space vehicles) to join together.

dock² (dok), *v.t.* **1.** to cut off the end of: *to dock a
tail.* **2.** to deduct from (wages).

dock³ (dok), *n.* the place in a courtroom where a
prisoner is placed during trial.

dock⁴ (dok), *n.* any of various weedy plants of the
buckwheat family.

dock•et (dok′it), *n.* **1.** a list of cases scheduled to be
heard in a court. **2.** any list of business to be transacted. —*v.t.* **3.** to enter in a docket.

dock′yard′, *n.* a waterside area containing docks,
workshops, etc., for building and repairing ships.

doc•tor (dok′tər), *n.* **1.** a person licensed to practice
medicine, as a physician, dentist, or veterinarian. **2.**
a person who has been awarded a doctor's degree. **3.**
DOCTOR OF THE CHURCH. —*v.t.* **4.** to give medical treatment to. **5.** to restore; repair. **6.** to tamper with. **7.**
to revise, alter, or adapt for a specific purpose: *to
doctor a play.* —*v.i.* **8.** to practice medicine. [< L:
teacher < *docēre* to teach] —**doc′tor•al,** *adj.*

doc′tor•ate (-it), *n.* DOCTOR'S DEGREE.

Doc′tor of the Church′, *n.* a title conferred on an
ecclesiastic for great learning and saintliness.

doc′tor's degree′, *n.* any of several degrees of the
highest rank awarded by universities, as the Ph.D.

doc•tri•naire (dok′trə nâr′), *n.* **1.** a stubborn adherent of a doctrine; dogmatist. —*adj.* **2.** dogmatic;
fanatical.

doc′trine (-trin), *n.* **1.** a particular principle, position, or policy taught or advocated, as of a religion
or government. **2.** a body of teachings. —**doc′tri•
nal,** *adj.*

doc•u•dra•ma (dok′yə drä′mə, -dram′ə), *n., pl.*
-mas. a fictionalized television drama depicting actual events. [*docu*(*mentary*) + *drama*]

doc•u•ment (*n.* dok′yə mənt; *v.* -ment′), *n.* **1.** a
written or printed paper furnishing information or evidence, as a passport. **2.** a computer data file. —*v.t.*
3. to furnish with or support by documents. —**doc′u•
men•ta′tion,** *n.*

doc′u•men′ta•ry, *adj., n., pl.* **-ries.** —*adj.* **1.** pertaining to, consisting of, or derived from documents.
2. depicting an actual event, life story, etc., without
fictional elements. —*n.* **3.** a documentary film, television program, etc.

dod•der (dod′ər), *v.i.* to shake; tremble; totter.
—**dod′der•ing,** *adj.*

dodge (doj), *v.,* **dodged, dodg•ing,** *n.* —*v.t.* **1.** to
avoid by a sudden shift of position or by strategy;
evade. —*v.i.* **2.** to move suddenly, as to avoid a
blow. **3.** to use evasive methods. —*n.* **4.** a quick,
evasive movement. **5.** a clever scheme or trick.
—**dodg′er,** *n.*

Dodg•son (doj′sən), *n.* **Charles Lutwidge** (*"Lewis
Carroll"*), 1832–98, English mathematician and writer
of children's books.

do•do (dō′dō), *n., pl.* **-dos, -does. 1.** a large, extinct, flightless bird. **2.** *Slang.* a dull-witted person.

dodo

doe (dō), *n., pl.* **does, doe.** the female of the deer,
antelope, rabbit, etc.

Do•eg (dō′eg), *n.* a servant of Saul who was ordered to put the priests of Nob to death. I Sam. 21:7;
22:9–19.

do•er (dōō′ər), *n.* a person who does something,
esp. one who gets things done efficiently.

does (duz), *v.* 3rd pers. sing. pres. indic. of DO¹.

doe′skin′, *n.* **1.** the skin of a doe. **2.** soft leather made from this.

does•n′t (duz′ənt), contraction of *does not.*

doff (dof, dôf), *v.t.* **1.** to take off, as clothing. **2.** to tip (the hat), as in greeting. **3.** to get rid of.

dog (dôg, dog), *n.*, *v.*, **dogged, dog•ging.** —*n.* **1.** a domesticated carnivore bred in many varieties. **2.** any animal belonging to the same family, including wolves and foxes. **3.** a despicable person. **4.** a fellow: *a lucky dog.* **5.** *Slang.* something of poor quality. **6.** *Slang.* an unattractive person. **7.** a mechanical device for holding something. —*v.t.* **8.** to follow or track like a dog; hound. —*Idiom.* **9. go to the dogs,** to deteriorate. **10. let sleeping dogs lie,** to leave an existing situation alone rather than risk provoking something worse.

dog′catch′er, *n.* a person employed to impound stray dogs, cats, etc.

dog′-ear′, *n.* **1.** a folded corner of a book page. —*v.t.* **2.** to fold down the corner of (a page). —**dog′-eared′,** *adj.*

dog′fight′, *n.* combat between enemy aircraft.

dog′fish′, *n.*, *pl.* **-fish, -fish•es.** any of several small sharks that are destructive to food fishes.

dog•ged (dô′gid, dog′id), *adj.* persistent; stubbornly tenacious. —**dog′ged•ly,** *adv.*

dog•ger•el (dô′gər əl, dog′ər-), *n.* crude or trivial poetry, usu. irregular in measure.

dog′gy or **-gie,** *n.*, *pl.* **-gies.** a little dog.

dog′gy bag′, *n.* a container provided by a restaurant for a customer to take home leftovers.

dog′house′, *n.* **1.** a shelter for a dog. —*Idiom.* **2. in the doghouse,** in disfavor.

do•gie (dō′gē), *n.* (in the Western U.S.) a motherless calf.

dog•ma (dôg′mə, dog′-), *n.*, *pl.* **-mas. 1.** a system of principles or tenets, as of a church. **2.** a specific tenet authoritatively put forth. **3.** an established belief or principle.

dog•mat′ic (-mat′ik), *adj.* **1.** of the nature of a dogma. **2.** arrogantly asserting opinions or beliefs. —**dog•mat′i•cal•ly,** *adv.*

dog′ma•tism, *n.* dogmatic assertion in matters of opinions. —**dog′ma•tist,** *n.*

do′-good′er, *n.* a well-intentioned but naive social reformer.

dog′trot′, *n.* a gentle trot.

dog′wood′, *n.* a tree or shrub with pink or white blossoms.

doi•ly (doi′lē), *n.*, *pl.* **-lies.** any small, ornamental mat, esp. one of embroidery or lace. [after a 17th-century London draper]

do′ing, *n.* **1.** performance; execution. **2. doings,** deeds; proceedings; events.

Dol•by (dōl′bē, dôl′-), *Trademark.* a system for reducing high-frequency noise in a tape recording.

dol•drums (dōl′drəmz, dol′-), *n.pl.* **1.** a state of inactivity or stagnation. **2.** a dull, depressed mood. **3. the doldrums,** a belt of calms near the equator.

dole (dōl), *n.*, *v.*, **doled, dol•ing.** —*n.* **1.** an allotment of money or food given by a charity or government to the needy. —*v.t.* **2.** to distribute in charity. **3.** to give out in small quantities.

dole′ful, *adj.* sorrowful; mournful. —**dole′ful•ly,** *adv.*

doll (dol), *n.* **1.** a child's toy representing a baby or other human being, esp. an attractive one. **2.** *Slang.* **a.** a physically attractive person. **b.** a generous or helpful person. —*v.* **3. doll up, a.** to dress in fancy clothing, elaborate makeup, etc. **b.** to decorate: *to doll up a room for a party.*

dol•lar (dol′ər), *n.* **1.** the basic monetary unit of the U.S., equal to 100 cents. **2.** the monetary unit of various other countries, as Canada and Australia. **3.** a coin or bill equivalent to one dollar.

dol•lop (dol′əp), *n.* **1.** a lump or blob of some substance. **2.** a small amount.

dol•ly (dol′ē), *n.*, *pl.* **-lies. 1.** *Informal.* a doll. **2.** a low truck or cart with small wheels for moving

heavy loads. **3.** a mobile platform for moving a movie or television camera about a set.

dol•men (dōl′men, -mən, dol′-), *n.* a prehistoric structure consisting of upright stones capped by a horizontal stone.

dolmen

do•lo•mite (dō′lə mīt′, dol′ə-), *n.* a common mineral, calcium magnesium carbonate, occurring in crystals and in masses.

do•lor•ous (dō′lər əs, dol′ər-), *adj.* full of or causing pain or sorrow. —**do′lor•ous•ly,** *adv.*

dol•phin (dol′fin, dôl′-), *n.* **1.** a marine mammal resembling a small whale, having a beaklike snout. **2.** either of two large, slender fishes of warm and temperate seas.

dolphin

dolt (dōlt), *n.* a blockhead; dunce. —**dolt′ish,** *adj.*

-dom, a suffix meaning: domain (*kingdom*); collection of persons (*officialdom*); rank or station (*earldom*); general condition (*freedom*).

do•main (dō mān′), *n.* **1.** a field of action, thought, influence, etc. **2.** the territory governed by a single ruler or government.

dome (dōm), *n.* **1.** a hemispheric vault, ceiling, or roof of a room or building. **2.** any covering thought to resemble a dome.

Dome′ of the Rock′, *Islam.* a shrine in Jerusalem at the site from which Muhammad ascended to the throne of God: built on the site of the Jewish Temple.

Domes′day (or **Dooms′day**) **Book′,** *n.* a record of a survey of the lands of England made by order of William the Conqueror about 1086.

do•mes•tic (də mes′tik), *adj.* **1.** of the home, family, or household affairs. **2.** devoted to home life. **3.** tame; domesticated. **4.** of one's own or a particular country: *domestic trade.* **5.** produced in one's own country. —*n.* **6.** a household servant. —**do•mes′ti•cal•ly,** *adv.*

do•mes′ti•cate′ (-kāt′), *v.t.*, **-cat•ed, -cat•ing. 1.** to tame, breed, or cultivate for human use. **2.** to accustom to household life. —**do•mes′ti•ca′tion,** *n.*

do•mes•tic•i•ty (dō′me stis′i tē), *n.*, *pl.* **-ties. 1.** the state of being domestic. **2.** home life. **3.** a domestic activity.

domes′tic part′ner, *n.* either member of an unmarried, cohabiting couple that seeks benefits usu. available only to spouses.

domes′tic vi′olence, *n.* acts of violence against a member of one's immediate family, esp. in the home.

dom•i•cile (dom′ə sīl′, -səl, dō′mə-), *n.*, *v.*, **-ciled, -cil•ing.** —*n.* **1.** a house or home. **2.** a permanent legal residence. —*v.t.* **3.** to establish in a domicile.

dom•i•nant (dom′ə nənt), *adj.* **1.** ruling or controlling; exerting chief authority or influence. **2.** noting or pertaining to one of a pair of hereditary traits that masks the other when both are present in an organism. —**dom′i•nance,** *n.* —**dom′i•nant•ly,** *adv.*

dom′i•nate′ (-nāt′), *v.*, **-nat•ed, -nat•ing.** —*v.t.* **1.** to rule over; control. **2.** to tower above. **3.** to be the major factor or influence in. —*v.i.* **4.** to exercise power or control; predominate. **5.** to occupy a commanding position. —**dom/i•na/tion,** *n.*

dom•i•neer (dom/ə nēr/), *v.i., v.t.* to rule arbitrarily or despotically; dominate. —**dom/i•neer/ing,** *adj.*

Dom•i•nic (dom/ə nik), *n.* **Saint,** 1170–1221, Spanish priest: founder of the Dominican order.

Dom•i•ni•ca (dom/ə nē/kə, də min/i kə), *n.* an island republic in the E West Indies. 83,226. —**Dom/i•ni/can,** *adj., n.*

Do•min/i•can Repub/lic (də min/i kən), *n.* a republic in the West Indies on the E part of Hispaniola. 6,700,000. —**Do•min/i•can,** *adj., n.*

dom•i•nie (dom/ə nē, dō/mə-), *n.* **1.** *Chiefly Scot.* a schoolmaster. **2.** a pastor in the Dutch Reformed Church. **3.** *Chiefly Hudson Valley.* a pastor or minister.

do•min•ion (də min/yən), *n.* **1.** sovereign authority. **2.** the act or fact of ruling. **3.** a domain or realm. **4.** (*often cap.*) a former title for a self-governing country belonging to the Commonwealth of Nations.

dom•i•no¹ (dom/ə nō/), *n., pl.* **-noes. 1.** a small, flat block marked with pips or dots. **2. dominoes,** a game played with dominoes.

dom•i•no² (dom/ə nō/), *n., pl.* **-noes, -nos. 1.** a hooded cloak worn with a half mask by persons in masquerade. **2.** the mask.

dom/ino the/ory, *n.* a theory that a particular event will precipitate similar ones elsewhere. Also called **dom/ino effect/, dom/ino reac/tion.**

don¹ (don; *Sp., It.* dôn), *n.* **1.** (*cap.*) Mr. or Sir: a Spanish title of respect. **2.** a Spanish lord or gentleman. **3.** (*cap.*) an Italian title of address, esp. for a priest. **4.** a fellow or tutor at an English university. **5.** the head of a Mafia family.

don² (don), *v.t.,* **donned, don•ning.** to put on or dress in.

Don (don), *n.* a river in W central Russian Federation, flowing S into the Black Sea.

Do•ña (dô/nyä), *n., pl.* **-ñas.** Madam or Lady; a Spanish title of respect.

do•nate (dō/nāt, dō nāt/), *v.t., v.i.,* **-nat•ed, -nat•ing.** to contribute or give. —**do•na/tion,** *n.*

done (dun), *v.* **1** pp. of *do.* —*adj.* **2.** finished; completed. **3.** cooked sufficiently. —*Idiom.* **4. done for, a.** dead or dying. **b.** exhausted. **c.** doomed to failure. **5. done in,** very tired; exhausted. —**Usage.** Usage guides occasionally object to DONE in the adjectival sense "finished," but the meaning is fully standard.

dong¹ (dông, dong), *n.* a deep sound like that of a large bell.

dong² (dông, dong), *n., pl.* **dong.** the basic monetary unit of Vietnam.

don•gle (dong/gəl, dông/-), *n.* a hardware device attached to a computer without which a given software program will not run: used to prevent unauthorized use.

Don Juan (don wän/, hwän/), *n.* a legendary Spanish nobleman famous for his seductions and dissolute life.

don•key (dong/kē, dông/-, dung/-), *n., pl.* **-keys. 1.** a domesticated ass. **2.** a representation of this animal as the emblem of the U.S. Democratic Party. **3.** a stupid, silly, or obstinate person.

Donne (dun), *n.* **John,** 1573–1631, English poet.

don•ny•brook (don/ē brŏŏk/), *n.* (*often cap.*) a brawl or free-for-all.

do•nor (dō/nər), *n.* **1.** one who donates. **2.** a provider of blood, an organ, or other biological tissue for transfusion or transplantation.

Don Quix•o•te (don/ kē hō/tē, -tā, don kwik/sət), *n.* the hero of a novel by Cervantes who was inspired by chivalrous but impractical ideals.

don't (dōnt), *v.* contraction of *do not.*

do•nut (dō/nət, -nut/), *n.* DOUGHNUT.

doo•dad (dōō/dad/), *n.* *Informal.* an unnamed gadget or trinket.

doo•dle (dōōd/l), *v.,* **-dled, -dling,** *n.* —*v.i., v.t.* **1.**

to draw or scribble idly. —*n.* **2.** a figure produced by doodling. —**doo/dler,** *n.*

doom (dōōm), *n.* **1.** fate or destiny, esp. adverse fate. **2.** ruin or death. **3.** an unfavorable judgment or sentence. —*v.t.* **4.** to destine to an adverse fate. **5.** to sentence; condemn.

dooms/day/, *n.* the day of the Last Judgment.

dooms/day cult/, *n.* a religious cult that anticipates the imminent end of the world.

door (dôr), *n.* **1.** a movable barrier for opening and closing an entrance, cabinet, etc. **2.** a doorway. **3.** any means of access.

door/bell/, *n.* a bell, chime, or buzzer at a doorway, rung to alert persons within.

door/man/ (-man/, -mən), *n., pl.* **-men.** an attendant at the door of an apartment house, nightclub, etc., who assists those entering and departing.

door/mat/, *n.* a mat placed before an entrance for wiping dirt from shoes.

door/step/, *n.* a step in front of an outside door.

door/way/, *n.* **1.** the entryway to a building, room, etc. **2.** any means of access.

door/yard/, *n.* a yard near the front door of a house.

do•pa (dō/pə), *n.* an amino acid: one form **(L-dopa)** is used as a drug to treat Parkinson's disease.

dope (dōp), *n., v.,* **doped, dop•ing.** —*n.* **1.** any thick liquid substance used to prepare a surface or coat a fabric. **2.** *Slang.* any narcotic or illicit drug. **3.** *Slang.* information; news. **4.** *Informal.* a stupid person. —*v.t.* **5.** *Slang.* to affect or treat with dope; drug. **6. dope out,** *Slang.* to figure out.

dop/ey or **dop/y,** *adj.,* **-i•er, i•est.** *Informal.* **1.** stupid; inane. **2.** sluggish or befuddled, as from the use of drugs.

Dor•cas (dôr/kəs), *n.* a Christian woman at Joppa who made clothing for the poor. Acts 9:36–41.

Dor•ic (dôr/ik, dor/-), *adj.* of or designating a style of classical architecture characterized by fluted columns with simple capitals.

dorm (dôrm), *n.* a dormitory.

dor•mant (dôr/mənt), *adj.* **1.** temporarily inactive, as in sleep; resting; torpid. **2.** undeveloped; latent. —**dor/man•cy,** *n.*

dor•mer (dôr/mər), *n.* **1.** Also called **dor/mer win/dow.** a vertical window in a projection built out from a sloping roof. **2.** the entire structure.

dormer

dor•mi•to•ry (dôr/mi tôr/ē), *n., pl.* **-ries. 1.** a building, as at a college, containing rooms and facilities for residents. **2.** a room serving as communal sleeping quarters.

dor•mouse (dôr/mous/), *n., pl.* **-mice.** a small, bushy-tailed Old World rodent.

dor•sal (dôr/səl), *adj.* of or situated at the back.

Dort•mund (dôrt/mənd), *n.* a city in W Germany. 583,600.

do•ry (dôr/ē), *n., pl.* **-ries.** a small, flat-bottomed boat with a high bow and flaring sides.

DOS (dôs, dos), *n.* an operating system for microcomputers.

dose (dōs), *n., v.,* **dosed, dos•ing.** —*n.* **1.** a quantity of medicine prescribed to be taken at one time. **2.** an intense and often disagreeable experience. **3.** the amount of radiation administered to or absorbed by living tissue. —*v.t.* **4.** to give a dose of medicine to. **5.** to administer in doses. —*Idiom.* **6. get a dose of one's own medicine,** to receive back what was given out. —**dos/age,** *n.*

do·sim·e·ter (dō sim′i tər), *n.* a device for measuring doses of ionizing radiation.

dos·si·er (dos′ē ā′, dô′sē ā′), *n.* a file of documents containing detailed information about a person or topic.

dost (dust), *v. Archaic.* 2nd pers. sing. pres. indic. of DO[1].

Dos·to·ev·sky or **Dos·to·yev·sky** (dos′tə yef′-skē, dus′-), *n.* **Fyodor Mikhailovich,** 1821–81, Russian novelist.

dot (dot), *n., v.,* **dot·ted, dot·ting.** —*n.* **1.** a small, roundish mark made with or as if with a pen. **2.** a small spot; speck. **3.** a signal of shorter duration than a dash, used to represent letters, as in Morse code. **4.** a period, esp. as used when pronouncing an Internet address. —*v.t.* **5.** to mark or cover with or as if with a dot or dots. —*Idiom.* **6. on the dot,** exactly at the time specified.

dot·age (dō′tij), *n.* a decline of mental faculties, esp. resulting from old age.

dote (dōt), *v.i.,* **dot·ed, dot·ing. 1.** to bestow excessive fondness or love. **2.** to be weak-minded or foolish, esp. from old age. —**dot′er,** *n.*

doth (duth), *v. Archaic.* 3rd pers. sing. pres. indic. of DO[1].

dot′-ma′trix, *adj.* pertaining to the formation of characters with dots from a matrix, as by some computer printers.

Dou′ay Bi′ble (dōō′ā), *n.* an English version of the Bible translated from the Vulgate by Roman Catholic scholars (New Testament 1582; Old Testament 1609). [after *Douay,* France]

dou·ble (dub′əl), *adj., n., v.,* **-bled, -bling,** *adv.* —*adj.* **1.** twice as large, as strong, as many, etc. **2.** composed of two like parts. **3.** suitable for two persons. **4.** twofold; dual. **5.** marked by duplicity. **6.** folded in two. **7.** (of flowers) having more than the normal number of petals. —*n.* **8.** something that is twice the usual size, quantity, strength, etc. **9.** a duplicate or counterpart. **10.** a fold or plait. **11.** an actor's substitute or understudy. **12.** a hit in baseball that enables the batter to reach second base. **13. doubles,** a game between two pairs of players, as in tennis. **14.** (in bridge) a doubling of an opponent's bid. —*v.t.* **15.** to make double or twice as great. **16.** to fold or bend with one part over another. **17.** to clench: *to double one's fists.* **18.** to repeat or duplicate. **19.** (in bridge) to challenge (an opponent's bid) by increasing the value of tricks won or lost. —*v.i.* **20.** to become double. **21.** to reverse direction sharply (often fol. by *back*). **22.** to serve in two capacities. **23.** to hit a double in baseball. **24. double up,** a. to share quarters. b. to bend over, as from pain. —*adv.* **25.** twofold. **26.** in pairs. —*Idiom.* **27. on the double,** without delay.

dou′ble-bar′reled, *adj.* **1.** (esp. of a shotgun) having two barrels side by side. **2.** serving a double purpose.

dou′ble bass′ (bās), *n.* the largest and lowest-pitched instrument of the violin family.

dou′ble-blind′, *adj.* of or being an experiment in which neither the researchers nor the subjects know who is receiving the tested medication or treatment.

dou′ble boil′er, *n.* a utensil consisting of two nested pots, the lower one for boiling water to cook food in the upper.

dou′ble-breast′ed, *adj.* (of a coat, jacket, etc.) having a front closure with a wide overlap.

dou′ble-click′, *v.i. Computers.* to click a mouse button twice in rapid succession, as to call up a program or select a file. —**dou′ble click′,** *n.*

dou′ble-cross′, *v.t.* to betray or swindle. —**dou′-ble-cross′er,** *n.*

dou′ble date′, *n.* a date on which two couples go together. —**dou′ble-date′,** *v.i.,* **-dat·ed, -dat·ing.**

Dou·ble·day (dub′əl dā′), *n.* **Abner,** 1819–93, U.S. army officer: sometimes credited with inventing baseball.

dou′ble-deal′ing, *n.* deception or duplicity.

dou′ble-deck′er, *n.* **1.** something with two decks,

levels, or the like. **2.** a sandwich of three slices of bread and two layers of filling.

dou′ble-dip′ping, *n.* the receiving of more than one form of compensation from the same employer.

dou·ble en·ten·dre (dub′əl än tän′drə, -tänd′; *Fr.* dōō blän tän′dR[ə]), *n., pl.* **-ten·dres** (-tän′draz, -tändz′; *Fr.* -tän′dR[ə]). a word or expression with two meanings, esp. when one meaning is risqué.

dou′ble·head′er, *n.* two games played on the same day in immediate succession.

dou′ble-joint′ed, *adj.* having especially flexible joints that can bend in unusual ways or to an unusually great extent.

dou′ble knit′, *n.* a fabric knitted with two sets of needles and yarns, having the same ribbing on the face and back.

dou′ble play′, *n.* a baseball play in which two players are put out.

dou′ble-reed′, *adj.* of or designating a wind instrument producing sounds through two reeds beating together, as the oboe.

dou′ble stand′ard, *n.* a moral code permitting men greater freedom than women, esp. in sexual conduct.

dou·blet (dub′lit), *n.* **1.** a close-fitting jacket worn by men in the Renaissance. **2.** a pair of like things. **3.** one of a pair of like things.

dou′ble take′, *n.* a delayed response, as to a person not recognized or a situation not grasped immediately.

dou′ble-talk′, *n.* **1.** speech using nonsense syllables along with real words. **2.** evasive or ambiguous language.

dou·bloon (du blōōn′), *n.* a former gold coin of Spain and Spanish America.

dou·bly (dub′lē), *adv.* **1.** to a double measure or degree. **2.** in a double manner.

doubt (dout), *v.t.* **1.** to be uncertain and undecided about. **2.** to distrust. —*v.i.* **3.** to be uncertain. —*n.* **4.** a feeling of uncertainty and indecision. **5.** distrust or suspicion. **6.** a situation causing uncertainty. —*Idiom.* **7. beyond** or **without doubt,** with certainty. **8. no doubt,** a. probably. b. certainly. —**doubt′er,** *n.*

doubt′ful, *adj.* **1.** of uncertain outcome. **2.** admitting of or causing doubt. **3.** unsettled in opinion or belief. —**doubt′ful·ly,** *adv.*

doubt′ing Thom′as, *n.* a person who refuses to believe without proof; skeptic. John 20:24–29.

doubt′less, *adv.* **1.** certainly. **2.** probably.

douche (dōōsh), *n., v.,* **douched, douch·ing.** —*n.* **1.** a jet of water, sometimes with a cleansing agent, applied to a body part or cavity. **2.** an instrument, as a syringe, for administering a douche. —*v.t., v.i.* **3.** to apply a douche (to).

dough (dō), *n.* **1.** flour or meal combined with water, milk, etc., in a pliable mass for baking into bread, pastry, etc. **2.** *Slang.* money. —**dough′y,** *adj.,* **-i·er, -i·est.**

dough·nut (dō′nət, -nut′), *n.* a small, usu. ring-shaped cake of sweetened dough fried in deep fat.

dough′ty (-tē), *adj.,* **-ti·er, -ti·est.** courageous and resolute.

Doug·las (dug′ləs), *n.* **Stephen A(rnold),** 1813–61, U.S. political leader.

Doug′las fir′ (dug′ləs), *n.* a giant North American evergreen tree of the pine family.

Doug·lass (dug′ləs), *n.* **Frederick,** 1817–95, U.S. exslave, abolitionist, and orator.

dour (dŏŏr, dou[ə]r, dou[ə]r), *adj.* **1.** sullen; gloomy. **2.** severe; stern. —**dour′ness,** *n.*

douse (dous), *v.t.,* **doused, dous·ing. 1.** to plunge into water or the like; drench. **2.** to throw water or other liquid on. **3.** to extinguish.

dove[1] (duv), *n.* **1.** any bird of the pigeon family. **2.** a symbol of peace. **3.** a person who advocates peace.

dove[2] (dōv), *v.* a pt. of DIVE.

Do·ver (dō′vər), *n.* **1.** a seaport in SE England. 104,300. **2.** the capital of Delaware. 23,512.

dove′tail′, *n.* **1.** a tapered tenon; pin. **2.** a joint formed of one or more such tenons fitting tightly within corresponding mortises. —*v.t., v.i.* **3.** to join together by means of a dovetail. **4.** to fit together compactly or harmoniously.

dow•a•ger (dou′ə jər), *n.* **1.** a woman who holds some title or property from her deceased husband. **2.** an elderly woman of stately dignity.

dow•dy (dou′dē), *adj.*, **-di•er, -di•est.** not neat or stylish in dress. —**dow′di•ness,** *n.*

dow•el (dou′əl), *n., v.*, **-eled, -el•ing** or (*esp. Brit.*) **-elled, -el•ling.** —*n.* **1.** a pin, usu. round, fitting into holes in two adjacent pieces to prevent their slipping or to align them. —*v.t.* **2.** to pin with dowels.

dow•er (dou′ər), *n.* **1.** the portion of a deceased husband's real property allowed to his widow for life. **2.** DOWRY. —*v.t.* **3.** to provide with a dower.

down[1] (doun), *adv.* **1.** toward or into a lower position or level. **2.** on or to the ground, floor, or bottom. **3.** to or in a sitting or lying position. **4.** to or toward the south. **5.** to a lower value or rate. **6.** to a lesser pitch or volume. **7.** in or to a calmer state. **8.** from an earlier to a later time. **9.** from a greater to a lesser strength, amount, etc. **10.** earnestly: *to get down to work.* **11.** on paper: *Write this down.* **12.** thoroughly; completely. **13.** in cash at the time of purchase: *$50 down.* **14.** into a condition of ill health. **15.** in or into a lower status or condition. —*prep.* **16.** in a descending or more remote direction on or along. —*adj.* **17.** directed downward. **18.** being at a low position or on the ground or bottom. **19.** downcast; depressed. **20.** ailing or bedridden. **21.** behind an opponent in points, games, etc. **22.** having lost the amount indicated: *to be down $10.* **23.** finished or taken care of: *five down and one to go.* **24.** not working: *The computer is down again.* —*n.* **25.** a downward movement; descent. **26.** a turn for the worse; reverse. **27.** *Football.* one of a series of plays during which a team must advance the ball. —*v.t.* **28.** to knock, throw, or bring down. **29.** to drink down, esp. quickly. —*Idiom.* **30. down and out,** destitute. **31. down on,** hostile to. **32. down with,** to do away with (used imperatively).

down[2] (doun), *n.* **1.** the soft plumage of birds. **2.** the under plumage of some birds, as geese and ducks, used for filling in quilts, clothing, etc., chiefly for warmth. **3.** the fine, soft hair on certain leaves and fruit. —*adj.* **4.** filled with down: *a down jacket.* —**down′y,** *adj.*, **-i•er, -i•est.**

down[3] (doun), *n.* Often, **downs.** open, rolling country usu. covered with grass.

down′beat′, *n.* the downward stroke of a conductor's arm indicating the first or accented beat of a measure.

down′cast′, *adj.* **1.** directed downward, as the eyes. **2.** dejected; depressed.

Down′ East′, *n.* (*often l.c.*) **1.** NEW ENGLAND. **2.** the state of Maine.

down′er, *n. Informal.* **1.** a depressing experience or person. **2.** a depressant or sedative drug.

down′fall′, *n.* **1.** overthrow; ruin. **2.** something causing this. **3.** a sudden fall of rain or snow.

down′grade′, *v.*, **-grad•ed, -grad•ing,** *n.* —*v.t.* **1.** to reduce in rank, income, importance, etc. —*n.* **2.** a downward slope.

down′heart′ed, *adj.* dejected; depressed.

down′hill′ (*adv.* -hil′; *adj.* -hil′), *adv.* **1.** down the slope of a hill. **2.** into a worse condition. —*adj.* **3.** going downward. **4.** free of obstacles; easy.

down′-home′, *adj.* characteristic of the rural southern U.S.; simple; earthy.

down′load′, *v.t.* to transfer (software or data) from a computer to a smaller computer or a peripheral device.

down′ pay′ment, *n.* an initial amount given as partial payment at the time of purchase.

down′pour′, *n.* a heavy, drenching rain.

down′right′, *adv.* **1.** completely; thoroughly. —*adj.* **2.** thorough; absolute. **3.** frank; straightforward.

down′scale′, *adj.* characteristic of or suitable for

people at the lower end of a social or economic scale.

down′size′, *v.t.*, **-sized, -siz•ing. 1.** to design or make a smaller version of. **2.** to reduce in size or number; cut back.

down′stage′ (*adv.* -stāj′; *adj.* -stāj′), *adv., adj.* at or toward the front of the stage.

down′stairs′ (*adv., n.* -stârz′; *adj.* -stârz′), *adv.* **1.** down the stairs. **2.** to or on a lower floor. —*adj.* **3.** pertaining to or situated on a lower floor. —*n.* **4.** the lower floor or floors of a building.

down′state′, *adj., adv.* in, characteristic of, or from the southern part of a state.

down′stream′, *adv., adj.* in the direction of the current of a stream.

down′swing′, *n.* **1.** a downward swing, as of a golf club. **2.** a downward trend, as of business.

Down′ (or **Down′s′**) **syn′drome,** *n.* a genetic disorder characterized by mental retardation, a wide, flattened skull, and slanting eyes. [after J. L. H. *Down* (1828–96), British physician]

down′-to-earth′, *adj.* practical and realistic.

down′town′, *adv., adj.* **1.** to, toward, or in the main business section of a city. —*n.* **2.** the main business section of a city.

down′trod′den, *adj.* tyrannized; oppressed.

down′turn′, *n.* a downward trend; decline.

down′ward, *adv.* **1.** Also, **down′wards.** from a higher to a lower level or condition. **2.** from a past time. —*adj.* **3.** moving to a lower level or condition.

down′wind′ (-wind′), *adv., adj.* in the direction toward which the wind is blowing.

dow•ry (dou′rē) *n., pl.* **-ries.** the money, goods, etc., that a wife brings to her husband at marriage.

dowse[1] (dous), *v.t.*, **dowsed, dows•ing.** DOUSE.

dowse[2] (douz), *v.i.*, **dowsed, dows•ing.** to search for underground sources of water, metal, etc., using a divining rod. —**dows′er,** *n.*

dox•ol•o•gy (dok sol′ə jē), *n., pl.* **-gies. 1.** a hymn of praise to God. **2. the Doxology,** the metrical formula beginning "Praise God from whom all blessings flow." —**dox′o•log′i•cal** (-sə log′i kəl), *adj.*

doy•en (doi en′, doi′ən), *n.* the senior member of a group, profession, etc.

Doyle (doil), *n.* **Sir Arthur Conan,** 1859–1930, British physician and writer.

doz., dozen.

doze (dōz), *v.*, **dozed, doz•ing,** *n.* —*v.i.* **1.** to sleep lightly and briefly; nap. —*n.* **2.** a nap.

doz•en (duz′ən), *n., pl.* **-ens, -en.** a group of 12. —**doz′enth,** *adj.*

dpi, dots per inch: a measure of resolution used esp. for printed text or images.

Dr., **1.** Doctor. **2.** Drive.

drab (drab), *adj.*, **drab•ber, drab•best,** *n.* —*adj.* **1.** lacking in brightness, spirit, etc.; dull. **2.** of the color drab. —*n.* **3.** a brownish gray. —**drab′ness,** *n.*

drach•ma (drak′mə, dräk′-), *n., pl.* **-mas, -mae** (-mē). **1.** the basic monetary unit of modern Greece. **2.** a coin of ancient Greece.

draft (draft, dräft), *n.* **1.** a drawing, sketch, or design. **2.** a preliminary form of any writing. **3.** a current of air in any enclosed space. **4.** a device for regulating the current of air in a fireplace, stove, etc. **5.** the act of pulling loads. **6.** something drawn or pulled. **7.** the force required to pull a load. **8.** the selection of persons for military service, an athletic team, etc. **9.** the persons so selected. **10.** a written order for payment of money. **11.** beer or ale drawn from a cask. **12.** the act of drinking or inhaling. **13.** a drink or dose. **14.** the depth to which a ship is immersed when bearing a given load. —*v.t.* **15.** to sketch. **16.** to compose. **17.** to select by draft, as for military service. —*adj.* **18.** used for drawing loads: *a draft horse.* **19.** drawn from a cask. **20.** being a preliminary outline or sketch. —*Idiom.* **21. on draft,** available from a cask: *beer on draft.* —**draft′er,** *n.*

draft•ee (draf tē′, dräf-), *n., pl.* **-ees.** a person who is drafted for military service.

drafts′man, *n., pl.* **-men. 1.** a person employed in

making mechanical drawings. **2.** an artist skilled in drawing. —**drafts′man•ship′,** n.

draft′y, adj., **-i•er, -i•est.** characterized by or admitting drafts of air. —**draft′i•ness,** n.

drag (drag), v., **dragged, drag•ging,** n. —v.t. **1.** to draw or pull slowly and with effort; haul. **2.** to search with a drag or grapnel. **3.** to introduce or insert, as an irrelevant matter. **4.** to protract tediously (often fol. by out). —v.i. **5.** to be drawn or hauled along. **6.** to trail on the ground. **7.** to move slowly and with great effort. **8.** to proceed or pass tediously. **9.** to lag behind. —n. **10.** any device for searching the bottom of a body of water to recover objects. **11.** a heavy harrow. **12.** Slang. a bore. **13.** the force exerted on an aerodynamic body that reduces forward motion. **14.** the act of dragging. **15.** something that retards progress. **16.** Slang. clothing characteristically worn by the opposite sex. **17.** a city street: the main drag.

drag′gy, adj., **-gi•er, -gi•est. 1.** lethargic; sluggish. **2.** boring; dull.

drag•net (drag′net′), n. **1.** a net to be drawn along the bottom of a stream to catch fish, or along the ground for small game. **2.** an interlinked system for finding or catching someone, as a wanted criminal.

drag•on (drag′ən), n. a mythical monster generally represented as a huge, winged reptile spouting fire.

drag′on•fly′, n., pl. **-flies.** an insect with a long, narrow body and four wings.

dragonfly

dra•goon (drə gōōn′), n. **1.** a heavily armed mounted soldier common in European armies from c1600 to World War I. —v.t. **2.** to pressure or coerce.

drag′ race′, n. a race between two or more automobiles accelerating from a standstill.

drain (drān), v.t. **1.** to draw off (a liquid) gradually. **2.** to empty by drawing off liquid. **3.** to exhaust or use up gradually. —v.i. **4.** to flow off or empty gradually. —n. **5.** a pipe, conduit, etc., by which a liquid drains. **6.** the act of draining. **7.** continuous outflow or depletion. —Idiom. **8. down the drain,** lost or wasted. —**drain′er,** n.

drain•age (drā′nij), n. **1.** the act or process of draining. **2.** a system of drains. **3.** an area drained, as by a river. **4.** something drained off.

drain′pipe′, n. a pipe that carries away water, sewage, etc.

drake (drāk), n. a male duck.

dram (dram), n. **1.** a unit of apothecaries' weight equal to 60 grains, or ⅛ ounce (3.89 grams). **2.** ¹/₁₆ ounce avoirdupois weight (27.34 grains; 1.77 grams).

dra•ma (drä′mə, dram′ə), n., pl. **-mas. 1.** a composition presenting a story in dialogue to be performed by actors; a play. **2.** the art of writing and producing plays. **3.** a series of vivid, exciting, or suspenseful events. **4.** the quality of being vivid or striking. —**dra•mat•ic** (drə mat′ik), adj. —**dra•mat′i•cal•ly,** adv.

Dram•a•mine (dram′ə mēn′), Trademark. a brand of antihistamine used to prevent motion sickness.

dra•mat•ics (drə mat′iks), n. **1.** (used with a sing. v.) the art of producing or acting dramas. **2.** (used with a pl. v.) overly emotional or insincere behavior.

dram•a•tist (dram′ə tist, drä′mə-), n. a writer of dramas; playwright.

dram′a•tize′, v.t., **-tized, -tiz•ing. 1.** to put into a form suitable for acting. **2.** to express or represent strikingly or vividly. —**dram′a•ti•za′tion,** n.

drank (drangk), v. pt. and a pp. of DRINK. ——**Usage.** See DRINK.

drape (drāp), v., **draped, drap•ing,** n. —v.t. **1.** to cover or hang with fabric, esp. in graceful folds. **2.** to adjust (fabric, clothes, etc.) into loose folds. **3.** to arrange, hang, or let fall carelessly. —n. **4.** a long, heavy curtain, esp. one of a pair. **5.** manner or style of hanging.

drap′er, n. Brit. a dealer in cloth, dry goods, and clothing.

drap′er•y, n., pl. **-er•ies. 1.** hangings, clothing, etc., arranged in loose folds. **2.** Usu., **-er•ies.** long curtains of heavy fabric. **3.** Brit. DRY GOODS.

dras•tic (dras′tik), adj. **1.** acting with force; violent. **2.** severe or harsh. —**dras′ti•cal•ly,** adv.

draught (draft, dräft), n., v.t., adj. Chiefly Brit. DRAFT.

draw (drô), v., **drew, drawn, draw•ing.** —v.t. **1.** to cause to move in a particular direction by or as if by pulling. **2.** to pull down or over, as to cover, or to pull up or aside, as to uncover: Please draw the curtain. He drew the blanket over him. **3.** to bring, take, or pull out, as from a receptacle or source. **4.** to attract. **5.** to sketch or depict with lines or words. **6.** to frame or formulate. **7.** to inhale or suck in. **8.** to deduce; infer: to draw a conclusion. **9.** to receive: to draw a salary. **10.** to withdraw (funds) from an account. **11.** to write (a check or draft). **12.** to produce; bring in: to draw interest. **13.** to choose or have assigned to one at random. **14.** to wrinkle or shrink by contraction. **15.** (of a ship) to need (a specific depth of water) to float. —v.i. **16.** to exert a pulling or attracting force. **17.** to move or pass, esp. continuously: The day draws near. **18.** to take out a sword, pistol, etc., for action. **19.** to hold a lottery: to draw for prizes. **20.** to sketch or to trace figures. **21.** to shrink or contract. **22.** to produce or permit a draft, as a pipe or flue. **23. draw on, a.** to utilize or make use of, esp. as a source: to draw on the imagination. **24. ~ out, a.** to pull out. **b.** to prolong. **c.** to persuade to speak. **25. ~ up, a.** to draft, esp. a legal or formal document. **b.** to put into order. **c.** to stop. —n. **26.** the act or result of drawing. **27.** something that attracts. **28.** something drawn. **29.** a contest that ends in a tie.

draw′back′, n. a disadvantageous feature.

draw′bridge′, n. a bridge that may be raised or moved aside to prevent access or permit passage of ships.

draw•er (drôr for 1, 2; drô′ər for 3), n. **1.** a sliding, lidless box, as in a desk or bureau. **2. drawers,** (used with a pl. v.) an undergarment with legs that covers the lower half of the body. **3.** one that draws.

draw′ing, n. **1.** the act of a person or thing that draws. **2.** the art of making a graphic representation with lines, as with a pencil or crayon. **3.** a picture or design thus produced. **4.** the drawing of lots; lottery.

draw′ing card′, n. a person or thing that attracts attention or patrons.

draw′ing room′, n. a formal reception room in a home.

drawl (drôl), v.t., v.i. **1.** to speak in a slow manner, usu. prolonging the vowels. —n. **2.** an act or utterance of a person who drawls.

drawn (drôn), v. **1.** pp. of DRAW. —adj. **2.** tense; haggard. **3.** eviscerated, as a fowl.

draw′string′, n. a string or cord that closes or tightens an opening, as of a bag or garment.

dray (drā), n. a low, strong cart without fixed sides, for carrying heavy loads.

dread (dred), v.t. **1.** to fear greatly. **2.** to be very reluctant to do, meet, or experience. —n. **3.** terror or apprehension. —adj. **4.** greatly feared. **5.** held in awe.

dread′ful, adj. **1.** causing dread or terror; terrible. **2.** extremely bad or unpleasant. —**dread′ful•ly,** adv.

dread′locks′, n.pl. a hairstyle of many long, ropelike locks.

dread′nought′ or **-naught′,** n. a type of battleship with heavy-caliber guns.

dream (drēm), n., v., **dreamed** or **dreamt, dream•ing.** —n. **1.** a succession of images or thoughts passing through the mind during sleep. **2.** a daydream or reverie. **3.** a goal; aim. **4.** a wild or vain fancy. **5.** something of unreal beauty or excellence. —v.i. **6.** to have a dream. **7.** to daydream. **8.** to conceive of something remotely (usu. fol. by *of*). —*v.t.* **9.** to see or imagine in a dream. **10.** to imagine as possible; conceive. **11.** to pass (time) in dreaming (often fol. by *away*). **12. dream up,** to conceive or devise. —**dream′er,** *n.* —**dream′like′,** *adj.*

dream′land′, *n.* **1.** a lovely land that exists only in dreams or the imagination. **2.** a state of sleep.

dream′ team′, *n.* a number of persons of the highest ability associated in some joint action: *a dream team at the Olympics; a dream team of lawyers.*

dream′ tick′et, *n.* a pair of candidates for president and vice president who appeal to most of the public.

dream′ world′, *n.* the realm of imagination or illusion.

dream′y, *adj.,* **-i•er, -i•est. 1.** full of dreams. **2.** vague; dim. **3.** soothing or restful. **4.** given to daydreaming. **5.** of the nature of dreams. **6.** wonderful; marvelous. —**dream′i•ly,** *adv.*

dredge¹ (drej), *n., v.,* **dredged, dredg•ing.** —*n.* **1.** any of various machines for scooping up mud or earth, as from a river bottom. —*v.t.* **2.** clear out or remove with a dredge. —*v.i.* **3.** to use a dredge. **4. dredge up,** to discover and reveal.

dredge² (drej), *v.t.,* **dredged, dredg•ing.** to coat (food) with a powdery substance, as flour.

dregs (dregz), *n.pl.* **1.** the sediment of liquids; grounds. **2.** the least valuable part of anything.

drei•del (drād′l), *n., pl.* **-dels, -del.** a four-sided top bearing Hebrew letters, used in a children's game played on Hanukkah.

dreidel

Drei•ser (drī′sər, -zər), *n.* **Theodore,** 1871–1945, U.S. novelist.

drench (drench), *v.t.* **1.** to wet thoroughly; soak. **2.** to cover completely; bathe.

Dres•den (drez′dən), *n.* a city in SE Germany. 518,057.

Dres′den chi′na, *n.* porcelain ware produced at Meissen, Germany, near Dresden, after 1710.

dress (dres), *n.* **1.** an outer garment for women, consisting of bodice and skirt in one piece. **2.** clothing; apparel. —*adj.* **3.** of or for dresses. **4.** of or for a formal occasion. —*v.t.* **5.** to put clothing upon; clothe. **6.** to decorate; adorn. **7.** to comb out and do up (hair). **8.** to prepare for cooking, as by removing feathers. **9.** to prepare for use; finish: *to dress leather.* **10.** to apply medication or a dressing to (a wound). **11.** to bring (troops) into line. —*v.i.* **12.** to put on one's clothes. **13.** to put on or wear formal clothes. **14.** to come into line, as troops. **15. dress down, a.** to reprimand; scold. **b.** to dress informally or less formally. **16. ~ up, a.** to put on one's best or fanciest clothing. **b.** to dress in costume.

dres•sage (drə säzh′, dre-), *n.* the art of training a horse in obedience and in precision of movement.

dress′ cir′cle, *n.* a semicircular division of seats in a theater, usu. the first gallery.

dress′ code′, *n.* a set of rules establishing the type of clothing to be worn in a given circumstance, as when on duty, or in a certain environment, as a classroom.

dress′er¹, *n.* **1.** someone or something that dresses. **2.** a person employed to dress others. **3.** a person who dresses in a particular manner.

dress′er², *n.* a chest of drawers; bureau.

dress′ing, *n.* **1.** the act of a person or thing that

dresses. **2.** a sauce, esp. for salad. **3.** stuffing for a fowl. **4.** material to dress a wound.

dress′ing-down′, *n.* a severe scolding.

dress′ing gown′, *n.* a robe worn when one is not fully dressed, as when resting.

dress′mak′er, *n.* a person who makes or alters women's dresses, coats, etc. —**dress′mak′ing,** *n.*

dress′ rehears′al, *n.* a final rehearsal, as of a play, with scenery and costumes.

dress′y, *adj.,* **-i•er, -i•est. 1.** appropriate to formal occasions. **2.** fancy or stylish. —**dress′i•ness,** *n.*

drew (drōō), *v.* pt. of DRAW.

Drey•fus (drā′fəs, drī′-), *n.* **Alfred,** 1859–1935, French army officer of Jewish descent: wrongfully convicted of treason; acquitted 1906.

drib•ble (drib′əl), *v.,* **-bled, -bling,** *n.* —*v.i., v.t.* **1.** to fall or let fall in drops. **2.** to drool. **3.** to advance (a ball or puck) by bouncing it or giving it short kicks or pushes. —*n.* **4.** a trickle or drop. **5.** a small quantity. **6.** the act of dribbling a ball or puck. —**drib′bler,** *n.*

drib′let (-lit), *n.* a small portion or sum.

dribs′ and drabs′, *n.pl.* small and usu. irregular amounts.

dried (drīd), *v.* pt. and pp. of DRY.

dri•er¹ (drī′ər), *n.* **1.** any additive that speeds the drying of paints, printing inks, etc. **2.** DRYER.

dri•er² (drī′ər), *adj.* comparative of DRY.

dri′est, *adj.* superlative of DRY.

drift (drift), *n.* **1.** an act or instance of being carried along by currents of water or air. **2.** a gradual deviation from a set course. **3.** a course or tendency: *a drift toward conservatism.* **4.** a meaning; intent: *the drift of a statement.* **5.** something heaped up by wind, as a snowdrift. —*v.i.* **6.** to be carried along, as by currents. **7.** to wander aimlessly. **8.** to be driven into heaps. —*v.t.* **9.** to cause to drift.

drift′er, *n.* a person who moves frequently from one place, job, etc., to another, as a hobo.

drift′ net′, *n.* a fishing net, usu. many miles in length, supported by floats that allow it to be carried with the current.

drift′wood′, *n.* wood floating on a body of water or cast ashore by it.

drill¹ (dril), *n.* **1.** a shaftlike tool for making holes in firm materials, esp. by rotation. **2.** training in formal marching or other precise military movements. **3.** any strict, methodical training or exercise: *a spelling drill.* —*v.t., v.i.* **4.** to pierce or bore with a drill. **5.** to perform or make perform training drills. —**drill′er,** *n.*

drill² (dril), *n.* **1.** a small furrow made in the soil in which to sow seeds. **2.** a machine for sowing in rows and for covering the seeds when sown.

drill³ (dril), *n.* a strong, twilled cotton fabric.

drill′mas′ter, *n.* **1.** a person who trains others by means of drills. **2.** a person who instructs in military drill.

drill′ press′, *n.* a drilling machine having a single vertical spindle.

drill′ team′, *n.* a group trained, esp. for exhibition purposes, in precision marching, the manual of arms, etc.

drink (dringk), *v.,* **drank, drunk** or, often, **drank, drink•ing,** *n.* —*v.i.* **1.** to take water or other liquid into the mouth and swallow it. **2.** to consume alcoholic drinks, esp. to excess. **3.** to propose or take part in a toast. —*v.t.* **4.** to take (a liquid) into the mouth and swallow. **5.** to absorb (a liquid). **6.** to take in through the senses, esp. with eagerness: *to drink in the beauty of a scene.* **7.** to swallow the contents of (a cup, glass, etc.). —*n.* **8.** any liquid for drinking; beverage. **9.** liquor; alcohol. **10.** indulgence in alcohol. **11.** a swallow or draft of liquid. —**drink′-a•ble,** *adj.* —**drink′er,** *n.* —**Usage.** The past tense of DRINK is normally DRANK. The past participle is normally DRUNK. DRANK often appears as the past participle: *Who has drank all the milk?* However, such usage is generally considered nonstandard.

drip (drip), *v.,* **dripped, drip•ping,** *n.* —*v.i.* **1.** to let drops fall; shed drops. **2.** to fall in drops, as a liquid. —*v.t.* **3.** to let fall in drops. —*n.* **4.** the act of dripping. **5.** liquid that drips. **6.** *Slang.* a boring or colorless person.

drip'-dry', *adj.* of or being a garment that dries unwrinkled when hung dripping wet.

drip'ping, *n.* Often, **-pings.** fat and juice exuded from meat in cooking.

drive (drīv), *v.*, **drove, driv•en, driv•ing**, *n.* —*v.t.* **1.** to send, expel, or otherwise force to move. **2.** to force in or down; make penetrate. **3.** to cause and guide the movement of (a vehicle, an animal, etc.). **4.** to convey in a vehicle. **5.** to force to work or act. **6.** to urge; compel. **7.** to carry vigorously through: *to drive a hard bargain.* **8.** to hit (a ball, puck, etc.) with force. —*v.i.* **9.** to cause and guide the movement of a vehicle or animal. **10.** to travel in a vehicle. **11.** to hit a ball or puck with force. **12.** to strive vigorously toward a goal. **13.** to be impelled. **14. drive at**, to intend to convey. **15. ~ in**, *Baseball.* to cause (a run) to be scored or (a runner) to score. —*n.* **16.** the act of driving. **17.** a trip in a vehicle. **18.** an impelling along, as of game or cattle, in a particular direction. **19.** an inner urge or instinctive need. **20.** a vigorous effort toward a goal. **21.** a strong military offensive. **22.** energy and initiative. **23.** a road for vehicles, esp. a scenic highway. **24.** a driving mechanism, as of an automobile. —**driv'er**, *n.*

drive'-by', *adj.*, *n.*, *pl.* **-bys.** —*adj.* **1.** occurring while driving past a person: *a drive-by shooting.* **2.** casual; superficial; offhand: *a drive-by news analysis.* **3.** involving a brief stay in a hospital, clinic, etc.: *a drive-by mastectomy.* —*n.* **4.** a drive-by shooting.

drive'-in', *n.* a facility or business, as a movie theater or restaurant, designed to accommodate patrons in automobiles.

driv•el (driv'əl), *n.*, *v.*, **-eled, -el•ing** or (*esp. Brit.*) **-elled, -el•ling.** —*n.* **1.** silly or meaningless talk; nonsense. —*v.i.*, *v.t.* **2.** to let (saliva) flow from the mouth. **3.** to talk childishly or idiotically.

drive' shaft', *n.* a shaft for imparting torque from a power source to machinery.

drive'way', *n.* a private road leading from a street to a house, garage, etc.

driz•zle (driz'əl), *v.*, **-zled, -zling**, *n.* —*v.i.*, *v.t.* **1.** to rain in fine drops; sprinkle. —*n.* **2.** a very light rain. —**driz'zly**, *adj.*

Dr. Jekyll and Mr. Hyde, (*The Strange Case of Dr. Jekyll and Mr. Hyde*) a novel (1886) by Robert Louis Stevenson.

drogue (drōg), *n.* a parachutelike device for braking an aircraft or spacecraft.

droll (drōl), *adj.*, **-er, -est.** amusing in an odd way. —**droll'er•y**, *n.*, *pl.* **-er•ies.** —**droll'ness**, *n.* —**drol'ly**, *adv.*

drom•e•dar•y (drom'i der'ē, drum'-), *n.*, *pl.* **-dar•ies.** the single-humped camel of Arabia and N Africa. [< LL *dromedārius* (*camēlus*) running (camel)]

dromedary

drone¹ (drōn), *n.* **1.** the male of the honeybee and other bees that is stingless and makes no honey. **2.** an aircraft or ship operated by remote control. **3.** a parasitic loafer.

drone² (drōn), *v.*, **droned, dron•ing**, *n.* —*v.i.* **1.** to make a continued, low, monotonous sound; hum. **2.** to speak or proceed in a montonous manner. —*v.t.* **3.** to say in a dull, monotonous tone. —*n.* **4.** a low, monotonous sound.

drool (drōōl), *v.i.* **1.** to water at the mouth, as in an-

ticipation of food; salivate. **2.** to talk foolishly. —*n.* **3.** saliva running down from one's mouth.

droop (drōōp), *v.i.* **1.** to sink, bend, or hang down, as from exhaustion. **2.** to fall into a weakened or dispirited state. —*v.t.* **3.** to let sink or drop. —*n.* **4.** a drooping. —**droop'y**, *adj.*, **-i•er, -i•est.** —**droop'i•ness**, *n.*

drop (drop), *n.*, *v.*, **dropped, drop•ping.** —*n.* **1.** a small quantity of liquid that falls in a more or less spherical mass. **2.** a small quantity of liquid. **3.** a minute quantity of anything. **4.** Usu., **drops.** liquid medicine given in drops. **5.** an act or instance of falling or dropping. **6.** the distance to which anything drops. **7.** a decline in amount, degree, value, etc. **8.** a spherical piece of candy. **9.** a depository where items are left: *a mail drop.* **10.** something resembling a drop, as an ornament. **11.** a dropping of persons or supplies by parachute. —*v.i.* **12.** to fall in drops. **13.** to fall vertically. **14.** to sink to the ground, as if inanimate. **15.** to fall lower or backward in position, degree, value, etc. **16.** to come to an end: *He let the matter drop.* **17.** to pass without effort into some condition or activity. **18.** to make an unexpected visit: *A neighbor dropped in last night.* **19.** to vanish: *to drop from sight.* —*v.t.* **20.** to let fall in drops. **21.** to let or cause to fall. **22.** to cause or allow to sink to a lower position. **23.** to reduce in value, quality, etc. **24.** to utter casually. **25.** to send: *Drop me a note.* **26.** to set down or unload. **27.** to omit; leave out. **28.** to abandon; forget. **29.** to remove or dismiss. **30.** (of animals) to give birth to. **31. drop off, a.** to fall asleep. **b.** to decline. **32. ~ out**, to withdraw, as from school or a race.

drop' kick', *n.* a kick made by dropping a football to the ground and kicking it as it starts to bounce up. —**drop'-kick'**, *v.t.*, *v.i.* —**drop'-kick'er**, *n.*

drop'let, *n.* a little drop.

drop'-off', *n.* **1.** a very steep descent. **2.** a decline; decrease. **3.** a place of delivery.

drop'out', *n.* a person who withdraws, esp. a student who leaves school before graduation.

drop'per, *n.* a small tube with a squeezable bulb at one end for drawing in a liquid and expelling it in drops.

drop•sy (drop'sē), *n.* (formerly) edema.

dross (drôs, dros), *n.* **1.** a waste product taken off molten metal during smelting. **2.** waste matter; refuse.

drought (drout), *n.* an extended period of dry weather, esp. one injurious to crops.

drove¹ (drōv), *v.* pt. of DRIVE.

drove² (drōv), *n.* **1.** a number of oxen, sheep, or swine driven in a group. **2.** Usu., **droves.** a large crowd of people, esp. in motion.

dro•ver (drō'vər), *n.* a person who drives cattle or sheep.

drown (droun), *v.i.* **1.** to die of suffocation under water or other liquid. —*v.t.* **2.** to kill by suffocation in water or other liquid. **3.** to flood. **4.** to render inaudible, as by a louder sound (often fol. by *out*).

drowse (drouz), *v.*, **drowsed, drows•ing**, *n.* —*v.i.* **1.** to be half asleep. —*n.* **2.** a sleepy condition.

drow'sy, *adj.*, **-si•er, -si•est. 1.** being half asleep. **2.** inducing sleepiness. —**drow'si•ness**, *n.*

drub (drub), *v.t.*, **drubbed, drub•bing. 1.** to beat, as with a stick. **2.** to defeat decisively, as in a game. —**drub'ber**, *n.*

drudge (druj), *n.*, *v.*, **drudged, drudg•ing.** —*n.* **1.** a person who does menial, dull, or hard work. —*v.i.* **2.** to perform such work. —**drudg'er•y**, *n.*, *pl.* **-er•ies.**

drug (drug), *n.*, *v.*, **drugged, drug•ging.** —*n.* **1.** a chemical substance used in medicines or as a medicine. **2.** any nonfood substance that, when taken, affects functions of the body or mind. **3.** a narcotic. —*v.t.* **4.** to stupefy or poison with a drug. **5.** to mix (food or drink) with a drug, esp. a stupefying or poisonous drug.

drug'gist, *n.* **1.** PHARMACIST. **2.** the owner or operator of a drugstore.

drug'store', *n.* the place of business of a pharmacist, usu. also selling toiletries, cosmetics, stationery, etc.

dru•id (droo'id), n. (often cap.) a member of a pre-Christian religious order among the ancient Celts of Gaul, Britain, and Ireland. —**dru'id•ism,** n.

drum (drum), n., v., **drummed, drum•ming.** —n. **1.** a percussion instrument consisting of a hollow, cylindrical body covered at one or both ends with a tightly stretched membrane, which is struck to produce a sound. **2.** the sound produced by a drum. **3.** the eardrum. **4.** any cylindrical object, esp. a large, metal receptacle for storing liquids. —v.i. **5.** to beat a drum. **6.** to tap one's fingers rhythmically. —v.t. **7.** to perform by beating a drum. **8.** to drive or force by persistent repetition: My parents drummed that idea into my head. **9. drum out,** to expel in disgrace. **10.** ~ **up,** to obtain or create (trade, interest, etc.) through vigorous effort.

drum•lin (drum'lin), n. a long, narrow or oval hill of unstratified glacial drift.

drum' ma'jor, n. the leader of a marching band.

drum' majorette', n. MAJORETTE.

drum'mer, n. **1.** a person who plays a drum. **2.** a traveling sales representative.

drum'stick', n. **1.** a stick for beating a drum. **2.** the meaty leg of a cooked fowl.

drunk (drungk), adj. **1.** having one's faculties impaired by an excess of alcoholic drink. **2.** overcome or dominated by a strong feeling. —n. **3. a.** a person who is drunk. **b.** DRUNKARD. **4.** a drinking spree. —v. **5.** pp. of DRINK. ——**Usage.** See DRINK.

drunk•ard (drung'kərd), n. a person who is habitually or frequently drunk.

drunk'en, adj. **1.** intoxicated; drunk. **2.** given to drunkenness. **3.** pertaining to, caused by, or marked by intoxication: a drunken quarrel. —**drunk'en•ly,** adv. —**drunk'en•ness,** n.

drupe (droop), n. a pulpy fruit, as a peach, having a hard inner shell that encloses a single seed.

Dru•sil•la (droo sil'ə). n. the daughter of Herod Agrippa and wife of Felix, who heard a discourse by the Apostle Paul. Acts 24:24–25.

dry (drī), adj., **dri•er, dri•est,** v., **dried, dry•ing,** n., pl. **drys, dries.** —adj. **1.** free from moisture or excess moisture; not wet. **2.** characterized by little or no rain. **3.** characterized by a deficiency of natural moisture. **4.** not under or on water. **5.** drained, depleted, or empty of liquid. **6.** not yielding milk. **7.** thirsty. **8.** of nonliquid substances or commodities. **9.** (esp. of wines) not sweet. **10.** not allowing the manufacture and sale of alcoholic beverages. **11.** sober. **12.** dull; uninteresting. **13.** expressed in a straight-faced, matter-of-fact way: dry humor. **14.** unproductive: dry years. —v.t., v.i. **15.** to make or become dry. —n. **16.** a prohibitionist. —**dry'ly, dri'ly,** adv. —**dry'ness,** n.

dry•ad (drī'əd, -ad), n. (often cap.) a nymph of the woods.

dry' cell', n. a cell in which the electrolyte exists in the form of a paste or is otherwise restrained from flowing.

dry' clean'ing, n. the cleaning of garments, fabrics, draperies, etc., with chemicals rather than with water. —**dry'-clean',** v.t. —**dry' clean'er,** n.

dry' dock', n. a structure able to contain a ship, leaving all parts of the hull accessible for repairs or construction.

dry'er, n. **1.** a machine or apparatus for removing moisture, as by heat. **2.** DRIER¹.

dry' farm'ing, n. farming in dry regions that uses moisture in the soil rather than irrigation.

dry' goods', n.pl. textile fabrics and related merchandise.

dry' ice', n. the solid form of carbon dioxide, used chiefly as a refrigerant.

dry' meas'ure, n. the system of volumetric units used in measuring dry commodities, as grain.

dry' run', n. a rehearsal or trial.

dry'wall', n. a material, as plasterboard, used to make an interior wall.

DST or **D.S.T.,** daylight-saving time.

DTP, 1. diphtheria, tetanus, and pertussis: a mixed vaccine. **2.** desktop publishing.

Du., Dutch.

du•al (doo'əl, dyoo'-), adj. **1.** of or noting two. **2.** composed or consisting of two together; twofold; double. —**du'al•ism,** n. —**du•al'i•ty,** n.

dub¹ (dub), v.t., **dubbed, dub•bing. 1.** to invest with a name, epithet, nickname, or title. **2.** to smooth by striking or rubbing, as leather. —**dub'-ber,** n.

dub² (dub), v.t., **dubbed, dub•bing. 1.** to furnish (a film or tape) with a new sound track, as one in another language. **2.** to add (music, speech, etc.) to a film or tape recording. —**dub'ber,** n.

Du•bai (doo bī'), n. an emirate in the NE United Arab Emirates. 419,104.

dub•bin (dub'in) also **-bing** (-ing), n. a mixture of tallow and oil used in dressing leather.

du•bi•e•ty (doo bī'i tē, dyoo-), n., pl. **-ties. 1.** doubtfulness; doubt. **2.** a matter of doubt.

du'bi•ous (-bē əs), adj. **1.** marked by or occasioning doubt. **2.** of doubtful quality or propriety; questionable. **3.** inclined to doubt; hesitant. —**du'bi•ous•ly,** adv.

Dub•lin (dub'lin), n. the capital of Ireland. 422,220.

du•cal (doo'kəl, dyoo'-), adj. of a duke or dukedom.

duc•at (duk'ət), n. any of several gold coins formerly issued in various parts of Europe.

duch•ess (duch'is), n. **1.** the wife or widow of a duke. **2.** a woman who rules a duchy.

duch•y (duch'ē), n., pl. **duch•ies.** the territory ruled by a duke or duchess.

duck¹ (duk), n., pl. **ducks, duck. 1.** any of numerous web-footed swimming birds characterized by a broad, flat bill. **2.** the flesh of this bird, eaten as food.

duck² (duk), v.i., v.t. **1.** to lower or bend (the head or body) suddenly. **2.** to evade (a blow, unpleasant task, etc.). **3.** to plunge momentarily under water.

duck³ (duk), n. **1.** a heavy cotton fabric for tents, clothing, etc. **2. ducks,** (used with a pl. v.) trousers made of this.

duck'bill', n. PLATYPUS. Also called **duck'bill plat'y-pus.**

duck'ling (-ling), n. a young duck.

duck'y, adj., **-i•er, -i•est.** Informal. fine or delightful.

duct (dukt), n. **1.** any tube, canal, pipe, or conduit by which a liquid, air, or other substance is conveyed. **2.** a single enclosed runway for electrical conductors or cables. —**duct'less,** adj.

duc•tile (duk'tl, -til), adj. **1.** capable of being hammered thin or drawn out into wire, as certain metals. **2.** capable of being molded or shaped; malleable. —**duc•til'i•ty,** n.

duct'less gland', n. an endocrine gland.

duct' tape', (duk, dukt), n. a strongly adhesive silver-gray cloth tape, used in plumbing, household repairs, etc.

dud (dud), n. **1.** a failure. **2.** a shell or missile that fails to explode after being fired.

dude (dood, dyood), n. **1.** a dandy or fop. **2.** Slang. a fellow. **3.** an urban Easterner who vacations on a ranch.

dude' ranch', n. a ranch operated as a vacation resort.

dudg•eon (duj'ən), n. anger: We left in high dudgeon.

due (doo, dyoo), adj. **1.** owing or owed: This bill is due. **2.** owing as a right. **3.** proper; fitting. **4.** adequate; sufficient. **5.** expected or scheduled. —n. **6.** something owed or naturally belonging to someone. **7.** Usu., **dues.** a regular fee, as for membership. —adv. **8.** directly or exactly: due east. —**Idiom. 9. due to, a.** attributable or ascribable to. **b.** because of. **10. pay one's dues,** to earn something, as a privilege. esp. by having worked hard.

du•el (doo'əl, dyoo'-), n., v., **-eled, -el•ing** or (esp. Brit.) **-elled, -el•ling.** —n. **1.** a prearranged combat between two persons, fought with deadly weapons, esp. to settle a private quarrel. **2.** any contest between two parties. —*v.t., v.i.* **3.** to fight in a duel. —**du•el•er, du•el•ist,** *n.*

due′ proc′ess of law′, *n.* the regular administration of a system of laws with respect to a person's rights and liberties. Also called **due′ proc′ess.**

du•et (dōō et′, dyōō-), *n.* **1.** a musical composition for two voices or instruments. **2.** the performers of a duet.

duf′fel bag′ (duf′əl), *n.* a large, cylindrical canvas bag for carrying clothing and other belongings.

duff•er (duf′ər), *n.* **1.** *Informal.* a plodding, incompetent person. **2.** a person inept at a specific sport, as golf.

dug (dug), *v.* a pt. and pp. of DIG.

dug′out′, *n.* **1.** a boat made by hollowing out a log. **2.** a roofed structure in which baseball players sit when not on the field. **3.** a rough shelter dug in the ground, esp. one used by soldiers.

duh (du; *often pronounced with a dentalized* d), *interj.* (used to express annoyance at the banality or obviousness of a previous comment.)

Duis•burg (dʏs′bŏŏʀk), *n.* a city in W Germany. 525,200.

du jour (də zhōōr′), *adj.* as prepared or offered on the particular day: *soup du jour.*

duke (dōōk, dyōōk), *n.* **1.** (in Continental Europe) the male ruler of a duchy. **2.** a nobleman ranking immediately below a prince. **3. dukes,** *Slang.* fists or hands. [< OF *duc* < L *dux* leader; *dukes* "fists" perh. of distinct origin] —**duke′dom,** *n.*

dul•cet (dul′sit), *adj.* pleasant to the ear; melodious.

dul•ci•mer (dul′sə mər), *n.* a musical instrument with metal strings that are struck with light hammers, plucked, or strummed.

dull (dul), *adj.,* -**er,** -**est. 1.** not sharp; blunt. **2.** causing boredom; tedious. **3.** not spirited; listless. **4.** not bright or clear; dim: *a dull day.* **5.** lacking richness or intensity of color. **6.** not brisk; sluggish. **7.** somewhat stupid. **8.** not intense or acute: *a dull pain.* —*v.t., v.i.* **9.** to make or become dull. —**dull′ness,** *n.* —**dul′ly,** *adv.*

dull′ard (-ərd), *n.* a stupid, insensitive person.

du•ly (dōō′lē, dyōō′-), *adv.* **1.** in a due manner; properly. **2.** in due season; punctually.

Du•mas (dōō mä′, dyōō-), *n.* **Alexandre** (*"Dumas père"*), 1802–70, and his son, **Alexandre** (*"Dumas fils"*), 1824–95, French novelists.

dumb (dum), *adj.,* -**er,** -**est, 1.** silly or stupid. **2.** lacking the power of speech: *a dumb animal.* **3.** not speaking; silent. **4.** lacking electronic processing power of its own: *a dumb computer terminal.* —*v.i.* **5. dumb down,** to reduce the intellectual or developmental level of. —**dumb′ness,** *n.*

Dum′bar•ton Oaks′ (dum′bär tn), *n.* an estate in the District of Columbia: site of conferences held to discuss proposals for creation of the United Nations, August–October, 1944.

dumb′bell′, *n.* **1.** a weight for exercising, consisting of two heavy balls or disks connected by a graspable bar. **2.** *Slang.* a stupid person.

dumb′found (dum found′, dum′found′), *v.t.* to make speechless with amazement; astonish.

dumb′wait′er, *n.* a small elevator used for moving food, garbage, etc.

dum•dum (dum′dum′), *n.* a hollow-nosed or soft-nosed bullet that expands on impact. Also called **dum′dum bul′let.**

dum′my, *n., pl.* -**mies,** *adj.* —*n.* **1.** an imitation or copy of something. **2.** a figure, made in the form of a person, as for displaying clothes in store windows. **3.** *Informal.* a stupid person. **4.** one put forward to act for others while ostensibly acting for oneself. **5.** (in bridge) the declarer's partner, whose hand is exposed and played by the declarer. —*adj.* **6.** counterfeit; sham; fictitious.

dump (dump), *v.t.* **1.** to drop or let fall in a heap or mass. **2.** to unload or empty out. **3.** to rid oneself of suddenly and irresponsibly; discard or dismiss. **4.** to put (goods or securities) on the market in large quantities and at an unusually low price. **5.** to output (computer data), esp. to diagnose a failure. **6.**

dump on, to criticize harshly; abuse. —*n.* **7.** a place where garbage, refuse, etc., is deposited. **8.** a collection of ammunition, military stores, etc. **9.** *Informal.* a dilapidated, dirty place.

dump′ling (-ling), *n.* **1.** a small mass of steamed or boiled dough served in soups or stews. **2.** a wrapping of dough enclosing fruit or a savory filling.

dumps (dumps), *n.pl.* a depressed state of mind (usu. prec. by *in the*).

dump′y, *adj.,* -**i•er,** -**i•est.** short and stout; squat.

dun¹ (dun), *v.,* **dunned, dun•ning,** *n.* —*v.t.* **1.** to make repeated demands upon, esp. for the payment of a debt. —*n.* **2.** a demand for payment.

dun² (dun), *adj.* dull grayish brown.

Dun•can (dung′kən), *n.* **Isadora,** 1878–1927, U.S. dancer.

dunce (duns), *n.* a dull-witted or ignorant person; dolt.

dune (dōōn, dyōōn), *n.* a sand hill or sand ridge formed by the wind.

dune′ bug′gy, *n.* a light automotive vehicle with oversize tires for traveling along sand.

dung (dung), *n.* excrement, esp. of animals; manure.

dun•ga•ree (dung′gə rē′), *n.* **1. dungarees,** work clothes, overalls, or trousers of blue denim. **2.** blue denim.

dun•geon (dun′jən), *n.* a strong, dark prison or cell, usu. underground.

dung′hill′, *n.* a heap of dung.

dunk (dungk), *v.t.* **1.** to dip (a doughnut, cake, etc.) into coffee, milk, or the like, before eating. **2.** to submerge briefly in a liquid. **3.** to thrust (a basketball) downward through the basket. —*v.i.* **4.** to submerge oneself in water.

Dun•kirk (dun′kûrk), *n.* a seaport in N France: site of the evacuation of Allied forces under German fire 1940. 73,618.

dunk′ shot′, *n.* a basketball shot whereby a player thrusts the ball downward through the basket.

du•o (dōō′ō, dyōō′ō), *n., pl.* **du•os. 1.** DUET. **2.** a couple or pair.

du•o•de•num (dōō′ə dē′nəm, dyōō′-; dōō od′n əm, dyōō-), *n., pl.* -**de•na** (-ə dē′nə; -od′n ə), -**o•de•nums.** the first portion of the small intestine, from the stomach to the jejunum. —**du′o•de′nal,** *adj.*

dupe (dōōp, dyōōp), *n., v.,* **duped, dup•ing.** —*n.* **1.** a person who is easily deceived or fooled. —*v.t.* **2.** to make a dupe of; deceive; delude. —**dup′er,** *n.*

du•ple (dōō′pəl, dyōō′-), *adj.* having two or sometimes a multiple of two beats in a measure.

du•plex (dōō′pleks, dyōō′-), *n.* **1.** an apartment with rooms on two floors. **2.** a house for two families. —*adj.* **3.** double; twofold.

du•pli•cate (*n., adj.* dōō′pli kit, dyōō′-; *v.* -kāt′), *n., v.,* -**cat•ed,** -**cat•ing,** *adj.* —*n.* **1.** an exact copy. **2.** anything corresponding in all respects to something else. —*v.t.* **3.** to make an exact copy of. **4.** to do again; repeat. —*adj.* **5.** exactly like or corresponding to something else. **6.** consisting of two identical or corresponding parts; double. —**du′pli•ca′tion,** *n.*

du′pli•ca′tor, *n.* a machine for making duplicates, as a mimeograph. Also called **du′plicating machine′.**

du•plic•i•ty (dōō plis′i tē, dyōō-), *n., pl.* -**ties.** deceitfulness in speech or conduct.

Du•Pont or **Du Pont** (dōō pont′, dyōō-, dōō′pont, dyōō′-), *n.* **Eleuthère Irénée,** 1771–1834, U.S. industrialist, born in France.

du•ra•ble (dŏŏr′ə bəl, dyŏŏr′-), *adj.* **1.** highly resistant to wear, decay, etc. **2.** lasting; enduring. —**du′ra•bil′i•ty,** *n.*

du•ra ma•ter (dŏŏr′ə mā′tər, dyŏŏr′ə), *n.* the tough, fibrous membrane forming the outermost covering of the brain and spinal cord.

dur•ance (dŏŏr′əns, dyŏŏr′-), *n.* imprisonment.

du•ra•tion (dōō rā′shən, dyōō-), *n.* **1.** the length of time something continues or exists. **2.** continuance in time.

Dur•ban (dûr′bən), *n.* a seaport in the E Republic of South Africa. 982,075.

Dü•rer (dŏor'ər, dyŏor'-), *n.* **Albrecht,** 1471–1528, German painter and engraver.

du•ress (dŏo res', dyŏo-, dŏor'is, dyŏor'-), *n.* **1.** compulsion by threat or force; coercion. **2.** forcible restraint, esp. imprisonment.

Dur•ham (dûr'əm, dur'-), *n.* a city in N North Carolina. 143,439.

dur•ing (dŏor'ing, dyŏor'-), *prep.* **1.** throughout the duration. **2.** at some point in the course of.

durst (dûrst), *v. Archaic.* pt. of DARE.

du•rum (dŏor'əm, dyŏor'-), *n.* a wheat, the grain of which yields flour used in making pasta.

Du•shan•be (dŏo shän'bə, -shäm'-, dyŏo-), *n.* the capital of Tajikistan. 595,000.

dusk (dusk), *n.* **1.** the period of partial darkness between day and night. **2.** partial darkness; gloom. —**dusk'y,** *adj.,* **-i•er, -i•est.**

Düs•sel•dorf (dŏos'əl dôrf'), *n.* a city in W Germany. 563,400.

dust (dust), *n.* **1.** earth or other matter in fine, dry particles. **2.** the ground; earth. **3.** the disintegrated remains of the dead. **4.** anything worthless. —*v.t.* **5.** to wipe the dust from. **6.** to sprinkle with a powder or dust. —*v.i.* **7.** to wipe dust from furniture, woodwork, etc. —*Idiom.* **8. bite the dust,** to die; be killed. —**dust'less,** *adj.* —**dust'y,** *adj.,* **-i•er, -i•est.**

Dust' Bowl', *n.* the region in the S central U.S. that suffered from dust storms in the 1930s.

dust' bowl', *n.* an arid region subject to storms of dust-filled wind.

dust'er, *n.* **1.** a person or thing that removes or applies dust or powder. **2.** a lightweight housecoat.

dust'pan', *n.* a short-handled shovellike utensil into which dust is swept.

Dutch (duch), *adj.* **1.** of the Netherlands, its inhabitants, or their language. —*n.* **2.** (*used with a pl. v.*) the people of the Netherlands. **3.** the Germanic language of the Netherlands and N and W Belgium. —*Idiom.* **4. go Dutch,** to pay one's own expenses, as on a date. —**Dutch'man,** *n., pl.* **-men.**

Dutch' door', *n.* a door that is horizontally divided so that each half can be opened separately.

Dutch door

Dutch' ov'en, *n.* a heavy pot with a close-fitting lid, used for pot roasts, stews, etc.

Dutch' treat', *n.* a meal or entertainment for which each person pays his or her own way.

Dutch' un'cle, *n.* a person, often a mentor, who criticizes with unsparing frankness.

du•te•ous (dŏo'tē əs, dyŏo'-), *adj.* dutiful; obedient. —**du'te•ous•ly,** *adv.*

du'ti•a•ble, *adj.* subject to customs duty.

du'ti•ful, *adj.* **1.** performing the duties expected or required of one. **2.** proceeding from a sense of duty. —**du'ti•ful•ly,** *adv.*

du'ty, *n., pl.* **-ties. 1.** something that one is expected or required to do by moral or legal obligation. **2.** moral or legal obligation. **3.** action required by one's position or occupation. **4.** the respectful and obedient conduct due a parent, elder, or superior. **5.** an as-

signed military task or service. **6.** tax imposed on the import or export of goods. —*Idiom.* **7. off duty,** not at one's work. **8. on duty,** at one's work.

DVD, an optical disc that can store a very large amount of digital data, as text or images. [orig. *d(igital) v(ideo) d(isk);* then *d(igital) v(ersatile) d(isk);* now an abbreviation only]

Dvo•řák (dvôr'zhäk, -zhak), *n.* **Antonín,** 1841–1904, Czech composer.

dwarf (dwôrf), *n., pl.* **dwarfs, dwarves** (dwôrvz), *adj., v.* —*n.* **1.** a person, animal, or plant of abnormally small size. **2.** (in folklore) a small man having magical powers. —*adj.* **3.** of unusually small size. —*v.t.* **4.** to cause to seem small by comparison. **5.** to prevent the growth of; stunt. —**dwarf'ish,** *adj.* —**dwarf'ism,** *n.*

dweeb (dwēb), *n. Slang.* a nerd; wimp.

dwell (dwel), *v.i.,* **dwelt** or **dwelled, dwell•ing. 1.** to live or stay as a resident; reside. **2. dwell on** or **upon,** to think, speak, or write about at length. —**dwell'er,** *n.*

dwell'ing, *n.* a place of residence; abode.

DWI, driving while intoxicated.

dwin•dle (dwin'dl), *v.i., v.t.,* **-dled, -dling.** to make or become smaller and smaller; diminish.

dyb•buk (dib'ək), *n.* (in Jewish folklore) the spirit of a dead person that enters and possesses a living person.

dye (dī), *n., v.,* **dyed, dye•ing.** —*n.* **1.** a substance used to color cloth, paper, hair, etc. **2.** color or hue produced by dyeing. —*v.t.* **3.** to color with a dye. —**dy'er,** *n.*

dyed'-in-the-wool', *adj.* through and through; complete.

dye'stuff', *n.* a material yielding or used as a dye.

dy'ing, *adj.* **1.** approaching death. **2.** given or uttered just before death. **3.** drawing to a close.

dyke (dīk), *n.* DIKE[1].

Dykes (dīks), *n.* **John B(acchus),** 1823–76, English musician and hymn writer.

dy•nam•ic (dī nam'ik), *adj.* **1.** forceful; energetic. **2.** of or pertaining to force or energy related to motion. —**dy•nam'i•cal•ly,** *adv.*

dy•nam'ics, *n.* **1.** (*used with a sing. v.*) the branch of mechanics that deals with the motion and equilibrium of systems under the action of forces. **2.** (*used with a pl. v.*) the motivating or driving forces in any field or system.

dy•na•mite (dī'nə mīt'), *n., v.,* **-mit•ed, -mit•ing,** *adj.* —*n.* **1.** a high explosive, orig. consisting of nitroglycerin mixed with an absorbent substance. —*v.t.* **2.** to blow up with dynamite. —*adj.* **3.** *Informal.* wonderful or exciting.

dy'na•mo' (-mō'), *n., pl.* **-mos. 1.** an electric generator, esp. for direct current. **2.** an energetic, forceful person.

dy•nas•ty (dī'nə stē), *n., pl.* **-ties.** a succession of rulers from the same family, stock, or group. —**dy•nas'tic** (-nas'tik), *adj.*

dys-, a combining form meaning ill or bad (*dysfunction*).

dys•en•ter•y (dis'ən ter'ē), *n.* any infectious disease of the large intestines marked by hemorrhagic diarrhea.

dys•func•tion (dis fungk'shən), *n.* impairment of function or malfunctioning, as of an organ of the body.

dys•lex•i•a (dis lek'sē ə), *n.* an impairment of the ability to read. —**dys•lex'ic,** *adj., n.*

dys•pep•sia (dis pep'shə, -sē ə), *n.* indigestion. —**dys•pep'tic,** *adj.*

dz., dozen.

E

E, e (ē), *n., pl.* **Es** or **E's, es** or **e's.** the fifth letter of the English alphabet, a vowel.
E, 1. east. **2.** eastern. **3.** English. **4.** excellent.
E, *Symbol.* **1.** the fifth in order or in a series. **2.** a grade or mark indicating unacceptable academic work. **3.** the third note of the ascending C major scale. **4.** *Physics.* energy.
E., 1. Earth. **2.** east. **3.** eastern. **4.** English.
e., 1. *Football.* end. **2.** *Baseball.* error.
ea., each.
each (ēch), *adj.* **1.** every one of two or more considered individually. —*pron.* **2.** every one individually. —*adv.* **3.** to, from, or for each; apiece. —**Usage.** When the adjective EACH follows a plural subject, the verb agrees with the subject: *The houses each have central heating.* When the pronoun, a singular form, is followed by an *of* phrase containing a plural noun or pronoun, strict usage requires the singular verb: *Each of the candidates has spoken on the issue.* However, plural verbs tend to occur frequently even in edited writing.
each′ oth′er, *pron.* each the other; one another: *They distrust each other.* —**Usage.** Usage guides advise that EACH OTHER be used only of two, and ONE ANOTHER only of three or more or of an indefinite number. In standard practice, however, these expressions are used interchangeably.
ea•ger (ē′gər), *adj.* characterized by or full of keen or enthusiastic desire or interest. —**ea′ger•ly,** *adv.* —**ea′ger•ness,** *n.*
ea•gle (ē′gəl), *n.* **1.** a robust, broad-winged bird of prey with a massive bill and talons. **2.** a former gold coin of the U.S., equal to ten dollars. **3.** a golf score of two below par for a single hole.
ea′gle eye′, *n.* unusually sharp visual powers. —**ea′gle-eyed′,** *adj.*
ea•glet (ē′glit), *n.* a young eagle.
ear¹ (ēr), *n.* **1.** the organ of hearing and equilibrium in vertebrates. **2.** the external part of the ear. **3.** the sense of hearing. **4.** attention; heed. **5.** a part that resembles an ear in position or form. —*Idiom.* **6. be all ears,** to listen intently. **7. by ear,** without reference to musical notation. **8. go in one ear and out the other,** to be heard but without understanding or effect. **9. play it by ear,** to improvise.
ear² (ēr), *n.* the spike of a cereal plant, as corn, containing the seed grains.
ear′ache′, *n.* a pain or ache in the ear.
ear′drum′, *n.* TYMPANIC MEMBRANE.
ear′flap′, *n.* a flap attached to a cap, for covering the ear in cold weather.
Ear•hart (âr′härt), *n.* **Amelia (Mary),** 1897–1937, U.S. aviator.
earl (ûrl), *n.* a British nobleman of a rank below marquis and above viscount. —**earl′dom,** *n.*
ear′lobe′ or **ear′ lobe′,** *n.* the soft, pendulous lower part of the external ear.
ear•ly (ûr′lē), *adv.* and *adj.,* **-li•er, -li•est.** —*adv.* **1.** in or during the first part, as of a period of time or series of events. **2.** before the usual or appointed time. **3.** far back in time. —*adj.* **4.** occurring early. **5.** occurring in the near future: *I look forward to an early reply.* —*Idiom.* **6. early on,** not long after the beginning. —*Proverb.* **7. Early to bed and early to rise, makes a man healthy, wealthy, and wise,** moderation is a key to success: saying popularized by Benjamin Franklin in *Poor Richard's Almanac.*
ear′ly bird′, *n.* **1.** a person who rises at an early hour. **2.** a person who arrives before others. —*Proverb.* **3. The early bird catches the worm,** success depends on being active early.
ear′mark′, *n.* **1.** an identifying or distinguishing mark or characteristic. —*v.t.* **2.** to set aside for a spe-

cific purpose, use, or recipient. **3.** to mark with an earmark.
ear′muff′, *n.* one of a pair of connected coverings for the ears in cold weather.
earn (ûrn), *v.t.* **1.** to gain in return for one's labor or service. **2.** to merit; deserve. **3.** to produce as return or profit. —**earn′er,** *n.*
ear•nest¹ (ûr′nist), *adj.* **1.** serious in intention, purpose, or effort. **2.** showing depth and sincerity of feeling. **3.** important; grave. —*n.* **4.** full seriousness, as of intention: *said in earnest.* —**ear′nest•ly,** *adv.* —**ear′nest•ness,** *n.*
ear•nest² (ûr′nist), *n.* **1.** something given or done as a pledge. **2.** money given by a buyer to a seller to bind a contract.
earn′ings, *n.pl.* money earned; wages or profits.
Earp (ûrp), *n.* **Wyatt (Berry Stapp),** 1848–1929, U.S. law officer.
ear′phone′, *n.* a sound receiver, as of a radio or telephone, that fits in or over the ear.
ear′plug′, *n.* a plug inserted into the opening of the outer ear, esp. to keep out water or noise.
ear•ring (ēr′ring′, ēr′ing), *n.* **1.** an ornament worn on the earlobe. **2.** a similar ornament decorating another part of the body.
ear′shot′, *n.* the range within which sound can be heard.
ear′split′ting, *adj.* extremely loud or shrill.
earth (ûrth), *n.* **1.** (*often cap.*) the planet third in order from the sun. **2.** the earth as the habitation of humans. **3.** the surface of the earth; ground. **4.** soil and dirt. —**earth′ward,** *adv., adj.*
earth′en, *adj.* **1.** composed of earth. **2.** made of baked clay.
earth′en•ware′, *n.* pottery of baked or hardened clay.
earth′ling (-ling), *n.* an inhabitant of earth; mortal.
earth′ly, *adj.,* **-li•er, -li•est. 1.** of the earth, esp. as opposed to heaven. **2.** possible or conceivable: *no earthly reason for it.* —**earth′li•ness,** *n.*
earth′quake′, *n.* a series of vibrations in the earth's crust.
earth′ sci′ence, *n.* a science, as geology, that deals with the earth.
earth′shak′ing, *adj.* imperiling, challenging, or significantly affecting something basic, as a belief.
earth′work′, *n.* a military construction formed chiefly of earth for protection against enemy fire.
earth′worm′, *n.* a segmented worm that burrows in soil.
earth′y, *adj.,* **-i•er, -i•est. 1.** of, like, or consisting of earth or soil. **2.** realistic; practical. **3.** coarse or unrefined. —**earth′i•ness,** *n.*
ear′wax′, *n.* a yellowish, waxlike secretion in the external auditory canal.
ear′wig′, *n.* any of numerous slender insects with horny pincers at the rear.
ease (ēz), *n., v.,* **eased, eas•ing.** —*n.* **1.** freedom from pain, concern, or anxiety. **2.** freedom from difficulty or great effort. **3.** freedom from stiffness, constraint, or formality. —*v.t.* **4.** to free from anxiety or care. **5.** to mitigate, lighten, or lessen. **6.** to make less difficult. —*v.i.* **7.** to become less painful, severe, or difficult.
ea•sel (ē′zəl), *n.* a stand or frame for supporting or displaying an artist's canvas, a blackboard, or a picture.
ease′ment, *n.* a right by one property owner to use the land of another for a limited and specific purpose.
eas•i•ly (ē′zə lē, ēz′lē), *adv.* **1.** in an easy manner. **2.** beyond question; by far. **3.** likely; well.

east (ēst), *n.* **1.** the cardinal point of the compass 90° to the right of north. **2.** the direction in which east lies. **3.** (*usu. cap.*) a region in the east. **4. the East, a.** the Orient. **b.** the eastern part of the U.S. —*adj.* **5.** lying toward or situated in the east. **6.** coming from the east. —*adv.* **7.** to, toward, or in the east.

East′ Berlin′, *n.* See under BERLIN.

East′ Chi′na Sea′, *n.* a part of the N Pacific, bounded by China and Japan.

Eas•ter (ē′stər), *n.* an annual Christian festival in commemoration of the resurrection of Jesus Christ.

east•er•ly (ē′stər lē), *adj., adv.* toward or from the east.

east′ern, *adj.* **1.** of, toward, or in the east. **2.** coming from the east. **3.** (*usu. cap.*) of the East. **4.** (*cap.*) of the Christian churches originating in countries of the eastern part of the Roman Empire. —**east′-ern•er,** *n.*

East′ern Estab′lishment, *n.* Americans living on the East Coast, considered to have national political influence.

East′ern Hem′isphere, *n.* the part of the globe east of the Atlantic, including Asia, Africa, Australia, and Europe.

East′ Ger′many, *n.* a former republic in central Europe. Compare GERMANY.

East′ In′dies (in′dēz), *n.pl.* the Malay Archipelago. —**East′ In′dian,** *adj., n.*

East•man (ēst′mən), *n.* **George,** 1854–1932, U.S. philanthropist and inventor in the field of photography.

east′ward (-wərd), *adv.* **1.** Also, **east′wards.** toward the east. —*adj.* **2.** moving, facing, or situated toward the east.

eas•y (ē′zē), *adj. and adv.,* **-i•er, -i•est.** —*adj.* **1.** not difficult. **2.** free from pain, worry, or care. **3.** easygoing; relaxed. **4.** not harsh or strict; lenient. **5.** not forced or hurried; moderate. **6.** not steep; gradual. —*adv.* **7.** in an easy manner; easily. —*Idiom.* **8. easy come, easy go,** what is acquired without effort is just as easily lost. —**eas′i•ness,** *n.*

eas′y chair′, *n.* an upholstered armchair.

eas′y-go′ing, *adj.* relaxed and rather casual.

eat (ēt), *v.,* **ate** (āt; *esp. Brit.* et), **eat•en** (ēt′n), **eat•ing,** *n.* —*v.t.* **1.** to take into the mouth and swallow for nourishment. **2.** to wear away; corrode. **3.** to use up, esp. wastefully; consume. **4.** to cause anxiety or irritation in: *What's eating you?* —*v.i.* **5.** to consume food; have a meal. —*n.* **6. eats,** *Informal.* food. —*Proverb.* **7. Eat, drink, and be merry,** enjoy life to the fullest. Isa. 22:13; Eccl. 8:15.

eat′er•y, *n., pl.* **-on•ies.** *Informal.* a restaurant.

eat′ing disor′der, *n.* any of various disorders, as anorexia or bulimia, characterized by severe disturbances in eating habits.

eaves (ēvz), *n.pl.* the overhanging lower edge of a roof.

eaves′drop′, *v.i.,* **-dropped, -drop•ping.** to listen secretly to a private conversation. —**eaves′drop′per,** *n.*

E•bal (ē′bəl), *n.* a mountaintop altar set up by Moses. Deut. 27:4–5; Josh. 8:30.

ebb (eb), *n.* **1.** the flowing back of the tide as the water returns to the sea. **2.** a point or state of decline. —*v.i.* **3.** to flow back or away. **4.** to decline or decay.

E•bed-Me•lech (ē′bed mē′lek), *n.* an Ethiopian who rescued the prophet Jeremiah from a cistern. Jer. 38:7–13.

E•bon•ics or **e•bon•ics** (i bon′iks), *n.* (*used with a sing. v.*) BLACK ENGLISH. [b. of EBONY and PHONICS]

eb•on•y (eb′ə nē), *n., pl.* **-ies,** *adj.* —*n.* **1.** a hard, heavy, dark wood from various tropical trees of Africa and Asia. —*adj.* **2.** made of ebony. **3.** of a deep, lustrous black.

e•bul•lient (i bul′yənt, i bŏŏl′-), *adj.* **1.** marked by enthusiasm, excitement, or vivacity. **2.** bubbling up; boiling. —**e•bul′lience,** *n.* —**e•bul′lient•ly,** *adv.*

eb•ul•li•tion (eb′ə lish′ən), *n.* **1.** a seething, as of feeling; overflow. **2.** the act or process of boiling up.

ec•ce ho•mo (ech′ā hō′mō, ek′ā), *Latin.* "Behold the man!": the words with which Pilate presented Christ to his accusers. John 19:5.

ec•cen•tric (ik sen′trik, ek-), *adj.* **1.** unconventional, as in behavior; odd. **2.** not having the same center. **3.** not situated in the center. **4.** having the axis away from the center. **5.** deviating from a circular form. —*n.* **6.** an eccentric person. **7.** a disk with an off-center axis of revolution that converts rotary motion to reciprocating motion. —**ec•cen•tric•i•ty** (ek′sen tris′i tē, -sən-), *n., pl.* **-ties.**

Eccl. or **Eccles.,** Ecclesiastes.

Ec•cle•si•as•tes (i klē′zē as′tēz), *n.* a book of the Bible, containing thoughts about life and its meaning. [LL < Gk *ekklēsiastḗs* person addressing an assembly]

ec•cle•si•as•tic (i klē′zē as′tik), *n.* **1.** a member of the clergy. —*adj.* **2.** ecclesiastical.

ec•cle•si•as•ti•cal, *adj.* of a church or the clergy.

Ec•cle•si•as•ti•cus (i klē′zē as′ti kəs), *n.* a book of the Apocrypha. Also called **Wisdom of Jesus, Son of Sirach.**

ech•e•lon (esh′ə lon′), *n.* **1.** a level of command, authority, or rank. **2.** a steplike formation of troops, airplanes, etc.

ech•o (ek′ō), *n., pl.* **-oes,** *v.,* **-oed, -o•ing.** —*n.* **1.** a repetition of sound produced by the reflection of sound waves from a surface. **2.** a sound so produced. **3.** a repetition or imitation of the ideas or words of another. —*v.i.* **4.** to resound with an echo. **5.** to be repeated by or as if by an echo. —*v.t.* **6.** to emit an echo of. **7.** to repeat in imitation.

ech′o•lo•ca′tion, *n.* a sonarlike system, as that used by bats, to detect objects by emitting sounds that reflect off the object and return to the source.

Eck•hart (ek′ärt), *n.* **Johannes,** ("*Meister Eckhart*"), c1260–1327?, Dominican theologian: founder of German mysticism.

é•clair (ā klâr′, ā′klâr), *n.* an elongated, usu. iced cream puff filled with custard or whipped cream. [< F: lit., lightning]

é•clat (ā klä′), *n.* **1.** brilliance, as of success. **2.** showy or elaborate display. **3.** acclamation; acclaim. [< F]

ec•lec•tic (i klek′tik), *adj.* selecting or made up of elements from various sources. —**ec•lec′ti•cal•ly,** *adv.* —**ec•lec′ti•cism,** *n.*

e•clipse (i klips′), *n., v.,* **e•clipsed, e•clips•ing.** —*n.* **1.** the partial or complete interception of the light of one heavenly body by another. **2.** a reduction or loss of splendor, status, or reputation. —*v.t.* **3.** to cause to undergo eclipse.

e•clip•tic (i klip′tik), *n.* the great circle formed by the intersection of the plane of the earth's orbit with the celestial sphere.

ec•logue (ek′lôg, -log), *n.* a pastoral poem, often in dialogue form.

eco-, a combining form meaning ecology, environment, or natural habitat (*ecocide*).

ec•o•cide (ek′ə sīd′, ē′kə-), *n.* the destruction of large areas of the natural environment, as by dumping harmful chemicals. —**ec′o•ci′dal,** *adj.*

ecol., **1.** ecological. **2.** ecology.

e•col•o•gy (i kol′ə jē), *n.* **1.** the branch of biology dealing with the interactions between organisms and their environment. **2.** the set of relationships existing between organisms and their environment. —**ec•o•log′i•cal** (ek′ə loj′i kəl, ē′kə-), **ec′o•log′ic,** *adj.* —**e•col′o•gist,** *n.*

econ., **1.** economic(s). **2.** economy.

ec•o•nom•ic (ek′ə nom′ik, ē′kə-), *adj.* **1.** pertaining to the production, distribution, and use of income, wealth, and commodities. **2.** of the science of economics. **3.** pertaining to personal finances.

ec′o•nom′i•cal, *adj.* **1.** avoiding waste or extravagance; thrifty. **2.** pertaining to economics. —**ec′o•nom′i•cal•ly,** *adv.*

ec′o•nom′ics, *n.* **1.** (*used with a sing. v.*) the science of the production, distribution, and consumption of goods and services. **2.** (*used with a pl. v.*) financial considerations. —**e•con•o•mist** (i kon′ə mist), *n.*

e·con·o·mize (i kon′ə mīz′), v.i., **-mized, -miz·ing.** to avoid waste or extravagance; be thrifty.

e·con′o·my, n., pl. **-mies,** adj. —n. **1.** thrifty management of money and materials. **2.** an act or instance of economy. **3.** the management of the resources of an area, as a nation. **4.** an organized system. **5.** the efficient or sparing use of something: economy of motion. —adj. **6.** intended to save money: an economy car.

ec·o·sys·tem (ek′ō sis′təm, ē′kō-), n. a system formed by the interaction of a community of organisms with its environment.

ec·ru or **éc·ru** (ek′rōō, ā′krōō), n., adj. BEIGE.

ec·sta·sy (ek′stə sē), n., pl. **-sies. 1.** rapturous delight. **2.** an overpowering emotion; a state of sudden, intense feeling. **3.** the frenzy of poetic inspiration. —**ec·stat′ic** (-stat′ik), adj. —**ec·stat′i·cal·ly,** adv.

-ectomy, a combining form meaning surgical excision of (tonsillectomy).

ec·to·plasm (ek′tə plaz′əm), n. a substance alleged to emanate from a medium and produce living forms.

Ec·ua·dor (ek′wə dôr′), n. a republic in NW South America. 11,690,535. —**Ec′ua·do′ran, Ec′ua·do′re·an, Ec′ua·do′ri·an,** adj., n.

ec·u·men·i·cal (ek′yōō men′i kəl; esp. Brit. ē′kyōō-) also **-men′ic,** adj. **1.** universal; worldwide. **2.** pertaining to, promoting, or fostering Christian unity throughout the world. —**ec′u·me·nism** (-mə-niz′əm), **ec′u·men′i·cism** (-men′ə siz′əm), n.

ec·ze·ma (ek′sə mə, eg′zə-, ig zē′-), n. a skin inflammation accompanied by itching and scaling.

-ed¹, a suffix forming the past tense of weak verbs (He waited).

-ed², a suffix forming the past participle of weak verbs (He had crossed the river) and participial adjectives (inflated balloons).

-ed³, a suffix forming adjectives from nouns (diseased).

ed., 1. pl. **eds.** edition. 2. pl. **eds.** editor. 3. education.

E·dam (ē′dəm, ē′dam), n. a mild yellow cheese produced in a round shape.

ed·dy (ed′ē), n., pl. **-dies,** v., **-died, -dy·ing.** —n. **1.** a current of water or air running counter to the main current. **2.** a whirlpool. —v.t., v.i. **3.** to whirl in eddies.

Ed·dy (ed′ē), n. **Mary (Morse) Baker,** 1821–1910, U.S. founder of the Christian Science Church.

e·del·weiss (ād′l vīs′, -wīs′), n. a small, flowering Alpine plant with white woolly leaves.

e·de·ma (i dē′mə), n., pl. **-mas, -ma·ta** (-mə tə). abnormal accumulation of fluid in the tissue spaces, cavities, or joint capsules of the body.

E·den (ēd′n), n. **1.** Also called **Garden of Eden.** the place where Adam and Eve lived before the Fall. Gen. 2:8–24. **2.** any delightful region; paradise.

edge (ej), n., v., **edged, edg·ing.** —n. **1.** the line at which something ends. **2.** a brink or verge: the edge of disaster. **3.** the thin, sharp side of a cutting blade. **4.** a quality of sharpness or keenness. **5.** an advantage. —v.t. **6.** to provide with an edge or border. **7.** to sharpen. **8.** to make (one's way) gradually. —v.i. **9.** to move gradually or cautiously. —**Idiom. 10.** on edge, **a.** tense; nervous. **b.** impatient. —**edg′er,** n.

edge′wise′ (-wīz′) also **-ways′** (-wāz′), adv. **1.** with the edge forward. **2.** sideways. —**Idiom. 3. get a word in edgewise,** to succeed in participating in a conversation when someone else is constantly talking.

edg′ing, n. something that forms or is placed along an edge.

edg′y, adj., **-i·er, -i·est. 1.** nervous or anxious; tense. **2.** sharp-edged. —**edg′i·ness,** n.

ed·i·ble (ed′ə bəl), adj. **1.** fit to be eaten. —n. **2.** Usu., **-bles.** something edible; food. —**ed′i·bil′i·ty, ed′i·ble·ness,** n.

e·dict (ē′dikt), n. a decree issued by an authority, as a sovereign.

ed·i·fi·ca·tion (ed′ə fi kā′shən), n. improvement or guidance, esp. in moral matters.

ed·i·fice (ed′ə fis), n. a building, esp. a large or imposing one.

ed′i·fy′, v.t., **-fied, -fy·ing.** to instruct and improve, esp. morally; enlighten. —**ed′i·fi′er,** n.

Ed·in·burgh (ed′n bûr′ə, -bur′ə; esp. Brit. -brə), n. the capital of Scotland. 470,085.

Ed·i·son (ed′ə sən), n. **Thomas Alva,** 1847–1931, U.S. inventor.

ed·it (ed′it), v.t. **1.** to supervise the preparation of (a publication). **2.** to prepare (a manuscript) for publication. **3.** to revise or correct, as a manuscript. **4.** to delete; eliminate (often fol. by out): to edit out all references to his family. **5.** to prepare (film or tape) by deleting, arranging, and splicing. **6.** to modify (computer data or text). —**ed′i·tor,** n.

edit., 1. edited. 2. edition. 3. editor.

e·di·tion (i dish′ən), n. **1.** the format in which a literary work is published. **2.** the whole number of impressions or copies, as of a book, printed at one time. **3.** a version of something.

ed·i·to·ri·al (ed′i tôr′ē əl), n. **1.** an article or statement, as in a newspaper or on a broadcast, presenting the opinion of the publishers, editors, or owners. —adj. **2.** of an editor or editing. **3.** of, resembling, or being an editorial. —**ed′i·to′ri·al·ly,** adv.

ed′i·to′ri·al·ize′, v.i., **-ized, -iz·ing. 1.** to set forth an opinion in an editorial. **2.** to inject opinions into a factual account.

Ed·mon·ton (ed′mən tən), n. the capital of Alberta, in SW Canada. 573,982.

E·dom (ē′dəm), n. an ancient country between the Dead Sea and the Gulf of Aqaba, bordering ancient Palestine.

EDP, electronic data processing.

Ed·sel (ed′səl), n. **1.** an unpopular automobile produced by the Ford Motor Company. **2.** Informal. any unpopular or untimely product.

EDT, Eastern daylight-saving time.

educ., 1. education. 2. educational.

ed·u·ca·ble (ej′ōō kə bəl), adj. capable of being educated or trained. —**ed′u·ca·bil′i·ty,** n.

ed′u·cate′ (-kāt′), v.t., **-cat·ed, -cat·ing. 1.** to develop the faculties and powers of (a person) by schooling; teach. **2.** to provide with training, knowledge, or information. —**ed′u·ca′tor,** n.

ed′u·ca′tion, n. **1.** the act or process of educating. **2.** the result produced by instruction, training, or study. **3.** the science or art of teaching. —**ed′u·ca′tion·al,** adj. —**ed′u·ca′tion·al·ly,** adv.

e·duce (i dōōs′, i dyōōs′), v.t., **e·duced, e·duc·ing. 1.** to bring out; elicit. **2.** to infer or deduce.

ed·u·tain·ment (ej′ōō tān′mənt), n. television programs, books, software, etc., that are both educational and entertaining, esp. those intended for school-age children.

-ee, a suffix denoting a person who is the object, beneficiary, or performer of an act (addressee; escapee).

EEC, European Economic Community.

EEG, electroencephalogram.

eel (ēl), n., pl. **eels, eel.** any of numerous elongated, snakelike marine or freshwater fishes.

EEO, equal employment opportunity.

e′er (âr), adv. Chiefly Literary. ever.

-eer, a suffix denoting a person who produces, handles, or is associated with something (auctioneer).

ee·rie or **-ry** (ēr′ē), adj., **-ri·er, -ri·est.** uncanny, so as to inspire superstitious fear; strange and mysterious. —**ee′ri·ly,** adv. —**ee′ri·ness,** n.

ef·face (i fās′), v.t., **-faced, -fac·ing. 1.** to do away with by or as if by rubbing out. **2.** to make (oneself) inconspicuous. —**ef·face′ment,** n. —**ef·fac′er,** n.

ef·fect (i fekt′), n. **1.** something produced by a cause; result. **2.** power to produce results; force. **3.** operation or execution. **4.** a mental or emotional impression. **5.** general meaning or purpose; intent. **6. effects,** personal property. —v.t. **7.** to bring about; accomplish or produce. —**Idiom. 8. in effect, a.** virtually; implicitly. **b.** essentially; basically. **c.** operating or functioning; in force. **9. take effect, a.** to begin to function. **b.** to produce a result. —**Usage.** See AFFECT¹.

ef•fec′tive, *adj.* **1.** producing the intended or expected effect. **2.** in operation or in force. **3.** producing a deep or vivid impression; striking. —**ef•fec′- tive•ly,** *adv.* —**ef•fec′tive•ness,** *n.*

ef•fec′tu•al (-chōō əl), *adj.* producing or capable of producing an intended effect.

ef•fec′tu•ate′ (-āt′), *v.t.,* **-at•ed, -at•ing.** to bring about; effect.

ef•fem•i•nate (i fem′ə nit), *adj.* (of a man or boy) having traits, as softness or delicacy, traditionally considered feminine. —**ef•fem′i•na•cy** (-nə sē), *n.*

ef•fen•di (i fen′dē), *n., pl.* **-dis.** **1.** a former Turkish title of respect. **2.** (in E Mediterranean countries) an aristocratic man.

ef•fer•ent (ef′ər ənt), *adj.* conveying or conducting away from a bodily organ or part.

ef•fer•vesce (ef′ər ves′), *v.i.,* **-vesced, -vesc•ing. 1.** to give off bubbles of gas, as a carbonated liquid does. **2.** to show enthusiasm or liveliness. —**ef′fer• ves′cence,** *n.* —**ef′fer•ves′cent,** *adj.*

ef•fete (i fēt′), *adj.* **1.** degenerate; decadent. **2.** exhausted of energy; worn out. —**ef•fete′ness,** *n.*

ef•fi•ca•cious (ef′i kā′shəs), *adj.* capable of having the desired result or effect; effective. —**ef′fi•ca′- cious•ly,** *adv.* —**ef′fi•ca•cy** (-kə sē), *n.*

ef•fi•cient (i fish′ənt), *adj.* performing or functioning effectively with the least waste of time, effort, or resources. —**ef•fi′cient•ly,** *adv.*

ef•fi•gy (ef′i jē), *n., pl.* **-gies.** an image, esp. a crude representation of someone disliked.

ef•flo•res•cence (ef′lə res′əns), *n.* **1.** the state or a period of flowering. **2.** an example or result of growth and development. —**ef′flo•res′cent,** *adj.*

ef•flu•ence (ef′lōō əns), *n.* **1.** the action or process of flowing out. **2.** something that flows out; emanation. —**ef′flu•ent,** *adj., n.*

ef•flu•vi•um (i flōō′vē əm), *n., pl.* **-vi•a** (-vē ə), **-vi• ums.** an often disagreeable or noxious exhalation, vapor, or odor.

ef•fort (ef′ərt), *n.* **1.** exertion of physical or mental power. **2.** an earnest or strenuous attempt. **3.** something achieved by exertion or hard work. —**ef′fort• less,** *adj.* —**ef′fort•less•ly,** *adv.*

ef•fron•ter•y (i frun′tə rē), *n., pl.* **-ter•ies. 1.** shameless or impudent boldness; audacity. **2.** an act or instance of this.

ef•ful•gent (i ful′jənt, i fōōl′-), *adj.* shining brilliantly; radiant. —**ef•ful′gence,** *n.*

ef•fu•sion (i fyōō′zhən), *n.* **1.** the act or result of pouring forth. **2.** an unrestrained expression, as of feelings. —**ef•fu′sive** (-siv), *adj.* —**ef•fu′sive•ly,** *adv.* —**ef•fu′sive•ness,** *n.*

EFT, electronic funds transfer.

e.g., for example. [< L *exemplī grātiā*]

e•gal•i•tar•i•an (i gal′i târ′ē ən), *adj.* **1.** asserting, resulting from, or characterized by belief in the equality of all people. —*n.* **2.** one who adheres to egalitarian beliefs. —**e•gal′i•tar′i•an•ism,** *n.*

egg (eg), *n.* **1.** the roundish reproductive body produced by the female of certain animals, as birds and most reptiles. **2.** an egg produced by a domestic bird, esp. the hen. **3.** the female gamete; ovum. **4.** *Informal.* a person: *He's a good egg.* —*Saying.* **5. Don't put all your eggs in one basket,** don't venture all that you possess in a single enterprise.

egg′beat′er, *n.* **1.** a small rotary beater for beating or whipping. **2.** *Slang.* a helicopter.

egg′head′, *n. Informal.* an intellectual.

egg′nog′ (-nog′), *n.* a drink made of eggs, milk or cream, sugar, and usu. rum.

egg′plant′, *n.* **1.** a plant cultivated for its edible, dark-purple fruit, used as a vegetable. **2.** the fruit.

egg′ roll′, *n.* a mixture of minced meat or shrimp and vegetables wrapped in egg dough and fried.

egg′shell′, *n.* the shell of a bird's egg.

e•gis (ē′jis), *n.* AEGIS.

eg•lan•tine (eg′lən tīn′, -tēn′), *n.* the sweetbrier.

Eg•lon (eg′lon), *n.* a Moabite king. Judg. 3:12–25.

e•go (ē′gō), *n., pl.* **e•gos. 1.** the self of a person. **2.** *Psychoanalysis.* the component of the psyche that ex-

periences and reacts to the outside world. **3.** egotism; conceit.

e′go•cen′tric (-sen′trik), *adj.* **1.** regarding the self as the center of all things. **2.** selfish. —**e′go•cen• tric′i•ty** (-tris′i tē), *n.*

e′go•ism, *n.* **1.** the view in ethics that morality ultimately rests on self-interest. **2.** egotism or conceit. —**e′go•ist,** *n.* —**e′go•is′tic, e′go•is′ti•cal,** *adj.*

e•go•tism (ē′gə tiz′əm), *n.* **1.** excessive reference to oneself. **2.** self-centeredness. —**e′go•tist,** *n.* —**e′go• tis′tic, e′go•tis′ti•cal,** *adj.* —**e′go•tis′ti•cal•ly,** *adv.*

e′go trip′, *n. Informal.* something done primarily to satisfy one's vanity.

e•gre•gious (i grē′jəs, -jē əs), *adj.* extraordinarily bad; flagrant; glaring. —**e•gre′gious•ly,** *adv.*

e•gress (ē′gres), *n.* a means or place of going out; exit.

e•gret (ē′grit, eg′rit), *n.* any of several usu. white herons having long, graceful plumes during the breeding season.

E•gypt (ē′jipt), *n.* a country in NE Africa, on the Mediterranean Sea. 64,791,891.

E•gyp•tian (i jip′shən), *n.* **1.** a native or inhabitant of Egypt. **2.** the extinct language of Egypt under the Pharaohs. —*adj.* **3.** of Egypt, its people, or their language.

E•hud (ē′hud), *n.* a Benjamite judge of Israel. Judg. 3:15–4:1.

ei•der•down (ī′dər doun′), *n.* **1.** down from the female eider duck. **2.** a quilt filled with eiderdown.

ei′der duck′, *n.* a large diving duck of northern seas.

eight (āt), *n.* **1.** a cardinal number, seven plus one. **2.** a symbol for this number, as 8 or VIII. —*adj.* **3.** amounting to eight in number. —**eighth,** *adj., n.*

eight′ball′, *n.* **1.** (in pool) a black ball bearing the number eight. —*Idiom.* **2. behind the eightball,** in a difficult situation; stymied.

eight•een (ā′tēn′), *n.* **1.** a cardinal number, ten plus eight. **2.** a symbol for this number, as 18 or XVIII. —*adj.* **3.** amounting to 18 in number. —**eight′eenth′,** *adj., n.*

Eight′fold Path′, *n. Buddhism.* the pursuits of one seeking enlightenment, comprising right understanding, motives, speech, action, means of livelihood, effort, intellectual activity, and contemplation.

800 number, *n.* a toll-free telephone number preceded by the three-digit code "800," used esp. by a business to receive orders from distant customers.

eight′y, *n., pl.* **eight•ies,** *adj.* —*n.* **1.** a cardinal number, ten times eight. **2.** a symbol for this number, as 80 or LXXX. —*adj.* **3.** amounting to 80 in number. —**eight′i•eth,** *adj., n.*

Ein•stein (īn′stīn), *n.* **Albert,** 1879–1955, German physicist, U.S. citizen from 1940: formulator of the theory of relativity. —**Ein•stein′i•an,** *adj.*

ein•stein′i•um (-stī′nē əm), *n.* a synthetic, radioactive metallic element. *Symbol:* Es; *at. no.:* 99.

Eir•e (âr′ə, ī′rə, âr′ē, ī′rē), *n.* the Irish name of IRE-LAND.

Ei•sen•how•er (ī′zən hou′ər), *n.* **Dwight David,** 1890–1969, U.S. general: 34th president of the U.S. 1953–61.

Ei′senhower Doc′trine, *n.* a foreign policy under Dwight D. Eisenhower that sought to prevent the spread of communism in the Middle East.

ei•ther (ē′thər, ī′thər), *adj.* **1.** one or the other of two: *Read either newspaper.* **2.** the one and the other: *There are trees on either side.* —*pron.* **3.** one or the other: *Either will do.* —*conj.* **4.** (used with *or* to indicate a choice): *Either call or write.* —*adv.* **5.** as well; likewise: *If you don't go, I won't either.* —**Usage.** When used as the subject, the pronoun EI-THER takes a singular verb even when followed by a prepositional phrase with a plural object: *Either of the shrubs grows well in this soil.* As a conjunction, EITHER often introduces a series of more than two: *pizza topped with either onions, peppers, or mushrooms.*

e•jac•u•late (i jak′yə lāt′), *v.t., v.i.,* **-lat•ed, -lat• ing. 1.** to eject (semen). **2.** to utter suddenly and briefly; exclaim. **—e•jac′u•la′tion,** *n.* **—e•jac′u•la• to′ry** (-lǝ tôr′ē), *adj.*

e•ject (i jekt′), *v.t.* to drive, force, or throw out. **—e•jec′tion,** *n.*

eke (ēk), *v.t.,* **eked, ek•ing.** to obtain, maintain, or supplement with great effort: *eked out her income with odd jobs.*

EKG, 1. electrocardiogram. **2.** electrocardiograph.

Ek•ron (ek′ron), *n.* the northernmost of the five chief Philistine cities. Josh. 15:45–46; I Sam. 17:52.

e•lab•o•rate (*adj.* i lab′ǝr it; *v.* -ǝ rāt′), *adj., v.,* **-rat•ed, -rat•ing. —adj. 1.** worked out in great detail; painstaking. **2.** ornate, showy, or gaudy. **—v.t. 3.** to work out in minute detail. **—v.i. 4.** to add details or information; expand: *Elaborate on your idea.* **—e•lab′o•rate•ly,** *adv.* **—e•lab′o•ra′tion,** *n.*

E•lam (ē′lǝm), *n.* an ancient kingdom E of Babylonia and N of the Persian Gulf.

é•lan (ā län′, ā län′), *n.* dash or vivacity; verve.

e•land (ē′lǝnd), *n., pl.* **e•lands, e•land.** a large African antelope with long, spirally twisted horns. [< Afrik]

e•lapse (i laps′), *v.i.,* **e•lapsed, e•laps•ing.** (of time) to slip or pass by.

e•las•tic (i las′tik), *adj.* **1.** capable of returning to an original length or shape after being stretched. **2.** flexible; adaptable. **3.** bouncy or springy. **4.** resilient, esp. after a setback. **—n. 5.** elastic fabric or material. **6.** RUBBER BAND. **—e•las•tic•i•ty** (i las tis′i tē, ē′las-), *n.* **—e•las′ti•cize′** (-tǝ sīz′), *v.t.,* **-cized, -ciz•ing.**

e•late (i lāt′), *v.t.,* **e•lat•ed, e•lat•ing.** to make extremely happy; overjoy. **—e•la′tion,** *n.*

E•lath (ē′lath), *n.* a town at the head of the Gulf of Aqaba. I Kings 9:26–28.

El•be (el′bǝ, elb), *n.* a river in central Europe, flowing from the Czech Republic through Germany to the North Sea. 725 mi. (1165 km) long.

el•bow (el′bō), *n.* **1.** the joint of the human arm between the upper arm and forearm. **2.** something bent like an elbow. **—v.t. 3.** to push aside with or as if with the elbow. **4.** to make (one's way) by elbowing.

el′bow grease′, *n.* hard work.

el′bow•room′, *n.* space in which to move or work freely.

eld•er¹ (el′dǝr), *adj. a compar. of* **old** *with* **eldest** *as superl.* **1.** older. **2.** of higher rank; senior. **3.** of former times; earlier. **—n. 4.** an older person. **5.** an older, influential member of a community. **6.** a lay member who is a governing officer of a church.

el•der² (el′dǝr), *n.* a shrub or tree of the honeysuckle family, bearing red, black, or yellow berries.

el′der•ber′ry, *n., pl.* **-ries. 1.** the fruit of the elder, used in making wine and jelly. **2.** ELDER².

eld′er•ly, *adj.* **1.** approaching old age. **2.** of persons in later life.

eld′er states′man, *n.* a respected older politician or political adviser.

eld′est (el′dist), *adj. a superl. of* **old** *with* **elder** *as compar.* of greatest age; oldest.

El Do•ra•do (el′ dǝ rä′dō, -rä′-), *n., pl.* **-dos.** a place offering great wealth.

e•lect (i lekt′), *v.t.* **1.** to select by vote, as for an office. **2.** to choose. **3.** (of God) to select for divine mercy or favor, esp. for salvation. **—adj. 4.** elected to office but not yet inducted: *the governor-elect.* **5.** select or choice. **6.** chosen by God, esp. for eternal life. [< L *ēlēctus* chosen] **—e•lect′a•ble,** *adj.*

e•lec•tion (i lek′shǝn), *n.* **1.** the act of electing. **2.** the fact of being elected.

e•lec′tion•eer′, *v.i.* to work for the success of a particular candidate or party in an election.

e•lec′tive (-tiv), *adj.* **1.** of or derived from the principle of election. **2.** chosen by election. **3.** empowered to elect. **4.** open to choice; optional. **—n. 5.** an elective academic course.

e•lec′tor (-tǝr), *n.* **1.** a qualified voter. **2.** a member of the electoral college. **—e•lec′tor•al,** *adj.*

elec′toral col′lege, *n.* a body of electors chosen to elect the president and vice-president of the U.S.

e•lec′tor•ate (-it), *n.* a body of persons entitled to vote.

e•lec•tric (i lek′trik) also **-tri•cal,** *adj.* **1.** pertaining to, derived from, produced by, or operated by electricity. **2.** thrilling; exciting. **—e•lec′tri•cal•ly,** *adv.*

elec′tric chair′, *n.* a chair used to electrocute condemned criminals.

elec′tric eye′, *n.* PHOTOELECTRIC CELL.

e•lec•tri•cian (i lek trish′ǝn, ē′lek-), *n.* a person who installs, operates, or repairs electric devices or wiring.

e•lec•tric′i•ty (-tris′i tē), *n.* **1.** a fundamental property of matter caused by the motion of electrons, protons, or positrons and manifesting itself as attraction, repulsion, luminous and heating effects, etc. **2.** electric current or power.

e•lec•tri•fy (i lek′trǝ fī′), *v.t.,* **-fied, -fy•ing. 1.** to charge with electricity. **2.** to supply with or equip for the use of electric power. **3.** to thrill. **—e•lec′tri•fi• ca′tion,** *n.* **—e•lec′tri•fi′er,** *n.*

electro-, a combining form meaning electric or electricity (*electromagnetic*).

e•lec•tro•car•di•o•gram (l lek′uō kär′dē ǝ gram′), *n.* the graphic record produced by an electrocardiograph.

e•lec′tro•car′di•o•graph′, *n.* a device that records variations in the electric potential that triggers the heartbeat. **—e•lec′tro•car′di•og′ra•phy,** *n.*

e•lec′tro•con•vul′sive ther′apy, *n.* the treatment of mental illness by inducing a seizure with electric current.

e•lec•tro•cute (i lek′trǝ kyōōt′), *v.t.,* **-cut•ed, -cut• ing. 1.** to kill by electricity. **2.** to execute (a criminal) by electricity. **—e•lec′tro•cu′tion,** *n.*

e•lec•trode (i lek′trōd), *n.* a conductor through which an electric current enters or leaves a nonmetallic portion of a circuit.

e•lec•tro•en•ceph•a•lo•gram (i lek′trō en sef′ǝ- lǝ gram′), *n.* the graphic record produced by an electroencephalograph.

e•lec′tro•en•ceph′a•lo•graph′, *n.* an instrument for measuring and recording the electric activity of the brain. **—e•lec′tro•en•ceph′a•log′ra•phy,** *n.*

e•lec•trol•o•gist (i lek trol′ǝ jist), *n.* a person trained in the use of electrolysis for removing moles, warts, or unwanted hair.

e•lec•trol′y•sis (-ǝ sis), *n.* **1.** the passage of an electric current through an electrolyte with subsequent migration of ions to the electrodes. **2.** the destruction of hair roots by an electric current.

e•lec′tro•lyte′ (-trǝ līt′), *n.* a substance that dissociates into ions when melted or dissolved and thus forms a conductor of electricity. **—e•lec′tro•lyt′ic** (-lit′ik), *adj.*

e•lec′tro•mag′net (i lek′trō-), *n.* a device consisting of an iron or steel core that is magnetized by an electric current in a coil that surrounds it.

elec′tromagnet′ic wave′, *n.* a wave propagated at the speed of light by the periodic variations of electric and magnetic fields.

e•lec′tro•mag′net•ism, *n.* **1.** the phenomena associated with the relations between electric current and magnetism. **2.** the science that studies electromagnetism. **—e•lec′tro•mag•net′ic,** *adj.*

e•lec′tro•mo′tive (i lek′trǝ-), *adj.* pertaining to or producing a flow of electricity.

elec′tromo′tive force′, *n.* the energy available for conversion to electric form per unit of charge passing through the source of the energy.

e•lec•tron (i lek′tron), *n.* an elementary particle that is a fundamental constituent of matter, has a negative charge, and exists outside the nucleus of an atom.

e•lec•tron•ic (i lek tron′ik, ē′lek-), *adj.* **1.** of electronics or devices and systems developed through electronics. **2.** of electrons. **—e•lec•tron′i•cal•ly,** *adv.*

electron′ic mail′, *n.* E-MAIL.

e•lec•tron′ics, *n.* the science dealing with the development of devices and systems involving the flow of electrons in a vacuum, in gaseous media, and in semiconductors.

elec′tron mi′croscope, *n.* a microscope of extremely high power that uses beams of electrons focused by magnetic lenses instead of rays of light.

elec′tron tube′, *n.* a sealed glass bulb containing two or more electrodes, used to generate, amplify, and rectify electric oscillations and alternating currents.

e•lec•tro•plate (i lek′trə plāt′), *v.t.,* **-plat•ed, -plat• ing.** to plate with a metal by electrolysis.

e•lec•tro•scope′, *n.* a device for detecting the presence and determining the sign of electric charges. **—e•lec′tro•scop′ic** (-skop′ik), *adj.*

e•lec′tro•shock′, *n.* ELECTROCONVULSIVE THERAPY.

e•lec′tro•stat′ics (-stat′iks), *n.* the branch of physics dealing with electric phenomena not associated with electricity in motion. **—e•lec′tro•stat′ic,** *adj.*

el•ee•mos•y•nar•y (el′ə mos′ə ner′ē, -moz′-, el′ē ə-), *adj.* supported by charity.

el•e•gant (el′i gənt), *adj.* **1.** splendid or luxurious, as in design. **2.** polished and graceful, as in form or movement. **3.** of superior quality; exceptional. **—el′• e•gance,** *n.* **—el′e•gant•ly,** *adv.*

el•e•gi•ac (el′i jī′ak, i lē′jē ak′) also **-gi′a•cal,** *adj.* **1.** of or resembling an elegy. **2.** mournful.

el•e•gy (el′i jē), *n., pl.* **-gies.** a mournful, melancholy, or plaintive poem, esp. a lament for the dead. **—el′e•gize′,** *v.t., v.i.,* **-gized, -giz•ing.**

el•e•ment (el′ə mənt), *n.* **1.** a component or constituent of a whole. **2.** a substance that cannot be separated into simpler substances by chemical means. **3.** a natural environment. **4. elements, a.** atmospheric forces; weather. **b.** the rudimentary principles, as of an art. **5.** *Math.* a member of a set.

el′e•men′tal (-men′tl), *adj.* **1.** of or being an element. **2.** starkly simple, primitive, or basic: *elemental emotions.* **—el′e•men′tal•ly,** *adv.*

el′e•men′ta•ry (-tə rē, -trē), *adj.* **1.** rudimentary, basic, or irreducible. **2.** of an elementary school.

el′emen′tary par′ticle, *n.* any of the fundamental units of matter or radiation; a subatomic particle.

elemen′tary school′, *n.* a school giving instruction in rudimentary subjects in five to eight grades.

el•e•phant (el′ə fənt), *n., pl.* **-phants, -phant. 1.** either of two very large mammals with a long prehensile trunk and large tusks. **2.** a representation of this animal, used in the U.S. since 1874 as the emblem of the Republican party.

African elephant

el•e•phan•ti•a•sis (el′ə fən tī′ə sis, -fan-), *n.* a chronic disease characterized by marked enlargement of the parts affected, esp. the legs and scrotum.

el•e•phan•tine (el′ə fan′tēn, -tīn, -tin), *adj.* **1.** of massive size; huge. **2.** ponderous; clumsy.

el•e•vate (el′ə vāt′), *v.t.,* **-vat•ed, -vat•ing. 1.** to raise to a higher place or position. **2.** to raise to a higher status or rank. **3.** to elate.

el′e•va′tion, *n.* **1.** the act of elevating or state of being elevated. **2.** the height to which something is elevated. **3.** altitude above sea or ground level. **4.** an elevated place.

el′e•va′tor, *n.* **1.** a moving platform or cage for carrying passengers or freight from one level to another. **2.** a building for the storage and discharge of grain. **3.** a hinged horizontal surface on an aircraft wing used to control inclination.

e•lev•en (i lev′ən), *n.* **1.** a cardinal number, ten plus one. **2.** a symbol for this number, as 11 or XI.

—*adj.* **3.** amounting to 11 in number. **—e•lev′enth,** *adj., n.*

elf (elf), *n., pl.* **elves** (elvz). a diminutive, mischievous being in folklore.

El Gre•co (el grek′ō), *n.* 1541–1614, Spanish painter, born in Crete.

E•li (ē′lī), *n.* a Hebrew judge and priest. I Sam. 1–4.

e•lic•it (i lis′it), *v.t.* to draw or bring out or forth; evoke. **—e•lic′i•ta′tion,** *n.* **—e•lic′i•tor,** *n.*

e•lide (i līd′), *v.t.,* **e•lid•ed, e•lid•ing. 1.** to omit (a vowel, consonant, or syllable) in pronunciation. **2.** to pass over; ignore. **—e•li•sion** (i lizh′ən), *n.*

el•i•gi•ble (el′i jə bəl), *adj.* **1.** being a proper or worthy choice. **2.** qualified, as to be elected to office. **—el′i•gi•bil′i•ty,** *n.*

El•i•hu (el′ə hyōō′, i lī′hyōō), *n.* a young man who entered into discourse with Job. Job 32–37.

E•li•jah (i lī′jə), *n.* a Hebrew prophet of the 9th century B.C. I Kings 17; II Kings 2.

Eli′jah's chair′, *n.* a chair customarily set apart in honor of the prophet Elijah at the Jewish rite of circumcision.

Eli′jah's cup′, *n.* a cup of wine customarily set apart in honor of the prophet Elijah at the Jewish Passover Seder.

E•lim•e•lech (i lim′ə lek′), *n.* the father-in-law of Ruth and husband of Naomi. Ruth 1:1–3.

e•lim•i•nate (i lim′ə nāt′), *v.t.,* **-nat•ed, -nat•ing. 1.** to get rid of; remove. **2.** to leave out; omit. **3.** to void or excrete from the body. [< L *ēlīminātus* turned out of doors] **—e•lim′i•na′tion,** *n.*

El•i•ot (el′ē ət, el′yət), *n.* **1. George** (*Mary Ann Evans*), 1819–80, English novelist. **2. John** (*"the Apostle of the Indians"*), 1604–90, American colonial missionary. **3. T(homas) S(tearns)** (stûrnz), 1888–1965, British poet and critic, born in the U.S.

El•i•phaz (el′ə faz′), *n.* a friend of Job. Job 2:11; 4:1.

E•lis•a•beth (i liz′ə bəth), *n.* the mother of John the Baptist. Luke 1:5–25.

E•li•sha (i lī′shə), *n.* a Hebrew prophet of the 9th century B.C., the successor of Elijah. II Kings 3–9.

e•lite or **é•lite** (i lēt′, ā lēt′), *n.* (*often with a pl. v.*) the choice, best, or most powerful members of a group, class, etc.

e•lit′ism, *n.* practice of or belief in rule by an elite. **—e•lit′ist,** *n., adj.*

e•lix•ir (i lik′sər), *n.* **1.** a sweetened solution of alcohol and water used as a medicinal medium. **2.** a preparation formerly believed capable of prolonging life indef. **3.** PANACEA.

E•liz•a•beth (i liz′ə bəth), *n.* **1. Elizabeth I,** (*Elizabeth Tudor*) 1533–1603, queen of England 1558–1603 (daughter of Henry VIII and Anne Boleyn). **2. Elizabeth II,** (*Elizabeth Alexandra Mary Windsor*) born 1926, queen of Great Britain since 1952.

E•liz′a•be′than (-bē′thən, -beth′ən), *adj.* of or characteristic of Elizabeth I of England or her reign.

elk (elk), *n.,pl.* **elks, elk. 1.** a large North American deer. **2.** the moose.

ell¹ (el), *n.* an extension usu. at right angles to a building or room.

ell² (el), *n.* a former measure of length, in England equal to 45 inches (114 cm).

el•lipse (i lips′), *n.* a closed plane curve shaped like an oval.

ellipse

el•lip•sis (i lip′sis), *n., pl.* **-ses** (-sēz). **1.** the omission from a grammatical construction of a word or phrase understandable from the context. **2.** a mark or series of marks (...) used to indicate an omission.

el•lip′soid (-soid), *n.* a solid figure whose plane sections are all ellipses or circles. —**el•lip•soi′dal**, *adj.*

el•lip′ti•cal (-ti kəl) also **-tic**, *adj.* **1.** of or having the form of an ellipse. **2.** of or marked by ellipsis. —**el•lip′ti•cal•ly**, *adv.*

El′lis Is′land, *n.* an island in upper New York Bay: a former U.S. immigrant examination station.

elm (elm), *n.* **1.** a shade tree characterized by gradually spreading branches. **2.** the wood of an elm.

El Ni•ño (el nēn′yō), *n.* a warm ocean current that develops after late December along the coast of Ecuador and Peru and sometimes causes catastrophic weather conditions. [< Sp: lit., the child, i.e., the Christ child, alluding to the appearance of the current near Christmas]

el•o•cu′tion (el′ə kyōō′shən), *n.* the study and practice of public speaking. —**el′o•cu′tion•ar′y** (-shə ner′ē), *adj.* —**el′o•cu′tion•ist**, *n.*

E•lo•him (el′ō hēm′, -him′, e lō′him), *n.* God. —**El′o•him′ic** (-him′ik), *adj.*

e•lon•gate (i lông′gāt, i long′-), *v.i., v.t.,* **-gat•ed, -gat•ing.** to increase in length. —**e•lon•ga′tion**, *n.*

e•lope (i lōp′), *v.i.,* **e•loped, e•lop•ing.** to run off secretly, esp. in order to be married. —**e•lope′ment**, *n.*

el•o•quent (el′ə kwənt), *adj.* **1.** skilled in or marked by fluent, forceful expression. **2.** forcefully expressive. —**el′o•quence**, *n.* —**el′o•quent•ly**, *adv.*

El Pas•o (el pas′ō), *n.* a city in W Texas. 597,307.

El Sal•va•dor (el sal′və dôr′), *n.* a republic in NW Central America. 5,661,827.

else (els), *adj.* **1.** other; different: *What else could I have done?* **2.** additional: *Who else was there?* —*adv.* **3.** if not: *Watch your step, or else you'll slip.* **4.** otherwise: *How else could I have acted?*

else′where′, *adv.* in or to another place.

e•lu•ci•date (i lōō′si dāt′), *v.t., v.i.,* **-dat•ed, -dat•ing.** to make clear, esp. by explaining. —**e•lu′ci•da′tion**, *n.* —**e•lu′ci•da′tor**, *n.*

e•lude (i lōōd′), *v.t.,* **e•lud•ed, e•lud•ing. 1.** to escape detection or capture by; evade. **2.** to escape the comprehension of. —**e•lud′er**, *n.*

e•lu•sive (i lōō′siv) also **-so•ry** (-sə rē), *adj.* **1.** eluding perception. **2.** skillfully evasive. —**e•lu′sive•ly**, *adv.* —**e•lu′sive•ness**, *n.*

el•ver (el′vər), *n.* a young eel.

elves (elvz), *n.* pl. of ELF.

El•y•mas (el′ə məs), *n.* Bar-Jesus.

E•ly•si•um (i lizh′ē əm, i liz′-), *n.* **1.** (in Greek mythology) the abode of the blessed after death. **2.** PARADISE (def. 3). —**E•ly•sian** (i lizh′ən), *adj.*

em (em), *n.* the square of any size of type used as the unit of measurement for printed matter: originally the portion of a line occupied by the letter M.

'em (əm), *pron. Informal.* them.

em-, var. of EN-.

e•ma•ci•ate (i mā′shē āt′), *v.t.,* **-at•ed, -at•ing.** to make abnormally thin. —**e•ma′ci•a′tion**, *n.*

e-mail or **email** or **E-mail** (ē′māl′), *n.* **1.** a system for sending messages via telecommunications links between computers. **2.** a message sent by e-mail: *Send me an e-mail on the idea.* —*v.t.* **3.** to send a message to by e-mail.

em•a•nate (em′ə nāt′), *v.i.,* **-nat•ed, -nat•ing.** to flow out or issue forth. —**em′a•na′tion**, *n.*

e•man•ci•pate (i man′sə pāt′), *v.t.,* **-pat•ed, -pat•ing. 1.** to free from restraint. **2.** to free (a slave) from bondage. —**e•man′ci•pa′tion**, *n.* —**e•man′ci•pa′tor**, *n.*

e•mas•cu•late (i mas′kyə lāt′), *v.t.,* **-lat•ed, -lat•ing. 1.** to castrate. **2.** to deprive of strength or vigor; weaken. —**e•mas′cu•la′tion**, *n.* —**e•mas′cu•la′tor**, *n.*

em•balm (em bäm′), *v.t.* to treat (a dead body) so as to preserve it, as with chemicals. —**em•balm′er**, *n.*

em•bank′, *v.t.* to enclose or protect with an embankment.

em•bank′ment, *n.* a bank or mound, as of earth or stone, raised to hold back water, carry a roadway, etc.

em•bar•go (em bär′gō), *n., pl.* **-goes**, *v.,* **-goed, -go•ing.** —*n.* **1.** a restriction on commerce, esp. a government order prohibiting the movement of merchant ships into or out of its ports. —*v.t.* **2.** to impose an embargo on. [< Sp, der. of *embargar* to hinder, embarrass]

em•bark (em bärk′), *v.i.* **1.** to board a ship or aircraft. **2.** to start on an enterprise. —*v.t.* **3.** to board (passengers) onto a ship or aircraft. —**em′bar•ka′tion**, *n.*

em•bar•rass (em bar′əs), *v.t.* **1.** to make ashamed or self-conscious; disconcert. **2.** to impede; hinder. **3.** to burden with debt. —**em•bar′rass•ing•ly**, *adv.* —**em•bar′rass•ment**, *n.*

em•bas•sy (em′bə sē), *n., pl.* **-sies. 1.** the official headquarters of an ambassador. **2.** the function or office of an ambassador. **3.** a mission headed by an ambassador.

em•bat′tled, *adj.* prepared for, engaged in, or beset by conflict.

em•bed′, *v.t., v.i.,* **-bed•ded, -bed•ding.** to fix or be fixed into a surrounding mass.

em•bel•lish (em bel′ish), *v.t.* **1.** to beautify with ornamentation; adorn. **2.** to enhance with elaborate additions. —**em•bel′lish•ment**, *n.*

em•ber (em′bər), *n.* **1.** a small live piece of coal or wood, as in a dying fire. **2. embers**, the smoldering remains of a fire.

em•bez•zle (em bez′əl), *v.t.,* **-zled, -zling.** to appropriate fraudulently to one's own use, as money entrusted to one's care. —**em•bez′zle•ment**, *n.* —**em•bez′zler**, *n.*

em•bit′ter, *v.t.* **1.** to cause to feel bitterness. **2.** to make bitter in taste.

em•bla•zon (em blā′zən), *v.t.* **1.** to adorn with heraldic devices or emblems. **2.** to decorate brilliantly. **3.** to extol. —**em•bla′zon•ment**, *n.*

em•blem (em′bləm), *n.* **1.** an object symbolizing something else; symbol. **2.** a figure or design that identifies something. —**em′blem•at′ic**, *adj.*

em•bod′y, *v.t.,* **-ied, -y•ing. 1.** to give concrete form to; personify or exemplify. **2.** to provide with a body; incarnate. **3.** to collect into a body; organize. —**em•bod′i•ment**, *n.*

em•bold•en (em bōl′dən), *v.t.* to make bold; encourage.

em•bo•lism (em′bə liz′əm), *n.* the occlusion of a blood vessel, as by a gas bubble or fat globule.

em•boss (em bôs′, -bos′), *v.t.* **1.** to raise (designs) in relief. **2.** to decorate (a surface) with raised ornament. —**em•boss′er**, *n.*

em•bou•chure (äm′bŏŏ shŏŏr′), *n.* **1.** the mouthpiece of a wind instrument. **2.** the adjustment of a player's mouth to an embouchure.

em•bow′er, *v.t.* to shelter in or as if in a bower.

em•brace (em brās′), *v.,* **-braced, -brac•ing**, *n.* —*v.t.* **1.** to clasp in the arms; hug. **2.** to accept or adopt willingly. **3.** to include or contain. —*v.i.* **4.** to join in an embrace. —*n.* **5.** an encircling hug with the arms. —**em•brace′a•ble**, *adj.*

em•bra•sure (em brā′zhər), *n.* **1.** an opening in a wall through which a cannon may be fired. **2.** a usu. sloped enlargement of a door or window. —**em•bra′sured**, *adj.*

em•bro•ca•tion (em′brō kā′shən, -brə-), *n.* **1.** the act of rubbing a bruised or diseased part of the body with a liniment. **2.** a liniment.

em•broi•der (em broi′dər), *v.t., v.i.* **1.** to decorate with or do embroidery. **2.** to embellish, as with fictitious details. —**em•broi′der•er**, *n.*

em•broi•der•y (-də rē, -drē), *n., pl.* **-der•ies. 1.** the art of ornamental needlework. **2.** embroidered work or ornamentation. **3.** elaboration, as in telling a story.

em•broil′, *v.t.* **1.** to involve in conflict. **2.** to throw into confusion. —**em•broil′ment**, *n.*

em•bry•o (em′brē ō′), *n., pl.* **-bry•os. 1.** an organism in the earliest stages of development, as in the womb. **2.** a beginning or rudimentary stage. —**em′bry•on′ic** (-on′ik), *adj.*

em•bry•ol•o•gy (em′brē ol′ə jē), *n.* the study of

the formation and development of embryos. —em′·bry·ol·o·gist, n.

em·cee (em′sē′), n., pl. -cees, v., -ceed, -cee·ing. —n. 1. a master of ceremonies. —v.i., v.t. 2. to serve or direct as master of ceremonies.

e·mend (i mend′), v.t. to change (a text), esp. by correcting; edit. —e·men·da·tion (ē′mən dā′shən), n.

em·er·ald (em′ər əld), n. 1. a green beryl that is valued as a gem. —adj. 2. of a clear, deep green.

e·merge (i mûrj′), v.i., e·merged, e·merg·ing. 1. to come forth into view. 2. to rise from or as if from water. 3. to come into existence. —e·mer′gence, n. —e·mer′gent, adj.

e·mer·gen·cy (i mûr′jən sē), n., pl. -cies. a sudden, urgent, usu. unexpected occurrence requiring immediate action.

e·mer·i·tus (i mer′i təs), adj. retired from active professional duty but retaining the title of one′s office or position: professor emeritus.

Em·er·son (em′ər sən), n. Ralph Waldo, 1803–82, U.S. essayist and poet. —Em′er·so′ni·an (-sō′nē-ən), adj.

em·er·y (em′ə rē), n. a granular corundum used for grinding and polishing.

e·met·ic (i met′ik), adj. 1. causing vomiting. —n. 2. an emetic medicine or agent.

emf or EMF, electromotive force.

-emia, a combining form denoting a condition of the blood (anemia).

em·i·grate (em′i grāt′), v.i., -grat·ed, -grat·ing. to leave one country or region to settle in another. —em′i·grant (-grənt), n., adj. —em′i·gra′tion, n.

é·mi·gré (em′i grā′, em′i grā′), n., pl. -grés. an emigrant, esp. one who flees for political reasons.

em·i·nence (em′ə nəns), n. 1. high station, rank, or repute. 2. a high place; hill or height. 3. (cap.) a title of honor applied to cardinals.

em′i·nent, adj. 1. high in station, rank, or repute; distinguished. 2. lofty; high. 3. prominent; conspicuous. —em′i·nent·ly, adv.

em′inent domain′, n. the power of the state to take private property for public use.

e·mir (ə mēr′, ā mēr′), n. a chieftain, prince, commander, or head of state in some Islamic countries. —em·ir·ate (em′ər it, ə mēr′-), n.

em·is·sar·y (em′ə ser′ē), n., pl. -sar·ies. a representative sent on a mission, esp. a secret mission.

e·mit (i mit′), v.t., e·mit·ted, e·mit·ting. 1. to send forth; discharge: a bonfire emitting heat. 2. to utter; voice. 3. to issue formally, as paper money. —e·mis·sion (i mish′ən), n. —e·mit′ter, n.

Em·man·u·el (i man′yōō əl), n. IMMANUEL.

Em·ma·us (ə mā′əs), n. a village near Jerusalem toward which two disciples were walking when they met the resurrected Jesus. Luke 24:13.

e·mol·lient (i mol′yənt), adj. 1. softening or soothing: an emollient lotion for the skin. —n. 2. an emollient substance.

e·mol·u·ment (i mol′yə mənt), n. compensation, as fees, from employment; recompense.

e·mote (i mōt′), v.i., e·mot·ed, e·mot·ing. to show emotion in or as if in acting. —e·mot′er, n.

e·mo·ti·con (i mō′ti kon′), n. an abbreviation or icon used on a computer network, as IMHO for "in my humble opinion" or :-), a sideways representation of a smiling face, to indicate amusement. [b. of EMOTION and ICON]

e·mo·tion (i mō′shən), n. 1. a strong feeling, as joy, sorrow, hate, or love. 2. strong agitation or excitement. —e·mo′tion·al, adj. —e·mo′tion·al·ism, n. —e·mo′tion·al·ly, adv.

em·pa·thize (em′pə thīz′), v.i., -thized, -thiz·ing. to experience empathy.

em′pa·thy (-thē), n. identification with or vicarious experiencing of the feelings or thoughts of another. —em′pa·thet′ic (-thet′ik), adj.

em·per·or (em′pər ər), n. 1. the male sovereign or supreme ruler of an empire. —Saying. 2. The emperor has no clothes on, the purported power of

well-known figures may be a sham. [from a fairy tale by Hans Christian Andersen]

em·pha·sis (em′fə sis), n., pl. -ses (-sēz′). 1. special stress or importance: an emphasis on reliability. 2. stress given to particular words or syllables.

em′pha·size′ (-sīz′), v.t., -sized, -siz·ing. to give emphasis to; stress.

em·phat·ic (-fat′ik), adj. 1. uttered or done with emphasis. 2. using emphasis in speech or action. —em·phat′i·cal·ly, adv.

em·phy·se·ma (em′fə sē′mə, -zē′-), n. a chronic lung disease characterized by abnormal enlargement and loss of elasticity of the air spaces.

em·pire (em′pīʳr), n. 1. a group of nations, states, or peoples ruled over by a powerful sovereign, esp. an emperor or empress. 2. sovereignty; dominion. 3. a powerful enterprise controlled by one person or group: a shipping empire. [< AF, OF < L imperium]

em·pir·i·cal (em pir′i kəl), adj. derived from or depending upon experience or observation alone. —em·pir′i·cal·ly, adv.

em·pir′i·cism (-siz′əm), n. 1. empirical method or practice. 2. the philosophic doctrine that all knowledge is derived from sense experience. —em·pir′i·cist, n., adj.

em·place′ment, n. a space or platform where heavy military equipment, esp. artillery, can be positioned.

em·ploy (em ploi′), v.t. 1. to engage the services of; hire. 2. to make use of. 3. to devote (time, energies, etc.) to a particular activity. —n. 4. employment; service. —em·ploy′a·ble, adj. —em·ploy′er, n.

em·ploy′ee or -ploy′e (-ploi′ē), n., pl -es or -ees. a person hired to work for another.

em·ploy′ment, n. 1. the act of employing or state of being employed. 2. an occupation or activity.

em·po·ri·um (em pôr′ē əm), n., pl. -po·ri·ums, -po·ri·a (-pôr′ē ə). a retail store selling a great variety of articles.

em·pow′er, v.t. 1. to give power or authority to. 2. to enable. —em·pow′er·ment, n.

em·press (em′pris), n. 1. a female ruler of an empire. 2. the consort of an emperor.

emp·ty (emp′tē), adj., -ti·er, -ti·est, v., -tied, -ty·ing, n., pl. -ties. —adj. 1. containing nothing. 2. not occupied; vacant. 3. lacking force, effect, or significance. —v.t., v.i. 4. to make or become empty. 5. to discharge: The river empties into the sea. —n. 6. an empty container. —emp′ti·ly, adv. —emp′ti·ness, n.

emp′ty-hand′ed, adj. 1. having nothing in the hands. 2. having achieved nothing.

emp′ty nest′ syn′drome, n. a depressed state felt by some parents after their children have grown up and left home.

em·py·re·an (em′pə rē′ən, em pir′ē ən), n. 1. the highest heaven. 2. the visible heavens; sky.

EMT, emergency medical technician.

e·mu (ē′myōō), n., pl. e·mus. a large, flightless bird of Australia that resembles the ostrich.

EMU or emu, electromagnetic unit.

em·u·late (em′yə lāt′), v.t., -lat·ed, -lat·ing. to imitate in an effort to equal or surpass. —em′u·la′tion, n. —em′u·la′tive, adj. —em′u·la′tor, n.

e·mul·si·fy (i mul′sə fī′), v.t., v.i., -fied, -fy·ing. to make into or form an emulsion. —e·mul′si·fi·ca′tion, n. —e·mul′si·fi′er, n.

e·mul·sion (-shən), n. 1. a colloidal suspension of one liquid in another. 2. a photosensitive coating on photographic film.

en (en), n. a space that is half the width of an em.

en-, a prefix meaning: to put into or on (enthrone); to cover or surround with (encircle); to make or cause to be (enlarge).

-en¹, a suffix meaning: to make or become (harden); to cause or come to have (strengthen).

-en², a suffix meaning made of or resembling (woolen).

en·a·ble (en ā′bəl), v.t., -bled, -bling. 1. to make able; authorize or empower. 2. to make possible or easy. —en·a′bler, n.

en•act′, *v.t.* **1.** to make into law. **2.** to represent in or as if in a play. —**en•act′ment,** *n.*

e•nam•el (i nam′əl), *n., v.,* -**eled, -el•ing** or (*esp. Brit.*) -**elled, -el•ling.** —*n.* **1.** an ornamental or protective glassy substance, usu. opaque, applied by fusion to the surface of metal, pottery, etc. **2.** a paint that dries to a hard, glossy finish. **3.** the hard, glossy covering of the crown of a tooth. —*v.t.* **4.** to inlay or overlay with enamel. —**e•nam′el•er,** *n.*

e•nam′el•ware′, *n.* metal utensils covered with enamel.

en•am•or (i nam′ər), *v.t.* to fill or inflame with love: *He was enamored of the princess.* Also, *esp. Brit.,* **en•am′our.**

en bloc (äN blôk′), *adv., adj. French.* as a whole; all together.

en•camp′, *v.t., v.i.* to lodge or settle in a camp. —**en•camp′ment,** *n.*

en•cap•su•late (en kap′sə lāt′, -syōō-), *v.t.,* -**lat•ed, -lat•ing. 1.** to place in or as if in a capsule. **2.** to summarize or condense. —**en•cap′su•la′tion,** *n.*

en•case′, *v.t.,* -**cased, -cas•ing.** to enclose in or as if in a case.

-ence, a suffix meaning: act or fact (*abhorrence*); state or quality (*absence*).

en•ceph•a•li•tis (en sef′ə lī′tis), *n.* inflammation of the brain. —**en•ceph′a•lit′ic** (-lit′ik), *adj.*

en•ceph′a•lon′ (-lon′, -lən), *n., pl.* -**lons, -la** (-lə) the brain.

en•chain′, *v.t.* to bind with or as if with chains; fetter.

en•chant (en chant′, -chänt′), *v.t.* **1.** to place under a spell; bewitch. **2.** to delight utterly; captivate. —**en•chant′er,** *n.* —**en•chant′ing•ly,** *adv.* —**en•chant′ment,** *n.*

en•chi•la•da (en′chə lä′də, -lad′ə), *n., pl.* -**das.** a tortilla rolled around a filling, as of meat or cheese, served usu. with a chili-flavored sauce.

en•ci′pher, *v.t.* to put (a message) into cipher. —**en•ci′pher•ment,** *n.*

en•cir′cle, *v.t.,* -**cled, -cling. 1.** to form a circle around. **2.** to make a circuit of. —**en•cir′cle•ment,** *n.*

encl., 1. enclosed. **2.** enclosure.

en•clave (en′klāv, än′-), *n.* a country or a portion of a country surrounded by foreign territory.

en•close′ (-klōz′), *v.t.,* -**closed, -clos•ing. 1.** to shut or hem in on all sides. **2.** to surround, as with a fence. **3.** to insert in the same envelope or package with something else. —**en•clo′sure,** *n.*

en•code′, *v.t.,* -**cod•ed, -cod•ing.** to convert (a message, etc.) into code. —**en•cod′er,** *n.*

en•co•mi•um (en kō′mē əm), *n., pl.* -**mi•ums, -mi•a** (-mē ə). a usu. formal expression of high praise.

en•com•pass (en kum′pəs), *v.t.* **1.** to encircle; surround. **2.** to enclose; envelop. **3.** to include comprehensively.

en•core (äng′kôr, än′-), *n., v.,* -**cored, -cor•ing.** —*n.* **1.** a demand by an audience for a repetition, as of a song. **2.** a performance in response to an encore. —*v.t.* **3.** to call for an encore from (a performer).

en•coun•ter (en koun′tər), *v.t.* **1.** to come upon or meet, esp. unexpectedly. **2.** to meet in conflict. —*n.* **3.** a meeting, esp. when casual or unexpected. **4.** a meeting between people or groups in conflict; battle.

en•cour•age (en kûr′ij, -kur′-), *v.t.,* -**aged, -ag•ing. 1.** to inspire with courage or confidence. **2.** to stimulate, as by approval. **3.** to promote; foster. —**en•cour′age•ment,** *n.* —**en•cour′ag•ing•ly,** *adv.*

en•croach (en krōch′), *v.i.* to trespass upon the property, domain, or rights of another, esp. gradually or stealthily. —**en•croach′ment,** *n.*

en•crust′, *v.t., v.i.* INCRUST. —**en′crus•ta′tion,** *n.*

en•cum•ber (en kum′bər), *v.t.* **1.** to impede or hinder. **2.** to weigh down; burden. —**en•cum′brance,** *n.*

-ency, a suffix meaning state or quality (*consistency*).

ency. or **encyc.** or **encycl.,** encyclopedia.

en•cyc•li•cal (en sik′li kəl, -sī′kli-), *n.* a letter from the pope to all the bishops of the church.

en•cy•clo•pe•di•a or **-pae•di•a** (en sī′klə pē′-

dē ə), *n., pl.* -**di•as.** a book or set of books covering all branches of knowledge or all aspects of one subject. [< NL < Gk *enkýklios paideía* circular (i.e., well-rounded) education] —**en•cy′clo•pe′dic,** *adj.*

en•cyst′, *v.t., v.i.* to enclose or become enclosed in a cyst. —**en•cyst′ment, en′cys•ta′tion,** *n.*

end (end), *n.* **1.** the last part; extremity. **2.** a point that indicates the full extent or limit of something. **3.** a part or place at an extremity. **4.** termination, as of life; conclusion. **5.** final status or condition. **6.** an intention or aim. **7.** an outcome or result. **8.** destruction or ruin. **9.** a remnant or fragment. **10.** a share or part. **11.** either of the linemen in football stationed farthest from the center. —*v.t., v.i.* **12.** to bring or come to an end. **13.** to form the end (of). **14.** to kill or die. —*Idiom.* **15. make (both) ends meet,** to live within one's means. **16. no end,** very much.

en•dan•ger, *v.t.* **1.** to expose to danger; imperil. **2.** to threaten with extinction. —**en•dan′ger•ment,** *n.*

endan′gered spe′cies, *n.* a species at risk of extinction.

en•dear′, *v.t.* to make dear or beloved. —**en•dear′ing•ly,** *adv.*

en•dear′ment, *n.* an utterance or action expressing affection.

en•deav•or (en dev′ər), *v.i.* **1.** to make an earnest effort; strive. —*n.* **2.** an earnest effort; attempt. Also, *esp. Brit.,* **en•deav′our.**

en•dem•ic (en dem′ik), *adj.* belonging exclusively or confined to a particular place or people.

end′ing, *n.* **1.** a concluding part. **2.** an inflection at the end of a word, esp. a suffix.

en•dive (en′dīv, än dēv′), *n.* **1.** a plant with curly-edged leaves used in salads. **2.** a plant with a narrow head of whitish, edible leaves.

end′less, *adj.* **1.** having or seeming to have no end. **2.** interminable or incessant. **3.** joined at the ends; continuous. —**end′less•ly,** *adv.* —**end′less•ness,** *n.*

end′most′, *adj.* most distant.

endo-, a combining form meaning within or internal (*endogenous*).

en•do•crine (en′də krin, -krīn′), *adj.* **1.** secreting internally into the blood or lymph. **2.** of or being a gland, as the thyroid, that secretes hormones directly into the blood or lymph.

en•do•cri•nol•o•gy (en′dō krə nol′ə jē, -krī-), *n.* the study of the endocrine glands and their secretions. —**en′do•cri•nol′o•gist,** *n.*

en•dog•e•nous (en doj′ə nəs), *adj.* originating, developing, or proceeding from within. —**en•dog′e•nous•ly,** *adv.*

En•dor (en′dôr), *n.* a town where King Saul consulted a medium. I Sam. 28:7.

en•dorse (en dôrs′), *v.t.,* -**dorsed, -dors•ing. 1.** to express approval or support of, esp. publicly. **2.** to designate oneself as payee of (a check) by signing, usu. on the reverse side. **3.** to sign one's name on (a check or commercial document). —**en•dorse′ment,** *n.* —**en•dors′er,** *n.*

en•do•scope (en′də skōp′), *n.* a tubular optical instrument for examining the interior of a body cavity or hollow organ. —**en′do•scop′ic** (-skop′ik), *adj.* —**en•dos′co•py,** *n.*

en•do•ther•mic (en′dō thûr′mik) also **-ther′mal,** *adj.* of or characterized by absorption of heat.

en•dow (en dou′), *v.t.* **1.** to provide with a permanent fund or source of income: *to endow a college.* **2.** to furnish with a talent, faculty, or quality; equip. —**en•dow′er,** *n.* —**en•dow′ment,** *n.*

end′ prod′uct, *n.* the final product, as of a process.

end′ ta′ble, *n.* a small table placed beside a chair or at the end of a sofa.

en•due (en dōō′, -dyōō′), *v.t.,* -**dued, -du•ing.** to invest or endow with a gift, quality, or faculty.

en•dur•ance (en dōōr′əns, -dyōōr′-), *n.* **1.** the ability to bear pain, hardship, or adversity. **2.** lasting quality; duration.

en•dure′, *v.,* -**dured, -dur•ing.** —*v.t.* **1.** to sustain without impairment or yielding; undergo. **2.** to bear patiently; tolerate. —*v.i.* **3.** to continue to exist; last. **4.** to suffer without yielding. —**en•dur′a•ble**, *adj.*

end′ways′ (-wāz′) also **-wise′** (-wīz′), *adv.* **1.** on end. **2.** with the end upward or forward. **3.** lengthwise.

ENE, east-northeast.

-ene, a suffix denoting an unsaturated hydrocarbon (*benzene*).

en•e•ma (en′ə mə), *n., pl.* **-mas. 1.** the injection of a fluid into the rectum. **2.** the fluid injected.

en•e•my (en′ə mē), *n., pl.* **-mies. 1.** a person who hates or fosters harmful designs against another. **2.** an opposing military force. **3.** something harmful or prejudicial.

en•er•get•ic (en′ər jet′ik), *adj.* possessing or exhibiting energy. —**en′er•get•i•cal•ly,** *adv.*

en′er•gize′ (-jīz′), *v.t.,* **-gized, -giz•ing.** to give energy to. —**en′er•giz′er,** *n.*

en′er•gy (-jē), *n., pl.* **-gies. 1.** the capacity for vigorous activity. **2.** Often **-gies.** an exertion of energy; effort. **3.** forcefulness of expression. **4.** *Physics.* the capacity to do work. **5.** a source of usable power, as fossil fuel.

En′ergy Star′ Pro′gram, *n.* a program of the U.S. Environmental Protection Agency encouraging the manufacture of electric and electronic devices that can reduce their energy consumption when left idle.

en•er•vate (en′ər vāt′), *v.t.,* **-vat•ed, -vat•ing.** to deprive of force or strength; weaken. —**en′er•va′-tion,** *n.* —**en′er•va′tor,** *n.*

en•fee′ble, *v.t.,* **-bled, -bling.** to make feeble; weaken. —**en•fee′ble•ment,** *n.*

en•fi•lade (en′fə lād′, -läd′), *n.* sweeping gunfire along the length of a line of enemy troops.

en•fold′, *v.t.* **1.** to wrap up; envelop. **2.** to hug or clasp; embrace.

en•force′, *v.t.,* **-forced, -forc•ing. 1.** to compel obedience to: *The police enforced the law.* **2.** to obtain by force or compulsion; compel: *to enforce attendance.* —**en•force′a•ble,** *adj.* —**en•force′ment,** *n.* —**en•forc′er,** *n.*

en•fran′chise, *v.t.,* **-chised, -chis•ing. 1.** to admit to citizenship, esp. to the right of voting. **2.** to set free, as from slavery; liberate. —**en•fran′chise•ment,** *n.*

Eng., England.

en•gage (en gāj′), *v.,* **-gaged, -gag•ing.** —*v.t.* **1.** to occupy the attention or efforts of; involve. **2.** to employ; hire. **3.** to attract and hold fast: *The book engaged my attention.* **4.** to bind by a pledge or promise, esp. by a pledge to marry. **5.** to enter into conflict with. **6.** to cause (gears) to become interlocked. —*v.i.* **7.** to be or become involved: *to engage in politics.* **8.** to assume an obligation. **9.** to enter into conflict. **10.** to interlock. —**en•gag′er,** *n.*

en•gage′ment, *n.* **1.** the act of engaging or state of being engaged. **2.** an appointment. **3.** an agreement to marry. **4.** employment. **5.** a conflict or battle.

en•gag′ing, *adj.* winning; attractive. —**en•gag′-ing•ly,** *adv.*

En•gels (eng′gəlz), *n.* **Friedrich,** 1820–95, German socialist in England.

en•gen•der (en jen′dər), *v.t.* **1.** to give rise to; cause. **2.** to beget; procreate.

en•gine (en′jən), *n.* **1.** a machine for converting energy into force and motion. **2.** a railroad locomotive. **3.** a mechanical contrivance.

en•gi•neer (en′jə nēr′), *n.* **1.** a person trained in engineering. **2.** a person who operates an engine or locomotive. **3.** a member of the military specially trained in engineering. —*v.t.* **4.** to plan, construct, or manage as an engineer. **5.** to arrange, manage, or carry through with subtle and often devious skill.

en′gi•neer′ing, *n.* **1.** the practical application of science and mathematics, as in the design of structures, roads, and systems. **2.** the work or profession of an engineer.

Eng•land (ing′glənd; *often* -lənd), *n.* a division of the United Kingdom, in S Great Britain. 55,780,000.

Eng•lish (ing′glish; *often* -lish), *n.* **1.** the Germanic language of England, the U.S., and regions formerly under British or U.S. dominion. **2.** (*used with a pl.*

v.) the inhabitants of England. —*adj.* **3.** of or characteristic of England, its inhabitants, or their language.

Eng′lish Chan′nel, *n.* an arm of the Atlantic between S England and N France.

Eng′lish Civ′il War′, *n.* the war (1642–46) between the Parliamentarians and the Royalists.

Eng′lish horn′, *n.* a woodwind instrument a fifth lower in pitch than the oboe.

Eng′lish•man or **-wom′an,** *n., pl.* **-men** or **-wom•en.** a native or inhabitant of England.

en•gorge (en gôrj′), *v.t., v.i.,* **-gorged, -gorg•ing. 1.** to swallow greedily; gorge. **2.** to fill or congest, esp. with blood. —**en•gorge′ment,** *n.*

en•gram (en′gram), *n.* a presumed encoding in neural tissue that provides a physical basis for the persistence of memory.

en•grave (en grāv′), *v.t.,* **-graved, -grav•ing. 1. a.** to cut or etch (letters or designs) into a surface. **b.** to print from such a surface. **2.** to mark or ornament with incised letters or designs. —**en•grav′er,** *n.*

en•grav′ing, *n.* **1.** the act or art of a person who engraves. **2. a.** an engraved plate or block. **b.** an impression or print from this.

en•gross (en grōs′), *v.t.* **1.** to occupy completely; absorb. **2.** to write or copy in a clear, large script. —**en•gross′ing,** *adj.* —**en•gross′ment,** *n.*

en•gulf′, *v.t.* **1.** to swallow up in or as if in a gulf. **2.** to overwhelm or envelop completely.

en•hance (en hans′, -häns′), *v.t.,* **-hanced, -hanc•ing. 1.** to raise to a higher degree; intensify. **2.** to increase the value, attractiveness, or quality of; improve. —**en•hance′ment,** *n.*

e•nig•ma (ə nig′mə), *n., pl.* **-mas. 1.** a puzzling or inexplicable person, occurrence, or situation. **2.** a riddle. —**en•ig•mat•ic** (en′ig mat′ik), *adj.*

en•jamb•ment or **-jambe•ment** (en jam′mənt), *n.* the running on of a thought from one poetic line, couplet, or stanza to the next without a syntactic break.

en•join (en join′), *v.t.* **1.** to direct or order; command. **2.** to prohibit or restrain by or as if by injunction. —**en•join′der,** *n.*

en•joy (en joi′), *v.t.* **1.** to take pleasure in. **2.** to have the use or benefit of. —**en•joy′a•ble,** *adj.* —**en•joy′er,** *n.* —**en•joy′ment,** *n.*

en•large′, *v.,* **-larged, -larg•ing.** —*v.t.* **1.** to make larger. —*v.i.* **2.** to grow larger. **3.** to speak or write at length; expatiate. —**en•large′a•ble,** *adj.* —**en•large′ment,** *n.* —**en•larg′er,** *n.*

en•light′en, *v.t.* **1.** to give intellectual or spiritual understanding to. **2.** to free of ignorance, false beliefs, or prejudice. —**en•light′en•ment,** *n.*

enlight′ened self′-in′terest, *n.* a belief that setting aside selfishness may eventually bring benefit.

en•light•en•ment (en līt′n mənt), *n.* **1.** the state of being enlightened. **2. the Enlightenment,** a philosophical movement of the 17th and 18th centuries, characterized by belief in the power of reason and by innovations in political, religious, and educational doctrine.

en•list′, *v.i., v.t.* **1.** to enroll or engage for military service. **2.** to enter into or secure for a cause or enterprise. —**en•list•ee′,** *n., pl.* **-ees.** —**en•list′ment,** *n.*

enlist′ed man′ (or **wom′an**), *n.* a member of the U.S. armed services ranking below a noncommissioned officer or a petty officer.

en•liv′en, *v.t.* to make vigorous, active, or lively; animate.

en masse (än mas′, än), *adv.* in a mass; all together. [< F]

en•mesh′, *v.t.* to catch in or as if in the meshes of a net; entangle. —**en•mesh′ment,** *n.*

en•mi•ty (en′mi tē), *n., pl.* **-ties.** a feeling of bitter hatred; ill will.

en•no′ble, *v.t.,* **-bled, -bling. 1.** to elevate, as in character; exalt. **2.** to confer a title of nobility on. —**en•no′ble•ment,** *n.*

en•nui (än wē′), *n.* a feeling of utter weariness and discontent; boredom.

E·noch (ē′nək), *n.* **1.** the father of Methuselah. Gen. 5:22. **2.** a son of Cain. Gen. 4:17.

e·nor·mi·ty (i nôr′mi tē), *n., pl.* **-ties. 1.** outrageous or heinous character. **2.** an outrageous or heinous act or offense. **3.** greatness of size or scope. —**Usage.** Many people feel that ENORMITY can only mean "outrageousness" or "atrociousness." The sense "greatness of size" occurs regularly in edited writing, but is often considered to be nonstandard.

e·nor′mous, *adj.* greatly exceeding the common size, extent, amount, or degree; huge. —**e·nor′mous·ly,** *adv.* —**e·nor′mous·ness,** *n.*

E·nos (ē′nəs), *n.* the son of Seth. Gen. 5:6.

e·nough (i nuf′), *adj.* **1.** sufficient for a purpose, want, or need. —*pron.* **2.** an adequate quantity or number. —*adv.* **3.** sufficiently. **4.** fully or quite. **5.** tolerably or passably.

en·plane′, *v.i.,* **-planed, -plan·ing.** to board an airplane.

en·quire (en kwī°r′), *v.i., v.t.,* **-quired, -quir·ing.** INQUIRE. —**en·quir·y** (en kwī°r′ē, en′kwə rē), *n., pl.* **-quir·ies.**

en·rage′, *v.t.,* **-raged, -rag·ing.** to put into a rage; infuriate.

en·rap′ture, *v.t.,* **-tured, -tur·ing.** to move to rapture; delight.

en·rich′, *v.t.* **1.** to make rich or richer. **2.** to add value or significance to. **3.** to adorn or decorate. **4.** to improve in quality, productivity, or nutritive value. —**en·rich′ment,** *n.*

en·roll or **-rol** (en rōl′), *v.,* **-rolled, -roll·ing** or **-rol·ling.** —*v.t.* **1.** to record in a roll or register. **2.** to enlist (oneself). —*v.i.* **3.** to enroll oneself or become enrolled. —**en·roll′ment,** *n.*

en route (än rōōt′, en, än), *adv.* on or along the way. [< F]

en·sconce (en skons′), *v.t.,* **-sconced, -sconc·ing.** to settle securely or snugly.

en·sem·ble (än säm′bəl, -sämb′, än-), *n.* **1.** all the parts of a thing taken together; set; whole. **2.** an entire outfit with all the parts in harmony. **3.** a group, as of singers or dancers, performing together.

en·shrine (en shrīn′), *v.t.,* **-shrined, -shrin·ing. 1.** to enclose in or as if in a shrine. **2.** to cherish as sacred. —**en·shrine′ment,** *n.*

en·shroud′, *v.t.* to shroud; conceal.

en·sign (en′sən; *for 1,2 also* -sīn), *n.* **1.** a flag or banner, as on a naval vessel. **2.** a badge of office or authority. **3.** the lowest commissioned officer in the U.S. Navy or Coast Guard.

en·si·lage (en′sə lij), *n.* SILAGE.

en·sile (en sīl′, en′sīl), *v.t.,* **-siled, -sil·ing.** to preserve (green fodder) in a silo.

en·slave′, *v.t.,* **-slaved, -slav·ing.** to make a slave of. —**en·slave′ment,** *n.*

en·snare′, *v.t.,* **-snared, -snar·ing.** to capture in or as if in a snare; entrap. —**en·snare′ment,** *n.*

en·sue (en sōō′), *v.i.,* **-sued, -su·ing.** to follow in order or as a consequence.

en·sure (en shŏŏr′, -shûr′), *v.t.,* **-sured, -sur·ing. 1.** to secure or guarantee. **2.** to make sure or certain. —**en·sur′er,** *n.*

-ent, a suffix meaning: a person or thing that performs or promotes (*president*); performing or being (*insistent*).

en·tail (en tāl′), *v.t.* **1.** to cause or involve by necessity or as a consequence. **2.** to limit the passage of (real property) to a specified line or category of heirs. —**en·tail′ment,** *n.*

en·tan·gle, *v.t.,* **-gled, -gling. 1.** to make tangled; ensnarl. **2.** to involve in difficulties, complications, or confusion. —**en·tan′gle·ment,** *n.*

en·tente (än tänt′), *n.* **1.** an understanding between nations agreeing to a particular policy. **2.** an alliance of parties to such an understanding.

en·tente cor·diale (än tänt′ kôr dyäl′, än tänt′), *n.* a friendly understanding, esp. between nations.

en·ter (en′tər), *v.t.* **1.** to come or go in or into. **2.** to become a member of; join. **3.** to begin; start. **4.** to become involved in; take part in. **5.** *Law.* **a.** to make

a formal record of (a fact). **b.** to occupy or take possession of (lands). **6.** to put forward, submit, or register, esp. formally: *to enter an objection.* —*v.i.* **7.** to come or go in. **8.** to be admitted, as into a school. **9.** to make a beginning. **10. enter into, a.** to participate in; engage in. **b.** to form a part or ingredient of.

en·ter·i·tis (en′tə rī′tis), *n.* inflammation of the intestines.

en·ter·prise (en′tər prīz′), *n.* **1.** a project undertaken, esp. one requiring originality, boldness, or energy. **2.** adventurous spirit or ingenuity. **3.** a business firm.

en′ter·pris′ing, *adj.* characterized by imagination, energy, and initiative.

en·ter·tain (en′tər tān′), *v.t.* **1.** to divert; amuse. **2.** to show hospitality to. **3.** to admit into or hold in the mind. —*v.i.* **4.** to show hospitality to guests. —**en′ter·tain′er,** *n.* —**en′ter·tain′ing,** *adj.* —**en′ter·tain′ment,** *n.*

en·thrall (en thrôl′), *v.t.* **1.** to captivate; spellbind. **2.** to enslave; subjugate.

en·throne′, *v.t.,* **-throned, -thron·ing. 1.** to place on or as if on a throne. **2.** to exalt. —**en·throne′·ment,** *n.*

en·thuse (en thōōz′), *v.,* **-thused, -thus·ing.** —*v.i.* **1.** to show enthusiasm. —*v.t.* **2.** to cause to become enthusiastic. —**Usage.** ENTHUSE, which first appeared in the early 19th century, is now standard in the speech and all but the most formal writing of educated persons in both Britain and the U.S. Despite its long history and frequent occurrence, however, ENTHUSE is still strongly disapproved of by many.

en·thu·si·asm (-thōō′zē az′əm), *n.* **1.** lively, absorbing interest or involvement. **2.** something inspiring enthusiasm. —**en·thu′si·ast′,** *n.* —**en·thu′si·as′tic,** *adj.* —**en·thu′si·as′ti·cal·ly,** *adv.*

en·tice (en tīs′), *v.t.,* **-ticed, -tic·ing.** to lead on by exciting hope or desire; allure. —**en·tice′ment,** *n.* —**en·tic′ing·ly,** *adv.*

en·tire (en tī°r′), *adj.* having all parts or elements; whole or complete. —**en·tire′ly,** *adv.*

en·tire·ty (-tī°r′tē -tī′ri-), *n., pl.* **-ties. 1.** the state of being entire. **2.** something entire; whole.

en·ti′tle, *v.t.,* **-tled, -tling. 1.** to give a right or claim to. **2.** to call by a title or name. —**en·ti′tle·ment,** *n.*

en·ti·ty (en′ti tē), *n., pl.* **-ties. 1.** something that has a real existence; thing. **2.** being or existence.

en·tomb′, *v.t.* to place in or as if in a tomb; bury. —**en·tomb′ment,** *n.*

en·to·mol·o·gy (en′tə mol′ə jē), *n.* the branch of zoology dealing with insects. —**en′to·mo·log′i·cal** (-mə loj′i kal), *adj.* —**en′to·mol′o·gist,** *n.*

en·tou·rage (än′tŏŏ räzh′), *n.* a group of attendants or associates.

en·tr′acte (än trakt′, än-), *n.* **1.** the interval between two acts of a play or opera. **2.** a performance, as of music, during such an interval.

en·trails (en′trālz, -trəlz), *n.pl.* inner organs, esp. intestines.

en·train′, *v.i., v.t.* to go or put aboard a train.

en·trance¹ (en′trans), *n.* **1.** the act of entering. **2.** a point or place of entering. **3.** the right, privilege, or permission to enter.

en·trance² (en trans′, -träns′), *v.t.,* **-tranced, -tranc·ing.** to fill with delight; enrapture. —**en·trance′ment,** *n.* —**en·tranc′ing·ly,** *adv.*

en·trant (en′trənt), *n.* a person who enters a competition or contest.

en·trap′, *v.t.,* **-trapped, -trap·ping.** to catch in or as if in a trap; ensnare. —**en·trap′ment,** *n.*

en·treat (en trēt′), *v.t., v.i.* to ask earnestly; implore. —**en·treat′ing·ly,** *adv.* —**en·treat′y,** *n., pl.* **-treat·ies.**

en·trée or **-tree** (än′trā), *n., pl.* **-trées** or **-trees. 1.** the main course of a meal. **2.** the privilege of entering; access.

en·trench (en trench′), *v.t.* **1.** to establish firmly or solidly. **2.** to surround with trenches. —**en·trench′ment,** *n.*

en·tre·pre·neur (än′trə prə nûr′), *n.* a person who

organizes and manages an enterprise, esp. a business, usu. with considerable risk. —**en′tre•pre•neur′i•al,** adj.

en•tro•py (en′trə pē), n. **1.** a measure of the energy that is not available for work in a thermodynamic process. **2.** (in data transmission and information theory) a measure of the loss of information in a transmitted signal. **3.** a hypothetical tendency for the universe to attain a state of maximum homogeneity.

en•trust′, v.t. **1.** to give to as a trust or responsibility. **2.** to give to another for protection, care, or handling.

en•try (en′trē), n., pl. **-tries. 1.** the act of entering. **2.** a place of entrance, as a vestibule. **3.** permission or right to enter. **4. a.** the act of entering something, as in a book. **b.** the item entered. **5.** an entrant in a contest or competition.

en•twine′, v.t., v.i., **-twined, -twin•ing.** to twine around or together.

e•nu•mer•ate (i nōō′mə rāt′, i nyōō′-), v.t., **-at•ed, -at•ing. 1.** to name one by one; list. **2.** to count. —**e•nu′mer•a•ble,** adj. —**e•nu′mer•a′tion,** n.

e•nun•ci•ate (i nun′sē āt′), v.t., v.i., **-at•ed, -at•ing. 1.** to pronounce (words), esp. in an articulate manner. **2.** to state definitely; proclaim. —**e•nun′ci•a′tion,** n.

en•u•re•sis (en′yə rē′sis), n. urinary incontinence; bed-wetting.

en•vel•op (en vel′əp), v.t. **1.** to wrap up in or as if in a covering. **2.** to surround entirely. —**en•vel′op•er,** n. —**en•vel′op•ment,** n.

en•ve•lope (en′və lōp′, än′-), n. **1.** a flat paper container, as for a letter. **2.** a wrapper or surrounding cover. **3.** the gasbag of a balloon.

en•ven•om (en ven′əm), v.t. **1.** to make poisonous. **2.** to embitter.

en•vi•a•ble (en′vē ə bəl), adj. worthy of envy; very desirable. —**en′vi•a•bly,** adv.

en′vi•ous, adj. feeling or expressing envy. —**en′vi•ous•ly,** adv. —**en′vi•ous•ness,** n.

en•vi•ron•ment (en vī′rən mənt, -vī′ərn-), n. **1.** surroundings; milieu. **2.** the external factors and forces surrounding and affecting an organism, person, or population. —**en•vi′ron•men′tal,** adj. —**en•vi′ron•men′tal•ly,** adv.

en•vi′ron•men′tal•ist, n. a person who advocates or works for the protection and preservation of natural resources. —**en•vi′ron•men′tal•ism,** n.

en•vi′rons, n.pl. surrounding districts, as of a city; outskirts.

en•vis•age (en viz′ij), v.t., **-aged, -ag•ing.** to visualize; envision.

en•vi′sion, v.t. to picture mentally.

en•voy (en′voi, än′-), n. **1.** a diplomatic representative. **2.** an accredited messenger or representative.

en•vy (en′vē), n., pl. **-vies,** v., **-vied, -vy•ing.** —n. **1.** discontent and resentment over or desire for another's advantages, possessions, or attainments. **2.** an object of envy. —v.t. **3.** to regard with envy. —**en′vy•ing•ly,** adv.

en•zyme (en′zīm), n. any of various proteins originating from living cells and capable of producing certain chemical changes in organic substances by catalytic action, as in digestion. —**en′zy•mat′ic,** adj.

e•o•li•an (ē ō′lē ən), adj. pertaining to, carried by, or arranged by the wind.

e.o.m., end of month.

e•on (ē′ən, ē′on), n. an indefinitely long period of time; age.

-eous, a suffix meaning resembling or having the nature of (gaseous).

EPA, Environmental Protection Agency.

ep•au•let or **-lette** (ep′ə let′, -lit, ep′ə let′), n. an ornamental shoulder piece, esp. on a uniform. [< Fr épaulette = épaule shoulder + -ette]

é•pée or **e•pee** (ā pā′, ep′ā), n., pl. **-pées** or **-pees.** a fencing rapier with a three-sided blade and a guard over the tip.

e•phed•rine (i fed′rin), n. a white, crystalline alka-

loid used esp. in the treatment of asthma, hay fever, and colds.

e•phem•er•al (i fem′ər əl), adj. lasting a very short time; transitory.

E•phe•sians (i fē′zhənz), n. a book of the New Testament, written by Paul.

Eph•e•sus (ef′ə səs), n. an ancient city in W Asia Minor: famous temple of Artemis, or Diana; early Christian community, site of one of the seven churches of Asia (Rev. 1:11). —**E•phe•sian** (i fē′zhən), adj., n.

E•phra•im (ē′frē əm, ē′frəm), n. **1.** the younger son of Joseph. Gen. 41:52. **2.** one of the 12 tribes of Israel. Gen. 48:1. **3.** the northern kingdom of Israel.

E•phra•im•ite (ē′frē ə mīt′, ē′frə-), n. **1.** a member of the tribe of Ephraim. **2.** an inhabitant of the northern kingdom of Israel.

epi-, a prefix meaning: on, at, or over (epidermis).

ep•ic (ep′ik), adj. **1.** of or resembling a long poem in which the great achievements of a hero are narrated in elevated style. **2.** impressively great; heroic. —n. **3.** an epic poem. **4.** a novel, film, etc., suggesting an epic.

ep•i•cen•ter (ep′ə sen′tər), n. a point directly above the true center of an earthquake from which the shock waves apparently radiate.

ep•i•cure (ep′i kyŏor′), n. a person with refined taste, esp. in food and wine; connoisseur.

ep′i•cu•re′an (-kyŏo rē′ən, -kyŏor′ē-), adj. **1.** fit for an epicure. —n. **2.** an epicure.

Ep•i•cu•rus (ep′i kyŏor′əs), n. 342?–270 B.C., Greek philosopher.

ep•i•dem•ic (ep′i dem′ik), adj. **1.** affecting many individuals at the same time. **2.** prevalent; widespread. —n. **3.** an epidemic disease. **4.** a rapid spread or increase. —**ep′i•dem′i•cal•ly,** adv.

ep′i•de′mi•ol′o•gy (-dē′mē ol′ə jē, -dem′ē-), n. the branch of medicine dealing with the incidence, prevalence, and control of disease in populations. —**ep′i•de′mi•ol′o•gist,** n.

ep′i•der′mis, n. the outermost layer of the skin. —**ep′i•der′mal, ep′i•der′mic,** adj.

ep′i•glot′tis, n. a flap of cartilage that helps close the opening to the windpipe during swallowing.

ep•i•gram (ep′i gram′), n. a terse, witty saying or poem. —**ep′i•gram•mat′ic** (-grə mat′ik), adj.

ep′i•graph′, n. **1.** an inscription, as on a building. **2.** an apt quotation at the beginning of a book or chapter.

e•pig•ra•phy (i pig′rə fē), n. the study of inscriptions, esp. ancient ones.

ep•i•lep•sy (ep′ə lep′sē), n. a nervous disorder usu. characterized by convulsions, often with loss of consciousness. —**ep′i•lep′tic** (-lep′tik), adj., n.

ep•i•logue or **-log** (ep′ə lôg′, -log′), n. **1.** a concluding part added to a literary work. **2.** a speech delivered by an actor at the conclusion of a play.

ep•i•neph•rine or **-rin** (ep′ə nef′rin), n. an adrenal hormone used in synthetic form chiefly as a heart stimulant and antiasthmatic.

E•piph•a•ny (i pif′ə nē), n., pl. **-nies.** a Christian festival, observed on Jan. 6, commemorating the manifestation of Christ to the gentiles in the persons of the Magi.

e•pis•co•pa•cy (i pis′kə pə sē), n., pl. **-cies. 1.** government of the church by bishops. **2.** EPISCOPATE.

e•pis′co•pal (-pəl), adj. **1.** of or governed by a bishop or bishops. **2.** (cap.) of or designating the Anglican Church or Protestant Episcopal Church.

E•pis′co•pa′lian (-pāl′yən, -pā′lē ən), adj. **1.** pertaining or adhering to the Protestant Episcopal Church. —n. **2.** a member of the Protestant Episcopal Church.

e•pis′co•pate (-pit, -pāt′), n. **1.** the office, rank, or term of a bishop. **2.** the order or body of bishops.

ep•i•sode (ep′ə sōd′, -zōd′), n. **1.** an incident in the course of a series of events. **2.** an incident or scene within a narrative. —**ep′i•sod′ic** (-sod′ik), adj.

ep•is•te•mol•o•gy (i pis′tə mol′ə jē), n. a branch

of philosophy that investigates the nature and limits of human knowledge.

e•pis•tle (i pis′əl), *n.* **1.** a letter. **2.** (*usu. cap.*) one of the apostolic letters in the New Testament. —**e•pis′to•lar/y** (-tl er′ē), *adj.*

ep•i•taph (ep′i taf′, -täf′), *n.* a commemorative inscription, esp. on a tomb.

ep•i•the•li•um (ep′ə thē′lē əm), *n., pl.* **-li•ums, -li•a** (-lē ə). a layer of tissue covering body surfaces or lining body cavities. —**ep/i•the/li•al,** *adj.*

ep•i•thet (ep′ə thet′), *n.* **1.** a characterizing word or phrase. **2.** an abusive or contemptuous word, phrase, or expression.

e•pit•o•me (i pit′ə mē), *n., pl.* **-mes. 1.** one that is typical of a whole class; embodiment. **2.** a summary; abstract.

e•pit′o•mize′ (-mīz′), *v.t.* **-mized, -miz•ing.** to make or serve as an epitome of.

ep•och (ep′ək; *esp. Brit.* ē′pok), *n.* **1.** a period of time marked by distinctive features, noteworthy events, or changed conditions. **2.** a memorable event, date, or state of affairs. **3.** any of several divisions of a geologic period. —**ep/och•al,** *adj.*

ep•ox•y (i pok′sē), *n., pl.* **-ox•ies.** any of a class of resins derived by polymerization, used chiefly in adhesives, coatings, and castings.

EPROM (ē′prom′), *n.* a memory chip that can be reprogrammed any number of times, as to correct bugs: used widely in the manufacture of personal computers. [*e*(*rasable*) *p*(*rogrammable*) *r*(*ead*-)*o*(*nly*) *m*(*emory*)]

ep•si•lon (ep′sə lon′, -lən; *esp. Brit.* ep sī′lən), *n.* the fifth letter of the Greek alphabet (E, ε).

Ep′som salts′, *n.pl.* hydrated magnesium sulfate, used esp. as a cathartic. [after their presence in the mineral water at *Epsom*, England]

Ep′stein-Barr′ vi′rus (ep′stīn bär′), *n.* a herpeslike virus that causes mononucleosis.

eq•ua•ble (ek′wə bəl, ē′kwə-), *adj.* **1.** free from change or variation; uniform. **2.** not easily annoyed or disturbed; calm. —**eq/ua•bil/i•ty,** *n.* —**eq/ua•bly,** *adv.*

e•qual (ē′kwəl), *adj., n., v.,* **e•qualed, e•qual•ing** or (*esp. Brit.*) **e•qualled, e•qual•ling.** —*adj.* **1.** being the same as another in quantity, degree, value, number, or quality. **2.** evenly proportioned or balanced. **3.** uniform in operation or effect: *equal laws.* **4.** having adequate powers, ability, or means: *equal to the task.* **5.** impartial or equitable. —*n.* **6.** a person or thing that is equal. —*v.t.* **7.** to be or become equal to; match. **8.** to do something equal to. —**e•qual/i•ty** (i kwol′i tē), *n., pl.* **-ties.** —**e′qual•ly,** *adv.*

e′qual•ize′, *v.t.* **-ized, -iz•ing.** to make equal or uniform. —**e/qual•i•za/tion,** *n.* —**e/qual•iz/er,** *n.*

E′qual Rights′ Amend′ment, *n.* a proposed amendment to the U.S. Constitution prohibiting discrimination on the basis of sex.

e′qual (or **e′quals**) **sign′,** *n.* the symbol (=) used to indicate that the terms it separates are equal.

e•qua•nim•i•ty (ē′kwə nim′i tē, ek′wə-), *n.* composure, esp. under strain; evenness.

e•quate (i kwāt′), *v.t.* **e•quat•ed, e•quat•ing.** to regard, treat, or represent as equivalent or comparable. —**e•quat/a•ble,** *adj.*

e•qua•tion (i kwā′zhən, -shən), *n.* **1.** the act of equating or state of being equated. **2.** an expression or a proposition, often algebraic, asserting the equality of two quantities.

e•qua•tor (-tər), *n.* the great circle of the earth that is equidistant from the North Pole and South Pole. —**e•qua•to•ri•al** (ē′kwə tôr′ē əl, ek′wə-), *adj.*

E′quato′rial Guin′ea, *n.* a republic in W equatorial Africa. 442,516.

eq•uer•ry (ek′wə rē, i kwer′ē), *n., pl.* **-ries. 1.** an officer of a royal or noble household, charged with the care of horses. **2.** an officer who attends a member of the British royal family.

e•ques•tri•an (i kwes′trē ən), *adj.* **1.** of horseback riding or horseback riders. **2.** representing a person mounted on a horse. —*n.* **3.** a person who rides horses. —**e•ques/tri•an•ism,** *n.*

e•ques′tri•enne′ (-en′), *n.* a woman who rides horses.

equi-, a combining form meaning equal (*equilateral*).

e•qui•dis•tant (ē′kwi dis′tənt, ek′wi-), *adj.* equally distant.

e′qui•lat′er•al, *adj.* having all the sides equal.

e′qui•lib′ri•um (-lib′rē əm), *n., pl.* **-ri•ums, -ri•a** (-rē ə). a state of balance between opposing forces, powers, or influences.

e•quine (ē′kwīn, ek′wīn), *adj.* **1.** of or resembling a horse. —*n.* **2.** a horse.

e•qui•nox (ē′kwə noks′, ek′wə-), *n.* one of the times when the sun crosses the equator, making night and day of approximately equal length all over the earth and occurring about March 21 and Sept. 22. —**e/qui•noc/tial** (-nok′shəl), *adj.*

e•quip (i kwip′), *v.t.* **e•quipped, e•quip•ping.** to provide with what is needed; fit out.

e•qui•page (ek′wə pij), *n.* a carriage, esp. one drawn by horses and attended by servants.

e•quip•ment (i kwip′mənt), *n.* **1.** the articles used or needed for a specific purpose or activity. **2.** the act of equipping or state of being equipped.

e•qui•poise (ē′kwə poiz′, ek′wə-), *n.* **1.** even balance; equilibrium. **2.** a counterpoise.

eq•ui•ta•ble (ek′wi tə bəl), *adj.* fair and impartial; just. —**eq/ui•ta•bly,** *adv.*

eq•ui•ta•tion (ek′wi tā′shən), *n.* the act or art of riding on horseback.

eq′ui•ty, *n., pl.* **-ties. 1.** the quality of being fair or impartial; fairness. **2.** (in England and the U.S.) a system of jurisprudence serving to supplement the common law. **3.** the value of a property or business beyond any amounts owed on it.

equiv., equivalent.

e•quiv•a•lent (i kwiv′ə lənt), *adj.* **1.** equal in value, measure, force, effect, or significance. —*n.* **2.** something equivalent. —**e•quiv/a•lence, e•quiv/a•len•cy,** *n., pl.* **-ces, -cies.** —**e•quiv/a•lent•ly,** *adv.*

e•quiv•o•cal (i kwiv′ə kəl), *adj.* **1.** deliberately ambiguous. **2.** uncertain or doubtful. **3.** questionable or dubious. —**e•quiv/o•cal•ly,** *adv.*

e•quiv/o•cate′ (-kāt′), *v.i.* **-cat•ed, -cat•ing.** to use ambiguous or evasive expressions. —**e•quiv/o•ca/tion,** *n.* —**e•quiv/o•ca/tor,** *n.*

ER, emergency room.

Er, *Chem. Symbol.* erbium.

-er¹, a suffix meaning: a person who is occupied with or works at something (*roofer*); a native or resident of a place (*southerner*); a person or thing associated with a particular characteristic or circumstance (*teenager*); one that performs or is used in performing an action (*fertilizer*).

-er², a suffix forming the comparative degree of adjectives (*smaller*) and adverbs (*faster*).

ERA, 1. Also, **era.** *Baseball.* earned run average. **2.** Equal Rights Amendment.

e•rad•i•cate (i rad′i kāt′), *v.t.* **-cat•ed, -cat•ing.** to remove or destroy utterly; extirpate. —**e•rad/i•ca•ble,** *adj.* —**e•rad/i•ca/tion,** *n.*

e•rase (i rās′), *v.t.* **e•rased, e•ras•ing. 1.** to rub or scrape out (written characters, recorded material, etc.); efface. **2.** to eliminate completely; obliterate. —**e•ras/a•ble,** *adj.* —**e•ras/er,** *n.* —**e•ra/sure** (-shər), *n.*

E•ras•mus (i raz′məs), *n.* **Desiderius,** 1466?–1536, Dutch humanist, scholar, and theologian. —**E•ras/mi•an,** *adj.*

er•bi•um (ûr′bē əm), *n.* a rare-earth element having pink salts. *Symbol:* Er; *at. wt.:* 167.26; *at. no.:* 68.

ere (âr), *prep., conj.* before.

e•rect (i rekt′), *adj.* **1.** upright in position or posture. —*v.t.* **2.** to build; construct. **3.** to raise and set in an upright position. **4.** to set up; establish. —**e•rect/ly,** *adv.* —**e•rect/ness,** *n.* —**e•rec/tor,** *n.*

e•rec•tile (i rek′tl, -til, -tīl), *adj.* capable of being distended with blood and becoming rigid, as tissue.

e•rec/tion (-shən), *n.* **1.** something erected. **2.** a distended and rigid state of an organ or part containing erectile tissue, esp. the penis.

ere•long′, *adv.* before long; soon.

er•e•mite (er′ə mīt′), *n.* a hermit.

erg (ûrg), *n.* the centimeter-gram-second unit of work or energy.

er•go (ûr′gō, er′gō), *conj., adv.* therefore. [< L]

er•go•nom•ics (ûr′gə nom′iks), *n.* an applied science that coordinates the design of devices and systems with the requirements of workers. —**er′go• nom′ic**, *adj.*

er•gos•ter•ol (ûr gos′tə rōl′, -rôl), *n.* a sterol that occurs in ergot and yeast and that is converted to vitamin D when irradiated with ultraviolet light.

er•got (ûr′gət, -got), *n.* **1.** a disease of cereal grasses, as rye, caused by a fungus. **2.** a medicinal alkaloid derived from a dried ergot fungus.

Er•ic•son or **Er•ics•son** (er′ik sən), *n.* **Leif,** fl. A.D. c1000, Norse mariner (son of Eric the Red).

Er′ic the Red′ (er′ik), *n.* born A.D. c950, Norse mariner: explorer and colonizer of Greenland c985.

E•rie (ēr′ē), *n.* **1. Lake,** the southernmost lake of the Great Lakes between the U.S. and Canada. **2.** a port in NW Pennsylvania. 108,398.

E′rie Canal′, *n.* a canal in New York between Albany and Buffalo, connecting the Hudson River with Lake Erie, completed in 1825.

Er•in (er′in), *n. Literary.* Ireland.

Er•i•tre•a (er′i trē′ə), *n.* a republic in NE Africa. 3,589,687. —**Er′i•tre′an**, *adj., n.*

er•mine (ûr′min), *n., pl.* **-mines, -mine. 1.** a weasel having a white coat with a black-tipped tail in the winter. **2.** the white winter fur of the ermine.

e•rode (i rōd′), *v.*, **e•rod•ed, e•rod•ing.** —*v.t.* **1.** to eat into or wear away, esp. slowly or gradually. —*v.i.* **2.** to become eroded. —**e•rod′i•ble**, *adj.*

e•rog•e•nous (i roj′ə nəs), *adj.* sensitive to sexual stimulation.

E•ros (ēr′os, er′os), *n.* the ancient Greek god of carnal love.

e•ro•sion (i rō′zhən), *n.* **1.** the act or process of eroding. **2.** the state of being eroded. —**e•ro′sive**, *adj.*

e•rot•ic (i rot′ik), *adj.* **1.** of or dealing with sexual love. **2.** arousing or satisfying sexual desire. [< Gk *erōtikós* pertaining to Eros] —**e•rot′i•cal•ly**, *adv.* —**e•rot′i•cism** (-ə siz′əm), *n.*

e•rot′i•ca (-i kə), *n.* (*used with a sing. or pl. v.*) erotic literature or art.

err (ûr, er), *v.i.* **1.** to be mistaken or incorrect. **2.** to go astray morally; sin.

er•rand (er′ənd), *n.* **1.** a short trip to accomplish a specific purpose, often for someone else. **2.** the purpose of an errand.

er•rant (er′ənt), *adj.* **1.** deviating from the regular or proper course. **2.** traveling, esp. in quest of adventure. **3.** moving in an aimless manner.

er•rat•ic (i rat′ik), *adj.* **1.** inconsistent or changeable; unpredictable. **2.** peculiar; eccentric. **3.** not fixed; wandering. —**er•rat′i•cal•ly**, *adv.*

er•ra•tum (i rä′təm, i rā′-, i rat′əm), *n., pl.* **-ta** (-tə). an error in writing or printing.

er•ro•ne•ous (ə rō′nē əs, e rō′-), *adj.* containing an error; incorrect. —**er•ro′ne•ous•ly**, *adv.*

er•ror (er′ər), *n.* **1.** a deviation from accuracy or correctness; mistake. **2.** belief in something untrue. **3.** the condition of believing what is not true. **4.** wrongdoing; sin. **5.** a defensive misplay in baseball.

er•satz (er′zäts, -säts), *adj.* serving as a substitute; synthetic or artificial.

erst (ûrst), *adv. Archaic.* formerly.

erst′while′, *adj.* **1.** former. —*adv.* **2.** *Archaic.* formerly.

ERT, estrogen replacement therapy.

e•ruct (i rukt′), *v.t., v.i.* to belch. —**e•ruc•ta•tion** (i ruk tā′shən, ē′ruk-), *n.*

er•u•dite (er′yŏŏ dīt′, er′ŏŏ-), *adj.* characterized by erudition; learned. —**er′u•dite′ly**, *adv.*

er•u•di′tion (-dish′ən), *n.* knowledge acquired by study or research; learning.

e•rupt (i rupt′), *v.i.* **1.** to burst forth. **2.** (of a volcano, geyser, etc.) to eject matter. **3.** to break out of

a pent-up state. **4.** to break out in a skin rash. —*v.t.* **5.** to cause to burst forth. —**e•rup′tion**, *n.* —**e•rup′tive**, *adj.*

-ery, a suffix meaning: things collectively (*machinery*); people collectively (*peasantry*); occupation, activity, or condition (*archery*); a place for (*winery*); characteristic conduct (*prudery*).

e•ryth•ro•cyte (i rith′rə sīt′), *n.* RED BLOOD CELL.

Es, *Chem. Symbol.* einsteinium.

-es¹, var. of -s¹.

-es², var. of -s².

E•sau (ē′sô), *n.* a son of Isaac and Rebekah, older twin of Jacob, to whom he sold his birthright. Gen. 25:21–25.

es•ca•late (es′kə lāt′), *v.i., v.t.*, **-lat•ed, -lat•ing.** to increase in intensity, magnitude, number, amount, or scope. —**es′ca•la′tion**, *n.*

es′ca•la′tor, *n.* a continuously moving stairway on an endless loop.

es•cal•lop (e skol′əp, e skal′-), *v.t.* **1.** to bake (food) in a sauce, often with breadcrumbs on top. —*n.* **2.** SCALLOP.

es•ca•pade (es′kə pād′, es′kə pād′), *n.* a reckless adventure or wild prank.

es•cape (i skāp′), *v.*, **-caped, -cap•ing,** *n., adj.* —*v.i.* **1.** to get away, as from confinement. **2.** to avoid a threatened evil. **3.** to issue from a confining enclosure, as a gas. —*v.t.* **4.** to get away from. **5.** to succeed in avoiding. **6.** to elude (one's memory or notice). **7.** to slip from or be expressed by inadvertently: *A sigh escaped her lips.* —*n.* **8.** an act or instance of escaping. **9.** a means of escape. **10.** avoidance of reality. **11.** leakage, as of gas. —*adj.* **12.** for or providing an escape.

es•cap•ee (i skā pē′, es′kā-), *n., pl.* **-ees.** a person who has escaped, esp. from prison.

es•cape•ment (i skāp′mənt), *n.* the portion of a watch or clock that measures beats and controls the speed of wheels in gear.

escape′ veloc′ity, *n.* the minimum speed an object must have to free itself from the gravitational pull of a celestial body.

es•cap′ism, *n.* the avoidance of reality by absorption of the mind in entertainment or fantasy. —**es• cap′ist**, *adj., n.*

es•ca•role (es′kə rōl′), *n.* a broad-leaved endive used in salads.

es•carp•ment (i skärp′mənt), *n.* a long, steep cliff-like ridge of land or rock.

-escence, a suffix meaning the state or process of becoming (*coalescence*).

-escent, a suffix meaning: beginning to be (*adolescent*); giving off light (*fluorescent*).

es•chew (es chōō′), *v.t.* to keep away from; avoid.

es•cort (*n.* es′kôrt; *v.* i skôrt′), *n.* **1.** a person or group accompanying another for protection or courtesy. **2.** a protective guard, as a body of warships. **3.** a man who accompanies a woman in public. —*v.t.* **4.** to accompany as an escort.

es•cri•toire (es′kri twär′), *n.* a writing desk.

es•crow (es′krō), *n.* a deed, funds, or property deposited with a third party to be transferred to the grantee when specified conditions have been fulfilled.

es•cu•do (e skōō′dō), *n., pl.* **-dos.** the basic monetary unit of Cape Verde and Portugal.

es•cutch•eon (i skuch′ən), *n.* a shield or shieldlike surface on which a coat of arms is depicted.

Es•dra•e•lon (es′drā ē′lon, -drā-, ez′-), *n.* a plain in N Israel, extending from the Mediterranean to the Jordan River. Also called **Plain of Jezreel.**

Es•dras (ez′drəs), *n.* either of the first two books of the Apocrypha, I Esdras or II Esdras.

ESE, east-southeast.

-ese, a suffix meaning: the inhabitants of a place or their language (*Japanese*); a characteristic jargon, style, or accent (*journalese*).

Esh•col (esh′kol), *n.* a valley north of Hebron, famous for fertility. Num. 13:24.

Es•ki•mo (es′kə mō′), *n., pl.* **-mo, -mos** for 1. **1.** a member of a people living in regions from Greenland through Canada and Alaska to NE Siberia. 2. the languages spoken by the Eskimos.

Es'kimo dog', *n.* a dog of arctic regions of North America, used for pulling sleds.

ESL, English as a second language.

e•soph•a•gus (i sof'ə gəs, ē sof'-), *n.*, *pl.* **-gi** (-jī', -gī'). a muscular tube for the passage of food from the pharynx to the stomach. —**e•soph•a•ge•al** (i sof'ə jē'əl, ē'sə faj'ē əl), *adj.*

es•o•ter•ic (es'ə ter'ik), *adj.* 1. understood by or meant for only a select few. 2. private; secret. —**es'o•ter'i•cal•ly,** *adv.*

ESP, extrasensory perception.

esp., especially.

es•pa•drille (es'pə dril'), *n.* a flat shoe with a cloth upper and a rope sole.

es•pal•ier (i spal'yər, -yā), *n.* 1. a trellis or framework on which fruit trees or shrubs are trained to grow flat. 2. a plant so trained.

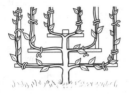

espalier

es•pe•cial (i spesh'əl), *adj.* special; particular. —**es•pe'cial•ly,** *adv.*

Es•pe•ran•to (es'pə rän'tō, -ran'-), *n.* an artificial language based on words common to the major European languages.

es•pi•o•nage (es'pē ə näzh', -nij), *n.* the act or practice of spying.

es•pla•nade (es'plə näd', -nād'), *n.* an open level space, esp. one serving for public walks.

es•pouse (i spouz', i spous'), *v.t.,* **-poused, -pous•ing.** 1. to adopt or embrace, as a cause; support. 2. to marry. —**es•pous'al,** *n.*

es•pres•so (e spres'ō), *n.,* *pl.* **-sos.** a strong coffee prepared by forcing hot water through finely ground coffee beans.

es•prit (e sprē'), *n.* sprightliness of spirit or wit.

es•prit' de corps' (də kôr'), *n.* a sense of unity and common purpose among the members of a group. [< F]

es•py (i spī'), *v.t.,* **-pied, -py•ing.** to catch sight of.

Esq., Esquire.

-esque, a suffix meaning: resembling (*Lincolnesque*); in the style or manner of (*Kafkaesque*).

es•quire (es'kwīr), *n.* 1. (*cap.*) a title of respect, in the U.S. chiefly applied to lawyers. 2. SQUIRE (def. 2). 3. a man of the English gentry ranking below a knight. 4. *Archaic.* SQUIRE (def. 1).

-ess, a suffix forming distinctively feminine nouns: *countess; goddess; lioness.* —**Usage.** The use of -ESS words has declined sharply in the latter half of the 20th century. Among those words that are rarely used or are either rejected or discouraged in modern American English are *ambassadress, ancestress, authoress, poetess, proprietress, sculptress,* and *stewardess.* Some nouns in -ESS are still current: *actress* (but some women prefer *actor*); *heiress* (largely in journalistic writing); *hostess* (but women who conduct radio and television programs are *hosts*); *millionairess; murderess; postmistress* (not in official U.S. government use); *seamstress;* and *waitress.*

es•say (*n.* es'ā *or, for 2,* e sā'; *v.* e sā'), *n.* 1. a short literary composition on a particular theme or subject. 2. an effort; attempt. —*v.t.* 3. to try; attempt. —**es•say'er,** *n.* —**es'say•ist,** *n.*

es•sence (es'əns), *n.* 1. the basic, real, and invariable nature of a thing; substance. 2. a concentrate of a substance. 3. a perfume; scent. 4. the true nature or constitution of something.

Es•sene (es'ēn, e sēn'), *n.* a member of a Jewish ascetic sect that flourished in ancient Palestine.

es•sen•tial (ə sen'shəl), *adj.* 1. absolutely necessary; indispensable. 2. of or constituting an essence. —*n.* 3. something basic, indispensable, or necessary. —**es•sen'tial•ly,** *adv.*

EST, Eastern Standard Time.

-est, a suffix forming the superlative degree of adjectives (*warmest*) and adverbs (*fastest*).

est., 1. established. 2. estimate. 3. estimated.

es•tab•lish (i stab'lish), *v.t.* 1. to bring into being; found. 2. to install or settle, as in a position or business. 3. to prove. 4. to cause to be accepted or recognized. 5. to enact or ordain on a permanent basis, as a law.

estab'lished church', *n.* a church that is recognized by law, and sometimes financially supported, as the official church of a nation. Compare NATIONAL CHURCH.

es•tab•lish•ment, *n.* 1. the act of establishing or state of being established. 2. **the Establishment,** the existing power structure in a society. 3. a place of residence or business including personnel, equipment, and property. 4. a permanent civil or military force or organization.

es•tate (i stāt'), *n.* 1. a piece of landed property, esp. one of large extent. 2. a. a person's property or possessions. b. the property of a deceased person. 3. a period or condition of life. 4. a major political or social group or class.

es•teem (i stēm'), *v.t.* 1. to regard with respect or admiration. 2. to consider as being; regard. —*n.* 3. respect or admiration.

es•ter (es'tər), *n.* a chemical compound produced by the reaction between an acid and an alcohol.

Es•ther (es'tər), *n.* 1. the Jewish wife of Ahasuerus. 2. a book of the Bible bearing her name.

es•thet•ics (es thet'iks), *n.* AESTHETICS. —**es'thete** (-thēt), *n.* —**es•thet'ic,** *adj.*

es•ti•ma•ble (es'tə mə bəl), *adj.* worthy of esteem.

es'ti•mate (*v.* -māt'; *n.* -mit, -māt'), *v.,* **-mat•ed, -mat•ing,** *n.* —*v.t.* 1. to form an approximate judgment regarding the worth, amount, size, etc., of. 2. to form an opinion of; judge. —*v.i.* 3. to make an estimate. —*n.* 4. an approximate judgment or calculation. 5. a judgment or opinion. 6. a statement of the approximate charge for doing work. —**es'ti•ma'tor,** *n.*

es'ti•ma'tion, *n.* 1. a judgment or estimate. 2. esteem; respect.

Es•to•ni•a (e stō'nē ə), *n.* a republic in N Europe, on the Baltic: formerly part of the USSR. 1,444,721. —**Es•to'ni•an,** *adj., n.*

es•trange (i strānj'), *v.t.,* **-tranged, -trang•ing.** to alienate the feelings or affections of; make unfriendly or hostile. —**es•trange'ment,** *n.*

es•tro•gen (es'trə jən), *n.* any of several female sex hormones capable of inducing estrus and producing secondary female sex characteristics.

es•trus (es'trəs), *n.* a recurring period of maximum sexual receptivity in most female mammals. —**es'trous,** *adj.*

es•tu•ar•y (es'chōō er'ē), *n., pl.* **-ar•ies.** the part of the lower course of a river at which the river's current meets the sea's tide.

-et, a suffix meaning little (*eaglet*).

ET, Eastern time.

e•ta (ā'tə, ē'tə), *n., pl.* **-tas.** the seventh letter of the Greek alphabet (H, η).

e•ta•gere *or* **é•ta•gère** (ā'tä zhâr', ā'tə-), *n.* a stand with open shelves for small objects.

et al. (et al', äl', ôl'), and others. [< L *et aliī*]

etc., et cetera.

et cet•er•a (et set'ər ə, se'trə), *adv.* and others, esp. of the same sort. [< L]

etch (ech), *v.t.* 1. to engrave furrows in, esp. with an acid. 2. to produce (a design, image, etc.) by etching. 3. to outline sharply; delineate. —**etch'er,** *n.*

etch'ing, *n.* 1. the act, art, or process of making

designs or pictures by the corrosive action of an acid. **2. a.** an impression taken from an etched plate. **b.** the design so produced.

e•ter•nal (i tûr′nl), adj. **1.** without beginning or end; lasting forever. **2.** perpetual; ceaseless. **3.** not subject to change; immutable. —**e•ter′nal•ly,** adv. —**e•ter′nal•ness,** n.

e•ter′ni•ty (-ni tē), n., pl. **-ties. 1.** infinite time. **2.** eternal existence. **3.** the timeless state after death. **4.** a seemingly endless period of time.

-eth, var. of -TH².

eth•ane (eth′ān), n. a colorless, odorless, flammable gas present in natural gas and crude petroleum, used chiefly as a fuel.

eth•a•nol (eth′ə nôl′, -nol′), n. ALCOHOL (def. 1).

e•ther (ē′thər), n. **1.** a colorless, highly volatile, flammable liquid used as a solvent and formerly as an anesthetic. **2.** the upper regions of space; the heavens. **3.** a substance formerly supposed to occupy all space.

e•the•re•al (i thēr′ē əl), adj. **1.** light or airy. **2.** extremely delicate or refined. **3.** heavenly; celestial. —**e•the′re•al•ly,** adv.

eth•ic (eth′ik), n. **1.** a body of moral principles or values. **2.** a moral precept or rule of conduct.

eth′i•cal, adj. **1.** pertaining to ethics. **2.** in accordance with standards for right conduct or practice, esp. those of a profession. —**eth′i•cal•ly,** adv.

eth′ics, n. **1.** (used with a sing. or pl. v.) a system of moral principles. **2.** (used with a sing. v.) the branch of philosophy dealing with right and wrong and the morality of motives and ends.

E•thi•o•pi•a (ē′thē ō′pē ə), n. a republic in E Africa. 58,732,577. —**E′thi•o′pi•an,** adj., n.

eth•nic (eth′nik), adj. **1.** of or pertaining to a people, esp. a group sharing a common and distinctive culture. —n. **2.** a member of an ethnic group or minority. —**eth′ni•cal•ly,** adv.

eth′nic cleans′ing, n. the elimination of an unwanted group from a society.

eth•nic′i•ty (-nis′i tē), n. ethnic traits or association.

eth•no•cen•trism (eth′nō sen′triz əm), n. belief in the inherent superiority of one's own ethnic group. —**eth′no•cen′tric,** adj.

eth•nol•o•gy (eth nol′ə jē), n. **1.** a branch of anthropology that analyzes and compares cultures. **2.** a branch of anthropology dealing with racial origins, distribution, and characteristics. —**eth′no•log′i•cal** (-nə loj′i kəl), **eth′no•log′ic,** adj. —**eth•nol′o•gist,** n.

e•thol•o•gy (ē thol′ə jē, i thol′-), n. the scientific study of animal behavior. —**e•tho•log•i•cal** (ē′thə loj′i kəl, eth′ə-), adj. —**e•thol′o•gist,** n.

e•thos (ē′thos, eth′ōs), n. the distinguishing character, spirit, or disposition of a person or group.

eth•yl (eth′əl), n. an antiknock fluid used in gasoline for more even combustion.

eth′yl al′cohol, n. ALCOHOL (def. 1).

eth•yl•ene (eth′ə lēn′), n. a colorless, flammable gas used to enhance the color of citrus fruits and as an inhalation anesthetic.

e•ti•ol•o•gy (ē′tē ol′ə jē), n., pl. **-gies. 1.** the study of causes, esp. of diseases. **2.** a cause or origin, esp. of a disease. —**e′ti•o•log′ic** (-ə loj′ik), **e′ti•o•log′i•cal,** adj. —**e′ti•ol′o•gist,** n.

et•i•quette (et′i kit, -ket′), n. conventional requirements for proper social or professional behavior.

Et•na (et′nə), n. **Mount,** an active volcano in E Sicily.

E•tru•ri•a (i trŏŏr′ē ə), n. an ancient country located in modern W Italy. —**E•tru′ri•an,** adj., n.

E•trus•can (i trus′kən), n. **1.** a member of a people inhabiting ancient Etruria. **2.** the extinct language of the Etruscans.

et seq., and the following. [< L et sequēns]

-ette, a suffix meaning: little (kitchenette); female or feminine (majorette). —**Usage.** English nouns in which -ETTE signifies a feminine identity have been

perceived as implying inferiority and are now avoided.

é•tude (ā′tōōd, ā′tyōōd), n. a musical composition practiced to improve a point of technique but also played for its artistic merit.

et•y•mol•o•gy (et′ə mol′ə jē), n., pl. **-gies. 1.** the history of a word or word element. **2.** an account of the origin and development of a word or word element. **3.** the study of historical linguistic change. —**et′y•mo•log′i•cal** (-mə loj′i kəl), adj. —**et′y•mol′o•gist,** n.

eu-, a combining form meaning good (eugenics).

Eu, Chem. Symbol. europium.

eu•ca•lyp•tus (yōō′kə lip′təs), n., pl. **-ti** (-tī), **-tus•es.** a tree of the myrtle family, having aromatic evergreen leaves.

Eu•cha•rist (yōō′kə rist), n. **1.** the sacrament of Holy Communion. **2.** the consecrated bread and wine used in this sacrament, esp. the bread. —**Eu′cha•ris′tic,** adj.

eu•chre (yōō′kər), n., v., **-chred, -chring.** —n. **1.** a card game usu. played with the 32 highest cards in the deck. —v.t. **2.** Slang. to cheat; swindle.

Eu•clid (yōō′klid), n. fl. c300 B.C., Greek geometrician and educator at Alexandria.

Eu•gene (yōō jēn′), n. a city in W Oregon. 118,122.

eu•gen•ics (yōō jen′iks), n. a science concerned with improving the genetic traits of a breed or species, esp. the human species. —**eu•gen′ic,** adj. —**eu•gen′i•cist** (-ə sist), n.

eu•lo•gize (yōō′lə jīz′), v.t., **-gized, -giz•ing.** to praise highly, esp. in a eulogy; extol. —**eu′lo•gist** (-jist), **eu′lo•giz′er,** n.

eu′lo•gy (-jē), n., pl. **-gies. 1.** a speech in praise of a person or thing, esp. a funeral oration. **2.** high praise. —**eu′lo•gis′tic,** adj.

eu•nuch (yōō′nək), n. a castrated man.

eu•phe•mism (yōō′fə miz′əm), n. **1.** the substitution of a mild or indirect expression for one thought to be offensive or harsh. **2.** the expression substituted. —**eu′phe•mis′tic,** adj. —**eu′phe•mis′ti•cal•ly,** adv.

eu•pho•ni•ous (yōō fō′nē əs), adj. agreeable to the ear. —**eu•pho′ni•ous•ly,** adv.

eu•pho•ny (yōō′fə nē), n., pl. **-nies.** agreeableness of sound, esp. a pleasing combination of words.

eu•pho•ri•a (yōō fôr′ē ə), n. a strong feeling of happiness, confidence, or well-being. —**eu•phor′ic** (-fôr′ik, -for′-), adj.

Eu•phra•tes (yōō frā′tēz), n. a river in SW Asia, flowing from Turkey through Syria and Iraq, into the Persian Gulf.

Eur., n. **1.** Europe. **2.** European.

Eur•a•sia (yōō rā′zhə), n. Europe and Asia considered together as one continent. —**Eur•a′sian,** adj., n.

eu•re•ka (yōō rē′kə, yə-), interj. an exclamation of triumph at a discovery. [< Gk heúrēka I have found (it)]

Eu•rip•i•des (yōō rip′i dēz′, yə-), n. c480–406? B.C., Greek dramatist.

eu•ro (yŏŏr′ō, yûr′-), n., pl. **-ros.** the official common currency of members of the European monetary Union, effective January 1, 1999. [by shortening and alter. of Eurocurrency]

Eu•ro•cur•ren•cy (yŏŏr′ō kûr′ən sē, -kur′-, yûr′-), n., pl. **-cies.** funds, esp. U.S. funds, deposited in a European bank and payable in the currency of that country.

Eu•ro•dol•lar (yŏŏr′ō dol′ər, yûr′-), n. a U.S. dollar deposited in or credited to a European bank.

Eu•rope (yŏŏr′əp, yûr′-), n. a continent in the W part of Eurasia, separated from Asia by the Ural Mountains. —**Eu•ro•pe′an** (-ə′ən), adj., n.

European Econom′ic Commu′nity, n. an association of European nations for economic cooperation.

European Monetary Union, n. an agreement by which most countries of W Europe have pooled currency reserves in order to trade their currencies at a fixed rate in preparation for the introduction of the euro on January 1, 1999: signed by Austria, Belgium, Finland, France, Germany, Ireland, Italy, Luxembourg, the Netherlands, Portugal, and Spain.

Eu•ro•pe•an plan', *n.* a system of paying a fixed hotel rate that covers lodging only.

Eu'ro•pe•an Un'ion, *n.* an association of European nations formed in 1993 for the purpose of achieving political and economic integration. *Abbr.:* EU

eu•ro•pi•um (yŏŏ rō'pē əm, ya-), *n.* a rare-earth metallic element. *Symbol:* Eu; *at. wt.:* 151.96; *at. no.:* 63.

Eu•sta'chian tube' (yŏŏ stā'shən, -stā'kē ən), *n.* (*often l.c.*) a canal between the middle ear and the pharynx. [after B. *Eustachio* (1524?-74), Italian anatomist]

eu•tha•na•sia (yŏŏ'thə nā'zhə), *n.* painless killing of a person or animal suffering from an incurable disease.

eu•then•ics (yŏŏ then'iks), *n.* a science concerned with improving the human species by changing the environment.

eu•troph•ic (yŏŏ trof'ik, -tŭō'fik), *adj.* (of a lake) characterized by an abundant accumulation of nutrients but shallow and depleted of oxygen in summer. —**eu•troph'i•ca'tion,** *n.*

Eu•ty•chus (yŏŏ'ti kəs), *n.* a young man whom the Apostle Paul restored to life. Acts 20:9–12.

eV or **ev,** electron-volt.

e•vac•u•ate (i vak'yŏŏ āt'), *v.,* -at•ed, -at•ing. —*v.t.* 1. to make empty. 2. to remove (persons or things) from (a place or area), esp. for safety. 3. to discharge from the bowels. —*v.i.* 4. to leave a place; withdraw. —**e•vac'u•a'tion,** *n.*

e•vac'u•ee' (-yŏŏ ē'), *n., pl.* -ees. a person who is evacuated from a place of danger.

e•vade (i vād'), *v.t., v.i.,* e•vad•ed, e•vad•ing. to escape or avoid, esp. by cleverness or trickery. —**e•vad'er,** *n.*

e•val•u•ate (i val'yŏŏ āt'), *v.t.,* -at•ed, -at•ing. to determine the value, quality, or significance of. —**e•val'u•a'tion,** *n.* —**e•val'u•a'tor,** *n.*

ev•a•nes•cent (ev'ə nes'ənt), *adj.* fading away; vanishing. —**ev'a•nes'cence,** *n.*

e•van•gel•i•cal (ē'van jel'i kəl, ev'ən-), *adj.* 1. of or in keeping with the Gospels. 2. of or belonging to the Christian churches that emphasize the authority of the Scriptures. 3. designating Christians who hold to a conservative but not necessarily literal interpretation of the Bible. 4. marked by fervor or zeal. —**e'van•gel'i•cal•ism,** *n.* —**e'van•gel'i•cal•ly,** *adv.*

e•van•ge•lism (i van'jə liz'əm), *n.* 1. the preaching of the Christian gospel. 2. missionary zeal.

e•van•ge•list, *n.* 1. a preacher of the Christian gospel, esp. a revivalist. 2. (*cap.*) one of the writers of the four Gospels. —**e•van'ge•lis'tic,** *adj.*

e•van•ge•lize' (-līz'), *v.,* -lized, -liz•ing. —*v.t.* 1. to convert to Christianity. —*v.i.* 2. to preach the gospel.

Ev•ans•ville (ev'ənz vil'), *n.* a city in SW Indiana. 126,272.

e•vap•o•rate (i vap'ə rāt'), *v.,* -rat•ed, -rat•ing. —*v.i.* 1. to change into or pass off in vapor. 2. to disappear; vanish; fade. —*v.t.* 3. to convert into vapor. 4. to extract moisture or liquid from, as by heat. —**e•vap'o•ra'tion,** *n.*

e•va•sion (i vā'zhən), *n.* 1. an act or instance of evading. 2. a means of evading. —**e•va'sive** (-siv), *adj.* —**e•va'sive•ly,** *adv.* —**e•va'sive•ness,** *n.*

eve (ēv), *n.* 1. (*sometimes cap.*) the evening or day before an event, esp. a holiday. 2. the period preceding an event. 3. evening.

Eve (ēv), *n.* the first woman: wife of Adam. Gen. 3:20.

e•ven (ē'vən), *adj.* 1. level; flat. 2. without irregularities; smooth. 3. on the same plane or line. 4. free from variations; uniform. 5. equal in measure or quantity. 6. divisible by two. 7. leaving no balance of debt on either side. 8. exact. 9. calm; placid. —*adv.* 10. still; yet: *even more suitable.* 11. (used to suggest an extreme case or an unlikely instance): *Even the slightest noise disturbs him.* 12. exactly;

just: *Even as help was coming, the troops surrendered.* 13. fully; quite: *was moved even to tears.* 14. indeed: *He is willing, even eager, to do it.* —*v.t., v.i.* 15. to make or become even. —**e'ven•ly,** *adv.* —**e'ven•ness,** *n.*

e'ven•hand'ed, *adj.* impartial; equitable. —**e'ven•hand'ed•ly,** *adv.* —**e'ven•hand'ed•ness,** *n.*

eve•ning (ēv'ning), *n.* the latter part of the day and early part of the night.

eve'ning star', *n.* a bright planet, esp. Venus, seen in the western sky at or soon after sunset.

e'ven mon'ey, *n.* equal odds in a wager.

e•vent (i vent'), *n.* 1. an occurrence, esp. one of some importance. 2. a possible occurrence. 3. a single sports contest within a scheduled program.

e•vent'ful, *adj.* 1. full of events or incidents. 2. very important; momentous. —**e•vent'ful•ly,** *adv.* —**e•vent'ful•ness,** *n.*

e•ven•tide (ē'vən tīd'), *n.* evening.

e•ven•tu•al (i ven'chŏŏ əl), *adj.* happening at an indefinite future time. —**e•ven'tu•al•ly,** *adv.*

e•ven'tu•al'i•ty, *n., pl.* -ties. a possible event, occurrence, or circumstance.

e•ven'tu•ate' (-āt'), *v.i.,* -at•ed, -at•ing. to be the outcome; result.

ev•er (ev'ər), *adv.* 1. at any time. 2. at all times; always. 3. in any possible case.

Ev•er•est (ev'ər ist), *n.* **Mount,** a mountain in S Asia, in the Himalayas: the highest mountain in the world. 29,028 ft. (8848 m).

ev'er•glade', *n.* a tract of low, swampy land.

ev'er•green', *adj.* 1. having green leaves throughout the year. —*n.* 2. an evergreen plant.

ev'er•last'ing, *adj.* 1. lasting forever; eternal. —*n.* 2. eternity.

ev'er•more', *adv.* always; forever.

Ev•ers (ev'ərz), *n.* **(James) Charles,** born 1922, and his brother **Med•gar (Wiley)** (med'gər), 1925–63, U.S. civil-rights leaders.

eve•ry (ev'rē), *adj.* 1. being one of a group taken collectively; each. 2. all possible: *every prospect of success.* —**Idiom. 3. every other,** every second; each alternate: *every other day.*

eve'ry•bod'y (-bod'ē, -bud'ē), *pron.* every person.

eve'ry•day', *adj.* 1. daily. 2. of or for ordinary days. 3. ordinary; commonplace.

eve'ry•one' (-wun', -wən), *pron.* 1. everybody. —*Proverb.* 2. Everyone to whom much is given, of him will much be required, one who has received blessings has great responsibilities. Luke 12:48.

eve'ry•place', *adv.* everywhere.

eve'ry•thing', *pron.* every particular of an aggregate or total; all.

eve'ry•where', *adv.* in every place or part.

e•vict (i vikt'), *v.t.* to expel (a tenant) from property by legal process. —**e•vic'tion,** *n.*

ev•i•dence (ev'i dəns), *n., v.,* -denced, -denc•ing. —*n.* 1. something that constitutes proof. 2. an indication or sign. 3. data presented in court to substantiate claims or allegations. —*v.t.* 4. to show clearly; manifest.

ev'i•dent, *adj.* clear to the sight or understanding. —**ev'i•dent•ly,** *adv.*

e•vil (ē'vəl), *adj.* 1. morally wrong or bad; wicked. 2. harmful; injurious. 3. unfortunate; disastrous. —*n.* 4. evil quality, intention, or conduct; wickedness or sin. 5. injury or harm. 6. something causing injury or harm. —*Proverb.* 7. Evil to him who evil thinks, may one who thinks of others receive retribution. —**e'vil•ly,** *adv.*

e'vil•do'er, *n.* a person who does evil or wrong. —**e'vil•do'ing,** *n.*

e'vil eye', *n.* a look thought capable of inflicting injury or harm.

E•vil-Me•ro•dach (ē'vil mi rō'dak), *n.* a king of Babylon. II Kings 25:27–30; Jer. 52:31–34.

Evil One', *n.* Satan, the devil. Matt. 13:19; John 17:15; I John 2:13–14; 5:18.

e•vince (i vins′), v.t., **e•vinced, e•vinc•ing.** to make evident; manifest.

e•vis•cer•ate (i vis′ə rāt′), v.t., **-at•ed, -at•ing, 1.** to remove the entrails of; disembowel. **2.** to deprive of vital or essential parts. —**e•vis′cer•a′tion,** n.

e•voke (i vōk′), v.t., **e•voked, e•vok•ing. 1.** to call up (memories, feelings, etc.). **2.** to draw forth; elicit: The comment evoked loud protests. —**ev•o•ca•tion** (ev′ə kā′shən, ē′vō-), n. —**e•voc•a•tive** (i vok′ə tiv, i vō′kə-), adj.

ev•o•lu•tion (ev′ə loo′shən; esp. Brit. ē′və-), n. **1.** a process of formation or growth; development. **2. a.** change in the gene pool of a population from generation to generation by such processes as mutation and natural selection. **b.** the theory that all existing organisms developed from earlier forms by natural selection. **3.** a pattern formed by a series of movements. —**ev′o•lu′tion•ar′y,** adj. —**ev′o•lu′tion•ism,** n. —**ev′o•lu′tion•ist,** n., adj.

e•volve (i volv′), v.t., v.i., **e•volved, e•volv•ing.** to develop gradually by or as if by a process of evolution. —**e•volve′ment,** n.

ewe (yoo; Dial. yō), n. a female sheep.

ew•er (yoo′ər), n. a pitcher or jug with a wide spout.

ex¹ (eks), prep. not including; without: ex dividend.

ex² (eks), n. Informal. a former spouse.

ex-, a prefix meaning: out of or from (export); utterly or thoroughly (exacerbate); former (ex-governor).

Ex., Exodus.

ex., 1. example. 2. except. 3. exception. 4. exchange.

ex•ac•er•bate (ig zas′ər bāt′, ek sas′-), v.t., **-bat•ed, -bat•ing.** to increase the severity, bitterness, or violence of; aggravate. —**ex•ac′er•ba′tion,** n.

ex•act (ig zakt′), adj. **1.** strictly accurate, correct, or precise. —v.t. **2.** to call for, demand, or require. **3.** to force the payment, yielding, or performance of. —**ex•ac′tion,** n. —**ex•act′ly,** adv. —**ex•act′ness,** n.

ex•act•ing, adj. **1.** severe in making demands or setting requirements. **2.** requiring close application and attention. —**ex•act′ing•ly,** adv.

ex•ac′ti•tude′ (-zak′ti tood′, -tyood′), n. the quality of being exact.

ex•ag•ger•ate (ig zaj′ə rāt′), v.t., v.i., **-at•ed, -at•ing.** to magnify beyond the limits of truth; overstate or overemphasize. —**ex•ag′ger•at′ed•ly,** adv. —**ex•ag′ger•a′tion,** n. —**ex•ag′ger•a′tor,** n.

ex•alt (ig zôlt′), v.t. **1.** to raise in rank, power, etc.; elevate. **2.** to praise; extol. —**ex′al•ta′tion,** n.

ex•am (ig zam′), n. Informal. an examination.

ex•am′i•na′tion (-ə nā′shən), n. **1.** the act of examining or state of being examined. **2.** a test to determine knowledge or qualifications.

ex•am′ine (-in), v.t., **-ined, -in•ing. 1.** to inspect or scrutinize carefully. **2.** to test the knowledge or qualifications of (a pupil, witness, etc.), as by questions. —**ex•am′in•er,** n.

ex•am•ple (ig zam′pəl, -zäm′-), n. **1.** one of a number of things taken to show the character of the whole. **2.** a pattern or model to be imitated or avoided. **3.** an instance illustrating a rule or method.

ex•as•per•ate (ig zas′pə rāt′), v.t., **-at•ed, -at•ing.** to irritate or provoke to a high degree. —**ex•as′per•a′tion,** n.

ex ca•the•dra (eks′ kə thē′drə, kath′i drə), adv., adj. from the seat of authority; with authority.

ex•ca•vate (eks′kə vāt′), v.t., **-vat•ed, -vat•ing. 1.** to make a hole or cavity in. **2.** to form by removing material. **3.** to dig out (earth, sand, etc.). **4.** to expose by or as if by digging; unearth. —**ex′ca•va′tion,** n. —**ex′ca•va′tor,** n.

ex•ceed (ik sēd′), v.t. **1.** to go beyond the bounds or limits of. **2.** to be superior to; surpass.

ex•ceed′ing•ly, adv. to an unusual degree; extremely.

ex•cel (ik sel′), v.i, v.t., **-celled, -cel•ling.** to be superior (to); surpass (others).

ex•cel•lence (ek′sə ləns), n. **1.** the fact or state of excelling. **2.** an excellent quality or feature.

Ex′cel•len•cy, n., pl. **-cies.** a title of honor given to certain high officials, as bishops and archbishops.

ex′cel•lent, adj. remarkably good; first-rate. —**ex′cel•lent•ly,** adv.

ex•cel•si•or (ik sel′sē ər, ek-), n. fine wood shavings used esp. for stuffing and packing. [formerly a trademark]

ex•cept¹ (ik sept′), prep. **1.** with the exclusion of; but. —conj. **2.** with the exception that; only.

ex•cept² (ik sept′), v.t. **1.** to leave out; exclude. —v.i. **2.** to object.

ex•cept′ing, prep. except.

ex•cep′tion, n. **1.** the act of excepting or fact of being excepted. **2.** something excluded from a general rule or class. **3.** an objection. —Idiom. **4. take exception, a.** to object. **b.** to take offense.

ex•cep′tion•a•ble, adj. liable to exception.

ex•cep′tion•al, adj. **1.** being an exception; unusual, esp. superior. **2.** needing special schooling, as because of a mental handicap. —**ex•cep′tion•al•ly,** adv.

ex•cerpt (n. ek′sûrpt; v. ik sûrpt′, ek′sûrpt), n. **1.** a passage or quotation taken or selected, as from a book. —v.t. **2.** to take or select (an excerpt) from.

ex•cess (ik ses′, ek′ses), n. **1.** the amount or degree by which one thing exceeds another. **2.** a superabundance or surplus. **3.** immoderate indulgence, as in eating. —adj. **4.** being more than what is necessary, usual, or specified; extra.

ex•ces′sive, adj. exceeding the usual, necessary, or proper limit or degree. —**ex•ces′sive•ly,** adv.

ex•change (iks chānj′), v., **-changed, -chang•ing,** n. —v.t. **1.** to give up (something) for an equivalent or substitute; trade. **2.** to give and receive reciprocally; interchange. —n. **3.** an act or instance of exchanging. **4.** something exchanged. **5.** a place where commodities, securities, or services are exchanged. **6.** a central office or station: a telephone exchange. **7.** the reciprocal transfer of equivalent sums of money, esp. in the currencies of two different countries. —**ex•change′a•ble,** adj.

ex•cheq•uer (eks′chek ər, iks chek′ər), n. **1.** a treasury, as of a nation. **2.** (often cap.) the British governmental department in charge of the public revenues. **3.** Informal. financial resources; funds.

ex•cise¹ (ek′sīz, -sīs), n. a tax on the manufacture, sale, or consumption of certain commodities, as liquor or tobacco, within a country.

ex•cise² (ik sīz′), v.t., **-cised, -cis•ing.** to remove by cutting out or off. —**ex•ci′sion** (-sizh′ən), n.

ex•cit•a•ble (ik sī′tə bəl), adj. easily excited. —**ex•cit′a•bil′i•ty,** n.

ex•cite (ik sīt′), v.t., **-cit•ed, -cit•ing. 1.** to stir up the emotions or feelings of; arouse. **2.** to arouse (emotions or feelings); awaken. **3.** to stir to action; stimulate. —**ex•ci•ta•tion** (ek′sī tā′shən), n. —**ex•cit′ed•ly,** adv. —**ex•cit′er,** n. —**ex•cit′ing,** adj.

ex•cite′ment, n. **1.** an excited state or condition. **2.** something that excites.

ex•claim (ik sklām′), v.i., v.t. to cry out or say suddenly and vehemently, as in surprise. —**ex•cla•ma•tion** (ek′sklə mā′shən), n. —**ex•clam•a•to•ry** (iksklam′ə tôr′ē), adj.

exclama′tion point′ (or **mark′**), n. the sign (!) used in writing after an exclamation or interjection.

ex•clude (ik sklood′), v.t., **-clud•ed, -clud•ing. 1.** to prevent the entrance of. **2.** to shut out, as from consideration. **3.** to expel; eject. —**ex•clu′sion** (-zhən), n.

ex•clu•sive (ik skloo′siv, -ziv), adj. **1.** excluding others, as from a part or share. **2.** expensive or fashionable. **3.** single or sole. **4.** resistant to the admission of outsiders, as to membership, association, or intimacy. **5.** not divided; entire: paid exclusive attention to business. —**ex•clu′sive•ly,** adv —**ex•clu′sive•ness, ex•clu•siv•i•ty** (eks′kloo siv′i tē), n.

ex•com•mu•ni•cate (eks′kə myoo′ni kāt′), v.t., **-cat•ed, -cat•ing.** to cut off from communion or membership, esp. from the sacraments of a church. —**ex′com•mu′ni•ca′tion,** n.

ex•co•ri•ate (ik skôr′ē āt′), v.t., **-at•ed, -at•ing. 1.**

to denounce or berate severely. **2.** to strip off or remove the skin of. —ex•co′ri•a′tion, *n.*

ex•cre•ment (ek′skrə mənt), *n.* waste matter, esp. feces, discharged from the body. —ex′cre•men′tal (-men′tl), *adj.*

ex•cres•cence (ik skres′əns), *n.* an abnormal outgrowth or addition. —ex•cres′cent, *adj.*

ex•cre•ta (ik skrē′tə), *n.pl.* excreted matter, as urine or sweat.

ex•crete (ik skrēt′), *v.t.,* -cret•ed, -cret•ing. to separate and eliminate (waste) from the body. —ex• cre′tion, *n.* —ex•cre•to•ry (ek′skri tôr′ē), *adj.*

ex•cru•ci•at•ing (ik skrōō′shē ā′ting), *adj.* **1.** causing intense suffering. **2.** intense or extreme. —ex• cru′ci•at′ing•ly, *adv.*

ex•cul•pate (ek′skul pāt′, ik skul′pāt), *v.t.,* -pat•ed, -pat•ing. to clear from a charge of guilt or fault; free from blame. —ex′cul•pa′tion, *n.*

ex•cur•sion (ik skûr′zhən), *n.* **1.** a short trip; outing. **2.** a trip, as on a train, at a reduced rate. **3.** a deviation or digression —ex•cur′sion•ist, *n.*

ex•cur•sive (-siv), *adj.* given to digression, as in speech; rambling. —ex•cur′sive•ly, *adv.* —ex•cur′-sive•ness, *n.*

ex•cur•sus (-səs), *n., pl.* -sus•es, -sus. a detailed discussion of a point in a book, esp. one added as an appendix.

ex•cuse (*v.* ik skyōōz′; *n.* -skyōōs′), *v.,* -cused, -cusing, *n.* —*v.t.* **1.** to pardon or forgive. **2.** to offer or serve as an apology for. **3.** to release from an obligation or duty. **4.** to allow to leave. —*n.* **5.** an explanation offered as a reason for being excused. **6.** a reason for excusing or being excused. **7.** an inferior specimen: *a poor excuse for a poem.* —ex•cus′a•ble, *adj.*

ex•e•cra•ble (ek′si krə bəl), *adj.* **1.** utterly detestable. **2.** very bad. —ex′e•cra•bly, *adv.*

ex•e•crate (ek′si krāt′), *v.t.,* -crat•ed, -crat•ing. **1.** to detest utterly as being evil or abhorrent. **2.** to denounce. —ex′e•cra′tion, *n.*

ex•e•cute (ek′si kyōōt′), *v.t.,* -cut•ed, -cut•ing. **1.** to carry out; accomplish. **2.** to perform or do. **3.** to put to death according to law. **4.** to produce in accordance with a plan or design. **5.** to give validity to (a legal instrument) by fulfilling requirements. **6.** to run (a computer program) or process (a command). —ex′e•cu′tion, *n.*

ex′e•cu′tion•er, *n.* an official who inflicts capital punishment in pursuance of a legal warrant.

ex•ec•u•tive (ig zek′yə tiv), *n.* **1.** a person or group having administrative or managerial authority in an organization. **2.** the executive branch of a government. —*adj.* **3.** of or suited for carrying out plans, duties, or policies. **4.** of or charged with the administration of laws or public affairs.

exec′utive branch′, *n.* the branch of the U.S. government whose powers are vested in the president.

exec′utive or′der, *n.* (*often caps.*) a regulation issued by the chief executive and having the force of law.

ex•ec•u•tor (-tər), *n.* a person named in a will to carry out its provisions.

ex•ec•u•trix (-triks), *n., pl.* ex•ec•u•tri•ces (ig zek′-yə trī′sēz), ex•ec•u•trix•es. a woman named in a will to carry out its provisions.

ex•e•ge•sis (ek′si jē′sis), *n., pl.* -ses (-sēz). critical explanation or interpretation, esp. of Scripture. —ex′-e•get′ic (-jet′ik), *adj.*

ex•em•plar (ig zem′plər, -plär), *n.* **1.** a model or pattern to be copied or imitated. **2.** a typical example or instance.

ex•em•pla•ry (-plə rē), *adj.* **1.** worthy of imitation; commendable. **2.** serving as a model or pattern.

ex•em′pli•fy′ (-plə fī′), *v.t.,* -fied, -fy•ing. **1.** to illustrate by example. **2.** to serve as an example of; typify. —ex•em′pli•fi•ca′tion, *n.*

ex•empt (ig zempt′), *v.t.* **1.** to free from an obligation or liability to which others are subject. —*adj.* **2.** released from or not subject to an obligation or liability. —ex•emp′tion, *n.*

ex•er•cise (ek′sər sīz′), *n., v.,* -cised, -cis•ing. —*n.*

1. bodily or mental exertion, esp. for the sake of training. **2.** something done for practice or training. **3.** a putting into action, use, or effect: *the exercise of caution.* **4.** Often, **-cises.** a traditional ceremony: *graduation exercises.* —*v.t.* **5.** to put through exercises. **6.** to put into action or use. **7.** to make uneasy; worry or annoy. —*v.i.* **8.** to take bodily exercise. —ex′er•cis′er, *n.*

ex•ert (ig zûrt′), *v.t.* **1.** to put forth: *to exert strength.* **2.** to put in force or operation: *exerted pressure on his father.* **3.** to put (oneself) into vigorous action or effort. —ex•er′tion, *n.*

ex•hale (eks hāl′), *v.i., v.t.,* -haled, -hal•ing. **1.** to breathe out. **2.** to pass or give off as vapor. —ex′ha-la′tion (-hə lā′shən), *n.*

ex•haust (ig zôst′), *v.t.* **1.** to drain of strength or energy; wear out. **2.** to use up completely; consume. **3.** to treat or study (a subject) thoroughly. **4.** to draw out or drain off completely. —*n.* **5. a.** the escape of steam or gases from an engine. **b.** the steam or gases ejected. **6.** the parts of an engine through which exhaust is ejected. —ex•haust′i•ble, *adj.* —ex•haus′-tion, *n.*

ex•haus′tive, *adj.* exhausting a subject; comprehensive.

ex•hib•it (ig zib′it), *v.t.* **1.** to offer or expose to view; display. **2.** to submit (a document, object, etc.) as evidence in a court. —*v.i.* **3.** to present something, as art, to public view. —*n.* **4.** an act or instance of exhibiting. **5.** something exhibited. **6.** a document or object exhibited as evidence. —ex•hi•bi•tion (ek′sə-bish′ən), *n.* —ex•hib′i•tor, *n.*

ex′hi•bi′tion•ism, *n.* a tendency to call attention to oneself, esp. by exhibiting the genitals. —ex′hi• bi′tion•ist, *n., adj.*

ex•hil•a•rate (ig zil′ə rāt′), *v.t.,* -rat•ed, -rat•ing. **1.** to enliven; invigorate. **2.** to make cheerful. —ex• hil′a•ra′tion, *n.*

ex•hort (ig zôrt′), *v.t., v.i.* to urge, advise, or caution earnestly; admonish urgently. —ex•hor•ta•tion (eg′zôr tā′shən, ek′sôr-), *n.*

ex•hume (ig zōōm′, -zyōōm′, eks hyōōm′), *v.t.,* -humed, -hum•ing. **1.** to remove from the earth; disinter. **2.** to revive or restore. —ex•hu•ma•tion (eks′-hyōō mā′shən), *n.*

ex•i•gen•cy (ek′si jən sē), *n., pl.* -cies. **1.** a state of urgency. **2.** Usu., **-cies.** something needed, demanded, or required in a specific circumstance. **3.** an emergency. —ex′i•gent, *adj.*

ex•ig•u•ous (ig zig′yōō əs), *adj.* scanty; meager.

ex•ile (eg′zīl, ek′sīl), *n., v.,* -iled, -il•ing. —*n.* **1. a.** expulsion from one's native land; banishment. **b.** the fact or state of such expulsion. **2.** a person banished or separated from his or her native land. —*v.t.* **3.** to expel (a person) from his or her country; banish.

ex•ist (ig zist′), *v.i.* **1.** to have being; be. **2.** to have life. **3.** to continue to be or live.

ex•ist′ence, *n.* **1.** the state or fact of existing. **2.** continuance in being or life. **3.** something that exists. —ex•ist′ent, *adj.*

ex•is•ten•tial (eg′zi sten′shəl, ek′si-), *adj.* **1.** of existence. **2.** of existentialism. —ex′is•ten′tial•ly, *adv.*

ex′is•ten′tial•ism, *n.* a philosophy that stresses self-determination and responsibility for one's actions. —ex′is•ten′tial•ist, *n., adj.*

ex•it (eg′zit, ek′sit), *n.* **1.** a way or passage out. **2.** a going out or away. **3.** a departure of an actor from the stage. —*v.i., v.t.* **4.** to leave. [< L *exitus* act or means of going out]

ex′it poll′, *n.* a survey taken of a percentage of voters as they leave the voting place.

exo-, a combining form meaning outside or outer (*exosphere*).

ex•o•bi•ol•o•gy (ek′sō bī ol′ə jē), *n.* the study of potential life beyond the earth's atmosphere.

ex•o•crine (ek′sə krin, -krīn′), *adj.* **1.** of an exocrine gland or its secretion. —*n.* **2.** EXOCRINE GLAND.

ex′ocrine gland′, *n.* a gland, as a salivary gland, that secretes externally through a duct.

Exod., Exodus.

ex•o•dus (ek′sə dəs), *n.* **1.** a mass departure or emigration. **2.** (*cap.*) the departure of the Israelites from Egypt under Moses. **3.** (*cap.*) the second book of the Old Testament.

ex of•fi•ci•o (eks′ ə fish′ē ō′), *adv.*, *adj.* by virtue of office or official position. [< L]

ex•og•e•nous (ek soj′ə nəs), *adj.* originating from outside; derived externally.

ex•on•er•ate (ig zon′ə rāt′), *v.t.*, **-at•ed, -at•ing.** to clear from accusation, guilt, or blame. —**ex•on′er•a′tion,** *n.* —**ex•on′er•a′tor,** *n.*

ex•or•bi•tant (ig zôr′bi tənt), *adj.* exceeding the bounds of custom, propriety, or reason. —**ex•or′bi•tance,** *n.* —**ex•or′bi•tant•ly,** *adv.*

ex•or•cise (ek′sôr sīz′, -sər-), *v.t.*, **-cised, -cis•ing. 1.** to seek to expel (an evil spirit) by religious or solemn ceremonies. **2.** to free of evil spirits. —**ex′or•cism** (-siz′əm), *n.* —**ex′or•cist,** *n.*

ex•o•sphere (ek′sō sfēr′), *n.* the highest region of the atmosphere.

ex•o•ther•mic (ek′sō thûr′mik) also **-ther′mal,** *adj.* pertaining to a chemical change accompanied by a liberation of heat.

ex•ot•ic (ig zot′ik), *adj.* **1.** not native; foreign. **2.** strikingly unusual or strange, as in appearance. —**ex•ot′i•cal•ly,** *adv.*

exp., 1. expenses. **2.** expired. **3.** export. **4.** express.

ex•pand (ik spand′), *v.t.*, *v.i.* **1.** to increase in extent, size, scope, or volume. **2.** to stretch out; spread. **3.** to express (something) in fuller form or in greater detail. —**ex•pand′a•ble, ex•pand′i•ble,** *adj.*

ex•panse (ik spans′), *n.* a broad, unbroken space or area.

ex•pan′sion (-span′shən), *n.* **1.** the act or process of expanding. **2.** the state, quality, or degree of being expanded. **3.** an expanded portion or form.

expan′sion card′, *n.* a card in a computer on which additional chips can be mounted to expand the computer's capabilities.

ex•pan′sion•ism, *n.* a policy of expansion, as of territory. —**ex•pan′sion•ist,** *n., adj.*

ex•pan′sive (-siv), *adj.* **1.** wide; extensive. **2.** cordial and open. **3.** tending to expand. **4.** causing expansion. —**ex•pan′sive•ly,** *adv.* —**ex•pan′sive•ness,** *n.*

ex parte (eks pär′tē), *adv., adj.* from or on one side only, as of a dispute.

ex•pa•ti•ate (ik spā′shē āt′), *v.i.*, **-at•ed, -at•ing.** to elaborate in discourse or writing. —**ex•pa′ti•a′tion,** *n.*

ex•pa•tri•ate (*v.* eks pā′trē āt′; *esp. Brit.* -pa′trē-; *n.* -it, -āt′), *v.*, **-at•ed, -at•ing.** *n.* —*v.t., v.i.* **1.** to send into or become an exile. —*n.* **2.** an expatriated person. —**ex•pa′tri•a′tion,** *n.*

ex•pect (ik spckt′), *v.t.* **1.** to anticipate the occurrence or coming of. **2.** to consider as due or justified. **3.** *Informal.* to suppose; surmise. —*Idiom.* **4. be expecting,** to be pregnant. —**Usage.** Objections are still occasionally made to the use of EXPECT to mean "to suppose," but this use is now, though informal, well established.

ex•pect′an•cy (-spek′tən sē), *n., pl.* **-cies.** EXPECTATION (defs. 1, 2).

ex•pect′ant, *adj.* **1.** marked by expectation. **2.** pregnant. —**ex•pect′ant•ly,** *adv.*

ex•pec•ta•tion (ek′spek tā′shən), *n.* **1.** the act or state of expecting. **2.** something expected. **3.** an expectant mental attitude. **4.** Often, **-tions.** a prospect, as of future benefit.

ex•pec•to•rant (ik spek′tər ənt), *n.* a medicine that promotes the discharge of fluid from the respiratory tract.

ex•pec′to•rate′ (-rāt′), *v.i., v.t.*, **-rat•ed, -rat•ing.** to spit. —**ex•pec′to•ra′tion,** *n.*

ex•pe•di•en•cy (ik spē′dē ən sē), *n., pl.* **-cies. 1.** the quality of being expedient. **2.** a regard for what is advantageous rather than for what is right. **3.** something expedient. Often, **ex•pe′di•ence.**

ex•pe′di•ent, *adj.* **1.** fit or suitable for a purpose. **2.** governed or marked by self-interest. —*n.* **3.** a handy means to an end. —**ex•pe′di•ent•ly,** *adv.*

ex•pe•dite (ek′spi dīt′), *v.t.*, **-dit•ed, -dit•ing. 1.** to

speed up the progress of. **2.** to perform promptly. —**ex′pe•dit′er, ex′pe•di′tor,** *n.*

ex•pe•di•tion (ek′spi dish′ən), *n.* **1. a.** a journey made for a specific purpose. **b.** the group engaged in such an activity. **2.** promptness. —**ex′pe•di′tion•ar′y,** *adj.*

ex′pe•di′tious, *adj.* characterized by promptness. —**ex′pe•di′tious•ly,** *adv.* —**ex′pe•di′tious•ness,** *n.*

ex•pel (ik spel′), *v.t.*, **-pelled, -pel•ling.** to drive or force out or away; eject.

ex•pend (ik spend′), *v.t.* **1.** to use up. **2.** to pay out; spend. —**ex•pend′er,** *n.*

ex•pend′a•ble, *adj.* **1.** capable of being expended. **2.** consumed in use. **3.** capable of being sacrificed in case of need.

ex•pend•i•ture (ik spen′di chər), *n.* **1.** the act of expending. **2.** something expended.

ex•pense (ik spens′), *n.* **1.** cost; charge. **2.** a cause of spending. **3. expenses,** charges incurred in connection with business. —*Idiom.* **4. at the expense of,** at the sacrifice or to the detriment of.

ex•pen′sive, *adj.* entailing great expense; costly. —**ex•pen′sive•ly,** *adv.*

ex•pe•ri•ence (ik spēr′ē əns), *n., v.*, **-enced, -enc•ing.** —*n.* **1.** something personally lived through or encountered. **2.** the observing, encountering, or undergoing of events as they occur in the course of time. **3.** knowledge or practical wisdom gained from this process. —*v.t.* **4.** to have experience of. —*Idiom.* **5. experience religion,** to undergo a spiritual conversion.

ex•pe′ri•enced, *adj.* wise or skillful through experience.

ex•per•i•ment (*n.* ik sper′ə mənt; *v.* -ment′), *n.* **1.** a test for the purpose of discovering something unknown or of testing a principle, supposition, or theory. —*v.i.* **2.** to conduct an experiment. —**ex•per′i•men′tal,** *adj.* —**ex•per′i•men′tal•ly,** *adv.* —**ex•per′i•men•ta′tion,** *n.* —**ex•per′i•ment′er,** *n.*

ex•pert (ek′spûrt; *adj.* also ik spûrt′), *n.* **1.** a person with special skill or knowledge in a particular field. —*adj.* **2.** possessing or showing special skill or knowledge. —**ex•pert′ly,** *adv.* —**ex•pert′ness,** *n.*

ex•per•tise (ek′spər tēz′), *n.* expert skill or knowledge.

ex•pi•ate (ek′spē āt′), *v.t.*, **-at•ed, -at•ing.** to make amends for. —**ex′pi•a′tion,** *n.* —**ex′pi•a′tor,** *n.* —**ex′pi•a•to′ry** (-ə tôr′ē), *adj.*

ex•pire (ik spīᵉr′), *v.i.*, **-pired, -pir•ing. 1.** to come to an end. **2.** to die. **3.** to breathe out. —**ex•pi•ra•tion** (ek′spə rā′shən), *n.*

ex•plain (ik splān′), *v.t.* **1.** to make clear or intelligible. **2.** to make known the cause of or reason for. —*v.i.* **3.** to give an explanation. —**ex•plain′a•ble,** *adj.* —**ex•plain′er,** *n.*

ex•pla•na•tion (ek′splə nā′shən), *n.* **1.** the act or process of explaining. **2.** something that explains.

ex•plan•a•to•ry (ik splan′ə tôr′ē), *adj.* serving to explain.

ex•ple•tive (ek′spli tiv), *n.* an often profane exclamation.

ex•pli•ca•ble (ek′spli kə bəl, ik splik′ə bəl), *adj.* capable of being explained.

ex′pli•cate′ (-kāt′), *v.t.*, **-cat•ed, -cat•ing.** to explain in detail. —**ex′pli•ca′tion,** *n.* —**ex′pli•ca′tor,** *n.*

ex•plic•it (ik splis′it), *adj.* fully and clearly expressed. —**ex•plic′it•ly,** *adv.* —**ex•plic′it•ness,** *n.*

ex•plode (ik splōd′), *v.*, **-plod•ed, -plod•ing.** —*v.i.* **1.** to burst suddenly, noisily, and violently, as from rapid chemical change or from internal pressure. **2.** to burst forth energetically; erupt. —*v.t.* **3.** to cause to explode. **4.** to discredit; disprove. —**ex•plod′er,** *n.*

explod′ed view′, *n.* a graphic representation that displays the parts of a mechanism separately while showing their spatial relationship.

ex•ploit¹ (ek′sploit, ik sploit′), *n.* a striking or notable deed; feat.

ex•ploit² (ik sploit′), *v.t.* **1.** to utilize, esp. for profit. **2.** to take advantage of. **3.** to use selfishly for one's own ends. —**ex•ploi•ta•tion** (ek′sploi tā′shən), *n.* —**ex•ploit′a•tive,** *adj.* —**ex•ploit′er,** *n.*

ex•plore (ik splôr′), *v.*, **-plored, -plor•ing.** —*v.t.* **1.** to range over (an area) for the purpose of discovery. **2.** to look into closely; investigate or examine. —*v.i.* **3.** to engage in exploring. —**ex•plo•ra•tion** (ek′splə-rā′shən), *n.* —**ex•plor′a•to′ry,** *adj.* —**ex•plor′er,** *n.*

ex•plo•sion (ik splō′zhən), *n.* **1.** an act or instance of exploding. **2.** the noise of an explosion. **3.** a sudden rapid increase.

ex•plo′sive (-siv), *adj.* **1.** tending to explode. **2.** pertaining to or of the nature of an explosion. —*n.* **3.** an explosive agent or substance. —**ex•plo′sive•ly,** *adv.* —**ex•plo′sive•ness,** *n.*

ex•po (ek′spō), *n.*, *pl.* **-pos.** an exposition.

ex•po•nent (ik spō′nənt *or, esp. for 3,* ek′spō-nənt), *n.* **1.** a person or thing that expounds or interprets. **2.** a representative, advocate, or symbol. **3.** *Math.* a symbol placed above and after another to denote the power to which the latter is to be raised. —**ex•po•nen′tial** (ek′spə nen′shəl), *adj.*

ex•port (*v.* ik spôrt′, ek′spôrt; *n.* ek′spôrt), *v.t.* **1.** to ship or transmit abroad. **2.** to save (electronic documents, data, etc.) in a format usable by another application program. —*n.* **3.** the act of exporting. **4.** something exported. —**ex′por•ta′tion,** *n.* —**ex•port′er,** *n.*

ex•pose (ik spōz′), *v.t.*, **-posed, -pos•ing. 1.** to lay open, as to danger. **2.** to uncover; bare. **3.** to present to view; exhibit. **4.** to make known; reveal. **5.** to subject to an influence or action.

ex•po•sé (ek′spō zā′), *n.*, *pl.* **-sés.** a public revelation of something discreditable.

ex•po•si•tion (ek′spə zish′ən), *n.* **1.** a large-scale public exhibition. **2.** the act of expounding or explaining. **3.** a statement of explanation; explanatory treatise.

ex•pos•i•tor (ik spoz′i tər), *n.* a person who expounds or explains.

ex•pos′i•to′ry (-tôr′ē), *adj.* serving to expound or explain.

ex post fac•to (eks′ pōst′ fak′tō), *adj.* made or done after the fact; retroactive. [< L: from a thing done afterward]

ex•pos•tu•late (ik spos′chə lāt′), *v.i.*, **-lat•ed, -lat•ing.** to reason earnestly with someone by way of warning or rebuke. —**ex•pos′tu•la′tion,** *n.*

ex•po•sure (ik spō′zhər), *n.* **1.** the act of exposing or state of being exposed. **2. a.** the act of subjecting a photosensitive surface to light. **b.** a photographic image produced. **3.** position with regard to weather or direction.

ex•pound (ik spound′), *v.t.* **1.** to set forth in detail; state. **2.** to explain; interpret. —*v.i.* **3.** to make a detailed statement. —**ex•pound′er,** *n.*

ex•press (ik spres′), *v.t.* **1.** to put into words. **2.** to show; reveal. **3.** to represent by a symbol. **4.** to send by express. **5.** to squeeze out. —*adj.* **6.** clearly stated; explicit. **7.** specific; particular: *an express purpose.* **8.** moving fast, esp. with few or no stops: *an express train.* —*n.* **9.** an express vehicle. **10.** a system for the rapid delivery of freight, parcels, and mail. —*adv.* **11.** by express. —**ex•press′i•ble,** *adj.* —**ex•press′ly,** *adv.*

ex•pres•sion (ik spresh′ən), *n.* **1.** the act of expressing. **2.** a particular word or phrase. **3.** the manner in which a thing is expressed. **4.** a facial look or vocal intonation expressing personal feeling. **5.** a mathematical symbol or combination of symbols representing a value, relation, or operation. —**ex•pres′sion•less,** *adj.*

ex•pres′sion•ism, *n.* (*often cap.*) a style in art, literature, etc., stressing the subjective element in experience and the symbolic aspects of objects. —**ex•pres′sion•ist,** *n.*, *adj.* —**ex•pres′sion•is′tic,** *adj.*

ex•pres•sive (ik spres′iv), *adj.* **1.** full of expression; meaningful. **2.** serving to express. **3.** of or pertaining to expression. —**ex•pres′sive•ly,** *adv.* —**ex•pres′sive•ness,** *n.*

ex•press′way′, *n.* a divided highway for high-speed traffic, having few if any intersections.

ex•pro•pri•ate (eks prō′prē āt′), *v.t.*, **-at•ed, -at•ing. 1.** to take possession of, esp. for public use. **2.** to dispossess (a person) of ownership. —**ex•pro′pri•a′tion,** *n.* —**ex•pro′pri•a′tor,** *n.*

ex•pul•sion (ik spul′shən), *n.* **1.** the act of expelling. **2.** the state of being expelled.

ex•punge (ik spunj′), *v.t.*, **-punged, -pung•ing.** to strike or blot out; obliterate or erase.

ex•pur•gate (ek′spər gāt′), *v.t.*, **-gat•ed, -gat•ing.** to amend by removing words or passages deemed objectionable. —**ex′pur•ga′tion,** *n.*

ex•quis•ite (ik skwiz′it, ek′skwi zit), *adj.* **1.** of special beauty, charm, delicacy, or excellence. **2.** intense; acute. **3.** keenly sensitive or responsive. **4.** of particular refinement. —**ex•quis′ite•ly,** *adv.* —**ex•quis′ite•ness,** *n.*

ex•tant (ek′stənt, ik stant′), *adj.* still existing; not destroyed or lost.

ex•tem•po•ra•ne•ous (ik stem′pə rā′nē əs), *adj.* done, spoken, or performed without preparation; impromptu: *an extemporaneous speech.* —**ex•tem′po•ra′ne•ous•ly,** *adv.* —**ex•tem′po•ra•ne′i•ty** (-rə nē′i tē), *n.*

ex•tem•po•re (ik stem′pə rē), *adv.* in an extemporaneous manner. [< L: lit., out of time, at the moment]

ex•tem′po•rize′, *v.i.*, *v.t.*, **-rized, -riz•ing.** to speak or perform extemporaneously.

ex•tend (ik stend′), *v.t.* **1.** to stretch or draw out or outward. **2.** to hold out; offer. **3.** to make longer; prolong. **4.** to enlarge, as in scope. **5.** to exert (oneself) to an unusual degree. —*v.i.* **6.** to stretch out; reach. —**ex•tend′er,** *n.* —**ex•tend′i•ble, ex•tend′-a•ble, ex•ten′si•ble,** *adj.*

extend′ed fam′ily, *n.* a kinship group consisting of a married couple, their children, and close relatives.

ex•ten•sion (ik sten′shən), *n.* **1.** an act or instance of extending. **2.** the state of being extended. **3.** an addition. **4.** an additional telephone that operates on a principal line.

ex•ten′sive (-siv), *adj.* of great extent; broad or thorough. —**ex•ten′sive•ly,** *adv.* —**ex•ten′sive•ness,** *n.*

ex•tent (ik stent′), *n.* **1.** the space or degree to which a thing extends. **2.** something having extension.

ex•ten•u•ate (ik sten′yōō āt′), *v.t.*, **-at•ed, -at•ing.** to make seem less serious, esp. by offering excuses. —**ex•ten′u•a′tion,** *n.*

ex•te•ri•or (ik stēr′ē ər), *adj.* **1.** being at the outer side or the outside. **2.** intended or suitable for outdoor use. —*n.* **3.** an exterior surface or part.

ex•ter•mi•nate (ik stûr′mə nāt′), *v.t.*, **-nat•ed, -nat•ing.** to get rid of by destroying. —**ex•ter′mi•na′tion,** *n.* —**ex•ter′mi•na′tor,** *n.*

ex•ter•nal (ik stûr′nl), *adj.* **1.** pertaining to or being on the outside or outer part. **2.** acting or coming from without. **3.** pertaining merely to outward appearance; superficial. **4.** pertaining to foreign countries. —*n.* **5. externals,** external features. —**ex•ter′nal•ly,** *adv.*

ex•tinct (ik stingkt′), *adj.* **1.** no longer in existence. **2.** no longer in use. **3.** no longer burning; extinguished. **4.** no longer active. —**ex•tinc′tion,** *n.*

ex•tin•guish (ik sting′gwish), *v.t.* **1.** to cause to stop burning; put out. **2.** to bring to an end; wipe out. —**ex•tin′guish•a•ble,** *adj.* —**ex•tin′guish•er,** *n.*

ex•tir•pate (ek′stər pāt′), *v.t.*, **-pat•ed, -pat•ing. 1.** to destroy totally. **2.** to pull up by or as if by the roots. —**ex′tir•pa′tion,** *n.*

ex•tol *or* **-toll** (ik stōl′, -stol′), *v.t.*, **-tolled, -tol•ling.** to praise highly; laud. —**ex•tol′ler,** *n.*

ex•tort (ik stôrt′), *v.t.* to obtain (money, information, etc.) by force, intimidation, or abuse of authority. —**ex•tor′tion,** *n.* —**ex•tor′tion•ist,** *n.*

ex•tor•tion•ate (ik stôr′shə nit), *adj.* excessive; exorbitant.

ex•tra (ek′strə), *adj.*, *n.*, *pl.* **-tras,** *adv.* —*adj.* **1.** being more or better than what is usual, expected, or necessary; additional or superior. —*n.* **2.** an additional feature. **3.** an additional expense or charge. **4.**

a special edition of a newspaper. **5.** an additional worker, esp. a performer hired to appear in the background action of a film. —*adv.* **6.** in excess of what is usual.

extra-, a prefix meaning outside or beyond (*extrasensory*).

ex•tract (*v.* ik strakt′; *n.* ek′strakt), *v.t.* **1.** to pull or draw out, usu. with effort. **2.** to take or copy out (an excerpt), as from a book. **3.** to separate or obtain by pressure, distillation, or treatment with solvents. —*n.* **4.** something extracted. **5.** an excerpt. **6.** a concentrate, as of a food, plant, or drug: *vanilla extract.* —ex•trac′tor, *n.*

ex•trac′tion, *n.* **1.** an act or instance of extracting. **2.** descent; ancestry. **3.** something extracted.

ex•tra•cur•ric•u•lar (ek′strə kə rik′yə lər), *adj.* outside a regular curriculum.

ex•tra•dite (ek′strə dīt′), *v.t.,* **-dit•ed, -dit•ing.** to surrender (an alleged fugitive or criminal) to another jurisdiction. —ex′tra•di′tion (-dish′ən), *n.*

ex′tra•le′gal, *adj.* beyond the authority of law.

ex′tra•mar′i•tal, *adj.* pertaining to sexual relations with someone other than one's spouse.

ex′tra•mu′ral (-myŏŏr′əl), *adj.* involving representatives of more than one school.

ex•tra•ne•ous (ik strā′nē əs), *adj.* **1.** coming from without. **2.** not essential or pertinent. —ex•tra′ne•ous•ly, *adv.*

ex•traor•di•nar•y (ik strôr′dn er′ē, ek′strə ôr′-), *adj.* being beyond what is usual; exceptional or remarkable. —ex•traor′di•nar′i•ly, *adv.*

ex•trap•o•late (ik strap′ə lāt′), *v.t., v.i.,* **-lat•ed, -lat•ing.** to infer (an unknown) from something that is known. —ex•trap′o•la′tion, *n.* —ex•trap′o•la′tor, *n.*

ex•tra•sen•so•ry (ek′strə sen′sə rē), *adj.* outside one's normal sense perception.

ex′tra•ter•res′tri•al, *adj.* **1.** existing or originating outside the limits of the earth. —*n.* **2.** an extraterrestrial being.

ex′tra•ter′ri•to′ri•al, *adj.* existing or occurring beyond local territorial jurisdiction.

ex′tra•ter′ri•to′ri•al•i•ty (-al′i tē), *n.* immunity from the jurisdiction of a nation, as granted to foreign diplomats.

ex•trav•a•gant (ik strav′ə gənt), *adj.* **1.** spending much more than is necessary or wise. **2.** exceeding the bounds of reason or moderation; excessive. —ex•trav′a•gance, *n.* —ex•trav′a•gant•ly, *adv.*

ex•trav′a•gan′za (-gan′zə), *n., pl.* **-zas.** a lavish or opulent production or entertainment.

ex•tra•ve•hic•u•lar (ek′strə vē hik′yə lər), *adj.* performed or occurring outside a vehicle, esp. an orbiting spacecraft.

ex•treme (ik strēm′), *adj.,* **-trem•er, -trem•est,** *n.* —*adj.* **1.** going well beyond the ordinary or average. **2.** farthest from the center. **3.** utmost. **4.** immoderate; radical. **5.** last; final. **6.** (esp. of a sport) very dangerous or difficult. —*n.* **7.** one of two things as different from each other as possible. **8.** an extreme degree, act, measure, or condition. **9.** *Math.* the first or the last term, as of a proportion. —ex•treme′ly, *adv.* —ex•treme′ness, *n.*

ex•trem′ism, *n.* a tendency to go to extremes, esp. in politics. —ex•trem′ist, *n., adj.*

ex•trem•i•ty (ik strem′i tē), *n., pl.* **-ties. 1.** the extreme or terminal point or part. **2.** a limb or the body, esp. a hand or foot. **3.** a condition of extreme need or danger. **4.** an utmost degree. **5.** a drastic measure or effort.

ex•tri•cate (ek′stri kāt′), *v.t.,* **-cat•ed, -cat•ing.** to free from entanglement; disengage. —ex′tri•ca•ble, *adj.* —ex′tri•ca′tion, *n.*

ex•trin•sic (ik strin′sik, -zik), *adj.* **1.** not essential or inherent; extraneous. **2.** being or coming from without; external. —ex•trin′si•cal•ly, *adv.*

ex•tro•vert (ek′strə vûrt′), *n.* an outgoing person who is concerned more with the physical and social

environment than with the self. —ex′tro•ver′sion (-vûr′zhən), *n.* —ex′tro•vert′ed, *adj.*

ex•trude (ik strŏŏd′), *v.t.,* **-trud•ed, -trud•ing. 1.** to force or press out. **2.** to shape (metal, plastic, etc.) by forcing through a die. —ex•tru′sion (-zhən), *n.* —ex•tru′sive (-siv), *adj.*

ex•u•ber•ant (ig zōō′bər ənt), *adj.* **1.** uninhibitedly enthusiastic. **2.** profuse, as in growth; abundant. —ex•u′ber•ance, *n.* —ex•u′ber•ant•ly, *adv.*

ex•ude (ig zŏŏd′, ik sŏŏd′), *v.i., v.t.,* **-ud•ed, -ud•ing. 1.** to ooze or cause to ooze out. **2.** to project abundantly; radiate. —ex•u•da•tion (eks′yŏŏ dā′shən), *n.*

ex•ult (ig zult′), *v.i.* to show or feel triumphant joy. —ex•ult′ant, *adj.* —ex•ul•ta•tion (eg′zul tā′shən, ek′sul-), *n.* —ex•ult′ing•ly, *adv.*

ex•urb (ek′sərb), *n.* a small, usu. prosperous community situated beyond the suburbs of a city. —ex•ur•ban (ek sûr′bən), *adj.* —ex•ur′ban•ite′, *n.*

ex•ur•bi•a (ek sûr′bē ə), *n., pl.* **-bi•as.** a generalized area comprising the exurbs.

-ey, var. of-y¹.

eye (ī), *n., v.,* **eyed, ey•ing** or **eye•ing.** —*n.* **1.** the organ of sight, in vertebrates one of a pair of spherical bodies in an orbit of the skull. **2.** sight; vision. **3.** appreciative or discriminating visual perception. **4.** a look, glance, or gaze. **5.** an attentive look; observation. **6.** judgment; opinion: *in the eyes of the law.* **7.** something suggesting an eye, as the bud of a potato or the hole in a needle. —*v.t.* **8.** to look at; view. —*Idiom.* **9. have an eye for,** to be discerning about. **10. keep one's eyes open,** to be alert or observant. **11. see eye to eye,** to agree. —eyed, *adj.* —eye′less, *adj.* —ey′er, *n.*

eye′ball′, *n.* **1.** the globe of the eye. —*v.t.* **2.** *Informal.* to examine closely.

eye′brow′, *n.* **1.** the bony arch or ridge forming the upper part of the orbit of the eye. **2.** the fringe of hair growing on the eyebrow.

eye′-catch′er, *n.* a person or thing that attracts the attention. —eye′-catch′ing, *adj.*

eye•ful (ī′fŏŏl), *n., pl.* **-fuls. 1.** a thorough view. **2.** *Informal.* a very good-looking person.

eye•glass′, *n.* **1. eyeglasses,** GLASS (def. 3). **2.** a single lens worn to aid vision.

eye′lash′, *n.* one of the short hairs growing on the edge of an eyelid.

eye•let (ī′lit), *n.* **1.** a small hole for the passage of a cord or lace or for decoration. **2.** a metal ring for lining a small hole.

eye′lid′, *n.* the movable lid of skin that covers and uncovers the eyeball.

eye•lin′er, *n.* a cosmetic applied in a line along the eyelids to accentuate the eyes.

eye′o′pen•er, *n.* an experience or disclosure that provides sudden enlightenment. —eye′o′pen•ing, *adj.*

eye′piece′, *n.* the lens or combination of lenses in an optical instrument through which the eye views the image.

eye′ shad′ow, *n.* a cosmetic coloring material applied to the eyelids.

eye′sight′, *n.* **1.** SIGHT (def. 1). **2.** SIGHT (def. 2).

eye′sore′, *n.* something unpleasant to look at.

eye′strain′, *n.* discomfort in the eyes caused by excessive or improper use.

eye′tooth′, *n., pl.* **-teeth.** a canine tooth of the upper jaw.

eye′wash′, *n.* **1.** a soothing solution for the eye. **2.** nonsense; bunk.

eye′wit′ness, *n.* a person who has actually seen an act or occurrence and can give a firsthand account of it.

ey•rie or **-ry** (âr′ē, ēr′ē), *n., pl.* **-ries.** AERIE.

E•ze•ki•el (i zē′kē əl), *n.* **1.** a Major Prophet of the 6th century B.C. **2.** a book of the Bible bearing his name.

Ez•ra (ez′rə), *n.* **1.** a Jewish scribe and prophet of the 5th century B.C. **2.** a book of the Bible bearing his name.

F

F, f (ef), *n.*, *pl.* **Fs** or **F's, fs** or **f's.** the sixth letter of the English alphabet, a consonant.
F, 1. female. **2.** franc. **3.** French.
F, 1. the sixth in order or in a series. **2.** a grade indicating academic work of the lowest quality. **3.** the fourth note of the C major scale. **4.** Fahrenheit. **5.** farad. **6.** *Chem.* fluorine. **7.** *Physics.* **a.** force. **b.** frequency.
f, *Symbol.* focal length.
F., 1. Fahrenheit. **2.** February. **3.** franc. **4.** France. **5.** French. **6.** Friday.
f., 1. farad. **2.** feet. **3.** female. **4.** feminine. **5.** folio. **6.** following. **7.** foot. **8.** franc.
fa (fä), *n.* the fourth tone of the diatonic scale.
FAA, Federal Aviation Administration.
fa•ble (fā′bəl), *n.* **1.** a short tale used to teach a moral, often with animals as characters. **2.** a story not founded on fact. **3.** a lie; falsehood.
fa′bled, *adj.* **1.** celebrated in fables. **2.** having no real existence; fictitious.
fab•ric (fab′rik), *n.* **1.** a cloth made by weaving, knitting, or felting fibers. **2.** framework; structure.
fab′ri•cate′ (-ri kāt′), *v.t.,* **-cat•ed, -cat•ing. 1.** to construct, esp. by assembling parts or sections; make. **2.** to invent; make up. —**fab′ri•ca′tion,** *n.*
fab•u•lous (fab′yə ləs), *adj.* **1.** almost impossible to believe; incredible. **2.** exceptionally good; marvelous. **3.** known through fables. —**fab′u•lous•ly,** *adv.*
fa•cade or **-çade** (fə säd′, fa-), *n.* **1.** the front of a building, esp. an imposing or decorative one. **2.** a superficial appearance; illusion.
face (fās), *n.,* *v.,* **faced, fac•ing.** —*n.* **1.** the front part of the head. **2.** a look or expression on the face. **3.** a grimace: *to make a face.* **4.** impudence; boldness. **5.** outward appearance. **6.** good reputation; prestige: *to lose face.* **7.** the surface of something: *the face of the earth.* **8.** the side upon which the use of a thing depends: *the face of a watch.* **9.** the most important or most frequently seen side; front. —*v.t.* **10.** to look toward. **11.** to have the front toward. **12.** to confront directly, courageously, or impudently. **13.** to cover with a different material in front. **14.** to finish the edge of (a garment) with facing. —*v.i.* **15.** to turn or be turned: *She faced toward the sea.* **16.** to be placed with the front in a certain direction: *The barn faces south.* **17. face up to, a.** to admit. **b.** to meet courageously. —*Idiom.* **18. face to face, a.** opposite one another; facing. **b.** confronting one another. **19. in the face of,** in the presence of. **20. to one's face,** in one's very presence. —**faced,** *adj.*
face′less, *adj.* lacking distinction or identity.
face′-lift′ or **face′lift′,** *n.* **1.** plastic surgery to eliminate facial sagging and wrinkles. **2.** a renovation, as of a building.
face′-off′, *n.* **1.** *Ice Hockey.* the act of putting the puck into play by dropping it between two opposing players. **2.** a direct confrontation.
face′-sav′ing, *adj.* serving to save one's prestige or dignity.
fac•et (fas′it), *n.,* *v.,* **-et•ed, -et•ing** or (*esp. Brit.*) **-et•ted, -et•ting.** —*n.* **1.** one of the small polished plane surfaces of a cut gem. **2.** an aspect; phase. —*v.t.* **3.** to cut facets on.
fa•ce•tious (fə sē′shəs), *adj.* **1.** not meant to be taken seriously or literally. **2.** amusing; humorous. —**fa•ce′tious•ly,** *adv.* —**fa•ce′tious•ness,** *n.*
face val•ue (fās′ val′yōō *for 1*; fās′ val′yōō *for 2*), *n.* **1.** the value printed on the face of a stock, bond, etc. **2.** apparent value.
fa•cial (fā′shəl), *adj.* **1.** of or for the face. —*n.* **2.** a treatment to beautify the face.
fac•ile (fas′il; *esp. Brit.* -īl), *adj.* **1.** easily accomplished or achieved. **2.** working or moving easily; fluent; effortless. **3.** superficial; shallow.
fa•cil•i•tate (fə sil′i tāt′), *v.t.,* **-tat•ed, -tat•ing.** to make easier; help forward. —**fa•cil′i•ta′tion,** *n.* —**fa•cil′i•ta′tor,** *n.*
fa•cil•i•ty (fə sil′i tē), *n.,* *pl.* **-ties. 1.** something designed, built, or installed for a specific purpose: *a research facility.* **2.** Usu., **-ties.** something that permits the easier performance of an action or process. **3.** ease due to skill, aptitude, or practice. **4.** the quality of being easily performed.
fac•ing (fā′sing), *n.* **1.** a covering in front, as an outer layer of stone on a brick wall. **2.** a lining applied along an edge of a garment.
fac•sim•i•le (fak sim′ə lē), *n.,* *pl.* **-les,** *v.,* **-led, -le•ing.** —*n.* **1.** an exact copy, as of a book. **2.** FAX. —*v.t.* **3.** to make a facsimile of. [< L *fac* make + *simile* similar]
fact (fakt), *n.* **1.** reality; actuality. **2.** something known to exist or to have happened. **3.** something known to be true. **4.** something said to be true. —*Idiom.* **5. after the fact,** done, made, or formulated after something has occurred. **6. in fact,** in truth; indeed.
fac•tion (fak′shən), *n.* **1.** a group or clique within a larger group. **2.** party strife and intrigue. —**fac′tion•al,** *adj.* —**fac′tion•al•ism,** *n.*
fac′tious, *adj.* **1.** given to faction. **2.** of or caused by faction. —**fac′tious•ness,** *n.*
fac•ti•tious (fak tish′əs), *adj.* artificial or contrived.
fac•toid (fak′toid), *n.* **1.** something fictitious or unsubstantiated that is presented as fact, devised esp. to gain publicity, and accepted because of constant repetition. **2.** an insignificant fact.
fac•tor (fak′tər), *n.* **1.** one of the elements contributing to a particular result. **2.** *Math.* one of two or more quantities that when multiplied together produce a given product. **3.** a person who transacts business for another. **4.** a gene. —*v.t.* **5.** to express (a mathematical quantity) as a product of two or more factors.
fac•to•ry (fak′tə rē, -trē), *n.,* *pl.* **-ries.** a building or group of buildings with facilities for the manufacture of goods.
fac•to•tum (fak tō′təm), *n.* an assistant who performs a wide range of tasks. [< L *fac* make, do + *tōtum* all]
fac•tu•al (fak′chōō əl), *adj.* **1.** of or concerning facts. **2.** based on facts. —**fac′tu•al•ly,** *adv.*
fac•ul•ty (fak′əl tē), *n.,* *pl.* **-ties. 1.** an ability for a particular kind of action. **2.** one of the powers of the mind, as speech. **3.** an inherent capability of the body. **4. a.** the teaching and administrative staff of a school. **b.** one of the departments of learning in a university.
fad (fad), *n.* a temporary fashion, esp. one followed enthusiastically by a group. —**fad′dish,** *adj.*

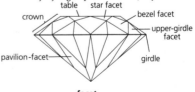

facet

fade (fād), *v.,* **fad•ed, fad•ing,** *n.* —*v.i.* **1.** to lose brightness or vividness of color. **2.** to become dim, as light. **3.** to lose freshness, vigor, strength, or health. **4.** to disappear gradually; die out. —*v.t.* **5.** to cause to fade. —*n.* **6.** an act or instance of fading. **7.** a hairstyle in which the hair is closely cropped at the sides and shaped into an upright block at the top.

fa•er•ie or **-er•y** (fā′ə rē, fâr′ē), *n., pl.* **-er•ies.** *Archaic.* **1.** fairyland. **2.** a fairy.

fag (fag), *n., v.,* **fagged, fag•ging.** —*n.* **1.** a drudge. —*v.t.* **2.** to tire by labor; exhaust.

fag′ end′, *n.* **1.** the very end of something. **2.** the unfinished end of a piece of cloth.

fag•got (fag′ət), *n. Brit.* FAGOT.

fag•ot (fag′ət), *n.* a bundle of sticks, twigs, or branches bound together and used esp. as fuel.

fag′ot•ing, *n.* embroidery in which some horizontal threads are drawn from a fabric and the remaining vertical threads are gathered into groups and tied.

Fahr•en•heit (far′ən hīt′), *adj.* pertaining to or being a temperature scale in which 32° represents the freezing point of water and 212° the boiling point. [after G. D. *Fahrenheit* (1686-1736), German physicist]

fa•ience or **-ïence** (fī äns′, -äns′, fā-), *n.* glazed earthenware.

fail (fāl), *v.i.* **1.** to fall short of success. **2.** to receive less than a passing academic grade. **3.** to be or become deficient; fall short. **4.** to become weak. **5.** to stop functioning. **6.** to dwindle or die away. **7.** to become bankrupt. —*v.t.* **8.** to be unsuccessful in the performance of. **9.** to prove of no use or help to: *His friends failed him.* **10.** to receive less than a passing grade or mark in. **11.** to give less than a passing grade to. —*Idiom.* **12. without fail,** with certainty.

fail′ing, *n.* **1.** a defect or fault; shortcoming. —*prep.* **2.** in the absence of.

faille (fīl, fāl), *n.* a ribbed fabric, esp. of silk or rayon.

fail′-safe′, *adj.* **1.** of or being a feature that ensures safety should a system fail to operate properly. **2.** guaranteed to work; totally reliable.

fail′ure (-yər), *n.* **1.** an act or instance of failing. **2.** nonperformance of something due or expected. **3.** an insufficiency. **4.** deterioration or decay. **5.** a condition of being bankrupt. **6.** a person or thing that has failed.

fain (fān), *Archaic.* *adv.* **1.** gladly; willingly. —*adj.* **2.** content; willing. **3.** constrained; obliged.

faint (fānt), *adj.,* **-er, -est,** *v., n* —*adj.* **1.** lacking brightness, vividness, or clarity. **2.** lacking strength; feeble. **3.** feeling weak or dizzy and about to lose consciousness. **4.** lacking courage; cowardly. —*v.i.* **5.** to lose consciousness. —*n.* **6.** a temporary loss of consciousness. —**faint′ly,** *adv.* —**faint′ness,** *n.*

faint′heart′ed, *adj.* lacking courage.

fair¹ (fâr), *adj.* and *adv.,* **-er, -est.** —*adj.* **1.** free from bias, dishonesty, or injustice. **2.** proper under the rules: *a fair fight.* **3.** moderately large: *a fair income.* **4.** moderately good: *fair health.* **5.** bright, sunny, and cloudless. **6.** not dark: *fair skin.* **7.** pleasing in appearance; attractive. **8.** likely; promising. **9.** free from blemish or imperfection. **10.** easy to read. —*adv.* **11.** in a fair manner. —**fair′ness,** *n.*

fair² (fâr), *n.* **1.** a usu. competitive exhibition, as of farm products. **2.** a periodic gathering of buyers and sellers in an appointed place. **3.** an exhibition and sale of articles to raise money, as for charity.

Fair′ Deal′, *n.* the principles of the liberal wing of the Democratic party under the leadership of President Harry S. Truman.

fair′ground′, *n.* Often, **-grounds.** an area where fairs are held, esp. one with exhibition buildings.

fair′-haired′, *adj.* **1.** having light-colored hair. —*Idiom.* **2. fair-haired boy,** a favorite.

fair′ly, *adv.* **1.** justly or impartially. **2.** moderately; tolerably. **3.** properly; legitimately. **4.** actually or completely.

fair′ shake′, *n.* a just and equal opportunity or treatment.

fair′way′, *n.* the part of a golf course where the grass is cut short between the tees and the putting greens.

fair•y (fâr′ē), *n., pl.* **-fair•ies.** an imaginary being

having a diminutive human form and possessing magical powers.

fair′y•land′, *n.* **1.** the imaginary realm of fairies. **2.** an enchantingly beautiful region or place.

fair′y tale′, *n.* **1.** a story, usu. for children, about magical creatures. **2.** an improbable story.

fait ac•com•pli (fe tA kôn plē′), *n., pl.* **faits ac•com•plis** (fe zA kôn plē′). *French.* something already done.

faith (fāth), *n.* **1.** confidence or trust in a person or thing. **2.** belief in God. **3.** a system of religious belief. **4.** loyalty or fidelity.

faith′ful, *adj.* **1.** steady in allegiance or affection; loyal. **2.** reliable or believable. **3.** true to fact, a standard, or an original. **4.** thorough in the performance of duty. —**faith′ful•ly,** *adv.* —**faith′ful•ness,** *n.*

faith′less, *adj.* **1.** not loyal. **2.** not trustworthy; unreliable. —**faith′less•ly,** *adv.* —**faith′less•ness,** *n.*

fa•ji•tas (fä hē′təz, fə-), *n.* (*used with a sing. or pl. v.*) a dish of thin strips of marinated and grilled meat, served with tortillas.

fake (fāk), *v.,* **faked, fak•ing,** *n., adj.* —*v.t.* **1.** to create or treat so as to mislead or defraud others. **2.** to pretend; simulate. **3.** to imitate convincingly; counterfeit. —*v.i.* **4.** to fake something; pretend. —*n.* **5.** a counterfeit; sham. **6.** one who fakes. —*adj.* **7.** counterfeit; sham. —**fak′er,** *n.*

fa•kir (fə kēr′, fā′kər), *n.* a Muslim or Hindu ascetic or mendicant considered to be a wonder-worker.

fal•con (fôl′kən, fal′-, fô′kən), *n.* any of various birds of prey that are capable of swift flight.

fal′con•ry, *n.* **1.** the sport of hunting with hawks. **2.** the art of training hawks to hunt. —**fal′con•er,** *n.*

fall (fôl), *v.,* **fell, fall•en, fall•ing,** *n.* —*v.i.* **1.** to drop under the force of gravity. **2.** to come down suddenly to a lower position, esp. from a standing or erect position. **3.** to decline, as in level, degree, or value. **4.** to hang down. **5.** to become directed downward: *His eyes fell.* **6.** to become lower in pitch or volume. **7.** to succumb to temptation or sin. **8.** to lose status, dignity, or position. **9.** to succumb to attack: *The city fell to the enemy.* **10.** to be overthrown, as a government. **11.** to drop down wounded or dead. **12.** to pass into a physical or emotional condition: *to fall in love.* **13.** to come as if by dropping: *Night fell.* **14.** to come by lot or chance: *The chore fell to me.* **15.** to occur at a certain time: *Christmas fell on a Monday.* **16.** to have its proper place: *The accent falls on the last syllable.* **17.** to come by right. **18.** to look disappointed: *The child's face fell.* **19.** to slope or extend downward. **20. fall back,** to recede; retreat. **21. ~ back on,** to have recourse to; rely on. **22. ~ for,** *Informal.* **a.** to be deceived by. **b.** to fall in love with. **23. ~ on** or **upon,** to assault. **24. ~ out,** to quarrel; disagree. **25. ~ through,** to fail to be accomplished. **26. ~ to, a.** to begin. **b.** to begin to eat. —*n.* **27.** an act or instance of falling. **28.** something that has fallen. **29.** autumn. **30.** the distance through which something falls: *a long fall to the ground.* **31.** Usu., **falls.** a cataract or waterfall. **32.** downward slope or declivity. **33.** a falling from an erect position, as to the ground. **34.** a succumbing to temptation or sin. **35.** surrender or capture, as of a city. **36.** a hairpiece of long hair that hangs freely. —*Idiom.* **37. fall by the wayside, a.** to fall from grace. 13:3-8; 18-23; Luke 8:5-15. **b.** to be defeated. **38. fall on stony ground,** to fail because of unfavorable conditions. Matt. 13:3-8, 18-23; Luke 8:5-15.

fal•la•cious (fə lā′shəs), *adj.* **1.** logically unsound. **2.** deceptive; misleading. —**fal•la′cious•ly,** *adv.*

fal•la•cy (fal′ə sē), *n., pl.* **-cies.** **1.** a misleading or false notion; misconception. **2.** a logically unsound argument. **3.** erroneous reasoning.

fall′en an′gel, *n.* an angel who has rebelled against God and been cast out of heaven. Rev. 12:7–9.

fal•li•ble (fal′ə bəl), *adj.* **1.** liable to be mistaken. **2.** liable to be erroneous. —**fal/li•bil′i•ty,** *n.* —**fal′li•bly,** *adv.*

fall′ing-out′, *n., pl.* **fall•ings-out, fall•ing-outs.** a quarrel or estrangement.

fall′ing star′, *n.* a shooting star; meteor.

fall′off′, *n.* a decline, as in quantity or vigor.

fal·lo′pi·an (or **Fal·lo′pi·an**) **tube′** (fə lō′pē-ən), *n.* either of a pair of long slender ducts in the female abdomen that transport ova from the ovary to the uterus. [< G. *Fallopio* (1523–62), Italian anatomist]

fall′out′, *n.* **1. a.** the settling to the ground of airborne radioactive particles that result from a nuclear explosion. **b.** the particles themselves. **2.** an incidental effect, outcome, or product.

fal·low (fal′ō), *adj.* **1.** (of land) plowed and left unseeded for a season or more; uncultivated. **2.** not in use; inactive.

fal′low deer′, *n.* a Eurasian deer with a yellowish coat that has spots in the summer.

false (fôls), *adj.*, **fals·er, fals·est,** *adv.* —*adj.* **1.** not true or correct. **2.** uttering what is untrue; lying. **3.** not faithful or loyal. **4.** tending to deceive or mislead. **5.** not genuine; counterfeit. **6.** based on mistaken ideas. *false pride.* **7.** inaccurate in pitch. —*adv.* **8.** dishonestly; treacherously. —**false′ly,** *adv.*

false′hood, *n.* **1.** a false statement; lie. **2.** lack of conformity to truth or fact; falsity.

false′-mem′ory syn′drome, *n.* a psychological condition in which a person believes that he or she remembers events that have not actually occurred.

fal·set·to (fôl set′ō), *n., pl.* **-tos. 1.** an artificially high-pitched voice, esp. in a man. **2.** a person who sings with a falsetto.

fal′si·fy′ (-sə fī′), *v.t.,* **-fied, -fy·ing. 1.** to make false, esp. so as to deceive. **2.** to fashion or alter fraudulently. **3.** to represent falsely. **4.** to show to be false. —**fal′si·fi·ca′tion,** *n.* —**fal′si·fi′er,** *n.*

fal′si·ty, *n., pl.* **-ties. 1.** the quality or condition of being false. **2.** something false; a falsehood.

fal·ter (fôl′tər), *v.i.* **1.** to hesitate or waver in action or intent. **2.** to speak hesitatingly. **3.** to move unsteadily; stumble. —*n.* **4.** the act of faltering. **5.** a faltering sound. —**fal′ter·ing·ly,** *adv.*

Fal·well (fôl′wel), *n.* Jerry L., born 1933, U.S. clergyman, founder of Moral Majority, now called the Liberty Foundation, and president since 1979.

fame (fām), *n.* widespread reputation, esp. of a favorable character; renown. —**famed,** *adj.*

fa·mil·ial (fə mil′yəl, -mil′ē əl), *adj.* of or characteristic of a family.

fa·mil·iar (fə mil′yər), *adj.* **1.** commonly or generally known or seen. **2.** thoroughly conversant; well-acquainted. **3.** informal; unceremonious. **4.** intimate or personal. **5.** unduly intimate; too personal. —*n.* **6.** a familiar friend or associate. —**fa·mil′iar·ly,** *adv.*

fa·mil′i·ar′i·ty (-ē ar′i tē), *n., pl.* **-ties. 1.** thorough knowledge or mastery of something. **2.** close acquaintance; intimacy. **3.** informality. **4.** undue intimacy.

fa·mil′iar·ize′ (-yə rīz′), *v.t.,* **-ized, -iz·ing. 1.** to make (oneself or another) thoroughly acquainted. **2.** to make (something) generally known. —**fa·mil′iar·i·za′tion,** *n.*

fam·i·ly (fam′ə lē, fam′lē), *n., pl.* **-lies. 1.** parents and their children considered as a group. **2.** a group of persons descended from a common progenitor. **3.** a group of persons who form a household, esp. under one head. **4.** a group of related things or individuals. **5.** a major subdivision of an order or suborder in the classification of plants or animals.

fam′ily leave′, *n.* an unpaid leave of absence from work in order to take care of a baby or an ailing family member.

fam′ily plan′ning, *n.* a program for determining the size of families through the spacing or prevention of pregnancies.

fam′ily tree′, *n.* a genealogical chart of a family.

fam′ily val′ues, *n.pl.* the moral and ethical principles traditionally upheld and transmitted within a family, as honesty, loyalty, industry, and faith.

fam·ine (fam′in), *n.* **1.** extreme and general scarcity of food. **2.** a general scarcity; dearth.

fam′ish, *v.t., v.i.* to suffer or cause to suffer extreme hunger.

fa·mous (fā′məs), *adj.* **1.** renowned; celebrated. **2.** first-rate; excellent. **3.** notorious.

fa′mous·ly, *adv.* in a splendid manner; very well.

fan¹ (fan), *n., v.,* **fanned, fan·ning.** —*n.* **1.** a device, as a triangular hand implement or an electric machine with blades, for producing a current of air. **2.** something resembling a fan. —*v.t.* **3.** to move (the air) with or as if with a fan. **4.** to cause air to blow upon. **5.** to stir to activity; incite: *to fan emotions.* **6.** to spread out like a fan. **7.** (of a baseball pitcher) to strike out (a batter). —*v.i.* **8.** to spread like a fan. [OE *fann* < L *vannus* winnowing basket]

fan² (fan), *n.* an enthusiastic devotee or follower, as of a sport. [short for *fanatic*]

fa·nat·ic (fə nat′ik), *n.* **1.** a person with an extreme enthusiasm or zeal, as in religion; zealot. —*adj.* **2.** fanatical. —**fa·nat′i·cism** (-ə siz′əm), *n.*

fa·nat′i·cal, *adj.* of or characteristic of a fanatic. —**fa·nat′i·cal·ly,** *adv.*

fan·ci·er (fan′sē ər), *n.* a person having an interest in something, esp. in breeding a particular animal or plant.

fan′ci·ful (-si fəl), *adj.* **1.** whimsical in appearance. **2.** imaginary or unreal. **3.** imaginative or inventive. —**fan′ci·ful·ly,** *adv.* —**fan′ci·ful·ness,** *n.*

fan′cy, *n., pl.* **-cies,** *adj.,* **-ci·er, -ci·est,** *v.,* **-cied, -cy·ing.** —*n.* **1.** imagination, esp. as exercised capriciously. **2.** a mental image or conception; notion. **3.** a caprice; whim. **4.** a preference, inclination, or liking. —*adj.* **5.** of exceptional quality. **6.** ornamental or decorative. **7.** depending on imagination or caprice. **8.** much too costly. —*v.t.* **9.** to picture to oneself; imagine. **10.** to believe without being absolutely certain. **11.** to have a liking for. —**fan′ci·ly,** *adv.*

fan′cy-free′, *adj.* free from emotional ties or influences, esp. from love.

fan′cy·work′, *n.* ornamental needlework.

fan·dan·go (fan dang′gō), *n., pl.* **-gos.** a lively Spanish or Spanish-American dance in triple time.

fan·fare (fan′fâr), *n.* **1.** a flourish played, esp. on a trumpet. **2.** an ostentatious display.

fang (fang), *n.* **1.** one of the long, sharp teeth of a venomous snake by which poison is injected. **2.** a long, sharp, projecting tooth, esp. a canine tooth. —**fanged,** *adj.*

fan′jet′, *n.* **1.** a jet engine with a large impeller that takes in air for use partly for the combustion of fuel and partly as exhaust. **2.** an airplane having a fanjet.

fan′ny, *n., pl.* **-nies.** *Informal.* the buttocks.

fan′ny pack′, *n.* a small zippered pouch suspended from a belt around the waist.

fan′tail′, *n.* **1.** a tail, end, or part shaped like a fan. **2.** a bird having a broad, upward-slanting tail.

fan·ta·sia (fan tā′zhə), *n., pl.* **-sias.** a dramatic, somewhat fanciful musical work, as for the piano.

fan′ta·size′ (-tə sīz′), *v.,* **-sized, -siz·ing.** —*v.i.* **1.** to conceive fanciful or extravagant notions. —*v.t.* **2.** to create in one's fancy or daydreams. —**fan′ta·siz′er,** *n.*

fan·tas′tic (-tas′tik) also **-ti·cal,** *adj.* **1.** conceived or seemingly conceived by an unrestrained imagination; bizarre or grotesque. **2.** fanciful or capricious. **3.** imaginary or groundless; irrational. **4.** extremely great or good. —**fan·tas′ti·cal·ly,** *adv.*

fan′ta·sy (-tə sē, -zē), *n., pl.* **-sies. 1.** imagination, esp. when unrestrained. **2.** a daydream or illusion. **3.** fiction based on highly imaginative characters and premises. **4.** a fantasia.

FAQ (fak, ef′ā′kyōō′), *n., pl.* **FAQs, FAQ's.** *Chiefly Computers.* a document that introduces newcomers to a technical topic, as in a newsgroup. [f(*requently*) a(*sked*) q(*uestions*)]

far (fär), *adv., adj.,* **far·ther** or **fur·ther, far·thest** or **fur·thest.** —*adv.* **1.** at or to a great distance or remote point. **2.** at or to a remote or advanced time. **3.** at or to a definite point or degree. **4.** much: *I need far more time.* —*adj.* **5.** being at a great distance. **6.** more distant of two: *the far corner.* —**Idiom. 7.** by **far,** by a great deal; very much. **8. far and away,** without doubt; decidedly. **9. far and wide,** over great distances; everywhere. **10. so far, a.** up to now. **b.** up to a certain point or extent.

far•ad (far′əd, -ad), *n.* a unit of capacitance equal to that of a capacitor having a potential of 1 volt when charged with 1 coulomb of electricity. [after M. *Faraday* (1791–1867), English physicist]

far′a•way′ (fär′-), *adj.* **1.** distant; remote. **2.** dreamy; preoccupied.

farce (färs), *n.* **1.** a comedy based on unlikely situations and exaggerated effects. **2.** humor of the type displayed in a farce. **3.** a foolish or meaningless show; sham or mockery. —**far′ci•cal**, *adj.*

fare (fâr), *n., v.,* **fared, far•ing.** —*n.* **1.** the price of conveying a passenger, as in a bus. **2.** a paying passenger. **3.** food; diet. **4.** something offered to the public, as for entertainment. —*v.i.* **5.** to get on; manage: *to fare well.*

Far′ East′, *n.* the countries of E Asia, including China, Japan, Korea, and sometimes adjacent areas.

fare′well′, *interj.* **1.** good-bye. —*n.* **2.** an expression of good wishes at parting. **3.** leave-taking; departure. —*adj.* **4.** parting; final: *a farewell performance.*

far′-fetched′ or **far′fetched′,** *adj.* not naturally pertinent; improbable.

far′-flung′, *adj.* **1.** extending over a great distance. **2.** widely distributed.

fa•ri•na (fə rē′nə), *n.* flour or meal made from cereal grains and cooked as cereal or used in puddings.

far•i•na•ceous (far′ə nā′shəs), *adj.* **1.** consisting or made of flour or meal. **2.** mealy in appearance or nature.

farm (färm), *n.* **1.** a tract of land on which crops and often livestock are raised. —*v.t.* **2.** to cultivate (land). —*v.i.* **3.** to cultivate the soil; operate a farm. **4. farm out,** to assign or subcontract (work) to another. —**farm′a•ble,** *adj.*

farm′er, *n.* a person who operates a farm or cultivates land.

Far•mer (fär′mər), *n.* **Fannie (Merritt),** 1857–1915, U.S. authority on cooking.

farm′er cheese′, *n.* a cheese similar to dry cottage cheese.

farm′hand′, *n.* a hired worker on a farm.

farm′house′, *n.* a house on a farm.

farm′yard′, *n.* a yard or enclosure surrounded by or connected with farm buildings.

far•o (fâr′ō), *n.* a gambling game in which players bet on cards.

far′-off′, *adj.* distant; remote.

far′-out′, *adj. Slang.* **1.** unconventional; offbeat. **2.** radical; extreme.

far•ra•go (fə rä′gō, -rā′-), *n., pl.* **-goes.** a confused mixture; medley.

Far•ra•gut (far′ə gət), *n.* **David Glasgow,** 1801–70, U.S. admiral for the Union in the U.S. Civil War.

far′-reach′ing, *adj.* extending far in influence or effect.

far•ri•er (far′ē ər), *n. Chiefly Brit.* BLACKSMITH.

far•row (far′ō), *n.* **1.** a litter of pigs. —*v.i.* **2.** to produce a farrow.

far′sight′ed (-sī′tid, -sī′-), *adj.* **1.** seeing distant objects more clearly than near ones. **2.** wise, as in foreseeing future developments. —**far′sight′ed•ness,** *n.*

far•ther (fär′thər), *adv., compar. of* **far. 1.** at or to a greater distance or more advanced point. **2.** at or to a greater degree or extent. —*adj., compar. of* **far. 3.** more distant or remote. **4.** additional. —**Usage.** While some usage guides advise that only FARTHER can be used for physical distance (*We walked farther than we planned*), both FARTHER and FURTHER are often used in this and other senses. However, only FURTHER can be used in the adverbial sense "moreover" (*Further, you hurt my feelings*) and in the adjectival senses "additional" and "more extended" (*no further comment*).

far′ther•most′ (-mōst′, -məst), *adj.* farthest.

far′thest (-thist), *adj., superl. of* **far. 1.** most distant or remote. **2.** most extended; longest. —*adv., superl. of* **far. 3.** at or to the greatest distance or most advanced point. **4.** at or to the greatest degree or extent.

far•thing (fär′thing), *n.* a former British coin equal to 1/4th of a penny.

fas•ci•cle (fas′i kəl), *n.* **1.** a section of a book being published in installments. **2.** a small bundle or tight cluster, as of flowers.

fas•ci•nate (fas′ə nāt′), *v.t.,* **-nat•ed, -nat•ing. 1.** to attract and hold, as by a unique power or a special quality; spellbind. **2.** to arouse the interest or curiosity of. —**fas′ci•na′tion,** *n.*

fas•cism (fash′iz əm), *n.* (*sometimes cap.*) **1.** a totalitarian governmental system led by a dictator and emphasizing aggressive nationalism, militarism, and often racism. **2.** the philosophy, principles, or methods of fascism. [< It *fascismo* = *fasc(io)* bundle, political group + *-ismo* -ISM] —**fas′cist,** *n., adj.* —**fa•scis•tic** (fə shis′tik), *adj.*

fash•ion (fash′ən), *n.* **1.** a prevailing custom or style, as of dress. **2.** conventional usage or conformity to it. **3.** manner; way. **4.** the make or form of something; shape. —*v.t.* **5.** to give shape or form to; make. **6.** to adjust; adapt. —*Idiom.* **7. after a fashion,** to some minimal extent. —**fash′ion•er,** *n.*

fash′ion•a•ble, *adj.* **1.** observant of or conforming to fashion; stylish. **2.** of or characteristic of the world of fashion. —**fash′ion•a•bly,** *adv.*

fast¹ (fast, fäst), *adj.* and *adv.,* **-er, -est.** —*adj.* **1.** acting or moving with speed. **2.** done in comparatively little time. **3.** (of a timepiece) ahead of the correct time. **4.** characterized by unrestrained conduct. **5.** resistant: *acid-fast.* **6.** firmly fixed, held, or tied. **7.** securely closed, as a shutter. **8.** loyal: *fast friends.* **9.** permanent or unchangeable: *a fast color.* **10.** deep and sound, as sleep. **11.** *Photog.* **a.** (of a lens) able to transmit a large amount of light in a short time. **b.** (of a film) requiring a relatively short exposure to attain a given density. —*adv.* **12.** quickly, swiftly, or rapidly. **13.** tightly; firmly: *to hold fast.* **14.** soundly: *fast asleep.* **15.** in a rash way; recklessly.

fast² (fast, fäst), *v.i.* **1.** to abstain from all food. **2.** to eat only sparingly or of certain kinds of food. —*n.* **3.** the act of fasting. **4.** a period of fasting.

fast′back′, *n.* an automobile having a back in the form of a single, unbroken curve from the top to the bumper.

fas•ten (fas′ən, fä′sən), *v.t.* **1.** to attach firmly or securely. **2.** to fix securely to something else; connect. **3.** to direct (the eyes, thoughts, etc.) intently. —*v.i.* **4.** to become fastened. —**fas′ten•er,** *n.*

fas′ten•ing, *n.* something that fastens, as a lock.

fast′-food′, *adj.* specializing in foods, as hamburgers, that can be prepared and served rapidly: *fast food restaurants.*

fas•tid•i•ous (fa stid′ē əs, fə-), *adj.* **1.** hard to please. **2.** requiring or characterized by excessive care or delicacy. —**fas•tid′i•ous•ly,** *adv.* —**fas•tid′i•ous•ness,** *n.*

fast′ness, *n.* a stronghold.

fast′-talk′, *v.t.* to persuade with clever, facile, or misleading talk.

fast′ track′, *n.* a career track offering unusually rapid advancement.

fat (fat), *n., adj.,* **fat•ter, fat•test.** —*n.* **1.** any of several oily substances that are the chief component of animal adipose tissue and many plant seeds. **2.** animal tissue containing much fat. **3.** obesity; corpulence. **4.** the richest or best part. **5.** an overabundance; excess. —*adj.* **6.** having too much fat; obese. **7.** plump; well-fed. **8.** containing fat. **9.** profitable; lucrative. **10.** broad or thick. —*Idiom.* **11. fat chance,** a very slight chance. —**fat′ness,** *n.*

fa•tal (fāt′l), *adj.* **1.** causing or capable of causing death. **2.** causing misfortune or ruin; calamitous. **3.** decisively important; fateful. —**fa′tal•ly,** *adv.*

fa′tal•ism, *n.* the doctrine that all events are subject to fate or inevitable predetermination. —**fa′tal•ist,** *n.* —**fa′tal•is′tic,** *adj.*

fa•tal•i•ty (fā tal′i tē, fə-), *n., pl.* **-ties. 1.** a death caused by a disaster. **2.** the quality of being deadly; deadliness. **3.** predetermined liability to disaster or misfortune.

fat′back′, *n.* the fat and fat meat from the upper part of a side of pork, usu. cured by salting.

fat′ cat′, *n. Slang.* a wealthy person, esp. one who makes large political campaign contributions.

fate (fāt), *n.* **1.** something that unavoidably befalls a person; fortune. **2.** the ultimate agency by which the order of things is presumably prescribed; destiny. **3.** the ultimate outcome. **4.** death or ruin. **5. Fates,** the three goddesses of destiny in Greek and Roman myth.

fat′ed, *adj.* subject to or guided by fate; destined.

fate′ful, *adj.* **1.** having momentous significance; decisively important. **2.** fatal, deadly, or disastrous. **3.** controlled by destiny. **4.** prophetic; ominous. —**fate′ful•ly,** *adv.* —**fate′ful•ness,** *n.*

fat′head′, *n.* a stupid person; fool.

fa•ther (fä′thər), *n.* **1.** a male who begets or rears offspring; male parent. **2.** a male ancestor; forefather. **3.** a person who has invented or created something; originator. **4.** one of the leading men in a city, town, etc. **5.** a priest or a title for a priest. **6.** (*cap.*) God. —*v.t.* **7.** to beget. **8.** to be the creator, founder, or author of. **9.** to act as a father toward. —**fa′ther•hood′,** *n.* —**fa′ther•less,** *adj.* —**fa′ther•ly,** *adj.*

fa′ther-in-law′, *n., pl.* **fa•thers-in-law.** the father of one's husband or wife.

fa′ther•land′, *n.* **1.** one's native country. **2.** the land of one's ancestors.

Fa′ther of his Coun′try, *n.* epithet of George Washington.

Fa′ther of the Constitu′tion, *n.* one who attended the constitutional convention at Philadelphia in 1787, esp. James Madison.

fath•om (fath′əm), *n., pl.* **-oms, -om,** *v.* —*n.* **1.** a nautical unit of length equal to 6 feet (1.8 m). —*v.t.* **2.** to measure the depth of by means of a sounding line. **3.** to penetrate deeply; understand. —**fath′om•a•ble,** *adj.* —**fath′om•less,** *adj.*

fa•tigue (fə tēg′), *n., v.,* **-tigued, -ti•guing.** —*n.* **1.** weariness from bodily or mental exertion. **2.** the weakening or breakdown of material subjected to repeated stress: *metal fatigue.* **3.** nonmilitary labor by military personnel. **4. fatigues,** military clothing worn for fatigue or field duty. —*v.t., v.i.* **5.** to weary with bodily or mental exertion.

fat′ten, *v.t., v.i.* to make or become fat.

fat′ty, *adj.,* **-ti•er, -ti•est. 1.** consisting of, containing, or like fat. **2.** characterized by excessive fat.

fat′ty ac′id, *n.* any of a class of organic acids found in animal and vegetable fats.

fat•u•ous (fach′ŏŏ əs), *adj.* complacently foolish or inane; silly. —**fa•tu•i•ty** (fə tōō′i tē, -tyōō′-), *n., pl.* **-ties.** —**fat′u•ous•ly,** *adv.* —**fat′u•ous•ness,** *n.*

fau•cet (fô′sit), *n.* a device for controlling the flow of liquid, as from a pipe, by opening or closing an orifice; tap.

Faulk•ner (fôk′nər), *n.* **William,** 1897–1962, U.S. novelist.

fault (fôlt), *n.* **1.** a defect or imperfection; flaw. **2.** responsibility for failure or a wrongful act. **3.** an error or mistake. **4.** an error in serving the ball in tennis. **5.** a fracture in a body of rock. —*v.i.* **6.** to commit a fault. **7.** *Geol.* to undergo a fault. —*v.t.* **8.** to accuse of a fault; criticize or blame. —*Idiom.* **9. at fault,** open to censure; blameworthy. **10. find fault,** to complain or be critical. **11. to a fault,** to an extreme degree. —**fault′less,** *adj.*

fault′find′er, *n.* a person who habitually finds fault or criticizes, esp. in a petty way. —**fault′find′-ing,** *n., adj.*

fault′y, *adj.,* **-i•er, -i•est.** having faults; imperfect.

faun (fôn), *n.* an ancient Roman deity of the countryside, part human and part goat.

fau•na (fô′nə), *n., pl.* **-nas, -nae** (-nē). the animals or animal life of a given region or period.

Fau•ré (fô rā′, fō-), *n.* **Gabriel Urbain,** 1845–1924, French composer.

Faust (foust), *n.* a magician in medieval German legend who sold his soul to the devil for knowledge and power. —**Faus′ti•an,** *adj.*

Fauve (fōv), *n.* (*sometimes l.c.*) any of a group of artists of the early 20th century whose works are characterized by the use of vivid colors and free forms. —**Fauv′ism,** *n.* —**Fauv′ist,** *n., adj.*

faux pas (fō pä′), *n., pl.* **faux pas** (fō päz′). a slip or blunder, esp. in manners or conduct. [< F]

fa•vor (fā′vər), *n.* **1.** a kind act. **2.** friendly regard; goodwill. **3.** popularity. **4.** preferential treatment; partiality. **5.** a gift bestowed as a token of regard or love. **6.** a small gift distributed to guests at a party. **7.** Usu., **-vors.** sexual intimacy. —*v.t.* **8.** to regard with favor. **9.** to treat with partiality; prefer. **10.** to show favor to; oblige. **11.** to be favorable to; facilitate. **12.** to treat or use gently: *to favor a sore wrist.* **13.** to bear a physical resemblance to. —*Idiom.* **14. in favor of, a.** in support of. **b.** to the advantage of. Also, *esp. Brit.,* **fa′vour.**

fa′vor•a•ble, *adj.* **1.** characterized by approval; positive. **2.** winning favor; pleasing. **3.** advantageous: *a favorable position.* **4.** boding well; promising. —**fa′vor•a•bly,** *adv.*

fa′vor•ite (-it), *n.* **1.** a person or thing regarded with special preference or approval. **2.** a competitor or contestant considered likely to win. —*adj.* **3.** being a favorite.

fa′vor•it•ism, *n.* the undue favoring of one person or group over others.

fawn¹ (fôn), *n.* **1.** a young deer, esp. an unweaned one. **2.** a light yellowish brown color.

fawn² (fôn), *v.i.* **1.** to seek notice or favor by servile behavior; toady. **2.** (esp. of a dog) to behave affectionately. —**fawn′er,** *n.* —**fawn′ing•ly,** *adv.*

fax (faks), *n.* **1. a.** a method or device for transmitting graphic matter, as documents or photographs, by telephone or radio for exact reproduction elsewhere. **b.** an exact copy or reproduction so transmitted. —*v.t.* **2.** to transmit by fax.

fax′ mo′dem, *n.* a modem that can fax data, as documents or pictures, directly from a computer.

fay (fā), *n.* FAIRY.

faze (fāz), *v.t.,* **fazed, faz•ing.** to cause to be disconcerted; daunt; fluster.

FBI, Federal Bureau of Investigation: a bureau in the U.S. Department of Justice charged with conducting investigations for the Attorney General and with safeguarding national security.

FCC, Federal Communications Commission.

FDA, Food and Drug Administration.

FDIC, Federal Deposit Insurance Corporation.

FDR, Franklin Delano Roosevelt.

Fe, *Chem. Symbol.* iron. [< L *ferrum*]

fe•al•ty (fē′əl tē), *n., pl.* **-ties. 1.** the fidelity of a feudal vassal to his lord. **2.** fidelity; loyalty.

fear (fēr), *n.* **1.** a distressing emotion aroused by impending danger, evil, or pain. **2.** a specific instance of or propensity for fear. **3.** concern or anxiety; solicitude. **4.** reverential awe, esp. toward God. —*v.t.* **5.** to regard with fear. **6.** to be worried or afraid. **7.** to have reverential awe of. —*v.i.* **8.** to be afraid. —*Saying.* **9. The only thing we have to fear is fear itself,** being afraid can so immobolize you that you can't move to solve the problems that are causing your fear. Franklin D. Roosevelt, March 4, 1933 —**fear′less,** *adj.* —**fear′less•ly,** *adv.* —**fear′less•ness,** *n.*

fear′ful, *adj.* **1.** causing fear. **2.** feeling fear. **3.** showing or caused by fear. **4.** extreme in size, intensity, or badness. —**fear′ful•ly,** *adv.* —**fear′ful•ness,** *n.*

fear′some (-səm), *adj.* **1.** causing fear. **2.** afraid; timid.

fea•si•ble (fē′zə bəl), *adj.* **1.** capable of being done, effected, or accomplished. **2.** probable; likely. **3.** suitable. —**fea′si•bil′i•ty,** *n.* —**fea′si•bly,** *adv.*

feast (fēst), *n.* **1.** a rich or abundant meal. **2.** a sumptuous meal for many guests. **3.** a periodic religious festival. —*v.i.* **4.** to partake of a feast. **5.** to dwell with delight, as on a picture. —*v.t.* **6.** to entertain with a feast. —*Proverb.* **7. After the feast comes the reckoning,** excessive pleasure exacts a toll.

Feast′ of Booths′, *n.* SUKKOTH.

feat (fēt), *n.* a noteworthy or extraordinary act or achievement.

feath•er (feth'ər), *n.* **1.** one of the horny epidermal structures that form the principal covering of birds. **2.** kind; character: *two boys of the same feather.* **3.** condition, esp. of spirits: *to be in fine feather. —v.t.* **4.** to provide (an arrow) with feathers. **5.** to clothe or cover with or as if with feathers. —*Idiom.* **6. a feather in one's cap,** a praiseworthy achievement; honor. —**feath'er•y,** *adj.*

feath•er•bed'ding, *n.* the practice of requiring an employer to hire more workers than are necessary or to limit production according to a union rule or a safety statute.

feath'er•weight', *n.* **1.** a professional boxer weighing up to 126 lb. (57 kg). **2.** an insignificant, shallow, or unintelligent person.

fea•ture (fē'chər), *n.*, *v.*, **-tured, -tur•ing.** —*n.* **1.** a prominent or conspicuous characteristic. **2.** something offered as a special attraction. **3.** the main motion picture in a program. **4.** a part of the face, as the nose. **5. features,** the face; countenance. **6.** the form or appearance of the face. **7.** a prominent story or article in a newspaper or magazine. —*v.t.* **8.** to give prominence to. **9.** to be a feature or distinctive mark of. **10.** to delineate the features of; depict. —*v.i.* **11.** to play a major part.

Feb or **Feb.,** February.

feb•ri•fuge (feb'rə fyōoj'), *n.* a medicine or agent serving to dispel or reduce fever.

fe•brile (fē'brəl, feb'rəl; *esp. Brit.* fē'brīl), *adj.* of or marked by fever.

Feb•ru•ar•y (feb'rōo er'ē, feb'yōo-), *n.*, *pl.* **-ar•ies.** the second month of the year, ordinarily containing 28 days but containing 29 days in leap years.

fe•ces (fē'sēz), *n.pl.* waste matter discharged from the intestines; excrement. —**fe'cal** (-kəl), *adj.*

feck•less (fek'lis), *adj.* **1.** ineffective; incompetent. **2.** irresponsible and lazy. —**feck'less•ly,** *adv.*

fe•cund (fē'kund, -kənd, fek'und, -ənd), *adj.* **1.** prolific or fruitful. **2.** very productive or creative. —**fe•cun•di•ty** (fi kun'di tē), *n.*

fe•cun•date (fē'kən dāt', fek'ən-), *v.t.,* **-dat•ed, -dat•ing. 1.** to make fecund. **2.** to impregnate or fertilize. —**fe'cun•da'tion,** *n.*

fed (fed), *v.* **1.** pt. and pp. of FEED. —*Idiom.* **2. fed up,** impatient, disgusted, or bored.

fed., **1.** federal. **2.** federated. **3.** federation.

fed•er•al (fed'ər əl), *adj.* **1. a.** pertaining to or of the nature of a union of states under a central government distinct from the individual governments of the separate states. **b.** of or involving such a government. **2.** (*cap.*) **a.** of or supporting the Federalist Party. **b.** supporting the Union in the Civil War. —*n.* **3.** (*cap.*) **a.** a Federalist. **b.** a soldier or supporter of the Union in the Civil War. [< L *foeder-*, s. of *foedus* league + -AL¹] —**fed'er•al•ly,** *adv.*

fed'er•al•ism, *n.* **1. a.** the federal principle of government. **b.** advocacy of this principle. **2.** (*cap.*) the principles of the Federalist Party. —**fed'er•al•ist,** *n.*, *adj.*

Fed'eralist Par'ty, *n.* a political party in early U.S. history advocating a strong central government.

fed'er•al•ize', *v.t.,* **-ized, -iz•ing. 1.** to bring under the control of a federal government. **2.** to bring together in a federal union. —**fed'er•al•i•za'tion,** *n.*

Fed'eral Repub'lic of Ger'many, *n.* official name of GERMANY.

fed•er•ate (fed'ə rāt'), *v.t., v.i,* **-at•ed, -at•ing.** to unite in a federation.

fed'er•a'tion, *n.* **1.** the act of federating. **2.** the formation of a federal political entity. **3.** a union. **4.** a number of societies or organizations.

fe•do•ra (fi dôr'ə), *n.*, *pl.* **-ras.** a soft felt hat with a curved brim.

fee (fē), *n.*, *pl.* **fees. 1.** a sum charged, as for professional services. **2.** *Law.* **a.** a heritable estate in land. **b.** an estate in land held of a feudal lord in return for services performed; fief.

fee•ble (fē'bəl), *adj.,* **-bler, -blest. 1.** weak, as from age or sickness; frail. **2.** lacking in substance, force, or effectiveness: *feeble arguments.* —**fee'ble•ness,** *n.* —**fee'bly,** *adv.*

fee'ble-mind'ed, *adj.* lacking normal intellectual powers. —**fee'ble-mind'ed•ness,** *n.*

feed (fēd), *v.,* **fed, feed•ing,** *n.* —*v.t.* **1.** to give food to. **2.** to serve as food for. **3.** to provide as food. **4.** to satisfy or gratify. **5.** to supply for growth, maintenance, development, or operation. —*v.i.* **6.** (esp. of animals) to take food; eat. —*n.* **7.** food, esp. for farm animals. **8.** a meal, esp. a lavish one. **9.** material or an amount of material for feeding a device or machine. **10.** a feeding mechanism. —**feed'er,** *n.*

feed'back', *n.* **1.** the return of part of the output of a circuit, system, or device to the input. **2.** a reaction or response, as to an activity.

feel (fēl), *v.,* **felt, feel•ing,** *n.* —*v.t.* **1.** to perceive by direct physical contact. **2.** to examine by touch. **3.** to have a physical sensation of. **4.** to find (one's way) by touching or cautious moves. **5.** to be or become conscious of. **6.** to be emotionally affected by. **7.** to experience. **8.** to think; believe. —*v.i.* **9.** to have perception by touch. **10.** to search with the hands or fingers; grope. **11.** to perceive a state of mind or a condition of body: *to feel happy.* **12.** to have a sensation of being: *to feel warm.* **13.** to feel sympathy or compassion. —*n.* **14.** a quality of something that is perceived by touching. **15.** the sense of touch: *soft to the feel.* **16.** native ability or acquired sensitivity: *to have a feel for teaching.* —*Idiom.* **17. feel like,** to be favorably disposed toward.

feel'er, *n.* **1.** a proposal, remark, or suggestion designed to elicit the opinions or reactions of others. **2.** an organ of touch, as an antenna.

feel'ing, *n.* **1.** the function or power of perceiving by touch. **2.** a sensation perceived by touch. **3.** an often vague awareness or consciousness. **4.** an emotion. **5.** capacity for emotion, esp. compassion. **6.** a sentiment or opinion. **7. feelings,** sensibilities; susceptibilities: *He hurt her feelings.* —*adj.* **8.** sensitive. **9.** readily affected by emotion. **10.** indicating or characterized by emotion. —**feel'ing•ly,** *adv.*

feet (fēt), *n.* pl. of FOOT.

feign (fān), *v.t.* **1.** to put on an appearance of: *to feign sickness.* —*v.i.* **2.** to make believe; pretend. —**feign'er,** *n.*

feint (fānt), *n.* **1.** a deceptive attack or blow aimed at one place or point to distract from the real target. —*v.i., v.t.* **2.** to make or deceive with a feint.

feist•y (fī'stē), *adj.,* **-i•er, -i•est. 1.** full of animation or energy; spirited. **2.** ill-tempered; pugnacious. —**feist'i•ly,** *adv.* —**feist'i•ness,** *n.*

feld•spar (feld'spär', fel'-), *n.* any of a group of crystalline minerals, principally silicates of aluminum with potassium, sodium, and calcium.

fe•lic•i•ta•tion (fi lis'i tā'shən), *n.* Often, **-tions.** an expression of good wishes; congratulation. —**fe•lic'i•tate',** *v.t.,* **-tat•ed, -tat•ing.**

fe•lic'i•tous (-təs), *adj.* **1.** well-suited for an occasion; apt. **2.** having a special ability for felicitous expression. **3.** enjoyable; pleasant. —**fe•lic'i•tous•ly,** *adv.*

fe•lic'i•ty, *n.*, *pl.* **-ties. 1.** the state of being happy, esp. to a high degree; bliss. **2.** a source of happiness. **3. a.** a faculty or capacity for skill or grace: *felicity of expression.* **b.** an instance or display of this.

fe•line (fē'līn), *adj.* **1.** of the cat family. **2.** sly, stealthy, or treacherous. —*n.* **3.** an animal of the cat family; cat.

Fe•lix (fē'liks), *n.* the husband of Drusilla who heard the Apostle Paul speak. Acts 24:24–25.

fell¹ (fel), *v.* pt. of FALL.

fell² (fel), *v.t.* **1.** to knock, strike, shoot, or cut down. **2.** (in sewing) to finish (a seam) by sewing the edge down flat.

fell³ (fel), *adj.* **1.** fierce; cruel. **2.** destructive; deadly.

fel•low (fel'ō), *n.* **1.** a man or boy. **2.** a comrade; associate. **3.** a person of the same rank or class; peer. **4.** one of a pair; mate. **5.** a graduate student who receives a stipend. **6.** a member of a learned society. —*adj.* **7.** united by the same occupation, interests, or circumstances.

fel'low•ship', *n.* **1.** friendly relationship; companionship. **2.** community of interest or feeling. **3.** an association of persons having similar interests or occupations. **4. a.** the position or stipend of an academic fellow. **b.** a foundation for the maintenance of such a fellow.

fel′low trav′eler, *n.* a nonmember who supports or sympathizes with a group or party, esp. the Communist Party.

fel•on[1] (fel′ən), *n.* a person who has committed a felony.

fel•on[2] (fel′ən), *n.* a painful inflammation of the tissues of a finger or toe, usu. near the nail.

fel′o•ny, *n., pl.* **-nies.** an offense, as murder or burglary, of graver character than a misdemeanor. —**fe•lo′ni•ous** (fə lō′nē əs), *adj.*

felt[1] (felt), *v.* pt. and pp. of FEEL.

felt[2] (felt), *n.* **1.** a nonwoven fabric of wool, fur, or hair, matted together by heat, moisture, and great pressure. **2.** a matted fabric or material that resembles felt.

fem., 1. female. **2.** feminine.

fe•male (fē′māl), *n.* **1.** a person of the sex that conceives and bears young. **2.** an organism of the sex or sexual phase that produces egg cells. **3.** a plant having pistils. —*adj.* **4.** of or being a female. **5.** of or characteristic of a girl or woman; feminine. **6.** having a recessed part into which a corresponding projecting part fits: *a female plug.* —**fe′male•ness,** *n.*

fem•i•nine (fem′ə nin), *adj.* **1.** of or characteristic of women or girls. **2.** of or belonging to the female sex. **3.** of or being the grammatical gender that has among its members most nouns referring to females. —*n.* **4.** the feminine gender. **5.** a word or form in the feminine gender. —**fem′i•nine•ly,** *adv.* —**fem′i•nin′i•ty,** *n.*

fem′i•nism, *n.* **1.** a doctrine advocating social, political, and economic rights for women equal to those of men. **2.** a movement for the attainment of the goals of feminism. —**fem′i•nist,** *n., adj.*

femme fa•tale (fem′ fə tal′, -täl′, fä-), *n., pl.* **femmes fa•tales** (fem′ fə talz′, -tälz′, fä-). a woman who is irresistibly attractive; siren. [< F: lit., fatal woman]

fe•mur (fē′mər), *n., pl.* **fe•murs, fem•o•ra** (fem′-ər ə). the long bone extending from the pelvis to the knee; thighbone. —**fem′o•ral,** *adj.*

fen (fen), *n.* low, boggy land; marsh.

fence (fens), *n., v.,* **fenced, fenc•ing.** —*n.* **1.** a barrier, usu. of posts and wire or wood, used to prevent entrance or mark a boundary. **2. a.** a person who receives and disposes of stolen goods. **b.** the place of business of such a person. —*v.t.* **3.** to enclose or separate with or as if with a fence. **4.** to keep in or out with a fence. **5.** to sell (stolen goods) to a fence. —*v.i.* **6.** to practice the sport of fencing. **7.** to try to avoid giving direct answers; hedge. —**Idiom. 8. on the fence,** uncommitted; undecided. —**Saying. 9. Good fences make good neighbors,** relationships are smoother when people respect one another's privacy: popularized by Robert Frost in *Mending Wall* (1914). —**fenc′er,** *n.*

fenc′ing, *n.* **1.** the art or sport in which a foil or saber is used for defense and attack. **2.** fences collectively. **3.** material for fences.

fend (fend), *v.t.* **1.** to ward off: *to fend off blows.* —*v.i.* **2.** to try to manage; shift: *to fend for oneself.*

fend′er, *n.* **1.** a part mounted over the wheels of a vehicle such as an automobile or bicycle to protect it, as from splashes. **2.** a low metal guard before an open fireplace.

fen•es•tra•tion (fen′ə strā′shən), *n.* the design and disposition of windows and doors of a building.

feng shui (fung′ shwā′), *n.* the Chinese practice of creating harmonious surroundings that enhance the balance of yin and yang. [< Chin: natural surroundings, lit., wind and water]

fen•nel (fen′l), *n.* **1.** a plant of the parsley family with aromatic feathery leaves. **2.** the aromatic seeds of the fennel, used in cooking.

fe•ral (fēr′əl, fer′-), *adj.* **1.** existing in a wild state; not domesticated or cultivated. **2.** having reverted to the wild state. **3.** ferocious; savage.

fer•ment (*n.* fûr′ment; *v.* fər ment′), *n.* **1.** a living

organism; as yeast, that causes fermentation. **2.** agitation or excitement; commotion: *political ferment.* —*v.i., v.t.* **3.** to undergo or cause to undergo fermentation. **4.** to be or cause to be agitated or excited.

fer′men•ta′tion, *n.* **1.** a chemical change brought about by a ferment, as the conversion of grape sugar into ethyl alcohol by yeast enzymes. **2.** agitation; excitement.

Fer•mi (fûr′mē, fâr′-), *n.* **Enrico,** 1901–54, U.S. physicist, born in Italy.

fer•mi•um (fûr′mē əm, fâr′-), *n.* a radioactive element artificially produced from plutonium or uranium. *Symbol:* Fm; *at. no.:* 100. [after E. FERMI]

fern (fûrn), *n.* a nonflowering vascular plant having fronds and reproducing by spores.

fe•ro•cious (fə rō′shəs), *adj.* **1.** savagely fierce or cruel; brutal. **2.** extreme or intense. —**fe•ro′cious•ly,** *adv.* —**fe•roc′i•ty** (-ros′i tē), **fe•ro′cious•ness,** *n.*

-ferous, a combining form meaning carrying, producing, or yielding (*coniferous*).

fer•ret (fer′it), *n.* **1.** a domesticated variety of the polecat used esp. in Europe for driving small mammals from their burrows. **2.** a North American prairie weasel with a black mask and black feet. —*v.t.* **3.** to drive out by or as if by using a ferret. **4.** to hunt with ferrets. **5.** to search out and bring to light.

fer•ric (fer′ik), *adj.* of or containing iron, esp. in the trivalent state.

Fer′ris wheel′ (fer′is), *n.* an amusement ride consisting of a large upright wheel rotating on a fixed stand and having seats suspended freely from its rim. [after G. W. G. *Ferris* (1859–96), U.S. engineer]

Ferris wheel

ferro-, a combining form meaning iron (*ferromagnetic*).

fer•ro•mag•net•ic (fer′ō mag net′ik), *adj.* noting a substance, as iron, that can possess magnetization in the absence of an external magnetic field.

fer•rous (fer′əs), *adj.* of or containing iron, esp. in the bivalent state.

fer•rule (fer′əl, -ōol), *n.* a band or ring put around the end of a post, cane, or handle to prevent splitting.

fer•ry (fer′ē), *n., pl.* **-ries,** *v.,* **-ried, -ry•ing.** —*n.* **1.** a service for transporting persons or things across a river, bay, etc. **2.** a ferryboat. **3.** a service for flying airplanes over a particular route. —*v.t.* **4.** to carry or convey over a fixed route in a boat or plane. **5.** to fly (an airplane) over a particular route, esp. for delivery. —*v.i.* **6.** to go in a ferry.

fer′ry•boat′, *n.* a boat used for ferrying.

fer•tile (fûr′tl; *esp. Brit.* -tīl), *adj.* **1.** producing or capable of producing abundantly; productive: *fertile soil; a fertile imagination.* **2.** bearing or capable of bearing offspring. **3.** capable of developing, as a seed or egg. —**fer•til•i•ty** (fər til′i tē), *n.*

Fer′tile Cres′cent, *n.* a crescent-shaped agricultural region of the ancient Near East beginning at the

Mediterranean Sea and extending between the Tigris and Euphrates rivers to the Persian Gulf.

fer′ti•lize′, v.t., -lized, -liz•ing. **1. a.** to render (a female gamete) capable of development through union with a male gamete. **b.** to impregnate (an animal or plant). **2.** to make fertile. —**fer′ti•li•za′tion**, n.

fer′ti•liz′er, n. a substance, esp. a commercial or chemical manure, used to fertilize the soil.

fer•ule (fer′əl, -ool), n. a rod, cane, or stick for punishing children.

fer•vent (fûr′vənt), adj. **1.** having or showing warmth or intensity of feeling; ardent. **2.** hot; glowing. —**fer′ven•cy**, n. —**fer′vent•ly**, adv.

fer′vid (-vid), adj. **1.** heated or vehement, as in spirit; impassioned. **2.** very hot; fiery. —**fer′vid•ly**, adv.

fer′vor, n. **1.** warmth or intensity of feeling; ardor. **2.** intense heat.

fes•cue (fes′kyoo), n. a kind of grass cultivated for pasture or lawns.

-fest, a combining form meaning an assembly of people engaged in a common activity (songfest).

fes•tal (fes′tl), adj. festive.

fes•ter (fes′tər), v.i. **1.** to form pus; suppurate. **2.** to rankle, as resentment or bitterness.

fes•ti•val (fes′tə vəl), n. **1.** a time of celebration marked by special ceremonies. **2.** a period or program of festive activities, cultural events, or entertainment.

fes′tive, adj. **1.** of or suitable for a feast or festival. **2.** joyous; merry. —**fes′tive•ly**, adv. —**fes′tive•ness**, n.

fes•tiv′i•ty, n., pl. -ties. **1.** a festive celebration. **2.** festivities, festive events or activities. **3.** festive character or quality.

fes•toon (fe stoon′), n. **1.** a string or chain, as of foliage, suspended in a curve between two points. **2.** a decorative representation of a festoon, as on pottery. —v.t. **3.** to adorn with or as if with festoons. **4.** to form into festoons.

fet•a (fet′ə), n. a white, brine-cured Greek cheese usu. made from sheep's or goat's milk.

fe•tal (fēt′l), adj. of or being a fetus.

fetch (fech), v.t. **1.** to go and return with. **2.** to cause to come. **3.** to sell for. **4.** to take (a breath). **5.** to utter (a sigh, groan, etc.). **6.** to deliver (a stroke or blow). —**fetch′er**, n.

fetch′ing, adj. charming; captivating. —**fetch′ing•ly**, adv.

fete or **fête** (fāt, fet), n., pl. fetes or fêtes, v., fet•ed or fêt•ed, fet•ing or fêt•ing. —n. **1.** a festive celebration or entertainment. **2.** a religious feast or festival. —v.t. **3.** to entertain at or honor with a fete.

fet•id (fet′id, fē′tid), adj. having an offensive odor; noisome. —**fet′id•ness**, n.

fet•ish (fet′ish, fē′tish), n. **1.** an object regarded as having magical power; talisman. **2.** something eliciting unquestioning reverence or devotion. —**fet′ish•ism**, n. —**fet′ish•ist**, n. —**fet′ish•is′tic**, adj.

fet•lock (fet′lok′), n. **1.** a projection on the leg of a horse behind the hoof, bearing a tuft of hair. **2.** the tuft of hair itself.

fet•ter (fet′ər), n. **1.** a chain or shackle placed on the feet. **2.** Usu., -ters. something that confines or restrains. —v.t. **3.** to put fetters on. **4.** to confine; restrain.

fet•tle (fet′l), n. state; condition: in fine fettle.

fe•tus (fē′təs), n., pl. -tus•es. the young of an animal in the womb or egg, esp. in the later stages of development.

feud (fyood), n. **1.** a state of bitter hostility, between families or clans, lasting for years or generations. —v.i. **2.** to carry on a feud.

feu•dal (fyood′l), adj. of or characteristic of feudalism.

feu′dal•ism, n. a system of social and economic organization in medieval Europe based on the holding of lands in fief and on the resulting relations between lord and vassal. —**feu′dal•is′tic**, adj.

fe•ver (fē′vər), n. **1.** an abnormally high body tem-

perature. **2.** a disease, as scarlet fever, in which high temperature is a prominent symptom. **3.** intense nervous excitement. —**fe′ver•ish**, adj. —**fe′ver•ish•ly**, adv.

few (fyoo), adj., -er, -est, n., pron. —adj. **1.** not many but more than one. —n. **2.** (used with a pl. v.) a small number. **3.** a special limited number: the privileged few. —pron. **4.** (used with a pl. v.) a small number of persons or things. ——Usage. See LESS.

fey (fā), adj. **1.** whimsical; strange. **2.** supernatural; enchanted. **3.** appearing to be under a spell. **4.** Chiefly Scot. doomed.

fez (fez), n., pl. fez•zes. a red, cone-shaped felt hat with a tassel, worn by men, esp. in Egypt. [< Turkish, after Fez, city in Morocco where originally made]

ff, **1.** folios. **2.** (and the) following (pages, verses, etc.).

fi•an•cé (fē′än sā′, fē än′sā), n., pl. -cés. a man engaged to be married.

fi•an•cée (fē′än sā′, fē än′sā), n., pl. -cées. a woman engaged to be married.

fi•as•co (fē as′kō), n., pl. -cos, -coes. a complete and ignominious failure.

fi•at (fē′ät, -at; fī′ət, -at), n. an authoritative decree, sanction, or order. [< L: let it be done]

fib (fib), n., v., fibbed, fib•bing. —n. **1.** a minor or trivial lie. —v.i. **2.** to tell a fib. —**fib′ber**, n.

fi•ber (fī′bər), n. **1.** a fine threadlike piece, as of cotton or asbestos. **2.** a slender filament. **3.** matter or material composed of filaments. **4.** essential character, quality, or strength. **5.** plant matter, as cellulose, that is bulky and stimulates peristalsis. Also, esp. Brit., **fi′bre**. —**fi′brous** (-brəs), adj.

fi′ber•board′, n. a building material made of plant fibers compressed into rigid sheets.

fi′ber•fill′, n. synthetic fibers, as polyester, used as a filling or insulating material, as in pillows.

fi′ber•glass′, n. a material consisting of fine filaments of glass, used for textiles, insulation, boat hulls, etc.

fi′ber op′tics, n. the technology of sending light and images, as around bends and corners, through transparent glass or plastic fibers. —**fi′ber-op′tic**, adj.

fi•bril (fī′brəl, fib′rəl), n. a small or fine fiber.

fi•bril•la•tion (fī′brə lā′shən, fib′rə-), n. chaotic contractions across the atrium of the heart, causing fast and irregular ventricular activity. —**fi′bril•late′**, v.i., v.t., -lat•ed, -lat•ing.

fi•brin (fī′brin), n. the insoluble protein end product of blood coagulation.

fi•brin′o•gen (-ə jən), n. a globulin occurring in blood and yielding fibrin in blood coagulation.

fi•broid (fī′broid), adj. resembling or composed of fibrous tissue: a fibroid tumor.

fi•bro′sis (-brō′sis), n. the development in an organ of excess fibrous connective tissue.

fib•u•la (fib′yə lə), n., pl. -lae (-lē′), -las. the outer and thinner of the two bones extending from the knee to the ankle. —**fib′u•lar**, adj.

-fic, a combining form meaning making, producing, or causing (honorific).

FICA (fī′kə, fē′-), Federal Insurance Contributions Act.

fiche (fēsh), n. MICROFICHE.

fich•u (fish′oo, fē′shoo), n., pl. fich•us. a woman's sheer triangular scarf worn over the shoulders.

fick•le (fik′əl), adj. not stable or constant; changeable. —**fick′le•ness**, n.

fic•tion (fik′shən), n. **1. a.** the class of literature comprising works of imaginative narration, esp. in prose form. **b.** works of this class, as novels. **2.** something invented or imagined, esp. a made-up story. —**fic′tion•al**, adj.

fic′tion•al•ize′, v.t., -ized, -iz•ing. to make into fiction; give a fictional version of: to fictionalize a biography. —**fic′tion•al•i•za′tion**, n.

fic•ti′tious (-tish′əs), adj. **1.** created or assumed for the sake of concealment; false. **2.** of or consisting of fiction; created by the imagination. —fic•ti′tious•ly, adv.

fic′tive, adj. 1. fictitious; imaginary. 2. of fiction.

fid•dle (fid′l), n., v., -dled, -dling. —n. 1. a violin. —v.i. 2. to play the fiddle. 3. to make nervous movements with the hands. 4. to touch something, as to adjust it. 5. to waste time; trifle. —fid′dler, n.

fid′dle•sticks′, interj. an exclamation of impatience, dismissal, etc.

fi•del•i•ty (fi del′i tē, fī-), n., pl. -ties. 1. loyalty; faithfulness. 2. adherence to fact or detail. 3. accuracy; exactness. 4. the degree of accuracy with which sound or images are recorded or reproduced.

fidg•et (fij′it), v.i. 1. to move about restlessly, nervously, or impatiently. —n. 2. Often, fidgets. the condition of being restless, nervous, or impatient. —fid′get•er, n. —fidg′et•y, adj.

fi•du•ci•ar•y (fi dōō′shē er′ē, -dyōō′-), n., pl. -ar•ies, adj. —n. 1. Law. a person who holds something in trust for the benefit of another. —adj. 2. Law. of or being a fiduciary. 3. of, based on, or in the nature of trust or confidence.

fief (fēf), n. an estate in land held of a feudal lord. —fief′dom, n.

field (fēld), n. 1. a piece of open or cleared land, esp. one suitable for pasture or tillage. 2. an area devoted to sports; playing field. 3. a sphere of activity or interest. 4. a job or research location away from regular work or study facilities. 5. a. a battleground. b. a battle. 6. an expanse of something: a field of ice. 7. a region characterized by a particular feature or natural resource: an oil field. 8. the background of a flag, shield, or coin. 9. all the competitors in a contest. 10. a region of space in which a force acts, as that around a magnet or a charged particle. —v.t. 11. a. (in baseball and cricket) to catch or pick up (the ball) in play. b. to place (a player or team) in the field to play. 12. to answer skillfully: to field questions. —Idiom. 13. play the field, Informal. to date a number of different persons. —field′er, n.

field′ day′, n. 1. a day devoted to outdoor sports or athletic contests. 2. an occasion or opportunity for unrestricted activity or enjoyment.

field′ glass′, n. Usu., field glasses. binoculars for use out- of-doors.

field′ goal′, n. 1. a three-point goal made by place-kicking a football above the opponent's crossbar. 2. a goal in basketball made while the ball is in play.

field′ hock′ey, n. a field game in which two teams use curved sticks to try to drive a ball into a netted goal.

Field•ing (fēl′ding), n. Henry, 1707–54, English novelist.

field′ mar′shal, n. a military officer of the highest rank, as in the British army.

Fields (fēldz), n. W. C., 1880–1946, U.S. vaudeville and motion-picture comedian.

field′-test′, v.t. to test (a device or product) under conditions of actual use.

fiend (fēnd), n. 1. an evil spirit; demon. 2. a diabolically cruel or wicked person. 3. Informal. a person who is addicted to a habit or practice: an opium fiend. 4. Informal. a person who is excessively interested in an activity; fan. —fiend′ish, adj. —fiend′ish•ly, adv. —fiend′ish•ness, n.

fierce (fērs), adj., fierc•er, fierc•est. 1. menacingly wild and savage. 2. violent in force or intensity. 3. furiously eager or intense: fierce competition. 4. Informal. extremely bad or severe. [< OF < L ferus wild] —fierce′ly, adv. —fierce′ness, n.

fier•y (fīər′ē, fī′ə rē), adj., -i•er, -i•est. 1. consisting of or characterized by fire. 2. intensely hot. 3. like or suggestive of fire: a fiery red. 4. intensely ardent or passionate. 5. easily angered or provoked. 6. inflamed, as a sore. —fier′i•ness, n.

fi•es•ta (fē es′tə), n., pl. -tas. a festival or festive celebration. [< Sp < L fēsta feast]

fife (fīf), n. a small high-pitched transverse flute. —fif′er, n.

FIFO (fī′fō), n. first-in, first-out: a method of inventory evaluation.

fif•teen (fif′tēn′), n. 1. a cardinal number, ten plus five. 2. a symbol for this number, as 15 or XV. —adj. 3. amounting to 15 in number. —fif′teenth′, adj., n.

fifth (fifth), adj. 1. next after the fourth; being the ordinal number for five. 2. being one of five equal parts. —n. 3. a fifth part. 4. the fifth member of a series. 5. a fifth part of a gallon of liquor or spirits; ⁴⁄₅ of a quart (about 750 milliliters). —adv. 6. in the fifth place. —fifth′ly, adv.

Fifth′ Amend′ment, n. an amendment to the U.S. Constitution providing chiefly that no person be required to testify against himself or herself in a criminal case.

fifth′ col′umn, n. a group of people within a country who act traitorously out of secret sympathy with an enemy.

fifth′ wheel′, n. a superfluous or unwanted person or thing.

fif•ty (fif′tē), n., pl. -ties, adj. —n. 1. a cardinal number, ten times five. 2. a symbol for this number, as 50 or L. —adj. 3. amounting to 50 in number. —fif′ti•eth, adj., n.

fif′ty-fif′ty, adj. 1. equally likely and unlikely or favorable and unfavorable: a fifty-fifty chance. —adv. 2. in an evenly or equally divided way.

fig (fig), n. 1. a tree or shrub of the mulberry family that bears a pear-shaped edible fruit. 2. its fruit. 3. a contemptibly trifling amount.

fig., 1. figurative. 2. figuratively. 3. figure.

fight (fīt), n., v., fought, fight•ing. —n. 1. a battle. 2. a contest or struggle. 3. an angry argument or disagreement. 4. a boxing bout. 5. ability, will, or inclination to combat, strive, or resist. —v.i. 6. to engage in battle or single combat. 7. to contend vigorously; strive. —v.t. 8. to contend with in or as if in battle or combat. 9. to carry on; wage. 10. to make (one's way) by fighting or striving.

fight′er, n. 1. a boxer. 2. an aircraft designed to seek out and destroy enemy aircraft. 3. a person with courage or spunk.

fig•ment (fig′mənt), n. a product of mental invention.

fig•u•ra•tion (fig′yə rā′shən), n. 1. the act of shaping into a particular figure. 2. a figure, outline, or shape.

fig′ur•a•tive (-yər ə tiv), adj. 1. of the nature of or involving a figure of speech, esp. a metaphor; metaphorical. 2. characterized by figures of speech. 3. representing by a figure or emblem; emblematic. —fig′ur•a•tive•ly, adv.

fig•ure (fig′yər; esp. Brit. fig′ər), n., v., -ured, -ur•ing. —n. 1. a numerical symbol; numeral. 2. an amount or value expressed in numbers. 3. figures, arithmetic. 4. a written symbol other than a letter. 5. the form or shape of something; outline. 6. the bodily form or frame. 7. a personage, esp. one of distinction. 8. the appearance or impression made by a person. 9. a figure of speech. 10. a pattern, as in cloth. 11. a movement or series of movements, as in dancing or skating. —v.t. 12. to compute or calculate. 13. to adorn with a design or pattern. 14. to picture or depict. 15. Informal. to conclude, reason, or think. —v.i. 16. to compute or work with numerical figures. 17. to be or appear, esp. conspicuously. 18. Informal. (of a situation, act, request, etc.) to be logical, expected, or reasonable. 19. figure on, a. to count on. b. to plan on. 20. ~ out, to come to understand; solve.

fig′ure•head′, n. 1. a person who is titular head, as of a group, but has no real authority. 2. a carved figure on the bow of a sailing ship.

fig′ure of speech′, n. an expression, as in metaphor, in which words are used in a nonliteral sense.

fig′ur•ine′ (-yə rēn′), n. a small ornamental figure, as of pottery or glass.

Fi•ji (fē′jē), n. a republic consisting of an archipelago (Fi′ji Is′lands) in the S Pacific. 715,375.

fil•a•ment (fil′ə mənt), n. 1. a very fine thread or threadlike structure. 2. a threadlike conductor in a light bulb that is heated to incandescence. —fil′a•men′tous (-men′təs), adj.

fil•bert (fil′bərt), n. 1. the thick-shelled edible nut of a European hazel. 2. a tree or shrub bearing filberts. [< AF, alluding to St. Philibert, near whose feast day these nuts ripen]

filch (filch), v.t. to steal (esp. something of small value). —filch′er, n.

file¹ (fīl), n., v., filed, fil•ing. —n. 1. a container, as a folder or cabinet, in which papers are arranged in order. 2. a collection of papers arranged in order. 3. a collection of related computer data or program records stored by name. 4. a line of persons or things one behind another. —v.t. 5. to place in a file. 6. to arrange in order for storage or reference. 7. to transmit (a news story), as by wire. 8. to submit or register: to file a petition. —v.i. 9. to march in a line. 10. to make application: to file for divorce. —Idiom. 11. on file, filed for easy retrieval. —fil′er, n.

file² (fīl), n., v., filed, fil•ing. —n. 1. a metal tool having rough surfaces for reducing or smoothing metal, wood, etc. —v.t. 2. to reduce, smooth, or remove with or as if with a file.

fi•let mi•gnon (fi lā′ min yon′, -yôn′), n., pl. fi•lets mi•gnons (fi lā′ min yonz′, -yôn′). a tender round of steak cut from the thick end of a beef tenderloin.

fil•i•al (fil′ē əl), adj. of or befitting a son or daughter.

fil•i•bus•ter (fil′ə bus′tər), n. 1. the use of obstructive tactics, as exceptionally long speeches, to prevent or delay the adoption of a legislative measure. —v.i., v.t. 2. to impede (legislation) by obstructive tactics. —fil′i•bus′ter•er, n.

fil•i•gree (fil′ə grē′), n., adj., v., -greed, -gree•ing. —n. 1. delicate ornamental work, as of fine silver or gold wire. —adj. 2. composed of or resembling filigree. —v.t. 3. to adorn with or form into filigree.

fil′ings, n.pl. particles removed by a file.

Fil•i•pi•no (fil′ə pē′nō), n., pl. -nos. a native or inhabitant of the Philippines.

fill (fil), v.t. 1. to put as much as can be held into. 2. to occupy to full capacity. 3. to feed fully; satiate. 4. to pervade completely. 5. to furnish (a vacancy or office) with an occupant. 6. to occupy and perform the duties of (a position or post). 7. to supply the requirements or contents of: got her prescription filled. 8. to meet satisfactorily: to fill a need. 9. to stop up; plug: to fill a cavity. —v.i. 10. to become full. 11. fill in, a. to supply (missing information). b. to complete by adding detail. c. to act as a substitute. 12. ~out, a. to complete (a document or form) by supplying required information. b. to become rounder and fuller, as the human figure. —n. 13. a full supply: to eat one's fill. 14. material such as earth or stones for building up the level of an area of ground.

fill′er, n. 1. a person or thing that fills. 2. a substance used to fill cracks. 3. a substance used to give solidity or bulk to another substance. 4. material used to stuff or pad something, as a quilt.

fil•let (fil′it; usually fi lā′ for 1, 3), n., v., fil•let•ed (fil′i tid) or, for 3 fil•leted (fi lād′), fil•let•ing. —n. 1. a boneless cut or slice of meat or fish. 2. a narrow strip, as of ribbon or fabric. —v.t. 3. to cut (meat or fish) into a fillet. 4. to bind or adorn with or as if with a fillet.

fill′-in′, n. a person or thing that fills in, as a substitute or replacement.

fill′ing, n. 1. an edible preparation used to fill sandwiches or pastry: pie filling. 2. a substance such as cement or amalgam used to fill a cavity in a tooth.

fill′ing sta′tion, n. SERVICE STATION.

fil•lip (fil′əp), v.t. 1. to strike with the nail of a finger snapped from the end of the thumb. —n. 2. an act or instance of filliping. 3. something that tends to rouse or stimulate.

Fill•more (fil′môr), n. Millard, 1800–74, 13th president of the U.S. 1850–53.

fil•ly (fil′ē), n., pl. -lies. a young female horse.

film (film), n. 1. a thin layer or coating. 2. a thin skin or membrane. 3. a thin sheet or strip coated

with a light-sensitive emulsion for taking photographs or motion pictures. 4. MOTION PICTURE. —v.t. 5. to cover with a film. 6. a. to photograph with a motion-picture camera. b. to make a motion picture of. —v.i. 7. to become covered with a film.

film′strip′, n. a strip of film with a series of transparencies for still projection.

film′y, adj., -i•er, -i•est. 1. thin and light like film; gauzy. 2. covered with a film. —film′i•ness, n.

Fi•lo•fax (fī′lə faks′), Trademark. a notebook with an appointment calendar, space for addresses, and specialized inserts, as maps and checklists.

fil•ter (fil′tər), n. 1. a substance, as cloth or charcoal, through which liquid or gas is passed to remove suspended impurities. 2. a device containing a substance for filtering. 3. a lens screen on a camera that controls the rendering of color or diminishes the intensity of light. 4. an electronic device that passes certain frequencies and blocks others. —v.t., v.i. 5. to remove by a filter. 6. to pass through or as if through a filter. —fil′ter•a•ble, fil′tra•ble, adj. —fil′ter•er, n.

filth (filth), n. 1. disgusting dirt or refuse; foul matter. 2. moral impurity or corruption. 3. vulgar or obscene language or thought. —filth′y, adj., -i•er, -i•est. —filth′i•ness, n.

fil•trate (fil′trāt), v., -trat•ed, -trat•ing, n. —v.t., v.i. 1. to filter. —n. 2. liquid that has been passed through a filter. —fil•tra′tion, n.

fin (fin), n. 1. a membranous winglike or paddlelike organ on the body of an aquatic animal, as a fish, used for propulsion, steering, or balancing. 2. a part, as of a mechanism, resembling a fin. 3. Usu., fins. FLIPPER (def. 2). —finned, adj.

fi•na•gle (fi nā′gəl), v.i., v.t., -gled, -gling. to practice or obtain by guile, trickery, or manipulation. —fi•na′gler, n.

fi•nal (fīn′l), adj. 1. pertaining to or coming at the end; last. 2. ultimate. 3. conclusive or decisive. —n. 4. the last and decisive game, match, or round in a series, as in sports. 5. the last examination in a course of study. —fi•nal′i•ty, n. —fi′nal•ly, adv.

fi•na•le (fi nal′ē, -nä′lē), n., pl. -les. the concluding part of something, esp. of a musical composition.

fi•nal•ist (fīn′l ist), n. a participant in the final round of a contest.

fi′nal•ize′, v.t., -ized, -liz•ing. to put into final form. —fi′nal•i•za′tion, n. —Usage. Although FINALIZE is regarded by many as being a recent, bureaucratic coinage, the word has been current in English since the 1920s.

fi•nance (fi nans′, fī′nans), n., v., -nanced, -nanc•ing. —n. 1. the management of funds, esp. those affecting the public. 2. finances, monetary resources, as of an individual or a government. —v.t. 3. to supply with money or capital. 4. to obtain money or credit for. —fi•nan′cial, adj. —fi•nan′cial•ly, adv.

fin•an•cier (fin′ən sēr′, fī′nan-), n. a person skilled or engaged in managing large financial operations.

finch (finch), n. any of various small songbirds with a short bill adapted for eating seeds.

find (fīnd), v., found, find•ing, n. —v.t. 1. to come upon by chance. 2. to locate, attain, or obtain by search or effort. 3. to recover (something lost). 4. to gain or regain the use of: to find one's tongue. 5. to ascertain by study or calculation. 6. to feel; perceive. 7. to determine after judicial inquiry. —v.i. 8. to determine an issue after judicial inquiry: The jury found for the plaintiff. 9. find out, to uncover and expose the true nature or identity of. —n. 10. the act of finding. 11. something found, esp. a valuable discovery. —find′er, n.

fin-de-siè•cle (Fr. faṅ də sye′klə), adj. of or characteristic of the final years of the 19th century, esp. in Europe.

find′ing, n. 1. Often, -ings. something found or ascertained. 2. a. a decision or verdict after a judicial inquiry. b. a U.S. presidential order authorizing an action.

fine¹ (fīn), adj., fin•er, fin•est, adv. —adj. 1. of superior quality; excellent. 2. consisting of minute particles: *fine sand.* **3.** very thin; slender: *fine thread.* **4.** sharp, as a tool. **5.** delicate, as in texture. **6.** highly skilled; accomplished. **7.** polished; refined: *fine manners.* **8.** delicate; subtle: *a fine distinction.* **9.** (of a precious metal or its alloy) free from impurities. —*adv.* **10.** very well; excellently. —**fine′ly,** *adv.* —**fine′ness,** *n.*

fine² (fīn), *n., v.,* **fined, fin•ing.** —*n.* **1.** a sum of money imposed as a penalty for an offense or dereliction. —*v.t.* **2.** to subject to or punish by a fine.

fine′ art′, *n.* art, as painting, created primarily for aesthetic purposes and valued for its beauty.

fin′er•y, *n.* fine or showy clothing and ornaments.

fine′spun′, *adj.* highly refined or subtle.

fi•nesse (fi ness′), *n.* **1.** delicacy or subtlety of performance or skill. **2.** skill and adroitness in handling a situation.

fine′-tune′, *v.t.,* **-tuned, -tun•ing. 1.** to adjust for optimal reception. **2.** to make delicate adjustments in so as to produce stability: *to fine-tune the nation's economy.*

fin•ger (fing′gər), *n.* **1.** one of the jointed terminal members of the hand, esp. one other than the thumb. **2.** something like a finger in form or use. —*v.t.* **3.** to touch with the fingers; handle. **4.** to play on (a musical instrument) with the fingers. —**Idiom. 5. keep one's fingers crossed,** to hope fervently for something. **6. put one's finger on, a.** to remember precisely. **b.** to locate exactly. **7. wrap around one's finger,** to exert complete control over, esp. through cajolery.

fin′ger•board′, *n.* the strip of wood on the neck of a stringed instrument against which the strings are stopped by the fingers.

fin′ger bowl′, *n.* a small bowl to hold water for rinsing the fingers at table.

fin′ger•ing, *n.* **1.** the act or method of using the fingers in playing a musical instrument. **2.** the indication of which fingers are to be used in playing a piece of music.

fin′ger•ling (-ling), *n.* a young or small fish.

fin′ger•nail′, *n.* the nail at the end of a finger.

fin′ger paint′, *n.* a jellylike paint used by children in painting with their fingers. —**fin′ger paint′ing,** *n.*

fin′ger•print′, *n.* **1.** an impression of the markings of the inner surface of the fingertip, esp. when made for purposes of identification. —*v.t.* **2.** to take or record the fingerprints of.

fin′ger•tip′, *n.* the tip of a finger.

fin•i•al (fin′ē əl), *n.* an ornamental terminal feature, as on a spire or a lamp.

fin•ick•y (fin′i kē) also **-i•cal** (-i kəl), *adj.* excessively particular or fastidious.

fin•is (fin′is, fē nē′, fī′nis), *n.* the end; conclusion.

fin•ish (fin′ish), *v.t.* **1.** to bring to an end. **2.** to come to the end of. **3.** to use completely. **4.** to destroy or kill. **5.** to complete and perfect in detail. **6.** to put a surface coating on (wood, metal, etc.). —*v.i.* **7.** to come to an end. —*n.* **8.** the final part or last stage; end or conclusion. **9.** educational or social polish. **10.** the surface coating or texture, as of wood. **11.** something that finishes, completes, or perfects a thing. —**fin′ish•er,** *n.*

fi•nite (fī′nīt), *adj.* **1.** having bounds or limits. **2. a.** (of a set of mathematical elements) capable of being completely counted. **b.** not infinite or infinitesimal. —**fi′nite•ly,** *adv.*

fink (fingk), *n. Slang.* **1.** a strikebreaker. **2.** an informer; stool pigeon. **3.** a contemptible person.

Fin•land (fin′lənd), *n.* a republic in N Europe, on the Baltic. 5,109,148.

Finn (fin), *n.* a native or inhabitant of Finland.

Finn or **Finn.,** Finnish.

fin•nan had•die (fin′ən had′ē), *n.* smoked haddock.

Finn•ish (fin′ish), *n.* **1.** the language of Finland. —*adj.* **2.** of Finland, the Finns, or Finnish.

fin′ny, *adj.,* **-ni•er, -ni•est. 1.** pertaining to or abounding in fish. **2.** having or resembling fins.

fiord (fyôrd, fē ôrd′), *n.* FJORD.

fir (fûr), *n.* **1.** an evergreen tree of the pine family with flat needles and erect cones. **2.** the wood of a fir.

fire (fīªr), *n., v.,* **fired, fir•ing.** —*n.* **1.** the light, heat, and flame given off by something burning. **2.** a burning mass of material, as in a furnace. **3.** a destructive burning, as of a building. **4.** brilliance, as of a gem. **5.** burning passion. **6.** the discharge of firearms: *enemy fire.* —*v.t.* **7.** to set on fire. **8.** to supply with fuel. **9.** to bake in a kiln. **10.** to fill with excitement or enthusiasm. **11.** to discharge; shoot: *to fire an arrow.* **12.** to dismiss from a job. —*v.i.* **13.** to take fire. **14.** to become excited or enthusiastic. **15.** to discharge a gun or hurl a projectile. —**Idiom. 16. under fire, a.** under attack, esp. by military forces. **b.** under censure or criticism. —**fir′er,** *n.*

fire′arm′, *n.* a weapon, as a pistol, from which a projectile is fired by gunpowder.

fire′ball′, *n.* **1.** a ball of fire. **2.** a luminous meteor, sometimes exploding. **3.** the highly luminous central portion of a nuclear explosion. **4.** an exceptionally energetic person.

fire′bomb′, *n.* **1.** an explosive device with incendiary effects. —*v.t.* **2.** to attack with firebombs.

fire′box′, *n.* **1.** a chamber, as in a furnace, containing a fire. **2.** a box with a device for notifying a fire station of an outbreak of fire.

fire′brand′, *n.* **1.** a piece of burning wood. **2.** a person who kindles strife or encourages unrest.

fire′break′, *n.* a strip of land cleared to check the spread of a fire.

fire′brick′, *n.* a brick made of a refractory clay.

fire′bug′, *n.* an arsonist; pyromaniac.

fire′crack′er, *n.* a paper cylinder having an explosive and a fuse and set off to make a noise.

fire′damp′, *n.* a combustible gas consisting chiefly of methane, formed esp. in coal mines.

fire′ en′gine, *n.* a vehicle equipped for firefighting.

fire′ escape′, *n.* a metal stairway down an outside wall for escaping from a burning building.

fire′fight′, *n.* an exchange of gunfire between two opposing military forces.

fire′fight′er, *n.* a person who fights destructive fires. —**fire′fight′ing,** *n., adj.*

fire′fly′, *n., pl.* **-flies.** a nocturnal beetle with a light-producing organ at the rear of the abdomen.

fire′house′, *n.* FIRE STATION.

fire′ i′rons, *n.pl.* implements used for tending a fire.

fire′man′, *n., pl.* **-men. 1.** a firefighter. **2.** a person employed to tend fires; stoker.

fire′place′, *n.* **1.** the part of a chimney that opens into a room and in which fuel is burned. **2.** an open structure for keeping a fire, as at a campsite.

fire′plug′, *n.* HYDRANT.

fire′pow′er, *n.* the capability, as of a military force or weapons system, to deliver effective fire to a target.

fire′proof′, *adj.* **1.** resistant to destruction by fire. —*v.t.* **2.** to make fireproof.

fire′side′, *n.* **1.** the space around a fire or hearth. **2.** home or family life.

fire′ sta′tion, *n.* a building in which firefighting apparatus and usu. firefighters are housed.

fire′ tow′er, *n.* a tower, as on a mountain, from which a watch for fires is kept.

fire′trap′, *n.* a building likely to burn and difficult to escape from.

fire′ truck′, *n.* FIRE ENGINE.

fire′ wall′ or **fire′wall′,** *n.* **1.** a partition built to prevent the spread of a fire. **2.** a collection of security measures designed to prevent unauthorized electronic access to a networked computer system.

fire′wa′ter, *n.* alcoholic drink; liquor.

fire′wood′, *n.* wood suitable for fuel.

fire′work′, *n.* Often, **-works.** a combustible or explosive device for producing a striking display of light or a loud noise.

fir′ing line′, *n.* **1.** the positions at which troops are stationed to fire on a target. **2.** the forefront of an action or activity.

fir'ing squad', *n.* a military detachment assigned to execute a condemned person by shooting.

firm¹ (fûrm), *adj.*, **-er, -est**, *v.* —*adj.* **1.** not soft or yielding when pressed. **2.** securely fixed in place. **3.** not shaking or trembling. **4.** not subject to change or fluctuation. **5.** indicating determination. —*v.t., v.i.* **6.** to make or become firm. —**firm'ly**, *adv.* —**firm'ness**, *n.*

firm² (fûrm), *n.* a commercial company; business.

fir•ma•ment (fûr'mə mənt), *n.* the arch or vault of heaven; sky.

first (fûrst), *adj.* **1.** being before all others; used as the ordinal number of *one.* —*adv.* **2.** before all others. **3.** for the first time. **4.** in preference to something else; rather: *I'd die first.* —*n.* **5.** the person or thing that is first, as in time, order, or rank. **6.** the beginning. **7.** low gear in an automotive vehicle. **8.** the winning position or rank in a competition.

first' aid', *n.* emergency treatment given before regular medical services can be obtained. —**first'-aid'**, *adj.*

first'born', *adj.* **1.** first in the order of birth; eldest. —*n.* **2.** a firstborn child.

first' class', *n.* **1.** the best or highest class or grade. **2.** the most expensive class of travel accommodation. **3.** the class of mail consisting of matter sealed against inspection. —**first'-class'**, *adj., adv.*

first'hand' or **first'-hand'**, *adj., adv.* from the first or original source.

first' la'dy, *n.* (*often caps.*) the wife of the president of the U.S. or of the governor of a state.

first' lieuten'ant, *n.* a military officer ranking next above second lieutenant.

first'ly, *adv.* in the first place.

first' mate', *n.* the officer of a merchant ship ranking next below the captain.

first' per'son, *n.* the form of a pronoun or verb that refers to the speaker.

first'-rate', *adj.* **1.** of the highest quality, rank, rate, or class. —*adv.* **2.** very well.

first' ser'geant, *n.* a noncommissioned officer ranking in the U.S. Army above a master sergeant and in the Marine Corps above a gunnery sergeant.

first'-string', *adj.* composed of regular members or participants, not substitutes. —**first'-string'er**, *n.*

firth (fûrth), *n.* an indentation of a seacoast.

fis•cal (fis'kəl), *adj.* **1.** of a public treasury or public revenues. **2.** of financial matters. —**fis'cal•ly**, *adv.*

fish (fish), *n., pl.* **fish, fish•es**, *v.* —*n.* **1.** any of various cold-blooded aquatic vertebrates having gills, fins, and typically scales. **2.** the flesh of a fish used as food. —*v.t.* **3.** to try to catch fish in. **4.** to draw as if fishing: *He fished a coin out of his pocket.* —*v.i.* **5.** to attempt to catch fish. **6.** to search carefully: *to fish through papers.* **7.** to seek to obtain something indirectly: *fishing for a compliment.* **8.** a symbol for Christ: from the Greek word *ichthys* and derived from the initials of the Greek words for "Jesus Christ, Son of God, Savior." **9.** a secret sign used by Christians to recognize one another during the days of persecution by the Romans.

fish'er, *n.* **1.** a fisherman. **2. a.** a dark-furred North American marten. **b.** the fur of the fisher.

fisher•man, *n., pl.* **-men. 1.** a person who fishes for profit or pleasure. **2.** a ship used in fishing.

fish'er•y, *n., pl.* **-er•ies. 1.** a fish hatchery. **2.** a place where fish are caught. **3.** the occupation or industry of catching or selling fish.

fish'hook', *n.* a barbed hook for catching fish.

fish'ing, *n.* the occupation or diversion of catching fish.

fish'ing rod', *n.* a flexible rod for use with a reel and line in catching fish.

fish' sto'ry, *n.* an exaggerated or incredible story.

fish'wife', *n., pl.* **-wives. 1.** a woman who sells fish. **2.** a coarse-mannered, raucous woman.

fish'y, *adj.*, **-i•er, -i•est. 1.** like a fish, esp. in smell

or taste. **2.** of questionable character; dubious: *a fishy excuse.* —**fish'i•ly**, *adv.* —**fish'i•ness**, *n.*

fis•sile (fis'əl), *adj.* **1.** capable of being split. **2.** capable of undergoing fission.

fis•sion (fish'ən), *n.* **1.** the act of cleaving into parts. **2.** the splitting of the nucleus of an atom into nuclei of lighter atoms, accompanied by the release of energy. —**fis'sion•a•ble**, *adj.*

fis•sure (fish'ər), *n.* a narrow opening, division, or groove.

fist (fist), *n.* **1.** the hand closed tightly with the fingers doubled into the palm. **2.** INDEX (def. 4).

fist'ful (-fŏol), *n., pl.* **-fuls.** a handful.

fist•i•cuff (fis'ti kuf'), *n.* **1.** a cuff or blow with the fist. **2. fisticuffs,** combat with the fists.

fis•tu•la (fis'chŏo lə), *n., pl.* **-las, -lae** (-lē'). a narrow passage or duct formed by disease or injury. —**fis'tu•lous,** *adj.*

fit¹ (fit), *adj.*, **fit•ter, fit•test**, *v.*, **fit•ted** or **fit, fit•ting**, *n.* —*adj.* **1.** adapted or suited; appropriate. **2.** proper or becoming. **3.** prepared or ready. **4.** in good physical condition; healthy. —*v.t.* **5.** to be adapted to or suitable for. **6.** to be proper or becoming for. **7.** to be of the right size or shape for. **8.** to make conform; adjust. **9.** to make qualified or competent. **10.** to make ready; prepare. **11.** to provide; equip. —*v.i.* **12.** to be suitable or proper. **13.** to be of the right size or shape. —*n.* **14.** the manner in which a thing fits. **15.** something that fits. —**fit'ly**, *adv.* —**fit'ness**, *n.* —**fit'ter**, *n.* —**Usage.** Both FIT and FITTED are standard as past tense and past participle of FIT. FITTED is somewhat more common in the sense "to make conform, adjust": *The tailor fitted the suit.* In the passive voice, FITTED is the more common past particple: *The door was fitted with a new handle.*

fit² (fit), *n.* **1.** a sudden acute attack, as of a disease or of convulsions. **2.** a sudden onset, as of emotion. —*Idiom.* **3. by fits and starts,** at irregular intervals.

fit'ful, *adj.* spasmodic; irregular. —**fit'ful•ly**, *adv.* —**fit'ful•ness**, *n.*

fit'ting, *adj.* **1.** suitable or appropriate. —*n.* **2.** an act or instance of trying on clothes that are being made or altered. **3.** an item provided as standard equipment. —**fit'ting•ly**, *adv.*

Fitz•ger•ald (fits jer'əld), *n.* **1. Ella,** 1917–96, U.S. jazz singer. **2. F(rancis) Scott (Key),** 1896–1940, U.S. novelist.

five (fīv), *n.* **1.** a cardinal number, four plus one. **2.** a symbol for this number, as 5 or V. —*adj.* **3.** amounting to five in number.

five'-and-ten', *n.* a store offering a wide assortment of inexpensive items. Also called **five'-and-dime'.**

fix (fiks), *v.t.* **1.** to repair; mend. **2.** to put in order; adjust. **3.** to make fast, firm, or stable. **4.** to settle definitely: *to fix a price.* **5.** to direct or hold steadily: *eyes fixed on the page.* **6.** to put into permanent form. **7.** to put or place; assign: *tried to fix the blame on me.* **8.** to arrange or influence the outcome of, esp. dishonestly: *to fix a game.* **9.** to get (a meal) ready. **10.** to get even with. **11.** to castrate or spay (an animal, esp. a pet). **12.** to make (a photographic image) permanent by removing light-sensitive silver halides. —*v.i.* **13.** to become fixed. **14. fix up, a.** to provide with an introduction to someone for a date. **b.** to repair. **c.** to refurbish. —*n.* **15.** a difficult situation; predicament. **16.** a charted position of a ship or aircraft. **17.** *Slang.* an underhand or illegal arrangement. —**fix'a•ble**, *adj.* —**fix'er**, *n.*

fix•a•tion (fik sā'shən), *n.* a strong preoccupation, as with one subject or person; obsession. —**fix'ate**, *v.t., v.i.*, **-at•ed, -at•ing.**

fix'a•tive (fik'sə tiv), *adj.* **1.** serving to fix, preserve, or stabilize. —*n.* **2.** a fixative substance, as a spray that prevents blurring on a drawing.

fixed, *adj.* **1.** firmly attached or placed; stationary. **2.** stable or permanent, as color. **3.** steadily directed; intent: *a fixed stare.* **4.** not fluctuating or varying: *a fixed income.* —**fix•ed•ly** (fik'sid lē, fikst'lē), *adv.*

fix'ings, *n.pl. Informal.* appropriate accompaniments; trimmings.

fix′i•ty, *n.* the state or quality of being fixed; stability.

fix′ture (-chər), *n.* **1.** something securely and usu. permanently attached: *a light fixture.* **2.** a person or thing long established in the same place or position.

fizz (fiz), *v.i.* **1.** to make a hissing or sputtering sound; effervesce. —*n.* **2.** a fizzing sound. **3.** an effervescent drink.

fiz•zle (fiz′əl), *v.,* **-zled, -zling,** *n.* —*v.i.* **1.** to fizz. **2.** to fail or expire feebly, esp. after a good start. —*n.* **3.** a failure; fiasco.

fjord (fyôrd, fē ôrd′), *n.* a long narrow arm of the sea bordered by steep cliffs.

FL, Florida.

fl., 1. floor. **2.** florin. **3.** (he or she) flourished. [< L *floruit*] **4.** fluid.

Fla., Florida.

flab (flab), *n.* loose, excessive flesh.

flab•ber•gast (flab′ər gast′), *v.t.* to overcome with surprise and bewilderment; astound.

flab•by (flab′ē), *adj.,* **-bi•er, -bi•est. 1.** lacking firmness; flaccid. **2.** lacking determination; weak-minded. —**flab′bi•ly,** *adv.* —**flab′bi•ness,** *n.*

flac•cid (flak′sid, flas′id), *adj.* not firm; soft and limp.

flack (flak), *n. Slang.* **1.** PRESS AGENT. **2.** PUBLICITY.

flac•on (flak′ən, fla kôn′), *n.* a small bottle or flask with a stopper.

flag¹ (flag), *n., v.,* **flagged, flag•ging.** —*n.* **1.** a piece of cloth of distinctive color and design that is used as a symbol, as of a nation, or as a signal. **2.** something, as a tag on a file card, used to attract attention. —*v.t.* **3.** to place a flag over or on. **4.** to signal or warn with or as if with a flag.

flag² (flag), *n.* any of various plants with long, sword-shaped leaves.

flag³ (flag), *v.i.,* **flagged, flag•ging. 1.** to fall off in vigor, energy, activity, or interest. **2.** to hang limply; droop.

flag⁴ (flag), *n.* FLAGSTONE.

flag•el•late (flaj′ə lāt′), *v.t.,* **-lat•ed, -lat•ing.** to punish by whipping; scourge. —**flag′el•la′tion,** *n.* —**flag′el•la′tor,** *n.*

fla•gel•lum (flə jel′əm), *n., pl.* **-gel•la** (-jel′ə), **-gel•lums.** a long, lashlike appendage serving as an organ of locomotion, as in protozoa.

flag•on (flag′ən), *n.* a container for liquids, esp. one with a handle, a spout, and a cover.

flag′pole′, *n.* a staff or pole on which a flag can be flown.

fla•grant (flā′grənt), *adj.* shockingly noticeable or evident; glaring. —**fla′gran•cy, fla′grance,** *n.* —**fla′grant•ly,** *adv.*

fla•gran•te de•lic•to (flə gran′tē di lik′tō), *adv.* in the very act of committing an offense.

flag′ship′, *n.* **1.** a ship carrying the commander of a fleet or squadron. **2.** the most important one of a group.

flag′staff′, *n.* a flagpole.

flag′stone′, *n.* a flat stone slab used esp. for paving.

flail (flāl), *n.* **1.** an instrument for threshing grain. —*v.t., v.i.* **2.** to beat or swing with or as if with a flail.

flair (flâr), *n.* **1.** natural talent or aptitude. **2.** smartness of style or manner.

flak (flak), *n.* **1.** antiaircraft fire. **2.** critical or hostile reaction.

flake (flāk), *n., v.,* **flaked, flak•ing.** —*n.* **1.** a small, flat, thin piece detached from a larger piece or surface. **2.** a small piece or mass, as of snow. —*v.i.* **3.** to peel off, fall in, or form into flakes. —*v.t.* **4.** to remove in flakes. —**flak′y,** *adj.,* **-i•er, -i•est.**

flam•bé (fläm bā′, flän-), *adj.* (of food) served in flaming liquor.

flam•boy•ant (flam boi′ənt), *adj.* **1.** strikingly bold or brilliant. **2.** florid; ornate. —**flam•boy′ance, flam•boy′an•cy,** *n.* —**flam•boy′ant•ly,** *adv.*

flame (flām), *n., v.,* **flamed, flam•ing.** —*n.* **1.** burning gas or vapor, as from ignited wood. **2.** Often,

flames. blazing combustion. **3.** a flamelike condition. **4.** brilliant light. **5.** intense ardor or passion. **6.** a sweetheart. **7.** an act or instance of angry criticism or disparagement, esp. on a computer network. —*v.i.* **8.** to burn with or burst into flames. **9.** to glow like flame. **10.** to behave in an offensive manner, esp. on a computer network.

fla•men•co (flä meng′kō, flə-), *n., pl.* **-cos.** a dance style of the Spanish Gypsies marked by stamping of the feet. [< Sp: pertaining to the Gypsies]

flame′-out′, *n.* the failure of a jet engine due to faulty combustion.

flame′throw′er, *n.* a device that sprays ignited incendiary fuel.

fla•min•go (flə ming′gō), *n., pl.* **-gos, -goes.** a wading bird with pinkish to scarlet plumage and very long legs.

flam•ma•ble (flam′ə bəl), *adj.* easily set on fire. —**flam′ma•bil′i•ty,** *n.*

Flan•ders (flan′dərz), *n.* a region in W Belgium and N France.

flange (flanj), *n.* a projecting rim, as on a pipe, to give strength or support or to enable attachment of objects.

flank (flangk), *n.* **1.** a side, esp. the side of an animal or a person between the ribs and hip. **2.** the right or left side of a military formation. —*v.t.* **3.** to stand or be placed at the flank of. **4.** to defend at the flank. **5.** to menace or attack the flank of. **6.** to pass around the flank of.

flan•nel (flan′l), *n.* **1.** a warm, soft, napped fabric of wool or cotton. **2. flannels,** trousers or underwear made of flannel.

flan′nel•et′ or **-ette′** (-et′), *n.* a soft cotton flannel.

flap (flap), *v.,* **flapped, flap•ping,** *n.* —*v.i., v.t.* **1.** to swing or cause to swing loosely, esp. with noise. **2.** to move up and down, as wings. **3.** to strike with something broad and flexible. —*n.* **4.** something flat and broad attached at one side only and hanging loose. **5.** a flapping motion or sound. **6.** *Informal.* a state of nervous excitement.

flap′jack′, *n.* a pancake.

flap′per, *n.* **1.** one that flaps. **2.** a young woman of the 1920s who flouted conventional behavior.

flare (flâr), *v.,* **flared, flar•ing,** *n.* —*v.i.* **1.** to blaze or burn with a sudden unsteady flame. **2.** to burst out in sudden, fierce emotion. **3.** to spread gradually outward, as the bottom of a wide skirt. —*n.* **4.** a flaring or swaying flame or light. **5. a.** a blaze of fire or light used as a signal or for illumination. **b.** a device producing such a blaze. **6.** a sudden burst, as of anger. **7.** outward curvature.

flare′up′, *n.* a sudden outburst or outbreak.

flash (flash), *n.* **1.** a brief, sudden burst of light. **2.** a sudden, brief outburst, as of wit. **3.** a brief moment; instant. **4.** a flashlight. **5.** ostentatious display. **6.** a brief preliminary news dispatch. **7.** a sudden thought or insight. —*v.i.* **8.** to break forth into sudden flame or light. **9.** to gleam; sparkle. **10.** to appear suddenly: *The answer flashed into his mind.* **11.** to move like a flash. —*v.t.* **12.** to emit (fire or light) in sudden flashes. **13.** to cause to flash. **14.** to communicate instantaneously, as by radio. **15.** to make an ostentatious display of. **16.** to display briefly: *to flash an ID card.* —*adj.* **17.** sudden and brief: *a flash fire.*

flash′back′, *n.* **1.** an earlier event inserted into the chronological structure of a literary or dramatic work. **2.** an abnormally vivid, often recurrent recollection of a disturbing past event.

flash′bulb′, *n.* a glass bulb filled with metal wire or foil that when electrically ignited illuminates a photographic subject momentarily.

flash′gun′, *n.* a device that discharges a flashbulb.

flash′ing, *n.* sheet metal used to cover and protect roof joints and angles against leakage.

flash′light′, *n.* a portable electric lamp powered by dry batteries.

flash′ point′, *n.* the lowest temperature at which a liquid will give off sufficient vapor to ignite momentarily on application of a flame.

flash′y, *adj.*, **-i•er, -i•est. 1.** briefly and superficially brilliant. **2.** ostentatious and tasteless; gaudy. —**flash′i•ly**, *adv.* —**flash′i•ness**, *n.*

flask (flask, fläsk), *n.* a flat metal or glass bottle, esp. for carrying in the pocket: *a flask of brandy.*

flat¹ (flat), *adj.*, **flat•ter, flat•test**, *n.*, *v.*, **flat•ted, flat•ting**, *adv.* —*adj.* **1.** horizontally level. **2.** level, even, or smooth in surface. **3.** lying at full length; prone. **4.** not deep or thick. **5.** spread out, as an unrolled map. **6.** deflated: *a flat tire.* **7.** absolute; downright: *a flat denial.* **8.** unvarying; fixed: *a flat rate.* **9.** lacking vitality or animation. **10.** lacking flavor, piquancy, or effervescence. **11.** pointless, as a joke. **12.** not shiny or glossy; matte. **13.** *Music.* **a.** lowered a half step in pitch. **b.** below an intended pitch. —*n.* **14.** something flat. **15.** a flat surface, side, or part. **16.** flat or level ground: *salt flats.* **17.** *Music.* **a.** a sign indicating a tone one half step below a given tone. **b.** a tone one half step below another. **18.** a deflated automobile tire. —*v.t., v.i.* **19.** to make or become flat. —*adv.* **20.** in a flat position or manner. **21.** completely; utterly: *flat broke.* **22.** exactly; precisely: *in two minutes flat.* **23.** *Music.* below the true pitch: *sang flat.* —**Idiom. 24. flat out**, *Informal.* **a.** directly or openly. **b.** at full speed or with maximum effort. —**flat′ly**, *adv.* —**flat′ness**, *n.*

flat² (flat), *n.* a residential apartment.

flat′bed′, *n.* a truck with a body in the form of an open platform.

flat′boat′, *n.* a flat-bottomed boat for use in shallow water.

flat′car′, *n.* a railroad car without sides or top.

flat′fish′, *n.*, *pl.* **-fish, -fish•es.** any of various fishes, including the flounders and soles, that have a flattened body with both eyes on the upper side.

flat′foot′, *n.*, *pl.* **-feet** for 1b, **-foots** for 2. **1. a.** a condition in which the arch of the foot is flattened. **b.** Usu., **-feet.** feet with flattened arches. **2.** *Slang.* a police officer. —**flat′foot′ed**, *adj.*

flat′i′ron, *n.* an iron for use in pressing clothes.

flat′-out′, *adj. Informal.* **1.** using full speed or all of one's resources. **2.** downright; thoroughgoing.

flat′ten, *v.t., v.i.* to make or become flat. —**flat′ten•er**, *n.*

flat′ter, *v.t.* **1.** to praise or compliment insincerely, effusively, or excessively. **2.** to represent or show favorably: *The portrait flatters her.* **3.** to feel satisfaction with (oneself), often mistakenly: *He flattered himself that the speech had gone well.* —**flat′ter•er**, *n.* —**flat′ter•ing•ly**, *adv.* —**flat′ter•y**, *n.*

flat′top′, *n.* **1.** *Informal.* an aircraft carrier. **2.** a crew cut.

flat•u•lent (flach′ə lənt), *adj.* **1.** having an accumulation of gas in the intestinal tract. **2.** inflated and empty; pompous. —**flat′u•lence**, *n.*

fla•tus (flā′təs), *n.* intestinal gas.

flat′ware′, *n.* **1.** table utensils, as knives, forks, and spoons. **2.** flat tableware, as plates and saucers.

Flau•bert (flō bâr′), *n.* **Gustave**, 1821–80, French novelist.

flaunt (flônt), *v.t.* **1.** to display ostentatiously; parade. **2.** to flout. —**flaunt′er**, *n.* —**flaunt′ing•ly**, *adv.* —**Usage.** Although definition 2 of FLAUNT, which stems from a simple confusion, does appear often in educated speech, it is widely considered to be nonstandard.

flau•tist (flô′tist, flou′-), *n.* FLUTIST.

fla•vor (flā′vər), *n.* **1.** the distinctive taste of something. **2.** a flavoring. **3.** the characteristic quality of a thing. —*v.t.* **4.** to give flavor to. Also, *esp. Brit.*, **fla′vour.** —**fla′vor•ful**, *adj.* —**fla′vor•less**, *adj.* —**fla′vor•some**, *adj.*

fla′vor•ing, *n.* a substance used to give a particular flavor to food or drink.

flaw (flô), *n.* **1.** a feature that mars the perfection of something; defect, weakness, or blemish. —*v.t.* **2.** to produce a flaw in. —**flaw′less**, *adj.* —**flaw′less•ly**, *adv.* —**flaw′less•ness**, *n.*

flax (flaks), *n.* **1.** a plant with blue flowers that is cultivated for its fiber, used for making linen yarn,

and for its seeds, which yield linseed oil. **2.** the fiber of this plant.

flax′en, *adj.* **1.** of or made of flax. **2.** pale yellow.

flay (flā), *v.t.*, **1.** to strip off the skin of. **2.** to criticize with scathing severity. —**flay′er**, *n.*

flea (flē), *n.* a small, bloodsucking, leaping insect parasitic upon mammals and birds.

flea′-bit′ten, *adj.* **1.** bitten by or infested with fleas. **2.** shabby; dilapidated.

flea′ mar′ket, *n.* a market, often outdoors, where used articles, curios, and antiques are sold.

fleck (flek), *n.* **1.** a small bit; speck. **2.** a small patch, as of color; spot. —*v.t.* **3.** to mark with flecks.

fledg•ling (flej′ling), *n.* **1.** a young bird that has recently acquired flight feathers. **2.** an inexperienced person. Also, *esp. Brit.*, **fledge′ling.**

flee (flē), *v.*, **fled, flee•ing.** —*v.i.* **1.** to run away, as from danger. **2.** to pass swiftly; fly. —*v.t.* **3.** to run away from.

fleece (flēs), *n.*, *v.*, **fleeced, fleec•ing.** —*n.* **1.** the coat of wool that covers a sheep. **2.** a warm fabric with a thick pile. —*v.t.* **3.** to cheat or swindle. **4.** to remove the fleece of (a sheep). —**fleec′er**, *n.* —**fleec′y**, *adj.*, **-i•er, -i•est.**

fleer (flēr), *v.i.* to grin or laugh coarsely or mockingly. —**fleer′ing•ly**, *adv.*

fleet¹ (flēt), *n.* **1.** the largest organization of warships under the command of a single officer. **2.** a large group of ships, airplanes, trucks, etc., under the same management or ownership.

fleet² (flēt), *adj.*, **-er, -est**, *v.* —*adj.* **1.** swift; rapid. —*v.i.* **2.** to move swiftly; fly. —**fleet′ly**, *adv.* —**fleet′ness**, *n.*

fleet′ ad′miral, *n.* the highest ranking officer in the U.S. Navy.

fleet′ing, *adj.* passing swiftly. —**fleet′ing•ly**, *adv.*

Flem•ing (flem′ing), *n.* **1.** a Flemish-speaking Belgian. **2.** a native or inhabitant of Flanders.

Flem•ish (flem′ish), *adj.* **1.** of Flanders, the Flemings, or their speech. —*n.* **2.** (*used with a pl. v.*) **a.** the Flemish-speaking inhabitants of Belgium; Flemings. **b.** the inhabitants of Flanders. **3.** the Dutch language as spoken in N and E Belgium and adjacent parts of France: one of the official languages of Belgium.

flesh (flesh), *n.* **1.** the soft substance of an animal's body, esp. muscular tissue. **2.** muscular and fatty tissue. **3.** meat, usu. excluding fish and fowl. **4.** the body as distinguished from the spirit or soul. **5.** HUMANKIND. **6.** living creatures in general. **7.** a person's family or relatives. **8.** the soft, pulpy portion of a fruit or vegetable. —*v.t.* **9.** to give dimension or substance to: *The playwright fleshed out the characters.* —**Idiom. 10. in the flesh**, present before one's eyes; in person.

flesh′ and blood′, *n.* **1.** offspring or relatives. **2.** the human body or nature. **3.** substance.

flesh′ly, *adj.*, **-li•er, -li•est. 1.** of the body; corporeal. **2.** carnal; sensual. **3.** worldly rather than spiritual.

flesh′pot′, *n.* a place of luxurious and unrestrained pleasure.

flesh′y, *adj.*, **-i•er, -i•est. 1.** plump; fat. **2.** consisting of or resembling flesh. **3.** pulpy, as a fruit.

fleur-de-lis

fleur-de-lis (flûr′dl ē′, -dl ēs′, flŏŏr′-), *n.*, *pl.* **fleurs-de-lis** (flûr′dl ēz′, flŏŏr′-). **1.** a stylized representation of an iris with three petals, used ornamentally and as a heraldic device. **2.** a symbol for the Trinity. **3.** a symbol for the Virgin Mary.

flew (flōō), v. a pt. of FLY¹.

flex (fleks), v.t., v.i. **1.** to bend. **2.** to tighten (a muscle) by contraction.

flex•dol•lars (fleks'dol'ərz), n.pl. money given by an employer that an employee can apply to any of various employee benefits.

flex'i•ble, adj. **1.** capable of being bent or flexed. **2.** susceptible of modification or change; adaptable. **3.** willing or disposed to yield; tractable. —**flex'i•bil'i•ty**, n. —**flex'i•bly**, adv.

flex'time' also **flex'i•time'** (flek'si-), n. a system that allows an employee to choose the hours for starting and leaving work.

flex•ure (flek'shər), n. **1.** the state of being flexed. **2.** a bent part; bend or fold.

flib•ber•ti•gib•bet (flib'ər tē jib'it), n. a flighty person.

flick¹ (flik), n. **1.** a sudden light blow or tap. **2.** the sound made by a flick. **3.** a light and rapid movement. —v.t. **4.** to strike, remove, propel, or operate with a flick. —v.i. **5.** to move rapidly or jerkily.

flick² (flik), n. Slang. a motion picture.

flick'er¹, v.i. **1.** to burn unsteadily. **2.** to flutter. —n. **3.** an unsteady flame or light. **4.** a flickering movement. **5.** a brief flurry: a flicker of interest.

flick'er², n. any of several North American woodpeckers with yellow or red underwings.

flied (flīd), v. a pt. and pp. of FLY¹.

fli•er (flī'ər), n. **1.** a person, animal, or thing that flies. **2.** a pilot. **3.** something that moves with great speed. **4.** a small handbill; circular. **5.** Informal. a risky or speculative venture.

flight¹ (flīt), n. **1.** the act, process, or power of flying. **2.** the distance covered or the course taken in a flight. **3.** a trip by or in an airplane. **4.** a number of beings or things flying together. **5.** swift movement, transition, or progression. **6.** a transcending of the ordinary bounds of the mind: a flight of fancy. **7.** a series of steps between one floor and the next.

flight² (flīt), n. an act or instance of fleeing.

flight' attend'ant, n. an airline employee who attends to passengers' comfort and safety.

flight' deck', n. **1.** the upper deck of an aircraft carrier. **2.** an elevated compartment in certain aircraft.

flight'less, adj. incapable of flying.

flight' path', n. the trajectory of a moving aircraft or spacecraft relative to a fixed reference.

flight'y, adj., -i•er, -i•est. **1.** frivolous and irresponsible. **2.** unstable; volatile. —**flight'i•ness**, n.

flim•flam (flim'flam'), n. Informal. **1.** a trick or deception, esp. a swindle. **2.** nonsense; twaddle.

flim•sy (flim'zē), adj., -si•er, -si•est. **1.** without material strength or solidity. **2.** not effective or convincing; implausible. —**flim'si•ly**, adv. —**flim'si•ness**, n.

flinch (flinch), v.i. **1.** to draw back, as from pain or danger; shrink. **2.** to shrink or tense under pain; wince.

fling (fling), v., flung, fling•ing, n. —v.t. **1.** to throw with force, violence, or abandon. **2.** to put or send suddenly or without preparation. **3.** to involve (oneself) vigorously in an undertaking. **4.** to throw aside or away. —v.i. **5.** to move with haste or violence. —n. **6.** an act or instance of flinging. **7.** a short period of unrestrained indulgence of one's desires. **8.** an attempt. **9.** a lively Scottish dance. —**fling'er**, n.

flint (flint), n. **1.** a hard stone that is a form of silica. **2.** a piece of flint, esp. as used for striking fire. —**flint'y**, adj., -i•er, -i•est.

Flint, n. a city in SE Michigan. 138,164.

flint' glass', n. an optical glass composed of alkalis, lead oxide, and silica.

flint'lock', n. **1.** an outmoded gunlock in which a flint ignites the charge. **2.** a firearm with a flintlock.

flip (flip), v., flipped, flip•ping, n., adj., flip•per, flip•pest. —v.t. **1.** to turn over by or as if by tossing.

2. to move or activate with a sudden stroke or jerk. **3.** to resell, esp. quickly, or refinance. —v.i. **4.** to read or look at rapidly or perfunctorily. **5.** Slang. **a.** to react with excitement. **b.** to become insane. —n. **6.** an act or instance of flipping. —adj. **7.** flippant; pert. —Idiom. **8. flip one's lid,** Slang. to lose control of one's temper.

flip'-flop', n. **1.** a sudden or unexpected reversal, as of opinion. **2.** a backward somersault. **3.** the sound or motion of something flapping. **4.** a flat backless shoe or slipper, esp. one of rubber with a thong between the first two toes.

flip•pant (flip'ənt), adj. frivolously disrespectful, shallow, or lacking in seriousness. —**flip'pan•cy**, n. —**flip'pant•ly**, adv.

flip•per (flip'ər), n. **1.** a broad, flat limb, as of a seal, specially adapted for swimming. **2.** a paddlelike device, usu. of rubber, worn on the foot as an aid in swimming.

flip' side', n. **1.** the reverse and usu. less popular side of a phonograph record. **2.** an opposite or reverse side.

flirt (flûrt), v.i. **1.** to act amorously without serious intentions. **2.** to trifle or toy, as with an idea. **3.** to move jerkily. —n. **4.** a person given to flirting. **5.** a sudden jerk. —**flir•ta'tion**, n. —**flir•ta'tious**, adj. —**flir•ta'tious•ly**, adv.

flit (flit), v.i., flit•ted, flit•ting. to fly, move, or pass swiftly, lightly, or irregularly from one place or condition to another.

float (flōt), v.i. **1.** to rest on the surface of a liquid. **2.** to move gently on or as if on the surface of a liquid; drift along: a balloon floating through the air. **3.** to move lightly and gracefully. **4.** to wander aimlessly. —v.t. **5.** to cause to float. **6.** to issue (stocks, bonds, etc.) in order to raise money. —n. **7.** something that floats, as a raft. **8.** a hollow ball that through its buoyancy automatically regulates the level of a liquid. **9.** a cork supporting a baited fishing line in the water. **10.** a vehicle bearing a display in a parade. **11.** a drink with ice cream floating in it. —**float'er**, n.

flock¹ (flok), n. **1.** a group of animals, as sheep or birds, that live, travel, or feed together. **2.** a large group, as of people. **3.** the congregation of a church. —v.i. **4.** to gather or go in a flock.

flock² (flok), n. finely powdered fiber, as of wool, used for producing a velvetlike pattern on wallpaper or cloth or for coating metal.

floe (flō), n. a sheet of floating ice.

flog (flog, flôg), v.t., flogged, flog•ging. to beat with a whip or stick. —**flog'ger**, n.

flood (flud), n. **1.** a great overflow of water, esp. over land not usu. submerged. **2.** a great outpouring: a flood of tears. **3. the Flood,** Bible. the great deluge that occurred in the time of Noah. Gen. 7. —v.t. **4.** to cover with or as if with a flood. **5.** to overwhelm with an abundance or excess. —v.i. **6.** to become flooded.

flood'gate', n. a gate designed to regulate a flow of water.

flood'light', n., v., -light•ed or -lit, -light•ing. —n. **1.** an artificial light that provides uniform illumination over a large area. —v.t. **2.** to illuminate with a floodlight.

flood' tide', n. the inflow of the tide.

floor (flôr), n. **1.** the surface of a room on which one walks. **2.** a story of a building. **3.** the lower or bottom surface: the ocean floor. **4. a.** the part of a legislative chamber where members sit and from which they speak. **b.** the right to speak from the floor. **5.** a minimum level. —v.t. **6.** to cover or furnish with a floor. **7.** to knock down. **8.** to overwhelm; shock. **9.** to confound; nonplus.

floor'board', n. **1.** any of the boards composing a floor. **2.** the floor of an automobile.

floor' ex'ercise, n. a competitive gymnastics event in which tumbling feats are performed without apparatus.

floor' fight', n. a debate that takes place on the floor of a political convention.

floor′ing, n. 1. a floor. 2. material for floors.

floor′ show′, n. a nightclub entertainment consisting of a series of acts.

floor′walk′er, n. a store employee who assists customers and supervises salespeople.

flop (flop), v., **flopped, flop•ping,** n. —v.i. 1. to move around, drop, or fall in a heavy, clumsy, or negligent manner. 2. to be a complete failure. —v.t. 3. to drop or move loosely or clumsily. —n. 4. an act or sound of flopping. 5. a complete failure.

flop′py, adj., **-pi•er, -pi•est,** n., pl. **-pies.** —adj. 1. tending to flop. —n. 2. FLOPPY DISK. —**flop′pi•ly,** adv. —**flop′pi•ness,** n.

flop′py disk′, n. a thin, usu. flexible plastic disk coated with magnetic material for storing computer data and programs.

flo•ra (flôr′ə), n., pl. **flo•ras, flo•rae** (flôr′ē). the plants or plant life of a particular region or period.

flo′ral, adj. of or consisting of flowers.

Flor•ence (flôr′əns, flor′-), n. a city in central Italy. 421,299. —**Flor′en•tine′** (-ən tēn′), adj., n.

flo•res•cence (flô res′əns, flə-), n. a state or period of flowering. —**flo•res′cent,** adj.

flo•ret (flôr′it), n. a small flower.

flor•id (flôr′id, flor′-), adj. 1. reddish in color; rosy. 2. excessively ornate; flowery.

Flor•i•da (flôr′i də, flor′-), n. a state in the SE United States. 14,399,985. Cap.: Tallahassee. Abbr.: FL, Fla. —**Flo•rid•i•an** (flə rid′ē ən), **Flor′i•dan,** adj., n.

flor•in (flôr′in, flor′-), n. 1. a former British coin equal to two shillings. 2. the guilder of the Netherlands.

flo•rist (flôr′ist, flor′-), n. a retailer of flowers and ornamental plants.

floss (flôs, flos), n. 1. **a.** short, untwisted silk filaments. **b.** embroidery thread of silk or fine cotton. 2. silky, filamentous matter, as the silk of corn. 3. DENTAL FLOSS. —v.i. 4. to use dental floss. —v.t. 5. to clean (the teeth) with dental floss.

floss′y, adj., **-i•er, -i•est.** 1. made of or resembling floss. 2. showily stylish; fancy.

flo•ta•tion (flō tā′shən), n. the act, process, or state of floating.

flo•til•la (flō til′ə), n., pl. **-las.** 1. a group of small ships. 2. a large group moving together.

flot•sam (flot′səm), n. wreckage of a ship and its cargo found floating on the water.

flounce¹ (flouns), v., **flounced, flounc•ing,** n. —v.i. 1. to go with exaggerated, impatient, or impetuous movements. 2. to throw the body about; flounder. —n. 3. an act or instance of flouncing.

flounce² (flouns), n. a strip of gathered or pleated material attached along one edge, as to the bottom of a skirt.

floun•der¹ (floun′dər), v.i., 1. to struggle to gain one's balance or to move. 2. to act or speak clumsily, helplessly, or falteringly.

floun•der² (floun′dər), n., pl. **-ders, -der.** any of various flatfishes valued as food.

flour (flouªr, flou′ər), n. 1. the finely ground meal of grain, esp. wheat. 2. a fine, soft powder resembling flour. —v.t. 3. to sprinkle or coat with flour. —**flour′y,** adj.

flour•ish (flûr′ish, flur′-), v.i. 1. to be in a vigorous state; thrive. 2. to be at the height of development. 3. to be successful; prosper. —v.t. 4. to brandish dramatically. —n. 5. a dramatic gesture or display. 6. a decoration or embellishment, esp. in writing. 7. an elaborate musical passage; fanfare. —**flour′ish•er,** n.

flout (flout), v.t., v.i. to treat with or show disdain or scorn; scoff (at). —**flout′er,** n. —**Usage.** See FLAUNT.

flow (flō), v.i. 1. to move in a stream. 2. to circulate, as blood. 3. to stream forth. 4. to issue from a source. 5. to proceed smoothly or easily. 6. to hang loosely and gracefully. 7. to abound. 8. to rise and advance, as the tide. —v.t. 9. to cause or permit to flow. —n. 10. the act of flowing. 11. movement in or as if in a stream. 12. the rate or volume of flow. 13.

something that flows. 14. an overflow; flood. 15. the rise of the tide. 16. a transference of energy.

flow′ chart′, n. a graphic representation of the successive steps in a procedure or system.

flow•er (flou′ər), n. 1. the blossom of a plant. 2. the part of a seed plant comprising the reproductive organs. 3. a plant cultivated for its blossom. 4. a state of efflorescence or bloom. 5. the finest or most flourishing period. 6. the best or finest member, product, or example. —v.i. 7. to produce flowers; blossom. 8. to develop fully; mature. —**flow′ered,** adj.

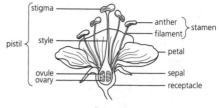

flower

flow′er•pot′, n. a container in which to grow plants.

flow′er•y, adj., **-i•er, -i•est.** 1. covered with or full of flowers. 2. rhetorically ornate or precious. —**flow′er•i•ness,** n.

flown (flōn), v. a pp. of FLY¹.

fl. oz., fluid ounce.

flu (flōō), n. influenza.

flub (flub), v.t., v.i., **flubbed, flub•bing.** to botch or bungle.

fluc•tu•ate (fluk′chōō āt′), v.i., **-at•ed, -at•ing.** to shift back and forth; vary irregularly. —**fluc′tu•a′tion,** n.

flue (flōō), n. a passage or duct for smoke, air, or gas.

flu•ent (flōō′ənt), adj. 1. spoken with ease: fluent French. 2. able to speak smoothly or readily. 3. flowing or capable of flowing: fluid. —**flu′en•cy,** n. —**flu′ent•ly,** adv.

fluff (fluf), n. 1. light, downy particles, as of cotton. 2. a soft, light, downy mass. 3. something light or frivolous. 4. a mistake, esp. an actor's memory lapse. —v.t., v.i. 5. to make or become fluffy. 6. to make a mistake (in).

fluff′y, adj., **-i•er, -i•est.** 1. of, like, or covered with fluff. 2. light or airy. 3. superficial or frivolous. —**fluff′i•ness,** n.

flu•id (flōō′id), n. 1. a substance, as a liquid or gas, that is capable of flowing and changing its shape when acted upon by a force. —adj. 2. flowing or capable of flowing. 3. not fixed or rigid: Our plans are fluid. 4. convertible into cash: fluid assets. —**flu•id′i•ty,** n. —**flu′id•ly,** adv.

flu′id ounce′, n. a measure of capacity equal to 1. 8047 cubic inches (29.573 milliliters) in the U.S. and to 1.7339 cubic inches (28.413 milliliters) in Great Britain.

fluke¹ (flōōk), n. 1. the part of an anchor that catches in the ground. 2. a barbed head, as of a spear. 3. either half of the tail of a whale.

fluke² (flōōk), n. a stroke of good luck. —**fluk′y,** adj., **-i•er, -i•est.**

fluke³ (flōōk), n. 1. any of several American flounders. 2. TREMATODE.

flume (flōōm), n. 1. a deep, narrow gorge containing a stream or torrent. 2. an artificial channel or trough for conducting water.

flum•mox (flum′əks), v.t. Informal. to confound; confuse.

flung (flung), v. pt. and pp. of FLING.

flunk (flungk), v.i., v.t. to fail, esp. in a course or examination.

flun•ky or **-key** (flung′kē), n., pl. **-kies** or **-keys.** 1. a liveried male servant. 2. one who does menial work. 3. a servile follower.

fluo·resce (flŏŏ res′, flô-), *v.i.*, **-resced, -resc·ing.** to exhibit fluorescence.

fluo·res′cence, *n.* **1.** the emission of radiation, esp. of visible light, by a substance during exposure to external radiation, as light or x-rays. **2.** the radiation so produced. **—fluo·res′cent,** *adj.*

fluores′cent lamp′, *n.* a tubular electric lamp in which light is produced by the fluorescence of phosphors coating the inside of the tube.

fluor·i·date (flŏŏr′i dāt′, flôr′-), *v.t.*, **-dat·ed, -dat·ing.** to add fluorides to (a water supply) to reduce tooth decay. **—fluor′i·da′tion,** *n.*

fluor′ide (-īd), *n.* a compound containing fluorine.

fluor′ine (-ēn), *n.* the most reactive nonmetallic element, a pale yellow, corrosive, toxic gas. *Symbol:* F; *at. wt.:* 18.9984; *at. no.:* 9.

fluo·rite (flŏŏr′īt, flôr′-), *n.* a mineral occurring in crystals.

fluor·o·car·bon (flŏŏr′ō kär′bən, flôr′-), *n.* any of a class of compounds containing fluorine and carbon and used chiefly as a lubricant and refrigerant.

fluor′o·scope′ (-ə skōp′), *n.* a device for viewing objects, esp. deep body structures, by means of x-rays. **—fluor′o·scop′ic** (-skop′ik), *adj.*

flur·ry (flûr′ē, flur′ē), *n.*, *pl.* **-ries,** *v.*, **-ried, -ry·ing.** **—n.** **1.** a light, brief shower of snow. **2.** sudden commotion, excitement, or bustle. **3.** a sudden gust of wind. **—v.t.** **4.** to make confused or agitated. **—v.i.** **5.** to move in a confused or agitated manner. [b. of *flutter* and *hurry*]

flush¹ (flush), *n.* **1.** a rosy glow; blush. **2.** a rushing flow, as of water. **3.** a sudden rise, esp. of emotion. **4.** glowing freshness or vigor. **5.** a sensation of heat. **—v.t.** **6.** to cause to blush. **7.** to wash out by a sudden rush of water. **8.** to excite; inflame. **—v.i.** **9.** to blush. **10.** to flow and spread suddenly with a rush.

flush² (flush), *adj.* **1.** even or level with an adjoining surface. **2.** in direct contact; immediately adjacent. **3.** well supplied, esp. with money. **4.** ruddy or reddish in color. **5.** full of vigor. **6.** full to overflowing. **7.** even with the right or left margin of a type page. **—adv.** **8.** so as to be on the same level or plane or in direct contact. **—v.t.** **9.** to make flush.

flush³ (flush), *v.t.* to cause to start up or fly off suddenly: *to flush a woodcock.*

flush⁴ (flush), *n.* a hand of cards all of one suit.

flus·ter (flus′tər), *v.t.* to put into a state of nervous or agitated confusion.

flute (flŏŏt), *n.* **1.** a wind instrument with a high range, consisting of a tube with a series of fingerholes or keys. **2.** a groove, as on the shaft of a column. **—flut′ed,** *adj.* **—flut′ing,** *n.*

flut′ist, *n.* a flute player.

flut·ter (flut′ər), *v.i.* **1.** to wave or flap about. **2.** to flap the wings rapidly. **3.** to move with quick, irregular motions. **4.** to beat rapidly, as the heart. **5.** to be tremulous or agitated. **—v.t.** **6.** to cause to flutter. **—n.** **7.** a fluttering movement. **8.** a state of nervous excitement or mental agitation. **9.** a stir; flurry. **—flut′ter·y,** *adj.*

flux (fluks), *n.* **1.** a flowing or flow. **2.** continuous change. **3.** a substance used to prevent oxidation of fused metal, as in soldering. **4.** an abnormal discharge of liquid matter from the bowels. **—v.t.** **5.** to make fluid; melt. **6.** to fuse with flux.

fly¹ (flī), *v.*, **flew** or, for 8, **flied, flown, fly·ing,** *n.*, *pl.* **flies.** **—v.i.** **1.** to move through the air using wings. **2.** to be carried through the air. **3.** to float or flutter in the air. **4.** to travel in or operate an aircraft or spacecraft. **5.** to move suddenly and quickly. **6.** to flee; escape. **7.** to pass swiftly. **8.** to bat a fly ball in baseball. **—v.t.** **9.** to cause to float or move through the air. **10.** to operate (an aircraft or spacecraft). **11.** to operate an aircraft over. **12.** to transport by air. **13.** to escape from. **—n.** **14.** a fold of material that conceals fasteners in a garment opening. **15.** a flap forming the door of a tent. **16.** an act of flying; flight. **17.** FLY BALL. **18.** flies, the space above the stage of a theater. **—Idiom.** **19. on the fly, a.** while in the air. **b.** without pausing. **—fly′a·ble,** *adj.*

fly² (flī), *n.*, *pl.* **flies.** **1.** any of numerous two-winged insects, esp. the common housefly. **2.** a fishhook dressed to resemble an insect.

fly′ ball′, *n.* a baseball batted high into the air.

fly′blown′, *adj.* tainted or contaminated; spoiled.

fly′by′ or **fly′-by′,** *n.*, *pl.* **-bys.** a flight of a spacecraft close enough to a celestial object to gather scientific data.

fly′-by-night′, *adj.* **1.** not reliable or stable, esp. in business. **2.** not lasting; transitory.

fly′catch′er, *n.* a bird that catches insects in the air.

fly·er (flī′ər), *n.* FLIER.

fly′ing but′tress, *n.* an arch or segment of an arch projecting from and supporting a wall.

fly′ing col′ors, *n.pl.* outstanding success; triumph.

fly′ing fish′, *n.* a fish with winglike fins that enable it to glide for some distance in the air.

fly′ing sau′cer, *n.* any of various disk-shaped objects reportedly seen flying at high speeds and altitudes.

fly′ing squir′rel, *n.* a tree squirrel with extensible folds of skin that permit long, gliding leaps.

fly′leaf′, *n.*, *pl.* **-leaves.** a blank leaf in the front or the back of a book.

fly′pa′per, *n.* paper that catches flies on its sticky, often poisonous surface.

fly′speck′, *n.* **1.** a speck of fly excrement. **2.** something minute.

fly′way′, *n.* a route taken by migrating birds.

fly′weight′, *n.* a boxer or weightlifter weighing up to 112 lb. (51 kg).

fly′wheel′, *n.* a heavy wheel that rotates on a shaft and regulates the speed of the shaft and connected machinery.

FM, 1. frequency modulation: a method of impressing a signal on a radio carrier wave by varying the frequency of the carrier wave. **2.** a system of radio broadcasting using FM.

Fm, *Chem. Symbol.* fermium.

f′-num′ber, *n.* a number corresponding to the ratio of the focal length to the diameter of a lens system, esp. a camera lens.

foal (fōl), *n.* **1.** the nursing young of a mammal of the horse family. **—v.i.** **2.** to give birth to a foal.

foam (fōm), *n.* **1.** a collection of minute bubbles formed on the surface of a liquid. **2.** a thick, frothy substance, as shaving cream. **3.** a lightweight material, as foam rubber, in which gas bubbles are dispersed in a solid. **—v.i.** **4.** to form or gather foam; froth. **—foam′y,** *adj.* **-i·er, -i·est.**

foam′ rub′ber, *n.* spongy rubber used esp. for mattresses and cushions.

fob¹ (fob), *n.* **1.** a short chain or ribbon attached to a pocket watch. **2.** an ornament on a fob.

fob² (fob), *v.t.*, **fobbed, fob·bing. fob off,** to dispose of (something inferior) by deception or trickery; palm off.

fob or **FOB,** free on board.

fo·cal (fō′kəl), *adj.* of or being a focus. **—fo′cal·ly,** *adv.*

fo′cal length′, *n.* the distance from the center of a lens or mirror to the focus.

fo′c's'le or **fo′c'sle** (fōk′səl), *n.* FORECASTLE.

fo·cus (fō′kəs), *n.*, *pl.* **-cus·es, -ci** (-sī, -kī), *v.*, **-cused, -cus·ing** or (*esp. Brit.*) **-cussed, -cus·sing.** **—n.** **1.** a central point, as of attraction, attention, or activity. **2.** a point at which rays of light, heat, etc., meet after being refracted or reflected. **3. a.** FOCAL LENGTH. **b.** the adjustment of an optical device necessary to produce a clear image: *in focus; out of focus.* **—v.t.** **4.** to bring to a focus or into focus. **5.** to concentrate. **—v.i.** **6.** to become focused.

fo′cus group′, *n.* a representative group of people questioned together, usually in a controlled setting, about their opinions on issues of politics, product marketing, etc.

fod·der (fod′ər), *n.* coarse food for livestock.

foe (fō), *n.* **1.** an enemy. **2.** an opponent, as in a contest.

foe•tus (fē′təs), *n., pl.* **-tus•es.** FETUS. **—foe′tal,** *adj.*

fog (fog, fôg), *n., v.,* **fogged, fog•ging. —***n.* **1.** a cloudlike mass or layer of minute water droplets near the surface of the earth, appreciably reducing visibility. **2.** a state of mental confusion. —*v.t., v.i.* **3.** to envelop or become enveloped with or as if with fog. **—fog′gy,** *adj.,* **-gi•er, -gi•est.**

fog′horn′, *n.* a horn for sounding warnings to ships in foggy weather.

fo•gy or **-gey** (fō′gē), *n., pl.* **-gies** or **-geys.** an old-fashioned or conservative person. **—fo′gy•ish,** *adj.*

foi•ble (foi′bəl), *n.* a minor weakness or failing of character.

foil[1] (foil), *v.t.* to prevent the success of; frustrate or thwart.

foil[2] (foil), *n.* **1.** metal in the form of very thin sheets: *aluminum foil.* **2.** a person or thing that makes another seem better by contrast.

foil[3] (foil), *n.* a flexible four-sided fencing sword with a blunt point.

foist (foist), *v.t.* to impose fraudulently; palm off.

fol., **1.** folio. **2.** followed. **3.** following.

fold[1] (fōld), *v.t.* **1.** to bend (cloth, paper, etc.) over upon itself. **2.** to make compact by folding: *She folded up the map.* **3.** to bring together and intertwine or cross. **4.** to bring (wings) close to the body, as a bird. **5.** to enclose, wrap, or envelop. **6.** to embrace. **7.** to blend (a cooking ingredient) into a mixture by turning one part over another. —*v.i.* **8.** to be folded. **9.** to fail, esp. to go out of business. —*n.* **10.** a part, as a pleat, that is folded. **11.** a line, crease, or hollow made by folding. **—fold′a•ble,** *adj.*

fold[2] (fōld), *n.* **1.** an enclosure for sheep. **2.** a flock of sheep. **3.** a group sharing common beliefs or values.

-fold, a combining form meaning: having a specified number of parts (*a fourfold plan*); multiplied the number of times specified (to increase *tenfold*).

fold′a•way′, *adj.* designed to be folded out of the way: *a foldaway bed.*

fold′er, *n.* **1.** a folded sheet of light cardboard used to hold papers. **2.** a printed sheet, as a circular, folded into a number of pages like sections.

fo•li•age (fō′lē ij), *n.* leaves, as of a tree or plant.

fo′lic ac′id (fō′lik, fol′ik), *n.* a vitamin of the vitamin B complex, used in treating anemia.

fo•li•o (fō′lē ō′), *n., pl.* **-li•os. 1. a.** a sheet of paper folded once to make two leaves, or four pages, of a book. **b.** a book having pages of the largest size, formerly made from such a sheet. **2.** a page number in a book.

folk (fōk), *n.* **1.** Usu., **folks.** (*used with a pl. v.*) people in general. **2.** Often, **folks.** (*used with a pl. v.*) people of a specified class or group: *poor folks.* **3.** (*used with a pl. v.*) a group of people as the carriers of a society's customs and traditions. **4. folks,** *Informal.* the members of one's family; relatives. —*adj.* **5.** of or originating among the common people: *folk music.*

folk′lore′, *n.* the traditional beliefs, legends, and customs of a people. **—folk′lor′ic,** *adj.* **—folk′lor′-ist,** *n.* **—folk′lor•is′tic,** *adj.*

folk′ song′, *n.* **1.** a song originating among the common people and marked by simple melody and stanzaic, narrative verse. **2.** a song of similar character written by a known composer. **—folk′ sing′er,** *n.*

folk′sy, *adj.,* **-si•er, -si•est. 1.** friendly; sociable. **2.** informal; unceremonious. **—folk′si•ness,** *n.*

foll., following.

fol•li•cle (fol′i kəl), *n. Anatomy.* a small cavity, sac, or gland.

fol•low (fol′ō), *v.t.* **1.** to come after in sequence or order; succeed. **2.** to go or come after. **3.** to act in accordance with; obey. **4.** to result from. **5.** to go in pursuit of. **6.** to engage in as a pursuit. **7.** to keep up with and understand. —*v.i.* **8.** to come next after something else in sequence or order. **9.** to occur as a consequence. **10. follow through,** to continue a mo-

tion, stroke, activity, or undertaking to its completion.

fol′low•er, *n.* **1.** one that follows. **2.** a disciple or adherent. **3.** an attendant, servant, or retainer.

fol′low•ing, *n.* **1.** a body of followers, adherents, admirers, or patrons. —*adj.* **2.** next in order or time; ensuing. **3.** that is now to follow.

fol′low-up′, *n.* something, as a letter or visit, that serves to reinforce the effectiveness of a previous action.

fol•ly (fol′ē), *n., pl.* **-lies. 1.** lack of understanding or sense. **2.** a foolish action, practice, or idea. **3.** a costly and foolish undertaking.

fo•ment (fō ment′), *v.t.* to foster; instigate: *to foment trouble.* **—fo′men•ta′tion,** *n.* **—fo•ment′er,** *n.*

fond (fond), *adj.,* **-er, -est. 1.** having a liking or affection: *fond of animals.* **2.** loving; affectionate. **3.** excessively tender; doting. **4.** cherished: *fond hopes.* **—fond′ly,** *adv.* **—fond′ness,** *n.*

fon•dant (fon′dənt), *n.* **1.** a thick, creamy sugar paste. **2.** a candy made of fondant.

fon•dle (fon′dl), *v.t.,* **-dled, -dling.** to handle or touch lovingly; caress. **—fon′dler,** *n.*

fon•due (fon dōō′, -dyōō′), *n.* a dish consisting of melted cheese, often with brandy, served hot with pieces of bread for dipping.

font[1] (font), *n.* **1.** a receptacle for holy water, esp. that used in baptism. **2.** a productive source.

font[2] (font), *n. Print.* a complete set of type of one style and size.

food (fōōd), *n.* **1.** a substance that is taken into the body to sustain life, provide energy, and promote growth. **2.** solid nourishment as distinguished from liquids. **3.** a particular kind of nourishment: *dog food.* **4.** something serving for consumption or use: *food for thought.*

food′ chain′, *n. Ecol.* a series of interrelated organisms in which the smallest is fed upon by a larger one, which in turn feeds a still larger one.

food′ court′, *n.* a space, as in a shopping mall, with a concentration of fast-food stalls and usu. a common eating area.

food′ie, *n. Slang.* a person keenly interested in food, esp. a gourmet.

food′ poi′soning, *n.* an illness caused by eating toxic or contaminated food.

food′ proc′essor, *n.* an electric appliance with interchangeable blades that can chop, shred, or otherwise process food at high speed.

food′ stamp′, *n.* a coupon sold or given under a federal program to eligible needy persons and redeemable for food at designated stores or markets.

food′stuff′, *n.* a substance capable of being used as food.

fool (fōōl), *n.* **1.** a silly or stupid person. **2.** a court jester. **3.** a person who has been tricked into appearing foolish. —*v.t.* **4.** to trick or deceive. —*v.i.* **5.** to act like a fool. **6.** to jest; joke. **7. fool around,** to putter aimlessly. **b.** to trifle or flirt. **8. ~ with,** to play with idly. [< OF < L *follis* bellows, bag]

fool′er•y, *n., pl.* **-er•ies. 1.** foolish action or conduct. **2.** a foolish act.

fool′har′dy, *adj.,* **-di•er, -di•est.** recklessly bold; rash. **—fool′har′di•ly,** *adv.* **—fool′har′di•ness,** *n.*

fool′ish, *adj.* **1.** resulting from or showing a lack of sense; unwise. **2.** silly; ridiculous; absurd. **—fool′-ish•ly,** *adv.* **—fool′ish•ness,** *n.*

fool′proof′, *adj.* **1.** involving no risk or harm even when tampered with. **2.** never-failing: *a foolproof method.*

fools•cap (fōōlz′kap′), *n.* a type of writing paper, esp. legal-size sheets bound in tablet form.

fool′s′ gold′, *n.* iron or copper pyrites, sometimes mistaken for gold.

fool′s′ par′adise, *n.* a state of illusory happiness.

foot (fōōt), *n., pl.* **feet,** *v.* —*n.* **1.** the terminal part of the leg on which the body stands. **2.** a part similar to a foot in position or function. **3.** a unit of length equal to 12 inches or 30.48 centimeters. **4.** the part, as of a stocking or sock, covering the foot. **5.** the lowest part, as of a hill; bottom. **6.** the part of something opposite the top or head. **7.** a group of syllables constituting a metrical unit of verse. —*v.i.* **8.** to go on foot; walk. **9.** to move the feet rhythmically, esp. in dance. —*v.t.* **10.** to pay or settle: *to foot the bill.* —*Idiom.* **11. on foot,** by walking or running. **12. under foot,** in the way.

foot′age (-ij), *n.* length or extent in feet.

foot′-and-mouth′ disease′, *n.* a contagious viral disease of hoofed animals, esp. cattle, characterized by blisters in the mouth and about the hoofs.

foot′ball′, *n.* **1.** a game in which two opposing teams of 11 players each defend goals at opposite ends of a field. **2.** the ball used in football. **3.** *Chiefly Brit.* **a.** RUGBY. **b.** SOCCER.

foot′bridge′, *n.* a bridge for pedestrians only.

foot′-can′dle, *n.* a unit equivalent to the illumination produced by a source of one candle at a distance of one foot.

foot′ed, *adj.* having a foot or feet: *a footed goblet; a four-footed animal.*

foot′fall′, *n.* the sound of a footstep.

foot′hill′, *n.* a low hill at the base of a mountain.

foot′hold′, *n.* **1.** a support for the feet. **2.** a firm basis for further progress.

foot′ing, *n.* **1.** a basis; foundation. **2.** a place or support for the foot; foothold. **3.** a firm placing of the feet; stability. **4.** mutual standing; status. **5. a.** the act of adding up a column of figures. **b.** the total of such a column.

foot′-in-mouth′ disease′, *n.* *Informal.* a tendency to use ill-chosen words.

foot′less, *adj.* **1.** lacking feet. **2.** having no basis; unsubstantial. **3.** awkward or inefficient.

foot′lights′, *n.pl.* **1.** the lights at the front of a stage floor. **2.** the acting profession.

foot′lock′er, *n.* a small trunk kept at the foot of a bed.

foot′loose′, *adj.* free to go or travel about.

foot′man, *n.,* *pl.* **-men.** a household servant who ranks below a butler.

foot′note′, *n.* **1.** an explanatory note, comment, or reference at the bottom of a page. **2.** a minor or tangential comment or event.

foot′path′, *n.* a path for people going on foot.

foot′-pound′, *n.* a unit of energy equal to the energy expended in raising one pound a distance of one foot.

foot′print′, *n.* a mark left by the foot, as in earth.

foot′rest′, *n.* a support for the feet.

foot′ sol′dier, *n.* an infantryman.

foot′sore′, *adj.* having sore or tender feet, as from much walking.

foot′step′, *n.* **1. a.** the setting down of a foot. **b.** the sound so produced. **2.** the distance covered by a footstep. **3.** FOOTPRINT.

foot′stool′, *n.* a low stool upon which to rest the feet.

foot′wear′, *n.* articles, as shoes, to be worn on the feet.

foot′work′, *n.* the use of the feet, as in tennis.

fop (fop), *n.* a man excessively concerned with his clothes; dandy. —**fop′per•y,** *n.* —**fop′pish,** *adj.* —**fop′pish•ness,** *n.*

for (fôr; *unstressed* fər), *prep.* **1.** with the purpose of: *He runs for exercise.* **2.** intended to benefit or be used by: *equipment for the baseball team; medicine for the aged.* **3.** in order to obtain: *to work for a salary.* **4.** in return for: *three for a dollar.* **5.** appropriate or adapted to: *clothes for travel.* **6.** with respect to: *pressed for time.* **7.** during the continuance of: *for two years.* **8.** in favor of: *rooted for the home team.* **9.** instead of: *a substitute for butter.* **10.** on behalf of: *to act for a client.* **11.** in exchange for: *blow for blow.* **12.** in honor of: *to give a dinner for a friend.* **13.** with the purpose of reaching: *to start for home.* **14.** in consideration of: *tall for his age.* **15.** as being: *knew it for a fact.* **16.** because of: *to shout for joy.* **17.** in spite of: *They're decent people for all their*

faults. **18.** to the extent of: *to walk for a mile.* **19.** (used to introduce a subject in an infinitive phrase): *It's time for me to go.* —*conj.* **20.** because.

for•age (fôr′ij, for′-), *n., v.,* **-aged, -ag•ing.** —*n.* **1.** food for horses or cattle; fodder. **2.** the seeking or obtaining of forage. —*v.i.* **3.** to wander or go in search of provisions. **4.** to search about; rummage. —*v.t.* **5.** to collect forage from. **6.** to obtain by foraging. —**for′ag•er,** *n.*

for•ay (fôr′ā, for′ā), *n.* **1.** a quick raid, usu. for spoils. **2.** a venture or attempt. —*v.i.* **3.** to make a raid.

for•bear¹ (fôr bâr′), *v.,* **-bore, -borne, -bear•ing.** —*v.t.* **1.** to refrain from. —*v.i.* **2.** to be patient or self-controlled. —**for•bear′ance,** *n.* —**for•bear′er,** *n.*

for•bear² (fôr′bâr′), *n.* FOREBEAR.

for•bid (fər bid′, fôr-), *v.t.,* **-bade** or **-bad** or **-bid, -bid•den** or **-bid, -bid•ding. 1.** to command (a person) not to do something. **2.** to prohibit (something); bar. **3.** to make impossible; prevent.

forbid′den fruit′, *n.* **1.** the fruit of the tree of knowledge of good and evil, tasted by Adam and Eve. Gen. 2:17; 3:3. **2.** any unlawful pleasure.

for•bid′ding, *adj.* **1.** grim; threatening. **2.** daunting; discouraging. —**for•bid′ding•ly,** *adv.*

force (fôrs), *n., v.,* **forced, forc•ing.** —*n.* **1.** physical power or strength. **2.** physical coercion; violence. **3.** vigor; energy. **4.** power to influence, convince, or persuade. **5.** Often, **forces.** military or fighting strength, esp. of a nation. **6.** a body of persons combined for joint action: *a sales force.* **7.** *Physics.* an influence on a body or system producing or tending to produce a change in movement or shape. —*v.t.* **8.** to compel to do something. **9.** to drive or propel against resistance. **10.** to bring about or effect by force. **11.** to bring about of necessity. **12.** to obtain by or as if by force. **13.** to break open: *forced the lock.* **14.** to cause (plants, fruits, etc.) to grow or mature at an increased rate by artificial means. —*Idiom.* **15. in force, a.** in operation; effective. **b.** in large numbers. —**forc′er,** *n.*

force′-feed′, *v.t.,* **-fed, -feed•ing. 1.** to compel to take food. **2.** to compel to absorb or assimilate.

force′ful, *adj.* full of force; powerful. —**force′ful•ly,** *adv.* —**force′ful•ness,** *n.*

for•ceps (fôr′saps, -seps), *n., pl.* **-ceps.** an instrument resembling pincers for seizing and holding objects firmly, as in surgical operations.

for•ci•ble (fôr′sə bəl), *adj.* **1.** done or effected by force. **2.** having or showing force; powerful. —**for′ci•bly,** *adv.*

ford (fôrd), *n.* **1.** a place where a body of water can be crossed by wading. —*v.t.* **2.** to cross at a ford. —**ford′a•ble,** *adj.*

Ford, *n.* **1. Gerald R(udolph, Jr.),** born 1913, 38th president of the U.S. 1974–77. **2. Henry,** 1863–1947, U.S. automobile manufacturer.

fore¹ (fôr), *adj.* **1.** situated in front. **2.** first in place, time, order, or rank. —*adv.* **3.** at or toward the bow of a ship. **4.** forward. —*n.* **5.** the front.

fore² (fôr), *interj.* a cry of warning on a golf course to persons in danger of being struck by a ball.

fore-, a prefix meaning: before (*forewarn*); front (*forehead*); preceding (*forefather*); superior (*foreman*).

fore′-and-aft′, *adj.* *Naut.* located along or parallel to a line from the stem to the stern.

fore′arm′¹, *n.* the part of the arm between the elbow and the wrist.

fore•arm′², *v.t.,* to arm beforehand; prepare.

fore′bear′, *n.* an ancestor; forefather.

fore•bode′, *v.t.,* **-bod•ed, -bod•ing. 1.** to foretell; portend. **2.** to have a presentiment of. —**fore•bod′-ing,** *n.*

fore′cast′, *v.,* **-cast** or **-cast•ed, -cast•ing,** *n.* —*v.t.* **1.** to predict (a future condition or occurrence). **2.** to serve as a prediction of; foreshadow. —*n.* **3.** a prediction, esp. of weather conditions. —**fore′cast′er,** *n.*

fore•cas•tle (fōk′səl, fôr′kas/əl, -kä′səl), *n.* **1.** a superstructure at or immediately aft of the bow of a ship. **2.** sailors' quarters located in the forward part of a ship.

fore•close′ (-klōz′), v., **-closed, -closing.** —v.t. **1.** to deprive (a mortgagor) of the right to redeem a property, esp. after a default in mortgage payments. **2.** to shut out; exclude. —v.i. **3.** to foreclose a mortgage.

fore•clo′sure, n. the act of foreclosing a mortgage.

fore•doom′, v.t. to doom beforehand.

fore′fa′ther, n. an ancestor; progenitor.

fore′fin′ger, n. the finger next to the thumb.

fore′foot′, n., pl. **-feet.** one of the front feet esp. of a quadruped.

fore′front′, n. **1.** the foremost part or place. **2.** the leading position; vanguard.

fore•go′¹, v.t., v.i., **-went, -gone, -go•ing.** to go before; precede.

fore•go′², v.t., **-went, -gone, -go•ing.** FORGO.

fore•go′ing, adj. previous; preceding.

fore′gone (fôr gôn′, -gon′, fōr′gôn′, -gon′), adj. having gone before; past.

fore′gone′ conclu′sion, n. an inevitable conclusion or result.

fore′ground′, n. **1.** the portion of a scene nearest to the viewer. **2.** a prominent position.

fore′hand′, adj. **1.** of or being a stroke, as in tennis, made with the palm of the hand facing the direction of movement. —n. **2.** a forehand stroke.

fore′head (fôr′id, for′-; fôr′hed′, for′-), n. the part of the face above the eyebrows.

for•eign (fôr′in, for′-), adj. **1.** of or from another country or nation. **2.** of contact or dealings with other countries. **3.** external to one's own country or nation. **4.** not belonging to the place or body where found. **5.** not related or connected; irrelevant.

for′eign•er, n. a person from a foreign country.

for′eign min′ister, n. a cabinet minister who conducts and supervises foreign affairs.

fore•knowl•edge (fôr′nol′ij), n. knowledge of something before it exists or happens; prescience. —**fore•know′,** v.t., **-knew, -known, -know•ing.**

fore′leg′, n. one of the front legs esp. of a quadruped.

fore′limb′, n. a front limb of an animal.

fore′lock′, n. a lock of hair that grows from the front part of the head.

fore′man or **-wom′an** or **-per′son,** n., pl. **-men** or **-wom•en** or **-per•sons. 1.** a person in charge of a department or group of workers. **2.** the chairperson of a jury.

fore′mast′, n. the mast nearest the bow of a ship.

fore′most′, adj., adv. first in place, rank, or importance.

fore•moth•er (fôr′muth′ər, fōr′-), n. a female ancestor.

fore′name′, n. a first name.

fore′named′, adj. named or mentioned before.

fore′noon′, n. the period of day before noon.

fo•ren•sic (fə ren′sik), adj. of, suited to, or used in courts of law or in public debate. —**fo•ren′si•cal•ly,** adv.

fore′or•dain′, v.t. to ordain or appoint beforehand; predestine.

fore′part′, n. the first, front, or early part.

fore′play′, n. sexual stimulation leading to intercourse.

fore′quar′ter, n. the forward end of half of a carcass, as of beef.

fore′run′ner, n. **1.** a predecessor or ancestor. **2.** an indication of something to follow; portent or harbinger.

fore′sail′ (-sāl′; Naut. -səl), n. the lowermost sail on a foremast.

fore•see′, v.t., **-saw, -seen, -see•ing.** to see or know in advance. —**fore•see′a•ble,** adj. —**fore•se′er,** n.

fore•shad′ow, v.t. to show or indicate beforehand. —**fore•shad′ow•er,** n.

fore•short′en, v.t. to reduce or distort (a repre-

sented object) in order to convey the illusion of depth.

fore′sight′, n. **1.** care or provision for the future. **2.** the act or power of foreseeing. **3.** an act of looking forward. —**fore′sight′ed,** adj. —**fore′sight′ed•ness,** n.

fore′skin′, n. the prepuce.

for•est (fôr′ist, for′-), n. **1.** a large tract of land covered with trees and underbrush. —v.t. **2.** to supply or cover with trees. —*Saying.* **3.** not see the forest for the trees, to fail to perceive the complete picture because of one's excessive attention to detail. —**for′est•ed,** adj.

fore•stall′, v.t. to prevent, hinder, or thwart by action in advance. **2.** to deal with or realize beforehand; anticipate. —**fore•stall′ment,** n.

for•est•a•tion (fôr′ə stā′shən, for′-), n. the planting of forests.

for′est•er, n. an expert in forestry.

for′est rang′er, n. an officer who supervises the care and preservation of forests, esp. public forests.

for′est•ry, n. the science of planting and taking care of forests.

fore•taste (n. fôr′tāst′; v. fôr tāst′), n., v., **-tast•ed, -tast•ing.** —n. **1.** a taste or sample of something to come. —v.t. **2.** to have a foretaste of.

fore•tell′, v.t., **-told, -tell•ing.** to tell of beforehand. —**fore•tell′er,** n.

fore′thought′, n. **1.** thoughtful advance provision. **2.** previous consideration or planning.

for•ev•er (fôr ev′ər, fər-), adv. **1.** without ever ending; eternally. **2.** without stopping; continually.

for•ev′er•more′, adv. forever hereafter.

fore•warn′, v.t. to warn in advance.

fore′word′, n. an introductory statement in a published work, as a book.

for•feit (fôr′fit), n. **1.** a fine or penalty. **2.** the act of forfeiting. **3.** something to which the right is lost, as for commission of a crime. —v.t. **4.** to lose as a forfeit.

for′fei•ture (-fi chər), n. **1.** the act of forfeiting. **2.** something forfeited.

for•gath′er, v.i. to gather together; convene.

for•gave (fər gāv′), v. pt. of FORGIVE.

forge¹ (fôrj), v., **forged, forg•ing,** n. —v.t. **1.** to shape (metal) by heating and hammering. **2.** to fashion, esp. by concentrated effort: *to forge a treaty.* **3.** to imitate fraudulently: *Someone forged his signature.* —n. **4.** a fireplace, hearth, or furnace in which metal is heated before shaping. —**forg′er,** n. —**forg′er•y,** n., pl. **-er•ies.**

forge² (fôrj), v.i., **forged, forg•ing. 1.** to move ahead slowly but steadily. **2.** to move ahead with increased speed and effectiveness.

for•get (fər get′), v., **-got, -got•ten** or **-got, -get•ting.** —v.t. **1.** to be unable to recall. **2.** to omit or neglect unintentionally. **3.** to fail to think of. —v.i. **4.** to cease or fail to think of something. —*Idiom.* **5.** forget oneself, to say or do something improper. —**for•get′ta•ble,** adj.

for•get′ful, adj. **1.** apt to forget. **2.** heedless; neglectful: *forgetful of others.* —**for•get′ful•ly,** adv. —**for•get′ful•ness,** n.

forget′-me-not′, n. a small plant with light blue flowers.

forg•ing (fôr′jing), n. a piece of forged work in metal.

for•give (fər giv′), v., **-gave, -giv•en, -giv•ing.** —v.t. **1.** to grant pardon for or to. **2.** to cancel (a debt or payment). **3.** to cease to feel resentment against. —v.i. **4.** to grant pardon. —**for•giv′a•ble,** adj. —**for•give′ness,** n. —**for•giv′er,** n.

for•giv′ing, adj. disposed to forgive.

for•go (fôr gō′), v.t., **-went, -gone, -go•ing.** to abstain or refrain from; give up. —**for•go′er,** n.

fork (fôrk), n. **1.** an instrument with two or more prongs for holding, digging, or lifting, esp. an implement for handling food. **2.** something resembling a fork. **3. a.** a division into branches. **b.** the point at which something branches. **c.** one of the branches.

—*v.t.* **4.** to pierce, raise, pitch, dig, or carry with a fork. —*v.i.* **5.** to divide into branches. **6.** *Informal.*
fork over, to deliver; pay; hand over. —**fork′ful** (-fŏŏl), *n., pl.* **-fuls.**
forked (fôrkt, fôr′kid), *adj.* having or shaped like a fork.
fork′lift′, *n.* a vehicle with two power-operated prongs at the front for lifting and moving heavy loads.
for•lorn (fôr lôrn′), *adj.* **1.** miserable; wretched. **2.** forsaken; desolate. **3.** hopeless; despairing. —**for•lorn′ly,** *adv.*
form (fôrm), *n.* **1.** shape as distinguished from color or material; configuration. **2.** a body, esp. of a human being. **3.** a model of the human body used for fitting or displaying clothing. **4.** a mold. **5.** the mode in which something appears or exists: *water in the form of ice.* **6.** a manner or style of arranging and coordinating parts, as in musical composition. **7.** the formal structure of a work of art. **8.** a kind, type, or variety. **9.** a prescribed or customary order or method of doing something. **10.** a set order of words, as in a legal document. **11.** a document with blank spaces to be filled in with particulars. **12.** procedure according to a set order or method. **13.** conformity to the usages of society; manners. **14.** a manner or method of performing. **15.** physical condition or fitness, as for performing. **16.** a particular shape of a word that occurs in more than one shape. **17.** a grade in a British secondary school or in certain U.S. private schools. —*v.t.* **18.** to construct or frame. **19.** to make or produce. **20.** to serve to make up; constitute. **21.** to arrange; organize. **22.** to frame (ideas, opinions, etc.) in the mind. **23.** to develop (habits, friendships, etc.). **24.** to give a particular form or shape to. **25.** to mold or develop by discipline or instruction. —*v.i.* **26.** to take form. **27.** to take a particular form or arrangement. —**form′less,** *adj.* —**form′less•ness,** *n.*
-form, a combining form meaning having the form of (*cruciform*).
for•mal (fôr′məl), *adj.* **1.** being in accordance with accepted custom; conventional. **2.** marked by form or ceremony. **3. a.** designed for wear or use at ceremonial events. **b.** requiring formal dress. **4.** prim; decorous. **5.** made or done in accordance with procedures that ensure validity. **6.** being such merely in name; nominal. —*n.* **7.** a social occasion, as a dance, that requires formal attire. —**for′mal•ly,** *adv.*
form•al•de•hyde (fôr mal′də hīd′, fər-), *n.* a toxic gas used chiefly as a disinfectant and preservative.
for′mal•ism, *n.* strict adherence to prescribed or traditional forms, as in music. —**for′mal•ist,** *n., adj.*
for•mal′i•ty (-mal′i tē), *n., pl.* **-ties. 1.** the condition or quality of being formal. **2.** strict adherence to established rules and procedures. **3.** a formal act or observance.
for′mal•ize, *v.t.,* **-ized, -iz•ing. 1.** to make formal, esp. for the sake of official acceptance. **2.** to give a definite form or shape to. —**for′mal•i•za′tion,** *n.*
for•mat (fôr′mat), *n., v.,* **-mat•ted, -mat•ting.** —*n.* **1.** the general appearance or style of a book, magazine, or newspaper. **2.** the organization and plan of something. **3.** the arrangement of data for computer input or output. —*v.t.* **4.** to plan or provide a format for. **5.** to produce in a specified format.
for•ma•tion (fôr mā′shən), *n.* **1.** the act or process of forming. **2.** the manner in which something is formed. **3.** an arrangement or disposition, as of troops or airplanes. **4.** something formed.
form•a•tive (fôr′mə tiv), *adj.* **1.** giving or capable of giving form or shape. **2.** pertaining to formation or development.
for•mer (fôr′mər), *adj.* **1.** preceding in time; earlier. **2.** being the first mentioned of two. **3.** having previously been.
for′mer•ly, *adv.* in time past; previously.
form′fit′ting, *adj.* designed to fit snugly.
for•mic (fôr′mik), *adj.* **1.** of ants. **2.** designating a colorless acid found esp. in ants and spiders.
For•mi•ca (fôr mī′kə), *Trademark.* a brand of lami-

nated plastic used esp. as a surface for kitchen counters.
for•mi•da•ble (fôr′mi də bəl *or, sometimes,* fər-mid′ə-), *adj.* **1.** causing fear, awe, or apprehension. **2.** of discouraging difficulty; intimidating. —**for′mi•da•bly,** *adv.*
form′ let′ter, *n.* a standardized letter that can be sent to any number of persons.
For•mo•sa (fôr mō′sə), *n.* TAIWAN.
for•mu•la (fôr′myə lə), *n., pl.* **-las, -lae** (-lē′). **1.** a set form of words, as for prescribed use on a ceremonial occasion. **2.** a conventional method or approach. **3.** a mathematical rule or principle, frequently expressed in algebraic symbols. **4.** an expression of the constituents of a chemical compound by symbols and figures. **5.** a recipe or prescription. **6.** a special nutritive mixture, esp. of milk or milk substitute, for feeding a baby. —**for′mu•la′ic** (-lā′ik), *adj.*
for′mu•late′, *v.t.,* **-lat•ed, -lat•ing. 1.** to express in precise form. **2.** to devise or develop. **3.** to express in a formula. —**for′mu•la′tion,** *n.* —**for′mu•la′tor,** *n.*
for•ni•ca•tion (fôr′ni kā′shən), *n.* **1.** voluntary sexual intercourse between two unmarried persons or two persons not married to each other. **2.** (in the Bible) **a.** adultery. **b.** idolatry. —**for•ni•ca•to•ry** (fôr′-ni kə tôr′ē, -tōr′ē), *adj.*
for•sake (fôr sāk′), *v.t.,* **-sook** (-sŏŏk′), **-sak•en, -sak•ing. 1.** to quit or leave entirely; abandon. **2.** to give up; renounce.
for•sooth (fôr sŏŏth′), *adv. Archaic.* in truth; indeed.
For•ster (fôr′stər), *n.* **E(dward) M(organ),** 1879–1970, English novelist.
for•swear′, *v.,* **-swore, -sworn, -swearing.** —*v.t.* **1.** to renounce under oath. **2.** to deny vehemently or under oath. —*v.i.* **3.** to commit perjury.
for•syth•i•a (fôr sith′ē ə, fər-), *n., pl.* **-syth•i•as.** a shrub bearing yellow flowers that blossom in early spring. [after W. *Forsyth* (1737–1804), English horticulturist]
fort (fôrt), *n.* **1.** a fortified location occupied by troops. **2.** a permanent army post.
forte[1] (fôrt, fôr′tā), *n.* an area in which a person excels; specialty.
for•te[2] (fôr′tā), *Music.* —*adj.* **1.** loud. —*adv.* **2.** loudly.
forth (fôrth), *adv.* **1.** onward, outward, or forward: *to go forth.* **2.** out into view: *Love shines forth in her eyes.*
forth′com′ing, *adj.* **1.** coming or about to come; approaching. **2.** ready or available.
forth′right′, *adj.* going straight to the point; direct; outspoken: *a forthright answer.* —**forth′right′ly,** *adv.* —**forth′right′ness,** *n.*
forth′with′, *adv.* immediately.
for•ti•fy (fôr′tə fī′), *v.t.,* **-fied, -fy•ing. 1.** to increase the defenses of. **2.** to impart strength or vigor to. **3.** to increase the effectiveness of, as by additional ingredients. **4.** to strengthen mentally or morally. —**for′ti•fi•ca′tion,** *n.* —**for′ti•fi′er,** *n.*
for•tis•si•mo (fôr tis′ə mō′), *Music.* —*adj.* **1.** very loud. —*adv.* **2.** very loudly.
for•ti•tude (fôr′ti tŏŏd′, -tyŏŏd′), *n.* strength in facing adversity, danger, or temptation courageously.
Fort′ Knox′ (noks), *n.* a military reservation in N Kentucky: federal gold depository.
Fort′ Lau′der•dale (lô′dər dāl′), *n.* a city in SE Florida. 162,842.
Fort′ Leav′en•worth, *n.* a military reservation and U.S. Army training center in E Kansas.
Fort′ McHen′ry, *n.* a fort in N Maryland, at the entrance to Baltimore harbor: Francis Scott Key wrote *The Star-Spangled Banner* during British bombardment in 1814.
fort′night′, *n.* two weeks. —**fort′night′ly,** *adj., adv.*
for•tress (fôr′tris), *n.* a fort or group of forts.
Fort′ Sum′ter, *n.* a fort in SE South Carolina: its

bombardment by the Confederates opened the Civil War on April 12, 1861.

for·tu·i·tous (fôr tōō'i təs, -tyōō'-), *adj.* **1.** happening or produced by chance; accidental. **2.** lucky. —**for·tu'i·tous·ly,** *adv.* —**Usage.** Some commentators object to the use of FORTUITOUS to mean "lucky." In modern standard use, however, the word almost always carries the senses both of chance and luck.

for·tu/i·ty, *n., pl.* **-ties. 1.** the state or quality of being fortuitous. **2.** an accidental occurrence.

for·tu·nate (fôr'chə nit), *adj.* **1.** having good fortune; lucky. **2.** bringing or indicating good fortune. —**for'tu·nate·ly,** *adv.*

for'tune, *n.* **1.** wealth; riches. **2.** chance; luck. **3. fortunes,** varied occurrences that happen or are to happen to a person in life. **4.** fate; destiny. [< OF < L *fortūna* chance, luck]

for'tune-tell/er, *n.* a person who claims the ability to predict the future. —**for'tune-tell'ing,** *n.*

Fort' Wayne' (wān), *n.* a city in NE Indiana. 183,359.

Fort' Worth', *n.* a city in N Texas. 451,814.

for·ty (fôr'tē), *n., pl.* **-ties,** *adj.* —*n.* **1.** a cardinal number, ten times four. **2.** a symbol for this number, as 40 or XL. —*adj.* **3.** amounting to 40 in number. —**for'ti·eth,** *adj., n.*

for'ty-five', *n.* **1.** a .45-caliber handgun. **2.** a 7-inch phonograph record played at 45 r.p.m.

for'ty-nin'er (-nī'nər), *n.* a person participating in the 1849 California gold rush.

For'ty-ninth' Par'allel, *n.* the line of latitude that marks the border between the United States and Canada.

for'ty winks', *n.* a short nap.

fo·rum (fôr'əm), *n.* **1.** the marketplace or public square of an ancient Roman city. **2.** a court; tribunal. **3.** a meeting place or medium for discussion of matters of public interest.

for·ward (fôr'wərd), *adv.* Also, **for'wards. 1.** toward or to what is in front. **2.** into view or consideration; forth. —*adj.* **3.** directed toward a point in advance. **4.** well-advanced. **5.** ready; eager. **6.** presumptuous; bold. **7.** situated in the front. **8.** of or for the future. **9.** radical or extreme. —*n.* **10.** a player stationed in front of others in a team, as in hockey. —*v.t.* **11.** to send onward, esp. to a new address. **12.** to promote; advance. —**for'ward·er,** *n.* —**for'ward·ly,** *adv.* —**for'ward·ness,** *n.*

for·went', *v.* pt. of FORGO.

Fos·dick (foz'dik), *n.* **Harry Emerson,** 1878–1969, U.S. preacher and author.

fos·sil (fos'əl), *n.* **1.** the preserved remains or imprint of a living organism, usu. of a former geologic age. **2.** an outdated or old-fashioned person or thing. —*adj.* **3.** like or being a fossil. **4.** formed from the remains of prehistoric life, as oil: *a fossil fuel.*

fos/sil·ize/, *v.t., v.i.,* **-ized, -iz·ing.** to convert into a fossil. —**fos/sil·i·za/tion,** *n.*

fos·ter (fô'stər, fos'tər), *v.t.* **1.** to promote the growth or development of. **2.** to bring up; rear. —*adj.* **3.** giving or receiving parental care though not kin by blood or related legally: *a foster parent.*

fought (fôt), *v.* pt. and pp. of FIGHT.

foul (foul), *adj.* **1.** grossly offensive to the senses. **2.** very dirty; filthy. **3.** clogged or obstructed with dirt. **4.** stormy; inclement. **5.** morally offensive. **6.** profane; obscene. **7.** contrary to the rules, as in a sport. **8. a.** indicating the limits of a baseball field: *foul lines.* **b.** hit outside the foul line: *a foul ball.* **9.** obstructed; entangled. —*adv.* **10.** in a foul manner. —*n.* **11.** a collision; entanglement. **12.** a violation of the rules of a sport or game. **13.** a foul ball. —*v.t.* **14.** to make foul. **15.** to clog; obstruct. **16.** to collide with. **17.** to cause to become entangled. **18.** to dishonor; disgrace. **19.** to hit (a pitched ball) foul. —*v.i.* **20.** to become foul. **21.** to commit a foul in a sport or game. **22.** to hit a foul ball. **23. foul up,** to bungle or spoil. —**foul'ly,** *adv.* —**foul'ness,** *n.*

fou·lard (fōō lärd', fə-), *n.* a lightweight silk, rayon, or cotton fabric with a printed pattern.

foul/mouthed/, *adj.* using obscene or scurrilous language.

foul/ play/, *n.* violent mischief, esp. murder.

foul/-up/, *n.* a condition of disorder brought on by inefficiency or stupidity.

found¹ (found), *v.* pt. and pp. of FIND.

found² (found), *v.t.* **1.** to establish on a firm basis or for enduring existence. **2.** to provide a firm basis for; ground. —**found/er,** *n.*

found³ (found), *v.t.* to melt and pour (metal) into a mold. —**found/er,** *n.*

foun·da/tion, *n.* **1.** basis; groundwork. **2.** the base on which a structure rests. **3.** the act of founding. **4.** the state of being founded. **5. a.** an institution financed by a donation or legacy. **b.** an endowment for such an institution. **6.** a corset or girdle.

foun·der (foun'dər), *v.i.* **1.** to fill with water and sink. **2.** to fail utterly. **3.** to stumble or go lame, as a horse.

found/ling, *n.* an abandoned infant without a known parent.

found/ry (foun'drē), *n., pl.* **-ries.** an establishment for producing castings in molten metal.

fount (fount), *n.* **1.** a fountain. **2.** a source.

foun·tain (foun'tn), *n.* **1.** a spring of water from the earth. **2.** a source; origin. **3.** a mechanically created jet or stream of water. **4.** a reservoir for a liquid to be supplied continuously.

foun/tain·head/, *n.* a source.

foun/tain pen/, *n.* a pen with a refillable reservoir that provides a continuous supply of ink to its point.

four (fôr), *n.* **1.** a cardinal number, three plus one. **2.** a symbol for this number, as 4 or IV. —*adj.* **3.** amounting to four in number.

4 × 4 or **four-by-four** (fôr'bī fôr, fōr'bī fōr'), *n.* a vehicle, as a small truck, that has four wheels and a four-wheel drive.

four/-flush/, *v.i.* to bluff. —**four/flush/er,** *n.*

four/fold/, *adj.* **1.** comprising four parts or members. **2.** four times as great or as much. —*adv.* **3.** in fourfold measure.

Four/ Horse/men of the Apoc/alypse, *n.pl.* four horsemen symbolizing pestilence, war, famine, and death. Rev. 6:2–8.

tour/-in-hand/, *n.* **1.** a necktie tied in a slipknot with the ends left hanging. **2.** a vehicle drawn by four horses and driven by one person. **3.** a team of four horses.

Four/ No/ble Truths/, *n.pl.* the doctrines of Buddha: all life is suffering, the cause of suffering is ignorant desire, this desire can be destroyed, the means to this is the Eightfold Path.

four/-o'clock/, *n.* a plant bearing tubular flowers that open in the late afternoon.

four/post/er, *n.* a bed with four corner posts, as for supporting a canopy.

four/score/, *adj.* four times twenty; eighty.

four/some (-səm), *n.* **1.** a company or set of four. **2.** a golf match between two pairs of players.

four/square/, *adj.* **1.** square in shape. **2.** firm; forthright. —*adv.* **3.** firmly; forthrightly.

four/teen/, *n.* **1.** a cardinal number, ten plus four. **2.** a symbol for this number, as 14 or XIV. —*adj.* **3.** amounting to 14 in number. —**four/teenth/,** *adj., n.*

fourth (fôrth), *adj.* **1.** next after the third; being the ordinal number for four. **2.** being one of four equal parts. —*n.* **3.** a fourth part. **4.** the fourth member of a series. —*adv.* **5.** in the fourth place.

fourth/ class/, *n.* a class of mail consisting of merchandise weighing one pound or more and not sealed against inspection. —**fourth/-class/,** *adj., adv.*

fourth/ dimen/sion, *n.* a dimension, usu. time, in addition to length, width, and depth.

fourth/ estate/, *n.* (*often caps.*) the journalistic profession or its members.

Fourth/ of July/, *n.* INDEPENDENCE DAY.

four/-wheel/, *adj.* **1.** having four wheels. **2.** functioning on or by four wheels: *a truck with four-wheel drive.*

four/-wheel/ drive/, *n.* a drive system in which

engine power is transmitted to all four wheels of a vehicle for improved traction.

fowl (foul), *n., pl.* **fowls, fowl,** *v.* —*n.* **1.** a domestic hen or rooster. **2.** a bird such as a turkey or pheasant. **3.** the meat of a domestic fowl. —*v.i.* **4.** to hunt wildfowl.

fox (foks), *n., pl.* **fox·es, fox,** *v.* —*n.* **1.** a small carnivore of the dog family with a sharply pointed muzzle and a long bushy tail. **2.** the fur of the fox. **3.** a cunning or crafty person. —*v.t.* **4.** to deceive or trick. —*Saying.* **5. let the fox guard the henhouse,** to give someone authority over a situation that he or she might exploit for personal gain.

foxed, *adj.* stained or spotted a yellowish brown.

fox′fire′ or **fox′-fire′,** *n.* organic luminescence, esp. from certain fungi on decaying wood.

fox′glove′, *n.* a plant with purple flowers on a tall spike and leaves that yield digitalis.

fox′hole′, *n.* a pit used as a shelter in a battle zone.

fox′hound′, *n.* any of several breeds of hounds trained to hunt foxes.

fox′ ter′rier, *n.* a small terrier with a long, narrow head and either a wiry or a smooth white coat.

fox′ trot′, *n.* a ballroom dance in duple meter. —fox′-trot′, *v.i.,* -trot·ted, -trot·ting.

fox′y, *adj.,* -i·er, -i·est. slyly clever; cunning.

foy·er (foi′ər, foi′ā), *n.* **1.** a lobby, esp. of a theater. **2.** an entrance hall.

FPO, 1. field post office. **2.** fleet post office.

fps, 1. feet per second. **2.** foot-pound-second.

Fr, *Chem. Symbol.* francium.

Fr., 1. Father. **2.** France. **3.** French. **4.** Friar. **5.** Friday.

fr, 1. fragment. **2.** *pl.* **fr, frs** franc. **3.** from.

fra·cas (frā′kəs, frak′əs), *n.* a disorderly disturbance.

frac·tion (frak′shən), *n.* **1. a.** a number usu. expressed in the form *a/b*. **b.** a ratio of algebraic quantities similarly expressed. **2.** a part of a whole; portion. **3.** a fragment. —frac′tion·al, *adj.*

frac·tious (frak′shəs), *adj.* **1.** rebellious; unruly. **2.** readily angered or annoyed. —frac′tious·ly, *adv.*

frac·ture (frak′chər), *n., v.,* -tured, -tur·ing. —*n.* **1.** the breaking of something, esp. a bone. **2.** a break; split. —*v.t., v.i.* **3.** to break; crack.

frag·ile (fraj′əl; *Brit.* -īl), *adj.* **1.** easily broken or damaged. **2.** lacking in substance; flimsy. —fra·gil·i·ty (frə jil′i tē), *n.* —frag′ile·ness, *n.*

fragile X syndrome, *n.* a widespread form of mental retardation caused by a faulty gene on the X chromosome.

frag·ment (*n.* frag′mənt; *v.* frag′ment), *n.* **1.** a part broken off or detached. **2.** an unfinished or incomplete part. —*v.i., v.t.* **3.** to break into fragments. —frag′men·ta′tion, *n.*

frag·men·tar·y (frag′mən ter′ē), *adj.* consisting of fragments; incomplete.

fra·grant (frā′grənt), *adj.* having a pleasing scent. —fra′grance, *n.* —fra′grant·ly, *adv.*

frail (frāl), *adj.,* -er, -est. **1.** not physically strong; delicate. **2.** easily broken; fragile. —frail′ly, *adv.*

frail·ty (frāl′tē, frā′əl-), *n., pl.* -ties. **1.** the quality or state of being frail. **2.** a fault resulting from moral weakness.

frame (frām), *n., v.,* framed, fram·ing. —*n.* **1.** a decorative border, as for a picture. **2.** a rigid supporting structure formed of joined parts, as in a building. **3.** the size and build of the human body. **4.** an enclosing structure or case: *a window frame.* **5.** form, constitution, or structure. **6.** a particular state: *an unhappy frame of mind.* **7.** one of the successive pictures on a strip of film. —*v.t.* **8.** to construct; shape. **9.** to devise; compose. **10.** to cause (an innocent person) to seem guilty. **11.** to provide with or put into a frame. —fram′er, *n.*

frame′-up′, *n.* a fraudulent incrimination of an innocent person.

frame′work′, *n.* **1.** a skeletal supporting or enclos-

ing structure. **2.** a structure composed of parts fitted together.

franc (frangk), *n.* the basic monetary unit of France, Belgium, Switzerland, Luxembourg, Guinea, Madagascar, Rwanda, Burundi, and Djibouti.

France (frans, fräns), *n.* **1. Anatole,** 1844–1924, French author. **2.** a republic in W Europe. 58,470,421.

fran·chise (fran′chīz), *n., v.,* -chised, -chis·ing. —*n.* **1.** a privilege conferred on an individual or group by a government. **2.** the right or license granted by a company to an individual or group to market its products or services. **3.** the right to vote. —*v.t.* **4.** to grant a franchise to. —fran′chise·ment (-chīz-mənt, -chiz-), *n.*

fran′chi·see′ (-chī zē′), *n., pl.* -sees. one to whom a franchise is granted.

fran′chis·er, *n.* **1.** Also, **fran′chi·sor.** one that grants a franchise. **2.** a franchisee.

Fran·cis·can (fran sis′kən), *adj.* **1.** of or pertaining to St. Francis or the Franciscans. —*n.* **2.** a member of the mendicant order founded by St. Francis in the 13th century.

Fran′cis of Assi′si, *n.* Saint (*Giovanni Francesco Bernardone*),1182?–1226, Italian friar: founder of the Franciscan order.

fran·ci·um (fran′sē əm), *n.* a radioactive element of the alkali metal group. *Symbol:* Fr; *at. no.:* 87.

Franck (frängk), *n.* **César,** 1822–90, French composer, born in Belgium.

Fran·co (frang′kō), *n.* **Francisco** (*Francisco Paulino Hermenegildo Teódulo Franco-Bahamonde*), 1892–1975, Spanish dictator: head of Spain 1939–75. —Fran′co·ist, *n.*

fran·gi·ble (fran′jə bəl), *adj.* easily broken. —fran′gi·bil′i·ty, *n.*

frank¹ (frangk), *adj.,* -er, -est, *n., v.* —*adj.* **1.** direct and unreserved in expression. —*n.* **2.** a stamp, printed marking, or signature on a piece of mail indicating that it can be sent postage free. —*v.t.* **3.** to mark (mail) with a frank. —frank′ly, *adv.* —frank′ness, *n.*

frank² (frangk), *n.* a frankfurter.

Frank·en·stein (frang′kən stīn′), *n.* **1.** a destructive agency that brings about its creator's ruin. **2.** a monster shaped like a human being. [after *Frankenstein,* creator of a monster in M. Shelley's novel of the same name (1818)]

Frank·fort (frangk′fərt), *n.* the capital of Kentucky. 25,973.

Frank·furt (frangk′fûrt, frängk′fŏŏrt), *n.* a city in W Germany. 618,500.

frank·furt·er (frangk′fər tər), *n.* a smoked sausage usu. of beef or beef and pork.

frank·in·cense (frang′kin sens′), *n.* an aromatic gum resin, used chiefly as an incense: one of three gifts, the other two being gold and myrrh, given by the Magi to the infant Jesus. Matt. 2:11.

Frank·lin (frangk′lin), *n.* **Benjamin,** 1706–90, American statesman and inventor.

fran·tic (fran′tik), *adj.* desperate or wild with emotion; frenzied. —fran′ti·cal·ly, *adv.*

frappe (frap, fra pā′), *n. Northeastern U.S.* a milk shake made with ice cream.

frap·pé (fra pā′), *n., pl.* -pés. **1.** a fruit juice mixture frozen to a mush. **2.** a liqueur poured over cracked ice. **3.** FRAPPE.

fra·ter·nal (frə tûr′nl), *adj.* **1.** of or befitting a brother. **2.** of or being a society of men associated in brotherly union. —fra·ter′nal·ism, *n.* —fra·ter′nal·ly, *adv.*

fra·ter·ni·ty, *n., pl.* -ties. **1.** a social organization of male college students. **2.** a group of persons with common purposes or interests: *the medical fraternity.* **3.** the quality or state of being brotherly; brotherhood.

frat·er·nize (frat′ər nīz′), *v.i.,* -nized, -niz·ing. **1.** to associate in a friendly way. **2.** to associate cordially with members of a hostile group. —frat′er·ni·za′tion, *n.* —frat′er·niz′er, *n.*

frat·ri·cide (fra′tri sīd′, frā′-), *n.* **1.** the act of killing one's brother. **2.** a person who kills his or her brother. —**frat′ri•cid′al,** adj.

fraud (frôd), n. **1.** deceit or trickery. **2.** a particular instance of deceit or trickery: mail fraud. **3.** a deceitful person; impostor.

fraud•u•lent (frô′jə lənt), adj. characterized by, involving, or proceeding from fraud. —**fraud′u•lence,** n. —**fraud′u•lent•ly,** adv.

fraught (frôt), adj. filled or accompanied: an undertaking fraught with danger.

fray¹ (frā), n. **1.** a fight; skirmish. **2.** a noisy quarrel.

fray² (frā), v.t. **1.** to wear (material) into loose threads at the edge. **2.** to wear out by rubbing. **3.** to cause strain on. —v.i. **4.** to become frayed.

fraz•zle (fraz′əl), v., **-zled, -zling,** n. —v.t., v.i. **1.** to make or become physically or mentally fatigued. **2.** to wear to threads; fray. —n. **3.** a state of physical or mental fatigue.

FRB or **F.R.B.,** Federal Reserve Board.

freak (frēk), n. **1.** an abnormal, unusual, or strange person, animal, or thing. **2.** a sudden and apparently causeless notion or turn of events. **3.** Slang. a devoted fan; enthusiast. —v.t., v.i. **4.** to make or become frightened, nervous, or excited. **5. freak out,** Slang. to lose or cause to lose emotional control. —**freak′ish,** adj. —**freak′y,** adj., **-i•er, -i•est.**

freck•le (frek′əl), n., v., **-led, -ling.** —n. **1.** a small brownish spot on the skin. —v.t., v.i. **2.** to cover or become covered with freckles —**freck′ly,** adj., **-li•er, -li•est.**

Fred•er•icks•burg (fred′riks bûrg′, fred′ər iks-), n. a city in NE Virginia: scene of a Confederate victory 1862. 15,322.

Fred′erick the Great′ (fred′rik, -ər ik), n. 1712-86, king of Prussia 1740-86.

Fred•er•ic•ton (fred′rik tən, fred′ər ik-), n. the capital of New Brunswick, in SE Canada. 44,352.

free (frē), adj., **fre•er, fre•est,** adv., v., **freed, free•ing.** —adj. **1.** enjoying personal liberty. **2.** possessing civil and political liberties. **3.** exempt from external restriction. **4.** able to do something at will. **5.** clear of obstructions or obstacles. **6.** not occupied or in use. **7.** unaffected by something; exempt or released. **8.** provided without a charge. **9.** not attached or tied; loose. **10.** lacking self-restraint. **11.** generous or lavish, as in giving **12.** not literal. a free translation. —adv. **13.** in a free manner. **14.** at no cost or charge. —v.t. **15.** to set at liberty. **16.** to relieve or rid. **17.** to disengage; clear. —**free′ly,** adv.

free•bie or **-bee** (frē′bē), n., pl. **-bies, -bees.** Informal. something given or received without charge.

free′boot′er, n. a pirate; buccaneer.

free′born′, adj. **1.** born free rather than in slavery. **2.** pertaining to or befitting freeborn persons.

freed′man or **-wom′an,** n., pl. **-men** or **-wom•en.** a person who has been freed from slavery.

free•dom (frē′dəm), n. **1.** the state of being free. **2.** political independence. **3.** personal liberty. **4.** exemption; immunity. **5.** ease or facility of movement or action. **6.** frankness, as of speech. **7.** a right, as of citizenship or membership. **8.** the right to frequent, enjoy, or use at will.

free′dom march′ or **Free′dom March′,** n. an organized march in support of racial integration in the U.S. in the 1960s. —**free′dom march′er,** n.

free′dom ride′ or **Free′dom Ride′,** n. (esp. in the 1960s) a bus trip made to the southern U.S. by persons engaging in efforts to integrate public facilities. —**free′dom rid′er,** n.

free′ en′terprise, n. the doctrine that a capitalist economy can regulate itself with a minimum of governmental interference.

free′ fall′, n. the fall of a body in which the only force acting upon it is gravity.

free′-for-all′, n. a fight or contest open to everyone and usu. without rules.

free′ hand′, n. unrestricted freedom or authority.

free′hand′, adj. drawn or done by hand without the aid of instruments or measurements.

free′hold′, n. an estate in land, inherited or held for life. —**free′hold′er,** n.

free′lance′ or **free′-lance′** (-lans′, -läns′), n., v., **-lanced, -lanc•ing,** adj., adv. —n. **1.** Also, **free′-lanc′er.** a person who sells services without working on a regular basis for any single employer. —v.i. **2.** to work as a freelance. —adj. **3.** of or being a freelance. —adv. **4.** as a freelance.

free′load′, v.i. Informal. to take advantage of the generosity of others for free food, lodging, etc. —**free′load′er,** n.

free′ love′, n. the practice of having sexual relations without marriage.

free′man, n., pl. **-men. 1.** a person who enjoys civil or political liberty. **2.** a person who is entitled to citizenship.

Free′ma′son, n. a member of a secret fraternal association for mutual assistance and the promotion of brotherly love. —**Free′ma′son•ry,** n.

Free′port Doc′trine, n. a policy advocated by Stephen Douglas in 1858 that would give a territory the right to bar slavery prior to the formation of a state constitution.

free′-range′, adj. **1.** permitted to graze or forage rather than being confined to an enclosure: free-range chickens. **2.** of, pertaining to, or produced by free-range animals: free-range eggs.

free′stand′ing, adj. not attached to a support; standing alone.

free′stone′, n. **1.** a fruit, as a peach, with a pit that does not cling to the pulp. **2.** a stone, as sandstone, that can be cut without splitting.

free′think′er, n. a person who forms opinions on the basis of reason alone, esp. in religious matters. —**free′think′ing,** adj., n.

Free′town′, n. the capital of Sierra Leone, in W Africa. 469,776.

free′ trade′, n. international trade free from protective duties and quotas.

free′ univer′sity, n. an institution run informally by college students, offering courses not included in the traditional college curriculum.

free′ verse′, n. verse with no fixed metrical pattern.

free′way′, n. an express highway with no intersections.

free′ weight′, n. a weight used for weightlifting, as a dumbbell, whose motion is not constrained by external apparatus.

free′wheel′ing, adj. **1.** moving about freely. **2.** not constrained by rules or responsibilities.

free′ will′, n. **1.** free and independent choice. **2.** the doctrine that human conduct expresses personal choice and is not determined by physical or divine forces.

free′will′, adj. voluntary.

freeze (frēz), v., **froze, fro•zen, freez•ing,** n. —v.i. **1.** to become hardened into ice. **2.** to become hard or stiffened because of loss of heat. **3.** to suffer the effects of intense cold. **4.** to be at the degree of cold at which water freezes. **5.** to lose warmth of feeling. **6.** to become immobilized, as through fear. **7.** to become obstructed by the formation of ice: The water pipes froze. **8.** to die or be injured because of frost or cold. **9.** to become unfriendly or aloof. **10.** to become temporarily inoperable; cease to function (often fol. by up): My keyboard froze. —v.t. **11.** to harden into ice. **12.** to form ice on the surface of. **13.** to harden or stiffen by cold. **14.** to subject to freezing temperature, as in a freezer. **15.** to cause to suffer the effects of intense cold. **16.** to kill or damage by frost or cold. **17.** to obstruct or clog by the formation of ice. **18.** to fix (rents, prices, or wages) at a particular level. **19.** to prevent (assets) from being liquidated or collected. **20.** to act toward in an unfriendly or aloof manner. —n. **21.** an act or instance of freezing. **22.** the state of being frozen. **23.** a period of very cold weather. —**freez′a•ble,** adj.

freeze′-dry′, v.t., **-dried, -dry•ing.** to preserve (foods, blood plasma, etc.) by freezing and then drying in a vacuum.

freez′er, n. **1.** a compartment, cabinet, or room for

freezing and storing food. **2.** a machine containing a refrigerant for making ice cream or sherbet.

freez′ing point′, *n.* the temperature at which a liquid freezes.

freight (frāt), *n.* **1.** goods or cargo transported for pay. **2. a.** transportation of goods provided by common carriers. **b.** the charges for such transportation. **3.** a train that carries freight. —*v.t.* **4.** to load with goods for transportation. **5.** to transport by freight.

freight′er, *n.* a ship or aircraft used mainly for carrying freight.

Fre•mont (frē′mont), *n.* a city in W California. 183,575.

French[1] (french), *n.* **1.** the Romance language of France. **2.** (*used with a pl. v.*) the natives or inhabitants of France. —*adj.* **3.** of or characteristic of France, its inhabitants, or their language. —**French′- man,** *n., pl.* **-men.** —**French′wom′an,** *n., pl.* **-wom′en.**

French[2] (french), *n.* **Daniel Chester,** 1850–1931, U.S. sculptor.

French′ door′, *n.* a door having glass panes throughout its length.

French′ dress′ing, *n.* **1.** a salad dressing made of oil, vinegar, and seasonings. **2.** a creamy, orange-colored salad dressing.

French′ (or **french′**) **fries′,** *n.pl.* strips of potato that have been deep-fried.

French′-fry′ or **french′-fry′,** *v.t.,* **-fried, -fry•ing.** to fry in deep fat.

French′ Gui•an′a (gē an′a, -ä′na), *n.* an overseas department of France, on the NE coast of South America. 73,012.

French′ horn′, *n.* a brass wind instrument with a long coiled tube and a flaring bell.

French′ leave′, *n.* a departure without ceremony, permission, or notice.

French′ Revolu′tion, *n.* the revolution in France that began in 1789, overthrew the Bourbon monarchy, and ended with Napoleon's seizure of power in 1799.

French′ toast′, *n.* bread dipped in egg and milk and sautéed.

fre•net•ic (fra net′ik), *adj.* frantic; frenzied. —**fre• net′i•cal•ly,** *adv.*

fren•zy (fren′zē), *n., pl.* **-zies. 1.** extreme agitation or wild excitement. **2.** a spell of mental derangement. **3.** agitated activity. —**fren′zied,** *adj.*

freq., **1.** frequency. **2.** frequent. **3.** frequently.

fre•quen•cy (frē′kwan sē), *n., pl.* **-cies. 1.** the state or fact of being frequent. **2.** rate of occurrence. **3.** *Physics.* the number of cycles or completed alternations per unit time of a wave or oscillation.

fre′quency modula′tion, *n.* See FM.

fre•quent (*adj.* frē′kwant; *v.* fri kwent′, frē′kwant), *adj.* **1.** happening at short intervals. **2.** constant, habitual, or regular. —*v.t.* **3.** to visit often or habitually. —**fre•quent′er,** *n.* —**fre′quent•ly,** *adv.*

fre′quent fli′er, *n.* an airline passenger registered with a program that provides bonuses, as free flights, based esp. on distance traveled.

fres•co (fres′kō), *n., pl.* **-coes, -cos. 1.** the art of painting on a moist plaster surface. **2.** a picture or design so painted.

fresh (fresh), *adj.,* **-er, -est,** *adv.* —*adj.* **1.** newly made or obtained. **2.** recently arrived. **3.** not previously known; new or novel. **4.** additional or further. **5.** not salty, as water. **6.** not stale or spoiled. **7.** not preserved by canning, pickling, etc. **8.** not fatigued; vigorous. **9.** not faded. **10.** pure, cool, or refreshing, as air. **11.** (of wind) brisk. **12.** inexperienced: *fresh recruits.* **13.** *Informal.* impertinent; impudent. —*adv.* **14.** newly; recently. —**fresh′ly,** *adv.* —**fresh′ness,** *n.*

fresh′en, *v.t., v.i.* **1.** to make or become fresh. **2.** **freshen up,** to make oneself feel refreshed, as by showering. —**fresh′en•er,** *n.*

fresh•et (fresh′it), *n.* a flooding of a stream caused by heavy rains or the rapid melting of snow and ice.

fresh′man, *n., pl.* **-men. 1.** a student in the first

year at a high school or college. **2.** a novice; beginner.

fresh′wa′ter, *adj.* **1.** of or living in water that is not salty. **2.** accustomed only to fresh water.

Fres•no (frez′nō), *n.* a city in central California. 386,551.

fret[1] (fret), *v.,* **fret•ted, fret•ting,** *n.* —*v.i., v.t.* **1.** to feel or cause to feel worry, annoyance, or discontent. **2.** to wear or cause to be worn away; corrode. **3.** to agitate or become agitated, as water. **4.** to form by wearing away. —*n.* **5.** an irritated state of mind; vexation. **6.** erosion or corrosion. **7.** a worn or eroded place.

fret[2] (fret), *n.* an angular design of intersecting bands within a border.

fret[3] (fret), *n.* a ridge of wood or metal set across the fingerboard of a stringed instrument, as a guitar.

fret′ful, *adj.* disposed to fret; irritable. —**fret′- ful•ly,** *adv.* —**fret′ful•ness,** *n.*

fret′work′, *n.* ornamental work consisting of interlacing parts, esp. work with the design formed by perforation.

Freud (froid), *n.* **Sigmund,** 1856–1939, Austrian neurologist: founder of psychoanalysis.

Fri., Friday.

fri•a•ble (frī′a bal), *adj.* easily crumbled or reduced to powder.

fri•ar (frī′ar), *n.* a member of a Roman Catholic religious order, esp. a mendicant order. [< OF < L *frāter* brother]

fri′ar•y, *n., pl.* **-ar•ies.** a monastery of friars.

fric•as•see (frik′a sē′), *n., pl.* **-sees,** *v.,* **-seed, -see• ing.** —*n.* **1.** pieces of meat, esp. chicken, stewed in a sauce. —*v.t.* **2.** to prepare as a fricassee.

fric•a•tive (frik′a tiv), *n.* a consonant sound, as (th) or (v), characterized by audible friction produced by forcing the breath through a constricted passage.

Frick (frik), *n.* **Henry Clay,** 1849–1919, U.S. industrialist and art patron.

fric•tion (frik′shan), *n.* **1.** surface resistance to relative motion, as of a body sliding or rolling. **2.** the rubbing of one surface against another. **3.** dissension or conflict, as between persons or nations. —**fric′- tion•al,** *adj.*

Fri•day (frī′dā, -dē), *n.* the sixth day of the week, following Thursday.

fried (frīd), *v.* pt. and pp. of FRY[1].

fried′cake′, *n.* a small cake fried in deep fat.

friend (frend), *n.* **1.** a person attached to another by affection or regard. **2.** a patron; supporter. **3.** a person who is not hostile. **4.** (*cap.*) a member of the Society of Friends; Quaker. —**Idiom. 5.** fair-weather friend, one who is unreliable. **6. make friends with,** to become a friend to. —**Proverb. 7. A friend in need is a friend indeed,** a true friend is one who helps no matter what the circumstances. —**friend′- less,** *adj.*

friend′ly, *adj.,* **-li•er, -li•est,** *n., pl.* **-lies.** —*adj.* **1.** characteristic of, like, or befitting a friend. **2.** favorably disposed. **3.** not hostile; amicable. **4.** easy to use, operate, understand, or experience: *viewer-friendly art; a friendly computer.* —*n.* **5.** a person who is friendly. —**friend′li•ness,** *n.*

friend′ship, *n.* **1.** the state of being a friend. **2.** friendly feeling or disposition.

frieze (frēz), *n.* a decorative, often carved band, as around the top of a wall.

frig•ate (frig′it), *n.* **1.** a fast ship of the late 18th and early 19th centuries. **2.** a modern warship larger than a destroyer.

fright (frīt), *n.* **1.** sudden and extreme fear. **2.** a shocking or grotesque person or thing.

fright′en, *v.t.* **1.** to make afraid; scare. **2.** to drive away or off by frightening. —*v.i.* **3.** to become frightened. —**fright′en•ing•ly,** *adv.*

fright′ful, *adj.* **1.** causing fright; alarming. **2.** horrible or shocking. **3.** *Informal.* unpleasant; disagreeable. **4.** *Informal.* very great; extreme. —**fright′ful•ly,** *adv.*

frig•id (frij′id), *adj.* **1.** very cold in temperature. **2.** lacking warmth of feeling. **3.** (of a woman) sexually unresponsive. —**fri•gid′i•ty,** *n.* —**frig′id•ly,** *adv.*

Frig′id Zone′, *n.* the regions between the Arctic Circle and the North Pole or between the Antarctic Circle and the South Pole.

frill (fril), *n.* **1.** a trimming, as a strip of lace, gathered at one edge. **2.** something superfluous; luxury. —**frill′i•ness,** *n.* —**frill′y,** *adj.,* **-i•er, -i•est.**

fringe (frinj), *n., v.,* **fringed, fring•ing.** —*n.* **1.** a decorative border of short threads, cords, or loops. **2.** something resembling a fringe; border. **3.** an outer edge; margin; periphery. **4.** something peripheral or marginal to something else. —*v.t.* **5.** to furnish with or as if with a fringe. **6.** to serve as a fringe for.

fringe′ ben′efit, *n.* a benefit, such as health insurance, received by an employee in addition to regular pay.

frip•per•y (frip′ə rē), *n., pl.* **-per•ies. 1.** finery in dress, esp. when gaudy. **2.** empty display; ostentation.

Fris•bee (friz′bē), *pl.* **-bees.** *Trademark.* a brand of plastic disk thrown back and forth in a catching game.

Fri′sian (frizh′ən, frē′zhən), *n.* **1.** a native or inhabitant of the Frisian Islands. **2.** the Germanic language of the Frisians.

Fri′sian Is′lands, *n.pl.* a chain of islands in the North Sea, extending along the coasts of the Netherlands, Germany, and Denmark.

frisk (frisk), *v.i.* **1.** to dance, leap, skip, or gambol; frolic. —*v.t.* **2.** to search (a person), as for concealed weapons, by feeling the person's clothing.

frisk′y, *adj.,* **-i•er, -i•est.** lively and playful. —**frisk′i•ly,** *adv.* —**frisk′i•ness,** *n.*

frit•ter¹ (frit′ər), *v.t.* **1.** to squander or disperse piecemeal. **2.** to break into small pieces.

frit•ter² (frit′ər), *n.* a small cake of fried batter, usu. containing corn, fruit, or meat.

friv•o•lous (friv′ə ləs), *adj.* **1.** characterized by lack of seriousness or sense. **2.** not worthy of serious notice; trivial. —**fri•vol•i•ty** (fri vol′i tē), *n., pl.* **-ties.** —**friv′o•lous•ly,** *adv.*

frizz (friz), *v.i., v.t.* **1.** to form into small crisp curls. *n.* **2.** something frizzed, as hair. —**frizz′y,** *adj.,* **-i•er, -i•est.**

friz′zle¹, *v.,* **-zled, -zling.** *n.* —*v.t., v.i.* **1.** to frizz. —*n.* **2.** a small crisp curl.

friz′zle², *v.,* **-zled, -zling.** —*v.i.* **1.** to make a sizzling noise in frying. —*v.t.* **2.** to make (food) crisp by frying.

fro (frō), *adv.* from; back (used esp. in the phrase *to and fro*).

frock (frok), *n.* **1.** a dress worn by a girl or woman. **2.** a smock worn by peasants and workers. **3.** a coarse outer garment worn by monks.

frock′ coat′, *n.* a man's close-fitting, knee-length coat.

frog¹ (frog, frôg), *n.* **1.** a tailless amphibian with smooth, moist skin and long hind legs used for leaping. **2.** a slight hoarseness.

frog² (frog, frôg), *n.* an ornamental fastening for the front of a garment, consisting of a button and a loop.

frog•man (frog′man′, -mən, frôg′-), *n., pl.* **-men** (-men′, -mən). a swimmer specially equipped for underwater operations, as demolition or scientific exploration.

frol•ic (frol′ik), *n., v.,* **-icked, -ick•ing.** —*n.* **1.** merriment; gaiety. **2.** playful behavior or action. —*v.i.* **3.** to play in a frisky manner; romp. **4.** to engage in merrymaking. —**frol′ick•er,** *n.* —**frol′ic•some,** *adj.*

from (frum, from; *unstressed* frəm), *prep.* **1.** (used to specify a starting point in space): *ran away from home.* **2.** (used to specify a starting point in an expression of limits): *works from 9 to 5.* **3.** (used to express removal or separation): *30 minutes from now.* **4.** (used to express discrimination or distinction): *differs from her father.* **5.** (used to indicate source, origin, agent, or cause): *came from the Midwest.*

frond (frond), *n.* an often large, finely divided leaf, esp. of a fern palm.

front (frunt), *n.* **1.** the forward part or surface. **2.** the part or side of something that faces or is directed forward. **3.** a place or position directly before something else. **4.** a place where combat operations are carried on. **5.** an area of activity or competition. **6.** land facing a road, river, etc. **7.** a person or thing that serves as a cover or disguise for an activity, esp. a disreputable one. **8.** bearing; demeanor: *a calm front.* **9. a.** the forehead. **b.** the entire face. **10.** a zone of transition between two dissimilar air masses. —*adj.* **11.** of or situated in or at the front. —*v.t., v.i.* **12.** to face. **13.** to serve as a front (for). —*Idiom.* **14. in front of, a.** ahead of. **b.** in the presence of. **15. up front,** *Informal.* **a.** before anything else. **b.** frank; open. —**fron′tal,** *adj.*

front•age (frun′tij), *n.* **1.** the front of a building or lot. **2.** the lineal extent of a frontage. **3.** FRONT (def. 6).

front′ burn′er, *n.* a condition of top priority.

fron•tier (frun tēr′), *n.* **1.** the part of a country that borders another country. **2.** land that forms the farthest extent of a country's settled regions. **3.** Often, **-tiers.** the limit of knowledge or achievement. —**fron•tiers′man,** *n., pl.* **-men.**

fron•tis•piece (frun′tis pēs′, fron′-), *n.* an illustrated leaf preceding the title page of a book.

front′ of′fice, *n.* the executive or administrative officers of an organization.

front′-run′ner or **front′ run′ner,** *n.* a person who leads in a competition.

front′-wheel′ drive′, *n.* a drive system in which engine power is transmitted through the front wheels only.

Frost (frôst, frost), *n.* **Robert (Lee),** 1874–1963, U.S. poet.

frost′bite′, *n., v.,* **-bit, -bit•ten, -bit•ing.** —*n.* **1.** injury to a part of the body from excessive exposure to extreme cold. —*v.t.* **2.** to injure by extreme cold.

frost′ing, *n.* **1.** a sweet, creamy mixture for coating baked goods; icing. **2.** a dull or lusterless finish, as on metal or glass.

froth (frôth, froth), *n.* **1.** an aggregation of bubbles, as on an agitated liquid; foam. **2.** a foam of saliva. **3.** something unsubstantial or trivial. —*v.t.* **4.** to cover with or give out froth. —**froth′y,** *adj.,* **-i•er, -i•est.**

frou•frou (frōō′frōō′), *n.* **1.** elaborate decoration, esp. on women's clothing. **2.** a rustling, as of silk.

fro•ward (frō′wərd, frō′ərd), *adj.* willfully contrary. —**fro′ward•ness,** *n.*

frown (froun), *v.i.* **1.** to contract the brow, as in displeasure; scowl. **2.** to view with disapproval: *They frown on gambling.* —*n.* **3.** a frowning look; scowl. —**frown′er,** *n.* —**frown′ing•ly,** *adv.*

frow•zy (frou′zē), *adj.,* **-i•er, -i•est.** dirty and untidy; slovenly. —**frowz′i•ly,** *adv.* —**frowz′i•ness,** *n.*

froze (frōz), *v.* pt. of FREEZE.

fro′zen, *v.* **1.** pp. of FREEZE. —*adj.* **2.** turned into, covered with, or obstructed by ice. **3.** very cold; frigid. **4.** chilly or cold in manner. **5.** preserved by freezing. **6.** not convertible into cash without substantial loss. **7.** not permitted to be changed; fixed: *frozen rents.*

fruc•ti•fy (fruk′tə fī′, frŏŏk′-, frōŏk′-), *v.,* **-fied, -fy•ing.** —*v.i.* **1.** to bear fruit. —*v.t.* **2.** to make fruitful or productive.

fruc′tose (-tōs), *n.* an extremely sweet sugar occurring in honey and many fruits.

fru•gal (frōō′gəl), *adj.* **1.** not wasteful; economical. **2.** marked by economy; sparse. —**fru•gal′i•ty,** *n., pl.* **-ties.** —**fru′gal•ly,** *adv.*

fruit (frōōt), *n., pl.* **fruits, fruit,** *v.* —*n.* **1.** the edible part of a plant developed from a flower, as a peach or banana. **2.** the developed ovary of a seed plant with its contents and accessory parts, as a nut or tomato. **3.** a product, result, or effect. —*v.i., v.t.* **4.** to bear or cause to bear fruit. —*Proverb.* **5. By their fruits shall ye know them,** people are known by their actions. Matt. 7:20.

fruit′cake′, *n.* a rich cake containing dried or candied fruit, nuts, and spices.

fruit' fly', *n.* any of numerous small flies whose larvae feed on fruit.

fruit'ful, *adj.* **1.** producing good results; productive. **2.** abounding in fruit. —**fruit'ful•ly,** *adv.* —**fruit'ful•ness,** *n.*

fru•i•tion (frōō ish'ən), *n.* **1.** attainment of something desired; realization. **2.** enjoyment, as of something attained. **3.** the state of bearing fruit.

fruit'less, *adj.* **1.** not producing results or success. **2.** bearing no fruit; barren. —**fruit'less•ly,** *adv.* —**fruit'less•ness,** *n.*

fruit'y, *adj.,* **-i•er, -i•est. 1.** resembling fruit, esp. in taste or smell. **2.** excessively sweet or sentimental; cloying. —**fruit'i•ness,** *n.*

frump (frump), *n.* a dowdy, drab, and unattractive woman. —**frump'y,** *adj.,* **-i•er, -i•est.**

Frun•ze (frōōn'zə), *n.* a former name (1926–91) of BISHKEK.

frus•trate (frus'trāt), *v.t.,* **-trat•ed, -trat•ing. 1.** to defeat (plans, efforts, etc.); block. **2.** to cause feelings of disappointment in; thwart. —**frus'trat•ing•ly,** *adv.* —**frus•tra'tion,** *n.*

frus•tum (frus'təm), *n., pl.* **-tums, -ta** (-tə). the part of a solid, as a cone, between two usu. parallel cutting planes.

fry¹ (frī), *v.,* **fried, fry•ing,** *n., pl.* **fries.** —*v.t.* **1.** to cook in fat or oil, usu. over direct heat. —*v.i.* **2.** to undergo frying. —*n.* **3.** a dish of fried food. **4.** a party or gathering at which fried food is served. [< OF < L *frīgere* to roast] —**fry'a•ble,** *adj.*

fry² (frī), *n., pl.* **fry. 1.** the young of fish. **2.** individuals, esp. children: *games for the small fry.* [ME: seed, descendant]

fry'er, *n.* **1.** something, esp. a young chicken, for frying. **2.** a pan for frying.

FSLIC, Federal Savings and Loan Insurance Corporation.

ft., **1.** feet. **2.** foot. **3.** fort.

FTC, Federal Trade Commission.

fuch•sia (fyōō'shə), *n., pl.* **-sias. 1.** a shrubby plant with pink to purplish drooping flowers. **2.** a bright purplish red color.

fud•dle (fud'l), *v.,* **-dled, -dling,** *n.* —*v.t.* **1.** to muddle or confuse. —*n.* **2.** a muddled state; confusion.

fud•dy-dud•dy (fud'ē dud'ē, -dud'ē), *n., pl.* **-dies.** a person who is stuffy, old-fashioned, conservative, or fussy about details.

fudge¹ (fuj), *n.* a soft candy made of sugar, butter, milk, and flavoring.

fudge² (fuj), *n.* nonsense or foolishness.

fudge³ (fuj), *v.,* **fudged, fudg•ing.** —*v.i.* **1.** to behave in a dishonest way; cheat or welsh. **2.** to avoid coming to grips with something. —*v.t.* **3.** to evade; dodge. **4.** to falsify; fake.

fu•el (fyōō'əl), *n., v.,* **-eled, -el•ing** or (*esp. Brit.*) **-elled, -el•ling.** —*n.* **1.** combustible matter, as coal, wood, or oil, used to create heat or power, or as an energy source for a nuclear reactor. **2.** something that sustains or stimulates. —*v.t., v.i.* **3.** to supply with or obtain fuel.

fu'el injec'tion, *n.* the spraying of liquid fuel into the cylinders or combustion chambers of an engine.

fu•gi•tive (fyōō'ji tiv), *n.* **1.** a person who flees, as from prosecution. —*adj.* **2.** having taken flight or run away. **3.** passing quickly; fleeting.

fugue (fyōōg), *n.* a polyphonic composition in which the themes are enunciated by different voices or parts in turn. —**fu'gal,** *adj.*

Fu•ji (fōō'jē), *n.* a dormant volcano in central Japan, on Honshu island: highest mountain in Japan. 12,395 ft. (3778 m).

-ful, a suffix meaning: full of or characterized by (*beautiful*); tending to or able to (*harmful*); as much as will fill (*spoonful*).

Ful•bright (fōōl'brīt'), *n.* **1. (James) William,** 1905–95, U.S. senator 1945–74. **2. a.** a grant awarded under the provisions of the Fulbright Act. **b.** a person who receives such a grant.

Ful'bright Act', *n.* an act of Congress (1946) that established funds for U.S. citizens to study or teach

abroad as well as for foreigners to pursue similar activities in the U.S. [after J. W. FULBRIGHT]

ful•crum (fōōl'krəm, ful'-), *n., pl.* **-crums, -cra** (-krə). the support or point of rest on which a lever turns.

ful•fill or **-fil** (fōōl fil'), *v.t.,* **-filled, -fill•ing** or **-fil•ling. 1.** to bring to realization. **2.** to carry out; perform. **3.** to satisfy (requirements, obligations, etc.). **4.** to bring to an end. —**ful•fill'er,** *n.* —**ful•full'ment,** *n.*

full¹ (fōōl), *adj.,* **-er, -est,** *adv., n.* —*adj.* **1.** filled to capacity. **2.** complete in all respects. **3.** of maximum size, amount, extent, or degree: *full pay.* **4.** having ample fabric: *a full skirt.* **5.** having an abundance; well supplied: *a cabinet full of medicine.* **6.** rounded in form: *a full figure.* **7.** engrossed; occupied: *full of her own anxieties.* **8.** of the highest rank: *a full professor.* **9.** ample and rich in sound. —*adv.* **10.** exactly or directly: *struck him full in the face.* **11.** very: *knew full well what I meant.* —*n.* **12.** the fullest state, amount, or degree. —**full'ness,** *n.*

full² (fōōl), *v.t.* to shrink and thicken (woolen cloth). —**full'er,** *n.*

full'back', *n.* (in football) a running back who lines up behind the quarterback.

full'-blood'ed, *adj.* **1.** of unmixed ancestry; thoroughbred. **2.** vigorous; hearty.

full'-blown', *adj.* **1.** completely developed. **2.** in full bloom.

full'-bod'ied, *adj.* of full strength, flavor, or richness.

full' disclo'sure, *n.* complete release of information.

full' dress', *n.* attire customarily worn for formal or ceremonial occasions.

Ful•ler (fōōl'ər), *n.* **R(ichard) Buckminster,** 1895–1983, U.S. engineer, designer, and architect.

full'-fledged', *adj.* **1.** of full rank or standing. **2.** fully developed.

full' moon', *n.* the moon when the whole of its disk is illuminated.

full'-scale', *adj.* **1.** having the exact size or proportions of an original. **2.** using all possible means; complete.

full'-time', *adj.* **1.** working or operating the customary number of hours in a given period. —*adv.* **2.** on a full-time basis. —**full'-tim'er,** *n.*

ful'ly, *adv.* **1.** entirely or wholly. **2.** at least; quite.

ful•mi•nate (ful'mə nāt'), *v.i.,* **-nat•ed, -nat•ing. 1.** to explode with a loud noise. **2.** to issue violent denunciation or strong condemnation. —**ful'mi•na'tion,** *n.* —**ful'mi•na'tor,** *n.*

ful•some (fōōl'səm, ful'-), *adj.* offensive to good taste, esp. as being excessive or insincere; sickening. —**ful'some•ly,** *adv.* —**ful'some•ness,** *n.*

Ful•ton (fōōl'tn), *n.* **Robert,** 1765–1815, U.S. engineer and inventor.

fum•ble (fum'bəl), *v.,* **-bled, -bling,** *n.* —*v.i.* **1.** to grope clumsily. **2.** to fail to hold a baseball or football after having touched or carried it. **3.** to do or handle something clumsily or ineffectively. —*v.t.* **4.** to handle clumsily; botch. **5.** to fail to hold (a ball). —*n.* **6.** the act of fumbling. **7.** a fumbled ball. —**fum'bler,** *n.* —**fum'bling•ly,** *adv.*

fume (fyōōm), *n., v.,* **fumed, fum•ing.** —*n.* **1.** a smokelike or vaporous exhalation, esp. of an irritating nature. —*v.t.* **2.** to treat with or expose to fumes. —*v.i.* **3.** to show irritation or anger. **4.** to emit fumes. —**fum'y,** *adj.,* **-i•er, -i•est.**

fu•mi•gant (fyōō'mi gənt), *n.* a chemical used in fumigating.

fu'mi•gate', *v.t.,* **-gat•ed, -gat•ing.** to expose to fumes, as in killing vermin. —**fu'mi•ga'tion,** *n.* —**fu'mi•ga'tor,** *n.*

fun (fun), *n.* **1.** something that provides mirth or amusement. **2.** enjoyment or playfulness. —*adj.* **3.** *Informal.* providing fun; enjoyable: *a fun thing to do.* —*Idiom.* **4. make fun of,** to ridicule; deride.

func•tion (fungk'shən), *n.* **1.** the kind of action or activity proper to a person or thing. **2.** the purpose for which something is designed or exists. **3.** a ceremonious public or social gathering or occasion. **4.** a factor related to or dependent upon other factors. **5.** *Math.* a relation between two sets in which one element of the second set is assigned to each element of the first set. —*v.i.* **6.** to work; operate. **7.** to perform a function; serve.

func'tion•al, *adj.* **1.** of a function. **2.** capable of functioning. **3.** having or serving a utilitarian purpose; practical. **4.** marked by impaired function without known organic or structural cause: *a functional disorder.* —**func'tion•al•ly,** *adv.*

func'tion•ar'y (-shə ner'ē), *n., pl.* **-ar•ies.** a person who functions in a specified capacity, esp. a government official.

func'tion word', *n.* a word, as a preposition, that chiefly expresses grammatical relationships.

fund (fund), *n.* **1.** a sum of money set aside for a specific purpose. **2.** a supply; stock. **3. funds,** money immediately available. **4.** an organization created to manage money contributed or invested. —*v.t.* **5.** to provide funds for. **6.** to provide a fund to pay the interest or principal of (a debt).

fun•da•men•tal (fun'də men'tl), *adj.* **1.** of or being a foundation or basis; basic. **2.** of great importance; essential. **3.** being an original or primary source. —*n.* **4.** something fundamental, as a principle or rule. —**fun'da•men'tal•ly,** *adv.*

fun'da•men'tal•ism, *n.* (*sometimes cap.*) a Protestant movement that stresses the infallibility of the Bible. —**fun'da•men'tal•ist,** *n., adj.*

fu•ner•al (fyōō'nər əl), *n.* the ceremonies for a dead person prior to burial or cremation.

fu'neral direc'tor, *n.* a person who supervises or arranges funerals.

fu'neral home', *n.* an establishment where the dead are prepared for burial or cremation and where funeral services are often held.

fu'ner•ar'y (-nə rer'ē), *adj.* of a funeral.

fu•ne're•al (-nēr'ē əl), *adj.* **1.** of or suitable for a funeral. **2.** gloomy; dismal. —**fu•ne're•al•ly,** *adv.*

fun•gi•cide (fun'jə sīd', fung'gə-), *n.* an agent that destroys fungi. —**fun'gi•cid'al,** *adj.*

fun•gus (fung'gəs), *n., pl.* **fun•gi** (fun'jī, fung'gī), **fun•gus•es.** any of a number of organisms, including mushrooms, molds, and mildews, that live by decomposing and absorbing the organic material in which they grow. —**fun'gal, fun'gous,** *adj.*

fu•nic•u•lar (fyōō nik'yə lər), *n.* a steep cable railway in which the ascending and descending cars are counterbalanced.

funk (fungk), *n.* **1.** a state of cowering fear. **2.** a dejected mood; depression.

funk'y, *adj.,* **-i•er, -i•est. 1.** having an earthy, blues-based character: *funky jazz.* **2.** *Slang.* offbeat or unconventional. —**funk'i•ness,** *n.*

fun•nel (fun'l), *n., v.,* **-neled, -nel•ing** or (*esp. Brit.*) **-nelled, -nel•ling.** —*n.* **1.** a cone-shaped utensil with a tube for channeling a substance through a small opening. **2.** a smokestack, esp. of a steamship. **3.** a flue or shaft. —*v.t., v.i.* **4.** to pass through or as if through a funnel.

fun•ny (fun'ē), *adj.,* **-ni•er, -ni•est,** *n., pl.* **-nies.** —*adj.* **1.** provoking laughter; comical. **2.** warranting suspicion; underhanded. **3.** strange; peculiar. —*n.* **4. funnies, a.** comic strips. **b.** the section of a newspaper reserved for comic strips. —**fun'ni•ly,** *adv.* —**fun'ni•ness,** *n.*

fun'ny bone', *n.* the part of the elbow where a blow to the nerve causes a tingling sensation.

fun'ny farm', *n. Slang.* a psychiatric hospital.

fun'ny mon'ey, *n. Slang.* **1.** counterfeit currency. **2.** currency of little value.

fur (fûr), *n.* **1.** the soft, thick, hairy coat of a mammal. **2.** the processed pelt of an animal, as a mink, used esp. for garments. **3.** a garment made of fur. **4.** a coating resembling fur. —**furred,** *adj.*

fur•be•low (fûr'bə lō'), *n.* **1.** a ruffle or flounce. **2.** a bit of showy trimming or finery.

fur•bish (fûr'bish), *v.t.* to restore to good condition; renovate.

fu•ri•ous (fyŏōr'ē əs), *adj.* **1.** full of fury or rage. **2.**

violent, as a storm. **3.** very intense: *furious activity.* —**fu'ri•ous•ly,** *adv.*

furl (fûrl), **1.** to gather into a roll and bind securely, as a flag against its staff. —*v.i.* **2.** to become furled.

fur•long (fûr'lông, -long), *n.* a unit of distance equal to 220 yards (201 m) or ¹⁄₈ of a mile (0.2 km).

fur•lough (fûr'lō), *n.* **1.** a leave of absence, esp. one granted to a person in the military. —*v.t.* **2.** to grant a furlough to.

fur•nace (fûr'nis), *n.* a structure or apparatus in which heat is generated, as for heating houses.

fur•nish (fûr'nish), *v.t.* **1.** to supply with what is necessary, esp. with furniture. **2.** to provide; give.

fur'nish•ings, *n.pl.* **1.** articles, esp. furniture, for a room. **2.** articles or accessories of dress.

fur'ni•ture (-chər), *n.* movable articles, as tables or chairs, required for use or ornament in a room.

fu•ror (fyŏōr'ôr, -ər), *n.* **1.** a general outburst of excitement; uproar. **2.** a fad or craze. **3.** fury; rage. Also, *esp. Brit.,* **fu'rore** (for defs. 1, 2).

fur•ri•er (fûr'ē ər), *n.* a fur dealer or fur dresser.

fur•ring (fûr'ing), *n.* strips of wood or metal attached to a surface, as a wall, to provide an even support or an air space.

fur•row (fûr'ō, fur'ō), *n.* **1.** a narrow groove made in the ground, esp. by a plow. **2.** a narrow groove-like depression, as a wrinkle. —*v.t.* **3.** to make furrows in. —*v.i.* **4.** to become furrowed.

fur•ry (fûr'ē), *adj.,* **-ri•er, -ri•est. 1.** consisting of or resembling fur. **2.** covered with fur. —**fur'ri•ness,** *n.*

fur•ther (fûr'ẖər), *adv., adj., compar.* of **far,** *v.* —*adv.* **1.** at or to a greater distance; farther. **2.** to a greater extent. **3.** in addition; moreover. —*adj.* **4.** more distant or remote; farther. **5.** more extended. **6.** additional; more. —*v.t.* **7.** to help forward; advance. —**fur'ther•ance,** *n.* —**Usage.** See FARTHER.

fur'ther•more', *adv.* in addition; moreover.

fur'ther•most', *adj.* most distant.

fur•thest (fûr'ẖist), *adj., adv., superl.* of **far.** FARTHEST.

fur•tive (fûr'tiv), *adj.* **1.** taken, done, or used by stealth; surreptitious. **2.** sly; shifty. —**fur'tive•ly,** *adv.* —**fur'tive•ness,** *n.*

fu•ry (fyŏōr'ē), *n., pl.* **-ries. 1.** unrestrained or violent anger; rage. **2.** a fit of such anger. **3.** violence; fierceness.

furze (fûrz), *n.* GORSE.

fuse¹ (fyōōz), *n.* **1.** a tube or cord filled or saturated with combustible matter for igniting an explosive. **2.** a mechanical or electronic device for detonating an explosive charge.

fuse² (fyōōz), *n., v.,* **fused, fus•ing.** —*n.* **1.** a safety device containing a conductor that melts when excess current runs through an electric circuit, breaking the circuit. —*v.t., v.i.* **2.** to blend or unite by or as if by melting together. **3.** to melt. —**fu'si•ble,** *adj.*

fu•see (fyōō zē'), *n., pl.* **-sees. 1.** a wooden friction match with a large head. **2.** a red flare light, used esp. on a railroad as a warning signal.

fu•se•lage (fyōō'sə läzh', -lij, -zə-), *n.* the central structure of an airplane, containing passenger and cargo compartments.

fu•sil•lade (fyōō'sə läd', -lād', -zə-), *n.* a simultaneous or continuous discharge of firearms.

fu•sion (fyōō'zhən), *n.* **1.** the act or process of fusing or the state of being fused. **2.** something that is fused. **3.** the joining of atomic nuclei in a reaction to form nuclei of heavier atoms.

fuss (fus), *n.* **1.** needless or useless bustle. **2.** a quarrel or dispute. **3.** a complaint, esp. about something unimportant. —*v.i.* **4.** to make a fuss. **5.** to complain, esp. about something unimportant.

fuss'budg'et, *n.* a fussy or needlessly faultfinding person.

fuss'y, *adj.,* **-i•er, -i•est. 1.** excessively anxious or particular about petty details. **2.** hard to satisfy or please. **3.** giving or calling for careful attention to details. **4.** excessively detailed. **5.** easily irritated. —**fuss'i•ly,** *adv.* —**fuss'i•ness,** *n.*

fus•tian (fus′chən), n. 1. a stout fabric of cotton and flax. 2. inflated or turgid writing or speech.

fus•ty (fus′tē), adj., -ti•er, -ti•est. 1. moldy; musty. 2. old-fashioned or out-of-date. —**fus′ti•ness,** n.

fut., future.

fu•tile (fyo͞ot′l, fyo͞o′tīl), adj. 1. incapable of producing a useful result; vain. 2. trifling; frivolous. —**fu′tile•ly,** adv. —**fu•til′i•ty,** n.

fu•ton (fo͞o′ton), n. a thin, quiltlike mattress placed on a floor for sleeping or used as seating.

fu•ture (fyo͞o′chər), n. 1. time that is to come hereafter. 2. something that will happen in the future. 3. a condition, esp. of success or failure, to come. 4. a. the future tense. b. a verb form in the future tense. 5. Usu., -tures. commodities bought and sold speculatively for future delivery. —adj. 6. being or coming hereafter. 7. of or being a verb tense that refers to events or states in time to come.

fu′tur•ism, n. (sometimes cap.) an artistic movement that attempted to express the dynamism and speed of industrial technology. —**fu′tur•ist,** n.

fu′tur•is′tic, adj. of the future or futurism.

fu•tu•ri•ty (fyo͞o to͞or′i tē, -tyo͞or′-, -cho͞or′-), n., pl. -ties. 1. future time. 2. a future event, possibility, or prospect. 3. the quality of being future.

fu′tur•ol′o•gy (-chə rol′ə jē), n. the study or forecasting of future trends or developments, as in science. —**fu′tur•ol′o•gist,** n.

futz (futs), v.i. Slang. to pass time idly; fool around.

fu•zee (fyo͞o zē′), n., pl. -zees. FUSEE.

fuzz¹ (fuz), n. loose, light, fibrous, or fluffy matter; down.

fuzz² (fuz), n. Slang. the police.

fuzz′y, adj., -i•er, -i•est. 1. resembling or covered with fuzz. 2. indistinct; blurred. —**fuzz′i•ly,** adv. —**fuzz′i•ness,** n.

FWD, 1. Also, **4WD** four-wheel drive. **2.** front-wheel drive.

fwd., 1. foreword. 2. forward.

-fy, a suffix meaning: to make or cause to be (purify); to become or be made (liquefy).

FYI, for your information.

G

G, g (jē), n., pl. **Gs** or **G's, gs** or **g's.** the seventh letter of the English alphabet, a consonant.

G, 1. general: a motion-picture rating advising that the film is suitable for all age groups. **2.** German.

G, Symbol. 1. the seventh in order or in a series. **2.** the fifth note of the C major scale.

g, 1. good. **2.** gram. **3.** gravity.

g, Symbol. acceleration of gravity.

GA, 1. general of the army. **2.** Georgia.

Ga, Chem. Symbol. gallium.

Ga., Georgia.

gab (gab), v., **gabbed, gab•bing,** n. Informal. —v.i. **1.** to talk idly; chatter. —n. **2.** idle talk. —**gab′ber,** n.

gab•ar•dine (gab′ər dēn′), n. a firm, woven fabric of worsted, cotton, or other fiber, with a twill weave.

gab•ble (gab′əl), v., **-bled, -bling,** n. —v.i., v.t. **1.** to speak or utter rapidly and unintelligibly. —n. **2.** rapid, unintelligible talk.

gab′by, adj., **-bi•er, -bi•est.** talkative; garrulous.

gab′fest′, n. Informal. **1.** a gathering at which there is a great deal of conversation. **2.** a long conversation.

Ga•ble (gā′bəl), n. **(William) Clark,** 1901–60, U.S. film actor.

Ga•bon (gA bôn′), n. a republic in W equatorial Africa. 1,190,159. —**Gab•o•nese** (gab′ə nēz′, -nēs′, gä′bə-), adj., n., pl. **-nese.**

Ga•bo•ro•ne (gä′bə rō′nē, gab′ə-), n. the capital of Botswana. 110,973.

Ga•bri•el (gā′brē əl), n. **1.** one of the archangels, appearing usu. as a divine messenger. Dan. 8:16; 9:21; Luke 1:19, 26. **2.** Islam. the angel of revelation and the intermediary between God and Muhammad.

gad (gad), v.i., **gad•ded, gad•ding.** to move aimlessly or restlessly about.

Gad (gad), n. **1.** a son of Jacob and Zilpah. Gen. 30:11. **2.** one of the twelve tribes of Israel. **3.** a Hebrew prophet and chronicler of the court of David. II Sam. 24:11–19.

gad′a•bout′, n. a person who moves about restlessly, esp. from one social activity to another.

Gad•a•ra (gad′ər ə), n. a town on the Sea of Galilee where Jesus compelled demons to enter a herd of swine (the **Gad′arene swine′**). Mark 5:1–13. —**Gad•a•rene** (gad′ə rēn′, gad′ə rēn′), adj.

gad′fly′, n., pl. **-flies. 1.** any of various flies that bite or annoy livestock. **2.** a person who persistently annoys or stirs up others.

gadg•et (gaj′it), n. a usu. small mechanical or electronic contrivance or device. —**gad′get•ry,** n.

gad•o•lin•i•um (gad′l in′ē əm), n. a rare-earth metallic element. Symbol: Gd; at. wt.: 157.25; at. no.: 64.

Gads′den Pur′chase, n. a tract of 45,535 sq. mi. (117,935 sq. km), now contained in New Mexico and Arizona, purchased for $10,000,000 from Mexico in 1853, the treaty being negotiated by James Gadsden.

Gael (gāl), n. a Gaelic-speaking inhabitant of Scotland or Ireland.

Gael′ic, n. **1.** SCOTTISH GAELIC. **2.** IRISH (def. 2). —adj. **3.** of the Gaels or Gaelic.

gaff¹ (gaf), n. **1.** an iron hook with a handle for landing large fish. **2.** a spar that supports the head of a fore-and-aft sail.

gaff² (gaf), n. Informal. harsh treatment, criticism, or ridicule (used esp. in the phrase stand the gaff).

gaffe (gaf), n. a social blunder.

gaf′fer, n. **1.** the chief electrician on a motion-picture or television production. **2.** Informal. an old man.

gag¹ (gag), v., **gagged, gag•ging,** n. —v.t. **1.** to stop up the mouth of (a person) by putting something in it, thus preventing speech, shouts, etc. **2.** to restrain from free speech. **3.** to cause to retch or choke. —v.i. **4.** to retch or choke. —n. **5.** something put into a person's mouth to prevent speech, shouting, etc. **6.** any suppression of free speech. **7.** a surgical instrument for holding the jaws open.

gag² (gag), n., v., **gagged, gag•ging.** Informal. —n. **1.** a joke. **2.** any contrived piece of wordplay or horseplay. —v.i. **3.** to tell jokes.

gage¹ (gāj), n. something, as a glove, thrown down

by a medieval knight in token of a challenge to combat.

gage² (gāj), *v.t.,* **gaged, gag•ing,** *n.* (chiefly in technical use) GAUGE.

gag•gle (gag′əl), *n.* **1.** a flock of geese when not flying. **2.** any disorderly group or gathering.

gai•e•ty (gā′i tē), *n., pl.* **-ties. 1.** the quality or state of being gay or cheerful; merriment. **2.** merrymaking or festivity. **3.** showiness; finery.

gai•ly (gā′lē), *adv.* **1.** merrily; cheerfully. **2.** brightly; showily.

gain (gān), *v.t.* **1.** to get (something desired), esp. as a result of one's efforts. **2.** to acquire as an increase or addition: *to gain speed.* **3.** to obtain as a profit or advantage. **4.** to win. **5.** to reach by effort. —*v.i.* **6.** to improve: *to gain in health.* **7.** to get nearer, as in pursuit: *Our horse gained on the favorite.* —*n.* **8.** profit or advantage. **9.** an increase or advance. **10.** **gains,** profits or winnings. —*Proverb.* **11. no gain without pain,** success requires considerable effort.

gain•ful, *adj.* profitable; lucrative. —**gain′ful•ly,** *adv.*

gain•say (gān′sā′, gān sā′), *v.t.,* **-said, -say•ing. 1.** to deny; contradict. **2.** to speak or act against. —**gain′say′er,** *n.*

gait (gāt), *n.* **1.** a manner of walking, stepping, or running. **2.** any of the manners in which a horse moves, as a trot, canter, or gallop.

gait′er, *n.* **1.** a cloth or leather covering for the ankle, instep, and lower leg. **2.** a cloth or leather shoe with elastic insertions at the sides.

gal (gal), *n. Informal.* a girl.

gal., gallon.

ga•la (gā′lə, gal′ə; *esp. Brit.* gä′lə), *adj., n., pl.* **-las.** —*adj.* **1.** festive; showy. —*n.* **2.** a festive occasion or celebration.

ga•lac•tose (gə lak′tōs), *n.* a white sugar obtained from lactose and vegetable mucilage.

Gal•a•had (gal′ə had′), *n. Sir,* a noble and pure knight of Arthurian legend, who gained the Holy Grail.

Ga•lá′pa•gos Is′lands (gə lä′pə gōs′, -gəs, -lap′-ə-), *n.pl.* an archipelago on the equator in the Pacific, ab. 600 mi. (965 km) W of and belonging to Ecuador: many unique species of animal life. 4058; 3029 sq. mi. (7845 sq. km)

Ga•la′tia (gə lā′shə, -shē ə), *n.* an ancient country in central Asia Minor: site of an early Christian community.

Ga•la•tians (gə lā′shənz), *n.* a book of the New Testament, written to the Christians in Galatia.

gal•ax•y (gal′ək sē), *n., pl.* **-ax•ies. 1. a.** a large system of stars held together by mutual gravitation. **b.** (*usu. cap.*) MILKY WAY. **2.** any large and brilliant assemblage of persons or things. [< Gk *galaxías (kýklos)* the Milky (Way)] —**ga•lac•tic** (gə lak′tik), *adj.*

Gal•braith (gal′brāth), *n.* **John Kenneth,** born 1908, U.S. economist, born in Canada.

gale (gāl), *n.* **1.** a very strong wind. **2.** a noisy outburst: *a gale of laughter.*

ga•le•na (gə lē′nə), *n.* a common heavy mineral: the principal ore of lead.

Gal•i•le•an (gal′ə lē′ən), *adj.* **1.** of Galilee. —*n.* **2.** an inhabitant of Galilee. **3.** a Christian. **4. the Galilean,** Jesus.

Gal•i•lee (gal′ə lē′), *n.* an ancient Roman province in what is now N Israel.

Gal•i•le•o (gal′ə lā′ō, -lē′ō), *n.* **1.** (*Galileo Galilei*), 1564–1642, Italian physicist and astronomer. **2.** a U.S. space probe to Jupiter, launched 1989.

gall¹ (gôl), *n.* **1.** impudence; effrontery. **2.** BILE (def. 1). **3.** something bitter or severe. **4.** bitterness of spirit; rancor.

gall² (gôl), *v.t.* **1.** to make sore by rubbing. **2.** to vex or irritate. —*n.* **3.** a sore on the skin, esp. of a horse, due to rubbing. **4.** something vexing or irritating. —**gall′ing,** *adj.*

gall³ (gôl), *n.* any abnormal swelling on a plant, as from insects.

gal•lant (gal′ənt; *for 2, 5 also* gə lant′, -länt′), *adj.* **1.** brave, spirited, or noble-minded. **2.** polite and attentive to women; chivalrous. **3.** stately; grand. **4.** showy or stylish. —*n.* **5.** a man exceptionally attentive to women. **6.** a stylish and dashing man. —**gal′lant•ly,** *adv.*

gal′lant•ry, *n., pl.* **-ries. 1.** dashing courage; heroic bravery. **2.** courteous attention to women. **3.** a gallant action or speech.

gall′blad′der, *n.* a membranous sac attached to the liver, in which bile is stored and concentrated.

gal•le•on (gal′ē ən, gal′yən), *n.* a large sailing ship of the 15th to 17th centuries.

gal•ler•y (gal′ə rē), *n., pl.* **-ler•ies. 1.** a balcony in a theater, church, or other public building. **2.** the uppermost of such balconies in a theater, usu. containing the cheapest seats. **3.** the occupants of these seats. **4.** a group of spectators, as at a legislative session. **5.** a room or building devoted to the exhibition of works of art. **6.** a long covered area used as a walk or corridor. **7.** a long porch; veranda. **8.** a large room or building used for photography, target practice, etc.

gal•ley (gal′ē), *n., pl.* **-leys. 1. a.** the kitchen area of a ship, plane, or camper. **b.** any small narrow kitchen. **2.** a seagoing ship propelled mainly by oars, used in ancient and medieval times. **3. a.** a tray for holding type that has been set. **b.** Also called **gal′ley proof′.** a proof printed from type in such a tray.

Gal•lic (gal′ik), *adj.* **1.** of the French or France; characteristically French. **2.** of the Gauls or Gaul.

Gal′li•cism (-ə siz′əm), *n.* (*sometimes l.c.*) a French idiom or trait.

gal•li•mau•fry (gal′ə mô′frē), *n., pl.* **-fries.** a hodgepodge; jumble; confused medley.

Gal•li•o (gal′ē ō′), *n.* a Roman proconsul before whom the Apostle Paul appeared on a mission to Corinth. Acts 18:12–17.

gal•li•um (gal′ē əm), *n.* a rare steel-gray metallic element used in high-temperature thermometers. *Symbol:* Ga; *at. wt.:* 69.72; *at. no.:* 31.

gal•li•vant (gal′ə vant′), *v.i.* to wander about, seeking pleasure or diversion.

gal•lon (gal′ən), *n.* a unit of capacity equal to four quarts or 231 cubic inches (3.7853 liters).

gal•lop (gal′əp), *n.* **1.** a fast gait of a horse or other quadruped in which all four feet are off the ground at once. —*v.i., v.t.* **2.** to move or cause to move at a gallop.

gal•lows (gal′ōz, -əz), *n., pl.* **-lows, -lows•es.** a frame consisting of two upright timbers with a crossbeam from which condemned persons are hanged.

gall′stone′, *n.* an abnormal stony mass in the gallbladder or the bile passages.

Gal•lup (gal′əp), *n.* **George Horace,** 1901–84, U.S. statistician.

ga•lore (gə lôr′), *adv.* in abundance; in plentiful amounts: *food and drink galore.*

ga•losh or **-loshe** (gə losh′), *n., pl.* **-losh•es.** a waterproof overshoe.

gal•va•nism (gal′və niz′əm), *n.* electricity, esp. as produced by chemical action. —**gal•van′ic** (-van′ik), *adj.*

gal′va•nize′, *v.t.,* **-nized, -niz•ing. 1.** to stimulate by an electric current. **2.** to stimulate or startle into sudden activity. **3.** to coat (iron or steel) with zinc.

gal′va•nom′e•ter (-nom′i tər), *n.* an instrument for detecting small electric currents and determining their strength.

Ga•ma (gam′ə, gä′mə), *n.* **Vasco da,** c1460–1524, Portuguese navigator.

Ga•ma•li•el (gə mā′lē əl, -māl′yəl), *n.* **1.** ("*the Elder*" or "*Gamaliel I*"), died A.D. 50?, the teacher of Paul (Acts 22:3); the grandson of Hillel. **2.** his grandson ("*the Younger*" or "*Gamaliel II*"), died A.D. 115?, leader of the Jews after the destruction of Jerusalem, A.D. 70.

Gam•bi•a (gam′bē ə), *n.* **the,** a republic in W Africa. 1,248,085. —**Gam′bi•an,** *n., adj.*

gam•bit (gam′bit), *n.* **1.** a chess opening to obtain some advantage by sacrificing a pawn or piece. **2.** any maneuver used to gain an advantage.

gam•ble (gam′bəl), v., **-bled, -bling,** n. —v.i. **1.** to play at a game of chance for money or other stakes. **2.** to stake or risk something of value on the outcome of something involving chance. —v.t. **3.** to lose by betting. **4.** to wager or risk (something of value). —n. **5.** any matter or thing involving risk. —**gam′bler,** n.

gam•bol (gam′bəl), v., **-boled, -bol•ing** or (esp. Brit.) **-bolled, -bol•ling,** n. —v.i. **1.** to skip about in play; frolic. —n. **2.** a skipping or frisking about.

gam′brel roof′, n. a gable roof, each side of which has a shallower slope above a steeper one.

game¹ (gām), n., adj., **gam•er, gam•est,** v., **gamed, gam•ing.** —n. **1.** an amusement or pastime. **2.** the equipment used in playing certain games. **3.** a competitive activity involving skill, chance, or endurance played according to rules. **4.** a single occasion of such an activity. **5.** the number of points required to win. **6.** a particular manner or style of playing. **7.** Informal. a business or profession. **8.** a trick or strategy. **9.** wild animals, including birds and fishes, hunted for food or sport. **10.** any object of attack, abuse, etc.: to be fair game for practical jokers. —adj. **11.** of or noting hunted animals or their flesh. **12.** having a fighting spirit; plucky. **13.** having the required spirit or will. —v.i. **14.** to play games of chance for stakes. **15. only game in town,** the only available choice. **16. play games,** to manipulate others **17. play the game,** to act in accordance with standards. —Saying. **18. The game is not worth the candle,** the effort required is more than the results are worth. —**game′ly,** adv. —**game′ness,** n.

game² (gām), adj. lame: a game leg.

game′cock′, n. a rooster bred and trained for fighting.

game′keep′er, n. a person employed to prevent poaching and provide for the conservation of game.

game′ plan′, n. a carefully planned strategy or course of action.

game′ point′, n. (in tennis, squash, etc.) a situation in which the next point scored could decide the winner.

games′man•ship′, n. skill in manipulating people or events so as to gain an advantage or outwit one's opponents.

game′ster (-stər), n. a person who plays games, esp. a gambler.

gam•ete (gam′ēt, gə mēt′), n. a mature sexual reproductive cell that unites with another cell to form a new organism.

gam•in (gam′in), n. **1.** a neglected boy left to run about the streets. **2.** GAMINE (def. 2).

gam•ine (gam′ēn, -in, gə mēn′), n. **1.** a neglected girl left to run about the streets. **2.** a diminutive girl who is playfully mischievous.

gam•ma (gam′ə), n., pl. **-mas.** the third letter of the Greek alphabet (Γ, γ).

gam′ma glob′ulin, n. a protein fraction of blood plasma that responds to stimulation of antigens by forming antibodies.

gam′ma ray′, n. a highly penetrating photon of high frequency.

gam•ut (gam′ət), n. **1.** the entire scale or range. **2.** the whole series of recognized musical notes.

gam•y (gā′mē), adj., **-i•er, -i•est. 1.** having the tangy flavor of game, esp. game kept uncooked until slightly tainted. **2.** plucky; game. **3.** risqué. —**gam′i•ness,** n.

gan•der (gan′dər), n. **1.** the male of the goose. **2.** Slang. a look; glance.

Gan•dhi (gän′dē, gan′-), n. **1. Indira,** 1917–84, prime minister of India 1966–77 and 1980–84 (daughter of Jawaharlal Nehru). **2. Mohandas Karamchand** ("Mahatma"), 1869–1948, Hindu religious leader and nationalist.

gang (gang), n. **1.** a group of people associated or working together. **2.** a group of persons associated for some criminal or other antisocial purpose. —v.t.,

v.i. **3.** to form into a gang. **4. gang up on,** to attack as a group.

Gan•ges (gan′jēz), n. a river in N India flowing into the Bay of Bengal. 1550 mi. (2495 km) long.

gang•land (gang′land′, -lənd), n. the world of organized crime; criminal underworld.

gan•gling (gang′gling) also **-gly** (-glē), adj. awkwardly tall and spindly.

gan•gli•on (gang′glē ən), n., pl. **-gli•a** (-glē ə), **-gli•ons.** a concentrated mass of interconnected nerve cells.

gang•plank (gang′plangk′), n. a movable bridgelike structure for use by persons boarding or leaving a ship.

gan•grene (gang′grēn, gang grēn′), n. necrosis of soft tissue due to obstructed circulation. —**gan′gre•nous** (-grə nəs), adj.

gang′ster, n. a member of a gang of criminals.

gang•way (n. gang′wā′; interj. gang′wā′), n. **1.** a passageway. **2. a.** an opening in the railing or bulwark of a ship. **b.** GANGPLANK. —interj. **3.** clear the way!

gant•let (gant′lit, gônt′-), n. GAUNTLET² (def. 1).

gan•try (gan′trē), n., pl. **-tries. 1.** a spanning framework, as a bridgelike portion of certain cranes. **2.** a frame consisting of scaffolds on various levels used to erect rockets.

gaol (jāl), n., v.t. Brit. JAIL. —**gaol′er,** n.

gap (gap), n. **1.** a break or opening, as in a fence or wall. **2.** an empty space or interval. **3.** a wide divergence or difference; disparity. **4.** a deep ravine or mountain pass.

gape (gāp, gap), v., **gaped, gap•ing,** n. —v.i. **1.** to stare with open mouth, as in wonder. **2.** to open the mouth wide involuntarily, as the result of sleepiness. **3.** to open as a gap. —n. **4.** a wide opening or gap. **5.** an act or instance of gaping.

gar (gär), n., pl. **gars, gar.** a North American freshwater fish with a long jaw and large teeth.

ga•rage (gə räzh′, -räj′; esp. Brit. gar′ij, -äzh), n., v., **-raged, -rag•ing.** —n. **1.** a structure for parking or storing motor vehicles. **2.** a commercial establishment for repairing and servicing motor vehicles. —v.t. **3.** to put or keep in a garage.

garage′ sale′, n. a sale of used household goods or personal items.

garb (gärb), n. **1.** a fashion or mode of dress, esp. of a distinctive, uniform kind. **2.** outward appearance or form. —v.t. **3.** to dress; clothe.

gar•bage (gär′bij), n. **1.** discarded matter, esp. kitchen refuse. **2.** anything worthless, inferior, or vile.

gar•ban•zo (gär bän′zō), n., pl. **-zos.** CHICKPEA.

gar•ble (gär′bəl), v.t., **-bled, -bling.** to distort or confuse (a report, message, etc.) so as to be misleading or unintelligible.

gar•çon (gar sôn′), n., pl. **-çons** (-sôn′). French. a waiter in a restaurant.

gar•den (gär′dn), n. **1.** a plot of ground where flowers, vegetables, fruits, or herbs are cultivated. **2.** a planted area used for public recreation. **3.** a fertile and delightful spot. —adj. **4.** of, for, or produced in a garden. —v.i. **5.** to tend a garden. [< OF jardin < Gmc] —**gar′den•er,** n.

Gar′den Grove′, n. a city in SW California. 147,958.

gar•de•nia (gär dē′nyə, -nē ə), n., pl. **-nias. 1.** an evergreen tree or shrub with shiny leaves and fragrant white flowers. **2.** its flower.

gar′den-vari′ety, adj. common or ordinary; unexceptional.

Gar•field (gär′fēld′), n. **James Abram,** 1831–81, 20th president of the U.S., 1881.

gar′fish′, n., pl. **-fish, -fish•es.** GAR.

gar•gan•tu•an (gär gan′chōō ən), adj. gigantic.

gar•gle (gär′gəl), v., **-gled, -gling,** n. —v.t., v.i. **1.** to rinse (the throat) with a liquid kept in motion by a stream of air from the lungs. —n. **2.** a liquid used for gargling.

gar·goyle (gär′goil), *n.* a grotesquely carved figure of a human or animal, often functioning as a water-spout, projecting from a building.

gargoyle

Gar·i·bal·di (gar′ə bôl′dē), *n.* **Giuseppe,** 1807–82, Italian patriot and general.

gar·ish (gâr′ish, gar′-), *adj.* crudely or tastelessly colorful, showy, or elaborate. —**gar′ish·ly,** *adv.* —**gar′ish·ness,** *n.*

gar·land (gär′lənd), *n.* **1.** a wreath or festoon of flowers, leaves, or other material. —*v.t.* **2.** to deck with garlands.

Gar′land, *n.* a city in NE Texas. 194,218.

gar·lic (gär′lik), *n.* a hardy plant of the amaryllis family, having a strongly pungent bulb that is used in cooking. —**gar′lick·y,** *adj.*

gar·ment (gär′mənt), *n.* any article of clothing.

gar·ner (gär′nər), *v.t.* **1.** to gather and store. **2.** to get or acquire.

gar·net (gär′nit), *n.* any of a group of deep red, brownish, or green vitreous minerals: several varieties are used as gems.

gar·nish (gär′nish), *v.t.* **1.** to provide with something ornamental. **2.** to provide (a food) with something that adds flavor, decorative color, etc. **3.** GARNISHEE. —*n.* **4.** something used to garnish a food.

gar·nish·ee (gär′ni shē′), *v.t.,* -eed, -ee·ing. *Law.* to attach (money or property) by garnishment.

gar′nish·ment, *n. Law.* a warning served on a third party to hold wages, property, etc., belonging to a debtor pending settlement in court.

gar·ret (gar′it), *n.* an attic, usu. a small, cramped one.

gar·ri·son (gar′ə sən), *n.* **1.** a body of troops stationed in a fortified place. **2.** any military post. —*v.t.* **3.** to station (troops) in a fort, post, etc.

Gar·ri·son (gar′ə sən), *n.* **William Lloyd,** 1805–79, U.S. leader in the abolition movement.

gar·rote or **-rotte** (gə rot′, -rōt′), *n., v.,* -rot·ed, -rot·ing or -rot·ted, -rot·ting. —*n.* **1.** a method of capital punishment of Spanish origin in which a person is strangled by an iron collar. **2.** strangulation, esp. in the course of a robbery. **3.** a cord or wire with attached handles, used to strangle a victim. —*v.t.* **4.** to strangle or throttle, as by a garrote.

gar·ru·lous (gar′ə ləs, gar′yə-), *adj.* **1.** excessively talkative in a rambling manner. **2.** wordy or diffuse. —**gar·ru·li·ty** (gə rōō′li tē), **gar′ru·lous·ness,** *n.* —**gar′ru·lous·ly,** *adv.*

gar·ter (gär′tər), *n.* a device for holding up a stocking or sock.

gar′ter snake′, *n.* a harmless, striped snake common in North and Central America.

Gar·y (gâr′ē, gar′ē), *n.* a port in NW Indiana. 114,256.

gas (gas), *n., pl.* **gas·es,** *v.,* **gassed, gas·sing.** —*n.* **1.** a fluid substance with the ability to expand indefinitely. **2.** any such fluid or mixture of fluids used as a fuel, anesthetic, asphyxiating agent, etc. **3. a.** gasoline. **b.** the accelerator of an automotive vehicle. **4.** FLATUS. —*v.t.* **5.** to overcome, poison, or asphyxiate with gas. **6.** to treat with gas. —**gas′e·ous** (gas′-ē əs, gash′əs), *adj.*

gas′ cham′ber, *n.* a room used for executing prisoners by poison gas.

gash (gash), *n.* **1.** a long, deep wound or cut. —*v.t.* **2.** to make a gash in.

gas·ket (gas′kit), *n.* a rubber, metal, or rope ring for packing a piston or placing around a joint to make it watertight.

gas′light′, *n.* light produced by the combustion of illuminating gas.

gas′ mask′, *n.* a masklike device that filters air to protect the wearer against noxious gases.

gas·o·hol (-hôl′, -hol′), *n.* a mixture of gasoline and ethyl alcohol, used as an automobile fuel. [*gas(oline)* + *(alc)ohol*]

gas·o·line (gas′ə lēn′, gas′ə lēn′), *n.* a volatile, flammable liquid mixture of hydrocarbons obtained from petroleum, used chiefly as fuel for internal-combustion engines.

gasp (gasp, gäsp), *n.* **1.** a sudden, short intake of breath. **2.** a short, convulsive utterance. —*v.i.* **3.** to struggle for breath with the mouth open; breathe convulsively. —*v.t.* **4.** to utter with gasps.

gas′ sta′tion, *n.* SERVICE STATION.

gas·tric (gas′trik), *adj.* pertaining to the stomach.

gas′tric juice′, *n.* the digestive fluid secreted by the glands of the stomach.

gas·tri·tis (ga strī′tis), *n.* inflammation of the stomach.

gas′tro·in·tes′ti·nal (gas′trō-), *adj.* of or affecting the stomach and intestines.

gas·tron·o·my (ga stron′ə mē), *n.* the art or science of good eating. —**gas·tro·nom·ic** (gas′trə-nom′ik), **gas′tro·nom′i·cal,** *adj.*

gas·tro·pod (gas′trə pod′), *n.* any of a class of mollusks including snails, slugs, etc., having a single shell and a muscular foot for locomotion.

gas′works′, *n., pl.* -works. (*used with a sing. v.*) a plant where heating and illuminating gas is manufactured and piped to consumers.

gate (gāt), *n.* **1.** a movable barrier closing an opening in a fence, wall, etc. **2.** any movable barrier, as at a tollbooth. **3.** any means of access or entrance. **4.** a sliding barrier for regulating the passage of water or steam. **5.** the total number of persons who pay for admission to a sports event, performance, etc. **6. the gate,** rejection.

-gate, a combining form extracted from WATERGATE, used in names of scandals arising from improprieties in government or business (*Irangate*).

gate′-crash′er, *n.* a person who attends a social function, performance, or sports event without an invitation or ticket.

gate′post′, *n.* the vertical post on which a gate is suspended by hinges.

gate′way′, *n.* **1.** an entrance or passage that may be closed by a gate. **2.** any means of entrance.

Gath (gath), *n.* a Philistine city on the coast of Palestine. I Sam. 17:4.

gath·er (gath′ər), *v.t.* **1.** to bring together into one group or place. **2.** to pick or harvest. **3.** to scoop up: *She gathered the child in her arms.* **4.** to increase gradually: *The car gathered speed.* **5.** to assemble or collect for an effort: *to gather one's strength.* **6.** to conclude from observation. **7.** to wrap or draw around, as a garment. **8.** to draw (cloth) into fine folds by means of stitches. —*v.i.* **9.** to come together or assemble. **10.** to increase. —*n.* **11.** Often, -ers. a fold or pucker. —**gath′er·er,** *n.* —**gath′er·ing,** *n.*

gauche (gōsh), *adj.* lacking social grace; tactless. —**gauche′ly,** *adv.*

gau·che·rie (gō′shə rē′), *n., pl.* -ries. **1.** lack of social grace; tactlessness. **2.** a gauche act or movement.

gau·cho (gou′chō), *n., pl.* -chos. a cowboy of the South American pampas.

gaud·y (gô′dē), *adj.,* -i·er, -i·est. showy in a tasteless way. —**gaud′i·ly,** *adv.* —**gaud′i·ness,** *n.*

gauge (gāj), *v.,* **gauged, gaug·ing,** *n.* —*v.t.* **1.** to determine the exact dimensions, capacity, quantity, or force of. **2.** to appraise or judge. —*n.* **3.** a standard of measure or measurement. **4.** any device for measuring or testing something. **5.** a means of estimating or judging. **6.** the internal diameter of a shotgun barrel. **7.** the distance between the two rails in a track. **8.** the thickness or diameter of various thin objects, as wire.

Gau•guin (gō gaN′), *n.* **(Eugène Henri) Paul,** 1848–1903, French painter.

Gaul (gôl), *n.* **1.** an ancient region of the Roman Empire, in W Europe. **2.** a native or inhabitant of Gaul. **3.** a native or inhabitant of France.

gaunt (gônt), *adj.,* **-er, -est. 1.** extremely thin and bony; haggard. **2.** bleak, desolate, or grim. **—gaunt′-ness,** *n.*

gaunt•let[1] (gônt′lit, gänt′-), *n.* **1.** a mailed glove worn with a suit of armor to protect the hand. **2.** a glove with an extended cuff. —**Idiom. 3.** throw down the gauntlet, to challenge someone to fight.

gaunt•let[2] (gônt′lit, gänt′-), *n.* **1.** a former military punishment in which the offender ran between two rows of men who struck at him as he passed. —**Idiom. 2.** run the gauntlet, to suffer severe criticism or tribulation.

Gau•ta•ma (gō′tə mə, gou′-), *n.* BUDDHA. Also called **Gau′tama Bud′dha.**

gauze (gôz), *n.* a thin, transparent fabric in a loose weave, used esp. for surgical dressings. **—gauz′y,** *adj.,* **-i•er, -i•est.**

gave (gāv), *v.* pt. of GIVE.

gav•el (gav′əl), *n.* a small mallet used, as by a judge, to signal for attention or order.

ga•votte (gə vot′), *n.* an old French dance in moderately quick quadruple meter.

gawk (gôk), *v.i.* to stare stupidly.

gawk′y, *adj.,* **-i•er, -i•est.** awkward or ungainly. **—gawk′i•ly,** *adv.* **—gawk′i•ness,** *n.*

gay (gā), *adj.,* **-er, -est,** *n.* —*adj.* **1.** having or showing a lively mood; merry. **2.** bright or showy: *gay colors.* **3.** homosexual. —*n.* **4.** a homosexual person, esp. a male.

gay′e•ty, *n., pl.* **-ties.** GAIETY.

gay′ly, *adv.* GAILY.

Ga′za Strip′, *n.* a coastal area on the E Mediterranean: formerly in the Palestine mandate, occupied by Israel 1967–94; since 1994 under Palestinian self-rule.

gaze (gāz), *v.,* **gazed, gaz•ing,** *n.* —*v.i.* **1.** to look steadily and intently. —*n.* **2.** a steady or intent look. **—gaz′er,** *n.*

ga•ze•bo (gə zā′bō, -zē′-), *n., pl.* **-bos, -boes.** a structure, as a pavilion, built on a site that provides an attractive view.

ga•zelle (gə zel′), *n., pl.* **-zelles, -zelle.** any of various small graceful antelopes of Africa and Asia.

ga•zette (gə zet′), *n., v.,* **-zet•ted, -zet•ting.** —*n.* **1.** a newspaper (now used chiefly in names). **2.** *Brit.* a government journal listing appointments, promotions, etc. —*v.t.* **3.** *Brit.* to announce or list in a gazette.

gaz•et•teer (gaz′i tēr′), *n.* a geographical dictionary.

G.B., Great Britain.

Gd, *Chem. Symbol.* gadolinium.

Ge, *Chem. Symbol.* germanium.

gear

gear (gēr), *n.* **1. a.** a part, esp. a wheel, having teeth that mesh with teeth in another part to transmit or receive force and motion. **b.** an assembly of such parts. **2.** implements, tools, or apparatus: *fishing gear.* **3.** portable items of personal property, including clothing. —*v.t.* **4.** to provide with or connect by gears. **5.** to put in gear. **6.** to adjust or regulate so as to match or conform to something: *to gear output to seasonal demands.* **7.** gear up, to get ready; prepare.

—*Idiom.* **8. in gear, a.** in the state in which gears are engaged. **b.** in proper working order. **9. out of gear,** in the state in which gears are disengaged.

gear′shift′, *n.* a lever used for engaging and disengaging the gears in a power-transmission system, esp. in a motor vehicle.

gear′wheel′, *n.* COGWHEEL.

Ged•a•li•ah (ged′l ī′ə, gi däl′yə), *n.* the governor of Judah after its conquest by Babylon. II Kings 25:22–26.

gee (jē), *interj.* an exclamation of surprise, disappointment, etc.

geek (gēk), *n. Slang.* **1.** a carnival performer billed as performing bizarre acts. **2.** a peculiar or offensive person, esp. one who is overly intellectual.

geese (gēs), *n.* pl. of GOOSE.

gee•zer (gē′zər), *n. Slang.* an odd or eccentric man.

ge•fil′te fish′ (gə fil′tə), *n.* cakes of chopped boned fish mixed with egg, matzo meal, etc., and simmered in a broth.

Ge•hen•na (gi hen′ə), *n.* **1.** the valley of Hinnom, near Jerusalem, where propitiatory sacrifices were made to Moloch. II Kings 23:10. **2.** HELL (def. 1). **3.** any place of extreme torment or suffering.

Geh•rig (ger′ig), *n.* **Henry Louis** (*"Lou"*), 1903–41, U.S. baseball player.

Gei′ger count′er (gī′gər), *n.* an instrument for detecting ionizing radiations, used chiefly to measure radioactivity.

Gei•sel (gī′zəl), *n.* **Theodor Seuss** (soos), (*"Dr. Seuss"*), 1904–91, U.S. humorist, illustrator, and author of children's books.

gei•sha (gā′shə, gē′-), *n., pl.* **-shas, -sha.** a Japanese woman trained as a professional singer, dancer, and companion for men.

gel (jel), *n., v.,* **gelled, gel•ling.** —*n.* **1.** a semirigid colloidal dispersion of a solid with a liquid or gas, as a jelly or glue. —*v.i.* **2.** to form or become a gel.

gel•a•tin or **-tine** (jel′ə tn), *n.* a glutinous substance obtained by boiling animal bones, ligaments, etc., or a similar vegetable substance, used in making jellies, glues, and the like. [< F *gélatine* < ML *gelātīna* < L *gelātus* frozen] **—ge•lat•i•nous** (jə lat′n əs), *adj.*

geld (geld), *v.t.* **geld•ed** or **gelt, geld•ing.** to castrate (esp. a horse).

geld′ing, *n.* a castrated horse.

gel•id (jel′id), *adj.* very cold; icy.

Gell-Mann (gel män′, -man′), *n.* **Murray,** born 1929, U.S. physicist.

gem (jem), *n.* **1.** a mineral, pearl, or other natural substance fine enough for use in jewelry. **2.** something prized because of its beauty or worth.

gem•i•nate (jem′ə nāt′), *v.t., v.i.,* **-nat•ed, -nat•ing.** to make or become doubled or paired. **—gem′i•nate•ly,** *adv.* **—gem′i•na′tion,** *n.*

Gem•i•ni (jem′ə nī′, -nē), *n.* the third sign of the zodiac. [< L: the twins]

gem•ol•o•gy or **gem•mol•o•gy** (je mol′ə jē), *n.* the science dealing with gemstones. **—gem•o•log′i•cal** (jem′ə loj′i kəl), *adj.* **—gem•ol′o•gist,** *n.*

gem′stone′, *n.* a mineral or crystal that can be cut and polished for use as a gem.

-gen, a suffix meaning something that produces (*carcinogen*).

Gen., **1.** General. **2.** Genesis.

gen•darme (zhän′därm; *Fr.* zhäN däRM′), *n.* a police officer, esp. in France.

gen•der (jen′dər), *n.* **1.** a set of grammatical categories applied to nouns, as masculine, feminine, or neuter, often correlated in part with sex or animateness. **2.** sex: *the feminine gender.*

gene (jēn), *n.* the basic physical unit of heredity, carried on a chromosome and transmitted from parent to offspring.

ge•ne•al•o•gy (jē′nē ol′ə jē, -al′-, jen′ē-), *n., pl.* **-gies. 1.** a record or account of the ancestry of a person, family, etc. **2.** the study of family ancestries. **3.** descent from an ancestor or progenitor. **—ge′ne•a•log′i•cal** (-ə loj′i kəl), *adj.* **—ge′ne•al′o•gist,** *n.*

gen•er•a (jen′ər ə), *n.* a pl. of GENUS.

gen•er•al (jen′ər əl), *adj.* **1.** of or affecting all persons or things belonging to a group or category. **2.** of or true of such persons or things in the main. **3.** not limited to one class, field, etc.: *the general public.* **4.** dealing with broad, universal, or important aspects: *general guidelines.* **5.** not specific or definite: *a general idea.* **6.** having superior rank: *the general manager.* —*n.* **7.** an officer ranking below a general of the army or general of the air force. **8.** an officer holding the highest rank in the U.S. Marine Corps. —*Idiom.* **9.** in general, **a.** as a whole. **b.** as a rule.

Gen′eral Assem′bly, *n.* **1.** the legislature in some states of the U.S. **2.** the main deliberative body of the United Nations.

gen′er•al•is′si•mo (-ə lis′ə mō′), *n., pl.* -mos. (in certain countries) the supreme commander of the armed forces.

gen′er•al′i•ty, *n., pl.* -ties. **1.** an indefinite or undetailed statement. **2.** a general principle or rule. **3.** the greater part or majority. **4.** the state or quality of being general.

gen′er•al•ize′, *v.,* -ized, -iz•ing. —*v.t.* **1.** to infer (a general principle) from particular facts or instances. **2.** to form a general opinion or conclusion from. **3.** to give a general character to. **4.** to bring into general use or knowledge. —*v.i.* **5.** to form general principles, opinions, etc. **6.** to think or speak in generalities. —**gen′er•al•i•za′tion,** *n.*

gen′eral practi′tioner, *n.* a medical practitioner whose practice is not limited to any specific branch of medicine.

gen′er•al•ship′, *n.* **1.** skill as a military commander. **2.** the rank or duties of a general. **3.** management or leadership.

gen′eral store′, *n.* a store, usu. in a rural area, that sells a wide variety of merchandise.

gen•er•ate (jen′ə rāt′), *v.t.,* -at•ed, -at•ing. **1.** to bring into existence. **2.** to reproduce; procreate. —**gen′er•a′tive,** *adj.*

gen′er•a′tion, *n.* **1.** the entire body of individuals born and living at about the same time. **2.** the average period between the birth of parents and the birth of their offspring. **3.** a single step in natural descent, as of human beings. **4.** a stage of technological development or production distinct from but based upon another stage. **5.** the act or process of generating. —**gen′er•a′tion•al,** *adj.*

Generation X (eks), *n.* the generation born in the U.S. after 1965. Also called **Gen X** (jen′ eks′). [after *Generation X,* a novel by Douglas Coupland] —**Generation X′er,** *n.*

gen′er•a′tor, *n.* **1.** a machine that converts mechanical energy into electrical energy, as a dynamo. **2.** one that generates.

ge•ner•ic (jə ner′ik), *adj.* **1.** of or applicable to all the members of a genus, class, group, or kind. **2.** of or constituting a genus. **3.** applicable or referring to both men and women: *a generic pronoun.* **4.** not protected by trademark registration. —*n.* **5.** a generic term. **6.** any product that can be sold without a brand name. —**ge•ner′i•cal•ly,** *adv.*

gen•er•ous (jen′ər əs), *adj.* **1.** liberal in giving or sharing. **2.** free from meanness or pettiness; magnanimous. **3.** large; abundant; ample. —**gen′er•os′i•ty** (-ə ros′i tē), *n.* —**gen′er•ous•ly,** *adv.*

gen•e•sis (jen′ə sis), *n., pl.* -ses (-sēz′). an origin or beginning.

Gen•e•sis (jen′ə sis), *n.* the first book of the Old Testament.

gene′ splic′ing, *n.* the act or process of recombining genes from different sources to form new genetic combinations.

Ge•net (zhə nā′), *n.* **Jean** (zhäN), 1910–86, French playwright and novelist.

gene′ ther′apy, *n.* the treatment of a disease by replacing aberrant genes with normal ones.

genet′ic code′, *n.* the biochemical instructions by which the four DNA bases are arranged, specifying the synthesis of particular proteins that determine hereditary traits.

genet′ic engineer′ing, *n.* the development and application of methods that permit direct manipulation of genetic material to alter the hereditary traits of a cell, organism, or population.

ge•net•ics (jə net′iks), *n.* the branch of biology that deals with heredity and with the genetic contribution to similarities and differences among related organisms. —**ge•net′ic,** *adj.* —**ge•net′i•cal•ly,** *adv.* —**ge•net′i•cist** (-ə sist), *n.*

Ge•ne•va (jə nē′və), *n.* a city in SW Switzerland. 160,900.

Gene′va Conven′tion, *n.* an international agreement establishing rules for the treatment of prisoners of war and of casualties in battle.

Gen•ghis Khan (jeng′gis kän′, geng′-), *n.* 1162–1227, Mongol conqueror.

gen•ial (jēn′yəl, jē′nē əl), *adj.* **1.** pleasantly cheerful; cordial. **2.** pleasantly warm; comfortably mild: *a genial climate.* —**ge′ni•al′i•ty** (-al′i tē), *n.* —**gen′ial•ly,** *adv.*

ge•nie (jē′nē), *n., pl.* -nies. **1.** JINN. —*Saying.* **let the genie out of the bottle,** to release a malign or mischievous force.

gen•i•tal (jen′i tl), *adj.* of or pertaining to reproduction or the sexual organs.

gen′i•ta′li•a (-tā′lē ə, -tāl′yə), *n.pl.* the organs of reproduction.

gen′i•tals, *n.pl.* GENITALIA.

gen•i•tive (jen′i tiv), *adj.* **1.** of or noting a grammatical case typically indicating possession, origin, or other close association. —*n.* **2.** the genitive case.

gen′i•to•u′ri•nar′y (jen′i tō-), *adj.* of the genital and urinary organs.

gen•ius (jēn′yəs), *n., pl.* -ius•es. **1.** an exceptional natural capacity of intellect. **2.** a person having such capacity. **3.** natural ability or talent. **4.** distinctive character or spirit, as of a nation or period.

Gen•nes•a•ret (ge nes′ə ret′), *n.* Galilee. Luke 5:1.

Gen•o•a (jen′ō ə), *n.* a seaport in NW Italy. 762,895.

gen•o•cide (jen′ə sīd′), *n.* the deliberate and systematic extermination of a national, racial, political, or cultural group.

ge•nome (jē′nōm), *n.* a full haploid set of chromosomes with all its genes; the total genetic constitution of a cell or organism.

gen•o•type (jen′ə tīp′, jē′nə-), *n.* **1.** the genetic makeup of an organism or group of organisms. **2.** the sum total of genes transmitted from parent to offspring.

gen•re (zhän′rə; *Fr.* zhäN′ʀ³), *n., pl.* -res. **1.** a class or category of artistic endeavor having a particular form, content, or technique. **2.** painting in which scenes of everyday life form the subject matter.

gent (jent), *n.* a gentleman.

gen•teel (jen tēl′), *adj.* **1.** belonging or suited to polite society. **2.** well-bred or refined. **3.** affectedly or pretentiously polite or delicate.

gen•tian (jen′shən), *n.* any of numerous plants having usu. blue but sometimes yellow, white, or red flowers.

gen•tile (jen′tīl), (*often cap.*) —*adj.* **1.** of or characteristic of any people not Jewish. —*n.* **2.** a person who is not Jewish, esp. a Christian.

gen•til•i•ty (jen til′i tē), *n.* **1.** good breeding or refinement. **2.** affected or pretentious politeness or elegance.

gen•tle (jen′tl), *adj.,* -tler, -tlest. **1.** kindly; amiable. **2.** not severe, rough, or violent: *a gentle tap.* **3.** moderate: *gentle heat.* **4.** not steep. **5.** of or characteristic of good birth. **6.** easily handled or managed. **7.** soft or low. **8.** polite or refined. —**gen′tle•ness,** *n.* —**gen′tly,** *adv.*

gen′tle•folk′ or **-folks′,** *n.pl.* persons of good family and breeding.

gen′tle•man, *n., pl.* -men. **1.** a man of good family or social position. **2.** (used as a polite term) a man. **3. gentlemen,** (used as a form of address): *Gentlemen, please follow me.* **4.** a civilized, educated, or well-mannered man. —**gen′tle•man•ly,** *adv.*

gen′tle•wom′an, *n., pl.* -wom•en. **1.** a woman of

good family or social position. **2.** a civilized, educated, or well-mannered woman.

gen'tri•fy' (-trə fī'), v.t., **-fied, -fy•ing.** to upgrade (a run-down urban neighborhood) by renovating or remodeling buildings. —**gen'tri•fi•ca'tion,** n.

gen'try, n. **1.** wellborn and well-bred people. **2.** (in England) the class below the nobility.

gen•u•flect (jen'yŏŏ flekt'), v.i. to bend or touch one knee to the floor in reverence or worship. —**gen'u•flec'tion,** n.

gen•u•ine (jen'yŏŏ in or, sometimes, -īn'), adj. **1.** possessing the claimed character, quality, or origin; real. **2.** free from pretense, affectation, or hypocrisy: genuine admiration. —**gen'u•ine•ly,** adv. —**gen'u•ine•ness,** n.

ge•nus (jē'nəs), n., pl. **gen•e•ra** (jen'ər ə), **ge•nus•es. 1.** the major subdivision of a biological family or subfamily, usu. consisting of more than one species. **2.** a kind; sort; class.

geo-, a combining form meaning the earth or ground (geography).

ge•o•cen•tric (jē'ō sen'trik), adj. **1.** having or representing the earth as a center. **2.** viewed or measured as from the center of the earth.

ge•ode (jē'ōd), n. a hollow nodular stone often lined with crystals.

ge•o•des•ic (jē'ə des'ik, -dē'sik), n. **1.** Also called **ge'odes'ic line'.** the shortest line on a curved surface connecting two given points. —adj. **2.** of a geodesic.

ge'odes'ic dome', n. a dome consisting of a framework of straight members that form a grid of polygonal faces.

geodesic dome

ge•od•e•sy (jē od'ə sē), n. the branch of applied mathematics that deals with the curvature, shape, and dimensions of the earth. —**ge•od'e•sist,** n.

ge•o•det•ic (jē'ə det'ik), adj. **1.** of geodesy. **2.** GEODESIC.

ge•og•ra•phy (jē og'rə fē), n., pl. **-phies. 1.** the science dealing with the earth's surface features and the climate, vegetation, population, etc., of its countries and other divisions. **2.** the topographical features of a region. —**ge•og'ra•pher,** n. —**ge'o•graph'i•cal** (-ə graf'i kəl), **ge'o•graph'ic,** adj. —**ge'o•graph'i•cal•ly,** adv.

ge•ol•o•gy (jē ol'ə jē), n., pl. **-gies. 1.** the science that deals with the earth's physical history and changes, its rocks, etc. **2.** these features and processes occurring in a given region on the earth or another celestial body. —**ge'o•log'ic** (-ə loj'ik), **ge'o•log'i•cal,** adj. —**ge'o•log'i•cal•ly,** adv. —**ge•ol'o•gist,** n.

ge•o•mag•net•ic (jē'ō mag net'ik), adj. of or characteristic of terrestrial magnetism. —**ge'o•mag'net•ism** (-ni tiz'əm), n.

ge•om•e•try (jē om'i trē), n. the branch of mathematics that deals with the deduction of the properties, measurement, and relationships of points, lines, angles, and figures in space. —**ge'o•met'ric** (-ə met'trik), **ge'o•met'ri•cal,** adj. —**ge'o•met'ri•cal•ly,** adv.

ge•o•phys•ics (jē'ō fiz'iks), n. the branch of geology that deals with the physics of the earth and its atmosphere, including oceanography, seismology, etc. —**ge'o•phys'i•cal,** adj.

ge'o•pol'i•tics, n. the study of the influence of physical geography on the politics, national power, or foreign policy of a state. —**ge'o•po•lit'i•cal** (-pə-lit'i kəl), adj.

George (jôrj), n. **Saint,** died A.D. 303?, Christian martyr: patron saint of England.

George III (jôrj), 1738–1820, king of England 1760–1820.

Geor•gia (jôr'jə), n. **1.** a state in the SE United States. 7,353,225. Cap.: Atlanta. Abbr.: GA, Ga. **2.** Also called **Geor'gian Repub'lic.** a republic in the Caucasus, bordering on the Black Sea: formerly a part of the USSR. 5,174,642. —**Geor'gian,** adj., n.

ge•o•sta•tion•ar•y (jē'ō stā'shə ner'ē), adj. designating a satellite traveling at the same speed as the earth does so as to remain in the same spot over the earth.

ge'o•syn'cline (-sin'klīn), n. a portion of the earth's crust subjected to downward warping.

ge'o•ther'mal also **-mic,** adj. of the internal heat of the earth.

Ger., Germ. 1. German. **2.** Germany.

ge•ra•ni•um (ji rā'nē əm), n. a common garden plant cultivated for its red, white, or pink flowers.

ger•bil (jûr'bəl), n. a small burrowing rodent with long hind legs.

ger•i•at•rics (jer'ē a'triks, jēr'-), n. the branch of medicine dealing with the diseases, debilities, and care of aged persons. —**ger'i•at'ric,** adj.

germ (jûrm), n. **1.** a microorganism, esp. when disease-producing. **2.** a bud or seed. **3.** the rudiment of a living organism. **4.** a source of development; origin. [< MF < L germen shoot, seed, sprout]

Ger•man (jûr'mən), n. **1.** a native or inhabitant of Germany. **2.** the Germanic language of Germany, Austria, and most of Switzerland. —adj. **3.** of Germany, its inhabitants, or their language.

ger•mane (jər mān'), adj. closely or significantly related.

Ger•man'ic (-man'ik), n. **1.** a family of languages, a branch of the Indo-European family, that includes English, Dutch, German, the Scandinavian languages, and Gothic. —adj. **2.** of Germanic or its speakers.

ger•ma•ni•um (jər mā'nē əm), n. a hard, metallic, grayish white element, used chiefly as a semiconductor. Symbol: Ge; at. wt.: 72.59; at. no.: 32.

Ger'man mea'sles, n. RUBELLA.

Ger'man shep'herd, n. one of a breed of large dogs with a thick, usu. gray or black-and-tan coat.

Ger'ma•ny, n. a republic in central Europe: formerly divided into East Germany and West Germany; reunited in 1990. 84,068,216. Official name, **Federal Republic of Germany.**

germ' cell', n. a sexual reproductive cell at any stage.

ger•mi•cide' (jûr'mə sīd'), n. an agent for killing germs or microorganisms. —**ger'mi•cid'al,** adj.

ger'mi•nal (-nl), adj. **1.** being in the earliest stage of development. **2.** of a germ or germs.

ger'mi•nate', v.i., v.t., **-nat•ed, -nat•ing.** to begin or cause to grow or develop; sprout. —**ger'mi•na'tion,** n.

Ge•ron•i•mo (jə ron'ə mō'), n. (Goyathlay), 1829–1909, American Apache Indian chief.

ger•on•tol•o•gy (jer'ən tol'ə jē, jēr'-), n. the study of aging and the problems and care of aged people. —**ger•on•to•log'i•cal** (jə ron'tl oj'i kəl), adj. —**ger'on•tol'o•gist,** n.

ger•ry•man•der (jer'i man'dər, ger'-), v.t. to divide (a state, county, etc.) into election districts so as to give one political party an unfair advantage.

Ger•shom (gûr'shəm), n. the elder son of Moses and Zipporah. Ex. 18:3.

Gersh•win (gûrsh'win), n. **1. George,** 1898–1937, U.S. composer. **2.** his brother, **Ira,** 1896–1983, U.S. lyricist.

ger•und (jer'ənd), n. the -ing form of an English verb when functioning as a noun.

Ge•sta•po (gə stä'pō), n. the German secret police during the Nazi regime. [< G (1933), acronym for Ge(heime) Sta(ats)po(lizei) secret state police]

ges•ta•tion (je stā'shən), n. the process, state, or period of carrying young in the womb. —**ges'tate,** v.t., v.i., **-tat•ed, -tat•ing.** —**ges•ta'tion•al,** adj.

ges•tic•u•late (je stik'yə lāt'), v.i., **-lat•ed, -lat•**

ing. to make or use gestures, esp. in an animated manner. —**ges•tic′u•la′tion,** *n.*

ges•ture (jes′chər), *n., v.,* **-tured, -tur•ing.** —*n.* **1.** a movement or position of the hand, arm, body, head, or face that is expressive of an idea, emotion, etc. **2.** any action or communication intended for effect or as a formality. —*v.i.* **3.** to make or use a gesture or gestures. —**ges′tur•al,** *adj.*

ge•sund•heit (gə zŏŏnt′hīt), *interj.* (used to wish good health, esp. to a person who has sneezed.)

get (get), *v.,* **got, got** or **got•ten, get•ting,** *n.* —*v.t.* **1.** to come to have possession, use, or enjoyment of; obtain; receive. **2.** to go after (something); fetch: *She got the trunk from the attic.* **3.** to cause or cause to become, to move, etc., as specified: *She got her hair cut.* **4.** to communicate with over a distance: *You can get me by phone.* **5.** to hear clearly: *I didn't get your name.* **6.** to understand: *I get your meaning.* **7.** to capture; seize. **8.** to receive as a punishment: *to get a year in jail.* **9.** to persuade: *Get him to go with us.* **10.** to prepare: *to get dinner.* **11.** (esp. of animals) to beget. **12.** to affect emotionally: *Her tears got me.* **13.** to hit. **14.** to take vengeance on. **15.** to catch or be afflicted with: *to get malaria.* **16.** to puzzle or annoy: *Their silly remarks get me.* —*v.i.* **17.** to come to or reach a specified place: *What time do we get there?* **18.** to become: *to get ready.* **19.** to succeed in coming, going, etc.: *I don't get into town very often.* **20.** to leave immediately: *He told us to get.* **21.** to start or enter upon the action of: *to get moving.* **22. get about, a.** to move about. **b.** to become known. **c.** to be socially active. **23. ~ across,** to make or become clearly understood. **24. ~ ahead,** to be successful. **25. ~ along, a.** to go away. **b.** to get on. **26. ~ around, a.** to circumvent. **b.** to ingratiate oneself with. **c.** to get about. **27. ~ at, a.** to reach. **b.** to hint at or imply. **c.** to discover; determine: *to get at the root of a problem.* **28. ~ away, a.** to escape. **b.** to start out. **29. ~ away with,** to do without detection or punishment. **30. ~ back, a.** to return. **b.** to recover. **31. ~ by,** to survive or manage minimally. **32. ~ down,** to concentrate; attend: *to get down to work.* **33. ~ in, a.** to enter. **b.** to arrive. **c.** to enter into close association: *He got in with the wrong crowd.* **34. ~ off, a.** to dismount from or leave. **b.** to escape or help to escape punishment. **35. ~ on, a.** to proceed; advance. **b.** to have sufficient means to manage or survive. **c.** to be on good terms. **36. ~ out, a.** to leave. **b.** to become publicly known. **c.** to produce or complete. **37. ~ over,** to recover from. **38. ~ through, a.** to complete. **b.** to make oneself understood. **c.** to bear or survive. **39. ~ to, a.** to contact. **b.** to affect. **40. ~ together, a.** to gather. **b.** to congregate; meet. **c.** to come to an accord. **41. ~ up, a.** to rise, as from bed. **b.** to prepare or organize. —*n.* **42.** the offspring, esp. of a male animal. —**Idiom. 43. get it, a.** to be punished. **b.** to understand something. **44. has** or **have got, a.** to possess: *Have you got the tickets?* **b.** must: *He's got to get to a doctor.* **c.** to suffer from: *Have you got a cold?*

get′a•way′, *n.* **1.** an escape. **2.** the start of a race. **3.** a place where one escapes for relaxation, a vacation, etc.

Geth•sem•a•ne (geth sem′ə nē) *n.* a garden E of Jerusalem, near the brook of Kidron: scene of Jesus' agony and betrayal. Matt. 26:36.

get′-togeth′er, *n.* **1.** an informal social gathering. **2.** a meeting or conference.

Get•ty (get′ē), *n.* **J(ean) Paul,** 1892–1976, U.S. oil magnate.

Get•tys•burg (get′iz bûrg′), *n.* a borough in S Pennsylvania: site of a major Civil War battle in 1863.

Get′tysburg Address′, *n.* the short speech made by President Lincoln on Nov. 19, 1863, at the dedication of the national cemetery at Gettysburg.

get′-up′, *n. Informal.* costume; outfit.

gew•gaw (gyŏŏ′gô, gŏŏ′-), *n.* something gaudy and useless.

gey•ser (gī′zər, -sər), *n.* a hot spring that intermittently sends up jets of water and steam into the air.

Gha•na (gä′nə, gan′ə), *n.* a republic in W Africa. 18,100,703. —**Gha′na•ian, Gha′ni•an,** *n., adj.*

ghast•ly (gast′lē, gäst′-), *adj.,* **-li•er, -li•est. 1.** shockingly frightful or dreadful; horrible. **2.** resembling a ghost, esp. in being very pale. —**ghast′li•ness,** *n.*

gher•kin (gûr′kin), *n.* the small immature fruit of a variety of cucumber, used in pickling.

ghet•to (get′ō), *n., pl.* **-tos, -toes. 1.** a section of a city inhabited predominantly by members of a minority group. **2.** (formerly, in certain European cities) a section in which all Jews were required to live. **3.** a situation or environment in which a group has been relegated or in which a group has segregated itself.

ghet′to•ize′, *v.t.,* **-ized, -iz•ing.** to segregate in or as if in a ghetto.

ghost (gōst), *n.* **1.** the disembodied spirit of a dead person imagined as wandering among or haunting the living. **2.** a mere shadow or semblance. **3.** a remote possibility: *not a ghost of a chance.* **4.** a secondary image, as on a television screen. —*v.t., v.i.* **5.** to ghostwrite. —**ghost′ly,** *adj.,* **-li•er, -li•est.**

ghost′writ′er, *n.* a person who writes a speech, book, etc., for another who is presumed to be the author. —**ghost′write′,** *v.t., v.i.,* **-wrote, -writ•ten, -writ•ing.**

ghoul (gōōl), *n.* an evil demon believed to rob graves, prey on corpses, etc. —**ghoul′ish,** *adj.*

GHQ, *Mil.* general headquarters.

GI (jē′ī′), *n., pl.* **GIs** or **GI's,** *adj.* —*n.* **1.** a member or former member of the U.S. armed forces, esp. an enlisted soldier. —*adj.* **2.** rigidly adhering to military regulations and practices. **3.** of a standardized style or type issued or required by the U.S. armed forces: *a GI haircut.*

Gia•co•met•ti (jä′kə met′ē), *n.* **Alberto,** 1901–66, Swiss sculptor and painter.

gi•ant (jī′ənt), *n.* **1.** (in folklore) a being with human form but superhuman size and strength. **2.** a person or thing of unusually great size, achievement, etc. —*adj.* **3.** unusually large; huge.

gi′ant•ess, *n.* (in folklore) a female being with human form but superhuman size and strength.

gib•ber (jib′ər, gib′-), *v.i.* to speak inarticulately or foolishly.

gib′ber•ish, *n.* meaningless or unintelligible talk or writing.

gib•bet (jib′it), *n.* **1.** a structure from which the bodies of executed criminals were hung for public display. **2.** a gallows. —*v.t.* **3.** to hang on a gibbet. **4.** to hold up to public scorn.

gib•bon (gib′ən), *n.* a small, slender arboreal ape of S Asia.

Gib•bon (gib′ən), *n.* **Edward,** 1737–94, English historian.

gibe (jīb), *v.,* **gibed, gib•ing,** *n.* —*v.i., v.t.* **1.** to mock; jeer. —*n.* **2.** a taunting or sarcastic remark.

GI Bill, *n.* any of various Congressional bills enacted to provide funds benefits for armed-services veterans. Also called **GI Bill of Rights.**

gib•let (jib′lit), *n.* Usu., **-lets.** the heart, liver, gizzard, etc., of a fowl.

Gi•bral•tar (ji brôl′tər), *n.* a seaport on a promontory near the S tip of Spain: a British crown colony. 29,934.

Gib•son (gib′sən), *n.* **Charles Dana,** 1867–1944, U.S. artist and illustrator.

gid•dy (gid′ē), *adj.,* **-di•er, -di•est. 1.** affected with or causing dizziness. **2.** frivolous and lighthearted. — **gid′di•ly,** *adv.* —**gid′di•ness,** *n.*

Gide (zhēd), *n.* **André,** 1869–1951, French writer.

Gid•e•on (gid′ē ən), *n.* a judge of Israel and conqueror of the Midianites. Judg. 6–8.

Gid′eons Interna′tional, *n.* a society organized in 1899 to place Bibles in hotel rooms. Formerly, **Gid′eon Soci′ety.**

gift (gift), *n.* **1.** something given voluntarily without payment in return. **2.** the act of giving. **3.** a special ability; talent. —*v.t.* **4.** to present with a gift.

gift'ed, *adj.* **1.** having a special ability; talented. **2.** having exceptionally high intelligence.

Gift' of the Ma'gi, *n.* one of three gifts—gold, frankincense, and myrrh—given by the Magi to the infant Jesus. Matt. 2:11.

gift' of tongues', *n.* SPEAKING IN TONGUES.

gig¹ (gig), *n.* **1.** a light, two-wheeled one-horse carriage. **2.** a light ship's boat.

gig² (gig), *n.* a spearlike device for fishing.

gig³ (gig), *n. Slang.* a single professional engagement, as of jazz or rock musicians.

gig•a•byte (gig'ə bīt', jig'-), *n.* a measure of data storage capacity equal to 1 billion (10⁹) bytes.

gi•gan•tic (jī gan'tik, ji-), *adj.* **1.** very large. **2.** of, like, or befitting a giant. —**gi•gan'ti•cal•ly,** *adv.*

gig•gle (gig'əl), *v.,* **-gled, -gling,** —*v.i.* **1.** to laugh in a silly, undignified way, esp. with short, repeated gasps. —*n.* **2.** a silly, spasmodic laugh. —**gig'gler,** *n.* —**gig'gly,** *adj.*

GIGO (gī'gō), *n.* the axiom that faulty data fed into a computer will result in distorted information. [*g(arbage) i(n) g(arbage) o(ut)*]

Gi'la mon'ster (hē'lə), *n.* a large, venomous lizard of the SW United States and NW Mexico.

gil•bert (gil'bərt), *n.* the centimeter-gram-second unit of magnetomotive force, equal to 0.7958 ampere-turns.

Gil•bert (gil'bərt), *n.* **1. Sir Humphrey,** 1509?–83, English navigator and colonizer in America. **2. Sir William Schwenck** 1836–1911, English dramatist and poet: collaborator with Sir Arthur Sullivan.

Gil•bo•a (gil bō'ə), *n.* a range of mountains between the plain of Jezreel and the Jordan Valley. I Chron. 10:1–6.

gild (gild), *v.t.,* **gild•ed** or **gilt, gild•ing.** **1.** to coat with gold, gold leaf, or a gold-colored substance. **2.** to give a bright, pleasing, or specious aspect to. —**gild'er,** *n.* —**gild'ing,** *n.*

Gil•gal (gil'gal), *n.* the name of several places in ancient Palestine. Josh. 4:19–24.

Gil•ga•mesh (gil'gə mesh'), *n.* a legendary Sumerian king, the hero of Sumerian and Babylonian epics.

gill¹ (gil), *n.* the respiratory organ of aquatic animals, as fish, that breathe oxygen dissolved in water.

gill² (jil), *n.* a unit of liquid measure equal to ¼ of a pint (118.2937 ml).

Gil•lette (ji let'), *n.* **King Camp,** 1855–1932, U.S. businessman: inventor of the safety razor.

gilt (gilt), *v.* **1.** a pt. and pp. of GILD. —*n.* **2.** the gold or other material applied in gilding. —*adj.* **3.** coated with gilt.

gilt'-edged' or **-edge',** *adj.* of the highest quality.

gim•bals (jim'bəlz, gim'-), *n.* (*used with a sing. v.*) a contrivance, consisting of pivoted rings, that permits a ship's compass or other object to remain horizontal.

gim•crack (jim'krak'), *n.* **1.** a showy, useless trifle. —*adj.* **2.** showy but useless.

gim•let (gim'lit), *n.* a small tool for boring holes, consisting of a shaft with a pointed screw at one end.

gim•mick (gim'ik), *n.* **1.** an ingenious or novel device or stratagem used to draw attention. **2.** a concealed disadvantage. **3.** a hidden mechanical device, as one used by a magician. —**gim'mick•ry,** *n., pl.* **-ries.** —**gim'mick•y,** *adj.*

gimp (gimp), *n. Slang.* **1.** a limp. **2.** a lame person. —**gimp'y,** *adj.*

gin¹ (jin), *n.* an alcoholic liquor distilled with juniper berries.

gin² (jin), *n., v.,* **ginned, gin•ning.** —*n.* **1.** COTTON GIN. **2.** a trap or snare for game. —*v.t.* **3.** to clear (cotton) of seeds with a cotton gin.

gin³ (jin), *n.* a variety of rummy for two players. Also called **gin' rum'my.**

gin•ger (jin'jər), *n.* **1.** a reedlike plant with a pungent, spicy rhizome used in cookery and medicine. **2.** the rhizome itself. **3.** piquancy; animation. —**gin'ger•y,** *adj.*

gin'ger ale', *n.* a carbonated soft drink flavored with ginger extract.

gin'ger•bread', *n.* **1.** a cake flavored with ginger and molasses. **2.** elaborate or gaudy architectural ornamentation.

gin'ger•ly, *adv.* **1.** with great care or caution. —*adj.* **2.** cautious or wary.

gin'ger•snap', *n.* a crisp cookie flavored with ginger and molasses.

ging•ham (ging'əm), *n.* a yarn-dyed, plain-weave cotton fabric, usu. striped or checked. [< D *gingang* < Malay *gəŋgaŋ* striped]

gin•gi•vi•tis (jin'jə vī'tis), *n.* inflammation of the gums.

gink•go or **ging•ko** (ging'kō, jing'-), *n., pl.* **-goes** or **-koes.** a shade tree native to China, with fanshaped leaves.

Gins•burg (ginz'bûrg), *n.* **Ruth Bader,** born 1933, associate justice of the U.S. Supreme Court since 1993.

gin•seng (jin'seng), *n.* **1.** a perennial plant with an aromatic root used medicinally. **2.** the root itself.

Giot•to (jot'ō), *n.* (*Giotto di Bondone*) 1266?–1337, Florentine painter, sculptor, and architect.

Gip•sy (jip'sē), *n., pl.* **-sies,** *adj. Chiefly Brit.* GYPSY.

gi•raffe (jə raf'; *esp. Brit.* -räf'), *n.* a tall, longnecked, spotted ruminant of Africa. [< F < It < dial. Ar *zirāfah*]

gird (gûrd), *v.t.,* **gird•ed** or **girt, gird•ing.** **1.** to encircle or bind with a belt or band. **2.** to surround. **3.** to prepare (oneself) for action. **4.** to equip or invest, as with power or strength.

gird'er, *n.* a large beam, as of steel or timber, for supporting masonry, joists, etc.

gir'dle, *n., v.,* **-dled, -dling.** —*n.* **1.** a woman's undergarment for supporting the abdomen, hips, and buttocks. **2.** a belt or sash worn about the waist. **3.** anything that encircles or confines. —*v.t.* **4.** to encircle with or as if with a belt.

girl (gûrl), *n.* **1.** a female child. **2.** a young, immature woman, esp. an unmarried one. **3.** a daughter: *My wife and I have two girls.* **4.** girlfriend; sweetheart. —**Usage.** Many women resent being called GIRLS or the less formal GALS. In business and professional offices, *the girl* or *my girl* in reference to one's secretary has decreased but not disappeared. Such terms as *the girls* for a group of women, GIRL or GAL FRIDAY for a female assistant, and BACHELOR GIRL for an unmarried woman are frequently regarded as offensive, and WORKING GIRL in the sense "a woman who works" is declining in use. See also LADY, WOMAN.

girl'friend', *n.* **1.** a frequent or favorite female companion; sweetheart. **2.** a female friend.

girl' scout', *n.* (*sometimes caps.*) a member of an organization of girls (**Girl' Scouts'**) that promotes character development, health, etc.

girt (gûrt), *v.* a pt. and pp. of GIRD.

girth (gûrth), *n.* **1.** the measure around a body or object; circumference. **2.** a band that passes underneath a horse or other animal to hold a saddle in place.

gis•mo (giz'mō), *n., pl.* **-mos.** *Informal.* a gadget.

gist (jist), *n.* the main or essential point of a matter.

give (giv), *v.,* **gave, giv•en, giv•ing,** *n.* —*v.t.* **1.** to present voluntarily and without expecting compensation. **2.** to hand to someone. **3.** to place in someone's care. **4.** to grant (permission, opportunity, etc.) to someone. **5.** to transmit or communicate. **6.** to pay or deliver in exchange. **7.** to furnish or proffer: *to give evidence.* **8.** to provide as an entertainment: *to give a party.* **9.** to administer: *to give medicine.* **10.** to put forth or utter: *to give a cry.* **11.** to produce or yield: *to give good results.* **12.** to make, do, or perform: *to give a concert.* **13.** to sacrifice: *to give one's life for a cause.* **14.** to assign or allot, as a name. **15.** to attribute or ascribe. **16.** to cause or occasion: *Strawberries give me a rash.* **17.** to devote: *to give one's attention to a problem.* **18.** to inflict as a punishment. **19.** to concede, as a point in an argument. —*v.i.* **20.** to make a gift. **21.** to yield under force, pressure, etc. **22.** to be warm and open in relationships. **23. give away, a.** to give as a present. **b.** to present (the bride) to the bridegroom. **c.** to disclose or betray. **24. ~ back,** to return or restore. **25. ~ in, a.** to acknowledge defeat. **b.** to hand in. **26. ~ off,** to put forth; emit. **27. ~ out, a.** to send out; emit. **b.** to make public. **c.** to distribute; issue. **d.** to become exhausted or used up. **28. ~ up, a.** to abandon hope. **b.** to desist from. **c.** to surrender. —*n.* **29.** the quality or state of being resilient. —*Proverb.* **30. It is more blessed to give than to receive,** giving, rather than taking, brings spiritual rewards. Acts 20:35. —**giv′er,** *n.*

give′-and-take′, *n.* **1.** a compromise or mutual concession; cooperation. **2.** good-natured exchange of talk, ideas, etc.

give′a•way′, *n.* **1.** something given away, esp. as a premium. **2.** an unintentional betrayal or disclosure. **3.** a radio or television program on which prizes are awarded to contestants.

giv′en, *v.* **1.** pp. of GIVE. —*adj.* **2.** stated or specified: *a given time.* **3.** inclined; disposed: *given to making snide remarks.* **4.** bestowed; conferred. **5.** granted or assumed. —*n.* **6.** something accepted as a fact.

giv′en name′, *n.* the name given to one, as distinguished from a surname.

giz•mo (giz′mō), *n.*, *pl.* **-mos.** GISMO.

giz•zard (giz′ərd), *n.* the muscular lower stomach of many birds and reptiles that grinds partially digested food.

Gk., Greek.

gla•cial (glā′shəl), *adj.* **1.** of or pertaining to glaciers or ice sheets. **2.** bitterly cold. **3.** happening or moving extremely slowly.

gla′cier, *n.* an extended mass of ice formed from snow falling and accumulating over the years and moving very slowly.

glad¹ (glad), *adj.*, **glad•der, glad•dest. 1.** feeling joy or pleasure. **2.** showing or causing joy or pleasure. **3.** very willing. —**glad′ly,** *adv.* —**glad′ness,** *n.*

glad² (glad), *n.* GLADIOLUS.

glad′den, *v.t.* to make glad.

glade (glād), *n.* an open space in a forest.

glad′ hand′, *n.* a hearty welcome or enthusiastic reception, esp. one that is hypocritical. —**glad′-hand′,** *v.t., v.i.* —**glad′-hand′er,** *n.*

glad•i•a•tor (glad′ē ā′tər), *n.* **1.** (in ancient Rome) an armed man compelled to fight to the death in an arena for the entertainment of spectators. **2.** someone who engages in a fight or controversy. —**glad′i•a•to′ri•al** (-ə tôr′ē əl), *adj.*

glad•i•o•lus (glad′ē ō′ləs), *n.*, *pl.* **-li** (-lī), **-lus.** a plant of the iris family with sword-shaped leaves and spikes of flowers. [< L: small sword]

glad′some, *adj.* glad.

Glad•stone (glad′stōn, -stən), *n.* **William Ew•art** (yōō′ərt), 1809–98, British prime minister four times between 1868 and 1894.

glam•or•ize (glam′ə rīz′), *v.t.*, **-ized, -iz•ing.** to make glamorous. —**glam′or•i•za′tion,** *n.*

glam′our or **-or** (glam′ər), *n.* **1.** alluring charm, fascination, and attractiveness. **2.** magic or enchantment. —**glam′or•ous, glam′our•ous,** *adj.*

glance (glans, gläns), *v.*, **glanced, glanc•ing,** *n.* —*v.i.* **1.** to look quickly or briefly. **2.** to gleam or flash. **3.** to strike a surface obliquely and bounce off at an angle. —*n.* **4.** a quick or brief look. **5.** a gleam or flash. **6.** a deflected movement or course.

gland (gland), *n.* any organ or group of cells specialized for producing secretions. —**glan•du•lar** (glan′jə lər), *adj.*

glans (glanz), *n.*, *pl.* **glan•des** (glan′dēz). the head of the penis or of the clitoris.

glare (glâr), *n.*, *v.*, **glared, glar•ing.** —*n.* **1.** a very harsh, dazzling light. **2.** a fiercely piercing stare. **3.** dazzling or showy appearance. —*v.i.* **4.** to shine with a very harsh, dazzling light. **5.** to stare with a fiercely piercing look. —*v.t.* **6.** to express with a glare.

glar′ing, *adj.* **1.** dazzlingly bright. **2.** very conspicu-

ous or obvious. **3.** staring fiercely. **4.** excessively or tastelessly showy. —**glar′ing•ly,** *adv.*

Glas•gow (glas′kō, glaz′gō), *n.* a seaport in SW Scotland. 880,617.

glass (glas, gläs), *n.* **1.** a hard, brittle, more or less transparent substance usu. produced by fusing silicates containing soda and lime, used for windows, bottles, etc. **2.** something made of glass, as a drinking container. **3. glasses,** a device to compensate for defective vision or to protect the eyes from light, dust, etc. **4.** GLASSWARE. **5.** an amount contained by a drinking glass. —*adj.* **6.** made of or fitted with glass. —*v.t.* **7.** to fit or enclose with glass. —*Proverb.* **8. People who live in glass houses shouldn't throw stones,** those who attack others should make sure they are not themselves vulnerable.

glass′ ceil′ing, *n.* an upper limit to professional advancement, esp. as imposed on women and other minorities, that is not readily perceived or acknowledged.

glass′ware′, *n.* articles of glass, esp. drinking glasses.

glass′y, *adj.*, **-i•er, -i•est. 1.** resembling glass, as in transparency. **2.** expressionless; dull: *glassy eyes.*

glau•co•ma (glô kō′mə, glou-), *n.* a condition of elevated fluid pressure within the eyeball, causing progressive loss of vision.

glaze (glāz), *v.*, **glazed, glaz•ing,** *n.* —*v.t.* **1.** to fit with glass, as a window. **2.** to cover (a ceramic or the like) with a smooth, glossy surface or coating. **3.** to coat (a food) with sugar syrup. —*v.i.* **4.** to become glazed or glassy. —*n.* **5.** a smooth, glossy surface or coating. **6.** the substance for producing such a coating.

gla′zier (glā′zhər), *n.* a person who fits windows with glass.

gleam (glēm), *n.* **1.** a flash or beam of light. **2.** a subdued or reflected light. **3.** a brief or slight manifestation. —*v.i.* **4.** to send forth a gleam. **5.** to appear suddenly and clearly.

glean (glēn), *v.t., v.i.* **1.** to gather (grain) after the reapers. **2.** to collect (facts or information) little by little or slowly.

glee (glē), *n.* open delight or pleasure. —**glee′ful,** *adj.*

glee′ club′, *n.* a chorus organized for singing choral music.

glen (glen), *n.* a small, narrow, secluded valley.

Glen•dale (glen′dāl′), *n.* **1.** a city in SW California. 178,481. **2.** a city in central Arizona. 168,439.

Glenn (glen), *n.* **John (Herschel),** born 1921, U.S. astronaut and senator: first U.S. orbital spaceflight 1962.

glib (glib), *adj.*, **glib•ber, glib•best.** readily fluent, often thoughtlessly or insincerely so. —**glib′ly,** *adv.* —**glib′ness,** *n.*

glide (glīd), *v.*, **glid•ed, glid•ing,** *n.* —*v.i.* **1.** to move smoothly and effortlessly along. **2.** to fly downward at an easy angle, with little or no engine power. —*v.t.* **3.** to cause to glide. —*n.* **4.** a gliding movement, as in dancing. **5. a.** a transitional sound heard during the articulation linking two contiguous speech sounds. **b.** a semivowel. **6.** the act of gliding.

glid′er, *n.* **1.** a motorless aircraft launched by towing or catapult. **2.** one that glides. **3.** a couchlike porch swing suspended from a steel framework.

glim•mer (glim′ər), *n.* **1.** a faint or unsteady light. **2.** a dim or faint perception; inkling. —*v.i.* **3.** to shine faintly or unsteadily. **4.** to appear faintly or dimly. —**glim′mer•ing,** *n.*

glimpse (glimps), *n.*, *v.*, **glimpsed, glimps•ing.** —*n.* **1.** a very brief, passing look. **2.** a vague idea; inkling. —*v.t.* **3.** to catch a glimpse of. —*v.i.* **4.** to look briefly.

glint (glint), *n.* **1.** a tiny, quick flash of light. **2.** a brief or slight manifestation or occurrence; trace. —*v.i.* **3.** to shine with a glint.

glis•san•do (gli sän′dō), *adj.*, *n.*, *pl.* **-di** (-dē), **-dos.** —*adj.* **1.** performed with a gliding effect by sliding fingers rapidly over piano keys or harp strings. —*n.* **2.** a glissando passage.

glis•ten (glis′ən), *v.i.* **1.** to reflect a sparkling light or a faint intermittent glow. —*n.* **2.** a glistening; sparkle.

glitch (glich), *n. Informal.* a defect, error, or malfunction, as in a machine or plan.

glit•ter (glit′ər), *v.i.* **1.** to reflect light with a brilliant, sparkling luster. **2.** to make a brilliant show. —*n.* **3.** a sparkling light or luster. **4.** showy splendor. **5.** small glittering ornaments. —**glit′ter•y,** *adj.*

glitz•y (glit′sē), *adj.,* **-i•er, -i•est.** *Informal.* pretentiously or tastelessly showy; flashy.

gloam•ing (glō′ming), *n.* twilight; dusk.

gloat (glōt), *v.i.* to indulge in malicious or excessive satisfaction.

glob (glob), *n.* **1.** a drop of a liquid. **2.** a rounded lump or mass.

glob•al (glō′bəl), *adj.* **1.** of or involving the whole world; universal. **2.** of or involving a whole; general. —**glob′al•ly,** *adv.*

glob′al•ism, *n.* the policy or doctrine of involving one's country in international affairs, alliances, etc. —**glob′al•ist,** *n.*

glo′bal warm′ing, *n.* an increase in the earth's average atmospheric temperature that causes changes in climate.

globe (glōb), *n.* **1.** the planet Earth. **2.** a sphere on which a map of the earth is depicted. **3.** anything more or less spherical.

globe′trot′ter, *n.* one who travels regularly all over the world.

glob•u•lar (glob′yə lər), *adj.* **1.** spherical. **2.** composed of globules.

glob•ule (glob′yōol), *n.* a small spherical body.

glob•u•lin (glob′yə lin), *n.* any of a group of plant and animal proteins that are soluble in salt solutions and coagulable by heat.

glock•en•spiel (glok′ən spēl′, -shpēl′), *n.* a musical instrument composed of a set of graduated steel bars struck with hammers. [< G, = *Glocken* bells + *Spiel* play]

gloom (glōom), *n.* **1.** total or partial darkness. **2.** a state of melancholy or depression. —**gloom′y,** *adj.,* **-i•er, -i•est.**

glop (glop), *n. Informal.* **1.** any gooey or gelatinous substance, esp. unappetizing food. **2.** sentimentality. —**glop′py,** *adj.,* **-pi•er, -pi•est.**

Glo•ri•a (glōr′ē ə, glōr′-), *n.* **1.** GLORIA IN EXCELSIS DEO. **2.** GLORIA PATRI.

Glo•ri•a in Ex•cel•sis De•o (glōr′ē ə in ek sel′sis dā′ō, glōr′-), *n.* the hymn beginning "Glory to God in the highest."

Glo•ri•a Pa•tri (glōr′ē ə pä′trē, glōr′-), *n.* the short hymn beginning "Glory be to the Father, and to the Son, and to the Holy Ghost."

glo•ri•fy (glōr′ə fī′), *v.t.,* **-fied, -fy•ing. 1.** to treat as more splendid or excellent than would normally be considered. **2.** to honor, extol, or worship. **3.** to give glory to. —**glor′i•fi•ca′tion,** *n.*

glo′ri•ous (-ē əs), *adj.* **1.** delightful; wonderful. **2.** conferring glory. **3.** full of glory. **4.** brilliantly beautiful or magnificent. —**glo′ri•ous•ly,** *adv.*

glo′ry, *n., pl.* **-ries,** *v.,* **-ried, -ry•ing.** —*n.* **1.** very great praise, honor, or distinction. **2.** a source of praise or honor. **3.** adoring praise given in worship. **4.** resplendent beauty or magnificence. **5.** a state of absolute happiness: *to be in one's glory.* **6.** the splendor and bliss of heaven. —*v.i.* **7.** to exult with triumph.

gloss¹ (glos, glôs), *n.* **1.** a superficial luster or shine. **2.** a deceptively good appearance. —*v.t.* **3.** to put a gloss upon. **4.** gloss over, to give a deceptively good appearance to: *to gloss over flaws.* —**gloss′y,** *adj.,* **-i•er, -i•est.**

gloss² (glos, glôs), *n.* **1.** a marginal or interlinear explanation or translation. —*v.t.* **2.** to insert glosses on; annotate. **3.** to give a misleading interpretation of.

glos•sa•ry (glos′ə rē, glô′sə-), *n., pl.* **-ries.** a list of difficult or specialized terms with accompanying definitions.

glos•so•la•li•a (glos′ə lā′lē ə, glô′sə-), *n.* incom-

prehensible speech sometimes occurring in an episode of religious ecstasy.

glot•tis (glot′is), *n.* the opening at the upper part of the larynx, between the vocal cords. —**glot′tal,** *adj.*

glove (gluv), *n., v.,* **gloved, glov•ing.** —*n.* **1.** a covering for the hand made with a separate sheath for each finger. **2.** any of various leather-padded coverings for the hand used in baseball, boxing, etc. —*v.t.* **3.** to cover with a glove.

glow (glō), *n.* **1.** a light emitted by or as if by a heated substance. **2.** brightness of color, esp. ruddiness. **3.** a sensation of bodily heat. **4.** warmth of emotion or passion. —*v.i.* **5.** to emit light and heat without flame. **6.** to shine like something intensely heated. **7.** to exhibit a bright, usu. ruddy color. **8.** to show emotion or elation: *to glow with pride.* —**glow′ing,** *adj.*

glow•er (glou′ər), *v.i.* **1.** to stare with sullen dislike or anger. —*n.* **2.** a look of sullen dislike or anger.

glow•worm (glō′wûrm′), *n.* the larva or wingless female of a beetle that emits a greenish light.

glu•cose (glōo′kōs), *n.* **1.** a simple sugar occurring in fruits and honey. **2.** a syrup obtained by the incomplete hydrolysis of starch.

glue (glōo), *n., v.,* **glued, glu•ing.** —*n.* **1.** a protein gelatin obtained by boiling animal substances in water, used as an adhesive. **2.** any of various similar preparations. —*v.t.* **3.** to join or attach firmly with or as if with glue. —**glue′y,** *adj.,* **glu•i•er, glu•i•est.**

glum (glum), *adj.,* **glum•mer, glum•mest.** sullenly or silently gloomy. —**glum′ly,** *adv.* —**glum′ness,** *n.*

glut (glut), *v.,* **glut•ted, glut•ting,** *n.* —*v.t.* **1.** to feed or fill to satiety or to excess. **2.** to flood (the market) with a particular item or service so that supply greatly exceeds demand. —*n.* **3.** an excessive amount.

glu•ten (glōot′n), *n.* a grayish, sticky component of wheat flour and other grain flours. [< L *glūten* glue] —**glu′ten•ous,** *adj.*

glu′ti•nous, *adj.* viscid; sticky. —**glu′ti•nous•ly,** *adv.*

glut•ton (glut′n), *n.* **1.** a person who eats and drinks excessively. **2.** a person with a great desire or capacity for something. —**glut′ton•ous,** *adj.* —**glut′ton•ous•ly,** *adv.* —**glut′ton•y,** *n.*

glyc•er•in (glis′ər in) also **-er•ine** (-ər in, -ə rēn′), *n.* GLYCEROL.

glyc′er•ol′ (-ə rôl′, -rol′), *n.* a colorless liquid made from fats, used as a sweetener, in skin emollients, etc.

gly•co•gen (glī′kə jən, -jen′), *n.* a substance constituting the principal carbohydrate stored by the animal body, converted to glucose when needed.

Gmc or **Gmc.,** Germanic.

gnarl (närl), *n.* **1.** a knotty protuberance on a tree. —*v.t.* **2.** to twist into a knotted form. —**gnarled,** *adj.*

gnash (nash), *v.t., v.i.* to grind (the teeth) together, esp. in rage or pain.

gnat (nat), *n.* any of certain small flies, most of which bite or suck.

gnaw (nô), *v.,* **gnawed, gnawed** or **gnawn, gnaw• ing.** —*v.t.* **1.** to bite on persistently. **2.** to wear away or corrode. **3.** to torment by constant annoyance. —*v.i.* **4.** to bite persistently. **5.** to cause corrosion. **6.** to cause an effect resembling corrosion: *Her mistake gnawed at her conscience.*

gneiss (nīs), *n.* a metamorphic rock, generally made up of bands that differ in color and composition.

gnome (nōm), *n.* any of a group of dwarflike beings believed to inhabit the interior of the earth. —**gnom′ish,** *adj.*

GNP, gross national product.

gnu (nōo, nyōo), *n., pl.* **gnus, gnu.** a stocky, oxlike African antelope.

go (gō), *v.,* **went, gone, go•ing,** *n., pl.* **goes,** *adj.* —*v.i.* **1.** to move or proceed, esp. to or from something. **2.** to leave a place. **3.** to function or operate: *The engine is going.* **4.** to become as specified: *to go mad.* **5.** to continue in a certain state: *to go barefoot.* **6.** to act so as to come into a certain state: *to go to sleep.* **7.** to be known: *to go by a false name.* **8.** to reach or extend: *This door goes outside.* **9.** (of time) to elapse. **10.** to be applied to a particular purpose. **11.** to be sold. **12.** to be considered usually: *He's tall, as jockeys go.* **13.** to conduce or tend. **14.** to result; turn out. **15.** to have a place: *The book goes here.* **16.** (of colors, styles, etc.) to harmonize. **17.** to be consumed, discarded, etc. **18.** to develop or proceed. **19.** to make a certain sound. **20.** to be phrased or composed. **21.** to resort: *to go to court.* **22.** to die. **23.** to fail or give way. **24.** to begin: *Go when you hear the bell.* **25.** to be able to be divided: *Three goes into fifteen five times.* **26.** to contribute to an end result. **27.** to have as one's goal; intend: *I am going to be a doctor.* **28.** to be approved or accepted: *Anything goes.* **29.** to be authoritative: *What I say goes!* **30.** to subject oneself: *Don't go to any trouble.* **31.** (used as an intensifier): *He had to go ask for a loan.* —*v.t.* **32.** to proceed along. **33.** to share in to the extent of: *to go halves.* **34.** *Informal.* to bet or bid. **35.** to assume the obligation of: *His father went bail for him.* **36.** *Informal.* to say. **37. go after,** to attempt to obtain. **38.** ~ **around, a.** to be sufficient for all. **b.** to pass or circulate. **39.** ~ **at, a.** to assault; attack. **b.** to begin vigorously. **40.** ~ **for, a.** to try for. **b.** to assault. **c.** to favor. **41.** ~ **in for,** to adopt as one's particular interest. **42.** ~ **into, a.** to discuss or investigate. **b.** to undertake as one's study or work. **43.** ~ **off, a.** to explode. **b.** to happen. **c.** to leave. **44.** ~ **on, a.** to happen. **b.** to continue. **c.** to talk effusively. **45.** ~ **out, a.** to cease to function. **b.** to participate in social activities. **46.** ~ **over, a.** to review. **b.** to be effective or successful. **c.** to examine. **47.** ~ **through, a.** to bear. **b.** to examine carefully. **c.** to use up. **48.** ~ **through with,** to bring to completion. **49.** ~ **under,** to fail or founder. —*n.* **50.** the act of going. **51.** energy or spirit. **52.** a try or attempt. **53.** a success. **54.** *Informal.* approval or permission. —*adj.* **55.** functioning properly; ready: *All systems are go.* —*Idiom.* **56. go together, a.** to be harmonious. **b.** to date steadily. **57. let go, a.** to free. **b.** to cease to employ. **58. let oneself go,** to free oneself of inhibitions. **59. no go,** *Informal.* **a.** futile. **b.** canceled. **60. on the go,** very busy. **61. to go,** (of food) for consumption off the premises where sold.

goad (gōd), *n.* **1.** a pointed stick for driving cattle, oxen, etc. **2.** anything that pricks or urges on. —*v.t.* **3.** to drive with or as if with a goad.

go'-a•head', *n.* a signal or permission to proceed.

goal (gōl), *n.* **1.** the result toward which effort is directed. **2.** the terminal point in a race. **3.** a place into which players of various games try to propel a ball or puck to score. **4.** the score made.

goal'ie, *n.*, *pl.* -**ies.** GOALKEEPER.

goal'keep'er, *n.* (in hockey, soccer, etc.) a player whose chief duty is to prevent the ball or puck from crossing the goal. —**goal'keep'ing**, *n.*

goat (gōt), *n.* an agile, hollow-horned ruminant closely related to the sheep.

goat•ee (gō tē'), *n.*, *pl.* -**ees.** a man's beard trimmed to a tuft on the chin.

goat'herd', *n.* a person who tends goats.

goat'skin', *n.* **1.** the skin or hide of a goat. **2.** leather made from it.

gob¹ (gob), *n.* **1.** a mass or lump. **2. gobs,** *Informal.* a large quantity.

gob² (gob), *n. Slang.* a sailor, esp. a seaman in the U.S. Navy.

gob•ble¹ (gob'əl), *v.t.*, *v.i.*, -**bled,** -**bling.** **1.** to eat hastily or hungrily. **2.** to seize eagerly.

gob•ble² (gob'əl), *v.*, -**bled,** -**bling,** *n.* —*v.i.* **1.** to make the throaty cry of a male turkey. —*n.* **2.** the cry itself.

gob•ble•dy•gook or -**de•gook** (gob'əl dē gook'), *n.* language characterized by circumlocution and jargon.

gob•bler (gob'lər), *n.* a male turkey.

go'-between', *n.* a person who acts as an intermediary between parties.

Go•bi (gō'bē), *n.* a desert in E Asia, mostly in Mongolia.

gob•let (gob'lit), *n.* a drinking glass with a foot and stem.

gob•lin (gob'lin), *n.* a grotesque, mischievous sprite or elf.

God (god), *n.* **1.** the creator and ruler of the universe. **2.** (*l.c.*) one of several immortal powers, esp. a male deity, presiding over some portion of worldly affairs. **3.** (*l.c.*) any deified person or object. —**god'-like'**, *adj.*

God' and mam'mon, *n.* contrasted spiritual and material life. Matt. 6:24.

god'child', *n.*, *pl.* -**chil•dren.** a child for whom a godparent serves as sponsor.

god'daugh'ter, *n.* a female godchild.

god'dess (-is), *n.* **1.** a female god. **2.** a woman admired for her great beauty.

god'fa'ther, *n.* **1.** a man who serves as sponsor for a child. **2.** the head of a Mafia family.

God'head', *n.* the essential being or nature of God.

god'hood, *n.* divine character or condition.

God' Incar'nate, *n.* Jesus Christ.

God' in Three' Per'sons, *n.* the Trinity.

Go•di•va (gə dī'və), *n.* ("Lady Godiva"), died 1057, an English noblewoman who, according to legend, rode naked through the streets to win relief for the people from a burdensome tax.

god'less, *adj.* **1.** acknowledging no god; atheistic. **2.** evil; sinful.

god'ly, *adj.*, -**li•er,** -**li•est.** **1.** devout; pious. **2.** coming from God; divine. —**god'li•ness**, *n.*

god'moth'er, *n.* a woman who serves as sponsor for a child.

god'par'ent, *n.* a godfather or godmother.

god'send', *n.* an unexpected thing or event that is particularly welcome and timely, as if sent by God.

god'son', *n.* a male godchild.

God's' Word', *n.* the Bible.

God' the Fa'ther, *n.* one of the three persons in the Trinity, the others being **God' the Son'** and **God' the Ho'ly Ghost'.**

God'win Aus'ten, *n.* See K2.

Goe•the (gœ'tə), *n.* **Johann Wolfgang von,** 1749–1832, German poet and dramatist. —**Goe•the•an,** **Goe'thi•an,** *adj.*

go•fer (gō'fər), *n. Slang.* an employee whose chief duty is running errands.

Gog and Ma•gog (gog' ən mā'gog), *n.pl.* nations led by Satan at Armageddon. Rev. 20:8.

go'-get'ter, *n. Informal.* an enterprising, aggressive person.

gog•gle (gog'əl), *n.*, *v.*, -**gled,** -**gling.** —*n.* **1. goggles,** large spectacles worn to protect the eyes from strong wind, flying objects, etc. **2.** a bulging or wide-open look of the eyes; stare. —*v.i.* **3.** to stare with bulging or wide-open eyes.

go'ings-on', *n.pl. Informal.* behavior or happenings, esp. when open to criticism.

goi•ter (goi'tər), *n.* an enlargement of the thyroid gland on the front and sides of the neck. Also, *esp. Brit.*, **goi'tre.**

Go'lan Heights' (gō'lan, -län), *n.pl.* a range of hills in northern Israel, formerly belonging to Syria and occupied by Israel in 1967.

gold (gōld), *n.* **1.** a precious yellow metallic element, highly malleable and ductile, and not subject to oxidation: one of three gifts, the other two being frankincense and myrrh, given by the Magi to the infant Jesus. Matt. 2:11. *Symbol:* Au; *at. wt.:* 196.967; *at. no.:* 79. **2.** money; riches. **3.** a bright yellow color. —*Proverb.* **4. All that glitters is not gold,** appearances can be deceiving.

Gold•berg (gōld'bûrg), *n.* **Reuben Lucius** ("Rube"), 1883–1970, U.S. cartoonist, whose work often depicts deviously complex and impractical inventions.

gold'brick', *Slang.* —*n.* **1.** Also, **gold'brick'er.** a person, esp. a soldier, who loafs on the job. —*v.i.* **2.** to shirk work.

gold'en, *adj.* **1.** of the color of gold. **2.** made or consisting of gold. **3.** exceptionally valuable. **4.** full of happiness or prosperity. **5.** destined for success:

television's golden boy. **6.** indicating the 50th year, as a wedding anniversary.

gold′en calf′, *n.* **1.** a golden idol set up by Aaron. Ex. 32. **2.** either of the two similar idols set up by Jeroboam. I Kings 12:28, 29.

gold′en hand′shake, *n.* an incentive, as severance pay, offered as an inducement to elect early retirement.

gold′en•rod′, *n.* a North American plant with small, yellow flower heads on wandlike stalks.

gold′en rule′, *n.* a rule of ethical conduct, usu. phrased "Do unto others as you would have others do unto you": found in various wordings in most major religions.

gold′finch′, *n.* a New World finch, the male of which has yellow body plumage in the summer.

gold′fish′, *n.*, **-fish,** **-fish•es.** a small, yellow or orange fish of the carp family, often kept in aquariums and pools.

gold′ leaf′, *n.* gold in the form of very thin foil, as for gilding.

gold′ med′al, *n.* a medal, traditionally of gold, awarded to a person or team finishing first in a competition. Compare BRONZE MEDAL, SILVER MEDAL. —**gold′ med′alist,** *n.*

gold′smith′, *n.* a person who makes or sells articles of gold.

gold′ stand′ard, *n.* a monetary system with gold of specified weight and fineness as the unit of value.

Gold•wa•ter (gōld′wô′tər, -wot′ər), *n.* **Barry Morris,** 1909–98, U.S. politician.

Gold•wyn (gōld′win), *n.* **Samuel** (*Samuel Goldfish*), 1882–1974, U.S. movie producer, born in Poland.

golf (golf, gôlf; *Brit.* also gof), *n.* **1.** a game in which clubs are used to hit a small ball into a series of 9 or 18 holes. —*v.i.* **2.** to play golf. —**golf′er,** *n.*

Gol•go•tha (gol′gə thə), *n.* CALVARY (defs. 1, 3). [< LL < Gk *golgothá* < Aram *gulgaltā,* akin to Heb *gulgōleth* skull]

Go•li•ath (gə lī′əth), *n.* the Philistine giant whom David killed with a slinghot. I Sam. 17:48–51.

gol•ly (gol′ē), *interj.* a mild exclamation of surprise, wonder, or the like.

Go•mor•rah (gə môr′ə, -mor′ə), *n.* an ancient city destroyed because of its wickedness. Gen. 19:24, 25.

Gom•pers (gom′pərz), *n.* **Samuel,** 1850–1924, U.S. labor leader, born in England.

-gon, a combining form meaning having a specified number or sort of angles (*polygon*).

go•nad (gō′nad, gon′ad), *n.* any organ or gland in which gametes are produced; an ovary or testis. —**go•nad′al,** *adj.*

gon•do•la (gon′dl ə *or, esp. for 1,* gon dō′lə), *n., pl.* **-las.** **1.** a long, narrow boat used on the canals in Venice, Italy. **2.** a passenger compartment suspended beneath a balloon or airship. **3.** a cabin suspended from a cable, used esp. to transport skiers. **4.** an open railroad freight car with low sides.

gondola

gon′do•lier′ (-ēr′), *n.* a person who rows or poles a gondola.

gone (gôn, gon), *v.* **1.** pp. of GO. —*adj.* **2.** departed. **3.** hopeless. **4.** ruined. **5.** dead. **6.** past. **7.** weak and faint. **8.** used up. **9.** *Slang.* pregnant.

gon′er, *n. Informal.* one that is dead, lost, or past recovery.

gong (gông, gong), *n.* a large bronze disk that produces a vibrant, hollow tone when struck.

gon•or•rhe•a (gon′ə rē′ə), *n.* a contagious, purulent inflammation of the urethra or the vagina. Also, *esp. Brit.,* **gon′or•rhoe′a.** —**gon′or•rhe′al,** *adj.*

goo (gōō), *n., pl.* **goos.** *Informal.* **1.** a thick or sticky substance. **2.** maudlin sentimentality. —**goo′ey,** *adj.,* **-i•er,** **-i•est.**

goo•ber (gōō′bər), *n. Chiefly Southern U.S.* the peanut.

good (gŏŏd), *adj.,* **bet•ter,** **best,** *n., interj., adv.* —*adj.* **1.** morally excellent; virtuous. **2.** satisfactory or superior in quality, quantity, or degree. **3.** proper, suitable, or right. **4.** well-behaved. **5.** kind or friendly. **6.** honorable or worthy. **7.** not counterfeit. **8.** sound or valid: *good judgment.* **9.** beneficial. **10.** healthy: *good teeth.* **11.** not spoiled or tainted. **12.** favorable: *good news.* **13.** agreeable; pleasant. **14.** attractive: *a good figure.* **15.** competent or skillful. **16.** full: *a good day's journey away.* **17.** fairly large; ample. —*n.* **18.** profit or advantage. **19.** kindness. **20.** moral righteousness; virtue. **21. goods, a.** personal property. **b.** merchandise. **22. the good,** good things or persons collectively. —*interj.* **23.** an exclamation of approval or satisfaction. —*adv.* **24.** *Informal.* well. —*Idiom.* **25. for good,** finally and permanently. **26. good and,** very: *good and hot.* **27. good for, a.** certain to repay (money owed). **b.** worth. **c.** serviceable or useful for. —**Usage.** GOOD is common as an adverb in informal speech, esp. after forms of *do: He did good on the test.* In careful speech or writing, WELL is used instead.

good′-bye′ *or* **-by′,** *interj., n., pl.* **-byes** *or* **-bys.** —*interj.* **1.** (a conventional expression used at parting.) —*n.* **2.** an act of saying good-bye; farewell. [contr. of *God be with ye*]

good′-for-noth′ing (-nuth′ing, -nuth′-), *adj.* **1.** worthless; of no use. —*n.* **2.** a worthless or useless person.

Good′ Fri′day, *n.* the Friday before Easter, commemorating the Crucifixion.

good′-heart′ed, *adj.* kind or generous. —**good′-heart′ed•ly,** *adv.* —**good′-heart′ed•ness,** *n.*

Good′ Hope′, *n.* **Cape of,** CAPE OF GOOD HOPE.

good′ hu′mor, *n.* a cheerful or amiable mood. —**good′-hu′mored,** *adj.*

good′-look′ing, *adj.* having an attractive appearance.

good′ly, *adj.,* **-li•er,** **-li•est.** **1.** of substantial size or amount. **2.** of good appearance.

good′-na′tured, *adj.* having or showing a pleasant, kindly disposition. —**good′-na′tured•ly,** *adv.*

good′ness, *n.* **1.** the state or quality of being good. **2.** virtue. **3.** kindness. **4.** the good part of anything. **5.** a euphemism for God: *Thank goodness!* —*interj.* **6.** an exclamation of surprise, alarm, etc.

Good′ News′ Bi′ble, *n.* a Bible (1976) produced by the American Bible Society.

good′ (*or* **Good′**) **Samar′itan,** *n.* a person who voluntarily helps to those in distress or need: a parable of Jesus. Luke 10:30–37.

Good′ Shep′herd, *n.* Jesus Christ. John 10:11–14.

good′ sol′dier, *n.* one who is willing to place a cause or concern ahead of personal interest.

good′will′ *or* **good′ will′,** *n.* **1.** friendly disposition. **2.** cheerful consent. **3.** an intangible, salable asset arising from the reputation of a business and its relations with its customers.

good′y, *n., pl.* **good•ies,** *interj.* —*n.* **1.** something pleasing to eat, as candy. —*interj.* **2.** a childish exclamation of delight.

Good•year (gŏŏd′yēr′), *n.* **Charles,** 1800–60, U.S. inventor.

good′y-good′y, *n., pl.* **-good•ies,** *adj.* —*n.* **1.** a person who is self-righteously good or virtuous. —*adj.* **2.** of or like a goody-goody.

goof (gŏŏf), *Informal.* —*v.i.* **1.** to make an error, misjudgment, etc. **2.** to waste time; evade work: *We goofed off all morning.* —*v.t.* **3.** to make a mess of. —*n.* **4.** a foolish or stupid person. **5.** a mistake or blunder. —**goof′y,** *adj.,* **-i•er,** **-i•est.**

goof′ball′, *n. Slang.* an extremely eccentric or silly person.

goof′-off′, *n. Informal.* a person who habitually shirks work or responsibility.

gook (gŏŏk, gōŏk), *n. Slang.* any grimy or viscid substance.

goon (gōōn), *n. Slang.* **1.** a hired hoodlum. **2.** a stupid, foolish, or awkward person.

goose (gōōs), *n., pl.* **geese. 1.** any of numerous web-footed swimming birds, most of which are larger and have a longer neck than the ducks. **2.** the female of this bird. **3.** the flesh of a goose, used as food. **4.** a silly or foolish person. —*Idiom.* **5. cook someone's goose,** *Informal.* to ruin someone's chances. —*Proverb.* **6. Don't kill the goose that laid the golden eggs,** don't destroy a sure source of future profit out of current greed.

goose′ber′ry (gōōs′-, gōōz′-), *n., pl.* **-ries. 1.** a small, sour, sometimes prickly fruit. **2.** the shrub it grows on.

goose′ flesh′, *n.* a bristling of the hair on the skin, as from cold or fear. Also called **goose′ pim′ples, goose′ bumps′.**

GOP or **G.O.P.,** Grand Old Party (an epithet of the Republican Party).

go•pher (gō′fər), *n.* any of various New World burrowing rodents with external cheek pouches.

Gor•ba•chev (gôr′bə chôf′, -chof′, gôr′bə chôf′, -chof′), *n.* **Mikhail S(ergeyevich),** born 1931, president of the Soviet Union 1988–91.

gore¹ (gôr), *n.* **1.** blood that is shed, esp. when clotted. **2.** bloodshed; violence.

gore² (gôr), *v.t.,* **gored, gor•ing.** to pierce with or as if with a horn or tusk.

gore³ (gôr), *n.* a triangular piece of material inserted in a garment, sail, etc.

Gore, *n.* **Albert Arnold, Jr.** (*Al*), born 1948, vice president of the U.S. since 1993.

gorge (gôrj), *n., v.,* **gorged, gorg•ing.** —*n.* **1.** a narrow ravine with steep, rocky walls. **2.** something that is swallowed. **3.** an obstructing mass: *an ice gorge.* **4.** the throat; gullet. **5.** strong disgust or anger. —*v.t., v.i.* **6.** to stuff (oneself) with food.

gor•geous (gôr′jəs), *adj.* **1.** splendid or magnificent. **2.** very attractive or beautiful. —**gor′geous•ly,** *adv.*

go•ril•la (gə ril′ə), *n., pl.* **-las.** the largest anthropoid ape, native to equatorial Africa.

Gor•ki (gôr′kē), *n.* former name of NIZHNI NOVGOROD.

gor•mand•ize (gôr′mən dīz′), *v.i., v.t.,* **-ized, -iz•ing.** to eat greedily. —**gor′mand•iz′er,** *n.*

gorse (gôrs), *n.* a spiny European evergreen shrub with yellow flowers.

gor•y (gôr′ē), *adj.,* **-i•er, -i•est. 1.** covered with gore. **2.** involving much bloodshed. **3.** unpleasant or sensational. —**gor′i•ness,** *n.*

gosh (gosh), *interj.* an exclamation of surprise, wonder, etc.

gos•hawk (gos′hôk′), *n.* a robust short-winged hawk of North America and Eurasia.

Go•shen (gō′shən), *n.* a pastoral region in Lower Egypt, occupied by the Israelites before the Exodus. Gen. 45:10.

gos•ling (goz′ling), *n.* a young goose.

gos•pel (gos′pəl), *n.* **1.** the teachings of Jesus and the apostles. **2.** (*usu. cap.*) any of the first four books of the New Testament. **3.** Also called **gos′pel truth′.** something absolutely or unquestionably true. **4.** impassioned rhythmic spiritual music, influential in the development of rhythm and blues.

gos•sa•mer (gos′ə mər), *n.* **1.** a fine, filmy cobweb. **2.** something extremely light, flimsy, or delicate. —*adj.* **3.** thin and light.

gos•sip (gos′əp), *n., v.,* **-siped** or **-sipped, -sip•ing** or **-sip•ping.** —*n.* **1.** idle talk or rumor, esp. about the private affairs of others. **2.** a person given to such talk. —*v.i.* **3.** to relate or spread gossip. —**gos′sip•y,** *adj.*

got (got), *v.* a pt. and pp. of GET.

Goth (goth), *n.* a member of a Germanic people

who, from the 3rd to 5th centuries, invaded parts of the Roman Empire.

Goth•ic (goth′ik), *adj.* **1.** noting a style of architecture of W Europe from the 12th to 16th centuries, marked by pointed arches, rich ornamentation, etc. **2.** of the Goths or their language. **3.** (*often l.c.*) noting a style of literature marked by a gloomy setting and mysterious or sinister events. —*n.* **4.** Gothic architecture. **5.** the extinct Germanic language of the Goths.

got′ten (got′n), *v.* a pp. of GET.

Gou•da (gou′də, gōō′-), *n.* a yellowish Dutch cheese, usu. coated with red wax.

gouge (gouj), *n., v.,* **gouged, goug•ing.** —*n.* **1.** a chisel with a partly cylindrical blade. **2.** a groove or hole made by or as if by a gouge. **3.** an act of extortion; swindle. —*v.t.* **4.** to scoop out with or as if with a gouge. **5.** to swindle or overcharge. —**goug′er,** *n.*

gou•lash (gōō′läsh, -lash), *n.* a stew of beef or veal and vegetables, seasoned with paprika. [< Hungarian *gulyás,* short for *gulyáshús* herdsman's meat]

gourd (gôrd, gōōrd), *n.* **1.** the hard-shelled fruit of a vine related to the squash, melon, etc. **2.** a plant bearing such a fruit. **3.** a dried gourd shell used as a bottle, dipper, etc.

gourde (*Fr.* gōōrd; *Eng.* gōōrd), *n.* the basic monetary unit of Haiti.

gour•mand (gōōr mänd′, gōōr′mənd), *n.* one who is fond of good eating, often to excess. [< OF *gourmant* a glutton]

gour•met (gōōr mā′, gōōr′mā), *n.* a connoisseur of fine food and drink.

gout (gout), *n.* a painful inflammation, esp. of the big toe, characterized by an excess of uric acid in the blood. —**gout•y,** *adj.,* **-i•er, -i•est.**

gov., **1.** government. **2.** governor.

gov•ern (guv′ərn), *v.t.* **1.** to rule by right of authority. **2.** to exercise a directing influence over. **3.** to hold in check; control. **4.** to serve as a law for. —*v.i.* **5.** to exercise the function of government. —**gov′ern•a•ble,** *adj.* —**gov′ern•ance** (-ər nəns), *n.*

gov′ern•ess, *n.* a woman employed in a private household to take charge of a child's upbringing and education.

gov′ern•ment (-ərn mənt, -ər mənt), *n.* **1.** the political direction and control exercised over communities, societies, and states. **2.** the form or system of rule by which a state, community, etc., is governed. **3.** a governing body of persons. **4.** direction; control; rule. —*Saying.* **5. Government of the people, by the people, and for the people,** democracy: a saying made popular by Abraham Lincoln in the Gettysburg Address (1863). —**gov′ern•men′tal** (-men′tl), *adj.*

gover•nor (-ər nər, -ə nər), *n.* **1.** the executive head of a state in the U.S. **2.** the head of an institution, society, etc. **3.** a ruler appointed to govern a province, town, or the like. **4.** a device for maintaining uniform speed in an engine. —**gov′er•nor•ship′,** *n.*

govt., government.

gown (goun), *n.* **1.** a woman's formal dress, esp. a full-length one. **2.** a nightgown or robe. **3.** a loose, flowing outer garment worn by judges, members of the clergy, etc.

Go•ya (goi′ə), *n.* **Francisco de,** 1746–1828, Spanish painter.

G.P., General Practitioner.

Gr., 1. Greece. **2.** Greek.

gr., 1. grade. **2.** grain. **3.** gram. **4.** grammar. **5.** gravity. **6.** gross. **7.** group.

grab (grab), *v.,* **grabbed, grab•bing,** *n.* —*v.t.* **1.** to seize suddenly, eagerly, or roughly. **2.** to seize forcibly or unscrupulously. **3.** to obtain and consume quickly: *Let's grab a sandwich.* **4.** *Informal.* to impress or affect. —*n.* **5.** the act of grabbing. —**grab′ber,** *n.*

grace (grās), *n., v.,* **graced, grac•ing.** —*n.* **1.** elegance or beauty of form, manner, or motion. **2.** a pleasing or attractive quality. **3.** favor or goodwill. **4.** mercy; clemency. **5.** favor shown in granting a delay. **6.** the favor and love of God. **7.** a short prayer before or after a meal. **8.** (*cap.*) a title for a duke, duchess, or archbishop. —*v.t.* **9.** to lend or add grace to. **10.** to favor or honor. —*Idiom.* **11. fall from grace, a.** to relapse into sin. Gal. 5:4. **b.** to lose favor with those in power. **12. in someone's good** (or **bad**) **graces,** regarded with favor (or disfavor) by someone. —**grace′ful,** *adj.* —**grace′ful•ly,** *adv.* —**grace′ful•ness,** *n.* —**grace′less,** *adj.* —**grace′-less•ly,** *adv.* —**grace′less•ness,** *n.*

Grace•land (grās′lənd), *n.* (Nashville, Tenn.) the former home of Elvis Presley.

gra•cious (grā′shəs), *adj.* **1.** pleasantly kind or courteous. **2.** characterized by good taste, comfort, or luxury. —**gra′cious•ly,** *adv.* —**gra′cious•ness,** *n.*

grack•le (grak′əl), *n.* any of several long-tailed North American blackbirds with iridescent black plumage.

grad (grad), *n. Informal.* a graduate.

gra•da•tion (grā dā′shən), *n.* **1.** a change taking place through a series of stages or by degrees. **2.** a stage or degree in such a series. **3.** the act of grading.

grade (grād), *n., v.,* **grad•ed, grad•ing.** —*n.* **1.** a degree in a scale, as of rank or quality. **2.** a class of persons or things; category. **3.** a step or stage in a course or process. **4.** any of the divisions corresponding to a year's work in school. **5.** a letter or number indicating the quality of a student's work. **6. a.** a slope of a road, railroad, etc. **b.** the degree of such slope. —*v.t.* **7.** to arrange in a series of grades. **8.** to assign a grade to (a student's work). **9.** to reduce the inclination of: *to grade a road.* —*Idiom.* **10. make the grade,** to succeed.

grade′ cross′ing, *n.* an intersection of a railroad track and another track, a road, etc., at the same level.

grade′ school′, *n.* ELEMENTARY SCHOOL.

gra•di•ent (grā′dē ənt), *n.* GRADE (def. 6).

grad•u•al (graj′ōō əl), *adj.* **1.** changing, moving, etc., by degrees or little by little. —*n.* **2.** an antiphon sung between the Epistle and the Gospel in the Eucharistic service. —**grad′u•al•ly,** *adv.*

grad′u•al•ism, *n.* the principle of achieving some goal by gradual steps rather than by drastic change.

grad′u•ate (*n., adj.* -it, -āt′; *v.* -āt′), *n., adj., v.,* -**at•ed, -at•ing.** —*n.* **1.** a person who has received an academic degree or diploma. —*adj.* **2.** of or involved in academic study beyond the bachelor's degree. **3.** having an academic degree or diploma. —*v.i.* **4.** to receive an academic degree or diploma: *to graduate from college.* —*v.t.* **5.** to grant an academic degree or diploma to. **6.** to receive a degree or diploma from. **7.** to arrange in grades or gradations. **8.** to divide into or mark with degrees or other divisions. —**Usage.** The active form of GRADUATE, occasionally objected to, is the most common construction today: *He graduated from Harvard.* The passive form, though once considered to be the only correct pattern, is now infrequent: *He was graduated from Yale.*

grad′u•a′tion, *n.* **1.** the act of graduating or state of being graduated. **2.** the ceremony of conferring degrees or diplomas. **3.** a mark or marks on an instrument or container for indicating degree or quantity.

graf•fi•to (grə fē′tō), *n., pl.* -**ti** (-tē). Usu., **-ti.** a drawing, message, etc., scrawled or painted on a wall or other public surface.

graft¹ (graft, gräft), *n.* **1. a.** a bud or shoot of a plant inserted into another plant in which it continues to grow. **b.** the plant resulting from this. **2.** a portion of living tissue transplanted to another part of the body or from one individual to another. —*v.t., v.i.* **3.** to insert (a graft). **4.** to transplant (a portion of living tissue) as a graft. —**graft′er,** *n.*

graft² (graft, gräft), *n.* **1.** the acquisition of money or advantage by dishonest means, esp. through political influence. **2.** the gain or advantage acquired. —*v.t., v.i.* **3.** to obtain by graft. —**graft′er,** *n.*

gra•ham (grā′əm, gram), *adj.* made of graham flour.

Gra•ham (grā′əm, gram), *n.* **1. Martha,** 1894–1991, U.S. dancer and choreographer. **2. William Franklin** ("*Billy*"), born 1918, U.S. evangelist.

gra′ham crack′er, *n.* a semisweet cracker made chiefly of whole-wheat flour.

Gra•hame (grā′əm), *n.* **Kenneth,** 1859–1932, Scottish writer.

Grail (grāl), *n.* (in medieval legend) the cup or chalice supposedly used at the Last Supper.

grain (grān), *n.* **1.** a small, hard seed of a food plant, esp. a cereal plant such as wheat or rye. **2.** the gathered seed of such plants. **3.** such plants collectively. **4.** any small, hard particle, as of sand. **5.** the smallest unit of weight in the U.S. and British systems. **6.** a tiny amount. **7.** the arrangement or direction of fibers in wood, meat, etc. **8.** texture: *sugar of fine grain.* **9.** temperament or natural character. —**grained,** *adj.*

grain′ al′cohol, *n.* ALCOHOL (def. 1).

grain′y, *adj.,* -**i•er, -i•est. 1.** of or resembling grain. **2.** (of a photograph) having a granular appearance. —**grain′i•ness,** *n.*

gram (gram), *n.* a metric unit of mass or weight equal to 15.432 grains, or ¹⁄₁₀₀₀ of a kilogram. Also, *esp. Brit.,* **gramme.**

-gram, a combining form meaning something written or drawn (*diagram*).

gram•mar (gram′ər), *n.* **1.** the study of the way the sentences of a language are constructed, esp. the study of morphology and syntax. **2.** a set of rules accounting for the features or constructions of a given language. **3.** knowledge or usage of the preferred forms in speaking or writing. —**gram•mar•i•an** (grə-mâr′ē ən), *n.* —**gram•mat′i•cal** (-mat′i kəl), *adj.* —**gram•mat′i•cal•ly,** *adv.*

gram′mar school′, *n. Older Use.* ELEMENTARY SCHOOL.

gra•na•ry (grā′nə rē, gran′ə-), *n., pl.* -**ries.** a storehouse or repository for grain.

grand (grand), *adj.,* **grand•er, grand•est,** *n., pl.* **grands** for 8, **grand** for 9. —*adj.* **1.** impressive in size, appearance, or effect. **2.** stately; dignified. **3.** highly ambitious. **4.** high in rank or official dignity. **5.** of great importance or pretension. **6.** complete; comprehensive: *a grand total.* **7.** first-rate; splendid. —*n.* **8.** GRAND PIANO. **9.** *Informal.* a thousand dollars. —**grand′ly,** *adv.* —**grand′ness,** *n.*

grand-, a combining form meaning one generation more remote (*grandmother*).

Grand′ Can′yon, *n.* a gorge of the Colorado River in N Arizona.

grand•child (gran′chīld′), *n., pl.* -**chil•dren.** a child of one's son or daughter.

grand′daugh′ter (gran′-), *n.* a daughter of one's son or daughter.

grand′ design′, *n.* a master plan.

grande dame (grän′ däm′, gränd′), *n., pl.* **grandes dames** (grän′ dämz′, gränd′). a usu. older woman of dignified bearing or great accomplishment.

gran•dee (gran dē′), *n., pl.* -**dees.** a man of high social rank, esp. a Spanish or Portuguese nobleman.

gran•deur (gran′jər, -jŏŏr), *n.* the quality or state of being grand.

grand′fa′ther (gran′-, grand′-), *n.* **1.** the father of one's father or mother. **2.** a male ancestor.

grand′father (or **grand′father's**) **clock′,** *n.* a pendulum floor clock having a case as tall as a person.

gran•dil•o•quence (gran dil′ə kwəns), *n.* speech that is lofty in tone and often bombastic. —**gran•dil′-o•quent,** *adj.*

gran•di•ose (gran′dē ōs′), *adj.* **1.** affectedly grand; pompous. **2.** grand in an imposing way.

grand′ ju′ry, *n.* a jury designated to determine if a law has been violated and whether the evidence warrants prosecution.

grand•ma (gran′mä′, -mô′, grand′-, gram′-), *n., pl.* -**mas.** *Informal.* GRANDMOTHER.

grand mal (gran′ mäl′, -mal′, grand′), *n.* severe epilepsy.

grand′moth′er (gran′-, grand′-, gram′-), *n.* the mother of one's father or mother.

grand′ op′era, *n.* a usu. tragic opera in which the text is set to music.

grand•pa (gran′pä′, -pô′, grand′-, gram′-), *n., pl.* **-pas.** *Informal.* GRANDFATHER.

grand′ pian′o, *n.* a piano having the frame supported horizontally on three legs.

Grand′ Rap′ids, *n.* a city in SW Michigan. 190,395.

grand′ slam′, *n.* **1.** the winning of or bid for all thirteen tricks of a deal in bridge. **2.** a home run with three runners on base.

grand′son′ (gran′-, grand′-), *n.* a son of one's son or daughter.

grand′stand′ (gran′-, grand′-), *n.* **1.** a main seating area, as of a stadium or racetrack. —*v.i.* **2.** to conduct oneself or perform showily to impress onlookers.

grange (grānj), *n.* **1.** a farm with its nearby buildings. **2.** (*cap.*) a U.S. farmers' organization, or one of its local branches.

gran•ite (gran′it), *n.* a coarse-grained igneous rock composed chiefly of feldspar and quartz. —**gra•nit•ic** (grə nit′ik), *adj.*

gran•ny or **-nie** (gran′ē), *n., pl.* **-nies. 1.** *Informal.* GRANDMOTHER. **2.** an elderly woman.

gra•no•la (grə nō′lə), *n., pl.* **-las.** a breakfast food of rolled oats, nuts, dried fruit, brown sugar, etc. [orig. a trademark]

grant (grant, gränt), *v.t.* **1.** to confer, esp. by a formal act. **2.** to give; accord: *to grant permission.* **3.** to agree to. **4.** to accept for the sake of argument. **5.** to transfer (property), esp. by deed. —*n.* **6.** something granted, as a right, a sum of money, or a tract of land. **7.** the act of granting. —*Idiom.* **8. take for granted, a.** to assume without question. **b.** to fail to appreciate. —**grant′er, gran′tor,** *n.*

Grant (grant, gränt), *n.* **Ulysses S(impson),** 1822–85, Union general: 18th president of the U.S. 1869–77.

gran•tee (gran tē′, grän-), *n., pl.* **-tees.** the receiver of a grant.

grants′man•ship′, *n.* skill in securing grants, as for research.

gran•u•lar (gran′yə lər), *adj.* **1.** of the nature of granules. **2.** composed of or bearing granules or grains. —**gran′u•lar′i•ty,** *n.*

gran′u•late′, *v.t., v.i.,* **-lat•ed, -lat•ing.** to form into granules or grains. —**gran′u•la′tion,** *n.*

gran′ule (-yōōl), *n.* **1.** a little grain. **2.** a small particle.

grape (grāp), *n.* **1.** an edible, smooth-skinned fruit that grows in clusters on a vine. **2.** GRAPEVINE (def. 1). **3.** a dark purplish red color.

grape′fruit′, *n.* a large, roundish, yellow-skinned, edible citrus fruit.

grape′ hy′acinth, *n.* a plant of the lily family, with round, blue, grapelike flowers.

grape′shot′, *n.* a cluster of small cast-iron balls formerly used as a charge for a cannon.

grape′vine′, *n.* **1.** a vine that bears grapes. **2.** a person-to-person method of spreading gossip or information.

graph (graf, gräf), *n.* **1.** a diagram representing a system of connections or interrelations among things, as by a number of dots or lines. —*v.t.* **2.** to represent by a graph.

-graph, a combining form meaning: something written or drawn (*autograph*); an instrument that writes or records (*seismograph*).

graph′ic, *adj.* Also, **graph′i•cal. 1.** giving a clear and effective picture; vivid. **2.** of or using diagrams or graphs. **3.** of or expressed by writing. **4.** of the graphic arts. —*n.* **5.** a product of the graphic arts, as a print. **6.** a graphic representation, as a picture or map. **7.** a computer-generated image. —**graph′i•cal•ly,** *adv.*

graph′ical us′er in′terface, *n.* a software interface designed to standardize and simplify the use of computer programs, as by using a mouse to manipu-

late text on a screen featuring icons and menus. Also called **GUI.**

graph′ic arts′, *n.pl.* **1.** the arts, as engraving or lithography, by which copies of a design are printed from a plate, block, or the like. **2.** the arts of drawing, painting, and printmaking.

graph′ics, *n.* **1.** (*used with a sing. v.*) the art of drawing, esp. in architecture, engineering, etc. **2.** (*used with a pl. v.*) GRAPHIC ARTS (def. 1). **3.** (*used with a sing. v.*) **a.** pictorial computer output produced, through the use of software, on a display screen or printer. **b.** the technique used to produce such output.

graph′ite (-īt), *n.* a soft carbon used for pencil leads, as a lubricant, etc.

graph•ol•o•gy (gra fol′ə jē), *n.* the study of handwriting, esp. to find clues to the writer's character. —**graph•ol′o•gist,** *n.*

-graphy, a combining form meaning: a process or form of writing, printing, recording, or describing (*biography*); an art or science concerned with such processes (*geography*).

grap•nel (grap′nl), *n.* **1.** a device consisting of one or more hooks for grasping or holding. **2.** a small anchor with three or more flukes.

grap•ple (grap′əl), *v.,* **-pled, -pling,** *n.* —*v.i.* **1.** to use a grapnel. **2.** to seize another in a firm grip, as in wrestling. **3.** to cope or struggle: *to grapple with a problem.* —*v.t.* **4.** to seize or hold. —*n.* **5.** GRAPNEL (def. 1). **6.** a seizing or gripping. **7.** a hand-to-hand fight.

grap′pling i′ron, *n.* GRAPNEL.

grasp (grasp, gräsp), *v.t.* **1.** to seize and hold with or as if with the hand. **2.** to seize upon. **3.** to comprehend; understand. —*v.i.* **4.** to make a motion of seizing. —*n.* **5.** the act of grasping. **6.** a hold or grip. **7.** one's power to seize; reach. **8.** mastery or comprehension. —**grasp′a•ble,** *adj.*

grasp′ing, *adj.* greedy; avaricious.

grass (gras, gräs), *n.* **1.** any of various plants that have jointed stems and bladelike leaves. **2.** such plants collectively. **3.** grass-covered ground. —**grass′y,** *adj.,* **-i•er, -i•est.**

grass′hop′per, *n.* any of numerous insects having the hind legs adapted for leaping.

grass′ roots′, *n.* (*used with a sing. or pl. v.*) **1.** ordinary citizens, as contrasted with the leadership or elite. **2.** the people inhabiting rural areas, esp. as a political group. —**grass′-roots′,** *adj.*

grass′ wid′ow, *n.* a woman who is separated or divorced from her husband.

grate¹ (grāt), *n.* **1.** a frame of metal bars for holding burning fuel, as in a fireplace. **2.** a framework of parallel or crossed bars used as a partition, guard, or cover.

grate² (grāt), *v.,* **grat•ed, grat•ing.** —*v.i.* **1.** to have an irritating effect. **2.** to make a sound of rough scraping. —*v.t.* **3.** to reduce to small particles by rubbing against a rough surface. **4.** to rub together with a harsh sound. **5.** to irritate; annoy. —**grat′er,** *n.*

grate′ful, *adj.* **1.** warmly or deeply appreciative; thankful. **2.** expressing gratitude. —**grate′ful•ly,** *adv.* —**grate′ful•ness,** *n.*

grat•i•fy (grat′ə fī′), *v.t.,* **-fied, -fy•ing. 1.** to give pleasure to. **2.** to satisfy, humor, or indulge. —**grat′i•fi•ca′tion,** *n.*

grat•ing¹ (grā′ting), *n.* GRATE¹ (def. 2).

grat•ing² (grā′ting), *adj.* **1.** irritating; abrasive. **2.** harsh; discordant.

grat•is (grat′is, grā′tis), *adv., adj.* without charge or payment.

grat•i•tude (grat′i tōōd′, -tyōōd′), *n.* the quality or feeling of being grateful or thankful.

gra•tu•i•tous (grə tōō′i təs, -tyōō′-), *adj.* **1.** given, done, or obtained without charge. **2.** being without apparent reason or justification.

gra•tu′i•ty, *n., pl.* **-ties.** a gift of money for service rendered; tip.

gra•va•men (grə vā′mən), *n., pl.* **-vam•i•na** (-vam′-ə nə). *Law.* the part of an accusation weighing most heavily against the accused.

grave[1] (grāv), *n.* **1.** an excavation made in the earth to bury a dead body. **2.** any place of interment.

grave[2] (grāv), *adj.,* **grav•er, grav•est. 1.** sedate or solemn. **2.** weighty; momentous. **3.** serious; critical. —**grave**/**ly,** *adv.* —**grave**/**ness,** *n.*

grave[3] (grāv), *v.t.,* **graved, grav•en** or **graved, grav•ing. 1.** to carve or engrave. **2.** to impress deeply.

grave/ **ac**/**cent** (grăv, gräv), *n.* a mark (`) placed over a vowel to show pronunciation, stress, etc.

grav•el (grav/əl), *n.* small stones and pebbles or a mixture of these with sand. —**grav**/**el•ly,** *adj.*

grave/**stone**/, *n.* a stone marking a grave.

grave/**yard**/, *n.* CEMETERY.

grave/**yard shift**/, *n.* a work shift usu. beginning about midnight.

grav•id (grav/id), *adj.* pregnant.

gra•vim•e•ter (grə vim/i tər), *n.* **1.** an instrument for measuring specific gravity. **2.** an instrument for measuring variations in the earth's gravitational field.

grav•i•tate (grav/i tāt/), *v.i.,* **-tat•ed, -tat•ing. 1.** to move under the influence of gravitational force. **2.** to be strongly attracted.

grav/**i•ta**/**tion,** *n.* **1.** the force of attraction between any two masses. **2.** a movement toward something or someone. —**grav**/**i•ta**/**tion•al,** *adj.*

grav/**i•ty,** *n., pl.* **-ties. 1.** the force of attraction by which terrestrial bodies tend to fall toward the center of the earth. **2.** gravitation in general. **3.** heaviness or weight. **4.** serious or critical nature.

gra•vy (grā/vē), *n., pl.* **-vies. 1.** the fat and juices of cooked meat, often used to make a sauce. **2.** *Slang.* profit or money easily or unexpectedly obtained.

gray (grā), *adj., n., v.,* **1.** of a color between white and black. **2.** dismal or gloomy. **3.** having gray hair. **4.** indeterminate in character. —*n.* **5.** any achromatic color. **6.** something of this color. **7.** (*often cap.*) a member of the Confederate army in the American Civil War, or the army itself. Compare BLUE (def. 3). —*v.t., v.i.* **8.** to make or become gray. —**gray**/**ish,** *adj.*

Gray (grā), *n.* **Thomas,** 1716–71, English poet.

gray/ **mat**/**ter,** *n.* **1.** a reddish gray nerve tissue of the brain and spinal cord. **2.** *Informal.* brains or intellect.

graze[1] (grāz), *v.,* **grazed, graz•ing.** —*v.i.* **1.** to feed on growing grass and herbage. **2.** *Informal.* **a.** to eat snacks in place of regular meals. **b.** to eat small portions of a variety of foods at one meal. —*v.t.* **3.** to put (livestock) out to graze. —**graz**/**er,** *n.*

graze[2] (grāz), *v.t., v.i.,* **grazed, graz•ing.** to touch, rub, or scrape (something) lightly in passing.

Gr. Br. or **Gr. Brit.,** Great Britain.

grease (*n.* grēs; *v.* grēs, grēz), *n., v.,* **greased, greas•ing.** —*n.* **1.** the melted fat of animals. **2.** fatty or oily matter in general. —*v.t.* **3.** to put grease on.

grease/ **paint**/, *n.* an oily makeup used by actors, clowns, etc.

greas•y (grē/sē, -zē), *adj.,* **-i•er, -i•est. 1.** soiled with grease. **2.** containing grease. —**greas**/**i•ness,** *n.*

great (grāt), *adj.,* **-er, -est,** *adv., n.* —*adj.* **1.** comparatively large in size or dimensions. **2.** large in number. **3.** considerable in degree, intensity, etc. **4.** first-rate; excellent. **5.** highly significant or consequential. **6.** distinguished; famous. **7.** of extraordinary ability or achievement. **8.** of marked duration. **9.** skillful; expert: *She's great at golf.* **10.** being of one generation more remote from the relative specified: *a great-grandson.* —*adv.* **11.** *Informal.* very well. —*n.* **12.** a person who has achieved importance or distinction. —**great**/**ly,** *adv.* —**great**/**ness,** *n.*

Great/ **Awak**/**ening,** *n.* the series of religious revivals among Protestants in the American colonies, esp. in New England, lasting from about 1725 to 1770.

Great/ **Bar**/**rier Reef**/, *n.* a coral reef parallel to the coast of Queensland, in NE Australia.

Great/ **Brit**/**ain,** *n.* an island of NW Europe, comprising England, Scotland, and Wales. Compare UNITED KINGDOM.

Great/ **Commis**/**sion, The,** *n.* Christ's command

to his disciples to go through the world teaching and baptizing. Matt. 28:18–20.

Great/ **Com**/**moner,** *n.* **1.** epithet of Henry Clay. **2.** epithet of William Jennings Bryan.

Great/ **Dane**/, *n.* a large and powerful shorthaired dog.

Great/**er Antil**/**les,** *n.pl.* See under ANTILLES.

great/**est show**/ **on earth**/, *n.* epithet for the circus: coined by P.T. Barnum.

great/**heart**/**ed,** *adj.* **1.** generous; magnanimous. **2.** high-spirited; courageous.

Great/ **Lakes**/, *n.pl.* a series of five lakes between the U.S. and Canada, comprising Lakes Erie, Huron, Michigan, Ontario, and Superior.

Great/ **Plains**/, *n.* a semiarid region E of the Rocky Mountains, in the U.S. and Canada.

Great/ **Salt**/ **Lake**/, *n.* a shallow salt lake in NW Utah.

great/ **seal**/, *n.* the principal seal of a government or state.

Great Seal of the United States

Great/ **Smok**/**y Moun**/**tains,** *n.pl.* a range of the Appalachian Mountains in North Carolina and Tennessee.

Great/ **Soci**/**ety,** *n.* the goal of the Democratic party under the leadership of President Lyndon B. Johnson.

Great/ **Tribula**/**tion, the,** *n.* a short period of great suffering at the end of time. Rev. 7:14.

grebe (grēb), *n.* a diving bird with a rudimentary tail and lobed toes.

Gre•cian (grē/shən), *adj.* **1.** of Greece, esp. ancient Greece. —*n.* **2.** a Greek.

Greece (grēs), *n.* a republic in S Europe. 10,583,126.

greed (grēd), *n.* excessive or rapacious desire, esp. for wealth.

greed/**y,** *adj.,* **-i•er, -i•est. 1.** excessively desirous of wealth, profit, etc. **2.** having a great desire for food or drink. —**greed**/**i•ly,** *adv.* —**greed**/**i•ness,** *n.*

Greek (grēk), *n.* **1.** a native or inhabitant of Greece. **2.** the Indo-European language of the Greeks. —*adj.* **3.** of Greece, the Greeks, or their language. **4.** of the Greek Orthodox Church.

Greek/ **Or**/**thodox Church**/, *n.* the branch of the Orthodox Church constituting the national church of Greece.

Gree•ley (grē/lē), *n.* **Horace,** 1811–72, U.S. journalist, editor, and political leader.

green (grēn), *adj.,* **-er, -est,** *n., v.* —*adj.* **1.** of the color of growing foliage, between yellow and blue in the spectrum. **2.** covered with foliage. **3.** made of green vegetables. **4.** not fully developed or matured. **5.** unseasoned: *green lumber.* **6.** immature or inexperienced. **7.** sickly or pale. —*n.* **8.** a color intermediate between yellow and blue. **9. greens,** the edible leaves and stems of certain plants, as spinach or lettuce. **10.** grassy land. **11.** the area of closely cropped grass surrounding each hole on a golf course. —*v.i., v.t.* **12.** to become or make green. —**green'ish,** *adj.*

green'back', *n.* a U.S. legal-tender note, printed in green on the back.

green' bean', *n.* the immature green pod of the kidney bean.

green'belt', *n.* an area of woods, parks, or open land surrounding a community.

Greene (grēn), *n.* **1. Graham,** 1904–91, English novelist and journalist. **2. Nathanael,** 1742–86, American Revolutionary general.

green'er•y, *n.* foliage or vegetation.

green'-eyed', *adj.* jealous; envious.

green'gro'cer, *n.* a retailer of fresh vegetables and fruit.

green'horn', *n.* **1.** an inexperienced person. **2.** a naive or gullible person.

green'house', *n.* a glass building with controlled temperature, used for cultivating plants.

green'house effect', *n.* heating of the atmosphere resulting from the absorption by certain gases of solar radiation.

Green'land (-lənd, -land'), *n.* a self-governing Danish island NE of North America: the largest island in the world. 53,733. —**Green'land•er,** *n.*

green' manure', *n.* a crop of growing plants plowed under to enrich the soil.

Green' Moun'tain Boys', *n.pl.* the soldiers from Vermont in the American Revolution.

green' on'ion, *n.* a young onion with a slender green stalk and a small bulb; scallion.

Green' Par'ty, *n.* a liberal political party focusing on environmental issues.

green' pep'per, *n.* the mild-flavored, unripe fruit of the bell or sweet pepper.

green'room', *n.* a lounge in a theater, television studio, etc., for use by performers.

Greens•bo•ro (grēnz'bûr'ō, -bur'ō), *n.* a city in N North Carolina. 196,167.

green'sward', *n.* green, grassy turf.

green' thumb', *n.* an exceptional skill for growing plants.

Green•wich (grin'ij, -ich, gren'-), *n.* a borough in SE London, England: located on the prime meridian. 216,600.

Green'wich Time', *n.* the time as measured on the prime meridian running through Greenwich, England: used as a worldwide standard of calculation.

Green'wich Vil'lage (gren'ich, grin'-), *n.* a section of New York City, in lower Manhattan.

green'wood', *n.* a wood or forest when green.

greet (grēt), *v.t.* **1.** to address with some form of salutation. **2.** to receive: *to greet a proposal with boos.* **3.** to manifest itself to: *Music greeted our ears.*

greet'ing, *n.* **1.** the act or words of one who greets. **2. greetings,** an expression of friendly regard.

gre•gar•i•ous (gri gâr'ē əs), *adj.* **1.** fond of the company of others. **2.** living in flocks or herds. —**gre•gar'i•ous•ly,** *adv.* —**gre•gar'i•ous•ness,** *n.*

Grego'rian cal'endar, *n.* the reformed Julian calendar now in use. [after Pope *Gregory* XIII (1502–85)]

grem•lin (grem'lin), *n.* an imaginary, mischievous being humorously alleged to cause disruptions in any activity.

Gre•na•da (gri nā'də), *n.* an island country in the E West Indies. 95,537. —**Gre•na'di•an** (-dē ən), *adj., n.*

gre•nade (gri nād'), *n.* a small shell containing an explosive, usu. thrown by hand.

gren•a•dier (gren'ə dēr'), *n.* **1.** a member of a British infantry regiment. **2.** (formerly) a soldier who threw grenades.

gren•a•dine (gren'ə dēn'), *n.* a syrup made from pomegranate juice.

Gren•a•dines (gren'ə denz', gren'ə dēnz'), *n.pl.* a chain of islands in the E West Indies.

grew (grōō), *v.* pt. of GROW.

grey (grā), *adj., n., v.t., v.i.,* GRAY.

grey'hound', *n.* a tall, slender shorthaired dog noted for its keen sight and swiftness.

grid (grid), *n.* **1.** a grating of crossed bars. **2.** a network of horizontal and perpendicular lines for locating points on a map, chart, etc. **3.** a system of electrical distribution serving a large area. **4.** a metallic framework in a storage battery for conducting the electric current. **5.** an electrode in a vacuum tube for controlling the flow of electrons.

grid•dle (grid'l), *n.* a flat pan for cooking pancakes, bacon, etc., over direct heat.

grid'dle•cake', *n.* a pancake.

grid'i'ron, *n.* **1.** a football field. **2.** a utensil consisting of parallel metal bars on which to broil food.

grid'lock', *n.* **1.** a complete stoppage of all vehicular movement due to traffic blocking key intersections. —*v.t., v.i.* **2.** to cause or undergo a gridlock.

grief (grēf), *n.* **1.** keen mental suffering over affliction or loss. **2.** a cause of keen distress or sorrow.

Grieg (grēg), *n.* **Edvard,** 1843–1907, Norwegian composer.

griev•ance (grē'vəns), *n.* **1.** a wrong considered as grounds for complaint. **2.** a complaint against an unjust act.

grieve (grēv), *v.i., v.t.,* **grieved, griev•ing.** to feel or cause to feel grief. —**griev'er,** *n.*

griev'ous, *adj.* **1.** causing or expressing grief. **2.** very serious; severe. **3.** burdensome or oppressive. —**griev'ous•ly,** *adv.*

grif•fin (grif'in), *n.* a fabled monster with the head and wings of an eagle and the body of a lion.

griffin

grill¹ (gril), *n.* **1.** an apparatus topped by a grated metal framework for cooking food over direct heat. **2.** GRIDIRON (def. 2). **3.** a flat metal surface for broiling food. **4.** a dish of grilled food. **5.** a restaurant serving grilled food. —*v.t.* **6.** to broil on a grill. **7.** to subject to severe and persistent questioning.

grill² (gril), *n.* GRILLE.

grille (gril), *n.* a grating or openwork barrier, as for a gate.

grim (grim), *adj.,* **grim•mer, grim•mest. 1.** stern and unyielding. **2.** of a sinister or ghastly character. **3.** having a harsh or forbidding air. —**grim'ly,** *adv.* —**grim'ness,** *n.*

grim•ace (grim'əs, gri mās'), *n., v.,* **-aced, -ac•ing.** —*n.* **1.** a facial expression that indicates disapproval, pain, etc. —*v.i.* **2.** to make grimaces.

grime (grīm), *n.* dirt or soot adhering to or embedded in a surface. —**grim'y,** *adj.,* **-i•er, -i•est.**

Grimm (grim), *n.* **Jakob Ludwig Karl,** 1785–1863, and his brother **Wilhelm Karl,** 1786–1859, German philologists and folklorists.

grin (grin), *v.,* **grinned, grin•ning,** *n.* —*v.i.* **1.** to smile broadly, as in amusement. **2.** to draw back the lips so as to show the teeth, as a snarling dog. —*n.* **3.** the act or expression of grinning.

grind (grīnd), *v.,* **ground, grind•ing,** *n.* —*v.t.* **1.** to wear, smooth, or sharpen by abrasion or friction. **2.** to reduce to fine particles. **3.** to oppress or crush. **4.** to rub together harshly or gratingly, as the teeth. **5.** to operate by turning a crank. **6. grind out,** to produce in a routine or mechanical way. —*n.* **7.** the act or sound of grinding. **8.** a grade of particle fineness. **9.** laborious, usu. uninteresting work. **10.** *Informal.* an excessively diligent student.

grind'er, *n.* **1.** a person or thing that grinds. **2.** HERO SANDWICH.

grind'stone', *n.* **1.** a rotating solid stone wheel used for sharpening, shaping, etc. —*Idiom.* **2.** keep one's nose to the grindstone, to work hard and steadily.

grip (grip), n., v., **gripped, grip•ping.** —n. **1.** the act of grasping firmly. **2.** the power of grasping. **3.** mastery or control. **4.** mental or intellectual hold. **5.** a device that seizes and holds. **6.** a handle or hilt. **7.** Older Use. a small traveling bag. —v.t. **8.** to grasp firmly. **9.** to hold the attention of: to grip the imagination. —v.i. **10.** to take firm hold. —**Idiom. 11. come to grips with,** to face and cope with. —**grip′per,** n.

gripe (grip), v., **griped, grip•ing,** n. —v.i. **1.** Informal. to complain naggingly or constantly. —v.t. **2.** to produce pain in the bowels of. **3.** to annoy or irritate. —n. **4.** Informal. a nagging complaint. **5.** Usu., **gripes.** a pain in the bowels. —**grip′er,** n.

grippe (grip), n. Older Use. INFLUENZA.

gris•ly (griz′lē), adj., **-li•er, -li•est.** causing a shudder or feeling of horror; gruesome.

grist (grist), n. **1.** grain to be ground. **2.** ground grain.

gris•tle (gris′əl), n. cartilage, esp. in meat. —**gris′tly,** adj., **-tli•er, -tli•est.**

grit (grit), n., v., **grit•ted, grit•ting.** —n. **1.** hard, abrasive particles, as of sand or gravel. **2.** firmness of character. —v.t. **3.** to clamp or grind (the teeth) together, as to show determination. —**grit′ty,** adj., **-ti•er, -ti•est.**

grits (grits), n. (used with a pl. v.) coarsely ground hominy.

griz•zled (griz′əld), adj. **1.** having gray hair. **2.** gray or partly gray.

griz′zly, adj., **-zli•er, -zli•est,** n., pl. **-zlies.** —adj. **1.** somewhat gray. **2.** gray-haired. —n. **3.** GRIZZLY BEAR.

griz′zly bear′, n. a large North American brown bear with coarse, gray-tipped fur.

groan (grōn), n. **1.** a low, mournful sound uttered in pain, grief, disapproval, etc. **2.** a creaking sound due to overburdening. —v.i., v.t. **3.** to utter (with) a groan.

groats (grōts), n. (used with a pl. v.) hulled, cracked grain, as wheat or oats.

gro•cer (grō′sər), n. the owner or operator of a store that sells general food supplies and articles of household use. [< OF gross(i)er wholesale merchant]

gro′cer•y, n., pl. **-cer•ies. 1.** a grocer's store. **2.** Usu., **-ceries.** the goods sold by a grocer.

grog′gy, adj., **-gi•er, -gi•est.** staggering or dazed, as from exhaustion or blows. —**grog′gi•ly,** adv. —**grog′gi•ness,** n.

groin (groin), n. **1.** the fold where the thigh joins the abdomen. **2.** the general region of this fold. **3.** Architecture. the curved edge formed by the intersection of two vaults.

grom•met (grom′it, grum′-), n. **1.** a reinforcing metal eyelet, as in cloth. **2.** a ring of rope or wire used to secure sails, oars, etc.

groom (grōom, grŏom), n. **1.** BRIDEGROOM. **2.** a man or boy in charge of horses or a stable. —v.t. **3.** to make neat or tidy. **4.** to clean and brush (a horse, dog, etc.). **5.** to prepare or train for a position. —**groom′er,** n.

groove (grōov), n., v., **grooved, groov•ing.** —n. **1.** a long, narrow cut in a surface. **2.** a fixed routine. **3.** Slang. an enjoyable time or experience. —v.t. **4.** to cut a groove in. —v.i. **5.** Slang. **a.** to take great pleasure. **b.** to interact well.

groov′y, adj., **-i•er, -i•est.** Slang. very pleasing or attractive.

grope (grōp), v., **groped, grop•ing,** n. —v.i. **1.** to feel about with the hands. **2.** to search uncertainly. —v.t. **3.** to seek (one's way) by groping. —**grop′er,** n.

gros•beak (grōs′bēk′), n. a finch with a thick, conical bill.

gros•grain (grō′grān′), n. a heavy, corded ribbon or cloth of silk or rayon.

gross (grōs), adj., **gross•er, gross•est,** n., pl. **gross** for 6, **gross•es** for 7, v. —adj. **1.** without deductions: gross earnings. **2.** flagrant and extreme. **3.** indelicate, coarse, or vulgar. **4.** very fat or large. **5.** broad or

general. —n. **6.** twelve dozen. **7.** total income, profits, etc., before deductions. —v.t. **8.** to earn as a total before deductions, as of taxes or expenses. —**gross′ly,** adv. —**gross′ness,** n.

gross′ na′tional prod′uct, n. the total monetary value of all goods and services produced in a country during one year.

gro•tesque (grō tesk′), adj. odd or unnatural in shape, appearance, or character; fantastically ugly or absurd. —**gro•tesque′ly,** adv.

grot•to (grot′ō), n., pl. **-toes, -tos. 1.** a cave or cavern. **2.** an artificial cavernlike recess or structure.

grouch (grouch), n. **1.** a sulky or complaining person. **2.** a sulky mood. —v.i. **3.** to be sulky or morose. —**grouch′y,** adj., **-i•er, -i•est.**

ground[1] (ground), n. **1.** the solid surface of the earth. **2.** earth or soil. **3.** Often, **grounds.** a tract of land: picnic grounds. **4.** Usu., **grounds.** the basis on which a belief or action rests. **5.** a subject for discussion. **6.** the background, as in a painting. **7. grounds,** dregs or sediment. **8. grounds,** the gardens, lawn, etc., surrounding and belonging to a building. **9.** a conducting connection between an electric circuit or equipment and the earth or some other conducting body. —adj. **10.** of, on, at, or near the ground. —v.t. **11.** to lay on the ground. **12.** to place on a foundation. **13.** to instruct in first principles. **14.** to establish a ground for (an electric circuit, device, etc.). **15.** to cause (a ship) to run aground. **16.** to restrict (an aircraft or pilot) to the ground. **17.** Informal. to restrict the activities, esp. the social activities, of. —v.i. **18.** to come to or strike the ground. **19. ground out,** Baseball. to be put out at first base after hitting a ground ball. —**Idiom. 20. from the ground up,** a. gradually from the most elementary level to the highest level. **b.** extensively; thoroughly. **21. gain** (or **lose**) **ground, a.** to advance (or fail to advance). **b.** to gain (or lose) approval or acceptance. **22. give ground,** to retreat. **23. hold** or **stand one's ground,** to maintain one's position. **24. off the ground,** into action or well under way: The play never got off the ground.

ground[2] (ground), v. pt. and pp. of GRIND.

ground′ ball′, n. a batted baseball that rolls or bounces along the ground. Also called **ground′er.**

ground′ cov′er, n. any of various low-growing plants and trailing vines used in place of grass.

ground′ floor′, n. **1.** the floor of a building at or nearest to ground level. **2.** Informal. an advantageous position in a new enterprise.

ground′ glass′, n. glass that has had its polished surface removed by fine grinding and that is used to diffuse light.

ground′hog′, n. WOODCHUCK.

ground′less, adj. without rational basis.

ground′ rule′, n. **1.** a basic or governing principle of conduct in a situation. **2.** a rule adopted for playing a game in a particular stadium or field.

ground′swell′, n. **1.** a broad, deep swell or rolling of the sea. **2.** a surge of feelings, esp. among the general public.

ground′work′, n. the foundation or basis of a project.

group (grōop), n. **1.** a number of persons, animals, or things gathered, classed, or acting together. —v.t., v.i. **2.** to form into a group or groups.

group′er, n., pl. **-ers, -er.** any of various large warm-water sea basses.

group′ie, n., pl. **-ies. 1.** a young female fan of rock musicians, who may follow them on tour. **2.** an ardent fan of any celebrity.

group′ ther′apy, n. psychotherapy in which a group of patients, usu. led by a therapist, discuss their problems.

grouse[1] (grous), n., pl. **grous•es, grouse.** a game bird related to the pheasant, with a short bill and feathered legs.

grouse[2] (grous), v., **groused, grous•ing,** n. Informal. —v.i. **1.** to grumble; complain. —n. **2.** a complaint.

grout (grout), n. **1.** a thin, coarse mortar used to fill crevices, as between tiles. —*v.t.* **2.** to fill or consolidate with grout.

grove (grōv), *n.* a small wood or orchard.

grov•el (grov'əl, gruv'-), *v.i.,* **-eled, -el•ing** or (*esp. Brit.*) **-elled, -el•ling. 1.** to humble oneself; act in an abject manner. **2.** to lie or crawl with the face downward, as in abject humility or fear. —**grov'el•er,** *esp. Brit.,* **grov'el•ler,** *n.*

grow (grō), *v.,* **grew, grown, grow•ing.** —*v.i.* **1.** to increase in size by a natural process of development. **2.** to arise or issue as a natural development. **3.** to increase gradually in size, amount, etc. **4.** to become united by or as if by growth. **5.** to become by degrees: *to grow old.* —*v.t.* **6.** to cause or allow to grow. **7. grow on,** to become gradually more liked or accepted by. **8. ~ up,** to be fully grown; attain maturity. —**grow'er,** *n.*

growl (groul), *v.i.* **1.** to utter a deep guttural sound of anger or hostility. **2.** to complain angrily. —*v.t.* **3.** to express by growling. —*n.* **4.** the act or sound of growling. —**growl'er,** *n.*

grown (grōn), *adj.* **1.** arrived at full growth or maturity. —*v.* **2.** pp. of GROW.

grown'-up', *adj.* **1.** having reached maturity; adult. **2.** of or suitable for adults.

grown'up', *n.* an adult.

growth (grōth), *n.* **1.** the act or process of growing. **2.** a size or stage of development: *to reach one's full growth.* **3.** something that has grown: *a growth of weeds.* **4.** an abnormal mass of tissue, as a tumor. —*adj.* **5.** of or noting a stock, industry, etc., that grows in value or earnings at a rate higher than average.

grub (grub), *n., v.,* **grubbed, grub•bing.** —*n.* **1.** a thick-bodied, sluggish larva, esp. of the beetle. **2.** *Slang.* food. —*v.t.* **3.** to clear of roots, stumps, etc. **4.** to uproot. **5.** *Slang.* to scrounge. —*v.i.* **6.** to search by digging. **7.** to lead a laborious life. —**grub'ber,** *n.*

grub'by, *adj.,* **-bi•er, -bi•est.** dirty; slovenly. —**grub'bi•ness,** *n.*

grub'stake', *n.* provisions, gear, etc., furnished to a prospector on condition of sharing in the profits of any discoveries.

grudge (gruj), *n., v.,* **grudged, grudg•ing.** —*n.* **1.** a feeling of ill will or resentment. —*v.t.* **2.** to give or permit with reluctance. **3.** to resent the good fortune of (another). —**grudg'ing•ly,** *adv.*

gru•el (grōō'əl), *n.* a thin cooked cereal.

gru•el•ing (grōō'ə ling, grōō'ling), *adj.* exhausting; arduously severe.

grue•some (grōō'səm), *adj.* causing horror and repugnance: *a gruesome murder.* —**grue'some•ly,** *adv.* —**grue'some•ness,** *n.*

gruff (gruf), *adj.,* **-er, -est. 1.** low and harsh. **2.** brusque or surly. —**gruff'ly,** *adv.* —**gruff'ness,** *n.*

grum•ble (grum'bəl), *v.,* **-bled, -bling,** *n.* —*v.i.* **1.** to mutter in discontent. **2.** to growl. **3.** to rumble. —*v.t.* **4.** to utter by grumbling. —*n.* **5.** an expression of discontent; complaint. —**grum'bler,** *n.*

grump•y (grum'pē), *adj.,* **-i•er, -i•est.** discontentedly or sullenly irritable. —**grump'i•ness,** *n.*

grunge (grunj), *n. Slang.* **1.** dirt; filth; rubbish. **2.** something of inferior quality. **3.** a style or fashion derived from a movement in rock music: in fashion characterized by unkempt clothing and in music by aggressive, nihilistic songs.

grun•gy (grun'jē), *adj.,* **-gi•er, -gi•est.** *Slang.* dirty or run-down.

grun•ion (grun'yən), *n.* a small food fish that lays its eggs on S California beaches.

grunt (grunt), *v.i., v.t.* **1.** to utter (with) the deep, guttural sound characteristic of a hog. —*n.* **2.** a sound of grunting.

Gru•yère (grōō yâr', gri ; *Fr.* gʀy yeʀ'), *n.* a firm yellow cheese, esp. of France and Switzerland, having small holes.

GU, Guam.

Gua•da•la•ja•ra (gwäd'l ə här'ə), *n.* a city in W Mexico. 2,244,715.

Guam (gwäm), *n.* an island in the W Pacific: an unincorporated U.S. territory. 120,000.

Guang•zhou (gwäng'jō'), *n.* a seaport in SE China. 3,290,000. Also called **Canton.**

gua•nine (gwä'nēn), *n.* a purine base that is a fundamental constituent of DNA and RNA.

gua•no (gwä'nō), *n.* a manure composed chiefly of the excrement of sea birds, valued as a fertilizer.

gua•ra•ni (gwär'ə nē'), *n., pl.* **-nis, -ni.** the basic monetary unit of Paraguay.

guar•an•tee (gar'ən tē'), *n., pl.* **-tees,** *v.,* **-teed, -tee•ing.** —*n.* **1.** an assurance, esp. one in writing, that something is of specified quality, content, etc., or will perform satisfactorily for a given time. **2.** GUARANTY (defs. 1, 2). **3.** something that assures a particular condition. **4.** GUARANTOR. —*v.t.* **5.** to make or give a guarantee for. **6.** to promise or make certain.

guar'an•tor' (-tôr', -tər), *n.* a person, group, etc., that guarantees.

guar'an•ty, *n., pl.* **-ties,** *v.,* **-tied, -ty•ing.** —*n.* **1.** a formal assurance given as security that another's debt or obligation will be fulfilled. **2.** something taken or given as security. **3.** the act of giving security. **4.** GUARANTOR. —*v.t.* **5.** to guarantee.

guard (gärd), *v.t.* **1.** to keep safe from harm or danger. **2.** to keep under close watch or control. **3.** (in sports) to try to impede the movement or progress of (an opponent). —*v.i.* **4.** to take precautions. **5.** to keep watch. —*n.* **6.** one that guards. **7.** a close watch, as over a prisoner. **8.** a device or attachment that prevents injury, loss, etc. **9.** a posture of defense or readiness, as in boxing. **10.** a football or basketball player who guards an opponent. —**guard'er,** *n.*

guard'ed, *adj.* **1.** cautious; prudent: *a guarded comment.* **2.** protected or restrained. —**guard'ed•ly,** *adv.*

guard'house', *n.* a building housing military guards or for the temporary detention of prisoners.

guard'i•an, *n.* **1.** a person who guards, protects, or preserves. **2.** a person legally entrusted with the care of another's person or property, as that of a minor. —**guard'i•an•ship',** *n.*

Gua•te•ma•la (gwä'tə mä'lə), *n.* **1.** a republic in N Central America. 11,588,407. **2.** Also called **Gua'tema'la Cit'y.** the capital of this republic. 1,500,000. —**Gua'te•ma'lan,** *adj., n.*

gua•va (gwä'və), *n., pl.* **-vas. 1.** a tropical tree of the myrtle family. **2.** its large yellow fruit.

gu•ber•na•to•ri•al (gōō'bər nə tôr'ē əl, gyōō'-), *adj.* of a state governor or the office of state governor.

Guern•sey (gûrn'zē), *n., pl.* **-seys** for 2. **1.** Isle of, one of the Channel Islands, in the English Channel. **2.** one of a breed of dairy cattle orig. raised on this island.

guer•ril•la or **gue•ril•la** (gə ril'ə), *n., pl.* **-las.** a member of a band of irregular soldiers that harasses the enemy, as by surprise raids. [< Sp: band of guerrillas, dim. of *guerra* war]

guess (ges), *v.t., v.i.* **1.** to risk a judgment or opinion about (something) without sufficient evidence. **2.** to figure out or judge correctly. **3.** to think or suppose. —*n.* **4.** an opinion reached by guessing. **5.** the act of guessing. —**guess'er,** *n.*

guest (gest), *n.* **1.** a person who spends time at another's home in a social activity. **2.** a person who patronizes a hotel, restaurant, etc. **3.** a person invited to appear in a program or performance. —*adj.* **4.** of or for guests. **5.** appearing as a guest.

guf•faw (gu fô', gə-), *n.* **1.** a loud, unrestrained burst of laughter. —*v.i.* **2.** to laugh loudly and boisterously.

Gug•gen•heim (gōōg'ən hīm', gōō'gən-), *n.* **Daniel,** 1856–1930, U.S. industrialist and philanthropist.

GUI (gōō'ē), *n., pl.* **GUIs, GUI's.** GRAPHICAL USER INTERFACE.

guid•ance (gīd'ns), *n.* **1.** the act or function of guiding. **2.** advice or counseling, esp. for students.

guide (gīd), *v.,* **guid•ed, guid•ing,** *n.* —*v.t.* **1.** to show the way to; lead. **2.** to direct the movement or course of. **3.** to lead or direct in any course or action. —*n.* **4.** a person who guides, esp. one hired to conduct tours. **5.** a mark, tab, or sign that guides. **6.** a guidebook. **7.** a device that directs motion or action: *a sewing-machine guide.* —**guid′er,** *n.*

guide′book′, *n.* a book of directions, advice, and information, as for tourists.

guid′ed mis′sile, *n.* a missile steered during its flight by radio signals, clockwork controls, etc.

guide′line′, *n.* any guide or indication of a future course of action.

guild (gild), *n.* **1.** an organization of persons with related interests, goals, etc. **2.** a medieval association of merchants or artisans.

guil•der (gil′dər), *n.,* *pl.* **-ders, -der.** the basic monetary unit of the Netherlands.

guile (gīl), *n.* insidious cunning or duplicity in attaining a goal. —**guile′ful,** *adj.* —**guile′less,** *adj.*

guil•lo•tine (gil′ə tēn′, gē′ə-; *esp. for v.* gil′ə tēn′, gē′ə-), *n.,* *v.,* **-tined, -tin•ing.** —*n.* **1.** a device for beheading a person, consisting of a heavy blade that drops between two posts. —*v.t.* **2.** to behead by the guillotine. [< F, after J. I. *Guillotin* (1738–1814), French physician who urged its use as a humane method of execution]

guilt (gilt), *n.* **1.** the fact or state of being guilty. **2.** a feeling of responsibility or remorse for some real or imagined offense, crime, wrong, etc. —**guilt′less,** *adj.*

guilt′y, *adj.,* **-i•er, -i•est. 1.** having committed an offense, crime, violation, or wrong. **2.** connected with or involving guilt. **3.** having or showing guilt. —**guilt′i•ly,** *adv.* —**guilt′i•ness,** *n.*

Guin•ea (gin′ē), *n.,* *pl.* **-eas** for 2. **1.** a republic on the W coast of Africa. 7,405,375. **2.** (*l.c.*) a former gold coin of Great Britain, worth 21 shillings. —**Guin′e•an,** *n., adj.*

Guin′ea-Bissau′, *n.* a republic on the W coast of Africa. 1,178,584.

guin′ea fowl′, *n.* an African game bird with spotted gray plumage.

guin′ea hen′, *n.* **1.** the female of the guinea fowl. **2.** any guinea fowl.

guin′ea pig′, *n.* **1.** a tailless rodent raised as a pet and for use in laboratories. **2.** the subject of any test or experiment.

Guin•e•vere (gwin′ə vēr′), *n.* the wife of King Arthur and mistress of Lancelot.

guise (gīz), *n.* **1.** general external appearance. **2.** assumed appearance or mere semblance.

gui•tar (gi tär′), *n.* a musical instrument with typically six strings plucked with the fingers or a plectrum. [< Sp *guitarra* ≪ Gk *kithára* lyre-like musical instrument] —**gui•tar′ist,** *n.*

gulch (gulch), *n.* a deep, narrow ravine, esp. one marking the course of a stream.

gulf (gulf), *n.* **1.** a portion of an ocean or sea partly enclosed by land. **2.** a chasm or abyss. **3.** any wide gap or divergence.

Gulf′ War′, *n.* a conflict (Jan.–Feb. 1991) between Iraq and the United States and its allies to expel Iraq from Kuwait.

gull¹ (gul), *n.* a long-winged aquatic bird, typically white with gray or black wings and back.

gull² (gul), *v.t.* **1.** to deceive, trick, or cheat. —*n.* **2.** a person who is easily deceived or cheated.

gul•let (gul′it), *n.* **1.** the esophagus. **2.** the throat or pharynx.

gul•li•ble (gul′ə bəl), *adj.* easily deceived or cheated. —**gul′li•bil′i•ty,** *n.*

gul•ly (gul′ē), *n.,* *pl.* **-lies.** a small valley or ravine formed by running water, esp. rainwater.

gulp (gulp), *v.i.* **1.** to gasp, as if taking large drafts of a liquid. —*v.t.* **2.** to swallow eagerly or hastily, or in large amounts. **3.** to choke back as if by swallowing. —*n.* **4.** the act of gulping. **5.** a mouthful.

gum¹ (gum), *n., v.,* **gummed, gum•ming.** —*n.* **1.** any of various sticky substances exuded from plants, hardening on exposure to air, and soluble in or forming a viscid mass with water. **2.** any of various similar substances, as resin. **3.** CHEWING GUM. —*v.t.* **4.** to smear,

stick together, or clog with gum. —*v.i.* **5.** to become clogged with or as if with gum. **6. gum up,** *Slang.* to spoil or ruin. —**gum′my,** *adj.,* **-mi•er, -mi•est.**

gum² (gum), *n., v.,* **gummed, gum•ming.** —*n.* **1.** Often, **gums.** the firm, fleshy tissue enveloping the bases of the teeth. —*v.t.* **2.** to chew with toothless gums.

gum′ ar′abic, *n.* a gum obtained from acacia trees, used chiefly as an emulsifier or adhesive.

gum•bo (gum′bō), *n., pl.* **-bos.** a soup of chicken or seafood, thickened with okra.

gump•tion (gump′shən), *n.* **1.** initiative; resourcefulness. **2.** courage or spunk.

gum′shoe′, *n., pl.* **-shoes. 1.** *Slang.* a detective. **2.** a rubber overshoe.

gun (gun), *n., v.,* **gunned, gun•ning.** —*n.* **1.** a weapon consisting of a metal tube from which projectiles are shot by the force of an explosive. **2.** any portable firearm. **3.** a long-barreled cannon. **4.** any device for shooting or ejecting something under pressure, as paint. —*v.t.* **5.** to shoot with a gun. **6.** to cause (an engine) to increase in speed very quickly by increasing the supply of fuel. —*v.i.* **7.** to shoot or hunt with a gun. **8. gun for,** to try earnestly to obtain. —*Idiom.* **9.** stick to one's guns, to maintain one's position in the face of opposition. **10. under the gun,** under pressure, as to meet a deadline. —**gun′ner,** *n.*

gun′boat′, *n.* a small armed warship of light draft.

gun′fight′, *n.* a battle between people using guns.

gun′fire′, *n.* the firing of guns.

gung-ho (gung′hō′), *adj. Informal.* wholeheartedly enthusiastic and loyal.

gun′lock′, *n.* the mechanism of a firearm by which the charge is exploded.

gun′man, *n., pl.* **-men.** a person armed with a gun, esp. a criminal.

gun•ner•y (gun′ə rē), *n.* the art and science of constructing and operating guns, esp. large guns.

gun′nery ser′geant, *n.* a noncommissioned officer in the U.S. Marine Corps ranking above a staff sergeant.

gun•ny (gun′ē), *n., pl.* **-nies.** a strong coarse material made commonly from jute.

gun′ny•sack′, *n.* a sack made of gunny or burlap.

gun′point′, *n.* **1.** the point or aim of a gun. —*Idiom.* **2. at gunpoint,** under threat of being shot.

gun′pow′der, *n.* an explosive mixture, as of potassium nitrate, sulfur, and charcoal, used in guns and for blasting.

gun′shot′, *n.* **1.** the shooting of a gun. **2.** a bullet or other shot fired from a gun.

gun′-shy′, *adj.* frightened by the sound of a gun firing.

gun′smith′, *n.* a person who makes or repairs firearms.

gun•wale (gun′l), *n.* the upper edge of the side or bulwark of a vessel.

gup•py (gup′ē), *n., pl.* **-pies.** a small freshwater fish often kept in aquariums.

gur•gle (gûr′gəl), *v.,* **-gled, -gling,** *n.* —*v.i.* **1.** to flow in a broken, irregular, noisy current. **2.** to make a sound as of water doing this. —*n.* **3.** the act or noise of gurgling.

gur•ney (gûr′nē), *n., pl.* **-neys.** a wheeled table or stretcher for transporting patients.

gu•ru (gōō′rōō, gŏō rōō′), *n., pl.* **-rus. 1.** (in Hinduism) one's personal religious or spiritual instructor. **2.** any person who counsels or advises; mentor. **3.** a leader in a particular field. [< Hindi *gurū* < Skt *guru* venerable]

gush (gush), *v.i.* **1.** to flow out or issue copiously or forcibly. **2.** to talk effusively. —*v.t.* **3.** to cause to gush. —*n.* **4.** a sudden copious outflow.

gush′er, *n.* **1.** one that gushes. **2.** a flowing oil well, usu. of large capacity.

gus•set (gus′it), *n.* a triangular piece of material inserted into a shirt, shoe, etc., to improve the fit or for reinforcement.

gus•sy (gus′ē), *v.t., v.i.,* **-sied, -sy•ing.** *Informal.* to dress up or decorate in a showy manner: *all gussied up for the celebration.*

gust (gust), *n.* **1.** a sudden strong blast of wind. **2.** an outburst of emotion. —*v.i.* **3.** to blow in gusts. —**gust′y,** *adj.,* **-i•er, -i•est.**

gus•ta•to•ry (gus′tə tôr′ē), *adj.* of taste or tasting.

gus•to (gus′tō), *n.* hearty enjoyment or enthusiasm.

gut (gut), *n., v.,* **gut•ted, gut•ting,** *adj.* —*n.* **1.** the alimentary canal, esp. the intestine. **2. guts,** *a.* the bowels or entrails. **b.** courage and fortitude. **3.** intestinal tissue or fiber. **4.** CATGUT. —*v.t.* **5.** to take out the entrails of. **6.** to destroy the interior of. —*adj.* **7. a.** basic or essential. **b.** based on instincts or emotions: *a gut reaction.* —**gut′less,** *adj.*

Gu•ten•berg (gōōt′n bûrg′), *n.* **Johannes,** (*Johann Gensfleisch*), c1400–68, German printer: first to print with movable type.

Gu′tenberg Bi′ble, *n.* an edition of the Vulgate printed at Mainz, Germany, before 1456, ascribed to Gutenberg and others.

guts′y, *adj.,* **-i•er, -i•est. 1.** daring or courageous. **2.** robust or lusty.

gut•ter (gut′ər), *n.* **1.** a channel for leading off water, as at the side of a road or along the eaves of a roof. —*v.i.* **2.** to flow in streams.

gut•tur•al (gut′ər əl), *adj.* **1.** of the throat. **2.** harsh; throaty. **3.** pronounced in the throat.

guy[1] (gī), *n.* **1.** a man or boy. **2. guys,** people.

guy[2] (gī), *n.* **1.** a rope, cable, or appliance used to guide and steady an object. —*v.t.* **2.** to guide or steady with a guy.

Guy•a•na (gī an′ə, -ä′nə), *n.* a republic on the NE coast of South America. 706,116. —**Guy′a•nese′** (-ə nēz′, -nēs′), *n., pl.* **-nese,** *adj.*

guz•zle (guz′əl), *v.i., v.t.,* **-zled, -zling.** to drink, or sometimes eat, greedily or excessively. —**guz′zler,** *n.*

gym (jim), *n.* **1.** a gymnasium. **2.** PHYSICAL EDUCATION.

gym•na′si•um (-nā′zē əm), *n., pl.* **-si•ums, -si•a** (-zē ə, -zhə). a building or room equipped for indoor sports, exercise, or physical education.

gym•nas′tics (-nas′tiks), *n.* **1.** (*used with a pl. v.*) physical exercises that develop and demonstrate strength, balance, and agility. **2.** (*used with a sing. v.*) the practice, art, or competitive sport of such exercises. —**gym′nast** (-nast, -nəst), *n.* —**gym•nas′tic,** *adj.*

gym•no•sperm (jim′nə spûrm′), *n.* any nonflow-ering plant having seeds not enclosed in fruit at the time of pollination.

gy•ne•col•o•gy (gī′ni kol′ə jē, jin′i-), *n.* the branch of medicine that deals with the health maintenance and diseases of women, esp. of the reproductive organs. —**gy′ne•co•log′ic** (-kə loj′ik), **gy′ne•co•log′i•cal,** *adj.* —**gy′ne•col′o•gist,** *n.*

gyp (jip), *v.,* **gypped, gyp•ping,** *n. Informal.* —*v.t., v.i.* **1.** to swindle or cheat. —*n.* **2.** a swindle or fraud. **3.** Also, **gyp′per, gyp′ster** (-stər). a swindler.

gyp•sum (jip′səm), *n.* a common soft mineral used to make plaster of Paris and as a fertilizer.

Gyp•sy (jip′sē), *n., pl.* **-sies. 1.** a member of a traditionally itinerant people, orig. of N India, now residing mostly in permanent communities in many countries. **2.** ROMANY. **3.** (*l.c.*) a person who resembles the stereotype of a Gypsy, as in an itinerant way of life.

gyp′sy moth′, *n.* a moth introduced into the U.S. from Europe, the larvae of which feed on the foliage of trees.

gy•rate (jī′rāt, jī rāt′), *v.i.,* **-rat•ed, -rat•ing.** to move in a circle or spiral. —**gy•ra′tion,** *n.*

gyr•fal•con (jûr′fôl′kən, -fal′-, -fô′kən), *n.* a large falcon of arctic and subarctic regions.

gy•ro (jēr′ō, yēr′ō), *n., pl.* **-ros. 1.** pressed beef or lamb roasted on a spit and sliced. **2.** a sandwich of this.

gy•ro•com•pass (jī′rō kum′pəs), *n.* a compass containing a gyroscope rotor that registers the direction of true north.

gyroscope

gy•ro•scope (jī′rə skōp′), *n.* a rotating wheel so mounted that its axis can turn freely in all directions, used to maintain equilibrium and to determine direction.

H

H, h (āch), *n., pl.* **Hs** or **H's, hs** or **h's.** the eighth letter of the English alphabet, a consonant.

H, high.

H, *Chem. Symbol.* hydrogen.

h. or **H., 1.** height. **2.** high. **3.** *Baseball.* hit. **4.** hour. **5.** hundred. **6.** husband.

ha (hä), *interj.* an exclamation of surprise, suspicion, triumph, etc.

Ha•bak•kuk (hə bak′ək, hab′ə kuk′, -kōōk′), *n.* **1.** a Minor Prophet of the 7th century B.C. **2.** a book of the Bible bearing his name.

ha•be•as cor•pus (hā′bē əs kôr′pəs), *n.* a writ requiring a person to be brought before a court to determine whether the person has been detained legally. [< L: lit., have the body (first words of writ)]

hab•er•dash•er (hab′ər dash′ər), *n.* a retail dealer in men's furnishings. —**hab′er•dash′er•y,** *n., pl.* **-er•ies.**

ha•bil•i•ment (hə bil′ə mənt), *n.* **1.** Usu., **habiliments.** clothing. **2. habiliments,** accouterments.

hab•it (hab′it), *n.* **1.** a pattern of behavior acquired as a result of frequent repetition. **2.** customary practice or use. **3.** addiction, esp. to narcotics. **4.** the garb of a particular profession, religious order, etc.

hab•it•a•ble (hab′i tə bəl), *adj.* capable of being inhabited. —**hab′it•a•bil′i•ty,** *n.*

hab′i•tat′ (-tat′), *n.* **1.** the natural environment of a plant or animal. **2.** the place where a person is usu. found.

hab•i•ta′tion, *n.* **1.** a dwelling; abode. **2.** the act of inhabiting.

hab′it-form′ing, *adj.* addictive, esp. through physiological dependence.

ha•bit•u•al (hə bich′ōō əl), *adj.* **1.** fixed by or resulting from habit. **2.** being such by habit; confirmed. **3.** common or usual; customary. —**ha•bit′u•al•ly,** *adv.* —**ha•bit′u•al•ness,** *n.*

ha•bit′u•ate′ (-āt′), *v.t.,* **-at•ed, -at•ing.** to accustom, as to a particular situation. —**ha•bit′u•a′tion,** *n.*

ha•bit•u•é (hə bich′ōō ā′), *n., pl.* **-és.** a habitual visitor to a place. [< F]

ha•ci•en•da (hä′sē en′də), *n., pl.* **-das.** (in Spanish

America) **1.** a large landed estate or ranch. **2.** the main house on such an estate.

hack[1] (hak), *v.t.* **1.** to cut or chop with crude, often heavy strokes. **2.** *Slang.* to deal or cope with. —*v.i.* **3.** to make rough cuts or notches. **4.** to cough harshly and dryly. —*n.* **5.** a cut or notch. **6.** a tool for hacking. **7.** a rasping, dry cough.

hack[2] (hak), *n.* **1.** a professional, esp. a writer, who does routine work primarily for money. **2.** a horse for hire. **3.** an old or worn-out horse. **4.** a carriage for hire; hackney. **5.** a taxicab. —*v.i.* **6.** to drive a taxi. **7.** to work as a hack. —*adj.* **8.** hired as a hack. **9.** trite; banal.

hack′er, *n. Slang.* **1.** a computer enthusiast who is especially proficient. **2.** a computer user who attempts to gain unauthorized access to computer systems.

hack•le (hak′əl), *n.* **1.** the neck plumage of a male bird, as the domestic rooster. **2. hackles, a.** the erectile hair on the back of an animal's neck. **b.** anger, esp. when aroused in a challenging or challenged manner: *with one's hackles up.*

hack′ney (-nē), *n., pl.* **-neys. 1.** a carriage for hire. **2.** a horse used for ordinary riding or driving.

hack′neyed, *adj.* made commonplace or trite.

hack′saw′ or **hack′ saw′,** *n.* a saw for cutting metal, consisting of a fine-toothed blade fixed in a frame.

had (had), *v.* pt. and pp. of HAVE.

had•dock (had′ək), *n., pl.* **-docks, -dock.** a fish of the cod family, of the N Atlantic.

Ha•des (hā′dēz), *n.* **1.** (in Greek myth) the underworld inhabited by the spirits of the dead. **2.** the ancient Greek god ruling over the underworld. **3.** (in the Revised Version of the New Testament) the abode or state of the dead. **4.** (*often l.c.*) hell.

had•n't (had′nt), contraction of *had not.*

hadst (hadst), *v. Archaic.* a 2nd pers. sing. pt. of HAVE.

haf•ni•um (haf′nē əm, häf′-), *n.* a toxic metallic element found in most zirconium minerals. *Symbol:* Hf; *at. wt.:* 178.49; *at. no.:* 72.

haft (haft, häft), *n.* a handle, esp. of a knife, sword, or dagger.

hag (hag), *n.* **1.** an ugly old woman, esp. a malicious one. **2.** a witch. —**hag′gish,** *adj.*

Ha•gar (hā′gär, -gər), *n.* the mother of Ishmael. Gen. 16.

hag•ga•dah or **hag•ga•da** (hə gô′də, hä′gä dä′), *n., pl.* **-dahs** or **-das, -doth, -dot** (-dôt′). **1.** a book containing the story of the Exodus, used at the Seder service on Passover. **2.** (*cap.*) AGGADAH. —**hag•gad′ic** (hə gad′ik, -gä′dik), **hag•gad′i•cal,** *adj.*

Hag•ga•i (hag′ē ī′, hag′ī), *n.* **1.** a Minor Prophet of the 6th century B.C. **2.** a book of the Bible bearing his name.

hag•gard (hag′ərd), *adj.* appearing gaunt, wasted, or exhausted. —**hag′gard•ly,** *adv.* —**hag′gard•ness,** *n.*

hag•gis (hag′is), *n.* a traditional Scottish pudding made of the heart, liver, etc., of a sheep or calf, minced with suet and oatmeal.

hag•gle (hag′əl), *v.,* **-gled, -gling,** *n.* —*v.i.* **1.** to bargain in a petty, quibbling manner. —*n.* **2.** the act of haggling. —**hag′gler,** *n.*

Hag•i•og•ra•pha (hag′ē og′rə fə, hā′jē-), *n.* (*used with a sing. v.*) the third of the three Jewish divisions of the Old Testament, usu. comprising the Psalms, Proverbs, Job, Song of Solomon, Ruth, Lamentations, Ecclesiastes, Esther, Daniel, Ezra, Nehemiah, and Chronicles. Also called **the Writings.** [< LL < Gk: sacred writings]

hag•i•og•ra•phy (hag′ē og′rə fē, hā′jē-), *n., pl.* **-phies.** the study of the lives of the saints. —**hag′i•og′ra•pher,** *n.*

Hague (hāg), *n.* **The,** a city in the W Netherlands: seat of the government. 444,313.

hah (hä), *interj.* HA.

ha-ha (hä′hä′, hä′hä′), *interj.* an exclamation of laughter.

hai•ku (hī′kōō), *n., pl.* **-ku.** a Japanese poem or verse form, consisting of 3 lines of 5, 7, and 5 syllables, respectively.

hail[1] (hāl), *v.t.* **1.** to salute or greet. **2.** to acclaim. **3.** to call out or signal to. —*v.i.* **4.** to call out. **5. hail from,** to come or be from. —*n.* **6.** a call or greeting. —*interj.* **7.** an exclamation of greeting or acclamation.

hail[2] (hāl), *n.* **1.** precipitation in the form of irregular pellets of ice. **2.** a shower of anything. —*v.i.* **3.** to pour down or fall like hail. —*v.t.* **4.** to pour down as or like hail.

Hail′ Mar′y, *n.* AVE MARIA.

hail′stone′, *n.* a pellet of hail.

hail′storm′, *n.* a storm with hail.

Hail′ to the Chief′, the official song of the President of the United States.

hair (hâr), *n.* **1.** any of the numerous fine filaments growing from the skin of mammals. **2.** an aggregate of such filaments. **3.** any fine, filamentous outgrowth. **4.** a very small amount, degree, etc. —*Idiom.* **5. get in someone's hair,** to annoy someone. **6. split hairs,** to make tiny, petty distinctions. —**haired,** *adj.* —**hair′less,** *adj.* —**hair′like′,** *adj.*

hair′ball′, *n.* a ball of hair accumulated in the stomach of a cat or other animal that licks its coat.

hair′breadth′ or **hairs′breadth′,** *n.* **1.** a very small space or distance. —*adj.* **2.** extremely narrow or close.

hair′brush′, *n.* a brush for grooming the hair.

hair′cut′, *n.* **1.** the act of cutting the hair. **2.** the style in which the hair is cut and worn.

hair′do′ (-dōō′), *n., pl.* **-dos.** the style in which hair is cut and arranged; coiffure.

hair′dress′er, *n.* a person who arranges or cuts hair. —**hair′dress′ing,** *n.*

hair′line′, *n.* **1.** a very slender line. **2.** the border along which a growth of hair emerges along the upper forehead.

hair′piece′, *n.* a toupee or wig.

hair′pin′, *n.* **1.** a slender U-shaped pin used to fasten up the hair. —*adj.* **2.** sharply curved back, as in a U shape: *a hairpin turn.*

hair′-rais′ing, *adj.* terrifying or horrifying.

hair′split′ting, *n.* **1.** the making of unnecessarily fine distinctions. —*adj.* **2.** quibbling. —**hair′split′ter,** *n.*

hair′spring′, *n.* a fine, usu. spiral spring used for oscillating the balance of a timepiece.

hair′style′, *n.* a way of cutting or arranging hair; hairdo. —**hair′styl′ist,** *n.*

hair′-trig′ger, *adj.* easily activated or set off.

hair′y, *adj.,* **-i•er, -i•est. 1.** covered with or as if with hair. **2.** *Slang.* difficult, frightening, or risky. —**hair′i•ness,** *n.*

Hai•ti (hā′tē), *n.* a republic in the West Indies occupying the W part of the island of Hispaniola. 6,611,407. —**Hai′tian** (-shən, -tē ən), *adj., n.*

hajj (haj), *n., pl.* **hajj•es.** the pilgrimage to Mecca, which every adult Muslim is supposed to make at least once. Also.

haj•ji or **hadj•i** or **haj•i** (haj′ē), *n., pl.* **haj•jis** or **hadj•is** or **haj•is.** a Muslim who has gone on a pilgrimage to Mecca. [< Ar]

hake (hāk), *n., pl.* **hakes, hake.** any of various codlike marine food fishes.

ha•lal (hə läl′), *adj.* (of an animal or its meat) prepared in the manner prescribed by Islamic law. [Ar *halāl* lawful]

hal•berd (hal′bərd, hôl′-) also **-bert** (-bərt), *n.* a shafted weapon with an axlike cutting blade, used esp. in the 15th and 16th centuries.

hal•cy•on (hal′sē ən), *adj.* peaceful; happy; carefree.

hale[1] (hāl), *adj.,* **hal•er, hal•est.** healthy; robust.

hale[2] (hāl), *v.t.,* **haled, hal•ing.** to compel (someone) to go.

Ha•ley (hā′lē), *n.* **Alex,** 1921–92, U.S. writer.

half (haf, häf), *n., pl.* **halves** (havz, hävz), *adj., adv.* —*n.* **1.** one of two equal parts of something. **2.** either of two equal periods of play in a game. **3.** one of a pair. —*adj.* **4.** being a half. **5.** partial or incomplete. —*adv.* **6.** in or to the extent of a half. **7.** in part; incompletely. —*Proverb.* **8. Half a loaf is better**

than none, it is preferable to accept something rather than nothing.

half′-and-half′, *n.* **1.** a mixture of two things in equal or nearly equal proportions, as of milk and cream. —*adj.* **2.** half one thing and half another. —*adv.* **3.** in two equal or nearly equal parts.

half′back′, *n. Football.* one of two backs who typically line up on each side of the fullback.

half′-baked′, *adj.* **1.** insufficiently cooked. **2.** insufficiently planned or prepared. **3.** foolish.

half′ broth′er, *n.* a male sibling related through one parent only.

half′-caste′, *n.* a person whose parents are of different races.

half′-cocked′, *adj.* ill-considered or ill-prepared.

half′heart′ed, *adj.* having or showing little enthusiasm: *a halfhearted attempt to work.* —**half′heart′edly,** *adv.* —**half′heart′ed•ness,** *n.*

half′-life′, *n., pl.* **-lives.** the time required for one half the atoms of a given amount of a radioactive substance to decay.

half′-mast′, *n.* a position approximately halfway down a mast, staff, etc.

half′ note′, *n.* a musical note equivalent in time value to half a whole note.

half•pen•ny (hā′pə nē, hāp′nē), *n., pl.* **half•pen•nies** for 1; **half•pence** (hā′pəns) for 2. **1.** a former British coin equal to half a penny. **2.** the sum of half a penny.

half′ sis′ter, *n.* a female sibling related through one parent only.

half′-slip′, *n.* a woman's skirtlike undergarment with an elasticized waistband.

half′ sole′, *n.* the sole of a shoe that extends from the shank to the end of the toe.

half′ step′, *n.* SEMITONE.

half′time′ or **half′-time′,** *n.* the intermission between the two halves of a football, basketball, or other game.

half′tone′, *n.* **1.** a printing process in which gradation of tone is obtained by a system of minute dots. **2.** the print obtained in such a process.

half′-track′, *n.* a motor vehicle with rear driving wheels on caterpillar treads, esp. an armored vehicle.

half′-truth′, *n.* a statement that is only partly true, esp. one intended to deceive.

half′way′ (-wā′, -wā′), *adv.* **1.** to the midpoint. **2.** partially or almost. —*adj.* **3.** midway. **4.** partial or inadequate. —**Idiom. 5. meet halfway,** to compromise with.

half′way house′, *n.* a residence for persons released from a hospital, prison, or other institution that eases their return to society.

half′-wit′, *n.* a feeble-minded or foolish person. —**half′-wit′ted,** *adj.*

hal•i•but (hal′ə bət, hol′-), *n., pl.* **-buts, -but.** any of various large, edible flounders.

Hal•i•fax (hal′ə faks′), *n.* the capital of Nova Scotia, in SE Canada. 113,577.

hal•ite (hal′īt, hā′līt), *n.* rock salt.

hal•i•to•sis (hal′i tō′sis), *n.* a condition of having offensive-smelling breath.

hall (hôl), *n.* **1.** a corridor in a building. **2.** the large entrance room of a house or building. **3.** a large room or building for public gatherings. **4.** a building at a college or university. **5.** the main house of a large estate.

Hal•lel (hä′lāl, hä lāl′), *n.* a Hebrew liturgical prayer consisting of all or part of Psalms 113–118. [< Heb *hallēl* praise]

hal•le•lu•jah or **hal•le•lu•iah** (hal′ə lōō′yə), *interj.* **1.** Praise ye the Lord! —*n.* **2.** an exclamation of "hallelujah!" **3.** a shout of joy, praise, or gratitude. **4.** a musical composition wholly or principally based upon the word "hallelujah."

Hal•ley (hal′ē; *sometimes* hā′lē), *n.* **Edmund** or **Edmond,** 1656–1742, English astronomer.

Hal′ley's com′et (hal′ēz *or, often,* hā′lēz), *n.* a comet with a period averaging 76 years: most re-

cently visible in 1986. [after E. HALLEY, who first predicted its return]

hall′mark′, *n.* **1.** any mark or indication of genuineness, quality, etc. **2.** any distinguishing characteristic.

hal•lo (hə lō′) also **-loo** (-lōō′), *interj., n., pl.* **-los** also **-loos.** —*interj.* **1.** a shout to attract someone's attention. —*n.* **2.** the cry "hallo!"

hal•low (hal′ō), *v.t.* to make or honor as holy. —**hal′low•er,** *n.*

Hal•low•een or **-e′en** (hal′ə wēn′, -ō ēn′, hol′-), *n.* the evening of October 31; the eve of All Saints' Day. [(*All)hallow(s) + e(v)en* evening]

hal•lu•ci•nate (hə lōō′sə nāt′), *v.i., v.t.,* **-nat•ed, -nat•ing.** to have or cause to have hallucinations.

hal•lu′ci•na′tion, *n.* **1.** a sensory experience, as of images or sounds, that does not exist outside the mind. **2.** an illusion or delusion. —**hal•lu′ci•na•to′ry** (-nə tôr′ē), *adj.*

hal•lu′ci•no•gen (-nə jən), *n.* a substance that produces hallucinations. —**hal•lu′ci•no•gen′ic** (-jen′ik), *adj.*

hall′way′, *n.* **1.** a corridor, as in a building. **2.** an entrance hall.

ha•lo (hā′lō), *n., pl.* **-los, -loes. 1.** a symbolic circle of radiant light around the head in pictures of holy personages. **2.** a bright circle or arc centered on the sun or moon.

hal•o•gen (hal′ə jən, -jen′, hā′lə-), *n.* any of the nonmetallic elements, fluorine, chlorine, iodine, bromine, and astatine.

hal′ogen lamp′, *n.* a high-intensity incandescent lamp containing a small amount of a halogen.

halt¹ (hôlt), *v.i.* **1.** to stop or cause to stop. —*n.* **2.** a stop or pause.

halt² (hôlt), *v.i.* **1.** to falter or hesitate. —*adj.* **2.** lame.

hal•ter (hôl′tər), *n.* **1.** a rope or strap for leading or restraining horses or cattle. **2.** a hangman's noose. **3.** a woman's top, tied behind the neck and across the back. —*v.t.* **4.** to put a halter on; restrain as by a halter.

halt′ing, *adj.* **1.** faltering or hesitating, esp. in speech. **2.** limping or lame. —**halt′ing•ly,** *adv.*

halve (hav, häv), *v.t.,* **halved, halv•ing. 1.** to divide into two equal parts. **2.** to share equally. **3.** to reduce to half.

halves, *n.* **1.** pl. of HALF. —*Idiom.* **2. by halves,** incompletely or halfheartedly. **3. go halves,** to share equally.

hal•yard (hal′yərd), *n.* any of various lines or tackles for hoisting a spar, sail, flag, etc.

Ham (ham), *n.* the second son of Noah. Gen. 10:1.

Ha•man (hā′mən), *n.* the chief minister of King Ahasuerus and an enemy of the Jews. Esther 3–7.

Ham•burg (ham′bûrg, häm′bŏŏrg), *n.* a seaport in N Germany. 1,593,600.

ham•burg•er (ham′bûr′gər), *n.* **1.** a patty of ground beef. **2.** a sandwich consisting of such a patty and a bun.

Ham•il•ton (ham′əl tən), *n.* **1. Alexander,** 1757–1804, American statesman. **2.** a seaport in SE Ontario, in SE Canada. 306,728.

ham•let (ham′lit), *n.* a small village.

Ham•mar•skjöld (ham′mər shōld′, -shəld, ham′ər-), *n.* **Dag Hjalmar,** 1905–61, Swedish statesman: Secretary General of the United Nations 1953–61; Nobel peace prize 1961.

ham•mer (ham′ər), *n.* **1.** a tool consisting of a solid head set crosswise on a handle, used for driving nails, beating metals, etc. **2.** something resembling this in form, action, or use. **3.** the part of a firearm that strikes the firing pin and causes the discharge. —*v.t., v.i.* **4.** to beat with a hammer, esp. repeatedly. **5.** to shape, drive, or work, as with a hammer. —**ham′mer•er,** *n.*

ham′mer•head′, *n.* **1.** the head of a hammer. **2.** a shark having a mallet-shaped head with an eye at each end.

ham′mer•lock′, *n.* a wrestling hold in which one

arm is twisted and forced upward behind the back by the opponent.

Ham·mer·stein (ham′ər stīn′), n. **1. Oscar,** 1847?–1919, U.S. theatrical manager, born in Germany. **2.** his grandson, **Oscar II,** 1895–1960, U.S. lyricist and librettist.

ham·mer·toe′, n. a deformed toe in which there is a permanent angular flexion of the joints.

ham·mock (ham′ək), n. a bed of canvas, cord, or the like that hangs between two supports.

ham·per¹ (ham′pər), v.t. to hold back; hinder; impede. —**ham′per·er,** n.

ham·per² (ham′pər), n. a large covered basket: *a picnic hamper.*

Hamp·ton (hamp′tən), n. a city in SE Virginia. 133,793.

ham·ster (ham′stər), n. a short-tailed, burrowing rodent with large cheek pouches.

ham′string′, n., v., **-strung, -string·ing.** —n. **1.** any of the tendons behind the knee. —v.t. **2.** to disable by cutting a hamstring. **3.** to make powerless, ineffective, etc.

Han·cock (han′kok), n. **John,** 1737–93, American statesman.

hand (hand), n. **1.** the terminal, prehensile part of the arm in humans and other primates. **2.** the corresponding part of the forelimb in any four-legged vertebrate. **3.** anything resembling a hand in shape or function, as a pointer. **4.** a manual worker or crew member. **5.** a person skilled or experienced at some job. **6.** skill or workmanship. **7.** Often, **hands.** possession or power; control or care: *in fate's hands.* **8.** means; agency. **9.** assistance; aid: *to lend a hand.* **10.** side; direction: *the left hand of the road.* **11.** handwriting. **12.** a round of applause. **13.** a promise of marriage. **14.** a linear measure equal to 4 inches (10.2 centimeters). **15.** Cards. **a.** the cards held by each player at one time. **b.** a single round of a game. —v.t. **16.** to deliver or pass with or as if with the hand. **17.** to help, guide, etc., with the hand. **18.** to give or provide with. **19. hand down,** to deliver or transmit. **20. ~ out,** to distribute. —adj. **21.** of, belonging to, using, or operated by the hand. —*Idiom.* **22. at hand,** near. **23. hand in hand,** close together. **24. hand it to,** to give credit to. **25. hand over fist,** speedily and abundantly. **26. hands down,** effortlessly; easily. **27. on hand,** available or present. **28. on the one hand,** from one perspective. **29. on the other hand,** from the opposing perspective. **30. wash one's hands of,** to abandon any further responsibility for. —*Proverb.* **31.** Idle hands are the devil's tools, idleness leads to mischief. **32.** Never let your left hand know what your right hand is doing, give freely to others without flaunting your generosity. Matt. 6:3.

Hand (hand), n. **Lear·ned** (lûr′nid), 1872–1961, U.S. jurist.

hand′bag′, n. a bag, usu. with a handle or strap, used by women to carry money, cosmetics, etc.

hand′ball′, n. a game in which players strike a small ball against a wall with the hand.

hand′bar′row, n. a frame with handles at each end by which it is carried.

hand′bill′, n. a small printed notice or announcement, usu. for distribution by hand.

hand′book′, n. a concise guide or reference book; manual.

hand′car′, n. a small railroad car or platform on four wheels propelled by hand.

hand′cart′, n. a small cart drawn or pushed by hand.

hand′clasp′, n. HANDSHAKE.

hand′craft′ (n. -kraft′, -kräft′; v. -kraft′, -kräft′), n. **1.** HANDICRAFT. —v.t. **2.** to make by manual skill.

hand′cuff′, n. **1.** a metal ring that can be locked around a prisoner's wrist, usu. one of a pair connected by a chain. —v.t. **2.** to put handcuffs on. **3.** to restrain or thwart.

hand′ed, adj. **1.** having or involving a hand or hands: *a two-handed backhand.* **2.** requiring a specified number of persons: *a four-handed game of* poker. **3.** preferring the use of a particular hand: *right-handed.*

Han·del (han′dl), n. **George Frideric,** 1685–1759, German composer in England after 1712.

hand′ful (-fŏŏl), n., pl. **-fuls. 1.** the quantity or amount that the hand can hold. **2.** a small amount or quantity. **3.** *Informal.* a person or thing that is hard to manage or control.

hand′gun′, n. any firearm that can be held and fired with one hand.

hand·i·cap (han′dē kap′), n., v., **-capped, -cap·ping.** —n. **1.** a contest in which disadvantages or advantages of weight, distance, etc., are given to competitors to equalize their chances of winning. **2.** the disadvantage or advantage itself. **3.** any disadvantage. **4.** a physical or mental disability. —v.t. **5.** to place at a disadvantage. **6.** to assign handicaps to. **7.** to predict the winner of (a contest, esp. a horse race). —**hand′i·cap′per,** n.

hand′i·capped′, adj. **1.** physically or mentally disabled. —n. **2. the handicapped,** handicapped persons collectively.

hand′i·craft′, n. **1.** manual skill. **2.** an art, craft, or trade requiring manual skill. **3.** the articles made by handicraft.

hand′i·work′, n. **1.** work done by hand. **2.** the work of a particular person.

hand·ker·chief (hang′kər chif, -chēf′), n. a small piece of fabric used for wiping the nose, eyes, etc.

han·dle (han′dl), n., v., **-dled, -dling.** —n. **1.** a part of a tool, vessel, etc., by which it is grasped or held by the hand. —v.t. **2.** to touch, pick up, carry, or feel with the hands. **3.** to manage or deal with. **4.** to train or control. **5.** to deal or trade in. —v.i. **6.** to perform in a particular way when operated: *The jet was handling poorly.* —**han′dler,** n.

han′dle·bar′, n. Usu., **-bars.** the curved steering bar of a bicycle, motorcycle, etc., gripped by the hands.

hand′made′, adj. made by hand, rather than by machine.

hand′maid′ or **-maid′en,** n. a female servant.

hand′-me-down′, n. a used item passed along for further use by another.

hand′out′, n. **1.** food, clothing, etc., given to a needy person. **2.** a press release. **3.** a flyer or other printed material distributed to a group. **4.** anything given away for nothing.

hand′pick′, v.t. **1.** to pick by hand. **2.** to select personally and with care.

hand′rail′, n. a rail serving as a support or guard at the side of a stairway, platform, etc.

hand′saw′, n. any common saw with a handle for manual operation.

hand′set′, n. a telephone having a mouthpiece and earpiece mounted at opposite ends of a handle.

hand′shake′, n. a gripping and shaking of each other's hand in greeting, agreement, etc.

hands′-off′, adj. characterized by nonintervention or noninterference.

hand·some (han′səm), adj., **-som·er, -som·est. 1.** attractive and well-proportioned, esp. in an imposing or manly way; good-looking. **2.** considerable or ample. **3.** gracious; generous. —*Proverb.* **4. Handsome is as handsome does,** actions are more important than appearance. —**hand′some·ly,** adv. —**hand′some·ness,** n.

hands′-on′, adj. characterized by or involving active personal participation.

hand′spring′, n. an acrobatic movement in which a person starts from a standing position and turns the body in a complete circle, landing first on the hands and then on the feet.

hand′stand′, n. an act of supporting the body in a vertical position by balancing on the palms of the hands.

hand′-to-hand′, adj. at close quarters: *hand-to-hand combat.*

hand′-to-mouth′, adj. providing barely enough to survive: *a hand-to-mouth existence.*

hand′work′, n. work done by hand.

hand′writ′ing, *n.* **1.** writing done by hand with a pen or pencil. **2.** a style or manner of such writing. —**hand′writ′ten** (-rit′n), *adj.*

hand′y, *adj.*, **-i•er, -i•est. 1.** within easy reach; accessible. **2.** easily used. **3.** skillful with the hands; dexterous. —**hand′i•ly**, *adv.* —**hand′i•ness**, *n.*

hand′y•man′, *n., pl.* **-men.** a person hired to do small maintenance or repair jobs.

hang (hang), *v.*, **hung** or (*esp. for 3, 11*) **hanged, hang•ing**, *n.* —*v.t.* **1.** to fasten or attach (a thing) so that it is supported from above or near its own top. **2.** to attach or suspend so as to allow free movement. **3.** to execute by suspending from a gallows or the like. **4.** to decorate with something suspended. **5.** to attach (wallpaper, pictures, etc.) to a wall. **6.** to let (one's head) droop. **7.** to bring (a jury) to a deadlock. —*v.i.* **8.** to be suspended; dangle. **9.** to swing freely. **10.** to incline downward, jut out, or lean over. **11.** to suffer death by hanging. **12.** to be contingent: *Our future hangs on their decision.* **13.** to fall or drape, as a garment. **14.** *Informal.* to hang out. **15. hang around**, *Informal.* **a.** to spend time in a certain place. **b.** to loiter. **16. ~ back**, to hesitate. **17. ~ in (there)**, *Informal.* to persevere or endure. **18. ~ on, a.** to cling tightly. **b.** to persevere or endure. **c.** to persist. **d.** to keep a telephone line open. **19. ~ out**, *Informal.* to spend one's time habitually. **20. ~ up, a.** to suspend, as on a hook. **b.** to stop or delay. **c.** to end a telephone call by breaking the connection. —*n.* **21.** the way in which a thing hangs. **22.** *Informal.* the precise manner of doing, using, etc., something. **23.** *Informal.* meaning or significance: *to get the hang of a subject.* —*Idiom.* **24. hang loose**, *Slang.* to remain relaxed or calm. **25. hang tough**, *Informal.* to be unyielding or inflexible. —**Usage.** HANGED, the historically older past tense and past participle, is rarely used except in the sense of putting to death, esp. legally: *The prisoner was hanged by the neck until dead.* But HUNG also appears in this sense, and is actually more frequent in contexts other than legal executions: *He hung himself in his cell.*

hang•ar (hang′ər), *n.* a structure for housing aircraft. [< F: shed, shelter]

hang′dog′, *adj.* abject or shamefaced.

hang′er, *n.* something by which things are hung, as a frame with a hook for hanging clothes.

hang′er-on′, *n., pl.* **hang•ers-on.** an opportunistic follower.

hang′ glid′ing, *n.* the sport of launching oneself from a steep incline and soaring through the air while harnessed to a kitelike glider **(hang′ glid′er).**

hang′ing, *n.* **1.** an act or instance of hanging a condemned criminal from a gallows or the like. **2.** something hung on a wall, as a drapery or tapestry.

hang′man, *n., pl.* **-men.** a person who hangs condemned criminals.

hang′nail′, *n.* a small piece of partly detached skin at the side or base of the fingernail.

hang′out′, *n. Informal.* a place that a person frequents, esp. for recreation.

hang′o′ver, *n.* **1.** the disagreeable physical aftereffects of drunkenness. **2.** something remaining from a former period or state.

hang′-up′, *n. Slang.* a psychological preoccupation or problem.

hank (hangk), *n.* **1.** SKEIN. **2.** a coil or loop: *a hank of hair.*

han•ker (hang′kər), *v.i.* to have a restless or incessant longing. —**han′ker•ing**, *n.*

han•ky or **-kie** (hang′kē), *n., pl.* **-kies.** a handkerchief.

han-ky-pan•ky (hang′kē pang′kē), *n. Informal.* mischief; deceit.

Han•nah (han′ə), *n.* the mother of Samuel. I Sam. 1:20.

Han•ni•bal (han′ə bəl), *n.* 247–183 B.C., Carthaginian general.

Ha•noi (ha noi′, hə-), *n.* the capital of Vietnam. 2,000,000.

Han′seat′ic League′, *n.* a medieval league of towns of N Germany and adjacent countries, formed for the protection of commerce.

han•som (han′səm), *n.* a two-wheeled, covered vehicle drawn by one horse, with the driver mounted on an elevated seat behind. Also called **han′som cab′**. [after J. A. *Hansom* (1803–82), English architect who designed it]

Ha•nuk•kah (hä′nə kə, KHä′-), *n.* an eight-day Jewish festival commemorating the rededication of the Temple in Jerusalem.

hap (hap), *n.* luck or lot.

hap•haz•ard (hap haz′ərd), *adj.* characterized by lack of order or planning; random. —**hap•haz′ard•ly**, *adv.*

hap′less, *adj.* luckless; unfortunate.

hap•loid (hap′loid), *adj.* **1.** pertaining to a single set of chromosomes. —*n.* **2.** an organism or cell having only one complete set of chromosomes.

hap′ly, *adv. Archaic.* perhaps; by chance.

hap•pen (hap′ən), *v.i.* **1.** to take place; come to pass; occur. **2.** to come to pass by chance. **3.** to have the fortune or occasion: *I happened to see him.* **4.** to meet or discover by chance. **5.** to be, come, go, etc., casually or by chance.

hap′pen•ing, *n.* **1.** an occurrence or event. **2.** a spontaneous or unconventional performance or entertainment.

hap′pen•stance′ (-stans′), *n.* a chance happening or event.

hap•py (hap′ē), *adj.*, **-pi•er, -pi•est. 1.** delighted or pleased. **2.** characterized by or indicative of pleasure or joy. **3.** favored by fortune. **4.** apt or felicitous. —**hap′pi•ly**, *adv.* —**hap′pi•ness**, *n.*

hap′py-go-luck′y, *adj.* carefree; easygoing.

hap′py hour′, *n.* a period at a bar when drinks are served at reduced prices.

ha•ra-ki•ri (här′ə kēr′ē), *n.* **1.** ceremonial suicide by cutting the abdomen. **2.** any self-destructive act. [< Japn. = *hara* belly + *kiri* cut]

ha•rangue (hə rang′), *n., v.*, **-rangued, -rangu•ing.** —*n.* **1.** a long, passionate, and pompous speech. —*v.t.* **2.** to address in a harangue. —*v.i.* **3.** to deliver a harangue.

Ha•ra•re (hə rär′ā), *n.* the capital of Zimbabwe. 675,000.

ha•rass (hə ras′, har′əs), *v.t.* **1.** to disturb persistently. **2.** to trouble by repeated attacks. —**ha•rass′er**, *n.* —**ha•rass′ment**, *n.*

Har•bin (här′bin′), *n.* a city in NE China. 2,630,000.

har•bin•ger (här′bin jər), *n.* one that heralds the approach of someone or something.

har•bor (här′bər), *n.* **1.** a sheltered part of a body of water along the shore deep enough for anchoring a ship. **2.** any place of shelter or refuge. —*v.t.* **3.** to give shelter to. **4.** to conceal. **5.** to hold in the mind: *to harbor suspicion.* —*v.i.* **6.** to take shelter. Also, *esp. Brit.*, **harbour.** —**har′bor•er**, *n.*

hard (härd), *adj.* and *adv.*, **-er, -est.** —*adj.* **1.** solid and firm to the touch. **2.** firmly formed; tight. **3.** difficult to do, deal with, understand, etc. **4.** involving a great deal of effort, energy, or persistence. **5.** energetic or persistent. **6.** violent or severe: *a hard fall.* **7.** bad or unbearable: *hard luck.* **8.** oppressive; harsh. **9.** undeniable: *hard facts.* **10.** factual: *hard information.* **11.** unfriendly; resentful: *hard feelings.* **12.** stern or searching: *a hard look.* **13.** (of water) containing mineral salts that interfere with the action of soap. **14.** in currency as distinguished from checks or promissory notes. **15.** (of paper money) readily convertible into foreign currency. —*adv.* **16.** with great exertion, vigor, or violence. **17.** earnestly or critically. **18.** harshly or severely. **19.** so as to be solid or firm: *frozen hard.* **20.** with force: *hit hard.* —*Idiom.* **21. hard by**, near. **22. hard up**, *Informal.* urgently in need of money. —**hard′ness**, *n.*

hard′-and-fast′, *adj.* unalterable; strict.

hard′back′, *n.* HARDCOVER.

hard′ball′, *n.* **1.** baseball, as distinguished from softball. —*adj.* **2.** tough or ruthless: *hardball politics.*

hard′-bit′ten, *adj.* tough; stubborn.

hard′-boiled′, *adj.* **1.** (of an egg) boiled long

enough for the yolk and white to solidify. **2.** unsentimental; tough.

hard′ ci′der, *n.* fermented cider.

hard′ cop′y, *n.* computer output printed on paper; printout.

hard′-core′, *adj.* **1.** absolute and uncompromising. **2.** persistent or chronic: *hard-core unemployment.*

hard′cov′er, *adj.* **1.** bound in cloth, leather, or the like, over stiff material. —*n.* **2.** a hardcover book.

hard′ disk′, *n.* a rigid computer disk for storing programs and large amounts of data.

hard′ drive′, *n.* a disk drive containing a hard disk.

hard′en, *v.t., v.i.* to make or become hard or unfeeling. —**hard′en•er,** *n.*

hard′ hat′, *n.* **1.** a protective helmet worn by construction workers, miners, etc. **2.** a construction worker.

hard′head′ed, *adj.* **1.** practical; shrewd. **2.** obstinate; willful. —**hard′head′ed•ly,** *adv.* —**hard′head′ed•ness,** *n.*

hard′heart′ed, *adj.* unfeeling; pitiless. —**hard′heart′ed•ly,** *adv.* —**hard′heart′ed•ness,** *n.*

har•di•hood (här′dē hŏŏd′), *n.* fortitude, vigor, or courage.

Har•ding (här′ding), *n.* **Warren G(amaliel),** 1865–1923, 29th president of the U.S. 1921–23.

hard′-line′ or **hard/line′,** *adj.* adhering rigidly to a set of principles or demands, as in politics. —**hard′-lin′er,** *n.*

hard′ly, *adv.* **1.** barely or scarcely. **2.** with little likelihood: *He will hardly come now.* —**Usage.** HARDLY, BARELY, SCARCELY all have a negative connotation, and the use of any of them with a supplementary negative (*I can't hardly remember*) is considered nonstandard.

hard′-nosed′, *adj. Informal.* practical and shrewd.

hard′ pal′ate, *n.* the anterior bony portion of the palate.

hard′ rock′, *n.* rock music dependent on a driving beat and amplified sound.

hard′ sell′, *n.* aggressively insistent selling or advertising.

hard′-shell′, *adj.* **1.** having a hard shell. **2.** rigid or uncompromising.

hard′ship, *n.* **1.** a condition that is difficult to endure, as poverty or illness. **2.** an instance or cause of this.

hard′stand′, *n.* a hard-surfaced area on which heavy vehicles or airplanes can be parked.

hard′tack′, *n.* a hard, saltless biscuit, formerly much used aboard ships.

hard′top′, *n.* a style of car having a rigid metal top and no center posts between windows.

hard′ware′, *n.* **1.** metalware, as tools, locks, or cutlery. **2.** the mechanical and electronic devices composing a computer system.

hard′wood′, *n.* **1.** the hard, compact wood or timber of various trees, as the oak or cherry. —*adj.* **2.** made of hardwood.

har•dy (här′dē), *adj.,* **-di•er, -di•est. 1.** sturdy; strong. **2.** bold or daring; courageous. —**har′di•ly,** *adv.* —**har′di•ness,** *n.*

Har•dy (här′dē), *n.* **1. Oliver,** 1892–1957, U.S. motion-picture comedian. **2. Thomas,** 1840–1928, English novelist and poet.

hare (hâr), *n., pl.* **hares, hare.** a mammal closely related to but usu. larger than the rabbit.

hare′brained′, *adj.* giddy; reckless.

Ha•re Krish•na (här′ē krish′nə), *n., pl.* **-nas** for 2. **1.** a religious sect based on Vedic scriptures; founded in the U.S. in 1966. **2.** a member of this sect.

har•em (hâr′əm, har′-), *n.* **1.** the part of a Muslim house reserved for the residence of women. **2.** the women in a Muslim household. [< Ar *ḥarīm* harem, lit., forbidden]

hark (härk), *v.i.* **1.** to listen attentively. **2. hark back,** to recollect a previous event or topic.

hark′en, *v.i., v.t.* HEARKEN.

Har•lem (här′ləm), *n.* a section of New York City, in N Manhattan.

har•le•quin (här′lə kwin, -kin), *n.* **1.** (*often cap.*) a character in comic theater and pantomime, usu. masked, dressed in multicolored, diamond-patterned tights. **2.** a buffoon.

har•lot (här′lət), *n.* a prostitute. —**har′lot•ry,** *n.*

harm (härm), *n.* **1.** injury or damage. —*v.t.* **2.** to cause harm to. —**Saying. 3. First, do no harm,** do not prescribe a medical treatment that does more damage than good: said to be the first principle of Hippocrates. —**harm′ful,** *adj.* —**harm′ful•ly,** *adv.* —**harm′less,** *adj.* —**harm′less•ly,** *adv.*

har•mon•ic (här mon′ik), *adj.* **1.** of or in musical harmony. —*n.* **2.** OVERTONE (def. 1). —**har•mon′i•cal•ly,** *adv.*

har•mon′i•ca (-i kə), *n., pl.* **-cas.** a wind instrument played by exhaling and inhaling air through a set of metal reeds.

har•mon′ics, *n.* the science of musical sounds.

har•mo•ni•ous (-mō′nē əs), *adj.* **1.** marked by agreement in feeling, attitude, etc. **2.** forming a pleasingly consistent whole. **3.** tuneful; melodious. —**har•mo′ni•ous•ly,** *adv.* —**har•mo′ni•ous•ness,** *n.*

har′mo•nize′ (-mə nīz′), *v.,* **-nized, -niz•ing.** —*v.t.* **1.** to bring into harmony or accord. —*v.i.* **2.** to be in accord. **3.** to sing in harmony. —**har′mo•ni•za′tion,** *n.* —**har′mo•niz′er,** *n.*

har′mo•ny, *n., pl.* **-nies. 1.** agreement; accord. **2.** a consistent or pleasing arrangement of parts. **3.** the simultaneous combination of tones, esp. when blended into chords pleasing to the ear. [< OF < L *harmonia* < Gk: joint, agreement, harmony]

har•ness (här′nis), *n.* **1.** the combination of straps, bands, and other parts forming the working gear of a draft animal. —*v.t.* **2.** to put a harness on. **3.** to gain control over for a particular end: *to harness water power.*

harp (härp), *n.* **1.** a musical instrument having strings stretched across a triangular frame, played by plucking with the fingers. —*v.i.* **2.** to play on a harp. **3. harp on** or **upon,** to repeat interminably and tediously. —**harp′ist,** *n.*

harp

Har′pers (or **Har′per's**) **Fer′ry** (här′pərz), *n.* a town in NE West Virginia at the confluence of the Shenandoah and Potomac rivers: site of John Brown's raid 1859. 361.

har•poon (här pōōn′), *n.* **1.** a barbed, spearlike missile attached to a rope, used to spear whales and large fish. —*v.t.* **2.** to strike with a harpoon. —**har•poon′er,** *n.*

harp•si•chord (härp′si kôrd′), *n.* a keyboard instrument, precursor of the piano, in which the strings are plucked by leather or quill points connected with the keys. —**harp′si•chord′ist,** *n.*

Har•py (här′pē), *n., pl.* **-pies. 1.** any of a group of winged supernatural beings of classical myth, portrayed by later authors as rapacious female monsters. **2.** (*l.c.*) a bad-tempered woman. **3.** (*l.c.*) a greedy person.

har•ri•dan (här′i dn), *n.* a scolding, vicious woman.

har•ri•er (har′ē ər), *n.* **1.** one of a breed of medium-sized hunting hounds. **2.** a cross-country runner.

Har•ris•burg (har′is bûrg′), n. the capital of Pennsylvania. 51,720.

Har•ri•son (har′ə sən), n. **1.** Benjamin, 1833–1901, 23rd president of the U.S. 1889–93. **2.** his grandfather, **William Henry**, 1773–1841, 9th president of the U.S. 1841.

har•row (har′ō), v.t. Archaic. (of Christ) to descend into (hell) to free the righteous held captive.

har•ry (har′ē), v.t., -ried, -ry•ing. **1.** to harass; torment. **2.** to ravage, as in war.

harsh (härsh), adj. -er, -est. **1.** ungentle in action or effect. **2.** grim; cruel. **3.** unpleasant to the senses. —harsh′ly, adv. —harsh′ness, n.

hart (härt), n., pl. harts, hart. a mature male European red deer.

Hart•ford (härt′fərd), n. the capital of Connecticut. 124,196.

har•um-scar•um (hâr′əm skâr′əm, har′əm skar′əm), adj. **1.** reckless; irresponsible. —adv. **2.** recklessly; wildly.

har•vest (här′vist), n. **1.** the gathering of crops. **2.** the season when ripened crops are gathered. **3.** a crop or yield of one growing season. **4.** the result of any act, process, etc. —v.t., v.i. **5.** to gather or reap. —har′vest•er, n.

has (haz; unstressed həz, əz), v. a 3rd pers. sing. pres. indic. of HAVE.

has′-been′, n. a person or thing that is no longer effective, successful, etc.

hash (hash), n. **1.** diced cooked meat and potatoes or other vegetables browned together. **2.** a mess or muddle. —v.t. **3.** to discuss or review thoroughly: to hash over a proposal. [< F hacher to cut up]

Ha•sid (hä′sid, KHä′-, KHô′-, KHä sēd′), n., pl. **Ha•sid•im** (hä sid′im, KHä-, KHä′sē dēm′). a member of a Jewish sect founded in Poland in the 18th century that emphasizes mysticism, ritual strictness, religious zeal, and joy. [< Heb ḥāsīd pious (person)] —Ha•sid•ic (hä sid′ik, hə-), adj. —Has•i•dism (has′i diz′əm, häs′si-), n.

has•n't (haz′ənt), contraction of has not.

hasp (hasp), n. a clasp for a door, lid, etc., esp. one passing over a staple and fastened by a pin or padlock.

has•sle (has′əl), n., v., -sled, -sling. Informal. —n. **1.** a disorderly dispute. **2.** a troublesome situation. —v.i. **3.** to quarrel. **4.** to be put to inconvenience, exertion, etc. —v.t. **5.** to bother or harass.

has•sock (has′ək), n. a thick, firm cushion used as a footstool.

hast (hast), v. Archaic. 2nd pers. sing. pres. indic. of HAVE.

haste (hāst), n. **1.** swiftness of motion; speed. **2.** unnecessarily quick or rash action. —Idiom. **3.** make haste, to hurry. —Proverb. **4.** Haste makes waste, rushing through a task may result in errors. —Saying. **5.** Make haste slowly, to move quickly but carefully.

has•ten (hā′sən), v.i. **1.** to move or act with haste. —v.t. **2.** to cause to hasten.

hast′y, adj., -i•er, -i•est. **1.** speedy; hurried. **2.** unduly quick; rash. —hast′i•ly, adv. —hast′i•ness, n.

hat (hat), n. **1.** a shaped covering for the head, usu. with a crown and brim. —Idiom. **2.** pass the hat, to ask for contributions of money. **3.** talk through one's hat, to make absurd statements. **4.** throw one's hat into the ring, to declare one's candidacy for political office. **5.** under one's hat, confidential.

hatch[1] (hach), v.t. **1.** to bring forth (young) from the egg. **2.** to cause young to emerge from (the egg), as by incubating. **3.** to devise; plot. —v.i. **4.** to be hatched.

hatch[2] (hach), n. **1.** an opening in the deck of a ship or in the floor or roof of a building, used as a passageway. **2.** the cover over such an opening.

hatch[3] (hach), v.t. to mark with closely set parallel lines, as for shading. —hatch′ing, n.

hatch′back′, n. a style of automobile in which the rear deck lid and window lift open as a unit.

hatch′er•y, n., pl. -er•ies. a place for hatching eggs of hens, fish, etc.

hatch•et (hach′it), n. a small, short-handled ax.

hatch′et job′, n. a maliciously destructive critique.

hatch′way′, n. HATCH[2] (def. 1).

hate (hāt), v., hat•ed, hat•ing, n. —v.t. **1.** to dislike intensely; detest. **2.** to be unwilling; dislike: I hate to accept it. —v.i. **3.** to feel hatred. —n. **4.** intense dislike or hostility. **5.** the object of hatred. —hat′er, n.

hate′ful, adj. arousing or deserving hate. —hate′ful•ly, adv. —hate′ful•ness, n.

hath (hath), v. Archaic. 3rd pers. sing. pres. indic. of HAVE.

ha•tred (hā′trid), n. intense dislike, aversion, or hostility.

hat′ter, n. a maker or seller of hats.

hau•berk (hô′bûrk), n. a medieval tunic of chain mail.

haugh•ty (hô′tē), adj., -ti•er, -ti•est. disdainfully proud; snobbish; arrogant. —haugh′ti•ly, adv. —haugh′ti•ness, n.

haul (hôl), v.t., v.i. **1.** to pull with force. **2.** to transport; carry. **3.** haul off, Informal. to draw back the arm in order to strike. —n. **4.** an act or instance of hauling. **5.** the load hauled. **6.** the distance over which anything is hauled. —Idiom. **7.** long (or short) haul, a relatively great (or small) period of time. —haul′er, n.

haunch (hônch, hänch), n. **1.** the hip or the fleshy part of the body about the hip. **2.** the leg and loin of an animal, used for food.

haunt (hônt, hänt), v.t. **1.** to visit habitually or appear to frequently as a spirit or ghost. **2.** to recur persistently to the consciousness of. **3.** to visit frequently. —n. **4.** a place frequently visited. —haunt′ed, adj. —haunt′er, n.

haunt′ing, adj. remaining in the consciousness; not quickly forgotten. —haunt′ing•ly, adv.

haute cou•ture (ōt′ kōō tŏŏr′), n. high fashion.

haute cui•sine (ōt′ kwi zēn′), n. gourmet cooking; food preparation as an art.

hau•teur (hō tûr′, ō tûr′), n. haughty manner or spirit.

Ha•van•a (hə van′ə), n., pl. -van•as for 2. **1.** the capital of Cuba. 2,014,800. **2.** a cigar made in Cuba.

have (hav; unstressed həv, əv; for 14 usually haf), v. and auxiliary v., had, hav•ing, n. —v.t. **1.** to possess; own; hold. **2.** to get or take: to have a part in a play. **3.** to experience: Have a good time. **4.** to hold in mind, sight, etc.: to have doubts. **5.** to cause to or cause to be: Have him come at five. **6.** to engage in: to have a talk. **7.** to eat or drink. **8.** to permit; allow. **9.** to assert or maintain: Rumor has it that she's moving. **10.** to give birth to. **11.** to hold an advantage over: He has you there. **12.** to outwit; cheat: We were had by a con artist. —auxiliary verb. **13.** (used with a past participle to form perfect tenses): She has gone. **14.** (used with an infinitive to express obligation or compulsion): I have to leave now. —n. **15.** Usu., haves. a wealthy individual or group. —Idiom. **16.** have had it, to be tired and disgusted. **17.** have it in for, to wish harm to. **18.** have it out, to reach an understanding through fighting or discussion.

ha•ven (hā′vən), n. **1.** a harbor; port. **2.** any place of shelter and safety.

have′-not′, n. Usu., -nots. an individual or group that is without wealth.

have•n't (hav′ənt), contraction of have not.

hav•er•sack (hav′ər sak′), n. a single-strapped shoulder bag for carrying supplies.

hav•oc (hav′ək), n. **1.** great destruction or devastation. —Idiom. **2.** play havoc with, to destroy; ruin.

haw[1] (hô), v.i. to hesitate while speaking (usu. in the phrase to hem and haw).

haw[2] (hô), n. **1.** the fruit of the hawthorn. **2.** the hawthorn.

Haw., Hawaii.

Ha•wai•i (hə wī′ē, -wä′ē), n. **1.** a state of the United States comprising a group of islands (**Hawai′ian Is′lands**) in the N Pacific. 1,183,723. Cap.: Honolulu. Abbr.: HI, Haw. **2.** the largest island of Hawaii, in the SE part. —**Ha•wai′ian** (-wī′ən, -wä′yən), *adj.*, *n.*

hawk¹ (hôk), *n.* **1.** any of various birds of prey, having a hooked beak, broad wings, and curved talons. **2.** a person who advocates war. —**hawk′ish**, *adj.*

hawk² (hôk), *v.t.* to offer for sale by calling aloud in public. —**hawk′er**, *n.*

hawk³ (hôk), *v.i.* **1.** to make an effort to raise phlegm from the throat. —*v.t.* **2.** to raise by hawking.

hawk′-eyed′, *adj.* having very keen sight.

Haw•king (hô′king), *n.* **Stephen William,** born 1942, English physicist.

haw•ser (hô′zər, -sər), *n.* a heavy rope for mooring or towing.

haw•thorn (hô′thôrn′), *n.* any of various small trees of the rose family, with stiff thorns and bright-colored fruit.

Haw•thorne (hô′thôrn′), *n.* **Nathaniel,** 1804–64, U.S. writer.

hay (hā), *n.* **1.** herbage, as grass or clover, dried for use as forage. —*v.i.* **2.** to cut grass, clover, etc., for use as forage. —*Proverb.* **3. make hay while the sun shines,** to take advantage of favorable circumstances.

hay′cock′, *n.* a small, conical pile of hay in a field.

Hay•dn (hīd′n), *n.* **Franz Joseph,** 1732–1809, Austrian composer.

Hayes (hāz), *n.* **Rutherford B(irchard),** 1822–93, 19th president of the U.S. 1877–81.

hay′ fe′ver, *n.* inflammation of the mucous membranes of the eyes and respiratory tract, caused by pollen of certain plants.

hay′loft′, *n.* a loft in a stable or barn for the storage of hay.

hay′mow′ (-mou′), *n.* **1.** hay stored in a barn. **2.** HAYLOFT.

hay′seed′, *n.* a yokel; hick.

hay′stack′, *n.* a stack of hay built up in the open air for preservation.

Hay•ward (hā′wərd), *n.* a city in central California. 115,590.

hay′wire′, *adj.* out of control; disordered; crazy.

ha•zan or **cha•zan** (кнä′zən, кнä zän′), *n.*, *pl.* **ha•za•nim** (кнä zô′nim, кнä′zä nēm′), *Eng.* **ha•zans.** *Hebrew.* a cantor of a synagogue.

haz•ard (haz′ərd), *n.* **1.** something causing danger, risk, etc. **2.** an obstacle on a golf course. —*v.t.* **3.** to venture or risk. —**haz′ard•ous,** *adj.* —**haz′ard•ous•ly,** *adv.*

haze¹ (hāz), *n.*, *v.*, **hazed, haz•ing.** —*n.* **1.** an aggregation in the atmosphere of very fine, widely dispersed particles, giving the air a blurred appearance. **2.** vagueness, as of the mind. —*v.t.*, *v.i.* **3.** to make or become hazy.

haze² (hāz), *v.t.*, **hazed, haz•ing.** to subject (freshmen, newcomers, etc.) to abusive or humiliating tricks and ridicule. —**haz′er**, *n.*

ha•zel (hā′zəl), *n.* **1.** a small tree or shrub of the birch family, with toothed ovate leaves and edible nuts. **2.** a light golden- or greenish-brown color.

ha′zel•nut′, *n.* the nut of the hazel; filbert.

ha•zy (hā′zē), *adj.*, **-zi•er, -zi•est. 1.** characterized by the presence of haze; misty. **2.** vague; indefinite. —**ha′zi•ly,** *adv.* —**ha′zi•ness,** *n.*

H′-bomb′, *n.* HYDROGEN BOMB.

HDL, high-density lipoprotein: a circulating lipoprotein that picks up cholesterol in the arteries and deposits it in the liver for reprocessing or excretion.

hdqrs., headquarters.

HDTV, high-definition television.

he (hē; *unstressed* ē), *pron.*, *n.*, *pl.* **hes.** —*pron.* **1.** the male person or animal last mentioned. **2.** anyone: *He who hesitates is lost.* —*n.* **3.** any male person or animal.

He, *Chem. Symbol.* helium.

head (hed), *n.* **1.** the upper part of the body, containing the skull with mouth, eyes, ears, nose, and brain. **2.** the mind; brain. **3.** a position of leadership or honor. **4.** a leader or chief. **5.** the uppermost part

of anything: *the head of a pin.* **6.** the foremost or forward part of anything: *at the head of a procession.* **7.** one of a number, herd, or group: *a dinner at $50 a head.* **8.** a culmination; crisis or climax. **9.** froth at the top of a liquid. **10.** any dense flower cluster or compact part of a plant, as that composed of leaves in the cabbage. **11.** the obverse of a coin. **12.** the source of a river or stream. **13.** HEADLINE. **14.** the stretched membrane covering the end of a drum. **15.** any of the parts of a tape recorder that record, play back, or erase magnetic signals. —*adj.* **16.** first in rank or position. **17.** of or for the head. **18.** situated at the top or front. **19.** moving or coming from the front: *head tide.* —*v.t.* **20.** to lead; precede. **21.** to be the chief of. **22.** to direct the course of. —*v.i.* **23.** to go in a certain direction: *to head east.* **24. head off,** to intercept. —*Idiom.* **25. come to a head, a.** to suppurate, as a boil. **b.** to reach a crisis; culminate. **26. go to one′s head, a.** to exhilarate or intoxicate. **b.** to fill one with conceit. **27. head over heels,** intensely; completely. **28. keep** (or **lose**) **one′s head,** to keep (or lose) one′s poise. **29. on one′s head,** as one′s responsibility or fault. **30. over one′s head,** beyond one′s comprehension. **31. turn someone′s head,** to make someone conceited. —**head′less,** *adj.*

head′ache′, *n.* **1.** a pain located in the head. **2.** an annoying person, situation, etc.

head′band′, *n.* a band worn around the head.

head′board′, *n.* a board forming the head of something, as a bed.

head′ cold′, *n.* a common cold characterized by nasal congestion and sneezing.

head′dress′, *n.* a covering or decoration for the head.

head′ed, *adj.* having a specified kind of head or number of heads: *levelheaded; two-headed.*

head′first′, *adv.* **1.** with the head in front. **2.** rashly; precipitately.

head′gear′, *n.* a covering for the head, as a hat.

head′hunt′ing, *n.* **1.** the practice of decapitating victims and preserving their heads as trophies. **2.** the recruiting of executives to fill high-level positions. —**head′hunt′er**, *n.*

head′ing, *n.* **1.** something that serves as a head, top, or front. **2.** a title or caption of a page, chapter, etc. **3.** the direction toward which a traveler or vehicle is moving.

head′land (-lənd), *n.* a promontory extending into a large body of water.

head′light′, *n.* a light with a reflector on the front of a motor vehicle.

head′line′, *n.*, *v.*, **-lined, -lin•ing.** —*n.* **1.** a heading in a newspaper for any written material. —*v.t.* **2.** to furnish with a headline. **3.** to be the star of (a show, nightclub act, etc.). —*v.i.* **4.** to be the star of an entertainment. —**head′lin′er**, *n.*

head′long′, *adv.* **1.** headfirst. **2.** hastily. **3.** rashly. —*adj.* **4.** hasty. **5.** done with the head foremost. **6.** rash; impetuous.

head′mas′ter or **-mis′tress,** *n.* a person in charge of a private school.

head′-on′, *adj.*, *adv.* with the front or head foremost.

head′phone′, *n.* Usu., **-phones.** a headset for use with a stereo system.

head′quar′ters, *n.*, *pl.* **-ters.** (*used with a sing. or pl. v.*) a center of operations from which orders are issued.

head′rest′, *n.* a support of any kind for the head.

head′room′, *n.* clear space overhead, as in a car.

head′set′, *n.* a device consisting of one or two earphones attached to a headband.

head′ start′, *n.* an advantage given or acquired in any competition, endeavor, etc.

head′stone′, *n.* a stone marker at the head of a grave.

head′strong′, *adj.* willful; stubborn.

head′wa′ters, *n.pl.* the upper tributaries of a river.

head′way′, *n.* **1.** forward movement. **2.** progress.

head′wind′, *n.* a wind opposed to the course of a moving aircraft, ship, etc.

head′y, *adj.,* **-i•er, -i•est. 1.** intoxicating: *heady perfume.* **2.** rashly impetuous.

heal (hēl), *v.t.* **1.** to restore to health or soundness. **2.** to repair or reconcile. —*v.i.* **3.** to effect a cure. **4.** to become well or sound. **—heal′er,** *n.*

health (helth), *n.* **1.** the general condition of the body or mind: *in poor health.* **2.** soundness of body or mind; freedom from disease or ailment. **3.** a wish for a person's health and happiness, as a toast. **4.** vigor; vitality: *economic health.*

health′ care′ or **health′care′,** *n.* any field or enterprise concerned with supplying services, equipment, information, etc., for the maintenance or restoration of health.

health′ful, *adj.* conducive to health; wholesome. **—health′ful•ly,** *adv.*

health′ main′tenance organiza′tion, *n.* See HMO.

health′y, *adj.,* **-i•er, -i•est. 1.** possessing good health. **2.** of or characteristic of good health. **3.** HEALTHFUL. **4.** fairly large: *a healthy distance.* **—health′i•ly,** *adv.* **—health′i•ness,** *n.*

heap (hēp), *n.* **1.** a group of things lying one on another. **2.** *Informal.* a great quantity or number. —*v.t.* **3.** to put in a heap; pile. **4.** to give in great quantity. **5.** to fill abundantly. —*v.i.* **6.** to become heaped.

hear (hēr), *v.,* **heard** (hûrd), **hear•ing.** —*v.t.* **1.** to perceive by the ear. **2.** to be informed of. **3.** to listen to. **4.** to consider officially, as a judge: *to hear a case.* —*v.i.* **5.** to be capable of perceiving sound by the ear. **6.** to receive information. **7.** to listen with favor or assent: *I will not hear of your going.* **—hear′er,** *n.*

hear′ing, *n.* **1.** the faculty or sense by which sound is perceived. **2.** the act of perceiving sound. **3.** an opportunity to be heard. **4.** a session in which testimony and arguments are presented, esp. before a judge. **5.** earshot.

heark•en (här′kən), *v.i.* to give heed or attention to what is said.

hear′say′, *n.* unverified information acquired from another.

hearse (hûrs), *n.* a vehicle for conveying a dead person to the place of burial.

Hearst (hûrst), *n.* **William Randolph,** 1863–1951, U.S. editor and publisher.

heart (härt), *n.* **1.** a muscular organ in vertebrates that receives blood from the veins and pumps it through the arteries to oxygenate the blood. **2.** the center of the personality, esp. with reference to emotion. **3.** capacity for sympathy; affection. **4.** spirit or courage. **5.** the central part of anything: *in the heart of Paris.* **6.** the essential part; core. **7.** a conventional figure shaped like the heart. **8.** any of a suit of playing cards bearing heart-shaped figures. —*Idiom.* **9. after one's own heart,** in accord with one's preference. **10. at heart,** fundamentally; basically. **11. by heart,** entirely from memory. **12. set one's heart on,** to wish for intensely. **13. take to heart, a.** to consider seriously. **b.** to grieve over.

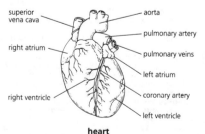

heart

heart′ache′, *n.* sorrow; grief.

heart′ attack′, *n.* any sudden insufficiency of oxygen supply to the heart that results in heart muscle damage.

heart′beat′, *n.* a pulsation of the heart.

heart′break′, *n.* great sorrow or anguish. **—heart′-break′ing,** *adj.* **—heart′bro′ken,** *adj.*

heart′burn′, *n.* a burning sensation in the stomach and esophagus, sometimes associated with the backflow of an acid fluid.

heart′en, *v.t.* to give courage or confidence to.

heart′felt′, *adj.* deeply felt.

hearth (härth), *n.* **1.** the floor of a fireplace, usu. of stone or brick. **2.** the fireside. **3.** home and family life.

heart′land′, *n.* any central or vital area, as of a state, nation, or continent.

heart′less, *adj.* lacking compassion or feeling; cruel. **—heart′less•ly,** *adv.* **—heart′less•ness,** *n.*

heart′rend′ing, *adj.* causing or expressing intense grief or anguish. **—heart′rend′ing•ly,** *adv.*

heart′sick′, *adj.* extremely depressed or unhappy. **—heart′sick′ness,** *n.*

heart′strings′, *n.pl.* the strongest feelings or affections.

heart′throb′, *n.* **1.** a rapid beat of the heart. **2.** a passionate or sentimental emotion. **3.** a person who inspires such emotion.

heart′-to-heart′, *adj.* frank; sincere and intimate.

heart′warm′ing, *adj.* tenderly moving.

heart′y, *adj.,* **-i•er, -i•est 1.** warm-hearted; cordial. **2.** genuine; sincere: *hearty dislike.* **3.** exuberant; unrestrained: *hearty laughter.* **4.** vigorous: *hale and hearty.* **5.** abundant or nourishing: *a hearty meal.* **—hear′ti•ly,** *adv.* **—heart′i•ness,** *n.*

heat (hēt), *n.* **1.** the condition or quality of being hot. **2.** degree of hotness. **3.** the sensation of hotness. **4.** energy that causes a rise in temperature, expansion, or other physical change. **5.** hot weather or climate. **6.** intensity of feeling. **7.** maximum intensity in an activity or condition: *the heat of battle.* **8.** *Slang.* coercive pressure: *to put the heat on someone.* **9.** a single division of a race or other contest. **10.** the period of sexual receptiveness in animals, esp. females. —*v.t., v.i.* **11.** to make or become hot or warm. **12.** to make or become excited emotionally. —*Saying.* **13. If you can't stand the heat, get out of the kitchen,** don't stay around if you can't handle stress: a saying popularized by President Harry Truman.

heat′ed, *adj.* excited or angry; impassioned. **—heat′ed•ly,** *adv.*

heat′er, *n.* an apparatus for heating, as one for heating the air in a room.

heath (hēth), *n.* **1.** a tract of open and uncultivated land. **2.** any of various shrubs common on such land.

hea•then (hē′thən), *n., pl.* **-thens, -then,** *adj.* —*n.* **1.** an unconverted individual of a people that do not acknowledge the God of the Bible or Koran. **2.** an irreligious or uncivilized person. —*adj.* **3.** pagan. **4.** irreligious or uncivilized. **—hea′then•ish,** *adj.*

heath•er (heth′ər), *n.* any of various heaths of England and Scotland, having small pinkish purple flowers.

heat′ light′ning, *n.* lightning too distant for thunder to be heard, seen on summer evenings.

heat′stroke′, *n.* a condition of headache, fever, etc., caused by exposure to excessive heat.

heave (hēv), *v.,* **heaved** or (*esp. Naut.*) **hove; heav•ing;** *n.* —*v.t.* **1.** to lift with effort. **2.** to lift and throw with effort. **3.** to utter laboriously. **4.** to haul or pull on (a rope, cable, etc.). —*v.i.* **5.** to rise and fall rhythmically. **6.** to breathe with effort; pant. **7.** to vomit; retch. **8.** to swell or bulge. **9.** to pull or haul on a rope, cable, etc. **10.** *Naut.* to move in a certain direction or into a certain position: *The ship hove into sight.* **11. heave to,** *Naut.* to come to a halt. —*n.* **12.** an act or effort of heaving. **—heav′er,** *n.*

heav•en (hev′ən), *n.* **1.** the abode of God, the angels, and the spirits of the righteous after death. **2.** (*cap.*) God. **3.** Usu., **-ens.** the sky or firmament. **4.** a place or state of supreme happiness. **—heav′en•ly,** *adj.* **—heav′en•ward,** *adv., adj.*

Heav′enly Cit′y, *n.* NEW JERUSALEM.

heav•y (hev′ē), adj., **-i•er, -i•est,** n., pl. **-ies,** adv.
—adj. **1.** of great weight. **2.** of great amount or size: a heavy vote. **3.** of great force or intensity: heavy fighting. **4.** of more than the usual or average weight. **5.** of high specific gravity: a heavy metal. **6.** grave; serious. **7.** deep or intense: a heavy slumber. **8.** designating the more powerful types of weapons: heavy artillery. **9.** burdensome; oppressive. **10.** being as indicated to an unusual degree: a heavy sleeper. **11.** broad, thick, or coarse: heavy lines. **12.** depressed; sad: a heavy heart. **13.** ponderous or clumsy. **14.** overcast or cloudy. **15.** not easily digested. **16.** producing or refining basic materials, as steel or coal: heavy industry. —n. **17.** a theatrical character or role that is unsympathetic or villainous. **18.** Slang. a very important person. —adv. **19.** in a heavy manner. —Idiom. **20. heavy with child,** in a state of advanced pregnancy. —heav′i•ly, adv. —heav′i•ness, n.

heav′y-du′ty, adj. made to withstand great strain or use.

heav′y-hand′ed, adj. **1.** clumsy; graceless. **2.** oppressive; harsh.

heav′y-heart′ed, adj. sorrowful; melancholy.

heav′y met′al, n. highly amplified, often harsh rock music with a heavy beat.

heav′y•set′, adj. stocky; stout.

heav′y•weight′, n. **1.** a professional boxer weighing more than 175 lb. (79.4 kg). **2.** a powerful or important person, company, etc.

Heb or **Heb., 1.** Hebrew. **2.** Bible. Hebrews.

He•bra•ic (hi brā′ik), adj. of or characteristic of the Hebrews or their culture. —**He•bra•ism** (hē′brā iz′əm, -brē-), n.

He•brew (hē′brōō), n. **1.** a member of any of a group of Semitic peoples who claimed descent from Abraham, Isaac, and Jacob. **2.** the Semitic language of the ancient Hebrews, revived as a vernacular in the 20th century. —adj. **3.** of the Hebrews or their language.

He′brews, n. a book of the New Testament.

Heb•ri•des (heb′ri dēz′), n.pl. a group of islands off the W coast of Scotland.

He•bron (hē′brən), n. an ancient city of Palestine, formerly in W Jordan; occupied by Israel 1967–97; since 1997 under Palestinian self-rule.

heck (hek), interj. a mild expression of annoyance, disgust, etc.

heck•le (hek′əl), v.t., **-led, -ling.** to harass (a public speaker or performer) with impertinent questions or gibes. —**heck′ler,** n.

hec•tare (hek′târ), n. a unit of surface or land measure equal to 10,000 square meters (2.471 acres).

hec•tic (hek′tik), adj. **1.** characterized by confusion, excitement, or hurried activity. **2.** feverish or flushed. —**hec′ti•cal•ly,** adv.

hecto-, a combining form meaning hundred (hectogram).

hec•tor (hek′tər), v.t. **1.** to harass or urge by bullying. —v.i. **2.** to act in a bullying way. —n. **3.** a bully.

Hec•tor (hek′tər), n. the eldest son of Priam and greatest Trojan hero in the Trojan War, in the course of which he was killed by Achilles.

he′d (hēd; unstressed ēd), **1.** contraction of he had. **2.** contraction of he would.

hedge (hej), n., v., **hedged, hedg•ing.** —n. **1.** a dense row of bushes or small trees forming a fence or boundary. **2.** any barrier or boundary. **3.** an act or means of hedging. —v.t. **4.** to surround or obstruct with or as if with a hedge. **5.** to mitigate a possible loss by counterbalancing (one's bets, investments, etc.). —v.i. **6.** to avoid commitment. —**hedg′er,** n.

hedge′hog′, n. **1.** an Old World insect-eating mammal with spiny hairs on the back and sides. **2.** the American porcupine.

he•don•ism (hēd′n iz′əm), n. devotion to pleasure and self-gratification as a way of life. —**he′don•ist,** n. —**he′don•is′tic,** adj.

heed (hēd), v.t., v.i. **1.** to give careful attention (to). —n. **2.** careful attention (usu. with give or take). —**heed′ful,** adj. —**heed′less,** adj. —**heed′less•ly,** adv. —**heed′less•ness,** n.

hee•haw (hē′hô′), n. **1.** the braying sound made by a donkey. —v.i. **2.** to bray.

heel¹ (hēl), n. **1.** the back part of the foot, below the ankle. **2.** the part of a stocking, shoe, etc., covering this part. **3.** a solid raised base attached to the back of the sole of a shoe. **4.** something resembling a heel in position or shape. —v.t. **5.** to furnish with heels. **6.** to follow closely. —v.i. **7.** (of a dog) to follow at one's heels on command. —Idiom. **8. down at (the) heel(s),** dressed shabbily. **9. kick up one's heels,** to have a lively time. **10. on** or **upon the heels of,** closely following.

heel² (hēl), v.i., v.t. to lean or cause to lean to one side, as a ship.

heel³ (hēl), n. a dishonorable or irresponsible person.

heeled (hēld), adj. provided with money: well-heeled.

heft (heft), n. **1.** weight; heaviness. **2.** significance; importance. —v.t. **3.** to test the weight of by lifting.

heft′y, adj., **-i•er, -i•est. 1.** heavy; weighty. **2.** big and strong; powerful; muscular. **3.** notably large or substantial. —**heft′i•ness,** n.

he•gem•o•ny (hi jem′ə nē, hej′ə mō′-), n., pl. **-nies.** leadership or domination, esp. of one nation over others.

He•gi•ra (hi jī′rə, hej′ər ə), n., pl. **-ras. 1.** (sometimes l.c.) HIJRA. **2.** (l.c.) Also, **hejira.** any flight or journey to a more desirable or congenial place.

Hei•del•berg (hīd′l bûrg′), n. a city in SW Germany: university, founded 1386. 127,500.

heif•er (hef′ər), n. a young cow that has not produced a calf.

Hei•fetz (hī′fits), n. **Ja•scha** (yä′shə), 1901–87, U.S. violinist, born in Russia.

height (hīt), n. **1.** extent or distance upward. **2.** the distance between the lowest and highest points of a person standing upright. **3.** great altitude or elevation. **4.** Often, **heights.** a high place; hill or mountain. **5.** the highest or most intense point: the height of pleasure.

height′en, v.t., v.i. **1.** to make or become higher. **2.** to increase in degree or amount.

Heim′lich maneu′ver (hīm′lik), n. a procedure to aid a choking victim by applying sudden pressure to the victim's upper abdomen to force an object from the windpipe.

hei•nous (hā′nəs), adj. utterly reprehensible or evil. —**hei′nous•ly,** adv. —**hei′nous•ness,** n.

heir (âr), n. **1.** a person who inherits or has a right to inherit the property, title, etc., of another.

heir′ appar′ent, n., pl. **heirs apparent.** an heir whose right cannot be taken away, provided he or she survives the ancestor.

heir′ess, n. a female heir, esp. to great wealth.

heir′loom′, n. a family possession handed down from generation to generation.

heist (hīst), n. Slang. **1.** a robbery. —v.t. **2.** to rob.

held (held), v. pt. and pp. of HOLD¹.

Hel•e•na (hel′ə nə), n. the capital of Montana. 23,938.

Hel′en of Troy′, n. the beautiful wife of Menelaus, the king of Sparta: her abduction by Paris caused the Trojan War.

hel•i•cal (hel′i kəl, hē′li-), adj. having the form of a helix.

hel•i•cop•ter (hel′i kop′tər, hē′li-), n. **1.** an aircraft that is lifted and sustained in the air horizontally by rotating blades turning on vertical axes. —v.i., v.t. **2.** to fly in a helicopter. [< F hélicoptère < Gk hélix spiral + pterón wing]

he•li•o•cen•tric (hē′lē ō sen′trik), adj. having or representing the sun as a center. —**he′li•o•cen•tric′i•ty** (-tris′i tē), n.

He•li•op•o•lis (hē′lē op′ə lis), n. Biblical name, **On.** an ancient ruined city in N Egypt, on the Nile delta.

he•li•o•trope (hē′lē ə trōp′), n. **1.** any of numerous plants cultivated for their small, fragrant, purple flowers. **2.** a light purple color.

hel·i·port (hel′ə pôrt′, hē′lə-), n. a takeoff and landing place for helicopters.

he·li·um (hē′lē əm), n. an inert, gaseous element present in natural gas, used in balloons and dirigibles. Symbol: He; at. wt.: 4.0026; at. no.: 2. [< NL < Gk hēlios the sun]

he·lix (hē′liks), n., pl. **hel·i·ces** (hel′ə sēz′), **he·lix·es.** a spiral.

hell (hel), n. **1.** the place or state of punishment of the wicked after death. **2.** any place, state, or cause of torment or misery.

he'll (hēl; unstressed ēl, hil, il), contraction of he will.

hell′bent′, adj. **1.** recklessly determined. **2.** going at terrific speed.

hell′cat′, n. a bad-tempered, spiteful woman.

hel·le·bore (hel′ə bôr′), n. any of various poisonous plants of the buttercup or lily family.

Hel·len·ic (he len′ik, -lē′nik), adj. **1.** of the ancient Greeks or their language, culture, thought, etc. **2.** GREEK (def. 1). —**Hel·len·ism** (hel′ə niz′əm), n. —**Hel′len·ist,** n.

Hel·len·is·tic (hel′ə nis′tik), adj. of Greek civilization after the death of Alexander the Great.

Hel·ler (hel′ər), n. **Joseph,** born 1923, U.S. novelist.

hel·lion (hel′yən), n. a troublesome or rowdy person.

hell′ish, adj. **1.** of or like hell; extremely unpleasant. **2.** devilishly bad; fiendish. —**hell′ish·ly,** adv.

Hell·man (hel′mən), n. **Lillian Florence,** 1905–84, U.S. playwright.

hel·lo (he lō′, hə-, hel′ō), interj. **1.** an exclamation of greeting. **2.** an exclamation used derisively to question the comprehension, intelligence, or sense of the person being addressed.

helm (helm), n. **1.** a wheel or tiller by which a ship is steered. **2.** the place or post of control.

hel·met (hel′mit), n. any of various forms of protective, rigid head covering worn by soldiers, football players, etc.

helms·man (helmz′mən), n., pl. **-men.** a person who steers a ship.

hel·ot (hel′ət, hē′lət), n. a serf or slave.

help (help), v.t. **1.** to provide what is necessary to accomplish a task or satisfy a need. **2.** to rescue. **3.** to facilitate or promote. **4.** to be useful to. **5.** to refrain from: I can't help teasing him. **6.** to prevent: The disagreement could not be helped. **7.** to remedy. **8.** to serve or wait on (a customer). —v.i. **9.** to give aid; be of service. **10. help out,** to assist, as during a time of need. —n. **11.** the act of helping. **12.** one that helps. **13.** a hired helper or helpers. **14.** relief or remedy. —**Idiom. 15. cannot** or **can't help but,** to be unable to refrain from or avoid; be obliged to: Still, you can't help but admire her. **16. help oneself to, a.** to serve oneself with. **b.** to take without asking permission. —**Proverb. 17. God helps those who help themselves,** one must make every effort to accomplish things on one's own. —**help′er,** n. —**Usage.** CANNOT HELP BUT has been condemned by some as ungrammatical, but it is so common in all types of speech and writing that it must be characterized as standard.

help′ful, adj. giving help. —**help′ful·ly,** adv. —**help′ful·ness,** n.

help′ing, n. a portion of food served to a person at one time.

help′less, adj. **1.** unable to help oneself. **2.** without aid or protection. **3.** deprived of strength or power. —**help′less·ly,** adv. —**help′less·ness,** n.

help′mate′, n. a companion and helper, esp. a spouse.

help′meet′, n. HELPMATE.

Hel·sin·ki (hel′sing kē), n. the capital of Finland. 490,034.

hel·ter-skel·ter (hel′tər skel′tər), adv. **1.** in headlong and disorderly haste. **2.** in a haphazard manner. —adj. **3.** disorderly.

helve (helv), n. the handle of an ax or the like.

Hel·ve·tia (hel vē′shə), n. Latin name of SWITZERLAND. —**Hel·ve′tian,** adj., n.

Hel·wys (hel′wis), n. **Thomas,** 1550–1616, English religious leader, founder of the first English Baptist church.

hem¹ (hem), v., **hemmed, hem·ming,** n. —v.t. **1.** to fold back and sew down the edge of (cloth, a garment, etc.). **2.** to enclose or confine: hemmed in by enemies. —n. **3.** an edge made by hemming. —**hem′-mer,** n.

hem² (hem), interj., n., v., **hemmed, hem·ming.** —interj., n. **1.** a sound resembling a clearing of the throat, used esp. to attract attention. —v.i. **2.** to make this sound. —**Idiom. 3. hem and haw,** to hesitate while speaking so as to avoid giving a direct answer.

he′-man′, n., pl. **-men.** Informal. a strong, tough, virile man.

he·ma·tite (hē′mə tīt′), n. a mineral, ferric oxide, that is the principal ore of iron.

he′ma·tol′o·gy (-tol′ə jē), n. the study of the nature and diseases of the blood and of blood-forming organs. —**he′ma·to·log′ic** (-tl oj′ik), **he′ma·to·log′i·cal,** adj. —**he′ma·tol′o·gist,** n.

he′ma·to′ma (-tō′mə), n., pl. **-mas, -ma·ta** (-mə tə). a circumscribed collection of blood, usu. clotted, in a tissue or organ.

heme (hēm), n. a deep-red, iron-containing pigment obtained from hemoglobin.

hemi-, a combining form meaning half (hemisphere).

Hem·ing·way (hem′ing wā′), n. **Ernest (Miller),** 1899–1961, U.S. novelist, short-story writer, and journalist.

hem·i·sphere (hem′i sfēr′), n. **1.** (often cap.) half of the terrestrial globe or celestial sphere, esp. one of the halves into which the earth is divided: Eastern Hemisphere. **2.** a half of a sphere. —**hem′i·spher′ic** (-sfer′ik), **hem′i·spher′i·cal,** adj.

hem′line′, n. the bottom edge of a coat, skirt, etc.

hem·lock (hem′lok′), n. **1.** a poisonous plant of the parsley family. **2.** a poisonous drink made from this plant. **3.** any of several tall coniferous trees of the pine family. **4.** the wood of a hemlock tree.

he·mo·glo·bin (hē′mə glō′bin, hem′ə-), n. a compound in red blood cells that transports oxygen from the lungs to the tissues.

he·mo·phil·i·a (hē′mə fil′ē ə), n. a genetic disorder, chiefly in males, characterized by prolonged or excessive bleeding. —**he′mo·phil′i·ac′** (-ak′), n.

hem·or·rhage (hem′ər ij), n., v., **-rhaged, -rhag·ing.** —n. **1.** a profuse discharge of blood. —v.i. **2.** to bleed profusely. —**hem′or·rhag′ic** (-ə raj′ik), adj.

hem·or·rhoid (hem′ə roid′), n. Usu. **-rhoids.** a usu. painful varicose vein in the region of the anal sphincter.

he·mo·stat (hē′mə stat′), n. an instrument or agent used to stop hemorrhage.

hemp (hemp), n. **1.** a tall, coarse Asian plant. **2.** its tough fiber, used for making rope, coarse fabric, etc. **3.** an intoxicating drug, as marijuana or hashish, prepared from the hemp plant. —**hemp′en,** adj.

hem′stitch′, v.t. **1.** to sew along a border from which threads have been drawn out, stitching the cross threads into little groups. —n. **2.** the stitch used in hemstitching.

hen (hen), n. **1.** the female of the domestic fowl. **2.** the female of any bird.

hence (hens), adv. **1.** as an inference from this fact; therefore. **2.** from this time: a month hence. **3.** from this source or origin. **4.** from this place; away.

hence·forth (hens′fôrth′, hens′fôrth′), adv. from now on.

hench·man (hench′mən), n., pl. **-men. 1.** an unscrupulous and ruthless subordinate. **2.** a political supporter, esp. one motivated by the hope of personal gain.

hen·na (hen′ə), n., pl. **-nas,** v., **-naed, -na·ing.** —n. **1.** an Asian shrub or small tree. **2.** a hair dye made from its leaves. **3.** a reddish brown color. —v.t. **4.** to tint or dye with henna.

hen'peck', *v.t.* to nag or regularly find fault with (one's husband).

Hen•ry¹ (hen'rē), *n.* **1. O.**, pen name of William Sidney PORTER. **2. Patrick**, 1736–99, American patriot and orator.

Hen•ry² (hen'rē), *n.* **1. Henry II**, 1133–89, king of England 1154–89: first king of the Plantagenets. **2. Henry IV**, **a.** (*Bolingbroke*) (*"Henry of Lancaster"*) 1367–1413, king of England 1399–1413. **b.** (*"Henry of Navarre"*) 1553–1610, king of France 1589–1610: first of the Bourbon kings. **3. Henry V**, 1387–1422, king of England 1413–22. **4. Henry VII**, (*Henry Tudor*) 1457–1509, king of England 1485–1509: first king of the house of Tudor. **5. Henry VIII**, (*"Defender of the Faith"*) 1491–1547, king of England 1509–47.

hep (hep), *adj.* Older Slang. HIP³.

hep•a•rin (hep'ə rin), *n.* a substance present in animal tissues, esp. the liver, that has anticoagulant properties.

he•pat•ic (hi pat'ik), *adj.* of or acting on the liver.

hep•a•ti•tis (hep'ə tī'tis), *n.* inflammation of the liver.

Heph•zi•bah (hef'zə bə, -sə-), *n.* **1.** the wife of Hezekiah and the mother of Manasseh. II Kings 21:1. **2.** a name applied to Jerusalem. Isa. 62:4.

Hep•ta•teuch (hep'tə tōōk', -tyōōk'), *n.* the first seven books of the Old Testament.

hep•tath•lon (hep tath'lən, -lon), *n.* an athletic contest for women comprising seven different track-and-field events.

her (hûr; *unstressed* hər, ər), *pron.* **1.** the objective case of SHE, used as a direct or indirect object. **2.** a form of the possessive case of SHE, used as an attributive adjective.

He•ra (hēr'ə, her'ə), *n.* an ancient Greek goddess, the wife and sister of Zeus.

her•ald (her'əld), *n.* **1.** a royal or official messenger. **2.** a forerunner; harbinger. **3.** one that proclaims or announces. —*v.t.* **4.** to announce; proclaim. **5.** to usher in.

he•ral•dic (he ral'dik, hə-), *adj.* of heralds or heraldry.

her•ald•ry (her'əl drē), *n.* **1.** the art of blazoning and granting armorial bearings, tracing genealogies, deciding precedence, etc. **2.** ceremonial splendor; pageantry.

herb (ûrb; *esp. Brit.* hûrb), *n.* **1.** a flowering plant whose stem above ground does not become woody. **2.** such a plant valued for its medicinal properties, flavor, or scent. —**her•ba•ceous** (hûr bā'shəs, ûr-), *adj.* —**herb•al** (ûr'bəl, hûr'-), *adj.*

herb•age (ûr'bij, hûr'-), *n.* **1.** nonwoody vegetation. **2.** the succulent parts of herbaceous plants, esp. when used for grazing.

herb•al•ist (hûr'bə list, ûr'-), *n.* a person who collects or deals in herbs.

Her•bert (hûr'bərt), *n.* **1. George**, 1593–1633, English cleric and poet. **2. Matthew**, 1662–1714, English clergyman and Bible commentator. **3. Victor**, 1859–1924, U.S. composer.

herb•i•cide (hûr'bə sīd', ûr'-), *n.* a substance or preparation for killing plants, esp. weeds. —**her'bi•cid'al**, *adj.*

her•bi•vore (hûr'bə vôr', ûr'-), *n.* a herbivorous animal.

her•biv•o•rous (hûr biv'ər əs, ûr-), *adj.* feeding on plants.

her•cu•le•an (hûr'kyə lē'ən, hûr kyōō'lē-), *adj.* **1.** requiring extraordinary strength or exertion. **2.** of enormous strength, courage, or size.

Her•cu•les (hûr'kyə lēz'), *n.* a hero of classical myth who possessed exceptional strength.

herd (hûrd), *n.* **1.** a number of animals feeding, traveling, or kept together. **2.** a crowd; mob. —*v.i., v.t.* **3.** to move or assemble as a herd. —**herd'er**, *n.*

herds'man, *n., pl.* **-men.** the keeper of a herd.

here (hēr), *adv.* **1.** in or at this place: *Put the pen here.* **2.** to or toward this place: *Come here.* **3.** at this point: *Here the speaker paused.* **4.** in the present life or existence. —*n.* **5.** this place or point: *It's a long*

way *from here.* —**Idiom. 6. neither here nor there**, without relevance. —**Usage.** See THERE.

here'a•bout' or **-a•bouts'**, *adv.* in this neighborhood.

here•af'ter, *adv.* **1.** in the future; from now on. **2.** in the life or world to come. —*n.* **3.** a life after death. **4.** the future.

here•by', *adv.* by means of this.

he•red•i•tar•y (hə red'i ter'ē), *adj.* **1.** passing, or capable of passing, genetically from parent to offspring. **2.** existing by reason of feelings or opinions held by predecessors: *a hereditary enemy.* **3.** holding title, rights, etc., by inheritance.

he•red'i•ty, *n.* **1.** the passing on of characters or traits from parents to offspring through genes. **2.** the genetic characters so transmitted.

here•in', *adv.* **1.** in or into this place. **2.** in view of this.

here•of', *adv.* **1.** of this. **2.** concerning this.

her•e•sy (her'ə sē), *n., pl.* **-sies. 1.** religious opinion at variance with the orthodox doctrine. **2.** any belief at variance with established beliefs, customs, etc.

her•e•tic (her'i tik), *n.* **1.** a professed believer who maintains religious opinions contrary to those of his or her church. **2.** anyone who does not conform to an established view, doctrine, etc. —**he•ret'i•cal**, *adj.*

here•to', *adv.* to this matter, document, etc.

here'to•fore', *adv.* before this time; until now.

here'up•on', *adv.* **1.** upon or on this. **2.** immediately following this.

here•with', *adv.* **1.** along with this. **2.** by means of this.

her•it•a•ble (her'i tə bəl), *adj.* capable of being inherited.

her•it•age (her'i tij), *n.* **1.** something that comes or belongs to one by reason of birth: *a heritage of democracy.* **2.** property, esp. land, that is passed on by inheritance.

her•maph•ro•dite (hûr maf'rə dīt'), *n.* an animal or plant in which reproductive organs of both sexes are present. —**her•maph'ro•dit'ic** (-dit'ik), *adj.*

Her•mes (hûr'mēz), *n.* an ancient Greek god, the herald and messenger of the other gods.

her•met•ic (hûr met'ik) also **-i•cal**, *adj.* made airtight by fusion or sealing. —**her•met'i•cal•ly**, *adv.*

her•mit (hûr'mit), *n.* a person living in seclusion; recluse.

her'mit•age (-mi tij), *n.* **1.** the habitation of a hermit. **2.** any secluded place of residence.

her•ni•a (hûr'nē ə), *n., pl.* **-ni•as, -ni•ae** (-nē ē'). the protrusion of an organ or tissue through an opening in its surrounding walls. —**her'ni•al**, *adj.*

her'ni•ate' (-āt'), *v.i.* **-at•ed, -at•ing.** to protrude so as to constitute a hernia. —**her'ni•a'tion**, *n.*

he•ro (hēr'ō), *n., pl.* **-roes;** for 4 also **-ros. 1.** a man who has performed brave deeds. **2.** any person admired for noble qualities or special achievements. **3.** the principal male character in a story, play, etc. **4.** HERO SANDWICH.

Her•od (her'əd), *n.* (*"the Great"*) 73?–4 B.C., king of Judea 37–4.

Her'od A•grip'pa (ə grip'ə), *n.* (*Julius Agrippa*) c10 B.C.–A.D. 44, king of Judea 41–44 (grandson of Herod the Great).

Her'od An'ti•pas (an'ti pas'), *n.* died after A.D. 39, ruler of Galilee A.D. 4–39.

He•ro•di•as (hə rō'dē əs), *n.* the second wife of Herod Antipas; mother of Salome.

He•rod•o•tus (hə rod'ə təs), *n.* 484?–425? B.C., Greek historian.

he•ro•ic (hi rō'ik), *adj.* **1.** of or characteristic of a hero; brave, daring, or noble. **2.** dealing with the deeds of heroes. —*n.* **heroics, 3.** flamboyant or extravagant language or behavior. **4.** heroic action. —**he•ro'i•cal•ly**, *adv.*

her•o•in (her'ō in), *n.* a white crystalline powder, derived from morphine, that is narcotic and addictive.

her•o•ine (her'ō in), *n.* **1.** a woman admired for her brave deeds, noble qualities, or special achievements. **2.** the principal female character in a story, play, etc.

her•o•ism (her′ō iz′əm), *n.* **1.** heroic qualities. **2.** heroic conduct.

her•on (her′ən), *n.* any of various long-legged, long-necked wading birds, usu. having a spearlike bill.

he′ro sand′wich, *n.* a large sandwich consisting of a small loaf of bread filled with cold cuts, cheese, etc.

her•pes (hûr′pēz), *n.* any of several viral diseases characterized by eruption of blisters on the skin or mucous membranes.

her′pes sim′plex (sim′pleks), *n.* a recurrent form of herpes that produces blisters on the mouth, lips, eyes, or genitalia.

her′pes zos′ter (zos′tər), *n.* SHINGLES.

her•pe•tol•o•gy (hûr′pi tol′ə jē), *n.* the branch of zoology dealing with reptiles and amphibians. —**her′pe•to•log′ic** (-tl oj′ik), **her′pe•to•log′i•cal,** *adj.* —**her′pe•tol′o•gist,** *n.*

Herr (heR; *Eng.* hâr), *n., pl.* **Her•ren** (heR′ən; *Eng.* hâr′ən). the German term of address for a man, corresponding to *Mr.* or *sir.*

her•ring (her′ing), *n., pl.* **-rings, -ring.** an important food fish of the N Atlantic.

her′ring•bone′, *n.* **1.** a pattern consisting of adjoining vertical rows of slanting lines, any two contiguous lines forming a V or inverted V. **2.** a fabric with this pattern.

hers (hûrz), *pron.* **1.** a form of the possessive case of SHE, used as a predicate adjective: *The red umbrella is hers.* **2.** that or those belonging to her: *Hers are the red ones.*

her•self′, *pron.* **1.** the reflexive form of HER: *She supports herself.* **2.** an intensive form of SHE: *She herself wrote the letter.* **3.** her normal self: *After some rest, she will be herself again.*

hertz (hûrts), *n., pl.* **hertz, hertz•es.** a unit of frequency equal to one cycle per second.

Her•zl (hûrt′səl, hârt′-), *n.* **Theodor,** 1860–1904, Hungarian-born Austrian Jewish writer and Zionist.

he's (hēz; *unstressed* ēz), **1.** contraction of *he is.* **2.** contraction of *he has.*

He•si•od (hē′sē əd, hes′ē-), *n.* fl. 8th century B.C., Greek poet.

hes•i•tant (hez′i tənt), *adj.* hesitating, undecided or doubtful. —**hes′i•tan•cy,** *n.* —**hes′i•tant•ly,** *adv.*

hes′i•tate′ (-tāt′), *v.i.* **-tat•ed, -tat•ing.** **1.** to wait to act because of fear, indecision, or disinclination. **2.** to be unwilling; have reservations. **3.** to pause. **4.** to falter in speaking. —**hes′i•tat′ing•ly,** *adv.* —**hes′i•ta′tion,** *n.*

Hes•se (hes′ə), *n.* **Hermann,** 1877–1962, German writer.

hetero-, a combining form meaning different or other (*heterodox*).

het•er•o•dox (het′ər ə doks′), *adj.* not in accordance with established doctrines, esp. in theology. —**het′er•o•dox′y,** *n., pl.* **-dox•ies.**

het•er•o•ge′ne•ous (-jē′nē əs), *adj.* **1.** different in kind. **2.** composed of parts of different kinds. —**het′er•o•ge•ne′i•ty** (-ə rō jə nē′i tē), **het′er•o•ge′ne•ous•ness,** *n.* —**het′er•o•ge′ne•ous•ly,** *adv.*

het•er•o•sex′u•al, *adj.* **1.** of or having sexual desire for persons of the opposite sex. **2.** pertaining to the opposite sex or to both sexes. —*n.* **3.** a heterosexual person. —**het′er•o•sex′u•al′i•ty,** *n.*

heu•ris•tic (hyŏŏ ris′tik; *often* yŏŏ-), *adj.* **1.** serving to indicate or point out. **2.** encouraging a person to learn, understand, etc., on his or her own, as by experimenting: *a heuristic teaching method.*

hew (hyōō; *often* yōō), *v.,* **hewed, hewed** or **hewn, hew•ing.** —*v.t.* **1.** to strike forcibly with a cutting instrument. **2.** to make or shape with or as if with cutting blows. —*v.i.* **3.** to conform: *to hew to the party line.* —**hew′er,** *n.*

hew′ers of wood′ and draw′ers of wa′ter, *n.pl.* performers of menial tasks. Josh. 9:21.

hex (heks), *v.t.* **1.** to practice witchcraft on. **2.** to bring bad luck to. —*n.* **3.** a spell; charm; jinx.

hexa-, a combining form meaning six (*hexagon*).

hex•a•em•er•on (hek′sə em′ə ron′), *n.* the Biblical account of the six days of creation. Gen. 1. —**hex′a•em′er•ic,** *adj.*

hex•a•gon (hek′sə gon′, -gən), *n.* a polygon having six angles and six sides. —**hex•ag′o•nal** (-sag′ə nl), *adj.*

hex•am•e•ter (hek sam′i tər), *n.* a line of verse having six metrical feet.

Hex•a•teuch (hek′sə tōōk′, -tyōōk′), *n.* the first six books of the Old Testament. —**Hex′a•teuch′al,** *adj.*

hey (hā), *interj.* an exclamation used to call attention or to express pleasure, surprise, etc.

hey•day (hā′dā′), *n.* the period of greatest vigor, success, etc.; prime.

Hez•bol•lah or **Hiz•bal•lah** (*Arabic.* кнes′bä lä′), *n.* a radical Shi'ite Muslim organization engaged in guerrilla warfare against Israel.

Hez•e•ki•ah (hez′ə kī′ə), *n.* a king of Judah of the 7th and 8th centuries B.C. II Kings 18.

Hf, *Chem. Symbol.* hafnium.

Hg, *Chem. Symbol.* mercury. [< NL *hydrargyrum*]

hgt., height.

hgwy., highway.

HHS, Department of Health and Human Services.

hi (hī), *interj. Informal.* an exclamation of greeting.

HI, Hawaii.

Hi•a•le•ah (hī′ə lē′ə), *n.* a city in SE Florida. 194,120.

hi•a•tus (hī ā′təs), *n., pl.* **-tus•es, -tus.** a break or interruption in the continuity of a work, series, action, etc.

hi•ba•chi (hi bä′chē), *n., pl.* **-chis.** a small charcoal brazier covered with a grill. [< Japn: fire pot]

hi•ber•nate (hī′bər nāt′), *v.i.* **-nat•ed, -nat•ing.** to spend the winter in a dormant condition, as certain animals. —**hi′ber•na′tion,** *n.* —**hi′ber•na′tor,** *n.*

hi•bis•cus (hī bis′kəs, hi-), *n., pl.* **-cus•es.** a woody plant of the mallow family, with large, showy flowers.

hic•cup or **-cough** (hik′up, -əp), *n., v.,* **-cuped** or **-cupped** or **-coughed, -cup•ing** or **cup•ping** or **-cough•ing.** —*n.* **1.** a quick inhalation that follows a spasm of the diaphragm and is checked by closure of the glottis, producing a short, sharp sound. **2.** Usu., **-cups.** the condition of having such spasms. —*v.i.* **3.** to make the sound of a hiccup.

hick (hik), *n.* an unsophisticated, provincial person.

hick•ey (hik′ē), *n., pl.* **-eys. 1.** *Slang.* a reddish mark left on the skin by a passionate kiss. **2.** any device or gadget whose name is unknown.

Hick•ok (hik′ok), *n.* **James Butler** ("*Wild Bill*"), 1837–76, U.S. frontiersman.

hick•o•ry (hik′ə rē), *n., pl.* **-ries. 1.** a North American tree of the walnut family, bearing edible nuts. **2.** the wood of this tree.

Hicks (hiks), *n.* **Edward,** 1780–1849, U.S. painter.

hide[1] (hīd), *v.,* **hid, hid•den** or **hid, hid•ing.** —*v.t.* **1.** to conceal from sight. **2.** to obstruct the view of. **3.** to keep secret. —*v.i.* **4.** to conceal oneself. **5.** to lie concealed. —*Proverb.* **6. Don't hide your light under a bushel,** don't conceal your talents. Matt. 5:15. —**hid′er,** *n.*

hide[2] (hīd), *n.* the raw or dressed pelt or skin of a large animal.

hide′a•way′, *n.* a place to which a person can retreat.

hide′bound′, *adj.* narrow and rigid in opinion.

hid•e•ous (hid′ē əs), *adj.* **1.** horrible or frightful to the senses. **2.** shocking to the moral sense. —**hid′e•ous•ly,** *adv.* —**hid′e•ous•ness,** *n.*

hide′out′, *n.* a safe place for hiding, esp. from the law.

hie (hī), *v.i., v.t.,* **hied, hie•ing** or **hy•ing.** to hasten (oneself).

hi•er•ar•chy (hī′ə rär′kē), *n., pl.* **-chies. 1.** any system of persons or things ranked one above another. **2.** government by ecclesiastical rulers. —**hi′er•ar′chi•cal, hi′er•ar′chic,** *adj.* —**hi′er•ar′chi•cal•ly,** *adv.*

hi•er•o•glyph•ic (hī′ər ə glif′ik, hī′rə-), *adj.* **1.** of or designating a pictographic script, as that of the ancient Egyptians, in which many of the symbols are conventionalized pictures of the things represented. —*n.* **2.** a hieroglyphic symbol. **3. hieroglyphics,** symbols that are difficult to decipher.

hi-fi (hī′fī′), *n., pl.* **-fis. 1.** high fidelity. **2.** a phonograph, radio, etc., possessing high fidelity.

high (hī), *adj.* and *adv.,* **-er, -est,** *n.* —*adj.* **1.** lofty; tall. **2.** having a specified height. **3.** situated above the ground or some base. **4.** greater than usual or normal in degree, force, etc.: *high speed.* **5.** expensive; costly. **6.** exalted, as in rank or station. **7.** elevated in pitch: *high notes.* **8.** extending to or performed from an elevation: *a high dive.* **9.** important; grave: *high crimes.* **10.** elated: *high spirits.* **11.** luxurious: *high living.* **12.** advanced to the utmost extent: *high tide.* **13.** haughty or arrogant. —*adv.* **14.** at or to a high point, place, or level. **15.** luxuriously; extravagantly. —*n.* **16.** an automotive transmission gear producing the highest speed. **17.** an atmospheric pressure system characterized by high pressure at its center. **18.** a high point, place, or level. —*Idiom.* **19. high and low,** everywhere. **20. high on,** enthusiastic about. **21. on high, a.** above. **b.** in heaven. —**high′ly,** *adv.*

high′ball′, *n.* a drink of whiskey mixed with club soda or ginger ale.

high′born′, *adj.* of high rank by birth.

high′boy′, *n.* a tall chest of drawers on legs.

high′brow′, *n.* **1.** a person who has or affects superior intellectual or cultural interests and tastes. —*adj.* **2.** of or characteristic of a highbrow.

high′chair′, *n.* a chair with very long legs, for use by a baby during meals.

high′-defini′tion tel′evision, *n.* a television system having a high number of scanning lines per frame, producing a sharper image and greater picture detail. *Abbr.:* HDTV

high′er-up′, *n. Informal.* a person in a position of high authority in an organization.

Highest, the, *n.* God. Luke 1:32,35.

high•fa•lu•tin (hī′fə loot′n), *adj. Informal.* pompous; pretentious.

high′ fidel′ity, *n.* sound reproduction over the full range of audible frequencies with little distortion of the original signal.

high′-five′, *n.* a gesture of greeting, triumph, etc., in which one person slaps the upraised palm of another.

high′-flown′, *adj.* **1.** extravagant in aims, pretensions, etc. **2.** pretentiously lofty.

high′ fre′quency, *n.* the range of frequencies in the radio spectrum between 3 and 30 megahertz.

High′ Ger′man, *n.* the group of Germanic dialects spoken in central and S Germany, Switzerland, and Austria.

high′-hand′ed, *adj.* overbearing and arbitrary; presumptuous. —**high′-hand′ed•ly,** *adv.* —**high′-hand′ed•ness,** *n.*

high′-hat′, *v.,* **-hat•ted, -hat•ting,** *adj. Informal.* —*v.t.* **1.** to snub or treat condescendingly. —*adj.* **2.** snobbish; haughty.

High′ Hol′idays, *n.pl.* the Jewish holidays of Rosh Hashanah and Yom Kippur. Also called **High′ Ho′ly Days′.**

high′land, *n.* **1.** an elevated region. **2. highlands,** a mountainous or hilly region of a country.

High′lands, *n.* **the,** a mountainous region in N Scotland. —**High′land•er,** *n.*

high′-lev′el, *adj.* **1.** of or involving participants having high status. **2.** having high status. **3.** (of a programming language) based on a vocabulary of Englishlike statements for writing program code.

high′light′, *v.t.* **1.** to make prominent. **2.** to create highlights in. —*n.* **3.** an important or conspicuous event, scene, etc. **4.** an area of contrasting lightness or brightness. —**high′light′er,** *n.*

high′-mind′ed, *adj.* having or showing exalted principles or feelings; noble. —**high′-mind′ed•ly,** *adv.* —**high′-mind′ed•ness,** *n.*

high′ness (-nis), *n.* **1.** the quality or state of being high. **2.** (*cap.*) a title given to members of a royal family (usu. prec. by *His, Your,* etc.).

high′-oc′cupancy ve′hicle, *n.* See HOV.

high′-pres′sure, *adj., v.,* **-sured, -sur•ing.** —*adj.* **1.** involving a pressure above the normal. **2.** involving a high degree of stress. **3.** persistent; aggressive. —*v.t.* **4.** to use aggressively forceful tactics on.

high′-rise′, *adj.* **1.** (of a building) having a comparatively large number of stories. —*n.* **2.** a high-rise building.

high′road′, *n.* **1.** *Chiefly Brit.* HIGHWAY. **2.** an easy or certain course. **3.** a moral or ethical course.

high′ school′, *n.* a school consisting of grades 9 or 10 through 12.

high′ sea′, *n.* Usu., **high seas.** the open ocean, esp. beyond the territorial waters of a country.

high′-sound′ing, *adj.* having an impressive or pretentious sound; grand: *high-sounding titles.*

high′-spir′ited, *adj.* **1.** characterized by energetic enthusiasm. **2.** boldly courageous.

high′-strung′, *adj.* being highly sensitive or nervous.

high′tail′, *v.i. Informal.* to leave rapidly.

high′-tech′, *n.* **1.** high technology. **2.** a style of interior design using industrial and commercial fixtures, materials, etc. —*adj.* **3.** of or suggesting high-tech.

high′ technol′ogy, *n.* technology that uses highly sophisticated equipment and advanced engineering techniques.

high′-ten′sion, *adj.* subjected to or operating under relatively high voltage: *high-tension wire.*

high′-test′, *adj.* (of gasoline) boiling at a relatively low temperature.

high′ tide′, *n.* the tide at its highest level of elevation.

high′ time′, *n.* the appropriate time or past the appropriate time.

high′ top′, *n.* a sneaker that covers the ankle.

high′way′, *n.* **1.** a main road, esp. one between towns or cities. **2.** any public road.

high′way′man, *n., pl.* **-men.** a holdup man who robbed travelers along a public road.

hi•jack (hī′jak′), *v.t.* **1.** to seize (an airplane or other vehicle in transit) by threat or force. **2.** to steal (cargo) from a vehicle in transit. —**hi′jack′er,** *n.*

Hij•ra (hij′rə), *n.* (*sometimes l.c.*) *Islam.* **1.** the flight of Muhammad from Mecca to Medina to escape persecution A.D. 622: regarded as the beginning of the Muslim Era. **2.** the Muslim Era itself. Also, **Hegira, Hij′rah.**

hike (hīk), *v.,* **hiked, hik•ing,** *n.* —*v.i.* **1.** to walk a great distance, esp. through rural areas. —*v.t.* **2.** to move or raise with a jerk: *to hike up one's socks.* **3.** to increase, often sharply: *to hike the price of milk.* —*n.* **4.** a long walk. **5.** a sharp increase. —**hik′er,** *n.*

hi•lar•i•ous (hi lâr′ē əs, -lar′-, hī-), *adj.* **1.** very funny. **2.** boisterously merry. —**hi•lar′i•ous•ly,** *adv.* —**hi•lar′i•ty,** *n.*

hill (hil), *n.* **1.** a natural elevation of the earth's surface, smaller than a mountain. **2.** an artificial heap, pile, or mound. —**hill′y,** *adj.,* **-i•er, -i•est.**

hill′bil′ly (-bil′ē), *n., pl.* **-lies.** *Informal.* a person from a backwoods area. [*hill + Billy,* familiar form of William]

Hil•lel (hil′el, -āl, hi lāl′), *n.* c60 B.C.–A.D. 9?, Palestinian rabbi and interpreter of Biblical law.

hill•ock (hil′ək), *n.* a small hill.

hill′side′, *n.* the side of a hill.

hill′top′, *n.* the top of a hill.

hilt (hilt), *n.* the handle of a sword, dagger, or tool.

him (him), *pron.* the objective case of HE, used as a direct or indirect object.

Him•a•la•yas (him′ə lā′əz, hi mäl′yəz), *n.pl.* **the,** a mountain range on the border between India and Tibet. —**Him′a•lay′an,** *adj.*

him•self (him self′; *medially often* im-), *pron.* **1.** the reflexive form of HIM: *He cut himself.* **2.** an intensive form of HE: *He himself told me.* **3.** his normal self: *He is himself again.*

hind¹ (hīnd), *adj.* situated in the rear; posterior.

hind² (hīnd), *n., pl.* **hinds, hind.** the female of the European red deer.

Hind., 1. Hindu. **2.** Hindustan.

Hin•de•mith (hin′də mith, -mit), *n.* **Paul,** 1895–1963, U.S. composer, born in Germany.

Hin•den•burg (hin′dən bûrg′), *n.* a giant German zeppelin that crashed and burned near Lakehurst, N.J., in 1937.

hin•der¹ (hin′dər), *v.t.* **1.** to cause delay or difficulty in; hamper; impede. **2.** to prevent from doing or happening. **—hin′der•er,** *n.*

hind•er² (hīn′dər), *adj.* situated at the rear; posterior.

Hin•di (hin′dē), *n.* a language of N India, having equal status with English as an official language throughout India.

hind′most′ (hīnd′-), *adj.* nearest the rear.

hind′quar′ter, *n.* **1.** hindquarters, the rear part of a quadruped. **2.** the posterior end of a halved carcass, as of a steer.

hin•drance (hin′drəns), *n.* the act of hindering or state of being hindered.

hind′sight′, *n.* recognition of the nature or requirements of a situation or event after its occurrence.

Hin•du (hin′dōo), *n., pl.* **-dus,** *adj.* **—n. 1.** an adherent of Hinduism. **—adj. 2.** of Hindus or Hinduism.

Hin′du•ism, *n.* the dominant religion of India.

Hin′du•stan′ (-stän′), *n.* **1.** a region of N India. **2.** the predominantly Hindu areas of India.

Hin′du•sta′ni (-stä′nē, -stan′ē), *n.* a standardized form of the Hindi language based on the speech of the Delhi region.

Hines (hīnz), *n.* **Earl** (*"Fatha"*), 1905–83, U.S. jazz pianist.

hinge (hinj), *n., v.,* **hinged, hing•ing. —n. 1.** a jointed device on which a door, lid, etc., moves. **2.** a natural anatomical joint, as that of the knee. **—v.i. 3.** to be contingent: *Everything hinges on her decision.* **—v.t. 4.** to attach by or as if by a hinge.

hint (hint), *n.* **1.** an indirect, covert, or helpful suggestion. **2.** a very slight amount. **—v.t., v.i. 3.** to give a hint (of). **—hint′er,** *n.*

hin•ter•land (hin′tər land′), *n.* **1.** the remote area of a country. **2.** the land lying behind a coastal region.

hip¹ (hip), *n.* the projecting part on each side of the body surrounding the hip joint.

hip² (hip), *n.* the fleshy fruit of a rose.

hip³ (hip), *adj.,* **hip•per, hip•pest.** *Slang.* **1.** familiar with the latest ideas, styles, etc. **—Idiom. 2. hip to,** knowledgeable about.

hip′bone′, *n.* either of the two bones forming the sides of the pelvis.

hip′-hop′, *n. Slang.* the popular subculture of usu. black urban youth, esp. as characterized by rap music.

hip′ joint′, *n.* the joint between the head of the femur and the hipbone.

hip•pie (hip′ē), *n., pl.* **-pies.** a young person of the 1960s who rejected established social values and wore long hair and unconventional clothes.

hip•po (hip′ō), *n., pl.* **-pos.** a hippopotamus.

Hip•poc•ra•tes (hi pok′rə tēz′), *n.* (*"Father of Medicine"*) c460–c377 B.C., Greek physician. **—Hip•po•crat•ic** (hip′ə krat′ik), *adj.*

Hip′pocrat′ic oath′, *n.* an oath embodying the duties and obligations of physicians, usu. taken by those about to enter upon the practice of medicine.

hip•po•drome (hip′ə drōm′), *n.* an arena for equestrian and other spectacles.

hip•po•pot•a•mus (hip′ə pot′ə məs), *n., pl.* **-mus•es, -mi** (-mī′). a large African mammal with a thick body and short legs, living in and alongside rivers. [< L < Gk *hippopótamos* river horse]

hire (hīr), *v.,* **hired, hir•ing.** *—v.t.* **1.** to engage the services of (a person) for a fee. **2.** to engage the temporary use of (a thing) at a set price. **—n. 3.** the act of hiring or condition of being hired. **4.** the price or compensation paid in hiring.

hire′ling (-ling), *n.* a person who works only for pay, esp. in a menial or boring job.

Hi•ro•shi•ma (hēr′ō shē′mə, hi rō′shə mə), *n.* a seaport on SW Honshu, in SW Japan: first military use of atomic bomb Aug. 6, 1945. 1,034,000.

hir•sute (hûr′sōot, hûr sōot′), *adj.* hairy; shaggy. **—hir′sute•ness,** *n.*

his (hiz; *unstressed* iz), *pron.* **1.** the possessive form of HE, used as an attributive or predicate adjective. **2.** that or those belonging to him: *His is the blue one.*

His•pan•ic (hi span′ik), *adj.* **1.** of Spain or Spanish-speaking countries. **2.** of Hispanics. **—n. 3.** a U.S. citizen or resident of Spanish or Latin-American descent.

His•pan•io•la (his′pən yō′lə), *n.* an island in the West Indies.

hiss (his), *v.i.* **1.** to make a sound like that of the letter *s* when prolonged. **2.** to express disapproval by making this sound. **—v.t. 3.** to express disapproval of by hissing. **—n. 4.** a hissing sound.

Hiss (his), *n.* **Alger,** 1904–96, U.S. public official, accused of espionage 1948 and imprisoned for perjury 1950–54.

his•ta•mine (his′tə mēn′, -min), *n.* an organic compound released from human tissues during allergic reactions.

his•tol•o•gy (hi stol′ə jē), *n.* the branch of biology dealing with the study of tissues. **—his•tol′o•gist,** *n.*

his•to•ri•an (hi stôr′ē ən), *n.* **1.** an authority on history. **2.** a writer of history.

his•tor′ic (-stôr′ik, -stor′-), *adj.* **1.** well-known or important in history. **2.** HISTORICAL.

his•tor′i•cal, *adj.* **1.** of or concerned with history. **2.** based on history or documented material from the past. **3.** HISTORIC. **—his•tor′i•cal•ly,** *adv.*

his•to•ric•i•ty (his′tə ris′i tē), *n.* historical authenticity.

his•to•ri•og•ra•phy (hi stôr′ē og′rə fē), *n., pl.* **-phies.** the body of techniques and principles of historical research. **—his•to′ri•og′ra•pher,** *n.*

his•to•ry (his′tə rē, -trē), *n., pl.* **-ries. 1.** the branch of knowledge dealing with past events. **2.** a systematic narrative of past events as relating to a particular people, country, etc. **3.** the record of past events. **4.** a past notable for its important events: *a ship with a history.*

his•tri•on•ic (his′trē on′ik), *adj.* **1.** overly dramatic in behavior or speech. **2.** of actors or acting. **—his′tri•on′i•cal•ly,** *adv.*

his′tri•on′ics, *n.* (*used with a sing. or pl. v.*) **1.** overly dramatic behavior or speech. **2.** dramatic representation.

hit (hit), *v.,* **hit, hit•ting. —v.t. 1.** to deal a blow to. **2.** to come against with an impact. **3.** to reach with a missile, weapon, etc. **4.** *Baseball.* to make (a base hit). **5.** to drive or propel by a stroke: *to hit a ball.* **6.** to have a marked effect on: *to be hit hard by inflation.* **7.** to reach (a specified level or amount): *Prices hit a new high.* **8.** to come upon: *to hit the right answer.* **9.** *Informal.* to begin to travel on: *Let's hit the road.* **—v.i. 10.** to strike; deal a blow. **11.** to come into collision. **12.** to come or light: *to hit on a new method.* **—n. 13.** a collision. **14.** a stroke that reaches an object; blow. **15.** BASE HIT. **16.** a success. **—Idiom. 17. hit it off,** to get along. **—hit′ter,** *n.*

hit′-and-run′, *adj.* fleeing the scene of an accident one has caused, esp. a vehicular accident.

hitch¹ (hich), *v.t.* **1.** to fasten or harness by means of a hook, rope, etc. **2.** to raise with jerks: *to hitch up one's trousers.* **3.** *Slang.* to unite in marriage. **—v.i. 4.** to become fastened. **5.** to move jerkily. **—n. 6.** any of various knots or loops made to attach a rope to something. **7.** a period of military service. **8.** an unexpected difficulty, delay, etc. **9.** a jerk or pull. **10.** a fastening; catch.

hitch² (hich), *v.i. Informal.* to hitchhike. **—hitch′er,** *n.*

Hitch•cock (hich′kok), *n.* **Sir Alfred (Joseph),** 1899–1980, U.S. film director, born in England.

hitch′hike′, *v.i.,* **-hiked, -hik•ing.** to travel by soliciting rides from passing vehicles. **—hitch′hik′er,** *n.*

hith•er (hiдth′ər), *adv.* **1.** to or toward this place. —*adj.* **2.** being on this side.

hith′er•to′, *adv.* until now.

Hit•ler (hit′lər), *n.* **Adolf,** 1889–1945, Nazi dictator of Germany 1934–45.

hit′-or-miss′, *adj.* careless; haphazard.

HIV, *n.* a retrovirus that invades and inactivates T cells and is a cause of AIDS. [*h(uman) i(mmunodeficiency) v(irus)*]

hive (hīv), *n., v.,* **hived, hiv•ing.** —*n.* **1.** a shelter for a colony of honeybees. **2.** the bees inhabiting a hive. **3.** a place swarming with busy occupants. **4.** a swarming multitude. —*v.t.* **5.** to gather into a hive. —*v.i.* **6.** (of bees) to enter a hive.

hives (hīvz), *n.* (*used with a sing. or pl. v.*) a transient eruption of large, itchy wheals on the skin.

HMO, *pl.* **HMOs, HMO′s.** health maintenance organization: a prepaid health plan in which subscribers receive comprehensive health services from member physicians, usually in a central facility.

HMS or **H.M.S.,** Her (or His) Majesty's Ship.

Ho, *Chem. Symbol.* holmium.

hoa•gy or **-gie** (hō′gē), *n., pl.* **-gies.** HERO SANDWICH.

hoard (hôrd), *n.* **1.** a supply that is hidden or carefully guarded for future use. —*v.t., v.i.* **2.** to accumulate a hoard (of). —**hoard′er,** *n.*

hoar′frost′ (hôr′frôst′, -frost′), *n.* FROST (def. 2).

hoarse (hôrs), *adj.,* **hoars•er, hoars•est. 1.** having a low and harsh vocal tone; husky. **2.** having a raucous voice. —**hoarse′ly,** *adv.* —**hoarse′ness,** *n.*

hoar•y (hôr′ē), *adj.,* **-i•er, -i•est. 1.** gray or white with age. **2.** ancient or venerable. —**hoar′i•ness,** *n.*

hoax (hōks), *n.* **1.** something intended to deceive or defraud. —*v.t.* **2.** to deceive by a hoax. —**hoax′er,** *n.*

hob (hob), *n.* **1.** a hobgoblin or elf. —*Idiom.* **2. play hob with,** to do mischief or harm to.

hob•ble (hob′əl), *v.,* **-bled, -bling,** *n.* —*v.i.* **1.** to walk lamely. —*v.t.* **2.** to cause to limp. **3.** to fasten together the legs of (a horse, mule, etc.) by a short rope to prevent free motion. **4.** to impede. —*n.* **5.** a limp. **6.** a rope, strap, etc., used to hobble an animal. —**hob′bler,** *n.*

hob•by (hob′ē), *n., pl.* **-bies. 1.** an activity pursued for pleasure, not as an occupation. **2.** a child's hobbyhorse. —**hob′by•ist,** *n.*

hob′by•horse′, *n.* **1.** a stick with a horse's head, or a rocking horse, ridden by children. **2.** a pet idea or project.

hob′gob′lin, *n.* **1.** something causing superstitious fear. **2.** a mischievous goblin.

hob′nail′, *n.* a large-headed nail for protecting the soles of heavy boots and shoes. —**hob′nailed′,** *adj.*

hob′nob′ (-nob′), *v.i.,* **-nobbed, -nob•bing.** to associate on very friendly terms.

ho•bo (hō′bō), *n., pl.* **-bos, -boes. 1.** a tramp or vagrant. **2.** a migratory worker.

Ho Chi Minh (hō′ chē′ min′), *n.* 1890?–1969, president of North Vietnam 1954–69.

Ho′ Chi′ Minh′ Cit′y, *n.* a seaport in S Vietnam. 4,000,000. Formerly, **Saigon.**

hock¹ (hok), *n.* the joint in the hind leg of a horse, cow, etc., corresponding to the ankle in humans.

hock² (hok), *v.t.* **1.** to pawn. —*n.* **2.** the state of being held as security. **3.** the condition of owing.

hock•ey (hok′ē), *n.* **1.** ICE HOCKEY. **2.** FIELD HOCKEY.

Hock•ney (hok′nē), *n.* **David,** born 1937, British artist.

hock′shop′, *n.* PAWNSHOP.

ho•cus-po•cus (hō′kəs pō′kəs), *n.* **1.** meaningless words used in conjuring. **2.** a sleight of hand. **3.** mysterious talk for covering up a deception. [pseudo-Latin rhyming formula used by magicians]

hod (hod), *n.* **1.** a portable trough for carrying bricks, mortar, etc., on the shoulder. **2.** a coal scuttle.

hodge•podge (hoj′poj′), *n.* a heterogeneous mixture; jumble.

Hodg′kin's disease′ (hoj′kinz), *n.* a malignant disorder characterized by enlargement of the lymph nodes and spleen.

hoe (hō), *n., v.,* **hoed, hoe•ing.** —*n.* **1.** a long-

handled implement with a thin, flat blade set transversely, used in breaking up the soil and in weeding. —*v.t., v.i.* **2.** to scrape or weed with a hoe. —**ho′er,** *n.*

hoe′down′, *n.* **1.** a community party featuring folk and square dances. **2.** the music typical of a hoedown.

hog (hôg, hog), *n., v.,* **hogged, hog•ging.** —*n.* **1.** any swine, esp. a domesticated adult swine raised for market. **2.** a selfish, gluttonous, or filthy person. —*v.t.* **3.** to take more than one's share of. —*Idiom.* **4. go (the) whole hog,** to do something thoroughly. **5. live high off (or on) the hog,** to live prosperously. —**hog′ger,** *n.* —**hog′gish,** *adj.* —**hog′gish•ly,** *adv.*

ho•gan (hō′gôn, -gən), *n.* a Navajo dwelling constructed of logs and sticks covered with mud or sod.

hogs′head′, *n.* **1.** a large cask holding from 63 to 140 gallons (238 to 530 liters). **2.** a liquid measure, esp. one equivalent to 63 gallons (238 liters).

hog′tie′, *v.t.,* **-tied, -ty•ing. 1.** to tie (an animal) with all four feet together. **2.** to hamper; thwart.

hog′wash′, *n.* **1.** refuse given to hogs; swill. **2.** nonsense; bunk.

hog′-wild′, *adj.* wildly enthusiastic.

hoi pol•loi (hoi′ pə loi′), *n.* the common people; the masses. [< Gk: the many]

hoist (hoist), *v.t.* **1.** to raise or lift, esp. by some mechanical appliance. —*n.* **2.** an apparatus for hoisting, as a crane. **3.** the act of hoisting; a lift.

hoke (hōk), *v.t.,* **hoked, hok•ing.** to alter so as to give a deceptively improved quality (usu. fol. by *up*).

hok′ey, *adj.,* **hok•i•er, hok•i•est. 1.** cloyingly sentimental; mawkish. **2.** contrived in an obvious way.

ho•kum (hō′kəm), *n.* **1.** utter nonsense; bunkum. **2.** elements of low comedy or stale melodrama introduced into a play or story.

Hol•bein (hōl′bīn), *n.* **1. Hans** ("*the Elder*"), 1465?–1524, German painter. **2.** his son, **Hans** ("*the Younger*"), 1497?–1543, German painter, chiefly in England.

hold¹ (hōld), *v.,* **held, hold•ing,** *n.* —*v.t.* **1.** to have in the hand; grasp. **2.** to bear or support. **3.** to keep in a specified state or relation: *He held them spellbound.* **4.** to conduct: *to hold a meeting.* **5.** to restrain. **6.** to possess or occupy: *to hold office.* **7.** to contain. **8.** to make accountable: *held her to her word.* **9.** to keep in the mind. **10.** to regard; consider: *They held him responsible.* **11.** to keep forcibly: *Enemy forces held the hill.* **12.** to decide legally. —*v.i.* **13.** to remain in a specified state or relation: *Hold still.* **14.** to maintain a grasp: *The clamp held.* **15.** to agree; sympathize: *She doesn't hold with new ideas.* **16.** to remain faithful: *to hold to one's purpose.* **17.** to remain valid: *The rule still holds.* **18. hold forth,** to speak at great length. **19. ~ out, a.** to offer. **b.** to last. **c.** to refuse to yield. **d.** *Informal.* to withhold something expected. **20. ~ over, a.** to keep for future consideration. **b.** to keep beyond the arranged period. **21. ~ up, a.** to support. **b.** to delay. **c.** to persevere. **d.** to display. **e.** to rob at gunpoint. —*n.* **22.** a grasp; grip. **23.** something to grasp, esp. for support. **24.** something that holds something else. **25.** a controlling force. **26.** a prison cell. —*Idiom.* **27. hold the fort,** to maintain a place or situation until someone else returns. **28. hold the line,** to maintain or restrain. **29. hold your horses,** to wait; be patient. **30. no holds barred,** without limits, rules, or restraints. —**hold′er,** *n.*

hold² (hōld), *n.* **1.** the cargo space in the hull of a vessel. **2.** the cargo compartment of an aircraft.

hold′ing, *n.* **1.** a section of land leased, esp. for agricultural purposes. **2.** Often, **-ings.** legally owned property, as securities.

hold′o′ver, *n.* a person or thing remaining from a former period.

hold′up′, *n.* **1.** a robbery at gunpoint. **2.** a delay.

hole (hōl), *n., v.,* **holed, hol•ing.** —*n.* **1.** an opening through something; gap. **2.** a hollow place in a solid mass; cavity. **3.** the burrow of an animal. **4.** a cramped or shabby place. **5.** an embarrassing predicament. **6.** a fault; flaw: *serious holes in your reason-*

ing. **7.** *Golf.* **a.** the cup in a green into which the ball is to be played. **b.** a part of a course leading to it. —*v.t., v.i.* **8.** to make a hole (in). **9. hole up, a.** to hibernate, as in a cave. **b.** to hide from or as if from pursuers. —*Idiom.* **10. in the hole,** in debt.

-holic, var. of -AHOLIC.

Hol•i•day (hol′i dā′), *n.* **Billie** (*"Lady Day"*), 1915–59, U.S. jazz singer.

ho′li•er-than-thou′ (hō′lē ər), *adj.* obnoxiously pious; sanctimonious.

ho′li•ness, *n.* **1.** the quality or state of being holy. **2.** (*cap.*) a title of the pope (usu. prec. by *His* or *Your*).

ho′liness church′, *n.* one of several Christian groups emphasizing that a state of sinlessness, sanctification, or holiness follows conversion and is needed for salvation.

ho•lis•tic (hō lis′tik), *adj.* **1.** pertaining to the theory that whole entities are more than the sum of their parts. **2.** of or using therapies that consider one's total physical and psychological state in the treatment of disease.

Hol•land (hol′ənd), *n.* the Netherlands. —**Hol′-land•er,** *n.*

hol′lan•daise sauce′ (hol′ən dāz′), *n.* a sauce of egg yolks, butter, lemon juice, and seasonings.

hol•ler (hol′ər), *v.i., v.t.* **1.** to shout; yell. —*n.* **2.** a shout.

hol•low (hol′ō), *adj.,* -**er, -est,** *n., v.* —*adj.* **1.** having a space inside; empty. **2.** having a concavity. **3.** sunken: *hollow cheeks.* **4.** not resonant: *a hollow voice.* **5.** meaningless: *a hollow victory.* **6.** insincere: *hollow compliments.* —*n.* **7.** a hole; cavity. **8.** a valley. —*v.t., v.i.* **9.** to make or become hollow. —**hol′-low•ness,** *n.*

hol•ly (hol′ē), *n., pl.* -**lies.** a tree or shrub with glossy leaves and red berries.

hol′ly•hock′ (-hok′, -hôk′), *n.* a tall Asian plant with a long cluster of showy, colored flowers.

Hol′ly•wood′, *n.* **1.** the NW part of Los Angeles, Calif.: center of the U.S. motion-picture industry. **2.** a city in SE Florida. 124,992.

Holmes (hōmz, hōlmz), *n.* **Oliver Wendell,** 1841–1935, U.S. jurist.

hol•mi•um (hōl′mē əm), *n.* a malleable rare-earth element. *Symbol:* Ho; *at. wt.:* 164.930; *at. no.:* 67.

hol•o•caust (hol′ə kôst′, hō′lə-), *n.* **1.** a great devastation, esp. by fire. **2. the Holocaust,** the systematic mass slaughter of European Jews by the Nazis.

Hol•o•cene (hol′ə sēn′, hō′lə-), *adj.* **1.** of the Recent epoch. —*n.* **2.** the Recent epoch.

Hol•o•fer•nes (hol′ə fûr′nez, hō′lə-), *n.* (in the Book of Judith) a general of Nebuchadnezzar killed by Judith.

hol•o•gram (hol′ə gram′, hō′lə-), *n.* a three-dimensional picture produced by recording the patterns of interference formed by a split laser beam on photographic film.

hol•o•graph (hol′ə graf′, -gräf′, hō′lə-), *n.* a document wholly written by the person in whose name it appears. —**hol′o•graph′ic,** *adj.*

ho•log•ra•phy (hə log′rə fē), *n.* the technique of making holograms.

Hol•stein (hōl′stīn, -stēn), *n.* a breed of large black-and-white dairy cattle.

hol•ster (hōl′stər), *n.* a case for a firearm, attached to a belt, shoulder sling, etc.

ho•ly (hō′lē), *adj.,* -**li•er, -li•est. 1.** recognized as sacred by religious use or authority: *holy ground.* **2.** spiritually pure: *a holy love.* **3.** venerated as sacred: *a holy relic.*

Ho′ly Ark′, *n.* a cabinet in a synagogue in the wall that faces toward Jerusalem, for keeping the Torah.

Ho′ly Cit′y, *n.* (*sometimes l.c.*) **1.** a city regarded as particularly sacred by the adherents of a religious faith. **2.** heaven. **3.** Jerusalem. Isa. 51:1.

Ho′ly Commun′ion, *n.* a Christian sacrament in which the Last Supper of Jesus is commemorated with consecrated bread and wine.

Ho′ly Fa′ther, *n.* a title of the pope.

Ho′ly Ghost′, *n.* the third person of the Trinity. Also called **Holy Spirit.**

Ho′ly Grail′ or **ho′ly grail′,** *n.* GRAIL.

Ho′ly Land′, *n.* PALESTINE.

Ho′ly Moth′er, *n.* honorific title of the Virgin Mary.

ho′ly of ho′lies, *n.* **1.** a place of special sacredness. **2.** the innermost chamber of the Biblical tabernacle and the Temple in Jerusalem, in which the ark of the covenant was kept. **3.** *Eastern Ch.* the bema. [trans. of LL *sanctum sanctōrum* (Vulgate), trans. of Gk *tò hágion tôn hagíon,* itself trans. of Heb *qōdesh haqqodāshīm*]

Ho′ly One′, *n.* **1.** God. Isa. 10:20. **2.** Jesus Christ, esp. as the Messiah. Mark 1:24; Acts 3:14.

ho′ly pla′ces, *n.pl.* the places in the Holy Land that are associated with Christ.

Ho′ly Ro′man Em′pire, *n.* a Germanic empire located chiefly in central Europe from A.D. 962 to 1806.

Ho′ly Rood′, *n.* the cross on which Jesus died.

Ho′ly See′, *n.* the see of the pope.

Ho′ly Sep′ulcher, *n.* the sepulcher in which the body of Jesus lay between His burial and His resurrection.

Ho′ly Spir′it, *n.* the third person of the Trinity.

Ho′ly Thurs′day, *n.* MAUNDY THURSDAY.

ho′ly war′, *n.* **1.** a war waged for what is proclaimed to be a holy purpose. **2.** any disagreement or argument between fanatical proponents of differing beliefs, opinions, etc.: *a holy war about welfare reform.*

ho′ly wa′ter, *n.* water blessed by a priest.

hom•age (hom′ij, om′-), *n.* respect, honor, or reverence given or shown: *to pay homage to one's forebears.*

hom•burg (hom′bûrg), *n.* a man's felt hat with a crown dented lengthwise and a slightly rolled brim.

home (hōm), *n., adj., adv., v.,* **homed, hom•ing.** —*n.* **1.** a house or other place of residence. **2.** the place in which one's domestic affections are centered. **3.** an institution for people with special needs: *a nursing home.* **4.** the place or region where something is native or most common. **5.** a person's native place or country. **6.** headquarters. —*adj.* **7.** of one's home. **8.** principal: *the home office.* —*adv.* **9.** to, toward, or at home. **10.** deep: *to the heart: The truth struck home.* **11.** to the point aimed at: *He drove the nail home.* —*v.i.* **12.** to go or return home. **13.** to proceed toward a specified point: *The missile homed in on the target.* —*Idiom.* **14. at home, a.** in one's home. **b.** at ease. **15. home free,** in a position assured of success or out of jeopardy. —**home′less,** *adj.*

home′bod′y, *n., pl.* -**bod•ies.** a person who prefers staying at home.

home′boy′, *n.* **1.** a person from the same locality

as oneself. **2.** *Slang.* a close friend or fellow gang member.

home'-care', *adj.* pertaining to care, esp. medical care, given or received at home.

home' econom'ics, *n.* the study of home management, including nutrition, household economics, etc.

home'land', *n.* one's native land.

home'ly, *adj.*, **-li•er**, **-li•est**. **1.** unattractive; plain. **2.** simple; unpretentious. —**home'li•ness**, *n.*

home'made', *adj.* made at home, locally, or on the premises.

home'mak'er, *n.* a person who manages a household.

ho•me•op•a•thy (hō'mē op'ə thē), *n.* a method of treating disease by minute doses of drugs that in a healthy person would produce symptoms similar to those of the disease. —**ho'me•o•path'ic** (-ə path'ik), *adj.*

ho•me•o•sta•sis (hō'mē ə stā'sis), *n.* the tendency of a system, esp. the physiological system of higher animals, to maintain internal stability. —**ho'me•o•stat'ic** (-stat'ik), *adj.*

home' page', *n.* *Computers.* the initial page of a Web site.

home' plate', *n.* the base in baseball at which the batter stands and which a runner must reach safely to score a run.

Ho•mer (hō'mər), *n.* **1.** 9th-century B.C. Greek epic poet. **2. Winslow,** 1836–1910, U.S. artist. —**Ho•mer'ic** (-mer'ik), *adj.*

home' run', *n.* a hit in baseball allowing the batter to circle the bases and score a run.

home•school•ing (hōm'skōō'ling), *n.* the practice of teaching one's own children at home.

home'sick', *adj.* longing for home while away from it. —**home'sick'ness**, *n.*

home'spun', *adj.* **1.** spun at home. **2.** made of homespun cloth. **3.** plain; simple. —*n.* **4.** a plain-weave cloth made of homespun yarn. **5.** any cloth of similar appearance.

home'stead' (-sted, -stid), *n.* a family dwelling with its land and buildings.

Home'stead Act', *n.* a special act of Congress (1862) that made public lands in the West available to settlers without payment, to be used as farms.

home'stretch', *n.* **1.** the straight part of a racetrack from the last turn to the finish line. **2.** the final phase of any endeavor.

Home', Sweet' Home', an American song by John Howard Payne.

home'ward (-wərd), *adv.* **1.** Also, **home'wards.** toward home. —*adj.* **2.** directed toward home.

home'work', *n.* **1.** schoolwork assigned to be done outside the classroom. **2.** thorough preparatory study of a subject.

hom'ey, *adj.*, **hom•i•er**, **hom•i•est**. comfortably informal and inviting; cozy. —**hom'ey•ness**, *n.*

hom•i•cide (hom'ə sīd', hō'mə-), *n.* **1.** the killing of one human being by another. **2.** a person who kills another. —**hom'i•cid'al**, *adj.*

hom•i•ly (hom'ə lē), *n.*, *pl.* **-lies. 1.** a sermon. **2.** an admonitory or moralizing discourse. —**hom'i•let'ic** (-let'ik), *adj.*

hom'ing pi'geon (hō'ming), *n.* a pigeon trained to carry messages and return home.

hom•i•nid (hom'ə nid), *n.* a member of a family of modern or extinct bipedal primates that includes humans.

hom•i•ny (hom'ə nē), *n.* hulled corn from which the bran and germ have been removed.

homo-, a combining form meaning same or identical (*homogeneous*).

ho•mo•ge•ne•ous (hō'mə jē'nē əs), *adj.* **1.** composed of parts all of the same kind. **2.** of the same kind or nature. —**ho'mo•ge•ne'i•ty** (-jə nē'i tē), *n.* —**ho'mo•ge•ne'ous•ly**, *adv.*

ho•mog•e•nize (hə moj'ə nīz', hō-), *v.t.*, **-nized, -niz•ing. 1.** to make homogeneous. **2.** to emulsify the fat globules in (milk), causing them to be distributed throughout. —**ho•mog'e•ni•za'tion**, *n.*

hom•o•graph (hom'ə graf', -gräf', hō'mə-), *n.* a word of the same written form as another but of different meaning and origin, whether pronounced the same way or not.

ho•mol•o•gous (hə mol'ə gəs, hō-), *adj.* corresponding, as in relative position or structure.

hom•o•nym (hom'ə nim), *n.* **1.** HOMOPHONE. **2.** a word the same as another in sound and spelling but different in meaning. **3.** HOMOGRAPH.

ho•mo•pho•bi•a (hō'mə fō'bē ə), *n.* unreasoning fear or hatred of homosexuals and homosexuality.

hom•o•phone (hom'ə fōn', hō'mə-), *n.* a word pronounced the same as another but differing in meaning, whether spelled the same way or not.

Ho•mo sa•pi•ens (hō'mō sā'pē ənz), *n.* the species of bipedal primates to which modern humans belong.

ho•mo•sex•u•al (hō'mə sek'shōō əl), *adj.* **1.** attracted sexually to members of one's own sex. —*n.* **2.** a homosexual person. —**ho'mo•sex'u•al'i•ty**, *n.*

Hon., 1. Honorable. **2.** Honorary.

Hon•du•ras (hon dŏŏr'əs, -dyŏŏr'-), *n.* a republic in NE Central America. 5,751,384. —**Hon•du'ran**, *adj.*, *n.*

hone (hōn), *n.*, *v.*, **honed, hon•ing.** —*n.* **1.** a whetstone for sharpening tools. —*v.t.* **2.** to sharpen on or as if on a hone. —**hon'er**, *n.*

hon•est (on'ist), *adj.* **1.** honorable in principles, intentions, and actions. **2.** gained fairly: *to earn an honest living.* **3.** sincere; frank: *an honest face.* **4.** truthful. —**hon'est•ly**, *adv.*

Hon'est Abe', *n.* epithet of Abraham Lincoln.

hon•es•ty (on'ə stē), *n.*, *pl.* **-ties. 1.** integrity; trustworthiness. **2.** truthfulness, sincerity, or frankness. **3.** freedom from deceit. **4.** a plant of the mustard family, having clusters of purple flowers and semitransparent satiny pods. —*Proverb.* **5. Honesty is the best policy,** deception or withholding the truth ultimately has no benefit.

hon•ey (hun'ē), *n.*, *pl.* **-eys. 1.** a sweet, viscid fluid produced by bees from the nectar collected from flowers. **2.** something sweet or delightful. **3.** *Informal.* sweetheart; darling. —*Proverb.* **4. You can catch more flies with honey than with vinegar,** pleasant words are more effective than harsh words. —**hon'eyed**, *adj.*

hon'ey•bee', *n.*, *pl.* **-bees.** any bee that collects and stores honey.

hon'ey•comb', *n.* **1.** a structure of hexagonal wax cells, formed by bees to store honey, pollen, and their eggs. **2.** anything resembling such a structure. —*adj.* **3.** having the appearance of a honeycomb. —*v.t.* **4.** to cause to be full of holes.

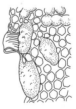

honeycomb

hon'ey•dew' mel'on, *n.* a winter melon with a pale greenish rind and light green flesh.

hon'ey•moon', *n.* **1.** a vacation taken by a newly married couple. **2.** any new relationship characterized by an initial period of harmony. —*v.i.* **3.** to spend one's honeymoon. —**hon'ey•moon'er**, *n.*

hon'ey•suck'le, *n.* an upright or climbing shrub cultivated for its fragrant flowers.

Hong Kong (hong' kong'), *n.* a former British dependent territory in SE China: reverted to Chinese sovereignty in 1997. 6,413,000.

Ho•ni•a•ra (hō'nē är'ə), *n.* the capital of the Solomon Islands, on N Guadalcanal. 26,000.

honk (hongk, hôngk), *n.* **1.** the cry of a goose. **2.**

any similar sound, as of an automobile horn. —*v.i., v.t.* **3.** to make or cause to make a honk. —**honk′er,** *n.*

honk•y-tonk (hong′kē tongk′, hông′kē tôngk′), *n.* **1.** a cheap, noisy nightclub. —*adj.* **2.** of or pertaining to music played on a tinny-sounding piano.

Hon•o•lu•lu (hon′ə lōō′lōō), *n.* the capital of Hawaii, on S Oahu. 385,881.

hon•or (on′ər), *n.* **1.** honesty or integrity in one's beliefs and actions. **2.** a source of credit or distinction. **3.** high respect. **4.** a token of respect: *the place of honor at the table.* **5.** high public esteem; glory. **6.** a privilege: *I have the honor of introducing this evening's speaker.* **7.** (*cap.*) a title of respect, as for judges (prec. by *His, Her,* or *Your*). **8.** chastity. —*v.t.* **9.** to hold in high respect. **10.** to treat with honor. **11.** to confer distinction upon. **12.** to accept or pay (a credit card, check, etc.). —*Idiom.* **13. do the honors,** to act as host. —*Proverb.* **14. Honor thy father and thy mother,** respect your parents: the Fifth Commandment. Ex. 20:12. Also, *esp. Brit.,* **hon′our.** —**hon′or•ee′,** *n.* —**hon′or•er,** *n.*

hon′or•a•ble, *adj.* **1.** characterized by principles of honor; upright. **2.** worthy of honor. **3.** bringing honor. —**hon′or•a•bly,** *adv.*

hon•o•rar•i•um (on′ə rȃr′ē əm), *n., pl.* **-rar•i•ums, -rar•i•a** (-rȃr′ē ə). a payment for professional services for which custom forbids a price to be set.

hon′or•ar′y (-rer′ē), *adj.* **1.** given for honor only: *an honorary degree.* **2.** holding a position conferred for honor only, without the usual compensation. —**hon′or•ar′i•ly** (-rȃr′ə lē), *adv.*

hon′or•if′ic (-rif′ik), *adj.* doing or conferring honor.

Hon•shu (hon′shōō), *n.* an island in central Japan: chief island of the country.

hood[1] (hŏŏd), *n.* **1.** a flexible covering for the head and neck, usu. attached to a coat. **2.** something resembling this. **3.** the part of an automobile body covering the engine. —**hood′ed,** *adj.*

hood[2] (hŏŏd, hōōd), *n. Slang.* a hoodlum.

Hood (hŏŏd), *n.* **1. Robin,** Robin Hood. **2. Mount,** a volcanic peak in N Oregon, in the Cascade Range. 11,253 ft. (3430 m).

-hood, a suffix meaning: state or condition (*childhood*); character or nature (*likelihood*); a body of persons of a particular class (*priesthood*).

hood•lum (hŏŏd′ləm, hōōd′-), *n.* **1.** a thug or gangster. **2.** a young street ruffian.

hoo•doo (hōō′dōō), *n., pl.* **-doos. 1.** voodoo. **2.** bad luck. **3.** a person or thing that brings bad luck.

hood•wink (hŏŏd′wingk′), *v.t.* to deceive or trick.

hoo•ey (hōō′ē), *n., interj. Informal.* nonsense; bunk.

hoof (hŏŏf, hōōf), *n., pl.* **hoofs** or **hooves,** *v.* —*n.* **1.** the horny covering protecting the ends of the digits or encasing the foot in certain animals, as the horse. **2.** the entire foot of a horse, donkey, etc. —*v.t. Slang.* to walk: *Let's hoof it.* —**hoofed,** *adj.*

hook (hŏŏk), *n.* **1.** a curved or angular piece of metal, etc., for catching, pulling, or suspending something. **2.** a fishhook. **3.** something having a sharp curve, bend, or angle at one end. **4.** the path described by a ball that curves in a direction opposite to the throwing hand. **5.** (in boxing) a short circular punch delivered with the elbow bent. —*v.t.* **6.** to seize, fasten, or catch hold of with or as if with a hook. **7.** *Slang.* to steal. —*v.i.* **8.** to become hooked. **9.** to curve or bend like a hook. **10. hook up,** to connect, as components of a machine. —*Idiom.* **11. by hook or by crook,** by any means whatsoever. **12. off the hook,** released from some difficulty.

hook•ah (hŏŏk′ə), *n.* a water pipe with a long flexible tube by which smoke is drawn through a jar of water and thus cooled.

hooked, *adj.* **1.** bent like a hook. **2.** made with a hook: *a hooked rug.* **3.** *Informal.* addicted to or obsessed with something. **4.** *Slang.* married.

Hook•er (hŏŏk′ər), *n.* **1. Joseph,** 1814–79, Union general in the U.S. Civil War. **2. Thomas,** 1586?–1647, English Puritan: founder of Connecticut.

hook′up′, *n.* an assembly and connection of parts

or apparatus into a circuit, network, machine, or system.

hook′worm′, *n.* a nematode worm, parasitic in the intestines.

hoo•li•gan (hōō′li gən), *n.* a hoodlum.

hoop (hōōp, hŏŏp), *n.* **1.** a rigid circular band, as of metal or wood, used esp. for holding together the staves of a barrel. **2.** a circular or ringlike object, part, or figure. —*v.t.* **3.** to fasten with or as if with a hoop.

hoop•la (hōōp′lä), *n. Informal.* **1.** commotion. **2.** sensational publicity.

hoop′ skirt′, *n.* a skirt made to stand out by a framework of flexible hoops.

hoo•ray (hŏŏ rā′), *interj., v.i., n.* hurrah.

hoose•gow (hōōs′gou), *n. Slang.* a jail. [< MexSp *juzgado* jail]

Hoo•sier (hōō′zhər), *n.* a native or inhabitant of Indiana.

hoot (hōōt), *v.i.* **1.** to shout in derision. **2.** to utter the cry characteristic of an owl. —*v.t.* **3.** to assail by hooting. —*n.* **4.** the cry of an owl. **5.** a shout of derision. —**hoot′er,** *n.*

hoot•en•an•ny (hōōt′n an′ē), *n., pl.* **-nies.** an informal concert at which folk singers perform.

Hoo•ver (hōō′vər), *n.* **Herbert (Clark),** 1874–1964, 31st president of the U.S. 1929–33.

hop[1] (hop), *v.,* **hopped, hop•ping,** *n.* —*v.i.* **1.** to make a short, bouncing leap. **2.** to leap on one foot. **3.** to make a short, quick trip. —*v.t.* **4.** to jump over. **5.** to board (a vehicle). —*n.* **6.** a short leap, esp. on one foot. **7.** a short trip, esp. by air. **8.** *Informal.* a dance.

hop[2] (hop), *n., v.,* **hopped, hop•ping.** —*n.* **1.** a twining plant of the hemp family. **2. hops,** its dried ripe cones, used in brewing, medicine, etc. —*v.* **hop up,** *Slang.* **3.** to excite. **4.** to add to the power of.

hope (hōp), *n., v.,* **hoped, hop•ing.** —*n.* **1.** the feeling that what is wanted can be had or that events will turn out well. **2.** a person or thing in which expectations are centered. **3.** something hoped for. —*v.t.* **4.** to look forward to with desire and reasonable confidence. **5.** to believe or trust: *I hope you will be happy.* —*v.i.* **6.** to have hope. —**hope′ful,** *adj.* —**hope′ful•ly,** *adv.* —**hope′ful•ness,** *n.* —**hope′less,** *adj.* —**hope′less•ly,** *adv.* —**hope′less•ness,** *n.*

Ho•pi (hō′pē), *n., pl.* **-pi, -pis.** a member of an American Indian people of NE Arizona.

hop•per (hop′ər), *n.* **1.** one that hops. **2.** any jumping insect. **3.** a bin in which loose material, as grain, is stored temporarily.

Hop′per, *n.* **1. Edward,** 1882–1967, U.S. painter. **2. Grace Murray,** 1906–92, U.S. naval officer and computer scientist.

hop′scotch′, *n.* a game in which a child hops around a diagram drawn on the ground to retrieve a small object.

Hor (hôr), *n.* **Mount,** the mountain where Aaron died and was buried. Num. 20:22–29; Deut. 32:50.

Hor•ace (hôr′is, hor′-), *n.* 65–8 b.c., Roman poet.

horde (hôrd), *n., v.,* **hord•ed, hord•ing.** —*n.* **1.** a large multitude; crowd. —*v.i.* **2.** to gather in a horde.

Ho•reb (hôr′eb, hōr′-), *n.* a mountain in the Bible sometimes identified with Mount Sinai. Ex. 3:1, 33:6.

hore•hound (hôr′hound′), *n.* **1.** a plant of the mint family containing a bitter juice. **2.** a lozenge flavored with horehound extract.

ho•ri•zon (hə rī′zən), *n.* **1.** the line that forms the apparent boundary between earth and sky. **2.** Usu. **-zons.** the scope of a person's interest, education, understanding, etc. [< L < Gk *horízōn (kýklos)* bounding (circle)]

hor•i•zon•tal (hôr′ə zon′tl, hor′-), *adj.* **1.** at right angles to the vertical; parallel to level ground. **2.** flat or level. **3.** near, on, or parallel to the horizon. —**hor′i•zon′tal•ly,** *adv.*

hor•mone (hôr′mōn), *n.* an internally secreted compound formed in endocrine glands that affects the functions of specifically receptive organs or tissues when transported to them. —**hor•mo′nal,** *adj.*

horn (hôrn), *n.* **1.** one of the hard, usu. paired

growths on the head of certain mammals, as goats. **2.** the substance of which horns are composed. **3.** any projection resembling an animal horn. **4.** a brass wind instrument, esp. a French horn. **5.** an instrument for sounding a warning: *an automobile horn.* —*v.* **6. horn in,** *Informal.* to thrust oneself forward obtrusively. —*horned, adj.* **7.** made of horn. —**horn′less,** *adj.* —**horn′y,** *adj.,* **-i•er, -i•est.**

Horn (hôrn), *n.* **Cape, CAPE HORN.**

horned′ toad′, *n.* a small lizard with hornlike spines on the head.

hor•net (hôr′nit), *n.* a large, stinging social wasp.

horn′ of plen′ty, *n.* CORNUCOPIA.

horn′pipe′, *n.* a lively jiglike dance, traditionally a favorite of sailors.

ho•rol•o•gy (hô rol′ə jē, hō-), *n.* the science of making timepieces or of measuring time. —**hor•o•log′ic** (hôr′o loj′ik, hor′-), *adj.* —**ho•rol′o•gist,** *n.*

hor•o•scope (hôr′ə skōp′, hor′-), *n.* a diagram of the position of planets and the signs of the zodiac, as at the moment of a person's birth, used to predict events in a person's life.

Hor•o•witz (hôr′ə wits, hor′), *n.* **Vladimir,** 1904–89, U.S. pianist, born in Russia.

hor•ren•dous (hə ren′dəs), *adj.* dreadful; horrible. —**hor•ren′dous•ly,** *adv.*

hor•ri•ble (hôr′ə bəl, hor′-), *adj.* **1.** causing horror. **2.** extremely unpleasant. —**hor′ri•ble•ness,** *n.* —**hor′ri•bly,** *adv.*

hor•rid (-id), *adj.* **1.** such as to cause horror. **2.** extremely disagreeable. —**hor′rid•ly,** *adv.* —**hor′rid•ness,** *n.*

hor•rif•ic (hô rif′ik, ho-), *adj.* causing horror.

hor′ri•fy, *v.t.,* **-fied, -fy•ing. 1.** to cause to feel horror. **2.** to distress greatly.

hor•ror (hôr′ər, hor′-), *n.* **1.** an overwhelming and painful feeling caused by something shocking or terrifying. **2.** anything that causes such a feeling. **3.** a strong aversion.

hors de com•bat (ôr də kôn bA′), *adj., adv.* *French.* out of the fight; disabled.

hors d'oeuvre (ôr dûrv′), *n., pl.* **hors d'oeuvre** (ôr dûrv′), **hors d'oeuvres** (ôr dûrvz′, dûrv′), a small portion of food served as an appetizer or as a snack with cocktails. [< F]

horse (hôrs), *n., pl.* **hors•es, horse,** *v.,* **horsed, hors•ing,** *adj.* —*n.* **1.** a large, solid-hoofed mammal, domesticated for pulling loads and for riding. **2.** a frame with legs on which something is mounted or supported. —*v.t.* **3.** to provide with a horse. **4.** to set on horseback. **5. horse around,** *Informal.* to fool around. —*adj.* **6.** of or for a horse. —*Idiom.* **7. from the horse's mouth,** from the original or a trustworthy source. **8. hold one's horses,** *Informal.* to be patient. **9. horse of another color,** something entirely different. Also, **horse of a different color. 10. look a gift horse in the mouth,** to be critical of a gift.

horse′back′, *n.* **1.** the back of a horse. —*adv.* **2.** on horseback.

horse′ chest′nut, *n.* a shrub or tree with large leaves and upright clusters of white flowers.

horse′ fly′, *n.* a large, bloodsucking fly that is a pest of horses, cattle, etc.

horse′hair′, *n.* **1.** hair from the mane or tail of a horse. **2.** a sturdy glossy fabric woven of this hair.

horse′hide′, *n.* **1.** the hide of a horse. **2.** leather made from the hide of a horse.

horse′laugh′, *n.* a loud, coarse laugh, esp. of derision.

horse′man or **-wo′man,** *n., pl.* **-men** or **-wo•men.** a person skilled in riding a horse. —**horse′man•ship′,** *n.*

horse′ op′era, *n.* WESTERN (def. 8).

horse′play′, *n.* rough or boisterous play.

horse′pow′er, *n.* a unit for computing the power of an engine, equivalent to 550 foot-pounds per second, or 745.7 watts.

horse′rad′ish, *n.* a cultivated plant of the mus-

tard family. **2.** the pungent root of this plant, grated and used as a condiment.

horse′ sense′, *n.* COMMON SENSE.

horse′shoe′, *n.* **1.** a U-shaped metal plate nailed to a horse's hoof to protect it. **2.** something U-shaped. **3. horseshoes,** a game in which horseshoes are tossed at an iron stake to encircle it.

horse′shoe crab′, *n.* a marine arthropod with a stiff tail and brown carapace curved like a horseshoe.

horse′tail′, *n.* a nonflowering plant with hollow, jointed stems.

horse′whip′, *n., v.,* **-whipped, -whip•ping.** —*n.* **1.** a whip for controlling horses. —*v.t.* **2.** to beat with a horsewhip.

hors′y, *adj.,* **-i•er, -i•est. 1.** of or characteristic of a horse. **2.** dealing with or interested in horses or sports involving them.

hor•ta•to•ry (hôr′tə tôr′ē), *adj.* urging to some course of conduct or action.

hor•ti•cul•ture (hôr′ti kul′chər), *n.* the science or art of cultivating flowers, fruits, vegetables, or ornamental plants. —**hor′ti•cul′tur•al,** *adj.* —**hor′ti•cul′tur•ist,** *n.*

ho•san•na (hō zan′ə), *interj.* an exclamation in praise of God.

hose (hōz), *n., pl.* **hos•es** for 1, **hose** for 2, *v.,* **hosed, hos•ing.** —*n.* **1.** a flexible tube for conveying a liquid, as water, to a desired point. **2.** (*used with a pl. v.*) stockings or socks. —*v.t.* **3.** to water, wash, or spray with a hose.

Ho•se•a (hō zē′ə, -zā′ə), *n.* **1.** a Minor Prophet of the 8th century B.C. **2.** a book of the Bible bearing his name.

ho•sier•y (hō′zhə rē), *n.* stockings or socks.

hos•pice (hos′pis), *n.* **1.** a shelter for pilgrims, strangers, etc., esp. one kept by a religious order. **2.** a facility for supportive care of the terminally ill.

hos•pi•ta•ble (hos′pi tə bəl, ho spit′ə-), *adj.* **1.** treating guests or strangers warmly and generously. **2.** favorably receptive or open: *hospitable to new ideas.* —**hos′pi•ta•bly,** *adv.*

hos•pi•tal (hos′pi tl), *n.* an institution in which sick or injured persons are given medical or surgical treatment.

hos′pi•tal′i•ty, *n., pl.* **-ties.** the friendly treatment of guests or strangers; an act or show of welcome.

hos′pi•tal•ize′, *v.t.,* **-ized, -iz•ing.** to place in a hospital for medical care. —**hos′pi•tal•i•za′tion,** *n.*

host¹ (hōst), *n.* **1.** a person who receives or entertains guests. **2.** an emcee or moderator for a television or radio program. **3.** a living animal or plant from which a parasite obtains nutrition. —*v.i., v.t.* **4.** to act as host (to).

host² (hōst), *n.* **1.** a multitude or great number. **2.** an army.

Host (hōst), *n.* the bread or wafer consecrated in the celebration of the Eucharist.

hos•tage (hos′tij), *n.* a person given or held as security for the fulfillment of certain conditions or terms.

hos•tel (hos′tl), *n.* an inexpensive, supervised lodging place for young travelers. [< OF < L *hospitāle* guesthouse]

hos′tel•ry, *n., pl.* **-ries.** an inn or hotel.

host•ess (hō′stis), *n.* **1.** a woman who receives or entertains guests. **2.** a woman employed in a restaurant or the like to seat patrons.

hos•tile (hos′tl; *esp. Brit.* -tīl), *adj.* **1.** of or characteristic of an enemy. **2.** opposed in feeling, action, or character; antagonistic. —**hos′tile•ly,** *adv.*

hos•til•i•ty (ho stil′i tē), *n., pl.* **-ties. 1.** a hostile state, condition, or attitude. **2.** a hostile act. **3. hostilities,** acts of warfare.

hos•tler (hos′lər, os′lər), *n.* a person who takes care of horses, esp. at an inn.

hot (hot), *adj.,* **hot•ter, hot•test. 1.** having a high temperature. **2.** having or causing a sensation of great bodily heat. **3.** peppery or pungent: *hot mustard.* **4.** showing intense or violent feeling: *a hot temper.* **5.** violent or intense: *a hot battle.* **6.** new; fresh:

hot off the press. **7.** following closely: *hot on the trail.* **8.** *Informal.* very good: *not so hot.* **9.** *Informal.* currently popular. **10.** *Informal.* performing exceedingly well or rapidly. **11.** actively conducting an electric current: *a hot wire.* —**hot′ly,** *adv.* —**hot′ness,** *n.*

hot′ air′, *n. Informal.* empty or exaggerated talk.

hot′bed′, *n.* **1.** a glass-covered bed of earth heated by electric cables or fermenting manure, for growing plants out of season. **2.** an environment favoring rapid growth, esp. of something unwanted.

hot′-blood′ed, *adj.* **1.** excitable; impetuous. **2.** ardent; passionate.

hot′-but′ton, *adj.* exciting strong feelings: *hot-button issues.*

hot′ cake′, *n.* **1.** a pancake. —*Idiom.* **2. sell like hot cakes,** to be disposed of very quickly.

hot′ dog′, *n.* a frankfurter, esp. one served in a split roll.

hot′-dog′, *v.i.* **-dogged, -dog•ging.** *Slang.* to perform intricate maneuvers in surfing or skiing.

ho•tel (hō tel′), *n.* a commercial establishment offering lodging to travelers and often having public restaurants, meeting rooms, etc. [< F *hôtel,* OF *hostel* HOSTEL]

ho•te•lier (ō′təl yā′, hōt′l ēr′, hō tel′yər), *n.* a manager or owner of a hotel.

hot′ flash′, *n.* a sudden, temporary sensation of heat experienced by some women during menopause.

hot′head′, *n.* an impetuous or short-tempered person. —**hot′head′ed,** *adj.* —**hot′head′ed•ly,** *adv.* —**hot′head′ed•ness,** *n.*

hot′house′, *n.* an artificially heated greenhouse for tender plants.

hot′ line′, *n.* **1.** a direct telecommunications link for immediate communication between heads of state in a crisis. **2.** a telephone number providing direct access to a company, agency, etc., as for information or counseling.

hot•link (hot′lingk′), *n.* a hypertext link.

hot′ plate′, *n.* a portable electrical appliance for cooking.

hot′ pota′to, *n. Informal.* a situation or issue that is unpleasant or risky to deal with.

hot′ rod′, *n.* an automobile specially built or altered for fast acceleration and increased speed. —**hot′ rod′der,** *n.*

hot′ seat′, *n. Slang.* **1.** ELECTRIC CHAIR. **2.** an uncomfortable or embarrassing situation.

hot′shot′, *n. Slang.* an impressively skillful and often vain person.

hot′ spot′, *n.* **1.** a region where dangerous political situations exist or may develop. **2.** any area of known danger, instability, etc. **3.** *Informal.* a nightclub.

hot′ tub′, *n.* a wooden tub, usu. big enough for several persons, filled with hot water.

hot′ wa′ter, *n. Informal.* trouble; a predicament.

Hou•di•ni (hoō dē′nē), *n.* **Harry** (*Erich Weiss*), 1874–1926, U.S. magician.

hound (hound), *n.* **1.** any of several breeds of dogs that pursue game either by sight or scent. **2.** any dog. **3.** an addict or devotee. —*v.t.* **4.** to hunt or track with hounds. **5.** to annoy or persecute relentlessly. —**hound′er,** *n.*

hour (ouᵊr, ou′ər), *n.* **1.** a period of time equal to $\frac{1}{24}$ of a day, equivalent to 60 minutes. **2.** any specific time of day: *What is the hour?* **3.** a customary or usual time: *dinner hour.* **4. hours,** time spent at a workplace or in working. **5.** one unit of academic credit.

hour′glass′, *n.* an instrument for measuring time by the draining of sand or mercury from a top to a bottom glass bulb.

hou•ri (hoŏr′ē, hou′r′ē), *n., pl.* **-ris.** one of the beautiful virgins of the Muslim paradise.

hour′ly, *adj.* **1.** of, occurring, or done each successive hour. **2.** using an hour as a basic unit of reckon-

ing. **3.** frequent; continual. —*adv.* **4.** once an hour. **5.** frequently.

house (*n.* hous; *v.* houz), *n., pl.* **hous•es** (hou′ziz), *v.,* **housed, hous•ing.** —*n.* **1.** a building in which people live. **2.** a household. **3.** (*often cap.*) a family, including ancestors and descendants. **4.** a building for any purpose: *a house of worship.* **5. a.** a theater or the like. **b.** the audience of a theater or the like. **6.** (*often cap.*) a legislative body. **7.** (*often cap.*) a commercial establishment: *a publishing house.* —*v.t.* **8.** to provide shelter or lodging for. **9.** to provide with a place to work or study. **10.** to store; hold: *This casing houses the batteries.* —*Idiom.* **11. keep house,** to maintain a home. **12. on the house,** as a gift from the management. —**house′ful,** *n., pl.* **-fuls.**

house′ arrest′, *n.* confinement of an arrested person to his or her home.

house′boat′, *n.* a flat-bottomed bargelike boat fitted for use as a floating dwelling.

house′break′, *v.t.,* **-broke, -bro•ken, -break•ing.** to train (a pet) to excrete outdoors or in a specific place.

house′break′er, *n.* a person who breaks into and enters a house with felonious intent. —**house′break′ing,** *n.*

house′fly′, *n., pl.* **-flies.** a medium-sized fly, common around human habitations.

house′hold′, *n.* **1.** the people of a house collectively. **2.** a home and its related affairs.

house′hold word′, *n.* a familiar name, phrase, or saying; byword.

house′hus′band, *n.* a married man who stays at home to manage the household.

house′keep′er, *n.* a person, often hired, who does or directs the domestic work in a home. —**house′keep′ing,** *n.*

house′keeping bill′, *n.* an act in a legislature that embodies a minor alteration to a law.

house′maid′, *n.* a female servant who does housework.

House′ of Bur′gesses, *n.* the popular branch of the colonial legislature of Virginia or Maryland.

House′ of Com′mons, *n.* the elective lower house of the Parliament of Great Britain, Canada, etc.

House′ of Lords′, *n.* the nonelective upper house of the British Parliament.

House′ of Represen′tatives, *n.* the lower house of many national and state legislatures, as in the U.S. and Mexico.

house′plant′, *n.* an ornamental plant that is grown indoors.

house′wares′, *n.pl.* articles of household equipment.

house′warm′ing, *n.* a party to celebrate a person's or family's move to a new home.

house′wife′, *n., pl.* **-wives.** a married woman who manages her own household as her principal occupation.

house′work′, *n.* the work of cleaning, cooking, etc., done in housekeeping.

hourglass

hous•ing (hou′zing), *n.* **1.** any lodging or dwelling place. **2.** houses collectively. **3.** the providing of houses or shelter. **4.** anything that covers or protects; casing.

Hous•ton (hyoō′stən), *n.* **Sam(uel),** 1793–1863, U.S. soldier: president of the Republic of Texas 1836–38.

HOV, high-occupancy vehicle: a bus, van, or car with two or more passengers.

hove (hōv), *v.* a pt. and pp. of HEAVE.

hov•el (huv′əl, hov′-), *n.* a small, mean dwelling.

hov•er (huv′ər, hov′-), *v.i.* **1.** to hang fluttering or suspended in the air. **2.** to wait near at hand. **3.** to waver: *to hover between life and death.*

HOV lane, *n.* a highway or street lane for high-occupancy vehicles.

how (hou), *adv.* **1.** in what way or manner? **2.** to what extent, degree, etc.?: *How difficult was the test?* **3.** in what state or condition? **4.** for what reason?: *How can you talk such nonsense?* **5.** with what meaning?: *How is one to interpret this?* **6.** what?: *How do you mean?* **7.** (used as an intensifier): *How nice!* —*conj.* **8.** the manner or way in which: *I knew how to solve the problem.* **9.** however: *You can dress how you please.* —*Idiom.* **10. how about,** what is your response to?

how•be•it (hou bē′it), *adv. Archaic.* nevertheless.

how•dah (hou′də), *n.* a seat placed on the back of an elephant.

Howe (hou), *n.* **1. Elias,** 1819–67, U.S. inventor of the sewing machine. **2. Julia Ward,** 1819–1910, U.S. writer and reformer.

how•ev′er, *adv.* **1.** nevertheless; yet. **2.** to whatever extent or degree. —*conj.* **3.** in whatever manner or state.

how•itz•er (hou′it sər), *n.* a short-barreled cannon for firing shells at an elevated angle.

howl (houl), *v.i.* **1.** to utter the loud, prolonged, mournful cry of a wolf, dog, etc. **2.** to utter a similar cry, as in pain. **3.** to utter a loud laugh. —*v.t.* **4.** to utter with howls. **5.** to drive or force by howls. —*n.* **6.** the cry of a dog, wolf, etc. **7.** any similar cry or sound. **8.** something that causes a laugh.

howl′er, *n.* **1.** one that howls. **2.** an embarrassing mistake.

how′so•ev′er, *adv.* **1.** to whatsoever extent or degree. **2.** in whatsoever manner.

hoy•den (hoid′n), *n.* a boisterous, bold girl; tomboy. —**hoy′den•ish,** *adj.*

Hoyle (hoil), *n.* **1. Edmond,** 1672–1769, English authority and writer on card games. **2. Sir Fred,** born 1915, British astronomer, mathematician, and educator. —*Idiom.* **3. according to Hoyle,** according to the rules or to the authority.

HP or **hp,** horsepower.

HQ or **hq,** headquarters.

hr., hour.

H.R., House of Representatives.

H.R.H., Her (or His) Royal Highness.

HRT, hormone replacement therapy.

H.S., High School.

ht., height.

HTML, HyperText Markup Language: a set of standards, a variety of SGML, used to tag the elements of a hypertext document on the World Wide Web.

Hts., Heights (used in place names).

http, hypertext transfer protocol: a protocol for transferring hypertext documents, the standard protocol for the World Wide Web.

hua•ra•che (wə rä′chē, -chä), *n., pl.* **-ches** (-chēz, -chäz). a Mexican sandal having the upper woven of leather strips.

hub (hub), *n.* **1.** the central part of a wheel, propeller, fan, etc. **2.** a center of activity.

Hub•ble (hub′əl), *n.* **Edwin Powell,** 1889–1953, U.S. astronomer: pioneer in extragalactic research.

hub•bub (hub′ub), *n.* tumult; uproar.

hub′cap′, *n.* a removable cover for the hub of an automobile wheel.

hu•bris (hyōō′bris, hōō′-), *n.* excessive pride or self-confidence.

huck•le•ber•ry (huk′əl ber′ē), *n., pl.* **-ries. 1.** the dark blue, edible berry of various shrubs of the heath family. **2.** a shrub bearing such fruit.

huck•ster (huk′stər), *n.* **1.** an aggressive seller or promoter. **2.** a peddler, esp. of fruits and vegetables.

HUD (hud), *n.* Department of Housing and Urban Development.

hud•dle (hud′l), *v.,* **-dled, -dling,** *n.* —*v.i., v.t.* **1.** to crowd together closely. **2.** to draw (oneself) together. —*n.* **3.** a closely gathered group or heap. **4.** a close gathering of football players to hear instructions for the next play. **5.** a conference or consultation, esp. a private one.

Hud•son (hud′sən), *n.* **1. Henry,** died 1611?, English navigator and explorer. **2.** a river in E New York, flowing S to New York Bay. 306 mi. (495 km) long.

Hud′son Bay′, *n.* a large inland sea in N Canada.

hue (hyōō), *n.* **1.** a gradation or variety of a color; tint. **2.** color. —**hued,** *adj.*

hue′ and cry′, *n.* public clamor or alarm.

huff (huf), *n.* **1.** a mood of sulking anger. —*v.i.* **2.** to puff or blow; breathe heavily. —**huff′y,** *adj.,* **-i•er, -i•est.**

hug (hug), *v.,* **hugged, hug•ging,** *n.* —*v.t.* **1.** to clasp tightly in the arms, esp. with affection. **2.** to cling firmly or fondly to: *to hug an opinion.* **3.** to keep close to: *to hug the shore.* —*n.* **4.** a tight clasp with the arms.

huge (hyōōj; *often* yōōj), *adj.,* **hug•er, hug•est.** extraordinarily large; gigantic; enormous. —**huge′ly,** *adv.* —**huge′ness,** *n.*

Hughes (hyōōz), *n.* **1. Charles Evans,** 1862–1948, Chief Justice of the U.S. 1930–41. **2. (James) Langston,** 1902–67, U.S. novelist and poet.

Hu•go (hyōō′gō *or, often,* yōō′-), *n.* **Victor (Marie, Viscount)** 1802–85, French poet, novelist, and dramatist.

Hu•gue•not (hyōō′gə not′; *often* yōō′-), *n.* a French Protestant in the 16th and 17th centuries.

huh (hu), *interj.* an exclamation of surprise, contempt, or interrogation.

hu•la (hōō′lə), *n., pl.* **-las.** a Hawaiian native dance with intricate arm movements.

Hul•dah (hul′də), *n.* a prophet at the time of King Josiah. II Kings 22:14–20; II Chron. 34:22–28.

hulk (hulk), *n.* **1.** the body of an old or dismantled ship. **2.** a bulky or unwieldy person or thing.

hulk′ing, *adj.* heavy and clumsy.

hull[1] (hul), *n.* **1.** the husk, shell, or outer covering of a seed or fruit. **2.** any covering or envelope. —*v.t.* **3.** to remove the hull of. —**hull′er,** *n.*

hull[2] (hul), *n.* the hollow, lowermost portion of a ship.

hul•la•ba•loo (hul′ə bə lōō′), *n., pl.* **-loos.** a clamorous noise or disturbance.

hum (hum), *v.,* **hummed, hum•ming,** *n.* —*v.i.* **1.** to make a low, continuous droning sound. **2.** to sing with closed lips, without articulating words. **3.** to be in a state of busy activity. —*v.t.* **4.** to utter by humming. —*n.* **5.** the act or sound of humming. —**hum′mer,** *n.*

hu•man (hyōō′mən; *often* yōō′-), *adj.* **1.** of, characteristic of, or having the nature of people. —*n.* **2.** Also called **hu′man be′ing.** a person. —**hu′man•ness,** *n.*

hu•mane′ (-mān′), *adj.* **1.** characterized by compassion and sympathy for others. **2.** of humanistic studies. —**hu•mane′ly,** *adv.* —**hu•mane′ness,** *n.*

hu′man•ism, *n.* **1.** any system of thought in which human interests, values, and dignity predominate. **2.** (*sometimes cap.*) the study of the cultures of ancient Rome and Greece as pursued by Renaissance scholars. —**hu′man•ist,** *n., adj.* —**hu•man•is′tic,** *adj.*

hu•man′i•tar′i•an (-man′i târ′ē ən), *adj.* **1.** having concern for the welfare of people. —*n.* **2.** a person engaged in promoting human welfare. —**hu•man′i•tar′i•an•ism,** *n.*

hu•man′i•ty, *n., pl.* **-ties. 1.** the human race. **2.** the quality or condition of being human or humane. **3. the humanities,** literature, philosophy, art, etc., as distinguished from the sciences.

hu′man•ize′ (-mə nīz′), *v.t., v.i.,* **-ized, -iz•ing.** to make or become human or humane. —**hu•man•i•za′tion,** *n.* —**hu′man•iz′er,** *n.*

hu′man•kind′, *n.* the human race; humanity.

hu′man•ly, *adv.* **1.** in the manner of human beings. **2.** within the limits of human capability.

hu′man•oid′ (-mə noid′), *adj.* **1.** resembling human beings. —*n.* **2.** a humanoid being.

hu′man resourc′es depart′ment, *n.* a department of an organization supervising matters of personnel. Also called **hu′man resourc′es.**

hum•ble (hum′bəl, um′-), *adj.,* **-bler, -blest,** *v.,* **-bled, -bling.** —*adj.* **1.** not proud or arrogant. **2.** low in status, condition, etc. **3.** respectful: *in my humble opinion.* —*v.t.* **4.** to lower in status or condition. **5.** to lower the pride of. —**hum′bly,** *adv.*

hum•bug (hum′bug′), *n.* **1.** something intended to deceive. **2.** an impostor. —*v.t.* **3.** to deceive; trick. —*interj.* **4.** nonsense!

hum•ding•er (hum′ding′ər), *n. Informal.* a person or thing of remarkable excellence or effect.

hum•drum (hum′drum′), *adj.* boring; dull.

hu•mer•us (hyōō′mər əs; *often* yōō′-), *n., pl.* **-mer•i** (-mə rī′). the bone of the upper arm or forelimb. —**hu′mer•al,** *adj.*

hu•mid (hyōō′mid; *often* yōō′-), *adj.* noticeably moist.

hu•mid′i•fy, *v.t.,* **-fied, -fy•ing.** to make humid. —**hu•mid′i•fi•ca′tion,** *n.* —**hu•mid′i•fi′er,** *n.*

hu•mid′i•ty, *n.* **1.** moistness; dampness. **2.** the amount of water vapor in the air.

hu′mi•dor′ (-mi dôr′), *n.* a container to keep tobacco moist.

hu•mil•i•ate (hyōō mil′ē āt′; *often* yōō-), *v.t.,* **-at•ed, -at•ing.** to cause (a person) a painful loss of pride or self-respect. —**hu•mil′i•at′ing•ly,** *adv.* —**hu•mil′i•a′tion,** *n.*

hu•mil′i•ty, *n.* the quality or state of being humble.

hum′ming•bird′, *n.* a tiny, colorful bird with narrow wings that beat very rapidly.

hum•mock (hum′ək), *n.* a knoll or hillock.

hu•mon•gous (hyōō mung′gəs, -mong′-; *often* yōō-), *Slang.* extraordinarily large. [expressive coinage, perh. reflecting *huge* and *monstrous,* with stress pattern of *tremendous*]

hu•mor (hyōō′mər; *often* yōō′-), *n.* **1.** a comic quality causing amusement. **2.** the faculty of perceiving and expressing what is amusing or comical. **3.** comical writing, talk, or actions. **4.** a mood or frame of mind. **5.** a whim. **6.** any animal or plant fluid, as bile. —*v.t.* **7.** to comply with the humor or mood of. Also, *esp. Brit.,* **hu′mour.** —**hu′mor•ist,** *n.* —**hu′mor•less,** *adj.*

hu′mor•ous, *adj.* characterized by humor; funny; comical; amusing. —**hu′mor•ous•ly,** *adv.* —**hu′mor•ous•ness,** *n.*

hump (hump), *n.* **1.** a rounded protuberance, esp. on the back, as of a camel. **2.** a low, rounded rise of ground. —*v.t.* **3.** to raise (the back) in a hump. —*Idiom.* **4. over the hump,** past the greatest difficulties.

hump′back′, *n.* **1.** a back that is humped. **2.** HUNCHBACK. **3.** a large whale with long, narrow flippers. —**hump′backed′,** *adj.*

Hum•phrey (hum′frē), *n.* **Hubert H(oratio),** 1911–78, U.S. vice president 1965–69.

hu•mus (hyōō′məs; *often* yōō′-), *n.* the dark organic material in soils, produced by the decomposition of vegetable or animal matter.

Hum•vee (hum′vē), *n., pl.* **-vees.** a military vehicle that combines the features of a jeep with those of a light truck. [from the pronunciation of the initials HMMWV for *H(igh)–M(obility) M(ultipurpose) W(heeled) V(ehicle)*]

Hun (hun), *n.* **1.** a member of a pastoral people of the Eurasian steppes who reached the height of their power in Europe in the mid-5th century A.D. **2.** (*often l.c.*) a barbarous, destructive person.

Hu•nan (hōō′nän′), *n.* a province in S China. 56,960,000.

hunch (hunch), *v.t.* **1.** to thrust out or up in a hump; arch. —*v.i.* **2.** to thrust oneself forward jerkily. —*n.* **3.** a premonition or suspicion.

hunch′back′, *n.* a person whose back is humped

because of abnormal spinal curvature. —**hunch′-backed′,** *adj.*

hun•dred (hun′drid), *n., pl.* **-dreds, -dred,** *adj.* —*n.* **1.** a cardinal number, ten times ten. **2.** a symbol for this number, as 100 or C. **3. hundreds,** a number between 100 and 999. —*adj.* **4.** amounting to 100 in number. —**hun′dredth,** *adj., n.*

hun′dred•fold′, *adj.* a hundred times as great or as much.

hun′dred•weight′, *n., pl.* **-weights, -weight.** a unit of weight equivalent to 100 pounds (45.359 kilograms) in the U.S.

Hun′dred Years′/ War′, *n.* the series of wars between England and France, 1337–1453.

hung (hung), *v.* **1.** a pt. and past part. of HANG. —*Idiom.* **2. hung over,** suffering from a hangover. **3. hung up,** *Slang.* beset by psychological problems. **4. hung up on,** *Slang.* obsessed by. —**Usage.** See HANG.

Hung., 1. Hungarian. **2.** Hungary.

Hun•gar•i•an (hung gâr′ē ən), *n.* **1.** a native or inhabitant of Hungary. **2.** the language of Hungary. —*adj.* **3.** of Hungary, its people, or their language.

Hun•ga•ry (hung′gə rē), *n.* a republic in central Europe. 9,935,774.

hun•ger (hung′gər), *n.* **1.** a compelling need or desire for food. **2.** discomfort caused by the need of food. **3.** any strong desire or craving. —*v.i.* **4.** to feel hunger. **5.** to have a strong desire. —**hun′gry,** *adj.,* **-gri•er, -gri•est.** —**hun′gri•ly,** *adv.*

hun′ger strike′, *n.* a deliberate refusal to eat, undertaken in protest, as against social injustice.

hunk (hungk), *n.* **1.** a large piece or lump. **2.** *Slang.* a handsome man with a well-developed physique.

hun•ker (hung′kər), *v.i.* **1.** to squat on one's heels. —*n.* **2. hunkers,** the haunches.

hunt (hunt), *v.t.* **1.** to chase or search for (game) to catch or kill. **2.** to pursue (a person) in order to capture. **3.** to scour (an area) in pursuit of game. **4.** to search for; seek. —*v.i.* **5.** to capture or kill wild animals for food or sport. **6.** to make a search. —*n.* **7.** the act of hunting game. **8.** a search or pursuit. **9.** a group of hunters. —**hunt′er,** *n.*

hunts′man, *n., pl.* **-men. 1.** a person who manages the hounds during a hunt. **2.** a hunter.

Hunts•ville (hunts′vil), *n.* a city in N Alabama. 160,325.

hur•dle (hûr′dl), *n., v.,* **-dled, -dling.** —*n.* **1.** a fencelike barrier over which runners or horses must leap in certain races. **2.** a difficulty to be overcome. —*v.t.* **3.** to leap over. **4.** to master (a difficulty). —**hur′dler,** *n.*

hur•dy-gur•dy (hûr′dē gûr′dē), *n., pl.* **-gur•dies.** a barrel organ or similar instrument played by turning a crank.

hurl (hûrl), *v.t.* **1.** to throw with great force. **2.** to throw down. **3.** to utter with vehemence. —**hurl′er,** *n.*

hurl•y-burl•y (hûr′lē bûr′lē), *n.* noisy disorder and confusion.

Hu•ron (hyōōr′ən, -on; *often* yōōr′-), *n., pl.* **-ron, -rons. 1.** a member of a confederacy of American Indian tribes formerly living east of Lake Huron. **2. Lake,** a lake between the U.S. and Canada: second largest of the Great Lakes.

hur•rah (hə rä′, -rô′) also **-ray** (-rā′), *interj.* **1.** an exclamation of joy, exultation, encouragement, etc. —*v.i.* **2.** to shout "hurrah." —*n.* **3.** an exclamation of "hurrah."

hur•ri•cane (hûr′i kān′, hur′-), *n.* a violent, tropical, cyclonic storm, esp. of the W North Atlantic. [< Sp *huracán* < Taino (West Indian language)]

hur•ry (hûr′ē, hur′ē), *v.,* **-ried, -ry•ing,** *n., pl.* **-ries.** —*v.i.* **1.** to move or act with haste. —*v.t.* **2.** to cause to move or act with speed. **3.** to hasten; urge forward. **4.** to impel or perform with undue haste; rush. —*n.* **5.** a state of urgency or eagerness. **6.** hurried movement or action. —**hur′ried•ly,** *adv.*

hurt (hûrt), *v.,* **hurt, hurt•ing,** *n., adj.* —*v.t.* **1.** to cause injury or pain to. **2.** to affect adversely; harm. **3.** to offend. —*v.i.* **4.** to feel or suffer pain. **5.** to cause pain, damage, or distress. —*n.* **6.** something that hurts, as a wound. **7.** injury, damage, or harm. —*adj.* **8.** injured or damaged. —**hurt′ful,** *adj.*

hur•tle (hûr′tl), *v.i., v.t.,* **-tled, -tling.** to move or fling with great speed or force.

Hus (hŏŏs, hus), *n.* **Jan** (yän), 1369?–1415, Czech religious reformer and martyr.

hus•band (huz′bənd), *n.* **1.** a married man. —*v.t.* **2.** to manage with economy.

hus′band•man, *n., pl.* **-men.** a farmer.

hus′band•ry, *n.* **1.** the cultivation of crops and the raising of livestock. **2.** careful or thrifty management.

hush (hush), *interj.* **1.** a command to be silent or quiet. —*v.i.* **2.** to become silent or quiet. —*v.t.* **3.** to make silent. **4.** to suppress mention of. **5.** to calm or quiet. —*n.* **6.** silence or quiet.

hush′-hush′, *adj.* highly secret.

hush′ pup′py, *n.* a small deep-fried ball of cornmeal dough.

husk (husk), *n.* **1.** the dry external covering of certain fruits or seeds, esp. of an ear of corn. **2.** the outer part of anything, esp. when dry or worthless. —*v.t.* **3.** to remove the husk from. —**husk′er,** *n.*

husk′y[1], *adj.,* **-i•er, -i•est. 1.** big and strong. **2.** (of the voice) somewhat hoarse. —**husk′i•ly,** *adv.* —**husk′i•ness,** *n.*

husk′y[2], *n., pl.* **-ies.** (*sometimes cap.*) a sturdy dog of arctic regions, used for pulling sleds.

hus•sar (hŏŏ zär′), *n.* a member of a class of European light cavalry, usu. with flamboyant uniforms. [< Hungarian « ML *cursārius* corsair]

hus•sy (hus′ē, huz′ē), *n., pl.* **-sies. 1.** a disreputable woman. **2.** a mischievous or impudent girl.

hus•tings (hus′tingz), *n.* (*used with a sing. or pl. v.*) **1.** any place from which political campaign speeches are made. **2.** the political campaign trail.

hus•tle (hus′əl), *v.,* **-tled, -tling,** *n.* —*v.i.* **1.** to proceed or work rapidly or energetically. **2.** to push or force one's way. **3.** to be aggressive or unethical in making money. —*v.t.* **4.** to force roughly or hurriedly. **5.** to urge or speed up. **6.** to obtain or sell by aggressive and often illicit means. **7.** to jostle or push roughly. —*n.* **8.** energetic activity. **9.** the act of hustling. —**hus′tler,** *n.*

hut (hut), *n.* a small or humble dwelling of simple construction.

hutch (huch), *n.* **1.** a pen or coop for small animals. **2.** a chestlike cabinet with open shelves above. **3.** a small cottage.

Hutch•in•son (huch′in sən), *n.* **1. Anne Marbury,** 1591–1643, American religious liberal, born in England. **2. Thomas,** 1711–80, American colonial administrator of Massachusetts 1769–74.

hutz•pa or **hutz•pah** (кнŏŏt′spə, hŏŏt′-), *n. Slang.* CHUTZPA.

Hux•ley (huks′lē), *n.* **Aldous (Leonard),** 1894–1963, English novelist, essayist, and critic.

huz•zah (hə zä′), *interj.* **1.** an exclamation of joy, applause, appreciation, etc. —*n.* **2.** the exclamation "huzzah."

hwy., highway.

hy•a•cinth (hī′ə sinth), *n.* a plant of the lily family, with a cylindrical cluster of colorful flowers.

hy•brid (hī′brid), *n.* **1.** the offspring of two animals or plants of different breeds, varieties, or species. **2.** anything derived from unlike sources or composed of disparate elements. —*adj.* **3.** of or characteristic of a hybrid. —**hy′brid•ism,** *n.*

hy′brid•ize′, *v.i., v.t.,* **-ized, -iz•ing.** to produce or cause to produce hybrids. —**hy′brid•i•za′tion,** *n.*

Hy•der•a•bad (hī′dər ə bäd′, -bad′), *n.* a city in S central India. 2,528,000.

hy•dra (hī′drə), *n., pl.* **-dras, -drae** (-drē). a freshwater polyp with a cylindrical body and tentacles around the mouth.

hy•dran•gea (hī drān′jə), *n., pl.* **-geas.** a shrub with large flower clusters of white, pink, or blue.

hy•drant (hī′drənt), *n.* an upright pipe with an outlet for drawing water from a water main.

hy′drate (-drāt), *n., v.,* **-drat•ed, -drat•ing.** —*n.* **1.** any of a class of compounds containing chemically

combined water. —*v.t., v.i.* **2.** to combine chemically with water. —**hy•dra′tion,** *n.* —**hy′dra•tor,** *n.*

hy•drau•lic (hī drô′lik, -drol′ik), *adj.* **1.** operated by water or other liquid under pressure. **2.** of hydraulics. —**hy•drau′li•cal•ly,** *adv.*

hy•drau′lics, *n.* the science that deals with the laws governing water or other liquids in motion and their applications in engineering.

hydro-[1], a combining form meaning water (*hydroplane*).

hydro-[2], a combining form representing HYDROGEN (*hydrocarbon*).

hy•dro•car•bon (hī′drə kär′bən), *n.* any of a class of compounds containing only hydrogen and carbon, as methane.

hy′dro•ceph′a•lus (-sef′ə ləs) also **-ceph′a•ly,** *n.* an abnormal accumulation of fluid within the cranium, often causing enlargement of the head. —**hy•dro•ce•phal•ic** (hī′drō sə fal′ik), *adj., n.*

hy′dro•chlo′ric ac′id (-klôr′ik), *n.* a corrosive, fuming liquid, used in petrochemical and industrial processes.

hy′dro•dy•nam′ics (hī′drō dī nam′iks, -di-), *n.* the science that deals with the forces in or motions of liquids. —**hy′dro•dy•nam′ic,** *adj.*

hy′dro•e•lec′tric, *adj.* pertaining to the generation and distribution of electricity derived from the energy of falling water. —**hy′dro•e•lec•tric′i•ty,** *n.*

hy•dro•foil (hī′drə foil′), *n.* **1.** a winglike structure that lifts the hull of a moving boat out of water when traveling at high speed. **2.** a boat with hydrofoils.

hy•dro•gen (hī′drə jən), *n.* a colorless, odorless, flammable gas, the lightest of the elements. *Symbol:* H; *at. wt.:* 1.00797; *at. no.:* 1. —**hy•drog′e•nous** (-droj′ə nəs), *adj.*

hy•dro•gen•ate (hī′drə jə nāt′, hī droj′ə-), *v.t.,* **-at•ed, -at•ing.** to combine with or treat with hydrogen. —**hy′dro•gen•a′tion,** *n.*

hy′drogen bomb′, *n.* a bomb, more powerful than an atomic bomb, that derives its explosive energy from the thermonuclear fusion reaction of hydrogen isotopes.

hy′drogen perox′ide, *n.* a colorless liquid used as an antiseptic and a bleaching agent.

hy•drol•o•gy (hī drol′ə jē), *n.* the science dealing with the circulation, distribution, and properties of the waters of the earth.

hy•drol′y•sis (-ə sis), *n., pl.* **-ses** (-sēz′). decomposition in which a compound is split into other compounds by reacting with water. —**hy′dro•lyt′ic** (-drə lit′ik), *adj.* —**hy′dro•lyze′** (-līz′), *v.t., v.i.,* **-lyzed, -lyz•ing.**

hy•drom•e•ter (hī drom′i tər), *n.* an instrument for determining the specific gravity of a liquid. —**hy•drom′e•try,** *n.*

hy•dro•pho•bi•a (hī′drə fō′bē ə), *n.* **1.** an abnormal dread of water. **2.** RABIES. [< LL < Gk: horror of water]

hy′dro•phone′, *n.* a device for detecting sounds transmitted through water.

hy′dro•plane′, *n.* **1.** a seaplane. **2.** a light, high-powered speedboat designed to plane along the surface of the water.

hy′dro•pon′ics (-pon′iks), *n.* the cultivation of plants by placing the roots in liquid nutrient solutions rather than soil. —**hy′dro•pon′ic,** *adj.*

hy′dro•sphere′, *n.* the water on or surrounding the surface of the globe.

hy′dro•ther′a•py, *n.* the use of water in the treatment of disease or injury.

hy•drous (hī′drəs), *adj.* containing water, esp. in some kind of chemical union.

hy•drox•ide (hī drok′sīd), *n.* a chemical compound of oxygen and hydrogen grouped together with one atom each.

hy•e•na (hī ē′nə), *n., pl.* **-nas.** a large carnivore of Africa and S Asia, feeding chiefly on carrion.

hy•giene (hī′jēn), *n.* **1.** the application of scientific knowledge to the preservation of health. **2.** a condition or practice conducive to health, as cleanliness.

—**hy′gi•en′ic** (-jē en′ik, -jen′-, -jē′nik), *adj.* —**hy′gi•en′i•cal•ly,** *adv.* —**hy•gien′ist** (-jē′nist, -jen′ist), *n.*

hy•grom•e•ter (hī grom′i tər), *n.* any instrument for measuring the water-vapor content of the atmosphere. —**hy•grom′e•try,** *n.*

hy•ing (hī′ing), *v.* a pres. part. of HIE.

hy•men (hī′mən), *n.* a fold of mucous membrane partly closing the external orifice of the vagina in a virgin.

hy•me•ne•al (hī′mə nē′əl), *adj.* of marriage.

hymn (him), *n.* a song in praise of God, a nation, etc.

hym•nal (him′nl), *n.* a book of hymns. Also called **hymn′book′.**

hype (hīp), *v.*, **hyped, hyp•ing,** *n. Informal.* —*v.t.* **1.** to stimulate or agitate. **2.** to create interest in by flamboyant methods. —*n.* **3.** intensive or exaggerated promotion. **4.** a flamboyant or questionable claim or method used in advertising.

hy•per (hī′pər), *adj. Informal.* very excitable.

hyper-, a prefix meaning over, above, or excessive (*hypersensitive*).

hy•per•ac•tive (hī′pər ak′tiv), *adj.* **1.** unusually active. **2.** (of children) displaying excessive physical activity. —**hy′per•ac•tiv′i•ty,** *n.*

hy•per•bo•la (hī pûr′bə lə), *n., pl.* **-las.** the set of points in a plane whose distances to two fixed points in the plane have a constant difference.

hy•per•bo•le (hī pûr′bə lē), *n., pl.* **-les.** obvious and intentional exaggeration not intended to be taken literally. —**hy′per•bol′ic** (-pər bol′ik), *adj.*

hy•per•gly•ce•mi•a (hī′pər glī sē′mē ə), *n.* an abnormally high level of glucose in the blood. —**hy′-per•gly•ce′mic,** *adj.*

hy′per•link′, *n.* a hypertext link.

hy′per•sen′si•tive, *adj.* **1.** excessively sensitive. **2.** allergic to a substance to which most people do not react. —**hy′per•sen′si•tiv′i•ty,** *n.*

hy′per•ten′sion, *n.* high blood pressure. —**hy′-per•ten′sive,** *adj., n.*

hy′per•text′, *n.* data, as text, graphics, or sound, stored in a computer so that a user can move nonsequentially through a link from one object or document to another.

hy′per•thy′roid•ism (-thī′roi diz′əm), *n.* overactivity of the thyroid gland. —**hy′per•thy′roid,** *adj.*

hy′per•ven′ti•la′tion, *n.* prolonged rapid or deep breathing, resulting in excessive oxygen levels in the blood. —**hy′per•ven′ti•late′,** *v.i.*, **-lat•ed, -lat•ing.**

hy•phen (hī′fən), *n.* **1.** a short line (-) used to connect the parts of a compound word or the parts of a word divided for any purpose. —*v.t.* **2.** to hyphenate. [< L < Gk: together]

hy′phen•ate′ (-fə nāt′), *v.t.*, **-at•ed, -at•ing. 1.** to join by a hyphen. **2.** to divide with a hyphen. —**hy′-phen•a′tion,** *n.*

hyp•no•sis (hip nō′sis), *n., pl.* **-ses** (-sēz). an artificially induced trance, characterized by heightened susceptibility to suggestion.

hyp•not′ic (-not′ik), *adj.* **1.** of or resembling hypnosis or hypnotism. **2.** inducing sleep. —*n.* **3.** an agent or drug that induces sleep. —**hyp•not′i•cal•ly,** *adv.*

hyp′no•tism (-nə tiz′əm), *n.* the study or practice of inducing hypnosis. —**hyp′no•tist,** *n.*

hyp′no•tize′, *v.t.*, **-tized, -tiz•ing.** to put in a state of hypnosis.

hy•po (hī′pō), *n., pl.* **-pos.** a hypodermic syringe or injection.

hypo-, a prefix meaning: under or beneath (*hypodermic*); lacking or insufficient (*hypothyroidism*).

hy′po•al′ler•gen′ic, *adj.* designed to minimize the likelihood of an allergic response.

hy•po•chon•dri•a (hī′pə kon′drē ə), *n.* an excessive preoccupation with one's health, usu. focusing on some particular symptom. —**hy′po•chon′dri•ac′,** *n., adj.*

hy•poc•ri•sy (hi pok′rə sē), *n., pl.* **-sies.** the professing of publicly approved qualities, beliefs, or feelings that one does not really possess.

hyp•o•crite (hip′ə krit), *n.* a person who practices hypocrisy. —**hyp′o•crit′i•cal,** *adj.* —**hyp′o•crit′i•cal•ly,** *adv.*

hy•po•der•mic (hī′pə dûr′mik), *adj.* **1.** introduced or injected under the skin. —*n.* **2.** a hypodermic injection. **3.** a hypodermic syringe or needle.

hypoder′mic syringe′, *n.* a small syringe having a detachable hollow needle (**hypoder′mic nee′dle**) for use in injecting solutions under the skin.

hy•po•gly•ce•mi•a (hī′pō glī sē′mē ə), *n.* an abnormally low level of glucose in the blood. —**hy′po•gly•ce′mic,** *adj.*

hy•pot•e•nuse (hī pot′n ōōs′, -yōōs′), *n.* the side of a right triangle opposite the right angle.

hypotenuse

hy•po•thal•a•mus (hī′pō thal′ə məs), *n., pl.* **-mi** (-mī′). a region of the brain that regulates visceral functions, as sleep cycles.

hy•po•ther•mi•a (hī′pə thûr′mē ə), *n.* subnormal body temperature.

hy•poth•e•sis (hī poth′ə sis, hi-), *n., pl.* **-ses** (-sēz′). a provisional theory or assumption set forth to explain some class of phenomena.

hy•poth′e•size′, *v.*, **-sized, -siz•ing.** —*v.i.* **1.** to form a hypothesis. —*v.t.* **2.** to assume by hypothesis.

hy•po•thet•i•cal (hī′pə thet′i kəl), *adj.* of or based on a hypothesis; conjectural. —**hy′po•thet′i•cal•ly,** *adv.*

hy•po•thy′roid•ism (-thī′roi diz′əm), *n.* deficient activity of the thyroid gland. —**hy′po•thy′roid,** *adj.*

hys•sop (his′əp), *n.* **1.** an aromatic plant of the mint family. **2.** an unidentified Biblical plant whose twigs were used in ceremonial sprinkling.

hys•ter•ec•to•my (his′tə rek′tə mē), *n., pl.* **-mies.** surgical excision of the uterus.

hys•te•ri•a (hi ster′ē ə, -stēr′-), *n., pl.* **-ri•as. 1.** a neurosis characterized by violent emotional outbreaks, sensory disturbances, etc. **2.** an uncontrollable emotional outburst, as from fear. —**hys•ter′i•cal,** *adj.* —**hys•ter′i•cal•ly,** *adv.*

hys•ter•ic (hi ster′ik), *n.* **1.** Usu., **-ics.** a fit of uncontrollable laughter or weeping. **2.** a person subject to hysteria.

Hz, hertz.

I

I, i (ī), *n., pl.* **Is** or **I's, is** or **i's.** the ninth letter of the English alphabet, a vowel.
I (ī), *pron.* the nominative singular pronoun used by a speaker or writer in referring to himself or herself.
I, interstate: *I-95.*
I, *Symbol.* **1.** the ninth in order or in a series. **2.** (*sometimes l.c.*) the Roman numeral for 1. **3.** *Chem.* iodine.
IA or **Ia.,** Iowa.
i•amb (ī′am, ī′amb), *n.* a prosodic foot of two syllables, an unstressed followed by a stressed one. —**i•am′bic,** *adj.*
-ian, var. of -AN[1].
I′ and Thou′, a book of religious philosophy (1923) by Martin Buber.
-iatrics, a combining form meaning medical care or treatment (*geriatrics*).
-iatry, a combining form meaning healing or medical practice (*psychiatry*).
I•ba•dan (ē bäd′n), *n.* a city in SW Nigeria. 1,060,000.
I•be•ri•a (ī bēr′ē ə), *n.* a peninsula in SW Europe, comprising Spain and Portugal. Also called **Ibe′rian Penin′sula.** —**I•be′ri•an,** *adj., n.*
i•bex (ī′beks), *n., pl.* **i•bex•es, ib•i•ces** (ib′ə sēz′, ī′bə-), **i•bex.** a wild goat of Eurasia and N Africa, with long, backward-curving horns.
ibid. (ib′id), ibidem.
i•bi•dem (ib′i dəm, i bī′dəm), *adv.* in the same book, chapter, page, etc., previously cited. [< L]
i•bis (ī′bis), *n., pl.* **i•bis•es, i•bis.** a large wading bird of warm regions.
-ible, var. of -ABLE.
Ib•sen (ib′sən), *n.* **Henrik,** 1828–1906, Norwegian dramatist.
i•bu•pro•fen (ī′byo͞o prō′fən), *n.* an anti-inflammatory drug, used esp. for reducing local pain and swelling.
-ic[1], an adjective suffix meaning: of or pertaining to (*prophetic*); like or characteristic of (*idyllic*); containing or made of (*alcoholic*); produced by or suggestive of (*Homeric*); showing the higher of two valences (*ferric*).
-ic[2], a noun suffix meaning: a person having (*arthritic*); an agent or drug (*cosmetic*); a follower or adherent (*Socratic*).
-ical, a combination of -IC[1] and -AL[1], used to form adjectives with a similar or somewhat different meaning from adjectives ending in -IC (*economical*).
ICBM, intercontinental ballistic missile.
ICC, Interstate Commerce Commission.
ice (īs), *n., v.,* **iced, ic•ing.** —*n.* **1.** the solid form of water, produced by freezing. **2.** a frozen dessert made of sweetened water and fruit juice. **3.** *Slang.* diamonds. —*v.t.* **4.** to change into ice; freeze. **5.** to cool with ice. **6.** to cover with icing. —*v.i.* **7.** to change to ice. **8.** to become coated with ice: *The windshield has iced up.* —***Idiom.*** **9. break the ice,** to overcome reserve or formality. **10. on thin ice,** in a precarious situation. —**iced,** *adj.*
Ice., **1.** Iceland. **2.** Icelandic.
ice′ age′, *n.* (*often caps.*) the Pleistocene Epoch, during which much of the Northern Hemisphere was covered by great ice sheets.
ice′ bag′, *n.* a waterproof bag filled with ice and applied to a part of the body, as to reduce swelling.
ice′berg (-bûrg), *n.* a large floating mass of ice detached from a glacier and carried out to sea.
ice′bound′, *adj.* obstructed or hemmed in by ice.
ice′box′, *n.* **1.** an insulated cabinet packed with ice, used for cooling food and beverages. **2.** a refrigerator.
ice′break′er, *n.* a ship used for breaking navigable passages through ice.
ice′cap′, *n.* a domelike cover of ice over an area.
ice′ cream′, *n.* a frozen dessert made with cream or milk, sweeteners, and flavoring.
ice′ floe′, *n.* FLOE.
ice′ hock′ey, *n.* a game played on ice between two teams, the object being to shoot a puck into the opponents' cage.
Ice′land, *n.* an island republic in the N Atlantic between Greenland and Scandinavia. 247,357. —**Ice′land′er,** *n.*
Ice•lan′dic (-lan′dik), *adj.* **1.** of Iceland, its inhabitants, or their language. —*n.* **2.** the Germanic language of Iceland.
ice′ milk′, *n.* a frozen dessert similar to ice cream but made with skim milk.
ice′ pick′, *n.* a tool for chipping ice.
ice′ skate′, *n.* a shoe or boot fitted with a metal blade, used for skating on ice. —**ice′-skate′,** *v.i.,* **-skat•ed, -skat•ing.** —**ice′ skat′er,** *n.*
ich•thy•ol•o•gy (ik′thē ol′ə jē), *n.* the branch of zoology dealing with fishes. —**ich′thy•ol′o•gist,** *n.*
i•ci•cle (ī′si kəl), *n.* a hanging piece of ice formed by the freezing of dripping water.
ic′ing, *n.* a mixture, as of sugar, liquid, butter, and flavoring, used to coat cakes, cookies, etc.
i•con (ī′kon), *n.* **1.** a picture, image, or other representation. **2.** (in the Eastern Church) a sacred image of Christ, a saint, etc. **3.** a small graphic image on a computer screen representing a file or a command.
i•con′o•clast′ (-ə klast′), *n.* a person who attacks cherished beliefs or traditional institutions. —**i•con′o•clas′tic,** *adj.*
-ics, a suffix meaning: an art, science, or field of knowledge (*physics*); activities or practices of a certain kind (*acrobatics*). —**Usage.** Nouns ending in -ICS that name fields of study, sciences, or the like usu. take a singular verb: *Acoustics deals with sound. Politics fascinates me.* In certain uses, often when preceded by a determiner like *the, his, her,* or *their,* most of these nouns can take a plural verb: *The acoustics* (sound-reflecting qualities) *of the hall are splendid. Their politics* (political opinions) *have antagonized everyone.*
ic•tus (ik′təs), *n., pl.* **-tus•es, -tus.** rhythmical or metrical stress.
ICU, intensive care unit.
i•cy (ī′sē), *adj.,* **i•ci•er, i•ci•est.** **1.** full of or covered with ice. **2.** resembling ice. **3.** very cold. **4.** lacking warmth of feeling. —**i′ci•ly,** *adv.* —**i′ci•ness,** *n.*
id (id), *n. Psychoanalysis.* the part of the psyche that is the source of unconscious and instinctive impulses.
ID (ī′dē′), *n., pl.* **IDs, ID's.** a document, card, or other means of identification.
ID or **Id.,** Idaho.
I'd (īd), contraction of *I would* or *I had.*
I.D., **1.** identification. **2.** identity. **3.** Intelligence Department.
Ida., Idaho.
I•da•ho (ī′də hō′), *n.* a state in the NW United States. 1,189,251. *Cap.:* Boise. *Abbr.:* ID, Id., Ida. —**I′da•ho′an,** *adj., n.*
i•de•a (ī dē′ə, ī dēə′), *n.* **1.** a conception existing in the mind as a result of mental activity. **2.** an opinion or belief. **3.** a plan. **4.** a purpose or guiding principle.
i•de•al (ī dē′əl, ī dēl′), *n.* **1.** a conception of something in its perfection. **2.** a standard of perfection. **3.** a person or thing regarded as conforming to such a standard. **4.** an ultimate aim. —*adj.* **5.** conforming to

an ideal. **6.** regarded as perfect. **7.** existing only in the imagination.

i·de′al·ism, *n.* **1.** the pursuit of one's ideals. **2.** the practice of idealizing. —**i·de′al·ist,** *n.* —**i·de′al·is′tic,** *adj.* —**i·de′al·is′ti·cal·ly,** *adv.*

i·de′al·ize′, *v.t.,* **-ized, -iz·ing.** to consider or represent as having qualities of ideal perfection. —**i·de′al·i·za′tion,** *n.*

i·de′al·ly, *adv.* **1.** in accordance with an ideal. **2.** in theory or principle.

i·dem (ī′dem, id′em), *pron., adj.* the same as previously given or mentioned. [< L]

i·den·ti·cal (ī den′ti kəl, i den′-), *adj.* **1.** similar or alike in every way. **2.** the very same. —**i·den′ti·cal·ly,** *adv.*

i·den·ti·fi·ca·tion (ī den′tə fi kā′shən, i den′-), *n.* **1.** the act of identifying or the state of being identified. **2.** something that identifies one.

i·den′ti·fy′, *v.t.,* **-fied, -fy·ing. 1.** to verify the identity of. **2.** to regard as identical. **3.** to associate closely. —**i·den′ti·fi′a·ble,** *adj.*

i·den′ti·ty (-tē), *n., pl.* **-ties. 1.** the state or fact of remaining the same. **2.** the condition of being oneself or itself and not another. **3.** the state or fact of being the same one as described. **4.** the sense of self.

id·e·o·gram (id′ē ə gram′, ī′dē-), *n.* a written symbol that represents an idea or object directly rather than a particular word.

i·de·ol·o·gy (ī′dē ol′ə jē, id′ē-), *n., pl.* **-gies. 1.** the body of doctrine or thought that guides an individual, social movement, institution, or group. **2.** such a body of doctrine or thought forming a political or social program. —**i′de·o·log′i·cal,** *adj.*

ides (īdz), *n.* (*often cap.*) (*used with a sing. or pl. v.*) (in the ancient Roman calendar) the 15th day of March, May, July, or October, or the 13th day of the other months.

id·i·o·cy (id′ē ə sē), *n., pl.* **-cies. 1.** utterly senseless or foolish behavior. **2.** the state of being an idiot.

id·i·om (id′ē əm), *n.* **1.** an expression whose meaning is not predictable from the usual meanings of its elements. **2.** a language, dialect, or style of speaking peculiar to a people, occupational group, etc. **3.** the manner of expression characteristic of a given language. —**id′i·o·mat′ic,** *adj.* —**id′i·o·mat′i·cal·ly,** *adv.*

id·i·o·path·ic (id′ē ə path′ik), *adj.* of unknown cause, as a disease.

id·i·o·syn·cra·sy (id′ē ə sing′krə sē, -sin′-), *n., pl.* **-sies.** a habit or mannerism peculiar to an individual. —**id′i·o·syn·crat′ic** (-ō sin krat′ik, -sing-), *adj.*

id·i·ot (id′ē ət), *n.* **1.** an utterly stupid or foolish person. **2.** (in a former classification of mental retardation) a person having a mental age of less than three years. —**id′i·ot′ic** (-ot′ik), *adj.* —**id′i·ot′i·cal·ly,** *adv.*

i·dle (īd′l), *adj.,* **i·dler, i·dlest,** *v.,* **i·dled, i·dling.** —*adj.* **1.** not working or active. **2.** not filled with activity: *idle hours.* **3.** lazy. **4.** of no real worth: *idle talk.* **5.** having no basis or reason: *idle fears.* —*v.i.* **6.** to pass time doing nothing. **7.** to move aimlessly. **8.** (of a machine, engine, or mechanism) to operate at a low speed. —*v.t.* **9.** to pass (time) doing nothing: *to idle away the afternoon.* **10.** to cause to be idle. —**i′dle·ness,** *n.* —**i′dler,** *n.* —**i′dly,** *adv.*

i·dol (īd′l), *n.* **1.** an image representing a deity and worshiped as such. **2.** a person or thing devotedly admired.

i·dol·a·try (ī dol′ə trē), *n., pl.* **-tries. 1.** the religious worship of idols. **2.** excessive admiration or devotion. —**i·dol′a·ter,** *n.* —**i·dol′a·trous,** *adj.*

i·dol·ize (īd′l īz′), *v.t.,* **-ized, -iz·ing. 1.** to regard with adoration or devotion. **2.** to worship as a god.

i·dyll or **i·dyl** (īd′l), *n.* **1.** a poem or prose composition that describes pastoral scenes or events or any charmingly simple episode. **2.** an episode or scene of charming simplicity. —**i·dyl·lic** (ī dil′ik), *adj.*

IE or **I.E.,** Indo-European.

i.e., that is. [< L *id est*]

-ier, var. of **-EER** (*financier*).

if (if), *conj.* **1.** in case that; granting or supposing that; on condition that: *I'll go if you do.* **2.** even though: *an enthusiastic if small audience.* **3.** whether: *She asked if I knew Spanish.*

if′fy, *adj.,* **-fi·er, -fi·est.** *Informal.* full of unresolved points or questions. —**if′fi·ness,** *n.*

igloo

ig·loo (ig′lōō), *n., pl.* **-loos.** an Eskimo dwelling usu. built of blocks of hard snow and shaped like a dome.

ig·ne·ous (ig′nē əs), *adj.* **1.** produced under intense heat, as rocks of volcanic origin. **2.** of or characteristic of fire.

ig·nite (ig nīt′), *v.,* **-nit·ed, -nit·ing.** —*v.t.* **1.** to set on fire. —*v.i.* **2.** to catch fire. —**ig·nit′a·ble, ig·nit′i·ble,** *adj.*

ig·ni′tion (-nish′ən), *n.* **1.** the act of igniting or the state of being ignited. **2.** a means for igniting. **3.** (in an internal-combustion engine) the process that ignites the fuel in the cylinder.

ig·no·ble (ig nō′bəl), *adj.* of low character. —**ig′no·bil′i·ty, ig·no′ble·ness,** *n.* —**ig·no′bly,** *adv.*

ig·no·min·i·ous (ig′nə min′ē əs), *adj.* **1.** marked by disgrace or dishonor. **2.** bearing or deserving contempt. —**ig′no·min′i·ous·ly,** *adv.* —**ig′no·min′y,** *n.*

ig·no·ra·mus (ig′nə rā′məs, -ram′əs), *n., pl.* **-mus·es.** an extremely ignorant person.

ig·no·rant (ig′nər ənt), *adj.* **1.** lacking in knowledge, education, or training. **2.** uninformed; unaware. **3.** showing lack of knowledge. —**ig′no·rance,** *n.* —**ig′no·rant·ly,** *adv.*

ig·nore (ig nôr′), *v.t.,* **-nored, -nor·ing.** to refrain from noticing or recognizing.

i·gua·na (i gwä′nə), *n., pl.* **-nas.** a large lizard of tropical America.

I′ have′ a dream′, a phrase in a speech by Martin Luther King, Jr. during a civil rights march on Washington on August 28, 1963.

IHS, 1. Jesus. [< LL < Gk: partial transliteration of the first three letters of *Iēsoûs* Jesus] **2.** Jesus Savior of Men. [< ML *Iēsus Hominum Salvātor*] **3.** in this sign (the cross) shalt thou conquer. [< L *In Hōc Signō Vincēs*] **4.** in this (cross) is salvation. [< L *In Hōc Salūs*]

Ike (īk), *n.* nickname for Dwight D. Eisenhower.

IL, Illinois.

il-¹, var. of IN-¹ before *l.*

il-², var. of IN-² before *l.*

il·e·i·tis (il′ē ī′tis), *n.* inflammation of the ileum.

il′e·um (-ē əm), *n., pl.* **-e·a** (-ē ə). the division of the small intestine extending from the jejunum to the large intestine.

Il·i·ad (il′ē əd), *n.* a Greek epic poem describing the siege of Troy, ascribed to Homer.

I′ like′ Ike′, a political slogan in support of Dwight D. Eisenhower.

il·i·um (il′ē əm), *n., pl.* **-i·a** (-ē ə). the broad upper portion of each hipbone.

ilk (ilk), *n.* family, class, or kind.

ill (il), *adj.,* **worse, worst,** *n., adv.* —*adj.* **1.** of unsound physical or mental health. **2.** objectionable; faulty. **3.** hostile; unkindly: *ill feeling.* **4.** evil; wicked: *of ill repute.* **5.** unfavorable; adverse. —*n.* **6.** trouble; misfortune. **7.** evil. **8.** sickness. —*adv.* **9.** unsatisfactorily; poorly: *It ill befits a man to betray old friends.* **10.** badly. **11.** with difficulty; scarcely:

an expense we can ill afford. —*Idiom.* **12. ill at ease,** uncomfortable; uneasy.

I'll (īl), contraction of *I will.*

Ill., Illinois.

ill'-ad•vised', *adj.* acting or done without due consideration.

ill'-bred', *adj.* unmannerly; rude.

il•le•gal (i lē'gəl), *adj.* **1.** forbidden by law. **2.** contrary to official rules or regulations. —il'le•gal'i•ty, *n.* —il•le'gal•ly, *adv.*

il•leg'i•ble, *adj.* impossible or hard to read. —il•leg'i•bil'i•ty, *n.* —il•leg'i•bly, *adv.*

il'le•git'i•mate (-mit), *adj.* **1.** born out of wedlock. **2.** not sanctioned by law or custom. —il'le•git'i•ma•cy (-mə sē), *n.* —il'le•git'i•mate•ly, *adv.*

ill'-fat'ed, *adj.* **1.** destined to an unhappy fate. **2.** bringing bad fortune.

ill'-got'ten, *adj.* acquired by dishonest or evil means.

ill'-hu'mor, *n.* a disagreeable or surly mood. —ill'-hu'mored, *adj.*

il•lib'er•al, *adj.* narrow-minded; bigoted.

il•lic'it, *adj.* not legally permitted. —il•lic'it•ly, *adv.* —il•lic'it•ness, *n.*

il•lim•it•a•ble (i lim'i tə bəl), *adj.* not limitable; boundless.

Il•li•nois (il'ə noi'; *sometimes* -noiz'), *n.* **1.** a state in the central United States. 11,846,544. *Cap.:* Springfield. *Abbr.:* IL, Ill. **2.** (*used with a pl. v.*) the members of a group of American Indian tribes formerly occupying parts of Illinois and adjoining regions westward.

il•lit'er•ate (-it), *adj.* **1.** unable to read and write. **2.** having little education. **3.** showing lack of culture. —*n.* **4.** an illiterate person. —il•lit'er•a•cy, *n.*

ill'-man'nered, *adj.* having bad manners.

ill'-na'tured, *adj.* having or showing an unpleasant disposition. —ill'-na'tured•ly, *adv.* —ill'-na'tured•ness, *n.*

ill'ness, *n.* **1.** the state of being ill. **2.** a particular ailment; sickness.

il•log'i•cal, *adj.* not logical; unreasonable.

ill'-starred', *adj.* unlucky; ill-fated.

ill'-treat', *v.t.* to treat badly. —ill'-treat'ment, *n.*

il•lu•mi•nate (i lōō'mə nāt'), *v.t.* -nat•ed, -nat•ing. **1.** to supply with light. **2.** to clarify. **3.** to enlighten. **4.** to decorate (a manuscript or book) with colors and gold or silver. —il•lu'mi•na'tion, *n.*

il•lu'mine (-min), *v.t.* -mined, -min•ing. to illumine.

illus., **1.** illustrated. **2.** illustration.

ill-use (*v.* il'yōōz'; *n.* -yōōs'), *v.,* -used, -us•ing, *n.* —*v.t.* **1.** to treat badly or unjustly. —*n.* **2.** Also, **ill'-us'age.** bad or unjust treatment.

il•lu•sion (i lōō'zhən), *n.* **1.** something that deceives by producing a false impression of reality. **2.** a misleading perception of visual stimuli.

il•lu'so•ry (-sə rē, -zə-), *adj.* causing or like an illusion.

il•lus•trate (il'ə strāt', i lus'trāt), *v.t.,* -trat•ed, -trat•ing. **1.** to furnish with drawings, pictures, or other artwork. **2.** to make intelligible with examples or analogies. —il'lus•tra'tor, *n.*

il'lus•tra'tion, *n.* **1.** something that illustrates, as a picture in a magazine. **2.** an example intended for explanation or corroboration. **3.** the act of illustrating.

il•lus•tra•tive (i lus'trə tiv), *adj.* serving to illustrate. —il•lus'tra•tive•ly, *adv.*

il•lus•tri•ous (i lus'trē əs), *adj.* distinguished; renowned. —il•lus'tri•ous•ly, *adv.* —il•lus'tri•ous•ness, *n.*

ill' will', *n.* hostile feeling.

I'm (īm), contraction of *I am.*

im-¹, var. of IN-¹ before *b, m, p.*

im-², var. of IN-² before *b, m, p.*

im•age (im'ij), *n., v.,* -aged, -ag•ing. —*n.* **1.** a physical likeness or representation of a person, animal, or thing. **2.** an optical counterpart of an object, as is produced by reflection from a mirror. **3.** a mental representation. **4.** form; semblance: *created in*

God's image. **5.** counterpart; copy: *That child is the image of his mother.* **6.** a general or public perception, as of a company. **7.** type; embodiment: *He was the image of frustration.* **8.** a figure of speech. —*v.t.* **9.** to picture in the mind. **10.** to reflect the likeness of.

im'age•ry, *n., pl.* -ries. **1.** mental images collectively. **2.** figurative description or illustration.

im•ag•i•na•ble (i maj'ə nə bəl), *adj.* capable of being imagined or conceived. —i•mag'i•na•bly, *adv.*

im•ag'i•nar'y (-ner'ē), *adj.* existing only in the imagination.

im•ag'i•na'tion (-nā'shən), *n.* **1.** the act or faculty of imagining. **2.** the ability to form mental images of things never experienced. **3.** creativity or resourcefulness. —im•ag'i•na•tive (-nə tiv), *adj.* —im•ag'i•na•tive•ly, *adv.*

im•ag'ine (-in), *v.t., v.i.,* -ined, -in•ing. **1.** to form a mental image of (something not actually present to the senses). **2.** to believe. **3.** to suppose or guess.

i•ma•go (i mā'gō, i mä'-), *n., pl.* -goes, -gi•nes (-gə nēz'). an adult insect.

i•mam (i mäm'), *n. Islam.* the title for a Muslim religious leader or chief. Also, **i•maum** (i mäm', i•môm'). —i•mam'ship, *n.*

im•bal•ance (im bal'əns), *n.* the state or condition of lacking balance.

im•be•cile (im'bə sil), *n.* **1.** (in a former classification of mental retardation) a person having a mental age of seven or eight years. **2.** a stupid person. —im'be•cil'ic, *adj.*

im•bibe (im bīb'), *v.,* -bibed, -bib•ing. —*v.t.* **1.** to consume (liquids) by drinking. **2.** to receive into the mind. —*v.i.* **3.** to drink, esp. alcoholic beverages. —im•bib'er, *n.*

im•bri•ca•tion (im'bri kā'shən), *n.* **1.** an overlapping, as of tiles or shingles. **2.** a pattern resembling this.

im•bro•glio (im brōl'yō), *n., pl.* -glios. **1.** a complicated misunderstanding or disagreement. **2.** an intricate and perplexing state of affairs.

im•bue (im byōō'), *v.t.,* -bued, -bu•ing. **1.** to permeate or inspire profoundly: *imbued with patriotism.* **2.** to saturate with moisture or color.

IMF, International Monetary Fund.

im•i•tate (im'i tāt'), *v.t.,* -tat•ed, -tat•ing. **1.** to follow as a model or example. **2.** to mimic; impersonate. **3.** to reproduce closely. **4.** to assume the appearance of. —im'i•ta'tor, *n.*

im'i•ta'tion, *n.* **1.** a result or product of imitating; copy. **2.** the act of imitating. —*adj.* **3.** designed to imitate something genuine.

im'i•ta'tive, *adj.* **1.** given to imitation. **2.** of or characterized by imitation. **3.** counterfeit. —im'i•ta'tive•ly, *adv.* —im'i•ta'tive•ness, *n.*

im•mac•u•late (i mak'yə lit), *adj.* **1.** free from spot or stain. **2.** free from moral blemish. **3.** free from errors. —im•mac'u•late•ly, *adv.* —im•mac'u•late•ness, *n.*

Immac'ulate Concep'tion, *n.* the Roman Catholic doctrine according to which the Virgin Mary was conceived in her mother's womb without the stain of original sin.

im•ma•nent (im'ə nənt), *adj.* **1.** remaining within; inherent. **2.** (of the Deity) indwelling the universe, time, etc. —im'ma•nence, im'ma•nen•cy, *n.* —im'ma•nent•ly, *adv.*

Im•man•u•el (i man'yōō əl), *n.* the name of the Messiah as prophesied by Isaiah. Isa. 7:14. [< Heb *'immānū'ēl* lit., God is with us]

im•ma•te•ri•al (im'ə tēr'ē əl), *adj.* **1.** not pertinent; unimportant. **2.** incorporeal; spiritual. —im'ma•te'ri•al•ly, *adv.* —im'ma•te'ri•al•ness, *n.*

im'ma•ture', *adj.* **1.** not yet mature or ripe. **2.** emotionally undeveloped; childish. —im'ma•ture'ly, *adv.* —im'ma•tu'ri•ty, *n.*

im•meas'ur•a•ble, *adj.* incapable of being measured; limitless. —im•meas'ur•a•bly, *adv.*

im•me•di•a•cy (i mē'dē ə sē), *n., pl.* -cies. **1.** the state or quality of being immediate. **2.** Often, -cies. an immediate need.

im•me′di•ate (-it), *adj.* **1.** occurring without delay. **2.** following or preceding without a lapse of time. **3.** having no object or space intervening; very close. **4.** of the present time. **5.** without intervening medium or agent. —**im•me′di•ate•ly,** *adv.*

im′me•mo′ri•al, *adj.* extending back beyond memory, record, or knowledge. —**im′me•mo′ri•al•ly,** *adv.*

im•mense (i mens′), *adj.* vast; immeasurable. —**im•mense′ly,** *adv.* —**im•men′si•ty,** *n.*

im•merse (i mûrs′), *v.t.,* -**mersed,** -**mers•ing. 1.** to plunge into or place under a liquid. **2.** to involve deeply; absorb. **3.** to baptize by submerging in the water. —**im•mers′i•ble,** *adj.*

im•mer•sion (i mûr′zhən, -shən), *n.* **1.** an act or instance of immersing. **2.** baptism in which the whole body of the person is submerged in the water.

im•mi•grant (im′i grənt), *n.* **1.** a person who immigrates. **2.** an organism found in a new habitat.

im′mi•grate′ (-grāt′), *v.i.,* -**grat•ed,** -**grat•ing.** to come to a country of which one is not a native, usu. for permanent residence. —**im′mi•gra′tion,** *n.*

im•mi•nent (im′ə nənt), *adj.* likely to occur at any moment. —**im′mi•nence,** *n.* —**im′mi•nent•ly,** *adv.*

im•mo•bile (i mō′bəl, -bēl), *adj.* **1.** incapable of moving or being moved. **2.** motionless. —**im′mo•bil′i•ty,** *n.* —**im•mo′bi•li•za′tion,** *n.* —**im•mo′bi•lize′,** *v.t.,* -**lized,** -**liz•ing.**

im•mod′er•ate (-it), *adj.* exceeding just or reasonable limits.

im•mod′est, *adj.* **1.** indecent; shameless. **2.** impudent. —**im•mod′est•ly,** *adv.* —**im•mod′es•ty,** *n.*

im•mo•late (im′ə lāt′), *v.t.,* -**lat•ed,** -**lat•ing.** to kill as a sacrificial victim, as by fire. —**im′mo•la′tion,** *n.*

im•mor′al, *adj.* **1.** violating moral principles. **2.** licentious; lascivious. —**im•mor′al•ly,** *adv.*

im′mo•ral′i•ty, *n., pl.* -**ties. 1.** immoral quality, character, or conduct. **2.** an immoral act.

im•mor′tal, *adj.* **1.** not subject to death. **2.** perpetual; everlasting. **3.** remembered through all time. —*n.* **4.** an immortal being. **5.** a person of enduring fame. —**im′mor•tal′i•ty,** *n.* —**im•mor′tal•ly,** *adv.*

im•mor′tal•ize′, *v.t.,* -**ized,** -**iz•ing.** to make immortal, esp. in fame.

im•mov•a•ble (i mōō′və bəl), *adj.* **1.** fixed; stationary. **2.** implacable; unyielding. —**im•mov′a•bil′i•ty,** *n.*

im•mune (i myōōn′), *adj.* **1.** protected from a disease or infection, as by inoculation. **2.** exempt or not susceptible. —**im•mu′ni•ty,** *n., pl.* -**ties.**

im•mu•nize (im′yə nīz′), *v.t.,* -**nized,** -**niz•ing.** to make immune. —**im′mu•ni•za′tion,** *n.*

im′mu•nol′o•gy (-nol′ə jē), *n.* the branch of science dealing with immunity, as to a disease. —**im′•mu•no•log′ic** (-nl oj′ik), **im′mu•no•log′i•cal,** *adj.* —**im′mu•nol′o•gist,** *n.*

im•mure (i myŏōr′), *v.t.,* -**mured,** -**mur•ing.** to enclose within or as if within walls.

im•mu′ta•ble, *adj.* not mutable; unchangeable. —**im•mu′ta•bil′i•ty,** *n.* —**im•mu′ta•bly,** *adv.*

imp (imp), *n.* **1.** a small devil or demon. **2.** a mischievous child.

imp., **1.** imperative. **2.** imperfect. **3.** imperial.

im•pact (*n.* im′pakt; *v.* im pakt′), *n.* **1.** the striking of one thing against another. **2.** influence; effect. **3.** a forcible impinging. —*v.t.* **4.** to drive or press firmly into something. **5.** to collide with. **6.** to have an effect on. —*v.i.* **7.** to make contact forcefully. **8.** to have an effect.

im•pact′ed, *adj.* (of a tooth) so confined in its socket as to be incapable of normal eruption.

im•pair (im pâr′), *v.t.* to make worse; weaken; damage. —**im•pair′ment,** *n.*

im•pal•a (im pal′ə, -pä′lä), *n., pl.* -**pal•as,** -**pal•a.** an African antelope, the male of which has lyre-shaped horns.

im•pale (im pāl′), *v.t.,* -**paled,** -**pal•ing.** to pierce or fix with something pointed. —**im•pale′ment,** *n.* —**im•pal′er,** *n.*

im•pal′pa•ble, *adj.* **1.** incapable of being perceived by the sense of touch. **2.** difficult for the mind to grasp readily. —**im•pal′pa•bly,** *adv.*

im•pan′el, *v.t.,* -**eled,** -**el•ing** or (*esp. Brit.*) -**elled,** -**el•ling. 1.** to enter on a panel for jury duty. **2.** to select (a jury) from a panel.

im•part (im pärt′), *v.t.* **1.** to make known. **2.** to give; bestow.

im•par′tial, *adj.* not partial or biased. —**im•par′ti•al′i•ty** (-shē al′i tē), *n.* —**im•par′tial•ly,** *adv.*

im•pass′a•ble, *adj.* not allowing passage.

im•passe (im′pas, im pas′), *n.* **1.** a position or situation from which there is no escape. **2.** a road or way that has no outlet.

im•pas′si•ble (-pas′ə bəl), *adj.* **1.** incapable of suffering pain. **2.** incapable of emotion. —**im•pas′si•bil′i•ty,** *n.* —**im•pas′si•bly,** *adv.*

im•pas′sioned, *adj.* filled with intense feeling or passion.

im•pas′sive, *adj.* showing or feeling no emotion. —**im•pas′sive•ly,** *adv.* —**im′pas•siv′i•ty,** *n.*

im•pas•to (im pas′tō, -pä′stō), *n.* **1.** the laying on of paint thickly. **2.** the paint so laid on.

im•pa′tience, *n.* **1.** intolerance of anything that thwarts, delays, or hinders. **2.** eager desire for relief or change.

im•pa•tiens (im pā′shənz), *n., pl.* -**tiens.** an annual plant with irregular, spurred flowers.

im•pa′tient, *adj.* **1.** not readily accepting interference. **2.** indicating lack of patience. **3.** restless in desire or expectation. —**im•pa′tient•ly,** *adv.*

im•peach (im pēch′), *v.t.* **1.** to accuse (a public official) of misconduct in office by bringing charges before an appropriate tribunal. **2.** to challenge the credibility of. —**im•peach′a•ble,** *adj.* —**im•peach′ment,** *n.*

im•pec•ca•ble (im pek′ə bəl), *adj.* **1.** faultless. **2.** not liable to sin. —**im•pec′ca•bil′i•ty,** *n.* —**im•pec′ca•bly,** *adv.*

im•pe•cu•ni•ous (im′pi kyōō′nē əs), *adj.* having little or no money. —**im′pe•cu′ni•ous•ly,** *adv.* —**im′pe•cu′ni•ous•ness,** *n.*

im•ped•ance (im pēd′ns), *n.* the total opposition to alternating current by an electric circuit.

im•pede (im pēd′), *v.t.,* -**ped•ed,** -**ped•ing,** to slow in movement or progress by means of obstacles or hindrances. —**im•ped′er,** *n.*

im•ped′i•ment (-ped′ə mənt), *n.* **1.** an obstruction; hindrance. **2.** any physical defect that impedes normal or easy speech.

im•ped′i•men′ta (-men′tə), *n.pl.* things that impede, as bulky equipment.

im•pel (im pel′), *v.t.,* -**pelled,** -**pel•ling. 1.** to drive or urge forward. **2.** to impart motion to. —**im•pel′ler,** *n.*

im•pend (im pend′), *v.i.* **1.** to be about to happen. **2.** to threaten; menace.

im•pen′e•tra•ble, *adj.* **1.** incapable of being penetrated, pierced, or entered. **2.** incapable of being understood. —**im•pen′e•tra•bil′i•ty,** *n.* —**im•pen′e•tra•bly,** *adv.*

im•pen′i•tent, *adj.* not feeling regret or remorse. —**im•pen′i•tence,** *n.*

imper., imperative.

im•per•a•tive (im per′ə tiv), *adj.* **1.** absolutely necessary or required. **2.** expressing a command. **3.** of or noting a grammatical mood that is used in commands, exhortations, etc. —*n.* **4.** something imperative. **5.** the imperative mood. —**im•per′a•tive•ly,** *adv.*

im′per•cep′ti•ble, *adj.* **1.** very slight, gradual, or subtle. **2.** not perceived by or affecting the senses. —**im′per•cep′ti•bil′i•ty,** *n.* —**im′per•cep′ti•bly,** *adv.*

im′per•cep′tive, *adj.* not perceptive.

imperf., imperfect.

im•per′fect, *adj.* **1.** of or characterized by defects or weaknesses. **2.** lacking completeness. **3.** of or noting a verb tense typically indicating a habitual, repeated, or continuing action or state in the past. —*n.*

4. the imperfect tense. —im•per′fect•ly, *adv.* —im•per′fect•ness, *n.*

im′per•fec′tion, *n.* **1.** a fault; flaw. **2.** the quality or state of being imperfect.

im•pe•ri•al[1] (im pēr′ē əl), *adj.* **1.** of or characteristic of an empire, emperor, or empress. **2.** characterizing the rule or authority of a sovereign state over its dependencies. **3.** regal; imperious. **4.** of superior size or quality. —im•pe′ri•al•ly, *adv.* —im•pe′ri•al•ness, *n.*

im•pe•ri•al[2] (im pēr′ē əl), *n.* a small, pointed beard beneath the lower lip.

impe′rial gal′lon, *n.* a British gallon equivalent to 1⅕ U.S. gallons.

im•pe′ri•al•ism, *n.* the policy of extending the rule or authority of a nation over foreign countries, or of acquiring colonies and dependencies. —im•pe′ri•al•ist, *n., adj.* —im•pe′ri•al•is′tic, *adj.*

impe′rial pres′idency, *n.* a presidency that wrongfully appropriates powers which are designated to other branches of government by the Constitution. [from a 1973 book of that name by Arthur M. Schlesinger]

im•per′il, *v.t.*, -iled, -il•ing or (*esp. Brit.*) -illed, -il•ling. to put in peril. —im•per′il•ment, *n.*

im•pe•ri•ous (im pēr′ē əs), *adj.* **1.** domineering in a haughty manner. **2.** urgent; imperative. —im•pe′ri•ous•ly, *adv.* —im•pe′ri•ous•ness, *n.*

im•per′ish•a•ble, *adj.* not perishable; enduring. —im•per′ish•a•bly, *adv.*

im•per′ma•nent, *adj.* not permanent. —im•per′ma•nence, *n.* —im•per′ma•nent•ly, *adv.*

im•per′me•a•ble, *adj.* **1.** not permeable or passable. **2.** not permitting the passage of a fluid. —im•per′me•a•bil′i•ty, *n.* —im•per′me•a•bly, *adv.*

im′per•mis′si•ble, *adj.* not permissible.

im•per′son•al, *adj.* **1.** lacking reference to a particular person. **2.** devoid of human character or traits. **3.** (of a verb) having only third person singular forms, usu. with the pronoun *it* as the subject. —im•per′son•al•ly, *adv.*

im•per•son•ate (im pûr′sə nāt′), *v.t.*, -at•ed, -at•ing. to assume the character or appearance of. —im•per′son•a′tion, *n.* —im•per′son•a′tor, *n.*

im•per′ti•nent, *adj.* **1.** boldly rude or disrespectful. **2.** not pertinent. —im•per′ti•nence, *n.* —im•per′ti•nent•ly, *adv.*

im′per•turb′a•ble, *adj.* incapable of being upset or agitated. —im′per•turb′a•bil′i•ty, *n.* —im′per•turb′a•bly, *adv.*

im•per•vi•ous (im pûr′vē əs), *adj.* **1.** not permitting penetration or passage. **2.** incapable of being influenced or affected. —im•per′vi•ous•ly, *adv.*

im•pe•ti•go (im′pi tī′gō), *n.* a contagious skin infection characterized by pustules.

im•pet•u•ous (im pech′ōō əs), *adj.* **1.** of or characterized by sudden or rash action or emotion. **2.** moving with great force. —im•pet′u•os′i•ty (-os′i tē), *n.* —im•pet′u•ous•ly, *adv.*

im•pe•tus (im′pi təs), *n., pl.* -tus•es. **1.** a driving force; impulse. **2.** the momentum of a moving body.

im•pi•e•ty, *n., pl.* -ties. **1.** the quality or state of being impious. **2.** an impious act.

im•pinge (im pinj′), *v.i.*, -pinged, -ping•ing. **1.** to encroach; infringe. **2.** to strike; collide. **3.** to make an impression. —im•pinge′ment, *n.*

im•pi•ous (im′pē əs, im pī′-), *adj.* **1.** not pious; irreligious. **2.** disrespectful. —im′pi•ous•ly, *adv.*

imp′ish, *adj.* mischievous. —imp′ish•ly, *adv.* —imp′ish•ness, *n.*

im•plac•a•ble (im plak′ə bəl, -plā′kə-), *adj.* not to be appeased, mollified, or pacified. —im•plac′a•bil′i•ty, *n.* —im•plac′a•bly, *adv.*

im•plant (*v.* im plant′, -plänt′; *n.* im′plant′, -plänt′), *v.t.* **1.** to establish firmly in the mind. **2.** to plant securely. **3.** to insert or graft (a tissue, organ, or inert substance) into the body. —*n.* **4.** a device or material used for repairing or replacing part of the body. —im•plant′a•ble, *adj.*

im•plau′si•ble, *adj.* not plausible; causing disbelief. —im•plau′si•bil′i•ty, *n.* —im•plau′si•bly, *adv.*

im•ple•ment (*n.* im′plə mənt; *v.* also -ment′), *n.* **1.** an instrument, tool, or utensil for accomplishing work. —*v.t.* **2.** to put into effect according to a plan or procedure. —im′ple•men•ta′tion, *n.*

im•pli•cate (im′pli kāt′), *v.t.*, -cat•ed, -cat•ing. **1.** to show to be involved, usu. in an incriminating manner. **2.** to imply.

im′pli•ca′tion, *n.* **1.** something implied or suggested. **2.** the act of implying or state of being implied. **3.** the act of implicating or state of being implicated.

im•plic•it (im plis′it), *adj.* **1.** not expressly stated; implied. **2.** unquestioning; absolute. **3.** potentially contained. —im•plic′it•ly, *adv.* —im•plic′it•ness, *n.*

im•plode (im plōd′), *v.i., v.t.*, -plod•ed, -plod•ing. to burst inward. —im•plo′sion (-plo′zhən), *n.* —im•plo′sive (-siv), *adj.*

im•plore (im plôr′), *v.t.*, -plored, -plor•ing. **1.** to beg urgently or piteously. **2.** to beg urgently or piteously for. —im•plor′ing•ly, *adv.*

im•ply (im plī′), *v.t.*, -plied, -ply•ing. **1.** to indicate or suggest without being explicitly stated. **2.** to involve as a necessary circumstance.

im′po•lite′, *adj.* not polite. —im′po•lite′ly, *adv.*

im•pol′i•tic, *adj.* not politic or expedient. —im•pol′i•tic•ly, *adv.*

im•pon′der•a•ble, *adj.* **1.** not susceptible to precise measurement or evaluation. —*n.* **2.** something imponderable.

im•port (*v.* im pôrt′; *n.* im′pôrt), *v.t.* **1.** to bring in from a foreign country or other source, esp. for resale. **2.** to mean or signify. **3.** to bring (electronic documents, data, etc.) into one application program from another. —*n.* **4.** something imported. **5.** consequence; importance. **6.** meaning; implication. —im•port′a•ble, *adj.* —im′por•ta′tion, *n.* —im•port′er, *n.*

im•por•tant (im pôr′tnt), *adj.* **1.** of much significance or consequence. **2.** of considerable authority or distinction. —im•por′tance, *n.* —im•por′tant•ly, *adv.*

im•por•tu•nate (im pôr′chə nit), *adj.* **1.** overly urgent or persistent in solicitation. **2.** annoying. —im•por′tu•nate•ly, *adv.*

im•por•tune (im′pôr tōōn′, -tyōōn′, im pôr′chən), *v.t., v.i.*, -tuned, -tun•ing. to urge or entreat with excessive persistence. —im′por•tun′i•ty, *n., pl.* -ties.

im•pose (im pōz′), *v.t.*, -posed, -pos•ing. **1.** to apply or establish by or as if by authority: *to impose taxes.* **2.** to thrust intrusively upon others. **3. impose on,** to take unfair advantage of. —im•pos′er, *n.* —im′po•si′tion (-pə zish′ən), *n.*

im•pos′ing, *adj.* impressive because of great size, stately appearance, etc. —im•pos′ing•ly, *adv.*

im•pos′si•ble, *adj.* **1.** incapable of being or happening. **2.** unable to be performed or effected. **3.** difficult beyond reason or propriety. **4.** utterly impracticable. **5.** hopelessly unsuitable or objectionable. —im•pos′si•bil′i•ty, *n., pl.* -ties. —im•pos′si•bly, *adv.*

im•post (im′pōst), *n.* a tax; duty.

im•pos•tor or **-post•er** (im pos′tər), *n.* a person who practices deception under an assumed identity or name.

im•pos′ture (-chər), *n.* the act or practice of using an assumed identity or name.

im•po•tent (im′pə tənt), *adj.* **1.** lacking power or ability. **2.** lacking force or effectiveness. **3.** (of a male) unable to attain or sustain an erection. —im′po•tence, im′po•ten•cy, *n.* —im′po•tent•ly, *adv.*

im•pound′, *v.t.* **1.** to shut up in or as if in a pound. **2.** to seize and retain in custody of the law.

im•pov•er•ish (im pov′ər ish, -pov′rish), *v.t.* **1.** to reduce to poverty. **2.** to exhaust the strength or vitality of. —im•pov′er•ish•ment, *n.*

im•prac′ti•ca•ble, *adj.* incapable of being put into practice or use.

im•prac′ti•cal, *adj.* **1.** not practical or useful. **2.** incapable of dealing sensibly with practical matters. **3.** impracticable. —im•prac′ti•cal′i•ty, *n.*

im·pre·cate (im′pri kāt′), v.t., -cat·ed, -cat·ing. to call down or invoke (evil or curses). —im′pre·ca′tion, n. —im′pre·ca′tor, n.

im·pre·cise′, adj. vague; inexact. —im′pre·cise′ly, adv. —im′pre·ci′sion, im′pre·cise′ness, n.

im·preg·na·ble (im preg′nə bəl), adj. **1.** strong enough to resist or withstand attack. **2.** irrefutable, as an argument. —im·preg′na·bil′i·ty, n. —im·preg′na·bly, adv.

im·preg′nate (-nāt), v.t., -nat·ed, -nat·ing. **1.** to make pregnant. **2.** to permeate or imbue. —im′preg·na′tion, n. —im·preg′na·tor, n.

im·pre·sa·ri·o (im′prə sär′ē ō′, -sâr′-), n., pl. -ri·os. one who organizes or manages public entertainments, as operas.

im·press¹ (v. im pres′; n. im′pres), v.t. **1.** to affect deeply or strongly; influence. **2.** to establish firmly in the mind. **3.** to produce (a mark) by pressure. **4.** to apply with pressure so as to leave a mark. —n. **5.** the act of impressing. **6.** a mark made by pressure. —im·press′er, n.

im·press² (im pres′), v.t. **1.** to press or force into public service, esp. into the navy. **2.** to take for public use.

im·press′i·ble, adj. impressionable. —im·press′i·bil′i·ty, n.

im·pres′sion, n. **1.** a strong effect produced on the intellect, feelings, or senses. **2.** the effect produced by an agency or influence. **3.** a somewhat vague awareness, notion, etc. **4.** a mark produced by pressure. **5.** a caricatured imitation of a famous person by an entertainer.

im·pres′sion·a·ble, adj. readily impressed.

im·pres′sion·ism, n. (often cap.) a style of 19th-century painting characterized by short brush strokes of bright colors to represent the effect of light on objects. —im·pres′sion·ist, n., adj. —im·pres′sion·is′tic, adj.

im·pres′sive, adj. arousing admiration or respect. —im·pres′sive·ly, adv. —im·pres′sive·ness, n.

im·pri·ma·tur (im′pri mä′tər, -mā′-), n. **1.** permission to print or publish a book, pamphlet, etc., granted by the Roman Catholic Church. **2.** sanction; approval.

im·print (n. im′print; v. im print′), n. **1.** a mark or indentation impressed on something. **2.** any impressed effect. **3.** the designation under which a publisher issues a given list of titles. —v.t. **4.** to mark by or as if by pressure. **5.** to produce (a mark) by pressure. **6.** to fix firmly on the mind. —im·print′er, n.

im·pris′on, v.t. to confine in or as if in a prison. —im·pris′on·ment, n.

im·prob′a·ble, adj. unlikely to be true or to happen. —im·prob′a·bil′i·ty, n. —im·prob′a·bly, adv.

im·promp·tu (im promp′tōō, -tyōō), adj., adv. without previous preparation.

im·prop′er, adj. **1.** not strictly suitable, applicable, or correct. **2.** not in accordance with propriety or regulations. —im·prop′er·ly, adv.

improp′er frac′tion, n. a fraction having the numerator greater than the denominator.

im′pro·pri′e·ty, n., pl. -ties. **1.** the quality or condition of being improper. **2.** an improper expression or act.

im·prove (im prōōv′), v., -proved, -prov·ing. —v.t. **1.** to bring into a more desirable or excellent condition; make better. **2.** to make (land) more useful or valuable, as by cultivation. —v.i. **3.** to increase in quality or value; become better. —im·prov′a·ble, adj.

im·prove′ment, n. **1.** the act of improving or state of being improved. **2.** a change or addition by which a thing is improved.

im·prov′i·dent, adj. neglecting to provide for future needs. —im·prov′i·dence, n. —im·prov′i·dent·ly, adv.

im·pro·vise (im′prə vīz′), v.t., v.i., -vised, -vis·ing. **1.** to perform, deliver, or compose without previous preparation. **2.** to make or provide from whatever materials are available. —im·prov′i·sa′tion (-prov′-

ə zā′shən), n. —im·prov′i·sa′tion·al, adj. —im′pro·vis′er, im′pro·vi′sor, n.

im·pru′dent, adj. not prudent; lacking discretion; rash. —im·pru′dence, n.

im·pu·dent (im′pyə dənt), adj. characterized by offensive boldness or disrespect. —im′pu·dence, n. —im′pu·dent·ly, adv.

im·pugn (im pyōōn′), v.t. to challenge as false; cast doubt upon. —im·pugn′er, n.

im·pulse (im′puls), n. **1.** the influence of a particular feeling or mental state. **2.** sudden inclination prompting to action. **3.** an impelling force; impetus. **4.** the motion caused by such an impetus. **5.** a sudden flow of electric current in one direction.

im·pul·sion (im pul′shən), n. **1.** the act of impelling. **2.** the resulting state or effect.

im·pul′sive, adj. **1.** actuated or swayed by impulse. **2.** inciting to action. —im·pul′sive·ly, adv. —im·pul′sive·ness, n.

im·pu·ni·ty (im pyōō′ni tē), n. exemption from punishment or detrimental effects.

im·pure′, adj. **1.** not pure; mixed with extraneous matter, esp. of an inferior nature. **2.** not morally pure; unchaste. —im·pure′ly, adv. —im·pur′i·ty, n., pl. -ties.

im·pute (im pyōōt′), v.t., -put·ed, -put·ing. to attribute or ascribe (esp. something discreditable) to someone or something. —im′pu·ta′tion (-pyōō tā′shən), n.

in (in), prep. **1.** (used to indicate inclusion within space or a place): walking in the park. **2.** (used to indicate inclusion within something immaterial): in politics. **3.** (used to indicate occurrence during a period of time): in ancient times. **4.** (used to indicate qualification, as of condition or manner): spoken in a whisper. **5.** (used to indicate means): written in French. **6.** into: Let's go in the house. **7.** (used to indicate purpose): a party in honor of the winner. —adv. **8.** in or into some place, position, etc. **9.** on the inside. **10.** in one's house or office. —adj. **11.** inner; internal. **12.** fashionable; stylish. **13.** comprehensible only to a special group. **14.** being in power. —n **15.** Usu., **ins.** persons in power. **16.** pull or influence. —Idiom. **17. in for,** certain to undergo (a disagreeable experience). **18. in that,** because; inasmuch as.

IN, Indiana.

In, Chem. Symbol. indium.

in-¹, a prefix meaning in, into, within, or toward (incarcerate).

in-², a prefix meaning not or lack of (inexperience).

-in, a combining form meaning any organized protest or social activity (sing-in).

in., inch.

in ab·sen·tia (in ab sen′shə, -shē ə), adv. Latin. in absence.

in·ac·ti·vate (in ak′tə vāt′), v.t., -vat·ed, -vat·ing. to make inactive. —in·ac′ti·va′tion, n.

in·ad·vert·ent (in′əd vûr′tnt), adj. **1.** unintentional. **2.** not attentive; heedless. —in′ad·vert′ence, n. —in′ad·vert′ent·ly, adv.

in·al·ien·a·ble, adj. not transferable or capable of being taken away: inalienable rights. —in·al′ien·a·bil′i·ty, n. —in·al′ien·a·bly, adv.

in·am·o·ra·ta (in am′ə rä′tə, in′am-), n., pl. -tas. a woman who loves or is loved.

in·ane (i nān′), adj. **1.** lacking sense, significance, or ideas. **2.** empty; void. —in·an·i·ty (i nan′i tē), n., pl. -ties.

in·an′i·mate (-mit), adj. **1.** not animate; lifeless. **2.** not animated; dull. —in·an′i·mate·ly, adv. —in·an′i·mate·ness, n.

in′ap·pre′ci·a·ble, adj. imperceptible; insignificant. —in′ap·pre′ci·a·bly, adv.

in′ar·tic′u·late (-lit), adj. **1.** lacking the ability to express oneself in clear and effective speech. **2.** unable to use articulate speech. **3.** not uttered with intelligible modulations. **4.** not fully expressed or expressible. —in′ar·tic′u·late·ly, adv. —in′ar·tic′u·late·ness, n.

in•as•much′ as′, *conj.* **1.** seeing that; since. **2.** to such a degree as.

in•at•ten′tion, *n.* **1.** lack of attention. **2.** an act of neglect. —**in•at•ten′tive,** *adj.*

in•au•gu•ral (in ô′gyər əl, -gər əl), *adj.* **1.** of an inauguration. **2.** marking the beginning of a new venture or series. —*n.* **3.** an address, as of a president, at the beginning of a term of office. **4.** an inaugural ceremony.

in•au′gu•rate′ (-rāt′), *v.t.,* -rat•ed, -rat•ing. **1.** to begin formally. **2.** to induct into office with formal ceremonies. **3.** to introduce into public use by some formal ceremony. —**in•au′gu•ra′tion,** *n.*

in′board′, *adj., adv.* **1.** located inside a hull or aircraft. **2.** located nearer the center, as of an airplane.

in′born′, *adj.* present at birth; innate.

in′bound′, *adj.* inward bound.

in′bred′, *adj.* **1.** innate. **2.** resulting from inbreeding.

in′breed′, *v.t.* to produce by the repeated breeding of closely related individuals. —**in′breed′ing,** *n.*

inc., **1.** incomplete. **2.** incorporated. **3.** increase.

In•ca (ing′kə), *n., pl.* -cas. a member of any of the groups of South American Indian peoples dominant in Peru prior to the Spanish conquest.

in•cal′cu•la•ble, *adj.* **1.** unable to be calculated. **2.** very numerous or great. **3.** uncertain; unpredictable. —**in•cal′cu•la•bly,** *adv.*

in•can•des•cent (in′kən des′ənt), *adj.* **1.** glowing or white with heat. **2.** extremely bright. —**in′can•des′cence,** *n.* —**in′can•des′cent•ly,** *adv.*

in′candes′cent lamp′, a lamp in which a filament in an evacuated glass bulb glows as an electric current passes through it.

in•can•ta′tion (in′kan tā′shən), *n.* **1.** the chanting or uttering of words purporting to have magical power. **2.** the formula employed.

in•ca′pa•ble, *adj.* **1.** not having the necessary ability, qualification, or strength. **2.** utterly incompetent. —**in•ca′pa•bil′i•ty,** *n.* —**in•ca′pa•bly,** *adv.*

in•ca•pac•i•tate (in′kə pas′i tāt′), *v.t.,* -tat•ed, -tat•ing. **1.** to deprive of ability, qualification, or strength. **2.** to deprive of legal power.

in′ca•pac′i•ty, *n.* **1.** lack of capacity or ability. **2.** lack of legal power to act.

in•car′cer•ate (in kär′sə rāt′), *v.t.,* -at•ed, -at•ing. to imprison. —**in•car′cer•a′tion,** *n.*

in•car•na•dine (in kär′nə dīn′, -din, -dēn′), *adj.* blood-red; crimson.

in•car•nate (*adj.* in kär′nit, -nāt; *v.* -nāt), *adj., v.,* -nat•ed, -nat•ing. —*adj.* **1.** given a bodily, esp. a human, form. **2.** personified; typified. —*v.t.* **3.** to give a bodily form to. **4.** to be the embodiment of.

in•car•na′tion (in′kär nā′shən), *n.* **1.** an incarnate being or form. **2. the Incarnation,** (*sometimes l.c.*) the doctrine that the second person of the Trinity assumed human form in the person of Jesus Christ. **3.** a person or thing regarded as embodying some quality. **4.** the act of incarnating. **5.** state of being incarnated.

in•cen•di•ar•y (in sen′dē er′ē), *adj., n., pl.* -ar•ies. —*adj.* **1.** used or adapted for setting property on fire. **2.** of arson. **3.** tending to arouse strife, sedition, etc. —*n.* **4.** a person who commits arson. **5.** a device that burns with an intense heat. **6.** a person who stirs up strife.

in•cense¹ (in′sens), *n.* **1.** an aromatic substance producing a sweet odor when burned. **2.** the perfume or smoke arising from incense.

in•cense² (in sens′), *v.t.,* -censed, -cens•ing. to arouse the wrath of.

in•cen•tive (in sen′tiv), *n.* something that incites to action or greater effort.

in•cep•tion (in sep′shən), *n.* beginning; commencement.

in•cer•ti•tude (in sûr′ti tōōd′, -tyōōd′), *n.* **1.** uncertainty; doubtfulness. **2.** instability; insecurity.

in•ces•sant (in ses′ənt), *adj.* continuing without interruption. —**in•ces′sant•ly,** *adv.*

in•cest (in′sest), *n.* sexual relations between persons so closely related that they are forbidden by law or religion to marry. —**in•ces′tu•ous** (-ses′chōō əs), *adj.*

inch (inch), *n.* **1.** a unit of length, ¹/₁₂ of a foot, equivalent to 2.54 centimeters. —*v.t., v.i.* **2.** to move by small degrees. —*Idiom.* **3. every inch,** in every respect. **4. within an inch of,** close to.

in•cho•ate (in kō′it), *adj.* **1.** not yet fully developed. **2.** just begun; incipient.

inch′worm′, *n.* a moth larva that moves in a looping motion.

in•ci•dence (in′si dəns), *n.* the rate or range of occurrence or influence.

in′ci•dent, *n.* **1.** an occurrence or event. **2.** a seemingly minor occurrence that can lead to serious consequences. —*adj.* **3.** likely to happen. **4.** falling or striking on something, as light rays.

in′ci•den′tal (-den′tl), *adj.* **1.** happening in fortuitous or subordinate conjunction with something else. **2.** incurred casually. —*n.* **3.** something that is incidental. **4. incidentals,** minor expenses.

in′ci•den′tal•ly (-den′tl ē *or, for 1,* -dent′lē), *adv.* **1.** apart or aside from the main subject. **2.** by chance.

in•cin•er•ate (in sin′ə rāt′), *v.t., v.i.,* -at•ed, -at•ing. to burn to ashes. —**in•cin′er•a′tion,** *n.*

in•cin′er•a′tor, *n.* a furnace or apparatus for incinerating.

in•cip•i•ent (in sip′ē ənt), *adj.* beginning to exist or appear. —**in•cip′i•ence,** *n.* —**in•cip′i•ent•ly,** *adv.*

in•cise (in sīz′), *v.t.,* -cised, -cis•ing. **1.** to cut marks or figures upon. **2.** to engrave.

in•ci′sion (in sizh′ən), *n.* **1.** a cut, gash, or notch. **2.** a surgical cut into a tissue or organ.

in•ci′sive (-sī′siv), *adj.* **1.** penetrating; cutting. **2.** mentally sharp; keen. —**in•ci′sive•ly,** *adv.* —**in•ci′sive•ness,** *n.*

in•ci•sor (in sī′zər), *n.* any of the four anterior teeth in each jaw, used for cutting.

in•cite (in sīt′), *v.t.,* -cit•ed, -cit•ing. to stimulate to action; urge on. —**in•cite′ment,** *n.* —**in•cit′er,** *n.*

in′ci•vil′i•ty, *n., pl.* -ties. **1.** the quality or state of being uncivil. **2.** an uncivil act.

incl., including.

in•clem′ent, *adj.* **1.** severe; stormy. **2.** not kind or merciful. —**in•clem′en•cy,** *n.*

in•cli•na•tion (in′klə nā′shən), *n.* **1.** a liking or preference. **2.** something to which one is inclined. **3.**

---

in′a•bil′i•ty, *n.*

in′ac•ces′si•ble, *adj.*

in•ac′cu•ra•cy, *n., pl.* -cies.

in•ac′cu•rate, *adj.*

in•ac′tion, *n.*

in•ac′tive, *adj.*

in′ac•tiv′i•ty, *n.*

in′ad•e′qua•cy, *n., pl.* -cies.

in′ad•e′quate, *adj.; -ly, adv.*

in′ad•mis′si•ble, *adj.*

in′ad•vis′a•bil′i•ty, *n.*

in′ad•vis′a•ble, *adj.*

in•ap′pli•ca•ble, *adj.*

in•ap•pro′pri•ate, *adj.; -ly, adv.*

in•au′di•ble, *adj.; -bly, adv.*

in′aus•pi′cious, *adj.*

in•cau′tious, *adj.*

in′com•mu′ni•ca•ble, *adj.*

in′com•pre•hen′si•ble, *adj.*

in′con•ceiv′a•ble, *adj.*

in′con•clu′sive, *adj.*

in′con•sist′en•cy, *n., pl.* -cies.

in′con•sist′ent, *adj.; -ly, adv.*

in′de•ter′mi•na•ble, *adj.*

in′dis•cern′i•ble, *adj.*

in′dis•tin′guish•a•ble, *adj.*

in′di•vis′i•ble, *adj.*

in•ed′i•ble, *adj.*

in•el′i•gi•bil′i•ty, *n.*

in•el′i•gi•ble, *adj.*

in•eq′ui•ta•ble, *adj.*

in•eq′ui•ty, *n., pl.* -ties.

in′ex•act′, *adj.*

in′ex•cus′a•ble, *adj.*

in′ex•pen′sive, *adj; -ly, adv.*

in•hos′pi•ta•ble, *adj.*

in•ju•di′cious, *adj.*

in•op′por•tune′, *adj.*

in′sig•nif′i•cance, *n.*

in′sig•nif′i•cant, *adj.*

in•solv′a•ble, *adj.*

in′suf•fi′cien•cy, *n., pl.* -cies.

in′suf•fi′cient, *adj.; -ly, adv.*

in′sur•mount′a•ble, *adj.*

in•var′i•a•ble, *adj., v.*

the act of inclining or state of being inclined. **4.** a tendency toward a certain condition, action, etc. **5.** an inclined surface.

in•cline (*v.* in klīn′; *n.* in′klīn, in klīn′), *v.*, **-clined, -clin•ing,** *n.* —*v.i.* **1.** to deviate from the vertical or horizontal. **2.** to have a mental tendency or preference. **3.** to tend in character or in course of action. **4.** to lean; bend. —*v.t.* **5.** to persuade; dispose. **6.** to cause to lean or bend in a particular direction. —*n.* **7.** a sloping surface.

in•close (in klōz′), *v.t.,* **-closed, -clos•ing.** ENCLOSE. —**in•clo′sure** (-klō′zhər), *n.*

in•clude (in klōōd′), *v.t.,* **-clud•ed, -clud•ing. 1.** to contain or encompass as part of a whole. **2.** to put in or consider as part of a group or category. —**in•clu′sion** (-klōō′zhən), *n.*

in•clu′sive (-siv), *adj.* **1.** including the stated limits: *from 6 to 9 inclusive.* **2.** including everything. —*Idiom.* **3. inclusive of,** including. —**in•clu′sive•ly,** *adv.* —**in•clu′sive•ness,** *n.*

in•cog•ni•to (in′kog nē′tō, in kog′ni tō′), *adv., adj.* with one's identity hidden or unknown.

in•co•her′ent, *adj.* lacking logical or meaningful connection. —**in′co•her′ence,** *n.* —**in′co•her′ent•ly,** *adv.*

in′com•bus′ti•ble, *adj.* incapable of being burned.

in•come (in′kum), *n.* the monetary payment received for goods or services, or from other sources, such as rents or investments.

in′come tax′, *n.* a tax levied on the annual incomes of individuals and corporations.

in′com′ing, *adj.* coming in: *the incoming class.*

in′com•men′su•rate, *adj.* not commensurate; disproportionate; inadequate. —**in′com•men′su•rate•ly,** *adv.*

in•com•mu•ni•ca•do (in′kə myōō′ni kä′dō), *adv., adj.* without means of communication with others.

in′com•pa•ra•ble, *adj.* **1.** fine beyond comparison. **2.** not fit for comparison.

in′com•pat′i•ble, *adj.* **1.** unable to exist together in harmony. **2.** incongruous; discordant. —**in′com•pat′i•bil′i•ty,** *n.* —**in′com•pat′i•bly,** *adv.*

in•com′pe•tent, *adj.* **1.** lacking qualification or ability. **2.** not legally qualified. —*n.* **3.** an incompetent person. —**in•com′pe•tence,** *n.* —**in•com′pe•tent•ly,** *adv.*

in′com•plete′, *adj.* **1.** lacking some part or parts. **2.** not finished. —**in′com•plete′ly,** *adv.* —**in′com•plete′ness,** *n.*

in•con′gru•ous, *adj.* **1.** out of keeping or place. **2.** not harmonious in character. —**in′con•gru′i•ty,** *n., pl.* **-ties.** —**in•con′gru•ous•ly,** *adv.*

in′con•se•quen′tial, *adj.* having little or no consequence or importance. —**in′con•se•quen′tial•ly,** *adv.*

in′con•sid′er•a•ble, *adj.* small, as in value, amount, or size.

in′con•sid′er•ate, *adj.* **1.** lacking regard for the rights or feelings of others. **2.** thoughtless; heedless. —**in′con•sid′er•ate•ly,** *adv.* —**in′con•sid′er•ate•ness, in′con•sid′er•a′tion,** *n.*

in′con•sol′a•ble, *adj.* not consolable.

in′con•spic′u•ous, *adj.* not conspicuous or noticeable. —**in′con•spic′u•ous•ly,** *adv.* —**in′con•spic′u•ous•ness,** *n.*

in•con′stant, *adj.* not constant; changeable. —**in•con′stan•cy,** *n.* —**in•con′stant•ly,** *adv.*

in′con•test′a•ble, *adj.* not open to dispute. —**in′con•test′a•bil′i•ty,** *n.* —**in′con•test′a•bly,** *adv.*

in•con′ti•nent, *adj.* **1.** unable to restrain natural discharges of urine or feces. **2.** lacking in moderation or control. —**in•con′ti•nence,** *n.*

in′con•tro•vert′i•ble, *adj.* not open to question.

in′con•ven′ience, *n., v.,* **-ienced, -ienc•ing.** —*n.* **1.** the quality or state of being inconvenient. **2.** an inconvenient circumstance or thing. —*v.t.* **3.** to put to trouble.

in′con•ven′ient, *adj.* **1.** not accessible or at hand. **2.** inopportune. **3.** not suiting one's needs or purposes. —**in′con•ven′ient•ly,** *adv.*

in•cor′po•rate′ (-pə rāt′), *v.,* **-rat•ed, -rat•ing.** —*v.t.* **1.** to form into a corporation. **2.** to introduce as an integral part. **3.** to include as a part. **4.** to combine into one body. —*v.i.* **5.** to form a corporation. **6.** to combine so as to form one body. —**in•cor′po•ra′tion,** *n.*

in′cor•po′re•al, *adj.* not corporeal or material.

in′cor•rect′, *adj.* **1.** not correct as to fact. **2.** improper; inappropriate. —**in′cor•rect′ly,** *adv.*

in•cor′ri•gi•ble (in kôr′i jə bəl, -kor′-), *adj.* bad beyond reform; uncontrollable: *an incorrigible liar.* —**in•cor′ri•gi•bil′i•ty,** *n.* —**in•cor′ri•gi•bly,** *adv.*

in′cor•rupt′i•ble, *adj.* **1.** not corruptible; honest. **2.** not susceptible to decay. —**in′cor•rupt′i•bil′i•ty,** *n.*

in•crease (*v.* in krēs′; *n.* in′krēs), *v.,* **-creased, -creas•ing,** *n.* —*v.t., v.i.* **1.** to make or become greater, as in number, size, or quality. —*n.* **2.** the act or process of increasing. **3.** an amount by which something is increased. —**in•creas′ing•ly,** *adv.*

in•cred′i•ble, *adj.* so extraordinary as to seem impossible or unbelievable. —**in•cred′i•bil′i•ty,** *n.* —**in•cred′i•bly,** *adv.*

in•cred′u•lous, *adj.* **1.** disinclined or indisposed to believe. **2.** indicating disbelief. —**in′cre•du′li•ty,** *n.*

in•cre•ment (in′krə mənt, ing′-), *n.* **1.** something added or gained. **2.** an amount by which something increases. —**in′cre•men′tal** (-men′tl), *adj.*

in•crim•i•nate (in krim′ə nāt′), *v.t.,* **-nat•ed, -nat•ing.** to accuse of or indicate involvement in a crime or fault. —**in•crim′i•na′tion,** *n.* —**in•crim•i•na•to•ry** (-nə tôr′ē), *adj.*

in•crust′, *v.t.* **1.** to cover with a crust or hard coating. —*v.i.* **2.** to form a crust. —**in′crus•ta′tion,** *n.*

in•cu•bate (in′kyə bāt′, ing′-), *v.t., v.i.,* **-bat•ed, -bat•ing. 1.** to sit on (eggs) for the purpose of hatching. **2.** to hatch (eggs), as by sitting on them or by artificial heat. **3.** to maintain under favorable conditions promoting development, as premature infants. **4.** to develop as if by hatching. —**in′cu•ba′tion,** *n.*

in′cu•ba′tor, *n.* **1.** an apparatus for hatching eggs. **2.** an apparatus in which premature infants are cared for in controlled conditions. **3.** an apparatus in which microorganisms are cultivated at a constant temperature.

in•cu•bus (in′kyə bəs, ing′-), *n., pl.* **-bus•es, -bi** (-bī′). **1.** an evil spirit supposed to descend upon sleeping persons. **2.** something that oppresses one like a nightmare.

in•cul•cate (in kul′kāt, in′kul kāt′), *v.t.,* **-cat•ed, -cat•ing.** to implant by repeated statement or admonition. —**in′cul•ca′tion,** *n.*

in•cul′pa•ble, *adj.* free from blame or guilt.

in•cul•pate (in kul′pāt, in′kul pāt), *v.t.,* **-pat•ed, -pat•ing.** to incriminate.

in•cum•ben•cy (in kum′bən sē), *n., pl.* **-cies. 1.** the quality or state of being incumbent. **2.** the position or term of an incumbent.

in•cum′bent, *adj.* **1.** currently holding an indicated office: *the incumbent president.* **2.** obligatory: *a duty incumbent upon me.* —*n.* **3.** the holder of an office.

in•cum′ber, *v.t.* ENCUMBER.

in•cu•nab•u•la (in′kyōō nab′yə lə, ing′-), *n.pl., sing.* **-lum** (-ləm). books printed before 1501.

in•cur (in kûr′), *v.t.,* **-curred, -cur•ring. 1.** to come into or acquire: *to incur debts.* **2.** to bring upon oneself: *incurred our displeasure.*

in•cur′a•ble, *adj.* incapable of being cured or remedied. —**in•cur′a•bly,** *adv.*

in•cu′ri•ous, *adj.* not inquisitive or observant.

in•cur•sion (in kûr′zhən, -shən), *n.* a hostile entrance into or invasion of a place or territory.

Ind., 1. India. **2.** Indiana.

ind., 1. independent. **2.** index. **3.** indicative. **4.** industry.

in•debt′ed, *adj.* **1.** obligated to repay money. **2.** obligated for favors or kindness received. —**in•debt′ed•ness,** *n.*

in•de′cent, *adj.* **1.** offensive to good taste or propriety. **2.** unbecoming; unseemly. —**in•de′cen•cy,** *n.* —**in•de′cent•ly,** *adv.*

in′de•ci′pher•a•ble, *adj.* incapable of being deciphered; illegible.

in′de•ci′sion, *n.* inability to decide.

in′de•ci′sive, *adj.* **1.** characterized by indecision. **2.** not decisive or conclusive. —**in′de•ci′sive•ly,** *adv.* —**in′de•ci′sive•ness,** *n.*

in•dec′o•rous, *adj.* unseemly; unbecoming.

in•deed (in dēd′), *adv.* **1.** in fact; truly. —*interj.* **2.** an exclamation of surprise or skepticism.

in•de•fat•i•ga•ble (in′di fat′i gə bəl), *adj.* incapable of being tired out. —**in′de•fat′i•ga•bly,** *adv.*

in•de•fea•si•ble (in′di fē′zə bəl), *adj.* not able to be annulled. —**in′de•fea′si•bly,** *adv.*

in′de•fen′si•ble, *adj.* **1.** not justifiable; inexcusable. **2.** incapable of being defended, as against attack. —**in′de•fen′si•bly,** *adv.*

in′de•fin′a•ble, *adj.* not readily identified, described, or analyzed.

in•def′i•nite, *adj.* **1.** having no fixed limit. **2.** not clearly defined or determined. **3.** uncertain; vague. —**in•def′i•nite•ly,** *adv.*

indef′inite ar′ticle, *n.* an article, as English *a* or *an*, that does not particularize the noun modified.

in•del•i•ble (in del′ə bəl), *adj.* **1.** making marks that cannot be removed. **2.** incapable of being removed or erased. —**in•del′i•bly,** *adv.*

in•del′i•cate, *adj.* **1.** offensive to propriety or decency. **2.** lacking sensitivity; tactless. —**in•del′i•ca•cy,** *n., pl.* **-cies.** —**in•del′i•cate•ly,** *adv.*

in•dem•ni•fy (in dem′nə fī′), *v.t.,* **-fied, -fy•ing. 1.** to compensate for damage or loss sustained. **2.** to secure against anticipated loss. —**in•dem′ni•fi•ca′tion,** *n.*

in•dem•ni•ty (in dem′ni tē), *n., pl.* **-ties. 1.** protection or security against damage or loss. **2.** compensation for damage or loss sustained.

in•dent¹ (in dent′), *v.t.* **1.** to form notches in the edge of. **2.** to set in from the margin: *Indent the first line of a paragraph.* —*v.i.* **3.** to form an indentation. **4.** to space in from the margin.

in•dent² (in dent′), *v.t.* to form a dent in.

in′den•ta′tion (-den tā′shən), *n.* **1.** a notch or recess. **2.** a series of notches. **3.** a notching or being notched.

in•den•ture (in den′chər), *n., v.,* **-tured, -tur•ing.** —*n.* **1.** a contract, esp. one by which an apprentice is bound to service. —*v.t.* **2.** to bind by indenture.

in′de•pend′ence, *n.* the quality or state of being independent.

In′de•pend′ence, *n.* a city in W Missouri. 112,301.

Independ′ence Day′, *n.* July 4, a U.S. holiday commemorating the adoption of the Declaration of Independence in 1776.

in′de•pend′ent, *adj.* **1.** not influenced or controlled by others. **2.** not depending upon something else. **3.** not relying on another for aid or support. **4.** not subject to another's authority or jurisdiction. **5.** free from political party commitments. **6.** capable of standing syntactically as a complete sentence: *an independent clause.* —*n.* **7.** an independent person, esp. a voter not committed to a party. —**in′de•pend′ent•ly,** *adv.*

in′-depth′, *adj.* intensive; thorough.

in′de•scrib′a•ble, *adj.* not describable; too extraordinary for description. —**in′de•scrib′a•bly,** *adv.*

in′de•struct′i•ble, *adj.* incapable of being destroyed. —**in′de•struct′i•bil′i•ty,** *n.* —**in′de•struct′i•bly,** *adv.*

in′de•ter′mi•nate (-nit), *adj.* not precisely fixed or determined; vague. **2.** not settled in advance. —**in′de•ter′mi•na•cy** (-nə sē), *n.* —**in′de•ter′mi•nate•ly,** *adv.*

in•dex (in′deks), *n., pl.* **-dex•es, -di•ces** (-də sēz′), *v.* —*n.* **1.** (in a printed work) an alphabetical list of names, places, and topics with the page numbers on which they are mentioned. **2.** a sign or indication: *an index of character.* **3.** a pointer, as on a dial. **4.** a

printed sign, a hand with extended index finger, used to point out a note or paragraph. **5.** a number or formula expressing a property or ratio: *index of growth.* **6.** INDEX NUMBER. —*v.t.* **7.** to provide with an index. **8.** to enter in an index. —**in′dex•er,** *n.*

in′dex fin′ger, *n.* FOREFINGER.

in′dex num′ber, *n.* a quantity whose variation over a period of time measures the change in some phenomenon.

in′dex of refrac′tion, *n.* the ratio of the speed of light in a vacuum or in air to that in the given medium.

In•di•a (in′dē ə), *n.* **1.** a republic in S Asia. 967,612,804. **2.** a subcontinent in S Asia, S of the Himalayas.

In′dia ink′, *n.* (*sometimes l.c.*) **1.** a black pigment made from lampblack. **2.** an ink made from this pigment.

In′di•an, *n.* **1.** AMERICAN INDIAN. **2.** any of the indigenous languages of the American Indians. **3.** a native or inhabitant of the Republic of India. —*adj.* **4.** of the American Indians or their languages. **5.** of India or S Asia.

In•di•an•a (in′dē an′ə), *n.* a state in the central United States. 5,840,528. *Cap.:* Indianapolis. *Abbr.:* IN, Ind. —**In′di•an′an, In′di•an′i•an,** *adj., n.*

In•di•an•ap•o•lis (in′dē ə nap′ə lis), *n.* the capital of Indiana. 752,279.

In′dian corn′, *n.* CORN¹ (def. 1).

In′dian file′, *n., adv.* SINGLE FILE.

In′dian O′cean, *n.* an ocean S of Asia, between Africa and Australia.

In′dian pipe′, *n.* a leafless plant with a solitary white flower.

In′dian sum′mer, *n.* a period of mild, dry weather in late fall or early winter.

in•di•cate (in′di kāt′), *v.t.,* **-cat•ed, -cat•ing. 1.** to be a sign of. **2.** to point out or point to. **3.** to express minimally. —**in′di•ca′tion,** *n.*

in•dic′a•tive (-dik′ə tiv), *adj.* **1.** pointing out; suggestive. **2.** of or noting the grammatical mood used for ordinary objective statements and questions. —*n.* **3.** the indicative mood. —**in•dic′a•tive•ly,** *adv.*

in′di•ca′tor (-di kā′tər), *n.* **1.** a person or thing that indicates. **2.** a pointing device, as a pointer on a dial.

in•dict (in dīt′), *v.t.* to charge with a crime or accuse of wrongdoing. —**in•dict′a•ble,** *adj.* —**in•dict′ment,** *n.*

in•dif′fer•ent, *adj.* **1.** without interest or concern. **2.** having no bias or preference. **3.** not particularly good. **4.** immaterial or unimportant. —**in•dif′fer•ence,** *n.* —**in•dif′fer•ent•ly,** *adv.*

in•dig•e•nous (in dij′ə nəs), *adj.* originating in and characteristic of a particular region or country.

in•di•gent (in′di jənt), *adj.* **1.** lacking the necessities of life because of poverty. —*n.* **2.** an indigent person. —**in′di•gence,** *n.* —**in′di•gent•ly,** *adv.*

in′di•gest′i•ble, *adj.* not easily digested.

in′di•ges′tion, *n.* **1.** a feeling of discomfort after eating, as of heartburn. **2.** inadequate or abnormal digestion.

in•dig•nant (in dig′nənt), *adj.* feeling, characterized by, or expressing indignation. —**in•dig′nant•ly,** *adv.*

in′dig•na′tion (-nā′shən), *n.* strong displeasure at something considered unjust, offensive, insulting, or base.

in•dig′ni•ty, *n., pl.* **-ties.** an injury to a person's dignity; slighting or contemptuous treatment.

in•di•go (in′di gō′), *n., pl.* **-gos, -goes. 1.** a blue dye obtained from plants or manufactured synthetically. **2.** a deep violet blue.

in′di•rect′, *adj.* **1.** deviating from a straight line, as a path. **2.** not resulting immediately, as consequences. **3.** not direct in action or procedure. **4.** devious. —**in′di•rect′ly,** *adv.* —**in′di•rect′ness,** *n.*

in′direct ob′ject, *n.* a word or words representing the person or thing with reference to which the action of a verb is performed.

in′direct tax′, *n.* a tax levied on a commodity that is paid by the consumer as part of the market price.

in′dis•creet′, *adj.* lacking prudence, good judgment, or circumspection. —**in′dis•creet′ly,** *adv.*

in′dis•cre′tion, *n.* **1.** lack of discretion. **2.** an indiscreet act, remark, etc.

in•dis•crim•i•nate (in′di skrim′ə nit), *adj.* **1.** not discriminating; lacking in care, judgment, selectivity, etc. **2.** thrown together; jumbled. —**in′dis•crim′i•nate•ly,** *adv.*

in′dis•pen′sa•ble, *adj.* absolutely necessary, essential, or requisite. —**in′dis•pen′sa•bil′i•ty,** *n.* —**in′dis•pen′sa•bly,** *adv.*

in′dis•posed′, *adj.* **1.** sick or ill, esp. mildly. **2.** disinclined or unwilling. —**in′dis•po•si′tion,** *n.*

in′dis•put′a•ble, *adj.* not disputable or deniable. —**in′dis•put′a•bly,** *adv.*

in•dis•sol•u•ble (in′di sol′yə bəl), *adj.* incapable of being dissolved, decomposed, undone, or destroyed.

in′dis•tinct′, *adj.* **1.** not clearly marked or defined. **2.** not clearly distinguishable or perceptible. —**in′dis•tinct′ly,** *adv.*

in•dite (in dīt′), *v.t.,* **-dit•ed, -dit•ing.** to compose or write.

in•di•um (in′dē əm), *n.* a rare metallic element that is soft, white, and malleable. *Symbol:* In; *at. wt.:* 114.82; *at. no.:* 49.

in•di•vid•u•al (in′də vij′ōō əl), *n.* **1.** a single human being, as distinguished from a group. **2.** a person. **3.** a distinct, indivisible entity. —*adj.* **4.** single; separate. **5.** intended for one person only. **6.** of or characteristic of a particular person or thing. **7.** distinguished by special characteristics. —**in′di•vid′u•al•ly,** *adv.*

in′di•vid′u•al•ism, *n.* **1.** a social theory advocating the liberty, rights, or interests of the individual. **2.** the principle of independent thought or action. —**in′di•vid′u•al•ist,** *n.*

in′di•vid′u•al′i•ty, *n., pl.* **-ties. 1.** the aggregate of qualities that distinguishes one person or thing from others. **2.** existence as a distinct individual.

in′di•vid′u•al•ize′, *v.t.,* **-ized, -iz•ing. 1.** to make individual or distinctive. **2.** to specify; particularize. —**in′di•vid′u•al•i•za′tion,** *n.*

in′di•vid′u•ate′ (-āt′), *v.t.,* **-at•ed, -at•ing. 1.** to form into a distinct entity. **2.** to give a distinctive character to. —**in′di•vid′u•a′tion,** *n.*

In•do•chi•na (in′dō chī′nə), *n.* a peninsula in SE Asia, S of China, comprising Vietnam, Cambodia, Laos, Thailand, W Malaysia, and Myanmar. —**In′do•chi•nese′,** *adj., n., pl.* **-nese.**

in•doc•tri•nate (in dok′trə nāt′), *v.t.,* **-nat•ed, -nat•ing.** to instruct in a doctrine or ideology, esp. dogmatically. —**in•doc′tri•na′tion,** *n.*

In•do-Eu•ro•pe•an (in′dō yŏŏr′ə pē′ən), *n.* **1.** a family of languages spoken or formerly spoken in Europe and SW, central, and S Asia. **2.** a member of any of the peoples speaking an Indo-European language. —*adj.* **3.** of or belonging to Indo-European.

in•do•lent (in′dl ənt), *adj.* lazy; slothful. —**in′do•lence,** *n.*

in•dom•i•ta•ble (in dom′i tə bəl), *adj.* incapable of being subdued or overcome. —**in•dom′i•ta•bly,** *adv.*

In•do•ne•sia (in′də nē′zhə), *n.* **Republic of,** a republic in the Malay Archipelago, consisting of Sumatra, Java, most of Borneo, and many small islands. 209,774,138. —**In′do•ne′sian,** *n., adj.*

in′door′, *adj.* located, used, or existing inside a building.

in•doors′, *adv.* in or into a building.

in•dorse (in dôrs′), *v.t.,* **-dorsed, -dors•ing.** ENDORSE.

in•du•bi•ta•ble (in dōō′bi tə bəl, -dyōō′-), *adj.* not to be doubted. —**in•du′bi•ta•bly,** *adv.*

in•duce (in dōōs′, -dyōōs′), *v.t.,* **-duced, -duc•ing. 1.** to lead or move by persuasion. **2.** to bring about: *It induces sleep.* **3.** to produce (magnetism or electric current) by induction. **4.** to infer by logical induction. —**in•duc′er,** *n.*

in•duce′ment (-mənt), *n.* **1.** something that induces. **2.** the act of inducing or state of being induced.

in•duct (in dukt′), *v.t.* **1.** to install in an office, esp. formally. **2.** to take (a draftee) into military service. **3.** to bring in as a member.

in•duct′ance, *n.* the property of a circuit by which a change in current induces an electromotive force.

in•duc•tee (in′duk tē′, in duk-), *n., pl.* **-tees.** a person inducted into military service or some other organization.

in•duc′tion, *n.* **1.** the act of inducing. **2.** formal installation in an office. **3. a.** any form of reasoning in which a general conclusion is reached from particular cases. **b.** a conclusion reached by this process. **4.** the process by which a body having electric or magnetic properties produces magnetism, an electric charge, or an electromotive force in a neighboring body without contact. —**in•duc′tive,** *adj.*

in•dulge (in dulj′), *v.,* **-dulged, -dulg•ing.** —*v.t.* **1.** to yield to or gratify (desires, feelings, etc.). **2.** to yield to the wishes or whims of (oneself or another). —*v.i.* **3.** to yield to an inclination or desire.

in•dul′gence, *n.* **1.** the act of indulging or state of being indulgent. **2.** something indulged in. **3.** (in Roman Catholicism) a partial remission of the temporal punishment still due for sin after absolution.

in•dul′gent, *adj.* inclined to indulge; lenient.

in•dus•tri•al (in dus′trē əl), *adj.* **1.** of, used in, or resulting from industry. **2.** having many and highly developed industries. —**in•dus′tri•al•ly,** *adv.*

indus′trial arts′, *n.pl.* the techniques of using tools and machinery.

in•dus′tri•al•ism, *n.* the economic organization of a society built largely on mechanized industry.

in•dus′tri•al•ist, *n.* a person who owns or manages an industrial enterprise.

in•dus′tri•al•ize′, *v.,* **-ized, -iz•ing.** —*v.t.* **1.** to introduce industry into on a large scale. —*v.i.* **2.** to become industrial. —**in•dus′tri•al•i•za′tion,** *n.*

indus′trial park′, *n.* an industrial complex, typically in a suburban area.

indus′trial revolu′tion, *n.* (*often caps.*) the complex of social and economic changes resulting from the mechanization of industry that began in England about 1760.

indus′trial-strength′, *adj.* unusually strong or effective.

in•dus′tri•ous, *adj.* working energetically and devotedly; hard-working. —**in•dus′tri•ous•ly,** *adv.* —**in•dus′tri•ous•ness,** *n.*

in•dus•try (in′də strē), *n., pl.* **-tries. 1.** the aggregate of manufacturing or technically productive enterprises. **2.** any general business activity: *the tourist industry.* **3.** energetic, devoted activity at any task.

in•dwell′, *v.t., v.i.,* **-dwelt, -dwell•ing.** to be or reside (within), as a guiding force or motivating principle.

-ine¹, an adjective suffix meaning: of or characteristic of (*Alpine*); made of or like (*crystalline*).

-ine², a noun suffix indicating: an organic compound, esp. a base (*caffeine*); a halogen element (*chlorine*).

in•e•bri•ate (*v.* in ē′brē āt′, i nē′-; *n.* -it), *v.,* **-at•ed, -at•ing,** *n.* —*v.t.* **1.** to make drunk. —*n.* **2.** a drunkard. —**in•e′bri•a′tion,** *n.*

in•ed′u•ca•ble, *adj.* incapable of being educated, esp. because of some condition, as mental retardation.

in•ef•fa•ble (in ef′ə bəl), *adj.* **1.** incapable of being expressed in words. **2.** not to be spoken. —**in•ef′fa•bly,** *adv.*

in′ef•fec′tive, *adj.* **1.** not producing results. **2.** inefficient or incompetent.

in′ef•fec′tu•al, *adj.* **1.** producing no satisfactory or decisive effect. **2.** unavailing; futile.

in′ef•fi′cient, *adj.* unable to achieve the desired result with reasonable economy of means. —**in′ef•fi′cien•cy,** *n., pl.* **-cies.** —**in′ef•fi′cient•ly,** *adv.*

in•el′e•gant, *adj.* lacking in refinement, gracefulness, or good taste. —**in•el′e•gant•ly,** *adv.*

in•e•luc•ta•ble (in′i luk′tə bəl), *adj.* incapable of being evaded. —**in′e•luc′ta•bly,** *adv.*

in•ept (in ept′, i nept′), *adj.* **1.** lacking skill or aptitude; incompetent. **2.** inappropriate; unsuitable. **3.** absurd or foolish. —**in•ept′i•tude′,** *n.* —**in•ept′ly,** *adv.* —**in•ept′ness,** *n.*

in′e•qual′i•ty, *n., pl.* **-ties. 1.** the condition of being unequal. **2.** injustice; partiality. **3.** unevenness, as of surface. **4.** a mathematical statement that two quantities are unequal.

in•er′rant, *adj.* free from error.

in•ert (in ûrt′, i nûrt′), *adj.* **1.** having no inherent power of action, motion, or resistance. **2.** *Chem.* having little or no ability to react. **3.** sluggish by habit or nature. —**in•ert′ly,** *adv.* —**in•ert′ness,** *n.*

in•er•tia (in ûr′shə, i nûr′-), *n.* **1.** inactivity; sluggishness. **2.** the property of matter by which it retains its state of rest or its velocity along a straight line so long as it is not acted upon by an external force. —**in•er′tial,** *adj.*

in•es•cap•a•ble (in′ə skā′pə bəl), *adj.* incapable of being escaped or avoided. —**in′es•cap′a•bly,** *adv.*

in•es′ti•ma•ble, *adj.* **1.** incapable of being estimated or assessed. **2.** too precious to be estimated or appreciated. —**in•es′ti•ma•bly,** *adv.*

in•ev•i•ta•ble (in ev′i tə bəl), *adj.* unable to be avoided or escaped. —**in•ev′i•ta•bil′i•ty,** *n.* —**in•ev′i•ta•bly,** *adv.*

in′ex•haust′i•ble, *adj.* **1.** incapable of being depleted. **2.** untiring; tireless. —**in′ex•haust′i•bly,** *adv.*

in•ex•o•ra•ble (in ek′sər ə bəl), *adj.* **1.** unyielding; unalterable. **2.** not to be persuaded or moved by entreaties. —**in•ex′o•ra•bly,** *adv.*

in′ex•pe′ri•ence, *n.* **1.** lack of experience. **2.** lack of knowledge, skill, or wisdom gained from experience. —**in′ex•pe′ri•enced,** *adj.*

in•ex•pert (in eks′pûrt, in′ik spûrt′), *adj.* not expert; unskilled.

in•ex•pi•a•ble (in eks′pē ə bəl), *adj.* not allowing for expiation or atonement.

in•ex′pli•ca•ble, *adj.* incapable of being explained. —**in•ex′pli•ca•bly,** *adv.*

in′ex•press′i•ble, *adj.* incapable of being uttered or described in words.

in′ex•tin′guish•a•ble, *adj.* incapable of being quenched or suppressed.

in ex•tre•mis (in eks trē′mēs; *Eng.* in ik strē′mis), *adv. Latin.* **1.** in extremity. **2.** near death.

in•ex′tri•ca•ble, *adj.* **1.** from which one cannot extricate oneself. **2.** incapable of being disentangled or loosed. **3.** hopelessly intricate or perplexing. —**in•ex′tri•ca•bly,** *adv.*

inf., **1.** inferior. **2.** infinitive.

in•fal′li•ble, *adj.* **1.** unfailing; sure. **2.** exempt from liability to error. —**in•fal′li•bil′i•ty,** *n.* —**in•fal′li•bly,** *adv.*

in•fa•mous (in′fə məs), *adj.* **1.** having an extremely bad reputation. **2.** causing an evil reputation.

in′fa•my, *n., pl.* **-mies. 1.** extremely bad reputation as the result of a shameful or outrageous act. **2.** infamous character or conduct. **3.** an infamous act.

in•fan•cy (in′fən sē), *n., pl.* **-cies. 1.** very early childhood. **2.** the earliest stage of anything.

in•fant (in′fant), *n.* **1.** a child during the earliest period of its life. —*adj.* **2.** of infants or infancy. **3.** being in the earliest stage.

in•fan′ti•cide′ (in fan′tə sīd′), *n.* **1.** the act of killing an infant. **2.** a person who kills an infant.

in′fan•tile′ (-fan tīl′, -til), *adj.* **1.** characteristic of or befitting an infant. **2.** of infants or infancy.

in′fantile paral′ysis, *n.* POLIOMYELITIS.

in•fan•try (in′fən trē), *n., pl.* **-tries.** a branch of an army composed of soldiers who fight on foot. —**in′fan•try•man,** *n., pl.* **-men.**

in•fat•u•ate (in fach′ō̄ āt′), *v.t.,* **-at•ed, -at•ing.** to inspire or possess with a foolish or unreasoning admiration or love. —**in•fat′u•a′tion,** *n.*

in•fect (in fekt′), *v.t.* **1.** to contaminate with disease-producing germs. **2.** to affect with disease. **3.** to af-

fect, esp. adversely, with a feeling, belief, etc. **4.** to affect with a computer virus.

in•fec′tion, *n.* **1.** the act of infecting or state of being infected. **2.** an infecting agency or influence. **3.** an infectious disease.

in•fec′tious, *adj.* **1.** communicable by infection. **2.** causing or communicating infection. **3.** tending to spread quickly: *infectious laughter.* —**in•fec′tious•ly,** *adv.* —**in•fec′tious•ness,** *n.*

in′fe•lic′i•tous, *adj.* inapt or inappropriate. —**in′fe•lic′i•ty,** *n., pl.* **-ties.**

in•fer (in fûr′), *v.t.* **-ferred, -fer•ring. 1.** to conclude by reasoning from premises or evidence. **2.** to guess; surmise. —**in′fer•ence** (-fər əns), *n.* —**in′fer•en′tial** (-fə ren′shəl), *adj.*

in•fe•ri•or (in fēr′ē ər), *adj.* **1.** lower in rank or importance. **2.** lower in quality or value. **3.** lower in place or position. **4.** poor in quality. —*n.* **5.** an inferior person. —**in•fe′ri•or′i•ty** (-ôr′i tē, -or′-), *n.*

in•fer•nal (in fûr′nl), *adj.* **1.** hellish; diabolical. **2.** of hell or the underworld.

in•fer′no (-nō), *n., pl.* **-nos. 1.** hell. **2.** a place that resembles hell.

in•fer′tile, *adj.* not fertile; unproductive; sterile; barren. —**in′fer•til′i•ty,** *n.*

in•fest (in fest′), *v.t.* to overrun in a troublesome manner, as vermin do. —**in′fes•ta′tion,** *n.*

in•fi•del (in′fi dl, -del′), *n.* **1.** a person who does not accept a particular religion, esp. Christianity or Islam. **2.** a person who has no religious faith.

in′fi•del′i•ty, *n., pl.* **-ties. 1.** marital unfaithfulness. **2.** disloyalty.

in′field′, *n.* **1.** the area of a baseball field bounded by the base lines. **2.** the infielders collectively.

in′field′er, *n. Baseball.* the first baseman, second baseman, shortstop, or third baseman.

in′fight′ing, *n.* **1.** fighting at close range. **2.** fighting between rivals or people closely associated. —**in′fight′er,** *n.*

in•fil•trate (in fil′trāt, in′fil trāt′), *v.t., v.i.* **-trat•ed, -trat•ing. 1.** to move into (an organization, enemy area, etc.) surreptitiously and with hostile intent. **2.** to filter into or through (a substance). —**in′fil•tra′tion,** *n.* —**in′fil•tra′tor,** *n.*

infin., infinitive.

in•fi•nite (in′fə nit), *adj.* **1.** immeasurably great. **2.** unbounded or unlimited. **3.** *Math.* not finite. —*n.* **4.** something infinite. —**in′fi•nite•ly,** *adv.*

in•fin•i•tes•i•mal (in′fin i tes′ə məl), *adj.* **1.** immeasurably or exceedingly small. —*n.* **2.** *Math.* a variable having zero as a limit. —**in′fin•i•tes′i•mal•ly,** *adv.*

in•fin•i•tive (in fin′i tiv), *n.* a verb form not inflected for person, number, or tense, and in English usu. preceded by *to.* —**in′fin•i•ti′val** (-tī′vəl), *adj.*

in•fin′i•tude′ (-i tōod′, -tyōod′), *n.* **1.** infinity. **2.** an infinite extent, amount, or number.

in•fin′i•ty, *n., pl.* **-ties. 1.** the quality or state of being infinite. **2.** infinite space, time, or quantity. **3.** an indefinitely great amount or number.

in•firm (in fûrm′), *adj.* **1.** feeble in body or health. **2.** not firm, solid, or strong.

in•fir′ma•ry (-fûr′mə rē), *n., pl.* **-ries.** a place for the care of the infirm, sick, or injured.

in•fir′mi•ty, *n., pl.* **-ties. 1.** a physical weakness or ailment. **2.** a moral weakness or failing.

in•flame′, *v.t., v.i.* **-flamed, -flam•ing. 1.** to kindle or excite (passions, desires, etc.). **2.** to affect or become affected with inflammation. **3.** to set aflame or afire.

in•flam′ma•ble, *adj.* **1.** capable of being set on fire. **2.** easily aroused to passion or anger. —**in•flam′ma•bil′i•ty,** *n.*

in•flam•ma•tion (in′flə mā′shən), *n.* redness, swelling, and fever in a local area of the body in reaction to an infection or an injury.

in•flam•ma•to•ry (in flam′ə tôr′ē), *adj.* **1.** tending to arouse anger, passion, etc. **2.** of or caused by inflammation.

in•flate (in flāt′), *v.,* **-flat•ed, -flat•ing.** —*v.t.* **1.** to expand or distend with or as if with air or gas. **2.** to puff up with pride, satisfaction, etc. **3.** to increase unduly, as prices. —*v.i.* **4.** to become inflated. —**in•flat′a•ble**, *adj.*

in•fla′tion, *n.* **1.** a steady rise in the level of prices related to an increased volume of money and credit and resulting in a loss of value of currency. **2.** the act of inflating or state of being inflated. —**in•fla′tion•ar′y** (-shə ner′ē), *adj.*

in•flect (in flekt′), *v.t.* **1.** to modulate (the voice). **2.** to change the form of (a word) by inflection.

in•flec′tion, *n.* **1.** modulation of the voice. **2.** the change in the form of a word to express grammatical or syntactic relations, as of case or number. Also, *esp. Brit.,* **in•flex′ion.** —**in•flec′tion•al**, *adj.*

in•flex′i•ble, *adj.* **1.** incapable of or resistant to being bent. **2.** of an unyielding temper, purpose, etc. **3.** not permitting change or variation. —**in•flex′i•bil′i•ty**, *n.* —**in•flex′i•bly**, *adv.*

in•flict (in flikt′), *v.t.* **1.** to impose (anything unwelcome). **2.** to deal or deliver, as a blow. —**in•flic′tion,** *n.* —**in•flic′tive**, *adj.*

in′-flight′, *adj.* done, served, or shown during flight in an aircraft.

in•flo•res′cence, *n.* **1.** a flowering or blossoming. **2. a.** the arrangement of flowers on the stem. **b.** a flower cluster. **c.** flowers collectively. —**in′flo•res′cent,** *adj.*

in′flow′, *n.* something that flows in.

in•flu•ence (in′flŏŏ əns), *n., v.,* -**enced, -enc•ing.** —*n.* **1.** the power to produce effects on others by intangible or indirect means. **2.** a person or thing that exerts influence. **3.** the power to persuade or obtain advantages resulting from one's status, wealth, etc. —*v.t.* **4.** to move or impel (a person) to some action. —**in′flu•en′tial** (-en′shəl), *adj.*

in•flu•en•za (in′flŏŏ en′zə), *n.* an acute, contagious viral disease characterized by respiratory symptoms, fever, muscular aches, etc.

in′flux′, *n.* a flowing or coming in.

in•fo (in′fō), *n. Informal.* information.

in•fold′, *v.t.* ENFOLD.

in•fo•mer•cial (in′fō mûr′shəl), *n.* a program-length television commercial cast in a standard format, as a documentary.

in•form (in fôrm′), *v.t.* **1.** to give knowledge of a fact or circumstance to. —*v.i.* **2.** to give information. **3.** to furnish incriminating evidence about someone. —**in•form′er,** *n.*

in•for′mal, *adj.* **1.** without formality or ceremony. **2.** not according to the prescribed or customary manner. **3.** suitable to or characteristic of casual or familiar speech or writing. —**in′for•mal′i•ty**, *n., pl.* -**ties.** —**in•for′mal•ly**, *adv.*

in•form′ant (-fôr′mənt), *n.* a person who gives information.

in′for•ma′tion (-fər mā′shən), *n.* **1.** knowledge communicated or received concerning a particular fact. **2.** knowledge gained through study, research, etc. **3.** computer data at any stage of processing. —**in′for•ma′tion•al**, *adj.*

in•form′a•tive (-fôr′mə tiv), *adj.* giving information.

in•fra (in′frə), *adv.* below, esp. when used in referring to parts of a text. [< L]

in•frac′tion (in frak′shən), *n.* a breach; violation.

in′fra•red′ (in′frə-), *n.* the part of the invisible spectrum contiguous to the red end of the visible spectrum.

in′fra•son′ic, *adj.* noting or pertaining to a sound wave with a frequency below the range of audible sound.

in′fra•struc′ture, *n.* **1.** the basic framework of a system or organization. **2.** fundamental facilities, as transportation and communication systems.

in•fre′quent, *adj.* **1.** happening or occurring at long intervals or rarely. **2.** not constant, habitual, or regular. —**in•fre′quen•cy, in•fre′quence,** *n.* —**in•fre′quent•ly**, *adv.*

in•fringe (in frinj′), *v.,* -**fringed, -fring•ing.** —*v.t.*

1. to commit a breach or infraction of. —*v.i.* **2.** to encroach or trespass: *to infringe on someone's privacy.* —**in•fringe′ment,** *n.*

in•fu•ri•ate (in fyŏŏr′ē āt′), *v.t.,* -**at•ed, -at•ing.** to make furious. —**in•fu′ri•at′ing•ly**, *adv.*

in•fuse (in fyŏŏz′), *v.t.,* -**fused, -fus•ing. 1.** to introduce, as if by pouring. **2.** to imbue or inspire. **3.** to steep or soak (leaves, bark, etc.) to extract the soluble properties. —**in•fus′er,** *n.* —**in•fu′sion** (-fyŏŏ′zhən), *n.*

-ing¹, a suffix meaning: action or process (*building*); an instance of such action (*listing*); material used in an action (*wadding*); something that performs or receives an action (*covering*).

-ing², a suffix forming the present participle of verbs (*thinking*), such participles being often used as participial adjectives: *warring factions.*

in•gen•ious (in jēn′yəs), *adj.* **1.** characterized by cleverness or originality. **2.** cleverly inventive; resourceful. —**in•gen′ious•ly**, *adv.* —**in•gen′ious•ness,** *n.*

in•gé•nue or **-ge•nue** (an′zhə nŏŏ′), *n.* **1.** the role of an artless, innocent young woman, esp. as represented on the stage. **2.** an actress who plays such a role.

in•ge•nu•i•ty (in′jə nŏŏ′i tē, -nyŏŏ′-), *n.* the quality of being cleverly inventive or resourceful.

in•gen•u•ous (in jen′yŏŏ əs), *adj.* **1.** free from deceit or disguise; open. **2.** artless; innocent. —**in•gen′u•ous•ly**, *adv.* —**in•gen′u•ous•ness,** *n.*

in•gest (in jest′), *v.t.* to take into the body, as food or liquid. —**in•ges′tion,** *n.*

In•gle•wood (ing′gəl wŏŏd′), *n.* a city in SW California. 109,602.

in•glo′ri•ous, *adj.* **1.** shameful; disgraceful. **2.** not famous or honored. —**in•glo′ri•ous•ly**, *adv.*

in•got (ing′gət), *n.* a mass of metal cast in a form for shaping, remelting, or refining.

in•grained′, *adj.* firmly fixed; deep-rooted; inveterate: *ingrained superstition.*

in•grate (in′grāt), *n.* an ungrateful person.

in•gra•ti•ate (in grā′shē āt′), *v.t.,* -**at•ed, -at•ing.** to establish (oneself) in the favor of others. —**In•gra′ti•a′tion,** *n.*

in•grat′i•tude′, *n.* the state of being ungrateful.

in•gre•di•ent (in grē′dē ənt), *n.* **1.** something that enters as an element into a mixture. **2.** a constituent element of anything.

in•gress (in′gres), *n.* the act of going in or entering.

in′grown′, *adj.* having grown into the flesh: *an ingrown toenail.*

in•gui•nal (ing′gwə nl), *adj.* of or situated in the groin.

in•hab•it (in hab′it), *v.t.* to live or dwell in. —**in•hab′it•a•ble,** *adj.*

in•hab′it•ant (-i tənt), *n.* a person or animal that inhabits a place.

in•hal•ant (in hā′lənt), *n.* a volatile medicine or other substance that is inhaled.

in•ha•la•tor (in′hə lā′tər), *n.* **1.** an apparatus to help one inhale anesthetics, medicinal vapors, etc. **2.** RESPIRATOR (def. 1).

in•hale (in hāl′), *v.t., v.i.,* -**haled, -hal•ing.** to draw in (air, smoke, etc.) by breathing. —**in′ha•la′tion** (-hə lā′shən), *n.*

in•hal′er, *n.* **1.** INHALATOR. **2.** a person who inhales.

in•here (in hēr′), *v.i.,* -**hered, -her•ing.** to belong intrinsically; be inherent.

in•her′ent (-hēr′ənt, -her′-), *adj.* existing in someone or something as a permanent and inseparable quality or attribute. —**in•her′ent•ly**, *adv.*

in•her•it (in her′it), *v.t., v.i.* **1.** to receive (property, a title, etc.) by succession or will, as an heir. **2.** to receive from predecessors. **3.** to receive (a genetic character) by heredity.

in•her′it•ance (-i təns), *n.* **1.** something that is or may be inherited. **2.** the genetic characters transmitted from parent to offspring. **3.** the act or fact of inheriting.

in•hib•it (in hib′it), *v.t.* to restrain, hinder, arrest, or check (an action, impulse, etc.).

in•hi•bi•tion (in′i bish′ən, in′hi-), *n.* **1.** the act of inhibiting or state of being inhibited. **2.** something that inhibits. **3.** the blocking or holding back of one psychological process by another.

in•hib•i•tor (in hib′i tər), *n.* a substance that slows or stops a chemical reaction.

in hoc sig•no vin•ces (in hōk′ sig′nō wing′kās; *Eng.* in hok′ sig′nō vin′sēz), *Latin.* in this sign shalt thou conquer: motto used by Constantine the Great.

in-house (*adj.* in′hous′; *adv.* -hous′), *adj., adv.* within or utilizing an organization's own staff or resources.

in•hu•man, *adj.* **1.** lacking sympathy, pity, warmth, or compassion. **2.** not human.

in′hu•mane′, *adj.* lacking humanity, kindness, compassion, etc. **—in′hu•mane′ly**, *adv.*

in′hu•man′i•ty, *n., pl.* **-ties. 1.** the state or quality of being inhuman or inhumane. **2.** an inhuman or inhumane act.

in•im•i•cal (i nim′i kəl), *adj.* **1.** adverse in tendency or effect. **2.** unfriendly; hostile. **—in•im′i•cal•ly**, *adv.*

in•im•i•ta•ble (i nim′i tə bəl), *adj.* incapable of being imitated or copied. **—in•im′i•ta•bly**, *adv.*

in•iq•ui•ty (i nik′wi tē), *n., pl.* **-ties. 1.** gross injustice or wickedness. **2.** a wicked act; sin. **—in•iq′ui•tous**, *adj.*

in•i•tial (i nish′əl), *adj., n., v.,* **-tialed, -tial•ing** or (*esp. Brit.*) **-tialled, -tial•ling.** **—adj. 1.** of or occurring at the beginning. **—n. 2.** an initial letter, as of a word. **3.** the first letter of a proper name. **—v.t. 4.** to mark or sign with initials. **—in•i′tial•ly**, *adv.*

in•i•ti•ate (*v.* i nish′ē āt′; *n.* -it, -āt′), *v.,* **-at•ed, -at•ing**, *n.* **—v.t. 1.** to begin, set going, or originate. **2.** to introduce into the knowledge of some art or subject. **3.** to admit into the membership of an organization or group. **—n. 4.** a person who has been initiated. **—in•i′ti•a′tion**, *n.* **—in•i′ti•a′tor**, *n.*

in•i•ti•a•tive (i nish′ē ə tiv, i nish′ə-), *n.* **1.** an introductory act or step. **2.** readiness and ability in initiating action. **3.** one's personal, responsible decision. **4.** a procedure by which a specified number of voters may propose legislation.

in•ject (in jekt′), *v.t.* **1.** to force (a fluid) into a passage, cavity, or tissue. **2.** to introduce or interject (a remark, suggestion, etc.), as into conversation. **—in•jec′tion**, *n.* **—in•jec′tor**, *n.*

in•junc•tion (in jungk′shən), *n.* **1.** a judicial order requiring a person or persons to do or refrain from doing a particular act. **2.** an act or instance of enjoining. **3.** a command; order.

in•jure (in′jər), *v.t.,* **-jured, -jur•ing. 1.** to do or cause harm of a kind to. **2.** to treat unjustly or unfairly. **—in′jur•er**, *n.*

in•ju•ry, *n., pl.* **-ries. 1.** harm or damage done or sustained, esp. bodily harm. **2.** wrong or injustice done or suffered. **—in•ju′ri•ous** (-jŏŏr′ē əs), *adj.*

in•jus′tice, *n.* **1.** the quality or fact of being unjust. **2.** an unjust act.

ink (ingk), *n.* **1.** a colored fluid used for writing or printing. **—v.t. 2.** to mark, stain, or smear with ink.

ink′blot′, *n.* a blot of ink forming an irregular pattern, one of a series used in the Rorschach test.

ink′-jet′ print′ing, *n.* a high-speed printing process in which charged droplets of ink issuing from nozzles are directed onto paper under computer control. **—ink′-jet′ print′er**, *n.*

ink•ling (ingk′ling), *n.* **1.** a slight suggestion. **2.** a vague idea.

ink′well′, *n.* a small container for ink.

ink′y, *adj.,* **-i•er, -i•est. 1.** black as ink. **2.** stained with ink. **3.** consisting of or containing ink. **—ink′i•ness**, *n.*

in•laid (in′lād′, in lād′), *adj.* decorated or made with a design set into the surface.

in•land (*adj.* in′lənd; *adv.,* *n.* -land′, -lənd), *adj.* **1.** of or situated in the interior part of a country or region. **—adv. 2.** in or toward the interior of a country. **—n. 3.** the interior part of a country.

in′-law′, *n.* a relative by marriage.

in•lay (*v.* in′lā′, in′lā′; *n.* in′lā′), *v.,* **-laid, -lay•ing**, *n.* **—v.t. 1.** to insert (pieces of wood, ivory, etc.) in the surface of an object. **2.** to decorate with such pieces. **—n. 3.** inlaid work. **4.** a filling of metal, porcelain, etc., that is cemented into a tooth cavity.

in′let, *n.* **1.** an indentation of a shoreline, usu. long and narrow. **2.** a narrow passage between islands.

in′-line′ skate′, *n.* a roller skate with four hard-rubber wheels in a straight line resembling the blade of an ice skate. **—in′-line skat′ing**, *n.*

in′mate′, *n.* a person confined in a prison, hospital, etc.

in me•mo•ri•am (in mə môr′ē əm), *prep.* in memory (of).

in′most′, *adj.* **1.** situated farthest within. **2.** most intimate.

inn (in), *n.* **1.** a small establishment that provides lodging and food for the public, esp. travelers. **2.** a tavern.

in•nards (in′ərdz), *n.pl.* **1.** the internal parts of the body. **2.** the internal parts, structure, etc., of something.

in•nate (i nāt′, in′āt), *adj.* **1.** existing in one from birth. **2.** inherent in the character of something. **—in•nate′ly**, *adv.* **—in•nate′ness**, *n.*

in•ner (in′ər), *adj.* **1.** situated within or farther within. **2.** more intimate or private. **3.** mental; spiritual: *the inner life.*

in′ner cit′y, *n.* a central part of a city, densely populated, and often deteriorating.

in′ner-direct′ed, *adj.* guided by one's own set of values rather than by external pressures.

in′ner ear′, *n.* the inner, liquid-filled, membranous portion of the ear, involved in hearing and balance.

In′ner Light′, *n.* (in Quakerism) the light of Christ in the soul of every person, considered as a guiding force. Also called **In′ner Word′, Inward Light, Christ Within.**

In′ner Mongo′lia, *n.* an autonomous region in NE China.

in′ner•most′, *adj.* INMOST.

in′ner•sole′, *n.* INSOLE.

in′ner•spring′, *adj.* having a number of enclosed coil springs within a padding, as a mattress.

in•ner•vate (i nûr′vāt, in′ər vāt′), *v.t.,* **-vat•ed, -vat•ing.** to furnish with nerves. **—in′ner•va′tion**, *n.*

in•ning (in′ing), *n.* **1.** *Baseball.* a division of a game during which each team has an opportunity to score. **2. innings**, (*used with a sing. v.*) *Cricket.* a unit of play in which each team has a turn at bat.

inn′keep′er, *n.* a person who owns or manages an inn.

in•no•cent (in′ə sənt), *adj.* **1.** free from moral wrong. **2.** free from legal or specific wrong. **3.** not involving evil intent. **4.** not causing physical or moral injury. **5.** without guile; ingenuous. **—n. 6.** an innocent person, as a child. **7.** a simpleton or idiot. **—in′no•cent•ly**, *adv.*

in•noc•u•ous (i nok′yŏŏ əs), *adj.* **1.** not harmful or injurious. **2.** not likely to irritate or offend. **—in•noc′u•ous•ly**, *adv.* **—in•noc′u•ous•ness**, *n.*

in•no•vate (in′ə vāt′), *v.i., v.t.,* **-vat•ed, -vat•ing.** to introduce (something new). **—in′no•va′tion**, *n.* **—in′no•va′tive**, *adj.* **—in′no•va′tor**, *n.*

in•nu•en•do (in′yŏŏ en′dō), *n., pl.* **-dos, -does.** an indirect intimation about a person or thing, esp. of a disparaging nature.

in•nu′mer•a•ble, *adj.* too numerous to be counted.

in•nu′mer•ate (-it), *adj.* unfamiliar with mathematical concepts and methods.

in•oc•u•late (i nok′yə lāt′), *v.t.,* **-lat•ed, -lat•ing.** to inject a vaccine, microorganism, etc., into (a person, animal, or plant) to protect against or study a disease. **—in•oc′u•la′tion**, *n.*

in′of•fen′sive, *adj.* **1.** causing no harm, trouble, or annoyance. **2.** not objectionable. **—in′of•fen′sive•ly**, *adv.*

in·op′er·a·ble, *adj.* **1.** not operable or practicable. **2.** incapable of being treated or cured by surgery.

in·op′er·a·tive, *adj.* **1.** not in operation. **2.** without effect.

in·or·di·nate (in ôr′dn it), *adj.* **1.** exceeding proper limits. **2.** not regulated or regular. —**in·or′di·nate·ly,** *adv.*

in·or·gan′ic, *adj.* **1.** not having the structure or organization characteristic of living bodies. **2.** noting or pertaining to chemical compounds that are not hydrocarbons or their derivatives.

in·pa′tient, *n.* a patient who stays in a hospital while receiving medical care or treatment.

in′put′, *n., v.,* **-put·ted** or **-put, -put·ting.** —*n.* **1.** something that is put in. **2.** the power or energy supplied to a machine. **3.** data entered into a computer for processing. **4.** contribution of ideas, opinions, etc. —*v.t.* **5.** to enter (data) into a computer for processing.

in′quest, *n.* a judicial inquiry, usu. before a jury, esp. one made by a coroner.

in·qui·e·tude (in kwī′i tōōd′, -tyōōd′), *n.* restlessness or uneasiness.

in·quire (in kwīᵊr′), *v.,* **-quired, -quir·ing.** —*v.i.* **1.** to seek information by questioning. **2.** to investigate: *They inquired into the incident.* —*v.t.* **3.** to seek to learn by asking. —**in·quir′er,** *n.*

in·quir·y (in kwīᵊr′ē, in′kwə rē), *n., pl.* **-quir·ies. 1.** a seeking for information or knowledge. **2.** an investigation. **3.** a question; query.

in·qui·si·tion (in′kwə zish′ən, ing′-), *n.* **1.** an official investigation, esp. one of a political or religious nature. **2.** any harsh or prolonged questioning. **3.** (*cap.*) *Roman Catholic Church.* a former special tribunal, engaged chiefly in combating and punishing heresy. —**in·quis′i·tor** (-kwiz′i tər), *n.*

in·quis′i·tive (-kwiz′i tiv), *adj.* **1.** given to inquiry or research. **2.** unduly curious. —**in·quis′i·tive·ly,** *adv.* —**in·quis′i·tive·ness,** *n.*

in re (in rē′, rā′), *prep.* in the matter of.

I.N.R.I., Jesus of Nazareth, King of the Jews. [< LL *Iēsūs Nazarēnus, Rēx Iūdaeōrum*]

in′road′, *n.* **1.** a damaging or serious encroachment: *inroads on our savings.* **2.** a hostile raid.

ins., **1.** inches. **2.** insurance.

in·sane (in sān′), *adj.* **1.** (*not in technical use*) mentally unsound or deranged. **2.** of or for persons who are mentally deranged. **3.** utterly senseless. —**in·sane′ly,** *adv.* —**in·san′i·ty** (-san′i tē), *n.*

in·sa·tia·ble (in sā′shə bəl, -shē ə-), *adj.* incapable of being satisfied.

in·scribe (in skrīb′), *v.t.,* **-scribed, -scrib·ing. 1.** to address or dedicate (a book, photograph, etc.) to someone. **2.** to mark (a surface) with words, characters, etc., esp. in a durable way. **3.** to write, print, or engrave (words, characters, etc.). **4.** to enroll, as on an official list. **5.** *Geom.* to draw (one figure) within another figure so as to touch at as many points as possible. —**in·scrib′er,** *n.* —**in·scrip′tion** (-skrip′shən), *n.*

in·scru·ta·ble (in skrōō′tə bəl), *adj.* **1.** incapable of being investigated or scrutinized. **2.** not easily understood; mysterious. —**in·scru′ta·bil′i·ty, in·scru′ta·ble·ness,** *n.* —**in·scru′ta·bly,** *adv.*

in′seam′, *n.* an inner seam of a garment, esp. of a trouser leg.

in·sect (in′sekt), *n.* any of a large class of small, air-breathing arthropods having the body divided into three parts and having three pairs of legs and usu. two pairs of wings.

in·sec′ti·cide′ (-sek′tə sīd′), *n.* a substance or preparation used for killing insects.

in′sec·tiv′o·rous (-tiv′ər əs), *adj.* feeding chiefly on insects. —**in·sec′ti·vore′** (-tə vôr′), *n.*

in·se·cure (in′si kyōŏr′), *adj.* **1.** subject to fears, doubts, etc. **2.** exposed or liable to risk or danger. **3.** not firmly or reliably placed or fastened. —**in′se·cure′ly,** *adv.* —**in′se·cu′ri·ty,** *n., pl.* **-ties.**

in·sem·i·nate (in sem′ə nāt′), *v.t.,* **-nat·ed, -nat·ing.** to inject semen into (the female reproductive tract). —**in·sem′i·na′tion,** *n.*

in·sen·sate (in sen′sāt, -sit), *adj.* **1.** not endowed with sensation. **2.** without feeling or sensitivity. **3.** without sense or judgment.

in·sen′si·ble, *adj.* **1.** incapable of feeling or perceiving. **2.** unaware; unconscious. **3.** not perceptible by the senses. —**in·sen′si·bil′i·ty,** *n.* —**in·sen′si·bly,** *adv.*

in·sen′si·tive, *adj.* **1.** not emotionally sensitive or sympathetic. **2.** not physically sensitive. —**in·sen′si·tive·ly,** *adv.* —**in·sen′si·tiv′i·ty,** *n.*

in·sen′ti·ent, *adj.* without sensation or feeling. —**in·sen′ti·ence,** *n.*

in·sep′a·ra·ble, *adj.* incapable of being separated, parted, or disjoined. —**in·sep′a·ra·bil′i·ty,** *n.* —**in·sep′a·ra·bly,** *adv.*

in·sert (*v.* in sûrt′; *n.* in′sûrt), *v.t.* **1.** to put or place in. **2.** to introduce into the body of something. —*n.* **3.** something inserted or to be inserted. —**in·ser′tion,** *n.*

in·set (*n.* in′set′; *v.* in set′), *n., v.,* **-set, -set·ting.** —*n.* **1.** an insert. —*v.t.* **2.** to set in or insert.

in′shore′, *adj.* **1.** situated or carried on close to the shore. —*adv.* **2.** toward the shore.

in·side (in′sīd′, in′sīd′), *prep.* **1.** on the inner side or part of. **2.** prior to. —*adv.* **3.** in or into the inner part. **4.** indoors. —*n.* **5.** the inner part. **6.** the inner side or surface. **7. insides,** *Informal.* the stomach and intestines. **8.** a position of power, prestige, etc. **9.** inward nature, thoughts, or feelings —*adj.* **10.** interior; internal. **11.** private; confidential. —*Idiom.* **12. inside of,** within the space or period of. **13. inside out, a.** with the inner side turned out. **b.** thoroughly; completely.

in·sid′er, *n.* **1.** a member of a certain organization, society, etc. **2.** a person who has influence, esp. one privy to confidential information.

in·sid·i·ous (in sid′ē əs), *adj.* **1.** stealthily treacherous or deceitful. **2.** operating or proceeding inconspicuously but with grave effect.

in′sight′, *n.* the act or power of apprehending the true nature of a thing, esp. through intuitive understanding. —**in·sight′ful,** *adj.*

in·sig·ni·a (in sig′nē ə), *n., pl.* **-ni·a** or **-ni·as. 1.** a badge or mark of office or honor. **2.** a distinguishing mark or sign of anything. Sometimes, **in·sig′ne** (-nē).

in′sin·cere′, *adj.* not honest in the expression of actual feeling. —**in′sin·cere′ly,** *adv.* —**in′sin·cer′i·ty,** *n.*

in·sin·u·ate (in sin′yōō āt′), *v.t.,* **-at·ed, -at·ing. 1.** to suggest or hint slyly. **2.** to instill or infuse subtly or artfully, as into the mind. **3.** to bring or introduce into a position by indirect or artful methods. —**in·sin′u·a′tion,** *n.* —**in·sin′u·a′tive** (-ā′tiv, -ə tiv), *adj.*

in·sip·id (in sip′id), *adj.* **1.** without distinctive or interesting qualities. **2.** without sufficient taste or flavor.

in·sist (in sist′), *v.i.* **1.** to be emphatic, firm, or resolute: *to insist on accuracy.* —*v.t.* **2.** to assert or demand firmly or persistently. —**in·sist′ing·ly,** *adv.*

in·sist′ent, *adj.* **1.** emphatic in dwelling upon or maintaining something. **2.** compelling attention or notice. —**in·sist′ence,** *n.* —**in·sist′ent·ly,** *adv.*

in si·tu (in sī′tōō, -tyōō), *adv., adj.* in its original place.

in′so·far′, *adv.* to such an extent: *insofar as I am able.*

in′sole′, *n.* **1.** the inner sole of a shoe or boot. **2.** a removable sole put inside a shoe for comfort.

in·so·lent (in′sə lənt), *adj.* boldly rude or disrespectful. —**in′so·lence,** *n.* —**in′so·lent·ly,** *adv.*

in·sol′u·ble, *adj.* **1.** incapable of being dissolved. **2.** incapable of being solved. —**in·sol′u·bil′i·ty,** *n.*

in·sol′vent, *adj.* unable to satisfy creditors or discharge liabilities. —**in·sol′ven·cy,** *n.*

in·som·ni·a (in som′nē ə), *n.* difficulty in falling or staying asleep, esp. when chronic. —**in·som′ni·ac′,** *n., adj.*

in′so·much′, *adv.* **1.** to such a degree (usu. fol. by *that*). **2.** inasmuch (usu. fol. by *as*).

in•sou•ci•ant (in sōō'sē ənt), *adj.* free from concern or anxiety. —**in•sou'ci•ance,** *n.*

in•spect (in spekt'), *v.t.* **1.** to look carefully at or over. **2.** to view or examine formally or officially. —**in•spec'tion,** *n.* —**in•spec'tor,** *n.*

in•spi•ra•tion (in'spə rā'shən), *n.* **1.** an inspiring or animating action or influence. **2.** something inspired, as an idea. **3.** the drawing of air into the lungs. **4.** the act of inspiring. —**in'spi•ra'tion•al,** *adj.*

in•spire (in spīr'), *v.,* **-spired, -spir•ing.** —*v.t.* **1.** to fill with an animating or exalting influence. **2.** to arouse or generate (a feeling, thought, etc.). **3.** to affect with a feeling, thought, etc. **4.** to guide or control by divine influence. —*v.i.* **5.** to give inspiration. **6.** to inhale.

in•spir'it, *v.t.* to infuse spirit or life into.

Inst., **1.** Instance. **2.** Institution.

in'sta•bil'i•ty, *n.* lack of stability or steadiness.

in•stall or **-stal** (in stôl'), *v.t.,* **-stalled, -stall•ing** or **-stal•ling.** **1.** to put in place or connect for service or use. **2.** to establish in a place. **3.** to induct into an office with formalities. —**in'stal•la'tion** (-stə lā'shən), *n.* —**in•stall'er,** *n.*

in•stall'ment¹ or **in•stal'ment,** *n.* **1.** any of several parts into which a debt is divided for payment at specified intervals. **2.** a single portion of something issued in parts at successive times.

in•stall'ment² or **in•stal'ment,** *n.* the act of installing or fact of being installed; installation.

install'ment plan', *n.* a system for paying for an item in installments.

in•stance (in'stəns), *n., v.,* **-stanced, -stanc•ing.** —*n.* **1.** a case or occurrence of something. **2.** an example put forth in proof or illustration. **3.** the institution and prosecution of a legal case. —*v.t.* **4.** to cite as an instance.

in'stant, *n.* **1.** a very short time; moment. **2.** a particular moment. —*adj.* **3.** immediate. **4.** pressing or urgent. **5.** processed so as to require minimal time to prepare: *instant coffee.*

in'stan•ta'ne•ous (-stən tā'nē əs), *adj.* occurring, done, or completed in an instant. —**in'stan•ta'ne•ous•ly,** *adv.*

in•stan•ter (in stan'tər), *adv.* at once.

in'stant•ly, *adv.* immediately; at once.

in•state', *v.t.,* **-stat•ed, -stat•ing.** to place in a state, position, or office. —**in•state'ment,** *n.*

in•stead (in sted'), *adv.* **1.** as a substitute or replacement. **2.** as a preferred or accepted alternative. —*Idiom.* **3. instead of,** in place of.

in'step', *n.* the arched upper surface of the human foot between the toes and the ankle.

in•sti•gate (in'sti gāt'), *v.t.,* **-gat•ed, -gat•ing.** **1.** to cause by incitement. **2.** to provoke to some action or course. —**in'sti•ga'tion,** *n.* —**in'sti•ga'tor,** *n.*

in•still or **-stil** (in stil'), *v.t.,* **-stilled, -still•ing** or **-stil•ling.** **1.** to infuse slowly, as into the mind. **2.** to put in drop by drop.

in•stinct (in'stingkt), *n.* **1.** an inborn pattern of activity or tendency to action common to a given biological species. **2.** a natural inclination or aptitude. **3.** natural intuitive power. —**in•stinc'tive, in•stinc'tu•al** (-stingk'chōō əl), *adj.*

in•sti•tute (in'sti tōōt', -tyōōt'), *v.,* **-tut•ed, -tut•ing,** *n.* —*v.t.* **1.** to set up; establish. **2.** to initiate; start. —*n.* **3.** a society for the promotion of the arts, scientific research, etc. **4. a.** a college for instruction in technical subjects. **b.** a unit within a university for advanced instruction and research. —**in'sti•tut'er, in'sti•tu'tor,** *n.*

in'sti•tu'tion, *n.* **1.** an organization devoted to the promotion of a cause or program, esp. one of a public character. **2.** the building occupied by such an organization. **3.** a place for the care or confinement of people, as mental patients. **4.** any established law, custom, etc. **5.** any familiar person, thing, or practice. —**in'sti•tu'tion•al,** *adj.*

in'sti•tu'tion•al•ize', *v.t.,* **-ized, -iz•ing.** **1.** to make into or treat as an institution. **2.** to confine in an institution. —**in'sti•tu'tion•al•i•za'tion,** *n.*

instr., **1.** instructor. **2.** instrument.

in•struct (in strukt'), *v.t.* **1.** to furnish with knowledge, esp. by a systematic method. **2.** to direct; command.

in•struc'tion, *n.* **1.** the act or practice of instructing or teaching. **2.** the knowledge imparted. **3.** Usu., **-tions.** orders or directions. **4.** a computer command. —**in•struc'tion•al,** *adj.*

in•struc'tive (-tiv), *adj.* serving to instruct or inform.

in•struc'tor, *n.* **1.** a person who instructs. **2.** a college teacher who ranks below an assistant professor.

in•stru•ment (in'strə mənt), *n.* **1.** a mechanical tool or implement, esp. one used for precision work. **2.** a device for producing musical sounds. **3.** a means by which something is done; agency. **4.** a mechanical or electronic device for monitoring or controlling, esp. one used in navigation. **5.** a formal legal document, as a bond. —*adj.* **6.** relying only on the observation of instruments for navigation: *instrument flying.* —*v.t.* **7.** to equip with instruments.

in'stru•men'tal (-men'tl), *adj.* **1.** serving as an instrument or means. **2.** performed on or written for a musical instrument or instruments. **3.** of an instrument or tool.

in'stru•men'tal•ist, *n.* a person who plays a musical instrument.

in'stru•men•tal'i•ty, *n., pl.* **-ties.** a means or agency.

in'stru•men•ta'tion (-tā'shən), *n.* **1.** the arranging of music for instruments, esp. for an orchestra. **2.** the use of, or work done by, instruments.

in'sub•or'di•nate (-dn it), *adj.* not submitting to authority. —**in'sub•or'di•na'tion,** *n.*

in'sub•stan'tial, *adj.* **1.** not substantial or real. **2.** not solid or firm; flimsy.

in•suf•fer•a•ble (in suf'ər ə bəl), *adj.* not to be endured; intolerable. —**in•suf'fer•a•bly,** *adv.*

in•su•lar (in'sə lər, ins'yə-), *adj.* **1.** of an island or islands. **2.** detached; isolated. **3.** narrow-minded or illiberal. —**in•su•lar'i•ty,** *n.*

in'su•late' (-lāt'), *v.t.,* **-lat•ed, -lat•ing.** **1.** to cover with a material that prevents or reduces the passage or transfer of heat, electricity, or sound. **2.** to place in an isolated situation. —**in'su•la'tion,** *n.* —**in'su•la'tor,** *n.*

in•su•lin (in'sə lin, ins'yə-), *n.* **1.** a hormone, secreted by the pancreas, that regulates the metabolism of glucose and other nutrients. **2.** a commercial preparation of this substance, used for treating diabetes.

in•sult (*v.* in sult'; *n.* in'sult), *v.t.* **1.** to treat insolently or with contemptuous rudeness. —*n.* **2.** an insolent or contemptuously rude action or remark. —*Saying.* **3. add insult to injury,** to inflict additional harm on a person who has already been hurt.

in•su•per•a•ble (in sōō'pər ə bəl), *adj.* incapable of being overcome or surmounted.

in'sup•port'a•ble, *adj.* **1.** unbearable; insufferable. **2.** incapable of being maintained or justified.

in•sur•ance (in shŏŏr'əns, -shûr'-), *n.* **1.** the act or business of insuring property, life, etc., against loss or harm, in return for payment. **2.** coverage by contract in which one party agrees to indemnify another for a specified loss. **3.** the contract itself. **4.** the amount for which anything is insured. **5.** any means of guaranteeing against loss or harm.

in•sure', *v.t.,* **-sured, -sur•ing.** **1.** to issue or obtain insurance on or for. **2.** to ensure. —**in•sur'a•ble,** *adj.*

in•sured', *n.* a person covered by an insurance policy.

in•sur'er, *n.* a person or company that insures or issues insurance.

in•sur•gent (in sûr'jənt), *n.* **1.** a person who takes part in forcible opposition to an established government or authority. **2.** a member of a group, esp. a political party, who revolts against the leadership. —*adj.* **3.** rebellious. —**in•sur'gence,** *n.* —**in•sur'gen•cy,** *n., pl.* **-cies.**

in•sur•rec•tion (in'sə rek'shən), *n.* the act of rising in arms or open rebellion against an established government or authority. —**in′sur•rec′tion•ist,** n.

int., 1. interest. **2.** interior. **3.** interjection. **4.** internal. **5.** international. **6.** intransitive.

in•tact (in takt′), adj. remaining uninjured, sound, or whole.

in•tagl•io (in tal′yō, -täl′-), n., pl. **-tagl•ios, -ta•gli** (-tal′yē, -täl′-). incised carving, as opposed to carving in relief.

in′take′, n. **1.** the place at which a fluid is taken into a channel, pipe, etc. **2.** the act of taking in. **3.** a quantity taken in.

in•tan′gi•ble, adj. **1.** incapable of being perceived by touch. **2.** not definite or clear to the mind. —n. **3.** something intangible, esp. an intangible asset, as goodwill. —**in•tan′gi•bil′i•ty,** n.

in•te•ger (in′ti jər), n. one of the positive or negative numbers 1, 2, 3, etc., or zero.

in•te•gral (in′ti grəl, in teg′rəl), adj. **1.** necessary to completeness; constituent. **2.** composed of parts that together constitute a whole. **3.** complete; whole.

in•te•grate (in′ti grāt′), v., **-grat•ed, -grat•ing.** —v.t. **1.** to bring together into a unified or interrelated whole. **2.** to combine to produce a whole or a larger unit. **3.** to make (a school, neighborhood, etc.) available to all racial and other ethnic groups. —v.i. **4.** to become integrated. —**in′te•gra′tion,** n. —**in′te•gra′tive,** adj.

in•teg•ri•ty (in teg′ri tē), n. **1.** uncompromising adherence to moral and ethical principles. **2.** the state of being whole or entire. **3.** a sound or unimpaired condition.

in•teg•u•ment (in teg′yə mənt), n. a natural covering, as a skin or shell.

in•tel•lect (in′tl ekt′), n. **1.** the faculty of the mind by which one knows or understands. **2.** a particular mind or intelligence, esp. of a high order. **3.** a highly intelligent person.

in′tel•lec′tu•al, adj. **1.** appealing to or engaging the intellect. **2.** developed by or relying on the intellect. **3.** showing mental capacity to a high degree. —n. **4.** a person who values or pursues intellectual interests. —**in′tel•lec′tu•al•ly,** adv.

in′tel•lec′tu•al•ize′, v.t., **-ized, -iz•ing.** to analyze intellectually or rationally, often ignoring the emotional significance. —**in′tel•lec′tu•al•i•za′tion,** n.

in′tellec′tual prop′erty, n. Law. property that results from original creative thought, as patents, copyright material, and trademarks.

in•tel•li•gence (in tel′i jəns), n. **1.** capacity for learning, reasoning, and understanding. **2.** manifestation of a high mental capacity. **3.** information received or imparted. **4. a.** secret information, esp. about an enemy. **b.** an organization engaged in gathering such information.

intel′ligence quo′tient, n. an intelligence test score obtained by dividing mental age by chronological age and multiplying by 100.

in•tel′li•gent, adj. having good understanding or a high mental capacity. —**in•tel′li•gent•ly,** adv.

in•tel′li•gent′si•a (-jent′sē ə, -gent′-), n.pl. intellectuals considered as a group.

in•tel′li•gi•ble (-jə bəl), adj. capable of being understood. —**in•tel′li•gi•bil′i•ty,** n. —**in•tel′li•gi•bly,** adv.

in•tem′per•ate, adj. **1.** given to immoderate indulgence in alcoholic beverages. **2.** immoderate in indulgence of appetite or passion. —**in•tem′per•ance,** n.

in•tend (in tend′), v.t. **1.** to have in mind as something to be done or brought about. **2.** to design for a particular purpose or use. **3.** to mean or signify.

in•tend′ed, n. Informal. the person one plans to marry.

in•tense (in tens′), adj. **1.** existing in a high or extreme degree. **2.** acute or vehement, as emotions. **3.** strenuous or earnest. **4.** having or showing great seriousness or strong feeling. —**in•tense′ly,** adv.

in•ten′si•fy′, v.t., v.i., **-fied, -fy•ing.** to make or become intense or more intense. —**in•ten′si•fi•ca′tion,** n. —**in•ten′si•fi′er,** n.

in•ten′si•ty (-si tē), n., pl. **-ties. 1.** the quality or

condition of being intense. **2.** great energy or vehemence, as of feeling. **3.** a high or extreme degree, as of heat. **4.** magnitude, as of energy or a force per unit of area, time, etc.

in•ten′sive, adj. **1.** of or characterized by intensity. **2.** (of a grammatical form or construction) indicating increased emphasis or force. —n. **3.** an intensive form or construction. —**in•ten′sive•ly,** adv. —**in•ten′sive•ness,** n.

inten′sive care′, n. the use of specialized equipment and personnel for continuous monitoring and care of the critically ill.

in•tent¹ (in tent′), n. **1.** something intended. **2.** the act of intending. **3.** meaning or significance. —**Idiom. 4. to** or **for all intents and purposes,** practically speaking.

in•tent² (in tent′), adj. **1.** firmly fixed or directed. **2.** having the attention sharply focused. **3.** determined or resolved: intent on revenge. —**in•tent′ly,** adv. —**in•tent′ness,** n.

in•ten′tion, n. **1.** the act of determining upon some action or result. **2.** the end or object intended. **3. intentions,** purpose or attitude toward the effect of one's actions.

in•ten′tion•al, adj. done with intention or on purpose. —**in•ten′tion•al•ly,** adv.

in•ter (in tûr′), v.t., **-terred, -ter•ring.** to place (a dead body) in a grave or tomb.

inter-, a prefix meaning: between or among (interdepartmental); mutual or reciprocally (interdependent).

inter., 1. intermediate. **2.** interrogation. **3.** interrogative.

in•ter•act (in′tər akt′), v.i. to act upon one another. —**in′ter•ac′tion,** n.

in′ter•ac′tive, adj. **1.** acting upon one another. **2.** (of a computer or program) characterized by immediate two-way communication between a source of information and a user, who can initiate or respond to queries.

in′ter•breed′, v.t., v.i., **-bred, -breed•ing.** to crossbreed (a plant or animal).

in′ter•cede′ (-sēd′), v.i., **-ced•ed, -ced•ing. 1.** to plead in behalf of one in trouble. **2.** to mediate.

in′ter•cept′ (-sept′), v.t. **1.** to stop or interrupt the course, progress, or transmission of. **2.** Math. to mark off or include, as between two points or lines. —**in′ter•cep′tion,** n. —**in′ter•cep′tor,** n.

in′ter•ces′sion (-sesh′ən), n. **1.** the act of interceding. **2.** a pleading on behalf of another person. **3.** a prayer to God on behalf of another. —**in′ter•ces′so•ry,** adj.

in•ter•change (v. in′tər chānj′; n. in′tər chānj′), v., **-changed, -chang•ing,** n. —v.t. **1.** to put each in the place of the other. **2.** to give and receive reciprocally; exchange. —n. **3.** an act or instance of interchanging. **4.** a multilevel highway intersection allowing vehicles to move without crossing the streams of traffic. —**in′ter•change′a•ble,** adj.

in′ter•col•le′giate, adj. taking place between or representing different colleges.

in′ter•com′ (-kom′), n. a communication system, as within a building, with a loudspeaker and microphone at each of two or more points.

in′ter•com•mu′ni•cate′, v.i., v.t., **-cat•ed, -cat•ing.** to communicate mutually. —**in′ter•com•mu′ni•ca′tion,** n.

in′ter•con•nect′, v.t., v.i. to connect or become connected with one another.

in′ter•con•ti•nen′tal, adj. **1.** between or among continents. **2.** capable of traveling between continents.

in′ter•cos′tal (-kos′tl, -kô′stl), adj. situated between the ribs.

in′ter•course′, n. **1.** dealings or communication between individuals, countries, etc. **2.** sexual relations or a sexual coupling, esp. coitus.

in′ter•de•nom′i•na′tion•al, adj. between or involving different religious denominations.

in′ter•de•part•men′tal, adj. involving or existing between two or more departments.

in′ter•de•pend′ent, *adj.* mutually dependent. —**in′ter•de•pend′ence,** *n.*

in•ter•dict′ (*n.* in′tər dikt′; *v.* in′tər dikt′), *n.* **1.** any prohibitory act or decree. —*v.t.* **2.** to prohibit officially. **3.** to impede the flow or use of by steady bombardment. —**in′ter•dic′tion,** *n.*

in′ter•dis′ci•pli•nar′y, *adj.* involving two or more academic disciplines.

in•ter•est (in′tər ist, -trist), *n.* **1.** a feeling of having one's attention or curiosity engaged by something. **2.** something that arouses such feelings. **3.** the power to excite such feelings. **4.** a business, cause, etc., in which a person has a share or concern. **5.** a legal share or right, as in a business. **6.** Often, **-ests.** a group involved in an enterprise, industry, etc. **7.** benefit; advantage. **8.** self-interest. **9. a.** a sum charged for borrowing money. **b.** the rate for such charge. —*v.t.* **10.** to excite the attention or curiosity of. **11.** to involve. —*Idiom.* **12. in the interest(s) of,** on behalf of. —**in′ter•est•ed,** *adj.*

in′terest group′, *n.* a group of people acting together because of a common interest, concern, or purpose.

in′ter•est•ing (-tər ə sting, -trə sting, -tə res′ting), *adj.* engaging the attention or curiosity.

in•ter•face (*n.* in′tər fās′; *v.* in′tər fās′), *n.*, *v.*, **-faced, -fac•ing.** —*n.* **1.** a surface regarded as the common boundary of two bodies or spaces. **2.** a common boundary between systems, equipment, concepts, or people. **3.** computer hardware or software designed to communicate information, as between a computer and a user. —*v.t.*, *v.i.* **4.** to bring into or be in an interface.

in′ter•faith′, *adj.* between or involving persons belonging to different religions.

in′ter•fere′ (-fēr′), *v.i.*, **-fered, -fer•ing. 1.** to come into opposition so as to hinder or obstruct action. **2.** to meddle. **3.** (in sports) to obstruct the action of an opposing player in an illegal way. —**in′ter•fer′ence,** *n.*

in•ter•fer•on (in′tər fēr′on), *n.* a protein produced by virus-infected cells that inhibits reproduction of the virus.

in•ter•ga•lac•tic (in′tər gə lak′tik), *adj.* of, existing, or occurring in the space between galaxies.

in•ter•im (in′tər əm), *n.* **1.** an intervening time. —*adj.* **2.** for an interim; temporary.

in•te•ri•or (in tēr′ē ər), *adj.* **1.** situated within. **2.** situated well inland from a coast. —*n.* **3.** the internal or inner part. **4.** a representation of the inside of a room or building. **5.** the inland parts of a region, country, etc. **6.** the domestic affairs of a country.

inte′rior decora′tion, *n.* the art or profession of designing and furnishing the interior of a house, office, etc. —**inte′rior dec′orator,** *n.*

inte′rior mon′ologue, *n.* a form of stream-of-consciousness writing that represents the inner thoughts of a character.

interj., interjection.

in′ter•ject′ (-jekt′), *v.t.* to insert, often abruptly, between other things.

in′ter•jec′tion, *n.* **1.** the act of interjecting. **2.** something interjected, as a remark. **3.** a word or expression typically used in grammatical isolation to express emotion.

in′ter•lace′, *v.i*, *v.t.*, **-laced, -lac•ing.** to unite by or as if by weaving together; intertwine.

in′ter•lard′, *v.t.* to diversify by interspersing something striking or contrasting.

in•ter•leu•kin (in′tər loo′kin), *n.* any of a family of proteins that participate in the body's defense system, esp. by promoting the growth of white blood cells.

in′ter•line′[1], *v.t.*, **-lined, -lin•ing.** to write or insert between the lines of writing or print.

in′ter•line′[2], *v.t.*, **-lined, -lin•ing.** to provide with an interlining.

in′ter•lin′ing, *n.* an inner lining placed between the ordinary lining and the outer fabric of a garment.

in′ter•lock′, *v.i.*, *v.t.* to lock, join, or fit together closely.

in•ter•loc•u•to•ry (in′tər lok′yə tôr′ē), *adj. Law.* (of a decision, decree, etc.) not finally decisive.

in′ter•lope′, *v.i.*, **-loped, -lop•ing. 1.** to thrust oneself into the affairs of others. **2.** to intrude into some field of trade without a proper license. —**in′ter•lop′er,** *n.*

in′ter•lude′, *n.* **1.** an intervening episode, period, or space. **2.** an entertainment between the acts of a play. **3.** an instrumental piece of music played between the parts of a song, church service, etc.

in′ter•mar′ry, *v.i.*, **-ried, -ry•ing. 1.** to become connected by marriage, as two families. **2.** to marry within one's family. **3.** to marry outside one's religion, ethnic group, etc. —**in′ter•mar′riage,** *n.*

in′ter•me′di•ar′y (-mē′dē er′ē), *n.*, *pl.* **-ar•ies,** *adj.* —*n.* **1.** an intermediate agent or agency. —*adj.* **2.** being between; intermediate. **3.** acting as an intermediary between persons or parties.

in′ter•me′di•ate (-it), *adj.* **1.** being or acting between two points, stages, etc. —*n.* **2.** something intermediate, as a form or class.

in•ter•ment (in tûr′mənt), *n.* the act or ceremony of interring.

in•ter•mez•zo (in′tər met′sō, -med′zō), *n.*, *pl.* **-mez•zos, -mez•zi** (-met′sē, -med′zē). a short musical composition, as between main divisions of an extended musical work.

in•ter•mi•na•ble (in tûr′mə nə bəl), *adj.* having no apparent limit or end. —**in•ter′mi•na•bly,** *adv.*

in′ter•min′gle, *v.t.*, *v.i.*, **-gled, -gling.** to mix together; mingle.

in′ter•mis′sion (-mish′ən), *n.* an interval between periods of action or activity, as between the acts of a play.

in′ter•mit′tent (-mit′nt), *adj.* alternately ceasing and beginning again.

in•tern[1] (in tûrn′), *v.t.* to confine within prescribed limits, as prisoners of war. —**in•tern′ment,** *n.*

in•tern[2] (in′tûrn), *n.* **1.** a recent medical school graduate serving under supervision in a hospital. **2.** someone working as a trainee to gain practical experience in an occupation. —*v.i.* **3.** to serve as an intern. —**in′tern•ship′,** *n.*

in•ter•nal (in tûr′nl), *adj.* **1.** of or on the inside or inner part. **2.** inherent or intrinsic. **3.** of the domestic affairs of a country. **4.** to be taken inside the body, esp. orally. —**in•ter′nal•ize′,** *v.t.*, **-ized, -iz•ing.** —**in•ter′nal•ly,** *adv.*

inter′nal-combus′tion en′gine, *n.* an engine in which the process of combustion takes place within the cylinder or cylinders.

inter′nal med′icine, *n.* the branch of medicine dealing with the diagnosis and nonsurgical treatment of diseases.

inter′nal rev′enue, *n.* the revenue of a government from any domestic source.

in′ter•na′tion•al, *adj.* **1.** between or among nations. **2.** of two or more nations or their citizens. **3.** pertaining to the relations between nations. **4.** having members or activities in several nations. —**in′ter•na′tion•al•ize′,** *v.t.*, *v.i.*, **-ized, -iz•ing.** —**in′ter•na′tion•al•ly,** *adv.*

In′terna′tional Court′ of Jus′tice, *n.* the chief judicial agency of the United Nations, established in 1945 to decide disputes arising between nations. Also called **World Court.**

In′terna′tional Date′ Line′, *n.* a theoretical line following approximately the 180th meridian, the regions to the east of which are counted as being one day earlier than those to the west.

in′ter•na′tion•al•ism, *n.* **1.** the principle of cooperation among nations. **2.** international character, relations, or control.

Interna′tional Phonet′ic Al′phabet, *n.* a set of phonetic symbols designed to provide a universally understood system for transcribing the speech sounds of any language.

in′ter•ne•cine (-nē′sēn, -sīn, -nes′ēn, -nes′īn), *adj.* **1.** involving conflict or struggle within a group. **2.** mutually destructive.

in•tern•ee (in′tûr nē′), *n.*, *pl.* **-ees**. a person who is interned, as a prisoner of war.

In•ter•net (in′tər net′), *n.* a large computer network linking smaller computer networks worldwide (usu. prec. by *the*).

in•tern•ist (in′tûr nist, in tûr′nist), *n.* a physician specializing in internal medicine.

in′ter•of′fice, *adj.* functioning or communicating between the offices of an organization.

in′ter•per•son•al, *adj.* between persons.

in′ter•play′, *n.* reciprocal relationship, action, or influence.

in•ter•po•late (in tûr′pə lāt′), *v.t.,* **-lat•ed, -lat•ing. 1.** to introduce (something extraneous) between other things or parts. **2.** to alter (a text) by the insertion of new matter, esp. without authorization. —**in•ter′po•la′tion,** *n.*

in′ter•pose′, *v.t., v.i.,* **-posed, -pos•ing. 1.** to place or come between (other things). **2.** to put in (a remark, question, etc.) in the midst of a conversation or discourse. **3.** to bring (influence, action, etc.) to bear between parties. —**in′ter•po•si′tion** (-pə-zish′ən), *n.*

in•ter•pret (in tûr′prit), *v.t.* **1.** to give the meaning of. **2.** to understand in a particular way. **3.** to translate orally. **4.** to perform (a song, role in a play, etc.) according to one's own understanding or sensitivity. —*v.i.* **5.** to translate orally. **6.** to explain. —**in•ter′pret•er,** *n.*

in•ter′pre•ta′tion, *n.* **1.** the act of interpreting. **2.** the meaning assigned to another's creative work, behavior, etc. **3.** the performing of a dramatic part, music, etc., to demonstrate one's conception of it.

in′ter•pre′tive, *adj.* of or serving to interpret.

in′ter•ra′cial, *adj.* of or involving members of different races.

in′ter•re•late′, *v.t., v.i.,* **-lat•ed, -lat•ing.** to bring or enter into reciprocal relation. —**in′ter•re•lat′ed,** *adj.*

in•ter•ro•gate (in ter′ə gāt′), *v.t., v.i.,* **-gat•ed, -gat•ing.** to ask questions of (a person), esp. formally and thoroughly: *to interrogate a suspect.* —**in•ter′ro•ga′tion,** *n.* —**in•ter′ro•ga′tor,** *n.*

International Date Line

in•ter•rog•a•tive (in′tə rog′ə tiv), *adj.* **1.** of or conveying a question. **2.** used in or to form a question: *an interrogative pronoun.* —*n.* **3.** an interrogative word or construction.

in′ter•rog′a•to′ry (-tôr′ē), *adj., n., pl.* **-to•ries.**

—*adj.* **1.** interrogative. —*n.* **2.** (in law) a formal or written question.

in•ter•rupt (in′tə rupt′), *v.t.* **1.** to break the continuity or uniformity of (a process, activity, etc.). **2.** to stop (a person) in the midst of something, esp. by an interjected remark. —*v.i.* **3.** to interfere with action or speech. —**in′ter•rup′tion,** *n.*

in′ter•scho•las′tic, *adj.* existing or occurring between schools.

in′ter•sect′ (-sekt′), *v.t.* **1.** to cut or divide by passing through or across. —*v.i.* **2.** to cross, as lines or wires.

in′ter•sec′tion, *n.* **1.** a place where two or more roads meet. **2.** the act or fact of intersecting.

in′ter•ses′sion, *n.* a period between two academic terms.

in′ter•sperse′ (-spûrs′), *v.t.,* **-spersed, -spers•ing. 1.** to scatter here and there. **2.** to diversify with something scattered.

in′ter•state′, *adj.* connecting or involving different states, esp. of the U.S.

in′ter•stel′lar, *adj.* situated or occurring between the stars.

in•ter•stice (in tûr′stis), *n., pl.* **-stic•es** (-stə sēz′, -siz). a small or narrow space between things or parts.

in′ter•twine′, *v.t., v.i.,* **-twined, -twin•ing.** to unite by twining together.

in′ter•ur′ban, *adj.* between cities.

in•ter•val (in′tər vəl), *n.* **1.** an intervening period of time. **2.** a space between things, points, etc. **3.** the difference in pitch between two tones. —*Idiom.* **4. at intervals, a.** now and then. **b.** here and there.

in′ter•vene′ (-vēn′), *v.i.,* **-vened, -ven•ing. 1.** to come between disputing people, groups, etc. **2.** to occur between other events or periods. **3.** to occur incidentally so as to modify. **4.** to interfere with force or a threat of force. —**in′ter•ven′tion** (-ven′shən), *n.*

in′ter•view′, *n.* **1.** a formal meeting in which a person questions or evaluates another. **2. a.** a conversation in which a writer or reporter obtains information from a person. **b.** the report of such a conversation. —*v.t.* **3.** to have an interview with. —**in′ter•view•ee′,** *n., pl.* **-ees.** —**in′ter•view′er,** *n.*

in′ter•vo•cal′ic, *adj.* immediately following a vowel and preceding a vowel, as the *v* in *cover.*

in′ter•weave′, *v.t., v.i.,* **-wove** or **-weaved; -wo•ven** or **-weaved; -weav•ing. 1.** to weave together. **2.** to blend as if by weaving.

in•tes•tate (in tes′tāt, -tit), *adj.* **1.** not having made a will: *to die intestate.* **2.** not disposed of by will. —**in•tes′ta•cy** (-tə sē), *n.*

in•tes•tine (in tes′tin), *n.* Usu., **-tines.** the lower part of the alimentary canal, extending from the pylorus to the anus and consisting of a narrow, longer part **(small intestine)** and a broad, shorter part **(large intestine).** —**in•tes′ti•nal,** *adj.*

in•ti•mate¹ (in′tə mit), *adj.* **1.** associated in close personal relations. **2.** characterized by warm friendship. **3.** private; closely personal. **4.** characterized by privacy; cozy. **5.** inmost or deep within. —*n.* **6.** an intimate friend. —**in′ti•ma•cy** (-mə sē), *n., pl.* **-cies.** —**in′ti•mate•ly,** *adv.*

in•ti•mate² (in′tə māt′), *v.t.,* **-mat•ed, -mat•ing.** to make known indirectly. —**in′ti•ma′tion,** *n.*

in•tim•i•date (in tim′i dāt′), *v.t.,* **-dat•ed, -dat•ing. 1.** to make timid or fearful. **2.** to force into or deter from some action by inducing fear. —**in•tim′i•da′tion,** *n.*

in•tinc•tion (in tingk′shən), *n.* (in a communion service) the act of dipping the bread into the wine.

in•to (in′tōō; *unstressed* -tōō, -tə), *prep.* **1.** to the inside of: *We walked into the room.* **2.** toward or in the direction of: *going into town.* **3.** to a point of contact with: *backed into a parked car.* **4.** to the state or form assumed or brought about: *lapsed into disrepair.* **5.** to the occupation, action, circumstance, or acceptance of: *coerced into complying.* **6.** (used to indicate a continuing extent in time or space): *lasted into the night.* **7.** *Informal.* interested or absorbed in: *She's into yoga.*

in•tol′er•a•ble, *adj.* **1.** unbearable; insufferable. **2.** excessive. —**in•tol′er•a•bly,** *adv.*

in•tol′er•ant, *adj.* **1.** not tolerating beliefs, manners, etc., different from one's own, as in religious matters. **2.** unable or unwilling to tolerate or endure: *intolerant of heat.* —**in•tol′er•ance,** *n.*

in•to•na•tion (in′tō nā′shən, -tə-), *n.* **1.** the pattern or melody of pitch changes in connected speech. **2.** the act of intoning. **3.** the ability to produce musical tones on pitch. **4.** something intoned or chanted.

in•tone′, *v.t.,* -toned, -ton•ing. **1.** to utter with a particular tone or voice modulation. **2.** to recite or chant in monotone. —**in•ton′er,** *n.*

in to•to (in tō′tō), *adv.* completely; entirely.

in•tox•i•cate (in tok′si kāt′), *v.t.,* -cat•ed, -cat•ing. **1.** to excite or stupefy with liquor. **2.** to elate; exhilarate. —**in•tox′i•cant** (-kənt), *n.* —**in•tox′i•ca′tion,** *n.*

intra-, a prefix meaning within (*intramural*).

in•trac′ta•ble, *adj.* not docile or manageable. —**in•trac′ta•bil′i•ty,** *n.*

in•tra•mu•ral (in′trə myoŏr′əl), *adj.* **1.** involving students at the same school: *intramural sports.* **2.** within the walls or confines, as of an institution.

in•tra•net (in′trə net′), *n.* a computer network with restricted access, as within a corporation, that uses software and protocols developed for the Internet.

in•tran•si•gent (in tran′si jənt), *adj.* refusing to agree or compromise. —**in•tran′si•gence,** *n.*

in•tran′si•tive, *adj.* of or being a verb that indicates a complete action without being accompanied by a direct object. —**in•tran′si•tive•ly,** *adv.*

in•tra•state (in′trə stāt′), *adj.* existing or occurring within a state, esp. of the U.S.

in′tra•u′ter•ine device′, *n.* any of various devices for insertion into the uterus as a contraceptive.

in′tra•ve′nous, *adj.* within or into a vein. —**in′tra•ve′nous•ly,** *adv.*

in•trench′, *v.t., v.i.* ENTRENCH.

in•trep•id (in trep′id), *adj.* fearless; dauntless. —**in•trep′id•ly,** *adv.*

in•tri•cate (in′tri kit), *adj.* **1.** having many interrelated parts or facets. **2.** hard to understand, work, or make. —**in′tri•ca•cy** (-kə sē), *n., pl.* -cies. —**in′tri•cate•ly,** *adv.*

in•trigue (*v.* in trēg′; *n.* also in′trēg), *v.,* -trigued, -tri•guing, *n.* —*v.t.* **1.** to arouse the curiosity or interest of. —*v.i.* **2.** to plot craftily or underhandedly. —*n.* **3.** a crafty or underhanded plot. **4.** the act of plotting. **5.** a secret love affair. —**in•tri′guing•ly,** *adv.*

in•trin•sic (in trin′sik, -zik), *adj.* belonging to a thing by its very nature. —**in•trin′si•cal•ly,** *adv.*

intro-, a prefix meaning inside or within (*introspection*).

in•tro•duce (in′trə doos′, -dyoos′), *v.t.,* -duced, -duc•ing. **1.** to present (a person) to another so as to make acquainted. **2.** to present (a person, product, etc.) to a group or to the public for the first time. **3.** to bring to first knowledge or experience of something: *He introduced me to skiing.* **4.** to bring into notice or use. **5.** to begin; preface. **6.** to insert. —**in′tro•duc′tion** (-duk′shən), *n.* —**in′tro•duc′to•ry** (-tə rē), *adj.*

in•tro•it (in′trō it, -troit), *n.* **1.** a part of a psalm with antiphon recited at the beginning of the Roman Catholic mass. **2.** a choral response sung at the beginning of a religious service.

in•tro•spec•tion (in′trə spek′shən), *n.* observation or examination of one's own emotional state and mental processes. —**in′tro•spec′tive,** *adj.*

in′tro•vert′ (-vûrt′), *n.* a shy person concerned primarily with inner thoughts and feelings. —**in′tro•ver′sion** (-vûr′zhən), *n.* —**in′tro•vert′ed,** *adj.*

in•trude (in trood′), *v.,* -trud•ed, -trud•ing. —*v.t.* **1.** to thrust in. —*v.i.* **2.** to come in without permission or welcome. —**in•trud′er,** *n.* —**in•tru′sion** (-troo′zhən), *n.* —**in•tru′sive** (-siv), *adj.* —**in•tru′sive•ly,** *adv.*

in•tu•it (in too′it, -tyoo′-), *v.t., v.i.* to know or understand by intuition.

in′tu•i′tion (-ish′ən), *n.* **1.** direct perception of

truth, fact, etc., independent of any reasoning process. **2.** a keen and quick insight. —**in•tu′i•tive** (-i tiv), *adj.* —**in•tu′i•tive•ly,** *adv.*

In•u•it (in′oo it, -yoo-), *n., pl.* -it, -its. **1. a.** a member of any of the Eskimo groups inhabiting an area from Greenland to W arctic Canada. **b.** ESKIMO (def. 1). **2.** the speech of the Eskimo groups from Greenland to NW Alaska.

in•un•date (in′ən dāt′, -un-), *v.t.,* -dat•ed, -dat•ing. **1.** to cover with a flood. **2.** to overwhelm with abundance. —**in′un•da′tion,** *n.*

in•ure (in yoŏr′, i noŏr′), *v.t.,* -ured, -ur•ing. to toughen or accustom by use or exposure.

in•vade (in vād′), *v.t.,* -vad•ed, -vad•ing. **1.** to enter forcefully as an enemy. **2.** to enter and affect injuriously. **3.** to intrude upon. —**in•vad′er,** *n.*

in•va•lid¹ (in′və lid), *n.* **1.** an infirm or sickly person. —*adj.* **2.** unable to care for oneself due to infirmity or disability. **3.** of or for invalids. —*v.t.* **4.** to make an invalid.

in•val•id² (in val′id), *adj.* **1.** without force or foundation. **2.** deficient in substance or cogency. **3.** without legal force, as a contract. —**in•va•lid′i•ty,** *n.*

in•val′i•date′ (-dāt′), *v.t.,* -dat•ed, -dat•ing. **1.** to make invalid. **2.** to deprive of legal force. —**in•val′i•da′tion,** *n.*

in•val′u•a•ble, *adj.* beyond calculable value. —**in•val′u•a•bly,** *adv.*

in•va•sion (in vā′zhən), *n.* **1.** an act or instance of invading, esp. by an army. **2.** infringement by intrusion: *invasion of privacy.* —**in•va′sive** (-siv), *adj.*

in•vec•tive (in vek′tiv), *n.* vehement denunciation, censure, or abuse.

in•veigh (in vā′), *v.i.* to protest strongly or attack vehemently with words.

in•vei•gle (in vā′gəl, -vē′-), *v.t.,* -gled, -gling. **1.** to entice or lure by artful talk. **2.** to obtain by such talk. —**in•vei′gler,** *n.*

in•vent (in vent′), *v.t.* **1.** to originate as a product of one's own ingenuity or contrivance. **2.** to make up or fabricate: *to invent excuses.* —**in•ven′tor,** *n.*

in•ven′tion, *n.* **1.** the act of inventing. **2.** a new process, machine, etc., that is recognized as the product of some unique intuition or genius. **3.** the power of inventing. **4.** something fabricated, as a false statement.

in•ven′tive, *adj.* **1.** apt at inventing, devising, or contriving. **2.** involving or showing invention. —**in•ven′tive•ness,** *n.*

in•ven•to•ry (in′vən tôr′ē), *n., pl.* -ries, *v.,* -ried, -ry•ing. —*n.* **1.** a complete list of stock on hand, raw materials, etc., made by a business. **2.** the items listed. **3.** the act of making such a list. —*v.t.* **4.** to make an inventory of.

in•verse (in vûrs′, in′vûrs), *adj.* **1.** reversed in position, direction, or tendency. —*n.* **2.** something inverse; the opposite. —**in•verse′ly,** *adv.*

in•ver′sion (-vûr′zhən, -shən), *n.* **1.** the act of inverting or state of being inverted. **2.** anything inverted. **3.** a condition in which the atmospheric temperature rises at higher altitudes.

in•vert′ (-vûrt′), *v.t.* **1.** to turn upside down. **2.** to reverse in position, direction, or relationship. **3.** to turn inside out.

in•ver′te•brate, *adj.* **1.** without a backbone or spinal column. —*n.* **2.** an invertebrate animal.

in•vest (in vest′), *v.t.* **1.** to put (money) to use in something offering profitable returns. **2.** to use or devote (time, talent, etc.), as to achieve something. **3.** to furnish with power, authority, etc. **4.** to install in office. **5.** to cover, adorn, or envelop. —*v.i.* **6.** to invest money. —**in•vest′ment,** *n.* —**in•ves′tor,** *n.*

in•ves•ti•gate (in ves′ti gāt′), *v.t., v.i.,* -gat•ed, -gat•ing. to search or inquire (into) systematically. —**in•ves′ti•ga′tion,** *n.* —**in•ves′ti•ga′tive,** *adj.* —**in•ves′ti•ga′tor,** *n.*

in•ves′ti•ture (-chər, -choŏr′), *n.* the act or process of investing, as with a rank or office.

in•vet•er•ate (in vet′ər it), *adj.* **1.** confirmed in a habit, feeling, or the like. **2.** firmly established by long continuance. —**in•vet′er•a•cy** (-ə sē), *n.*

in•vid•i•ous (in vid′ē əs), *adj.* **1.** calculated to create ill will. **2.** offensively or unfairly discriminating. —in•vid′i•ous•ly, *adv.* —in•vid′i•ous•ness, *n.*

in•vig•or•ate (in vig′ə rāt′), *v.t.,* -at•ed, -at•ing. to fill with life and energy. —in•vig′or•a′tion, *n.*

in•vin′ci•ble, *adj.* incapable of being conquered, defeated, or subdued. —in•vin′ci•bil′i•ty, *n.*

in•vi′o•la•ble, *adj.* **1.** secure from destruction, infringement, or desecration. **2.** incapable of being violated; unassailable. —in•vi′o•la•bil′i•ty, *n.*

in•vi′o•late (-lit, -lāt′), *adj.* free from violation, injury, or desecration.

in•vis′i•ble, *adj.* **1.** not perceptible by the eye. **2.** out of sight. **3.** not perceptible or discernible by the mind. —in•vis′i•bil′i•ty, *n.* —in•vis′i•bly, *adv.*

invis′ible gov′ernment, *n.* a group that creates public policy without being responsible to the electorate.

in•vi•ta•tion (in′vi tā′shən), *n.* **1.** the act of inviting. **2.** the written or spoken form with which a person is invited.

in′vi•ta′tion•al, *adj.* restricted to participants who have been invited.

in•vite′ (-vīt′), *v.t.,* -vit•ed, -vit•ing. **1.** to request the presence or participation of. **2.** to request politely or formally. **3.** to act so as to bring on or make probable. **4.** to attract or entice. —in′vi•tee′, *n.*

in•vit′ing, *adj.* attractive, alluring, or tempting.

in vi•tro (in vē′trō), *adj.* (of a biological entity or process) developed or maintained in a controlled, nonliving environment, as a laboratory vessel.

in•vo•ca•tion (in′və kā′shən), *n.* **1.** the act of invoking a deity, spirit, etc. **2.** a prayer at the beginning of a public or religious ceremony.

in•voice (in′vois), *n., v.,* -voiced, -voic•ing. —*n.* **1.** an itemized list of goods sold or services provided, containing prices, terms, etc. —*v.t.* **2.** to present an invoice to or for.

in•voke (in vōk′), *v.t.,* -voked, -vok•ing. **1.** to call for with earnest desire. **2.** to call on (a deity, Muse, etc.), as in prayer. **3.** to declare to be binding or in effect: *to invoke the law.* **4.** to petition for help or aid. **5.** to call forth or upon (a spirit) by incantation. **6.** to cause or bring about.

in•vol′un•tar′y, *adj.* **1.** independent of one's will. **2.** unintentional; unconscious. **3.** functioning without volition: *involuntary muscles.* —in•vol′un•tar′i•ly, *adv.*

in•vo•lu•tion (in′və lōō′shən), *n.* **1.** the act of involving or state of being involved. **2.** something complicated.

in•volve (in volv′), *v.t.,* -volved, -volv•ing. **1.** to include as a necessary circumstance, condition, or consequence. **2.** to include within itself or its scope. **3.** to make intricate. **4.** to bring into a troublesome matter. **5.** to absorb fully; preoccupy. —in•volved′, *adj.* —in•volve′ment, *n.*

in•vul′ner•a•ble, *adj.* **1.** incapable of being wounded or damaged. **2.** proof against attack. —in•vul′ner•a•bil′i•ty, *n.*

in•ward (in′wərd), *adv.* Also, **in′wards. 1.** toward the inside, as of a place. **2.** toward the mind or soul. —*adj.* **3.** directed toward the inside. **4.** situated within. **5.** mental or spiritual.

In′ward Light′, *n.* INNER LIGHT.

in′ward•ly, *adv.* **1.** in, on, or with reference to the inside. **2.** privately; secretly. **3.** mentally or spiritually. **4.** toward the inside or interior.

in′-your′-face′, *adj. Informal.* involving confrontation; defiant; provocative.

Io., Iowa.

I/O, *Computers.* input/output.

i•o•dide (ī′ə dīd′, -did), *n.* a salt or compound consisting of two elements, one of which is iodine.

i•o•dine (ī′ə dīn′, -din; *in Chem. also* -dēn′), *n* a nonmetallic halogen element occurring as a grayish-black crystalline solid, used in medicine and dyes. *Symbol:* I; *at. wt.:* 126.904; *at. no.:* 53.

i′o•dize′ (-dīz′), *v.t.,* -dized, -diz•ing. to treat with iodine or an iodide.

i•on (ī′ən, ī′on), *n.* an electrically charged atom or atom group. —i•on′ic, *adj.*

-ion, a suffix meaning: action or process (*inspection*); result of action (*creation*); state or condition (*depression*).

Io•nes•co (yə nes′kō, ē ə-), *n.* **Eugène,** 1912–94, French playwright, born in Romania.

I•on•ic (ī on′ik), *adj.* noting a style of ancient Greek architecture characterized by slender, scroll-shaped capitals.

i•on•ize (ī′ə nīz′), *v.,* -ized, -iz•ing. —*v.t.* **1.** to separate or change into ions. **2.** to produce ions in. —*v.i.* **3.** to become ionized. —i′on•i•za′tion, *n.* —i′on•iz′er, *n.*

i•on•o•sphere (ī on′ə sfēr′), *n.* the outermost region of the earth's atmosphere, consisting of several ionized layers. —i•on′o•spher′ic (-sfer′ik), *adj.*

i•o•ta (ī ō′tə), *n., pl.* -tas. **1.** a very small quantity. **2.** the ninth letter of the Greek alphabet (I, ι).

IOU, *n., pl.* **IOUs, IOU's.** a written acknowledgment of a debt.

-ious, variant of -ous.

I•o•wa (ī′ə wə), *n.* a state in the central United States. 2,851,792. *Cap.:* Des Moines. *Abbr.:* IA, Ia., Io. —I′o•wan, *n., adj.*

IPA, International Phonetic Alphabet.

ip•e•cac (ip′i kak′), *n.* **1.** a tropical South American shrubby plant. **2.** the dried root of this plant, used as an emetic.

ip•so fac•to (ip′sō fak′tō), *adv.* by the fact itself. [< L]

IQ or **I.Q.,** intelligence quotient.

Ir or **Ir., 1.** Ireland. **2.** Irish.

Ir, *Chem. Symbol.* iridium.

ir-¹, var. of IN-¹ before *r.*

ir-², var. of IN-² before *r.*

IRA or **I.R.A., 1.** individual retirement account: a personal savings plan that offers tax advantages to set aside money for retirement. **2.** Irish Republican Army.

I•ran (i ran′, i rän′, ī ran′), *n.* a republic in SW Asia. 67,540,002. Formerly, **Persia.** —I•ra•ni•an (i rā′nē ən), *adj., n.*

Iran′-Con′tra Affair′, *n.* a secret initiative by members of the National Security Council and the Central Intelligence Agency, revealed in 1986 and 1987, to sell arms to Iran in exchange for hostages held there from 1979 to 1981, the revenue diverted to buy military assistance for the Contras in Nicaragua.

I•raq (i rak′, i räk′), *n.* a republic in SW Asia, W of Iran. 22,219,289. —I•ra•qi (i rak′ē, i rä′kē), *adj., n., pl.* -qis.

i•ras•ci•ble (i ras′ə bəl), *adj.* **1.** easily provoked to anger. **2.** produced by anger. —i•ras′ci•bil′i•ty, *n.*

i•rate (ī rāt′, ī′rāt), *adj.* **1.** angry. **2.** arising from or characterized by anger. —i•rate′ly, *adv.* —i•rate′ness, *n.*

ire (ī°r), *n.* intense anger. —ire′ful, *adj.* —ire′ful•ly, *adv.*

Ire., Ireland.

Ire•land (ī°r′lənd), *n.* **1.** an island of the British Isles, W of Great Britain, comprising Northern Ireland and the Republic of Ireland. **2. Republic of,** a republic occupying most of the island of Ireland. 3,555,500.

i•ren•ic (ī ren′ik, ī rē′nik), *adj.* tending to promote peace or reconciliation. —i•ren′i•cal•ly, *adv.*

ir•i•des•cent (ir′i des′ənt), *adj.* displaying a play of lustrous colors like those of the rainbow. —ir′i•des′cence, *n.*

i•rid•i•um (i rid′ē əm), *n.* a precious metallic element resembling platinum: used in alloys. *Symbol:* Ir; *at. wt.:* 192.2; *at. no.:* 77.

I•ri•jah (ī rī′jə), *n.* a soldier who arrested Jeremiah while the Babylonians were besieging Jerusalem. Jer. 37:11–14.

i•ris (ī′ris), *n., pl.* **i•ris•es;** esp. for 1 **ir•i•des** (ir′i dēz′, ī′ri-). **1.** the circular diaphragm forming the colored portion of the eye. **2.** a plant having flowers with three upright petals and three drooping, petal-like sepals.

I•rish (ī′rish), *n.* **1.** (*used with a pl. v.*) the natives or inhabitants of Ireland. **2.** the Celtic language of Ireland. —*adj.* **3.** of Ireland, its inhabitants, or their language.

I′rish•man or **-wom′an,** *n., pl.* **-men** or **-wom•en.** a native or inhabitant of Ireland.

I′rish Repub′lican Ar′my, *n.* an underground Irish nationalist organization founded to work for Irish independence from England. *Abbr.:* IRA, I.R.A.

I′rish Sea′, *n.* a part of the Atlantic between Ireland and England.

irk (ûrk), *v.t.* to irritate, annoy, or exasperate.

irk′some (-səm), *adj.* annoying; exasperating; tiresome. —**irk′some•ly,** *adv.*

i•ron (ī′ərn), *n.* **1.** a ductile, malleable, silver-white metallic element, used for making tools, machinery, etc. *Symbol:* Fe; *at. wt.:* 55.847; *at. no.:* 26. **2.** something hard, strong, or unyielding: *hearts of iron.* **3.** something made of iron. **4.** an appliance with a flat metal bottom, used to press clothes and linens. **5.** any of a series of iron-headed golf clubs. **6. irons,** shackles or fetters. —*adj.* **7.** made of iron. **8.** resembling iron. —*v.t., v.i.* **9.** to press with a heated iron. **10.** iron out, to clear away (difficulties).

I′ron Age′, *n.* a period of human history following the Stone Age and the Bronze Age, marked by the use of implements and weapons made of iron.

i′ron•clad′, *adj.* **1.** covered or cased with iron plates, as a ship. **2.** very rigid or exacting: *an ironclad contract.*

i′ron cur′tain, *n.* a barrier to the exchange of information and ideas, esp. such a barrier between the Soviet bloc and other countries after World War II.

i•ron•ic (ī ron′ik) also **-i•cal,** *adj.* **1.** of or characterized by irony. **2.** using or prone to irony. —**i•ron′i•cal•ly,** *adv.*

i′ron lung′, *n.* a chamber that encloses the body except the head and in which alternate pulsations of high and low pressure force air into and out of the lungs.

i′ron•ware′, *n.* articles of iron, as pots or tools.

i′ron•work′, *n.* objects or parts made of iron.

i•ro•ny (ī′rə nē, ī′ər-), *n., pl.* **-nies. 1.** the use of words to convey a meaning that is the opposite of its literal meaning. **2.** an outcome of events contrary to what was, or might have been, expected.

Ir•o•quois (ir′ə kwoi′, -kwoiz′), *n., pl.* **-quois.** a member of a confederacy of American Indian peoples formerly centered in New York. —**Ir′o•quoi′an,** *n., adj.*

ir•ra•di•ate (i rā′dē āt′), *v.t.,* **-at•ed, -at•ing. 1.** to shed rays of light upon. **2.** to illumine intellectually. **3.** to radiate. **4.** to expose to radiation, as for medical treatment. —**ir•ra′di•a′tion,** *n.*

ir•ra′tion•al, *adj.* **1.** lacking the faculty of reason. **2.** lacking sound judgment. **3.** not governed by reason. **4.** (of a number) not capable of being expressed exactly as a ratio of two integers. —**ir•ra′tion•al′i•ty,** *n.* —**ir•ra′tion•al•ly,** *adv.*

ir′re•claim′a•ble, *adj.* incapable of being reclaimed or rehabilitated.

ir′rec′on•cil′a•ble, *adj.* **1.** incapable of being brought into harmony or adjustment. **2.** incapable of being made to acquiesce or compromise.

ir′re•cov′er•a•ble, *adj.* **1.** incapable of being recovered or regained. **2.** unable to be remedied or rectified.

ir′re•deem′a•ble, *adj.* **1.** incapable of being bought back or paid off. **2.** beyond redemption or reform. **3.** (of paper money) not convertible into gold or silver.

ir•ref′u•ta•ble, *adj.* incapable of being refuted.

ir′re•gard′less, *adv. Nonstandard.* regardless.

ir•reg′u•lar, *adj.* **1.** lacking symmetry, even shape, etc. **2.** not conforming to established rules, methods, etc. **3.** not conforming to the prevalent pattern of formation, inflection, etc., in a language. —*n.* **4.** a combatant not of a regular military force, as a guerrilla. —**ir•reg′u•lar′i•ty,** *n., pl.* **-ties.**

ir•rel′e•vant, *adj.* not relevant or pertinent. —**ir•rel′e•vance,** *n.*

ir′re•li′gious, *adj.* **1.** not practicing a religion and feeling no religious impulses. **2.** showing a lack of religion. **3.** showing hostility to religion.

ir′re•me′di•a•ble, *adj.* not admitting of remedy, cure, or repair. —**ir′re•me′di•a•bly,** *adv.*

ir′rep•a•ra•ble (i rep′ər ə bəl), *adj.* incapable of being rectified, remedied, or made good.

ir′re•place′a•ble, *adj.* incapable of being replaced.

ir′re•press′i•ble (ir′i pres′ə bəl), *adj.* incapable of being repressed or restrained.

ir′re•proach•a•ble (ir′i prō′chə bəl), *adj.* free from blame.

ir′re•sist•i•ble (ir′i zis′tə bəl), *adj.* **1.** incapable of being resisted or withstood. **2.** enticing; tempting. —**ir′re•sist′i•bly,** *adv.*

ir′res′o•lute′, *adj.* doubtful; infirm of purpose. —**ir•res′o•lute′ly,** *adv.* —**ir•res′o•lu′tion,** *n.*

ir′re•spec′tive, *adj.* without regard to: *Irrespective of the weather, I should go.*

ir′re•spon′si•ble, *adj.* **1.** characterized by a lack of a sense of responsibility. **2.** not capable of responsibility. —**ir′re•spon′si•bil′i•ty,** *n.* —**ir′re•spon′si•bly,** *adv.*

ir′re•triev′a•ble (ir′i trē′və bəl), *adj.* incapable of being retrieved or recovered.

ir•rev′er•ence, *n.* **1.** lack of reverence or respect. **2.** an irreverent act or statement. —**ir•rev′er•ent,** *adj.*

ir′re•vers′i•ble, *adj.* incapable of being reversed or changed.

ir•rev′o•ca•ble (i rev′ə kə bəl), *adj.* not to be revoked or recalled. —**ir•rev′o•ca•bly,** *adv.*

ir•ri•gate (ir′i gāt′), *v.t.,* **-gat•ed, -gat•ing. 1.** to supply (land) with water by artificial means, as by diverting streams. **2.** to wash (an orifice, wound, etc.) with liquid. —**ir′ri•ga•ble,** *adj.* —**ir′ri•ga′tion,** *n.*

ir•ri•ta•ble (ir′i tə bəl), *adj.* **1.** easily irritated or annoyed. **2.** abnormally sensitive to stimulation. —**ir′ri•ta•bil′i•ty,** *n.* —**ir′ri•ta•bly,** *adv.*

ir′ri•tant (-tnt), *adj.* **1.** tending to cause irritation. —*n.* **2.** something that irritates.

ir′ri•tate′ (-tāt′), *v.t.,* **-tat•ed, -tat•ing. 1.** to excite to impatience or anger. **2.** to make sore, red, or swollen. —**ir′ri•ta′tion,** *n.*

ir•rupt (i rupt′), *v.i.* to break or burst in. —**ir•rup′tion,** *n.* —**ir•rup′tive,** *adj.*

IRS, Internal Revenue Service.

Ir•vine (ûr′vīn), *n.* a city in SW California. 110,330.

Ir•ving (ûr′ving), *n.* **Washington,** 1783–1859, U.S. essayist, story writer, and historian.

is (iz), *v.* 3rd pers. sing. pres. indic. of BE.

is., 1. island. **2.** isle.

I•saac (ī′zək), *n.* a son of Abraham and Sarah, and father of Jacob. Gen. 21:1–4.

I•sa•iah (ī zā′ə), *n.* **1.** a Hebrew prophet of the 8th century B.C. **2.** a book of the Bible bearing his name.

Is•car•i•ot (i skar′ē ət), *n.* the surname of Judas, the betrayer of Jesus. Mark 3:19; 14:10, 11. [< LL *Iscariōta* < Gk *Iskariótēs* < Heb *īsh-qərīyōth* man of *Kerioth* a village in Palestine]

-ise, *Chiefly Brit.* var. of -IZE.

-ish, a suffix meaning: of or belonging to (*British*); like or having the characteristics of (*babyish*); inclined to (*bookish*); near or about (*fiftyish*); somewhat (*reddish*).

Ish•ma•el (ish′mē əl, -mā-), *n.* the son of Abraham and Hagar. Gen. 16:11, 12.

Ish•ma•el•ite (ish′mē ə līt′, -mā ə-, -mə-), *n.* a member of a Biblical people descended from Ishmael, who is regarded in Muslim tradition as the progenitor of the Arabs.

i•sin•glass (ī′zən glas′, -gläs′, ī′zing-), *n.* **1.** a gelatin obtained from the air bladders of certain fish. **2.** mica in thin, translucent sheets.

I•sis (ī′sis), *n.* the ancient Egyptian goddess of fertility.

Is•lam (is läm′, is′ləm, iz′-), *n.* **1.** the religion of the Muslims, as set forth in the Koran. **2.** the whole body of Muslim believers and countries. —**Is•lam′ic,** *adj.*

Is•lam•a•bad (is lä′mə bäd′), *n.* the capital of Pakistan. 201,000.

is•land (ī′lənd), *n.* **1.** a tract of land completely surrounded by water and not large enough to be called a continent. **2.** something resembling an island, esp. in being isolated. —*Proverb.* **3. No man is an island,** everyone is an interdependent part of society. John Donne, *Meditation XVII.*

is′land•er, *n.* a native or inhabitant of an island.

isle (īl), *n.* **1.** a small island. **2.** any island.

is•let (ī′lit), *n.* a very small island.

ism (iz′əm), *n.* a distinctive doctrine, theory, or system.

-ism, a suffix meaning: action or practice (*baptism*); state or condition (*barbarism*); doctrine or principle (*Marxism*); distinctive feature or usage (*witticism*).

isn′t (iz′ənt), contraction of *is not.*

iso-, a combining form meaning equal or identical (*isobar*).

i•so•bar (ī′sə bär′), *n.* a line on a map that connects points at which the barometric pressure is the same. —**i′so•bar′ic** (-bär′-), *adj.* —**i′so•bar′ism,** *n.*

i•so•late (ī′sə lāt′), *v.t.,* **-lat•ed, -lat•ing.** to detach or separate so as to be alone. —**i′so•la′tion,** *n.*

i′so•la′tion•ism, *n.* the policy of isolating one's country from alliances and commitments with other countries. —**i′so•la′tion•ist,** *n., adj.*

i•so•mer (ī′sə mər), *n.* any of two or more chemical compounds composed of the same kinds and numbers of atoms but having different structural arrangements. —**i′so•mer′ic** (-mer′ik), *adj.* —**i•som•er•ism** (ī som′ə riz′əm), *n.*

i•so•met•ric (ī′sə me′trik), *adj.* **1.** having equality of measure. **2.** of isometrics. —*n.* **3. isometrics,** exercise in which muscles are tensed against other muscles or against an immovable object. —**i′so•met′ri•cal•ly,** *adv.*

i•sos•ce•les (ī sos′ə lēz′), *adj.* (of a straight-sided plane figure) having two sides equal.

i•so•tope (ī′sə tōp′), *n.* one of two or more forms of a chemical element having the same atomic number but different atomic weights. —**i′so•top′ic** (-top′ik), *adj.*

Is•ra•el (iz′rē əl, -rā-), *n.* **1.** a republic in SW Asia, on the Mediterranean. 4,440,000. **2.** the descendants of Jacob; the Jewish people. **3.** a name given to Jacob. Gen. 32:28. **4.** the northern kingdom of the Hebrews. **5.** a group considered as God's chosen people.

Is•rae′li (-rā′lē), *n., pl.* **-lis, -li,** *adj.* —*n.* **1.** a native or inhabitant of modern Israel. —*adj.* **2.** of modern Israel or its inhabitants.

Is′ra•el•ite′ (-rē ə līt′, -rā-), *n.* a member of the Hebrew people who inhabited ancient Israel.

Is•sa•char (is′ə kär′), *n.* **1.** a son of Jacob and Leah. Gen. 30:18. **2.** one of the 12 tribes of Israel.

is•su•ance (ish′ōō əns), *n.* the act of issuing.

is•sue (ish′ōō; *esp. Brit.* is′yōō), *n., v.,* **-sued, -su•ing.** —*n.* **1.** the act of sending out or putting forth. **2.** one thing or a series of things printed, published, or distributed at one time. **3.** a matter in dispute, the resolution of which is of special or public importance. **4.** something proceeding from any source, as a consequence. **5.** offspring; progeny. **6.** an outlet or exit. **7.** a discharge of blood, pus, or the like. —*v.t.* **8.** to mint, print, or publish for sale or distribution. **9.** to distribute (food, clothing, etc.). **10.** to send out; discharge. —*v.i.* **11.** to go, pass, or flow out. **12.** to be printed or published. **13.** to arise as a result. —*Idiom.* **14. at issue,** being disputed. **15. take issue,** to disagree.

-ist, a suffix meaning: one who makes or produces (*novelist*); one who operates or practices (*machinist*); one skilled in (*cellist*); advocate or supporter (*socialist*).

Is•tan•bul (is′tän bōōl′, -tan-), *n.* a seaport in NW Turkey. 5,494,900. Formerly, **Constantinople.**

isth•mus (is′məs), *n., pl.* **-mus•es, -mi** (-mī). a narrow strip of land, bordered on both sides by water,

connecting two larger bodies of land. —**isth′mi•an** (-mē ən), *adj.*

it (it), *pron., nom.* **it,** *poss.* **its,** *obj.* **it,** *pl. nom.* **they,** *poss.* **their** or **theirs,** *obj.* **them,** *n.* —*pron.* **1.** (used to represent an inanimate thing understood, previously mentioned, or present in the context). **2.** (used to represent a person or animal whose gender is unknown). **3.** (used to represent a group of persons). **4.** (used to represent a concept or abstract idea). **5.** (used as the impersonal subject of the verb *to be*): *It is six o'clock.* **6.** (used in referring to an implied action, condition, or situation). **7.** (used as an anticipatory subject or object): *It is necessary that you do your duty.* —*n.* **8.** (in children's games) the player who is to perform some task, as the one who must catch the others in tag.

It. or **Ital.,** **1.** Italian. **2.** Italy.

ital., italic.

I•tal•ian (i tal′yən), *n.* **1.** a native or inhabitant of Italy. **2.** the Romance language of Italy. —*adj.* **3.** of Italy, its people, or their language.

i•tal•ic (i tal′ik, ī tal′-), *adj.* **1.** designating a printing type in which the letters slope to the right, used esp. for emphasis. —*n.* **2.** Often, **-ics.** italic type.

i•tal′i•cize′ (-ə sīz′), *v.t.,* **-cized, -ciz•ing.** to print in italics. —**i•tal′i•ci•za′tion,** *n.*

It•a•ly (it′l ē), *n.* a republic in S Europe. 57,534,088.

itch (ich), *v.i.* **1.** to feel a tingling irritation of the skin that causes a desire to scratch the part affected. **2.** to have a desire to do or get something. —*n.* **3.** the sensation of itching. **4.** a restless longing. —**itch′y,** *adj.,* **-i•er, -i•est.** —**itch′i•ness,** *n.*

-ite, a suffix meaning: inhabitant (*Tokyoite*); follower (*Mennonite*); mineral or fossil (*bauxite*); commercial product (*dynamite*).

i•tem (ī′təm), *n.* **1.** a separate article or particular. **2.** a piece of information or news.

i′tem•ize′, *v.t.,* **-ized, -iz•ing.** to state or present by items. —**i′tem•i•za′tion,** *n.*

it•er•ate (it′ə rāt′), *v.t.,* **-at•ed, -at•ing.** to say or do again. —**it′er•a′tion,** *n.*

i•tin•er•ant (ī tin′ər ənt, i tin′-), *adj.* **1.** traveling from place to place, esp. on a circuit: *an itinerant preacher.* —*n.* **2.** an itinerant person.

i•tin′er•ar′y (-ə rer′ē), *n., pl.* **-ar•ies. 1.** a detailed plan for a journey. **2.** a line of travel. **3.** an account of a journey.

-itis, a suffix meaning inflammation of a specified body part (*appendicitis*).

it′ll (it′l), a contraction of *it will.*

its (its), *pron.* the possessive form of IT (used as an attributive adjective): *The book has lost its jacket.*

it′s (its), **1.** contraction of *it is.* **2.** contraction of *it has.*

it•self′, *pron.* **1.** a reflexive form of IT: *The battery recharges itself.* **2.** (used as an intensive of IT or a noun): *The land itself was not for sale.* **3.** its normal self: *The injured cat was never quite itself again.*

it•ty-bit•ty (it′ē bit′ē) also **it•sy-bit•sy** (it′sē-bit′sē), *adj. Informal.* very small; tiny.

IUD, intrauterine device.

IV (ī′vē′), *n., pl.* **IVs, IV′s.** an apparatus for intravenous delivery of medicines, nutrients, etc.

Ivan IV, *n.* ("*Ivan the Terrible*") 1530–84, first czar of Russia 1547–84.

I′ve (īv), contraction of *I have.*

-ive, a suffix meaning: tending to (*destructive*); of the nature of (*festive*).

Ives (īvz), *n.* **1. Burl,** 1909–95, U.S. folk singer and actor. **2. Charles Edward,** 1874–1954, U.S. composer. **3. James Merritt,** 1824–95, U.S. lithographer. Compare CURRIER.

i•vo•ry (ī′və rē, ī′vrē), *n., pl.* **-ries,** *adj.* —*n.* **1.** the hard white substance composing the main part of the tusks of the elephant, walrus, etc. **2.** any substance resembling ivory. **3. ivories,** *Slang.* **a.** the keys of a piano. **b.** dice. **4.** a creamy or yellowish white. —*adj.* **5.** made of ivory. **6.** of the color ivory.

I′vory Coast′, *n.* a republic in W Africa. 11,630,000. Also called **Côte d'Ivoire.**

i′vory tow′er, *n.* **1.** a place remote from worldly

affairs. **2.** an attitude of aloofness from worldly affairs.

i•vy (ī′vē), *n., pl.* **i•vies. 1.** a climbing vine with smooth, shiny evergreen leaves. **2.** any of various other climbing plants. —**i′vied,** *adj.*

I•wo Ji•ma (ē′wə jē′mə, ē′wō), *n.* one of the Vol-

cano Islands, in the N Pacific, S of Japan: under U.S. administration after 1945; returned to Japan 1968.

-ize, a suffix meaning: to practice or engage in (*economize*); to treat in a certain way (*idolize*); to become or form into (*unionize*); to make or cause to be (*civilize*).

J

J, j (jā), *n., pl.* **Js** or **J's, js** or **j's.** the tenth letter of the English alphabet, a consonant.

jab (jab), *v.,* **jabbed, jab•bing,** *n.* —*v.t., v.i.* **1.** to poke sharply, as with a point. **2.** to punch, esp. with a short, quick blow. —*n.* **3.** a sharp, quick thrust. **4.** a short, quick punch.

jab•ber (jab′ər), *v.i., v.t.* **1.** to speak rapidly, indistinctly, or nonsensically. —*n.* **2.** gibberish. —**jab′-ber•er,** *n.*

Jab•bok (jab′ək), *n.* a tributary of the Jordan River, near where Jacob wrestled with God. Gen. 32:22.

ja•bot (zha bō′, ja-), *n.* a ruffle extending down the front of a blouse, dress, etc.

jack (jak), *n.* **1.** any of various devices for lifting heavy objects short heights: *an automobile jack.* **2.** a playing card bearing the picture of a soldier or servant. **3.** a connecting device in an electrical circuit designed for the insertion of a plug: *a telephone jack.* **4.** one of a set of small, six-pointed metal objects used in a game (**jacks**). **5.** a small national flag flown at the bow of a ship. —*v.t.* **6.** to lift with a jack. **7.** to increase or raise: *to jack up prices.* —**Saying. 8. jack of all trades and master of none,** one who can do many things fairly well but none of them expertly.

jack•al (jak′əl), *n.* any of several wild dogs of Asia and Africa.

jack′ass′, *n.* **1.** a male donkey. **2.** a foolish or stupid person.

jack′boot′, *n.* a man's sturdy leather boot reaching up over the knee.

jack′daw′ (-dô′), *n.* a small Eurasian crow with a gray nape.

jack•et (jak′it), *n.* **1.** a short coat, usu. opening down the front. **2.** a protective outer covering: *a book jacket.* —**jack′et•ed,** *adj.*

Jack′ Frost′, *n.* frost or freezing cold personified.

jack′ham′mer, *n.* a portable drill operated by compressed air and used to drill rock, concrete, etc.

jack′-in-the-box′, *n., pl.* **-box•es.** a toy consisting of a box from which a figure springs up when the lid is opened.

jack′-in-the-pul′pit, *n., pl.* **-pul•pits.** a plant with an upright spadix arched over by a spathe.

jack-in-the-pulpit

jack′knife′, *n., pl.* **-knives,** *v.,* **-knifed, -knif•ing.** —*n.* **1.** a large pocketknife. **2.** a dive during which the diver bends to touch the toes and then straightens out. —*v.i.* **3.** to bend over from the middle. **4.** (of a trailer truck) to have the cab and trailer swivel until they form a **V.** —*v.t.* **5.** to cause to jackknife.

jack′-of-all′-trades′, *n., pl.* **jacks-of-all-trades.** a person who is adept at many different kinds of work.

jack′-o′-lan′tern (-ə lan′tərn), *n.* a hollowed pumpkin with openings cut to represent a face and a candle or other light inside.

jack′pot′, *n.* the cumulative stakes in a contest, lottery, or the like.

jack′ rab′bit, *n.* a large hare of W North America, having long hind legs and long ears.

Jack•son (jak′sən), *n.* **1. Andrew** (*"Old Hickory"*), 1767–1845, U.S. general: 7th president of the U.S. 1829–37. **2. Helen Hunt** (*Helen Maria Fiske*), 1830–85, U.S. novelist and poet. **3. Jesse L(ouis),** born 1941, U.S. Baptist minister and civil-rights and political activist. **4. Mahalia,** 1911–72, U.S. gospel singer. **5. Thomas Jonathan** (*"Stonewall Jackson"*), 1824–63, Confederate general in the American Civil War.

Jack′son•ville′ (-vil′), *n.* a seaport in NE Florida. 655,070.

Ja•cob (jā′kəb), *n.* a son of Isaac and Rebekah, younger twin of Esau, and father of the 12 patriarchs. Gen. 24:24–34.

Ja′cob's well′, *n.* a well where Jesus spoke to a Samaritan woman. John 4:1–26.

jac•quard (jak′ärd, jə kärd′), *n.* (*often cap.*) a fabric with an elaborately woven pattern.

Ja•cuz•zi (jə kōō′zē), *pl.* **-zis.** *Trademark.* a brand name for a device for a whirlpool bath and related products.

jade¹ (jād), *n.* either of two minerals, jadeite or nephrite, sometimes green, used for carvings, jewelry, etc.

jade² (jād), *n., v.,* **jad•ed, jad•ing.** —*n.* **1.** a broken-down, worthless horse. **2.** a disreputable woman. —*v.t., v.i.* **3.** to make or become dull or weary, as from overwork. —**jad′ed•ly,** *adv.* —**jad′ed•ness,** *n.*

jade•ite (jā′dīt), *n.* a colorless, green, or black mineral, the most precious type of jade.

Ja•el (jā′əl), *n.* a woman who killed Sisera by hammering a tent pin into his head as he slept. Judg. 4:17–22.

Jaf•fa (jaf′ə, jä′fə; *locally* yä′fä) also **Yafo,** *n.* a former seaport in W Israel, part of Tel Aviv-Jaffa since 1950: ancient Biblical town. Ancient, **Joppa.**

jag¹ (jag), *n.* a sharp projection on an edge or surface.

jag² (jag), *n.* a spree; binge: *a crying jag.*

jag•ged (jag′id), *adj.* having ragged notches or points. —**jag′ged•ly,** *adv.* —**jag′ged•ness,** *n.*

jag•uar (jag′wär), *n.* a large, powerful cat of tropical America.

jaguar

jai a•lai (hī′ lī′, hī′ ə lī′), *n.* a game resembling handball, played on a three-walled court with wicker, basketlike rackets.

jail (jāl), *n.* **1.** a prison, esp. one for persons awaiting trial or convicted of minor offenses. —*v.t.* **2.** to confine in a jail.

jail′break′, *n.* an escape from prison.

jail′er or **jail′or**, *n.* a person in charge of a jail.

Ja•kar•ta (jə kär′tə), *n.* the capital of Indonesia, on the NW coast of Java. 6,503,449.

ja•la•pe•ño (hä′lə pān′yō), *n.*, *pl.* **-ños.** a hot pepper used esp. in Mexican cooking.

ja•lop•y (jə lop′ē), *n.*, *pl.* **-lop•ies.** an old, decrepit automobile.

jal•ou•sie (jal′ə sē′), *n.*, *pl.* **-sies.** a blind or shutter made with adjustable horizontal slats.

jam¹ (jam), *v.*, **jammed, jam•ming,** *n.* —*v.t.* **1.** to squeeze into a confined space. **2.** to crush by squeezing. **3.** to fill tightly; cram. **4.** to push violently against something: *He jammed his foot on the brake.* **5.** to block up by crowding. **6.** to make unworkable by causing parts to become stuck or blocked. **7.** to interfere with (radio signals or the like) by sending out other signals of approximately the same frequency. —*v.i.* **8.** to become stuck, wedged, etc. **9.** to press or push, as into a confined space. **10.** to become unworkable, as through the jamming of a part. **11.** to participate in a jam session. —*n.* **12.** the act of jamming or state of being jammed. **13.** *Informal.* a difficult situation.

jam² (jam), *n.* a preserve of slightly crushed fruit boiled with sugar.

Jam., Jamaica.

Ja•mai•ca (jə mā′kə), *n.* an island republic in the West Indies, S of Cuba. 2,300,000. —**Ja•mai′can**, *n.*, *adj.*

jamb (jam), *n.* either of the vertical sides of a doorway or other opening.

jam•bo•ree (jam′bə rē′), *n.*, *pl.* **-rees. 1.** any noisy merrymaking. **2.** a large gathering of the Boy Scouts or Girl Scouts.

James (jāmz), *n.* **1.** Also called **James′ the Great′.** one of the 12 apostles, brother of the apostle John. Matt. 4:21. **2. a.** the person identified in Gal. 1:19 as a brother of Jesus. **b.** one of the books or epistles of the New Testament ascribed to him. **3.** Also called **James′ the Less′.** (*"James the son of Alphaeus"*) one of the 12 apostles. **4. Henry,** 1843–1916, U.S. writer in England.

James′town′, *n.* a village in E Virginia: first permanent English settlement in North America 1607.

jam′-pack′, *v.t.* to fill or pack as tightly as possible.

jam′ ses′sion, *n.* a meeting of musicians, esp. jazz musicians, to play for their own enjoyment.

Jan or **Jan.,** January.

Ja•ná•ček (yä′nə chek′), *n.* **Le•oš** (lā′ôsh), 1854–1928, Czech composer.

Jane′ Doe′ (jān′ dō′), *n.* a fictitious name used in legal proceedings for a female party whose true name is not known. Compare JOHN DOE.

jan•gle (jang′gəl), *v.*, **-gled, -gling,** *n.* —*v.i.* **1.** to produce a harsh, usu. metallic sound. —*v.t.* **2.** to cause to jangle. **3.** to cause to become irritated. —*n.* **4.** a harsh, usu. metallic sound. —**jan′gler,** *n.*

jan•i•tor (jan′i tər), *n.* a person employed to clean the public areas of a building and do minor repairs. —**jan′i•to′ri•al** (-tôr′ē əl), *adj.*

Jan•u•ar•y (jan′yōō er′ē), *n.*, *pl.* **-ar•ies.** the first month of the year, containing 31 days.

Jap., **1.** Japan. **2.** Japanese.

ja•pan (jə pan′), *n.*, *v.*, **-panned, pan•ning. 1.** a black varnish, orig. from Japan, for coating metal or other surfaces. —*v.t.* **2.** to varnish with japan.

Ja•pan′, *n.* **1.** a constitutional monarchy on a chain of islands off the E coast of Asia. 125,716,637. **2. Sea of,** the part of the Pacific Ocean between Japan and mainland Asia.

Jap•a•nese (jap′ə nēz′, nēs′), *n.*, *pl.* **-nese,** *adj.* —*n.* **1.** a native or inhabitant of Japan. **2.** the language of Japan. —*adj.* **3.** of Japan, its people, or their language.

Jap′anese bee′tle, *n.* an iridescent green beetle, native to Japan, established in North America as a plant pest.

jape (jāp), *v.*, **japed, jap•ing,** *n.* —*v.i.* **1.** to jest; joke. —*n.* **2.** a joke or trick. —**jap′er•y,** *n.*

Ja•pheth (jā′fith), *n.* a son of Noah. Gen. 5:32.

Japn or **Japn., 1.** Japan. **2.** Japanese.

jar¹ (jär), *n.* a broad-mouthed container, usu. of glass or earthenware.

jar² (jär), *v.*, **jarred, jar•ring,** *n.* —*v.t.* **1.** to have a sudden and unpleasant effect on. **2.** to cause to vibrate or shake. —*v.i.* **3.** to have a harshly unpleasant effect, as on the nerves. **4.** to produce a harsh, grating sound. **5.** to vibrate or shake. —*n.* **6.** a jolt or shake. **7.** an unpleasant effect; shock. **8.** a harsh or discordant sound.

jar•di•niere (jär′dn ēr′, zhär′dn yâr′), *n.* an ornamental receptacle or stand for plants or flowers.

jar•gon (jär′gən, -gon), *n.* **1.** the vocabulary peculiar to a particular profession or group. **2.** unintelligible language.

jas•mine (jaz′min, jas′-), *n.* any of numerous shrubs or vines with fragrant flowers.

jas•per (jas′pər), *n.* an opaque variety of quartz, usu. red or brown.

ja•to or **JATO** (jā′tō), *n.*, *pl.* **ja•tos** or **JATOs.** a jet-assisted takeoff of an aircraft, esp. with auxiliary rocket motors.

jaun•dice (jôn′dis, jän′-), *n.* yellow discoloration of the skin, whites of the eyes, etc., due to an increase of bile pigments in the blood.

jaun′diced, *adj.* **1.** affected with jaundice. **2.** distorted or prejudiced, as by envy or resentment.

jaunt (jônt, jänt), *n.* **1.** a short journey, esp. for pleasure. —*v.i.* **2.** to make such a journey.

jaun•ty (jôn′tē, jän′-), *adj.*, **-ti•er, -ti•est. 1.** easy and sprightly in manner or bearing. **2.** smartly trim, as clothing. —**jaun′ti•ly,** *adv.* —**jaun′ti•ness,** *n.*

Ja•va (jä′və; *esp. for 2* jav′ə), *n.* **1.** the main island of Indonesia. **2.** (*l.c.*) *Slang.* coffee. **3.** *Trademark.* a programming language used to create interactive applications running on the Internet. —**Jav•a•nese** (jav′ə nēz′, -nēs′, jä′və-), *n.*, *pl.* **-nese,** *adj.*

jave•lin (jav′lin, jav′ə-), *n.* a light spear, usu. thrown by hand.

jaw (jô), *n.* **1.** either of two tooth-bearing bones that form the framework of the vertebrate mouth. **2.** one of two or more parts, as of a machine, that grasp or hold something. —*v.i.* **3.** *Slang.* to chat; gossip. —**jawed,** *adj.* —**jaw′less,** *adj.*

jaw′bone′, *n.*, *v.*, **-boned, -bon•ing.** —*n.* **1.** any bone of a jaw, esp. a mandible. —*v.t.* **2.** to influence by persuasion, esp. by public appeal.

jaw′break′er, *n.* **1.** a word that is hard to pronounce. **2.** a very hard candy.

jay (jā), *n.* **1.** any of various typically noisy, gregarious songbirds of the family Corvidae, mostly of the Northern Hemisphere, having blue or gray plumage. **2.** *Slang.* **a.** a talkative person; chatterer. **b.** a fop.

Jay (jā), *n.* **John,** 1745–1829, first Chief Justice of the U.S. 1789–95.

jay′walk′, *v.i.* to cross a street at a place other than a regular crossing. —**jay′walk′er,** *n.*

jazz (jaz), *n.* **1.** music originating in New Orleans, marked by propulsive rhythms, ensemble playing, and improvisation. **2.** *Slang.* insincere or pretentious talk. —*v.t.* **3. jazz up,** *Slang.* **a.** to enliven. **b.** to embellish.

jazz′y, *adj.*, **-i•er, -i•est. 1.** of or suggestive of jazz music. **2.** *Slang.* fancy or flashy.

J.D., 1. Doctor of Jurisprudence; Doctor of Law. [< NL *Jūris Doctor*] **2.** Doctor of Laws. [< NL *Jūrum Doctor*] **3.** Justice Department.

jeal•ous (jel′əs), *adj.* **1.** resentful and envious, as of someone's success. **2.** inclined to suspicions of rivalry, unfaithfulness, etc. **3.** watchful in guarding something: *She is jealous of her independence.* —**jeal′ous•ly,** *adv.* —**jeal′ous•y,** *n.*, *pl.* **-ous•ies.**

jean (jēn), *n.* **1.** a sturdy twilled cloth, usu. of cotton. **2. jeans,** (*used with a pl. v.*) trousers made of this or a similar cloth.

Jed•da (jed′ə), *n.* JIDDA.

Jeep (jēp), *Trademark.* a small, rugged utility vehicle with four-wheel drive.

jeer (jēr), *v.i., v.t.* **1.** to speak or shout derisively (at). —*n.* **2.** a jeering utterance. —**jeer′ing•ly,** *adv.*

Jef•fer•son (jef′ər sən), *n.* **Thomas,** 1743–1826, 3rd president of the U.S. 1801–09. —**Jef′fer•so′ni•an** (-sō′nē ən), *adj., n.*

Jef′ferson Cit′y, *n.* the capital of Missouri. 33,619.

Je•ho•a•haz (jē hō′ə haz′), *n.* **1.** a king of Israel. II Kings 10:35. **2.** a ruler of Judah. II Kings 23:30–34.

Je•hoi•a•chin (jē hoi′ə kin), *n.* a king of Judah. II Kings 24:8–16; 25:27–30.

Je•hosh•a•phat (ji hosh′ə fat′, -hos′-), *n.* a king of Judah. I Kings 22:41–50.

Je•ho•vah (ji hō′və), *n.* **1.** a name of God in the Old Testament, a rendering of the ineffable name, JHVH, in the Hebrew Scriptures. **2.** (in modern Christian use) God. —**Je•ho′vic,** *adj.*

Jeho′vah's Wit′nesses, *n.* a Christian sect that believes in the imminent destruction of the world's wickedness and the establishment of a theocracy under God's rule.

Je•hu (jē′hyōō *or, often,* -hōō), *n., pl.* **-hus. 1.** a king of Israel noted for his furious chariot attacks. II Kings 9. **2.** (*l.c.*) **a.** the driver of a cab or coach. **b.** a fast driver.

je•june (ji jōōn′), *adj.* **1.** lacking interest or significance; insipid. **2.** lacking maturity; childish.

je•ju•num (ji jōō′nəm), *n.* the middle portion of the small intestine.

jell (jel), *v.i., v.t.* **1.** to become or cause to become jellylike in consistency. **2.** to become or cause to become clear or definite.

jel•ly (jel′ē), *n., pl.* **-lies,** *v.,* **-lied, -ly•ing.** —*n.* **1.** a sweet spread of fruit juice boiled with sugar and sometimes pectin. **2.** any substance having such consistency. —*v.i., v.t.* **3.** JELL (def. 1).

jel′ly•bean′, *n.* a small, bean-shaped, chewy candy.

jel′ly•fish′, *n., pl.* **-fish, -fish•es. 1.** a stinging, jellylike marine animal with trailing tentacles. **2.** an indecisive or weak person.

jel′ly roll′, *n.* a thin layer of sponge cake spread with jelly and rolled up.

jeop•ard•ize (jep′ər dīz′), *v.t.,* **-ized, -iz•ing.** to put in jeopardy.

jeop′ard•y (-dē), *n.* exposure to loss, harm, death, or injury.

Jer., *Bible.* Jeremiah.

jer•e•mi•ad (jer′ə mī′əd, -ad), *n.* a prolonged lament; complaint.

Jer•e•mi•ah (jer′ə mī′ə), *n.* **1.** a Hebrew prophet of the 6th and 7th centuries B.C. **2.** a book of the Bible bearing his name. *Abbr.:* Jer.

Jer•i•cho (jer′i kō′), *n.* an ancient city of Palestine, N of the Dead Sea.

jerk (jûrk), *n.* **1.** a quick, sharp pull, thrust, or the like. **2.** a sudden involuntary muscle contraction, as of a reflex. **3.** *Slang.* a contemptibly naive or stupid person. —*v.t.* **4.** to pull, thrust, etc., with a jerk. —*v.i.* **5.** to move spasmodically.

jer•kin (jûr′kin), *n.* a close-fitting jacket or short coat, usu. sleeveless.

jerk′wa′ter, *adj.* insignificant and out-of-the-way.

jerk′y¹, *adj.,* **-i•er, -i•est. 1.** characterized by jerks; spasmodic. **2.** *Slang.* silly; foolish. —**jerk′i•ly,** *adv.*

jer′ky², *n.* meat preserved by being cut into strips and dried in the sun.

Jer•o•bo•am (jer′ə bō′əm), *n.* the first king of the Biblical kingdom of the Hebrews in N Palestine. I Kings 11:26–40; 14:20.

Je•rome (jə rōm′), *n.* **Saint** (*Eusebius Hieronymus*), A.D. c340–420, Christian ascetic and Biblical scholar: chief preparer of the Vulgate.

jer′ry-built′ (jer′ē-), *adj.* **1.** built cheaply and flimsily. **2.** developed haphazardly.

jer•sey (jûr′zē), *n., pl.* **-seys. 1.** a machine-made fabric, characteristically soft and elastic. **2.** a close-fitting knitted sweater or shirt. **3.** (*cap.*) one of a

breed of dairy cattle, raised orig. on Jersey, one of the Channel Islands.

Jer′sey Cit′y, *n.* a seaport in NE New Jersey, opposite New York City. 226,022.

Je•ru•sa•lem (ji rōō′sə ləm, -zə-), *n.* an ancient holy city for Jews, Christians, and Muslims: the capital of Israel. 482,700. —**Je•ru′sa•lem•ite′,** *adj., n.*

jes•sa•mine (jes′ə min), *n.* JASMINE.

Jes•se (jes′ē), *n.* the father of David. I Sam. 16.

jest (jest), *n.* **1.** a joke or witty remark. **2.** a taunt; jeer. **3.** sport or fun. **4.** the object of laughter. —*v.i.* **5.** to joke or banter. **6.** to gibe or scoff.

jest′er, *n.* **1.** a person given to jesting. **2.** a professional fool, esp. at a medieval court.

Je•su (jē′zōō, -sōō, jā′-, yā′-), *n.* JESUS (def. 1). [ME < L *Iēsu,* form of *Iēsus* < Gk *Iēsoû;* see JESUS]

Jes•u•it (jezh′ōō it, -yōō it, jez′-), *n.* a member of the Society of Jesus, a Roman Catholic religious order for men founded in 1534.

Je•sus (jē′zəs, -zəz), *n.* **1.** Also called **Je′sus Christ′, Je′sus of Naz′areth.** born 4? B.C., crucified A.D. 29?, the source of the Christian religion. **2.** ("*the Son of Sirach*") the author of the Apocryphal book of Ecclesiasticus, who lived in the 3rd century B.C. **3.** *Christian Science.* the supreme example of God's nature expressed through human beings. [ME < L *Iēsus* < Gk *Iēsoûs* < Heb *Yēshūa′,* var. of *Yəhōshūa′* God is help]

jet¹ (jet), *n., v.,* **jet•ted, jet•ting,** *adj.* —*n.* **1.** a stream of liquid or gas shooting forth from a nozzle, orifice, etc. **2.** a spout or nozzle for emitting liquid or gas. **3.** Also called **jet′ plane′.** an airplane moved by jet propulsion. —*v.i., v.t.* **4.** to travel or transport by jet plane. **5.** to shoot (something) forth in a stream. —*adj.* **6.** of or powered by jet propulsion.

jet² (jet), *n.* **1.** a hard black coal, polished and used in jewelry. **2.** a deep black. —*adj.* **3.** of the color jet.

jet′ en′gine, *n.* an engine that produces forward motion by the exhaust of a jet of fluid or heated air and gases.

Jeth•ro (jeth′rō), *n.* the father-in-law of Moses. Ex. 3:1. Also called **Reuel.** Ex. 2:18.

jet′ lag′, *n.* a temporary disruption of the body's biological rhythms after high-speed air travel through several time zones.

jet′ propul′sion, *n.* the propulsion of a body by its reaction to a force ejecting a gas or a liquid from it. —**jet′-propelled′,** *adj.*

jet•sam (jet′səm), *n.* goods cast overboard to lighten a ship in an emergency.

jet′ set′, *n.* an international social set of wealthy people who travel frequently by jet plane to parties and resorts. —**jet′-set′ter,** *n.*

Jet′ Ski′, *Trademark.* a brand of personal watercraft.

jet′ stream′, *n.* strong, generally westerly winds concentrated in a narrow, shallow stream in the upper troposphere.

jet•ti•son (jet′ə sən, -zən), *v.t.* **1.** to cast (cargo) overboard. **2.** to discard.

jet•ty (jet′ē), *n., pl.* **-ties. 1.** a structure projecting into a body of water to protect a harbor, deflect the current, etc. **2.** a wharf or landing pier.

Jew (jōō), *n.* **1.** a member of a people who trace their descent from the Israelites of the Bible. **2.** a person whose religion is Judaism.

jew•el (jōō′əl), *n., v.,* **-eled, -el•ing** or (*esp. Brit.*) **-elled, -el•ling.** —*n.* **1.** a precious stone; gem. **2.** a valuable piece of jewelry. **3.** a person or thing that is treasured. **4.** a bearing made of natural or synthetic precious stone, used in timepieces. —*v.t.* **5.** to adorn with jewels.

jew′el•er, *n.* a person who makes, sells, or repairs jewelry. Also, *esp. Brit.,* **jew′el•ler.**

jew′el•ry, *n.* objects of personal adornment made of precious metals, gems, etc., or imitation materials. Also, *esp. Brit.,* **jew′el•ler•y.**

Jew•ish (jōō′ish), *adj.* **1.** of or pertaining to Jews or Judaism. —*n.* **2.** *Informal.* Yiddish. —**Jew′ish•ness,** *n.*

Jew′ish cal′endar, *n.* a calendar used by Jews, as for determining religious holidays, that is reckoned from the traditional date of the Creation (corresponding to 3761 B.C.).

Jew•ry (jōō′rē), *n.* the Jewish people collectively.

Jez•e•bel (jez′ə bel′, -bəl), *n.* the wife of Ahab, king of Israel. I Kings 16:31.

Jez•re•el (jez′rē əl, -el′), *n.* **Plain of,** ESDRAELON. —Jez′re•el•ite′, *n.*

jib (jib), *n.* a triangular sail set forward of a mast.

jibe¹ (jīb), *v.i.,* **jibed, jib•ing. 1.** to shift from one side to the other, as a fore-and-aft sail. **2.** to alter course so that a fore-and-aft sail shifts in this manner.

jibe² (jīb), *v.i., v.t.,* **jibed, jib•ing,** *n.* GIBE.

jibe³ (jīb), *v.i.,* **jibed, jib•ing.** to be in harmony or accord.

Jid•da (jid′də), *n.* a seaport in W Saudi Arabia, on the Red Sea. 1,500,000.

jif•fy (jif′ē), *n., pl.* **-fies.** *Informal.* a very short time.

jig¹ (jig), *n.* a plate, box, or open frame for holding work and for guiding a machine tool to the work.

jig² (jig), *n., v.,* **jigged, jig•ging.** —*n.* **1.** a lively dance, usu. in triple meter. —*v.t., v.i.* **2.** to dance (a jig). —*Idiom.* **3. in jig time,** rapidly.

jig′ger, *n.* **1.** a measure of 1½ oz. (45 ml) used in cocktail recipes. **2.** a small whiskey glass holding this amount.

jig′gle, *v.,* **-gled, -gling,** *n.* —*v.t., v.i.* **1.** to move up and down or to and fro with short, quick jerks. —*n.* **2.** a jiggling movement. —**jig′gly,** *adj.,* **-gli•er, -gli•est.**

jig′saw′, *n.* a saw with a narrow, vertically mounted blade, for cutting curves, complex patterns, etc.

jig′saw puz′zle, *n.* a set of irregularly cut pieces of pasteboard or the like that form a picture when fitted together.

ji•had (ji häd′), *n.* a holy war undertaken as a sacred duty by Muslims.

jilt (jilt), *v.t.* to reject or cast aside (a lover or sweetheart). —**jilt′er,** *n.*

Jim′ Crow′ (jim), *n.* (*sometimes l.c.*) a practice or policy of segregating or discriminating against blacks. —Jim′-Crow′, *adj.*

jim•my (jim′ē), *n., pl.* **-mies,** *v.,* **-mied, -my•inq.** —*n.* **1.** a short crowbar. —*v.t.* **2.** to force open with or as if with a jimmy.

jim•son•weed (jim′sən wēd′), *n.* a coarse weed with poisonous leaves and tubular flowers.

jin•gle (jing′gəl), *v.,* **-gled, -gling,** *n.* —*v.i., v.t.* **1.** to make or cause to make clinking or tinkling sounds. —*n.* **2.** a jingling sound. **3.** a short verse or song with a catchy succession of repetitious sounds.

jin•go•ism (jing′gō iz′əm), *n.* chauvinism marked by the advocacy of an aggressive foreign policy. —**jin′go•ist,** *n.* —**jin′go•is′tic,** *adj.*

jinn (jin) also **jin•ni** (ji nē′, jin′ē), *n., pl.* **jinns** also **jin•nis.** (in Islamic myth) a spirit capable of influencing humankind for good or evil.

jin•rik•i•sha or **-rik•sha** (jin rik′shô, -shä), *n., pl.* **-shas.** a two-wheeled passenger vehicle pulled by one person, formerly used in Japan and China.

jinx (jingks), *n.* **1.** one thought to bring bad luck. —*v.t.* **2.** to bring bad luck to.

jit•ney (jit′nē), *n., pl.* **-neys.** a small passenger bus following a regular route.

jit•ter•bug (jit′ər bug′), *n., v.,* **-bugged, -bug•ging.** —*n.* **1.** a strenuously acrobatic jazz dance. —*v.i.* **2.** to dance the jitterbug. —**jit′ter•bug′ger,** *n.*

jit′ters, *n.pl.* a feeling of fright or uneasiness (usu. prec. by *the*). —**jit′ter•y,** *adj.*

jive (jīv), *n., v.,* **jived, jiv•ing.** —*n.* **1.** swing music or early jazz. **2.** *Slang.* deceptive or meaningless talk. —*v.t., v.i.* **3.** *Slang.* to fool or kid (someone).

Jo•ab (jō′ab), *n.* a commander of David's army and the slayer of Absalom. II Sam. 3:27; 18:14.

Joan of Arc (jōn′ əv ärk′), *n.* **Saint** (*"the Maid of Orléans"*), 1412?–31, French martyr who raised the siege of Orléans.

job (job), *n., v.,* **jobbed, job•bing.** —*n.* **1.** a piece of

work done as part of one's occupation or for a price. **2.** a post of employment. **3.** any task or project. **4.** the material or item being worked upon. —*v.i.* **5.** to work at jobs or odd pieces of work. **6.** to do business as a jobber. —*v.t.* **7.** to assign (work) in separate portions, as to different contractors. —**job′hold′er,** *n.* —**job′less,** *adj.* —**job′less•ness,** *n.*

Job (jōb), *n.* **1.** the central figure in an Old Testament parable of the righteous sufferer. **2.** a book of the Bible bearing his name.

job′ ac′tion, *n.* a work slowdown or other protest by employees to win specified demands.

job′ber, *n.* **1.** a wholesale merchant, esp. one selling to retailers. **2.** a person who does piecework.

job′ lot′, *n.* a large assortment of goods sold as a single unit.

Joch•e•bed (jok′ə bed′), *n.* the mother of Aaron, Moses, and Miriam. Ex. 6:20.

jock (jok), *n.* **1.** a jockstrap. **2.** *Informal.* an athlete. **3.** *Informal.* an enthusiast: *a computer jock.*

jock•ey (jok′ē), *n., pl.* **-eys,** *v.,* **-eyed, -ey•ing.** —*n.* **1.** a person who rides horses professionally in races. —*v.t.* **2.** to ride (a horse) as a jockey. **3.** to move by skillful maneuvering. —*v.i.* **4.** to aim at an advantage by skillful maneuvering.

jock′strap′, *n.* an elasticized belt with a pouch for the genitals, worn by men while participating in athletics.

jo•cose (jō kōs′, jə-), *adj.* given to or characterized by joking. —**jo•cose′ly,** *adv.* —**jo•cos′i•ty** (-kos′i-tē), **jo•cose′ness,** *n.*

joc•u•lar (jok′yə lər), *adj.* given to or characterized by joking or jesting. —**joc′u•lar′i•ty,** *n.* —**joc′u•lar•ly,** *adv.*

joc•und (jok′ənd, jō′kənd), *adj.* cheerful; merry; jolly. —**jo•cun•di•ty** (jō kun′di tē), *n.* —**joc′und•ly,** *adv.*

jodh•purs (jod′pərz), *n.pl.* riding breeches cut very full over the hips and tightfitting below the knees.

Jo•el (jō′əl), *n.* **1.** a Minor Prophet of the postexilic period. **2.** a book of the Bible bearing his name.

jog¹ (jog), *v.,* **jogged, jog•ging.** —*v.t.* **1.** to move or shake with a push or jerk. **2.** to stir into activity or alertness: *to jog one's memory.* —*v.i.* **3.** to run at a slow, steady pace, esp. as an exercise. —*n.* **4.** a slight push; nudge. **5.** an act or instance of jogging. —**jog′ger,** *n.*

jog² (jog), *n., v.,* **jogged, jog•ging.** —*n.* **1.** an irregularity of line or surface. **2.** a bend or turn. —*v.i.* **3.** to bend or turn.

jog′gle, *v.,* **-gled, -gling,** *n.* —*v.t., v.i.* **1.** to shake slightly. —*n.* **2.** a slight shake or jolt.

Jo•an•na (jō an′ə), *n.* a member of the household of Herod Antipas, who witnessed the empty tomb after Jesus' resurrection. Luke 24:1–10.

Jo•han•nes•burg (jō han′is bûrg′), *n.* a city in NE South Africa. 1,609,408.

john (jon), *n.* *Informal.* a toilet.

John,¹ *n.* **1.** a Christian apostle, believed to be the author of the fourth Gospel. **2.** the fourth Gospel. **3.** any of the three Epistles of John; I, II, or III John. **4.** JOHN THE BAPTIST. **5.** (*John Lackland*) 1167?–1216, king of England 1199–1216: signer of the Magna Carta 1215.

John² (jon), **John XXIII,** (*Angelo Giuseppe Roncalli*) 1881–1963, Italian ecclesiastic: pope 1958–63.

John′ Birch′ Soci′ety, *n.* an ultraconservative organization, founded in 1958, to combat alleged Communist activities in the U.S.

John′ Bull′, *n.* **1.** the English people. **2.** the typical Englishman.

John′ Doe′ (dō), *n.* a fictitious name used in legal proceedings for a male party whose true name is not known.

John Paul II, *n.* (*Karol Wojtyła*) born 1920, Polish ecclesiastic: pope since 1978.

Johns (jonz), *n.* **Jasper,** born 1930, U.S. painter.

John•son (jon′sən), *n.* **1. Andrew,** 1808–75, 17th president of the U.S. 1865–69. **2. James Weldon,** 1871–1938, U.S. poet, essayist, editor, and social reformer. **3. J(ohn) Rosamond,** U.S. composer (brother of James Weldon Johnson). **4. Lyndon Baines,** 1908–73, 36th president of the U.S. 1963–69. **5. Samuel** (*"Dr. Johnson"*), 1709–84, English lexicographer and writer.

Johns/town Flood/ (jonz/toun/), *n.* a disastrous flood (1889) that killed 2,200 people at Johnstown, Pa.

John/ the Bap/tist, *n.* the forerunner and baptizer of Jesus. Matt. 3.

joie de vi•vre (zhwAd³ vē/vR³), *n. French.* a delight in being alive.

join (join), *v.t., v.i.* **1.** to put together or in contact. **2.** to come into contact or union (with). **3.** to become a member of (a club, society, etc.). **4.** to participate with (someone) in some act or activity.

join/er, *n.* **1.** a carpenter, esp. one who constructs doors and other permanent woodwork. **2.** a person given to joining organizations. **—join/er•y,** *n.*

joint (joint), *n.* **1.** the place at which two things are joined. **2.** the place of union between two bones or elements of a skeleton. **3.** a large piece of meat, usu. with a bone. **4.** *Slang.* a cheap or disreputable place of public entertainment. **—adj. 5.** shared by or common to two or more. **6.** sharing or acting in common: *joint authorship.* **—v.t. 7.** to unite by a joint. **8.** to provide with joints. **9.** to cut (meat) at the joints. **—Idiom. 10. out of joint, a.** dislocated, as a bone. **b.** disordered. **—joint/ly,** *adv.*

joist (joist), *n.* one of a number of small parallel beams that support a floor or ceiling.

joist

joke (jōk), *n., v.,* **joked, jok•ing. —n. 1.** a short humorous anecdote with a punch line. **2.** anything said or done to cause amusement. **3.** an object of laughter or ridicule. **4.** a trifling matter: *The loss was no joke.* **—v.i. 5.** to make or tell jokes. **6.** to say something in fun rather than in earnest. **—jok/ing•ly,** *adv.*

jok/er, *n.* **1.** one who jokes. **2.** an extra playing card used in some games. **3.** a seemingly minor clause inserted in a document to change its effect.

jol•li•ty (jol/i tē), *n., pl.* **-ties.** a jolly mood, condition, or activity.

jol•ly (jol/ē), *adj.,* **-li•er, -li•est,** *v.,* **-lied, -ly•ing. —adj. 1.** in good spirits; merry. **2.** cheerfully festive. **—v.t. 3.** to try to keep (a person) in good humor (usu. fol. by *along*). **4.** to tease, esp. good-naturedly. **—jol/li•ly,** *adv.* **—jol/li•ness,** *n.*

jolt (jōlt), *v.t.* **1.** to shake up roughly. **2.** to shock or startle. **—v.i. 3.** to move with sharp jerks. **—n. 4.** a jolting movement or blow. **5.** a psychological shock.

Jo•nah (jō/nə), *n.* **1.** a Hebrew prophet who was thrown overboard and swallowed by a large fish, and later cast up unharmed. **2.** a book of the Bible bearing his name.

Jon•a•than¹ (jon/ə thən), *n.* a son of Saul and friend of David. I Sam. 18–20.

Jon•a•than² (jon/ə thən), *n.* a variety of red apple. [after *Jonathan* Hasbrouck (d. 1846), U.S. jurist]

Jones (jōnz), *n.* **1. Inigo,** 1573–1652, English architect. **2. John Paul** (*John Paul*), 1747–92, American naval commander in the Revolutionary War, born in Scotland. **3. Mary Harris** (*"Mother Jones"*), 1830–1930, U.S. labor leader, born in Ireland. **4. Rufus Matthew,** 1863–1948, U.S. Quaker, teacher, author, and humanitarian. **5. Sam(uel Porter),** 1847–1906, U.S. evangelist.

jon•quil (jong/kwil, jon/-), *n.* a narcissus with yellow or white flowers.

Jon•son (jon/sən), *n.* **Ben,** 1573?–1637, English dramatist and poet. **—Jon•so/ni•an** (-sō/nē ən), *adj.*

Jop•lin (jop/lin), *n.* **Scott,** 1868–1917, U.S. ragtime pianist and composer.

Jop•pa (jop/ə), *n.* ancient name of JAFFA.

Jo•ram (jôr/am, jōr/-) also **Jehoram,** *n.* **1.** a king of Judah, the son of Jehoshaphat. II Kings 8:16–24. **2.** a king of Israel, son of Ahab and Jezebel; slain by Jehu. II Kings 3:1–6; 9:14–26.

Jor•dan (jôr/dn), *n.* **1.** a kingdom in SW Asia, E of Israel. 4,324,638. **2.** a river in SW Asia, flowing through Jordan into the Dead Sea. **—Jor•da/ni•an** (-dā/nē ən), *n., adj.*

Jo•seph (jō/zəf, -səf), *n.* **1.** a son of Jacob and Rachel who was sold into slavery by his jealous brothers. Gen. 30:22–24; 37. **2.** the husband of Mary, the mother of Jesus. Matt. 1:16–25.

Jo/seph of Ar•i•ma•thae/a (ar/ə mə thē/ə), *n.* a member of the Sanhedrin who placed the body of Jesus in the tomb. Matt. 27:57–60; Mark 15:43.

josh (josh), *v.t., v.i.* to tease in a bantering way. **—josh/er,** *n.*

Josh•u•a (josh/ōō ə), *n.* **1.** the successor of Moses as leader of the Israelites. Deut. 31:14, 23; 34:9. **2.** a book of the Bible bearing his name.

jos•tle (jos/əl), *v.,* **-tled, -tling,** *n.* **—v.t., v.i. 1.** to bump or shove roughly or rudely, as in a crowd. **—n. 2.** the act of jostling.

jot (jot), *v.,* **jot•ted, jot•ting,** *n.* **—v.t. 1.** to write down quickly or briefly (usu. fol. by *down*). **—n. 2.** a little bit. **—jot/ter,** *n.*

jot/ting, *n.* a quickly written or brief note.

joule (jōol, joul), *n.* a unit of work or energy, equal to the work done by a force of one newton acting through a distance of one meter.

jounce (jouns), *v.,* **jounced, jounc•ing,** *n.* **—v.t., v.i. 1.** to move joltingly. **—n. 2.** a jouncing movement. **—jounc/y,** *adj.*

jour•nal (jûr/nl), *n.* **1.** a daily record of occurrences or observations. **2.** a newspaper, esp. a daily one. **3.** a professional or academic periodical. **4.** a record of proceedings, as of a legislative body. **5.** (in bookkeeping) a book into which all transactions are entered before being posted into the ledger. **6.** the portion of a shaft or axle contained by a bearing.

jour/nal•ese/ (-ēz/, -ēs/), *n.* a style of writing regarded as typical of newspapers and magazines.

jour/nal•ism, *n.* the occupation of gathering, writing, editing, and publishing or broadcasting news. **—jour/nal•ist,** *n.* **—jour/nal•is/tic,** *adj.*

jour•ney (jûr/nē), *n., pl.* **-neys,** *v.,* **-neyed, -ney•ing. —n. 1.** a traveling from one place to another, usu. taking a long time. **—v.i. 2.** to make a journey. **—jour/ney•er,** *n.*

jour/ney•man, *n., pl.* **-men. 1.** a person who has served an apprenticeship at a trade. **2.** a competent but routine worker or performer.

joust (joust, just), *n.* **1.** a combat between two mounted knights armed with lances. **—v.i. 2.** to engage in a joust. **—joust/er,** *n.*

jo•vi•al (jō/vē əl), *adj.* characterized by hearty, joyous humor. **—jo/vi•al/i•ty,** *n.* **—jo/vi•al•ly,** *adv.*

jowl¹ (joul), *n.* **1.** a jaw, esp. the lower jaw. **2.** the meat of the cheek of a hog.

jowl² (joul), *n.* a fold of flesh hanging from the jaw, as of a fat person. **—jowl/y,** *adj.,* **-i•er,** -i•est.

joy (joi), *n.* **1.** a feeling of great delight or happiness; elation. **2.** a cause of keen pleasure or delight. **—joy/less,** *adj.*

Joyce (jois), *n.* **James,** 1882–1941, Irish writer. **—Joyc/e•an,** *adj., n.*

joy/ful, *adj.* **1.** full of joy. **2.** showing or causing joy. **—joy/ful•ly,** *adv.* **—joy/ful•ness,** *n.*

joy/ous, *adj.* joyful; jubilant. **—joy/ous•ly,** *adv.* **—joy/ous•ness,** *n.*

joy/ride/, *n.* a pleasure ride in an automobile, esp. when the vehicle is driven recklessly. **—joy/rid/er,** *n.*

joy/stick/, *n.* **1.** *Informal.* the control stick of an airplane or other vehicle. **2.** a lever used to control the movement of a cursor or other graphic element, as in a video game.

JP, Justice of the Peace.

Jpn. or **Jpn, 1.** Japan. **2.** Japanese.

Jr. or **jr.,** junior.

Ju•bal (jōō′bəl), *n.* a descendant of Cain: the progenitor of musicians. Gen. 4:21.

ju•bi•lant (jōō′bə lənt), *adj.* showing great joy or triumph; exultant. —**ju′bi•lant•ly,** *adv.*

ju′bi•la′tion, *n.* **1.** a feeling of joy or exultation. **2.** a joyful celebration.

ju•bi•lee (jōō′bə lē′), *n.*, *pl.* **-lees. 1.** the celebration of any of certain anniversaries, as the 25th, 50th, or 75th. **2.** any season or occasion of rejoicing. **3.** rejoicing or jubilation.

Ju•dah (jōō′də), *n.* **1.** the fourth son of Jacob and Leah. Gen. 29:35. **2.** one of the 12 tribes of Israel. **3.** the Biblical kingdom of the Hebrews in S Palestine.

Ju•da•ic (jōō dā′ik) also **Ju•da′i•cal,** *adj.* of or pertaining to Judaism or the Jews; Jewish. —**Ju•da′i•cal•ly,** *adv.*

Ju•da•i•ca (jōō dā′i kə), *n.pl.* things pertaining to Jewish life and customs.

Ju•da•ism (jōō′dē iz′əm, -də-), *n.* the monotheistic religion of the Jews, based on the precepts of the Old Testament and the teachings and commentaries of the rabbis as found chiefly in the Talmud.

Ju•das (jōō′dəs), *n.* **1.** Judas Iscariot, the disciple who betrayed Jesus. Mark 3:19. **2.** a person treacherous enough to betray a friend. **3.** Also called **Saint Judas** or **Saint Jude.** one of the 12 apostles (not Judas Iscariot). Luke 6:16; Acts 1:13. **4.** a brother of James and possibly of Jesus. Matt. 13:55.

Ju′das Maccabae′us, *n.* Maccabaeus, Judas.

Jude (jōōd), *n.* **1.** a book of the New Testament. **2.** the author of this book, sometimes identified with Judas, the brother of James.

Ju•de•a (jōō dē′ə), *n.* the S region of ancient Palestine: existed under Persian, Greek, and Roman rule; divided between Israel and Jordan in 1948; occupied by Israel since 1967. —**Ju•de′an,** *adj.*, *n.*

Ju•de•o-Chris•tian (jōō dā′ō kris′chən, -dē′-), *adj.* of or pertaining to the religious writings, beliefs, values, or traditions held in common by Judaism and Christianity.

judge (juj), *n.*, *v.*, **judged, judg•ing.** —*n.* **1.** a public officer authorized to hear and decide cases in a court of law. **2.** a person appointed to decide in a competition or contest. **3.** a person qualified to pass critical judgment. **4.** an administrative head of Israel in the period between the death of Joshua and the accession to the throne by Saul. —*v.t.* **5.** to pass legal judgment on. **6.** to form a judgment or opinion concerning. **7.** to decide or settle authoritatively. **8.** to think or hold as an opinion. **9.** to act as a judge in. —*v.i.* **10.** to act as a judge. **11.** to form an opinion. —*Proverb.* **12. Judge not according to appearances,** things are not always what they seem. John 7:24. **13. Judge not, that ye be not judged,** remember that you are likely to be measured by the same criteria you apply to others. Matt. 7:1. —**judge′ship,** *n.*

Judg•es (juj′iz), *n.* (*used with a sing. v.*) a book of the Bible containing the history of Israel from the death of Joshua to the accession of Saul.

judg′ment, *n.* **1.** the act of judging. **2.** the ability to judge objectively or wisely. **3.** an opinion formed. **4. a.** a judicial decision. **b.** the certificate embodying such a decision. **5.** (*cap.*) Last Judgment. Also, *esp. Brit.,* **judge′ment.**

judg•men′tal, *adj.* tending to make judgments, esp. moral judgments.

Judg′ment Day′, *n.* the day of the Last Judgment; doomsday.

ju•di•ca•to•ry (jōō′di kə tôr′ē), *n.*, *pl.* **-to•ries,** *adj.* —*n.* **1.** a court of law and justice. —*adj.* **2.** pertaining to the administration of justice.

ju′di•ca′ture (-kā′chər, -kə chŏŏr′), *n.* **1.** the administration of justice. **2.** the jurisdiction of a judge or court. **3.** a body of judges.

ju•di′cial (-dish′əl), *adj.* **1.** pertaining to courts of law or to judges. **2.** proper to the character of a

judge. **3.** decreed, sanctioned, or enforced by a court. —**ju•di′cial•ly,** *adv.*

judi′cial branch′, *n.* the branch of the U.S. government whose powers are vested in the Supreme Court and the federal court system.

ju•di′ci•ar′y (-dish′ē er′ē, -dish′ə rē), *n.*, *pl.* **-ar•ies,** *adj.* —*n.* **1.** the judicial branch of government. **2.** the system of courts in a country. **3.** judges collectively. —*adj.* **4.** pertaining to the judicial branch or system or to judges.

ju•di′cious, *adj.* having, exercising, or characterized by good judgment. —**ju•di′cious•ly,** *adv.* —**ju•di′cious•ness,** *n.*

Ju•dith (jōō′dith), *n.* **1.** a Jewish woman who saved her town from the besieging Assyrian army by cutting off the head of its commander, Holofernes, while he slept. **2.** a book of the Apocrypha and Douay Bible bearing her name.

ju•do (jōō′dō), *n.* a martial art based on jujitsu but banning dangerous throws and blows.

jug (jug), *n.* **1.** a container for liquid, having a handle and a narrow neck. **2.** *Slang.* a jail; prison.

jug•ger•naut (jug′ər nôt′, -not′), *n.* any large, overpowering, destructive force or object.

jug•gle (jug′əl), *v.*, **-gled, -gling.** —*v.t.* **1.** to keep (several objects, as balls) in the air simultaneously by tossing and catching. **2.** to manipulate in order to deceive: *to juggle the accounts.* **3.** to handle the requirements of (two or more activities) simultaneously: *to juggle the obligations of work and school.* —*v.i.* **4.** to juggle objects. —**jug′gler,** *n.* —**jug′gler•y,** *n.*

jug•u•lar (jug′yə lər), *adj.* **1.** of the throat or neck. —*n.* **2.** any of several veins of the neck that convey blood from the head to the heart.

juice (jōōs), *n.*, *v.*, **juiced, juic•ing.** —*n.* **1.** the natural fluid in a plant, esp. a fruit. **2.** the natural fluids of an animal body: *gastric juices.* **3.** strength or vitality. **4.** *Slang.* **a.** electricity. **b.** gasoline or fuel oil. —*v.t.* **5.** to extract juice from.

juic′er, *n.* an appliance for extracting juice from fruits and vegetables.

juic′y, *adj.*, **-i•er, -i•est. 1.** full of juice. **2.** very profitable or satisfying. **3.** very interesting, esp. when slightly scandalous. —**juic′i•ly,** *adv.* —**juic′i•ness,** *n.*

Ju•jit•su (jōō jit′sōō) also **-jut′su** (-jut′sōō, -jōōt′-), *n.* a Japanese method of defending oneself without weapons by using the strength and weight of one's adversary to disable him or her.

ju•jube (jōō′jōōb, jōō′jōō bē′), *n.* a chewy fruit-flavored lozenge.

juke•box (jōōk′boks′), *n.* a coin-operated phonograph having records selected by push button.

Jul or **Jul., July.**

ju•lep (jōō′lip), *n.* mint julep.

ju•li•enne (jōō′lē en′), *adj.* (of vegetables) cut into thin strips.

Ju•ly (jōō lī′, jə-), *n.*, *pl.* **-lies.** the seventh month of the year, containing 31 days.

jum•ble (jum′bəl), *v.*, **-bled, -bling,** *n.* —*v.t.*, *v.i.* **1.** to mix or be mixed in a confused mass. —*n.* **2.** a mixed or disordered mass.

jum•bo (jum′bō), *n.*, *pl.* **-bos,** *adj.* —*n.* **1.** a very large person, animal, or thing. —*adj.* **2.** very large.

jump (jump), *v.i.* **1.** to spring from the ground or other support by a sudden muscular effort. **2.** to move or jerk suddenly, as from shock. **3.** *Informal.* to be full of activity. **4.** to rise suddenly: *Prices jumped.* **5.** to proceed abruptly: *to jump to a conclusion.* **6.** to take eagerly; seize: *We jumped at the offer.* —*v.t.* **7.** to leap or spring over. **8.** to cause to leap. **9.** to skip or bypass. **10.** to move or start before (a signal); anticipate. **11.** to increase suddenly. **12.** to attack without warning, as from ambush. **13.** to flee from: *to jump town.* —*n.* **14.** an act or instance of jumping. **15.** a sudden rise in amount, price, etc. **16.** an abrupt transition. **17.** a sudden start, as from nervous excitement. —*Idiom.* **18. get** or **have the jump on,** to have an initial advantage over. **19. jump ship,** to escape from or desert a ship.

—*Saying.* **20. jump from the frying pan into the fire,** to go from a bad situation to a worse one.
jump′er[1], *n.* **1.** one that jumps. **2.** a short wire used to make a temporary electrical connection. **3.** either of a pair of electric cables for starting the engine of a vehicle whose battery is dead.

jump′er[2], *n.* **1.** a sleeveless dress worn over a blouse. **2.** a loose jacket.

jump′-start′, *n.* **1.** the starting of an internal-combustion engine by means of jumpers. —*v.t.* **2.** to give a jump-start to. **3.** to enliven or revive: *to jump-start a sluggish economy.*

jump′suit′, *n.* **1.** a one-piece suit worn by parachutists. **2.** a garment fashioned after it.

jump′y, *adj.*, **-i•er, -i•est. 1.** nervous or apprehensive; jittery. **2.** characterized by sudden jerks. —**jump′i•ness,** *n.*

Jun or **Jun.,** June.

jun•co (jung′kō), *n., pl.* **-cos.** any of several small North American finches.

junc•tion (jungk′shən), *n.* **1.** the act of joining or state of being joined. **2.** a place where things meet or cross.

junc′ture (-chər), *n.* **1.** a point of time, esp. one made critical by circumstances. **2.** a crisis. **3.** the point at which two bodies are joined.

June (jōōn), *n.* the sixth month of the year, containing 30 days.

Ju•neau (jōō′nō), *n.* the capital of Alaska. 19,528.

Jung (yŏŏng), *n.* **Carl Gustav,** 1875–1961, Swiss psychiatrist and psychologist. —**Jung′i•an,** *adj., n.*

jun•gle (jung′gəl), *n.* **1.** wild land overgrown with dense vegetation, esp. in the tropics. **2.** a place of violence, struggle, or ruthless competition.

jun•ior (jōōn′yər), *adj.* **1.** younger (designating a son named after his father; often written as *Jr.* following the name). **2.** of more recent election, appointment, or admission. **3.** of lower rank. **4.** of juniors in school. —*n.* **5.** a person who is younger or of lower rank than another. **6.** a student in the next to the last year at a high school or college.

jun′ior col′lege, *n.* a school offering courses only through the first two years of college.

jun′ior high′ school′, *n.* a secondary school usu. consisting of grades seven through nine.

ju•ni•per (jōō′nə pər), *n.* an evergreen shrub or tree with berrylike cones that yield an oil used to flavor gin.

junk[1] (jungk), *n.* **1.** old or discarded material or objects. **2.** something regarded as worthless. —*v.t.* **3.** to discard as junk. —**junk′y,** *adj.*, **-i•er, -i•est.**

junk[2] (jungk), *n.* a seagoing ship used primarily in Chinese waters, having a flat bottom.

junk′ bond′, *n.* a corporate bond with a low rating and a high yield, often involving high risk.

junk′er, *n. Informal.* a car in bad enough repair to be scrapped.

Jun•ker (yŏŏng′kər), *n.* a member of a politically conservative class of Prussian landowners.

jun•ket (jung′kit), *n.* **1.** a custardlike dessert of flavored milk curdled with rennet. **2.** a pleasure excursion. **3.** a trip by a government official at public expense, ostensibly to obtain information. —*v.i.* **4.** to go on a junket. —**jun′ke•teer′** (-ki tēr′), **jun′ket•er,** *n.*

junk′ food′, *n.* food that is high in calories but of little nutritional value.

junk′ mail′, *n.* unsolicited commercial material, as advertisements, mailed in bulk.

Ju•no (jōō′nō), *n.* a Roman goddess, the wife and sister of Jupiter: associated with women and childbirth.

jun•ta (hŏŏn′tə, jun′-, hun′-), *n., pl.* **-tas.** a small group ruling a country, esp. immediately after a coup d'état.

Ju•pi•ter (jōō′pi tər), *n.* **1.** the supreme deity of the ancient Romans, associated with the sky and rain. **2.** the largest planet in the solar system, fifth in order from the sun.

Ju•ras•sic (jŏŏ ras′ik), *adj.* pertaining to a period of the Mesozoic Era, characterized by the presence of dinosaurs.

ju•rid•i•cal (jŏŏ rid′i kəl) also **-rid′ic,** *adj.* of or pertaining to law or jurisprudence.

ju•ris•dic•tion (jŏŏr′is dik′shən), *n.* **1.** the right, power, or authority to administer justice. **2.** power; authority; control. **3.** the territory over which authority is exercised. —**ju′ris•dic′tion•al,** *adj.*

ju′ris•pru′dence, *n.* **1.** the science or philosophy of law. **2.** a system of laws. **3.** a branch of law.

ju′rist, *n.* a person versed in the law, as a judge.

ju•ror (jŏŏr′ər, -ôr), *n.* a member of a jury.

ju′ry, *n., pl.* **-ries. 1.** a group of persons selected and sworn to examine the evidence in a case and render a verdict to a court. **2.** a group of persons chosen to adjudge prizes, awards, etc. —*Idiom.* **3. the jury is still out,** a decision or opinion is yet to be rendered: *The jury is still out on his job performance.*

just (just), *adv.* **1.** within a brief preceding time: *The sun just came out.* **2.** precisely: *That's just what I mean.* **3.** barely: *just in time.* **4.** merely: *just a child.* **5.** at this moment: *The movie is just ending.* **6.** simply: *We'll just have to wait and see.* —*adj.* **7.** guided by reason and fairness. **8.** proper: *a just reply.* **9.** lawful: *a just claim.* **10.** true; correct: *a just analysis.* **11.** deserved: *a just punishment.* **12.** proper or right: *just proportions.* **13.** righteous. —**just′ly,** *adv.* —**just′ness,** *n.*

jus•tice (jus′tis), *n.* **1.** the quality of being just; moral rightness. **2.** rightfulness or lawfulness, as of a claim. **3.** the administering of deserved punishment or reward. **4.** the administration of what is just according to law. **5.** a judge or magistrate. —*Idiom.* **6. do justice to, a.** to act fairly toward. **b.** to appreciate properly. —*Proverb.* **7. Justice is blind,** the law should be impartial.

jus′tice of the peace′, *n.* a local public officer having authority to try minor cases, solemnize marriages, etc.

jus′ti•fy′, *v.t.*, **-fied, -fy•ing. 1.** to show to be just, right, or reasonable. **2.** to uphold as warranted: *Don't try to justify his rudeness.* **3.** to absolve of guilt. —**jus′ti•fi′a•ble,** *adj.* —**jus′ti•fi′a•bly,** *adv.* —**jus′ti•fi•ca′tion,** *n.*

Jus•tin•i•an I (ju stin′ē ən), *n.* A.D. 483–565, Byzantine emperor 527–565.

jut (jut), *v.*, **jut•ted, jut•ting,** *n.* —*v.i., v.t.* **1.** to project; protrude. —*n.* **2.** something that juts out.

jute (jōōt), *n.* **1.** a strong fiber used for making burlap, cordage, etc., obtained from two East Indian plants. **2.** either of these plants.

ju•ve•nile (jōō′və nl, -nīl′), *adj.* **1.** characteristic of or suitable for young people. **2.** young. **3.** immature; childish. —*n.* **4.** a young person. **5.** an actor or actress who plays youthful roles. **6.** a book for children.

ju′venile delin′quency, *n.* illegal or antisocial behavior by a minor. —**ju′venile delin′quent,** *n.*

jux•ta•pose (juk′stə pōz′, juk′stə pōz′), *v.t.*, **-posed, -pos•ing.** to place close together or side by side, as for contrast. —**jux′ta•po•si′tion** (-pə zish′ən), *n.*

K

K, k (kā), *n., pl.* **Ks** or **K's, ks** or **k's.** the 11th letter of the English alphabet, a consonant.

K, 1. *Computers.* **a.** the number 1024 or 2^{10}. **b.** kilobyte. **2.** the number 1000: *a \$50K salary*. **3.** kindergarten.

K, *Symbol.* **1.** *Chem.* potassium. [< NL *kalium*] **2.** Kelvin. **3.** strikeout.

k. or **k, 1.** karat. **2.** kilogram.

K2 (kā′tōō′), *n.* a mountain in N Kashmir: second highest peak in the world. 28,250 ft. (8611 m). Also called **Godwin Austen.**

ka·bu·ki (kə bōō′kē, kä′bōō kē′), *n.* a popular drama of Japan characterized by stylized acting and the performance of all roles by male actors. [< Japn: song-and-dance art]

Ka·bul (kä′bŏŏl, -bəl, kə bōōl′), *n.* the capital of Afghanistan. 913,164.

kad·dish (kä′dish), *n. Judaism.* (*often cap.*) **1.** a prayer glorifying God that is recited during the daily services. **2.** a form of this prayer recited by mourners.

kaf·fee·klatsch (kä′fē kläch′, -klach′, kô′-), *n.* a social gathering for informal conversation and coffee.

Kaf·ka (käf′kə), *n.* **Franz,** 1883–1924, Austrian writer, born in Prague.

Kah·lo (kä′lō), *n.* **Frida,** 1910–54, Mexican painter.

kai·ser (kī′zər), *n.* a German emperor: the title used from 1871 to 1918.

kale (kāl), *n.* a cabbagelike plant with wrinkled leaves.

ka·lei·do·scope (kə lī′də skōp′), *n.* **1.** a tubular optical toy in which bits of colored glass are reflected by mirrors to display changing patterns. **2.** a continually shifting pattern, scene, etc. —**ka·lei·do·scop·ic** (-skop′ik), *adj.*

ka·mi·ka·ze (kä′mi kä′zē), *n., pl.* **-zes. 1.** (in World War II) a Japanese pilot charged with suicidal missions against U.S. warships. **2.** an airplane filled with explosives and flown by a kamikaze.

Kam·pa·la (käm pä′lə, kam-), *n.* the capital of Uganda. 458,423.

Kam·pu·che·a (kam′pōō chē′ə), *n.* former name of CAMBODIA. —**Kam′pu·che′an,** *adj., n.*

Kan., Kansas.

Kan·din·sky (kan din′skē), *n.* **Wassily** or **Vasili,** 1866–1944, Russian painter.

kan·ga·roo (kang′gə rōō′), *n., pl.* **-roos.** a herbivorous leaping marsupial of Australia and adjacent islands, with short forelimbs and powerful hind legs.

kangaroo

kan′garoo court′, *n.* a self-appointed tribunal that disregards existing principles of law or human rights.

Kans., Kansas.

Kan·sas (kan′zəs), *n.* a state in the central United States. 2,572,150. *Cap.:* Topeka. *Abbr.:* KS, Kans., Kan., Kas. —**Kan′san,** *n., adj.*

Kan′sas Cit′y, *n.* **1.** a city in W Missouri. 443,878. **2.** a city in NE Kansas. 142,630.

Kan′sas-Nebras′ka Act′, *n.* an act of Congress (1854) annulling the Missouri Compromise, providing for the organization of the territories of Kansas and Nebraska, and permitting these territories self-determination on the question of slavery.

Kant (kant, känt), *n.* **Immanuel,** 1724–1804, German philosopher.

ka·o·lin or **-line** (kā′ə lin), *n.* a fine white clay used in making porcelain.

ka·pok (kā′pok), *n.* the silky down that covers the seeds of a tropical tree, used for stuffing pillows, life jackets, etc.

kap·pa (kap′ə), *n., pl.* **-pas.** the tenth letter of the Greek alphabet (K, κ).

ka·put (kä pŏŏt′, -pōŏt′, kə-), *adj. Slang.* ruined or broken.

Ka·ra·chi (kə rä′chē), *n.* a seaport in S Pakistan. 5,208,170.

kar·a·kul (kar′ə kəl), *n.* **1.** an Asian sheep, the young of which have black, curly fleece. **2.** the fur from this fleece.

ka·ra·o·ke (kar′ē ō′kē), *n.* the act of singing along to a music video, esp. one from which the original vocals have been eliminated. [< Japn, = *kara* empty + *oke* orchestra]

kar·at (kar′ət), *n.* a unit for measuring the fineness of gold, pure gold being 24 karats fine.

ka·ra·te (kə rä′tē), *n.* a Japanese method of self-defense using fast, hard blows with the hands, elbows, knees, or feet. [< Japn, = *kara* empty + *te* hand(s)]

kar·ma (kär′mə), *n.* (in Hinduism and Buddhism) action seen as bringing upon oneself inevitable results, either in this life or in a reincarnation.

kart (kärt), *n.* a small, low-slung vehicle, powered by a gasoline engine.

Kas., Kansas.

Kash·mir (kash mēr′), *n.* a region in SW Asia, in N India.

kash·ruth or **kash·rut** (käsh rōōt′, käsh′root), *n.* **1.** the Jewish dietary laws. **2.** fitness for use with respect to Jewish law.

Kat·man·du (kät′män dōō′, kat′man-), *n.* the capital of Nepal. 235,160.

ka·ty·did (kā′tē did), *n.* any of several large, usu. green, American grasshoppers.

Ka·ua·i (kä wä′ē, kou′ī), *n.* an island in NW Hawaii.

kay·ak (kī′ak), *n.* **1.** an Eskimo canoe with a skin cover on a light framework. **2.** a small boat resembling this, used in sports.

kay·o (kā′ō′, kā′ō′), *n., pl.* **-os,** *v.t.,* **-oed, -o·ing.** See KO.

Ka·zakh·stan (kä′zäk stän′), *n.* a republic in central Asia, NE of the Caspian Sea: formerly a part of the USSR. 16,898,572.

ka·zoo (kə zōō′), *n., pl.* **-zoos.** a tubular musical toy with a membrane that vibrates with a buzz when one hums into it.

kc, kilocycle.

K.C., Kansas City.

Kea·ton (kēt′n), *n.* **Buster** (*Joseph Francis Keaton*), 1895–1966, U.S. film comedian and director.

Keats (kēts), *n.* **John,** 1795–1821, English poet.

ke·bab or **-bob** (kə bob′), *n.* small pieces of meat, marinated and broiled on a skewer.

Ke·ble (kē′bəl), *n.* **John,** 1792–1866, English clergyman and poet.

Ke·dar (kē′dər), *n.* the second son of Ishmael. Gen. 25:13.

keel (kēl), *n.* **1.** a central structural member in the bottom of a ship's hull, extending from the stem to the stern. —*v.* **2. keel over, a.** to capsize. **b.** to fall or cause to fall over without warning. —*Idiom.* **3. on an even keel,** in a stable or calm state.

keen¹ (kēn), *adj.*, **-er, -est. 1.** finely sharpened: *a keen razor.* **2.** sharp or piercing: *a keen wind.* **3.** highly sensitive or perceptive: *keen ears.* **4.** shrewdly intelligent: *a keen observer.* **5.** intense: *keen desire.* **6.** eager: *keen to go swimming.* —**keen′ly,** *adv.* —**keen′ness,** *n.*

keen² (kēn), *n.* **1.** a wailing lament for the dead. —*v.t., v.i.* **2.** to wail in lamentation for (the dead).

keep (kēp), *v.*, **kept, keep•ing,** *n.* —*v.t.* **1.** to retain in one's possession. **2.** to hold in a given place: *to keep mints in a dish.* **3.** to cause to continue in a given position, state, etc.: *to keep a light burning.* **4.** to maintain in good condition: *to keep meat by freezing it.* **5.** to detain. **6.** to maintain in one's service or for one's use: *to keep a chauffeur.* **7.** to take care of or support. **8.** to refrain from disclosing: *to keep a secret.* **9.** to restrain or prevent: *to keep a pipe from leaking.* **10.** to record regularly: *to keep attendance figures.* **11.** to obey or fulfill (a law, promise, etc.). **12.** to observe with formalities: *to keep the Sabbath.* **13.** to protect: *He kept her from harm.* —*v.i.* **14.** to continue in a specified position, state, etc.: *to keep cool.* **15.** to continue or go on: *Keep trying.* **16.** to stay in good condition. **17.** to refrain: *Try to keep from smiling.* **18. keep up, a.** to perform as swiftly or successfully as others. **b.** to continue. **c.** to maintain in good condition. **d.** to stay informed. —*n.* **19.** subsistence; support. **20.** the innermost and strongest structure of a medieval castle. —*Idiom.* **21. for keeps,** permanently. **22. keep to oneself, a.** to remain aloof from others. **b.** to hold as secret. —**keep′er,** *n.*

keep′ing, *n.* agreement or conformity: *actions in keeping with one's words.*

keep′sake′, *n.* anything kept, or given to be kept, as a token of friendship.

keg (keg), *n.* **1.** a small cask. **2.** a unit of weight equal to 100 pounds (45 kg), used for nails.

Kel•ler (kel′ər), *n.* **Helen (Adams),** 1880–1968, U.S. lecturer and author: blind and deaf from infancy.

Kel•logg (kel′ôg, -og), *n.* **1. Frank Billings,** 1856–1937, U.S. statesman: Secretary of State 1925–29; Nobel peace prize 1929. **2. W(ill) K(eith),** 1860–1951, U.S. philanthropist and manufacturer of prepared cereals.

Kel′logg-Bri•and′ Pact′ (kel′ôg brē änd′), *n.* a treaty (1928) renouncing war as an instrument of national policy and urging peaceful means for the settlement of international disputes.

Kel•ly (kel′ē), *n.* **Gene** (*Eugene Curran*), 1912–96, U.S. dancer, choreographer, actor, and director.

kelp (kelp), *n.* any large, brown, cold-water seaweed.

Kelt (kelt), *n.* CELT.

Kel•vin (kel′vin), *adj.* of or noting an absolute scale of temperature in which 0° equals -273.16° Celsius. [after 1st Baron *Kelvin* (1824–1907), English physicist]

Ken (ken), *n.* **Thomas,** 1631–1711, English clergyman and hymn writer.

Ke•nite (kē′nīt), *n.* one of a nomadic tribe who fought the Israelites. Num. 24:21–22.

Ken•ne•dy (ken′i dē), *n.* **1. John Fitzgerald,** 1917–63, 35th president of the U.S. 1961–63. **2. Robert Francis,** 1925–68, U.S. political leader and government official. **3. Cape,** former name (1963–73) of Cape CANAVERAL.

ken•nel (ken′l), *n., v.,* **-neled, -nel•ing** or (*esp. Brit.*) **-nelled, -nel•ling.** —*n.* **1.** a shelter for a dog or cat. **2.** Often, **-nels.** an establishment where dogs or cats are bred, trained, or boarded. —*v.t.* **3.** to put or keep in a kennel.

Kent (kent), *n.* **Rockwell,** 1882–1971, U.S. illustrator and painter.

Ken•tuck•y (kən tuk′ē), *n.* a state in the E central United States. 3,883,723. *Cap.:* Frankfort. *Abbr.:* KY, Ken., Ky. —**Ken•tuck′i•an,** *adj., n.*

Ken•ya (ken′yə, kēn′-), *n.* a republic in E Africa. 28,803,085. —**Ken′yan,** *adj., n.*

Kep•ler (kep′lər), *n.* **Johann,** 1571–1630, German astronomer.

kept (kept), *v.* **1.** pt. and pp. of KEEP. —*adj.* **2.** financially supported by another in exchange for sexual services.

ker•a•tin (ker′ə tin), *n.* a tough, insoluble protein that is the main constituent of hair, nails, horn, etc.

kerb (kûrb), *n. Brit.* CURB (def. 1).

ker•chief (kûr′chif, -chēf), *n.* **1.** a woman's square scarf worn as a covering for the head or neck. **2.** HANDKERCHIEF.

Kern (kûrn), *n.* **Jerome (David),** 1885–1945, U.S. composer.

ker•nel (kûr′nl), *n.* **1.** the softer, usu. edible part of a nut or fruit pit. **2.** the body of a seed within its husk. **3.** the central or most important part of anything.

ker•o•sene (ker′ə sēn′), *n.* a white oily liquid obtained by distilling petroleum, used as a fuel and cleaning solvent.

ke•ryg•ma (ki rig′mə), *n.* the preaching of the gospel of Christ. [< Gk *kḗrygma* proclamation, preaching] —**ker•yg•mat•ic** (ker′ig mat′ik), *adj.*

kes•trel (kes′trəl), *n.* any of various small falcons that hover as they hunt.

ketch (kech), *n.* a sailing ship rigged fore and aft on two masts.

ketch•up (kech′əp, kach′-), *n.* a condiment consisting of puréed tomatoes, onions, vinegar, sugar, and spices. [< Malay *kachap* fish sauce, perh. < dial. Chin]

ket•tle (ket′l), *n.* a metal container in which to boil liquids or cook foods.

ket′tle•drum′, *n.* a drum consisting of a hollow hemisphere of brass, copper, or fiberglass over which is stretched a skin.

Ke•tur•ah (ki tŏŏr′ə), *n.* the second wife of Abraham. Gen. 25:1.

key¹ (kē), *n., pl.* **keys,** *adj., v.,* **keyed, key•ing.** —*n.* **1.** a metal instrument inserted into a lock to move its bolt. **2.** any device resembling or functioning like a key. **3.** something that affords a means to achieve something else: *the key to happiness.* **4.** something that serves to clarify, solve, etc., as a list of answers to a test. **5.** one of a set of levers or buttons pressed by the fingers in operating a typewriter, computer, piano, etc. **6.** the principal tonality of a musical composition: *a symphony in the key of C minor.* **7.** degree of intensity, as of feeling. —*adj.* **8.** chief; major; essential. —*v.t.* **9.** to adjust (actions, speech, etc.) to a particular state or activity. **10.** to regulate the pitch of. **11.** to provide with a key. **12.** to keyboard: *to key in data.* **13. key up,** to increase tension in.

key² (kē), *n., pl.* **keys.** a reef or low island.

Key, *n.* **Francis Scott,** 1780–1843, U.S. lawyer: author of *The Star-Spangled Banner.*

key′board′, *n.* **1.** the row or set of keys on a piano, computer, etc. **2.** a musical instrument with a pianolike keyboard. —*v.t., v.i.* **3.** to enter (data) into a computer by means of a keyboard. —**key′board′er,** *n.*

key′hole′, *n.* a hole for inserting a key in a lock.

key′note′, *n., v.,* **-not•ed, -not•ing.** —*n.* **1.** the note on which a key or system of tones is founded; tonic. **2.** the basic idea, principle, or theme. —*v.t.* **3.** to deliver a keynote address at. —**key′not′er,** *n.*

key′note address′, *n.* a speech, as at a political convention, that presents important issues, policies, etc.

key′punch′, *n.* a machine, operated by a keyboard, for coding information by punching holes in cards. —**key′punch′er,** *n.*

key′stone′, *n.* **1.** the wedge-shaped piece at the summit of an arch. **2.** something on which associated things depend.

Key′ West′, *n.* an island off S Florida, in the Gulf of Mexico.

kg, kilogram.

KGB, the Soviet secret police responsible for intelligence and internal security. [< Russ, for *K(omitét) g(osudárstvennoĭ) b(ezopásnosti)* Committee for State Security]

Kha·cha·tu·ri·an (kä′chə tŏŏr′ē ən, kach′ə-), n. Aram Ilich, 1903–78, Armenian composer.

khak·i (kak′ē, kä′kē), n., pl. **-khak·is. 1.** a dull yellowish brown. **2.** a stout, twilled fabric of this color. **3.** Usu., **khakis.** a uniform or trousers made of khaki. —adj. **4.** made of khaki. [< Urdu < Pers khāki dusty]

khan (kän, kan), n. **1.** a title of rulers of the empire founded by Genghis Khan, and of the states that succeeded his empire. **2.** a title of respect used in numerous Asian countries.

Khar·kov (kär′kôf, -kof), n. a city in E Ukraine. 1,611,000.

Khar·toum (kär tŏŏm′), n. the capital of the Sudan, on the Nile. 476,218.

kHz, kilohertz.

KIA, killed in action.

kib·butz (ki bŏŏts′, -bŏŏts′), n., pl. **-but·zim** (-bŏŏt-sēm′). a collective, usu. agricultural settlement in Israel. [< ModHeb qibbūṣ lit., gathering]

kib·itz·er (kib′it sər), n. Informal. **1.** a spectator at a card game who gives unsolicited advice. **2.** a giver of unsolicited advice; busybody. —**kib′itz,** v.i.

ki·bosh (kī′bosh, ki bosh′), n. Slang. —**Idiom. put the kibosh on,** to put an end to; squelch; check.

kick (kik), v.t. **1.** to strike with the foot. **2.** to drive or force by or as if by kicks. **3.** Football. to score (a field goal) by kicking the ball. **4.** Slang. to give up (a habit). —v.i. **5.** to make a rapid, forceful thrust with the foot. **6.** to object or complain. **7.** (of a firearm) to recoil. **8. kick in,** to contribute as one's share. **9. ~ over,** (of an internal-combustion engine) to begin ignition. —n. **10.** the act of kicking. **11.** an objection or complaint. **12.** Slang. **a.** pleasurable excitement or stimulation. **b.** a strong but temporary interest: Photography is her latest kick. **13.** a recoil of a gun. —**kick′er,** n.

kick′back′, n. a portion of an income given to someone as payment for having made the income possible.

kick′off′, n. **1.** a kick that puts the ball into play in football or soccer. **2.** the start of something.

kick′stand′, n. a pivoting bar for holding a bicycle or motorcycle upright when not in use.

kick′y, adj., **-i·er, -i·est.** Slang. pleasurably exciting.

kid¹ (kid), n. **1.** Informal. a child. **2.** a young goat. **3.** leather made from the skin of a young goat.

kid² (kid), v.t., v.i., **kid·ded, kid·ding.** Informal. **1.** to tease. **2.** to deceive as a joke. —**kid′der,** n.

kid·die (kid′ē), n. Informal. a child.

Kid·dush (kid′əsh, ki dŏŏsh′), n. Judaism. a blessing recited over a cup of wine or over bread. [< Heb qiddūsh lit., sanctification]

kid·nap (kid′nap), v.t., **-napped** or **-naped, -nap·ping** or **-nap·ing.** to carry off (a person) by force or fraud, esp. for ransom. —**kid′nap·per, kid′nap·er,** n.

kid·ney (kid′nē), n., pl. **-neys. 1.** one of a pair of organs that filter waste from the blood and excrete uric acid or urea. **2.** an animal's kidney used as food. **3.** temperament. **4.** kind; sort.

kid′ney bean′, n. **1.** a bean plant cultivated in many varieties for its edible seeds. **2.** its mature seed.

kid′ney stone′, n. a mineral concretion formed abnormally in the kidney.

Ki·dron (kē′drən, kid′rən), n. a ravine E of Jerusalem: traditionally identified by Jewish, Christian, and Muslim religions as the Valley of Decision, the place of final judgment. Joel 3:2, 12. Also, **Kedron.**

kiel·ba·sa (kil bä′sə, kēl-), n., pl. **-sas, -sy** (-sē). a smoked Polish sausage.

Kier·ke·gaard (kēr′ki gärd′, -gôr′), n. Søren Aabye, 1813–55, Danish philosopher and theologian.

Ki·ev (kē′ef, -ev), n. the capital of Ukraine. 2,587,000. —**Ki′ev·an,** adj., n.

Ki·ga·li (kē gä′lē), n. the capital of Rwanda. 156,650.

Kil·i·man·ja·ro (kil′ə mən jär′ō), n. a volcanic mountain in NE Tanzania: highest peak in Africa. 19,321 ft. (5889 m).

kill (kil), v.t. **1.** to cause the death of; slay. **2.** to destroy; extinguish. **3.** to spend (time) unprofitably. **4.** Informal. to cause discomfort to. **5.** to cancel publication of. **6.** to defeat or veto (a legislative bill, etc.). **7.** to turn off: to kill an engine. —n. **8.** the act of killing, esp. game. **9.** an animal or animals killed. —**kill′er,** n.

kill′er in′stinct, n. a willingness to capitalize on another's weakness.

kill′er whale′, n. a large, predatory, black-and-white dolphin.

kill′ing, n. **1.** the act of a person or thing that kills. **2.** a quick, large profit. —adj. **3.** fatal. **4.** exhausting.

kill′-joy′, n. a person who spoils the pleasure of others.

kiln (kil, kiln), n. a furnace or oven for burning, baking, or drying something, esp. one for firing pottery.

ki·lo (kē′lō, kil′ō), n., pl. **-los. 1.** a kilogram. **2.** a kilometer.

kilo-, a combining form meaning thousand (kilowatt).

kil·o·byte (kil′ə bīt′), n. Computers. **1.** 1024 bytes. **2.** (loosely) 1000 bytes.

kil′o·cy·cle, n. KILOHERTZ: no longer in technical use.

kil′o·gram′, n. the basic unit of mass in the metric system, equal to 1000 grams.

kil′o·hertz′, n., pl. **-hertz, -hertz·es.** a unit of frequency equal to 1000 cycles per second.

kil·o·me·ter (ki lom′i tər, kil′ə mē′-), n. a unit of length equal to 1000 meters.

kil·o·ton (kil′ə tun′), n. **1.** a unit of weight equal to 1000 tons. **2.** an explosive force equal to that of 1000 tons of TNT.

kil′o·watt′, n. a unit of power equal to 1000 watts.

kilt (kilt), n. **1.** a pleated, knee-length tartan skirt worn by Scotsmen in the Highlands. **2.** a woman's skirt modeled on this.

kil·ter (kil′tər), n. good condition: The engine was out of kilter.

ki·mo·no (kə mō′nə, -nō), n., pl. **-nos. 1.** a loose, wide-sleeved Japanese robe, fastened with a broad sash. **2.** a woman's dressing gown.

kin (kin), n. all of a person's relatives.

-kin, a suffix meaning little or diminutive (lambkin).

kind¹ (kīnd), adj., **-er, -est.** gentle; considerate; benevolent.

kind² (kīnd), n. **1.** a class or group of animals, objects, etc., classified on the basis of common traits. **2.** nature or character. **3.** variety; sort. —**Idiom. 4. in kind, a.** in the same way. **b.** in goods or services rather than money. **5. kind of,** Informal. somewhat. —**Usage.** KIND (or SORT) as a modifier meaning "somewhat" is common in informal speech and writing, but a synonym such as RATHER, QUITE, or SOMEWHAT is preferred in formal use.

kin·der·gar·ten (kin′dər gär′tn, -dn), n. a class or school for young children, usu. five-year-olds. —**kin′der·gart′ner, kin′der·gar′ten·er** (-gärt′nər, -gärd′-), n. [< G]

kind′heart′ed, adj. having or showing kindness. —**kind′heart′ed·ly,** adv. —**kind′heart′ed·ness,** n.

kin·dle (kin′dl), v., **-dled, -dling.** —v.t. **1.** to set fire to or ignite. **2.** to excite or arouse. —v.i. **3.** to begin to burn. **4.** to become aroused or animated.

kin′dling, n. material that can be readily ignited, used in starting a fire.

kind′ly, adj., **-li·er, -li·est,** adv. —adj. **1.** kind or sympathetic. **2.** pleasant or beneficial. —adv. **3.** in a kind manner. **4.** cordially: We thank you kindly. **5.** obligingly; please: Kindly close the door. **6.** with liking; favorably: to take kindly to an idea. —**kind′li·ness,** n.

kind′ness, n. **1.** the state or quality of being kind. **2.** a kind act.

kin·dred (kin′drid), n. **1.** a person's relatives collectively; kin. —adj. **2.** related or similar.

ki·net·ic (ki net′ik, kī-), adj. of or caused by motion.

kin′folk′ or **-folks′,** n.pl. relatives or kindred.

King (king), *n.* **Martin Luther, Jr.,** 1929–68, U.S. Baptist minister: civil-rights leader.

king'dom (-dəm), *n.* **1.** a state having a king or queen as its head. **2.** anything constituting an independent realm: *the kingdom of thought.* **3.** one of the three broad divisions of natural objects: *the animal, vegetable, and mineral kingdoms.*

King'dom Hall', *n.* a meeting place of Jehovah's Witnesses.

king'fish'er, *n.* a fish- or insect-eating bird with a long, stout bill.

King' James' Ver'sion, *n.* an English version of the Bible prepared in England under James I and published in 1611. Also called the **Authorized Version.**

King' of kings' (or **Kings'**), *n.* **1.** Christ; Jesus. **2.** God; Jehovah.

king'pin, *n.* **1.** (in bowling) the pin at the center. **2.** *Informal.* a person or thing of chief importance.

Kings (kingz), *n.* (*used with a sing. v.*) either of two books of the Bible, I Kings or II Kings, which contain the history of the kings of Israel and Judah.

king'-size' or **-sized',** *adj.* larger or longer than the usual size.

Kings•ton (kingz'tən, king'stən), *n.* the capital of Jamaica. 600,000.

kink (kingk), *n.* **1.** a twist or curl, as in a thread or hair. **2.** a muscular stiffness or soreness, as in the neck. **3.** a flaw likely to hinder the operation of something. **4.** a mental twist; eccentricity. —*v.i., v.t.* **5.** to form or cause to form a kink or kinks. —**kink'y,** *adj.,* **-i•er, -i•est.**

Kinkaid' Act', *n.* an act of Congress (1904) providing for the granting of 640-acre homesteads to settlers in western Nebraska.

kins•folk (kinz'fōk'), *n.pl.* KINFOLK.

Kin•sha•sa (kin shä'sə), *n.* the capital of the Democratic Republic of the Congo. 2,653,558.

kin'ship, *n.* **1.** family relationship. **2.** affinity; likeness.

kins'man or **-wom'an,** *n., pl.* **-men** or **-wom•en.** a relative.

ki•osk (kē'osk, kē osk'), *n.* a small, open structure used as a newsstand, refreshment stand, etc. [< F *kiosque* stand in a public park « Turkish *köşk* < Pers *küshk* palace, villa]

Kip•ling (kip'ling), *n.* **(Joseph) Rud•yard** (rud'yərd), 1865–1936, English author.

kip•per (kip'ər), *v.t.* **1.** to cure (herring or salmon) by salting and drying or smoking. —*n.* **2.** a kippered fish.

Kir•ghi•zia (kir gē'zhə), *n.* former name of KYRGYZSTAN.

Ki•ri•ba•ti (kēr'ē bä'tē, kēr'ə bas'), *n.* a republic on a group of islands in the central Pacific Ocean. 66,250.

Kir•jath Ar•ba (kēr'jath är'bə), *n.* **1.** Hebron. Gen. 23:2. **2.** an Israeli settlement near Hebron.

kirk (kûrk, kirk), *n. Chiefly Scot.* a church.

Ki•shi•nev (kish'ə nef', -nôf', -nof'), *n.* the capital of Moldova. 565,000.

kis•met (kiz'mit, -met, kis'-), *n.* fate; destiny.

kiss (kis), *v.t., v.i.* **1.** to touch with the lips or join lips, as in affection, greeting, etc. **2.** to touch gently or lightly. —*n.* **3.** an act or instance of kissing. **4.** a slight touch. **5.** a chocolate candy. —**kiss'a•ble,** *adj.*

kiss'-and-tell', *adj.* disclosing secrets; gossipy.

kiss' of peace', *n.* **1.** a ceremonial greeting given as a token of Christian love. **2.** a ceremonial kiss formerly given, esp. at a baptism or Eucharistic service, as a token of Christian love and unity. Also called **pax.**

kit (kit), *n.* **1.** a set of tools or materials for a specific purpose: *a first-aid kit.* **2.** a container for these. **3.** a set of materials or parts from which something can be assembled. —*Idiom.* **4. the whole kit and caboodle,** all the persons or things concerned.

kitch•en (kich'ən), *n.* a room or place equipped for cooking or preparing food.

kitch'en cab'inet, *n.* a group of unofficial advisers on whom a head of government relies.

Kitch•e•ner (kich'ə nər), *n.* a city in S Ontario, in SE Canada. 150,604.

kitch'en•ette' (-ə net'), *n.* a very small, compact kitchen.

kite (kīt), *n.* **1.** a light frame covered with some thin material, to be flown in the wind at the end of a string. **2.** any of various slim, graceful hawks with long, pointed wings.

kith (kith), *n.* acquaintances, friends, or neighbors: *kith and kin.*

kitsch (kich), *n.* something of tawdry design or content created to appeal to undiscriminating taste. —**kitsch'y,** *adj.*

kit•ten (kit'n), *n.* a young cat. —**kit'ten•ish,** *adj.*

kit•ty[1] (kit'ē), *n., pl.* **-ties. 1.** a kitten. **2.** a pet name for a cat.

kit•ty[2] (kit'ē), *n., pl.* **-ties. 1.** a pool or reserve of money for a particular purpose. **2.** (in poker) the pot.

kit'ty-cor'nered or **-cor'ner,** *adj., adv.* CATER-CORNERED.

Kit'ty Hawk', *n.* a village in NE North Carolina: Wright brothers' airplane flight 1903.

ki•wi (kē'wē), *n., pl.* **-wis. 1.** any of several flightless birds of New Zealand. **2.** a brown, egg-sized berry with an edible, green pulp.

kiwi

K.J.V., King James Version.

KKK, Ku Klux Klan.

Klee (klā), *n.* **Paul,** 1879–1940, Swiss painter.

klep•to•ma•ni•a (klep'tə mā'nē ə), *n.* a compulsion to steal having no relation to need or the value of the object. —**klep'to•ma'ni•ac',** *n., adj.*

klieg' light' (klēg), *n.* a powerful arc light once widely used in motion-picture studios.

Klon•dike (klon'dīk), *n.* a region of the Yukon territory in NW Canada: gold rush 1897–98.

klutz (kluts), *n. Slang.* a clumsy or stupid person. —**klutz'y,** *adj.,* **-i•er, -i•est.** —**klutz'i•ness,** *n.*

km, kilometer.

knack (nak), *n.* **1.** a special skill or talent. **2.** a clever way of doing something.

knack•wurst (näk'wûrst, -woorst), *n.* a short, thick, highly seasoned sausage.

knap•sack (nap'sak'), *n.* a fabric or leather bag for carrying clothes or other supplies on the back.

knave (nāv), *n.* **1.** an unprincipled or dishonest person. **2.** (in cards) the jack. —**knav'er•y,** *n.* —**knav'ish,** *adj.*

knead (nēd), *v.t.* **1.** to work (dough, clay, etc.) into a uniform mixture by pressing and stretching. **2.** to manipulate by similar movements, as the body in a massage.

knee (nē), *n., v.,* **kneed, knee•ing.** —*n.* **1.** the joint of the human leg that allows for movement between the femur and tibia. **2.** something resembling a bent knee. —*v.t.* **3.** to strike or touch with the knee.

knee'cap', *n., v.,* **-capped, -cap•ping.** —*n.* **1.** the patella. —*v.t.* **2.** to cripple (a person) by shooting in the knee.

knee'-deep', *adj.* **1.** up to the knees. **2.** deeply involved: *knee-deep in trouble.*

knee'-jerk', *adj. Informal.* reacting in an automatic, habitual manner.

knee'-jerk' lib'eral, *n. Slang.* a political liberal who reacts without thinking.

kneel (nēl), *v.i.,* **knelt** or **kneeled, kneel•ing.** to go down or rest on the knees or a knee.

knell (nel), *n.* **1.** the sound made by a bell rung slowly, as at a funeral. **2.** a sound or sign announcing someone's death or the end of something. —*v.i.* **3.** (of a bell) to ring slowly. **4.** to give forth a mournful or ominous sound. —*v.t.* **5.** to proclaim or summon by a knell.

knelt (nelt), *v.* a pt. and pp. of KNEEL.

knew (nōō, nyōō), *v.* pt. of KNOW.

knick•ers (nik′ərz), *n.* (*used with a pl. v.*) loosefitting short trousers gathered in at the knees.

knick•knack (nik′nak′), *n.* an ornamental trinket.

knife (nīf), *n., pl.* **knives** (nīvz), *v.,* **knifed, knif• ing.** —*n.* **1.** a cutting instrument having a sharpedged blade fitted with a handle. **2.** any blade for cutting, as in a machine. —*v.t.* **3.** to cut or stab with a knife. **4.** to undermine in an underhanded way. —*Idiom.* **5. under the knife,** undergoing surgery.

knight (nīt), *n.* **1.** (in the Middle Ages) a man raised to honorable military rank and bound to chivalrous conduct. **2.** a man honored by a sovereign with a nonhereditary rank and dignity. **3.** a chess piece shaped like a horse's head. —*v.t.* **4.** to make (a man) a knight. —**knight′hood,** *n.* —**knight′ly,** *adj.*

knight′-er′rant, *n., pl.* **knights-errant.** a knight who traveled in search of adventures.

knish (knish), *n.* a baked turnover filled usu. with mashed potato.

knit (nit), *v.,* **knit•ted** or **knit, knit•ting,** *n.* —*v.t.* **1.** to make (a garment, fabric, etc.) by interlocking loops of yarn with needles. **2.** to join or grow together closely and firmly. **3.** to contract into wrinkles, as the brow. —*n.* **4.** a fabric or garment produced by knitting. —**knit′ter,** *n.*

knit′wear′, *n.* clothing made of knitted fabric.

knob (nob), *n.* **1.** a rounded projecting part forming a handle, as on a door, or a control device, as on a radio. **2.** a rounded lump or protuberance on the surface of something.

knock (nok), *v.i.* **1.** to strike a sounding blow. **2.** to strike in collision: *to knock into a table.* **3.** to make a pounding noise: *The engine is knocking.* —*v.t.* **4.** to give a sounding blow to. **5.** to make or drive by striking: *to knock a hole in the wall.* **6.** to strike (a thing) against something else. **7.** *Informal.* to criticize. **8. knock around** or **about,** to wander. **9. ~ down, a.** to cause to fall by striking. **b.** to dismantle. **c.** to lower (a price). **d.** to sell at auction. **10. ~ off, a.** to cease. **b.** *Informal.* to do or produce quickly or with ease. **c.** *Slang.* to murder. **d.** to deduct. **11. ~ out, a.** to defeat by a knockout. **b.** to make unconscious. **c.** to make exhausted. **d.** to damage or destroy. —*n.* **12.** the act or sound of knocking. **13.** a blow or thump. **14.** *Informal.* an adverse criticism. **15.** a pounding noise in an engine.

knock′er, *n.* **1.** one that knocks. **2.** a hinged knob, bar, etc., on a door, for use in knocking.

knock′-knee′, *n.* inward curvature of the legs at the knees. —**knock′-kneed′,** *adj.*

knock′out′, *n.* **1.** the act of knocking out or state of being knocked out. **2.** (in boxing) a blow that knocks an opponent to the canvas and immobilizes him for a certain time. **3.** *Informal.* a person or thing overwhelmingly attractive or successful.

knock•wurst (nok′wûrst, -wŏŏrst), *n.* KNACKWURST.

knoll (nōl), *n.* a small, rounded hill or mound.

knot (not), *n., v.,* **knot•ted, knot•ting.** —*n.* **1.** an interlacing of a cord, rope, etc., drawn tight into a knob. **2.** an ornamental bow of ribbon. **3.** a cluster of persons or things. **4.** the hard, cross-grained mass of wood where a branch joins a tree trunk. **5.** a part of this mass showing in a piece of lumber. **6.** a complicated problem. **7.** a unit of speed equal to one nautical mile, or about 1.15 statute miles per hour. **8.** a bond or tie: *the knot of matrimony.* —*v.t.* **9.** to form a knot in. —*v.i.* **10.** to become tied or tangled in a knot. **11.** to form knots. —**knot′ty,** *adj.,* **-ti•er, -ti•est.**

knot′hole′, *n.* a hole in a board or plank formed by the falling out of a knot.

know (nō), *v.,* **knew, known, know•ing.** —*v.t.* **1.** to perceive or understand as fact or truth. **2.** to have

fixed in the mind or memory. **3.** to be aware of. **4.** to be acquainted or familiar with. **5.** to understand from experience or practice: *to know how to make bread.* **6.** to be able to distinguish or recognize: *to know right from wrong.* —*v.i.* **7.** to have knowledge, as of fact or truth. **8.** to be aware, as of some occurrence. —*Idiom.* **9. in the know,** privy to information. —**know′a•ble,** *adj.*

know′-how′, *n.* knowledge of how to do something.

know′ing, *adj.* **1.** revealing knowledge of private information: *a knowing glance.* **2.** having knowledge or information. **3.** intentional; deliberate. —**know′- ing•ly,** *adv.*

know′-it-all′, *n.* a person who acts as though he or she knows a great deal.

knowl•edge (nol′ij), *n.* **1.** familiarity, understanding, or information gained by study or experience. **2.** the fact or state of knowing. **3.** something that is or may be known. **4.** the body of truths or facts accumulated in the course of time. **5.** the sum of what is known.

knowl′edge•a•ble (-i jə bəl), *adj.* possessing or exhibiting knowledge.

Knox (noks), *n.* **John,** c1510–72, Scottish religious reformer and historian.

Knox•ville (noks′vil), *n.* a city in E Tennessee. 169,311.

knuck•le (nuk′əl), *n., v.,* **-led, -ling.** —*n.* **1.** a joint of a finger, esp. one of the joints at the roots of the fingers. —*v.t.* **2.** to rub or press with the knuckles. **3. knuckle down,** to apply oneself earnestly. **4. ~ under,** to submit; yield.

knuck′le•head′, *n.* *Informal.* a stupid, inept person.

knurl (nûrl), *n.* **1.** one of a series of small ridges or beads, as on the edge of a thumbscrew for a firm grip. **2.** a knotty growth, as on a tree. —*v.t.* **3.** to make knurls on.

KO (*n.* kā′ō′, kā′ō′; *v.* kā′ō′), *n., pl.* **KOs** or **KO′s,** *v.,* **KO′d, KO′•ing.** —*n.* **1.** a knockout in boxing. —*v.t.* **2.** to knock out in boxing.

ko•a•la (kō ä′lə), *n., pl.* **-las.** a gray, tree-dwelling Australian marsupial.

koalas

Ko•be (kō′bē, -bā), *n.* a seaport on S Honshu, in S Japan. 1,413,000.

Ko•dá•ly (kō′dī, -dä ē), *n.* **Zoltán,** 1882–1967, Hungarian composer.

kohl•ra•bi (kōl rä′bē, -rab′ē), *n., pl.* **-bies.** a cultivated cabbage with an edible bulblike stem.

ko•la (kō′lə), *n., pl.* **-las. 1.** a tropical African tree grown for kola nuts. **2.** COLA[1].

ko′la nut′, *n.* the brown seed of the kola tree: its extract is used in soft drinks.

kook (kōōk), *n.* *Slang.* an eccentric, strange, or crazy person. —**kook′y,** *adj.,* **-i•er, -i•est.** —**kook′i•ness,** *n.*

ko•peck (kō′pek), *n.* a monetary unit of Russia, the Soviet Union, and its successor states, equal to $\frac{1}{100}$ of the ruble.

Ko•ran (kə rän′, -ran′, kô-), *n.* the sacred text of Islam. [< Ar *qur'ān* book, reading]

Ko•re•a (kə rē′ə), *n.* **1. Democratic People's Republic of,** official name of NORTH KOREA. **2. Republic of,** official name of SOUTH KOREA.

Ko•re•an (kə rē′ən), *n.* **1.** a native or inhabitant of

Korea. **2.** the language of this people. —*adj.* **3.** of Korea, the Koreans, or their language.

Kore′an War′, *n.* the war (1950–53) between North Korea, aided by Communist China, and South Korea, aided by the U.S. and other United Nations members.

ko•sher (kō′shər), *adj.* **1. a.** fit to be eaten or used according to Jewish dietary laws. **b.** adhering to these laws. **2.** *Informal.* proper; legitimate.

kow•tow (kou′tou′, -tou′, kō′-), *v.i.* **1.** to act in a fawning or servile manner. **2.** to touch the forehead to the ground while kneeling, as an act of worship, respect, etc. [< Chin *kòutóu* lit., knock (one's) head]

KP (kā′pē′), *n.* **1.** enlisted soldiers detailed to assist in kitchen duties. **2.** their work. [*k(itchen) p(olice)*]

Kr, *Chem. Symbol.* krypton.

Kra•ków (krak′ou), *n.* a city in S Poland. 716,000.

Krem•lin (krem′lin), *n.* **1. the Kremlin,** the government of Russia or of the Soviet Union. **2.** the citadel of Moscow, housing the government offices.

Krish•na (krish′nə), *n.* **1.** an avatar of Vishnu and one of the most popular of Hindu deities. **2.** Formerly, **Kistna.** a river in S India, flowing E from the Western Ghats to the Bay of Bengal. 800 mi. (1290 km) long.

kro•na (krō′nə), *n., pl.* **-nor** (-nôr). the basic monetary unit of Sweden.

kró•na (krō′nə), *n., pl.* **-nur** (-nər). the basic monetary unit of Iceland.

kro•ne (krō′nə), *n., pl.* **-ner** (-nər). the basic monetary unit of Denmark and Norway.

kryp•ton (krip′ton), *n.* an inert gaseous element, present in very small amounts in the atmosphere. *Symbol:* Kr; *at. wt.:* 83.80; *at. no.:* 36.

KS, Kansas.

kt., **1.** karat. **2.** kiloton. **3.** knot.

Kua•la Lum•pur (kwä′lə loo͞m poo͞r′), *n.* the capital of Malaysia. 937,875.

ku•dos (ko͞o′dōz, -dōs, -dos, kyo͞o′-), *n.* honor; glory; acclaim.

kud•zu (ko͞od′zo͞o), *n., pl.* **-zus.** a fast-growing vine, planted for fodder and to retain soil.

Ku Klux Klan (ko͞o′ kluks′ klan′), *n.* **1.** a secret, chiefly antiblack, terrorist organization in the southern U.S., active after the Civil War. **2.** a secret organization founded in 1915 and directed against blacks, Catholics, Jews, and other groups.

kum•quat (kum′kwot), *n.* a small, orange-colored citrus fruit with a sweet rind and acid pulp.

kung fu (kung′ fo͞o′, ko͞ong′), *n.* a Chinese martial art based on the use of fluid movements of the arms and legs. [< Chin *gōngfú* lit., skill]

Kurd (kûrd, ko͞ord), *n.* a member of a people of SW Asia, the principal inhabitants of Kurdistan.

Kur•di•stan (kûr′də stan′, -stän′), *n.* a mountain and plateau region in SE Turkey, NW Iran, and N Iraq, inhabited largely by Kurds.

Ku•wait (ko͞o wāt′), *n.* **1.** a sovereign monarchy in NE Arabia. 2,076,805. **2.** its capital. 167,750. —**Ku•wai′ti** (-wā′tē), *n., pl.* **-tis,** *adj.*

kW or **kw,** kilowatt.

Kwang•chow (*Chin.* gwäng′jō′), *n.* GUANGZHOU.

Kwan•zaa or **Kwan•za** (kwän′zə), *n., pl.* **-zaas** or **-zas.** a harvest festival celebrated from Dec. 26 until Jan. 1 in some African-American communities. [< Swahili *kwanza* first]

KY or **Ky.,** Kentucky.

Kyo•to (kē ō′tō, kyō′-), *n.* a city on S Honshu, in central Japan. 1,472,993.

Kyr•gyz•stan (kēr′gi stan′, -stän′), *n.* a republic in central Asia: formerly a part of the USSR. 4,540,185. Formerly, **Kirghizia.**

Kyr•i•e e•le•i•son (kēr′ē ā′ e lā′ə sôn′, -son′, -sən;), *n.* **1.** the brief response or petition in services in various Christian Churches, beginning with the words, "Lord, have mercy upon us." **2.** Also called **Kyr′i•e′.** a musical setting of this. [< Late Gk *Kýrie eléēson* Lord, have mercy]

Kyu•shu (kē o͞o′sho͞o, kyo͞o′-), *n.* an island in SW Japan.

L

L, l (el), *n., pl.* **Ls** or **L's, ls** or **l's.** **1.** the 12th letter of the English alphabet, a consonant. **2.** something shaped like an L.

L or **L.,** **1.** lake. **2.** large. **3.** Latin. **4.** left. **5.** length. **6.** *Brit.* pound. [< L *lībra*] **7.** long.

L, *Symbol.* the Roman numeral for 50.

l. or **l,** **1.** left. **2.** length. **3.** *pl.* **ll.** line. **4.** liter.

la (lä), *n. Music.* the sixth tone of a diatonic scale.

LA or **La.,** Louisiana.

La, *Chem. Symbol.* lanthanum.

L.A., **1.** Latin America. **2.** Los Angeles.

lab (lab), *n.* laboratory.

La•ban (lā′bən), *n.* the father of Leah and Rachel and the father-in-law of Jacob. Gen. 24:29; 29:16–30.

la•bel (lā′bəl), *n., v.,* **-beled, -bel•ing** or (*esp. Brit.*) **-belled, -bel•ling.** —*n.* **1.** a slip of paper or other material attached to something to indicate its manufacturer, nature, destination, etc. **2.** a short word or phrase descriptive of a person, group, etc. —*v.t.* **3.** to affix a label to. **4.** to designate or describe by or on a label.

la•bi•al (lā′bē əl), *adj.* **1.** of the lips or labia. **2.** (of a speech sound) articulated using one or both lips, as (p), (v), (m), or (w).

la•bile (lā′bəl, -bīl), *adj.* apt to change.

la•bi•um (lā′bē əm), *n., pl.* **-bi•a** (-bē ə). **1.** a lip or liplike part. **2.** any of the folds of skin bordering the vulva.

la•bor (lā′bər), *n.* **1.** productive activity, esp. for economic gain. **2.** the body of persons engaged in such activity, esp. those working for wages. **3.** physical or mental work; toil. **4.** a job or task. **5.** the uterine contractions of childbirth. —*v.i.* **6.** to perform labor. **7.** to strive, as toward a goal. **8.** to move slowly and with effort. **9.** to function at a disadvantage: *to labor under a misapprehension.* **10.** to undergo childbirth. —*v.t.* **11.** to develop in excessive detail: *Don't labor the point.* —*Idiom.* **12. labor of love, a.** a task done for satisfaction rather than for profit. **b.** labor done out of the love of God. Also, *esp. Brit.,* **la′bour.** —**la′bor•er,** *n.*

lab•o•ra•to•ry (lab′rə tôr′ē, lab′ər ə-), *n., pl.* **-ries.** a place equipped to conduct scientific experiments, tests, etc.

La′bor Day′, *n.* a legal holiday observed on the first Monday in September in honor of labor.

la′bored, *adj.* done with difficulty; strained; forced: *labored breathing.*

la•bo•ri•ous (lə bôr′ē əs), *adj.* **1.** requiring much work or exertion. **2.** industrious. —**la•bo′ri•ous•ly,** *adv.*

la′bor un′ion, *n.* an organization of workers for mutual aid and protection, esp. by collective bargaining.

Lab•ra•dor (lab′rə dôr′), *n.* **1.** a peninsula in E Canada between Hudson Bay and the Atlantic, containing the provinces of Newfoundland and Quebec. **2.** the E portion of this peninsula, constituting the mainland part of Newfoundland. —**Lab′ra•dor′e•an, Lab′ra•dor′i•an,** *adj., n.*

Lab′rador retriev′er, *n.* one of a breed of retrievers with a short, dense black, yellow, or chocolate coat.

la•bur•num (lə bûr′nəm), *n.* a poisonous tree or shrub with drooping clusters of yellow flowers.

lab•y•rinth (lab′ə rinth), *n.* an intricate combination of paths or passages in which it is difficult to find one's way. —**lab′y•rin′thine** (-rin′thin, -thīn), *adj.*

labyrinth

lac (lak), *n.* a resinous deposit secreted on certain S Asian trees by a scale insect: used in varnishes.

lace (lās), *n., v.,* **laced, lac•ing.** —*n.* **1.** a netlike ornamental fabric made of threads. **2.** a string for holding or drawing together opposite edges. —*v.t.* **3.** to fasten by means of a lace. **4.** to interlace; intertwine. **5.** to beat; thrash. —*v.i.* **6.** to attack physically or verbally (usu. fol. by *into*). —**lac′y,** *adj.,* -i•er, -i•est.

lac•er•ate (las′ə rāt′), *v.t.* -at•ed, -at•ing. to tear roughly. —**lac′er•a′tion,** *n.*

La•chish (lā′kish), *n.* a Canaanite city captured by Joshua. Josh. 10:31–34.

lach•ry•mal (lak′rə məl), *adj.* **1.** of or characterized by tears. **2.** LACRIMAL.

lach′ry•mose′ (-mōs′), *adj.* **1.** tending to cause tears; mournful. **2.** given to shedding tears readily.

lack (lak), *n.* **1.** deficiency or absence of something needed or desirable. **2.** something missing or wanted. —*v.t., v.i.* **3.** to be wanting or deficient (in).

lack•a•dai•si•cal (lak′ə dā′zi kəl), *adj.* being without vigor or spirit; listless. —**lack′a•dai′si•cal•ly,** *adv.*

lack•ey (lak′ē), *n., pl.* -eys. **1.** a servile follower. **2.** a liveried manservant.

lack′lus′ter, *adj.* lacking brilliance or vitality.

la•con•ic (lə kon′ik), *adj.* using few words; terse. —**la•con′i•cal•ly,** *adv.*

lac•quer (lak′ər), *n.* **1.** a protective coating consisting of a resin, cellulose ester, or both, dissolved in a volatile solvent. **2.** any of various resinous varnishes, esp. one obtained from a Japanese tree. —*v.t.* **3.** to coat with lacquer.

lac•ri•mal (lak′rə məl), *adj.* of or situated near the glands that secrete tears.

la•crosse (lə krôs′, -kros′), *n.* a game played by two teams using a small ball and long-handled sticks with netted pockets. [< CanF: lit., the crook]

lac•tate (lak′tāt), *v.i.,* -tat•ed, -tat•ing. to secrete milk. —**lac•ta′tion,** *n.*

lac′te•al (-tē əl), *adj.* of, consisting of, or resembling milk.

lac′tic, *adj.* of or obtained from milk.

lac′tic ac′id, *n.* a syrupy liquid produced in the fermentation of milk or carbohydrates.

lac′tose (-tōs), *n.* a sweet crystalline substance present in milk, used in infant foods, confections, etc.

la•cu•na (lə kyōō′nə), *n., pl.* -nae (-nē), -nas. a gap or missing part, as in a manuscript.

lad (lad), *n.* a boy or youth.

lad•der (lad′ər), *n.* **1.** a structure for climbing, consisting of two sidepieces between which a series of rungs are set. **2.** a graded series of stages or levels.

lade (lād), *v.t., v.i.,* **lad•ed, lad•en** or **lad•ed, lad•ing. 1.** to load (a ship or cargo). **2.** to ladle (a liquid).

lad•en (lād′n), *adj.* burdened.

lad•ing (lā′ding), *n.* a load; cargo.

la•dle (lād′l), *n., v.,* -**dled, -dling.** —*n.* **1.** a long-handled utensil with a cup-shaped bowl for dipping or conveying liquids. —*v.t.* **2.** to dip or convey with a ladle.

la•dy (lā′dē), *n., pl.* -dies, *adj.* —*n.* **1.** a woman who is refined, polite, and well-spoken. **2.** a woman of high social position or economic class. **3.** any woman. **4.** (*cap.*) a British title for the wives or daughters of certain nobles. —**Usage.** In the meanings "refined, polite woman" and "woman of high social position" the noun LADY is the parallel of *gentleman*. Except in chivalrous or literary contexts, the singular is now usu. perceived as rude: *Where do you want the air conditioner, lady?* Other uses that are commonly disliked include LADY in phrases referring to occupation or position (*cleaning lady; forelady*) and as a modifier (*lady doctor*). Increasingly, sex-neutral terms replace LADY (*cleaner; supervisor*). When it is relevant to specify the sex of the performer or practitioner, *woman* rather than LADY is used, the parallel term being *man*: *Men doctors outnumber women doctors on the staff by three to one.* See also -PERSON, -WOMAN.

la′dy•bug′, *n.* any of numerous small, round, often brightly colored and spotted beetles.

la′dy•fin′ger, *n.* a small finger-shaped sponge cake.

la′dy-in-wait′ing, *n., pl.* **la•dies-in-wait•ing.** a lady who is in attendance upon a queen or princess.

la′dy•like′, *adj.* befitting a lady; well-bred; proper.

la′dy•love′, *n.* a sweetheart.

la′dy•ship′, *n.* **1.** (*often cap.*) the form used in speaking of or to a woman having the title of *Lady* (usu. prec. by *her* or *your*). **2.** the rank of a lady.

la′dy's-slip′per or **la′dy-slip′per,** *n.* an orchid having a slipper-shaped flower lip.

La′dy with′ the Lamp′, *n.* epithet of Florence Nightingale.

La•fa•yette (laf′ē et′, laf′ā-, lä′fē-, -fä-), *n.* **Marie Joseph Paul Yves Roch Gilbert du Motier, Marquis de,** 1757–1834, French statesman and general.

La Fon•taine (lä′ fon ten′, -tän′), *n.* **Jean de** (zhän), 1621–95, French poet and fabulist.

lag (lag), *v.,* **lagged, lag•ging,** *n.* —*v.i.* **1.** to fail to maintain a desired pace or speed. **2.** to decrease gradually; flag. —*n.* **3.** a lagging or falling behind. **4.** an interval of time.

la•ger (lä′gər, lô′-), *n.* a light beer aged from six weeks to six months.

lag•gard (lag′ərd), *n.* **1.** one that lags. —*adj.* **2.** moving or responding slowly. —**lag′gard•ly,** *adj., adv.*

la•gniappe or **-gnappe** (lan yap′, lan′yap), *n.* **1.** a small gift given with a purchase. **2.** a gratuity.

la•goon (lə gōōn′), *n.* **1.** an area of shallow water separated from the sea by low sand dunes. **2.** any pondlike body of water, esp. one connected with a larger body of water.

La•gos (lā′gōs, lä′gos), *n.* a seaport in Nigeria: former capital. 1,097,000.

La•hore (lə hôr′), *n.* a city in NE Pakistan. 2,922,000.

laid (lād), *v.* pt. and pp. of LAY¹.

laid′-back′, *adj. Informal.* relaxed; easygoing.

lain (lān), *v.* pp. of LIE².

lair (lâr), *n.* a den or retreat, esp. of a wild animal.

lais•sez faire (les′ā fâr′), *n.* the theory that government should intervene as little as possible in the direction of economic affairs. [< F: lit., allow to act]

la•i•ty (lā′i tē), *n.* **1.** the body of religious worshipers, as distinguished from the clergy. **2.** the people outside of a particular profession.

lake (lāk), *n.* **1.** an inland body of water of considerable size. **2.** a pool of any liquid, as oil.

Lake′wood′, *n.* a city in central Colorado. 126,031.

lal•ly•gag (lä′lē gag′, lal′ē-), *v.i.,* **-gagged, -gag•ging.** *Informal.* to spend time idly; loaf.

lam (lam), *n., v.,* **lammed, lam•ming.** *Slang.* —*n.* **1.**

a hasty escape; flight. —*v.i.* **2.** to escape; flee. —*Idiom.* **3.** **on the lam,** in flight from the police.

la•ma (läⁱmə), *n., pl.* **-mas.** a monk in Lamaism.

La′ma•ism, *n.* the Buddhism of Tibet and Mongolia. —**La′ma•ist,** *n.*

la′ma•ser′y (-ser′ē), *n., pl.* **-ser•ies.** a monastery of lamas.

La•maze′ meth′od (lə mäz′), *n.* a method by which an expectant mother is prepared for childbirth by education, breathing exercises, etc.

lamb (lam), *n.* **1.** a young sheep. **2.** the meat of a young sheep. **3.** a person who is gentle, meek, or innocent.

lam•baste (lam bāst′, -bast′), *v.t.,* **-bast•ed, -bast•ing.** *Informal.* **1.** to beat severely. **2.** to reprimand harshly.

lamb•da (lamⁱdə), *n., pl.* **-das.** the 11th letter of the Greek alphabet (Λ, λ).

lam•bent (lamⁱbənt), *adj.* **1.** moving lightly over a surface: *lambent tongues of flame.* **2.** dealing lightly and gracefully with a subject: *lambent wit.* **3.** softly bright or radiant. —**lamⁱben•cy,** *n.* —**lamⁱbent•ly,** *adv.*

lamb•kin (lamⁱkin), *n.* a little lamb.

Lamb′ of God′, *n.* Jesus Christ. John 1:29, 36.

lame (lām), *adj.,* **lam•er, lam•est,** *v.,* **lamed, lam•ing.** —*adj.* **1.** crippled or physically disabled, esp. in the foot or leg. **2.** stiff and sore. **3.** weak; inadequate: *lame excuses.* —*v.t.* **4.** to make lame or defective. —**lameⁱly,** *adv.* —**lameⁱness,** *n.*

la•mé (la mā′, lä-), *n., pl.* **-més.** an ornamental fabric interwoven with metallic threads.

lameⁱbrain′, *n. Informal.* a stupid person.

lame′ duck′, *n.* an elected official who is completing a term after the election of a successor.

la•ment (lə mentⁱ), *v.t., v.i.* **1.** to express grief or regret (for or over). —*n.* **2.** a vocal expression of grief. **3.** an elegy; dirge. —**la•mentⁱa•ble,** *adj.* —**lam•en•taⁱtion** (lamⁱən tāⁱshən), *n.*

Lam•en•ta•tions (lamⁱən tāⁱshənz), *n.* (*used with a sing. v.*) a book of the Bible, traditionally ascribed to Jeremiah.

lam•i•na (lamⁱə nə), *n., pl.* **-nae** (-nē′), **-nas.** a thin plate, scale, or layer. —**lamⁱi•nar,** *adj.*

lam•i•nate (*v.* lamⁱə nāt′; *adj.* -nāt′, -nit), *v.,* **-nat•ed, -nat•ing,** *adj.* —*v.t.* **1.** to construct from layers of material bonded together. **2.** to cover with laminae. —*adj.* **3.** Also, **lamⁱi•natⁱed.** composed of or having laminae. —**lamⁱi•naⁱtion,** *n.*

lamp (lamp), *n.* **1.** a device furnishing artificial light, as by electricity or gas. **2.** a device furnishing heat, ultraviolet, or other radiation.

lampⁱblack′, *n.* a fine black pigment consisting of almost pure carbon.

lam•poon (lam pōōn′), *n.* **1.** a broad, often harsh satire directed against an individual or institution. —*v.t.* **2.** to ridicule in a lampoon.

lampⁱpost′, *n.* a post supporting an outdoor lamp.

lam•prey (lamⁱprē), *n., pl.* **-preys.** an eellike jawless fish with a round, sucking mouth.

LAN (lan), *n.* LOCAL-AREA NETWORK.

Lan•cas•ter (langⁱkə stər), *n.* a member of the English royal family that reigned 1399–1461.

lance (lans, läns), *n., v.,* **lanced, lanc•ing.** —*n.* **1.** a long wooden spear with a metal head. **2.** LANCER. **3.** LANCET. —*v.t.* **4.** to open with a lancet. **5.** to pierce with a lance.

Lan•ce•lot (lanⁱsə lət, -lot′, län′-), *n.* **Sir,** the greatest of King Arthur's knights.

lancⁱer, *n.* a cavalry soldier armed with a lance.

lan•cet (lanⁱsit, län′-), *n.* a sharp-pointed surgical instrument, usu. with two edges.

land (land), *n.* **1.** any part of the earth's surface not covered by water. **2.** an area of ground: *arable land.* **3.** any part of the earth's surface that can be owned as property. **4.** a region or country. —*v.t.* **5.** to bring to or set on land. **6.** to bring to a particular place or condition: *His behavior will land him in jail.* **7.** *Informal.* to secure or gain: *to land a job.* —*v.i.* **8.** to come to land or shore. **9.** to go or come ashore from

a ship. **10.** to alight upon a surface. **11.** to come to rest or arrive in a particular place or condition.

landⁱed, *adj.* **1.** owning land: *landed gentry.* **2.** consisting of land: *landed property.*

landⁱfall′, *n.* **1.** an approach to or sighting of land. **2.** the land sighted or reached.

landⁱfill′, *n.* **1.** a low area of land that is built up from deposits of solid refuse in layers covered by soil. **2.** the solid refuse itself.

land′ grant′, *n.* a tract of land given by the government, as for a college or railroad.

landⁱhold′er, *n.* a holder, owner, or occupant of land.

landⁱing, *n.* **1.** the act of one that lands. **2.** a place where persons or goods are landed. **3.** the level floor between flights of stairs.

landⁱing gear′, *n.* the wheels, floats, etc., of an aircraft, upon which it lands and moves on ground or water.

landⁱla′dy, *n., pl.* **-dies.** a woman who owns and leases apartments, houses, land, etc., to others.

landⁱlocked′, *adj.* **1.** shut in completely, or almost completely, by land: *a landlocked bay.* **2.** having no direct access to the sea: *a landlocked country.* **3.** living in waters shut off from the sea, as some fish.

landⁱlord′, *n.* **1.** a person or organization that owns and leases land, buildings, apartments, etc. **2.** a person who runs an inn.

landⁱlub′ber (-lubⁱər), *n.* an unseasoned sailor; someone unfamiliar with the sea.

landⁱmark′, *n.* **1.** a prominent object on land that serves as a guide. **2.** a building or site of historical or cultural importance. **3.** a significant or historic event, achievement, etc.

landⁱmass′, *n.* a large area of land having a distinct identity, as a continent.

land′ of′fice, *n.* a government office for the transaction of business relating to public lands.

land′-of′fice busi′ness, *n.* a booming business.

Land′ of the Mid′night Sun′, *n.* **1.** a country containing land within the Arctic Circle where there is a midnight sun in midsummer. **2.** LAPLAND.

Land′ of the Ris′ing Sun′, *n.* JAPAN.

landⁱscape′ (-skāp′), *n., v.,* **-scaped, -scap•ing.** —*n.* **1.** an expanse of natural scenery that can be seen from a single viewpoint. **2.** a picture representing such scenery. —*v.t.* **3.** to improve the appearance of (an area of land), as by planting shrubs. —**landⁱscap′er,** *n.*

landⁱslide′, *n.* **1.** the sliding of a mass of soil or rock from a steep slope. **2.** the mass itself. **3.** an overwhelming victory, esp. in an election.

landⁱward′ (-wərd), *adv.* **1.** Also, **landⁱwards.** toward the land. —*adj.* **2.** lying or tending toward the land.

lane (lān), *n.* **1.** a narrow way or passage, as between houses. **2.** any well-defined path, route, or channel.

lan•guage (langⁱgwij), *n.* **1.** a body of words and systems for their use common to a people of the same community or nation. **2.** communication using a system of vocal sounds or written symbols in conventional ways. **3.** any system of symbols, sounds, or gestures used for communication. **4.** the vocabulary used by a particular group. **5.** a set of symbols and syntactic rules by means of which a computer can be given directions. [< AF < L *lingua* language, tongue]

lan•guid (langⁱgwid), *adj.* **1.** lacking in vigor or vitality. **2.** lacking in spirit or interest. **3.** drooping from weakness or fatigue.

lan•guish (-gwish), *v.i.* **1.** to be or become weak; droop. **2.** to suffer neglect or hardship: *to languish in prison.* **3.** to pine; long. **4.** to assume an expression of sentimental melancholy.

lan′guor (-gər), *n.* **1.** lack of energy or vitality. **2.** lack of spirit or interest. —**lan′guor•ous,** *adj.*

lank (langk), *adj.,* **-er, -est.** **1.** (of hair) straight and limp. **2.** lean; thin.

lankⁱy, *adj.,* **-i•er, -i•est.** ungracefully tall and thin. —**lankⁱi•ness,** *n.*

lan•o•lin (lan′l in), *n.* a fatty substance extracted from wool, used in ointments, cosmetics, etc.

Lan•sing (lan′sing), *n.* the capital of Michigan. 119,590.

lan•tern (lan′tərn), *n.* a portable, transparent case for enclosing and protecting a light.

lan′tern jaw′, *n.* a long, thin jaw. —**lan′tern-jawed′**, *adj.*

lan•tha•num (lan′thə nəm), *n.* a rare-earth metallic element allied to aluminum. *Symbol:* La; *at. wt.:* 138.91; *at. no.:* 57.

lan•yard (lan′yərd), *n.* a short rope used on ships to secure riggings.

La•od•i•ce•a (lā od′ə sē′ə, lā′ə də-), *n.* ancient name of Latakia: the site of one of the seven churches of Asia (Rev. 1:11).

La•os (lä′ōs), *n.* a country in SE Asia. 5,116,959. —**La•o•tian** (lā ō′shən), *n., adj.*

Lao-tzu or **Lao-tse** or **Lao•zi** (lou′dzu′), *n.* 6th-century B.C. Chinese philosopher; reputed founder of Taoism.

lap¹ (lap), *n.* **1.** the front part of the human body from the waist to the knees when in a sitting position. **2.** the part of the clothing that covers this. **3.** a place or situation of rest or nurture: *the lap of luxury.* **4.** an area of care, charge, or control: *They dropped the problem right in my lap.* **5.** a part of a garment that extends over another.

lap² (lap), *v.*, **lapped, lap•ping,** *n.* —*v.t.* **1.** to fold over or around something. **2.** to enwrap in something. **3.** to lay (something) partly over something underneath. **4.** to overlap. **5.** to get a lap ahead of (a competitor) in racing. —*v.i.* **6.** to fold or wind around something. **7.** to extend beyond a limit. —*n.* **8.** the act of lapping. **9.** a complete circuit of a course in racing. **10.** an overlapping part.

lap³ (lap), *v.*, **lapped, lap•ping,** *n.* —*v.t., v.i.* **1.** (of water) to wash against (something) with a light, splashing sound. **2.** to take in (liquid) with the tongue. **3. lap up,** to receive enthusiastically. —*n.* **4.** the act or sound of lapping.

La Paz (lə päz′, päs′), *n.* a city in and the administrative capital of Bolivia. 992,592.

lap′board′, *n.* a board held on the lap and used as a table or writing surface.

lap′ dog′, *n.* a small dog that can be held in the lap.

la•pel (lə pel′), *n.* the front part of a garment that is folded back and forms a continuous piece with the collar.

lap•i•dar•y (lap′i der′ē), *n., pl.* **-dar•ies.** a worker who cuts, polishes, and engraves precious stones.

lap•in (lap′in), *n.* rabbit fur, esp. when trimmed and dyed.

lap•is laz•u•li (lap′is laz′ŏŏ lē, -lī′, laz′yŏŏ-), *n., pl.* **-lis. 1.** a deep blue semiprecious gemstone. **2.** a sky-blue color; azure.

Lap•land (lap′land′), *n.* a region in N Norway, N Sweden, and N Finland.

Lapp (lap), *n.* a member of a people inhabiting Lapland. Also called **Lap′land′er.**

lap•pet (lap′it), *n.* a small flap or loosely hanging part of a garment or headdress.

lapse (laps), *n., v.*, **lapsed, laps•ing.** —*n.* **1.** a slip or error, often of a trivial sort. **2.** an interval of time. **3.** a moral fall. **4.** a decline to a lower condition or degree. **5.** the termination of a right or privilege, as through neglect to exercise it. —*v.i.* **6.** to fall or deviate from a previous standard. **7.** to come to an end: *We let our subscription lapse.* **8.** to fall, slip, or sink: *to lapse into silence.* **9.** to fall spiritually. **10.** to pass away, as time. **11.** to become void.

lap′top′, *n.* a portable, usu. battery-powered microcomputer small enough to rest on the lap.

lap′wing′, *n.* any of several large plovers of Eurasia and N Africa, having a long, upcurved crest.

lar•board (lär′bōrd′, -bərd), *n., adj. Naut. Obs.* PORT².

lar•ce•ny (lär′sə nē), *n., pl.* **-nies.** the wrongful taking of the personal goods of another; theft. —**lar′ce•nist,** *n.* —**lar′ce•nous,** *adj.*

larch (lärch), *n.* **1.** a deciduous conifer yielding a tough, durable wood. **2.** its wood.

lard (lärd), *n.* **1.** the rendered fat of hogs. —*v.t.* **2.** to insert strips of fat in (lean meat) before cooking. **3.** to supplement or enrich: *a literary work larded with mythological allusions.*

lar•der (lär′dər), *n.* **1.** a room or place where food is kept; pantry. **2.** a supply of food.

La•re•do (lə rā′dō), *n.* a city in S Texas. 149,914.

large (lärj), *adj.*, **larg•er, larg•est. 1.** of more than average size, quantity, degree, etc. **2.** on a great scale. **3.** of great scope or range. —*Idiom.* **4.** at **large,** a. not incarcerated. **b.** as a whole; in general. **c.** Also **at-large.** representing the whole of a political division rather than one part of it. —**large′ness,** *n.*

large′ cal′orie, *n.* See under CALORIE.

large′heart′ed, *adj.* having or showing generosity or kindness.

large′ intes′tine, *n.* See under INTESTINE.

large′ly, *adv.* **1.** to a great extent; generally. **2.** in great quantity.

large′-scale′, *adj.* **1.** very extensive. **2.** made to a large scale.

lar•gess or **-gesse** (lär jes′, lär′jis), *n.* **1.** generous giving of gifts. **2.** the gift or gifts so given.

lar•go (lär′gō), *adj., adv. Music.* in a slow, dignified style.

lar•i•at (lar′ē ət), *n.* **1.** a lasso. **2.** a rope used to picket grazing animals.

lark¹ (lärk), *n.* any of numerous, chiefly Old World songbirds, esp. the skylark.

lark² (lärk), *n.* **1.** a merry, carefree adventure. —*v.i.* **2.** to have fun; frolic.

lark′spur′, *n.* any of several plants characterized by the spur-shaped formation of the calyx and petals.

lar•va (lär′və), *n., pl.* **-vae** (-vē). **1.** the immature, wingless, feeding stage of an insect that undergoes complete metamorphosis. **2.** any animal in an analogous immature form. —**lar′val,** *adj.*

lar•yn•gi•tis (lar′ən jī′tis), *n.* inflammation of the larynx, often with accompanying loss of voice.

lar•ynx (lar′ingks), *n., pl.* **la•ryn•ges** (lə rin′jēz), **lar•ynx•es.** a muscular structure at the upper part of the trachea, in which the vocal cords are located. —**la•ryn•ge•al** (lə rin′jē əl, lar′ən jē′əl), *adj.*

la•sa•gna (lə zän′yə, lä-), *n.* a baked dish of wide strips of pasta layered with cheese, tomato sauce, and usu. meat.

las•civ•i•ous (lə siv′ē əs), *adj.* **1.** inclined to or expressive of lustfulness; lewd. **2.** arousing sexual desire. —**las•civ′i•ous•ness,** *n.*

la•ser (lā′zər), *n.* a device that produces a narrow beam of intense light by exciting atoms and causing them to radiate their energy in phase. [l(ight) a(mplification by) s(timulated) e(mission of) r(adiation)]

la′ser disc′, *n.* OPTICAL DISC.

la′ser print′er, *n.* a high-speed, high-resolution computer printer that uses a laser to form dot-matrix patterns and an electrostatic process to print page.

lash¹ (lash), *n.* **1.** the flexible extremity of a whip. **2.** a swift stroke or blow, as with a whip. **3.** an eyelash. —*v.t.* **4.** to strike or beat, as with a whip. **5.** to attack severely with words. **6.** to dash or switch suddenly and swiftly. —*v.i.* **7.** to strike vigorously. **8.** to attack with harsh words: *to lash out at injustice.*

lash² (lash), *v.t.* to bind or fasten with a rope, cord, etc.

lass (las), *n.* a girl or young woman.

las•sie (las′ē), *n., pl.* **-sies.** a young girl; lass.

las•si•tude (las′i tŏŏd′, -tyŏŏd′), *n.* weariness of body or mind, as from strain.

las•so (las′ō, la sŏŏ′), *n., pl.* **-sos, -soes,** *v.*, **-soed, -so•ing.** —*n.* **1.** a long rope with a running noose at one end, used for roping horses, cattle, etc. —*v.t.* **2.** to catch with or as if with a lasso.

last¹ (last, läst), *adj.* **1.** occurring after all others, as in time or place. **2.** most recent: *last week.* **3.** being the only remaining: *my last dollar.* **4.** conclusive; definitive. **5.** least likely or probable: *the last person we'd want to represent us.* —*adv.* **6.** after all others.

7. on the most recent occasion. **8.** in the end. —n. **9.** a person or thing that is last. —*Idiom.* **10.** at **(long) last,** after considerable delay. —**last/ly,** *adv.*

last² (last, läst), *v.i.* **1.** to continue in time, force, etc. **2.** to be enough: *Will the food last?* **3.** to remain in usable condition.

last³ (last, läst), *n.* a foot-shaped form on which shoes are shaped or repaired.

last/ing, *adj.* continuing or enduring a long time. —**last/ing•ly,** *adv.*

Last/ Judg/ment, *n.* God's final judgment of all people at the end of the world.

last/ straw/, *n.* the last of a succession of troubles that leads to a loss of patience.

Last/ Sup/per, *n.* the supper of Jesus and His disciples on the eve of His Crucifixion.

Las Ve•gas (läs vā/gəs), *n.* a city in SE Nevada. 327,878.

Lat., Latin.

lat., latitude.

Lat•a•ki•a (lat/ə kē/ə *or, esp. for 1,* lä/tä kē/ä), *n.* **1.** Ancient, **Laodicea.** a seaport in NW Syria, on the Mediterranean. 191,329. **2.** a coastal district in Syria, in the W part. 389,552.

latch (lach), *n.* **1.** a device for holding a door, gate, etc., closed. —*v.t., v.i.* **2.** to close or fasten with a latch. **3. latch onto, a.** to obtain. **b.** to attach oneself to.

late (lāt), *adj.* and *adv.,* **lat•er, lat•est.** —*adj.* **1.** occurring or coming after the usual or proper time. **2.** at the end of the day or well into the night: *a late hour.* **3.** recent: *a late bulletin.* **4.** recently deceased: *the late Mr. Phipps.* —*adv.* **5.** after the usual or proper time. **6.** at or to an advanced time. **7.** recently but no longer. —*Idiom.* **8. of late,** lately. —**late/ness,** *n.*

late/com/er, *n.* one that arrives late.

late/ly, *adv.* recently; not long since.

la•tent (lāt/nt), *adj.* present but not visible, actualized, or active. —**la/ten•cy,** *n.*

lat•er•al (lat/ər əl), *adj.* of, at, from, or to a side. —**lat/er•al•ly,** *adv.*

la•tex (lā/teks), *n., pl.* **lat•i•ces** (lat/ə sēz/), **la•tex•es.** **1.** a milky liquid in certain plants, as milkweeds. **2.** an emulsion in water of particles of synthetic rubber or plastic, used in paints.

lath (lath, läth), *n., pl.* **laths** (lathz, laths, läthz, läths). **1.** a thin, narrow strip of wood, used as a backing for plaster or stucco. **2.** any building material used for a similar purpose.

lathe (lāth), *n., v.,* **lathed, lath•ing.** —*n.* **1.** a machine for use in working a piece of wood, metal, etc., by rotating it against a tool that shapes it. —*v.t.* **2.** to cut or shape on a lathe.

lathe

lath•er (lath/ər), *n.* **1.** foam made by a soap stirred or rubbed in water. **2.** foam formed in profuse sweating, as on a horse. **3.** *Informal.* a state of excitement. —*v.i., v.t.* **4.** to form or cover with lather.

Lat•in (lat/n), *n.* **1.** the language of ancient Rome. **2.** a member of any of the Latin peoples. **3.** a native or inhabitant of ancient Rome. —*adj.* **4.** pertaining to those peoples speaking languages descended from Latin. **5.** of ancient Rome or its inhabitants.

Lat/in Amer/ica, *n.* the part of the American continents south of the United States in which Romance languages are spoken. —**Lat/in-Amer/ican,** *adj.* —**Lat/in A•mer/i•can,** *n.*

La•ti•no (lə tē/nō, la-), *n., pl.* **-nos.** HISPANIC.

lat•i•tude (lat/i tōōd/, -tyōōd/), *n.* **1. a.** the angular distance north or south from the equator of a point on the earth's surface, expressed in degrees. **b.** a region as marked by this distance. **2.** freedom from narrow restrictions. —**lat/i•tu/di•nal** (-tōōd/n l, -tyōōd/-), *adj.*

la•trine (lə trēn/), *n.* a communal toilet, esp. in a military installation.

lat•te (lä/tā), *n.* hot espresso served mixed with hot milk. [< It *(caffè) latte* (coffee with) milk]

lat•ter (lat/ər), *adj.* **1.** being the second mentioned of two. **2.** more advanced in time. **3.** near to the end. —**lat/ter•ly,** *adv.*

lat/ter-day/, *adj.* **1.** of a later or following period. **2.** of the present period or time.

Lat/ter-day/ Saint/, *n.* a member of the Church of Jesus Christ of Latter-day Saints.

lat•tice (lat/is), *n.* a structure of crossed wooden or metal strips usu. arranged to form a diagonal pattern of open spaces. —**lat/ticed,** *adj.*

lat/tice•work/, *n.* **1.** work consisting of lattices. **2.** a lattice.

Lat•vi•a (lat/vē ə, lät/-), *n.* a republic in N Europe, on the Baltic: formerly a part of the USSR. 2,437,649. —**Lat/vi•an,** *adj., n.*

laud (lôd), *v.t.* to praise highly.

laud/a•ble, *adj.* praiseworthy. —**laud/a•bly,** *adv.*

lau•da•num (lôd/n əm, lôd/nəm), *n.* a tincture of opium.

laud/a•to/ry (-tôr/ē), *adj.* containing or expressing praise.

laugh (laf, läf), *v.i.* **1.** to express mirth, derision, etc., with inarticulate sounds and facial or bodily movements. —*v.t.* **2.** to drive, bring, etc., by or with laughter: *They laughed him out of town.* **3. laugh at, a.** to ridicule. **b.** to find amusing. —*n.* **4.** the act or sound of laughing. **5.** one that provokes laughter. —**laugh/ing•ly,** *adv.*

laugh/a•ble, *adj.* such as to cause laughter. —**laugh/a•bly,** *adv.*

laugh/ing gas/, *n.* NITROUS OXIDE.

laugh/ing•stock/, *n.* an object of ridicule.

laugh/ter (-tər), *n.* **1.** the action or sound of laughing. —*Saying.* **2. Laughter is the best medicine,** laughter can provide a respite from one's troubles.

launch¹ (lônch, länch), *v.t.* **1.** to float (a newly constructed ship). **2.** to send forth forcefully: *to launch a spacecraft.* **3.** to set going; start: *to launch a new product.* **4.** *Computers.* to start (an application program). —*v.i.* **5.** to plunge boldly into action, speech, etc. **6.** to start out or forth. —*n.* **7.** the act of launching. —**launch/er,** *n.*

launch² (lônch, länch), *n.* a heavy, open or half-decked boat.

launch/ (or **launch/ing) pad/,** *n.* the platform on which a rocket, missile, etc., is launched.

laun•der (lôn/dər, län/-), *v.t., v.i.* **1.** to wash or wash and iron (clothes or linens). **2.** *Informal.* to disguise the source of (illegal money), as by transmitting it through a foreign bank. —**laun/der•er,** *n.* —**laun/dress** (-dris), *n.*

laun/der•ette/ (-də ret/), *n.* a self-service laundry having coin-operated washers and driers.

Laun/dro•mat/ (-drə mat/), *Trademark.* a type of launderette.

laun/dry, *n., pl.* **-dries. 1.** articles of clothing, linens, etc., that have been or are to be washed. **2.** a place where articles are laundered. —**laun/dry•man/** or **-wom/an,** *n., pl.* **-men** or **-wom•en.**

lau•re•ate (lôr/ē it, lor/-), *n.* **1.** a person who has been honored in a particular field: *a poet laureate.* —*adj.* **2.** crowned with laurel as a mark of honor.

lau•rel (lôr/əl, lor/-), *n.* **1.** a small European evergreen tree with dark, glossy leaves. **2.** any of various similar trees or shrubs. **3.** the foliage of the laurel as an emblem of victory or distinction. **4.** a wreath of laurel foliage. **5.** Usu., **-rels.** honor won, as for achievement in a field or activity.

Lau•rel (lôr′əl, lor′-), *n.* **Stan** (*Arthur Stanley Jefferson*), 1890–1965, U.S. motion-picture comedian, born in England.

la•va (lä′və, lav′ə), *n., pl.* **-vas. 1.** the molten rock that issues from a volcano. **2.** the rock formed when this solidifies. [< It: avalanche ≪ L *lābēs* a sliding down]

La•val (lə val′), *n.* a city in S Quebec, in E Canada. 284,164.

lav•a•liere or **-lier** (lav′ə lēr′, lä′və-), *n.* an ornamental pendant worn on a chain around the neck.

lav•a•to•ry (lav′ə tôr′ē), *n., pl.* **-ries.** a room fitted with washbowls and toilets.

lave (lāv), *v.t., v.i.,* **laved, lav•ing.** to wash; bathe.

lav•en•der (lav′ən dər), *n.* **1.** a pale bluish purple. **2.** an Old World plant with spikes of pale purple flowers. **3.** its dried flowers placed among linen, clothes, etc., for scent.

lav•ish (lav′ish), *adj.* **1.** bestowed or occurring in abundance. **2.** using or giving in great amounts. —*v.t.* **3.** to expend or give in great amounts. —**lav′-ish•ly,** *adv.*

law (lô), *n.* **1.** a rule or system of rules established by a government or other authority and applicable to a people. **2.** the condition of society brought about by observance of such rules: *maintaining law and order.* **3.** the field of knowledge concerned with these rules; jurisprudence. **4.** the profession that deals with law and legal procedure. **5.** any rule or injunction that must be obeyed. **6.** (in philosophy, science, etc.) a statement of a relation or sequence of phenomena invariable under the same conditions. **7.** a commandment or a revelation from God.

law′-abid′ing, *adj.* obedient to law.

law′break′er, *n.* a person who violates the law. —**law′break′ing,** *n., adj.*

law′ful, *adj.* **1.** allowed by law. **2.** sanctioned or recognized by law. —**law′ful•ly,** *adv.* —**law′ful•ness,** *n.*

law′giv′er, *n.* a person who promulgates a law or a code of laws.

law′less, *adj.* **1.** without regard for the law. **2.** uncontrolled by law; unruly. **3.** illegal. —**law′less•ness,** *n.*

law′mak′er, *n.* a person who makes or enacts law; legislator.

lawn¹ (lôn), *n.* a stretch of grass-covered land, esp. one closely mowed, as near a house.

lawn² (lôn), *n.* a sheer linen or cotton fabric.

lawn′ bowl′ing, *n.* a game played on a bowling green by rolling a ball toward a stationary ball.

lawn′ mow′er, *n.* a machine for cutting grass.

Law′ of Mo′ses, *n.* the ancient law of the Hebrews, ascribed to Moses and contained in the Pentateuch.

Law•rence (lôr′əns, lor′-), *n.* **1. D(avid) H(erbert),** 1885–1930, English novelist. **2. Ernest O(rlando),** 1901–58, U.S. physicist. **3. Gertrude,** 1901?–52, English actress. **4. Saint,** died A.D. 258?, early church martyr. **5. T(homas) E(dward)** (*T. E. Shaw*) (*"Lawrence of Arabia"*), 1888–1935, English soldier and writer.

law•ren•ci•um (lô ren′sē əm), *n.* a synthetic, radioactive metallic element. *Symbol:* Lr; *at. no.:* 103.

law′suit′, *n.* a case brought before a court.

law•yer (lô′yər, loi′ər), *n.* a person who represents clients in court or advises them in legal matters.

lax (laks), *adj.,* **-er, -est. 1.** not strict or severe; careless or negligent. **2.** loose or slack. —**lax′i•ty, lax′-ness,** *n.* —**lax′ly,** *adv.*

lax•a•tive (lak′sə tiv), *n.* **1.** an agent for relieving constipation. —*adj.* **2.** of or constituting a laxative.

lay¹ (lā), *v.,* **laid, lay•ing,** *n.* —*v.t.* **1.** to place in a horizontal position. **2.** to strike or throw to the ground. **3.** to put or place. **4.** to place in proper position: *to lay bricks.* **5.** to present for notice or consideration: *I laid my case before the commission.* **6.** to bring forward, as a claim. **7.** to attribute or ascribe:

to lay blame. **8.** to bring forth and deposit (an egg). **9.** to devise, as a plan. **10.** to wager; stake. **11.** to quiet or allay. **12. lay aside,** to save for use at a later time. **13. ~ away,** to reserve for later use. **14. ~ off, a.** to dismiss (an employee), esp. temporarily. **b.** *Informal.* to cease or quit. **15. ~ open, a.** to cut open. **b.** to expose. **16. ~ out, a.** to spread out in order; arrange. **b.** to ready (a corpse) for burial. **c.** *Informal.* to spend or contribute (money). **17. ~ over,** to make a stopover. **18. ~ up, a.** to put away for future use. **b.** to confine to bed. —*n.* **19.** the way or position in which a thing is laid or lies: *the lay of the land.* —**Usage.** See LIE².

lay² (lā), *v.* pt. of LIE¹.

lay³ (lā), *adj.* **1.** of or involving the laity. **2.** not belonging to or connected with a profession.

lay⁴ (lā), *n.* **1.** a short narrative or other poem. **2.** a song.

Lay•a•mon (lā′ə mən, lä′yə-), *n.* fl. c1200, English poet and chronicler.

lay′a•way plan′, *n.* a method of purchasing by which an item is reserved by the store until the customer has completed payments.

lay′er, *n.* **1.** a thickness of some material laid on or spread over a surface. **2.** one that lays, as a hen.

lay•ette (-et′), *n.* an outfit of clothing, bedding, etc., for a newborn baby.

lay′ing on′ of hands′, *n.* a rite in which a cleric's hands touch the person to be ordained, healed, etc.

lay′man or **-wom′an** or **-per′son,** *n., pl.* **-men** or **-wom•en** or **-per•sons. 1.** a person who is not a member of the clergy. **2.** a person who is not a member of a given profession.

lay′off′, *n.* the act of dismissing employees.

lay′out′, *n.* **1.** an arrangement or plan. **2.** a plan or sketch for an advertisement or other printed matter.

lay′o′ver, *n.* STOPOVER.

Laz•a•rus (laz′ər əs), *n.* **1.** the diseased beggar in a parable of Jesus. Luke 16:19–31. **2.** a man whom Jesus raised from the dead. John 11:1–44; 12:1–18. **3. Emma,** 1849–87, U.S. poet.

laze (lāz), *v.i., v.t.,* **lazed, laz•ing.** to pass (time) lazily.

la•zy (lā′zē), *adj.,* **-zi•er, -zi•est. 1.** averse to work or activity; indolent. **2.** slow-moving; sluggish. —**la′-zi•ly,** *adv.* —**la′zi•ness,** *n.*

la′zy•bones′, *n. Informal.* a lazy person.

la′zy (or **La′zy**) **Su′san,** *n.* a revolving tray for foods or condiments.

lb., *pl.* **lbs., lb.** pound. [< L *lībra*]

LBJ, Lyndon Baines Johnson.

l.c., lowercase.

LCD, *pl.* **LCDs, LCD's.** liquid-crystal display: a display of information, as on digital watches, using a crystal-line liquid film.

L.C.D., least common denominator; lowest common denominator.

l′cha•im (lə κнä′yim, lə κнä yēm′), *interj. Hebrew.* (used as a drinking toast.) [*ləhayyīm* lit., to life]

L.C.M., least common multiple; lowest common multiple.

LDL, low-density lipoprotein: a plasma protein that is the major carrier of cholesterol in the blood, with high levels being associated with atherosclerosis.

L-do•pa (el′dō′pə), *n.* See under DOPA.

lea (lē, lā), *n.* a meadow.

leach (lēch), *v.t.* **1.** to dissolve out soluble constituents from (ashes, soil, etc.) by percolation. **2.** to cause (a liquid) to percolate through something. —*v.i.* **3.** to undergo the action of percolating water. —**leach′er,** *n.*

lead¹ (lēd), *v.,* **led, lead•ing,** *n.* —*v.t.* **1.** to go before or with to show the way. **2.** to conduct by holding and guiding: *to lead a horse by a rope.* **3.** to influence or induce. **4.** to live: *to lead a full life.* **5.** to be in control or command of; direct. **6.** to be or go at the head of: *The mayor will lead the parade.* **7.** to have the advantage over. —*v.i.* **8.** to act as a guide. **9.** to afford passage to a place: *That path leads to the house.* **10.** to be or go first. **11.** to result in: *The incident led to her resignation.* **12.** to make the first play in a card game. **13. lead off,** to begin. **14.** ~ **on,** to mislead. —*n.* **15.** the position in advance of others. **16.** the extent of such advance. **17.** one that leads. **18.** a tip or clue. **19.** the principal part in a play. **20.** the right of playing first in a card game. —*Idiom.* **21. lead up to,** to prepare the way for. —**lead′er,** *n.* —**lead′er•ship′,** *n.*

lead² (led), *n.* **1.** a heavy, comparatively soft, malleable, bluish-gray metal. *Symbol:* Pb; *at. wt.:* 207.19; *at. no.:* 82. **2.** a plummet of lead for taking soundings. **3.** bullets collectively. **4.** a small stick of graphite, as used in pencils. **5.** a thin strip of metal used for increasing the space between lines of type. —*v.t.* **6.** to cover, weight, or treat with lead.

lead•ed (led′id), *adj.* (of gasoline) containing tetraethyllead.

lead•en (led′n), *adj.* **1.** heavy like lead: *leaden feet.* **2.** dull or gloomy. **3.** of a dull gray color. **4.** sluggish. **5.** made of lead.

lead•ing¹ (lē′ding), *adj.* **1.** principal; most important. **2.** directing, guiding.

lead•ing² (led′ing), *n.* LEAD² (def. 5).

lead′ing ques′tion (lē′ding), *n.* a question so worded as to suggest the proper or desired answer.

lead′ poi′soning (led), *n.* a toxic condition produced by ingestion, inhalation, or skin absorption of lead or lead compounds.

lead′ time′ (lēd), *n.* the period of time between the initial phase of a process and the emergence of results.

leaf (lēf), *n., pl.* **leaves** (lēvz), *v.* —*n.* **1.** one of the expanded, usu. green organs borne by the stem of a plant. **2.** a sheet of paper, one side of each sheet constituting a page. **3.** a thin sheet of metal. **4.** a hinged or detachable flat part, as of a tabletop. —*v.i.* **5.** to put forth leaves. **6.** to turn pages quickly (usu. fol. by *through*). —**leaf′less,** *adj.* —**leaf′y,** *adj.,* **-i•er, -i•est.**

leaf′let (-lit), *n.* **1.** a small flat or folded sheet of printed matter. **2.** a small leaf.

league¹ (lēg), *n., v.,* **leagued, lea•guing.** —*n.* **1.** an association of persons, states, etc., for the promotion of common interests or for mutual assistance. **2.** a group of athletic teams organized to compete chiefly among themselves. —*v.t., v.i.* **3.** to unite in a league.

league² (lēg), *n.* a unit of distance, roughly 3 miles (4.8 kilometers).

League′ of Na′tions, *n.* an international organization created in 1919 to promote world peace and cooperation: dissolved in 1946.

Le•ah (lē′ə), *n.* the first wife of Jacob. Gen. 29:23–26.

leak (lēk), *n.* **1.** an unintended hole, crack, etc., through which fluid or light enters or escapes. **2.** any means of unintended entrance or escape. **3.** a disclosure of secret information. —*v.i.* **4.** to let a fluid or light enter or escape through a leak. **5.** to pass in or out in this manner. **6.** to become known unintentionally: *The news leaked out.* —*v.t.* **7.** to let (fluid or light) enter or escape. **8.** to allow to become known. —**leak′y,** *adj.,* **-i•er, -i•est.**

leak•age (lē′kij), *n.* **1.** the act of leaking. **2.** the thing or amount that leaks.

lean¹ (lēn), *v.,* **leaned** or *(esp. Brit.)* **leant** (lent), **lean•ing.** —*v.i.* **1.** to incline or bend from a vertical position. **2.** to incline in feeling, opinion, etc. **3.** to rest or lie for support: *to lean against a wall.* **4.** to depend or rely. —*v.t.* **5.** to cause to lean.

lean² (lēn), *adj.,* **-er, -est. 1.** without much flesh or fat. **2.** lacking in richness, quantity, etc.: *lean years.* **3.** spare; economical. —**lean′ness,** *n.*

lean′ing, *n.* inclination; tendency.

lean′-to′, *n., pl.* **-tos. 1.** a roof of a single pitch with the higher end abutting a wall. **2.** a structure with such a roof.

leap (lēp), *v.,* **leaped** or **leapt** (lept, lēpt), **leap•ing,** *n.* —*v.i.* **1.** to spring from one point to another; jump. **2.** to move or act quickly or suddenly: *to leap at an opportunity.* —*v.t.* **3.** to jump over. **4.** to cause to leap. —*n.* **5.** a spring or jump. **6.** the distance covered in a leap. **7.** an abrupt transition. —**leap′er,** *n.*

leap′frog′, *n., v.,* **-frogged, -frog•ging.** —*n.* **1.** a game in which players take turns leaping over another player bent over from the waist. —*v.t., v.i.* **2.** to jump over (a person or thing) in or as if in leapfrog.

leap′ year′, *n.* a year occurring every four years that contains 366 days, with February 29 as an additional day.

learn (lûrn), *v.,* **learned** (lûrnd) or **learnt, learn•ing.** —*v.t.* **1.** to acquire knowledge of or skill in by study, instruction, or experience. **2.** to become informed of. **3.** to memorize. —*v.i.* **4.** to acquire knowledge or skill. **5.** to become informed: *to learn of an accident.* —**learn′er,** *n.*

learn•ed (lûr′nid), *adj.* having much knowledge; scholarly; erudite.

learn′ing, *n.* **1.** knowledge acquired by systematic study. **2.** the act or process of acquiring knowledge or skill. —**Proverb. 3. A little learning (or knowledge) is a dangerous thing,** partial knowledge of a subject is sometimes worse than ignorance.

learn′ing disabil′ity, *n.* any of several conditions characterized by difficulty in reading, writing, etc., and associated with impairment of the central nervous system. —**learn′ing-disa′bled,** *adj.*

lease (lēs), *n., v.,* **leased, leas•ing.** —*n.* **1.** a contract renting property to another for a specified period in consideration of rent. —*v.t.* **2.** to grant or hold by lease. —**leas′er,** *n.*

lease′hold′, *n.* **1.** property acquired under a lease. **2.** a tenure under a lease. —**lease′hold′er,** *n.*

leash (lēsh), *n.* **1.** a chain, strap, etc., for controlling a dog or other animal. —*v.t.* **2.** to secure or control by or as if by a leash.

least (lēst), *adj., a superl. of* **little** *with* **less** *or* **lesser** *as compar.* **1.** smallest in size, amount, degree, etc. **2.** lowest in consideration or importance. —*n.* **3.** the least amount, quantity, degree, etc. —*adv., superl. of* **little** *with* **less** *as compar.* **4.** to the smallest extent, amount, or degree. —*Idiom.* **5. at least, a.** at the lowest estimate. **b.** in any case. **6. not in the least,** not at all. —**Proverb. 7. Least said, soonest mended,** apologies may only worsen a mistake.

least′ com′mon denom′inator, *n.* the smallest number that is a common denominator of a given set of fractions.

least′ com′mon mul′tiple, *n.* LOWEST COMMON MULTIPLE.

least′wise′, *adv. Informal.* at least; at any rate.

leath•er (leth′ar), *n.* **1.** the skin of an animal with the hair removed, prepared for use by tanning or a similar process. —*adj.* **2.** of or made of leather. —**leath′er•y,** *adj.*

leath′er•neck′, *n. Informal.* a U.S. marine.

leave¹ (lēv), *v.,* **left, leav•ing.** —*v.t.* **1.** to go away from, as a place. **2.** to depart from permanently; quit. **3.** to let remain behind: *The bear left tracks.* **4.** to let stay or be as specified: *to leave a motor running.* **5.** to let remain in a position to do something without interference: *We left him to his work.* **6.** to give up or abandon. **7.** to give for use after one's death. —*v.i.* **8.** to go away or depart. **9.** ~ **off,** to stop; cease. **10.** ~ **out,** to omit. —**leav′er,** *n.*

leave² (lēv), *n.* **1.** permission to do something. **2.** permission to be absent, as from military duty. **3.** the time this permission lasts. —*Idiom.* **4. take leave of,** to part or separate from. **5. take one's leave,** to depart.

leav•en (lev′ən), *n.* **1.** a substance, as yeast, that causes fermentation and expansion of dough. **2.** an element that produces an altering or transforming influence. —*v.t.* **3.** to make (dough) rise with a leaven. **4.** to permeate with an altering or transforming element.

leav′en•ing, *n.* **1.** the process of causing fermentation by leaven. **2.** LEAVEN.

leaves (lēvz), *n.* pl. of LEAF.

leave′-tak′ing, *n.* a saying farewell.

leav′ings, *n.pl.* leftovers or remains; refuse.

Leb•a•non (leb′ə non, -non′), *n.* a republic at the E end of the Mediterranean. 3,858,736. —**Leb′a•nese′** (-nēz′, -nēs′), *adj., n., pl.* **-nese.**

lec·i·thin (les′ə thin), *n.* any of a group of fatty substances found in nerve tissue and egg yolk, used in foods, cosmetics, etc.

Le Cor·bu·sier (lə kôr′bY zyā′), *n.* 1887–1965, Swiss architect in France.

lec·tern (lek′tərn), *n.* a stand with a slanted top, used to hold a book, speech, etc., for a standing speaker.

lec·tion·ar·y (lek′shə ner′ē), *n., pl.* **-ar·ies.** a book of readings for a divine service.

lec·ture (lek′chər), *n., v.,* **-tured, -tur·ing.** —*n.* **1.** a discourse delivered before an audience or class, esp. for instruction. **2.** a long, tedious reprimand. —*v.i.* **3.** to give a lecture. —*v.t.* **4.** to deliver a lecture to. **5.** to reprimand at length. —**lec′tur·er,** *n.*

led (led), *v.* pt. and pp. of LEAD[1].

LED, *pl.* **LEDs, LED′s.** light-emitting diode: a semiconductor diode that emits light when conducting current, used for displays on digital watches, calculators, etc.

ledge (lej), *n.* **1.** a narrow, horizontal, shelflike projection on a wall or cliff. **2.** a reef or ridge of rocks in the sea.

ledg·er (lej′er), *n.* an account book in which business transactions are recorded in final form.

Lee (lē), *n.* **1. Ann,** 1736–84, British mystic: founder of Shaker sect in U.S. **2. Francis Lightfoot,** 1734–97, American Revolutionary statesman. **3. Gypsy Rose** (*Rose Louise Hovick*), 1914–70, U.S. entertainer. **4. Henry** (*"Light-Horse Harry"*), 1756–1818, American Revolutionary general (father of Robert E. Lee). **5. Robert E(dward),** 1807–70, Confederate general in the Civil War (son of Henry Lee).

leech (lēch), *n.* **1.** a bloodsucking annelid worm, once used for bloodletting. **2.** a person who clings to another for personal gain. —*v.i.* **3.** to hang on to a person in the manner of a leech.

leek (lēk), *n.* a plant related to the onion, used in cookery.

leer (lēr), *v.i.* **1.** to look with a sideways glance suggestive of lascivious interest or malicious intention. —*n.* **2.** a lascivious or sly look.

leer′y (lēr′ē), *adj.,* **-i·er, -i·est.** wary; suspicious. —**leer′i·ness,** *n.*

lees (lēz), *n.pl.* sediment or dregs, esp. of wine.

lee·ward (lē′wərd; *Naut.* lōō′ərd), *adj.* **1.** at or toward the quarter toward which the wind blows. —*n.* **2.** the lee side. —*adv.* **3.** toward the lee.

Lee′ward Is′lands (lē′wərd), *n.pl.* a group of islands in the Lesser Antilles of the West Indies.

lee′way′, *n.* **1.** extra time, space, etc., within which to act. **2.** a degree of freedom of action or thought. **3.** the drift of a ship leeward from its heading.

left[1] (left), *adj.* **1.** of, on, or near the side of a person or thing that is toward the west when the subject is facing north. **2.** (*often cap.*) of or belonging to the political Left. —*n.* **3.** the left side. **4.** a turn toward the left. **5. the Left,** those individuals or groups advocating liberal reform or revolutionary change in the established order. —*adv.* **6.** toward the left.

left[2] (left), *v.* pt. and pp. of LEAVE.[1]

left′-hand′, *adj.* **1.** on or to the left. **2.** of, for, or with the left hand.

left′-hand′ed, *adj.* **1.** having the left hand more effective than the right. **2.** adapted to or performed by the left hand. **3.** ambiguous and often derogatory: *a left-handed compliment.* —*adv.* **4.** with the left hand. —**left′-hand′ed·ness,** *n.*

left′ist, *n.* (*sometimes cap.*) **1.** a member of the political Left. —*adj.* **2.** of the political Left. —**left′ism,** *n.*

left′o′ver, *n.* Often, **-vers.** a portion remaining unused, as food uneaten at the end of a meal.

left′ wing′, *n.* the liberal or radical element in a political party or other group. —**left′-wing′,** *adj.* —**left′-wing′er,** *n.*

left′y, *n., pl.* **-ies.** *Informal.* a left-handed person.

leg (leg), *n.* **1.** either of the two lower limbs of a biped, or any of the paired legs of an animal, that support and move the body. **2.** something resembling a leg in use, position, or appearance. **3.** the

part of a garment that covers the leg. **4.** one of the distinct sections of any course: *the last leg of a trip.*

leg·a·cy (leg′ə sē), *n., pl.* **-cies. 1.** a gift of money or property left to someone in a will. **2.** anything handed down from the past, as from an ancestor.

le·gal (lē′gəl), *adj.* **1.** permitted by law. **2.** of or established by law. **3.** of or characteristic of lawyers. —**le·gal′i·ty,** *n., pl.* **-ties.** —**le′gal·ly,** *adv.*

le′gal·ese′ (-gə lēz′, -lēs′), *n.* language containing an excessive amount of legal terminology or jargon.

le′gal hol′iday, *n.* a public holiday established by law.

le′gal·ism, *n.* strict adherence to law, esp. to the letter rather than the spirit. —**le′gal·is′tic,** *adj.*

le′gal·ize′, *v.t.,* **-ized, -iz·ing.** to make legal; authorize. —**le′gal·i·za′tion,** *n.*

le′gal ten′der, *n.* currency that may be lawfully tendered in payment of a debt, as paper money or coins.

leg·ate (leg′it), *n.* **1.** an ecclesiastic delegated by the pope as his representative. **2.** an envoy or emissary.

leg·a·tee (leg′ə tē′), *n., pl.* **-tees.** a person to whom a legacy is bequeathed.

le·ga·tion (li gā′shən), *n.* **1.** a diplomatic minister and staff in a foreign mission. **2.** the official headquarters of a diplomatic minister.

le·ga·to (lə gä′tō), *adj., adv. Music.* smooth and connected; without breaks between tones.

leg·end (lej′ənd), *n.* **1.** an unverifiable story or collection of stories handed down by tradition and popularly accepted as historical. **2.** an inscription on a monument, coin, etc. **3.** a table on a map, chart, or illustration explaining the symbols used. **4.** an admirable person about whom stories are told. —**leg′en·dar′y** (-ən der′ē), *adj.*

leg·er·de·main (lej′ər də mān′), *n.* **1.** sleight of hand. **2.** trickery; deception.

leg·ged (leg′id, legd), *adj.* having a specified number or kind of legs: *two-legged; long-legged.*

leg′ging, *n.* **1.** a covering for the leg, usu. from ankle to knee. **2. leggings, a.** close-fitting knit pants. **b.** the pants of a two-piece snowsuit.

leg′gy, *adj.,* **-gi·er, -gi·est. 1.** having awkwardly long legs. **2.** having long, attractively shaped legs.

Leg·horn (leg′hôrn′, -ərn), *n.* one of a breed of chickens that are prolific layers of eggs.

leg·i·ble (lej′ə bəl), *adj.* capable of being read with ease, as writing. —**leg′i·bil′i·ty,** *n.* —**leg′i·bly,** *adv.*

le·gion (lē′jən), *n.* **1.** the largest unit of the ancient Roman army. **2.** a great number of persons or things. —*adj.* **3.** very great in number: *His followers were legion.* —**le′gion·ar′y** (-jə ner′ē), *adj., n., pl.* **-ar·ies.** —**le′gion·naire′** (-nâr′), *n.*

leg·is·late (lej′is lāt′), *v.,* **-lat·ed, -lat·ing.** —*v.i.* **1.** to make or enact laws. —*v.t.* **2.** to create or control by legislation: *attempts to legislate morality.* —**leg′is·la′tor,** *n.*

leg′is·la′tion, *n.* **1.** the act of legislating. **2.** a law or a body of laws enacted.

leg′is·la′tive, *adj.* **1.** having the function of making laws. **2.** pertaining to a legislature or legislation.

leg′islative branch′, *n.* the branch of the U.S. government whose powers are vested in the Congress.

leg′is·la′ture (-chər), *n.* a body of persons empowered to make, change, or repeal laws.

le·git·i·mate (*adj.* li jit′ə mit; *v.* -māt′), *adj., v.,* **-mat·ed, -mat·ing.** —*adj.* **1.** according to law. **2.** in accordance with established rules, standards, etc. **3.** born of legally married parents. **4.** valid; logical: *a legitimate conclusion.* **5.** justified: *a legitimate complaint.* **6.** of stage plays, as distinguished from burlesque, vaudeville, etc. —*v.t.* **7.** to make lawful or legal. **8.** to sanction or authorize. —**le·git′i·ma·cy** (-mə sē), *n.* —**le·git′i·mate·ly,** *adv.*

le·git′i·ma·tize′, *v.t.,* **-tized, -tiz·ing.** LEGITIMATE.

le·git′i·mize′, *v.t.,* **-mized, -miz·ing.** LEGITIMATE. —**le·git′i·mi·za′tion,** *n.*

leg′man′ (-man′, -mən), *n., pl.* **-men. 1.** a person

employed to gather information, run errands, etc. **2.** a reporter who gathers news firsthand.

leg′room′, *n.* space sufficient for keeping one's legs in a comfortable position, as in an automobile.

leg·ume (leg′yoōm, li gyoōm′), *n.* **1.** any of a large family of plants having pods that split open when dry, comprising beans, peas, etc. **2.** the pod or seed of such a plant. —**le·gu′mi·nous,** *adj.*

leg′work′, *n.* work involving extensive walking or traveling about.

lei (lā, lā′ē), *n., pl.* **leis.** (in Hawaii) a wreath of flowers worn around the neck.

Leip·zig (līp′sig), *n.* a city in E central Germany. 545,307.

lei·sure (lē′zhər, lezh′ər), *n.* **1.** freedom from the demands of work or duty. **2.** free or unoccupied time. —*adj.* **3.** free or unoccupied. **4.** having leisure.

lei′sure·ly, *adj.* **1.** acting or done without haste. —*adv.* **2.** in a leisurely manner.

leit·mo·tif (līt′mō tēf′), *n.* a theme associated throughout a music drama with a particular person, situation, or idea.

lem·ming (lem′ing), *n.* any of various small, mainly arctic rodents, noted for periodic mass migrations.

lem·on (lem′ən), *n.* **1.** the yellowish, acid fruit of a subtropical citrus tree. **2.** the tree itself. **3.** *Informal.* a person or thing that is defective or unsatisfactory. —*lem′on·y,* *adj.*

lem′on·ade′ (-ə nād′), *n.* a beverage of lemon juice, sweetener, and water.

Lem·u·el (lem′yoō əl), *n.* a Hebrew king whose mother's teachings are recorded in Proverbs 31.

le·mur (lē′mər), *n.* a small, arboreal primate with large eyes and a foxlike face.

lend (lend), *v.,* **lent, lend·ing.** —*v.t.* **1.** to grant the use of (something) on condition that it will be returned. **2.** to give (money) temporarily, usu. at interest. **3.** to adapt: *The building lends itself to remodeling.* **4.** to give or impart. —*v.i.* **5.** to make a loan. —**lend′er,** *n.*

L'En·fant (län fän′), *n.* **Pierre Charles,** 1754–1825, U.S. engineer and architect, born in France: designer of Washington, D.C.

L'En·gle (leng′gəl), *n.* **Madeleine,** born 1918, U.S. novelist and Christian essayist.

length (lengkth, length, lenth), *n.* **1.** the longest extent of anything as measured from end to end. **2.** extent in time or space. **3.** a piece of a certain extent: *a length of rope.* **4.** a large extent or expanse of something. —*Idiom.* **5. at length, a.** finally. **b.** fully; in detail.

length′en, *v.t., v.i.* to make or become greater in length.

length′wise′, *adv., adj.* in the direction of the length.

length′y, *adj.,* **-i·er, -i·est. 1.** very long. **2.** excessively long.

le·ni·ent (lē′nē ənt, lēn′yənt), *adj.* agreeably tolerant; not strict or severe. —*le′ni·en·cy,* *n.* —*le′ni·ent·ly,* *adv.*

Le·nin (len′in), *n.* **V(ladimir) I(lyich),** 1870–1924, Russian revolutionary leader: Soviet premier 1918–24. —**Le′nin·ism,** *n.* —**Le′nin·ist,** *adj., n.*

Le′nin·grad′ (-grad′), *n.* a former name of ST. PETERSBURG.

len·i·tive (len′i tiv), *adj.* soothing or mitigating, as medicines.

lens (lenz), *n., pl.* **lens·es. 1.** a curved piece of transparent substance, usu. glass, used in optical devices for changing the convergence of light rays, as for magnification or correcting vision defects. **2.** some analogous device, as for affecting sound waves, electromagnetic radiation, etc. **3.** a transparent body in the eye that focuses light on the retina.

lent (lent), *v.* pt. and pp. of LEND.

Lent (lent), *n.* (in the Christian religion) a season of fasting and penitence, lasting the 40 weekdays from Ash Wednesday to Easter. —**Lent′en, lent′en,** *adj.*

len·til (len′til, -tl), *n.* **1.** a legume having flattened seeds used as food. **2.** the seed itself.

Le·o (lē′ō), *n.* the fifth sign of the zodiac. [< L: lion]

Le·o·nar·do da Vin·ci (lē′ə närd′dō də vin′chē, dä vin′-, lā′-), *n.* 1452–1519, Italian artist, architect, and engineer.

Le·on·ca·val·lo (lā′ōn kə vä′lō), *n.* **Ruggiero,** 1858–1919, Italian operatic composer and librettist.

le·o·nine (lē′ə nīn′), *adj.* of or resembling a lion.

leop·ard (lep′ərd), *n.* **1.** a large, powerful Asian or African cat, usu. tawny with black spots. —*Proverb.* **2. A leopard can't change its spots,** someone's intrinsic nature can't be altered. Jer. 13:23.

le·o·tard (lē′ə tärd′), *n.* a skintight one-piece garment for the torso, worn by acrobats, dancers, etc.

lep·er (lep′ər), *n.* a person who has leprosy.

lep·re·chaun (lep′rə kôn′, -kon′), *n.* a sprite of Irish folklore, often represented as a little old man.

lep·ro·sy (lep′rə sē), *n.* a mildly infectious disease marked by ulcerations, destruction of tissue, loss of sensation, etc. —**lep′rous,** *adj.*

lep·ton (lep′ton), *n.* any of a class of weakly interacting elementary particles. —**lep·ton′ic,** *adj.*

Ler·ner (lûr′nər), *n.* **Alan Jay,** 1918–86, U.S. lyricist and librettist.

les·bi·an (lez′bē ən), *n.* a female homosexual. —**les′bi·an·ism,** *n.*

lese maj·es·ty or **lèse maj·es·té** (lēz′ maj′əs tē), *n.* **1.** an offense against the dignity of a ruler. **2.** an attack on any revered custom, institution, etc.

le·sion (lē′zhən), *n.* any localized area of diseased or injured tissue or of abnormal structural change.

Le·so·tho (lə soō′toō, -sō′tō), *n.* a monarchy in S Africa. 2,007,814.

less (les), *adv., a compar. of* **little** *with* **least** *as superl.* **1.** to a smaller extent, amount, or degree. —*adj., a compar. of* **little** *with* **least** *as superl.* **2.** smaller in size, amount, or degree. **3.** lower in consideration, rank, etc.: *no less a person than the mayor.* **4.** fewer. —*n.* **5.** a smaller amount or quantity. —*prep.* **6.** minus. —*Idiom.* **7. less and less,** to a decreasing extent or degree. —*Saying.* **8. Less is more,** simplicity in art, fashion, etc., is more effective than excess. —*Usage.* Many modern usage guides say that FEWER should be used before plural nouns specifying individuals or distinguishable units (*fewer words; no fewer than 31 states*). LESS should modify only singular mass nouns (*less sugar*) or abstract nouns (*less doubt*). It should modify plural nouns only when they suggest combination into a unit, group, or aggregation (*less than $50; less than three miles*).

-less, a suffix meaning: without (*childless*); not able to (*sleepless*); not able to be (*useless*).

les·see (le sē′), *n., pl.* **-sees.** a person to whom a lease is granted.

less′en, *v.t., v.i.* to make or become less.

less′er, *adj., a compar. of* **little** *with* **least** *as superl.* smaller, as in size, value, or importance.

Less′er Antil′les, *n.pl.* See under ANTILLES.

Les·sing (les′ing), *n.* **Doris (May),** born 1919, British author.

les·son (les′ən), *n.* **1.** a section into which a course of study is divided. **2.** a chapter, exercise, etc., assigned to a student for study. **3.** something learned or studied. **4.** an instructive example. **5.** a reproof or punishment. **6.** a portion of Scripture read at a divine service.

les·sor (les′ôr, le sôr′), *n.* a person who grants a lease.

lest (lest), *conj.* for fear that.

let¹ (let), *v.,* **let, let·ting.** —*v.t.* **1.** to allow or permit. **2.** to cause to; make: *to let her know the truth.* **3.** (used as an auxiliary expressive of a request, warning, etc.): *Let me see.* **4.** to rent or lease. —*v.i.* **5.** to be rented or leased. **6. let down, a.** to disappoint or betray. **b.** to lower. **7. ~ off, a.** to release explosively. **b.** to release without punishment. **8. ~ on, a.** to reveal, as information. **b.** to pretend. **9. ~ out, a.**

to release, as from confinement. **b.** to alter (a garment) so as to make larger. **10.** ~ **up, a.** to abate. **b.** to cease. —*Idiom.* **11. let be,** to refrain from interfering with.

let[2] (let), *n.* **1.** (in tennis, badminton, etc.) any shot or action that must be replayed. **2.** *Chiefly Law.* an obstacle: *to act without let or hindrance.*

-let, a suffix meaning: small (*booklet*); an article worn on (*anklet*).

let'down', *n.* **1.** a disappointment. **2.** a decrease in volume, force, energy, etc.

le•thal (lē′thəl), *adj.* deadly; fatal. —**le′thal•ly,** *adv.*

leth•ar•gy (leth′ər jē), *n.* the quality or state of being drowsy; apathetic or sluggish inactivity. —**le•thar•gic** (lə thär′jik), *adj.* —**le•thar′gi•cal•ly,** *adv.*

let's (lets), contraction of *let us.*

let•ter (let′ər), *n.* **1.** a written communication usu. transmitted by mail. **2.** a character that is part of an alphabet. **3.** literal meaning: *the letter of the law.* **4. letters, a.** literature in general. **b.** learning; knowledge, esp. of literature. —*v.t.* **5.** to mark with letters. —**let′ter•er,** *n.*

let′ter car′rier, *n.* MAIL CARRIER.

let′tered, *adj.* **1.** educated or learned. **2.** literate. **3.** marked with letters.

let′ter•head′, *n.* **1.** a printed heading on stationery giving a name and address. **2.** a sheet of paper bearing a letterhead.

let′ter•ing, *n.* **1.** the act of marking with or forming letters. **2.** the letters themselves.

let′ter-per′fect, *adj.* precise in every detail.

let′ter•press′, *n.* the process of printing from letters or type in relief.

let′ter-qual′i•ty, *adj.* designating or producing type equal in sharpness and resolution to that produced by an electric typewriter.

let′ters pat′ent, *n.pl.* an instrument issued by a government conferring an exclusive right, as to make and sell an invention.

let•tuce (let′is), *n.* a cultivated plant with succulent leaves used for salads.

let′up′, *n.* cessation; pause; relief.

leu•ke•mi•a (lōō kē′mē ə), *n.* any of several cancers of the bone marrow characterized by an abnormal increase of white blood cells. —**leu•ke′mic,** *adj.*

leu•ko•cyte (lōō′kə sīt′), *n.* WHITE BLOOD CELL.

lev•ee (lev′ē), *n., pl.* **-ees. 1.** an embankment designed to prevent the flooding of a river. **2.** a landing place for ships; quay.

lev•el (lev′əl), *adj., n., v.,* **-eled, -el•ing** or (*esp. Brit.*) **-elled, -el•ling.** —*adj.* **1.** having a flat or even surface. **2.** being parallel to the horizon. **3.** equal, as in height or status. **4.** steady or uniform: *a level voice.* **5.** sensible; rational: *a level head.* —*n.* **6.** the horizontal line or plane in which anything is situated, with regard to its elevation: *a shelf at eye level.* **7.** elevation; height: *The water rose to a level of 30 feet.* **8.** a position in a graded scale of values: *an average level of skill.* **9.** a horizontal surface: *the upper level of the bridge.* **10.** a surveying instrument used for establishing a horizontal. —*v.t.* **11.** to make level or even. **12.** to bring to the level of the ground: *to level trees.* **13.** *Informal.* to knock down (a person). **14.** to make equal, as in status. **15.** to aim (a weapon, criticism, etc.) at a mark. **16. level with,** to be frank with. —*v.i.* **17.** to bring persons or things to a common level. —**lev′el•er, lev′el•ler,** *n.*

lev′el•head′ed, *adj.* having common sense and sound judgment. —**lev′el•head′ed•ness,** *n.*

lev′el play′ing field′, *n.* a state of equality; an equal opportunity.

lev•er (lev′ər, lē′vər), *n.* **1.** a rigid bar that pivots about one point and is used to move an object at a second point by a force applied at a third. **2.** a means to an end.

lev′er•age (-ij), *n.* **1.** the mechanical advantage gained by using a lever. **2.** power to act effectively or to influence people.

lev′eraged buy′out, *n.* the purchase of a company with borrowed money, using the company's assets as collateral.

Le•vi (lē′vī, lā′vē), *n.* **1.** a son of Jacob and Leah. Gen. 29:34. **2.** one of the 12 tribes of Israel. **3.** original name of MATTHEW (def. 1). **4.** a Levite.

le•vi•a•than (li vī′ə thən), *n.* **1.** (*often cap.*) *Bible.* a sea monster. Ps. 104:26 **2.** something of immense size or power. [< LL ≪ Heb *liwyāthān*]

Le•vi's (lē′vīz), (*used with a pl. v.*) *Trademark.* a brand of jeans, esp. blue jeans.

lev•i•tate (lev′i tāt′), *v.i., v.t.,* **-tat•ed, -tat•ing.** to rise or cause to rise in the air, esp. in apparent defiance of gravity. —**lev′i•ta′tion,** *n.*

Le•vite (lē′vīt), *n.* a member or a descendant of the tribe of Levi, having honorific religious duties.

Le•vit•i•cus (li vit′i kəs), *n.* the third book of the Bible, containing laws chiefly concerning the priests and Jewish ceremonial observance.

lev•i•ty (lev′i tē), *n.* lightness of mind, character, or behavior.

lev•y (lev′ē), *n., pl.* **-ies,** *v.,* **-ied, -y•ing.** —*n.* **1.** an imposing or collecting, as of a tax, by authority or force. **2.** the amount collected. **3.** the conscription of troops. **4.** the troops conscripted. —*v.t.* **5.** to impose (a tax, fine, etc.). **6.** to conscript (troops). **7.** to wage (war). —**lev′i•er,** *n.*

lewd (lōōd), *adj.,* **-er, -est. 1.** inclined to or inciting to lust or lechery. **2.** obscene or indecent. —**lewd′ly,** *adv.* —**lewd′ness,** *n.*

Lew•is (lōō′is), *n.* **1. C(live) S(taples)** ("*Clive Hamilton*"), 1898–1963, English novelist, literary historian, and Christian essayist. **2. (Harry) Sinclair,** 1885–1951, U.S. writer. **3. John L(lewellyn),** 1880–1969, U.S. labor leader. **4. Meriwether,** 1774–1809, U.S. explorer: leader of the Lewis and Clark expedition 1804–06.

lex•i•cog•ra•phy (lek′si kog′rə fē), *n.* the writing, editing, or compiling of dictionaries. —**lex′i•cog′ra•pher,** *n.* —**lex′i•co•graph′ic** (-kə graf′ik), **lex′i•co•graph′i•cal,** *adj.*

lex′i•con′ (-kon′, -kən), *n.* **1.** a dictionary, esp. of Greek, Latin, or Hebrew. **2.** the vocabulary of a particular language, field, etc. —**lex′i•cal,** *adj.*

Lex•ing•ton (lek′sing tən), *n.* a city in N Kentucky. 204,165.

lg., 1. large. **2.** long.

Lha•sa (lä′sə, -sä, las′ə), *n.* the capital of Tibet, in SW China. 310,000.

Li, *Chem. Symbol.* lithium.

L.I., Long Island.

li•a•bil•i•ty (lī′ə bil′i tē), *n., pl.* **-ties. 1.** liabilities, debts or monetary obligations. **2.** something disadvantageous. **3.** the state or quality of being liable.

li′a•ble, *adj.* **1.** legally responsible. **2.** subject or susceptible. **3.** likely or apt. —**Usage.** Some usage guides say that LIABLE can be used only in contexts in which the outcome is undesirable: *The picnic is liable to be spoiled by rain.* This use occurs often in formal writing but not to the exclusion of use in contexts in which the outcome is desirable: *liable to stimulate the economy.*

li•ai•son (lē ā′zən, -zon), *n.* **1.** the contact maintained between military or organizational units. **2.** a person who maintains such a contact. **3.** an illicit sexual relationship.

li•ar (lī′ər), *n.* a person who tells lies.

lib (lib), *n. Informal.* liberation: *women's lib.*

li•ba•tion (lī bā′shən), *n.* **1.** a pouring out of wine or other liquid in honor of a deity. **2.** the liquid poured out.

li•bel (lī′bəl), *n., v.,* **-beled, -bel•ing** or (*esp. Brit.*) **-belled, -bel•ling.** —*n.* **1. a.** defamation by written or printed matter, rather than by spoken words. **b.** the crime of publishing such matter. —*v.t.* **2.** to publish a libel against. —**li′bel•er, li/bel•ler,** *n.* —**li′bel•ous, li′bel•lous,** *adj.*

lib•er•al (lib′ər əl, lib′rəl), *adj.* **1.** favoring progress or reform. **2.** free from prejudice; tolerant. **3.** characterized by generosity. **4.** ample or abundant. **5.** not strict or literal. **6.** of the liberal arts. —*n.* **7.** a person of liberal principles or views. —**lib′er•al•ism,** *n.* —**lib′er•al•ly,** *adv.*

lib′eral arts′, *n.pl.* college courses comprising the

arts, humanities, natural sciences, and social sciences.

lib′er•al•ize′, *v.t.*, *v.i.*, **-ized, -iz•ing.** to make or become liberal. —**lib′er•al•i•za′tion**, *n.*

lib′er•ate′ (-ə rāt′), *v.t.*, **-at•ed, -at•ing. 1.** to set free, as from bondage or foreign control. **2.** to free (a group or individual) from social or economic constraints. **3.** to set free from combination, as a gas. —**lib′er•a′tion**, *n.* —**lib′er•a′tor**, *n.*

libera′tion theol′ogy, *n.* a modern Christian theology stressing liberation from racial, economic, and political oppression. —**libera′tion theolo′gian,** *n.*

Li•be•ri•a (lī bēr′ē ə), *n.* a republic in W Africa: founded by freed American slaves 1822. 2,602,068. —**Li•be′ri•an,** *adj., n.*

lib•er•tar•i•an (lib′ər târ′ē ən), *n.* a person who advocates liberty, esp. with regard to thought or conduct.

lib′er•tine′ (-tēn′, -tin), *n.* **1.** a person who is morally or sexually unrestrained. —*adj.* **2.** dissolute; licentious.

lib′er•ty, *n., pl.* **-ties. 1.** freedom from arbitrary or despotic government. **2.** freedom from external or foreign rule. **3.** freedom from captivity, confinement, etc. **4.** permission granted to a sailor to go ashore. **5.** impertinent freedom in action or speech: *to take liberties.* —*Idiom.* **6. at liberty, a.** free from captivity. **b.** free to do or be as specified. —*Saying.* **7. Give me liberty or give me death!** death is preferable to tyranny: a statement (1775) by Patrick Henry.

Lib′erty Bell′, *n.* the bell of Independence Hall in Philadelphia, rung on July 8, 1776, to proclaim the adoption of the Declaration of Independence.

Lib′erty Founda′tion, *n.* a political action group formed mainly of Protestant fundamentalists to further strict conservative aims. Formerly, **Moral Majority.**

li•bid•i•nous (li bid′n əs), *adj.* lustful; lascivious.

li•bi•do (li bē′dō), *n., pl.* **-dos. 1.** *Psychoanalysis.* all of the instinctual energies and desires derived from the id. **2.** sexual drive. —**li•bid′i•nal** (-bid′n l), *adj.*

Li•bra (lē′brə, lī′-), *n.* the seventh sign of the zodiac. [< L: pair of scales]

li•brar•i•an (lī brâr′ē ən), *n.* a person in charge of a library.

li•brar•y (lī′brer′ē, -brə rē, -brē), *n., pl.* **-brar•ies. 1.** a place containing books, films, etc., arranged and cataloged in a fixed way. **2.** any collection of books, or the space containing them.

li•bret•to (li bret′ō), *n., pl.* **-bret•tos, -bret•ti** (-bret′ē). **1.** the text of an opera or similar work. **2.** a book containing such a text. —**li•bret′tist,** *n.*

Lib•y•a (lib′ē ə), *n.* a republic in N Africa. 5,648,359. —**Lib′y•an,** *adj., n.*

lice (līs), *n.* pl. of LOUSE.

li•cense (lī′səns), *n., v.,* **-censed, -cens•ing.** —*n.* **1.** formal permission from a constituted authority to do something, as to carry on some business. **2.** a certificate of such permission. **3.** deviation from rule, fact, etc., as for the sake of literary effect: *poetic license.* —*v.t.* **4.** to issue or grant a license to or for.

li′cen•see′ (-sən sē′), *n., pl.* **-sees.** a person to whom a license is granted.

li•cen′ti•ate (-sen′shē it, -āt′), *n.* a person who has received a license, as from a university, to practice a profession.

li•cen′tious, *adj.* sexually unrestrained; lascivious. —**li•cen′tious•ly,** *adv.* —**li•cen′tious•ness,** *n.*

li•chen (lī′kən), *n.* an organism composed of a fungus in union with an alga, commonly forming patches on rocks and trees.

Lich•ten•stein (lik′tən stēn′), *n.* **Roy,** 1923–97, U.S. artist.

lic•it (lis′it), *adj.* legal; lawful. —**lic′it•ly,** *adv.*

lick (lik), *v.t.* **1.** to pass the tongue over the surface of. **2.** (of waves, flames, etc.) to pass lightly over. **3.** *Informal.* **a.** to hit or beat. **b.** to defeat. —*n.* **4.** a stroke of the tongue over something. **5.** SALT LICK. **6.** *Informal.* **a.** a blow. **b.** a brief, brisk burst of activity. **c.** a small amount. —*Idiom.* **7. lick and a promise,** a perfunctory performance of a chore.

lick′e•ty-split′ (lik′i tē), *adv. Informal.* at great speed.

lick′ing, *n. Informal.* **1.** a beating or thrashing. **2.** a defeat or setback.

lic•o•rice (lik′ər ish, -ə ris), *n.* **1.** the sweet-tasting, dried root of a Eurasian plant, or an extract made from it. **2.** a candy flavored with licorice root.

lid (lid), *n.* **1.** a movable cover, as for a jar. **2.** an eyelid. **3.** a restraint or curb, as on prices or news. —**lid′ded,** *adj.*

lie¹ (lī), *n., v.,* **lied, ly•ing.** —*n.* **1.** a false statement made with deliberate intent to deceive. —*v.i.* **2.** to tell a lie. —*v.t.* **3.** to bring about or affect by lying.

lie² (lī), *v.,* **lay, lain, ly•ing.** *n.* —*v.i.* **1.** to be in or assume a horizontal or recumbent position. **2.** to rest on a surface in a horizontal position. **3.** to remain in a state of inactivity, restraint, etc.: *to lie in ambush.* **4.** to be situated: *land lying along the coast.* **5.** to be found; exist: *The fault lies here.* —*n.* **6.** the manner, position, or direction in which something lies. —*Idiom.* **7. lie down on the job,** *Informal.* to do less than one could or should do. **8. take lying down,** to accept without remonstrance. —**Usage.** LIE and LAY, though often confused, are different verbs. LAY takes an object, and means "to put or place": *Lay the folders on the desk. She laid the baby in the crib.* LIE does not take an object; its past tense is identical with the present tense of LAY: *Lie down, children. Yesterday the dog lay in the shade all afternoon.*

Liech•ten•stein (lik′tən stīn′, liкн′-), *n.* a small principality in central Europe between Austria and Switzerland. 31,461.

lied (lēd, lēt), *n., pl.* **lied•er** (lē′dər). a typically 19th-century German song.

lie′ detec′tor, *n.* a polygraph used to determine the truth or falsity of a person's answers under questioning.

lief (lēf), *adv.* gladly; willingly: *I would as lief go south as not.*

liege (lēj, lēzh), *n.* **1.** a feudal lord. **2.** a feudal vassal or subject.

lien (lēn, lē′ən), *n.* the legal right to hold another's property, esp. to satisfy a debt.

lieu (lōō), *n.* **1.** place; stead. —*Idiom.* **2. in lieu of,** instead of.

lieu•ten•ant (lōō ten′ənt; *in Brit. use, except in the navy,* lef ten′ənt), *n.* **1. a.** FIRST LIEUTENANT. **b.** SECOND LIEUTENANT. **2.** a naval officer ranking above a lieutenant junior grade. **3.** a person who acts in the place of a superior. —**lieu•ten′an•cy,** *n.*

lieuten′ant colo′nel, *n.* a military officer ranking above a major.

lieuten′ant comman′der, *n.* a commissioned officer in the U.S. Navy or Coast Guard ranking above a lieutenant.

lieuten′ant gen′eral, *n.* a military officer ranking above a major general.

lieuten′ant gov′ernor, *n.* an official next in rank to the governor of a state.

lieuten′ant jun′ior grade′, *n.* a naval officer ranking above an ensign.

life (līf), *n., pl.* **lives** (līvz). —*n.* **1.** the condition that distinguishes organisms from inorganic objects and dead organisms, being manifested by metabolism, growth, reproduction, etc. **2.** the animate existence or period of animate existence of an individual. **3.** the period of existence or activity of something inanimate. **4.** a living being. **5.** living things collectively: *insect life.* **6.** a particular aspect of existence: *enjoyed an active physical life.* **7.** the sum of experiences and actions that constitute a person's existence. **8.** a biography. **9.** animation; liveliness. **10.** a manner of living. —*Idiom.* **11. for dear life,** with the most desperate effort possible. **12. not on your life,** absolutely not. **13. take one's life in one's hands,** to risk death knowingly. **14. to the life,** in perfect imitation; exactly. —**life′less,** *adj.* —**life′like′,** *adj.*

life′ belt′, *n.* a beltlike life preserver.

life′blood′, *n.* **1.** the blood, considered as essential to life. **2.** a vital or animating element.

life′boat′, *n.* a ship's boat designed to rescue persons from a sinking ship.

life′-care′ or **life′care′**, *adj.* designed to provide for the basic needs of elderly residents: *a life-care facility.*

life′guard′, *n.* an expert swimmer employed, as at a beach, to protect bathers from drowning.

life′ insur′ance, *n.* insurance providing for cash payment to a named beneficiary upon the death of the policyholder.

life′ jack′et, *n.* a life preserver in the form of a sleeveless jacket.

Life′, lib′erty, and the pursuit′ of hap′-piness, inalienable rights of human beings, as stated in the U.S. Declaration of Independence (1776).

life′line′, *n.* **1.** a rope for saving life, as one attached to a lifeboat. **2.** the line by which a diver is lowered and raised. **3.** a route over which needed supplies are sent.

life′long′, *adj.* lasting through all of one's life.

life′ preserv′er, *n.* a buoyant device for keeping a person afloat.

lif′er, *n. Informal.* a person serving a term of life imprisonment.

life′ raft′, *n.* a raft for use in emergencies at sea.

life′sav′er, *n.* **1.** one who rescues another from danger of death. **2.** one that saves a person, as from a difficult situation. —**life′sav′ing**, *adj., n.*

life′-size′ or **-sized′**, *adj.* of the natural size of an object, person, etc.

life′style′ or **life′ style′**, *n.* the typical way of living of an individual or group.

life′time′, *n.* the time that the life of someone or something continues.

life′work′, *n.* the complete or principal work of a lifetime.

LIFO (lī′fō), *n.* last-in, first-out: a method of inventory evaluation.

lift (lift), *v.t.* **1.** to bring up to a higher position. **2.** to raise or direct upward: *to lift one's head.* **3.** to rescind or stop, as a curfew or blockade. **4.** to raise in rank, condition, etc. **5.** *Informal.* to steal. **6.** to pay off (a debt). —*v.i.* **7.** to go up. **8.** to strain upward in raising something. —*n.* **9.** the act of lifting. **10.** the distance that anything is raised. **11.** a lifting force. **12.** the quantity lifted. **13.** a ride, esp. one given to a pedestrian. **14.** a feeling of exaltation. **15.** a device for lifting. **16.** *Brit.* ELEVATOR (def. 1). **17.** the component of the aerodynamic forces exerted on an airfoil perpendicular to the forward motion and opposing gravity.

lift′off′, *n.* **1.** the vertical ascent by a spacecraft or aircraft. **2.** the instant of this.

lig•a•ment (lig′ə mənt), *n.* a band of strong tissue that connects bones or holds organs in place.

lig•a•ture (lig′ə chər, -chŏŏr′), *n.* **1.** the act of binding or tying up. **2.** a tie or bond. **3.** a character or type combining two or more letters, as *fl.* **4.** a thread or wire for surgical constriction of blood vessels.

light¹ (līt), *n., adj.,* **light•er, light•est,** *v.,* **light•ed** or **lit, light•ing.** —*n.* **1.** something that makes things visible or affords illumination. **2. a.** electromagnetic radiation to which the organs of sight react. **b.** ultraviolet or infrared radiation. **3.** an illuminating source, as the sun or a lamp. **4.** radiance or illumination. **5.** daybreak or dawn. **6.** a means of igniting, as a spark. **7.** the aspect in which a thing is regarded: *saw things in a new light.* **8.** mental or spiritual enlightenment. **9.** a window or a windowpane. —*adj.* **10.** having light or illumination. **11.** pale. —*v.t.* **12.** to set burning, as a fire. **13.** to turn on (an electric light). **14.** to give light to. **15.** to brighten. —*v.i.* **16.** to become kindled. **17.** to ignite a cigar, cigarette, or pipe (usu. fol. by *up*). **18.** to become illuminated. **19.** to brighten. —*Idiom.* **20. in (the) light of,** considering. **21. light at the end of the tunnel,** a prospect of success, relief, or redemption. **22. see the light, a.** to come into existence or prominence. **b.** to understand something at last. —*Saying.* **23. Better to light one little candle than to curse the darkness,** even small actions help to dispel the wrongs of

the world. **24. Let there be light,** God's command to create the universe out of the void. Gen. 1:3. —**light′ness,** *n.*

light² (līt), *adj.* and *adv.,* **-er, -est.** —*adj.* **1.** of little weight. **2.** of little weight in proportion to bulk. **3.** of less than the usual weight, force, intensity, etc. **4.** not difficult or burdensome. **5.** not profound or serious. **6.** of little importance. **7.** easily digested: *light food.* **8.** (esp. of beer and wine) having fewer calories than the standard product. **9.** airy or buoyant in movement. **10.** cheerful; carefree: *a light heart.* **11.** dizzy. **12.** using small-scale machinery primarily for the production of consumer goods: *light industry.* —*adv.* **13.** without much baggage: *to travel light.* —**light′ly,** *adv.* —**light′ness,** *n.*

light³ (līt), *v.i.,* **light•ed** or **lit, light•ing. 1.** to come to rest; land. **2.** to come by chance: *to light on a clue.* **3. light into,** to attack physically or verbally.

light′en¹, *v.t.* to make or become lighter or less dark; brighten. —**light′en•er,** *n.*

light′en², *v.t., v.i.* **1.** to make or become lighter in weight. **2.** to make or become less burdensome. **3.** to make or become less gloomy.

light′er¹, *n.* a device used in lighting cigarettes, cigars, or pipes.

light′er², *n.* a large barge used to load or unload ships or to transport goods short distances.

light′face′, *n.* a printing type characterized by thin, light lines. —**light′-faced′,** *adj.*

light′-fin′gered, *adj.* skillful at or given to pilfering.

Light•foot (līt′fŏŏt′), *n.* **Joseph Barber,** 1828–89, English clergyman and Bible scholar.

light′-foot′ed, *adj.* stepping lightly or nimbly.

light′head′ed, *adj.* **1.** giddy or dizzy. **2.** having a frivolous disposition.

light′heart′ed, *adj.* carefree; cheerful. —**light′-heart′ed•ly,** *adv.* —**light′heart′ed•ness,** *n.*

light′ heav′yweight, *n.* a professional boxer weighing up to 175 lb. (80 kg).

light′house′, *n.* a tower displaying a light for the guidance of mariners.

lighthouse

light′ing, *n.* **1.** the act of igniting or illuminating. **2.** the arrangement of lights to achieve particular effects.

light′ me′ter, *n.* an instrument that measures the intensity of light in a certain place and indicates proper photographic exposure.

light′ning (-ning), *n.* **1.** a luminous electric spark discharge in the atmosphere. —*adj.* **2.** of or resembling lightning, esp. in regard to speed. —*Saying.* **3. Lightning never strikes twice in the same place,** events are unique in their timing and circumstances.

light′ning bug′, *n.* FIREFLY.

light′ning rod′, *n.* a metal rod installed to divert lightning away from a structure by providing a direct path to the ground.

Light′ of the World′, *n.* Jesus Christ. John 8:12; 9:5; 12:46.

light′ op′era, *n.* OPERETTA.

light′weight′, *adj.* **1.** light in weight. **2.** trivial or trifling. —*n.* **3.** *Informal.* a person of little influence, importance, etc. **4.** a professional boxer weighing up to 135 lb. (61 kg).

light′-year′, *n.* the distance traversed by light in one year, about 5.88 trillion mi. (9.46 trillion km).

lig·ne·ous (lig′nē əs), *adj.* of the nature of or resembling wood.

lik·a·ble or **like·a·ble** (lī′kə bəl), *adj.* readily or easily liked. —**lik′a·ble·ness, lik′a·bil′i·ty,** *n.*

like¹ (līk), *adj.* **1.** of the same form, appearance, kind, etc. —*prep.* **2.** similarly to: *She works like a beaver.* **3.** resembling: *Your necklace is like mine.* **4.** characteristic of: *It would be like him to be late.* **5.** indicative of: *It looks like rain.* **6.** disposed or inclined to: *to feel like going to bed.* —*adv.* **7.** *Informal.* likely or probably: *like as not.* —*conj.* **8.** as: *It happened like you said it would.* **9.** as if: *He acted like he was afraid.* **10.** *Informal.* (used esp. after forms of *be* to introduce reported speech or thought): *She's like, "I don't believe it,"* and *I'm like, "No, it's true!"* —*n.* **11.** a counterpart, match, or equal: *No one has seen her like in a long time.* **12. the like,** something of a similar nature: *They grow oranges, lemons, and the like.* —*Idiom.* **13. something like,** approximately the same as. **14. the like** or **likes of,** the equal of. —**Usage.** Since the mid-19th century, there have been many objections to the use of LIKE as a conjunction meaning "as" or "as if": *She talks like you do. It looks like it will rain.* However, such uses have existed for more than 500 years and are almost universal today except in the most formal speech and writing.

like² (līk), *v.,* **liked, lik·ing,** *n.* —*v.t.* **1.** to find agreeable or congenial to one's taste. **2.** to regard with favor. **3.** to wish or want. —*v.i.* **4.** to feel inclined: *Stay if you like.* —*n.* **5.** Usu., **likes.** the things a person likes.

-like, a suffix meaning like or characteristic of (*childlike*).

like/li·hood′ (-lē hood′), *n.* the state of being likely; probability.

like/ly, *adj.,* **-li·er, -li·est,** *adv.* —*adj.* **1.** probably destined: *something not likely to happen.* **2.** seeming like truth or fact: *a likely story.* **3.** apparently suitable: *a likely place to live.* —*adv.* **4.** probably: *We will most likely stay home.*

like/-mind′ed, *adj.* having a similar opinion, disposition, etc. —**like′-mind′ed·ness,** *n.*

lik′en, *v.t.* to represent as similar or like.

like′ness, *n.* **1.** a portrait or copy. **2.** the state or fact of being similar. **3.** the semblance of something; guise.

like/wise′, *adv.* **1.** in addition. **2.** in like manner; similarly.

lik′ing, *n.* **1.** preference, inclination, or favor. **2.** pleasure or taste.

li·lac (lī′lək, -läk, -lak), *n.* **1.** a shrub with large clusters of fragrant purple or white flowers. **2.** pale reddish purple.

Lil·li·pu·tian (lil′i pyoo′shən), *adj.* **1.** extremely small. **2.** petty; trivial.

Li·long·we (li lông′wä), *n.* the capital of Malawi, in the SW part. 186,800.

lilt (lilt), *n.* **1.** a rhythmic swing or cadence. **2.** a light, cheerful song or tune. —**lilt′ing,** *adj.*

lil·y (lil′ē), *n., pl.* **lil·ies,** *adj.* —*n.* **1.** any of various scaly-bulbed plants with funnel-shaped or bellshaped flowers. **2.** the flower of such a plant. **3.** any similar plant, as the water lily. —*adj.* **4.** white as a lily.

lil′y-liv′ered, *adj.* cowardly.

lil′y of the val′ley, *n., pl.* **lilies of the valley. 1.** a plant with an elongated cluster of bell-shaped, fragrant white flowers. **2.** a plant mentioned in the Bible. Song of Solomon 2:10.

lil′y pad′, *n.* the large, floating leaf of a water lily.

Li·ma (lē′mə), *n.* the capital of Peru. 4,605,043.

li′ma bean′ (lī′mə), *n.* **1.** a bean with a broad, flat, edible seed. **2.** the seed.

limb (lim), *n.* **1.** one of the paired bodily appendages of animals, as a leg, arm, or wing. **2.** a main branch

of a tree. —*Idiom.* **3. out on a limb,** in a risky situation. —**limb/less,** *adj.*

lim·ber (lim′bər), *adj.* **1.** characterized by ease in bending the body; supple. **2.** bending readily; flexible. —*v.t., v.i.* **3.** to make or become limber: *to limber up before the game.* —**lim′ber·ness,** *n.*

lim·bo¹ (lim′bō), *n., pl.* **-bos. 1.** (*often cap.*) *Theology.* a region for the souls of unbaptized infants and of the righteous who died before the coming of Christ. **2.** a place or state of oblivion. **3.** an intermediate state or place. [< ML *in limbo* on hell's border (L: on the edge)]

lim·bo² (lim′bō), *n., pl.* **-bos.** a West Indian dance done by bending backward to pass under a successively lowered horizontal bar. [cf. Jamaican E *limba* limber]

Lim·burg·er (lim′bûr′gər), *n.* a soft cheese with a strong odor and flavor. Also called **Lim′burger cheese′.**

lime¹ (līm), *n., v.,* **limed, lim·ing.** —*n.* **1.** a white or grayish white solid, calcium oxide, used in mortars, plasters, and cements and as a fertilizer. —*v.t.* **2.** to treat or cover with lime. —**lim/y,** *adj.*

lime² (līm), *n.* **1.** the small, greenish yellow, acid fruit of a citrus tree. **2.** the tree itself.

lime·ade (līm′ād′, līm′ād′), *n.* a beverage of lime juice, sweetener, and water.

lime/light′, *n.* **1.** a position at the center of public attention. **2.** (formerly) a spotlight unit for the stage, using a flame of mixed gases directed at a cylinder of lime.

lim·er·ick (lim′ər ik), *n.* a humorous, often nonsensical poem of five lines. [alluding to *Limerick,* county and city in Ireland]

lime/stone′, *n.* a sedimentary rock consisting predominantly of calcium carbonate.

lim·it (lim′it), *n.* **1.** the final or furthest boundary or point as to extent, amount, continuance, etc. **2. limits,** the premises enclosed within boundaries. —*v.t.* **3.** to restrict by establishing limits. **4.** to confine within limits. —**lim/i·ta/tion,** —**lim/it·less,** *adj.*

lim/it·ed, *adj.* **1.** confined within limits. **2.** (of trains, buses, etc.) making only a limited number of stops en route.

limn (lim), *v.t.,* **limned, limn·ing** (lim′ing, -ning). **1.** to represent in drawing or painting. **2.** to describe. —**lim/ner** (-nər), *n.*

lim·o (lim′ō), *n., pl.* **lim·os.** *Informal.* a limousine.

Li·moges (li mōzh′), *n.* a type of fine porcelain manufactured at Limoges, France. Also called **Limoges′ ware′.**

lim·ou·sine (lim′ə zēn′, lim′ə zēn′), *n.* **1.** a large, luxurious automobile, esp. one driven by a chauffeur. **2.** a small bus for transporting passengers to and from an airport, train station, etc.

limp¹ (limp), *v.i.* **1.** to walk with a labored movement, as when lame. **2.** to progress with difficulty. —*n.* **3.** a lame movement or gait.

limp² (limp), *adj.,* **-er, -est. 1.** lacking stiffness or rigidity. **2.** lacking force or energy. —**limp/ly,** *adv.* —**limp/ness,** *n.*

lim·pet (lim′pit), *n.* any of various marine gastropods, usu. adhering to rocks.

lim·pid (lim′pid), *adj.* clear or transparent, as water. —**lim·pid/i·ty, lim/pid·ness,** *n.* —**lim/pid·ly,** *adv.*

lin·age (lī′nij), *n.* the number of printed lines covered by a magazine article, advertisement, etc.

linch·pin (linch′pin′), *n.* a pin inserted through the end of an axle to keep the wheel on.

Lin·coln (ling′kən), *n.* **1. Abraham,** 1809–65, 16th president of the U.S. 1861–65. **2.** the capital of Nebraska, in the SE part. 203,076.

Lin′coln's Sec′ond Inau′gural Address′, *n.* a speech given by Abraham Lincoln on March 4, 1865, during which he urged that the nation should deal with the aftermath of the Civil War "with malice toward none, with charity for all."

Lind·bergh (lind′bûrg, lin′-), *n.* **Charles Augustus,** 1902–74, U.S. aviator.

lin·den (lin/dən), *n.* any of various trees with fragrant yellowish white flowers and heart-shaped leaves.

line¹ (līn), *n., v.,* **lined, lin·ing.** —*n.* **1.** a long, thin mark made with a pen, tool, etc., on a surface. **2.** the trace of a moving point. **3.** a number of persons or things arranged along an imaginary line. **4.** a wrinkle on the face or neck. **5.** an indication of demarcation; boundary. **6.** a unit in the metrical structure of a poem. **7.** Usu., **lines.** the words of an actor's part. **8.** a short written message. **9.** a transportation company or system, or one of its routes. **10.** a course of movement or progress: *the line of march.* **11.** a course of action, thought, etc.: *a conservative line.* **12.** a piece of information: *I've got a line on a good used car.* **13.** a series of persons descended from a common ancestor: *a line of kings.* **14.** a person's occupation or business. **15.** *Informal.* a mode of conversation intended to impress. **16.** outline or contour. **17.** a telephone connection. **18.** a stock of goods of the same general class. **19.** *Mil.* **a.** a series of fortifications. **b.** a formation of troops or ships drawn up for battle. **20.** a string, cord, wire, etc. **21.** a pipe or hose: *a steam line.* **22.** the football players stationed on the line of scrimmage. —*v.i.* **23.** to take a position in a line: *to line up for play.* —*v.t.* **24.** to bring into a line. **25.** to mark with lines. **26.** to form a line along. —*Idiom.* **27. draw the line,** to impose a limit. **28. hold the line,** to maintain the status quo. **29. into line,** into conformity or alignment. **30. on line,** actively linked to a computer.

line² (līn), *v.t.,* **lined, lin·ing,** to cover the inner side or surface of.

lin·e·age (lin/ē ij), *n.* **1.** lineal descent from an ancestor. **2.** family or stock.

lin/e·al (-əl), *adj.* **1.** being in a direct line: *a lineal descendant.* **2.** of or transmitted by lineal descent. **3.** LINEAR.

lin/e·a·ment (-ə mənt), *n.* Often, **-ments.** a distinguishing feature or detail, esp. of the face.

lin/e·ar (-ər), *adj.* **1.** of, consisting of, or using lines. **2.** involving measurement in one dimension only. **3.** narrow and elongated. —**lin/e·ar·ly,** *adv.*

line/back/er, *n.* a football player on defense who takes a position close behind the linemen.

line/ drive/, *n.* a batted baseball that travels low, fast, and straight.

line/man, *n., pl.* **-men. 1.** a person who installs or repairs telephone, telegraph, or other wires. **2.** one of the football players in the defensive line.

lin·en (lin/ən), *n.* **1.** fabric woven from flax yarns. **2.** Often, **-ens.** bedding, tablecloths, etc., made of linen or a substitute, as cotton.

line/ of scrim/mage, *n.* an imaginary line on a football field along which opposing teams line up to start a play.

lin·er¹ (lī/nər), *n.* **1.** a ship or airplane operated by a transportation company. **2.** EYELINER.

lin·er² (lī/nər), *n.* **1.** something serving as a lining. **2.** a person who fits or provides linings.

lines/man, *n., pl.* **-men. 1.** an official in tennis and soccer who indicates when the ball goes out of bounds. **2.** an official in football who marks the distances gained or lost.

line/up/, *n.* **1.** an arrangement of persons or things in a line, as to allow identification. **2.** a list of the participating players in a game.

-ling, a suffix meaning: a person connected with (*hireling*); little (*duckling*).

lin·ger (ling/gər), *v.i.* **1.** to remain in a place longer than is usual or expected. **2.** to dwell in thought or enjoyment. **3.** to be tardy in action. —**lin/ger·er,** *n.* —**lin/ger·ing·ly,** *adv.*

lin·ge·rie (län/zhə rā/, -jə-, lan/zhə rē/), *n.* women's undergarments.

lin·go (ling/gō), *n., pl.* **-goes. 1.** the jargon of a particular field, group, etc. **2.** language, esp. if strange or foreign.

lin·gua fran·ca (ling/gwə frang/kə), *n., pl.* **lin·gua fran·cas, lin·guae fran·cae** (ling/gwē fran/sē,

frang/kē). any language widely used as a means of communication among speakers of other languages.

lin·gual (ling/gwəl), *adj.* of or articulated with the aid of the tongue.

lin/guist (-gwist), *n.* **1.** a specialist in linguistics. **2.** a person skilled in several languages.

lin·guis/tics, *n.* the study of language. —**lin·guis/tic,** *adj.*

lin·i·ment (lin/ə mənt), *n.* a liquid preparation for rubbing on the skin, as to relieve soreness.

lin·ing (lī/ning), *n.* something used to line the inner side of something, as a garment.

link (lingk), *n.* **1.** one of the separate pieces forming a chain. **2.** a bond or tie. **3.** any of a number of connected sausages. **4.** *Computers.* an object, as text or graphics, linked through hypertext to a document, another object, etc. —*v.t., v.i.* **5.** to join by or as if by links; unite.

link·age (ling/kij), *n.* **1.** the act of linking, or the state or manner of being linked. **2.** a system of links.

link/ing verb/, *n.* COPULA.

links, *n.pl.* a golf course.

link/up/, *n.* **1.** a contact established, as between military units. **2.** something serving as a linking element or system.

Lin·nae·us (li nē/əs), *n.* **Carolus,** 1707–78, Swedish botanist.

lin·net (lin/it), *n.* a small Old World finch.

li·no·le·um (li nō/lē əm), *n.* a hard, washable floor covering. [< L *līn(um)* flax, linen + *oleum* oil]

lin·seed (lin/sēd/), *n.* the seed of flax.

lin/seed oil/, *n.* a drying oil obtained by pressing linseed, used in making paints, inks, etc.

lint (lint), *n.* **1.** minute shreds or ravelings of yarn. **2.** staple cotton fiber used to make yarn. —**lint/y,** *adj.,* **-i·er, -i·est.**

lin·tel (lin/tl), *n.* a horizontal piece supporting the weight above an opening, as a door.

li·on (lī/ən), *n.* **1.** a large, usu. tawny-yellow cat of Africa and S Asia. **2.** a person of great strength or courage. **3.** a prominent or influential person. —*Proverb.* **4. The lion shall lie down with the lamb,** there shall be peace among enemies (based on Isa. 11:6).

li/on·ess, *n.* a female lion.

li/on·heart/ed, *adj.* exceptionally courageous.

li/on·ize/, *v.t.,* **-ized, -iz·ing.** to treat (a person) as a celebrity.

lip (lip), *n.* **1.** either of the two fleshy folds forming the margins of the mouth. **2.** an edge or rim, as of a pitcher or canyon. **3.** *Slang.* impudent talk. **4.** a liplike anatomical part; labium. —*Idiom.* **5. keep a stiff upper lip,** to face misfortune bravely. —**lipped,** *adj.*

lip·id (lip/id, lī/pid), *n.* any of a group of organic compounds comprising fats, waxes, and similar substances.

lip·o·pro·tein (lip/ə prō/tēn, -tē in, lī/pə-), *n.* any of the class of proteins that contain a lipid combined with a simple protein.

lip·o·suc·tion (lip/ə suk/shən, lī/pə-), *n.* the surgical withdrawal of excess fat from local areas under the skin.

lip·read/ing, *n.* a method, as used by a deaf person, of understanding spoken words by interpreting the speaker's lip movements. —**lip/read/,** *v.t., v.i.,* **-read** (-red/), **-read·ing.** —**lip/read/er,** *n.*

lip/ serv/ice, *n.* insincere profession of friendship, admiration, etc.

lip/stick/, *n.* a crayonlike cosmetic for coloring the lips.

lip/-sync/ or **-synch/,** *v.t., v.i.* to match lip movements with (recorded speech or singing).

liq·ue·fy (lik/wə fī/), *v.t., v.i.,* **-fied, -fy·ing.** to make or become liquid. —**liq/ue·fac/tion** (fak/shən), *n.*

li·queur (li kûr/, -kyŏŏr/), *n.* a strong, sweet, and highly flavored alcoholic liquor.

liq·uid (lik/wid), *adj.* **1.** composed of freely moving molecules that do not tend to separate; neither gaseous nor solid. **2.** of or consisting of liquids. **3.** flowing like water. **4.** clear or bright: *liquid eyes.* **5.** (of sounds or movements) smooth; flowing freely. **6.** readily convertible into cash: *liquid assets.* —*n.* **7.** a liquid substance. —**li•quid/i•ty,** *n.*

liq/ui•date/ (-wi dāt/), *v.t.,* -**dat•ed, -dat•ing. 1.** to settle or pay (a debt). **2.** to dissolve (a business or estate) by apportioning the assets to offset the liabilities. **3.** to convert (assets) into cash. **4.** to get rid of, esp. by killing. —**liq/ui•da/tion,** *n.* —**liq/ui•da/tor,** *n.*

liq/uid•ize/, *v.t.,* -**ized, -iz•ing.** to make liquid.

liq•uor (lik/ər), *n.* **1.** a distilled beverage, as brandy or whiskey. **2.** any liquid substance.

li•ra (lēr/ə), *n., pl.* **li•re** (lēr/ā), **li•ras.** the basic monetary units of Italy, Malta, and Turkey.

Lis•bon (liz/bən), *n.* the capital of Portugal. 807,937.

lisle (līl), *n.* a fine, hard-twisted cotton thread.

lisp (lisp), *n.* **1.** a speech defect consisting in pronouncing *s* and *z* like the *th*-sounds of *thin* and *this,* respectively. **2.** the act or sound of lisping. —*v.t., v.i.* **3.** to speak with a lisp. **4.** to speak imperfectly, esp. in a childish manner. —**lisp/er,** *n.*

lis•some or **-som** (lis/əm), *adj.* **1.** lithe; supple. **2.** agile or nimble.

list¹ (list), *n.* **1.** a series of items written together in a meaningful sequence. —*v.t.* **2.** to set down or enter in a list.

list² (list), *n.* **1.** a leaning to one side, as of a ship. —*v.i., v.t.* **2.** to incline or to cause to incline to one side.

lis•ten (lis/ən), *v.i.* **1.** to give attention for the purpose of hearing. **2.** to heed; obey. —**lis/ten•er,** *n.*

list/ing, *n.* **1.** a list. **2.** the act of making a list. **3.** something included in a list.

list/less (-lis), *adj.* having little interest in anything; languid. —**list/less•ly,** *adv.* —**list/less•ness,** *n.*

list/ price/, *n.* the price at which a product is usu. sold to the public.

list/ serv/er, *n. Computers.* any program that distributes messages to a mailing list.

Liszt (list), *n.* **Franz,** 1811–86, Hungarian composer and pianist.

lit¹ (lit), *v.* a pt. and pp. of LIGHT¹.

lit² (lit), *v.* a pt. and pp. of LIGHT³.

lit., 1. literally. **2.** literature.

lit•a•ny (lit/n ē), *n., pl.* **-nies. 1.** a prayer consisting of a series of invocations with responses. **2.** a prolonged or tedious account: *a litany of complaints.*

li•tchi (lē/chē), *n., pl.* **-tchis.** the fruit of a Chinese tree, consisting of a thin shell enclosing a sweet pulp and a single seed.

li•ter (lē/tər), *n.* a metric unit of liquid capacity equivalent to 1.0567 liquid quarts.

lit•er•a•cy (lit/ər ə sē), *n.* the quality or state of being literate.

lit/er•al (-əl), *adj.* **1.** in accordance with the strict meaning of a word or text. **2.** following the words of the original very closely: *a literal translation.* **3.** true to fact: *a literal description.* **4.** tending to construe words in an unimaginative way. —**lit/er•al•ly,** *adv.* —**lit/er•al•ness,** *n.*

lit•er•ar•y (lit/ə rer/ē), *adj.* **1.** of or characteristic of literature. **2.** versed in literature; well-read.

lit/er•ate (-ər it), *adj.* **1.** able to read and write. **2.** educated. **3.** having knowledge or skill: *computer-literate.* —*n.* **4.** a literate person. —**lit/er•ate•ly,** *adv.*

lit•e•ra•ti (lit/ə rä/tē, -rā/-), *n.pl.* persons of scholarly or literary attainments.

lit•er•a•ture (lit/ər ə chər, -chŏŏr/, li/trə-), *n.* **1.** writing in prose or verse regarded as having permanent worth through its intrinsic excellence. **2.** the entire body of writings of a specific language, period, etc. **3.** the writings dealing with a particular subject. **4.** any kind of printed material.

lithe (līth), *adj.,* **lith•er, lith•est.** bending readily; supple.

lith•i•um (lith/ē əm), *n.* a soft, silver-white metallic element. *Symbol:* Li; *at. wt.:* 6.939; *at. no.:* 3.

lith•o•graph (lith/ə graf/, -gräf/), *n.* **1.** a print pro-

duced by lithography. —*v.t.* **2.** to produce by lithography. —**li•thog/ra•pher** (li thog/rə fər), *n.*

li•thog•ra•phy (li thog/rə fē), *n.* a printing technique by which an image is fixed on a stone or metal plate with a combination of ink-absorbent and ink-repellent vehicles. —**lith•o•graph•ic** (lith/ə graf/ik), *adj.*

lith•o•sphere (lith/ə sfēr/), *n.* the crust and upper mantle of the earth.

Lith•u•a•ni•a (lith/ōō ā/nē ə), *n.* a republic in N Europe, on the Baltic: formerly a part of the USSR. 3,635,932. —**Lith/u•a/ni•an,** *n., adj.*

lit•i•gant (lit/i gənt), *n.* a person engaged in a lawsuit.

lit/i•gate/ (-gāt/), *v.,* -**gat•ed, -gat•ing.** —*v.t.* **1.** to make the subject of a lawsuit. —*v.i.* **2.** to carry on a lawsuit. —**lit/i•ga/tion,** *n.* —**lit/i•ga/tor,** *n.*

li•ti•gious (li tij/əs), *adj.* **1.** of litigation. **2.** inclined to litigate. **3.** argumentative. —**li•ti/gious•ness,** *n.*

lit•mus (lit/məs), *n.* a coloring matter obtained from lichens that turns blue in alkaline solution and red in acid solution.

lit/mus pa/per, *n.* a strip of paper impregnated with litmus, used as a chemical indicator.

li•tre (lē/tər), *n. Chiefly Brit.* LITER.

Litt. D., Doctor of Letters; Doctor of Literature. [< L *Lit(t)erārum Doctor*]

lit•ter (lit/ər), *n.* **1.** scattered objects, rubbish, etc. **2.** a number of young brought forth by an animal at one birth. **3.** a stretcher for transporting a sick or wounded person. **4.** a vehicle carried by people or animals, consisting of a couch suspended between shafts. **5.** straw, hay, etc., used as bedding for animals. **6.** any of various absorbent materials used for lining a box (**lit/ter box/**) in which a cat can eliminate waste. —*v.t.* **7.** to strew (a place) with litter. **8.** to scatter (objects) in disorder. —**lit/ter•er,** *n.*

lit/ter•bug/, *n.* a person who litters public places with trash.

lit•tle (lit/l), *adj.,* **lit•tler** or **less** or **less•er, lit•tlest** or **least,** *adv.,* **less, least,** *n.* —*adj.* **1.** small in size, amount, degree, scale, etc. **2.** short in duration. **3.** minor; unimportant. **4.** mean or narrow: *a little mind.* —*adv.* **5.** not at all: *He little knows what awaits him.* **6.** slightly. **7.** seldom; infrequently. —*n.* **8.** a small amount, quantity, or degree. —*Idiom.* **9.** **little by little,** gradually. **10. too little, too late,** belated and inadequate. —**lit/tle•ness,** *n.*

Lit/tle Cor/poral, *n.* epithet of Napoleon I.

Lit/tle Dip/per, *n.* See under DIPPER (def. 2b).

Lit/tle Gi/ant, *n.* epithet of Stephen Douglas.

lit/tle•neck/, *n.* the quahog clam when young and small.

Lit/tle Rock/, *n.* the capital of Arkansas. 178,136.

lit•to•ral (lit/ər əl), *adj.* of the shore of a lake, sea, or ocean.

lit•ur•gy (lit/ər jē), *n., pl.* **-gies.** a form of public worship; ritual. —**li•tur•gi•cal** (li tûr/ji kəl), *adj.* —**lit/ur•gist,** *n.*

liv•a•ble or **live•a•ble** (liv/ə bəl), *adj.* **1.** suitable for living in. **2.** worth living. —**liv/a•bil/i•ty,** *n.*

live¹ (liv), *v.,* **lived** (livd), **liv•ing.** —*v.i.* **1.** to be alive. **2.** to remain alive. **3.** to continue in existence, operation, memory, etc. **4.** to maintain one's existence; subsist: *to live on one's income.* **5.** to reside. **6.** to pass life in a specified manner. —*v.t.* **7.** to pass or spend: *to live a life of ease.* **8.** to exhibit in one's life: *to live one's philosophy.* **9. ~ down,** to live so as to allow (a mistake, disgrace, etc.) to be forgotten or forgiven. **10. ~ up to,** to behave so as to satisfy (an ideal or standard). —*Proverb.* **11. Live and learn,** to learn from experience. **12. Live and let live,** to be tolerant of others.

live² (līv), *adj.* **1.** being alive; living. **2.** of or during the life of a living being. **3.** full of life, energy, or activity. **4.** burning or glowing: *live coals.* **5.** being in play, as a football. **6.** unexploded: *live ammunition.* **7.** broadcast while happening or being performed. **8.** of current interest: *live issues.* **9.** electrically connected or charged: *a live wire.*

lived (līvd, livd), *adj.* having life, a life, or lives, as specified: *a many-lived cat.*

live•li•hood (līv′lē hŏŏd′), *n.* a means of supporting one's existence, esp. financially.

live′long′ (liv′-), *adj.* entire, esp. when tediously long: *to fret the livelong day.*

live•ly (līv′lē), *adj.*, **-li•er, -li•est. 1.** full of life or energy; vigorous. **2.** animated; sprightly. **3.** stirring or exciting. **4.** strong or keen. **5.** rebounding quickly: *a lively tennis ball.* —**live′li•ness,** *n.*

liv•en (lī′vən), *v.t., v.i.* to make or become more lively (usu. fol. by *up*).

liv•er (liv′ər), *n.* **1.** a glandular organ in vertebrates, functioning in the secretion of bile and in metabolic processes. **2.** this organ of an animal used as food.

Liv•er•pool (liv′ər pōōl′), *n.* a seaport in NW England. 476,000. —**Liv′er•pud′li•an** (-pud′lē ən), *n., adj.*

liv′er•wurst′ (-wûrst′), *n.* a cooked sausage containing a large percentage of liver.

liv•er•y (liv′ə rē, liv′rē), *n., pl.* **-er•ies. 1.** a uniform worn by servants. **2.** the care and feeding of horses for pay. **3.** a stable where horses and vehicles are kept for hire. **4.** a company that rents out automobiles, boats, etc. —**liv′er•ied,** *adj.*

lives (līvz), *n.* pl. of LIFE.

live•stock (līv′stok′), *n.* the animals raised on a farm or ranch.

live′ wire′ (līv), *n. Informal.* an energetic, keenly alert person.

liv•id (liv′id), *adj.* **1.** having a discolored, bluish appearance caused by a bruise. **2.** furiously angry. **3.** deathly pale. —**liv′id•ly,** *adv.*

liv•ing (liv′ing), *adj.* **1.** being alive. **2.** in actual existence or use: *living languages.* **3.** of or suitable for life: *living conditions.* **4.** of living persons: *within living memory.* **5.** lifelike; true to life. **6.** sufficient for living: *a living wage.* —*n.* **7.** the act or condition of one that lives. **8.** livelihood. **9.** a particular manner of life. **10. the living,** living persons collectively.

Liv′ing Bi′ble, *n.* a U.S. Bible paraphrase (New Testament 1962, Bible 1971).

liv′ing room′, *n.* a room in a home used for leisure activities, entertaining guests, etc.

liv′ing will′, *n.* a document stipulating that no extraordinary measures be used to prolong the signer's life during a terminal illness.

Li•vo•ni•a (li vō′nē ə), *n.* a city in SE Michigan, near Detroit. 101,415.

liz•ard (liz′ərd), *n.* any of various scaly reptiles typically having a long body, long tail, and four legs.

Lju•blja•na (lōō′blē ä′nə, -nä), *n.* the capital of Slovenia. 305,211.

'll, a contraction of *shall* or *will: I'll answer the phone.*

LL or **L.L.,** Late Latin.

ll., lines.

lla•ma (lä′mə, yä′-), *n., pl.* **-mas.** a South American ruminant related to the camel.

lla•no (lä′nō, yä′-), *n., pl.* **-nos.** (in the southwestern U.S. and Spanish America) an extensive grassy plain.

LL.B., Bachelor of Laws. [< L *Lēgum Baccalaureus*]

LL.D., Doctor of Laws. [< L *Lēgum Doctor*]

lo (lō), *interj.* look! see!

load (lōd), *n.* **1.** a quantity carried or supported at one time. **2.** the normal maximum amount of something carried by a vehicle, ship, etc. **3.** the amount of work assigned to a person, team, machine, etc. **4.** something that weighs down like a burden. **5. loads,** *Informal.* a great quantity or number. **6.** a commission charged to buyers of mutual-fund shares. —*v.t.* **7.** to put a load on or in. **8.** to supply abundantly. **9.** to weigh down or burden. **10.** to insert ammunition into (a firearm). **11.** to place film, tape, etc., into (a camera or other device). **12.** to bring (a program or data) into a computer's RAM, as from a disk.

load′ed, *adj.* **1.** (of a word, statement, etc.) charged with associations that prevent rational communication. **2.** *Slang.* rich.

load′star′, *n.* LODESTAR.

load′stone′, *n.* LODESTONE.

loaf[1] (lōf), *n., pl.* **loaves. 1.** a portion of bread baked in an oblong mass. **2.** a shaped or molded mass of food, as of ground meat.

loaf[2] (lōf), *v.i.* **1.** to idle away time. **2.** to lounge lazily and idly. —**loaf′er,** *n.*

Loaf′er, *Trademark.* a moccasinlike slip-on shoe.

loam (lōm), *n.* a rich soil containing sand, silt, and clay. —**loam′y,** *adj.*

loan (lōn), *n.* **1.** the act of lending. **2.** something lent, esp. a sum of money lent at interest. —*v.t., v.i.* **3.** to lend. —**loan′er,** *n.* —**Usage.** Despite occasional objections that LOAN cannot be used as a verb referring to things other than money, the word is standard in all contexts but is perhaps most common in financial ones.

loan′ shark′, *n. Informal.* a person who lends money at excessively high rates of interest; usurer.

loan′word′, *n.* a word in one language that has been borrowed from another language.

loath (lōth, lōth), *adj.* unwilling; reluctant.

loathe (lōth), *v.t.*, **loathed, loath•ing.** to feel intense aversion or dislike for; abhor.

loath•ing (lō′thing), *n.* intense aversion.

loath•some (lōth′səm, lōth′-), *adj.* causing loathing; repulsive. —**loath′some•ness,** *n.*

loaves (lōvz), *n.* pl. of LOAF[1].

lob (lob), *v.*, **lobbed, lob•bing,** *n.* —*v.t., v.i.* **1.** to hit (a ball) in a high arc. —*n.* **2.** a lobbed ball. —**lob′ber,** *n.*

lob•by (lob′ē), *n., pl.* **-bies,** *v.*, **-bied, -by•ing.** —*n.* **1.** an entrance hall, as in a public building. **2.** a group of persons who try to influence legislators to vote in favor of a special interest. —*v.i.* **3.** to try to influence legislation. —*v.t.* **4.** to try to influence the votes of (legislators). **5.** to urge the passage of (legislation) by lobbying. —**lob′by•ist,** *n.*

lobe (lōb), *n.* **1.** a roundish projection or division, as of an organ or a leaf. **2.** EARLOBE. —**lo•bar** (lō′bər, -bär), *adj.*

lo•bot•o•my (lə bot′ə mē, lō-), *n., pl.* **-mies.** a surgical incision into or across a lobe of the brain to treat a mental disorder. —**lo•bot′o•mize′** (-mīz′), *v.t.*, **-mized, -miz•ing.**

lob•ster (lob′stər), *n., pl.* **-sters, -ster.** an edible marine crustacean with large pincers.

lo•cal (lō′kəl), *adj.* **1.** of, characteristic of, or restricted to a particular place. **2.** stopping at most or all stations: *a local train.* **3.** of or affecting a particular part of the body. —*n.* **4.** a local train, bus, etc. **5.** a local branch of a union, fraternity, etc. —**lo′cal•ly,** *adv.*

lo′cal-ar′ea net′work, *n.* a computer network confined to a limited area, linking esp. personal computers so that programs, data, etc., can be shared. Also called **LAN.**

lo•cale (lō kal′, -käl′), *n.* a locality, esp. with reference to events or circumstances connected with it.

lo•cal•i•ty, *n., pl.* **-ties.** a specific place or area; location.

lo′cal•ize′ (-kə līz′), *v.t.*, **-ized, -iz•ing.** to confine or restrict to a particular place. —**lo′cal•i•za′tion,** *n.*

lo•cate (lō′kāt, lō kāt′), *v.*, **-cat•ed, -cat•ing.** —*v.t.* **1.** to discover the place of. **2.** to establish in a position or place. **3.** to assign a particular place to. —*v.i.* **4.** to become settled. —**lo′ca•tor,** *n.*

lo•ca′tion, *n.* **1.** a place, position, or situation. **2.** a site outside a movie studio used for filming: *shot on location.*

loc. cit. (lok′ sit′), in the place cited. [< L *locō citātō*]

loch (lok, loкн), *n. Scot.* **1.** a lake. **2.** a narrow arm of the sea.

lock[1] (lok), *n.* **1.** a device for fastening or securing a door, lid, etc. **2.** (in a firearm) the mechanism that explodes the charge. **3.** a chamber in a canal, dam, etc., with gates for raising or lowering ships by admitting or releasing water. —*v.t.* **4.** to fasten or secure with a lock. **5.** to shut in by or as if by means of a lock. **6.** to make fast or immovable. **7.** to interlink: *to lock arms.* —*v.i.* **8.** to become locked. **9.** to become fastened, fixed, or interlocked.

lock² (lok), *n.* **1.** a curl of hair. **2. locks,** the hair of the head. **3.** a tuft of wool, cotton, etc.

lock'er, *n.* **1.** a chest, compartment, etc., that can be locked. **2.** a large compartment for keeping frozen foods.

lock'et (-it), *n.* a small case for a keepsake, usu. worn on a necklace.

lock'jaw', *n.* tetanus in which the jaws become firmly locked together.

lock'out', *n.* the temporary closing of a business during a labor dispute until employees accept the employer's terms.

lock'smith', *n.* a person who makes or repairs locks and keys.

lock'step', *n.* **1.** a way of marching in very close file. **2.** a rigidly inflexible pattern or process.

lock'up', *n.* a jail.

lo•co (lō'kō), *adj. Slang.* insane; crazy.

lo•co•mo•tion (lō'kə mō'shən), *n.* the act or power of moving from place to place.

lo'co•mo'tive, *n.* **1.** a self-propelled vehicular engine for pulling a railroad train. —*adj.* **2.** of locomotion.

lo'co•weed' (lō'kō-), *n.* any of various plants of the southwestern U.S. and Mexico, causing a disease in livestock.

lo•cus (lō'kəs), *n.*, *pl.* **-ci** (-sī, -kē, -kī). **1.** a place; locality. **2.** *Math.* the set of all points, lines, or surfaces that satisfy a given requirement.

lo•cust (lō'kəst), *n.* **1.** a grasshopper commonly migrating in swarms that strip the vegetation from large areas. **2.** any of various cicadas, as the seventeen-year locust. **3.** a North American tree with clusters of fragrant white flowers.

lo•cu•tion (lō kyōō'shən), *n.* **1.** a word, phrase, or expression. **2.** a style of speech or verbal expression.

lode (lōd), *n.* a veinlike deposit of ore.

lo•den (lōd'n), *n.* a sturdy, water-repellent cloth used for coats and jackets.

lode'star', *n.* a star that shows the way, esp. Polaris.

lode'stone', *n.* a variety of magnetite that possesses magnetic polarity.

lodge (loj), *n.*, *v.*, **lodged, lodg•ing.** —*n.* **1.** a makeshift or rough shelter. **2.** a temporary residence, as in the hunting season. **3.** a resort hotel or motel. **4.** the meeting place of a branch of certain fraternal organizations. —*v.i.* **5.** to live in a place temporarily. **6.** to live in rented quarters. **7.** to be fixed in a place or position: *The bullet lodged in the wall.* —*v.t.* **8.** to furnish with living quarters, esp. temporarily. **9.** to bring into a particular place or position. **10.** to vest (power, authority, etc.). **11.** to put (a complaint, etc.) before a court or other authority.

lodg'er, *n.* a person who lives in rented quarters in another's house.

lodg'ing, *n.* **1.** a temporary place to stay. **2. lodgings,** a room or rooms rented for residence in another's house.

Loewe (lō), *n.* **Frederick,** born 1904, U.S. composer, born in Austria.

loft (lôft, loft), *n.* **1.** a room or space under a sloping roof; attic. **2.** a gallery in a church, hall, etc.: *a choir loft.* **3.** an upper story of a warehouse usu. not partitioned into rooms. **4.** Also called **loft' bed'.** a platform built over a living area and used for sleeping. —*v.t.* **5.** to hit or throw aloft.

loft'y, *adj.*, **-i•er, -i•est. 1.** extending high in the air. **2.** exalted in rank, dignity, or character. **3.** elevated in style, tone, or sentiment. **4.** haughty. —**loft'i•ness,** *n.*

log¹ (lôg, log), *n.*, *v.*, **logged, log•ging.** —*n.* **1.** a portion of the trunk or of a large limb of a felled tree. **2.** a detailed record, esp. of the trip of a ship or aircraft. **3.** a device for determining the speed of a ship. —*v.t.* **4.** to cut (trees) into logs. **5.** to enter in a log. **6.** to travel for (a certain distance or a certain amount of time). —*v.i.* **7.** to cut down trees and get

out logs for timber. **8. log in** or **on,** to gain access to a computer system by keying in identifying information. **9.** ~ **off** or **out,** to end a session on a computer system. —**log'ger,** *n.*

log² (lôg, log), *n.* LOGARITHM.

-log, var. of -LOGUE.

lo•gan•ber•ry (lō'gən ber'ē), *n.*, *pl.* **-ries. 1.** a dark red, tart berry of a hybrid blackberry bush. **2.** the plant itself.

log•a•rithm (lô'gə riṯh'əm, log'ə-), *n.* the exponent of the power to which a base number must be raised to equal a given number. —**log'a•rith'mic,** *adj.*

loge (lōzh), *n.* (in a theater) a box or the front section of the lowest balcony.

log•ger•head (lô'gər hed', log'ər-), *n.* **1.** a stupid person. —*Idiom.* **2. at loggerheads,** in conflict.

log•gi•a (lō'jē ə, loj'ə), *n.*, *pl.* **-gi•as.** a gallery or arcade open to the air on at least one side.

loggia

log•ic (loj'ik), *n.* **1.** the science that investigates the principles governing correct inference. **2.** a particular method of reasoning. **3.** reason or sound judgment. **4.** any connection between facts that seems reasonable. **5.** the arrangement of circuitry in a computer. —**lo•gi•cian** (lō jish'ən), *n.*

log'i•cal, *adj.* **1.** according to the principles of logic. **2.** reasonable; to be expected. —**log'i•cal•ly,** *adv.*

lo•gis•tics (lō jis'tiks, lə-), *n.* (*used with a sing. or pl. v.*) **1.** the military science dealing with the procurement of equipment, movement of personnel, etc. **2.** the planning and implementation of the details of any operation. —**lo•gis'tic, lo•gis'ti•cal,** *adj.* —**lo•gis'ti•cal•ly,** *adv.*

log'jam', *n.* **1.** a pileup of logs, as in a river, causing a blockage. **2.** a blockage or impasse.

lo•go (lō'gō), *n.*, *pl.* **-gos.** logotype.

lo•gos (lō'gos, -gōs, log'os), *n.* **1.** (in Greek philosophy) the rational principle that governs the universe. **2.** (in Christian theology) the divine word incarnate in Jesus Christ. John 1:1–14.

log•o•type (lô'gə tīp', log'ə-), *n.* a graphic representation or symbol of a company name, trademark, etc.

log'roll'ing, *n.* the exchange of support or favors, esp. by legislators for mutual political gain.

-logue, a combining form meaning a specified kind of spoken or written discourse (*monologue*).

lo•gy (lō'gē), *adj.*, **-gi•er, -gi•est.** lacking vitality; sluggish. —**lo'gi•ness,** *n.*

-logy, a combining form meaning: the science or study of (*theology*); speaking or expression (*tautology*).

loin (loin), *n.* **1.** Usu., **loins.** the part of the body between the ribs and hipbone. **2.** a cut of meat from this region. **3. loins,** the hips and groin regarded as the seat of physical strength and generative power.

loin'cloth', *n.* a cloth worn around the loins or hips.

Lo•is (lō'is), *n.* a Christian woman, the grandmother of Timothy. II Tim. 1:5.

loi•ter (loi'tər), *v.i.* **1.** to linger aimlessly in or about a place. **2.** to move in a slow, idle manner. **3.** to dawdle. —**loi'ter•er,** *n.*

loll (lol), *v.i.* **1.** to recline in a relaxed or lazy manner. **2.** to hang loosely; droop. —*v.t.* **3.** to allow to droop.

Lol•lard (lol'ərd), *n.* a follower of the religious teachings of John Wycliffe. [late ME < MD *lollaert* mumbler (of prayers)] —**Lol′lard•y, Lol′lard•ry, Lol′lard•ism,** *n.*

lol•li•pop (lol′ē pop′), *n.* a piece of hard candy attached to the end of a stick.

lol•ly•gag (lol′ē gag′), *v.i.,* **-gagged, -gag•ging.** LALLYGAG.

Lon•don (lun′dən), *n.* **1. Jack,** 1876–1916, U.S. writer. **2.** a metropolis in SE England: capital of the United Kingdom. 6,770,400. **3.** a city in S Ontario, in SE Canada. 269,140. —**Lon′don•er,** *n.*

lone (lōn), *adj.* **1.** being alone; solitary. **2.** standing apart; isolated. **3.** sole; only.

lone•ly (lōn′lē), *adj.,* **-li•er, -li•est. 1.** affected with or causing a depressing feeling of being alone. **2.** lone; solitary. —**lone′li•ness,** *n.*

lon′er, *n.* a person who is or prefers to be alone.

lone′some (-səm), *adj.* **1.** depressed because of the lack of companionship. **2.** attended with or causing such a feeling. **3.** remote or isolated. —**lone′some•ness,** *n.*

Lone′ Star′ State′, *n.* Texas (used as a nickname).

lone′ wolf′, *n. Informal.* a person who prefers to live, act, or work alone or independent of others.

long¹ (lông, long), *adj.* and *adv.,* **long•er** (lông′gər, long′-), **long•est** (lông′gist, long′-), *n.* —*adj.* **1.** having considerable extent in space or duration in time. **2.** totaling a number of specified units: *eight miles long.* **3.** containing many items or units. **4.** taking a long time; slow. **5.** broad; considering all aspects: *to take a long view.* **6.** having an ample supply: *long on brains.* —*adv.* **7.** for a great extent of time. **8.** for or throughout a specified period of time: *How long did he stay?* **9.** at a distant point in time: *long before.* —*n.* **10.** a comparatively long time: *They haven't been gone for long.* —*Idiom.* **11. as long as, a.** provided that. **b.** seeing that; since. **c.** during the time that; while. **12. before long,** soon.

long² (lông, long), *v.i.* to have a strong desire; yearn.

long., longitude.

Long′ Beach′, *n.* a city in SW California. 433,852.

long′ dis′tance, *n.* telephone service between distant places. —**long′-dis′tance,** *adj., adv.*

lon•gev•i•ty (lon jev′i tē, lôn-), *n.* **1.** long life. **2.** length of life.

long′ face′, *n.* an unhappy expression. —**long′-faced′,** *adj.*

Long•fel•low (lông′fel′ō, long′-), **Henry Wads•worth** (wodz′wərth), 1807–82, U.S. poet.

long′hair′, *Informal.* —*n.* **1.** *Sometimes Disparaging.* an intellectual. **2.** a lover of classical music. —*adj.* **3.** of or characteristic of longhairs or their tastes.

long′hand′, *n.* writing in which words are written out in full by hand.

long′ house′, *n.* a communal structure, mainly of the Iroquois, orig. consisting of a wooden, barkcovered framework: formerly used as a dwelling.

long′ing, *n.* **1.** strong desire or craving. —*adj.* **2.** characterized by earnest desire. —**long′ing•ly,** *adv.*

Long′ Is′land, *n.* an island in SE New York.

lon•gi•tude (lon′ji tōōd′, -tyōōd′), *n.* angular distance east or west from the meridian of some particular place to the prime meridian at Greenwich, England.

lon•gi•tu•di•nal (-tōōd′n l, -tyōōd′-), *adj.* **1.** of longitude or length. **2.** lengthwise. —**lon′gi•tu′di•nal•ly,** *adv.*

long′ jump′, *n.* a jump for distance from a running start.

long′-lived′ (-līvd′, -livd′), *adj.* having a long life or duration.

long′-play′ing, *adj.* of or pertaining to microgroove phonograph records played at 33⅓ revolutions per minute.

long′-range′, *adj.* **1.** considering or extending into the future. **2.** designed to cover or operate over a long distance.

long′shore′man, *n., pl.* **-men.** a person employed

on the wharves of a port, as in loading and unloading ships.

long′ shot′, *n.* **1.** a horse, team, etc., that has little chance of winning. **2.** an undertaking that offers much but has little chance for success.

Longs′ Peak′ (lôngz, longz), *n.* a peak in N central Colorado, in Rocky Mountain National Park. 14,255 ft. (4345 m).

long′stand′ing, *adj.* existing for a long time.

long′-suf′fering, *adj.* enduring trouble, provocation, etc., long and patiently.

long′-term′, *adj.* covering or involving a relatively long period of time.

long′time′, *adj.* longstanding.

long′ ton′, *n.* See under TON¹.

long′-wind′ed, *adj.* **1.** talking or writing at tedious length. **2.** (of speech or writing) continued to a tedious length. —**long′-wind′ed•ness,** *n.*

look (lōōk), *v.i.* **1.** to turn one's eyes toward something in order to see. **2.** to use one's sight in searching, examining, etc. **3.** to appear to the eye: *to look pale.* **4.** to appear to the mind: *It looks promising.* **5.** to face or afford a view: *The room looks out on the garden.* —*v.t.* **6.** to give (someone) a look. **7.** to have an appearance appropriate to: *to look one's age.* **8.** **look after,** to take care of. **9.** ~ **down on** or **upon,** to regard with contempt. **10.** ~ **for, a.** to seek. **b.** to anticipate. **11.** ~ **forward to,** to anticipate with pleasure. **12.** ~ **in (on),** to visit briefly. **13.** ~ **into,** to investigate. **14.** ~ **out,** to be careful. **15.** ~ **over,** to examine. **16.** ~ **to, a.** to pay attention to. **b.** to depend on. **17.** ~ **up,** to search for, as in a reference book. **18.** ~ **up to,** to admire. —*n.* **19.** the act of looking. **20.** the way in which a person or thing appears; aspect. **21. looks, a.** general appearance. **b.** personal appearance. —*Proverb.* **22. Look before you leap,** consider matters carefully before taking action.

look′er-on′, *n., pl.* **look•ers-on.** an onlooker; spectator.

look′ing glass′, *n.* a mirror.

look′out′, *n.* **1.** the act of keeping watch. **2.** a person keeping a watch. **3.** a place from which a watch is kept.

look′-see′, *n. Informal.* a quick visual inspection.

loom¹ (lōōm), *n.* **1.** an apparatus for weaving fabrics. —*v.t.* **2.** to weave on a loom.

loom

loom² (lōōm), *v.i.* **1.** to come into view in indistinct and enlarged form. **2.** to assume form as an impending event.

loon¹ (lōōn), *n.* a large, ducklike diving bird of the Northern Hemisphere.

loon² (lōōn), *n.* a crazy or simple-minded person.

loon′y, *adj.,* **-i•er, -i•est.** *Informal.* **1.** lunatic; insane. **2.** extremely foolish.

loon′y bin′, *n. Informal.* an insane asylum.

loop (lōōp), *n.* **1.** a portion of a cord, ribbon, etc., folded or doubled upon itself so as to leave an opening between the parts. **2.** anything shaped like a loop. **3.** INTRAUTERINE DEVICE. —*v.t.* **4.** to form into a loop. **5.** to make a loop in. —*v.i.* **6.** to make or form a loop. —*Idiom.* **7. out of the loop,** excluded from the circle of people having power.

loop′hole′, *n.* **1.** a narrow opening in a wall for

looking or shooting through. **2.** a means of escape or evasion.

loop'y, adj., **-i•er, -i•est.** Slang. **1.** crazy; dotty. **2.** befuddled; confused.

loose (lōōs), adj., **loos•er, loos•est,** adv., v., **loosed, loos•ing.** —adj. **1.** not firmly fastened or attached: a loose tooth. **2.** free from confinement or restraint. **3.** not firm or taut: loose skin. **4.** relaxed or limber: a loose, open stride. **5.** not compact: a loose weave. **6.** not strict or exact: a loose translation. **7.** lacking in restraint: a loose tongue. **8.** sexually promiscuous. —adv. **9.** in a loose manner. —v.t. **10.** to let loose; set free. **11.** to unfasten or untie. **12.** to shoot; discharge: to loose missiles. **13.** to make less tight. —v.i. **14.** to let go a hold. —Idiom. **15.** on the loose, free; unconfined. —loose'ly, adv. —loose'ness, n.

loose' can'non, n. a person whose reckless behavior endangers the efforts or welfare of others.

loose'-leaf', adj. having sheets or pages that can be easily inserted or removed.

loos'en, v.t. **1.** to make less tight. **2.** to unfasten, as a bond. —v.i. **3.** to become loose or looser. **4.** loosen up, to become less tense or formal.

loot (lōōt), n. **1.** plunder taken in war. **2.** anything taken by dishonesty, force, etc. **3.** Slang. money or gifts. —v.t., v.i. **4.** to take (as) loot. —loot'er, n.

lop¹ (lop), v.t., **lopped, lop•ping. 1.** to cut off (branches, twigs, etc.) from a tree or other plant. **2.** to cut off. **3.** to eliminate as unnecessary.

lop² (lop), v.i., **lopped, lop•ping.** to hang loosely; droop.

lope (lōp), v., **loped, lop•ing,** n. —v.i. **1.** to move or run with a long, easy stride. —n. **2.** a long, easy stride.

lop'sid'ed, adj. heavier, larger, or more developed on one side. —lop'sid'ed•ly, adv. —lop'sid'ed•ness, n.

lo•qua•cious (lō kwā'shəs), adj. exceedingly talkative. —lo•qua'cious•ness, lo•quac'i•ty (-kwas'i tē), n.

lord (lôrd), n. **1.** a master or ruler. **2.** the proprietor of a feudal manor. **3.** a titled nobleman or peer. **4.** (cap.) God. **5.** (cap.) Jesus Christ. —v. Idiom. **6. lord it (over),** to behave in a domineering manner (toward). —Proverb. **7. The Lord giveth and the Lord taketh away,** the will of God is paramount. Job: 1:21.

lord'ly, adj., **-li•er, -li•est,** adv. —adj. **1.** grand or magnificent. **2.** haughty; arrogant. —adv. **3.** in the manner of a lord.

lord'ship, n. **1.** (often cap.) (in Great Britain) a term of respect used when speaking of or to judges or certain noblemen (usu. prec. by his or your). **2.** the authority or power of a lord. **3.** the domain of a lord.

Lord's' Prayer' (prâr), n. **the,** the prayer beginning with the words Our Father. Matt. 6:9-13; Luke 11:2-4.

lore (lôr), n. the body of knowledge, esp. of a traditional nature, on a particular subject.

lor•gnette (lôrn yet'), n. eyeglasses or opera glasses mounted on a handle.

lorn (lôrn), adj. forsaken; desolate; bereft.

lor•ry (lôr'ē, lor'ē), n., pl. **-ries.** Chiefly Brit. a large motor truck.

Los Al•a•mos (lôs al'ə mōs', los), n. a town in central New Mexico: atomic research center. 11,039.

Los An•ge•les (lôs an'jə ləs, -lēz', los; sometimes ang'gə-), n. a seaport in SW California. 3,448,613.

lose (lōōz), v., **lost, los•ing.** —v.t. **1.** to come to be without through accident, misfortune, etc. **2.** to fail to retain or maintain: to lose one's balance. **3.** to have slip from sight or awareness: We lost him in the crowd. **4.** to stray from: to lose one's way. **5.** to waste: to lose time in waiting. **6.** to fail to win. **7.** to cause the loss of: The delay lost them the battle for them. **8.** to allow (oneself) to become engrossed. —v.i. **9.** to suffer loss. **10. lose out,** to suffer defeat or loss. —Idiom. **11. lose it,** to fail to maintain control. —Saying. **12. I only regret that I have but one**

life to lose for my country, the last words (1776) of the American patriot Nathan Hale. —los'er, n.

loss (lôs, los), n. **1.** the act of losing. **2.** disadvantage or deprivation from loss. **3.** one that is lost. **4.** an amount lost. —Idiom. **5. at a loss,** bewildered or uncertain.

lost (lôst, lost), adj. **1.** no longer possessed. **2.** no longer to be found. **3.** having gone astray. **4.** not used to good purpose. **5.** not won. **6.** destroyed; ruined. **7.** preoccupied; rapt. —v. **8.** pt. and pp. of LOSE.

lost' tribes', n.pl. the members of the 10 tribes of ancient Israel taken into captivity in 722 B.C. by Sargon II and believed never to have returned to Palestine.

lot (lot), n. **1.** one of a set of objects, as straws or pebbles, drawn or thrown to decide a question by chance. **2.** the casting or drawing of such objects. **3.** the decision made by such a method. **4.** allotted share; portion. **5.** fate; destiny. **6.** a distinct piece of land. **7.** a distinct parcel of merchandise. **8.** number of things or persons. **9.** kind; sort: He's a bad lot. **10.** Often, **lots.** Informal. a great many or a great deal: a lot of books.

Lo•thar•i•o (lō thâr'ē ō'), n., pl. **-thar•i•os.** (often l.c.) a man who obsessively seduces women.

lo•tion (lō'shən), n. a liquid preparation applied to the skin, as for cleansing or soothing.

lot•ter•y (lot'ə rē), n., pl. **-ter•ies. 1.** a gambling game in which a large number of tickets are sold and a drawing is held for prizes. **2.** a drawing of lots.

lot•to (lot'ō), n., pl. **-tos. 1.** a game in which a leader randomly draws numbers and players cover the corresponding numbers on cards, the winner being the first to cover a row. **2.** a lottery in which players choose numbers that are matched against those of the official drawing.

lo•tus (lō'təs), n., pl. **-tus•es. 1.** (in Greek legend) a plant whose fruit induced a state of contented forgetfulness. **2.** any of several water lilies.

lo'tus posi'tion, n. a standard seated posture for yoga with legs intertwined, left foot over right thigh and right foot over left thigh.

loud (loud), adj. and adv., **-er, -est.** —adj. **1.** having exceptional volume or intensity. **2.** making strongly audible sounds. **3.** clamorous; noisy. **4.** emphatic; insistent. **5.** garish; ostentatious. **6.** vulgar; coarse. —adv. **7.** in a loud manner. —loud'ly, adv. —loud'ness, n.

loud'mouth', n. a person given to loud or indiscreet talk. —loud'mouthed', adj.

loud'speak'er, n. any of various devices that convert amplified electronic signals into audible sound.

Lou•is¹ (lōō'is), n. Joe (Joseph Louis Barrow), 1914-81, U.S. boxer: world heavyweight champion 1937-49.

Lou•is² (lōō'ē; Fr. lwē), n. **1. Louis XIV,** 1638-1715, king of France 1643-1715. **2. Louis XV,** 1710-74, king of France 1715-74. **3. Louis XVI,** 1754-93, king of France 1774-92.

Lou•i•si•an•a (lōō ē'zē an'ə), n. a state in the S United States. 4,350,579. Cap.: Baton Rouge. Abbr.: LA, La. —Lou•i'si•an'an, Lou•i'si•an'i•an, adj., n.

Louisiana Purchase

Loui′sian′a Pur′chase, *n.* the territory that the U.S. purchased from France in 1803, extending from the Mississippi River to the Rocky Mountains and from the Gulf of Mexico to Canada.

Lou•is•ville (lōō′ē vil′, -ə vəl), *n.* a port in N Kentucky. 270,308.

lounge (lounj), *v.,* **lounged, loung•ing,** *n.* —*v.i.* **1.** to pass time indolently. **2.** to recline indolently. —*n.* **3.** a backless sofa having a headrest at one end. **4.** a public room for waiting, socializing, etc.

Lourdes (lōōrd, lōōrdz; *Fr.* lōōrd), *n.* a city in SW France: Roman Catholic shrine famed for miraculous cures. 18,096.

louse (*n.* lous; *v. also* louz), *n., pl.* **lice** (līs) for 1, 2, **lous•es** for 3, *v.,* **loused, lous•ing.** —*n.* **1.** any of various small, wingless insects that are parasitic on humans and other animals. **2.** APHID. **3.** *Slang.* a contemptible person. —*v.* **4. louse up,** *Slang.* to spoil; botch.

lous•y (lou′zē), *adj.,* **-i•er, -i•est. 1.** infested with lice. **2.** *Informal.* **a.** mean; contemptible. **b.** wretchedly bad; miserable. —*Idiom.* **3. lousy with,** *Slang.* well supplied with. —**lous′i•ness,** *n.*

lout (lout), *n.* a clumsy, boorish person. —**lout′ish,** *adj.*

lou•ver (lōō′vər), *n.* **1.** a window or opening having a series of slanting, overlapping slats, adjustable for admitting light and air while shutting out rain. **2.** one of these slats. —**lou′vered,** *adj.*

love (luv), *n., v.,* **loved, lov•ing.** —*n.* **1.** a profoundly tender, passionate affection for another person. **2.** an intense personal attachment or affection. **3.** a person toward whom love is felt. **4.** a strong enthusiasm or liking. **5.** a score of zero in tennis. —*v.t., v.i.* **6.** to have love or affection (for). —*Idiom.* **7. in love (with),** feeling love (for). **8. make love, a.** to have sexual relations. **b.** to embrace and kiss. —**lov′a•ble, love′a•ble,** *adj.* —**love′less,** *adj.*

love′bird′, *n.* any of various small parrots of Africa, noted for the affection shown between mates.

love′ feast′, *n.* **1.** (among the early Christians) a meal eaten in token of brotherly love; agape. **2.** a rite in imitation of this; a fellowship meal. **3.** a gathering to promote good feeling, honor a special guest, etc.

love′lorn′, *adj.* being without love or a lover.

love•ly (luv′lē), *adj.,* **-li•er, -li•est. 1.** charmingly or gracefully beautiful. **2.** very pleasing; delightful. —**love′li•ness,** *n.*

lov′er, *n.* **1.** a person who is in love with another. **2.** a person who has a sexual relationship with another. **3.** a devotee: *a lover of music.*

love′ seat′, *n.* a small upholstered sofa for two persons.

love′sick′, *adj.* languishing with love.

lov′ing, *adj.* warmly affectionate. —**lov′ing•ly,** *adv.*

lov′ing cup′, *n.* a large drinking cup with two handles, often given as a prize.

low¹ (lō), *adj.* and *adv.,* **-er, -est,** *n.* —*adj.* **1.** not far above the ground or floor. **2.** of small extent upward. **3.** lying below the general level: *low ground.* **4.** of less than normal height or depth: *The river is low.* **5.** ranked near the bottom on a scale of measurement: *a low income bracket.* **6.** depressed or dejected. **7.** of small number, degree, force, etc. **8.** not loud. **9.** deep in pitch. **10.** humble: *of low birth.* **11.** of inferior quality: *a low grade of fabric.* **12.** base; disreputable. **13.** coarse; vulgar. —*adv.* **14.** in or to a low position, degree, level, etc. —*n.* **15.** a low point, place, or level. **16.** a transmission gear producing the lowest speed and maximum power. **17.** an atmospheric low pressure system. —*Idiom.* **18. lay low,** to overpower or kill. **19. lie low,** to hide oneself. —**low′ness,** *n.*

low² (lō), *v.i.* **1.** to utter the deep sound characteristic of cattle; moo. —*n.* **2.** the act or sound of lowing.

Low (lō), *n.* **Juliette,** 1860–1927, U.S. founder of the Girl Scouts.

low′brow′, *n.* a person with little interest in matters of intellect or culture.

low-cal (lō′kal′, -kal′), *adj.* containing fewer calories than usual or standard: *a low-cal diet.*

Low′ Coun′tries, *n.pl.* Belgium, Luxembourg, and the Netherlands.

low•down (*n.* lō′doun′; *adj.* -doun′), *n.* **1.** the real and unadorned facts. —*adj.* **2.** contemptible; mean.

low•er¹ (lō′ər), *v.t.* **1.** to cause to descend. **2.** to make lower in height or level. **3.** to reduce in amount, degree, etc. **4.** to bring down in rank or estimation. —*v.i.* **5.** to become lower. —*adj.* **6.** comparative of LOW¹. —**low′er•most′,** *adj.*

low•er² (lou′ər, lou²r), *v.i.* **1.** to be dark and threatening. **2.** to scowl; glower. —**low′er•ing•ly,** *adv.*

low′er•case′ (lō′ər-), *adj.* **1.** (of an alphabetical letter) of a form often different from and smaller than its corresponding capital letter. —*n.* **2.** a lowercase letter.

low′er class′, *n.* a class of people below the middle class, characterized by low income and lack of education. —**low′er-class′,** *adj.*

low′er house′, *n.* one of two branches of a legislature, generally larger and more representative than the upper branch.

low′est com′mon denom′inator, *n.* LEAST COMMON DENOMINATOR.

low′est com′mon mul′tiple, *n.* the smallest number that is a common multiple of a given set of numbers.

low-fat, *adj.* of or being a food or style of cooking that contains or uses very little butter, oil, or other fat.

low′ fre′quency, *n.* a radio frequency between 30 and 300 kilohertz.

Low′ Ger′man, *n.* the Germanic dialects of N Germany, forming with Dutch a single dialect complex distinct from the High German dialects.

low′-key′, *adj.* restrained; understated.

low′land, *n.* **1.** land that is low or level in comparison with the adjacent country. **2. the Lowlands,** a low region in S, central, and E Scotland.

low′life′, *n., pl.* **-lifes.** a disreputable or degenerate person.

low′ly, *adj.,* **-li•er, -li•est,** *adv.* —*adj.* **1.** having a low status or rank. **2.** humble; meek. —*adv.* **3.** in a low position, manner, or degree. —**low′li•ness,** *n.*

low′-mind′ed, *adj.* having or showing coarse or vulgar taste or interests.

low′ pro′file, *n.* a deliberately inconspicuous manner.

low′-spir′ited, *adj.* depressed; dejected.

low′ tide′, *n.* the tide at the point of maximum ebb.

lox¹ (loks), *n.* brine-cured salmon.

lox² or **LOX** (loks), *n.* liquid oxygen, used in liquid rocket propellants.

loy•al (loi′əl), *adj.* **1.** faithful to one's allegiance, as to a government or friends. **2.** faithful to one's oath or obligations. **3.** characterized by faithfulness. —**loy′al•ly,** *adv.* —**loy′al•ty,** *n., pl.* **-ties.**

loy′al•ist, *n.* a person who remains loyal, esp. to an existing government.

loy′al opposi′tion, *n.* a political opposition whose action is consistent with patriotism or loyalty to the nation.

loy′alty oath′, *n.* a pledge of fealty to, and promise to avoid subversion against, a group, esp. a government.

loz•enge (loz′inj), *n.* **1.** a small flavored tablet, often medicated. **2.** a diamond-shaped heraldic charge.

LP, *pl.* **LPs, LP's.** a phonograph record played at 33⅓ r.p.m.; long-playing record.

LPN, licensed practical nurse.

Lr, *Chem. Symbol.* lawrencium.

Lt., lieutenant.

Ltd. or **ltd.,** limited.

Lu, *Chem. Symbol.* lutetium.

Lu•an•da (lōō an′də, -än′-), *n.* the capital of Angola. 1,200,000.

lu•au (lōō′ou), *n., pl.* **-aus.** an outdoor feast of Hawaiian food.

Lu·ba·vitch·er (lōō′bə vich′ər, lōō bä′vi chər), *n.* a member of a missionary Hasidic movement.

lub·ber (lub′ər), *n.* **1.** a big, clumsy, stupid person. **2.** an awkward or unskilled sailor. —**lub′ber·ly,** *adj., adv.*

Lub·bock (lub′ək), *n.* a city in NW Texas. 188,090.

lube (lōōb), *n. Informal.* **1.** lubricant. **2.** an application of a lubricant to a vehicle.

lu·bri·cant (lōō′bri kənt), *n.* **1.** a substance, as oil or grease, for lessening friction, esp. in the working parts of a mechanism. —*adj.* **2.** capable of lubricating.

lu′bri·cate′ (-kāt′), *v.,* -**cat·ed, -cat·ing.** —*v.t.* **1.** to apply a lubricant to in order to diminish friction; make slippery. —*v.i.* **2.** to act as a lubricant. —**lu′bri·ca′tion,** *n.* —**lu′bri·ca′tor,** *n.*

lu·bri·cious (lōō brish′əs), *adj.* **1.** arousing or expressive of sexual desire; lustful; lecherous. **2.** smooth and slippery. —**lu·bric′i·ty** (-bris′i tē), *n.*

Lu·cas (lōō′kəs), *n.* **George,** born 1945, U.S. film director.

Luce (lōōs), *n.* **1. Clare Boothe,** 1903–87, U.S. writer, politician, and diplomat. **2. Henry Robinson,** 1898–1967, U.S. publisher and editor (husband of Clare Boothe Luce).

lu·cid (lōō′sid), *adj.* **1.** easily understood. **2.** rational; sane. **3.** luminous. **4.** clear; transparent. —**lu·cid′i·ty,** *n.* —**lu′cid·ly,** *adv.*

Lu·ci·fer (lōō′sə fər), *n.* a rebellious archangel, identified with Satan, who fell from heaven.

Lu·cite (lōō′sīt), *Trademark.* a transparent plastic.

luck (luk), *n.* **1.** the force that seems to operate for good or ill in a person's life. **2.** good fortune. —*v.* **3. luck out,** *Informal.* to have an occasion of good luck. —**luck′less,** *adj.*

luck′y, *adj.,* -**i·er, -i·est. 1.** having good luck. **2.** happening fortunately. **3.** believed to bring good luck. —**luck′i·ly,** *adv.* —**luck′i·ness,** *n.*

lu·cra·tive (lōō′krə tiv), *adj.* profitable; moneymaking. —**lu′cra·tive·ly,** *adv.* —**lu′cra·tive·ness,** *n.*

lu·cre (lōō′kər), *n.* monetary reward or gain.

lu·cu·brate (lōō′kyōō brāt′), *v.i.,* -**brat·ed, -brat·ing.** to work, write, or study laboriously, esp. at night. —**lu′cu·bra′tion,** *n.*

lu·di·crous (lōō′di krəs), *adj.* causing or deserving laughter because of absurdity; ridiculous. —**lu′di·crous·ly,** *adv.* —**lu′di·crous·ness,** *n.*

luff (luf), *v.i.* to bring the head of a sailing ship closer to the wind.

lug¹ (lug), *v.t., v.i.,* **lugged, lug·ging.** to pull or carry with effort.

lug² (lug), *n.* **1.** a projecting piece by which anything is held or supported. **2.** *Slang.* an awkward, clumsy fellow.

luge (lōōzh), *n., v.,* **luged, lug·ing.** —*n.* **1.** a one- or two-person sled for coasting or racing down a chute, used esp. in Europe. —*v.i.* **2.** to go or race on a luge. —**lug′er,** *n.*

lug′gage (-ij), *n.* suitcases, trunks, etc.; baggage.

lug′ nut′, *n.* a large nut, esp. for attaching a wheel to an automobile.

lu·gu·bri·ous (lōō gōō′brē əs, -gyōō′-), *adj.* mournful or gloomy, esp. exaggeratedly so. —**lu·gu′bri·ous·ly,** *adv.* —**lu·gu′bri·ous·ness,** *n.*

Luke (lōōk), *n.* **1.** an early Christian disciple, believed to be the author of the third Gospel. **2.** the third Gospel.

luke·warm (lōōk′wôrm′), *adj.* **1.** moderately warm. **2.** having little ardor or enthusiasm.

lull (lul), *v.t.* **1.** to put to sleep or rest by soothing means. **2.** to give a false sense of safety. —*v.i.* **3.** to quiet down; subside. —*n.* **4.** a temporary calm.

lull′a·by′ (-ə bī′), *n., pl.* -**bies.** a song used to lull a child to sleep.

lum·ba·go (lum bā′gō), *n.* pain in the lower back.

lum·bar (lum′bər, -bär), *adj.* of the loin or loins.

lum·ber¹ (lum′bər), *n.* **1.** timber sawed into planks, boards, etc. —*v.i.* **2.** to cut timber and prepare it for market. —**lum′ber·er,** *n.* —**lum′ber·man,** *n., pl.* -**men.**

lum·ber² (lum′bər), *v.i.* to move clumsily or heavily.

lum′ber·jack′, *n.* a person who works at lumbering.

lum′ber·yard′, *n.* a yard where lumber is stored for sale.

lu·mi·nar·y (lōō′mə ner′ē), *n., pl.* -**nar·ies. 1.** a celestial body that gives light, as the sun or moon. **2.** a person who has attained eminence in a field.

lu·mi·nes·cence (lōō′mə nes′əns), *n.* the emission of light occurring at a temperature below that of incandescent bodies. —**lu′mi·nes′cent,** *adj.*

lu·mi·nous (lōō′mə nəs), *adj.* **1.** radiating or reflecting light. **2.** clear; readily intelligible. —**lu′mi·nos′i·ty** (-nos′i tē), *n.*

lum·mox (lum′əks), *n. Informal.* a clumsy, stupid person.

lump¹ (lump), *n.* **1.** a piece or mass of no particular shape. **2.** a protuberance or swelling. **3. lumps,** *Informal.* harsh criticism, punishment, or defeat. —*adj.* **4.** in the form of a lump or lumps. **5.** made up of a number of items taken together: *a lump sum.* —*v.t.* **6.** to unite into one collection or mass. **7.** to deal with, consider, etc., in a lump or mass. —*v.i.* **8.** to form a lump or lumps. —**lump′y,** *adj.,* -**i·er, -i·est.** —**lump′i·ness,** *n.*

lump² (lump), *v.t. Informal.* to put up with: *If you don't like it, you can lump it.*

lu·na·cy (lōō′nə sē), *n.* **1.** insanity. **2.** extreme foolishness.

lu′nar (-nər), *adj.* of the moon.

lu·na·tic (-tik), *n.* **1.** an insane person. —*adj.* **2.** insane; crazy. **3.** recklessly foolish. **4.** for the insane. [< OF *lunatique* < LL *lūnāticus* moonstruck]

lunch (lunch), *n.* **1.** a light midday meal between breakfast and dinner. —*v.i.* **2.** to eat lunch. —*Idiom.* **3. out to lunch,** *Slang.* inattentive or unaware.

lunch·eon (lun′chən), *n.* a lunch, esp. a formal one.

lunch′eon·ette′ (-chə net′), *n.* a small restaurant where light meals are served.

lunch′eon meat′, *n.* any of various molded loaf meats, sliced and served cold.

lung (lung), *n.* either of the two saclike respiratory organs in the thorax of humans and other airbreathing vertebrates.

lunge (lunj), *n., v.,* **lunged, lung·ing.** —*n.* **1.** a sudden forward thrust, as with a sword. **2.** any sudden forward movement. —*v.i., v.t.* **3.** to move or cause to move with a lunge.

lunk·head (lungk′hed′), *n. Slang.* a dull or stupid person. Also called **lunk.**

lu·pine¹ (lōō′pin), *n.* a leguminous plant with tall, dense clusters of blue, pink, or white flowers.

lu·pine² (lōō′pīn), *adj.* of or resembling the wolf.

lu·pus (lōō′pəs), *n.* any of several diseases characterized by skin eruptions or inflammation.

lurch¹ (lûrch), *n.* **1.** a sudden tip or roll to one side, as of a ship or a staggering person. —*v.i.* **2.** (of a ship) to roll or pitch suddenly. **3.** to stagger or sway.

lurch² (lûrch), *n.* an uncomfortable or difficult situation: *Our supervisor resigned and left us in the lurch.*

lure (lŏŏr), *n., v.,* **lured, lur·ing.** —*n.* **1.** anything that entices or allures. **2.** an artificial bait used in fishing or trapping. —*v.t.* **3.** to attract, entice, or tempt.

lu·rid (lŏŏr′id), *adj.* **1.** gruesome; revolting. **2.** wildly sensational; shocking. **3.** shining with an unnatural, fiery glow. —**lu′rid·ly,** *adv.* —**lu′rid·ness,** *n.*

lurk (lûrk), *v.i.* **1.** to lie hidden, as in ambush. **2.** to go furtively.

Lu·sa·ka (lōō sä′kə), *n.* the capital of Zambia. 818,994.

lus·cious (lush′əs), *adj.* **1.** highly pleasing to the taste or smell. **2.** richly satisfying to the senses or the mind. —**lus′cious·ly,** *adv.* —**lus′cious·ness,** *n.*

lush (lush), *adj.,* -**er, -est. 1.** characterized by luxuriant vegetation. **2.** characterized by abundance, opulence, etc. —**lush′ness,** *n.*

lust (lust), *n.* **1.** intense sexual desire or appetite. **2.** an overwhelming desire: *a lust for power.* **3.** ardent enthusiasm: *a lust for life.* —*v.i.* **4.** to have a strong desire. —**lust′ful**, *adj.*

lus•ter (lus′tər), *n.* **1.** the state or quality of shining by reflecting light; sheen or gloss. **2.** radiant or luminous brightness. **3.** radiance of beauty, excellence, distinction, or glory. Also, *esp. Brit.,* **lus′tre.** —**lus′ter•less**, *adj.* —**lus′trous**, *adj.*

lust′y, *adj.,* -i•er, -i•est. full of healthy vigor. —**lust′i•ly**, *adv.* —**lust′i•ness**, *n.*

lute (lo͞ot), *n.* a stringed instrument having a long, fretted neck and a hollow, pear-shaped body. —**lu•te•nist, lu•ta•nist** (lo͞ot′n ist), *n.*

lute

lu•te•ti•um (lo͞o tē′shē əm), *n.* a trivalent rare-earth element. *Symbol:* Lu; *at. wt.:* 174.97; *at. no.:* 71.

Lu•ther (lo͞o′thər), *n.* **Martin,** 1483–1546, German leader of the Protestant Reformation.

Lu•ther•an (lo͞o′thər ən), *adj.* **1.** of or pertaining to Luther, adhering to his doctrines, or belonging to one of the Protestant churches that bear his name. —*n.* **2.** a follower of Luther or an adherent of his doctrines; a member of the Lutheran Church. —**Lu′ther•an•ism**, *n.*

Lux•em•bourg or **-burg** (luk′səm bûrg′), *n.* a grand duchy in W Europe. 422,474.

lux•u•ri•ant (lug zho͝or′ē ənt, luk sho͝or′-), *adj.* **1.** abundant in growth, as vegetation. **2.** producing abundantly, as soil. **3.** florid, as ornamentation. —**lux•u′ri•ance**, *n.* —**lux•u′ri•ant•ly**, *adv.*

lux•u′ri•ate′ (-āt′), *v.i.,* -at•ed, -at•ing. **1.** to indulge in luxury. **2.** to grow abundantly. **3.** to take great delight. —**lux•u′ri•a′tion**, *n.*

lux•u′ri•ous, *adj.* **1.** characterized by luxury. **2.** given or inclined to luxury. —**lux•u′ri•ous•ly**, *adv.* —**lux•u′ri•ous•ness**, *n.*

lux•u•ry (luk′shə rē, lug′zhə-), *n.,* *pl.* -ries, *adj.* —*n* **1.** an object, service, etc., conducive to physical comfort or sumptuous living. **2.** indulgence in the pleasures afforded by such things. —*adj.* **3.** of or providing luxury.

Lu•zon (lo͞o zon′), *n.* the chief island of the Philippines.

-ly, a suffix meaning: in a specified manner (*loudly*); in or according to (*theoretically*); to or from a specified direction (*inwardly*); like or characteristic of (*saintly*); every (*hourly*).

Lyc•a•o•ni•a (lik′ā ō′nē ə, -ōn′yə, lī′kā-), *n.* an ancient country in S Asia Minor.

ly•ce•um (lī sē′əm), *n.* **1.** an institution for popular education, providing lectures, concerts, etc. **2.** a building for such activities.

Lyd•i•a (lid′ē ə), *n.* an ancient kingdom in W Asia Minor: during the reign of Croesus (560–546 B.C.), a

wealthy empire including most of Asia Minor. *Cap.:* Sardis.

lye (lī), *n.* a white, powerful alkaline substance used for washing and in making soap.

ly•ing¹ (lī′ing), *n.* **1.** the telling of lies. —*adj.* **2.** telling or containing lies.

ly•ing² (lī′ing), *v.* pres. part. of LIE².

ly′ing-in′, *n.,* *pl.* **ly•ings-in, ly•ing-ins**, *adj.* —*n.* **1.** the confinement of a woman giving birth. —*adj.* **2.** of or for childbirth.

Lyme′ disease′ (līm), *n.* a tick-transmitted disease characterized by joint pains, fatigue, and sometimes neurological disturbances.

lymph (limf), *n.* a yellowish fluid containing lymphocytes and fats that surrounds body cells and carries away their wastes.

lym•phat•ic (lim fat′ik), *adj.* **1.** of, containing, or conveying lymph. **2.** flabby or sluggish. —*n.* **3.** a lymphatic vessel.

lymph′ node′, *n.* any of the glandlike masses of tissue in the lymphatic vessels containing cells that become lymphocytes.

lym′pho•cyte′ (-fə sīt′), *n.* a type of white blood cell important in the production of antibodies.

lym′phoid (-foid), *adj.* of or resembling lymph or the tissue of the lymph nodes.

lym•pho•ma (lim fō′mə), *n.,* *pl.* -mas, -ma•ta (-mə tə). a tumor arising from any of the cellular elements of lymph nodes.

lynch (linch), *v.t.* to put to death, esp. by hanging, by mob action and without legal authority. [shortening of *lynch law,* after the self-instituted tribunals presided over by William *Lynch* (1742–1820) of Virginia] —**lynch′er**, *n.*

lynx (lingks), *n.,* *pl.* **lynx•es, lynx.** a wildcat having long limbs and a short tail.

Ly•ons (lē ôN′) also **Lyon** (*Fr.* lyôn), *n.* a city in E France. 418,476.

lyre (līər), *n.* a small harplike musical instrument of ancient Greece.

lyre

lyr•ic (lir′ik), *adj.* Also, **lyr′i•cal. 1.** (of a poem) having the form of a song expressing the writer's feelings. **2.** expressing strong, spontaneous feeling: *lyric writing.* **3.** having a voice of light volume and modest range: *a lyric soprano.* —*n.* **4.** a lyric poem. **5.** Usu., **-ics.** the words of a song. —**lyr′i•cal•ly**, *adv.* —**lyr′i•cism** (-ə siz′əm), *n.*

lyr′i•cist (-ə sist), *n.* a person who writes lyrics.

-lysis, a combining form meaning a breaking down, loosening, or decomposition (*hydrolysis*).

Lys•tra (lis′trə), *n.* a city in Lycaonia. Acts 16:1–2; 14:6–19.

M

M, m (em), *n., pl.* **Ms** or **M's, ms** or **m's.** the 13th letter of the English alphabet, a consonant.

M, 1. major. **2.** Medieval. **3.** medium. **4.** Middle.

M, *Symbol.* the Roman numeral for 1000.

m, 1. *Physics.* mass. **2.** medieval. **3.** medium. **4.** meter. **5.** middle. **6.** minor.

M., 1. majesty. **2.** meridian. **3.** noon. [< L *merīdiēs*] **4.** Monday. **5.** *pl.* **MM.** monsieur.

m., 1. male. **2.** married. **3.** masculine. **4.** *Physics.* mass. **5.** medium. **6.** noon. **7.** meter. **8.** mile. **9.** minute. **10.** month.

ma (mä), *n., pl.* **mas.** mother.

MA, Massachusetts.

M.A., Master of Arts. [< L *Magister Artium*]

ma'am (mam, mäm; *unstressed* məm), *n.* (*often cap.*) MADAM (def. 1).

ma•ca•bre (mə kä′brə, -käb′), *adj.* gruesome in character; ghastly.

mac•ad•am (mə kad′əm), *n.* **1.** a road or pavement of compacted broken stone, often with asphalt or tar. **2.** broken stone used for macadam. —**mac•ad′am•ize′,** *v.t.,* **-ized, -iz•ing.**

Ma•cao (mə kou′), *n.* a Chinese territory under Portuguese administration, in S China. 426,400.

ma•caque (mə kak′, -käk′), *n.* a chiefly Asian monkey with cheek pouches and usu. a short tail.

ma•ca•re•na (mä′kə rä′nə, -ren′ə), *n.* (*often cap.*) a dance performed in a group line or solo and following a rhythmic pattern of arm, hand, and hip movements in time to a Spanish song.

mac•a•ro•ni (mak′ə rō′nē), *n.* small tubular pasta made of wheat flour.

mac•a•roon (mak′ə rōōn′), *n.* a cookie made of beaten egg whites, sugar, and almond paste or coconut.

Ma•cau•lay (mə kô′lē), *n.* **Thomas Babington, 1st Baron,** 1800–59, English historian and statesman.

ma•caw (mə kô′), *n.* a large, long-tailed parrot of the New World tropics.

Mac•beth (mək beth′), *n.* died 1057, king of Scotland 1040–57: subject of a tragedy by Shakespeare.

Mac•ca•bae•us (mak′ə bē′əs), *n.* **Judas** or **Judah** ("the Hammer"), died 160 B.C., Judean patriot.

mace¹ (mās), *n.* **1.** a clublike armor-breaking weapon used chiefly in the Middle Ages. **2.** a ceremonial staff symbolic of office.

mace² (mās), *n.* a spice made from the inner husk of the nutmeg.

Mace (mās), *v.,* **Maced, Mac•ing. 1.** *Trademark.* a chemical spray that causes severe eye and skin irritation. —*v.t.* **2.** (*sometimes l.c.*) to spray with Mace.

Mac•e•do•ni•a (mas′i dō′nē ə), *n.* **1.** an ancient kingdom in SE Europe. **2.** a republic in SE Europe: formerly part of Yugoslavia. 2,113,866. —**Mac′e•do′ni•an,** *n., adj.*

mac•er•ate (mas′ə rāt′), *v.t.,* **-at•ed, -at•ing. 1.** to soften or separate into parts by steeping in a liquid. **2.** to cause to waste away. —**mac′er•a′tion,** *n.*

ma•chet•e (mə shet′ē, -chet′ē), *n., pl.* **-es.** a heavy swordlike knife used esp. as a cutting implement.

Mach•i•a•vel•li (mak′ē ə vel′ē), *n.* **Niccolò di Bernardo,** 1469–1527, Italian political philosopher.

Mach•i•a•vel•li•an (mak′ē ə vel′ē ən), *adj.* **1.** characterized by unscrupulous cunning, deception, or expediency. —*n.* **2.** a follower of Machiavelli's principles. [after N. *Machiavelli*]

mach•i•na•tion (mak′ə nā′shən), *n.* Usu., **-tions.** a crafty scheme or maneuver.

ma•chine (mə shēn′), *n., v.,* **-chined, -chin•ing.** —*n.* **1.** an apparatus consisting of interrelated parts with separate functions, used in the performance of some kind of work. **2.** a device, as a pulley, that transmits or modifies force or motion. **3.** an automobile or airplane. **4.** an electric, mechanical, or electronic device, as a vending machine. **5.** a group of persons that controls a political party. —*v.t.* **6.** to make, prepare, or finish with a machine.

machine′ gun′, *n.* a firearm capable of shooting a continuous stream of bullets. —**ma•chine′-gun′,** *v.t.,* **-gunned, -gun•ning.**

machine′ lan′guage, *n.* a numerical coding system specific to the hardware of a given computer model, requiring no translation before being used.

machine′-read′able, *adj.* (of data) in a form suitable for direct acceptance and processing by computer.

ma•chin′er•y, *n., pl.* **-er•ies. 1.** machines collectively. **2.** the parts of a machine. **3.** a system by which action is maintained or a result is obtained.

ma•chin′ist, *n.* a person who makes, repairs, or operates machinery.

ma•chis•mo (mä chēz′mō), *n.* an exaggerated sense of manliness.

Mach′ (or **mach′) num′ber** (mäk), *n.* the ratio of the speed of an object to the speed of sound in the surrounding atmosphere.

ma•cho (mä′chō), *adj., n., pl.* **-chos.** —*adj.* **1.** characterized by machismo. —*n.* **2.** MACHISMO. **3.** an assertively virile or domineering male.

Mac•ken•zie (mə ken′zē), *n.* a river in NW Canada, flowing to the Arctic Ocean. 1120 mi. (1800 km) long.

mack•er•el (mak′ər əl), *n., pl.* **-els, -el.** a food fish of the N Atlantic.

mack•i•naw (mak′ə nô′), *n.* a short, double-breasted coat of heavy, usu. plaid wool.

mack•in•tosh or **mac•in•tosh** (mak′in tosh′), *n. Chiefly Brit.* RAINCOAT.

Ma•con (mā′kən), *n.* a city in central Georgia. 109,191.

mac•ra•mé (mak′rə mā′), *n.* lacelike webbing made of knotted cord or yarn.

macro-, a combining form meaning large (*macrocosm*).

mac•ro•bi•ot•ics (mak′rō bī ot′iks), *n.* a program emphasizing harmony with nature, esp. through a restricted, primarily vegetarian diet. —**mac′ro•bi•ot′ic,** *adj.*

mac•ro•cosm (mak′rə koz′əm), *n.* the universe considered as a whole.

ma•cron (mā′kron, mak′ron), *n.* a horizontal line used over a vowel to show that it is long, as (ā) in *fate* (fāt).

mac•ro•scop•ic (mak′rə skop′ik) also **-i•cal,** *adj.* **1.** visible to the naked eye. **2.** pertaining to large units; comprehensive.

mad (mad), *adj.,* **mad•der, mad•dest. 1.** very angry; enraged. **2.** mentally disturbed; deranged. **3.** affected with rabies. **4.** extremely foolish; imprudent. **5.** impetuous: frantic. **6.** brimming with enthusiasm. **7.** wildly frivolous; hilarious. —**mad′ly,** *adv.* —**mad′ness,** *n.* —**Usage.** Critics occasionally reject the sense "very angry, enraged." This use has been in existence for about 700 years and is found in Shakespeare and the Bible, but ANGRY is sometimes substituted for MAD in formal contexts.

Mad•a•gas•car (mad′ə gas′kər), *n.* an island republic in the Indian Ocean, off the SE coast of Africa. 14,061,627. —**Mad′a•gas′can,** *n., adj.*

mad•am (mad′əm), *n., pl.* **mes•dames** (mā dam′, -däm′) (*often cap.*) a polite term of address to a woman. [< OF, orig. *ma dame* my lady]

mad•ame (mad′əm, mə dam′, -däm′, ma-), *n., pl.*

mes•dames (mā dam′, -däm′). (often cap.) a French title equivalent to Mrs.

mad′cap′, adj. **1.** recklessly impulsive; rash. —n. **2.** a madcap person.

mad′ cow′ disease′, n. BOVINE SPONGIFORM ENCEPHALOPATHY.

mad′den, v.t., v.i. to make or become mad. —**mad′den•ing**, adj.

mad•der (mad′ər), n. **1.** a plant with clusters of small yellowish flowers. **2.** the root of the madder. **3.** a reddish dye derived from the root.

mad′ding, adj. tumultuous: the madding crowd.

made (mād), v. pt. and pp. of MAKE.

Ma•dei•ra (mə dēr′ə, -dâr′ə), n., pl. **-ras**. (often l.c.) a fortified amber-colored wine.

mad•e•moi•selle (mad′ə mə zel′, mad′mwə-, mam zel′), n., pl. **mad•e•moi•selles, mes•de•moi•selles** (mã′də mə zel′, -zelz′, mād′mwə-). (often cap.) a French title equivalent to Miss.

made′-to-or′der, adj. **1.** made to individual order. **2.** perfectly suited.

made′-up′, adj. **1.** falsely fabricated; concocted. **2.** wearing facial makeup.

mad′house′, n. **1.** a hospital for the mentally disturbed. **2.** a disorderly, often noisy place.

Mad•i•son (mad′ə sən), n. **1.** Dolly or Dolley (Dorothea Payne), 1768–1849, wife of James Madison. **2.** James, 1751–1836, 4th president of the U.S. 1809–17. **3.** the capital of Wisconsin. 191,262.

mad′man′ or **-wom′an**, n., pl. **-men** or **-wom•en.** an insane person.

Ma•don•na (mə don′ə), n., pl. **-nas. 1.** the Virgin Mary. **2.** a picture or statue representing the Virgin Mary. [< It: my lady]

mad•ras (mad′rəs, mə dras′, -dräs′), n. a light cotton fabric, esp. one in multicolored plaid or stripes.

Ma•dras (mə dras′, -dräs′), n. a seaport in SE India. 4,277,000.

Ma•drid (mə drid′), n. the capital of Spain. 3,123,713.

mad•ri•gal (mad′ri gəl), n. an unaccompanied polyphonic vocal composition, esp. of the 16th and 17th centuries.

mael•strom (māl′strəm), n. **1.** a powerful whirlpool. **2.** a tumultuous state of affairs.

mae•nad (mē′nad), n. **1.** a female votary of Dionysus. **2.** a frenzied or raging woman.

maes•tro (mī′strō), n., pl. **-tros. 1.** an eminent composer, teacher, or conductor of music. **2.** a master of an art.

Ma•fi•a (mä′fē ə, maf′ē ə), n. a secret organization allegedly engaged in criminal activities internationally. [< dial. It (Sicily): courage, boldness]

ma•fi•o•so (mä′fē ō′sō), n., pl. **-si** (-sē), **-sos.** (often cap.) a member of the Mafia.

mag•a•zine (mag′ə zēn′), n. **1.** a periodical publication typically containing essays, stories, and poems. **2.** a room for keeping explosives, as gunpowder. **3.** a military depot for arms or provisions. **4.** a receptacle on a gun for holding cartridges. **5.** a compartment in a camera for holding film.

Ma•gel•lan (mə jel′ən), n. **Ferdinand,** c1480–1521, Portuguese navigator.

Ma•gen Da•vid (mä′gən dā′vid, mä gen′ dä vēd′), n. STAR OF DAVID. [< Heb māghēn dāwīd lit., shield of David]

ma•gen•ta (mə jen′tə), n., pl. **-tas.** a purplish red.

mag•got (mag′ət), n. the soft-bodied, legless larva of certain flies. —**mag′got•y,** adj.

Ma•gi (mā′jī), n.pl., sing. **-gus** (-gəs). (sometimes l.c.) the three wise men who paid homage to the infant Jesus.

mag•ic (maj′ik), n. **1.** the art of producing illusions, esp. by sleight of hand. **2.** the use of techniques such as incantation to exert alleged control over the supernatural or the forces of nature. **3.** an extraordinary influence or power. —adj. **4.** done by or employed in magic. **5.** mysteriously enchanting. —**mag′i•cal,** adj. —**mag′i•cal•ly,** adv.

ma•gi•cian (mə jish′ən), n. a person who performs magic.

mag•is•te•ri•al (maj′ə stēr′ē əl), adj. **1.** of or befitting a master or a magistrate. **2.** imperious; domineering. —**mag′is•te′ri•al•ly,** adv.

mag′is•trate′ (-strāt′, -strit), n. **1.** a civil officer charged with the administration of the law. **2.** a minor judicial officer, as a justice of the peace.

mag•ma (mag′mə), n. molten material beneath or within the earth's crust, from which igneous rock is formed.

Mag•na Car•ta (or **Char•ta**) (mag′nə kär′tə), n. the charter of liberties forced from King John by the English barons in 1215.

mag•nan•i•mous (mag nan′ə məs), adj. **1.** generous in forgiving. **2.** showing noble sensibility; highminded. —**mag′na•nim′i•ty** (-nə nim′i tē), n. —**mag•nan′i•mous•ly,** adv.

mag′nate (-nāt, -nit), n. a person of great influence, importance, or standing.

mag•ne•sia (mag nē′zhə), n. a white tasteless substance used as an antacid and laxative.

mag•ne′si•um (-zē əm, -zhəm), n. a ductile, silverwhite metallic element that burns with a dazzling light. Symbol: Mg; at. wt.: 24.312; at. no.: 12.

mag•net (mag′nit), n. **1.** a body that possesses the property of attracting certain substances, as iron. **2.** LODESTONE. **3.** a person or thing that attracts.

mag•net′ic (-net′ik), adj. **1.** of a magnet or magnetism. **2.** having the properties of a magnet. **3.** capable of being magnetized. **4.** pertaining to the earth's magnetic field. **5.** exerting a strong attractive power or charm. —**mag•net′i•cal•ly,** adv.

magnet′ic field′, n. a region of space near a magnet, electric current, or moving charged particle in which a magnetic force acts.

magnet′ic res′onance im′aging, n. a process of producing images of the body by means of a strong magnetic field and low-energy radio waves.

magnet′ic tape′, n. a ribbon of material coated with a magnetically sensitive substance for recording sound, images, or data.

mag′net•ism, n. **1.** the properties of attraction possessed by magnets. **2.** the agency producing magnetic phenomena. **3.** strong attractive power.

mag′net•ite′ (-ni tīt′), n. a common black iron oxide, an important iron ore.

mag′net•ize′, v.t., **-ized, -iz•ing. 1.** to impart magnetic properties to. **2.** to exert an attracting influence upon. —**mag′net•i•za′tion,** n.

mag•ne′to (nē′tō), n., pl. **-tos.** a small electric generator in which permanent magnets provide the magnetic field.

mag′ne•tom′e•ter (-ni tom′i tər), n. an instrument for measuring the intensity of a magnetic field.

mag•nif•i•cent (mag nif′ə sənt), adj. **1.** splendid or impressive, esp. in appearance; superb. **2.** noble; sublime. —**mag•nif′i•cence,** n. —**mag•nif′i•cent•ly,** adv.

mag•ni•fy (mag′nə fī′), v.t., **-fied, -fy•ing. 1.** to increase the apparent or actual size of; enlarge. **2.** to exaggerate; overstate. **3.** to intensify; heighten. **4.** to praise. —**mag′ni•fi•ca′tion,** n. —**mag′ni•fi′er,** n.

mag•nil•o•quent (mag nil′ə kwənt), adj. speaking or expressed in a lofty or grandiose style; bombastic. —**mag•nil′o•quence,** n.

mag′ni•tude′ (-ni tōōd′, -tyōōd′), n. **1.** size; extent. **2.** great importance or consequence. **3.** greatness of size or amount. **4.** the brightness of a celestial body as expressed on a logarithmic scale.

mag•no•lia (mag nōl′yə, -nō′lē ə), n., pl. **-lias.** a shrub or tree bearing large, usu. fragrant flowers.

mag•num (mag′nəm), n. a large wine bottle having a capacity of 1.5 liters (1.6 quarts).

mag′num o′pus, n. a great work, esp. the chief work of a writer, composer, or artist.

mag•pie (mag′pī′), n. a noisy, black-and-white bird of the jay family.

Mag•yar (mag′yär, mäg′-), n. HUNGARIAN (def. 2).

Ma·ha·na·im (mā'hə nā'im), *n.* a town in Gilead, headquarters for David. II Sam. 17:24.

ma·ha·ra·jah or **-ja** (mä'hə rä'jə, -zhə), *n., pl.* **-jahs** or **-jas.** a former ruling prince in India.

ma·ha·ra·nee or **-ni** (-nē), *n., pl.* **-nees** or **-nis.** 1. the wife of a maharajah. 2. a former Indian princess being sovereign in her own right.

ma·ha·ri·shi (mä hə rē'shē, mə här'ə-), *n., pl.* **-shis.** a Hindu religious sage.

ma·hat·ma (mə hät'mə, -hat'-), *n., pl.* **-mas.** (*sometimes cap.*) a person, esp. in India, who is held in the highest esteem for wisdom and saintliness.

Ma·hi·can (mə hē'kən), *n., pl.* **-can, -cans.** a member of an American Indian people who formerly lived in the Hudson River valley.

mah-jongg or **mah·jong** (mä'jông', -jong', -zhông', -zhong'), *n.* a game of Chinese origin played with dominolike tiles.

Mah·ler (mä'lər), *n.* **Gustav,** 1860–1911, Austrian composer.

ma·hog·a·ny (mə hog'ə nē), *n., pl.* **-nies.** 1. any of several tropical American trees yielding hard, reddish brown wood used for making furniture. 2. the wood of a mahogany.

Ma·hom·et (mə hom'it), *n.* MUHAMMAD.

ma·hout (mə hout'), *n.* the keeper and driver of an elephant.

maid (mād), *n.* 1. a female servant. 2. a girl or young unmarried woman.

maid'en, (-ən), *n.* 1. MAID (def. 2). —*adj.* 2. of or befitting a maiden. 3. a. unmarried. b. virgin. 4. first: *a maiden flight.* —**maid'en·hood'**, *n.* —**maid'en·ly,** *adj.*

maid'en·hair', *n.* a fern with slender stalks and finely divided fronds.

maid'en·head', *n.* 1. HYMEN. 2. maidenhood; virginity.

maid'en name', *n.* a woman's surname before marriage.

maid' of hon'or, *n.* an unmarried woman who is the chief attendant of a bride.

maid'serv'ant, *n.* a female servant.

mail[1] (māl), *n.* 1. matter, as letters, sent or delivered by a postal service. 2. a single collection or delivery of mail. 3. Also, **mails.** a system, usu. operated by a government, for sending or delivering mail. —*v.t.* 4. to send by mail. —**mail'er,** *n.*

mail[2] (māl), *n.* flexible armor of metal rings or plates. —**mailed,** *adj.*

mail'box', *n.* 1. a public box in which mail is placed for pickup. 2. a private box into which mail is delivered.

mail' car'rier, *n.* a person employed to deliver mail.

mail'ing list', *n.* 1. a list of addresses to which mail, esp. advertisements, can be sent. 2. a list of e-mail addresses to which messages, usu. on a specific topic, are sent; a discussion group whose messages are distributed through e-mail.

Mail·lol (mä yôl', -yōl', ma-), **Aristide,** 1861–1944, French sculptor.

mail·lot (mä yō', ma-), *n.* a close-fitting, one-piece bathing suit for women.

mail'man', *n., pl.* **-men.** MAIL CARRIER.

mail' or'der, *n.* an order for goods received or shipped through the mail. —**mail'-or'der,** *adj.*

maim (mām), *v.t.* 1. to deprive of the use of a part of the body, esp. by wounding. 2. to impair; disfigure.

main (mān), *adj.* 1. chief, as in importance; principal. 2. syntactically independent. 3. sheer; utmost: *by main strength.* —*n.* 4. a principal distributing pipe or duct in a utility system. 5. physical strength or force: *might and main.* 6. the chief part or point. 7. the open ocean. —**main'ly,** *adv.*

Maine (mān), *n.* a state in the NE United States, on the Atlantic coast. 1,243,316. *Cap.:* Augusta. *Abbr.:* ME, Me. —**Main'er,** *n.*

main'frame', *n.* a large computer, often the hub of a system serving many users.

main'land' (-land', -lənd), *n.* the principal land of a continent, country, or region.

main' line', *n.* a principal highway or railway line.

main'mast' (-mast', -mäst'; *Naut.* -məst), *n.* the principal mast of a sailing ship.

main'sail', *n.* the lowermost sail on a mainmast.

main'spring', *n.* 1. the principal spring in a mechanism, as in a watch. 2. the chief motive power; the impelling cause.

main'stay', *n.* 1. a chief support. 2. the stay that secures the mainmast forward.

main'stream', *n.* 1. the principal or dominant course, tendency, or trend. —*adj.* 2. of or characteristic of a mainstream. —*v.t.* 3. to place in regular school classes: *to mainstream disabled children.*

main·tain (mān tān'), *v.t.* 1. to keep in existence or continuance. 2. to keep in due condition, operation, or force. 3. to affirm; assert. 4. to support or defend. 5. to provide for the upkeep of. —**main·tain'a·ble,** *adj.* —**main'te·nance** (-tə nəns), *n.*

maî·tre (or **mai·tre**) **d'** (mā'tər dē', mā'trə, me'trə), *n., pl.* **maître** (or **maitre**) **d's.** MAÎTRE D'HÔTEL.

maî·tre d'hô·tel (mā'trə dō tel'; *Fr.* me tR⁹ dō-tel'), *n., pl.* **maî·tres d'hôtel** (mā'trəz; *Fr.* me tR⁹). 1. a headwaiter. 2. a steward or butler.

maize (māz), *n.* CORN[1] (def. 1).

Maj., Major.

maj·es·ty (maj'ə stē), *n., pl.* **-ties.** 1. regal, lofty, or stately dignity. 2. supreme greatness or authority. 3. (*usu. cap.*) a title of a sovereign. —**ma·jes·tic** (mə-jes'tik), *adj.* —**ma·jes'ti·cal·ly,** *adv.*

ma·jol·i·ca (mə jol'i kə, mə yol'-), *n.* Italian earthenware with an opaque glaze of tin oxide.

ma·jor (mā'jər), *n.* 1. a commissioned military officer ranking next above a captain. 2. a. a field of study in which a student specializes. b. a student specializing in such a field. —*adj.* 3. greater in size, extent, or amount. 4. marked by risk; serious: *a major operation.* 5. *Music.* of, based on, or being a scale with half steps between the third and fourth and seventh and eighth degrees. —*v.i.* 6. to follow an academic major.

ma'jor-do'mo (-dō'mō), *n., pl.* **-mos.** 1. a man in charge of a great household, as that of a sovereign. 2. a steward; butler.

ma'jor·ette' (-jə ret'), *n.* a girl or woman who twirls a baton with or leads a marching band.

ma'jor gen'eral, *n.* a military officer ranking next above a brigadier general.

ma·jor·i·ty (mə jôr'i tē, -jor'-), *n., pl.* **-ties.** 1. a. a number larger than half of a total. b. the amount by which this greater number surpasses the remainder. 2. the state or time of being of full legal age. 3. the military rank of a major.

major'ity lead'er, *n.* the floor leader of the majority party in a legislature.

Ma'jor Proph'et, *n.* any of a group of Old Testament prophets, including Isaiah, Jeremiah, and Ezekiel. Compare MINOR PROPHET.

make (māk), *v.,* **made, mak·ing,** *n.* —*v.t.* 1. to create by shaping, changing, or combining material: *to make a dress.* 2. to cause to exist or happen: *made trouble.* 3. to cause to become: *to make someone happy.* 4. to appoint; name. 5. to put in proper condition, as for use; prepare: *Make your bed.* 6. to force; compel: *made them do it.* 7. to produce, earn, or win: *made many friends.* 8. to draw up; draft: *to make a will.* 9. to establish; enact: *to make laws.* 10. to develop into; become: *You'll make a good lawyer.* 11. to form in the mind: *to make a decision.* 12. to interpret or judge: *What do you make of that remark?* 13. to amount to: *Two plus two makes four.* 14. to constitute: *a table made of wood.* 15. to assure the success of: *The book made her reputation.* 16. to deliver; utter: *to make a speech.* 17. to reach; attain: *didn't make the station in time.* —*v.i.* 18. to cause someone or something to be as specified: *to make sure.* 19. to act in a certain way: *to make merry.* 20. **make away with,** to carry off; steal. 21. **~ for, a.** to move toward. **b.** to promote or result in: *Calm makes for fewer arguments.* 22. **~ out, a.** to write out. **b.** to perceive the meaning of. **c.** to see with effort; discern. **d.** to suggest or impute: *made me out to be a liar.* **e.** to manage; fare: *How are you making out in school?* **23.** ~ **over,** to remodel; alter. **24.** ~ **up, a.** to concoct; invent. **b.** to compensate. **c.** to settle; decide: *Make up your mind.* **d.** to become reconciled. **e.** to apply cosmetics. —*n.* **25.** the style or manner in which something is made. **26.** brand: *a foreign make of car.* —*Idiom.* **27. make believe,** to pretend; imagine. **28. make do,** to manage with whatever is available. **29. make it,** to achieve success. —**mak′er,** *n.*

make′-believe′, *n.* **1.** pretense, esp. of an innocent or playful kind. —*adj.* **2.** pretended; imaginary.

make′-do′, *adj., n., pl.* **-dos.** —*adj.* **1.** used as a substitute; makeshift. —*n.* **2.** something makeshift.

Ma•kem•ie (mə kem′ē, -kā′mē), *n.* **Francis,** 1658–1708, the Irish founder of the Presbyterian Church in America.

make′shift′, *n.* **1.** a temporary expedient or substitute. —*adj.* **2.** being or serving as a makeshift.

make′up′ or **make′-up′,** *n.* **1.** cosmetics, esp. for the face. **2.** the total ensemble of items, as cosmetics and costumes, used by a theatrical performer. **3.** the manner of being put together; composition. **4.** physical or mental constitution.

make′-work′, *n.* work created to keep a person from being idle.

mak′ings, *n.pl.* material from which something is or may be made.

mal-, a combining form meaning bad, wrongful, or ill (*malfunction*).

Mal•a•chi (mal′ə kī′), *n.* **1.** a Minor Prophet of the 5th century B.C. **2.** the book of the Bible bearing his name.

mal•a•chite (mal′ə kīt′), *n.* a green mineral that is an ore of copper, used for making ornamental articles.

mal•ad•just•ed (mal′ə jus′tid), *adj.* badly adjusted, as to one's social circumstances. —**mal′ad•just′-ment,** *n.*

mal•a•droit′, *adj.* lacking in adroitness; awkward. —**mal′a•droit′ly,** *adv.*

mal•a•dy (mal′ə dē), *n., pl.* **-dies.** a disorder or disease of the body.

ma•laise (ma lāz′, -lez′, mə-), *n.* a vague feeling of discomfort or unease.

mal•a•mute (mal′ə myoot′), *n.* one of an Alaskan breed of large dogs, raised orig. for pulling sleds.

mal•a•prop•ism (mal′ə prop iz′əm), *n.* a usu. ludicrous confusion of words that are similar in sound.

mal•ap•ro•pos (mal′ap rə pō′), *adj.* **1.** inappropriate; inopportune. —*adv.* **2.** inappropriately; inopportunely.

ma•lar•i•a (mə lâr′ē ə), *n.* a disease characterized by recurring chills, fever, and sweating and transmitted by an anopheles mosquito. [< It, contr. of *mala aria* bad air] —**ma•lar′i•al,** *adj.*

ma•lar•key (mə lär′kē), *n. Informal.* nonsensical speech or writing.

mal•a•thi•on (mal′ə thī′on, -ən), *n.* an organic insecticide of relatively low toxicity for mammals.

Ma•la•wi (mə lä′wē), *n.* a republic in SE Africa. 9,609,081. —**Ma•la′wi•an,** *adj., n.*

Ma•lay (mā′lā, mə lā′), *n.* **1.** a member of a people of Southeast Asia comprising the principal inhabitants of the Malay Peninsula and adjacent islands. **2.** the language of the Malays.

Mal•a•ya•lam (mal′ə yä′ləm), *n.* a language spoken mainly in extreme SW India.

Ma′lay Archipel′ago, *n.* an extensive island group in the Indian and Pacific oceans, SE of Asia.

Ma′lay Penin′sula, *n.* a peninsula in SE Asia.

Ma•lay•sia (mə lā′zhə), *n.* a constitutional monarchy in SE Asia. 20,376,235. —**Ma•lay′sian,** *adj., n.*

Mal•chus (mal′kəs), *n.* a servant whose ear was cut off by Peter in the Garden of Gethsemane. John 18:10.

Mal•colm X (mal′kəm eks′), *n.* (*Malcolm Little*), 1925–65, U.S. civil-rights activist and religious leader.

mal•con•tent (mal′kən tent′), *adj.* **1.** not satisfied with current conditions. —*n.* **2.** a malcontent person.

Mal•dives (môl′dēvz, mal′dīvz), *n.* a republic on a group of islands in the Indian Ocean, SW of Sri Lanka. 280,391. —**Mal•div′i•an** (-div′ē ən), *adj., n.*

male (māl), *n.* **1.** an individual or organism of the sex or sexual phase that normally produces a sperm cell or male gamete. —*adj.* **2.** of or being a male. **3.** of or characteristic of a boy or man; masculine. **4.** made to fit into a corresponding open or recessed part: *a male plug.* —**male′ness,** *n.*

mal•e•dic•tion (mal′i dik′shən), *n.* a curse; imprecation.

mal•e•fac•tor (mal′ə fak′tər), *n.* **1.** a person who violates the law; criminal. **2.** an evildoer. —**mal′e•fac′tion,** *n.*

ma•lef•ic (mə lef′ik), *adj.* productive of evil; malign.

ma•lef′i•cent (-ə sənt), *adj.* evil or harmful. —**ma•lef′i•cence,** *n.*

ma•lev•o•lent (-lev′ə lənt), *adj.* **1.** wishing evil or harm to others; malicious. **2.** producing evil or harm; injurious. —**ma•lev′o•lence,** *n.*

mal•fea•sance (mal fē′zəns), *n.* misconduct or wrongdoing, esp. by a public official.

mal′for•ma′tion, *n.* a faulty or anomalous formation or structure. —**mal•formed′,** *adj.*

mal•func′tion, *n.* **1.** failure to function properly. —*v.i.* **2.** to fail to function properly.

Ma•li (mä′lē), *n.* a republic in W Africa. 9,945,383. —**Ma′li•an,** *n., adj.*

mal•ice (mal′is), *n.* **1.** a desire to inflict harm or suffering on another. **2.** *Law.* malevolence, deliberate lying, or recklessness in the commission of a wrong. —**ma•li•cious** (mə lish′əs), —**ma•li′cious•ly,** *adv.*

ma•lign (mə līn′), *v.t.* **1.** to speak harmful untruths about. —*adj.* **2.** evil in effect. **3.** evil in disposition.

ma•lig•nant (mə lig′nənt), *adj.* **1.** inclined to cause harm, suffering, or distress. **2.** dangerous or harmful in influence or effect. **3.** tending to produce death, as a tumor. —**ma•lig′nan•cy,** *n., pl.* **-cies.** —**ma•lig′ni•ty** (-ni tē), *n.*

ma•lin•ger (mə ling′gər), *v.i.* to pretend illness, esp. in order to shirk duty or work. —**ma•lin′ger•er,** *n.*

mall (môl), *n.* **1.** a large retail shopping complex. **2.** an urban street lined with shops and closed to motor vehicles. **3.** a large shaded public walk or promenade. **4.** a strip of land separating two roadways.

mal•lard (mal′ərd), *n., pl.* **-lards, -lard.** a common wild duck from which domestic ducks are descended.

mal•le•a•ble (mal′ē ə bəl), *adj.* **1.** capable of being extended or shaped by hammering or pressure from rollers. **2.** adaptable; tractable. —**mal′le•a•bil′i•ty,** *n.*

mal•let (mal′it), *n.* **1.** a hammerlike tool with an enlarged head for driving another tool or striking a surface without causing damage. **2.** a wooden implement used to strike a ball, as in croquet.

mal•low (mal′ō), *n.* any of various plants with lobed leaves and purple, pink, or white flowers.

mal•nour•ished (mal nûr′isht, -nur′-), *adj.* poorly nourished.

mal′nu•tri′tion, *n.* inadequate or unbalanced nutrition.

mal′oc•clu′sion, *n.* irregular contact of opposing teeth in the upper and lower jaws.

mal•o′dor•ous, *adj.* having a foul odor.

mal•prac′tice, *n.* dereliction of professional duty, as by a physician or lawyer, esp. when injury or loss follows.

malt (môlt), *n.* **1.** germinated grain used esp. in brewing and distilling. **2.** an alcoholic beverage, as beer, fermented from malt. —**malt′y,** *adj.,* **-i•er, -i•est.**

Mal•ta (môl′tə), *n.* an island republic in the Mediterranean, south of Sicily. 379,365. —**Mal•tese′** (-tēz′, -tēs′), *n., pl.* -**tese**, *adj.*

malt′ed milk′, *n.* **1.** a soluble powder made of dehydrated milk and a malt extract. **2.** a beverage made by dissolving malted milk in milk and usu. adding ice cream and flavoring.

malt•ose (môl′tōs), *n.* a sugar formed by the action of an enzyme on starch.

mal•treat (mal trēt′), *v.t.* to treat badly or roughly. —**mal•treat′ment**, *n.*

ma•ma or **mam•ma** (mä′mə, mə mä′), *n., pl.* -**mas.** MOTHER. [nursery word, with parallels in other European languages]

mam•ba (mäm′bä), *n., pl.* -**bas.** any of several long slender tree snakes of Africa.

mam•bo (mäm′bō), *n., pl.* -**bos.** a ballroom dance of Caribbean origin similar to the rumba and cha-cha.

mam•mal (mam′əl), *n.* a warm-blooded vertebrate of the class that nourishes its young with milk from maternal mammary glands. —**mam•ma•li•an** (mə-mā′lē ən, -māl′yən), *n., adj.*

mam•ma•ry (mam′ə rē), *adj.* of or pertaining to a gland in the female breast that secretes milk.

mam•mo•gram (mam′ə gram′), *n.* an x-ray photograph obtained by mammography.

mam•mog•ra•phy (ma mog′rə fē), *n.* x-ray photography of a breast, esp. for detection of tumors.

mam•mon (mam′ən), *n.* riches or material wealth, esp. as an influence for evil or immorality. Matt. 6:24; Luke 16:9, 11, 13. [< LL < Gk < Aram *māmōnā* riches]

mam•moth (mam′əth), *n.* **1.** an extinct Pleistocene elephant with hairy skin. —*adj.* **2.** very large; enormous.

mammoth

man (man), *n., pl.* **men,** *v.,* **manned, man•ning.** —*n.* **1.** an adult male person. **2.** the human race; humankind. **3.** a human being; person. **4.** a husband. **5.** a male having qualities considered appropriately masculine. **6.** a male servant or attendant. **7.** a playing piece used in certain games, as chess. —*v.t.* **8.** to supply with people, as for service. **9.** to take one's place at, as to defend or operate. —**Usage.** The use of MAN or the combining form -MAN to refer to humans in general is now often considered sexist, especially in occupational titles. Many prefer gender-neutral alternatives: *human being(s); humankind; spokesperson; chair* or *chairperson; firefighter.* See also -PERSON.

Man (man), *n.* **Isle of,** an island of the British Isles, in the Irish Sea.

Man., Manitoba.

man•a•cle (man′ə kəl), *n., v.,* -**cled, -cling.** —*n.* **1.** a shackle for the hand. —*v.t.* **2.** to handcuff; fetter. **3.** to hamper; restrain.

man•age (man′ij), *v.,* -**aged, -ag•ing.** —*v.t.* **1.** to succeed in accomplishing. **2.** to take or be in charge or control of. **3.** to dominate or influence, esp. by tact. —*v.i.* **4.** to be in charge or control of an undertaking. **5.** to get along; function. —**man′age•a•ble,** *adj.*

man′aged care′, *n.* a health plan or system that seeks to control medical costs by contracting with a network of providers and by requiring preauthorization for visits to specialists.

man′age•ment, *n.* **1.** the act or process of managing. **2.** executive ability. **3.** the persons managing an enterprise.

man′ag•er, *n.* a person who manages, as one who directs the activities of an athlete or team. —**man′a•ge′ri•al** (-i jēr′ē əl), *adj.*

Ma•na•gua (mə nä′gwä), *n.* the capital of Nicaragua. 682,111.

Ma•na•ma (mə nam′ə), *n.* the capital of Bahrain. 151,500.

ma•ña•na (mä nyä′nä), *n., adv. Spanish.* tomorrow.

Ma•nas•sas (mə nas′əs), *n.* a town in NE Virginia, near which the first and second Battles of Bull Run (known in the South as the **Battle of Manassas**) were fought in 1861 and 1862.

Ma•nas•seh (mə nas′ə), *n.* **1.** the first son of Joseph. Gen. 41:51. **2.** one of the 12 tribes of Israel. Gen. 48:14–19. **3.** a king of Judah of the 7th century B.C. II Kings 21.

man•a•tee (man′ə tē′), *n., pl.* -**tees.** a plant-eating aquatic mammal of Caribbean and W African waters.

Man•ches•ter (man′ches′tər, -chə stər), *n.* a city in NW England. 451,000.

Man•chu (man chōō′), *n., pl.* -**chu, -chus. 1.** a member of a people of Manchuria who conquered China and established a dynasty there (1644–1912). **2.** the language of the Manchu.

Man•chu•ri•a (man chŏŏr′ē ə), *n.* a historic region in NE China. —**Man•chu′ri•an,** *adj., n.*

man•da•la (mun′dl ə), *n., pl.* -**las.** a schematized representation of the cosmos in Hindu and Buddhist iconography.

Man•da•lay (man′dl ā′, man′dl ā′), *n.* a city in central Myanmar. 532,985.

man•da•mus (man dā′məs), *n., pl.* -**mus•es.** *Law.* a writ from a superior court commanding that a specified thing be done.

man•da•rin (man′də rin), *n.* **1.** a member of any of the nine ranks of public officials in the Chinese Empire. **2.** (*cap.*) the principal dialect of Chinese. **3.** a small, loose-skinned citrus fruit.

man•date (man′dāt), *n.* **1.** an authorization to act given by an electorate to a representative. **2.** an authoritative order or command. **3.** a commission given by the League of Nations to a member nation to administer a former Turkish territory or German colony.

man•da•to•ry (man′də tôr′ē), *adj.* **1.** of, containing, or being a command. **2.** having received a mandate, as a nation.

Man•de•la (man del′ə), *n.* **Nelson (Rolihlahla),** born 1918, president of South Africa since 1994.

man•di•ble (man′də bəl), *n.* **1.** the bone comprising the lower jaw of vertebrates. **2.** the lower part of a bird's bill. —**man•dib′u•lar** (-dib′yə lər), *adj.*

man•do•lin (man′dl in, man′dl in′), *n.* a stringed musical instrument with a pear-shaped body and a fretted neck.

man•drake (man′drāk, -drik), *n.* a narcotic plant with a fleshy, forked root somewhat resembling a human form.

man•drel or **-dril** (man′drəl), *n.* a shaft or bar inserted into a piece of work to hold it during machining.

man•drill (man′dril), *n.* a large W African baboon, the male of which has a ribbed blue and scarlet muzzle.

mane (mān), *n.* the long hair around or at the back of the neck of some animals, as the horse or lion. —**maned,** *adj.*

ma•nège or **-nege** (ma nezh′, -nāzh′), *n.* the art of training and riding horses.

Ma•net (ma nā′), *n.* **Édouard,** 1832–83, French painter.

ma•neu•ver (mə nōō′vər), *n.* **1.** a planned movement of troops, warships, etc. **2. maneuvers,** a series of tactical military exercises. **3.** a physical movement or procedure, esp. when carried out skillfully. **4.** a clever or crafty tactic; ploy. —*v.i., v.t.* **5.** to perform or cause to perform a maneuver. **6.** to position, manipulate, or steer skillfully or adroitly. [< F ≪ L, = *manū operārī* to work with the hands] —**ma•neu′ver•a•ble,** *adj.* —**ma•neu′ver•a•bil′i•ty,** *n.*

man′ Fri′day, *n., pl.* **men Friday.** a reliable male assistant.

man′ful, *adj.* having or showing boldness, courage, or strength. —**man′ful•ly,** *adv.*

man•ga•nese (mang′gə nēs′, -nēz′), *n.* a hard, brittle, grayish white metallic element, used chiefly in strengthening steel. *Symbol:* Mn; *at. wt.:* 54.938; *at. no.:* 25.

mange (mānj), *n.* a skin disease, esp. of animals, characterized by hair loss and scabby eruptions. —**mang′y,** *adj.,* -**i•er,** -**i•est.**

man•ger (mān′jər), *n.* a trough from which livestock eat.

man•gle¹ (mang′gəl), *v.t.,* -**gled,** -**gling. 1.** to injure, disfigure, or mutilate by cutting, slashing, or crushing. **2.** to spoil; ruin.

man•gle² (mang′gəl), *n.* a machine for pressing laundry by passing it between heated rollers.

man•go (mang′gō), *n., pl.* -**goes,** -**gos. 1.** the oblong sweet fruit of a tropical tree of the cashew family. **2.** a tree bearing mangoes.

man•grove (mang′grōv, man′-), *n.* a tropical tree growing in marshes or tidal shores, noted for its interlacing above-ground roots.

man•han•dle (man′han′dl), *v.t.,* -**dled,** -**dling. 1.** to handle roughly. **2.** to move by human strength alone.

Man•hat•tan (man hat′n, mən-), *n.* a borough of New York City. 1,427,533.

Manhat′tan Proj′ect, *n.* the unofficial designation for the U.S. War Department's secret program to explore the production of an atomic bomb.

man′hole′, *n.* a hole giving access to a sewer, drain, or conduit.

man′hood, *n.* **1.** the state or time of being a man. **2.** traditional manly qualities. **3.** men collectively.

man′-hour′, *n.* a unit of measurement based on an ideal amount of work accomplished by one person in an hour.

man′hunt′, *n.* an intensive search for a person, esp. a criminal or fugitive.

ma•ni•a (mā′nē ə), *n., pl.* -**ni•as. 1.** an excessive enthusiasm; craze. **2.** a pathological state characterized by euphoria, excessive activity, and impaired judgment.

ma•ni•ac′, *n.* **1.** an insane person; lunatic. —*adj.* **2.** insane; mad. —**ma•ni•a•cal** (mə nī′ə kəl), *adj.*

man•ic (man′ik), *adj.* pertaining to or affected by mania.

man′ic-depres′sive, *adj.* **1.** suffering from a mental disorder marked by periods of mania alternating with depression. —*n.* **2.** a manic-depressive person.

man•i•cure (man′i kyŏōr′), *n., v.,* -**cured,** -**cur•ing.** —*n.* **1.** a cosmetic treatment of the hands or fingernails. —*v.t.* **2.** to apply manicure treatment to. **3.** to trim or cut meticulously. —**man′i•cur′ist,** *n.*

man•i•fest (man′ə fest′), *adj.* **1.** readily perceived; evident. —*v.t.* **2.** to make evident; show. —*n.* **3.** a list of cargo or passengers. —**man′i•fest′ly,** *adv.*

man′i•fes•ta′tion (-fə stā′shən, -fe-), *n.* **1.** the act of manifesting or state of being manifested. **2.** outward or perceptible indication.

Man′ifest Des′tiny, *n.* the 19th-century belief that it was inevitable for the U.S. to expand to the Pacific coast.

man′i•fes′to (-fes′tō), *n., pl.* -**tos,** -**toes.** a public declaration of intentions, opinions, or purposes.

man•i•fold (man′ə fōld′), *adj.* **1.** of many kinds; varied. **2.** having numerous different parts, features, or forms. —*n.* **3.** a pipe with several openings for funneling the flow of liquids or gases. —*v.t.* **4.** to make many copies of.

man•i•kin (man′i kin), *n.* **1.** a little man; dwarf. **2.** MANNEQUIN.

Ma•nil•a (mə nil′ə), *n.* the capital of the Philippines, on SW Luzon. 1,630,485.

Manil′a (or **manil′a**) **hemp′,** *n.* the fiber from a Philippine plant, used for rope, fabric, etc.

Manil′a (or **manil′a**) **pa′per,** *n.* strong, light brown or buff paper orig. made from Manila hemp.

man′ in the street′, *n.* an ordinary person.

man•i•oc (man′ē ok′, mä′nē-), *n.* CASSAVA.

ma•nip•u•late (mə nip′yə lāt′), *v.t.,* -**lat•ed,** -**lat•ing. 1.** to manage or influence skillfully and often unfairly. **2.** to handle or use, esp. with skill. **3.** to examine or treat by skillful use of the hands. —**ma•nip′u•la′tion,** *n.* —**ma•nip′u•la′tive,** *adj.* —**ma•nip′u•la′tor,** *n.*

Man•i•to•ba (man′i tō′bə), *n.* a province in central Canada. 1,063,016. *Cap.:* Winnipeg. *Abbr.:* MB, Man.

man•kind (man′kīnd′ for 1; man′kīnd′ for 2), *n.* **1.** human beings collectively. **2.** men as distinguished from women.

man′ly, *adj.,* -**li•er,** -**li•est,** *adv.* —*adj.* **1.** having qualities traditionally ascribed to men; virile. **2.** suitable for males. —*adv.* **3.** in a manly manner. —**man′li•ness,** *n.*

man′-made′, *adj.* produced or made by humans.

Mann (man *for 1;* man, män *for 2*), *n.* **1. Horace,** 1796–1859, U.S. educational reformer. **2. Thomas,** 1875–1955, German novelist, in the U.S. 1938–52.

man•na (man′ə), *n.* **1.** the food miraculously supplied to the Israelites in the wilderness. Ex. 16:14-36. **2.** a sudden or unexpected source of help or gratification.

manned, *adj.* carrying or operated by a person: *a manned spacecraft.*

man•ne•quin (man′i kin), *n.* **1.** a three-dimensional model of the human form, as that used for fitting clothes. **2.** a person employed to model clothing.

man•ner (man′ər), *n.* **1.** a way of doing, being done, or happening. **2. manners, a.** the prevailing customs of a people, class, or period. **b.** ways of behaving with reference to polite standards. **3.** customary way of doing or making. **4.** kind; sort. **5.** characteristic style in art or literature.

man′nered, *adj.* **1.** having manners of a specified kind: *ill-mannered.* **2.** not natural; affected: *a mannered walk.*

man′ner•ism, *n.* **1.** a habitual or characteristic manner of doing something. **2.** excessive or affected adherence to a particular manner.

man′ner•ly, *adj.* showing good manners, courteous.

man•ni•kin (man′i kin), *n.* MANIKIN.

man•nish (man′ish), *adj.* being typical or suggestive of a man rather than a woman. —**man′nish•ly,** *adv.* —**man′nish•ness,** *n.*

Ma•no•ah (mə nō′ə), *n.* the father of Samson. Judg. 13.

ma•noeu•vre (mə nōō′vər), *n., v.i., v.t.,* -**vred,** -**vring.** *Chiefly Brit.* MANEUVER.

Man′ of Gal′ilee, *n.* Jesus.

Man′ of Sor′rows, *n.* (in Christian exegesis) an appellation of Jesus as the suffering Savior. Isa. 53:3.

man′-of-war′, *n., pl.* **men-of-war. 1.** WARSHIP. **2.** PORTUGUESE MAN-OF-WAR.

ma•nom•e•ter (mə nom′i tər), *n.* an instrument for measuring the pressure of a fluid.

man•or (man′ər), *n.* **1.** a feudal estate. **2.** (in England) the landed estate of a lord. **3.** the main house on an estate. —**ma•no•ri•al** (mə nôr′ē əl), *adj.*

man′pow′er, *n.* power in terms of people available or required for work or military service.

man•qué (mäng kā′, män-), *adj.* unsuccessful; unfulfilled: *a poet manqué.* [< F]

man•sard (man′särd), *n.* a roof having four sides, each with two slopes, the lower slope being steeper than the upper.

manse (mans), *n.* the house occupied by a minister.

man′serv′ant, *n., pl.* **men•serv•ants.** a male servant.

man•sion (man′shən), *n.* a very large or stately residence.

man′-sized′ or **-size′,** *adj.* generous in size; big.

man′slaugh′ter, *n.* the unlawful killing of a human being without malice.

man′slay′er, *n.* a person who kills another human being.

man•sue•tude (man′swi tŏŏd′, -tyŏŏd′), n. mildness; gentleness.

man•ta (man′tə, män′-), n., pl. **-tas.** a huge ray with pectoral fins resembling wings. Also called **man′ta ray′.**

man•tel (man′tl), n. **1.** a decorative construction framing the opening of a fireplace. **2.** a shelf above a fireplace.

man′tel•piece′, n. MANTEL (def. 2).

man•til•la (man til′ə, -tē′ə), n., pl. **-las.** a woman's silk or lace scarf worn over the head and shoulders, esp. in Spain or Latin America.

man•tis (man′tis), n., pl. **-tis•es, -tes** (-tēz). any of several insects typically holding the forelegs upraised as if in prayer.

man•tis•sa (man tis′ə), n., pl. **-sas.** the decimal part of a common logarithm.

man•tle (man′tl), n., v., **-tled, -tling. —n. 1.** a long, loose, sleeveless cloak. **2.** something that covers or conceals. **3.** the portion of the earth between the crust and the core. **4.** an incombustible hood that gives off a brilliant light when placed around a flame. **5.** MANTEL. —v.i. **7.** to flush; blush.

man•tra (man′trə, män′-), n., pl. **-tras.** (in Hinduism and Buddhism) a sacred word or formula repeated as an incantation.

man•u•al (man′yŏŏ əl), adj. **1.** operated by hand. **2.** involving or requiring human effort; physical. **3.** of the hands. —n. **4.** a small book, esp. one giving information or instructions. **5.** the prescribed drill in handling a rifle. **6.** a keyboard, esp. of a pipe organ. —**man′u•al•ly,** adv.

man•u•fac•ture (man′yə fak′chər), v., **-tured, -tur•ing,** n. —v.t. **1.** to make by hand or machinery, esp. on a large scale. **2.** to make up; invent: *to manufacture an excuse.* —n. **3.** the making of goods or wares by hand or machinery, esp. on a large scale. **4.** something manufactured. —**man′u•fac′tur•er,** n.

man•u•mit (man′yə mit′), v.t., **-mit•ted, -mit•ting.** to release from slavery. —**man′u•mis′sion,** n.

ma•nure (mə nŏŏr′, -nyŏŏr′), n., v., **-nured, -nur•ing.** —n. **1.** a substance, esp. animal excrement, used for fertilizing the soil. —v.t. **2.** to fertilize (land) with manure.

man•u•script (man′yə skript′), n. **1.** a written, typewritten, or computer-produced text. **2.** writing as distinguished from print.

Manx (mangks), n. **1.** (*used with a pl. v.*) the inhabitants of the Isle of Man. **2.** the moribund Celtic language of the Isle of Man.

man•y (men′ē), adj., **more, most,** n., pron. —adj. **1.** constituting or forming a large number. —n. **2.** a large number. —pron. **3.** many persons or things. —*Proverb.* **4. Many are called, but few are chosen,** only the most qualified people will be selected (to do God's work). Matt. 22:11-14.

Mao•ism (mou′iz əm), n. the theories and policies of Mao Zedong. —**Mao′ist,** n., adj.

Ma•o•ri (mou′rē), n., pl. **-ri, -ris. 1.** a member of the Polynesian people who are the aboriginal inhabitants of New Zealand. **2.** their language.

Mao Ze•dong (mou′ zə dŏŏng′, dzə-) also **Mao Tse-tung** (mou′ tsə tŏŏng′, dzə dŏŏng′), n. 1893-1976, chairman of the People's Republic of China 1949-59 and of the Chinese Communist party 1943-76.

map (map), n., v., **mapped, map•ping.** —n. **1.** a representation, usu. on a flat surface, of all or a part of the earth or the heavens. —v.t. **2.** to represent on a map. **3.** to sketch or plan: *mapped out a financial strategy.* —**map′mak′er,** n. —**map′per,** n.

ma•ple (mā′pəl), n. **1.** any of numerous trees or shrubs grown for shade or ornament, for timber, or for sap. **2.** the wood of a maple.

ma′ple sug′ar, n. sugar produced by boiling down maple syrup.

ma′ple syr′up, n. a syrup produced by partially boiling down the sap of a maple tree.

Ma•pu•to (mə pŏŏ′tō), n. the capital of Mozambique. 491,800.

mar (mär), v.t., **marred, mar•ring.** to damage the attractiveness or appeal of; impair.

Mar or **Mar.,** March.

mar•a•bou (mar′ə bŏŏ′), n., pl. **-bous. 1.** any of several bare-headed storks. **2.** material made from the feathers of marabous, used to trim women's clothing.

ma•rac•a (mə rä′kə, -rak′ə), n., pl. **-rac•as.** a gourd-shaped rattle filled with seeds or pebbles and used as a rhythm instrument.

Mar•a•cai•bo (mar′ə kī′bō), n. a seaport in NW Venezuela. 890,553.

Ma•rah (mâr′ə), n. a pool or well that was the first place the Israelites stopped after crossing the Red Sea. Num. 33:8-9.

mar•a•schi•no (mar′ə skē′nō, -shē′-), n., pl. **-nos.** a cordial distilled from a wild cherry.

mar′aschi′no cher′ry, n. a cherry preserved in maraschino or imitation maraschino.

mar•a•thon (mar′ə thon′, -thən), n. **1.** a foot race of 26 mi. 385 yd. (42 km 195 m). **2.** a long-distance race. **3.** a contest or event requiring great endurance. —**mar′a•thon′er,** n.

ma•raud (mə rôd′), v.i., v.t. to rove in quest of plunder; raid. —**ma•raud′er,** n.

mar•ble (mär′bəl), n., adj., v., **-bled, -bling. —n. 1.** a limestone that takes a high polish and is used esp. in sculpture and architecture. **2.** something resembling marble, as in hardness. **3. a.** a small ball, as of agate, for use in games. **b. marbles,** any of various children's games played with marbles. —adj. **4.** consisting of or resembling marble. —v.t. **5.** to color or stain in imitation of marble, as book edges. —**mar′bly,** adj.

mar′ble•ize′, v.t., **-ized, -iz•ing.** MARBLE.

mar•bling (mär′bling), n. the intermixture of fat with lean in a cut of meat.

Mar•bur•y v. Madison (mär′ber ē, -bə rē), n. a U.S. Supreme Court decision of 1803 that affirmed the Court's power to judge the constitutionality of laws passed by Congress.

march¹ (märch), v.i. **1.** to walk with regular, measured steps, as soldiers in military formation. **2.** to proceed in a deliberate manner. **3.** to advance. —v.t. **4.** to cause to march. —n. **5.** the act or course of marching. **6.** the distance covered in marching. **7.** advance; progress. **8.** a piece of music with a rhythm suited to accompany marching. —**march′er,** n.

march² (märch), n. a border district; frontier.

March, n. the third month of the year, containing 31 days.

mar•chion•ess (mär′shə nis, -nes′), n. **1.** the wife or widow of a marquess. **2.** a woman holding a rank equal to that of a marquess.

March′ on Wash′ington, n. a civil-rights rally held in Washington, D.C., on August 28, 1963.

Mar•co•ni (mär kō′nē), n. **Guglielmo,** 1874-1937, Italian physicist and inventor.

Mar•di Gras (mär′dē grä′, grä′), n. the day before Ash Wednesday, often celebrated as a day of carnival.

mare¹ (mâr), n. a female equine animal, esp. a horse.

ma•re² (mär′ā, mâr′ē), n., pl. **ma•ri•a** (mär′ē ə, mâr′-). any of several large, dark plains on the moon and Mars.

mare's′-nest′, n. **1.** a discovery that proves to be a delusion or hoax. **2.** a confused or disordered situation.

mar•ga•rine (mär′jər in), n. a butterlike product made of vegetable oils emulsified usu. with water or milk.

mar•gin (mär′jin), n. **1.** the space around the printed or written matter on a page. **2.** a border; edge. **3.** an amount beyond what is necessary. **4.** an amount or degree of difference. —**mar′gin•al,** adj. —**mar′gin•al•ly,** adv.

mar′gi•na′li•a (-jə nā′lē ə), n.pl. marginal notes.

mar•gue•rite (mär′gə rēt′), n. any of several daisy-like chrysanthemums.

ma•ri•a•chi (mär′ē ä′chē), *n., pl.* **-chis. 1.** a Mexican band of itinerant street musicians. **2.** a member of a mariachi. **3.** the dance music played by a mariachi.

Mar•i•an (mâr′ē ən), *adj.* of the Virgin Mary.

Ma•rie An•toi•nette (mə rē′ an′twə net′, an′tə-), *n.* 1755–93, queen of France 1774–93: wife of Louis XVI.

mar•i•gold (mar′i gōld′), *n.* a plant with golden or orange flowers and strong-scented foliage.

ma•ri•jua•na or **-hua•na** (mar′ə wä′nə), *n.* **1.** the dried leaves and flowers of the hemp plant used esp. in cigarette form as an intoxicant. **2.** HEMP (def. 1).

ma•rim•ba (mə rim′bə), *n., pl.* **-bas.** a kind of xylophone, often with resonators beneath the bars to reinforce the sound. [< Pg < a Bantu language]

ma•ri•na (mə rē′nə), *n., pl.* **-nas.** a boat basin offering dockage and services for small craft.

mar•i•nade (mar′ə nād′), *n.* a pungent liquid mixture in which food is steeped before cooking.

mar′i•nate′, *v.t.,* **-nat•ed, -nat•ing.** to steep (food) in a marinade. —**mar′i•na′tion,** *n.*

ma•rine (mə rēn′), *adj.* **1.** of the sea. **2.** of navigation or shipping. **3.** of the marines. —*n.* **4.** (*sometimes cap.*) a member of the U.S. Marine Corps. **5.** a soldier serving both on shipboard and on land. **6.** seagoing ships.

Marine′ Corps′, *n.* a branch of the U.S. armed forces trained for sea-launched assaults on land targets.

mar•i•ner (mar′ə nər), *n.* a sailor.

mar•i•on•ette (mar′ē ə net′), *n.* a puppet manipulated by strings attached to its jointed limbs.

mar•i•tal (mar′i tl), *adj.* of marriage. —**mar′i•tal•ly,** *adv.*

mar•i•time (mar′i tīm′), *adj.* **1.** of navigation or shipping on the sea. **2.** of or bordering on the sea.

mar•jo•ram (mär′jər əm), *n.* an aromatic herb of the mint family with leaves used as a seasoning.

mark¹ (märk), *n.* **1.** a visible impression on a surface, as a scratch. **2.** a symbol used in writing or printing: *a punctuation mark.* **3.** a token or indication; sign. **4.** a lasting effect; imprint. **5.** a distinctive or characteristic trait. **6.** a device or symbol serving to identify or indicate origin or ownership. **7.** TRADEMARK. **8.** a symbol used in rating a student's achievement; grade. **9.** an object or sign serving to indicate position. **10.** a recognized or required standard. **11.** a target; goal. **12.** distinction; note. **13.** an object of derision or abuse. **14.** the starting line in a race. —*v.t.* **15.** to be a distinguishing feature of. **16.** to put a mark or marks on. **17.** to rate or grade. **18.** to designate by or as if by marks. **19.** to make manifest. **20.** to give heed to: *Mark my words.* **21. mark down,** to reduce the price of. **22. ~ up,** to raise the price of. —*Idiom.* **23. make one's mark,** to achieve success. **24. mark time, a.** to function in an unproductive way. **b.** to move the feet alternately as if marching but without advancing. —**mark′er,** *n.*

mark² (märk), *n.* the basic monetary unit of Germany.

Mark (märk), *n.* **1.** an early Christian disciple, believed to be the author of the second Gospel. **2.** the second Gospel.

mark′down′, *n.* **1.** a reduction in price. **2.** the amount by which a price is reduced.

marked, *adj.* striking; conspicuous. —**mark′ed•ly,** *adv.*

mar•ket (mär′kit), *n.* **1.** a place where buyers and sellers convene for trade. **2.** a store for the sale of food. **3.** a meeting of people for buying and selling. **4.** demand for a commodity. **5.** a particular group of potential buyers. **6.** a region in which goods and services are bought or used. —*v.i.* **7.** to buy provisions for the home. —*v.t.* **8.** to offer for sale. **9.** to sell. —**mar′ket•a•ble,** *adj.* —**mar′ket•er,** *n.*

mar′ket•place′, *n.* **1.** an open area in a town where a market is held. **2.** the world of business, trade, and economics.

Mark•ham (mär′kəm), *n.* a town in SE Ontario, in S Canada. 114,597.

mark•ka (märk′kä), *n., pl.* **-kaa** (-kä). the basic monetary unit of Finland.

mark′ of the beast′, *n.* **1.** the mark put on the forehead of those who worship the beast, the symbol of opposition to God. **2.** the stain of apostasy. Rev. 13:16.

marks′man, *n., pl.* **-men.** a person skilled in shooting at a target. —**marks′man•ship′,** *n.*

mark′up′, *n.* **1.** an increase in price. **2.** the difference between cost and selling price. **3.** a set of instructions on a manuscript or tags in an electronic document to determine type styles, page makeup, etc.

marl (märl), *n.* an earthy deposit used esp. as a fertilizer for soils deficient in lime.

mar•lin (mär′lin), *n., pl.* **-lins, -lin.** a large saltwater game fish with a spearlike upper jaw.

mar•line•spike (mär′lin spīk′), *n.* a pointed iron implement used in separating strands of rope, as in splicing.

mar•ma•lade (mär′mə lād′), *n.* a jellylike preserve containing pieces of citrus fruit and rind.

mar•mo•set (mär′mə zet′, -set′), *n.* a squirrel-sized South and Central American monkey.

mar•mot (mär′mət), *n.* a stocky burrowing rodent, as the woodchuck.

ma•roon¹ (mə rōōn′), *n.* a dark brownish red.

ma•roon² (mə rōōn′), *v.t.* **1.** to put ashore and abandon on a desolate island or coast. **2.** to isolate without aid or resources.

marque (märk), *n.* a product model or type, as of a racing car.

mar•quee (mär kē′), *n., pl.* **-quees. 1.** a projecting structure over an entrance, as to a theater. **2.** a large tent, as for an outdoor reception.

mar•quess (mär′kwis), *n.* **1.** a British nobleman ranking below a duke and above an earl. **2.** MARQUIS.

mar•que•try (mär′ki trē), *n.* inlaid work forming a picture or pattern, esp. in furniture.

mar•quis (mär′kwis, mär kē′), *n.* a European nobleman ranking below a duke and above a count.

mar•quise (mär kēz′), *n.* **1.** the wife or widow of a marquis. **2.** a woman holding a rank equal to that of a marquis.

mar•qui•sette (mär′kə zet′, -kwə-), *n.* a lightweight open mesh fabric.

mar•riage (mar′ij), *n.* **1.** the state, condition, or relationship of being married. **2.** the ceremony that formalizes marriage. **3.** an intimate association or union. —**mar′riage•a•ble,** *adj.*

mar•row (mar′ō), *n.* the soft, fatty, vascular tissue in the cavities of bones.

mar•ry (mar′ē), *v.,* **-ried, -ry•ing.** —*v.t.* **1.** to take as a husband or wife. **2.** to join in wedlock. **3.** to join or unite intimately. —*v.i.* **4.** to take a husband or wife.

Mars (märz), *n.* **1.** the ancient Roman god of war. **2.** the planet fourth in order from the sun.

Mar•seilles or **-seille** (mär sā′), *n.* a seaport in SE France. 1,110,511.

marsh (märsh), *n.* a tract of waterlogged soil. —**marsh′y,** *adj.,* **-i•er, -i•est.**

mar•shal (mär′shəl), *n., v.,* **-shaled, -shal•ing** or (*esp. Brit.*) **-shalled, -shal•ling.** —*n.* **1.** an officer of a U.S. judicial district with duties similar to those of a sheriff. **2.** the chief of a police or fire department. **3.** an official who leads special ceremonies, as a parade. **4.** an army officer of the highest rank, as in France. —*v.t.* **5.** to arrange in proper or effective order. **6.** to usher or lead ceremoniously.

Mar•shall (mär′shəl), *n.* **1. John,** 1755–1835, Chief Justice of the U.S. 1801–35. **2. Thurgood,** 1908–93, associate justice of the U.S. Supreme Court 1967–91.

marsh′ gas′, *n.* a gaseous decomposition product of organic matter, consisting primarily of methane.

marsh′mal′low (-mel′ō, -mal′ō), *n.* a spongy confection made from gelatin, sugar, corn syrup, and flavoring.

marsh′ mar′igold, *n.* a yellow-flowered plant of the buttercup family.

mar·su·pi·al (mär sōō′pē əl), n. a mammal, as an opossum or kangaroo, bearing immature young that complete their development in a pouch on the mother's abdomen. [< NL marsupiālis pertaining to a pouch]

mart (märt), n. a trading center; market.

mar·ten (mär′tn), n., pl. -tens, -ten. 1. a carnivore of the weasel family with soft, glossy fur. 2. the fur of a marten.

Mar·tha (mär′thə), n. the sister of Mary and Lazarus. Luke 10:38–42; John 11:1–44.

mar·tial (mär′shəl), adj. 1. inclined to war. 2. of or suitable for war or the armed forces. 3. characteristic of or befitting a warrior.

mar′tial art′, n. any of the traditional forms of East Asian self-defense or combat, as karate or judo.

mar′tial law′, n. law imposed, as in occupied territory, by military forces.

Mar·tian (mär′shən), adj. 1. of the planet Mars or its hypothetical inhabitants. —n. 2. a supposed inhabitant of the planet Mars.

mar·tin (mär′tn), n. any of various small swallows.

mar·ti·net (mär′tn et′), n. a strict disciplinarian.

mar·tin·gale (mär′tn gāl′), n. a strap fastened at one end to the girth and at the other to the noseband or reins to steady a horse's head.

Mar·ti·nique (mär′tn ēk′), n. an island in the E West Indies; an overseas department of France. 336,000.

mar·tyr (mär′tər), n. 1. a person who willingly suffers death rather than renounce his or her religion. 2. a person who suffers on behalf of a cause. 3. a person who undergoes severe suffering. —v.t. 4. to make a martyr of. 5. to torment; torture. —mar′tyr·dom, n.

mar·vel (mär′vəl), n., v., -veled, -vel·ing or (esp. Brit.) -velled, -vel·ling. —n. 1. something that arouses wonder, admiration, or astonishment. 2. a feeling of wonder. —v.t. 3. to wonder at. —v.i. 4. to be filled with wonder.

mar′vel·ous, adj. 1. superbly fine. 2. arousing wonder, admiration, or astonishment. Also, esp. Brit., **mar′vel·lous.** —mar′vel·ous·ly, adv.

Marx (märks), n. Karl, 1818–83, German economist, philosopher, and socialist.

Marx′ism, n. the system of thought developed by Karl Marx. —Marx′ist, n., adj.

Mar·y (mâr′ē), n. 1. the mother of Jesus. 2. the sister of Lazarus and Martha. John 2. 3. the mother of James. Mark 15:40.

Mar·y·land (mer′ə lənd), n. a state in the E United States. 5,071,604. Cap.: Annapolis. Abbr.: MD, Md. —Mar′y·land·er, n.

Mar′y Mag′dalene, n. Mary of Magdala: traditionally identified with the repentant woman whom Jesus forgave. Luke 7:37–50.

mar·zi·pan (mär′zə pan′), n. a confection of almond paste and sugar.

masc., masculine.

mas·car·a (ma skar′ə), n., pl. -car·as. a cosmetic for darkening the eyelashes.

mas·cot (mas′kot, -kət), n. an animal, person, or thing thought to bring good luck.

mas·cu·line (mas′kyə lin), adj. 1. of or characteristic of a man. 2. having qualities traditionally ascribed to men; manly. 3. of or being the grammatical gender that has among its members most nouns referring to males. 4. (of a woman) mannish. —n. 5. the masculine gender. 6. a word or form in the masculine gender. —mas′cu·lin·i·ty, n.

ma·ser (mā′zər), n. a device for producing or amplifying electromagnetic waves.

Ma·se·ru (mä′sə rōō′, maz′ə rōō′), n. the capital of Lesotho. 109,382.

mash (mash), v.t. 1. to reduce to a soft pulpy mass. 2. to crush. —n. 3. a soft pulpy mass. 4. a mixture of boiled grain, bran, or meal, fed to livestock. 5. crushed malt or meal mixed with hot water to form wort. —mash′er, n.

MASH (mash), n. mobile army surgical hospital.

Mash·had (mash had′), n. a city in NE Iran: Muslim shrine. 1,463,508.

mask (mask, mäsk), n. 1. a covering for the face, worn esp. for concealment or protection. 2. something that disguises or conceals. 3. a likeness of a face cast in a mold. 4. a molded or carved covering for the face of an actor in Greek drama. 5. the face or head of an animal, as a fox. 6. MASQUE. —v.t. 7. to disguise, cover, conceal, or shield with or as if with a mask. —masked, adj. —mask′er, n.

mas·och·ism (mas′ə kiz′əm, maz′-), n. 1. a disorder in which sexual gratification is derived from pain or degradation. 2. the tendency to find pleasure in suffering. [after L. von Sacher-Masoch (1836–95), Austrian novelist] —mas′och·ist, n. —mas′och·is′tic, adj. —mas′och·is′ti·cal·ly, adv.

ma·son (mā′sən), n. 1. a person whose trade is building with firm units, as stones or bricks. 2. (cap.) FREEMASON.

Ma·son·ic (mə son′ik), adj. of Freemasons or Freemasonry.

ma·son·ry (mā′sən rē), n., pl. -ries. 1. work, esp. stonework, constructed by a mason. 2. the trade of a mason. 3. (cap.) the principles of Freemasonry.

masque (mask, mäsk), n. an elaborate court entertainment in 16th- and 17th-century England combining pantomime, dialogue, music, etc.

mas·quer·ade (mas′kə rād′), n., v., -ad·ed, -ad·ing. —n. 1. a. a festive gathering of people wearing masks and costumes. b. a costume worn at such a gathering. 2. false show; pretense. —v.i. 3. to represent oneself falsely. 4. to take part in a masquerade. —mas′quer·ad′er, n.

mass¹ (mas), n. 1. a body of coherent matter, usu. of indefinite shape. 2. aggregate; whole. 3. a considerable number or quantity. 4. bulk; massiveness. 5. the greater part. 6. Physics. the quantity of matter as determined from its weight or from Newton's second law of motion. 7. the masses, the ordinary or common people as a whole. —adj. 8. of or affecting the masses. 9. done on a large scale: mass destruction. —v.i., v.t. 10. to form or assemble in a mass.

mass² (mas), n. (often cap.) the liturgy or celebration of the Eucharist.

Mass., Massachusetts.

Mas·sa·chu·setts (mas′ə chōō′sits), n. a state in the NE United States. 6,016,425. Cap.: Boston. Abbr.: MA, Mass.

mas·sa·cre (mas′ə kər), n., v., -cred, -cring. —n. 1. the wanton killing of a large number of human beings. 2. a general slaughter. —v.t. 3. to kill in a massacre; slaughter.

mas·sage (mə säzh′, -säj′), n., v., -saged, -sag·ing. —n. 1. manipulation of the body, esp. by rubbing or kneading, to stimulate circulation or relieve tension. —v.t. 2. to treat by massage.

mas·seur (mə sûr′, -sōōr′), n. a man who provides massage as an occupation. [< F]

mas·seuse (mə sōōs′, -sōōz′), n. a woman who provides massage as an occupation. [< F]

mas·sive (mas′iv), adj. 1. consisting of or forming a large mass. 2. imposingly large or prominent. 3. large in scale, amount, or degree. —mas′sive·ly, adv. —mas′sive·ness, n.

mass′ me′dia, n.pl. the means of communication, as television and newspapers, that reach great numbers of people.

mass′ noun′, n. a noun, as water or happiness, that refers to an indefinitely divisible substance or an abstract notion.

mass′ num′ber, n. the number of nucleons in an atomic or isotopic nucleus.

mass′-produce′, v.t., -duced, -duc·ing. to produce (goods) in large quantities, esp. by machine. —mass′ produc′tion, n.

mast (mast, mäst), n. 1. a spar rising above the upper portions of a ship to hold sails, spars, and rigging. 2. an upright pole.

mas·tec·to·my (ma stek′tə mē), n., pl. -mies. surgical removal of a breast.

mas·ter (mas′tər, mä′stər), n. 1. a person with the

ability or power to control. **2.** a person highly skilled in an art, craft, etc. **3.** a male teacher. **4.** a person who commands a merchant ship. **5.** a person with a master's degree. **6.** a boy or young man (used as a term of address). **7.** an original, as of a document, from which copies can be made. —*adj.* **8.** of or being a master. —*v.t.* **9.** to make oneself an expert in. **10.** to conquer; overcome.

mas′ter•ful, *adj.* **1.** having or showing the qualities of a master. **2.** dominating; imperious. —**mas′ter•ful•ly,** *adv.*

mas′ter key′, *n.* a key that will open a number of different locks.

mas′ter•ly, *adj.* befitting a master.

mas′ter•mind′, *v.t.* **1.** to plan and direct skillfully. —*n.* **2.** a person who originates or oversees a project.

mas′ter of cer′emonies, *n.* a person who conducts events, as at a formal occasion or entertainment.

mas′ter•piece′, *n.* **1.** a person's greatest piece of work, as in an art. **2.** a fine example of skill or excellence.

mas′ter's degree′, *n.* an academic degree awarded to a student who has completed at least one year of graduate study.

mas′ter ser′geant, *n.* a noncommissioned officer ranking in the U.S. Army above a sergeant first class, in the Air Force above a technical sergeant, and in the Marine Corps above a gunnery sergeant.

mas′ter•stroke′, *n.* an extremely skillful action.

mas′ter•work′, *n.* MASTERPIECE.

mas′ter•y, *n., pl.* **-ter•ies. 1.** command; grasp. **2.** superiority; dominance. **3.** expert skill or knowledge.

mast′head′, *n.* **1.** a box or column in a newspaper or magazine giving the names of the owners and staff members. **2.** the head of a mast.

mas•tic (mas′tik), *n.* **1.** a bituminous preparation used as an adhesive or seal. **2.** a pasty cement used for filling holes, as in plaster.

mas•ti•cate (mas′ti kāt′), *v.t., v.i.,* **-cat•ed, -cat• ing.** to chew. —**mas′ti•ca′tion,** *n.*

mas•tiff (mas′tif, mä′stif), *n.* a large, powerful shorthaired dog.

mas•to•don (mas′tə don′), *n.* any of numerous extinct elephantlike mammals.

mastodon

mas•toid (mas′toid), *n.* a bony prominence on the base of the skull behind the ear.

mas•tur•ba•tion (mas′tər bā′shən), *n.* stimulation of the genitals, esp. to orgasm. —**mas′tur•bate′,** *v.i., v.t.,* **-bat•ed, -bat•ing.**

mat¹ (mat), *n., v.,* **mat•ted, mat•ting.** —*n.* **1.** a piece of fabric, as of plaited fiber, used esp. as a floor covering. **2.** a floor pad used to protect wrestlers and gymnasts. **3.** a thick tangled mass, as of hair or weeds. —*v.t., v.i.* **4.** to form into a mat.

mat² (mat), *n., v.,* **mat•ted, mat•ting.** —*n.* **1.** material serving as a border for a picture. —*v.t.* **2.** to provide with a mat.

mat³ (mat), *adj., n.* MATTE.

mat•a•dor (mat′ə dôr′), *n.* the bullfighter who traditionally kills the bull.

Ma•ta Ha•ri (mä′tə här′ē, mat′ə har′ē), *n.* (*Gertrud Margarete Zelle*) 1876–1917, Dutch dancer in France: executed as a spy by the French.

match¹ (mach), *n.* a slender piece of flammable material tipped with a chemical substance that ignites by friction.

match² (mach), *n.* **1.** a person or thing that equals or resembles another. **2.** a corresponding or suitably associated pair. **3.** a game or contest with two or more contestants or teams. **4.** a person considered as a marriage partner: *a good match.* **5.** a marriage. —*v.t.* **6.** to equal. **7.** to be the match or counterpart of. **8.** to cause to correspond. **9.** to fit together. **10.** to place in opposition or conflict. **11.** to unite in marriage. —*v.i.* **12.** to be equal or suitable. **13.** to correspond.

match′book′, *n.* a small folder of paper matches.

match′less, *adj.* having no equal.

match′mak′er, *n.* a person who arranges marriages.

mate (māt), *n., v.,* **mat•ed, mat•ing.** —*n.* **1.** a husband or wife. **2.** one of a pair of mated animals. **3.** one of a pair. **4.** an associate or companion. **5.** FIRST MATE. —*v.t., v.i.* **6.** to join as mates. **7.** to bring or come together for breeding.

ma•té or **-te** (mä′tā, mat′ā, mä tā′), *n., pl.* **-tés** or **-tes.** a tealike South American beverage.

ma•te•ri•al (mə tēr′ē əl), *n.* **1.** the substance of which something is made or composed. **2.** something that can be further developed. **3.** a constituent element. **4.** a textile. **5.** Often, **-als.** apparatus needed to make or do something: *writing materials.* —*adj.* **6.** of or consisting of matter: *the material world.* **7.** physical rather than spiritual or intellectual: *material comforts.* **8.** of substantial import; significant. **9.** pertinent; essential. —**ma•te′ri•al•ly,** *adv.*

ma•te•ri•al•ism, *n.* **1.** preoccupation with material as opposed to spiritual or intellectual values. **2.** the philosophical theory that regards matter as constituting the universe, and all phenomena, including those of mind, as due to material agencies. —**ma•te′ri•a• list,** *n., adj.* —**ma•te′ri•al•is′tic,** *adj.*

ma•te′ri•al•ize′, *v.,* **-ized, -iz•ing.** —*v.i.* **1.** to come into actual existence. **2.** to appear, esp. unexpectedly. **3.** to assume material form. —*v.t.* **4.** to give material form to. —**ma•te′ri•al•i•za′tion,** *n.*

ma•té•ri•el or **-te•ri•el** (mə tēr′ē el′), *n.* the aggregate of equipment and supplies used by an organization, as the military.

ma•ter•nal (mə tûr′nl), *adj.* **1.** of or resembling a mother. **2.** related through, derived from, or inherited from a mother. —**ma•ter′nal•ly,** *adv.*

ma•ter′ni•ty (-ni tē), *n.* **1.** the state of being a mother; motherhood. —*adj.* **2.** applicable immediately before, during, and just after childbirth: *maternity leave.* **3.** designed for wear by pregnant women.

math (math), *n.* mathematics.

math′e•mat′ics (-ə mat′iks), *n.* the systematic treatment of magnitude, relationships between figures and forms, and relations between quantities expressed symbolically. —**math′e•mat′i•cal,** *adj.* —**math′e•mat′i•cal•ly,** *adv.* —**math′e•ma•ti′cian** (-mə tish′ən), *n.*

mat•i•née (mat′n ā′), *n., pl.* **-nées** or **nees.** a dramatic or musical performance held in the afternoon. [< F: morning]

mat•ins (mat′nz), *n.* **1.** (*often cap.*) (*used with a sing. or pl. v.*) prayers read at midnight or daybreak. **2.** the service of morning prayer in Anglican churches.

Ma•tisse (mə tēs′, ma-), *n.* **Henri,** 1869–1954, French painter.

ma•tri•arch (mā′trē ärk′), *n.* the female head of a family or tribe. —**ma′tri•ar′chal,** *adj.* —**ma′tri•ar′chy,** *n., pl.* **-chies.**

mat•ri•cide (ma′tri sīd′, mā′-), *n.* **1.** the act of killing one's mother. **2.** a person who kills his or her mother. —**mat′ri•cid′al,** *adj.*

ma•tric•u•late (mə trik′yə lāt′), *v.t., v.i.,* **-lat•ed, -lat•ing.** to enroll as a student in a college or university. —**ma•tric′u•la′tion,** *n.*

mat•ri•mo•ny (ma′trə mō′nē), *n., pl.* **-nies. 1.** the state of being married. **2.** the ceremony of marriage. —**mat′ri•mo′ni•al,** *adj.*

ma•trix (mā′triks, ma′-), *n., pl.* **-tri•ces** (-tri sēz′),

-trix•es. 1. a place or point within which something else originates. 2. a mold for casting typefaces.
ma•tron (mā′trən), n. 1. a married woman, esp. one who is mature and dignified. 2. a woman officer, as in a prison for women. —ma′tron•ly, adj.
ma′tron of hon′or, n. a married woman who is the chief attendant of a bride.
Matt., Matthew.
matte or matt (mat), adj. 1. having a dull or luster-less surface. —n. 2. a dull surface or finish.
mat•ter (mat′ər), n. 1. the substance of which a physical object consists or is composed. 2. something that occupies space. 3. a situation, subject, or affair. 4. an approximate amount or extent: a matter of 10 miles. 5. something written or printed. 6. things sent by mail. 7. a substance, esp. pus, discharged by a living body. —v.i. 8. to be of importance; signify. —Idiom. 9. as a matter of fact, in reality; actually. 10. no matter, regardless of. 11. to be the matter, to be amiss or awry: What's the matter with you?
mat′ter-of-fact′, adj. adhering strictly to fact. —mat′ter-of-fact′ly, adv. —mat′ter-of-fact′ness, n.
Mat•thew (math′yōo), n. 1. one of the four Evange-lists; one of the 12 apostles. 2. the first Gospel.
Mat•thi•as (mə thī′əs), n. a disciple chosen to take the place of Judas Iscariot as one of the apostles. Acts 1:23–26.
mat′ting, n. 1. material for mats. 2. mats collec-tively.
mat•tock (mat′ək), n. a digging tool shaped like a pickax.
mat•tress (ma′tris), n. a cloth case filled with straw, cotton, foam rubber, etc., used as or on a bed.
ma•ture (mə tŏor′, -tyŏor′, -chŏor′, -chûr′), adj. -tur•er, -tur•est, v., -tured, -tur•ing. —adj. 1. fully developed. 2. complete in natural growth or develop-ment. 3. fully aged: mature wine. 4. payable; due: a mature bond. —v.t., v.i. 5. to make or become ma-ture. —mat•u•ra•tion (mach′ə rā′shən), n. —ma•ture′ly, adv. —ma•tu′ri•ty, n.
mat•zo (mät′sə), n., pl. -zos (-səz), -zoth, -zot (-sōt, -sōs). unleavened bread eaten by Jews during Passover.
maud•lin (môd′lin), adj. embarrassingly sentimen-tal.
Mau•i (mou′ē), n. an island in central Hawaii.
maul (môl), n. 1. a heavy hammer used esp. for driving stakes or wedges. —v.t. 2. to handle roughly. 3. to injure by rough treatment. —maul′er, n.
maun•der (môn′dər), v.i. 1. to talk ramblingly or unintelligibly. 2. to wander.
Maun′dy Thurs′day (môn′dē), n. the Thursday of Holy Week, commemorating Jesus' Last Supper.
Mau•pas•sant (mō′pə sän′), n. Guy de (gē də), 1850–93, French writer.
Mau•ri•ta•ni•a (môr′i tā′nē ə), n. a republic in NW Africa. 2,411,317. —Mau′ri•ta′ni•an, adj., n.
Mau•ri•tius (mô rish′əs), n. an island republic in the Indian Ocean, E of Madagascar. 1,151,272. —Mau•ri′tian, adj., n.
mau•so•le•um (mô′sə lē′əm, -zə-), n., pl. -le•ums, -le•a (-lē′ə). a large and stately tomb.
mauve (mōv, môv), n. a pale bluish purple.
ma•ven or -vin (mā′vən), n. an expert; connois-seur. [< Yiddish < Heb]
mav•er•ick (mav′ər ik), n. 1. an unbranded animal. 2. a person who thinks and acts independently of others.
maw (mô), n. the mouth, throat, or stomach, esp. of a voracious carnivore.
mawk•ish (mô′kish), adj. sentimental; maudlin. —mawk′ish•ly, adv.
max•i (mak′sē), n., pl. max•is. an ankle-length coat or skirt.
max•il•la (mak sil′ə), n., pl. max•il•lae (mak sil′ē). an upper jaw or jawbone. —max′il•lar′y (-sə ler′ē), adj.
max•im (mak′sim), n. a pithy saying; aphorism.
max•i•mal (mak′sə məl), adj. of or being a maxi-mum. —max′i•mal•ly, adv.

max′i•mize′, v.t., -mized, -miz•ing. to increase to the maximum.
max′i•mum (-məm), n., pl. -mums, -ma (-mə), adj. —n. 1. the highest amount, value, or degree. 2. an upper limit allowed by law or regulation. —adj. 3. of or being a maximum.
may (mā), auxiliary v., pres. may; past might; im-perative, infinitive, and participles lacking. 1. (used to express possibility): It may rain. 2. (used to ex-press opportunity or permission): You may enter. 3. (used to express contingency, concession, or pur-pose): I may be old, but I'm energetic. 4. (used to ex-press wish or prayer): Long may you live! —Usage. See CAN¹.
May (mā), n. the fifth month of the year, having 31 days.
Ma•ya (mä′yə), n., pl. -ya, -yas. a member of a group of American Indian peoples of Mexico and Central America whose civilization flourished c300 B.C.–A.D. 900. —Ma′yan, adj., n.
may′ ap′ple, n. a North American plant bearing an edible, yellowish, egg-shaped fruit.
may•be, adv. perhaps; possibly.
May′ Day′, n. the first day of May, variously cele-brated with festivities and observances.
may′flow′er, n. 1. any of various plants, as the ar-butus, that blossom in May. 2. (cap. italic) the ship on which the Pilgrims sailed from England to the New World in 1620.
may′fly′, n., pl. -flies. an insect with large transpar-ent forewings that lives only briefly as an adult.
may•hem (mā′hem, -əm), n. the crime of willfully crippling or mutilating another.
May•o (mā′ō), n. Charles Horace, 1865–1939, and his brother William James, 1861–1939, U.S. sur-geons.
may•on•naise (mā′ə nāz′), n. a thick dressing of egg yolks, vinegar or lemon juice, oil, and season-ings.
may•or (mā′ər), n. the chief executive official of a municipality. —may′or•al, adj. —may′or•al•ty, n., pl. -ties.
May′pole′, n. (often l.c.) a pole, decorated with flowers, around which people dance on May Day.
maze (māz), n. 1. a confusing network of paths or passages; labyrinth. 2. an intricate system that daunts or perplexes.
ma•zel tov (mä′zəl tôv′, tôf′, tōv′), interj. (used to express congratulations. [< Heb mazzāl tōbh good luck]
ma•zur•ka (mə zûr′kə, -zŏor′-), n., pl. -kas. 1. a Polish dance in moderately quick triple meter. 2. music for the mazurka.
MB, Manitoba.
MBA or M.B.A., Master of Business Administration.
MC, 1. master of ceremonies. 2. Member of Con-gress.
Mc-, a combining form, used esp. to form nonce words, with the meaning "generic; homogenized": reading McNews instead of a serious newspaper. [< Mc(Donald's), chain of fast-food restaurants]
Mc•Car•thy (mə kär′thē), n. Joseph R(aymond), 1909–57, U.S. politician.
Mc•Car•thy•ism (mə kär′thē iz′əm), n. the use of unsubstantiated accusations or unfair investigative techniques in an attempt to expose disloyalty. [after J. R. McCARTHY] —Mc•Car′thy•ite′, n.
Mc•Clel•lan (mə klel′ən), n. George Brinton, 1826–85, Union general in the American Civil War.
Mc•Cor•mick (mə kôr′mik), n. Cyrus Hall, 1809–84, U.S. inventor.
Mc•Coy (mə koi′), n. the genuine thing or person: the real McCoy.
Mc•Cul•lers (mə kul′ərz), n. Carson, 1917–67, U.S. author.
Mc•Cul•loch v. Maryland (mə kul′ək, -əкн), n. a U.S. Supreme Court decision in 1819 that asserted the authority of the federal government over the states.

Mc•Guf•fey (mə guf'ē), n. **William Holmes,** 1800–73, U.S. educator.

McJob (mək job'), n. an unstimulating, low-wage job, esp. in a service industry.

Mc•Kin•ley (mə kin'lē), n. **1. William,** 1843–1901, 25th president of the U.S. 1897–1901. **2. Mount,** a mountain in central Alaska: highest peak in North America, 20,320 ft. (6194 m).

Mc•Pher•son (mək fûr'sən, -fēr'-), n. **Aimee Semple,** 1890–1944, U.S. evangelist, born in Canada.

MD, 1. Maryland. **2.** Doctor of Medicine. [< NL *Medicīnae Doctor*] **3.** Middle Dutch.

Md, *Chem. Symbol.* mendelevium.

Md., Maryland.

mdse., merchandise.

me (mē), *pron.* the objective case of I.

ME, 1. Maine. **2.** Middle English.

Me., Maine.

mead[1] (mēd), n. an alcoholic drink of fermented honey and water.

mead[2] (mēd), n. *Archaic.* a meadow.

Mead (mēd), n. **Margaret,** 1901–78, U.S. anthropologist.

Meade (mēd), n. **George Gordon,** 1815–72, Union general in the American Civil War.

mead•ow (med'ō), n. a tract of low vegetation dominated by grasses.

mead'ow•lark', n. a North American songbird with a brown-streaked back and a yellow breast.

mea•ger (mē'gər), *adj.* **1.** deficient in quantity or quality; scanty. **2.** lean; thin. Also, *esp. Brit.,* **mea'gre. —mea'ger•ly,** *adv.* **—mea'ger•ness,** n.

meal[1] (mēl), n. **1.** the food served and eaten at one time. **2.** the time or an occasion for eating a meal.

meal[2] (mēl), n. **1.** coarse powder ground from the edible seeds of a grain. **2.** a ground or powdery substance. **—meal'y,** *adj.,* **-i•er, -i•est.**

meal'y•bug', n. any of several insects that are covered with a powdery wax secretion and feed on plants.

meal'y-mouthed', *adj.* avoiding the use of plain or honest language.

mean[1] (mēn), *v.,* **meant, mean•ing. —v.t. 1.** to have in mind as a purpose; intend. **2.** to intend to express or indicate: *What do you mean by "perfect"?* **3.** to have as a signification; denote. **4.** to bring as a result. **5.** to have the value or importance of: *Money means everything to them.* **—v.i. 6.** to have specified intentions: *We meant well.*

mean[2] (mēn), *adj.,* **-er, -est. 1.** uncharitable; malicious. **2.** small-minded; ignoble. **3.** stingy; miserly. **4.** inferior in quality or character. **5.** bad-tempered. **6.** excellent; topnotch: *plays a mean game of tennis.* **—mean'ly,** *adv.* **—mean'ness,** n.

mean[3] (mēn), n. **1. means,** (*used with a sing. or pl. v.*) an agency or method used to attain an end. **2. means,** resources, esp. money; wealth. **3.** something midway between two extremes. **4.** an average, esp. the arithmetic mean. **—adj. 5.** occupying a middle position or intermediate place. **—Idiom. 6. by all means,** certainly. **7. by means of,** by the agency of; through. **8. by no means,** not at all.

me•an•der (mē an'dər), *v.i.* **1.** to proceed by a winding course. **2.** to wander aimlessly. **—n. 3.** a winding path or course.

mean'ing, n. **1.** what is intended to be expressed or indicated; import. **2.** the end, purpose, or significance of something. **—mean'ing•ful,** *adj.* **—mean'ing•less,** *adj.*

meant (ment), *v.* pt. and pp. of MEAN[1].

mean'time', n. **1.** the intervening time. **—adv. 2.** MEANWHILE.

mean'while', n. **1.** MEANTIME. **—adv. 2.** in the intervening time.

Mean•y (mē'nē), n. **George,** 1894–1980, U.S. labor leader.

mea•sles (mē'zəlz), n. (*used with a sing. or pl. v.*) an acute infectious disease characterized by small red spots, fever, and coldlike symptoms.

mea•sly (mē'zlē), *adj.,* **-sli•er, -sli•est.** contemptibly small: *a measly salary.*

meas•ure (mezh'ər), *n., v.,* **-ured, -ur•ing. —n. 1.** a unit of measurement. **2.** a system of measurement. **3.** an instrument for measuring. **4.** the extent, dimensions, quantity, or capacity of something ascertained esp. by comparison with a standard. **5.** the act or process of measuring; measurement. **6.** a standard of comparison; criterion. **7.** a moderate amount. **8.** reasonable bounds or limits: *spending without measure.* **9.** a legislative bill or enactment. **10.** Usu., **-ures.** means to an end. **11.** rhythmical movement or structure, as in poetry. **12.** the music between two bar lines; bar. **—v.t. 13.** to ascertain the extent, dimensions, quantity, or capacity of. **14.** to mark off by way of measurement. **15.** to judge or appraise by comparison. **16.** to serve as the measure of. **—v.i. 17.** to take measurements. **18.** to be of a specified measure. **19. measure up, a.** to attain equality. **b.** to have the right qualifications. **—Idiom. 20. for good measure,** as an extra. **—meas'ur•a•ble,** *adj.* **—meas'ur•a•bly,** *adv.*

meas'ure•ment, n. **1.** the act or process of measuring. **2.** an extent, dimension, quantity, or capacity ascertained by measuring.

meat (mēt), n. **1.** the flesh of animals used for food. **2.** the edible part of something, as a nut. **3.** the essential point or part. **4.** solid food: *meat and drink.* **—Proverb. 5. One man's meat is another man's poison,** tastes differ. **—meat'y,** *adj.,* **-i•er, -i•est.**

meat'ball', n. a small ball of seasoned ground meat.

Mec•ca (mek'ə), *n., pl.* **-cas. 1.** a city in W Saudi Arabia: birthplace of Muhammad; spiritual center of Islam. 550,000. **2.** (*often l.c.*) a place that attracts many people.

me•chan•ic (mə kan'ik), n. **1.** a person who repairs machinery. **2.** a worker skilled in the use of tools and equipment.

me•chan•i•cal (mə kan'i kəl), *adj.* **1.** of machinery or tools. **2.** operated, caused, or produced by machinery. **3.** lacking spontaneity; routine. **4.** of the science of mechanics. **—me•chan'i•cal•ly,** *adv.*

mechan'ical draw'ing, n. drawing, as of machinery, done with the aid of instruments.

me•chan'ics, n. **1.** (*used with a sing. v.*) the branch of physics that deals with the action of forces on bodies and with motion. **2.** (*used with a sing. v.*) the theoretical and practical application of mechanics, as to machinery. **3.** (*used with a pl. v.*) the technical aspect of something: *knew little about the mechanics of managing an orchestra.*

mech•an•ism (mek'ə niz'əm), n. **1.** a system of parts performing a function. **2.** an agency or means by which a purpose is accomplished. **3.** a mechanical appliance; machine. **4.** the structure or arrangement of parts of a device, as a machine. **—mech'a•nis'tic** (-nis'tik), *adj.*

mech'a•nize', *v.t.,* **-nized, -niz•ing. 1.** to make mechanical. **2.** to introduce machinery into, esp. in order to replace manual labor. **3.** to equip with armored vehicles, as tanks. —**mech′a•ni•za′tion,** *n.*

med•al (med′l), *n.* **1.** a flat piece of metal issued as a token of commemoration or as an award, as for merit. **2.** a piece of metal bearing a religious image.

med′al•ist, *n.* **1.** a person who has been awarded a medal. **2.** a designer, engraver, or maker of medals. Also, *esp. Brit.,* **med′al•list.**

me•dal•lion (mə dal′yən), *n.* **1.** a large medal. **2.** something, as an ornament, resembling a medal.

Med′al of Hon′or, *n.* a Congressional award for exceptional bravery in combat: the highest U.S. military decoration.

med•dle (med′l), *v.i.,* **-dled, -dling.** to involve oneself in a matter without right or invitation; interfere. —**med′dler,** *n.* —**med′dle•some,** *adj.*

Me•del•lín (mā′də yēn′), *n.* a city in W Colombia. 1,468,089.

me•di•a (mē′dē ə), *n.* **1.** a pl. of MEDIUM. **2.** (*usu. with a pl. v.*) the means of communication, as radio, television, and newspapers, with wide reach and influence.

me•di•al (mē′dē əl), *adj.* **1.** of or being in the middle. **2.** ordinary or average.

me′di•an, *adj.* **1.** pertaining to a plane that divides something into two equal parts. **2.** situated in the middle; medial. —*n.* **3.** the middle number in a sequence, or the average of the middle two numbers when the sequence has an even number of numbers. **4.** a straight line from a vertex of a triangle to the midpoint of the opposite side. **5.** Also called **me′dian strip′.** a strip in the middle of a highway that separates opposing lanes of traffic.

me•di•ate (*v.* mē′dē āt′; *adj.* -it), *v.,* **-at•ed, -at•ing,** *adj.* —*v.t.* **1.** to settle (a dispute) as an intermediary. —*v.i.* **2.** to act as an intermediary. —*adj.* **3.** involving an intermediate agency; not direct. —**me′di•a′tion,** *n.* —**me′di•a′tor,** *n.*

med•ic (med′ik), *n.* **1.** a member of the medical corps trained to give first aid in battle. **2.** a doctor or intern.

Med•i•caid (med′i kād′), *n.* (*sometimes l.c.*) a federal and state program of medical insurance for persons with very low incomes.

med′i•cal, *adj.* of the science or practice of medicine. —**med′i•cal•ly,** *adv.*

me•dic•a•ment (mə dik′ə mənt, med′i kə-), *n.* a healing substance; medicine.

Med•i•care (med′i kâr′), *n.* (*sometimes l.c.*) a U.S. government program of medical insurance for aged or disabled persons.

med′i•cate′, *v.t.,* **-cat•ed, -cat•ing.** to treat with medicine. —**med′i•ca′tion,** *n.*

me•dic•i•nal (mə dis′ə nl), *adj.* of or having the properties of a medicine. —**me•dic′i•nal•ly,** *adv.*

med•i•cine (med′ə sin), *n.* **1.** a substance used in treating disease or illness. **2.** the art or science of preserving health and treating disease.

med′icine ball′, *n.* a heavy, leather-covered ball tossed for exercise.

med′icine man′, *n.* a person believed to possess magical powers, esp. among North American Indians.

me•di•e•val or **-ae•val** (mē′dē ē′vəl, mid ē′-), *adj.* of, like, or characteristic of the Middle Ages. —**me′di•e′val•ist,** *n.*

Me′die′val Lat′in, *n.* the Latin language as used in the Middle Ages, from c700 to c1500.

me•di•o•cre (mē′dē ō′kər), *adj.* of only ordinary or moderate quality; barely adequate. —**me′di•oc′ri•ty** (-ok′ri tē), *n.*

med•i•tate (med′i tāt′), *v.,* **-tat•ed, -tat•ing.** —*v.i.* **1.** to engage in contemplation; reflect. —*v.t.* **2.** to plan; intend. —**med′i•ta′tion,** *n.* —**med′i•ta′tive,** *adj.*

Med•i•ter•ra•ne•an (med′i tə rā′nē ən), *n.* **1.** Also called **Med′iter′ra′nean Sea′.** a sea surrounded by Africa, Europe, and Asia. —*adj.* **2.** of the Mediterranean Sea and its islands and countries.

me•di•um (mē′dē əm), *n., pl.* **-di•a** (-dē ə) except for 7, **-di•ums,** *adj.* —*n.* **1.** a middle state or condition. **2.** something intermediate. **3.** an intervening or

surrounding substance, as air. **4.** surrounding conditions or influences; environment. **5.** a means or instrument by which something is conveyed or accomplished. **6.** a means or channel of communication, information, or entertainment, as television. **7.** a person through whom the spirits of the dead are alleged to be able to contact the living. **8.** the material or technique with which an artist works. —*adj.* **9.** halfway between extremes in degree, quantity, position, or quality.

med•ley (med′lē), *n., pl.* **-leys. 1.** a heterogeneous mixture; jumble. **2.** a piece of music combining passages from various sources.

me•dul•la (mə dul′ə), *n., pl.* **-dul•las, -dul•lae** (-dul′ē). **1.** the soft marrowlike center of an organ, as the kidney. **2.** MEDULLA OBLONGATA.

medul′la ob•long•a′ta (ob′lông gä′tə, -long-), *n., pl.* **medulla oblongatas.** the lowest or hindmost part of the vertebrate brain.

meek (mēk), *adj.,* **-er, -est. 1.** humbly patient or docile. **2.** overly submissive or compliant. —*Proverb.* **3. The meek shall inherit the earth,** the humble shall be rewarded at the end. Matt. 5:5. —**meek′ly,** *adv.* —**meek′ness,** *n.*

meer•schaum (mēr′shəm, -shôm), *n.* **1.** a white, claylike mineral used esp. for pipes. **2.** a tobacco pipe made of meerschaum. [< G, = *Meer* sea + *Schaum* foam]

meet¹ (mēt), *v.,* **met, meet•ing,** *n.* —*v.t.* **1.** to come upon; encounter. **2.** to be introduced to. **3.** to be present at the arrival of. **4.** to come to the apprehension of: *A strange sight met my eyes.* **5.** to come into physical contact with. **6.** to oppose; fight. **7.** to deal effectively with: *met the challenge.* **8.** to comply with: *to meet a deadline.* —*v.i.* **9.** to come together. **10.** to assemble for action or conference. **11.** to come into contact or form a junction. **12. meet with,** to encounter; experience. —*n.* **13.** an assembly, esp. for sports competition.

meet² (mēt), *adj.* suitable; fitting.

meet′ing, *n.* **1.** the act of coming together. **2.** an assembly of persons. **3.** a place or point of contact.

mega-, a combining form meaning: large or great (*megalopolis*); 1,000,000 times a given unit of measure (*megaton*).

meg•a•byte (meg′ə bīt′), *n. Computers.* **1.** 2^{20} (1,048,576) bytes. **2.** (loosely) one million bytes.

meg•a•cy•cle (meg′ə sī′kəl), *n.* MEGAHERTZ.

meg′a•hertz′, *n., pl.* **-hertz, -hertz•es.** a unit of frequency equal to one million cycles per second.

meg•a•lo•ma•ni•a (meg′ə lō mā′nē ə), *n.* a highly exaggerated or delusional concept of one's own importance. —**meg′a•lo•ma′ni•ac,** *n.*

meg•a•lop•o•lis (meg′ə lop′ə lis), *n.* a very large urban region.

Meg′an's Law′ (mā′gənz), *n.* any of various laws aimed at people convicted of sex-related crimes, requiring community notification of the release of offenders, establishment of a registry of offenders, etc. [after *Megan* Kanka, girl killed by ex-convict]

meg′a•phone′, *n.* a cone-shaped device for amplifying the voice.

meg′a•ton′, *n.* an explosive force equal to that of one million tons of TNT.

Me•gid•do (mə gid′ō), *n.* an ancient city in N Israel, on the plain of Esdraelon: often identified with the Biblical Armageddon.

mei•o•sis (mī ō′sis), *n.* part of the process of gamete formation, consisting of two cell divisions after which the chromosome number is reduced by half. —**mei•ot′ic** (-ot′ik), *adj.*

Me•ir (mā ēr′, mī′ər), *n.* **Golda** (*Goldie Mabovitch, Goldie Myerson*), 1898–1978, prime minister of Israel 1969–74, born in Russia.

Me•kong (mā′kông, -kong), *n.* a river rising in SW China, flowing into the South China Sea. 2600 mi. (4200 km) long.

mel•a•mine (mel′ə mēn′), *n.* a crystalline solid used esp. in manufacturing resins.

mel•an•cho•li•a (mel′ən kō′lē ə), *n.* a severe form

of depression characterized typically by weight loss and insomnia.

mel′an•chol′ic (-kol′ik), *adj.* **1.** of melancholia. **2.** gloomy; dejected.

mel′an•chol′y, *n., pl.* -chol•ies. **1.** a gloomy state of mind; dejection. —*adj.* **2.** affected with melancholy; depressed. **3.** causing melancholy.

Mel•a•ne•sia (mel′ə nē′zhə), *n.* an island group in the S Pacific, NE of Australia. —**Mel′a•ne′sian,** *adj., n.*

mé•lange (mā länzh′, -länj′), *n.* a mixture; medley.

mel•a•nin (mel′ə nin), *n.* a pigment that accounts for the dark color of skin, hair, fur, scales, and feathers.

mel′a•nism, *n.* an unusually high concentration of melanin in the skin, plumage, etc., of an animal.

mel′a•no′ma (-nō′mə), *n., pl.* -mas, -ma•ta (-mə-tə). a darkly pigmented malignant skin tumor.

Mel′ba toast′ (mel′bə), *n.* thinly sliced crisp toast.

Mel•bourne (mel′bərn), *n.* a seaport in SE Australia. 2,942,000.

Mel•chior (mel′kyôr, -kē ôr′), *n.* one of the three Magi.

Mel•chiz•e•dek (mel kiz′i dek′), *n.* **1.** a priest and king of Salem. Gen. 14:18. **2.** the higher order of priests in the Church of Jesus Christ of Latter-day Saints.

meld (meld), *v.t., v.i.* **1.** to announce and display (a combination of playing cards) for a score. —*n.* **2.** a combination of cards to be melded.

me•lee or **mê•lée** (mā′lā), *n., pl.* -lees or lées. **1.** a confused hand-to-hand fight. **2.** a state of tumultuous confusion.

mel•io•rate (mēl′yə rāt′), *v.t., v.i.* -rat•ed, -rat•ing. AMELIORATE. —**mel′io•ra′tion,** *n.* —**mel′io•ra′-tive** (-yə rā′tiv, -yər ə tiv), *adj.*

mel•lif•lu•ous (mə lif′lōō əs), *adj.* sweetly or smoothly flowing. —**mel•lif′lu•ous•ly,** *adv.*

Mel•lon (mel′ən), *n.* **Andrew William,** 1855–1937, U.S. financier.

mel•low (mel′ō), *adj.,* -er, -est, *v.* —*adj.* **1.** sweet and full-flavored from ripeness, as fruit. **2.** soft and rich, as sound or colors. **3.** made gentle by age or maturity. **4.** pleasantly intoxicated. **5.** free from tension or discord. —*v.t., v.i.* **6.** to make or become mellow.

me•lo•di•ous (mə lō′dē əs), *adj.* **1.** of or characterized by melody. **2.** sweet-sounding; musical. —**me•lo′di•ous•ly,** *adv.* —**me•lo′di•ous•ness,** *n.*

mel•o•dra•ma (mel′ə drä′mə, -dram′ə), *n., pl.* -mas. a dramatic form that exaggerates emotion and emphasizes plot or action at the expense of characterization. —**mel′o•dra•mat′ic,** *adj.*

mel′o•dra•mat′ics, *n.pl.* exaggeratedly emotional or sentimental writing or behavior.

mel•o•dy (mel′ə dē), *n., pl.* -dies. **1.** musical sounds in agreeable succession. **2.** a rhythmical succession of musical tones. —**me•lod•ic** (mə lod′ik), *adj.* —**me•lod′i•cal•ly,** *adv.*

mel•on (mel′ən), *n.* the fruit of any of various plants of the gourd family, as the muskmelon or watermelon.

melt (melt), *v.i., v.t.* **1.** to change to a liquid state by heat. **2.** to dissolve. **3.** to diminish to nothing; dissipate. **4.** to pass or cause to pass gradually; blend. **5.** to soften in feeling.

melt′down′, *n.* the melting of a nuclear-reactor core due to inadequate cooling of the fuel elements.

melt′ing pot′, *n.* a locality in which a blending of races, peoples, or cultures takes place.

Mel•ville (mel′vil), *n.* **Herman,** 1819–91, U.S. novelist.

mem•ber (mem′bər), *n.* **1.** an individual belonging to or forming part of a group. **2.** a part of an animal or plant body. **3.** a constituent part of a structural or composite whole.

mem′ber•ship′, *n.* **1.** the state of being a member. **2.** the status of a member. **3.** the total number of members of a group.

mem•brane (mem′brān), *n.* a thin, pliable sheet or

layer of animal or vegetable tissue. —**mem′bra•nous** (-brə nəs), *adj.*

me•men•to (mə men′tō), *n., pl.* -tos, -toes. something that serves as a reminder or warning.

mem•o (mem′ō), *n., pl.* mem•os. memorandum.

mem•oir (mem′wär, -wôr), *n.* **1.** a record of events based on the writer's personal observation. **2.** Usu., -oirs. **a.** an autobiography. **b.** the published proceedings of a learned society.

mem′o•ra•bil′i•a (-ər ə bil′ē ə, -bil′yə), *n.pl.* **1.** mementos; souvenirs. **2.** matters or events worth remembering.

mem′o•ra•ble, *adj.* worth remembering; notable. —**mem′o•ra•bly,** *adv.*

mem•o•ran•dum (mem′ə ran′dəm), *n., pl.* -dums, -da (-də). **1.** a short note written as a reminder. **2.** a written message, esp. one circulated within a company.

me•mo•ri•al (mə môr′ē əl), *n.* **1.** something, as a monument, designed to preserve the memory of a person or event. **2.** a statement of facts presented to a governing body, often with a petition. —*adj.* **3.** serving to keep a memory alive. —**me•mo′ri•al•ize′,** *v.t.,* -ized, -iz•ing.

Memo′rial Day′, *n.* the last Monday in May, a U.S. holiday in memory of members of the armed forces killed in war.

mem•o•rize (mem′ə rīz′), *v.t., v.i.* -rized, -riz•ing. to commit to memory. —**mem′o•ri•za′tion,** *n.*

mem′o•ry, *n., pl.* -ries. **1.** the faculty or process of retaining or recalling past experiences. **2.** the act or fact of remembering. **3.** the length of time over which recollection extends. **4.** the state or fact of being remembered. **5.** a person or thing remembered. **6.** commemorative remembrance. **7. a.** the capacity of a computer to store information subject to recall. **b.** the components of the computer in which such information is stored.

Mem•phis (mem′fis), *n.* a port in SW Tennessee, on the Mississippi. 614,289.

men (men), *n. pl.* of MAN.

men•ace (men′is), *n., v.,* -aced, -ac•ing. —*n.* **1.** something that threatens. **2.** an annoying person. —*v.t., v.i.* **3.** to threaten or be threatening. —**men′ac•ing•ly,** *adv.*

mé•nage or **me•nage** (mā näzh′), *n.* a household.

me•nag•er•ie (mə naj′ə rē, -nazh′-), *n., pl.* -ies. a collection of wild or unusual animals, esp. for exhibition.

Menck•en (meng′kən), *n.* **H(enry) L(ouis),** 1880–1956, U.S. writer, editor, and critic.

mend (mend), *v.t.* **1.** to make whole, sound, or usable by repairing. **2.** to set right; correct. —*v.i.* **3.** to progress toward recovery; heal. —*n.* **4.** the act of mending. **5.** a mended place. —*Idiom.* **6. on the mend,** improving, esp. in health. —**mend′er,** *n.*

men•da•cious (men dā′shəs), *adj.* telling lies, esp. habitually; untruthful. —**men•da′cious•ly,** *adv.* —**men•dac′i•ty** (-das′i tē), *n.*

Men•del (men′dl), *n.* **Gregor Johann,** 1822–84, Austrian botanist.

men•de•le•vi•um (men′dl ē′vē əm), *n.* a synthetic, radioactive metallic element. *Symbol:* Md, Mv; *at. no.:* 101.

Men•dels•sohn (men′dl sən), *n.* **Felix** (*Jacob Ludwig Felix Mendelssohn-Bartholdy*), 1809–47, German composer.

men•di•cant (men′di kənt), *adj.* **1.** asking for or living on alms; begging. —*n.* **2.** a beggar. **3.** a mendicant friar. —**men′di•can•cy,** *n.*

men•ha•den (men hād′n), *n., pl.* -den. a herring-like W Atlantic fish important as a source of oil and fertilizer.

me•ni•al (mē′nē əl), *adj.* **1.** servile; degrading. **2.** of or suitable for servants. —*n.* **3.** a domestic servant. —**me′ni•al•ly,** *adv.*

me•nin•ges (mi nin′jēz), *n.pl., sing.* **me•ninx** (mē′-ningks), the three membranes covering the brain and spinal cord. —**me•nin′ge•al** (-jē əl), *adj.*

men•in•gi•tis (men′in jī′tis), *n.* inflammation of the meninges.

me·nis·cus (mi nis/kəs), *n., pl.* **-nis·ci** (-nis/ī, -nis/kī, -kē), **-nis·cus·es.** **1.** a crescent or a crescent-shaped body. **2.** the convex or concave upper surface of a column of liquid. **3.** a lens with a crescent-shaped section. —**me·nis/coid,** *adj.*

Men·non·ite (men/ə nīt/), *n.* a member of a Protestant sect that refuses oaths and the bearing of arms and is noted for simplicity of living. [< G *Mennonit,* after *Menno* Simons (1492–1559), Frisian religious leader] —**Men/no·nit·ism,** *n.*

men·o·pause (men/ə pôz/), *n.* the period of natural cessation of menstruation. —**men/o·pau/sal,** *adj.*

me·nor·ah (mə nôr/ə), *n.* a candelabrum used during the Jewish festival of Hanukkah.

menorah

Me·not·ti (mə not/ē), *n.* **Gian Carlo,** born 1911, U.S. composer, born in Italy.

men·ses (men/sēz), *n.* (*used with a sing. or pl. v.*) the menstrual flow or period.

men/stru·a/tion (-strōō ā/shən, -strā/-), *n.* the discharge of blood and mucosal tissue from the uterus, occurring approximately monthly in nonpregnant female primates. —**men/stru·al,** *adj.* —**men/stru·ate/,** *v.i.,* **-at·ed, -at·ing.**

men·su·ra·tion (men/shə rā/shən, -sə-), *n.* the act or process of measuring. —**men/su·ra·ble,** *adj.*

-ment, a suffix meaning: an action or resulting state (*abridgment*); a product (*fragment*); a means (*ornament*).

men·tal (men/tl), *adj.* **1.** of, performed by, or existing in the mind. **2.** of or affected by a disorder of the mind. **3.** for persons with a psychiatric disorder. —**men·tal·ly,** *adv.*

men·tal/i·ty, *n., pl.* **-ties. 1.** mental capacity or endowment. **2.** mental inclination; outlook.

men/tal retarda/tion, *n.* a developmental disorder characterized by impaired ability to learn.

men·thol (men/thôl, -thol), *n.* a colorless alcohol obtained from peppermint oil. —**men/tho·lat/ed** (-thə lā/tid), *adj.*

men·tion (men/shən), *v.t.* **1.** to refer briefly to. **2.** to cite formally for merit or achievement. —*n.* **3.** a brief reference. **4.** a formal citation for merit or achievement. —**men/tion·a·ble,** *adj.*

men·tor (men/tôr, -tər), *n.* a wise and trusted counselor or teacher.

men·u (men/yōō, mā/nyōō), *n., pl.* **men·us. 1.** a list of the dishes that can or will be served at a meal. **2.** the dishes served. **3.** a list of options available to a user, as displayed on a computer screen.

me·ow (mē ou/, myou), *n.* **1.** the characteristic sound a cat makes. —*v.i.* **2.** to make a meow.

Me·phib·o·sheth (mə fib/ə sheth/), *n.* a son of Jonathan, and the grandson of Saul. II Sam. 4:4.

Me·rab (mēr/ab), *n.* the older daughter of King Saul, promised in marriage to anyone who killed Goliath. I Sam. 14:49; 17:25.

mer·can·tile (mûr/kən tēl/, -tīl/, -til), *adj.* of or pertaining to merchants or trade.

mer/ce·nar/y (-sə ner/ē), *adj., n., pl.* **-nar·ies.** —*adj.* **1.** working or acting merely for money or material reward. —*n.* **2.** a professional soldier hired to serve in a foreign army.

mer·cer (mûr/sər), *n. Brit.* a dealer in fine textiles and fabrics.

mer/cer·ize/, *v.t.,* **-ized, -iz·ing.** to treat (cotton yarn or fabric) with alkali in order to increase strength, luster, and affinity for dye. —**mer/cer·i·za/tion,** *n.*

mer·chan·dise (*n.* mûr/chən dīz/, -dīs/; *v.* -dīz/), *n., v.,* **-dised, -dis·ing.** —*n.* **1.** goods bought and sold; commodities. —*v.i.* **2.** to carry on trade. —*v.t.* **3.** to buy and sell. **4.** to promote the sale of. —**mer/chan·dis/er,** *n.*

mer/chant (-chənt), *n.* **1.** a person whose business is buying and selling goods for profit. **2.** a storekeeper; retailer.

mer/chant·man, *n., pl.* -men. a trading ship.

mer/chant marine/, *n.* **1.** the ships of a nation that are engaged in commerce. **2.** the officers and crews of such ships.

mer·cu·ri·al (mər kyōōr/ē əl), *adj.* **1.** changeable and erratic. **2.** of, containing, or caused by the metal mercury.

mer·cu/ric, *adj.* of or containing bivalent mercury.

mer·cu/rous, *adj.* of or containing univalent mercury.

mer·cu·ry (mûr/kyə rē), *n., pl.* **-ries. 1.** a heavy, silver-white metallic element used in barometers, thermometers, and pharmaceuticals. *Symbol:* Hg; *at. wt.:* 200.59; *at. no.:* 80. **2.** (*cap.*) the Roman god of commerce and science and messenger to the other gods. **3.** (*cap.*) the planet nearest the sun and the smallest in the solar system.

mer·cy (mûr/sē), *n., pl.* **-cies. 1.** compassion shown toward an offender or an enemy. **2.** the disposition to be compassionate or forbearing. **3.** a cause for gratitude; blessing: *It was a mercy they weren't hurt.* —**mer/ci·ful,** *adj.* —**mer/ci·ful·ly,** *adv.* —**mer/ci·less,** *adj.* —**mer/ci·less·ly,** *adv.*

mer/cy kill/ing, *n.* EUTHANASIA.

mere (mēr), *adj., superl.* **mer·est.** being nothing more nor better than what is specified: *a mere child.* —**mere/ly,** *adv.*

mer·e·tri·cious (mer/i trish/əs), *adj.* **1.** vulgarly attractive; tawdry. **2.** based on pretense or insincerity. —**mer/e·tri/cious·ly,** *adv.*

mer·gan·ser (mər gan/sər), *n., pl.* **-sers, -ser.** a fish-eating diving duck with a narrow bill.

merge (mûrj), *v.i., v.t.,* **merged, merg·ing. 1.** to combine, coalesce, or unite into a single entity. **2.** to lose or cause to lose identity by gradual blending.

merg/er, *n.* **1.** combination of two or more corporations into a single corporation. **2.** an act or instance of merging.

me·rid·i·an (mə rid/ē ən), *n.* **1. a.** a great circle of the earth passing through the poles and any given point on the earth's surface. **b.** the half of such a circle included between the poles. **2.** the greatest or highest point or period.

me·ringue (mə rang/), *n.* egg whites stiffly beaten with sugar and browned in the oven, often used as topping, as for pies.

me·ri·no (mə rē/nō), *n., pl.* **-nos. 1.** (*often cap.*) one of a breed of sheep valued for their fine wool. **2.** wool from a merino. **3.** a yarn or fabric made from this wool.

mer·it (mer/it), *n.* **1.** claim to respect and praise; worth. **2.** a commendable quality. **3. merits,** the inherent rights and wrongs of a matter, as a legal case. **4.** (*pl.*) **-its.** the fact of deserving; desert. —*v.t.* **5.** to be worthy of; deserve.

mer/i·to/ri·ous (-i tôr/ē əs), *adj.* deserving praise, reward, or esteem. —**mer/i·to/ri·ous·ly,** *adv.*

Mer·lin (mûr/lin), *n.* a magician and seer in Arthurian legend.

mer·maid (mûr/mād/), *n.* (in folklore) a marine creature with the head and torso of a woman and the tail of a fish.

mer/man/, *n., pl.* **-men.** (in folklore) a marine creature with the head and torso of a man and the tail of a fish.

Mer·ri·mack (mer/ə mak/), *n.* (*italics*) Also, **Mer/ri·mac/.** a Union steamer that the Confederates converted into an ironclad warship, renamed the *Virginia,* and used against the *Monitor* in 1862 in the first battle between ironclads.

mer·ri·ment (mer/i mənt), *n.* cheerful or high-spirited gaiety; hilarity.

mer/ry, *adj.,* **-ri·er, -ri·est. 1.** full of cheer or gaiety; joyous. **2.** characterized by festive conviviality. —*Proverb.* **3. A merry heart makes a cheerful coun-**

tenance, how one looks is affected by how one feels. Prov. 15:13. —mer′ri•ly, adv. —mer′ri•ness, n.

mer′ry-go-round′, n. 1. a revolving circular platform with seats often formed like animals on which people ride, as at an amusement park. 2. a busy round, as of activities.

mer′ry•mak′ing, n. 1. indulgence in gaiety or conviviality. 2. a merry party; festivity; revel. —mer′ry•mak′er, n.

me•sa (mā′sə), n., pl. -sas. a land formation with steep walls and a relatively flat top.

Me•sa, n. a city in central Arizona. 280,360.

mé•sal•li•ance (mā′zə lī′əns, -zal yäns′), n., pl. -li•anc•es (-lī′ən siz, -zal yäns′). a marriage with someone considered socially inferior. [< F]

mes•cal (me skal′), n. 1. a. an alcoholic beverage distilled from certain species of agave. b. any agave yielding this. 2. a spineless, dome-shaped cactus of Texas and N Mexico.

mes•ca•line (mes′kə lēn′, -lin), n. a hallucinogenic powder obtained from the mescal cactus.

mesc•lun (mes′klən), n. a salad consisting esp. of young, tender mixed greens.

mes•dames (mā däm′, -dämz′, -dam′, -damz′), n. 1. a pl. of MADAM. 2. pl. of MADAME.

mes•de•moi•selles (mā′də mə zel′, -zelz′, mād′-mwə-), n. a pl. of MADEMOISELLE.

mesh (mesh), n. 1. a knit, woven, or knotted fabric of open texture. 2. an interwoven or intertwined structure; network. 3. a. one of the open spaces between the cords or wires of a net. b. meshes, the cords or wires that bind such spaces. 4. something that catches or holds fast. 5. the engagement of gear teeth. —v.t., v.i. 6. to entangle or become entangled in or as if in a net. 7. to engage or become engaged, as gear teeth. 8. to match; coordinate.

Me•shach (mē′shak), n. a companion of Daniel. Compare SHADRACH. Dan. 3:12–30.

Me•shed (me shed′), n. MASHHAD.

mes•mer•ize (mez′mə rīz′, mes′-), v.t., -ized, -iz•ing. 1. to hypnotize. 2. to spellbind; fascinate. [after F. A. Mesmer (1733–1815), Austrian physician] —mes′mer•ism, n. —mes′mer•iz′er, n.

Mes•o•lith•ic (mez′ə lith′ik, mes′-), adj. noting or pertaining to a transitional period of the Stone Age.

Mes•o•po•ta•mi•a (mes′ə pə tā′mē ə), n. an ancient region in W Asia between the Tigris and Euphrates rivers: now part of Iraq. —Mes′o•po•ta′mi•an, adj., n.

mes•o•sphere (mez′ə sfēr′, mes′-), n. the atmospheric region between the stratosphere and the thermosphere.

Mes•o•zo•ic (mez′ə zō′ik, mes′-), adj. noting or pertaining to a geologic era occurring between 230 and 65 million years ago, characterized by flowering plants and dinosaurs.

mes•quite (me skēt′, mes′kēt), n. a spiny tree or shrub of W North America bearing beanlike pods.

mess (mes), n. 1. a dirty, untidy, unpleasant, or confused condition. 2. a dirty or untidy accumulation; jumble. 3. a. a group regularly taking meals together. b. the meal taken. 4. a quantity of food. —v.t. 5. to make dirty or untidy. 6. to make a muddle of; bungle. —v.i. 7. to eat in company, esp. as a member of a mess. 8. mess around, a. to waste time. b. to involve oneself; associate. —mess′y, adj., -i•er, -i•est. —mess′i•ly, adv. —mess′i•ness, n.

mes•sage (mes′ij), n. 1. a written or spoken communication delivered esp. by an intermediary. 2. the main point, moral, or meaning, as of a speech.

mes•sei•gneurs (Fr mā se nyœr′). n. (sometimes cap.) pl. of MONSEIGNEUR.

mes•sen•ger (mes′ən jər), n. 1. a person who conveys messages or parcels. —v.t. 2. to send by messenger.

messenger RNA, n. an RNA that is synthesized in the nucleus from DNA and then enters the cytoplasm, carrying the genetic code required for protein synthesis.

Mes•si•ah (mi sī′ə), n. 1. the promised and ex-

pected deliverer of the Jews. 2. Jesus Christ. John 4:25, 26. 3. (italics) an oratorio (1742) by George Frideric Handel. —Mes•si•an•ic (mes′ē an′ik), adj.

mes•sieurs (me syœ′). n. pl. of MONSIEUR.

mess′mate′, n. a person with whom one regularly takes meals, as in an army camp.

Messrs. (mes′ərz), pl. of MR.

mes•ti•zo (me stē′zō), n., pl. -zos, -zoes. a person of racially mixed ancestry, esp. of mixed American Indian and European ancestry.

met (met), v. pt. and pp. of MEET¹.

meta-, a prefix meaning: after (metaphysics); beyond (metalinguistics); behind (metacarpus); change (metamorphosis).

me•tab•o•lism (mə tab′ə liz′əm), n. the sum of the processes in an organism by which its substance is produced, maintained, and destroyed and by which energy is made available. —met•a•bol•ic (met′ə bol′ik), adj. —me•tab′o•lize′, v.t., v.i., -lized, -liz•ing.

me•tab′o•lite′ (-līt′), n. a product of metabolism.

met•a•car•pus (met′ə kär′pəs), n., pl. -pi (-pī). the bones of a vertebrate forelimb between the wrist and the fingers. —met′a•car′pal, adj., n.

met•al (met′l), n. 1. any of a class of elementary substances, such as gold, that are typically characterized by opacity, ductility, conductivity, and luster. 2. an alloy of metals, as brass. 3. METTLE. —me•tal•lic (mə tal′ik), adj.

met•al•lur•gy (met′l ûr′jē), n. the technology or science of metals. —met′al•lur′gic, met′al•lur′gi•cal, adj. —met′al•lur′gist, n.

met•a•mor•phism (met′ə môr′fiz əm), n. a change in the constitution of a rock by natural means, as pressure and heat. —met′a•mor′phic, adj.

met′a•mor′phose (-fōz, -fōs), v.t, v.i., -phosed, -phos•ing. to subject to or undergo metamorphosis or metamorphism.

met′a•mor′pho•sis (-fə sis), n., pl. -ses (-sēz′). 1. a change in form from one stage to the next in the life of an organism, as from pupa to butterfly. 2. a change of form, structure, or substance, as by magic. 3. a remarkable change, as in appearance. [< L < Gk: transformation]

met•a•phor (met′ə fôr′, -fər), n. the application of a word or phrase to an object or concept it does not literally denote in order to suggest comparison, as in "A mighty fortress is our God." —met′a•phor′i•cal (-fôr′i kəl, -for′-), met′a•phor′ic, adj. —met′a•phor′i•cal•ly, adv.

met•a•phys•i•cal (met′ə fiz′i kəl), adj. 1. of metaphysics. 2. highly abstract or abstruse. 3. incorporeal or supernatural.

met′a•phys′ics, n. 1. the branch of philosophy that treats of the ultimate nature of existence, reality, and experience. 2. philosophy, esp. in its more abstruse branches.

me•tas•ta•sis (mə tas′tə sis), n., pl. -ses (-sēz′). the spread of disease-producing organisms or malignant cells from one to another part of the body. —met•a•stat•ic (met′ə stat′ik), adj.

me•tas•ta•size (mə tas′tə sīz′), v.i., -sized, -siz•ing. 1. to spread by or as if by metastasis: Street gangs have metastasized in our city. 2. to transform, esp. into a dangerous form: Truth metastasized into lurid fantasy.

met•a•tar•sus (met′ə tär′səs), n., pl. -si (-sī). the bones of a vertebrate hind limb between the tarsus and the toes. —met′a•tar′sal, adj., n.

me•tath•e•sis (mə tath′ə sis), n., pl. -ses (-sēz′). transposition of sounds in a word.

mete (mēt), v.t., met•ed, met•ing. to distribute by measure; dole: to mete out punishment.

me•tem•psy•cho•sis (mə tem′sə kō′sis, -temp′-, met′əm sī-), n., pl. -ses (-sēz). the passage of the soul after death into the body of another being.

me•te•or (mē′tē ər, -ôr′), n. 1. a meteoroid that has entered the earth's atmosphere. 2. a transient fiery streak in the sky produced by passage of a meteor.

me•te•or•ic (-ôr′ik, -or′-), *adj.* **1.** of meteors. **2.** resembling a meteor in transient brilliance: *a meteoric rise in politics.*

me•te•or•ite′ (-ə rīt′), *n.* the remains of a meteoroid that has reached the earth.

me′te•or•oid′, *n.* any of the small bodies of rock or metal traveling through space.

me′te•or•ol′o•gy (-ə rol′ə jē), *n.* the science dealing with the atmosphere, weather, and climate. —me′te•or•ol′o•gist, *n.*

me•ter[1] (mē′tər), *n.* the basic unit of length in the metric system, equivalent to 39.37 inches.

me•ter[2] (mē′tər), *n.* the rhythmic element in music and poetry.

me•ter[3] (mē′tər), *n.* **1.** an instrument for measuring and recording something, as amount or time. —*v.t.* **2.** to measure by means of a meter. **3.** to process (mail) by means of a postage meter.

-meter, a combining form meaning measuring instrument (*barometer*).

me′ter-kil′ogram-sec′ond, *adj.* of or being a system of measurement in which the meter, kilogram, and second are the basic units of length, mass, and time.

meth•a•done (meth′ə dōn′) also **-don′** (-don′), *n.* a synthetic narcotic used in the treatment of heroin addiction.

meth•ane (meth′ān), *n.* a colorless, odorless, flammable gas that is the main constituent of marsh gas and is obtained commercially from natural gas.

meth•a•nol (meth′ə nôl′, -nol′), *n.* METHYL ALCOHOL.

me•thinks (mi thingks′), *v. impersonal; pt.* **-thought** (-thôt′), *Archaic.* it seems to me.

meth•od (meth′əd), *n.* **1.** a procedure, technique, or planned way of doing something. **2.** orderly or systematic arrangement. —**me•thod•i•cal** (mə thod′i kəl), *adj.* —**me•thod′i•cal•ly,** *adv.*

Meth•od•ist (meth′ə dist), *n.* a member of a Protestant denomination that developed out of John Wesley's religious revival. —**Meth′od•ism,** *n.*

meth′od•ol′o•gy (-ə dol′ə jē), *n., pl.* **-gies.** a set or system of methods, principles, and rules, as in the sciences. —**meth′od•o•log′i•cal** (-dl oj′i kəl), *adj.* —**meth′od•ol′o•gist,** *n.*

Me•thu•se•lah (mə thōō′zə lə), *n.* a patriarch who lived 969 years. Gen. 5:27.

meth•yl (meth′əl), *n.* the univalent group derived from methane.

meth′yl al′cohol, *n.* a colorless, poisonous liquid used chiefly as a solvent, fuel, and antifreeze.

me•tic•u•lous (mə tik′yə ləs), *adj.* taking or showing extreme care about minute details. —**me•tic′u•lous•ly,** *adv.* —**me•tic′u•lous•ness,** *n.*

mé•tier or **me•tier** (mā′tyā), *n.* a field of activity in which one has special ability.

me•tre (mē′tər), *n. Chiefly Brit.* METER.

met•ric[1] (me′trik), *adj.* pertaining to the meter or to the metric system.

met•ric[2] (me′trik), *adj.* METRICAL.

met′ri•cal, *adj.* **1.** pertaining to or composed in rhythmic meter. **2.** pertaining to measurement. —**met′ri•cal•ly,** *adv.*

met′ri•ca′tion, *n.* conversion to the metric system. —**met′ri•cate′,** *v.i., v.t.,* **-cat•ed, -cat•ing.**

met′ric sys′tem, *n.* a decimal system of weights and measures based on the meter for length and the kilogram for mass.

met′ric ton′, *n.* a unit of 1000 kilograms, equivalent to 2204.62 avoirdupois pounds.

met•ro (me′trō), *n., pl.* **-ros.** (*often cap.*) a subway.

met•ro•nome (me′trə nōm′), *n.* an instrument that makes repeated clicks for marking rhythm, esp. in practicing music.

me•trop•o•lis (mi trop′ə lis), *n.* a large, busy city, esp. the chief city of a country or region. [< L < Gk: mother state or city] —**met′ro•pol′i•tan** (me′trə pol′i tn), *adj.*

met•tle (met′l), *n.* **1.** courage and fortitude. **2.** disposition or temperament.

met′tle•some (-səm), *adj.* spirited; courageous.

mew[1] (myōō), *n.* **1.** the high-pitched cry of a cat. —*v.i.* **2.** to emit a mew.

mew[2] (myōō), *n.* **mews,** (*usu. with a sing. v.*) **1.** stables and usu. servants' quarters built around a courtyard. **2.** a street with apartments converted from stables.

mewl (myōōl), *v.i.* to cry plaintively; whimper.

Mex., **1.** Mexican. **2.** Mexico.

Mex•i•co (mek′si kō′), *n.* **1.** a republic in S North America. 97,573,374. **2.** Gulf of, an arm of the Atlantic surrounded by the U.S., Cuba, and Mexico. —**Mex′i•can,** *n., adj.*

Mex′ico Cit′y, *n.* the capital of Mexico. 18,748,000.

mez•za•nine (mez′ə nēn′, mez′ə nēn′), *n.* **1.** the lowest balcony or forward part of such a balcony in a theater. **2.** a low-ceilinged story between two stories of greater height in a building. [< F < It *mezzanino,* dim. of *mezzano* middle < L *mediānus* median]

mez′zo-sopran′o (met′sō-, med′zō-), *n., pl.* **-pran•os.** a voice, voice part, or singer intermediate in range between soprano and contralto.

mfg., manufacturing.

mfr., *pl.* **mfrs.** manufacturer.

Mg, *Chem. Symbol.* magnesium.

mg, milligram.

Mgr or **mgr,** manager.

MHz, megahertz.

mi (mē), *n. Music.* the third tone of a diatonic scale.

MI, Michigan.

mi., mile.

MIA, missing in action.

Mi•am•i (mī am′ē, -am′ə), *n.* a city in SE Florida. 373,024. —**Mi•am′i•an,** *n.*

mi•as•ma (mī az′mə, mē-), *n., pl.* **-mas, -ma•ta** (-mə tə). **1.** a noxious exhalation from putrescent organic matter. **2.** a dangerous or corruptive influence or atmosphere.

mi•ca (mī′kə), *n., pl.* **-cas.** one of a group of minerals that separate readily into thin, often transparent sheets.

Mi•cah (mī′kə), *n.* **1.** a Minor Prophet of the 8th century B.C. **2.** a book of the Bible bearing his name.

mice (mīs), *n.* pl. of MOUSE.

Mich., Michigan.

Mi•chael (mī′kəl), *n.* a militant archangel. Dan. 10:13; Rev. 12:7.

Mi•chel•an•ge•lo (mī′kəl an′jə lō′, mik′əl-), *n.* (*Michelangelo Buonarroti*), 1475–1564, Italian artist, architect, and poet.

Mich•i•gan (mish′i gən), *n.* **1.** a state in the N central United States. 9,328,784. *Cap.:* Lansing. *Abbr.:* MI, Mich. **2. Lake,** a lake between Wisconsin and Michigan: one of the five Great Lakes. —**Mich′i•gan′der** (-gan′dər), **Mich′i•gan•ite′,** *n.*

micro-, a combining form meaning: very small (*microfilm*); microscopic (*microorganism*); one millionth (*micron*).

mi•crobe (mī′krōb), *n.* a microorganism, esp. a disease-causing bacterium.

mi•cro•bi•ol•o•gy (mī′krō bī ol′ə jē), *n.* the branch of biology dealing with microorganisms. —**mi′cro•bi•ol′o•gist,** *n.*

mi′cro•chip′, *n.* CHIP (def. 5).

mi′cro•com•put′er, *n.* a compact computer with less capability than a minicomputer.

mi•cro•cosm (mī′krə koz′əm), *n.* **1.** a world in miniature. **2.** something regarded as a microcosm.

mi•cro•fi•ber (mī′krō fī′bər), *n.* a very fine polyester fiber, weighing less than one denier per filament, used esp. for clothing.

mi′cro•fiche′ (-fēsh′), *n., pl.* **-fiche, -fich•es.** a flat sheet of microfilmed printed or graphic matter.

mi′cro•film′, *n.* **1.** a film bearing a miniature photographic copy of printed or graphic matter. —*v.t.* **2.** to make a microfilm of.

mi′cro•groove′, *n.* a very narrow spiral needle groove on a long-playing record.

mi′cro•man′age, *v.t.,* **-aged, -ag•ing.** to manage or control with excessive attention to minor details:

The executive had no time to micromanage every facet of the business. —**mi′cro•man′age•ment,** *n.*

mi•crom•e•ter (mī krom′i tər), *n.* a device for measuring minute distances, used esp. with a telescope or microscope.

mi•cron (mī′kron), *n., pl.* **-crons, -cra** (-krə). the millionth part of a meter.

Mi•cro•ne•sia (mī′krə nē′zhə), *n.* **1.** the small Pacific islands N of the equator and E of the Philippines. **2. Federated States of,** a group of islands in the W Pacific: a self-governing area associated with the U.S. 127,616. —**Mi′cro•ne′sian,** *adj., n.*

mi′cro•or′gan•ism (mī′krō-), *n.* an organism, as a bacterium, too small to be viewed by the unaided eye.

mi•cro•phone (mī′krə fōn′), *n.* an instrument for transforming sound waves into changes in electric currents, used in recording or transmitting sound.

mi•cro•proc•es•sor (mī′krō pros′es ər, -ə sər; *esp. Brit.* -prō′ses ər, -sə sər), *n.* an integrated computer circuit that performs all the functions of a CPU.

mi•cro•scope (mī′krə skōp′), *n.* an optical instrument for magnifying objects too small to be seen by the unaided eye. —**mi•cros′co•py** (-kros′kə pē), *n.*

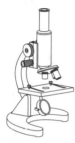

microscope

mi′cro•scop′ic (-skop′ik) also **-i•cal,** *adj.* **1.** too small to be visible without the use of a microscope. **2.** of or requiring the use of a microscope. —**mi′cro•scop′i•cal•ly,** *adv.*

mi•cro•sur•ger•y (mī′krō sûr′jə rē), *n.* surgery performed under magnification with very small specialized instruments.

mi′cro•wave′, *n., v.,* **-waved, -wav•ing.** —*n.* **1.** an electromagnetic wave with wavelengths from 1 mm to 30 cm. **2.** MICROWAVE OVEN. —*v.t.* **3.** to cook or heat in a microwave oven. —**mi′cro•wav′a•ble,** *adj.*

mi′crowave ov′en, *n.* an oven that uses microwaves to generate heat within the food.

mid¹ (mid), *adj.* being at or near the middle.

mid² or **′mid** (mid), *prep.* AMID.

mid•air′, *n.* a point in the air not contiguous with the earth.

mid′day′ (-dā′, -dā′), *n.* the middle of the day; noon.

mid•den (mid′n), *n.* a dunghill or refuse heap.

mid•dle (mid′l), *adj.* **1.** equally distant from the extremes; central. **2.** intermediate or intervening. **3.** (*cap.*) intermediate between linguistic periods classified as Old and New or Modern: *Middle English.* —*n.* **4.** a middle point, part, or position. **5.** the human waist.

mid′dle age′, *n.* the period of human life between about 45 and 65. —**mid′dle-aged′,** *adj.*

Mid′dle Ag′es, *n.* the time in European history from the late 5th century to about 1500.

Mid′dle Amer′ica, *n.* average or conventional middle-class Americans as a group. —**Mid′dle Amer′ican,** *n., adj.*

mid′dle•brow′, *n.* a moderately cultivated person.

mid′dle class′, *n.* a class of people intermediate between the upper and the lower class. —**mid′dle-class′,** *adj.*

mid′dle ear′, *n.* the middle portion of the ear consisting of the eardrum and an air-filled chamber lined with mucous membrane.

Mid′dle East′, *n.* the area from Libya east to Afghanistan. —**Mid′dle East′ern,** *adj.*

Mid′dle Eng′lish, *n.* the English language of the period c1150–c1475.

Mid′dle High′ Ger′man, *n.* the High German dialects of c1100 to c1500. *Abbr.:* MHG

mid′dle•man′, *n., pl.* **-men.** an intermediary, esp. one person who buys goods from the producer and resells them to the retailer or consumer.

mid′dle•most′, *adj.* MIDMOST.

mid′dle-of-the-road′, *adj.* following or favoring a position between extremes, esp. in politics; moderate.

Mid′dle Path′, *Buddhism.* the conduct of life in such a way as to avoid the extremes of luxury and asceticism.

mid′dle school′, *n.* a school encompassing grades five or six through eight.

mid′dle•weight′, *n.* a boxer weighing up to 160 pounds (72.5 kg).

Mid′dle West′, *n.* MIDWEST. —**Mid′dle West′ern,** *adj.*

mid′dling, *adj.* **1.** medium, moderate, or average in size, quantity, or quality. **2.** not first-rate; mediocre.

mid′dy, *n., pl.* **-dies. 1.** *Informal.* a midshipman. **2.** a loose blouse with a sailor collar.

Mid′east′, *n.* MIDDLE EAST. —**Mid′east′ern,** *adj.*

midge (mij), *n.* a minute insect somewhat resembling a mosquito.

midg•et (mij′it), *n.* **1.** a very small person. **2.** something, as an animal, that is very small for its kind.

mid•i (mid′ē), *n., pl.* **mid •is.** a garment, as a coat, of mid-calf length.

Mid•i•an (mid′ē ən), *n.* a son of Abraham. Gen. 25:1–4.

mid′land (-lənd), *n.* the middle or interior part of a country.

mid′most′, *adj.* being in or near the very middle.

mid′night′, *n.* **1.** twelve o'clock at night. —*adj.* **2.** of or resembling midnight.

mid′night sun′, *n.* the sun visible at midnight in summer in arctic and antarctic regions.

mid′point′, *n.* a point at or near the middle.

mid•rash (mē dräsh′), *n., pl.* **mid•ra•shim** (mē′drä-shēm′). an early Jewish interpretation of or commentary on a Biblical text. [< Heb *midrāsh* lit., exposition]

mid′rib′, *n.* the central or middle rib of a leaf.

mid′riff (-rif), *n.* **1.** DIAPHRAGM (def. 1). **2.** the middle portion of the human body, between the chest and the waist.

mid′ship′man, *n., pl.* **-men.** a student in training for commission as an officer in the U.S. Navy or Marine Corps.

midst¹ (midst), *n.* **1.** a position among other persons, things, or parts. **2.** the state of being surrounded or involved: *in the midst of work.* **3.** the middle or central point or part.

midst² (midst), *prep.* among; amidst.

mid′stream′, *n.* the middle of a stream.

mid′sum′mer (-sum′ər, -sum′-), *n.* **1.** the middle of summer. **2.** the summer solstice, around June 21.

mid′term′, *n.* **1.** the halfway point of a school term. **2.** an examination given at midterm.

mid′town′ (-toun′, -toun′), *n.* the central part of a city or town.

mid•way (*adv., adj.* mid′wā′; *n.* -wā′), *adv., adj.* **1.** in the middle of the way or distance. —*n.* **2.** a way, as at a carnival, along which amusements and concessions are located.

mid′week′ (-wēk′, -wēk′), *n.* the middle of the week. —**mid′week′ly,** *adj., adv.*

Mid′west′, *n.* a region in the N central United States, bounded on the W by the Rocky Mountains and on the E by the Ohio River. —**Mid′west′ern,** *adj.* —**Mid′west′ern•er,** *n.*

mid·wife′, *n., pl.* **-wives.** a person who assists women in childbirth. —**mid·wife′ry** (-wif′ə rē), *n.*

mid′win′ter (-win′tər, -win′-), *n.* **1.** the middle of winter. **2.** the winter solstice, around December 22.

mid·year (mid′yēr′, -yēr′), *n.* **1.** the middle of a year. **2.** an examination at the middle of a school year.

mien (mēn), *n.* bearing or demeanor, esp. as showing character or feeling.

miff (mif), *v.t.* to put into an irritable mood, esp. by offending.

might[1] (mīt), *auxiliary v., pres. sing. and pl.* **might;** *past* **might. 1.** pt. of MAY. **2.** (used to express possibility): *I might stay home.* **3.** (used to express obligation): *They might at least have tried.* **4.** (used to express contingency, concession, or purpose): *difficult as it might be.* **5.** (used in polite requests for permission): *Might I speak to you now?*

might[2] (mīt), *n.* **1.** physical strength. **2.** power or strength; force.

might′y, *adj.,* **-i·er, -i·est,** *adv.* —*adj.* **1.** having or showing power or strength. **2.** of great size; huge. **3.** great, as in importance; exceptional. —*adv.* **4.** *Informal.* very; extremely. —**might′i·ly,** *adv.* —**might′i·ness,** *n.*

might′y men′, *n.pl.* brave soldiers loyal to David. II Sam. 23:8–39; I Chron. 11:10–47.

mi·gnon·ette (min′yə net′), *n.* a plant with clusters of small, fragrant flowers.

mi·graine (mī′grān), *n.* a severe, recurrent headache often accompanied by nausea.

mi·grant (mī′grənt), *adj.* **1.** migrating. —*n.* **2.** a person or animal that migrates. **3.** a person who moves from place to place to find seasonal work.

mi′grate (-grāt), *v.i.,* **-grat·ed, -grat·ing. 1.** to move from one country, region, or place to another. **2.** to pass periodically from one region or climate to another, as certain birds. —**mi·gra′tion,** *n.* —**mi′gra·to′ry** (-grə tôr′ē), *adj.*

mi·ka·do (mi kä′dō), *n., pl.* **-dos.** an emperor of Japan.

mike (mīk), *n.* a microphone.

mil (mil), *n.* a unit of length equal to 0.001 of an inch (0.0254 mm).

Mi·lan (mi lan′, -län′), *n.* a city in N Italy. 1,478,505. —**Mil·an·ese** (mil′ə nēz′, -nēs′), *n., pl.* **-ese,** *adj.*

milch (milch), *adj.* yielding milk: *a milch cow.*

mild (mīld), *adj.,* **-er, -est. 1.** gentle in feeling, behavior, or manner. **2.** not cold, severe, or extreme; temperate. **3.** gentle in force or effect; moderate. —**mild′ly,** *adv.* —**mild′ness,** *n.*

mil·dew (mil′dōō′, -dyōō′), *n.* **1.** a cottony, usu. whitish coating caused by a fungus and appearing on plants and materials such as fabrics and leather. —*v.t., v.i.* **2.** to affect or become affected with mildew.

mile (mīl), *n.* **1.** a unit of distance equal to 5280 feet, or 1760 yards (1.609 kilometers). **2.** NAUTICAL MILE. —*Idiom.* **3. go the extra mile,** to make an extra effort.

mile·age (mī′lij), *n.* **1.** the aggregate number of miles traveled in a given time. **2.** the average number of miles a vehicle can travel on a specified quantity of fuel. **3.** an allowance for traveling expenses at a fixed rate per mile.

mile′post′, *n.* a post showing the distance in miles to or from a place.

mil′er, *n.* a participant in a one-mile race.

mile′stone′, *n.* **1.** a stone functioning as a milepost. **2.** a significant event or point in development.

mi·lieu (mil yōō′, mēl-; *Fr.* mē lyœ′), *n., pl.* **mi·lieus** (mil yōōz′, mēl-), **mi·lieux** (*Fr.* mē lyœ′). surroundings; environment.

mil·i·tant (mil′i tənt), *adj.* **1.** vigorously active, often combative, esp. in support of a cause. **2.** engaged in warfare. —*n.* **3.** a militant person. —**mil′i·tan·cy,** *n.* —**mil′i·tant·ly,** *adv.*

mil′i·ta·rism (-tə riz′əm), *n.* **1.** strong military spirit. **2.** the principle or policy of maintaining a large military establishment. —**mil′i·ta·rist,** *n.* —**mil′i·ta·ris′tic,** *adj.*

mil′i·ta·rize′, *v.t.,* **-rized, -riz·ing. 1.** to equip with armed forces and military supplies. **2.** to imbue with militarism. —**mil′i·ta·ri·za′tion,** *n.*

mil′i·tar′y (-ter′ē), *adj., n., pl.* **-tar·y.** —*adj.* **1.** of or for the army, the armed forces, soldiers, or war. **2.** performed by soldiers. —*n.* **3.** the armed forces of a nation. **4.** military personnel. —**mil′i·tar′i·ly,** *adv.*

mil′itary police′, *n.* soldiers who perform police duties within the army.

mil′i·tate′ (-tāt′), *v.i.,* **-tat·ed, -tat·ing.** to have a substantial effect; weigh heavily.

mi·li·tia (mi lish′ə), *n.* a body of citizens enrolled for military service but called out only in emergencies. —**mi·li′tia·man,** *n., pl.* **-men.**

milk (milk), *n.* **1.** a white liquid secreted by the mammary glands of female mammals and serving to nourish their young. **2.** a liquid resembling milk, as the liquid within a coconut. —*v.t.* **3.** to draw milk from the udder or breast of. **4.** to draw out as if by milking; extract. —**milk′y,** *adj.,* **-i·er, -i·est.** —**milk′i·ness,** *n.*

milk′ glass′, *n.* an opaque white glass.

milk′maid′, *n.* a dairymaid.

milk′man′, *n., pl.* **-men.** a person who sells or delivers milk.

milk′ of magne′sia, *n.* a milky suspension in water of magnesium hydroxide, used as an antacid or laxative.

milk′shake′, *n.* a beverage of cold milk, flavoring, and often ice cream, blended in a mixer.

milk′sop′, *n.* a weak or ineffectual person.

milk′ tooth′, *n.* one of the temporary teeth of a mammal that are replaced by the permanent teeth.

milk′weed′, *n.* a plant with milky juice and pods filled with silky tufted seeds.

Milk′y Way′, *n.* the galaxy containing the solar system, visible as a luminous band stretching across the night sky and composed of approximately a trillion stars.

mill[1] (mil), *n.* **1.** a factory, as one for the manufacture of paper or steel. **2.** a building equipped with machinery for grinding grain into meal or flour. **3.** a device for grinding, crushing, or pulverizing: *a coffee mill.* **4.** any of various machines that modify the shape or size of a piece of work by rotating tools or the work. —*v.t.* **5.** to grind, work, treat, or shape in or with a mill. —*v.i.* **6.** to move around aimlessly or confusedly.

mill[2] (mil), *n.* a money of account equal to .001 of a U.S. dollar.

mill′age (-ij), *n.* a tax rate assessed in mills per dollar.

Mil·lay (mi lā′), *n.* **Edna St. Vincent,** 1892–1950, U.S. poet.

mil·len·ni·um (mi len′ē əm), *n., pl.* **-ni·ums, -ni·a** (-nē ə). **1.** a period of 1000 years. **2.** the period of 1000 years during which Christ is to reign on earth. Rev. 20:1–7. **3.** a period of general happiness. **4.** a thousandth anniversary. —**mil·len′ni·al,** *adj.*

mill′er, *n.* **1.** a person who owns or operates a mill, esp. a flour mill. **2.** a moth with wings that appear powdery.

mil′let (-it), *n.* **1.** any of various cereal grasses cultivated as food and fodder. **2.** the grain of a millet.

milli-, a combining form meaning: thousand (*millipede*); thousandth (*millimeter*).

mil·liard (mil′yərd, -yärd), *n. Brit.* one billion.

mil·li·gram (mil′i gram′), *n.* a unit of mass or weight equal to ¹⁄₁₀₀₀ of a gram.

mil′li·li·ter, *n.* a unit of capacity equal to ¹⁄₁₀₀₀ of a liter.

mil′li·me·ter, *n.* a unit of length equal to ¹⁄₁₀₀₀ of a meter.

mil·li·ner (mil′ə nər), *n.* a person who creates or sells hats for women.

mil′li·ner′y (-ner′ē, -nə rē), *n.* **1.** women's hats and related articles. **2.** the business or trade of a milliner.

mil•lion (mil'yən), *n.*, *pl.* **-lions, -lion. 1.** a cardinal number, 1000 times 1000. **2.** a symbol for this number, as 1,000,000. **3.** a very great number or amount. —**mil'lionth,** *adj.*, *n.*

mil•lion•aire or **mil•lion•naire** (mil'yə nâr'), *n.* a person whose wealth amounts to a million or more, as in pounds or dollars.

mil•li•pede (mil'ə pēd'), *n.* an arthropod with a body composed of many segments, each with two pairs of legs.

mill'race', *n.* a channel for the current of water driving a mill wheel.

mill'stone', *n.* **1.** either of a pair of circular stones between which grain is ground, as in a mill. **2.** a heavy burden.

mill'stream', *n.* the stream in a millrace.

mill' wheel', *n.* a waterwheel for driving a mill.

mill'wright', *n.* a person who designs and erects mills and installs mill machinery.

milque•toast (milk'tōst'), *n.* (*often cap.*) a timid or unassertive person.

milt (milt), *n.* **1.** the sperm-containing secretion of fish testes. **2.** fish testes and sperm ducts when filled with milt.

Mil•ton (mil'tn), *n.* **John,** 1608–74, English poet.

Mil•wau•kee (mil wô'kē), *n.* a port in SE Wisconsin, on Lake Michigan. 617,044.

mime (mīm, mēm), *n.*, *v.*, **mimed, mim•ing.** —*n.* **1.** the art or technique of character portrayal or narration by gestures and body movements. **2.** an actor who specializes in mime. **3.** MIMIC (def. 3). —*v.t.* **4.** to mimic. **5.** to act out in mime. —*v.i.* **6.** to engage in mime.

mim•e•o•graph (mim'ē ə graf', -gräf'), *n.* **1.** a machine for making copies from a stencil on an ink-fed drum. —*v.t.* **2.** to duplicate by means of a mimeograph.

mi•met•ic (mi met'ik, mī-), *adj.* characterized by, exhibiting, or of the nature of mimicry.

mim•ic (mim'ik), *v.*, **-icked, -ick•ing,** *n.* —*v.t.* **1.** to imitate, as in action or speech, often playfully or derisively. **2.** to resemble closely. —*n.* **3.** a person or thing that mimics, esp. a performer who mimics others. —**mim'ick•er,** *n.*

mim'ic•ry (-rē), *n.*, *pl.* **-ries. 1.** the act, practice, or art of mimicking. **2.** a resemblance of one organism to a different one that confers a benefit, as concealment from predators.

mi•mo•sa (mi mō'sə, -zə), *n.*, *pl.* **-sas.** a plant, shrub, or tree of warm regions that bears small flowers in globular heads.

min., 1. minim. **2.** minimum. **3.** minor. **4.** minute.

min•a•ret (min'ə ret'), *n.* a lofty, slender tower attached to a mosque.

minaret

min•a•to•ry (min'ə tôr'ē), *adj.* menacing; threatening.

mince (mins), *v.*, **minced, minc•ing.** —*v.t.* **1.** to cut or chop into small pieces. **2.** to moderate (words) esp. for the sake of decorum. —*v.i.* **3.** to move with short, affectedly dainty steps. —**minc'ing,** *adj.*

mince'meat', *n.* a diced mixture, as of apples, raisins, and sometimes meat, for filling a pie.

mind (mīnd), *n.* **1.** the part or process in a conscious being that reasons, thinks, feels, wills, perceives, and judges. **2.** intellectual power; intelligence. **3.** sound mental condition; sanity: *lost his mind.* **4.** opinion, view, or sentiments: *Don't change your mind again.* **5.** inclination, intention, or desire: *He was of a mind to listen.* **6.** recollection; memory. **7.** attention; thoughts: *He can't keep his mind on his studies.* —*v.t.* **8.** to pay attention to. **9.** to heed or obey. **10.** to attend to. **11.** to look after; tend. **12.** to be careful or wary about. **13.** to care about. **14.** to object to: *I don't mind the interruption.* —*v.i.* **15.** to pay attention. **16.** to obey. **17.** to be careful or wary. **18.** to care or object.

mind'-blow'ing, *adj.* **1.** overwhelming; astounding. **2.** producing a hallucinogenic effect.

mind'-bod'y, *adj.* taking into account the physiological, psychic, and spiritual connections between the state of the body and that of the mind: *mind-body medicine.*

mind'ed, *adj.* **1.** having a certain kind of mind: *broad-minded.* **2.** inclined or disposed.

mind'ful, *adj.* attentive; aware. —**mind'ful•ly,** *adv.* —**mind'ful•ness,** *n.*

mind' games', *n.pl.* psychological manipulation or strategy.

mind'less, *adj.* **1.** showing, using, or requiring no intelligence or thought. **2.** unmindful; heedless. —**mind'less•ly,** *adv.* —**mind'less•ness,** *n.*

mind's' eye', *n.* the hypothetical site of recollection or imagination.

mine[1] (mīn), *pron.* **1.** a form of the possessive case of I: *The yellow sweater is mine.* **2.** that or those belonging to me: *Mine is on the left.*

mine[2] (mīn), *n.*, *v.*, **mined, min•ing.** —*n.* **1.** an excavation made in the earth for extracting mineral substances, as ore. **2.** a natural deposit of mineral substances. **3.** an abundant source: *a mine of information.* **4.** an explosive device for blowing up enemy shipping, personnel, or vehicles. **5.** a passage dug under an enemy position. —*v.i.* **6.** to dig a mine. **7.** to extract a mineral substance from a mine. —*v.t.* **8.** to dig in (earth) to extract a mineral substance. **9.** to extract from a mine. **10.** to place military mines under or in. **11.** to undermine. —**min'er,** *n.*

min•er•al (min'ər əl), *n.* **1.** a natural inorganic substance, as quartz, of definite chemical composition and usu. of definite crystal structure. **2.** an ore. **3.** a substance that is neither animal nor vegetable. —*adj.* **4.** of or containing minerals.

min'er•al•o•gy (-ə rol'ə jē, -ral'ə-), *n.* the science or study of minerals. —**min'er•al•o•gist,** *n.*

min'eral oil', *n.* an oil obtained from petroleum by distillation and used esp. as a laxative.

min'eral wa'ter, *n.* water containing dissolved mineral salts or gases.

Mi•ner•va (mi nûr'və), *n.* the Roman goddess of wisdom and the arts.

min•e•stro•ne (min'ə strō'nē), *n.*, *pl.* **-nes.** a thick vegetable soup.

mine'sweep'er, *n.* a ship used to remove or destroy explosive mines.

min•gle (ming'gəl), *v.*, **-gled, -gling.** —*v.i.* **1.** to become mixed, blended, or united. **2.** to mix in company. —*v.t.* **3.** to put together in a mixture; blend.

min•i (min'ē), *n.*, *pl.* **min•is. 1.** MINISKIRT. **2.** something small of its kind.

mini-, a combining form meaning: smaller than others of its kind (*minibike*); very short (*miniskirt*).

min•i•a•ture (min'ē ə chər, min'ə-), *n.* **1.** a representation of something on a small or reduced scale. **2.** something small of its class or kind. **3.** a very small painting, as on ivory. —*adj.* **4.** represented or being on a small or reduced scale: *a miniature poodle.* —**min'i•a•tur•ist,** *n.*

min'i•a•tur•ize', *v.t.*, **-ized, -iz•ing.** to make in greatly reduced size. —**min'i•a•tur•i•za'tion,** *n.*

min•i•bike (min'ē bīk'), *n.* a small, lightweight motorcycle.

min'i•bus', *n.* a small bus typically used for short distances.

min′i·com·put′er, *n.* a computer with processing and storage capabilities smaller than those of a mainframe but larger than those of a microcomputer.

min·im (min′əm), *n.* the smallest unit of liquid measure, ¹⁄₆₀ of a fluid dram.

min·i·mal (min′ə məl), *adj.* **1.** of or constituting a minimum. **2.** minimalism. —**min′i·mal·ly,** *adv.*

min′i·mal·ism, *n.* a style or method, as in art or music, that is spare, simple, and often repetitious. —**min′i·mal·ist,** *n.*

min′i·mize′ (-mīz′), *v.t.,* **-mized, -miz·ing. 1.** to reduce to the minimum. **2.** to represent as being of minimum value or importance, often in a disparaging way. —**min′i·miz′er,** *n.*

min′i·mum (-məm), *n., pl.* **-mums, -ma** (-mə), *adj.* —*n.* **1.** the least amount possible or allowable. **2.** the lowest amount, value, or degree attained or recorded. —*adj.* **3.** of or being a minimum.

min·ion (min′yən), *n.* **1.** a servile follower. **2.** a minor official. **3.** a favored person.

min·is·cule (min′ə skyōōl′), *adj.* MINUSCULE.

min′i·se′ries (min′ē-), *n., pl.* **-ries.** a television film broadcast in consecutive parts over a span of days or weeks.

min′i·skirt′, *n.* a skirt ending several inches above the knee.

min·is·ter (min′ə stər), *n.* **1.** a member of the clergy, esp. the Protestant clergy. **2.** a high officer of state, esp. one who heads an administrative department. **3.** a diplomatic representative, usu. ranking below an ambassador. **4.** an agent for another. —*v.i.* **5.** to perform the functions of a religious minister. **6.** to give service, care, or aid. —**min′is·te′ri·al** (-stēr′ē əl), *adj.* —**min′is·trant** (-strənt), *adj., n.* —**min′is·tra′tion,** *n.*

min′is·try, *n., pl.* **-tries. 1.** the service, functions, or profession of a minister. **2.** the body of ministers of religion; clergy. **3.** the body of ministers of state. **4.** an administrative department headed by a minister of state. **5.** ministration; service.

min·i·tow·er (min′ē tou′ər), *n.* a vertical case, smaller than a tower, designed to house a computer system standing on a floor or desk.

min·i·van (min′ē van′), *n.* a small passenger van.

mink (mingk), *n., pl.* **minks, mink. 1.** a semiaquatic weasel of North America and Eurasia. **2.** the soft, lustrous fur of the mink.

Minn., Minnesota.

Min·ne·ap·o·lis (min′ē ap′ə lis), *n.* a city in SE Minnesota on the Mississippi. 354,590.

min·ne·sing·er (min′ə sing′ər), *n.* one of a class of lyric poets and singers of medieval Germany. [< G, = *Minne* love + *Singer* singer]

Min·ne·so·ta (min′ə sō′tə), *n.* a state in the N central United States. 4,657,758. *Cap.:* St. Paul. *Abbr.:* MN, Minn. —**Min′ne·so′tan,** *adj., n.*

min·now (min′ō), *n., pl.* **-nows,** (*Rare*) **-now.** a small freshwater fish often used as bait.

Mi·no·an (mi nō′ən, mī-), *adj.* of or pertaining to the Bronze Age civilization of Crete, c2400–1400 B.C.

mi·nor (mī′nər), *adj.* **1.** lesser, as in size, extent, amount, or importance. **2.** under full legal age. **3.** *Music.* of, based on, or being a scale with half steps between the second and third and fifth and sixth degrees. —*n.* **4.** a person under full legal age. **5.** an academic subject pursued secondarily to a major. —*v.i.* **6.** to choose or study as an academic minor.

mi·nor·i·ty (mi nôr′i tē, -nor′-, mī-), *n., pl.* **-ties. 1.** a number, part, or amount forming less than half of a whole. **2.** a group differing, esp. in race, religion, or ethnic background, from the majority of a population. **3.** the state or period of being under full legal age.

minor′ity lead′er, *n.* the floor leader of the minority party in a legislature.

Mi′nor Proph′et, *n.* any of a group of Old Testament prophets including Hosea, Joel, Amos, Obadiah, Jonah, Micah, Nahum, Habakkuk, Zephaniah, Haggai, Zechariah, and Malachi. Compare MAJOR PROPHET.

min·ox·i·dil (mi nok′si dil′), *n.* a drug used for treating hypertension and applied topically to promote hair growth in some types of baldness.

Minsk (minsk), *n.* the capital of Belarus, and the Commonwealth of Independent States. 1,589,000.

min·strel (min′strəl), *n.* **1.** an often itinerant medieval poet, singer, and musician. **2.** a performer in a minstrel show. —**min′strel·sy,** *n.*

min′strel show′, *n.* a variety show in which whites in blackface performed comic dialogue and songs based on stereotypes of blacks.

mint¹ (mint), *n.* **1.** an aromatic herb with leaves used as flavoring. **2.** a mint-flavored candy. —**mint′y,** *adj.,* **-i·er, -i·est.**

mint² (mint), *n.* **1.** a place where coins are produced, esp. under government authority. **2.** a vast amount, esp. of money. —*adj.* **3.** being in pristine condition as if newly made: *a book in mint condition.* —*v.t.* **4.** to make coins by stamping metal. —**mint′er,** *n.*

min·u·end (min′yōō end′), *n.* a number from which another is subtracted.

min·u·et (min′yōō et′), *n.* a slow, stately dance in triple meter.

mi·nus (mī′nəs), *prep.* **1.** less by the subtraction of: *Ten minus six is four.* **2.** lacking or without: *a book minus a page.* —*adj.* **3.** involving subtraction. **4.** algebraically negative: *a minus quantity.* **5.** less than; just below: *got C minus on the test.* —*n.* **6.** MINUS SIGN. **7.** a minus quantity. **8.** a deficiency or loss.

mi·nus·cule (min′ə skyōōl′, mi nus′kyōōl), *adj.* very small.

mi′nus sign′, *n.* a symbol (–) denoting subtraction or a negative quantity.

min·ute¹ (min′it), *n.* **1.** the sixtieth part (¹⁄₆₀) of an hour. **2.** a short space of time. **3.** an exact point in time. **4.** minutes, the official record of the proceedings at a meeting. **5.** *Geom.* the sixtieth part of a degree of angular measure.

mi·nute² (mī nōōt′, -nyōōt′, mi-), *adj.,* **-nut·er, -nut·est. 1.** extremely small. **2.** of minor importance. **3.** attentive to small details. —**mi·nute′ly,** *adv.* —**mi·nute′ness,** *n.*

Min·ute·man (min′it man′), *n., pl.* **-men.** (*sometimes l.c.*) an American militiaman during the Revolutionary War who remained ready for instant military service.

min′ute steak′ (min′it), *n.* a thin, quickly sautéed slice of beefsteak.

mi·nu·ti·a (mi nōō′shē ə, -shə, -nyōō′-), *n., pl.* **-ti·ae** (-shē ē′). Usu., **minutiae.** precise details; small or trifling matters.

minx (mingks), *n.* a pert or flirtatious girl.

min·yan (min′yən, min yän′), *n., pl.* **min·yans, min·yan·im** (min′yə nēm′). the quorum of ten adult Jewish males required to be present for public prayers.

Mi·o·cene (mī′ə sēn′), *adj.* noting or pertaining to the fourth epoch of the Tertiary Period, when grazing mammals became widespread.

mir·a·cle (mir′ə kəl), *n.* **1.** an extraordinary occurrence that is ascribed to a divine or supernatural cause, esp. to God. **2.** a superb example; marvel. —**mi·rac·u·lous** (mi rak′yə ləs), *adj.* —**mi·rac′u·lous·ly,** *adv.*

mi·rage (mi räzh′), *n.* **1.** an optical phenomenon by which reflected images of distant objects are seen, often distorted. **2.** something illusory.

mire (mī°r), *n., v.,* **mired, mir·ing.** —*n.* **1.** an area of wet, swampy ground. **2.** deep mud. —*v.i., v.t.* **3.** to sink or stick in or as if in mire. —**mir′y,** *adj.*

Mir·i·am (mir′ē əm), *n.* the sister of Moses and Aaron. Num. 26:59.

Mi·ró (mē rō′), *n.* **Jo·an** (zhōō än′, hwän), 1893–1983, Spanish painter.

mir·ror (mir′ər), *n.* **1.** a reflecting surface, usu. of glass with a silvery backing. **2.** something that gives a faithful representation. —*v.t.* **3.** to reflect in or as if in a mirror.

mirth (mûrth), *n.* gaiety or jollity, esp. when accompanied by laughter. —**mirth′ful,** *adj.* —**mirth′less,** *adj.*

MIRV (mûrv), *n.* a missile carrying several nuclear warheads, each of which can be directed to a different target. [*m(ultiple) i(ndependently targetable) r(eentry) v(ehicle)*]

mis-, a prefix meaning: wrong (*misconduct*); wrongly (*misjudge*); lack of (*mistrust*).

mis•ad•ven•ture (mis′əd ven′chər), *n.* a misfortune; mishap.

mis′al•li′ance, *n.* an incompatible association, esp. in marriage.

mis•an•thrope (mis′ən thrōp′, miz′-) also **mis•an′thro•pist** (-an′thrə pist), *n.* a hater of humankind. —**mis′an•throp′ic** (-throp′ik), *adj.* —**mis•an′thro•py** (-an′thrə pē), *n.*

mis′ap•pre•hend′ (mis′-), *v.t.* MISUNDERSTAND. —**mis′ap•pre•hen′sion** (-hen′shən), *n.*

mis′ap•pro′pri•ate′ (-āt′), *v.t.,* -**at•ed,** -**at•ing.** to appropriate wrongfully or dishonestly. —**mis′ap•pro′pri•a′tion,** *n.*

mis′be•got′ten, *adj.* unlawfully or irregularly begotten; illegitimate.

mis′be•have′, *v.i., v.t.,* -**haved,** -**hav•ing.** to behave badly or improperly. —**mis′be•hav′ior,** *n.*

misc., **1.** miscellaneous. **2.** miscellany.

mis•call′, *v.t.* to call by a wrong name.

mis•car•ry (mis kar′ē; *for 1 also* mis′kar′ē), *v.i.,* -**ried,** -**ry•ing. 1.** to give birth to a fetus before it is viable. **2.** to be unsuccessful. **3.** to go astray. —**mis•car′riage** (-kar′ij), *n.*

mis•cast′, *v.t.* to cast in an unsuitable role.

mis•ceg•e•na•tion (mi sej′ə nā′shən, mis′i jə-), *n.* marriage or cohabitation between individuals of different races, esp. between a black and a white.

mis•cel•la•ne•ous (mis′ə lā′nē əs), *adj.* consisting of members or elements of different kinds.

mis•cel•la•ny (mis′ə lā′nē), *n., pl.* -**nies. 1.** a collection of various items or parts. **2.** a collection of literary works on various topics.

mis•chance′, *n.* **1.** a mishap. **2.** bad luck.

mis•chief (mis′chif), *n.* **1.** conduct or activity that causes annoyance. **2.** harm or trouble. **3.** an injury caused by a person or thing. **4.** a source of harm or annoyance.

mis′chie•vous (-chə vəs), *adj.* **1.** causing annoyance or trouble. **2.** roguishly or slyly teasing. **3.** harmful; injurious. —**mis′chie•vous•ly,** *adv.* —**mis′chie•vous•ness,** *n.*

mis•ci•ble (mis′ə bəl), *adj.* capable of being mixed.

mis′con•ceive′, *v.t., v.i.,* -**ceived,** -**ceiv•ing.** to interpret wrongly; misunderstand. —**mis′con•cep′tion,** *n.*

mis•con′duct (-kon′dukt), *n.* **1.** improper behavior. **2.** unlawful conduct, as by a public official.

mis′con•strue (mis′kən strōō′), *v.t.,* -**strued,** -**stru•ing.** to misunderstand the meaning of; misinterpret.

mis•count (*v.* mis kount′; *n.* mis′kount′), *v.i., v.t.* **1.** to count erroneously. —*n.* **2.** an erroneous counting.

mis•cre•ant (mis′krē ənt), *adj.* **1.** depraved; villainous. —*n.* **2.** a vicious or depraved person.

mis•cue′, *n., v.,* -**cued,** -**cu•ing.** —*n.* **1.** a mistake; blunder. —*v.i.* **2.** to make a mistake.

mis•deed′, *n.* an immoral deed.

mis′de•mean′or, *n.* **1.** a criminal offense less serious than a felony. **2.** a misdeed.

mis•di•rect′, *v.t.* to direct or guide wrongly. —**mis′di•rec′tion,** *n.*

mis•do′ing, *n.* Often, -**ings.** a wrongful or improper act.

mise-en-scène (mē zän sen′), *n., pl.* -**scènes** (-sens′, -sen′). **1.** the placement of actors, scenery, and properties on a stage. **2.** a stage setting. **3.** surroundings; environment.

mi•ser (mī′zər), *n.* a person who hoards money. —**mi′ser•ly,** *adj.* —**mi′ser•li•ness,** *n.*

mis•er•a•ble (miz′ər ə bəl), *adj.* **1.** wretchedly unhappy. **2.** of wretched character or quality; contemptible. **3.** causing misery. **4.** worthy of pity. —**mis′er•a•bly,** *adv.*

Mis•e•re•re (miz′ə rârʹē, -rērʹē), *n.* **1.** the 51st

Psalm or a musical setting for it. **2.** (*l.c.*) an appeal for mercy. [< L *miserēre* lit., have pity, first word of the psalm]

mis′er•y, *n., pl.* -**er•ies. 1.** suffering caused by privation or poverty. **2.** great emotional distress. **3.** a source of distress.

mis•fea•sance (mis fē′zəns), *n.* the wrongful and injurious exercise of lawful authority.

mis•fire (*v.* mis fīʳr′; *n.* mis′fīʳr′), *v.,* -**fired,** -**fir•ing,** *n.* —*v.i.* **1.** to fail to fire, explode, or ignite. **2.** to fail to achieve a desired result or effect. —*n.* **3.** an act or instance of misfiring.

mis•fit (mis fit′, mis′fit′ *for 1;* mis′fit′ *for 2*), *n.* **1.** something, as a garment, that fits badly. **2.** a person who is unable to adjust to a situation.

mis•for′tune, *n.* **1.** bad luck. **2.** an instance of bad luck.

mis•giv′ing, *n.* Often, -**ings.** a feeling of doubt, distrust, or apprehension.

mis•guide′, *v.t.,* -**guid•ed,** -**guid•ing.** to guide wrongly. —**mis•guid′ance,** *n.*

mis•han•dle, *v.t.,* -**dled,** -**dling. 1.** to handle roughly. **2.** to manage badly.

mis•hap (mis′hap, mis hap′), *n.* an unfortunate accident.

mish•mash (mish′mäsh′, -mash′), *n.* a confused mess; hodgepodge.

mis′in•form′, *v.t.* to give false or misleading information to. —**mis′in•for•ma′tion,** *n.*

mis′in•ter′pret, *v.t., v.i.* **1.** to interpret, explain, or understand incorrectly. —**mis′in•ter′pre•ta′tion,** *n.*

mis•judge′, *v.t., v.i.,* -**judged,** -**judg•ing.** to judge or estimate wrongly or unjustly. —**mis•judg′ment,** *n.*

mis•lay′, *v.t.,* -**laid,** -**lay•ing.** to lose temporarily; misplace.

mis•lead′ (-lēd′), *v.t.,* -**led,** -**lead•ing. 1.** to lead in the wrong direction. **2.** to lead into error, as of conduct. —**mis•lead′ing,** *adj.*

mis•man′age, *v.t., v.i.,* -**aged,** -**ag•ing.** to manage incompetently or dishonestly. —**mis•man′age•ment,** *n.*

mis•match (mis mach′; *for 2 also* mis′mach′), *v.t.* **1.** to match badly or unsuitably. —*n.* **2.** a bad or unsuitable match.

mis•no•mer (mis nō′mər), *n.* an incorrect name or designation.

mi•sog•a•my (mi sog′ə mē, mī-), *n.* hatred of marriage. —**mi•sog′a•mist,** *n.*

mi•sog•y•ny (mi soj′ə nē, mī-), *n.* hatred of or hostility toward women. —**mi•sog′y•nist,** *n.* —**mi•sog′y•nous,** *adj.*

mis•place′, *v.t.,* -**placed,** -**plac•ing. 1.** to put in a wrong place. **2.** to mislay. **3.** to place unsuitably or unwisely.

mis•play (*n.* mis plā′, mis′plā′; *v.* mis plā′), *n.* **1.** a wrong or bad play, as in a game. —*v.t., v.i.* **2.** to play wrongly or badly.

mis•print (*n.* mis′print′, mis print′; *v.* mis print′), *n.* **1.** a mistake in printing. —*v.t.* **2.** to print incorrectly.

mis•pri•sion (mis prizh′ən), *n.* a neglect or violation of official duty by one in office.

mis′pro•nounce′, *v.t., v.i.,* -**nounced,** -**nounc•ing.** to pronounce incorrectly. —**mis′pro•nun′ci•a′tion,** *n.*

mis•quote′, *v.,* -**quot•ed,** -**quot•ing,** *n.* —*v.t., v.i.* **1.** to quote incorrectly. —*n.* **2.** Also, **mis′quo•ta′tion.** an incorrect quotation.

mis•read′ (-rēd′), *v.t., v.i.,* -**read** (-red′), -**read•ing. 1.** to read wrongly. **2.** to misinterpret.

mis′rep•re•sent′, *v.t.* to represent incorrectly, improperly, or falsely. —**mis′rep•re•sen•ta′tion,** *n.*

mis•rule′, *n., v.,* -**ruled,** -**rul•ing.** —*n.* **1.** bad or unwise rule. **2.** disorder. —*v.t.* **3.** to rule badly.

miss¹ (mis), *v.t.* **1.** to fail to hit, encounter, meet, or catch. **2.** to fail to take advantage of. **3.** to fail to be present at or for. **4.** to notice or regret the absence or loss of. **5.** to escape or avoid: *just missed being caught.* **6.** to fail to understand. **7.** to leave out;

omit. —*v.i.* **8.** to fail to hit something. **9.** to be unsuccessful; fail. **10.** to misfire. —*n.* **11.** a failure, esp. a failure to hit something. **12.** MISFIRE.

miss² (mis), *n.* **1.** (*cap.*) a title of respect prefixed to the name of an unmarried woman. **2.** a young unmarried woman. [short for *mistress*]

Miss., Mississippi.

mis•sal (mis′əl), *n.* a book containing the prayers and rites of the Roman Catholic mass over the course of the year.

mis•shape (mis shāp′, mish-), *v.t.,* **-shaped, -shaped** or **-shap•en, -shap•ing.** to shape badly or wrongly; deform. —**mis•shap′en,** *adj.*

mis•sile (mis′əl; *esp. Brit.* -īl), *n.* **1.** an object or weapon that is thrown, shot, or propelled at a target. **2.** GUIDED MISSILE. **3.** BALLISTIC MISSILE.

mis•sile•ry or **-sil•ry** (mis′əl rē), *n.* **1.** the science of making and using missiles. **2.** missiles collectively.

miss′ing, *adj.* lacking, absent, or lost.

mis•sion (mish′ən), *n.* **1.** a group of persons sent by a government to a foreign country, as to conduct negotiations. **2.** a task to be performed. **3.** a permanent diplomatic establishment abroad. **4.** a group of missionaries sent out by a church. **5.** the place of work of religious missionaries.

mis•sion•ar′y (-ə ner′ē), *n., pl.* **-ar•ies,** *adj.* —*n.* **1.** a person sent by a church into an area to carry on religious or humanitarian work. —*adj.* **2.** of religious missions or missionaries.

Mis•sis•sau•ga (mis′ə sô′gə), *n.* a city in SE Ontario, in S Canada. 374,005.

Mis•sis•sip•pi (mis′ə sip′ē), *n.* **1.** a state in the S United States. 2,716,115. *Cap.:* Jackson. *Abbr.:* MS, Miss. **2.** a river flowing S from N Minnesota to the Gulf of Mexico. 2470 mi. (3975 km) long. —**Mis′sis•sip′pi•an,** *adj., n.*

mis•sive (mis′iv), *n.* a written message; letter.

Mis•sour•i (mi zŏŏr′ē, -zŏŏr′ə), *n.* **1.** a state in the central United States. 5,358,692. *Cap.:* Jefferson City. *Abbr.:* MO, Mo. **2.** a river flowing from SW Montana into the Mississippi N of St. Louis, Mo. 2723 mi. (4382 km) long. —**Mis•sour′i•an,** *adj., n.*

Missour′i Com′promise, *n.* a group of U.S. laws (1820–21) that admitted Missouri as a slave state and Maine as a free state to the Union, and prohibited slavery in the Louisiana Purchase north of latitude 36°30′N, except in Missouri.

mis•spell′, *v.t., v.i.,* **-spelled** or **-spelt, -spell•ing.** to spell incorrectly. —**mis•spell′ing,** *n.*

mis•spend′, *v.t.,* **-spent, -spend•ing.** to squander; waste.

mis•state′, *v.t.,* **-stat•ed, -stat•ing.** to state wrongly or misleadingly. —**mis•state′ment,** *n.*

mis•step′, *n.* **1.** a wrong step. **2.** an error, as in conduct.

mist (mist), *n.* **1.** a foglike mass of minute globules of water suspended in or falling from the atmosphere. **2.** something that dims, obscures, or blurs. —*v.t., v.i.* **3.** to make or become misty.

mis•take (mi stāk′), *n., v.,* **-took, -tak•en, -tak•ing.** —*n.* **1.** an error in action, opinion, or judgment. **2.** a misunderstanding or misconception. —*v.t.* **3.** to regard, identify, understand, or interpret wrongly. —**mis•tak′a•ble,** *adj.*

mis•tak′en, *adj.* **1.** wrongly conceived, held, or done. **2.** erroneous; wrong. **3.** being in error. —**mis•tak′en•ly,** *adv.*

mis•ter (mis′tər), *n.* **1.** (*cap.*) a title of respect prefixed to a man's name or position (usu. written *Mr.*). **2.** (used by itself as an informal term of address to a man).

mis•tle•toe (mis′əl tō′), *n.* a parasitic plant that bears white berries, used in Christmas decorations.

mis•treat′, *v.t.* to treat badly or abusively. —**mis•treat′ment,** *n.*

mis•tress (mis′tris), *n.* **1.** a woman who has authority, as over a household or institution. **2.** a woman who has a continuing extramarital sexual relationship with a man. **3.** something regarded as feminine that has supremacy: *Great Britain, mistress of the seas.* **4.** (*cap.*) a former term of address corresponding to Mrs., Miss, or Ms.

mis•tri′al, *n.* a trial terminated without conclusion, esp. because of a prejudicial error in the proceedings.

mis•trust′, *n.* **1.** lack of trust or confidence. —*v.t.* **2.** to regard with mistrust. —**mis•trust′ful,** *adj.*

mist′y, *adj.,* **-i•er, -i•est. 1.** covered or obscured by or as if by mist. **2.** consisting of or resembling mist. —**mist′i•ly,** *adv.* —**mist′i•ness,** *n.*

mis•un•der•stand′, *v.t., v.i.,* **-stood, -stand•ing.** to understand or interpret incorrectly.

mis•un•der•stand′ing, *n.* **1.** a failure to understand or interpret correctly. **2.** a disagreement or quarrel.

mis•use (*n.* mis yŏŏs′; *v.* -yŏŏz′), *n., v.,* **-used, -us•ing.** —*n.* **1.** wrong or improper use. —*v.t.* **2.** to use incorrectly or improperly. **3.** to treat badly; mistreat.

Mitch•ell (mich′əl), *n.* **1. John,** 1870–1919, U.S. labor leader. **2. Margaret,** 1900–49, U.S. novelist. **3. Maria,** 1818–89, U.S. astronomer. **4. William,** 1879–1936, U.S. general: pioneer in the field of aviation.

mite¹ (mīt), *n.* any of numerous tiny arachnids that are often parasitic on animals and plants.

mite² (mīt), *n.* **1.** a very small sum of money. **2.** a very small creature, person, or thing.

mi•ter (mī′tər), *n.* **1.** a headdress worn by a bishop or abbot. **2.** Also called **mi′ter joint′.** a joint formed by two pieces of wood whose beveled edges fit together at an angle. —*v.t.* **3.** to join with a miter joint. Also, *esp. Brit.,* **mi′tre.**

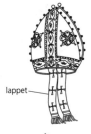

lappet

miter

mit•i•gate (mit′i gāt′), *v.t., v.i.,* **-gat•ed, -gat•ing.** to make or become less severe, intense, or painful. —**mit′i•ga′tion,** *n.*

mi•to•sis (mī tō′sis), *n.* the method of cell division in which chromosomes separate into two parts, one part of each chromosome being retained in each of

mis′ad•dress′, *v.t.*
mis′ad•vise′, *v.t.,* -vised, -vis•ing.
mis′a•ligned′, *adj.*
mis′a•lign′ment, *n.*
mis•al′pha•bet•ize′, *v.t.,* -ized, -iz•ing.
mis′ap•ply′, *v.t.,* -plied, -ply•ing.
mis•cal′cu•late′, *v.,* -lat•ed, -lat•ing.
mis′cal•cu•la′tion, *n.*
mis•clas′si•fy′, *v.t.,* -fied, -fy•ing.
mis•cop′y, *v.,* -ied, -y•ing.

mis′de•fine′, *v.t.,* -fined, -fin•ing.
mis′di•ag•nose′, *v.,* -nosed, -nos•ing.
mis•di′al, *v.,* -aled, -al•ing or (*esp. Brit.*) -alled, -al•ling.
mis′em•ploy′, *v.t.*
mis•file′, *v.t.,* -filed, -fil•ing.
mis•gauge′, *v.t.,* -gauged, -gaug•ing.
mis•gov′ern, *v.t.*
mis•hear′, *v.t.,* -heard, -hear•ing.
mis′i•den′ti•fi•ca′tion, *n.*

mis′i•den′ti•fy′, *v.t.,* -fied, -fy•ing.
mis•la′bel, *v.t.,* -beled, -bel•ing or (*esp. Brit.*) -belled, -bel•ling.
mis•name′, *v.t.,* -named, -nam•ing.
mis•num′ber, *v.*
mis′re•port′, *v.t., n.*
mis•throw′, *v.,* -threw, -thrown, -throw•ing.
mis•time′, *v.t.,* -timed, -tim•ing.
mis•ti′tle, *v.t.,* -tled, -tling.
mis′trans•late′, *v.t.,* -lat•ed, -lat•ing.

the two new daughter cells. —**mi•tot•ic** (mī tot′ik), *adj.*

mitt (mit), *n.* **1.** a thickly padded glove used by baseball catchers. **2.** *Slang.* a hand. **3.** a woman's glove that leaves the lower ends of the fingers bare.

mit′ten, *n.* a hand covering enclosing the four fingers together and the thumb separately.

mix (miks), *v.t.* **1.** to combine into one mass. **2.** to combine or unite. **3.** to form or make by combining ingredients. **4.** to crossbreed. —*v.i.* **5.** to associate or mingle, as in company. **6. mix up, a.** to confuse completely. **b.** to involve or entangle. —*n.* **7.** the result of mixing. **8.** a commercial mixture of dry food or drink ingredients. —**mix′a•ble,** *adj.* —**mix′er,** *n.*

mixed′ mul′titude, *n.* in the Bible, a crowd of different races and nationalities. Ex. 12:38; Num. 11:4; Neh. 13:3; Jer. 25:20–24.

mixed′ num′ber, *n.* a number consisting of a whole number and a fraction or decimal, as 4½ or 4.5.

mixed′-up′, *adj.* confused or unstable: *a mixed-up kid.*

mix′ture (-chər), *n.* **1.** a product of mixing. **2.** the act of mixing or state of being mixed.

mix′-up′, *n.* a state of confusion.

Miz•pah (miz′pə), *n.* a mound of stones set up by Jacob in Gilead. Gen. 31:49.

miz•zen (miz′ən), *n.* **1.** a fore-and-aft sail set on a mizzenmast. **2.** MIZZENMAST.

miz′zen•mast′ (-mast′, -mäst′; *Naut.* -məst), *n.* the third mast from forward in a ship with three or more masts.

mks or **MKS,** meter-kilogram-second.

ml, milliliter.

Mlle., Mademoiselle.

mm, millimeter.

MM., Messieurs.

Mme., Madame.

MN, Minnesota.

Mn, *Chem. Symbol.* manganese.

mne•mon•ic (ni mon′ik), *adj.* **1.** assisting or intended to assist the memory. —*n.* **2.** a mnemonic device, as a verse. **3.** a short form, as a symbol, used as a computer code or function.

Mne•mos•y•ne (nē mos′ə nē′, -moz′-), *n.* the ancient Greek goddess of memory, the mother by Zeus of the Muses.

MO, 1. Missouri. **2.** modus operandi.

Mo, *Chem. Symbol.* molybdenum.

Mo., 1. Missouri. **2.** Monday.

mo., *pl.* **mos.** month.

M.O. or **m.o., 1.** mail order. **2.** modus operandi. **3.** money order.

Mo•ab (mō′ab), *n.* an ancient kingdom E of the Dead Sea, in what is now Jordan. —**Mo′ab•ite′,** *n., adj.*

moan (mōn), *n.* **1.** a prolonged, low sound of pain or suffering. —*v.i., v.t.* **2.** to make or utter with a moan. **3.** to complain or lament.

moat (mōt), *n.* a deep, wide trench, usu. filled with water, surrounding a fortress or castle.

mob (mob), *n., v.,* **mobbed, mob•bing.** —*n.* **1.** a disorderly, riotous, or lawless crowd. **2.** the common people; masses. **3.** *Informal.* a criminal gang. —*v.t.* **4.** to crowd around and harass or attack. **5.** to fill with people; crowd.

mo•bile (mō′bəl, -bēl *for 1–4;* -bēl *for 5*), *adj.* **1.** capable of moving or being moved. **2.** utilizing a motor vehicle for ready movement: *a mobile library.* **3.** changing easily, as in expression or mood. **4.** permitting relatively free movement from one social class or level to another. —*n.* **5.** an abstract sculpture with delicately balanced units that move independently, as when stirred by a breeze. —**mo•bil′i•ty** (-bil′i tē), *n.*

Mo•bile (mō bēl′, mō′bēl), *n.* a seaport in SW Alabama. 204,490.

mo′bile home′, *n.* a trailer designed for year-round living in one place.

mo′bile phone′, *n.* any wireless telephone that

operates over a relatively large area, as a cellular phone.

mo•bi•lize (mō′bə līz′), *v.t., v.i.,* **-lized, -liz•ing.** to assemble and organize for action or use, esp. for war. —**mo′bi•li•za′tion,** *n.* —**mo′bi•liz′er,** *n.*

mob•ster (mob′stər), *n.* a member of a criminal mob.

Mo•by Dick (mō′bē dik′), a novel (1851) by Herman Melville.

moc•ca•sin (mok′ə sin, -zən), *n.* **1.** a heelless shoe made of soft leather. **2.** a hard-soled shoe resembling a moccasin. **3.** COTTONMOUTH.

mo•cha (mō′kə), *n.* **1.** a choice variety of coffee orig. grown in Arabia. **2.** a flavoring obtained by blending coffee with chocolate.

mock (mok), *v.t.* **1.** to treat with ridicule or contempt. **2.** to mimic or imitate, esp. derisively. **3.** to challenge; defy. —*v.i.* **4.** to scoff; jeer. —*adj.* **5.** feigned: *a mock battle.* —**mock′er,** *n.* —**mock′er•y,** *n., pl.* **-er•ies.** —**mock′ing•ly,** *adv.*

mock′ing•bird′, *n.* any of several New World songbirds that mimic the calls of other birds.

mock′-up′ or **mock′up′,** *n.* a model, often full-size, for study, testing, or teaching.

mod (mod), *adj.* very modern, as in style or dress.

mod′al auxil′iary, *n.* any of a group of auxiliary verbs, in English including *can, could, may, might, shall, should, will, would,* and *must,* used with the base form of another verb to express distinctions of mood.

mode[1] (mōd), *n.* **1.** a manner of acting or doing; method. **2.** a particular type or form of something. —**mod′al,** *adj.* —**mo•dal′i•ty,** *n., pl.* **-ties.**

mode[2] (mōd), *n.* fashion or style, as in manners or dress.

mod•el (mod′l), *n., adj., v.,* **-eled, -el•ing** or (*esp. Brit.*) **-elled, -el•ling.** —*n.* **1.** a standard or example for imitation or comparison. **2.** a representation, usu. in miniature. **3.** an image, as in clay, to be reproduced in more durable material. **4.** a person whose occupation is posing for artists or photographers. **5.** a person employed to wear and display clothing. **6.** a style or design of a particular product. —*adj.* **7.** serving as or worthy to serve as a model. **8.** being a miniature version of something: *a model ship.* —*v.t.* **9.** to form or plan according to a model. **10.** to make a miniature model of. **11.** to display, esp. by wearing: *to model dresses.* —*v.i.* **12.** to be employed as a model. —**mod′el•er,** *n.*

mo•dem (mō′dəm, -dem), *n.* **1.** an electronic device that makes possible the transmission of data to or from a computer via telephone or other communication lines. —*v.t.* **2.** to send (information, data, or the like) via a modem. [*mo(dulator)-dem(odulator)*]

mod•er•ate (*adj., n.* mod′ər it; *v.* -ə rāt′), *adj., n., v.,* **-at•ed, -at•ing.** —*adj.* **1.** not extreme, excessive, or intense. **2.** average in quantity, extent, or amount. **3.** mediocre or fair. **4.** calm or mild, as of the weather. —*n.* **5.** a person who holds moderate opinions, as in politics. —*v.t., v.i.* **6.** to make or become moderate. **7.** to preside over or act as moderator. —**mod′er•ate•ly,** *adv.* —**mod′er•a′tion,** *n.*

mod′er•a′tor, *n.* a person who presides over a meeting, discussion, or debate.

mod•ern (mod′ərn), *adj.* **1.** of or characteristic of present and recent time; contemporary. —*n.* **2.** a person of modern times. **3.** a person with modern views and tastes. —**mo•der′ni•ty,** *n.* —**mod′ern•ly,** *adv.* —**mod′ern•ness,** *n.*

Mod′ern Eng′lish, *n.* the English language since c1475.

mod′ern•ism, *n.* **1.** modern character, tendencies, or values. **2.** a modern usage or characteristic. **3.** estrangement or divergence from the past in the arts or literature occurring esp. in the 20th century. —**mod′ern•ist,** *n., adj.* —**mod′ern•is′tic,** *adj.*

mod′ern•ize, *v.t., v.i.,* **-ized, -iz•ing.** to make or become modern. —**mod′ern•i•za′tion,** *n.*

mod•est (mod′ist), *adj.* **1.** having or showing a moderate estimate of oneself. **2.** free from ostentation; unpretentious. **3.** having or showing regard for the decencies of behavior, speech, and dress. **4.** limited in amount, size, or extent. —**mod′est•ly,** *adv.* —**mod′es•ty,** *n.*

Mo•des•to (mə des′tō), *n.* a city in central California. 176,357.

mod•i•cum (mod′i kəm), *n.* a moderate or small amount.

mod•i•fy (mod′ə fī′), *v.t.,* **-fied, -fy•ing. 1.** to change somewhat; alter partially. **2.** (of a word, phrase, or clause) to limit or particularize the meaning of. **3.** to reduce in degree or extent. —**mod′i•fi•ca′tion,** *n.* —**mod′i•fi′er,** *n.*

Mo•di•glia•ni (mō dē′lē ä′nē, mō′dēl yä′-), *n.* Amedeo, 1884–1920, Italian painter in France.

mod•ish (mō′dish), *adj.* fashionable; stylish. —**mod′ish•ness,** *n.*

mod•u•lar (moj′ə lər), *adj.* **1.** of a module. **2.** composed of standardized units or sections.

mod′u•late′ (-lāt′), *v.,* **-lat•ed, -lat•ing.** —*v.t.* **1.** to regulate by or adjust to a proper measure or proportion. **2.** to cause the amplitude, frequency, phase, or intensity of (a carrier wave) to vary. —*v.i.* **3.** to move harmonically from one musical key to a related one. —**mod′u•la′tion,** *n.* —**mod′u•la′tor,** *n.*

mod•ule (moj′ōōl), *n.* **1.** a component, frequently interchangeable with others, for assembly into an integrated system. **2.** a self-contained segment of a spacecraft, designed for a particular task.

mo•dus op•e•ran•di (mō′dəs op′ə ran′dē, -dī), *n., pl.* **mo•di operandi** (mō′dē, -dī). a method of working or operating. [< L]

Mo•ga•di•shu (mō′gə dē′shōō), *n.* the capital of Somalia, in the S part. 444,882.

mo•gul¹ (mō′gəl), *n.* a bump on a ski slope.

mo•gul² (mō′gəl), *n.* a powerful or influential person.

mo•hair (mō′hâr′), *n.* **1.** the hair of the Angora goat. **2.** a fabric made from mohair.

Mo•ham•med (mōō ham′id, -hä′mid, mō-), *n.* MUHAMMAD.

Mo•ham′med•an (-i dn), *adj.* **1.** of Muhammad or Islam; Muslim. —*n.* **2.** an adherent of Islam; Muslim. —**Mo•ham′med•an•ism,** *n.* —**Usage.** See MUSLIM.

Mo•hawk (mō′hôk), *n., pl.* **-hawk, -hawks.** a member of an American Indian people orig. residing in the Mohawk River valley in New York.

Mo•he•gan (mō hē′gən), *n., pl.* **-gan, -gans.** a member of an American Indian people of E Connecticut.

Mo•hi′can (-hē′kən), *n., pl.* **-can, -cans.** MOHEGAN.

moi•e•ty (moi′i tē), *n., pl.* **-ties. 1.** a half. **2.** a portion, part, or share.

moil (moil), *v.i.* to work hard; drudge.

moi•ré (mwä rā′, mô-), *n., pl.* **-rés.** a fabric, as of silk, with a watery or wavelike appearance.

moist (moist), *adj.,* **-er, -est.** slightly wet; damp. —**moist′ly,** *adv.* —**moist′ness,** *n.*

mois•ten (moi′sən), *v.t., v.i.* to make or become moist. —**moist′en•er,** *n.*

mois′ture (-chər), *n.* condensed or diffused liquid, esp. water.

mois′tur•ize′, *v.t.,* **-ized, -iz•ing.** to add moisture to. —**mois′tur•iz′er,** *n.*

Mo•ja′ve (or **Mo•ha′ve**) **Des′ert** (mō hä′vē), *n.* a desert in SE California.

mo•lar (mō′lər), *n.* **1.** a tooth with a broad biting surface adapted for grinding. —*adj.* **2.** of the molar teeth.

mo•las•ses (mə las′iz), *n.* a thick syrup produced during the refining of sugar.

mold¹ (mōld), *n.* **1.** a hollow form for shaping something in a molten or plastic state. **2.** something formed in or on a mold. **3.** a frame on which something is formed or made. **4.** proper form. **5.** distinctive nature, character, or type. —*v.t.* **6.** to shape or form in or as if in a mold. —**mold′a•ble,** *adj.* —**mold′er,** *n.*

mold² (mōld), *n.* **1.** an often downy or furry growth of minute fungi on vegetable or animal matter. **2.** a

fungus that produces mold. —*v.i.* **3.** to become moldy.

mold³ (mōld), *n.* loose, crumbly earth rich in organic matter.

Mol•da•vi•a (mol dā′vē ə), *n.* **1.** a region in NE Romania. **2.** former name of MOLDOVA. —**Mol•da′vi•an,** *adj., n.*

mold′board′, *n.* the curved metal plate in a plow that turns over the earth.

mold′er, *v.i.* to turn to dust by natural decay; crumble.

mold′ing, *n.* **1.** the act or process of shaping in a mold. **2.** something molded. **3.** an ornamental strip of contoured material, esp. wood.

Mol•do•va (môl dō′və), *n.* a republic in SE Europe, NE of Romania: formerly a part of the USSR. 4,475,232. —**Mol•do′van,** *adj., n.*

mold′y, *adj.,* **-i•er, -i•est. 1.** overgrown or covered with mold. **2.** musty, as from decay or age. —**mold′i•ness,** *n.*

mole¹ (mōl), *n.* **1.** a small burrowing mammal with velvety fur and very small eyes. **2.** a spy who is part of and works from within the ranks of an enemy governmental staff or intelligence agency.

mole² (mōl), *n.* a small, usu. dark-colored, slightly elevated blemish on the human skin.

mole³ (mōl), *n.* a massive stone structure set up in the sea as a breakwater, pier, or jetty.

mol•e•cule (mol′ə kyōōl′), *n.* the smallest physical unit of an element or compound, consisting of one or more like atoms in an element and two or more different atoms in a compound. —**mo•lec•u•lar** (mə-lek′yə lər), *adj.*

mole′hill′, *n.* a small mound of earth dug up by a mole.

mole′skin′, *n.* **1.** the fur of the mole. **2.** a strong, heavy cotton fabric with a suedelike finish.

mo•lest (mə lest′), *v.t.* **1.** to bother or annoy. **2.** to make indecent sexual advances to. —**mo•les•ta•tion** (mō′le stā′shən, mol′e-), *n.* —**mo•lest′er,** *n.*

Mo•lière (mōl yâr′), *n.* (*Jean Baptiste Poquelin*) 1622–73, French playwright.

moll (mol), *n. Slang.* a female companion of a criminal.

mol•li•fy (mol′ə fī′), *v.t.,* **-fied, -fy•ing. 1.** to soften in feeling or temper. **2.** to mitigate; reduce. —**mol′li•fi•ca′tion,** *n.*

mol•lusk (mol′əsk), *n.* any of a large group of invertebrates with a soft body usu. protected by a shell, and including snails, squids, and octopuses.

mol•ly•cod•dle (mol′ē kod′l), *v.,* **-dled, -dling,** *n.* —*v.t.* **1.** to coddle; pamper. —*n.* **2.** a coddled man or boy. —**mol′ly•cod′dler,** *n.*

Mo•loch (mō′lok, mol′ək), *n.* a deity who was propitiated by the sacrificial burning of children. II Kings 23:10; Jer. 32:35.

molt (mōlt), *v.i.* **1.** to cast or shed an outer layer or covering, as feathers or skin, in the process of renewal or growth. —*n.* **2.** the act or process of molting. —**molt′er,** *n.*

mol′ten, *adj.* liquefied or fused by heat.

mo•lyb•de•num (mə lib′də nəm), *n.* a silver-white metallic element used as an alloy. *Symbol:* Mo; *at. wt.:* 95.94; *at. no.:* 42.

mom (mom), *n. Informal.* mother.

mo•ment (mō′mənt), *n.* **1.** a very short period of time; instant. **2.** a particular time, esp. the present. **3.** importance or consequence. **4.** a time of success, excellence, or satisfaction.

mo•men•tar•i•ly (mō′mən târ′ə lē, mō′mən ter′-), *adv.* **1.** for a moment. **2.** at any moment. **3.** instantly.

mo′men•tar′y, *adj.* **1.** lasting but a moment. **2.** likely to occur at any moment.

mo′ment of truth′, *n.* the moment at which one's character, skill, etc., is put to an extreme test; critical moment.

mo•men′tous, *adj.* of great importance or consequence. —**mo•men′tous•ly,** *adv.* —**mo•men′tous•ness,** *n.*

mo•men'tum (-təm), n., pl. -ta (-tə), -tums. 1. force or speed of movement; impetus. 2. the product of the mass of a body and its velocity.

mom•my (mom'ē), n., pl. -mies. Informal. mother.

mom'my track', n. a career path for women who are willing to forgo some promotions or raises so as to spend more time with their children.

Mon., 1. Monday. 2. Monsignor.

Mon•a•co (mon'ə kō', mə nä'kō), n. a principality on the Mediterranean coast, bordering SE France. 31,892.

mon•arch (mon'ərk, -ärk), n. 1. a hereditary sovereign, as a king or emperor. 2. one holding a dominant position. 3. a large, deep orange butterfly with black and white markings. [< LL < Gk monárchēs sole ruler] —mo•nar•chi•cal (mə när'ki kəl), mo•nar'chic, adj.

mon'ar•chism, n. advocacy of monarchy. —mon'ar•chist, n., adj. —mon'ar•chist'ic, adj.

mon'ar•chy, n., pl. -chies. 1. government by a monarch. 2. a state ruled by a monarch.

mon•as•ter•y (mon'ə ster'ē), n., pl. -ter•ies. a residence for a community of persons, esp. monks, under religious vows.

mo•nas•tic (mə nas'tik), adj. of or characteristic of monks, nuns, or monasteries. —mo•nas'ti•cism, n.

mon•au•ral (mon ôr'əl), adj. MONOPHONIC.

Mon•day (mun'dā, -dē), n. the second day of the week.

mon•de•green (mon'di grēn'), n. a word or phrase resulting from a misinterpretation of one that has been heard. [coined by author S. Wright fr. the line laid him on the green, interpreted as Lady Mondegreen, in a Scottish ballad]

mon•do (mon'dō), Slang. —adv. 1. very; extremely: mondo cool. —adj. 2. large; big: a mondo history paper.

Mon•dri•an (môn'drē än', mon'-), n. Piet (pēt), 1872–1944, Dutch painter.

Mo•net (mō nā'), n. Claude, 1840–1926, French painter.

mon•e•tar•y (mon'i ter'ē, mun'-), adj. 1. of the coinage or currency of a country. 2. of money; pecuniary. —mon'e•tar'i•ly (-tär'ə lē), adv.

mon•ey (mun'ē), n., pl. mon•eys, mon•ies. 1. a circulating medium of exchange, including coins and paper money. 2. money or property as a measure of wealth. —Proverb. 3. Money begets money, those who have money are likely to accumulate more.

mon'ey•bag', n. 1. a bag for money. 2. moneybags, (used with a sing. v.) Informal. a wealthy person.

mon'eyed, adj. 1. having much money; wealthy. 2. of the wealthy.

mon'ey•lend'er, n. one whose business is lending money at interest.

mon'ey•mak'er, n. 1. a person who is successful at making money. 2. something that yields a large profit. —mon'ey•mak'ing, adj., n.

mon'ey or'der, n. an order for the payment of money, as one issued by one bank or post office and payable at another.

mon•ger (mung'gər, mong'-), n. 1. a person involved with something in a petty or contemptible way: a gossipmonger. 2. Chiefly Brit. a dealer or trader: fishmongers.

Mon•gol (mong'gəl, -gōl, mon'-), n. 1. a member of one of the pastoral tribes of Mongolia. 2. MONGOLOID (def. 3). 3. MONGOLIAN (def. 2).

Mon'gol Em'pire, n. an empire founded in the 12th century by Genghis Khan, encompassing the larger part of Asia and extending westward to the Dnieper River in E Europe.

Mon•go•li•a (mong gō'lē ə, mon-), n. a region in Asia including Inner Mongolia in China and the Mongolian People's Republic.

Mon•go'li•an, n. 1. a native of Mongolia. 2. a family of languages spoken in Mongolia. 3. MONGOLOID (def. 3). —adj. 4. of Mongolia, its inhabitants, or their languages. 5. MONGOLOID (def. 1).

Mongo'lian Peo'ple's Repub'lic, n. a republic in E central Asia. 2,538,211.

Mon•gol'ic (-gol'ik), adj. MONGOLOID (def. 1).

mon•gol•ism (mong'gə liz'əm, mon'-), n. (sometimes cap.) DOWN SYNDROME.

Mon•gol•oid (mong'gə loid', mon'-), adj. 1. of, designating, or characteristic of one of the traditional racial divisions of humankind, marked by yellowish complexion, straight black hair, and high cheekbones, and including the Mongols, Chinese, Japanese, etc. 2. (often l.c.) of or affected with Down syndrome. —n. 3. a member of the Mongoloid race. 4. (often l.c.) a person affected with Down syndrome.

mon•goose (mong'gōōs', mon'-), n., pl. -goos•es. a ferretlike carnivore of India that is noted for its ability to kill cobras.

mon•grel (mung'grəl, mong'-), n. an animal or plant, esp. a dog, resulting from an uncontrolled or accidental crossing of breeds or varieties.

mon•ied (mun'ēd), adj. MONEYED.

mon'ies, n. a pl. of MONEY.

mon•i•ker or mon•ick•er (mon'i kər), n. Slang. a name or nickname.

mon•ism (mon'iz əm, mō'niz əm), n. a metaphysical theory that reality consists of a single element. —mon'ist, n. —mo•nis•tic (mə nis'tik, mō-), adj.

mo•ni•tion (mə nish'ən, mō-), n. an admonition; warning.

mon•i•tor (mon'i tər) n. 1. a student appointed to assist a teacher. 2. a device for observing, detecting, or recording the operation of a machine or system. 3. Radio and Television. a receiver for monitoring transmissions. 4. a component with a display screen for viewing computer data. 5. a. a former U.S. steam-propelled, armored warship of very low freeboard. b. (cap., italics) the first of such warships, used by Union forces against the Merrimack in 1862. —v.t. 6. to check the quality of (transmitted signals) on a receiving set. 7. to observe, record, or detect with instruments. 8. to watch closely; keep track of.

mon•i•to•ry (mon'i tôr'ē), adj. serving to warn; admonitory.

monk (mungk), n. a man who is a member of a religious order and usu. lives in a monastery.

mon•key (mung'kē), n., pl. -keys, v., -keyed, -key•ing. —n. 1. a primate mammal, excluding humans, characterized by a flattened face and usu. a long tail. —v.i. 2. Informal. to trifle idly; fool.

mon'key busi'ness, n. mischievous or improper behavior.

mon'key•shine', n. Often, -shines. a playful trick.

Mon'key Tri'al, n. See under SCOPES.

mon'key wrench', n. a wrench with an adjustable jaw.

mon•o¹ (mon'ō), n. MONONUCLEOSIS.

mon•o² (mon'ō), adj. MONOPHONIC.

mono-, a combining form meaning one, single, or lone (monochromatic).

mon•o•chro•mat•ic (mon'ə krō mat'ik, -ō krə-), adj. 1. of or having one color. 2. of or consisting of radiation of a single wavelength.

mon•o•chrome (mon'ə krōm'), adj. being or made in shades of a single color.

mon•o•cle (mon'ə kəl), n. an eyeglass for one eye. —mon'o•cled, adj.

mon•o•clo•nal (mon'ə klōn'l), adj. pertaining to cells or cell products derived from a single biological clone: monoclonal antibodies.

mon•o•cot•y•le•don (mon'ə kot'l ēd'n), n. a plant characterized by an embryo containing a single seed leaf. —mon'o•cot'y•le'don•ous, adj.

mo•noc•u•lar (mə nok'yə lər), adj. 1. having one eye. 2. of or for the use of only one eye.

mon•o•dy (mon'ə dē), n., pl. -dies. a poem in which the poet or speaker laments another's death. —mo•nod•ic (mə nod'ik), adj. —mon'o•dist, n.

mo•nog•a•my (mə nog'ə mē), n. the practice or condition of having only one spouse at a time. —mo•nog'a•mist, n. —mo•nog'a•mous, adj. —mo•nog'a•mous•ly, adv.

mon·o·gram (mon'ə gram'), *n.*, *v.*, **-grammed, -gram·ming.** —*n.* **1.** a design consisting of the combined initials of a name. —*v.t.* **2.** to decorate with a monogram.

mon'o·graph', *n.* a learned treatise on a particular subject.

mon'o·lin'gual, *adj.* knowing, able to use, spoken, or written in only one language.

mon'o·lith (-lith), *n.* **1.** a single block of stone, esp. one formed into an obelisk or column. **2.** something having a uniform, massive, or inflexible quality or character. —**mon'o·lith'ic**, *adj.*

mon'o·logue' or **-log'** (-lôg', -log'), *n.* **1. a.** a dramatic or comic piece delivered by a single performer. **b.** SOLILOQUY (def. 1). **2.** a prolonged talk or discourse by a single speaker. —**mon·o·log·ist** (mon'ə lô'gist, -log'ist, mə nol'ə jist), **mon·o·logu·ist** (mon'ə-lô'gist, -log'ist), *n.*

mon'o·ma'ni·a, *n.* an obsessive zeal for or interest in a single thing. —**mon'o·ma'ni·ac'**, *n.*

mon·o·mer (mon'ə mər), *n.* a molecule capable of reacting with others to form a polymer.

Mo·non·ga·he·la (mə nong'gə hē'lə), *n.* a river flowing from N West Virginia through SW Pennsylvania into the Ohio River. 128 mi. (205 km) long.

mon'o·nu'cle·o'sis (-noo'klē ō'sis, -nyoo'-), *n.* an infectious disease characterized by fever, swelling of lymph nodes, and an abnormally large number of certain leukocytes in the blood.

mon'o·phon'ic (-fon'ik), *adj.* of or noting a system of sound recording and reproduction using only a single channel.

mo·nop·o·ly (mə nop'ə lē), *n.*, *pl.* **-lies. 1.** exclusive control, as of a commodity or service. **2.** a commodity or service controlled by one individual or group. **3.** an individual or group that has a monopoly. —**mo·nop'o·list**, *n.* —**mo·nop'o·lis'tic**, *adj.* —**mo·nop'o·li·za'tion**, *n.* —**mo·nop'o·lize'**, *v.t.*, **-lized, -liz·ing.**

mon·o·rail (mon'ə rāl'), *n.* a single rail functioning as a track for wheeled vehicles.

mon·o·so·di·um glu·ta·mate (mon'ə sō'dē əm gloo'tə māt'), *n.* a white crystalline powder used to intensify the flavor of foods.

mon'o·syl'la·ble, *n.* a word of one syllable. —**mon'o·syl·lab'ic**, *adj.*

mon'o·the·ism, *n.* the doctrine or belief that there is only one God. —**mon'o·the'ist**, *n.*, *adj.* —**mon'o·the·is'tic**, *adj.*

mon'o·tone', *n.* a vocal utterance or series of speech sounds in one unvaried tone.

mo·not·o·nous (mə not'n əs), *adj.* **1.** tediously unvarying. **2.** sounded or uttered in one unvarying tone. —**mo·not'o·nous·ly**, *adv.* —**mo·not'o·ny**, *n.*

mon·ox·ide (mon ok'sīd, mə nok'-), *n.* an oxide containing one oxygen atom in each molecule.

Mon·roe (mən rō'), *n.* **James,** 1758–1831, 5th president of the U.S. 1817–25.

Monroe' Doc'trine, *n.* the doctrine, stated by President Monroe in 1823, that the U.S. opposed further European intervention in the Western Hemisphere.

Mon·ro·vi·a (mən rō'vē ə), *n.* the capital of Liberia. 425,000.

mon·sei·gneur (môn se nyœr'), *n.*, *pl.* **mes·sei·gneurs** (mā se nyœr'). a French title of honor for princes and bishops.

mon·sieur (mə syœ'), *n.*, *pl.* **mes·sieurs** (me syœ'). a French title corresponding to *Mr.* or *sir.*

mon·si·gnor (mon sē'nyər, mon'sē nyôr', môn'-), *n.*, *pl.* **mon·si·gnors, mon·si·gno·ri** (môn'sē nyôr'ē). a title conferred on certain Roman Catholic prelates.

mon·soon (mon soon'), *n.* **1.** a seasonal wind of the Indian Ocean and S Asia. **2.** the season during which the SW monsoon blows. —**mon·soon'al**, *adj.*

mon·ster (mon'stər), *n.* **1.** a grossly anomalous or markedly malformed animal or plant. **2.** an imaginary creature of strange appearance. **3.** a wicked or cruel person. **4.** a huge animal or thing. —**mon·**

stros'i·ty (-stros'i tē), *n.*, *pl.* **-ties.** —**mon'strous**, *adj.* —**mon'strous·ly**, *adv.*

mon·strance (mon'strəns), *n.* a receptacle used in the Roman Catholic Church for the display of the consecrated Host.

Mont., Montana.

mon·tage (mon täzh'; *Fr.* môn tAzh'), *n.*, *pl.* **-tag·es** (-tä'zhiz; *Fr.* -tazh'). **1.** the combining of pictorial or other artistic elements from different sources in a single composition. **2.** *Motion Pictures, Television.* juxtaposition or partial superimposition of several shots to form a single image.

Mon·taigne (mon tān'), *n.* **Michel de,** 1533–92, French essayist.

Mon·tan·a (mon tan'ə), *n.* a state in the NW United States. 879,372. *Cap.*: Helena. *Abbr.*: MT, Mont. —**Mon·tan'an**, *adj.*, *n.*

Mont·calm (mont käm'; *Fr.* môn-), *n.* **Louis Joseph,** 1712–59, French general in Canada.

Mon·te Car·lo (mon'tē kär'lō, -ti), *n.* a town in Monaco: gambling resort. 13,154.

Mon·te'go Bay' (mon tē'gō), *n.* a city in NW Jamaica: seaside resort. 70,265.

Mon·te·ne·gro (mon'tə nē'grō, -neg'rō), *n.* a constituent republic of Yugoslavia, in the SW part. 615,267. —**Mon'te·ne'grin** (-nē'grin, -neg'rin), *adj.*, *n.*

Mon·ter·rey (mon'tə rā'), *n.* a city in NE Mexico. 1,916,472.

Mon·tes·so·ri (mon'tə sôr'ē), *n.* **Maria,** 1870–1952, Italian educator.

Montesso'ri meth'od, *n.* a system for teaching children to be self-motivated learners, with special emphasis on sensory training. Also called **Montesso'ri sys'tem.**

Mon·te·vi·de·o (mon'tə vi dā'ō), *n.* the capital of Uruguay. 1,309,100.

Mont·gom·er·y (mont gum'ə rē), *n.* the capital of Alabama. 195,471.

month (munth), *n.* **1.** any of the 12 parts into which the calendar year is divided. **2.** a period of four weeks or 30 days.

month'ly, *adj.*, *n.*, *pl.* **-lies**, *adv.* —*adj.* **1.** done, happening, or appearing once a month. **2.** computed or payable by the month. —*n.* **3.** a monthly periodical. —*adv.* **4.** once a month.

Mon·ti·cel·lo (mon'ti chel'ō, -sel'ō), *n.* the estate and residence of Thomas Jefferson, in central Virginia, near Charlottesville.

Mont·pel·ier (mont pēl'yər), *n.* the capital of Vermont. 8,247.

Mont·re·al (mon'trē ôl', mun'-), *n.* a port in S Quebec, in E Canada. 1,015,420.

mon·u·ment (mon'yə mənt), *n.* **1.** something, as a pillar, erected in memory of a person or event. **2.** something, as a building, surviving from a past age and preserved for its historical or archaeological importance.

mon'u·men'tal, *adj.* **1.** of or serving as a monument. **2.** exceptionally great: *monumental egotism.* **3.** of enduring significance. —**mon'u·men'tal·ly**, *adv.*

moo (moo), *n.*, *pl.* **moos**, *v.*, **mooed, moo·ing.** —*n.* **1.** the deep, low sound characteristic of a cow. —*v.i.* **2.** to utter a moo.

mooch (mooch), *v.t.*, *v.i. Slang.* to scrounge; cadge. —**mooch'er**, *n.*

mood[1] (mood), *n.* **1.** a person's emotional state or outlook. **2.** a prevailing emotional tone or general attitude.

mood[2] (mood), *n.* a set of categories of the verb serving to indicate whether the verb expresses a fact, possibility, wish, or command.

mood'y, *adj.*, **-i·er, -i·est. 1.** given to moods, esp. gloomy or sullen moods. **2.** gloomy; sullen. —**mood'i·ly**, *adv.* —**mood'i·ness**, *n.*

moon (moon), *n.* **1.** the earth's natural satellite. **2.** a planetary satellite. **3.** something shaped like an orb or a crescent. —*v.i.* **4.** to act abstractedly or dreamily.

moon'beam', *n.* a ray of moonlight.

moon'light', *n.* **1.** the light of the moon. —*v.i.* **2.**

to work at an additional job after one's regular one. —**moon′light′er**, *n.* —**moon′lit′** (-lit′), *adj.*

moon′scape′ (-skāp′), *n.* the appearance or an artistic representation of the surface of the moon.

moon′shine′, *n.* **1.** *Informal.* smuggled or illicitly distilled liquor. **2.** empty or foolish talk. **3.** MOONLIGHT.

moon′shot′, *n.* the launching of a rocket or spacecraft to the moon.

moon′stone′, *n.* an opalescent, pearly blue variety of feldspar used as a gem.

moon′struck′, *adj.* **1.** mentally deranged. **2.** dreamily romantic or bemused.

moon′walk′, *n.* an exploratory walk by an astronaut on the surface of the moon.

moor[1] (mŏŏr), *n.* a tract of open, peaty wasteland, often overgrown with heath.

moor[2] (mŏŏr), *v.t., v.i.* to secure or be secured in place, as by cables and anchors or by lines.

Moor (mŏŏr), *n.* a member of a North African people of mixed Arab and Berber descent who conquered Spain in the 8th century. —**Moor′ish**, *adj.*

Moore (mŏŏr, môr, mōr), *n.* **Clement Clarke,** 1779–1863, U.S. scholar and writer.

moor′ing, *n.* **1. moorings,** a place where a ship, boat, or aircraft may be moored. **2.** Usu., **moorings.** a source of stability or security.

moose (mōōs), *n., pl.* **moose.** a large deer of the Northern Hemisphere.

moot (mōōt), *adj.* **1.** open to discussion or debate. **2.** of little or no practical value or meaning; purely academic.

mop (mop), *n., v.,* **mopped, mop•ping.** —*n.* **1.** a device consisting of absorbent material, as a sponge, fastened to a handle and used esp. for washing floors. **2.** a thick mass of hair. —*v.t.* **3.** to clean or remove with or as if with a mop. **4. mop up,** to complete or finish.

mope (mōp), *v.i.,* **moped, mop•ing.** to be sunk in dejection or apathy; brood. —**mop′er,** *n.* —**mop′ey, mop′y,** *adj.,* **-i•er, -i•est.** —**mop′ish,** *adj.*

mo•ped (mō′ped′), *n.* a motorized bicycle with pedals. [≪ Sw *(trampcykel med) mo(tor och) ped-(aler)* pedal cycle with engine and pedals]

mop•pet (mop′it), *n.* a young child.

mo•raine (mə rān′), *n.* a deposit of material such as boulders, gravel, and sand left by a glacier.

mor•al (môr′əl, mor′-), *adj.* **1.** of or concerned with the principles of right and wrong conduct. **2.** conforming to principles of right conduct. **3.** capable of recognizing and conforming to the rules of right conduct. **4.** acting on the mind, feelings, will, or character: *moral support.* **5.** based on strong probability: *a moral certainty.* —*n.* **6.** a moral teaching or practical lesson, as in a fable. **7. morals,** principles or habits with respect to right or wrong conduct. —**mor′al•ly,** *adv.*

mo•rale (mə ral′), *n.* emotional or mental condition, as of cheerfulness, with respect to work or a duty.

mor•al•ist (môr′ə list, mor′-), *n.* **1.** a person who teaches morals. **2.** a person concerned with regulating the morals of others. —**mor′al•is′tic,** *adj.*

mo•ral•i•ty (mə ral′i tē, mô-), *n., pl.* **-ties. 1.** conformity to the rules of right conduct. **2.** moral quality or conduct. **3.** a doctrine of morals.

mor•al•ize (môr′ə līz′, mor′-), *v.i.,* **-ized, -iz•ing.** to reflect on or discuss moral matters, esp. in a self-righteous or tiresome way. —**mor′al•i•za′tion,** *n.* —**mor′al•iz′er,** *n.*

Mor′al Major′ity, *n.* former name of the LIBERTY FOUNDATION.

mo•rass (mə ras′), *n.* **1.** a marsh or bog. **2.** something from which it is difficult to free oneself.

mor•a•to•ri•um (môr′ə tôr′ē əm, mor′-), *n., pl.* **-to•ri•a** (-tôr′ē ə), **-to•ri•ums.** a suspension of activity.

Mo•ra•vi•a (mō rä′vē ə, -rä′-, mō-), *n.* a region in the E part of the Czech Republic.

Mo•ra•vi•an (mô rä′vē ən, mō-), *n.* a member of a

Christian denomination descended from the Bohemian Brethren.

mo•ray (môr′ā, mô rā′), *n., pl.* **-rays.** a tropical eel lacking pectoral fins.

mor•bid (môr′bid), *adj.* **1.** suggesting an unhealthy mental attitude; unwholesomely gloomy. **2.** gruesome; grisly. **3.** of or characteristic of disease. —**mor′bid•ly,** *adv.* —**mor•bid′i•ty, mor′bid•ness,** *n.*

mor•dant (môr′dnt), *adj.* **1.** sharply caustic; biting. **2.** burning; corrosive. —**mor′dan•cy,** *n.*

Mor•de•cai (môr′di kī′, -KHĪ′), *n.* the cousin of Esther who delivered the Jews from destruction. Esther 2–8.

More (môr, mōr), *n.* **Sir Thomas,** 1478–1535, English statesman and author: canonized in 1935.

mo•rel (mə rel′), *n.* an edible mushroom with a deeply furrowed cap.

mo•rel•lo (mə rel′ō), *n., pl.* **-los.** a variety of sour cherry having dark-colored skin and juice.

Mo•re′no Val′ley (mə rē′nō), *n.* a city in SW California. 139,311.

more•o′ver, *adv.* in addition; besides.

mo•res (môr′āz, -ēz), *n.pl.* the fundamental moral views of a social group.

Mor•gan[1] (môr′gən), *n.* any of a breed of light carriage and saddle horses descended from the stallion Justin Morgan. [after the original sire, owned by J. *Morgan* (1747–98)]

Mor•gan[2] (môr′gən), *n.* **1. J(ohn) P(ierpont),** 1837–1913, U.S. financier and philanthropist. **2.** his son **John Pierpont,** 1867–1943, U.S. financier.

morgue (môrg), *n.* **1.** a place in which dead bodies are kept pending identification or burial. **2.** a reference file, as of clippings, esp. in a newspaper office.

Mo•ri•ah (mô rī′ə, mō-), *n.* **1.** a mountainous region in S Palestine, where Abraham prepared to sacrifice Isaac. Gen. 22:3. **2.** a site identified with Zion, where Solomon built the Temple. II Chron. 3:1.

mor•i•bund (môr′ə bund′, mor′-), *adj.* dying.

Mor•mon (môr′mən), *n.* the popular name given to a member of the Church of Jesus Christ of Latter-day Saints. —**Mor′mon•ism,** *n.*

morn (môrn), *n.* morning.

morn′ing, *n.* **1.** the first part of the day, from dawn or from midnight to noon. **2.** an early period; beginning.

morn′ing glo′ry, *n.* a twining plant with funnel-shaped flowers that often open only in the morning.

morn′ing sick′ness, *n.* nausea occurring esp. in the early part of the day during the first months of pregnancy.

morn′ing star′, *n.* a bright planet, esp. Venus, seen in the east immediately before sunrise.

Mo•roc•co (mə rok′ō), *n.* **1.** a kingdom in NW Africa. 30,391,423. **2.** (*l.c.*) a pebble-grained leather made from goatskin. —**Mo•roc′can,** *n., adj.*

mo•ron (môr′on), *n.* **1.** a stupid person. **2.** (in a former classification of mental retardation) a person having an intelligence quotient of 50 to 69. —**mo•ron′ic** (mə ron′ik), *adj.* —**mo•ron′i•cal•ly,** *adv.*

mo•rose (mə rōs′), *adj.* **1.** gloomily or sullenly ill-humored. **2.** gloomy or sullen. —**mo•rose′ly,** *adv.* —**mo•rose′ness,** *n.*

mor•pheme (môr′fēm), *n.* a minimal grammatical unit that cannot be divided into smaller meaningful parts. —**mor•phe′mic,** *adj.*

mor•phine (môr′fēn), *n.* an addictive narcotic obtained from opium, used as a pain reliever or sedative.

morph•ing (môr′fing), *n.* the smooth transformation of one image into another by computer, as in a motion picture.

mor•phol•o•gy (môr fol′ə jē), *n.* **1.** the branch of biology that deals with the form and structure of organisms. **2.** the study of patterns of word formation in a language. —**mor′pho•log′i•cal,** *adj.*

Mor•ris (môr′is, mor′-), *n.* **1. Gouv•er•neur** (guv′-ər nēr′), 1752–1816, U.S. statesman. **2. Robert,** 1734–1806, U.S. financier and statesman, born in

England. **3. William,** 1834–96, English artist, poet, and writer.

Mor·ri·son (môr′ə sən, mor′-), *n.* **Toni** (*Chloe Anthony Wofford*), born 1931, U.S. novelist.

mor·row (môr′ō, mor′ō), *n. Literary.* the next day.

Morse (môrs), *n.* **Samuel F(inley) B(reese),** 1791–1872, U.S. artist and developer of the telegraph.

Morse′ code′, *n.* either of two systems of dots and dashes, short and long sounds, or flashes of light used to represent letters, numerals, etc.: used esp. in telegraphy. [after S. F. B. *Morse* (1791–1872), U.S. inventor]

mor·sel (môr′səl), *n.* **1.** a small piece or amount, esp. of food; bit. **2.** an appetizing dish; treat.

mor·tal (môr′tl), *adj.* **1.** subject to death. **2.** of human beings. **3.** implacable; relentless: *a mortal enemy.* **4.** severe; grievous: *mortal fear.* **5.** causing death; fatal: *a mortal wound.* **6.** involving spiritual death: *a mortal sin.* —*n.* **7.** a human being. —**mor′tal·ly,** *adv.*

mor·tal/i·ty, *n., pl.* **-ties. 1.** the state or condition of being subject to death. **2.** the relative frequency of deaths in a population.

mor′tal sin′, *n. Rom. Cath. Ch.* a willfully committed sin, as murder, serious enough to deprive the soul of divine grace. Compare VENIAL SIN.

mor·tar[1] (môr′tər), *n.* **1.** a bowl-shaped receptacle in which substances can be pounded or ground with a pestle. **2.** a short-barreled cannon for throwing shells at high angles.

mor·tar[2] (môr′tər), *n.* a mixture, esp. of lime or cement with sand and water, used as a bonding agent, as between bricks.

mor′tar·board′, *n.* **1.** a board, usu. square, used by masons to hold mortar. **2.** an academic cap with a square, flat top and a tassel.

mort·gage (môr′gij), *n., v.,* **-gaged, -gag·ing.** —*n.* **1.** a conveyance of an interest in property as security for the repayment of a loan. **2.** the deed by which a mortgage is effected. —*v.t.* **3.** to convey or place (property) under a mortgage. **4.** to place under an obligation; pledge. —**mort′ga·gee′** (-gə jē′), *n., pl.* **-gees.** —**mort′ga·gor, mort′gag·er,** *n.*

mor·ti·cian (môr tish′ən), *n.* FUNERAL DIRECTOR.

mor·ti·fy (môr′tə fī′), *v.t.,* **-fied, -fy·ing. 1.** to humiliate or shame. **2.** to subjugate (the body, passions, etc.) by abstinence, ascetic discipline, or self-inflicted suffering. —**mor′ti·fi·ca′tion,** *n.*

mor·tise (môr′tis), *n.* a notch, hole, or slot made in a piece of wood to receive a tenon.

Mor·ton (môr′tn), *n.* **1. Jelly Roll** (*Ferdinand Morton*), 1885–1941, U.S. jazz pianist, composer, and band leader. **2. William Thomas Green,** 1819–68, U.S. dentist: first to employ ether as an anesthetic.

mor·tu·ar·y (môr′chōō er′ē), *n., pl.* **-ar·ies.** FUNERAL HOME.

mos., months.

mo·sa·ic (mō zā′ik), *n.* **1.** a picture or decoration made of small, usu. colored inlaid pieces, as of stone or glass. **2.** the process of producing a mosaic. **3.** something resembling a mosaic.

Mosa′ic Law′, *n.* the ancient law of the Hebrews; the Law of Moses.

Mos·cow (mos′kō, -kou), *n.* the capital of the Russian Federation. 8,967,000.

Mo·ses (mō′ziz, -zis), *n.* the Hebrew prophet who led the Israelites out of Egypt and delivered the Law during their years in the desert.

mo·sey (mō′zē), *v.i., Informal.* to stroll in a leisurely way.

Mos·lem (moz′ləm, mos′-), *adj., n., pl.* **-lems, -lem.** MUSLIM. —**Usage.** See MUSLIM.

mosque (mosk, môsk), *n.* a Muslim place of public worship.

mos·qui·to (mə skē′tō), *n., pl.* **-toes, -tos.** an insect, the female of which sucks the blood of animals and humans.

moss (môs, mos), *n.* a tiny, leafy-stemmed plant that grows in tufts or mats, esp. on moist ground, tree trunks, and rocks. —**moss′y,** *adj.,* **-i·er, -i·est.**

moss′back′, *n. Informal.* a person holding very antiquated notions.

most (mōst), *adj., superl. of* **much** *or* **many** *with* **more** *as compar.* **1.** greatest, as in number: *the most votes.* **2.** the majority of: *most people.* —*n.* **3.** the greatest amount or degree: *the most we can do.* —*pron.* **4.** (*used with a sing. or pl. v.*) the greatest part; majority: *Most were pleased with the decision.* —*adv., superl. of* **much** *with* **more** *as compar.* **5.** in or to the greatest extent or degree: *most wisely.* **6.** very: *most puzzling.*

Most′ High′, *n.* God. Ps. 21:7; 91:1.

most·ly, *adv.* for the most part; in the main.

mote (mōt), *n.* a small particle or speck, esp. of dust.

mo·tel (mō tel′), *n.* a hotel for motorists, typically with rooms adjacent to an outside parking area.

mo·tet (mō tet′), *n.* an unaccompanied polyphonic choral composition usu. on a sacred text.

moth (môth, moth), *n., pl.* **moths** (môthz, mothz, môths, moths). any of numerous insects related to but distinguished from the butterflies by their feathery antennae and nocturnal habits.

moth′ball′, *n.* **1.** a small ball, esp. of naphthalene, placed in storage areas to repel moths from clothing. **2. in mothballs, a.** in storage. **b.** in a state of disuse.

moth·er (muth′ər), *n.* **1.** a female who bears or rears offspring; female parent. **2.** a woman in authority. **3.** something that gives rise to something else; source. —*adj.* **4.** of, characteristic of, or being a mother. —*v.t.* **5.** to give birth, origin, or rise to. **6.** to care for or protect like a mother. —**moth′er·hood′,** *n.* —**moth′er·less,** *adj.*

moth′er-in-law′, *n., pl.* **mothers-in-law.** the mother of one's husband or wife.

moth′er·land′, *n.* **1.** one's native land. **2.** the land of one's ancestors.

moth′er·ly, *adj.* of, characteristic of, or befitting a mother. —**moth′er·li·ness,** *n.*

Moth′er of God′, *n.* a title of the Virgin Mary.

moth′er-of-pearl′, *n.* a hard, iridescent substance that forms the inner layer of certain mollusk shells.

mo·tif (mō tēf′), *n.* a recurring subject, theme, or idea, esp. in a literary, artistic, or musical work.

mo·tile (mōt′l, mō′til), *adj. Biol.* capable of moving spontaneously. —**mo·til/i·ty,** *n.*

mo·tion (mō′shən), *n.* **1.** the action or process of moving. **2.** an expressive bodily movement; gesture. **3.** a formal proposal, esp. one made to a deliberative assembly. **4. in motion,** in active operation; moving. —*v.t., v.i.* **5.** to direct by or make a meaningful motion. —**mo′tion·less,** *adj.*

mo′tion pic′ture, *n.* **1.** a sequence of photographic images projected onto a screen in such rapid succession as to give the illusion of natural movement. **2.** a story, incident, etc., presented in this form.

mosque

mo′tion sick′ness, *n.* nausea and dizziness resulting from the effect of motion, as during car travel.

mo·ti·vate (mō′tə vāt′), *v.t.,* **-vat·ed, -vat·ing.** to provide with a motive; spur. —mo′ti•va′tion, n. —mo′ti•va′tion•al, adj. —mo′ti•va′tor, n.

mo′tive (-tiv), n. **1.** something that causes a person to act; incentive. **2.** MOTIF. —adj. **3.** of or causing motion. **4.** prompting to action.

mot•ley (mot′lē), adj., -li•er, -li•est. **1.** exhibiting diversity of elements; heterogeneous. **2.** being of different colors combined; variegated.

mo•to•cross (mō′tō krôs′, -kros′), n. a motorcycle race over a course of very rough terrain.

mo•tor (mō′tər), n. **1.** a comparatively small engine, esp. an internal-combustion engine, as in an automobile. **2.** something that imparts motion. **3.** a machine that converts electrical energy into mechanical energy. —adj. **4.** equipped with or operated by a motor. **5.** of, by, or for motor vehicles or motorists. **6.** causing or producing motion. **7.** of or involving muscular movement. —v.i. **8.** to ride in an automobile.

mo′tor•bike′, n. a small, lightweight motorcycle.

mo′tor•boat′, n. a boat propelled by an inboard or outboard motor.

mo′tor•cade′ (-kād′), n. a procession or parade of motor vehicles.

mo′tor•car′, n. AUTOMOBILE.

mo′tor•cy′cle, n. a two-wheeled motor vehicle. —mo′tor•cy′clist, n.

mo′tor home′, n. a van or trucklike vehicle outfitted as living quarters.

mo′tor•ist, n. a person who drives or travels in an automobile.

mo′tor•ize′, v.t., -ized, -iz•ing. **1.** to furnish with a motor. **2.** to supply with motor vehicles.

mo′tor•man, n., pl. -men. a person who drives an electrically operated vehicle, as a subway train.

mo′tor scoot′er, n. SCOOTER (def. 2).

mo′tor ve′hicle, n. a motor-driven conveyance, as an automobile, truck, or bus.

mot•tle (mot′l), v.t., -tled, -tling. to mark with blotches of a different color; spot.

mot•to (mot′ō), n., pl. -toes, -tos. **1.** a pithy expression of a guiding principle. **2.** a sentence, phrase, or word inscribed on something to express its spirit or purpose. [< It < LL muttum sound, utterance]

moue (mōō), n., pl. moues (mōō). a pouting grimace.

mould (mōld), n., v.t., v.i. Chiefly Brit. MOLD.

moult (mōlt), v.i., n. Chiefly Brit. MOLT.

mound (mound), n. **1.** a natural elevation of earth; knoll. **2.** an artificial elevation of earth; embankment. **3.** the slightly raised ground on which a baseball pitcher stands.

mount[1] (mount), v.t. **1.** to go up; ascend. **2.** to get up on (a platform, a horse, etc.). **3.** to place at an elevation. **4.** to organize and launch (an attack, campaign, etc.). **5.** to put into position for use. **6.** to fix on or in a support, backing, or setting: to mount a photograph. **7.** to prepare for exhibition or study as a specimen. —v.i. **8.** to increase in amount or intensity. **9.** to rise; ascend. **10.** to get up on something, as a platform. —n. **11.** a horse or other animal for riding. **12.** a support, backing, or setting on or in which something is mounted. —mount′a•ble, adj. —mount′er, n.

mount[2] (mount), n. a mountain.

moun•tain (moun′tn), n. **1.** a natural elevation of land higher than a hill. **2.** a huge amount.

moun′tain ash′, n. a small tree of the rose family, with white flowers and bright red to orange berries.

moun′tain bike′, n. a sturdy bicycle designed for off-road use.

moun′tain•eer′, n. **1.** an inhabitant of a mountainous district. **2.** a climber of mountains, esp. for sport. —v.i. **3.** to climb mountains.

moun′tain goat′, n. ROCKY MOUNTAIN GOAT.

moun′tain lau′rel, n. a North American shrub bearing clusters of rose to white flowers.

moun′tain li′on, n. COUGAR.

moun′tain•ous, adj. **1.** abounding in mountains. **2.** resembling a mountain; very large.

moun′tain•top′, n. the top of a mountain.

moun•te•bank (moun′tə bangk′), n. a charlatan.

mount′ing, n. a support or setting; mount.

mourn (môrn), v.i., v.t. to feel or express sorrow or grief (for). —mourn′er, n.

mourn′ers′ bench′, n. (at religious revival meetings) a seat at the front of the room, set apart for mourners or penitent sinners seeking salvation.

mourn′ful, adj. **1.** feeling, expressing, or causing sorrow or grief. **2.** gloomy or somber; sad. —mourn′ful•ly, adv. —mourn′ful•ness, n.

mourn′ing, n. **1.** the act of one who mourns. **2.** the manifestation of sorrow for a person's death, as the wearing of black. **3.** the period during which one grieves.

mouse (n. mous; v. also mouz), n., pl. mice, v., moused, mous•ing. —n. **1.** any of numerous small rodents with small ears and a long, thin tail. **2.** a quiet, timid person. **3.** a palm-sized device used to select items on a computer display screen and to control the cursor. —v.i. **4.** to hunt for or catch mice.

mouse′ pad′, n. a small typically foam rubber sheet used to provide a stable surface on which a computer mouse can be moved.

mous•er (mou′zər), n. an animal that catches mice.

mouse′trap′, n. a trap for catching mice.

mousse (mōōs), n. **1.** a sweetened dessert made with whipped cream, egg whites, and gelatin and chilled in a mold. **2.** a foamy preparation used to style the hair.

mous•tache (mus′tash, mə stash′), n. MUSTACHE.

mous•y or **-ey** (mou′sē, -zē), adj., -i•er, -i•est. resembling a mouse, as in being drab and colorless or meek and timid. —mous′i•ness, n.

mouth (n. mouth; v. mouth), n., pl. mouths (mouthz), v. **1.** the opening through which an animal takes in food. **2.** something, as an opening, resembling a mouth: the mouth of a cave. —v.t. **3.** to utter in a sonorous or pompous manner. **4.** to form (a word, sound, etc.) silently or indistinctly with the mouth. —Idiom. **5. down in** or **at the mouth,** dejected.

mouth′ful, n., pl. -fuls. **1.** the amount a mouth can hold. **2.** the amount taken into the mouth at one time. **3.** a remark of great truth or relevance.

mouth′ or′gan, n. HARMONICA.

mouth′piece′, n. **1.** a part, as of a musical instrument, applied to or held in the mouth. **2.** one that voices the opinions of others.

mouth′wash′, n. a solution, often containing an antiseptic or astringent, for cleaning the mouth.

mouth′-wa′tering, adj. appetizing, as in appearance or aroma.

mouth•y (mou′thē, -thē), adj., -i•er, -i•est. talkative, often in a bombastic manner. —mouth′i•ness, n.

mou•ton (mōō′ton), n. sheepskin processed to resemble seal or beaver.

mov•a•ble or **move•a•ble** (mōō′və bəl), adj. **1.** capable of being moved. **2.** Law. (of property) personal as distinguished from real. —n. **3.** something that is not fixed in place. **4.** Often, -bles. Law. an article of personal property.

move (mōōv), v., moved, mov•ing, n. —v.i. **1.** to pass from one place or position to another. **2.** to change one's place of residence or business. **3.** to advance or progress. **4.** to be active. **5.** to take action; proceed. **6.** to make a formal request, application, or proposal. —v.t. **7.** to cause to go from one place or position to another. **8.** to set or keep in motion. **9.** to prompt or impel to take action. **10.** to arouse the feelings of. **11.** to evacuate (the bowels). **12.** to propose formally, as for consideration by a deliberative assembly. **13. move in,** to begin to occupy a residence or workplace. —n. **14.** an act or instance of moving. **15.** an action toward an objective. **16.** (in chess, checkers, etc.) a player's right or turn to make a play. —Idiom. **17. on the move, a.** busy; active. **b.** moving from place to place. **c.** making progress; advancing.

move′ment, n. **1.** the act, process, or result of

moving. **2.** a shift in the position of troops or ships. **3.** a series of actions directed toward a particular end. **4.** a course, tendency, or trend. **5.** a group of people or organizations working toward or favoring a common goal. **6.** an evacuation of the bowels. **7.** the working parts of a mechanism, as a watch. **8.** *Music.* a principal division or section of a composition, as a sonata or symphony.

mov′er, *n.* **1.** one that moves. **2.** a person or company that moves household effects or office equipment from one place to another.

mov•ie (mōō′vē), *n.* **1.** MOTION PICTURE. **2. movies, a.** the motion-picture industry. **b.** the showing of a motion picture.

mow¹ (mō), *v.t.,* **mowed, mowed** or **mown, mow• ing. 1.** to cut down (grass, grain, etc.) with a scythe or a machine. **2.** to cut grass, grain, etc., from. **3. mow down, a.** to destroy or kill in great numbers. **b.** to overwhelm. —**mow′er,** *n.*

mow² (mou), *n.* the place in a barn where hay or grain is stored.

Mo•zam•bique (mō′zam bēk′, -zəm-), *n.* a republic in SE Africa. 18,165,476. —**Mo′zam•bi′can,** *n., adj.*

Mo•zart (mōt′särt), *n.* **Wolfgang Amadeus,** 1756– 91, Austrian composer. —**Mo•zar′te•an, Mo•zar′- ti•an,** *adj.*

moz•za•rel•la (mot′sə rel′lə, mōt′-), *n., pl.* **-las.** a mild, white, semisoft cheese.

MP, 1. Member of Parliament. **2.** Military Police.

mp, melting point.

mpg, miles per gallon.

mph, miles per hour.

Mr. (mis′tər), *pl.* **Messrs.** (mes′ərz). mister: a title of respect prefixed to a man's name or position. [abbr. of *mister*]

MRI, magnetic resonance imaging.

Mrs. (mis′iz, miz′iz), *pl.* **Mmes.** (mā däm′, -dam′). a title of respect prefixed to the name of a married woman.

MS, 1. Also, **ms, ms.** manuscript. **2.** Mississippi. **3.** multiple sclerosis.

Ms. (miz), *pl.* **Mses.** (miz′əz). a title of respect prefixed to a woman's name: unlike *Miss* or *Mrs.,* it does not indicate marital status. [b. of *Miss* and *Mrs.*]

M.S., Master of Science.

MSG, monosodium glutamate.

Msgr., 1. Monseigneur. **2.** Monsignor.

MST, Mountain Standard Time.

MT, 1. Montana. **2.** Mountain Time.

Mt. or **mt., 1.** mount. **2.** mountain.

mtg., 1. meeting. **2.** Also, **mtge.** mortgage.

mu (myōō, mōō), *n., pl.* **mus.** the 12th letter of the Greek alphabet (M, μ).

much (much), *adj.,* **more, most,** *n., pron., adv.,* **more, most.** —*adj.* **1.** great in quantity, measure, or degree: *too much cake.* —*n., pron.* **2.** a great quantity, measure, or degree: *not much to do.* **3.** a great, important, or notable thing or matter: *not much to look at.* —*adv.* **4.** to a great extent or degree: *much earlier.* **5.** nearly or about: *much like the others.*

mu•ci•lage (myōō′sə lij), *n.* a sticky, usu. liquid preparation used as an adhesive. —**mu′ci•lag′i•nous** (-laj′ə nəs), *adj.*

muck (muk), *n.* **1.** moist dung; manure. **2.** a highly organic dark or black soil. **3.** mire; mud. **4.** filth; dirt. —**muck′y,** *adj.,* **-i•er, -i•est.**

muck′rake′, *v.i.,* **-raked, -rak•ing.** to search for and expose real or alleged corruption, esp. in politics. —**muck′rak′er,** *n.*

mu•cous (myōō′kəs), *adj.* **1.** of, consisting of, or resembling mucus. **2.** containing or secreting mucus.

mu′cous mem′brane, *n.* a mucus-secreting membrane lining all bodily passages that are open to the air.

mu′cus (-kəs), *n.* a viscous protective and lubricating solution secreted by mucous membranes.

mud (mud), *n.* wet, soft earth; mire.

mud•dle (mud′l), *v.,* **-dled, -dling,** *n.* —*v.t.* **1.** to

mess up; bungle. **2.** to confuse mentally with or as if with liquor; stupefy. —*v.i.* **3.** to think or act in a confused manner. —*n.* **4.** a confused mental state. **5.** a confused state of affairs; mess.

mud′dle•head′ed, *adj.* confused in one's thinking.

mud′dy, *adj.,* **-di•er, -di•est,** *v.,* **-died, -dy•ing.** —*adj.* **1.** full of or covered with mud. **2.** not clear or pure: *muddy colors.* **3.** confused or vague, as in thought. —*v.t.* **4.** to make muddy. —**mud′di•ness,** *n.*

mud′sling′ing, *n.* efforts to discredit an opponent by malicious or scandalous attacks. —**mud′sling′er,** *n.*

muen•ster (mun′stər, mŏōn′-), *n.* (*often cap.*) a semisoft cheese made from whole milk.

mu•ez•zin (myōō ez′in, mŏō-), *n.* a crier who calls Muslims to prayer.

muff (muf), *n.* **1.** a thick tubular case for warming the hands. **2.** a bungled action or performance. —*v.t., v.i.* **3.** to handle or act clumsily.

muf•fin (muf′in), *n.* a small quick bread baked in a cuplike mold.

muf•fle (muf′əl), *v.t.,* **-fled, -fling. 1.** to wrap with something to deaden sound. **2.** to wrap or envelop, esp. for warmth or protection. **3.** to suppress; stifle.

muf′fler, *n.* **1.** a scarf worn around the neck for warmth. **2.** a device for deadening sound.

muf•ti (muf′tē), *n.* civilian clothes.

mug (mug), *n., v.,* **mugged, mug•ging.** —*n.* **1.** a cylindrical drinking cup with a handle. **2.** *Slang.* **a.** the face. **b.** a thug. —*v.t.* **3.** to assault with intent to rob. **4.** to photograph (a suspect or criminal). —*v.i.* **5.** to make exaggerated faces; grimace. —**mug′ger,** *n.*

mug′gy, *adj.,* **-gi•er, -gi•est.** oppressively damp and close. —**mug′gi•ness,** *n.*

mug•wump (mug′wump′), *n.* **1.** a Republican who refused to support the party nominee in the presidential campaign of 1884. **2.** a person who takes an independent position.

Mu•ham•mad (mŏō ham′əd, -hä′məd), *n.* A.D. 570–632, Arab prophet: founder of Islam.

Mu•ham′mad•an (-ham′ə dn), *adj.* **1.** of Muhammad or Islam. —*n.* **2.** a follower of Muhammad; an adherent of Islam. —**Mu•ham′mad•an•ism,** *n.* —Usage. See MUSLIM.

Muh•len•berg (myōō′lən bûrg′), *n.* **1. Frederick Augustus Conrad,** 1750–1801, U.S. clergyman and statesman: first Speaker of the House 1789–91, 1793– 95. **2.** his father, **Henry Melchior,** 1711–87, American Lutheran clergyman, born in Germany.

Muir (myŏŏr), *n.* **John,** 1838–1914, U.S. naturalist, explorer, and writer; born in Scotland.

muk•luk (muk′luk), *n.* **1.** a soft boot worn by Eskimos, usu. made of sealskin or reindeer skin. **2.** a slipper or lounging boot resembling a mukluk.

mu•lat•to (mə lat′ō, -lä′tō), *n., pl.* **-toes. 1.** the offspring of one white and one black parent. **2.** a person of mixed Negro and Caucasian ancestry.

mul•ber•ry (mul′ber′ē, -bə rē), *n., pl.* **-ries. 1.** a tree bearing edible, dark-purple, berrylike fruit. **2.** the fruit of the mulberry.

mulch (mulch), *n.* **1.** a covering, as of straw or compost, spread on the ground around plants, esp. to prevent evaporation or erosion and enrich the soil. —*v.t.* **2.** to cover with mulch.

mulct (mulkt), *v.t.* **1.** to defraud; swindle. **2.** to punish by a fine. —*n.* **3.** a fine.

mule¹ (myōōl), *n.* **1.** the offspring of a female horse and a male donkey. **2.** a stubborn person.

mule² (myōōl), *n.* a backless lounging slipper.

mule′ deer′, *n.* a deer of W North America with large ears and a gray coat.

mu•le•teer (myōō′lə tēr′), *n.* a driver of mules.

mul′ish, *adj.* unyieldingly stubborn; obstinate.

mull¹ (mul), *v.t.* to think about carefully; ponder: *mulled over the advice.*

mull² (mul), *v.t.* to heat, sweeten, and spice (ale, wine, or cider).

mul•lah (mul′ə, mŏŏl′ə, mōō′lə), *n.* a Muslim teacher of the sacred law.

mul•lein or **-len** (mul′ən), *n.* a tall plant with woolly leaves and a dense spike of yellow flowers.

mul•let (mul′it), *n.*, *pl.* **-lets, -let.** an edible marine or freshwater fish with spiny fins.

mul′li•gan stew′ (mul′i gən), *n.* a stew made of any ingredients that are available.

mul•li•ga•taw•ny (mul′i gə tô′nē) a curry-flavored soup made usu. with chicken stock.

mul•lion (mul′yən), *n.* a vertical member separating the lights of a window.

multi-, a combining form meaning: many (*multiform*); many times (*multimillionaire*); more than two (*multinational*).

mul•ti•cul•tur•al•ism (mul′tē kul′chər ə liz′əm, mul′tī-), *n.* the existence, recognition, or preservation of different cultures or cultural identities within a unified society. —**mul′ti•cul′tur•al,** *adj.*

mul•ti•far•i•ous (mul′tə fâr′ē əs), *adj.* having many different parts, elements, or forms; varied. —**mul′ti•far′i•ous•ly,** *adv.* —**mul′ti•far′i•ous•ness,** *n.*

mul′ti•form′, *adj.* having many shapes or kinds.

mul′ti•me′di•a (mul′tē-, mul′tī-), *n.* (*used with a sing. v.*) **1.** the combined use of several media, as music and video in computer applications, or radio and newspapers. —*adj.* **2.** of or involving the use of several media.

mul′ti•mil′lion•aire′, *n.* one whose wealth amounts to several million, as in dollars.

mul′ti•na′tion•al, *n.* **1.** a large corporation with operations and subsidiaries in several nations. —*adj.* **2.** of or involving several nations or multinationals.

mul•ti•ple (mul′tə pəl), *adj.* **1.** consisting of, having, or involving several or many; manifold. —*n.* **2.** a number that contains another number an integral number of times without a remainder.

mul′tiple-choice′, *adj.* consisting of several possible answers from which the correct one must be selected.

mul′tiple sclero′sis, *n.* a disease marked by destruction of small areas of the brain and spinal cord, leading to neural and muscular impairments.

mul•ti•plex (mul′tə pleks′), *adj.* **1.** manifold; multiple. **2.** of or using equipment permitting the simultaneous transmission of two or more signals or messages over a single channel.

mul′ti•pli•cand′ (-pli kand′), *n.* a number to be multiplied by another.

mul′ti•pli•ca′tion, *n.* **1.** the act or process of multiplying. **2.** the addition of a number to itself as often as is indicated by another number, as in 5 × 10.

multiplica′tion sign′, *n.* a symbol (·), (×), or (∗) denoting multiplication.

mul′ti•plic′i•ty (-plis′i tē), *n.*, *pl.* **-ties.** a large number or variety.

mul′ti•pli′er (-plī′ər), *n.* **1.** a person or thing that multiplies. **2.** a number by which another is multiplied.

mul′ti•ply′, *v.t.*, *v.i.*, **-plied, -ply•ing. 1.** to increase in number or quantity. **2.** to perform the process of multiplication (on).

mul′ti•stage (mul′ti stāj′), *adj.* (of a rocket or guided missile) having more than one stage.

mul•ti•tude (mul′ti tōōd′, -tyōōd′), *n.* a great number. —**mul′ti•tu′di•nous,** *adj.*

mul•ti•vi•ta•min (mul′ti vī′tə min, mul′ti vī′-), *adj.* containing or consisting of several vitamins.

mum¹ (mum), *adj.* silent: *kept mum.*

mum² (mum), *n.* CHRYSANTHEMUM.

mum•ble (mum′bəl), *v.,* **-bled, -bling,** *n.* —*v.i.,* *v.t.* **1.** to speak softly and indistinctly. —*n.* **2.** a soft, indistinct utterance. —**mum′bler,** *n.*

mum•ble-ty•peg (mum′bəl tē peg′) also **mum′-ble-the-peg′** (-ᵺə-), *n.* a game in which a pocketknife is flipped so that its blade sticks into the ground.

mum•bo jum•bo (mum′bō jum′bō), *n.* **1.** meaningless incantation or ritual. **2.** senseless or confusing language.

mum•mer (mum′ər), *n.* **1.** a person who wears a

mask or fantastic costume while merrymaking, as at Christmas. **2.** an actor, esp. a pantomimist. —**mum′-mer•y,** *n.*, *pl.* **-mer•ies.**

mum•mi•fy (mum′ə fī′), *v.t.*, *v.i.*, **-fied, -fy•ing.** to make into or shrivel up like a mummy. —**mum′mi•fi•ca′tion,** *n.*

mum•my (mum′ē), *n.*, *pl.* **-mies.** a dead body preserved by or as if by the ancient Egyptian embalming process.

mumps (mumps), *n.* (*used with a sing. v.*) an infectious viral disease characterized by inflammatory swelling of the salivary glands.

mun., 1. municipal. **2.** municipality.

munch (munch), *v.t.*, *v.i.* to chew steadily and often audibly.

mun•dane (mun dān′, mun′dān), *adj.* **1.** of this world. **2.** common; ordinary. —**mun•dane′ly,** *adv.*

Mu•nich (myōō′nik), *n.* a city in SW Germany. 1,188,800.

mu•nic•i•pal (myōō nis′ə pəl), *adj.* of a municipality or its local government. —**mu•nic′i•pal•ly,** *adv.*

mu•nic′i•pal′i•ty (-pal′i tē), *n.*, *pl.* **-ties.** a city, town, village, or borough with corporate status and usu. its own local government.

mu•nif•i•cent (myōō nif′ə sənt), *adj.* characterized by great generosity. —**mu•nif′i•cence,** *n.*

mu•ni•tions (myōō nish′ənz), *n.pl.* materials, esp. weapons and ammunition, used in war.

mu•ral (myōōr′əl), *n.* **1.** a picture painted directly on a wall. —*adj.* **2.** of or like a wall. —**mu′ral•ist,** *n.*

mur•der (mûr′dər), *n.* **1.** the unlawful killing of a person, esp. when deliberate or premeditated. **2.** *Informal.* something very difficult, dangerous, or unpleasant. —*v.t.* **3.** to kill by an act constituting murder. **4.** to spoil or mar through incompetence: *The singer murdered the aria.* **5.** *Informal.* to defeat thoroughly. —**mur′der•er,** *n.* —**mur′der•ess,** *n.*

mur•der•ous, *adj.* **1.** of the nature of or involving murder. **2.** guilty of, bent on, or capable of murder. **3.** *Informal.* very difficult, dangerous, or unpleasant.

mu′ri•at′ic ac′id (myōōr′ē at′ik, myōōr′-), *n.* HYDROCHLORIC ACID.

murk (mûrk), *n.* darkness; gloom.

murk′y, *adj.*, **-i•er, -i•est. 1.** dark; gloomy. **2.** vague; unclear. —**murk′i•ly,** *adv.* —**murk′i•ness,** *n.*

mur•mur (mûr′mər), *n.* **1.** a low and indistinct continuous sound. **2.** a mumbled or private expression of discontent. **3.** an abnormal sound heard within the body, esp. in the heart valves. —*v.i.*, *v.t.* **4.** to make or express in a murmur. **mur′mur•er,** *n.* —**mur′mur•ous,** *adj.*

mur•rain (mûr′in), *n.* a disease or pestilence of domestic animals or plants.

mus•cat (mus′kət, -kat), *n.* a variety of grape with a pronounced sweet aroma and flavor, used esp. for making wine.

Mus•cat (mus kat′), *n.* the capital of Oman. 250,000.

mus•ca•tel (mus′kə tel′), *n.* a sweet wine made from muscat grapes.

mus•cle (mus′əl), *n.*, *v.,* **-cled, -cling.** —*n.* **1.** bodily tissue composed of elongated cells that contract to produce movement. **2.** muscular strength; brawn. **3.** power or force, esp. of a coercive nature. —*v.i.* **4.** *Informal.* to make one's way by force.

mus′cle•bound′, *adj.* having enlarged and inelastic muscles, as from excessive exercise.

mus′cu•lar (-kyə lər), *adj.* **1.** of or consisting of muscle. **2.** having well-developed muscles; brawny. —**mus′cu•lar′i•ty,** *n.*

mus′cular dys′tro•phy (dis′trə fē), *n.* a hereditary disease characterized by gradual wasting of the muscles.

mus′cu•la•ture (-lə chər, -chōōr′), *n.* the muscular system of the body or of its parts.

muse (myōōz), *v.,* **mused, mus•ing.** —*v.i.* **1.** to meditate quietly; reflect. —*v.t.* **2.** to say or think meditatively. —**mus′er,** *n.*

Muse (myōōz), *n.* **1.** one of the nine Greek goddesses, daughters of Zeus and Mnemosyne, who presided over the arts: Calliope, Clio, Erato, Euterpe, Melpomene, Polyhymnia, Terpsichore, Thalia, and Urania. **2.** (*sometimes l.c.*) the inspiration that motivates a poet, artist, or thinker.

mu•sette (myo͞o zet′), *n.* a small leather or canvas bag with a shoulder strap. Also called **musette′ bag′.**

mu•se•um (myo͞o zē′əm), *n.* a building or place where objects of permanent value, as works of art, are kept and displayed. [< L *museum* place sacred to the Muses]

mush¹ (mush *or, esp. for 2, 3,* mo͞osh), *n.* **1.** meal, esp. cornmeal, boiled in water or milk. **2.** a thick, soft mass. **3.** mawkish sentimentality. —**mush′y,** *adj.,* **-i•er, -i•est.** —**mush′i•ness,** *n.*

mush² (mush), *v.i.* to go or travel, esp. over snow with a dog team and sled.

mush•room (mush′ro͞om, -ro͝om), *n.* **1.** any of various fleshy fungi, including toadstools, puffballs, and morels. —*v.i.* **2.** to spread, grow, or develop quickly.

mu•sic (myo͞o′zik), *n.* **1.** the art of ordering sounds into cohesive and structured forms. **2.** sounds organized to have melody, rhythm, harmony, and dynamics. **3.** the score of a musical composition. **4.** musical quality.

mu′si•cal, *adj.* **1.** of or producing music. **2.** melodious; harmonious. **3.** fond of or skilled in music. —*n.* **4.** a play or motion picture in which the plot is developed by songs and dances. —**mu′si•cal•i•ty,** *n.* —**mu′si•cal•ly,** *adv.*

mu′si•cale′ (-kal′), *n.* a social occasion featuring music.

mu•si′cian (-zish′ən), *n.* a person who performs or composes music. —**mu•si′cian•ly,** *adj.* —**mu•si′cian•ship,** *n.*

mu′si•col′o•gy (-zi kol′ə jē), *n.* the scholarly or scientific study of music. —**mu′si•col′o•gist,** *n.*

mu′sic vid′eo, *n.* a videotape featuring a dramatized rendition of a popular song.

musk (musk), *n.* a pungent glandular secretion of an Asiatic deer: used in perfumery. —**musk′y,** *adj.,* **-i•er, -i•est.** —**musk′i•ness,** *n.*

mus•keg (mus′keg), *n.* a bog of N North America, esp. one with sphagnum mosses.

mus•kel•lunge (mus′kə lunj′), *n., pl.* **-lung•es, -lunge.** a large North American game fish of the pike family.

mus•ket (mus′kit), *n.* a heavy, large-caliber smoothbore gun: predecessor of the modern rifle. —**mus′ket•eer′,** *n.*

mus′ket•ry, *n.* **1.** the fire of muskets. **2.** muskets collectively. **3.** musketeers collectively.

musk′mel′on, *n.* a round or oblong melon with sweet, edible flesh.

musk′ox′ or **musk′ ox′,** *n., pl.* **-ox•en.** a large, shaggy, oxlike mammal of arctic regions of North America.

musk′rat′, *n., pl.* **-rats, -rat. 1.** a large, aquatic North American rodent with glossy dark-brown fur. **2.** the fur of a muskrat.

Mus•lim (muz′lim, mo͝oz′-, mo͝os′-), *adj., n., pl.* **-lims, -lim.** —*adj.* **1.** of the religion, law, or civilization of Islam. —*n.* **2.** an adherent of Islam. —**Usage.** MOSLEM, once the more widely used form, still has currency but has declined in favor of MUSLIM. The use of MUHAMMADAN in reference to Islam or its adherents is rejected by Muslims themselves, as is MUHAMMADANISM for Islam.

mus•lin (muz′lin), *n.* a plain-weave cotton fabric used esp. for sheets.

muss (mus), *v.t.* **1.** to put into disorder. —*n.* **2.** a state of disorder; untidiness.

mus•sel (mus′əl), *n.* any of various bivalve mollusks, esp. an edible marine bivalve.

Mus•so•li•ni (mo͞os′ə lē′nē, mo͞o′sə-), *n.* **Benito** ("*Il Duce*"), 1883–1945, Italian Fascist leader: premier of Italy 1922–43.

Mus•sorg•sky (mo͞o sôrg′skē, -zôrg′-), *n.* **Modest Petrovich,** 1839–81, Russian composer.

must¹ (must), *auxiliary v.* **1.** (used to express obliga-

tion, compulsion, or necessity): *The rules must be obeyed.* **2.** (used to express strong probability or reasonable expectation): *He must be at least 70.* **3.** (used to express inevitability): *Human beings must die.* —*n.* **4.** something necessary or required: *Getting enough sleep is a must.*

must² (must), *n.* (in winemaking) the juice of grapes or other fruit during fermentation.

must³ (must), *n.* mold; moldiness; mustiness: *a castle harboring the must of centuries.*

mus•tache (mus′tash, mə stash′), *n.* the hair growing on the upper lip. —**mus′tached,** *adj.*

mus•tang (mus′tang), *n.* a small, hardy horse of the American plains. [< Sp *mestengo* stray or ownerless beast]

mus•tard (mus′tərd), *n.* **1.** any of various acrid or pungent plants with yellow flowers. **2.** a pungent powder or paste prepared from the seed of the mustard plant and used as a condiment.

mus′tard gas′, *n.* an oily liquid used in warfare for its irritating, blinding, and poisonous properties.

mus•ter (mus′tər), *v.t.* **1.** to bring together, as for inspection. **2.** to summon up; gather. —*v.i.* **3.** to come together; assemble. **4. muster out,** to discharge from military service. —*n.* **5.** an assembling, as for formal inspection. **6.** an assemblage, as of troops. —*Idiom.* **7. pass muster,** to be found acceptable.

must•n′t (mus′ənt), contraction of *must not.*

mus•ty (mus′tē), *adj.,* **-ti•er, -ti•est. 1.** having an odor or flavor suggestive of mold, as old buildings. **2.** outdated; antiquated. —**mus′ti•ness,** *n.*

mu•ta•ble (myo͞o′tə bəl), *adj.* **1.** liable or subject to change or alteration. **2.** given to changing; inconstant. —**mu′ta•bil′i•ty,** *n.* —**mu′ta•bly,** *adv.*

mu•tant (myo͞ot′nt), *n.* **1.** an organism resulting from mutation. —*adj.* **2.** undergoing or resulting from mutation.

mu•tate (myo͞o′tāt), *v.i., v.t.,* **-tat•ed, -tat•ing.** to undergo or cause to undergo mutation. —**mu′ta•tive** (-tā′tiv), *adj.*

mu•ta′tion, *n.* **1.** *Biol.* **a.** a sudden change in a heritable characteristic. **b.** an individual or species characterized by such a change. **2.** a change or alteration, as in form. —**mu•ta′tion•al,** *adj.*

mute (myo͞ot), *adj., n., v.,* **mut•ed, mut•ing.** —*adj.* **1.** not speaking; silent. **2.** incapable of speech. —*n.* **3.** a person incapable of speech. **4.** a mechanical device for muffling the tone of a musical instrument. —*v.t.* **5.** to deaden or muffle the sound of. —**mute′ly,** *adv.* —**mute′ness,** *n.*

mu•ti•late (myo͞ot′l āt′), *v.t.,* **-lat•ed, -lat•ing. 1.** to injure or disfigure by irreparably damaging parts. **2.** to deprive (a person or animal) of an essential part, as a limb. —**mu′ti•la′tion,** *n.* —**mu′ti•la′tor,** *n.*

mu•ti•ny (myo͞ot′n ē), *n., pl.* **-nies,** *v.,* **-nied, -ny•ing.** —*n.* **1.** rebellion against constituted authority, esp. by sailors or soldiers against their officers. —*v.i.* **2.** to commit mutiny. —**mu′ti•neer′,** *n.* —**mu′ti•nous,** *adj.*

mutt (mut), *n. Slang.* a mongrel dog.

mut•ter (mut′ər), *v.i., v.t.* **1.** to speak or utter indistinctly or in a barely audible tone. **2.** to grumble. —*n.* **3.** the act or utterance of a person who mutters.

mut•ton (mut′n), *n.* the flesh of a mature sheep.

mut′ton•chops′, *n.pl.* side whiskers that are narrow at the temples and broad and trimmed short at the jawline.

mu•tu•al (myo͞o′cho͞o əl), *adj.* **1.** exchanged in equal measure; reciprocal: *mutual respect.* **2.** having the same relation each toward the other: *mutual enemies.* **3.** held in common; shared: *mutual interests.* —**mu′tu•al′i•ty,** *n.* —**mu′tu•al•ly,** *adv.*

mu′tual fund′, *n.* an investment company that invests its pooled funds in a diversified list of securities.

muz•zle (muz′əl), *n., v.,* **-zled, -zling.** —*n.* **1.** the projecting part of an animal's head, including jaws, mouth, and nose. **2.** the open end of the barrel of a gun. **3.** a device placed over an animal's muzzle to prevent the animal from biting or eating. —*v.t.* **4.** to put a muzzle on (an animal). **5.** to restrain from speech or expression.

Mv, *Chem. Symbol.* mendelevium.

MVP, most valuable player.

MX, missile, experimental: a ten-warhead U.S. inter-continental ballistic missile.

my (mī), *pron.* **1.** a form of the possessive case of I used as an attributive adjective. —*interj.* **2.** an exclamation of mild surprise or dismay.

My•an•mar (mī än′mär), *n.* a republic in SE Asia. 39,840,000. Formerly, **Burma.**

my•as•the•ni•a (mī′əs thē′nē ə), *n.* muscle weakness. —**my′as•then′ic** (-then′ik), *adj.*

My•ce•nae (mī sē′nē), *n.* an ancient city in S Greece, in Argolis: important ruins.

My•ce•nae•an or **My•ce•ne•an** (mī′si nē′ən), *adj.* pertaining to the Bronze Age civilization at Mycenae, dating from c2000 to c1100 B.C.

my•col•o•gy (mī kol′ə jē), *n.* the branch of biology dealing with fungi. —**my•col′o•gist,** *n.*

my•e•li•tis (mī′ə līʹtis), *n.* **1.** inflammation of the spinal cord. **2.** inflammation of the bone marrow.

My Lai (mē′ līʹ), *n.* a hamlet in S Vietnam: U.S. forces' massacre of South Vietnamese civilians 1968.

My•lar (mī′lär), *Trademark.* a brand of strong, thin polyester film used in photography, recording tapes, and insulation.

my•na or **-nah** (mī′nə), *n.,* *pl.* **-nas** or **-nahs.** any of various Asian birds of the starling family, esp. those with the ability to mimic human speech.

my•o•pi•a (mī ōʹpē ə), *n.* **1.** a condition of the eye in which objects are seen distinctly only at short distances. **2.** lack of foresight. —**my•op′ic** (-op′ik, -ō′pik), *adj.*

myr•i•ad (mir′ē əd), *n.* **1.** an indefinitely great number. —*adj.* **2.** consisting of a myriad; innumerable.

myr•mi•don (mûr′mi don′, -dn), *n.* a person who carries out orders without question or scruple.

myrrh (mûr), *n.* an aromatic gum resin obtained from plants and used chiefly in making incense and perfumes: one of three gifts, the other two being gold and frankincense, given by the Magi to the infant Jesus. Matt. 2:11.

myr•tle (mûr′tl), *n.* a plant of S Europe with evergreen leaves, fragrant white flowers, and aromatic

berries. **2.** any of certain unrelated plants, as the periwinkle.

my•self′, *pron.* **1.** the reflexive form of ME: *I cut myself.* **2.** (used as an intensive of I or ME): *I myself don't like it.* **3.** my normal self: *I wasn't myself when I said that.*

mys•te•ri•ous (mi stēr′ē əs), *adj.* **1.** of or full of mystery. **2.** puzzling; inexplicable. —**mys•te′ri•ous•ly,** *adv.* —**mys•te′ri•ous•ness,** *n.*

mys•ter•y (mis′tə rē), *n.,* *pl.* **-ter•ies.** **1.** something unexplained or inexplicable. **2.** a person or thing having qualities that arouse curiosity or speculation. **3.** a fictional work that involves the solving of a puzzle, esp. a crime. **4.** the quality of being obscure or enigmatic. **5.** a truth unknowable except by divine revelation. **6.** (in the Christian religion) **a.** a sacramental rite. **b.** the Eucharist. **7. mysteries, a.** ancient religions with secret rites and rituals known only to initiates. **b.** any rites or secrets known only to initiates.

mys•tic (mis′tik), *adj.* **1.** of or characterized by esoteric or otherworldly practices or content. **2.** of occult character or significance. **3.** of mystics or mysticism. —*n.* **4.** a person who claims insight into mysteries transcending ordinary human knowledge.

mys′ti•cal, *adj.* **1.** mystic; occult. **2.** of mystics or mysticism. **3.** spiritually symbolic. —**mys′ti•cal•ly,** *adv.*

mys′ti•cism (-tə siz′əm), *n.* the doctrine of an immediate spiritual intuition of truths, or of a direct, intimate union of the soul with God through contemplation or spiritual ecstasy.

mys′ti•fy′, *v.t.,* **-fied, -fy•ing. 1.** to perplex or bewilder. **2.** to make mysterious. —**mys′ti•fi•ca′tion,** *n.*

mys•tique (mi stēk′), *n.* **1.** a framework of attitudes and beliefs constructed around a person or object. **2.** an aura of mystery or mystical power surrounding a particular occupation or pursuit.

myth (mith), *n.* **1.** a traditional or legendary story, esp. one that involves gods and heroes and explains a cultural practice or natural phenomenon. **2.** a fictitious person, story, etc. **3.** an unproven or false belief. —**myth′i•cal,** *adj.*

my•thol•o•gy (mi thol′ə jē), *n.,* *pl.* **-gies. 1.** a body of myths as that of a particular people. **2.** the study of myths. —**myth•o•log•i•cal** (mith′ə loj′i kəl), *adj.* —**my•thol′o•gist,** *n.*

N

N, n (en), *n.,* *pl.* **Ns** or **N's, ns** or **n's.** the 14th letter of the English alphabet, a consonant.

N, 1. north. **2.** northern.

N, *Chem. Symbol.* nitrogen.

N., 1. Navy. **2.** north. **3.** northern. **4.** November.

n., 1. name. **2.** neuter. **3.** new. **4.** nominative. **5.** noon. **6.** north. **7.** northern. **8.** noun. **9.** number.

Na, *Chem. Symbol.* sodium. [< NL *natrium*]

N.A., 1. North America. **2.** not applicable.

NAACP, National Association for the Advancement of Colored People.

Na•a•man (nā′ə mən), *n.* a leper who was healed by Elisha. II Kings 5:1–14.

nab (nab), *v.t.,* **nabbed, nab•bing.** *Informal.* **1.** to arrest or capture. **2.** to snatch or seize.

NAB, New American Bible.

Na•bal (nā′bəl), *n.* a wealthy Calcbite, husband of Abigail, who refused rightful tribute to King David for protecting Nabal's flocks. I Sam. 25.

na•bob (nā′bob), *n.* any very wealthy, influential, or powerful person.

Na•bo•kov (nə bô′kəf, nab′ə kôf′, -kof′), *n.* **Vladimir,** 1899–1977, U.S. writer born in Russia.

na•cre (nā′kər), *n.* MOTHER-OF-PEARL. —**na′cre•ous** (-krē əs), *adj.*

na•dir (nā′dər, -dēr), *n.* **1.** the point on the celestial

sphere directly beneath a given position or observer and diametrically opposite the zenith. **2.** the lowest point.

nae (nā), *Scot. and North Eng.* —*adv.* **1.** no; not. —*adj.* **2.** no.

NAFTA (naf′tə), *n.* North American Free Trade Agreement.

nag¹ (nag), *v.,* **nagged, nag•ging,** *n.* —*v.t.* **1.** to annoy by persistent faultfinding, complaints, etc. **2.** to be a constant source of unease to. —*v.i.* **3.** to find fault or complain persistently. —*n.* **4.** a person who nags. —**nag′ger,** *n.*

nag² (nag), *n.* an old or worthless horse.

Na•ga•sa•ki (nä′gə sä′kē, nag′ə sak′ē), *n.* a seaport in SW Japan: second military use of the atomic bomb 1945. 447,000.

Na•go•ya (nə goi′ə), *n.* a city on S Honshu, in central Japan. 2,091,884.

Na•hum (nā′həm), *n.* **1.** a Minor Prophet of the 7th century B.C. **2.** a book of the Bible bearing his name.

nai•ad (nā′ad, -əd, nī′-), *n.,* *pl.* **-ads, -a•des** (-ə dēz′). (in Greek myth) a nymph presiding over a river or spring.

nail (nāl), *n.* **1.** a piece of metal with a pointed tip and flattened head, hammered into wood as a fastener. **2.** a thin, horny plate growing on the upper side of the end of a finger or toe. —*v.t.* **3.** to fasten with a nail. **4.** *Informal.* to catch or seize. **5. nail down,** to make final; settle once and for all. —*Idiom.* **6. hit the nail on the head,** to say or do exactly the right thing. —*Proverb.* **7. For want of a nail the kingdom was lost,** no detail is so small as to be insignificant.

nail-bit•er (nāl/bī/tər), *n.* a situation marked by anxiety or tension.

Nai•ro•bi (nī rō/bē), *n.* the capital of Kenya. 827,775.

na•ive or **-ïve** (nä ēv/), *adj.* **1.** having unaffected simplicity of nature. **2.** lacking in experience, judgment, or information. [< F < L *nātīvus* native] —**na•ive/ly,** *adv.*

na•ive•té or **-ïve•té** (nä ēv tā/, -ēv/tā, -ē/və-), *n.* **1.** the quality or state of being naive. **2.** a naive action, remark, etc. [< F]

na•ked (nā/kid), *adj.* **1.** being without clothing; nude. **2.** without covering: *a naked sword.* **3.** (of the eye, sight, etc.) unassisted by an optical instrument. **4.** plain; unadorned: *the naked truth.* —**na/ked•ly,** *adv.* —**na/ked•ness,** *n.*

nam•by-pam•by (nam/bē pam/bē), *adj., n., pl.* **-bies.** —*adj.* **1.** irresolute. **2.** wanting in character. **3.** insipid. —*n.* **4.** a namby-pamby person or thing.

name (nām), *n., v.,* **named, nam•ing,** *adj.* —*n.* **1.** a word or phrase by which a person or thing is designated. **2.** mere designation rather than fact: *a king in name only.* **3.** an abusive epithet. **4.** reputation or fame. —*v.t.* **5.** to give a name to. **6.** to identify by name. **7.** to designate or nominate for office. **8.** to specify: *Name your price.* —*adj.* **9.** well-known. —*Idiom.* **10. in the name of, a.** with appeal to. **b.** by the authority of. **11. name names,** to specify or accuse people by name. **12. to one's name,** within one's resources: *not a penny to his name.* —*Proverb.* **13. A good name is better than precious ointment,** reputation is one's most important possession. Eccl. 7:1. —**name/a•ble,** *adj.*

name/less, *adj.* **1.** having no name. **2.** not referred to by name. **3.** incapable of being described.

name/ly, *adv.* that is to say; specifically.

name/sake/, *n.* **1.** a person named after another. **2.** a person having the same name as another.

Na•mib•i•a (nə mib/ē ə), *n.* a republic in SW Africa. 1,727,183. —**Na•mib/i•an,** *n., adj.*

Nan•jing (nän/jing/) also **-king/** (-king/), *n.* a city in E China: a former capital of China. 2,250,000.

nan•ny (nan/ē), *n., pl.* **-nies.** a person employed to take care of a young child in the home.

nan/ny goat/, *n.* a female goat.

nan/ny tax/, *n.* the portion of Social Security and Medicare taxes paid by the employer of a household worker.

nan•o•sec•ond (nan/ə sek/ənd, nā/nə-), *n.* one billionth of a second.

Na•o•mi (nā ō/mē), *n.* the mother-in-law of Ruth. Ruth 1.

nap[1] (nap), *v.,* **napped, nap•ping,** *n.* —*v.i.* **1.** to sleep for a short time. **2.** to be off one's guard: *The question caught him napping.* —*n.* **3.** a brief period of sleep. —**nap/per,** *n.*

nap[2] (nap), *n.* the short fuzzy ends of fibers on the surface of cloth. —**nap/less,** *adj.* —**napped,** *adj.*

na•palm (nā/päm), *n.* **1.** a highly incendiary jellylike substance used in firebombs, flamethrowers, etc. —*v.t.* **2.** to bomb or attack with napalm.

nape (nāp, nap), *n.* the back of the neck.

Naph•ta•li (naf/tə lī/), *n.* **1.** the sixth son of Jacob and Bilhah. Gen. 30:7, 8. **2.** one of the 12 tribes of Israel.

naph•tha (naf/thə, nap/-), *n.* a colorless, volatile petroleum distillate, used as a solvent and a fuel. —**naph/thous,** *adj.*

naph/tha•lene/ (-lēn/), *n.* a white crystalline hydrocarbon obtained from coal tar: used in making dyes and as a moth repellent.

nap•kin (nap/kin), *n.* a small piece of cloth or paper used to wipe the lips and fingers and to protect the clothes while eating.

Na•ples (nā/pəlz), *n.* a seaport in SW Italy. 1,200,958.

Na•po•le•on (nə pō/lē ən, -pōl/yən), *n.* **1. Napoleon I,** (*Napoléon Bonaparte*) (*"the Little Corporal"*) 1769–1821, French general born in Corsica: emperor of France 1804–15. **2. Napoleon III,** (*Louis Napoléon*) (*Charles Louis Napoléon Bonaparte*) 1808–73, president of France 1848–52, emperor of France 1852–70 (nephew of Napoleon I). —**Na•po•le•on•ic** (nə pō/lē on/ik), *adj.*

narc (närk), *n. Slang.* a government narcotics agent.

nar•cis•sism (när/sə siz/em), *n.* inordinate fascination with oneself; excessive self-love. —**nar/cis•sist,** *n.* —**nar/cis•sis/tic,** *adj.*

nar•cis•sus (när sis/əs), *n., pl.* **-cis•sus, -cis•sus•es, -cis•si** (-sis/ē, -sis/ī). **1.** any of various bulbous plants with showy yellow or white flowers and a cup-shaped corona. **2.** (*cap.*) (in Greek myth) a youth who fell in love with his own reflection in a pool and was transformed into the narcissus flower.

nar•co•sis (när kō/sis), *n.* a state of drowsiness or stupor.

nar•cot•ic (-kot/ik), *n.* **1.** any addictive substance that blunts the senses and can cause confusion, stupor, coma, and death. —*adj.* **2.** pertaining to narcotics or their use.

nar/co•tize/ (-kə tīz/), *v.t.,* **-tized, -tiz•ing.** to subject to a narcotic. —**nar/co•ti•za/tion,** *n.*

nark (närk), *n.* NARC.

nar•rate (nar/āt, na rāt/), *v.t., v.i.,* **-rat•ed, -rat•ing. 1.** to tell or relate (a story, event, etc.). **2.** to add a spoken commentary to (a film or television program). —**nar•ra/tion,** *n.* —**nar/ra•tor,** *n.*

nar/ra•tive (-ə tiv), *n.* **1.** a story or account, whether true or fictitious. **2.** the art or process of narrating. —*adj.* **3.** of a narrative or narration.

nar•row (nar/ō), *adj.,* **-er, -est,** *v., n.* —*adj.* **1.** of little breadth or width. **2.** limited in range or scope. **3.** lacking breadth of view or sympathy. **4.** barely adequate or successful: *a narrow escape.* —*v.i., v.t.* **5.** to become or make narrower in width or scope. —*n.* **6.** narrows, a narrow part of a body of water. —**nar/row•ly,** *adv.* —**nar/row•ness,** *n.*

nar/row-mind/ed, *adj.* having a closed mind; prejudiced. —**nar/row-mind/ed•ness,** *n.*

nar•whal (när/wəl), *n.* a small arctic whale, the male of which has a long, twisted tusk.

nar•y (nâr/ē), *adj.* not any.

NASA (nas/ə), *n.* National Aeronautics and Space Administration.

na•sal (nā/zəl), *adj.* **1.** of the nose. **2.** (of a speech sound) pronounced with the voice issuing through the nose. —**na•sal/i•ty,** *n.* —**na/sal•ly,** *adv.*

na/sal•ize/, *v.,* **-ized, -iz•ing.** —*v.t.* **1.** to give a nasal sound to. —*v.i.* **2.** to produce nasal sounds. —**na/sal•i•za/tion,** *n.*

nas•cent (nas/ənt, nā/sənt), *adj.* beginning to exist or develop. —**nas/cence,** *n.*

Nash•ville (nash/vil), *n.* the capital of Tennessee. 481,380.

Nas•sau (nas/ô), *n.* the capital of the Bahamas. 132,000.

Nast (nast), *n.* **Thomas,** 1840–1902, U.S. illustrator and cartoonist.

nas•tur•tium (nə stûr/shəm, na-), *n.* a garden plant with shield-shaped leaves and bright, irregular flowers.

nas•ty (nas/tē), *adj.,* **-ti•er, -ti•est. 1.** filthy. **2.** indecent or obscene. **3.** highly unpleasant. **4.** vicious or spiteful. —**nas/ti•ly,** *adv.* —**nas/ti•ness,** *n.*

na•tal (nāt/l), *adj.* of a person's birth.

Na•than (nā/thən), *n.* a prophet during the reigns of David and Solomon. II Sam. 12; I Kings 1:34.

Na•than•a•el (nə than/ē əl, -than/yəl), *n.* a disciple of Jesus, possibly Bartholomew. John 1:45–51.

na•tion (nā/shən), *n.* **1.** a body of people associated with a particular territory and possessing its own government. **2.** the territory or country itself. **3.** an American Indian people or tribe. —**na/tion•hood/,** *n.*

Na•tion (nā'shən), *n.* **Carry** or **Carrie (Amelia Moore)**, 1846–1911, U.S. temperance leader.

na•tion•al (nash'ə nl), *adj.* **1.** of or belonging to a nation. **2.** peculiar or common to a nation. —*n.* **3.** a citizen or subject of a particular nation. —**na'tion•al•ly,** *adv.*

Na'tional Aeronau'tics and Space' Administra'tion, *n.* the federal agency that administers programs that deal with aeronautical research. *Abbr.:* NASA

Na'tional Associa'tion for the Advance'ment of Col'ored Peo'ple, *n.* an interracial U.S. organization working for equality of black people: organized in 1910. *Abbr.:* NAACP

na'tional church', *n.* an independent church within a country, usually representing the prevalent religion. Compare ESTABLISHED CHURCH.

Na'tional Endow'ment for the Arts', *n.* an independent agency that stimulates the arts in the U.S. by awarding grants. *Abbr.:* NEA

Na'tional Endow'ment for the Human'ities, *n.* an independent agency that stimulates the study of the humanities in the U.S. by awarding grants. *Abbr.:* NEH

Na'tional Guard', *n.* a state military force that is subject to call by the state or federal government in emergencies.

na'tion•al•ism, *n.* **1.** devotion to one's nation; patriotism. **2.** the desire for national advancement or independence. —**na'tion•al•ist,** *adj., n.* —**na'tion•al•is'tic,** *adj.*

na'tion•al'i•ty, *n., pl.* **-ties. 1.** the status of belonging to a particular nation by birth or naturalization. **2.** a nation or people.

na'tion•al•ize', *v.t.,* **-ized, -iz•ing. 1.** to bring under the ownership or control of a nation, as an industry or land. **2.** to make national in extent or scope. —**na'tion•al•i•za'tion,** *n.*

Na'tional La'bor Rela'tions Act', *n.* an act of Congress (1935) that forbade any interference by employers with labor unions.

Na'tional Organiza'tion for Wom'en, *n.* a women's rights organization founded in 1966. *Abbr.:* NOW

Na'tional Ri'fle Associa'tion, *n.* a U.S. association of gun-owners, founded in 1871, that supports the right to bear arms. *Abbr.:* NRA

Na'tional Secur'ity Coun'cil, *n.* the council that determines how best to safeguard the national security. *Abbr.:* NSC

Na'tional Transporta'tion Safe'ty Board', *n.* an independent agency that promotes safe transportation in the U.S. *Abbr.:* NTSB

Na'tion of Islam', *n.* an organization composed chiefly of American blacks, advocating the teachings of Islam: members are known as Black Muslims.

na•tion•wide (nā'shən wīd'), *adj.* extending throughout the nation.

na•tive (nā'tiv), *adj.* **1.** being the place of origin of a person or thing. **2.** belonging to a person by birth or to a thing by nature. **3.** belonging to the original inhabitants of a region. **4.** born in a particular place. **5.** originating naturally in a particular region. —*n.* **6.** one of the people indigenous to a place. **7.** a person born in a particular place. **8.** an indigenous animal or plant. [< MF < L *nātīvus* inborn, natural]

Na'tive Amer'ican, *n.* AMERICAN INDIAN.

na•tiv•i•ty (nə tiv'i tē, nā-), *n., pl.* **-ties. 1.** birth. **2.** (*cap.*) the birth of Christ.

natl., national.

NATO (nā'tō), *n.* an organization formed in 1949 for the purpose of collective defense: originally comprising Belgium, Canada, Denmark, France, Iceland, Italy, Luxembourg, the Netherlands, Norway, Portugal, the United Kingdom, and the United States, and later joined by Greece, Turkey, Germany, Spain, the Czech Republic, Hungary, and Poland. [*N(orth) A(tlantic) T(reaty) O(rganization)*]

nat•ty (nat'ē), *adj.,* **-ti•er, -ti•est.** neatly or trimly smart. —**nat'ti•ly,** *adv.*

nat•u•ral (nach'ər əl), *adj.* **1.** existing in or formed by nature. **2.** of or pertaining to nature. **3.** inborn; innate. **4.** free from affectation. **5.** to be expected: *a natural result.* **6.** true to or closely imitating nature. **7.** *Music.* neither sharp nor flat. —*n.* **8.** a person or thing that is likely to be successful. **9.** *Music.* a sign placed before a note, canceling the effect of a sharp or flat. —**nat'u•ral•ness,** *n.*

nat'ural child'birth, *n.* childbirth involving little or no use of drugs or anesthesia.

nat'ural gas', *n.* a mixture of gaseous hydrocarbons that accumulates in porous sedimentary rocks, used as a fuel.

nat'ural his'tory, *n.* the study of organisms and natural objects.

nat•u•ral•ism (-ər ə liz'əm), *n.* an artistic or literary style that represents objects and events as they occur in nature or real life. —**nat'u•ral•is'tic,** *adj.*

nat•u•ral•ist, *n.* **1.** a person who studies natural history. **2.** an adherent of naturalism.

nat•u•ral•ize', *v.t.,* **-ized, -iz•ing.** to confer citizenship upon (an alien). —**nat'u•ral•i•za'tion,** *n.*

nat•u•ral•ly, *adv.* **1.** in a natural manner. **2.** by nature. **3.** of course.

nat'ural re'source, *n.* a source of wealth occurring in nature, as a forest or water.

nat'ural sci'ence, *n.* a science of objects or processes observable in nature, as biology or physics.

nat'ural selec'tion, *n.* the process by which forms of life having traits that better enable them to adapt to environmental pressures will survive and reproduce in greater numbers than others of their kind.

na•ture (nā'chər), *n.* **1.** the natural world as it exists without human beings. **2.** the universe, with all its phenomena. **3.** the inherent character of a person, animal, or thing. **4.** kind or sort. **5.** the primitive condition of humankind. —**Proverb. 6. Nature abhors a vacuum,** something always fills a vacant space.

naught (nôt), *n.* **1.** nothing. **2.** a cipher (0); zero.

naugh•ty (nô'tē), *adj.,* **-ti•er, -ti•est. 1.** disobedient; mischievous. **2.** improper or indecent. —**naugh'ti•ly,** *adv.* —**naugh'ti•ness,** *n.*

Na•u•ru (nä ōō'rōō), *n.* an island republic in the W Pacific. 8042. —**Na•u'ru•an,** *n., adj.*

nau•se•a (nô'zē ə, -zhə, -sē ə, -shə), *n.* **1.** sickness at the stomach, accompanied by an involuntary impulse to vomit. **2.** extreme disgust.

nau'se•ate' (-zē āt', -zhē-, -sē-, -shē-), *v.t.,* **-at•ed, -at•ing.** to affect with nausea. —**nau'se•at'ing•ly,** *adv.*

nau'seous (-shəs, -zē əs), *adj.* **1.** affected with nausea. **2.** causing nausea. —**nau'seous•ness,** *n.*

nau•ti•cal (nô'ti kəl, not'i-), *adj.* of sailors, ships, or navigation. —**nau'ti•cal•ly,** *adv.*

nau'tical mile', *n.* a unit of distance at sea or in the air equal to 1.852 kilometers.

nau•ti•lus (nôt'l əs, not'-), *n., pl.* **nau•ti•lus•es, nau•ti•li** (nôt'l ī', not'-). a deep-sea mollusk having a spiral, chambered shell.

nautilus

Nav•a•jo or **-ho** (nav'ə hō', nä'və-), *n., pl.* **-jo, -jos, -joes** or **-ho, -hos, -hoes.** a member of an American Indian people of the U.S. Southwest.

na•val (nā'vəl), *adj.* of, for, or possessing a navy.

nave (nāv), *n.* the principal area of a church, from the main entrance to the chancel.

na•vel (nā'vəl), *n.* the depression in the surface of the abdomen where the umbilical cord was connected with the fetus.

na'vel or'ange, *n.* a seedless orange having a navellike formation at the apex.

nav·i·ga·ble (nav′i gə bəl), *adj.* **1.** deep and wide enough for the passage of ships. **2.** capable of being steered. —**nav′i·ga·bil′i·ty,** *n.*

nav′i·gate′ (-gāt′), *v.t., v.i.,* **-gat·ed, -gat·ing. 1.** to move on or through (water, air, or land) in a ship or aircraft. **2.** to direct or manage (a ship or aircraft) on its course. **3.** to walk or find one's way (in or across). —**nav′i·ga′tion,** *n.* —**nav′i·ga′tor,** *n.*

na·vy (nā′vē), *n., pl.* **-vies. 1.** the warships belonging to a country. **2.** (*often cap.*) the complete body of such warships, together with their personnel, equipment, etc. **3.** NAVY BLUE.

na′vy bean′, *n.* a small, white kidney bean.

na′vy blue′, *n.* a dark blue.

nay (nā), *adv.* **1.** and not only so but: *many good, nay, noble qualities.* —*n.* **2.** a denial or refusal. **3.** a negative vote or voter.

nay′say′er, *n.* a person who habitually expresses negative views.

Naz·a·rene (naz′ə rēn′, naz′ə rēn′), *n.* **1.** a native or inhabitant of Nazareth. **2.** a member of a sect of early Jewish converts to Christianity who retained the Mosaic ritual. **3. the Nazarene,** JESUS (def. 1). —*adj.* **4.** of or pertaining to Nazareth or the Nazarenes. [< LL *Nazarēnus* < Gk *Nazarēnós,* der. of *Nazar(ét)* NAZARETH]

Naz·a·reth (naz′ər əth), *n.* a town in N Israel: the childhood home of Jesus. 45,600.

Na·zi (nät′sē, nat′-), *n., pl.* **-zis.** a member of the fascist political party which controlled Germany from 1933 to 1945 under Adolf Hitler. —**Na′zism** (-siz əm), **Na′zi·ism,** *n.*

NB or **N.B., 1.** New Brunswick. **2.** nota bene.

Nb, *Chem. Symbol.* niobium.

NBS or **N.B.S.,** National Bureau of Standards.

NC or **N.C., 1.** network computer. **2.** no charge. **3.** North Carolina.

NCO, Noncommissioned Officer.

NC-17 (en′sē′sev′ən tēn′), *Trademark.* no children under 17: a motion-picture rating advising that persons under 17 will not be admitted.

ND or **N.D.,** North Dakota.

Nd, *Chem. Symbol.* neodymium.

N.Dak., North Dakota.

nde, near-death experience. Also, **NDE.**

N′Dja·me·na (ən jä mā′nä), *n.* the capital of Chad. 511,700.

NE, 1. Nebraska. **2.** northeast. **3.** northeastern.

Ne, *Chem. Symbol.* neon.

NEA or **N.E.A., 1.** National Education Association. **2.** National Endowment for the Arts.

Ne·an·der·thal (nē an′dər thôl′), *adj.* **1.** of Neanderthal man. **2.** (*often l.c.*) primitive or unenlightened. —*n.* **3.** NEANDERTHAL MAN. **4.** (*often l.c.*) an unenlightened person.

Nean′derthal man′, *n.* a member of an extinct subspecies of humans that lived in the Stone Age.

neap (nēp), *adj.* **1.** designating those tides that attain the least height. —*n.* **2.** neap tide.

Ne·a·pol·i·tan (nē′ə pol′i tn), *adj.* **1.** of Naples. —*n.* **2.** a native or inhabitant of Naples.

near (nēr), *adv.* and *adj.,* **-er, -est,** *prep., v.* —*adv.* **1.** at a short distance in space or time. **2.** close in relation. **3.** almost. —*adj.* **4.** close in distance or time. **5.** closely related or connected. **6.** intimate or familiar. **7.** narrow or close: *a near escape.* —*prep.* **8.** close to. —*v.t., v.i.* **9.** to come near (to). —**near′ness,** *n.*

near′by′, *adj., adv.* close at hand.

near′-death′ expe′rience, *n.* any experience involving a vision, as of the afterlife, reported by a resuscitated person.

Near′ East′, *n.* the countries of SW Asia, the Arabian Peninsula, and Egypt.

near′ly, *adv.* almost.

near′sight′ed (-sī′tid, -sī′-), *adj.* seeing distinctly at a short distance only; myopic. —**near′sight′ed·ness,** *n.*

neat (nēt), *adj.,* **-er, -est. 1.** orderly and clean. **2.** trim and graceful. **3.** skillful; adroit. **4.** *Slang.* great;

wonderful. **5.** undiluted. —**neat′ly,** *adv.* —**neat′ness,** *n.*

neath or **'neath** (nēth, nēth), *prep. Chiefly Literary.* BENEATH.

Neb., Nebraska.

Nebr., Nebraska.

Ne·bras·ka (nə bras′kə), *n.* a state in the central United States. 1,652,093. *Cap.:* Lincoln. *Abbr.:* NE, Nebr., Neb. —**Ne·bras′kan,** *n., adj.*

Neb·u·chad·nez·zar (neb′ə kəd nez′ər, neb′yōō-), *n.* Also, **Neb′u·chad·rez′zar** (-rez′ər), died 562? B.C., king of Babylonia 605?–562? B.C.: conqueror of Jerusalem. II Kings 24, 25.

neb·u·la (neb′yə lə), *n., pl.* **-lae** (-lē′, -lī′), **-las.** a cloud of interstellar gas and dust. —**neb′u·lar,** *adj.*

neb·u·lous (neb′yə ləs), *adj.* **1.** hazy or vague. **2.** of or resembling a nebula or nebulae.

nec·es·sar·i·ly (nes′ə sâr′ə lē, -ser′-), *adv.* **1.** by or of necessity. **2.** as a necessary result.

nec′es·sar′y (-ser′ē), *adj., n., pl.* **-sar·ies.** —*adj.* **1.** essential; indispensable. **2.** unavoidable. **3.** acting or proceeding from compulsion or obligation. —*n.* **4.** something necessary.

ne·ces·si·tate (nə ses′i tāt′), *v.t.,* **-tat·ed, -tat·ing. 1.** to make necessary or unavoidable. **2.** to compel or oblige.

ne·ces′si·ty, *n., pl.* **-ties. 1.** something necessary or indispensable. **2.** an imperative requirement or need. **3.** the state or fact of being necessary. **4.** a compulsion to do something. **5.** poverty. —*Idiom.* **6.** of necessity, inevitably; unavoidably. —*Proverb.* **7. Necessity is the mother of invention,** ingenuity will fill a need.

neck (nek), *n.* **1.** the part of the body that connects the head and the trunk. **2.** the part of a garment closest to the neck. **3.** a slender part that resembles a neck, as on a bottle or vase. **4.** a narrow strip of land. —*v.i.* **5.** *Informal.* to embrace, kiss, and caress amorously. —*Idiom.* **6. neck and neck,** just even or very close.

neck·er·chief (nek′ər chif, -chēf′), *n.* a cloth or scarf worn around the neck.

neck′lace (-lis), *n.* a piece of jewelry worn around the neck, as a string of pearls or beads.

neck′line′, *n.* the contour of the neck of a garment.

neck′tie′, *n.* a band of decorative fabric worn around the neck and tied in front with a knot or bow.

ne·crol·o·gy (nə krol′ə jē, ne-), *n., pl.* **-gies.** a list of persons who have died within a certain time.

nec·ro·man·cy (nek′rə man′sē), *n.* **1.** a method of divination through invocation of the dead. **2.** black magic; sorcery. —**nec′ro·man′cer,** *n.*

ne·cro·sis (nə krō′sis), *n.* death of a portion of animal or plant tissue. —**ne·crot′ic** (-krot′ik), *adj.*

nec·tar (nek′tər), *n.* **1.** the saccharine secretion of a plant, which attracts the insects or birds that pollinate the flower. **2.** (in Greek myth) the life-giving drink of the gods. **3.** any delicious drink.

nec·tar·ine (nek′tə rēn′, nek′tə rēn′), *n.* a variety of peach having a smooth skin.

nee or **née** (nā), *adj.* born (used to introduce the maiden name of a married woman): *Mrs. Jones, nee Berg.*

need (nēd), *n.* **1.** a requirement or obligation. **2.** a lack of something wanted or deemed necessary. **3.** urgent want, as of something requisite. **4.** a situation or time of difficulty. **5.** destitution; poverty. —*v.t.* **6.** to have need of. —*v.i.* **7.** to be in need. —*auxiliary v.* **8.** (used to express obligation or necessity, esp. in interrogative or negative statements): *Need I say more?* —*Idiom.* **9. if need be,** should the necessity arise.

need′ful, *adj.* necessary or required.

nee·dle (nēd′l), *n., v.,* **-dled, -dling.** —*n.* **1.** a small, slender, steel implement with a point at one end and a hole for thread at the other, used in sewing. **2.** any of various larger implements for making stitches, as in knitting. **3.** a hypodermic needle. **4.** the pointer on a dial or compass. **5.** a slender, pointed device used to transmit vibrations from the groove of a phonographic record. **6.** a needle-shaped leaf, as of a pine. —*v.t.* **7.** *Informal.* **a.** to prod or goad. **b.** to tease. —*Idiom.* **8. needle in a haystack,** something very difficult to locate.

nee′dle•point′, *n.* **1.** embroidery on canvas. —*adj.* **2.** noting a lace in which a needle works out the design on paper.

need′less, *adj.* not needed; unnecessary. —**need′-less•ly,** *adv.*

nee′dle•work′, *n.* the art or product of working with a needle, esp. in embroidery or needlepoint.

need•n′t (nēd′nt), contraction of *need not.*

needs (nēdz), *adv.* of necessity (usu. prec. or fol. by *must*): *It needs must be.*

need′y, *adj.,* **-i•er, -i•est.** extremely poor; destitute. —**need′i•ness,** *n.*

ne′er (nâr), *adv. Literary.* never.

ne′er′-do-well′, *n.* an idle, worthless person.

ne•far•i•ous (ni fâr′ē əs), *adj.* extremely wicked or villainous: *a nefarious plot.* —**ne•far′i•ous•ly,** *adv.* —**ne•far′i•ous•ness,** *n.*

Nef•er•ti•ti (nef′ər tē′tē) also **Nef•re•te•te** (nef′-ri-), *n.* fl. early 14th century B.C., Egyptian queen: wife of Akhenaton.

ne•gate (ni gāt′, neg′āt), *v.t.,* **-gat•ed, -gat•ing. 1.** to deny the existence or truth of (something). **2.** to nullify or invalidate (something).

ne•ga′tion, *n.* **1.** the act of denying. **2.** the absence or opposite of something considered positive. **3.** a negative idea or concept.

neg•a•tive (neg′ə tiv), *adj., n., v.,* **-tived, -tiv•ing.** —*adj.* **1.** expressing negation or denial. **2.** expressing refusal or resistance. **3.** lacking positive attributes. **4.** lacking in constructiveness or helpfulness. **5.** *Math.* expressing a quantity less than zero. **6.** *Photog.* noting an image in which the light and dark tones are reversed. **7.** of or pertaining to the electric charge of a body that has an excess of electrons. **8.** *Med.* failing to show a positive result in a diagnostic test. —*n.* **9.** a negative answer, word, etc. **10.** a negative quality or characteristic. **11.** *Photog.* a negative image, as on a film. —*v.t.* **12.** to deny; contradict. **13.** to veto. —*Idiom.* **14. in the negative,** in the form of a negative response. —**neg′a•tive•ly,** *adv.* —**neg′a•tive•ness, neg′a•tiv′i•ty,** *n.*

neg•a•tiv•ism, *n.* a negative or pessimistic attitude.

ne•glect (ni glekt′), *v.t.* **1.** to pay too little attention to; disregard. **2.** to be remiss in the care of. **3.** to fail to carry out or perform. —*n.* **4.** an act or instance of neglecting. **5.** the fact or state of being neglected. —**ne•glect′ful,** *adj.* —**ne•glect′ful•ly,** *adv.*

neg•li•gee (neg′li zhā′, neg′li zhā′), *n., pl.* **-gees.** a woman's dressing gown of sheer, soft fabric.

neg•li•gent (neg′li jənt), *adj.* **1.** guilty of or characterized by neglect. **2.** careless and indifferent. —**neg′li•gence,** *n.* —**neg′li•gent•ly,** *adv.*

neg′li•gi•ble (-jə bəl), *adj.* so small or unimportant as to be safely disregarded.

ne•go•ti•a•ble (ni gō′shē ə bəl, -shə bəl), *adj.* **1.** capable of being negotiated. **2.** (esp. of securities) transferable by delivery. —**ne•go′ti•a•bil′i•ty,** *n.*

ne•go′ti•ate′ (-shē āt′), *v.,* **-at•ed, -at•ing.** —*v.i.* **1.** to deal or bargain with another or others. —*v.t.* **2.** to arrange for by discussion and settlement of terms. **3.** to move through in a satisfactory manner: *to negotiate a sharp curve.* **4.** to transfer (a draft, promissory note, etc.) to a new owner by delivery. —**ne•go′ti•a′tion,** *n.* —**ne•go′ti•a′tor,** *n.*

Neg•ri•tude (neg′ri tōōd′, -tyōōd′, nē′gri-), *n.* (*sometimes l.c.*) prideful recognition by black peoples of their cultural heritage.

Ne•gro¹ (nē′grō), *adj., n., pl.* **-groes.** *Sometimes Offensive.* —*adj.* **1.** of, designating, or characteristic of one of the traditional racial divisions of humankind, marked by brown to black skin and including esp. the indigenous peoples of sub-Saharan Africa. —*n.* **2.** a member of the Negro race. [< Sp and Pg *negro* black < L] —**Usage.** See BLACK.

Ne•gro² (nā′grō), *n.* a river in NW South America, flowing SE from Colombia into the Amazon. 1400 mi. (2255 km) long.

Ne′groid, *adj.* of or characteristic of the Negro race.

NEH, National Endowment for the Humanities.

Neh., Nehemiah.

Ne•he•mi•ah (nē′ə mī′ə), *n.* **1.** a Hebrew leader of the 5th century B.C. **2.** a book of the Bible bearing his name.

Neh•ru (nā′rōō, nâr′ōō), *n.* **Jawaharlal,** 1889–1964, first prime minister of India 1947–64.

neigh (nā), *n.* **1.** the high-pitched, snorting sound of a horse. —*v.i.* **2.** to utter such a sound.

neigh•bor (nā′bər), *n.* **1.** a person who lives near another. **2.** a person or thing that is near another. **3.** one's fellow human being. —*v.t., v.i.* **4.** to live or be situated nearby. Also, *esp. Brit.,* **neigh′bour.** —**neigh′bor•ing,** *adj.*

neigh′bor•hood′, *n.* **1.** a district or locality, often with reference to its character. **2.** a number of persons living in a particular locality. —*Idiom.* **3. in the neighborhood of,** approximately; about.

neigh′bor•ly, *adj.* showing qualities befitting a neighbor; friendly. —**neigh′bor•li•ness,** *n.*

nei•ther (nē′ðʰər, nī′-), *conj.* **1.** not either: *Neither John nor Betty is at home.* **2.** nor: *Bob can't go; neither can I.* —*adj.* **3.** not either: *neither path.* —*pron.* **4.** not either: *Neither is to be trusted.*

nem•a•tode (nem′ə tōd′), *n.* an unsegmented worm with an elongated, cylindrical body; roundworm.

nem•e•sis (nem′ə sis), *n., pl.* **-ses** (-sēz′). **1.** a source of harm or failure. **2.** an unconquerable opponent. **3.** an agent or act of retribution.

neo-, a combining form meaning new, recent, or revived (*neoclassic*).

ne•o•clas•sic (nē′ō klas′ik) also **-si•cal,** *adj.* noting or pertaining to a revival or adaptation of classical styles, principles, etc., as in art or architecture. —**ne′o•clas′si•cism** (-ə siz′əm), *n.*

ne′o•co•lo′ni•al•ism, *n.* the policy by which a nation exerts control over a less powerful independent nation.

ne•o•dym•i•um (nē′ō dim′ē əm), *n.* a rare-earth element occurring with cerium and other rare-earth metals. *Symbol:* Nd; *at. wt.* 144.24; *at. no.:* 60.

Ne•o•lith•ic (nē′ə lith′ik), *adj.* noting or pertaining to the last phase of the Stone Age.

ne•ol•o•gism (nē ol′ə jiz′əm), *n.* a new word or phrase or an existing word used in a new sense.

ne•on (nē′on), *n.* an inert gaseous element occurring in small amounts in the earth's atmosphere, used chiefly in a type of electrical lamp. *Symbol:* Ne; *at. wt.:* 20.183; *at. no.:* 10.

ne•o•nate (nē′ə nāt′), *n.* a newborn child. —**ne′o•na′tal,** *adj.*

ne•o•or•tho•dox•y or **ne•o-or•tho•dox•y** (nē′-ō ôr′thə dok′sē), *n.* a 20th-century movement in Protestant theology reacting against liberal theology and reaffirming doctrines of the Reformation. —**ne′o•or′tho•dox,** *adj.*

ne′o•phyte′ (-fīt′), *n.* **1.** a beginner or novice. **2.** a new convert to a belief.

ne′o•plasm (-plaz′əm), *n.* a new growth of abnormal tissue; tumor. —**ne′o•plas′tic** (-plas′tik), *adj.*

ne′o•prene′ (-prēn′), *n.* an oil-resistant synthetic rubber, used in putty, paint, etc.

Ne•pal (nə pôl′, -päl′), *n.* a constitutional monarchy in the Himalayas. 22,641,061. —**Nep•a•lese** (nep′ə-lēz′, -lēs′), *n., pl.* **-lese,** *adj.*

ne•pen•the (ni pen′thē), *n., pl.* **-thes.** anything inducing a pleasurable sensation of forgetfulness.

neph•ew (nef′yōō; *esp. Brit.* nev′yōō), *n.* **1.** a son of one's brother or sister. **2.** a son of one's spouse's brother or sister.

Neph•i•lim (nef′ə lim), *n.pl.* a race of giants. Gen. 6:4; Num. 13:33.

neph•rite (nef′rīt), *n.* a whitish to dark green form of jade.

ne•phri•tis (nə frī′tis), *n.* inflammation of the kidneys. —**ne•phrit′ic** (-frit′ik), *adj.*

ne plus ul•tra (nē′ plus′ ul′trə, nā′), *n.* the highest point or stage. [< L: not further beyond]

nep•o•tism (nep′ə tiz′əm), *n.* favoritism based on family relationship. —**nep′o•tist,** *n.*

Nep•tune (nep′tōon, -tyōon), *n.* **1.** the Roman god of the sea. **2.** the planet eighth in order from the sun.

nep•tu•ni•um (nep tōo′nē əm, -tyōo′-), *n.* a radioactive element produced in nuclear reactors by the neutron bombardment of uranium. *Symbol:* Np; *at. no.:* 93; *at. wt.:* 237.

nerd (nûrd), *n. Slang.* a dull, ineffectual, or unattractive person.

Ne•ro (nēr′ō), *n.* A.D. 37–68, emperor of Rome 54–68.

nerve (nûrv), *n., v.,* **nerved, nerv•ing.** —*n.* **1.** one or more bundles of fibers that convey impulses between the brain or spinal cord and other parts of the body. **2.** courage. **3.** boldness; impudence. **4.** **nerves,** nervousness. —*v.t.* **5.** to give courage to. —*Idiom.* **6. get on someone's nerves,** to irritate someone.

nerve′ cell′, *n.* NEURON.

nerve′ cen′ter, *n.* a control center.

nerve′ gas′, *n.* any of several poison gases that interfere with nerve conduction and respiration.

nerve′less, *adj.* **1.** calm. **2.** lacking vigor; weak. —**nerve′less•ly,** *adv.*

nerve′-rack′ing or **-wrack′ing,** *adj.* producing great tension or irritation.

nerv′ous, *adj.* **1.** uneasy; fearful; timid. **2.** highly excitable or agitated. **3.** of or affecting the nerves: *nervous tension.* —**nerv′ous•ly,** *adv.* —**nerv′ous•ness,** *n.*

nerv′ous break′down, *n.* (not in technical use) any disabling mental or emotional disorder.

nerv′ous sys′tem, *n.* a system involved in receiving and transmitting stimuli and controlling bodily activities: in vertebrates it includes the brain, spinal cord, nerves, etc.

nerv′y, *adj.,* **-i•er, -i•est. 1.** brashly presumptuous. **2.** showing courage.

-ness, a suffix meaning: quality or state (*goodness*); something exemplifying a quality or state (*kindness*).

Ness (nes), *n.* **Loch,** a lake in SW Scotland. 23 mi. (37 km) long.

nest (nest), *n.* **1.** a structure of twigs, grasses, and mud prepared by a bird for incubating eggs and rearing young. **2.** any structure used for depositing eggs or raising young. **3.** a snug retreat or refuge. **4.** a set of items that fit one within another: *a nest of tables.* **5.** a place where something bad flourishes: *a nest of thieves.* —*v.i., v.t.* **6.** to build or settle in a nest. **7.** to fit one within another.

nest′ egg′, *n.* money saved and held for emergencies, retirement, etc.

nes•tle (nes′əl), *v.,* **-tled, -tling.** —*v.i.* **1.** to lie close and snug. **2.** to be located in a sheltered spot. —*v.t.* **3.** to settle snugly. **4.** to press affectionately.

nest•ling (nest′ling), *n.* a bird too young to leave the nest.

net¹ (net), *n., v.,* **net•ted, net•ting.** —*n.* **1.** a fabric with a uniform open mesh. **2.** a contrivance of such fabric, for catching fish or other animals. **3.** a piece of meshed fabric used to divide a court, as in tennis. **4.** anything serving to catch or ensnare. **5.** a computer or telecommunications network. **6. the Net,** the Internet. —*v.t.* **7.** to catch or ensnare.

net² (net), *adj., n., v.,* **net•ted, net•ting.** —*adj.* **1.** remaining after deductions, as for expenses. —*n.* **2.** net income, profit, etc. —*v.t.* **3.** to gain as clear profit.

Neth., Netherlands.

neth•er (neth′ər), *adj.* lying beneath; lower or under.

Neth•er•lands (neth′ər ləndz), *n.* **the,** a kingdom in W Europe. 14,715,000. —**Neth′er•land′er** (-lan′-dər, -lən-), *n.*

neth′er•most′, *adj.* lowest; farthest down.

net•i•quette (net′i kit, -ket′), *n.* the etiquette of computer networks, esp. the Internet.

net′ na′tional prod′uct, *n.* the gross national product less depreciation of capital goods.

net′ting, *n.* a net fabric.

net′tle, *n., v.,* **-tled, -tling.** —*n.* **1.** a plant covered with stinging hairs. —*v.t.* **2.** to irritate or annoy.

net′tle•some, *adj.* **1.** causing irritation or annoyance. **2.** easily provoked or annoyed.

net′work′, *n.* **1.** any combination of intersecting filaments, lines, etc. **2.** a group of broadcasting stations linked together so that the same program can be carried by all. **3.** any system of interconnected elements. **4.** a computer or telecommunications system linked to permit exchange of information. —*v.i.* **5.** to engage in networking. —*v.t.* **6.** to place in or connect to a network. **7.** to organize into a network.

net′work comput′er, *n.* a computer with minimal processing power, designed primarily to provide access to networks, as the Internet.

net′work′ing, *n.* **1.** the informal sharing of information among individuals linked by a common interest. **2.** the design, establishment, or utilization of a computer network.

neu•ral (nōor′əl, nyōor′-), *adj.* of a nerve or the nervous system. —**neu′ral•ly,** *adv.*

neu•ral•gia (nōo ral′jə, nyōo-), *n.* sharp and paroxysmal pain along a nerve. —**neu•ral′gic,** *adj.*

neur•as•the•ni•a (nōor′əs thē′nē ə, nyōor′-), *n.* a pattern of symptoms, including chronic fatigue, often linked with depression. —**neur′as•then′ic** (-then′ik), *adj., n.*

neu•ri•tis (nōo rī′tis, nyōo-), *n.* inflammation of a nerve.

neuro-, a combining form meaning nerve or nervous system (*neurology*).

neu•rol•o•gy (-rol′ə jē), *n.* the branch of medicine dealing with the nervous system. —**neu•ro•log•i•cal** (nōor′ə loj′i kəl), *adj.* —**neu•rol′o•gist,** *n.*

neu•ron (nōor′on, nyōor′-), *n.* a cell that is the functional unit of the nervous system, consisting of the cell body and its processes. —**neu•ron•al** (nōor′-ə nl, nyōor′-, nōo rōn′l, nyōo-), *adj.*

neu•ro•sis (nōo rō′sis, nyōo-), *n., pl.* **-ses** (-sēz) a disorder in which anxiety, obsessional thoughts, compulsive acts, etc., dominate the personality. —**neu•rot′ic** (-rot′ik), *adj., n.* —**neu•rot′ic•al•ly,** *adv.*

neu•ro•sur•ger•y (nōor′ō sûr′jə rē, nyōor′-), *n.* surgery of the brain or other nerve tissue. —**neu′ro•sur′geon** (-jən), *n.*

neu′ro•trans′mit•ter, *n.* any of several chemical substances that transmit nerve impulses across a synapse.

neu•ter (nōo′tər, nyōo′-), *adj.* **1.** of or being a grammatical gender that refers to things classed as neither masculine nor feminine. **2.** having no organs of reproduction; asexual. **3.** *Zool.* having imperfectly developed sexual organs, as worker bees. —*v.t.* **4.** to spay or castrate (a dog, cat, etc.).

neu•tral (nōo′trəl, nyōo′-), *adj.* **1.** not taking the part of either side in a dispute or war. **2.** of no particular kind, characteristics, etc.: *a neutral personality.* **3.** (of a color) **a.** without hue. **b.** matching well with most other colors. —*n.* **4.** a neutral person or nation. **5.** the position of gears when not engaged. **6.** a neutral color. —**neu′tral•ly,** *adv.*

neu′tral•ism, *n.* the policy of neutrality in foreign affairs. —**neu′tral•ist,** *n., adj.*

neu•tral′i•ty, *n.* **1.** the state of being neutral. **2.** the policy or status of a neutral nation.

neu′tral•ize′, *v.t.,* **-ized, -iz•ing. 1.** to make neutral or ineffective. **2.** to declare neutral in wartime. —**neu′tral•i•za′tion,** *n.* —**neu′tral•iz′er,** *n.*

neu•tri•no (nōo trē′nō, nyōo-), *n., pl.* **-nos.** a nearly massless electrically neutral lepton.

neu•tron (nōo′tron, nyōo′-), *n.* an elementary particle having no charge and a mass slightly greater than that of a proton.

neu′tron bomb′, *n.* a nuclear weapon designed to release an intense burst of neutrons and gamma rays, with a weaker blast than other nuclear bombs.

Nev., Nevada.

Ne•vad•a (nə vad′ə, -vä′də), *n.* a state in the W

United States. 1,603,163. *Cap.*: Carson City. *Abbr.*: NV, Nev. —**Ne·vad′an,** *adj., n.*

nev·er (nev′ər), *adv.* **1.** not ever; at no time. **2.** absolutely not: *This will never do.*

nev′er·more′, *adv.* never again.

nev′er·the·less′, *adv.* however; in spite of that.

Ne·vis (nē′vis, nev′is), *n.* an island in the E West Indies: part of St. Kitts-Nevis.

ne·vus (nē′vəs), *n., pl.* **-vi** (-vī). any congenital anomaly of the skin, as a birthmark.

new (nōō, nyōō), *adj.*, **-er, -est,** *adv., n.* —*adj.* **1.** of recent origin, production, purchase, etc.; having but lately come or been brought into being: *a new book.* **2.** of a kind now appearing for the first time; novel: *a new concept of the universe.* **3.** having but lately or but now become known: *a new elementary particle.* **4.** unfamiliar or strange (often fol. by *to*): *ideas new to us; to explore new worlds.* **5.** having but lately come to a place, position, status, etc.: *a new minister.* **6.** unaccustomed (usu. fol. by *to*): *people new to such work.* **7.** further; additional: *new gains.* **8.** fresh or unused: *a new sheet of paper.* **9.** different and better in physical or moral quality: *It made a new man of him.* **10.** other than the former or the old: *a new era.* **11.** being the later or latest of two or more things of the same kind: *a new edition of Shakespeare.* **12.** (*cap.*) (of a language) in its latest known period, esp. as a living language at the present time: *New High German.* —*adv.* **13.** recently or freshly (usu. used in combination): *new-mown hay.* —*n.* **14.** something new: *Ring out the old, ring in the new.* —*Proverb.* **15. There is nothing new under the sun,** everything has happened at least once before. Eccl. 1:9. —**new′ness,** *n.*

New′ Age′, *adj.* **1.** pertaining to a movement espousing a range of beliefs and practices traditionally viewed as occult or supernatural. **2.** pertaining to an unintrusive style of popular music using both acoustic and electronic instruments.

New′ Am′ster·dam (am′stər dam′), *n.* a former Dutch town on Manhattan Island: renamed New York by the British in 1664.

New·ark (nōō′ərk, nyōō′-), *n.* a city in NE New Jersey. 258,751.

new·bie (nōō′bē, nyōō′-), *n.* a newcomer, esp. an inexperienced user of the Internet or of computers in general.

new′born′, *adj., n., pl.* **-born, -borns.** —*adj.* **1.** recently born. —*n.* **2.** a newborn infant.

New′ Bruns′wick, *n.* a province in SE Canada. 709,442. *Cap.*: Fredericton. *Abbr.*: NB, N.B.

New·cas·tle (nōō′kas′əl, -kä′səl, nyōō′-), *n.* **1.** Also called **New′cas·tle-up·on′-Tyne′.** a seaport in NE England, on the Tyne River: coal center. 282,700. —*Saying.* **2. carry coals to Newcastle,** to provide something already present in abundance.

new′com′er, *n.* a person or thing that has recently arrived.

New′ Deal′, *n.* the economic and social policies and programs introduced by President Franklin D. Roosevelt. —**New′ Deal′er,** *n.*

New′ Del′hi (del′ē), *n.* the capital of India, adjacent to Delhi. 271,990.

new·el (nōō′əl, nyōō′-), *n.* **1.** Also called **new′el post′.** the post supporting the handrail at the top or bottom of a flight of stairs. **2.** a central pillar from which the steps of a winding stair radiate.

New′ Eng′land, *n.* an area in the NE United States, including Connecticut, Maine, Massachusetts, New Hampshire, Rhode Island, and Vermont. —**New′ Eng′land·er,** *n.*

Newf., Newfoundland.

new′fan′gled (-fang′gəld, -fang′-), *adj.* of a new kind or fashion.

New·found·land (nōō′fən lənd, -land′, -fənd-, nyōō′-), *n.* **1.** a large island in E Canada. **2.** a province in E Canada, composed of this island and Labrador. 568,349. *Cap.*: St. John's. *Abbr.*: NF, N.F., NFD.

New′ Fron′tier, *n.* the policies of the liberal wing of the Democratic party under the leadership of President John F. Kennedy.

New′ Guin′ea, *n.* a large island N of Australia.

New′ Hamp′shire (hamp′shər, -shēr), *n.* a state in the NE United States. 1,162,481. *Cap.*: Concord. *Abbr.*: NH, N.H. —**New′ Hamp′shir·ite′,** *n.*

New′ Ha′ven, *n.* a seaport in S Connecticut. 119,604.

New′ Heb′rides, *n.* former name of VANUATU.

New′ Interna′tional Bi′ble, *n.* a Bible in modern English: first published in 1978 under the direction of the New York Bible Society.

New′ Jer′sey, *n.* a state in the E United States. 7,987,933. *Cap.*: Trenton. *Abbr.*: NJ, N.J. —**New′ Jer′sey·an, New′ Jer′sey·ite′,** *n.*

New′ Jeru′salem, *n.* the abode of God and His saints; heaven.

New′ King′ James′ Ver′sion, *n.* a revision of the KING JAMES VERSION, published in 1982, that eliminated many archaic expressions.

New′ Lat′in, *n.* the Latin of literature and learned writing from c1500 to the present.

new′ly, *adv.* **1.** recently; lately. **2.** anew or afresh.

new′ly·wed′, *n.* a person who has recently married.

New·man (nōō′mən, nyōō′-), *n.* **John Henry, Cardinal,** 1801–90, English Roman Catholic theologian and author.

New′ Mex′ico, *n.* a state in the SW United States. 1,713,407. *Cap.*: Santa Fe. *Abbr.*: NM, N.M., N. Mex.

new′ moon′, *n.* the moon either when in conjunction with the sun or soon after, being either invisible or visible as a slender crescent.

New′ Or′le·ans (ôr′lē əns, -lənz, ôr lēnz′), *n.* a seaport in SE Louisiana. 484,149.

New′port News′ (nōō′pôrt′, -pərt, nyōō′-), *n.* a seaport in SE Virginia. 179,127.

New′ Revised′ Stand′ard Ver′sion, *n.* a revision of the 1952 REVISED STANDARD VERSION: published in 1989.

news (nōōz, nyōōz), *n.* **1.** a report of a recent event. **2.** a report on recent events in a newspaper or on radio or television. **3.** such reports taken collectively.

news′boy′, *n.* a person who sells or delivers newspapers.

news′cast′, *n.* a broadcast of news on radio or television. —**news′cast′er,** *n.*

news′group′, *n.* a discussion group on a specific set of topics, maintained on a computer network.

news′let′ter, *n.* an informational report issued periodically by an organization to employees, contributors, etc.

news′man′ or **-wom′an,** *n., pl.* **-men** or **-wom·en.** a person employed to gather and report news.

news′pa′per (nōōz′-, nyōōz′-, nōōs′-, nyōōs′-), *n.* a publication, usu. issued daily or weekly, containing news, comment, features, and advertising.

news′pa′per·man′ or **-wom′an,** *n., pl.* **-men** or **-wom·en. 1.** a person employed by a newspaper or wire service as a reporter, writer, or editor. **2.** the owner of a newspaper.

news′print′, *n.* a low-grade paper used chiefly for newspapers.

news′reel′, *n.* a short motion picture presenting current or recent events.

news′stand′, *n.* a stall or stand at which newspapers and periodicals are sold.

news′wor′thy, *adj.* of sufficient interest to warrant press coverage. —**news′wor′thi·ness,** *n.*

news′y, *adj.,* **-i·er, -i·est.** full of news.

newt (nōōt, nyōōt), *n.* any of several brilliantly colored, semiaquatic salamanders.

New′ Tes′tament, *n.* the collection of the books of the Christian Bible, comprising the Gospels, Acts of the Apostles, the Epistles, and the Revelation of St. John the Divine.

new·ton (nōōt′n, nyōōt′n), *n.* the SI unit of force, equal to the force that produces an acceleration of one meter per second per second on a mass of one kilogram. [after I. NEWTON]

New·ton (nōōt′n, nyōōt′n), *n.* **Sir Isaac,** 1642–1727, English physicist and mathematician.

new′ wave′, *n.* (*often caps.*) a movement, esp. in French filmmaking of the 1950s, that breaks with traditional values, techniques, etc.

New′ World′, *n.* Western Hemisphere.

New′ Year′s′ Day′, *n.* January 1.

New′ Year′s′ Eve′, *n.* the night of December 31.

New′ York′, *n.* **1.** a state in the NE United States. 18,184,774. *Cap.:* Albany. *Abbr.:* NY, N.Y. **2.** Also called **New′ York′ Cit′y.** a seaport in SE New York. 7,333,253. —**New′ York′er,** *n.*

New′ Zea′land (zē′lənd), *n.* a country in the S Pacific, SE of Australia, consisting of two large islands. 3,587,275. —**New′ Zea′land•er,** *n.*

next (nekst), *adj.* **1.** immediately following in time, order, etc. **2.** nearest in place or position. —*adv.* **3.** in the nearest place, time, order, etc. **4.** on the first occasion to follow. —*Idiom.* **5. next to, a.** adjacent to: *Sit next to me.* **b.** almost; nearly: *next to impossible.* **c.** aside from: *Next to me, you're the best.*

next′-door′, *adj.* situated in the next house, apartment, etc.

nex•us (nek′səs), *n., pl.* **nex•us.** a means of connection; tie; link.

Nez Percé (nez′ pûrs′), *n., pl.* **Nez Percé, Nez Per•cés.** a member of an American Indian people of Idaho, SE Washington, and NE Oregon.

NF or **N.F.,** Newfoundland.

NFD. or **Nfd.** or **Nfld.,** Newfoundland.

N.G., 1. National Guard. **2.** no good.

NH or **N.H.,** New Hampshire.

Ni, *Chem. Symbol.* nickel.

ni•a•cin (nī′ə sin), *n.* nicotinic acid.

Niag′ara Falls′, *n.* the falls on a river **(Niag′ara Riv′er)** flowing from Lake Erie into Lake Ontario.

Nia•mey (nyä mā′), *n.* the capital of Niger. 399,100.

nib (nib), *n.* **1.** the writing end of a pen. **2.** any pointed end.

nib′ble, *v.,* **-bled, -bling,** *n.* —*v.t., v.i.* **1.** to eat small bits of (something). **2.** to bite gently. —*n.* **3.** a small or gentle bite. —**nib′bler,** *n.*

nibs (nibz), *n.* **his** or **her nibs,** *Informal.* a haughty person in authority.

Ni•cae•a (nī sē′ə), *n.* an ancient city in NW Asia Minor: Nicene Creed formulated here A.D. 325.

Nic•a•ra•gua (nik′ə rä′gwə), *n.* a republic in Central America. 4,386,399. —**Nic′a•ra′guan,** *n., adj.*

nice (nīs), *adj.,* **nic•er, nic•est. 1.** pleasing; agreeable. **2.** amiable; pleasant; kind. **3.** requiring or displaying great skill, tact, or precision. **4.** fine or subtle: *a nice distinction.* **5.** refined in manners, language, etc. —*Idiom.* **6. nice and,** (used as an intensifier to indicate sufficiency, pleasure, comfort, or the like): *It's nice and warm in here.* [< OF: silly, simple < L *nescius* ignorant] —**nice′ly,** *adv.* —**nice′-ness,** *n.*

Nice (nēs), *n.* a seaport in SE France. 338,486.

Ni′cene Creed′, *n.* a formal statement of Christian belief, adopted by the first Nicene Council.

ni•ce•ty (nī′si tē), *n., pl.* **-ties. 1.** a delicate or fine point. **2.** exactness, as in workmanship. **3.** Usu., **-ties.** refined or fine things or manners.

niche (nich), *n.* **1.** a recess in a wall, as for a decorative object. **2.** a suitable place or position. **3.** the position of a particular population in an ecological community.

Nich•o•las (nik′ə ləs, nik′ləs), *n.* **Saint,** fl. 4th century A.D., bishop in Asia Minor: patron saint of Russia; protector of children and prototype of Santa Claus.

nick (nik), *n.* **1.** a small notch, groove, etc., cut into a surface. —*v.t.* **2.** to injure slightly. **3.** to make a nick in. —*Idiom.* **4. in the nick of time,** at the last possible moment.

nick•el (nik′əl), *n.* **1.** a hard, silvery white metallic element, used in alloys and in electroplating. *Symbol:* Ni; *at. wt.:* 58.71; *at. no.:* 28. **2.** a copper and nickel coin of the U.S., equal to five cents.

nick•el•o•de•on (nik′ə lō′dē ən), *n.* **1.** an early jukebox. **2.** an early motion-picture theater.

nick•er (nik′ər), *n., v.i.* neigh.

nick′name′, *n., v.,* **-named, -nam•ing.** —*n.* **1.** a name substituted for the proper name of a person, place, etc. **2.** a familiar form of a proper name, as *Jim* for *James.* —*v.t.* **3.** to give a nickname to.

Nic•o•de•mus (nik′ə dē′məs), *n.* a Pharisee and member of the Sanhedrin who became a secret follower of Jesus. John 3:1–21; 7:50–52; 19:39.

Nic•o•si•a (nik′ə sē′ə), *n.* the capital of Cyprus. 164,500.

nic•o•tine (nik′ə tēn′), *n.* a highly toxic liquid alkaloid found in tobacco.

nic′o•tin′ic ac/id (nik′ə tin′ik, -tē′nik, nik′ə-), *n.* a crystalline acid that is a component of the vitamin B complex.

niece (nēs), *n.* **1.** a daughter of one's brother or sister. **2.** a daughter of one's spouse's brother or sister.

Nie•tzsche (nē′chə, -chē), *n.* **Friedrich Wilhelm,** 1844–1900, German philosopher.

nif•ty (nif′tē), *adj.,* **-ti•er, -ti•est.** *Informal.* **1.** fine; excellent. **2.** stylish or smart.

Ni•ger (nī′jər, nē zhâr′), *n.* **1.** a republic in NW Africa. 9,388,859. **2.** a river in W Africa. 2600 mi. (4185 km) long. —**Ni•ge•ri•en** (nī jēr′ē en′), *adj., n.*

Ni•ge•ri•a (nī jēr′ē ə), *n.* a republic in W Africa. 107,129,469. —**Ni•ge′ri•an,** *n., adj.*

nig•gard (nig′ərd), *n.* **1.** an extremely stingy person. —*adj.* **2.** stingy. —**nig′gard•ly,** *adv.* —**nig′-gard•li•ness,** *n.*

nig•gling (nig′ling), *adj.* **1.** petty; trivial. **2.** demanding too much care, time, etc. —**nig′gler,** *n.*

nigh (nī), *adv., adj.,* **-er, -est,** *prep.* near.

night (nīt), *n.* **1.** the period of darkness between sunset and sunrise. **2.** a condition or time of ignorance, misfortune, etc. —*Idiom.* **3. night and day,** unceasingly; continually.

night′ blind′ness, *n.* abnormally poor vision in dim light.

night′cap′, *n.* **1.** an alcoholic drink taken at the end of the day. **2.** a cap worn in bed.

night′clothes′, *n.pl.* garments for wearing in bed.

night′club′, *n.* an establishment open at night, offering food, drink, and entertainment.

night′ crawl′er, *n.* an earthworm.

night′fall′, *n.* the coming of night; dusk.

night′gown′, *n.* a loose gown, worn in bed by women or children.

night′hawk′, *n.* any of several long-winged, nightflying birds related to the whippoorwill.

night′ie, *n., pl.* **-ies.** *Informal.* nightgown.

Night•in•gale (nīt′n gāl′, nī′ting-), *n.* **Florence,** 1820–1910, English nurse.

night′life′, *n.* the activity of people seeking nighttime diversion, as at a nightclub or theater.

night′ly, *adj.* **1.** occurring each night or at night. **2.** of or characteristic of night. —*adv.* **3.** on every night. **4.** at or by night.

night′mare′ (-mâr′), *n.* **1.** a terrifying dream. **2.** a thought or experience suggestive of a nightmare. —**night′mar′ish,** *adj.*

night′ owl′, *n.* a person who often stays up late at night.

night′shade′, *n.* **1.** any of various plants related to the potato and tomato and bearing black or red berries, some species of which are poisonous. **2.** belladonna (def. 1).

night′shirt′, *n.* a loose shirtlike garment for wearing in bed.

night′spot′, *n.* nightclub.

night′ stick′, *n.* a billy carried by police officers.

night′ ta′ble, *n.* a small table set next to a bed.

night′time′, *n.* the time between evening and morning.

ni•hil•ism (nī′ə liz′əm, nē′-), *n.* **1.** total rejection of established laws and institutions. **2.** the belief that all existence is senseless and that there is no possibility of an objective basis for truth. —**ni′hil•ist,** *n., adj.* —**ni′hil•is′tic,** *adj.*

Ni•hon (nē′hôn′), *n.* Japanese name of Japan (def. 1).

Ni•ko•la•yev or **-la•ev** (nik′ə lä′yəf), *n.* a city in S Ukraine. 501,000.

nil (nil), *n.* nothing; zero.

Nile (nīl), *n.* a river in E Africa, the longest in the world, flowing N through Egypt to the Mediterranean. 3473 mi. (5592 km) long.

nim•ble (nim′bəl), *adj.,* **-bler, -blest. 1.** quick and light in movement; agile. **2.** quick to understand, devise, etc. —**nim′ble•ness,** *n.* —**nim′bly,** *adv.*

nim•bus (nim′bəs), *n., pl.* **-bi** (-bī), **-bus•es. 1.** HALO (def. 1). **2.** a rain cloud.

NIMBY or **Nim•by** (*usu.* nim′bē), not in my backyard (used to refer to persons that oppose the introduction into their neighborhood of an objectionable institution, as a prison).

Nim•rod (nim′rod), *n.* the great-grandson of Noah: noted as a hunter. Gen. 10:8–10.

nin•com•poop (nin′kəm poōp′, ning′-), *n.* a fool or simpleton.

nine (nīn), *n.* **1.** a cardinal number, eight plus one. **2.** a symbol for this number, as 9 or IX. —*adj.* **3.** amounting to nine. **4. the Nine,** the Muses. **5. nine days' wonder,** a fad or transient trend. —**ninth,** *adj., n.*

900 number, *n.* a telephone number preceded by the three-digit code "900," used to provide information or entertainment for a fee charged directly to the caller.

nine′pins′, *n.* tenpins played without the head pin.

nine′teen′, *n.* **1.** a cardinal number, ten plus nine. **2.** a symbol for this number, as 19 or XIX. —*adj.* **3.** amounting to 19. —**nine′teenth′,** *adj., n.*

nine′ty, *n., pl.* **-ties,** *adj.* —*n.* **1.** a cardinal number, ten times nine. **2.** a symbol for this number, as 90 or XC. —*adj.* **3.** amounting to 90. —**nine′ti•eth,** *adj., n.*

Nin•e•veh (nin′ə və), *n.* the ancient capital of Assyria, on the Tigris River, in what is now N Iraq.

nin•ny (nin′ē), *n., pl.* **-nies.** a fool or simpleton.

ni•o•bi•um (nī ō′bē əm), *n.* a steel-gray metallic element, used chiefly in alloy steels. *Symbol:* Nb; *at. no.:* 41; *at. wt.:* 92.906.

nip (nip), *v.,* **nipped, nip•ping,** *n.* —*v.t.* **1.** to pinch; bite. **2.** to sever by pinching, biting, or snipping. **3.** to check in growth or development. **4.** to affect painfully, as cold does. —*n.* **5.** the act of nipping. **6.** a biting quality, as of frosty air. **7.** sharp cold. **8.** a small quantity of anything. —*Idiom.* **9. nip and tuck,** closely contested.

nip′per, *n.* **1.** a person or thing that nips. **2.** Usu., **-pers.** a device for nipping, as pincers or forceps. **3.** the claw of a crustacean. **4.** a small boy.

nip′ple, *n.* **1.** a protuberance of the breast where, in the female, the milk ducts discharge. **2.** something resembling it, as the mouthpiece of a nursing bottle.

Nip•pon (ni pon′, nip′on), *n.* Japanese name of JAPAN (def. 1).

nip′py, *adj.,* **-pi•er, -pi•est. 1.** chilly; cold. **2.** sharp; pungent.

nir•va•na (nir vä′nə, -van′ə, nər-), *n.* **1.** (*often cap.*) (in Buddhism) release from the cycle of reincarnations as a result of the extinction of individual passion, hatred, and delusion. **2.** a state of freedom from pain and worry.

Ni•sei (nē′sā, nē sā′), *n., pl.* **-sei.** (*sometimes l.c.*) a child of Japanese immigrants, born and educated in North America. [< Japn: lit., second generation]

nit (nit), *n.* **1.** the egg of a parasitic insect, esp. of a louse. **2.** the young of such an insect.

ni•ter (nī′tər), *n.* **1.** POTASSIUM NITRATE. **2.** SODIUM NITRATE. Also, *esp. Brit.,* **ni′tre.**

nit′pick′, *v.i.* to be critical of inconsequential details. —**nit′pick′er,** *n.*

ni•trate (*n.* nī′trāt, -trit; *v.* -trāt), *n., v.,* **-trat•ed, -trat•ing.** —*n.* **1.** a salt or ester of nitric acid. —*v.t.* **2.** to treat with nitric acid or a nitrate.

ni′tric ac′id, *n.* a caustic liquid used in the manufacture of explosives, fertilizers, etc.

ni′tri•fy′, *v.t.,* **-fied, -fy•ing. 1.** to oxidize (ammonia, ammonium compounds, or nitrogen) to nitrites or nitrates, esp. by bacterial action. **2.** to combine with nitrogen or its compounds. —**ni′tri•fi•ca′tion,** *n.*

ni•trite (nī′trīt), *n.* a salt or ester of nitrous acid.

ni•tro•cel•lu•lose (nī′trə sel′yə lōs′), *n.* any of a group of compounds produced by adding sulfuric and nitric acids to cellulose, used in the manufacture of lacquers and explosives.

ni•tro•gen (nī′trə jən), *n.* a colorless, odorless, gaseous element that constitutes about four-fifths of the volume of the atmosphere. *Symbol:* N; *at. wt.:* 14. 0067; *at. no.:* 7. —**ni•trog′e•nous** (-troj′ə nəs), *adj.*

ni•tro•glyc•er•in (nī′trə glis′ər in) also **-er•ine** (-ə rin, -ə rēn′), *n.* a highly explosive oily liquid used in explosives and as a vasodilator.

ni′trous ac′id, *n.* an unstable compound of nitrogen known only in solution.

ni′trous ox′ide (nī′trəs), *n.* a colorless, sweet-smelling gas, used in dentistry for mild anesthesia.

nit′ty-grit′ty (nit′e-), *n., pl.* **-ties.** the crux of a matter.

nit′wit′, *n.* a slow-witted or foolish person.

nix (niks), *n.* **1.** nothing. —*adv.* **2.** no. —*v.t.* **3.** to veto.

Nix•on (nik′sən), *n.* **Richard M(ilhous),** 1913–94, 37th president of the U.S. 1969–74 (resigned).

Nizh•ni Nov•go•rod (nizh′nē nov′gə rod′), *n.* a city in the W Russian Federation on the Volga. 1,438,000.

NJ or **N.J.,** New Jersey.

NM or **N.M.,** New Mexico.

N. Mex., New Mexico.

no[1] (nō), *adv., n., pl.* **noes, nos.** —*adv.* **1.** (a negative expressing dissent, denial, or refusal.) **2.** not at all: *He is no better.* —*n.* **3.** a denial or refusal. **4.** a negative vote or voter.

no[2] (nō), *adj.* **1.** not any. **2.** far from being: *He is no genius.*

No, *Chem. Symbol.* nobelium.

no. or **No., 1.** north. **2.** northern. **3.** number. [< L *numero*]

No•ah (nō′ə), *n.* the patriarch who built a ship (**No′-ah's Ark′**) in which he, his family, and animals of every species survived the Flood. Gen. 5–9.

No•bel (nō bel′), *n.* **Alfred Bernhard,** 1833–96, Swedish engineer, manufacturer, and philanthropist.

No•bel′ist, *n.* a winner of a Nobel prize.

no•bel•i•um (nō bel′ē əm, -bē′lē-), *n.* a synthetic radioactive element. *Symbol:* No; *at. no.:* 102.

No′bel prize′, *n.* any of various awards made annually from funds established by Alfred B. Nobel for achievements in physics, chemistry, medicine or physiology, literature, and the promotion of peace.

no•bil•i•ty (nō bil′i tē), *n., pl.* **-ties. 1.** the noble class in a country. **2.** the state or quality of being noble. **3.** noble birth or rank.

no•ble (nō′bəl), *adj.*, **-bler, -blest**, *n.* —*adj.* **1.** of or belonging to a hereditary class distinguished by high birth, rank, or status. **2.** of an exalted moral character. **3.** imposing in appearance. **4.** of an admirably high quality. —*n.* **5.** a person of noble birth or rank. —**no′ble•ness**, *n.* —**no′bly**, *adv.*

no•ble•man or **-wom′an**, *n.*, *pl.* **-men** or **-wom•en.** a person of noble birth or rank.

no•blesse o•blige (nō bles′ ō blēzh′), *n.* the moral obligation of the rich or highborn to display honorable and generous conduct.

no•bod•y (nō′bod′ē, -bud′ē, -bə dē), *pron.*, *n.*, *pl.* **-bod•ies.** —*pron.* **1.** no person. —*n.* **2.** a person of no importance or influence.

no′-brain′er, *n. Informal.* something requiring little thought or effort.

noc•tur•nal (nok tûr′nl), *adj.* **1.** of or occurring in the night. **2.** active at night. —**noc•tur′nal•ly**, *adv.*

noc′turne (-tûrn), *n.* a dramatic, brooding piano composition.

Nod (nod), *n.* the land east of Eden where Cain went to dwell. Gen. 4:16.

node (nōd), *n.* **1.** a protuberance or swelling. **2.** a part of a stem that bears a leaf or branch. —**nod′al**, *adj.*

nod•ule (noj′ōōl), *n.* **1.** a small node. **2.** a small, rounded mass or lump. —**nod′u•lar**, *adj.*

No•el (nō el′), *n.* CHRISTMAS.

no′-fault′, *adj.* **1.** of or being a form of automobile insurance entitling a policyholder to collect basic compensation without determination of liability. **2.** holding neither party responsible: *a no-fault divorce.*

nog•gin (nog′ən), *n.* **1.** a small mug. **2.** *Informal.* a person's head.

no′-good′, *adj.* worthless or undependable.

noise (noiz), *n.*, *v.*, **noised, nois•ing.** —*n.* **1.** sound, esp. of a loud or harsh kind. **2.** loud shouting or clamor. —*v.t.* **3.** to spread, as a report or rumor. [< OF < L *nausea* seasickness] —**noise′less**, *adj.* —**noise′less•ly**, *adv.* —**nois′y**, *adj.* **-i•er, -i•est.** —**nois′i•ly**, *adv.* —**nois′i•ness**, *n.*

noi•some (noi′səm), *adj.* **1.** offensive, as an odor. **2.** harmful or injurious to health.

no•mad (nō′mad), *n.* **1.** a member of a people that has no permanent abode but moves about in search of pasturage or food. **2.** any wanderer. —**no•mad′ic**, *adj.*

no′ man's′ land′, *n.* an area between warring armies that no one controls.

nom de plume (nom′ də plōōm′), *n.*, *pl.* **noms de plume.** PEN NAME.

no•men•cla•ture (nō′mən klā′chər), *n.* a system of terms, as those of a particular science or art.

-nomics a combining form abstracted from *economics* to indicate someone's economic policies or practices: *Reaganomics.*

nom•i•nal (nom′ə nl), *adj.* **1.** being such in name only. **2.** trifling in comparison with the actual value: *a nominal fee.* **3.** of or constituting a name or names. —**nom′i•nal•ly**, *adv.*

nom′i•nate′ (-nāt′), *v.t.*, **-nat•ed, -nat•ing.** to name as a candidate for an office or honor. —**nom′i•na′tion**, *n.* —**nom′i•na′tor**, *n.*

nom•i•na•tive (nom′ə nə tiv), *adj.* **1.** noting the grammatical case typically indicating the subject of a finite verb. —*n.* **2.** the nominative case. **3.** a word in the nominative case.

nom′i•nee′, *n.*, *pl.* **-nees.** a person nominated, as for an office.

non-, a prefix meaning not (*nonaligned*).

non•age (non′ij, nō′nij), *n.* **1.** the period of legal minority. **2.** any period of immaturity.

non•a•ge•nar•i•an (non′ə jə nâr′ē ən, nō′nə-), *adj.* **1.** of the age of 90 years, or between 90 and 100 years old. —*n.* **2.** a nonagenarian person.

non•a•ligned (non′ə līnd′), *adj.* not politically aligned, esp. with either one of two opposing powers. —**non′a•lign′ment**, *n.*

non′ap•pear′ance, *n.* failure to appear.

nonce (nons), *n.* the immediate occasion or purpose.

nonce′ word′, *n.* a word coined and used only for a particular occasion.

non•cha•lant (non′shə länt′), *adj.* coolly unconcerned. —**non′cha•lance′**, *n.* —**non′cha•lant′ly**, *adv.*

non•com (non′kom′), *n. Informal.* NONCOMMISSIONED OFFICER.

non•com•bat•ant (non′kəm bat′nt, non kom′-bə tnt), *n.* **1.** a member of a military force who is not a fighter, as a chaplain. **2.** a civilian in wartime.

non′commis′sioned of′ficer, *n.* an enlisted person holding a rank below commissioned or warrant officer in the armed forces.

non′com•mit′tal, *adj.* having or giving no particular view, feeling, etc. —**non′com•mit′tal•ly**, *adv.*

non com•pos men•tis (non′ kom′pəs men′tis), *adj. Law.* not of sound mind. [< L]

non′con•duc′tor, *n.* a substance that does not readily conduct heat, sound, or electricity.

non′con•form′ist, *n.* **1.** one who refuses to conform, as to established customs. **2.** (*often cap.*) a Protestant in England who is not a member of the Church of England. —**non′con•form′i•ty**, *n.*

non•dair′y, *adj.* containing no dairy ingredients.

non•de•script (non′di skript′), *adj.* **1.** undistinguished or dull. **2.** of no recognized or specific type or kind.

none (nun), *pron.* **1.** no one; not one. **2.** not any. **3.** no part; nothing: *I'll have none of that.* **4.** (*used with a pl. v.*) not any persons or things: *None were left when I came.* —*adv.* **5.** not at all: *We saw the ceremony none too well.* —**Usage.** Many people insist that NONE is always singular and must take a singular verb. However, it has been used as a singular and a plural since the 9th century, and the plural is actually more common when the meaning is "not any persons or things": *The rescue party searched for survivors, but none were found.*

non•en′ti•ty, *n.*, *pl.* **-ties.** a person or thing of no importance.

none′such′, *n.* a person or thing without equal.

none′the•less′, *adv.* nevertheless.

non•e•vent (non′i vent′), *n.* **1.** a well-publicized event that does not occur or occurs with little impact; anticlimax. **2.** an occasion that creates little or no interest.

non′fat′, *adj.* having the fat solids removed.

non•fic′tion, *n.* literature comprising works that are not fictional. —**non•fic′tion•al**, *adj.*

non′in•ter•ven′tion, *n.* **1.** abstention by a nation from interference in the affairs of other nations. **2.** failure or refusal to intervene.

non•met′al, *n.* an element not having the character of a metal, as carbon or nitrogen.

non•mil•len•ni•al•ism (non′mi len′ē ə liz′əm), *n.* AMILLENNIALISM.

no′-non′sense, *adj.* **1.** serious; businesslike. **2.** practical.

non•pa•reil (non′pə rel′), *adj.* **1.** having no equal; peerless. —*n.* **2.** a person or thing having no equal.

non•par′ti•san, *adj.* **1.** not partisan. **2.** not affiliated with any of the established political parties.

non•per′son, *n.* UNPERSON.

non•plus (non plus′, non′plus), *v.t.*, **-plussed** or **-plused, -plus•sing** or **-plus•ing.** to render utterly perplexed.

non•prof′it, *adj.* not established for the purpose of making a profit.

non′pro•lif′er•a′tion, *n.* the practice of curbing proliferation, esp. of nuclear weapons.

non′rep•re•sen•ta′tion•al, *adj.* not resembling any object in nature: *a nonrepresentational painting.*

non•res′i•dent, *adj.* **1.** not resident in a particular place. —*n.* **2.** a person who is nonresident.

non′re•stric′tive, *adj.* noting a word, phrase, or clause that describes a modified element but is not essential to its meaning, usu. set off by commas.

non•sched′uled, *adj.* (of an airline or plane) authorized to operate between specified points as demand warrants, rather than on a regular schedule.

non′sec•tar′i•an, *adj.* not affiliated with a specific religious denomination.

non•sense (non′sens, -səns), *n.* **1.** meaningless or absurd words or actions. **2.** anything trifling or of little use. —**non•sen′si•cal**, *adj.* —**non•sen′si•cal•ly**, *adv.*

non se•qui•tur (non sek′wi tər, -tŏŏr′), *n.* **1.** a conclusion that does not follow from the premises. **2.** a comment that is unrelated to a preceding one. [< L: it does not follow]

non•sex′ist, *adj.* not showing, advocating, or involving sexism.

non′skid′, *adj.* resistant to skidding.

non′stand′ard, *adj.* not conforming in pronunciation, grammar, etc., to the usage considered acceptable by educated native speakers.

non•start•er (non stär′tər), *n.* **1.** someone or something that does not start. **2.** an inoperative idea or proposal.

non′stick′, *adj.* having a finish that prevents food from sticking during cooking.

non′stop′, *adj.* **1.** being without a single stop en route. **2.** happening without a pause: *nonstop meetings.*

non′sup•port′, *n.* failure to provide financial support for a dependent.

non•un′ion, *adj.* **1.** not belonging to a labor union. **2.** not recognizing labor unions. **3.** not produced by union workers.

non•vi′o•lence, *n.* the policy of refraining from the use of violence, as in protesting injustice. —**non•vi′o•lent**, *adj.*

noo•dle¹ (nōōd′l), *n.* a dried strip of egg dough that is boiled and served in soups, casseroles, etc.

noo•dle² (nōōd′l), *n. Slang.* the head.

nook (nŏŏk), *n.* **1.** a corner, as in a room. **2.** any remote or sheltered spot.

noon (nōōn), *n.* twelve o'clock in the daytime.

no′ one′, *pron.* not anyone.

noose (nōōs), *n.* a loop with a running knot, as in a lasso, that tightens as the rope is pulled.

nor (nôr; *unstressed* nər), *conj.* **1.** (used in negative phrases, esp. after *neither*, to introduce the following member or members of a series): *Neither he nor I will go.* **2.** (used to continue the force of a preceding negative phrase): *I never saw him again, nor did I care.*

Nor•dic (nôr′dik), *adj.* having the physical features associated with the peoples of northern Europe, typically tall stature, blond hair, and blue eyes.

Nor•folk (nôr′fək, -fôk), *n.* a seaport in SE Virginia. 241,426.

norm (nôrm), *n.* **1.** a standard, model, or pattern. **2.** the general level or average.

nor•mal (nôr′məl), *adj.* **1.** conforming to the standard or the common type; usual. **2.** average in any psychological trait, as intelligence or personality. **3.** free from any mental disorder. —*n.* **4.** the average or mean. **5.** the standard or common type. —**nor′mal•cy**, **nor•mal′i•ty**, *n.* —**nor′mal•ize′**, *v.t., v.i.,* -ized, -iz•ing. —**nor′mal•ly**, *adv.*

Nor•man (nôr′mən), *n.* **1.** any of the Scandinavian raiders who conquered Normandy in the 10th century. **2.** one of the mixed Scandinavian and French people who inhabited Normandy and conquered England in 1066. **3.** a native of Normandy. —*adj.* **4.** of Normandy, the Normans, or their speech.

Nor′man Con′quest, *n.* the conquest of England by the Normans in 1066.

Nor•man•dy (nôr′mən dē), *n.* a historic region in NW France along the English Channel.

nor•ma•tive (nôr′mə tiv), *adj.* of or tending to establish a norm.

Nor•plant (nôr′plant′, -plänt′), *Trademark.* a longterm contraceptive for women, consisting of capsules of a progesteronelike substance implanted under the skin.

Norse (nôrs), *adj.* **1.** of medieval Scandinavia, its in-

habitants, or their speech. —*n.* **2.** the inhabitants of medieval Scandinavia.

Norse′man, *n., pl.* -men. a native of medieval Scandinavia during the Viking period.

north (nôrth), *n.* **1.** a cardinal point of the compass, lying to the left of a person facing the rising sun. **2.** the direction in which north lies. **3.** (*usu. cap.*) a region situated in this direction. **4. the North,** the northern area of the United States, esp. the states that fought to preserve the Union in the Civil War. —*adj.* **5.** lying toward or situated in the north. **6.** coming from the north. —*adv.* **7.** to, toward, or in the north.

North′ Amer′ica, *n.* the northern continent of the Western Hemisphere. —**North′ Amer′ican**, *n., adj.*

North′ Car•o•li′na, *n.* (kar′ə lī′nə), *n.* a state in the SE United States. 6,628,637. *Cap.:* Raleigh. *Abbr.:* NC, N.C. —**North′ Car•o•lin′i•an** (-lin′ē ən), *n., adj.*

North′ Dako′ta, *n.* a state in the N central United States. 638,800. *Cap.:* Bismarck. *Abbr.:* ND, N.D., N. Dak. —**North′ Dako′tan**, *n., adj.*

north′east′, *n.* **1.** a point on the compass midway between north and east. **2.** a region in this direction. **3. the Northeast,** the northeastern part of the United States. —*adj.* **4.** in, toward, or facing the northeast. **5.** coming from the northeast. —*adv.* **6.** toward or from the northeast. —**north′east′er•ly**, *adj., adv.* —**north′east′ern**, *adj.*

north′east′er, *n.* a storm from the northeast.

north•er•ly (nôr′thər lē), *adj., adv.* **1.** toward the north. **2.** from the north.

north′ern, *adj.* **1.** toward or in the north. **2.** from the north. **3.** (*often cap.*) of the North, esp. the northern U.S. —**north′ern•most′**, *adj.*

north′ern•er, *n.* (*often cap.*) a native or inhabitant of the north.

North′ern Hem′isphere, *n.* the half of the earth between the North Pole and the equator.

North′ern Ire′land, *n.* a political division of the United Kingdom, in the NE part of Ireland. 1,575,200.

north′ern king′dom, *n.* Israel under King Jeroboam.

north′ern lights′, *n.pl.* AURORA BOREALIS.

North′ern Rhode′sia, *n.* former name of ZAMBIA.

North′ Kore′a, *n.* a country in E Asia. 24,317,004. *Cap.:* Pyongyang. Official name, **Democratic People's Republic of Korea.** Compare SOUTH KOREA. —**North′ Kore′an**, *n., adj.*

North′ Pole′, *n.* the end of the earth's axis of rotation, marking the northernmost point on earth.

North′ Sea′, *n.* an arm of the Atlantic between Great Britain and the European mainland.

North′-South′ divide′, *n.* the difference in living standards between the economically developed nations, chiefly in the northern hemisphere, and the undeveloped nations of the southern hemisphere.

North′ Star′, *n.* POLARIS.

North′ Vietnam′, *n.* See under VIETNAM.

north′ward (-wərd), *adv.* **1.** Also, **north′wards.** toward the north. —*adj.* **2.** moving, facing, or situated toward the north.

north′west′, *n.* **1.** a point on the compass midway between north and west. **2.** a region in this direction. **3. the Northwest,** the northwestern part of the United States. —*adj.* **4.** in, toward, or facing the northwest. **5.** coming from the northwest. —*adv.* **6.** toward or from the northwest. —**north′west′er•ly**, *adj.,adv.* —**north′west′ern**, *adj.*

North′west Or′dinance, *n.* the act of Congress in 1787 providing for the government of the Northwest Territory.

North′west Ter′ritories, *n.* a territory in N Canada. 52,238. *Cap.:* Yellowknife. *Abbr.:* NWT, N. W.T.

North′west Ter′ritory, *n.* the region north of the Ohio River, comprising present-day Ohio, Indiana, Illinois, Michigan, Wisconsin, and the eastern part of Minnesota.

North' York', *n.* a city in SE Ontario, in S Canada. 556,297.

Norw or **Norw.**, 1. Norway. 2. Norwegian.

Nor•way (nôr′wā), *n.* a kingdom in N Europe. 4,404,456.

Nor•we′gian (-wē′jən), *n.* 1. a native or inhabitant of Norway. 2. the language of Norway. —*adj.* 3. of Norway, its inhabitants, or their language.

nos. or **Nos.**, numbers.

nose (nōz), *n.*, *v.*, **nosed, nos•ing.** —*n.* 1. the part of the face that contains the nostrils and organs of smell and that functions as a passage for air in respiration. 2. the sense of smell. 3. anything resembling a nose. 4. a faculty of detecting: *a nose for news.* —*v.t.* 5. to perceive by or as if by smell. 6. to move or push forward with or as if with the nose. 7. to nuzzle. —*v.i.* 8. to move or push forward. 9. to meddle or pry. 10. **nose out, a.** to defeat by a narrow margin. **b.** to discover by prying. —*Idiom.* 11. **on the nose,** precisely; exactly.

nose′bleed′, *n.* bleeding from the nostril.

nose′ cone′, *n.* the cone-shaped forward section of a rocket or guided missile.

nose′dive′, *n.*, *v.*, **-dived** or **-dove, -dived, -div•ing.** —*n.* Also, **nose′ dive′.** 1. a plunge of an aircraft with the forward point pointing downward. 2. a sudden drop or decline. —*v.i.* Also, **nose′-dive′.** 3. to go into a nosedive.

nose′gay′, *n.* a small bunch of flowers.

nosh (nosh), *Informal.* —*v.i.*, *v.t.* 1. to snack (on). —*n.* 2. a snack. [< Yiddish *nashn*] —**nosh′er,** *n.*

no′-show′, *n.* a person who neither uses nor cancels a reservation.

nos•tal•gia (no stal′jə), *n.* a sentimental longing for something in the past. —**nos•tal′gic,** *adj.*

Nos•tra•da•mus (nos′trə dä′məs, -dä′-, nō′strə-), *n.*, 1503-66, French astrologer.

nos•tril (nos′trəl), *n.* either of the two external openings of the nose.

nos•trum (nos′trəm), *n.* 1. a quack medicine. 2. a pet remedy, esp. for social ills.

nos•y (nō′zē), *adj.*, **-i•er, -i•est.** unduly curious; prying. —**nos′i•ly,** *adv.* —**nos′i•ness,** *n.*

not (not), *adv.* 1. (used to express negation, denial, refusal, prohibition, etc.): *It's not far from here.* 2. *Slang.* (used jocularly to indicate that a previous statement is untrue): *That's a lovely dress. Not!*

no•ta be•ne (nō′tə ben′ē), *Latin.* note well.

no•ta•ble (nō′tə bəl), *adj.* 1. worthy of notice. 2. prominent; distinguished. —*n.* 3. a prominent or distinguished person. —**no′ta•bly,** *adv.*

no•ta•rize (nō′tə rīz′), *v.t.*, **-rized, -riz•ing.** to certify (a contract or other document) through a notary public. —**no′ta•ri•za′tion,** *n.*

no′ta•ry pub′lic (-tər ē), *n.*, *pl.* **no•ta•ries public.** a person authorized to take affidavits, authenticate contracts, etc.

no•ta•tion (nō tā′shən), *n.* 1. a system of graphic symbols for a specialized use: *musical notation.* 2. the process of writing down by means of such a system. 3. a short note.

notch (noch), *n.* 1. a V-shaped cut or indentation. 2. a narrow pass between mountains. 3. a step; degree. —*v.t.* 4. to make a notch in.

note (nōt), *n.*, *v.*, **not•ed, not•ing.** —*n.* 1. a brief written record, as to assist the memory. 2. a short, informal letter. 3. **notes,** a written summary or outline of something heard, read, etc. 4. an annotation of a text. 5. distinction or importance. 6. notice or observation. 7. a distinctive quality, mood, etc. 8. *Music.* a symbol used to represent a tone, its position and form indicating the pitch and duration of the tone. 9. a written promise to pay a specified sum of money at a fixed time. —*v.t.* 10. to write down. 11. to make particular mention of. 12. to annotate. 13. to observe carefully.

note′book′, *n.* 1. a book with blank pages on which to write notes. 2. a small, lightweight laptop computer.

not′ed, *adj.* well-known; renowned.

note′wor′thy, *adj.* worthy of notice or attention.

noth•ing (nuth′ing), *pron.* 1. no thing; not anything. 2. no part or trace: *The house showed nothing of its former splendor.* 3. something of no importance or value: *Money is nothing to him.* —*n.* 4. a person of no importance. 5. nonexistence; nothingness. 6. a zero; naught. —*adv.* 7. not at all. —*Idiom.* 8. **for nothing, a.** free of charge. **b.** for no reason. **c.** futilely. —*Proverb.* 9. **Nothing ventured, nothing gained,** rewards require taking risks.

noth′ing•ness, *n.* 1. lack of being. 2. unconsciousness or death. 3. absence of meaning or worth.

no•tice (nō′tis), *n.*, *v.*, **-ticed, -tic•ing.** —*n.* 1. information or warning. 2. a written statement conveying information or warning to the public. 3. a formal notification of one's intention to terminate an agreement. 4. observation or attention. 5. a brief review of a book, play, etc. —*v.t.* 6. to become aware of or observe. 7. to mention or refer to.

no′tice•a•ble, *adj.* attracting notice or attention. —**no′tice•a•bly,** *adv.*

no′ti•fy′, *v.t.*, **-fied, -fy•ing.** to inform; give notice to. —**no′ti•fi•ca′tion,** *n.* —**no′ti•fi′er,** *n.*

no•tion (nō′shən), *n.* 1. a general or vague idea. 2. an opinion or belief. 3. a whim. 4. **notions,** small articles, as buttons or thread, displayed for sale. —**no′tion•al,** *adj.*

no•to•ri•ous (nō tôr′ē əs, nə-), *adj.* widely and unfavorably known. —**no′to•ri′e•ty** (-tə rī′i tē), *n.* —**no•to′ri•ous•ly,** *adv.*

no′-trump′, *n.* the bid in bridge to play a contract without a trump suit.

not′with•stand′ing, *prep.* 1. in spite of. —*adv.* 2. nevertheless. —*conj.* 3. although.

Nouak•chott (nwäk shot′), *n.* the capital of Mauritania. 500,000.

nou•gat (nōō′gət), *n.* a candy containing nuts and sometimes fruit.

nought (nôt), *n.*, *adj.*, *adv.* NAUGHT.

noun (noun), *n.* a word that refers to a person, place, thing, state, or quality.

nour•ish (nûr′ish, nur′-), *v.t.* 1. to sustain with food or nutriment. 2. to strengthen or promote. —**nour′ish•ing,** *adj.*

nour′ish•ment, *n.* 1. something that nourishes. 2. the act of nourishing or state of being nourished.

nou•veau riche (nōō′vō rēsh′), *n.*, *pl.* **nou•veaux riches** (nōō′vō rēsh′). a person who is newly rich, esp. when ostentatious or uncultivated. [< F]

nou•velle′ cuisine′ (nōō vel′), *n.* a style of cooking that emphasizes the use of fresh ingredients, light sauces, and the artful presentation of food. [< F]

Nov or **Nov.,** November.

no•va (nō′və), *n.*, *pl.* **-vas, -vae** (-vē). a star that suddenly becomes thousands of times brighter and then gradually fades.

No′va Sco′tia, *n.* a peninsula and province in SE Canada. 873,176. *Cap.:* Halifax. *Abbr.:* NS, N.S. —**No′va Sco′tian,** *n.*, *adj.*

nov•el¹ (nov′əl), *n.* a fictitious prose narrative of considerable length. —**nov′el•ist,** *n.* —**nov′el•is′tic,** *adj.* —**nov′el•i•za′tion,** *n.* —**nov′el•ize′,** *v.t.*, **-ized, -iz•ing.**

nov•el² (nov′əl), *adj.* of a new kind.

nov′el•ette′ (-ə let′), *n.* a brief novel.

no•vel•la (nō vel′ə), *n.*, *pl.* **-las.** a short novel.

nov•el•ty (nov′əl tē), *n.*, *pl.* **-ties.** 1. the state or quality of being novel. 2. a novel occurrence, experience, etc. 3. a small decorative or amusing article.

No•vem•ber (nō vem′bər), *n.* the 11th month of the year, containing 30 days.

no•ve•na (nō vē′nə, nə-), *n.*, *pl.* **-nae** (-nē), **-nas.** a Roman Catholic devotion occurring on nine consecutive days.

nov•ice (nov′is), *n.* 1. a person who is new to a situation or position; beginner. 2. a person admitted into a religious order for a probation period before taking vows.

no•vi•ti•ate (nō vish′ē it, -āt′), *n.* the state or period of being a novice.

No•vo•caine (nō′və kān′), *Trademark.* a brand of procaine.

No•vo•si•birsk (nō′və sə bērsk′), *n.* a city in the central Russian Federation in Asia, on the Ob. 1,436,000.

now (nou), *adv.* **1.** at the present time or moment. **2.** without further delay; immediately: *Do it now or not at all.* **3.** at the time being referred to: *The case was now ready for the jury.* **4.** in the very recent past: *I saw them just now.* **5.** in these times; nowadays. **6.** under the present circumstances: *I see now what you meant.* **7.** (used to introduce a statement or question): *Now, may I ask you something?* **8.** (used to strengthen a command, entreaty, or the like): *Now stop that!* —*conj.* **9.** inasmuch as; since (often fol. by *that*): *Now that you're here, stay for dinner.* —*n.* **10.** the present time or moment. —*adj.* **11.** current; very fashionable: *the now look.* —**Idiom.** **12. now and again,** occasionally. Also, **now and then.** **13. now you see it, now you don't,** (said of a quick disappearance.)

NOW (nou), National Organization for Women.

now′a•days′ (-ə dāz′), *adv.* at the present time.

no′ way′, *adv. Informal.* absolutely not; no.

no′way′ also **-ways′,** *adv.* in no way; not at all.

no′where′, *adv.* **1.** not anywhere. —*n.* **2.** a state or place of nonexistence. —**Idiom.** **3.** nowhere near, not nearly.

no′-win′, *adj.* denoting a condition in which one cannot succeed.

no′wise′, *adv.* not at all.

nox•ious (nok′shəs), *adj.* **1.** harmful to health. **2.** morally harmful.

noz•zle (noz′əl), *n.* a spout serving as an outlet, as of a hose.

Np, *Chem. Symbol.* neptunium.

N.P., notary public.

NRA, National Rifle Association.

NS or **N.S.,** Nova Scotia.

-n′t, a contraction of NOT: *didn't.*

NT, New Testament.

nth (enth), *adj.* **1.** being the last in a series of infinitely decreasing or increasing values, amounts, etc. **2.** utmost: *to the nth degree.*

nt. wt., net weight.

nu (nōō, nyōō), *n., pl.* **nus.** the 13th letter of the Greek alphabet (N, ν).

nu•ance (nōō′äns, nyōō′-), *n.* a subtle distinction, as in color, expression, or meaning. —**nu′anced,** *adj.*

nub (nub), *n.* **1.** the point or gist of something. **2.** a knob or lump. —**nub′by,** *adj.*, **-bi•er, -bi•est.**

nub•bin (nub′in), *n.* **1.** a small stunted piece. **2.** an imperfect ear of corn.

nu•bile (nōō′bil, -bīl, nyōō′-), *adj.* **1.** (of a young woman) marriageable. **2.** (of a young woman) sexually attractive.

nu•cle•ar (nōō′klē ər, nyōō′-; *by metathesis* -kyə-lər), *adj.* **1.** of or involving atomic weapons. **2.** operated or powered by atomic energy. **3.** having atomic weapons. **4.** of or forming a nucleus.

nu′clear en′ergy, *n.* energy released by reactions within atomic nuclei, as in nuclear fission or fusion.

nu′clear fam′ily, *n.* a social unit composed of father, mother, and children.

nu′clear phys′ics, *n.* the branch of physics that deals with atomic nuclei.

Nu′clear Reg′ulatory Commis′sion, *n.* an independent agency that regulates the nonmilitary use of nuclear energy. *Abbr.:* NRC

Nu′clear Test′-Ban′ Trea′ty, *n.* an agreement signed by 99 nations in 1963, committing them to halt atmospheric tests of nuclear weapons.

nu′clear win′ter, *n.* the worldwide devastation, darkness, and cold that conceivably could result from a nuclear war.

nu•cle•ate (*adj.* nōō′klē it, -āt′, nyōō′-; *v.* -āt′), *adj., v.,* **-at•ed, -at•ing.** —*adj.* **1.** having a nucleus. —*v.t., v.i.* **2.** to form into a nucleus. —**nu′cle•a′tion,** *n.*

nu•cle′ic ac′id (nōō klē′ik, -klā′-, nyōō-), *n.* any of a group of complex acids, either DNA or various types of RNA, that carry genetic information.

nu•cle•o•lus (nōō klē′ ləs, nyōō-), *n., pl.* **-li** (-lī′). a small, rounded body within the cell nucleus.

nu•cle•on (nōō′klē on′, nyōō′-), *n.* a proton or neutron, esp. when considered as a component of a nucleus.

nu′cle•us (-klē əs), *n., pl.* **-cle•i** (-klē ī′), **-cle•us•es.** **1.** a central part about which other parts are grouped; core. **2.** a specialized, usu. spherical mass of protoplasm found in most living cells, containing most of the genetic material. **3.** the positively charged mass within an atom, composed of neutrons and protons.

nude (nōōd, nyōōd), *adj.,* **nud•er, nud•est,** *n.* —*adj.* **1.** unclothed, as a person or the body. —*n.* **2.** an unclothed human figure, esp. in a work of art. **3.** the condition of being unclothed: *to sleep in the nude.* —**nu′di•ty,** *n.*

nudge (nuj), *v.,* **nudged, nudg•ing,** *n.* —*v.t.* **1.** to push gently with the elbow, esp. to get someone's attention. —*n.* **2.** a gentle push with the elbow.

nud•ism (nōō′diz əm, nyōō′-), *n.* the practice of going nude. —**nud′ist,** *n., adj.*

nu•ga•to•ry (nōō′gə tôr′ē, nyōō′-), *adj.* **1.** trifling or worthless. **2.** ineffective or futile.

nug•get (nug′it), *n.* **1.** a lump, esp. of native gold. **2.** anything small but of great value.

nui•sance (nōō′səns, nyōō′-), *n.* **1.** an annoying person, thing, etc. **2.** *Law.* harm, injury, or disturbance.

nuke (nōōk, nyōōk), *n., v.,* **nuked, nuk•ing.** *Informal.* —*n.* **1.** a nuclear weapon. —*v.t.* **2.** to attack with nuclear weapons.

null (nul), *adj.* **1.** without value or significance. **2.** amounting to nothing. —**Idiom.** **3. null and void,** not valid. —**nul′li•ty,** *n., pl.* **-ties.**

nul′li•fy′, *v.t.,* **-fied, -fy•ing. 1.** to render or declare legally void. **2.** to deprive of value or effectiveness. [< LL *nūllificāre* to despise] —**nul′li•fi•ca′tion,** *n.*

numb (num), *adj.,* **-er, -est,** *v.* —*adj.* **1.** deprived of sensation, as by anesthesia. —*v.t.* **2.** to make numb. —**numb′ly,** *adv.* —**numb′ness,** *n.*

num•ber (num′bər), *n.* **1.** a mathematical unit used to express an amount, quantity, etc. **2.** a numeral. **3.** the total of a collection of persons or things. **4.** a numeral or numerals assigned to an object, person, etc., for identification or classification. **5.** an imprecise but considerable quantity. **6. numbers, a.** many. **b.** numerical superiority. **c.** arithmetic. **7.** a distinct performance within a show, as a song. **8.** a category of inflection or other variation in the form of a word that indicates whether the word has one or more than one referent. —*v.t.* **9.** to mark with numbers. **10.** to amount to in number. **11.** to include in a number: *I number myself among his friends.* **12.** to count; enumerate. **13.** to fix the number of. —*v.i.* **14.** to be numbered. —**Idiom.** **15. without number,** of countless number; vast. —**Usage.** See AMOUNT.

num′ber•less, *adj.* innumerable; countless.

num′ber of the beast′, *n.* the number 666, considered to represent the Antichrist. Rev. 13:18.

Num′bers, *n.* the fourth book of the Old Testament.

num′bers game′, *n.* a misleading use of statistics.

nu•mer•al (nōō′mər əl, nyōō′-), *n.* a word, letter, or figure representing a number. —*adj.* **2.** of or noting a number or numbers.

nu′mer•ate (*v.* -mə rāt′; *adj.* -mər it), *v.,* **-at•ed, -at•ing,** *adj.* —*v.t.* **1.** ENUMERATE (def. 2). —*adj.* **2.** able to use or understand numerical techniques of mathematics. —**nu′mer•a•cy,** *n.*

nu′mer•a′tor, *n.* the term of a fraction written above or below the line.

nu•mer•i•cal (nōō mer′i kəl, nyōō-) also **-ic,** *adj.* **1.** of numbers. **2.** expressed in numbers. —**nu•mer′i•cal•ly,** *adv.*

nu•mer•ol•o•gy (nōō′mə rol′ə jē, nyōō′-), *n.* the study of numbers, as one's year of birth, to determine their supernatural meaning. —**nu′mer•ol′o•gist,** *n.*

nu/mer·ous, adj. 1. very many. 2. comprising a great number of units or individuals.

nu·mi·nous (nōō/mə nəs, nyōō/-), adj. spiritual or supernatural.

nu·mis·mat·ics (nōō/miz mat/iks, -mis-, nyōō/-), n. the study or collecting of money, medals, etc. —**nu/mis·mat/ic,** adj. —**nu·mis/ma·tist** (-mə tist), n.

num·skull or **numb·skull** (num/skul/), n. a dull-witted or stupid person.

nun (nun), n. a woman bound to a religious order, esp. by vows of poverty, chastity, and obedience.

nun·ci·o (nun/shē ō/, -sē ō/, nōōn/-), n., pl. **-ci·os.** a papal diplomatic representative in a foreign capital.

nun·ner·y (nun/ə rē), n., pl. **-ner·ies.** a convent for nuns.

nup·tial (nup/shəl, -chəl), adj. 1. of marriage or a wedding. —n. 2. Usu., **-tials.** a wedding or marriage.

Nu·rem·berg (nōōr/əm bûrg/, nyōōr/-), n. a city in SE Germany: site of international trials (1945–46) of Nazis accused of war crimes. 471,800.

Nu·re·yev (nōō rā/ef, -ev), n. **Rudolf,** 1938–93, Austrian ballet dancer, born in Russia.

nurse (nûrs), n., v., **nursed, nurs·ing.** —n. 1. a person trained in the care of the sick or infirm. 2. a woman who has the general care of a child. 3. WET NURSE. —v.t. 4. to minister to in sickness, infirmity, etc. 5. to try to cure (an ailment) by taking care of oneself. 6. to suckle (an infant). 7. to use slowly or carefully: to nurse a drink. 8. to promote the growth and development of. —v.i. 9. to suckle a child. 10. (of a child) to suckle. 11. to tend the sick or infirm. —**nurs/er,** n.

nurse/maid/, n. a woman employed to care for children.

nurs/er·y, n., pl. **-er·ies.** 1. a room set apart for young children. 2. a nursery school or day nursery. 3. a place where young trees or other plants are raised.

nurs/er·y·man, n., pl. **-men.** a person who owns or conducts a plant nursery.

nurs/ery rhyme/, n. a short, simple poem or song for very young children.

nurs/ery school/, n. a prekindergarten school for children.

nurs/ing home/, n. a residential institution caring for the aged or infirm.

nurs/ling (-ling), n. 1. a nursing infant or young animal. 2. any person or thing that is carefully nurtured.

nur·ture (nûr/chər), v., **-tured, -tur·ing,** n. —v.t. 1. to feed and protect. 2. to support and encourage. 3. to bring up; train; educate. —n. 4. upbringing; training; education. 5. development. 6. something that nourishes. —**nur/tur·er,** n.

nut (nut), n. 1. a dry fruit consisting of an edible kernel enclosed in a woody shell. 2. the kernel itself. 3. a hard, one-seeded fruit, as the acorn. 4. a metal block perforated with a threaded hole so that it can

be screwed onto a bolt. 5. Slang. a devotee or zealot. 6. Slang. an insane or eccentric person.

nut/crack/er, n. an instrument for cracking the shells of nuts.

nut/hatch/, n. a small, sharp-beaked songbird that seeks food along tree trunks.

nut/meat/, n. the kernel of a nut, usu. edible.

nut/meg (-meg), n. the hard, aromatic seed of an East Indian tree, used as a spice.

nut/pick/, n. a sharp-pointed implement for removing the edible kernels from nuts.

nu·tri·a (nōō/trē ə, nyōō/-), n., pl. **-tri·as.** 1. a large South American aquatic rodent. 2. the fur of this animal.

nu·tri·ent (nōō/trē ənt, nyōō/-), adj. 1. providing nourishment or nutriment. —n. 2. a nutrient substance.

nu/tri·ment (-trə mənt), n. something that nourishes, as food.

nu·tri/tion (-trish/ən), n. 1. the study of dietary requirements for proper health and development. 2. the process by which organisms take in and utilize food. 3. food; nutriment. —**nu·tri/tion·al,** adj. —**nu·tri/tion·al·ly,** adv. —**nu·tri/tion·ist,** n. —**nu/tri·tive** (-tri tiv), adj.

nu·tri/tious, adj. providing nourishment, esp. to a high degree. —**nu·tri/tious·ly,** adv. —**nu·tri/tious·ness,** n.

nuts (nuts), Slang. —interj. 1. an exclamation of disgust, defiance, etc. —adj. 2. insane; crazy. —**Idiom.** 3. be nuts about, a. to love deeply. b. to be wildly enthusiastic about.

nut/shell/, n. 1. the shell of a nut. —**Idiom.** 2. in a nutshell, briefly.

nut/ty, adj., **-ti·er, -ti·est.** 1. abounding in or producing nuts. 2. nutlike in flavor. 3. Slang. crazy. —**nut/ti·ness,** n.

nuz·zle (nuz/əl), v.t., v.i., **-zled, -zling.** 1. to touch or rub with the nose, snout, etc. 2. to cuddle or snuggle. —**nuz/zler,** n.

NV, Nevada.

NW or **N.W.,** 1. northwest. 2. northwestern.

NWT or **N.W.T.,** Northwest Territories.

n. wt., net weight.

NY or **N.Y.,** New York.

NYC or **N.Y.C.,** New York City.

ny·lon (nī/lon), n. 1. a strong, elastic synthetic material used for yarn, fabrics, and bristles. 2. **nylons,** stockings made of nylon. [coined by the du Pont Chemical Co.]

nymph (nimf), n. 1. any of a class of female deities in mythology, inhabiting waters or forests. 2. a beautiful young woman. 3. the young of an insect that undergoes incomplete metamorphosis.

nym·pho·ma·ni·a (nim/fə mā/nē ə), n. abnormal, uncontrollable sexual desire in a female. —**nym/pho·ma/ni·ac/,** n., adj.

N.Z. or **N. Zeal.,** New Zealand.

O

O, o (ō), n., pl. **Os** or **O's, os** or **o's** or **oes.** the 15th letter of the English alphabet, a vowel.

O (ō), interj. 1. (used in direct address, esp. in solemn or poetic language): Hear, O Israel! 2. OH.

O, Symbol. 1. the Arabic numeral; zero. 2. a major blood group. 3. Chem. oxygen.

oaf (ōf), n. a stupid or clumsy person. —**oaf/ish,** adj. —**oaf/ish·ly,** adv. —**oaf/ish·ness,** n.

O·a·hu (ō ä/hōō), n. an island in central Hawaii.

oak (ōk), n. 1. a tree of the beech family, bearing the acorn as fruit. 2. the wood of the oak. —**Proverb.** 3. Great oaks from little acorns grow,

mighty people or projects may develop from small beginnings. —**oak/en,** adj.

Oak/land/, n. a seaport in W California. 366,926.

Oak/ Ridge/, n. a city in E Tennessee, near Knoxville: atomic research center. 27,310.

oa·kum (ō/kəm), n. loose fiber obtained by picking apart old ropes, used for caulking.

oar (ōr), n. 1. a long shaft with a broad blade at one end, used for rowing or steering a boat. —**Idiom.** 2. rest on one's oars, to cease to make further effort. —**oars/man,** n., pl. **-men.**

oar/lock/, n. a U-shaped device providing a pivot for an oar in rowing.

OAS, Organization of American States.

o•a•sis (ō ā′sis), *n., pl.* **-ses** (-sēz). a fertile area in a desert region, usu. having a spring or well.

oat (ōt), *n.* **1.** a cereal grass cultivated for its edible grain. **2.** Usu., **oats.** the grain of this plant. —**oat′en,** *adj.*

oat•cake (ōt′kāk′), *n.* a small, thin cake made of oatmeal.

oath (ōth), *n., pl.* **oaths** (ōŧhz, ōths). **1.** a solemn appeal to a deity to witness one's determination to speak the truth or keep a promise. **2.** a blasphemous use of the name of God. **3.** any profane expression or utterance.

oat′meal′, *n.* **1.** meal made from oats. **2.** a cooked breakfast food made from this.

Ob (ōb, ob), *n.* a river in the Russian Federation in Asia. 2500 mi. (4025 km) long.

OB, 1. obstetrician. **2.** obstetrics.

ob-, a prefix meaning: toward or to (*object*); on or over (*obscure*); against (*obstruct*).

O•ba•di•ah (ō′bə dī′ə), *n.* **1.** a Minor Prophet. **2.** a book of the Bible bearing his name.

ob•bli•ga•to (ob′li gä′tō), *n., pl.* **-tos, -ti** (-tē). a musical line performed by a single instrument in accompaniment to a solo part.

ob•du•rate (ob′dŏŏ rit, -dyŏŏ-), *adj.* **1.** stubborn and unyielding. **2.** stubbornly resistant to moral influence; impenitent. —**ob′du•ra•cy** (-rə sē), **ob′du•rate•ness,** *n.* —**ob′du•rate•ly,** *adv.*

o•be•di•ent (ō bē′dē ənt), *adj.* complying with or submissive to authority. —**o•be′di•ence,** *n.*

o•bei•sance (ō bā′səns, ō bē′-), *n.* **1.** a bodily movement, as a bow, expressing respect or deferential courtesy. **2.** deference; homage. —**o•bei′sant,** *adj.*

ob•e•lisk (ob′ə lisk), *n.* a four-sided shaft of stone that tapers to a pyramidal apex.

obelisk

o•bese (ō bēs′), *adj.* very fat. —**o•be′si•ty,** *n.*

o•bey (ō bā′), *v.t.* **1.** to comply with the commands of. **2.** to comply with: *to obey orders.* **3.** to submit or conform to. —*v.i.* **4.** to be obedient.

ob•fus•cate (ob′fə skāt′, ob fus′kāt), *v.t.,* **-cat•ed, -cat•ing. 1.** to confuse. **2.** to darken. —**ob′fus•ca′tion,** *n.*

ob•i•ter dic•tum (ob′i tər dik′təm), *n., pl.* **obiter dic•ta** (dik′tə). an incidental remark or opinion.

o•bit•u•ar•y (ō bich′ŏŏ er′ē), *n., pl.* **-ar•ies.** a notice of the death of a person, often with a biographical sketch.

obj., 1. object. **2.** objective.

ob•ject (*n.* ob′jikt, -jekt; *v.* əb jekt′), *n.* **1.** anything that is visible or tangible. **2.** a thing or person to which thought or action is directed. **3.** a goal; objective. **4.** a noun, noun phrase, or pronoun representing the goal or recipient of the action of a verb or the goal of a preposition. **5.** *Computers.* any item that can be individually selected or manipulated, as a picture or piece of text. —*v.i.* **6.** to offer a reason in opposition. **7.** to express or

feel disapproval or dislike. —*v.t.* **8.** to state or cite in opposition. —**ob•jec′tor,** *n.*

ob•jec•tion (əb jek′shən), *n.* **1.** a reason or argument offered in opposition. **2.** the act of objecting. **3.** a feeling of disapproval, dislike, or disagreement. —**ob•jec′tion•a•ble,** *adj.*

ob•jec′tive, *n.* **1.** a purpose; goal. **2.** the lens, as in a telescope, that first receives the rays from an observed object and forms its image. —*adj.* **3.** not influenced by personal feelings; unbiased. **4.** existing without regard to thought, imagination, etc.; real. **5.** of or being a grammatical case that indicates the object of a transitive verb or preposition. —**ob•jec′tive•ly,** *adv.* —**ob•jec•tiv•i•ty** (ob′jik tiv′i tē, -jek-), **ob•jec′tive•ness,** *n.*

ob′ject les′son, *n.* a practical or concrete illustration of a principle.

ob•jet d′art (ob′zhä där′), *n., pl.* **ob•jets d′art** (ob′zhä där′). an object of artistic worth or interest.

ob•late (ob′lāt, o blāt′), *adj.* flattened at the poles, as a spheroid.

ob•la•tion (o blā′shən), *n.* an offering made to a deity.

ob•li•gate (ob′li gāt′), *v.t.,* **-gat•ed, -gat•ing.** to bind or oblige morally or legally.

ob′li•ga′tion, *n.* **1.** a moral or legal duty. **2.** a binding promise, contract, etc. **3.** the act of obligating oneself. **4.** a debt of gratitude.

o•blig•a•to•ry (ə blig′ə tôr′ē, ob′li gə-), *adj.* **1.** required as a matter of obligation; mandatory. **2.** incumbent or compulsory.

o•blige (ə blīj′), *v.t.,* **o•bliged, o•blig•ing. 1.** to bind morally or legally. **2.** to place under a debt of gratitude for a favor. **3.** to do a favor for: *He obliged us with a song.* —**o•blig′ing,** *adj.*

o•blique (ə blēk′, ō blēk′), *adj.* **1.** neither perpendicular nor parallel to a given line or surface; slanting. **2.** indirectly stated or expressed. —**o•blique′ly,** *adv.* —**o•bliq•ui•ty** (ə blik′wi tē, ō blik′-), **o•blique′ness,** *n.*

ob•lit•er•ate (ə blit′ə rāt′), *v.t.,* **-at•ed, -at•ing. 1.** to remove or destroy all traces of. **2.** to blot out. —**ob•lit′er•a′tion,** *n.*

ob•liv•i•on (ə bliv′ē ən), *n.* **1.** the state of being completely forgotten. **2.** the state of forgetting completely.

ob•liv′i•ous, *adj.* **1.** unmindful or unaware (usu. fol. by *to* or *of*). **2.** forgetful. —**ob•liv′i•ous•ness,** *n.*

ob•long (ob′lông′, -long′), *adj.* **1.** in the form of a rectangle one of whose dimensions is greater than the other. —*n.* **2.** an oblong figure.

ob•lo•quy (ob′lə kwē), *n., pl.* **-quies. 1.** censure or blame. **2.** discredit or disgrace.

ob•nox•ious (əb nok′shəs), *adj.* highly objectionable or offensive.

o•boe (ō′bō), *n.* a woodwind instrument having a slender conical body and a double-reed mouthpiece. [< It < F *hautbois* = *haut* high + *bois* wood] —**o′bo•ist,** *n.*

obs., obsolete.

ob•scene (əb sēn′), *adj.* **1.** offensive to morality or decency; indecent; lewd. **2.** abominable; disgusting. —**ob•scen′i•ty** (-sen′i-, -sē′ni-), *n., pl.* **-ties.**

ob•scu•rant•ism (əb skyōōr′ən tiz′əm), *n.* **1.** opposition to the increase and spread of knowledge. **2.** deliberate evasion of clarity. —**ob•scu′rant•ist,** *n., adj.*

ob•scure (əb skyōōr′), *adj.,* **-scur•er, -scur•est,** *v.,* **-scured, -scur•ing.** —*adj.* **1.** not clear to the understanding; ambiguous or vague. **2.** not readily seen, heard, etc. **3.** not easily noticed; inconspicuous. **4.** not famous; unknown. **5.** dark; dim. —*v.t.* **6.** to make obscure. —**ob•scure′ly,** *adv.* —**ob•scur′i•ty,** *n.*

ob•se•qui•ous (əb sē′kwē əs), *adj.* servilely complaisant or deferential; fawning.

ob•se•quy (ob′si kwē), *n., pl.* **-quies.** Usu., **obsequies.** a funeral rite or ceremony.

ob•serv•ance (əb zûr′vəns), *n.* **1.** the act of observing a law, custom, etc. **2.** a keeping or celebration of a holiday or ritual.

ob•serv′ant, adj. **1.** quick to perceive; alert. **2.** regarding attentively. **3.** careful in the observing of a law, religious ritual, etc.

ob•ser•va′tion (ob′zûr vā′shən), n. **1.** the act or faculty of observing. **2.** a remark based on what one has observed. **3.** the condition of being observed.

ob•serv•a•to•ry (əb zûr′və tôr′ē), n., pl. **-ries.** a place used for making observations of astronomical or other natural phenomena.

ob•serve′, v.t., **-served, -serv•ing. 1.** to see or notice. **2.** to regard with attention. **3.** to watch or note for a scientific or other special purpose. **4.** to remark. **5.** to obey or conform to: to observe laws. **6.** to celebrate, as a holiday, in an appropriate way. —**ob•serv′a•ble,** adj. —**ob•serv′er,** n.

ob•sess (əb ses′), v.t. **1.** to excessively preoccupy the thoughts or feelings of. —v.i. **2.** to think about something unceasingly. —**ob•sess′ive,** adj. —**ob•sess′ive•ly,** adv.

ob•ses′sion, n. **1.** the domination of one's thoughts or feelings by a persistent idea, desire, etc. **2.** the idea, desire, etc., itself.

ob•sid•i•an (əb sid′ē ən), n. a dark volcanic glass similar in composition to granite.

ob•so•les•cent (ob′sə les′ənt), adj. becoming obsolete. —**ob′so•les′cence,** n.

ob′so•lete′ (-lēt′), adj. **1.** no longer in general use. **2.** out-of-date.

ob•sta•cle (ob′stə kəl), n. something that obstructs or hinders progress.

ob•stet•rics (əb ste′triks), n. the branch of medicine concerned with pregnancy and childbirth. —**ob•stet′ric, ob•stet′ri•cal,** adj. —**ob•ste•tri•cian** (ob′stitrish′ən), n.

ob•sti•nate (ob′stə nit), adj. **1.** stubbornly adhering to a purpose, opinion, etc. **2.** not easily treated, as a disease. —**ob′sti•na•cy** (-nə sē), n.

ob•strep•er•ous (əb strep′ər əs), adj. resisting control in a noisy and difficult manner; unruly. —**ob•strep′er•ous•ly,** adv.

ob•struct (əb strukt′), v.t. **1.** to block with an obstacle. **2.** to hinder the passage, progress, etc., of. **3.** to block from sight. —**ob•struc′tion,** n. —**ob•struc′tive,** adj.

ob•struc′tion•ist, n. a person who deliberately obstructs progress. —**ob•struc′tion•ism,** n.

ob•tain (əb tān′), v.t. **1.** to get, as through effort or request. —v.i. **2.** to be prevalent or customary: the morals that obtained in Rome. —**ob•tain′a•ble,** adj.

ob•trude (əb trōōd′), v., **-trud•ed, -trud•ing.** —v.t. **1.** to thrust forward without warrant or invitation. **2.** to push out. —v.i. **3.** to thrust oneself unduly; intrude. —**ob•tru′sion** (-trōō′zhən), n. —**ob•tru′sive,** adj. —**ob•tru′sive•ness,** n.

ob•tuse (əb tōōs′, -tyōōs′), adj. **1.** not quick in perception, feeling, or intellect. **2.** not sharp or pointed; blunt.

obtuse′ an′gle, n. an angle greater than 90° but less than 180°.

ob•verse (n. ob′vûrs; adj. ob vûrs′, ob′vûrs), n. **1.** the side, as of a coin, that bears the principal design. **2.** a counterpart. —adj. **3.** facing the observer. **4.** corresponding to something else as a counterpart.

ob•vi•ate (ob′vē āt′), v.t., **-at•ed, -at•ing.** to anticipate and prevent by effective measures. —**ob′vi•a′tion,** n.

ob•vi•ous (ob′vē əs), adj. **1.** easily seen or understood. **2.** lacking in subtlety.

oc•a•ri•na (ok′ə rē′nə), n., pl. **-nas.** a simple musical wind instrument with a mouthpiece and finger holes.

O′Ca•sey (ō kā′sē), n. Sean (shôn), 1880–1964, Irish playwright.

oc•ca•sion (ə kā′zhən), n. **1.** a particular time, esp. as marked by certain occurrences. **2.** a special or important time, event, etc. **3.** a convenient or favorable time. **4.** the immediate or incidental cause or reason. —v.t. **5.** to cause; bring about. —**Idiom. 6. on occasion,** once in a while.

oc•ca′sion•al, adj. **1.** occurring or appearing at infrequent intervals. **2.** of or intended for a special occasion. —**oc•ca′sion•al•ly,** adv.

Oc•ci•dent (ok′si dənt), n. **1. the Occident, a.** the West; the countries of Europe and America. **b.** WESTERN HEMISPHERE. **2.** (l.c.) the west. —**Oc′ci•den′tal,** **oc′ci•den′tal,** adj., n.

oc•clude (ə klōōd′), v., **-clud•ed, -clud•ing.** —v.t. **1.** to close or stop up (a passage or opening). **2.** to shut in, out, or off. —v.i. **3.** (of a tooth) to make contact with the surface of an opposing tooth when the jaws are closed. —**oc•clu′sion,** n. —**oc•clu′sive,** adj.

oc•cult (ə kult′, ok′ult), adj. **1.** pertaining to any system claiming knowledge of supernatural agencies. **2.** beyond ordinary knowledge. **3.** secret; disclosed only to the initiated. **4.** hidden from view.

oc•cu•pant (ok′yə pənt), n. **1.** a person or group that occupies something. **2.** a tenant of a house, office, etc. —**oc′cu•pan•cy,** n., pl. **-cies.**

oc•cu•pa•tion (-pā′shən), n. **1.** a person's usual or principal work in earning a living. **2.** any activity in which a person is engaged. **3.** the seizure and control of an area by military forces. —**oc′cu•pa′tion•al,** adj.

occupa′tional ther′apy, n. therapy that utilizes useful activities to facilitate psychological or physical rehabilitation.

oc′cu•py′, v.t., **-pied, -py•ing. 1.** to take or fill up (time, space, etc.). **2.** to be a resident of; dwell in. **3.** to employ or engage; busy. **4.** to take possession and control of (a place), as by military invasion. **5.** to hold (a position, office, etc.).

oc•cur (ə kûr′), v.i., **-curred, -cur•ring. 1.** to happen; take place. **2.** to be found; appear. **3.** to come to mind.

oc•cur•rence (ə kûr′əns, ə kur′-), n. **1.** the action or fact of occurring. **2.** something that happens.

o•cean (ō′shən), n. **1.** the body of salt water that covers almost three-fourths of the earth's surface. **2.** any of the geographical divisions of this body: the Atlantic, Pacific, Indian, Arctic, and Antarctic oceans. **3.** a vast quantity. —**o•ce•an•ic** (ō′shē an′ik), adj.

O•ce•an•i•a (ō′shē an′ē ə, -ä′nē ə), n. the islands of the central and S Pacific, including Micronesia, Melanesia, and Polynesia. —**O′ce•an′i•an,** adj., n.

o•cea•nog•ra•phy (ō′shə nog′rə fē, ō′shē ə-), n. the branch of physical geography dealing with the ocean and marine life. —**o′cea•nog′ra•pher,** n. —**o′cea•no•graph′ic** (-nə graf′ik), adj.

o′cea•nol′o•gy (-nol′ə jē), n. the science concerned with the practical application of oceanography.

O′cean•side′, n. a city in SW California. 146,229.

oc•e•lot (os′ə lot′, ō′sə-), n. a spotted wildcat, ranging from Texas through South America.

o•cher or **o•chre** (ō′kər), n. a mixture of hydrated oxide of iron with various earthy materials, ranging in color from yellow to orange and red, and used as a pigment.

Ochs (oks), n. **Adolph Simon,** 1858–1935, U.S. newspaper publisher.

o′clock (ə klok′), adv. of, by, or according to the clock.

O′Con•nor (ō kon′ər), n. **1. (Mary) Flannery,** 1925–64, U.S. author. **2. Sandra Day,** born 1930, associate justice of the U.S. Supreme Court since 1981.

Oct or **Oct.,** October.

oc•ta•gon (ok′tə gon′, -gən), n. a polygon having eight angles and eight sides. —**oc•tag′o•nal** (-tag′ə nl), adj.

oc•tane (ok′tān), n. any of 18 isomeric saturated hydrocarbons.

oc′tane num′ber, n. a designation of antiknock quality of gasoline.

oc•tave (ok′tiv, -tāv), n. **1. a.** a tone on the eighth degree from a given musical tone. **b.** the interval encompassed by such tones. **c.** the harmonic combination of such tones. **d.** a series of tones, or of keys of an instrument, extending through this interval. **2.** a series or group of eight. **3. a.** a group of eight lines of verse, esp. the first eight lines of a sonnet in the

Italian form. **b.** a stanza of eight lines. **4. a.** the eighth day from a religious festival. **b.** the period of eight days beginning with such a day. —**oc•ta•val** (ok tā′vəl, ok′tə-), *adj.*

oc•ta•vo (ok tā′vō, -tä′-), *n., pl.* **-vos. 1.** a book size of about 6 × 9 in. (16 × 23 cm), determined by printing on sheets folded to form 8 leaves or 16 pages. **2.** a book of this size.

oc•tet or **-tette** (ok tet′), *n.* **1.** a company of eight singers or musicians. **2.** a musical composition for an octet.

Oc•to•ber (ok tō′bər), *n.* the tenth month of the year, containing 31 days.

Octo′ber surprise′, *n.* a surprising, last-minute development that may affect esp. a presidential election in November.

oc•to•ge•nar•i•an (ok′tə jə nâr′ē ən), *n.* **1.** a person between 80 and 90 years old. —*adj.* **2.** between 80 and 90 years old.

oc•to•pus (ok′tə pəs), *n., pl.* **-pus•es, -pi** (-pī′) a marine mollusk having a soft, oval body and eight sucker-bearing arms. [< NL < Gk *oktōpous* eight-footed]

oc•u•lar (ok′yə lər), *adj.* **1.** of or for the eyes. **2.** performed or perceived by eyesight.

oc′u•list (-list), *n.* an ophthalmologist.

O.D., Doctor of Optometry.

o•da•lisque (ōd′l isk), *n.* a female slave or concubine in a harem.

odd (od), *adj.,* **-er, -est. 1.** differing in nature from what is usual or expected. **2.** peculiar or eccentric. **3.** leaving a remainder of 1 when divided by 2. **4.** more or less: *sixty-odd dollars.* **5.** being part of a pair or set of which the rest is lacking: *an odd glove.* **6.** remaining after all others are grouped. **7.** not regular or full-time: *odd jobs.*

odd′ball′, *n. Informal.* a peculiar person or thing.

odd′i•ty, *n., pl.* **-ties. 1.** an odd person, thing, or event. **2.** the quality of being odd.

odds (odz), *n.* (*usu. with a pl. v.*) **1.** the probability that something is so or is more likely to occur than something else. **2.** this probability, expressed as a ratio: *The odds are two-to-one that it will rain today.* **3.** an equalizing allowance, as that given the weaker player in a contest. **4.** an advantage favoring one of two contestants. —***Idiom.*** **5. at odds,** in disagreement.

odds′ and ends′, *n.pl.* **1.** miscellaneous items, matters, etc. **2.** remnants; scraps.

odds′-on′, *adj.* being the one most likely to achieve something: *the odds-on favorite.*

ode (ōd), *n.* a lyric poem expressing exalted or enthusiastic emotion.

O•des•sa (ō des′ə), *n.* a seaport in S Ukraine, on the Black Sea. 1,115,000.

O•din (ō′din), *n.* the principal Norse god, associated with war, poetry, and wisdom.

o•di•ous (ō′dē əs), *adj.* **1.** deserving or causing hatred. **2.** highly offensive; disgusting.

o′di•um (-əm), *n.* **1.** intense hatred. **2.** the reproach, discredit, etc., attaching to some discreditable action.

o•dom•e•ter (ō dom′i tər), *n.* an instrument for measuring distance traveled, as by an automobile.

o•dor (ō′dər), *n.* **1.** the property of a substance that activates the sense of smell. **2.** a smell or scent. **3.** a quality suggestive of something: *an odor of suspicion.* **4.** repute: *in bad odor.* Also, *esp. Brit.,* **odour.** —*o′dor•ous, adj.*

o•dor•if•er•ous (ō′də rif′ər əs), *adj.* yielding an odor, esp. an unpleasant one.

O•dys•se•us (ō dis′ē əs, ō dis′yōōs), *n.* a legendary king of Ithaca, the protagonist of Homer's *Odyssey.*

Od•ys•sey (od′ə sē), *n., pl.* **-seys. 1.** (*italics*) an epic poem attributed to Homer, describing Odysseus's adventures after the Trojan War. **2.** (*l.c.*) any long, adventurous journey.

OE or **O.E.,** Old English.

OED or **O.E.D.,** Oxford English Dictionary.

oed•i•pal (ed′ə pəl, ē′də-), *adj.* (*often cap.*) of or resulting from the Oedipus complex.

Oed•i•pus (ed′ə pəs, ē′də-), *n.* a legendary king of Thebes who unwittingly killed his father and married his mother.

Oed′ipus com′plex, *n.* libidinous feelings toward the parent of the opposite sex, esp. toward the mother.

oe•nol•o•gy (ē nol′ə jē), *n.* the science of winemaking.

oe•no•phile (ē′nə fīl′), *n.* a connoisseur of wine.

o′er (ôr), *prep., adv.* over.

oeu•vre (Fr. œ′vrə), *n., pl.* **oeu•vres** (Fr. œ′vrə). the works of a writer, painter, etc., taken as a whole.

of (uv, ov; *unstressed* əv or, *esp. before consonants,* ə), *prep.* **1.** from or away from: *within a mile of the house.* **2.** by or coming from: *the songs of Gershwin.* **3.** owing to: *dead of hunger.* **4.** containing or consisting of: *a book of poems.* **5.** ruling or possessing: *the king of Spain.* **6.** possessed or ruled by: *property of the church.* **7.** (used to indicate inclusion in a whole): *one of us.* **8.** (used to indicate the object of action following a noun, verb, or adjective): *the ringing of bells.* **9.** having particular attributes: *a woman of courage.* **10.** so as to be left without: *robbed of one's money.* **11.** before; until: *ten minutes of one.* **12.** on the part of: *It was nice of you to come.* **13.** set aside for: *a minute of prayer.* **14.** about: *There is talk of peace.* **15.** named: *the city of London.* **16.** belonging to: *the sleeve of a dress.*

off (ôf, of), *adv.* **1.** so as to be no longer attached: *The button came off.* **2.** so as to be no longer covering: *Pull the wrapping off.* **3.** so as to be away or on one's way: *to start off early.* **4.** from a charge or price: *Take 10 percent off.* **5.** at a distance in space or future time: *Summer is only a week off.* **6.** out of operation: *Turn the lights off.* **7.** in absence from work, service, etc.: *to get two days off.* —*prep.* **8.** so as no longer to be supported by, resting on, etc.: *Wipe the dirt off your shoes.* **9.** deviating from: *to be off course.* **10.** below the usual level or standard: *20 percent off the marked price.* **11.** disengaged or resting from: *to be off duty.* **12.** abstaining from: *He's off gambling.* **13.** located apart from: *a village off the main road.* **14.** by means of: *living off his parents.* —*adj.* **15.** in error. **16.** less than sane: *a little off, but harmless.* **17.** no longer in effect: *The agreement is off.* **18.** in a specified state, circumstance, etc.: *to be badly off for money.* **19.** free from work or duty: *one's off hours.* **20.** of less than the ordinary activity: *an off-season in the tourist trade.* **21.** unlikely: *on the off chance she's at home.* **22.** starting on one's way: *I'm off to Europe.* —*Idiom.* **23. off and on,** intermittently. **24. off of,** off: *Take your feet off of the table!* —*Usage.* The phrase **off of,** which has existed for about 400 years, is usu. considered redundant by usage guides. Widespread in speech, it is rare in edited writing.

of•fal (ô′fəl, of′əl), *n.* **1.** the viscera or inedible remains of a butchered animal. **2.** refuse or rubbish.

off′beat′ (*adj.* -bēt′; *n.* -bēt′), *adj.* **1.** unconventional. —*n.* **2.** an unaccented beat of a measure in music.

off′-col′or, *adj.* **1.** not having the usual color. **2.** of doubtful propriety or taste.

Of•fen•bach (ô′fən bäk′, of′ən-), *n.* **Jacques,** 1819–80, French composer.

of•fend (ə fend′), *v.t.* **1.** to irritate, annoy, or anger; insult. **2.** to affect (the sense, taste, etc.) disagreeably. —*v.i.* **3.** to cause resentful displeasure. **4.** to err in conduct.

of•fense (ə fens′ or, for 6, 7, ô′fens, of′ens), *n.* **1.** a breaking of a social or moral rule. **2.** a transgression of the law; misdemeanor. **3.** something that offends. **4.** the act of offending. **5.** a feeling of resentful displeasure: *to give offense.* **6.** aggression or assault. **7.** the side that is attacking or attempting to score in a game. Also, *esp. Brit.,* **of•fence′.**

of•fen•sive (ə fen′siv or, for 4, ô′fen-, of′en-), *adj.* **1.** causing resentful displeasure. **2.** unpleasant or disagreeable to the senses. **3.** repugnant to the moral sense, good taste, etc. **4.** pertaining to offense or attack. —*n.* **5.** the position or attitude of aggression or attack. **6.** an aggressive movement or attack.

of•fer (ô′fər, of′ər), *v.t.* **1.** to present for acceptance or rejection. **2.** to propose for consideration. **3.** to present as an act of worship. **4.** to present for sale. **5.** to tender or bid as a price. **6.** to put forth; exert: *to offer resistance.* —*v.i.* **7.** to present itself; occur. —*n.* **8.** the act of offering. **9.** something offered.

of•fer•ing, *n.* **1.** something offered in worship. **2.** anything offered as a gift or contribution. **3.** the act of one who offers.

of•fer•to•ry (ô′tôr′ē), *n., pl.* **-ries. 1.** (*sometimes cap.*) the offering to God of the unconsecrated elements in a Eucharistic service. **2. a.** the verses or music accompanying the offerings made at a religious service. **b.** that part of a service at which offerings are made.

off′hand′, *adv.* **1.** without previous thought or preparation. —*adj.* **2.** casual or curt. **3.** done or made offhand. —**off′hand′ed•ness,** *n.*

of•fice (ô′fis, of′is), *n.* **1.** a place where business is conducted. **2.** the staff that works in a place of business. **3.** a position of duty, trust, or authority: *the office of president.* **4.** position as an official: *to seek office.* **5.** the duty or function of a person or agency. **6.** Often, **-fices.** something done or said for or to another: *the good offices of a friend.* **7. a.** the prescribed form for a church service or for devotional use. **b.** the services so prescribed.

of′fice•hold′er, *n.* a public official.

of•fi•cer, *n.* **1.** a person holding a commission in the armed services. **2.** a member of a police department. **3.** a person holding a position of authority in some organization.

of•fi•cial (ə fish′əl), *n.* **1.** a person holding an office or charged with certain duties. —*adj.* **2.** of an office or position of authority. **3.** appointed or authorized by a government or organization. **4.** public and formal. —**of•fi′cial•dom,** *n.* —**of•fi′cial•ism,** *n.* —**of•fi′cial•ly,** *adv.*

of•fi•ci•ant (ə fish′ē ənt), *n.* a person who officiates at a religious service.

of•fi′ci•ate′ (-āt′), *v.i.* **-at•ed, -at•ing. 1.** to perform the duties or function of some office or position. **2.** to perform the office of a cleric, as at a divine service.

of•fi′cious, *adj.* objectionably aggressive in offering unwanted help or advice.

off•ing (ô′fing, of′ing), *n.* **1.** the distant part of the sea seen from the shore. —*Idiom.* **2. in the offing, a.** at a distance but within sight. **b.** in the projected future.

off′-key′, *adj.* out of tune.

off′-lim′its, *adj.* forbidden to be patronized, used, etc., by certain persons.

off′-line′ or **off′line′,** *adj.* operating independently of, or disconnected from, an associated computer.

off′load′, *v.t., v.i.* UNLOAD.

off′-put′ting, *adj.* provoking uneasiness, dislike, annoyance, etc.

off′-sea′son, *n.* a time of year other than the busiest one for a specific activity.

off•set (*n.* ôf′set′, of′-; *v.* ôf′set′, of′-), *n., v.,* **-set, -set•ting.** —*n.* **1.** something that compensates for something else. **2.** a process in which a lithographic plate is used to make an inked impression on a rubber blanket that transfers it to the paper being printed. —*v.t.* **3.** to compensate for. **4.** to print by the process of offset lithography.

off′shoot′, *n.* **1.** a branch from a main stem, as of a plant. **2.** anything conceived of as or proceeding from a main stock.

off′shore′, *adv.* **1.** off or away from the shore. **2.** at a distance from the shore. **3.** in a foreign country. —*adj.* **4.** moving or tending away from the shore. **5.** located or operating at some distance from the shore. **6.** registered or located in a foreign country.

off′side′, *adj., adv.* illegally beyond a prescribed area or in advance of the ball or puck during play.

off′spring′, *n., pl.* **-spring, -springs.** children or young of a particular parent or progenitor.

off′stage′, *adv., adj.* away from the view of the audience.

off′-the-cuff′, *adj.* with little or no preparation; impromptu.

off′-the-rec′ord, *adj.* not to be published or quoted.

off′-the-wall′, *adj. Informal.* markedly unconventional; bizarre.

off′track′, *adj.* occurring away from a racetrack: *offtrack betting.*

off′-white′, *adj.* white mixed with a small amount of gray, yellow, or other light color.

off′ year′, *n.* **1.** a year without a major, esp. presidential, election. **2.** a year marked by reduced or inferior production or activity.

oft (ôft, oft), *adv.* OFTEN.

of•ten (ô′fən, of′ən; ôf′tən, of′-), *adv.* many times; frequently.

Og (og), *n.* the king of Bashan. Deut. 3:1–4.

o•gle (ō′gəl), *v.,* **o•gled, o•gling,** *n.* —*v.t., v.i.* **1.** to look (at) amorously or flirtatiously. —*n.* **2.** an amorous or flirtatious look.

O•gle•thorpe (ō′gəl thôrp′), *n.* **James Edward,** 1696–1785, British general: founder of the colony of Georgia.

o•gre (ō′gər), *n.* **1.** a monster in fairy tales who feeds on human flesh. **2.** a monstrously ugly or cruel person.

oh (ō), *interj., n., pl.* **ohs, oh's.** —*interj.* **1.** an exclamation of surprise, pain, sympathy, etc. —*n.* **2.** the exclamation "oh."

OH, Ohio.

O. Hen•ry (ō hen′rē), *n.* pen name of William S. PORTER.

O•hi•o (ō hī′ō), *n.* **1.** a state in the NE central United States. 11,172,782. *Cap.:* Columbus. *Abbr.:* OH **2.** a river flowing SW from Pittsburgh, Pa., to the Mississippi. 981 mi. (1580 km) long. —**O•hi′o•an,** *adj., n.*

ohm (ōm), *n.* a unit of electrical resistance.

o•ho (ō hō′), *interj.* an exclamation of surprise, exultation, etc.

-oid, a suffix meaning resembling or like (*humanoid*).

oil (oil), *n.* **1.** any of various unctuous, viscous, combustible substances that are not soluble in water. **2.** petroleum. **3. a.** OIL COLOR. **b.** OIL PAINTING. —*v.t.* **4.** to smear, lubricate, or supply with oil. —*adj.* **5.** of or resembling oil. —*Idiom.* **6. pour oil on troubled waters,** to attempt to calm a difficult or tense situation. —*Proverb.* **7. Oil and water don't mix,** very different things are incompatible.

oil′cloth′, *n.* a cotton fabric made waterproof by treatment with oil.

oil′ col′or, *n.* a paint made by grinding a pigment in oil.

oil′ paint′ing, *n.* **1.** the art of painting with oil colors. **2.** a painting in oil colors.

oil′skin′, *n.* **1.** a cotton fabric made waterproof by treatment with oil. **2.** Often, **-skins.** a garment made of this, as a raincoat.

oil′ well′, *n.* a well drilled to obtain petroleum.

oil′y, *adj.,* **-i•er, -i•est. 1.** smeared or covered with oil. **2.** of or containing oil. **3.** smooth or unctuous, as in manner. —**oil′i•ness,** *n.*

oink (oingk), *n.* **1.** the grunting sound made by a hog. —*v.i.* **2.** to utter such a sound.

oint•ment (oint′mənt), *n.* a soft, unctuous preparation, often medicated, for application to the skin.

O•jib•wa (ō jib′wä, -wə) also **-way** (-wā), *n., pl.* **-wa, -was** also **-way, -ways.** a member of an American Indian people of Canada and the U.S., living in a region around Lakes Huron and Superior.

OK, Oklahoma.

OK or **O.K.** or **o•kay** (ō′kā′, ō′kā′, ō′kā′), *adj., adv., n., pl.* **OKs, OK's** or **O.K.'s** or **o•kays,** *v.,* **OK'd** or **O.K.'ed** or **o•kayed, OK'ing** or **O.K.'ing** or **o•kay•ing.** —*adj., adv.* **1.** all right or all correct.

correct or acceptable. —*n.* **3.** an approval, agreement, or endorsement. —*v.t.* **4.** to endorse or indicate approval of. [initials of *oll korrect*, facetious spelling of *all correct*]

O'Keeffe (ō kēf′), *n.* **Georgia**, 1887–1986, U.S. painter.

O•ki•na•wa (ō′kə nou′wə, -nä′wə), *n.* the largest of the Ryukyu Islands, in the N Pacific. —**O′ki•na′-wan**, *adj., n.*

Okla., Oklahoma.

O•kla•ho•ma (ō′klə hō′mə), *n.* a state in the S central United States. 3,300,902. *Cap.:* Oklahoma City. *Abbr.:* OK, Okla. —**O′kla•ho′man**, *adj., n.*

O′klaho′ma Cit′y, *n.* the capital of Oklahoma. 463,201.

o•kra (ō′krə), *n., pl.* **o•kras. 1.** a shrub bearing sticky pods. **2.** the pods, used in soups, stews, etc.

old (ōld), *adj.,* **old•er, old•est** or **eld•er, eld•est,** *n.* —*adj.* **1.** having lived or existed for a long time. **2.** of the latter part of life or existence. **3.** having lived or existed for a specified time: *a six-month-old company.* **4.** deteriorated through age or use: *old clothes.* **5.** of long standing: *an old friend.* **6.** former: *an old classmate.* **7.** of an earlier period: *old maps.* **8.** ancient: *old civilizations.* **9.** (*cap.*) (of a language) in its oldest known period: *Old English.* **10.** experienced: *an old sailor.* —*n.* **11. the old,** old persons collectively. **12.** time long past: *days of old.*

old′en, *adj.* ancient; old.

Old′ Eng′lish, *n.* the English language before c1150.

old′-fash′ioned, *adj.* reflecting or favoring the styles, customs, or methods of the past.

old′ fo′gy (or **fo′gey**), *n.* an excessively old-fashioned person.

Old′ French′, *n.* the French language of the 9th through the 13th centuries.

Old′ Glo′ry, *n.* the national flag of the U.S.

Old′ Guard′, *n.* (*sometimes l.c.*) the conservative members of any group.

old′ hand′, *n.* a person with long experience in a subject, area, etc.

old′ hat′, *adj.* old-fashioned; dated.

Old′ Hick′ory, *n.* epithet of Andrew Jackson.

Old′ High′ Ger′man, *n.* the High German dialects before c1100.

old′ie, *n., pl.* **-ies.** *Informal.* a popular song, movie, etc., of the past.

old′-line′, *adj.* following traditional ideas, customs, etc.

old′ mas′ter, *n.* **1.** an eminent artist of the 15th to 18th centuries. **2.** a work by such an artist.

Old′ Norse′, *n.* the Germanic language of medieval Scandinavia.

Old′ Sax′on, *n.* Low German before c1100.

old′ school′, *n.* supporters of established custom or of conservatism.

Old′ Tes′tament, *n.* the complete Bible of the Jews, being the first of the two main divisions of the Christian Bible.

old′-time′, *adj.* **1.** of old or former times, methods, etc. **2.** being long established.

old′-tim′er, *n.* a person whose residence, membership, etc., dates from long ago.

old′ wives′ tale′, *n.* a traditional, often superstitious, belief or story.

Old′ World′, *n.* **1.** Europe, Asia, and Africa. **2.** EASTERN HEMISPHERE.

old′-world′, *adj.* old-fashioned; traditional.

o•lé (ō lā′), *interj.* a shout of approval, triumph, or encouragement.

o•le•ag•i•nous (ō′lē aj′ə nəs), *adj.* **1.** having the nature or qualities of oil. **2.** unctuous; fawning.

o•le•an•der (ō′lē an′dər), *n.* a poisonous evergreen shrub with clusters of pink, red, or white flowers.

o•le•o (ō′lē ō′), *n., pl.* **-os.** *Older Use.* MARGARINE.

o′le•o•mar′ga•rine, *n. Older Use.* MARGARINE.

o•les•tra (ō les′trə), *n.* a synthetic oil used as a substitute for dietary fat: not digested or absorbed by the human body.

ol•fac•to•ry (ol fak′tə rē, ōl-), *adj.* of the sense of smell. —**ol•fac′tion,** *n.*

ol•i•gar•chy (ol′i gär′kē), *n., pl.* **-chies. 1.** a form of government in which power is vested in a few persons. **2.** a state so ruled. **3.** the persons so ruling. —**ol′i•garch′,** *n.* —**ol′i•gar′chic,** *adj.*

Ol•i•go•cene (ol′i gō sēn′), *adj.* noting or pertaining to the third epoch of the Tertiary Period.

ol•ive (ol′iv), *n.* **1.** an evergreen tree of Mediterranean and other warm regions. **2.** the small, oval fruit of this tree, eaten as a relish and used as a source of oil. **3.** the dull yellow-green of the unripe fruit.

ol′ive branch′, *n.* a branch of the olive tree as an emblem of peace.

O•lym•pi•a (ə lim′pē ə), *n.* the capital of Washington. 27,447.

O•lym′pic Games′ (ə lim′pik), *n.pl.* **1.** the greatest of the national festivals of ancient Greece. **2.** Also called **O•lym′pics.** a modern international sports competition with Summer Games and Winter Games alternating every two years.

O•lym′pus (ə lim′pəs), *n.* **Mount,** a mountain in NE Greece, mythical abode of the Greek gods. 9730 ft. (2966 m). —**O•lym′pi•an,** *adj.*

Om (ōm), *n.* a sacred syllable used as a mantra in Hinduism and Buddhism.

O•ma•ha (ō′mə hô′, -hä′), *n.* a city in E Nebraska. 345,033.

O•man (ō män′), *n.* an independent sultanate in SE Arabia. 2,264,590. —**O•ma•ni** (ō mä′nē), *n., pl.* **-nis,** *adj.*

O•mar Khay•yám (ō′mär kī yäm′, -yam′, ō′mər), *n.* died 1123?, Persian poet and mathematician.

om•buds•man (om′bədz mən, ôm′-, om boodz′-, ôm-), *n., pl.* **-men. 1.** a public official who investigates complaints by citizens against government agencies or officials. **2.** a person who investigates and resolves complaints. [< Sw: legal representative]

o•me•ga (ō mē′gə, ō meg′ə), *n., pl.* **-gas.** the 24th and last letter of the Greek alphabet (Ω, ω).

o•me′ga-3 fat′ty ac′id, *n.* a fatty acid found esp. in fish oil and valuable in reducing blood cholesterol levels.

om•e•let or **-lette** (om′lit, om′ə-), *n.* a dish of beaten eggs cooked and served folded, often around a filling.

o•men (ō′mən), *n.* any event believed to portend something good or evil.

om•i•cron (om′i kron′, ō′mi-), *n.* the 15th letter of the Greek alphabet (O, o).

om•i•nous (om′ə nəs), *adj.* portending evil or harm.

o•mit (ō mit′), *v.t.,* **o•mit•ted, o•mit•ting. 1.** to leave out; fail to include. **2.** to fail (to do, make, use, etc.). —**o•mis′sion,** *n.*

omni-, a combining form meaning all (*omnipotent*).

om•ni•bus (om′nə bus′, -bəs), *n., pl.* **-bus•es, bus•ses,** *adj.* —*n.* **1.** BUS¹ (def. 1). —*adj.* **2.** dealing with numerous items at once.

om•nip•o•tent (om nip′ə tənt), *adj.* **1.** having unlimited authority or power. —*n.* **2. the Omnipotent,** GOD. —**om•nip′o•tence,** *n.*

om•ni•pres•ent (om′nə prez′ənt), *adj.* present everywhere at the same time. —**om′ni•pres′ence,** *n.*

om•nis•cient (om nish′ənt), *adj.* **1.** having complete knowledge, awareness, or understanding. —*n.* **2. the Omniscient,** GOD. —**om•nis′cience,** *n.*

om•niv•o•rous (om niv′ər əs), *adj.* **1.** eating all kinds of foods, esp. both animals and plants. **2.** taking in everything, as with the mind: *an omnivorous reader.* —**om′ni•vore** (-nə vôr′), *n.*

on (on, ôn), *prep.* **1.** so as to be attached to, supported by, or suspended from: *a package on a chair.* **2.** so as to be in contact with. **3.** connected or associated with: *to serve on a jury.* **4.** having as a place, location, etc.: *a scar on the face.* **5.** in proximity to: *a house on the lake.* **6.** in the direction of: *to sail on a southerly course.* **7.** by the agency or means of: *drunk on wine.* **8.** about: *a book on birds.* **9.** in a condition or process of: *on strike.* **10.** engaged in or occupied with: *I'm on the second chapter.* **11.** having as a source or agent: *to depend on friends for support.* **12.** having as a basis or ground: *on my word of honor.* **13.** at the time or occasion of: *on Sunday.* **14.** paid for by: *Dinner is on me.* **15.** regularly taking or addicted to: *on drugs.* —*adv.* **16.** in, into, or onto a position of being supported or attached: *Sew the buttons on.* **17.** toward a place, point, activity, or object: *to look on while others work.* **18.** forward, onward, or along: *further on.* **19.** with continuous activity: *to work on.* **20.** into or in operation: *Turn the gas on.* —*adj.* **21.** operating or in use: *Is the radio on?* —*Idiom.* **22. on and off,** intermittently. **23. on and on,** at great length.

ON, Ontario.

once (wuns), *adv.* **1.** formerly: *a once powerful nation.* **2.** a single time: *I go once a week.* —*n.* **3.** a single occasion: *Once is enough.* —*conj.* **4.** as soon as: *Once you're finished, you can leave.* —*Idiom.* **5. at once, a.** simultaneously. **b.** immediately. **6. once and for all,** decisively; finally. **7. once in a while,** occasionally.

once'-o'ver, *n.* a quick look.

on•co•gene (ong′kə jēn′), *n.* any gene that is a causative factor in the initiation of cancerous growth.

on•col′o•gy (-kol′ə jē), *n.* the branch of medical science dealing with tumors. —**on•col′o•gist,** *n.*

on′com′ing, *adj.* approaching; nearing.

one (wun), *adj.* **1.** being a single unit or individual. **2.** of the same kind, nature, or condition: *of one mind.* **3.** a certain: *One John Smith was chosen.* **4.** being a unique individual or item: *the one person I can trust.* —*n.* **5.** the first and lowest whole number, being a cardinal number. **6.** a symbol of this number, as 1 or I. **7.** a single person or thing. —*pron.* **8.** a person or thing of a number or kind: *one of the Elizabethan poets.* **9.** any person or thing indefinitely: *as good as one could desire.* **10.** something or someone of the kind just mentioned: *The portraits are good ones.* —*Idiom.* **11. at one,** united in thought or feeling. **12. one by one,** singly and successively.

one'-house' bill', *n.* a piece of legislation not expected to pass both houses of the legislature, intended only to create a good impression.

one'-house' ve'to, *n.* a provision in a law that enables either the House of Representatives or the Senate to cancel presidential actions.

O•nei•da (ō nī′də), *n., pl.* **-da, -das.** a member of an American Indian people orig. inhabiting central New York.

O'Neill (ō nēl′), *n.* **Eugene (Gladstone),** 1888–1953, U.S. playwright.

one'-lin'er, *n.* a brief joke or witty remark.

one' man', one' vote', *adj.* of a system of legislative representation in which each member represents the same number of people.

one′ness, *n.* **1.** the quality of being one. **2.** unity of thought, feeling, etc.

one'-on'-one', *adj.* **1.** consisting of direct individual communication, confrontation, etc. —*adv.* **2.** in direct encounter.

one'-par'ty press', *n.* favoritism considered to be shown by the media toward one political party.

one'-par'ty rule', *n.* prolonged domination by one party.

on•er•ous (on′ər əs, ō′nər-), *adj.* burdensome or oppressive.

one•self (wun self′, wunz-), *pron.* **1.** a person's self (used as a reflexive or emphatic form of ONE). —*Idiom.* **2. be oneself, a.** to be in one's normal state. **b.** to be unpretentious. **3. by oneself,** alone.

one'-sid'ed, *adj.* **1.** considering but one side of a matter or question; partial or unfair. **2.** unequal: *a one-sided fight.* —**one'-sid'ed•ness,** *n.*

O•nes•i•mus (ō nes′ə məs), *n.* a slave of Philemon who was converted to Christianity. Col. 4:9; Philem. 10.

one'-time', *adj.* **1.** former. **2.** occurring, done, etc., only once.

one'-track', *adj.* unable to cope with more than one idea, subject, etc., at a time: *a one-track mind.*

one'-up', *v.t.,* **-upped, -up•ping.** to gain an advantage over.

one'-up'man•ship (-up′mən ship′), *n.* the practice of maneuvering for advantage in a competitive relationship.

one'-way', *adj.* moving or allowing movement in one direction only.

on′go′ing, *adj.* continuing without interruption.

on•ion (un′yən), *n.* **1.** a plant with an edible, pungent bulb. **2.** this bulb.

on′ion•skin′, *n.* a thin, translucent glazed paper.

on'-line' or **on'line',** *adj.* **1.** operating under the direct control of, or connected to, a main computer. **2.** connected by computer to one or more other computers or networks, as through a commercial database service or the Internet. **3.** using a computer. —*adv.* **4.** with or through a computer, esp. over a network.

on′look′er, *n.* a spectator.

on•ly (ōn′lē), *adv.* **1.** solely; exclusively. **2.** no more than; merely; just: *only on weekends.* **3.** as recently as: *only yesterday.* **4.** in the final outcome: *That will only make matters worse.* —*adj.* **5.** being the single one of the kind; lone; sole. —*conj.* **6.** but: *I would have gone, only you objected.* —*Idiom.* **7. only too,** very; extremely.

on•o•mat•o•poe•ia (on′ə mat′ə pē′ə, -mä′tə-), *n.* the formation of a word, as *boom,* by imitation of a sound. —**on′o•mat′o•poe′ic, on′o•mat′o•po•et′ic** (-pō et′ik), *adj.*

On•on•da•ga (on′ən dô′gə, -dä′-, -dā′-), *n., pl.* **-ga, -gas.** a member of an American Indian people of central New York.

on′rush′, *n.* a strong forward rush, flow, etc. —**on′rush′ing,** *adj.*

on′set′, *n.* **1.** a beginning or start. **2.** an assault or attack.

on•slaught (on′slôt′, ôn′-), *n.* a vigorous assault.

Ont., Ontario.

On•tar•i•o (on târ′ē ō′), *n.* **1.** a province in S Canada. 9,101,694. *Cap.:* Toronto. *Abbr.:* ON, Ont. **2. Lake,** a lake between the NE United States and S Canada: the smallest of the Great Lakes. **3.** a city in SW California. 134,825. —**On•tar′i•an,** *adj., n.*

on′to, *prep.* **1.** to a position on. **2.** *Informal.* aware of the true nature of: *I'm onto your tricks.*

on•tog•e•ny (on toj′ə nē), *n.* the development of an individual organism.

o•nus (ō′nəs), *n., pl.* **o•nus•es. 1.** an annoying or unfair burden. **2.** blame; responsibility.

on′ward (-wərd), *adv.* **1.** Also, **on′wards.** toward a point ahead; forward. —*adj.* **2.** directed or moving onward.

on•yx (on′iks, ō′niks), *n.* a variety of chalcedony having parallel bands of alternating colors.

oo•dles (ōōd′lz), *n.pl. Informal.* a large quantity.

ooze¹ (ōōz), *v.,* **oozed, ooz•ing,** *n.* —*v.i.* **1.** to flow or exude slowly, as through holes. —*v.t.* **2.** to exude (moisture, air, etc.) slowly. —*n.* **3.** something that oozes.

ooze² (ōōz), *n.* **1.** mud composed chiefly of the shells of one-celled organisms, found on the ocean bottom. **2.** soft mud or slime.

o•pal (ō′pəl), *n.* **1.** a mineral found in many varieties and colors. **2.** a gemstone made of this, esp. of an iridescent variety.

o•pal•es•cent (ō′pə les′ənt), *adj.* exhibiting a play of colors like that of the opal. —**o′pal•es′cence,** *n.*

o•paque (ō pāk′), *adj.* **1.** not allowing light to pass through. **2.** dark; dull. **3.** hard to understand. —**o•pac′i•ty** (ō pas′i tē), *n.* —**o•paque′ly,** *adv.*

op′ art′ (op), *n.* a style of art in which lines, forms, and space are distributed so as to produce optical effects.

op. cit. (op′ sit′), (in the work cited. [< L *opere citātō*]

OPEC (ō′pek), *n.* Organization of Petroleum Exporting Countries.

Op'-Ed', *n.* a newspaper page or section devoted to

signed articles, letters, etc. [*op(posite)-ed(itorial page)*]

o•pen (ō′pən), *adj.* **1.** not closed, covered, or barred. **2.** having large or numerous spaces or intervals: *open ranks of soldiers*. **3.** relatively unoccupied by buildings, trees, etc.: *open country*. **4.** extended or unfolded: *an open newspaper*. **5.** without restrictions as to who may participate: *an open session*. **6.** accessible or available: *Which job is open?* **7.** ready to carry on normal business: *The new store is now open*. **8.** exposed to general view or knowledge: *open disregard of the rules*. **9.** candid or frank. **10.** generous. **11.** liable or subject: *open to question*. **12.** undecided: *an open question*. **13.** without legal or moral regulations: *an open town*. —*v.t., v.i.* **14.** to make or become open. **15.** to make or become accessible or available. **16.** to begin, start, or commence. **17.** to expand or spread out. **18.** to make or become less compact or closely spaced. **19.** to reveal or become revealed. **20.** to make or become receptive to knowledge, sympathy, etc. —**o′pen•er,** *n.*

o′pen air′, *n.* the outdoors.

o′pen-and-shut′, *adj.* easily decided.

o′pen-end′ed, *adj.* **1.** unrestricted. **2.** having no fixed answer: *an open-ended question*.

o′pen-faced′ *adj.* **1.** having a frank or ingenuous face. **2.** (of a sandwich) without a slice of bread on top.

o′pen•hand′ed, *adj.* generous; liberal.

o′pen-heart′ed, *adj.* **1.** candid or frank. **2.** kindly; benevolent.

o′pen-heart′ sur′gery, *n.* surgery performed on the exposed heart with the aid of a mechanical device that pumps the blood.

o′pen house′, *n.* **1.** a party during which a person's home is open to visitors. **2.** a time during which an institution is open to the public.

o′pen•ing, *n.* **1.** an unobstructed or unoccupied space or place. **2.** a hole in solid matter. **3.** the act of beginning; start. **4.** the initial stage of anything. **5.** an employment vacancy. **6.** an opportunity; chance.

o′pen-mind′ed, *adj.* **1.** having a mind receptive to new ideas. **2.** unprejudiced; impartial.

o′pen shop′, *n.* a business in which union membership is not a condition of employment.

o′pen-skies′, *adj.* relatively unrestricted aircraft traffic across international boundaries.

o′pen•work′, *n.* any kind of ornamental work having open spaces in the material.

op•er•a¹ (op′ər ə, op′rə), *n.* a dramatic work in which the parts are sung to orchestral accompaniment. —**op′er•at′ic,** *adj.*

o•pe•ra² (ō′pər ə, op′ər ə), *n.* a pl. of OPUS.

op•er•a•ble (op′ər ə bəl), *adj.* **1.** treatable by a surgical operation. **2.** capable of being put into use or practice.

op′era glass′es, *n.pl.* small, low-power binoculars.

op•er•and (op′ə rand′), *n.* a quantity upon which a mathematical operation is performed.

op′er•ate′ (-ə rāt′), *v.,* **-at•ed, -at•ing.** —*v.i.* **1.** to work or function, as a machine does. **2.** to exert force or influence. **3.** to perform a surgical procedure. —*v.t.* **4.** to manage or use (a machine, device, etc.). **5.** to put or keep in operation.

op′erating sys′tem, *n.* the software that directs a computer's operations, as by controlling and scheduling the execution of other programs.

op′er•a′tion, *n.* **1.** the act, process, or manner of operating. **2.** the state of being operative: *a rule no longer in operation*. **3.** the exertion of force or influence. **4.** a process of a practical or mechanical nature. **5.** a surgical procedure aimed at restoring or improving the health of a patient. —**op′er•a′tion•al,** *adj.*

op′er•a•tive (-ər ə tiv, -ə rā′tiv), *n.* **1.** a person engaged or skilled in some branch of work. **2.** a secret agent; spy. —*adj.* **3.** exerting force or influence. **4.** being in operation. **5.** significant; key.

op′er•a′tor (-ə rā′tər), *n.* **1.** a person who operates a machine or apparatus, as a telephone switchboard. **2.** a person who manages an industrial establish-

ment. **3.** a person who accomplishes his or her purposes by cleverness or devious means.

op•er•et•ta (op′ə ret′ə), *n., pl.* **-tas.** a short opera of a light and amusing character.

oph•thal•mol•o•gy (of′thal mol′ə jē, -thə-, -thal-, op′-), *n.* the branch of medicine dealing with the eye. —**oph′thal•mol′o•gist,** *n.*

o•pi•ate (ō′pē it, -āt′), *n.* **1.** a drug containing opium or its derivatives. **2.** anything that soothes the feelings.

o•pine (ō pīn′), *v.t., v.i.,* **o•pined, o•pin•ing.** to express or hold (an opinion).

o•pin•ion (ə pin′yən), *n.* **1.** a belief based on grounds insufficient to produce certainty. **2.** a personal attitude or appraisal. **3.** the formal expression of a professional judgment. **4.** a favorable estimate; esteem.

o•pin′ion•at′ed (-yə nā′tid), *adj.* obstinate regarding the merit of one's own opinions.

O′ Pioneers!, a novel (1913) by Willa Cather.

o•pi•um (ō′pē əm), *n.* a narcotic prepared from the condensed juice of a certain poppy.

o•pos•sum (ə pos′əm, pos′əm), *n., pl.* **-sums, -sum.** a marsupial of the eastern U.S., noted for feigning death when in danger.

op•po•nent (ə pō′nənt), *n.* a person who is on an opposing side; adversary.

op•por•tune (op′ər tōōn′, -tyōōn′), *adj.* **1.** suitable; apt. **2.** occurring at an appropriate time.

op′por•tun′ism, *n.* the practice of adapting actions, decisions, etc., to expediency without regard to moral principles or consequences. —**op′por•tun′-ist,** *n.*

op′por•tun•is′tic, *adj.* **1.** practicing opportunism. **2. a.** (of a microorganism) causing disease only under certain conditions, as when a person's immune system is impaired. **b.** (of a disease or infection) caused by such an organism.

op′por•tu′ni•ty, *n., pl.* **-ties. 1.** an appropriate or favorable time or occasion. **2.** a condition favorable for attainment of a goal. **3.** a good chance, as for success. —**Proverb. 4. Opportunity knocks but once,** seize a chance when it occurs or you may not get another.

op•pose (ə pōz′), *v.t.,* **-posed, -pos•ing. 1.** to resist; combat. **2.** to be hostile or averse to. **3.** to set (something) opposite something else.

op•po•site (op′ə zit, -sit), *adj.* **1.** situated in corresponding positions across an intervening line, space, etc. **2.** radically different; opposed. —*n.* **3.** a person or thing that is opposite or contrary. —*prep.* **4.** across from.

op′po•si′tion (-zish′ən), *n.* **1.** the action of opposing. **2.** antagonism or hostility. **3.** a person or group that opposes, criticizes, or protests. **4.** (*sometimes cap.*) the major political party opposed to the party in power.

op•press (ə pres′), *v.t.* **1.** to exercise harsh authority or power over. **2.** to lie heavily on; weigh down. —**op•pres′sor,** *n.*

op•pres′sion, *n.* **1.** the exercise of authority or power in a cruel or unjust manner. **2.** something that oppresses. **3.** the feeling of being oppressed.

op•pres′sive, *adj.* **1.** unjustly harsh or tyrannical. **2.** causing discomfort. **3.** distressing or grievous. —**op•pres′sive•ly,** *adv.*

op•pro•bri•um (ə prō′brē əm), *n.* **1.** the disgrace incurred by shameful conduct. **2.** the cause of such disgrace. —**op•pro′bri•ous,** *adj.*

opt (opt), *v.i.* to make a choice: *They opted for compromise.*

op•tic (op′tik), *adj.* of the eye or sight.

op′ti•cal, *adj.* **1.** of or applying optics. **2.** of the eye or sight. **3.** constructed to assist sight. —**op′ti•cal•ly,** *adv.*

op′tical disc′, *n.* a disk on which digital data, as text or music, is stored and read by a laser.

op′tical scan′ner, *n.* a device capable of scanning printed text or illustrations and converting the information into digital form.

op•ti•cian (op tish′ən), *n.* a person who makes or

sells eyeglasses, contact lenses, and other optical goods.

op'tics, *n.* the branch of physical science that deals with light and vision.

op•ti•mism (op'tə miz'əm), *n.* **1.** a tendency to look on the more favorable side of events or conditions. **2.** the belief that good will ultimately triumph over evil. —**op'ti•mist,** *n.* —**op'ti•mis'tic,** *adj.*

op'ti•mum (-məm), *n., pl.* **-ma** (-mə), **-mums,** *adj.* —*n.* **1.** the most favorable point, degree, or amount of something for obtaining a given result. —*adj.* **2.** Also, **op'ti•mal.** most favorable; best.

op•tion (op'shən), *n.* **1.** the power or right of choosing. **2.** something that may be chosen; choice. **3.** the act of choosing. **4.** part of a legal agreement giving one the right to buy property, use services, etc., within a specified time. —**op'tion•al,** *adj.*

op•tom•e•try (op tom'i trē), *n.* the profession of examining the eyes for defects of vision in order to prescribe corrective lenses. —**op•tom'e•trist,** *n.*

op•u•lent (op'yə lənt), *adj.* **1.** wealthy or rich. **2.** richly supplied; plentiful. —**op'u•lence,** *n.*

o•pus (ō'pəs), *n., pl.* **o•pus•es, o•pe•ra** (ō'pər ə, op'ər ə). a musical or literary work or composition.

O'pus De'i (dā'ē), *n.* an international Roman Catholic order.

or (ôr; *unstressed* ər), *conj.* **1.** (used to connect words representing alternatives): *to be or not to be.* **2.** (used to connect alternative terms for the same thing): *the tympanic membrane, or eardrum.* **3.** (used in correlation): *Either we go now or wait till tomorrow.*

OR, 1. operating room. **2.** Oregon.

-or¹, a suffix meaning condition or quality (*pallor*).

-or², a suffix meaning a person or thing that does something (*orator*).

or•a•cle (ôr'ə kəl, or'-), *n.* **1.** (in the ancient world) **a.** a shrine at which inquiries were made of a deity. **b.** the priest who answered the inquiry. **c.** the response of the deity. **2.** a person who delivers authoritative or wise pronouncements. —**o•rac•u•lar** (ô rak'yə lər), *adj.*

o•ral (ôr'əl), *adj.* **1.** uttered by the mouth; spoken. **2.** of or using speech. **3.** of or involving the mouth. —**Usage.** See VERBAL.

or•ange (ôr'inj, or'-), *n.* **1.** any of various reddish yellow, edible citrus fruits. **2.** a tree bearing such fruit. **3.** a color between yellow and red.

Or'ange, *n.* a city in SW California. 116,785.

Or'ange Free' State', *n.* a province in central Republic of South Africa. 1,863,327.

o•rang•u•tan (ô rang'ŏŏ tan', ə rang'-), *n.* a large, mostly arboreal, long-armed anthropoid ape of Borneo and Sumatra.

o•rate (ô rāt', ôr'āt), *v.i.,* **-rat•ed, -rat•ing.** to deliver an oration, esp. to speak pompously.

o•ra'tion, *n.* a formal public speech, esp. for a special occasion.

or•a•tor (ôr'ə tər, or'-), *n.* a public speaker of great eloquence.

or•a•to•ri•o (ôr'ə tôr'ē ō', or'-), *n., pl.* **-ri•os.** a musical work for voices and orchestra, usu. based on a religious theme.

or'a•to•ry,¹ *n.* **1.** eloquence in public speaking. **2.** the art of public speaking. —**or'a•tor'i•cal** (ôr'ə tôr'-), *adj.*

or•a•to•ry² (ôr'ə tôr'ē, -tôr'ē, or'-), *n., pl.* **-ries.** a place of prayer, as a small chapel.

orb (ôrb), *n.* a sphere or globe. —**or•bic•u•lar** (ôr bik'yə lər), *adj.*

or•bit (ôr'bit), *n.* **1.** the curved path, usu. elliptical, described by a planet, satellite, etc., around a celestial body. **2.** a sphere of influence, as of a nation. —*v.t., v.i.* **3.** to travel in or send into an orbit. —**or'bit•al,** *adj.*

or•chard (ôr'chərd), *n.* **1.** land devoted to the cultivation of fruit or nut trees. **2.** a group of such trees.

or•ches•tra (ôr'kə strə, -kes trə), *n., pl.* **-tras. 1.** a group of performers who play various musical instru-

ments together. **2.** (in a theater) **a.** the space reserved for the musicians, usu. the front part of the main floor. **b.** the front section of seats on the main floor. —**or•ches'tral,** *adj.*

or•ches•trate (ôr'kə strāt'), *v.t.,* **-trat•ed, -trat•ing. 1.** to compose or arrange (music) for an orchestra. **2.** to arrange the elements of to achieve a goal or effect. —**or'ches•tra'tion,** *n.*

or•chid (ôr'kid), *n.* **1.** any of various chiefly tropical plants having showy flowers with three petals, the lowest of which is enlarged. **2.** the flower of an orchid. **3.** a bluish to reddish purple.

or•dain (ôr dān'), *v.t.* **1.** to invest with ministerial or priestly functions. **2.** to decree; give orders for. —*v.i.* **3.** to command. —**or•dain'ment,** *n.*

or•deal (ôr dēl', ôr'dēl), *n.* any extremely severe or trying experience.

or•der (ôr'dər), *n.* **1.** an authoritative instruction; command. **2.** a succession or sequence: *alphabetical order.* **3.** a methodical or harmonious arrangement. **4.** state or condition generally: *in working order.* **5.** conformity or obedience to established authority: *to maintain law and order.* **6.** customary mode of procedure. **7.** a direction or commission to make or provide something. **8.** goods purchased or sold. **9.** a class, kind, or sort: *talents of a high order.* **10.** a major subdivision of a class in the classification of organisms, consisting of one or more families. **11.** a body or society of persons living under the same religious, moral, or social regulations. **12.** *Archit.* any of five styles of column and entablature typical of classical architecture. **13. orders,** the rank of an ordained Christian minister. —*v.t., v.i.* **14.** to give an order (to). **15.** to place an order (for). **16.** to put (things) in order. —**Idiom. 17. in order, a.** appropriate. **b.** properly arranged. **c.** correct according to the rules. **18. in order to,** with the purpose of. **19. in short order,** rapidly. **20. out of order, a.** not in correct arrangement. **b.** inappropriate. **c.** not operating properly. **d.** incorrect according to the rules. **21. to order,** according to the purchaser's requirements.

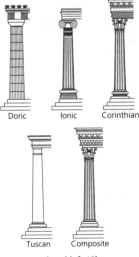

Doric   Ionic   Corinthian

Tuscan   Composite

orders (def. 12)

or'der•ly, *adj., n., pl.* **-lies,** *adv.* —*adj.* **1.** arranged in a tidy manner. **2.** observant of law, rule, or discipline. —*n.* **3.** a hospital attendant. **4.** an enlisted soldier assigned to perform various chores for an officer. —*adv.* **5.** methodically. **6.** according to established order. —**or'der•li•ness,** *n.*

or•di•nal (ôr'dn əl), *adj.* **1.** of or showing order in a series. —*n.* **2.** an ordinal number.

or'dinal num'ber, *n.* any of the numbers that express position in a series, as *first* and *second.*

or•di•nance (ôr'dn əns), *n.* a public regulation, esp. a municipal one.

or•di•nar•i•ly (ôr'dn âr'ə lē), *adv.* generally; usually.

or'di•nar'y (-er'ē), *adj.* **1.** commonplace; unexceptional. **2.** customary; usual; normal. —*Idiom.* **3. out of the ordinary,** unusual. —**or'di•nar'i•ness,** *n.*

or•di•nate (ôr'dn it', -āt'), *n.* (in plane Cartesian coordinates) the y-coordinate of a point: its distance from the x-axis measured parallel to the y-axis.

or•di•na•tion (ôr'dn ā'shən), *n.* **1.** the act of ordaining as a priest, minister, etc. **2.** the fact or state of being ordained.

ord•nance (ôrd'nəns), *n.* **1.** artillery. **2.** military weapons with their equipment, ammunition, etc.

Or•do•vi•cian (ôr'də vish'ən), *adj.* noting or pertaining to a geologic period of the Paleozoic Era, notable for the advent of fish.

or•dure (ôr'jər, -dyŏŏr), *n.* dung; excrement.

ore (ôr), *n.* a mineral or rock that is the source of a valuable metal or nonmetallic substance.

Ore., Oregon.

Oreg., Oregon.

o•reg•a•no (ə reg'ə nō'), *n., pl.* **-nos.** an aromatic herb with leaves used as seasoning.

Or•e•gon (ôr'i gən, -gon', or'-), *n.* a state in the NW United States. 3,203,735. *Cap.:* Salem. *Abbr.:* OR, Ore., Oreg. —**Or'e•go'ni•an** (-gō'nē ən), *adj., n.*

Or'egon Trail', *n.* a route used during the U.S. westward migrations, esp. 1840 to 1860, starting in Missouri and ending in Oregon. ab. 2000 mi. (3200 km) long.

or•gan (ôr'gən), *n.* **1.** a musical instrument having sets of pipes actuated by keyboard and sounded by compressed air. **2.** a grouping of animal or plant tissues into a distinct structure that performs a specialized task. **3.** a periodical representing a special group. **4.** a means of action.

or•gan•dy (ôr'gən dē), *n., pl.* **-dies.** a fine, thin cotton fabric with a crisp finish.

or•gan•elle (ôr'gə nel'), *n.* a specialized cell structure that has a specific function.

or•gan•ic (ôr gan'ik), *adj.* **1.** of or noting a class of chemical compounds containing carbon. **2.** of, characteristic of, or derived from living organisms. **3.** raised or grown without synthetic fertilizers, pesticides, or drugs. **4.** of the organs of an animal or plant. **5.** organized; systematic. **6.** fundamental; inherent. —**or•gan'i•cal•ly,** *adv.*

or'gan•ism (-gə niz'əm), *n.* any individual life form.

or'gan•ist, *n.* a person who plays the organ.

or•gan•i•za•tion (ôr'gə nə zā'shən), *n.* **1.** the act or process of organizing. **2.** the state or manner of being organized. **3.** something organized. **4.** a group of persons organized for some end or work. —**or'gan•i•za'tion•al,** *adj.*

organiza'tion man', *n.* a person who conforms

and is loyal to the standards and values of an organization. [from a 1972 novel of that name by William H. Whyte, Jr.]

or'gan•ize', *v.,* **-ized, -iz•ing.** —*v.t.* **1.** to form as or into a whole, esp. for united action. **2.** to systematize; order. **3.** to give organic structure or character to. **4.** to enlist the employees of (a business) into a labor union. —*v.i.* **5.** to become organized. —**or'gan•iz'er,** *n.*

or•gan•za (ôr gan'zə), *n., pl.* **-zas.** a sheer fabric of rayon, nylon, or silk with a crisp finish.

or•gasm (ôr'gaz əm), *n.* the sensation experienced at the peak of sexual excitation; climax. —**or•gas'mic, or•gas'tic** (-gas'tik), *adj.*

or•gy (ôr'jē), *n., pl.* **-gies. 1.** drunken or licentious revelry. **2.** any actions or proceedings marked by unbridled indulgence of passions: *an orgy of killing.*

o•ri•el (ôr'ē əl), *n.* a bay window projecting out from a wall, supported by brackets.

oriel

o•ri•ent (*n.* ôr'ē ənt, -ē ent'; *v.* ôr'ē ent'), *n.* **1. the Orient,** the countries of Asia, esp. East Asia. **2.** the east. —*v.t.* **3.** to familiarize with new surroundings or circumstances. **4.** to place in a position with reference to the points of the compass. **5.** to place so as to face the east, esp. to build (a church) with the chief altar to the east and the chief entrance to the west. —**o'ri•en•ta'tion,** *n.*

O•ri•en•tal (ôr'ē en'tl), (*sometimes l.c.*) —*adj.* **1.** of or characteristic of the Orient. —*n.* **2.** *Sometimes Offensive.* a native or inhabitant of East Asia, or a person of East Asian descent.

or•i•fice (ôr'ə fis, or'-), *n.* a mouthlike opening or hole.

o•ri•ga•mi (ôr'i gä'mē), *n.* the Japanese art of folding paper into decorative or representational forms. [< Japn: folding paper]

or•i•gin (ôr'i jin, or'-), *n.* **1.** the source from which anything arises or is derived. **2.** the beginning of something. **3.** ancestry; parentage.

o•rig•i•nal (ə rij'ə nl), *adj.* **1.** of or belonging to the beginning of something. **2.** inventive; novel. **3.** capable of or given to thinking or acting in an independent, creative, or individual manner: *an original thinker.* **4.** undertaken or presented for the first time. **5.** being that from which a copy, translation, etc., is made. —*n.* **6.** a primary type from which varieties are derived. **7.** an original work, document, etc. —**o•rig'i•nal'i•ty,** *n.* —**o•rig'i•nal•ly,** *adv.*

orig'inal sin', *n.* a tendency to evil, held to be innate in humankind in consequence of Adam's sin.

o•rig'i•nate', *v.,* **-nat•ed, -nat•ing.** —*v.i.* **1.** to take or have origin; arise. —*v.t.* **2.** to give origin or rise to; initiate. —**o•rig'i•na'tion,** *n.* —**o•rig'i•na'tor,** *n.*

o•ri•ole (ôr'ē ōl'), *n.* any of various songbirds, the males of which are usu. black and orange or yellow.

O•ri•on (ə rī'ən), *n.* a constellation lying on the celestial equator.

Or•lan•do (ôr lan'dō), *n.* a city in central Florida. 176,948.

Or•lon (ôr'lon), *Trademark.* a brand of acrylic textile fiber.

or•mo•lu (ôr′mə lōō′), n., pl. **-lus.** an alloy of copper and zinc used to imitate gold.

or•na•ment (n. ôr′nə mənt; v. -ment′, -mənt), n. **1.** an object or feature that embellishes; decoration. **2.** a person or thing that adds to the credit or glory of a society, era, etc. **3.** a tone or group of tones applied as decoration to a principal melodic tone. —v.t. **4.** to embellish; decorate. —**or′na•men′tal,** adj. —**or′na•men•ta′tion,** n.

or•nate (ôr nāt′), adj. elaborately adorned, often excessively so. —**or•nate′ly,** adv. —**or•nate′ness,** n.

or•ner•y (ôr′nə rē), adj., **-i•er, -i•est. 1.** disagreeable in disposition. **2.** stubborn. —**or′ner•i•ness,** n.

or•ni•thol•o•gy (ôr′nə thol′ə jē), n. the branch of zoology that deals with birds. —**or′ni•thol′o•gist,** n.

o•ro•tund (ôr′ə tund′), adj. **1.** (of the voice or speech) strong, full, and clear. **2.** (of speech or writing) pompous or bombastic. —**o′ro•tun′di•ty,** n.

or•phan (ôr′fən), n. **1.** a child who has lost both parents through death. —adj. **2.** bereft of parents. **3.** of or for orphans. **4.** lacking sponsorship or funding: an orphan disease. —v.t. **5.** to cause to become an orphan.

or′phan•age (-fə nij), n. an institution for the housing and care of orphans.

Or•phe•us (ôr′fē əs, -fyŏos), n. a poet and lyre-player of Greek legend whose music charmed beasts, trees, and rocks.

or•ris (ôr′is, or′-), n. an iris with a fragrant root-stock.

or•tho•don•tics (ôr′thə don′tiks) also **-don′tia** (-don′shə), n. a branch of dentistry dealing with the prevention and correction of irregular teeth. —**or′tho•don′tic,** adj. —**or′tho•don′tist,** n.

or•tho•dox (ôr′thə doks′), adj. **1.** conforming to the approved form of any doctrine, philosophy, etc. **2.** conforming to generally approved beliefs, attitudes, etc. **3.** sound or correct in matters of theological doctrine or opinion. **4.** conforming to the Christian faith as represented in the creeds of the early church. **5.** (cap.) of the Eastern Church, esp. the Greek Orthodox Church. **6.** (cap.) conforming to or characteristic of Orthodox Judaism. [< LL orthodoxus < Gk orthódoxos = ortho- straight, right, correct + dóxa belief, opinion] —**or′tho•dox′y,** n., pl. **-dox•ies.**

or•thog•ra•phy (ôr thog′rə fē), n., pl. **-phies. 1.** the art of spelling according to accepted usage. **2.** language study concerned with spelling. —**or′tho•graph′ic** (-thə graf′ik), adj.

or•tho•pe•dics (ôr′thə pē′diks), n. the medical specialty concerned with correction of deformities or disorders of the skeletal system. —**or′tho•pe′dic,** adj. —**or′tho•pe′dist,** n.

Or•well (ôr′wel, -wəl), n. **George** (Eric Arthur Blair), 1903–50, English novelist and essayist. —**Or•well′i•an,** adj.

-ory¹, an adjective suffix meaning of, characterized by, or serving to (excretory).

-ory², a noun suffix meaning a place or instrument for (crematory).

Os, Chem. Symbol. osmium.

O•sage (ō′sāj, ō sāj′), n., pl. **O•sage, O•sag•es.** a member of an American Indian people who formerly inhabited Missouri.

O•sa•ka (ō sä′kə, ō′sä kä′), n. a city on S Honshu, in S Japan. 2,546,000.

os•cil•late (os′ə lāt′), v.i., **-lat•ed, -lat•ing. 1.** to swing to and fro. **2.** to waver or vacillate. **3.** Physics. to vary between maximum and minimum values, as of a cycle. —**os′cil•la′tion,** n. —**os′cil•la′tor,** n.

os•cil•lo•scope (ə sil′ə skōp′), n. a device that uses a cathode-ray tube to display on a screen periodic changes in an electric quantity.

os•cu•late (os′kyə lāt′), v.t., v.i., **-lat•ed, -lat•ing.** to kiss. —**os′cu•la′tion,** n.

-ose¹, an adjective suffix meaning given to, abounding in, or like (verbose).

-ose², a noun suffix forming the name of sugars and other carbohydrates (fructose).

OSHA (ō′shə), n. Occupational Safety and Health Administration.

Osh•a•wa (osh′ə wə), n. a city in SE Ontario, in S Canada. 123,651.

o•sier (ō′zhər), n. **1.** any of various willows with tough, flexible twigs used for wickerwork. **2.** a twig from such a willow.

-osis, a suffix meaning: action or condition (osmosis); a disorder or abnormal state (tuberculosis).

Os•lo (oz′lō, os′-), n. the capital of Norway. 453,700.

os•mi•um (oz′mē əm), n. a hard, heavy metallic element, used chiefly as a catalyst and in alloys. Symbol: Os; at. wt.: 190.2; at. no.: 76.

os•mo•sis (oz mō′sis, os-), n. **1.** the tendency of a fluid to pass through a membrane into a solution where the solvent concentration is higher, thus equalizing the concentrations of materials on either side. **2.** a subtle or gradual absorption: to learn by osmosis. —**os•mot′ic** (-mot′ik), adj.

os•prey (os′prē, -prā), n., pl. **-preys.** a large bird of prey that feeds on fish.

os•si•fy (os′ə fī′), v.t., v.i., **-fied, -fy•ing. 1.** to convert into bone. **2.** to make or become rigid in habits, opinions, etc. —**os′si•fi•ca′tion,** n.

os•ten•si•ble (o sten′sə bəl), adj. outwardly appearing as such. —**os•ten′si•bly,** adv.

os•ten•ta•tion (os′ten tā′shən, -tən-), n. pretentious display. —**os′ten•ta′tious,** adj.

os•te•o•ar•thri•tis (os′tē ō är thrī′tis), n. arthritis marked by chronic breakdown of cartilage in the joints.

os•te•op•a•thy (os′tē op′ə thē), n. a system of medical practice emphasizing the manipulation of muscles and bones to relieve certain disorders. —**os′te•o•path′** (-ə path′), n.

os•te•o•po•ro•sis (os′tē ō pə rō′sis), n. a disorder in which the bones become increasingly porous, brittle, and subject to fracture.

os•tra•cize (os′trə sīz′), v.t., **-cized, -ciz•ing.** to exclude, by general consent, from society, privileges, etc. —**os′tra•cism,** n.

os•trich (ô′strich, os′trich), n. a two-toed, swift-footed, flightless bird, orig. of Africa and SW Asia.

ostrich

Os•wald (oz′wôld), n. **Lee Harvey,** 1939–63, determined by a presidential commission to be the lone assassin of John F. Kennedy.

OT, 1. Old Testament. **2.** overtime.

OTC, over-the-counter.

oth•er (uth′ər), adj. **1.** additional or further: one other person. **2.** different from the one mentioned: in some other city. **3.** different in nature or kind: I would not have him other than he is. **4.** being the remaining one or ones of a number: the other men. **5.** not long past: the other night. —pron. **6.** Usu., **-ers.** other persons or things. **7.** some person or thing else. —adv. **8.** otherwise: We can't collect the rent other than by suing.

oth′er•wise′, adv. **1.** under other circumstances. **2.** in another manner. **3.** in other respects. —adj. **4.** of a different kind.

oth′er•world′ly, adj. concerned with the world of imagination or the world to come.

o•ti•ose (ō′shē ōs′, ō′tē-), *adj.* **1.** idle. **2.** futile or useless.

O•tis (ō′tis), *n.* James, 1725–83, American Revolutionary lawyer and public official.

Ot•ta•wa (ot′ə wə), *n.* the capital of Canada, in SE Ontario. 300,763.

ot•ter (ot′ər), *n.*, *pl.* **-ters, -ter. 1.** any of several aquatic, furbearing mammals with webbed feet. **2.** the fur of an otter.

ot•to•man (ot′ə mən), *n.*, *pl.* **-mans. 1.** a cushioned footstool. **2.** a cushioned seat or sofa without back or arms.

Oua•ga•dou•gou (wä′gə dōō′gōō), *n.* the capital of Burkina Faso. 442,223.

ouch (ouch), *interj.* an exclamation of sudden pain or dismay.

ought (ôt), *auxiliary verb.* **1.** (used to express duty or moral obligation): *Every citizen ought to help.* **2.** (used to express justice or moral rightness): *He ought to be punished.* **3.** (used to express propriety or appropriateness): *We ought to bring her flowers.* **4.** (used to express probability): *That ought to be our train now.*

ounce (ouns), *n.* **1.** a unit of weight equal to ¹⁄₁₆ of a pound (28.349 grams) avoirdupois. **2.** a unit of weight equal to ¹⁄₁₂ of a pound (31.103 grams) troy. **3.** a fluid ounce. **—Proverb. 4. An ounce of prevention is worth a pound of cure,** taking the right measures beforehand is easier than correcting a problem later.

our (ou°r, ou′ər; *unstressed* är), *pron.* a form of the possessive case of WE used as an attributive adjective: *Our team won.*

ours, *pron.* **1.** a form of the possessive case of WE used as a predicate adjective: *Which house is ours?* **2.** that or those belonging to us: *Ours are the pink ones.*

our•selves′, *pron.pl.* **1.** the reflexive form of WE: *We deceived ourselves.* **2.** an intensive form of WE: *We ourselves decided.* **3.** our normal selves: *We were ourselves again after a nap.*

-ous, a suffix meaning full of, characterized by, or having (*glorious*).

oust (oust), *v.t.* to expel from a place or position occupied.

oust′er, *n.* expulsion from a place or position occupied.

out (out), *adv.* **1.** not in the usual place, position, etc. **2.** in or into the outdoors. **3.** to the end or conclusion: *Please hear me out.* **4.** to a state of depletion, nonexistence, or extinction: *a practice on the way out.* **5.** in or into neglect, disuse, etc.: *That style has gone out.* **6.** in or into public notice: *The truth is out.* **7.** so as to project or extend: *to stretch out.* **8.** from a specified source or material: *made out of scraps.* **9.** aloud or loudly: *to cry out.* **10.** thoroughly; completely: *tired out.* **11.** in or into activity, existence, or manifestation: *A riot broke out.* **12.** from a number, stock, or store: *to pick out.* —*adj.* **13.** not at one's home or place of work. **14.** not in effective operation, use, etc. **15.** not fashionable. **16.** *Baseball.* not succeeding in getting on base. **17.** beyond fixed or usual limits. **18.** having a financial loss: *I'm out ten dollars.* **19.** inaccurate: *calculations out by $27.* **20.** external; outer. —*prep.* **21.** out from or through: *She ran out the door.* **22.** out along or on: *Let's drive out the old parkway.* —*n.* **23.** a means of escape, as from responsibility. **24.** Usu., **outs.** those persons or groups lacking status, power, etc. **25.** *Baseball.* an instance of putting out a batter or base runner. —*Idiom.* **26. on the outs,** quarreling; at odds. **27. out for,** determined to acquire, achieve, etc. **28. out of, a.** not within. **b.** beyond the reach of: *out of hearing.* **c.** not in a condition of: *out of danger.* **d.** without or lacking. **e.** from within or among. **f.** because of: *out of loyalty.*

out-, a prefix meaning: outward or external (*outburst*); outside or at a distance from (*outpost*); to surpass (*outbid*).

out•age (ou′tij), *n.* an interruption or failure in the supply of power, esp. electricity.

out′-and-out′, *adj.* complete; absolute.

out′back′, *n.* the back country or remote settlements, esp. in Australia.

out′bal′ance, *v.t.* **-anced, -anc•ing.** to outweigh.

out′board′, *adj.* located on the exterior of a hull or aircraft.

out′bound′, *adj.* outward bound.

out′break′, *n.* a sudden occurrence; eruption.

out′build′ing, *n.* a detached building subordinate to a main building.

out′burst′, *n.* a sudden and violent release or outpouring.

out′cast′, *n.* **1.** a person who is rejected, as from society. —*adj.* **2.** cast out or rejected.

out′class′, *v.t.* to surpass in excellence.

out′come′, *n.* a final product or end result.

out′crop′, *n.* **1.** an emergence of a rock stratum or mineral vein at the surface of the earth. **2.** the exposed portion of such a stratum or vein.

out′cry′, *n.*, *pl.* **-cries. 1.** a strong and public expression of protest. **2.** a loud cry or shout.

out′dat′ed, *adj.* outmoded.

out′dis′tance, *v.t.* **-tanced, -tanc•ing.** to leave behind, as in running.

out′do′, *v.t.* **-did, -done, -do•ing.** to surpass in execution or performance.

out′door′, *adj.* located, occurring, or belonging outdoors.

out′doors′, *adv.* **1.** in the open air. —*n.* **2.** the world outside of or away from buildings; open air.

out′er, *adj.* **1.** situated on or toward the outside. **2.** situated farther out.

out′er•most′, *adj.* farthest out.

out′er space′, *n.* **1.** space beyond the earth's atmosphere. **2.** space beyond the solar system.

out′er•wear′, *n.* garments, as overcoats, worn over other clothing.

out′field′, *n.* **1.** the part of a baseball field beyond the diamond. **2.** the players (**out′field′ers**) positioned there.

out′fit′, *n.*, *v.*, **-fit•ted, -fit•ting.** —*n.* **1.** the gear for a particular task or role. **2.** a set of harmonious garments worn together. **3.** a group or team of people, as a business firm or military unit. —*v.t.* **4.** to furnish with an outfit. —**out′fit′ter,** *n.*

out′flank′, *v.t.* **1.** to go or extend beyond the flank of (an enemy force). **2.** to outmaneuver.

out′flow′, *n.* **1.** the act of flowing out. **2.** something that flows out.

out′fox′, *v.t.* to outsmart.

out′go′, *n.*, *pl.* **-goes.** money paid out.

out′go′ing (-gō′ing *or, for 3,* -gō′-), *adj.* **1.** departing. **2.** retiring from a position or office. **3.** friendly; sociable.

out′grow′, *v.t.*, **-grew, -grown, -grow•ing. 1.** to grow too large for. **2.** to discard or lose in the course of development. **3.** to surpass in growing.

out′growth′, *n.* an additional, supplementary result.

out′house′, *n.* an outbuilding serving as a toilet.

out′ing, *n.* a pleasure trip, picnic, etc.

out•land′ish (-lan′dish), *adj.* grotesquely strange or odd.

out′last′, *v.t.* to endure or last longer than.

out′law′, *n.* **1.** a habitual criminal. —*v.t.* **2.** to make illegal.

out•lay (*n.* out′lā′; *v.* out′lā′), *n.*, *v.*, **-laid, -lay•ing.** —*n.* **1.** an expending, as of money. **2.** an amount expended. —*v.t.* **3.** to expend.

out′let (-let, -lit), *n.* **1.** an opening by which anything is let out. **2.** a point on a wiring system at which current may be taken to supply electric devices. **3.** a means of expression: *an outlet for sorrow.* **4.** a store selling the goods of a particular manufacturer.

out′line′, *n.*, *v.*, **-lined, -lin•ing.** —*n.* **1.** the line by which a figure or object is bounded. **2.** a drawing restricted to line without shading. **3.** a general report, indicating only the main features. —*v.t.* **4.** to draw in outline. **5.** to indicate the main features of.

out/live/, *v.t.,* **-lived, -liv•ing.** to live or last longer than.

out/look/, *n.* **1.** the view from a place. **2.** mental attitude; point of view. **3.** prospect for the future.

out/ly/ing, *adj.* lying at a distance from the main body; remote.

out/ma•neu/ver, *v.t.* to outwit by maneuvering.

out/mod/ed (-mō/did), *adj.* **1.** no longer fashionable. **2.** obsolete.

out/num/ber, *v.t.* to exceed in number.

out/-of-bod/y, *adj.* of or characterized by the sensation that the mind or soul has left the body and is acting on its own.

out/-of-date/, *adj.* outmoded.

out-of-door, *adj.* OUTDOOR.

out/-of-doors/, *adv., n.* OUTDOORS.

out/-of-the-way/, *adj.* **1.** remote; isolated. **2.** unusual.

out/pa/tient, *n.* a person who receives treatment at a hospital but is not hospitalized.

out/place/ment, *n.* assistance in finding a new job, provided by a company for an employee who is being let go.

out/post/, *n.* **1.** a station established at a distance from an army to protect it from surprise attack. **2.** the body of troops stationed there. **3.** a post in a foreign environment.

out/put/, *n., v.* **-put•ted** or **-put, -put•ting.** —*n.* **1.** the quantity of something produced in a specified period. **2.** the material produced. **3.** the current, voltage, or power produced by an electrical or electronic device. **4. a.** any information made available by computer. **b.** the process of transferring such information from computer memory to or by means of an output device. —*v.t.* **5.** to transfer (computer output). **6.** to produce; yield.

out/rage (-rāj), *n., v.,* **-raged, -rag•ing.** —*n.* **1.** an act of wanton violence. **2.** anything that strongly offends the feelings. **3.** great anger. —*v.t.* **4.** to subject to grievous violence. **5.** to anger or offend.

out•ra/geous (-rā/jəs), *adj.* **1.** of or involving gross injury or wrong. **2.** grossly offensive to the sense of right or decency. **3.** passing reasonable bounds: *an outrageous price.* —**out•ra/geous•ly,** *adv.*

out/rank/, *v.t.* to have a higher rank than.

ou•tré (ōō trā/), *adj.* unconventional; bizarre.

out•reach (*v.* out/rēch/; *n., adj.* out/rēch/), —*v.t.* **1.** to reach beyond; exceed. —*v.i.* **2.** to reach out. —*n.* **3.** an act or instance of reaching out. —*adj.* **4.** concerned with extending community services: *outreach programs in education.*

out/rig/ger (-rig/ər), *n.* a framework supporting a float extended from the side of a boat for increasing stability.

out/right/ (*adj.* -rīt/; *adv.* -rīt/, -rīt/), *adj.* **1.** complete; total. **2.** downright; unqualified. —*adv.* **3.** entirely. **4.** openly. **5.** at once.

out/run/, *v.t.,* **-ran, -run, -run•ning. 1.** to run faster or farther than. **2.** to exceed; surpass.

out/sell/, *v.t.,* **-sold, -sell•ing.** to exceed in number of sales.

out/set/, *n.* beginning; start.

out/shine/, *v.t.,* **-shone** or **-shined, -shin•ing. 1.** to shine more brightly than. **2.** to surpass in excellence, achievement, etc.

out•side (*n.* out/sīd/, -sīd/; *adj.* out/sīd/, out/-; *adv.* out/sīd/; *prep.* out/sīd/, out/sīd/), *n.* **1.** the outer side, surface, or part; exterior. **2.** the external appearance. **3.** the space beyond an enclosure or boundary. —*adj.* **4.** of, situated on, or coming from the outside. **5.** not belonging to a specified group: *outside influences.* **6.** extremely unlikely: *an outside chance.* **7.** extreme or maximum: *an outside estimate.* —*adv.* **8.** on or to the outside. —*prep.* **9.** on the outside of. **10.** beyond the confines of. —**Idiom. 11. outside of,** other than.

out/sid/er, *n.* a person who is not part of a particular group.

out/size/, *n.* **1.** an uncommon size, esp. one larger than average. —*adj.* **2.** being unusually large, heavy, etc.

out/skirt/, *n.* Often, **-skirts.** the outlying district, as of a city.

out/smart/, *v.t.* to outwit.

out/spo/ken, *adj.* **1.** expressed with frankness. **2.** unreserved in speech.

out/spread/, *v.t., v.i.,* **-spread, -spread•ing.** to spread out; extend.

out/stand/ing, *adj.* **1.** prominent; conspicuous. **2.** excellent; distinguished. **3.** remaining unpaid, unresolved, etc.: *outstanding debts.* **4.** projecting.

out/stretch/, *v.t.* **1.** to stretch forth; extend. **2.** to stretch beyond.

out/strip/, *v.t.,* **-stripped, -strip•ping. 1.** to surpass or exceed. **2.** to get ahead of in a race.

out/take/, *n.* a segment of film or a part of a recording edited out of the final version.

out/vote/, *v.t.,* **-vot•ed, -vot•ing.** to defeat in voting.

out/ward (-wərd), *adj.* **1.** proceeding or directed toward the outside or exterior. **2.** pertaining to surface qualities only; superficial. **3.** of or situated on the outside. —*adv.* **4.** Also, **out/wards.** toward the outside. —**out/ward•ly,** *adv.*

out/weigh/, *v.t.* **1.** to exceed in value or importance. **2.** to exceed in weight.

out/wit/, *v.t.,* **-wit•ted, -wit•ting.** to get the better of by cleverness.

o•va (ō/və), *n.* pl. of OVUM.

o•val (ō/vəl), *adj.* **1.** egg-shaped. **2.** ellipsoidal or elliptical. —*n.* **3.** something oval in shape.

O/val Of/fice, *n.* the office of the president of the United States, located in the White House.

o•va•ry (ō/və rē), *n., pl.* **-ries. 1.** the female reproductive gland, in which the ova develop. **2.** the enlarged lower part of the pistil in flowering plants enclosing the new seeds. —**o•var•i•an** (ō vâr/ē ən), *adj.*

o•vate (ō/vāt), *adj.* egg-shaped.

o•va•tion (ō vā/shən), *n.* an enthusiastic public acclamation, marked by loud, prolonged applause.

ov•en (uv/ən), *n.* a chamber, as in a stove, for baking, roasting, etc.

o•ver (ō/vər), *prep.* **1.** above in place or position. **2.** above and to the other side of: *to leap over a wall.* **3.** above in authority, rank, etc. **4.** so as to cover: *Throw a sheet over the bed.* **5.** throughout: *to travel over Europe.* **6.** on or to the other side of: *to go over a bridge.* **7.** in excess of. **8.** in preference to. **9.** throughout the duration of: *over the years.* **10.** concerning: *to quarrel over a matter.* —*adv.* **11.** so as to cover or affect the whole surface: *to paint the room over.* **12.** through a region or area: *known the world over.* **13.** from one side to another or across an intervening space: *to sail over.* **14.** across or beyond an

---

o/ver•a•bun/dant, *adj.;* -ly, *adv.*
o/ver•ac/tive, *adj.*
o/ver•an/a•lyze/, *v.,* -lyzed, -lyz•ing.
o/ver•anx/ious, *adj.*
o/ver•ar/gu•men/ta•tive, *adj.*
o/ver•as•ser/tive, *adj.;* -ness, *n.*
o/ver•as•sured/, *adj.*
o/ver•at•ten/tive, *adj.;* -ness, *n.*
o/ver•bid/, *v.,* -bid, -bid•ding.
o/ver•bold/, *adj.*
o/ver•bur/den, *v.t.*

o/ver•buy/, *v.,* -bought, -buy•ing.
o/ver•cau/tious, *adj.*
o/ver•com/pen•sate/, *v.,* -sat•ed, -sat•ing.
o/ver•com•pet/i•tive, *adj.*
o/ver•com•pla/cen•cy, *n.*
o/ver•com•pla/cent, *adj.*
o/ver•con/fi•dent, *adj.*
o/ver•con/sci•en/tious, *adj.*
o/ver•con•sid/er•ate, *adj.*
o/ver•cook/, *v.t.*
o/ver•cool/, *adj., v.t.*

o/ver•crit/i•cal, *adj.*
o/ver•crowd/, *v.*
o/ver•cu/ri•ous, *adj.*
o/ver•dec/o•rate/, *v.,* -rat•ed, -rat•ing.
o/ver•de•fen/sive, *adj.*
o/ver•de•pend/ent, *adj.*
o/ver•de•vel/op, *v.*
o/ver•dram/a•tize/, *v.,* -tized, -tiz•ing.
o/ver•dress/, *v.*
o/ver•ea/ger, *adj.*

edge or rim: *The soup boiled over.* **15.** from beginning to end: *Think it over.* **16.** from one person to another: *He made the property over to his brother.* **17.** from one opinion or belief to another: *won them over.* **18.** on the other side, as of a sea or any space: *over in Japan.* **19.** from an upright position: *to knock over a glass.* **20.** to a reversed position: *The dog rolled over.* **21.** once more: *Do the work over.* **22.** in repetition or succession: *20 times over.* **23.** in excess or addition. —*adj.* **24.** upper; higher up. **25.** surplus; extra. **26.** too great. **27.** ended; past: *when the war was over.*

over-, a prefix meaning: too or too much (*overact*); over or above (*overflow*); higher in authority or rank (*overlord*).

o′ver•a•chieve′, *v.i.,* -chieved, -chiev•ing. **1.** to perform academically above the potential indicated by tests of one's ability. **2.** to perform better than is expected. —**o′ver•a•chiev′er,** *n.*

o′ver•act′, *v.t., v.i.* to perform (a role) in an exaggerated manner.

o•ver•age¹ (ō′vər āj′), *adj.* beyond the acceptable, desired, or usual age.

o•ver•age² (ō′vər ij), *n.* an excess supply of merchandise.

o•ver•all (*adv.* ō′vər ôl′; *adj., n.* ō′vər ôl′), *adv., adj.* **1.** from one end to the other. **2.** including everything. —*n.* **3.** overalls, (*used with a pl. v.*) loose, sturdy trousers, usu. having a bib with attached shoulder straps.

o′ver•awe′, *v.t.,* -awed, -aw•ing. to restrain or subdue by inspiring awe.

o′ver•bal′ance, *v.t.,* -anced, -anc•ing. **1.** to outweigh. **2.** to cause to lose balance.

o′ver•bear′ing, *adj.* domineering; arrogant.

o′ver•bite′, *n.* occlusion in which the upper incisor teeth overlap the lower ones.

o′ver•blown′, *adj.* **1.** overdone or excessive. **2.** pretentious.

o′ver•board′, *adv.* **1.** over the side of a ship into the water. —*Idiom.* **2. go overboard,** to go to extremes.

o′ver•cast′ (-kast′, -käst′, -kast′, -käst′), *adj.* overspread with clouds: *an overcast sky.*

o•ver•charge (*v.* ō′vər chärj′; *n.* ō′vər chärj′), *v.,* -charged, -charg•ing, *n.* —*v.t., v.i.* **1.** to charge too high a price. **2.** to overload. —*n.* **3.** a charge in excess of a just price. **4.** an excessive load.

o′ver•class′, *n.* a social stratum consisting of educated and wealthy persons considered to control the economic power of a country.

o′ver•coat′, *n.* a coat worn over the ordinary indoor clothing.

o′ver•come′, *v.,* -came, -come, -com•ing. —*v.t.* **1.** to get the better of in a conflict. **2.** to prevail over (opposition, temptations, etc.). **3.** to overpower or overwhelm in body or mind. —*v.i.* **4.** to win.

o′ver•do′, *v.,* -did, -done, -do•ing. —*v.t.* **1.** to do to excess. **2.** to exaggerate. **3.** to overcook. —*v.i.* **4.** to do too much; go to extremes.

o•ver•dose (*n.* ō′vər dōs′; *v.* ō′vər dōs′, ō′vər-dōs′), *n., v.,* -dosed, -dos•ing. —*n.* **1.** an excessive dose of a drug. —*v.i.* **2.** to take an excessive dose. —*v.t.* **3.** to give an excessive dose to.

o′ver•draft′, *n.* **1.** the act of overdrawing a checking account. **2.** an overdrawn check. **3.** the amount overdrawn.

o′ver•draw′, *v.t.,* -drew, -drawn, -draw•ing. to draw upon (an account) in excess of the balance.

o′ver•due′, *adj.* past due, as a bill remaining unpaid.

o•ver•flow (*v.* ō′vər flō′; *n.* ō′vər flō′), *v.i.* **1.** to flow or run over, as water. **2.** to be supplied with in great measure. —*v.t.* **3.** to flow over; flood. **4.** to flow over the edge or brim of. —*n.* **5.** an overflowing. **6.** a superabundance. **7.** an outlet for excess liquid.

o′ver•grow′, *v.,* -grew, -grown, -grow•ing. —*v.t.* **1.** to cover with growth. —*v.i.* **2.** to grow too fast or too large. —**o′ver•grown′,** *adj.* —**o′ver•growth′,** *n.*

o′ver•hand′, *adj., adv.* with the hand and part or all of the arm raised over the shoulder.

o•ver•hang (*v.* ō′vər hang′; *n.* ō′vər hang′), *v.,* -hung, -hang•ing, *n.* —*v.t., v.i.* **1.** to hang or project over (something). —*n.* **2.** something that extends or juts out over.

o•ver•haul (*v.* ō′vər hôl′, ō′vər hôl′; *n.* ō′vər hôl′), *v.t.* **1.** to restore to working condition. **2.** to examine thoroughly and revise or refurbish. **3.** to gain on or catch up with. —*n.* **4.** a general examination and repair.

o′ver•head′ (*adv.* -hed′; *adj., n.* -hed′), *adv.* **1.** above one's head; up in the sky. —*adj.* **2.** situated or operating above or over the head. —*n.* **3.** the general, fixed costs of running a business, as rent and lighting.

o′ver•hear′, *v.t.,* -heard, -hear•ing. to hear (speech or a speaker) without the speaker's intention or knowledge.

o′ver•joy′, *v.t.,* to cause to feel great joy. —**o′ver•joyed′,** *adj.*

o′ver•kill′, *n.* **1.** the capacity of a nation to destroy by nuclear weapons more of an enemy than would be necessary for a victory. **2.** an excess of what is required or suitable.

o′ver•land′ (-land′, -lənd), *adv., adj.* by, over, or across land.

O′ver•land Park′ (-lənd), *n.* a town in E Kansas. 125,225.

o•ver•lap (*v.* ō′vər lap′; *n.* ō′vər lap′), *v.,* -lapped, -lap•ping, *n.* —*v.t., v.i.* **1.** to extend over and cover a part (of). **2.** to coincide in part (with). —*n.* **3.** the extent or state of overlapping. **4.** an overlapping part.

o′ver•lay′, *v.t.,* -laid, -lay•ing. **1.** to lay or place (one thing) over or upon another. **2.** to finish with a superimposed decorative layer.

o′ver•lie′, *v.t.,* -lay, -lain, -ly•ing. to lie over or on.

o′ver•look′, *v.t.* **1.** to fail to notice. **2.** to disregard indulgently. **3.** to excuse; pardon. **4.** to look over, as from a higher position. **5.** to supervise.

o′ver•lord′, *n.* a person who is lord over other lords.

o′ver•ly, *adv.* excessively; too.

o′ver•much′, *adj., n., adv.* too much.

o′ver•night′ (*adv.* -nīt′; *adj.* -nīt′), *adv.* **1.** for or during the night. **2.** very quickly; suddenly. —*adj.* **3.** done or continuing during the night. **4.** for one night. **5.** sudden: *an overnight sensation.*

o′ver•pass′, *n.* a road, walkway, or bridge providing access over another route.

o′ver•play′, *v.t.* **1.** to exaggerate (one's role, an emotion, etc.). —*Idiom.* **2. overplay one's hand,** to overestimate the strength of one's position.

---

o′ver•eat′, *v.i.,* -ate, -eat•en, -eat•ing.

o′ver•ed′u•cate′, *v.t.,* -cat•ed, -cat•ing.

o′ver•em′pha•sis, *n.*

o′ver•em′pha•size′, *v.t.,* -sized, -siz•ing.

o′ver•em•phat′ic, *adj.*

o′ver•en•dowed′, *adj.*

o′ver•es•thu′si•as′tic, *adj.*

o′ver•es′ti•mate′, *v.t.,* -mat•ed, -mat•ing.

o′ver•ex•cit′a•ble, *adj.*

o′ver•ex•cite′, *v.t.,* -cit•ed, -cit•ing.

o′ver•ex•ert′, *v.*

o′ver•ex•pose′, *v.t.,* -posed, -pos•ing.

o′ver•ex•tend′, *v.t.*

o′ver•feed′, *v.,* -fed, -feed•ing.

o′ver•fond′, *adj.*

o′ver•full′, *adj.*

o′ver•fur′nish, *v.*

o′ver•gen′er•al•ize′, *v.,* -ized, -iz•ing.

o′ver•gen′er•ous, *adj.*

o′ver•graze′, *v.t.,* -grazed, -graz•ing.

o′ver•heat′, *v.*

o′ver•in•dulge′, *v.,* -dulged, -dulg•ing.

o′ver•in′flu•en′tial, *adj.*

o′ver•in•sist′ence, *n.*

o′ver•in•sist′ent, *adj.*

o′ver•in•sure′, *v.t.,* -sured, -sur•ing.

o′ver•large′, *adj.*

o'ver·pow'er, *v.t.* **1.** to overcome by superior force. **2.** to affect or impress excessively.

o'ver·qual'i·fied', *adj.* having more education or experience than is required for a job.

o'ver·reach', *v.t.* **1.** to reach or extend over or beyond. **2.** to defeat (oneself) by excessive eagerness.

o'ver·ride', *v.t.,* **-rode, -rid·den, -rid·ing. 1.** to prevail over; overrule. **2.** to set aside or nullify. **3.** to ride over or across.

o'ver·rid'ing, *adj.* most important; primary.

o'ver·rule', *v.t.,* **-ruled, -rul·ing. 1.** to rule against; reject. **2.** to prevail over.

o·ver·run (*v.* ō'vər run'; *n.* ō'vər run'), *v.,* **-ran, -run, -run·ning,** *n.* —*v.t.* **1.** to swarm over in great numbers. **2.** to defeat decisively and occupy the position of. **3.** to exceed, as a budget. **4.** to overflow. —*n.* **5.** an act or instance of overrunning. **6.** an amount in excess of that needed or ordered.

o·ver·seas (*adv.* ō'vər sēz'; *adj.* ō'vər sēz'), *adv.* **1.** over, across, or beyond the sea. —*adj.* **2.** across or over the sea. **3.** of, from, or located in places across the sea; foreign.

o'ver·see', *v.t.,* **-saw, -seen, -see·ing.** to supervise; manage. —**o'ver·se'er,** *n.*

o'ver·shad'ow, *v.t.* **1.** to exceed in importance. **2.** to cast a shadow over.

o'ver·shoe', *n.* a shoe or boot worn over another for protection in wet or cold weather.

o'ver·shoot', *v.t.,* **-shot, -shoot·ing. 1.** to shoot or go over or beyond so as to miss. **2.** to pass or go beyond.

o'ver·sight', *n.* **1.** a careless omission or error. **2.** the act of overseeing; supervision.

o'ver·size' also **-sized',** *adj.* of a size larger than is usual or necessary.

o'ver·sleep', *v.i.,* **-slept, -sleep·ing.** to sleep beyond the intended time of waking.

o·ver·soul (ō'vər sōl'), *n.* (esp. in transcendentalism) a supreme reality or mind.

o'ver·state', *v.t.,* **-stat·ed, -stat·ing. 1.** to state too strongly; exaggerate.

o'ver·stay', *v.t.,* to stay beyond the time or duration of.

o'ver·step', *v.t.,* **-stepped, -step·ping.** to go beyond; exceed.

o'ver·stuffed', *adj.* **1.** stuffed or filled to excess. **2.** (of furniture) covered by thick upholstery: *an overstuffed sofa.*

o'ver·sub·scribe', *v.t.,* **-scribed, -scrib·ing.** to subscribe for more of than is available, expected, or required.

o·vert (ō vûrt', ō'vûrt), *adj.* open to view or knowledge; not concealed. —**o·vert'ly,** *adv.*

o'ver·take', *v.t.,* **-took, -tak·en, -tak·ing. 1.** to catch up with or pass. **2.** to befall suddenly.

o'ver-the-count'er, *adj.* **1.** not listed on or transacted through an organized securities exchange. **2.** sold legally without a prescription.

o·ver·throw (*v.* ō'vər thrō'; *n.* ō'vər thrō'), *v.,* **-threw, -thrown, -throw·ing,** *n.* —*v.t.* **1.** to depose, as from power. **2.** to overturn; topple. **3.** to throw past or over. —*n.* **4.** an act or instance of overthrowing or being overthrown.

o'ver·time', *n.* **1.** working time before or after one's regular working hours. **2.** pay for such time. —*adv.* **3.** during overtime. —*adj.* **4.** of or for overtime.

o'ver·tone', *n.* **1.** an acoustical frequency higher than and simultaneous with the fundamental in a complex musical tone. **2.** an additional, usu. implicit meaning or quality.

o·ver·ture (ō'vər chər, -chŏŏr'), *n.* **1.** an initiating move in a negotiation, relationship, etc. **2.** an orchestral prelude to a musical work, as an opera.

o'ver·turn', *v.t.* **1.** to cause to turn over on the side, face, or back. **2.** to destroy the power of. —*v.i.* **3.** to turn over; capsize.

o'ver·view', *n.* a general outline of a subject or situation.

o'ver·ween'ing, *adj.* **1.** presumptuously conceited, overconfident, or proud. **2.** excessive.

o'ver·whelm', *v.t.* **1.** to overpower in mind or feeling. **2.** to overpower with superior force. **3.** to bury beneath a mass of something.

o·ver·wrought (ō'vər rôt', ō'vər-), *adj.* **1.** extremely excited or agitated. **2.** excessively complex or ornate.

Ov·id (ov'id), *n.* (*Publius Ovidius Naso*) 43 B.C.–A.D. 17?, Roman poet.

o·vi·duct (ō'vi dukt'), *n.* a tube through which ova are transported from the ovary to the uterus.

o·vip·a·rous (ō vip'ər əs), *adj.* producing eggs that hatch outside the body.

o·void (ō'void), *adj.* **1.** egg-shaped. —*n.* **2.** an ovoid body.

ov·u·late (ov'yə lāt', ō'vyə-), *v.i.,* **-lat·ed, -lat·ing.** to produce and discharge eggs from an ovary. —**ov'u·la'tion,** *n.*

ov·ule (ov'yōōl, ō'vyōōl), *n.* **1.** the structure in seed plants that develops into a seed after fertilization. **2.** a small egg. —**ov·u·lar** (ov'yə lər, ō'vyə-), *adj.*

o·vum (ō'vəm), *n., pl.* **o·va** (ō'və). a female reproductive cell.

ow (ou), *interj.* an expression of pain.

owe (ō), *v.t.,* **owed, ow·ing. 1.** to be under obligation to pay or render. **2.** to be in debt to. **3.** to be indebted for: *to owe one's fame to good fortune.*

Ow·ens (ō'ənz), *n.* **Jesse** (*John Cleveland*), 1913–80, U.S. athlete.

ow'ing, *adj.* **1.** owed, unpaid, or due for payment. —*Idiom.* **2. owing to,** because of.

owl (oul), *n.* a nocturnal bird of prey with large eyes. —**owl'ish,** *adj.*

own (ōn), *adj.* **1.** of or belonging to oneself or itself: *his own money.* —*pron.* **2.** something that belongs to oneself. —*v.t.* **3.** to have as one's own. **4.** to acknowledge or admit. —*v.i.* **5.** to confess: *He owned to being uncertain.* —*Idiom.* **6. on one's own, a.** through one's own efforts. **b.** living independently. —**own'er,** *n.* —**own'er·ship',** *n.*

ox (oks), *n., pl.* **ox·en.** any bovine animal, esp. a castrated adult bull used as a draft animal.

ox'blood', *n.* a deep, dull red color.

ox'bow' (-bō'), *n.* the U-shaped part of a yoke that is placed under and around the neck of an ox.

ox·ford (oks'fərd), *n.* **1.** a low shoe laced over the instep. **2.** a cotton or synthetic fabric with a plain or basket weave.

Ox'ford, *n.* a city in S England, NW of London: university. 115,800. —**Ox·o·ni·an** (ok sō'nē ən), *adj., n.*

ox·i·dant (ok'si dənt), *n.* a chemical agent that oxidizes.

---

o'ver·load', *v.t.*
o'ver·load', *n.*
o'ver·long', *adj., adv.*
o'ver·pay', *v.t.,* -paid, -pay·ing.
o'ver·pop'u·late', *v.t.,* -lat·ed, -lat·ing.
o'ver·praise', *v.t.,* -praised, -prais·ing, *n.*
o'ver·price', *v.t.,* -priced, -pric·ing.
o'ver·print', *v.t.*
o'ver·pro·duce', *v.,* -duced, -duc·ing.

o'ver·pro·tect', *v.t.*
o'ver·rate', *v.t.*
o'ver·re·act', *v.i.*
o'ver·ripe', *adj.*
o'ver·salt', *v.t.*
o'ver·scru'pu·lous, *adj.*
o'ver·sell', *v.,* -sold, -sell·ing.
o'ver·sen'si·tive, *adj.*
o'ver·sim'pli·fy', *v.,* -fied, -fy·ing.
o'ver·so·lic'i·tous, *adj.*
o'ver·spend', *v.,* -spent, -spend·ing.

o'ver·stim'u·late', *v.,* -lat·ed, -lat·ing.
o'ver·stock', *v.t.*
o'ver·stock', *n.*
o'ver·strict', *adj.*
o'ver·tax', *v.t.*
o'ver·tire', *v.,* -tired, -tir·ing.
o'ver·use', *v.t.*
o'ver·use', *n.*
o'ver·weight', *adj.*
o'ver·work', *v.t.*
o'ver·zeal'ous, *adj.*

ox•i•da'tion (-dā'shən), n. the process or result of oxidizing.

ox•ide (ok'sīd, -sid), n. a compound containing oxygen and another element or radical. —**ox•id'ic** (-sid'ik), adj.

ox•i•dize (ok'si dīz'), v., -dized, -diz•ing. —v.t. 1. to combine chemically with oxygen. —v.i. 2. to become oxidized. —**ox'i•diz'er,** n.

Ox•nard (oks'närd), n. a city in SW California. 145,863.

ox•y•a•cet•y•lene (ok'sē ə set'l ēn', -in), n. a mixture of oxygen and acetylene, used in a blowtorch.

ox•y•gen (ok'si jən), n. a colorless, odorless, gaseous element constituting about one-fifth of the volume of the atmosphere. Symbol: O; at. wt.: 15.9994; at. no.: 8. —**ox'y•gen'ic** (-jen'ik), **ox•yg'e•nous** (-sij'ə nəs), adj.

ox'y•gen•ate' (-jə nāt'), v.t., -at•ed, -at•ing. to treat, combine, or enrich with oxygen. —**ox'y•gen•a'tion,** n.

ox•y•mo•ron (ok'si môr'on), n., pl. -mo•ra (-môr'ə). a figure of speech that uses seeming contradictions, as "cruel kindness."

oys•ter (oi'stər), n. any of several edible, marine, bivalve mollusks having an irregularly shaped shell.

oz., ounce.

O'zark Moun'tains (ō'zârk), n.pl. a group of low mountains in S Missouri, N Arkansas, and NE Oklahoma. Also called **O'zarks.**

o•zone (ō'zōn, ō zōn'), n. a form of oxygen produced when an electric spark passes through air: used for bleaching, sterilizing, etc.

o'zone hole', n. any part of the ozone layer that has become depleted by atmospheric pollution, resulting in excess ultraviolet radiation passing through the atmosphere.

o'zone lay'er, n. the layer of the upper atmosphere where most atmospheric ozone is concentrated, serving to absorb much solar ultraviolet radiation.

P

P, p (pē), n., pl. **Ps** or **P's, ps** or **p's.** the 16th letter of the English alphabet, a consonant.

P, Chem. Symbol. phosphorus.

p., 1. page. 2. participle. 3. past. 4. per. 5. pint.

pa (pä, pô), n., pl. **pas.** Informal. father.

PA, 1. Parents' Association. 2. Pennsylvania. 3. public-address system.

Pa, Chem. Symbol. protactinium.

Pa., Pennsylvania.

PAC (pak), n., pl. **PAC's, PACs.** political action committee.

pace¹ (pās), n., v., **paced, pac•ing.** —n. 1. a rate of movement in stepping or walking. 2. a rate of activity, progress, etc. 3. a single step. 4. the distance covered in a step. 5. a manner of stepping; gait. 6. a gait of a horse in which the feet on the same side are lifted and put down together. —v.t. 7. to set the pace for, as in racing. 8. to traverse with slow, regular steps. 9. to measure by paces. 10. to train to a certain pace. —v.i. 11. to take slow, regular steps. 12. (of a horse) to go at a pace. —**Idiom.** 13. **put through one's paces,** to cause to demonstrate a set of skills. —**pac'er,** n.

pa•ce² (pā'sē, pä'chā), prep. with all due respect to.

pace'mak'er, n. 1. an electronic device implanted beneath the skin to provide a normal heartbeat. 2. PACESETTER.

pace'set'ter, n. a person or group that serves as a model to be imitated or followed.

pach•y•derm (pak'i dûrm'), n. any large, thickskinned, hoofed mammal, as the elephant or rhinoceros.

pach•y•san•dra (pak'ə san'drə), n., pl. -dras. a low-growing evergreen plant, grown as a ground cover.

pa•cif•ic (pə sif'ik), adj. 1. tending to make or preserve peace. 2. calm; tranquil. —n. 3. (cap.) PACIFIC OCEAN.

Pacif'ic O'cean, n. an ocean bordered by the American continents, Asia, and Australia: largest ocean in the world.

pac•i•fi•er (pas'ə fī'ər), n. 1. one that pacifies. 2. a device, often shaped like a nipple, for a baby to suck on.

pac'i•fism (-fiz'əm), n. opposition to war or violence as a method of settling disputes. —**pac'i•fist,** n., adj.

pac'i•fy', v.t., -fied, -fy•ing. 1. to bring or restore to a state of peace or tranquillity. 2. to reduce to a submissive state. —**pac'i•fi•ca'tion,** n.

pack¹ (pak), n. 1. a group of things wrapped or tied together for easy handling or carrying. 2. a definite quantity of merchandise together with its wrapping: a pack of cigarettes. 3. a group of people or things: a pack of lies. 4. a group of animals of the same kind: a pack of wolves. —v.t. 5. to make into a pack. 6. to fill compactly with anything: to pack a trunk. 7. to put into a case, trunk, etc., as for traveling. 8. to press or crowd together within: The crowd packed the room. 9. to make airtight or watertight by stuffing. 10. to carry: to pack a gun. 11. Informal. to be able to deliver: to pack a mean punch. —v.i. 12. to pack goods in compact form, as for shipping. 13. to place clothes in luggage preparatory to traveling. 14. to crowd together. 15. to become compacted: Wet snow packs readily. 16. **pack off,** to send away with dispatch: packed the kids off to camp. —adj. 17. used in carrying a load: pack animals.

pack² (pak), v.t. to choose (cards, persons, etc.) so as to serve one's own purposes: to pack a jury.

pack'age (-ij), n., v., -aged, -ag•ing. —n. 1. a bundle of something that is packed and wrapped or boxed; parcel. 2. a container in which something is packed. 3. a group of related elements offered as a single unit: a tax package. —v.t. 4. to make or put into a package.

pack'er, n. a person or thing that packs, esp. a person or company that packs food for market.

pack'et (-it), n. 1. a small package. 2. a small ship that carries mail, passengers, and goods regularly on a fixed route.

pack'ing, n. 1. the act or work of a person or thing that packs. 2. material used to cushion or protect goods packed in a container.

pack' rat', n. 1. a North and Central American rat noted for carrying off shiny articles to its nest. 2. Informal. a person who saves useless small items.

pack'sad'dle, n. a saddle designed for supporting the load on a pack animal.

pact (pakt), n. an agreement or compact.

pad¹ (pad), n., v., pad•ded, pad•ding. —n. 1. a cushionlike mass of soft material used for comfort, protection, or stuffing. 2. a number of sheets of paper glued together at one edge to form a tablet. 3. any of the cushionlike parts on the feet of vertebrates. 4. the large floating leaf of a water lily. 5. Slang. one's living quarters. —v.t. 6. to furnish or stuff with a pad or padding. 7. to expand unnecessarily or dishonestly: to pad an expense account.

pad² (pad), n., v., pad•ded, pad•ding. —n. 1. a dull, muffled sound, as of footsteps on the ground. —v.i. 2. to walk with a dull, muffled sound.

pad'ding, n. 1. material used to pad something. 2. something added unnecessarily or dishonestly.

pad·dle¹ (pad′l), *n., v.,* **-dled, -dling.** —*n.* **1.** a short, flat-bladed oar for propelling a canoe or small boat. **2.** a similar implement used for mixing, stirring, or beating. **3.** a short-handled racket, as that used in table tennis. **4.** a blade of a paddle wheel. —*v.i., v.t.* **5.** to propel (a canoe or the like) with a paddle. **6.** to stir or beat with a paddle.

pad·dle² (pad′l), *v.i.,* **-dled, -dling.** to move the feet or hands playfully in shallow water.

pad′dle wheel′, *n.* a wheel for propelling a ship, having a number of projecting paddles.

pad·dock (pad′ək), *n.* **1.** a small, enclosed field near a stable for pasturing or exercising animals. **2.** the enclosure in which horses are saddled and mounted before a race.

pad·dy (pad′ē), *n., pl.* **-dies.** a rice field.

pad′dy wag′on, *n.* an enclosed van used by the police to transport prisoners.

pad·lock′, *n.* **1.** a detachable lock with a sliding shackle that can be passed through a link, ring, etc. —*v.t.* **2.** to fasten with or as if with a padlock.

pa·dre (pä′drā, -drē), *n., pl.* **-dres.** a clergyman, esp. a priest. [< Sp, Pg, It: father < L *pater*]

pae·an (pē′ən), *n.* a song of praise, joy, or triumph.

pa·gan (pā′gən), *n.* **1.** one of a people observing a polytheistic religion, as the ancient Romans. **2.** a person who is not a Christian, Jew, or Muslim; heathen. **3.** an irreligious person. —*adj.* **4.** of pagans or their religion. —**pa′gan·ism,** *n.*

Pa·ga·ni·ni (pag′ə nē′nē, pä′gə-), *n.* **Niccolò,** 1784–1840, Italian composer and violinist.

page¹ (pāj), *n., v.,* **paged, pag·ing.** —*n.* **1.** one side of a leaf of something printed or written, as a book. **2.** the entire leaf. **3.** a block of computer memory up to 4,096 bytes long. —*v.t.* **4.** to number the pages of. —*v.i.* **5.** to turn pages (usu. fol. by *through*).

page² (pāj), *n., v.,* **paged, pag·ing.** —*n.* **1.** a boy servant or attendant. **2.** an employee who carries messages, runs errands, etc., as in a hotel. —*v.t.* **3.** to summon (a person) in a public place by calling out his or her name.

pag·eant (paj′ənt), *n.* **1.** a costumed procession or parade forming part of public festivities. **2.** a public spectacle illustrative of the history of a place, institution, etc. **3.** a show or exhibition: *a beauty pageant.* —**pag′eant·ry,** *n., pl.* **-ries.**

pag·er (pā′jər), *n.* BEEPER.

pag·i·na·tion (paj′ə nā′shən), *n.* the figures by which the leaves of a book, manuscript, etc., are marked to indicate their sequence. —**pag′i·nate′,** *v.t.,* **-nat·ed, -nat·ing.**

pa·go·da (pə gō′də), *n., pl.* **-das.** a temple of the Far East, usu. a tower having an upward-curving roof over each story.

paid (pād), *v.* a pt. and pp. of PAY¹.

pail (pāl), *n.* a cylindrical container with a handle; bucket. —**pail′ful′,** *n., pl.* **-fuls.**

pain (pān), *n.* **1.** physical suffering typically from injury or illness. **2.** severe mental or emotional distress. **3. pains,** diligent care: *Take pains with your work.* —*v.t.* **4.** to cause pain to. —*Idiom.* **5. on** or **under pain of,** subject to the penalty of. —**pain′ful,** *adj.* —**pain′ful·ly,** *adv.* —**pain′less,** *adj.* —**pain′less·ly,** *adv.*

Paine (pān), *n.* **Thomas,** 1737–1809, U.S. patriot and political writer, born in England.

pain′kill′er, *n.* something that relieves pain, esp. an analgesic. —**pain′kill′ing,** *adj.*

pains·tak·ing (pānz′tā′king, pān′stā′-), *adj.* expending or showing diligent care; careful. —**pains′-tak·ing·ly,** *adv.*

paint (pānt), *n.* **1.** a mixture of solid coloring matter and a liquid, applied as a protective or decorative coating to various surfaces or to an artist's canvas. **2.** the dried surface pigment. —*v.t.* **3.** to coat, cover, or decorate with paint. **4.** to produce (a picture or design) in paint. **5.** to represent in paint. **6.** to describe vividly in words. —*v.i.* **7.** to engage in painting as an art. —**paint′er,** *n.*

paint′brush′, *n.* a brush for applying paint.

paint′ing, *n.* **1.** a picture or design executed in

paints. **2.** the act, art, or work of a person who paints.

pair (pâr), *n., pl.* **pairs, pair,** *v.* —*n.* **1.** two corresponding things that are matched for use together: *a pair of gloves.* **2.** something having two pieces joined together: *a pair of scissors.* **3.** two individual persons or things that are in some way associated: *a pair of horses.* —*v.t., v.i.* **4.** to form (into) a pair. **5.** (of animals) to mate or cause to mate.

pais·ley (pāz′lē), *adj.* (*often cap.*) having a pattern of colorful, minutely detailed, usu. curving figures.

pa·ja·mas (pə jä′məz, -jam′əz), *n.* (*used with a pl. v.*) nightclothes consisting of loose-fitting trousers and a jacket.

Pak·i·stan (pak′ə stan′, pä′kə stän′), *n.* a republic in S Asia, between India and Afghanistan. 132,185,299. —**Pak′i·stan′i,** *n., pl.* **-stan·is, -stan·i,** *adj.*

pal (pal), *n. Informal.* a close friend.

pal·ace (pal′is), *n.* **1.** the official residence of a sovereign or other exalted personage. **2.** a large and stately building.

pal·a·din (pal′ə din), *n.* any knightly or heroic champion.

pal·an·quin (pal′ən kēn′), *n.* an enclosed litter suspended from poles and carried by several men, formerly used in E Asia.

pal·at·a·ble (pal′ə tə bəl), *adj.* **1.** acceptable to the palate or taste. **2.** acceptable to the mind or feelings.

pal′a·tal (-ə tl), *adj.* **1.** pertaining to the palate. **2.** (of a speech sound, esp. a consonant) articulated with the blade of the tongue held close to or touching the hard palate. —*n.* **3.** a palatal consonant. **pal′a·tal·ize′,** *v.t.,* **-ized, -iz·ing.** to change into a palatal sound. —**pal′a·tal·i·za′tion,** *n.*

pal′ate (-it), *n.* **1.** the roof of the mouth in mammals. **2.** the sense of taste.

pa·la·tial (pə lā′shəl), *adj.* **1.** of or resembling a palace. **2.** suitable for a palace; magnificent.

pa·lat·i·nate (pə lat′n āt′, -it), *n.* the territory under a palatine.

pal·a·tine (pal′ə tīn′, -tin), *adj.* **1.** having royal privileges. **2.** of a palatine or palatinate. —*n.* **3.** a vassal exercising royal privileges in a province. **4.** a high official of an imperial court.

pa·lav·er (pə lav′ər, -lä′vər), *n.* **1.** profuse and idle talk. —*v.i.* **2.** to talk profusely and idly. [< Pg *palavra* word, speech]

pale¹ (pāl), *adj.,* **pal·er, pal·est,** *v.,* **paled, pal·ing.** —*adj.* **1.** lacking intensity of color. **2.** approaching white or gray: *pale yellow.* —*v.t., v.i.* **3.** to make or become pale. —**pale′ness,** *n.*

pale² (pāl), *n.* **1.** a stake or picket, as of a fence. **2.** limits; bounds: *outside the pale of my jurisdiction.*

pale′face′, *n. Slang.* a white person, esp. as distinguished from a North American Indian.

Pa·le·o·cene (pā′lē ə sēn′; *esp. Brit.* pal′ē-), *adj.* noting or pertaining to an epoch of the Tertiary Period.

Pa′le·o·lith′ic (-ō lith′ik), *adj.* noting or pertaining to the early phase of the Stone Age.

pa′le·on·tol′o·gy (-ən tol′ə jē), *n.* the science of the forms of life existing in former geologic periods, as represented by their fossils. —**pa′le·on·tol′o·gist,** *n.*

Pa′le·o·zo′ic (-ə zō′ik), *adj.* noting or pertaining to a geologic era occurring between 570 million and 230 million years ago, when fish, insects, and reptiles first appeared.

Pa·ler·mo (pə lûr′mō, -lâr′-), *n.* the capital of Sicily. 701,782.

Pal·es·tine (pal′ə stīn′), *n.* Biblical name, **Canaan.** an ancient country in SW Asia, on the E coast of the Mediterranean.

Pal′estine Libera′tion Organiza′tion, *n.* an umbrella organization for several Arab groups dedicated to the recovery of Palestine from the state of Israel and the return of refugees from the area to their homeland. *Abbr.:* PLO

pal·ette (pal′it), *n.* **1.** a thin board used by painters for holding and mixing colors. **2.** the set of colors on such a board.

pal•frey (pôl′frē), *n., pl.* **-freys.** *Archaic.* a saddle horse particularly suitable for a woman.

pal•i•mo•ny (pal′ə mō′nē), *n.* a form of alimony awarded to one member of an unmarried couple who separated after a period of living together.

pal•imp•sest (pal′imp sest′), *n.* a parchment or the like from which writing has been partially or completely erased to make room for another text.

pal•in•drome (pal′in drōm′), *n.* a word, verse, etc., reading the same backward as forward, as *madam.*

pal•ing (pā′ling), *n.* **1.** a fence of pales. **2.** pales collectively.

pal•i•sade (pal′ə sād′), *n.* **1.** a fence of pales or stakes, as for defense. **2. palisades,** a line of cliffs.

pall[1] (pôl), *n.* **1.** something that covers with darkness or gloom. **2.** a cloth for spreading over a coffin.

pall[2] (pôl), *v.i.* **1.** to have a wearying effect. **2.** to become satiated or cloyed with something.

pal•la•di•um (pə lā′dē əm), *n.* a rare metallic element, used chiefly as a catalyst and in alloys. *Symbol:* Pd; *at. wt.:* 106.4; *at. no.:* 46.

pall′bear′er, *n.* one of several persons who carry or attend the coffin at a funeral.

pal•let[1] (pal′it), *n.* **1.** a bed or mattress of straw. **2.** a small or makeshift bed.

pal•let[2] (pal′it), *n.* a low, portable platform on which goods are placed for storage or moving.

pal•li•ate (pal′ē āt′), *v.t.* **-at•ed, -at•ing. 1.** to relieve without curing. **2.** to try to mitigate the gravity of (an offense) by excuses, apologies, etc. **—pal′li•a′tion,** *n.* **—pal′li•a′tive** (-ā′tiv, -ə tiv), *adj., n.*

pal•lid (pal′id), *adj.* **1.** faint or deficient in color. **2.** lacking in vitality or interest.

pal•lor (pal′ər), *n.* extreme paleness, as from fear or ill health.

palm[1] (päm), *n.* **1.** the inner surface of the hand between the wrist and the fingers. **—v.t. 2.** to conceal in the palm, as in sleight of hand. **3.** to pick up stealthily. **4. palm off,** to foist upon someone, as by fraud.

palm[2] (päm), *n.* **1.** any of numerous tropical plants, most of which are tall, unbranched trees with a crown of large leaves. **2.** a leaf of such a tree, formerly carried to signify victory.

pal•met•to (pal met′ō, päl-, pä-), *n., pl.* **-tos, -toes.** any of various palms with fan-shaped leaves.

palm•is•try (pä′mə strē), *n.* the practice of reading fortunes and character from the lines on the palm of a person's hand. **—palm′ist,** *n.*

Palm′ Sun′day, *n.* the Sunday before Easter, commemorating Christ's triumphal entry into Jerusalem.

palm•top (päm′top′), *n.* a battery-powered microcomputer small enough to fit in the palm.

palm′y, *adj.,* **-i•er, -i•est. 1.** prosperous or flourishing. **2.** abounding in palms.

pal•o•mi•no (pal′ə mē′nō), *n., pl.* **-nos.** a horse with a golden coat and a white mane and tail.

pal•pa•ble (pal′pə bəl), *adj.* **1.** readily or plainly seen or perceived; obvious. **2.** capable of being touched or felt; tangible. **—pal′pa•bly,** *adv.*

pal•pate (pal′pāt), *v.t.* **-pat•ed, -pat•ing.** to examine by touch, esp. for the purpose of diagnosing disease or illness. **—pal•pa′tion,** *n.*

pal•pi•tate (pal′pi tāt′), *v.i.* **-tat•ed, -tat•ing. 1.** to pulsate, as the heart, with unusual rapidity. **2.** to quiver; throb. **—pal′pi•ta′tion,** *n.*

pal•sy (pôl′zē), *n., pl.* **-sies.** any of several conditions characterized by paralysis or tremors. **—pal′sied,** *adj.*

pal•try (pôl′trē), *adj.,* **-tri•er, -tri•est. 1.** ridiculously small. **2.** utterly worthless. **—pal′tri•ness,** *n.*

pam•pas (pam′pəz; *attributively* -pəs), *n.pl., sing.* **-pa.** the vast grassy plains of S South America, esp. in Argentina.

pam•per (pam′pər), *v.t.* to treat with excessive indulgence, kindness, or care.

pam•phlet (pam′flit), *n.* a short unbound publica-

tion, often on a contemporary or controversial subject. **—pam′phlet•eer′** (-fli tēr′), *n.*

pan[1] (pan), *n., v.,* **panned, pan•ning. —n. 1.** a broad, shallow container used for cooking, washing, etc. **2.** any similar receptacle or part, as the scales of a balance. **—v.t. 3.** *Informal.* to criticize harshly, as in a review. **4.** to wash (gravel, sand, etc.) in a pan to separate gold. **—v.i. 5.** to wash gravel, sand, etc., in a pan in seeking gold. **6. pan out,** *Informal.* to have an outcome, esp. a successful one.

pan[2] (pan), *v.,* **panned, pan•ning,** *n.* **—v.i., v.t. 1.** to swivel (a television or motion-picture camera) horizontally to keep a moving subject in view or record a panorama. **—n. 2.** the act of panning a camera.

Pan, *n.* an ancient Greek god of shepherds and hunters, usu. represented as a man with the legs of a goat.

pan-, a combining form meaning: all (*pantheism*); the union of all branches of a group (*Pan-American*).

Pan., Panama.

pan•a•ce•a (pan′ə sē′ə), *n., pl.* **-ce•as. 1.** a remedy for all ills. **2.** a solution for all difficulties.

pa•nache (pə nash′, -näsh′), *n.* **1.** a grand or flamboyant manner; flair. **2.** a plume, esp. on a helmet.

Pan•a•ma (pan′ə mä′, -mô′), *n., pl.* **-mas** for 3. **1.** a republic in S Central America. 2,693,417. **2.** Also called **Pan′ama Cit′y.** the capital of Panama. 386,393. **3.** (*sometimes l.c.*) PANAMA HAT. **—Pan′a•ma′ni•an** (-mä′nē ən), *adj., n.*

Pan′ama Canal′, *n.* a canal extending SE from the Atlantic to the Pacific across Panama.

Pan′ama hat′, *n.* a hat made of finely plaited young leaves of a palmlike tropical plant.

Pan′-A•mer′i•can, *adj.* of or representing all the countries or people of North, Central, and South America.

pan′cake′, *n.* a thin, flat cake of batter fried on a griddle or in a frying pan.

pan′chro•mat′ic, *adj.* sensitive to all visible colors, as a photographic film.

pan•cre•as (pan′krē əs, pang′-), *n.* a large gland that secretes digestive enzymes into the intestine and insulin into the bloodstream. **—pan′cre•at′ic** (-at′ik), *adj.*

pan•da (pan′də), *n., pl.* **-das. 1.** a white-and-black bearlike mammal, now restricted to central China. **2.** a reddish brown, raccoonlike mammal of the Himalayas and adjacent regions.

giant panda

pan•dem•ic (pan dem′ik), *adj.* (of a disease) epidemic over a large area.

pan•de•mo•ni•um (pan′də mō′nē əm), *n.* wild uproar or disorder; tumult or chaos.

pan•der (pan′dər), *n.* **1.** a procurer; pimp. **2.** a person who caters to or profits from the weaknesses or vices of others. **—v.i. 3.** to cater basely.

Pan•do•ra (pan dôr′ə), *n.* (in Greek myth) the first woman: she opened a box and released all the evils that might plague humankind.

pane (pān), *n.* one of the divisions of a window or the like, consisting of a single plate of glass in a frame.

pan•e•gyr•ic (pan′i jir′ik, -jī′rik), *n.* **1.** a lofty oration or writing in praise of a person or thing. **2.** elaborate praise.

pan•el (pan′l), *n., v.,* **-eled, -el•ing** or (*esp. Brit.*) **-elled, -el•ling. —n. 1.** a distinct section of a wall, wainscot, door, etc. **2.** a group of persons gathered to conduct a public discussion, judge a contest, etc. **3.** a list of persons summoned for service as jurors. **4.** a surface on a machine on which controls and dials are mounted. **5.** a strip of material set vertically in a dress, skirt, etc. —*v.t.* **6.** to arrange in or furnish with panels.

pan'el·ing, *n.* **1.** wood or other material made into panels. **2.** panels collectively. Also, *esp. Brit.,* **pan'el·ling.**

pan'el·ist, *n.* a member of a panel convened for public discussion, judging, etc.

pan'el truck', *n.* a small truck having a fully enclosed body.

pang (pang), *n.* **1.** a sudden feeling of mental or emotional distress. **2.** a sudden sharp physical pain.

pan'han'dle¹, *n.* a long, narrow, projecting strip of a larger territory.

pan'han'dle², *v.i., v.t.,* **-dled, -dling.** *Informal.* to accost (passers-by) on the street and beg (from). —**pan'han'dler,** *n.*

pan·ic (pan'ik), *n., v.,* **-icked, -ick·ing.** —*n.* **1.** a sudden, overwhelming fear that can spread quickly. **2.** *Informal.* someone or something considered hilariously funny. —*v.t.* **3.** to affect with panic. **4.** *Informal.* to keep (an audience or the like) highly amused. —*v.i.* **5.** to be stricken with panic. —**pan'ick·y,** *adj.*

pan·nier (pan'yər, -ē ər), *n.* **1.** a large basket for carrying goods, provisions, etc. **2.** one of a pair of baskets to be slung across the back of a pack animal.

pan·o·ply (pan'ə plē), *n., pl.* **-plies. 1.** a wide-ranging and impressive array or display. **2.** a complete suit of armor.

pan·o·ram·a (pan'ə ram'ə, -rä'mə), *n., pl.* **-ram·as. 1.** a wide, unobstructed view of an extensive area. **2.** a continuously changing scene or unfolding of events: *the panorama of Chinese history.* —**pan'o·ram'ic,** *adj.*

pan·sy (pan'zē), *n., pl.* **-sies.** a violet with richly and variously colored flowers.

pant (pant), *v.i.* **1.** to breathe hard and quickly, as after exertion. **2.** to long eagerly; yearn. —*v.t.* **3.** to breathe or utter gaspingly. —*n.* **4.** a short, quick, labored breath; gasp.

pan·ta·loons (pan'tl ōōnz'), *n.* (*used with a pl. v.*) a man's close-fitting trousers, worn esp. in the 19th century.

pan·the·ism (pan'thē iz'əm), *n.* any religious belief or philosophical doctrine that identifies God with the universe. —**pan'the·ist,** *n.* —**pan'the·is'tic,** *adj.*

pan·the·on (pan'thē on'), *n.* **1.** a public building containing tombs or memorials of the illustrious dead of a nation. **2.** the realm of the heroes of any group, movement, etc. **3.** a temple dedicated to all the gods.

pan·ther (pan'thər), *n., pl.* **-thers, -ther. 1.** the cougar. **2.** any leopard in the black color phase.

pant·ies (pan'tēz), *n.* (*used with a pl. v.*) short underpants for women and children.

pan·to·mime (pan'tə mīm'), *n., v.,* **-mimed, -miming.** —*n.* **1.** an entertainment in which the performers express themselves by gesture alone. **2.** significant gesture without speech. —*v.t., v.i.* **3.** to express (oneself) in pantomime. —**pan'to·mim'ic** (-mim'ik), *adj.* —**pan'to·mim'ist** (-mī'mist), *n.*

pan·try (pan'trē), *n., pl.* **-tries.** a room or closet, usu. near a kitchen, in which food, dishes, etc., are kept.

pants (pants), *n.* (*used with a pl. v.*) **1.** TROUSERS. **2.** PANTIES.

pant'suit', *n.* a woman's suit consisting of trousers and a matching jacket.

pant'y·hose', *n.* (*used with a pl. v.*) a one-piece woman's garment combining panties and stockings.

pap (pap), *n.* **1.** soft food for infants or invalids. **2.** ideas, writings, etc., lacking substance or real value.

pa·pa (pä'pə, pə pä'), *n., pl.* **-pas.** FATHER.

pa·pa·cy (pä'pə sē), *n., pl.* **-cies. 1.** the office or jurisdiction of the pope. **2.** the system of Roman Catholic government. **3.** the period during which a pope is in office.

pa·pal (pä'pəl), *adj.* **1.** of the pope or the papacy. **2.** of the Roman Catholic Church.

pa·paw (pô'pô, pə pô'), *n.* PAWPAW.

pa·pa·ya (pə pä'yə), *n., pl.* **-yas. 1.** a small tropical American tree bearing a yellow, melonlike fruit. **2.** the fruit itself.

pa·per (pä'pər), *n.* **1.** a substance made from wood pulp or other fibrous material, usu. in thin sheets, used for writing, wrapping, etc. **2.** a piece or sheet of this. **3.** a newspaper or journal. **4.** a scholarly essay, article, or dissertation. **5.** a written piece of schoolwork, as a report. **6.** a document verifying identity, status, etc. **7.** WALLPAPER. —*v.t.* **8.** to cover with paper, esp. wallpaper. —*adj.* **9.** made of paper. **10.** like paper, as in being thin. —*Saying.* **11. not worth the paper it's written on,** worthless. —**pa'per·er,** *n.* —**pa'per·y,** *adj.*

pa'per·back', *n.* a book bound in a flexible paper cover.

pa'per clip', *n.* a flat clip that holds sheets of paper between two loops.

pa'per·hang'er, *n.* a person whose job is covering walls with wallpaper. —**pa'per·hang'ing,** *n.*

pa'per ti'ger, *n.* a person, nation, etc., that has the appearance of power but is actually weak and ineffectual.

pa'per trail', *n.* a written or printed record, as of transactions, esp. when used to incriminate someone.

pa'per·weight', *n.* a small, heavy object placed on papers to keep them from scattering.

pa'per·work', *n.* written or clerical work forming an incidental but necessary part of some work or job.

pa·pier-mâ·ché (pā'pər mə shā', pä pyä'-), *n.* moistened paper pulp mixed with glue, molded when moist to form various articles and becoming hard when dry. [< F: lit., chewed paper]

pa·pil·la (pə pil'ə), *n., pl.* **-pil·lae** (-pil'ē). any small, nipplelike projection, as on the tongue. —**pap·il·lar·y** (pap'ə ler'ē), *adj.*

pa·poose (pa pōōs', pə-), *n.* a North American Indian baby.

pap·ri·ka (pa prē'kə, pə-, pä-, pap'ri kə), *n.* a red, powdery condiment derived from dried, ripe sweet peppers.

Pap' test' (pap), *n.* a test for cancer of the cervix. [after G. *Papanicolaou* (1883–1962), U.S. cytologist]

Pap'u·a New' Guin'ea (pap'yōō ə, pä'pōō ä), *n.* a country comprising the E part of the island of New Guinea and nearby islands. 4,496,221. —**Pap'ua New' Guin'ean,** *n., adj.*

pa·py·rus (pə pī'rəs), *n., pl.* **-ri** (-rī, -rē), **-py·rus·es. 1.** a tall, aquatic plant, native to the Nile valley. **2.** a writing material made from the pith of this plant, used by ancient peoples.

par (pär), *n.* **1.** an equality in value or standing. **2.** an average or normal amount, degree, etc. **3.** the number of golf strokes set as a standard for one hole or a complete course. **4. a.** the value of the monetary unit of one country in terms of that of another. **b.** the face value of a note, stock, or bond. —*adj.* **5.** average or normal.

par., 1. paragraph. **2.** parish.

para-, a prefix meaning: beside (*paradigm*); beyond (*parapsychology*); auxiliary (*paralegal*).

par·a·ble (par'ə bəl), *n.* a short allegorical story designed to teach some truth or moral lesson.

pa·rab·o·la (pə rab'ə lə), *n., pl.* **-las.** a plane curve formed by the intersection of a right circular cone with a plane parallel to a generator of the cone. —**par·a·bol·ic** (par'ə bol'ik), *adj.*

par·a·chute (par'ə shōōt'), *n., v.,* **-chut·ed, -chut·ing.** —*n.* **1.** a folding, umbrellalike device for allowing a person, object, etc., to descend slowly from a height, esp. from an aircraft. —*v.t., v.i.* **2.** to drop by parachute. —**par'a·chut'ist,** *n.*

par·a·clete (par'ə klēt'), *n.* **1.** an advocate or intercessor. **2.** (*cap.*) the Holy Spirit.

pa·rade (pə rād'), *n., v.,* **-rad·ed, -rad·ing.** —*n.* **1.** a public procession held in honor of an event, person, etc. **2.** a military ceremony involving the formation and marching of troops. **3.** an ostentatious display. —*v.t.* **4.** to walk up and down on. **5.** to display ostentatiously. —*v.i.* **6.** to march in a procession. **7.** to promenade in a public place. —**pa·rad'er,** *n.*

par·a·digm (par′ə dīm′, -dim), *n.* **1.** a set of all the inflected forms of a word based on a single stem or root. **2.** an example serving as a model. —**par′a·dig·mat′ic** (-dig mat′ik), *adj.*

par′adigm shift′, *n.* a great change in overall thinking.

par·a·dise (par′ə dīs′, -dīz′), *n.* **1.** heaven. **2.** (*often cap.*) EDEN (def. 1). **3.** a place or state of supreme happiness. —**par′a·di·sa′i·cal** (-di sā′i kəl, -zā′-, -dī-), *adj.*

par·a·dox (par′ə doks′), *n.* **1.** a seemingly contradictory statement that expresses a possible truth. **2.** a self-contradictory and false proposition. **3.** a person or situation exhibiting an apparently contradictory nature. —**par′a·dox′i·cal,** *adj.* —**par′a·dox′i·cal·ly,** *adv.*

par·af·fin (par′ə fin), *n.* a waxy, solid substance, used in candles and sealing materials.

par·a·gon (par′ə gon′, -gən), *n.* a model of excellence.

par′a·graph′, *n.* **1.** a distinct portion of written matter, beginning on a new line that is usu. indented. —*v.t.* **2.** to divide into paragraphs.

Par·a·guay (par′ə gwī′, -gwā′), *n.* a republic in central South America. 5,651,634. —**Par′a·guay′an,** *n., adj.*

par·a·keet (par′ə kēt′), *n.* any of various small to medium-sized parrots with a long, graduated tail.

par′a·le′gal, *n.* an attorney's assistant trained to perform certain legal tasks but not licensed to practice law.

par·al·lax (par′ə laks′), *n.* the apparent displacement of an observed object due to a change in the position of the observer.

par·al·lel (par′ə lel′, -ləl), *adj., n., v.,* **-leled, -lel·ing** or (*esp. Brit.*) **-lelled, -lel·ling.** —*adj.* **1.** extending in the same direction, equidistant at all points, and never converging or diverging. **2.** having the same direction, nature, etc.; similar or corresponding. —*n.* **3.** a parallel line or plane. **4.** anything parallel or similar to something else. **5.** any of the imaginary lines on the earth's surface, parallel to the equator, that mark the latitude. **6.** a comparison made between things. —*v.t.* **7.** to provide a parallel for; match. **8.** to be in a parallel course to. **9.** to form a parallel to; equal. **10.** to compare. [< L *parallēlus* < Gk *parállēlos* side by side] —**par′al·lel·ism,** *n.*

par′al·lel′o·gram′ (-lel′ə gram′), *n.* a quadrilateral having both pairs of opposite sides parallel to each other.

pa·ral·y·sis (pə ral′ə sis), *n., pl.* **-ses** (-sēz′). **1.** a loss or impairment of movement or sensation in a body part. **2.** a state of helpless stoppage or inability to act. —**par·a·lyt·ic** (par′ə lit′ik), *adj., n.*

par·a·lyze (par′ə līz′), *v.t.,* **-lyzed, -lyz·ing. 1.** to affect with paralysis. **2.** to make powerless or helplessly inactive.

par·a·me·ci·um (par′ə mē′shē əm, -sē əm), *n., pl.* **-ci·a** (-shē ə, -sē ə). an oval, freshwater protozoan with a fringe of cilia.

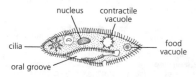

nucleus — contractile vacuole — cilia — oral groove — food vacuole

paramecium

par′a·med′ic, *n.* a person trained to assist a physician or to give medical treatment in the absence of a physician.

par′a·med′i·cal, *adj.* related to the medical profession in a supplementary capacity.

pa·ram·e·ter (pə ram′i tər), *n.* **1.** a constant or variable term in a mathematical function that determines the specific form of the function but not its general nature. **2.** Usu., **-ters.** limits or boundaries;

guidelines. **3.** a determining characteristic. —**par·a·met·ric** (par′ə me′trik), *adj.*

par·a·mil·i·tar·y (par′ə mil′i ter′ē), *adj.* of or noting an organization operating in place of or as a supplement to a regular military force.

par·a·mount (par′ə mount′), *adj.* chief in importance, rank, etc.

par·a·mour (par′ə mŏŏr′), *n.* **1.** an illicit lover. **2.** any lover.

Pa·ra·ná (par′ə nä′, pär′-), *n.* a river flowing from Brazil along the border of Paraguay into Argentina. 2050 mi. (3300 km) long.

par·a·noi·a (par′ə noi′ə), *n.* **1.** a mental disorder characterized by delusions ascribing hostile intentions to others. **2.** baseless or excessive distrust of others. —**par′a·noid′,** *adj., n.*

par·a·pet (par′ə pit, -pet′), *n.* **1.** a wall or elevation in a fortification. **2.** any low protective wall or barrier at the edge of a balcony, roof, etc.

par′a·pher·na′lia (-fər nāl′yə, -fə nāl′-), *n.* (*used with a sing. or pl. v.*) **1.** equipment, apparatus, etc., used in a particular activity. **2.** personal belongings.

par′a·phrase′, *n., v.,* **-phrased, -phras·ing.** —*n.* **1.** a restatement of a passage giving the meaning in another form, as for clearness. —*v.t., v.i.* **2.** to render in or make a paraphrase. —**par′a·phras′er,** *n.*

par·a·ple·gi·a (-plē′jē ə, -jə), *n.* paralysis of both lower limbs. —**par·a·ple′gic** (-plē′jik, -plej′ik), *adj., n.*

par′a·pro·fes′sion·al, *n.* a person trained to assist a doctor, lawyer, or other professional.

par′a·psy·chol′o·gy, *n.* the branch of psychology that studies psychic phenomena, as clairvoyance. —**par′a·psy·chol′o·gist,** *n.*

par·a·site (par′ə sīt′), *n.* **1.** an organism that lives on or within a plant or animal of another species, from which it obtains nutrients. **2.** one who receives support or advantage from another without giving any useful return. —**par′a·sit′ic** (-sit′ik), *adj.*

par·a·sol (par′ə sôl′, -sol′), *n.* a lightweight umbrella used as a sunshade.

par′a·sym′pa·thet′ic, *adj.* pertaining to that part of the autonomic nervous system that functions in regulatory opposition to the sympathetic system, as in slowing heartbeat.

par·a·thi·on (par′ə thī′on), *n.* a poisonous liquid used as an insecticide.

par·a·thy′roid gland′ (par′ə thī′roid), *n.* any of several small paired glands that lie near the thyroid gland and secrete a hormone that helps regulate the blood levels of calcium and phosphate.

par′a·troop′er, *n.* a member of an infantry unit trained to land in combat areas by parachuting from airplanes.

par·boil (pär′boil′), *v.t.* to boil partially or for a short time.

par·cel (pär′səl), *n., v.,* **-celed, -cel·ing** or (*esp. Brit.*) **-celled, -cel·ling.** —*n.* **1.** an object or objects wrapped to form a small bundle; package. **2.** a distinct, continuous tract of land. —*v.t.* **3.** to divide into or distribute in portions (usu. fol. by *out*).

par′cel post′, *n.* (in the U.S. Postal Service) parcels weighing one pound or more sent at fourth-class rates.

parch (pärch), *v.t.* **1.** to make extremely dry, as heat, sun, and wind do. **2.** to make thirsty. —*v.i.* **3.** to suffer from heat or thirst.

parch·ment (pärch′mənt), *n.* **1.** the skin of sheep, goats, etc., prepared for writing on. **2.** a manuscript on such material. **3.** a stiff off-white paper treated to resemble this material.

par·don (pär′dn), *n.* **1.** a legal release from the penalty of an offense. **2.** forgiveness of an offense or discourtesy. —*v.t.* **3.** to excuse or make courteous allowance for. **4.** to release from liability for an offense. **5.** to remit the penalty of (an offense). —**par′don·a·ble,** *adj.* —**par′don·er,** *n.*

pare (pâr), *v.t.,* **pared, par·ing. 1.** to cut off the outer coating, layer, etc., of. **2.** to reduce gradually. —**par′er,** *n.*

par•e•gor•ic (par′i gôr′ik, -gor′-), *n.* an opium derivative used as a mild sedative and to treat diarrhea.

par•ent (pâr′ənt, par′-), *n.* **1.** a father or mother. **2.** a source, origin, or cause. **3.** any organism that produces another. —*adj.* **4.** of or noting an enterprise that owns controlling interests in a subsidiary. —*v.t.* **5.** to be or act as parent of. —**pa•ren•tal** (pə ren′tl), *adj.* —**par′ent•hood′,** *n.*

par′ent•age (-ən tij), *n.* derivation or descent from parents or ancestors.

pa•ren•the•sis (pə ren′thə sis), *n.,* *pl.* -ses (-sēz′). **1.** either or both of a pair of signs ( ) used to mark off an interjected explanatory or qualifying remark. **2.** a qualifying or explanatory word, phrase, or clause that interrupts a syntactic construction without otherwise affecting it. —**par•en•thet•ic** (par′ənthet′ik), **par′en•thet′i•cal,** *adj.*

par′ent•ing, *n.* the rearing of children by parents.

pa•re•sis (pə rē′sis, par′ə sis), *n.* **1.** partial motor paralysis. **2.** a late manifestation of syphilis, characterized by dementia and paralysis. —**pa•ret′ic** (-ret′ik, -rē′tik), *n.,* *adj.*

pa•re•ve (pär′ə və, pär′və) also **parve,** *adj. Judaism.* containing neither meat nor milk and thus permissible for use with either meat or dairy meals in accordance with the dietary laws.

par ex•cel•lence (pär ek′sə läns′), *adj.* being an example of excellence; superior. [< F]

par•fait (pär fā′), *n.* **1.** a dessert of layered ice cream, fruit, syrup, and whipped cream. **2.** a frozen dessert of flavored whipped cream or custard.

pa•ri•ah (pə rī′ə), *n.* OUTCAST.

par•i•mu•tu•el (par′i myōō′chōō əl), *n.* a form of betting on horse races in which the winners divide the total amount bet in proportion to their wagers.

par•ing (pâr′ing), *n.* a piece or part pared off: *apple parings.*

Par•is¹ (par′is; *Fr.* PA Rē′), *n.* **1.** the capital of France, in the N part, on the Seine. 2,188,918. **2. Treaty of, a.** a treaty signed in 1763 by France, Spain, and Great Britain that ended the Seven Years' War and the French and Indian War. **b.** a treaty signed in 1783 by the United States and Great Britain that ended the American Revolution. **c.** a treaty signed in 1898 by the United States and Spain that ended the Spanish-American War. —**Pa•ri•sian** (pərē′zhən, -rizh′ən), *adj., n.*

Par•is² (par′is), *n.* a Trojan prince, son of King Priam and his wife, Hecuba: his abduction of Helen led to the Trojan War.

par•ish (par′ish), *n.* **1.** an ecclesiastical district having its own church and cleric. **2.** a local church with its field of activity. **3.** (in Louisiana) a county.

pa•rish•ion•er (pə rish′ə nər), *n.* a member or inhabitant of a parish.

par•i•ty (par′i tē), *n.,* *pl.* -ties. **1.** equality, as in amount, status, or character. **2.** equivalent value at a fixed ratio between different currencies. **3.** a system of regulating prices of farm commodities to provide farmers with the same purchasing power they had in a selected base period.

park (pärk), *n.* **1.** a public area of land, usu. in a natural state, having facilities for recreation. **2.** an enclosed area or a stadium used for sports. **3.** a setting in an automatic transmission in which the transmission is in neutral and the brake is engaged. —*v.t., v.i.* **4.** to put or leave (a vehicle) in a place temporarily.

par•ka (pär′kə), *n.,* *pl.* -kas. a hooded jacket made of materials that protect against very cold temperatures.

Par′kin•son's disease′ (pär′kin sənz), *n.* a neurologic disease characterized by tremors, esp. of the fingers and hands, muscle rigidity, and a shuffling gait. [after J. *Parkinson* (1755–1824), English physician]

Par′kinson's law′, *n.* any of various facetious statements about business and office management, as that work expands to fill the time allotted. [after C. N. *Parkinson* (b. 1909), English historian]

park′way′, *n.* a broad thoroughfare with a dividing strip or side strips planted with grass, trees, etc.

par•lance (pär′ləns), *n.* a way or manner of speaking; vernacular: *legal parlance.*

par•lay (pär′lā, -lē), *v.,* —*v.t.* **1.** to bet (an original amount and its winnings) on a subsequent contest. **2.** to use (assets) to achieve a relatively great gain: *to parlay a modest inheritance into a fortune.* —*n.* **3.** a bet parlayed.

par•ley (pär′lē), *n.* **1.** a discussion; conference. **2.** a conference between enemies under a truce. —*v.i.* **3.** to hold a parley.

par•lia•ment (pär′lə mənt), *n.* **1.** (*cap.*) the national legislature in various countries, esp. Great Britain. **2.** an assembly on public or national affairs. —**par′lia•men′ta•ry** (-men′tə rē, -trē), *adj.*

par′lia•men•tar′i•an (-men târ′ē ən, -mən-), *n.* **1.** an expert in parliamentary rules. **2.** (*cap.*) a partisan of the British Parliament in opposition to King Charles I.

par•lor (pär′lər), *n.* **1.** a room in a home for receiving visitors; living room. **2.** a shop or business establishment: *an ice-cream parlor.*

Par•me•san (pär′mə zän′, -zan′, -zən), *n.* (*sometimes l.c.*) a hard, dry Italian cheese.

par•mi•gia•na (pär′mə zhä′nə, -zhän′), *adj.* cooked with Parmesan cheese.

Par•nell (pär nel′, pär′nl), *n.* **Charles Stewart,** 1846–91, Irish political leader. —**Par•nell′ite,** *n.*

pa•ro•chi•al (pə rō′kē əl), *adj.* **1.** of a parish. **2.** of very limited or narrow scope; provincial. —**pa•ro′chi•al•ism,** *n.*

paro′chial school′, *n.* a primary or secondary school maintained by a religious organization.

par•o•dy (par′ə dē), *n.,* *pl.* -dies, *v.,* -died, -dy•ing. —*n.* **1.** a humorous or satirical imitation of a serious piece of literature or music. —*v.t.* **2.** to imitate (a composition, author, etc.) for purposes of ridicule or satire.

pa•role (pə rōl′), *n., v.,* -roled, -rol•ing. —*n.* **1.** the conditional release of a person from prison prior to the end of the sentence imposed. —*v.t.* **2.** to place or release on parole. [< MF, short for *parole d'honneur* word of honor] —**pa•rol•ee′** (-rō lē′), *n., pl.* -ees.

par•ox•ysm (par′ək siz′əm), *n.* **1.** any sudden, violent outburst, as of emotion. **2.** a severe attack of a disease, usu. recurring periodically.

par•quet (pär kā′), *n., v.,* -queted (-kād′), -quet•ing (-kā′ing). —*n.* **1.** a floor made of parquetry. **2.** the part of the main floor of a theater for spectators. —*v.t.* **3.** to construct (a floor) of parquetry.

par′que•try (-ki trē) *n.* mosaic work of wood used for floors, wainscoting, etc.

par•ri•cide (par′ə sīd′), *n.* **1.** the killing of one's father, mother, or other close relative. **2.** a person who commits such an act. —**par′ri•cid′al,** *adj.*

par•rot (par′ət), *n.* **1.** any of numerous brilliantly colored birds of warmer regions, some of which can mimic speech. **2.** a person who mindlessly repeats the words of another. —*v.t.* **3.** to repeat without thought or understanding.

par•ry (par′ē), *v.,* -ried, -ry•ing, *n., pl.* -ries. —*v.t.* **1.** to ward off (a sword blow, weapon, etc.). **2.** to turn aside; dodge. —*n.* **3.** an act or instance of parrying.

parse (pärs), *v.,* parsed, pars•ing. —*v.t.* **1.** to analyze (a sentence) grammatically, identifying parts of speech, syntactic relations, etc. —*v.i.* **2.** to admit of being parsed.

par•si•mo•ny (pär′sə mō′nē), *n.* excessive economy or frugality; stinginess. —**par′si•mo′ni•ous,** *adj.*

pars•ley (pär′slē), *n.* an herb with either curled leaf clusters or flat compound leaves.

pars•nip (pär′snip), *n.* **1.** a plant with a large, white, edible root. **2.** its root.

par•son (pär′sən), *n.* a member of the Protestant clergy.

par′son•age (-sə nij), *n.* the residence provided by a parish for its parson.

part (pärt), *n.* **1.** a portion or division of a whole that is separate or distinct. **2.** an essential or integral quality. **3.** an allotted portion; share. **4.** Usu., **parts.** a region or district. **5.** either of the opposing sides in a contest, contract, etc. **6.** the dividing line formed in separating the hair when combing it. **7.** a constituent piece of a machine or tool. **8.** the score for one of the instruments or voices in concerted music. **9.** participation or concern in something; role. **10.** a role given to an actor or actress. —*v.t.* **11.** to divide into parts. **12.** to comb (the hair) away from a dividing line. **13.** to put or keep apart; separate. —*v.i.* **14.** to be or become divided into parts. **15.** to go apart from one another, as persons. **16.** to break apart. **17.** to depart. **18. part with,** to relinquish. —*adj.* **19.** partial. —*adv.* **20.** partly. —*Idiom.* **21. for one's part,** as far as concerns one. **22. in part,** in some measure or degree. **23. take part,** to participate.

par•take (pär tāk′), *v.i.* **-took, -tak•en, -tak•ing. 1.** to participate: *to partake in a celebration.* **2.** to receive, take, or have a portion: *to partake of a meal.* —**par•tak′er,** *n.*

par•terre (pär târ′), *n.* **1.** the rear section of theater seats under the balcony. **2.** an arrangement of ornamental flower beds separated by walks.

par•the•no•gen•e•sis (pär′thə nō jen′ə sis), *n.* development of an egg without fertilization.

Par•the•non (pär′thə non′, -nən), *n.* a Doric temple of Athena on the Acropolis in Athens.

par•tial (pär′shəl), *adj.* **1.** incomplete. **2.** favoring one person, group, etc., over another. —*Idiom.* **3. partial to,** especially fond of. —**par′ti•al′i•ty** (-shē-al′i tē), *n.* —**par′tial•ly,** *adv.*

par•tic•i•pate (pär tis′ə pāt′), *v.i.* **-pat•ed, -pat• ing.** to take part or have a share, as with others. —**par•tic′i•pant,** *n.* —**par•tic′i•pa′tion,** *n.* —**par• tic′i•pa′tor,** *n.* —**par•tic′i•pa•to′ry** (-pə tôr′ē), *adj.*

par•ti•ci•ple (pär′tə sip′əl, -sə pəl), *n.* a verbal form that can function as an adjective or be used with an auxiliary to form certain tenses. —**par′ti• cip′i•al** (-sip′ē əl), *adj.*

par•ti•cle (pär′ti kəl), *n.* **1.** a minute portion, piece, or amount. **2.** one of the extremely small constituents of matter, as an atom or proton. **3.** a small word having functional or relational rather than lexical use, as *to* used in forming the infinitive.

par•ti-col•ored (pär′tē kul′ərd), *adj.* having different colors in different areas.

par•tic•u•lar (pər tik′yə lər, pə tik′-), *adj.* **1.** pertaining to a single or specific person, thing, etc. **2.** considered separately from others; specific. **3.** special; unusual. **4.** exacting; fussy. —*n.* **5.** an individual or distinct part, as an item of a list. —*Idiom.* **6. in particular,** particularly; especially. —**par•tic′u• lar′i•ty,** *n., pl.* **-ties.**

par•tic′u•lar•ize′, *v.,* **-ized, -iz•ing.** —*v.t.* **1.** to state or treat in detail. —*v.i.* **2.** to give details; be specific. —**par•tic′u•lar•i•za′tion,** *n.*

par•tic′u•lar•ly, *adv.* **1.** especially. **2.** specifically. **3.** in detail.

par•tic•u•late (pər tik′yə lit, -lāt′, pär-), *adj.* of or composed of distinct particles.

part′ing, *n.* **1.** a division; separation. **2.** departure; leave-taking. —*adj.* **3.** given, taken, or done at parting: *a parting glance.* **4.** departing.

par•ti•san (pär′tə zən, -sən), *n.* **1.** an adherent or supporter of a person, cause, etc. **2.** a member of a guerrilla band fighting an occupying army. —*adj.* **3.** of or characteristic of partisans. —**par′ti•san•ship′,** *n.*

par•ti•tion (pär tish′ən, pər-), *n.* **1.** a division into portions. **2.** something that separates or divides. —*v.t.* **3.** to divide into portions. **4.** to divide or separate by a partition. —**par•ti′tioned,** *adj.*

part′ly, *adv.* partially.

part•ner (pärt′nər), *n.* **1.** a person who is associated with another in some endeavor; associate. **2.** a spouse or lover. **3.** either of two people who dance together. **4.** a player on the same team as another. —**part′ner•ship′,** *n.*

part′ of speech′, *n.* any of the classes into which words can be divided on the basis of their meaning, form, or syntactic function.

par•tridge (pär′trij), *n., pl.* **-tridg•es, -tridge. 1.** any of various birds of the pheasant family. **2.** any game bird resembling the partridge, as the bobwhite.

part′-song′, *n.* a song with parts for several voices, esp. one sung without accompaniment.

part′-time′ (*adj.* -tīm′; *adv.* -tīm′), *adj.* **1.** involving, working, or studying less than the usual or full time. —*adv.* **2.** on a part-time basis. —**part′-tim′er,** *n.*

par•tu•ri•tion (pär′tŏŏ rish′ən, -tyŏŏ-), *n.* childbirth.

part′way′ (-wā′, -wä′), *adv.* in some degree; partly.

par•ty (pär′tē), *n., pl.* **-ties,** *v.,* **-tied, -ty•ing.** —*n.* **1.** a social gathering for conversation, entertainment, etc. **2.** a group gathered for some special purpose: *a search party.* **3.** a political group organized for gaining governmental control. **4.** a person or group that participates in some action, plan, etc.: *He was a party to the merger deal.* **5.** one of the litigants in a legal proceeding. **6.** a specific individual. —*v.i.* **7.** to go to or give parties.

par′ty eld′ers, *n.pl.* veteran, respected members of a political party.

par′ty faith′ful, *n.* (*used with a pl. v.*) loyal supporters of a political party.

par•ty line (pär′tē līn′ *for 1;* līn′ *for 2*), *n.* **1.** the guiding policy, tenets, or practices of a political party. **2.** a telephone line connecting the telephones of a number of subscribers.

par•ve•nu (pär′və nōō′, -nyōō′), *n., pl.* **-nus.** a person who has newly acquired wealth or influence but not the social acceptance associated with it.

Pas•a•de•na (pas′ə dē′nə), *n.* **1.** a city in SW California. 134,170. **2.** a city in SE Texas. 116,880.

Pas•cal (pa skal′), *n.* **1. Blaise,** 1623–62, French philosopher and mathematician. **2.** Also, **PASCAL** a high-level computer language for facilitating structured programming.

pas•chal (pas′kəl), *adj.* **1.** of Easter. **2.** of Passover.

pas′chal lamb′, *n.* **1.** a lamb slaughtered and eaten by the ancient Hebrews at Passover. **2.** (*caps.*) JESUS. **3.** (*caps.*) any of several symbolic representations of Christ.

pa•sha (pä′shə, pə shä′), *n., pl.* **-shas.** a former title placed after the name of high officials in countries under Turkish rule.

pass (pas, päs), *v.t.* **1.** to move past. **2.** to cause or allow to go through a barrier, obstacle, etc. **3.** to go across or over. **4.** to undergo successfully: *to pass a test.* **5.** to go beyond; surpass. **6.** to cause to go or move onward. **7.** to allow to elapse: *How did you pass the time?* **8.** to circulate or transmit: *to pass rumors.* **9.** to approve, esp. by vote. **10.** to obtain the approval of: *The bill passed the Senate.* **11.** to express; pronounce: *to pass judgment.* **12.** to transfer (a ball or puck) to a teammate. —*v.i.* **13.** to go or move onward. **14.** to elapse. **15.** to come to an end. **16.** to die (often fol. by *away* or *on*). **17.** to take place. **18.** to go by or move past. **19.** to be transferred, as by inheritance. **20.** to go or get through a barrier, test, etc., successfully. **21.** to go unchallenged: *I let the insult pass.* **22.** to pronounce judgment. **23.** to obtain the approval of a committee or the like. **24.** to make a pass, as in football. **25.** *Cards.* to forgo one's opportunity to bid. **26. pass off,** to present or sell by deceit. **27. ~ out, a.** to faint. **b.** to give out. **28. ~ over,** to disregard; ignore. **29. ~ up,** to refuse or neglect to take advantage of. —*n.* **30.** the act of passing. **31.** a road or other means of passage, as through an obstructed region. **32.** a permission to go, come, or enter. **33.** permission given a soldier to be absent briefly from a station. **34.** a free ticket or permit. **35.** a particular stage or state of affairs. **36.** a single movement or effort: *We made a pass at the enemy airfield.* **37.** the transfer of a ball or puck from one teammate to another. —*Idiom.* **38. bring to pass,** to cause to happen. **39. come to pass,** to happen.

pass′a•ble, *adj.* **1.** capable of being passed, penetrated, or crossed. **2.** marginally acceptable; adequate. —**pass/a•bly,** adv.

pas•sage (pas'ij), n. **1.** a portion of a written work or musical composition. **2.** an act or instance of passing from one place, condition, etc., to another. **3.** the right or freedom to pass. **4.** the route or course by which a person or thing passes or travels. **5.** the enactment into law of a legislative measure.

pas/sage•way/, n. a way affording passage, as a corridor or alley.

pass/book/, n. BANKBOOK.

pas•sé (pa sā'), adj. **1.** old-fashioned; out-of-date. **2.** past one's prime.

pas•sel (pas'əl), n. a group of indeterminate number.

pas•sen•ger (pas'ən jər), n. a person traveling in an automobile, train, etc. who is not the operator.

pass•er•by (pas'ər bī', -bī', pä'sər-), n., pl. **pass•ers•by.** a person passing by.

pas•sim (pas'im), adv. here and there (used in bibliographic references).

pass/ing, adj. **1.** going past; elapsing. **2.** brief: a passing fancy. **3.** superficial: a passing mention. **4.** satisfactory: a passing grade. —n. **5.** the act of a person or thing that passes. **6.** death. —Idiom. **7.** in passing, incidentally. —**pass/ing•ly,** adv.

pas•sion (pash'ən), n. **1.** any compelling emotion. **2.** strong amorous feeling. **3.** strong sexual desire. **4.** a strong fondness or enthusiasm. **5.** the object of one's passion. **6.** violent anger; wrath. **7.** (often cap.) **a.** the sufferings of Christ on the cross or subsequent to the Last Supper. **b.** the Gospel narrative of Christ's sufferings or a musical setting of this. —**pas/sion•less,** adj.

pas/sion•ate (-ə nit), adj. **1.** having or compelled by intense emotion. **2.** ardently sensual. **3.** intense or vehement, as emotions. **4.** easily moved to anger. —**pas/sion•ate•ly,** adv.

pas•sive (pas'iv), adj. **1.** acted upon by some external force, agency, etc. **2.** submitting without resistance. **3.** noting a voice, verb form, or construction having a subject represented as undergoing the action expressed by the verb. —**pas/sive•ly,** adv. —**pas•siv/i•ty,** n.

pas/sive resist/ance, n. opposition to a government or to specific laws by the use of noncooperation or other nonviolent methods.

pas/sive smok/ing, n. the inhaling of the cigarette, cigar, or pipe smoke of others.

pass/key/, n. **1.** MASTER KEY. **2.** SKELETON KEY.

Pass•o•ver (pas'ō'vər, päs'-), n. a Jewish festival that commemorates the Exodus of the Israelites from Egypt.

pass/port/, n. a governmental document issued to a citizen, authenticating the bearer's identity and right to travel to other countries.

pass/word/, n. a secret word used by authorized persons to gain access, information, etc.

past (past, päst), adj. **1.** gone by or elapsed in time. **2.** of a previous time; bygone. **3.** gone by just before the present time. **4.** previous; earlier. **5.** designating a verb tense referring to events or states in times gone by. —n. **6.** the time gone by. **7.** the history of a person, nation, etc. **8.** an earlier period of a person's life that is characterized by questionable conduct. —adv. **9.** so as to pass by or beyond. —prep. **10.** beyond in space, time, amount, scope, etc. —Proverb. **11. Those who cannot remember the past are condemned to repeat it,** the study of history can teach how to avoid mistakes. George Santayana, Life of Reason (1905-06).

pas•ta (pä'stə), n., pl. -tas. a food preparation of thin, unleavened dough, processed into a variety of forms, as spaghetti or ravioli.

paste (pāst), n., v., past•ed, past•ing. —n. **1.** a mixture of flour and water, often with starch, used as an adhesive. **2.** any soft, smooth material or preparation. **3.** dough, esp. when prepared with shortening. **4.** a brilliant, heavy glass used for making artificial gems. —v.t. **5.** to fasten or stick with paste or the like. **6.** Slang. to hit (a person) hard.

paste/board/, n. a stiff board made of sheets of paper pasted or layers of paper pulp pressed together.

pas•tel (pa stel'), n. **1.** a paste made of ground pigment. **2.** a crayon made from such paste. **3.** a drawing made with such crayons. **4.** a color having a soft, subdued shade.

pas•tern (pas'tərn), n. the part of the foot of a horse, cow, etc., between the fetlock and the hoof.

Pas•ter•nak (pas'tər nak'), n. **Boris (Leonidovich),** 1890–1960, Russian poet, novelist, and translator.

Pas•teur (pa stûr'), n. **Louis,** 1822–95, French chemist and bacteriologist.

pas•teur•ize (pas'chə rīz', pas'tə-), v.t., -ized, -iz•ing. to expose (a food) to a high temperature to destroy harmful or undesirable microorganisms. —**pas/teur•i•za/tion,** n.

pas•tiche (pa stēsh', pä-), n. a literary, musical, or artistic piece consisting of motifs or techniques from borrowed sources.

pas•time (pas'tīm', päs'-), n. something, as a hobby, that makes time pass agreeably.

past/ mas/ter, n. one who is thoroughly skilled in a profession or art; expert.

pas•tor (pas'tər, pä'stər), n. a minister or priest in charge of a church. —**pas/tor•ate** (-it), n.

pas/to•ral, adj. **1.** having the simplicity, serenity, etc., attributed to rural areas. **2.** rural; rustic. **3.** of shepherds. **4.** of a pastor or the duties of a pastor.

Pas/toral Epis/tles, n.pl. the Epistles I and II Timothy and Titus.

past/ par/ticiple, n. a participle used to express a past action or state, to form the passive voice, or as an adjective.

pas•tra•mi (pə strä'mē), n. a brisket of beef cured in seasonings and smoked before cooking. [< Yiddish < Romanian pastramă pressed, cured meat]

pas•try (pā'strē), n., pl. -tries. **1.** a sweet baked food, esp. one made with a crust of dough. **2.** PASTE (def. 3).

pas/tur•age (pas'chər ij, päs'-), n. PASTURE.

pas/ture, n., v., -tured, -tur•ing. —n. **1.** ground suitable for the grazing of livestock. **2.** grass or other plants for feeding livestock. —v.t. **3.** to put out (livestock) to graze on pasture.

past•y (pā'stē), adj., -i•er, -i•est. of or like paste, as in texture or color. —**past/i•ness,** n.

pat¹ (pat), v., pat•ted, pat•ting, n. —v.t. **1.** to strike lightly or tap gently, as with the hand or a small object. —n. **2.** a light stroke or gentle tap. **3.** the sound of a light stroke. **4.** a small piece, usu. flat and square: a pat of butter. —Idiom. **5. pat on the back,** praise, congratulations, or encouragement.

pat² (pat), adj. **1.** exactly to the point. **2.** excessively glib. **3.** mastered perfectly: to have something pat. —Idiom. **4. stand pat,** to cling firmly to one's decision, beliefs, etc.

pat., **1.** patent. **2.** patented.

patch (pach), n. **1.** a small piece of material used to mend a tear, cover a hole, etc. **2.** a piece of material used to cover an injured part. **3.** a small piece or area: a patch of ice. **4.** a small plot of land: a cabbage patch. —v.t. **5.** to mend or cover with a patch. **6.** to repair in a hasty way (usu. fol. by up). **7.** to settle or smooth over: to patch up a quarrel.

patch/ test/, n. a test for allergy in which a patch impregnated with an allergen is applied to the skin.

patch/work/, n. **1.** something made up of incongruous pieces or parts. **2.** sewn work made of pieces of material in various colors or shapes.

patch/y, adj., -i•er, -i•est. **1.** made up of patches. **2.** irregular in quality, distribution, etc.: patchy fog. —**patch/i•ness,** n.

pate (pāt), n. the crown of the head.

pâ•té (pä tā', pa-), n., pl. -tés. a paste of puréed or chopped meat, liver, etc.

pa•tel•la (pə tel'ə), n., pl. -tel•las, -tel•lae (-tel'ē). the flat, movable bone at the front of the knee; kneecap.

pat•ent (pat'nt; for 6 pāt'-), n. **1.** the exclusive right granted to an inventor to manufacture or sell an invention for a specified number of years. **2.** an invention or process protected by this right. **3.** an official document conferring such a right. —*adj.* **4.** protected by a patent. **5.** dealing with patents. **6.** evident; obvious. —*v.t.* **7.** to obtain a patent on.

pat′ent leath′er (pat′nt, pat′n), *n.* a hard, glossy, smooth leather used esp. for shoes and accessories.

pat′ent med′icine, *n.* a nonprescription drug that is protected by the trademark of a company.

pa•ter•nal (pə tûr′nl), *adj.* **1.** of, characteristic of, or befitting a father. **2.** related on the father's side. **3.** inherited from a father. —**pa•ter′nal•ly,** *adv.*

pa•ter′nal•ism, *n.* the practice of managing individuals, businesses, etc., in the manner of a father dealing with his children. —**pa•ter′nal•is′tic,** *adj.*

pa•ter′ni•ty (-ni tē), *n.* **1.** the state of being a father. **2.** derivation or descent from a father.

Pat•er•son (pat′ər sən), *n.* a city in NE New Jersey. 138,290.

path (path, päth), *n., pl.* **paths** (paŧhz, päŧhz, paths, päths). **1.** a way formed by the feet of persons or animals. **2.** a narrow walk or way: *a bicycle path.* **3.** a route along which something moves. **4.** a course of action, conduct, or procedure.

pa•thet•ic (pə thet′ik), *adj.* evoking pity, either sympathetically or contemptibly. —**pa•thet′i•cal•ly,** *adv.*

pathet′ic fal′lacy, *n.* the endowment of nature, inanimate objects, etc., with human traits, as in *the smiling skies.*

path′find′er, *n.* a person who finds a path or way, esp. through a wilderness.

path•o•gen (path′ə jən, -jen′), *n.* any disease-producing agent, esp. a microorganism. —**path′o•gen′ic,** *adj.*

pa•thol•o•gy (pə thol′ə jē), *n., pl.* **-gies. 1.** the science of the origin, nature, and course of diseases. **2.** any deviation from a healthy or normal condition. —**path•o•log•i•cal** (path′ə loj′i kəl), *adj.* —**pa•thol′o•gist,** *n.*

pa•thos (pā′thos, -thōs), *n.* the quality or power of evoking pity or compassion.

path′way′, *n.* a path, course, route, or way.

-pathy, a combining form meaning: feeling (*antipathy*); suffering or disease (*psychopathy*); method of treating a disease (*homeopathy*).

pa•tience (pā′shəns), *n.* the quality or capacity of being patient.

pa′tient, *n.* **1.** a person who is under medical care. —*adj.* **2.** tolerating delay, provocation, annoyance, etc., without complaint or anger. **3.** persevering or diligent. —**pa′tient•ly,** *adv.*

pat•i•na (pat′n ə, pə tē′nə), *n., pl.* **-nas.** a green film produced by oxidation on the surface of old bronze.

pat•i•o (pat′ē ō′, pä′tē ō′), *n., pl.* **-i•os. 1.** a paved area adjoining a house and used for outdoor lounging, dining, etc. **2.** a courtyard enclosed by low buildings or walls.

pat•ois (pat′wä, pä′twä), *n., pl.* **pat•ois** (pat′wäz, pä′twäz). a regional form of a language, esp. of French.

pat. pend., patent pending.

pa•tri•arch (pā′trē ärk′), *n.* **1.** the male head of a family or tribal line. **2.** any of the three great progenitors of the Israelites: Abraham, Isaac, and Jacob. **3.** the head of any of the Eastern Orthodox sees of Alexandria, Antioch, Constantinople, or Jerusalem. **4.** a venerable old man. —**pa′tri•ar′chal,** *adj.*

pa′tri•arch′ate (-är′kit, -kāt), *n.* the office, jurisdiction, or residence of an ecclesiastical patriarch.

pa′tri•arch′y, *n., pl.* **-arch•ies. 1.** a form of social organization in which the father is the head of the family, clan, or tribe and descent is reckoned in the male line. **2.** an institution or organization in which power is held by males.

pa•tri•cian (pə trish′ən), *n.* a person of noble or high rank; aristocrat.

pat•ri•cide (pa′trə sīd′), *n.* **1.** the act of killing one's father. **2.** a person who commits such an act.

Pat•rick (pa′trik), *n.* **Saint,** A.D. 389?–461?, British

missionary and bishop in Ireland: patron saint of Ireland.

pat•ri•mo•ny (pa′trə mō′nē), *n., pl.* **-nies.** an estate inherited from one's father or ancestors. —**pat′ri•mo′ni•al,** *adj.*

pa•tri•ot (pā′trē ət, -ot′; *esp. Brit.* pa′trē ət), *n.* a person who loves, supports, and defends his or her country. [< MF < LL < Gk *patriōtēs* fellow-countryman] —**pa′tri•ot′ic,** *adj.* —**pa′tri•ot•ism,** *n.*

pa•trol (pə trōl′), *v.,* **-trolled, -trol•ling,** *n.* —*v.t., v.i.* **1.** to pass regularly through or along (a specified area or route) in order to maintain order and security. —*n.* **2.** a person or group that patrols. **3.** the act of patrolling.

patrol′ car′, *n.* SQUAD CAR.

pa•trol′man or **-wom•an,** *n., pl.* **-men** or **-wom•en.** a police officer who patrols a specific route or area.

patrol′ wag′on, *n.* PADDY WAGON.

pa•tron (pā′trən), *n.* **1.** a person who is a customer, client, etc., esp. a regular one. **2.** a person who supports an artist, charity, etc., with money or efforts. **3.** PATRON SAINT.

pa•tron•age (pā′trə nij, pa′-), *n.* **1.** the business provided to a store or the like by customers, clients, etc. **2. a.** the power of public officials to make appointments to government jobs or grant other favors. **b.** the jobs or favors so distributed. **3.** the support of a patron, as toward an artist.

pa′tron•ize′, *v.t.,* **-ized, -iz•ing. 1.** to give (a store, restaurant, etc.) one's patronage. **2.** to behave in a condescending manner toward. **3.** to act as a patron toward; support. —**pa′tron•iz′er,** *n.*

pa′tron saint′, *n.* a saint regarded as the special guardian of a person, group, etc.

pat•ro•nym•ic (pa′trə nim′ik), *n.* a name derived from the name of a father or ancestor, as *Williamson* (son of *William*). —**pat′ro•nym′i•cal•ly,** *adv.*

pat•sy (pat′sē), *n., pl.* **-sies.** *Slang.* **1.** a person who is easily swindled or manipulated. **2.** a person upon whom the blame for something falls.

pat•ter¹ (pat′ər), *v.i.* **1.** to make a rapid succession of light taps. —*n.* **2.** a rapid succession of light tapping sounds. **3.** the act of pattering.

pat•ter² (pat′ər), *n.* **1.** glib and rapid talk used to attract attention, entertain, etc. —*v.i., v.t.* **2.** to speak glibly or rapidly.

pat•tern (pat′ərn), *n.* **1.** a decorative design composed of elements in a regular arrangement. **2.** a combination of qualities, acts, etc., forming a characteristic arrangement: *behavior patterns.* **3.** a model considered for or deserving of imitation. **4.** anything designed to serve as a model for something to be made. —*v.t.* **5.** to make or fashion after a pattern.

Pat•ton (pat′n), *n.* George S(mith), 1885–1945, U.S. general.

pat•ty (pat′ē), *n., pl.* **-ties. 1.** a thin, round piece of ground or minced food, as of meat. **2.** a little pie.

pau•ci•ty (pô′si tē), *n.* **1.** smallness of quantity; scarcity. **2.** smallness or insufficiency of number.

Paul (pôl), *n.* **Saint,** died A.D. c67, a missionary and apostle to the gentiles: author of several of the Epistles. Compare SAUL (def. 2).

Paul′ Bun′yan (bun′yən), *n.* a legendary giant lumberjack of the American frontier.

Paul•ine (pô′līn, -lēn), *adj.* pertaining to the apostle Paul or to his doctrines.

Paul•ing (pô′ling), *n.* **Linus Carl,** 1901–94, U.S. chemist.

paunch (pônch, pänch), *n.* a large and protruding belly; potbelly. —**paunch′y,** *adj.,* **-i•er, -i•est.**

pau•per (pô′pər), *n.* a very poor person. —**pau′per•ism,** *n.* —**pau′per•ize′,** *v.t.,* **-ized, -iz•ing.**

pause (pôz), *v., n., v.,* **paused, paus•ing.** —*n.* **1.** a temporary stop or rest. **2.** a break in speaking or writing to emphasize or clarify meaning. —*v.i.* **3.** to make a pause.

Pa•va•rot•ti (pav′ə rot′ē, pä′və rô′tē), *n.* **Luciano,** born 1935, Italian operatic tenor.

pave (pāv), *v.t.,* **paved, pav•ing. 1.** to cover or lay (a road, walk, etc.) with concrete, stones, or asphalt.

—*Idiom.* **2. pave the way for,** to prepare the way for.

pave/ment (-mənt), *n.* a paved surface, as a sidewalk.

pa•vil•ion (pə vil/yən), *n.* **1.** a light, usu. open building, used for concerts, exhibits, etc. **2.** any of a number of separate or attached buildings forming a hospital or the like. **3.** a large, elaborate tent.

pav/ing, *n.* **1.** a pavement. **2.** material for paving.

Pav•lov (pav/lof, -lôf), *n.* **Ivan Petrovich,** 1849–1936, Russian physiologist. —**Pav•lov/i•an** (-lō/vē-ən), *adj.*

paw (pô), *n.* **1.** the foot of an animal that has claws. **2.** *Informal.* the human hand. —*v.t., v.i.* **3.** to strike or scrape with the paws. **4.** to handle clumsily, rudely, or with unwelcome familiarity.

pawl (pôl), *n.* a pivoted bar adapted to engage with the teeth of a wheel so as to prevent movement or impart motion.

pawn¹ (pôn), *v.t.* **1.** to deposit as security, as for money borrowed. **2.** to stake; risk. —*n.* **3.** the state of being pawned. **4.** something pawned.

pawn² (pôn), *n.* **1.** a chess piece of the lowest value. **2.** someone used to further another's purposes.

pawn/bro/ker, *n.* a person whose business is lending money at interest on personal property deposited until redeemed.

pawn/shop/, *n.* a pawnbroker's shop.

paw•paw (pô/pô/, pə pô/), *n.* **1.** a tree of the eastern U.S. with large, oblong leaves and purplish flowers. **2.** the fleshy, edible fruit of this tree. **3.** PAPAYA.

pax (paks, päks), *n.* **1.** KISS OF PEACE. **2.** (*often cap.*) a period in history marked by general peace.

pax/ Americа/na, *n.* a peace imposed by the United States upon hostile nations.

pay (pā), *v.,* **paid, pay•ing,** *n., adj.* —*v.t.* **1.** to settle (a debt or obligation). **2.** to give over (money) in exchange for something. **3.** to transfer money to (a person or organization) for work done or services rendered. **4.** to be profitable to. **5.** to give (attention, a compliment, etc.), as if due or fitting. **6.** to make (a call, visit, etc.). —*v.i.* **7.** to transfer money, goods, etc., as in making a purchase or settling a debt. **8.** to be worthwhile: *It pays to be courteous.* **9. pay back, a.** to repay. **b.** to retaliate against. **10. ~ off, a.** to pay everything that is due. **b.** to pay (a debt) in full. **c.** *Informal.* to bribe. **d.** to result in success. **11. ~ up,** to pay fully. —*n.* **12.** wages, salary, or a stipend. —*adj.* **13.** requiring payment for service or use: *a pay phone.* —**pay/a•ble,** *adj.* —**pay•ee/,** *n., pl.* **-ees.** —**pay/er,** *n.*

pay/ dirt/, 1. soil, gravel, or ore that can be mined profitably. **2.** *Informal.* any source of wealth.

pay/load/, *n.* **1.** the part of a cargo producing revenue. **2.** the bomb load, warhead, cargo, or passengers of an aircraft, rocket, etc.

pay/mas/ter, *n.* a person in charge of paying out wages or salaries.

pay/ment (-mənt), *n.* **1.** something paid. **2.** the act of paying. **3.** reward or punishment.

Payne (pān), *n.* **John Howard,** 1791–1852, U.S. actor and dramatist.

pay/off/, *n.* **1.** the payment of a salary, debt, etc. **2.** the outcome of a series of events; climax. **3.** a settlement or reckoning, as in retribution or reward. **4.** *Informal.* BRIBE.

pay•o•la (pā ō/lə), *n.* secret payment in return for the promotion of a product, service, etc., through the abuse of one's position.

pay/roll/, *n.* **1.** a list of employees to be paid, with the amount due to each. **2.** the sum total of these amounts.

Pb, *Chem. Symbol.* lead. [< L *plumbum*]

PBS, Public Broadcasting System.

PBX, a telephone facility within an office, building, etc., that is connected to the public telephone network. [*P(rivate) B(ranch) E)x(change)*]

PC, 1. Peace Corps. **2.** *pl.* **PCs** or **PC's.** personal computer. **3.** politically correct.

PCB, *pl.,* **PCBs, PCB's.** any of a family of highly toxic,

possibly carcinogenic compounds formerly used in industry. [*p(oly)c(hlorinated) b(iphenyl)*]

PCS, Personal Communications Service: a system of digital wireless communications.

pct., percent.

Pd, *Chem. Symbol.* palladium.

pd., paid.

p/e, price-earnings ratio.

PE, Prince Edward Island.

pea (pē), *n., pl.* **peas. 1.** the round edible seed of a widely cultivated plant of the legume family. **2.** the plant itself.

peace (pēs), *n.* **1.** freedom from war. **2.** a state of harmony between people or groups. **3.** freedom from civil commotion. **4.** a state of tranquillity or serenity. **5.** (*often cap.*) an agreement that ends a war. —*Idiom.* **6. hold** or **keep one's peace,** to keep silent. —*Proverb.* **7. If you want peace, prepare for war,** a strong defense is the best safeguard against the outbreak of hostilities. —**peace/a•ble,** *adj.* —**peace/ful,** *adj.* —**peace/ful•ly,** *adv.*

Peace/ Corps/, *n.* a civilian organization, sponsored by the U.S. government, that sends volunteers to instruct citizens of underdeveloped countries.

peace/ div/idend, *n.* money cut by a government from its defense budget as a result of the cessation of hostilities with other countries.

peace/ful coexist/ence, *n.* competition without war, or a policy of peace between nations of widely differing political systems and ideologies.

peace/mak/er, *n.* a person, group, or nation that attempts to make peace. —**peace/mak/ing,** *n., adj.*

peace/ of/fering, *n.* **1.** any offering made to procure peace. **2.** a sacrificial offering made to assure communion with God. Ex. 20:24; Lev. 7:11–18.

peace/ of/ficer, *n.* a civil officer appointed to preserve the public peace, as a sheriff.

peace/ pipe/, *n.* CALUMET.

peace/time/, *n.* a period of freedom from war.

peach (pēch), *n.* **1.** a round, pink-to-yellow, fuzzy-skinned fruit. **2.** the tree bearing this fruit. **3.** *Informal.* a person or thing that is especially attractive or well-liked.

pea/cock/, *n., pl.* **-cocks, -cock.** the male peafowl, having long, iridescent tail feathers that can be spread in a fan.

peacock

pea/fowl/, *n.* a large Asiatic bird of the pheasant family.

pea/hen/, *n.* the female peafowl.

pea/ jack/et, *n.* a short, double-breasted coat of navy-blue wool, worn orig. by seamen.

peak (pēk), *n.* **1.** the pointed top of a mountain or ridge. **2.** a mountain with a pointed summit. **3.** the pointed top of anything. **4.** the highest or most important point or level. —*v.i.* **5.** to attain a peak of activity, popularity, etc. —*adj.* **6.** attaining or being at the highest or maximum level, point, etc.

peak•ed (pē/kid), *adj.* pale and drawn.

peal (pēl), *n.* **1.** a loud, prolonged ringing of bells. **2.** a set of bells tuned to one another. **3.** any loud, sustained sound, as of thunder. —*v.t., v.i.* **4.** to sound or sound forth in a peal.

pea/nut/ (-nut/, -nət), *n.* **1.** the pod or the enclosed edible seed of a plant of the legume family. **2.** the plant itself. **3. peanuts,** *Informal.* a very small amount of money.

pea/nut but/ter, *n.* a food paste made from ground roasted peanuts.

pear (pâr), *n.* **1.** an edible fruit, usu. rounded but elongated and growing smaller toward the stem. **2.** the tree bearing this fruit.

pearl (pûrl), *n.* **1.** a smooth, rounded bead formed within the shells of oysters and other mollusks, valued as a gem. **2.** something similar in form or luster. **3.** something precious or choice. **4.** a very pale bluish gray. **5.** MOTHER-OF-PEARL. —**pearl′y,** *adj.,* -i•er, -i• est.

Pearl′ Har′bor, *n.* a harbor near Honolulu, on S Oahu, in Hawaii: surprise attack by Japan on U.S. naval base Dec. 7, 1941.

Pea•ry (pēr′ē), *n.* **Robert Edwin,** 1856–1920, U.S. admiral and arctic explorer.

peas•ant (pez′ənt), *n.* **1.** a small farmer or farm laborer, as in Europe, Asia, or Latin America. **2.** a boorish, uneducated person. —**peas′ant•ry,** *n.*

peat (pēt), *n.* partially decayed vegetable matter found in bogs, cut and then dried for use as fuel.

peat′ moss′, *n.* any moss from which peat may form, used chiefly as a mulch.

peb•ble (peb′əl), *n.* a small, rounded stone, esp. one worn by the action of water. —**peb′bly,** *adj.*

pe•can (pi kän′, -kan′, pē′kan), *n.* **1.** a hickory tree of the southern U.S. and Mexico, cultivated for its edible nuts. **2.** a nut of this tree.

pec•ca•dil•lo (pek′ə dil′ō), *n., pl.* -loes, -los. a slight sin or offense.

pec•ca•ry (pek′ə rē), *n., pl.* -ries. a piglike New World mammal having a dark gray coat with a white collar.

peck¹ (pek), *n.* a dry measure of 8 quarts; the fourth part of a bushel.

peck² (pek), *v.t.* **1.** to strike with the beak or with some pointed instrument. **2.** to make (a hole) by doing this. **3.** to take (food) bit by bit. —*v.i.* **4.** to make strokes with the beak or a pointed instrument. **5. peck at,** *a.* to nibble indifferently at (food). **b.** to nag or carp at. —*n.* **6.** a quick stroke. **7.** a quick kiss.

peck′ing or′der, *n.* a hierarchy of status or authority in a social or business group.

Pe′cos Bill′, *n.* a legendary cowboy of the American frontier who performed such fabulous feats as digging the Rio Grande.

pec•tin (pek′tin), *n.* a carbohydrate present in ripe fruits: used in jellies for its thickening and emulsifying properties.

pec•to•ral (pek′tər əl), *adj.* of, in, or on the chest or breast.

pec•u•late (pek′yə lāt′), *v.t., v.i.,* -lat•ed, -lat•ing. to embezzle (money, esp. public funds). —**pec′u•la′• tion,** *n.* —**pec′u•la′tor,** *n.*

pe•cu•liar (pi kyōōl′yər), *adj.* **1.** strange; odd. **2.** distinctive in nature or character from others. **3.** belonging exclusively to some person, group, or thing. —**pe•cu′li•ar′i•ty** (-kyōō′lē ar′i tē), *n., pl.* -ties. —**pe•cu′liar•ly,** *adv.*

pe•cu•ni•ar•y (pi kyōō′nē er′ē), *adj.* of or consisting of money.

ped•a•gogue (ped′ə gog′, -gôg′), *n.* **1.** a teacher. **2.** a person who is pedantic and dogmatic.

ped′a•go′gy (-gō′jē, -goj′ē), *n.* the art or science of teaching.

ped•al (ped′l), *n., v.,* -aled, -al•ing or (*esp. Brit.*) -alled, -al•ling. —*n.* **1.** a foot-operated lever used to control power to various mechanisms. —*v.i.* **2.** to work or use pedals, as in riding a bicycle. —*v.t.* **3.** to work the pedals of.

ped•ant (ped′nt), *n.* **1.** a person who makes an excessive display of learning. **2.** a person who overemphasizes rules or minor details. —**pe•dan•tic** (pə-dan′tik), *adj.* —**ped′ant•ry,** *n., pl.* -ries.

ped•dle (ped′l), *v.t., v.i.,* -dled, -dling. to carry (small articles) from place to place for sale. —**ped′• dler,** *n.*

ped•es•tal (ped′ə stl), *n.* an architectural support for a column, statue, etc.

pe•des•tri•an (pə des′trē ən), *n.* **1.** a person who travels on foot. —*adj.* **2.** going or performed on foot. **3.** of or intended for walking.

pe•di•at•rics (pē′dē a′triks), *n.* the branch of medicine concerned with the development, care, and dis-

eases of children. —**pe′di•at′ric,** *adj.* —**pe′di•a•tri′• cian** (-ə trish′ən), *n.*

ped•i•cab (ped′i kab′), *n.* (esp. in Southeast Asia) a three-wheeled public conveyance operated by pedals.

ped•i•cure (ped′i kyŏŏr′), *n.* professional care of the feet, as the trimming of toenails. —**ped′i•cur′ist,** *n.*

ped•i•gree (ped′i grē′), *n., pl.* -grees. **1.** an ancestral line; lineage. **2.** a genealogical record, esp. of a purebred animal. —**ped′i•greed′,** *adj.*

ped•i•ment (ped′ə mənt), *n.* (in classical architecture) a low triangular gable surmounting a colonnade, an end wall, etc.

pe•dom•e•ter (pə dom′i tər), *n.* an instrument that measures the distance walked.

pe•dun•cle (pi dung′kəl, pē′dung-), *n.* the stalk that supports a flower cluster.

peek (pēk), *v.i.* **1.** to look quickly or furtively. —*n.* **2.** a quick or furtive look.

peel (pēl), *v.t.* **1.** to strip (something) of its skin, rind, etc. **2.** to strip away from something. —*v.i.* **3.** (of skin, paint, etc.) to come off in pieces. **4.** to lose the skin, paint, etc. —*n.* **5.** the skin or rind of a fruit or vegetable. —**peel′er,** *n.*

Peel (pēl), *n.* **Sir Robert,** 1788–1850, British statesman: founder of the London constabulary; prime minister 1834–35, 1841–46.

peel′ing, *n.* a piece, as of skin or rind, peeled off.

peen (pēn), *n.* the wedgelike or spherical end of a hammerhead opposite the face.

peep¹ (pēp), *v.i.* **1.** to look through a small opening or from a concealed location. **2.** to come partially into view. —*n.* **3.** a quick or furtive look. —**peep′er,** *n.*

peep² (pēp), *n.* **1.** a short, shrill cry, as of a young bird. —*v.i.* **2.** to utter a short, shrill cry.

peep′hole′, *n.* a small hole, as in a door, through which to look.

peer¹ (pēr), *n.* **1.** a person who is the equal of another in abilities, social status, etc. **2.** a member of the nobility in Great Britain. —**peer′age,** *n.*

peer² (pēr), *v.i.* **1.** to look searchingly, as in the effort to discern clearly. **2.** to appear slightly; peep out.

peer′less, *adj.* having no equal.

peeve (pēv), *v.,* peeved, peev•ing, *n.* —*v.t.* **1.** to make peevish. —*n.* **2.** a source of annoyance or irritation. **3.** a peevish mood.

pee•vish (pē′vish), *adj.* cross, querulous, or fretful. —**pee′vish•ly,** *adv.* —**pee′vish•ness,** *n.*

pee•wee (pē′wē′), *n., pl.* -wees. *Informal.* a person or thing that is unusually small.

peg (peg), *n., v.,* pegged, peg•ging. —*n.* **1.** a pin driven or fitted into something as a fastening, support, stopper, or marker. **2.** a notch or degree. **3.** *Informal.* a hard throw, esp. in baseball. —*v.t.* **4.** to fasten or mark with pegs. **5.** to keep (a price) at a set level. **6.** *Informal.* to throw (a ball) forcefully. **7.** *Informal.* to identify or classify. —*v.i.* **8.** to work persistently: *pegging away at homework.*

Peg•a•sus (peg′ə səs), *n.* a winged horse of Greek myth.

peg′ leg′, *n.* **1.** an artificial leg, esp. a wooden one. **2.** a person with an artificial leg.

P.E.I., Prince Edward Island.

peign•oir (pān wär′, pen-), *n.* a woman's loose dressing gown.

Pei•ping (pā′ping′, bā′-), *n.* former name of BEIJING.

pe•jo•ra•tive (pi jôr′ə tiv, -jor′-), *adj.* **1.** having a disparaging effect or force. —*n.* **2.** a pejorative form or word, as *poetaster.* —**pej′o•ra′tion** (pej′ə rā′shən), *n.*

Pe•kah (pē′kä, -kə), *n.* an idolatrous king of Israel. II Kings 15:25–31; II Chron. 28:5–31.

Pe•king (pē′king′, pā′-), *n.* BEIJING.

Pe•king•ese or **-kin•ese** (pē′kə nēz′, -nēs′) *n., pl.* -ese. one of a Chinese breed of small, long-haired dogs having a flat, wrinkled muzzle.

pe•koe (pē′kō), *n.* a black tea from Sri Lanka, India, and Java.

pe•lag•ic (pə laj′ik), *adj.* of the open seas or oceans.

pelf (pelf), *n.* money, esp. of questionable source.

pel•i•can (pel'i kən), *n.* a large, web-footed, fish-eating bird with an expandable throat pouch.

pel•la•gra (pə lag'rə, -lā'grə, -lä'-), *n.* a disease caused by a deficiency of niacin in the diet, characterized by skin changes, nerve dysfunction, and mental symptoms.

pel•let (pel'it), *n.* 1. a small, rounded body, as of food or medicine. 2. one of a charge of small shot, as for a shotgun.

pell-mell (pel'mel'), *adv.* 1. in a recklessly hurried manner. 2. in a disordered mass. —*adj.* 3. disorderly or confused. 4. overhasty or precipitate.

pel•lu•cid (pə lōō'sid), *adj.* 1. allowing the maximum passage of light, as glass. 2. clear in meaning.

pelt[1] (pelt), *v.t.* 1. to attack with or as if with repeated blows or missiles. —*v.i.* 2. to beat or pound unrelentingly.

pelt[2] (pelt), *n.* the untanned skin of an animal.

pel•vis (pel'vis), *n.*, *pl.* **-vis•es, -ves** (-vēz). 1. the basinlike cavity in the lower trunk of the body. 2. the bones forming this cavity. [< L: basin] —**pel'-vic,** *adj.*

pen[1] (pen), *n.*, *v.*, **penned, pen•ning.** —*n.* 1. any of various instruments for writing or drawing with ink. 2. the pen as a symbol of authorship. —*v.t.* 3. to write or draw with a pen. —*Proverb.* **4. The pen is mightier than the sword,** words have more lasting influence than violence.

pen[2] (pen), *n.*, *v.*, **penned, pen•ning.** —*n.* 1. a small enclosure for domestic animals. —*v.t.* 2. to confine in or as if in a pen.

Pen. or **pen.,** peninsula.

pe•nal (pēn'l), *adj.* 1. of or involving punishment. 2. prescribing punishment.

pe'nal•ize', *v.t.*, **-ized, -iz•ing.** to subject to a penalty. —**pe'nal•i•za'tion,** *n.*

pen•al•ty (pen'l tē), *n.*, *pl.* **-ties.** 1. a punishment for a violation of law or rule. 2. something forfeited, as a sum of money.

pen'ance (-əns), *n.* a punishment undergone as penitence for sin.

pence (pens), *n. Brit.* a pl. of PENNY.

pen•chant (pen'chənt), *n.* a strong taste or liking for something.

pen•cil (pen'səl), *n.*, *v.*, **-ciled, -cil•ing** or (*esp. Brit.*) **-cilled, -cil•ling.** —*n.* 1. a slender tube of wood, metal, etc., containing a core of graphite or crayon, used for writing or drawing. —*v.t.* 2. to write, draw, or mark with a pencil.

pend•ant (pen'dənt), *n.* a hanging ornament, as a jewel suspended from a necklace.

pend•ent (pen'dənt), *adj.* 1. hanging or suspended. 2. overhanging; jutting. 3. (esp. of a lawsuit) pending.

pend'ing, *prep.* 1. while awaiting. 2. during: *pending the trial.* —*adj.* 3. awaiting decision or settlement. 4. about to happen.

pen•du•lous (pen'jə ləs, pen'dyə-), *adj.* hanging down loosely.

pen'du•lum (-ləm), *n.* a body so suspended from a fixed point as to move to and fro by the action of gravity and acquired momentum.

pen•e•trate (pen'i trāt'), *v.t.*, *v.i.*, **-trat•ed, -trat•ing.** 1. to pierce or pass into or through (something). 2. to permeate. 3. to comprehend. 4. to affect deeply. —**pen'e•tra•ble,** *adj.* —**pen'e•tra'tion,** *n.*

pen'e•trat'ing, *adj.* 1. able to penetrate; piercing; sharp. 2. acute; discerning.

pen•guin (peng'gwin, pen'-), *n.* a flightless aquatic bird of the Southern Hemisphere, having webbed feet and flippers.

pen•i•cil•lin (pen'ə sil'in), *n.* any of several antibiotics widely used to prevent and treat bacterial infection and other diseases.

pen•in•su•la (pə nin'sə lə, -nins'yə lə), *n.*, *pl.* **-las.** an area of land almost completely surrounded by water. [< L *paenīnsula = paene* almost + *īnsula* island] —**pen•in'su•lar,** *adj.*

pe•nis (pē'nis), *n.*, *pl.* **-nis•es, -nes** (-nēz). the male organ of copulation and urination. —**pe•nile** (pēn'l, pē'nīl), *adj.*

pen•i•tent (pen'i tənt), *adj.* 1. feeling sorrow for sin or wrongdoing and disposed to atonement. —*n.* 2. a penitent person. —**pen'i•tence,** *n.* —**pen'i•ten'tial** (-ten'shəl), *adj.* —**pen'i•tent•ly,** *adv.*

pen•i•ten•tia•ry (-ten'shə rē), *n.*, *pl.* **-ries,** *adj.* —*n.* 1. a state or federal prison for serious offenders. —*adj.* 2. punishable by imprisonment in a penitentiary.

pen'knife', *n.*, *pl.* **-knives.** a small pocketknife.

pen'light', *n.* a flashlight similar in size and shape to a fountain pen.

pen'man, *n.*, *pl.* **-men.** 1. a scribe; copyist. 2. a writer or author.

pen'man•ship', *n.* 1. the art of handwriting. 2. a person's style of handwriting.

Penn (pen), *n.* **William,** 1644–1718, English Quaker: founder of Pennsylvania.

Penn. or **Penna.,** Pennsylvania.

pen' name', *n.* a writer's pseudonym.

pen•nant (pen'ənt), *n.* 1. a long, tapering flag. 2. a flag serving as an emblem of championship, esp. in baseball.

pen•ni•less (pen'i lis), *adj.* totally without money.

pen•non (pen'ən), *n.* 1. a flag formerly borne on the lance of a knight. 2. any flag or banner.

Penn•syl•va•nia (pen'səl vān'yə), *n.* a state in the E United States. 12,056,112. *Cap.:* Harrisburg. *Abbr.:* PA, Pa., Penn., Penna. —**Penn'syl•va'nian,** *adj.*, *n.*

pen•ny (pen'ē), *n.*, *pl.* **pen•nies** for 1, **pence** for 2, 3. 1. a monetary unit of the U.S. or Canada, equal to $1/100$ of a dollar. 2. a monetary unit of the United Kingdom, equal to $1/100$ of a pound. 3. a monetary unit equal to $1/12$ of the former British shilling.

pen'ny arcade', *n.* an area that contains coin-operated entertainment devices.

pen'ny pinch'er, *n.* a stingy person. —**pen'ny-pinch'ing,** *n.*, *adj.*

pen'ny•weight', *n.* (in troy weight) a unit of 24 grains or $1/20$ of an ounce (1.555 grams).

pe•nol•o•gy (pē nol'ə jē), *n.* 1. the study of the punishment of crime. 2. the study of the management of prisons. —**pe•nol'o•gist,** *n.*

pen' pal', *n.* a person with whom one keeps up an exchange of letters.

pen•sion (pen'shən), *n.* 1. a fixed amount, other than wages, paid regularly to a person for past services, injury sustained, etc. —*v.t.* 2. to grant or pay a pension to. —**pen'sion•er,** *n.*

pen•sive (pen'siv), *adj.* dreamily or wistfully thoughtful. —**pen'sive•ly,** *adv.*

penta-, a combining form meaning five (*pentagon*).

pen•ta•cle (pen'tə kəl), *n.* PENTAGRAM.

pen•ta•gon (pen'tə gon'), *n.* 1. a polygon having five angles and five sides. **2. the Pentagon,** the U.S. Department of Defense; the U.S. military establishment. —**pen•tag'o•nal** (-tag'ə nl), *adj.*

penguin

pen'ta•gram' (-gram'), *n.* a five-pointed, star-shaped figure, used as an occult symbol.

pen•tam•e•ter (pen tam'i tər), *n.* a line of verse consisting of five metrical feet.

Pen•ta•teuch (pen'tə tōōk', -tyōōk'), *n.* the first five books of the Old Testament: Genesis, Exodus,

Leviticus, Numbers, and Deuteronomy. Compare HAGIOGRAPHA, PROPHETS.

pen•tath•lon (pen tath′lən, -lon), *n.* an athletic contest comprising five different track and field events.

Pen•te•cost (pen′ti kôst′, -kost′), *n.* **1.** a Christian festival celebrated on the seventh Sunday after Easter, commemorating the descent of the Holy Ghost upon the apostles. **2.** SHAVUOTH. [< OE < LL < Gk *pentēkostē (hēméra)* fiftieth (day)]

Pen′te•cos′tal, *adj.* **1.** of Pentecost. **2.** noting or pertaining to various fundamentalist Christian groups that emphasize inspiration by the Holy Spirit.

pent•house (pent′hous′), *n.* **1.** an apartment on the roof of a building. **2.** any specially designed apartment on the top floor of a building.

pent′-up′, *adj.* not vented or expressed.

pe•nu•che (pə nōō′chē), *n.* a fudge made of brown sugar, butter, milk, and esp. nuts.

Pe•nu•el (pi nōō′el, -nyōō′-) also **Pe•ni•el** (pi nī′-el), *n.* a place where Jacob wrestled with God. Gen. 32:30; Judg. 8:17.

pe•nul•ti•mate (pi nul′tə mit), *adj.* next to the last.

pe•nu•ri•ous (pə nōōr′ē əs, -nyōōr′-), *adj.* **1.** extremely stingy. **2.** extremely poor. —**pe•nu′ri•ous•ly,** *adv.* —**pe•nu′ri•ous•ness,** *n.*

pen•u•ry (pen′yə rē), *n.* extreme poverty.

pe•on (pē′ən, pē′on), *n.* **1.** (in Spanish America) a farm worker or unskilled laborer. **2.** (formerly, esp. in Mexico) a person held in servitude to work off debts. **3.** any person of low social status. —**pe′on•age** (-ə nij), *n.*

pe•o•ny (pē′ə nē), *n., pl.* **-nies.** a plant with large showy flowers.

peo•ple (pē′pəl), *n., pl.* **-ples** for 2, *v.,* **-pled, -pling.** —*n.* **1.** persons indefinitely or collectively. **2.** the body of persons who constitute a group by virtue of a common culture, religion, or the like. **3.** the persons of any particular group or number: *educated people.* **4.** the ordinary persons; populace. **5.** a person's family or relatives. —*v.t.* **6.** to populate.

Peo′ple's Repub′lic of Chi′na, *n.* CHINA (def. 1).

Pe•o•ri•a (pē ôr′ē ə), *n.* a city in central Illinois. 113,504.

pep (pep), *n., v.,* **pepped, pep•ping.** —*n.* **1.** lively spirits or energy. —*v.* **2. pep up,** to make or become spirited or vigorous. —**pep′py,** *adj.,* **-pi•er, -pi•est.**

pep•per (pep′ər), *n.* **1. a.** the pungent dried berries of a tropical climbing shrub, used as a condiment. **b.** the shrub itself. **2. a.** the usu. green or red fruit of any of several plants, ranging from mild to pungent in flavor. **b.** any of these plants. —*v.t.* **3.** to season or sprinkle with or as if with pepper. **4.** to pelt with missiles.

pep′per•corn′, *n.* the dried berry of the pepper plant.

pep′per mill′, *n.* a hand-held device for grinding peppercorns.

pep′per•mint′ (-mint′, -mənt), *n.* **1.** an aromatic herb of the mint family, having lance-shaped leaves. **2.** its oil, used as a flavoring. **3.** a confection flavored with peppermint.

pep•per•o•ni (pep′ə rō′nē), *n., pl.* **-nis.** a highly seasoned, hard sausage.

pep′per•y, *adj.* **1.** full of or tasting like pepper. **2.** sharp or stinging. **3.** easily angered.

pep•sin (pep′sin), *n.* an enzyme, produced in the stomach, that promotes the digestion of proteins.

pep′ talk′, *n.* a vigorous talk intended to arouse enthusiasm, determination, etc.

pep•tic (pep′tik), *adj.* **1.** of or promoting digestion. **2.** of or due to the action of pepsin.

per (pûr; *unstressed* pər), *prep.* **1.** for or in each: *$10 per yard.* **2.** according to: *per your instructions.* **3.** by means of: *Send it per messenger.* —**Usage.** In nontechnical use, A is often preferred in the sense "for each": *$5 a year.*

Per., 1. Persia. **2.** Persian.

per•am•bu•late (pər am′byə lāt′), *v.,* **-lat•ed, -lat•**

ing. —*v.t.* **1.** to walk through, about, or over. —*v.i.* **2.** to stroll.

per•am′bu•la′tor, *n.* BABY CARRIAGE.

per an•num (pər an′əm), *adv.* yearly.

per•cale (pər kāl′), *n.* a smooth, plain-weave cotton cloth, used esp. for bedsheets.

per cap•i•ta (pər kap′i tə), *adj., adv.* by or for each person.

per•ceive (pər sēv′), *v.t.,* **-ceived, -ceiv•ing. 1.** to become aware of by means of the senses. **2.** to recognize or understand. —**per•ceiv′a•ble,** *adj.*

per•cent (pər sent′), *n.* **1.** one one-hundredth part; ¹⁄₁₀₀. **2.** PERCENTAGE (defs. 1, 3). —*adj.* **3.** figured or expressed on the basis of a rate or proportion per hundred. [short for ML *per centum* by the hundred]

per•cent′age (-sen′tij), *n.* **1.** a rate or proportion per hundred. **2.** an allowance, commission, or rate of interest calculated by percent. **3.** a proportion in general. **4.** profit; advantage.

per•cen•tile (-tīl, -til), *n.* one of the values of a statistical variable that divides the distribution of the variable into 100 groups having equal frequencies.

per•cep•ti•ble (pər sep′tə bəl), *adj.* capable of being perceived. —**per•cep′ti•bly,** *adv.*

per•cep′tion, *n.* **1.** the act or faculty of perceiving. **2.** intuitive recognition or appreciation; insight. **3.** the result or product of perceiving.

per•cep′tive, *adj.* **1.** having or showing keenness of perception. **2.** of perception. —**per•cep′tive•ly,** *adv.* —**per•cep′tive•ness,** *n.*

per•cep′tu•al (-chōō əl), *adj.* of or involving perception.

perch¹ (pûrch), *n.* **1.** a horizontal pole or rod serving as a roost for birds. **2.** an elevated position, resting place, or the like. —*v.i., v.t.* **3.** to rest or set on or as if on a perch.

perch² (pûrch), *n., pl.* **perch•es, perch. 1.** a small freshwater fish with a spiny anterior dorsal fin. **2.** any of various related or similar fishes.

per•chance (pər chans′, -chäns′), *adv.* **1.** perhaps. **2.** *Archaic.* by chance.

per•co•late (pûr′kə lāt′), *v.,* **-lat•ed, -lat•ing.** —*v.t.* **1.** to cause (a liquid) to pass through a porous body; filter. **2.** to brew (coffee) in a percolator. —*v.i.* **3.** to pass through a porous substance; filter. —**per′co•la′tion,** *n.*

per′co•la′tor, *n.* a coffeepot in which boiling water is forced up a hollow stem and filters down through ground coffee.

per•cus•sion (pər kush′ən), *n.* **1.** the striking of one body against another with some sharpness. **2.** the percussion instruments of an orchestra.

percus′sion in′strument, *n.* a musical instrument, as the drum or cymbal, that is struck to produce a sound.

per•cus′sion•ist, *n.* a musician who plays percussion instruments.

per di•em (pər dē′əm, dī′əm), *adv.* **1.** by the day. —*n.* **2.** a daily allowance for living expenses, as while traveling on business. [< L]

per•di•tion (pər dish′ən), *n.* **1.** a state of final spiritual ruin. **2.** hell.

per•dur•a•ble (pər dōōr′ə bəl, -dyōōr′-), *adj.* very durable.

per•e•gri•nate (per′i grə nāt′), *v.,* **-nat•ed, -nat•ing.** —*v.i.* **1.** to travel or journey, esp. on foot. —*v.t.* **2.** to travel over or through. —**per′e•gri•na′tion,** *n.*

per′e•grine fal′con (per′i grin, -grēn′), *n.* a cosmopolitan falcon that feeds on birds taken in flight.

per•emp•to•ry (pə remp′tə rē), *adj.* **1.** leaving no opportunity for denial or refusal. **2.** imperious or dictatorial. **3.** *Law.* decisive or final.

per•en•ni•al (pə ren′ē əl), *adj.* **1.** lasting for an indefinitely long time. **2.** (of plants) living more than two years. **3.** continuing throughout the entire year, as a stream. **4.** continuing; recurrent. —*n.* **5.** a perennial plant. —**per•en′ni•al•ly,** *adv.*

per•fect (*adj.* n. pûr′fikt; *v.* pər fekt′), *adj.* **1.** conforming absolutely to an ideal type: *a perfect gentleman.* **2.** excellent or complete beyond improvement.

3. without flaws. **4.** accurate in every detail. **5.** thorough; utter: *perfect strangers.* **6.** designating a verb tense that indicates an action or state brought to a close prior to some temporal point of reference. —*v.t.* **7.** to make perfect. —*n.* **8.** the perfect tense. **9.** a verb form in the perfect tense. —**per'fect•ly,** *adv.* —**Usage.** Some commentators object to the use of comparative terms such as *most, more,* and *rather* with PERFECT on the grounds that PERFECT describes an absolute condition that cannot exist in degrees. However, such uses have been fully standard since the first appearance of the word in the language.

per•fect•i•ble (par fek'ta bal), *adj.* capable of becoming or being made perfect.

per•fec'tion, *n.* **1.** the state or quality of being perfect. **2.** the highest degree of excellence. **3.** a perfect embodiment of something. **4.** the act or fact of perfecting.

per•fec'tion•ism, *n.* a personal standard that demands perfection. —**per•fec'tion•ist,** *n., adj.*

per•fi•dy (pûr'fi dē), *n., pl.* **-dies.** deliberate breach of faith or trust; treachery. —**per•fid•i•ous** (par fid'ē əs), *adj.*

per•fo•rate (pûr'fa rāt'), *v.,* **-rat•ed, -rat•ing.** —*v.t.* **1.** to make a hole or holes through, as by boring or punching. **2.** to pierce with a row of small holes to facilitate separation. —*v.i.* **3.** to penetrate. —**per'fo•ra'tion,** *n.*

per•force (par fôrs'), *adv.* of necessity; necessarily.

per•form (par fôrm'), *v.t.* **1.** to carry out; do. **2.** to carry into effect; fulfill: *to perform a contract.* **3.** to present (a play, musical work, etc.) before an audience. —*v.i.* **4.** to execute or do something. **5.** to give a performance. —**per•form'er,** *n.*

per•for'mance (-fôr'mans), *n.* **1.** an entertainment presented before an audience. **2.** the act of performing. **3.** the execution of work, feats, etc. **4.** a particular action, deed, etc.

perform'ing arts', *n.pl.* arts or skills that require public performance, as acting and singing.

per•fume (*n.* pûr'fyōōm, par fyōōm'; *v.* par fyōōm', pûr'fyōōm), *n., v.,* **-fumed, -fum•ing.** —*n.* **1.** a substance that imparts an agreeable smell, esp. a fluid containing fragrant oils extracted from flowers. **2.** an agreeable scent. —*v.t.* **3.** to fill with perfume or a pleasant fragrance.

per•fum'er•y, *n., pl.* **-er•ies. 1.** perfumes collectively. **2.** a place where perfumes are made or sold.

per•func•to•ry (par fungk'ta rē), *adj.* **1.** performed merely as a routine duty. **2.** lacking interest or enthusiasm. —**per•func'to•ri•ly,** *adv.*

Per•ga (pûr'ga), *n.* the capital of Pamphylia. Acts 13:13–14; 14:25.

Per•ga•mum (pûr'ga mam), *n.* the ancient capital of the kingdom of Pergamum, on the coast of Asia Minor, the site of one of the seven churches of Asia (Rev. 1:11): now the site of Bergama, in W Turkey.

per•haps (par haps'), *adv.* maybe; possibly.

peri-, a prefix meaning: about or around (*periscope*); enclosing or surrounding (*peritoneum*); near (*perigee*).

per•i•car•di•um (per'i kär'dē əm), *n., pl.* **-di•a** (-dē ə). the membranous sac enclosing the heart.

Per•i•cles (per'i klēz'), *n.* c495–429 B.C., Athenian statesman.

per•i•gee (per'i jē'), *n., pl.* **-gees.** the point in the orbit of the moon or an artificial satellite at which it is nearest to the earth.

per•i•he•li•on (per'a hē'lē ən), *n., pl.* **-he•li•a** (-hē'lē ə). the point in the orbit of a planet or comet at which it is nearest to the sun.

per•il (per'al), *n., v.,* **-iled, -il•ing** or (*esp. Brit.*) **-illed, -il•ling.** —*n.* **1.** grave risk; jeopardy. **2.** something that may cause injury, loss, or destruction. —*v.t.* **3.** to expose to peril. —**per'il•ous,** *adj.* —**per'il•ous•ly,** *adv.*

pe•rim•e•ter (pa rim'i tar), *n.* **1.** the outer boundary of a two-dimensional figure. **2.** the length of such a boundary.

per•i•ne•um (per'a nē'am), *n., pl.* **-ne•a** (-nē'ə). the area in front of the anus extending to the genitals.

pe•ri•od (pēr'ē əd), *n.* **1.** an interval of time marked by particular qualities, conditions, or events: *a period of illness.* **2.** any of the parts of equal length into which something, as a sports contest, is divided. **3.** the time during which something runs its course. **4.** the character (.) used to mark the end of a declarative sentence or indicate an abbreviation. **5.** an occurrence of menstruation. **6.** the basic unit of geologic time, comprising two or more epochs and included with other periods in an era.

pe'ri•od'ic (-od'ik), *adj.* **1.** occurring at regular intervals. **2.** recurring irregularly; intermittent. —**pe'ri•od'i•cal•ly,** *adv.* —**pe'ri•o•dic'i•ty** (-ə dis'i tē), *n.*

pe'ri•od'i•cal, *n.* **1.** a publication, as a magazine, that is issued under the same title at regular intervals. —*adj.* **2.** of such publications. **3.** published at regular intervals. **4.** PERIODIC.

pe'ri•od'ic ta'ble, *n.* a table in which the chemical elements, arranged according to their atomic numbers, are shown in related groups.

per•i•o•don•tal (per'ē ə don'tl), *adj.* of or concerning the bone, connective tissue, and gums surrounding and supporting the teeth.

per•i•pa•tet•ic (per'ə pə tet'ik), *adj.* walking or traveling about; itinerant.

pe•riph•er•al (pə rif'ər əl), *adj.* **1.** of, on, or constituting the periphery. **2.** comparatively superficial or unessential. —*n.* **3.** an external hardware device, as a printer, connected to a computer's CPU.

pe•riph'er•y, *n., pl.* **-er•ies. 1.** the boundary of any surface or area. **2.** the external surface of a body. **3.** a surrounding region or area.

pe•riph•ra•sis (pə rif'rə sis), *n., pl.* **-ses** (-sēz'). the use of a verbose or roundabout form of expression. —**per•i•phras•tic** (per'ə fras'tik), *adj.*

per•i•scope (per'ə skōp'), *n.* an optical instrument for viewing objects in an obstructed field of vision, used esp. in submarines.

per•ish (per'ish), *v.i.* **1.** to die as a result of violence, privation, etc. **2.** to suffer destruction or ruin.

per'ish•a•ble, *adj.* **1.** subject to decay or destruction. —*n.* **2.** Usu., **-bles.** something perishable, esp. food.

per•i•stal•sis (per'ə stôl'sis, -stal'-), *n., pl.* **-ses** (-sēz). waves of muscle contractions and relaxations that move matter along certain tubelike organs, as food along the alimentary canal. —**per'i•stal'tic** (-tik), *adj.*

per•i•to•ne•um (per'i tn ē'əm), *n., pl.* **-to•ne•ums, -to•ne•a** (-tn ē'ə). the serous membrane lining the abdominal cavity. —**per'i•to•ne'al,** *adj.*

per'i•to•ni'tis (-ī'tis), *n.* inflammation of the peritoneum.

per•i•wig (per'i wig'), *n.* a wig, esp. a peruke.

per•i•win•kle¹ (per'i wing'kal), *n.* a small edible sea snail.

per•i•win•kle² (per'i wing'kal), *n.* any of various plants with glossy evergreen foliage and blue-violet flowers.

per•jure (pûr'jar), *v.t.,* **-jured, -jur•ing.** to make (oneself) guilty of perjury. —**per'jur•er,** *n.*

per'ju•ry, *n., pl.* **-ries.** the willful giving of false testimony under oath.

perk¹ (pûrk), *v.i.* **1.** to become lively, vigorous, etc., again (usu. fol. by *up*). —*v.t.* **2.** to enhance or enliven (often fol. by *up*). **3.** to raise smartly or briskly: *The dog perked up his ears.* —**perk'y,** *adj.,* **-i•er, -i•est.** —**perk'i•ness,** *n.*

perk² (pûrk), *v.t., v.i.* to percolate.

perk³ (pûrk), *n.* perquisite.

per•ma•frost (pûr'ma frôst', -frost'), *n.* (in arctic or subarctic regions) permanently frozen subsoil.

per•ma•nent (pûr'ma nant), *adj.* **1.** existing perpetually. **2.** intended to serve, function, etc., for a long, indefinite period. —*n.* **3.** a wave or curl set into the hair by the application of chemicals or heat and lasting for a number of months. —**per'ma•nence,** *n.* —**per'ma•nent•ly,** *adv.*

per'manent press', *n.* a process in which a fabric is chemically treated to make it wrinkle-resistant.

per•me•a•ble (pûr'mē ə bəl), *adj.* capable of being permeated. —per•me•a•bil/i•ty, *n.*

per'me•ate' (-āt'), *v.t., v.i.,* -at•ed, -at•ing. 1. to penetrate through the pores or interstices (of). 2. to be or become diffused through; spread throughout.

Per•mi•an (pûr'mē ən), *adj.* noting or pertaining to the last period of the Paleozoic Era.

per•mis•si•ble (pər mis/ə bəl), *adj.* capable of being permitted; allowable.

per•mis'sion (-mish/ən), *n.* authorization to do something; formal consent.

per•mis'sive, *adj.* 1. tolerant of something that others might disapprove or forbid. 2. granting or expressing permission. —per•mis/sive•ly, *adv.* —per•mis'sive•ness, *n.*

per•mit (*v.* pər mit/; *n.* pûr'mit, pər mit/), *v.,* -mit•ted, -mit•ting, *n.* —*v.t.* 1. to allow to do something. 2. to allow to be done or occur. —*v.i.* 3. to afford opportunity: *when time permits.* —*n.* 4. an authoritative certificate of permission; license.

per•mu•ta•tion (pûr'myoō tā/shən), *n.* 1. alteration or transformation. 2. *Math.* a. the act of changing the order of set elements arranged in a particular way, as *abc* into *acb.* b. any of the resulting arrangements.

per•ni•cious (pər nish/əs), *adj.* causing insidious harm or ruin. —per•ni/cious•ly, *adv.* —per•ni/cious•ness, *n.*

per•o•ra•tion (per/ə rā/shən), *n.* 1. the concluding part of a speech, which recapitulates the principal points. 2. a long, highly rhetorical speech.

per•ox•ide (pə rok/sīd), *n., v.,* -id•ed, -id•ing. —*n.* 1. a. hydrogen peroxide. b. an oxide in which two oxygen atoms are bonded to each other. —*v.t.* 2. to bleach with peroxide.

per•pen•dic•u•lar (pûr'pən dik/yə lər), *adj.* 1. vertical; straight up and down. 2. meeting a given line or surface at right angles. —*n.* 3. a perpendicular line, plane, or position.

per•pe•trate (pûr'pi trāt/), *v.t.,* -trat•ed, -trat•ing. to carry out; commit. —per'pe•tra/tion, *n.* —per'pe•tra/tor, *n.*

per•pet•u•al (pər pech/oō əl), *adj.* 1. continuing forever. 2. lasting an indefinitely long time. 3. continuing without interruption. —per•pet/u•al•ly, *adv.*

per•pet'u•ate' (-āt'), *v.t.,* -at•ed, -at•ing. to make perpetual; preserve from extinction or oblivion. —per•pet/u•a/tion, *n.*

per•pe•tu•i•ty (pûr'pi toō/i tē, -tyoō/-), *n., pl.* -ties. 1. the state or character of being perpetual. 2. endless duration or existence.

per•plex (pər pleks/), *v.t.* to cause to be puzzled or bewildered. —per•plex/ing, *adj.* —per•plex/i•ty, *n., pl.* -ties.

per•qui•site (pûr'kwə zit), *n.* a payment, benefit, or privilege over and above regular income or salary.

Per•ry (per/ē), *n.* 1. **Matthew Calbraith,** 1794–1858, U.S. commodore. 2. his brother, **Oliver Hazard,** 1785–1819, U.S. naval officer.

Pers or Pers., 1. Persia. 2. Persian.

per se (pûr sā/, sē/, pər), *adv.* by, of, for, or in itself; intrinsically.

per•se•cute (pûr'si kyoōt/), *v.t.,* -cut•ed, -cut•ing. to subject to harassing or cruel treatment, as because of religion, race, or beliefs. —per'se•cu/tion, *n.* —per'se•cu/tor, *n.*

per•se•vere (pûr'sə vēr/), *v.i.,* -vered, -ver•ing. to persist in pursuing something in spite of obstacles or opposition. —per'se•ver/ance, *n.*

Per•shing (pûr'shing, -zhing), *n.* **John Joseph** ("*Blackjack*"), 1860–1948, U.S. general in World War I.

Per•sia (pûr'zhə), *n.* 1. Also called **Persian Em/pire.** an ancient empire located in W and SW Asia. 2. former official name (until 1935) of Iran.

Per'sian, *adj.* 1. of ancient, medieval, or modern Persia, its people, or their language. —*n.* 2. a native or inhabitant of Persia. 3. the Iranian language of Iran and much of Afghanistan.

Per'sian cat', *n.* a long-haired variety of domestic cat.

Per'sian Gulf', *n.* an arm of the Arabian Sea, between SW Iran and Arabia.

Per'sian lamb', *n.* 1. the lamb of the Karakul sheep. 2. its tightly curled fur.

per•si•flage (pûr'sə fläzh/, pâr/-), *n.* light, bantering talk.

per•sim•mon (pər sim/ən), *n.* 1. any of several trees bearing a plumlike, orange, edible fruit. 2. the fruit itself.

per•sist (pər sist/, -zist/), *v.i.* 1. to continue steadily in some purpose or course of action in spite of opposition. 2. to endure tenaciously: *The legend of King Arthur still persists.* 3. to be insistent in a request, question, etc. —per•sist/ence, *n.* —per•sist/ent, *adj.*

per•snick•et•y (pər snik/i tē), *adj. Informal.* 1. excessively particular; fussy. 2. requiring painstaking care.

per•son (pûr'sən), *n.* 1. a human being. 2. the individual personality of a human being. 3. the body of a living human being. 4. a human being or other entity, as a corporation, recognized by law as having rights and duties. 5. a grammatical category applied esp. to pronouns and verbs, used to distinguish between the speaker, the person addressed, and the people or things spoken about. —*Idiom.* 6. in person, in one's own bodily presence.

-person, a combining form of PERSON, replacing such paired, sex-specific forms as -MAN and -WOMAN: *salesperson.* —**Usage.** The -PERSON compounds are used, esp. by the media and in government and business, to avoid specifying an individual's sex. A number of alternatives have won acceptance, as *anchor* and *chair;* other coinages, as *congressmember,* have had only marginal use.

per'son•a•ble, *adj.* having an agreeable personality.

per'son•age (-nij), *n.* a person of distinction or importance.

per'son•al (-nl), *adj.* 1. of or concerning a particular person: *a personal opinion.* 2. referring to a particular person, esp. in an offensive manner: *personal remarks.* 3. done, carried out, etc., in person. 4. of the body, clothing, or appearance. 5. of or indicating grammatical person. 6. *Law.* pertaining to property consisting of movable articles. —*n.* 7. a. a brief, private message to a particular person, placed in a newspaper or magazine. b. a notice placed by a person seeking companionship, marriage, etc.

per'sonal comput/er, *n.* a microcomputer designed for individual use, as for word processing.

per'sonal effects/, *n.pl.* privately owned articles consisting chiefly of items for intimate use, as clothing.

per'son•al/i•ty, *n., pl.* -ties. 1. the visible aspect of one's character as it impresses others. 2. the sum total of the distinctive characteristics of an individual. 3. pleasingly distinctive qualities in a person. 4. a prominent person.

per'son•al•ize/, *v.t.,* -ized, -iz•ing. 1. to have marked with one's initials or name. 2. to make personal.

per'son•al•ly, *adv.* 1. in person. 2. as if directed at oneself: *Don't take this personally.* 3. as regards oneself: *Personally, I don't care.* 4. as a person: *I like her personally.*

per'sonal train/er, *n.* a person who works one-on-one with a client to plan or implement an exercise or fitness regimen.

per'son•al•ty (-te), *n., pl.* -ties. personal estate or property.

per'sonal wa/tercraft, *n.* a jet-propelled boat or boats ridden like a motorcycle.

per•so•na non gra•ta (pər sō/nə non grä/tə), *adj.* not being personally acceptable or welcome.

per•son•i•fy (pər son/ə fī/), *v.t.,* -fied, -fy•ing. 1. to attribute a human character to (an idea or thing). 2. to be an embodiment of; typify. —per•son/i•fi•ca/tion, *n.*

per·son·nel (pûr′sə nel′), *n.* **1.** the body of persons employed in an organization. **2.** an organizational department supervising matters of personnel.

per·spec·tive (pər spek′tiv), *n.* **1.** a technique of depicting spatial relationships on a flat surface. **2.** the manner in which objects appear to the eye in respect to their relative positions and distance. **3.** the ability to see all the relevant data in a meaningful relationship. **4.** a mental view or prospect.

per·spi·ca·cious (pûr′spi kā′shəs), *adj.* having keen mental perception and understanding. —**per′·spi·ca′cious·ly**, *adv.* —**per′spi·cac′i·ty** (-kas′i tē), *n.*

per·spic·u·ous (pər spik′yōō əs), *adj.* clearly expressed; lucid. —**per·spi·cu·i·ty** (pûr′spi kyōō′i tē), *n.*

per·spire (pər spīʳr′), *v.i.* **-spired, -spir·ing.** to secrete a salty, watery fluid from the sweat glands; sweat. —**per·spi·ra·tion** (pûr′spə rā′shən), *n.*

per·suade (pər swād′), *v.t.* **-suad·ed, -suad·ing.** **1.** to prevail on (a person) to do something, as by advising or urging. **2.** to induce to believe; convince. —**per·suad′er**, *n.*

per·sua·sion (-zhən), *n.* **1.** the act of persuading or state of being persuaded. **2.** power to persuade. **3.** a deep conviction. **4.** a system of religious belief.

per·sua·sive (-siv, -ziv), *adj.* able to persuade. —**per·sua′sive·ly**, *adv.*

pert (pûrt), *adj.* **-er, -est. 1.** impertinent; saucy. **2.** jaunty and stylish. **3.** lively; sprightly. —**pert′ly**, *adv.* —**pert′ness**, *n.*

per·tain (pər tān′), *v.i.* **1.** to have reference or relation. **2.** to belong or be connected as a part, attribute, etc. **3.** to be appropriate.

per·ti·na·cious (pûr′tn ā′shəs), *adj.* **1.** holding tenaciously to a purpose, opinion, etc. **2.** stubbornly persistent. —**per′ti·na′cious·ly**, *adv.* —**per′ti·nac′·i·ty** (-tn as′i tē), *n.*

per′ti·nent (-tn ənt), *adj.* pertaining directly to the matter at hand; relevant. —**per′ti·nence**, *n.*

per·turb (pər tûrb′), *v.t.* to disturb or disquiet greatly in mind; agitate. —**per·turb′a·ble**, *adj.* —**per·tur·ba·tion** (pûr′tər bā′shən), *n.*

Pe·ru (pə rōō′), *n.* a republic in W South America. 24,949,512. —**Pe·ru′vi·an** (-vē ən), *adj., n.*

pe·ruke (pə rōōk′), *n.* a man's wig of the 17th and 18th centuries.

pe·ruse (pə rōōz′), *v.t.* **-rused, -rus·ing. 1.** to read through thoroughly or carefully. **2.** to read in an often desultory way. —**pe·rus′al**, *n.*

per·vade (pər vād′), *v.t.* **-vad·ed, -vad·ing.** to become spread throughout all parts of. —**per·va′sive** (-siv), *adj.*

per·verse (pər vûrs′), *adj.* **1.** willfully determined not to do what is expected or desired. **2.** wayward or cantankerous. **3.** turned away from what is right, good, or proper. —**per·verse′ly**, *adv.* —**per·verse′·ness**, *n.* —**per·ver′si·ty**, *n., pl.* **-ties.**

per·ver′sion (-zhən, -shən), *n.* the act of perverting or state of being perverted.

per·vert (pər vûrt′), *v.t.* **1.** to lead astray morally. **2.** to turn to an improper use. **3.** to misinterpret, esp. deliberately; distort. **4.** to debase. —**per·vert′ed**, *adj.*

pe·se·ta (pə sā′tə), *n., pl.* **-tas.** the basic monetary unit of Spain.

pes·ky (pes′kē), *adj.* **-ki·er, -ki·est.** annoying; troublesome. —**pesk′i·ly**, *adv.* —**pesk′i·ness**, *n.*

pe·so (pā′sō), *n., pl.* **-sos.** the basic monetary unit of Argentina, Chile, Colombia, Cuba, the Dominican Republic, Guinea-Bissau, Mexico, the Philippines, and Uruguay.

pes·si·mism (pes′ə miz′əm), *n.* **1.** the tendency to see only what is gloomy or to anticipate the worst. **2.** the belief that the evil in the world outweighs any goodness. —**pes′si·mist**, *n.* —**pes′si·mis′tic**, *adj.* —**pes′si·mis′ti·cal·ly**, *adv.*

pest (pest), *n.* a troublesome or destructive person, animal, or thing.

pes·ter (pes′tər), *v.t.* to bother persistently with petty annoyances.

pes·ti·cide (pes′tə sīd′), *n.* a chemical for destroying plant, fungal, or animal pests.

pes·tif·er·ous (pe stif′ər əs), *adj.* **1.** bearing disease. **2.** pernicious; dangerous. **3.** troublesome; annoying.

pes·ti·lence (pes′tl əns), *n.* **1.** a deadly epidemic disease. **2.** something regarded as harmful.

pes′ti·lent also **pes′ti·len′tial** (-len′shəl), *adj.* **1.** producing or tending to produce an epidemic disease. **2.** destructive to life. **3.** injurious to peace, morals, etc. **4.** troublesome or annoying.

pes·tle (pes′əl, pes′tl), *n.* a tool for pounding or grinding substances in a mortar.

pes·to (pes′tō), *n., pl.* **-tos.** a pasta sauce of basil ground together with pine nuts, garlic, olive oil, and cheese.

pet (pet), *n., adj., v.*, **pet·ted, pet·ting.** —*n.* **1.** any domesticated animal kept as a companion. **2.** a person or thing especially cherished. —*adj.* **3.** kept or treated as a pet. **4.** favorite; preferred: *a pet theory.* **5.** showing affection: *pet names.* —*v.t.* **6.** to treat as a pet. **7.** to fondle or caress: *I like to pet the cat and listen to her purr.* —*v.i.* **8.** to engage in amorous caressing.

pet·al (pet′l), *n.* one of the segments of the corolla of a flower.

pe·tard (pi tärd′), *n.* **1.** an explosive device formerly used to blow in a door, gate, etc. —*Idiom.* **2. hoist by** or **with one's own petard,** caught by the very device one had contrived to hurt another.

pe·ter (pē′tər), *v.i.* **1.** to tire; become exhausted (usu. fol. by *out*). **2. peter out,** to diminish gradually and stop.

Pe·ter (pē′tər), *n.* **1.** Also called **Simon Peter.** died A.D. 67?, one of the 12 apostles and the reputed author of two of the Epistles. **2.** either of these two Epistles in the New Testament, I Peter or II Peter.

Peter I, *n.* (*"Peter the Great"*), 1672–1725, czar of Russia 1682–1725.

pet·i·ole (pet′ē ōl′), *n.* the slender stalk by which a leaf is attached to the stem.

pe·tite (pə tēt′), *adj.* (of a woman) short and having a trim figure.

pet·it four (pet′ē fôr′), *n., pl.* **pet·its fours** (pet′ē fôrz′). a small frosted teacake.

pe·ti·tion (pə tish′ən), *n.* **1.** a formal request signed by those endorsing it and addressed to a person or persons in authority. **2.** a respectful or humble request. **3.** something that is sought by request or entreaty. —*v.t.* **4.** to address a petition to (a sovereign, legislature, etc.). **5.** to ask by petition for (something). —*v.i.* **6.** to present a petition. —**pe·ti′·tion·er**, *n.*

pet′it ju′ry (pet′ē), *n.* PETTY JURY.

pet·rel (pe′trəl), *n.* any of various oceanic tube-nosed seabirds.

pet·ri·fy (pe′trə fī′), *v.t.* **-fied, -fy·ing. 1.** to convert into stone or a stony substance. **2.** to benumb with strong emotion, as fear. **3.** to harden; deaden. —**pet′ri·fac′tion** (-fak′shən), *n.*

petro-¹, a combining form meaning rock or stone (*petrology*).

petro-², a combining form meaning petroleum (*petrodollars*).

pet·ro·chem·i·cal (pe′trō kem′i kəl), *n.* a chemical substance obtained from petroleum or natural gas, as gasoline.

pet′ro·dol′lars, *n.pl.* revenues in dollars that are accumulated by petroleum-exporting countries.

pet·rol (pe′trəl), *n. Brit.* GASOLINE.

pet·ro·la·tum (pe′trə lā′təm, -lä′-), *n.* a gelatinous mass obtained from petroleum, used as a lubricant, protective dressing, etc.

pe·tro·le·um (pə trō′lē əm), *n.* an oily naturally occurring liquid that is a form of bitumen or a mixture of various hydrocarbons: used as fuel or separated by distillation into gasoline, paraffin, etc.

petro′leum jel′ly, *n.* PETROLATUM.

pe·trol·o·gy (pi trol′ə jē), *n.* the scientific study of rocks. —**pe·trol′o·gist**, *n.*

PET scan, *n.* an examination performed with a device that produces computerized cross-sectional images of biochemical activity in the brain, using radioactive tracers. [*p(ositron) e(mission) t(omography)*]

pet•ti•coat (pet′ē kōt′), *n.* an underskirt, often trimmed and ruffled.

pet•ti•fog (pet′ē fog′, -fôg′), *v.i.,* **-fogged, -fog•ging. 1.** to quibble over trifles. **2.** to carry on an unethical law business. —**pet′ti•fog′ger,** *n.*

pet•tish (pet′ish), *adj.* petulant; peevish.

pet•ty (pet′ē), *adj.,* **-ti•er, -ti•est. 1.** of little or no importance. **2.** of lesser importance or merit; minor. **3.** having or showing narrow ideas, interests, etc. **4.** showing meanness of spirit. —**pet′ti•ness,** *n.*

pet′ty cash′, *n.* a cash fund for paying minor expenses, as in an office.

pet′ty ju′ry, *n.* a jury, usu. of 12 persons, impaneled to render a verdict in a civil or criminal proceeding.

pet′ty of′fi•cer, *n.* a noncommissioned officer in the navy or coast guard.

pet•u•lant (pech′ə lənt), *adj.* showing sudden irritation, esp. over some trifling annoyance. —**pet′u•lance,** *n.* —**pet′u•lant•ly,** *adv.*

pe•tu•nia (pi tōō′nyə, -nē ə, -tyōō′-), *n., pl.* **-nias.** a garden plant with funnel-shaped flowers of various colors.

pew (pyōō), *n.* one of a number of fixed benches with backs in a church.

pe•wee (pē′wē), *n., pl.* **-wees.** any of several New World flycatchers.

pew•ter (pyōō′tər), *n.* **1.** any of various alloys in which tin is the chief constituent. **2.** articles made of pewter.

pe•yo•te (pā ō′tē), *n., pl.* **-tes. 1.** MESCAL (def. 2). **2.** MESCALINE.

pf., (of stock) preferred.

Pfc. or **PFC,** private first class.

PG, parental guidance: a motion-picture rating indicating that some material may be unsuitable for children.

PG-13 (pē′jē′thûr′tēn′), a motion-picture rating indicating that some material may be unsuitable for children under 13.

pg., page.

pH, the symbol used to describe the acidity or alkalinity of a chemical solution on a scale of 0 (more acidic) to 14 (more alkaline).

pha•e•ton (fā′i tn), *n.* **1.** a light, four-wheeled carriage used in the 19th century. **2.** an early type of open automobile.

phag•o•cyte (fag′ə sīt′), *n.* any cell that ingests foreign particles, bacteria, or cell debris.

pha•lan•ger (fə lan′jər), *n.* a tree-dwelling Australian marsupial, including mouselike, squirrellike, and lemurlike forms.

pha•lanx (fā′langks, fal′angks), *n., pl.* **pha•lanx•es** for 1, 2, **pha•lan•ges** (fə lan′jēz) for 3. **1.** (in ancient Greece) a group of heavily armed infantry formed in close ranks and files. **2.** a compact body of persons, animals, or things. **3.** a bone of a finger or toe.

phal•lus (fal′əs), *n., pl.* **phal•li** (fal′ī), **phal•lus•es. 1.** a representation of the penis as a symbol of male generative powers. **2.** PENIS. —**phal′lic,** *adj.*

phan•tasm (fan′taz əm), *n.* **1.** a creation of the imagination; fantasy. **2.** an illusory likeness of something.

phan•tas′ma•go′ri•a (-mə gôr′ē ə), *n., pl.* **-ri•as.** a shifting series of phantasms or deceptive appearances, as in a dream.

phan′ta•sy (-tə sē, -zē), *n., pl.* **-sies.** FANTASY.

phan′tom (-təm), *n.* **1.** an apparition or specter. **2.** an illusion without material substance. —*adj.* **3.** illusory. **4.** nonexistent; fictitious.

Phar•aoh (fâr′ō, far′ō), *n.* a title of an ancient Egyptian king.

Phar•i•see (far′ə sē′), *n., pl.* **-sees. 1.** a member of an ancient Jewish sect that emphasized liberal interpretation of the Bible and strict adherence to oral

laws and traditions. **2.** (*l.c.*) a self-righteous or hypocritical person. —**Phar′i•sa′ic** (-sā′ik), **Phar′i•sa′i•cal,** *adj.*

phar•ma•ceu•ti•cal (fär′mə sōō′ti kəl), *adj.* **1.** of pharmacy or pharmacists. —*n.* **2.** a pharmaceutical preparation.

phar′ma•ceu′tics, *n.* PHARMACY (def. 2).

phar′ma•cist (-sist), *n.* a person licensed to prepare and dispense drugs and medicines.

phar′ma•col′o•gy (-kol′ə jē), *n.* the science dealing with the preparation, uses, and effects of drugs. —**phar′ma•col′o•gist,** *n.*

phar′ma•co•poe′ia (-kə pē′ə), *n., pl.* **-ias. 1.** a book containing a list of drugs, their formulas, and other related information. **2.** a stock of drugs.

phar′ma•cy (-sē), *n., pl.* **-cies. 1.** DRUGSTORE. **2.** the art and science of preparing and dispensing drugs and medicines.

phar•yn•gi•tis (far′in jī′tis), *n.* inflammation of the mucous membrane of the pharynx.

phar•ynx (far′ingks), *n., pl.* **pha•ryn•ges** (fə rin′jēz), **phar•ynx•es.** the portion of the alimentary canal that connects the mouth and nasal passages with the larynx. —**pha•ryn•ge•al** (fə rin′jē əl), *adj.*

phase (fāz), *n., v.,* **phased, phas•ing.** —*n.* **1.** any of the major aspects in which a thing of varying modes or conditions manifests itself. **2.** a stage in a process of change or development. **3.** a side, aspect, or point of view. **4.** the particular appearance presented by the moon or a planet at a given time. —*v.* **5. phase in,** to put into use gradually. **6. ~ out,** to bring to an end gradually.

phase′out′, *n.* a phasing out; planned discontinuation or expiration.

phat (fat), *adj. Slang.* great; wonderful.

Ph.D., Doctor of Philosophy. [< NL *Philosophiae Doctor*]

pheas•ant (fez′ənt), *n.* any of numerous large, long-tailed game birds.

phe•nac•e•tin (fə nas′i tin), *n.* a white, crystalline solid formerly used to relieve pain and fever.

phe•no•bar•bi•tal (fē′nō bär′bi tôl′, tal′, -nə-), *n.* a white, crystalline powder used as a sedative and hypnotic.

phe•nol (fē′nôl, -nol), *n.* a white, crystalline, poisonous substance used as a disinfectant, as an antiseptic, and in organic synthesis.

phe•nom•e•non (fi nom′ə non′, -nən), *n., pl.* **-na** (-nə) or, esp. for 3, **-nons. 1.** a fact, occurrence, or circumstance observed or observable. **2.** something remarkable or extraordinary. **3.** a remarkable or exceptional person. —**phe•nom′e•nal,** *adj.*

phe•no•type (fē′nə tīp′), *n.* **1.** the observable constitution of an organism. **2.** the appearance of an organism resulting from the interaction of the genotype and the environment.

pher•o•mone (fer′ə mōn′), *n.* any chemical substance released by an animal that influences physiology or behavior of other members of the species.

phi (fī), *n., pl.* **phis.** the 21st letter of the Greek alphabet (Φ, φ).

phi•al (fī′əl), *n.* VIAL.

Phila., Philadelphia.

Phil•a•del•phi•a (fil′ə del′fē ə), *n.* **1.** a city in SE Pennsylvania, on the Delaware River. 1,524,249 **2.** a city of Lydia, the site of one of the seven churches of Asia. Rev. 1:11.

Philadel′phia law′yer, *n.* a lawyer skilled at exploiting legal fine points and technicalities.

phi•lan•der (fi lan′dər), *v.i.* (of a man) to make love with a woman one cannot or will not marry. —**phi•lan′der•er,** *n.*

phi•lan•thro•py (fi lan′thrə pē), *n , pl.* **-pies. 1.** altruistic concern for human beings manifested by donations to institutions advancing human welfare. **2.** a philanthropic act or donation. **3.** a philanthropic institution. —**phil•an•throp•ic** (fil′ən throp′ik), *adj.* —**phi•lan′thro•pist,** *n.*

phi•lat•e•ly (fi lat′l ē), *n.* the collection and study of postage stamps and related material. —**phil•a•tel• ic** (fil′ə tel′ik), *adj.* —**phil•lat′e•list,** *n.*

-phile, a combining form meaning one that loves or has a strong enthusiasm for (*bibliophile*).

Phi•le•mon (fi lē′mən, fī-), *n.* **1.** an Epistle written by Paul. **2.** a person who was probably a convert of Paul and to whom this Epistle is addressed.

Phi•le•tus (fi lē′təs), *n.* a false teacher of the early Christian church. II Tim. 2:17–18.

phil•har•mon•ic (fil′här mon′ik), *n.* (*often cap.*) a symphony orchestra.

Phil•ip (fil′ip), *n.* **1.** one of the 12 apostles. Mark 3:18; John 1:43–48, 6:5–7. **2.** Prince, Duke of Edin- burgh, born 1921, consort of Elizabeth II.

Phi•lip•pi (fi lip′ī, fil′ə pī′), *n.* a ruined city in NE Greece, in Macedonia.

Phi•lip•pi•ans (fi lip′ē ənz), *n.* an Epistle written by Paul to the Christians in Philippi.

phi•lip•pic (fi lip′ik), *n.* a bitter verbal denuncia- tion.

Phil•ip•pines (fil′ə pēnz′), *n.pl.* a republic compris- ing an archipelago of 7083 islands **(Phil′ippine Is′- lands)** in the Pacific, SE of China. 76,103,564. —**Phil′ip•pine′,** *adj.*

phil•is•tine (fil′ə stēn′, -stīn′, fi lis′tin, -tēn), *n.* **1.** (*sometimes cap.*) a person lacking in or smugly indif- ferent to culture, aesthetic refinement, etc. **2.** (*cap.*) a member of a people who controlled SW Palestine from c1200 to 604 B.C.

phil•o•den•dron (fil′ə den′drən), *n.,* *pl.* -**drons, -dra.** a tropical American climbing plant, grown as a houseplant.

phi•lol•o•gy (fi lol′ə jē), *n.* **1.** the study and analy- sis of literary works and other written records. **2.** (esp. in older use) linguistics, esp. historical and comparative linguistics. —**phil•o•log•i•cal** (fil′ə loj′i- kəl), *adj.* —**phi•lol′o•gist,** *n.*

phi•los•o•pher (fi los′ə fər), *n.* **1.** a student of or expert in philosophy. **2.** a person who regulates his or her life by the light of philosophy or reason. **3.** a person who is calm or rational under trying circum- stances.

phi•los′o•phize′ (-fīz′), *v.i.,* -**phized, -phiz•ing. 1.** to theorize in a superficial or imprecise manner. **2.** to reason as a philosopher.

phi•los′o•phy, *n.,* *pl.* -**phies. 1.** the rational inves- tigation of the truths and principles of being, knowl- edge, or conduct. **2.** a system of philosophical doc- trine. **3.** the study of the basic concepts of a particular branch of knowledge: *the philosophy of sci- ence.* **4.** a system of principles for guidance in practi- cal affairs: *a philosophy of life.* **5.** a calm or rational attitude. —**phil•o•soph•i•cal** (fil′ə sof′i kəl), **phil′o• soph′ic,** *adj.*

phil•ter (fil′tər), *n.* a potion or charm, esp. one sup- posed to cause a person to fall in love.

Phin•e•as (fin′ē əs), *n.* **1.** the third high priest of Is- rael. Ex. 6:25; Num. 25:13. **2.** a son of Eli who was killed in battle with the Philistines. I Sam. 1:3; 2:12– 17, 22–25.

phle•bi•tis (flə bī′tis), *n.* inflammation of a vein.

phlegm (flem), *n.* **1.** thick mucus secreted in the respiratory passages and discharged through the mouth, as during a cold. **2.** sluggishness or apathy.

phleg•mat•ic (fleg mat′ik), *adj.* having a calm or apathetic temperament.

phlo•em (flō′em), *n.* the complex vascular tissue through which dissolved food passes to all parts of a plant.

phlox (floks), *n.,* *pl.* **phlox, phlox•es.** a North American plant, certain species of which are culti- vated for their showy flowers.

Phnom Penh (nom′ pen′, pə nôm′), *n.* the capital of Cambodia. 500,000.

-phobe, a combining form meaning one who hates or fears (*Anglophobe*).

pho•bi•a (fō′bē ə), *n.,* *pl.* -**bi•as.** a persistent, irra- tional fear of a specific object, activity, or situation. —**pho′bic,** *adj., n.*

-phobia, a combining form meaning fear, dread, or aversion (*xenophobia*).

phoe•be (fē′bē), *n.,* *pl.* -**bes.** any of several New World flycatchers.

Phoe•ni•cia (fi nish′ə, -nē′shə), *n.* an ancient king- dom on the E Mediterranean. —**Phoe•ni′cian,** *n., adj.*

phoe•nix (fē′niks), *n.* a fabulous bird that after a life of five centuries burns itself to death and rises from the ashes.

Phoe′nix, *n.* the capital of Arizona. 1,048,949.

phone (fōn), *n., v.t., v.i.,* **phoned, phon•ing.** tele- phone.

phone′ card′, *n.* CALLING CARD (def. 2).

pho•neme (fō′nēm), *n.* any of the minimal units of speech sound in a language that can distinguish one word from another. —**pho•ne′mic** (fə-, fō-), *adj.*

phone′ tag′, *n.* TELEPHONE TAG.

pho•net•ics (fə net′iks, fō-), *n.* the study of speech sounds and their production, classification, and tran- scription. —**pho•net′ic,** *adj.* —**pho•ne•ti•cian** (fō′- ni tish′ən), *n.*

phon•ics (fon′iks), *n.* a method of teaching reading and spelling based upon the phonetic interpretation of ordinary spelling. —**phon′ic,** *adj.* —**phon′i• cal•ly,** *adv.*

phono-, a combining form meaning sound or voice (*phonology*).

pho•no•graph (fō′nə graf′, -gräf′), *n.* any sound- reproducing machine using records in the form of grooved disks. —**pho′no•graph′ic,** *adj.*

pho•nol•o•gy (fə nol′ə jē, fō-), *n.,* *pl.* -**gies. 1.** the system of speech sounds of a language. **2.** the study of sound changes in a language. —**pho•no•log•i•cal** (fōn′l oj′i kəl), *adj.* —**pho•nol′o•gist** (-jist), *n.*

pho•ny or -**ney** (fō′nē), *adj.,* -**ni•er, -ni•est,** *n., pl.* -**nies** or -**neys.** —*adj.* **1.** not real or genuine; fake. **2.** false or deceiving. —*n.* **3.** something that is phony. **4.** an insincere or affected person. —**pho′ni•ness,** *n.*

Pho′ny War′, *n.* the period of World War II be- tween the fall of Poland in 1939 and the German at- tack on Norway and Denmark in the spring of 1940.

phoo•ey (fōō′ē), *interj. Informal.* an exclamation of contempt or disgust.

phos•phate (fos′fāt), *n.* **1.** (loosely) a salt or ester of phosphoric acid. **2.** a fertilizer containing com- pounds of phosphorus. **3.** a carbonated drink of wa- ter and fruit syrup.

phos•phor (fos′fər, -fôr), *n.* a substance that exhib- its luminescence when struck by light of certain wavelengths.

phos′pho•res′cence (-fə res′əns), *n.* **1.** the prop- erty of being luminous at temperatures below incan- descence. **2.** any luminous radiation emitted from a substance after the removal of the exciting agent. —**phos′pho•res′cent,** *adj.*

phos•phor′ic ac′id, (fos fôr′ik, -for′-), *n.* any of three acids containing phosphorus and oxygen.

phos′pho•rus (-fər əs), *n., pl.* -**pho•ri** (-fə rī′). a nonmetallic element used, in combined form, in matches and fertilizers. *Symbol:* P; *at. wt.:* 30.974; *at. no.:* 15.

photo-, a combining form meaning: light (*photo- graph*); photograph or photographic (*photoengrav- ing*).

pho•to•ag•ing (fō′tō ā′jing), *n.* damage to the skin, as wrinkles, caused by prolonged exposure to sunlight.

pho•to•cop•y (fō′tə kop′ē), *n., pl.* -**ies,** *v.,* -**ied, -y•ing.** —*n.* **1.** a photographic reproduction of a doc- ument or the like. —*v.t.* **2.** to make a photocopy of. —**pho′to•cop′i•er,** *n.*

pho•to•e•lec•tric (fō′tō i lek′trik), *adj.* pertaining to electronic effects produced by light.

pho′toelec′tric cell′, *n.* an electronic device that converts light into electrical energy or uses light to regulate the flow of current.

pho′to•en•grav′ing, *n.* a photographic process of preparing printing plates for letterpress printing. —**pho′to•en•grave′,** *v.t.,* -**graved, -grav•ing.** —**pho′to•en•grav′er,** *n.*

pho′to fin′ish, *n.* a finish of a race so close as to

require scrutiny of a photograph to determine the winner.

pho•to•gen•ic (fō′tə jen′ik), *adj.* forming an appealing subject for photography or looking attractive in a photograph.

pho′to•graph′, *n.* **1.** a picture produced by photography. —*v.t.* **2.** to take a photograph of. —*v.i.* **3.** to be photographed.

pho•tog•ra•phy (fə tog′rə fē), *n.* the process or art of producing images of objects on sensitized surfaces by the chemical action of light. —**pho•tog′ra•pher,** *n.* —**pho•to•graph•ic** (fō′tə graf′ik), *adj.* —**pho′to•graph′i•cal•ly,** *adv.*

pho•to•jour•nal•ism (fō′tō jûr′nl iz′əm), *n.* journalism in which the story is told largely in captioned photographs. —**pho′to•jour′nal•ist,** *n.*

pho•ton (fō′ton), *n.* a quantum of electromagnetic radiation. —**pho•ton′ic,** *adj.*

pho′to-off′set, *n.* a method of printing in which the inked image is transferred from the metal plate to a rubber surface and then to the paper.

pho•to•sen•si•tive (fō′tō sen′si tiv), *adj.* sensitive to light or similar radiation.

Pho•to•stat (fō′tə stat′), *n.*, *v.*, **-stat•ed** or **-stat•ted,** **-stat•ing** or **-stat•ting.** **1.** *Trademark.* a camera for making facsimile copies of documents, drawings, etc., in the form of paper negatives. —*n.* **2.** (*often l.c.*) a copy so made. —*v.t.* **3.** (*l.c.*) to copy with this camera.

pho′to•syn′the•sis, *n.* the production of carbohydrates from carbon dioxide and water, using sunlight as the source of energy and with the aid of chlorophyll. —**pho′to•syn′the•size′,** *v.i.*, *v.t.*, **-sized, -siz•ing.** —**pho′to•syn•thet′ic,** *adj.*

phrase (frāz), *n.*, *v.*, **phrased, phras•ing.** —*n.* **1.** a sequence of two or more grammatically related words that does not contain a subject and predicate. **2.** a brief utterance or remark. **3.** a division of a musical composition, commonly a passage of four or eight measures. —*v.t.* **4.** to express in a particular way. **5.** to express in words. —**phras′al,** *adj.*

phra•se•ol•o•gy (frā′zē ol′ə jē), *n.* style of verbal expression; characteristic language.

phre•nol•o•gy (fri nol′ə jē, fre-), *n.* a system of character analysis based upon the configurations of the skull.

Phryg•i•a (frij′ē ə), *n.* an ancient country in central and NW Asia Minor.

phy•lac•ter•y (fi lak′tə rē), *n.*, *pl.* **-ter•ies.** either of two leather cubes containing parchment inscribed with Biblical verses: worn by Jewish men during morning prayers, one strapped to the left arm, the other to the head above the hairline.

phylactery

phy•log•e•ny (fī loj′ə nē), *n.* the development or evolution of a particular group of organisms. —**phy•log′e•nist,** *n.*

phy•lum (fī′ləm), *n.*, *pl.* **-la** (-lə). the primary subdivision of a taxonomic kingdom, grouping together all classes of organisms that have the same body plan.

phys•ic (fiz′ik), *n.* a medicine that purges.

phys′i•cal, *adj.* **1.** of the body. **2.** of that which is material: *the physical universe.* **3.** of or noting the properties of matter and energy other than those peculiar to living matter. —*n.* **4.** an examination of

one's body by a physician to determine one's state of health. —**phys′i•cal•ly,** *adv.*

phys′ical anthropol′ogy, *n.* the branch of anthropology dealing with the evolutionary changes in human body structure and the classification of modern races.

phys′ical educa′tion, *n.* instruction in sports, exercise, and hygiene, esp. as part of a school program.

phys′ical sci′ence, *n.* any of the natural sciences dealing with inanimate matter or energy, as physics or chemistry.

phys′ical ther′apy, *n.* the treatment of physical disability or pain by physical techniques, as exercise or massage. —**phys′ical ther′apist,** *n.*

phy•si•cian (fi zish′ən), *n.* **1.** a doctor of medicine. —*Proverb.* **2.** Physician, heal thyself, one should look after one's own problems first. Luke 4:23.

phys•ics (fiz′iks), *n.* the science that deals with matter, energy, motion, and force. —**phys′i•cist** (-ə sist), *n.*

phys•i•og•no•my (fiz′ē og′nə mē, -on′ə-), *n.*, *pl.* **-mies.** the face, esp. when considered as an index to character.

phys′i•og′ra•phy (-og′rə fē), *n.* the branch of geography concerned with natural features and phenomena of the earth's surface.

phys′i•ol′o•gy (-ol′ə jē), *n.* the branch of biology dealing with the functions and activities of living organisms and their parts. —**phys′i•o•log′i•cal** (-ə loj′i kəl), *adj.* —**phys′i•ol′o•gist,** *n.*

phys′i•o•ther′a•py (fiz′ē ō-), *n.* PHYSICAL THERAPY. —**phys′i•o•ther′a•pist,** *n.*

phy•sique (fi zēk′), *n.* bodily structure and appearance.

pi¹ (pī), *n.*, *pl.* **pis. 1.** the 16th letter of the Greek alphabet (Π, π). **2. a.** the letter π, used as the symbol for the ratio of the circumference of a circle to its diameter. **b.** the ratio itself: 3.14159 +.

pi² (pī), *n.*, *pl.* **pies.** printing type mixed together indiscriminately.

pi•a•nis•si•mo (pē′ə nis′ə mō′, pyä-), *Music.* —*adj.* **1.** very soft. —*adv.* **2.** very softly.

pi•an•ist (pē an′ist, pyan′-, pē′ə nist), *n.* a person who plays the piano.

pi•an•o¹ (pē an′ō, pyan′ō), *n.*, *pl.* **-an•os.** a musical instrument in which felt-covered hammers, operated from a keyboard, strike metal strings.

pi•an•o² (pē ä′nō, pyä′-), *Music.* —*adj.* **1.** soft. —*adv.* **2.** softly.

pi•an•o•forte (pē an′ə fôrt′, pē an′ə fôr′tē), *n.* PIANO¹.

pi•as•ter or **-tre** (pē as′tər, -ä′stər), *n.* a monetary unit of Egypt, Lebanon, Sudan, and Syria, equal to ¹/₁₀₀ of a pound.

pi•az•za (pē az′ə, or, for 1, -ät′sə), *n.*, *pl.* **-zas. 1.** an open public square, esp. in Italy. **2.** *Chiefly New Eng. and Southern U.S.* a large porch.

pi•broch (pē′brокн), *n.* a series of martial or dirgelike variations for the bagpipe.

pic•a•resque (pik′ə resk′), *adj.* of or noting a form of prose fiction that humorously describes the adventures of a roguish hero.

Pi•cas•so (pi kä′sō, -kas′ō), *n.* **Pablo,** 1881–1973, Spanish painter and sculptor in France.

pic•a•yune (pik′ē yōōn′, pik′ə-), *adj.* **1.** of little value or account. **2.** petty, carping, or prejudiced.

pic•ca•lil•li (pik′ə lil′ē), *n.*, *pl.* **-lis.** a relish of chopped vegetables, mustard, vinegar, and hot spices.

pic•co•lo (pik′ə lō′), *n.*, *pl.* **-los.** a small flute sounding an octave higher than the ordinary flute. [< *It:* small]

pick¹ (pik), *v.t.* **1.** to choose or select. **2.** to provoke: *to pick a fight.* **3.** to steal the contents of: *to pick a pocket.* **4.** to open (a lock) with a device other than the key. **5.** to pierce, dig into, or break up with a pointed instrument. **6.** to use a pointed instrument or the fingers on to remove adhering matter: *to pick one's teeth.* **7.** to prepare by removing feathers: *to pick a fowl.* **8.** to detach piece by piece with the fingers: *to pick meat from the bones.* **9.** to pluck one by one: *to pick flowers.* **10.** to separate or pull to pieces: *to pick fibers.* **11.** to pluck (the strings of a musical instrument). —*v.i.* **12.** to use a pointed instrument on something. **13.** to select carefully or fastidiously. **14. pick at,** to eat sparingly. **15. ~ off, a.** to remove by plucking off. **b.** to single out and shoot. **16. ~ on,** to criticize, tease, or harass. **17. ~ out,** to select. **18. ~ up, a.** to lift or take up. **b.** to obtain or learn casually. **c.** to take on as a passenger. **d.** to accelerate. **e.** to improve. **f.** to become acquainted with casually, often in hope of a sexual relationship. —*n.* **19.** the act of choosing. **20.** a person or thing selected. **21.** the choicest part or example. —**pick′er,** *n.*

pick² (pik), *n.* **1.** a heavy tool with a curved metal head pointed at one or both ends, mounted on a handle, and used for breaking up soil, rock, etc. **2.** any of various other pointed tools for picking: *an ice pick.* **3.** PLECTRUM.

pick•ax or **-axe** (pik′aks′), *n., pl.* **-ax•es.** PICK² (def. 1).

pick•er•el (pik′ər əl), *n., pl.* **-els, -el.** any of several small pikes.

pick•et (pik′it), *n.* **1.** a stake driven into the ground for use in a fence or to fasten down a tent. **2.** a person stationed by a striking union outside a factory, store, etc., to dissuade workers or customers from entering. **3.** a person engaged in any similar demonstration. **4.** a soldier or soldiers posted to warn against an enemy advance. —*v.t.* **5.** to enclose within a picket fence. **6.** to tether to a picket. **7.** to place pickets at (a factory, embassy, etc.) **8.** to guard with pickets. —*v.i.* **9.** to stand or march as a picket. —**pick′et•er,** *n.*

pick′et line′, *n.* a line of strikers or other pickets.

pick•le (pik′əl), *n., v.,* **-led, -ling.** —*n.* **1.** a vegetable, esp. a cucumber, that has been preserved and flavored in brine, vinegar, or the like. **2.** a brine or marinade. **3.** a troublesome situation; predicament. —*v.t.* **4.** to preserve or steep in brine or other liquid.

pick′pock′et, *n.* a person who steals from people's pockets, purses, etc., as in a crowd.

pick′up′, *n.* **1.** an improvement, as in health or business. **2.** acceleration, or the capacity for acceleration. **3.** a small truck with a low-sided open body. **4.** a device in a phonograph that translates the movement of the stylus into a changing electrical voltage.

pick′y, *adj.,* **-i•er, -i•est.** extremely fussy or finicky.

pic•nic (pik′nik), *n., v.,* **-nicked, -nick•ing.** —*n.* **1.** an excursion in which the participants eat a meal in the open air. —*v.i.* **2.** to go on a picnic. —**pic′nick•er,** *n.*

pi•cot (pē′kō), *n.* one of a number of small decorative loops along the edge of lace, ribbon, etc.

pic•to•graph (pik′tə graf′, -gräf′), *n.* **1.** a single pictorial symbol, as in a system of picture writing. **2.** a graph or chart consisting of pictorial symbols.

pic•to•ri•al (pik tôr′ē əl), *adj.* **1.** of or expressed in pictures. **2.** having the visual appeal or imagery of a picture. —**pic•to′ri•al•ly,** *adv.*

pic•ture (pik′chər), *n., v.,* **-tured, -tur•ing.** —*n.* **1.** a visual representation of a person, object, or scene, as a painting or photograph. **2.** a graphic or vivid description. **3.** MOTION PICTURE (def. 2). **4.** the perfect likeness of someone else: *She is the picture of her father.* **5.** a concrete embodiment of some quality or condition: *the picture of health.* **6.** a situation or set of circumstances: *the economic picture.* **7.** the image on a television or motion-picture screen. —*v.t.* **8.** to represent pictorially. **9.** to form a mental picture of. **10.** to describe graphically.

pic′tur•esque′ (-chə resk′), *adj.* visually charming, as if resembling a painting.

pic′ture tube′, *n.* a cathode-ray tube with a screen at one end on which televised images are reproduced.

pic′ture win′dow, *n.* a large, usu. single-paned window.

pid•dle (pid′l), *v.i.,* **-dled, -dling.** to waste time; dawdle.

pid′dling, *adj.* trifling; negligible.

pidg•in (pij′ən), *n.* an auxiliary language that has developed from the need of speakers of two different

languages to communicate and is primarily a simplified form of one of the languages.

pie¹ (pī), *n.* **1.** a pastry crust filled with fruit, meat, etc., and baked, often with a top crust. —*Idiom.* **2. easy as pie,** extremely easy.

pie² (pī), *n.* PI².

pie•bald (pī′bôld′), *adj.* **1.** having patches of two colors. —*n.* **2.** a piebald animal.

piece (pēs), *n., v.,* **pieced, piec•ing.** —*n.* **1.** a quantity of some material forming a separate entity. **2.** a portion or quantity of a whole: *a piece of pie.* **3.** an artistic work, as a painting or musical composition. **4.** an example, specimen, or instance of something. —*v.t.* **5.** to mend by adding a piece or pieces. **6.** to make by or as if by joining pieces. —*Idiom.* **7. go to pieces, a.** to break into fragments. **b.** to lose control of oneself.

pièce de ré•sis•tance (pyes də RĀ zē stäns′), *n., pl.* **pièces de ré•sis•tance** (pyes də RĀ zē stäns′), *French.* **1.** the principal dish of a meal. **2.** the principal item of a series.

piece′ goods′, *n.pl.* goods, esp. fabrics, sold at retail by linear measure.

piece′meal′, *adv.* **1.** one piece at a time. —*adj.* **2.** done piecemeal.

piece′work′, *n.* work done and paid for by the piece.

pie′ chart′, *n.* a data display in which sectors of a circle correspond in area to the relative size of the quantities represented.

pied (pīd), *adj.* having patches of two or more colors.

pied-à-terre (pyä′də târ′, -dä-), *n., pl.* **pieds-à-terre** (pyä′də târ′, -dä-). an apartment for part-time use. [< F: lit., foot on ground]

pier (pēr), *n.* **1.** a structure built on posts over water, used as a landing place for ships, an entertainment area, etc. **2.** (in a bridge or the like) a support for the ends of adjacent spans. **3.** a pillar or post on which a gate or door is hung. **4.** a support of masonry or steel for sustaining vertical pressure.

pierce (pērs), *v.,* **pierced, pierc•ing.** —*v.t.* **1.** to penetrate (something), as a pointed object does. **2.** to make a hole in. **3.** to force a way into or through. **4.** to penetrate with the eye or mind. **5.** to sound sharply through (the air, stillness, etc.), as a cry. —*v.i.* **6.** to force a way into or through something.

Pierce (pērs), *n.* **Franklin,** 1804–69, 14th president of the U.S. 1853–57.

Pierre (pēr), *n.* the capital of South Dakota. 11,973.

pi•e•ty (pī′i tē), *n., pl.* **-ties. 1.** reverence for God or devout fulfillment of religious obligations. **2.** dutiful respect for parents, homeland, etc. **3.** a pious act, belief, etc.

pif•fle (pif′əl), *n. Informal.* nonsense, as idle talk. —**pif′fling,** *adj.*

pig (pig), *n., v.,* **pigged, pig•ging.** —*n.* **1.** any swine, esp. a young domesticated hog weighing less than 120 lb. (54 kg). **2.** a person who is gluttonous or slovenly. **3.** an oblong mass of metal run while still molten into a mold. —*v.* **4. pig out,** *Slang.* to overindulge in eating. —*Saying.* **5. pig in a poke,** something of undetermined value, as an offering or purchase.

pi•geon (pij′ən), *n.* **1.** any of numerous birds having a plump body and small head. **2.** *Slang.* a person who is easily fooled or cheated.

pi′geon•hole′, *n., v.,* **-holed, -hol•ing.** —*n.* **1.** one of a series of small, open compartments, as in a desk, for filing papers, letters, etc. —*v.t.* **2.** to assign to a definite place in an orderly system. **3.** to put aside for the present. **4.** to place in a pigeonhole.

pi′geon-toed′, *adj.* having the toes or feet turned inward.

pig•gish (pig′ish), *adj.* gluttonous or slovenly. —**pig′gish•ness,** *n.*

pig′gy, *n., pl.* **-gies,** *adj.,* **-gi•er, -gi•est.** —*n.* **1.** a small pig. —*adj.* **2.** PIGGISH.

pig′gy•back′, *adv.* **1.** on the back or shoulders. —*adj.* **2.** astride the back or shoulders. **3.** attached to or allied with something else: *a piggyback clause.* **4.**

noting or pertaining to the carrying of truck trailers on flatcars.

pig′head′ed, *adj.* stupidly obstinate.

pig′ i′ron, *n.* iron cast into pigs for conversion into steel, cast iron, etc.

pig•ment (pig′mənt), *n.* **1.** a coloring matter or substance. **2.** a biological substance that produces color in the tissues of organisms.

pig′men•ta′tion, *n.* coloration with or deposition of pigment.

pig′pen′, *n.* **1.** a pen for keeping pigs. **2.** a filthy or flagrantly untidy place.

pig′skin′, *n.* **1.** leather made from the skin of a pig. **2.** FOOTBALL (def. 2).

pig′sty′, *n., pl.* **-sties.** PIGPEN.

pig′tail′, *n.* a braid of hair hanging down the back of the head.

pike[1] (pīk), *n., pl.* **pikes, pike.** a large, slender, freshwater fish with a long, flat snout.

pike[2] (pīk), *n.* a shafted weapon with a pointed head, formerly used by infantry.

pike[3] (pīk), *n.* a turnpike.

pik′er, *n.* a person who does anything in a contemptibly small or cheap way.

Pikes′ Peak′, *n.* a mountain in central Colorado: a peak of the Rocky Mountains. 14,108 ft. (4300 m).

pi•laf or **-laff** (pē′läf, pi läf′), *n.* a Middle Eastern dish of rice cooked in bouillon.

pi•las•ter (pi las′tər), *n.* a shallow rectangular feature projecting from a wall, usu. imitating the form of a column.

Pi•late (pī′lət), *n.* **Pon•tius** (pon′shəs, -tē əs), fl. early 1st century A.D., Roman procurator of Judea A.D. 26–36?.

pil•chard (pil′chərd), *n.* a marine fish, related to the herring but smaller and rounder.

pile[1] (pīl), *n., v.,* **piled, pil•ing.** —*n.* **1.** an assemblage of things lying one upon the other. **2.** a large amount of anything. **3.** a pyre. **4.** a large building or group of buildings. —*v.t.* **5.** to lay or dispose in a pile. **6.** to accumulate (often fol. by *up*). **7.** to cover or load with a pile. —*v.i.* **8.** to accumulate (usu. fol. by *up*). **9.** to move as a group in a confused, disorderly cluster: *They piled off the train.*

pile[2] (pīl), *n.* a long beam of wood, steel, etc., hammered vertically into soil to form part of a foundation or retaining wall.

pile[3] (pīl), *n.* a soft surface on cloth, rugs, etc., formed by upright yarns that have been cut straight across or left standing in loops. —**piled,** *adj.*

pile[4] (pīl), *n.* Usu., **piles.** HEMORRHOID.

pile′up′, *n.* **1.** a collision of several moving vehicles. **2.** an accumulation, as of chores or bills.

pil•fer (pil′fər), *v.i., v.t.* to steal, esp. in small quantities. —**pil′fer•age** (-ij), *n.* —**pil′fer•er,** *n.*

pil•grim (pil′grim, -grəm), *n.* **1.** a person who journeys to some sacred place as an act of religious devotion. **2.** a traveler or wanderer. **3.** (*cap.*) one of the band of Puritans who founded the colony of Plymouth, Mass., in 1620.

pil′grim•age (-grə mij), *n.* **1.** a journey of a pilgrim. **2.** any long journey.

pill (pil), *n.* **1.** a small tablet or capsule of medicine. **2.** *Slang.* a tiresomely disagreeable person. **3. the pill,** (*sometimes cap.*) an oral contraceptive.

pil•lage (pil′ij), *v.,* **-laged, -lag•ing,** *n.* —*v.t., v.i.* **1.** to strip of money or goods by violence, as in war. —*n.* **2.** the act of plundering. **3.** booty or spoil.

pil•lar (pil′ər), *n.* **1.** an upright, slender structure used as a building support or as a monument. **2.** a person who is a chief supporter of a state, institution, etc.

pil′lar of salt′, *n.* the object into which Lot's wife was turned after she looked back at the cities of Sodom and Gomorrah. Gen. 19:26.

Pil′lars of Is′lam, *n.* the five bases of the Islamic faith: shahada (confession of faith), salat (prayer), zakat (almsgiving), sawm (fasting, esp. during the month of Ramadan), and hajj (the pilgrimage to Mecca). Also called **Pil′lars of the Faith′.**

pill′box′, *n.* **1.** a small box for holding pills. **2.** a small, boxlike fortification for machine guns or anti-tank weapons.

pil•lion (pil′yən), *n.* **1.** a cushion attached behind the saddle of a horse, esp. as a seat for a woman. **2.** a cushion or saddle used as a passenger seat, as on a motorcycle.

pil•lo•ry (pil′ə rē), *n., pl.* **-ries,** *v.,* **-ried, -ry•ing.** —*n.* **1.** a wooden framework with holes for securing the head and hands, formerly used to expose an offender to public derision. —*v.t.* **2.** to set in the pillory. **3.** to expose to public derision.

pil•low (pil′ō), *n.* **1.** a cloth case filled with soft material, used to cushion the head during sleep. **2.** a similar cushion used for decoration, as on a sofa. —*v.t.* **3.** to rest on or as if on a pillow. **4.** to serve as a pillow for.

pil′low•case′, *n.* a removable covering drawn over a pillow. Also called **pil′low•slip′.**

pi•lot (pī′lət), *n.* **1.** a person qualified to operate an aircraft. **2.** a person qualified to steer ships into or out of a harbor. **3.** a person who steers a ship. **4.** a guide or leader. **5.** a television program serving to introduce a possible new series. —*v.t.* **6.** to act as pilot on, in, or over. **7.** to lead or guide. —*adj.* **8.** serving as a trial undertaking prior to full-scale operation or use.

pi′lot•house′, *n.* an enclosed structure on the deck of a ship from which it can be navigated.

pi′lot light′, *n.* a small flame burning continuously, as in a gas stove, to relight the main burners.

pi•men•to (pi men′tō), *n., pl.* **-tos.** the red, mild-flavored fruit of a sweet pepper.

pi•mien′to (-myen′tō, -men′-), *n., pl.* **-tos.** PIMENTO.

pimp (pimp), *n.* **1.** a person who solicits customers for a prostitute. —*v.i.* **2.** to act as a pimp.

pim•per•nel (pim′pər nel′, -nl), *n.* a plant with scarlet or white flowers that close at the approach of bad weather.

pim•ple (pim′pəl), *n.* a small, usu. inflammatory swelling of the skin. —**pim′ply,** *adj.,* **-pli•er, -pli•est.**

pin (pin), *n., v.,* **pinned, pin•ning.** —*n.* **1.** a small, slender, often pointed piece of metal, wood, etc., used as a fastener or support. **2.** a short, slender piece of wire with a point at one end, used for fastening things together. **3.** an ornament or badge consisting essentially or partly of a penetrating wire. **4.** one of the rounded wooden clubs set up as the target in bowling. —*v.t.* **5.** to fasten with or as if with a pin. **6.** to hold fast in a spot or position. **7. pin down,** to force (someone) to deal with a situation or come to a decision. —*Idiom.* **8. pin something on someone,** *Informal.* to ascribe the blame for something to a person.

PIN (pin), *n.* an identification number assigned to an individual to gain access to a computer system via an ATM or other device.

pin•a•fore (pin′ə fôr′), *n.* a sleeveless, apronlike garment worn over a dress or with a blouse.

pin′ball′, *n.* a game in which a spring-driven ball is shot to the top of a sloping board and rolls down against pins and through holes that record one's score.

pince-nez (pans′nā′, pins′-), *n., pl.* **pince-nez.** a pair of glasses held on the face by a spring that grips the nose.

pin•cers (pin′sərz), *n.* (*usu. with a pl. v.*) **1.** a gripping tool consisting of a pair of jaws and a pair of handles. **2.** a grasping organ, as the claw of a lobster.

pinch (pinch), *v.t.* **1.** to squeeze between the finger and thumb, the jaws of an instrument, etc. **2.** to squeeze painfully, as a tight shoe does. **3.** to make unnaturally constricted: *a face pinched with fear.* **4.** to affect with sharp discomfort or distress, as hunger does. **5.** *Slang.* **a.** to steal. **b.** to arrest. —*v.i.* **6.** to squeeze painfully. **7.** to economize unduly. —*n.* **8.** the act of pinching. **9.** an amount taken up between the finger and thumb. **10.** sharp or painful stress. **11.**

an emergency. —*Idiom.* **12. pinch pennies,** to be frugal with expenditures.

pinch′-hit′, *v.i.* **-hit, -hit•ting. 1.** to substitute at bat for a teammate in baseball. **2.** to substitute for someone in an emergency. —**pinch′ hit′ter,** *n.*

pin′ curl′, *n.* a curl of dampened hair secured by a hairpin until it dries.

pin′cush′ion, *n.* a small cushion into which pins are stuck until needed.

pine¹ (pīn), *n.* **1.** an evergreen tree with needlelike leaves and woody cones enclosing winged seeds. **2.** the wood of a pine.

pine² (pīn), *v.i.,* **pined, pin•ing. 1.** to yearn deeply. **2.** to fail in health or vitality from grief, regret, etc.

pin′e•al gland′ (pin′ē əl), *n.* an endocrine organ in the posterior forebrain, involved in biorhythms and gonadal development.

pine′ap′ple, *n.* **1.** the edible, juicy fruit of a tropical plant having spiny-edged leaves. **2.** the plant itself.

pine′ tar′, *n.* a viscid, blackish brown liquid obtained by the distillation of pine wood, used in paints, as an antiseptic, etc.

pin′feath′er, *n.* an undeveloped feather just coming through the skin.

ping (ping), *v.i.* **1.** to produce a sharp sound like that of a bullet striking metal. —*n.* **2.** a pinging sound.

ping-pong (ping′pong′, -pông′), *v.t., v.i.* to move back and forth.

Ping′-Pong′, *Trademark.* TABLE TENNIS.

pin′head′, *n.* **1.** the head of a pin. **2.** a stupid person.

pin′hole′, *n.* **1.** a small hole made by or as if by a pin. **2.** a hole for a pin to go through.

pin•ion¹ (pin′yən), *n.* a gear with a small number of teeth that engages a rack or larger gear.

pin•ion² (pin′yən), *n.* **1.** the terminal segment of a bird's wing. **2.** the wing of a bird. —*v.t.* **3.** to cut off the pinion of (a wing) or bind (the wings), so as to prevent a bird from flying. **4.** to bind (a person's arms or hands) so they cannot be used.

pink¹ (pingk), *n., adj.,* **-er, -est.** —*n.* **1.** a pale reddish purple. **2.** any of several garden plants with pink, white, or red flowers resembling carnations. **3.** the highest form or degree: *in the pink of condition.* —*adj.* **4.** of the color pink.

pink² (pingk), *v.t.* **1.** to pierce with a rapier or the like. **2.** to cut (fabric) at the edge with a notched pattern.

pink′eye′, *n.* a contagious, epidemic form of acute conjunctivitis.

pink′ie or **pink′y,** *n., pl.* **pink•ies.** *Informal.* the little finger.

pink′ing shears′, *n.* (*used with a pl. v.*) shears with notched blades, for simultaneously cutting and pinking fabric.

pin′ mon′ey, *n.* any small sum set aside for minor expenditures.

pin•na•cle (pin′ə kəl), *n.* **1.** the highest or culminating point, as of success. **2.** any pointed, towering formation, as of rock. **3.** a relatively small upright structure, commonly terminating in a pyramid or cone.

pin•nate (pin′āt, -it), *adj.* (of a leaf) having leaflets on each side of a common stalk.

pi•noch•le (pē′nuk əl, -nok-), *n.* a card game played with a 48-card deck.

pin′point′, *v.t.* to locate or describe exactly.

pin′prick′, *n.* **1.** any minute puncture made by a pin or the like. **2.** a negligible annoyance.

pins′ and nee′dles, *n.pl.* **1.** a tingly, prickly sensation in a limb that is recovering from numbness. —*Idiom.* **2. on pins and needles,** in a state of nervous anticipation.

pin′set′ter, *n.* a person or machine in a bowling alley that positions the pins.

pin′stripe′, *n.* a very thin stripe in fabrics. —**pin′-striped,** *adj.*

pint (pīnt), *n.* a liquid and dry measure of capacity,

equal to one half of a quart, approximately 35 cubic inches (0.6 liter).

Pin•ter (pin′tər), *n.* **Harold,** born 1930, English playwright.

pin•to (pin′tō, pēn′-), *adj., n., pl.* **-tos.** —*adj.* **1.** marked with spots of white and other colors. —*n.* **2.** a pinto horse.

pin′up′, *n.* **1.** a large photograph of a sexually attractive person, suitable for pinning on a wall. **2.** a person in such a photograph. —*adj.* **3.** of, suitable for, or appearing in a pinup.

pin′wheel′, *n.* **1.** a toy consisting of a wheel with vanes attached to a stick, designed to revolve when blown. **2.** a firework that makes a wheel of sparks.

pin•yin (pin′yin′), *n.* (*sometimes cap.*) a system for transliterating Chinese into the Latin alphabet.

pi•o•neer (pī′ə nēr′), *n.* **1.** a person who is among those who first enter or settle a region. **2.** one who is among the earliest in any field of inquiry, enterprise, etc. —*v.i.* **3.** to act as a pioneer. —*v.t.* **4.** to be a pioneer of or in. [< MF < OF *peonier* foot soldier]

pi•ous (pī′əs), *adj.* **1.** having or showing reverence for God or an earnest wish to fulfill religious obligations. **2.** characterized by a hypocritical concern with virtue or religious devotion. —**pi′ous•ly,** *adv.*

pip¹ (pip), *n.* one of the spots on dice, playing cards, or dominoes.

pip² (pip), *n.* a contagious disease of birds, esp. poultry.

pip³ (pip), *n.* a small seed of a fleshy fruit, as an orange.

pipe (pīp), *n., v.,* **piped, pip•ing.** —*n.* **1.** a hollow cylinder, as of metal, used to convey water, gas, etc. **2.** a tube with a small bowl at one end, used for smoking tobacco, opium, etc. **3. a.** a musical wind instrument, as a flute, constructed of a single tube. **b.** one of the tubes from which the tones of an organ are produced. **c.** *pipes,* BAGPIPE. **4.** a tubular organ or passage. —*v.i.* **5.** to play on a pipe. **6.** to utter a shrill sound like that of a pipe. —*v.t.* **7.** to convey by or as if by pipes. **8.** to play (music) on a pipe. **9.** to utter in a shrill tone. **10. pipe down,** *Slang.* to stop talking; be quiet. **11. pipe up,** to make oneself heard, esp. as to assert oneself. —**pip′er,** *n.*

pipe′ dream′, *n.* an unrealistic hope or plan.

pipe′line′, *n.* **1.** a linked series of pipes used to transport crude oil, water, etc., over great distances. **2.** a route along which supplies pass. **3.** a channel of information.

pipe′ or′gan, *n.* ORGAN (def. 1).

pip•er (pī′pər), *n.* **1.** a person who plays on a pipe. **2.** a bagpiper. —*Idiom.* **3. pay the piper, a.** to pay the cost of something. **b.** to bear the unfavorable consequences of one's actions. —*Proverb.* **4. He who pays the piper calls the tune,** financial control dictates what decisions are made.

pip•ing, *n.* **1.** pipes collectively. **2.** a shrill sound. **3.** the music of pipes. **4.** a narrow band of ornamental material used for trimming the edges of clothing, upholstery, etc. —*Idiom.* **5. piping hot,** (of food or drink) very hot.

pip•pin (pip′in), *n.* any of numerous varieties of apple.

pip•squeak (pip′skwēk′), *n.* *Informal.* a small or unimportant person.

pi•quant (pē′kənt, -känt), *adj.* **1.** agreeably pungent in taste. **2.** interestingly provocative. —**pi′quan•cy,** *n.* —**pi′quant•ly,** *adv.*

pique (pēk), *v.,* **piqued, piqu•ing,** *n.* —*v.t.* **1.** to affect with sharp irritation and resentment. **2.** to excite or arouse. —*n.* **3.** a feeling of irritation or resentment.

pi•qué or **-que** (pi kā′, pē-), *n., pl.* **-qués** or **-ques.** a fabric of cotton, rayon, or silk, woven with lengthwise cords or with an overall design.

pi•ra•cy (pī′rə sē), *n., pl.* **-cies. 1.** robbery or illegal violence at sea. **2.** the unauthorized reproduction or use of copyrighted material, a patented invention, etc.

pi•ra•nha (pi rän′yə, -ran′-, -rä′nə, -ran′ə), *n., pl.* **-nhas, -nha.** any of several small, predatory South

American freshwater fishes with sharp interlocking teeth: dangerous when swimming in schools.

pi•rate (pī′rət), *n.*, *v.*, **-rat•ed, -rat•ing.** —*n.* **1.** a person who practices piracy. —*v.t.* **2.** to take by piracy. **3.** to use or reproduce (a book, invention, etc.) without authorization or legal right. —**pi•rat•i•cal** (pī rat′i kəl, pi-), *adj.*

pir•ou•ette (pir′o͞o et′), *n.*, *v.*, **-et•ted, -et•ting.** —*n.* **1.** a whirling about on one foot or on the points of the toes, as in ballet dancing. —*v.i.* **2.** to perform a pirouette.

pis•ca•to•ry (pis′kə tôr′ē) also **pis′ca•to′ri•al,** *adj.* of fishermen or fishing.

Pis•ces (pī′sēz, pis′ēz), *n.* the 12th sign of the zodiac. [< NL, L *piscēs,* pl. of *piscis* fish]

pis•mire (pis′mīr′, piz′-), *n.* an ant.

pis•tach•i•o (pi stash′ē ō′, -stä′shē ō′), *n.*, *pl.* **-os.** **1.** Also, **pistach′io nut′.** the nut of a Eurasian tree containing an edible, greenish kernel. **2.** the tree itself.

pis•til (pis′tl), *n.* the seed-bearing organ of a flower. —**pis′til•late** (-it, -āt′), *adj.*

pis•tol (pis′tl), *n.* a short firearm held and fired with one hand.

pis′tol-whip′, *v.t.*, **-whipped, -whip•ping.** to beat with a pistol.

pis•ton (pis′tən), *n.* a disk or cylinder moving within a longer cylinder and exerting pressure on, or receiving pressure from, a fluid or gas.

pit[1] (pit), *n.*, *v.*, **pit•ted, pit•ting.** —*n.* **1.** a deep hole in the ground. **2.** a trap; pitfall. **3. the pits,** *Slang.* a very unpleasant place, condition, etc. **4.** a hollow or indentation in a surface, as of the body. **5.** POCKMARK. **6.** an enclosure for staging fights, esp. between dogs or cocks. **7.** ORCHESTRA (def. 2a). **8.** an area at a racing track for servicing and refueling the cars. —*v.t.* **9.** to mark or indent with pits. **10.** to set in opposition or combat. —*v.i.* **11.** to become marked with pits.

pit[2] (pit), *n.*, *v.*, **pit•ted, pit•ting.** —*n.* **1.** the stone of a fruit, as of a cherry. —*v.t.* **2.** to remove the pit from.

pi•ta (pē′tä, -tə), *n.*, *pl.* **-tas.** a round, flat Middle Eastern bread having a pocket that can be filled to make a sandwich. Also called **pi′ta bread′.**

pit•a•pat (pit′ə pat′), *adv.* **1.** with a quick succession of beats or taps. —*n.* **2.** the movement or sound of something going pitapat.

pitch[1] (pich), *v.t.* **1.** to set up (a tent, camp, etc.). **2.** to put or set in a fixed place. **3.** to throw or toss. **4.** *Baseball.* **a.** to throw (the ball) to the batter. **b.** to serve as pitcher of (a game). **5.** to set at a certain point, degree, etc. —*v.i.* **6.** to fall forward or headlong. **7.** *Baseball.* **a.** to throw the ball to the batter. **b.** to serve as pitcher. **8.** to slope downward; dip. **9.** to plunge with alternate fall and rise of bow and stern. **10. pitch in,** *Informal.* to contribute to a common cause. —*n.* **11.** relative point or degree: *a high pitch of excitement.* **12.** the degree of slope. **13.** the degree of height or depth of a tone or of sound. **14.** the act or manner of pitching. **15.** a throw or toss. **16.** *Informal.* a sales talk.

pitch[2] (pich), *n.* any of various dark, viscous substances for caulking and paving, distilled from coal tar or wood tar.

pitch′-black′, *adj.* extremely black.

pitch•blende (pich′blend′), *n.* a black mineral that is a major ore of uranium and radium.

pitch′-dark′, *adj.* extremely dark.

pitch′er[1], *n.* a container, usu. with a handle and spout or lip, for holding and pouring liquids.

pitch′er[2], *n.* **1.** *Baseball.* the player who throws the ball to the batter. —*Proverb.* **2. Little pitchers have big ears,** adults should be careful what they say when children are around.

pitch′er plant′, *n.* any of various insectivorous plants with pitcher-shaped leaves in which insects are trapped.

pitch′fork′, *n.* a large, long-handled fork for lifting and pitching hay, stalks of grain, etc.

pitch′man, *n.*, *pl.* **-men. 1.** a person who makes a sales pitch. **2.** an itinerant hawker of small wares.

pitch′ pipe′, *n.* a small pipe producing one or more pitches when blown into.

pit•e•ous (pit′ē əs), *adj.* evoking or deserving pity; pathetic. —**pit′e•ous•ly,** *adv.* —**pit′e•ous•ness,** *n.*

pit′fall′, *n.* **1.** a lightly covered and unnoticeable pit for trapping people or animals. **2.** any danger for the unwary.

pith (pith), *n.* **1.** the soft, spongy central tissue in the stems of dicotyledonous plants. **2.** the important or essential part.

Pi•thom (pī′thəm), *n.* one of the two cities built by Israelite slaves in Egypt. Ex. 1:11. Compare RAAMSES.

pith′y, *adj.*, **-i•er, -i•est. 1.** brief, forceful, and meaningful in expression. **2.** of, like, or abounding in pith. —**pith′i•ly,** *adv.*

pit•i•ful (pit′i fal), *adj.* **1.** evoking or deserving pity. **2.** arousing contempt by smallness, poor quality, etc. —**pit′i•ful•ly,** *adv.*

pit′i•less, *adj.* feeling or showing no pity; merciless.

pi•ton (pē′ton), *n.* a metal spike with an eye through which a rope may be passed, used in mountain climbing.

pit•tance (pit′ns), *n.* **1.** a small amount or share. **2.** a small allowance of money.

pit•ter-pat•ter (pit′ər pat′ər), *n.* the sound of a rapid succession of light beats or taps, as of rain.

Pitts•burgh (pits′bûrg), *n.* a city in SW Pennsylvania. 358,883.

pitu′itary gland′ (pi to͞o′i ter′ē, -tyo͞o′-), *n.* the master endocrine gland, attached to the base of the brain, affecting all hormonal functions of the body.

pit′ vi′per, *n.* any of various vipers, as the rattlesnake, that have a heat-sensitive pit above each nostril.

pit•y (pit′ē), *n.*, *pl.* **-ies,** *v.*, **-ied, -y•ing.** —*n.* **1.** sympathetic sorrow evoked by the suffering of another. **2.** a cause or reason for pity, sorrow, or regret. —*v.t.*, *v.i.* **3.** to feel pity (for). —**pit′i•a•ble,** *adj.*

piv•ot (piv′ət), *n.* **1.** a pin or short shaft on which something turns or around which something rotates. **2.** a person or thing on which something depends. **3.** a whirling around on one foot. —*v.i.* **4.** to turn on or as if on a pivot. —*v.t.* **5.** to provide with a pivot. —**piv′ot•al,** *adj.*

pix•el (pik′səl, -sel), *n.* the smallest element of an image that can be individually processed in a video display system.

pix•ie (pik′sē), *n.* a mischievous fairy or sprite.

pi•zazz or **piz•zazz** (pə zaz′), *n. Informal.* **1.** energy; vigor. **2.** dash; flair.

piz•za (pēt′sə), *n.*, *pl.* **-zas.** a baked, open-faced pie consisting of a thin layer of dough topped with tomato sauce, cheese, etc.

piz′ze•ri′a (-rē′ə), *n.*, *pl.* **-ri•as.** a place where pizzas are made and sold.

piz•zi•ca•to (pit′si kä′tō), *adj. Music.* played by plucking the strings with the finger, as on a violin.

pj′s or **p.j.′s** (pē′jāz′), *n.* (*used with a pl. v.*) *Informal.* PAJAMAS.

pk or **pk.,** peck.

pkg., package.

pkwy., parkway.

PL, Public Law: *PL #480.*

pl., 1. place. **2.** plural.

P/L, profit and loss.

plac•ard (plak′ärd, -ərd), *n.* **1.** a sign or notice, as one posted in a public place. —*v.t.* **2.** to display placards on or in.

pla•cate (plā′kāt, plak′āt), *v.t.*, **-cat•ed, -cat•ing.** to appease or pacify. —**pla•ca′tion,** *n.*

place (plās), *n.*, *v.*, **placed, plac•ing.** —*n.* **1.** a particular portion of space, as that occupied by a person or thing. **2.** any part of a body or surface. **3.** a space or seat for a person, as in a theater. **4.** position or situation. **5.** a proper or appropriate location, position, or time. **6.** a post or office. **7.** a function or duty. **8.** a region or area of habitation. **9.** a short street or court. **10.** a building, location, etc., set aside for a specific purpose. **11.** a residence or dwelling. **12.** lieu; substitution: *Use milk in place of cream.* **13.** a step or point in order of proceeding: *in the first place.* **14.** the position of the competitor who comes in second in a horse race. —*v.t.* **15.** to put in a particular position, situation, or condition. **16.** to put in a suitable place for some purpose: *to place an ad.* **17.** to appoint to a post or office. **18.** to find employment or living quarters for. **19.** to assign a certain position or rank to. **20.** to identify: *to place a face.* **21.** to make (a bet, phone call, etc.). —*v.i.* **22.** to finish second in a horse race. **23.** to earn a specified standing, as in a competition. —*Proverb.* **24. A place for everything and everything in its place,** everything should be neat and in proper order.

pla•ce•bo (plə sē′bō), *n., pl.* **-bos, -boes.** a substance having no pharmacological effect but given to placate a patient or as a control in testing a drug.

place′ mat′, *n.* a mat set beneath an individual table setting.

place′ment, *n.* **1.** the act of placing or state of being placed. **2.** location; arrangement.

pla•cen•ta (plə sen′tə), *n., pl.* **-tas, -tae** (-tē). the organ in the lining of the uterus that provides for the nourishment of the fetus. —**pla•cen′tal,** *adj.*

plac•er (plas′ər), *n.* a natural concentration of heavy metal particles, as gold or platinum, in sand or gravel.

plac•id (plas′id), *adj.* pleasantly calm or peaceful. —**pla•cid•i•ty** (plə sid′i tē), *n.* —**plac′id•ly,** *adv.*

plack•et (plak′it), *n.* a slit at the neck, waist, or wrist of a garment for ease in putting it on or taking it off.

pla•gia•rize (plā′jə rīz′), *v.t., v.i.,* **-rized, -riz•ing.** to take and use (ideas, passages, etc.) from (another's work), representing them as one's own. —**pla′gia•rism,** *n.* —**pla′gia•rist,** *n.*

plague (plāg), *n., v.,* **plagued, pla•guing.** —*n.* **1.** an epidemic disease that causes high mortality. **2.** any widespread affliction or calamity. —*v.t.* **3.** to torment in any manner. **4.** to smite with a plague. —*Saying.* **5. A plague on both your houses,** may both of you be cursed. William Shakespeare, *Romeo and Juliet.*

plaid (plad), *n.* **1.** any fabric woven of differently colored yarns in a cross-barred pattern. **2.** a pattern of this kind.

plain (plān), *adj.,* **-er, -est,** *adv., n.* —*adj.* **1.** clear or distinct to the eye or ear. **2.** easily understood. **3.** sheer; utter: *plain stupidity.* **4.** free from ambiguity or evasion: *the plain truth.* **5.** without pretensions; ordinary: *plain people.* **6.** not beautiful: *a plain face.* **7.** without intricacies. **8.** with little or no decoration. —*adv.* **9.** clearly and simply. —*n.* **10.** an area of land with relatively minor differences in elevation. —**plain′ly,** *adv.* —**plain′ness,** *n.*

plain′clothes′man, *n., pl.* **-men.** a police officer who wears ordinary civilian clothes while on duty.

Plain′ Peo′ple, *n.pl.* members of the Amish, the Mennonites, or the Dunkers: so named because they stress simple living.

plains′man, *n., pl.* **-men.** an inhabitant of the plains.

plain′song′, *n.* the ancient traditional unisonal music of the Christian Church.

plaint (plānt), *n.* **1.** a complaint. **2.** a lament.

plain•tiff (plān′tif), *n.* one who brings a suit in a court.

plain•tive (plān′tiv), *adj.* expressing sorrow or melancholy; mournful. —**plain′tive•ly,** *adv.*

plait (plāt, plat), *n.* **1.** a braid, esp. of hair or straw. **2.** a pleat. —*v.t.* **3.** to braid. **4.** to pleat.

plan (plan), *n., v.,* **planned, plan•ning.** —*n.* **1.** a scheme or method of acting, proceeding, etc., developed in advance. **2.** a drawing made to scale to represent a horizontal section of a structure or machine. **3.** an outline, diagram, or sketch. —*v.t.* **4.** to formulate a plan for. **5.** to draw a plan of, as a build-

ing. **6.** to have in mind as an intention. —*v.i.* **7.** to make plans. —**plan′ner,** *n.*

plane¹ (plān), *n.* **1.** a flat or level surface. **2.** *Geom.* a surface generated by a straight line moving at a constant velocity with respect to a fixed point. **3.** a level of dignity, character, etc.: *a high moral plane.* **4.** an airplane or hydroplane. —*adj.* **5.** flat or level. **6.** of planes or plane figures. —**pla•nar** (plā′nər), *adj.*

plane² (plān), *n., v.,* **planed, plan•ing.** —*n.* **1.** a woodworking instrument for paring, truing, or smoothing. —*v.t.* **2.** to smooth or dress with a plane.

plan•et (plan′it), *n.* **1.** any of the nine large heavenly bodies revolving about the sun. **2.** a similar body revolving about a star other than the sun. —**plan′e•tar′y** (-i ter′ē), *adj.*

plan•e•tar•i•um (-i târ′ē əm), *n., pl.* **-i•ums, -i•a** (-ē ə). **1.** a model representing the planetary system. **2.** a device that simulates the heavens by use of moving projectors. **3.** the building or room housing such a device.

plane′ tree′, *n.* any of several large, spreading shade trees, esp. the North American sycamore.

plan•gent (plan′jənt), *adj.* resounding loudly, esp. with a plaintive sound.

plank (plangk), *n.* **1.** a long, flat piece of timber, thicker than a board. **2.** one of the principles or objectives in the platform of a political party. —*v.t.* **3.** to lay or cover with planks. **4.** to bake or broil and serve (steak, fish, etc.) on a board. **5.** PLUNK (def. 2).

plank′ing, *n.* **1.** planks collectively. **2.** the act of laying or covering with planks.

plank•ton (plangk′tən), *n.* the passively floating organisms in a body of water, primarily comprising microscopic algae and protozoa.

Pla•no (plā′nō), *n.* a town in N Texas. 157,394.

plant (plant, plänt), *n.* **1.** a multicellular organism that produces food from sunlight and inorganic matter by photosynthesis and has rigid cell walls containing cellulose. **2.** an herb or other small vegetable growth, in contrast with a tree or shrub. **3.** the buildings, equipment, etc., necessary to carry on any industrial business. —*v.t.* **4.** to put in the ground for growth. **5.** to establish or implant (ideas, principles, etc.). **6.** to place or set firmly. **7.** to place or station covertly for purposes of deception: *to plant a spy.*

Plan•tag•e•net (plan taj′ə nit), *n.* a member of the royal house that ruled England from 1154 to 1485.

plan•tain¹ (plan′tin, -tn), *n.* **1.** a tropical plant resembling the banana. **2.** its fruit.

plan•tain² (plan′tin, -tn), *n.* a weed with large, spreading basal leaves and long spikes of small flowers.

plan•tar (plan′tər), *adj.* of the sole of the foot.

plan•ta•tion (plan tā′shən), *n.* **1.** a large estate, esp. in a tropical country, on which crops are cultivated, usu. by resident laborers. **2.** a group of planted trees.

plant′er, *n.* **1.** an implement for planting seeds. **2.** the owner or manager of a plantation. **3.** a container for growing ornamental plants.

plant′ louse′, *n.* APHID.

plaque (plak), *n.* **1.** a thin, flat plate or tablet of metal, porcelain, etc., intended for ornament, as on a wall. **2.** an inscribed commemorative tablet, as on a monument. **3.** a soft, sticky film formed on tooth surfaces.

plash (plash), *n.* **1.** a gentle splash. —*v.t., v.i.* **2.** to splash gently.

plas•ma (plaz′mə), *n.* **1.** the fluid part of blood or lymph. **2.** a highly ionized gas containing an approximately equal number of positive ions and electrons.

plas•ter (plas′tər, plä′stər), *n.* **1.** a composition, as of lime, sand, and water, applied in a pasty form to walls, ceilings, etc., and allowed to harden and dry. **2.** PLASTER OF PARIS. **3.** a preparation spread on cloth and applied to the body for some healing purpose. —*v.t.* **4.** to cover or fill with plaster. **5.** to lay flat (often fol. by *down*). **6.** to apply a plaster to (the body). **7.** to overspread with something, esp. excessively: *to plaster a wall with posters.* —**plas′ter•er,** *n.*

plas′ter·board′, *n.* a material used for insulating or covering walls, consisting of paper-covered sheets of gypsum and felt.

plas′ter of Par′is, *n.* calcined gypsum in white, powdery form, used in making plasters and casts.

plas′tic, *n.* **1.** any of a group of synthetic or natural organic materials that may be shaped when soft and then hardened. **2.** a credit card, or credit cards collectively. —*adj.* **3.** made of plastic. **4.** capable of being molded. **5.** having the power to mold or shape material. [< L *plasticus* that may be molded < Gk *plastikós*] —**plas·tic′i·ty** (-tis′i tē), *n.*

plas′tic sur′gery, *n.* the branch of surgery dealing with the repair, replacement, or reshaping of malformed, injured, or lost parts of the body. —**plas′tic sur′geon,** *n.*

plat (plat), *n., v.,* **plat·ted, plat·ting.** —*n.* **1.** a plot of ground. **2.** a plan or map, as of land. —*v.t.* **3.** to make a plat of.

plate (plāt), *n., v.,* **plat·ed, plat·ing.** —*n.* **1.** a shallow dish from which food is eaten. **2.** the contents of such a dish. **3.** household dishes, utensils, etc., of or plated with gold or silver. **4.** a thin, flat sheet of metal. **5.** a sheet of metal, plastic, etc., on which a picture or text has been engraved, used as a printing surface. **6.** a printed impression from such a surface. **7.** the part of a denture that conforms to the mouth and contains the teeth. **8. the plate,** HOME PLATE. **9.** a sheet of glass or metal coated with a sensitized emulsion, used for taking a photograph. —*v.t.* **10.** to coat (metal) with a thin film of gold, silver, etc. **11.** to cover or overlay with metal plates for protection. —**plat′ed,** *adj.*

pla·teau (pla tō′), *n., pl.* **-teaus. 1.** a level land area considerably raised above adjoining land. **2.** a period of little growth or decline.

plate′ glass′, *n.* smooth, polished glass used in large windows, mirrors, etc.

plat·en (plat′n), *n.* **1.** a flat plate in a printing press for pressing the paper against an inked surface. **2.** the roller of a typewriter or computer printer.

plate′ tecton′ics, *n.* a geologic theory that the earth's crust is divided into rigid plates whose movement accounts for continental drift and earthquakes.

plat·form (plat′fôrm), *n.* **1.** a raised flooring or other horizontal surface for use as a stage. **2.** the raised area between or alongside the tracks of a railroad station. **3.** a set of principles on which a political party or other group takes a public stand. **4.** the underlying hardware or software for a computer system.

plat·ing (plā′ting), *n.* **1.** a thin coating of gold, silver, etc. **2.** an external layer of metal plates.

plat·i·num (plat′n əm), *n.* a heavy, grayish white metallic element, resistant to most chemicals: used for making scientific apparatus and in jewelry. *Symbol:* Pt; *at. wt.:* 195.09; *at. no.:* 78.

plat·i·tude (plat′i tōōd′, -tyōōd′), *n.* a dull or trite remark. —**plat′i·tu′di·nous** (-n əs), *adj.*

Pla·to (plā′tō), *n.* 427–347 B.C., Greek philosopher.

Pla·ton·ic (plə ton′ik), *adj.* **1.** of or characteristic of Plato or his philosophy. **2.** (*usu. l.c.*) free from sensual desire; purely spiritual: *a platonic relationship.*

pla·toon (plə tōōn′), *n.* **1.** a military unit consisting of two or more squads and a headquarters. —*v.t.* **2.** *Sports.* to use (a player) at a position in a game alternately with another player.

Platte (plat), *n.* a river flowing E from the junction of the North and South Platte rivers in central Nebraska to the Missouri River S of Omaha. 310 mi. (500 km) long.

plat·ter (plat′ər), *n.* a large, shallow dish for holding and serving food.

plat·y (plat′ē), *n., pl.* **plat·ys, plat·ies, plat·y.** PLATYFISH.

plat′y·fish′, *n., pl.* **-fish, -fish·es.** any of several small freshwater fishes common in home aquariums.

plat·y·pus (plat′i pəs, -pōōs′), *n., pl.* **-pus·es, -pi** (-pī′), **-pus.** an aquatic, egg-laying mammal of Australia and Tasmania, having webbed feet and a ducklike bill.

plau·dit (plô′dit), *n.* Usu., **-dits. 1.** an enthusiastic expression of approval. **2.** a round of applause.

plau·si·ble (plô′zə bəl), *adj.* credible; believable. —**plau′si·bil′i·ty,** *n.* —**plau′si·bly,** *adv.*

play (plā), *n.* **1.** a dramatic composition or performance; drama. **2.** activity engaged in for recreation. **3.** fun or jest, as opposed to earnest. **4.** the action or conduct of a game. **5.** one's turn to play. **6.** action of a specified kind: *fair play.* **7.** action or operation: *the play of fancy.* **8.** brisk, light, or changing movement: *the play of a water fountain.* **9.** freedom for movement or activity. **10.** attention; coverage. —*v.t.* **11.** to portray; enact: *to play Macbeth.* **12.** to act the part of in real life: *to play the fool.* **13.** to engage in (a game, pastime, etc.). **14.** to contend against in a game. **15.** to employ in a game: *to play a high card.* **16.** to use as if in playing a game: *He played his brothers against each other.* **17.** to bet on. **18.** to imitate, as for recreation: *to play house.* **19.** to perform on (a musical instrument). **20.** to perform (music) on an instrument. **21.** to cause to produce sound or pictures: *played the VCR.* **22.** to perform or do in sport: *to play tricks.* —*v.i.* **23.** to occupy oneself in amusement or recreation. **24.** to do something that is not to be taken seriously. **25.** to toy; trifle. **26.** to take part in a game. **27.** to conduct oneself in a specified way: *to play fair.* **28.** to act on or as if on the stage. **29.** to perform on a musical instrument. **30.** to give forth sound. **31.** to be performed or shown. **32.** to move about lightly or quickly: *A smile played about her lips.* **33. play down,** to treat as of little importance. **34. ~ out,** to use up; exhaust. **35. ~ up,** to emphasize. **36. ~ up to,** to try to please; flatter. —*Saying.* **37. But will it play in Peoria?** will it appeal to people in Middle America?

play′act′, *v.i.* **1.** to engage in make-believe. **2.** to be insincere or affected in speech, manner, etc. —**play′act′ing,** *n.*

play′back′, *n.* **1.** the act of reproducing a sound or video recording. **2.** the apparatus used in producing playbacks.

play′bill′, *n.* a program or announcement of a play.

play′boy′ or **-girl′,** *n.* a person who pursues a life of pleasure without responsibility or attachments.

play′ date′, *n.* an appointment made by parents from separate families to have their young children play together.

play′er, *n.* **1.** a person who takes part in some game or sport. **2.** a stage actor. **3.** a musician. **4.** a sound– or image–reproducing machine: *a videodisc player.*

play′ful (-fəl), *adj.* **1.** full of play or fun. **2.** pleasantly humorous or jesting. —**play′ful·ly,** *adv.* —**play′ful·ness,** *n.*

play′go′er, *n.* a person who attends the theater often.

play′ground′, *n.* an area used by children for outdoor recreation.

play′house′, *n.* **1.** THEATER (def. 1). **2.** a small house for children to play in.

play′ing card′, *n.* one of a set of 52 cards in four suits, used in playing various games.

play′mate′, *n.* a companion, esp. of a child, in play or recreation.

play′off′, *n.* **1.** an extra game, inning, etc., played to settle a tie. **2.** a series of games played to decide a championship.

play′ on words′, *n.* a pun.

platypus

play′pen′, *n.* a small, portable enclosure in which a baby can play.

play′thing′, *n.* a toy.

play′wright′ (-rīt′), *n.* a writer of plays.

pla•za (plä′zə, plaz′ə), n., pl. -zas. 1. a public square or open space in a city or town. 2. a shopping center. 3. an area along an expressway where public facilities are available.

plea (plē), n., pl. **pleas.** 1. an appeal or entreaty. 2. something that is alleged, urged, or pleaded in defense or justification. 3. an excuse; pretext. 4. a defendant's answer to a charge.

plea′ bar′gaining, n. a practice in which a criminal defendant pleads guilty to a lesser charge rather than risk conviction for a graver crime. —**plea′-bar′gain,** v.i.

plead (plēd), v., **plead•ed** or **pled; plead•ing.** —v.i. 1. to entreat earnestly; beg. 2. to put forward a plea in a law court. —v.t. 3. to offer as an excuse: *to plead ignorance.* 4. a. to argue (a case) before a court. b. to make a plea of: *to plead guilty.*

pleas•ant (plez′ənt), adj. 1. giving pleasure; agreeable or enjoyable. 2. having a pleasing manner, appearance, etc. —**pleas′ant•ly,** adv. —**pleas′ant•ness,** n.

pleas•ant•ry, n., pl. -ries. 1. a humorous action or remark. 2. a courteous remark used to facilitate conversation.

please (plēz), adv., v., **pleased, pleas•ing.** —adv. 1. (used in polite requests) be so kind as to: *Please come here.* 2. to give pleasure to. 3. to be the pleasure of: *May it please your Majesty.* —v.i. 4. to like or wish: *Do as you please.* 5. to give pleasure or satisfaction.

pleas′ing, adj. giving pleasure; agreeable. —**pleas′ing•ly,** adv.

pleas•ur•a•ble (plezh′ər ə bəl), adj. enjoyable; agreeable; pleasant. —**pleas′ur•a•bly,** adv.

pleas′ure, n. 1. enjoyment or satisfaction; gratification. 2. a source of enjoyment or delight. 3. one's will or desire. —**pleas′ure•ful,** adj.

pleat (plēt), n. 1. a fold of even width made by doubling cloth or the like upon itself. —v.t. 2. to arrange in pleats.

ple•be•ian (pli bē′ən), adj. 1. of the common people. 2. common or vulgar. —n. 3. a member of the common people.

pleb•i•scite (pleb′ə sīt′, -sit), n. a direct vote of the qualified voters of a state on some public question.

plec•trum (plek′trəm), n., pl. -tra (-trə), -trums. a small piece of metal, plastic, etc., for plucking the strings of a musical instrument.

pled (pled), v. a pt. and pp. of PLEAD.

pledge (plej), n., v., **pledged, pledg•ing.** —n. 1. a solemn promise or agreement. 2. something delivered as security, as for the fulfillment of a promise. 3. the state of being given or held as security. 4. a person accepted for membership in a club, fraternity, etc., but not yet formally approved. —v.t. 5. to bind by a pledge. 6. to promise solemnly. 7. to give as a pledge.

Pleis•to•cene (plī′stə sēn′), adj. noting or pertaining to the geologic epoch forming the earlier half of the Quaternary Period, characterized by the advent of modern humans.

ple•na•ry (plē′nə rē, plen′ə-), adj. 1. full; complete: *plenary powers.* 2. attended by all qualified members.

plen•i•po•ten•ti•ar•y (plen′ə pə ten′shē er′ē, -shə rē), n., pl. -ar•ies, adj. —n. 1. a person, esp. a diplomatic agent, invested with full authority to transact business. —adj. 2. invested with full power or authority.

plen•i•tude (plen′i tōōd′, -tyōōd′), n. 1. fullness; abundance. 2. the state of being full or complete.

plen•te•ous (plen′tē əs), adj. plentiful; abundant.

plen′ti•ful (-ti fəl), adj. existing or yielding in abundance. —**plen′ti•ful•ly,** adv.

plen′ty, n., pl. -ties, adv. —n. 1. a full or abundant supply or amount. 2. the state or quality of being plentiful. —adv. 3. Informal. fully; quite.

Plessy v. Ferguson (ples′ē; fûr′gə sən), n. a U.S. Supreme Court decision of 1896 that upheld segregation, thereby establishing the "separate but equal" doctrine.

pleth•o•ra (pleth′ər ə), n. an overabundance; excess.

pleu•ra (plŏŏr′ə), n., pl. **pleu•rae** (plŏŏr′ē). one of a pair of membranes that cover the lungs and line the chest wall.

pleu′ri•sy (-ə sē), n. inflammation of the pleura.

Plex•i•glas (plek′si glas′, -gläs′), Trademark. a lightweight, transparent plastic material, used for signs, windows, etc.

plex•us (plek′səs), n., pl. -us•es, -us. a network, as of nerves or blood vessels.

pli•a•ble (plī′ə bəl), adj. 1. easily bent; flexible. 2. easily influenced or persuaded. 3. adaptable. —**pli′a•bil′i•ty,** n.

pli′ant (-ənt), adj. 1. bending readily; pliable. 2. adapting readily to different situations. —**pli′an•cy,** n.

pli•ers (plī′ərz), n. (used with a sing. or pl. v.) small pincers for bending wire, holding small objects, etc.

plight¹ (plīt), n. a distressing condition or situation.

plight² (plīt), v.t. to give in pledge, as one's word, or to pledge, as one's honor.

plinth (plinth), n. a slab beneath the base of a column, pedestal, or pier.

Pli•o•cene (plī′ə sēn′), adj. noting or pertaining to the latest epoch of the Tertiary Period.

PLO, Palestine Liberation Organization.

plod (plod), v.i., **plod•ded, plod•ding.** 1. to walk heavily or move laboriously. 2. to work with steady and monotonous perseverance. —**plod′der,** n.

plop (plop), v., **plopped, plop•ping.** —v.t., v.i. 1. to drop with a sound like that of an object striking water without a splash. 2. to drop with direct impact: *to plop into a chair.* —n. 3. a plopping sound or fall.

plot (plot), n., v., **plot•ted, plot•ting.** —n. 1. a secret plan, usu. evil or unlawful. 2. the main story of a literary or dramatic work. 3. a small piece of ground. —v.t. 4. to plan secretly or conspiratorially. 5. to mark on a map or chart, as the course of a ship. —v.i. 6. to plan secretly; conspire. —**plot′ter,** n.

plov•er (pluv′ər, plō′vər), n. any of various shorebirds with a compact body and pigeonlike head.

plow (plou), n. 1. an agricultural implement used for cutting and turning up soil. 2. any of various implements resembling this, as a snowplow. —v.t. 3. to turn up (soil) with a plow. 4. to make with or as if with a plow: *to plow furrows.* —v.i. 5. to work with a plow. 6. to move forcefully: *to plow through a crowd.* 7. to proceed laboriously: *to plow through a pile of reports.* Also, esp. Brit., **plough.** —**plow′man,** n., pl. -men.

plow′share′, n. the cutting part of a plow.

ploy (ploi), n. a stratagem to gain the advantage.

pluck (pluk), v.t. 1. to pull off or out from the place of growth, as flowers. 2. to grasp or grab. 3. to remove feathers or hair from by pulling: *to pluck a chicken.* 4. to sound (the strings of an instrument) by pulling at them. —v.i. 5. to pull or tug sharply. —n. 6. the act of plucking. 7. courage.

pluck′y, adj., -i•er, -i•est. courageous; brave. —**pluck′i•ness,** n.

plug (plug), n., v., **plugged, plug•ging.** —n. 1. a piece of wood or other material used to stop up a hole. 2. an attachment at the end of an electrical cord that allows its insertion into an outlet. 3. a cake of pressed tobacco. 4. the favorable mention of a product, performer, etc., as in a television interview. 5. an artificial fishing lure. —v.t. 6. to stop with or as if with a plug. 7. to mention (a product or the like) favorably. —v.i. 8. to work with stubborn persistence. 9. **plug in,** to connect to an electrical power source: *Plug in the toaster.*

Plug′ and Play′, n. (sometimes l.c.) a standard for the production of compatible computers, peripherals, and software that facilitates installation and enables automatic configuration of the system.

plum (plum), n. 1. a round fruit with a smooth skin and an oblong stone. 2. the tree that bears this fruit. 3. a raisin, as in a cake. 4. a deep purple. 5. an excellent or desirable thing.

plum•age (plōō′mij), *n.* the entire feathery covering of a bird.

plumb (plum), *n.* **1.** a small mass of lead suspended by a line (**plumb′ line′**) and used to measure the depth of water or to ascertain a vertical line. —*adj.* **2.** true according to a plumb line; perpendicular. —*adv.* **3.** in a perpendicular or vertical direction. **4.** exactly or precisely. **5.** completely or absolutely. —*v.t.* **6.** to test or adjust by a plumb line. **7.** to examine closely in order to understand. [< L *plumbum* lead]

plumb′er, *n.* a person who installs and repairs piping, fixtures, etc., of a water or drainage system.

plumb′er's help′er, *n.* PLUNGER (def. 2).

plumb′ing, *n.* **1.** the system of pipes and other apparatus of a water or drainage system. **2.** the work of a plumber.

plume (plōōm), *n.*, *v.*, **plumed, plum•ing.** —*n.* **1.** a large or conspicuous feather. **2.** any plumelike part or formation. —*v.t.* **3.** to adorn with plumes. **4.** to preen. —**plumed,** *adj.* —**plum′y,** *adj.*

plum•met (plum′it), *n.* **1.** the weight attached to a plumb line. —*v.i.* **2.** to fall straight down; plunge.

plump[1] (plump), *adj.*, **-er, -est.** well filled out or rounded in form; fleshy. —**plump′ness,** *n.*

plump[2] (plump), *v.i.*, *v.t.* **1.** to drop heavily or suddenly. **2. plump for,** to support enthusiastically. —*n.* **3.** a heavy or sudden fall. **4.** the sound of such a fall. —*adv.* **5.** heavily or suddenly. **6.** straight down.

plun•der (plun′dər), *v.t.* **1.** to rob of goods by force, as in war. **2.** to rob or fleece. —*v.i.* **3.** to take plunder. —*n.* **4.** plundering or pillage. **5.** that which is taken in plundering.

plunge (plunj), *v.*, **plunged, plung•ing,** *n.* —*v.t.* **1.** to cast or thrust forcibly or suddenly into something. —*v.i.* **2.** to fall or cast oneself into water, from a great height, etc. **3.** to rush or dash with haste. **4.** to bet or speculate recklessly. **5.** to descend abruptly. —*n.* **6.** the act of plunging. —*Idiom.* **7. take the plunge,** to enter upon a course of action, esp. after hesitation.

plung′er, *n.* **1.** a pistonlike part moving within the cylinder of a pump or hydraulic device. **2.** a device consisting of a handle with a rubber suction cup at one end, used to free clogged drains.

plunk (plungk), *v.t.* **1.** PLUCK (def. 4). **2.** to throw, drop, etc., heavily or suddenly. —*v.i.* **3.** to give forth a twanging sound. **4.** to drop heavily or suddenly. —*n.* **5.** the act or sound of plunking. —**plunk′er,** *n.*

plu•ral (plŏŏr′əl), *adj.* **1.** of or involving more than one. **2.** of or belonging to the grammatical category of number indicating that a word has more than one referent. —*n.* **3.** the plural number. **4.** a word or other form in the plural.

plu′ral•ism, *n.* a condition in which minority groups participate fully in the dominant society, yet maintain their cultural differences. —**plu′ral•is′tic,** *adj.*

plu•ral•i•ty (plŏŏ ral′i tē), *n.*, *pl.* **-ties. 1.** (in an election involving three or more candidates) the excess of votes received by the leading candidate over those received by the next candidate. **2.** a majority. **3.** the state or fact of being plural or numerous.

plu′ral•ize′, *v.t.*, *v.i.*, **-ized, -iz•ing.** to make or become plural. —**plu′ral•i•za′tion,** *n.*

plus (plus), *prep.* **1.** increased by: *Ten plus two is twelve.* **2.** in addition to. —*adj.* **3.** involving or noting addition. **4.** positive: *on the plus side.* **5.** more or greater than: *A plus for effort.* **6.** and more: *She has personality plus.* —*n.* **7.** a plus quantity. **8.** Also called **plus′ sign′.** the symbol (+) indicating addition or a positive quantity. **9.** something additional. **10.** an advantage or gain.

plush (plush), *n.*, *adj.*, **-er, -est.** —*n.* **1.** a fabric resembling velvet but having a deeper pile. —*adj.* **2.** luxurious.

Plu•tarch (plōō′tärk), *n.* A.D. c46–c120, Greek biographer. —**Plu•tarch′i•an,** *adj.*

Plu•to (plōō′tō), *n.* **1.** the ancient Greek and Roman god of the underworld. **2.** the planet ninth in order from the sun.

plu•toc•ra•cy (plōō tok′rə sē), *n.*, *pl.* **-cies. 1.** a government in which the wealthy class rules. **2.** a class ruling by virtue of its wealth. —**plu′to•crat′** (-tə krat′), *n.* —**plu′to•crat′ic,** *adj.*

plu•to•ni•um (plōō tō′nē əm), *n.* a radioactive metallic element with a fissile isotope of mass number 239 that can be produced from nonfissile uranium 238. *Symbol:* Pu; *at. no.:* 94.

plu•vi•al (plōō′vē əl), *adj.* **1.** of rain. **2.** formed by the action of rain.

ply[1] (plī), *v.*, **plied, ply•ing.** —*v.t.* **1.** to work with diligently: *to ply the needle.* **2.** to carry on busily or steadily: *to ply a trade.* **3.** to assail persistently. **4.** to offer something pressingly to: *to ply a person with drink.* **5.** to pass over or along (a river, stream, etc.) steadily or regularly. —*v.i.* **6.** to travel regularly between certain places, as a boat. **7.** to perform one's work busily or steadily.

ply[2] (plī), *n.*, *pl.* **plies. 1.** a thickness or layer. **2.** a strand of yarn or rope.

Plym•outh (plim′əth), *n.* a city in SE Massachusetts: the oldest town in New England, founded by the Pilgrims 1620. 35,913.

Plym′outh Breth′ren, *n.* a loosely organized body of Christians founded in Plymouth, England, about 1830.

Plym′outh Rock′, *n.* a rock at Plymouth, Mass., on which the Pilgrims who sailed on the *Mayflower* are said to have stepped ashore when they landed in America in 1620.

ply′wood′, *n.* a building material consisting of wood veneers glued over each other.

Pm, *Chem. Symbol.* promethium.

p.m. or **P.M., 1.** after noon. **2.** the period between noon and midnight. [< L *post merīdiem*]

PMS, premenstrual syndrome: the physical and emotional changes that may be experienced in the several days before menstruation.

pneu•mat•ic (nŏŏ mat′ik, nyŏŏ-), *adj.* **1.** of air, gases, or wind. **2.** filled with or operated by compressed air, as a tire. —**pneu•mat′i•cal•ly,** *adv.*

pneu•mo•nia (nŏŏ mōn′yə, nyŏŏ-), *n.* **1.** inflammation of the lungs with congestion. **2.** an acute infection of the lungs.

Po (pō), *n.* a river in Italy, flowing from the Alps to the Adriatic. 418 mi. (669 km) long.

Po, *Chem. Symbol.* polonium.

P.O., post office.

poach[1] (pōch), *v.i.*, *v.t.* **1.** to trespass on (private property) in order to hunt or fish. **2.** to take (game or fish) illegally. —**poach′er,** *n.*

poach[2] (pōch), *v.t.* to cook (eggs, fish, etc.) in a hot liquid just below the boiling point.

pock (pok), *n.* **1.** a pustule on the body caused by an eruptive disease, as smallpox. **2.** a pockmark. —**pocked,** *adj.*

pock•et (pok′it), *n.* **1.** a small pouch attached to a garment, used for carrying small articles. **2.** financial resources. **3.** any pouchlike receptacle or cavity. **4.** an isolated group, area, or element: *pockets of resistance.* —*adj.* **5.** small enough for carrying in the pocket. **6.** relatively small: *a pocket war.* —*v.t.* **7.** to put into one's pocket. **8.** to take as one's own, often dishonestly. **9.** to conceal or suppress: *to pocket one's pride.* **10.** to enclose; confine. —**pock′et•ful′,** *n.*, *pl.* **-fuls.**

poc′ket•book′, *n.* **1.** a woman's purse or handbag. **2.** financial resources.

pock′et•knife′, *n.*, *pl.* **-knives.** a small knife with one or more blades that fold into the handle.

pock′et ve′to, *n.* an automatic veto of a bill, occurring when Congress adjourns within the ten-day period allowed for presidential action on the bill and the president has retained it unsigned.

pock′mark′, *n.* a scar left by a pustule of smallpox, chickenpox, etc.

pod (pod), *n.* an elongated seed vessel, as that of the pea or bean.

Pod•go•ri•ca (pod′gə rēt′sə), *n.* the capital of Montenegro, in SW Yugoslavia. 132,290.

po·di·a·try (pə dī′ə trē, pō-), *n.* the diagnosis and treatment of foot disorders. —**po·di′a·trist,** *n.*

po·di·um (pō′dē əm), *n., pl.* **-di·ums, -di·a** (-dē ə). **1.** a small platform, as for an orchestra conductor. **2.** LECTERN (def. 2).

Poe (pō), *n.* **Edgar Allan,** 1809–49, U.S. short-story writer and poet.

po·em (pō′əm), *n.* a composition in verse, esp. one characterized by the use of heightened language and rhythm.

po′e·sy (-ə sē, -zē), *n., pl.* **-sies.** poetry.

po′et (-it), *n.* one who writes poetry.

po′et·as′ter (-as′tər), *n.* an inferior poet.

po·et′ic (-et′ik), *adj.* Also, **po·et′i·cal. 1.** possessing the qualities of poetry. **2.** of or characteristic of a poet or poetry. —**po·et′i·cal·ly,** *adv.*

poet′ic jus′tice, *n.* a particularly fitting distribution of rewards and punishments.

poet′ic li′cense, *n.* liberty, esp. as taken by a poet or other writer, in deviating from conventional form, fact, etc., to produce a desired effect.

po′et·ry (-i trē), *n.* **1.** poems collectively. **2.** the art of writing poems. **3.** poetic qualities however manifested.

po·grom (pə grum′, -grom′, pō-), *n.* an organized massacre, esp. of Jews. [< Russ *pogróm* destruction]

poi (poi), *n.* a Hawaiian food made of taro root pounded into a paste.

poign·ant (poin′yənt), *adj.* **1.** keenly distressing to the feelings. **2.** affecting the emotions. **3.** pungent to the smell. —**poign′an·cy,** *n.* —**poign′ant·ly,** *adv.*

poin·ci·an·a (poin′sē an′ə), *n., pl.* **-an·as.** any of several tropical trees with showy red, orange, or yellow flowers.

poin·set·ti·a (poin set′ē ə, -set′ə), *n., pl.* **-ti·as.** a plant, native to Mexico and Central America, having scarlet, pink, or white petallike bracts.

point (point), *n.* **1.** a sharp or tapering end. **2.** a projecting part of anything. **3.** something that has position but not extension, as the intersection of two lines. **4.** a dot used in writing, esp. a period. **5.** any of 32 horizontal directions on a compass. **6.** a degree or stage. **7.** a particular instant of time. **8.** a place or locality. **9.** the main idea or purpose. **10.** a strikingly effective fact, idea, etc. **11.** an individual element or item. **12.** a distinguishing mark or quality. **13.** a unit in counting, measuring, or scoring a game. **14.** a unit of price quotation, as one dollar in stock transactions. **15.** *Print.* a unit of type measurement equal to $1/72$ inch. —*v.t.* **16.** to direct (the finger, a weapon, etc.); aim. **17.** to direct attention to; indicate: *to point out advantages.* **18.** to furnish with a point; sharpen. **19.** to give added force to: *to point up the need for caution.* —*v.i.* **20.** to indicate position or direction or call attention, as with the finger. **21.** to be directed; tend: *Conditions point to inflation.* —*Idiom.* **22. beside the point,** irrelevant. **23. to the point,** relevant. —**point′y,** *adj.,* **-i·er, -i·est.**

point′-blank′, *adj.* **1.** aimed or fired straight at the mark, esp. from close range. **2.** straightforward or explicit. —*adv.* **3.** with a direct aim. **4.** bluntly; frankly.

point′ed, *adj.* **1.** having a point. **2.** sharp or piercing: *pointed wit.* **3.** aimed at a particular person: *a pointed remark.* **4.** marked; emphasized. —**point′ed·ly,** *adv.*

point′er, *n.* **1.** a long, tapering stick used in pointing things out, as on a blackboard. **2.** the hand on a watch dial, scale, etc. **3.** a large, shorthaired hunting dog. **4.** a piece of advice.

poin·til·lism (pwan′tl iz′əm), *n.* (*sometimes cap.*) a technique in painting of using dots of pure color that are optically mixed into the resulting hue by the viewer. —**poin′til·list,** *n., adj.*

point′less, *adj.* **1.** without relevance or force; meaningless. **2.** without a point. —**point′less·ly,** *adv.* —**point′less·ness,** *n.*

point′ of no′ return′, *n.* the critical point in an undertaking where one has committed oneself irrevocably to a course of action.

point′ of view′, *n.* **1.** a specified manner of consideration or appraisal. **2.** an opinion or attitude.

poise (poiz), *n., v.,* **poised, pois·ing.** —*n.* **1.** a state of balance or equilibrium. **2.** a dignified, self-confident manner or bearing. **3.** the way of being poised or carried. —*v.t., v.i.* **4.** to balance or be balanced.

poi·son (poi′zən), *n.* **1.** a substance that has an inherent tendency to destroy life or impair health. —*v.t.* **2.** to kill or injure with or as if with poison. **3.** to put poison into or upon. **4.** to ruin or corrupt. —**poi′son·ous,** *adj.* —**poi′son·ous·ly,** *adv.*

poi′son i′vy, *n.* **1.** a vine or shrub with trifoliate leaves and whitish berries: may cause dermatitis when touched. **2.** the rash caused by poison ivy.

poi′son pill′, *n.* a means of preventing a corporate takeover, as by implementing a policy that would be costly to a buyer.

poke (pōk), *v.,* **poked, pok·ing,** *n.* —*v.t.* **1.** to prod or push, as with something pointed. **2.** to make by or as if by poking. **3.** to thrust or push: *She poked her head out of the window.* —*v.i.* **4.** to make a thrusting movement, as with the finger. **5.** to thrust oneself obtrusively. **6.** to search curiously; pry. **7.** to proceed in a slow or aimless way. —*n.* **8.** a thrust or push. —*Idiom.* **9. poke fun at,** to ridicule.

pok·er¹ (pō′kər), *n.* a metal rod for stirring a fire.

pok·er² (pō′kər), *n.* a card game in which the players bet on the value of their cards.

pok′er face′, *n.* a face that shows no emotion or intention. —**pok′er-faced′,** *adj.*

pok′y or **-ey,** *adj.,* **-i·er, -i·est. 1.** slow; dawdling. **2.** (of a place) small and cramped.

pol (pol), *n. Informal.* a politician.

Pol., 1. Poland. **2.** Polish.

Po·land (pō′lənd), *n.* a republic in E central Europe. 38,700,291.

po·lar (pō′lər), *adj.* **1.** of or near the North or South Pole. **2.** of the poles of a magnet, sphere, etc.

po′lar bear′, *n.* a large white bear of arctic regions.

Po·lar·is (pō lâr′is, -lar′-, pə-), *n.* the bright star close to the north pole of the heavens.

po·lar·i·ty (pō lar′i tē, pə-), *n., pl.* **-ties. 1.** the property that produces unequal physical effects at different points in a body or system, as a magnet or storage battery. **2.** the presence of two contrasting principles or tendencies.

po·lar·i·za′tion (-lər ə zā′shən), *n.* **1.** a sharp division of a group into opposing factions. **2.** a state, or the production of a state, in which rays of light or similar radiation exhibit different properties in different directions.

po′lar·ize′, *v.,* **-ized, -iz·ing.** —*v.t.* **1.** to cause polarization in. **2.** to divide into sharply opposing factions. **3.** to give polarity to. —*v.i.* **4.** to become polarized.

Po·lar·oid (pō′lə roid′), *Trademark.* **1.** a brand of glare-reducing material that produces polarized light. **2.** the first brand of instant camera.

pole¹ (pōl), *n., v.,* **poled, pol·ing.** —*n.* **1.** a long, cylindrical, slender piece of wood, metal, etc. —*v.t., v.i.* **2.** to push or propel (a boat, raft, etc.) with a pole.

pole² (pōl), *n.* **1.** each of the extremities of the axis of the earth or of any spherical body. **2.** one of two opposite principles or tendencies. **3.** either of the two regions of an electric battery, magnet, etc., that exhibits electrical or magnetic polarity.

Pole (pōl), *n.* a native or inhabitant of Poland.

pole′cat′, *n., pl.* **-cats, -cat. 1.** a European weasel that ejects a fetid fluid when attacked or disturbed. **2.** any of various North American skunks.

po·lem·ic (pə lem′ik, pō-), *n.* **1.** a controversial argument, as one against some opinion, doctrine, etc. —*adj.* **2.** Also, **po·lem′i·cal.** of a polemic.

po·lem′ics, *n.* the art or practice of disputation. —**po·lem′i·cist** (-ə sist), *n.*

pole·star (pōl′stär′), *n.* **1.** POLARIS. **2.** a guiding principle.

pole′ vault′, *n.* a field event in which a vault over a crossbar is performed with the aid of a long pole. —**pole′-vault′,** *v.i.* —**pole′-vault′er,** *n.*

po•lice (pə lēs′), *n.*, *v.*, **-liced, -lic•ing.** —*n.* **1.** an organized civil force for maintaining order, preventing and detecting crime, and enforcing the laws. **2.** (*used with a pl. v.*) members of such a force. **3.** people who seek to regulate a specified activity, practice, etc.: *the language police.* —*v.t.* **4.** to regulate or keep in order with or as if with police. **5.** to clean and keep clean (a military camp, post, etc.).

po•lice′man or **-wom′an,** *n.*, *pl.* **-men** or **-wom•en.** a member of a police force.

police′ state′, *n.* a totalitarian state in which a national police force suppresses any act conflicting with government policy.

pol•i•cy¹ (pol′ə sē), *n.*, *pl.* **-cies. 1.** a course of action adopted and pursued by a government, corporation, etc. **2.** prudence or practical wisdom.

pol•i•cy² (pol′ə sē), *n.*, *pl.* **-cies.** a document embodying a contract of insurance.

pol′i•cy•hold′er, *n.* the individual or firm in whose name an insurance policy is written.

pol′icy wonk′, *n. Slang.* an obsessive student of public policy.

po•li•o•my•e•li•tis (pō′lē ō mī′ə lī′tis), *n.* an infectious viral disease of the spinal cord, sometimes resulting in paralysis. Also called **po′li•o′.**

pol•ish (pol′ish), *v.t.* **1.** to make smooth and glossy, esp. by rubbing. **2.** to make refined or elegant. —*v.i.* **3.** to become smooth and glossy through polishing. **4.** polish off, to finish or dispose of quickly. —*n.* **5.** a substance used to give smoothness or gloss. **6.** smoothness and gloss of surface. **7.** refinement; elegance. —**pol′ish•er,** *n.*

Po•lish (pō′lish), *n.* **1.** the Slavic language of Poland. —*adj.* **2.** of Poland, its inhabitants, or their language.

po•lite (pə līt′), *adj.*, **-lit•er, -lit•est. 1.** showing good manners; courteous. **2.** refined or cultured: *polite society.* —**po•lite′ly,** *adv.* —**po•lite′ness,** *n.*

pol•i•tesse (pol′i tes′, pô′lĕ-), *n.* politeness; courtesy. [< F]

pol•i•tic (pol′i tik), *adj.* **1.** shrewd or prudent in practical matters. **2.** expedient: *a politic reply.*

po•lit•i•cal (pə lit′i kəl), *adj.* of or concerned with government or politics. **po•lit′i•cal•ly,** *adv.*

polit′ical an′imal, *n.* a human being, considered as a member of society.

polit′ically correct′, *adj.* marked by a typically progressive orthodoxy on issues involving race, gender, ecology, etc. *Abbr.:* PC, P.C. —**polit′ical correct′ness,** *n.*

polit′ical sci′ence, *n.* a social science dealing with political institutions and with the principles and conduct of government.

pol•i•ti•cian (pol′i tish′ən), *n.* a person who is active in politics, esp. as a career.

po•lit•i•cize (pə lit′ə sīz′), *v.t.*, **-cized, -ciz•ing.** to give a political character or bias to.

pol•i•tick•ing (pol′i tik′ing), *n.* political activity, esp. campaigning.

po•lit•i•co (pə lit′i kō′), *n.*, *pl.* **-cos.** POLITICIAN.

pol•i•tics (pol′i tiks), *n.* (*used with a sing. or pl. v.*) **1.** the science or art of government. **2.** political affairs. **3.** political methods. **4.** political opinions. **5.** the use of strategy or intrigue in obtaining power or status.

pol′i•ty, *n.*, *pl.* **-ties. 1.** a particular form of government. **2.** a state or other organized community.

Polk (pōk), *n.* **James Knox,** 1795–1849, the 11th president of the U.S. 1845–49.

pol•ka (pōl′kə, pō′kə), *n.*, *pl.* **-kas. 1.** a lively couple dance of Bohemian origin. **2.** a piece of music for such a dance. [≪ Czech: lit., Polish woman]

pol′ka dot′ (pō′kə), *n.* a round spot repeated to form a pattern, esp. on a fabric.

poll (pōl), *n.* **1.** a sampling or collection of opinions on a subject, as in a public survey. **2.** the act of voting in an election. **3.** Usu., **polls.** the place where votes are cast. **4.** the number of votes cast. **5.** a list of individuals, as for purposes of taxing or voting. **6.** the head. —*v.t.* **7.** to take a sampling of the opinions of. **8.** to receive at the polls, as votes. **9.** to register

the votes of. **10.** to cast at the polls, as a vote. **11.** to cut short or cut off the hair or wool of (an animal) or the horns of (cattle). —**poll′er,** *n.*

pol•len (pol′ən), *n.* the fertilizing element of flowering plants, consisting of fine, powdery, yellowish grains.

pol′len count′, *n.* a count of the pollen in the air at a given time.

pol•li•nate (-ə nāt′), *v.t.*, **-nat•ed, -nat•ing.** to convey pollen to the stigma of (a flower). —**pol′li•na′tion,** *n.* —**pol′li•na′tor,** *n.*

pol•li•wog or **-ly•wog** (pol′ē wog′), *n.* TADPOLE.

Pol•lock (pol′ək), *n.* **Jackson,** 1912–56, U.S. painter.

poll•ster (pōl′stər), *n.* a person whose occupation is the taking of public-opinion polls.

poll′ tax′, *n.* a capitation tax, sometimes levied as a prerequisite for voting.

pol•lute (pə lōōt′), *v.t.*, **-lut•ed, -lut•ing.** to make foul or unclean, esp. with harmful chemical or waste products; contaminate. —**pol•lu′tant,** *n.* —**pol•lut′er,** *n.* —**pol•lu′tion,** *n.*

po•lo (pō′lō), *n.* a game played on horseback between two teams, who score points by driving a ball into the opponents' goal with a long-handled mallet.

Po•lo (pō′lō), *n.* **Marco,** c1254–1324, Venetian traveler to Asia.

pol•o•naise (pol′ə nāz′, pō′lə-), *n.* **1.** a slow dance of Polish origin. **2.** music for such a dance.

po•lo•ni•um (pə lō′nē əm), *n.* a radioactive chemical element. *Symbol:* Po; *at. no.:* 84; *at. wt.:* about 210.

pol•ter•geist (pōl′tər gīst′), *n.* a spirit supposed to manifest its presence by noises, knockings, etc.

pol•troon (pol trōōn′), *n.* a wretched coward; craven.

poly-, a combining form meaning much or many (*polygamy*).

pol•y•clin•ic (pol′ē klin′ik), *n.* a clinic or a hospital dealing with various diseases.

pol•y•es•ter (pol′ē es′tər), *n.* a polymer used to make resins, plastics, and textile fibers.

pol•y•eth•yl•ene (pol′ē eth′ə lēn′), *n.* a plastic polymer of ethylene used chiefly for containers, electrical insulation, and packaging.

po•lyg•a•my (pə lig′ə mē), *n.* the practice or condition of having more than one spouse, esp. a wife, at one time. —**po•lyg′a•mist,** *n.* —**po•lyg′a•mous,** *adj.*

pol•y•glot (pol′ē glot′), *adj.* **1.** able to speak, write, or read several languages. **2.** written in several languages. —*n.* **3.** a polyglot person. **4.** a book containing the same text in several languages.

pol•y•gon (pol′ē gon′), *n.* a closed plane figure having three or more, usu. straight, sides. —**po•lyg•o•nal** (pə lig′ə nl), *adj.*

pol•y•graph (pol′ē graf′, -gräf′), *n.* **1.** an instrument for recording tracings of variations in certain body activities. **2.** LIE DETECTOR.

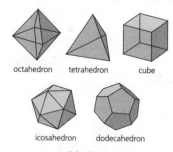

octahedron   tetrahedron   cube

icosahedron   dodecahedron

polyhedrons

pol•y•he•dron (pol′ē hē′drən), *n.*, *pl.* **-drons, -dra** (-drə). a solid figure having many faces. —**pol′y•he′dral,** *adj.*

pol•y•math (pol′ē math′), *n.* a person of great learning in several fields.

pol•y•mer (pol′ə mər), *n.* a compound of high molecular weight derived by the addition of many smaller molecules or by the condensation of many smaller molecules with the elimination of water, alcohol, or the like. —**pol′y•mer′ic** (-mer′ik), *adj.*

pol′y•mer•i•za′tion, *n.* the act or process of forming a polymer or polymeric compound. —**pol′y•mer•ize′,** *v.t., v.i.,* -**ized, -iz•ing.**

Pol•y•ne•sia (pol′ə nē′zhə), *n.* a series of island groups in the Pacific lying E of Micronesia. —**Pol′y•ne′sian,** *adj., n.*

pol•y•no•mi•al (pol′ə nō′mē əl), *n.* an algebraic expression consisting of the sum of two or more terms.

pol•yp (pol′ip), *n.* **1.** the cylindrical body form in the life cycle of a cnidarian, having stinging tentacles around the mouth. **2.** a projecting growth from a mucous surface, as of the nose.

po•lyph•o•ny (pə lif′ə nē), *n.* a musical style in which two or more melodic lines are in equitable juxtaposition. —**pol•y•phon•ic** (pol′ē fon′ik), *adj.*

pol•y•sty•rene (pol′ē stī′rēn, -stēr′ēn), *n.* a clear plastic or stiff foam, used in molded objects and as an insulator.

pol′y•syl•lab′ic, *adj.* **1.** consisting of four or more syllables. **2.** characterized by polysyllabic words. —**pol′y•syl′la•ble,** *n.*

pol•y•tech•nic (pol′ē tek′nik), *adj.* of or offering instruction in a variety of industrial arts, applied sciences, or technical subjects.

pol′y•the•ism, *n.* the doctrine of or belief in more than one god. —**pol′y•the′ist,** *n., adj.* —**pol′y•the•is′tic,** *adj.*

pol′y•un•sat′u•rat′ed, *adj.* of or noting a class of fats of animal or vegetable origin, associated with a low cholesterol content.

pol′y•vi′nyl, *adj.* pertaining to or derived from a vinyl polymer.

pol′yvi′nyl chlo′ride, *n.* a white, water-insoluble, thermoplastic resin, used for thin coatings, insulation, and piping.

po•made (po mād′, -mäd′, pō-), *n.* a scented ointment, as for the hair.

pome•gran•ate (pom′gran′it, pom′i-, pum′-), *n.* **1.** a round fruit with a leathery red rind, tart red pulp, and many seeds. **2.** the tree that bears this fruit.

pom•mel (pum′əl, pom′-), *n., v.,* -**meled, -mel•ing** or *(esp. Brit.)* -**melled, -mel•ling.** —*n.* **1.** a knob, as on the hilt of a sword. **2.** the protuberant part at the front and top of a saddle. —*v.t.* **3.** PUMMEL.

Po•mo•na (pə mō′nə), *n.* a city in SW California. 143,870.

pomp (pomp), *n.* **1.** stately or splendid display. **2.** ostentatious display.

pom•pa•dour (pom′pə dôr′, -dōōr′), *n.* an arrangement of hair in which it is brushed up high from or raised over the forehead.

pom•pa•no (pom′pə nō′), *n., pl.* -**nos, -no.** a deep-bodied food fish inhabiting waters off the S Atlantic and Gulf states.

Pom•peii (pom pā′), *n.* an ancient city in SW Italy, buried by an eruption of Mount Vesuvius in A.D. 79. —**Pom•pe′ian, Pom•pei′ian,** *n., adj.*

pom•pom (pom′pom′) also -**pon** (-pon′), *n.* an ornamental tuft, as of feathers or wool, used esp. on clothing.

pomp•ous (pom′pəs), *adj.* **1.** characterized by an ostentatious display of importance. **2.** ostentatiously lofty or high-flown. **3.** characterized by stately splendor. —**pom•pos′i•ty** (-pos′i tē), **pom′pous•ness,** *n.* —**pomp′ous•ly,** *adv.*

Ponce de Le•ón (pons′ də lē′ən, pon′sä dā lē ōn′), *n.* **Juan,** c1460–1521, Spanish explorer.

pon•cho (pon′chō), *n., pl.* -**chos.** a blanketlike cloak with a center opening for the head, esp. a waterproof one worn as a raincoat.

pond (pond), *n.* a body of water smaller than a lake.

pon•der (pon′dər), *v.i., v.t.* to consider (something) carefully and thoroughly. —**pon′der•er,** *n.*

pon•der•o′sa pine′ (pon′də rō′sə, pon′-), *n.* **1.** a large pine of W North America, having yellowish brown bark. **2.** its wood.

pon•der•ous (pon′dər əs), *adj.* **1.** heavy; massive. **2.** awkward or unwieldy. **3.** dull and labored. —**pon′der•ous•ly,** *adv.*

pone (pōn), *n. Chiefly Southern U.S.* an oval-shaped bread, esp. corn bread.

pon•gee (pon jē′), *n., pl.* -**gees.** silk of a slightly uneven weave, usu. having a natural tan color.

pon•iard (pon′yərd), *n.* a small, slender dagger.

pon•tiff (pon′tif), *n.* **1.** the pope. **2.** any high or chief priest. —**pon•tif′i•cal,** *adj.*

pon•tif•i•cate (*v.* pon tif′i kāt′; *n.* -kit, -kāt′), *v.,* -**cat•ed, -cat•ing,** *n.* —*v.i.* **1.** to speak in a pompous or dogmatic manner. **2.** to discharge the duties of a pontiff. —*n.* **3.** the office or term of office of a pontiff.

Pon′tius Pi′late (pon′shəs, -tē əs), *n.* PILATE, Pontius.

pon•toon (pon tōōn′), *n.* **1.** a boat or other float used as one of the supports for a temporary bridge. **2.** a float for a derrick, landing stage, etc. **3.** a seaplane float.

po•ny (pō′nē), *n., pl.* -**nies. 1.** a small horse of any of several breeds. **2.** *Informal.* a literal translation of a text, used illicitly as an aid in schoolwork. **3.** a small glass holding about one ounce (30 ml) of liqueur.

po′ny•tail′, *n.* a hairstyle in which the hair is gathered and fastened at the back of the head, so as to hang freely there.

pooch (pōōch), *n. Informal.* a dog.

poo•dle (pōōd′l), *n.* one of a breed of dogs with long, thick, frizzy or curly hair.

pooh (pōō, pōō), *interj.* an exclamation of disdain or contempt.

pooh-pooh (pōō′pōō′), *v.t., v.i.* to express disdain or contempt (for).

pool[1] (pōōl), *n.* **1.** a small pond. **2.** any small collection of liquid on a surface: *a pool of blood.* **3.** a large artificial basin filled with water for swimming.

pool[2] (pōōl), *n.* **1.** any of various games played on a table (**pool′ ta′ble**) with a cue ball and 15 other balls that are driven into pockets. **2.** the total amount staked by a combination of bettors. **3.** a combination of resources, funds, etc., for common advantage. **4.** a facility or service shared by a group of people: *a car pool.* —*v.t., v.i.* **5.** to combine in a common fund.

poop[1] (pōōp), *n.* **1.** a superstructure at the stern of a ship. **2.** a weather deck on top of a poop.

poop[2] (pōōp), *v.t. Informal.* to cause to become exhausted.

poop[3] (pōōp), *n. Slang.* a candid factual report; lowdown.

poor (pōōr), *adj.,* -**er, -est,** *n.* —*adj.* **1.** having little or no money or other means of support. **2.** characterized by poverty. **3.** lacking in resources, ability, etc. **4.** wretched; unfortunate. —*n.* **5. the poor,** poor persons collectively. —**poor′ly,** *adv.*

poncho

poor′house′, *n.* (formerly) an institution in which paupers were maintained at public expense.

poor′-mouth′, *v.i. Informal.* to plead or complain about poverty, usu. as an excuse.

Poor′ Rich′ard′s Al′manac, an almanac (1732–58) written and published by Benjamin Franklin.

pop¹ (pop), *v.,* **popped, pop•ping,** *n.* —*v.i.* **1.** to make or burst open with a sudden, explosive sound. **2.** to come or go quickly or suddenly. **3.** (of eyes) to protrude from the sockets. —*v.t.* **4.** to cause to pop. **5.** to put or thrust quickly: *Pop the muffins into the oven.* **6. pop up,** to hit a pop fly. —*n.* **7.** a short, quick, explosive sound. **8.** SODA POP.

pop² (pop), *adj.* **1.** of popular songs. **2.** of pop art. **3.** reflecting or aimed at the tastes of the general public: *pop culture.* —*n.* **4.** popular music.

pop., **1.** popular. **2.** population.

pop′ art′, *n.* art in which everyday objects and subjects are depicted with the flat naturalism of advertising or comic strips. —**pop′ ar′tist,** *n.*

pop′corn′, *n.* **1.** a variety of corn whose kernels burst open and puff out when heated. **2.** such corn when popped.

pope (pōp), *n.* (*often cap.*) the bishop of Rome as head of the Roman Catholic Church.

Pope, *n.* **Alexander,** 1688–1744, English poet.

pop′ fly′, *n., pl.* **pop flies.** *Baseball.* a high fly ball hit to the infield.

pop′gun′, *n.* a toy gun from which a pellet is shot by compressed air.

pop•in•jay (pop′in jā′), *n.* a vain, shallow person.

pop•lar (pop′lər), *n.* **1.** any of several rapidly growing softwood trees of the willow family. **2.** the wood of any such tree.

pop•lin (pop′lin), *n.* a finely corded fabric of cotton, rayon, silk, or wool.

pop′o′ver, *n.* a puffy, hollow muffin.

pop•py (pop′ē), *n., pl.* **-pies.** any of various plants with showy, usu. red flowers.

pop′py•cock′, *n.* nonsense; foolishness.

pop•u•lace (pop′yə ləs), *n.* **1.** (in a community or nation) the common people. **2.** the inhabitants of a place.

pop′u•lar (-lər), *adj.* **1.** approved or favored by people in general: *a popular preacher.* **2.** of or representing the people as a whole: *popular government.* **3.** prevailing among the people generally: *a popular superstition.* **4.** appealing to the public at large: *popular music.* —**pop′u•lar′i•ty** (-lar′i tē), *n.* —**pop′u•lar•ly,** *adv.*

pop′u•lar•ize′, *v.t.,* **-ized, -iz•ing.** to make popular. —**pop′u•lar•i•za′tion,** *n.*

pop′u•late′ (-lāt′), *v.t.,* **-lat•ed, -lat•ing. 1.** to inhabit. **2.** to furnish with inhabitants.

pop′u•la′tion, *n.* **1.** the total number of persons inhabiting a country, city, etc. **2.** the number of inhabitants of a particular group or class in a place: *the working-class population.* **3.** the things or individuals subject to a statistical study. **4.** the act or process of populating.

popula′tion explo′sion, *n.* a rapid increase in population attributed to an accelerating birthrate, an increase in life expectancy, etc.

pop′u•lism, *n.* a political philosophy or movement that promotes the interests of the common people. —**pop′u•list,** *n., adj.*

Pop′u•list Par′ty, *n.* a U.S. political party (1891–1904) advocating agrarian interests, expansion of currency, state control of railroads, and a graduated income tax. Also called **People's Party.**

pop′u•lous, *adj.* **1.** heavily populated: *a populous area.* **2.** crowded with people. —**pop′u•lous•ness,** *n.*

por•ce•lain (pôr′sə lin, pôrs′lin), *n.* a strong, vitreous, translucent ceramic material.

porch (pôrch), *n.* **1.** a covered approach or vestibule to a doorway. **2.** an open or enclosed room attached to the outside of a house.

por•cine (pôr′sīn, -sin), *adj.* of or resembling swine.

por•cu•pine (pôr′kyə pīn′), *n.* a large rodent with stiff, sharp, erectile quills.

pore¹ (pôr), *v.i.,* **pored, por•ing. 1.** to read or study with steady attention: *to pore over old manuscripts.* **2.** to ponder.

pore² (pôr), *n.* a minute opening, as in the skin or a leaf, for perspiration, absorption, etc.

pork (pôrk), *n.* the flesh of a hog or pig used as food. [< OF < L *porcus* hog]

pork′ bar′rel, *n.* government appropriations for local improvements designed to ingratiate legislators with their constituents.

por•nog•ra•phy (pôr nog′rə fē), *n.* writings, photographs, etc., intended to arouse sexual desire. —**por′no•graph′ic** (-nə graf′ik), *adj.* —**por′no•graph′i•cal•ly,** *adv.*

po•rous (pôr′əs), *adj.* **1.** permeable by water, air, etc. **2.** full of pores. —**po•ros•i•ty** (pô ros′i tē, pə-), *n.*

por•phy•ry (pôr′fə rē), *n., pl.* **-ries.** a very hard purplish red rock containing small crystals of feldspar.

por•poise (pôr′pəs), *n., pl.* **-pois•es, -poise.** any of certain toothed cetaceans having a blunt, rounded snout.

por•ridge (pôr′ij, por′-), *n.* a thick cereal made of oatmeal boiled in water or milk.

por•rin•ger (pôr′in jər, por′-), *n.* a low dish or cup, often with a handle, for soup, porridge, etc.

port¹ (pôrt), *n.* **1.** a city, town, or other place where ships load or unload. **2.** a harbor. —*Proverb.* **3. Any port in a storm,** any place of safety will do in an emergency.

port² (pôrt), *n.* **1.** the left-hand side of a ship or aircraft, facing forward. —*adj.* **2.** of or located on this side.

port³ (pôrt), *n.* a very sweet, dark red wine.

port⁴ (pôrt), *n.* **1.** an opening in a ship for admitting air and light or for taking on cargo. **2.** an aperture in a cylinder, as in machinery, for the passage of steam, air, etc. **3.** a data connection in a computer to which a peripheral device can be attached.

port⁵ (pôrt), *v.t.* to carry (a rifle or other weapon) diagonally in front of the body, with the muzzle pointing upward to the left.

Port., **1.** Portugal. **2.** Portuguese.

port′a•ble, *adj.* **1.** capable of being carried. **2.** easily carried by hand. —*n.* **3.** something portable. —**port′a•bil′i•ty,** *n.*

por•tage (pôr′tij, pôr täzh′), *n., v.,* **-taged, -tag•ing.** —*n.* **1.** the carrying of boats, supplies, etc., overland from one navigable water to another. **2.** the route over which this is done. —*v.i., v.t.* **3.** to carry (boats, supplies, etc.) over a portage.

por′tal (-tl), *n.* a door, gate, or entrance, esp. one of imposing appearance. —**por′taled, por′talled,** *adj.*

Port-au-Prince (pôrt′ō prins′, -praNs′), *n.* the capital of Haiti. 763,188.

port•cul•lis (pôrt kul′is), *n.* a strong iron grating at the gateway of a castle that can be let down to prevent passage.

portcullis

por•tend (pôr tend′), *v.t.* **1.** to indicate in advance, as an omen does. **2.** to signify; mean.

por′tent (-tent), *n.* **1.** an indication or omen of something momentous about to happen. **2.** threatening or disquieting significance.

por•ten′tous, *adj.* **1.** ominously significant. **2.** solemnly self-important. **3.** marvelous; amazing. —**por•ten′tous•ly,** *adv.*

Por•ter (pôr′tər, pōr′-), *n.* **1. Cole,** 1893–1964, U.S. composer. **2. Katherine Anne,** 1890–1980, U.S. writer. **3. William Sydney** ("*O. Henry*"), 1862–1910, U.S. short-story writer.

por•ter•house′, *n.* a choice cut of beef between the prime ribs and the sirloin.

port•fo•li•o (pôrt fō′lē ō′), *n., pl.* **-li•os. 1.** a flat, portable case for carrying loose papers, drawings, etc. **2.** a collection of drawings, photographs, etc., representative of a person's work. **3.** the securities held by an investor. **4.** the office or post of a minister of state.

port′hole′, *n.* a small, round window in the side of a ship.

por•ti•co (pôr′ti kō′), *n., pl.* **-coes, -cos.** a porchlike structure consisting of a roof supported by columns.

por•tiere or **-tière** (pôr tyâr′, -têr′), *n.* a curtain hung in a doorway.

por•tion (pôr′shən), *n.* **1.** a part of a whole; segment. **2.** the part of a whole allotted to a person or group; share. **3.** a person's fate or lot. **4.** a dowry. —*v.t.* **5.** to divide into portions. **6.** to furnish with a portion.

Port′land, *n.* a seaport in NW Oregon. 450,777.

Port′ Lou′is (lōō′is, lōō′ē), *n.* the capital of Mauritius. 139,038.

port′ly, *adj.,* **-li•er, -li•est.** rather heavy or fat.

port•man•teau (pôrt man′tō), *n., pl.* **-teaus, -teaux** (-tōz, -tō). *Chiefly Brit.* a leather trunk that opens into two halves.

Port′ Mores′by (môrz′bē), *n.* the capital of Papua New Guinea. 152,100.

port′ of en′try, *n.* any place where goods, travelers, or immigrants may enter a country subject to inspection.

Port′-of-Spain′, *n.* the capital of Trinidad and Tobago. 58,400.

Por•to No•vo (pôr′tō nō′vō), *n.* the capital of Benin. 208,258.

Por•to Ri•co (pôr′tə rē′kō), *n.* former name of PUERTO RICO.

por•trait (pôr′trit, -trāt), *n.* **1.** a painting or photograph of a person, esp. of the face. **2.** a verbal description.

por′trait•ist, *n.* a person who makes portraits.

por′trai•ture (-chər), *n.* the art or practice of making portraits.

por•tray (pôr trā′), *v.t.* **1.** to make a likeness of by drawing, painting, etc. **2.** to depict in words. **3.** to represent dramatically, as on the stage. —**por•tray′al,** *n.*

Ports•mouth (pôrts′məth), *n.* a seaport in SE Virginia. 103,464.

Por•tu•gal (pôr′chə gəl), *n.* a republic in SW Europe. 9,867,654.

Por•tu•guese′ (-gēz′, -gēs′), *n., pl.* **-guese,** *adj.* —*n.* **1.** a native or inhabitant of Portugal. **2.** a Romance language spoken in Portugal, Brazil, the Azores, and Madeira. —*adj.* **3.** of Portugal, its people, or their language.

Por′tuguese man′-of-war′, *n.* a large colonial marine animal having a buoyant sac from which dangle poisonous stinging tentacles.

por•tu•lac•a (pôr′chə lak′ə), *n., pl.* **-as.** a fleshy annual plant with showy, variously colored flowers.

pose (pōz), *v.,* **posed, pos•ing,** *n.* —*v.i.* **1.** to assume or hold a physical position or attitude, as for an artistic purpose. **2.** to pretend to be what one is not: *to pose as a police officer.* **3.** to behave in an affected manner. —*v.t.* **4.** to place in a particular position, as for a picture. **5.** to state or put forward: *That poses a problem.* —*n.* **6.** a bodily attitude or posture, esp. one assumed for an artistic purpose. **7.** a mental posture that is assumed for effect.

Po•sei•don (pō sīd′n, pə-), *n.* the ancient Greek god of the sea and of horses.

pos′er, *n.* a person who poses.

po•seur (pō zûr′), *n.* a person who affects a character, manner, etc., to impress others.

posh (posh), *adj.* stylishly elegant; luxurious.

pos•it (poz′it), *v.t.* to lay down or assume as a fact or principle; postulate.

po•si•tion (pə zish′ən), *n.* **1.** the location or place of a person or thing at a given moment. **2.** the

proper or usual place: *out of position.* **3.** situation or condition with relation to circumstances: *The question put me in an awkward position.* **4.** status or standing; rank. **5.** a post of employment; job. **6.** the manner of being placed, disposed, or arranged. **7.** attitude or opinion. —*v.t.* **8.** to put in a particular position.

pos•i•tive (poz′i tiv), *adj.* **1.** confident in opinion or assertion; sure. **2.** showing approval or agreement. **3.** affirmative: *a positive answer.* **4.** constructive: *a positive attitude.* **5.** explicitly stated, stipulated, etc.: *a positive denial.* **6.** certain: *positive proof.* **7.** overconfident or dogmatic. **8.** possessing an actual force, existence, etc. **9.** proceeding in a direction assumed as beneficial, auspicious, etc.: *a positive trend.* **10. a.** noting or pertaining to the electricity in a body or substance that is deficient in electrons. **b.** indicating a point in a circuit that has a higher potential than that of another point. **11.** (of a diagnostic test) indicating the presence of the disease, condition, etc., tested for. **12.** noting a numerical quantity greater than zero. **13.** designating the initial degree of grammatical comparison, used with reference to the base form of an adjective or adverb, as *good* or *smoothly.* **14.** of or noting a photographic print showing the brightness values as they are in the subject. —*n.* **15.** something positive. **16. a.** the positive degree in grammatical comparison. **b.** the positive form of an adjective or adverb. **17.** a positive photographic image. —**pos′i•tive•ly,** *adv.*

pos•i•tron (poz′i tron′), *n.* an elementary particle with the same mass as an electron but a positive charge.

poss., 1. possessive. **2.** possibly.

pos•se (pos′ē), *n., pl.* **-ses.** a body of persons given legal authority to assist a peace officer, esp. in an emergency.

pos•sess (pə zes′), *v.t.* **1.** to have as property; own. **2.** to have as a faculty, quality, or the like. **3.** to have a powerful influence on; control or dominate: *possessed by an idea.* —**pos•ses′sor,** *n.*

pos•sessed′, *adj.* controlled or moved by a strong feeling, madness, or a supernatural power.

pos•ses′sion, *n.* **1.** the act of possessing or state of being possessed. **2.** a thing possessed or owned. **3. possessions,** property or wealth. **4.** a territorial dominion of a state.

pos•ses′sive, *adj.* **1.** desiring to dominate or be the only influence on someone. **2.** of possession or ownership. **3.** (of a word, construction, or grammatical case) indicating possession, ownership, origin, etc., as *Jane's* in *Jane's coat.* —*n.* **4.** the possessive case. **5.** a possessive form or construction. —**pos•ses′sive•ly,** *adv.* —**pos•ses′sive•ness,** *n.*

pos•si•ble (pos′ə bəl), *adj.* **1.** that may or can exist, happen, be done, etc. **2.** capable of being true: *It is possible that she has gone.* —**pos′si•bil′i•ty,** *n., pl.* **-ties.** —**pos′si•bly,** *adv.*

pos•sum (pos′əm), *n., pl.* **-sums, -sum.** OPOSSUM.

post¹ (pōst), *n.* **1.** a piece of timber or metal set upright as a support, a point of attachment, etc. **2.** the point where a race begins or ends. **3.** *Computers.* a message sent to a newsgroup. —*v.t.* **4.** to affix (a notice) to a post, wall, etc. **5.** to bring to public notice, as by a poster: *to post a reward.* **6.** to publish the name of in a list. **7.** to put up signs on (property) forbidding trespass. **8.** *Computers.* to send (a message) to a newsgroup.

post² (pōst), *n.* **1.** a position of duty, employment, or trust: *a diplomatic post.* **2.** a military station with permanent buildings. **3.** the body of troops occupying a military station. —*v.t.* **4.** to station at a post. **5.** to provide, as bail.

post³ (pōst), *n.* **1.** *Chiefly Brit.* **a.** a single delivery of mail. **b.** the mail itself. —*v.t.* **2.** to supply with up-to-date information: *Keep me posted on your activities.* **3.** *Chiefly Brit.* to send by mail. **4.** *Bookkeeping.* to transfer (an entry or item) from a journal to a ledger. **5.** to travel with speed; hasten.

post-, a prefix meaning: subsequent to or after (*post-date*); at the rear of or behind (*postnasal*).

post•age (pō′stij), *n.* the charge for the conveyance of matter sent by mail.

post•al (pōs′tl), *adj.* **1.** of or pertaining to the post office or mail service. —**Idiom. 2. go postal,** *Slang.* to lose control or go crazy.

post′al card′, *n.* a card sold by the post office with a stamplike motif and value printed on it.

post′card′, *n.* **1.** a small card usu. having a picture on one side and space for a stamp, address, and message on the other. **2.** POSTAL CARD.

post•date (pōst dāt′, pōst′-), *v.t.* **-dat•ed, -dat•ing. 1.** to date (a check, invoice, etc.) with a date later than the current or actual date. **2.** to follow in time.

post′er, *n.* a placard or bill for posting in a public place, as for advertising.

post′er child′, *n.* a person or thing that exemplifies or represents: *She could be a poster child for good sportsmanship.*

pos•te•ri•or (po stēr′ē ər, pō-), *adj.* **1.** situated behind or at the rear of. **2.** coming after in order or in time. —*n.* **3.** the buttocks.

pos•ter•i•ty (po ster′i tē), *n.* **1.** future generations collectively. **2.** all the descendants of one person.

post′ exchange′, *n.* a retail store on a military post.

post•grad•u•ate (pōst graj′ōō it, -āt′), *adj.* **1.** of or consisting of postgraduates. —*n.* **2.** a student who is taking advanced work after graduation.

post′haste′, *adv.* with the greatest possible speed.

post•hu•mous (pos′chə məs, -chōō-), *adj.* **1.** occurring after one's death. **2.** published after the death of the author. **3.** born after the death of the father. —**post′hu•mous•ly,** *adv.*

post•hyp•not•ic (pōst′hip not′ik), *adj.* (of a suggestion) made during hypnosis so as to be effective after awakening.

pos•til•ion (po stil′yən, po-), *n.* a person who rides the leading left horse of those drawing a carriage. Also, *esp. Brit.,* **pos•til′lion.**

post′in•dus′tri•al, *adj.* of or characteristic of the era following large-scale industrialization.

post′lude (-lōōd), *n.* a concluding piece of music.

post′man, *n., pl.* **-men.** MAIL CARRIER.

post′mark′, *n.* **1.** an official mark stamped on mail passed through a postal system, showing the place and date of sending. —*v.t.* **2.** to stamp with a postmark.

post′mas′ter, *n.* the official in charge of a post office.

post′master gen′eral, *n., pl.* **postmasters general.** the executive head of the postal system of a country.

post′me•rid′i•an, *adj.* occurring after noon.

post′ me•rid′i•em (mə rid′ē əm, -em′), *adj.* See P.M.

post′mis′tress, *n.* a woman in charge of a post office.

post•mod′ern, *adj.* (*sometimes cap.*) pertaining to any of various movements in the arts or literature developing in the late 20th century in reaction to modernism.

post•mor′tem (-môr′təm), *adj.* **1.** of or occurring in the time following death. **2.** pertaining to examination of the body after death. —*n.* **3.** a postmortem examination; autopsy. **4.** an evaluation after the end or fact of something.

post•na′sal drip′, *n.* a trickling of mucus onto the pharyngeal surface from the posterior portion of the nasal cavity.

post•na′tal, *adj.* subsequent to childbirth.

post′ of′fice, *n.* **1.** an office of a government postal system at which mail is handled, stamps are sold, and other services rendered. **2.** (*often caps.*) the department of a government in charge of the mail.

post•op′er•a•tive, *adj.* occurring after a surgical operation.

post′paid′, *adj., adv.* with the postage prepaid.

post•par′tum (-pär′təm), *adj.* following childbirth.

post•pone (pōst pōn′, pōs-), *v.t.* **-poned, -pon•ing.** to put off to a later time. —**post•pone′ment,** *n.*

post•pran•di•al (pōst pran′dē əl), *adj.* after a meal.

post•script (pōst′skript′, pōs′-), *n.* a note added to a letter that has already been signed.

pos•tu•late (*v.* pos′chə lāt′; *n.* -lit, -lāt′), *v.,* **-lat•ed, -lat•ing,** *n.* —*v.t.* **1.** to assume the existence or truth of as a basis for reasoning or arguing. **2.** to assume without proof; take for granted. —*n.* **3.** something postulated. **4.** a necessary condition; prerequisite. —**pos′tu•la′tion,** *n.*

pos•ture (pos′chər), *n., v.,* **-tured, -tur•ing.** —*n.* **1.** the position or carriage of the body. **2.** an affected or unnatural attitude. **3.** a policy or stance, as that adopted by a government. —*v.i.* **4.** to act in an affected or artificial manner.

post′war′, *adj.* following a war.

po•sy (pō′zē), *n., pl.* **-sies.** a flower or bouquet.

pot (pot), *n., v.,* **pot•ted, pot•ting.** —*n.* **1.** a container of earthenware, metal, etc., usu. round and deep, used for cooking, serving, etc. **2.** such a container with its contents. **3.** FLOWERPOT. **4.** all the money bet at a single time. —*v.t.* **5.** to put into a pot. **6.** to cook or preserve in a pot. —*Saying.* **7. go to pot,** to become ruined. —*Saying.* **8. pot calling the kettle black,** hypocrisy. —**pot′ful′,** *n., pl.* **-fuls.**

po•ta•ble (pō′tə bəl), *adj.* **1.** fit for drinking. —*n.* **2.** Usu., **-bles.** drinkable liquids. —**po′ta•bil′i•ty,** *n.*

pot•ash (pot′ash′), *n.* a potassium compound obtained from wood ashes, used in making soap, glass, etc.

po•tas•si•um (pə tas′ē əm), *n.* a silvery white metallic element whose compounds are used in industry and medicine. *Symbol:* K; *at. wt.:* 39.102; *at. no.:* 19.

potas′sium ni′trate, *n.* a crystalline compound used in gunpowders, fertilizers, and preservatives.

po•ta•to (pə tā′tō, -tə), *n., pl.* **-toes. 1.** the edible tuber of a cultivated plant of the nightshade family. **2.** the plant itself.

pota′to chip′, *n.* a thin slice of potato fried until crisp and usu. salted.

pot′bel′ly, *n., pl.* **-lies.** a protuberant belly. —**pot′bel′lied,** *adj.*

pot′boil′er, *n.* a mediocre work of literature or art produced merely for financial gain.

po•tent (pōt′nt), *adj.* **1.** powerful; mighty. **2.** cogent; persuasive. **3.** producing powerful physical or chemical effects. **4.** (of a male) capable of sexual intercourse. —**po′ten•cy,** *n.*

po•ten•tate (-tāt′), *n.* a person who possesses great power, as a monarch.

po•ten•tial (pə ten′shəl), *adj.* **1.** possible, as opposed to actual. **2.** capable of being or becoming. —*n.* **3.** something potential; possibility. **4.** a latent excellence or ability that may or may not be developed. **5.** the relative electrification of a point or body

---

post′ad•o•les′cent, *adj., n.*
post′-Ar•is•to•te′lian, *n.*
post•clas′si•cal, *adj.*
post′col•le′giate, *adj.*
post′co•lo′ni•al, *adj.*
post′con•so•nan′tal, *adj.*
post-cor′o•nar′y, *adj.*
post′-Dar•win′i•an, *adj.*
post′de•liv′er•y, *adj.*
post′de•vel′op•men′tal, *adj.*
post′di•ag•nos′tic, *adj.*

post′di•ges′tive, *adj.*
post•doc′tor•al, *adj.*
post′e•lec′tion, *adj.*
post-Freud′i•an, *adj.*
post•gla′cial, *adj.*
Post′-Im•pres′sion•ism, *n.*
post′launch′, *adj.*
post-Marx′i•an, *adj.*
post′men•o•pau′sal, *adj.*
post′mil•len′ni•al, *adj.*
post′-Na•po′le•on′ic, *adj.*
post•na′sal, *adj.*

post′-New•to′ni•an, *adj.*
post•nup′tial, *adj.*
post•pri′ma•ry, *adj.*
post′pu′ber•ty, *adj.*
post′pu•bes′cence, *n.*
post′pu•bes′cent, *n., adj.*
post′-Ref•or•ma′tion, *n.*
post′-Rev•o•lu′tion•ar′y, *adj.*
post•sea′son, *adj., n.*
post•sea′son•al, *adj.*
post′sur′gi•cal, *adj.*
post′-Vic′to′ri•an, *adj.*

with respect to some other electrification, as that of the earth. —**po•ten′ti•al′i•ty** (-shē al′i tē), *n., pl.* -ties. —**po•ten′tial•ly,** *adv.*

poth•er (poth′ər), *n.* **1.** commotion; uproar. —*v.t., v.i.* **2.** to worry; bother.

pot′herb′, *n.* any herb boiled for use as a vegetable or added as a seasoning.

pot′hold′er, *n.* a thick piece of material used in handling hot pots and dishes.

pot′hole′, *n.* a hole formed in pavement.

pot′hook′, *n.* **1.** a hook for suspending a pot over an open fire. **2.** an S-shaped stroke in writing.

po•tion (pō′shan), *n.* a drink, esp. one having or reputed to have medicinal, poisonous, or magical powers.

Pot•i•phar (pot′ə fər), *n.* the Egyptian officer whose wife tried to seduce Joseph. Gen. 39:1–20.

pot′luck′, *n.* **1.** a meal that happens to be available without special preparation. **2.** Also called **pot′luck sup′per.** a meal to which participants bring food to be shared.

Po•to•mac (pə tō′mək), *n.* a river flowing SE from West Virginia to the Chesapeake Bay. 287 mi. (460 km) long.

pot′pie′ (-pī′, -pī′), *n.* a deep-dish pie of meat or chicken and vegetables topped with a crust.

pot•pour•ri (pō′pŏŏ rē′), *n., pl.* -ris. **1.** a fragrant mixture of dried flower petals and spices. **2.** any miscellaneous grouping.

pot′ roast′, *n.* a cut of beef stewed in one piece.

pot′sherd′ (-shûrd′), *n.* a pottery fragment, esp. one of archaeological value.

pot′shot′, *n.* **1.** a shot at an animal or person within easy range. **2.** a casual or aimless shot. **3.** a random or incidental criticism.

pot•tage (pot′ij), *n.* a thick soup made of vegetables, with or without meat.

pot′ted, *adj.* transplanted into or grown in a pot.

pot′ter, *n.* a person who makes pottery.

Pot•ter (pot′ər), *n.* **Beatrix,** 1866–1943, English writer and illustrator of children's books.

pot′ter's field′, *n.* (*sometimes caps.*) a burial place for unidentified persons and the poor. Matt. 27:7.

pot′ter's wheel′, *n.* a rotating disk upon which clay is molded by a potter.

pot′ter•y, *n., pl.* -ies. **1.** ceramic ware, esp. earthenware and stoneware. **2.** the art or business of a potter. **3.** a place where earthen vessels are made.

pouch (pouch), *n.* **1.** a small bag or similar receptacle: *a tobacco pouch.* **2.** a bag for carrying mail. **3.** a baglike anatomical structure, as the receptacle for the young of marsupials. —*v.t.* **4.** to put into a pouch. —*v.i.* **5.** to form a pouch or pouchlike cavity.

poul•tice (pōl′tis), *n., v.,* -ticed, -tic•ing. —*n.* **1.** a soft, moist mass of cloth, meal, herbs, etc., applied as a medicament to the body. —*v.t.* **2.** to apply a poultice to.

poul•try (pōl′trē), *n.* domesticated fowl valued for their meat and eggs, as chickens and turkeys.

pounce (pouns), *v.,* pounced, pounc•ing, *n.* —*v.i.* **1.** to swoop down or spring suddenly. **2.** to seize eagerly or suddenly. —*n.* **3.** a sudden swoop or spring.

pound¹ (pound), *v.t.* **1.** to strike repeatedly with great force, as with the fist. **2.** to crush into a powder or paste by beating repeatedly. —*v.i.* **3.** to strike heavy blows repeatedly. **4.** to throb violently, as the heart. **5.** to walk or go with heavy steps.

pound² (pound), *n., pl.* pounds, pound. **1. a.** an avoirdupois unit of weight equal to 7000 grains, divided into 16 ounces (0.453 kg). **b.** a troy unit of weight equal to 5760 grains, divided into 12 ounces (0.373 kg). **2.** Also called **pound′ ster′ling.** the basic monetary unit of the United Kingdom, formerly equal to 20 shillings or 240 pence: equal to 100 new pence after decimalization in 1971. **3.** the basic monetary unit of Cyprus, Egypt, Ireland, Lebanon, and Syria.

pound³ (pound), *n.* an enclosure maintained by public authorities for confining stray or homeless animals.

pound′ cake′, *n.* a rich cake made with flour, butter, sugar, and eggs.

pour (pôr), *v.t.* **1.** to send (a liquid, fluid, etc.) flowing, as from one container to another. **2.** to emit, propel, or utter continuously or rapidly. —*v.i.* **3.** to move or proceed in great quantity or number. **4.** to flow forth or along; stream. **5.** to rain heavily.

pout (pout), *v.i.* **1.** to thrust out the lips, esp. in displeasure or sullenness. **2.** to look or be sullen. —*n.* **3.** the act of pouting. **4.** a fit of sullenness: *to be in a pout.* —**pout′er,** *n.* —**pout′ing•ly,** *adv.*

pov•er•ty (pov′ər tē), *n.* **1.** the state or condition of being poor. **2.** deficiency of necessary or desirable ingredients, qualities, etc. **3.** scantiness; insufficiency.

pov′erty-strick′en, *adj.* extremely poor.

POW, *pl.* POWs, POW's. prisoner of war.

pow•der (pou′dər), *n.* **1.** matter reduced to a state of fine, loose particles by grinding, disintegration, etc. **2.** a preparation in this form, as face powder. **3.** loose, fresh snow that is not granular, wet, or packed. —*v.t.* **4.** to reduce to powder; pulverize. **5.** to sprinkle or cover with powder. —**pow′der•y,** *adj.*

pow′der keg′, *n.* **1.** a barrellike container for gunpowder. **2.** a dangerously explosive situation.

pow′der room′, *n.* a public lavatory for women.

Pow•ell (pou′əl), *n.* **1. Adam Clayton, Jr.,** 1908–72, U.S. clergyman, politician, and civil-rights leader: congressman 1945–67, 1969–71. **2. Co•lin** (kō′lin, kol′in), born 1937, U.S. general.

pow•er (pou′ər), *n.* **1.** ability to do or act. **2.** strength; might; force. **3.** the possession of control over others; authority. **4.** legal ability or authority. **5.** a person or thing that possesses authority or influence. **6.** a nation having international authority or influence. **7.** Often, **powers.** a deity; divinity: *the heavenly powers.* **8. powers,** an order of angels.Compare ANGEL (def. 1). **9.** mechanical or physical energy: *hydroelectric power.* **10.** Math. the product obtained by multiplying a quantity by itself one or more times. **11.** the magnifying capacity of a microscope, telescope, etc. —*v.t.* **12.** to supply with electricity or other means of power. —*adj.* **13.** operated by a motor or electricity. **14.** operated by a procedure in which manual effort is supplemented or replaced by hydraulic, mechanical, or electric means: *power brakes.* **15.** conducting electricity. **16.** Informal. involving or characteristic of those having power or authority: *a power breakfast.*

pow′er curve′, *n.* Informal. the capacity to sustain influence.

pow′er•ful (-fəl), *adj.* having or exerting great power, strength, authority, influence, etc. —**pow′er•ful•ly,** *adv.*

pow′er•house′, *n.* **1.** a building where electricity is generated. **2.** a person or group with great energy or potential for success.

pow′er•less, *adj.* **1.** unable to produce an effect; ineffective. **2.** lacking power to act; helpless. —**pow′er•less•ly,** *adv.*

pow′er lunch′, *n.* a meal at which business or political matters are discussed.

pow′er of attor′ney, *n.* written legal authorization for another person to act in one's place.

pow′er of the purse′, *n.* the influence of money.

pow•wow (pou′wou′), *n.* **1.** a council or conference of or with North American Indians. **2.** Informal. any conference.

pox (poks), *n.* **1.** a disease characterized by multiple skin pustules, as smallpox. **2.** syphilis.

pp., **1.** pages. **2.** past participle.

P.P., 1. parcel post. **2.** postpaid. **3.** prepaid.

ppd., 1. postpaid. **2.** prepaid.

ppr. or **p.ppr.,** present participle.

P.P.S. or **p.p.s.,** an additional postscript.

PR or **P.R., 1.** public relations. **2.** Puerto Rico.

Pr, Chem. Symbol. praseodymium.

Pr., Provençal.

prac•ti•ca•ble (prak′ti kə bəl), *adj.* **1.** capable of being put into practice. **2.** capable of being used. —**prac′ti•ca•bil′i•ty,** *n.* —**prac′ti•ca•bly,** *adv.*

prac·ti·cal, *adj.* **1.** of, involving, or resulting from practice or action. **2.** adapted or suited for actual use: *practical instructions.* **3.** inclined toward or fitted for action or useful activities. **4.** engaged or experienced in actual practice or work: *a practical politician.* **5.** matter-of-fact; prosaic. **6.** being such in practice or effect: *a practical certainty.* —**prac'ti·cal'·i·ty,** *n., pl.* **-ties.**

prac'tical joke', *n.* a playful trick in which the victim is placed in an embarrassing position. —**prac'tical jok'er,** *n.*

prac'ti·cal·ly, *adv.* **1.** in a practical manner. **2.** from a practical point of view. **3.** almost; nearly.

prac'tical nurse', *n.* a nurse with less training than a registered nurse, usu. licensed by the state.

prac'tice (-tis), *n., v.,* **-ticed, -tic·ing.** —*n.* **1.** habitual or customary course of action or way of doing something. **2.** repeated performance or exercise in order to acquire skill. **3.** skill so gained. **4.** the action of doing something: *to put a scheme into practice.* **5.** the exercise or pursuit of a profession. —*v.t.* **6.** to perform or do habitually or usually. **7.** to pursue as a profession. **8.** to perform or exercise repeatedly in order to acquire skill. —*v.i.* **9.** to do something repeatedly in order to acquire skill. —*Proverb.* **10. Practice makes perfect,** practice improves skill. **11. Practice what you preach,** do what you tell others to do. Also, *Brit.,* **prac'tise** (for defs. 6–9).

prac'ticed, *adj.* skilled or proficient through practice.

prac'ti·cum (-ti kəm), *n.* a course of study devoted to practical experience in a field.

prac·ti'tion·er (-tish'ə nər), *n.* a person engaged in the practice of a profession or occupation.

prae·tor (prē'tər), *n.* an ancient Roman magistrate subordinate to a consul. —**prae·to'ri·an** (-tôr'ē ən), *adj.*

prag·mat·ic (prag mat'ik), *adj.* **1.** concerned with practical considerations or consequences. **2.** of philosophical pragmatism. —**prag·mat'i·cal·ly,** *adv.*

prag'ma·tism (-mə tiz'əm), *n.* **1.** emphasis on practical results or concerns. **2.** a philosophical system stressing practical consequences as constituting the essential criterion in determining truth or value. —**prag'ma·tist,** *n., adj.*

Prague (prag), *n.* the capital of the Czech Republic. 1,215,000.

prai·rie (prâr'ē), *n., pl.* **-ries.** an extensive, grassy, level or rolling tract of land.

prai'rie dog', *n.* a burrowing squirrel of W North American and N Mexican plains and prairies.

prai'rie schoon'er, *n.* a covered wagon used by pioneers in crossing the plains of North America.

praise (prāz), *n., v.,* **praised, prais·ing.** —*n.* **1.** an expression of approval or admiration. **2.** the offering of grateful homage as an act of worship. —*v.t.* **3.** to express approval or admiration of. **4.** to offer grateful homage to (God or a deity). —*Saying.* **5. Praise the Lord and pass the ammunition,** rely on your own efforts as well as on God: title of a popular song during World War II.

praise'wor'thy, *adj.* deserving of praise. —**praise'wor'thi·ness,** *n.*

pra·line (prā'lēn, prä'-), *n.* a confection made of nuts and sugar cooked until caramelized.

prance (prans, präns), *v.,* **pranced, pranc·ing,** *n.* —*v.i.* **1.** to move in a lively or spirited manner; caper. **2.** to move in a proud or insolent manner. **3.** (esp. of a horse) to spring from the hind legs, or move by springing. —*n.* **4.** the act of prancing. —**pranc'er,** *n.*

prank (prangk), *n.* a playful, sometimes malicious, trick. —**prank'ster,** *n.*

pra·se·o·dym·i·um (prā'zē ō dim'ē əm, prā'sē-), *n.* a rare-earth metallic element. *Symbol:* Pr; *at. wt.:* 140.91; *at. no.:* 59.

prate (prāt), *v.i., v.t.,* **prat·ed, prat·ing.** to talk excessively and pointlessly. —**prat'er,** *n.*

prat·fall (prat'fôl'), *n.* a fall on the buttocks, often regarded as comical or humiliating.

prat·tle (prat'l), *v.,* **-tled, -tling,** *n.* —*v.i., v.t.* **1.** to

talk in a childish or simple-minded way. —*n.* **2.** chatter; babble.

prawn (prôn), *n.* any of various shrimplike crustaceans, some of which are used as food.

pray (prā), *v.t.* **1.** to offer devout petition, praise, thanks, etc., to (God or an object of worship). **2.** to make earnest petition to (a person). —*v.i.* **3.** to engage in prayer. **4.** to make entreaty to a person or for a thing.

prayer (prâr), *n.* **1.** a devout petition to or spiritual communion with God or an object of worship. **2.** the act of praying. **3.** a formula of words used in praying. **4. prayers,** a religious observance consisting mainly of prayer. **5.** something prayed for. **6.** a petition; entreaty. **7.** a negligible hope or chance.

Prayer' of Manas'seh, *n.* a book of the Apocrypha.

pray'ing man'tis, *n.* MANTIS.

PRC, People's Republic of China.

pre-, a prefix meaning: before or earlier than (*precook*); in front or ahead of (*preface*); above or surpassing (*preeminent*).

preach (prēch), *v.t.* **1.** to deliver (a sermon). **2.** to advocate (moral principles, conduct, etc.) as right or advisable. —*v.i.* **3.** to deliver a sermon. **4.** to give advice in an insistent, tedious, or moralizing way. —**preach'er,** *n.* —**preach'ment,** *n.* —**preach'y,** *adj.,* **-i·er, -i·est.**

pre·am·ble (prē'am'bəl, prē am'-), *n.* an introductory statement, as of a statute or constitution, stating the intent of what follows.

pre'ar·range', *v.t.,* **-ranged, -rang·ing.** to arrange in advance. —**pre'ar·range'ment,** *n.*

Pre·cam·bri·an (prē kam'brē ən, -kām'-), *adj.* noting or pertaining to the earliest era of earth history, during which the earth's crust formed and life first appeared.

pre·can'cer·ous, *adj.* showing pathological changes that may be preliminary to malignancy.

pre·car·i·ous (pri kâr'ē əs), *adj.* **1.** dependent on circumstances beyond one's control; uncertain. **2.** dangerous because insecure or unsteady. —**pre·car'·i·ous·ly,** *adv.*

pre·cau·tion (pri kô'shən), *n.* a measure taken in advance to avert possible harm. —**pre·cau'tion·ar'y,** *adj.*

pre·cede (pri sēd'), *v.t., v.i.,* **-ced·ed, -ced·ing.** to go or come before, as in place, rank, importance, or time.

prec·e·dence (pres'i dəns, pri sēd'ns), *n.* the act, fact, or right of preceding.

prec·e·dent (*n.* pres'i dənt; *adj.* pri sēd'nt, pres'i-dənt), *n.* **1.** an act, decision, or case that may serve as an example, guide, or justification for subsequent ones. **2.** established practice; custom. —*adj.* **3.** preceding; prior.

pre·ced·ing (pri sē'ding), *adj.* that precedes; previous.

pre·cept (prē'sept), *n.* an injunction as to moral conduct; maxim.

pre·cep·tor (pri sep'tər, prē'sep-), *n.* a teacher; tutor.

pre·cinct (prē'singkt), *n.* **1.** a district, as of a city, marked out for administrative purposes or for police protection. **2.** the police station in such a district. **3.** one of a fixed number of voting districts of a city, town, etc. **4. precincts,** environs. **5.** a bounded space within which a building or place is situated.

pre·ci·os·i·ty (presh'ē os'i tē), *n., pl.* **-ties.** fastidious or carefully affected refinement.

pre·cious (presh'əs), *adj.* **1.** of high price or great value. **2.** dear; beloved. **3.** affectedly or excessively refined. —**pre'cious·ly,** *adv.* —**pre'cious·ness,** *n.*

prec·i·pice (pres'ə pis), *n.* a cliff with a vertical or overhanging face.

pre·cip·i·tant (pri sip'i tənt), *adj.* hasty, sudden, or headlong.

pre·cip·i·tate (*v.* -tāt'; *adj., n.* -tit, -tāt'), *v.,* **-tat·ed, -tat·ing,** *adj., n.* —*v.t.* **1.** to hasten the occurrence of. **2.** to fling or hurl down. **3.** to separate (a substance) in solid form from a solution. —*v.i.* **4.** to condense from vapor and fall to the earth's surface as rain, snow, etc. **5.** to separate from a solution as a precipitate. —*adj.* **6.** overhasty; rash. **7.** exceedingly sudden or abrupt. —*n.* **8.** a substance precipitated from a solution. —**pre•cip/i•tate•ly,** *adv.*

pre•cip/i•ta/tion, *n.* **1. a.** falling products of condensation in the atmosphere, as rain or snow. **b.** the amount of rain, snow, etc., that has fallen at a given place within a given period. **2.** the act of precipitating. **3.** the precipitating of a substance from a solution. **4.** sudden or rash haste.

pre•cip/i•tous, *adj.* **1.** extremely steep. **2.** PRECIPITATE.

pré•cis (prā sē/, prā/sē), *n.,* *pl.* **-cis** (-sēz/, -sēz). a concise summary.

pre•cise (pri sīs/), *adj.* **1.** definitely or strictly stated, defined, or fixed. **2.** exact in measuring, recording, etc. **3.** excessively or rigidly particular. —**pre•cise/ly,** *adv.* —**pre•cise/ness,** *n.*

pre•ci/sion (-sizh/ən), *n.* **1.** the state or quality of being precise. —*adj.* **2.** of or characterized by precision: *precision instruments.*

pre•clude (pri klōōd/), *v.t.,* **-clud•ed, -clud•ing. 1.** to make impossible. **2.** to exclude or debar. —**pre•clu/sion** (-klōō/zhən), *n.*

pre•co•cious (pri kō/shəs), *adj.* unusually advanced in mental development or talent. —**pre•coc/i•ty** (-kos/i tē), *n.*

pre•cog•ni•tion (prē/kog nish/ən), *n.* knowledge of a future event through extrasensory means. —**pre•cog/ni•tive** (-kog/ni tiv), *adj.*

pre/-Co•lum/bi•an, *adj.* of the period before the arrival of Columbus in the Americas.

pre/con•ceive/, *v.t.,* **-ceived, -ceiv•ing.** to form (an idea or opinion) beforehand. —**pre/con•cep/tion,** *n.*

pre/con•di/tion, *n.* **1.** something that is necessary to a subsequent result. —*v.t.* **2.** to subject to a special treatment in preparation for a subsequent experience, process, etc.

pre•cur•sor (pri kûr/sər, prē/kûr-), *n.* **1.** a person or thing that precedes, as in a job or method; forerunner. **2.** a harbinger. —**pre•cur/so•ry,** *adj.*

pre/date/, *v.t.,* **-dat•ed, -dat•ing. 1.** to date before the actual time. **2.** to precede in time.

pred•a•to•ry (pred/ə tôr/ē), *adj.* **1.** preying upon other organisms for food. **2.** characterized by plunder, robbery, or exploitation. —**pred/a•tor,** *n.*

pre•de•cease (prē/di sēs/), *v.t.,* **-ceased, -ceas•ing.** to die before (another person).

pred•e•ces•sor (pred/ə ses/ər), *n.* a person who precedes another in an office, position, etc.

pre•des•ti•na•tion (pri des/tə nā/shən, prē/des-), *n.* **1.** fate; destiny. **2.** the foreordination by God of whatever comes to pass, esp. the salvation and damnation of souls.

pre•des•tine (pri des/tin), *v.t.,* **-tined, -tin•ing.** to destine in advance; foreordain.

pre•de•ter•mine (prē/di tûr/min), *v.t.,* **-mined, -min•ing. 1.** to decide in advance. **2.** to ordain in advance; predestine. —**pre/de•ter/mi•na/tion,** *n.*

pre•dic•a•ment (pri dik/ə mənt), *n.* an unpleasantly difficult or perplexing situation.

pred•i•cate (*v.* pred/i kāt/; *adj., n.* -kit), *v.,* **-cat•ed, -cat•ing,** *adj., n.* —*v.t.* **1.** to declare or assert as an assumed quality or attribute. **2.** to found or derive (a statement, action, etc.); base: *to predicate one's behavior on faith in humanity.* —*adj.* **3.** belonging to the predicate of a sentence. —*n.* **4.** a syntactic unit

that expresses the action performed by or the state attributed to the subject. —**pred/i•ca/tion,** *n.* —**pred/i•ca/tive** (-kā/tiv, -kə-), *adj.*

pre•dict (pri dikt/), *v.t., v.i.* to tell (what will happen) in advance; foretell. —**pre•dict/a•ble,** *adj.* —**pre•dic/tion,** *n.* —**pre•dic/tor,** *n.*

pre•di•gest (prē/di jest/, -dī-), *v.t.* to treat (food) by an artificial process analogous to digestion so that, when eaten, it is more easily digestible.

pre•di•lec•tion (pred/l ek/shən, prēd/-), *n.* a partiality; preference.

pre•dis•pose (prē/di spōz/), *v.t.,* **-posed, -pos•ing. 1.** to make susceptible or liable. **2.** to dispose beforehand; incline. —**pre•dis/po•si/tion,** *n.*

pre•dom•i•nant (pri dom/ə nənt), *adj.* **1.** having authority or influence over others. **2.** preponderant; prominent. —**pre•dom/i•nance,** *n.* —**pre•dom/i•nant•ly,** *adv.*

pre•dom/i•nate/ (-nāt/), *v.i.,* **-nat•ed, -nat•ing. 1.** to have numerical superiority or advantage. **2.** to have or exert controlling power.

pre•em•i•nent (prē em/ə nənt), *adj.* eminent above or before others. —**pre•em/i•nence,** *n.* —**pre•em/i•nent•ly,** *adv.*

pre•empt (prē empt/), *v.t.* **1.** to occupy (land) in order to establish a prior right to buy. **2.** to acquire or appropriate before someone else can. **3.** to take the place of; supplant: *A news report preempted the game show.* —**pre•emp/tion,** *n.* —**pre•emp/tive,** *adj.*

preen (prēn), *v.t.* **1.** to trim or dress (feathers, fur, etc.) with the beak or tongue. **2.** to dress (oneself) carefully or smartly; primp. **3.** to pride (oneself) on something.

pref., **1.** preface. **2.** preferred.

pre•fab (prē/fab/), *Informal.* —*adj.* **1.** prefabricated. —*n.* **2.** something prefabricated, as a building.

pre•fab/ri•cate/, *v.t.,* **-cat•ed, -cat•ing.** to manufacture in standardized sections ready for quick assembly, as a house. —**pre/fab•ri•ca/tion,** *n.*

pref•ace (pref/is), *n., v.,* **-aced, -ac•ing.** —*n.* **1.** an introductory statement, as of a book or speech. **2.** a prayer of thanksgiving, the introduction to the canon of the Mass. —*v.t.* **3.** to provide with or introduce by a preface. —**pref/a•to/ry** (-ə tôr/ē), *adj.*

pre•fect (prē/fekt), *n.* a chief magistrate or administrative official. —**pre/fec•ture** (-fek chər), *n.*

pre•fer (pri fûr/), *v.t.,* **-ferred, -fer•ring. 1.** to like better. **2.** to promote or advance, as in rank or office. —*Idiom.* **3.** prefer charges, to make an accusation of misconduct, wrongdoing, etc., against another.

pref•er•a•ble (pref/ər ə bəl), *adj.* more desirable. —**pref/er•a•bly,** *adv.*

pref•er•ence (pref/ər əns), *n.* **1.** the act of preferring or state of being preferred. **2.** something preferred. **3.** an advantage given to one person or country over others. —**pref/er•en/tial** (-ə ren/shəl), *adj.*

pre•fer•ment (pri fûr/mənt), *n.* advancement or promotion, esp. in the church.

pre•fig•ure (prē fig/yər), *v.t.,* **-ured, -ur•ing.** to foreshadow.

pre•fix (*n.* prē/fiks; *v. also* prē fiks/), *n.* **1.** an affix placed before a word or stem. —*v.t.* **2.** to put before or in front. **3.** to add as a prefix.

preg•nant (preg/nənt), *adj.* **1.** having a child or other offspring developing in the body. **2.** fraught or abounding (usu. fol. by *with*). **3.** fertile; rich. **4.** full of meaning. —**preg/nan•cy,** *n., pl.* **-cies.**

---

pre/ad•dress/, *v.t.*
pre/ad•o•les/cence, *n.*
pre/ap•pli•ca/tion, *n.*
pre/ap•ply/, *v.t.,* **-plied, -ply•ing.**
pre/as•sem/ble, *v.t.,* **-bled, -bling.**
pre/as•signed/, *adj.*
pre•bake/, *v.,* **-baked, -bak•ing.**
pre•book/, *v.*
pre•can/cel, *v.t.*
pre•col/lege, *adj.*
pre/co•lo/ni•al, *adj.*
pre/con•ces/sion, *n.*

pre•con/scious, *adj.*
pre•cook/, *v.t.*
pre•cut/, *adj.*
pre/des•ig•na/tion, *n.*
pre/di•ag•nos/tic, *adj.*
pre•din/ner, *adj.*
pre/e•lec/tion, *n., adj.*
pre/en•list/ment, *adj., n.*
pre/es•tab/lish, *v.t.*
pre/ex•ist/, *v.i.*
pre•game/, *adj.*
pre•gla/cial, *adj.*

pre•heat/, *v.t.*
pre/in•au/gu•ral, *adj.*
pre/in•dus/tri•al, *adj.*
pre/kin/der•gar/ten, *n., adj.*
pre•nup/tial, *adj.*
pre•plan/, *v.,* **-planned, -plan•ning.**
pre•reg/is•ter, *v.*
pre/rev•o•lu/tion•ar/y, *adj.*
pre/se•lect/, *v.t.*
pre•sort/, *v.t.*
pre/sur/gi•cal, *adj.*
pre•tri/al, *n., adj.*

pre·hen·sile (pri hen′sil, -sīl), *adj.* adapted for taking hold of something: *a prehensile tail.*

pre·his·tor·ic (prē′hi stôr′ik, -stor′-, prē′i-), *adj.* of the time prior to recorded history.

pre·judge′, *v.t.*, **-judged, -judg·ing.** to judge prematurely or without sufficient investigation. —**pre·judg′ment**, *n.*

prej·u·dice (prej′ə dis), *n., v.,* **-diced, -dic·ing.** —*n.* **1.** an opinion, esp. an unfavorable one, formed beforehand or without knowledge or thought. **2.** unreasonable, hostile attitudes regarding a racial, religious, or national group. **3.** damage or injury. —*v.t.* **4.** to affect with a prejudice. —**prej′u·di′cial** (-dish′əl), *adj.*

prel·ate (prel′it), *n.* an ecclesiastic of high rank, as a bishop.

pre·lim·i·nar·y (pri lim′ə ner′ē), *adj., n., pl.* **-nar·ies.** —*adj.* **1.** leading up to the main part or business. —*n.* **2.** something preliminary, as an introductory or preparatory step.

pre·lit·er·ate (prē lit′ər it), *adj.* lacking a written language.

prel·ude (prel′yōōd, prā′lōōd), *n.* **1.** a preliminary to an action, work, etc., of broader scope and higher importance. **2.** *Music.* **a.** a short, independent instrumental composition. **b.** a piece that is introductory to another piece.

pre·mar·i·tal (prē mar′i tl), *adj.* preceding marriage.

pre·ma·ture (prē′mə chŏŏr′, -tŏŏr′, -tyŏŏr′), *adj.* **1.** occurring, coming, or done too soon. **2.** born before gestation is complete. —**pre′ma·ture′ly**, *adv.*

pre·med·i·tate (pri med′i tāt′), *v.t., v.i.,* **-tat·ed, -tat·ing.** to consider or plan beforehand. —**pre·med′i·ta′tion**, *n.*

pre·mier (pri mēr′, -myēr′), *n.* **1.** the head of the cabinet in France and certain other countries; prime minister. —*adj.* **2.** first in rank; chief.

pre·miere (pri mēr′, -myâr′), *n., v.,* **-miered, -mier·ing.** —*n.* **1.** a first public performance of a play, opera, etc. —*v.t., v.i.* **2.** to present or perform publicly for the first time. [< F: lit., first]

prem·ise (prem′is), *n., v.,* **-ised, -is·ing.** —*n.* **1.** a proposition supporting or helping to support a conclusion or argument. **2. premises,** a tract of land including its buildings. —*v.t.* **3.** to state or assume as a premise.

pre·mi·um (prē′mē əm), *n.* **1.** a bonus given as an inducement, as to purchase products. **2.** a sum additional to the usual price, wages, etc. **3.** the amount usu. paid in installments by a policyholder for coverage under a contract. **4.** great value or esteem: *She puts a premium on loyalty.*

pre·mo·lar (prē mō′lər), *n.* **1.** any of eight teeth located in pairs on each side of the upper and lower jaws in front of the molars. —*adj.* **2.** of the premolars.

pre·mo·ni·tion (prem′ə nish′ən, prē′mə-), *n.* an intuitive anticipation of a future event; presentiment. —**pre·mon′i·to·ry** (pri mon′i tôr′ē), *adj.*

pre·na·tal (prē nāt′l), *adj.* previous to birth or to giving birth.

pre·oc·cu·py′, *v.t.,* **-pied, -py·ing. 1.** to engross to the exclusion of other things. **2.** to occupy beforehand or before others. —**pre·oc′cu·pa′tion**, *n.*

pre·or·dain′, *v.t.* to ordain or decree beforehand.

prep (prep), *adj., v.,* **prepped, prep·ping.** —*adj.* **1.** preparatory: *a prep school.* —*v.t.* **2.** to prepare (a person), as for a surgical procedure. —*v.i.* **3.** to prepare; get ready.

prep., **1.** preparatory. **2.** preposition.

pre·pack′age, *v.t.,* **-aged, -ag·ing.** to package (foodstuffs or manufactured goods) before retail sale.

prep·a·ra·tion (prep′ə rā′shən), *n.* **1.** a plan, measure, etc., by which one prepares for something. **2.** the act of preparing or state of being prepared. **3.** something prepared or manufactured: *a preparation for burns.*

pre·par·a·to·ry (pri par′ə tôr′ē, -pâr′-, prep′ər ə-), *adj.* **1.** serving to prepare. **2.** introductory.

prepar′atory school′, *n.* a private secondary school providing a college-preparatory education.

pre·pare (pri pâr′), *v.,* **-pared, -par·ing.** —*v.t.* to

put in readiness. **2.** to put together, as a meal. **3.** to provide with what is necessary. —*v.i.* **4.** to put things or oneself in readiness.

pre·par·ed·ness (-pâr′id nis, -pârd′nis), *n.* the state of being prepared or ready, esp. for war.

pre·pay (prē pā′), *v.t.,* **-paid, -pay·ing.** to pay beforehand or before due. —**pre·pay′ment**, *n.*

pre·pon·der·ate (pri pon′də rāt′), *v.i.,* **-at·ed, -at·ing.** to be superior in power, force, number, etc. —**pre·pon′der·ance**, *n.* —**pre·pon′der·ant**, *adj.*

prep·o·si·tion (prep′ə zish′ən), *n.* a word used before a noun, pronoun, or other substantive to form a phrase. —**prep′o·si′tion·al**, *adj.*

pre·pos·sess (prē′pə zes′), *v.t.* **1.** to prejudice, esp. favorably. **2.** to impress favorably at the outset.

pre′pos·sess′ing, *adj.* impressing favorably.

pre·pos·ter·ous (pri pos′tər əs), *adj.* completely senseless or foolish.

prep·py or **-pie** (prep′ē), *n., pl.* **-pies,** *adj.,* **-pi·er, -pi·est.** —*n.* **1.** a student or graduate of a preparatory school. —*adj.* **2.** of or characteristic of a preppy.

pre·puce (prē′pyōōs), *n.* the fold of skin that covers the head of the penis.

pre·quel (prē′kwəl), *n.* a sequel to a film, play, etc., that prefigures the original.

pre·re·cord (prē′ri kôrd′), *v.t.* to record beforehand, as a television program before broadcast.

pre·req·ui·site (pri rek′wə zit, prē-), *adj.* **1.** required beforehand. —*n.* **2.** something prerequisite.

pre·rog·a·tive (pri rog′ə tiv, pə rog′-), *n.* an exclusive right or privilege, exercised by virtue of rank, office, etc.

pres., **1.** present. **2.** president.

pres·age (pres′ij; *v. also* pri sāj′), *v.,* **-aged, -ag·ing,** *n.* —*v.t.* **1.** to portend; foreshadow. **2.** to forecast; predict. —*n.* **3.** presentiment; foreboding. **4.** something that portends a future event; omen.

pres·by·o·pi·a (prez′bē ō′pē ə, pres′-), *n.* farsightedness, usu. associated with aging.

pres·by·ter (prez′bi tər, pres′-), *n.* **1.** (in the early Christian church) an office bearer who exercised teaching, priestly, and administrative functions. **2.** (in hierarchical churches) a priest. **3.** an elder in a Presbyterian church.

Pres·by·te·ri·an (prez′bi tēr′ē ən, pres′-), *adj.* **1.** designating various churches governed by presbyters and professing modified forms of Calvinism. —*n.* **2.** a member of a Presbyterian church.

pres·by·ter·y (prez′bi ter′ē, pres′-), *n., pl.* **-ter·ies. 1.** (in Presbyterian churches) an assembly consisting of all the ministers and one or two presbyters from each congregation. **2.** the churches under the jurisdiction of a presbytery. **3.** the part of a church appropriated to the clergy. **4.** *Rom. Cath. Ch.* RECTORY. [Late ME *presbetory* priests' bench < LL *presbyterium* group of elders < Gk *presbytérion,* der. of *presbyteros* elder, priest]

pre·school (*adj.* prē′skōōl′; *n.* prē′skōōl′), *adj.* **1.** of or for a child between infancy and kindergarten age. —*n.* **2.** a school or nursery for preschool children. —**pre′school′er**, *n.*

pre·science (presh′əns, -ē əns, prē′shəns, -shē əns), *n.* knowledge of things before they exist or happen. —**pre′scient·ly**, *adv.*

pre·scribe (pri skrīb′), *v.t.,* **-scribed, -scrib·ing. 1.** to lay down as a rule or course of action to be followed. **2.** to order the use of (a medicine, remedy, etc.).

pre·script (prē′skript), *n.* something prescribed, as a rule or precept. —**pre·scrip′tive**, *adj.*

pre·scrip·tion (pri skrip′shən), *n.* **1. a.** a written direction by a physician for the preparation and use of a medicine. **b.** the medicine prescribed. **2.** the act of prescribing. **3.** something prescribed.

pres·ence (prez′əns), *n.* the state or fact of being present. **2.** immediate vicinity. **3.** personal appearance or bearing, esp. of a dignified or imposing kind.

pres′ence of mind′, *n.* the ability to think clearly and act appropriately, as during a crisis.

pres·ent¹ (prez′ənt), *adj.* **1.** existing or occurring now. **2.** designating a verb tense used to refer to an action or state occurring or existing at the moment of speaking or to a habitual event. **3.** being in a specified or understood place: *to be present at the wedding.* **4.** being actually under consideration: *the present topic.* —*n.* **5.** the present time. **6. a.** the present tense. **b.** a verb form in the present tense. —*Idiom.* **7. for the present,** for now; temporarily.

pre•sent[2] (*v.* pri zent′; *n.* prez′ənt), *v.t.* **1.** to furnish with a gift or the like, esp. by formal act. **2.** to offer or give in a formal way: *to present one's credentials.* **3.** to introduce (a person) to another, esp. in a formal manner. **4.** to bring before the public: *to present a play.* **5.** to offer for consideration: *to present a plan.* —*n.* **pres•ent 6.** a gift. —**pre•sent′er,** *n.*

pre•sent•a•ble (pri zen′tə bəl), *adj.* **1.** capable of being presented. **2.** fit to be seen.

pres•en•ta•tion (prez′ən tā′shən, prē′zen-), *n.* **1.** the act of presenting or state of being presented. **2.** an exhibition or performance, as of a play. **3.** a demonstration, lecture, or welcoming speech.

pres′ent-day′, *adj.* current; modern.

pre•sen•ti•ment (pri zen′tə mənt), *n.* a feeling that something is about to happen, esp. something evil.

pres•ent•ly (prez′ənt lē), *adv.* **1.** in a little while; soon. **2.** at the present time: *He is presently on sabbatical leave.* —**Usage.** PRESENTLY, meaning "at the present time, now," dates back to the 15th century. Despite occasional objection, it is currently in standard use in all varieties of speech and writing.

pre•sent•ment (pri zent′mənt), *n.* PRESENTATION (def. 1).

pres′ent par′ticiple, *n.* a participle form, in English having the suffix -*ing,* denoting repetition or duration of an activity or event.

pres•er•va•tion•ist (prez′ər vā′shə nist), *n.* one who advocates preservation, esp. of wildlife, natural areas, or historical places.

pre•serv•a•tive (pri zûr′və tiv), *n.* **1.** a chemical substance used to preserve foods or other organic materials from decomposition or fermentation. —*adj.* **2.** tending to preserve.

pre•serve (pri zûrv′), *v.,* -**served, -serv•ing,** *n.* —*v.t.* **1.** to keep alive or in existence: *to preserve our liberties.* **2.** to keep safe from harm or injury. **3.** to keep up; maintain. **4.** to prepare (any perishable substance) so as to resist decomposition or fermentation. **5.** to prepare (fruit, vegetables, etc.) by pickling, canning, etc. —*n.* **6.** Usu., **-serves.** fruit, vegetables, etc., prepared by cooking with sugar. **7.** a place set apart for protection of game or fish. —**pres•er•va′tion** (prez′ər vā′shən), *n.* —**pre•serv′er,** *n.*

pre•set (prē set′), *v.t.,* -**set, -set•ting.** to set beforehand.

pre•side (pri zīd′), *v.i.,* -**sid•ed, -sid•ing. 1.** to have charge of an assembly, meeting, etc. **2.** to exercise management or control.

pres•i•dent (prez′i dənt), *n.* **1.** (*often cap.*) the chief of state of a modern republic, as the United States. **2.** the chief officer of a university, corporation, etc. —**pres′i•den•cy,** *n., pl.* -**cies.** —**pres′i•den′tial** (-den′shəl), *adj.*

pres′iden′tial tim′ber, *n.* one with the abilities to become president.

pres′ident pro tem′pore, *n.* a senator who is chosen to preside over the Senate in the absence of the vice president. Also called **pres′ident pro tem′.**

pre•sid•i•um (pri sid′ē əm), *n., pl.* -**i•ums, -i•a** (-ē ə). an executive board or committee.

Pres•ley (pres′lē, prez′-), *n.* Elvis (Aron), 1935–77, U.S. rock-and-roll singer.

press[1] (pres), *v.t.* **1.** to act upon with steadily applied weight or force. **2.** to compress or squeeze. **3.** to hold closely, as in an embrace. **4.** to make smooth by ironing. **5.** to extract juice or contents from by pressure. **6.** to trouble or oppress, as by lack of something. **7.** to beset; harass. **8.** to urge insistently. **9.** to propound forcefully. **10.** to urge onward. —*v.i.* **11.** to exert weight or force. **12.** to bear heavily, as upon the mind. **13.** to push forward with force or haste. **14.** to crowd; throng. —*n.* **15.** PRINTING PRESS.

16. printed publications collectively, esp. newspapers and periodicals. **17.** their editorial employees. **18.** the consensus of critical commentary. **19.** an establishment for printing books, magazines, etc. **20.** any of various devices for exerting pressure, stamping, or crushing. **21.** a crowding together. **22.** the smooth effect caused by ironing. **23.** urgency, as of business. **24.** a large upright cupboard for holding clothes, linens, etc. —**press′er,** *n.*

press[2] (pres), *v.t.* to force into service, esp. naval or military service.

press′ a′gent, *n.* a person employed to promote a client by obtaining favorable publicity.

press′ con′ference, *n.* an interview with reporters held by a government official or prominent person.

press′ing, *adj.* demanding immediate attention.

press′man, *n., pl.* -**men.** a person who operates a printing press.

press′ release′, *n.* a statement or news story distributed to the press by a public relations firm, governmental agency, etc.

pres•sure (presh′ər), *n., v.,* -**sured, -sur•ing.** —*n.* **1.** the exertion of force upon a surface by an object, fluid, etc., in contact with it. **2.** *Physics.* force per unit area. **3.** harassment; stress. **4.** a constraining or compelling force or influence. **5.** urgency, as of business: *He works well under pressure.* —*v.t.* **6.** to put pressure on.

pres′sure cook′er, *n.* a cooking pot with an airtight lid for cooking food quickly by steam maintained under pressure.

pres′sure group′, *n.* an interest group that attempts to influence legislation.

pres•sur•ize, *v.t.,* -**ized, -iz•ing.** to produce or maintain normal air pressure in (an airplane, spacesuit, etc.) at high altitudes. —**pres′sur•i•za′tion,** *n.* —**pres′sur•iz′er,** *n.*

pres•ti•dig•i•ta•tion (pres′ti dij′i tā′shən), *n.* sleight of hand.

pres•tige (pre stēzh′, -stēj′), *n.* reputation or influence arising from success, achievement, rank, etc. —**pres•tig′ious** (-stij′əs), *adj.*

pres•to (pres′tō), *adv.* **1.** quickly or immediately. **2.** *Music.* at a rapid tempo. —*adj.* **3.** quick or rapid. **4.** *Music.* executed at a rapid tempo. [< It: quick, quickly < L *praestō* ready, at hand]

pre•sume (pri zōōm′), *v.,* -**sumed, -sum•ing.** —*v.t.* **1.** to take for granted, assume, or suppose. **2.** to undertake (to do something) without right or permission. —*v.i.* **3.** to go too far in acting with unjustifiable boldness; take liberties. —**pre•sum′a•ble,** *adj.* —**pre•sum′a•bly,** *adv.*

pre•sump′tion (-zump′shən), *n.* **1.** the act of presuming. **2.** something presumed; assumption. **3.** a reason for presuming. **4.** unjustifiable; or impertinent boldness. —**pre•sump′tive,** *adj.*

pre•sump′tu•ous (-chōō əs), *adj.* excessively or impertinently bold.

pre•sup•pose (prē′sə pōz′), *v.t.,* -**posed, -pos•ing. 1.** to suppose or assume beforehand. **2.** to require as an antecedent condition. —**pre′sup•po•si′tion** (-sup ə zish′ən), *n.*

pre•teen′, *n.* a child between the ages of 10 and 13.

pre•tend (pri tend′), *v.t.* **1.** to feign: *to pretend illness.* **2.** to make believe: *The children pretended they were cowboys.* **3.** to presume; venture. **4.** to claim or profess falsely: *He pretended not to know.* —*v.i.* **5.** to make believe, as in play. **6.** to lay claim: *to pretend to the throne.* —**pre•tend′er,** *n.*

pre•tense (pri tens′, prē′tens), *n.* **1.** a false show of something: *a pretense of friendship.* **2.** a pretending or feigning. **3.** a false claim or justification; pretext. **4.** a claim; pretension.

pre•ten•sion (pri ten′shən), *n.* **1.** a claim to something. **2.** Often, **-sions.** an unwarranted or false claim, as to merit, importance, or wealth.

pre•ten′tious, *adj.* **1.** characterized by the assumption of dignity, importance, artistic distinction, etc. **2.** making an exaggerated outward show; ostentatious. —**pre•ten′tious•ly,** *adv.* —**pre•ten′tious•ness,** *n.*

pret•er•it or **-ite** (pret′ər it), *n.* **1.** a verb tense referring to a past or completed action or state. **2.** a verb form in this tense. —*adj.* **3.** expressing a past action or state.

pre·ter·nat·u·ral (prē′tər nach′ər əl), *adj.* **1.** being outside the ordinary course of nature; exceptional or abnormal. **2.** supernatural.

pre·test (*n.* prē′test′; *v.* prē test′), *n.* **1.** an advance testing or trial. —*v.t., v.i.* **2.** to give a pretest (to).

pre·text (prē′tekst), *n.* something put forward to conceal a true purpose.

Pre·to·ri·a (pri tôr′ē ə), *n.* the administrative capital of the Republic of South Africa. 822,925.

pret·ti·fy (prit′ə fī′), *v.t.,* **-fied, -fy·ing.** to make pretty in a small, petty way.

pret·ty (prit′ē), *adj.,* **-ti·er, -ti·est,** *adv., v.,* **-tied, -ty·ing.** —*adj.* **1.** attractive in a delicate or graceful way. **2.** fine; grand (often used ironically): *a pretty mess!* **3.** *Informal.* fairly great: *a pretty sum.* —*adv.* **4.** moderately: *a pretty good time.* —*v.t.* **5.** to make pretty: *to pretty up a room.* —**pret′ti·ly,** *adv.* —**pret′ti·ness,** *n.* ——**Usage.** The qualifying adverb PRETTY, meaning "fairly or moderately," has been in general use for about 400 years. Although most common in informal speech and writing, it is far from restricted to these contexts.

pret·zel (pret′səl), *n.* a crisp, dry biscuit, typically in the form of a knot or stick, salted on the outside.

pre·vail (pri vāl′), *v.i.* **1.** to be widespread or current. **2.** to occur as the most important or frequent element. **3.** to prove superior in power or influence: *to prevail over one's enemies.* **4.** to succeed. **5.** to use persuasion successfully: *Can you prevail on him to go?*

pre·vail·ing, *adj.* **1.** most frequent or common. **2.** having superior power or influence.

prev·a·lent (prev′ə lənt), *adj.* **1.** widespread. **2.** dominant. —**prev′a·lence,** *n.*

pre·var·i·cate (pri var′i kāt′), *v.i.,* **-cat·ed, -cat·ing.** to speak falsely or misleadingly; equivocate; lie. —**pre·var′i·ca′tion,** *n.* —**pre·var′i·ca′tor,** *n.*

pre·vent (pri vent′), *v.t.* **1.** to keep from occurring. **2.** to stop from doing something. —**pre·vent′a·ble, pre·vent′i·ble,** *adj.* —**pre·ven′tion,** *n.*

pre·ven·tive also **-vent′a·tive** (-tə tiv), *adj.* **1.** serving to prevent or hinder: *preventive medicine.* —*n.* **2.** a preventive agent or measure.

pre·view (prē′vyoo′), *n.* **1.** an earlier or advance view. **2.** an advance showing of a motion picture, play, etc., before its public opening. **3.** a showing of brief scenes from a motion picture for purposes of advertisement. —*v.t.* **4.** to view or show beforehand or in advance.

pre·vi·ous (prē′vē əs), *adj.* **1.** coming or occurring before something else; prior. ——*Idiom.* **2. previous to,** before. —**pre′vi·ous·ly,** *adv.*

pre′war′, *adj.* existing, occurring, etc., before a particular war.

prey (prā), *n.* **1.** an animal hunted or seized for food by a carnivorous animal. **2.** any victim. **3.** the action or habit of preying: *a beast of prey.* —*v.i.* (usu. fol. by *on* or *upon*) **4.** to seize and devour prey. **5.** to make attacks for plunder. **6.** to exert a harmful and often obsessive influence: *The problem preyed upon his mind.* **7.** to victimize others.

Pri·am (prī′əm), *n.* a legendary king of Troy, the father of Paris, Cassandra, and Hector.

pri·ap·ic (prī ap′ik), *adj.* or or resembling a phallus.

price (prīs), *n., v.,* **priced, pric·ing.** —*n.* **1.** the amount of money for which anything is bought or sold. **2.** that which must be given, done, or undergone to obtain something. —*v.t.* **3.** to fix the price of. **4.** to find out the price of.

price′less, *adj.* having a value beyond all price; invaluable.

prick (prik), *n.* **1.** a puncture made by a needle, thorn, or the like. **2.** a sharp pain or feeling of discomfort; twinge. —*v.t.* **3.** to pierce with a sharp point. **4.** to affect with sharp pain. **5.** to cause sharp mental pain to. **6.** to cause to point upward: *The dog pricked up its ears.*

prick′le, *n., v.,* **-led, -ling.** —*n.* **1.** a small, sharp

projection, as on a plant. **2.** a pricking sensation. —*v.t.* **3.** to cause a pricking or tingling sensation in. —*v.i.* **4.** to tingle. —**prick′ly,** *adj.,* **-li·er, -li·est.**

prick′ly heat′, *n.* a skin eruption accompanied by an itching sensation, due to an inflammation of the sweat glands.

pride (prīd), *n., v.,* **prid·ed, prid·ing.** —*n.* **1.** self-respect; self-esteem. **2.** gratification arising from association with something laudable. **3.** conceit; arrogance. **4.** something that causes one to be proud. **5.** a group of lions. —*v.t.* **6.** to indulge (oneself) in a feeling of pride: *He prides himself on his good memory.* —*Proverb.* **7. Pride goes before a fall,** excessive pride leads to humiliation. Prov. 16:18. —**pride′ful,** *adj.* —**pride′ful·ly,** *adv.*

pri·er (prī′ər), *n.* a person who pries.

priest (prēst), *n.* **1.** (in certain Christian, esp. Catholic, churches) a member of the clergy ranking below a bishop. **2.** a person whose office it is to perform religious rites. —**priest′hood′,** *n.* —**priest′ly,** *adj.*

priest·ess (prē′stis), *n.* a woman who officiates in sacred rites.

prig (prig), *n.* a person self-righteously concerned with the rigid observance of proprieties. —**prig′gish,** *adj.*

prim (prim), *adj.,* **-mer, -mest.** formally precise or proper; prissy. —**prim′ly,** *adv.* —**prim′ness,** *n.*

pri·ma·cy (prī′mə sē), *n., pl.* **-cies.** **1.** the state of being first in order, rank, importance, etc. **2.** the office or rank of an ecclesiastical primate.

pri·ma don·na (prē′mə don′ə, prim′ə), *n., pl.* **prima don·nas. 1.** a principal female singer in an opera. **2.** a vain, temperamental person.

pri·ma fa·ci·e (prī′mə fā′shē ē′, fā′shē), *adj.* sufficient to establish a fact unless rebutted: *prima facie evidence.*

pri·mal (prī′məl), *adj.* **1.** first; original. **2.** of first importance.

pri·mar·i·ly (prī mâr′ə lē, -mer′-), *adv.* **1.** essentially; chiefly. **2.** at first; originally.

pri·ma·ry (prī′mer ē, -mə rē), *adj., n., pl.* **-ries.** —*adj.* **1.** first in importance; chief. **2.** first in order or time. **3.** being of the most basic order of its kind: *a primary classification.* **4.** immediate or direct: *primary perceptions.* —*n.* **5.** something first in order or importance. **6.** a preliminary election in which voters of each party nominate candidates for office, party officers, etc.

pri′mary care′, *n.* medical care by a physician who is the patient's first contact with the health-care system and who may recommend a specialist if necessary. —**pri′mary-care′,** *adj.*

pri′mary school′, *n.* an elementary school, esp. one covering the first three or four grades and sometimes kindergarten.

pri′mary stress′, *n.* the strongest degree of stress in a word or phrase. Also called **pri′mary ac′cent.**

pri·mate (prī′māt *or, esp. for 1,* -mit), *n.* **1.** an archbishop or bishop ranking first among the bishops of a province or country. **2.** any of an important order of mammals including humans, the apes, monkeys, and lemurs.

prime (prīm), *adj., n., v.,* **primed, prim·ing.** —*adj.* **1.** of the first rank or importance. **2.** of the greatest value or best quality. **3.** first in order of time or development. **4.** basic; fundamental. **5.** (of any two or more numbers) having no common divisor except unity. —*n.* **6.** the most flourishing stage or state. **7.** the choicest part of anything. **8.** the earliest stage of any period. —*v.t.* **9.** to prepare; make ready. **10.** to supply (a firearm) with powder. **11.** to pour liquid into (a pump) to expel air and prepare for action. **12.** to cover (a surface) with an undercoat of paint or the like. **13.** to supply with needed information, facts, etc.

prime′ merid′ian, *n.* the meridian running through Greenwich, England, from which longitude east and west is reckoned.

prime′ min′ister, *n.* the head of government and of the cabinet in parliamentary systems.

prim·er¹ (prim′ər; *esp. Brit.* prī′mər), *n.* **1.** an elementary book for teaching children to read. **2.** any book of elementary principles.

prim•er[2] (prī′mər), *n.* **1.** one that primes. **2.** an explosive cap, cylinder, etc., used to ignite a charge of powder. **3.** a first coat of paint, size, etc.

prime′ rate′, *n.* the minimum interest rate charged by a commercial bank on business loans to large, best-rated customers.

prime′ time′, *n.* the hours, generally between 7 and 11 P.M., considered to have the largest television audience.

pri•me•val (prī mē′vəl), *adj.* of the first ages of the world; primordial.

prim•i•tive (prim′i tiv), *adj.* **1.** being the first or earliest of the kind: *primitive forms of life.* **2.** characteristic of early ages or of an early state of human development. **3.** simple or crude: *primitive equipment.* —*n.* **4.** someone or something primitive.

pri•mo•gen•i•ture (prī′mə jen′i chər, -chŏŏr′), *n.* **1.** the state of being the firstborn of the same parents. **2.** inheritance by the eldest son.

pri•mor•di•al (prī môr′dē əl), *adj.* existing at or from the very beginning.

primp (primp), *v.t., v.i.* to dress or groom (oneself) with care.

prim•rose (prim′rōz′), *n.* any of several plants with showy, five-lobed flowers in a variety of colors.

prim′rose path′, *n.* **1.** a way of life devoted to irresponsible hedonism. **2.** any irresponsible course of action.

Prince, The (prins), (Italian, *Il Principe*), a treatise on statecraft (1513) by Niccolò Machiavelli.

prince′ con′sort, *n.* a prince who is the husband of a reigning female sovereign.

Prince′ Ed′ward Is′land, *n.* an island province of SE Canada. 126,646. *Cap.:* Charlottetown. *Abbr:* PE, P.E.I.

prince′ly, *adj.,* -li•er, -li•est. **1.** lavish; magnificent. **2.** of a prince. —**prince′li•ness,** *n.*

Prince′ of Dark′ness, *n.* Satan.

Prince′ of Peace′, *n.* the Messiah. Isa. 9:6.

Prince′ of Wales′, *n.* a title conferred by the British sovereign on the male heir apparent.

prin•cess (prin′sis, -ses), *n.* **1.** a nonreigning female member of a royal family, esp. a daughter of the sovereign. **2.** the consort of a prince.

prin•ci•pal (prin′sə pəl), *adj.* **1.** first in rank, importance, value, etc. —*n.* **2.** a chief or head. **3.** the head of a school. **4.** a chief actor or performer. **5.** a person who authorizes another to act for him or her. **6.** a capital sum, as distinguished from interest or profit. —**prin′ci•pal•ly,** *adv.*

prin•ci•pal•i•ty (-pal′i tē), *n., pl.* -ties. a state ruled by a prince.

prin′cipal parts′, *n.* a set of inflected forms of a verb from which all the other inflected forms can be derived, as *sing, sang, sung.*

Prín•ci•pe (prin′sə pə, -pä′), *n.* See under São Tomé AND Príncipe.

prin•ci•ple (prin′sə pəl), *n.* **1.** a rule of conduct. **2.** a fundamental law, axiom, or doctrine. **3.** a guiding sense of the requirements of right conduct: *a man of principle.* **4.** a law exemplified in natural phenomena, the operation of a machine, etc.: *the principle of capillary attraction.* **5.** a method of formation, operation, or procedure: *a family organized on the patriarchal principle.* —**prin′ci•pled,** *adj.*

print (print), *v.t., v.i.* **1.** to produce (a text, picture, etc.) by applying inked type or plates to paper or other material. **2.** to publish in printed form. **3.** to write in letters like those used in print. **4.** *Photog.* to produce a positive picture from (a negative). **5. print out,** *Computers.* to produce (data) in printed form. —*n.* **6.** printed lettering. **7.** printed material. **8.** an indentation, mark, etc., made by the pressure of one thing on another. **9.** a cloth displaying a stamped design or pattern. **10.** a photograph, esp. a positive made from a negative. —*Idiom.* **11. in** (or **out of**) **print,** (of a book or the like) still (or no longer) available from the publisher. —**print′a•ble,** *adj.*

print′ed cir′cuit, *n.* a circuit in which the inter-

connecting conductors and some of the components have been printed, etched, etc., onto an insulating sheet.

print′er, *n.* **1.** a person or firm engaged in the business of printing. **2.** a computer output device that produces a paper copy of data or graphics.

print′ing, *n.* **1.** the skill, process, or business of producing printed material. **2.** the act of a person or thing that prints. **3.** the total number of copies of a publication printed at one time. **4.** writing in which the letters resemble printed ones.

print′ing press′, *n.* a machine for printing on paper or the like from type, plates, etc.

print′out′, *n.* computer output produced by a printer.

pri•or[1] (prī′ər), *adj.* **1.** preceding in time or order. **2.** preceding in importance or privilege. —*Idiom.* **3. prior to,** preceding.

pri•or[2] (prī′ər), *n.* an officer in a religious house.

pri•or•ess (prī′ər is), *n.* a woman holding a position corresponding to that of a prior.

pri•or•i•tize (prī ôr′i tīz′, -or′-), *v.t.,* -tized, -tiz•ing. to arrange or do in order of priority.

pri•or•i•ty, *n., pl.* -ties. **1.** the state or quality of being earlier in time or occurrence. **2.** the right to take precedence in obtaining something. **3.** the right to precede others in rank, privilege, etc. **4.** something given special or prior attention.

pri•o•ry (prī′ə rē), *n., pl.* -ries. a religious house governed by a prior or prioress.

Pris•cil•la (pri sil′ə), *n.* a Christian of Corinth who was a leader in the early church. Acts 18:2.

prism (priz′əm), *n.* **1.** a transparent solid body used for dispersing light into a spectrum or for reflecting rays of light. **2.** a solid having bases or ends that are parallel, congruent polygons and sides that are parallelograms. —**pris•mat′ic** (-mat′ik), *adj.*

pris•on (priz′ən), *n.* a building for the confinement of persons convicted of crimes or awaiting trial.

pris′on•er, *n.* a person confined in prison or kept in custody.

pris•sy (pris′ē), *adj.,* -si•er, -si•est. excessively or affectedly proper. —**pris′si•ly,** *adv.* —**pris′si•ness,** *n.*

pris•tine (pris′tēn, pri stēn′), *adj.* **1.** uncorrupted or unsullied. **2.** of the earliest period or state.

prith•ee (prith′ē), *interj. Archaic.* (I) pray thee.

pri•va•cy (prī′və sē; *Brit. also* priv′ə-), *n., pl.* -cies. **1.** the state of being private. **2.** freedom from the intrusion of others in one's private life. **3.** secrecy.

pri•vate (prī′vit), *adj.* **1.** of or belonging to some particular person or persons. **2.** confined to or intended for only one person. **3.** not of an official or public character: *to return to private life.* **4.** personal; secret. **5.** not open to the general public. **6.** preferring privacy; retiring. **7.** not maintained under public funds: *a private school.* —*n.* **8.** a soldier of one of the three lowest enlisted ranks. **9. privates,** the external genital organs. —*Idiom.* **10. in private,** not publicly. —**pri′vate•ly,** *adv.*

pri•va•teer (prī′və tēr′), *n.* **1.** a privately owned ship commissioned to fight or harass enemy ships. **2.** the captain or a crew member of such a ship.

pri′vate eye′, *n. Informal.* a private detective.

pri•va•tion (prī vā′shən), *n.* lack of the usual comforts or necessaries of life.

priv•et (priv′it), *n.* an evergreen shrub commonly grown as a hedge.

priv•i•lege (priv′ə lij, priv′lij), *n., v.,* -leged, -leg•ing. —*n.* **1.** a right, immunity, or benefit enjoyed by a particular person or group. —*v.t.* **2.** to grant a privilege to.

priv′i•leged, *adj.* **1.** enjoying a privilege or privileges. **2.** restricted to a select group: *privileged information.* **3.** *Law.* (of communications) protected against being used as evidence in court.

priv•y (priv′ē), *adj.,* -i•er, -i•est, *n., pl.* -ies. —*adj.* **1.** having knowledge of something private or secret: *Many people were privy to the plot.* —*n.* **2.** OUTHOUSE.

priv′y coun′cil, *n.* a board or select body of personal advisers, as of a sovereign.

prize¹ (prīz), *n.* **1.** a reward for victory or superiority, as in a contest or competition. **2.** anything striven for or worth striving for. —*adj.* **3.** having won a prize. **4.** worthy of a prize. **5.** awarded as a prize.

prize² (prīz), *v.t.,* **prized, priz•ing.** to value or esteem highly.

prize/fight/, *n.* a professional boxing match. —**prize/fight/er,** *n.*

pro¹ (prō), *adv., n., pl.* **pros.** —*adv.* **1.** in favor of a proposition, opinion, etc. —*n.* **2.** a person who upholds the affirmative in a debate. **3.** an argument or vote in favor of something.

pro² (prō), *adj., n., pl.* **pros.** professional.

pro-¹, a prefix meaning: favoring or supporting (*prowar*); forth or forward (*proceed*); in place of (*pronoun*).

pro-², a prefix meaning: before or beforehand (*prognosis*); in front of (*proscenium*).

prob., **1.** probably. **2.** problem.

prob•a•bil•i•ty (prob/ə bil/i tē), *n., pl.* **-ties. 1.** the quality or fact of being probable. **2.** a probable event, circumstance, etc.

prob/a•ble, *adj.* **1.** likely to occur or prove true. **2.** having more evidence for than against, but not proven conclusively. —**prob/a•bly,** *adv.*

pro•bate (prō/bāt), *n., adj., v.,* **-bat•ed, -bat•ing.** —*n.* **1.** the official proving of a will as authentic or valid. —*adj.* **2.** of or involving probate. —*v.t.* **3.** to establish the authenticity or validity of (a will).

pro•ba/tion, *n.* **1.** the testing of a person's conduct, character, etc. **2.** the period of such testing. **3.** the conditional release of an offender under supervision. —**pro•ba/tion•al, pro•ba/tion•ar/y,** *adj.*

pro•ba/tion•er, *n.* a person undergoing probation.

probe (prōb), *v.,* **probed, prob•ing,** *n.* —*v.t.* **1.** to search into thoroughly. **2.** to examine or explore with a probe. —*v.i.* **3.** to examine or explore something with or as if with a probe. —*n.* **4.** a slender surgical instrument for exploring a wound, sinus, etc. **5.** an investigation of suspected illegal activity. **6.** a spacecraft designed to explore the solar system and transmit data back to earth.

pro•bi•ty (prō/bi tē, prob/i-), *n.* integrity and uprightness. [< L *probitās*]

prob•lem (prob/ləm), *n.* **1.** any question or matter involving doubt, uncertainty, or difficulty. **2.** a question proposed for solution or discussion. **3.** a source of difficulty or trouble.

prob/lem•at/ic (-lə mat/ik) also **-i•cal,** *adj.* of the nature of a problem; doubtful; uncertain.

pro•bos•cis (prō bos/is, -kis), *n.* **1.** the trunk of an elephant. **2.** any long flexible snout.

pro•caine (prō kān/, prō/kān), *n.* a compound used chiefly as a local and spinal anesthetic.

pro•ce•dure (prə sē/jər), *n.* the act or manner of proceeding in any action. —**pro•ce/dur•al,** *adj.*

pro•ceed (*v.* prə sēd/; *n.* prō/sēd), *v.i.* **1.** to go forward or onward, esp. after stopping. **2.** to carry on any action. **3.** to initiate a legal action (often fol. by *against*). **4.** to come forth; issue (often fol. by *from*). —*n.* **5. proceeds,** the amount or profit derived from a sale or other transaction.

pro•ceed•ing (prə sē/ding), *n.* **1.** a particular action or course of action. **2. proceedings, a.** a record of the business discussed at a meeting, as of an academic society. **b.** legal action. **3.** the act of a person or thing that proceeds.

proc•ess (pros/es; *esp. Brit.* prō/ses), *n., pl.* **proc•ess•es** (pros/es iz, -ə siz, -ə sēz/; *esp. Brit.* prō/ses-, prō/sə-), *v.* —*n.* **1.** a systematic series of actions directed to some end: *a process for homogenizing milk.* **2.** a continuous action or series of changes taking place in a definite manner: *the process of decay.* **3.** the summons by which a defendant is brought to court. **4.** *Anatomy.* a natural outgrowth or projection. **5.** the action of going forward or on. —*v.t.* **6.** to treat or prepare by some particular process, as in manufacturing. **7.** to handle (persons, papers, etc.) according to a routine procedure.

pro•ces•sion (prə sesh/ən), *n.* **1.** the act of pro-

ceeding in an orderly succession or a ceremonious manner. **2.** a line of persons, vehicles, etc., moving in such a manner.

pro•ces/sion•al, *n.* a piece of music suitable for accompanying a procession.

pro-choice (prō chois/), *adj.* supporting the right to legalized abortion.

pro•claim (prō klām/, prə-), *v.t.* to announce officially or formally. —**proc•la•ma•tion** (prok/lə mā/shən), *n.*

pro•cliv•i•ty (prō kliv/i tē), *n., pl.* **-ties.** a natural or habitual inclination or tendency.

pro•cras•ti•nate (prō kras/tə nāt/, prə-), *v.i., v.t.,* **-nat•ed, -nat•ing.** to defer or delay (action). —**pro•cras/ti•na/tion,** *n.* —**pro•cras/ti•na/tor,** *n.*

pro•cre•ate (prō/krē āt/), *v.t., v.i.,* **-at•ed, -at•ing.** to beget or generate (offspring). —**pro/cre•a/tion,** *n.* —**pro/cre•a/tive,** *adj.*

Pro•crus•te•an (prō krus/tē ən), *adj.* (*often l.c.*) tending to produce conformity by violent or arbitrary means.

Pro•crus•tes (prō krus/tēz), *n.* (in Greek myth) a robber who stretched or amputated the limbs of travelers to make them conform to the length of his bed.

proc•tol•o•gy (prok tol/ə jē), *n.* the branch of medicine dealing with the rectum and anus. —**proc•tol/o•gist,** *n.*

proc•tor (prok/tər), *n.* **1.** a person who keeps watch over students at examinations. —*v.t., v.i.* **2.** to supervise or monitor.

proc•u•ra•tor (prok/yə rā/tər), *n.* (in ancient Rome) an imperial agent with fiscal or administrative powers, esp. in a province.

pro•cure (prō kyoor/, prə-), *v.t.,* **-cured, -cur•ing. 1.** to obtain by effort. **2.** to obtain (a person) for the purpose of prostitution. —**pro•cur/a•ble,** *adj.* —**pro•cure/ment,** *n.* —**pro•cur/er,** *n.*

prod (prod), *v.,* **prod•ded, prod•ding,** *n.* —*v.t.* **1.** to jab with or as if with something pointed. **2.** to nag; goad. —*n.* **3.** a poke or jab. **4.** any pointed instrument used as a goad.

prod•i•gal (prod/i gəl), *adj.* **1.** wastefully or recklessly extravagant. **2.** lavishly abundant. —*n.* **3.** one who is wastefully extravagant. —**prod/i•gal/i•ty** (-gal/i tē), *n.*

prod/igal son/, *n.* a wayward son who squanders his inheritance but returns home to find that his father forgives him. Luke 15:11–32.

pro•di•gious (prə dij/əs), *adj.* **1.** extraordinary in size, amount, etc. **2.** arousing admiration or amazement. —**pro•di/gious•ly,** *adv.*

prod•i•gy (prod/i je), *n., pl.* **-gies.** a person, esp. a child, having extraordinary talent or ability.

pro•duce (*v.* prə dōōs/, -dyōōs/; *n.* prod/ōōs, -yōōs, prō/dōōs, -dyōōs), *v.,* **-duced, -duc•ing,** *n.* —*v.t.* **1.** to bring about; give rise to. **2.** to bring into existence by intellectual or creative ability. **3.** to make or manufacture. **4.** to bear or yield. **5.** to present; exhibit: *to produce one's credentials.* **6.** to bring (a play, motion picture, etc.) before the public. —*v.i.* **7.** to yield products, offspring, etc. —*n.* **prod•uce 8.** agricultural products collectively, esp. vegetables and fruits. —**pro•duc/er,** *n.* —**pro•duc/i•ble,** *adj.*

prod•uct (prod/əkt, -ukt) *n.* **1.** a thing produced, as by labor. **2.** a person or thing seen as resulting from a process, as a historical one. **3.** *Math.* the result obtained by multiplying two or more quantities together.

pro•duc•tion (prə duk/shən), *n.* **1.** the act of producing. **2.** something produced; product. **3.** the total amount produced. —**pro•duc/tive,** *adj.* —**pro•duc/tive•ly,** *adv.* —**pro•duc/tive•ness,** *n.*

prof (prof), *n. Informal.* professor.

Prof., Professor.

pro•fane (prə fān/, prō-), *adj., v.,* **-faned, -fan•ing.** —*adj.* **1.** showing irreverence toward God or sacred things. **2.** not devoted to holy purposes; secular. —*v.t.* **3.** to misuse (anything sacred); defile. —**prof•a•na•tion** (prof/ə nā/shən), *n.* —**pro•fane/ly,** *adv.* —**pro•fane/ness,** *n.*

pro•fan/i•ty (-fan/i tē), *n., pl.* **-ties. 1.** the quality of being profane. **2.** irreverent or blasphemous speech.

pro•fess (prə fes/), v.t. **1.** to lay claim to, often insincerely; pretend to. **2.** to declare openly; affirm. **3.** to affirm one's faith in (a religion, God, etc.). —**pro•fessed/,** adj.

pro•fes/sion, n. **1.** an occupation requiring extensive education, as law. **2.** the body of persons engaged in such an occupation. **3.** the act of professing.

pro•fes/sion•al, adj. **1.** following an occupation as a means of livelihood. **2.** of or engaged in a profession. **3.** following as a business something usu. regarded as a pastime: *a professional golfer.* —n. **4.** a member of a profession. **5.** a person who earns a living in a sport or other occupation frequently engaged in by amateurs. **6.** an expert. —**pro•fes/sion•al•ly,** adv.

pro•fes/sion•al•ism, n. professional character, spirit, or methods.

pro•fes/sor, n. a college or university teacher, esp. one of the highest rank. —**pro•fes•so•ri•al** (prō/fə-sôr/ē əl), adj.

prof•fer (prof/ər), v.t. to offer.

pro•fi•cient (prə fish/ənt), adj. fully competent in any endeavor; skilled. —**pro•fi/cien•cy** (-sē), n. —**pro•fi/cient•ly,** adv.

pro•file (prō/fīl), n. **1.** the outline of the human face viewed from one side. **2.** a picture or representation of this. **3.** an outline of an object. **4.** an informal biographical sketch.

prof•it (prof/it), n. **1.** the monetary surplus left after all expenses of a business transaction or venture have been met. **2.** advantage; benefit; gain. —v.i., v.t. **3.** to gain or cause to gain a profit. —**prof/it•a•ble,** adj. —**prof/it•a•bly,** adv.

prof/it•eer/, n. **1.** a person who makes excessive profits on the sale of scarce or rationed goods. —v.i. **2.** to act as a profiteer.

prof•li•gate (prof/li git, -gāt/), adj. **1.** utterly and shamelessly immoral. **2.** recklessly prodigal. —n. **3.** a profligate person. —**prof/li•ga•cy** (-gə sē), n.

pro for•ma (prō fôr/mə), adj. done as a matter of form or for the sake of form.

pro•found (prə found/), adj., -er, -est. **1.** showing deep insight or understanding. **2.** originating in the depths of one's being: *profound grief.* **3.** complete and pervasive: *a profound silence.* **4.** extending far beneath the surface: *the profound depths of the ocean.* —**pro•found/ly,** adv. —**pro•fun/di•ty** (-fun/-di tē), n.

pro•fuse (-fyōōs/), adj. **1.** extravagantly generous. **2.** made or done freely and abundantly. —**pro•fuse/ly,** adv. —**pro•fu/sion** (-fyōō/zhən), n.

pro•gen•i•tor (prō jen/i tər), n. **1.** a biologically related ancestor. **2.** a precursor.

prog•e•ny (proj/ə nē), n., pl. -nies. offspring collectively.

pro•ges•ter•one (prō jes/tə rōn/), n. a female hormone, produced in the ovary or prepared synthetically.

prog•na•thous (prog/nə thəs), adj. having protrusive jaws.

prog•no•sis (prog nō/sis), n., pl. -ses (-sēz). a forecast, esp. of the probable course and outcome of a disease. —**prog•nos/tic** (-nos/tik), adj.

prog•nos/ti•cate/ (-nos/ti kāt/), v.t., -cat•ed, -cat•ing. to forecast or prophesy from present signs or indications; foretell. —**prog•nos/ti•ca/tion,** n. —**prog•nos/ti•ca/tor,** n.

pro•gram (prō/gram, -grəm), n., v., -grammed or -gramed, -gram•ming or -gram•ing. —n. **1.** a plan of action to accomplish a specified end. **2.** a schedule to be followed. **3.** a radio or television production. **4.** a list of pieces, performers, etc., in an entertainment. **5.** a sequence of instructions enabling a computer to perform a task. —v.t. **6.** to schedule as part of a program. **7.** to provide a program for. **8.** to insert (instructions) into a machine or apparatus. Also, esp. Brit., **pro/gramme.** —**pro/gram•ma•ble,** adj. —**pro/gram•mat/ic** (-grə mat/ik), adj. —**pro/-gram•mer,** n.

pro/gram trad/ing, n. the use of computer programs that automatically buy and sell large quantities of stock.

prog•ress (n. prog/res, -rəs; esp. Brit. prō/gres; v. prə gres/), n. **1.** advancement toward a goal or to a higher stage. **2.** continuous improvement. **3.** forward or onward movement. —v.i. **pro•gress 4.** to go forward or onward in space or time. **5.** to grow or develop.

pro•gres•sion (prə gresh/ən), n. **1.** the act of progressing; advance. **2.** a succession or series. **3.** Math. a succession of quantities in which there is a constant relation between each member and the one succeeding it.

pro•gres/sive, adj. **1.** advocating progress or reform, esp. in political and social matters. **2.** noting or characterized by progress. **3.** advancing step by step. **4.** of or designating a verb form that indicates a continuing action or state. —n. **5.** a person who favors progress or reform. —**pro•gres/sive•ly,** adv.

pro•hib•it (prō hib/it), v.t. **1.** to forbid by authority or law. **2.** to prevent; hinder. —**pro•hib/i•tive, pro•hib/i•to/ry** (-i tôr/ē), adj.

pro•hi•bi•tion (prō/ə bish/ən), n. **1.** the act of prohibiting. **2.** the legal prohibiting of the manufacture, sale, and transportation of alcoholic beverages. —**pro/hi•bi/tion•ist,** n.

proj•ect (n. proj/ekt, -ikt; esp. Brit. prō/jekt; v. prə-jekt/), n. **1.** a plan or scheme. **2.** a large or important undertaking. —v.t. **pro•ject 3.** to propose or plan. **4.** to throw or impel forward or outward. **5.** to cast onto a surface or into space, as a shadow. **6.** to cause to jut out or protrude. —v.i. **pro•ject 7.** to jut out; protrude. —**pro•jec/tion,** n.

pro•jec•tile (prə jek/til, -tīl), n. **1.** an object fired from a gun, as a bullet. **2.** a body projected or impelled forward.

pro•jec/tion•ist, n. an operator of a motion-picture or slide projector.

pro•jec/tor, n. an apparatus for throwing an image onto a screen.

Pro•ko•fiev (prə kô/fē əf, -ef/, -kō/-), n. **Sergei Sergeevich,** 1891–1953, Russian composer.

pro•le•tar•i•at (prō/li târ/ē ət), n. the working class, esp. industrial wage earners. —**pro/le•tar/i•an,** adj., n.

pro•life/, adj. opposed to legalized abortion.

pro•lif•er•ate (prə lif/ə rāt/), v.i., v.t., -at•ed, -at•ing. to increase in number or spread rapidly. —**pro•lif/er•a/tion,** n.

pro•lif/ic, adj. **1.** producing offspring, fruit, etc., abundantly. **2.** highly productive. —**pro•lif/i•cal•ly,** adv.

---

pro/ad•min/is•tra/tion, adj.
pro/-A•mer/i•can, adj., n.
pro•busi/ness, adj.
pro•cap/i•tal•ist, n., adj.
pro•church/, adj.
pro•cler/i•cal, adj.
pro•com/mu/nism, n., adj.
pro•com/mun•ist, adj., n.
pro•com/pro•mise/, adj.
pro/con•ser•va/tion, adj.
pro/dem•o•crat/ic, adj.
pro/dis•ar/ma•ment, adj.

pro-Eng/lish, adj.
pro/en•vi/ron•men/tal, adj.
pro•fas/cist, adj., n.
pro•fem/i•nist, n., adj.
pro•gov/ern•ment, adj.
pro•gun/, adj.
pro/im•mi•gra/tion, adj.
pro•in/dus•try, adj.
pro/in•ter•ven/tion, adj.
pro•la/bor, adj.
pro•mar/riage, adj.
pro•mil/i•tar/y, adj.

pro/mi•nor/i•ty, adj.
pro•mod/ern, adj.
pro•mon/ar•chist, n., adj.
pro•na/tion•al•ist, adj., n.
pro•nu/cle•ar, adj.
pro/re•form/, adj.
pro/rev•o•lu/tion•ar/y, adj.
pro•slav/er•y, adj.
pro•trade/, adj.
pro•un/ion, adj.
pro•war/, adj.
pro-West/, adj.

pro•lix (prō liks′, prō′liks), *adj.* tediously long and wordy. —**pro•lix′i•ty,** *n.* —**pro•lix′ly,** *adv.*

pro•logue (prō′lôg, -log) *n.* **1.** an introductory part of a discourse, poem, or novel. **2.** anything that serves as an introduction.

pro•long (prə lông′, -long′), *v.t.* to extend the duration or spatial extent of. —**pro•lon•ga•tion** (prō′-lông gā′shən), *n.*

prom (prom), *n.* a formal dance held by a high school or college class. [short for *promenade*]

prom•e•nade (prom′ə nād′, -näd′), *n., v.,* -**nad•ed,** -**nad•ing.** —*n.* **1.** a leisurely walk in a public place. **2.** an area used for such walking. **3.** a march of guests opening a formal ball. —*v.i., v.t.* **4.** to take a promenade (through or about).

Pro•me•the•us (prə mē′thē əs, -thyŏos), *n.* a Titan in Greek myth who stole fire from Olympus and gave it to humankind.

prom•i•nent (prom′ə nənt), *adj.* **1.** conspicuous. **2.** projecting. **3.** well-known; eminent. —**prom′i•nence,** *n.* —**prom′i•nent•ly,** *adv.*

pro•mis•cu•ous (prə mis′kyŏo əs), *adj.* **1.** characterized by or having numerous sexual partners on a casual basis. **2.** consisting of a disordered mixture of various elements. —**prom•is•cu•i•ty** (prom′is kyŏo′-i tē), *n.* —**pro•mis′cu•ous•ly,** *adv.*

prom•ise (prom′is), *n., v.,* -**ised, -is•ing.** —*n.* **1.** a declaration that something will or will not be done, given, etc. **2.** indication of future excellence or achievement. **3.** something promised. —*v.t., v.i.* **4.** to make a promise of (something). **5.** to afford ground for expecting.

Prom′ised Land′, *n.* Canaan, the land promised by God to Abraham and his descendants. Gen. 12:7.

prom′is•ing, *adj.* likely to turn out well.

prom•is•so•ry (prom′ə sôr′ē), *adj.* containing or implying a promise.

prom′issory note′, *n.* a written promise to pay a specified sum of money at a fixed time or on demand.

prom•on•to•ry (prom′ən tôr′ē), *n., pl.* -**ries.** a high point of land projecting into water; headland.

pro•mote (prə mōt′), *v.t.,* -**mot•ed, -mot•ing. 1.** to encourage to exist or flourish: *to promote peace.* **2.** to advance in rank, position, etc. **3.** to encourage the sales, acceptance, or recognition of, esp. through advertising. —**pro•mot′er,** *n.* —**pro•mo′tion,** *n.* —**pro•mo′tion•al,** *adj.*

prompt (prompt), *adj.,* -**er, -est,** *v.* —*adj.* **1.** done, performed, delivered, etc., without delay. **2.** quick to act or respond. **3.** punctual. —*v.t.* **4.** to induce to action. **5.** to give rise to or inspire. **6.** to give a cue to; remind. —**prompt′er,** *n.* —**prompt′ly,** *adv.* —**prompt′ness,** *n.*

prom•ul•gate (prom′əl gāt′, prō mul′gāt), *v.t.,* -**gat•ed, -gat•ing. 1.** to put into operation by formal proclamation, as a law. **2.** to set forth publicly, as a doctrine. —**prom′ul•ga′tion,** *n.*

pron., 1. pronoun. **2.** pronunciation.

prone (prōn), *adj.* **1.** having a natural tendency toward something. **2.** lying facedown.

prong (prông, prong), *n.* **1.** one of the pointed tines of a fork. **2.** any pointed, projecting part, as of an antler. —**pronged,** *adj.*

prong′horn′, *n., pl.* -**horns, -horn.** a fleet, antelopelike ruminant of the plains of W North America.

pro•noun (prō′noun′), *n.* a word used as a substitute for a noun or noun phrase. —**pro•nom′i•nal** (-nom′ə nl), *adj., n.*

pro•nounce (prə nouns′), *v.t.,* -**nounced, -nounc•ing. 1.** to enunciate or articulate (sounds, words, etc.). **2.** to utter or deliver formally or officially. —**pro•nounce′a•ble,** *adj.* —**pro•nun′ci•a′tion** (-nun′sē ā′shən), *n.*

pro•nounced′, *adj.* **1.** clearly apparent. **2.** decided; unequivocal.

pro•nounce′ment, *n.* a formal or official statement.

pron•to (pron′tō), *adv.* promptly; quickly.

proof (prŏof), *n.* **1.** evidence sufficient to establish a

thing as true or believable. **2.** the establishment of a truth or fact. **3.** the strength of an alcoholic liquor with reference to a standard. **4.** *Photog.* a trial print from a negative. **5.** *Print.* a trial impression taken to correct errors and make alterations. —*adj.* **6.** impervious or invulnerable: *proof against attack.* **7.** of standard strength, as an alcoholic liquor. —*Proverb.* **8. The proof of the pudding is in the eating,** the worth of something is proved by experience and results.

-**proof,** a combining form meaning: resistant or impervious to (*waterproof*); protected against (*bulletproof*).

proof′read′ (-rēd′), *v.t., v.i.,* -**read** (-red′), -**read•ing.** to read (printers' proofs, copy, etc.) to detect and mark errors to be corrected. —**proof′read′er,** *n.*

prop[1] (prop), *n., v.,* **propped, prop•ping.** —*n.* **1.** a stick or other rigid support. **2.** a person or thing serving as a support or stay. —*v.t.* **3.** to support with or as if with a prop. **4.** to rest (a thing) against a support.

prop[2] (prop), *n.* PROPERTY (def. 5).

prop[3] (prop), *n.* a propeller.

prop., 1. properly. **2.** property. **3.** proposition. **4.** proprietor.

prop•a•gan•da (prop′ə gan′də), *n.* **1.** information or ideas methodically spread to promote or injure a cause, nation, etc. **2.** the deliberate spreading of such information or ideas. —**prop′a•gan′dist,** *n.* —**prop′a•gan′dize,** *v.t., v.i.,* -**dized, -diz•ing.**

prop•a•gate (prop′ə gāt′), *v.,* -**gat•ed, -gat•ing.** —*v.t.* **1.** to cause (an organism) to multiply by natural reproduction. **2.** to reproduce (itself, its kind, etc.), as an organism does. **3.** to transmit (hereditary features or elements) to or through offspring. **4.** to spread (a doctrine, practice, etc.) from person to person; disseminate. —*v.i.* **5.** to multiply by natural reproduction. —**prop′a•ga′tion,** *n.*

pro•pane (prō′pān), *n.* a colorless, flammable gas, used as a fuel and in organic synthesis.

pro•pel (prə pel′), *v.t.,* -**pelled, -pel•ling.** to drive forward or onward.

pro•pel•lant or -**lent** (prə pel′ənt), *n.* **1.** a propelling agent. **2.** a substance for propelling a rocket.

aircraft propeller   outboard-engine propeller

marine propeller

propellers

pro•pel′ler, *n.* a device having a revolving hub with radiating blades, for propelling an airplane, ship, etc.

pro•pen•si•ty (prə pen′si tē), *n., pl.* -**ties.** a natural inclination or tendency.

prop•er (prop′ər), *adj.* **1.** appropriate to the purpose or circumstances. **2.** correct or decorous. **3.** fitting; right. **4.** belonging exclusively to a person, thing, or group. **5.** noting a particular person, place, or thing: *a proper noun.* **6.** in the strict sense: *Boston proper.* —**prop′er•ly,** *adv.*

prop•er•ty (prop′ər tē), *n., pl.* -**ties. 1.** that which a person owns. **2.** land or real estate. **3.** ownership; right of possession. **4.** an essential or distinctive attribute or quality of a thing. **5.** a usu. movable item used onstage or in a film set. —**prop′er•tied′,** *adj.*

proph•e•cy (prof′ə sē), *n.*, *pl.* **-cies. 1.** the foretelling of what is to come. **2.** something declared by a prophet. **3.** any prediction.

proph′e•sy′ (-sī′), *v.t.*, *v.i.* **-sied, -sy•ing. 1.** to foretell or predict (future events). **2.** to foretell (something) by divine inspiration. —**proph′e•si′er,** *n.*

proph•et (prof′it), *n.* **1.** a person who speaks by divine inspiration. **2.** (in the Old Testament) **a.** a person chosen to speak for God and to guide the people of Israel. **b.** (*often cap.*) one of the Major or Minor Prophets. **c.** one of a band of ecstatic visionaries claiming divine inspiration. **3.** one of a class of persons in the early Christian church inspired to utter special revelations and predictions. 1 Cor. 12:28. **4. the Prophet,** Muhammad, the founder of Islam. —*Proverb.* **5. A prophet is not without honor, save in his own country,** one is often valued less by those close to one than by the world at large. Matt. 13:57.

pro•phet•ic (prə fet′ik), *adj.* **1.** of a prophet. **2.** of the nature of or containing prophecy. —**pro•phet′i•cal•ly,** *adv.*

pro•phy•lac•tic (prō′fə lak′tik), *adj.* **1.** preventive or protective, esp. from disease or infection. —*n.* **2.** a prophylactic medicine, measure, or device.

pro′phy•lax′is (-lak′sis), *n.* the prevention of disease, as by protective measures or treatment.

pro•pin•qui•ty (prō ping′kwi tē), *n.* **1.** nearness in time or place. **2.** nearness of relation.

pro•pi•ti•ate (prə pish′ē āt′), *v.t.*, **-at•ed, -at•ing.** to make favorably inclined; appease. —**pro•pit′i•a′tion,** *n.* —**pro•pi′ti•a•to′ry** (-ə tôr′ē), *adj.*

pro•pi′tious (-pish′əs), *adj.* **1.** presenting favorable conditions. **2.** indicative of favor; auspicious. **3.** favorably disposed.

pro•po•nent (prə pō′nənt), *n.* **1.** a person who puts forward a proposition. **2.** an adherent of a cause or doctrine.

pro•por•tion (prə pôr′shən), *n.* **1.** comparative relation between things or magnitudes. **2. proportions,** dimensions or size. **3.** a portion or part in its relation to the whole. **4.** symmetry or balance. —*v.t.* **5.** to adjust in proper proportion or relation. **6.** to balance or harmonize the proportions of. —**pro•por′tion•al, pro•por′tion•ate** (-shə nit), *adj.*

pro•pose (prə pōz′), *v.*, **-posed, -pos•ing.** —*v.t.* **1.** to offer for consideration, action, etc. **2.** to offer (a toast). **3.** to plan; intend. —*v.i.* **4.** to make an offer of marriage. —*Proverb.* **5. Man proposes, God disposes,** things do not always work out according to plan. —**pro•pos′al,** *n.*

prop•o•si•tion (prop′ə zish′ən), *n.* **1.** the act of proposing or a plan proposed. **2.** an offer of terms for a transaction, as in business. **3.** a matter to be dealt with: *a tough proposition.* **4.** anything stated for discussion. **5.** *Math.* a formal statement of a truth to be demonstrated or an operation to be performed.

pro•pound (prə pound′), *v.t.* to put forward for consideration.

pro•pri•e•tar•y (prə prī′i ter′ē), *adj.* **1.** of or belonging to a proprietor. **2.** manufactured and sold only by the owner of the patent, trademark, etc.: *proprietary medicine.*

pro•pri′e•tor, *n.* the owner of a business establishment, property, etc. —**pro•pri′e•tor•ship′,** *n.*

pro•pri′e•ty, *n.*, *pl.* **-ties.** conformity to established standards of proper behavior or manners.

pro•pul•sion (prə pul′shən), *n.* **1.** the act of propelling or the state of being propelled. **2.** a propelling force, impulse, etc. —**pro•pul′sive** (-siv), *adj.*

pro•rate (prō rāt′, prō′rāt′), *v.t.*, *v.i.*, **-rat•ed, -rat•ing.** to divide, distribute, or calculate proportionately.

pro•sa•ic (prō zā′ik), *adj.* commonplace or dull.

pro•sce•ni•um (prō sē′nē əm, prə-), *n.*, *pl.* **-ni•ums, -ni•a** (-nē ə). **1.** Also called **prosce′nium arch′.** the arch that separates a stage from the auditorium. **2.** (formerly) the apron or, esp. in ancient theater, the stage itself.

pro•scribe (prō skrīb′), *v.t.*, **-scribed, -scrib•ing. 1.**

to condemn (a thing) as harmful or odious; prohibit. **2.** to outlaw. **3.** to banish or exile. —**pro•scrip′tion** (-skrip′shən), *n.*

prose (prōz), *n.* ordinary language, as distinguished from poetry or verse.

pros•e•cute (pros′i kyoot′), *v.t.*, **-cut•ed, -cut•ing. 1.** to conduct legal proceedings against. **2.** to carry forward (an undertaking), usu. to completion: *to prosecute a war.* —**pros′e•cu′tion,** *n.* —**pros′e•cu′tor,** *n.*

pros•e•lyt•ize (pros′ə li tīz′), *v.t.*, *v.i.*, **-ized, -iz•ing.** to attempt to convert (someone) to another opinion, religious belief, etc. —**pros′e•lyte′** (-līt′), *n.* —**pros′e•lyt•iz′er,** *n.*

pros•o•dy (pros′ə dē), *n.* the study of poetic meters and versification.

pros•pect (pros′pekt), *n.* **1.** Usu., **-pects. a.** the probability of success, profit, etc. **b.** the outlook for the future. **2.** anticipation; expectation. **3.** a potential customer, candidate, etc. **4.** a view, esp. of scenery. **5.** a mental view or survey. —*v.t.*, *v.i.* **6.** to search (a region), as for gold. —**pros′pec•tor,** *n.*

pro•spec•tive (prə spek′tiv), *adj.* potential or likely.

pro•spec′tus (-təs), *n.*, *pl.* **-tus•es.** a document describing a proposed business venture, literary work, etc., for evaluation by prospective investors, participants, or buyers.

pros•per (pros′pər), *v.i.* to be successful or fortunate, esp. financially.

pros•per•i•ty (pro sper′i tē), *n.* success, esp. financial success.

pros•per•ous (pros′pər əs), *adj.* having or characterized by success or wealth. —**pros′per•ous•ly,** *adv.*

pros′tate gland′ (pros′tāt), *n.* a gland surrounding the urethra of males that secretes a fluid that makes up part of the semen.

pros•the•sis (pros thē′sis), *n.*, *pl.* **-ses** (-sēz). a device that substitutes for or supplements a missing or defective part of the body. —**pros•thet′ic** (-thet′ik), *adj.*

pros•ti•tute (pros′ti toot′, -tyoot′), *n.*, *v.*, **-tut•ed, -tut•ing.** —*n.* **1.** a person who engages in sexual acts for money. —*v.t.* **2.** to offer (oneself) as a prostitute. **3.** to put (one's talent or ability) to unworthy use. —**pros′ti•tu′tion,** *n.*

pros•trate (pros′trāt), *v.*, **-trat•ed, -trat•ing,** *adj.* —*v.t.* **1.** to cast (oneself) facedown on the ground, as in humility. **2.** to reduce to helplessness, weakness, or exhaustion. —*adj.* **3.** lying flat on the ground. **4.** lying facedown on the ground. **5.** helpless, weak, or exhausted. —**pros•tra′tion,** *n.*

pros•y (prō′zē), *adj.*, **-i•er, -i•est.** prosaic; dull.

prot•ac•tin•i•um (prō′tak tin′ē əm), *n.* a radioactive metallic element. *Symbol:* Pa; *at. no.:* 91.

pro•tag•o•nist (prō tag′ə nist), *n.* the leading character of a literary work.

pro•te•an (prō′tē ən, prō tē′-), *adj.* readily assuming different forms or characters.

pro•tect (prə tekt′), *v.t.* to defend from attack, loss, etc.; shield. —**pro•tec′tor,** *n.*

pro•tec′tion, *n.* **1.** the act of protecting or state of being protected. **2.** a thing, person, or group that protects.

pro•tec′tion•ism, *n.* the practice of protecting domestic industries from foreign competition by imposing import duties.

pro•tec′tive (-tiv), *adj.* **1.** tending to protect. **2.** of or favoring protectionism. —**pro•tec′tive•ness,** *n.*

pro•tec′tor•ate (-tər it), *n.* a weak state or territory that is protected and partly controlled by a stronger state.

pro•té•gé (prō′tə zhā′), *n.*, *pl.* **-gés.** a person under the patronage or protection of someone interested in his or her career or welfare.

pro•tein (prō′tēn, -tē in), *n.* any of numerous organic molecules constituting a large portion of the mass of every life form, composed of amino acids linked in chains.

pro tem·po·re (prō′ tem′pə rē′, -rā′), *adv.* **1.** temporarily. —*adj.* **2.** temporary.

pro·test (*n.* prō′test; *v.* prə test′, prō′test), *n.* **1.** an expression or declaration of objection, disapproval, or dissent. —*v.i., v.t.* **2.** to make a protest or remonstrance (against). **3.** to make solemn or earnest declaration (of). —**prot·es·ta·tion** (prot′ə stā′shən, prō′te-), *n.* —**pro·test′er,** *n.*

Prot·es·tant (prot′ə stənt), *n.* **1.** (loosely) any Christian not an adherent of a Catholic, Anglican, or Eastern church. **2.** an adherent of one of the Christian churches arising from the Reformation. —*adj.* **3.** belonging or pertaining to Protestants or their religion. —**Prot′es·tant·ism,** *n.*

proto-, a combining form meaning: earliest or original (*prototype*); foremost or essential (*protoplasm*).

pro·to·col (prō′tə kôl′, -kol′, -kōl′), *n.* **1.** the customs and regulations dealing with diplomatic formality, precedence, and etiquette. **2.** an original draft from which a document, esp. a treaty, is prepared. **3.** a set of rules governing the format of messages that are exchanged between computers.

pro·ton (prō′ton), *n.* a positively charged elementary particle found in all atomic nuclei.

pro·to·plasm (prō′tə plaz′əm), *n.* the colloidal and liquid substance of which cells are formed. —**pro′to·plas′mic,** *adj.*

pro′to·type′, *n.* the original or model on which something is based; pattern.

pro′to·zo′an (-zō′ən), *n., pl.* **-zo·ans, -zo·a** (-zō′ə). any of various one-celled organisms that usu. obtain nourishment by ingesting food particles rather than by photosynthesis. —**pro′to·zo′ic,** *adj.*

pro·tract (prō trakt′, prə-), *v.t.* to draw out or lengthen, esp. in time. —**pro·trac′tion,** *n.*

pro·trac′tor, *n.* (in surveying, mathematics, etc.) an instrument having a graduated arc for plotting or measuring angles.

pro·trude (prō trōōd′, prə-), *v.i., v.t.,* **-trud·ed, -trud·ing.** to jut out or cause to jut out. —**pro·tru′sion,** *n.*

pro·tru′sile (-trōō′sil, -sīl), *adj.* capable of being thrust forth or extended.

pro·tu′ber·ance (-tōō′bər əns, -tyōō′-), *n.* a part or thing that protrudes. —**pro·tu′ber·ant,** *adj.*

proud (proud), *adj.,* **-er, -est. 1.** feeling satisfaction over something regarded as creditable to oneself. **2.** having or showing self-esteem. **3.** giving a sense of pride: *a proud moment.* **4.** highly honorable or creditable: *a proud achievement.* **5.** arrogant; haughty. **6.** stately or magnificent: *proud cities.* —**proud′ly,** *adv.*

Proust (prōōst), *n.* **Marcel,** 1871–1922, French novelist. —**Proust′i·an,** *adj.*

prove (prōōv), *v.,* **proved, proved** or **prov·en, prov·ing.** —*v.t.* **1.** to establish the truth, genuineness, or validity of. **2.** to establish the quality or worth of, as by a test. —*v.i.* **3.** to turn out: *The experiment proved to be successful.* **4.** to be found to be: *His story proved false.* —**prov′a·ble,** *adj.* —**prov′a·bil′i·ty,** *n.* —**Usage.** Either PROVED or PROVEN is standard as the past participle of PROVE. As a modifier, PROVEN is by far the more common: *a proven fact.*

prov·e·nance (prov′ə nəns, -näns′), *n.* place or source of origin.

Pro·ven·çal (prō′vən säl′, prov′ən-; *Fr.* prô vän-säl′), *n.* the Romance speech of S France, including the dialects of Provence and other regions.

prov·en·der (prov′ən dər), *n.* **1.** dry food for livestock. **2.** food.

prov·erb (prov′ərb), *n.* a short popular saying expressing some commonplace truth. —**pro·ver·bi·al** (prə vûr′bē əl), *adj.*

Prov′erbs, *n.* a book of the Bible containing the sayings of sages.

pro·vide (prə vīd′), *v.,* **-vid·ed, -vid·ing.** —*v.t.* **1.** to make available; furnish. **2.** to supply or equip. **3.** to stipulate beforehand. —*v.i.* **4.** to take measures with due foresight. **5.** to supply means of support: *to provide for one's children.* —**pro·vid′er,** *n.*

pro·vid′ed or **-vid′ing,** *conj.* on the condition or understanding (that).

prov·i·dence (prov′i dəns), *n.* **1.** (*often cap.*) the foreseeing care and guidance of God or nature. **2.** (*cap.*) God. **3.** foresight; provident care.

Prov′i·dence, *n.* the capital of Rhode Island. 150,639.

prov·i·dent (-dənt), *adj.* **1.** providing carefully for the future. **2.** frugal; thrifty. —**prov′i·dent·ly,** *adv.*

prov·i·den′tial (-den′shəl), *adj.* **1.** of or resulting from divine providence. **2.** fortunate or lucky. —**prov·i·den′tial·ly,** *adv.*

prov·ince (prov′ins), *n.* **1.** an administrative division or unit of a country. **2. the provinces,** the parts of a country outside of the capital or the largest cities. **3.** a territory, district, or region. **4.** a sphere of activity or authority.

pro·vin·cial (prə vin′shəl), *adj.* **1.** belonging to a particular province. **2.** of the provinces. **3.** unsophisticated; parochial. —**pro·vin′cial·ism,** *n.*

prov′ing ground′ (prōō′ving), *n.* any place, context, or area for testing something.

pro·vi·sion (prə vizh′ən), *n.* **1.** the act of providing or supplying. **2.** something provided or supplied. **3.** an arrangement made beforehand. **4.** a legal or formal stipulation; proviso. **5. provisions,** supplies of food.

pro·vi′sion·al, *adj.* **1.** temporary. **2.** accepted or adopted tentatively; conditional. —**pro·vi′sion·al·ly,** *adv.*

pro·vi·so (prə vī′zō), *n., pl.* **-sos, -soes. 1.** a clause, as in a contract, by which a condition is introduced. **2.** a stipulation or condition.

prov·o·ca·tion (prov′ə kā′shən), *n.* **1.** the act of provoking. **2.** something that provokes.

pro·voc·a·tive (prə vok′ə tiv), *adj.* serving to provoke; stimulating, exciting, or vexing. —**pro·voc′a·tive·ly,** *adv.*

pro·voke′ (-vōk′), *v.t.,* **-voked, -vok·ing. 1.** to anger or vex. **2.** to stir up or call forth (feelings, desires, or activity). **3.** to incite to action. **4.** to induce or bring about. —**pro·vok′er,** *n.*

pro·vost (prō′vōst), *n.* **1.** a person appointed to superintend or preside. **2.** a high-ranking administrative officer of some colleges and universities. [< OF, < ML *prōpositus* abbot, lit., (one) placed before < L]

pro′vost mar′shal (prō′vō), *n.* an officer in the army charged with police functions within a command.

prow (prou), *n.* the forepart of a ship or boat.

prow·ess (prou′is), *n.* **1.** exceptional ability or skill. **2.** exceptional bravery, esp. in battle.

prowl (proul), *v.i., v.t.* **1.** to rove about stealthily, as in search of prey or something to steal. —*n.* **2.** the act of prowling. —**prowl′er,** *n.*

prox·im·i·ty (prok sim′i tē), *n.* nearness in place, time, relation, etc.

prox·y (prok′sē), *n., pl.* **prox·ies. 1.** the function or power of a person authorized to act for another. **2.** the person so authorized.

Pro·zac (prō′zak), *Trademark.* a brand of antidepressant.

prude (prōōd), *n.* one who is excessively proper or modest, esp. in matters involving sex. —**prud′er·y,** *n.* —**prud′ish,** *adj.*

pru·dent (prōōd′nt), *adj.* **1.** wise or judicious in practical affairs. **2.** cautious. **3.** careful in providing for the future. —**pru′dence,** *n.* —**pru·den·tial** (prōō den′shəl), *adj.* —**pru′dent·ly,** *adv.*

prune¹ (prōōn), *n.* any plum when dried.

prune² (prōōn), *v.t.,* **pruned, prun·ing. 1.** to cut off undesired twigs, branches, or roots from. **2.** to remove (anything undesirable). —**prun′er,** *n.*

pru·ri·ent (prōōr′ē ənt), *adj.* **1.** having lascivious or lustful desires. **2.** causing lasciviousness or lust. —**pru′ri·ence,** *n.*

Prus·sia (prush′ə), *n.* a former state in N Europe: became a military power in the 18th century and in 1871 led the formation of the German empire. —**Prus′sian,** *adj., n.*

pry¹ (prī), *v.i.,* **pried, pry·ing. 1.** to inquire impertinently into something. **2.** to look closely or curiously.

pry² (prī), *v.*, **pried, pry•ing**, *n.*, *pl.* **pries.** —*v.t.* **1.** to move, raise, or open by leverage. **2.** to obtain with difficulty. —*n.* **3.** a tool, as a crowbar, for raising, moving, or opening something by leverage. **4.** the leverage exerted.

P.S., 1. Also, **p.s.** postscript. **2.** Public School.

PSA, prostate specific antigen: a protein, produced by the prostate, elevated levels of which may indicate the presence of cancer.

psalm (säm), *n.* **1.** a sacred song or hymn. **2.** (*cap.*) any of the songs, hymns, or prayers contained in the Book of Psalms. —**psalm′ist,** *n.*

Psalms (sämz), *n.* a book of the Bible composed of 150 psalms.

Psal•ter (sôl′tər), *n.* **1.** the Book of Psalms. **2.** (*sometimes l.c.*) a book containing Psalms for devotional use.

psal•ter•y (sôl′tə rē), *n.*, *pl.* **-ter•ies.** an ancient musical instrument similar to a zither.

PSAT, *Trademark.* Preliminary SAT/National Merit Qualifying Test.

pseud•e•pig•ra•pha (soo′də pig′rə fə), *n.pl.* certain writings other than the canonical books and the Apocrypha professing to be Biblical in character.

pseu•do (soo′dō), *adj.* false or spurious.

pseudo-, a combining form meaning false or pretended (*pseudonym*).

pseu•do•nym (sood′n im), *n.* a fictitious name used by an author to conceal his or her identity. —**pseu•don•y•mous** (soo don′ə məs), *adj.*

pshaw (shô), *interj.* an exclamation of impatience, contempt, or disbelief.

psi (sī, psī), *n.*, *pl.* **psis.** the 23rd letter of the Greek alphabet (ψ, ψ).

psit•ta•co•sis (sit′ə kō′sis), *n.* a disease affecting parrots and other birds and transmissible to humans.

pso•ri•a•sis (sə rī′ə sis), *n.* a chronic, inflammatory skin disease characterized by scaly patches.

psst (pst), *interj.* (used to attract someone's attention in an unobtrusive manner.)

PST, Pacific Standard Time.

psych (sīk), *v.t.* **1.** to intimidate or frighten psychologically (often fol. by *out*). **2.** to prepare psychologically: *psyched herself up for the test.*

psych-, var. of PSYCHO-.

psych., psychology.

psy•che (sī′kē), *n.* **1.** the human soul, spirit, or mind. **2.** the mental structure of a person, esp. as a motive force.

psy•che•del•ic (sī′ki del′ik), *adj.* **1.** of or noting a mental state of intensified sensory perception. **2.** of or noting any drug that produces this state.

psy•chi•a•try (si kī′ə trē, sī-), *n.* the branch of medicine concerned with the study, diagnosis, and treatment of mental disorders. —**psy•chi•at•ric** (sī′kē a′trik), *adj.* —**psy•chi•a•trist,** *n.*

psy•chic (sī′kik), *adj.* Also, **psy′chi•cal. 1.** of the human soul or mind. **2.** outside of natural or scientific knowledge. **3.** sensitive to influences of a nonphysical or supernatural nature. —*n.* **4.** a person who is sensitive to psychic influences. —**psy′chi•cal•ly,** *adv.*

psy•cho (sī′kō), *n.*, *pl.* **-chos,** *adj. Slang.* —*n.* **1.** a psychopathic or psychotic person. —*adj.* **2.** psychopathic or psychotic.

psycho-, a combining form meaning: the mind (*psychology*); mental processes or disorders (*psychotherapy*).

psy′cho•ac′tive, *adj.* significantly affecting mood or mental state, as a drug.

psy′cho•a•nal′y•sis, *n.* a professional technique for investigating unconscious mental processes and treating mental illness. —**psy′cho•an′a•lyst** (-an′l-ist), *n.* —**psy′cho•an′a•lyze′,** *v.t.*, **-lyzed, -lyz•ing.**

psy•cho•gen•ic (sī′kə jen′ik), *adj.* having origin in the mind or in a mental condition or process.

psy•chol•o•gy (sī kol′ə jē), *n.*, *pl.* **-gies. 1.** the science of the mind or of mental states and processes. **2.** the science of human and animal behavior. —**psy′cho•log′i•cal** (-kə loj′i kəl), *adj.* —**psy•chol′o•gist,** *n.*

psy•cho•neu•ro•sis (sī′kō noo rō′sis, -nyoo-), *n.*, *pl.* **-ses** (-sēz). NEUROSIS.

psy•cho•path (sī′kə path′), *n.* a person having a character disorder distinguished by amoral or antisocial behavior. —**psy′cho•path′ic,** *adj.* —**psy•chop′a•thy** (-kop′ə thē), *n.*, *pl.* **-thies.**

psy•cho•sis (sī kō′sis), *n.*, *pl.* **-ses** (-sēz). a severe mental disorder characterized by symptoms, as delusions or hallucinations, that indicate impaired contact with reality. —**psy•chot′ic** (-kot′ik), *adj.*, *n.*

psy•cho•so•mat′ic, *adj.* of or noting a physical disorder caused or influenced by emotional factors.

psy′cho•ther′a•py, *n.*, *pl.* **-pies.** the treatment of psychological disorders or maladjustments by a professional technique, as psychoanalysis. —**psy′cho•ther′a•pist,** *n.*

psy′cho•tro′pic (-trō′pik), *adj.* affecting mental activity, behavior, or perception, as a mood-altering drug.

Pt, *Chem. Symbol.* platinum.

pt., 1. part. **2.** pint. **3.** point. **4.** preterit.

PTA, Parent-Teacher Association.

ptar•mi•gan (tär′mi gən), *n.*, *pl.* **-gans, -gan.** any of several grouses of mountainous and cold northern regions.

pter•o•dac•tyl (ter′ə dak′til), *n.* an extinct flying reptile with membranous wings supported by one elongated finger on each hand.

pterodactyl

Ptol•e•my (tol′ə mē), *n.* fl. A.D. 127–151, Greek mathematician and astronomer. —**Ptol′e•ma′ic** (-mā′ik), *adj.*

pto•maine (tō′mān), *n.* any of a class of nitrogenous substances produced by bacteria during putrefaction of protein, formerly thought to cause food poisoning.

Pu, *Chem. Symbol.* plutonium.

pub (pub), *n.* a bar or tavern.

pu•ber•ty (pyoo′bər tē), *n.* the period of life during which an individual becomes capable of sexual reproduction. —**pu′ber•tal,** *adj.*

pu•bes′cent (-bes′ənt), *adj.* arriving or arrived at puberty. —**pu•bes′cence,** *n.*

pu′bic, *adj.* of or situated near the genitalia.

pub•lic (pub′lik), *adj.* **1.** of or affecting a population or community as a whole: *a public nuisance.* **2.** done, acting, etc., for the community: *public prosecution.* **3.** open to all persons: *a public meeting.* **4.** maintained by or for a community: *a public library.* **5.** generally known. **6.** devoted to the welfare or well-being of the community: *public spirit.* —*n.* **7.** the people constituting a community, state, etc. **8.** a group of people with a common interest, aim, etc.: *the book-buying public.* —*Idiom.* **9. in public,** not in private; openly. —**pub′lic•ly,** *adv.*

pub′li•ca′tion, *n.* **1.** the act of publishing a book, piece of music, etc. **2.** something published, esp. a periodical.

pub′lic defend′er, *n.* a lawyer appointed to represent indigents in criminal cases at public expense.

pub′lic domain′, *n.* the legal status of material never or no longer protected by a copyright or patent.

pub′li•cist (-sist), *n.* a person who publicizes, as a public-relations consultant.

pub•lic•i•ty (pu blis′i tē), *n.* **1.** extensive mention in the news or other media. **2.** public notice so gained. **3.** the process or business of securing public notice. **4.** information, articles, etc., issued to secure public notice.

pub′li•cize′, *v.t.*, **-cized, -ciz•ing.** to give publicity to.

pub·lic rela'tions, *n.pl.* the actions of a corporation, organization, etc., in promoting goodwill with the public.

pub'lic school', *n.* **1.** (in the U.S.) a primary or secondary school maintained at public expense. **2.** (in England) a private secondary boarding school that prepares private students for the universities or for public service.

pub'lic serv'ant, *n.* a person holding a government office or job.

pub/lic-spir'ited, *adj.* having or showing an unselfish interest in the public welfare.

pub'lic trough', *n. Informal.* the self-interested use of public funds.

pub'lic util'ity, *n.* a business enterprise, as a gas company, performing an essential public service and regulated by the government.

Pub'lic Works' Administra'tion, *n.* the U.S. federal agency (1933–44) that administered projects for the construction of public works. *Abbr.:* PWA, P.W.A.

pub·lish (pub'lish), *v.t.* **1.** to issue (printed or otherwise reproduced textual or graphic material) for sale. **2.** to make publicly or generally known. —*v.i.* **3.** to issue newspapers, books, etc. **4.** to have one's work published. —**pub'lish·a·ble,** *adj.* —**pub'lish·er,** *n.*

Puc·ci·ni (pōō chē'nē), *n.* **Giacomo,** 1858–1924, Italian composer.

puck (puk), *n.* a black rubber disk that is hit into the goal in ice hockey.

puck·er (puk'ər), *v.t., v.i.* **1.** to draw or gather into wrinkles or irregular folds. —*n.* **2.** an irregular fold; wrinkle.

puck·ish (puk'ish), *adj.* mischievous.

pud·ding (pōōd'ing), *n.* a soft, thickened dessert, typically made with milk, sugar, flour, and flavoring. —**pud'ding·like',** *adj.*

pud·dle (pud'l), *n.* a small pool of water, as of rainwater on the ground.

pudg·y (puj'ē), *adj., -i·er, -i·est.* short and fat or thick.

pueb·lo (pweb'lō), *n., pl.* **-los. 1.** a communal dwelling of certain Indians of the southwestern U.S., consisting of adjoining houses of stone or adobe. **2.** (*cap.*) a member of an Indian people living in pueblos.

pu·er·ile (pyōō'ər il, -ə rīl', pyōōr'il, -īl), *adj.* immature; silly. —**pu/er·ile·ly,** *adv.* —**pu/er·il'i·ty,** *n.*

Puer·to Ri·co (pwer'tə rē'kō, pwer'tō, pôr'tə), *n.* an island in the central West Indies: a commonwealth associated with the U.S. 3,196,520. *Cap.:* San Juan. *Abbr.:* PR, P.R. —**Puer'to Ri'can,** *n., adj.*

puff (puf), *n.* **1.** a short, quick blast or emission of air, smoke, etc. **2.** an act of inhaling and exhaling, as on a cigarette. **3.** a light pastry filled with whipped cream, custard, etc. **4.** an exaggerated commendation of a book, performance, etc. **5.** a ball or pad of soft material. —*v.i.* **6.** to blow with puffs. **7.** to breathe quick and hard. **8.** to take puffs in smoking. **9.** to become inflated or distended (usu. fol. by *up*). —*v.t.* **10.** to send forth in puffs. **11.** to smoke (a cigar, cigarette, etc.). **12.** to inflate or make fluffy. **13.** to inflate with pride or vanity (often fol. by *up*). —**puff'y,** *adj., -i·er, -i·est.* —**puff'i·ness,** *n.*

puff'ball', *n.* any of various globular stalkless fungi that emit a cloud of spores when pressed or broken.

puffin

puf·fin (puf'in), *n.* any of several sea birds with a short neck and a colorful, triangular bill.

pug (pug), *n.* one of a breed of small, squarely built dogs with a deeply wrinkled face.

pu·gi·lism (pyōō'jə liz'əm), *n.* the practice of fighting with the fists; boxing. —**pu'gi·list,** *n.* —**pu'gi·lis'tic,** *adj.*

pug·na·cious (pug nā'shəs), *adj.* inclined to quarrel or fight readily. —**pug·na'cious·ly,** *adv.* —**pug·nac'i·ty** (-nas'i tē), *n.*

pug' nose', *n.* a short, broad, somewhat turned-up nose. —**pug'-nosed',** *adj.*

Pul (pul, pōōl), *n.* TIGLATH-PILESER.

pul·chri·tude (pul'kri tōōd', -tyōōd'), *n.* beauty; comeliness.

pule (pyōōl), *v.i.,* **puled, pul·ing.** to cry in a thin voice; whine.

Pu·litz·er (pōōl'it sər, pyōō'lit-), *n.* **Joseph,** 1847–1911, U.S. journalist and publisher, born in Hungary.

Pu'litzer Prize', *n.* any of the annual prizes, as in journalism, literature, or music, established by Joseph Pulitzer

pull (pōōl), *v.t.* **1.** to use force to cause (something) to move toward or after oneself or itself. **2.** to rip; tear. **3.** to dislodge or extract, as a tooth. **4.** to draw out (a weapon). **5.** to perform; carry out: *They pulled a spectacular coup.* **6.** to strain (a muscle). —*v.i.* **7.** to exert a drawing, tugging, or hauling force. **8.** to become or come as specified, by being pulled. **9.** to move or go: *The train pulled away from the station.* **10. pull for,** to support actively. **11. ~ off,** *Informal.* to perform successfully. **12. ~ out, a.** to depart. **b.** to abandon abruptly. **13. ~ through,** to come safely through (a crisis, illness, etc.). **14. ~ up, a.** to bring or come to a halt. **b.** to bring or draw closer. —*n.* **15.** the act of pulling. **16.** force used in pulling. **17.** influence, as with persons able to grant favors. **18.** a part or thing to be pulled, as a handle. **19.** the ability to attract; drawing power. —*Idiom.* **20. pull oneself together,** to regain command of one's emotions. —**pull'er,** *n.*

pull'back', *n.* the act of pulling back, esp. a retreat or a strategic withdrawal of troops.

pul·let (pōōl'it), *n.* a hen less than one year old.

pul·ley (pōōl'ē), *n., pl.* **-leys.** a wheel for supporting, guiding, or transmitting force to or from a moving rope or cable that rides in a groove in its edge.

Pull·man (pōōl'mən), *pl.* **-mans,** *Trademark.* a railroad sleeping car or parlor car. [after G. M. *Pullman* (1831–97), U.S. inventor]

pull'out', *n.* **1.** a withdrawal, as of troops or funds. **2.** a section of a newspaper or magazine that can be pulled out.

pull'o'ver, *adj.* **1.** designed to be put on by being drawn over the head. —*n.* **2.** a pullover garment, esp. a sweater.

pul·mo·nar·y (pul'mə ner'ē, pōōl'-), *adj.* of or affecting the lungs.

pulp (pulp), *n.* **1.** the soft, juicy, edible part of a fruit. **2.** the pith of a plant stem. **3.** the inner substance of the tooth, containing blood vessels and nerves. **4.** a soft, moist mass, as of linen or wood, used in making paper. **5.** a magazine or book printed on low-quality paper, usu. containing lurid material. —**pulp'y,** *adj., -i·er, -i·est.*

pul·pit (pōōl'pit, pul'-), *n.* **1.** a raised structure in a church, from which the sermon is delivered or the service is conducted. **2. the pulpit,** the clerical profession; ministry.

pul·sar (pul'sär), *n.* any of several hundred known celestial objects that emit regular pulses of radiation, esp. radio waves.

pul·sate (pul'sāt), *v.i.,* **-sat·ed, -sat·ing. 1.** to expand and contract rhythmically. **2.** to vibrate; quiver. —**pul·sa'tion,** *n.*

pulse (puls), *n., v.,* **pulsed, puls·ing.** —*n.* **1.** the regular throbbing of the arteries, caused by the successive contractions of the heart. **2.** a stroke or vibration, or a rhythmic series of these. **3.** a momentary, sudden fluctuation in an electrical quantity. —*v.i.* **4.** to beat or throb.

pul·ver·ize (pul'və rīz'), *v.t., v.i.,* **-ized, -iz·ing.** to reduce or become reduced to dust or powder, as by pounding. —**pul'ver·i·za'tion,** *n.*

pu·ma (pyōō'mə, pōō'-), *n., pl.* **-mas.** COUGAR.

pum•ice (pum′is), *n.* a porous or spongy form of volcanic glass, used as an abrasive.

pum•mel (pum′əl), *v.t.* **-meled, -mel•ing** or (*esp. Brit.*) **-melled, -mel•ling.** to beat or thrash with or as if with the fists.

pump¹ (pump), *n.* **1.** an apparatus or machine for driving or compressing fluids or gases, as by means of a piston. —*v.t.* **2.** to drive with a pump. **3.** to force or inject as a pump does. **4.** to remove the liquid from by means of a pump. **5.** to operate or move by an up-and-down action. **6.** to question persistently so as to elicit information. **7. pump up, a.** to inflate with a pump: *to pump up a tire.* **b.** to infuse with enthusiasm. —*Idiom.* **8. pump iron,** to lift weights as an exercise. —**pump′er,** *n.*

pump² (pump), *n.* a woman's lightweight, low-cut shoe without fastenings.

pum•per•nick•el (pum′pər nik′əl), *n.* a coarse, dark, slightly sour rye bread.

pump•kin (pump′kin *or, commonly,* pung′kin), *n.* a large, edible, orange-yellow fruit borne by a coarse vine.

pun (pun), *n., v.,* **punned, pun•ning.** —*n.* **1.** the humorous use of a word or phrase so as to suggest its different meanings or the use of words that are nearly alike in sound but different in meaning. —*v.i.* **2.** to make puns.

punch¹ (punch), *n.* **1.** a thrusting blow with the fist. **2.** forcefulness or effectiveness. —*v.t.* **3.** to hit with the fist. **4.** to drive (cattle). **5.** to prod, as with a stick. **6.** to strike or hit in operating: *to punch an elevator button.* **7. punch in** (or **out**), to record one's time of arrival (or departure) by punching a time clock. —**punch′er,** *n.*

punch² (punch), *n.* **1.** a tool or machine for perforating materials, driving nails, etc. —*v.t.* **2.** to perforate, drive, etc., with a punch. **3.** to make (a hole) with a punch.

punch³ (punch), *n.* **1.** a beverage of wine or spirits mixed with fruit juice, soda, etc. **2.** a beverage of two or more fruit juices, sugar, and water.

punch′-drunk′, *adj.* **1.** (of a boxer) showing symptoms of cerebral injury, as unsteadiness, caused by repeated blows to the head. **2.** befuddled; dazed.

pun•cheon (pun′chən), *n.* a large cask of varying capacity.

punch′ line′, *n.* the climactic phrase or sentence in a joke that produces the desired effect.

punch′y, *adj.,* **-i•er, -i•est. 1.** punch-drunk. **2.** vigorously effective; forceful.

punc•til•i•ous (pungk til′ē əs), *adj.* strict or exact in the observance of the formalities of conduct. —**punc•til′i•ous•ly,** *adv.* —**punc•til′i•ous•ness,** *n.*

punc•tu•al (pungk′chōō əl), *adj.* arriving or happening at the time appointed; prompt. —**punc′tu•al′i•ty,** *n.* —**punc′tu•al•ly,** *adv.*

punc′tu•ate′ (-āt′), *v.t.,* **-at•ed, -at•ing. 1.** to mark or divide (something written) with punctuation marks. **2.** to interrupt at intervals. **3.** to give emphasis or force to.

punc′tu•a′tion, *n.* the use of certain conventional marks (**punctua′tion marks′**) in writing or printing in order to separate elements and make the meaning clear.

punc•ture (pungk′chər), *n., v.,* **-tured, -tur•ing.** —*n.* **1.** the act of piercing with a pointed object. **2.** a hole so made. —*v.t., v.i.* **3.** to pierce or be pierced, as with something sharp.

pun•dit (pun′dit), *n.* a learned person; an expert or authority.

pun•gent (pun′jənt), *adj.* **1.** sharply affecting the organs of taste or smell; biting. **2.** incisive; forceful and sharp. —**pun′gen•cy,** *n.* —**pun′gent•ly,** *adv.*

pun•ish (pun′ish), *v.t.* **1.** to subject to pain, loss, etc., as a penalty for some offense or fault. **2.** to inflict such a penalty for (an offense or fault). **3.** to treat harshly. —**pun′ish•a•ble,** *adj.*

pun′ish•ment, *n.* **1.** the act of punishing or fact of being punished. **2.** a penalty inflicted for an offense or fault. **3.** severe treatment.

pu•ni•tive (pyōō′ni tiv), *adj.* concerned with or inflicting punishment. —**pu′ni•tive•ly,** *adv.*

punk¹ (pungk), *n.* **1.** any prepared substance that will smolder and can be used to light fireworks, fuses, etc. **2.** dry, decayed wood that can be used as tinder.

punk² (pungk), *n.* **1.** *Slang.* **a.** something or someone worthless or unimportant. **b.** a young ruffian; hoodlum. **2.** a style characterized by bizarre clothing, hairstyles, etc., and the defiance of social norms. —*adj.* **3.** *Informal.* poor in quality.

pun•ster (pun′stər), *n.* one who makes puns frequently.

punt¹ (punt), *n.* **1.** a kick, as in football, executed by dropping the ball and kicking it before it touches the ground. —*v.t., v.i.* **2.** to kick (a dropped ball) before it touches the ground. —**punt′er,** *n.*

punt² (punt), *n.* **1.** a small, flat-bottomed boat propelled by a pole. —*v.t., v.i.* **2.** to propel (a punt) by a pole. —**punt′er,** *n.*

punt³ (pōōnt, punt), *n., pl.* **punt.** the basic monetary unit of the Republic of Ireland.

pu•ny (pyōō′nē), *adj.,* **-ni•er, -ni•est. 1.** of less than normal size and strength. **2.** unimportant; insignificant. —**pu′ni•ness,** *n.*

pup (pup), *n.* **1.** a young dog. **2.** the young of certain other animals, as the seal.

pu•pa (pyōō′pə), *n., pl.* **-pae** (-pē), **-pas.** an insect in the transformation stage between the larva and the adult. —**pu′pal,** *adj.*

pu•pil¹ (pyōō′pəl), *n.* a person, usu. young, who is learning under the supervision of a teacher.

pu•pil² (pyōō′pəl), *n.* the expanding and contracting opening in the iris of the eye.

pup•pet (pup′it), *n.* **1.** a small figure of a person or animal, manipulated by the hand or by rods, wires, etc. **2.** a person or group whose actions are controlled by another. —**pup′pet•ry,** *n.*

pup′pet•eer′, *n.* a person who manipulates puppets.

pup•py (pup′ē), *n., pl.* **-pies.** a young dog.

pup′ tent′, *n.* a small tent for two persons.

pur•blind (pûr′blīnd′), *adj.* **1.** partially blind. **2.** deficient in understanding or imagination.

pur•chase (pûr′chəs), *v.,* **-chased, -chas•ing.** *n.* —*v.t.* **1.** to acquire by the payment of money; buy. —*n.* **2.** acquisition by the payment of money. **3.** something purchased. **4.** an effective hold for applying power in moving or raising a heavy object; leverage. —**pur′chas•a•ble,** *adj.* —**pur′chas•er,** *n.*

pure (pyōōr), *adj.,* **pur•er, pur•est. 1.** free from adulterating or extraneous matter. **2.** absolute; utter. **3.** being that and nothing else: *a pure accident.* **4.** clear; spotless. **5.** abstract or theoretical: *pure science.* **6.** untainted with evil or guilt. **7.** physically chaste; virgin. —**pure′ly,** *adv.* —**pure′ness,** *n.*

pure•bred (*adj.* pyōōr′bred′; *n.* pyōōr′bred′), *adj.* **1.** of an individual whose ancestors derive over many generations from a recognized breed. —*n.* **2.** a purebred animal.

pu•rée (pyōō rā′, -rē′), *n., pl.* **-rées,** *v.* **-réed, -rée•ing.** —*n.* **1.** a thick liquid prepared from cooked food passed through a sieve or broken down in a blender. **2.** a soup made of puréed ingredients. —*v.t.* **3.** to make a purée of. [< F < *purer* to strain, lit., make pure]

pur•ga•tive (pûr′gə tiv), *adj.* **1.** purging or cleansing, esp. by causing evacuation of the bowels. —*n.* **2.** a purgative medicine or agent.

pur′ga•to′ry (pûr′gə tôr′ē), *n., pl.* **-ries. 1.** (esp. in Roman Catholic belief) a place or state following death in which penitent souls are purified and thereby are made ready for heaven. **2.** any condition or place of temporary punishment or expiation. —**pur′ga•to′ri•al,** *adj.*

purge (pûrj), *v.,* **purged, purg•ing,** *n.* —*v.t.* **1.** to rid of impurities. **2.** to clear of imputed guilt. **3.** to clear (the stomach or intestines) by inducing vomiting or evacuation. **4.** to eliminate (undesirable members) from a government, political organization, etc.

—*n.* **5.** the act or process of purging. **6.** something that purges, as a purgative medicine. —**purg′er,** *n.*

pu•ri•fy (pyŏŏr′ə fī′), *v.*, **-fied, -fy•ing.** —*v.t.* **1.** to make pure. **2.** to free from guilt or evil. —*v.i.* **3.** to become pure. —**pu′ri•fi•ca′tion,** *n.* —**pu′ri•fi′er,** *n.*

Pu•rim (pŏŏr′im), *n.* a Jewish festival commemorating the deliverance of the Jews in Persia from destruction.

pu•rine (pyŏŏr′ēn, -in), *n.* **1.** a white, crystalline compound, from which is derived a group of compounds including uric acid and caffeine. **2.** one of several purine derivatives, esp. the bases adenine and guanine.

pur•ism (pyŏŏr′iz əm), *n.* strict observance of or insistence on purity or correctness in language, style, etc. —**pur′ist,** *n.*

Pu•ri•tan (pyŏŏr′i tn), *n.* **1.** a member of a group of Protestants that arose in the 16th century within the Church of England, demanding the simplification of doctrine and worship. **2.** (*l.c.*) a person who is excessively strict in moral or religious matters. —**pur′i• tan′i•cal,** *adj.* —**Pur′i•tan•ism, pur′i•tan•ism,** *n.*

pu•ri•ty (pyŏŏr′i tē), *n.* the condition or quality of being pure.

purl¹ (pûrl), *n.* **1.** a basic stitch in knitting, the reverse of the knit. —*v.i., v.t.* **2.** to knit with a purl stitch.

purl² (pûrl), *v.i.* **1.** to flow with rippling motion. **2.** to flow with a murmuring sound. —*n.* **3.** the action or sound of purling.

pur•lieu (pûr′lŏŏ, pûrl′yŏŏ), *n., pl.* **-lieus. 1.** purlieus, environs or neighborhood. **2.** an outlying district of a city.

pur•loin (pər loin′, pûr′loin), *v.t., v.i.* to take dishonestly; steal. —**pur•loin′er,** *n.*

pur•ple (pûr′pəl), *n., adj.,* **-pler, -plest.** —*n.* **1.** any color having components of both red and blue, esp. one deep in tone. **2.** cloth or clothing of this hue, esp. as formerly worn distinctively by royalty. —*adj.* **3.** of the color purple. **4.** imperial or regal. **5.** full of exaggerated literary devices and effects. **6.** profane or shocking, as language. —**pur′plish,** *adj.*

pur•port (*v.* pər pôrt′; *n.* pûr′pôrt), *v.t.* **1.** to profess or claim. **2.** to convey; express or imply. —*n.* **3.** the meaning or sense. **4.** a purpose or intention. —**pur′• port•ed,** *adj.* —**pur′port•ed•ly,** *adv.*

pur•pose (pûr′pəs), *n., v.,* **-posed, -pos•ing.** —*n.* **1.** the reason for which something exists or is done, made, etc. **2.** an intended or desired result. **3.** determination; resoluteness. —*v.t., v.i.* **4.** to intend; design; resolve. —*Idiom.* **5. on purpose,** intentionally. —**pur′pose•ful,** *adj.* —**pur′pose•less,** *adj.*

purr (pûr), *n.* **1.** the low, continuous, vibrating sound a cat makes. **2.** any similar sound. —*v.i.* **3.** to utter such a sound. **4.** to speak in a murmuring tone. —*v.t.* **5.** to express in or as if in a purr.

purse (pûrs), *n., v.,* **pursed, purs•ing.** —*n.* **1.** a woman's handbag. **2.** a small bag or case for carrying money. **3.** a sum of money offered as a prize or collected as a gift. **4.** financial resources. —*v.t.* **5.** to pucker. —*Proverb.* **6. You can't make a silk purse out of a sow's ear,** one cannot make something good out of inferior material.

purs′er, *n.* an officer in charge of the accounts and documents of a ship.

pur•su•ance (pər sŏŏ′əns), *n.* the carrying out of some plan, course, etc.

pur•su′ant, *adj.* **1.** pursuing. —*Idiom.* **2. pursuant to,** in accordance with.

pur•sue (pər sŏŏ′), *v.t.* **-sued, -su•ing. 1.** to follow in order to overtake, capture, etc. **2.** to strive to attain or accomplish. **3.** to follow or carry out. **4.** to carry on or engage in: *to pursue one's studies.* —**pur• su′er,** *n.*

pur•suit′ (-sŏŏt′), *n.* **1.** the act of pursuing. **2.** an occupation or regular pastime.

pu•ru•lent (pyŏŏr′ə lant, pyŏŏr′yə-), *adj.* containing, forming, or discharging pus. —**pu′ru•lence,** *n.*

pur•vey (pər vā′), *v.t.* to supply (esp. food), usu. as a business. —**pur•vey′or,** *n.*

pur•view (pûr′vyŏŏ), *n.* **1.** the range of operation,

authority, or concern. **2.** the range of vision, insight, or understanding.

pus (pus), *n.* a yellow-white, viscid substance produced by suppuration and found in abscesses, sores, etc.

Pu•san (pŏŏ′sän′), *n.* a seaport in SE South Korea. 3,516,768.

push (pŏŏsh), *v.t.* **1.** to press against (a thing) with force in order to move it. **2.** to make (one's way) by pushing. **3.** to urge to some action or course. **4.** to press (an action, proposal, etc.) insistently. **5.** to press the use, sale, etc., of. —*v.i.* **6.** to exert a thrusting force upon something. **7.** to proceed by force or effort. **8.** to put forth persistent efforts. —*n.* **9.** the act of pushing. **10.** a vigorous effort. **11.** a vigorous advance or military attack. **12.** *Informal.* persevering energy; enterprise. —**push′er,** *n.*

push′ but′ton, *n.* a button or knob that opens or closes an electric circuit when depressed or released.

push′o′ver, *n.* **1.** anything done easily. **2.** a person who is easily persuaded or influenced.

push′-up′, *n.* an exercise in which a person lying prone, with the hands palms down under the shoulders, raises and lowers the body using only the arms.

push′y, *adj.,* **-i•er, -i•est.** obnoxiously self-assertive. —**push′i•ness,** *n.*

pu•sil•lan•i•mous (pyŏŏ′sə lan′ə məs), *adj.* lacking courage or resolve; cowardly. —**pu′sil•la•nim′i• ty** (-lə nim′i tē), *n.*

puss (pŏŏs), *n.* a cat.

puss′y, *n., pl.* **-puss•ies.** a cat, esp. a kitten.

puss′y•foot′, *v.i.* **1.** to move in a stealthy or cautious manner. **2.** to act timidly or irresolutely.

puss′y wil′low, *n.* a small willow with silky catkins.

pus•tule (pus′chŏŏl), *n.* a small elevation of the skin containing pus.

put (pŏŏt), *v.,* **put, put•ting.** —*v.t.* **1.** to move (anything) into a specific location or position. **2.** to bring into some condition, relation, etc. **3.** to set to a task or action. **4.** to assign or attribute: *to put the blame on others.* **5.** to estimate (distance, time, etc.). **6.** to bet or wager. **7.** to express or state: *to put it honestly.* **8.** to apply (knowledge, skill, etc.) to a purpose. **9.** to submit for answer, consideration, etc. **10.** to impose (a tax, charge, etc.). **11.** to throw or cast: *to put the shot.* —*v.i.* **12.** to go or proceed: *to put out to sea.* **13. put across,** to cause to be understood or received favorably. **14. ~ aside** or **by,** to store up; reserve. **15. ~ down, a.** to write down. **b.** to suppress. **c.** to humiliate or embarrass. **d.** to pay as a deposit. **16. ~ in for,** to apply for or request. **17. ~ off, a.** to postpone. **b.** to get rid of by evasion. **18. ~ on, a.** to clothe oneself in. **b.** to stage, as a show. **c.** *Informal.* to deceive (someone) as a joke. **19. ~ out, a.** to extinguish, as a fire. **b.** to subject to inconvenience. **c.** *Baseball.* to prevent from reaching base or scoring. **20. ~ through, a.** to bring about; effect. **b.** to cause to suffer or endure. **21. ~ up, a.** to construct. **b.** to can or preserve (food). **c.** to set (the hair). **d.** to provide (money). **e.** to lodge. **f.** to offer, esp. for public sale. **22. ~ up with,** to endure; tolerate. —*Idiom.* **23. stay put,** to remain in the same position.

pu•ta•tive (pyŏŏ′tə tiv), *adj.* commonly regarded as such.

put′-down′, *n. Informal.* a disparaging or snubbing remark.

Put•nam (put′nəm), *n.* **1. Israel,** 1718–90, American Revolutionary general. **2. Rufus,** 1738–1824, American Revolutionary officer: engineer and colonizer in Ohio.

put-on (*n.* pŏŏt′on′, -ôn′; *adj.* -on′, -ôn′), *n. Informal.* **1.** a hoax or spoof. —*adj.* **2.** feigned or assumed.

pu•tre•fy (pyŏŏ′trə fī′), *v.t., v.i.* **-fied, -fy•ing.** to make or become putrid; rot. —**pu′tre•fac′tion** (-fak′shən), *n.*

pu•tres′cent (-tres′ənt), *adj.* becoming putrid. —**pu•tres′cence,** *n.*

pu′trid (-trid), *adj.* (of organic material) in a state of foul decay or decomposition.

putsch (pŏŏch), *n.* a sudden political revolt or uprising.

putt (put), *v.t., v.i.* **1.** to strike (a golf ball) gently so as to make it roll into the hole. —*n.* **2.** a stroke made in putting.

put·ter¹ (put′ər), *v.i.* to occupy oneself in a leisurely or ineffective manner. —**put′ter·er,** *n.*

putt·er² (put′ər), *n.* a golf club used in putting.

put·ty (put′ē), *n., pl.* **-ties,** *v.,* **-tied, -ty·ing.** —*n.* **1.** a compound of whiting and linseed oil used to secure windowpanes, patch woodwork, etc. —*v.t.* **2.** to secure, cover, etc., with putty.

puz·zle (puz′əl), *n., v.,* **-zled, -zling.** —*n.* **1.** a toy, game, or problem designed to amuse by presenting difficulties to be solved. **2.** a puzzling question, matter, or person. —*v.t.* **3.** to mystify; baffle. —*v.i.* **4.** to ponder over some perplexing problem. **5. puzzle out,** to solve by careful study or effort. —**puz′zle·ment,** *n.* —**puz′zler,** *n.*

PVC, polyvinyl chloride.

Pvt., Private.

PWA or **P.W.A.,** Public Works Administration.

PX, *pl.* **PXs.** post exchange.

Pyg·my (pig′mē), *n., pl.* **-mies,** *adj.* —*n.* **1.** a member of any of several small-statured peoples of Africa and SE Asia. **2.** (*l.c.*) a small person or thing. —*adj.* **3.** of the Pygmies. **4.** (*l.c.*) of very small size.

pyg′my chimpanzee′, *n.* BONOBO.

py·jam·as (pə jä′məz, -jam′əz), *n.* (*used with a pl. v.*) *Chiefly Brit.* PAJAMAS.

py·lon (pī′lon), *n.* **1.** a tower for guiding aviators. **2.** a monumental gateway, as to an ancient Egyptian temple. **3.** a steel tower used as a support. [< Gk: gateway]

py·lo·rus (pī lôr′əs, pi-), *n., pl.* **-lo·ri** (-lôr′ī). the opening between the stomach and the start of the intestine. —**py·lor′ic** (-lôr′ik, -lor′-), *adj.*

Pyong·yang (pyung′yang′), *n.* the capital of North Korea. 2,639,448.

py·or·rhe·a (pī′ə rē′ə), *n.* severe periodontitis, characterized by bleeding of the gums and loosening of the teeth.

pyr·a·mid (pir′ə mid), *n.* **1.** a massive masonry structure having four sloping sides meeting at an apex, as a tomb of ancient Egypt. **2.** any object or arrangement of objects shaped like a pyramid. **3.** a solid having a polygonal base and triangular sides that meet in a point. —*v.i., v.t.* **4.** to arrange or build in the form of a pyramid. **5.** to increase gradually. —**py·ram′i·dal** (-ram′i dl), *adj.*

Pyr′a·mus and This′be (pir′ə məs), two young lovers of classical legend: mistakenly believing that Thisbe is dead, Pyramus kills himself, and Thisbe, in turn, kills herself upon finding his body.

pyre (pīªr), *n.* a pile of wood for burning a dead body.

Pyr·e·nees (pir′ə nēz′), *n.pl.* a mountain range between Spain and France.

Py·rex (pī′reks), *Trademark.* a brand name for a heat- and chemical-resistant glassware.

py·rim·i·dine (pī rim′i dēn′, pi-), *n.* **1.** a compound that is the basis of several important biochemical substances. **2.** one of several pyrimidine derivatives, esp. the bases cytosine, thymine, and uracil.

py·rite (pī′rīt), *n.* a brass-yellow mineral containing sulfur and iron.

pyro-, a combining form meaning fire or heat (*pyromania*).

py·ro·ma·ni·a (pī′rə mā′nē ə), *n.* a compulsion to set things on fire. —**py′ro·ma′ni·ac,** *n.*

py′ro·tech′nics (-tek′niks), *n.pl.* **1.** a display of fireworks. **2.** a brilliant or sensational display, as of musicianship. —**py′ro·tech′nic,** *adj.*

Pyr′rhic vic′tory, *n.* a victory or goal achieved at too great a cost.

Py·thag·o·ras (pi thag′ər əs), *n.* c582–c500 B.C., Greek philosopher and mathematician. —**Py·thag′o·re′an** (-rē′an), *adj., n.*

Pythag′ore′an the′orem, *n.* the theorem that the square of the hypotenuse of a right triangle is equal to the sum of the squares of the other two sides.

py·thon (pī′thon, -thən), *n.* any of several Old World snakes that crush their prey to death in their coils.

pyx (piks), *n.* the vessel in which the reserved Eucharist is kept.

Q

Q, q (kyōō), *n., pl.* **Qs** or **Q's, qs** or **q's.** the 17th letter of the English alphabet, a consonant.

q., 1. farthing. [< L *quadrāns*] **2.** quart. **3.** query. **4.** question. **5.** quintal. **6.** quire.

Qa·tar (kä′tär, kə tär′), *n.* an independent emirate on the Persian Gulf. 665,485. —**Qa·tar′i,** *adj., n.*

QC, Quebec.

Q.E.D., which was to be shown or demonstrated. [< L *quod erat dēmōnstrandum*]

Qing·dao or **Tsing·tao** (ching′dou′), *n.* a seaport in E China. 1,250,000.

qq. v., which (words, things, etc.) see. [< L *quae vidē*]

qt., 1. quantity. **2.** *pl.* **qt., qts.** quart.

q.t. or **Q.T.,** *Informal.* **1.** quiet. —*Idiom.* **2. on the q.t.,** stealthily.

qty., quantity.

qua (kwā, kwä), *adv.* in the character or capacity of.

quack¹ (kwak), *n.* **1.** the harsh, throaty cry of a duck. —*v.i.* **2.** to utter a quack.

quack² (kwak), *n.* **1.** a fraudulent pretender to medical skill. **2.** a charlatan. —*adj.* **3.** being or befitting a quack. —**quack′er·y,** *n.*

quad¹ (kwod), *n.* a quadrangle.

quad² (kwod), *n.* a quadruplet.

quad′ran·gle (-rang′gəl), *n.* **1.** a plane figure having four angles and four sides. **2.** a square or court surrounded by buildings, as on a college campus.

quad′rant (-rənt), *n.* **1.** a quarter of a circle; an arc of 90°. **2.** one of the four parts into which a plane, as the face of a heavenly body, is divided by two perpendicular lines. **3.** an instrument used, as in astronomy, for measuring altitudes.

quad′ra·phon′ic (-rə fon′ik), *adj.* of the recording, reproduction, or transmission of sound by means of four channels.

quad·rat·ic (kwo drat′ik), *adj. Algebra.* involving the square and no higher power of an unknown quantity.

quad·ren·ni·al (kwo dren′ē əl), *adj.* **1.** occurring every four years. **2.** of or lasting for four years.

quad·ren·ni·um (kwo dren′ē əm), *n., pl.* **quad·ren·ni·ums, quad·ren·ni·a** (kwo dren′ē ə). a period of four years.

quadri-, a combining form meaning four (*quadrilateral*).

quad·ri·cen·ten·ni·al (kwod′rə sen ten′ē əl), *n.* a 400th anniversary or its celebration.

quad·ri·lat·er·al (kwod′rə lat′ər əl), *adj.* **1.** having four sides. —*n.* **2.** *Geom.* a polygon with four sides.

quad·rille (kwo dril′, kwə-), *n.* a square dance for four couples.

quad·ril·lion (kwo dril'yən), *n., pl.* **-lions, -lion.** a cardinal number represented in the U.S. by 1 followed by 15 zeros, and in Great Britain by 1 followed by 24 zeros.

quad·ri·ple·gi·a (kwod'rə plē'jē ə, -jə), *n.* paralysis of the entire body below the neck. —**quad'ri·ple'gic,** *n., adj.*

quad·riv·i·um (kwo driv'ē əm), *n., pl.* **quad·riv·i·a** (kwo driv'ē ə). (during the Middle Ages) the more advanced division of the seven liberal arts, comprising arithmetic, geometry, astronomy, and music.

quad·ru·ped (kwod'rōō ped'), *n.* an animal, esp. a mammal, that has four feet.

quad·ru·ple (kwo drōō'pəl, -drup'əl, kwod'rōōpəl), *adj., n., v.,* **-pled, -pling.** —*adj.* **1.** consisting of four parts. **2.** four times as great. —*n.* **3.** a number or amount four times as great as another. —*v.t., v.i.* **4.** to make or become four times as great.

quad·ru·plet (kwo drup'lit, -drōō'plit), *n.* **1.** a group or combination of four. **2.** one of four children or offspring born of one pregnancy.

quad·ru·pli·cate (*n., adj.* kwo drōō'pli kit; *v.* -kāt'), *n., adj., v.,* **-cat·ed, -cat·ing.** —*n.* **1.** one of four copies or identical items. —*adj.* **2.** consisting of four identical parts. **3.** noting a fourth item or copy. —*v.t.* **4.** to produce in quadruplicate. **5.** to make four times as great. —**quad·ru'pli·ca'tion,** *n.*

quaff (kwof, kwaf), *v.i., v.t.* **1.** to drink copiously and with hearty enjoyment. —*n.* **2.** a beverage quaffed.

quag·mire (kwag'mīªr', kwog'-), *n.* **1.** miry or boggy ground whose surface yields under the tread. **2.** a difficult situation.

qua·hog or **-haug** (kwô'hôg, -hog, kō'-), *n.* a thick-shelled, edible clam of North American Atlantic coasts.

quail¹ (kwāl), *n., pl.* **quails, quail. 1.** any of various small, plump New World birds of the pheasant family. **2.** any of various Old World birds similar to the quail.

quail² (kwāl), *v.i.* to shrink in fear.

quaint (kwānt), *adj.,* **-er, -est. 1.** having an oldfashioned charm. **2.** peculiar or unusual in an interesting or amusing way; oddly picturesque. —**quaint'ly,** *adv.* —**quaint'ness,** *n.*

quake (kwāk), *v.,* **quaked, quak·ing,** *n.* —*v.i.* **1.** to quiver, as from cold or fear. **2.** to tremble, as from shock or instability. —*n.* **3.** an earthquake. **4.** the act of quaking. —**quak'y,** *adj.,* **-i·er, -i·est.**

Quak·er (kwā'kər), *n.* a member of the Society of Friends. —**Quak'er·ism,** *n.*

qual·i·fi·ca·tion (kwol'ə fi kā'shən), *n.* **1.** a quality or accomplishment that fits a person for a function, office, or position. **2.** the act of qualifying or state of being qualified. **3.** modification, limitation, or restriction.

qual'i·fy', *v.,* **-fied, -fy·ing.** —*v.t.* **1.** to provide with proper or necessary skills, knowledge, or credentials. **2.** to make less general; modify or limit. **3.** to make less violent or severe; moderate. **4.** *Gram.* MODIFY (def. 2). —*v.i.* **5.** to be fit or competent, as for a position. **6.** to demonstrate the required ability in a preliminary contest. —**qual'i·fied',** *adj.*

qual·i·ta·tive (kwol'i tā'tiv), *adj.* of or concerned with quality or qualities. —**qual'i·ta'tive·ly,** *adv.*

qual'i·ty, *n., pl.* **-ties.** —*n.* **1.** an essential characteristic, property, or attribute. **2.** character or nature belonging to or distinguishing a thing. **3.** degree of excellence or fineness. **4.** superiority; excellence. **5.** a personality or character trait. —*adj.* **6.** of or having superior quality.

qual'ity time', *n.* time devoted exclusively to nurturing a cherished person or activity.

qualm (kwäm, kwôm), *n.* **1.** a pang of conscience; compunction. **2.** a sudden feeling of apprehension; misgiving. **3.** a sudden onset of illness, esp. of nausea.

quan·da·ry (kwon'də rē, -drē), *n., pl.* **-ries.** a state of perplexity or uncertainty.

quan·ti·fy (kwon'tə fī'), *v.t.,* **-fied, -fy·ing.** to determine, indicate, or express the quantity of.

quan'ti·ta'tive (-tā'tiv), *adj.* of or involving quantity.

quan'ti·ty, *n., pl.* **-ties. 1.** an indefinite or aggregate amount. **2.** an exact or specified amount or measure. **3.** a considerable or great amount.

quan'tum (-təm), *n., pl.* **-ta** (-tə), *adj.* —*n.* **1.** quantity or amount. **2.** *Physics.* a very small, indivisible quantity of energy. —*adj.* **3.** sudden and significant: *a quantum increase in productivity.*

quar·an·tine (kwôr'ən tēn', kwor'-), *n., v.,* **-tined, -tin·ing.** —*n.* **1.** strict isolation imposed to prevent the spread of disease. **2.** a period of detention imposed upon ships, people, animals, or plants suspected of carrying a contagious disease. **3.** a place where quarantine is imposed. —*v.t.* **4.** to subject to quarantine.

quark (kwôrk, kwärk), *n.* any of a group of subatomic particles having a fractional electric charge and thought to form the basis of all matter. [coined by U.S. physicist M. Gell-Mann, who associated it with a word in Joyce's *Finnegans Wake*]

quar·rel (kwôr'əl, kwor'-), *n., v.,* **-reled, -rel·ing** or (*esp. Brit.*) **-relled, -rel·ling.** —*n.* **1.** an angry dispute or altercation. **2.** a cause of dispute, complaint, or hostile feeling. —*v.i.* **3.** to disagree angrily. **4.** to make a complaint. —**quar'rel·er,** *n.* —**quar'rel·some,** *adj.*

quar·ry¹ (kwôr'ē, kwor'ē), *n., pl.* **-ries,** *v.,* **-ried, -ry·ing.** —*n.* **1.** a usu. open excavation or pit from which building stone or slate is obtained. —*v.t.* **2.** to obtain from or as if from a quarry.

quar·ry² (kwôr'ē, kwor'ē), *n., pl.* **-ries. 1.** an animal or bird hunted or pursued. **2.** an object of search, pursuit, or attack.

quart (kwôrt), *n.* **1.** a unit of liquid measure equal to one fourth of a gallon, or 57.749 cubic inches (0.946 liter). **2.** a unit of dry measure equal to one eighth of a peck, or 67.201 cubic inches (1.101 liters).

quar·ter (kwôr'tər), *n.* **1.** one of four equal or equivalent parts. **2. a.** one fourth of a U.S. or Canadian dollar, equivalent to 25 cents. **b.** a coin of this value. **3.** one fourth of an hour; 15 minutes. **4.** one fourth of a calendar or fiscal year. **5.** one of the four equal periods of play in certain games, as basketball. **6.** a district of a city or town. **7.** Usu., **-ters.** housing accommodations. **8.** Often, **-ters.** an unspecified source. **9.** mercy or indulgence: *gave no quarter.* —*v.t.* **10.** to divide into four equal or equivalent parts. **11.** to furnish with lodging. —*adj.* **12.** being one of four equal or equivalent parts.

quar'ter·back', *n.* **1.** a back in football who directs the offense of the team. —*v.t.* **2.** to direct the offense of (a team). **3.** to lead; direct.

quar'ter·deck', *n.* the rear part of a ship's weather deck.

quar'ter horse', *n.* one of an American breed of strong, agile horses capable of great speed over short distances.

quar'ter·ly, *adj., n., pl.* **-lies,** *adv.* —*adj.* **1.** occurring, done, paid, or issued at the end of every quarter of a year. —*n.* **2.** a periodical issued every three months. —*adv.* **3.** once each quarter of a year.

quar'ter·mas'ter, *n.* **1.** a military officer charged with providing quarters, clothing, and food for troops. **2.** a petty officer in charge of a ship's helm and navigating apparatus.

quar·tet or **-tette** (kwôr tet'), *n.* **1.** a group of four singers or players. **2.** a musical composition for a quartet. **3.** a group of four.

quar·to (kwôr'tō), *n., pl.* **-tos. 1.** a book size of about 9½ × 12 in. (24 × 30 cm), determined by folding printed sheets twice to form four leaves or eight pages. **2.** a book of this size.

quartz (kwôrts), *n.* a common mineral that is a form of silica and is the chief component of sand.

qua·sar (kwā'zär, -zər), *n.* any of numerous starlike celestial objects that may be the most distant and brightest objects in the universe.

quash (kwosh), *v.t.* **1.** to put down or suppress completely; quell. **2.** to set aside (a law, indictment, etc.).

qua•si (kwä′zī, -sī, kwä′sē, -zē), adj. resembling; seeming to be: a quasi liberal.

quasi-, a combining form meaning in part or somewhat (quasi-scientific).

qua′si-stel′lar ob′ject, n. QUASAR.

Quat•er•nar•y (kwot′ər ner′ē, kwə tûr′nə rē), adj. noting or pertaining to the present geologic period forming the latter part of the Cenozoic Era.

quat•rain (kwo′trān), n. a stanza or poem of four lines.

qua•ver (kwā′vər), v.i. **1.** to shake tremulously. **2.** to sound, speak, or sing tremulously. —n. **3.** a quivering or trembling. **4.** a quavering tone or utterance. —qua′ver•y, adj.

quay (kē, kā, kwā), n. a landing place, esp. one of solid masonry; wharf.

Que., Quebec.

quea•sy (kwē′zē), adj., -si•er, -si•est. **1.** feeling or causing nausea. **2.** uneasy; uncomfortable. —quea′si•ness, n.

Que•bec (kwi bek′, ki-), n. **1.** a province in E Canada. 6,532,461. Abbr.: QC, Que. **2.** the capital of this province. 164,580. —Que•bec′er, Que•beck′er, n.

queen (kwēn), n. **1.** a female sovereign or monarch. **2.** the wife or consort of a king. **3.** a woman preeminent in a particular respect. **4.** a playing card bearing a picture of a queen. **5.** the most powerful chess piece. **6.** a fertile female ant, bee, termite, or wasp. —queen′ly, adj., -li•er, -li•est.

Queens (kwēnz), n. a borough of New York City, on Long Island. 1,951,598.

queen′-size′ or **-sized′**, adj. larger than a double bed but smaller than king-size, usu. 60 in. (152 cm) wide and 80 in. (203 cm) long.

queer (kwēr), adj., -er, -est, v., n. —adj. **1.** strange or odd from a conventional viewpoint; eccentric. **2.** questionable in nature or character; suspicious. **3.** Slang. bad, worthless, or counterfeit. —v.t. **4.** to spoil; ruin. —queer′ly, adv. —queer′ness, n.

quell (kwel), v.t. **1.** to suppress; crush. **2.** to quiet; allay.

quench (kwench), v.t. **1.** to satisfy (thirst, desires, etc.); allay. **2.** to put out (fire, flames, etc.); extinguish. **3.** to cool suddenly by plunging into a liquid, as in tempering steel. **4.** to overcome; quell.

quer•u•lous (kwer′ə ləs, kwer′yə-), adj. **1.** full of complaints; petulant. **2.** characterized by complaint; peevish. —quer′u•lous•ly, adv.

que•ry (kwēr′ē), n., pl. -ries, v., -ried, -ry•ing. —n. **1.** a question. **2.** QUESTION MARK. —v.t. **3.** to question.

quest (kwest), n. **1.** a search. **2.** an adventurous expedition, as by knights in medieval romances.

ques•tion (kwes′chən), n. **1.** a sentence in interrogative form intended to elicit a reply. **2.** a matter for discussion, dispute, or investigation. **3.** a matter of some difficulty; problem. **4.** a proposal to be voted on, as in a meeting. —v.t. **5.** to ask questions of; interrogate. **6.** to make a question of; doubt. **7.** to challenge; dispute. —v.i. **8.** to ask questions. —Idiom. **9.** out of the question, not to be considered; impossible. **10.** the $64,000 question, the most difficult question. [so called from a 1950s television quiz show in which the top prize was $64,000]

ques′tion•a•ble, adj. **1.** of doubtful propriety, honesty, or morality. **2.** open to question; uncertain.

ques′tion mark′, n. a punctuation mark (?) indicating a question.

ques′tion•naire′ (-chə nâr′), n. a list of questions submitted to obtain information.

queue (kyoō), n., v., queued, queu•ing. —n. **1.** a braid of hair worn hanging down behind. **2.** a line, esp. of people. **3.** a sequence of items waiting for electronic action in a computer system. —v.i., v.t. **4.** to form in or arrange in a queue.

quib•ble (kwib′əl), n., v., -bled, -bling. —n. **1.** a petty or carping criticism. **2.** an evasion of a point at

issue. —v.i. **3.** to bicker, carp, or cavil. **4.** to use evasive language; equivocate. —quib′bler, n.

quiche (kēsh), n. a pie containing unsweetened custard baked with other ingredients, as cheese.

quick (kwik), adj. and adv., -er, -est, n. —adj. **1.** done, proceeding, or occurring with promptness; rapid. **2.** finished or completed in a short time. **3.** moving or able to move with speed. **4.** easily provoked or excited. **5.** keenly responsive; acute. **6.** acting with rapidity. **7.** prompt or swift in doing, perceiving, or understanding. —n. **8.** living persons: the quick and the dead. **9.** tender, sensitive flesh, esp. under the nails. **10.** the vital or most important part. —adv. **11.** in a quick manner. —quick′ly, adv. —quick′ness, n. —Usage. Both QUICK and QUICKLY are acceptable adverbial forms. QUICKLY is the usual form in all types of writing, while QUICK is used in short spoken sentences: He turned quickly and fled. Come quick! The roof is leaking!

quick′ and the dead′, n. the living and the dead: a phrase from the Apostles′ Creed.

quick′ bread′, n. bread made with a leavening agent that permits immediate baking.

quick′en, v.t. **1.** to make more rapid; accelerate. **2.** to give or restore vigor to; stimulate. —v.i. **3.** to become more rapid. **4.** to come to life; revive. **5.** to begin to manifest signs of life.

quick′-freeze′, v.t., -froze, -fro•zen, -freez•ing. to freeze (food) rapidly so that it can be stored at freezing temperatures.

quick′ie, n. something produced, done, or enjoyed in only a short time.

quick′lime′, n. LIME¹ (def. 1).

quick′sand′, n. a deep bed of loose sand saturated with water that yields under weight and into which objects tend to sink.

quick′sil′ver, n. MERCURY (def. 1).

quick′-tem′pered, adj. easily angered; touchy.

quick′-wit′ted, adj. having an alert mind; keen.

quid¹ (kwid), n. a portion of something, esp. tobacco, for chewing.

quid² (kwid), n., pl. quid. Brit. Informal. one pound sterling.

quid pro quo (kwid′ prō kwō′), n., pl. quid pro quos, quids pro quo. something given or taken for something else. [< L: lit., something for something]

qui•es•cent (kwē es′ənt, kwī-), adj. being at rest; quiet. —qui•es′cence, n.

qui•et¹ (kwī′it), adj., -er, -est, v. —adj. **1.** making little or no noise or sound; silent. **2.** free from noise. **3.** free from disturbance or tumult; tranquil. **4.** mild; gentle. **5.** not showy or obtrusive. —v.t., v.i. **6.** to make or become quiet. —Saying. **7.** All quiet on the Potomac, everything is calm; there is no fighting: phrase popularized during the Civil War. —qui′et•ly, adv. —qui′et•ness, n.

qui•et² (kwī′it), n. **1.** freedom from noise. **2.** freedom from disturbance or tumult.

qui′e•tude′ (-i tōōd′, -tyōōd′), n. the state of being quiet; tranquillity.

qui•e•tus (kwī ē′təs), n., pl. -tus•es. **1.** a final settlement, as of a debt. **2.** discharge or release from life.

quill (kwil), n. **1.** one of the large wing or tail feathers of a bird. **2.** the hard, hollow, tubular part of a feather. **3.** a feather, as of a goose, used as a pen for writing. **4.** one of the hollow spines on a porcupine or hedgehog.

quilt (kwilt), n. **1.** a padded bed coverlet made of two layers of fabric. —v.t. **2.** to stitch together (two pieces of cloth and a soft interlining). **3.** to pad or line like a quilt. —v.i. **4.** to make quilts. —quilt′ed, adj. —quilt′er, n. —quilt′ing, n.

quince (kwins), n. **1.** a small tree bearing hard, yellowish fruit used esp. for making preserves. **2.** the fruit of a quince.

qui•nine (kwī′nīn), n. a white crystalline alkaloid obtained from cinchona bark and used chiefly for treating malaria.

quin•sy (kwin′zē), n. an abscess between the tonsil

and the pharynx accompanied by a severe sore throat and fever.

quint (kwint), *n.* a quintuplet.

quin·tes·sence (kwin tes'əns), *n.* **1.** the pure and concentrated essence of a substance. **2.** the most perfect embodiment of something. —**quin'tes·sen'tial** (-tə sen'shəl), *adj.*

quin·tet or **-tette** (kwin tet'), *n.* **1.** a set or group of five. **2.** a group of five singers or players. **3.** a musical composition for a quintet.

quin·tu·ple (kwin too'pəl, -tyoo'-, -tup'əl, kwin'-too pəl, -tyoo-), *adj.*, *n.*, *v.*, **-pled, -pling.** —*adj.* **1.** consisting of five parts. **2.** five times as great. —*n.* **3.** a number or amount five times as great as another. —*v.t.*, *v.i.* **4.** to make or become five times as great.

quin·tu·plet (kwin tup'lit, -too'plit, -tyoo'-), *n.* **1.** a group or combination of five. **2.** five children or offspring born of one pregnancy.

quip (kwip), *n.*, *v.*, **quipped, quip·ping.** —*n.* **1.** a clever or witty remark. —*v.i.* **2.** to utter a quip. —**quip'ster** (-stər), *n.*

quire (kwīᵊr), *n.* a set of 24 uniform sheets of paper.

Qui·rin·i·us (kwī rin'ē əs), *n.* CYRENIUS.

quirk (kwûrk), *n.* **1.** a peculiarity of action, behavior, or personality. **2.** a sudden twist or turn. —**quirk'y,** *adj.*, **-i·er, i·est.** —**quirk'i·ness,** *n.*

quirt (kwûrt), *n.* a riding whip with a short, stout stock and a lash of braided leather.

quis·ling (kwiz'ling), *n.* a person who betrays his or her country by aiding an invading enemy. [after V. *Quisling* (1887–1945), pro-Nazi Norwegian leader]

quit (kwit), *v.*, **quit** or **quit·ted, quit·ting.** —*v.t.* **1.** to stop, cease, or discontinue. **2.** to depart from; leave. **3.** to let go; relinquish. **4.** to conduct (oneself). —*v.i.* **5.** to cease from doing something. **6.** to give up or resign one's job or position. **7.** to acknowledge defeat.

quit'claim', *n.* a transfer of one's interest in a property, esp. without a warranty of title.

quite (kwīt), *adv.* **1.** completely, wholly, or entirely. **2.** actually, really, or truly. **3.** to a considerable extent or degree.

Qui·to (kē'tō), *n.* the capital of Ecuador. 1,110,248.

quits (kwits), *adj.* **1.** being on equal terms, as by retaliation. —*Idiom.* **2. call it quits,** to end an activity or relationship.

quit·tance (kwit'ns), *n.* **1.** recompense or requital. **2.** discharge from a debt or obligation.

quit'ter, *n.* a person who gives up easily.

quiv·er¹ (kwiv'ər), *v.t.*, *v.i.* **1.** to shake with a slight but rapid motion. —*n.* **2.** the act of quivering. —**quiv'er·y,** *adj.*

quiv·er² (kwiv'ər), *n.* a case for arrows.

quix·ot·ic (kwik sot'ik), *adj.* extravagantly chivalrous or romantic but impractical. [after Don *Quixote,* hero of Cervantes' novel of the same name]

quiz (kwiz), *n.*, *pl.* **quiz·zes,** *v.*, **quizzed, quiz·zing.** —*n.* **1.** an informal test or examination. —*v.t.* **2.** to

examine or test (a student or class) informally by questions. —**quiz'zer,** *n.*

quiz'zi·cal, *adj.* **1.** odd or comical. **2.** questioning or puzzled. —**quiz'zi·cal·ly,** *adv.*

quoin (koin, kwoin), *n.* **1.** an external solid angle, as of a wall. **2.** a stone forming a quoin; cornerstone. **3.** a wedge of wood or metal for locking type in a chase.

quoit (kwoit, koit), *n.* **1. quoits,** (*used with a sing. v.*) a game in which rope or metal rings are thrown at an upright peg. **2.** a ring used in quoits.

quon·dam (kwon'dəm, -dam), *adj.* former; onetime. [< L]

Quon'set hut' (kwon'sit), *Trademark.* a semicylindrical metal shelter.

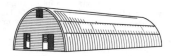

Quonset hut

quo·rum (kwôr'əm), *n.* the number of members of a group required to be present to transact business.

quo·ta (kwō'tə), *n.*, *pl.* **-tas. 1.** a proportional part of a total; share. **2.** the number or percentage of persons of a specified kind admitted to a college, country, etc.

quo·ta·tion (kwō tā'shən), *n.* **1.** the act of quoting. **2.** the words quoted. **3.** the quoted or current price of a commodity or security.

quota'tion mark', *n.* one of a pair of punctuation marks used to enclose a quotation, usu. shown as (") at the beginning and (") at the end.

quote, *v.*, **quot·ed, quot·ing,** *n.* —*v.t.* **1.** to repeat (a passage, phrase, etc.), as from a book or speech. **2.** to repeat words from (a book, author, etc.). **3.** to state the price of (a stock, bond, etc.). **4.** to state (a price). —*n.* **5.** something quoted. **6.** QUOTATION MARK. —**quot'a·ble,** *adj.*

quoth (kwōth), *v. Archaic.* said (used with first- and third-person pronouns and always before the subject).

quo·tid·i·an (kwō tid'ē ən), *adj.* **1.** daily. **2.** ordinary; everyday.

quo·tient (kwō'shənt), *n.* the result obtained by dividing one quantity by another.

q.v., *pl.* **qq.v.** which (word, thing, etc.) see. [< L *quod vidē*]

qy., query.

R

R, r (är), *n.*, *pl.* **Rs** or **R's, rs** or **r's.** the 18th letter of the English alphabet, a consonant.

R, 1. *Chem.* radical. **2.** *Math.* ratio. **3.** restricted: a motion-picture rating advising that children under 17 will not be admitted unless accompanied by an adult. **4.** right. **5.** roentgen. **6.** *Baseball.* run.

R, *Symbol.* **1.** registered trademark: written as superscript ® following a name. **2.** *Elect.* resistance.

r, 1. radius. **2.** roentgen.

R., 1. radius. **2.** railroad. **3.** railway. **4.** Republican. **5.** right. **6.** river. **7.** road.

r., 1. railroad. **2.** railway. **3.** range. **4.** right. **5.** river. **6.** road. **7.** rod.

Ra, *Chem. Symbol.* radium.

Ra·am·ses (rā am'sēz), *n.* a city that was built for the Pharaoh by the Israelites and from which the Exodus began. Ex. 1:11. Compare PITHOM.

Ra·bat (rä bät', rə-), *n.* the capital of Morocco. 518,616.

rab·bet (rab'it), *n.* **1.** a deep notch formed in the edge of a board, esp. so that something else can be fitted into it. —*v.t.* **2.** to cut a rabbet in. **3.** to join by means of a rabbet.

rab·bi (rab'ī), *n.*, *pl.* **-bis. 1.** the ordained chief religious official of a synagogue. **2.** a Jewish scholar or teacher. —**rab·bin·i·cal** (rə bin'i kəl), **rab·bin'ic,** *adj.*

rab•bin•ate (rab'ə nit, -nāt'), *n.* **1.** the office of a rabbi. **2.** rabbis collectively.

rab•bit (rab'it), *n., pl.* **-bits, -bit.** any of several large-eared hopping mammals resembling but usu. smaller than the hares.

rab'bit punch', *n.* a short, sharp blow to the nape of the neck.

rab•ble (rab'əl), *n.* **1.** a disorderly crowd; mob. **2.** the common people.

rab'ble-rous'er (-rou'zər), *n.* a person who stirs up the passions or prejudices of the public; demagogue.

Rab•e•lais (rab'ə lā'), *n.* **François,** c1490–1553, French satirist and humorist.

rab•id (rab'id), *adj.* **1.** irrationally extreme. **2.** furious or raging; violent. **3.** affected with rabies. —**rab'id•ly,** *adv.*

ra•bies (rā'bēz), *n.* an infectious, usu. fatal viral disease transmitted by the bite of an infected animal.

Ra•bin (rä bēn'), *n.* **Yitz•hak** (yits кнäk'), 1922–95, Israeli military and political leader: prime minister 1974–77 and 1992–95: Nobel peace prize 1994.

rac•coon (ra kōōn'), *n., pl.* **-coons, -coon.** **1.** a North American nocturnal carnivore with a masklike black stripe across the eyes and a ringed tail. **2.** the fur of the raccoon.

race[1] (rās), *n., v.,* **raced, rac•ing.** —*n.* **1.** a contest of speed. **2.** a competition, esp. to achieve superiority. **3.** onward movement or course. **4. a.** a strong current of water. **b.** the channel of such a current. —*v.i.* **5.** to run a race. **6.** to run, move, or go swiftly. —*v.t.* **7.** to run a race against. **8.** to enter in a race. **9.** to cause to run or go at high speed. —*Proverb.* **10. The race is not to the swift,** the expected winner may not succeed. —**rac'er,** *n.*

race[2] (rās), *n.* **1.** a group of people related by common descent. **2.** a classification of human beings based on physical characteristics or genetic markers. **3.** a people united by common history, language, etc. **4.** any group of people, animals, or plants having common characteristics.

race'horse', *n.* a horse bred or kept for racing.

ra•ceme (rā sēm', rə-), *n.* an inflorescence in which the flowers are borne on short stalks lying along the main stem.

race'track', *n.* a usu. oval course for horse racing.

race'way', *n.* **1.** a racetrack on which harness races are held. **2.** a channel for water.

Ra•chel (rā'chəl), *n.* Jacob's favorite wife, the mother of Joseph and Benjamin. Gen. 29–35.

ra•chi•tis (rə kī'tis), *n.* RICKETS. —**ra•chit'ic** (-kit'ik), *adj.*

ra•cial (rā'shəl), *adj.* **1.** of, characteristic of, or based on race. **2.** between races. —**ra'cial•ly,** *adv.*

rac•ism (rā'siz əm), *n.* **1.** a belief that one's own race is superior. **2.** a policy or practice based on racism. —**rac'ist,** *n., adj.*

rack[1] (rak), *n.* **1.** a framework, as of bars, on which articles are placed or arranged. **2.** a bar with teeth that engage with the teeth of a pinion. **3.** an instrument of torture on which a victim was stretched. **4.** a cause or state of intense suffering. —*v.t.* **5.** to distress acutely. **6.** to strain, as if in mental effort. **7.** to torture on a rack.

rack[2] (rak), *n.* wreckage or destruction: *to go to rack and ruin.*

rack•et[1] (rak'it), *n.* **1.** loud noise; din. **2.** an organized illegal activity. **3.** a dishonest scheme, business, or activity.

rack•et[2] or **rac•quet** (rak'it), *n.* a light bat with netting stretched in an oval frame, used in tennis, badminton, etc.

rack'et•eer', *n.* a person engaged in an organized illegal activity, as extortion. —**rack'et•eer'ing,** *n.*

rac•on•teur (rak'on tûr', -tōōr', -ən-), *n.* a person skilled in telling anecdotes.

rac'quet•ball', *n.* a game similar to handball that is played with rackets on a four-walled court.

rac•y (rā'sē), *adj.,* **-i•er, -i•est.** **1.** slightly improper; risqué. **2.** lively; spirited. **3.** piquant; pungent. **4.**

having an agreeably peculiar taste, as fruit. —**rac'i•ly,** *adv.* —**rac'i•ness,** *n.*

ra•dar (rā'där), *n.* a device for determining the presence and location of an object by measuring the direction and timing of radio waves. [ra(dio) d(etecting) a(nd) r(anging)]

ra'dar•scope', *n.* the viewing screen of radar equipment.

ra•di•al (rā'dē əl), *adj.* **1.** arranged or having parts arranged like radii or rays. **2.** of a radius or a ray. —**ra'di•al•ly,** *adv.*

ra'dial tire', *n.* a motor-vehicle tire in which the fabric plies are put straight across at a right angle to the direction of travel.

ra'di•ant (-ənt), *adj.* **1.** emitting rays of light. **2.** bright with joy, hope, or happiness. **3.** *Physics.* emitted or propagated by radiation. —**ra'di•ance,** *n.* —**ra'di•ant•ly,** *adv.*

ra'diant en'ergy, *n.* energy transmitted in wave motion, esp. electromagnetic wave motion.

ra'di•ate' (-āt'), *v.,* **-at•ed, -at•ing.** —*v.i.* **1.** to extend, spread, or move from a center like rays or radii. **2.** to emit rays, as of light or heat. —*v.t.* **3.** to emit in or as if in rays.

ra'di•a'tion, *n.* **1.** the process in which energy is emitted as particles or waves, transmitted, and absorbed. **2.** the act or process of radiating. **3.** something radiated. —**ra'di•a'tion•al,** *adj.*

radia'tion sick'ness, *n.* sickness caused by irradiation with x-rays or radioactive materials.

ra'di•a'tor, *n.* **1.** a heating device, as a series of pipes through which steam or hot water passes. **2.** a device for cooling circulating water, as in an automobile engine.

rad•i•cal (rad'i kəl), *adj.* **1.** of or going to a root or origin; fundamental. **2.** thoroughgoing or extreme. **3.** favoring drastic political, economic, or social reforms. —*n.* **4.** a person who advocates drastic reforms. **5.** *Math.* **a.** a quantity expressed as a root of another quantity. **b.** RADICAL SIGN. **6.** *Chem.* a group of atoms that act together as a single unit. —**rad'i•cal•ism,** *n.* —**rad'i•cal•ly,** *adv.*

rad'i•cal•ize', *v.t.,* **-ized, -iz•ing.** to make radical, esp. in politics. —**rad'i•cal•i•za'tion,** *n.*

rad'ical sign', *n. Math.* the symbol √ or ⌐ indicating extraction of a root of the quantity that follows it.

ra•di•i (rā'dē ī'), *n.* a pl. of RADIUS.

ra•di•o (rā'dē ō'), *n., pl.* **-os,** *adj., v.,* **-oed, -o•ing.** —*n.* **1.** a telecommunication system employing electromagnetic waves to transmit speech or other sound over long distances without wires. **2.** an apparatus for receiving or transmitting radio broadcasts. —*adj.* **3.** of, used in, or sent by radio. —*v.t.* **4.** to transmit by radio. **5.** to send a message to by radio.

radio-, a combining form meaning: radiant energy (*radiometer*); radio waves (*radiotelephone*); emission of rays as a result of the breakup of atomic nuclei (*radioactivity*).

ra'di•o•ac•tiv'i•ty, *n.* the property of certain elements of spontaneously emitting radiation as a result of changes in the nuclei of atoms of the element. —**ra'di•o•ac'tive,** *adj.*

ra'dio astron'omy, *n.* the branch of astronomy that uses radio waves rather than visible light to study the universe.

ra'di•o•car'bon, *n.* a radioactive isotope of carbon with mass number 14, used in the dating of organic materials.

ra'dio fre'quency, *n.* a frequency within the range of radio transmission, from about 15,000 to 10^{11} hertz.

ra'di•o•gram', *n.* a message transmitted by radiotelegraphy.

ra'di•o•i'so•tope', *n.* a usu. artificially produced radioactive isotope.

ra'di•ol'o•gy (-ol'ə jē), *n.* the use of radiation, as x-rays, and various imaging techniques for medical diagnosis and treatment. —**ra'di•ol'o•gist,** *n.*

ra'di•om'e•ter (-om'i tər), *n.* an instrument for detecting and measuring radiant energy. —**ra'di•o•met'ric** (-ō me'trik), *adj.* —**ra'di•om'e•try,** *n.*

ra′di•o•phone′, *n.* RADIOTELEPHONE.

ra′di•o•tel′e•graph′, *n.* a telegraph in which messages or signals are sent by radio waves rather than through wires. —**ra′di•o•te•leg′ra•phy**, *n.*

ra′di•o•tel′e•phone′, *n.* a telephone in which sound is transmitted by radio waves instead of through wires.

ra′dio tel′escope, *n.* an antenna used to detect radio waves emitted by sources in space.

ra′di•o•ther′a•py, *n.* the treatment of disease by means of x-rays or radioactive substances. —**ra′di•o•ther′a•pist**, *n.*

rad•ish (rad′ish), *n.* **1.** the crisp, pungent, edible root of a plant of the mustard family. **2.** the plant itself.

ra•di•um (rā′dē əm), *n.* a highly radioactive metallic element whose decay yields radon gas and alpha rays. *Symbol:* Ra; *at. wt.:* 226; *at. no.:* 88.

ra•di•us (rā′dē əs), *n., pl.* **-di•i** (-dē ī′), **-di•us•es. 1.** a straight line extending from the center of a circle or sphere to the circumference or surface. **2.** a circular area whose extent is determined by the length of its radius. **3.** the bone of the forearm on the thumb side. [< L: staff, spoke]

ra•don (rā′don), *n.* a chemically inert radioactive gaseous element produced by the decay of radium. *Symbol:* Rn; *at. no.:* 86; *at. wt.:* 222.

RAF, Royal Air Force.

raf•fi•a (raf′ē ə), *n., pl.* **-fi•as.** a fiber obtained from the leaves of a palm and used esp. for making mats and baskets.

raff•ish (raf′ish), *adj.* **1.** jaunty; rakish. **2.** gaudily vulgar or cheap; tawdry. —**raff′ish•ly**, *adv.* —**raff′ish•ness**, *n.*

raf•fle (raf′əl), *n., v.,* **-fled, -fling.** —*n.* **1.** a form of lottery in which a number of persons buy chances to win a prize. —*v.t.* **2.** to dispose of by a raffle.

raft¹ (raft, räft), *n.* **1.** a floating platform made of buoyant materials. **2.** a collection of logs or planks fastened together for floating on water. —*v.t.* **3.** to transport or travel by raft. —*v.i.* **4.** to go or travel on a raft.

raft² (raft, räft), *n. Informal.* a great quantity or number.

raf•ter (raf′tər, räf′-), *n.* a usu. sloping timber for supporting a roof.

rag¹ (rag), *n.* a worthless piece of cloth, esp. one that is torn or worn.

rag² (rag), *v.t.,* **ragged, rag•ging.** *Informal.* **1.** to scold. **2.** to tease.

rag³ (rag), *n.* a musical composition in ragtime.

ra•ga (rä′gə), *n., pl.* **-gas.** one of the traditional melodic formulas of Hindu music.

rag•a•muf•fin (rag′ə muf′in), *n.* a ragged, dirty person, esp. a child.

rage (rāj), *n., v.,* **raged, rag•ing.** —*n.* **1.** violent anger; fury. **2.** a fit of violent anger. **3.** an object of current popularity; fad. —*v.i.* **4.** to show or feel violent anger. **5.** to move or act with violent force or intensity. —**rag′ing•ly**, *adv.*

rag•ged (rag′id), *adj.* **1.** clothed in tattered garments. **2.** torn or tattered. **3.** shaggy, as an animal's coat. **4.** rough, uneven, or imperfect. —**rag′ged•ly**, *adv.* —**rag′ged•ness**, *n.*

rag•lan (rag′lən), *n.* a loose overcoat with raglan sleeves.

rag′lan sleeve′, *n.* a set-in sleeve with a long, slanting seam from neckline to armhole.

ra•gout (ra gōō′), *n.* a highly seasoned stew of meat or fish.

rag′time′, *n.* **1.** rhythm marked by an accompaniment in strict two-four time and a syncopated melody. **2.** music in ragtime rhythm.

rag′weed′, *n.* a plant with ragged leaves whose pollen is the chief cause of hay fever.

rah (rä), *interj.* an exclamation of encouragement.

raid (rād), *n.* **1.** a sudden assault or attack. —*v.t., v.i.* **2.** to make a raid (on). —**raid′er**, *n.*

Raikes (rāks), *n.* **Robert,** 1735–1811, English pub-

lisher and philanthropist who organized the first Sunday school.

rail¹ (rāl), *n.* **1.** a horizontal bar fixed to upright posts and forming a support, barrier, fence, or railing. **2.** one of a pair of steel bars forming the running surfaces for the wheels of railroad cars. **3.** railroad: *traveled by rail.* —*v.t.* **4.** to furnish or enclose with a rail or railing.

rail² (rāl), *v.i.* to utter bitter complaints.

rail³ (rāl), *n.* any of numerous short-winged marsh birds.

rail′ing, *n.* **1.** a fencelike barrier of horizontal rails. **2.** rails collectively.

rail′ler•y, *n., pl.* **ler•ies.** good-humored ridicule; banter.

rail′road′, *n.* **1.** a permanent road laid with rails forming a track on which locomotives and cars are run. **2.** an entire system of railroads together with its property and equipment. —*v.t.* **3.** to transport by railroad. **4.** to push (a law or bill) too hastily through a legislature. **5.** to convict hastily and unfairly. —*v.i.* **6.** to work on a railroad. —**rail′road′er**, *n.* —**rail′road′ing**, *n.*

rail′way′, *n., pl.* **-ways. 1.** a railroad. **2.** a line of rails forming a road for wheeled equipment.

rai•ment (rā′mənt), *n.* clothing; apparel.

rain (rān), *n.* **1.** water condensed from atmospheric vapor that falls to earth in drops. **2.** a heavy and continuous descent: *a rain of blows.* —*v.i.* **3.** (of rain) to fall. **4.** to fall like rain. —*v.t.* **5.** to send down. **6.** to offer or bestow in great quantity. **7. rain out,** to cancel or postpone because of rain. —**rain′y**, *adj.,* **-i•er, -i•est.**

rain′bow′ (-bō′), *n.* an arc of prismatic colors appearing opposite the sun and caused by the refraction and reflection of the sun's rays in raindrops.

rain′ check′, *n.* **1.** postponement of an invitation. **2.** a ticket for future admission to an event that has been postponed or interrupted by rain.

rain′coat′, *n.* a waterproof or water-repellent coat.

rain′drop′, *n.* a drop of rain.

rain′fall′, *n.* **1.** a fall of rain. **2.** the amount of water falling within a given time and area.

rain′ for′est, *n.* a tropical forest, usu. of tall, broad-leaved evergreens, in an area of high annual rainfall.

rain′mak′er, *n.* one who induces or tries to induce rainfall by artificial means. —**rain′mak′ing**, *n.*

rain′storm′, *n.* a storm with heavy rain.

rain′wa′ter, *n.* water fallen as rain.

raise (rāz), *v.,* **raised, rais•ing**, *n.* —*v.t.* **1.** to move to a higher position; lift. **2.** to set upright. **3.** to increase in amount, degree, intensity, pitch, or force. **4.** to grow or breed: *to raise corn.* **5.** to bring up; rear. **6.** to present for consideration; put forward. **7.** to build; erect: *to raise a house.* **8.** to give rise to; provoke. **9.** to give vigor to; animate: *raised our spirits.* **10.** to advance in rank or position. **11.** to assemble or collect: *to raise money.* **12.** to cause (dough or bread) to rise. —*n.* **13.** an increase in amount, as of wages. —**Usage.** RAISE and RISE, though similar in form and meaning, are two different words. RAISE is used transitively. RISE is intransitive in its standard uses. Both RAISE and REAR are used in the U.S. to refer to the upbringing of children. Although RAISE was once condemned in this sense, it is now standard.

rai•sin (rā′zin), *n.* a dried sweet grape.

rai•son d'ê•tre (rā′zōn de′trə, rez′ŌN′), *n., pl.* **rai•sons d'ê•tre** (rā′zŌNZ, rez′ŌN). reason or justification for existence. [< F]

ra•jah or **-ja** (rä′jə), *n., pl.* **-jahs** or **-jas.** a prince in India.

rake¹ (rāk), *n., v.,* **raked, rak•ing.** —*n.* **1.** an agricultural implement with a long handle and row of teeth or tines, as for gathering hay. —*v.t.* **2.** to gather, smooth, or remove with or as if with a rake. **3.** to gather in abundance: *raked in money.* **4.** to fire guns along the length of (a body of troops, a ship, etc.). —*v.i.* **5.** to use a rake.

rake² (rāk), *n.* a dissolute and licentious man.

rake³ (rāk), *v.*, **raked, rak•ing,** *n.* —*v.i., v.t.* **1.** to incline from the vertical or horizontal. —*n.* **2.** inclination away from the vertical or horizontal.

rake′-off′, *n.* a share or amount taken or received, esp. illicitly.

rak•ish¹ (rā′kish), *adj.* like a dissolute rake. —**rak′ish•ly,** *adv.*

rak•ish² (rā′kish), *adj.* **1.** jaunty; dashing. **2.** (of a ship) having an appearance suggesting speed.

Ra•leigh (rô′lē, rä′-), *n.* **1.** Also, **Ra′legh. Sir Walter,** 1552?–1618, English explorer and writer. **2.** the capital of North Carolina. 236,707.

ral•ly¹ (ral′ē), *v.*, **-lied, -ly•ing,** *n., pl.* **-lies.** —*v.t., v.i.* **1.** to bring or come together for common action or effort. **2.** to bring or come into order. **3.** to revive or recover, as from illness. —*n.* **4.** a renewal or recovery, as of strength or activity. **5.** a mass meeting to support a common cause. **6.** a sharp rise in stock prices or trading after a declining market. **7.** a long-distance automobile race, esp. for sports cars. —**ral′li•er,** *n.*

ral•ly² (ral′ē), *v.t.*, **-lied, -ly•ing.** to ridicule in a good-natured way.

ram (ram), *n., v.*, **rammed, ram•ming.** —*n.* **1.** a male sheep. **2.** any of various devices for battering, crushing, or forcing something. —*v.t.* **3.** to drive or force by heavy blows. **4.** to strike against with great force. **5.** to cram; stuff.

RAM (ram), *n.* random-access memory: volatile computer memory for creating, loading, and running programs and manipulating and temporarily storing data.

Ram•a•dan (ram′ə dän′), *n.* **1.** the ninth month of the Islamic calendar. **2.** the daily fast enjoined from dawn until sunset during this month.

ram•ble (ram′bəl), *v.*, **-bled, -bling,** *n.* —*v.i.* **1.** to wander around in a leisurely, aimless manner. **2.** to grow or spread in a random fashion, as a vine. **3.** to talk or write in a discursive, aimless manner. —*n.* **4.** a leisurely walk without a definite route.

ram′bler, *n.* **1.** one that rambles. **2.** a climbing rose with clusters of small flowers.

ram•bunc•tious (ram bungk′shəs), *adj.* difficult to control or handle; wildly boisterous. —**ram•bunc′tious•ness,** *n.*

ram•e•kin or **-quin** (ram′i kin), *n.* a small open baking dish.

ram•i•fy (ram′ə fī′), *v.t., v.i.*, **-fied, -fy•ing.** to divide or spread out into branches or branchlike parts. —**ram′i•fi•ca′tion,** *n.*

ram′jet′, *n.* a jet engine operated by fuel injected into a stream of air compressed by the aircraft's forward speed.

Ra′moth-Gil′ead (rā′moth), *n.* a city in Gad near the border of Israel and Syria, one of the cities of refuge. Deut. 4:43; Josh. 20:8.

ramp (ramp), *n.* **1.** a sloping surface connecting two levels. **2.** a movable staircase for entering or leaving an airplane.

ram•page (ram′pāj; *v.* also ram pāj′), *n., v.*, **-paged, -pag•ing.** —*n.* **1.** an eruption of violently uncontrolled, reckless, or destructive behavior. —*v.i.* **2.** to rush or act furiously or violently. —**ram•pag′er,** *n.*

ramp•ant (ram′pənt), *adj.* **1.** prevailing or unchecked; widespread. **2.** growing luxuriantly, as weeds. —**ramp′an•cy,** *n.* —**ramp′ant•ly,** *adv.*

ram•part (ram′pärt, -pərt), *n.* a mound, as of earth, raised as a fortification.

ram′rod′, *n.* **1.** a rod for ramming down the charge of a muzzleloading firearm. **2.** a rod for cleaning the barrel of a firearm.

ram′shack′le, *adj.* loosely made or held together; rickety.

ran (ran), *v.* pt. of RUN.

ranch (ranch), *n.* **1.** an establishment for raising livestock under range conditions. **2.** a farm that raises a single crop or animal. —*v.i.* **3.** to manage or work on a ranch. —**ranch′er,** *n.*

ranch′ house′, *n.* a usu. one-story house with a low-pitched roof.

Ran•cho Cu•ca•mon•ga (ran′chō kōō′kə mung′gə, -mong′-), *n.* a city in SE California. 114,799.

ran•cid (ran′sid), *adj.* having a rank, unpleasant smell or taste. —**ran•cid′i•ty, ran′cid•ness,** *n.*

ran•cor (rang′kər), *n.* bitter resentment or ill will; malice. Also, *esp. Brit.,* **ran′cour.** —**ran′cor•ous,** *adj.* —**ran′cor•ous•ly,** *adv.*

rand (rand), *n., pl.* **rand.** the basic monetary unit of South Africa.

R&B, rhythm and blues.

R&D, research and development.

Ran•dolph (ran′dolf, -dəlf), *n.* **1. A(sa) Philip,** 1889–1979, U.S. labor leader: president of the Brotherhood of Sleeping Car Porters 1925–68. **2. Edmund Jennings** (jen′ings), 1753–1813, U.S. statesman: first U.S. Attorney General 1789–94; Secretary of State 1794–95.

ran•dom (ran′dəm), *adj.* **1.** occurring or done without definite aim, reason, or pattern. —*Idiom.* **2. at random,** in a random manner. —**ran′dom•ly,** *adv.*

ran′dom•ize′, *v.t.*, **-ized, -iz•ing.** to perform, arrange, select, or distribute in a random manner. —**ran′dom•i•za′tion,** *n.*

R and R, 1. rest and recreation. **2.** rest and recuperation.

rang (rang), *v.* pt. of RING².

range (rānj), *n., v.*, **ranged, rang•ing.** —*n.* **1.** the limits between which variation is possible. **2.** extent; scope: *one's range of vision.* **3.** the distance of a target from a weapon. **4.** an area with targets for shooting practice. **5.** an area for flight-testing missiles. **6.** a rank, class, or order. **7.** a row, line, or series, as of persons or things. **8.** the act of moving around over an area or region. **9.** an open region where livestock can roam or graze. **10.** the region over which a population or species is distributed. **11.** a chain of mountains. **12.** a large stove with burners and an oven. —*v.t.* **13.** to arrange in rows or lines, esp. in an orderly way. **14.** to place in a particular class. **15.** to pass over or through (an area or region), as in exploring. —*v.i.* **16.** to vary within specified limits. **17.** to roam or wander. **18.** to extend in a certain direction.

rang′er, *n.* **1.** FOREST RANGER. **2.** one of a body of armed guards who patrol a region. **3.** (*often cap.*) a soldier trained for making surprise raids.

Ran•goon (rang gōōn′), *n.* former name of YANGON.

rang•y (rān′jē), *adj.*, **-i•er, -i•est.** slender and long-limbed. —**rang′i•ness,** *n.*

rank¹ (rangk), *n.* **1.** a social or official position or standing. **2.** high position or station. **3.** relative position or standing: *a writer of the first rank.* **4.** a row or series. **5. ranks,** enlisted soldiers as a group. **6.** an orderly arrangement; array. **7.** a line of soldiers standing abreast. —*v.t.* **8.** to arrange in ranks or in regular formation. **9.** to assign to a particular position or class. **10.** to outrank. —*v.i.* **11.** to hold a certain rank or position. **12.** to be the senior in rank.

rank² (rangk), *adj.*, **-er, -est. 1.** growing with excessive luxuriance. **2.** having an offensive smell. **3.** utter; absolute: *a rank amateur.* —**rank′ly,** *adv.* —**rank′ness,** *n.*

rank′ and file′, *n.* **1.** the members of an organization, apart from its leaders or officers. **2.** the enlisted soldiers of an army.

rank′ing, *adj.* **1.** senior in rank or position. **2.** highly regarded; renowned.

ran•kle (rang′kəl), *v.i., v.t.*, **-kled, -kling.** to cause keen irritation or bitter resentment (in).

ran•sack (ran′sak), *v.t.* **1.** to search thoroughly or vigorously through. **2.** to search through for plunder; pillage.

ran•som (ran′səm), *n.* **1.** the redemption for a price of a prisoner or captive. **2.** the price paid or demanded. —*v.t.* **3.** to redeem, as from detention, by paying a demanded price. —**ran′som•er,** *n.*

rant (rant), *v.i.* **1.** to talk in a wild or vehement way; rave. —*n.* **2.** wild or vehement talk. —**rant′er,** *n.*

rap (rap), *v.*, **rapped, rap•ping,** *n.* —*v.t.* **1.** to strike with a quick, smart blow. **2.** to utter sharply or vigorously. **3.** *Slang.* to criticize severely. —*v.i.* **4.** to knock smartly or vigorously. **5.** *Slang.* to talk; chat. —*n.* **6.** a quick, smart blow. **7.** *Slang.* blame or punishment. **8.** *Slang.* a criminal charge. **9.** *Slang.* talk; conversation. **10.** a kind of popular music marked by the rhythmical intoning of rhymed verses to an insistent beat. —**rap′per,** *n.*

ra•pa•cious (rə pā′shəs), *adj.* **1.** extremely greedy. **2.** subsisting on living prey; predatory. —**ra•pac′i•ty** (-pas′i tē), *n.*

rape¹ (rāp), *n., v.,* **raped, rap•ing.** —*n.* **1.** the unlawful act of forcing a person, esp. a female, to have sexual intercourse. **2.** an act of plunder or despoliation. —*v.i., v.t.* **3.** to commit rape (on). —**rap′ist,** *n.*

rape² (rāp), *n.* a plant whose leaves are used as fodder and whose seeds yield oil.

Raph•a•el (raf′ē əl, rä′fī el′), *n.* 1483–1520, Italian painter.

rap•id (rap′id), *adj.,* **-er, -est,** *n.* —*adj.* **1.** characterized by speed; swift. —*n.* **2.** Usu., **rapids.** a part of a river where the current runs very swiftly. —**ra•pid•i•ty** (rə pid′i tē), **rap′id•ness,** *n.* —**rap′id•ly,** *adv.*

rap′id tran′sit, *n.* a system of rapid public transportation, as a subway, in a metropolitan area.

ra•pi•er (rā′pē ər), *n.* a sword with a double-edged blade.

rap•ine (rap′in, -īn), *n.* the violent seizure and carrying off of another's property.

rap•port (ra pôr′, rə-), *n.* a relation, esp. a harmonious or sympathetic one.

rap•proche•ment (rap′rōsh män′), *n.* an establishment or renewal of harmonious relations.

rap•scal•lion (rap skal′yən), *n.* a rascal; rogue.

rap′ sheet′, *n. Slang.* a record of a person's arrests and convictions.

rapt (rapt), *adj.* **1.** deeply engrossed; absorbed. **2.** transported with emotion. —**rapt′ly,** *adv.* —**rapt′-ness,** *n.*

rap•ture (rap′chər), *n.* **1.** ecstatic joy or delight. **2.** religious or spiritual ecstasy. **3. the Rapture,** the experience, anticipated by some fundamentalist Christians, of meeting Christ midway in the air upon his return to earth. —**rap′tur•ous,** *adj.*

ra•ra a•vis (râr′ə ā′vis), *n., pl.* **ra•rae a•ves** (râr′ē ā′vēz). a rare person or thing; rarity. [< L rare bird]

rare¹ (râr), *adj.,* **rar•er, rar•est. 1.** occurring or found infrequently; uncommon. **2.** having component parts loosely compacted; thin: *rare gases.* **3.** unusually great; extraordinary. —**rare′ly,** *adv.* —**rare′-ness,** *n.* —**rar′i•ty,** *n., pl.* **-ties.**

rare² (râr), *adj.,* **rar•er, rar•est.** (of meat) cooked just slightly. —**rare′ness,** *n.*

rare•bit (râr′bīt), *n.* WELSH RABBIT.

rare′-earth′ el′ement, *n.* any of a group of related metallic elements of atomic numbers 57 through 71.

rar•e•fy (râr′ə fī′), *v.t., v.i.,* **-fied, -fy•ing.** to make or become rare or less dense; thin. —**rar′e•fac′tion** (-fak′shən), *n.*

rar′ing, *adj.* very eager or anxious: *raring to go.*

ras•cal (ras′kəl), *n.* **1.** a dishonest or unscrupulous person. **2.** a mischievous person or animal. —**ras′-cal•ly,** *adj.*

rash¹ (rash), *adj.,* **-er, -est.** marked by or resulting from reckless or ill-considered haste. —**rash′ly,** *adv.* —**rash′ness,** *n.*

rash² (rash), *n.* **1.** a skin eruption. **2.** multiple occurrences; outbreak: *a rash of robberies.*

rash′er (rash′ər), *n.* **1.** a thin slice of bacon or ham for frying or broiling. **2.** a serving of three or four slices, esp. of bacon.

rasp (rasp, räsp), *v.t.* **1.** to scrape with or as if with a rough instrument. **2.** to grate upon or irritate. —*v.i.* **3.** to speak with a grating sound. —*n.* **4.** a rasping sound. **5.** a coarse file with separate conical teeth. —**rasp′y,** *adj.,* **-i•er, -i•est.**

rasp•ber•ry (raz′ber′ē, -bə rē, räz′-), *n., pl.* **-ries. 1.** the small, juicy red, black, or pale yellow fruit of a prickly shrub of the rose family. **2.** a shrub bearing raspberries. **3.** a vulgar noise made with the lips and tongue to express contempt.

rat (rat), *n., v.,* **rat•ted, rat•ting.** —*n.* **1.** any of several long-tailed rodents resembling but larger than the mouse. **2.** *Slang.* **a.** a person who betrays associates. **b.** an informer. **3.** *Slang.* a person who frequents a specified place: *mall rat.* —*v.i.* **4.** *Slang.* to inform on one's associates; squeal. **5.** to hunt or catch rats. —*Proverb.* **6.** Rats desert a sinking ship, the cowardly flee during a crisis. —**rat′like′,** *adj.*

ratch•et (rach′it), *n.* **1.** a toothed bar or wheel with which a pawl engages. **2.** a mechanism consisting of a ratchet with a pawl.

rate¹ (rāt), *n., v.,* **rat•ed, rat•ing.** —*n.* **1.** a price, charge, or payment fixed with reference to a scale or standard. **2.** a certain amount of one thing, as speed, considered in relation to a unit of another, as time. **3.** degree of speed or progress. **4.** position in a class; rank. —*v.t.* **5.** to estimate the value or worth of. **6.** to esteem, consider, or regard. **7.** to deserve; merit. **8.** to place in a rank or class. —*v.i.* **9.** to have value or standing. —*Idiom.* **10. at any rate, a.** in any event. **b.** at least.

rate² (rāt), *v.t., v.i.,* **rat•ed, rat•ing.** to scold vehemently. —**rat′er,** *n.*

rath•er (rath′ər, rä′thər), *adv.* **1.** to some extent. **2.** more properly or justly. **3.** sooner: *to die rather than yield.* **4.** more truly. **5.** on the contrary.

raths•kel•ler (rät′skel′ər, rat′-, rath′-), *n.* a restaurant or bar usu. below street level.

rat•i•fy (rat′ə fī′), *v.t.,* **-fied, -fy•ing.** to confirm by expressing approval or formal sanction. —**rat′i•fi•ca′tion,** *n.* —**rat′i•fi′er,** *n.*

rat•ing (rā′ting), *n.* **1.** classification according to grade or rank. **2.** the credit standing of a person or firm. **3.** a percentage indicating the number of listeners to or viewers of a radio or television broadcast.

ra•tio (rā′shō, -shē ō′), *n., pl.* **-tios. 1.** the relation between two similar magnitudes with respect to the number of times the first contains the second. **2.** proportional relation; rate. [< L *ratiō* reckoning, proportion]

ra•ti•oc•i•nate (rash′ē os′ə nāt′, -ō′sə-, rat′ē-), *v.i.,* **-nat•ed, -nat•ing.** to reason logically. —**ra′ti•oc′i•na′tion,** *n.*

ra•tion (rash′ən, rā′shən), *n.* **1.** a fixed allowance of food, esp. for one day. **2.** an allotted amount. —*v.t.* **3.** to distribute as or provide with rations. **4.** to restrict consumption of.

ra•tion•al (rash′ə nl), *adj.* **1.** based on, agreeable to, or exercising reason. **2.** sane; lucid. **3.** *Math.* capable of being expressed exactly by a ratio of two integers: *a rational number.* —**ra′tion•al′i•ty,** *n., pl.* **-ties.** —**ra′tion•al•ly,** *adv.*

ra•tion•ale (-nal′), *n.* **1.** a fundamental reason. **2.** a statement of reasons or principles.

ra•tion•al•ism, *n.* the principle or habit of accepting reason as the sole authority in matters of opinion, belief, or conduct. —**ra′tion•al•ist,** *n.* —**ra′tion•al•is′tic,** *adj.*

ra•tion•al•ize′, *v.,* **-ized, -iz•ing.** —*v.t.* **1.** to ascribe (one's actions) to plausible but spurious causes. **2.** to cause to conform to reason. —*v.i.* **3.** to invent plausible but spurious explanations. —**ra′tion•al•i•za′tion,** *n.*

rat•line or **-lin** (rat′lin), *n.* any of the small ropes that cross the shrouds of a ship horizontally and serve as steps for going aloft.

rat′ race′, *n.* an exhausting and usu. competitive routine activity.

rat•tan (ra tan′, rə-), *n.* any of various Asian climbing palms with tough stems used esp. for wickerwork and canes.

rat•tle (rat′l), *v.,* **-tled, -tling,** *n.* —*v.i.* **1.** to make a rapid succession of short, sharp sounds. **2.** to move noisily. **3.** to chatter. —*v.t.* **4.** to cause to make a rattling noise. **5.** to utter or perform in a rapid or lively manner. **6.** to disconcert; confuse. —*n.* **7.** a rapid succession of short, sharp sounds. **8.** a baby's toy that rattles when shaken. **9.** the series of horny rings at the end of a rattlesnake's tail.

rat′tle•brain′, *n.* a silly or easily distracted person. —**rat′tle•brained′**, *adj.*

rat′tler, *n.* a rattlesnake.

rat′tle•snake′, *n.* any of several New World pit vipers with a rattle at the end of the tail.

rat′tle•trap′, *n.* a shaky, rattling object, esp. a rickety vehicle.

rat′tling, *adj.* **1.** brisk. **2.** splendid; fine. —*adv.* **3.** very: *a rattling good time.*

rat′trap′, *n.* **1.** a device for catching rats. **2.** a run-down, filthy place.

rat′ty, *adj.*, **-ti•er**, **-ti•est**. **1.** full of rats. **2.** of or characteristic of rats. **3.** wretched; shabby.

rau•cous (rô′kəs), *adj.* **1.** harsh; strident. **2.** rowdy; disorderly. —**rau′cous•ly**, *adv.* —**rau′cous•ness**, *n.*

raun•chy (rôn′chē, rän′-), *adj.*, **-chi•er**, **-chi•est**. **1.** vulgar; smutty. **2.** dirty; grubby. —**raun′chi•ly**, *adv.* —**raun′chi•ness**, *n.*

rav•age (rav′ij), *v.*, **-aged**, **-ag•ing**, *n.* —*v.t.*, *v.i.* **1.** to do ruinous damage (to); devastate. —*n.* **2.** ruinous damage. —**rav′ag•er**, *n.*

rave (rāv), *v.*, **raved**, **rav•ing**, *n.* —*v.i.* **1.** to talk irrationally, as in delirium. **2.** to talk or write with extravagant enthusiasm. —*n.* **3.** the act of raving. **4.** an extravagantly approving appraisal.

rav•el (rav′əl), *v.*, **-eled**, **-el•ing** or (*esp. Brit.*) **-elled**, **-el•ling**, *n.* —*v.t.* **1.** to disentangle the threads or fibers of; unravel. **2.** to make clear; unravel. **3.** to entangle; confuse. —*v.i.* **4.** to become unwound; fray. —*n.* **5.** a tangle.

Ra•vel (rə vel′), *n.* **Maurice**, 1875–1937, French composer.

ra•ven (rā′vən), *n.* **1.** a large black bird, related to the crow, having a loud, harsh call. —*adj.* **2.** lustrous black: *raven hair.*

rav•en•ing (rav′ə ning), *adj.* greedy for prey.

rav•en•ous, *adj.* **1.** extremely hungry. **2.** predatory. **3.** intensely eager. —**rav′en•ous•ly**, *adv.*

ra•vine (rə vēn′), *n.* a narrow, steep-sided valley.

rav•ing (rā′ving), *adj.* **1.** talking wildly; delirious. **2.** extraordinary in degree: *a raving beauty.* —*adv.* **3.** furiously; wildly: *raving mad.* —**rav′ing•ly**, *adv.*

ra•vi•o•li (rav′ē ō′lē), *n.* (*used with a sing. or pl. v.*) small pockets of pasta filled esp. with cheese or meat.

rav•ish (rav′ish), *v.t.* **1.** to transport with strong emotion, esp. joy. **2.** to rape. **3.** to seize and carry off by force. —**rav′ish•er**, *n.* —**rav′ish•ment**, *n.*

rav•ish•ing, *adj.* extremely beautiful or attractive.

raw (rô), *adj.*, **-er**, **-est**. **1.** not cooked. **2.** not processed, finished, or refined: *raw cotton.* **3.** unnaturally or painfully exposed: *raw flesh.* **4.** indelicate; crude: *raw jokes.* **5.** inexperienced; untrained: *a raw recruit.* **6.** brutally harsh or unfair: *a raw deal.* **7.** damp and chilly: *a raw day.* —*Idiom.* **8. in the raw, a.** in the natural or unrefined state. **b.** nude; naked. —**raw′ness**, *n.*

raw′boned′, *adj.* lean and bony.

raw′hide′, *n.* **1.** the untanned skin of cattle. **2.** a rope or whip made of rawhide.

ray¹ (rā), *n.* **1.** a narrow beam of light or other radiation. **2.** a slight manifestation: *a ray of hope.* **3.** one of the lines or streams in which light appears to radiate from a luminous body. **4.** one of a system of straight lines emanating from a point. **5.** a stream of radioactive particles. **6.** a radiating body part, as the arm of a starfish.

ray² (rā), *n.* a fish with a flattened body and greatly enlarged pectoral fins.

ray•on (rā′on), *n.* **1.** a textile filament made esp. from cellulose treated with caustic soda and passed through spinnerets. **2.** a fabric or yarn of rayon.

raze (rāz), *v.t.*, **razed**, **raz•ing**. to level to the ground; tear down.

ra•zor (rā′zər), *n.* a sharp-edged instrument used esp. for shaving.

razz (raz), *v.t.* to make fun of; mock.

raz′zle-daz′zle (raz′əl), *n.* showy or virtuosic technique or effect.

Rb, *Chem. Symbol.* rubidium.

RBI, *Baseball.* run batted in.

R.C.Ch., Roman Catholic Church.

rcpt., receipt.

rd, rod.

Rd., Road.

rd., **1.** road. **2.** round.

RD, Rural Delivery.

re¹ (rā), *n.* the second tone in the diatonic scale.

re² (rē, rā), *prep.* with reference to; regarding.

Re, *Chem. Symbol.* rhenium.

re-, a prefix meaning: back or backward (*repay*); again or anew (*recapture*).

reach (rēch), *v.t.* **1.** to get to; arrive at. **2.** to succeed in touching or seizing. **3.** to hold out; stretch. **4.** to extend as far as. **5.** to establish communication with. **6.** to amount to. —*v.i.* **7.** to make a stretch with or as if with the hand. **8.** to extend, as in operation or effect. —*n.* **9.** an act or instance of reaching. **10.** the extent or distance of reaching. **11.** range, as of effective action. **12.** a continuous extent, as of land. —*Proverb.* **13.** One's reach should exceed one's grasp, one should strive for as much as possible. —**reach′a•ble**, *adj.*

re•act (rē akt′), *v.i.* **1.** to act in response to an agent, influence, or stimulus. **2.** to act reciprocally. **3.** to act in a reverse manner, esp. to return to a prior condition. **4.** to act in opposition. **5.** to undergo a chemical reaction.

re•ac•tance (rē ak′təns), *n.* the opposition of inductance and capacitance to alternating electrical current.

re•ac′tant, *n.* a substance that undergoes a change in a chemical reaction.

re•ac′tion, *n.* **1.** a reverse movement or tendency. **2.** a movement toward extreme political conservatism. **3.** action in response to an agent, influence, or stimulus. **4.** a chemical change. **5.** a change in the nucleus of an atom.

re•ac′tion•ar′y (-shə ner′ē), *adj.*, *n.*, *pl.* **-ar•ies.** —*adj.* **1.** of, marked by, or favoring reaction, esp. in politics. —*n.* **2.** a reactionary person.

re•ac′tor, *n.* **1.** one that reacts. **2.** an apparatus in which a nuclear-fission chain reaction is sustained and controlled.

read¹ (rēd), *v.*, **read** (red), **read•ing** (rē′ding), *n.* —*v.t.* **1.** to look at and understand the meaning of (something written or printed). **2.** to utter aloud (something written or printed). **3.** to recognize and understand the meaning of: *to read an x-ray.* **4.** to foretell or predict. **5.** to register, as a thermometer. **6.** to learn or interpret by or as if by reading: *to read a person's thoughts.* **7.** to obtain (data or programs) from an external storage medium and place in a computer's memory. **8.** to study (a subject). —*v.i.* **9.** to read written or printed matter. **10.** to learn about something by reading. **11.** to be capable of being interpreted when read: *a rule that reads two different ways.* —*n.* **12.** something read: *Her new novel is a good read.* —*Idiom.* **13. read between the lines,** to understand from implications only. —**read′a•bil′i•ty**, *n.* —**read′a•ble**, *adj.* —**read′er**, *n.*

read² (red), *adj.* knowledgeable from reading: *a well-read person.*

read•er•ship (rē′dər ship′), *n.* the people who read a particular publication.

read•ing (rē′ding), *n.* **1.** the action of a person who reads. **2.** matter read or for reading. **3.** the form of a given passage in a particular text. **4.** a public recitation of a text. **5.** an interpretation, as of a musical composition. **6.** the indication of a graduated instrument, as a gauge.

read′-on′ly (rēd), *adj.* noting or pertaining to computer files or memory that can be read but cannot normally be changed.

read′out′ (rēd), *n.* the output in readable form of information from a computer.

read•y (red′ē), *adj.*, **-i•er**, **-i•est**, *v.*, **-ied**, **-y•ing.** —*adj.* **1.** prepared for action or use. **2.** not hesitant; willing. **3.** prompt, as in comprehending. **4.** showing skill or dexterity: *a ready wit.* **5.** inclined; disposed. **6.** likely at any moment. **7.** immediately available for use: *ready cash.* —*v.t.* **8.** to make ready; prepare. —**read/i•ly,** *adv.* —**read/i•ness,** *n.* —**Usage.** See ALREADY.

read/y-made/, *adj.* made in advance for sale to any purchaser.

Rea•gan (rā/gən), *n.* **Ronald (Wilson),** born 1911, 40th president of the U.S. 1981-89.

re•a•gent (rē ā/jənt), *n. Chem.* a substance that because of the reactions it causes is used in analysis and synthesis.

re•al (rē/əl, rēl), *adj.* **1.** true rather than ostensible. **2.** actual rather than imaginary, ideal, or fictitious. **3.** not artificial; genuine. **4.** *Law.* of immovable or permanent things, as land or buildings. —*adv.* **5.** *Informal.* very or extremely. —*Idiom.* **6. for real, a.** in reality; actually. **b.** genuine; sincere. —**re/al•ness,** *n.*

re/al estate/, *n.* property, esp. in land and buildings.

re/al•ism, *n.* **1.** the tendency to see things as they really are. **2.** the representation of things as they really are in art or literature. —**re/al•ist,** *n.* —**re/al•is/tic,** *adj.* —**re/al•is/ti•cal•ly,** *adv.*

re•al•i•ty (rē al/i tē), *n., pl.* **-ties. 1.** the state or quality of being real. **2.** a real thing or fact. **3.** real things, facts, or events as a whole. —*Idiom.* **4. in reality,** in fact; actually.

real/ity check/, *n.* a corrective confronting of reality, in order to counteract one's expectations, prejudices, or the like.

re/al•ize/, *v.t.,* **-ized, -iz•ing. 1.** to grasp or understand clearly. **2.** to give reality to (a hope, plan, etc.); fulfill. **3.** to gain; obtain: *realized a profit.* **4.** to bring as proceeds, as from a sale. —**re/al•iz/a•ble,** *adj.* —**re/al•i•za/tion,** *n.*

re/al•ly, *adv.* **1.** actually. **2.** genuinely; truly. **3.** indeed.

realm (relm), *n.* **1.** a royal domain; kingdom. **2.** a sphere, domain, or province.

re/al num/ber, *n.* a rational number or the limit of a sequence of rational numbers.

re/al time/, *n.* the actual time during which a process takes place.

re/al-time/, *adj.* of or involving computer applications or processes that can respond immediately to ... input.

Re/al•tor, *Trademark.* a real-estate broker belonging to the National Association of Real Estate Boards.

re/al•ty, *n.* real estate.

ream[1] (rēm), *n.* **1.** a standard quantity of paper consisting of 480, 500, or 516 sheets. **2.** Usu., **reams.** a large quantity.

ream[2] (rēm), *v.t.* **1.** to enlarge by means of a reamer. **2.** to remove, press out, or clean with a reamer.

ream/er, *n.* **1.** a rotary tool for finishing or enlarging holes. **2.** a juice extractor with a grooved cone in the center.

reap (rēp), *v.t.* **1.** to cut (wheat, rye, etc.) with a sickle, reaper, etc. **2.** to gather or take (a crop, harvest, etc.). **3.** to get as a return, recompense, or result.

reap/er, *n.* **1.** a machine for cutting standing grain. **2.** a person who reaps.

rear[1] (rēr), *n.* **1.** the back of something. **2.** a space or position at the back of something. **3.** the buttocks; rump. **4.** the hindmost portion, as of an army. —*adj.* **5.** situated at the rear.

rear[2] (rēr), *v.t.* **1.** to take care of up to maturity. **2.** to breed and raise (livestock). **3.** to raise by building; erect. **4.** to raise to an upright position. —*v.i.* **5.** to rise on the hind legs, as a horse. **6.** to rise high. —**Usage.** See RAISE.

rear/ ad/miral, *n.* a commissioned officer in the U.S. Navy or Coast Guard ranking above a captain.

rear/most/, *adj.* farthest in the rear.

rear/ward (-wərd), *adv.* **1.** Also, **rear/wards.** toward or in the rear. —*adj.* **2.** located in or directed toward the rear.

rea•son (rē/zən), *n.* **1.** a basis or cause for a belief, action, fact, or event. **2.** a statement presented in justification or explanation. **3.** the mental power concerned with forming conclusions or inferences. **4.** sound judgment; good sense. **5.** soundness of mind. —*v.i.* **6.** to use the power of reason; think. **7.** to argue in a logical manner. —*v.t.* **8.** to think through logically. **9.** to conclude or infer. —*Idiom.* **10. within reason,** in accord with reason; justifiable. —**rea/son•er,** *n.* —**reas/on•ing,** *n.* —**Usage.** Most usage critics advise against the constructions THE REASON IS BECAUSE or THE REASON WHY, claiming that they are redundant. Although they both are common in speech and writing, it is generally advised to use *that* instead of *because* or *why: The reason for the delay is that the driver got lost. The reason that the bill passed was the support of three key senators.*

rea•son•a•ble (rē/zə nə bəl, rēz/nə-), *adj.* **1.** in accord with reason; logical. **2.** not excessive; moderate. **3.** not expensive. **4.** endowed with reason; rational. —**rea/son•a•bly,** *adv.*

re•as•sure (rē/ə shoŏr/, -shûr/), *v.t.,* **-sured, -sur•ing. 1.** to restore to assurance or confidence. **2.** to assure again. —**re/as•sur/ance,** *n.* —**re/as•sur/ing•ly,** *adv.*

re•bate (rē/bāt; *v.* also ri bāt/), *n., v.,* **-bat•ed, -bat•ing.** —*n.* **1.** a return of part of an original payment, as for merchandise. —*v.t.* **2.** to allow a rebate of or on. —**re/bat•er,** *n.*

Re•bek•ah (ri bek/ə), *n.* the wife of Isaac, and mother of Esau and Jacob. Gen. 24-27.

reb•el (*n., adj.* reb/əl; *v.* ri bel/), *n., adj., v.,* **-belled, -bel•ling** .. *n.* **1.** a person who rises in arms against a government or ruler. **2.** a person who resists authority, control, or tradition. —*adj.* **3.** rebellious; defiant. **4.** of rebels. —*v.i.* **re•bel 5.** to act as a rebel. **6.** to show or feel utter repugnance.

re•bel/lion (-bel/yən), *n.* **1.** armed resistance to a government or ruler. **2.** defiance of any authority.

re•bel/lious, *adj.* **1.** defying or resisting authority. **2.** of or characteristic of rebels or rebellion. —**re•bel/lious•ly,** *adv.* —**re•bel/lious•ness,** *n.*

re•birth (rē bûrth/, rē/bûrth/), *n.* **1.** a new or second birth. **2.** a renaissance; revival.

re•bound (*v.* ri bound/, rē/bound/; *n.* rē/bound/, ri-bound/), *v.i.* **1.** to spring back from force of impact. **2.** to recover, as from ill health. —*n.* **3.** the act of rebounding. —*Idiom.* **4. on the rebound,** after being rejected by another: *to marry on the rebound.*

re•buff (*n.* ri buf/, rē/buf; *v.* ri buf/), *n.* **1.** a blunt or abrupt rejection or refusal. **2.** a check to action or progress. —*v.t.* **3.** to give a rebuff to.

re•buke (ri byoŏk/), *v.,* **-buked, -buk•ing,** *n.* —*v.t.* **1.** to express sharp, stern disapproval to; reprove. —*n.* **2.** a sharp reproof; reprimand. —**re•buk/ing•ly,** *adv.*

---

re/ab•sorb/, *v.t.*
re/ab•sorp/tion, *n.*
re/ac•quaint/, *v.t.*
re/ac•quire/, *v.t.,* -quired, -quir•ing.
re/a•dapt/, *v.*
re/ad•dress/, *v.t.*
re/ad•just/, *v.t.*
re/ad•mit/, *v.,* -mit•ted, -mit•ting.
re/af•firm/, *v.t.*
re/a•lign/, *v.*
re/a•lign/ment, *n.*
re•an/a•lyze/, *v.t.,* -lyzed, -lyz•ing.

re/ap•pear/, *v.i.*
re/ap•pear/ance, *n.*
re/ap•ply/, *v.,* -plied, -ply•ing.
re/ap•point/, *v.t.*
re/ap•por/tion, *v.t.*
re/ap•prais/al, *n.*
re/ar•range/, *v.,* -ranged, -rang•ing.
re/ar•range/ment, *n.*
re/as•sem/ble, *v.,* -bled, -bling.
re/as•sess/, *v.t.*
re/as•sign/, *v.t.*

re/as•sign/ment, *n.*
re/at•tach/, *v.*
re/at•tempt/, *v.t.*
re•build/, *v.,* -built, -build•ing.
re•charge/, *v.t.,* -charged, -charg•ing.
re•charge/a•ble, *adj.*
re•clas/si•fy/, *v.t.,* -fied, -fy•ing.
re/com•bine/, *v.,* -bined, -bin•ing.
re/com•pose/, *v.t.,* -posed, -pos•ing.
re/con•di/tion, *v.t.*

re•bus (rē′bəs), *n.*, *pl.* **-bus•es.** a representation of a word or phrase by means of pictures.

re•but (ri but′), *v.t.*, **-but•ted, -but•ting.** to refute by evidence or argument. —**re•but′tal,** *n.*

rec (rek), *n.* recreation.

re•cal•ci•trant (ri kal′si trənt), *adj.* **1.** resisting authority or control; refractory. **2.** hard to deal with, manage, or operate. —**re•cal′ci•trance,** *n.*

re•call (*v.* ri kôl′; *n.* ri kôl′, rē′kôl for 4, 5; rē′kôl for 6, 7), *v.t.* **1.** to recollect; remember. **2.** to call or order back. **3.** to revoke or withdraw. —*n.* **4.** the act of recalling. **5.** recollection; remembrance. **6.** the removal of or right to remove a public official from office by popular vote. **7.** a summons by a manufacturer for the return of a defective product.

re•cant (ri kant′), *v.t.*, *v.i.* to withdraw (a statement, opinion, etc.), esp. formally. —**re•can•ta•tion** (rē′kan tā′shən), *n.*

re•cap¹ (*v.* rē′kap′, rē kap′; *n.* rē′kap′), *v.*, **-capped, -cap•ping,** *n.* —*v.t.* **1.** to recondition (a worn tire) by cementing on and vulcanizing a strip of rubber. —*n.* **2.** a recapped tire.

re•cap² (rē′kap′), *n.*, *v.*, **-capped, -cap•ping.** —*n.* **1.** a recapitulation. —*v.t.*, *v.i.* **2.** to recapitulate.

re′ca•pit′u•late′, *v.t.*, *v.i.*, **-lat•ed, -lat•ing.** to sum up; summarize. —**re′ca•pit′u•la′tion,** *n.*

re•cap′ture, *v.*, **-tured, -tur•ing,** *n.* —*v.t.* **1.** to capture again; retake. **2.** to experience anew. —*n.* **3.** recovery or retaking by capture.

recd. or **rec′d.,** received.

re•cede (ri sēd′), *v.i.*, **-ced•ed, -ced•ing. 1.** to move back or away. **2.** to become or seem to become more distant. **3.** to slope backward.

re•ceipt (ri sēt′), *n.* **1.** a written acknowledgment of having received money or goods. **2. receipts,** an amount or quantity received. **3.** the act of receiving. **4.** a recipe. —*v.t.* **5.** to acknowledge the receipt of. **6.** to give a receipt for.

re•ceiv•a•ble (ri sē′və bəl), *adj.* **1.** awaiting receipt of payment; due. **2.** capable of being received.

re•ceive (ri sēv′), *v.*, **-ceived, -ceiv•ing.** —*v.t.* **1.** to take (something offered, given, or sent); get. **2.** to hold, bear, or contain. **3.** to take into the mind. **4.** to meet with; experience. **5.** to welcome or accept as a guest, member, etc. **6.** to accept as true, valid, or approved. —*v.i.* **7.** to welcome visitors.

re•ceiv′er, *n.* **1.** one that receives. **2.** an apparatus that receives electrical signals and makes them visible or audible. **3.** a person appointed by a court to take charge of a business or property in bankruptcy or litigation. **4.** *Football.* a player on the offensive team who is eligible to catch a forward pass.

re•ceiv′er•ship′, *n.* **1.** the condition of being in the hands of a receiver. **2.** the position or function of a receiver.

re•cent (rē′sənt), *adj.* **1.** lately happening, done, or made. **2.** of or belonging to a time not long past. **3.** (*cap.*) *Geol.* noting or pertaining to the present geological epoch. —**re′cent•ly,** *adv.*

re•cep•ta•cle (ri sep′tə kəl), *n.* **1.** a container or holder. **2.** a contact device with a socket installed at an electrical outlet.

re•cep•tion (ri sep′shən), *n.* **1.** the act of receiving or the state of being received. **2.** a manner of being received. **3.** a function or occasion when persons are formally received. **4.** the fidelity of a radio or television broadcast.

re•cep′tion•ist, *n.* a person employed to receive callers in an office.

re•cep′tive, *adj.* **1.** able or quick to receive. **2.** willing or inclined to receive.

re•cep′tor, *n.* a sensory nerve ending or sense organ that is sensitive to stimuli.

re•cess (ri ses′, rē′ses), *n.* **1. a.** a temporary cessation of work or activity; break. **b.** a period of such cessation. **2.** an indentation, as in a coastline. **3. recesses,** a secluded or inner area or part. —*v.t.* **4.** to place in a recess. **5.** to make a recess in. —*v.i.* **6.** to take a recess.

re•ces•sion (ri sesh′ən), *n.* **1.** a period of economic decline. **2.** the act of receding. **3.** a withdrawing procession, as at the end of a religious service. —**re•ces′sion•ar′y,** *adj.*

re•ces′sion•al, *n.* a piece of music played at the end of a religious service.

re•ces′sive, *adj.* **1.** tending to recede; receding. **2.** noting or pertaining to one of a pair of hereditary traits that is masked by the other when both are present in an organism.

re•cher•ché (rə shâr′shā, rə shâr shā′), *adj.* **1.** very rare or choice. **2.** affectedly refined.

re•cid•i•vism (ri sid′ə viz′əm), *n.* repeated or habitual relapse, as into crime. —**re•cid′i•vist,** *n.*, *adj.*

rec•i•pe (res′ə pē), *n.*, *pl.* **-pes. 1.** a set of instructions for preparing food or drink. **2.** a method for attaining a desired end.

re•cip•i•ent (ri sip′ē ənt), *n.* one that receives.

re•cip•ro•cal (ri sip′rə kəl), *adj.* **1.** given or felt by each toward the other; mutual. **2.** given or felt in return. **3.** inversely related; opposite. —*n.* **4.** one that is reciprocal to another. **5.** *Math.* the ratio of unity to a given quantity or expression. —**re•cip′ro•cal•ly,** *adv.*

re•cip′ro•cate′ (-kāt′), *v.t.*, *v.i.*, **-cat•ed, -cat•ing. 1.** to give or feel in return. **2.** to give and receive reciprocally; interchange. **3.** to move alternately backward and forward. —**re•cip′ro•ca′tion,** *n.*

rec•i•proc•i•ty (res′ə pros′i tē), *n.*, *pl.* **-ties. 1.** a reciprocal state or relation. **2.** a trade policy between countries by which corresponding advantages or privileges are granted by each country.

re•cit•al (ri sīt′l), *n.* **1.** a musical or dance performance, esp. by one artist. **2.** a public demonstration of progress by dance or music students. **3.** an act or instance of reciting, esp. from memory. **4.** a detailed statement or account. —**re•cit′al•ist,** *n.*

rec•i•ta•tion (res′i tā′shən), *n.* **1.** the act of reciting. **2.** a formal or public reciting of something from memory. **3.** oral response by pupils on a prepared lesson.

rec•i•ta•tive (res′i tə tēv′), *n.* a style of vocal music intermediate between speaking and singing.

re•cite (ri sīt′), *v.t.*, *v.i.*, **-cit•ed, -cit•ing. 1.** to repeat (something) exactly, esp. from memory and before an audience. **2.** to narrate (something) in detail. **3.** to answer a teacher's questions on (a lesson).

reck•less (rek′lis), *adj.* heedless of danger or consequences; rash; careless. —**reck′less•ly,** *adv.* —**reck′less•ness,** *n.*

reck•on (rek′ən), *v.t.* **1.** to compute or calculate. **2.** to regard as; deem. **3.** *Chiefly Dial.* to think or suppose. —*v.i.* **4.** to make a computation. **5.** to depend or rely. **6. reckon with,** to consider.

---

re′con•firm′, *v.t.*
re′con•fir•ma′tion, *n.*
re′con•nect′, *v.t.*
re′con•sol′i•date′, *v.*, -dat•ed, -dat•ing.
re′con•vene′, *v.*, -vened, -ven•ing.
re•dec′o•rate′, *v.*, -rat•ed, -rat•ing.
re•ded′i•cate′, *v.t.*, -cat•ed, -cat•ing.
re′de•fine′, *v.t.*, -fined, -fin•ing.
re′de•liv′er, *v.t.*
re′de•sign′, *v.*

re′de•vel′op, *v.*
re′di•rect′, *v.t.*
re′dis•cov′er, *v.t.*
re′dis•trib′ute, *v.t.*, -ut•ed, -ut•ing.
re′di•vide′, *v.*, -vid•ed, -vid•ing.
re•do′, *v.t.*, -did, -done, -do•ing.
re•dou′ble, *v.*, -bled, -bling.
re′draft′, *v.t.*
re′e•lect′, *v.t.*
re′e•lec′tion, *n.*
re′en•act′, *v.t.*
re′en•act′ment, *n.*

re′en•list′, *v.t.*
re′en•list′ment, *n.*
re•en′ter, *v.*
re′es•tab′lish, *v.t.*
re′es•tab′lish•ment, *n.*
re′e•val′u•ate′, *v.t.*, -at•ed, -at•ing.
re′ex•am′ine, *v.t.*, -ined, -in•ing.
re•fas′ten, *v.t.*
re′fi•nance′, *v.t.*, -nanced, -nanc•ing.
re•fin′ish, *v.t.*
re•fire′, *v.*, -fired, -fir•ing.

reck'on•ing, *n.* **1.** count; computation. **2.** a settlement of accounts.

re•claim (ri klām'), *v.t.* **1.** to bring (land) into a condition for cultivation or other use. **2.** to recover (substances) in a pure or usable form from refuse or waste. **3.** to bring back to a more wholesome way of life; reform. —**rec•la•ma•tion** (rek'lə mā'shən), *n.*

re•cline (ri klīn'), *v.i., v.t.,* **-clined, -clin•ing.** to lean or cause to lean back; lie or lay.

re•clin'er, *n.* an easy chair with an adjustable back and footrest.

rec•luse (rek'lōōs, ri klōōs'), *n.* a person who lives in seclusion or apart from society. —**re•clu'sive,** *adj.*

rec•og•ni•tion (rek'əg nish'ən), *n.* **1.** the act of recognizing or state of being recognized. **2.** acknowledgment, as of achievement. **3.** formal acknowledgment, esp. of the existence of a state or government. **4.** the automated conversion of words or images into a form that can be processed by a computer.

re•cog•ni•zance (ri kog'nə zəns, -kon'ə-), *n.* an obligation of record that binds a person to do something, as to appear for trial.

rec•og•nize (rek'əg nīz'), *v.t.,* **-nized, -niz•ing. 1.** to identify as previously seen or known. **2.** to identify from knowledge of appearance or characteristics: *to recognize a swindler.* **3.** to perceive or acknowledge as existing, true, or valid. **4.** to acknowledge as being entitled to speak. **5.** to acknowledge as entitled to treatment as a political unit. **6.** to show appreciation of. —**rec'og•niz'a•ble,** *adj.*

re•coil (*v.* ri koil'; *n.* rē'koil', ri koil'), *v.i.* **1.** to shrink back, as in horror or disgust. **2.** to spring or fly back, as a firearm when discharged. —*n.* **3.** an act or instance of recoiling.

rec•ol•lect (rek'ə lekt'), *v.t., v.i.* to remember; recall. —**rec'ol•lec'tion,** *n.*

re•com•bi•nant DNA (rē kom'bə nənt), *n.* DNA in which segments have been inserted by laboratory manipulation from a different molecule or from another part of the same molecule.

rec•om•mend (rek'ə mend'), *v.t.* **1.** to present as worthy of confidence, acceptance, or use. **2.** to urge or suggest as appropriate or beneficial. **3.** to make desirable or attractive. —**rec'om•mend'a•ble,** *adj.* **rec'om•men•da'tion,** *n.*

rec•om•pense (rek'əm pens'), *v.,* **-pensed, -pens•ing,** *n.* —*v.t.* **1.** to make payment to, as for work done. **2.** to make restitution for; compensate. —*n.* **3.** a repayment, requital, or reward. **4.** compensation; reparation.

rec•on•cile (rek'ən sīl'), *v.t.,* **-ciled, -cil•ing. 1.** to cause to accept something not desired. **2.** to cause to become friendly again. **3.** to settle (a quarrel, dispute, etc.). **4.** to make compatible or consistent: *reconciled her bank statement.* —**rec'on•cil'a•ble,** *adj.* —**rec'on•cil'i•a'tion** (-sil'ē ā'shən), *n.*

rec•on•dite (rek'ən dīt'), *adj.* **1.** very profound, difficult, or abstruse. **2.** known by relatively few; esoteric.

re•con•nais•sance (ri kon'ə səns, -zəns), *n.* a general survey of a region, esp. in order to gain information for military purposes.

re•con•noi•ter (rē'kə noi'tər, rek'ə-), *v.t., v.i.* to make a reconnaissance (of).

re'con•sid'er, *v.t., v.i.* to consider again, esp. with a view to a change of decision or action. —**re'con•sid'er•a'tion,** *n.*

re•con'sti•tute', *v.t.,* **-tut•ed, -tut•ing. 1.** to constitute again. **2.** to return (a dehydrated or concentrated food) to the liquid state by adding water.

re'con•struct', *v.t.* to construct again; rebuild.

re'con•struc'tion, *n.* **1.** the act of reconstructing. **2.** (*cap.*) the period during which the seceded states were reorganized as part of the Union after the Civil War.

re•cord (*v.* ri kôrd'; *n., adj.* rek'ərd), *v.t.* **1.** to set down, esp. in writing, for the purpose of preserving. **2.** to register or indicate. **3.** to register (sound or images) on a disk or tape for reproduction. —*n.* **rec•ord 4.** an account of facts or events preserved esp. in writing. **5.** information or knowledge about a person's achievements or performance. **6.** something, as a disk, on which sound or images have been recorded. **7.** standing with respect to contests won, lost, and tied. **8.** the best performance of its kind to date. —*adj.* **rec•ord 9.** surpassing all others. —*Idiom.* **10. off the record,** not for publication. **11. on record,** having stated one's position publicly.

re•cord'er, *n.* **1.** a person who records, esp. as an official duty. **2.** a recording apparatus or device. **3.** a flute with a mouthpiece like a whistle and eight finger holes.

re•cord'ing, *n.* **1.** sound recorded on a disk or tape. **2.** a disk or tape on which something is recorded.

rec'ord play'er, *n.* PHONOGRAPH.

re-count (*v.* rē kount'; *n.* rē'kount', rē kount'), *v.t.* **1.** to count again. —*n.* **2.** a second or additional count.

re•count (ri kount'), *v.t.* to tell in detail; relate.

re•coup (ri kōōp'), *v.t.* **1.** to get back the equivalent of. **2.** to regain; recover.

re•course (rē'kôrs, ri kôrs'), *n.* **1.** a resorting to a person or thing for help or protection. **2.** a source of help or protection.

re•cov•er (ri kuv'ər), *v.t.* **1.** to get back; regain. **2.** to make up for. **3.** to regain the strength, composure, or balance of (oneself). **4.** to regain (a substance) in usable form; reclaim. —*v.i.* **5.** to regain health, strength, composure, or balance. **6.** to obtain a favorable judgment in a lawsuit. —**re•cov'er•a•ble,** *adj.* —**re•cov'er•y,** *n., pl.* **-er•ies.**

rec•re•ant (rek'rē ənt), *adj.* **1.** cowardly. **2.** unfaithful; disloyal. —*n.* **3.** a cowardly or disloyal person.

re-cre•ate (rē'krē āt'), *v.t.* **-at•ed, -at•ing.** to create anew.

rec•re•ate (rek'rē āt'), *v.t.,* **-at•ed, -at•ing.** to refresh physically or mentally.

rec•re•a•tion (rek'rē ā'shən), *n.* **1.** mental or physical refreshment after work, as by means of a pastime. **2.** a means of enjoyable relaxation. —**rec're•a'tion•al,** *adj.*

re•crim•i•nate (ri krim'ə nāt'), *v.t.,* **-nat•ed, -nat•ing.** to bring a countercharge against (an accuser). —**re•crim'i•na'tion,** *n.*

re•cru•des•cence (rē'krōō des'əns), *n.* a breaking out again after inactivity. —**re'cru•des'cent,** *adj.*

re•cruit (ri krōōt'), *n.* **1.** a new member, esp. a newly enlisted or drafted member of the armed forces. —*v.t.* **2.** to enlist for military service. **3.** to supply (an armed force) with new members. **4.** to seek to hire, enroll, or enlist: *to recruit executives.* —*v.i.* **5.** to enlist new members. —**re•cruit'er,** *n.* —**re•cruit'ment,** *n.*

---

re•flow', *v.i.*
re•for'mu•late', *v.t.,* **-lat•ed, -lat•ing.**
re•fu'el, *v.*
re•heat', *v.*
re•hire', *v.t.,* **-hired, -hir•ing.**
re•ig•nite', *v.t.,* **-nit•ed, -nit•ing.**
re'in•fu'sion, *n.*
re'in•sert', *v.t.*
re'in•ser'tion, *n.*
re'in•spect', *v.t.*

re'in•ter'pret, *v.*
re'in•tro•duce', *v.t.,* **-duced, -duc•ing.**
re'in•vent', *v.t.*
re'in•vest', *v.t.*
re'in•ves'ti•gate', *v.,* **-gat•ed, -gat•ing.**
re'in•vest'ment, *n.*
re•kin'dle, *v.,* **-dled, -dling.**
re•load', *v.*
re'make', *v.t.,* **-made, -mak•ing.**
re'make', *n.*

re•mar'riage, *n.*
re•mar'ry, *v.,* **-ried, -ry•ing.**
re•name', *v.t.,* **-named, -nam•ing.**
re•ne'go•ti•ate', *v.,* **-at•ed, -at•ing.**
re'no•ti•fi•ca'tion, *n.*
re•num'ber, *v.t.*
re•oc'cu•py', *v.t.,* **-pied, -py•ing.**
re'oc•cur', *v.i.,* **-curred, -cur•ring.**
re'oc•cur'rence, *n.*
re•o'pen, *v.*
re•or'der, *v.t., v.i.*
re•pack'age, *v.t.,* **-aged, -ag•ing.**

rec·tal (rek/tl), *adj.* of or for the rectum. —**rec/tal·ly,** *adv.*

rec·tan·gle (rek/tang/gəl), *n.* a parallelogram with four right angles. —**rec·tan/gu·lar** (-tang/gyə lər), *adj.*

rec·ti·fy (rek/tə fī/), *v.t.,* **-fied, -fy·ing. 1.** to set right; correct. **2.** to change (alternating current) into direct current. —**rec·ti·fi/a·ble,** *adj.* —**rec/ti·fi·ca/tion,** *n.* —**rec/ti·fi/er,** *n.*

rec·ti·lin·e·ar (rek/tl in/ē ər), *adj.* **1.** forming or moving in a straight line. **2.** characterized by straight lines.

rec·ti·tude (rek/ti tōōd/, -tyōōd/), *n.* **1.** moral virtue; righteousness. **2.** correctness.

rec·to (rek/tō), *n., pl.* **-tos.** a right-hand page of an open book.

rec·tor (rek/tər), *n.* **1.** a member of the clergy in charge of a parish. **2.** the head of certain universities, colleges, or schools.

rec/to·ry, *n., pl.* **-ries.** a rector's house; parsonage.

rec·tum (rek/təm), *n., pl.* **-tums, -ta** (-tə). the terminal section of the large intestine, ending in the anus.

re·cum·bent (ri kum/bənt), *adj.* lying down.

re·cu·per·ate (ri kōō/pə rāt/, -kyōō/-), *v.,* **-at·ed, -at·ing.** —*v.i.* **1.** to regain health or strength. —*v.t.* **2.** to get back; recover. —**re·cu/per·a/tion,** *n.* —**re·cu/per·a/tive,** *adj.*

re·cur (ri kûr/), *v.i.,* **-curred, -cur·ring. 1.** to occur again, as an event. **2.** to return to the mind. —**re·cur/rence,** *n.* —**re·cur/rent,** *adj.* —**re·cur/rent·ly,** *adv.*

re·cy·cle (rē sī/kəl), *v.t.,* **-cled, -cling. 1.** to treat or process (used or waste materials) so as to make suitable for reuse. **2.** to use again with minimal alteration. **3.** to cause to pass through a cycle again. —**re·cy/cla·ble,** *adj.*

red (red), *n., adj.,* **red·der, red·dest.** —*n.* **1.** any of various colors resembling the color of blood. **2.** (*often cap.*) a radical leftist in politics, esp. a communist. —*adj.* **3.** of the color red. **4.** (*often cap.*) radically left politically, esp. communist. —**Idiom. 5. in the red,** being in debt. —**red/dish,** *adj.* —**red/ness,** *n.*

re·dact (ri dakt/), *v.t.* to edit. —**re·dac/tion,** *n.* —**re·dac/tor,** *n.*

red/ blood/ cell/, *n.* any of the blood cells that contain hemoglobin and carry oxygen to the cells and tissues.

red/-blood/ed, *adj.* vigorous; virile.

red/cap/, *n.* a baggage porter, as at a railroad station.

red/ car/pet, *n.* a display of courtesy, as that shown to persons of high station. —**red/-car/pet,** *adj.*

red/coat/, *n.* a British soldier, esp. during the American Revolution.

Red/ Cross/, *n.* an international organization to care for victims of war or disasters.

red/ deer/, *n.* a deer of Europe and Asia with a reddish brown summer coat.

red/den, *v.t., v.i.* to make or become red.

re·deem (ri dēm/), *v.t.* **1.** to pay off, as a mortgage. **2.** to recover (something pawned or mortgaged) by payment. **3.** to exchange (bonds, coupons, etc.) for money or goods. **4.** to fulfill (a pledge, promise, etc.). **5.** to make up for. **6.** to set free or save, as a sinner. —**re·deem/a·ble,** *adj.*

re·deem·er (ri dē/mər), *n.* **1.** a person who redeems. **2.** (*cap.*) Jesus Christ.

re·demp/tion (-demp/shən), *n.* the act of redeeming or state of being redeemed. —**re·demp/tive,** *adj.*

red/-hand/ed, *adj., adv.* in the very act of wrongdoing. —**red/-hand/ed·ly,** *adv.*

red/head/, *n.* a person with red hair. —**red/head/ed,** *adj.*

red/ her/ring, *n.* something intended to divert attention from the real problem or matter at hand.

red/-hot/, *adj.* **1.** red with heat. **2.** violent; furious. **3.** very fresh or new.

re·dis·trict (rē dis/trikt), *v.t.* to divide anew into districts, esp. for electoral purposes.

red/-let/ter, *adj.* of special importance; memorable.

red/lin/ing, *n.* a discriminatory practice in which mortgages or insurance are withheld in areas considered to be deteriorating. [as if such areas had been outlined in red on a map] —**red/line/,** *v.t.,* **-lined, -lin·ing.**

red·o·lent (red/l ənt), *adj.* **1.** having a pleasant odor. **2.** having a particular odor: *redolent of garlic.* **3.** suggestive; reminiscent. —**red/o·lence,** *n.*

re·doubt (ri dout/), *n.* an earthwork inside or outside a larger fortification.

re·doubt/a·ble, *adj.* **1.** evoking fear; formidable. **2.** commanding respect. —**re·doubt/a·bly,** *adv.*

re·dound (ri dound/), *v.i.* **1.** to have a good or bad effect. **2.** to result or accrue.

red/ pep/per, *n.* **1.** CAYENNE. **2.** the mild, ripe fruit of the sweet pepper.

re·dress (*n.* rē/dres, ri dres/; *v.* ri dres/), *n.* **1.** the setting right of what is wrong. **2.** relief from wrong. **3.** compensation for wrong. —*v.t.* **4.** to set right; remedy. **5.** to compensate.

Red/ Sea/, *n.* an arm of the Indian Ocean, extending NW between Africa and Arabia.

red/ snap/per, *n.* a large food fish of the Gulf of Mexico.

red/ tape/, *n.* bureaucratic routine that delays or prevents action.

red/ tide/, *n.* a brownish red discoloration of marine waters caused by an aggregation of flagellates lethal to shellfish.

re·duce (ri dōōs/, -dyōōs/), *v.,* **-duced, -duc·ing.** —*v.t.* **1.** to bring down, as to a smaller size or amount. **2.** to lower, as in degree or intensity. **3.** to demote to a lower rank or authority. **4.** to treat analytically. **5.** to act destructively upon. **6.** to bring to a certain state. **7.** to change the denomination or form but not the value of (a fraction, polynomial, etc.). —*v.i.* **8.** to become reduced. **9.** to lose weight, as by dieting. —**re·duc/er,** *n.* —**re·duc/tive** (-duk/tiv), *adj.*

re·duc/tion (-duk/shən), *n.* **1.** the act of reducing or state of being reduced. **2.** the amount by which something is reduced. **3.** something produced by reducing.

re·dun·dant (ri dun/dənt), *adj.* **1.** characterized by unnecessary repetition; wordy. **2.** exceeding what is usual or necessary. —**re·dun/dan·cy,** *n., pl.* **-cies.**

red/wood/, *n.* **1.** a coniferous tree native to California and noted for its great height. **2.** its brownish red timber.

reed (rēd), *n.* **1. a.** the straight stalk of any of various tall marsh grasses. **b.** any of the plants themselves. **2. a.** a flexible piece of cane, wood, metal, or

---

re·paint/, *v.t.*

re·pave/, *v.t.,* **-paved, -pav·ing.**

re·phrase/, *v.t.,* **-phrased, -phras·ing.**

re·pop·u·late/, *v.t.,* **-lat·ed, -lat·ing.**

re·pub/lish, *v.t.*

re·read/, *v.,* **-read, -read·ing.**

re·route/, *v.,* **-rout·ed, -rout·ing.**

re·sched/ule, *v.t.,* **-uled, -ul·ing.**

re·seal/a·ble, *adj.*

re·set/tle, *v.,* **-tled, -tling.**

re·set/tle·ment, *n.*

re·stage/, *v.t.,* **-staged, -stag·ing.**

re·start/, *v.*

re·stock/, *v.*

re·string/, *v.t.,* **-strung, -string·ing.**

re·struc/ture, *v.,* **-tured, -tur·ing.**

re·sub·mit/, *v.,* **-mit·ted, -mit·ting.**

re·sup·ply/, *v.t.,* **-plied, -ply·ing.**

re·sur/face, *v.t.,* **-faced, -fac·ing.**

re·tell/, *v.,* **-told, -tell·ing.**

re·think/, *v.t.,* **-thought, -think·ing.**

re·train/, *v.*

re·trans·late/, *v.t.,* **-lat·ed, -lat·ing.**

re·u·ni·fi·ca/tion, *n.*

re·u/ni·fy/, *v.t.,* **-fied, -fy·ing.**

re·u·nite/, *v.,* **-nited, -nit·ing.**

re·us/a·ble, *adj.*

re·use/, *v.,* **-used, -us·ing,** *n.*

re·val/u·a/tion, *n.*

re·vis/it, *v.t.*

re·wind/, *v.t.,* **-wound, -wind·ing.**

re·wire/, *v.t.,* **-wired, -wir·ing.**

re·work/, *v.,* **-worked or -wrought, -work·ing.**

plastic attached to the mouth of various wind instruments and set into vibration to produce a tone. **b.** a wind instrument played with a reed. **3.** an ancient unit of length, equal to 6 cubits. Ezek. 40:5. —**reed′y,** *adj.,* -**i•er,** -**i•est.** —**reed′i•ness,** *n.*

Reed (rēd), *n.* **Walter C.,** 1851–1902, U.S. army surgeon.

reef[1] (rēf), *n.* a ridge of rocks, sand, or coral at or near the surface of the water.

reef[2] (rēf), *n.* **1.** a part of a sail that is rolled and tied down to reduce the area exposed to the wind. —*v.t.* **2.** to shorten (a sail) by tying in one or more reefs.

reek (rēk), *v.i.* **1.** to smell strongly and unpleasantly. **2.** to be strongly pervaded with something unpleasant. —*v.t.* **3.** to give off; emit. —*n.* **4.** a strong, unpleasant smell.

reel[1] (rēl), *n.* **1.** a device, as a cylinder, that turns on an axis and is used to wind up or let out wire, rope, or film. **2.** a quantity of something wound on a reel. —*v.t.* **3.** to wind on a reel. **4.** to pull by winding a line on a reel: *to reel in a fish.* **5. reel off,** to say or write fluently and quickly.

reel[2] (rēl), *v.i.* **1.** to sway or fall back from or as if from a blow. **2.** to sway in standing or walking. **3.** to whirl. **4.** to have a sensation of whirling. —*n.* **5.** a reeling movement.

reel[3] (rēl), *n.* a lively Scottish dance.

re•en•try (rē en′trē), *n., pl.* -**tries.** **1.** a second entry. **2.** the return into the earth's atmosphere of a satellite, spacecraft, or rocket.

ref (ref), *n., v.t., v.i.,* **reffed, ref•fing.** REFEREE.

re•face (rē fās′), *v.t.,* -**faced,** -**fac•ing.** to renew, restore, or repair the face or surface of.

re•fec•tion (ri fek′shən), *n.* **1.** the fact of being refreshed, esp. with food or drink. **2.** food and drink; repast.

re•fec′to•ry (-tə rē), *n., pl.* -**ries.** a dining hall, esp. in a monastery.

re•fer (ri fûr′), *v.,* -**ferred,** -**fer•ring.** —*v.t.* **1.** to direct a person or place, as for information or aid. **2.** to direct the attention of. **3.** to submit for decision, consideration, etc. —*v.i.* **4.** to direct attention. **5.** to have recourse, as for information. **6.** to make reference or allusion. —**re•fer′rer,** *n.*

ref•er•ee (ref′ə rē′), *n., pl.* -**ees,** *v.,* -**eed,** -**ee•ing.** —*n.* **1.** a person to whom something is referred for decision or settlement. **2.** a judge in certain games and sports; umpire. —*v.t., v.i.* **3.** to preside over or act as referee.

ref•er•ence (ref′ər əns), *n.* **1.** the act of referring. **2.** mention or allusion. **3.** a direction of the attention, as in a book, to another book or passage. **4.** use or recourse for purposes of information. **5.** a source of facts or information. **6. a.** a person to whom one can refer for testimony as to another's character or abilities. **b.** a statement regarding a person's character or abilities. **7.** regard or relation: *without reference to age.*

ref•er•en•dum (ref′ə ren′dəm), *n., pl.* -**dums,** -**da** (-də). **1.** the practice of referring legislative measures to the vote of the electorate for approval or rejection. **2.** a vote on a measure thus referred.

ref•er•ent (ref′ər ənt), *n.* the object or event to which a term or symbol refers.

re•fer•ral (ri fûr′əl), *n.* **1.** an act or instance of referring. **2.** a person referred to someone or for something.

re•fill (*v.* rē fil′; *n.* rē′fil′), *v.t., v.i.* **1.** to fill again. —*n.* **2.** a material or supply to replace something used up. —**re•fill′a•ble,** *adj.*

re•fine (ri fīn′), *v.t., v.i.,* -**fined,** -**fin•ing.** **1.** to bring or come to a pure state; purify. **2.** to make or become more elegant or polished. —**re•fin′er,** *n.*

re•fined′, *adj.* **1.** having or showing good breeding; cultured. **2.** freed from impurities. **3.** very subtle.

re•fine′ment, *n.* **1.** fineness or elegance of feeling, taste, or manners. **2.** the act of refining or state of being refined. **3.** the quality or state of being refined. **4.** a subtle distinction. **5.** an improvement.

re•fin′er•y, *n., pl.* -**er•ies.** an establishment for refining something, as sugar or petroleum.

re•flect (ri flekt′), *v.t.* **1.** to cast back (light, sound, etc.) from a surface. **2.** to give back an image of. **3.** to cast or bring (credit, discredit, etc.). —*v.i.* **4.** to be cast back, as light. **5.** to ponder or meditate. **6.** to bring reproach or discredit. **7.** to give a particular aspect or impression. —**re•flec′tive,** *adj.* —**re•flec′-tive•ly,** *adv.*

re•flec′tion, *n.* **1.** the act of reflecting or state of being reflected. **2.** something reflected. **3.** careful thought or consideration. **4.** an unfavorable remark or observation; reproach.

re•flec′tor, *n.* **1.** one that reflects. **2.** a body, surface, or device that reflects light, heat, or sound.

re•flex (rē′fleks), *adj.* **1.** of or caused by an involuntary response to a stimulus. **2.** bent or turned back. —*n.* **3.** movement caused by a reflex response.

re•flex•ive (ri flek′siv), *adj.* **1. a.** (of a verb) taking a subject and object with identical referents, as *cut* in *I cut myself.* **b.** (of a pronoun) used as an object with the same referent as the subject of a verb, as *myself* in *I cut myself.* —*n.* **2.** a reflexive verb or pronoun. —**re•flex′ive•ly,** *adv.*

re•for•est (rē fôr′ist, -for′-), *v.t., v.i.* to replant trees on (land denuded by cutting, fire, etc.). —**re′for•est•a′tion,** *n.*

re-form (rē fôrm′), *v.t., v.i.* to form again.

re•form (ri fôrm′), *v.t.* **1.** the improvement of what is wrong, corrupt, or unsatisfactory. **2.** improvement, as of conduct or belief. —*v.t.* **3.** to change to a better state or form. **4.** to cause to abandon wrong or evil ways of life or conduct. —*v.i.* **5.** to abandon evil conduct or error.

ref•or•ma•tion (ref′ər mā′shən), *n.* **1.** the act of reforming or state of being reformed. **2.** (*cap.*) the 16th-century movement that resulted in the establishment of the Protestant churches.

re•form•a•to•ry (ri fôr′mə tôr′ē), *adj., n., pl.* -**ries.** —*adj.* **1.** serving or designed to reform. —*n.* **2.** Also called **reform′ school′.** a penal institution for reforming young offenders, esp. minors.

re•formed (ri fôrmd′), *adj.* **1.** amended or improved. **2.** (*cap.*) pertaining to Protestant churches, esp. Calvinist as distinguished from Lutheran. —**re•form′ed•ly,** *adv.*

re•form′er, *n.* a person devoted to bringing about reform, as in politics.

re•fract (ri frakt′), *v.t.* to subject to refraction.

re•frac′tion, *n.* the change of direction of a ray, as of light, in passing obliquely from one medium into another in which its wave velocity is different. —**re•frac′tive,** *adj.*

re•frac•to•ry (ri frak′tə rē), *adj.* **1.** difficult to manage; stubbornly disobedient. **2.** difficult to fuse, reduce, or work, as an ore.

re•frain[1] (ri frān′), *v.i.* to keep oneself from doing or saying something.

re•frain[2] (ri frān′), *n.* a phrase or verse recurring at intervals in a song or poem.

re•fresh (ri fresh′), *v.t.* **1.** to provide new vigor and energy to, as by rest. **2.** to stimulate (the memory). **3.** to freshen, as in appearance. —*v.i.* **4.** to become fresh again; revive. —**re•fresh′er,** *n.* —**re•fresh′-ing,** *adj.*

re•fresh′ment, *n.* **1.** something that refreshes. **2. refreshments,** food and drink, esp. for a light meal. **3.** the act of refreshing or state of being refreshed.

re•frig•er•ate (ri frij′ə rāt′), *v.t.,* -**at•ed,** -**at•ing.** to make or keep cold or cool, esp. for preservation. —**re•frig′er•ant,** *adj., n.* —**re•frig′er•a′tion,** *n.*

re•frig′er•a′tor, *n.* a cabinet or room in which food and drink are kept cool by refrigeration.

ref•uge (ref′yōōj), *n.* **1.** shelter from danger or trouble. **2.** a place of shelter or safety.

ref•u•gee (ref′yōō jē′, ref′yōō jē′), *n., pl.* -**gees.** a person who flees for refuge, as in time of political upheaval or war.

re•ful•gent (ri ful′jənt), *adj.* shining brightly; radiant. —**re•ful′gence,** *n.*

re•fund (*v.* ri fund′, rē′fund; *n.* rē′fund), *v.t.* **1.** to give back or restore (esp. money); repay. —*n.* **2.** the act of refunding. **3.** an amount refunded. —**re•fund′a•ble,** *adj.*

re•fur•bish (rē fûr′bish), *v.t.* to furbish again; renovate. —**re•fur′bish•ment,** *n.*

re•fuse¹ (ri fyōoz′), *v.,* **-fused, -fus•ing.** —*v.t.* **1.** to decline to accept, give, do, or comply. —*v.i.* **2.** to decline acceptance, consent, or compliance. —**re•fus′al,** *n.*

ref•use² (ref′yōos), *n.* something discarded as worthless or useless; rubbish.

re•fute (ri fyōot′), *v.t.,* **-fut•ed, -fut•ing.** to prove to be false or erroneous. —**re•fut′a•ble,** *adj.* —**ref•u•ta•tion** (ref′yōo tā′shən), *n.*

re•gain (rē gān′), *v.t.* **1.** to get again; recover. **2.** to succeed in reaching again.

re•gal (rē′gəl), *adj.* **1.** of, befitting, or resembling a king or queen. **2.** stately; splendid. —**re′gal•ly,** *adv.*

re•gale (ri gāl′), *v.t.,* **-galed, -gal•ing. 1.** to entertain agreeably; divert. **2.** to entertain with choice food or drink. —**re•gale′ment,** *n.*

re•ga•lia (ri gāl′yə), *n.pl.* **1.** the ensigns or emblems of royalty, as the crown and scepter. **2.** the decorations, insignia, or ceremonial clothes of an office or order. **3.** fancy clothing; finery.

re•gard (ri gärd′), *v.t.* **1.** to look at or think of in a particular way; consider. **2.** to have or show respect for. **3.** to think highly of; esteem. **4.** to relate to; concern. —*n.* **5.** reference; relation. **6.** an aspect, point, or particular. **7.** thought or attention. **8.** respect or esteem. **9. regards,** sentiments of esteem or affection. —*Idiom.* **10. as regards,** concerning; about.

re•gard′ing, *prep.* with regard to; concerning.

re•gard′less, *adj.* **1.** heedless; unmindful. —*adv.* **2.** despite everything; anyway. —*Idiom.* **3. regardless of,** in spite of.

re•gat•ta (ri gat′ə, -gä′tə), *n.,* *pl.* **-tas. 1.** a boat race, as of yachts. **2.** an organized series of such races.

re•gen•cy (rē′jən sē), *n.,* *pl.* **-cies. 1.** the office, jurisdiction, or control of a regent or regents. **2.** a body of regents. **3.** the term of office of a regent.

re•gen•er•ate (*v.* ri jen′ə rāt′; *adj.* -ər it), *v.,* **-at•ed, -at•ing,** *adj.* —*v.t.* **1.** to effect a complete moral or spiritual reform in. **2.** to make over, esp. in a better form. **3.** to bring into existence again. **4.** to restore (a body part) by the growth of new tissue. —*v.i.* **5.** to be formed again. **6.** to become spiritually renewed. —*adj.* **7.** made over; reconstituted. **8.** born again spiritually. —**re•gen′er•a•cy** (-ər ə sē), *n.* —**re•gen′er•a′tion,** *n.* —**re•gen′er•a′tive,** *adj.*

re•gent (rē′jənt), *n.* **1.** a person who rules a kingdom during the minority, absence, or disability of the sovereign. **2.** a member of a governing board, as of a state educational system.

reg•gae (reg′ā), *n.* a style of Jamaican music blending blues, calypso, and rock.

reg•i•cide (rej′ə sīd′), *n.* **1.** the killing of a king. **2.** a person who kills a king.

re•gime or **ré•gime** (rə zhēm′, rā-), *n.* **1.** a mode or system of government. **2.** a government in power. **3.** REGIMEN (def. 1).

reg•i•men (rej′ə mən), *n.* **1.** a regulated course, as of diet or exercise, to preserve or restore health. **2.** government or rule. [< L: rule]

reg•i•ment (*n.* rej′ə mənt; *v.* -ment′), *n.* **1.** a military unit of ground forces consisting of two or more battalions. —*v.t.* **2.** to subject to strict discipline. **3.** to organize, usu. for the purpose of rigid or complete control. —**reg′i•men′tal,** *adj.* —**reg′i•men•ta′tion,** *n.*

Re•gi•na (ri jī′nə), *n.* the capital of Saskatchewan, in S Canada. 175,064.

re•gion (rē′jən), *n.* **1.** an often extensive, continuous part of a surface, space, or body; area. **2.** a part of the body: *the abdominal region.* —**re′gion•al,** *adj.* —**re′gion•al•ly,** *adv.*

re′gion•al•ism, *n.* a feature, as a speech form, that is peculiar to or characteristic of a geographical region.

reg•is•ter (rej′ə stər), *n.* **1. a.** a book in which records, as of events, are kept. **b.** a list or record of

such items. **2.** a mechanical device by which certain data are automatically recorded. **3.** CASH REGISTER. **4.** the range of a voice or an instrument. **5.** a device for controlling the flow of warmed or cooled air through an opening. —*v.t.* **6.** to enter in a register. **7.** to cause (mail) to be recorded at a post office as a safeguard against loss. **8.** to enroll (a student, voter, etc.). **9.** to indicate on or as if on a scale. **10.** to show (an emotion). —*v.i.* **11.** to enter one's name in a register. **12.** to show: *A smile registered on her face.* **13.** to make an impression. —**reg′is•trant,** *n.*

reg′istered nurse′, *n.* a graduate nurse who has passed a state board examination and been licensed to practice.

reg′is•trar (-strär′), *n.* a person who keeps records, as at a school or college.

reg′is•tra′tion, *n.* **1.** the act of registering. **2.** the group or number registered. **3.** a certificate attesting to the fact that someone or something has been registered.

reg′is•try, *n.,* *pl.* **-tries. 1.** registration. **2.** an office of registration. **3.** an official record; register. **4.** the state of being registered.

reg•nant (reg′nənt), *adj.* **1.** reigning; ruling. **2.** exercising authority. **3.** prevalent; widespread.

re•gress (*v.* ri gres′; *n.* rē′gres), *v.i.* **1.** to move backward. **2.** to revert to an earlier or less advanced state or form. —*n.* **3.** the act of regressing. —**re•gres′sive,** *adj.*

re•gres•sion (ri gresh′ən), *n.* **1.** the act of regressing. **2.** *Psychoanalysis.* reversion to an earlier, less adaptive emotional state or behavior pattern.

re•gret (ri gret′), *v.,* **-gret•ted, -gret•ting,** *n.* —*v.t.* **1.** to feel sorrow or remorse for. **2.** to think of with a sense of loss. —*n.* **3.** a sense of loss. **4.** a feeling of sorrow or remorse, as for a fault. **5. regrets,** a polite, usu. formal refusal of an invitation. —**re•gret′ful,** *adj.* —**re•gret′ta•ble,** *adj.*

re•group (rē grōop′), *v.t., v.i.* to form into a new or restructured group.

reg•u•lar (reg′yə lər), *adj.* **1.** usual; customary. **2.** evenly or uniformly arranged. **3.** characterized by fixed principle or procedure. **4.** recurring at fixed intervals. **5.** adhering to a rule or procedure; methodical. **6.** habitual or long-standing: *a regular user.* **7.** legitimate or proper: *a regular doctor.* **8.** *Informal.* **a.** decent; nice: *a regular guy.* **b.** absolute; thoroughgoing: *a regular rascal.* **9.** conforming to the most prevalent pattern of formation or inflection in a language: *a regular verb.* **10.** *Math.* having all sides and angles equal. **11.** of or belonging to the standing army of a state. **12.** belonging to a religious or monastic order. —*n.* **13.** a long-standing or habitual customer or client. **14.** a professional soldier. **15.** a faithful party member. **16.** an athlete who plays in most games, usu. from the start. —**reg′u•lar′i•ty,** *n.* —**reg′u•lar•ize′,** *v.t.,* **-ized, -iz•ing.** —**reg′u•lar•ly,** *adv.*

reg′u•late′ (-lāt′), *v.t.,* **-lat•ed, -lat•ing. 1.** to control or direct by a rule, principle, or method. **2.** to adjust in accordance with a standard or requirement. **3.** to adjust so as to ensure accuracy of operation. **4.** to put in good order. —**reg′u•la′tive, reg′u•la•to′ry** (-lə tôr′ē), *adj.* —**reg′u•la′tor,** *n.*

reg′u•la′tion, *n.* **1.** a law or rule, esp. to regulate conduct. **2.** the act of regulating or state of being regulated. —*adj.* **3.** prescribed by or conforming to regulation.

re•gur•gi•tate (ri gûr′ji tāt′), *v.i., v.t.,* **-tat•ed, -tat•ing. 1.** to rush or cause to rush back. **2.** to vomit. —**re•gur′gi•ta′tion,** *n.*

re•hab (rē′hab′), *n., v.,* **-habbed, -hab•bing.** —*n.* **1.** rehabilitation. **2.** a rehabilitated building. —*v.t.* **3.** to rehabilitate.

re•ha•bil•i•tate (rē′hə bil′i tāt′, rē′ə-), *v.t.,* **-tat•ed, -tat•ing. 1.** to restore to a condition of good health, ability to work, etc. **2.** to restore to good condition, operation, or management. **3.** to restore to former rank, rights, or privileges. —**re′ha•bil′i•ta′tion,** *n.* —**re′ha•bil′i•ta′tive,** *adj.*

re•hash (*v.* rē hash′; *n.* rē′hash′), *v.t.* **1.** to rework or reuse in a new form without significant change. —*n.* **2.** the act of rehashing. **3.** something rehashed.

re•hears•al (ri hûr′səl), *n.* **1.** a usu. private practice session in preparation for a public performance. **2.** a repeating or relating: *a rehearsal of grievances.*

re•hearse′, *v.t., v.i.,* -hearsed, -hears•ing. **1.** to practice (a play, musical piece, etc.) before public presentation. **2.** to train by rehearsal. **3.** to relate the facts or particulars (of).

Rehn•quist (ren′kwist), *n.* **William H(ubbs),** born 1924, Chief Justice of the U.S. Supreme Court since 1986.

Re•ho•bo•am (rē′ə bō′əm), *n.* the successor of Solomon and the first king of Judah, reigned 922?–915? B.C. I Kings 11:43.

Re•ho•both (ri hō′both), *n.* a well dug by Isaac. Gen. 26:22.

Reich (rīk, rīкн), *n.* the German state during the period 1871–1945. [< G: kingdom]

reign (rān), *n.* **1.** the period during which a sovereign occupies a throne. **2.** royal rule or authority. —*v.i.* **3.** to exercise sovereign power or authority; rule. **4.** to be prevalent; prevail.

Reign′ of Ter′ror, *n.* **1.** a period of the French Revolution (1793–94) during which many persons were ruthlessly executed by the ruling faction. **2.** (*l.c.*) any period or situation of ruthless oppression or violence.

re•im•burse (rē′im bûrs′), *v.t.,* -bursed, -burs•ing. to pay back; repay. —**re′im•burse′ment,** *n.*

rein (rān), *n.* **1.** Often, **reins.** a leather strap fastened to a bridle and used by a rider or driver to control an animal, esp. a horse. **2.** a means of curbing or controlling. —*v.t.* **3.** to check or guide with or as if with reins. —*Idiom.* **4.** **give (free) rein to,** to give complete freedom to.

re•in•car•na•tion (rē′in kär nā′shən), *n.* rebirth of the soul in a new body. —**re′in•car′nate,** *v.i., v.t.,* -nat•ed, -nat•ing.

rein•deer (rān′dēr′), *n., pl.* -deer, (*occasionally*) -deers. a large deer of arctic regions.

reindeer

re•in•force (rē′in fôrs′), *v.t.,* -forced, -forc•ing. **1.** to strengthen with added support or material. **2.** to strengthen (a military force) with additional personnel or equipment. —**re′in•force′ment,** *n.*

re•in•state (rē′in stāt′), *v.t.,* -stat•ed, -stat•ing. to put back into a former position or state. —**re′in•state′ment,** *n.*

re•it•er•ate (rē it′ə rāt′), *v.t.,* -at•ed, -at•ing. to say or do again or repeatedly. —**re•it′er•a′tion,** *n.* —**re•it′er•a′tive** (-ə rā′tiv, -ər ə tiv), *adj.*

re•ject (*v.* ri jekt′; *n.* rē′jekt), *v.t.* **1.** to refuse to have, take, or use. **2.** to refuse to grant; deny. **3.** to refuse to accept or admit; rebuff. **4.** to discard as useless or unsatisfactory. —*n.* **5.** one that is rejected. —**re•ject′er,** *n.* —**re•jec′tion,** *n.*

re•joice (ri jois′), *v.i., v.t.,* -joiced, -joic•ing. to feel or cause to feel joy; delight. —**re•joic′ing,** *n.*

re•join¹ (rē join′), *v.t., v.i.* to join together again; reunite.

re•join² (ri join′), *v.t.* to say in response; answer.

re•join′der (-dər), *n.* an answer to a reply; response.

re•ju•ve•nate (ri jōō′və nāt′), *v.t.,* -nat•ed, -nat•

ing. to restore to youthful vigor or appearance; make young again. —**re•ju′ve•na′tion,** *n.*

rel., 1. relating. **2.** relative.

re•lapse (*v.* ri laps′; *n. also* rē′laps), *v.,* -lapsed, -laps•ing, *n.* —*v.i.* **1.** to fall back into a former state, esp. into illness after apparent recovery. —*n.* **2.** an act or instance of relapsing.

re•late (ri lāt′), *v.,* -lat•ed, -lat•ing. —*v.t.* **1.** to give an account of; tell. **2.** to connect in thought or meaning. —*v.i.* **3.** to have reference or relation. **4.** to establish a sympathetic relationship. —**re•lat′er,** *n.*

re•lat′ed, *adj.* **1.** associated; connected. **2.** allied by kinship, marriage, or common origin. —**re•lat′ed•ness,** *n.*

re•la′tion, *n.* **1.** a significant association; connection. **2. relations, a.** connections or dealings, as between countries. **b.** sexual intercourse. **3.** connection by blood or marriage; kinship. **4.** a relative. **5.** the act of narrating. **6.** regard; reference. —**re•la′tion•al,** *adj.*

re•la•tion•ship (ri lā′shən ship′), *n.* **1.** a connection, association, or involvement. **2.** kinship. **3.** an emotional or other connection between people.

rel•a•tive (rel′ə tiv), *n.* **1.** a person related to another by blood or marriage. **2.** something related to something else. **3.** a relative pronoun, adjective, or adverb. —*adj.* **4.** considered or existing only in relation to something else; comparative. **5.** having relation or connection. **6.** having reference; relevant. **7.** introducing a subordinate clause and referring to an antecedent. —**rel′a•tive•ly,** *adv.*

rel′ative humid′ity, *n.* the amount of water vapor in the air expressed as a percentage of the maximum amount that the air could hold at the same temperature.

rel′a•tiv′i•ty, *n.* **1.** the state or fact of being relative. **2.** *Physics.* Einstein's two-part theory that mass and energy are equivalent, that space and time are relative concepts, and that gravitational and inertial forces are equivalent.

re•lax (ri laks′), *v.t., v.i.* **1.** to make or become less tense, rigid, or firm. **2.** to make or become less strict or severe. **3.** to relieve or find relief from inhibition, worry, or tension. —**re•lax′er,** *n.*

re•lax′ant (-lak′sənt), *adj.* **1.** of or causing relaxation. —*n.* **2.** a relaxant drug.

re•lax•a•tion (rē′lak sā′shən), *n.* **1.** relief from work or effort. **2.** an activity or recreation that provides relaxation. **3.** the act of relaxing or state of being relaxed.

re•lay (rē′lā; *v. also* ri lā′), *n.* **1.** a crew or team, as of persons or animals, relieving one another or taking turns. **2.** a race between teams in which each contestant runs part of the distance. **3.** an electrical device that responds to a change of current or voltage in one circuit by making or breaking a connection in another. —*v.t.* **4.** to carry or convey by or as if by relays. **5.** to provide with fresh relays.

re•lease (ri lēs′), *v.,* -leased, -leas•ing, *n.* —*v.t.* **1.** to free from confinement, obligation, pain, or restraint. **2.** to allow to be known, issued, done, or seen. **3.** to surrender (a legal right, claim, etc.). —*n.* **4.** a releasing, as from confinement or restraint. **5.** a device that holds and releases a mechanism, as a catch. **6.** permission to publish, use, or sell something. **7. a.** the releasing of something to the public. **b.** a film, record, etc., that is released. **8.** a document by which one surrenders a legal right.

rel•e•gate (rel′i gāt′), *v.t.,* -gat•ed, -gat•ing. **1.** to send or consign to an inferior position, place, or condition. **2.** to turn over (a matter, task, etc.) to someone. **3.** to assign to a particular class or kind. **4.** to send into exile. —**rel′e•ga′tion,** *n.*

re•lent (ri lent′), *v.i.* to become more mild, compassionate, or forgiving.

re•lent′less, *adj.* unyieldingly severe, strict, or harsh. —**re•lent′less•ly,** *adv.* —**re•lent′less•ness,** *n.*

rel•e•vant (rel′ə vənt), *adj.* bearing upon the matter at hand; pertinent. —**rel′e•vance, rel′e•van•cy,** *n.*

re•li•a•ble (ri lī′ə bəl), *adj.* capable of being relied on; dependable. —**re•li′a•bil′i•ty,** *n.* —**re•li′a•bly,** *adv.*

re•li′ance (-əns), *n.* **1.** dependence. **2.** confidence. **3.** something or someone relied on. —**re•li′ant,** *adj.*

rel•ic (rel′ik), *n.* **1.** something surviving from the past. **2.** a surviving trace; vestige. **3.** relics, remaining parts or fragments. **4.** a souvenir; memento. **5.** an object associated with a saint and venerated as sacred.

re•lief¹ (ri lēf′), *n.* **1.** alleviation of or deliverance from pain or distress. **2.** help, as money or food, given to those in poverty or need. **3.** something affording a pleasing change, as from monotony. **4. a.** release from a post or duty, as by a replacement. **b.** the person or persons acting as replacement. **5.** the rescue of a besieged town, fort, etc.

re•lief² (ri lēf′), *n.* **1.** prominence or distinctness due to contrast. **2.** projection of a figure from its background, as in sculpture. **3.** differences in elevation and slope in a land surface.

re•lieve (ri lēv′), *v.t.,* -**lieved,** -**liev•ing. 1.** to ease or free from (pain, distress, etc.). **2.** to give aid to. **3.** to free from a burden, wrong, or oppression. **4.** to make less tedious or unpleasant. **5.** to release (a person on duty) by being or providing a replacement. **6.** to release from an obligation or position: *He was relieved of his post.*

re•li•gion (ri lij′ən), *n.* **1.** a set of beliefs concerning the nature and purpose of the universe, esp. when considered as the creation of a superhuman agency. **2.** an institutionalized system of religious beliefs and worship: *the Christian religion.* **3.** something a person believes in devotedly.

re•li′gious (*adj., n., pl.* -**gious.** —*adj.* **1.** of or concerned with religion. **2.** pious; devout. **3.** scrupulously faithful; conscientious. —*n.* **4.** a member of a religious order. —**re•li′gious•ly,** *adv.*

relig′ious right′, *n.* conservatives who support and promote fundamentalist Christian values in society, including prayer in the schools and opposition to legalized abortion.

re•lin•quish (ri ling′kwish), *v.t.* **1.** to give up (a possession, right, etc.); surrender. **2.** to put aside or desist from. **3.** to let go of; release. —**re•lin′quish•ment,** *n.*

rel•i•quar•y (rel′i kwer′ē), *n., pl.* -**quar•ies.** a receptacle for religious relics.

rel•ish (rel′ish), *n.* **1.** enjoyment of the taste of something. **2.** pleasurable appreciation; liking. **3.** something savory, as pickles, added to a meal. **4.** flavor, esp. when appetizing. —*v.t.* **5.** to take pleasure in; enjoy. **6.** to like the taste of.

re•live (rē liv′), *v.t.,* -**lived,** -**liv•ing. 1.** to experience again. **2.** to live (one's life) again. —**re•liv′a•ble,** *adj.*

re•lo′cate, *v.t., v.i.,* -**cat•ed,** -**cat•ing.** to move to a different location. —**re′lo•ca′tion,** *n.*

re•luc•tant (ri luk′tənt), *adj.* **1.** not willing; disinclined. **2.** marked by unwillingness. —**re•luc′tance,** *n.* —**re•luc′tant•ly,** *adv.*

re•ly (ri lī′), *v.i.,* -**lied,** -**ly•ing.** to depend confidently.

rem (rem), *n.* the quantity of ionizing radiation whose biological effect is equal to that produced by one roentgen of x-rays.

REM (rem), *n.* quick, darting movement of the eyes during sleep, esp. during dreams. [*r(apid) e(ye) m(ovement)*]

re•main (ri mān′), *v.i.* **1.** to continue to be as specified. **2.** to stay behind or in the same place. **3.** to be left after the removal or destruction of all else. **4.** to be left to be done, told, etc. —*n.* **5.** Usu., **remains.** something that remains or is left over. **6.** remains, a dead body; corpse.

re•main′der (-dər), *n.* **1.** something that remains or is left. **2.** *Math.* **a.** the quantity that remains after subtraction. **b.** the portion of the dividend that is not evenly divisible by the divisor. **3.** a book discounted by its publisher when sales have practically ceased.

re•mand (ri mand′, -mänd′), *v.t.* to send back, esp.

to return to custody, as to await further proceedings. —**re•mand′ment,** *n.*

re•mark (ri märk′), *v.t.* **1.** to say as a comment or observation. **2.** to note; observe. —*v.i.* **3.** to make a comment or observation. —*n.* **4.** notice, comment, or mention. **5.** a casual or brief expression of thought or opinion.

re•mark′a•ble, *adj.* notably unusual; noteworthy. —**re•mark′a•bly,** *adv.*

Rem•brandt (rem′brant, -bränt), *n.* (*Rembrandt Harmenszoon van Rijn* or *van Ryn*) 1606–69, Dutch painter.

re•me•di•al (ri mē′dē əl), *adj.* **1.** affording remedy. **2.** intended to improve poor skills: *remedial reading.* —**re•me′di•al•ly,** *adv.*

rem•e•dy (rem′i dē), *n., pl.* -**dies,** *v.,* -**died, -dy•ing.** —*n.* **1.** something, as a medicine, that cures or relieves a bodily disorder. **2.** something that corrects or removes an evil or error. —*v.t.* **3.** to cure or relieve. **4.** to put right; rectify.

re•mem•ber (ri mem′bər), *v.t.* **1.** to recall to the mind. **2.** to retain in the mind. **3.** to bear in mind as deserving a gift or reward. **4.** to mention (a person) to another as sending greetings. —*v.i.* **5.** to have or use the faculty of memory.

Remem′ber the Al′amo!, ——*Saying.* a battle cry uttered by Col. Sidney Sherman (1805–73) at the Battle of San Jacinto during the Texan war for independence.

re•mem′brance (-brəns), *n.* **1.** a recollection; memory. **2.** the act of remembering or state of being remembered. **3.** the ability to remember. **4.** the length of time over which memory extends. **5.** something that serves as a reminder. **6.** a gift given as a token of friendship.

re•mind (ri mīnd′), *v.t.* to cause to remember. —**re•mind′er,** *n.*

Rem•ing•ton (rem′ing tən), *n.* **Frederic,** 1861–1909, U.S. artist.

rem•i•nisce (rem′ə nis′), *v.i.,* -**nisced, -nisc•ing.** to recall or talk about past experiences.

rem′i•nis′cence, *n.* **1.** the act or process of reminiscing. **2.** a memory. **3.** Often, -**cences.** a recollection narrated or told. **4.** something that recalls or suggests something else. —**rem′i•nis′cent,** *adj.*

re•miss (ri mis′), *adj.* **1.** negligent or careless in performing a duty or task. **2.** characterized by negligence or carelessness. —**re•miss′ness,** *n.*

re•mis•sion (ri mish′ən), *n.* **1.** the act of remitting. **2.** forgiveness, as of sins. **3. a.** a subsidence of manifestations of a disease. **b.** a period of such a subsidence.

re•mit (ri mit′), *v.t.,* -**mit•ted, -mit•ting. 1.** to send (money), usu. in payment. **2.** to refrain from inflicting, enforcing, or exacting. **3.** to forgive (a sin, offense, etc.). **4.** to slacken; abate. —**re•mit′tance,** *n.*

rem•nant (rem′nənt), *n.* **1.** a remaining, usu. small part or number. **2.** a small unsold or unused piece of fabric. **3.** a trace; vestige.

re•mod•el (rē mod′l), *v.t.,* -**eled, -el•ing** or (*esp. Brit.*) -**elled, -el•ling.** to alter in structure or form; make over.

re•mon•strate (ri mon′strāt), *v.t., v.i.,* -**strat•ed, -strat•ing.** to reason or plead in protest, objection, or complaint. —**re•mon′strance** (-strəns), *n.* —**re•mon′strant,** *adj.*

re•morse (ri môrs′), *n.* deep and painful regret for wrongdoing. —**re•morse′ful,** *adj.* —**re•morse′less,** *adj.*

re•mote (ri mōt′), *adj.,* -**mot•er, -mot•est,** *n.* —*adj.* **1.** far away; distant. **2.** distant in time or relationship. **3.** slight or faint: *a remote chance.* **4.** reserved and distant in manner. —*n.* **5.** REMOTE CONTROL (def. 2). —**re•mote′ly,** *adv.*

remote′ control′, *n.* **1.** control of an apparatus from a distance, as by radio signals. **2.** a device used to control a machine or apparatus from a distance. —**remote′-control′,** *adj.*

re•move (ri mōōv′), *v.,* -**moved, -mov•ing,** *n.* —*v.t.* **1.** to move from one place or position to another. **2.** to take off; shed. **3.** to dismiss from a position; discharge. **4.** to do away with; eliminate. —*n.* **5.** the act of removing. **6.** a distance by which one person or thing is separated from another. **7.** a degree of difference. —**re•mov′a•ble,** *adj.* —**re•mov′al,** *n.*

re•mu•ner•ate (ri myo͞o′nə rāt′), *v.t.,* **-at•ed, -at•ing.** to pay for work, services, or trouble. —**re•mu′-ner•a′tion,** *n.* —**re•mu′ner•a′tive,** *adj.*

Ren•ais•sance (ren′ə säns′, -zäns′), *n.* **1.** the great revival of art, literature, and learning in Europe from the 14th to the 17th centuries. **2.** (*l.c.*) renewal; rebirth. [< F, MF: rebirth]

re•nal (rēn′l), *adj.* of or near the kidneys.

Re•nas•cence (ri nas′əns, -nā′səns), *n.* (*sometimes l.c.*) RENAISSANCE.

rend (rend), *v.t.,* **rent, rend•ing. 1.** to tear apart with force or violence. **2.** to distress with painful feelings. —**rend′er,** *n.*

ren•der[1] (ren′dər), *v.t.* **1.** to cause to be or become; make. **2.** to do; perform. **3.** to furnish; provide. **4.** to present, as for payment; submit. **5.** to translate. **6.** to depict, as in painting. **7.** to give in return. **8.** to melt down: *to render fat.* —*Proverb.* **9. Render unto Caesar the things that are Caesar's and unto God the things that are God's,** one should distinguish between one's duty to Caesar and one's duty to state. Matt. 22:19-21.

rend•er[2] (ren′dər), *n.* a person or thing that rends.

ren•dez•vous (rän′də vo͞o′, -dā-), *n., pl.* **-vous** (-vo͞oz′), *v.,* **-voused** (-vo͞od′), **-vous•ing** (-vo͞o′ing). —*n.* **1. a.** an agreement to meet at a certain time and place. **b.** the meeting itself. **2.** a place designated for a meeting, esp. of ships. **3.** a meeting of spacecraft in outer space. **4.** a popular gathering place. —*v.t., v.i.* **5.** to assemble at an agreed time and place. [< MF *rendez-vous* betake yourselves]

ren•di•tion (ren dish′ən), *n.* **1.** the act of rendering. **2.** a translation. **3.** an interpretation, as of a role.

ren•e•gade (ren′i gād′), *n.* a person who deserts a party, cause, or religion for another.

re•nege (ri nig′, -neg′), *v.i.,* **-neged, -neg•ing. 1.** to go back on one's word. **2.** to play a card that is not of the suit led when one can follow suit. —**re•neg′er,** *n.*

re•new (ri no͞o′, -nyo͞o′), *v.t.* **1.** to begin or take up again; resume. **2.** to make effective for an additional period. **3.** to restore, revive, or replenish. **4.** to make, say, or do again. —**re•new′a•ble,** *adj.* —**re•new′al,** *n.*

ren•net (ren′it), *n.* **1.** the lining membrane of the stomach of a young animal, esp. a calf. **2.** an extract of the rennet membrane used esp. in making cheese.

ren•nin (ren′in), *n.* a coagulating enzyme that forms the active principle of rennet and is able to curdle milk.

Re•no (rē′nō), *n.* a city in W Nevada. 145,029.

Re•noir (ren′wär, ren wär′), *n.* **1. Jean** (zhän), 1894–1979, French film director. **2.** his father, **Pierre Auguste,** 1841–1919, French painter.

re•nounce (ri nouns′), *v.t.,* **-nounced, -nounc•ing. 1.** to give up, esp. by formal declaration. **2.** to repudiate; disown. —**re•nounce′ment,** *n.*

ren•o•vate (ren′ə vāt′), *v.t.,* **-vat•ed, -vat•ing.** to restore to good condition. —**ren′o•va′tion,** *n.*

re•nown (ri noun′), *n.* widespread and high repute; fame. —**re•nowned′,** *adj.*

rent[1] (rent), *n.* **1.** a payment made periodically in return for the use of another's land or property. —*v.t.* **2.** to grant the possession and use of in return for rent. **3.** to take and hold in return for rent. —*v.i.* **4.** to be leased or let for rent. —*Idiom.* **5. for rent,** available to be rented. —**rent′er,** *n.*

rent[2] (rent), *n.* **1.** an opening made by rending. **2.** a breach of relations; schism.

rent[3] (rent), *v.* pt. and pp. of REND.

rent′al, *n.* **1.** an amount received or paid as rent. **2.** the act of renting. **3.** property offered or occupied for rent. —*adj.* **4.** of or available for rent.

re•nun•ci•a•tion (ri nun′sē ā′shən, -shē-), *n.* an act or instance of renouncing.

rep (rep), *n.* a horizontally ribbed fabric.

Rep., 1. Representative. **2.** Republic. **3.** Republican.

re•pair[1] (ri pâr′), *v.t.* **1.** to restore to sound condition; mend. **2.** to restore or renew. **3.** to make up for; remedy. —*n.* **4.** an act, instance, or result of repairing. **5.** condition with respect to soundness and usability.

re•pair[2] (ri pâr′), *v.i.* to betake oneself; go: *They repaired to the living room.*

re•pair′man′ (-man′, -mən), *n., pl.* **-men** (-men′, -mən). one whose work is the making of repairs.

rep•a•ra•tion (rep′ə rā′shən), *n.* **1.** the making of amends for wrong or injury. **2.** Usu., **-tions.** compensation payable by a defeated nation for damages or loss caused during war.

rep•ar•tee (rep′ər tē′, -tā′, -är-), *n., pl.* **-tees. 1.** a quick, witty reply. **2.** conversation full of such replies.

re•past (ri past′, -päst′), *n.* **1.** food and drink for a meal. **2.** a meal.

re•pa•tri•ate (rē pā′trē āt′), *v.t., v.i.,* **-at•ed, -at•ing.** to send or go back to the country of birth or citizenship. —**re•pa′tri•a′tion,** *n.*

re•pay (ri pā′), *v.t.,* **-paid, -pay•ing. 1.** to pay back; refund. **2.** to make return for or to. —**re•pay′ment,** *n.*

re•peal (ri pēl′), *v.t.* **1.** to revoke or annul formally or officially. —*n.* **2.** the act of repealing.

re•peat (ri pēt′), *v.t.* **1.** to say or do again. **2.** to say in reproducing the words or inflections of another. **3.** to tell (something heard) to another. —*v.i.* **4.** to say or do something again. —*n.* **5.** the act of repeating. **6.** something repeated, as a rerun on television. —**re•peat′er,** *n.*

re•peat′ed, *adj.* said or done again and again. —**re•peat′ed•ly,** *adv.*

re•pel (ri pel′), *v.t.,* **-pelled, -pel•ling. 1.** to drive or force back or away. **2.** to fail to mix with. **3.** to resist the absorption of: *This coat repels rain.* **4.** to cause distaste or aversion in.

re•pel′lent (-pel′ənt), *adj.* **1.** causing distaste or aversion. **2.** serving or tending to ward off or drive away. **3.** impervious or resistant to something: *moth-repellent.* —*n.* **4.** something that repels, as a substance that keeps away insects.

re•pent (ri pent′), *v.i., v.t.* **1.** to feel contrite (for); regret. **2.** to be penitent (for) and determine to change for the better. —**re•pent′ance,** *n.* —**re•pent′ant,** *adj.*

re•per•cus•sion (rē′pər kush′ən), *n.* **1.** an effect or result of a previous action or event. **2.** a rebounding or recoil after impact. **3.** reverberation; echo.

rep•er•toire (rep′ər twär′, -twôr′, rep′ə-), *n.* **1.** all the works that a performing company or artist is prepared to present. **2.** the skills, techniques, and devices used or required in a field or occupation.

rep•er•to•ry (rep′ər tôr′ē), *n., pl.* **-ries. 1. a.** a theater at which a company performs several works regularly or in alternate sequence in one season. **b.** a theatrical company at such a theater. **2.** REPERTOIRE.

rep•e•ti•tion (rep′i tish′ən), *n.* **1.** the act of repeating. **2.** something repeated. —**rep′e•ti′tious,** *adj.* —**re•pet•i•tive** (ri pet′i tiv), *adj.*

repet′itive strain′ in′jury, *n.* any of a group of debilitating disorders, esp. of the hand and arm, caused by the stress of repeated movements. Also called **repet′itive strain′ disor′der.**

Reph•i•dim (ref′i dim), *n.* the last encampment of the Israelites during the Exodus from Egypt before they reached Mount Sinai. Ex. 17:1–8.

re•pine (ri pīn′), *v.i.,* **-pined, -pin•ing. 1.** to fret or complain. **2.** to yearn for something.

re•place (ri plās′), *v.t.,* **-placed, -plac•ing. 1.** to assume the function of; substitute for. **2.** to provide a substitute or equivalent for. **3.** to restore to the proper place. —**re•place′a•ble,** *adj.* —**re•place′ment,** *n.*

re•play (*v.* rē plā′; *n.* rē′plā′), *v.t.* **1.** to play (a record, tape, etc.) again. —*n.* **2.** an act or instance of replaying. **3.** something replayed.

re•plen•ish (ri plen′ish), *v.t.* **1.** to make full or complete again. **2.** to supply again or anew. —**re•plen′ish•ment,** *n.*

re•plete (ri plēt'), *adj.* **1.** abundantly supplied. **2.** stuffed with food. —**re•ple'tion,** *n.*

rep•li•ca (rep'li kə), *n., pl.* -**cas. 1.** a close copy, as of a work of art. **2.** a reproduction.

rep•li•cate (rep'li kāt'), *v.t.,* -**cat•ed, -cat•ing.** to repeat, duplicate, or reproduce.

rep'li•ca'tion, *n.* **1.** a reply; answer. **2.** a copy; replica. **3.** the act or process of replicating.

re•ply (ri plī'), *v.,* -**plied, -ply•ing,** *n., pl.* -**plies.** —*v.i., v.t.* **1.** to give or return as an answer; respond. —*n.* **2.** an answer; response.

re•port (ri pôrt'), *n.* **1.** a usu. detailed account, as of an event. **2.** rumor or gossip. **3.** a loud noise, as from an explosion. **4.** repute; reputation. —*v.t.* **5.** to carry and repeat (an answer or message). **6.** to give an account or statement of. **7.** (of a committee) to return (a bill) to a legislative body with findings. **8.** to make a charge against (a person), as to a superior. **9.** to make known the presence, absence, or condition of. **10.** to relate; tell. —*v.i.* **11.** to make a report. **12.** to work as a reporter. **13.** to present oneself as ordered: *to report for duty.* —**re•port'ed•ly,** *adv.*

re•port•age (ri pôr'tij, rep'ôr tāzh'), *n.* **1.** the act of reporting news. **2.** reported news.

report' card', *n.* a periodic written report of a pupil's grades.

re•port'er, *n.* **1.** a person who reports. **2.** a person employed to gather and report news, as for a newspaper.

re•pose[1] (ri pōz'), *n., v.,* -**posed, -pos•ing.** —*n.* **1.** the state of being at rest. **2.** tranquillity; calm. **3.** absence of movement or animation. —*v.i.* **4.** to lie at rest. **5.** to lie dead. —*v.t.* **6.** to lay to rest. —**re•pose'ful,** *adj.*

re•pose[2] (ri pōz'), *v.t.,* -**posed, -pos•ing.** to put (confidence, trust, etc.) in a person or thing.

re•pos•i•tor•y (ri poz'i tôr'ē), *n., pl.* -**tor•ies. 1.** a place where things are deposited, stored, or offered for sale. **2.** a person to whom something is entrusted or confided.

re•pos•sess (rē'pə zes'), *v.t.* to take possession of again, esp. for nonpayment of money that is due. —**re/pos•ses'sion,** *n.*

rep•re•hend (rep'ri hend'), *v.t.* to find fault with; criticize. —**rep/re•hen'sion** (-hen'shən), *n.*

rep/re•hen'si•ble (-hen'sə bəl), *adj.* deserving rebuke or censure; blameworthy. —**rep/re•hen'si•bly,** *adv.*

rep•re•sent (rep'ri zent'), *v.t.* **1.** to serve to stand for; denote or symbolize. **2.** to act or speak for, esp. as an elected representative. **3.** to portray; depict. **4.** to set forth with a view to influencing opinion. **5.** to impersonate, as in acting. **6.** to serve as an example of.

rep/re•sen•ta/tion (-zen tā'shən, -zən-), *n.* **1.** the act of representing or state of being represented. **2.** a body of representatives of a constituency. **3.** something, as a picture, that stands for or depicts something else. **4.** a statement made esp. to influence opinion. —**rep/re•sen•ta/tion•al,** *adj.*

rep/re•sent/a•tive (-tə tiv), *n.* **1.** a person who represents another or others. **2.** a person who represents a constituency in a legislative body, esp. in the U.S. House of Representatives. **3.** a typical example. —*adj.* **4.** serving to represent. **5.** made up of representatives. **6.** of or founded on representation of the people in government. **7.** exemplifying a group or kind.

re•press (ri pres'), *v.t.* **1.** to check or inhibit. **2.** to keep down; suppress. **3.** to suppress (memories, emotions, etc.) unconsciously. —**re•pres'sion,** *n.* —**re•pres'sive,** *adj.*

re•prieve (ri prēv'), *v.,* -**prieved, -priev•ing.** —*v.t.* **1.** to delay the punishment of. **2.** to relieve temporarily. —*n.* **3.** the act of reprieving or state of being reprieved.

rep•ri•mand (rep'rə mand', -mänd'; *v. also* rep'rə mand', -mänd'), *n.* **1.** a severe rebuke, esp. an official one. —*v.t.* **2.** to rebuke severely, esp. officially.

re•pris•al (ri prī'zəl), *n.* retaliation against another by the infliction of equal or greater injuries.

re•prise (rə prēz', ri prīz'), *n.* a repeated occurrence, esp. a repetition of a musical theme or subject.

re•proach (ri prōch'), *v.t.* **1.** to express disapproval of; censure. —*n.* **2.** blame or censure. **3.** an expression of blame or censure. —**re•proach/a•ble,** *adj.* —**re•proach'ful,** *adj.* —**re•proach'ful•ly,** *adv.*

rep•ro•bate (rep'rə bāt'), *n.* **1.** a depraved or wicked person. —*adj.* **2.** depraved; wicked.

re•pro•duce (rē'prə dōōs', -dyōōs'), *v.,* -**duced, -duc•ing.** —*v.t.* **1.** to make a copy of; duplicate. **2.** to produce again or anew. **3.** to produce by a process of generation or propagation. —*v.i.* **4.** to bear offspring. —**re/pro•duc/i•ble,** *adj.* —**re/pro•duc/tion,** *n.* —**re/pro•duc/tive,** *adj.*

re•proof (ri prōōf'), *n.* an act or expression of reproving.

re•prove (ri prōōv'), *v.t.,* -**proved, -prov•ing. 1.** to criticize or correct, esp. gently. **2.** to express disapproval of; censure. —**re•prov'ing•ly,** *adv.*

rep•tile (rep'tĭl, -tīl), *n.* an air-breathing vertebrate, as a snake, lizard, or turtle, characterized by a bony skeleton and a covering of dry scales or horny plates. —**rep•til/i•an** (-til'ē ən), *adj.*

re•pub•lic (ri pub'lik), *n.* **1.** a state in which the supreme power rests in the citizens entitled to vote and is exercised by their chosen representatives. **2. a.** a state in which the head of government is not a monarch but is usu. a president. **b.** the form of government of such a state. [< F < L *rēs pūblica* public affairs, the state]

re•pub/li•can, *adj.* **1.** of or of the nature of a republic. **2.** favoring a republic. **3.** (*cap.*) of or belonging to the Republican Party. —*n.* **4.** one who favors a republican form of government. **5.** (*cap.*) a member of the Republican Party. —**re•pub/li•can•ism,** *n.*

Repub/lican Par/ty, *n.* one of the two major political parties in the U.S.

re•pu•di•ate (ri pyōō'dē āt'), *v.t.,* -**at•ed, -at•ing. 1.** to reject as having no authority or binding force. **2.** to refuse to accept; disown. **3.** to refuse to acknowledge and pay (a debt). —**re•pu/di•a/tion,** *n.*

re•pug•nant (ri pug'nənt), *adj.* **1.** objectionable or offensive. **2.** not consistent or compatible. —**re•pug/nance,** *n.*

re•pulse (ri puls'), *v.,* -**pulsed, -puls•ing,** *n.* —*v.t.* **1.** to drive back; repel. **2.** to repel with rudeness or denial. **3.** to cause repulsion in; disgust. —*n.* **4.** the act of repelling. **5.** a refusal or rejection. **6.** the fact of being repelled.

re•pul/sion (-pul'shən), *n.* **1.** the act of repulsing or state of being repulsed. **2.** a feeling of distaste or aversion. **3.** the force that tends to separate bodies of like electric charge or magnetic polarity.

re•pul/sive, *adj.* **1.** causing repugnance or aversion. **2.** tending or serving to repulse. —**re•pul/sive•ly,** *adv.* —**re•pul/sive•ness,** *n.*

rep•u•ta•ble (rep'yə tə bəl), *adj.* held in good repute; respectable. —**rep/u•ta•bil/i•ty,** *n.* —**rep/u•ta•bly,** *adv.*

rep/u•ta/tion, *n.* **1.** the estimation in which a person or thing is generally held. **2.** favorable repute.

re•pute (ri pyōōt'), *n., v.,* -**put•ed, -put•ing.** —*n.* **1.** reputation. —*v.t.* **2.** to consider; believe: *He was reputed to be a millionaire.*

re•put/ed, *adj.* reported or supposed to be such: *the reputed author.* —**re•put/ed•ly,** *adv.*

re•quest (ri kwest'), *n.* **1.** an act or instance of asking for something. **2.** something asked for. —*v.t.* **3.** to ask for. **4.** to ask (someone) to do something.

req•ui•em (rek'wē əm, rē'kwē-, rā'-), *n.* **1.** (*often cap.*) **a.** a mass for the dead. **b.** a celebration of this mass. **2.** a musical service or hymn for the repose of the dead.

re•quire (ri kwīr'), *v.t.,* -**quired, -quir•ing. 1.** to have need of. **2.** to order to do something. **3.** to call for as necessary or indispensable; demand. **4.** to place under an obligation. —**re•quire/ment,** *n.*

req•ui•site (rek'wə zit), *adj.* **1.** required. —*n.* **2.** something required.

req/ui•si/tion (-zish/ən), *n.* **1.** a formal or official written request for something, as supplies. **2.** the state of being in or required for use. —*v.t.* **3.** to demand or take, as for military purposes.

re•quite (ri kwīt′), *v.t.*, **-quit•ed, -quit•ing. 1.** to make repayment for (service, benefits, etc.). **2.** to retaliate for; avenge. **3.** to give or do in return. —**re•quit′al,** *n.* —**re•quit′er,** *n.*

re•run (rē′run′), *n.* **1.** the showing of a motion picture or television program after its initial run. **2.** the motion picture or television program shown.

re•sale (rē′sāl′, rē sāl′), *n.* the act of selling a second time, esp. of selling something secondhand.

re•scind (ri sind′), *v.t.* to revoke, annul, or repeal. —**re•scis′sion** (-sizh′ən), *n.*

res•cue (res′kyoō), *v.*, **-cued, -cu•ing,** *n.* —*v.t.* **1.** to free from confinement or danger. —*n.* **2.** the act of rescuing. —**res′cu•er,** *n.*

re•search (ri sûrch′, rē′sûrch), *n.* **1.** diligent and systematic inquiry into a subject in order to discover facts or revise theories. **2.** a particular instance or piece of research. —*v.i., v.t.* **3.** to investigate carefully. —**re•search′er,** *n.*

re•sec•tion (ri sek′shən), *n.* the surgical excision of part of an organ or tissue.

re•sem•blance (ri zem′bləns), *n.* the state or fact of resembling; similarity.

re•sem′ble, *v.t.*, **-bled, -bling.** to be like or similar to.

re•sent (ri zent′), *v.t.* to feel or show displeasure or indignation at. —**re•sent′ful,** *adj.* —**re•sent′ful•ly,** *adv.* —**re•sent′ment,** *n.*

res•er•va•tion (rez′ər vā′shən), *n.* **1.** the act of reserving. **2.** an exception or qualification. **3.** a tract of public land set apart for a special purpose. **4.** a prior arrangement to secure accommodations, as at a restaurant.

re•serve (ri zûrv′), *v.*, **-served, -serv•ing,** *n., adj.* —*v.t.* **1.** to keep back, esp. for future use; save. **2.** to retain or secure by prior arrangement. **3.** to set apart for oneself. —*n.* **4.** cash or assets held aside to meet unexpected demands. **5.** something kept for future use or need; stock. **6.** a resource not normally called upon but available if needed. **7.** RESERVATION (def. 3). **0.** the act of reserving. **9, 8.** a military force held in readiness. **b.** reserves, the enrolled but not regular components of the U.S. Army. **10.** formality and self-restraint. —*adj.* **11.** kept in reserve. —*Idiom.* **12. in reserve,** put aside for future need; reserved.

re•served′, *adj.* **1.** kept, held, or set apart for future use. **2.** formal and self-restrained. —**re•serv′ed•ly,** *adv.*

re•serv′ist, *n.* a member of a military reserve.

res•er•voir (rez′ər vwär′, -vwôr′, rez′ə-), *n.* **1.** a place where water is collected and stored for future use. **2.** a receptacle for holding a fluid. **3.** a large supply or stock.

re•side (ri zīd′), *v.i.*, **-sid•ed, -sid•ing. 1.** to live in a place as one's home; dwell. **2.** to be present; be inherent. **3.** to be vested, as powers.

res•i•dence (rez′i dəns), *n.* **1.** the place, esp. the house, in which a person resides; home. **2.** the act or fact of residing. **3.** the time during which a person resides in a place.

res′i•den•cy, *n., pl.* **-cies. 1.** RESIDENCE (def. 2). **2.** the position or tenure of a medical resident.

res′i•dent, *n.* **1.** one who resides in a place. **2.** a physician receiving specialized training at a hospital. —*adj.* **3.** residing; dwelling. **4.** living or staying at a place in discharge of duty. —**res′i•den′tial** (-den′-shəl), *adj.*

re•sid•u•al (ri zij′oō al), *adj.* **1.** of or being a residue or remainder. —*n.* **2.** a residual quantity; remainder. **3.** Usu., **-als.** a fee paid, as to an actor or composer, for each repeated broadcast after an original presentation.

res•i•due (rez′i doō′, -dyoō′), *n.* something that remains after a part is removed, disposed of, or used; remainder.

re•sid•u•um (ri zij′oō əm), *n., pl.* **-u•a** (-oō ə). a remainder or residue.

re•sign (ri zīn′), *v.i., v.t.* **1.** to give up (an office or

position), esp. formally. **2.** to relinquish (a right, claim, etc.). **3.** to submit (oneself, one's mind, etc.) without resistance.

res•ig•na•tion (rez′ig nā′shən), *n.* **1.** the act of resigning. **2.** a formal statement or document that one has resigned. **3.** an accepting, unresisting attitude or state; submission.

re•signed (ri zīnd′), *adj.* submissive or acquiescent. —**re•sign′ed•ly,** *adv.*

re•sil•ient (ri zil′yənt), *adj.* **1.** capable of springing back to an original form and size after compression, bending, or stretching; elastic. **2.** recovering readily, as from adversity or illness; buoyant. —**re•sil′ience, re•sil′ien•cy,** *n.*

res•in (rez′in), *n.* **1.** a substance obtained from certain plants or made artificially, used in making varnishes and plastics. **2.** ROSIN.

re•sist (ri zist′), *v.t.* **1.** to strive against; oppose. **2.** to withstand the action or effect of. **3.** to refrain or abstain from, esp. with difficulty. —*v.i.* **4.** to act or make efforts in opposition. —**re•sist′er,** *n.*

re•sist′ance, *n.* **1.** the act or power of resisting. **2.** the tendency of a conductor to oppose the flow of electric current. —**re•sist′ant,** *adj.*

re•sis′tor, *n.* a device designed to introduce resistance into an electric circuit.

re•sole (rē sōl′), *v.t.*, **-soled, -sol•ing.** to put a new sole on.

res•o•lute (rez′ə loōt′), *adj.* determined; resolved. —**res′o•lute′ly,** *adv.*

res•o•lu′tion, *n.* **1.** a formal expression of opinion or intention by a group, as a legislature. **2.** the act or process of resolving. **3.** the state or quality of being resolute; determination. **4.** a solution, as of a problem. **5.** the degree of sharpness of a computer-generated image as measured by the number of dots per linear inch in a printout or the number of pixels across and down on a screen.

re•solve (ri zolv′), *v.*, **-solved, -solv•ing,** *n.* —*v.t.* **1.** to come to a firm decision about; determine. **2.** to separate into constituent parts. **3.** to state in a formal resolution. **4.** to settle or solve (a question, controversy, etc.). **5.** to dispel (doubts, fears, etc.). —*v.i.* **6.** to make up one's mind. **7.** to break up into constituent parts. —*n.* **8.** a resolution or decision. **9.** firmness of purpose; determination. —**re•solv′a•ble,** *adj.*

re•solved′, *adj.* determined.

res•o•nance (rez′ə nəns), *n.* **1.** the state or quality of being resonant. **2.** an increase or prolongation of a sound caused by sympathetic vibration.

res′o•nant, *adj.* **1.** continuing to resound. **2.** deep and full in sound. **3.** producing resonance. —**res′o•nant•ly,** *adv.*

res′o•nate′ (-nāt′), *v.i.*, **-nat•ed, -nat•ing. 1.** to resound. **2.** to produce or exhibit resonance.

res′o•na′tor, *n.* **1.** something that resonates. **2.** an appliance for increasing sound by resonance.

re•sort (ri zôrt′), *v.i.* **1.** to turn for help, solution, etc.; have recourse: *resorted to violence.* **2.** to go frequently or customarily. —*n.* **3.** a place with facilities for vacationers. **4.** recourse. **5.** a person or thing resorted to.

re•sound (ri zound′), *v.i.* **1.** to ring with sound; reverberate. **2.** to sound loudly. —**re•sound′ing,** *adj.* —**re•sound′ing•ly,** *adv.*

re•source (rē′sôrs, ri sôrs′), *n.* **1.** a source of supply, support, or aid, esp. one that can be readily drawn upon when needed. **2. resources,** a country's means of producing wealth. **3.** Usu., **resources.** money or property; assets. **4.** capability in dealing with a situation or in meeting difficulties. —**re•source′ful,** *adj.* —**re•source′ful•ness,** *n.*

re•spect (ri spekt′), *n.* **1.** a particular; detail. **2.** relation; reference: *inquiries with respect to a route.* **3.** esteem; admiration. **4.** proper courtesy. **5.** the condition of being esteemed. **6. respects,** a formal expression of esteem or deference. —*v.t.* **7.** to hold in esteem. **8.** to refrain from intruding upon: *to respect a person's privacy.* **9.** to have reference to; concern. —**re•spect′ful,** *adj.* —**re•spect′ful•ly,** *adv.*

re•spect′a•ble, *adj.* **1.** worthy of respect. **2.** good enough to be seen or used. **3.** of moderate excellence. **4.** appreciable in size, number, or amount. —re•spect′a•bil′i•ty, *n.* —re•spect′a•bly, *adv.*

re•spect′ing, *prep.* regarding; concerning.

re•spec′tive, *adj.* pertaining individually to each of a number; particular.

re•spec′tive•ly, *adv.* in precisely the order given.

res•pi•ra•tion (res′pə rā′shən), *n.* the act or process of respiring; breathing. —res′pi•ra•to′ry (-rə-tôr′ē), *adj.*

res′pi•ra′tor, *n.* **1.** an apparatus to produce artificial respiration. **2.** a device worn over the nose and mouth to prevent inhalation of harmful substances.

re•spire (ri spīr′), *v.i.,* *v.t.,* **-spired, -spir•ing.** to inhale and exhale; breathe.

res•pite (res′pit), *n.* **1.** an interval of relief. **2.** a temporary suspension; stay.

re•splend•ent (ri splen′dənt), *adj.* shining brilliantly. —re•splend′ence, *n.* —re•splend′ent•ly, *adv.*

re•spond (ri spond′), *v.i.,* *v.t.* **1.** to answer; reply. **2.** to react, esp. favorably.

re•spond′ent, *n.* **1.** a person who responds. **2.** a defendant, esp. in divorce proceedings.

re•sponse′ (-spons′), *n.* **1.** an answer; reply. **2.** a reaction to a stimulus.

re•spon′si•bil′i•ty, *n., pl.* **-ties. 1.** the state or fact of being responsible. **2.** a person or thing for which one is responsible.

re•spon′si•ble, *adj.* **1.** accountable, as for something within one's power. **2.** involving duties or obligations. **3.** being the source or cause of something. **4.** having the capacity to make moral decisions. **5.** able to discharge obligations or pay debts. **6.** reliable or dependable. —re•spon′si•bly, *adv.*

re•spon′sive, *adj.* responding readily and sympathetically. —re•spon′sive•ly, *adv.* —re•spon′sive•ness, *n.*

rest¹ (rest), *n.* **1.** the quiet or repose of sleep. **2.** ease or inactivity after exertion or labor. **3.** relief or freedom, esp. from trouble. **4.** a period of rest. **5.** cessation or absence of motion. **6.** *Music.* **a.** an interval of silence between notes. **b.** a sign indicating it. **7.** a shelter or lodging. **8.** a supporting piece or device. —*v.i.* **9.** to refresh oneself, as by lying down. **10.** to cease from motion or activity. **11.** to lie, sit, lean, or be set. **12.** to be based or founded. **13.** to be found: *The blame rests with them.* **14.** to be fixed on something. —*v.t.* **15.** to give rest to. **16.** to lay or place for rest or support. **17.** to direct or cast. —rest′ful, *adj.* —rest′ful•ly, *adv.*

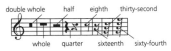

rests

rest² (rest), *n.* **1.** a part that is left; remainder. **2.** the others: *All the rest are going.* —*v.i.* **3.** to continue to be: *Rest assured that all is well.*

res•tau•rant (res′tər ənt, -tə ränt′), *n.* an establishment where meals are served to customers.

res′tau•ra•teur′ (-ə tûr′), *n.* the owner or manager of a restaurant.

rest′ home′, *n.* a residential establishment that provides care for convalescents and the aged.

res•ti•tu•tion (res′ti tōō′shən, -tyōō′-), *n.* **1.** compensation for loss, damage, or injury. **2.** the restoration of something, as property, to the rightful owner.

res•tive (res′tiv), *adj.* **1.** restless; uneasy. **2.** stubborn; balky. —res′tive•ly, *adv.* —res′tive•ness, *n.*

rest′less, *adj.* **1.** marked by inability to remain at rest. **2.** unquiet; uneasy. **3.** perpetually agitated or in motion. **4.** without rest or restful sleep. —rest′less•ly, *adv.* —rest′less•ness, *n.*

res•to•ra•tion (res′tə rā′shən), *n.* **1.** the act of restoring or state of being restored. **2.** something restored, as by renovating.

re•stor•a•tive (ri stôr′ə tiv), *adj.* **1.** of or for restoration. **2.** capable of restoring health or strength. —*n.* **3.** a restorative agent or means.

re•store′, *v.t.,* **-stored, -stor•ing. 1.** to bring back into existence or use. **2.** to bring back to an original or a former, more desirable condition. **3.** to put back in a former place or rank. **4.** to give back.

re•strain (ri strān′), *v.t.* **1.** to hold back; check or control. **2.** to deprive of liberty. **3.** to limit or hamper. —re•strained′, *adj.*

re•straint′ (-strānt′), *n.* **1.** a restraining action or influence. **2.** a means of restraining. **3.** a restraining device. **4.** the act of restraining or state of being restrained. **5.** caution or reserve, as in feelings.

re•strict (ri strikt′), *v.t.* to keep within limits, as of choice. —re•strict′ed, *adj.* —re•stric′tion, *n.*

re•stric′tive, *adj.* **1.** tending or serving to restrict. **2.** of or being a word, phrase, or clause that identifies or limits the meaning of a modified element. —re•stric′tive•ly, *adv.*

rest′ room′, *n.* a room in a public building having washbowls and toilets.

re•sult (ri zult′), *v.i.* **1.** to arise or proceed as a consequence. **2.** to end in a particular manner. —*n.* **3.** something that results. **4.** Often, **-sults.** a desirable outcome. **5.** *Math.* a quantity or expression obtained by calculation. —re•sult′ant, *adj., n.*

re•sume (ri zōōm′), *v.,* **-sumed, -sum•ing.** —*v.t.* **1.** to begin again after interruption. **2.** to take, occupy, or assume again. —*v.i.* **3.** to continue after interruption. —re•sump′tion (-zump′shən), *n.*

ré•su•mé or **re•su•me** or **re•su•mé** (rez′ŏŏ mā′, rez′ŏŏ mā′), *n.* **1.** SUMMARY. **2.** an account of one's education, employment, etc., submitted to a potential employer.

re•sur•gent (ri sûr′jənt), *adj.* rising or tending to rise again. —re•sur′gence, *n.*

res•ur•rect (rez′ə rekt′), *v.t.* **1.** to raise from the dead. **2.** to bring back, as into use or practice.

res′ur•rec′tion, *n.* **1.** a rising again, as from disuse; revival. **2.** (*cap.*) the rising of Christ after His death and burial. **3.** (*cap.*) the rising of the dead on Judgment Day.

re•sus•ci•tate (ri sus′i tāt′), *v.t.,* **-tat•ed, -tat•ing.** to revive, esp. from apparent death. —re•sus′ci•ta′-tion, *n.* —re•sus′ci•ta′tor, *n.*

re•tail (rē′tāl), *n.* the sale of goods to ultimate consumers, usu. in small quantities. —*adj.* **2.** connected with or engaged in sale at retail. —*adv.* **3.** at a retail price. —*v.t.,* *v.i.* **4.** to sell or be sold at retail. —re′tail•er, *n.*

re•tain (ri tān′), *v.t.* **1.** to keep possession of. **2.** to continue to use, practice, or hold. **3.** to keep in mind. **4.** to hold in place or position. **5.** to hire, esp. by payment of a retainer.

re•tain′er¹, *n.* **1.** one that retains. **2.** a servant or attendant.

re•tain′er², *n.* a fee paid to secure services, as of a lawyer.

re•take (*v.* rē tāk′; *n.* rē′tāk′), *v.,* **-took, -tak•en, -tak•ing,** *n.* —*v.t.* **1.** to take again. **2.** to photograph or film again. —*n.* **3.** a picture or scene photographed or filmed again.

re•tal•i•ate (ri tal′ē āt′), *v.i.,* **-at•ed, -at•ing.** to return like for like, esp. evil for evil. —re•tal′i•a′tion, *n.* —re•tal′i•a′tive, re•tal′i•a•to′ry (-ə tôr′ē), *adj.*

re•tard (ri tärd′), *v.t.* to delay the progress of. —re′-tar•da′tion, *n.*

re•tard′ant, *n.* **1.** a substance capable of slowing the speed of a chemical reaction. —*adj.* **2.** retarding or tending to retard.

re•tard′ed, *adj.* characterized by slowness or limitation in intellectual or emotional development.

retch (rech), *v.i.* to make efforts to vomit.

re•ten•tion (ri ten′shən), *n.* **1.** the act of retaining or state of being retained. **2.** the power to retain, esp. in the mind. —re•ten′tive, *adj.* —re•ten′tive•ness, *n.*

ret•i•cent (ret′ə sənt), *adj.* disposed to be silent or not to speak freely. —ret′i•cence, *n.*

ret•i•na (ret′n ə), *n., pl.* **-i•nas, -i•nae** (-n ē′). the innermost coat of the posterior part of the eyeball that receives the image produced by the lens. —**ret′i•nal**, adj.

ret•i•nue (ret′n oo′, -yoo′), n. a body of retainers attending an important personage.

re•tire (ri tīᵊr′), v., **-tired, -tir•ing.** —v.i. **1.** to withdraw to a place of privacy, shelter, or seclusion. **2.** to go to bed. **3.** to give up an office, occupation, or career, usu. because of age. **4.** to retreat, as from battle. —v.t. **5.** to withdraw (bonds, bills, etc.) from circulation. **6.** to withdraw (troops, ships, etc.), as from battle. **7.** to remove from an office or active service. **8.** Sports. to put out (a batter, side, etc.). —**re•tire′ment,** n.

re•tired′, adj. **1.** withdrawn from an office, occupation, or career. **2.** due or given a retired person. **3.** secluded or sequestered.

re•tir′ing, adj. reserved; shy.

re•tool (rē tool′), v.t., v.i. to replace the tools and machinery (of).

re•tort¹ (ri tôrt′), v.t. **1.** to reply to, esp. sharply. **2.** to return (an accusation, epithet, etc.) upon the person uttering it. —v.i. **3.** to reply, esp. sharply. —n. **4.** a sharp, incisive, or witty reply. **5.** the act of retorting.

re•tort² (ri tôrt′), n. a glass bulb with a long neck bent downward, used for distilling or decomposing substances by heat.

re•touch (rē tuch′), v.t. to improve, as with new touches, details, or corrections; touch up.

re•trace (ri trās′), v.t., **-traced, -trac•ing. 1.** to trace backward. **2.** to go back over.

re•tract¹ (ri trakt′), v.t. to draw back or in, as claws or fangs.

re•tract² (ri trakt′), v.t. to withdraw (a statement, promise, etc.); recant. —**re•trac′tion,** n.

re•tread (v. rē tred′; n. rē′tred′), v.t. **1.** to put a new tread on (a worn pneumatic tire casing). —n. **2.** a retreaded tire.

re•treat (ri trēt′), n. **1.** the forced or strategic withdrawal of a military force. **2.** the act of withdrawing, as into privacy. **3.** a place of refuge, seclusion, or privacy. **4.** a period of withdrawal, as for religious meditation. **5. a.** a military flag-lowering ceremony held at sunset. **b.** the bugle call for this. —v.i. **6.** to make a retreat. **7.** to slope backward.

re•trench (ri trench′), v.t., v.i. to reduce (expenses); economize. —**re•trench′ment,** n.

ret•ri•bu•tion (re′trə byoo′shən), n. requital according to merits or deserts, esp. for evil. —**re•trib•u•tive** (ri trib′yə tiv), adj.

re•trieve (ri trēv′), v., **-trieved, -triev•ing.** n. —v.t. **1.** to recover or regain. **2.** to make amends for; make good. **3.** (of hunting dogs) to fetch (killed or wounded game). **4.** to locate and read (data) from computer storage. —v.i. **5.** to retrieve game. —n. **6.** the act of retrieving. —**re•triev′al,** n.

re•triev′er, n. a dog trained to retrieve game.

retro-, a prefix meaning back or backward (retro-rocket).

ret•ro•ac•tive (re′trō ak′tiv), adj. effective as of a past date. —**ret′ro•ac′tive•ly,** adv.

ret′ro•fire′, v.t., **-fired, -fir•ing.** to ignite (a retro-rocket).

ret′ro•fit′, v.t., **-fit•ted** or **-fit, -fit•ting.** to furnish (an automobile, airplane, etc.) with parts or equipment made available only after manufacture.

ret•ro•grade (re′trə grād′), adj., v., **-grad•ed, -grad•ing.** —adj. **1.** moving backward. **2.** Chiefly Biol. exhibiting degeneration or deterioration. —v.i. **3.** to move backward. **4.** Chiefly Biol. to degenerate.

ret•ro•gress (re′trə gres′, re′trə gres′), v.i. to go backward, esp. into an earlier and usu. worse condition. —**ret′ro•gres′sion,** n. —**ret′ro•gress′ive,** adj.

ret•ro•nym (re′trə nim), n. a term, such as acoustic guitar, coined in modification of the original referent that was used alone, such as guitar, to distinguish it from a later contrastive development, such as electric guitar.

ret•ro•rock•et (re′trō rok′it), n. an auxiliary rocket engine used esp. for decelerating a larger rocket.

ret•ro•spect (re′trə spekt′), n. contemplation of the

past. —**ret′ro•spec′tion,** n. —**ret′ro•spec′tive,** adj. —**ret′ro•spec′tive•ly,** adv.

ret′ro•vi′rus, n., pl. **-rus•es.** any of various RNA-containing viruses, including the one that causes AIDS.

re•turn (ri tûrn′), v.i. **1.** to go or come back. **2.** to reply or retort. —v.t. **3.** to put, bring, take, give, or send back. **4.** to do or give in reciprocation, recompense, or requital. **5.** to yield (a profit, revenue, etc.). **6.** to report officially. **7.** to reelect, as to a legislative body. —n. **8.** the act of returning or fact of being returned. **9.** something returned. **10.** a recurrence. **11.** reciprocation, repayment, or requital. **12.** response or reply. **13.** Often, **-turns.** a yield or profit. **14.** a formal report of income and taxes due. **15.** Usu., **-turns.** a report on a count of votes or candidates elected. —adj. **16.** of or being a return. **17.** sent, given, or done in return. —**re•turn′a•ble,** adj.

re•turn•ee (ri tûr nē′, -tûr′nē), n., pl. **-ees.** a person who has returned, as from overseas military duty.

Reu•ben (roo′bən), n. **1.** the eldest son of Jacob and Leah. Gen. 29, 30. **2.** one of the 12 tribes of Israel.

Reu′ben sand′wich (roo′bən), n. a grilled sandwich of corned beef, Swiss cheese, and sauerkraut on rye bread.

Reu•el (roo′el), n. JETHRO.

re•un•ion (rē yoon′yan), n. **1.** the act of uniting again or state of being united again. **2.** a gathering of relatives, friends, or associates after separation.

rev (rev), n., v., **revved, rev•ving.** —n. **1.** a revolution of a rotating part in an engine. —v.t. **2.** to accelerate sharply the speed of (an internal-combustion engine). [short for revolution]

Rev., 1. Revelation; Revelations. **2.** Reverend.

re•vamp (rē vamp′), v.t. to renovate, revise, or restructure; redo.

re•veal (ri vēl′), v.t. **1.** to make known; disclose. **2.** to lay open to view; display.

rev•eil•le (rev′ə lē), n. a bugle call in the early morning to awaken military personnel.

rev•el (rev′əl), v., **-eled, -el•ing** or (esp. Brit.) **-elled, -el•ling,** n. v.i. **1.** to take great pleasure; delight. **2.** to make merry. —n. **3.** boisterous merry-making. —**rev′el•er;** esp. Brit., **rev′el•ler,** n. —**rev′el•ry,** n., pl. **-ries.**

rev•e•la•tion (rev′ə lā′shən), n. **1.** the act of revealing. **2.** something revealed, esp. a striking disclosure. **3.** Theol. **a.** God's disclosure of Himself and His will. **b.** something that contains such disclosure, as the Bible. **4.** (cap.) Usu., **Revelations.** Also called **The Revelation of St. John the Divine.** the last book in the New Testament; the Apocalypse.

re•venge (ri venj′), v., **-venged, -veng•ing,** n. —v.t. **1.** to inflict pain or harm in return for; avenge. —n. **2.** the act of revenging. **3.** something done in vengeance. **4.** the desire to revenge. —**re•venge′ful,** adj.

rev•e•nue (rev′ən yoo′, -ə noo′), n. **1.** the income of a government from taxation and other sources. **2.** the return or yield from investments; income.

re•ver•ber•ate (ri vûr′bə rāt′), v.i., v.t., **-at•ed, -at•ing. 1.** to reecho or resound. **2.** to rebound or recoil. —**re•ver′ber•a′tion,** n. —**re•ver′ber•a′tor,** n.

re•vere (ri vēr′), v.t., **-vered, -ver•ing.** to regard with respect tinged with awe; venerate.

Re•vere′, n. **Paul,** 1735–1818, American silversmith and patriot.

rev•er•ence (rev′ər əns), n., v., **-enced, -enc•ing.** —n. **1.** deep respect tinged with awe; veneration. **2.** a manifestation or gesture indicative of reverence. —v.t. **3.** to regard or treat with reverence. —**rev′er•ent, rev′er•en′tial** (-ə ren′shəl), adj. —**rev′er•ent•ly,** adv.

rev′er•end, adj. **1.** (cap.) (used as a title of respect prefixed to the name of a member of the clergy). **2.** worthy of being revered. —n. **3.** a member of the clergy.

rev•er•ie (rev′ə rē), n., pl. **-ies. 1.** a state of dreamy meditation. **2.** a daydream.

re•vers (ri vēr′, -vâr′), n., pl. **-vers** (-vērz′, -vârz′).

a part of a garment, esp. a lapel, turned back to show the facing.

re•verse (ri vûrs′), *adj., n., v.,* **-versed, -vers•ing.** —*adj.* **1.** opposite or contrary in position, direction, order, or character. **2.** with the back or rear part toward the observer. **3.** producing backward movement: *reverse gear.* —*n.* **4.** the opposite or contrary of something. **5.** the back or rear of something, as of a coin. **6.** an adverse change of fortune. **7.** a reversing mechanism. —*v.t.* **8.** to turn in an opposite position, direction, or order. **9.** to turn inside out or upside down. **10.** to cause (a mechanism) to run in a reverse direction. **11.** to revoke or annul (a decree, judgment, etc.). —*v.i.* **12.** to shift into reverse gear. **13.** to turn or move in the opposite or contrary direction. —**re•ver′sal,** *n.* —**re•vers′i•ble,** *adj.* —**re•vers′i•bly,** *adv.*

re•vert′ (-vûrt′), *v.i.* **1.** to return to a former habit, practice, belief, or condition. **2.** to return to a former owner or that person's heirs. **3.** to return to an ancestral type or characteristic. —**re•ver′sion** (-vûr′zhən), *n.* —**re•vert′i•ble,** *adj.*

re•vet•ment (ri vet′mənt), *n.* a facing, as of masonry, esp. for protecting an embankment.

re•view (ri vyoo′), *n.* **1.** a critical report, as on a book or play. **2.** the process of going over a subject again in study or recitation. **3.** a general survey, esp. in words. **4.** an inspection, esp. a formal military inspection. **5.** a periodical containing articles on current affairs, books, etc. **6.** a judicial reexamination, as by a higher court. —*v.t.* **7.** to go over (lessons, studies, etc.) in review. **8.** to inspect, esp. formally. **9.** to survey mentally. **10.** to evaluate in a critical review. **11.** to look back upon. **12.** to reexamine judicially. —**re•view′er,** *n.*

re•vile (ri vīl′), *v.t., v.i.,* **-viled, -vil•ing.** to speak (of) abusively. —**re•vile′ment,** *n.* —**re•vil′er,** *n.*

re•vise (ri vīz′), *v.,* **-vised, -vis•ing,** *n.* —*v.t.* **1.** to amend or alter. **2.** to correct or improve (something written or printed). —*n.* **3.** a revised form of something. —**re•vi′sion** (-vizh′ən), *n.*

Revised′ Stand′ard Ver′sion, *n.* an American revision of the Bible completed in 1952.

Revised′ Ver′sion, *n.* a critical revision of the KING JAMES VERSION. The New Testament was published in 1881, and the Old Testament in 1885.

re•vi•sion•ism (ri vizh′ə niz′əm), *n.* advocacy of revision, esp. of some authoritative or generally accepted doctrine, theory, or practice. —**re•vi′sion•ist,** *n., adj.*

re•vi•tal•ize (rē vīt′l īz′), *v.t.,* **-ized, -iz•ing.** to give new life, vitality, or vigor to. —**re•vi′tal•i•za′tion,** *n.*

re•viv•al (ri vī′vəl), *n.* **1.** a new presentation of an old play or motion picture. **2.** an evangelistic service to effect a religious awakening. **3.** the act of reviving or state of being revived. —**re•viv′al•ist,** *n.*

re•vive′, *v.,* **-vived, -viv•ing.** —*v.t.* **1.** to restore to life, consciousness, or vigor. **2.** to present (an old play or motion picture) again. **3.** to bring back into use, acceptance, or currency. **4.** to renew in the mind. —*v.i.* **5.** to return to life, consciousness, or vigor.

re•viv′i•fy′, *v.t.,* **-fied, -fy•ing.** to give new life to. —**re•viv′i•fi•ca′tion,** *n.*

re•voke (ri vōk′), *v.t.,* **-voked, -vok•ing.** to take back or withdraw; annul or cancel. —**rev•o•ca•ble** (rev′ə kə bəl), *adj.* —**rev′o•ca′tion** (-kā′shən), *n.*

re•volt (ri vōlt′), *v.i.* **1.** to break away from or rise against constituted authority; rebel. **2.** to turn away in disgust or abhorrence. —*v.t.* **3.** to affect with disgust or abhorrence. —*n.* **4.** an uprising; rebellion. —**re•volt′ing,** *adj.*

rev•o•lu•tion (rev′ə loo′shən), *n.* **1.** the overthrow and replacement of an established government or political system by the people governed. **2.** a sudden, complete, or radical change. **3.** rotation on or as if on an axis. **4.** the orbiting of one heavenly body around another. **5.** a single cycle in a rotation or orbit. —**rev′o•lu′tion•ar′y,** *adj., n., pl.* **-ar•ies.** —**rev′o•lu′tion•ist,** *n.*

revolu′tionary prax′is, *n.* the practical actions required to overthrow an existing political system.

Revolu′tionary War′, *n.* AMERICAN REVOLUTION.

rev′o•lu′tion•ize′, *v.t.,* **-ized, -iz•ing.** to effect a radical change in.

re•volve (ri volv′), *v.,* **-volved, -volv•ing.** —*v.i.* **1.** to move in a circular course or orbit. **2.** to rotate. **3.** to occur in cycles; recur. —*v.t.* **4.** to cause to revolve. **5.** to turn over in the mind; consider. —**re•volv′a•ble,** *adj.*

re•volv′er, *n.* a handgun with a revolving chambered cylinder for holding cartridges.

re•vue (ri vyoo′), *n.* a theatrical show featuring skits, dances, and songs.

re•vul•sion (ri vul′shən), *n.* **1.** a strong feeling of repugnance or distaste. **2.** a sudden and violent change of feeling or response.

re•ward (ri wôrd′), *n.* **1.** a sum of money offered, as for the recovery of lost property. **2.** something given or received in return for service, merit, etc. —*v.t.* **3.** to give a reward to or for.

re•ward′ing, *adj.* affording satisfaction; gratifying.

re•word (rē wûrd′), *v.t.* to put into other words.

re•write′, *v.t.,* **-wrote, -writ•ten, -writ•ing.** **1.** to write in a different form; revise. **2.** to write again. **3.** to write (news submitted by a reporter) for inclusion in a newspaper.

Rey•kja•vik (rā′kyə vik, -vēk′), *n.* the capital of Iceland. 93,245.

Re•zin (rē′zin), *n.* the last king of Syria. II Kings 15:37; 16:5–9; Isa. 7:4.

RFD, rural free delivery.

Rh, *Chem. Symbol.* rhodium.

rhap•so•dize (rap′sə dīz′), *v.i.,* **-dized, -diz•ing.** to talk with extravagant enthusiasm.

rhap′so•dy (-sə dē), *n., pl.* **-dies. 1.** a musical composition irregular in form and suggestive of improvisation. **2.** an ecstatic expression of feeling or enthusiasm. —**rhap•sod′ic** (-sod′ik), *adj.*

rhe•a (rē′ə), *n., pl.* **rhe•as.** a flightless ostrichlike bird of South America.

rhe•o•stat (rē′ə stat′), *n.* an adjustable resistor that controls the electric current in a circuit.

rhe′sus mon′key (rē′səs), *n.* a macaque of India that is used in biological and medical research.

rhet•o•ric (ret′ər ik), *n.* **1.** the art of effectively using language in speech or writing. **2.** the use of exaggerated language; bombast. —**rhe•tor•i•cal** (ri tôr′i-kəl), *adj.* —**rhet′o•ri′cian** (-ə rish′ən), *n.*

rhetor′ical ques′tion, *n.* a question asked for effect, not to elicit a reply.

rheum (room), *n.* a thin discharge of the mucous membranes. —**rheum′y,** *adj.*

rheumat′ic fe′ver, *n.* an acute disease, usu. affecting children, that is characterized by fever, arthritis, and heart disturbances.

rheu•ma•tism (roo′mə tiz′əm), *n.* any of several disorders characterized by pain and stiffness in the joints or muscles. —**rheu•mat′ic** (-mat′ik), *adj., n.* —**rheu′ma•toid′,** *adj.*

rheu′matoid arthri′tis, *n.* a chronic autoimmune disease characterized by inflammation and progressive deformity of the joints.

Rh factor (är′āch′), *n.* an antigen present in blood cells that may induce a severe reaction in an individual lacking the antigen. [so called because first found in the blood of *rhesus* monkeys]

Rhine (rīn), *n.* a river flowing from SE Switzerland through Germany and the Netherlands into the North Sea. 820 mi. (1320 km) long.

rhine•stone (rīn′stōn′), *n.* an artificial gemstone of brilliant glass or paste, esp. one cut in imitation of a diamond.

rhi•ni•tis (rī nī′tis), *n.* inflammation of the nose or its mucous membrane.

rhi•no (rī′nō), *n., pl.* **-nos, -no.** a rhinoceros.

rhi•noc•er•os (rī nos′ər əs), *n., pl.* **-os•es, -os.** a large, thick-skinned mammal of Africa and Asia, with one or two upright horns on the snout.

rhi•zome (rī′zōm), *n.* a rootlike stem that usu. produces roots below and sends up shoots from the upper surface.

rho (rō), *n., pl.* **rhos.** the 17th letter of the Greek alphabet (P, ρ).

Rho•da (rō′də), *n.* a girl in the household of Mary, mother of Mark. Acts 12:13.

Rhode′ Is′land (rōd), *n.* a state of the NE United States, on the Atlantic coast. 990,225. *Cap.:* Providence. *Abbr.:* RI, R.I. —**Rhode′ Is′lander,** *n.*

Rhodes (rōdz), *n.* a Greek island in the SE Aegean.

Rho•de•sia (rō dē′zhə), *n.* former name of ZIMBABWE. —**Rho•de′sian,** *n., adj.*

rho•di•um (rō′dē əm), *n.* a metallic element used esp. to electroplate scientific instruments. *Symbol:* Rh; *at. wt.:* 102.905; *at. no.:* 45.

rho•do•den•dron (rō′də den′drən), *n.* an evergreen shrub or tree with showy pink, purple, or white flowers.

rhom•boid (rom′boid), *n.* an oblique-angled parallelogram with only the opposite sides equal.

rhom′bus (-bəs), *n., pl.* **-bus•es, -bi** (-bī). an equilateral parallelogram with oblique angles.

Rhone or **Rhône** (rōn), *n.* a river flowing from S Switzerland through SE France into the Mediterranean. 504 mi. (810 km) long.

rhu•barb (rōō′bärb), *n.* **1.** a plant with edible leafstalks often used in making pies. **2.** *Slang.* a quarrel or squabble.

rhyme (rīm), *n., v.,* **rhymed, rhym•ing.** —*n.* **1.** identity in terminal sounds of words or lines of verse. **2.** a word agreeing with another in terminal sound. **3.** verse or poetry having correspondence in the terminal sounds of the lines. —*v.t.* **4.** to turn into rhyme. **5.** to use as a rhyme. —*v.i.* **6.** to make rhymes. **7.** to form a rhyme. —**rhym′er,** *n.*

rhythm (rith′əm), *n.* **1.** movement or procedure with uniform or patterned recurrence of an element. **2.** the pattern of pulses in music resulting from the occurrence of strong and weak melodic and harmonic beats. **3.** the pattern of recurrent strong and weak accents and long and short syllables in speech. —**rhyth′mic** (-mik), **rhyth′mi•cal,** *adj.* —**rhyth′mi•cal•ly,** *adv.*

rhythm′ and blues′, *n.* a folk-based form of black popular music.

rhythm′ meth′od, *n.* a method of birth control consisting of abstention from sexual intercourse during ovulation.

RI or **R.I.,** Rhode Island.

ri•al (rē ôl′, -äl′), *n.* the basic monetary unit of Iran, Oman, and the Republic of Yemen.

rib¹ (rib), *n., v.,* **ribbed, rib•bing.** —*n.* **1.** one of a series of curved bones that are attached to the spine, occur in pairs, and form the thoracic wall. **2.** something resembling a rib: *the ribs of an umbrella.* **3.** a ridge in cloth, esp. in knitted fabrics. —*v.t.* **4.** to furnish or strengthen with ribs. **5.** to mark with riblike ridges or markings.

rib² (rib), *v.t.,* **ribbed, rib•bing.** to make fun of; tease. —**rib′ber,** *n.*

rib•ald (rib′əld; *spelling pron.* rī′bəld), *adj.* vulgar or indecent, as in language; coarse. —**rib′ald•ry,** *n.*

rib•bon (rib′ən), *n.* **1.** a woven strip or band of fine material used esp. for ornament. **2.** ribbons, torn or ragged strips; shreds: *torn to ribbons.* **3.** a band of inked material, as that used in a typewriter.

ri•bo•fla•vin (rī′bō flā′-, -bə-), *n.* a vitamin B complex factor essential for growth and abundant in milk, meat, eggs, and leafy vegetables.

ri′bo•nu•cle′ic ac′id (rī′bō nōō klē′ik, -klā′-, -nyōō-, rī′-), *n.* See RNA.

rice (rīs), *n., v.,* **riced, ric•ing.** —*n.* **1.** the edible starchy seeds or grain of a grass cultivated in warm climates. —*v.t.* **2.** to reduce to a form resembling rice: *to rice potatoes.* —**ric′er,** *n.*

rich (rich), *adj.,* **-er, -est,** *n.* —*adj.* **1.** abundantly supplied with resources, means, or funds; wealthy. **2.** abounding: *rich in beauty.* **3.** of great value or worth; costly. **4.** abounding in sugar or fat. **5.** (of color) deep or vivid. **6.** full and mellow in tone. **7.** producing or yielding abundantly. **8.** abundant; plentiful. —*n.* **9. the rich,** rich persons collectively. —**rich′ly,** *adv.* —**rich′ness,** *n.*

Rich•ard I (rich′ərd), *n.* (*"Richard the Lion-Hearted"*), 1157–99, king of England 1189–99.

rich′es, *n.pl.* abundant and valuable possessions.

Rich•mond (rich′mənd), *n.* the capital of Virginia. 201,108.

Rich′ter scale′ (rik′tər), *n.* a logarithmic scale for indicating the intensity of an earthquake. [after C. F. *Richter* (1900–85), U.S. seismologist]

rick (rik), *n.* a large stack of hay, straw, etc., in a field.

Rick•en•back•er (rik′ən bak′ər), *n.* **Edward Vernon** (*"Eddie"*), 1890–1973, U.S. aviator and aviation executive.

rick•ets (rik′its), *n.* a childhood disease in which the bones soften from an inadequate intake of vitamin D.

rick•et•y (rik′i tē), *adj.,* **-i•er, -i•est. 1.** likely to fall or collapse; shaky. **2.** affected with rickets.

Rick•o•ver (rik′ō vər), *n.* **Hyman George,** 1900–86, U.S. naval officer, born in Poland; helped to develop the nuclear submarine.

rick•rack (rik′rak′), *n.* a narrow zigzag braid used as a trim.

rick•shaw (rik′shô, -shä), *n.* JINRIKISHA.

ric•o•chet (rik′ə shā′), *n., v.,* **-cheted** (-shād′), **-chet•ing** (-shā′ing). —*n.* **1.** the rebound of an object after it hits a glancing blow against a surface. —*v.i.* **2.** to move with or as if with ricochets.

ri•cot•ta (ri kot′ə, -kô′tə), *n., pl.* **-tas.** a soft Italian cheese that resembles cottage cheese.

rid (rid), *v.t.,* **rid** or **rid•ded, rid•ding. 1.** to free of something objectionable. —*Idiom.* **2. be** or **get rid of,** to be or become free of.

rid•dance (rid′ns), *n.* relief or deliverance.

rid′den, *v.* pp. of RIDE.

rid•dle¹ (rid′l), *n.* **1.** a question requiring ingenuity to be answered. **2.** a puzzling thing or person.

rid•dle² (rid′l), *v.t.,* **-dled, -dling.** to pierce with or as if with many holes.

ride (rīd), *v.,* **rode, rid•den, rid•ing,** *n.* —*v.i.* **1.** to be carried on the back of an animal or in a vehicle. **2.** to move along as if by vehicle. **3.** to continue without interruption or interference. **4.** to turn or rest on something. **5.** to float or seem to float. **6.** to lie at anchor. —*v.t.* **7.** to sit on and manage (a horse, bicycle, etc.) so as to be carried along. **8.** to be carried along on: *The ship rode the waves.* **9.** to ride over, along, or through (a road, region, etc.). **10.** to ridicule or harass. **11.** to control or dominate: *a man ridden by fear.* —*n.* **12.** a journey on a horse, camel, etc., or in a vehicle. **13.** a vehicle or device, as a roller coaster, on which people ride for amusement.

rid′er, *n.* **1.** a person who rides. **2.** an additional, usu. unrelated clause attached to a legislative bill. **3.** an addition or amendment to a document.

rid′er•ship′, *n.* the number of passengers who use a given public transportation system.

ridge (rij), *n., v.,* **ridged, ridg•ing.** —*n.* **1.** a long, narrow elevation of land. **2.** a long, narrow upper edge, as of a wave; crest. **3.** a raised, narrow strip, as on cloth. **4.** the horizontal line in which the tops of the rafters of a roof meet. —*v.t., v.i.* **5.** to provide with or form ridges. —**ridg′y,** *adj.,* **-i•er, -i•est.**

ridge′pole′, *n.* the horizontal member at the top of a roof to which the rafters are fastened.

rid•i•cule (rid′i kyōōl′), *n., v.,* **-culed, -cul•ing.** —*n.* **1.** speech or action intended to cause contemptuous laughter; derision. —*v.t.* **2.** to make fun of.

ri•dic•u•lous (ri dik′yə ləs), *adj.* causing or worthy of ridicule; laughable. —**ri•dic′u•lous•ly,** *adv.* —**ri•dic′u•lous•ness,** *n.*

rife (rīf), *adj.* **1.** of common or frequent occurrence; prevalent. **2.** abundant; abounding.

riff (rif), *n.* **1.** a constantly repeated melodic phrase in jazz or rock music. —*v.i.* **2.** to perform a riff.

riff•raff (rif′raf′), *n.* the lowest classes; rabble.

ri•fle¹ (rī′fəl), *n., v.,* **-fled, -fling.** —*n.* **1.** a shoulder firearm with a rifled bore. —*v.t.* **2.** to cut spiral grooves within (a gun barrel, pipe, etc.). —**ri′fle•man,** *n., pl.* **-men.**

ri•fle² (rī′fəl), *v.t.*, **-fled, -fling.** to ransack and rob. —**ri′fler,** *n.*

rift (rift), *n.* **1.** a fissure; cleft. **2.** a break in friendly relations. **3.** *Geol.* a fault. —*v.t., v.i.* **4.** to burst open; split.

rig (rig), *v.*, **rigged, rig•ging,** *n.* —*v.t.* **1.** to fit (a ship, mast, etc.) with rigging. **2.** to furnish with equipment or clothing. **3.** to assemble or install. **4.** to manipulate fraudulently. —*n.* **5.** the arrangement of masts, spars, and sails on a ship. **6.** apparatus; equipment. **7.** a tractor-trailer. **8.** a carriage with its horse. **9.** costume; clothing.

Ri•ga (rē′gə), *n.* the capital of Latvia. 915,000.

rig•a•ma•role (rig′ə mə rōl′), *n.* RIGMAROLE.

rig′ging, *n.* **1.** the ropes, chains, and tackle used to support and work the masts, sails, etc., of a ship. **2.** lifting or hauling tackle.

right (rīt), *adj.* **1.** in accordance with what is good, proper, or just. **2.** in conformity with fact or reason; correct. **3.** appropriate; suitable; desirable. **4.** of or located on the side of a person or thing that is turned toward the east when the subject is facing north. **5.** sound; sane. **6.** principal, front, or upper: *right side up.* **7.** (*often cap.*) of or belonging to the political Right. —*n.* **8.** something to which a person is entitled, as by just claim or legal guarantee. **9.** that which is morally, legally, or ethically proper. **10.** the right side. **11.** a right-hand turn. **12. the Right,** those individuals or groups holding conservative or reactionary political views. —*adv.* **13.** in a straight or direct line. **14.** quite; completely. **15.** immediately; promptly. **16.** exactly; precisely. **17.** correctly or accurately. **18.** righteously; properly. **19.** on or to the right. **20.** (*often cap.*) very (used in certain titles): *the right reverend.* —*v.t.* **21.** to put in an upright position. **22.** to bring into conformity with fact. **23.** to redress. —*Idiom.* **24. right away** or **off,** without hesitation; immediately. **25. right on,** *Slang.* exactly right. —**right′ly,** *adv.* —**right′ness,** *n.*

right′ an′gle, *n.* an angle of 90°.

right•eous (rī′chəs), *adj.* **1.** acting in an upright, moral way. **2.** morally right or justifiable: *righteous indignation.* —**right′eous•ly,** *adv.* —**right′eous• ness,** *n.*

right′ful, *adj.* **1.** having or held by a valid or just claim; legitimate. **2.** equitable or just. —**right′ful•ly,** *adv.* —**right′ful•ness,** *n.*

right′-hand′, *adj.* **1.** located on the right. **2.** RIGHT-HANDED. **3.** being of great assistance: *my right-hand man.*

right′-hand′ed, *adj.* **1.** using the right hand or arm more easily than the left. **2.** adapted to or performed by the right hand. —*adv.* **3.** with the right hand. —**right′-hand′edness,** *n.*

right′ist, *n.* (*sometimes cap.*) a member of the political Right.

right′-mind′ed, *adj.* having proper principles or opinions.

right′ of way′ or **right′-of-way′,** *n., pl.* **rights of way, right of ways** or **rights-of-way, right-of-ways. 1.** the right of a vehicle to proceed ahead of another. **2.** a right of passage over another's land. **3.** land acquired by a railroad for tracks. **4.** land covered by a public road.

right′size′, *v.t.*, **-sized, -siz•ing.** to adjust to an appropriate size: *Layoffs will be necessary to rightsize our workforce.*

right′-to-life′, *adj.* pertaining to or advocating laws making abortion illegal. —**right′-to-lif′er,** *n.*

right′ tri′angle, *n.* a triangle having a right angle.

right′ wing′, *n.* the conservative or reactionary element in a political party or organization. —**right′-wing′,** *adj.* —**right′-wing′er,** *n.*

rig•id (rij′id), *adj.* **1.** not pliant; stiff. **2.** firmly fixed or set. **3.** strict; severe. —**ri•gid′i•ty, rig′id•ness,** *n.* —**rig′id•ly,** *adv.*

rig•ma•role (rig′mə rōl′) *n.* **1.** a complicated procedure. **2.** confused or meaningless talk.

rig•or (rig′ər), *n.* **1.** the quality of being strict; inflexibility. **2.** harshness, as of attitude; severity. **3.** hardship; austerity. **4.** scrupulous accuracy; preci-

sion. Also, *esp. Brit.,* **rig′our.** —**rig′or•ous,** *adj.* —**rig′or•ous•ly,** *adv.*

rig•or mor•tis (rig′ər môr′tis), *n.* the stiffening of the body after death.

Riis (rēs), *n.* **Jacob August,** 1849–1914, U.S. journalist and social reformer, born in Denmark.

rile (rīl), *v.t.*, **riled, ril•ing. 1.** to irritate; vex. **2.** to make turbulent; roil.

rill (ril), *n.* a small rivulet or brook.

rim (rim), *n., v.,* **rimmed, rim•ming.** —*n.* **1.** the outer, often curved edge of something. **2.** the outer circle of a wheel. —*v.t.* **3.** to furnish with a rim.

rime¹ (rīm), *n.* FROST (def. 2). —**rim′y,** *adj.*, **-i•er, -i•est.**

rime² (rīm), *n., v.t., v.i.,* **rimed, rim•ing.** RHYME.

Rim•sky-Kor•sa•kov (rim′skē kôr′sə kôf′, -kof′), *n.* **Nicolai Andreevich,** 1844–1908, Russian composer.

rind (rīnd), *n.* a thick and firm outer coat or covering: *watermelon rind.*

ring¹ (ring), *n.* **1.** a circular band, as of gold, worn on the finger esp. as an ornament. **2.** something shaped like a ring. **3.** a circular line, mark, or course. **4.** a number of persons or things situated in a circle. **5.** an enclosed area, often circular, for a sports contest or exhibition: *a circus ring.* **6.** the sport of boxing. **7.** a group of persons cooperating for unethical or illegal purposes. —*v.t.* **8.** to surround with a ring. **9.** to form into a ring. —*Idiom.* **10. run rings around,** to surpass; outdo.

ring² (ring), *v.*, **rang, rung, ring•ing,** *n.* —*v.i.* **1.** to give forth a clear resonant sound. **2.** to cause a bell to sound, esp. as a signal. **3.** to resound; reecho. **4.** (of the ears) to have the sensation of a continued ringing sound. **5.** to seem to be; appear: *a story that rings true.* —*v.t.* **6.** to cause to ring. **7.** to announce by or as if by the sound of a bell. **8.** to telephone. **9. ring up,** to register (the amount of a sale) on a cash register. —*n.* **10.** a ringing sound. **11.** a sound like that of a ringing bell: *the ring of laughter.* **12.** a telephone call. **13.** an act or instance of ringing a bell. **14.** a characteristic sound or quality: *the ring of truth.* —*Idiom.* **15. ring a bell,** to evoke a memory.

ring′er¹, *n.* a quoit or horseshoe thrown so as to encircle the peg.

ring′er², *n.* **1.** one that rings or makes a ringing noise. **2.** a person that closely resembles another. **3.** a racehorse or athlete entered in a competition under false representation.

ring′lead′er, *n.* a person who leads others, esp. in unlawful activities.

ring′let (-lit), *n.* a curled lock of hair.

ring′mas′ter, *n.* a person in charge of the performances in a circus ring.

ring′side′, *n.* the area occupied by the first row of seats around a ring, as at a prizefight.

ring′worm′, *n.* a contagious skin disease caused by a fungus and characterized by ring-shaped patches.

rink (ringk), *n.* **1.** a smooth expanse of ice for ice-skating. **2.** a smooth floor, usu. of wood, for roller-skating.

rinse (rins), *v.*, **rinsed, rins•ing,** *n.* —*v.t.* **1.** to wash lightly, as by dipping in water. **2.** to drench in clean water as a final stage in washing. **3.** to remove (soap, dirt, etc.) by rinsing. —*n.* **4.** an act or instance of rinsing. **5.** the water used for rinsing. **6.** a preparation used, esp. after washing, to tint or condition the hair.

Ri•o de Ja•nei•ro (rē′ō dā zhə nâr′ō), *n.* a seaport in SE Brazil. 5,184,292.

Ri′o Grande′ (grand, grän′dā), *n.* a river flowing from SW Colorado into the Gulf of Mexico. 1800 mi. (2900 km) long.

ri•ot (rī′ət), *n.* **1.** a noisy, violent public disorder. **2.** disturbance of the public peace. **3.** a profuse outpouring or display. **4.** something or someone hilariously funny. —*v.i.* **5.** to take part in a riot. —**ri′ot•er,** *n.* —**ri′ot•ous,** *adj.*

rip (rip), *v.*, **ripped, rip•ping,** *n.* —*v.t.* **1.** to cut or tear apart roughly. **2.** to tear away or off in a rough manner. **3.** to saw (wood) in the direction of the grain. —*v.i.* **4.** to become torn apart. **5.** to move with great speed. **6. rip into,** to attack physically or verbally. **7.** ~ **off,** *Slang.* **a.** to steal. **b.** to steal from or exploit. —*n.* **8.** a tear made by ripping. —**rip'per,** *n.*

R.I.P., may he, she, or they rest in peace. [< L *requiēsca(n)t in pāce*]

rip' cord', *n.* a cord that when pulled opens a parachute.

ripe (rīp), *adj.,* **rip•er, rip•est. 1.** completely matured and developed: *ripe grain; a ripe peach.* **2.** sufficiently aged for use, as cheese. **3.** ready, as for action or use. **4.** ready enough; auspicious: *The time is ripe for a new policy.* —**ripe'ly,** *adv.* —**ripe'ness,** *n.*

rip'en, *v.t., v.i.* to make or become ripe.

rip'-off', *n. Slang.* **1.** a theft or exploitation. **2.** a copy; imitation.

ri•poste (ri pōst'), *n.* **1.** a quick, sharp reply or reaction. **2.** *Fencing.* a quick thrust given after parrying a lunge.

rip•ple (rip'əl), *v.,* **-pled, -pling,** *n.* —*v.i.* **1.** (of a liquid surface) to form small waves. **2.** (of sound) to move with a rising and falling tone or inflection. —*v.t.* **3.** to form small waves on. —*n.* **4.** a small wave. **5.** a sound as of water rippling: *a ripple of laughter.* —**rip'ply,** *adj.*

rip'ple effect', *n.* a spreading effect caused by a single action or event.

rip'-roar'ing, *adj.* boisterously wild and exciting; riotous.

rip'saw', *n.* a saw for cutting wood with the grain.

rip'tide', *n.* a tide that opposes other tides, causing a violent disturbance in the sea.

rise (rīz), *v.,* **rose, ris•en** (riz'ən), **ris•ing,** *n.* —*v.i.* **1.** to get up from a lying, sitting, or kneeling posture. **2.** to get up from bed. **3.** to revolt or rebel. **4.** to come into existence. **5.** to move from a lower to a higher position; ascend. **6.** to ascend above the horizon, as the sun. **7.** to extend or slope upward. **8.** to attain a higher level, as of importance. **9.** to prove oneself equal to a demand or emergency: *rose to the occasion.* **10.** to increase, as in amount or intensity. **11.** to puff up, as dough. **12.** to return from the dead. —*n.* **13.** an act or instance of rising. **14.** an increase or elevation, as in amount. **15.** origin or beginning. **16.** extension upward. **17.** upward slope, as of ground. **18.** a piece of rising ground. ——**Usage.** See RAISE.

ris'er, *n.* **1.** a person who rises, esp. from bed. **2.** the vertical face of a stair step.

ris•i•ble (riz'ə bəl), *adj.* **1.** causing laughter. **2.** able or disposed to laugh. —**ris'i•bil'i•ty,** *n., pl.* **-ties.**

risk (risk), *n.* **1.** exposure to the chance of injury or loss; danger. —*v.t.* **2.** to expose to the chance of injury or loss; hazard. **3.** to take the chance of. —**risk'y,** *adj.,* **-i•er, -i•est.**

ris•qué (ri skā'), *adj.* daringly close to indelicacy or impropriety.

rite (rīt), *n.* a formal ceremony or act prescribed or customary in religious use.

rite' of pas'sage, *n.* an act or event marking a passage from one stage of life to another.

rit•u•al (rich'ōo əl), *n.* **1.** an established procedure for a religious rite. **2.** a practice or pattern of behavior regularly performed in a set manner. —*adj.* **3.** of, being, or practiced as a ritual. —**rit'u•al•ism,** *n.* —**rit'u•al•is'tic,** *adj.* —**rit'u•al•ly,** *adv.*

ritz•y (rit'sē), *adj.,* **-i•er, -i•est.** swanky; elegant. [after the *Ritz* hotels founded by Swiss-born hotelier César Ritz (1850–1918)]

ri•val (rī'vəl), *n., adj., v.,* **-valed, -val•ing** or (*esp. Brit.*) **-valled, -val•ling.** —*n.* **1.** a person who competes with or tries to outdo another. **2.** a person or thing that equals another. —*adj.* **3.** competing. —*v.t.* **4.** to prove to be a worthy rival of. **5.** to equal (another); match. **6.** to compete with. —**ri'val•ry,** *n., pl.* **-ries.**

rive (rīv), *v.t., v.i.,* **rived, rived** or **riv•en, riv•ing. 1.** to tear apart. **2.** to split or break.

riv•er (riv'ər), *n.* a fairly large natural stream of water.

Ri•ve•ra (ri vâr'ə), *n.* **Diego,** 1886–1957, Mexican painter.

riv•er•bed (riv'ər bed'), *n.* the channel in which a river flows or formerly flowed.

riv'er•side', *n.* a bank of a river.

Riv'er•side', *n.* a city in SW California. 241,664.

riv•et (riv'it), *n., v.,* **-et•ed, -et•ing** or (*esp. Brit.*) **-et•ted, -et•ting.** —*n.* **1.** a metal pin for passing through holes in two or more pieces to hold them together, usu. made with a head at one end. —*v.t.* **2.** to fasten with a rivet. **3.** to hold (the eye, attention, etc.) firmly. —**riv'et•er,** *n.*

Riv•i•er•a (riv'ē âr'ə), *n.* a resort area along the Mediterranean coast, extending from SE France to NW Italy.

riv•u•let (riv'yə lit), *n.* a small stream.

Ri•yadh (rē yäd'), *n.* the capital of Saudi Arabia. 1,500,000.

ri•yal (rē yôl', -yäl'), *n.* the basic monetary unit of Qatar and Saudi Arabia.

rm., **1.** ream. **2.** room.

Rn, *Chem. Symbol.* radon.

RN or **R.N.,** registered nurse.

RNA, ribonucleic acid: any of a class of single-stranded nucleic acid molecules important in protein synthesis and in the transmission of genetic information transcribed from DNA.

roach[1] (rōch), *n.* a cockroach.

roach[2] (rōch), *n., pl.* **roach•es, roach.** a European freshwater fish of the carp family.

road (rōd), *n.* **1.** an open way for passage or travel, as by motor vehicle. **2.** a way or course. **3.** Often, **roads,** a sheltered place where ships may ride or anchor. ——*Idiom.* **4. down the road,** at some future time. **5. on the road,** traveling or touring.

road'bed', *n.* **1.** the bed or foundation for the track of a railroad. **2.** the material of which a road is composed.

road'block', *n.* **1.** an obstruction placed across a road for halting or hindering traffic. **2.** an obstruction to progress.

road' com'pany, *n.* a touring theatrical group.

road' kill', *n.* the body of an animal killed on a road by a motor vehicle.

road'run'ner, *n.* a large terrestrial cuckoo of the western U.S.

road' show', *n.* a show, as a play, performed by a touring group of actors.

road'side', *n.* the side of a road.

road'ster (-stər), *n.* an automobile with an open body and a single seat.

road' war'rior, *n. Slang.* a person who travels extensively on business.

road'way', *n.* **1.** the land over which a road is built. **2.** the part of a road over which vehicles travel.

road′work′, *n.* conditioning for an athlete, esp. a boxer, consisting of running long distances.

roam (rōm), *v.i., v.t.* to walk or travel (over or through) without purpose or direction; wander. —**roam′er,** *n.*

roan (rōn), *adj.* **1.** (chiefly of horses) of the color sorrel, chestnut, or bay sprinkled with gray or white. —*n.* **2.** an animal with a roan coat.

roar (rôr), *v.i.* **1.** to utter a loud, deep, extended sound. **2.** to laugh loudly. **3.** to make a loud din, as thunder. —*v.t.* **4.** to utter or express in a roar. —*n.* **5.** a roaring sound.

Roar′ing Twen′ties, *n.pl.* the 1920s regarded as a boisterous era of prosperity, fast cars, jazz, speakeasies, and wild youth.

roast (rōst), *v.t.* **1.** to cook (food) by dry heat, as in an oven. **2.** to parch (coffee beans, chestnuts, etc.) by exposure to heat. **3.** to heat excessively. **4.** to criticize severely. —*v.i.* **5.** to roast food. **6.** to undergo the process of becoming roasted. —*n.* **7.** a piece of meat for roasting. **8.** something roasted. **9.** an outdoor get-together at which food is roasted. —*adj.* **10.** roasted: *roast beef.* —**roast′er,** *n.*

rob (rob), *v.,* **robbed, rob•bing.** —*v.t.* **1.** to steal from. **2.** to deprive of something unjustly or injuriously. —*v.i.* **3.** to commit robbery. —**rob′ber,** *n.* —**rob′ber•y,** *n., pl.* **-ber•ies.**

robe (rōb), *n., v.,* **robed, rob•ing.** —*n.* **1.** a long, loose or flowing outer garment, esp. one worn as ceremonial dress. **2.** a bathrobe or dressing gown. **3.** a piece of fur or fabric used as a blanket or wrap. —*v.t., v.i.* **4.** to clothe with or put on a robe.

Rob•erts (rob′ərts), *n.* **Oral,** born 1918, U.S. evangelist.

Robe•son (rōb′sən), *n.* **Paul,** 1898–1976, U.S. singer and actor.

rob•in (rob′in), *n.* **1.** a large North American thrush with a chestnut-red breast. **2.** any of several small Old World birds with a reddish breast.

Rob′in Hood′, *n.* a legendary 12th-century English outlaw who robbed the rich to give to the poor.

Rob•in•son (rob′in sən), *n.* **1. Edward G.** (*Emanuel Goldenberg*), 1893–1973, U.S. actor, born in Romania. **2. Jack Roosevelt** (*Jackie*), 1919–72, U.S. baseball player. **3. Ray** (*Walker Smith*) ("*Sugar Ray*"), 1921–89, U.S. boxer.

ro•bot (rō′bət, -bot), *n.* **1.** a machine that resembles a human and does mechanical, routine tasks on command. **2.** a person who acts and responds in a mechanical, routine manner. **3.** an automatic machine or device. [coined by Karel Čapek (1890–1938), Czech playwright, in his play *R.U.R.,* from Czech *robota* labor] —**ro•bot′ic,** *adj.*

ro•bot•ics, *n.* the technology connected with using computer-controlled robots.

ro•bust (rō bust′, rō′bust), *adj.* **1.** strong and healthy; vigorous. **2.** rich and full-bodied: *a robust flavor.* —**ro•bust′ly,** *adv.* —**ro•bust′ness,** *n.*

Roch•es•ter (roch′es tər, -ə stər), *n.* a city in W New York. 231,170.

rock[1] (rok), *n.* **1. a.** a large mass of stone. **b.** a piece of stone. **2.** mineral matter assembled in masses in nature. **3.** something resembling a rock, as in firmness or support. **4.** *Slang.* a diamond. —*Idiom.* **5. on the rocks,** *Informal.* ruined or destroyed.

rock[2] (rok), *v.i., v.t.* **1.** to move to and fro or from side to side. **2.** to shake or disturb violently. —*n.* **3.** a rocking movement. **4.** popular music derived from blues and folk music and marked by an accented beat.

rock′a•bil/ly (-ə bil′ē), *n.* music combining features of rock and hillbilly music.

rock′-and-roll′ or **rock′-′n′-roll′,** ROCK[2] (def. 4).

rock′ bot′tom, *n.* the very lowest level.

rock′bound′, *adj.* hemmed in or covered by rocks.

rock′ can′dy, *n.* sugar in large, hard crystals.

Rock•e•fel•ler (rok′ə fel′ər), *n.* **1. John D(avison),** 1839–1937, and his son **John D(avison), Jr.,** 1874–1960, U.S. oil magnates and philanthropists. **2. Nelson A(ldrich),** 1908–79, vice president of the U.S. 1974–77 (son of John D. Rockefeller, Jr.).

rock′er, *n.* **1.** one of the curved pieces on which a cradle or a rocking chair rocks. **2.** Also called **rock′-ing chair′.** a chair mounted on rockers. —*Idiom.* **3. off one′s rocker,** *Slang.* insane; crazy.

rock•et (rok′it), *n.* **1.** any of various tubelike devices containing combustibles that on being ignited propel the tube through the air. **2.** a space capsule or vehicle put into orbit by a rocket. **3.** an engine with its own solid or liquid fuel and oxidizer. —*v.i., v.t.* **4.** to move like or by a rocket.

rock′et•ry, *n.* the science of rocket design, development, and flight.

rock′et sci′entist, *n.* **1.** a specialist in rocketry. **2.** a highly intelligent person, esp. one with mathematical ability. —**rock′et sci′ence,** *n.*

Rock•ford (rok′fərd), *n.* a city in N Illinois. 143,263.

rock′ gar′den, *n.* a garden on rocky ground or among rocks.

rock′ing horse′, *n.* a toy horse mounted on rockers or springs.

Rock•ne (rok′nē), *n.* **Knute (Kenneth)** (nōōt), 1888–1931, U.S. football coach, born in Norway.

rock′-ribbed′, *adj.* **1.** having ribs or ridges of rock. **2.** unyielding; uncompromising.

rock′ salt′, *n.* common salt occurring in rocklike masses.

Rock•well (rok′wel′, -wəl), *n.* **Norman,** 1894–1978, U.S. illustrator.

rock′ wool′, *n.* a woollike material made from molten slag or rock, used for insulation.

rock′y[1], *adj.,* **-i•er, -i•est. 1.** full of or consisting of rocks. **2.** rocklike, as in steadfastness. **3.** unfeeling. —**rock′i•ness,** *n.*

rock′y[2], *adj.,* **-i•er, -i•est. 1.** wobbly; unsteady. **2.** full of hazards; uncertain.

Rock′y Moun′tain goat′, *n.* a long-haired wild goat of W North America with short black horns.

Rock′y Moun′tains, *n.pl.* a mountain system in W North America, extending NW from central New Mexico through W Canada to N Alaska. Also called **Rock′ies.**

Rock′y Moun′tain sheep′, *n.* BIGHORN.

ro•co•co (rə kō′kō, rō′kə kō′), *n.* **1.** an artistic style marked by studied elegance and delicate ornamentation. —*adj.* **2.** of or characteristic of rococo. **3.** ornate or florid.

rod (rod), *n.* **1.** a straight bar or stick. **2. a.** a stick for measuring. **b.** a unit of linear measure, 5½ yards (5.03 m). **3.** a stick used as an instrument of punishment. **4.** punishment. **5.** a staff or scepter carried as a symbol of office or authority. **6.** FISHING ROD. **7.** *Bible.* a branch of a family; tribe. Ps. 74:2; Jer. 10:16.

rode (rōd), *v.* pt. of RIDE.

ro•dent (rōd′nt), *adj.* **1.** of or being a gnawing or nibbling mammal characterized by four continually growing incisors. —*n.* **2.** a rodent mammal, as a mouse.

ro•de•o (rō′dē ō′, rō dā′ō), *n., pl.* **-os. 1.** a public exhibition of cowboy skills. **2.** a roundup of cattle.

Rodg•ers (roj′ərz), *n.* **Richard,** 1902–79, U.S. composer of popular music.

Ro•din (rō dan′, -daN′), *n.* **Auguste,** 1840–1917, French sculptor.

roe[1] (rō), *n.* the eggs of a fish.

roe[2] (rō), *n., pl.* **roes, roe.** a small, agile Eurasian deer with three-pointed antlers.

roe′buck′, *n., pl.* **-bucks, -buck.** a male roe deer.

roent•gen (rent′gən, -jən, runt′-), *n.* the international unit for measuring radiation dosage.

Roe v. Wade (rō; wād), *n.* a U.S. Supreme Court case in 1973 that legalized abortions in the U.S.

rog•er (roj′ər), *interj.* **1.** *Informal.* all right; OK. **2.** message received and understood (a response to radio communications).

Rog•ers (roj′ərz), *n.* **1. Ginger,** 1911–95, U.S. dancer and actress. **2. Will(iam Penn Adair),** 1879–1935, U.S. actor and humorist.

rogue (rōg), *n.* **1.** a dishonest person; scoundrel. **2.**

a playfully mischievous person. —**ro′guer•y,** *n.* —**ro′guish,** *adj.*

roil (roil), *v.t.* **1.** to make (a fluid) cloudy by stirring up sediment. **2.** to disturb or disquiet; irritate.

roist•er (roi′stər), *v.i.* to revel noisily or without restraint. —**roist′er•er,** *n.*

role or **rôle** (rōl), *n.* **1.** a part or character played by an actor or singer. **2.** the proper or customary function of a person or thing.

role′ mod′el, *n.* a person whose behavior is imitated by others.

role′-play′ing, *n.* a method of psychotherapy in which participants act out roles relevant to real-life situations.

roll (rōl), *v.i.* **1.** to move along a surface by turning over and over. **2.** to move on wheels. **3.** to advance with an undulating motion, as waves. **4.** to extend in undulations, as land. **5.** to elapse, as time. **6.** to move as in a cycle, as seasons. **7.** to make a deep, prolonged sound, as thunder. **8.** (of the eyes) to rotate. **9.** (of a ship) to rock from side to side in open water. **10.** to walk with a swinging gait. —*v.t.* **11.** to cause to move along a surface by turning over and over. **12.** to move along on wheels. **13.** to utter or give forth with a full, continuous sound. **14.** to trill: *He rolls his r′s.* **15.** to cause to turn over. **16.** to rotate, as the eyes. **17.** to cause to rock from side to side. **18.** to wrap around an axis or around itself; wind. **19.** to wrap or envelop, as in a covering. **20.** to spread out or flatten, as with a rolling pin. **21.** to throw (dice). **22. roll back,** to reduce (prices, wages, etc.) to a former level. **23. ~ over,** to reinvest (funds). —*n.* **24.** something that is rolled up. **25.** a register or list, as of members. **26.** something rolled up in a cylindrical form. **27.** a rounded mass: *rolls of fat.* **28.** a small cake of bread sometimes folded over before baking. **29.** an act or instance of rolling. **30.** a deep, prolonged sound, as of thunder. **31.** a rolling motion or gait.

roll′back′, *n.* a return to a lower level, as of prices.

roll′ call′, *n.* the calling of a list of names for checking attendance.

roll′er, *n.* **1.** one that rolls. **2.** a cylinder, wheel, or caster upon which something is rolled along. **3.** a cylindrical object upon which something is rolled up. **4.** a cylindrical object for spreading, crushing, curling, or flattening something. **5.** a long, swelling wave.

Roll′er•blade′, *v.,* -blad•ed, -blad•ing. **1.** *Trademark.* a brand of in-line skates. —*v.i.* **2.** (*often l.c.*) to skate on in-line skates. —**roll′er•blad′er,** *n.*

roll′er coast′er, *n.* a small railroad, esp. in an amusement park, that moves along a high, sharply winding trestle with steep inclines.

roll′er skate′, *n.* a skate with wheels for use on a surface such as a sidewalk. —**roll′er-skate′,** *v.i.,* -skat•ed, -skat•ing. —**roll′er skat′er,** *n.*

rol•lick (rol′ik), *v.i.* to move or act in a carefree, frolicsome manner. —**rol′lick•ing,** *adj.*

roll′ing pin′, *n.* a cylinder, as of wood, for rolling out dough.

roll′o′ver, *n.* the reinvestment of funds.

roll′-top desk′, *n.* a desk with a flexible sliding cover for the working surface.

ro•ly-po•ly (rō′lē pō′lē, -pō′lē), *adj.* short and plumply round.

ROM (rom), *n.* read-only memory: nonmodifiable computer memory containing programmed instructions to the system.

Rom., 1. Roman. **2.** Also, **Rom** Romance. **3.** Romania. **4.** Romanian.

ro•maine (rō mān′, rə-), *n.* a variety of lettuce with a cylindrical head of long, loose leaves.

Ro•man (rō′mən), *adj.* **1.** of or typical of ancient or modern Rome or its inhabitants. **2.** (*usu. l.c.*) of or noting the upright style of printing types most commonly used. **3.** of the Roman Catholic Church. —*n.* **4.** a native, inhabitant, or citizen of ancient or modern Rome. **5.** (*usu. l.c.*) roman type or lettering.

Ro′man can′dle, *n.* a firework consisting of a tube that sends out sparks and balls of fire.

Ro′man Cath′olic, *adj.* **1.** of the Roman Catholic Church. —*n.* **2.** a member of the Roman Catholic Church. —**Ro′man Cathol′icism,** *n.*

Ro′man Cath′olic Church′, *n.* the Christian church of which the pope is the supreme head.

ro•mance (*n., adj.* rō mans′, rō′mans; *v.* rō mans′), *n., v.,* -manced, -manc•ing, *adj.* —*n.* **1.** a story depicting heroic or marvelous deeds, pageantry, and romantic exploits. **2.** a medieval narrative treating of heroic, fantastic, or supernatural events. **3.** a romantic spirit, sentiment, or quality. **4.** a love affair. —*v.i.* **5.** to indulge in fanciful stories or daydreams. —*v.t.* **6.** to court romantically. —*adj.* **7.** (*cap.*) of or noting the languages descended from Latin, including French, Spanish, Portuguese, Italian, and Romanian. —**ro•manc′er,** *n.*

Ro′man Em′pire, *n.* the empire of the ancient Romans lasting from 27 B.C. to A.D. 395.

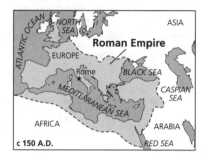

Ro•man•esque (rō′mə nesk′), *adj.* of the style of architecture prevailing in W and S Europe from the 9th through the 12th centuries.

Ro•ma•ni•a (rō mā′nē ə), *n.* a republic in SE Europe. 21,399,114. —**Ro•ma′ni•an,** *n., adj.*

Ro′man nu′meral, *n.* any of the numerals in the ancient Roman system of notation, still used occasionally. The basic symbols are **I** (=1), **V** (=5), **X**

ROMAN NUMERALS

Arabic Numeral	Roman Numeral	Arabic Numeral	Roman Numeral
1	I	29	XXIX
2	II	30	XXX
3	III	31	XXXI
4	IV	32	XXXII
5	V	40	XL
6	VI	41	XLI
7	VII	50	L
8	VIII	60	LX
9	IX	70	LXX
10	X	80	LXXX
11	XI	90	XC
12	XII	100	C
13	XIII	101	CI
14	XIV	102	CII
15	XV	200	CC
16	XVI	300	CCC
17	XVII	400	CD
18	XVIII	500	D
19	XIX	600	DC
20	XX	700	DCC
21	XXI	800	DCCC
22	XXII	900	CM
23	XXIII	1000	M
24	XXIV	2000	MM
25	XXV	5000	$\overline{\text{V}}$
26	XXVI	10,000	$\overline{\text{X}}$
27	XXVII	100,000	$\overline{\text{C}}$
28	XXVIII	1,000,000	$\overline{\text{M}}$

(=10), **L** (=50), **C** (=100), **D** (=500), and **M** (=1000).

Ro•ma•nov or **Ro•ma•noff** (rō′mə nôf′, -nof′, rōmä′nəf), *n.* a member of the imperial dynasty of Russia that ruled from 1613 to 1917.

Ro•mans (rō′mənz), *n.* an Epistle of the New Testament, written by Paul to the Christian community in Rome.

ro•man•tic (rō man′tik), *adj.* **1.** of or marked by romance. **2.** impractical or unrealistic. **3.** imbued with idealism; utopian. **4.** preoccupied with love or by the idealizing of love. **5.** passionate; fervent. **6.** (*often cap.*) of or characteristic of a style of literature and art that subordinates form to content and emphasizes imagination and emotion. —*n.* **7.** a romantic person. —**ro•man′ti•cal•ly,** *adv.*

ro•man′ti•cism (-tə siz′əm), *n.* (*often cap.*) the Romantic style in literature and art. —**ro•man′ti•cist,** *n.*

ro•man′ti•cize′, *v.,* -cized, -ciz•ing. —*v.t.* **1.** to invest with a romantic character. —*v.i.* **2.** to hold romantic notions.

Roman′tic Move′ment, *n.* a movement that led to the establishment of Romantic principles in art and literature around 1800.

Rom•a•ny (rom′ə nē, rō′mə-), *n.* the Indo-Aryan language of the Gypsies.

Rome (rōm), *n.* **1.** the capital of Italy. 2,817,227. **2.** the ancient Italian kingdom, republic, and empire whose capital was the city of Rome. —**Proverb. 3. Rome was not built in a day,** worthwhile projects take time to complete. **4. When in Rome, do as the Romans do,** one should follow the customs of one's hosts.

Ro•me•o (rō′mē ō′), *n.,* *pl.* -me•os. a romantic male lover.

Rom•mel (rom′əl, rum′-), *n.* **Erwin** ("the Desert Fox"), 1891–1944, German field marshal.

romp (romp), *v.i.* **1.** to play in a lively or boisterous manner; frolic. **2.** to win easily. —*n.* **3.** a lively or boisterous frolic. **4.** an easy victory.

romp′er, *n.* **1.** one that romps. **2.** Usu., -pers. (*used with a pl. v.*) a one-piece children's garment combining a shirt and short, bloomerlike pants.

rood (rōōd), *n.* **1.** a crucifix, esp. a large one. **2.** a unit of land measure equal to 40 square rods or ¼ acre.

roof (rōōf, rŏŏf), *n.* **1.** the external upper covering of a building. **2.** something like a roof in form or function. —*v.t.* **3.** to provide with a roof. —**roof′er,** *n.* —**roof′less,** *adj.*

roof′ing, *n.* material for roofs.

roof′top′, *n.* the roof of a building.

rook[1] (rŏŏk), *n.* **1.** a black, bare-faced Eurasian crow. —*v.t.* **2.** to cheat or swindle.

rook[2] (rŏŏk), *n.* a chess piece that may move any number of unobstructed squares horizontally or vertically.

rook′er•y, *n.,* *pl.* -er•ies. a colony or breeding place of gregarious creatures, esp. rooks.

rook′ie, *n.,* *pl.* -ies. **1.** an inexperienced recruit. **2.** a novice; beginner.

room (rōōm, rŏŏm), *n.* **1.** an enclosed or partitioned portion of space within a building. **2. rooms,** lodgings or quarters. **3.** the persons present in a room. **4.** an extent of space occupied by or available for something. **5.** opportunity or scope: *room for improvement.* —*v.i.* **6.** to occupy rooms; lodge. —**room′ful,** *n.,* *pl.* -fuls. —**room′y,** *adj.,* -i•er, -i•est. —**room′i•ness,** *n.*

room′ and board′, *n.* lodging and meals.

room′er, *n.* a person living in a rented room.

room•ette (rōō met′, rŏŏ-), *n.* a small private compartment in the sleeping car of a train.

room′ing house′, *n.* a house with furnished rooms to rent.

room′mate′, *n.* a person who shares a room or apartment with another or others.

roor•back or **roor•bach** (rōōr′bak′), *n.* a false and more or less damaging report circulated for political effect. [after a fictitious Baron von *Roorback,* in

whose travelogue occurred an account of an incident damaging to the character of James K. Polk]

Roo•se•velt (rō′zə velt′), *n.* **1. (Anna) Eleanor,** 1884–1962, U.S. diplomat and author (wife of Franklin Delano Roosevelt). **2. Franklin Delano** ("FDR"), 1882–1945, 32nd president of the U.S. 1933–45. **3. Theodore** (Teddy, "T.R."), 1858–1919, 26th president of the U.S. 1901–09.

roost (rōōst), *n.* **1.** a perch upon which birds or fowl rest at night. —*v.i.* **2.** to sit or rest on or as if on a roost.

roost′er, *n.* the male of the domestic fowl.

root[1] (rōōt, rŏŏt), *n.* **1.** a plant part that grows downward into the soil, anchoring the plant and absorbing nutriment and moisture. **2.** any underground plant part, as a rhizome. **3.** the embedded portion of a hair, tooth, nail, etc. **4.** a fundamental or essential part. **5.** a source or origin. **6. roots, a.** a person's original home, environment, and culture. **b.** the relationships, habits, etc., that make a locale one's true home. **7.** a quantity that when multiplied by itself a certain number of times produces a given quantity. **8.** a morpheme that underlies an inflectional or derivational paradigm, as *dance,* the root in *danced* and *dancer.* —*v.i.* **9.** to become fixed or established. —*v.t.* **10.** to fix by or as if by roots. **11.** to pull, tear, or dig up by the roots. **12.** to remove completely; extirpate. —**root′less,** *adj.*

tap (ragweed), fibrous (plantain),
Ambrosia trifida *Plantago major*

fleshy (carrot), tuberous (rue anemone),
Daucus carota *Anemonella thalictroides*

roots

root[2] (rōōt, rŏŏt), *v.i.* **1.** to turn up the soil with the snout. **2.** to poke, pry, or search. —*v.t.* **3.** to turn over with the snout.

root[3] (rōōt or, sometimes, rŏŏt), *v.i.* **1.** to encourage a team or contestant by cheering enthusiastically. **2.** to lend moral support. —**root′er,** *n.*

Root (rōōt), *n.* **Elihu,** 1845–1937, U.S. statesman.

root′ beer′, *n.* a carbonated beverage flavored with extracts of roots, barks, and herbs.

root′ canal′, *n.* the root portion of the pulp cavity of a tooth.

root′ cel′lar, *n.* a cellar, often underground and usu. covered with dirt, where root crops and other vegetables are stored.

Roots (rōōts, rŏŏts), a nonfiction work (1976) by Alex Haley, tracing the history of black Americans.

rope (rōp), *n.,* *v.,* **roped, rop•ing.** —*n.* **1.** a strong line or cord of twisted or braided strands, as of hemp. **2. ropes,** the operations of a business or the details of an undertaking: *to learn the ropes.* **3.** a hangman's noose. **4.** material or objects twisted or strung together in the form of a cord. —*v.t.* **5.** to tie, bind, or fasten with a rope. **6.** to enclose or mark with a rope. **7.** to catch with a lasso. **8. rope in,** to lure, esp. by trickery.

Roque•fort (rōk′fərt), *Trademark.* a strong-flavored cheese veined with mold, made from sheep's milk.

Ror′schach test′ (rôr′shäk), *n.* a diagnostic test of personality based on the viewer's interpretations of a standard series of inkblot designs.

ro•sa•ry (rō'zə rē), *n., pl.* **-ries. 1.** a series of prayers recited by Roman Catholics as a private devotion. **2.** a string of beads used in counting these prayers. [< ML *rosārium* rose garden]

rose[1] (rōz), *n.* **1.** any of various prickly-stemmed shrubs with showy, often fragrant flowers. **2.** the flower of a rose. **3.** a pinkish red, purplish pink, or light crimson. **4.** an ornament shaped like a rose. —*adj.* **5.** of the color rose.

rose[2] (rōz), *v.* pt. of RISE.

ro•sé (rō zā'), *n.* a pink wine.

ro•se•ate (rō'zē it, -āt'), *adj.* **1.** tinged with rose; rosy. **2.** incautiously optimistic.

rose'bud', *n.* the bud of a rose.

rose'bush', *n.* a shrub that bears roses.

rose'-col'ored, *adj.* **1.** of the color rose; rosy. **2.** optimistic; sanguine.

rose' fe'ver, *n.* a form of hay fever caused by rose pollen.

rose•mar•y (rōz'mâr'ē, -mə rē), *n., pl.* **-mar•ies.** an aromatic evergreen shrub of the mint family, with leaves used as a seasoning and in perfumes.

rose' of Shar'on, *n.* **1.** Also called **althea.** a shrub having showy white, reddish, or purplish flowers. **2.** a plant mentioned in the Bible. Song of Solomon 2:1.

Roset'ta stone', *n.* a stone slab, found in 1799 near Rosetta, Italy, with parallel inscriptions in Greek, Egyptian hieroglyphic, and demotic characters, enabling the decipherment of ancient Egyptian hieroglyphics.

ro•sette (rō zet'), *n.* **1.** a rose-shaped ornament or badge, esp. of ribbon. **2.** an architectural ornament resembling a rose.

rose' wa'ter, *n.* water containing oil distilled from roses, used in perfume.

rose' win'dow, *n.* a circular window decorated with tracery symmetrical about the center.

rose'wood', *n.* **1.** the reddish, often fragrant cabinet wood yielded by certain tropical trees. **2.** a tree yielding rosewood.

Rosh Ha•sha•nah (or **Ha•sha•na**) (rôsh' hə shä'nə, -shô'-, rōsh'), *n.* the Jewish New Year, celebrated in September or October.

ros•in (roz'in), *n.* a brittle resin left after distilling the turpentine from pine pitch, used in making varnish and for rubbing on violin bows.

Ros•set•ti (rō set'ē, -zet'ē, rə-), *n.* **1. Christina Georgina,** 1830–94, English poet. **2.** her brother, **Dante Gabriel** (*Gabriel Charles Dante Rossetti*), 1828–82, English poet and painter.

Ros•si•ni (rō sē'nē, rô-), *n.* **Gio•ac•chi•no Antonio** 1792–1868, Italian composer.

ros•ter (ros'tər), *n.* a list of persons or groups, as of military personnel.

ros•trum (ros'trəm), *n., pl.* **-trums, -tra** (-trə) a platform or stage for public speaking.

ros•y (rō'zē), *adj.,* **-i•er, i•est. 1.** pink or pinkish red; roseate. **2.** bright or promising: *a rosy future.* —**ros'i•ly,** *adv.* —**ros'i•ness,** *n.*

rot (rot), *v.,* **rot•ted, rot•ting,** *n.* —*v.i., v.t.* **1.** to undergo or cause to undergo decomposition; decay. —*n.* **2.** the process of rotting. **3.** the state of being rotten. **4.** rotting or rotten matter. **5.** an animal or plant disease caused by a fungal or bacterial infection and characterized by decay.

ro•ta•ry (rō'tə rē), *adj., n., pl.* **-ries.** —*adj.* **1.** turning or capable of turning on an axis. **2.** having a rotating part or parts. —*n.* **3.** TRAFFIC CIRCLE.

ro•tate (rō'tāt), *v.i., v.t.,* **-tat•ed, -tat•ing. 1.** to turn around on or as if on an axis; revolve. **2.** to proceed or cause to proceed in a fixed routine of succession. —**ro•ta'tion,** *n.* —**ro'ta•to'ry** (-tə tôr'ē), *adj.*

ROTC (är'ō tē sē', rot'sē), Reserve Officers Training Corps.

rote (rōt), *n.* **1.** a fixed, habitual, or mechanical course of procedure. —*Idiom.* **2. by rote,** from memory, without thought of the meaning.

ro•tis•ser•ie (rō tis'ə rē), *n., pl.* **-ies.** a cooking unit with a spit for barbecuing.

ro•to•gra•vure (rō'tə grə vyŏor'), *n.* **1.** a process by which an image to be reproduced is printed from an intaglio copper cylinder. **2.** a section of a newspaper consisting of rotogravure pages.

ro•tor (rō'tər), *n.* **1.** a rotating member of a mechanical or electrical device. **2.** a system of rotating airfoils, as the horizontal ones of a helicopter.

ro•to•till•er (rō'tə til'ər), *n.* a motorized device with spinning blades for tilling soil.

rot•ten (rot'n), *adj.,* **-er, -est. 1.** having rotted. **2.** foul-smelling; putrid. **3.** morally offensive; corrupt. **4.** wretchedly bad; miserable. —*Proverb.* **5. A rotten apple spoils the barrel,** one bad person or thing may corrupt or damage those nearby. —**rot'ten• ness,** *n.*

Rot•ter•dam (rot'ər dam'), *n.* a seaport in SW Netherlands. 574,299.

ro•tund (rō tund'), *adj.* **1.** rounded. **2.** plump. **3.** full-toned; sonorous. —**ro•tun'di•ty, ro•tund'ness,** *n.*

ro•tun•da (rō tun'də), *n., pl.* **-das. 1.** a round building, esp. one with a dome. **2.** a large circular hall or room.

rotunda

rou•é (rōō ā', rōō'ā), *n., pl.* **-és,** a licentious man; rake. [< F]

rouge (rōōzh), *n., v.,* **rouged, roug•ing.** —*n.* **1.** a red cosmetic for coloring the cheeks or lips. **2.** a reddish powder used for polishing metal, glass, and gems. —*v.t., v.i.* **3.** to use rouge (on).

rough (ruf), *adj.,* **-er, -est,** *n., adv., v.,* —*adj.* **1.** having a coarse or uneven surface. **2.** shaggy or coarse. **3.** characterized by violence. **4.** characterized by turbulence. **5.** tempestuous. **6.** lacking in gentleness, care, or consideration. **7.** unmannerly; rude. **8.** difficult or unpleasant: *had a rough time of it.* **9.** lacking culture or refinement. **10.** not elaborated, perfected, or corrected; unpolished. **11.** approximate or tentative: *a rough guess.* —*n.* **12.** something rough, esp. rough ground. **13.** a part bordering a golf fairway on which the grass is not trimmed. —*adv.* **14.** in a rough manner. —*v.t.* **15.** to roughen. **16.** to subject to physical violence. **17.** to make or do roughly in haste. —*Idiom.* **18. rough it,** to live without customary comforts or conveniences. —*Saying.* **19. take the rough with the smooth,** one must accept bad times as well as good. —**rough'ly,** *adv.* —**rough'ness,** *n.*

rough'age (-ij), *n.* FIBER (def. 5).

rough'-and-read'y, *adj.* rude or crude but good enough for the purpose.

rough'-and-tum'ble, *adj.* **1.** violent, random, and disorderly. —*n.* **2.** rough-and-tumble competition or fighting.

rough'en, *v.t., v.i.* to make or become rough or rougher.

rough'-hew', *v.t.,* **-hewed, -hewed** or **-hewn, -hew•ing. 1.** to hew (timber, stone, etc.) roughly or without smoothing. **2.** to shape roughly.

rough'house', *n., v.,* **-housed, -hous•ing.** —*n.* **1.** rough, disorderly play. —*v.i.* **2.** to engage in roughhouse. —*v.t.* **3.** to handle roughly but playfully.

rough′neck′, *n.* **1.** a rough, coarse person. **2.** a laborer on an oil-drilling rig.

Rough′ Rid′er, *n.* a member of a volunteer cavalry organized by Theodore Roosevelt in the Spanish-American War (1898).

rough′shod′, *adj.* **1.** shod with horseshoes having projecting points. —*Idiom.* **2. ride roughshod over**, to treat harshly.

rou•lette (rōō let′), *n.* **1.** a game of chance in which a small ball is spun on a wheel. **2.** a small wheel, esp. one with sharp teeth for making rows of marks or perforations.

Rou•ma•ni•a (rōō mā′nē ə), *n.* ROMANIA. —**Rou•ma′ni•an**, *adj., n.*

round (round), *adj.*, **-er, -est,** *n., adv., prep., v.* —*adj.* **1.** circular in form. **2.** curved like part of a circle. **3.** cylindrical. **4.** spherical or globular. **5.** consisting of full, curved lines or shapes, as handwriting. **6.** full or complete: *a round dozen.* **7.** expressed by a whole number with no fraction. **8.** considerable in amount; ample. **9.** brought to completeness or perfection. **10.** full and sonorous, as sound. **11.** plain or candid; outspoken. —*n.* **12.** any round shape or object. **13.** a completed course of time or series of events or operations. **14.** a complete course, series, or succession: *a round of talks.* **15.** Often, **rounds.** a habitual or definite circuit. **16.** a single outburst, as of applause. **17.** a single discharge of shot by each of a number of guns. **18.** ammunition for a single shot. **19.** a single serving of drink to everyone present. **20.** movement in a circle. **21.** a cut of beef below the rump and above the leg. **22.** a short musical canon in which the voices enter at equally spaced intervals of time. **23.** one of a series of periods, as in a boxing match. —*adv.* **24.** throughout. **25.** Also, **'round.** around. —*prep.* **26.** throughout. **27.** around. —*v.t.* **28.** to make round. **29.** to pass or travel around. **30.** to express as a round number. **31.** to encircle or surround. —*v.i.* **32.** to become round. **33.** to make a turn or circuit. **34.** to turn around as if on an axis. **35. round up**, to bring together; assemble. —*Idiom.* **36. in the round, a.** (of a theater) having a stage completely surrounded by seats. **b.** (of sculpture) freestanding. —**round′ness**, *n.*

round′a•bout′, *adj.* circuitous or indirect, as a statement.

roun•de•lay (roun′dl ā′), *n.* a song in which a phrase or line is continually repeated.

Round•head (round′hed′), *n.* a Puritan supporter of Parliament during the English Civil War: so called in derision by the Cavaliers because they wore their hair cut short.

round′house′, *n.* a building for the servicing and repair of locomotives.

round′ly, *adv.* **1.** in a round manner. **2.** vigorously. **3.** outspokenly or unsparingly. **4.** completely or fully.

round′-shoul′dered, *adj.* having the shoulders bent forward.

round′ ta′ble or **round′ta′ble**, *n.* a group gathered for a conference.

round′-the-clock′, *adj.* continuing without interruption.

round′ trip′, *n.* a trip to a given place and back again. —**round′-trip′**, *adj.*

round′up′, *n.* **1.** the driving together of cattle, as for branding or shipping to market. **2.** a gathering together of scattered items or people. **3.** a summary, as of news.

round′worm′, *n.* a nematode that infests the intestine of mammals.

rouse (rouz), *v.t., v.i.,* **roused, rous•ing. 1.** to bring or come out of a state of sleep, unconsciousness, or inactivity. **2.** to stir or be stirred up.

Rous•seau (rōō sō′), *n.* **Jean Jacques** (zhän), 1712–78, French philosopher and social reformer.

roust•a•bout (roust′ə bout′), *n.* an unskilled laborer, as at a circus or in an oil field.

rout¹ (rout), *n.* **1.** a disorderly flight. **2.** an overwhelming defeat. —*v.t.* **3.** to disperse in disorderly flight. **4.** to defeat decisively.

rout² (rout), *v.t.* **1.** to find or get by searching or rummaging. **2.** to force or drive out. **3.** to make a hollow in; furrow.

route (rōōt, rout), *n., v.,* **rout•ed, rout•ing.** —*n.* **1.** a way for passage or travel. **2.** a regular line of passage or travel. **3.** a specific itinerary or regular round of stops. —*v.t.* **4.** to fix the route of. **5.** to send by a particular route. [< OF < L *rupta (via)* broken (i.e., freshly made) (way)]

rou•tine (rōō tēn′), *n.* **1.** a customary or regular course of procedure. **2.** habitual, unvarying, or unimaginative procedure. **3.** a set of instructions directing a computer to perform a specific task. —*adj.* **4.** of, adhering to, or being routine. **5.** dull or uninteresting; commonplace. —**rou•tine′ly**, *adv.* —**rou•tin′ize**, *v.t.,* **-ized, -iz•ing.**

rove (rōv), *v.i., v.t.,* **roved, rov•ing.** to wander (over or through) aimlessly or at random. —**rov′er**, *n.*

row¹ (rō), *n.* **1.** a number of persons or things arranged in a line. **2.** a line of adjacent seats facing the same way, as in a theater. **3.** a street formed by two continuous lines of buildings.

row² (rō), *v.t., v.i.* **1.** to propel (a boat) with oars. **2.** to convey in a rowboat. —*n.* **3.** an act or period of rowing. **4.** an excursion in a rowboat. —**row′er**, *n.*

row³ (rou), *n.* **1.** a noisy dispute or quarrel. —*v.i.* **2.** to quarrel noisily.

row′boat′ (rō′-), *n.* a small boat designed for rowing.

row•dy (rou′dē), *adj.,* **-di•er, -di•est,** *n., pl.* **-dies.** —*adj.* **1.** rough and disorderly. —*n.* **2.** a rough, disorderly person. —**row′di•ness**, *n.* —**row′dy•ism**, *n.*

row•el (rou′əl), *n.* a small wheel with radiating points that forms the extremity of a spur.

row′ house′ (rō), *n.* one of a row of houses sharing a sidewall with a neighboring house.

row′ing machine′ (rō′ing), *n.* an exercise machine that allows the user to go through the motions of rowing in a racing shell.

roy•al (roi′əl), *adj.* **1.** of a king or queen. **2.** appropriate to or befitting a sovereign; magnificent. —**roy′al•ly**, *adv.*

roy′al blue′, *n.* a deep blue.

roy′al•ist, *n.* **1.** a supporter of a monarch or royal government. **2.** (*cap.*) a supporter of King Charles I of England; Cavalier. **3.** (*often cap.*) a loyalist in the American Revolution; Tory.

roy′al•ty, *n., pl.* **-ties. 1.** royal persons collectively. **2.** royal status, dignity, or power. **3.** compensation paid to the owner of a right, as a patent, for the use of it. **4.** an agreed portion of the income from a work paid to its author or composer.

rpm, revolutions per minute.

rps, revolutions per second.

RR, 1. railroad. **2.** rural route.

RSD, repetitive strain disorder.

RSFSR or **R.S.F.S.R.,** Russian Soviet Federated Socialist Republic.

RSI, repetitive strain injury.

RSV, Revised Standard Version (of the Bible).

RSVP or **R.S.V.P.,** please reply. [< F *r(épondez) s('il) v(ous) p(laît)*]

rte., route.

Ru, *Chem. Symbol.* ruthenium.

rub (rub), *v.,* **rubbed, rub•bing,** *n.* —*v.t.* **1.** to subject to pressure and friction, as in polishing. **2.** to move, spread, or apply with pressure and friction. **3.** to move (two things) with pressure and friction over each other. **4.** to make sore from friction. **5.** to remove or erase by pressure and friction. —*v.i.* **6.** to rub something. **7.** to move with pressure against something. **8. rub down**, to massage. **9. ~ out, a.** to obliterate; erase. **b.** *Slang.* to murder. —*n.* **10.** an act or instance of rubbing. **11.** something annoying or irritating. **12.** an annoying experience or circumstance. **13.** an obstacle or difficulty. —*Idiom.* **14. rub the wrong way**, to irritate; annoy.

rub•ber¹ (rub′ər), *n.* **1.** a highly elastic solid substance obtained from the milky juice of various tropical trees and plants. **2.** a similar substance made synthetically. **3.** an eraser of rubber. **4.** a low overshoe of rubber. **5.** one that rubs. —*adj.* **6.** made of or coated with rubber. —**rub′ber•y,** *adj.*

rub•ber² (rub′ər), *n.* **1.** a series or round, as in bridge, played until one side has won two out of three games. **2.** a deciding contest when a competition is tied.

rub′ber band′, *n.* a band of rubber used esp. for holding things together.

rub′ber cement′, *n.* a liquid adhesive consisting of unvulcanized rubber dispersed in benzene or gasoline.

rub′ber•ize′, *v.t.,* **-ized, -iz•ing.** to coat or impregnate with rubber.

rub′ber•neck′, *Informal.* —*v.i.* **1.** to look about or stare with curiosity. —*n.* **2.** a curious onlooker. **3.** a sightseer or tourist.

rub′ber stamp′, *n.* **1.** a stamp with a rubber printing surface used for imprinting names, standard messages, etc. **2.** a person or group that gives approval automatically or routinely. **3.** such approval. —**rub′ber-stamp′,** *v.t., adj.*

rub•bish (rub′ish), *n.* **1.** worthless material; trash. **2.** nonsense, as in writing.

rub•ble (rub′əl), *n.* broken bits and pieces, as of something demolished.

rub′down′, *n.* a massage.

rube (rōōb), *n. Informal.* an unsophisticated country person; hick.

ru•bel•la (rōō bel′ə), *n.* a usu. mild viral infection that may cause fetal damage if contracted during pregnancy.

Ru•bens (rōō′bənz), *n.* **Peter Paul,** 1577–1640, Flemish painter.

ru•bi•cund (rōō′bi kund′), *adj.* red or reddish; ruddy.

ru•bid•i•um (rōō bid′ē əm), *n.* an active metallic element resembling potassium. *Symbol:* Rb; *at. wt.:* 85.47; *at. no.:* 37.

ru•ble (rōō′bəl), *n.* the basic monetary unit of Russia, the Soviet Union, and its successor states.

ru•bric (rōō′brik), *n.* **1.** a title or heading, as in a manuscript, esp. when written or printed in red. **2.** a direction for the conduct of divine service. **3.** a class or category.

ru•by (rōō′bē), *n., pl.* **-bies,** *adj.* —*n.* **1.** a red variety of corundum used as a gem. **2.** a deep red. —*adj.* **3.** ruby-colored.

ruck•sack (ruk′sak′, rōōk′-), *n.* a type of knapsack.

ruck•us (ruk′əs), *n.* a noisy commotion; uproar.

rud•der (rud′ər), *n.* a vertical blade or flap that can be turned to steer a boat or an airplane.

rud•dy (rud′ē), *adj.,* **-di•er, -di•est.** **1.** having a fresh, healthy red color. **2.** red or reddish. —**rud′di•ness,** *n.*

rude (rōōd), *adj.,* **rud•er, rud•est.** **1.** discourteous; impolite. **2.** lacking culture or refinement. **3.** crude in behavior; uncouth. **4.** not gentle; harsh. **5.** roughly built or made. —**rude′ly,** *adv.* —**rude′ness,** *n.*

ru•di•ment (rōō′də mənt), *n.* **1.** Usu., **-ments. a.** the elements or first principles of a subject. **b.** an undeveloped or imperfect form of something. **2.** an incompletely developed part. —**ru′di•men′ta•ry** (-men′tə rē), *adj.*

rue¹ (rōō), *v.i., v.t.,* **rued, ru•ing.** to feel sorrow or remorse (for). —**rue′ful,** *adj.* —**rue′ful•ly,** *adv.*

rue² (rōō), *n.* a strongly scented plant with yellow flowers and leaves formerly used in medicine.

ruff (ruf), *n.* **1.** a gathered or pleated collar worn in the 16th and 17th centuries. **2.** a collarlike growth of hairs or feathers on the neck of an animal. —**ruffed,** *adj.*

ruf•fi•an (ruf′ē ən, ruf′yən), *n.* a tough, lawless person.

ruf•fle (ruf′əl), *v.,* **-fled, -fling,** *n.* —*v.t.* **1.** to destroy the evenness of. **2.** to erect (the feathers), as a bird in anger. **3.** to vex or irritate. **4.** to turn (pages) rapidly. **5.** to draw up (cloth, lace, etc.) into gathers or pleats. —*v.i.* **6.** to become ruffled. —*n.* **7.** a strip of fabric gathered along one edge and used as a trim-

ming. **8.** vexation; irritation. —**ruf′fler,** *n.* —**ruf′fly,** *adj.*

rug (rug), *n.* **1.** a piece of thick fabric for covering part of a floor. **2.** *Chiefly Brit.* a lap robe.

Rug•by (rug′bē), *n. (sometimes l.c.)* a form of football characterized by continuous action and prohibition against the use of substitute players.

rug•ged (rug′id), *adj.* **1.** having a rough or jagged surface. **2.** (of a face) wrinkled or furrowed. **3.** rough, harsh, or severe. **4.** capable of enduring; strong. **5.** requiring great endurance, determination, or stamina. **6.** tempestuous; stormy. —**rug′ged•ly,** *adv.* —**rug′ged•ness,** *n.*

rug′ged individ′ualism, *n.* a way of living defined by economic freedom and private initiative.

Ruhr (rōōr), *n.* **1.** a river in W Germany. 144 mi. (232 km) long. **2.** a mining and industrial area in the region of this river.

ru•in (rōō′in), *n.* **1. ruins,** the remains of something destroyed or decaying. **2.** downfall, decay, or destruction. **3.** complete loss, as of means or position. **4.** something that causes destruction; blight. **5.** the act of causing destruction. —*v.t.* **6.** to reduce to ruin. **7.** to bankrupt. **8.** to injure (a thing) irretrievably. —*v.i.* **9.** to come to ruin. —**ru′in•a′tion,** *n.* —**ru′in•ous,** *adj.*

rule (rōōl), *n., v.,* **ruled, rul•ing.** —*n.* **1.** a principle or regulation governing conduct. **2.** the customary or normal circumstance, occurrence, or practice. **3.** control, government, or dominion. **4.** RULER (def. 2). —*v.t., v.i.* **5.** to exercise dominating power, authority, or influence (over); govern. **6.** to decide judicially or authoritatively. **7.** to mark with lines, esp. with the aid of a ruler. **8.** to be superior or preeminent (in). **9. rule out,** to eliminate from consideration.

rule′ of law′, *n.* conformity by the country's leaders to common or constitutional law.

rule′ of thumb′, *n.* a rough, practical method of procedure.

rul′er, *n.* **1.** a person who rules; sovereign. **2.** a strip of material, as wood, that has a straight edge and is used for drawing lines and measuring.

rules′ commit′tee, *n.* a special committee of a legislature, having the authority to establish rules for expediting legislative action.

rul′ing, *n.* **1.** an authoritative decision, as one by a judge. —*adj.* **2.** governing or dominating. **3.** controlling; predominating.

rum (rum), *n.* an alcoholic liquor distilled from a fermented sugarcane product, esp. molasses.

Ru•ma•ni•a (rōō mā′nē ə), *n.* ROMANIA. —**Ru•ma′ni•an,** *adj., n.*

rum•ba (rum′bə, rōōm′-, rōōm′-), *n., pl.* **-bas** (-bəz), *v.,* **-baed** (-bəd), **-ba•ing** (-bə ing). —*n.* **1.** a dance of Cuban origin. —*v.i.* **2.** to dance the rumba. [< AmerSp]

rum•ble (rum′bəl), *v.,* **-bled, -bling,** *n.* —*v.i.* **1.** to make a deep, somewhat muffled, continuous sound, as thunder. **2.** to move or travel with a rumbling sound. —*n.* **3.** a rumbling sound. **4.** *Slang.* a street fight between rival teenage gangs.

rum′bling, *n.* **1.** Often, **-blings.** the first signs of dissatisfaction or grievance. **2.** RUMBLE (def. 3).

ru•mi•nant (rōō′mə nənt), *n.* **1.** an even-toed hoofed mammal, as a cow or camel, characterized by cud-chewing. —*adj.* **2.** chewing the cud. **3.** contemplative; meditative. —**ru′mi•nant•ly,** *adv.*

ru′mi•nate′ (-nāt′), *v.i., v.t.,* **-nat•ed, -nat•ing. 1.** to chew (the cud). **2.** to meditate (on); ponder. —**ru′mi•na′tion,** *n.* —**ru′mi•na′tive,** *adj.*

rum•mage (rum′ij), *v.,* **-maged, -mag•ing,** *n.* —*v.i., v.t.* **1.** to search thoroughly (through); esp. by moving around or turning over contents. —*n.* **2.** odds and ends. **3.** a rummaging search.

rum′mage sale′, *n.* a sale of miscellaneous articles, esp. items contributed to raise money for charity.

rum•my (rum′ē), *n.* any of various card games in which the object is to match cards into sets and sequences.

ru•mor (rōō′mər), *n.* **1.** a story or statement in general circulation without confirmation or certainty as to facts. **2.** gossip; hearsay. —*v.t.* **3.** to report or circulate by rumor. Also, *esp. Brit.*, **ru′mour.**

rump (rump), *n.* **1.** the fleshy hind part of an animal's body. **2.** a cut of beef from the rump. **3.** the lower back part of the human trunk; the buttocks. **4.** a remnant.

rum•ple (rum′pəl), *v.*, **-pled, -pling,** *n.* —*v.t.*, *v.i.* **1.** to crumple or wrinkle. —*n.* **2.** a wrinkle or crease. —**rum′ply,** *adj.*

rum•pus (rum′pəs), *n.* a noisy or violent disturbance; commotion.

run (run), *v.*, **ran, run, run•ning,** *n.* —*v.i.* **1.** to go quickly by moving the legs more rapidly than at a walk. **2.** to move or pass quickly. **3.** to depart quickly; flee. **4.** to make a quick trip or visit. **5.** to move freely and without restraint. **6.** to take part in a race or contest. **7.** to be a candidate for election. **8.** (of fish) to migrate, as for spawning. **9.** to go regularly; ply. **10.** to unravel, as a fabric. **11.** to flow in or as if in a stream. **12.** to include a specific range of variations: *Your work runs from fair to bad.* **13.** to spread on being applied, as a liquid. **14.** to undergo a spreading of colors: *materials that run when washed.* **15.** to operate or function. **16.** to encounter a certain condition: *to run into difficulties.* **17.** to amount; total. **18.** to be stated or worded. **19.** to continue or extend. **20.** to appear, as in print or on a stage. **21.** to spread or circulate. **22.** to recur persistently: *Musical ability runs in my family.* **23.** to tend to have or be a specified size, quality, etc. —*v.t.* **24.** to move along (a surface, path, etc.). **25.** to perform or compete in by or as if by running. **26.** to convey or transport. **27.** to cause to move or pass quickly. **28.** to get past or through: *to run a blockade.* **29.** to smuggle. **30.** to operate or drive. **31.** to print or publish. **32.** to sponsor as a candidate for election. **33.** to manage or conduct. **34.** to process (the instructions in a program) by computer. **35.** to expose oneself to (danger, a risk, etc.). **36.** to cause (a liquid) to flow. **37.** to bring into a certain condition. **38.** to drive or force. **39.** to extend in a particular direction: *to run a cable under the road.* **40.** to cost. **41. run across,** to meet or find accidentally. **42.** ~ **along,** to go away; leave. **43.** ~ **away,** to flee or escape, esp. with no intent to return. **44.** ~ **down, a.** to strike and knock down, esp. with a vehicle. **b.** to chase after and seize. **c.** to cease operation. **d.** to speak disparagingly of. **45.** ~ **in, a.** to pay a casual visit. **b.** to arrest. **46.** ~ **off, a.** to create quickly and easily. **b.** to print or duplicate. **47.** ~ **on, a.** to continue without interruption. **b.** to add at the end of a text. **48.** ~ **out,** to become used up. **49.** ~ **out of,** to use up a supply of. **50.** ~ **over, a.** to hit and drive over with a vehicle. **b.** to repeat; review. **51.** ~ **through, a.** to pierce as with a sword. **b.** to consume or squander. **c.** to practice or rehearse. **52.** ~ **up, a.** to sew rapidly. **b.** to amass; incur. —*n.* **53.** an act or instance of running. **54.** a fleeing; flight. **55.** a running pace. **56.** a distance covered, as in running. **57.** a quick trip. **58.** a routine or regular trip. **59. a.** a period of continuous operation of a machine. **b.** the amount of something produced in such a period. **60.** a ravel, as in a stocking. **61.** trend or tendency: *the normal run of events.* **62.** freedom to move around in or use something: *has the run of the house.* **63.** a continuous series, course, or extent. **64.** an extensive and continued demand: *a run on umbrellas.* **65.** a series of sudden and urgent demands for payment, as on a bank. **66.** a small stream; brook. **67.** the typical or ordinary kind. **68.** an inclined course, as on a slope: *a bobsled run.* **69.** an enclosure for domestic animals: *a sheep run.* **70.** large numbers of migrating fish. **71.** *Baseball.* a score made by running around all the bases. —*Idiom.* **72. in the long run,** in the course of long experience. **73. on the run, a.** scurrying about. **b.** while rushing to get somewhere.

run′a•bout′, *n.* a small, light automobile or motorboat.

run′a•round′, *n.* an indecisive or evasive response.

run′a•way′, *n.* **1.** one that runs away. **2.** the act of running away. —*adj.* **3.** having run away; fugitive. **4.** (of a contest) easily won. **5.** unchecked; rampant.

run′-down′, *adj.* **1.** fatigued; exhausted. **2.** in poor health. **3.** in dilapidated condition. **4.** (of a clock, watch, etc.) unwound.

run′down′, *n.* a short summary.

rune (rōōn), *n.* **1.** a character of an ancient alphabet used for writing Germanic languages. **2.** something written in runes. **3.** something secret or mysterious. —**run′ic,** *adj.*

rung¹ (rung), *v.* pt. and pp. of RING².

rung² (rung), *n.* **1.** one of the usu. rounded crosspieces forming the steps of a ladder. **2.** a rounded piece fixed horizontally between the legs of a chair. **3.** a spoke of a wheel.

run′-in′, *n.* a quarrel; argument.

run•nel (run′l) also **run′let** (-lit), *n.* a small stream; rivulet.

run′ner, *n.* **1.** one that runs, esp. as a racer. **2.** a messenger. **3.** *Baseball.* a player on base or trying to reach a base. **4.** either of the long strips of metal or wood on which a sled or sleigh slides. **5.** the blade of an ice skate. **6.** a long, narrow rug. **7.** a guiding or supporting strip for a drawer or sliding door. **8. a.** a slender, trailing stem that sends out roots at the nodes, as in the strawberry. **b.** a plant that spreads by such stems.

run′ner-up′, *n.*, *pl.* **run•ners-up.** the competitor, player, or team finishing in second place.

run′ning, *n.* **1.** the act of one that runs. —*adj.* **2.** that runs. **3.** (of measurement) in a straight line; linear. **4.** flowing or fluid. **5.** carried on continuously: *a running commentary.* **6.** performed with or during a run: *a running leap.* —*adv.* **7.** in succession; consecutively. —*Idiom.* **8. in the running,** competing. **9. out of the running,** not competing.

run′ning light′, *n.* a light displayed by a ship or aircraft operating at night.

run′ny, *adj.*, **-ni•er, -ni•est.** tending to run or drip.

run′off′, *n.* a final contest held to break a tie or eliminate semifinalists.

run′-of-the-mill′, *adj.* merely average; mediocre.

run′-on′, *adj.* **1.** of or being something that is added or run on. —*n.* **2.** run-on matter.

runt (runt), *n.* **1.** a small animal, esp. the smallest of a litter. **2.** a small and contemptible person. —**runt′ish,** *adj.*, **-runt′y,** *adj.*, **-i•er, -i•est.**

run′-through′, *n.* a trial or practice performance, esp. an uninterrupted rehearsal.

run′way′, *n.* **1.** a way along which something runs. **2.** a strip on which planes land and take off. **3.** a narrow ramp extending from a stage into an aisle, as in a theater.

ru•pee (rōō pē′, rōō′pē), *n.*, *pl.* **-pees.** the basic monetary unit of India, Mauritius, Nepal, and Pakistan.

ru•pi•ah (rōō pē′ə), *n.* the basic monetary unit of Indonesia.

rup•ture (rup′chər), *n.*, *v.*, **-tured, -tur•ing.** —*n.* **1.** the act of breaking or bursting. **2.** the state of being broken or burst. **3.** hernia, esp. abdominal hernia. —*v.i.*, *v.t.* **4.** to suffer or cause to suffer a rupture.

ru•ral (rōōr′əl), *adj.* of or characteristic of the country, country life, or country people; rustic.

ruse (rōōz), *n.* a trick, stratagem, or artifice.

rush¹ (rush), *v.i.*, *v.t.* **1.** to move or cause to move, act, or progress with speed, impetuosity, or violence. **2.** to carry with haste. **3.** to attack suddenly and violently; charge. —*n.* **4.** rapid, impetuous, or violent forward movement. **5.** hurried activity. **6.** a hurried state. **7.** an eager rushing of numbers of persons to a region: *the California gold rush.* —*adj.* **8.** requiring or done in haste.

rush² (rush), *n.* a grasslike marsh plant with pithy or hollow stems used esp. for making chair bottoms and baskets.

rush′ hour′, *n.* a time of day at which large numbers of people are in transit.

rusk (rusk), *n.* a slice of sweet raised bread dried and baked again.

Russ or **Russ.,** **1.** Russia. **2.** Russian.

Rus•sell (rus′əl), *n.* **1.** Bertrand, 1872–1970, English philosopher and mathematician. **2.** Charles Taze (*"Pastor Russell"*), 1852–1916, U.S. founder of Jehovah's Witnesses.

rus•set (rus′it), *n.* **1.** a yellowish or reddish brown. **2.** a winter apple with a rough brownish skin. —*adj.* **3.** of the color russet.

Rus•sia (rush′ə), *n.* **1.** RUSSIAN FEDERATION. **2.** Also called **Rus′sian Em′pire.** a former empire in E Europe and N Asia: overthrown by the Russian Revolution 1917. **3.** UNION OF SOVIET SOCIALIST REPUBLICS.

Rus′sian, *n.* **1. a.** a native or inhabitant of Russia or the Russian Federation. **b.** the Slavic language of Russia or the Russian Federation. —*adj.* **2.** of Russia, its inhabitants, or their language.

Rus′sian Federa′tion, *n.* a republic extending from E Europe to N Asia: formerly a part of the USSR. 147,987,101. Also called **Russia, Rus′sian Repub′lic.** Formerly, **Rus′sian So′viet Fed′erated So′cialist Repub′lic.**

rust (rust), *n.* **1.** the red or orange coating that forms on the surface of iron exposed to air and moisture. **2.** a plant disease characterized by reddish, brownish, or black pustules. **3.** a reddish brown. —*v.i., v.t.* **4.** to form rust (on). **5.** to deteriorate, as through inaction or disuse. —**rust′y,** *adj.,* **-i•er, -i•est.**

rus•tic (rus′tik), *adj.* **1.** of or appropriate for the country; rural. **2.** simple or unsophisticated. **3.** uncouth, rude, or boorish. —*n.* **4.** a country person. —**rus′ti•cal•ly,** *adv.* —**rus•tic•i•ty** (ru stis′i tē), *n.*

rus′ti•cate′ (-ti kāt′), *v.i., v.t.,* **-cat•ed, -cat•ing. 1.** to go or send to the country. **2.** to make or become rustic. —**rus′ti•ca′tion,** *n.*

rus•tle (rus′əl), *v.,* **-tled, -tling,** *n.* —*v.i., v.t.* **1.** to make or cause to make the slight, soft sounds of gentle rubbing, as of leaves. **2.** to move, proceed, or work energetically. **3.** to steal (livestock, esp. cattle).

4. rustle up, *Informal.* to find or gather by search. —*n.* **5.** a rustling sound. —**rus′tler,** *n.*

rut[1] (rut), *n., v.,* **rut•ted, rut•ting.** —*n.* **1.** a furrow or track in the ground, esp. one made by the passage of vehicles. **2.** a fixed, usu. dull way of proceeding. —*v.t.* **3.** to make a rut in; furrow. —**rut′ty,** *adj.,* **-ti•er, -ti•est.**

rut[2] (rut), *n.* the periodically recurring sexual excitement of the male of animals such as the deer. —**rut′tish,** *adj.*

ru•ta•ba•ga (rōō′tə bā′gə), *n., pl.* **-gas.** a turnip with a yellow- or white-fleshed edible tuber.

Ruth[1] (rōōth), *n.* **1.** a Moabite who married Boaz and became an ancestor of David: the daughter-in-law of Naomi. **2.** a book of the Bible bearing her name.

Ruth[2] (rōōth), *n.* George Herman (*"Babe"*), 1895–1948, U.S. baseball player.

ru•the•ni•um (rōō thē′nē əm), *n.* a rare metallic element of the platinum group. *Symbol:* Ru; *at. wt.:* 101.07; *at. no.:* 44.

ruth•less (rōōth′lis), *adj.* without pity or compassion; merciless. —**ruth′less•ly,** *adv.* —**ruth′less•ness,** *n.*

RV, 1. recreational vehicle. **2.** Revised Version (of the Bible).

Rwan•da (rōō än′də), *n.* a republic in central Africa. 7,737,537. —**Rwan′dan,** *adj., n.*

Rx, prescription.

-ry, var. of -ERY.

ry•a (rē′ə, rī′ə), *n., pl.* **-ry•as.** a handwoven Scandinavian rug with a thick pile and usu. a colorful design.

rye (rī), *n.* **1.** a widely cultivated cereal grass raised for its seeds and grain. **2.** a whiskey distilled from a mash containing rye grain.

Ryu′kyu Is′lands (rē ōō′kyōō), *n.pl.* a chain of Japanese islands in the W Pacific between Japan and Taiwan.

S

S, s (es), *n., pl.* **Ss** or **S's, ss** or **s's. 1.** the 19th letter of the English alphabet, a consonant. **2.** something shaped like an S.

S, 1. satisfactory. **2.** sentence. **3.** signature. **4.** small. **5.** soft. **6.** Also, **s** south. **7.** southern.

S, *Chem. Symbol.* sulfur.

's[1], an ending used to form the possessive of most singular nouns and of plural nouns not ending in *s: man's; women's.*

's[2], **1.** contraction of *is: She's here.* **2.** contraction of *has: He's been there.* **3.** contraction of *does: What's he look like?*

's[3], contraction of *us: Let's go.*

-s[1], an ending marking the third person sing. present indicative of verbs: *walks.*

-s[2], an ending marking nouns as plural: *weeks.*

S., 1. Sabbath. **2.** Saint. **3.** Saturday. **4.** Sea. **5.** Senate. **6.** September. **7.** south. **8.** southern. **9.** Sunday.

s., 1. school. **2.** section. **3.** series. **4.** shilling. **5.** singular. **6.** small. **7.** son. **8.** south. **9.** southern.

SA or **S.A., 1.** Salvation Army. **2.** seaman apprentice. **3.** South Africa. **4.** South America.

Saar (zär, sär), *n.* **1.** a river in W Europe, in NE France and W Germany. 150 mi. (240 km) long. **2.** Also called **Saar′ Ba′sin.** a coal-mining region in W Germany, in the Saar River valley.

Sab•a•oth (sab′ē oth′, -ôth′, sab′ā-, sə bā′ōth), *n.* (*used with a pl. v.*) armies; hosts. Rom. 9:29; James 5:4.

Sab•bath (sab′əth), *n.* **1.** the seventh day of the week, Saturday, as the day of rest and religious observance among Jews and some Christians. Ex. 20:8–11. **2.** the first day of the week, Sunday, observed by most Christians in commemoration of the Resurrec-

tion of Christ. [OE < L *sabbatum* < Gk *sábbaton* < Heb *shabbāth* rest]

sab•bat•i•cal (sə bat′i kəl), *adj.* **1.** (*cap.*) of or appropriate to the Sabbath. **2.** pertaining to a sabbatical year. —*n.* **3.** SABBATICAL YEAR.

sabbat′ical year′, *n.* a year, usu. every seventh, of release from normal teaching duties granted to a professor, as for research.

sa•ber (sā′bər), *n.* a one-edged sword, usu. slightly curved, used esp. by cavalry. Also, *esp. Brit.,* **sa′bre.**

sa′ber saw′, *n.* a portable electric jigsaw.

sa•bin (sā′bin), *n.* a unit of sound absorption, equal to the absorption of one square foot (929 square centimeters) of a perfectly absorptive surface. [after W.C. *Sabine* (1868–1919), U.S. physicist]

Sa•bin (sā′bin), *n.* Albert Bruce, 1906–93, U.S. physician, born in Russia: developed the Sabin vaccine.

Sa′bin vaccine′, *n.* an orally administered vaccine of live viruses for immunization against poliomyelitis. [after A. B. *Sabin*]

sa•ble (sā′bəl), *n., pl.* **-bles, -ble. 1.** a dark-colored Eurasian marten valued for its fur. **2.** the fur of the sable.

sab•o•tage (sab′ə täzh′), *n., v.,* **-taged, -tag•ing.** —*n.* **1.** deliberate damage of equipment or interference with production, as by disgruntled employees. **2.** destruction or obstruction intended to undermine a national military effort. **3.** undermining of a cause. —*v.t.* **4.** to injure or attack by sabotage.

sab′o•teur′ (-tûr′), *n.* a person who commits sabotage.

sa•bra (sä′brə), *n., pl.* **-bras.** an Israeli Jew born in Israel.

sac (sak), *n.* a baglike structure in an animal, plant, or fungus.

sac•cha•rin (sak′ər in), *n.* a synthetic powder used as a noncaloric sugar substitute.

sac′cha•rine (-ər in, -ə rēn′), *adj.* **1.** of, resembling, or containing sugar. **2.** cloyingly sweet or sentimental.

sac•er•do•tal (sas′ər dōt′l), *adj.* of priests; priestly.

sa•chem (sā′chəm), *n.* a North American Indian tribal chief.

sa•chet (sa shā′), *n.* a small bag containing scented powder or fragrant flower parts.

sack¹ (sak), *n.* **1.** a large bag of strong, coarsely woven material. **2.** a bag. **3.** *Slang.* dismissal from a job. **4.** a loose-fitting coat or jacket. —*v.t.* **5.** to put into a sack. **6.** *Slang.* to dismiss from a job. —**sack′ful,** *n., pl.* **-fuls.**

sack² (sak), *v.t.* **1.** to loot (a place) after capture; plunder. —*n.* **2.** the plundering of a captured place. —**sack′er,** *n.*

sack′cloth′, *n.* **1.** SACKING. **2.** a coarse cloth worn to show repentance or grief.

sack′ing, *n.* coarsely woven material, as of hemp or jute, used chiefly for sacks.

sac•ra•ment (sak′rə mənt), *n.* **1.** a rite, as baptism, considered to have been established by Christ as a channel for grace. **2.** (*often cap.*) the Eucharist. **3.** something regarded as possessing a sacred character or mysterious significance. [< ML *sacrāmentum* obligation, oath < L *sacrāre* to consecrate]

Sac•ra•men•to (sak′rə men′tō), *n.* the capital of California. 373,924.

sa•cred (sā′krid), *adj.* **1.** devoted or dedicated to a deity or to a religious purpose. **2.** meriting veneration or religious respect. **3.** of or connected with religion. **4.** dedicated to some person, purpose, or object. **5.** regarded with reverence. —**sa′cred•ly,** *adv.* —**sa′cred•ness,** *n.*

sa′cred cow′, *n.* one considered exempt from criticism or questioning.

sac•ri•fice (sak′rə fīs′), *n., v.,* **-ficed, -fic•ing.** —*n.* **1.** the offering of something to a deity, as in propitiation. **2.** something so offered. **3.** the surrender or destruction of something valued for the sake of something else. **4.** a loss incurred in selling something below its value. —*v.t., v.i.* **5.** to make a sacrifice (of). **6.** to surrender for the sake of something else. —**sac′ri•fi′cial** (-fish′əl), *adj.*

sac•ri•lege (sak′rə lij), *n.* violation or profanation of something sacred. —**sac′ri•le′gious** (-lij′əs, -lē′jəs), *adj.* —**sac′ri•le′gious•ly,** *adv.*

sac•ris•tan (sak′ri stən), *n.* an official in charge of a sacristy.

sac′ris•ty (-ri stē), *n., pl.* **-ties.** a room in a church in which sacred vessels and vestments are kept.

sac•ro•il•i•ac (sak′rō il′ē ak′, sā′krō-), *n.* the joint where the sacrum and ilium meet.

sac•ro•sanct (sak′rō sangkt′), *adj.* sacred; inviolable. —**sac′ro•sanct′ness,** *n.*

sac•rum (sak′rəm, sā′krəm), *n., pl.* **sac•ra** (sak′rə, sā′krə)• a bone forming the posterior wall of the pelvis.

sad (sad), *adj.,* **sad•der, sad•dest. 1.** affected by unhappiness or grief. **2.** expressive of, characterized by, or causing sorrow. **3.** deplorably bad; sorry: *a sad attempt.* —**sad′ly,** *adv.* —**sad′ness,** *n.*

sad′den, *v.t., v.i.* to make or become sad.

sad•dle (sad′l), *n., v.,* **-dled, -dling.** —*n.* **1.** a seat for a rider, as on the back of a horse or other animal. **2.** a cut of meat, as lamb, comprising both loins. —*v.t.* **3.** to put a saddle on. **4.** to load or charge, as with a burden.

sad′dle•bag′, *n.* a pouch laid over the back of a horse behind the saddle or mounted over the rear wheel of a bicycle or motorcycle.

sad′dle horse′, *n.* a horse bred or trained for riding.

sad′dle shoe′, *n.* an oxford-type shoe with a strip of contrasting color across the instep.

Sad•du•cee (saj′ə sē′, sad′yə-), *n., pl.* **-cees.** a member of an ancient Jewish sect that opposed the Pharisees.

sa•dism (sā′diz əm, sad′iz-), *n.* **1.** a disorder in which sexual gratification is derived by causing pain or degradation to others. **2.** pleasure in being cruel. [after D. A. F. de *Sade* (1740–1814), Fr. novelist] —**sa′dist,** *n., adj.* —**sa•dis•tic** (sə dis′tik), *adj.* —**sa•dis′ti•cal•ly,** *adv.*

sa•fa•ri (sə fär′ē), *n., pl.* **-ris. 1.** an expedition for hunting, esp. in East Africa. **2.** a long expedition.

safe (sāf), *adj.,* **saf•er, saf•est,** —*adj.* **1.** offering security from harm or danger. **2.** free from injury or risk. **3.** dependable; trustworthy. —*n.* **4.** a steel or iron box or repository for valuable items. —**safe′ly,** *adv.* —**safe′ness,** *n.*

safe′-con′duct, *n.* a document authorizing safe passage through a region, esp. in time of war.

safe′-de•pos′it, *adj.* providing safekeeping for valuables.

safe′guard′, *n.* **1.** something that serves as a protection or defense. —*v.t.* **2.** to guard; protect.

safe′ house′, *n.* a place for refuge or clandestine activities.

safe′keep′ing, *n.* the act of keeping safe or state of being kept safe.

safe′ty, *n., pl.* **-ties. 1.** the state of being safe. **2.** a device to prevent injury. **3. a.** a football play in which a player on the offensive team downs the ball in his own end zone. **b.** a defensive player farthest behind the line of scrimmage.

safe′ty glass′, *n.* shatter-resistant glass consisting of two sheets of glass with a layer of plastic between them.

safe′ty match′, *n.* a match that ignites only when rubbed on a specially prepared surface.

safe′ty pin′, *n.* a pin bent back on itself to form a spring, with a guard to cover the point.

safe′ty ra′zor, *n.* a razor with a blade guard to prevent serious cuts.

saf•flow•er (saf′lou′ər), *n.* a thistlelike plant with orange-red flower heads and seeds from which a cooking oil is extracted.

saf•fron (saf′rən), *n.* **1.** a crocus bearing showy purple flowers. **2.** an orange-colored condiment consisting of dried saffron stigmas used to color and flavor foods.

sag (sag), *v.,* **sagged, sag•ging,** *n.* —*v.i.* **1.** to sink downward by or as if by weight or pressure. **2.** to wane in vigor or intensity. **3.** to decline in value. —*n.* **4.** a place where something sags. —**sag′gy,** *adj.,* **-gi•er, -gi•est.**

sa•ga (sä′gə), *n., pl.* **-gas. 1.** a medieval Scandinavian narrative of historical or legendary events. **2.** a narrative of heroic exploits.

sa•ga•cious (sə gā′shəs), *adj.* having acute mental discernment and keen practical sense; shrewd. —**sa•gac′i•ty** (-gas′i tē), *n.*

Sa•gan (sā′gən), *n.* **Carl (Edward),** 1934–96, U.S. astronomer and writer.

sage¹ (sāj), *n., adj.,* **sag•er, sag•est.** —*n.* **1.** a profoundly wise person. —*adj.* **2.** wise, judicious, or prudent.

sage² (sāj), *n.* **1.** a plant or shrub of the mint family with aromatic grayish green leaves used in cooking. **2.** sagebrush.

English saddle and Western saddle

sage′brush′, *n.* any of several sagelike, bushy plants common on the dry plains of the western U.S.

Sag•it•tar•i•us (saj′i târ′ē əs), *n.* the ninth sign of the zodiac. [< L: archer]

sa•go (sā′gō), *n., pl.* **-gos.** a starch derived from the pith of a tropical Asian palm.

sa•gua•ro (sə wär′ō, -gwär′ō), *n., pl.* **-ros.** a tall, horizontally branched cactus of Arizona and neighboring regions.

Sa•har•a (sə har′ə), *n.* a desert in N Africa. —**Sa•har′an, Sa•har′i•an,** *adj.*

said (sed), *v.* pt. and pp. of SAY.

Sai•gon (sī gon′), *n.* former name of HO CHI MINH CITY: capital of South Vietnam 1954–76.

sail (sāl), *n.* **1.** a piece of fabric, as canvas, that catches the wind to propel a boat or ship. **2.** something similar to a sail. **3.** a trip in a sailing craft. —*v.i.* **4.** to travel on water in a sailing craft. **5.** to manage a sailboat. **6.** to begin a journey by water. **7.** to move along in a stately, effortless way. —*v.t.* **8.** to sail upon, over, or through. **9.** to navigate (a boat or ship).

sail′boat′, *n.* a boat propelled principally by sails.

sail′cloth′, *n.* any of various fabrics, as of cotton, for boat sails or tents.

sail′fish′, *n., pl.* **-fish, -fish•es.** a large marlinlike fish with a long, high dorsal fin.

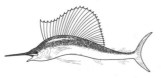

sailfish

sail′or, *n.* **1.** a person whose occupation is sailing or navigation. **2.** a seaman below the rank of officer.

saint (sānt), *n.* **1.** a person formally recognized by the Christian Church, esp. by canonization, as being exceptionally holy. **2.** a person of great virtue or benevolence. —**saint′hood′,** *n.* —**saint′li•ness,** *n.* —**saint′ly,** *adj.,* **-li•er, -li•est.**

Saint. For entries beginning with this word, see also ST., STE.

Saint′ Bernard′, *n.* one of a breed of very large dogs used, esp. formerly, to rescue travelers in the Swiss Alps.

Saint-Ex•u•pé•ry (SAN teg ZY pā RĒ′), *n.* **Antoine de,** 1900–45, French author and aviator.

Saint′ Pat′rick's Day′, *n.* March 17, observed in honor of St. Patrick, the patron saint of Ireland.

Saint′ Val′entine's Day′, *n.* VALENTINE'S DAY.

saith (seth, sā′əth), *v. Archaic.* third pers. sing. pres. of SAY.

sake¹ (sāk), *n.* **1.** benefit or well-being: *for the sake of all students.* **2.** purpose; end: *art for art's sake.*

sa•ke² (sä′kē), *n.* a mildly alcoholic Japanese beverage made from fermented rice.

sa•laam (sə läm′), *n.* **1.** a salutation used esp. in Islamic countries. **2.** a very low bow with the palm of the right hand on the forehead.

sa•la•cious (sə lā′shəs), *adj.* grossly indecent; lewd. —**sa•la′cious•ly,** *adv.* —**sa•la′cious•ness, sa•lac′i•ty** (-las′i tē), *n.*

sal•ad (sal′əd), *n.* **1.** a usu. cold dish of vegetables or fruit, served with a dressing. **2.** a mixture of chopped food and mayonnaise: *egg salad.*

sal′ad bar′, *n.* an assortment of salad ingredients and dressings, as in a restaurant, from which one can serve oneself.

sal•a•man•der (sal′ə man/dər), *n.* a tailed amphibian with soft, moist, scaleless skin.

sa•la•mi (sə lä′mē), *n., pl.* **-mis.** a spicy, garlic-flavored sausage.

Sal•a•mis (sal′ə mis, sä′lä mēs′), *n.* **1.** an island off the SE coast of Greece, W of Athens. **2.** an ancient city on Cyprus, in the E Mediterranean. Acts 13:5.

sal•a•ry (sal′ə rē), *n., pl.* **-ries.** fixed compensation paid periodically for work or services. —**sal′a•ried′,** *adj.*

sale (sāl), *n.* **1.** the act of selling. **2.** a special offering of goods at reduced prices. **3.** transfer of property for money or credit. **4.** opportunity to sell; demand. **5.** an auction. —**sal′a•ble, sale′a•ble,** *adj.*

Sa•lem (sā′ləm), *n.* **1.** a seaport in NE Massachusetts: founded 1626; execution of persons accused of witchcraft 1692. 38,220. **2.** the capital of Oregon. 107,786. **3.** an ancient city of Canaan, later identified with Jerusalem. Gen. 14:18; Ps. 76:2.

sales′clerk′, *n.* a person who sells goods in a store.

sales′girl′, *n.* a woman who sells goods in a store.

sales′man or **-wom′an** or **-per′son,** *n., pl.* **-men** or **-wom•en** or **-per•sons.** a person who sells goods or services.

sales′man•ship′, *n.* the skill or technique of selling a product or idea.

sales′peo′ple, *n.pl.* people engaged in selling.

sales′ represent′ative, *n.* a person authorized to solicit business for a company, esp. one who travels in an assigned territory.

sal′i•cyl′ic ac′id (sal′ə sil′ik), *n.* a white crystalline substance used in the manufacture of aspirin.

sa•li•ent (sā′lē ənt, sāl′yənt), *adj.* **1.** prominent or conspicuous. **2.** projecting or pointing outward. —*n.* **3.** a salient angle or part. —**sa′li•ence,** *n.* —**sa′li•ent•ly,** *adv.*

Sa•li•nas (sə lē′nəs), *n.* a city in W California. 119,814.

sa•line (sā′lēn, -līn), *adj.* **1.** of, containing, or tasting of salt; salty. —*n.* **2.** a saline solution. —**sa•lin•i•ty** (sə lin′i tē), *n.*

sa•li•va (sə lī′və), *n.* a viscid, watery secretion that moistens the mouth and starts the digestion of starches. —**sal•i•var•y** (sal′ə ver/ē), *adj.*

sal•i•vate (sal′ə vāt′), *v.i.,* **-vat•ed, -vat•ing.** to produce saliva. —**sal′i•va′tion,** *n.*

Salk (sôk, sôlk), *n.* **Jonas E(dward),** 1914–95, U.S. bacteriologist.

Salk′ vaccine′ (sôk), *n.* a vaccine for injection against poliomyelitis. [after J. E. *Salk* (1914–95), U.S. bacteriologist]

sal•low (sal′ō), *adj.,* **-er, -est.** of a sickly yellowish color. —**sal′low•ness,** *n.*

sal•ly (sal′ē), *n., pl.* **-lies,** *v.,* **-lied, -ly•ing.** —*n.* **1.** a sortie of troops from a besieged place against an enemy. **2.** an excursion. **3.** a witty remark; quip. —*v.i.* **4.** to make a sally.

salm•on (sam′ən), *n., pl.* **ons, -on** for 1. **1.** a marine and freshwater food fish with pink flesh. **2.** a light yellowish pink.

sal•mo•nel•la (sal′mə nel′ə), *n., pl.* **-nel•lae** (-nel′-ē), **-nel•las.** any of several rod-shaped bacteria that enter the digestive tract in contaminated food, causing food poisoning.

Sa•lo•me or **Sa•lo•mé** (sə lō′mē), *n.* **1.** one of the women who was present at the Crucifixion and on Easter morning. Matt. 27:56; Mark 15:40; 16:1. **2.** assumed to be the daughter of Herodias who danced for Herod Antipas and was granted the head of John the Baptist. Mark 6:22–25.

Sal•o•mon (sal′ə mən), *n.* **Haym** (hīm), 1740?–85, American financier and patriot, born in Poland.

sa•lon (sə lon′; *Fr.* SA lôN′), *n.* **1.** a drawing room in a large house. **2.** an assembly of leaders, as in the arts, esp. as a regular event. **3.** a specialized shop catering to fashionable clients.

sa•loon (sə lōōn′), *n.* **1.** a place where alcoholic drinks are sold and consumed. **2.** a large public room, as on a passenger ship.

sal•sa (säl′sə, -sä), *n., pl.* **-sas. 1.** Latin American music with elements of jazz, rock, and soul. **2.** a sauce, esp. a hot sauce containing chilies. [< AmerSp: sauce]

salt (sôlt), *n.* **1.** a crystalline compound of sodium and chlorine, sodium chloride, used for seasoning food and as a preservative. **2.** a chemical compound formed by neutralization of an acid by a base. **3.** a sailor. —*v.t.* **4.** to season, cure, sprinkle, or preserve with salt. **5.** salt away, to save for future use. —*adj.* **6.** containing or tasting of salt. **7.** cured or preserved with salt. —*Idiom.* **8.** take with a grain of salt, to be skeptical about. —**salt′ed,** *adj.* —**salt′y,** *adj.,* **-i•er, -i•est.** —**salt′i•ness,** *n.*

SALT (sôlt), *n.* Strategic Arms Limitation Talks (or Treaty).

salt'cel'lar, *n.* a shaker or dish for salt.

sal•tine (sôl tēn'), *n.* a crisp, salted cracker.

Salt' Lake' Cit'y, *n.* the capital of Utah. 171,849.

salt' lick', *n.* a place to which animals go to lick naturally occurring salt deposits.

salt' of the earth', *n.* an individual or group considered to embody the noblest human qualities.

salt'pe'ter or **-pe'tre** (-pē'tər), *n.* POTASSIUM NITRATE.

salt' pork', *n.* fat pork cured with salt.

salt'shak'er, *n.* a shaker for salt.

salt'wa'ter, *adj.* of or inhabiting salt water.

sa•lu•bri•ous (sə lōō'brē əs), *adj.* favorable to health.

sal•u•tar•y (sal'yə ter'ē), *adj.* promoting health; healthful.

sal'u•ta'tion, *n.* **1.** something uttered, written, or done by way of greeting, welcome, or recognition. **2.** a word or phrase serving as the prefatory greeting in a letter or speech.

sa•lute (sə lōōt'), *n., v.,* **-lut•ed, -lut•ing.** —*n.* **1.** a formal gesture of respect, as raising the hand to the head or firing cannon. **2.** a greeting or welcome. —*v.t., v.i.* **3.** to give a salute (to).

Sal•va•dor (sal'və dôr'), *n.* EL SALVADOR. —**Sal'va•do'ran, Sal'va•do'ri•an,** *adj., n.*

sal•vage (sal'vij), *n., v.,* **-vaged, -vag•ing.** —*n.* **1.** the saving of a ship or its cargo. **2. a.** the saving of property from destruction. **b.** the property saved. **3.** compensation given to those who save a ship or its cargo. —*v.t.* **4.** to save from peril, as shipwreck. —**sal'vage•a•ble,** *adj.*

sal•va'tion (-vā'shən), *n.* **1.** the act of saving or state of being saved, as from harm or loss. **2.** a means of being saved. **3.** *Theology.* deliverance from the power and penalty of sin.

salve (sav, säv), *n., v.,* **salved, salv•ing.** —*n.* **1.** a medicinal ointment for treating wounds, burns, and sores. —*v.t.* **2.** to soothe with or as if with salve; ease.

sal•ver (sal'vər), *n.* a tray, esp. one for serving food or drinks.

sal•vo (sal'vō), *n., pl.* **-vos, -voes.** a simultaneous or successive discharge of guns.

SAM (sam), *n.* surface-to-air missile.

Sa•mar•i•a (sə mâr'ē ə), *n.* **1.** a district in ancient Palestine N of Judea: later part of the Roman province of Syria; taken by Jordan 1948; occupied by Israel 1967. **2.** the northern kingdom of the ancient Hebrews. **3.** the ancient capital of this kingdom.

Sa•mar•i•tan (sə mar'i tn), *n.* **1.** an inhabitant of Samaria. **2.** a member of a religious sect of Samaria that split from Judaism in the 4th century B.C. **3.** (*often l.c.*) GOOD SAMARITAN.

sa•mar•i•um (sə mâr'ē əm), *n.* a rare-earth metallic element. *Symbol:* Sm; *at. wt.:* 150.35; *at. no.:* 62.

sam•ba (sam'bə, säm'-), *n., pl.* **-bas,** *v.,* **-baed, -ba•ing.** —*n.* **1.** a Brazilian dance of African origin. —*v.i.* **2.** to dance the samba.

same (sām), *adj.* **1.** identical with what has just been mentioned. **2.** agreeing, as in kind; corresponding. **3.** unchanged, as in character or condition. —*pron.* **4.** the same person, thing, or kind of thing. **5. the same,** in the same manner. —**same'ness,** *n.*

Sa•mo•a (sə mō'ə), *n.* a group of islands in the S Pacific: divided into American Samoa and Western Samoa. —**Sa•mo'an,** *adj., n.*

sam•o•var (sam'ə vär'), *n.* a metal urn used esp. in Russia for heating water to make tea.

sam•pan (sam'pan), *n.* a small boat of the Far East, esp. one propelled by a single scull over the stern.

sam•ple (sam'pəl, säm'-), *n., adj., v.,* **-pled, -pling.** —*n.* **1.** a part of or selection from something that shows the quality, style, or nature of the whole. **2.** a sound of short duration, as a drumbeat, digitally stored in a synthesizer for playback. —*adj.* **3.** serving as a specimen. —*v.t.* **4.** to take a sample of.

sam'pler, *n.* a piece of cloth embroidered with various stitches to show a beginner's skill.

Sam•son (sam'sən), *n.* a judge of Israel famous for his great strength. Judg. 13-16.

Sam•u•el (sam'yōō əl), *n.* **1.** a judge and prophet of Israel. I Sam. 1-3; 8-15. **2.** either of two books of the Bible bearing his name.

sam•u•rai (sam'ōō rī'), *n., pl.* **-rai.** (in feudal Japan) a member of the hereditary warrior class.

Sa•n'a or **Sa•naa** (sä nä'), *n.* the political capital of Yemen. 150,000.

San' An•dre'as fault' (san' an drā'əs), *n.* an active geological fault extending from San Francisco to S California. [after *San Andreas* Lake, located in the rift, in San Mateo County]

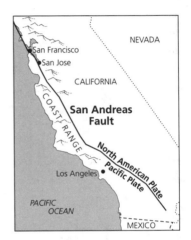

San An•to•ni•o (san' an tō'nē ō'), *n.* a city in S Texas. 998,905. —**San' An•to'ni•an,** *n., adj.*

san•a•to•ri•um (san'ə tôr'ē əm), *n., pl.* **-to•ri•ums, -to•ri•a** (-tôr'ē ə). **1.** a hospital for the treatment of chronic diseases, as tuberculosis. **2.** SANITARIUM.

San Ber•nar•di•no (san' bûr'nər dē'nō, -bûr'nə-), *n.* a city in S California. 164,164.

sanc•ti•fy (sangk'tə fī'), *v.t.,* **-fied, -fy•ing. 1.** to make holy; consecrate. **2.** to purify or free from sin. —**sanc'ti•fi'ca'tion,** *n.*

sanc•ti•mo•ni•ous (sangk'tə mō'nē əs), *adj.* hypocritically religious or virtuous. —**sanc'ti•mo'ni•ous•ly,** *adv.*

sanc'ti•mo'ny, *n.* pretended, affected, or hypocritical piety or virtue.

sanc•tion (sangk'shən), *n.* **1.** authoritative permission or approval. **2.** a provision of a law requiring a penalty for disobedience. **3.** action by a state or states to force another state to comply with an obligation. —*v.t.* **4.** to authorize, approve, or allow. **5.** to ratify or confirm.

sanc•ti•ty (sangk'ti tē), *n., pl.* **-ties. 1.** holiness, saintliness, or godliness. **2.** sacred or hallowed character.

sanc•tu•ar•y (sangk'chōō er'ē), *n., pl.* **-ar•ies. 1.** a sacred or holy place. **2.** an esp. holy place in a temple or church, as the chancel. **3.** a church or other sacred place formerly providing refuge, esp. immunity from arrest. **4.** any place of refuge. **5.** a tract of land where wildlife can live in safety from hunters; preserve.

sanc'tum (-təm), *n., pl.* **-tums, -ta** (-tə). **1.** a sacred place. **2.** an inviolably private place or retreat.

Sanc•tus (sangk'təs), *n.* the hymn with which the Eucharistic preface culminates. Isa. 6:3. [< L *sānctus* inviolate, holy]

sand (sand), *n.* **1.** small, loose grains of rock debris. —*v.t.* **2.** to smooth or polish with an abrasive, esp. sandpaper. **3.** to sprinkle or fill with sand.

—**sand′er,** *n.* —**sand′y,** *adj.,* **-i•er, -i•est.** —**sand′i• ness,** *n.*

san•dal (san′dl), *n.* **1.** a shoe consisting of a sole fastened to the foot by thongs or straps. **2.** a low shoe or slipper.

san′dal•wood′, *n.* the fragrant reddish yellow heartwood of an Indian tree used for incense and ornamental carving.

sand′bag′, *n.* a bag filled with sand that is used in fortification, as ballast, or as a weapon.

sand′bank′, *n.* a large mass of sand, as on a shoal.

sand′ bar′, *n.* a bar of sand formed in a river or sea by the action of tides or currents.

sand′blast′, *n.* **1.** a blast of air or steam laden with sand, used to clean, grind, cut, or decorate hard surfaces. —*v.t.* **2.** to clean, decorate, etc., with a sandblast. —**sand′blast′er,** *n.*

sand′box′, *n.* a box or receptacle holding sand for children to play in.

Sand•burg (sand′bûrg, san′-), *n.* **Carl,** 1878–1967, U.S. author.

sand′ dol′lar, *n.* any of various flat, disklike sea animals that live on sandy ocean bottoms.

sand′hog′, *n.* a person who digs underwater tunnels.

San Di•e•go (san′ dē ā′gō), *n.* a seaport in SW California. 1,151,977.

San•di•nis•ta (san′də nē′stə), *n., pl.* **-tas.** a member of the Nicaraguan revolutionary organization that controlled Nicaragua from 1979 to 1989.

S&L, savings and loan (association).

sand′lot′, *n.* **1.** a vacant lot used by youngsters for games or sports. —*adj.* **2.** of or played in a sandlot.

sand′man′, *n., pl.* **-men.** a being of folklore who puts sand in the eyes of children to make them sleepy.

sand′pa′per, *n.* **1.** strong paper coated with a layer of abrasive, esp. sand, used for smoothing or polishing. —*v.t.* **2.** to smooth or polish with sandpaper.

sand′pi′per (-pī′pər), *n.* a plump, thin-billed shorebird.

sandpiper

sand′stone′, *n.* a sedimentary rock consisting of sand cemented together by various substances, as by silica.

sand′storm′, *n.* a windstorm that blows along clouds of sand.

sand′ trap′, *n.* a golf hazard consisting of a shallow pit partly filled with sand.

sand•wich (sand′wich, san′-), *n.* **1.** two or more slices of bread with a filling, as of meat, between them. **2.** something that resembles a sandwich. —*v.t.* **3.** to insert or squeeze between two other things. [after John Montagu, fourth Earl of *Sandwich* (1718–1792)]

sand′wich genera′tion, *n.* the generation of people still raising their children while having to care for their aging parents.

sane (sān), *adj.,* **san•er, san•est. 1.** free from mental derangement. **2.** reasonable; sensible. —**sane′ly,** *adv.*

San•for•ized (san′fə rīzd′), *Trademark.* (of a fabric) specially processed to resist shrinking.

San Fran•cis•co (san′ frən sis′kō, fran-), *n.* a seaport in W central California. 734,676. —**San′ Fran• cis′can,** *n., adj.*

San′ Francis′co Bay′, *n.* an inlet of the Pacific in W central California: the harbor of San Francisco.

sang (sang), *v.* pt. of SING.

sang-froid (*Fr.* sän frwA′), *n.* coolness of mind; composure. [< F: lit., cold blood]

San•gre de Cris•to (sang′grē də kris′tō), *n.* a mountain range in S Colorado and N New Mexico: a part of the Rocky Mountains.

san•gri•a or **-gri•a** (sang grē′ə, san-), *n.* an iced drink typically of red wine, sugar, sliced fruit and fruit juice, soda water, and spices.

san•gui•nar•y (sang′gwə ner′ē), *adj.* **1.** characterized by bloodshed; bloody. **2.** eager to shed blood; bloodthirsty.

san′guine (-gwin), *adj.* **1.** cheerfully optimistic, hopeful, or confident. **2.** reddish; ruddy.

San•hed•rin (san hed′rin, -hē′drin, sän-, san′i drin) also **San•he•drim** (san′hi drim, san′i-), *n.* the supreme legislative council and ecclesiastical and secular tribunal of the ancient Jews.

san•i•tar•i•an (san′i târ′ē ən), *n.* a specialist in public sanitation and health.

san′i•tar′i•um (-ē əm), *n., pl.* **-i•ums, -i•a** (-ē ə). a health resort.

san′i•tar′y (-ter′ē), *adj.* **1.** of health or the conditions affecting health. **2.** free from dirt and bacteria.

san′itary nap′kin, *n.* a disposable pad worn by women to absorb menstrual flow.

san•i•ta′tion, *n.* **1.** the application of sanitary measures for the protection of public health. **2.** the disposal of sewage and solid waste.

san′i•tize′, *v.t.,* **-tized, -tiz•ing. 1.** to free from dirt and bacteria. **2.** to make less offensive by eliminating unwholesome or objectionable elements.

san•i•ty (san′i tē), *n.* the state of being sane.

San Jo•se (san′ hō zā′), *n.* a city in W California. 816,884.

San Jo•sé (san′ hō zā′), *n.* the capital of Costa Rica. 241,464.

San′ Juan′ (wän, hwän), *n.* the capital of Puerto Rico. 431,227.

San′ Juan′ Hill′, *n.* a hill in SE Cuba: captured by U.S. forces during the Spanish-American War in 1898.

sank (sangk), *v.* a pt. of SINK.

San′ Ma•ri′no (mə rē′nō), *n.* a small republic in E Italy. 24,714.

sans (sanz), *prep.* without.

San Sal′va•dor (sal′və dôr′), *n.* the capital of El Salvador. 452,614.

San•skrit (san′skrit), *n.* an ancient language retained in India in a classical form as a language of literature and Hinduism.

San•ta An•a (san′tə an′ə), *n.* a city in SW California. 293,742.

San′ta Claus′ (klôz), *n.* a white-bearded, plump, red-suited man of folklore who brings gifts to well-behaved children at Christmas.

San′ta Fe′ (fā), *n.* the capital of New Mexico. 59,300. —**San′ta Fe′an,** *n., adj.*

San′ta Fe′ Trail′, *n.* a trade route between Independence, Mo., and Santa Fe, N.M., used from about 1821 to 1880.

San′ta Ro′sa (rō′zə), *n.* a city in W California. 116,962.

San•ti•a•go (san′tē ä′gō), *n.* the capital of Chile. 4,858,342.

San•to Do•min•go (san′tō də ming′gō), *n.* the capital of the Dominican Republic. 1,313,172.

São Pau•lo (souɴ′ pou′lō, -lŏō), *n.* a city in SE Brazil. 7,032,547.

São′ To•mé′ and Prín′cipe or **Sao′ To•me′ and Prin′cipe** (souɴ′ tŏō mā′), *n.* a republic in W Africa, comprising two islands (**São Tomé** and **Príncipe**). 106,900.

sap¹ (sap), *n.* **1.** a fluid containing mineral salts and sugar that circulates through the tissues of a plant. **2.** energy; vitality. **3.** a fool; dupe. —**sap′less,** *adj.*

sap² (sap), *v.t.,* **sapped, sap•ping. 1.** to dig below (an enemy fortification). **2.** to weaken or destroy insidiously.

sa•pi•ent (sā′pē ənt), *adj.* having or showing great wisdom. —**sa′pi•ence,** *n.*

sap•ling (sap′ling), *n.* a young tree.

sap•phire (saf′īᵊr), *n.* **1.** a blue gem variety of corundum. **2.** a deep blue.

Sap•po•ro (sə pôr′ō), *n.* a city on W Hokkaido, in N Japan. 1,555,000.

sap•py (sap′ē), *adj.,* -pi•er, -pi•est. **1.** abounding in sap. **2.** foolish; silly. —**sap′pi•ness,** *n.*

sap•ro•phyte (sap′rə fīt′), *n.* an organism that lives on dead organic matter. —**sap′ro•phyt′ic** (-fit′ik), *adj.*

sap′suck′er, *n.* a North American woodpecker that drills holes in trees for sap.

Sar•a•cen (sar′ə sən), *n.* any of the Muslim opponents of the Crusaders in the Middle Ages.

Sar•ah (sâr′ə), *n.* the wife of Abraham and mother of Isaac. Gen. 17:15–22.

Sa•ra•je•vo (sar′ə yā′vō), *n.* the capital of Bosnia and Herzegovina. 448,519.

sa•ran (sə ran′), *n.* a tough thermoplastic resin used esp. in thin sheets for packaging.

sar•casm (sär′kaz əm), *n.* **1.** harsh or bitter derision or irony. **2.** a sneering or cutting remark. —**sar•cas′tic** (-kas′tik), *adj.* —**sar•cas′ti•cal•ly,** *adv.*

sar•co•ma (sär kō′mə), *n., pl.* -mas, -ma•ta (-mə-tə). a malignant tumor resembling embryonic connective tissue.

sar•coph•a•gus (sär kof′ə gəs), *n., pl.* -gi (-jī′, -gī′), -gus•es. a stone coffin.

sar•dine (sär dēn′), *n., pl.* -dines, -dine. a fish of the herring family, often canned in oil.

Sar•din•i•a (sär din′ē ə, -din′yə), *n.* an Italian island in the Mediterranean, W of Italy. 1,594,175.

Sar•dis (sär′dis) also **Sar•des** (-dēz), *n.* an ancient city in W Asia Minor: the capital of Lydia and site of one of the seven churches of Asia (Rev. 1:11).

sar•don•ic (sär don′ik), *adj.* scornfully derisive or mocking; cynical. —**sar•don′i•cal•ly,** *adv.*

Sar•gent (sär′jənt), *n.* **John Singer,** 1856–1925, U.S. painter.

sa•ri (sär′ē), *n., pl.* -ris. a woman's garment, worn esp. in India, consisting of a long cloth wrapped around the body.

sa•rong (sə rông′, -rong′), *n.* a loose-fitting skirtlike garment worn by both sexes in the Malay Archipelago and some Pacific islands.

sar•sa•pa•ril•la (sas′pə ril′ə, sär′sə pə-, sär′spə-), *n., pl.* -las. **1.** the root of a tropical American vine used medicinally and as a flavoring. **2.** a soft drink, as root beer, flavored with extract of sarsaparilla.

sar•to•ri•al (sär tôr′ē əl), *adj.* **1.** of tailors or their trade. **2.** of clothing or style of dress. —**sar•to′ri•al•ly,** *adv.*

Sar•tre (SAR′tR²), *n.* **Jean-Paul** (zhän), 1905–80, French philosopher and writer.

SASE, self-addressed stamped envelope.

sash¹ (sash), *n.* a long band worn over one shoulder or around the waist.

sash² (sash), *n.* a framework, as in a window, in which panes of glass are set.

sa•shay (sa shā′), *v.i.* **1.** to walk, move, or proceed easily or nonchalantly. **2.** to strut.

Sask., Saskatchewan.

Sas•katch•e•wan (sa skach′ə won′, -wən), *n.* **1.** a province in W Canada. 1,009,613. *Abbr.:* SK, Sask. *Cap.:* Regina. **2.** a river in SW Canada. 1205 mi. (1940 km) long.

Sas•ka•toon (sas′kə tōōn′), *n.* a city in S Saskatchewan, in SW Canada. 177,641.

sass (sas), *Informal.* —*n.* **1.** impudent back talk. —*v.t.* **2.** to answer back in an impudent manner.

sas•sa•fras (sas′ə fras′), *n.* **1.** an E North American tree of the laurel family. **2.** the aromatic bark of the sassafras root, used esp. as a flavoring agent.

sas′sy, *adj.,* -si•er, -si•est. impudent; fresh.

sat (sat), *v.* a pt. and pp. of sɪт.

SAT, *Trademark.* college admissions tests sponsored by the College Entrance Examination Board.

Sat., **1.** Saturday. **2.** Saturn.

Sa•tan (sāt′n), *n.* **1.** the devil. —*Proverb.* **2.** Get thee behind me, Satan, temptation must be resisted. Matt. 16:23.

sa•tan•ic (sə tan′ik, sā-) also **-i•cal,** *adj.* **1.** of or like Satan. **2.** extremely evil or wicked; fiendish. —**sa•tan′i•cal•ly,** *adv.*

satch•el (sach′əl), *n.* a small bag, sometimes with a shoulder strap.

sate (sāt), *v.t.,* sat•ed, sat•ing. **1.** to satisfy fully. **2.** to supply or indulge to excess; surfeit.

sa•teen (sa tēn′), *n.* a strong, lustrous cotton fabric in satin weave.

sat•el•lite (sat′l īt′), *n.* **1.** a natural body that revolves around a planet. **2.** a device designed to orbit a celestial body, as the earth. **3.** a country under the domination or influence of another. **4.** an often obsequious attendant or follower.

sa•ti•ate (sā′shē āt′), *v.t.,* -at•ed, -at•ing. **1.** to supply to excess; surfeit. **2.** to satisfy in the full. —**sa′ti•a′tion,** *n.*

sa•ti•e•ty (sə tī′i tē), *n.* the state of being satiated.

sat•in (sat′n), *n.* a fabric with a glossy finish and a soft, slippery texture. —**sat′in•y,** *adj.*

sat′in•wood′, *n.* **1.** a satiny wood used to make furniture. **2.** a tree yielding satinwood.

sat•ire (sat′īᵊr), *n.* **1.** the use of irony, sarcasm, or ridicule in exposing vice or folly. **2.** a literary composition or genre marked by satire. —**sa•tir•i•cal** (sə-tir′i kəl), *adj.* —**sat′i•rist** (-ər ist), *n.*

sat•i•rize (sat′ə rīz′), *v.t.,* -rized, -riz•ing. to attack or ridicule with satire.

sat•is•fac•tion (sat′is fak′shən), *n.* **1.** the state or feeling of being satisfied; contentment. **2.** a source of fulfillment or contentment. **3.** reparation, as for a wrong; compensation. **4.** payment, as of a debt.

sat′is•fac′to•ry (-tə rē), *adj.* serving to satisfy; adequate. —**sat′is•fac′to•ri•ly,** *adv.*

sat′is•fy′ (-fī′), *v.t.,* -fied, -fy•ing. **1.** to fulfill the desires, needs, or demands of; content. **2.** to fulfill the requirements or conditions of. **3.** to overcome the doubts of; convince. **4.** to discharge (an obligation) fully. **5.** to make reparation to or for. **6.** to pay (a creditor).

sa•to•ri (sə tôr′ē), *n.* sudden enlightenment in Zen.

sa•trap (sā′trap, sa′-), *n.* a subordinate ruler, often a despotic one.

sat•u•rate (sach′ə rāt′), *v.t.,* -rat•ed, -rat•ing. **1.** to load, fill, treat, or charge to the utmost. **2.** to soak, impregnate, or imbue thoroughly. —**sat′u•ra′tion,** *n.*

Sat•ur•day (sat′ər dā′, -dē), *n.* the seventh day of the week.

Sat′urday-night′ spe′cial, *n.* a cheap handgun that is easily obtained and concealed.

Sat•urn (sat′ərn), *n.* **1.** a Roman god of agriculture. **2.** the planet sixth in order from the sun and second largest in the solar system.

sat•ur•nine (sat′ər nīn′), *adj.* gloomy or morose in temperament; sullen.

sa•tyr (sā′tər, sat′ər), *n.* **1.** a lascivious ancient Greek woodland deity, part human and part horse or goat. **2.** a lascivious man. —**sa•tyr•ic** (sə tir′ik), *adj.*

sa•ty•ri•a•sis (sā′tə rī′ə sis, sat′ə-), *n.* abnormal, uncontrollable sexual desire in a male. Compare NYMPHOMANIA.

sauce (sôs), *n., v.,* sauced, sauc•ing. —*n.* **1.** a liquid or semiliquid preparation, as gravy, eaten as an accompaniment to food. **2.** stewed fruit. **3.** *Informal.* impertinence. —*v.t.* **4.** to dress or prepare with a sauce. **5.** *Informal.* to speak impertinently to; sass. —*Proverb.* **6. What's sauce for the goose is sauce for the gander,** people should be treated equally.

sauce′pan′, *n.* a cooking pan with a handle.

sau•cer (sô′sər), *n.* a round, shallow dish for holding a cup.

sau•cy (sô′sē), *adj.,* -ci•er, -ci•est. **1.** impertinent; insolent. **2.** pert; jaunty. —**sau′ci•ly,** *adv.* —**sau′ci•ness,** *n.*

Sau′di Ara′bia (sou′dē, sô′-, sä ōō′-), *n.* a kingdom occupying most of Arabia. 20,087,965. —**Sau′di,** *n., pl.* -dis, *adj.*

sau•er•kraut (souᵊr′krout′, sou′ər-), *n.* finely cut salted and fermented cabbage. [< G: sour greens]

Saul (sôl), n. **1.** the first king of Israel. I Sam. 9. **2.** Also called **Saul′ of Tar′sus.** the original name of the apostle Paul. Acts 9:1–30; 22:3.

sau•na (sô′nə, sou′-), n., pl. **-nas. 1.** a bath that uses dry heat to induce perspiration. **2.** a bath in which steam is produced by pouring water on heated stones. [< Fin]

saun•ter (sôn′tər, sän′-), v.i. **1.** to stroll. —n. **2.** a stroll.

sau•ri•an (sôr′ē ən), adj. of or resembling a lizard.

sau•ro•pod (sôr′ə pod′), n. any of various huge dinosaurs, including the brontosaur, with small heads and very long necks and tails.

sau•sage (sô′sij; esp. Brit. sos′ij), n. finely chopped, seasoned meat, usu. stuffed into a casing.

sau•té (sō tā′, sô-), v.t., **-téed** (-tād′), **-té•ing** (-tā′ing). to fry in a small amount of fat.

Sau•ternes (sō tûrn′, sô-), n. a sweet white table wine.

sav•age (sav′ij), adj. **1.** wild; untamed. **2.** uncivilized; barbarous. **3.** fierce, brutal, or cruel. —n. **4.** an uncivilized person. **5.** a fierce, brutal, or cruel person. —**sav′age•ly,** adv. —**sav′age•ry,** n., pl. **-ries.**

sa•van•na or **-nah** (sə van′ə), n., pl. **-nas** or **-nahs.** a grassy plain with scattered tree growth.

Sa•van′nah, n. a seaport in E Georgia. 140,597.

sa•vant (sa vänt′, sav′ənt; Fr. sa vän′), n., pl. **sa•vants** (sa vänts′, sav′ənts; Fr. sa vän′). a person of profound learning.

save[1] (sāv), v., **saved, sav•ing.** —v.t. **1.** to rescue from danger, harm, or loss. **2.** to keep safe, intact, or unhurt. **3.** to prevent the spending, consumption, loss, or waste of. **4.** to set aside in reserve; lay by. **5.** to deliver from sin. **6.** to copy (computer data) onto a hard or floppy disk, a tape, etc. —v.i. **7.** to set aside money. **8.** to be economical in expenditure. —**sav′a•ble, save′a•ble,** adj. —**sav′er,** n.

save[2] (sāv), prep. **1.** with the exception of; except; but. —conj. **2.** except; but.

sav′ing, n. **1.** a reduction in expenditure or outlay. **2. savings,** sums of money set aside. —prep. **3.** with the exception of. —conj. **4.** except.

sav•ior or **-iour** (sāv′yər), n. **1.** a person who saves. **2.** (cap.) Jesus Christ.

sa•voir-faire (sav′wär fâr′; Fr. sa vwar feR′), n. knowledge of just what to do in any situation.

sa•vor (sā′vər), n. **1.** a particular taste or odor. **2.** distinctive quality or property. —v.i. **3.** to have a particular savor. —v.t. **4.** to taste with relish. Also, esp. Brit., **sa′vour.** —**sa′vor•y,** adj.

sav•vy (sav′ē), n., adj., **-vi•er, -vi•est,** v., **-vied, -vy•ing.** —n. **1.** practical understanding: political savvy. —adj. **2.** shrewd and well-informed; canny. —v.t., v.i. **3.** to know; understand.

saw[1] (sô), n., v., **sawed, sawed** or **sawn, saw•ing.** —n. **1.** a cutting tool consisting of a thin serrated metal blade. —v.t., v.i. **2.** to cut or divide with or as if with a saw.

saw[2] (sô), v. pt. of see[1].

saw[3] (sô), n. a familiar saying; proverb.

saw′buck′, n. **1.** a sawhorse. **2.** Slang. a ten-dollar bill.

saw′dust′, n. fine particles of wood produced in sawing.

saw′horse′, n. a movable frame or trestle for supporting wood while it is being sawed.

saw′mill′, n. a mill where timber is sawed.

saw•yer (sô′yər, soi′ər), n. a person who saws wood, esp. as an occupation.

sax (saks), n. a saxophone.

Sax•on (sak′sən), n. **1.** a member of a Germanic people, groups of whom invaded Britain in the 5th–6th centuries. —adj. **2.** of the Saxons.

Sax•o•ny (sak′sə nē), n. **1.** a state in E central Germany. 4,900,000; 6561 sq. mi. (16,990 sq. km). Cap.: Dresden. **2.** a medieval division of N Germany: extended at its height from the Rhine to E of the Elbe.

sax•o•phone (sak′sə fōn′), n. a wind instrument with a conical tube, keys or valves, and a reed mouthpiece. —**sax′o•phon′ist,** n.

say (sā), v., **said, say•ing,** n. —v.t. **1.** to pronounce; speak. **2.** to express in words; state. **3.** to state as an opinion or judgment. **4.** to recite or repeat. **5.** to report or allege. **6.** to indicate or show: What does your watch say? —n. **7.** what a person says or has to say. **8.** the right or opportunity to state an opinion or exercise influence. —**Idiom. 9. that is to say,** in other words.

Say•ers (sā′ərz, sârz), n. **Dorothy L(eigh),** 1893–1957, English detective-story writer, essayist, translator, and Christian apologist.

say′ing, n. something said, esp. a proverb or maxim.

say′-so′, n., pl. **say-sos. 1.** the right of final authority. **2.** an authoritative statement.

Sb, Chem. Symbol. antimony. [< L stibium]

SC or **S.C.,** South Carolina.

Sc, Chem. Symbol. scandium.

s.c., Print. small capitals.

scab (skab), n., v., **scabbed, scab•bing.** —n. **1.** an incrustation that forms over a healing sore or wound. **2.** a worker who refuses to join a labor union or takes a striking worker's place on the job. —v.i. **3.** to become covered with a scab. **4.** to act or work as a scab. —**scab′by,** adj., **-bi•er, -bi•est.** —**scab′bi•ness,** n.

scab•bard (skab′ərd), n. a sheath for a sword, bayonet, or dagger.

sca•bies (skā′bēz, -bē ēz′), n. a form of mange caused by a mite that burrows into the skin.

scab•rous (skab′rəs), adj. **1.** having a rough surface, as because of minute projections. **2.** indecent; obscene.

scad (skad), n. Usu., **scads.** a great number or quantity.

scaf•fold (skaf′əld, -ōld), n. **1.** a raised platform for holding workers and materials, as during the erection of a building. **2.** an elevated platform on which a criminal is executed.

scaf′fold•ing, n. **1.** a system of scaffolds. **2.** materials for scaffolds.

scal•a•wag (skal′ə wag′), n. a white Southerner who supported Republican policy during Reconstruction.

scald (skôld), v.t. **1.** to burn with or as if with hot liquid or steam. **2.** to heat to a temperature just short of the boiling point. —n. **3.** a burn caused by scalding.

scale[1] (skāl), n., v., **scaled, scal•ing.** —n. **1.** one of the thin flat plates forming the covering of certain animals, as snakes or fishes. **2.** a thin flake, as one that peels off from the skin. **3.** a thin coating, as of rust. —v.t. **4.** to remove the scales from. —v.i. **5.** to come off in scales. —**scal′y,** adj., **-i•er, -i•est.**

scale[2] (skāl), n. **1.** Often, **scales.** a balance or other device for weighing. **2.** either of the pans or dishes of a balance.

scale[3] (skāl), n., v., **scaled, scal•ing.** —n. **1.** a progression or series of steps or degrees. **2.** a series of marks laid down at regular intervals along a line, used for measuring. **3.** a measuring instrument with such markings. **4.** the proportion that a representation bears to what it represents. **5.** a graduated line, as on a map, representing proportionate size. **6.** relative size or extent. **7.** a succession of musical tones ascending or descending at fixed intervals. —v.t. **8.** to climb by or as if by a ladder. **9.** to make according to a scale. **10.** to adjust to a standard or measure.

scale′ in′sect, n. any of numerous small, plant-sucking insects, the females of which secrete waxy scales.

sca•lene (skā lēn′), adj. (of a triangle) having three unequal sides.

Sca•li•a (skə lē′ə), n. **Antonin,** born 1936, associate justice of the U.S. Supreme Court since 1986.

scal•lion (skal′yən), n. an onion that does not form a large bulb.

scal•lop (skol′əp, skal′-), n. **1.** a bivalve mollusk with a fluted shell. **2.** the fleshy muscle of a scallop, used as food. **3.** the shell of a scallop. **4.** any of a series of curved projections cut along an edge, as of fabric. —*v.t.* **5.** to finish (an edge) with scallops. **6.** to escallop.

scalp (skalp), *n.* **1.** the skin of the top and back of the head, usu. covered with hair. —*v.t.* **2.** to cut or tear the scalp from. **3.** to resell at inflated prices: *to scalp tickets.* —**scalp′er,** *n.*

scal•pel (skal′pəl), *n.* a small, usu. straight knife used in surgery.

scam (skam), *n., v.,* scammed, scam•ming. —*n.* **1.** a fraudulent scheme; swindle. —*v.t.* **2.** to cheat; defraud.

scamp (skamp), *n.* **1.** an unscrupulous person; rascal. **2.** a playful or mischievous young person.

scamp′er, *v.i.* **1.** to run hastily or playfully. —*n.* **2.** an act or instance of scampering.

scam•pi (skam′pē, skäm′-), *n., pl.* **-pi. 1.** a large shrimp. **2.** a dish of scampi cooked esp. in butter and garlic. [< It, pl. of *scampo* a type of shrimp]

scan (skan), *v.,* scanned, scan•ning. —*v.t.* **1.** to examine minutely. **2.** to glance at hastily. **3.** to observe repeatedly or sweepingly. **4.** to analyze (verse) for metrical structure. **5.** to read (data) for use by a computer, esp. using an optical scanner. **6.** to traverse with a radar beam. —*v.i.* **7.** (of verse) to conform to the rules of meter. —*n.* **8.** an act or instance of scanning. —**scan′ner,** *n.*

Scan. or **Scand., 1.** Scandinavia. **2.** Scandinavian.

scan•dal (skan′dl), *n.* **1.** a disgraceful or discreditable action or circumstance. **2.** damage to reputation; disgrace. **3.** malicious gossip. —**scan′dal•ous,** *adj.* —**scan′dal•ous•ly,** *adv.*

scan′dal•ize′, *v.t.,* -ized, -iz•ing. to shock by being immoral or disgraceful.

scan′dal•mon′ger, *n.* a person who spreads scandal.

Scan•di•na•vi•a (skan′də nā′vē ə), *n.* Norway, Sweden, Denmark, and sometimes Finland and Iceland. —**Scan′di•na′vi•an,** *adj., n.*

scan•sion (skan′shən), *n.* the metrical analysis of verse.

scant (skant), *adj.,* -er, -est. **1.** barely sufficient. **2.** amounting to a bit less than indicated. **3.** having an inadequate or limited supply. —**scant′ly,** *adv.* —**scant′ness,** *n.*

scant′y, *adj.,* -i•er, -i•est. insufficient, as in amount. —**scant′i•ly,** *adv.* —**scant′i•ness,** *n.*

scape•goat (skāp′gōt′), *n.* **1.** a person or group made to bear the blame for others. —*v.t.* **2.** to make a scapegoat of.

scape′grace′, *n.* a persistent rascal.

scap•u•la (skap′yə lə), *n., pl.* -las, -lae (-lē′). either of two flat triangular bones forming the back part of the shoulder. —**scap′u•lar,** *adj.*

scar (skär), *n., v.,* scarred, scar•ring. —*n.* **1.** a mark left by a healed wound. **2.** a trace or lasting aftereffect of damage. —*v.t., v.i.* **3.** to mark with or form a scar.

scar•ab (skar′əb), *n.* **1.** a large beetle with a dark shell. **2.** a representation of a scarab.

scarce (skârs), *adj.,* scarc•er, scarc•est. **1.** insufficient to satisfy a need or demand. **2.** rarely encountered. —**scar′ci•ty,** scarce′ness, *n.*

scarce′ly, *adv.* **1.** not quite; barely. **2.** definitely not. **3.** probably not. ——Usage. See HARDLY.

scare (skâr), *v.,* scared, scar•ing, *n.* —*v.t., v.i.* **1.** to frighten or become frightened, esp. suddenly. **2.** **scare up,** to find or get despite difficulties. —*n.* **3.** a sudden fright. **4.** a condition of alarm.

scare′crow′, *n.* an object, usu. a figure of a person, set up to frighten birds away from crops.

scarf (skärf), *n., pl.* scarfs, scarves (skärvz). **1.** a long, sometimes broad strip of cloth worn about the neck, shoulders, or head. **2.** a long ornamental cloth, as for a bureau.

scar•i•fy (skar′ə fī′), *v.t.,* -fied, -fy•ing. **1.** to make scratches or superficial cuts in. **2.** to wound with severe criticism. —**scar′i•fi•ca′tion,** *n.*

scar•let (skär′lit), *n.* a bright red.

scar′let fe′ver, *n.* a contagious febrile disease characterized by a red rash.

scar•y (skâr′ē), *adj.,* -i•er, -i•est. **1.** causing fright. **2.** easily frightened. —**scar′i•ly,** *adv.* —**scar′i•ness,** *n.*

scat¹ (skat), *v.i.,* scat•ted, scat•ting. to go off hastily.

scat² (skat), *n.* jazz singing with improvised nonsense syllables.

scath•ing (skā′thing), *adj.* bitterly severe. —**scath′ing•ly,** *adv.*

sca•tol•o•gy (skə tol′ə jē), *n.* preoccupation with excrement or obscenity. —**scat•o•log•i•cal** (skat′l oj′i kal), *adj.*

scat•ter (skat′ər), *v.t.* **1.** to throw loosely about. **2.** to cause to disperse. —*v.i.* **3.** to separate and disperse.

scat′ter•brain′, *n.* a person incapable of serious, connected thought. —**scat′ter•brained′,** *adj.*

scat′ter rug′, *n.* a small rug.

scav•enge (skav′inj), *v.,* -enged, -eng•ing. —*v.t.* **1.** to take or gather (something usable) from discarded material. —*v.i.* **2.** to act as a scavenger.

scav′en•ger, *n.* **1.** an animal that feeds on dead organic matter. **2.** a person who searches through refuse for useful material.

sce•nar•i•o (si när′ē ō′, -när′-), *n., pl.* -os. **1.** an outline of the plot of a dramatic work. **2.** the outline of a motion picture or television program. **3.** an imagined sequence of events. —**sce•nar′ist,** *n.*

scene (sēn), *n.* **1.** the place where an action or event occurs. **2.** a view or picture. **3.** an incident or situation. **4.** an embarrassing display of emotion, esp. in public. **5.** a division of a play, film, etc., representing a single episode. **6.** the setting of a story or drama. **7.** SCENERY (def. 2). **8.** a sphere of activity or interest.

scen•er•y (sē′nə rē), *n.* **1.** all the features that give character to a landscape. **2.** the hangings, draperies, and structures used on a stage to represent the scene of action.

sce•nic (sē′nik, sen′ik), *adj.* **1.** of natural scenery. **2.** marked by beautiful scenery. **3.** of the stage or stage scenery. —**sce′ni•cal•ly,** *adv.*

scent (sent), *n.* **1.** a distinctive odor, esp. when agreeable. **2.** an odor left in passing, by means of which an animal can be tracked. **3.** a perfume. **4.** the sense of smell. —*v.t.* **5.** to perceive by or as if by the sense of smell. **6.** to fill with an odor; perfume. —**scent′ed,** *adj.*

scep•ter (sep′tar), *n.* a rod or wand held as an emblem of regal or imperial power. Also, *esp. Brit.,* **scep′tre.**

scep•tic (skep′tik), *n., adj.* SKEPTIC.

sched•ule (skej′ool, -ōol; *Brit.* shed′yool, shej′ōol), *n., v.,* -uled, -ul•ing. —*n.* **1.** a plan of procedure listing the sequence of events and the time allotted for each. **2.** a series of things to be done; agenda. **3.** a timetable. **4.** a statement of details. —*v.t.* **5.** to make a schedule of. **6.** to enter in a schedule. **7.** to plan for a certain date.

sche•mat•ic (skē mat′ik, ski-), *adj.* of or in the form of a diagram or scheme.

scheme (skēm), *n., v.,* schemed, schem•ing. —*n.* **1.** a plan or program of action. **2.** an underhand plot; intrigue. **3.** a system of correlated things or parts. —*v.t., v.i.* **4.** to devise a scheme (for); plan or plot. —**schem′er,** *n.* —**schem′ing,** *adj.*

scher•zo (skert′sō), *n., pl.* scher•zos, scher•zi (skert′sē). a playful musical movement.

Schick′ test′ (shik), *n.* a diphtheria immunity test. [after B. *Schick* (1877–1967), U.S. pediatrician]

schil•ling (shil′ing), *n.* the basic monetary unit of Austria.

schism (siz′am, skiz′-), *n.* **1.** division or disunion, esp. into mutually opposed parties. **2.** a division within or separation from a religious body. —**schis•mat′ic** (-mat′ik), *adj.*

schist (shist), *n.* a crystalline metamorphic rock. —**schis′tose** (-tōs), **schis′tous** (-tas), *adj.*

schiz•oid (skit′soid), *adj.* **1.** of or noting a personality disorder marked by passivity, indifference, etc. **2.** of schizophrenia. —*n.* **3.** a schizoid person.

schiz•o•phre•ni•a (skit/sə frē/nē ə), *n.* a severe mental disorder typically marked by disorganized behavior, delusions, and hallucinations. —**schiz/o•phren/ic** (-fren/ik), *adj., n.*

schle•miel (shlə mēl/), *n. Slang.* an awkward and unlucky person for whom things never turn out right. [< Yiddish *shlemil*]

schlep (shlep), *v.,* **schlepped, schlep•ping,** *n. Slang.* —*v.t., v.i.* **1.** to carry or move with great effort. —*n.* **2.** a slow or awkward person. **3.** a tedious journey. [< Yiddish *shlepn* to pull, drag]

Schles•in•ger (shles/in jər, shlā/zing ər), *n.* **1. Arthur (Meier),** 1888–1965, U.S. historian. **2.** his son, **Arthur (Meier), Jr.,** born 1917, U.S. historian and writer.

schlock (shlok), *n. Slang.* something of cheap or inferior quality. [< Yiddish *shlak* apoplectic stroke, evil, nuisance] —**schlock/y,** *adj.*

schmaltz (shmälts, shmôlts), *n. Informal.* exaggerated sentimentalism, as in music. [< Yiddish *shmalts* fat, grease] —**schmaltz/y,** *adj.,* **-i•er, -i•est.**

schnau•zer (shnou/zər), *n.* a dog with a wiry coat and a rectangular head with beardlike whiskers.

schnoz (shnoz) also **schnoz/zle,** *n. Slang.* a nose.

schol•ar (skol/ər), *n.* **1.** a learned or erudite person. **2.** a student; pupil. —**schol/ar•ly,** *adj.*

schol/ar•ship/, *n.* **1.** the qualities, knowledge, or attainments of a scholar. **2.** money given to enable a student to pursue his or her studies.

scho•las•tic (skə las/tik), *adj.* of schools, scholars, or education. —**scho•las/ti•cal•ly,** *adv.*

school[1] (skool), *n.* **1.** an institution for teaching. **2.** the activity of teaching or of learning, esp. at a school. **3.** the body of persons belonging to a school. **4.** a place, as a building, housing a school. **5.** a group of persons having common attitudes or beliefs. —*v.t.* **6.** to educate in or as if in a school.

school[2] (skool), *n.* a large number of marine animals, as fish, feeding or migrating together.

school/ board/, *n.* a local board in charge of public education.

school/boy/, *n.* a boy attending school.

school/girl/, *n.* a girl attending school.

school/house/, *n.* a building used as a school.

school/marm/ (-märm/), *n.* a female schoolteacher, esp. an old-fashioned type.

school/mas/ter, *n.* a man who directs or teaches in a school.

school/mate/, *n.* a companion at school.

school/mis/tress, *n.* a woman who directs or teaches in a school.

school/room/, *n.* a room in which pupils are taught.

school/teach/er, *n.* a teacher in a school.

school/work/, *n.* material studied in or for school.

school/yard/, *n.* a playground or sports field near a school.

school/ year/, *n.* the months of the year when school is open.

schoon•er (skoo/nər), *n.* **1.** a sailing ship with fore-and-aft sails. **2.** a very tall glass, as for beer.

Schu•bert (shoo/bərt, -bert), *n.* **Franz,** 1797–1828, Austrian composer.

Schul•er (shoo/lər), *n.* **Robert,** born 1916, U.S. evangelist.

Schulz (shoolts), *n.* **Charles M(onroe),** born 1922, U.S. cartoonist.

Schu•mann (shoo/män), *n.* **1. Clara,** (*Clara Wieck*), 1819–96, German pianist and composer (wife of Robert Schumann). **2. Robert,** 1810–56, German composer.

schuss (shoos, shoos), *n.* **1.** a straight downhill ski run at high speed. —*v.i.* **2.** to execute a schuss.

schuss/boom/er (-boo/mər), *n. Informal.* a skier who is skilled at schussing.

Schuy•ler (skī/lər), *n.* **Philip John,** 1733–1804, American statesman and general in the Revolutionary War.

schwa (shwä), *n.* **1.** the neutral vowel sound typical of unstressed syllables in English, as the *a* in *alone*. **2.** the symbol ə used to represent the schwa.

Schweit•zer (shwīt/sər, shvīt/-), *n.* **Albert,** 1875–1965, Alsatian writer, missionary, doctor, and musician in Africa.

sci., **1.** science. **2.** scientific.

sci•at•ic (sī at/ik), *adj.* of, near, or affecting the back of the hip or its nerves.

sci•at/i•ca (-i kə), *n.* pain in the lower back and along the back of the thigh.

sci•ence (sī/əns), *n.* **1.** a branch of knowledge or study dealing with a body of facts systematically arranged and showing the operation of general laws. **2.** systematic knowledge of the physical or material world gained through observation and experimentation. —**sci/en•tif/ic** (-ən tif/ik), *adj.* —**sci/en•tif/i•cal•ly,** *adv.* —**sci/en•tist** (-tist), *n.*

sci/ence fic/tion, *n.* a form of fiction that draws imaginatively on scientific knowledge and speculation.

sci-fi (sī/fī/), *n., adj. Informal.* science fiction.

scim•i•tar (sim/i tər), *n.* a curved, single-edged sword.

scin•til•la (sin til/ə), *n., pl.* **-las.** a minute particle; trace.

scin/til•late/ (-tl āt/), *v.i.,* **-lat•ed, -lat•ing. 1.** to emit sparks; flash. **2.** to be animated; sparkle. —**scin/til•la/tion,** *n.*

sci•on (sī/ən), *n.* **1.** a descendant, esp. of an illustrious family. **2.** a plant shoot or twig, esp. one cut for grafting.

scis•sor (siz/ər), *v.t.* **1.** to cut or clip out with scissors. —*n.* **2.** SCISSORS.

scis/sors, *n.* (*used with a sing. or pl. v.*) a cutting instrument consisting of two blades so pivoted together that their sharp edges work one against the other. —**scis/sor•like/,** *adj.*

scis/sors kick/, *n.* a swimmer's scissorlike motion of the legs.

scle•ro•sis (skli rō/sis), *n., pl.* **-ses** (-sēz). a hardening of a body tissue or part, as of an artery. —**scle•rot/ic** (-rot/ik), *adj.*

scoff (skôf, skof), *v.i.* **1.** to express derision, mockery, or scorn. —*n.* **2.** an expression of derision, mockery, or scorn.

scoff/law/, *n.* a person who flouts the law.

scold (skōld), *v.t.* **1.** to find fault with angrily. —*v.i.* **2.** to find fault angrily; rebuke. —*n.* **3.** a person who is constantly scolding. —**scold/ing,** *n.*

sco•li•o•sis (skō/lē ō/sis, skol/ē-), *n.* lateral curvature of the spine.

sconce (skons), *n.* a wall bracket for candles or electric lights.

scone (skōn, skon), *n.* a biscuitlike quick bread baked on a griddle.

scoop (skoop), *n.* **1.** a small shovel for taking up flour, sugar, etc. **2.** a utensil for dishing out balls of ice cream or other soft food. **3.** the bucket of a dredge or steam shovel. **4.** the quantity held in a scoop. **5.** the act of scooping. **6.** a news item revealed in one information medium before all others. —*v.t.* **7.** to take out or form with or as if with a scoop. **8.** to make a hollow in. **9.** to reveal a news item before (one's competitors).

scoot (skoot), *v.i.* to go swiftly or hastily.

scoot/er, *n.* **1.** a child's two-wheeled vehicle steered by a handlebar and propelled by pushing one foot against the ground. **2.** a motor vehicle similar to but larger and heavier than a scooter.

scope (skōp), *n.* **1.** extent or range of view, outlook, or understanding. **2.** opportunity or freedom for movement or activity. **3.** extent in space.

-scope, a combining form meaning instrument for viewing (*telescope*).

Scopes (skōps), *n.* **John Thomas,** 1901–70, U.S. high-school teacher whose teaching of the Darwinian theory of evolution became a cause célèbre **(Scopes/ Tri/al** or **Monkey Trial)** in 1925.

scor·bu·tic (skôr byōō'tik), *adj.* of, like, or having scurvy.

scorch (skôrch), *v.t.* **1.** to burn slightly so as to affect color or taste. **2.** to parch or shrivel with heat. —*v.i.* **3.** to become scorched. —*n.* **4.** a superficial burn.

score (skôr), *n., pl.* **scores; score** for 6; *v.,* **scored, scor·ing.** —*n.* **1.** a record of points made by competitors, as in a game. **2.** performance on an examination or test expressed by a symbol. **3.** a notch, scratch, or mark, esp. for keeping a record. **4.** an account showing indebtedness. **5.** an amount due. **6.** a group or set of 20. **7. scores,** a great many. **8.** a reason, ground, or cause. **9.** *Informal.* the basic facts of a situation. **10. a.** a musical composition with all the vocal and instrumental parts written or printed on staves. **b.** the music for a movie, play, or television show. —*v.t.* **11.** to make, gain, or earn in or as if in a game. **12.** to evaluate and assign a score to. **13.** *Music.* to compose a score for. **14.** to make notches, cuts, marks, or lines in, into, or on. **15.** to record the score of. —*v.i.* **16.** to make, gain, or earn points, as in a game. **17.** to keep score, as of a game. **18.** to achieve success. —**score'less,** *adj.* —**scor'er,** *n.*

score'board', *n.* a large board, as in a ballpark, that shows the score.

scorn (skôrn), *n.* **1.** open or unqualified contempt; disdain. —*v.t.* **2.** to treat or regard with scorn; disdain. —**scorn'ful,** *adj.* —**scorn'ful·ly,** *adv.*

Scor·pi·o (skôr'pē ō'), *n.* the eighth sign of the zodiac. [< L: scorpion]

scor·pi·on (skôr'pē ən), *n.* **1.** an arachnid with a long, upcurved tail ending in a venomous stinger. **2.** *Bible.* a whip or scourge. I Kings 12:11.

scorpion (def. 1)

Scot (skot), *n.* a native or inhabitant of Scotland. —**Usage.** See SCOTCH.

Scot., 1. Scotland. **2.** Scottish.

scotch (skoch), *v.t.* to put an end to; crush: *to scotch a rumor.*

Scotch (skoch), *adj.* **1.** of Scottish origin; characteristic of Scotland or the Scottish people: *Scotch plaid.* **2.** *Sometimes Offensive.* SCOTTISH. —*n.* **3.** (*used with a pl. v.*) *Sometimes Offensive.* the inhabitants of Scotland. **4.** (*often l.c.*) Also called **Scotch' whis'ky.** a whiskey distilled in Scotland from malted barley. —**Usage.** The natives of Scotland refer to themselves as SCOTS or, in the singular, SCOT, SCOTSMAN, or SCOTSWOMAN. SCOTCH as a noun or adjective is objected to except when referring to whisky or in certain set phrases.

Scotch' tape', *Trademark.* a brand name for various transparent or semitransparent adhesive tapes.

scot'-free' (skot'-), *adj.* free from harm, punishment, or obligation.

Scot'land, *n.* a division of the United Kingdom in the N part of Great Britain. 5,035,315.

Scot'land Yard', *n.* the police of London, England, esp. the branch engaged in crime detection.

Scots (skots), *n.* **1.** the dialect of English spoken in Scotland. —*adj.* **2.** SCOTTISH.

Scots'man, *n., pl.* -men. a native or inhabitant of Scotland. —**Usage.** See SCOTCH.

Scots'wom'an, *n., pl.* -wom·en. a woman who is a native or inhabitant of Scotland. —**Usage.** See SCOTCH.

Scott (skot), *n.* **1. Dred,** 1795?–1858, a black slave whose suit for freedom (1857) was denied by the U.S. Supreme Court. **2. Robert Falcon,** 1868–1912, British naval officer and explorer. **3. Sir Walter,** 1771–1832, Scottish author. **4. Winfield,** 1786–1866, U.S. general.

Scot·tish (skot'ish), *adj.* **1.** of Scotland or its inhab-

itants. —*n.* **2.** (*used with a pl. v.*) the inhabitants of Scotland. **3.** SCOTS.

Scot'tish (or **Scots'**) **Gael'ic,** *n.* a Celtic language spoken in the Hebrides and the Highlands of Scotland.

Scot'tish Psal'ter, *n.* a collection (1650) of metrical psalms published in Scotland.

Scotts·dale (skots'dāl'), *n.* a city in central Arizona. 152,439.

scoun·drel (skoun'drəl), *n.* an unprincipled, dishonorable person; villain.

scour¹ (skou°r), *v.t., v.i.* **1.** to cleanse or polish by rubbing, as with an abrasive. **2.** to remove by rubbing. **3.** to clear or dig out by or as if by the force of water.

scour² (skou°r), *v.t.* **1.** to range over, as in search. **2.** to pass quickly over or along.

scourge (skûrj), *n., v.,* **scourged, scourg·ing.** —*n.* **1.** a whip or lash. **2.** a cause of affliction or calamity. —*v.t.* **3.** to whip or lash. **4.** to punish or chastise severely.

scout (skout), *n.* **1.** a person, ship, or airplane employed in reconnoitering. **2.** a person sent out to obtain information. **3.** a person employed to discover new talent. **4.** (*sometimes cap.*) a Boy Scout or Girl Scout. —*v.t., v.i.* **5.** to reconnoiter as a scout. **6.** to search (for). **7.** to find by searching.

scout'mas'ter, *n.* the adult leader of a troop of Boy Scouts.

scow (skou), *n.* a boat having a flat-bottomed rectangular hull with sloping ends.

scowl (skoul), *v.i.* **1.** to draw down or contract the brows in a sullen, displeased, or angry manner. —*n.* **2.** a scowling expression.

scrab·ble (skrab'əl), *v.i., v.t.,* -bled, -bling. **1.** to scratch, scrape, or dig frantically. **2.** to scramble. **3.** to scrawl; scribble. —**scrab'bler,** *n.*

scrag·gly (skrag'lē), *adj.,* -gli·er, -gli·est. **1.** irregular; uneven. **2.** shaggy; unkempt.

scram (skram), *v.i.,* **scrammed, scram·ming.** *Informal.* to go away quickly.

scram·ble (skram'bəl), *v.,* -bled, -bling, *n.* —*v.i.* **1.** to climb or move quickly, esp. on the hands and knees. **2.** to compete or struggle for possession or gain. —*v.t.* **3.** to mix together confusedly. **4.** to cook (eggs) while stirring together whites and yolks. **5.** to make (a radio, telephonic, or television signal) unintelligible to interceptors. —*n.* **6.** a quick climb or progression. **7.** a disorderly struggle, as for possession or gain. —**scram'bler,** *n.*

scrap¹ (skrap), *n., v.,* **scrapped, scrap·ping.** —*n.* **1.** a small piece; fragment. **2. scraps,** bits of food, esp. of leftover food. **3.** discarded or leftover material, esp. metal that can be reworked. —*v.t.* **4.** to make into scrap. **5.** to discard as useless. —**scrap'py,** *adj.,* -pi·er, -pi·est.

scrap² (skrap), *n., v.,* **scrapped, scrap·ping.** *Informal.* —*n.* **1.** a fight or quarrel. —*v.i.* **2.** to engage in a scrap. —**scrap'per,** *n.* —**scrap'py,** *adj.,* -pi·er, -pi·est.

scrap'book', *n.* an album in which keepsakes, as clippings, can be pasted or mounted.

scrape (skrāp), *v.,* **scraped, scrap·ing,** *n.* —*v.t.* **1.** to draw something rough or sharp over (a surface), as to smooth it. **2.** to remove by scraping. **3.** to injure or mar by brushing against something rough or sharp. **4.** to collect laboriously or with difficulty. —*v.i.* **5.** to rub against something gratingly. **6.** to produce a grating sound. **7.** to get by with difficulty. **8.** to be very frugal; economize. —*n.* **9.** an act or instance of scraping. **10.** a grating sound. **11.** a scraped place. **12.** a distressing situation. —**scrap'er,** *n.*

scratch (skrach), *v.t.* **1.** to mar or mark the surface of with something sharp, as the fingernails. **2.** to rub or scrape slightly to relieve itching. **3.** to strike out or cancel by or as if by drawing a line through. **4.** to withdraw (an entry) from a race. —*v.i.* **5.** to use nails or claws, as for tearing or digging. **6.** to relieve itching by rubbing, esp. with the nails. —*n.* **7.** an injury or mark caused by scratching. **8.** the act or sound of scratching. —*adj.* **9.** used for hasty writing or figuring: *scratch paper.* **10.** gathered hastily and indiscriminately: *a scratch crew.* —*Idiom.* **11. from scratch,** from the very beginning or from nothing. **12. up to scratch,** meeting a standard; satisfactory. —**scratch′y,** *adj.,* **-i•er, -i•est.** —**scratch′i•ness,** *n.*

scrawl (skrôl), *v.t., v.i.* **1.** to write awkwardly, carelessly, or illegibly. —*n.* **2.** awkward, careless, or illegible handwriting. —**scrawl′y,** *adj.*

scrawn•y (skrô′nē), *adj.,* **-i•er, -i•est.** excessively thin; skinny. —**scrawn′i•ness,** *n.*

scream (skrēm), *v.i.* **1.** to utter a loud, sharp, piercing cry. **2.** to emit a shrill, piercing sound. —*v.t.* **3.** to utter with or as if with a scream. —*n.* **4.** a loud, sharp, piercing cry or sound. **5.** *Informal.* someone or something that is hilariously funny. —**scream′er,** *n.*

screech (skrēch), *v.t., v.i.* **1.** to utter with or make a harsh, shrill cry or sound. —*n.* **2.** a harsh, shrill cry or sound. —**screech•y,** *adj.,* **-i•er, -i•est.**

screen (skrēn), *n.* **1.** a movable or fixed device that provides protection or concealment or serves as a partition. **2.** a surface on which motion pictures or slides can be projected. **3. a.** motion pictures collectively. **b.** the motion-picture industry. **4.** the part of a television or computer on which a picture or information is displayed. **5.** something that shelters, protects, or conceals. **6.** a frame holding a mesh of wire, used in a window or doorway to exclude insects. **7.** a sieve used to separate smaller from larger particles. —*v.t.* **8.** to shelter, protect, or conceal with or as if with a screen. **9.** to provide with a screen. **10.** to sift, sort, or separate by or as if by passing through a screen. **11.** to project (a motion picture, slide, etc.) on a screen.

screen′play′, *n.* the outline or full script of a motion picture.

screen′writ′er, *n.* a writer of screenplays.

screw (skrōō), *n.* **1.** a metal fastener with a spirally threaded shank and slotted head that is driven into wood or the like by rotating. **2.** something having a spiral form. **3.** PROPELLER. —*v.t.* **4.** to fasten or attach with a screw. **5.** to attach, detach, or adjust by a twisting motion. **6.** to contort as if by twisting; distort. —*v.i.* **7.** to become attached, detached, or adjusted by being twisted. **8. ~ up,** *Slang.* to make a mess of; botch. —*Idiom.* **9. put the screws on,** to use coercion on.

screw′ball′, *n.* **1.** *Slang.* an eccentric or wildly whimsical person. **2.** a pitched baseball that veers toward the side from which it was thrown.

screw′driv′er, *n.* a hand tool for tightening or loosening a screw.

screw′worm′, *n.* the larva of a blow fly that infests the nostrils and open sores of livestock.

screw′y, *adj.,* **-i•er, -i•est.** *Slang.* **1.** crazy; nutty. **2.** absurd; odd. —**screw′i•ness,** *n.*

scrib•ble (skrib′al), *v.,* **-bled, -bling,** *n.* —*v.t., v.i.* **1.** to write or draw hastily or carelessly. —*n.* **2.** hasty, careless, or illegible drawing or writing. —**scrib′bler,** *n.*

scribe (skrīb), *n.* **1.** a professional copyist of manuscripts. **2.** one of a group of scholars of Jewish law and tradition, active from the 5th century B.C. to the 1st century A.D., who transcribed, edited, and interpreted the Bible. **3.** a writer, esp. a journalist. —**scrib′al,** *adj.*

scrim (skrim), *n.* a cotton or linen fabric of open weave.

scrim•mage (skrim′ij), *n., v.,* **-maged, -mag•ing.** *Football.* —*n.* **1. a.** the action from the snap of the ball to the end of a play. **b.** a practice session or informal game. —*v.i.* **2.** to engage in a scrimmage.

scrimp (skrimp), *v.i., v.t.* to be sparing (of) or frugal (with).

scrim•shaw (skrim′shô′), *n.* **1.** carved or engraved articles, esp. of whale ivory or whalebone. **2.** the art or technique of producing scrimshaw.

scrip (skrip), *n.* **1.** paper currency issued for temporary use. **2.** a certificate representing a fraction of a share of stock.

script (skript), *n.* **1.** handwriting. **2.** the written text of a play, motion picture, or radio or television program.

Scrip•ture (skrip′char), *n.* **1.** Often, **-tures.** the sacred writings of the Old or New Testament or both together. **2.** (*often l.c.*) a sacred or religious writing or book. —**scrip′tur•al,** *adj.*

script′writ′er, *n.* a writer of scripts.

scriv•ener (skriv′nar), *n.* a scribe.

scrod (skrod), *n.* a young Atlantic codfish or haddock.

scrof•u•la (skrof′ya la), *n.* tuberculosis of the lymphatic glands, esp. of the neck. —**scrof′u•lous,** *adj.*

scroll (skrōl), *n.* **1.** a roll of parchment, paper, or other material, esp. one with writing on it. **2.** a spiral or coiled ornament resembling a partly unrolled scroll. —*v.i.* **3.** to move a cursor smoothly, vertically or sideways, gradually causing new data to replace old on a computer screen.

scro•tum (skrō′tam), *n., pl.* **-ta** (-ta), **-tums.** the pouch of skin that contains the testes. —**scro′tal,** *adj.*

scrounge (skrounj), *v.,* **scrounged, scroung•ing.** —*v.t.* **1.** to take with no intention of repaying. **2.** to get by or as if by foraging. —*v.i.* **3.** to look around for what is needed. —**scroung′er,** *n.*

scrub[1] (skrub), *v.,* **scrubbed, scrub•bing,** *n.* —*v.t.* **1.** to rub hard in washing. **2.** to remove by scrubbing. **3.** *Informal.* to cancel; eliminate. —*v.i.* **4.** to cleanse something by hard rubbing. —*n.* **5.** an act or instance of scrubbing. —**scrub′ber,** *n.*

scrub[2] (skrub), *n.* **1.** low trees or shrubs collectively. **2.** an area covered with scrub. **3.** a domestic animal of inferior breeding. **4.** something undersized or inferior. **5.** *Sports.* a player not on the first-string team. —**scrub′by,** *adj.,* **-bi•er, -bi•est.**

scruff (skruf), *n.* the back of the neck; nape.

scruff•y (skruf′ē), *adj.,* **-i•er, -i•est.** untidy; shabby.

scrump•tious (skrump′shas), *adj.* extremely pleasing, esp. to the taste.

scrunch•y or **scrunch•ie** (skrun′chē), *n., pl.* **scrunch•ies.** a round elasticized fabric band, used to fasten the hair.

scru•ple (skrōō′pal), *n., v.,* **-pled, -pling.** —*n.* **1.** a moral or ethical consideration that inhibits action. **2.** a unit of apothecaries' weight equal to 20 grains. —*v.i.* **3.** to hesitate because of scruples.

scru•pu•lous (skrōō′pya las), *adj.* **1.** having scruples; principled. **2.** rigorously precise; exact. —**scru′pu•los′i•ty** (-los′i tē), *n.* —**scru′pu•lous•ly,** *adv.*

scru•ti•nize (skrōōt′n īz′), *v.t.,* **-nized, -niz•ing.** to examine minutely.

scru•ti•ny (skrōōt′n ē), *n., pl.* **-nies. 1.** a minute examination. **2.** a close and searching look.

scu•ba (skōō′ba), *n., pl.* **-bas.** a portable breathing device for free-swimming divers. [*s(elf)-c(ontained) u(nderwater) b(reathing) a(pparatus)*]

scu′ba div′ing, *n.* the activity of diving or exploring underwater through use of a scuba. —**scu′ba div′er,** *n.*

scud (skud), *v.,* **scud•ded, scud•ding.** —*v.i.* **1.** to run or move quickly. —*n.* **2.** clouds, spray, or mist driven by the wind.

scuff (skuf), *v.t., v.i.* **1.** to mar or become marred by scraping or hard use. **2.** to scrape (the feet) over or back and forth over something. —*n.* **3.** a flat-heeled slipper open at the back. **4.** a mar or scratch caused by scuffing.

scuf′fle, *v.,* **-fled, -fling,** *n.* —*v.i.* **1.** to struggle or fight in a rough, confused manner. **2.** to walk with a shuffle. —*n.* **3.** a rough, confused struggle or fight. **4.** a shuffle.

scull (skul), *n.* **1.** an oar mounted on the stern of a boat and moved from side to side to propel the boat. **2.** either of a pair of oars for one rower. **3.** a light, narrow racing boat. —*v.t., v.i.* **4.** to propel (a boat) by means of sculls.

scul•ler•y (skul′a rē), *n., pl.* **-ler•ies.** a room off a kitchen where cooking utensils are cleaned and stored.

scul′lion (-yan), *n.* a kitchen servant.

sculpt (skulpt), *v.t.*, *v.i.* to sculpture.

sculp/tor, *n.* a person who sculptures.

sculp/ture (-chər), *n.*, *v.*, **-tured, -tur•ing.** —*n.* **1.** the art of carving, modeling, or welding works of art in three dimensions. **2.** works of sculpture collectively. **3.** an individual work of sculpture. —*v.t.* **4.** to carve, model, or weld (a piece of sculpture). **5.** to represent in sculpture. —*v.i.* **6.** to work as a sculptor. —**sculp/tur•al,** *adj.*

scum (skum), *n.* **1.** a film of foul matter that forms on the surface of a liquid. **2.** waste material; refuse. **3.** low, worthless persons; dregs. —**scum/my,** *adj.*, **-mi•er, -mi•est.**

scup•per (skup/ər), *n.* an opening at the edge of a ship's deck that allows accumulated water to drain away.

scurf (skûrf), *n.* **1.** loose scales of skin. **2.** scaly matter on a surface. —**scurf/y,** *adj.*, **-i•er, -i•est.**

scur•ril•ous (skûr/ə ləs, skur/-), *adj.* grossly or obscenely abusive. —**scur•ril•i•ty** (skə ril/i tē), *n.* —**scur/ril•ous•ly,** *adv.*

scur•ry (skûr/ē, skur/ē), *v.i.*, **-ried, -ry•ing.** to move in haste.

scur•vy (skûr/vē), *n.*, *adj.*, **-vi•er, -vi•est.** —*n.* **1.** a disease caused by a lack of vitamin C and marked by swollen and bleeding gums and livid spots on the skin. —*adj.* **2.** contemptible; despicable.

scutch•eon (skuch/ən), *n.* ESCUTCHEON.

scut•tle¹ (skut/l), *n.* a deep bucket for carrying coal.

scut•tle² (skut/l), *v.i.*, **-tled, -tling.** to run with short, quick steps.

scut•tle³ (skut/l), *n.*, *v.*, **-tled, -tling.** —*n.* **1.** a small hatch with a cover in the deck, side, or bottom of a ship. —*v.t.* **2.** to sink (a ship) deliberately by making openings in the bottom.

scut•tle•butt (skut/l but/), *n. Informal.* rumor; gossip.

scuzz•y (skuz/ē), *adj.*, **-i•er, -i•est.** *Slang.* repulsive; disgusting.

scythe (sīth), *n.*, *v.*, **scythed, scyth•ing.** —*n.* **1.** a tool with a long, curving blade for cutting grass or grain by hand. —*v.t.* **2.** to cut or mow with a scythe.

scythe

SD or **S.D.,** **1.** South Dakota. **2.** special delivery.

S. Dak., South Dakota.

SE, 1. southeast. **2.** southeastern. **3.** Standard English.

Se, *Chem. Symbol.* selenium.

sea (sē), *n.* **1.** the salt waters that cover much of the earth's surface. **2.** an ocean. **3.** water turbulence, as caused by the wind. **4.** a large wave. **5.** a great or overwhelming quantity: *a sea of faces.* —*Idiom.* **6. at sea,** perplexed; uncertain.

sea/ anem/one, *n.* a solitary marine polyp with flowerlike tentacles.

sea/bed/, *n.* the ocean floor.

sea/board/, *n.* a region bordering a seacoast.

sea/coast/, *n.* land immediately adjacent to the sea.

sea/far/er (-fâr/ər), *n.* a sailor. —**sea/far/ing,** *adj.*

sea/food/, *n.* edible marine fish or shellfish.

sea/go/ing, *adj.* designed or fit for going to sea.

sea/ gull/, *n.* a gull, esp. one of the marine species.

sea/ horse/, *n.* a fish with an elongated snout and a head bent at right angles to the body.

seal¹ (sēl), *n.* **1.** an emblem or symbol used as evidence of authenticity. **2. a.** a device, as a stamp, engraved with a seal for impressing wax or clay. **b.** the impression obtained. **3.** an authenticating mark on a legal document. **4.** an adhesive used to close or fasten an envelope, door, etc. **5.** anything that closes or fastens securely, as a rubber gasket. **6.** a stamplike label: *an Easter seal.* **7.** anything that serves as assurance or confirmation. —*v.t.* **8.** to affix a seal to. **9.** to assure or confirm with or as if with a seal. **10.** to fasten or close by or as if by a seal. **11.** to decide irrevocably: *His fate was sealed.* —**seal/er,** *n.*

seal² (sēl), *n.*, *pl.* **seals, seal,** *v.* —*n.* **1.** any of numerous marine carnivores with limbs like flippers. **2.** the skin or fur of a seal. —*v.i.* **3.** to hunt, kill, or capture seals. —**seal/er,** *n.*

seal•ant (sē/lənt), *n.* a substance that dries to form a watertight coating.

sea/ legs/, *n.pl.* the ability to adjust one's balance to the motion of a ship.

sea/ lev/el, *n.* the position of the sea's surface at mean level between high and low tide.

sea/ li/on, *n.* a large eared seal of the N Pacific.

seal/skin/, *n.* the skin or fur of a seal.

seam (sēm), *n.* **1.** the line formed by sewing together pieces, as of cloth. **2.** a line formed by abutting edges. **3.** a wrinkle or scar. **4.** *Geol.* a thin stratum, as of coal. —*v.t.* **5.** to join together in a seam. **6.** to mark with lines, as wrinkles. —**seam/less,** *adj.*

sea/man, *n.*, *pl.* **-men. 1.** a person who assists in the handling of a ship; sailor. **2.** an enlisted person in the U.S. Navy ranking below petty officer. —**sea/man•ship/,** *n.*

seam•stress (sēm/stris), *n.* a woman whose occupation is sewing.

seam/y, *adj.*, **-i•er, -i•est.** sordid; disagreeable: *the seamy side of life.*

sé•ance (sā/äns), *n.* a meeting in which a spiritualist attempts to communicate with the spirits of the dead.

sea/plane/, *n.* an airplane with floats for water takeoffs and landings.

sea/port/, *n.* a port or harbor for seagoing ships.

sear (sēr), *v.t.* **1.** to burn or char the surface of. **2.** to mark with a branding iron. **3.** to dry up or wither.

search (sûrch), *v.t.* **1.** to look through carefully in order to find something. **2.** to examine carefully; scrutinize or probe. **3.** to uncover or find by examination or exploration. **4.** to command software to find specified characters or codes in (an electronic file). —*v.i.* **5.** to conduct a search. —*n.* **6.** an act or instance of searching. —**search/er,** *n.* —**search/ing,** *adj.*

search/light/, *n.* **1.** a device for projecting a powerful beam of light. **2.** a beam of light so projected.

sea/scape/ (-skāp/), *n.* **1.** a painting or photograph of the sea. **2.** a view of the sea.

sea/shell/, *n.* the shell of a marine mollusk.

sea/shore/, *n.* land along the sea.

sea/sick/ness, *n.* nausea induced by the motion of a ship or boat at sea. —**sea/sick/,** *adj.*

sea/side/, *n.* SEASHORE.

sea horse

sea•son (sē/zən), *n.* **1.** one of the four periods of the year: spring, summer, autumn, and winter. **2.** a period of the year marked by a particular condition, activity, or event: *the baseball season.* —*v.t.* **3.** to flavor (food) by adding seasoning. **4.** to add piquancy to; enhance. **5.** to make fit by experience. **6.** to prepare for use, as by drying. —*v.i.* **7.** to become seasoned. —*Proverb.* **8. To everything there is a season and a time to every purpose under the heaven,** everything that happens has its appointed time. Eccl. 3:1-8.

sea′son•a•ble, *adj.* **1.** suitable to the season. **2.** timely.

sea′son•al, *adj.* of, dependent on, or affected by the season. —**sea′son•al•ly,** *adv.*

sea′son•ing, *n.* something, as a spice, for enhancing the flavor of food.

seat (sēt), *n.* **1.** something, as a chair, for a person to sit on. **2.** the part of something on which a person sits. **3.** the buttocks. **4.** a place in which something is established: *a seat of learning.* **5.** a place in which administrative power is centered: *the seat of government.* **6.** a right to sit as a member, as in a legislative body. —*v.t.* **7.** to place in or on a seat. **8.** to accommodate with seats.

seat′ belt′, *n.* straps designed to keep a passenger secure in the seat of a vehicle.

Se•at•tle (sē at′l), *n.* a seaport in W Washington. 520,947.

sea′ ur′chin, *n.* a small, round sea animal with a spiny shell.

sea′ward (-wərd), *adv.* **1.** Also, **sea′wards.** toward the sea. —*adj.* **2.** facing toward the sea. **3.** coming from the sea.

sea′way′, *n.* a waterway giving oceangoing ships access to a landlocked port.

sea′weed′, *n.* **1.** any of numerous marine algae. **2.** any of various marine plants.

sea′wor′thy, *adj.,* **-thi•er, -thi•est.** (of a ship) fit for a voyage at sea.

se•ba•ceous (si bā′shəs), *adj.* of, resembling, or secreting a fatty substance.

seb•or•rhe•a (seb′ə rē′ə), *n.* abnormally heavy discharge from the sebaceous glands. —**seb′or•rhe′ic,** *adj.*

SEC, Securities and Exchange Commission.

sec., 1. second. **2.** secondary. **3.** secretary. **4.** section. **5.** sector.

se•cede (si sēd′), *v.i.,* **-ced•ed, -ced•ing,** to withdraw formally from an alliance, federation, or association.

se•ces′sion (-sesh′ən), *n.* **1.** an act or instance of seceding. **2.** (*often cap.*) the withdrawal from the Union of 11 southern states in 1860–61. —**se•ces′sion•ist,** *n.*

se•clude (si klōōd′), *v.t.,* **-clud•ed, -clud•ing. 1.** to remove from contact with others; isolate. **2.** to shut off; keep apart.

se•clu′sion (-klōō′zhən), *n.* the act of secluding or state of being secluded. —**se•clu′sive,** *adj.*

sec•ond¹ (sek′ənd), *adj.* **1.** being the ordinal number for two. **2.** next after the first, as in place, time, value, or rank. **3.** alternate: *every second week.* **4.** other; another: *a second Shakespeare.* **5.** of or being the gear transmission ratio at which drive shaft speed is greater than that of low gear. —*n.* **6.** a second part. **7.** the second member of a series. **8.** a person who aids or supports another, as in boxing. **9.** second gear. **10. seconds,** an additional helping of food. **11.** Usu., **seconds.** goods of inferior quality. —*v.t.* **12.** to assist or support. **13.** to express formal support of (a motion, proposal, etc.) before further discussion or voting. —*adv.* **14.** in the second place. —**sec′ond•ly,** *adv.*

sec•ond² (sek′ənd), *n.* **1.** the sixtieth part of a minute of time. **2.** a moment or instant. **3.** the sixtieth part of a minute of angular measure.

sec′ond•ar′y (-ən der′ē), *adj.* **1.** second in order, rank, or time. **2.** not primary or original. **3.** of minor or lesser importance. —**sec′ond•ar′i•ly,** *adv.*

sec′ondary school′, *n.* a school between a primary school and a college or university.

sec′ondary stress′, *n.* a degree of stress weaker than primary stress but stronger than lack of stress. Also called **sec′ondary ac′cent.**

sec′ond class′, *n.* **1.** the class of accommodations inferior to first class but superior to third class. **2.** the class of mail consisting of newspapers and periodicals.

sec′ond-class′, *adj.* **1.** of a secondary class or quality. **2.** second-rate.

Sec′ond Com′ing, *n.* the coming of Christ on Judgment Day.

sec′ond-guess′, *v.t.* **1.** to use hindsight in criticizing or correcting. **2.** to outguess.

sec′ond-hand′, *adj.* **1.** not directly known or experienced. **2.** previously used or owned. **3.** dealing in used goods. —*adv.* **4.** after another user or owner. **5.** indirectly.

sec′ondhand smoke′, *n.* tobacco smoke involuntarily inhaled.

sec′ond lieuten′ant, *n.* an officer in the U.S. Army, Air Force, or Marines of the lowest commissioned rank.

sec′ond na′ture, *n.* a deeply ingrained habit or tendency.

sec′ond per′son, *n.* a pronoun or verb form that refers to the one or ones being addressed.

sec′ond-rate′, *adj.* of lesser or minor quality or importance.

sec′ond-sto′ry man′, *n.* a burglar who enters through an upstairs window.

sec′ond string′, *n.* the squad of players available to replace or relieve those who start a game. —**sec′ond-string′er,** *n.*

sec′ond thought′, *n.* Often, **second thoughts.** reservation about a previous action or decision.

Sec′ond Vat′ican Coun′cil, *n.* the twenty-first Roman Catholic ecumenical council (1962–65) convened by Pope John XXIII. Its documents redefined the nature of the church and increased lay participation. Also called **Vatican II.**

sec′ond wind′ (wind), *n.* energy for a renewed effort.

se•cre•cy (sē′krə sē), *n., pl.* **-cies. 1.** the state or condition of being secret. **2.** the habit or characteristic of being secretive.

se•cret (sē′krit), *adj.* **1.** done, made, or carried out without the knowledge of others. **2.** kept from general knowledge. **3.** hidden from sight, concealed. **4.** close-mouthed; secretive. —*n.* **5.** something that is secret, hidden, or concealed. **6.** a mystery. **7.** a reason or explanation not readily apparent. —**se′cret•ly,** *adv.*

sec•re•tar•i•at (sek′ri târ′ē ət), *n.* **1.** the office or the officials entrusted with overseeing administrative duties for a governmental department. **2.** a group or department of secretaries.

sec′re•tar′y (-ter′ē), *n., pl.* **-tar•ies. 1.** a person in charge of records and correspondence for an organization. **2.** a person employed to do clerical work, as typing. **3.** (*often cap.*) an officer of state who heads a governmental department. **4.** a writing desk. —**sec′re•tar′i•al** (-târ′ē əl), *adj.*

se•crete¹ (si krēt′), *v.t.,* **-cret•ed, -cret•ing.** to discharge, generate, or release by secretion.

se•crete² (si krēt′), *v.t.,* **-cret•ed, -cret•ing.** to place out of sight; hide.

se•cre′tion, *n.* (in a cell or gland) the process or product of separating, elaborating, and releasing a substance that fulfills a function within the organism or undergoes excretion.

se•cre•tive (sē′kri tiv, si krē′-), *adj.* having or showing a disposition to secrecy. —**se′cre•tive•ly,** *adv.* —**se′cre•tive•ness,** *n.*

Se′cret Serv′ice, *n.* a branch of the U.S. Treasury Department responsible for protecting the president and apprehending counterfeiters.

sect (sekt), *n.* **1.** a religious denomination. **2.** a religious group deviating from a generally accepted tradition. **3.** a group united by a specific doctrine or under a particular leader.

sec•tar•i•an (sek târ′ē ən), *adj.* **1.** of or belonging to a sect. **2.** limited in interest, purpose, or scope. —*n.* **3.** a sectarian person. —**sec•tar′i•an•ism,** *n.*

sec′ta•ry (-tə rē), *n., pl.* **-ries.** a member of a sect.

sec•tion (sek/shən), *n.* **1.** a distinct subdivision, as of a community. **2.** a distinct part, as of a newspaper. **3.** a part that is cut off or separated. **4.** an act or instance of cutting apart. **5.** a representation of an object as it would appear if cut by a plane, showing its internal structure. —*v.t.* **6.** to cut or divide into sections.

sec/tion•al, *adj.* **1.** of or limited to a particular region or area. **2.** composed of sections: *a sectional sofa.* —**sec/tion•al•ism,** *n.*

sec•tor (sek/tər), *n.* **1.** a plane figure bounded by two radii and the included arc of a circle. **2.** an area that a particular military unit is assigned to defend. **3.** a distinct part.

sec•u•lar (sek/yə lər), *adj.* **1.** of worldly or nonreligious things or subjects; temporal. **2.** not relating to or concerned with religion. **3.** not bound by monastic vows. —**sec/u•lar•ism,** *n.* —**sec/u•lar•ist,** *n.*

sec/ular hu/manism, *n.* any set of beliefs that promotes human values without specific allusion to religious doctrines. —**sec/ular hu/manist,** *n.*

sec/u•lar•ize/, *v.t.,* -ized, -iz•ing. **1.** to make secular. **2.** to transfer from ecclesiastical to civil possession or use. —**sec/u•lar•i•za/tion,** *n.*

se•cure (si kyŏor/), *adj.,* -cur•er, -cur•est, *v.,* -cured, -cur•ing. —*adj.* **1.** free from danger or harm; safe. **2.** not liable to fail or yield; firm. **3.** free from care or anxiety. **4.** certain; assured. —*v.t.* **5.** to get hold of; obtain. **6.** to keep from danger or harm; make safe. **7.** to make certain of; ensure. **8.** to make fast. **9.** to assure payment of (a debt) by pledging property. —**se•cure/ly,** *adv.*

se•cu/ri•ty (-kyŏor/i tē), *n., pl.* -ties. **1.** freedom from danger or risk; safety. **2.** freedom from care, anxiety, or doubt. **3.** something that protects, shelters, or makes safe. **4.** precautions taken against crime, sabotage, escape, or attack. **5.** something given as surety for the fulfillment of an obligation. **6.** securities, stocks or bonds.

secu/rity blan/ket, *n.* something, as an object, that gives a feeling of security.

secy or **sec'y,** secretary.

se•dan (si dan/), *n.* **1.** an enclosed automobile with two or four doors and seats for four or more persons. **2.** an enclosed chair carried on poles by two persons.

se•date (si dāt/), *adj., v.,* -dat•ed, -dat•ing. —*adj.* **1.** calm, dignified, and composed. —*v.t.* **2.** to treat with a sedative. —**se•date/ly,** *adv.* —**se•da/tion,** *n.*

sed•a•tive (sed/ə tiv), *adj.* **1.** tending to calm or to lessen irritability or excitement. —*n.* **2.** a sedative drug.

sed•en•tar•y (sed/n ter/ē), *adj.* characterized by or requiring much sitting.

Se•der (sā/dər), *n., pl.* **Se•ders, Se•da•rim** (sä/dä-rēm/). *Judaism.* a ceremonial dinner, held on the first night or first two nights of Passover, that includes the reading of the haggadah and the eating of foods symbolic of the Israelites' slavery and the Exodus from Egypt.

sedge (sej), *n.* a grasslike plant that grows in wet places.

sed•i•ment (sed/ə mənt), *n.* **1.** the matter that settles to the bottom of a liquid. **2.** *Geol.* matter deposited by water, air, or ice. —**sed/i•men/ta•ry** (-men/-tə rē), *adj.* —**sed/i•men•ta/tion,** *n.*

se•di•tion (si dish/ən), *n.* incitement of discontent or rebellion against a government. —**se•di/tious,** *adj.*

se•duce (si dōōs/, -dyōōs/), *v.t.,* -duced, -duc•ing. **1.** to lead astray, as from duty. **2.** to induce to have sexual intercourse. —**se•duc/er,** *n.* —**se•duc/tion** (-duk/shən), *n.* —**se•duc/tive,** *adj.*

sed•u•lous (sej/ə ləs), *adj.* diligent; persevering. —**sed/u•lous•ly,** *adv.*

see¹ (sē), *v.,* saw, seen, see•ing. —*v.t.* **1.** to perceive with the eyes; look at. **2.** to perceive mentally; understand. **3.** to have a mental image of; visualize. **4.** to be cognizant of; recognize. **5.** to find out; ascertain. **6.** to have experience of. **7.** to make sure: *See that the door is locked.* **8.** to meet and converse with. **9.** to visit. **10.** to escort or accompany: *He saw her*

home. —*v.i.* **11.** to have the power of sight. **12.** to have insight; understand. **13. see after,** to attend to; take care of. **14. ~ through, a.** to ascertain the true nature of. **b.** to remain with until completion.

see² (sē), *n.* the authority, office, or jurisdiction of a bishop.

seed (sēd), *n., pl.* **seeds, seed,** *v.* —*n.* **1.** a fertilized, matured plant ovule containing an embryo or rudimentary plant. **2.** a propagative part of a plant, as a tuber or a bulb. **3.** the germ or source of something. **4.** offspring; progeny. —*v.t.* **5.** to sow with seed. **6.** to remove the seeds from. **7.** to rank (players or teams) so that the most superior competitors will not meet in early rounds. —*v.i.* **8.** to produce or shed seed. —*Idiom.* **9. go** or **run to seed, a.** to pass to the stage of yielding seed. **b.** to deteriorate, as in appearance. —**seed/er,** *n.* —**seed/less,** *adj.*

seed/ling (-ling), *n.* **1.** a plant or tree grown from a seed. **2.** any young plant.

seed/ mon/ey, *n.* capital for the initial stages of an enterprise.

seed/y, *adj.,* -i•er, -i•est. **1.** containing or bearing seeds. **2.** poorly kept; run-down. **3.** shabbily dressed. —**seed/i•ness,** *n.*

see/ing, *conj.* inasmuch as; considering.

seek (sēk), *v.t.,* sought, seek•ing. **1.** to try to find, discover, or obtain. **2.** to try; attempt. —**seek/er,** *n.*

seem (sēm), *v.i.* **1.** to appear to be. **2.** to appear to one's own senses or judgment. **3.** to appear to be true or probable.

seem/ing, *adj.* apparent; ostensible. —**seem/ing•ly,** *adv.*

seem/ly, *adj.,* -li•er, -li•est. fitting or proper; appropriate. —**seem/li•ness,** *n.*

seen (sēn), *v.* pp. of SEE¹.

seep (sēp), *v.i.* to pass, flow, or ooze gradually, as through a porous substance. —**seep/age,** *n.*

seer (sēr), *n.* a person who prophesies future events; prophet.

seer•suck•er (sēr/suk/ər), *n.* a cotton or cottonlike fabric, usu. striped and having a crinkled texture.

see•saw (sē/sô/), *n.* **1.** a balanced plank on which two children alternately ride up and down while seated at opposite ends. **2.** an alternating up-and-down or back-and-forth movement or procedure. —*v.i., v.t.* **3.** to move on or as if on a seesaw.

seethe (sēth), *v.i.,* seethed, seeth•ing. **1.** to surge or foam as if boiling. **2.** to be in a state of agitation or excitement.

see/-through/, *adj.* transparent.

seg•ment (*n.* seg/mənt; *v.* seg/ment, seg ment/), *n.* **1.** one of the parts into which something is divided; section. **2.** *Geom.* a part cut off from a figure, esp. a circle or sphere, by a line or plane. —*v.t., v.i.* **3.** to separate or divide into segments. —**seg/men•ta/tion,** *n.*

seg•re•gate (seg/ri gāt/), *v.t.,* -gat•ed, -gat•ing. **1.** to set apart from others; isolate. **2.** to require the separation of (a specific racial, religious, or other group) from the body of society. —**seg/re•ga/tion,** *n.* —**seg/re•ga/tion•ist,** *n.*

se•gue (sā/gwā, seg/wā), *v.i.,* -gued, -gue•ing, *n.* —*v.i.* **1.** to continue at once with the next section (used as a musical direction). **2.** to make a smooth transition, as from one topic to another. —*n.* **3.** a smooth, uninterrupted transition from one thing or part to another.

sei•gnior (sēn/yər, sān/-), *n.* (*sometimes cap.*) a lord, esp. a feudal lord. —**sei•gnio/ri•al, sei•gno/ri•al** (-yôr/ē əl), *adj.*

Seine (sān, sen), *n.* a river in N France. 480 mi. (773 km) long.

Se•ir (sē/ir), *n.* a mountainous area between the Dead Sea and the Red Sea. Deut. 2:12, 29.

seis•mic (sīz/mik, sīs/-), *adj.* of, resembling, or caused by an earthquake. —**seis/mi•cal•ly,** *adv.*

seis/mo•graph/ (-mə graf/, -gräf/), *n.* an instrument for measuring and recording the vibrations of earthquakes. —**seis•mog/ra•pher** (-mog/rə fər), *n.* —**seis/mo•graph/ic** (-graf/ik), *adj.* —**seis•mog/ra•phy,** *n.*

seis•mol/ogy (-mol/ə jē), *n.* the science of earthquakes and their phenomena. —seis′mo•log′ic (-mə loj′ik), seis′mo•log′i•cal, adj. —seis•mol′o•gist, n.

seize (sēz), v.t., seized, seiz•ing. 1. to take hold of suddenly or forcibly. 2. to grasp mentally; understand. 3. to take complete control of; possess. 4. to take legal possession of. 5. to capture or arrest. 6. to take prompt advantage of. —*Proverb.* 7. Seize the day, take full advantage of each moment.

sei•zure (sē′zhər), n. 1. an act or instance of seizing. 2. a sudden attack, as of epilepsy.

se•lah (sē′lə, sel′ə), n., interj. an expression that occurs frequently in the Psalms and whose meaning is uncertain: thought to be a liturgical or musical note.

sel•dom (sel′dəm), adv. on only a few occasions; rarely.

se•lect (si lekt′), v.t., v.i. 1. to choose in preference to others. —adj. 2. chosen in preference to others; choice. 3. careful in choosing. 4. carefully chosen. —se•lect′ness, n. —se•lec′tor, n.

se•lec′tion, n. 1. an act or instance of selecting or the state of being selected. 2. something selected. 3. a process that results in some members of a population having greater success in perpetuating their genetic traits. —se•lec′tive, adj. —se•lec•tiv′i•ty, n.

selec′tive serv′ice, n. compulsory military service.

se•lect′man, n., pl. -men. (in most New England states) one of a board of officers chosen to manage town affairs.

sel•e•nite (sel′ə nīt′, si lē′nīt), n. a variety of gypsum found in transparent crystals.

se•le•ni•um (si lē′nē əm), n. a nonmetallic element with an electrical resistance that varies under the influence of light. Symbol: Se; at. wt.: 78.96; at. no.: 34.

sel•e•nog•ra•phy (sel′ə nog′rə fē), n. the branch of astronomy that deals with the charting of the moon's surface. —sel′e•nog′ra•pher, n.

self (self), n. and pron., pl. selves, adj. —n. 1. a person or thing referred to with respect to complete individuality. 2. a person's nature or character. 3. personal interest. —pron. 4. myself, himself, etc. —adj. 5. being the same throughout.

self-, a combining form meaning: of the self (self-image); by oneself or itself (self-imposed); to, with, toward, for, on, or in oneself or itself (self-absorbed); independent (self-government); automatic (self-winding).

self′-absorbed′, adj. preoccupied with one's own thoughts or interests.

self′-addressed′, adj. addressed for return to the sender.

self′-aggran′dizement, n. aggressive increase of one's own power, wealth, etc. —self′-aggran′-dizing, adj.

self′-appoint′ed, adj. appointed by oneself, esp. without the approval of others.

self′-asser′tion, n. an expression of one's own importance, opinions, etc. —self′-asser′tive, adj.

self′-assur′ance, n. confidence in oneself; self-confidence. —self′-assured′, adj.

self′-cen′tered, adj. engrossed in oneself; selfish.

self′-confessed′, adj. openly admitting to being a person of a specified type.

self′-con′fidence, n. faith in one's own judgment, ability, etc. —self′-con′fident, adj.

self′-con′scious, adj. excessively aware of being observed by others; embarrassed or uneasy. —self′-con′sciously, adv. —self′-con′sciousness, n.

self′-contained′, adj. 1. containing within itself all that is necessary. 2. reserved in behavior. 3. having or showing self-control.

self′-contradic′tion, n. 1. an act or instance of contradicting oneself or itself. 2. a statement containing contradictory elements. —self′-contradict′ing, adj.

self′-control′, n. restraint of one's actions or feelings. —self′-controlled′, adj.

self′-defeat′ing, adj. serving to thwart one's own intention or interests.

self′-defense′, n. 1. the act of defending oneself or one's own interests or property. 2. a plea that the use of force was necessary in defending one's own person.

self′-deni′al, n. the sacrifice or restraint of one's own desires.

self′-destruct′, v.i. to destroy itself or oneself. —self′-destruc′tion, n. —self′-destruc′tive, adj.

self′-determina′tion, n. 1. freedom to act as one chooses without consulting others. 2. freedom of a people to determine the way in which they shall be governed. —self′-deter′mined, adj.

self′-dis′cipline, n. discipline or control of oneself for personal improvement. —self′-dis′ciplined, adj.

self′-doubt′, n. lack of confidence in one's own abilities.

self′-ed′ucated, adj. educated by one's own efforts, with little or no formal training.

self′-effac′ing, adj. keeping oneself in the background, as in humility. —self′-efface′ment, n.

self′-employed′, adj. earning one's living from one's own business or profession. —self′-employ′-ment, n.

self′-esteem′, n. 1. self-respect. 2. an exaggeratedly favorable opinion of oneself.

self′-ev′ident, adj. evident in itself without proof or demonstration.

self′-explan′atory, adj. needing no explanation; obvious.

self′-expres′sion, n. the expression of one's own personality, as in painting.

self′-fertiliza′tion, n. fertilization of the ovum by a male gamete of the same individual.

self′-fulfill′ing, adj. 1. characterized by fulfillment of oneself. 2. happening or brought about as a result of being foretold or expected.

self′-gov′ernment, n. government of a state, community, or region by its own people. —self′-gov′-erning, adj.

self′-help′, adj. (of a book, course, etc.) offering individuals counseling and information on how to help themselves attain certain goals.

self′-im′age, n. the conception one has of oneself.

self′-impor′tant, adj. having or showing an exaggerated opinion of one's own importance. —self′-impor′tance, n.

self′-imposed′, adj. imposed on oneself voluntarily.

self′-induced′, adj. induced by oneself or itself.

self′-indul′gent, adj. satisfying one's own desires, whims, etc., often without regard for others. —self′-indul′gence, n.

self′-inflict′ed, adj. done to one's person by oneself.

self′-in′terest, n. 1. regard for one's own interest or advantage, esp. with disregard for others. 2. personal interest or advantage.

self•ish (sel′fish), adj. 1. caring chiefly for oneself or one's own interests, regardless of others. 2. characterized by concern only for oneself. —self′ish•ly, adv. —self′ish•ness, n.

self′-knowl′edge, adj. knowledge or understanding of oneself and one's character, abilities, etc.

self′less, adj. having little concern for oneself; unselfish. —self′less•ly, adv. —self′less•ness, n.

self′-made′, adj. having succeeded in life unaided: a self-made man.

self′-pit′y, n. pity for oneself.

self′-pollina′tion, n. the transfer of pollen from the anther to the stigma of the same flower.

self′-por′trait, n. a portrait of oneself done by oneself.

self′-posses′sion, n. control of one's feelings, behavior, etc., esp. when under pressure. —self′-possessed′, adj.

self′-preserva′tion, n. the instinctive desire to preserve one's own life and safety.

self′-proclaimed′, adj. proclaimed by oneself.

self′-propelled′, adj. propelled by its own engine or motor.

self'-reg'ulating, *adj.* regulating itself without outside interference, controls, or regulations.

self'-reli'ance, *n.* reliance on one's own powers or resources. —**self'-reli'ant,** *adj.*

self'-respect', *n.* proper respect for the dignity of one's character. —**self'-respect'ing,** *adj.*

self'-restraint', *n.* self-control.

self'-right'eous, *adj.* confident of one's own righteousness; smugly moralistic. —**self'-right'eously,** *adv.* —**self'-right'eousness,** *n.*

self'-sac'rifice, *n.* sacrifice of oneself or one's interests for others. —**self'-sac'rificing,** *adj.*

self•same (self'sām', -sām'), *adj.* being the very same; identical.

self'-sat'isfied, *adj.* feeling or showing a usu. smug satisfaction with oneself or one's achievements. —**self'-satisfac'tion,** *n.*

self'-seek'ing, *n.* **1.** the selfish seeking of one's own interests or ends. —*adj.* **2.** given to or characterized by self-seeking. —**self'-seek'er,** *n.*

self'-serv'ice, *adj.* **1.** of or being a commercial establishment, as a restaurant, in which customers serve themselves. **2.** designed to be used without the aid of an attendant.

self'-serv'ing, *adj.* serving to further one's own selfish interests.

self'-start'er, *n.* a person who shows initiative. —**self'-start'ing,** *adj.*

self'-styled', *adj.* called or considered by oneself.

self'-suffi'cient, *adj.* able to supply one's own needs without external assistance. —**self'-suffi'ciency,** *n.*

self'-support', *n.* complete support of oneself without reliance on outside help. —**self'-support'ing,** *adj.*

self'-taught', *adj.* taught or learned by oneself without formal instruction.

self'-will', *n.* stubborn willfulness; obstinacy. —**self'-willed',** *adj.*

self'-wind'ing (-wīn'ding), *adj.* (of a timepiece) wound by an automatic mechanism.

sell (sel), *v.,* **sold, sell•ing,** *n.* —*v.t.* **1.** to transfer (goods or property) or render (services) in exchange for money. **2.** to offer for sale; deal in. **3.** to promote or effect the sale, acceptance, or approval of. —*v.i.* **4.** to engage in selling. **5.** to be offered for sale. **6.** to be in demand by buyers. **7. sell out, a.** to dispose of entirely by selling. **b.** to betray. —*n.* **8.** an act or method of selling. —*Idiom.* **9. sell down the river,** to betray someone. —**sell'er,** *n.*

sell'out', *n.* **1.** an entertainment for which all the seats are sold. **2.** a person who sells out; traitor.

selt•zer (selt'sər), *n.* **1.** effervescent mineral water. **2.** carbonated tap water.

sel•vage or **-vedge** (sel'vij), *n.* the edge of woven fabric finished to prevent raveling. —**sel'vaged,** *adj.*

selves (selvz), *n.* pl. of SELF.

se•man•tics (si man'tiks), *n.* **1.** the study of meaning in language, including historical changes in meaning and form. **2.** the branch of semiotics dealing with the relationship between signs or symbols and what they denote. —**se•man'tic,** *adj.* —**se•man'ti•cist** (-tə sist), *n.*

sem•a•phore (sem'ə fôr'), *n., v.,* **-phored, -phor•ing.** —*n.* **1.** an apparatus for visual signaling, as by a light whose position may be changed. **2.** a system of signaling by a flag held in each hand. —*v.t., v.i.* **3.** to signal by or as if by semaphore.

sem•blance (sem'bləns), *n.* **1.** outward appearance. **2.** assumed or unreal appearance. **3.** a likeness; image.

se•men (sē'mən), *n.* a fluid produced in the male reproductive organs, containing sperm.

se•mes•ter (si mes'tər), *n.* an academic session constituting half of the academic year.

sem•i (sem'ē, sem'ī), *n., pl.* **sem•is. 1.** a semitrailer. **2.** a semifinal contest or round.

semi-, a combining form meaning: half (*semiannual*); partially or somewhat (*semiautomatic*). —**Usage.** See BI-.

sem•i•an•nu•al (sem'ē an'yo͞o əl, sem'ī-), *adj.* **1.** occurring or published twice a year. **2.** lasting for half a year. —**sem'i•an'nu•al•ly,** *adv.*

sem'i•au•to•mat'ic, *adj.* (of a firearm) automatically ejecting a spent cartridge case and loading the next cartridge but requiring a squeeze of the trigger to fire each shot.

sem•i•cir•cle (sem'i sûr'kəl), *n.* half of a circle. —**sem'i•cir'cu•lar,** *adj.*

sem'i•co'lon, *n.* a punctuation mark (;) used to indicate a more distinct separation than is indicated by a comma.

sem'i•con•duc'tor (sem'ē-, sem'ī-), *n.* a substance, as silicon, with electrical conductivity intermediate between that of an insulator and a conductor.

sem'i•con'scious, *adj.* not fully conscious.

sem'i•fi'nal, *adj.* **1.** being the next to last round in an elimination tournament. —*n.* **2.** a semifinal round or bout. —**sem'i•fi'nal•ist,** *n.*

sem'i•month'ly, *adj.* **1.** occurring or published twice a month. —*adv.* **2.** twice a month.

sem•i•nal (sem'ə nl), *adj.* **1.** of or consisting of semen. **2.** influencing future development; original and creative.

sem•i•nar (sem'ə när'), *n.* **1.** a group of advanced students undertaking original research under a faculty member. **2.** a course of study for advanced students.

sem•i•nar•y (sem'ə ner'ē), *n., pl.* **-nar•ies. 1.** a school that prepares students for the priesthood, ministry, or rabbinate. **2.** a secondary school for young women. —**sem'i•nar'i•an,** *n.*

Sem•i•nole (sem'ə nōl'), *n., pl.* **-nole, -noles.** a member of an American Indian people of Florida and Oklahoma.

se•mi•ot•ics (sē'mē ot'iks, sem'ē-), *n.* the study of signs and symbols as elements of communicative behavior.

sem'i•per'me•a•ble (sem'ē-, sem'ī-), *adj.* permeable only to certain small molecules.

sem'i•pre'cious, *adj.* having commercial value as a gem but not classified as precious.

sem'i•pri'vate, *adj.* affording a degree of privacy but not fully private, as a hospital room.

sem'i•pro•fes'sion•al, *adj.* **1.** engaging in a field or sport for pay but on a part-time basis. **2.** engaged in by semiprofessional people. —*n.* **3.** a semiprofessional person.

sem'i•skilled', *adj.* having or requiring limited training.

sem'i•sol'id, *adj.* having a somewhat firm consistency.

Sem•ite (sem'īt; *esp. Brit.* sē'mīt), *n.* a member of a people speaking a Semitic language.

Se•mit•ic (sə mit'ik), *n.* **1.** a branch of the Afroasiatic language family that includes Hebrew and Arabic. —*adj.* **2.** of the Semitic languages or their speakers.

sem'i•tone', *n.* a musical pitch halfway between two whole tones.

sem•i•trail•er (sem'i trā'lər), *n.* a detachable freight trailer with the forward end supported by a tractor.

sem'i•trop'i•cal (sem'ē-, sem'ī-), *adj.* SUBTROPICAL.

sem•i•vow•el (sem'i vou'əl), *n.* a speech sound of vowel quality used as a consonant, as (w) in *wet* or (y) in *yet.*

sem'i•week'ly (sem'ē-, sem'ī-), *adj.* **1.** occurring or published twice a week. —*adv.* **2.** twice a week.

sen or **sen., 1.** senate. **2.** senator. **3.** senior.

sen•ate (sen'it), *n.* **1.** (*sometimes cap.*) the upper house of a national or state legislature, as in the U.S. and Canada. **2.** the supreme council of state of ancient Rome. **3.** a governing body, as at some universities.

sen'a•tor (-ə tər), *n.* a member of a senate. —**sen'a•to'ri•al** (-tôr'ē əl), *adj.*

senato'rial dis'trict, *n.* one of a fixed number of districts into which a state of the U.S. is divided, each electing one member to the state senate. Compare ASSEMBLY DISTRICT, CONGRESSIONAL DISTRICT.

send (send), *v.t.*, **sent, send•ing. 1.** to cause or enable to go. **2.** to cause to be conveyed to a destination. **3.** to propel or drive. **4.** to emit or utter. **5.** *Slang.* to delight; excite. **6. send for,** to summon. —**send′er,** *n.*

send′-off′, *n.* **1.** a demonstration of good wishes, as for a person beginning a new venture. **2.** a start; impetus.

Sen•e•ca (sen′i kə), *n., pl.* **-ca, -cas.** a member of an American Indian people orig. residing in W central New York.

Sen′eca Falls′ Conven′tion, *n.* a women's rights convention held at Seneca Falls, N.Y., in 1848.

Sen•e•gal (sen′i gôl′, -gäl′), *n.* a republic in W Africa. 9,403,546. —**Sen′e•ga•lese′** (-gə lēz′, -lēs′), *adj., n., pl.* **-lese.**

se•nes•cent (si nes′ənt), *adj.* growing old; aging. —**se•nes′cence,** *n.*

se•nile (sē′nīl, sen′īl), *adj.* **1.** showing a deterioration in mental functioning as a result of old age. **2.** of or resulting from old age. —**se•nil•i•ty** (si nil′i tē), *n.*

sen•ior (sēn′yər), *adj.* **1.** older or elder (written as *Sr.* following the name of a father with the same name as his son). **2.** of higher rank or longer service. **3.** of or for seniors. —*n.* **4.** a person who is older than another. **5.** a person of higher rank or longer service than another. **6.** a student in the final year at a high school or college.

sen′ior cit′izen, *n.* an older person, esp. one who is retired.

sen′ior high′ school′, *n.* a school usu. including grades 10 through 12.

sen•ior•i•ty (sēn yôr′i tē, -yor′-), *n., pl.* **-ties. 1.** the state of being senior. **2.** precedence conferred by length of service.

sen•na (sen′ə), *n., pl.* **-nas. 1.** a tropical plant, shrub, or tree of the legume family. **2.** a cathartic consisting of the dried leaflets of a senna.

se•ñor (sān yôr′), *n., pl.* **se•ñors, se•ño•res** (sān-yôr′ās). a Spanish term of address for a man, equivalent to *sir* or *Mr.*

se•ño•ra (sān yôr′ə), *n., pl.* **-ras.** a Spanish term of address for a married woman, equivalent to *Mrs.*

se•ño•ri•ta (sān′yə rē′tə), *n., pl.* **-tas.** a Spanish term of address for a girl or unmarried woman, equivalent to *miss.*

sen•sa•tion (sen sā′shən), *n.* **1.** perception of stimuli through the senses. **2.** a mental process or physical feeling from stimulation of a sense organ. **3.** the faculty of perceiving stimuli. **4.** a general feeling: *sensation of anxiety.* **5. a.** widespread excitement or interest. **b.** a cause of such feeling.

sen•sa′tion•al, *adj.* **1.** producing a startling or scandalous effect. **2.** extraordinarily good. **3.** of the senses or sensation. —**sen•sa′tion•al•ly,** *adv.*

sen•sa′tion•al•ism, *n.* the use of sensational subject matter or style.

sense (sens), *n., v.*, **sensed, sens•ing.** —*n.* **1.** one of the faculties, sight, hearing, smell, taste, or touch, by which humans and animals perceive stimuli. **2.** a feeling or perception based on one of the senses: *a sense of cold.* **3.** a special capacity for perception, estimation, or appreciation: *a sense of humor.* **4.** Often, **senses.** sound judgment; practical intelligence. **5.** an often vague perception or impression. **6.** meaning, as of a word or phrase. —*v.t.* **7.** to perceive by or as if by the senses. **8.** to detect (physical phenomena) mechanically, electrically, or photoelectrically.

sense′less, *adj.* **1.** unconscious. **2.** stupid; foolish. **3.** meaningless; nonsensical. —**sense′less•ly,** *adv.*

sen•si•bil•i•ty (sen′sə bil′i tē), *n., pl.* **-ties. 1.** capacity for feeling. **2.** mental responsiveness. **3.** Often, **-ties.** capacity for intellectual and aesthetic discrimination.

sen′si•ble, *adj.* **1.** having, using, or showing good sense. **2.** cognizant; aware. **3.** capable of being perceived by the senses or the mind. **4.** capable of feeling or perceiving. —**sen′si•bly,** *adv.*

sen′si•tive, *adj.* **1.** endowed with sensation. **2.** readily or excessively affected by external influences. **3.** responsive to the feelings of others. **4.** easily hurt or offended. —**sen′si•tive•ly,** *adv.* —**sen′si•tiv′i•ty, sen′si•tive•ness,** *n.*

sen′si•tize′ (-tīz′), *v.t., v.i.,* **-tized, -tiz•ing.** to make or become sensitive. —**sen′si•ti•za′tion,** *n.*

sen•sor (sen′sôr, -sər), *n.* a device sensitive to light, temperature, or radiation level that transmits a signal to a measuring or control instrument.

sen′so•ry (-sə rē), *adj.* of the senses or sensation.

sen•su•al (sen′shŌŌ əl), *adj.* **1.** arousing the senses. **2.** preoccupied with gratification of the senses, esp. the sexual appetite. **3.** sensory. —**sen′su•al′i•ty,** *n.* —**sen′su•al•ly,** *adv.*

sen′su•ous, *adj.* **1.** of, perceived by, or affecting the senses. **2.** readily affected through the senses. —**sen′su•ous•ly,** *adv.* —**sen′su•ous•ness,** *n.*

sent (sent), *v.* pt. and pp. of SEND.

sen•tence (sen′tns), *n., v.,* **-tenced, -tenc•ing.** —*n.* **1.** a structurally independent grammatical unit that typically consists of a subject and predicate and expresses a statement, question, request, command, or exclamation. **2.** a judicial decision, esp. one decreeing punishment to be inflicted. —*v.t.* **3.** to pronounce sentence upon. [< OF < L *sententia* opinion, decision]

sen•ten•tious (sen ten′shəs), *adj.* **1.** given to or abounding in pithy aphorisms. **2.** given to excessive moralizing.

sen•tient (sen′shənt), *adj.* capable of perceiving through the senses.

sen•ti•ment (sen′tə mənt), *n.* **1.** an attitude, feeling, or opinion. **2.** refined or tender emotion. **3.** a thought influenced by or based on emotion.

sen′ti•men′tal (-men′tl), *adj.* **1.** expressive of or appealing to the tender emotions. **2.** nostalgic. **3.** weakly emotional; mawkish. —**sen′ti•men′tal•ism,** *n.* —**sen′ti•men•tal′i•ty,** *n.* —**sen′ti•men′tal•ly,** *adv.*

sen′ti•men′tal•ize′, *v.i., v.t.,* **-ized, -iz•ing.** to indulge in or look upon with sentiment. —**sen′ti•men′tal•i•za′tion,** *n.*

sen•ti•nel (sen′tn l, -tə nl), *n.* one that stands watch; sentry.

sen•try (sen′trē), *n., pl.* **-tries.** a guard, esp., a soldier.

Seoul (sōl), *n.* the capital of South Korea. 9,645,824.

se•pal (sē′pəl), *n.* one of the individual leaves of a flower calyx.

sep•a•ra•ble (sep′ər ə bəl), *adj.* capable of being separated.

sep•a•rate (*v.* sep′ə rāt′; *adj., n.* -ər it), *v.,* **-rat•ed, -rat•ing,** *adj., n.* —*v.t.* **1.** to put or keep apart by or as if by a barrier; divide or disconnect. **2.** to extract: *to separate metal from ore.* —*v.i.* **3.** to withdraw from an association; part. **4.** to come apart. **5.** to go in different directions. —*adj.* **6.** not connected or joined; distinct. **7.** existing or maintained independently. **8.** not shared; individual: *separate checks.* —*n.* **9.** Usu., **-rates.** women's garments designed to be worn with other garments in various combinations. —**sep′a•rate•ly,** *adv.* —**sep′a•rate•ness,** *n.*

sep′arate but e′qual, *adj.* pertaining to a racial policy by which blacks may be segregated if granted equal opportunities and facilities. Compare PLESSY v. FERGUSON.

sep′a•ra′tion, *n.* **1.** the act of separating or state of being separated. **2.** a place, line, or point of parting. **3.** something that separates or divides.

sep′a•ra•tist (-ər ə tist, -ə rā′-), *n.* an advocate of separation, as from a church. —**sep′a•ra•tism,** *n.*

sep′a•ra′tor, *n.* a person or thing that separates, esp. a device for separating cream from milk.

Se•phar•di (sə fär′dē, -fär dē′), *n., pl.* **-phar•dim** (-fär′dim, -fär dēm′). a Jew of Spanish or Portuguese origin. Compare ASHKENAZI. —**Se•phar′dic,** *adj.*

se•pi•a (sē′pē ə), *n., pl.* **-pi•as. 1.** a brown pigment. **2.** a dark brown.

sep•sis (sep′sis), *n.* invasion of the body by pathogenic microorganisms or their toxins.

Sept., September.

Sep•tem•ber (sep tem′bər), *n.* the ninth month of the year, containing 30 days.

sep•tet (sep tet′), *n.* **1.** a group of seven, esp. a group of seven musicians. **2.** a musical composition for a septet.

sep•tic (sep′tik), *adj.* **1.** pertaining to or of the nature of sepsis. **2.** causing or caused by sepsis.

sep•ti•ce•mi•a (sep′tə sē′mē ə), *n.* the presence of pathogenic bacteria in the bloodstream.

sep′tic tank′, *n.* a tank in which sewage is decomposed by bacteria.

sep•tu•a•ge•nar•i•an (sep′chōō ə jə när′ē ən, -tōō-, -tyōō-), *n.* a person between 70 and 80 years of age.

Sep•tu•a•gint (sep′chōō ə jint′, -tōō-, -tyōō-), *n.* the oldest Greek version of the Old Testament.

sep•tum (sep′təm), *n.*, *pl.* **-ta** (-tə). a dividing wall or membrane in a plant or animal structure.

sep•ul•cher (sep′əl kər), *n.* **1.** a burial place; tomb. —*v.t.* **2.** to place in a sepulcher.

se•pul•chral (sə pul′krəl), *adj.* **1.** pertaining to tombs or burial. **2.** funereal; dismal.

seq., **1.** sequel. **2.** the following (one). [< L *sequēns*]

se•quel (sē′kwəl), *n.* **1.** a literary or filmic work that continues the narrative of a preceding work. **2.** a subsequent development. **3.** a result; consequence.

se′quence (-kwəns), *n.* **1.** the following of one thing after another. **2.** order of succession. **3.** a continuous connected series. **4.** a series of related scenes or shots that make up one episode of a film narrative. —**se•quen•tial** (si kwen′shəl), *adj.*

se′quenc•ing, *n.* the interruption of a career by a woman to bear and care for children.

se•ques•ter (si kwes′tər), *v.t.* **1.** to remove or withdraw into solitude or retirement. **2.** to set apart; separate. —**se•ques•tra•tion** (sē′kwes trā′shən), *n.*

se•quin (sē′kwin), *n.* a small shiny disk used for ornamentation, as on clothing. —**se′quined,** *adj.*

se•quoi•a (si kwoi′ə), *n.*, *pl.* **-quoi•as.** either of two extremely large coniferous trees of California.

ser., **1.** serial. **2.** series. **3.** sermon.

se•ra (sēr′ə), *n.* a pl. of SERUM.

se•ra•glio (si ral′yō, -räl′-), *n.*, *pl.* **-glios.** **1.** a harem. **2.** a sultan's palace.

se•ra•pe (sə rä′pē), *n.*, *pl.* **-pes.** a blanketlike shawl of brightly colored wool worn esp. in Mexico.

ser•aph (ser′əf), *n.*, *pl.* **-aphs, -a•phim** (-ə fim). **1.** one of the celestial beings hovering above God's throne in Isaiah's vision. Isa. 6. **2.** a member of the highest order of angels. —**se•raph•ic** (si raf′ik), *adj.*

Serb (sûrb), *n.* **1.** a native or inhabitant of Serbia and adjacent areas. **2.** Serbo-Croatian.

Ser•bi•a (sûr′bē ə), *n.* a constituent republic of Yugoslavia. 9,660,000.

Ser′bi•an, *n.* **1.** SERB (def. 1). **2.** Serbo-Croatian as spoken by Serbs. —*adj.* **3.** of Serbia, Serbs, or their language.

Ser′bo-Cro•a′tian (sûr′bō-), *n.* a Slavic language spoken by Serbs and Croats.

sere (sēr), *adj.* dry; withered.

ser•e•nade (ser′ə nād′), *n.*, *v.*, **-nad•ed, -nad•ing.** —*n.* **1.** music performed in the open air at night, as by a lover to his lady. —*v.t., v.i.* **2.** to entertain with or perform a serenade.

ser•en•dip•i•ty (ser′ən dip′i tē), *n.* an aptitude for making desirable discoveries by accident. —**ser′en• dip′i•tous,** *adj.*

se•rene (sə rēn′), *adj.* **1.** peaceful; tranquil. **2.** clear; fair: *serene weather.* —**se•rene′ly,** *adv.* —**se•ren′- i•ty** (-ren′i tē), **se•rene′ness,** *n.*

Ser•en•get•i (ser′ən get′ē), *n.* a plain in NW Tanzania.

serf (sûrf), *n.* a person in feudal servitude, attached to a lord's land and transferred with it from one owner to another. [< MF < L *servus* slave] —**serf′- dom,** *n.*

serge (sûrj), *n.* a twill-weave fabric with a characteristic diagonal wale.

ser•geant (sär′jənt), *n.* **1.** a noncommissioned officer in the U.S. Army and Marine Corps ranking above a corporal. **2.** a noncommissioned officer in the U.S. Air Force ranking above airman first class. **3.** a police officer ranking below a captain or lieutenant.

ser′geant at arms′, *n.* an officer whose chief duty is to preserve order, as in a legislative body.

ser′geant first′ class′, *n.* a noncommissioned officer in the U.S. Army ranking above a staff sergeant.

ser′geant ma′jor, *n.* **1.** a noncommissioned officer in the U.S. Army and Marine Corps ranking above a first sergeant. **2.** the chief administrative assistant in a military headquarters.

se•ri•al (sēr′ē əl), *n.* **1.** something that appears in installments at regular intervals. —*adj.* **2.** of or being a serial. **3.** of, arranged in, or occurring in a series. —**se′ri•al•i•za′tion,** *n.* —**se′ri•al•ize′,** *v.t.,* **-ized, -iz•ing.**

se′rial num′ber, *n.* a number, usu. one of a series, assigned for identification.

se•ries (sēr′ēz), *n.*, *pl.* **-ries.** a number of related or similar objects, events, etc., arranged or occurring in order or succession.

ser•if (ser′if), *n.* a smaller line used to finish off a main stroke of a letter.

ser•i•graph (ser′i graf′, -gräf′), *n.* a silkscreen print.

se•ri•ous (sēr′ē əs), *adj.* **1.** of, requiring, or characterized by deep thought. **2.** grave or somber. **3.** not trifling; earnest. **4.** weighty, important, or significant. **5.** giving cause for apprehension; critical or threatening. —**se′ri•ous•ly,** *adv.* —**se′ri•ous•ness,** *n.*

ser•mon (sûr′mən), *n.* **1.** a religious discourse, usu. delivered by a cleric during services. **2.** a long, tedious speech, esp. on a moral issue. —**ser′mon•ize′,** *v.i.,* **-ized, -iz•ing.**

Ser′mon on the Mount′, *n.* a discourse delivered by Jesus, containing fundamentals of Christian teachings, including the BEATITUDES, the GOLDEN RULE, and the LORD'S PRAYER. Matt. 5–7; Luke 6:20–49.

se•rol•o•gy (si rol′ə jē), *n.* the science dealing with the immunological properties and actions of serum. —**se•rol′o•gist,** *n.*

se•rous (sēr′əs), *adj.* of or resembling serum.

ser•pent (sûr′pənt), *n.* **1.** a snake. **2.** the Devil; Satan. Gen. 3:1–5.

ser′pen•tine′ (-pən tēn′, -tīn′), *adj.* **1.** of or resembling a serpent, as in form or movement. **2.** having a winding course, as a road; sinuous.

Ser•ra (ser′ə), *n.* **Ju•ní•pe•ro** (hōō nē′pə rō′) (*Miguel José Serra*), 1713–84, Spanish missionary in California and Mexico.

ser•rate (ser′āt), *adj.* notched on the edge like a saw: *a serrate leaf.* —**ser′rat•ed,** *adj.*

ser•ried (ser′ēd), *adj.* pressed together; compacted.

se•rum (sēr′əm), *n.*, *pl.* **se•rums, se•ra** (sēr′ə). **1.** the clear, pale yellow liquid that separates from the clot in the coagulation of blood. **2.** a watery animal fluid.

serv•ant (sûr′vənt), *n.* a person employed by another, esp. to perform domestic duties.

serve (sûrv), *v.*, **served, serv•ing,** *n.* —*v.i.* **1.** to act as a servant. **2.** to distribute food or drink. **3.** to give assistance; help. **4.** to go through a term of service. **5.** to have definite use. **6.** to answer a purpose. **7.** (in tennis, badminton, etc.) to put the ball or shuttlecock in play. —*v.t.* **8.** to work for as a servant. **9.** to be of service to; help. **10.** to go through (a term of service, imprisonment, etc.). **11.** to render homage or obedience to (God, a sovereign, etc.). **12.** to answer the requirements of. **13.** to wait upon at table. **14.** to distribute (food or drink) to another. **15.** to offer (a person) food or drink. **16.** to provide with a supply of something. **17.** (in tennis, badminton, etc.) to put (the ball or shuttlecock) in play. **18.** to make legal delivery of (a process or writ). —*n.* **19.** the act, manner, or right of serving, as in tennis.

serv′er, *n.* **1.** a person who serves. **2.** a utensil for dishing out individual portions of vegetables, cake, etc. **3.** a computer that makes services, as access to programs and peripheral devices, available to workstations on a network.

serv•ice (sûr'vis), *n., v.,* **-iced, -ic•ing.** —*n.* **1.** an act of helpful activity. **2.** the supplying or supplier of a utility, as electricity, that meets a public need. **3.** the providing or a provider of maintenance or repair. **4.** the performance of duties or the duties performed. **5. a.** a department of public employment. **b.** the personnel in it. **6.** the work of a servant. **7. a.** the armed forces. **b.** a branch of the armed forces. **8.** a meeting, ritual, or form for religious worship. **9.** a set of dishes or utensils. **10.** (in tennis, badminton, etc.) the act or manner of serving the ball or shuttlecock. —*v.t.* **11.** to maintain, repair, or restore. **12.** to supply with services.

serv'ice•a•ble, *adj.* **1.** being of service; useful. **2.** wearing well; durable.

serv'ice•man' (-man', -mən), *n., pl.* **-men** (-men', -mən). **1.** a member of the armed forces. **2.** a person whose occupation is to maintain or repair equipment.

serv'ice mark', *n.* a proprietary term, similar to a trademark, that distinguishes the seller or provider of a service.

serv'ice sta'tion, *n.* a place for servicing automobiles, as by selling gasoline.

ser•vile (sûr'vil, -vīl), *adj.* **1.** slavishly submissive. **2.** of or suitable for slaves. —**ser•vil'i•ty,** *n.*

serv'ing, *n.* a single portion of food or drink.

ser•vi•tor (sûr'vi tər), *n.* a servant or attendant.

ser'vi•tude' (-tōōd', -tyōōd'), *n.* slavery; bondage.

ser•vo (sûr'vō), *n., pl.* **-vos. 1.** SERVOMECHANISM. **2.** SERVOMOTOR.

ser'vo•mech'an•ism, *n.* an electronic system in which a controlling mechanism is actuated by a low-energy signal.

ser'vo•mo'tor, *n.* a motor forming part of a servomechanism.

ses•a•me (ses'ə mē), *n.* **1.** a tropical plant whose edible seeds yield an oil. **2.** the seeds of the sesame.

ses•qui•cen•ten•ni•al (ses'kwi sen ten'ē əl), *adj.* **1.** of or marking the completion of 150 years. —*n.* **2.** a 150th anniversary or its celebration.

ses•sion (sesh'ən), *n.* **1. a.** a meeting, as of a court or legislature, for the transaction of business. **b.** a series of such meetings. **2.** a period of instruction at a school or college. **3.** a meeting or period of time for a particular activity.

set (set), *v.,* **set, set•ting,** *n., adj.* —*v.t.* **1.** to put in a particular place, position, or posture. **2.** to cause to pass into a certain condition. **3.** to fix definitely; establish. **4.** to place or plant firmly. **5.** to establish for others to follow: *Try to set a good example.* **6.** to arrange or prepare for use: *Please set the table.* **7.** to style (the hair), as by using rollers. **8.** to adjust (a clock or watch) to accord with a standard. **9.** to fix (a gem) in a setting. **10.** to cause to sit; seat. **11.** to put (a broken or dislocated bone) back in position. **12.** to fit (words) to music. **13.** to spread (a sail) to catch the wind. **14.** to arrange (type) for printing. —*v.i.* **15.** to sink below the horizon: *The sun has set.* **16.** to decline; wane. **17.** to become firm, solid, or permanent, as dye. **18.** to sit on eggs, as a hen. **19.** to have a certain direction, as a wind. **20. set about,** to begin. **21.** ~ **aside, a.** to put to one side; reserve. **b.** to discard or annul. **22.** ~ **back, a.** to hinder; impede. **b.** *Informal.* to cost. **23.** ~ **forth, a.** to state or describe. **b.** to begin a journey. **24.** ~ **off, a.** to cause to explode. **b.** to begin; start. **c.** to intensify by contrast. **25.** ~ **on** or **upon,** to attack or cause to attack. **26.** ~ **out, a.** to begin a journey. **b.** to undertake; attempt. **27.** ~ **up, a.** to put upright; raise. **b.** to inaugurate or establish. —*n.* **28.** the act of setting or state of being set. **29.** a collection of articles for use together. **30.** a group of similar things. **31.** a group of persons associated esp. by common interests. **32.** fixed direction, bent, or inclination. **33.** an apparatus for receiving radio or television programs. **34.** a construction representing the site of the action in a play or film. **35.** *Tennis.* a unit of a match consisting of six or more games. **36.** *Math.* a collection of objects or elements classed together.

—*adj.* **37.** fixed or prescribed beforehand. **38.** customary: *set phrases.* **39.** fixed; rigid. **40.** resolved or determined. **41.** prepared; ready.

set'back', *n.* a check to progress; a reverse or defeat.

Seth (seth), *n.* the third son of Adam. Gen. 4:25.

set•tee (se tē'), *n., pl.* **-tees.** a long seat with a back and usu. arms.

set•ter (set'ər), *n.* a long-haired hunting dog with feathering on the tail.

set'ting, *n.* **1.** the act of one that sets. **2.** the position of something, as a thermostat, that has been set. **3.** surroundings or scenery. **4.** a mounting, as for a jewel. **5.** the locale and period of a story, play, etc.

set•tle (set'l), *v.,* **-tled, -tling.** —*v.t.* **1.** to put in order. **2.** to pay (a bill, debt, etc.). **3.** to cause to take up residence. **4.** to furnish with inhabitants. **5.** to quiet or calm. **6.** to determine or decide; resolve: *to settle a dispute.* **7.** to establish in a permanent position or on a permanent basis. —*v.i.* **8.** to come to an agreement, arrangement, or decision. **9.** to take up residence. **10.** to come to rest. **11.** to become fixed, as in a particular place. **12.** to sink gradually. **13.** to become clear by the sinking of suspended particles, as a liquid. **14.** to become firm or compact by sinking, as the ground. —**set'tler,** *n.*

set'tle•ment, *n.* **1.** the act of settling or state of being settled. **2.** an arrangement or adjustment, as of a disagreement. **3.** establishment of a person, as in a new country. **4.** a colony, esp. in its early stages. **5.** a small community. **6.** the satisfying of a debt, claim, or demand. **7.** an establishment providing aid in an underprivileged area.

set'-to' (-tōō'), *n., pl.* **-tos.** a usu. brief, sharp fight or argument.

set'up', *n.* **1.** organization; arrangement. **2.** glass, ice, mixer, etc., for patrons who provide their own liquor. **3.** an undertaking or contest deliberately made easy.

sev•en (sev'ən), *n.* **1.** a cardinal number, 6 plus 1. **2.** a symbol for this number, as 7 or VII. —*adj.* **3.** amounting to seven in number. —**sev'enth,** *adj., n.*

Sev'en Church'es of A'sia, *n pl.* the ancient Christian churches of Ephesus, Smyrna, Pergamum, Thyatira, Sardis, Philadelphia, and Laodicea. Rev. 1:2.

Sev'en Dead'ly Sins', *n.pl.* DEADLY SINS.

Sev'en Gifts' of the Spir'it, *n.pl.* wisdom, understanding, counsel, fortitude, knowledge, righteousness, and fear of the Lord.

Sev'en Pil'lars of Wis'dom, a military chronicle (1926) by T.E. Lawrence. Prov. 9:1.

sev'en•teen', *n.* **1.** a cardinal number, 10 plus 7. **2.** a symbol for this number, as 17 or XVII. —*adj.* **3.** amounting to 17 in number. —**sev'en•teenth',** *adj., n.*

seventeen'-year' lo'cust, *n.* a cicada of the eastern U.S., having nymphs that live in the soil for 17 years in the North and 13 years in the South.

Sev'enth-Day', *adj.* (*sometimes l.c.*) designating certain Christian denominations that make Saturday their chief day of rest and religious observance: *Seventh-Day Adventists.*

sev'enth heav'en, *n.* **1.** (esp. in Islam and the cabala) the highest heaven, where God and the most exalted angels dwell. **2.** a state of intense happiness; bliss.

sev'en•ty, *n., pl.* **-ties,** *adj.* —*n.* **1.** a cardinal number, 10 times 7. **2.** a symbol for this number, as 70 or LXX. —*adj.* **3.** amounting to 70 in number. —**sev'en•ti•eth,** *adj., n.*

Sev'en Vir'tues, *n.pl.* faith, hope, charity, justice, fortitude, prudence, and temperance.

Sev'en Won'ders of the World', *n.pl.* the seven structures considered the most remarkable of ancient times: the Egyptian pyramids, the Mausoleum at Halicarnassus, the Temple of Artemis at Ephesus, the Hanging Gardens of Babylon, the Colossus of Rhodes, the statue of Zeus by Phidias at Olympia, and the Pharos or lighthouse at Alexandria.

Sev'en Years'/ War', *n.* the war (1756–63) in

which England and Prussia defeated France, Austria, Russia, Sweden, and Saxony.

sev•er (sev′ər), v.t., v.i. to separate, divide, or break off. —**sev′er•ance,** n.

sev•er•al (sev′ər əl, sev′rəl), adj. **1.** being more than two but fewer than many. **2.** respective; individual: They went their several ways. —n. **3.** several persons or things. —**sev′er•al•ly,** adv.

se•vere (sə vēr′), adj., **-ver•er, -ver•est. 1.** causing distress; harsh. **2.** serious or stern, as in manner. **3.** austere, as in style; plain. **4.** extreme, intense, or violent. **5.** difficult or rigorous. **6.** rigidly exact; demanding. —**se•vere′ly,** adv. —**se•vere′ness, se•ver′i•ty** (-ver′i tē), n.

Se•ville (sə vil′), n. a port in SW Spain. 668,356. —**Se•vil′lian** (-yən), adj., n.

sew (sō), v., **sewed, sewn** or **sewed, sew•ing.** —v.t. **1.** to make, repair, join, or attach by stitches. —v.i. **2.** to work with a needle and thread or with a sewing machine. **3. sew up,** Informal. to get, accomplish, or control successfully or completely. —**sew′er** (sō′ər), n.

sew•age (sōō′ij), n. waste matter that passes through sewers.

Sew•ard (sōō′ərd), n. **William Henry,** 1801–72, U.S. Secretary of State 1861–69.

Sew′ard's Fol′ly, n. the purchase of Alaska in 1867, through the negotiations of Secretary of State W. H. Seward.

sew•er (sōō′ər), n. an artificial conduit, usu. underground, for carrying off waste water and refuse.

sew′er•age (-ər ij), n. **1.** a system of sewers. **2.** SEWAGE.

sew•ing (sō′ing), n. **1.** the act or work of one who sews. **2.** something sewn or to be sewn.

sew′ing machine′, n. any of various foot-operated or electric machines for sewing.

sex (seks), n. **1.** either the female or the male division of a species, esp. as differentiated by reproductive function. **2.** the structural and functional differences by which the female and male are distinguished. **3.** SEXUAL INTERCOURSE. —**sex′less,** adj.

sex-, a combining form meaning six (sextet).

sex•a•ge•nar•i•an (sek′sə jə nâr′ē ən), adj. **1.** of the age of 60 years or between 60 and 70 years old. —n. **2.** a sexagenarian person.

sex′ appeal′, n. the ability to excite people sexually.

sex′ chro′mosome, n. a chromosome that determines the sex of an individual.

sex•ism, n. discrimination, esp. against women, based on sex. —**sex′ist,** adj., n.

sex•tant (sek′stənt), n. an instrument used to determine latitude and longitude at sea by measuring angular distances, esp. of sun, moon, and stars.

sex•tet (seks tet′), n. **1.** a group of six. **2. a.** a group of six musicians. **b.** a musical composition for six voices or instruments.

sex•ton (sek′stən), n. an official who maintains church property.

sex•tu•ple (seks tōō′pəl, -tyōō′-, -tup′əl, seks′tōō-pəl, -tyōō-), adj., v., **-pled, -pling.** —adj. **1.** consisting of six parts. **2.** six times as great or as many. —v.t., v.i. **3.** to make or become six times as great.

sex•u•al (sek′shōō əl), adj. of or involving sex, the two sexes, or the sex organs. —**sex′u•al′i•ty,** n. —**sex′u•al•ly,** adv.

sex′ual harass′ment, n. unwelcome sexual advances, esp. by an employer or superior.

sex′ual in′tercourse, n. genital contact or coupling between individuals, esp. involving penetration of the penis into the vagina.

sex′ually transmit′ted disease′, n. any disease characteristically transmitted by sexual contact, as gonorrhea.

sex′y, adj., **-i•er, -i•est.** sexually interesting or exciting; erotic. —**sex′i•ly,** adv. —**sex′i•ness,** n.

Sey•chelles (sā shel′, -shelz′), n. (used with a pl. v.) a republic comprising a group of islands in the Indian Ocean, NE of Madagascar. 78,142.

SF or **sf,** science fiction.

Sfc, Sergeant first class.

SGML, Standard Generalized Markup Language: a set of standards enabling a user to create a markup scheme for tagging the elements of an electronic document.

Sgt., Sergeant.

sh (usu. an extended sh sound), interj. hush!

shab•by (shab′ē), adj., **-bi•er, -bi•est. 1.** showing signs of long or hard use; worn or run-down. **2.** wearing worn clothes. **3.** mean; contemptible. —**shab′bi•ly,** adv. —**shab′bi•ness,** n.

shack (shak), n. a rough cabin; shanty.

shack•le (shak′əl), n., v., **-led, -ling.** —n. **1.** a metal fastening for securing the wrist or ankle; fetter. **2.** a fastening or coupling device. **3.** Often, **-les.** something that serves to inhibit thought or action. —v.t. **4.** to confine, restrain, or inhibit by or as if by shackles.

shad (shad), n., pl. **shad.** an edible marine fish that spawns in rivers upstream from the sea.

shade (shād), n., v., **shad•ed, shad•ing.** —n. **1.** comparative darkness caused by the screening of rays of light. **2.** a place or area sheltered from light, esp. sunlight. **3.** something used to reduce or shut out light or heat: a window shade. **4. shades,** Informal. sunglasses. **5.** comparative obscurity. **6.** a ghost; specter. **7.** the degree of darkness of a color. **8.** a slight amount or degree. —v.t. **9.** to dim or darken. **10.** to screen or protect from light, heat, or view. **11.** to introduce degrees of darkness into (a drawing or painting). —v.i. **12.** to change by degrees.

shad′ing, n. **1.** a slight variation or difference, as of color. **2.** the representation of shade in a painting or drawing.

shad•ow (shad′ō), n. **1.** a dark figure or image cast on a surface by a body intercepting light. **2.** comparative darkness. **3.** a slight suggestion; trace. **4.** a specter or ghost. **5.** the dark part of a picture. **6.** a cause or period of gloom or unhappiness. —v.t. **7.** to cover with shadow; shade. **8.** to follow and watch (a person) secretly. **9.** to represent faintly or prophetically. —**shad′ow•y,** adj., **-i•er, -i•est.**

shad′ow•box′, v.i. to go through the motions of boxing without an opponent, as in training.

Shad•rach (shad′rak, shā′drak), n. a companion of Daniel who, with Meshach and Abednego, was thrown into the fiery furnace of Nebuchadnezzar and came out unharmed. Dan. 3:12–30.

shad′y, adj., **-i•er, -i•est.** abounding in or giving shade. —**shad′i•ness,** n.

shaft (shaft, shäft), n. **1.** the long, slender body of a weapon, as a lance. **2.** a ray or beam. **3.** the handle of a tool or implement. **4.** a rotating rod that transmits motion. **5.** a monument in the form of a column or obelisk. **6.** either of the parallel bars between which a draft animal is hitched. **7.** a vertical enclosed space, as in a building: an elevator shaft. **8.** a vertical or sloping underground passageway, as in a mine. **9.** Slang. harsh or unfair treatment. —v.t. **10.** Slang. to treat in a harsh or unfair manner.

shag¹ (shag), n. **1.** a rough, matted mass, as of hair or wool. **2.** a long, thick pile or nap. —**shag′gy,** adj., **-gi•er, -gi•est.** —**shag′gi•ness,** n.

shag² (shag), v.t., **shagged, shag•ging.** to retrieve and throw back (a fly ball) in batting practice.

shah (shä, shô), n. (often cap.) (formerly, in Iran) king; sovereign.

shake (shāk), v., **shook, shak•en, shak•ing,** n. —v.i., v.t. **1.** to move up and down or back and forth with short, quick movements. **2.** to tremble or cause to tremble. **3.** to clasp (another's hand), as in greeting. **4.** to brandish, esp. menacingly. **5.** to come or force off or out by short, quick movements. **6.** to agitate or disturb profoundly. **7.** to weaken. **8. shake down, a.** to cause to descend by shaking. **b.** to extort money from. **c.** to search for concealed weapons. —n. **9.** an act or instance of shaking. **10. shakes,** (used with a sing. v.) a state or spell of trembling, as from fever or cold. **11.** MILK SHAKE. **12.** treatment; deal: a fair shake. —**Idiom. 13. no great shakes,** not exceptional; ordinary.

shake′down′, n. **1.** extortion, as by blackmail. **2.** a thorough search. **3.** a test cruise or flight for familiarizing the crew with a craft's operation and remedying problems.

shak′er, *n.* **1.** a container with a perforated top from which salt, sugar, etc., is shaken onto food. **2.** (*cap.*) a member of a religious sect practicing celibacy and a strict and simple way of life. **3.** a person or thing that shakes.

Shake•speare (shāk′spēr), *n.* **William,** 1564–1616, English poet and dramatist. —**Shake•spear′e•an,** *n., adj.*

shake′-up′, *n.* a thorough change of administration in an organization.

shak′y, *adj.,* **-i•er, -i•est. 1.** tending to shake. **2.** liable to break down or give way; insecure or wavering. —**shak′i•ly,** *adv.* —**shak′i•ness,** *n.*

shale (shāl), *n.* a rock of laminated structure formed from clay.

shale′ oil′, *n.* petroleum distilled from oil shale.

shall (shal; *unstressed* shǝl), *auxiliary v., pres.* **shall;** *past* **should. 1.** plan to or intend to: *I shall go later.* **2.** will have to or is determined to: *You shall do it.* **3.** (in laws, directives, etc.) is or are obliged to; must: *Council meetings shall be public.* **4.** (used interrogatively): *Shall we go?* ——**Usage.** Today, WILL is used in place of SHALL to indicate future time in all three persons and in all types of speech and writing. SHALL has some use, chiefly in formal contexts, to express determination: *I shall return. We shall overcome.* SHALL also occurs in the language of law and in directives: *All visitors shall observe posted regulations.*

shal•lot (shal′ǝt, shǝ lot′), *n.* an onionlike plant with an edible bulb used in cooking.

shal•low (shal′ō), *adj.,* **-er, -est,** *n.* —*adj.* **1.** of little depth. **2.** lacking depth of intellect or emotion; superficial. —*n.* **3.** Usu., **-lows.** (*used with a sing. or pl. v.*) a shallow part of a body of water.

shalt (shalt), *v. Archaic.* 2nd pers. sing. of SHALL.

sham (sham), *n., adj., v.,* **shammed, sham•ming.** —*n.* **1.** a spurious imitation. **2.** a person who gives a false impression. **3.** a decorative cover, esp. for a pillow. —*adj.* **4.** not real; pretended. —*v.t., v.i.* **5.** to make a false show (of); pretend.

sha•man (shä′mǝn, shā′-, sham′ǝn), *n.* (esp. among certain tribal peoples) a person who uses magic to cure illness, foretell the future, and control spiritual forces. —**sha•man•ic** (shǝ man′ik), *adj.*

sham•ble (sham′bǝl), *v.,* **-bled, -bling,** *n.* —*v.i.* **1.** to walk awkwardly with a shuffle. —*n.* **2.** a shambling gait.

sham′bles, *n.* (*used with a sing. or pl. v.*) **1.** a slaughterhouse. **2.** a scene or condition of great destruction or disorder.

shame (shām), *n., v.,* **shamed, sham•ing.** —*n.* **1.** the painful feeling of having done something dishonorable or improper. **2.** disgrace; ignominy. **3.** a cause for regret or disappointment. —*v.t.* **4.** to cause to feel shame. **5.** to motivate through shame. **6.** to cause to suffer disgrace. —*Idiom.* **7. put to shame,** to outdo; surpass. —**shame′ful,** *adj.* —**shame′ful•ly,** *adv.* —**shame′ful•ness,** *n.*

shame′faced′, *adj.* **1.** feeling or showing shame. **2.** modest or bashful.

shame′less, *adj.* lacking a sense of shame; brazen. —**shame′less•ly,** *adv.* —**shame′less•ness,** *n.*

Sham•gar (sham′gǝr), *n.* a judge of Israel who killed 600 Philistines with an ox goad. Judg. 3:31.

sham•poo (sham pōō′), *n., pl.* **-poos,** *v.,* **-pooed, -poo•ing.** —*n.* **1.** a special cleansing preparation that produces suds. **2.** an act of washing or cleansing with shampoo. —*v.t.* **3.** to wash (the hair), esp. with shampoo. **4.** to clean (rugs, upholstery, etc.) with shampoo. —**sham•poo′er,** *n.*

sham•rock (sham′rok), *n.* any of several trifoliate plants, esp. a small clover that is the national emblem of Ireland.

shang•hai (shang′hī, shang hī′), *v.t.,* **-haied, -hai•ing.** to coerce (a sailor) to join the crew of a ship.

Shang•hai (shang hī′), *n.* a seaport in E China. 6,980,000.

shank (shangk), *n.* **1. a.** the part of the human leg

between the knee and ankle. **b.** a corresponding part in other vertebrates. **2.** a cut of meat from the leg. **3.** a straight, shaftlike part of an implement or tool that connects two more important or complex parts. **4.** *Informal.* the early part of a period of time.

shan′t (shant, shänt), contraction of *shall not.*

shan•tung (shan′tung′), *n.* a plain-weave silk with an irregular or uneven texture.

shan•ty (shan′tē), *n., pl.* **-ties.** a crudely built hut, cabin, or house.

shape (shāp), *n., v.,* **shaped, shap•ing.** —*n.* **1.** the outline or form of the external surface of something. **2.** something seen in outline, as in silhouette. **3.** an imaginary form; phantom. **4.** organized form or orderly arrangement. **5.** condition or state of repair. **6.** the figure or physique of a person. —*v.t.* **7.** to give definite shape to. **8.** to adjust; adapt. **9.** to direct (one's course, future, etc.). **10. shape up,** to improve or develop. ——*Idiom.* **11. take shape,** to assume a fixed or more complete form.

shape′less, *adj.* **1.** lacking definite shape or form. **2.** lacking a pleasing shape. —**shape′less•ness,** *n.*

shape′ly, *adj.,* **-li•er, -li•est.** having a pleasing shape. —**shape′li•ness,** *n.*

shard (shärd), *n.* a fragment, esp. of broken earthenware.

share¹ (shâr), *n., v.,* **shared, shar•ing.** —*n.* **1.** a portion allotted to one person. **2.** one of the equal parts into which the capital stock of a corporation is divided. —*v.t.* **3.** to divide and distribute in shares; apportion. **4.** to use, participate in, or receive jointly. —*v.i.* **5.** to have a share.

share² (shâr), *n.* a plowshare.

share′crop′per, *n.* a tenant farmer who pays as rent a share of the crop.

share′hold′er, *n.* one that owns shares of stock, as in a corporation.

shark¹ (shärk), *n.* any of various predatory fishes with a rough scaleless skin.

shark² (shärk), *n.* **1.** a person who preys greedily on others. **2.** *Informal.* one with unusual ability in a particular field.

shark′skin′, *n.* **1.** a smooth fabric, orig. of rayon, with a dull surface. **2.** a fine worsted fabric in twill weave used for suits.

sharp (shärp), *adj.,* **-er, -est,** *v., adv., n.* —*adj.* **1.** having a thin cutting edge or a fine point. **2.** not blunt or rounded. **3.** involving an abrupt change in direction or course. **4.** clearly defined; distinct. **5.** pungent or biting in taste. **6.** piercing or shrill in sound. **7.** keenly cold, as weather. **8.** felt acutely; intense. **9.** merciless, caustic, or harsh. **10.** alert or vigilant. **11.** mentally acute. **12.** shrewd, often to the point of dishonesty. **13.** *Music.* **a.** raised a half step in pitch. **b.** above the correct pitch. **14.** *Informal.* very stylish. —*v.t., v.i.* **15.** *Music.* to make or become sharp. —*adv.* **16.** keenly or acutely. **17.** abruptly or suddenly. **18.** punctually. **19.** *Music.* above the correct pitch. —*n.* **20.** SHARPER. **21.** *Music.* a sign indicating a tone one half step above a given tone. —**sharp′ly,** *adv.* —**sharp′ness,** *n.*

sharp′en, *v.t., v.i.* to make or become sharp or sharper. —**sharp′en•er,** *n.*

sharp′er, *n.* a shrewd swindler.

sharp′-eyed′, *adj.* having keen sight or perception.

sharp•ie or **sharp•y** (shär′pē), *n., pl.* **-ies. 1.** SHARPER. **2.** a very alert person.

sharp′shoot′er, *n.* a person skilled in shooting, esp. with a rifle. —**sharp′shoot′ing,** *n.*

sharp′-tongued′, *adj.* harsh or sarcastic in speech.

shat•ter (shat′ǝr), *v.t., v.i.* to break or burst into pieces or fragments.

shat′ter•proof′, *adj.* made to resist shattering.

shave (shāv), *v.,* **shaved, shaved** or (*esp. in combination*) **shav•en, shav•ing,** *n.* —*v.i.* **1.** to remove hair or a beard with a razor. —*v.t.* **2.** to remove hair from (the face, legs, etc.) close to the skin. **3.** to cut off (hair, esp. the beard) close to the skin. **4.** to cut or scrape away the surface of. **5.** to reduce to shavings. **6.** to come very near to; graze. —*n.* **7.** the act, process, or result of shaving.

shav•er, *n.* **1.** a person who shaves. **2.** an electric razor. **3.** *Informal.* a small boy; youngster.

shav•ing, *n.* **1.** a very thin slice, as of wood. **2.** the act of one who shaves.

Sha•vu•oth or **Sha•vu•ot** (shə vōō′ōs, shä vōō-ôt′), *n.* a Jewish festival that commemorates God's giving of the Ten Commandments to Moses. Also called **Feast of Weeks, Pentecost.**

Shaw (shô), *n.* **George Bernard,** 1856–1950, Irish writer. —**Sha•vi•an** (shā′vē ən), *adj., n.*

shawl (shôl), *n.* a piece of fabric worn, esp. by women, around the shoulders or head.

Shaw•nee (shô nē′), *n., pl.* **-nee, -nees.** a member of an American Indian people probably orig. of the upper Ohio River valley.

shay (shā), *n. Chiefly Dial.* a chaise.

she (shē), *pron., n., pl.* **shes.** —*pron.* **1.** the female person or animal last mentioned. **2.** something considered to be feminine. —*n.* **3.** a female person or animal.

sheaf (shēf), *n., pl.* **sheaves. 1.** a bundle of cut stalks of a cereal plant. **2.** a bundle, cluster, or collection, as of papers.

shear (shēr), *v.,* **sheared, sheared** or **shorn, shear•ing,** *n.* —*v.t.* **1.** to cut (something). **2.** to remove or deprive by or as if by cutting. **3.** to clip the hair, fleece, or wool from. —*n.* **4. shears,** (*used with a pl. v.*) **a.** large scissors. **b.** any of various cutting implements resembling scissors. **5.** the act or process of shearing. **6.** the tendency of a force applied to a solid body to cause deformation or rupture along a plane parallel to the force. —**shear′er,** *n.*

sheath (shēth), *n., pl.* **sheaths** (shēthz). **1.** a case for a blade, as of a dagger. **2.** a closely enveloping part or structure, as in an animal. **3.** a close-fitting dress.

sheathe (shēth), *v.t.,* **sheathed, sheath•ing. 1.** to put into a sheath. **2.** to cover or provide with a protective layer or sheathing.

sheath•ing (shē′thing), *n.* **1.** a covering, as of metal plates on a ship's bottom. **2.** material for sheathing.

she•bang (shə bang′), *n. Informal.* an organization, contrivance, or affair: *threw the whole shebang away.*

shed¹ (shed), *n.* a slight or rude structure built for shelter or storage.

shed² (shed), *v.,* **shed, shed•ding.** —*v.t.* **1.** to pour forth; let fall. **2.** to give forth (light, influence, etc.). **3.** to resist being penetrated by: *cloth that sheds water.* **4.** to cast off (leaves, skin, etc.) by a natural process. —*v.i.* **5.** to cast off a natural covering.

she'd (shēd), **1.** contraction of *she had.* **2.** contraction of *she would.*

sheen (shēn), *n.* luster; brightness.

sheep (shēp), *n., pl.* **sheep. 1.** a ruminant mammal related to the goat and bred for wool and meat. **2.** a meek or easily led person.

sheep′ dog′, *n.* a dog trained to herd and guard sheep.

sheep′fold′, *n.* an enclosure for sheep.

sheep′ish, *adj.* **1.** embarrassed or shamefaced. **2.** like a sheep, as in meekness. —**sheep′ish•ly,** *adv.* —**sheep′ish•ness,** *n.*

sheep′skin′, *n.* **1.** the skin of a sheep, esp. when dressed with the wool on. **2.** leather or parchment made from sheepskin. **3.** *Informal.* a diploma.

sheer¹ (shēr), *adj.,* **-er, -est,** *adv.* —*adj.* **1.** transparent and thin; diaphanous. **2.** unqualified; utter: *sheer nonsense.* **3.** almost vertical; very steep. —*adv.* **4.** completely; quite. **5.** very steeply. —**sheer′ness,** *n.*

sheer² (shēr), *v.i., v.t.* to turn from a course; swerve.

sheet¹ (shēt), *n.* **1.** a large rectangular piece of fabric, as cotton, used as an article of bedding. **2.** a broad, thin layer or covering: *a sheet of ice.* **3.** a relatively thin, usu. rectangular piece, as of glass or metal. **4.** a rectangular piece of paper.

sheet² (shēt), *n.* a rope or wire used to secure or adjust a ship's sail.

sheet′ing, *n.* fabric, esp. a firm muslin, used for making bedsheets.

sheet′ met′al, *n.* metal in sheets.

sheet′ mu′sic, *n.* music printed on unbound sheets of paper.

sheik or **sheikh** (shēk, shāk), *n.* (in Arab countries) the patriarch of a tribe or family; chief: also used as a term of polite address. —**sheik′dom,** *n.*

shek•el (shek′əl), *n.* **1.** the basic monetary unit of Israel. **2.** a coin of the ancient Hebrews. **3. shekels,** *Slang.* money; cash.

shelf (shelf), *n., pl.* **shelves** (shelvz). **1.** a slab, as of wood or metal, fixed horizontally to a wall to hold objects. **2.** something resembling a shelf, as a rock ledge or a sandbank. —*Idiom.* **3. on the shelf,** inactive or useless.

shelf′ life′, *n.* the period during which a stored commodity remains suitable for use.

shell (shel), *n.* **1.** a hard outer covering of an animal, as a clam or turtle. **2.** the hard outer covering of a seed, fruit, nut, or egg. **3.** a hollow projectile filled with an explosive charge. **4.** a metallic cartridge used in small arms. **5.** an unfilled pastry crust. **6.** a light, long, and narrow racing boat for rowing. **7.** a computer program with an interface designed to simplify use of the operating system. —*v.t.* **8.** to remove the shell of. **9.** to fire shells at, on, or among; bombard. **10. shell out,** *Informal.* to pay (money).

she'll (shēl; *unstressed* shil), contraction of *she will.*

shel•lac or **-lack** (shə lak′), *n., v.,* **-lacked, -lack•ing.** —*n.* **1.** a purified lac used for making varnish. **2.** a varnish made by dissolving shellac in alcohol. —*v.t.* **3.** to coat or treat with shellac. **4.** *Slang.* to defeat; trounce.

Shel•ley (shel′ē), *n.* **1. Mary Wollstonecraft (Godwin),** 1797–1851, English author (wife of Percy Bysshe Shelley). **2. Percy Bysshe** (bish), 1792–1822, English poet.

shell′fire′, *n.* the firing of explosive shells.

shell′fish′, *n., pl.* **-fish, -fish•es.** an aquatic animal having a shell, as a clam or lobster.

shell′ shock′, *n.* COMBAT FATIGUE. —**shell′-shocked′,** *adj.*

shel•ter (shel′tər), *n.* **1.** something that affords cover or protection; refuge. **2.** the protection or refuge afforded by a shelter. —*v.t.* **3.** to provide with a shelter. —*v.i.* **4.** to take shelter.

shelve (shelv), *v.t.,* **shelved, shelv•ing. 1.** to place on a shelf. **2.** to put off or aside. **3.** to remove from active use or service. **4.** to furnish with shelves.

shelves, *n. pl.* of SHELF.

shelv′ing, *n.* **1.** material for shelves. **2.** shelves collectively.

Shem (shem), *n.* the eldest of the three sons of Noah. Gen. 10:21.

Shen•an•do•ah (shen′ən dō′ə), *n.* a river flowing NE from N Virginia to the Potomac at Harpers Ferry, West Virginia. ab. 200 mi. (322 km) long.

she•nan•i•gan (shə nan′i gən), *n. Informal.* **1.** Usu. **-gans. a.** mischief; prankishness. **b.** deceit; trickery. **2.** a deceitful trick.

Shen•yang (shun′yäng′), *n.* a city in NE China. 4,200,000.

She•ol (shē′ōl), *n. Judaism.* **1.** the abode of the dead. **2.** (*l.c.*) hell.

Shep•ard (shep′ərd), *n.* **Alan Bartlett, Jr.,**1923–98, U.S. astronaut.

shep•herd (shep′ərd), *n.* **1.** a person who herds and tends sheep. —*v.t.* **2.** to tend as or like a shepherd.

sher•bet (shûr′bit), *n.* a frozen, fruit-flavored ice with milk, egg white, or gelatin added.

Sher•i•dan (sher′i dn), *n.* **Philip Henry,** 1831–88, U.S. general.

sher•iff (sher′if), *n.* a county law-enforcement officer.

Sher•man (shûr′mən), *n.* **William Tecumseh,** 1820–91, Union general in the Civil War.

Sher′man Antitrust′ Act′, *n.* an act of Congress (1890) prohibiting any contract, or combination of business interests in restraint of trade. Compare CLAYTON ANTITRUST ACT.

Sher•pa (sher′pə, shûr′-), *n.*, *pl.* **-pas.** a member of a people living in the Himalayas of E Nepal.

sher•ry (sher′ē), *n.*, *pl.* **-ries.** a fortified, amber-colored wine. [< Sp (*vino de*) *Xeres* (wine of) Jerez, a city in Spain]

Sher′wood For′est, *n.* a forest in central England, chiefly in Nottinghamshire: the traditional haunt of Robin Hood.

she's (shēz), **1.** contraction of *she is.* **2.** contraction of *she has.*

shew (shō), *v.i.*, *v.t.*, **shewed, shewn, shew•ing,** *n.* *Archaic.* SHOW.

shib•bo•leth (shib′ə lith, -leth′), *n.* **1.** a peculiarity of pronunciation or usage that distinguishes a particular group. **2.** a slogan; catchword. [< Heb *shibbōleth* lit., freshet, a word used by the Gileadites as a test to detect the fleeing Ephraimites, who could not pronounce the sound *sh* (Judg. 12:4–6)]

shied (shīd), *v.* pt. and pp. of SHY.

shield (shēld), *n.* **1.** a broad piece of armor carried on the arm or in the hand. **2.** a person or thing that guards, protects, or defends. **3.** something shaped like a shield. —*v.t.* **4.** to protect or conceal with or as if with a shield. —**shield′er,** *n.*

shift (shift), *v.t.* **1.** to move from one place, position, or direction to another. **2.** to replace by another; exchange. **3.** to change (gears) from one ratio to another in a motor vehicle. —*v.i.* **4.** to move from one place, position, or direction to another. **5.** to manage to get along. **6.** to change gears in a motor vehicle. —*n.* **7.** a change or transfer from one place, position, or direction to another. **8. a.** a person's scheduled period of work. **b.** a group scheduled to work together during such a period. **9.** a gearshift. **10.** a straight, loose-fitting dress. **11.** an ingenious device for getting something done; expedient. **12.** an evasion or trick.

shift′less, *adj.* lacking incentive, ambition, or aspiration; lazy. —**shift′less•ness,** *n.*

shift′y, *adj.*, **-i•er, -i•est.** evasive or crafty. —**shift′i•ly,** *adv.* —**shift′i•ness,** *n.*

Shi•ite or **Shi•ite** (shē′īt), also **Shi′ah, Shi•′i** (shē ē′, shē′ē), *n.* a member of one of the divisions of Islam that regards Ali, the son in law of Muhammad, as the legitimate successor of Muhammad. Compare SUNNI (def. 1). —**Shi•′ism** (shē′iz əm), *n.* —**Shi•′it•ic** (shē it′ik), *adj.*

shill (shil), *n.* a person who poses as a customer in order to decoy others into participating, as at a gambling house.

shil•le•lagh (shə lā′lē, -lə), *n.* a cudgel.

shil•ling (shil′ing), *n.* **1.** a coin and former monetary unit of the United Kingdom, the 20th part of a pound, equal to 12 pence. **2.** the basic monetary unit of Kenya, Somalia, Tanzania, and Uganda.

shil•ly-shal•ly (shil′ē shal′ē), *v.i.*, **-shal•lied, -shal•ly•ing.** **1.** to show indecision or hesitation; vacillate. **2.** to waste time.

shim (shim), *n.* a thin wedge, as of wood, for driving into crevices or for leveling something.

Shim•e•i (shim′ē ī), *n.* a Benjamite who insulted David and disobeyed Solomon. II Sam. 16:5–13; I Kings 2:8.

shim•mer (shim′ər), *v.i.* **1.** to shine with or reflect a soft, tremulous light. —*n.* **2.** a soft, tremulous light. —**shim′mer•y,** *adj.*

shim•my (shim′ē), *n.*, *pl.* **-mies,** *v.*, **-mied, -my•ing.** —*n.* **1.** excessive wobbling in the front wheels of a motor vehicle. —*v.i.* **2.** to wobble excessively.

shin (shin), *n.*, *v.*, **shinned, shin•ning.** —*n.* **1.** the front part of the leg from the knee to the ankle. —*v.t.*, *v.i.* **2.** to climb (a pole, tree, etc.) by gripping with the legs after pulling oneself up with the hands.

shin′bone′, *n.* the tibia.

shin•dig (shin′dig′), *n.* *Informal.* an elaborate and usu. large party.

shine (shīn), *v.*, **shone** or, esp. for 6, **shined; shin•ing;** *n.* —*v.i.* **1.** to give forth or glow with light. **2.** to glisten or sparkle. **3.** to be outstanding; excel. —*v.t.* **4.** to cause to shine. **5.** to direct the light of (a lamp, mirror, etc.). **6.** to polish (shoes, silverware, etc.).

—*n.* **7.** radiance or brightness. **8.** a polish given to shoes. **9.** fair weather: *rain or shine.* —*Idiom.* **10.** **take a shine to,** to develop a liking for.

shin′er, *n.* *Informal.* BLACK EYE.

shin•gle¹ (shing′gəl), *n.*, *v.*, **-gled, -gling.** —*n.* **1.** a thin piece of wood, asbestos, etc., laid in overlapping rows to cover the roofs or outside walls of buildings. **2.** a small signboard. —*v.t.* **3.** to cover with shingles.

shin•gle² (shing′gəl), *n.* **1.** waterworn pebbles lying loose esp. on a beach. **2.** a beach or riverbank covered with shingle.

shin′gles, *n.* (*used with a sing. or pl. v.*) a viral disease characterized by skin eruptions and pain along the course of involved nerves.

shin′ny, *v.i.*, **-nied, -ny•ing.** to shin.

shin′ splints′, *n.* (*used with a pl. v.*) a painful condition of the front lower leg associated with strenuous activity.

Shin•to (shin′tō), *n.* the native religion of Japan, primarily a system of nature and ancestor worship. Also, **Shin′to•ism.** [< Japn: the way of the gods] —**Shin′to•ist,** *n.*, *adj.* —**Shin′to•is′tic,** *adj.*

shin•y (shī′nē), *adj.*, **-i•er, -i•est.** bright or glossy; shining. —**shin′i•ness,** *n.*

ship (ship), *n.*, *v.*, **shipped, ship•ping.** —*n.* **1.** a vessel, esp. a large oceangoing one, for navigating in water. **2.** the crew and passengers of a ship. **3.** an airship, airplane, or spacecraft. —*v.t.* **4.** to transport by ship, rail, truck, or plane. **5.** to take in (water) over the side of a ship. **6.** to put in place for use on a ship or boat: *Ship the oars.* **7.** to send away. —*v.i.* **8.** to go on board ship. —**ship′per,** *n.*

-ship, a suffix meaning: state or quality (*friendship*); office or position (*governorship*); rank or title (*lordship*); skill or art (*horsemanship*); all people involved (*ridership*).

ship′board′, *n.* **1.** the deck or side of a ship. **2.** a ship.

ship′build′er, *n.* one who designs or constructs ships. —**ship′build′ing,** *n.*

ship′mate′, *n.* a fellow sailor.

ship′ment (-mənt), *n.* **1.** the act of shipping something, as cargo, that is shipped.

ship′ping, *n.* **1.** the act or business of transporting goods. **2.** ships, esp. merchant ships, taken as a whole.

ship′shape′, *adj.* in good order; trim or tidy.

ship′wreck′, *n.* **1.** the destruction of a ship. **2.** the remains of a wrecked ship. **3.** ruin or destruction. —*v.i.*, *v.t.* **4.** to suffer or cause to suffer shipwreck.

ship′yard′, *n.* a place where ships are built or repaired.

shire (shī‵r), *n.* one of the counties of Great Britain.

shirk (shûrk), *v.t.*, *v.i.* to evade (work, duty, etc.). —**shirk′er,** *n.*

shirr (shûr), *v.t.* **1.** to draw up or gather (fabric) on parallel threads. **2.** to bake (eggs), esp. in individual dishes. —*n.* **3.** Also, **shirr′ing.** an ornamental gathering of fabric.

shirt (shûrt), *n.* **1.** a garment for the upper part of the body, usu. having a collar and a front opening. **2.** an undershirt. —*Idiom.* **3. keep one's shirt on,** *Informal.* to remain calm.

shirt′ing, *n.* fabric, as broadcloth, used to make shirts.

shirt′tail′, *n.* the part of a shirt below the waistline.

shirt′waist′, *n.* a tailored blouse for women.

shish ke•bab (shish′ kə bob′), *n.* cubes of meat, as lamb, broiled on a skewer.

shiv (shiv), *n.* *Slang.* a knife.

Shi•va (shē′və), *n.* "the Destroyer," the third member of the Hindu Trinity, along with Brahma and Vishnu.

shiv•er¹ (shiv′ər), *v.i.* **1.** to shake or tremble, as with cold or excitement. —*n.* **2.** a tremble or quiver. —**shiv′er•er,** *n.* —**shiv′er•y,** *adj.*

shiv•er² (shiv′ər), *v.t.*, *v.i.* to break or split into fragments.

shle•miel (shlə mēl′), *n.* SCHLEMIEL.

shlep (shlep), *v.t., v.i.,* **shlepped, shlep•ping,** *n.* SCHLEP.

shlock (shlok), *n.* SCHLOCK.

shmaltz (shmälts, shmålts), *n.* SCHMALTZ.

shoal[1] (shōl), *n.* **1.** a shallow place in a body of water. **2.** a sandbank or sand bar.

shoal[2] (shōl), *n.* **1.** a large number or group. **2.** a school of fish.

shoat (shōt), *n.* a young, weaned pig.

shock[1] (shok), *n.* **1.** a sudden or violent disturbance of the emotions or sensibilities. **2.** a sudden and violent blow or impact. **3.** gravely diminished blood circulation caused by severe trauma and characterized by pallor and weak pulse. **4.** the effect produced by the passage of an electric current through the body. **5.** a shock absorber. —*v.t.* **6.** to affect with intense surprise, horror, or outrage. **7.** to give an electric shock to.

shock[2] (shok), *n.* a thick, bushy mass, as of hair.

shock′ absorb′er, *n.* a device for damping sudden and rapid motion, as the recoil of a spring-mounted object from shock.

shock′er, *n.* **1.** a person or thing that shocks. **2.** a sensational novel, play, or movie.

shock′ing, *adj.* **1.** causing intense surprise, horror, or outrage. **2.** very bad.

shock′ jock′, *n.* a radio disc jockey who features offensive or controversial material.

shock′proof′, *adj.* capable of undergoing shock without damage.

shock′ ther′apy, *n.* the use of a drug or electricity to induce convulsions for symptomatic relief in certain mental disorders.

shock′ troops′, *n.pl.* troops specially trained for engaging in assault.

shod (shod), *v.* a pt. and pp. of SHOE.

shod•dy (shod′ē), *adj.,* **-di•er, -di•est,** *n., pl.* **-dies.** —*adj.* **1.** of inferior quality or workmanship. **2.** shabby. —*n.* **3. a.** fiber made of reclaimed wool. **b.** a low-grade fabric made from this. **4.** inferior products or merchandise. —**shod′di•ly,** *adv.* —**shod′di•ness,** *n.*

shoe (shoo), *n., v.,* **shod** or **shoed, shoe•ing.** —*n.* **1.** an external covering for the human foot. **2.** a horseshoe. **3.** the outer casing of an automobile tire. —*v.t.* **4.** to provide with a shoe or shoes.

shoe′horn′, *n.* a curved device used to make a shoe slip on more easily.

shoe′lace′, *n.* a string or lace for fastening a shoe.

shoe′mak′er, *n.* a person who makes or mends shoes.

shoe′string′, *n.* **1.** SHOELACE. **2.** a very small amount of money.

shoe′tree′, *n.* a foot-shaped device placed inside a shoe to preserve its shape.

sho•far (shō′fər; *Heb.* shô fär′), *n., pl.* **-fars,** *Heb.* **-froth, -frot** (-frôt′). *Judaism.* a ram's horn used as a wind instrument, sounded in Biblical times as a signal and in modern times at synagogue services on Rosh Hashanah and Yom Kippur.

shofar

sho•gun (shō′gən, -gun), *n.* one of the chief military commanders of Japan from the 8th to 12th centuries. —**sho′gun•ate** (-gə nit, -nāt′), *n.*

shone (shōn), *v.* a pt. and pp. of SHINE.

shoo (shoo), *interj., v.,* **shooed, shoo•ing.** —*interj.* **1.** (used to scare or drive away chickens, birds, etc.). —*v.t.* **2.** to drive away by shouting "shoo."

shoo′-in′, *n.* a candidate, competitor, etc., regarded as certain to win.

shook (shook), *v.* **1.** pt. of SHAKE. —*adj.* **2.** Also, **shook′ up′.** *Informal.* emotionally unsettled.

shoot (shoot), *v.,* **shot, shoot•ing,** *n.* —*v.t.* **1.** to hit, wound, or kill with a missile, as a bullet. **2.** to send forth (a missile) from a weapon. **3.** to discharge (a weapon). **4.** to send forth rapidly or suddenly. **5.** to direct toward a target or goal. **6.** to pass rapidly through, over, or down: *to shoot the rapids.* **7.** to emit (a ray, as of light). **8.** to variegate with streaks or flecks of another color. **9.** to thrust forward. **10.** to take a picture of; photograph. —*v.i.* **11.** to send forth a missile, as from a bow. **12.** to hunt with a gun for sport. **13.** to move or pass suddenly or swiftly. **14.** to put forth buds or shoots. **15.** to project; jut. **16.** to dart through the body, as pain. **17.** **shoot for** or **at,** to attempt to obtain or accomplish. **18.** **~ up,** to grow rapidly or suddenly. —*n.* **19.** a shooting expedition or contest. **20.** new or young growth from a plant. —**shoot′er,** *n.*

shoot′ing star′, *n.* METEOR (def. 1).

shoot′out′, *n.* a gunfight.

shop (shop), *n., v.,* **shopped, shop•ping.** —*n.* **1.** a retail store, esp. a small one. **2.** a workshop. **3.** a factory, office, or business. —*v.i.* **4.** to visit stores for the purpose of purchasing or examining goods. —*Idiom.* **5. talk shop,** to talk about a shared trade, profession, or business. —**shop′per,** *n.*

shop′keep′er, *n.* a person who owns or operates a shop.

shop′lift′er, *n.* a person who steals goods from a retail store. —**shop′lift′,** *v.t., v.i.*

shoppe (shop), *n.* a shop (used chiefly on store signs for quaint effect).

shop′ping cen′ter, *n.* a group of stores within a single complex, esp. in a suburban area.

shop′talk′, *n.* conversation about one's work or occupation.

shop′worn′, *adj.* worn or marred, as goods exposed and handled in a store.

shore[1] (shôr), *n.* the land along the edge of a sea, lake, or river.

shore[2] (shôr), *n., v.,* **shored, shor•ing.** —*n.* **1.** a supporting post or beam; prop. —*v.t.* **2.** to support with or as if with a shore; prop.

shore′bird′, *n.* a bird, as a plover, that frequents seashores.

shore′line′, *n.* the line where shore and water meet.

shore′ patrol′, *n.* U.S. Navy, Coast Guard, or Marine Corps personnel performing police duties on shore.

shorn (shôrn), *v.* a pp. of SHEAR.

short (shôrt), *adj.,* **-er, -est,** *adv., n., v.* —*adj.* **1.** having little length or height. **2.** brief in duration. **3.** concise, as writing. **4.** rudely brief; abrupt. **5.** not sufficient; scanty. **6.** not reaching a mark, target, or standard. **7.** made with a large amount of shortening; crisp and flaky. **8.** noting a sale of securities or commodities that the seller does not possess, depending for profit on a decline in prices. —*adv.* **9.** abruptly or suddenly. **10.** briefly; curtly. **11.** on the near side of an intended or particular point. —*n.* **12.** something that is short. **13. shorts, a.** short trousers. **b.** undershorts. **14.** SHORT CIRCUIT. **15.** SHORT SUBJECT. —*v.i., v.t.* **16.** to form a short circuit (in). —*Idiom.* **17. in short,** in brief. —**short′ness,** *n.*

short•age (shôr′tij), *n.* a deficiency in quantity.

short′bread′, *n.* a rich, short butter cookie.

short′cake′, *n.* a rich biscuit or cake topped with fruit and whipped cream.

short′change′, *v.t.,* **-changed, -chang•ing. 1.** to give less than the correct change to. **2.** to cheat; defraud.

short′ cir′cuit, *n.* a condition of relatively low resistance between two points of differing potential in an electric circuit, usu. resulting in a flow of excess current. —**short′-cir′cuit,** *v.t., v.i.*

short′com′ing, *n.* a defect or deficiency, as in conduct.

short′cut′, *n.* **1.** a shorter way to get somewhere. **2.** a quicker method of accomplishing something.

short′en, *v.t., v.i.* to make or become short or shorter.

short·en·ing (shôrt′ning, shôr′tn ing), *n.* a fat, as butter, used to make pastry or bread crisp and flaky.

short′hand′, *n.* a method of rapid handwriting using simple strokes, abbreviations, or symbols to designate letters, words, or phrases.

short′-hand′ed, *adj.* not having the necessary number of workers.

Short′horn′, *n.* one of an English breed of beef cattle with short horns.

short′-lived′ (līvd, livd), *adj.* living or lasting only a little while.

short′ly, *adv.* 1. in a short time; soon. 2. briefly; concisely.

short′ or′der, *n.* an order for food that can be quickly prepared. —**short′-or′der,** *adj.*

short′-range′, *adj.* of limited extent, as in distance or time.

short′ shrift′, *n.* little attention or consideration.

short′sight′ed, *adj.* 1. nearsighted. 2. lacking in foresight. —**short′sight′ed·ly,** *adv.* —**short′sight′ed·ness,** *n.*

short′stop′, *n. Baseball.* the player or position of the player covering the area between second and third base.

short′ sto′ry, *n.* a piece of prose fiction, usu. under 10,000 words.

short′ sub′ject, *n.* a short film, as one shown with a feature-length film.

short′-tem′pered, *adj.* having a quick, hasty temper; irascible.

short′-term′, *adj.* covering or involving a relatively short period of time.

short′ ton′, *n.* See under TON¹.

short′-waist′ed, *adj.* of less than average length between shoulders and waistline.

short′wave′, *n.* a radio wave corresponding to frequencies of over 1600 kilohertz that is used for long-distance reception or transmission.

short′-wind′ed, *adj.* short of breath.

Sho·sho·ne or **-ni** (shō shō′nē), *n., pl.* **-ne, -nes** or **-ni, -nis.** a member of an American Indian people or group living mainly in Nevada, Utah, Idaho, and Wyoming.

shot¹ (shot), *n., pl.* **shots** or, for 4, 5, **shot.** 1. the discharge of a weapon, as a firearm. 2. an act or instance of shooting. 3. reach or range. 4. small balls or pellets of lead for a shotgun. 5. **a.** a projectile for discharge from a firearm. **b.** such projectiles collectively. 6. a marksman. 7. a heavy metal ball used in the shot put. 8. a stroke or throw in certain games. 9. an attempt or try. 10. a hypodermic injection. 11. a photograph, esp. a snapshot. 12. *Motion Pictures, Television.* a single unit of action photographed without interruption by one camera.

shot² (shot), *v.* 1. pt. and pp. of SHOOT. —*adj.* 2. in hopelessly bad condition.

shot′gun′, *n.* a smoothbore gun for firing small shot.

shot′ put′, *n.* a field event in which a heavy metal ball is thrown for distance. —**shot′-put′ter,** *n.* —**shot′-put′ting,** *n.*

should (shŏŏd), *auxiliary v.* 1. pt. of SHALL. 2. (used to indicate duty, propriety, or expediency): *You should not do that.* 3. (used to express condition): *Were he to arrive, I should be pleased.*

shoul·der (shōl′dər), *n.* 1. the part of the human body, from the base of the neck to the upper arm, where the arm joins the trunk. 2. a corresponding part in animals. 3. a shoulderlike part or projection. 4. a border alongside a roadway. —*v.t.* 5. to push or carry with or as if with the shoulder. 6. to assume as a responsibility.

shoul′der blade′, *n.* SCAPULA.

should·n′t (shŏŏd′nt), contraction of *should not.*

shout (shout), *v.i., v.t.* 1. to call or cry out loudly. —*n.* 2. a loud call or cry. —**shout′er,** *n.*

shove (shuv), *v.,* **shoved, shov·ing,** *n.* —*v.t., v.i.* 1.

to push roughly or rudely. 2. **shove off,** to go away; depart. —*n.* 3. an act or instance of shoving.

shov·el (shuv′əl), *n., v.,* **-eled, -el·ing** or (*esp. Brit.*) **-elled, -el·ling.** —*n.* 1. an implement consisting of a scoop attached to a long handle, used for lifting or throwing loose matter. —*v.t.* 2. to take up and throw with a shovel. 3. to dig, move, or clear with or as if with a shovel. —*v.i.* 4. to use a shovel. —**shov′el·ful,** *n., pl.* **-fuls.**

show (shō), *v.,* **showed, shown** or **showed, showing,** *n.* —*v.t.* 1. to cause or allow to be seen; display. 2. to point out; indicate. 3. to guide; escort. 4. to make known; explain. 5. to reveal; demonstrate. 6. to offer; grant: *to show mercy.* —*v.i.* 7. to be or become visible. 8. to finish third, as in a horse race. 9. **show off, a.** to display to advantage. **b.** to present with pride. **c.** to seek attention by ostentatious behavior. 10. **~ up, a.** to come to a place; arrive. **b.** to make (another) seem inferior by comparison. —*n.* 11. a theatrical production or performance. 12. a radio or television program. 13. a public exhibition. 14. ostentatious and often false display. 15. third place, as in a horse race. 16. appearance; impression. —*Idiom.* 17. **show the flag,** to make one's presence known.

show′boat′, *n.* 1. a boat, esp. a paddle-wheel steamer, used as a traveling theater. —*v.i.* 2. to perform or behave flamboyantly.

show′case′, *n., v.,* **-cased, -cas·ing.** —*n.* 1. a glass case for displaying and protecting articles. 2. a setting or vehicle for displaying something on a trial basis. —*v.t.* 3. to exhibit to best advantage.

show′down′, *n.* a conclusive confrontation or settlement of a matter.

show·er (shou′ər), *n.* 1. a brief fall of rain, hail, or snow. 2. a bath in which water is sprayed on the body. 3. something resembling a shower. 4. a party at which presents are given to the honoree. —*v.t.* 5. to give or give to in abundance. —*v.i.* 6. to rain in a shower. 7. to bathe in a shower. —**show′er·y,** *adj.*

show′ing, *n.* 1. the act of putting something on display. 2. performance or record: *a good showing at the polls.*

show′man, *n., pl.* **-men.** 1. a theatrical producer. 2. a person gifted in dramatic presentation. —**show′man·ship′,** *n.*

shown (shōn), *v.* a pp. of SHOW.

show′-off′, *n.* a person given to showing off.

show′piece′, *n.* something worthy of being exhibited as a fine example of its kind.

show′place′, *n.* a place, as a mansion, notable for its beauty or historical interest.

show′room′, *n.* a room for the display of merchandise.

show′ win′dow, *n.* a display window in a store.

show′y, *adj.,* **-i·er, -i·est.** 1. making an imposing display. 2. ostentatious; gaudy. —**show′i·ly,** *adv.* —**show′i·ness,** *n.*

shpt., shipment.

shrank (shrangk), *v.* a pt. of SHRINK.

shrap·nel (shrap′nl), *n.* 1. fragments from a shell, mine, or bomb. 2. a hollow projectile containing bullets and a bursting charge that explodes in the air. [after its inventor, H. *Shrapnel* (1761–1842), English army officer]

shred (shred), *n., v.,* **shred·ded** or **shred, shred·ding.** —*n.* 1. a piece cut or torn off, esp. in a narrow strip. 2. a bit; scrap. —*v.t., v.i.* 3. to cut, tear, or fragment into shreds. —**shred′der,** *n.*

Shreve·port (shrēv′pôrt′), *n.* a city in NW Louisiana. 198,525.

shrew¹ (shrōō), *n.* a scolding woman; nag. —**shrew′ish,** *adj.*

shrew² (shrōō), *n.* a small, mouselike mammal with a long, sharp snout.

shrewd (shrōōd), *adj.,* **-er, -est.** 1. clever or sharp in practical matters. 2. marked by cleverness, perceptiveness, etc. —**shrewd′ly,** *adv.* —**shrewd′ness,** *n.*

shriek (shrēk), *n.* 1. a loud, sharp, shrill cry. —*v.i., v.t.* 2. to utter or utter with a shriek.

shrift (shrift), *n. Archaic.* 1. the imposition of penance by a priest. **2.** remission of sins granted after confession and penance.

shrike (shrīk), *n.* a predatory songbird with a sharply hooked bill that often impales its prey on thorns.

shrill (shril), *adj.*, **-er, -est,** *v.* —*adj.* **1.** high-pitched and piercing. —*v.t., v.i.* **2.** to cry shrilly. —**shrill′-ness,** *n.* —**shrill′ly,** *adv.*

shrimp (shrimp), *n., pl.* **shrimps** or, for 1, **shrimp. 1.** any of various small, chiefly marine, often edible crustaceans. **2.** a small or insignificant person.

shrine (shrīn), *n.* **1.** a place consecrated to a saint or deity. **2.** the tomb of a saint. **3.** a place or object hallowed by its history or associations. **4.** a receptacle for sacred relics.

shrink (shringk), *v.,* **shrank** or, often, **shrunk; shrunk** or **shrunk•en; shrink•ing;** *n.* —*v.i.* **1.** to contract in size. **2.** to become reduced, esp. in value. **3.** to draw back; recoil. —*v.t.* **4.** to cause to shrink. —*n.* **5.** *Slang.* a psychiatrist. —**shrink′a•ble,** *adj.*

shrink•age (shring′kij), *n.* **1.** the process of shrinking. **2.** the amount or degree of shrinking.

shrink′ing vi′olet, *n.* a shy or modest person.

shrink′-wrap′, *v.,* **-wrapped, -wrap•ping,** *n.* —*v.t.* **1.** to wrap and seal in a plastic film that when exposed to heat shrinks tightly around the thing it covers. —*n.* **2.** the plastic used to shrink-wrap something.

shrive (shrīv), *v.t.,* **shrove** or **shrived, shriv•en** or **shrived, shriv•ing. 1.** to impose penance on. **2.** to grant absolution to.

shriv•el (shriv′əl), *v.t., v.i.,* **-eled, -el•ing** or (*esp. Brit.*) **-elled, -el•ling.** to shrink and wrinkle, as from dryness.

shroud (shroud), *n.* **1.** a cloth in which a corpse is wrapped for burial. **2.** something that covers, conceals, or protects. **3.** any of the ropes that converge from a ship's masthead to keep the mast from swaying. —*v.t.* **4.** to hide from view; cover.

Shrove′ Tues′day, *n.* the Tuesday before Ash Wednesday.

shrub (shrub), *n.* a woody plant smaller than a tree, usu. having multiple permanent stems. —**shrub′by,** *adj.,* **-bi•er, -bi•est.**

shrub′ber•y, *n., pl.* **-ber•ies. 1.** a planting of shrubs. **2.** shrubs collectively.

shrug (shrug), *v.,* **shrugged, shrug•ging,** *n.* —*v.t., v.i.* **1.** to raise and contract (the shoulders), as to express ignorance or indifference. **2. shrug off, a.** to disregard; minimize. **b.** to rid oneself of. —*n.* **3.** the act of shrugging.

shrunk (shrungk), *v.* a pp. and pt. of SHRINK.

shrunk′en, *v.* a pp. of SHRINK.

shtick (shtik), *n. Slang.* a show-business routine or bit. [< Yiddish *shtik* pranks, whims, lit., piece]

shuck (shuk), *n.* **1.** a husk, as of corn, or shell, as of an oyster. —*v.t.* **2.** to remove the shucks from. **3.** to peel off; remove.

shud•der (shud′ər), *v.i.* **1.** to tremble convulsively, as from horror. —*n.* **2.** a convulsive trembling.

shuf•fle (shuf′əl), *v.,* **-fled, -fling,** *n.* —*v.i.* **1.** to walk or dance without lifting the feet. **2.** to intermix playing cards. —*v.t.* **3.** to move (the feet) along the ground or floor without lifting. **4.** to move this way and that or from one place to another. **5.** to rearrange in random order: *to shuffle playing cards.* —*n.* **6.** an act or instance of shuffling. —**shuf′fler,** *n.*

shuf′fle•board′, *n.* a game in which disks are pushed with cues toward scoring sections marked on a floor or deck.

shun (shun), *v.t.,* **shunned, shun•ning.** to take pains to keep away from; avoid.

shunt (shunt), *v.t., v.i.* **1.** to turn aside or out of the way. **2.** to switch (railroad rolling stock) from one track to another. —*n.* **3.** the act of shunting. **4.** a railroad switch.

shush (shush), *interj.* **1.** hush! —*v.t.* **2.** to order to be silent; hush.

shut (shut), *v.,* **shut, shut•ting.** —*v.t.* **1.** to move into a closed position. **2.** to close the doors of. **3.** to close by bringing together the parts of. **4.** to confine;

enclose. **5.** to cause to suspend operations: *The factory was shut down for two weeks.* —*v.i.* **6.** to become shut. **7. shut off, a.** to stop the passage of. **b.** to isolate; separate. **8. ~ out, a.** to keep from entering; exclude. **b.** to prevent (an opponent) from scoring. **9. ~ up,** to stop or cause to stop talking.

shut′down′, *n.* a suspension or stoppage of function or operation.

shut′eye′, *n. Slang.* sleep.

shut′-in′, *n.* a person confined by infirmity or disease to the house, a hospital, etc.

shut′out′, *n.* a game in which one side does not score.

shut′ter, *n.* **1.** a solid or louvered movable cover for a window or door. **2.** a mechanical device for opening and closing the aperture of a camera lens to expose the film. —*v.t.* **3.** to close or provide with shutters.

shut′ter•bug′, *n.* an amateur photographer.

shut•tle (shut′l), *n., v.,* **-tled, -tling.** —*n.* **1.** a device in a loom for passing the filling thread back and forth through the warp. **2.** a public conveyance, as a train, that travels back and forth at regular intervals over a short route. **3.** (*often cap.*) SPACE SHUTTLE. —*v.i., v.t.* **4.** to move or cause to move to and fro.

shut′tle•cock′, *n.* the conical feathered cork device used in badminton.

shy¹ (shī), *adj.,* **shy•er** or **shi•er, shy•est** or **shi•est,** *v.,* **shied, shy•ing.** —*adj.* **1.** bashful; retiring. **2.** easily frightened; timid. **3.** distrustful; wary. **4.** deficient; lacking. —*v.i.* **5.** to start back or aside in alarm. **6.** to draw back; recoil. —**shy′ly,** *adv.* —**shy′ness,** *n.*

shy² (shī), *v.t., v.i.,* **shied, shy•ing.** to throw with a swift, sudden movement.

shy•lock (shī′lok), *n.* a cruel moneylender.

shy•ster (shī′stər), *n.* a lawyer who uses unprofessional or questionable methods.

Si, *Chem. Symbol.* silicon.

S.I., Staten Island.

Si•am (sī am′, sī′am), *n.* former name of THAILAND.

Si•a•mese (sī′ə mēz′, -mēs′), *adj., n., pl.* **-mese.** —*adj.* **1.** of Siam or its inhabitants. —*n.* **2.** a native or inhabitant of Siam. **3.** THAI (def. 2).

Si′amese cat′, *n.* one of a breed of slender short-haired cats with blue eyes and a pale fawn or grayish body.

Si′amese twins′, *n.pl.* twins who are congenitally joined together.

Si•be•li•us (si bā′lē əs, -bāl′yəs;), *n.* **Jean (Julius Christian),** 1865–1957, Finnish composer.

Si•be•ri•a (sī bēr′ē ə), *n.* a part of the Russian Federation in N Asia, from the Ural Mountains to the Pacific. —**Si•be′ri•an,** *adj., n.*

sib•i•lant (sib′ə lənt), *adj.* **1.** of, producing, or being a hissing sound. —*n.* **2.** a sibilant speech sound, as (s).

sib•ling (sib′ling), *n.* a brother or sister.

sib•yl (sib′əl), *n.* a female prophet. —**sib′yl•line** (-ə lēn′, -līn′), *adj.*

sic (sik), *v.t.,* **sicked, sick•ing.** to incite (a dog) to attack.

sic (sēk; *Eng.* sik), *adv. Latin.* so; thus: used within brackets to indicate that a wording has been quoted exactly though it may appear incorrect.

Si•chuan (sich′wän′, sich′o͞o än′) also **Szechwan, Szechuan,** *n.* a province in S central China. 103,200,000.

Sic•i•ly (sis′ə lē), *n.* an Italian island in the Mediterranean. 5,141,343. —**Si•cil•ian** (si sil′yən), *n., adj.*

sick (sik), *adj.,* **-er, -est. 1.** not healthy; ill. **2.** affected with nausea. **3.** deeply affected, as with sorrow. **4.** mentally or emotionally unsound. **5.** gruesome; sadistic. **6.** of or for use during sickness: *sick benefits.* **7.** disgusted; chagrined. —**sick′ish,** *adj.*

sick′ bay′, *n.* a hospital or dispensary, esp. aboard ship.

sick′bed′, *n.* a sick person's bed.

sick′en, *v.t., v.i.* to make or become sick. —**sick′en•ing,** *adj.*

sick•le (sik′əl), *n.* a curved, hooklike blade mounted in a short handle, for cutting grain or grass.

sick′le cell′ ane′mia, *n.* a chronic hereditary anemia, primarily affecting blacks, in which oxygen-deficient blood cells assume a crescent shape.

sick′ly, *adj.,* **-li•er, -li•est. 1.** not well; ailing. **2.** of or arising from ill health. **3.** nauseating. **4.** maudlin; mawkish. **5.** faint or feeble.

sick′ness, *n.* **1.** a particular disease or malady. **2.** the state of being sick; illness. **3.** nausea.

sick′out′, *n.* an organized absence from work by employees on the pretext of sickness.

sick′room′, *n.* a room in which a sick person is confined.

side (sīd), *n., adj., v.,* **sid•ed, sid•ing. —***n.* **1.** one of the surfaces forming the outside of something. **2.** either of the two surfaces of a thin flat object, as a door. **3.** either of the two lateral parts or areas of a thing. **4.** the right or left half of the body. **5.** an aspect; phase. **6.** region, direction, or position with reference to a central point. **7.** one of two or more contesting teams or groups. **8.** the position or course of a person or group opposing another. **9.** line of descent through either parent. **10.** the space immediately adjacent: *Stand at my side.* —*adj.* **11.** at or on one side. **12.** from or toward one side. **13.** subordinate; incidental: *a side issue.* —*v.i.* **14. side with** (or **against**), to support (or oppose), as in a dispute. —*Idiom.* **15. side by side,** next to one another. **16. take sides,** to support one party in a dispute.

side′ arm′, *n.* a weapon, as a pistol, carried at the side or in the belt.

side′arm′, *adv.* **1.** with a swinging sideways motion of the arm at or below shoulder level. —*adj.* **2.** thrown or performed sidearm.

side′bar′, *n.* a short news feature alongside and highlighting a longer story.

side′board′, *n.* a piece of furniture, as in a dining room, for holding articles of table service.

side′burns′, *n.pl.* projections of the hairline forming a border in front of each ear.

side′car′, *n.* a one-passenger car attached to the side of a motorcycle.

side′ dish′, *n.* a food that accompanies a main course.

side′ effect′, *n.* an often adverse secondary effect, as of a drug.

side′kick′, *n.* **1.** a close friend. **2.** a confederate or assistant.

side′light′, *n.* an item of incidental information.

side′line′, *n.* **1.** a business or activity pursued in addition to one's primary business. **2.** an additional line of goods. **3.** either of the two lines defining the side boundaries of an athletic field or court.

side′long′, *adj.* **1.** directed to one side. —*adv.* **2.** toward the side; obliquely.

side′man′ (-man′, -mən), *n., pl.* **-men** (-men′, -mən). an instrumentalist in a jazz band or orchestra.

side′piece′, *n.* a piece forming a side or a part of a side of something.

si•de•re•al (sī dēr′ē əl), *adj.* of or determined by or from the stars.

side′sad′dle, *n.* **1.** a saddle for women on which the rider sits with both feet on the same side of the horse. —*adv.* **2.** on a sidesaddle.

side′show′, *n.* **1.** a minor show in connection with a principal one, as at a circus. **2.** a subordinate event or spectacle.

side′split′ting, *adj.* **1.** convulsively uproarious. **2.** extremely funny.

side′step′, *v.i., v.t.,* **-stepped, -step•ping. 1.** to step to one side (of). **2.** to dodge by or as if by stepping aside.

side′stroke′, *n.* a swimming stroke in which the body is turned sideways in the water, the hands pull alternately, and the legs perform a scissors kick.

side′swipe′, *v.,* **-swiped, -swip•ing,** *n.* —*v.t.* **1.** to strike with a glancing blow in passing. —*n.* **2.** a glancing blow in passing.

side′track′, *v.t., v.i.* **1.** to move from a main railroad track to a siding. **2.** to move or distract from a main subject or course. —*n.* **3.** a railroad siding.

side′walk′, *n.* a usu. paved walk at the side of a roadway.

side′wall′, *n.* the part of a pneumatic tire between the edge of the tread and the rim of the wheel.

side′ways′, *adv.* **1.** with one side forward. **2.** toward or from one side. —*adj.* **3.** moving, facing, or directed toward one side. Also, **side′wise′.**

sid′ing, *n.* **1.** a short railroad track opening onto a main track. **2.** any of several varieties of weatherproof facing for frame buildings.

si•dle (sīd′l), *v.i.,* **-dled, -dling.** to move sideways, esp. in a furtive manner.

SIDS, sudden infant death syndrome.

siege (sēj), *n.* **1.** the surrounding and attacking of a fortified place to compel its surrender. **2.** a series of besetting illnesses or troubles. **3.** a prolonged period of trouble.

si•er•ra (sē er′ə), *n., pl.* **-ras.** a chain of hills or mountains whose peaks suggest the teeth of a saw. [< Sp: lit., saw < L]

Si•er′ra Le•o′ne (lē ō′nē, lē ōn′), *n.* a republic in W Africa, 4,891,546.

Sier′ra Nevad′a, *n.* a mountain range in E California.

si•es•ta (sē es′tə), *n., pl.* **-tas.** a midday or afternoon rest or nap.

sieve (siv), *n.* a utensil with a meshed or perforated surface for sifting or straining.

sift (sift), *v.t.* **1.** to pass through a sieve. **2.** to scatter by means of a sieve. **3.** to separate by or as if by a sieve. **4.** to examine closely. —*v.i.* **5.** to pass or fall as if through a sieve. —**sift′er,** *n.*

sigh (sī), *v.i.* **1.** to let out the breath audibly, as from sorrow or weariness. **2.** to yearn or long; pine. —*n.* **3.** the act or sound of sighing.

sight (sīt), *n.* **1.** the power, faculty, or act of seeing. **2.** one's range of vision. **3.** a view; glimpse. **4.** something seen or worth seeing. **5.** one that is unusual, shocking, or distressing to see. **6.** a viewing device, as on a firearm, for aiding the eye in aiming. —*v.t.* **7.** to see or observe. **8.** to aim by a sight. —*Idiom.* **9. on sight,** immediately upon seeing. **10. out of sight, a.** *Informal.* exceedingly high. **b.** *Slang.* fantastic; marvelous. **11. sight unseen,** without previous examination. —*Proverb.* **12. Out of sight, out of mind,** one easily forgets persons or things that are not constantly noticeable.

sight′ed, *adj.* having functional vision; not blind.

sight′less, *adj.* unable to see; blind.

sight′ly, *adj.,* **-li•er, -li•est.** pleasing to the sight.

sight′-read′ (rēd), *v.t., v.i.,* **-read** (red), **-read•ing.** to read or perform without previous practice, rehearsal, or study. —**sight′-read′er,** *n.*

sight′see′ing, *n.* **1.** the act of visiting and seeing places and things of interest. —*adj.* **2.** participating in or used for sightseeing. —**sight′se′er,** *n.*

sig•ma (sig′mə), *n., pl.* **-mas.** the 18th letter of the Greek alphabet (Σ, σ, ς).

sign (sīn), *n.* **1.** a token; indication. **2.** a conventional mark, figure, or symbol used instead of the word or words it represents. **3.** a motion or gesture used to convey information. **4.** an inscribed board, placard, or plate bearing a warning, advertisement, etc. **5.** a trace; vestige. **6.** an omen; portent. **7.** one of the 12 divisions of the zodiac. —*v.t.* **8.** to affix a signature to. **9.** to write as a signature. **10.** to engage by written agreement. **11.** to communicate by means of a sign. —*v.i.* **12.** to write one's signature. **13. sign in** (or **out**), to record one's arrival (or departure) by signing a register. **14. ~ off, a.** to cease radio or television broadcasting. **b.** to indicate one's approval explicitly if not formally. **15. ~ up,** to enlist, as in an organization. —**sign′er,** *n.*

sig•nal (sig′nl), *n., adj., v.,* **-naled, -nal•ing** or (*esp. Brit.*) **-nalled, -nal•ling.** —*n.* **1.** something, as a gesture, that serves to indicate, warn, direct, or command. **2.** something agreed upon as the indication for concerted action. **3.** an electrical quantity or effect, as current or voltage, that can be varied to convey information. —*adj.* **4.** serving as a signal. **5.** notable; outstanding. —*v.t., v.i.* **6.** to make a signal (to). **7.** to communicate by a signal.

sig′nal•ize, *v.t.,* -**ized,** -**iz•ing. 1.** to make conspicuous. **2.** to point out particularly. —**sig′nal•i•za′tion,** *n.*

sig′nal•ly, *adv.* conspicuously; notably.

sig•na•to•ry (sig′nə tôr′ē), *n., pl.* -**ries.** one of the signers of a document.

sig•na•ture (sig′nə chər), *n.* **1.** a person's name as signed personally. **2.** *Music.* a sign or set of signs following a clef to indicate the key or the meter of a piece.

sign′board′, *n.* a board bearing a sign.

sig•net (sig′nit), *n.* a small seal, as on a finger ring.

sig•nif•i•cance (sig nif′i kəns), *n.* **1.** importance; consequence. **2.** meaning; import. **3.** the quality of being significant.

sig•nif′i•cant, *adj.* **1.** of consequence; important. **2.** having or expressing a meaning, esp. a special, secret, or disguised meaning. —**sig•nif′i•cant•ly,** *adv.*

signif′icant oth′er, *n.* **1.** a person, as a parent, who has great influence on one's behavior and self-esteem. **2.** a spouse or cohabiting lover.

sig′ni•fy′, *v.,* -**fied,** -**fy•ing.** —*v.t.* **1.** to make known by or as if by a sign. **2.** to mean; denote. —*v.i.* **3.** to be of importance. —**sig′ni•fi•ca′tion,** *n.*

sign′ of the cross′, *n.* a movement of the hand to indicate a cross, as from forehead to breast and left shoulder to right or, in the Eastern Orthodox Church, from right shoulder to left.

si•gnor (sēn yôr′, sin-), *n., pl.* -**gnors,** -**gno•ri** (-yôr′ē). an Italian term of address for a man, equivalent to *sir* or *Mr.*

si•gno•ra (sēn yôr′ə, sin-), *n., pl.* -**gno•ras,** -**gno•re** (-yôr′ā). an Italian term of address for a married woman, equivalent to *Mrs.*

si•gno•ri•na (sēn′yô rē′nə), *n., pl.* -**nas,** -**ne** (-nā). an Italian term of address for a girl or unmarried woman.

sign′post′, *n.* a post bearing a sign.

Sikh (sēk), *n.* a member of a monotheistic religion of India that refuses to recognize the Hindu caste system. —**Sikh′ism,** *n.*

si•lage (sī′lij), *n.* fodder preserved through fermentation in a silo.

Si•las (sī′ləs), *n.* a prophet who accompanied Barnabas and the Apostle Paul to Antioch. Acts 15:22–35.

si•lence (sī′ləns), *n., v.,* -**lenced,** -**lenc•ing. 1.** absence of sound or noise. **2.** the state of being silent. **3.** absence or omission of mention. **4.** secrecy. —*v.t.* **5.** to put or bring to silence; still. **6.** to put (doubts, fears, etc.) to rest.

si′lenc•er, *n.* a device for deadening the report of a firearm.

si′lent, *adj.* **1.** making no sound. **2.** refraining from speech. **3.** speechless; mute. **4.** not inclined to speak. **5.** unspoken; tacit. **6.** (of a letter) not pronounced, as the *b* in *doubt.* **7.** (of a film) not having a soundtrack. —**si′lent•ly,** *adv.*

Si′lent Cal′ (kal), *n.* nickname of Calvin Coolidge.

si′lent major′ity, *n.* the majority of a country's citizens, regarded as not politically vocal.

sil•hou•ette (sil′ōō et′), *n., v.,* -**et•ted,** -**et•ting.** —*n.* **1.** a representation of the outline of an object, as a person's profile, filled in with black or another color. **2.** the outline of something. —*v.t.* **3.** to show in or as if in a silhouette.

sil•i•ca (sil′i kə), *n., pl.* -**cas.** the dioxide form of silicon occurring esp. as quartz sand, flint, and agate. —**si•li•ceous** (sə lish′əs), *adj.*

sil′i•cate (-kit, -kāt′), *n.* a mineral, as quartz, consisting of silicon and oxygen with a metal.

sil′i•con (-kən, -kon′), *n.* a nonmetallic element occurring in a combined state in minerals and rocks and constituting more than one fourth of the earth's crust. *Symbol:* Si; *at. wt.:* 28.086; *at. no.:* 14.

sil′i•cone′ (-kōn′), *n.* any of a number of polymers containing alternate silicon and oxygen atoms, very

resistant to heat and water: used in adhesives, lubricants, etc.

Sil′icon Val′ley, *n.* an area in N California where high-technology companies in the semiconductor industry are concentrated.

sil′i•co′sis (-kō′sis), *n.* a lung disease caused by the inhaling of silica particles.

silk (silk), *n.* **1.** the soft, lustrous fiber obtained from the cocoon of the silkworm. **2.** thread or cloth made from silk. **3.** a fiber or filament resembling silk. —**silk′en,** *adj.* —**silk′y,** *adj.,* -**i•er,** -**i•est.**

silk′screen′, *n.* **1.** a printmaking technique in which color is forced through the pores of a mesh cloth in areas not blocked out by a glue sizing. —*v.t.* **2.** to print by silkscreen.

silk′worm′, *n.* any of several moth caterpillars that spin a silken cocoon.

sill (sil), *n.* a horizontal member forming the bottom of a window or door.

sil•ly (sil′ē), *adj.,* -**li•er,** -**li•est. 1.** lacking good sense; stupid or foolish. **2.** absurd; ridiculous. **3.** stunned; dazed: *knocked me silly.* —**sil′li•ness,** *n.*

si•lo (sī′lō), *n., pl.* -**los. 1.** a pit or cylindrical structure in which fodder or forage is kept. **2.** an underground installation that houses a ballistic missile.

Si•lo•am (si lō′əm, sī-), *n.* a spring near Jerusalem. John 9:7.

silt (silt), *n.* **1.** earthy matter or fine sand carried by water and deposited as sediment. —*v.t., v.i.* **2.** to fill or choke up with silt. —**silt′y,** *adj.*

Si•lu•ri•an (si lŏŏr′ē ən, sī-), *adj.* of or noting the third period of the Paleozoic Era, marked by the advent of land plants.

sil•ver (sil′vər), *n.* **1.** a white, ductile metallic element used for making coins, table utensils, etc. *Symbol:* Ag; *at. wt.:* 107.870; *at. no.:* 47. **2.** coins made of silver. **3.** silverware. **4.** a lustrous grayish white. —*adj.* **5.** made of or plated with silver. **6.** of the color silver. **7.** eloquent; persuasive. —*v.t.* **8.** to coat with or as if with silver. —*Idiom.* **9.** thirty pieces of silver, payment for a betrayal. Matt. 26:14-16.

sil′ver bul′let, *n.* a quick solution to a difficult problem. [from the belief that supernatural beings, as werewolves, can be killed with a silver bullet]

sil′ver•fish′, *n.* a wingless, silvery-gray insect that feeds on starch, damaging books, wallpaper, etc.

sil′ver lin′ing, *n.* a prospect of hope or comfort.

sil′ver med′al, *n.* a medal, traditionally of silver, awarded to a person or team finishing second in a competition. Compare BRONZE MEDAL, GOLD MEDAL. —**sil′ver med′alist,** *n.*

sil′ver ni′trate, *n.* a corrosive, poisonous powder used in making photographic emulsions and as an antiseptic and astringent.

sil′ver•smith′, *n.* a person who makes and repairs articles of silver.

sil′ver-tongued′, *adj.* persuasive; eloquent.

sil′ver•ware′, *n.* articles, esp. eating utensils, made of silver, silver-plated metals, or stainless steel.

sil′ver•y, *adj.* **1.** resembling silver in luster or color. **2.** having a clear, ringing sound.

Sim•e•on (sim′ē ən), *n.* **1.** a son of Jacob and Leah. Gen. 29:33. **2.** one of the 12 tribes of Israel.

sim•i•an (sim′ē ən), *adj.* **1.** of or characteristic of an ape or monkey. —*n.* **2.** an ape or monkey.

sim•i•lar (sim′ə lər), *adj.* characterized by likeness or resemblance. —**sim′i•lar′i•ty,** *n., pl.* -**ties.** —**sim′i•lar•ly,** *adv.*

sim•i•le (sim′ə lē), *n., pl.* -**les.** a figure of speech in which two distinct things are compared by using "like" or "as," as in "a mouth like a rosebud." [< L: image, likeness]

si•mil•i•tude (si mil′i tōōd′, -tyōōd′), *n.* likeness; resemblance.

Si•mi′ Val′ley (si mē′, sē′mē), *n.* a city in SW California. 106,949.

sim•mer (sim′ər), *v.i.* **1.** to cook just at or below the boiling point. **2.** to be in a state of barely contained agitation. —*v.t.* **3.** to keep just at or below the boiling point. **4. simmer down,** to become calm or quiet. —*n.* **5.** the state or process of simmering.

Si•mon (sī′mən), *n.* **1.** the original name of the apostle Peter. Compare PETER. **2.** (*"Simon the Canaanite"* or *"Simon the Zealot"*) one of the 12 apostles. Matt. 10:4; Mark 3:18; Luke 6:15. **3.** a relative, perhaps a brother, of Jesus: sometimes identified with Simon the Canaanite. Matt. 13:55; Mark 6:3. **4.** (*"Simon Magus"*) a Samaritan sorcerer who was converted by the apostle Philip. Acts 8:9–24.

si•mon•ize (sī′mə nīz′), *v.t.,* **-ized, -iz•ing.** to polish, esp. with wax. [after *Simoniz,* trademark of an automobile wax]

Si′mon Pe′ter, *n.* PETER¹ (def. 1).

si′mon-pure′ (sī′mən), *adj.* untainted; pure.

si•mo•ny (sī′mə nē, sim′ə-), *n.* the buying or selling of ecclesiastical preferments or benefices.

sim•pa•ti•co (sim pä′ti kō′, -pat′i-), *adj.* congenial or like-minded.

sim•per (sim′pər), *v.i.* **1.** to smile in a silly, self-conscious way. —*n.* **2.** a silly, self-conscious smile.

sim•ple (sim′pəl), *adj.,* **-pler, -plest. 1.** not difficult; easy. **2.** not elaborate, complicated, or ornate; plain. **3.** not affected; unassuming. **4.** mere; bare: *the simple truth.* **5.** humble or lowly. **6.** lacking intelligence or sense. **7.** naive; artless. **8.** *Chem.* composed of only one substance or element. **9.** *Bot.* not divided. **10.** *Zool.* not compound. —**sim′ple•ness,** *n.*

sim′ple in′terest, *n.* interest payable only on the principal.

sim′ple-mind′ed, *adj.* **1.** lacking in complexity or subtlety; artless or unsophisticated. **2.** mentally deficient.

sim′ple•ton (-tən), *n.* a foolish person.

sim•plic•i•ty (-plis′i tē), *n., pl.* **-ties. 1.** freedom from complexity or intricacy. **2.** absence of luxury or pretentiousness; plainness. **3.** freedom from guile; artlessness. **4.** lack of mental acuteness.

sim′pli•fy′ (-plə fī′), *v.t.,* **-fied, -fy•ing.** to make simple or simpler. —**sim′pli•fi•ca′tion,** *n.*

sim•plis′tic (-plis′tik), *adj.* characterized by excessive simplification. —**sim•plis′ti•cal•ly,** *adv.*

sim′ply, *adv.* **1.** in a simple manner. **2.** merely; only. **3.** absolutely; really.

Simp•son (simp′sən), *n.* **Albert Benjamin,** 1844–1919, U.S. clergyman, founder of the Christian and Missionary Alliance.

sim•u•late (sim′yə lāt′), *v.t.,* **-lat•ed, -lat•ing. 1.** to create a model of. **2.** to make a pretense of; feign. **3.** to create the appearance or characteristics of: *simulated leather.* —**sim′u•la′tion,** *n.* —**sim′u•la′tor,** *n.*

si•mul•cast (sī′məl kast′, -käst′), *n., v.,* **-cast, -cast•ed, -cast•ing.** —*n.* **1.** a program broadcast simultaneously on radio and television. —*v.t., v.i.* **2.** to broadcast (in) a simulcast.

si•mul•ta•ne•ous (sī′məl tā′nē əs), *adj.* existing, occurring, or operating at the same time. —**si′mul•ta′ne•ous•ly,** *adv.*

sin (sin), *n., v.,* **sinned, sin•ning.** —*n.* **1.** a transgression of divine law. **2.** a willful violation of a moral principle. **3.** a serious fault or offense. —*v.i.* **4.** to commit a sin. —**sin′ful,** *adj.* —**sin′ner,** *n.*

Si•nai (sī′nī, sī′nē ī′), *n.* **1.** Also called **Si′nai Penin′sula.** a peninsula in NE Egypt, at the N end of the Red Sea between the Gulf of Suez and the Gulf of Aqaba. **2. Mount,** the mountain, of uncertain identity, on which Moses received the Law. Ex. 19.

Si•na•tra (si nä′trə), *n.* **Frank,** 1915–98, U.S. singer.

since (sins), *adv.* **1.** from then until now. **2.** after a particular past time; subsequently. **3.** before now; ago: *long since.* —*prep.* **4.** continuously from. **5.** between a past time and the present. —*conj.* **6.** in the period following the time when. **7.** inasmuch as; because.

sin•cere (sin sēr′), *adj.,* **-cer•er, -cer•est. 1.** free of deceit or hypocrisy. **2.** genuine; real. —**sin•cere′ly,** *adv.* —**sin•cer′i•ty** (-ser′i tē), *n.*

si•ne•cure (sī′ni kyŏŏr′, sin′i-), *n.* an office or position that pays well but requires little or no work.

si•ne di•e (sī′nē dī′ē, sin′ā dē′ā), *adv.* without fix-

ing a day for future action. [< L: without (a fixed) day]

si•ne qua non (sin′ā kwä nōn′, non′, kwä), *n.* an indispensable condition or element. [< LL: without which not]

sin•ew (sin′yōō), *n.* **1.** a tendon. **2.** strength; power. —**sin′ew•y,** *adj.*

sing (sing), *v.,* **sang** or, often, **sung; sung; sing•ing.** —*v.i.* **1.** to use the voice to produce musical sounds. **2.** to make a whistling, ringing, or whizzing sound. **3.** to produce a melodious sound: *nightingales singing.* **4.** *Slang.* to confess or act as an informer. —*v.t.* **5.** to utter with musical modulations of the voice. **6.** to proclaim enthusiastically: *sang his praises.* **7.** to chant or intone: *to sing mass.* —**sing′a•ble,** *adj.* —**sing′er,** *n.*

sing., singular.

Sin•ga•pore (sing′gə pôr′, sing′ə-), *n.* an island republic in the South China Sea, off the S tip of the Malay Peninsula. 3,461,929. —**Sin′ga•po′re•an,** *n., adj.*

singe (sinj), *v.,* **singed, singe•ing,** *n.* —*v.t.* **1.** to burn superficially or slightly; scorch. **2.** to remove hair, bristles, feathers, or down from by subjecting to flame. —*n.* **3.** a superficial burn. **4.** the act of singeing.

Singh (siN′h²), *n.* **Sadhu Sundar,** 1889–1929, Sikh Christian evangelist in India.

sin•gle (sing′gəl), *adj., v.,* **-gled, -gling.** —*adj.* **1.** one only; sole. **2.** intended or suitable for one person only. **3.** not married. **4.** consisting of only one part, element, or member. **5.** separate, particular, or distinct; individual. —*v.t.* **6.** to pick or choose (one) from others. —*v.i.* **7.** to hit a single in baseball. —*n.* **8.** a single person or thing; individual. **9.** an accommodation or ticket for one person only. **10.** an unmarried person. **11.** a one-dollar bill. **12.** (in baseball) a hit that enables a batter to reach first base. **13. singles,** (*used with a sing. v.*) a match, as in tennis, with one player on each side.

sin′gle-breast′ed, *adj.* (of a coat, jacket, etc.) having a center closure with a narrow overlap and a single button or row of buttons.

sin′gle file′, *n.* a line of persons or things one behind the other.

sin′gle-hand′ed, *adj.* **1.** accomplished by one person alone. **2.** by one's own effort; unaided. —*adv.* **3.** by one person alone; without aid. —**sin′gle-hand′ed•ly,** *adv.*

sin′gle-is′sue pol′itics, *n.* reduction of political discussion to one issue.

sin′gle-mind′ed, *adj.* having or showing a single aim or purpose. —**sin′gle-mind′ed•ly,** *adv.* —**sin′gle-mind′ed•ness,** *n.*

sin′gle•ton (-tən), *n.* a playing card that is the only one of a suit in a hand.

sin′gle-track′, *adj.* ONE-TRACK.

sin′gle-tree′, *n.* WHIFFLETREE.

sin′gly, *adv.* **1.** separately. **2.** one at a time. **3.** single-handed.

sing′song′, *n.* a monotonous, rhythmical rising and falling in pitch of the voice when speaking.

sin′gu•lar (-gyə lər), *adj.* **1.** extraordinary; remarkable. **2.** strange; odd. **3.** unique. **4.** of or belonging to the grammatical category denoting one person, place, thing, or instance. —*n.* **5.** the singular number. **6.** a form in the singular. —**sin′gu•lar′i•ty,** *n.* —**sin′gu•lar•ly,** *adv.*

Sin•ha•lese (sin′hə lēz′, -lēs′), *n., pl.* **-lese,** *adj.* —*n.* **1.** a member of a people comprising the majority of the inhabitants of Sri Lanka. **2.** the language of the Sinhalese. —*adj.* **3.** of the Sinhalese or their language.

sin•is•ter (sin′ə stər), *adj.* **1.** threatening or portending evil; ominous. **2.** evil or malevolent; wicked.

sink (singk), *v.,* **sank** or, often, **sunk; sunk** or **sunk•en; sink•ing;** *n.* —*v.i.* **1.** to fall, drop, or descend gradually to a lower level, position, or state. **2.** to fail in physical strength or health. **3.** to decrease in amount, extent, or intensity. **4.** to become lower in volume or pitch. **5.** to slope downward; dip. —*v.t.* **6.**

to cause to sink. **7.** to cause to penetrate. **8.** to dig or excavate (a shaft, well, etc.). **9.** to invest, esp. with the hope of profit. **10. sink in,** to enter or permeate the mind. —*n.* **11.** a basin connected with a water supply and drainage system. **12.** SINKHOLE (def. 2). **13.** a drain or sewer. **14.** a cesspool. —**sink′a•ble,** *adj.*

sink′er, *n.* **1.** one that sinks. **2.** a weight for sinking a fishing line or net.

sink′hole′, *n.* **1.** a hole in soluble rock through which surface water drains into an underground passage. **2.** a depressed area in which waste or drainage collects.

sink′ing fund′, *n.* a fund for extinguishing an indebtedness.

Sinn Fein (shin′ fān′), *n.* an Irish nationalist organization founded about 1905, existing today as the political wing of the Irish Republican Army. —**Sinn′ Fein′er,** *n.*

Sino-, a combining form meaning China or Chinese (*Sino-Tibetan*).

sin•u•ous (sin′yo͞o əs), *adj.* having many curves or turns; winding. —**sin′u•os′i•ty** (-os′i tē), *n.*

si•nus (sī′nəs), *n.* **1.** a bodily cavity or passage, as a channel for venous blood. **2.** one of the hollow cavities in the skull connecting with the nasal cavities.

si′nus•i′tis (-nə sī′tis), *n.* inflammation of a sinus, esp. of the skull.

Sioux (so͞o), *n., pl.* **Sioux** (so͞o, so͞oz). DAKOTA (defs. 3, 4).

Sioux′ Falls′, *n.* a city in SE South Dakota. 109,174.

sip (sip), *v.,* **sipped, sip•ping,** *n.* —*v.t., v.i.* **1.** to drink a little at a time. —*n.* **2.** an act or instance of sipping. **3.** a quantity taken by sipping. —**sip′per,** *n.*

si•phon (sī′fən), *n.* **1.** a U-shaped pipe that uses atmospheric pressure to draw liquid from one container, place, or level to another. —*v.t., v.i.* **2.** to draw or pass through or as if through a siphon.

sir (sûr), *n.* **1.** a respectful or formal term of address for a man, used without the name. **2.** (*cap.*) the distinctive title of a knight or baronet.

sire (sī″r), *n., v.,* **sired, sir•ing.** —*n.* **1.** the male parent of a quadruped. **2.** a respectful term of address for a male sovereign. **3.** *Archaic.* a father or forefather. —*v.t.* **4.** to beget; procreate.

si•ren (sī′rən), *n.* **1.** any of several beings in Greek legend, part woman and part bird, whose seductive singing lured mariners to destruction. **2.** a seductively beautiful woman. **3.** an acoustical device that produces a loud piercing sound and is used esp. as a warning signal.

sir•loin (sûr′loin), *n.* the portion of the loin of beef in front of the rump.

si•roc•co (sə rok′ō), *n., pl.* **-cos.** a hot, dry, dust-laden wind blowing from N Africa and affecting parts of S Europe.

sir•up (sir′əp, sûr′-), *n.* SYRUP.

sis (sis), *n.* sister.

si•sal (sī′səl, sis′əl), *n.* a fiber yielded by an agave and used esp. for making rope or rugs.

Sis•er•a (sis′ər ə), *n.* a commander of the Canaanite army: killed by Jael. Judg. 4:14–22.

sis•sy (sis′ē), *n., pl.* **-sies. 1.** an effeminate boy or man. **2.** a timid person. —**sis′si•fied′** (-ə fīd′), *adj.*

sis•ter (sis′tər), *n.* **1.** a female having both parents in common with another offspring. **2.** HALF SISTER. **3.** STEPSISTER. **4.** a woman connected, as by race, to another. **5.** a female member of a religious order. —*adj.* **6.** being in close relationship with another: *our sister cities.* —**sis′ter•ly,** *adj.*

sis′ter•hood′, *n.* **1.** the state of being a sister. **2.** a group or organization of sisters.

sis′ter-in-law′, *n., pl.* **sis•ters-in-law. 1.** the sister of one's spouse. **2.** the wife of one's brother. **3.** the wife of the brother of one's spouse.

Sis•y•phus (sis′ə fəs), *n.* a legendary ruler of Corinth punished by being compelled to roll up a slope a stone that always rolls back down again.

sit (sit), *v.,* **sat, sat, sit•ting.** —*v.i.* **1.** to rest with the body supported by the buttocks. **2.** to be located or

situated. **3.** to pose, as for an artist. **4.** to remain quiet or inactive. **5.** (of a bird) to cover eggs for hatching. **6.** to occupy an official seat, as a legislator. **7.** to be convened or in session. **8.** to baby-sit. **9.** to have a particular effect. —*v.t.* **10.** to cause to sit. **11.** to keep one's seat on (an animal, esp. a horse). **12. sit in on,** to be a spectator, observer, or visitor at. **13. ~ out,** to fail to participate in. **14. ~ up, a.** to be awake and active after one's usual sleep time. **b.** to become interested; take notice. —**sit′ter,** *n.*

si•tar (si tär′), *n.* an Indian lute with a pear-shaped body and a long, fretted neck. —**si•tar′ist,** *n.*

sit•com (sit′kom′), *n. Informal.* a situation comedy.

sit′-down′, *n.* a strike in which workers occupy their place of employment and refuse to work.

site (sīt), *n.* position or location, as of a town or building.

sit′-in′, *n.* an organized protest in which demonstrators occupy and refuse to leave a public place.

sit′ting, *n.* **1.** the act of one that sits. **2.** a period of being seated. **3.** a session, as of a court or legislature.

sit′ting duck′, *n.* a helpless or easy target or victim.

sit•u•ate (sich′o͞o āt′), *v.t.,* **-at•ed, -at•ing.** to put in or on a particular site or place; locate.

sit′u•a′tion, *n.* **1.** location or position. **2.** state of affairs; circumstances. **3.** a position of employment; job.

sit′ua′tion com′edy, *n.* a television comedy series consisting of episodes with a fixed group of characters.

sit′-up′, *n.* an exercise in which a person lies on the back, rises to a sitting position, and then lies flat again without changing leg position.

sitz′ bath′ (sits, zits), *n.* a bath in which only the thighs and hips are immersed.

six (siks), *n.* **1.** a cardinal number, five plus one. **2.** a symbol for this number, as 6 or VI. —*adj.* **3.** amounting to six in number. —*Idiom.* **4. at sixes and sevens, a.** in disorder or confusion. **b.** in disagreement or dispute. **5. six of one and half dozen of the other,** both work out to be the same. —**sixth,** *adj., n.*

six′-pack′, *n.* a package of six items, as cans of beer, sold as a unit.

six′-shoot′er (-sho͞o′tər, -sho͞o′-), *n.* a revolver that can fire six shots without being reloaded.

six′teen′, *n.* **1.** a cardinal number, ten plus six. **2.** a symbol for this number, as 16 or XVI. —*adj.* **3.** amounting to 16 in number. —**six′teenth′,** *adj., n.*

sixth′ sense′, *n.* the power of intuition.

six′ty, *n., pl.* **-ties,** *adj.* —*n.* **1.** a cardinal number, ten times six. **2.** a symbol for this number, as 60 or LX. —*adj.* **3.** amounting to 60 in number. —**six′ti•eth,** *adj., n.*

siz•a•ble or **size•a•ble** (sī′zə bəl), *adj.* of considerable size; fairly large.

size¹ (sīz), *n., v.,* **sized, siz•ing.** —*n.* **1.** spatial dimensions, proportions, magnitude, or extent. **2.** one of a series of graduated measures for articles of manufacture or trade. —*v.t.* **3.** to separate or sort according to size. **4. size up,** to form an estimate of; judge.

size² (sīz), *n., v.,* **sized, siz•ing.** —*n.* **1.** a gelatinous or glutinous substance used for filling pores in surfaces, as of cloth or paper. —*v.t.* **2.** to coat or treat with size.

sized, *adj.* having a specified size: *middle-sized.*

siz′ing, *n.* SIZE².

siz•zle (siz′əl), *v.,* **-zled, -zling,** *n.* —*v.i.* **1.** to make a hissing sound, as in frying. **2.** to be very hot. **3.** to be very angry. —*n.* **4.** a sizzling sound.

S.J., Society of Jesus.

SK, Saskatchewan.

skate¹ (skāt), *n., v.,* **skat•ed, skat•ing.** —*n.* **1.** ICE SKATE. **2.** ROLLER SKATE. —*v.i.* **3.** to glide or move on or as if on skates. —**skat′er,** *n.*

skate² (skāt), *n., pl.* **skates, skate.** a ray with wing-like pectoral fins.

skate′board′, *n.* **1.** a board mounted on roller-skate wheels. —*v.i.* **2.** to ride a skateboard.

ske•dad•dle (ski dad′l), *v.i.*, **-dled, -dling.** *Informal.* to run away hurriedly; flee.

skeet (skēt), *n.* a form of trapshooting in which targets are hurled so as to simulate the angles of flight taken by game birds.

skein (skān), *n.* a loose coil of thread or yarn.

skel•e•ton (skel′i tn), *n.* **1.** the bones of a vertebrate that form the body's internal framework. **2.** a supporting framework, as of a building. **3.** an outline, as of a literary work. [< Gk: mummy] —**skel′e•tal,** *adj.*

skel′eton key′, *n.* a key that opens various simple locks.

skep•tic (skep′tik), *n.* **1.** a person who questions the validity or truth of religion or religious tenets. **2.** a person with a doubting attitude. **3.** one who maintains that real knowledge is impossible. —**skep′ti•cal,** *adj.* —**skep′ti•cal•ly,** *adv.*

skep′ti•cism (-tə siz′əm), *n.* **1.** a questioning or doubting attitude. **2.** doubt regarding religion. **3.** the philosophical doctrine or belief that real knowledge is impossible.

sketch (skech), *n.* **1.** a simply or hastily executed drawing. **2.** a rough plan or draft, as of a book. **3.** a short piece of writing, often descriptive. **4. a.** a short comic routine. **b.** a brief dramatic scene. —*v.i., v.t.* **5.** to make a sketch (of). —**sketch′y,** *adj.,* **-i•er, -i•est.** —**sketch′i•ly,** *adv.* —**sketch′i•ness,** *n.*

skew (skyōō), *v.i., v.t.* **1.** to turn aside; swerve or slant. —*n.* **2.** a slanting movement, direction, or position.

skew′er, *n.* **1.** a long pin for holding together pieces of meat while they cook. —*v.t.* **2.** to fasten with or as if with a skewer.

ski (skē), *n., pl.* **skis, ski,** *v.,* **skied, ski•ing.** —*n.* **1.** one of a pair of long, slender runners used in gliding over snow. **2.** WATER SKI. —*v.i.* **3.** to travel on skis. —*v.t.* **4.** to travel on skis over. —**ski′er,** *n.*

skid (skid), *n., v.,* **skid•ded, skid•ding.** —*n.* **1.** a plank, bar, or platform on which something can be slid, rolled along, or stored. **2.** a plank on or by which a load is supported. **3.** a device for preventing a wheel from rotating. **4.** an unexpected or uncontrollable sideways slide on a surface. —*v.i.* **5.** to slide without rotating, as a wheel. **6.** to slip or slide, esp. sideways; lose traction.

skid′ row′, *n.* a run-down urban area frequented by alcoholics and vagrants.

skiff (skif), *n.* a small, light sailboat or rowboat.

ski′ lift′, *n.* a usu. motor-driven device that carries skiers up a slope.

skill (skil), *n.* **1.** the ability to do something well. **2.** expertness or dexterity in performance. **3.** a craft, trade, or job, esp. one requiring manual dexterity. —**skilled,** *adj.* —**skill′ful,** *adj.* —**skill′ful•ly,** *adv.*

skil•let (skil′it), *n.* a frying pan.

skim (skim), *v.,* **skimmed, skim•ming.** —*v.t.* **1. a.** to remove (floating matter) from the surface of a liquid. **b.** to clear (liquid) thus: *to skim milk.* **2.** to move lightly over or along. **3.** to read superficially or hastily. —*v.i.* **4.** to move lightly over, along, or near a surface. **5.** to read something superficially or hastily.

skim′ milk′, *n.* milk with the cream removed.

skimp (skimp), *v.i., v.t.* to scrimp.

skimp′y, *adj.,* **-i•er, -i•est.** lacking in size or fullness; scanty. —**skimp′i•ly,** *adv.* —**skimp′i•ness,** *n.*

skin (skin), *n., v.,* **skinned, skin•ning.** —*n.* **1.** the external covering of an animal body. **2.** a pelt or hide. **3.** an outer covering, casing, or layer, as the rind of fruit. —*v.t.* **4.** to strip or deprive of skin. **5.** to scrape a small piece of skin from (a part of the body). —*Idiom.* **6. by the skin of one's teeth,** by an extremely narrow margin; just barely; scarcely.

skin′ div′ing, *n.* underwater swimming with a face mask and flippers and sometimes with scuba. —**skin′ div′er,** *n.*

skin′flint′, *n.* a stingy person; miser.

skin′head′, *n. Slang.* **1.** a person with a bald head or closely cropped hair. **2.** an antisocial person who affects a hairless head as a symbol of rebellion or racism.

skin′ny, *adj.,* **-ni•er, -ni•est.** very lean or thin. —**skin′ni•ness,** *n.*

skin′ny-dip′, *v.,* **-dipped, -dip•ping,** *n. Informal.* —*v.i.* **1.** to swim in the nude. —*n.* **2.** a swim in the nude.

skin′tight′, *adj.* fitting almost as tightly as skin.

skip (skip), *v.,* **skipped, skip•ping,** *v.i.* **1.** to bound along with alternate hops on each foot. **2.** to pass from one point to another, disregarding what intervenes. **3.** to leave hastily and secretly. **4.** to ricochet or bounce. —*v.t.* **5.** to jump lightly over. **6.** to pass over without taking notice or action. **7.** to be advanced beyond (a grade or class) in school. **8.** to go away from hastily and secretly: *They skipped town.* —*n.* **9.** a skipping movement or gait.

skip′per, *n.* the master or captain of a ship.

skir•mish (skûr′mish), *n.* **1.** a fight between small bodies of troops. **2.** a minor conflict or encounter. —*v.i.* **3.** to engage in a skirmish.

skirt (skûrt), *n.* **1.** the part of a dress or coat that extends downward from the waist. **2.** a woman's one-piece garment extending downward from the waist. —*v.t.* **3.** to lie or pass along the border of. **4.** to avoid. —*v.i.* **5.** to move or lie along the border of something.

skit (skit), *n.* a short, usu. comical theatrical scene or act.

ski′ tow′, *n.* a ski lift.

skit•ter (skit′ər), *v.i.* to go, run, or glide lightly or rapidly.

skit′tish, *adj.* **1.** apt to start or shy: *a skittish horse.* **2.** frisky; lively. **3.** fickle; uncertain.

skiv•vy (skiv′ē), *n., pl.* **-vies. 1.** a man's cotton T-shirt. **2. skivvies,** men's underwear consisting of a T-shirt and shorts.

Skop•je (skôp′ye), *n.* the capital of Macedonia. 504,932.

skul•dug•ger•y or **skull•dug•ger•y** (skul dug′ə-rē), *n.* dishonorable or deceitful behavior.

skulk (skulk), *v.i.* **1.** to lie or keep in hiding, as for some evil reason. **2.** to move stealthily; slink. —**skulk′er,** *n.*

skull (skul), *n.* the bony or cartilaginous framework of the vertebrate head, enclosing the brain.

skull′cap′, *n.* a small, brimless, close-fitting cap.

skunk (skungk), *n., pl.* **skunks, skunk,** *v.* —*n.* **1.** a bushy-tailed New World mammal with black and white fur that sprays a fetid defensive fluid. **2.** a thoroughly contemptible person. —*v.t.* **3.** *Slang.* to defeat thoroughly in a game.

sky (skī), *n., pl.* **skies. 1.** the upper atmosphere of the earth. **2.** the celestial heaven.

sky′cap′, *n.* a porter at an airport.

sky′div′ing, *n.* the sport of jumping from an airplane and descending in free fall for a considerable distance before opening a parachute.

sky′-high′, *adv., adj.* very high.

sky′jack′, *v.t.* to hijack (an airliner). —**sky′jack′er,** *n.* —**sky′jack′ing,** *n.*

sky′lark′, *n.* **1.** a Eurasian lark famed for its melodious song. —*v.i.* **2.** to frolic; sport.

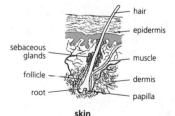

skin

sky′light′, *n.* a glass-fitted opening in a roof or ceiling.

sky′line′, *n.* **1.** the apparent horizon. **2.** an outline, esp. of buildings, seen against the sky.

sky′ mar′shal, *n.* an armed federal marshal responsible for preventing skyjacking.

sky′rock′et, *n.* **1.** a rocket firework that explodes high in the air, usu. in brilliant and colorful sparks. —*v.i., v.t.* **2.** to rise or cause to rise rapidly or suddenly.

sky′scrap′er, *n.* a tall building of many stories.

sky′ward (-wərd), *adv.* **1.** Also, **sky′wards.** toward the sky. —*adj.* **2.** directed toward the sky.

sky′writ′ing, *n.* writing in the sky formed by smoke released from an airplane. —**sky′writ′er,** *n.*

slab (slab), *n.* a broad, flat, somewhat thick piece.

slack (slak), *adj.* **-er, -est,** *v.* —*adj.* **1.** not tight or taut; loose. **2.** negligent; careless. **3.** slow, sluggish, or indolent. **4.** not active or busy. —*n.* **5.** a slack condition or part. **6.** a period of decreased activity. —*v.t., v.i.* **7.** to slacken. —**slack′ly,** *adv.* —**slack′ness,** *n.*

slack′en, *v.t., v.i.* **1.** to make or become less active, intense, etc. **2.** to make or become looser.

slack′er, *n.* a person who evades work or military service.

slacks, *n.* (*used with a pl. v.*) trousers for informal or casual wear.

slag (slag), *n.* the fused and vitrified matter separated during the reduction of a metal from its ore.

slain (slān), *v.* pp. of SLAY.

slake (slāk), *v.t.,* **slaked, slak•ing. 1.** to allay (thirst, desire, etc.) by satisfying; quench. **2.** to cause disintegration of (lime) by treatment with water.

sla•lom (slä′ləm, -lōm), *n.* a downhill ski race over a winding and zigzag course.

slam[1] (slam), *v.,* **slammed, slam•ming,** *n.* —*v.t., v.i.* **1.** to shut with force and noise. **2.** to strike, throw, or move with violence or noisy force. —*n.* **3.** the act or sound of slamming.

slam[2] (slam), *n.* the winning of all or all but one of the tricks in a deal of cards.

slam′-bang′, *adv.* **1.** with noisy violence. —*adj.* **2.** noisy and violent. **3.** excitingly fast-paced.

slam′ dance′, *n.* a dance performed to punk rock by groups of people who slam into one another. —**slam′-dance′,** *v.i.,* **-danced, -danc•ing.**

slam′ dunk′, *n.* a forceful, often dramatic dunk shot in basketball.

slan•der (slan′dər), *n.* **1.** a malicious, false, and defamatory statement or report. —*v.t.* **2.** to utter slander against; defame. —**slan′der•er,** *n.* —**slan′der•ous,** *adj.*

slang (slang), *n.* very informal vocabulary that is characteristically more metaphorical, playful, vivid, and ephemeral than ordinary language. —**slang′y,** *adj.,* **-i•er, -i•est.**

slant (slant, slänt), *v.i.* **1.** to turn at an angle away from a given level or line; slope. —*v.t.* **2.** to cause to slant. **3.** to present in a way that favors a particular viewpoint or appeals to a particular group. —*n.* **4.** a slanting direction, line, or surface. **5.** a particular viewpoint, opinion, or attitude. —**slant′wise′,** *adj., adv.*

slap (slap), *n., v.,* **slapped, slap•ping.** —*n.* **1.** a sharp blow, esp. with the open hand. **2.** a sharp or sarcastic rebuke or comment. —*v.t.* **3.** to strike sharply, esp. with the open hand. **4.** to put, place, or cast forcibly.

slap′dash′, *adj.* hasty and careless; offhand.

slap′hap′py, *adj.,* **-pi•er, -pi•est. 1.** severely befuddled. **2.** agreeably giddy or foolish.

slap′stick′, *n.* boisterous comedy characterized by broad farce and horseplay.

slash (slash), *v.t.* **1.** to cut with a violent sweeping stroke, as of a knife. **2.** to reduce sharply. **3.** to make slits in (a garment). —*n.* **4.** a violent sweeping stroke. **5.** a cut or mark made with a slash. **6.** VIRGULE. —**slash′er,** *n.*

slat (slat), *n.* a long, narrow strip, as of wood or metal.

slate (slāt), *n., v.,* **slat•ed, slat•ing.** —*n.* **1.** a fine-grained rock that tends to split along parallel cleavage planes. **2.** a thin piece or plate of slate used esp. for roofing or as a writing surface. **3.** a list of candidates for nomination or election. —*v.t.* **4.** to cover with slate. **5.** to set down for nomination or appointment.

slath•er (slath′ər), *v.t.* to spread or spread on thickly.

slat•tern (slat′ərn), *n.* a slovenly, untidy woman. —**slat′tern•ly,** *adj.*

slaugh•ter (slô′tər), *n.* **1.** the killing of animals for food. **2.** brutal or violent killing, esp. of great numbers of people. —*v.t.* **3.** to butcher (animals) for food. **4.** to kill brutally or in great numbers. —**slaugh′ter•er,** *n.*

slaugh′ter•house′, *n.* a building where animals are butchered.

Slaugh′ter of the In′nocents, *n.* the slaughter of male children in Bethlehem by order of Herod the Great. Matt. 2:16.

Slav (släv, slav), *n.* a member of a Slavic-speaking people.

slave (slāv), *n., v.,* **slaved, slav•ing.** —*n.* **1.** a person who is the property of and wholly subject to another. **2.** a person entirely under the domination of an influence or person. —*v.i.* **3.** to work like a slave; drudge.

slave′ driv′er, *n.* **1.** an overseer of slaves. **2.** a demanding taskmaster.

slav•er (slav′ər, slā′vər, slä′-), *v.i.* to slobber; drool.

slav•er•y (slā′və rē), *n.* **1.** the condition of a slave; bondage. **2.** the keeping of slaves as a practice or institution. **3.** toil; drudgery.

Slav•ic (slä′vik, slav′ik), *n.* **1.** a branch of the Indo-European language family that includes Polish, Czech, and Russian. —*adj.* **2.** of the Slavs or their languages.

slav•ish (slā′vish), *adj.* **1.** of or resembling a slave. **2.** deliberately imitative. —**slav′ish•ly,** *adv.* —**slav′ish•ness,** *n.*

slaw (slô), *n.* coleslaw.

slay (slā), *v.t.,* **slew, slain, slay•ing.** to kill by violence. —**slay′er,** *n.*

sleaze (slēz), *n.* **1.** sleazy quality, character, or appearance. **2.** *Slang.* a contemptible or vulgar person.

slea•zy (slē′zē), *adj.,* **-zi•er, -zi•est. 1.** contemptibly low or disreputable. **2.** squalid; tawdry. **3.** thin and limp in texture. —**slea′zi•ly,** *adv.* —**slea′zi•ness,** *n.*

sled (sled), *n., v.,* **sled•ded, sled•ding.** —*n.* **1.** a platform on runners, used by children for sliding over snow or ice. **2.** a sledge. —*v.i., v.t.* **3.** to ride on or convey by sled. —**sled′der,** *n.*

sledge[1] (slej), *n.* a heavy vehicle on runners for conveying people or loads over snow or ice.

sledge[2] (slej), *n.* SLEDGEHAMMER.

sledge′ham′mer, *n.* a large, heavy hammer wielded with both hands.

sleek (slēk), *adj.,* **-er, -est. 1.** smooth and glossy, as hair. **2.** well-fed or well-groomed. **3.** finely contoured; streamlined. —*v.t.* **4.** to make sleek. —**sleek′ly,** *adv.* —**sleek′ness,** *n.*

sleep (slēp), *v.,* **slept, sleep•ing,** *n.* —*v.i.* **1.** to take the rest afforded by the natural suspension of consciousness; cease being awake. **2.** to be dormant, quiescent, or inactive. **3. ~ away,** to pass (time) in sleep. **4. ~ off,** to get rid of (a headache, hangover, etc.) by sleeping. —*n.* **5.** the state of one that sleeps. **6.** a state, as dormancy, resembling sleep. —**sleep′less,** *adj.* —**sleep′less•ness,** *n.*

sleep′er, *n.* **1.** one that sleeps. **2.** SLEEPING CAR. **3.** an unexpected success.

sleep′ing bag′, *n.* a warmly lined bag in which a person can sleep, esp. outdoors.

sleep′ing car′, *n.* a railroad car equipped with sleeping accommodations.

sleep′ing gi′ant, *n.* an unrealized source of power and strength, esp. a group of nations.

sleep′ing pill′, *n.* a pill or capsule containing a drug for inducing sleep.

sleep′ing sick′ness, *n.* an infectious, usu. fatal

disease of Africa, characterized by wasting and progressive lethargy.

sleep/walk/ing, *n.* the act or state of walking while asleep; somnambulism. —**sleep/walk/,** *v.i.* —**sleep/walk/er,** *n.*

sleep/wear/, *n.* garments worn for sleeping.

sleep/y, *adj.*, **-i•er, -i•est. 1.** ready or inclined to sleep; drowsy. **2.** lethargic; inactive. —**sleep/i•ly,** *adv.* —**sleep/i•ness,** *n.*

sleet (slēt), *n.* **1.** precipitation created by the freezing of rain as it falls. —*v.i.* **2.** to send down or fall as sleet. —**sleet/y,** *adj.*

sleeve (slēv), *n.* **1.** the part of a garment that covers the arm. **2.** a tubular piece fitting over another part. —*Idiom.* **3. up one's sleeve,** kept hidden for future use. —**sleeve/less,** *adj.*

sleigh (slā), *n.* a horse-drawn vehicle on runners, used for conveying people over snow or ice.

sleight/ of hand/, *n.* **1.** skill in feats or tricks requiring manual dexterity. **2.** any such feat or trick.

slen•der (slen/dər), *adj.*, **-der•er, -der•est. 1.** narrow or small in circumference in proportion to height or length. **2.** thin, esp. gracefully slim. **3.** not adequate; meager. —**slen/der•ness,** *n.*

slen/der•ize/, *v.t., v.i.*, **-ized, -iz•ing.** to make or become slender.

slept (slept), *v.* pt. and pp. of SLEEP.

Sles•sor (sles/ər), *n.* **Mary,** 1848–1915, Scottish missionary in Africa.

sleuth (slōōth), *n.* a detective.

slew¹ (slōō), *v.* pt. of SLAY.

slew² (slōō), *n. Informal.* a large number or quantity.

slice (slīs), *n., v.*, **sliced, slic•ing.** —*n.* **1.** a thin, flat piece cut from something. **2.** a part or portion. **3.** the path described by a ball, as a golf ball, that curves toward the side from which it was struck. —*v.t.* **4.** to cut into slices. **5.** to cut off or remove a slice from. **6.** to hit (a ball) so as to result in a slice. —**slic/er,** *n.*

slick¹ (slik), *adj.*, **-er, -est,** *n.* —*adj.* **1.** smooth and slippery. **2.** shrewdly adroit; sly. **3.** ingenious; clever. **4.** having surface appeal but shallow or glib. —*n.* **5.** a smooth or slippery place or spot. —**slick/ly,** *adv.* —**slick/ness,** *n.*

slick² (slik), *v.t.* **1.** to make sleek or smooth. **2.** *Informal.* to make smart or spruce.

slick/er, *n.* **1.** a loose oilskin raincoat. **2.** *Informal.* a swindler.

slide (slīd), *v.*, **slid** (slid), **slid•ing.** —*v.i.* **1.** to move along in continuous contact with a smooth or slippery surface. **2.** to slip or skid. **3.** to glide or pass smoothly. —*v.t.* **4.** to cause to slide. **5.** to hand or pass along quietly or furtively. —*n.* **6.** an act or instance of sliding. **7.** a smooth surface for sliding on. **8.** a part that functions by sliding. **9.** a mass of matter, as earth, sliding down. **10.** a transparency, as a frame of positive film, mounted for projection on a screen. **11.** a plate of glass on which objects are placed for microscopic examination.

slide/ fas/tener, *n.* ZIPPER.

slid/er, *n.* **1.** one that slides. **2.** a fast-pitched baseball that curves slightly.

slid/ing scale/, *n.* a scale, as of wages or prices, that varies with such conditions as the cost of living or the ability of individuals to pay.

slight (slīt), *adj.*, **-er, -est,** *v., n.* —*adj.* **1.** small in amount or degree. **2.** of little importance or influence. **3.** slender or slim. **4.** frail; delicate. —*v.t.* **5.** to treat as unimportant. **6.** to treat with indifference; snub. **7.** to do negligently. —*n.* **8.** an instance of slighting; indifference or discourtesy. —**slight/ly,** *adv.* —**slight/ness,** *n.*

slim (slim), *adj.*, **slim•mer, slim•mest,** *v.*, **slimmed, slim•ming.** —*adj.* **1.** slender, as in form. **2.** meager; scanty. —*v.t., v.i.* **3.** to make or become slim. —**slim/ness,** *n.*

slime (slīm), *n.* **1.** thin, glutinous mud. **2.** a ropy or viscous liquid substance, esp. of a foul kind. —**slim/y,** *adj.*, **-i•er, -i•est.**

sling (sling), *n., v.*, **slung, sling•ing.** —*n.* **1.** a strap with a string at each end that is whirled around to hurl a missile, esp. a stone. **2.** a strap or band forming a loop by which something is suspended, supported, or carried. —*v.t.* **3.** to throw or hurl; fling. **4.** to place in or move by a sling.

sling/shot/, *n.* a Y-shaped stick with an elastic strip between the prongs for shooting small missiles.

slink (slingk), *v.i.*, **slunk, slink•ing. 1.** to move or go in a furtive, abject manner. **2.** to walk in a sinuous, provocative way. —**slink/y,** *adj.*, **-i•er, -i•est.**

slip¹ (slip), *v.*, **slipped, slip•ping,** *n.* —*v.i.* **1.** to move smoothly or easily. **2.** to slide suddenly and accidentally. **3.** to pass without having been done or used. **4.** to elapse quickly or imperceptibly. **5.** to move or go quietly or unobtrusively. **6.** to make a mistake. **7.** to decline; deteriorate. —*v.t.* **8.** to cause to move with a smooth or sliding motion. **9.** to put, pass, or insert quickly or stealthily. **10.** to put on or take off (a garment). **11.** to pass from or escape (the memory, attention, etc.). —*n.* **12.** an act or instance of slipping. **13.** a sudden, accidental slide. **14.** a mistake or blunder. **15.** a woman's undergarment worn under the outer dress. **16.** a pillowcase. **17.** a space for a ship between two wharves or in a dock.

slip² (slip), *n.* **1.** a piece suitable for propagation cut from a plant. **2.** a long, narrow strip, as of paper.

slip/case/, *n.* a box open at one end for a book or set of books.

slip/cov/er, *n.* an easily removable cover, esp. of cloth, for a piece of furniture.

slip/knot/ or **slip/ knot/,** *n.* a knot that slips easily along the cord or line around which it is made.

slip•page (slip/ij), *n.* **1.** an act or instance of slipping. **2.** an amount or extent of slipping.

slipped/ disk/, *n.* an abnormal protrusion of a spinal disk between vertebrae.

slip/per, *n.* a light, low-cut shoe into which the foot slips easily.

slip•per•y (slip/ə rē), *adj.*, **-i•er, -i•est. 1.** tending or liable to cause slipping or sliding. **2.** likely to slip away or escape. **3.** not trustworthy; shifty or tricky. —**slip/per•i•ness,** *n.*

slip/shod/, *adj.* careless, untidy, or slovenly.

slip/-up/, *n.* a mistake, blunder, or oversight.

slit (slit), *v.*, **slit, slit•ting,** *n.* —*v.t.* **1.** to make a long cut or opening in. **2.** to cut into strips. —*n.* **3.** a straight, narrow cut or opening.

slith•er (slith/ər), *v.i.* to move, walk, or slide like a snake. —**slith/er•y,** *adj.*

sliv•er (sliv/ər), *n.* **1.** a small, slender, often sharp piece, as of glass; splinter. —*v.t., v.i.* **2.** to cut or split into slivers.

slob (slob), *n.* a slovenly or boorish person.

slob•ber (slob/ər), *v.i.* **1.** to let saliva dribble from the mouth; drool. —*n.* **2.** saliva dribbling from the mouth.

sloe (slō), *n.* the small, sour, blackish fruit of the blackthorn.

sloe/-eyed/, *adj.* **1.** having very dark eyes. **2.** having slanted eyes.

slog (slog), *v.i.*, **slogged, slog•ging. 1.** to walk heavily; plod. **2.** to work long and hard; toil.

slo•gan (slō/gən), *n.* a distinctive phrase identified with a group, cause, or product; motto or catchword. [< ScotGael *sluagh-ghairm* army cry]

sloop (slōōp), *n.* a single-masted, fore-and-aft-rigged sailing boat.

slop (slop), *v.*, **slopped, slop•ping,** *n.* —*v.t., v.i.* **1.** to spill or splash (liquid). —*n.* **2.** kitchen waste used as feed for swine. **3.** unappetizing food or drink. **4.** liquid mud. **5.** spilled liquid.

slope (slōp), *v.*, **sloped, slop•ing,** *n.* —*v.i., v.t.* **1.** to incline or cause to incline; slant. —*n.* **2.** ground that has a natural incline. **3. a.** inclination or slant, esp. downward or upward. **b.** amount or degree of slant.

slop/py, *adj.*, **-pi•er, -pi•est. 1.** muddy, slushy, or very wet. **2.** untidy; slovenly. **3.** careless; slipshod. **4.** overly emotional; gushy. —**slop/pi•ness,** *n.*

slosh (slosh), *v.i.* **1.** to splash or move through water, mud, or slush. **2.** (of a liquid) to move about actively within a container.

slot (slot), *n.*, *v.*, **slot•ted, slot•ting.** —*n.* **1.** a long, narrow opening, esp. one for receiving something, as a letter. **2.** a place or position, as in a sequence or series. —*v.t.* **3.** to make a slot in. **4.** to place or fit into a slot.

sloth (slôth; *esp. for 2* slōth), *n.* **1.** indolence; laziness. **2.** a slow-moving, arboreal tropical American mammal that usually hangs upside down. —**sloth′ful,** *adj.* —**sloth′ful•ness,** *n.*

sloth

slot′ machine′, *n.* a gambling or vending machine operated by inserting coins into a slot.

slouch (slouch), *v.i.* **1.** to sit, stand, or walk with an awkward, drooping posture. —*n.* **2.** an awkward, drooping posture, carriage, or gait. **3.** a lazy, inept person. —**slouch′er,** *n.* —**slouch′y,** *adj.*, **-i•er, -i•est.**

slough¹ (slou), *n.* **1.** an area of soft, muddy ground. **2.** a swamp or swamplike region. **3.** a condition of despair.

slough² (sluf), *n.* **1.** something, as the outer layer of a snake's skin, that is shed or cast off. —*v.t.* **2.** to cast off as or like a slough; shed.

Slo•vak (slō′väk, -vak), *n.* **1.** a member of a Slavic people living in Slovakia. **2.** the Slavic language of the Slovaks.

Slo•va•ki•a (slō vä′kē ə, -vak′ē ə), *n.* a republic in central Europe: formerly part of Czechoslovakia. 5,393,016. Also called **Slo′vak Repub′lic.** —**Slo•va′-ki•an,** *n.*, *adj.*

slov•en (sluv′ən), *n.* a person who is habitually unclean or untidy.

Slo•ve•ni•a (slō vē′nē ə), *n.* a republic in SE Europe: formerly part of Yugoslavia. 1,945,998. —**Slo•ve′ni•an, Slo′vene,** *adj.*, *n.*

slov•en•ly (sluv′ən lē), *adj.*, **-li•er, -li•est. 1.** untidy or unclean. **2.** slipshod; negligent. —**slov′en•li•ness,** *n.*

slow (slō), *adj.* and *adv.*, **-er, -est,** *v.* —*adj.* **1.** moving or proceeding with little or less than usual speed. **2.** characterized by lack of speed. **3.** taking or requiring a longer time than usual. **4.** mentally dull. **5.** not busy; slack. **6.** running at less than the proper rate of speed, as a clock. **7.** tedious. —*adv.* **8.** in a slow manner. —*v.t.*, *v.i.* **9.** to make or become slow or slower. —*Proverb.* **10. Slow but steady wins the race,** a task is best accomplished slowly and methodically. —**slow′ly,** *adv.* —**slow′ness,** *n.*

slow′ burn′, *n. Informal.* a gradual building up of anger.

slow′down′, *n.* a slowing down, as in progress, action, or pace.

slow′ mo′tion, *n.* the process or technique of projecting or replaying a motion-picture or television sequence so that the action appears to be slowed down.

slow′-mo′tion, *adj.* photographed, appearing, or proceeding in or as if in slow motion.

slow′poke′, *n. Informal.* a person who moves, works, or acts very slowly.

slow′-wit′ted, *adj.* slow in comprehension; dull.

SLR, single-lens reflex: a camera in which the image passes through the same lens to both the viewfinder and the film.

sludge (sluj), *n.* **1.** mud, mire, or ooze; slush. **2.** a mudlike deposit, esp. sediment produced during the treatment of sewage.

slue (slōō), *v.i.*, *v.t.*, **slued, slu•ing.** to turn or swing around.

slug¹ (slug), *n.* **1.** a snaillike terrestrial gastropod mollusk having no shell. **2.** a metal disk used as a

coin or token. **3.** a piece of metal, esp. lead, for firing from a gun. **4.** a shot of liquor.

slug² (slug), *v.*, **slugged, slug•ging,** *n.* —*v.t.* **1.** to strike hard, esp. with the fist. —*n.* **2.** a hard blow or hit, esp. with the fist. —**slug′ger,** *n.*

slug•gard (slug′ərd), *n.* a habitually inactive or lazy person.

slug′gish, *adj.* **1.** lazy; indolent. **2.** slow to function, act, flow, or respond. **3.** slack, as sales. —**slug′-gish•ly,** *adv.* —**slug′gish•ness,** *n.*

sluice (slōōs), *n.*, *v.*, **sluiced, sluic•ing.** —*n.* **1.** an artificial channel for water with a gate (**sluice′ gate′**) for regulating the flow. **2.** a channel, esp. one carrying off surplus water. **3.** a long, sloping trough, as for washing ores. —*v.t.* **4.** to let out (water) by opening a sluice. **5.** to flush or cleanse with a rush of water.

slum (slum), *n.*, *v.*, **slummed, slum•ming.** —*n.* **1.** a run-down part of a city, usu. thickly populated by poor people. —*v.i.* **2.** to visit slums, esp. out of curiosity.

slum•ber (slum′bər), *v.i.* **1.** to sleep, esp. lightly. **2.** to be in a state of inactivity, quiescence, or calm. —*n.* **3.** sleep, esp. light sleep. **4.** a state of inactivity, quiescence, or calm. —**slum′ber•ous,** *adj.*

slum′lord′, *n.* a landlord who charges exorbitant rents in slum buildings.

slump (slump), *v.i.* **1.** to fall or drop heavily. **2.** to slouch. **3.** to decline markedly. —*n.* **4.** an act or instance of slumping.

slung (slung), *v.* pt. and pp. OF SLING.

slunk (slungk), *v.* pt. and pp. OF SLINK.

slur¹ (slûr), *v.*, **slurred, slur•ring,** *n.* —*v.t.* **1.** to pronounce (a syllable, word, etc.) indistinctly. **2.** to pass over without due mention or consideration. **3.** to sing or play (two or more tones of different pitch) without a break. —*n.* **4.** a slurred utterance or sound. **5.** a curved mark indicating that two or more tones of different pitch are to be slurred.

slur² (slûr), *n.* a disparaging remark; slight.

slurp (slûrp), *v.t.*, *v.i.* **1.** to eat or drink with loud sucking noises. —*n.* **2.** a slurping sound.

slush (slush), *n.* **1.** partly melted snow. **2.** liquid mud; mire. **3.** silly, sentimental talk or writing. —**slush′y,** *adj.*, **-i•er, -i•est.**

slush′ fund′, *n.* money used for illicit or corrupt political purposes.

sly (slī), *adj.*, **sly•er** or **sli•er, sly•est** or **sli•est,** *n.* —*adj.* **1.** cunning or wily. **2.** stealthy; surreptitious. **3.** mischievous or roguish. —*n.* **Idiom. 4. on the sly,** secretly. —**sly′ly,** *adv.* —**sly′ness,** *n.*

Sm, *Chem. Symbol.* samarium.

smack¹ (smak), *n.* **1.** a slight or distinctive taste or flavor. **2.** a trace or suggestion. —*v.i.* **3.** to have a smack.

smack² (smak), *v.t.* **1.** to strike or kiss with a loud sound. **2.** to close and open (the lips) with a sharp sound. —*n.* **3.** a loud blow or kiss. **4.** a smacking of the lips. —*adv.* **5.** suddenly and violently. **6.** directly; straight.

smack³ (smak), *n.* a fishing boat, esp. one with a well for keeping the catch alive.

smack′er, *n. Slang.* a dollar.

s′-mail′, *n.* SNAIL MAIL.

small (smôl), *adj.* and *adv.*, **-er, -est,** *n.* —*adj.* **1.** not big; little. **2.** not great, as in amount or extent. **3.** carrying on an activity on a limited scale: *a small business.* **4.** of minor importance. **5.** humble or modest. **6.** mean-spirited; petty. **7.** very young: *a small boy.* —*adv.* **8.** in a small manner. **9.** into small pieces. —*n.* **10.** a small or narrow part, as of the back. —**small′ish,** *adj.* —**small′ness,** *n.*

small′ arm′, *n.* a firearm held in the hand while being fired.

small′ cal′orie, *n.* See under CALORIE.

small′ fry′, *n.pl.* **1.** young children. **2.** unimportant persons.

small′ intes′tine, *n.* See under **intestine.**

small′-mind′ed, *adj.* selfish, petty, or narrowminded.

small′pox′, *n.* an acute, highly contagious viral disease characterized by fever and pustular eruptions.

small′-scale′, *adj.* **1.** of limited extent or scope. **2.** (of a map, model, etc.) being a relatively small version of an original.

small′ talk′, *n.* light conversation.

small′-time′, *adj.* of little or no importance or influence.

smart (smärt), *v., adj.,* **-er, -est,** *n.* —*v.i.* **1.** to cause or feel a sharp, stinging pain. **2.** to suffer from wounded feelings, shame, or distress. —*adj.* **3.** having or showing quick intelligence. **4.** clever or witty. **5.** neat or trim in appearance. **6.** elegant or fashionable. **7.** brisk or vigorous. **8.** sharp or keen. **9.** equipped with electronic control devices, as a missile. **10.** containing built-in electronic processing power: *a smart terminal.* —*n.* **11.** a sharp, stinging pain, as from a wound. **12. smarts,** *Informal.* intelligence. —**smart′ly,** *adv.* —**smart′ness,** *n.*

smart′ al′eck (or **al′ec**) (al′ik), *n. Informal.* an obnoxiously conceited person.

smart′ bomb′, *n.* an air-to-surface missile guided to its target by television or a laser beam.

smart′en, *v.t., v.i.* to make or become smart or smarter.

smash (smash), *v.t., v.i.* **1.** to break into pieces with violence. **2.** to destroy or be destroyed completely. **3.** to hit, dash, collide, or strike with force. —*n.* **4.** the act or sound of smashing. **5.** a blow, hit, or slap. **6.** a destructive collision; crash. **7.** a state of collapse or ruin, esp. financial failure. **8.** *Informal.* a great success; hit. **9.** (in racket sports) a powerful, downward overhand stroke. —**smash′er,** *n.*

smash′ing, *adj.* impressive or wonderful.

smash′-up′, *n.* a complete smash, esp. a collision of motor vehicles.

smat•ter•ing (smat′ər ing), *n.* slight or superficial knowledge.

smear (smēr), *v.t.* **1.** to spread or apply (an oily, viscous, or dirty substance). **2.** to spread or stain with an oily, viscous, or dirty substance. **3.** to defame or slander. **4.** to smudge or blur. —*n.* **5.** a stain or spot made by smearing. **6.** defamation or slander. —**smear′y,** *adj.,* **-i•er, -i•est.**

smell (smel), *v., smelled or smelt, smell•ing, n.* —*v.t.* **1.** to perceive the odor of through the nose. **2.** to perceive, detect, or discover by shrewdness. —*v.i.* **3.** to give off or have an odor. —*n.* **4.** the faculty of smelling. **5.** odor; scent. **6.** an act or instance of smelling.

smell′ing salts′, *n.* (*used with a sing. or pl. v.*) a preparation, essentially an ammonia compound, used as a stimulant and restorative.

smell′y, *adj.,* **-i•er, -i•est.** emitting an unpleasant odor. —**smell′i•ness,** *n.*

smelt¹ (smelt), *v.t.* **1.** to fuse or melt (ore) in order to separate the metal contained. **2.** to refine (metal) by smelting.

smelt² (smelt), *n., pl.* **smelts, smelt.** a small, silvery food fish of cold northern waters.

smelt³ (smelt), *v.* a pt. and pp. of SMELL.

smelt′er, *n.* **1.** one that smelts. **2.** a place where ores are smelted.

Sme•ta•na (smet′n ə), *n.* **Be•dřich** (bed′ər zhiкн, -zhik), 1824–84, Czech composer.

smid•gen or **-gin** or **-geon** (smij′ən), *n.* a very small amount.

smi•lax (smī′laks), *n.* **1.** any of a number of mostly woody-stemmed vines of the lily family. **2.** a delicate, twining plant with glossy egg-shaped leaves.

smile (smīl), *v., smiled, smil•ing, n.* —*v.i.* **1.** to assume a facial expression indicating pleasure, amusement, derision, or scorn. **2.** to regard with or show favor. —*v.t.* **3.** to express by a smile. —*n.* **4.** an act or instance of smiling. **5.** a smiling facial expression. —**smil′ing•ly,** *adv.*

smil•ey (smīlē), *n., pl.* **-eys.** a sideways representation of a smiling face, :-), or similar combination of symbols, as ;-), a winking face, or :-(, a sad face, used to communicate humor, sarcasm, sadness, etc., in an electronic message.

smirch (smûrch), *v.t.* **1.** to discolor or soil with or as if with soot. **2.** to disgrace; discredit. —*n.* **3.** a dirty mark or smear. **4.** a stain, as on reputation.

smirk (smûrk), *v.i.* **1.** to smile in an affected, smug, or offensively familiar way. —*n.* **2.** the facial expression of one who smirks.

smite (smīt), *v.t.,* **smote, smit•ten** (smit′n) or **smote, smit•ing. 1.** to hit hard with or as if with the hand. **2.** to injure or slay by striking hard. **3.** to affect strongly and suddenly.

smith (smith), *n.* **1.** a worker in metal. **2.** BLACK-SMITH.

Smith (smith), *n.* **1. Adam,** 1723–90, Scottish economist. **2. Alfred E(manuel),** 1873–1944, U.S. political leader. **3. John,** 1580–1631, English adventurer and colonist in Virginia. **4. Joseph,** 1805–44, U.S. religious leader: founded the Church of Jesus Christ of Latter-day Saints. **5. Margaret Chase,** 1897–1995, U.S. politician.

smith•er•eens (smith′ə rēnz′), *n.pl.* small pieces; bits.

smith•y (smith′ē, smith′ē), *n., pl.* **smith•ies.** the workshop of a smith, esp. a blacksmith.

smock (smok), *n.* **1.** a loose overgarment worn esp. to protect the clothing while working. —*v.t.* **2.** to gather (fabric) into a honeycomb pattern with diamond-shaped recesses.

smog (smog, smôg), *n.* atmospheric pollutants, esp. smoke, combined with fog. [*sm(oke)* + *(f)og*] —**smog′gy,** *adj.,* **-gi•er, -gi•est.**

smoke (smōk), *n., v.,* **smoked, smok•ing.** —*n.* **1.** the visible vapor and gases given off by a burning substance. **2.** something, as mist, resembling smoke. **3.** the act of smoking something. **4.** a cigarette, cigar, or pipe. —*v.i.* **5.** to give off smoke. **6.** to inhale and puff out tobacco smoke. —*v.t.* **7.** to inhale and puff out the smoke of: *He smoked a cigar.* **8.** to cure (meat, fish, etc.) by exposure to smoke. **9. smoke out, a.** to drive out by means of smoke. **b.** to expose to public view or knowledge. —**Proverb. 10. Where there's smoke, there's fire,** even if untrue, a rumor indicates that something is wrong. —**smoke′less,** *adj.* —**smok′er,** *n.* —**smok′y,** *adj.,* **-i•er, -i•est.**

smoke′ detec′tor, *n.* an alarm activated by the presence of smoke.

smoke′house′, *n.* a building or place in which meat or fish is cured with smoke.

smoke′ screen′, *n.* **1.** a mass of dense smoke for concealing an area, ship, or plane from an enemy. **2.** something intended to conceal or deceive.

smoke′stack′, *n.* a pipe for escape of smoke or combustion gases, as on a locomotive.

smol•der or **smoul•der** (smōl′dər), *v.i.* **1.** to burn without flame. **2.** to exist in a suppressed state. **3.** to show repressed feelings, as of anger.

smooch (smōōch), *Informal.* —*v.i.* **1.** to kiss. —*n.* **2.** a kiss.

smooth (smōōth), *adj.,* **-er, -est,** *adv., v.* —*adj.* **1.** having an even surface; not rough. **2.** of uniform consistency; free from lumps. **3.** allowing or marked by an even, uninterrupted movement or flow. **4.** free from hindrances or difficulties. **5.** elegant or polished. **6.** ingratiatingly polite; suave. **7.** bland or mellow. —*adv.* **8.** in a smooth manner. —*v.t.* **9.** to make smooth of surface. **10.** to free from hindrances or difficulties. **11.** to refine or polish. **12.** to calm or soothe. —**smooth′ly,** *adv.* —**smooth′ness,** *n.*

smor•gas•bord or **smör•gås•bord** (smôr′gəs-bôrd′; *often* shmôr′-), *n.* a buffet meal consisting of a number of hot and cold dishes. [< Sw: sandwich table]

smote (smōt), *v.* pt. and a pp. of SMITE.

smoth•er (smuth′ər), *v.t.* **1.** to stifle or suffocate. **2.** to cover closely or thickly; envelop. **3.** to suppress or repress. —*v.i.* **4.** to be stifled or suffocated.

smudge (smuj), *n., v.,* **smudged, smudg•ing.** —*n.* **1.** a dirty mark or smear. **2.** stifling smoke. —*v.t., v.i.* **3.** to make or become dirty with streaks or smears. —**smudg′y,** *adj.,* **-i•er, -i•est.**

smug (smug), *adj.,* **smug•ger, smug•gest.** full of

self-satisfaction; complacent. —**smug′ly,** *adv.* —**smug′ness,** *n.*

smug•gle (smug′əl), *v.*, **-gled, -gling.** —*v.t.* **1.** to import or export secretly, in violation of the law, esp. without paying legal duty. **2.** to bring, take, or put secretly. —*v.i.* **3.** to engage in smuggling. —**smug′gler,** *n.*

smut (smut), *n.* **1.** sooty matter. **2.** a black or dirty mark; smudge. **3.** indecent language or writing; obscenity. **4.** a fungous disease of plants, characterized by black, powdery masses. —**smut′ty,** *adj.,* **-ti•er, -ti•est.** —**smut′ti•ness,** *n.*

Smyr•na (smûr′nə), *n.* former name of IZMIR: site of one of the seven churches of Asia (Rev. 1:11).

Sn, *Chem. Symbol.* tin. [< L *stannum*]

snack (snak), *n.* **1.** a light meal, esp. one eaten between regular meals. —*v.i.* **2.** to eat a snack.

snack′ bar′, *n.* a lunchroom or restaurant where snacks are sold.

snaf•fle (snaf′əl), *n.* a usu. jointed horse's bit without a curb.

snag (snag), *n.*, *v.*, **snagged, snag•ging.** —*n.* **1.** a tree or part of a tree held fast in the bottom of a body of water. **2.** a sharp or rough projection. **3.** a tear, pull, or run in a fabric. **4.** an obstacle or impediment. —*v.t.* **5.** to run, catch up, or damage on a snag. **6.** to obstruct or impede. **7.** to grab; seize.

snail (snāl), *n.* a slow-moving mollusk with a spirally coiled shell and a muscular foot.

snail′ mail′, *n.* standard postal service, as contrasted with e-mail.

snake (snāk), *n.*, *v.*, **snaked, snak•ing.** —*n.* **1.** a limbless, scaly, elongate reptile. **2.** a treacherous person. —*v.i.* **3.** to move, twist, or wind like a snake. —*v.t.* **4.** to wind or make (one's course, way, etc.) like a snake. —**snake′like′,** *adj.* —**snak′y,** *adj.,* **-i•er, -i•est.**

Snake′ Riv′er, *n.* a river flowing from NW Wyoming to the Columbia River in SE Washington. 1038 mi. (1670 km) long.

snap (snap), *v.*, **snapped, snap•ping,** *n.*, *adj.*, *adv.* —*v.i.*, *v.t.* **1.** to make or cause to make a sudden, sharp, cracking sound. **2.** to move, shut, or catch with a sharp sound, as a door. **3.** to break suddenly with a sharp, cracking sound. **4.** to move or cause to move with quick or abrupt motions. **5.** to grasp or seize with or as if with a quick bite. **6.** to speak or say quickly and sharply. **7.** to flash, as the eyes. **8.** to take a snapshot (of). **9.** *Football.* to put (the ball) into play. —*n.* **10.** a quick, sudden action or movement. **11.** a short, sharp sound. **12.** a fastener that snaps when it closes. **13.** *Informal.* vigor or energy. **14.** a brittle cookie. **15.** a short spell of cold weather. **16.** *Informal.* an easy task, duty, etc. **17.** *Football.* the act of snapping the ball. —*adj.* **18.** made, done, or taken suddenly or offhand: *a snap judgment.* **19.** easy: *a snap course.* —*adv.* **20.** in a brisk, sudden manner. —**snap′per,** *n.* —**snap′pish,** *adj.* —**snap′py,** *adj.,* **-pi•er, -pi•est.**

snap′ bean′, *n.* a crisp bean pod, as a green bean.

snap′drag′on, *n.* a plant cultivated for its spikes of showy, two-lipped flowers.

snap′shot′, *n.* an informal photograph, esp. one taken with a hand-held camera.

snare¹ (snâr), *n.*, *v.*, **snared, snar•ing.** —*n.* **1.** a device, often consisting of a noose, for capturing small game. **2.** something that entraps or entangles. —*v.t.* **3.** to catch with or as if with a snare.

snare² (snâr), *n.* a gut or metal string stretched across the skin of a drum.

snarl¹ (snärl), *v.i.* **1.** to growl angrily or viciously, esp. with bared teeth. **2.** to speak in an angry or nasty manner. —*n.* **3.** an act or sound of snarling. —**snarl′ing•ly,** *adv.*

snarl² (snärl), *n.* **1.** a tangle, as of thread. **2.** a complicated or confused condition. —*v.i.*, *v.t.* **3.** to become or cause to become tangled or confused. —**snarl′y,** *adj.*

snatch (snach), *v.i.* **1.** to make a sudden effort to seize something. —*v.t.* **2.** to seize by a sudden or hasty grasp. —*n.* **3.** an act or instance of snatching.

4. a bit, scrap, or fragment. **5.** a brief spell, as of activity. —**snatch′er,** *n.*

sneak (snēk), *v.*, **sneaked** or **snuck, sneak•ing,** *n.*, *adj.* —*v.i.*, *v.t.* **1.** to go, act, move, or take in a stealthy or furtive manner. —*n.* **2.** a sneaking or underhand person. **3.** a sneaking act or move. —*adj.* **4.** stealthy; furtive. —**sneak′y,** *adj.,* **-i•er, -i•est.**

—**Usage.** As a past tense and past participle, SNUCK is especially frequent in fiction, in journalism, and on television, whereas SNEAKED is more likely in formal speech and writing. SNUCK has occasionally been considered nonstandard, but is now so common that it can no longer be so regarded.

sneak′er, *n.* a sports shoe of fabric, esp. canvas, with a flat rubber or synthetic sole.

sneak′ pre′view, *n.* a preview of a motion picture, often shown in addition to an announced film.

sneer (snēr), *v.i.* **1.** to smile, laugh, or contort the face in a manner that shows scorn or contempt. —*n.* **2.** a sneering look, expression, or remark.

sneeze (snēz), *v.*, **sneezed, sneez•ing,** *n.* —*v.i.* **1.** to expel the breath suddenly and audibly by involuntary spasmodic action. —*n.* **2.** an act or sound of sneezing.

snick•er (snik′ər), *v.i.* **1.** to laugh in a half-suppressed or disrespectful manner. —*n.* **2.** a snickering laugh.

snide (snīd), *adj.,* **snid•er, snid•est.** derogatory in a nasty, insinuating manner. —**snide′ness,** *n.*

sniff (snif), *v.i.*, *v.t.* **1.** to inhale audibly through the nose. **2.** to show disdain or contempt. **3.** to perceive by or as if by sniffing. —*n.* **4.** an act or sound of sniffing. **5.** an amount sniffed. —**sniff′er,** *n.*

snif•fle (snif′əl), *v.*, **-fled, -fling,** *n.* —*v.i.* **1.** to sniff repeatedly, as in repressing tears. —*n.* **2.** an act or sound of sniffling. **3. the sniffles,** a cold marked by sniffling.

snif•ter (snif′tər), *n.* a pear-shaped glass for brandy or liqueur.

snig•ger (snig′ər), *v.i.*, *n.* SNICKER.

snip (snip), *v.*, **snipped, snip•ping,** *n.* —*v.t.*, *v.i.* **1.** to cut or remove with small, quick strokes. —*n.* **2.** the act of snipping. **3.** a small piece snipped off. **4.** a small piece; bit. **5.** *Informal.* a small or insignificant person.

snipe (snīp), *n.*, *pl.* **snipes, snipe,** *v.*, **sniped, snip•ing.** —*n.* **1.** any of several long-billed sandpipers inhabiting marshy areas. —*v.i.* **2.** to shoot at individuals, esp. enemy soldiers, from a concealed or distant position. **3.** to make a petulant or snide attack. —**snip′er,** *n.*

snip•pet (snip′it), *n.* a small bit, scrap, or fragment.

snip′py, *adj.,* **-pi•er, -pi•est.** sharp or curt, esp. in a contemptuous or haughty way. —**snip′pi•ness,** *n.*

snit (snit), *n.* an agitated or irritated state.

snitch¹ (snich), *v.t. Informal.* to steal; pilfer.

snitch² (snich), *Informal.* —*v.i.* **1.** to turn informer; tattle. —*n.* **2.** an informer.

sniv•el (sniv′əl), *v.i.*, **-eled, -el•ing** or (*esp. Brit.*) **-elled, -el•ling. 1.** to weep or cry with sniffling. **2.** to have a runny nose.

snob (snob), *n.* a person who imitates, cultivates, or slavishly admires social superiors and is condescending to others. —**snob′ber•y, snob′bish•ness,** *n.* —**snob′bish,** *adj.*

snood (snood), *n.* a netlike hat or part of a hat that holds or covers the back of a woman's hair.

snoop (snoop), *Informal.* —*v.i.* **1.** to prowl or pry in a sneaking way. —*n.* **2.** an act or instance of snooping. **3.** a person who snoops. —**snoop′er,** *n.* —**snoop′y,** *adj.,* **-i•er, -i•est.**

snoot (snoot), *n. Informal.* **1.** the nose. **2.** a snob.

snoot′y, *adj.,* **-i•er, -i•est.** *Informal.* snobbish; condescending. —**snoot′i•ly,** *adv.* —**snoot′i•ness,** *n.*

snooze (snooz), *v.*, **snoozed, snooz•ing,** *n.* —*v.i.* **1.** to sleep for a short time; nap. —*n.* **2.** a short sleep; nap. —**snooz′er,** *n.*

snore (snôr), *v.*, **snored, snor•ing,** *n.* —*v.i.* **1.** to breathe during sleep with hoarse or harsh sounds. —*n.* **2.** an act or sound of snoring. —**snor′er,** *n.*

snor•kel (snôr′kəl), *n.* **1.** a tube through which a

swimmer can breathe while moving face down at or just below the surface of the water. —*v.i.* **2.** to swim while using a snorkel. [< G] —**snor'kel•er,** *n.*

snort (snôrt), *v.i.* **1.** to force the breath violently and noisily through the nostrils with a loud, harsh sound, as a horse. **2.** to express contempt, indignation, or annoyance by snorting. —*n.* **3.** an act or sound of snorting. —**snort'er,** *n.*

snot (snot), *n. Informal.* an impudently disagreeable person, esp. a youth. —**snot'ty,** *adj.,* **-ti•er, -ti•est.**

snout (snout), *n.* the part of an animal's head projecting forward and containing the nose and jaws; muzzle.

snow (snō), *n.* **1. a.** precipitation in the form of ice crystals formed directly from water vapor freezing in air. **b.** a layer or fall of snow. **2.** something, as white spots on a television screen, resembling snow. —*v.i.* **3.** to fall as or like snow. —*v.t.* **4.** to let fall as or like snow. **5.** to cover, obstruct, or confine with snow. **6.** *Slang.* to persuade or deceive by insincere talk. —**snow'y,** *adj.,* **-i•er, -i•est.**

snow'ball', *n.* **1.** a ball of snow pressed or rolled together. —*v.i., v.t.* **2.** to increase or cause to increase at an accelerating rate.

Snow'belt' or **Snow' Belt',** *n.* the northern parts of the U.S., esp. the Midwest and the Northeast.

snow•board (snō'bôrd', -bōrd'), *n.* a board for gliding on snow, resembling a wide ski, that one rides in a standing position. —**snow'board'er,** *n.* —**snow'board'ing,** *n.*

snow'bound', *adj.* shut in or immobilized by snow.

snow'drift', *n.* a mound or bank of snow driven together by the wind.

snow'drop', *n.* an early-blooming plant with drooping white flowers.

snow'fall', *n.* **1.** a fall of snow. **2.** the amount of snow at a particular place or in a given time.

snow'flake', *n.* a small crystal or flake of snow.

snow'man', *n., pl.* **-men.** a figure of a person made out of packed snow.

snow'mo•bile' (-mə bēl'), *n.* a motor vehicle with a tread in the rear and skis in the front, for traveling over snow.

snow'plow', *n.* a machine for clearing away snow.

snow'shoe', *n.* a racket-shaped contrivance for the foot for walking on deep snow without sinking.

snow'storm', *n.* a storm accompanied by a heavy fall of snow.

snow'suit', *n.* a child's warmly insulated outer garment for cold weather.

snow' tire', *n.* a tire with a deep tread for increased traction on snow or ice.

snub (snub), *v.,* **snubbed, snub•bing,** *n.* —*v.t.* **1.** to treat with contempt, esp. by ignoring. **2.** to check or stop (a rope or cable that is running out), esp. by means of a rope around a fixed object. —*n.* **3.** an affront, slight, or rebuff.

snub'-nosed', *adj.* having a nose that is short and turned up at the tip.

snuck (snuk), *v.* a pp. and pt. of SNEAK. —**Usage.** See SNEAK.

snuff¹ (snuf), *v.t., v.i.* **1.** to inhale noisily; sniff. **2.** to perceive by or as if by smelling. —*n.* **3.** a sniff. **4.** powdered tobacco inhaled through the nostrils or placed between cheek and gum. —*Idiom.* **5. up to snuff,** *Informal.* up to a certain standard.

snuff² (snuf), *v.t.* **1.** to cut off or remove the charred portion of (a candle). **2. snuff out,** to suppress; crush. —**snuff'er,** *n.*

snuff'box', *n.* a small box for holding snuff.

snuf'fle, *v.,* **-fled, -fling,** *n.* —*v.i.* **1.** to sniff or snuff. **2.** to draw the breath or mucus through the nostrils audibly or noisily. —*n.* **3.** an act or sound of snuffling.

snug (snug), *adj.,* **snug•ger, snug•gest. 1.** warmly comfortable or cozy. **2.** fitting closely, as a garment. **3.** trim or compactly arranged, as a ship. **4.** concealed; well-hidden. —**snug'ly,** *adv.* —**snug'ness,** *n.*

snug'gle, *v.i., v.t.,* **-gled, -gling.** to lie or draw comfortably close; nestle or cuddle.

so¹ (sō), *adv.* **1.** in the manner indicated; thus: *Hold the racket so.* **2.** to the extent or degree indicated: *Don't walk so fast.* **3.** very: *I'm so happy.* **4.** to such a degree or extent: *so far as I know.* **5.** hence; therefore: *She was ill, and so stayed home.* **6.** indeed; truly: *I was so at the party!* **7.** likewise; also: *If he is going, then so am I.* **8.** then; subsequently: *and so to bed.* —*conj.* **9.** in order that: *Study so you won't fail.* **10.** with the result that. —*pron.* **11.** such as has been stated: *If you're leaving, do so now.* **12.** about or near the person or thing in question: *a cup or so of sugar.* —*adj.* **13.** true: *Say it isn't so.* —**Usage.** The intensive *so* meaning "very" is used mainly in informal speech. In writing and formal speech, intensive *so* is most often followed by a completing *that* clause: *Everything is so expensive that families cannot afford necessities.*

so² (sō), *n. Music.* SOL.

soak (sōk), *v.i.* **1.** to lie in and become saturated with a liquid. **2.** to pass through or as if through pores or holes. —*v.t.* **3.** to wet thoroughly; saturate. **4.** to take in; absorb. **5.** *Slang.* to overcharge. —*n.* **6.** the act of soaking. **7.** the liquid in which something is soaked.

so'-and-so', *n., pl.* **so-and-sos.** a person or thing not definitely named.

soap (sōp), *n.* **1.** a cleansing substance usu. made by treating a fat with an alkali. **2.** *Informal.* SOAP OPERA. —*v.t.* **3.** to rub or treat with soap. —*Idiom.* **4. no soap,** *Informal.* useless or unacceptable. —**soap'y,** *adj.,* **-i•er, -i•est.** —**soap'i•ness,** *n.*

soap'box', *n.* an improvised platform, as one on a street, on which a speaker stands.

soap' op'era, *n.* an often melodramatic radio or television series depicting the interconnected lives of many characters. [so called because soap manufacturers were among the original sponsors of such programs]

soap'stone', *n.* a variety of talc with a soapy feel.

soar (sōr), *v.i.* **1.** to fly or glide high in the air. **2.** to rise or ascend to a higher or more exalted level.

sob (sob), *v.,* **sobbed, sob•bing,** *n.* —*v.i., v.t.* **1.** to weep or utter with a convulsive catching of the breath. —*n.* **2.** an act or sound of sobbing. —**sob'bing•ly,** *adv.*

so•ber (sō'bər), *adj.,* **-ber•er, -ber•est,** *v.* —*adj.* **1.** not drunk. **2.** habitually temperate, esp. in the use of liquor. **3.** serious or solemn. **4.** free from excess, extravagance, or exaggeration; restrained. —*v.t., v.i.* **5.** to make or become sober. —**so'ber•ly,** *adv.* —**so'ber•ness,** *n.*

so•bri•e•ty (sə brī'i tē, sō-), *n.* the state or quality of being sober.

so•bri•quet (sō'bri kā', -ket'), *n.* a nickname. Also, **so'bri•quet'.**

Soc. or **soc.,** **1.** socialist. **2.** society. **3.** sociology.

so'-called', *adj.* called thus, esp. incorrectly.

soc•cer (sok'ər), *n.* a form of football in which the ball may be kicked or bounced off any part of the body but the arms and hands.

soc'cer mom', *n.* a typical American suburban woman with school-age children. [so called from her practice of driving her children to soccer games]

so•cia•ble (sō'shə bəl), *adj.* **1.** inclined to enjoy the company of others; companionable. **2.** characterized by agreeable companionship. —**so'cia•bil'i•ty,** *n.* —**so'cia•bly,** *adv.*

so•cial (sō'shəl), *adj.* **1.** of or characterized by friendly relations or companionship. **2.** of or connected with fashionable society. **3.** living or disposed to live with others in a community. **4.** of or based on status in a society. **5.** of the life and welfare of human beings in a community. **6.** living together in colonies, hives, etc., as bees. —*n.* **7.** a social gathering. —**so'cial•ly,** *adv.*

so'cial•ism, *n.* a theory or system of social organization in which the means of production and distribution of goods are owned and controlled collectively or by the government. —**so'cial•ist,** *n.* —**so'cial•is'tic,** *adj.*

so′cial·ite′ (-shə līt′), *n.* a socially prominent person.

so′cial·ize′, *v.*, **-ized, -iz·ing.** —*v.t.* **1.** to make fit for life in society. **2.** to establish or regulate according to the theories of socialism. —*v.i.* **3.** to mingle sociably with others. —**so′cial·i·za′tion**, *n.*

so′cialized med′icine, *n.* a system to provide a nation with complete medical care through government subsidization.

so′cial sci′ence, *n.* a field of study, as economics, dealing with an aspect of society or forms of social activity.

so′cial secu′rity, *n.* (*often caps.*) a federal program of old age, unemployment, health, disability, and survivors' insurance.

so′cial work′, *n.* services or activities designed to improve social conditions among poor, sick, or troubled persons. —**so′cial work′er**, *n.*

so·ci·e·ty (sə sī′i tē), *n., pl.* **-ties.** —*n.* **1.** a group of persons associated together by religion, culture, or shared interests or purposes. **2.** a body of individuals living as members of a community. **3.** human beings collectively. **4.** companionship; company. **5.** the social class comprising wealthy or fashionable persons. —**so·ci′e·tal**, *adj.*

Soci′ety of Friends′, *n.* a Christian sect, founded in England, that is opposed to oath-taking and war.

Soci′ety of Je′sus, *n.* See under JESUIT (def. 1).

so′ci·o·ec·o·nom′ic (sō′sē ō-, sō′shē ō-), *adj.* of or involving a combination of social and economic factors.

so·ci·ol·o·gy (sō′sē ol′ə jē, sō′shē-), *n.* the study of the origin, development, organization, and functioning of human society. —**so′ci·o·log′i·cal** (-ə loj′i kəl), *adj.* —**so′ci·ol′o·gist**, *n.*

so·ci·o·path (sō′sē ə path′, sō′shē-), *n.* PSYCHO-PATH.

sock¹ (sok), *n., pl.* **socks;** sometimes **sox.** a short stocking reaching to the calf or just above the ankle.

sock² (sok), *v.t.* **1.** to strike or hit hard. **2. sock away,** to put into savings or reserve. —*n.* **3.** a hard blow.

sock·et (sok′it), *n.* a hollow or concave part or piece that holds a complementary part.

Soc·ra·tes (sok′rə tēz′), 469?–399 B.C., Athenian philosopher. —**So·crat·ic** (sə krat′ik), *adj., n.* —**So·crat′i·cal·ly**, *adv.*

sod (sod), *n., v.,* **sod·ded, sod·ding.** —*n.* **1.** the surface of the ground when covered with grass. **2.** a section of sod. —*v.t.* **3.** to cover with sod.

so·da (sō′də), *n., pl.* **-das. 1.** any of several compounds containing sodium. **2.** SODA WATER. **3.** a drink made with soda water, flavored syrup, and often ice cream. **4.** a carbonated, flavored and sweetened soft drink.

so′da crack′er, *n.* a crisp cracker made with a yeast dough containing baking soda.

so′da foun′tain, *n.* a counter, as in a drugstore, at which sodas, ice cream, etc., are served.

so′da pop′, *n.* SODA (def. 4).

so′da wa′ter, *n.* water charged with carbon dioxide.

sod·den (sod′n), *adj.* **1.** saturated with liquid or moisture. **2.** soggy, as poorly cooked food. **3.** torpid or listless. —**sod′den·ly**, *adv.*

sod′ house′, *n.* a house built of strips of sod, laid like brickwork, and used esp. by settlers on the Great Plains.

so·di·um (sō′dē əm), *n.* a soft, silver-white, chemically active metallic element that occurs naturally only in combination. *Symbol:* Na; *at. wt.:* 22.9898; *at. no.:* 11.

so′dium bicar′bonate, *n.* a white water-soluble powder used esp. as an antacid and in baking.

so′dium car′bonate, *n.* **1.** a grayish white, water-soluble powder used esp. in the manufacture of glass, ceramics, and soaps. **2.** a crystalline, hydrated form of this compound, used in cleansers.

so′dium chlo′ride, *n.* SALT¹ (def. 1).

so′dium hydrox′ide, *n.* a white, solid substance used esp. to make soap and as a caustic.

so′dium ni′trate, *n.* a crystalline, water-soluble compound that occurs naturally and is used in fertilizers and explosives.

Sod·om (sod′əm), *n.* **1.** an ancient city destroyed because of its wickedness. Gen. 18–19. **2.** any corrupt, vice-ridden place.

sod·om·y (sod′ə mē), *n.* **1.** anal or oral copulation with a member of the same sex or the opposite sex. **2.** sexual relations between a person and an animal. —**sod′om·ite′** (-mīt′), *n.*

so·ev·er (sō ev′ər), *adv.* **1.** of any kind or in any way. **2.** at all; whatever.

so·fa (sō′fə), *n., pl.* **-fas.** an upholstered couch with a back and arms.

so′fa bed′ or **so′fa·bed′**, *n.* a sofa that can be converted into a bed.

So·fi·a (sō′fē ə, sō fē′ə), *n.* the capital of Bulgaria. 1,128,859.

soft (sôft, soft), *adj.* and *adv.,* **-er, -est.** —*adj.* **1.** yielding readily to touch or pressure. **2.** relatively deficient in hardness, as metal. **3.** not rough in texture; smooth. **4.** not harsh or unpleasant to the senses. **5.** gentle or mild: *soft breezes.* **6.** SOFT-HEARTED. **7.** not strong or robust. **8.** not demanding; easy: *a soft job.* **9.** (of water) relatively free from mineral salts that interfere with the action of soap. **10.** (of the landing of a space vehicle) executed with deceleration. **11.** foolish or stupid: *soft in the head.* —*adv.* **12.** in a soft manner. —**soft′ly**, *adv.* —**soft′ness**, *n.*

soft′ball′, *n.* **1.** a form of baseball played with a larger and softer ball. **2.** the ball itself.

soft′-boiled′, *adj.* (of an egg) boiled only until the yolk is partially set.

soft′ coal′, *n.* BITUMINOUS COAL.

soft′ drink′, *n.* a nonalcoholic and often carbonated beverage.

soft·en (sô′fən, sof′ən), *v.t., v.i.* to make or become soft or softer. —**soft′en·er**, *n.*

soft′-heart′ed, *adj.* very sympathetic or responsive.

soft′ lens′, *n.* a nonrigid contact lens made of porous plastic.

soft′ mon′ey, *n.* money contributed to a political candidate or party that is not subject to federal regulations.

soft′ pal′ate, *n.* See under PALATE (def. 1).

soft′-ped′al, *v.t.,* **-aled, -al·ing** or (*esp. Brit.*) **-alled, -al·ling.** to make less obvious, important, or objectionable.

soft′ sell′, *n.* a quietly persuasive method of selling.

soft′ soap′, *n.* persuasive talk; flattery. —**soft′-soap′**, *v.t.*

soft′ware′, *n.* programs for directing the operation of a computer or for processing electronic data.

soft′wood′, *n.* a coniferous tree or its wood.

soft′y or **soft′ie**, *n., pl.* **-ties.** *Informal.* a person easily stirred to sentiment.

sog·gy (sog′ē), *adj.,* **-gi·er, -gi·est. 1.** thoroughly wet. **2.** damp and heavy, as poorly baked bread. —**sog′gi·ly**, *adv.* —**sog′gi·ness**, *n.*

soi·gné or **-gnée** (swän yā′; *Fr.* swa nyā′), *adj.* **1.** elegantly designed or done. **2.** well-groomed.

soil¹ (soil), *n.* **1.** the portion of the earth's surface consisting of disintegrated rock and humus. **2.** ground; earth. **3.** a country, land, or region.

soil² (soil), *v.t.* **1.** to make dirty. **2.** to sully, as with disgrace. —*v.i.* **3.** to become soiled. —*n.* **4.** a spot or stain. **5.** foul matter, esp. sewage or excrement.

soi·ree or **-rée** (swä rā′), *n., pl.* **-rees, -rées.** an evening party.

so·journ (*n.* sō′jûrn; *v. also* sō jûrn′), *n.* **1.** a temporary stay: *a week's sojourn in Paris.* —*v.i.* **2.** to stay temporarily. —**so·journ·er**, *n.*

sol (sōl), *n.* the musical syllable for the fifth tone of the diatonic scale.

Sol (sol), *n.* the Roman god of the sun.

sol·ace (sol′is), *n., v.,* **-aced, -ac·ing.** —*n.* **1.** comfort in sorrow or misfortune. **2.** a source of solace. —*v.t.* **3.** to comfort; console. —**sol′ac•er,** *n.*

so•lar (sō′lər), *adj.* **1.** of, determined by, or proceeding from the sun. **2.** utilizing, operated by, or depending on solar energy.

so′lar cell′, *n.* a photovoltaic cell that converts sunlight directly into electricity.

so•lar•i•um (sə lâr′ē əm, sō-), *n., pl.* **-lar•i•ums, -lar•i•a** (-lâr′ē ə). a glass-enclosed room exposed to the sun's rays.

so′lar plex′us, *n.* **1.** a network of nerves in the upper abdomen behind the stomach. **2.** a point on the stomach wall just below the sternum.

so′lar sys′tem, *n.* the sun with all the celestial bodies that revolve around it.

sold (sōld), *v.* pt. and pp. of SELL.

sol•der (sod′ər), *n.* **1.** an alloy fused and applied to the joint between metal objects to unite them. —*v.t., v.i.* **2.** to join with or as if with solder. —**sol′der•er,** *n.*

sol•dier (sōl′jər), *n.* **1.** a person, esp. an enlisted person, engaged in military service. **2.** a person dedicated to a cause. —*v.i.* **3.** to act or serve as a soldier. **4.** to idle while pretending to work. —**sol′dier•ly,** *adj.*

sol′dier of for′tune, *n.* a person who seeks riches or pleasure through a military career.

sole¹ (sōl), *adj.* being the only one. —**sole′ly,** *adv.*

sole² (sōl), *n., v.,* **soled, sol•ing.** —*n.* **1.** the undersurface of a foot. **2.** the undersurface of a shoe. —*v.t.* **3.** to furnish with a sole.

sole³ (sōl), *n., pl.* **sole, soles.** any of various chiefly marine flatfishes used for food.

sol•e•cism (sol′ə siz′əm, sō′lə-), *n.* **1.** a nonstandard or ungrammatical usage. **2.** a breach of etiquette.

sol•emn (sol′əm), *adj.* **1.** grave; mirthless. **2.** serious; earnest. **3.** formal or ceremonious in character. **4.** marked by or observed with religious rites. —**so•lem•ni•ty** (sə lem′ni tē), *n.* —**sol′emn•ly,** *adv.*

sol′em•nize′ (-nīz′), *v.t.,* **-nized, -niz•ing. 1.** to observe with ceremony or formality. **2.** to perform the ceremony of (marriage).

so•le•noid (sō′lə noid′, sol′ə-), *n.* a coil of wire that when carrying current magnetically attracts a sliding iron core.

so•lic•it (sə lis′it), *v.t.* **1.** to try to obtain by earnest plea. **2.** to entreat; petition. **3.** to lure; entice. —*v.i.* **4.** to solicit something desired, as orders or trade. —**so•lic′i•ta′tion,** *n.*

so•lic′i•tor (-i tar), *n.* **1.** a person who solicits. **2.** a legal officer of a city, town, or state. **3.** (in England and Wales) a lawyer who advises clients and prepares cases for barristers.

so•lic′i•tous, *adj.* **1.** anxious or concerned. **2.** anxiously desirous. —**so•lic′i•tous•ly,** *adv.* —**so•lic′i•tous•ness,** *n.*

so•lic′i•tude′ (-tōōd′, -tyōōd′), *n.* the state of being solicitous.

sol•id (sol′id), *adj.* **1.** not hollow. **2.** having or involving three dimensions. **3.** having no openings or breaks. **4.** firm or compact: *solid ground.* **5.** not liquid or gaseous. **6.** serious in character: *solid scholarship.* **7.** consisting entirely of one substance or material: *solid gold.* **8.** real; genuine: *solid comfort.* **9.** sound or reliable: *a solid citizen.* **10.** written without a hyphen, as a compound word. **11.** unanimous: *a solid majority.* —*n.* **12.** a body or object having three dimensions. **13.** a solid substance. —**so•lid•i•ty** (sə-lid′i tē), *n.* —**sol′id•ly,** *adv.* —**sol′id•ness,** *n.*

sol′i•dar′i•ty (-i dar′i tē), *n.* unanimity of attitude or purpose among members of a group.

so•lid•i•fy (sə lid′ə fī′), *v.t., v.i.,* **-fied, -fy•ing.** to make or become solid. —**so•lid′i•fi•ca′tion,** *n.*

sol′id-state′, *adj.* of or being an electronic device, as a transistor, that can control current without the use of moving parts, heated filaments, or vacuum gaps.

so•lil•o•quy (sə lil′ə kwē), *n., pl.* **-quies. 1.** a speech in a drama in which a character reveals inner thoughts as if alone. **2.** the act of talking to oneself.

—**so•lil′o•quize′** (-kwīz′), *v.i., v.t.,* **-quized, -quiz•ing.**

sol•i•taire (sol′i târ′), *n.* **1.** a card game for one person. **2.** a precious stone, esp. a diamond, set by itself.

sol•i•tar•y (sol′i ter′ē), *adj.* **1.** lacking or avoiding the society of others. **2.** marked by or done in the absence of companions. **3.** being the only one; sole. **4.** secluded; remote. —**sol′i•tar′i•ness,** *n.*

sol′i•tude′ (-tōōd′, -tyōōd′), *n.* **1.** the state of being alone; seclusion. **2.** a lonely, unfrequented place.

so•lo (sō′lō), *n., pl.* **-los** or, for 1, **-li** (-lē), *adj., adv., v.,* **-loed, -lo•ing.** —*n.* **1.** a musical composition for one performer with or without accompaniment. **2.** a performance by one person. —*adj.* **3.** of or being a solo. —*adv.* **4.** on one's own; alone. —*v.i.* **5.** to perform a solo. [< It < L *sōlus* alone] —**so′lo•ist,** *n.*

Sol•o•mon (sol′ə mən), *n.* **1.** fl. 10th century B.C., king of Israel (son of David). **2.** an extraordinarily wise man; a sage.

Sol′omon Is′lands, *n.pl.* a country on an archipelago in the W Pacific Ocean, E of New Guinea. 426,855. —**Sol′omon Is′lander,** *n.*

So•lon (sō′lən), *n.* **1.** c638–c558 B.C., Athenian statesman. **2.** (*often l.c.*) a wise lawgiver.

so′ long′, *interj. Informal.* good-bye.

sol•stice (sol′stis, sōl′-), *n.* either of the two times a year, about June 21 and about Dec. 22, when the sun is at its greatest distance from the celestial equator.

sol•u•ble (sol′yə bəl), *adj.* **1.** capable of being dissolved. **2.** capable of being solved. —**sol′u•bil′i•ty,** *n.*

sol•ute (sol′yōōt, sō′lōōt), *n.* a dissolved substance.

so•lu•tion (sə lōō′shən), *n.* **1.** the act or process of solving a problem. **2.** an answer to a problem. **3. a.** the process by which a gas, liquid, or solid is dispersed homogeneously in a gas, liquid, or solid without chemical change. **b.** the mixture thus formed.

solve (solv), *v.t.,* **solved, solv•ing.** to find the answer for or solution to. —**solv′a•ble,** *adj.* —**solv′er,** *n.*

sol•vent (sol′vənt), *adj.* **1.** able to pay all just debts. **2.** having the power of dissolving. —*n.* **3.** a substance that dissolves another to form a solution. —**sol′ven•cy,** *n.*

So•ma•li•a (sō mä′lē ə), *n.* a republic on the E coast of Africa. 9,940,232. —**So•ma′li•an,** *adj., n.*

so•mat•ic (sō mat′ik, sə-), *adj.* of or affecting the body; physical.

somat′ic cell′, *n.* one of the cells that take part in the formation of the body, becoming differentiated into the various tissues, organs, etc.

som•ber (som′bər), *adj.* **1.** gloomily dark. **2.** downcast; glum. **3.** extremely serious; grave. Also, *esp. Brit.,* **som′bre.** —**som′ber•ly,** *adv.*

som•bre•ro (som brâr′ō), *n., pl.* **-ros.** a broadbrimmed straw or felt hat worn esp. in Mexico and the southwestern U.S.

some (sum; *unstressed* səm), *adj.* **1.** being an undetermined or unspecified one: *Some salesman called.* **2.** unspecified in number, amount, or degree: *Have some popcorn.* **3.** *Informal.* remarkable of its type: *That was some storm.* —*pron.* **4.** an unspecified number or amount: *Some of the books are damaged.* —*adv.* **5.** approximately; about: *Some 300 were present.* **6.** to some degree or extent: *I like baseball some.*

-some¹, a suffix meaning: like (*burdensome*); tending to: (*quarrelsome*).

-some², a suffix meaning a group of a certain number (*threesome*).

-some³, a combining form meaning body (*chromosome*).

some•bod•y (sum′bod′ē, -bud′ē, -bə dē), *pron., n., pl.* **-bod•ies.** —*pron.* **1.** some person. —*n.* **2.** a person of importance.

some′day′, *adv.* at an indefinite future time.

some′how′, *adv.* in a way not specified, apparent, or known.

some′one′ (-wun′, -wən), *pron.* some person; somebody.

some′place′, *adv.* somewhere.

som•er•sault (sum′ər sôlt′), *n.* **1.** an acrobatic movement in which the body rolls end over end, making a complete revolution. —*v.i.* **2.** to perform a somersault.

some′thing′, *pron.* **1.** an undetermined or unspecified thing. **2.** (used in combination to indicate an additional amount, as of years, that is unknown or forgotten): *fortysomething.* —*adv.* **3.** to some extent; somewhat: *The bird looked something like a hawk.*

some′time′, *adv.* **1.** at an indefinite or indeterminate time. **2.** at an indefinite future time. —*adj.* **3.** having been formerly. **4.** being so only at times or in some ways.

some′times′, *adv.* on some occasions; now and then.

some′way′ also **-ways′,** *adv.* somehow.

some′what′, *adv.* **1.** to some extent or degree. —*pron.* **2.** some part, portion, or degree.

some′where′, *adv.* **1.** in, at, or to an unspecified or unknown place. **2.** in the neighborhood of; approximately: *somewhere around 60 years old.*

som•nam•bu•lism (som nam′byə liz′əm, səm-), *n.* SLEEPWALKING. —**som•nam′bu•list,** *n.*

som•no•lent (som′nə lənt), *adj.* **1.** sleepy; drowsy. **2.** tending to cause sleep. —**som′no•lence,** *n.*

son (sun), *n.* **1.** a male child or person in relation to his parents. **2.** a male descendant. **3. the Son,** Jesus Christ.

so•nar (sō′när), *n.* a method or apparatus for detecting and locating objects submerged in water by means of the sound waves they reflect or produce. [*so(und) na(vigation) r(anging)*]

so•na•ta (sə nä′tə), *n., pl.* **-tas.** an instrumental composition typically in three or four movements in contrasting forms and keys.

song (sông, song), *n.* **1.** an often short metrical composition for singing. **2.** poetry. **3.** the art or act of singing. **4.** a patterned, sometimes elaborate vocal signal produced by an animal, as a bird. —*Idiom.* **5. for a song,** at a very low price.

song′bird′, *n.* a bird that sings.

song′fest′, *n.* an informal gathering at which people sing.

Song′ of Sol′omon, The, *n.* a book of the Bible, consisting of a series of love poems. Also called **Song′ of Songs′.**

song′ster (-stər), *n.* one who sings; singer.

son•ic (son′ik), *adj.* of or pertaining to sound or the speed of sound.

son′ic bar′rier, *n.* SOUND BARRIER.

son′ic boom′, *n.* a loud noise caused by an aircraft moving at supersonic speed.

son′-in-law′, *n., pl.* **sons-in-law.** the husband of one's daughter.

son•net (son′it), *n.* a poem of 14 lines, usu. in iambic pentameter, with rhymes arranged in a fixed scheme.

son•ny (sun′ē), *n.* little son (used in addressing a boy).

Son′ of God′, *n.* Jesus Christ, esp. as the Messiah.

Son′ of Man′, *n.* Jesus Christ, esp. at the Last Judgment.

Son′ of Mar′y, *n.* Jesus.

so•no•rous (sə nôr′əs, son′ər əs), *adj.* **1.** resonant or resonating with sound. **2.** rich and full in sound. **3.** high-flown; grandiloquent. —**so•nor′i•ty** (-nôr′i tē, -nor′-), *n.*

Sons′ of Lib′erty, *n.* any of several patriotic societies that opposed the Stamp Act and supported moves for American independence.

soon (soon), *adv.,* **-er, -est. 1.** before long. **2.** promptly; quickly. **3.** readily or willingly.

soot (soot, soot), *n.* a powdery black carbonaceous substance produced during incomplete combustion, as of coal. —**soot′y,** *adj.,* **-i•er, -i•est.**

sooth (sooth), *n. Archaic.* truth, reality, or fact.

soothe (sooth), *v.t.,* **soothed, sooth•ing. 1.** to offer reassurance or comfort to. **2.** to make less severe; allay. —**sooth′er,** *n.* —**sooth′ing, —sooth′ing•ly,** *adv.*

sooth•say•er (sooth′sā′ər), *n.* a person who foretells events. —**sooth′say′ing,** *n.*

sop (sop), *n., v.,* **sopped, sop•ping.** —*n.* **1.** something offered to conciliate, pacify, or bribe. —*v.t.* **2.** to dip or soak in liquid. **3.** to drench. **4.** to take up by absorption.

SOP, Standard Operating Procedure; Standing Operating Procedure.

soph•ism (sof′iz əm), *n.* a specious but plausible argument. —**soph′ist,** *n.*

so•phis•ti•cate (sə fis′ti kit, -kāt′), *n.* a sophisticated person.

so•phis′ti•cat′ed, *adj.* **1.** not naive; worldly-wise. **2.** appealing to cultivated tastes. **3.** complex; intricate. —**so•phis′ti•ca′tion,** *n.*

soph•ist•ry (sof′ə strē), *n., pl.* **-ries.** subtle, plausible, but fallacious reasoning or argumentation.

Soph•o•cles (sof′ə klēz′), *n.* 495?–406? B.C., Greek dramatist.

soph•o•more (sof′ə môr′), *n.* a student in the second year at a high school or college. [earlier *sophumer,* perh. = *sophum* sophism + -ER¹]

soph′o•mor′ic (-môr′ik, -mor′-), *adj.* **1.** of or like a sophomore. **2.** intellectually pretentious but immature and ill-informed.

sop•o•rif•ic (sop′ə rif′ik, sō′pə-), *adj.* **1. a.** causing or tending to cause sleep. **b.** sleepy; drowsy. —*n.* **2.** something soporific, as a drug.

sop•py (sop′ē), *adj.,* **-pi•er, -pi•est. 1.** very wet; drenched. **2.** sentimental; mawkish.

so•pran•o (sə pran′ō, -prä′nō), *n., pl.* **-os. 1. a.** the highest singing voice in women and boys. **b.** a singer with such a voice. **2.** a part for a soprano.

sor•bet (sôr bā′, sôr′bit), *n.* a fruit or vegetable ice, often served between courses.

sor•cer•y (sôr′sə rē), *n., pl.* **-cer•ies.** the exercise of supernatural powers granted by evil spirits. —**sor′cer•er,** *n.* —**sor′cer•ess,** *n.*

sor•did (sôr′did), *adj.* **1.** morally base; vile. **2.** filthy; squalid. —**sor′did•ly,** *adv.* —**sor′did•ness,** *n.*

sore (sôr), *adj.,* **sor•er, sor•est,** *n.* —*adj.* **1.** physically painful or sensitive. **2.** suffering physical or mental pain. **3.** causing distress, sorrow, misery, or hardship. **4.** annoyed; irritated. —*n.* **5.** a sore spot on the body. **6.** a source of grief or distress. —**sore′ly,** *adv.* —**sore′ness,** *n.*

sore′head′, *n. Informal.* a disgruntled or vindictive person.

sor•ghum (sôr′gəm), *n.* **1.** a cereal grass with a tall stem bearing grain. **2.** syrup made from sorghum.

so•ror•i•ty (sə rôr′i tē, -ror′-), *n., pl.* **-ties.** a society or club of women, esp. in a college.

sor•rel¹ (sôr′əl, sor′-), *n.* **1.** a light reddish brown. **2.** a horse of this color.

sor•rel² (sôr′əl, sor′-), *n.* any of several plants with edible acid leaves.

sor•row (sor′ō, sôr′ō), *n.* **1.** distress, as that caused by loss; grief. **2.** a cause or occasion of grief. **3.** the expression of grief. —*v.i.* **4.** to feel or express sorrow. —**sor′row•ful,** *adj.* —**sor′row•ful•ly,** *adv.*

sor•ry (sor′ē, sôr′ē), *adj.,* **-ri•er, -ri•est. 1.** feeling regret, compunction, or sorrow. **2.** regrettable or deplorable; unfortunate. **3.** wretched, poor, or useless. —**sor′ri•ly,** *adv.* —**sor′ri•ness,** *n.*

sort (sôrt), *n.* **1.** a particular kind, class, or group; category. **2.** character, quality, or nature. **3.** manner, fashion, or way. —*v.t.* **4.** to arrange according to kind or class. **5.** to place (computerized data) in order numerically or alphabetically. —*Idiom.* **6. out of sorts, a.** irritable or depressed. **b.** indisposed; ill. **7. sort of,** *Informal.* somewhat; rather. —**sort′er,** *n.* —**Usage.** See KIND.

sor•tie (sôr′tē), *n., v.,* **-tied, -tie•ing.** —*n.* **1.** an attack of troops from a besieged place on the enemy. **2.** a combat mission or raid by an airplane. —*v.i.* **3.** to go on a sortie.

SOS (es′ō′es′), *n., pl.* **SOSs, SOS's. 1.** a radiotelegraphic distress signal, used esp. by ships. **2.** a call for help.

so′-so′, *adj.* **1.** neither very good nor very bad; mediocre. —*adv.* **2.** in a passable manner.

sot•to vo•ce (sot′ō vō′chē), *adv.* in a low voice; softly. [< It: lit., under (the) voice]

sou•brette (sōō bret′), *n.* **1.** a coquettish maidservant in a play or opera. **2.** an actress playing the role of a soubrette.

souf•flé (sōō flā′), *n., pl.* -flés. a light, puffed-up baked dish made fluffy with stiffly beaten egg whites.

sough (sou, suf), *v.i.* **1.** to make a rushing, rustling, or murmuring sound. —*n.* **2.** a soughing sound.

sought (sôt), *v.* pt. and pp. of SEEK.

soul (sōl), *n.* **1.** the spiritual part of a human being that is believed to survive death. **2.** the seat of human feelings. **3.** a person: *a brave soul.* **4.** an essential or central element or part. **5.** the embodiment of a quality: *He was the very soul of tact.* **6.** shared ethnic awareness and pride among black Americans. **7.** deeply felt emotion, as conveyed by a performer. —*adj.* **8.** of or typical of black Americans or their culture: *soul food.*

soul•ful, *adj.* expressive of deep feeling. —**soul′ful•ly,** *adv.* —**soul′ful•ness,** *n.*

sound[1] (sound), *n.* **1.** the sensation produced by stimulation of the organs of hearing. **2.** vibrations transmitted through an elastic medium, esp. air, that can be perceived by the ear. **3.** something heard, as noise or a musical tone. **4.** the distance within which something can be heard. —*v.i.* **5.** to make a sound. **6.** to convey a certain impression; seem: *The report sounds true.* —*v.t.* **7.** to cause to sound. **8.** to announce or order by a sound. **9.** to pronounce clearly.

sound[2] (sound), *adj.,* -**er,** -**est,** *adv.* —*adj.* **1.** free from injury, damage, defect, or disease. **2.** strong, secure, or reliable. **3.** competent or sensible. **4.** having a logical basis. **5.** uninterrupted and untroubled: *sound sleep.* **6.** thorough or severe. **7.** having no legal defect: *a sound title.* —*adv.* **8.** deeply: *sound asleep.* —**sound′ly,** *adv.* —**sound′ness,** *n.*

sound[3] (sound), *v.t.* **1.** to measure the depth of (water), esp. with a weighted line. **2.** to seek to ascertain the views of, esp. by subtle or indirect inquiries. —**sound′ing,** *n.*

sound[4] (sound), *n.* **1.** a relatively narrow passage of water between larger bodies of water or between the mainland and an island. **2.** an inlet or arm of the sea.

sound′ bar′rier, *n.* an abrupt increase in drag experienced by an aircraft approaching the speed of sound.

sound′ bite′, *n.* a brief, striking statement excerpted from an audiotape or videotape for insertion in a broadcast news story.

sound′ing board′, *n.* **1.** a thin board placed in a musical instrument to enhance resonance. **2.** a person whose reactions reveal the acceptability of an idea or plan.

sound′proof′, *adj.* **1.** impervious to sound. —*v.t.* **2.** to make soundproof. —**sound′proof′ing,** *n.*

sound′track′, *n.* the band on a strip of motion-picture film on which sound is recorded.

soup (sōōp), *n.* **1.** a liquid food made by simmering vegetables, seasonings, and often meat or fish. —*v.* **2. soup up,** *Slang.* to increase the power or speed of.

soup•çon (sōōp sôn′), *n.* a slight trace.

soup′y, *adj.,* -**i•er,** -**i•est. 1.** resembling soup in consistency. **2.** very thick; dense. **3.** overly sentimental.

sour (sou°r), *adj.,* -**er,** -**est,** *v.* —*adj.* **1.** acid in taste, as vinegar or lemon juice; tart. **2.** spoiled or fermented. **3.** distasteful or disagreeable. —*v.t., v.i.* **4.** to make or become sour. —**sour′ish,** *adj.* —**sour′ly,** *adv.* —**sour′ness,** *n.*

source (sôrs), *n.* **1.** any thing or place from which something comes or is obtained. **2.** the beginning of a stream or river. **3.** a book, person, or document that supplies information.

sour′dough′, *n.* fermented dough used as a leavening agent.

sour′ grapes′, *n.* pretended disdain for something unattainable.

sour′puss′, *n. Informal.* a grouchy person.

Sou•sa (sōō′zə, -sə), *n.* **John Philip,** 1854–1932, U.S. band conductor and composer.

souse (sous), *v.,* **soused, sous•ing,** *n.* —*v.t., v.i.* **1.** to plunge into liquid. **2.** to steep in brine; pickle. **3.** to make or become wet all over. —*n.* **4.** the act of sousing. **5.** something, as pigs' feet, steeped in pickle. **6.** a liquid for pickling.

Sou•ter (sōō′tər), *n.* **David H.,** born 1939, associate justice of the U.S. Supreme Court since 1990.

south (south), *n.* **1.** a cardinal point of the compass lying directly opposite north. **2.** the direction in which south lies. **3.** (*usu. cap.*) a region situated in this direction. **4. the South, a.** the area south of Pennsylvania and the Ohio River and east of the Mississippi. **b.** the Confederacy. —*adj.* **5.** lying toward or situated in the south. **6.** coming from the south. —*adv.* **7.** to, toward, or in the south.

South′ Af′rica, *n.* **Republic of,** a country in S Africa. 42,327,458. —**South′ Af′rican,** *adj., n.*

South′ Amer′ica, *n.* a continent in the S part of the Western Hemisphere. —**South′ Amer′ican,** *n., adj.*

South′ Bend′, *n.* a city in N Indiana. 105,092.

South′ Car•o•li′na (kar′ə lī′nə), *n.* a state in the SE United States. 3,698,746. *Cap.:* Columbia. *Abbr.:* SC, S.C. —**South′ Car•o•lin′ian** (-lin′ē ən), *n., adj.*

South′ Chi′na Sea′, *n.* a part of the W Pacific, bounded by SE Asia and the Philippines.

South′ Dako′ta, *n.* a state in the N central United States. 732,405. *Cap.:* Pierre. *Abbr.:* SD, S.D., S. Dak. —**South′ Dako′tan,** *n., adj.*

south′east′, *n.* **1.** the point or direction midway between south and east. **2.** a region in this direction. **3. the Southeast,** the southeast region of the United States. —*adj.* **4.** in, toward, or facing the southeast. **5.** coming from the southeast. —*adv.* **6.** toward or from the southeast. —**south′east′er•ly,** *adj., adv.* —**south′east′ern,** *adj.*

South′east A′sia, *n.* a region including Indochina, the Malay Peninsula, and the Malay Archipelago. —**South′east A′sian,** *n., adj.*

south•er•ly (suth′ər lē), *adj., adv.* **1.** toward the south. **2.** from the south.

south•ern (suth′ərn), *adj.* **1.** in or toward the south. **2.** from the south. **3.** (*often cap.*) of the south or South. —**south′ern•most′,** *adj.*

south′ern•er, *n.* **1.** a native or inhabitant of the south. **2.** (*cap.*) a native or inhabitant of the southern U.S.

South′ern Hem′isphere, *n.* the half of the earth between the South Pole and the equator.

south′ern king′dom, *n.* Judah under King Rehoboam.

south′ern lights′, *n.pl.* AURORA AUSTRALIS.

South′ern Rhode′sia, *n.* a former name of ZIMBABWE.

South′ Kore′a, *n.* a country in E Asia. 45,948,811. Official name, **Republic of Korea.** Compare NORTH KOREA. —**South′ Kore′an,** *n., adj.*

south′paw′, *n. Informal.* a left-handed person, esp. a left-handed baseball pitcher.

South′ Pole′, *n.* the southern end of the earth's axis, the southernmost point on earth.

South′ Sea′ Is′lands, *n.pl.* the islands in the S Pacific Ocean.

South′ Vietnam′, *n.* See under VIETNAM.

south′ward (-wərd), *adj.* **1.** moving, facing, or situated toward the south. —*adv.* **2.** Also, **south′wards.** toward the south.

south′west′, *n.* **1.** the point or direction midway between south and west. **2.** a region in this direction. **3. the Southwest,** the southwest region of the United States. —*adj.* **4.** in, toward, or facing the southwest. **5.** coming from the southwest. —*adv.* **6.** toward or from the southwest. —**south′west′er•ly,** *adj., adv.* —**south′west′ern,** *adj.*

south′west′er, *n.* a wind or storm from the southwest.

sou•ve•nir (sōō′və nēr′), *n.* an article kept as a reminder, as of a place visited; memento.

sov•er•eign (sov′rin, -ər in), *n.* **1.** a supreme ruler, as a monarch. **2.** a former British gold coin equal to one pound sterling. —*adj.* **3.** supreme in rank, power, or authority. **4.** having independence; autonomous: *a sovereign state.* **5.** surpassing all others in quality.

sov·er·eign·ty, *n., pl.* **-ties. 1.** the status, dominion, power, or authority of a sovereign. **2.** supreme and independent power or authority in a state.

So·vi·et (sō′vē et′, -it), *n.* **1.** Usu., **Soviets.** the governing officials and citizens of the Soviet Union. **2.** (*l.c.*) an elected governmental council in the Soviet Union. —*adj.* **3.** of the Soviet Union or the Soviets. [< Russ *sovét* council, advice]

So′viet Un′ion, *n.* UNION OF SOVIET SOCIALIST REPUBLICS.

sow¹ (sō), *v.,* **sowed, sown** or **sowed, sow·ing.** —*v.t.* **1.** to scatter (seed) for growth. **2.** to scatter seed over (land, earth, etc.). **3.** to implant or introduce; disseminate. —*v.i.* **4.** to sow seed. —*Idiom.* **5. sow one's wild oats,** to have a youthful fling at reckless behavior. —*Proverb.* **6. As you sow, so shall you reap,** people bear responsibility for the results of their actions. Gal. 6:7. —**sow′er,** *n.*

sow² (sou), *n.* an adult female swine.

So·we·to (sə wet′ō, -wā′tō), *n.* a group of black townships in NE South Africa.

sox (soks), *n.* a pl. of SOCK¹.

soy (soi), *n.* **1.** the soybean. **2.** Also called **soy′ sauce′.** a salty sauce made from fermented soybeans.

soy′bean′, *n.* **1.** a plant of the legume family grown chiefly for forage and its edible seed. **2.** the seed of the soybean.

Sp or **Sp., 1.** Spain. **2.** Spanish.

spa (spä), *n., pl.* **spas. 1.** a mineral spring. **2.** a luxurious resort, esp. one with a spa.

space (spās), *n., v.,* **spaced, spac·ing.** —*n.* **1.** the unlimited three-dimensional expanse in which all material objects are located. **2.** a portion or extent of space. **3.** OUTER SPACE. **4.** an available or allocated place: *a parking space.* **5.** an extent, period, or interval of time. **6.** a blank area, as in a text. **7.** freedom, as to express oneself or fulfill one's needs. —*v.t.* **8.** to divide into or separate by spaces.

Space′ Age′, *n.* (*sometimes l.c.*) the period marked by space exploration, considered as beginning Oct. 4, 1957, when the Soviet Union launched the first sputnik.

space′-age′, *adj.* **1.** of or pertaining to the Space Age. **2.** using the latest or most advanced technology or design. **3.** very modern; up-to-date; forward-looking: *space-age architecture.*

space′craft′, *n., pl.* **-crafts, -craft.** a vehicle designed to operate beyond the earth's atmosphere or orbit the earth.

space′flight′, *n.* flight in outer space.

space′ heat′er, *n.* a device for heating a limited area.

space′man′ (-man′, -mən), *n., pl.* **-men** (-men′, -mən). **1.** an astronaut. **2.** an extraterrestrial.

space′port′, *n.* a site at which spacecraft are tested and launched.

space′ship′, *n.* a spacecraft.

space′ shut′tle, *n.* a reusable spacecraft for shuttling passengers and cargo into orbit and back.

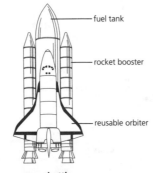

fuel tank

rocket booster

reusable orbiter

space shuttle

space′ sta′tion, *n.* a manned spacecraft or satellite orbiting the earth and serving as a base for research.

space′suit′, *n.* a pressurized suit designed to allow the wearer to survive in outer space.

space′walk′, *n.* **1.** the act of maneuvering in space outside a spacecraft. —*v.i.* **2.** to execute a spacewalk.

spa·cious (spā′shəs), *adj.* containing much space; roomy. —**spa′cious·ly,** *adv.* —**spa′cious·ness,** *n.*

Spack·le (spak′əl), *Trademark.* a brand of plasterlike material for patching cracks.

spade¹ (spād), *n., v.,* **spad·ed, spad·ing.** —*n.* **1.** a digging tool with a long handle and a flat blade. —*v.t.* **2.** to dig or cut with a spade. —**spade′ful,** *n., pl.* **-fuls.**

spade² (spād), *n.* **1.** a black figure shaped like an inverted heart with a short stem, used on playing cards. **2.** a card of the suit bearing spades.

spade′work′, *n.* preliminary work on which further activity is to be based.

spa·dix (spā′diks), *n., pl.* **spa·di·ces** (spā dī′sēz, spā′də sēz′). a fleshy or thickened spike of minute flowers, usu. enclosed in a spathe.

spa·ghet·ti (spə get′ē), *n.* pasta in the form of long strings.

Spain (spān), *n.* a kingdom in SW Europe. 39,244,195.

spake (spāk), *v. Archaic.* a pt. of SPEAK.

Spam (spam), *n., v.,* **spammed, spam·ming. 1.** *Trademark.* a canned food product consisting esp. of pork. —*n.* **2.** (*l.c.*) a disruptive message posted on a computer network. —*v.t.* **3.** (*l.c.*) to send spam to. —*v.i.* **4.** (*l.c.*) to send spam. [(def. 1) < SP(ICED) + (H)AM; (other defs.) ref. to a comedy routine on *Monty Python's Flying Circus,* Brit. TV series]

span¹ (span), *n., v.,* **spanned, span·ning.** —*n.* **1.** the full extent or reach of something. **2.** a short period of time. **3.** the distance or space between two supports, as of a bridge. **4.** the distance, about 9 inches, between the tips of the thumb and the little finger of a fully extended hand. —*v.t.* **5.** to extend or reach across. **6.** to measure by the span of the hand.

span² (span), *n.* a pair of animals, as horses, driven together.

Span., Spanish.

span·dex (span′deks), *n.* an elastic synthetic fiber used esp. in garments.

span·gle (spang′gəl), *n., v.,* **-gled, -gling.** —*n.* **1.** a small, thin piece of glittering metal used esp. for decorating garments. —*v.t.* **2.** to decorate with or as if with spangles.

Span·iard (span′yərd), *n.* a native or inhabitant of Spain.

span·iel (span′yəl), *n.* any of several dogs usu. having drooping ears and a long, silky coat.

Span·ish (span′ish), *n.* **1.** the Romance language of Spain, Mexico, and most of Central and South America. **2.** (*used with a pl. v.*) the inhabitants of Spain. —*adj.* **3.** of Spain, its inhabitants, or their language.

Span′ish Amer′ica, *n.* the Spanish-speaking countries south of the U.S.

Span′ish Amer′ican, *n.* **1.** a resident of the U.S. of Spanish birth or descent. **2.** a native or inhabitant of Spanish America. —**Span′ish-Amer′ican,** *adj.*

Span′ish moss′, *n.* a plant that grows in long strands over trees, esp. in the southeastern U.S.

spank (spangk), *v.t.* **1.** to strike on the buttocks with the open hand. —*n.* **2.** a blow given in spanking.

spank·ing, *adj.* **1.** quick and vigorous; brisk: *a spanking breeze.* —*adv.* **2.** extremely; very: *spanking clean.* —*n.* **3.** several quick slaps on the buttocks given as punishment.

spar¹ (spär), *n.* a stout pole, as a mast or yard, for supporting sails.

spar² (spär), *v.i.,* **sparred, spar·ring. 1.** to box with light blows, esp. as a part of training. **2.** to engage in a dispute.

spare (spâr), *v.,* **spared, spar·ing,** *adj.,* **spar·er, spar·est,** *n.* —*v.t.* **1.** to refrain from harming, punishing, or killing. **2.** to save, as from discomfort. **3.** to refrain from using; do without. **4.** to use or give frugally: *Don't spare the whipped cream! —adj.* **5.** kept in reserve: *a spare part.* **6.** exceeding present needs; extra: *spare time.* **7.** restricted; meager. **8.** lean or thin. *—n.* **9.** a spare thing or part, esp. a spare tire. **10.** the knocking down of all the bowling pins with two bowls. **—spare/ly,** *adv.* **—spare/ness,** *n.*

spare/ribs/, *n.pl.* a cut of meat from the ribs, esp. of pork, with some meat adhering to the bones.

spar/ing, *adj.* economical; frugal. **—spar/ing•ly,** *adv.*

spark (spärk), *n.* **1.** an ignited or glowing particle, as one thrown off by burning wood or produced by friction. **2.** the light produced by a sudden discharge of electricity. **3.** something that activates or stimulates. **4.** a small amount or trace. *—v.i.* **5.** to emit sparks. *—v.t.* **6.** to kindle, animate, or stimulate.

spar/kle, *v.,* **-kled, -kling,** *n.* *—v.i.* **1.** to give off or shine with flashes of light; glitter. **2.** to be brilliant or vivacious. **3.** to effervesce, as wine. *—n.* **4.** brilliance or vivacity. **5.** a little spark. **6.** effervescence. **—spar/kler,** *n.* **—spar/kly,** *adj.*

spark/ plug/, *n.* a device that ignites the fuel mixture in an internal-combustion engine.

spar•row (spar/ō), *n.* any of numerous small, typically gray-brown New World songbirds.

sparse (spärs), *adj.,* **spars•er, spars•est.** thinly scattered or distributed; not dense. **—sparse/ly,** *adv.* **—sparse/ness, spar/si•ty,** *n.*

Spar•ta (spär/tə), *n.* an ancient city in S Greece, famous for strict discipline and military power.

Spar/tan, *adj.* **1.** of Sparta or its inhabitants. **2.** sternly disciplined and austere. *—n.* **3.** a native or inhabitant of Sparta. **4.** a person of Spartan character.

spasm (spaz/əm), *n.* **1.** a sudden involuntary muscular contraction. **2.** a sudden burst of energy, activity, or feeling.

spas•mod•ic (spaz mod/ik), *adj.* **1.** of or characterized by spasms. **2.** fitful or intermittent. **—spas• mod/i•cal•ly,** *adv.*

spas•tic (spas/tik), *adj.* **1.** of, characterized by, or afflicted with muscular spasms. *—n.* **2.** a person afflicted with spasms.

spat¹ (spat), *n., v.,* **spat•ted, spat•ting.** *—n.* **1.** a petty quarrel. *—v.i.* **2.** to engage in a spat.

spat² (spat), *v.* a pt. and pp. of SPIT¹.

spat³ (spat), *n.* a short gaiter worn over the instep.

spat⁴ (spat), *n.* the spawn of a shellfish, as an oyster.

spate (spāt), *n.* a sudden outpouring.

spathe (spāth), *n.* a bract, often large, enclosing a spadix or spike of flowers.

spa•tial (spā/shəl), *adj.* of, existing in, or occurring in space. **—spa/tial•ly,** *adv.*

spat•ter (spat/ər), *v.t., v.i.* **1.** to scatter or spout in drops. **2.** to splash in or as if in a shower. *—n.* **3.** an act or sound of spattering. **4.** a splash or spot spattered.

spat•u•la (spach/ə lə), *n., pl.* **-las.** an implement with a flexible blade used for blending or spreading substances such as food.

spav•in (spav/in), *n.* a disease of horses marked by enlargement of the hock joint. **—spav/ined,** *adj.*

spawn (spôn), *n.* **1.** the eggs deposited in water by aquatic creatures, as fishes. **2.** progeny, esp. when numerous. *—v.i., v.t.* **3.** to deposit or produce (spawn). **4.** to bring forth; produce.

spay (spā), *v.t.* to remove the ovaries of (an animal).

speak (spēk), *v.,* **spoke, spo•ken, speak•ing.** *—v.i.* **1.** to utter words; talk. **2.** to communicate one's emotions or thoughts by or as if by speaking. **3.** to deliver an address or speech. *—v.t.* **4.** to utter (words). **5.** to express with or as if with the voice. **6.** to use or be able to use (a language) in oral utterance. *—Saying.* **7. Speak softly and carry a big stick,** refrain from aggressiveness, but let it be known the strength is there: a saying popularized by Theodore Roosevelt.

speak/eas/y, *n., pl.* **-eas•ies.** a place selling alcoholic beverages illegally.

speak/er, *n.* **1.** a person who speaks. **2.** (*usu. cap.*) the presiding officer of a legislative assembly. **3.** LOUDSPEAKER.

speak/ing in tongues/, *n.* a form of glossolalia in which a person experiencing religious ecstasy utters incomprehensible sounds believed to be of divine inspiration. Also called **gift of tongues.**

spear¹ (spēr), *n.* **1.** a weapon for thrusting or throwing that consists of a long shaft with a sharp-pointed head. **2.** a similar implement for use in fishing. *—v.t.* **3.** to pierce with or as if with a spear.

spear² (spēr), *n.* a sprout or shoot of a plant, as a blade of grass.

spear/head/, *n.* **1.** the sharp-pointed head of a spear. **2.** a person or force that leads an undertaking. *—v.t.* **3.** to act as a spearhead for.

spear/mint/, *n.* an aromatic herb of the mint family that is used for flavoring.

spe•cial (spesh/əl), *adj.* **1.** distinct or particular in kind; unique. **2.** intended for a specific function, purpose, or occasion. **3.** not ordinary or usual. **4.** exceptional. **5.** particularly valued. *—n.* **6.** a special person or thing. **—spe/cial•ly,** *adv.*

spe/cial deliv/ery, *n.* mail delivery by special messenger for an extra fee.

spe/cial•ist, *n.* a person devoted to one particular pursuit or branch of a subject.

spe/cial•ize/, *v.i.,* **-ized, -iz•ing.** to pursue a specialty. **—spe/cial•i•za/tion,** *n.*

spe/cial•ty, *n., pl.* **-ties. 1.** a subject of study, line of work, or activity on which one concentrates. **2.** an article, product, or service of superior quality. **3.** a special point, item, or feature.

spe•cie (spē/shē, -sē), *n.* coined money; coin.

spe•cies (spē/shēz, -sēz), *n., pl.* **-cies. 1.** a distinct sort or kind. **2.** a basic category of biological classification composed of related individuals that are able to breed among themselves.

spe/cies•ism, *n.* discrimination in favor of one species over another, esp. of the human species in the exploitation of other animals.

specif., **1.** specific. **2.** specifically.

spe•cif•ic (spi sif/ik), *adj.* **1.** clearly specified; precise or explicit. **2.** peculiar, proper, or limited to someone or something, as a characteristic. **3.** of or being a species. **4.** effective in the prevention or cure of a certain disease. *—n.* **5.** something specific. **—spe•cif/i•cal•ly,** *adv.* **—spec/i•fic/i•ty** (spes/ə fis/i tē), *n.*

spec•i•fi•ca•tion (spes/ə fi kā/shən), *n.* **1.** Usu., **-tions.** a detailed statement, as of requirements for a proposed building. **2.** something specified.

specif/ic grav/ity, *n.* the ratio of the density of a substance to the density of a standard substance, water being the standard for liquids and solids.

spec/i•fy/, *v.t.,* **-fied, -fy•ing. 1.** to mention or name explicitly. **2.** to set forth as a specification.

spec•i•men (spes/ə mən), *n.* **1.** a part or an individual taken as exemplifying a whole or group. **2.** a sample, esp. of urine, for examination.

spe•cious (spē/shəs), *adj.* apparently true, right, or attractive but lacking real merit. **—spe/cious•ly,** *adv.*

speck (spek), *n.* **1.** a small spot. **2.** a small amount; bit. *—v.t.* **3.** to mark with specks.

speck/le, *n., v.,* **-led, -ling.** *—n.* **1.** a small speck. *—v.t.* **2.** to mark with speckles.

specs (speks), *n.pl. Informal.* **1.** spectacles; eyeglasses. **2.** specifications.

spec•ta•cle (spek/tə kəl), *n.* **1.** something presented to the sight or view. **2.** a public display, esp. on a large scale. **3. spectacles,** eyeglasses.

spec•tac/u•lar (-tak/yə lər), *adj.* **1.** dramatic or impressive. *—n.* **2.** an impressive spectacle. **—spec• tac/u•lar•ly,** *adv.*

spec•ta•tor (spek/tā tər), *n.* a person who looks on or watches; observer.

spec•ter (spek/tər), *n.* a ghost; phantom. Also, *esp. Brit.,* **spec/tre.**

spec/tral (-tral), *adj.* **1.** of or resembling a specter. **2.** of or produced by a spectrum.

spec•tro•scope (spek/trə skōp/), *n.* an optical device for observing a spectrum of light or radiation. —**spec′tro•scop′ic** (-skop′ik), *adj.* —**spec•tros′-co•py** (-tros′kə pē), *n.*

spec′trum (-trəm), *n.*, *pl.* -**tra** (-trə), -**trums.** **1.** a band or series of colors produced by the dispersion of radiant energy, as by a prism. **2.** a broad range or sequence.

spec•u•late (spek′yə lāt′), *v.i.*, -**lat•ed**, -**lat•ing.** **1.** to engage in thought, esp. conjectural thought. **2.** to engage in a risky business transaction in the hope of making a large profit. —**spec′u•la′tion**, *n.* —**spec′u•la′tive**, *adj.* —**spec′u•la′tor**, *n.*

speech (spēch), *n.* **1.** the faculty of speaking. **2.** the act or manner of speaking. **3.** something spoken. **4.** an address by a speaker to an audience. **5.** a language or dialect.

speech′less, *adj.* **1.** temporarily deprived of speech, as by fear. **2.** lacking the faculty of speech.

speed (spēd), *n.*, *v.*, **sped** or **speed•ed**, **speed•ing.** —*n.* **1.** rapidity; swiftness. **2.** relative rate of motion or progress. **3.** a gear ratio in a motor vehicle or bicycle. —*v.t.* **4.** to promote the progress of. **5.** to increase the rate of speed of. —*v.i.* **6.** to go or proceed fast. **7.** to drive fast, esp. at an illegal rate of speed. **8.** to go faster; accelerate. —**speed′er**, *n.* —**speed′i•ly**, *adv.* —**speed′y**, *adj.*, -**i•er**, -**i•est.**

speed′boat′, *n.* a motorboat designed for high speeds.

speed•om•e•ter (spē dom′i tər, spi-), *n.* an instrument on an automobile or other vehicle for indicating speed.

speed′ster (-stər), *n.* one that travels at high speed.

speed′way′, *n.* **1.** an automobile or motorcycle racetrack. **2.** a road for fast driving.

speed′well′, *n.* a plant of the figwort family with spikes of small flowers.

spe•le•ol•o•gy (spē′lē ol′ə jē), *n.* the exploration and study of caves. —**spe′le•ol′o•gist**, *n.*

spell¹ (spel), *v.*, **spelled** or **spelt**, **spell•ing.** —*v.t.* **1.** to name or write the letters in order. **2.** (of letters) to form (a word, syllable, etc.). **3.** to signify; mean. —*v.i.* **4.** to spell words. **5. spell out,** to make the meaning of unmistakable.

spell² (spel), *n.* **1.** a word or phrase supposed to have magic power. **2.** a state of enchantment. **3.** an irresistible influence; fascination.

spell³ (spel), *n.* **1.** a continuous period of activity: *a spell at the wheel.* **2.** a turn at work. **3.** a bout, fit, or attack: *a coughing spell.* **4.** an indefinite period of time. **5.** a period of weather of a particular kind. —*v.t.* **6.** to take the place of for a time.

spell′bind′, *v.t.*, -**bound**, -**bind•ing.** to hold by or as if by a spell; enchant. —**spell′bind′er**, *n.*

spell′bound′, *adj.* held by or as if by a spell; enchanted.

spell′-check′, *v.t.* to process (a document) with a spell checker; check the spelling of.

spell′ (or **spell′ing**) **check′er**, *n.* a computer program for checking the spelling of words in an electronic document.

spell′down′, *n.* a spelling bee.

spell′er, *n.* **1.** a person who spells words. **2.** a textbook to teach spelling.

spell′ing, *n.* **1.** the order in which letters form a word. **2.** a group of letters composing a word.

spell′ing bee′, *n.* a spelling competition.

spe•lunk•er (spi lung′kər), *n.* a person who explores caves.

spend (spend), *v.*, **spent**, **spend•ing.** —*v.t.* **1.** to pay out (money). **2.** to expend (labor, thought, etc.) on an undertaking. **3.** to pass (time). **4.** to use up; exhaust. —*v.i.* **5.** to spend money, energy, resources, or time. —**spend′a•ble**, *adj.* —**spend′er**, *n.*

spend′ing cap′, *n.* an upper limit on expenditures, esp. by a government.

spend′thrift′, *n.* a person who spends extravagantly and wastefully.

Spen•ser (spen′sər), *n.* **Edmund**, c1552–99, English poet. —**Spen•se′ri•an** (-sēr′ē ən), *adj.*, *n.*

spent (spent), *v.* **1.** pt. and pp. of SPEND. —*adj.* **2.** worn-out; exhausted.

sperm (spûrm), *n.* **1.** a spermatozoon. **2.** semen. —**sper•mat′ic** (spûr mat′ik), *adj.*

sper•mat•o•zo•on (spûr mat′ə zō′ən, -on), *n.*, *pl.* -**zo•a** (-zō′ə). a mature male reproductive cell.

sper′mi•cide′ (-mə sīd′), *n.* a sperm-killing agent.

sperm′ whale′, *n.* a large, toothed whale with a cavity in the head containing a valuable oil.

spew (spyōō), *v.i.*, *v.t.* **1.** to vomit. **2.** to gush or pour out violently or copiously. —**spew′er**, *n.*

sp. gr., specific gravity.

sphere (sfēr), *n.* **1.** a solid geometric figure whose surface is at all points equidistant from the center. **2.** any rounded, globular body. **3.** a heavenly body. **4.** surroundings; environment. **5.** field; domain. [< L *sphaera* globe < Gk *sphaîra*] —**spher•i•cal** (sfer′kəl, sfēr′-), *adj.*

sphe•roid (sfēr′oid), *n.* a solid figure, as an ellipsoid, similar in shape to a sphere. —**sphe•roi′dal**, *adj.*

sphinc•ter (sfingk′tər), *n.* a circular band of muscle that closes a bodily orifice.

sphinx (sfingks), *n.*, *pl.* **sphinx•es, sphin•ges** (sfin′jēz). **1.** an ancient Egyptian figure with a lion's body and a human or animal head. **2.** (*cap.*) (in Greek myth) a winged monster with a woman's head and a lion's body that killed wayfarers unable to answer the riddle it posed. **3.** a mysterious, inscrutable person.

sphinx

spice (spīs), *n.*, *v.*, **spiced**, **spic•ing.** —*n.* **1.** an aromatic vegetable substance, as pepper or cinnamon, used to season food. **2.** something that gives zest or piquancy. —*v.t.* **3.** to season with spice. **4.** to give zest to. —**spic′y**, *adj.*, -**i•er**, -**i•est.** —**spic′i•ness**, *n.*

spick-and-span (spik′ən span′), *adj.* **1.** spotlessly clean. **2.** perfectly new.

spic•ule (spik′yōōl), *n.* a small, needlelike part or process.

spi•der (spī′dər), *n.* **1.** any of numerous arachnids with a body divided into two parts and silk-secreting spinnerets for spinning webs. **2.** a frying pan, orig. one with legs. —**spi′der•y**, *adj.*

spiel (spēl, shpēl), *n. Informal.* a glib and usu. extravagant talk or speech, esp. one used to persuade.

spiff•y (spif′ē), *adj.*, -**i•er**, -**i•est.** *Informal.* smart; fine.

spig•ot (spig′ət), *n.* **1.** a plug for stopping the vent of a cask. **2.** a faucet.

spike¹ (spīk), *n.*, *v.*, **spiked**, **spik•ing.** —*n.* **1.** a long thick nail. **2.** a naillike metal projection, as on the sole of a shoe, for improving traction. —*v.t.* **3.** to fasten or secure with spikes. **4.** to pierce with or impale on a spike. **5.** to suppress or thwart: *We spiked the rumor.* —**spik′y**, *adj.*, -**i•er**, -**i•est.**

spike² (spīk), *n.* **1.** an ear of grain. **2.** an elongated flower cluster.

spill (spil), *v.*, **spilled** or **spilt**, **spill•ing**, *n.* —*v.t.* **1.** to cause or allow to run, flow, or escape from a container, esp. accidentally. **2.** to shed (blood), as in wounding. **3.** to throw off: *spilled by a horse.* —*v.i.* **4.** to run, flow, or escape from or as if from a container. —*n.* **5.** a spilling, as of liquid. **6.** a quantity spilled. **7.** a fall, as from a horse. —**spill′age** (-ij), *n.*

spill′way′, *n.* a passageway through which surplus water escapes, as from a reservoir.

spin (spin), *v.*, **spun**, **spin•ning**, *n.* —*v.t.* **1.** to make (yarn) by drawing out and twisting fibers. **2.** to form (fibers) into yarn. **3.** to produce (a web, cocoon, etc.) by extruding a viscous filament that hardens in the air. **4.** to cause to rotate rapidly; twirl. **5.** to produce or fabricate slowly and bit by bit: *to spin a tale.* **6.** to draw out; protract. —*v.i.* **7.** to rotate rapidly. **8.** to extrude a viscous filament, as a spider. **9.** to spin yarn or thread. **10.** to move or travel rapidly. **11.** to have a sensation of whirling; reel. **12. spin off,** to create or derive from something already in existence. —*n.* **13.** a spinning motion. **14.** a short ride in a motor vehicle. **15.** *Slang.* a viewpoint or bias, esp. in the media. —**spin′ner,** *n.* —**spin′ning,** *n.*

spin•ach (spin′ich), *n.* a plant cultivated for its edible green leaves.

spi•nal (spīn′l), *adj.* of or pertaining to the spine or spinal cord.

spi′nal col′umn, *n.* the series of vertebrae forming the axis of the skeleton in vertebrates.

spi′nal cord′, *n.* the cord of nerve tissue extending through a canal in the spinal column.

spin′ control′, *n. Slang.* an attempt to give a bias to news coverage, esp. of a political event.

spin•dle (spin′dl), *n.* **1.** a rounded, tapered rod on which fibers are twisted and thread is wound in spinning. **2.** a rod or pin that turns or on which something turns. **3.** something, as a turned piece of wood, that resembles a spindle.

spin′dly, *adj.,* **-dli•er, -dli•est.** long, thin, and usu. frail.

spin′ doc′tor, *n. Slang.* a press agent skilled at spin control.

spine (spīn), *n.* **1.** SPINAL COLUMN. **2.** a stiff-pointed process on a plant or animal. **3.** the back of a book binding. —**spin′y,** *adj.,* **-i•er, -i•est.**

spine′less, *adj.* **1.** having no backbone or spines. **2.** lacking resolution or courage.

spin•et (spin′it), *n.* a small upright piano.

spin•na•ker (spin′ə kər), *n.* a large, usu. triangular sail used esp. when running before the wind.

spin′ning wheel′, *n.* a device used for spinning yarn or thread that consists of a single spindle driven by a large wheel.

spin′-off′ or **spin′off′,** *n.* a by-product or incidental outgrowth of something preexisting.

Spi•no•za (spi nō′zə), *n.* **Baruch** or **Benedict de,** 1632–77, Dutch philosopher.

spin•ster (spin′stər), *n.* an unmarried woman beyond the conventional age for marriage. —**spin′ster•hood′,** *n.* —**spin′ster•ish,** *adj.*

spin′y lob′ster, *n.* an edible crustacean differing from the lobster in having a spiny shell and lacking large pincers.

spi•ra•cle (spī′rə kəl, spir′ə-), *n.* an opening for breathing, as a blowhole.

spi•ral (spī′rəl), *n., adj., v.,* **-raled, -ral•ing** or (*esp. Brit.*) **-ralled, -ral•ling.** —*n.* **1.** a plane curve generated by a point moving around a fixed point while constantly receding from or approaching it. **2.** a single circle of a spiral object. **3.** something resembling a spiral. **4.** a continuously accelerating increase or decrease. —*adj.* **5.** of, shaped like, or being a spiral. —*v.i., v.t.* **6.** to take or cause to take a spiral form or course.

spire (spī°r), *n.* **1.** a tall, acutely pointed roof forming the top of a tower or steeple. **2.** a tall, sharp-pointed part; tip. —**spir′y,** *adj.*

spi•re•a or **-rae•a** (spī rē′ə), *n., pl.* **-re•as** or **-rae•as.** a shrub of the rose family with clusters of small white or pink flowers.

spir•it (spir′it), *n.* **1.** the animating principle of life, esp. of humans. **2.** the incorporeal part of humans, esp. the mind or soul. **3.** a supernatural being: *evil spirits.* **4.** (*cap.*) the Holy Spirit. **5.** Often, **-its.** temper, mood, or disposition. **6.** an individual; person: *a few brave spirits.* **7.** dominant tendency or character: *the spirit of the age.* **8.** vigorous sense of group membership: *college spirit.* **9.** general meaning or intent: *the spirit of the law.* **10.** Often, **-its.** a distilled alcoholic liquor. —*v.t.* **11.** to carry off mysteriously or secretly. —***Proverb.* 12. The spirit is willing, but the flesh is weak,** physical temptation may overcome virtue. Matt. 26:4. —**spir′it•less,** *adj.*

spir•it•ed, *adj.* having or showing courage or animation.

spir•it•u•al (-chōō əl), *adj.* **1.** of the spirit or the soul. **2.** of sacred matters; religious. **3.** of a church; ecclesiastical. —*n.* **4.** a religious song originating among blacks in the southern U.S. —**spir′it•u•al′i•ty,** *n.* —**spir′it•u•al•ly,** *adv.*

spir•it•u•al•ism, *n.* the belief that the spirits of the dead communicate with the living, esp. through a medium. —**spir′it•u•al•ist,** *n.* —**spir′it•u•al•is′tic,** *adj.*

spir•it•u•ous, *adj.* containing alcohol; alcoholic.

spi•ro•chete (spī′rə kēt′), *n.* any of various mobile, spiral bacteria including a species that causes syphilis.

spit¹ (spit), *v.,* **spit** or **spat, spit•ting,** *n.* —*v.i.* **1.** to eject saliva from the mouth. —*v.t.* **2.** to eject from the mouth. **3.** to send forth like saliva. —*n.* **4.** saliva, esp. when ejected. **5.** the act of spitting.

spit² (spit), *n., v.,* **spit•ted, spit•ting.** —*n.* **1.** a pointed rod for skewering and holding meat over a fire. **2.** a narrow point of land projecting into the water. —*v.t.* **3.** to pierce with or as if with a spit.

spit′ball′, *n.* **1.** a ball of chewed paper used as a missile. **2.** an illegal baseball pitch made to curve by moistening the ball with saliva.

spite (spīt), *n., v.,* **spit•ed, spit•ing.** —*n.* **1.** a malicious, usu. petty desire to harm, annoy, or humiliate another. —*v.t.* **2.** to treat with spite. —***Idiom.* 3. in spite of,** notwithstanding; despite. —**spite′ful,** *adj.* —**spite′ful•ly,** *adv.* —**spite′ful•ness,** *n.*

spit′fire′, *n.* a person with a fiery temper.

spit′tle, *n.* saliva; spit.

spit•toon (spi tōōn′), *n.* a cuspidor.

splash (splash), *v.t.* **1.** to wet or soil by dashing water, mud, etc., upon. **2.** to dash (water, mud, etc.) about in scattered masses. —*v.i.* **3.** to fall, move, or go with a splash. —*n.* **4.** an act or sound of splashing. **5.** a spot caused by splashing. **6.** a striking show or impression. —**splash′y,** *adj.,* **-i•er, -i•est.**

splash′down′, *n.* the landing of a space vehicle in the ocean.

splat¹ (splat), *n.* a broad piece, as of wood, forming part of a chair back.

splat² (splat), *n.* a sound made by splattering or slapping.

splat′ter, *v.t., v.i.* **1.** to spatter. —*n.* **2.** a spatter.

splay (splā), *v.t., v.i.* **1.** to spread out. **2.** to slant. —*adj.* **3.** spread or turned outward.

splay′foot′, *n., pl.* **-feet.** a broad foot that turns outward. —**splay′foot′ed,** *adj.*

spleen (splēn), *n.* **1.** a vascular organ near the stomach that destroys worn-out red blood cells and stores blood. **2.** ill humor, peevish temper, or spite.

splen•did (splen′did), *adj.* **1.** magnificent or sumptuous. **2.** distinguished or glorious. **3.** very good. **4.** brilliant, as in appearance or color. —**splen′did•ly,** *adv.*

splen′dor (-dər), *n.* **1.** grandeur; magnificence. **2.** great brightness or luster; brilliance. Also, *esp. Brit.,* **splen′dour.** —**splen′dor•ous,** *adj.*

sple•net•ic (spli net′ik), *adj.* **1.** of or affecting the spleen. **2.** irritable, peevish, or spiteful.

splice (splīs), *v.,* **spliced, splic•ing,** *n.* —*v.t.* **1.** to unite (two ropes) by the interweaving of strands. **2.** to unite (timbers, spars, etc.) by overlapping and binding their ends. **3.** to unite (film, magnetic tape, etc.) as if by splicing. —*n.* **4.** a union, joint, or junction made by splicing. —**splic′er,** *n.*

splint (splint), *n.* **1.** a piece of rigid material, as wood, used to immobilize a fractured or dislocated bone. **2.** a thin strip of wood interwoven with others, as to make a basket.

splin′ter, *n.* **1.** a thin, sharp piece, as of wood or bone, split or broken off from a main body. —*v.t., v.i.* **2.** to split into splinters. —**splin′ter•y,** *adj.*

split (split), *v.,* **split, split•ting,** *n.* —*v.t., v.i.* **1.** to divide or separate from end to end or into layers. **2.** to burst or break into parts or pieces. **3.** to divide or separate into different factions. **4.** to divide and share. —*n.* **5.** the act of splitting. **6.** a crack or break caused by splitting. **7.** a breach or rupture, as between persons.

split'-lev'el, *adj.* **1.** (of a house) having rooms about a half story above or below adjacent rooms. —*n.* **2.** a split-level house.

split' pea', *n.* a dried green pea, split and used esp. for soup.

split' personal'ity, *n.* a mental disorder in which a person acquires several personalities that function independently.

split'ting, *adj.* violent or severe, as a headache.

splotch (sploch), *n.* **1.** a large, irregular spot. —*v.t.* **2.** to mark or cover with splotches. —**splotch'y,** *adj.*, **-i•er, -i•est.**

splurge (splûrj), *v.*, **splurged, splurg•ing,** *n.* —*v.i.* **1.** to indulge oneself in a luxury or pleasure. **2.** to show off. —*n.* **3.** an ostentatious display. **4.** a bout of extravagant spending.

splut•ter (splut'ər), *v.i.* **1.** to talk rapidly and confusedly. **2.** to make a sputtering sound. —*v.t.* **3.** to sputter. —*n.* **4.** an act or sound of spluttering.

spoil (spoil), *v.*, **spoiled** or **spoilt, spoil•ing,** *n.* —*v.t.* **1.** to harm severely; ruin. **2.** to impair the quality of. **3.** to impair the character of by coddling. **4.** *Archaic.* to plunder; rob. —*v.i.* **5.** to become unfit for use, as food. —*n.* **6.** Often, **spoils.** booty, loot, or plunder. —*Idiom.* **7. be spoiling for,** *Informal.* to be eager for. —**spoil•age** (spoi'lij), *n.* —**spoil'er,** *n.*

spoil'sport', *n.* a person whose conduct spoils the pleasure of others.

spoils' sys'tem, *n.* the process by which party loyalists are rewarded after their side has achieved electoral success.

Spo•kane (spō kan'), *n.* a city in E Washington. 192,781.

spoke[1] (spōk), *v.* **1.** a pt. of SPEAK. **2.** *Archaic.* a pp. of SPEAK.

spoke[2] (spōk), *n.* **1.** one of the bars or rods radiating from the hub of a wheel and supporting the rim. **2.** a rung of a ladder.

spo'ken, *v.* **1.** a pp. of SPEAK. —*adj.* **2.** expressed by speaking; oral. **3.** speaking as specified: *soft-spoken.*

spokes'man, or **-wom'an** or **-per'son,** *n.*, *pl.* **-men** or **-wom•en** or **-per•sons.** a person who speaks for another or for a group.

spo•li•a•tion (spō'lē ā'shən), *n.* an act or instance of plundering.

sponge (spunj), *n.*, *v.*, **sponged, spong•ing.** —*n.* **1.** an aquatic animal with a porous skeleton. **2.** the absorbent skeleton of a sponge used esp. for cleaning or wiping. **3.** any of various absorbent materials resembling a sponge. —*v.t.* **4.** to wipe, rub, clean, or absorb with or as if with a sponge. **5.** to get by imposing on another's good nature. —*v.i.* **6.** to live at the expense of others. —**spong'er,** *n.* —**spong'y,** *adj.*, **-i•er, -i•est.**

sponge' cake', *n.* a light cake containing no shortening.

spon•sor (spon'sər), *n.* **1.** a person who is responsible for a person or thing. **2.** a person or firm that finances a radio or television program by buying time for advertising. **3.** a person who answers for the infant at baptism; godparent. —*v.t.* **4.** to act as sponsor for. —**spon'sor•ship',** *n.*

spon•ta•ne•ous (spon tā'nē əs), *adj.* **1.** coming or resulting from a natural impulse or tendency. **2.** arising from internal forces or causes. —**spon'ta•ne'i•ty** (-tə nē'i tē, -nā'-), *n.* —**spon•ta'ne•ous•ly,** *adv.*

sponta'neous combus'tion, *n.* the ignition of a substance or body without heat from an external source.

spoof (spōof), *n.* **1.** a lighthearted imitation; parody. **2.** a hoax; prank. —*v.t.*, *v.i.* **3.** to make fun (of) lightly and good-humoredly; kid.

spook (spōok), *n.* **1.** a ghost; specter. **2.** *Informal.* a spy. —*v.t.*, *v.i.* **3.** to frighten or become frightened. —**spook'y,** *adj.*, **-i•er, -i•est.**

spool (spōol), *n.* a cylinder on which something, as thread, is wound.

spoon (spōon), *n.* **1.** an eating or cooking utensil consisting of a small, shallow bowl with a handle. **2.** a fishing lure consisting of a spoon-shaped piece of metal. —*v.t.* **3.** to eat with or take up in or as if in a spoon. —**spoon'ful,** *n.*, *pl.* **-fuls.**

spoon'bill', *n.* a large wading bird having a long, flat bill with a spoonlike tip.

spoon•er•ism (spōo'nə riz'əm), *n.* the inadvertent transposition of usu. initial sounds of words, as in *a blushing crow* for *a crushing blow.* [after W. A. Spooner (1844–1930), English clergyman noted for such slips]

spoon'-feed', *v.t.*, **-fed, -feed•ing. 1.** to feed with a spoon. **2.** to provide so fully with information that independent thought or action is prevented.

spoor (spōor, spôr), *n.* a track or trail, esp. of a wild animal.

spo•rad•ic (spə rad'ik), *adj.* appearing or happening at irregular intervals or in isolated instances. —**spo•rad'i•cal•ly,** *adv.*

spore (spôr), *n.* the asexual reproductive body of a fungus or nonflowering plant.

sport (spôrt), *n.* **1.** an often competitive athletic activity requiring skill or physical prowess. **2.** diversion; recreation. **3.** jest; pleasantry. **4.** mockery; ridicule: *They made sport of his haircut.* **5.** LAUGHINGSTOCK. **6.** a sportsmanlike person. **7.** a debonair person; bon vivant. **8.** an organism that shows a genetic deviation; mutation. —*adj.* Also, **sports. 9.** of or used in sports. **10.** suitable for informal wear: *sport clothes.* —*v.i.* **11.** to amuse oneself pleasantly. —*v.t.* **12.** to wear or display, esp. with ostentation.

sport'ing, *adj.* **1.** engaging in or used in sports. **2.** befitting a sportsman; fair. **3.** of or connected with gambling. **4.** involving a tolerable degree of risk.

spor'tive, *adj.* playful; frolicsome.

sports' car', *n.* a low, small, high-powered automobile.

sports'cast', *n.* a radio or television broadcast of sports news. —**sports'cast'er,** *n.*

sports'man, *n.*, *pl.* **-men. 1.** a person who engages in sports, esp. hunting and fishing. **2.** a person who shows fairness and grace in winning and defeat. —**sports'man•like',** *adj.* —**sports'man•ship',** *n.*

sport'-util'ity ve'hicle, *n.* a rugged vehicle with a light-truck chassis and four-wheel drive, designed for occasional off-road use. *Abbr.:* SUV

sport'y, *adj.*, **-i•er, -i•est. 1.** flashy; showy. **2.** like or befitting a sportsman. **3.** designed for or suitable for sport.

spot (spot), *n.*, *v.*, **spot•ted, spot•ting,** *adj.* —*n.* **1.** a discolored mark; stain. **2.** a blemish or flaw. **3.** a small part, as of a surface, differing from the rest. **4.** a place; locality. **5.** a position, esp. an awkward or difficult one. —*v.t.* **6.** to stain or mark with spots. **7.** to notice, recognize, or detect. —*v.i.* **8.** to make a spot; stain. —*adj.* **9.** made, paid, or delivered at once: *a spot sale.* —**spot'less,** *adj.* —**spot'less•ly,** *adv.* —**spot'ted,** *adj.*

spot' check', *n.* a random sampling or investigation. —**spot'-check',** *v.t.*, *v.i.*

spot'light', *n.* **1. a.** an intense light focused on an object, person, or group, as on a stage. **b.** a lamp producing such a light. **2.** conspicuous public attention.

spot'ter, *n.* **1.** a civilian who watches for enemy airplanes. **2.** a person who spots targets.

spot'ty, *adj.*, **-ti•er, -ti•est. 1.** marked with spots; spotted. **2.** uneven in quality or character. —**spot'ti•ness,** *n.*

spouse (spous), *n.* a husband or wife. —**spous•al** (spou'zal), *adj.*

spout (spout), *v.t.*, *v.i.* **1.** to discharge or issue in a stream or jet. **2.** to say or speak volubly or pompously. —*n.* **3.** a pipe or tube through which a liquid spouts. **4.** a jet or stream of liquid.

sprain (sprān), *v.t.* **1.** to wrench and injure (the ligaments around a joint) without fracture or dislocation. —*n.* **2.** the act of spraining or condition of being sprained.

sprang (sprang), *v.* a pt. of SPRING.

sprat (sprat), *n.*, *pl.* **sprats, sprat.** a herring of the E North Atlantic.

sprawl (sprôl), v.i. **1.** to sit or lie with limbs spread out. **2.** to spread out or be distributed irregularly. —n. **3.** an act or instance of sprawling.

spray[1] (sprā), n. **1.** liquid, as water, blown or falling through the air in minute droplets. **2. a.** a jet of fine particles of liquid, as from an atomizer. **b.** a device for discharging such a jet. —v.t., v.i. **3.** to apply in a spray (to). **4.** to scatter or discharge as spray. —spray′er, n.

spray[2] (sprā), n. a branch or arrangement of leaves, flowers, or berries.

spray′ can′, n. a can whose contents are in aerosol form.

spray′ gun′, n. a device from which liquid, as paint, can be sprayed.

spread (spred), v., **spread, spread•ing**, n. —v.t., v.i. **1.** to stretch or open out, esp. over a flat surface. **2.** to force or move apart. **3.** to distribute or extend over an area. **4.** to apply in a layer or coating. **5.** to set (a table) for a meal. **6.** to become or cause to become widely known. —n. **7.** the act or process of spreading. **8.** expanse; extent. **9.** a distance or range between two points. **10.** a cloth covering for a bed. **11.** Informal. an abundance of food; feast. **12.** a food for spreading, as peanut butter. **13.** two facing pages, as of a newspaper. —spread′a•ble, adj. —spread′er, n.

spread′-ea′gle, adj., v., -gled, -gling. —adj. **1.** having or suggesting the form of an eagle with outspread wings. —v.t. **2.** to stretch out in a spread-eagle position.

spread′sheet′, n. **1.** an outsize ledger sheet used by accountants. **2.** such a sheet simulated electronically by computer software, used esp. for financial planning.

spree (sprē), n., pl. **sprees. 1.** a period, spell, or bout of indulgence. **2.** a binge; carousal.

sprig (sprig), n. a small shoot, twig, or spray.

spright•ly (sprīt′lē), adj., -li•er, -li•est. animated; lively. —spright′li•ness, n.

spring (spring), v., **sprang** or, often, **sprung; sprung; spring•ing**; n. —v.i. **1.** to rise, leap, or move suddenly. **2.** to move suddenly with resilience. **3.** to issue or occur suddenly or forcefully. **4.** to come into being; arise. —v.t **5.** to cause to spring. **6.** to cause the sudden operation of: to spring a trap. **7.** to cause to work loose, warp, or split. **8.** to develop: sprang a leak. **9.** to produce by surprise: to spring a joke. **10.** Slang. to secure the release of from confinement. —n. **11.** the act of springing. **12.** an elastic quality. **13.** an issue of water from the ground. **14.** a source; fountainhead. **15.** an elastic contrivance or body that recovers its shape after being compressed, bent, or stretched. **16.** the season between winter and summer. —spring′y, adj., -i•er, -i•est. —spring′i•ness, n.

spring′board′, n. **1.** a flexible board used in diving and gymnastics. **2.** a starting point.

spring′ fe′ver, n. a listless, lazy, or restless feeling commonly associated with the beginning of spring.

Spring•field (spring′fēld′), n. **1.** a city in S Massachusetts. 150,320. **2.** a city in SW Missouri. 149,164. **3.** the capital of Illinois. 105,938.

spring′time′, n. the season of spring.

sprin•kle (spring′kəl), v., -kled, -kling, n. —v.t., v.i. **1.** to scatter in drops or particles. **2.** to disperse or distribute here and there. **3.** to rain slightly in scattered drops. —n. **4.** an act or instance of sprinkling. **5.** a light rain. —sprin′kler, n.

sprin′kling, n. a small quantity scattered here and there.

sprint (sprint), v.i. **1.** to race or move at full speed for a short distance. —n. **2.** a short race at full speed. **3.** a burst of speed. —sprint′er, n.

sprite (sprīt), n. an elf, fairy, or goblin.

spritz (sprits, shprits), v.t. to spray briefly; squirt. —n. **2.** a brief spray; squirt.

sprock•et (sprok′it), n **1.** a toothed wheel engaging with a chain. **2.** a tooth on a sprocket.

sprout (sprout), v.i. **1.** to begin to grow. **2.** to put forth buds or shoots. —n. **3.** a shoot of a plant. **4.** a new growth, as from a seed.

spruce[1] (sprōōs), n. **1.** an evergreen coniferous tree with short needle-shaped leaves. **2.** the wood of a spruce.

spruce[2] (sprōōs), adj., **spruc•er, spruc•est,** v., **spruced, spruc•ing.** —adj. **1.** trim in appearance; neat. —v.t., v.i. **2.** to make or become spruce.

sprung (sprung), v. a pt. and pp. of SPRING.

spry (sprī), adj., **spry•er** or **spri•er, spry•est** or **spri•est.** nimbly energetic; agile. —spry′ly, adv. —spry′-ness, n.

spud (spud), n. **1.** Informal. a potato. **2.** a spadelike digging instrument.

spume (spyōōm), n. foamy matter on a liquid; froth.

spu•mo•ni or **-ne** (spə mō′nē), n. variously flavored and colored ice cream containing candied fruit and nuts.

spun (spun), v. pt. and pp. of SPIN.

spunk (spungk), n. spirit; mettle. —spunk′y, adj., -i•er, -i•est.

spur (spûr), n., v., **spurred, spur•ring.** —n. **1.** a device with a pointed projection that is secured to the heel of a rider's boot and used to urge a horse forward. **2.** something that goads to action. **3.** a stiff, often sharp process or projection, as on the leg of the domestic rooster. **4.** a ridge projecting from a mountain. **5.** a short branch track connecting with a main railroad track. —v.t. **6.** to incite or urge on with or as if with spurs. —Idiom. **7. on the spur of the moment,** impulsively; suddenly. —spurred, adj.

spurge (spûrj), n. any of numerous plants having milky juice and flowers with no petals or sepals.

spu•ri•ous (spyŏŏr′ē əs), adj. not genuine; counterfeit. —spu′ri•ous•ly, adv. —spu′ri•ous•ness, n.

spurn (spûrn), v.t. to reject with disdain; scorn.

spurt (spûrt), n. **1.** a sudden, forceful gush, as of liquid. **2.** a sudden brief increase in activity or effort. —v.i., v.t. **3.** to gush, expel in, or make a spurt.

sput•nik (spŏŏt′nik, sput′-), n. a Soviet earth-orbiting satellite. [< Russ: satellite, traveling companion]

sput•ter (sput′ər), v.i. **1.** to make explosive, popping sounds. **2.** to eject particles of saliva, food, etc., as when speaking angrily **3.** to talk explosively or incoherently. —v.t. **4.** to utter by sputtering. —n. **5.** an act or sound of sputtering.

spu•tum (spyōō′təm), n., pl. **-ta** (-tə). expectorated matter, as saliva mixed with mucus.

spy (spī), n., pl. **spies,** v., **spied, spy•ing.** —n. **1.** a person employed by a government to obtain intelligence about another, usu. hostile country. **2.** a person who keeps secret watch on others. —v.i **3.** to act as a spy. —v.t. **4.** to catch sight of; espy.

spy′glass′, n. a small telescope.

sq., **1.** sequence. **2.** the following one. [< L sequēns] **3.** squadron. **4.** square.

sqq., the following ones. [< L sequentia]

squab (skwob), n., pl. **squabs, squab.** a nestling, unfledged pigeon.

squab•ble (skwob′əl), v., -bled, -bling, n. —v.i. to engage in a petty quarrel. —n. **2.** a petty quarrel.

squad (skwod), n. **1.** the smallest military unit. **2.** a small group, as of police officers, engaged in a common task.

squad′ car′, n. a police car with a radiotelephone for communicating with headquarters.

squad′ron (-rən), n. any of various units of troops, ships, or airplanes.

squal•id (skwol′id, skwô′lid), adj. **1.** filthy and repulsive. **2.** degraded; sordid.

squall[1] (skwôl), n. a sudden, violent wind, often with rain, snow, or sleet.

squall[2] (skwôl), v.i. **1.** to cry out loudly; scream. —n. **2.** an act or sound of squalling.

squal•or (skwol′ər, skwô′lər), n. the condition of being squalid.

squa•mous (skwā′məs), adj. covered with, formed of, or resembling scales.

squan•der (skwon′dər), v.t. to spend or use extravagantly or wastefully.

Squan•to (skwon′tō), n. died 1622, North American

Indian of the Narragansett tribe: interpreter for the Pilgrims. Also called **Tisquantum.**

square (skwâr), *n.*, *v.*, **squared, squar•ing**, *adj.*, **squar•er, squar•est**, *adv.* —*n.* **1.** a rectangle with four sides of equal length and four right angles. **2.** something shaped like a square. **3.** an open area formed by intersecting streets. **4.** an instrument for drawing or testing right angles. **5.** the product obtained when a number is multiplied by itself. **6.** *Slang.* a conventional or conservative person. —*v.t.* **7.** to make square in form. **8.** to multiply (a number or quantity) by itself. **9.** to make straight, level, erect, or even. **10.** to adjust harmoniously or satisfactorily. **11.** to pay off; settle. —*v.i.* **12.** to accord; agree. **13. square off**, to assume a fighting stance. —*adj.* **14.** forming a right angle. **15.** having four equal sides and four right angles. **16.** having the form of a square and designated by a unit of linear measurement forming a side of the square: *one square foot.* **17.** solid and substantial. **18.** having all accounts settled. **19.** fair; honest. **20.** *Slang.* conventional or conservative. —*adv.* **21.** in a square shape. **22.** at right angles. **23.** fairly or honestly. —*Proverb.* **24. You can't fit a square peg into a round hole**, a person should not be expected to do a task for which he or she is not suited. —**square′ly**, *adv.* —**square′ness**, *n.*

square′ dance′, *n.* a dance by a set of four couples arranged in a square. —**square′-dance′,** *v.i.*, **-danced, -danc•ing.**

Square′ Deal′, *n.* the stated policy of President Theodore Roosevelt, promising fairness in all dealings with labor and management.

square′-rigged′, *adj.* having square sails as the principal sails.

square′ root′, *n.* a quantity of which a given quantity is the square.

squash¹ (skwosh, skwôsh), *v.t.* **1.** to press into a flat mass or pulp; crush. **2.** to suppress; quash. —*n.* **3.** an act or sound of squashing. **4.** a squashed mass. **5.** a game played on a four-walled court with rackets and a rubber ball. —**squash′y,** *adj.*, **-i•er, -i•est.**

squash² (skwosh, skwôsh), *n.*, *pl.* **squash•es, squash. 1.** the fruit of any of various plants of the gourd family, used as a vegetable. **2.** a plant that bears squash.

squat (skwot), *v.*, **squat•ted, squat•ting,** *adj.*, **squat•ter, squat•test,** *n.* —*v.i.* **1.** to sit on the haunches or heels. **2.** to occupy another's property without right or title. **3.** to settle on public land in order to acquire title to it. —*adj.* **4.** short and thickset. —*n.* **5.** the act, position, or posture of squatting. —**squat′ness,** *n.* —**squat′ter,** *n.*

squawk (skwôk), *v.i.* **1.** to utter a loud, harsh cry, as a duck. **2.** to complain loudly. —*n.* **3.** a loud, harsh cry. **4.** a loud complaint.

squeak (skwēk), *n.* **1.** a short, shrill or high-pitched sound. **2.** an escape, as from danger. —*v.i.*, *v.t.* **3.** to utter (with) a squeak. **4. squeak by** or **through,** to succeed or survive by a narrow margin. —**squeak′y,** *adj.*, **-i•er, -i•est.**

squeal (skwēl), *n.* **1.** a somewhat prolonged, sharp, shrill cry. —*v.i.* **2.** to utter a squeal. **3.** *Slang.* **a.** to turn informer. **b.** to protest or complain. —*v.t.* **4.** to utter with a squeal. —**squeal′er,** *n.*

squeam•ish (skwē′mish), *adj.* **1.** easily nauseated or disgusted. **2.** excessively particular or scrupulous in moral matters. —**squeam′ish•ness,** *n.*

squee•gee (skwē′jē), *n.*, *pl.* **-gees.** an implement with a rubber edge used esp. for removing water from windows after washing.

squeeze (skwēz), *v.*, **squeezed, squeez•ing,** *n.* —*v.t.* **1.** to press forcibly together; compress. **2.** to extract by applying pressure. **3.** to force, force out, or obtain by pressure. —*v.i.* **4.** to exert pressure. **5.** to force one's way. —*n.* **6.** an act or instance of squeezing. **7.** a troubled financial condition. **8.** a quantity obtained by squeezing. —**squeez′a•ble,** *adj.*

squeeze′ bot′tle, *n.* a flexible plastic bottle whose contents are forced out by squeezing.

squelch (skwelch), *v.t.* **1.** to put down or silence, as with a crushing reply. —*n.* **2.** a crushing reply.

squib (skwib), *n.* **1.** a short witty or sarcastic saying or writing. **2.** a firecracker that burns with a hissing noise but does not explode.

squid (skwid), *n.*, *pl.* **squid, squids.** a ten-armed marine animal with a slender, elongated body.

squig•gle (skwig′əl), *n.*, *v.*, **-gled, -gling.** —*n.* **1.** a short, irregular curve or twist, as in writing. —*v.i.*, *v.t.* **2.** to move in or form squiggles. —**squig′gly,** *adj.*

squint (skwint), *v.i.* **1.** to look with the eyes partly closed. **2.** to be cross-eyed. **3.** to look sidewise. —*n.* **4.** an act or instance of squinting. **5.** CROSS-EYE. **6.** a quick glance. —**squint′y,** *adj.*

squire (skwīr), *n.*, *v.*, **squired, squir•ing.** —*n.* **1.** an English country gentleman. **2.** a young man of noble birth who served a knight. **3.** a man who accompanies or escorts a woman. **4.** a local dignitary, as a justice of the peace. —*v.t.* **5.** to attend as a squire; escort.

Squire′ of Hyde′ Park′, *n.* epithet of Franklin D. Roosevelt.

squirm (skwûrm), *v.i.* **1.** to wriggle or writhe, as in embarrassment or pain. —*n.* **2.** the act of squirming. —**squirm′y,** *adj.*, **-i•er, -i•est.**

squir•rel (skwûr′əl, skwur′-), *n.*, *pl.* **-rels, -rel.** —*n.* **1.** an arboreal, bushy-tailed rodent with thick, soft fur. **2.** its fur.

squirt (skwûrt), *v.i.* **1.** to eject liquid in a thin jet or spurt. —*v.t.* **2.** to cause to squirt. **3.** to wet by squirting. —*n.* **4.** a jet or spurt of liquid. **5.** an amount squirted. **6.** *Informal.* an impudent youngster. **7.** an instrument for squirting.

squish (skwish), *v.t.* **1.** to squash. —*v.i.* **2.** (of water, soft mud, etc.) to make a gushing sound when walked in. —*n.* **3.** a squishing sound.

Sr, *Chem. Symbol.* strontium.

Sr., 1. Senior. **2.** Sister. [< L *Soror*]

Sri Lan•ka (srē′ läng′kə, lang′kə, shrē′), *n.* an island republic in the Indian Ocean, S of India. 16,600,000. Formerly, **Ceylon.** —**Sri′ Lan′kan,** *adj.*, *n.*

SRO, 1. single-room occupancy. **2.** standing room only.

SS, 1. social security. **2.** steamship. **3.** supersonic.

SSE, south-southeast.

SSN, Social Security number.

SST, supersonic transport.

SSW, south-southwest.

St., 1. Saint. **2.** Strait. **3.** Street.

Sta., Station.

stab (stab), *v.*, **stabbed, stab•bing,** *n.* —*v.t.*, *v.i.* **1.** to pierce or wound with or as if with a pointed weapon. **2.** to thrust, plunge, or penetrate. —*n.* **3.** a thrust with or as if with a pointed weapon. **4.** an attempt; try. **5.** a wound made by stabbing.

stab′bing, *adj.* penetrating; piercing.

sta•bi•lize (stā′bə līz′), *v.t.*, *v.i.*, **-lized, -liz•ing. 1.** to make or become stable, firm, or steadfast. **2.** to maintain or remain at an unfluctuating level. —**sta′bi•li•za′tion,** *n.* —**sta′bi•liz′er,** *n.*

sta•ble¹ (stā′bəl), *n.*, *v.*, **-bled, -bling.** —*n.* **1.** a building for the lodging and feeding of animals, esp. horses or cattle. **2.** the group of racehorses belonging to one owner. —*v.t.*, *v.i.* **3.** to put or stay in or as if in a stable.

sta•ble² (stā′bəl), *adj.*, **-bler, -blest. 1.** not likely to give way; steady. **2.** firmly established; enduring. **3.** not wavering in purpose; steadfast. **4.** mentally sound. **5.** resistant to physical or chemical change. —**sta•bil′i•ty** (stə bil′i tē), *n.*

stac•ca•to (stə kä′tō), *adj.* **1.** shortened and detached when played or sung: *staccato notes.* **2.** having short breaks between notes.

stack (stak), *n.* **1.** a usu. orderly pile or heap. **2.** a large, usu. conical pile of hay or straw. **3.** Often, **stacks.** a set of shelves for books, as in a library. **4.** SMOKESTACK. **5.** a great quantity. **6.** a linear list, as in a computer, in which the last item stored is the first retrieved. —*v.t.* **7.** to pile or arrange in a stack. **8.** to fix or arrange to force a desired result: *to stack a jury.* **9. stack up,** to measure up; compare.

sta•di•um (stā′dē əm), *n., pl.* **-di•ums, -di•a** (-dē ə). a sports arena, usu. oval or horseshoe-shaped, with tiers of seats for spectators. [< L < Gk *stádion* running track]

staff (staf, stäf), *n., pl.* **staffs** for 1–3; **staves** (stāvz) or **staffs** for 4, 5; *v.* —*n.* **1.** a group of personnel, as of a business establishment. **2.** a group of assistants to a manager, superintendent, or executive. **3.** a body of military officers concerned with administration rather than combat. **4.** a stick or rod used for support, as a weapon, or as a symbol of office or authority. **5.** the set of five horizontal lines on which music is written. —*v.t.* **6.** to provide with a staff. **7.** to serve on the staff of.

staff′er, *n.* a member of a staff, as at a newspaper.

staff′ ser′geant, *n.* a noncommissioned officer in the U.S. Army, Marine Corps, and Air Force ranking above a sergeant.

stag (stag), *n.* **1.** an adult male deer. —*adj.* **2.** of or for men only: *a stag dinner.* —*adv.* **3.** without a companion or date.

stage (stāj), *n., v.,* **staged, stag•ing.** —*n.* **1.** a phase, degree, or step in a process, development, or series. **2.** a raised platform, esp. one on which actors perform in a theater. **3. the stage,** the theater, esp. acting, as a profession. **4.** the scene of an action. **5.** a stagecoach. **6.** a place of rest on a journey. **7.** a section of a rocket, usu. designed to separate after burnout. —*v.t.* **8.** to represent, produce, or exhibit on or as if on a stage. **9.** to plan, organize, and carry out.

stage′coach′, *n.* a horse-drawn passenger and mail coach that formerly traveled regularly over a fixed route.

stage′hand′, *n.* a worker who deals with properties, lighting, and scenery in a theater.

stage′ left′, *n.* the part of the stage that is left of center as one faces the audience.

stage′ right′, *n.* the part of the stage that is right of center as one faces the audience.

stage′struck′ or **stage′-struck′,** *adj.* obsessed with the desire to become an actor or actress.

stag•ger (stag′ər), *v.i.* **1.** to walk or move unsteadily; totter. —*v.t.* **2.** to cause to stagger. **3.** to astonish or shock. **4.** to arrange in an alternating or overlapping pattern: *to stagger lunch hours.* —*n.* **5.** a reeling or tottering movement. **6. staggers,** (*used with a sing. v.*) any of several diseases of livestock characterized by a staggering gait. —**stag′ger•ing,** *adj.*

stag•nant (stag′nənt), *adj.* **1.** not flowing or moving, as water. **2.** stale, as air. **3.** inactive or sluggish.

stag′nate (-nāt), *v.i.,* **-nat•ed, -nat•ing.** to stay or become stagnant. —**stag•na′tion,** *n.*

staid (stād), *adj.* **1.** decorous, sedate, or solemn. —*v.* **2.** *Archaic.* a pt. and pp. of STAY¹. —**staid′ly,** *adv.*

stain (stān), *n.* **1.** an often permanent discoloration produced by foreign matter; spot. **2.** a cause of reproach; stigma. **3.** a dye, esp. one for coloring wood. —*v.t.* **4.** to discolor. **5.** to color with a stain; dye. **6.** to bring reproach upon; stigmatize. —*v.i.* **7.** to produce a stain. **8.** to become stained. —**stain′less,** *adj.*

stain′less steel′, *n.* steel alloyed with chromium to resist rust and corrosion.

stair (stâr), *n.* **1.** one of a flight or series of steps for going from one level to another. **2.** Usu., **stairs.** a flight of steps.

stair′case′, *n.* a flight or series of flights of stairs with its framework, banisters, etc.

stair′way′, *n.* a passageway with a series of stairs.

stair′well′, *n.* a vertical shaft containing a stairway.

stake¹ (stāk), *n., v.,* **staked, stak•ing.** —*n.* **1.** a pointed stick or post driven into the ground as a mark or support. **2. a.** a post to which a person is bound for execution by burning. **b.** death by burning. —*v.t.* **3.** to mark with or as if with stakes. **4.** to support or fasten with a stake. **5. stake out,** to keep under police surveillance.

stake² (stāk), *n., v.,* **staked, stak•ing.** —*n.* **1.** something wagered, as in a race. **2.** an investment or share, as in an undertaking. **3.** Often, **stakes.** a prize or reward in a contest. —*v.t.* **4.** to risk; gamble. **5.** to furnish with resources, esp. money. —*Idiom.* **6. at stake,** in danger; at risk.

stake′out′, *n.* surveillance of a location, by the police.

sta•lac•tite (stə lak′tīt), *n.* an icicle-shaped mineral deposit hanging from the roof of a cave.

stalactite

stalagmite

stalactite and stalagmite

sta•lag•mite (stə lag′mīt), *n.* a mineral deposit resembling an inverted stalactite formed on the floor of a cave.

stale (stāl), *adj.,* **stal•er, stal•est,** *v.,* **staled, stal•ing.** —*adj.* **1.** not fresh; flat, dry, or tasteless. **2.** musty; stagnant. **3.** hackneyed; trite. **4.** lacking interest, initiative, or enthusiasm, as from boredom. —*v.t., v.i.* **5.** to make or become stale. —**stale′ness,** *n.*

stale′mate′ (-māt′), *n., v.,* **-mat•ed, -mat•ing.** —*n.* **1.** a situation permitting no further action or progress; deadlock. —*v.t., v.i.* **2.** to subject to or result in a stalemate.

Sta•lin (stä′lin), *n.* **Joseph V.,** 1879–1953, premier of the U.S.S.R. 1941–53. —**Sta′lin•ism,** *n.* **Sta′lin•ist,** *n., adj.*

stalk¹ (stôk), *n.* **1.** the stem or main axis of a plant. **2.** a slender supporting part.

stalk² (stôk), *v.i.* **1.** to walk with stiff or haughty strides. —*v.t.* **2.** to pursue prey or quarry stealthily. —*n.* **3.** a stiff or haughty stride or gait.

stall¹ (stôl), *n.* **1.** a compartment in a stable for one animal. **2.** a booth or stand in which merchandise is displayed for sale. **3.** an enclosed seat in a church choir or chancel. **4.** a pew. **5.** a small compartment: *a shower stall.* **6.** a condition, caused by a poor fuel supply or overload, in which an engine stops functioning. —*v.t., v.i.* **7.** to put or keep in a stall. **8.** to bring or come to a standstill, esp. unintentionally.

stall² (stôl), *v.i., v.t.* **1.** to delay, esp. by evasion or deception. —*n.* **2.** a tactic, as a ruse, used to delay.

stal•lion (stal′yən), *n.* an uncastrated adult male horse.

stal•wart (stôl′wərt), *adj.* **1.** sturdy and robust. **2.** strong and brave. **3.** firm; steadfast. —*n.* **4.** a stalwart person.

sta•men (stā′mən), *n.* the pollen-bearing organ of a flower.

Stam•ford (stam′fərd), *n.* a city in SW Connecticut. 107,199.

stam•i•na (stam′ə nə), *n.* power to endure; strength.

stam•mer (stam′ər), *v.i., v.t.* **1.** to speak with involuntary pauses and spasmodic repetitions of sounds. —*n.* **2.** a speech defect or utterance marked by stammering. —**stam′mer•er,** *n.*

stamp (stamp), *v.t.* **1.** to strike with a forcible downward thrust of the foot. **2.** to bring (the foot) down forcibly. **3.** to crush, extinguish, etc., by or as if by stamping: *to stamp out crime.* **4.** to impress with a mark or device. **5.** to impress (a design, mark, etc.) on something. **6.** to affix a postage stamp to. —*v.i.* **7.** to bring the foot down forcibly. **8.** to walk with heavy, forcible steps. —*n.* **9.** a gummed printed label officially used as evidence of the payment of postage. **10.** a die or block for impressing or imprinting. **11.** a design made by imprinting. **12.** an official mark or seal indicating validity or payment of a tax or fee. **13.** a distinctive mark or impression. —**stamp′er,** *n.*

Stamp′ Act′, *n.* an act of the British Parliament (1765) for raising revenue in the American colonies by requiring that documents, newspapers, etc., bear an official stamp.

stam•pede (stam pēd′), *n.*, *v.*, **-ped•ed, -ped•ing.** —*n.* **1.** a sudden, frenzied rush or flight, esp. of a herd of frightened animals. —*v.i.,* *v.t.* **2.** to flee or cause to flee in a stampede. **3.** to act or cause to act in an unreasoning, often frantic rush.

stamp′ing ground′, *n.* a habitual or favorite haunt.

stance (stans), *n.* **1.** the position of the body while standing. **2.** a mental or emotional position.

stanch¹ (stônch, stanch, stänch), *v.t.* **1.** to stop the flow of (a liquid, esp. blood). —*v.i.* **2.** to stop flowing, as blood.

stanch² (stônch, stänch, stanch), *adj.,* **-er, -est.** STAUNCH².

stan•chion (stan′shən), *n.* an upright bar, beam, post, or support.

stand (stand), *v.,* **stood, stand•ing,** *n.* —*v.i.* **1.** to rise to, be in, or remain in an upright position on the feet. **2.** to take an indicated position: *I stood aside.* **3.** to rest in an upright position. **4.** to be located or situated. **5.** to remain unchanged. **6.** to be or remain in a specified state or condition. —*v.t.* **7.** to set upright. **8.** to submit to; undergo. **9.** to endure or withstand. **10. stand by, a.** to abide by; uphold. **b.** to be loyal to. **c.** to wait, esp. in anticipation. **11. ~ for, a.** to represent; symbolize. **b.** to tolerate; allow. **12. ~ out, a.** to project; protrude. **b.** to be conspicuous or prominent. **13. ~ up, a.** to be or remain convincing. **b.** to be durable or serviceable. **c.** to fail to keep an appointment with. —*n.* **14.** the act of standing. **15.** a policy, position, or attitude. **16.** the place occupied by a witness testifying in court. **17.** a raised platform, as for a speaker. **18. stands,** a raised section of seats for spectators. **19.** a framework or rack for supporting or displaying something. **20.** a stall or booth where goods are sold. **21.** a place occupied by vehicles for hire. **22.** a standing growth of trees. **23.** a stop on a tour for a performance. —*Idiom.* **24. stand on your own two feet,** to be self-reliant. —*Saying.* **25. Here I stand, I can do no other, God help me,** I must obey my conscience: said by Martin Luther 1521. —**stand′er,** *n.*

stand•ard (stan′dərd), *n.* **1.** something accepted as a basis of comparison. **2.** a rule used as a basis for judgment. **3.** the authorized exemplar of a unit of weight or measure. **4.** a flag, as one indicating the presence of a sovereign. **5.** an upright support. —*adj.* **6.** being or meeting a standard. **7.** of recognized excellence or authority: *a standard reference book.* **8.** usual or customary.

stand′ard-bear′er, *n.* the leader of a movement, political party, or cause.

stand′ard•ize′, *v.t.,* **-ized, -iz•ing.** to cause to conform with a standard. —**stand′ard•i•za′tion,** *n.*

stand′ard of liv′ing, *n.* a level of subsistence and comfort in daily life maintained by a community, class, or individual.

stand′ard time′, *n.* the civil time officially adopted for a country or region, under a system that divides the world into 24 time zones.

stand′by′, *n.,* *pl.* **-bys. 1.** a person or thing that can be relied on. **2.** one held ready to serve as a substitute.

stand•ee′, *n.,* *pl.* **-ees.** a person who stands, as in a theater.

stand′-in′, *n.* a substitute, as for an actor during the preparation of lighting and cameras.

stand′ing, *n.* **1.** rank, status, or position in an occupation or in society. **2.** good reputation. **3.** length of continuance; duration. —*adj.* **4.** erect; upright. **5.**

performed in or from an erect position. **6.** not flowing; still. **7.** lasting or permanent.

Stan•dish (stan′dish), *n.* **Myles** or **Miles,** c1584–1656, American settler, born in England.

stand′off′, *n.* a tie or draw, as in a game.

stand′off′ish, *adj.* tending to be aloof.

stand′out′, *n.* one that is conspicuously superior to others.

stand′pipe′, *n.* a vertical pipe into which water is pumped to obtain a required pressure.

stand′point′, *n.* the mental attitude from which a person views and judges things.

stand′still′, *n.* a halt; stop.

stand′-up′, *adj.* **1.** erect; upright. **2.** performing a comic monologue while standing alone before an audience or camera.

stank (stangk), *v.* a pt. of STINK.

stan•za (stan′zə), *n.,* *pl.* **-zas.** a number of lines forming a division of a poem.

staph (staf), *n.* staphylococcus.

staph•y•lo•coc•cus (staf′ə lə kok′əs), *n.,* *pl.* **-ci** (-sī, -sē). any of several spherical bacteria occurring in clusters, certain species of which are pathogenic.

sta•ple¹ (stā′pəl), *n.,* *v.,* **-pled, -pling.** —*n.* **1.** a short, thin bracket-shaped piece of wire driven through sheets of paper to bind and clinch them. **2.** a U-shaped piece of metal with pointed ends driven into a surface to hold something, as a hook. —*v.t.* **3.** to secure or fasten by a staple. —**sta′pler,** *n.*

sta•ple² (stā′pəl), *n.* **1.** a principal raw material or commodity of a locality. **2.** a basic or necessary item, as of food. **3.** a fiber, as of cotton or rayon, with respect to length and fineness. —*adj.* **4.** regularly and plentifully produced. **5.** basic, chief, or principal.

star (stär), *n.,* *adj.,* *v.,* **starred, star•ring.** —*n.* **1.** a hot, gaseous, self-luminous celestial body, as the sun. **2.** a celestial body that appears as a fixed point of light in the night sky. **3.** Usu., **stars.** a heavenly body regarded as an astrological influence on human affairs. **4.** a conventionalized figure representing a star, usu. having five radiating points. **5. a.** an actor or actress who plays the leading role. **b.** a famous or gifted performer. **6.** an asterisk. —*adj.* **7.** distinguished; preeminent. **8.** of or being a star. —*v.t.* **9.** to decorate with stars. **10.** to feature as a star. **11.** to mark with an asterisk. —*v.i.* **12.** to be brilliant or outstanding. **13.** to perform as a star. —**star′dom,** *n.* —**star′less,** *adj.* —**star′ry,** *adj.,* **-ri•er, -ri•est.**

star′board′ (-bərd, -bôrd′), *n.* **1.** the right-hand side of a ship or aircraft facing forward. —*adj.* **2.** of or located to the starboard.

starch (stärch), *n.* **1.** a white, tasteless, solid carbohydrate found in rice, corn, wheat, potatoes, and many other vegetables. **2.** a commercial preparation of starch used esp. to stiffen fabrics in laundering. —*v.t.* **3.** to stiffen with or as if with starch. —**starch′y,** *adj.,* **-i•er, -i•est.**

star′-crossed′, *adj.* thwarted or opposed by the stars; ill-fated: *star-crossed lovers.*

stare (stâr), *v.,* **stared, star•ing,** *n.* —*v.i.* **1.** to gaze fixedly and intently, esp. with wide-open eyes. —*v.t.* **2.** to stare at. —*n.* **3.** a staring gaze. —**star′er,** *n.*

star′fish′, *n.,* *pl.* **-fish, -fish•es.** a star-shaped sea animal with five or more radiating arms.

starfish

star′ fruit′, *n.* CARAMBOLA (def. 2).

star′gaze′, *v.i.,* **-gazed, -gaz•ing. 1.** to gaze at the stars. **2.** to daydream. —**star′gaz′er,** *n.*

stark (stärk), *adj.,* **-er, -est,** *adv.* —*adj.* **1.** complete; utter: *stark madness.* **2.** grim or desolate. **3.** extremely simple or severe. **4.** blunt; harsh: *stark real-*

ity. —*adv.* **5.** completely; utterly: *stark mad.*
—**stark′ly,** *adv.* —**stark′ness,** *n.*
star′let (-lit), *n.* a young actress, esp. in motion pictures.
star′light′, *n.* the light emanating from the stars. —**star′lit′,** *adj.*
star′ling (-ling), *n.* a Eurasian songbird with seasonally speckled iridescent black plumage.
Star′ of Beth′lehem, *n.* the star that guided the Magi to the manger of the infant Jesus in Bethlehem. Matt. 2:1–10.
Star′ of Da′vid, *n.* a hexagram used as a symbol of Judaism. Also called **Magen David, Shield of David.**

Star of David

star′ry-eyed′, *adj.* overly romantic or idealistic.
Stars′ and Bars′, *n.* the flag adopted by the Confederate States of America.
Stars′ and Stripes′, *n.* the national flag of the U.S.
Star′-Span′gled Ban′ner, The, *n.* **1.** Stars and Stripes. **2.** (*italics*) the national anthem of the U.S.
start (stärt), *v.i.* **1.** to begin to move, go, or act. **2.** to become active, manifest, or operative. **3.** to give a sudden involuntary jerk or jump, as from shock. —*v.t.* **4.** to set moving, going, or acting. **5.** to establish or found. **6.** to cause to be an entrant in a game or contest. —*n.* **7.** a beginning, as of a journey. **8.** a place from which to begin. **9.** a sudden involuntary movement of the body. **10.** a lead or advance, as over competitors. —**start′er,** *n.*
star′tle, *v.,* **-tled, -tling.** —*v.t.* **1.** to surprise or alarm suddenly and usu. briefly. —*v.i.* **2.** to become startled. —**star′tling,** *adj.*
Star′ Trek′, a U.S. science-fiction television series, progenitor of other similarly named series.
starve (stärv), *v.,* **starved, starv•ing.** —*v.i.* **1.** to weaken, waste, or die from lack of food. **2.** to be extremely hungry. **3.** to feel a strong need or desire. —*v.t.* **4.** to cause to starve. **5.** to subdue or force by hunger. —**star•va′tion** (-vā′shən), *n.*
starve′ling (-ling), *n.* a starving person, animal, or plant.
Star′ Wars′, *n.* **1.** a research program begun by the U.S. in 1983 to explore technologies for destroying incoming missiles. Also called **Strategic Defense Initiative. 2.** (*italics*) a U.S. science-fiction film (1977) directed by George Lucas.
stash (stash), *v.t.* **1.** to put by or away in a secret place. —*n.* **2.** something stashed away. **3.** a hiding place.
stat (stat), *n.* a statistic.
state (stāt), *n., adj., v.,* **stat•ed, stat•ing.** —*n.* **1.** the condition of a person or thing, as with respect to circumstances. **2.** the condition of matter, as with respect to form. **3.** status or position in life. **4.** a particular emotional condition. **5.** an unusually tense or perturbed condition: *in a state over losing his job.* **6. a.** a politically unified people occupying a definite territory. **b.** the territory or government of a state. **7.** one of the political units making up a federal union. —*adj.* **8.** of a state or a government. **9.** marked by or involving ceremony. —*v.t.* **10.** to express in speech or writing. **11.** to fix or settle, as by authority. —**state′hood′,** *n.*
state′craft′, *n.* the art of government and diplomacy.
state′house′, *n.* the building in which a state legislature sits.
state′less, *adj.* lacking nationality.

state′ly, *adj.,* **-li•er, -li•est. 1.** majestic; imposing. **2.** dignified. —**state′li•ness,** *n.*
state′ment, *n.* **1.** something stated; declaration or assertion. **2.** an abstract of a financial account. **3.** the act or manner of stating.
Stat′en Is′land (stat′n), *n.* an island borough of New York City. 378,977.
state′ of the art′, *n.* the most sophisticated or advanced stage of a technology, art, or science. —**state′-of-the-art′,** *adj.*
State′ of the Un′ion address′, *n.* an annual message to Congress by the President: required by the Constitution (Article II, Section 3). Also called **State′ of the Un′ion mes′sage.**
state′room′, *n.* a private room on a ship or train.
state′side′, *adj.* **1.** of or being in the continental U.S. —*adv.* **2.** in or toward the continental U.S.
states′man or **-wom′an,** *n., pl.* **-men** or **-wom•en.** a highly respected and influential political leader who shows devotion to public service. —**states′man•like′,** *adj.* —**states′man•ship′,** *n.*
stat•ic (stat′ik), *adj.* **1.** of bodies or forces at rest or in equilibrium. **2.** not moving; stationary. **3.** showing little or no change. **4.** pertaining to stationary electrical charges. —*n.* **5. a.** static or atmospheric electricity. **b.** interference, as with radio broadcasts, caused by such electricity. **6.** resistance or hostility, as to one's actions. —**stat′i•cal•ly,** *adv.*
sta•tion (stā′shən), *n.* **1.** the place or position where a person or thing is located. **2.** a regular stopping place, as for trains or buses. **3.** the headquarters of a public service. **4.** social position or standing. **5.** an assigned position, place, or office. **6.** a place from which radio or television broadcasts originate. —*v.t.* **7.** to assign a station to.
sta′tion•ar•y (-shə ner′ē), *adj.* **1.** not moving or movable; fixed. **2.** remaining in the same condition; not changing.
sta′tion break′, *n.* an interval in a radio or TV program for station identification.
sta′tion•er, *n.* a seller of stationery.
sta′tion•er•y (-shə ner′ē), *n.* **1.** writing paper. **2.** writing materials, as with pens and ink
sta′tions of the cross′ or **Sta′tions of the Cross′,** *n.pl.* a series of 14 representations of successive incidents from the Passion of Christ, visited in sequence, for prayer and meditation.
sta′tion wag′on, *n.* an automobile with folding or removable seats and space into which cargo can be loaded through a tailgate.
sta•tis•tic (stə tis′tik), *n.* a numerical fact or datum.
sta•tis•tics (stə tis′tiks), *n.* **1.** (*used with a sing. v.*) the science that deals with the analysis and interpretation of numerical data. **2.** (*used with a pl. v.*) a collection of numerical data. —**sta•tis′ti•cal,** *adj.* —**sta•tis′ti•cal•ly,** *adv.* —**stat•is•ti•cian** (stat′is tish′ən), *n.*
stat•u•ar•y (stach′ōō er′ē), *n., pl.* **-ar•ies.** statues collectively.
stat•ue (stach′ōō), *n.* a carved, molded, cast, or sculpted three-dimensional work of art.
stat′u•esque′ (-esk′), *adj.* like a statue, as in dignity or grace.
stat′u•ette′ (-et′), *n.* a small statue.
stat′ure (-ər), *n.* **1.** height, as of a person. **2.** esteem or status based on qualities or achievements.
sta•tus (stā′təs, stat′əs), *n.* **1.** the position or rank of an individual in relation to others; standing. **2.** high standing; prestige. **3.** state of affairs.
sta′tus quo′ (kwō), *n.* the existing state or condition.
sta′tus sym′bol, *n.* a possession that is believed to indicate high social status.
stat•ute (stach′ōōt, ōōt), *n.* a formal enactment by a legislature; law.
stat′ute mile′, *n.* MILE (def. 1).
stat′ute of limita′tions, *n.* a statute defining the period within which legal action may be taken.
stat′u•to′ry (-ōō tôr′ē), *adj.* **1.** pertaining to a stat-

ute. **2.** prescribed, authorized, or regulated by statute.

staunch[1] (stônch), *v.t.*, *v.i.* STANCH[1].

staunch[2] (stônch, stänch), *adj.*, **-er, -est. 1.** firm or steadfast. **2.** strong; substantial. **3.** impervious to water or other liquids. —**staunch/ly,** *adv.*

stave (stāv), *n.*, *v.*, **staved** or **stove, stav•ing.** —*n.* **1.** one of the thin, narrow pieces of wood that form the sides of a vessel, as a barrel. **2.** a stick, rod, or pole. **3.** a verse or stanza of a poem or song. —*v.t.* **4.** to break in the staves of. **5.** to break a hole in. **6. stave off,** to keep off or prevent.

staves (stāvz), *n.* **1.** a pl. of STAFF[1]. **2.** pl. of STAVE.

stay[1] (stā), *v.i.* **1.** to remain in a place, condition, or situation; continue. **2.** to live; dwell. **3.** to wait briefly; pause. **4.** to be steadfast; persevere. **5.** to keep up, as with a competitor. **6.** to stop or halt. —*v.t.* **7.** to stop or halt. **8.** to hold back or restrain. **9.** to suspend or delay. **10.** to satisfy temporarily the hunger of. **11.** to remain through or during. —*n.* **12.** a stop, halt, or pause. **13.** a sojourn or temporary residence. **14.** a suspension of a judicial proceeding.

stay[2] (stā), *n.* **1.** something used as a support; prop. **2.** a flat strip, as of steel or whalebone, used esp. for stiffening corsets. **3. stays,** a corset. —*v.t.* **4.** to hold up with or as if with stays; prop.

stay[3] (stā), *n.* **1.** a strong rope or wire for steadying something, as a mast. —*v.t.* **2.** to secure with stays.

stay/ing pow/er, *n.* endurance; stamina.

St. Cath•ar•ines (kath/ər inz, kath/rinz), *n.* a city in SE Ontario, in SE Canada. 123,455.

St. Chris•to•pher (kris/tə fər), *n.* ST. KITTS.

St. Christopher-Nevis, *n.* ST. KITTS-NEVIS.

STD, sexually transmitted disease.

std., standard.

Ste., (referring to a woman) Saint. [< F *Sainte*]

stead (sted), *n.* **1.** the function or place of a person or thing as occupied by a substitute. —*Idiom.* **2. stand in good stead,** to prove useful to.

stead/fast/, *adj.* **1.** fixed in place, position, or direction. **2.** firm in purpose, resolution, or faith; unwavering. —**stead/fast/ly,** *adv.* —**stead/fast/ness,** *n.*

stead/y, *adj.*, **-i•er, -i•est,** *n.*, *pl.* **-ies,** *v.*, **-ied, -y• ing,** *adv.* —*adj.* **1.** firmly placed or fixed. **2.** free from change, variation, or interruption. **3.** constant, regular, or habitual. **4.** free from excitement or agitation; calm. **5.** firm; unfaltering. **6.** steadfast or unwavering. **7.** sober and dependable. —*n.* **8.** a person whom one dates exclusively. **9.** a steady customer. —*v.t.*, *v.i.* **10.** to make or become steady. —*adv.* **11.** in a steady manner. —*Idiom.* **12. go steady,** to date one person exclusively. —**stead/i•ly,** *adv.* —**stead/i•ness,** *n.*

stead/y state/ the/ory, *n.* the theory that the average temperature and density of the universe are held constant through the creation of new matter and energy as the universe expands.

steak (stāk), *n.* a fleshy slice of meat, esp. beef, or of fish. [< ON]

steal (stēl), *v.*, **stole, sto•len, steal•ing,** *n.* —*v.t.* **1.** to take (another's property) without permission or right. **2.** to take or get insidiously or surreptitiously. **3.** *Baseball.* to gain (a base) by running while the ball is being pitched to the batter. —*v.i.* **4.** to commit theft. **5.** to move or pass secretly, imperceptibly, or gradually. —*n.* **6.** the act of stealing. **7.** a bargain.

stealth (stelth), *n.* **1.** secret or surreptitious procedure or action. —*adj.* **2.** (*often cap.*) having or providing the capacity to evade detection by radar: *Stealth planes.* **3.** secret; not openly acknowledged: *stealth issues.* —**stealth/y,** *adj.*, **-i•er, -i•est.** —**stealth/i•ly,** *adv.* —**stealth/i•ness,** *n.*

steam (stēm), *n.* **1.** water in the form of an invisible gas or vapor. **2.** water changed to steam by boiling and used to generate mechanical power and heat. **3.** the mist formed when the gas or vapor from boiling water condenses. **4.** power or energy. —*v.i.* **5.** to emit or pass off in the form of steam. **6.** to become covered with condensed steam. **7.** to move by or as if by the agency of steam. —*v.t.* **8.** to expose to or

treat with steam, as in cooking. —*adj.* **9.** employing or operated by steam. —**steam/y,** *adj.*, **-i•er, -i•est.**

steam/boat/, *n.* a steam-driven boat.

steam/ en/gine, *n.* an engine worked by steam, typically one in which a sliding piston in a cylinder is moved by the expansive action of steam.

steam/er, *n.* **1.** a steamship. **2.** a device or container in which something is steamed.

steam/fit/ter, *n.* one who installs and repairs steam pipes and their accessories. —**steam/fit/ting,** *n.*

steam/roll/er, *n.* **1.** a heavy steam-powered vehicle with a roller used esp. in paving roads. —*v.t.* **2.** to crush, flatten, or overwhelm with or as if with a steamroller.

steam/ship/, *n.* a large commercial ship driven by steam.

steam/ shov/el, *n.* a steam-powered machine for digging or excavating.

steed (stēd), *n.* a horse, esp. a spirited one.

steel (stēl), *n.* **1.** a hard, strong alloy consisting principally of iron and containing carbon and sometimes other metals. **2.** something, as a knife sharpener, made of steel. —*adj.* **3.** of, made of, or resembling steel. —*v.t.* **4.** to cause to be unyielding or determined. —**steel/y,** *adj.*, **-i•er, -i•est.**

steel/ wool/, *n.* a mass of stringlike steel shavings used esp. for scouring and smoothing.

steel•yard (stēl/yärd/, stil/yərd), *n.* a balance with two arms, the longer one having a movable counterpoise and the shorter one a hook for holding the object to be weighed.

steep[1] (stēp), *adj.*, **-er, -est. 1.** having an almost vertical slope or gradient. **2.** unduly high; exorbitant. —**steep/ly,** *adv.* —**steep/ness,** *n.*

steep[2] (stēp), *v.t.* **1.** to soak in a liquid, as to extract some constituent. **2.** to saturate: *an incident steeped in mystery.* —*v.i.* **3.** to lie soaking in a liquid.

stee•ple (stē/pəl), *n.* **1.** a structure ending in a spire, erected on a tower of a church or public building. **2.** a tower with a steeple.

steeple

stee/ple•chase/, *n.* a horse race over a course with artificial obstacles, as ditches.

stee/ple•jack/, *n.* a person who builds or repairs steeples or towers.

steer[1] (stēr), *v.t.* **1.** to guide the course of (something in motion), as by a rudder. **2.** to pursue (a particular course). **3.** to direct; guide. —*v.i.* **4.** to steer a vessel or vehicle. **5.** to pursue a course of action. —*Idiom.* **6. steer clear of,** to stay away from; avoid. —**steer/a•ble,** *adj.*

steer[2] (stēr), *n.*, *pl.* **steers, steer.** a castrated male bovine, esp. one raised for beef.

steer/age (-ij), *n.* **1.** accommodations in a passenger ship for travelers who pay the cheapest fare. **2.** management; direction.

steg•o•saur (steg/ə sôr/), *n.* a plant-eating dinosaur with bony plates along the back.

stein (stīn), *n.* an earthenware mug, esp. for beer.

Stein (stīn), *n.* **Gertrude,** 1874–1946, U.S. author in France.

Stein·beck (stīn′bek), *n.* **John (Ernst),** 1902–68, U.S. novelist.

Stein·way (stīn′wā′), *n.* **Henry Engelhard,** (*Heinrich Engelhard Steinweg*), 1797–1871, U.S. piano manufacturer, born in Germany.

stel·lar (stel′ər), *adj.* **1.** of or consisting of stars. **2.** of, befitting, or like a star performer; preeminent or outstanding.

stem¹ (stem), *n., v.,* **stemmed, stem·ming.** —*n.* **1.** the ascending axis of a plant. **2.** the stalk that supports a leaf, flower, or fruit. **3.** something resembling a stem. **4.** the line of descent of a family. **5.** the underlying form of a word to which inflectional endings may be added. —*v.i.* **6.** to arise or originate.

stem² (stem), *v.t.,* **stemmed, stem·ming.** to stop or check by or as if by damming.

stem³ (stem), *n., v.,* **stemmed, stem·ming.** —*n.* **1.** the forward part of a ship. —*v.t.* **2.** to make headway or progress against.

stem′ware′, *n.* glassware with footed stems.

stench (stench), *n.* an offensive smell.

sten·cil (sten′səl), *n., v.,* **-ciled, -cil·ing** or (*esp. Brit.*) **-cilled, -cil·ling.** —*n.* **1.** a thin sheet of material into which letters or designs have been cut so that they can be reproduced on another surface when ink or paint is applied over the cutout areas. —*v.t.* **2.** to mark or make with a stencil.

sten·o (sten′ō), *n., pl.* **sten·os. 1.** a stenographer. **2.** stenography.

ste·nog·ra·phy (stə nog′rə fē), *n.* the art of writing in shorthand. —**ste·nog′ra·pher,** *n.* —**sten·o·graph·ic** (sten′ə graf′ik), *adj.*

sten·to·ri·an (sten tôr′ē ən), *adj.* very loud.

step (step), *n., v.,* **stepped, step·ping.** —*n.* **1.** a movement made by lifting the foot and setting it down in a new position. **2.** the distance covered by a step. **3.** the sound made by the foot in taking a step. **4.** a footprint. **5.** a manner of walking. **6.** a stage in a process. **7.** rank or degree in a series or scale. **8.** a support for the foot in ascending or descending. **9.** a short distance. —*v.i.* **10.** to move in steps **11.** to walk a short distance. **12.** to go briskly. **13.** to come easily and naturally: *to step into a fortune.* **14.** to press with the foot. —*v.t.* **15.** to measure by steps. **16. step down, a.** to decrease by degrees. **b.** to resign or retire. **17. ~ up, a.** to increase by degrees. **b.** to advance. —*Idiom.* **18. in (or out of) step,** in (or not in) harmony or agreement. —**step′per,** *n.*

step′broth′er, *n.* one's stepparent's son by a previous marriage.

step′child′, *n., pl.* **-chil·dren.** a child of one's spouse by a previous marriage.

step′daugh′ter, *n.* a daughter of one's spouse by a previous marriage.

step′-down′, *n.* a decrease in rate or quantity.

step′fa′ther, *n.* the husband of one's mother by a later marriage.

Ste·phen (stē′vən), *n.* **Saint,** died A.D. c35, first Christian martyr.

step′lad′der, *n.* a ladder with flat steps and a hinged supporting frame.

step′moth′er, *n.* the wife of one's father by a later marriage.

step′par′ent, *n.* a stepfather or stepmother.

steppe (step), *n.* a vast treeless plain, esp. in SE Europe and Asia.

step′ping·stone′, *n.* **1.** a stone for stepping on, as in crossing a stream. **2.** a means of advancement.

step′sis′ter, *n.* one's stepparent's daughter by a previous marriage.

step′son′, *n.* a son of one's spouse by a previous marriage.

step′-up′, *n.* an increase in rate or quantity.

-ster, a suffix meaning: one who is (*youngster*); one who is associated with (*gangster*); one who makes or does (*trickster*).

ster·e·o (ster′ē ō′, stēr′-), *n., pl.* **ster·e·os,** *adj.* —*n.* **1.** a stereophonic sound system. **2.** stereophonic

reproduction. **3.** a stereoscopic photograph. —*adj.* **4.** stereophonic. **5.** stereoscopic.

stereo-, a combining form meaning three dimensions (*stereoscope*).

ster·e·o·phon·ic (ster′ē ə fon′ik, stēr′-), *adj.* of or being a system of recording and reproducing sound in which two channels are used instead of one to enhance realism.

ster′e·o·scope′ (-skōp′), *n.* an optical instrument in which two pictures of an object from slightly different points of view are merged into a single three-dimensional image. —**ster′e·o·scop′ic** (-skop′ik), *adj.*

ster′e·o·type′, *n., v.,* **-typed, -typ·ing.** —*n.* **1.** a printing plate cast from a mold of composed type. **2.** an idea, expression, etc., lacking in originality. **3.** a simplified and standardized conception or image shared by members of a group. —*v.t.* **4.** to make a stereotype of. —**ster′e·o·typed′,** *adj.* —**ster′e·o·typ′ic** (-tip′ik), **ster′e·o·typ′i·cal,** *adj.*

ster·ile (ster′il; *esp. Brit.* -īl), *adj.* **1.** free from microorganisms. **2.** incapable of producing offspring or vegetation. **3.** not productive; fruitless. —**ste·ril·i·ty** (stə ril′i tē), *n.*

ster′i·lize′, *v.t.,* **-lized, -liz·ing.** to make sterile. —**ster′i·li·za′tion,** *n.* —**ster′i·liz′er,** *n.*

ster·ling (stûr′ling), *adj.* **1.** of or noting the currency of Great Britain. **2.** (of silver) having the standard fineness of 0.925. **3.** made of sterling silver. **4.** thoroughly excellent. —*n.* **5.** British currency. **6.** sterling silver.

Ster′ling Heights′, *n.* a city in SE Michigan, near Detroit. 119,505.

stern¹ (stûrn), *adj.,* **-er, -est. 1.** firm, strict, or uncompromising. **2.** hard, harsh, or severe. **3.** unpleasantly serious; rigorous or austere. **4.** grim or forbidding. —**stern′ly,** *adv.* —**stern′ness,** *n.*

stern² (stûrn), *n.* the after part of a ship or boat.

ster·num (stûr′nəm), *n., pl.* **-na** (-nə), **-nums.** the bony plate or series of bones to which the ribs are attached.

ste·roid (stēr′oid, ster′-), *n.* any of a large group of fat-soluble organic compounds, as the sex hormones.

ster·to·rous (stûr′tər əs), *adj.* characterized by heavy snoring or noisy breathing.

stet (stet), *v.,* **stet·ted, stet·ting.** —*v.i.* **1.** let it stand (used as a direction on a printer's proof or manuscript to retain material previously deleted). —*v.t.* **2.** to mark with the word "stet."

steth·o·scope (steth′ə skōp′), *n.* an instrument used to detect sounds in the body, esp. in the chest.

Stet·son (stet′sən), *Trademark.* a brand of felt hat with a broad brim and high crown.

ste·ve·dore (stē′vi dôr′), *n.* one engaged in the loading or unloading of ships.

Ste·vens (stē′vənz), *n.* **1. John Paul,** born 1920, associate justice of the U.S. Supreme Court since 1975. **2. Thaddeus,** 1792–1868, U.S. abolitionist and political leader. **3. Wallace,** 1879–1955, U.S. poet.

Ste·ven·son (stē′vən sən), *n.* **Robert Louis,** 1850–94, Scottish writer.

stew (stōō, styōō), *v.t.* **1.** to cook by slow boiling. —*v.i.* **2.** to fret or worry. —*n.* **3.** a dish, esp. of meat and vegetables, cooked by stewing. **4.** a state of agitation or worry.

stew·ard (stōō′ərd, styōō′-), *n.* **1.** a person who manages another's property or finances. **2.** a person in charge of running a large estate. **3.** an employee in charge of the table, wine, and servants in a club or restaurant. **4.** an employee on a ship, train, or airplane who serves passengers. —**stew′ard·ship′,** *n.*

St. He·le·na (hə lē′nə), *n.* **1.** a British island in the S Atlantic: Napoleon's place of exile 1815–21. **2.** a British colony comprising this island, Ascension Island, and the Tristan da Cunha group. 5,564; 126 sq. mi. (326 sq. km). *Cap.:* Jamestown.

St. Hel·ens (hel′ənz), *n.* **Mount,** an active volcano in SW Washington, part of the Cascade Range: major eruptions 1980. 8364 ft. (2549 m).

stick¹ (stik), *n.* **1.** a cut or broken-off branch or shoot of a tree or shrub. **2.** a long, slender piece of wood. **3.** a rod, wand, or baton. **4.** a long, slender piece or part: *a stick of celery.* **5. the sticks,** *Informal.* the rural districts.

stick² (stik), *v.,* **stuck, stick•ing,** *n.* —*v.t.* **1.** to pierce with something pointed. **2.** to thrust (something pointed) into or through. **3.** to fasten in position by or as if by something thrust through. **4.** to impale. **5.** to thrust or poke: *She stuck her head out the window.* **6.** to attach with or as if with glue. **7.** to keep from moving or proceeding. **8.** to puzzle. **9.** *Informal.* to impose something disagreeable upon. —*v.i.* **10.** to be fastened in position by something pointed. **11.** to remain attached by or as if by adhesion. **12.** to remain firm or faithful. **13.** to persevere or persist. **14.** to become obstructed or jammed. **15.** to be unable to move or proceed. **16.** to be puzzled. **17.** to extend or protrude. **18. stick around,** *Informal.* to wait around; linger. **19. ~ up,** *Informal.* to rob, esp. at gunpoint. **20. ~ up for,** to defend or support. —*n.* **21.** a thrust with a pointed instrument.

stick′er, *n.* **1.** one that sticks. **2.** an adhesive label.

stick′-in-the-mud′, *n.* someone who avoids new activities, ideas, or attitudes.

stick•le•back (stik′əl bak′), *n.* a small, pugnacious, spiny-backed fish.

stick•ler (stik′lər), *n.* **1.** a person who insists on something unyieldingly. **2.** a puzzling or difficult problem.

stick′pin′, *n.* an ornamental pin, esp. one for holding a necktie in place.

stick′ shift′, *n.* a manual transmission for a motor vehicle.

stick′up′, *n. Informal.* a holdup; robbery.

stick′y, *adj.,* **-i•er, -i•est. 1.** having the property of adhering; adhesive. **2.** tending to adhere. **3.** hot and humid. **4.** awkwardly difficult. —**stick′i•ness,** *n.*

stiff (stif), *adj.,* **-er, -est,** *adv.* —*adj.* **1.** difficult to bend or flex. **2.** not moving or working easily. **3.** not supple. **4.** strong; powerful. **5.** rigidly formal in manner. **6.** harsh; as a penalty. **7.** excessive; unusually high: *a stiff price.* **8.** relatively firm in consistency: *a stiff cake batter.* —*adv.* **9.** completely or extremely: *scared stiff.* —**stiff′ly,** *adv.* —**stiff′ness,** *n.*

stiff′-arm′, *v.t.* STRAIGHT-ARM.

stiff′en, *v.t., v.i.* to make or become stiff. —**stiff′-en•er,** *n.*

stiff′-necked′, *adj.* haughty and obstinate.

sti•fle (stī′fəl), *v.,* **-fled, -fling.** —*v.t.* **1.** to suppress, curb, or withhold. **2.** to kill by impeding respiration; smother. —*v.i.* **3.** to suffocate. —**sti′fling,** *adj.*

stig•ma (stig′mə), *n., pl.* **stig•ma•ta** (stig′mə tə, stig mä′tə, -mat′ə), **stig•mas. 1.** a mark of reproach or disgrace. **2.** the part of a pistil that receives the pollen. **3. stigmata,** marks resembling the wounds of the crucified body of Christ. —**stig•mat′ic** (-mat′ik), *adj.*

stig′ma•tize′ (-tīz′), *v.t.,* **-tized, -tiz•ing. 1.** to set a mark of disgrace or discredit upon. **2.** to mark with a stigma.

stile (stīl), *n.* steps for scaling a wall or fence.

sti•let•to (sti let′ō), *n., pl.* **-tos, -toes.** a short dagger with a slender blade.

still (stil), *adj.,* **-er, -est,** *n., adv., conj., v.* —*adj.* **1.** motionless; stationary. **2.** free from sound or noise; quiet. **3.** free from turbulence; calm. **4.** of or being a single photograph. —*n.* **5.** calmness or silence. **6.** a still photograph. —*adv.* **7.** at or up to this or that time. **8.** even; yet. **9.** even then; nevertheless. **10.** without sound or movement; quietly. —*conj.* **11.** and yet; nevertheless. —*v.t., v.i.* **12.** to make or become still. —*Saying.* **13. Still waters run deep,** quietness may conceal complexity or passion. —**still′-ness,** *n.*

still′birth′, *n.* the birth of a dead fetus.

still′born′, *adj.* dead when born.

still′ life′, *n., pl.* **still lifes.** a picture of inanimate objects.

stilt (stilt), *n.* **1.** one of two poles, each with a foot support, enabling the wearer to walk above the ground. **2.** a post supporting a structure above the surface of land or water.

stilt′ed, *adj.* stiffly dignified or formal.

Stil•ton (stil′tn), *Trademark.* a rich white cheese veined with mold.

stim•u•lant (stim′yə lənt), *n.* **1.** an agent that temporarily quickens the functional activity of an organ or part. **2.** an alcoholic beverage.

stim′u•late′ (-lāt′), *v.t.,* **-lat•ed, -lat•ing. 1.** to rouse to action or effort; incite. **2.** to excite (a nerve, gland, etc.) to functional activity. —**stim′u•la′tion,** *n.*

stim′u•lus (-ləs), *n., pl.* **-li** (-lī′). something that stimulates.

sting (sting), *v.,* **stung, sting•ing.** —*v.t.* **1.** to prick painfully with a sharp-pointed, often venom-bearing organ. **2.** to cause to feel a sharp physical or mental pain. **3.** *Slang.* to cheat, esp. to overcharge. —*v.i.* **4.** to use or wound with a sting. **5.** to feel or cause a sharp, smarting pain. —*n.* **6.** the act of stinging. **7.** a wound or pain caused by or as if by stinging. **8.** a sharp-pointed, often venom-bearing organ, as of a bee, capable of inflicting a painful wound. —**sting′er,** *n.*

sting′ray′, *n.* a ray with a flexible tail armed with a bony, usu. poisonous spine.

stin•gy (stin′jē), *adj.,* **-gi•er, -gi•est. 1.** reluctant to give or spend. **2.** meager. —**stin′gi•ly,** *adv.* —**stin′-gi•ness,** *n.*

stink (stingk), *v.,* **stank** or, often, **stunk; stunk; stink•ing;** *n.* —*v.i.* **1.** to emit a strong offensive smell. **2.** *Informal.* to be disgustingly inferior. —*n.* **3.** a strong offensive smell. **4.** *Informal.* an unpleasant fuss. —**stink′er,** *n.* —**stink′ing,** *adj.*

stint (stint), *v.i.* **1.** to be frugal or sparing. —*v.t.* **2.** to limit, often unduly. —*n.* **3.** a period of time spent doing something. **4.** limitation or restriction. **5.** a limited or prescribed amount of work. —**stint′ing,** *adj.*

sti•pend (stī′pend), *n.* a periodic fixed payment, as a scholarship allowance.

stip•ple (stip′əl), *v.t.,* **-pled, -pling.** to paint, engrave, or draw by means of dots or small strokes.

stip•u•late (stip′yə lāt′), *v.t.,* **-lat•ed, -lat•ing. 1.** to specify in the terms of an agreement. **2.** to require as an essential condition of an agreement. —**stip′u•la′tion,** *n.*

stir¹ (stûr), *v.,* **stirred, stir•ring,** *n.* —*v.t., v.i.* **1.** to agitate (a substance) with a continuous or repeated movement of an implement. **2.** to affect or be moved strongly. **3.** to incite, instigate, or prompt. **4.** to move, esp. in a slight way. **5.** to rouse or be roused, as from inactivity. —*n.* **6.** the act of stirring. **7.** a state of excitement; commotion. —**stir′rer,** *n.*

stir² (stûr), *n. Slang.* prison.

stir′-cra′zy, *adj. Slang.* restless or frantic from long confinement.

stir′-fry′, *v.t.,* **-fried, -fry•ing.** to fry quickly while stirring constantly in a small amount of oil over high heat.

stir′ring, *adj.* **1.** rousing or exciting. **2.** active or lively.

stir•rup (stûr′əp, stir′-), *n.* **1.** a loop or ring suspended from the saddle of a horse to support the rider's foot. **2. a.** a strap of fabric or elastic at the bottom of a pair of pants, worn around and under the foot. **b.** stirrups, (*used with a pl. v.*) close-fitting knit pants with such straps.

stitch (stich), *n.* **1. a.** one complete movement of a threaded needle in sewing. **b.** a loop or portion of thread left after a stitch. **2.** the least bit, as of clothing. **3.** a sudden, sharp pain, esp. in the side. —*v.t.* **4.** to join or mend with stitches. **5.** to ornament with stitches. —*v.i.* **6.** to sew. —*Proverb.* **7. A stitch in time saves nine,** dealing with problems when they occur prevents future trouble.

stitch′er•y, *n.* NEEDLEWORK.

St. John's (or **John**), *n.* **1.** the capital of Newfoundland. 96,216. **2.** the capital of Antigua and Barbuda. 30,000.

St. Kitts (kits), *n.* an island in the E West Indies.

St. Kitts-Nevis, *n.* a twin-island state in the E West Indies, consisting of St. Kitts and Nevis. 44,400.

St. Lawrence, *n.* a river in SE Canada, flowing NE from Lake Ontario into the Atlantic. 760 mi. (1225 km) long.

St. Lawrence Seaway, *n.* a series of channels, locks, and canals between Montreal and the mouth of Lake Ontario: developed jointly by the U.S. and Canada.

St. Lou•is (lōō′is, lōō′ē), *n.* a port in E Missouri, on the Mississippi. 368,215.

St. Lu•cia (lōō′shə, -sē ə), *n.* an island country in the E West Indies. 159,639. —**St. Lu′cian,** *n., adj.*

stoat (stōt), *n.* the European ermine, esp. in its brown summer coat.

stock (stok), *n.* **1.** a supply of goods kept on hand, as by a merchant or manufacturer. **2.** a quantity accumulated, as for future use. **3.** LIVESTOCK. **4.** a stock company. **5. a.** the shares of a company or corporation. **b.** a certificate showing ownership of one or more shares. **6.** the type from which a group of animals or plants has been derived. **7.** a race, breed, or family, as of animals or plants. **8.** a line of descent. **9.** a wooden supporting structure, as the handle of a whip or the piece to which the barrel of a rifle is attached. **10. stocks,** a framework with holes for the ankles and, sometimes, the wrists, formerly used to expose an offender to public derision. **11.** raw material. **12.** the broth from boiled meat, fish, or poultry. —*adj.* **13.** kept regularly on hand. **14.** common or ordinary; standard. —*v.t.* **15.** to furnish with stock; supply. **16.** to lay up in store, as for future use. —*v.i.* **17.** to lay in a stock of something. —*Idiom.* **18. take** or **put stock in,** to believe; trust. **19. take stock, a.** to make an inventory of stock on hand. **b.** to appraise resources or prospects.

stock•ade (sto kād′), *n.* **1.** a defensive barrier of upright stakes or timbers driven into the ground one beside the other. **2.** an enclosure consisting of stockades. **3.** a military prison.

stock′brok′er, *n.* a broker who buys and sells securities for customers.

stock′ car′, *n.* **1.** a standard automobile modified for racing. **2.** a boxcar for livestock.

stock′ com′pany, *n.* a theatrical company acting a repertoire of plays, usu. at its own theater.

stock′ exchange′, *n.* **1.** a place where securities are bought and sold. **2.** an association of stockbrokers.

stock′hold′er, *n.* an owner of stock in a corporation.

Stock•holm (stok′hōm, -hōlm), *n.* the capital of Sweden. 666,810.

stock•i•nette or **-net** (stok′ə net′), *n.* a stretchy machine-knitted fabric used esp. for infants' wear.

stock′ing, *n.* a close-fitting knitted covering for the foot and leg.

stock′ing cap′, *n.* a conical knitted cap with a tassel or pompom.

stock′ mar′ket, *n.* **1.** STOCK EXCHANGE (def. 1). **2.** the market for stocks throughout a nation.

stock′pile′, *n., v.,* **-piled, -pil•ing.** —*n.* **1.** a supply of an essential material held in reserve. —*v.t., v.i.* **2.** to store or accumulate in a stockpile.

stock′-still′, *adj.* completely still; motionless.

Stock•ton (stok′tən), *n.* a city in central California. 222,633.

stock′y, *adj.,* **-i•er, -i•est.** sturdy and usu. short; thickset. —**stock′i•ness,** *n.*

stock′yard′, *n.* an enclosure for the temporary housing of livestock.

stodg•y (stoj′ē), *adj.,* **-i•er, -i•est. 1.** dull or uninteresting; boring. **2.** unduly formal and traditional. —**stodg′i•ness,** *n.*

sto•gy or **-gie** (stō′gē), *n., pl.* **-gies.** a long, slender, inexpensive cigar.

Sto•ic (stō′ik), *adj.* **1.** of or noting an ancient Greek school of philosophy teaching that people should be free of passion and submit without complaint to unavoidable necessity. **2.** (*l.c.*) stoical. —*n.* **3.** a member of the Stoic school of philosophy. **4.** (*l.c.*) a stoical person. —**Sto′i•cism** (-ə siz′əm), *n.*

sto′i•cal, *adj.* **1.** marked by a calm, austere fortitude

befitting the Stoics; impassive. **2.** (*cap.*) of the Stoics. —**sto′i•cal•ly,** *adv.*

stoke (stōk), *v.t., v.i.,* **stoked, stok•ing. 1.** to poke, stir up, and feed (a fire). **2.** to tend the fire of (a furnace). —**stok′er,** *n.*

STOL (es′tōl′), *n.* an aircraft that can become airborne after a short takeoff run. [*s(hort) t(ake)o(ff and) l(anding)*]

stole¹ (stōl), *v.* pt. of STEAL.

stole² (stōl), *n.* **1.** a narrow strip of material worn over the shoulders by some clergymen. **2.** a woman's long shoulder scarf of fur or other material.

sto•len (stō′lən), *v.* pp. of STEAL.

stol•id (stol′id), *adj.* not easily moved emotionally; impassive. —**sto•lid•i•ty** (stə lid′i tē), *n.* —**stol′-id•ly,** *adv.*

stom•ach (stum′ək), *n.* **1.** the saclike enlargement of the alimentary canal in which food is stored and partially digested. **2.** the belly; abdomen. **3.** appetite for food. **4.** desire; inclination. —*v.t.* **5.** to endure or tolerate; bear.

stom′ach•ache′, *n.* pain in the stomach or abdomen.

stom′ach•er, *n.* a 15th- and 16th-century ornamented garment or panel covering the stomach or chest.

stomp (stomp), *v.t., v.i.* to tread on or step heavily; trample.

stone (stōn), *n., pl.* **stones** for 1–3, 5, 6, **stone** for 4, *v.,* **stoned, ston•ing.** —*n.* **1.** the hard substance, formed of mineral matter, of which rocks consist. **2.** a small piece of rock. **3.** a gemstone. **4.** a British unit of weight equivalent to 14 pounds (6.4 kg). **5.** a hard seed, as of a date; pit. **6.** a calculous concretion in the body, as in the kidney. —*v.t.* **7.** to pelt or kill by pelting with stones. **8.** to remove stones from (fruit). —*Proverb.* **9. A rolling stone gathers no moss,** a wanderer acquires no responsibilities. —*Saying.* **10. Let him who is without sin cast the first stone,** one should examine one's own faults before condemning others. John 8:7. —**ston′y,** *adj.,* **-i•er, -i•est.**

Stone (stōn), *n.* **Lucy,** 1818–93, U.S. suffragist.

Stone′ Age′, *n.* the early period of human history characterized by the use of stone implements and weapons.

Stone•henge (stōn′henj), *n.* a prehistoric megalithic monument in S England.

stone′s′ throw′, *n.* a short distance.

stone′wall′, *v.i.* to be evasive or uncooperative; use obstructive tactics.

stood (stŏŏd), *v.* pt. and pp. of STAND.

stooge (stōōj), *n.* **1.** an entertainer who feeds lines to the main comedian. **2.** an underling, assistant, or accomplice.

stool (stōōl), *n.* **1.** a simple armless and backless seat. **2.** a low support on which to kneel or rest the feet. **3.** fecal matter.

stoop¹ (stōōp), *v.i.* **1.** to bend the body forward and downward. **2.** to bow the head and shoulders forward habitually. **3.** to descend from one's level of dignity; condescend. —*n.* **4.** the act of stooping. **5.** a stooping position or posture.

stoop² (stōōp), *n.* a small porch at the entrance of a house.

stop (stop), *v.,* **stopped, stop•ping,** *n.* —*v.t.* **1.** to desist from; discontinue. **2.** to cause to cease. **3.** to interrupt or check. **4.** to cut off, intercept, or withhold. **5.** to prevent from proceeding, acting, or operating. **6.** to block (an opening) by closing, filling, or obstructing. —*v.i.* **7.** to come to a halt. **8.** to cease proceeding, acting, or operating. **9.** to halt for a stay or visit. **10. stop by** or **in,** to make a brief visit. **11. ~ over,** to stop briefly in the course of a journey. —*n.* **12.** the act of stopping. **13.** a cessation; end. **14.** a stay or visit. **15.** a place where trains or other vehicles stop. **16.** a plug; stopper. **17.** an obstacle, impediment, or hindrance. **18. a.** a set of organ pipes producing tones of the same quality. **b.** a knob or handle that controls such a set. **19.** a consonant sound made with complete closure at some part of the vocal tract, usu. followed by sudden release of the interrupted air. **20.** a punctuation mark, esp. a period.

stop/cock/, *n.* COCK¹ (def. 2).

stop/gap/, *n.* something serving as a temporary substitute; makeshift.

stop/light/, *n.* **1.** a taillight that lights up as the driver of a vehicle applies the brakes. **2.** TRAFFIC LIGHT.

stop/o/ver, *n.* a stop in the course of a journey.

stop•page (stop′ij), *n.* **1.** an act or instance of stopping. **2.** the state of being stopped.

stop/per, *n.* something, as a plug or cork, used to close an opening or hole.

stop•ple (stop′əl), *n., v.,* **-pled, -pling.** —*n.* **1.** a stopper, esp. for a bottle. —*v.t.* **2.** to close or fit with a stopple.

stop/watch/, *n.* a watch with a hand that can be stopped or started at any instant, used for precise timing.

stor•age (stôr′ij), *n.* **1.** the act of storing or state of being stored. **2.** capacity for storing. **3.** MEMORY (def. 7).

stor/age bat/tery, *n.* a voltaic battery capable of being recharged by an electric current.

store (stôr), *n., v.,* **stored, stor•ing.** —*n.* **1.** a retail establishment where merchandise is sold. **2.** a supply or stock, esp. for future use. **3.** *Chiefly Brit.* a storehouse or warehouse. **4.** a great quantity; abundance. —*v.t.* **5.** to supply or furnish. **6.** to put away for future use. **7.** to deposit, as in a storehouse, for safekeeping. **8.** to put or retain (data) in a computer memory unit. —*Idiom.* **9. in store, a.** in reserve. **b.** about to happen. **10. set store by,** to have regard for; value.

store/front/, *n.* **1.** the side of a store facing a street. **2.** a street-level store that has frontage on a street.

store/house/, *n.* **1.** a building in which things are stored; warehouse. **2.** a source of abundant supplies.

store/keep/er, *n.* a person who owns or operates a store.

store/room/, *n.* a room in which supplies or goods are stored.

sto•rey (stôr′ē), *n., pl.* **-reys.** *Chiefly Brit.* STORY².

sto•ried (stôr′ēd), *adj.* celebrated in history or story.

stork (stôrk), *n., pl.* **storks, stork.** a large wading bird with long legs and a long neck and bill.

storm (stôrm), *n.* **1.** an atmospheric disturbance marked by strong winds and often accompanied by rain, snow, or hail. **2.** a violent military assault. **3.** a violent outburst or outbreak: *a storm of abuse.* —*v.i.* **4.** to blow, rain, snow, or hail heavily. **5.** to be furious; rage. **6.** to rush angrily. —*v.t.* **7.** to attack or assault.

storm/y, *adj.,* **-i•er, -i•est. 1.** indicative of or marked by storms. **2.** full of turmoil or strife. —**storm/i•ly**, *adv.* —**storm/i•ness**, *n.*

sto•ry¹ (stôr′ē), *n., pl.* **-ries. 1.** a written or spoken account of something that has happened. **2.** a fictitious tale shorter than a novel. **3.** the plot of a literary or dramatic work. **4.** a news report. **5.** a lie; fabrication.

sto•ry² (stôr′ē), *n., pl.* **-ries.** a complete horizontal section of a building.

sto/ry•board/, *n.* a panel with sketches depicting changes of action and scene, as for a motion picture.

sto/ry•book/, *n.* a book of stories, esp. for children.

sto/ry•tell/er, *n.* a person who tells stories. —**sto/ry•tell/ing**, *n.*

stoup (stōōp), *n.* a basin for holy water.

stout (stout), *adj.,* **-er, -est,** *n.* —*adj.* **1.** overweight; fat. **2.** courageous; brave. **3.** firm; resolute. **4.** strong of body; sturdy. **5.** substantial; solid. —*n.* **6.** a dark, sweet ale. —**stout/ly**, *adv.* —**stout/ness**, *n.*

stout/-heart/ed, *adj.* brave and resolute.

stove¹ (stōv), *n.* an apparatus that furnishes heat for warmth or cooking and uses fuel or electricity for power.

stove² (stōv), *v.* a pt. and pp. of STAVE.

stove/pipe/, *n.* a pipe serving as a stove chimney or to connect a stove with a flue.

stow (stō), *v.t.* **1.** to put away, esp. in an orderly fashion. **2. stow away, a.** to conceal oneself on a conveyance as a means of getting transportation. **b.** to hide away. —**stow/age** (-ij), *n.*

stow/a•way/, *n.* a person who stows away.

Stowe (stō), *n.* **Harriet Beecher,** 1811–96, U.S. abolitionist and novelist.

St. Paul, *n.* a port in and the capital of Minnesota. 262,071.

St. Pe•ters•burg (pē′tərz bûrg′), *n.* **1.** Formerly, **Leningrad.** a seaport in the NW Russian Federation. 5,020,000. **2.** a city in W Florida. 238,585.

strad•dle (strad′l), *v., pl.* **-dled, -dling,** *n.* —*v.i.* **1.** to stand or sit astride (of). **2.** to favor or appear to favor both sides (of). —*n.* **3.** an act or instance of straddling. —**strad/dler**, *n.*

Stra•di•va•ri (strad′ə vâr′ē, -vär′ē), *n.* **Antonio,** 1644?–1737, Italian violinmaker.

strafe (strāf, sträf), *v.t.,* **strafed, straf•ing.** to attack (ground troops or installations) with fire from low-flying airplanes. [< G propaganda slogan *(Gott) strafe (England) (may God) punish (England)*] —**straf/er**, *n.*

strag•gle (strag′əl), *v.i.,* **-gled, -gling. 1.** to stray from the road or course. **2.** to wander about or ramble. **3.** to spread at irregular intervals. —**strag/gler**, *n.* —**strag/gly**, *adj.,* **-gli•er, -gli•est.**

straight (strāt), *adj.,* **-er, -est,** *adv., n.* —*adj.* **1.** without a bend, angle, wave, or curve. **2.** direct in character; candid. **3.** honest; upright. **4.** cogent; rational: *straight thinking.* **5.** in the proper order or condition. **6.** continuous; unbroken. **7.** thoroughgoing; complete. **8.** *Informal.* **a.** heterosexual. **b.** traditional; conventional. —*adv.* **9.** in a straight manner. —*n.* **10.** the condition of being straight. **11.** a straight form, part, or position. **12.** a sequence of five consecutive cards in poker. —*Idiom.* **13. straight off** or **away,** without delay; immediately. —**straight/ly**, *adv.* —**straight/ness**, *n.*

straight/-arm/, *v.t.* to deflect (an opponent) by pushing away with the arm held straight.

straight/ ar/row, *n.* an often righteously conventional person.

straight/a•way/, *n.* a straight stretch, as of a highway.

straight/edge/, *n.* a bar, as of wood or metal, with a straight edge for use in drawing or testing straight lines.

straight/en, *v.t., v.i.* **1.** to make or become straight. **2. straighten out, a.** to free or become free of confusion or difficulties. **b.** to improve in conduct or character. —**straight/en•er**, *n.*

straight/ face/, *n.* a facial expression that conceals one's feelings. —**straight/-faced/**, *adj.*

straight/for/ward, *adj.* **1.** going or directed straight ahead. **2.** free from deceit; honest. —*adv.* **3.** Also, **straight/for/wards.** straight ahead.

straight/ man/, *n.* an entertainer who acts as a foil for a comedian.

strain (strān), *v.t.* **1.** to draw tight; make taut. **2.** to exert to the utmost. **3.** to injure (a muscle, tendon, etc.) by overexertion. **4.** to stretch beyond the proper limit. **5.** to cause to pass through a strainer. —*v.i.* **6.** to make strenuous efforts. **7.** to filter, percolate, or ooze. —*n.* **8.** great effort in pursuit of a goal. **9.** an injury, as to a muscle, due to overexertion. **10.** deformation of a solid body or structure in response to application of a force. **11.** severe or fatiguing pressure or exertion. —*Saying.* **12. strain at a gnat and swallow a camel,** to pay attention to small wrongs but neglect big ones. Matt. 23:24.

strained, *adj.* not natural or spontaneous.

strain/er, *n.* a filter or sieve for straining liquids.

strait (strāt), *n.* **1.** Often, **straits.** (*used with a sing. v.*) a narrow passage of water connecting two large bodies of water. **2.** Usu., **straits.** a position of difficulty, distress, or need. —*adj.* *Archaic.* **3.** narrow or confined. **4.** strict.

strait/en, *v.t.* **1.** to put into difficulties, esp. financial ones. **2. a.** to make narrow. **b.** to confine narrowly.

strait/jack/et, *n.* a garment made of strong material and designed to bind the arms of a violent person.

strait/-laced/, *adj.* excessively strict in conduct or morality.

strand[1] (strand), *v.t.* **1.** to drive or run onto a shore. **2.** to leave in a helpless position. —*n.* **3.** land bordering a body of water; shore.

strand[2] (strand), *n.* **1.** one of the fibers or wires plaited or twisted together to form a rope, cable, cord, or string. **2.** a filament, as of hair. **3.** a length of cord or string.

strange (strānj), *adj.,* **strang•er, strang•est. 1.** exciting curiosity or wonder; odd. **2.** estranged; alienated. **3.** unfamiliar; foreign. **4.** unaccustomed; inexperienced. **5.** reserved; aloof. —**strange/ly,** *adv.* —**strange/ness,** *n.*

strange/ bed/fellows, *n.pl. Informal.* odd or incongruous allies.

stran•ger (strān/jər), *n.* **1.** a person with whom one is not personally acquainted. **2.** a newcomer. **3.** an outsider. **4.** a person unacquainted with or unaccustomed to something.

strang/er rape/, *n.* sexual intercourse forced by an assailant upon a person he does not know.

stran•gle (strang/gəl), *v.,* **-gled, -gling.** —*v.t.* **1.** to kill by choking; throttle. **2.** to stifle or suppress. —*v.i.* **3.** to become strangled. —**stran/gler,** *n.*

stran/gle•hold/, *n.* **1.** an illegal wrestling hold by which an opponent is choked. **2.** a restrictive force or influence.

stran•gu•late/ (-gyə lāt/), *v.t.,* **-lat•ed, -lat•ing.** to constrict (a duct, intestine, vessel, etc.) so as to prevent circulation. —**stran/gu•la/tion,** *n.*

strap (strap), *n., v.,* **strapped, strap•ping.** —*n.* **1.** a narrow strip of flexible material, esp. leather, as for fastening or holding things together. —*v.t.* **2.** to secure or fasten with a strap.

strap/less, *adj.* **1.** lacking straps. **2.** lacking shoulder straps.

strapped, *adj.* needy; wanting.

strap/ping, *adj.* powerfully built, robust.

stra•ta (strā/tə, strat/ə, strä/tə), *n.* a pl. of STRATUM.

strat•a•gem (strat/ə jəm), *n.* **1.** a scheme or maneuver for surprising or deceiving an enemy. **2.** a trick or ruse.

Strate/gic Defense/ Ini/tiative, *n.* STAR WARS (def. 1).

strat•e•gy (strat/i jē), *n., pl.* **-gies. 1.** the science or art of planning and directing large-scale military movements and operations. **2.** a plan or method for achieving a goal. —**stra•te•gic** (strə tē/jik), *adj.* —**stra•te/gi•cal•ly,** *adv.* —**strat/e•gist,** *n.*

Strat/ford-upon-A/von or **Strat/ford-on-A/von,** *n.* a town in central England: birthplace and burial place of Shakespeare. 107,200.

strat•i•fy (strat/ə fī/), *v.t., v.i.,* **-fied, -fy•ing.** to form into or become arranged in layers or strata. —**strat/i•fi•ca/tion,** *n.*

strat•o•sphere (strat/ə sfēr/), *n.* the region of the upper atmosphere extending from about 12 to 30 miles (20–50 km) above the earth. —**strat/o•spher/ic** (-sfer/ik), *adj.*

Strat•ton (strat/n), *n.* **Charles Sherwood** ("*General Tom Thumb*"), 1838–83, U.S. midget who performed in the circus of P. T. Barnum.

stra•tum (strā/təm, strat/əm), *n., pl.* **stra•ta** (strā/tə, strat/ə), **stra•tums. 1.** a layer of material, often formed once upon another. **2.** a single bed of sedimentary rock. **3.** a social or cultural level.

Strauss (strous, shtrous), *n.* **1. Johann,** 1804–49, Austrian composer. **2.** his son **Johann** ("*The Waltz King*"), 1825–99, Austrian composer. **3. Ri•chard** (rikн/ärt), 1864–1949, German composer.

Stra•vin•sky (strə vin/skē), *n.* **Igor (Fëdorovich),** 1882–1971, U.S. composer, born in Russia.

straw (strô), *n.* **1. a.** a single stalk of grass, esp. of a cereal grass. **b.** a mass of such stalks after drying and threshing. **2.** something of negligible value. **3.** a tube for sucking up a beverage. —*adj.* **4.** of, resembling, or made of straw. **5.** of the color of straw; pale yellow. **6.** of little value; inconsequential. —*Idiom.* **7. catch, clutch,** or **grasp at a straw** or **at straws,** to pursue even the slightest hope or possibility out of desperation. **8. straw in the wind,** a piece of information foreshadowing future events. —*Saying.* **9. straw that breaks the camel's back,** a final burden that makes a situation intolerable.

straw•ber•ry (strô/ber/ē, -bə rē), *n., pl.* **-ries. 1.** the red, juicy fruit of a plant of the rose family. **2.** the plant itself.

straw/ boss/, *n.* an assistant foreman, as in a logging camp.

straw/ vote/, *n.* an unofficial vote taken to determine the general trend of opinion. Also called **straw/ poll/.**

stray (strā), *v.i.* **1.** to deviate from a direct or proper course. **2.** to wander; roam. **3.** to become distracted. —*n.* **4.** a lost, homeless, or friendless person or animal. —*adj.* **5.** straying or having strayed. **6.** incidental; occasional.

streak (strēk), *n.* **1.** a long, narrow mark or band of color. **2.** a vein; stratum: *streaks of fat in bacon.* **3.** a trace: *a streak of humor.* **4. a.** a spell; run. **b.** an uninterrupted series. **5.** a bolt of lightning. —*v.t.* **6.** to mark with streaks. —*v.i.* **7.** to become streaked. **8.** to run, go, or work rapidly. —**streak/y,** *adj.,* **-i•er, -i•est.**

stream (strēm), *n.* **1.** a body of water, as a brook, flowing in a channel. **2.** a flow or current, as of fluid. **3.** a continuous succession: *a stream of words.* —*v.i.* **4.** to flow, pass, or issue in or as if in a stream. **5.** to emit a fluid copiously. **6.** to wave, as a flag in the wind. —*v.t.* **7.** to discharge in a stream.

stream/er, *n.* **1.** a long narrow flag; pennant. **2.** a long narrow strip, as a ribbon. **3.** a stream of light, as from the aurora borealis. **4.** BANNER (def. 2).

stream/line/, *v.t.,* **-lined, -lin•ing. 1.** to make streamlined. **2.** to make more efficient or simple.

stream/lined/, *adj.* **1.** contoured to offer the least resistance to a current, as of air or water. **2.** designed or organized for maximum efficiency. **3.** modernized.

stream/ of con/sciousness, *n.* a style of writing in which a character's thoughts are represented by disregarding logical sequence, normal syntax, or distinctions in the levels of reality.

street (strēt), *n.* **1.** a usu. paved public road, as in a town or city. **2.** a street together with the sidewalks and adjacent property. **3.** the inhabitants or frequenters of a street.

street/car/, *n.* a public vehicle on rails running regularly along city streets.

street/ smarts/, *n.pl.* shrewd awareness of how to survive in an urban environment. —**street/-smart/,** *adj.*

street/wise/, *adj.* possessing street smarts.

strength (strengkth, strength, strenth), *n.* **1.** the quality or state of being strong; physical power. **2.** intellectual or moral force. **3.** force in numbers, as of an organization. **4.** effective force or cogency. **5.** power of resisting strain, force, etc. **6.** degree of potency or concentration. **7.** intensity, as of light. **8.** a strong or valuable attribute. **9.** a source of power; sustenance. —*Idiom.* **10. on the strength of,** on the basis of.

strength/en, *v.t., v.i.* to make or grow stronger.

stren•u•ous (stren/yŏō əs), *adj.* **1.** characterized by or calling for vigorous exertion. **2.** intensely active; energetic. —**stren/u•ous•ly,** *adv.* —**stren/u•ous•ness,** *n.*

strep (strep), *n.* streptococcus.

strep/ throat/, *n.* an acute sore throat caused by streptococci.

strep•to•coc•cus (strep/tə kok/əs), *n., pl.* **-ci** (-sī, -sē). any of several spherical bacteria occurring in pairs or chains, some of which cause serious diseases. —**strep/to•coc/cal,** *adj.*

strep/to•my/cin (-mī′sin), *n.* an antibiotic used chiefly to treat tuberculosis.

stress (stres), *n.* **1.** importance or significance. **2.** prominent relative loudness of a speech sound. **3.** physical force, as pressure, exerted on one thing by another. **4.** the action on a body of a system of forces that results in deformation. **5.** a stimulus, as pain, that disturbs the equilibrium. **6.** physical, mental, or emotional tension. —*v.t.* **7.** to emphasize. **8.** to accent. **9.** to subject to strain or tension. —**stress/ful,** *adj.*

stretch (strech), *v.t.* **1.** to spread out fully. **2.** to extend or cause to extend from one point or place to another. **3.** to draw tight or taut. **4.** to extend or enlarge beyond normal or proper limits. —*v.i.* **5.** to recline at full length. **6.** to extend one's limbs or body. **7.** to extend over a distance or in time. **8.** to become stretched without breaking. —*n.* **9.** the act of stretching or state of being stretched. **10.** a continuous length. **11.** the homestretch of a racetrack. **12.** an extent in time. —*adj.* **13.** capable of being stretched. —**stretch/a•ble,** *adj.* —**stretch/y,** *adj.*, **-i•er, -i•est.**

stretch/er, *n.* **1.** a litter, as of canvas, for carrying a sick or dead person. **2.** one that stretches.

strew (strōō), *v.t.*, **strewed, strewn** (strōōn) or **strewed, strew•ing. 1.** to scatter freely; sprinkle. **2.** to overspread by scattering. **3.** to disseminate.

stri•a (strī′ə), *n.*, *pl.* **stri•ae** (strī′ē). a slight or narrow furrow, ridge, stripe, or line. —**stri/at•ed** (-ā-tid), *adj.* —**stri•a/tion,** *n.*

strick•en (strik′ən), *v.* **1.** a pp. of STRIKE. —*adj.* **2.** wounded by or as if by a missile. **3.** afflicted, as with disease or sorrow.

strict (strikt), *adj.*, **-er, -est. 1.** closely conforming to requirements or principles. **2.** stringent; exacting. **3.** rigorously enforced. **4.** exact; precise. **5.** narrowly limited. **6.** absolute; complete. —**strict/ly,** *adv.* —**strict/ness,** *n.*

stric•ture (strik′chər), *n.* **1.** an abnormal contraction of a bodily passage or duct. **2.** limitation; restriction. **3.** an adverse criticism.

stride (strīd), *v.*, **strode, strid•den** (strid′n), **strid•ing,** *n.* —*v.i.*, *v.t.* **1.** to walk (over or along) with long steps. **2.** to take or pass over in one long step. —*n.* **3.** a striding manner or gait. **4.** a long step. **5.** the distance covered in a stride. **6.** a step forward, as in development.

stri•dent (strīd′nt), *adj.* harsh and loud in sound; grating. —**stri/dent•ly,** *adv.*

strife (strīf), *n.* **1.** violent or bitter conflict. **2.** a struggle; clash. **3.** competition; rivalry.

strike (strīk), *v.*, **struck; struck** or (*esp. for 14–16*) **strick•en; strik•ing;** *n.* —*v.t.* **1.** to deal a blow to with or as if with the fist. **2.** to inflict; deliver: *struck a blow.* **3.** to produce by percussion or friction. **4.** to ignite (a match) by friction. **5.** to collide with. **6.** to enter the mind of. **7.** to impress strongly. **8.** to happen upon; find: *struck oil.* **9.** to arrive at; achieve: *to strike a compromise.* **10.** to lower: *to strike a sail.* **11.** to cross out; cancel. **12.** to stamp: *to strike a medal.* **13.** to mark by or as if by chimes: *The clock struck 12.* **14.** to afflict suddenly: *stricken with fever.* **15.** to overwhelm emotionally. **16.** to implant; induce: *struck fear in our hearts.* **17.** to take on; assume: *struck a pose.* —*v.i.* **18.** to deal a blow. **19.** to make an attack. **20.** to hit or collide. **21.** to come suddenly: *struck on a new method.* **22.** to sound by percussion: *The clock strikes.* **23.** to go on strike against an employer. **24. strike out, a.** to put or be put out by a strikeout in baseball. **b.** to set out; venture forth. **25. ~ up, a.** to begin to play or sing. **b.** to bring into being. —*n.* **26.** an act or instance of striking. **27.** a group work stoppage to compel changes in working conditions. **28.** a baseball pitch that is swung at and missed or in the strike zone but not swung at. **29.** the knocking down of all the bowling pins with the first bowl. **30.** the discovery of a rich mineral deposit. **31.** an attack, esp. by military aircraft. —**strik/er,** *n.*

strike/out/, *n. Baseball.* an out made by a batter to whom three strikes have been charged.

strike/ zone/, *n. Baseball.* the area above home plate extending from the batter's knees to the armpits.

strik/ing, *adj.* **1.** conspicuously attractive or impressive. **2.** noticeable; conspicuous.

string (string), *n.*, *v.*, **strung, string•ing.** —*n.* **1.** a slender cord or thick thread for binding or tying. **2.** a collection of objects threaded on a string: *a string of pearls.* **3.** a series of things arranged in or as if in a line: *a string of questions.* **4. a.** the tightly stretched cord or wire of a musical instrument. **b. strings,** stringed instruments, esp. those played with a bow. **5.** a plant fiber. **6.** Usu., **strings.** conditions or limitations: *no strings attached.* —*v.t.* **7.** to furnish with a string. **8.** to extend or stretch like a string. **9.** to thread on or as if on a string. **10.** to arrange in a series or succession. **11.** to strip the strings from: *to string beans.* **12.** to make tense. —**string/y,** *adj.*, **-i•er, -i•est.**

string/ bean/, *n.* a bean, as the green bean, whose unripe pods are used as food.

stringed, *adj.* fitted with strings: *violins and other stringed instruments.*

strin•gent (strin′jənt), *adj.* rigorously binding or exacting; strict. —**strin/gen•cy,** *n.* —**strin/gent•ly,** *adv.*

string/er, *n.* **1.** a long horizontal timber connecting upright posts. **2.** a part-time news reporter.

strip¹ (strip), *v.*, **stripped, strip•ping.** —*v.t.* **1.** to deprive of covering or clothing. **2.** to take off; remove. **3.** to take away; divest. **4.** to clear out; empty. **5.** to shear or damage the thread or teeth of: *to strip gears.* —*v.i.* **6.** to remove one's clothes. —**strip/per,** *n.*

strip² (strip), *n.* **1.** a long, narrow piece. **2.** an airstrip.

strip/ crop/ping, *n.* the growing of different crops on alternate strips of ground to minimize erosion.

stripe (strīp), *n.*, *v.*, **striped, strip•ing.** —*n.* **1.** a narrow band differing in color, material, or texture from the background. **2.** a strip of braid or fabric worn on a uniform to indicate length of service or rank. **3.** variety; sort. —*v.t.* **4.** to mark or furnish with stripes.

strip•ling (strip′ling), *n.* a youth.

strip/ mall/, *n.* a retail complex consisting of stores or restaurants in adjacent spaces in one long building.

strip/ mine/, *n.* a mine in an open pit formed by removing the earth and rock covering a mineral deposit. —**strip/-mine/,** *v.t.*, *v.i.*, **-mined, -min•ing.**

strip/-search/, *v.t.* to search (a suspect who has been required to remove all clothing).

strive (strīv), *v.i.*, **strove** or **strived, striv•en** (striv′ən) or **strived, striv•ing. 1.** to make a strenuous effort. **2.** to contend in opposition; struggle.

strobe (strōb), *n.* **1.** Also called **strobe/ light/.** an electronic flash that produces rapid, brilliant bursts of light. **2.** a stroboscope.

stro•bo•scope (strō′bə skōp′, strob′ə-), *n.* a device for studying the motion of a body by making it appear to slow down or stop, as by periodic illumination.

strode (strōd), *v.* pt. of STRIDE.

stroke¹ (strōk), *n.* **1.** an act or instance of striking. **2.** the sound of striking, as of a bell. **3.** a blockage or hemorrhage of a blood vessel leading to the brain, causing loss of consciousness and often long-term impairment. **4.** a sudden vigorous action or movement. **5.** a single complete movement, esp. one continuously repeated, as in swimming. **6.** a single mark made by a pen, pencil, or brush. **7.** a feat; achievement: *a stroke of genius.* **8.** a sudden or chance happening: *a stroke of luck.* —*Saying.* **9. different strokes for different folks,** people have different tastes.

stroke² (strōk), *v.*, **stroked, strok•ing,** *n.* —*v.t.* **1.** to pass the hand or an instrument over gently, as in caressing. —*n.* **2.** an act or instance of stroking.

stroll (strōl), *v.i.*, *v.t.* **1.** to walk leisurely (along or through); ramble. —*n.* **2.** a leisurely walk.

stroll/er, *n.* **1.** one who strolls. **2.** a chairlike carriage in which small children are pushed.

strong (strông, strong), *adj.*, **strong•er** (strông'gər, strông'-), **strong•est** (strông'gist, strong'-). **1.** physically powerful; vigorous or robust. **2.** mentally or morally powerful. **3.** powerful in influence, authority, or resources. **4.** of great force, effectiveness, or potency. **5.** able to resist strain, force, or wear. **6.** strenuous or energetic; vigorous: *strong efforts.* **7.** not weak; intense or concentrated: *strong tea.* **8.** of a designated number: *an army 20,000 strong.* —**strong'ly,** *adv.*

strong'-arm', *adj.* **1.** using or involving physical force. —*v.t.* **2.** to use physical force on.

strong'box', *n.* a strongly made box or chest for valuables or money.

strong'hold', *n.* a well-fortified place; fortress.

strong'-mind'ed, *adj.* having strong and vigorous mental powers.

stron•ti•um (stron'shē əm, -shəm, -tē əm), *n.* a metallic chemical element whose compounds are used in fireworks. *Symbol:* Sr; *at. wt.:* 87.62; *at. no.:* 38.

strop (strop), *n.*, *v.*, **stropped, strop•ping.** —*n.* **1.** a strip of flexible material, esp. leather, for sharpening razors. —*v.t.* **2.** to sharpen on or as if on a strop.

stro•phe (strō'fē), *n.*, *pl.* **-phes.** a separate section or extended movement of a poem. —**stroph•ic** (strof'ik, strō'fik), *adj.*

strove (strōv), *v.* a pt. of STRIVE.

struck (struk), *v.* **1.** pt. and a pp. of STRIKE. —*adj.* **2.** closed or affected by a strike of workers.

struc•ture (struk'chər), *n.*, *v.*, **-tured, -tur•ing.** —*n.* **1.** the manner in which something is constructed. **2.** the manner in which the elements of something are organized or interrelated. **3.** something constructed, as a bridge. **4.** something composed of organized or interrelated elements. —*v.t.* **5.** to give structure to. —**struc'tur•al,** *adj.*

stru•del (strōōd'l; *Ger.* shtʀōōd'l), *n.* a pastry consisting of fruit or cheese rolled in a paper-thin sheet of dough and baked. [< G: lit., whirlpool]

strug•gle (strug'əl), *v.*, **-gled, -gling,** *n.* —*v.i.* **1.** to contend vigorously, as with an adversary or problem. **2.** to advance with great effort. —*n.* **3.** an act or instance of struggling. **4.** a war, fight, conflict, or contest.

strum (strum), *v.t.*, *v.i.*, **strummed, strum•ming.** to play on (a stringed instrument) by running the fingers lightly across the strings.

strung (strung), *v.* pt. and pp. of STRING.

strut¹ (strut), *v.*, **strut•ted, strut•ting,** *n.* —*v.i.* **1.** to walk with a vain, pompous bearing. —*n.* **2.** a strutting walk or gait.

strut² (strut), *n.* any of various structural members for resisting longitudinal compression.

strych•nine (strik'nin, -nēn, -nīn), *n.* a colorless crystalline poison formerly used as a central nervous system stimulant.

Stu•art (stōō'ərt, styōō'-), *n.* a member of the royal family that ruled in Scotland from 1371 to 1714 and in England from 1603 to 1714.

stub (stub), *n.*, *v.*, **stubbed, stub•bing.** —*n.* **1.** a short remaining piece, as of a pencil or cigar. **2.** the short detachable part of a check or receipt kept as a record. **3.** the returned portion of a ticket. **4.** a tree stump. —*v.t.* **5.** to strike (one's toe or foot) accidentally against something. **6.** to put out (a cigarette or cigar) by crushing. —**stub'by,** *adj.*, **-bi•er, -bi•est.**

stub•ble (stub'əl), *n.* **1.** the stumps of grain and other stalks left in the ground when the crop is cut. **2.** a short, rough growth, as of beard. —**stub'bly,** *adj.*

stub•born (stub'ərn), *adj.* **1.** unreasonably or perversely obstinate; unyielding. **2.** fixed, as in purpose; resolute. **3.** difficult to handle, treat, or manage. —**stub'born•ly,** *adv.* —**stub'born•ness,** *n.*

stuc•co (stuk'ō), *n.*, *pl.* **-coes, -cos,** *v.*, **-coed, -co•ing.** —*n.* **1.** a plasterlike finish for exterior walls. —*v.t.* **2.** to cover with stucco.

stuck (stuk), *v.* pt. and pp. of STICK².

stuck'-up', *adj. Informal.* snobbishly conceited.

stud¹ (stud), *n.*, *v.*, **stud•ded, stud•ding.** —*n.* **1.**

something, as a knob or nailhead, projecting from a surface. **2.** a buttonlike device on a shank used as an ornament or fastener: *a collar stud.* **3.** one of the slender, upright posts forming the frame of a wall and covered with plasterwork, paneling, etc. —*v.t.* **4.** to set with or as if with studs. **5.** to be scattered over the surface of.

stud² (stud), *n.* a male animal, esp. a stallion, kept for breeding.

stud'book', *n.* a book giving the pedigree of pure-bred animals, esp. horses or dogs.

stud'ding, *n.* **1.** studs, as in a wall. **2.** material for use as studs.

stu•dent (stōōd'nt, styōōd'-), *n.* **1.** a person who studies, esp. at a school or college. **2.** a person who investigates, observes, or examines thoughtfully.

stud•ied (stud'ēd), *adj.* marked by conscious effort; intentional. —**stud'ied•ly,** *adv.*

stu•di•o (stōō'dē ō', styōō'-), *n.*, *pl.* **-di•os. 1.** the workroom of an artist, as a painter. **2.** a place for instruction in one of the performing arts. **3.** a place equipped for producing radio or television programs, films, or recordings.

stu'dio couch', *n.* a couch, usu. without a back or arms, convertible into a bed.

stu•di•ous (stōō'dē əs, styōō'-), *adj.* **1.** disposed or given to diligent study. **2.** giving or showing careful attention. —**stu'di•ous•ly,** *adv.*

stud•y (stud'ē), *n.*, *pl.* **-ies,** *v.*, **-ied, -y•ing.** —*n.* **1.** application of the mind to the acquisition of knowledge. **2.** Often, **-ies.** a student's work at school or college. **3.** a detailed investigation and analysis, as of a subject. **4.** a branch of learning or knowledge. **5.** a room set apart for study, reading, or writing. —*v.i.* **6.** to apply the mind to the acquisition of knowledge. **7.** to think deeply; reflect. —*v.t.* **8.** to apply the mind to acquiring knowledge of (a subject). **9.** to examine or investigate carefully and in detail.

stuff (stuf), *n.* **1.** the material of which something is made. **2.** material to be used in making something. **3.** matter, objects, or items of an unspecified kind. **4.** personal belongings or equipment. **5.** inward character, qualities, or capabilities. **6.** a specialty or special skill: *did his stuff.* **7.** worthless or foolish ideas, talk, or writing. **8.** *Chiefly Brit.* woven material or fabric, esp. wool. —*v.t.* **9.** to fill by packing the contents in. **10.** to thrust or cram into a receptacle or opening. **11.** to fill or cram with food. **12.** to fill with stuffing. **13.** to pack tightly; crowd. **14.** to stop up or plug.

stuffed' shirt', *n.* a pompous, self-satisfied, and inflexible person.

stuff'ing, *n.* **1.** material used to stuff something. **2.** a filling, as seasoned breadcrumbs, used to stuff poultry, vegetables, etc.

stuff'y, *adj.*, **-i•er, -i•est. 1.** poorly ventilated; close. **2.** blocked or stopped up: *a stuffy nose.* **3.** dull or tedious. **4.** self-important; pompous. —**stuff'i•ly,** *adv.* —**stuff'i•ness,** *n.*

stul•ti•fy (stul'tə fī'), *v.t.*, **-fied, -fy•ing. 1.** to cause to appear foolish or ridiculous. **2.** to make futile or ineffectual. —**stul'ti•fi•ca'tion,** *n.*

stum•ble (stum'bəl), *v.*, **-bled, -bling,** *n.* —*v.i.* **1.** to trip in walking or running. **2.** to walk or go unsteadily. **3.** to make a slip or blunder, esp. a sinful one. **4.** to discover or meet with by chance. —*n.* **5.** the act of stumbling. —**stum'bler,** *n.*

stum'bling block', *n.* an obstacle; hindrance.

stump (stump), *n.* **1.** the lower end of a tree trunk or plant left after the upper part falls or is cut off. **2.** the part of a bodily limb remaining after the rest has been cut off. **3.** a part of a broken or decayed tooth left in the gum. **4.** the figurative place of political speechmaking. —*v.t.* **5.** to baffle or perplex. **6.** to make political campaign speeches to or in. —*v.i.* **7.** to walk heavily or clumsily. **8.** to make political campaign speeches. —**stump'y,** *adj.*, **-i•er, -i•est.**

stun (stun), *v.t.*, **stunned, stun•ning. 1.** to deprive of consciousness, feeling, or strength by or as if by a blow. **2.** to shock or amaze.

stung (stung), *v.* a pt. and pp. of STING.

stunk (stungk), *v.* a pt. and pp. of STINK.

stun′ning, *adj.* of striking beauty or excellence. —**stun′ning•ly,** *adv.*

stunt[1] (stunt), *v.t.* to stop, slow down, or hinder the growth or development of.

stunt[2] (stunt), *n.* **1.** a feat displaying skill, dexterity, or daring. **2.** a feat performed chiefly to attract attention.

stu•pe•fy (stoo′pə fī′, styoo′-), *v.t.,* **-fied, -fy•ing. 1.** to put into a stupor. **2.** to astound; astonish. —**stu′pe•fac′tion** (-fak′shən), *n.*

stu•pen•dous (stoo pen′dəs, styoo-), *adj.* **1.** causing amazement; astounding. **2.** amazingly large or great.

stu•pid (stoo′pid, styoo′-), *adj.,* **-er, -est. 1.** lacking intelligence; dull. **2.** showing or proceeding from a lack of intelligence. **3.** tediously dull. —**stu•pid′i•ty,** *n., pl.* **-ties.** —**stu′pid•ly,** *adv.*

stu•por (stoo′pər, styoo′-), *n.* **1.** a state marked by suspension or great diminution of sensibility. **2.** mental torpor; apathy.

stur•dy (stûr′dē), *adj.,* **-di•er, -di•est. 1.** strongly built; robust. **2.** firm; determined. —**stur′di•ly,** *adv.* —**stur′di•ness,** *n.*

stur•geon (stûr′jən), *n., pl.* **-geons, -geon.** any of several large food fishes valued as a source of caviar.

stut•ter (stut′ər), *v.i., v.t.* **1.** to speak or say with repetitions, blocks or spasms, or prolongations of sounds. —*n.* **2.** an act or instance of stuttering. **3.** a speech defect marked by stuttering. —**stut′ter•er,** *n.*

Stutt•gart (stut′gärt, stoot′-), *n.* a city in SW Germany. 552,300.

Stuy•ve•sant (stī′və sənt), *n.* **Peter,** 1592–1672, last Dutch governor of New Netherland 1646–64.

St. Vin′cent and the Gren′adines (vin′sənt; gren′ə dēnz′), *n.* a country in the SE West Indies, comprising an island (**St. Vincent**) and the N Grenadines. 119,092.

sty[1] (stī), *n., pl.* **sties. 1.** a pen or enclosure for swine; pigpen. **2.** a filthy place or abode.

sty[2] or **stye** (stī), *n., pl.* **sties** or **styes.** a swelling of a gland on the edge of the eyelid.

Styg•i•an (stij′ē ən), *adj.* **1.** of the river Styx. **2.** (*often l.c.*) dark or gloomy.

style (stīl), *n., v.,* **styled, styl•ing.** —*n.* **1.** a particular or characteristic manner of acting, speaking, or writing. **2.** the prevailing fashion, as in dress. **3.** a fashionable or luxurious mode of living. **4.** a mode of design, construction, or execution, esp. as characteristic of a person, group, or period. **5.** elegance or flair. **6.** STYLUS (defs. 1, 2). **7.** the rules or customs of spelling, punctuation, and the like, observed by a publisher. —*v.t.* **8.** to designate; name. **9.** to design in accordance with a given or new style.

styl′ish, *adj.* conforming to the current style.

styl′ist, *n.* **1.** a designer or consultant on style, as in hairdressing, clothing, etc. **2.** a person who cultivates or maintains a distinctive style, esp. in writing. —**sty•lis′tic,** *adj.* —**sty•lis′ti•cal•ly,** *adv.*

styl′ize, *v.t.,* **-ized, -iz•ing.** to cause to conform to a conventionalized style.

sty•lus (stī′ləs), *n., pl.* **-li** (-lī), **-lus•es. 1.** a pointed instrument used by the ancients for writing on wax tablets. **2.** any of various pointed, pen-shaped instruments used esp. in artwork. **3.** a phonograph needle.

sty•mie or **-my** (stī′mē), *v.,* **-mied, -mie•ing** or **-my•ing,** *n., pl.* **-mies.** —*v.t.* **1.** to hinder, block, or thwart. —*n.* **2.** *Golf.* an instance of a ball's lying on a direct line between the cup and the ball of an opponent about to putt.

styp•tic (stip′tik), *adj.* serving to check bleeding. —**styp′sis** (-sis), *n.*

Sty•ro•foam (stī′rə fōm′), *Trademark.* a lightweight plastic made from polystyrene.

Styx (stiks), *n.* (in Greek myth) a river in the underworld over which the souls of the dead were ferried.

sua•sion (swā′zhən), *n.* persuasion.

suave (swäv), *adj.,* **suav•er, suav•est.** smoothly agreeable or polite. —**suave′ly,** *adv.* —**suav′i•ty,** *n.*

sub (sub), *n., v.,* **subbed, sub•bing.** —*n.* **1.** a submarine. **2.** a substitute. —*v.i.* **3.** to act as a substitute for another.

sub-, a prefix meaning: under, below, or beneath (*subway*); just outside of or near (*subtropical*); less than or not quite (*subteen*); secondary or subordinate (*subcommittee*).

sub., 1. subordinated. **2.** subscription. **3.** substitute. **4.** suburb. **5.** suburban. **6.** subway.

sub•a•tom•ic (sub′ə tom′ik), *adj.* **1.** of a process that occurs within an atom. **2.** noting particles, as electrons, contained in an atom.

sub•cat′e•go′ry, *n., pl.* **-ries.** a subdivision of a category.

sub′com•mit′tee, *n., pl.* **-tees.** a secondary committee appointed out of a main committee.

sub•com′pact, *n.* an automobile smaller than a compact.

sub•con′scious, *adj.* **1.** existing or operating in the mind beneath or beyond conscious awareness. —*n.* **2.** subconscious mental processes. —**sub•con′scious•ly,** *adv.*

sub•con•ti•nent (sub kon′tn ənt, sub′kon′-), *n.* a very large subdivision of a continent.

sub•con•tract (sub kon′trakt, sub′kon′-; *v. also* sub′kən trakt′), *n.* **1.** a contract by which a third party agrees to provide services or materials necessary to fulfill an original contract. —*v.t., v.i.* **2.** to make a subcontract (for). —**sub•con′trac•tor,** *n.*

sub•cul′ture, *n.* a group having social, economic, or other traits distinctive enough to distinguish it from others within the same culture or society.

sub•cu•ta•ne•ous, *adj.* situated or introduced under the skin.

sub•di•vide (sub′di vīd′, sub′di vīd′), *v.t., v.i.,* **-vid•ed, -vid•ing. 1.** to divide into smaller parts. **2.** to divide (land) into building lots. —**sub′di•vi′sion,** *n.*

sub•due (səb doo′, -dyoo′), *v.t.,* **-dued, -du•ing. 1.** to conquer and subjugate. **2.** to bring under control. **3.** to reduce the intensity, force, or vividness of.

sub•fam•i•ly (sub fam′ə lē, sub′fam′ə lē), *n., pl.* **-lies. 1.** *Biol.* a category of related genera within a family. **2.** a group of related languages within a family.

sub′group′, *n.* a subdivision of a group.

sub′head′ also **-head′ing,** *n.* **1.** a heading of a subdivision, as of a chapter. **2.** a subordinate division of a title or heading.

sub•hu′man, *adj.* less than or not quite human.

subj., 1. subject. **2.** subjective. **3.** subjunctive.

sub•ject (*n., adj.* sub′jikt; *v.* səb jekt′), *n.* **1.** a person or thing forming the basis of thought, discussion, or investigation. **2.** a course of study. **3.** something or someone represented, as in a work of art. **4.** a person owing allegiance to or under the domination of a sovereign or state. **5.** a word or phrase referring to the one performing the action or being in the state expressed by the predicate. **6.** one that undergoes a treatment or experiment. —*adj.* **7.** being under the domination or control of another. **8.** open or exposed: *subject to ridicule.* **9.** dependent upon something: *subject to your approval.* **10.** liable; prone: *subject to headaches.* —*v.t.* **11.** to bring under domination or control. **12.** to cause to undergo. **13.** to make liable or vulnerable. —**sub•jec′tion,** *n.*

sub•jec′tive, *adj.* **1.** of or belonging to the thinking subject rather than to the object of thought. **2.** of or characteristic of an individual; personal. —**sub′jec•tiv′i•ty,** *n.*

sub•join (səb join′), *v.t.* to add at the end; append.

sub•ju•gate (sub′jə gāt′), *v.t.,* **-gat•ed, -gat•ing. 1.** to bring under complete control; conquer. **2.** to make submissive; enslave. —**sub′ju•ga′tion,** *n.*

sub•junc•tive (səb jungk′tiv), *adj.* **1.** of or being a grammatical mood typically used for subjective, doubtful, hypothetical, or grammatically subordinate statements or questions. —*n.* **2.** the subjunctive mood. **3.** a verb form in the subjunctive mood.

sub•lease (*n.* sub′lēs′; *v.* sub lēs′), *n., v.,* **-leased, -leas•ing.** —*n.* **1.** a lease granted to another by the lessee of a property. —*v.t., v.i.* **2.** to grant, take, or hold a sublease (of).

sub·let (sub let′, sub′let′), v.t., v.i., **-let, -let·ting. 1.** to sublease. **2.** to subcontract.

sub·li·mate (sub′lə māt′), v.t., **-mat·ed, -mat·ing. 1.** to divert the energy of (a sexual or other biological impulse) into more socially acceptable activities. **2.** to sublime. —**sub′li·ma′tion,** n.

sub·lime (sə blīm′), adj., v., **-limed, -lim·ing.** —adj. **1.** elevated, as in thought; lofty. **2.** inspiring awe or veneration. —v.t. **3.** to convert (a solid substance) by heat into a vapor that on cooling condenses again to solid form. —**Proverb. 4. From the sublime to the ridiculous is but a step,** only a small detail may separate the great and the laughable. —**sub·lim′i·ty** (-blim′i tē), n.

sub·lim·i·nal (sub lim′ə nl), adj. existing or operating below the threshold of consciousness.

sub′ma·chine′ gun′, n. an automatic firearm fired from the shoulder or hip.

sub·mar′gin·al, adj. below a required minimum.

sub·ma·rine (sub′mə rēn′, sub′mə rēn′), n. **1.** a naval boat that can be submerged and navigated under water. **2.** a hero sandwich. —adj. **3.** situated, operating, or living under the surface of the sea.

sub·merge (səb mûrj′), v.t., v.i., **-merged, -merg·ing. 1.** to put or sink below the surface of water. **2.** to cover or be covered with or as if with water. —**sub·mer′gence,** n.

sub·merse (səb mûrs′), v.t., **-mersed, -mers·ing.** to submerge. —**sub·mers′i·ble,** adj. —**sub·mer′sion** (-mûr′zhən, -shən), n.

sub·mi·cro·scop·ic (sub′mī krə skop′ik), adj. too small to be seen through a microscope.

sub·mit (səb mit′), v., **-mit·ted, -mit·ting.** —v.t. **1.** to give over or yield to the power or authority of another. **2.** to present for approval or consideration. **3.** to state as an opinion. —v.i. **4.** to yield oneself to the power or authority of another. —**sub·mis′sion,** n. —**sub·mis′sive,** adj.

sub·nor·mal (sub nôr′məl), adj. being below normal, as in intelligence.

sub′note′book, n. a laptop computer smaller and lighter than a notebook, typically weighing less than 5 pounds (2.3 kg).

sub·or′bit·al, adj. making less than a complete orbit, as of the earth.

sub·or·di·nate (adj., n. sə bôr′dn it; v. -dn āt′), adj., n., v., **-nat·ed, -nat·ing.** —adj. **1.** belonging to a lower order or rank. **2.** subject to or under the authority of a superior. **3.** of or noting a clause that is syntactically dependent on another clause. —n. **4.** a subordinate person or thing. —v.t. **5.** to place in a lower order or rank. **6.** to make subservient or dependent. —**sub·or′di·na′tion,** n.

sub·orn (sə bôrn′), v.t. to induce (a witness) to give false testimony. —**sub·or·na·tion** (sub′ôr nā′shən), n.

sub·plot (sub′plot′), n. a secondary plot, as in a novel.

sub·poe·na or **-pe·na** (sə pē′nə, səb-), n., pl. **-nas,** v., **-naed, -na·ing.** —n. **1.** a writ to summon witnesses or evidence before a court. —v.t. **2.** to serve with a subpoena.

sub ro·sa (sub rō′zə), adv. secretly; privately. [< L: lit., under the rose]

sub·scribe (səb skrīb′), v.t., v.i., **-scribed, -scrib·ing. 1.** to pay or pledge (money) as a contribution or investment. **2.** to sign one's name to (a document), as in approval. **3.** to obtain a subscription, as to a publication. **4.** to give one's consent (to). —**sub·scrib′er,** n.

sub·script (sub′skript), n. a letter, number, or symbol written or printed low on a line of text.

sub·scrip·tion (səb skrip′shən), n. **1.** a sum of money subscribed. **2.** the right to receive a publication or service or to attend a series of performances for a sum paid.

sub·sec·tion (sub′sek′shən), n. a part of a section.

sub·se·quent (sub′si kwənt), adj. following, as in order; succeeding. —**sub′se·quent·ly,** adv.

sub·ser·vi·ent (səb sûr′vē ənt), adj. **1.** subordinate. **2.** servile; obsequious. —**sub·ser′vi·ence,** n.

sub·set (sub′set′), n. Math. a set consisting of elements of a given set that can be the same as the given set or smaller.

sub·side (səb sīd′), v.i., **-sid·ed, -sid·ing. 1.** to sink to a lower level. **2.** to become quiet, less active, or less violent. **3.** to sink to the bottom; settle. —**sub·sid′ence** (səb sīd′ns, sub′si dns), n.

sub·sid·i·ar·y (səb sid′ē er′ē), adj., n., pl. **-ar·ies.** —adj. **1.** serving to assist or supplement. **2.** subordinate or secondary. —n. **3.** a subsidiary thing or person. **4.** a company owned and controlled by another company.

sub·si·dize (sub′si dīz′), v.t., **-dized, -diz·ing.** to furnish or aid with a subsidy. —**sub′si·di·za′tion,** n.

sub′si·dy, n., pl. **-dies.** direct financial aid furnished by a government, as to a private enterprise or another government.

sub·sist (səb sist′), v.i. **1.** to continue in existence. **2.** to remain alive, as on food.

sub·sist′ence, n. **1.** the state or fact of subsisting. **2.** means of supporting life.

sub·soil (sub′soil′), n. the stratum of earth immediately under the surface soil.

sub·son·ic, adj. **1.** of or being a speed less than that of sound. **2.** INFRASONIC.

sub·stance (sub′stəns), n. **1.** physical matter or material. **2.** matter of definite chemical composition: a metallic substance. **3.** substantial or solid quality. **4.** consistency; body. **5.** the essential part, as of speech; gist. **6.** means or wealth.

sub·stand′ard, adj. below a standard.

sub·stan·tial (səb stan′shəl), adj. **1.** considerable, as in amount; ample. **2.** corporeal or material in nature; real. **3.** firm, stout, or strong. **4.** being such essentially: stories in substantial agreement. **5.** wealthy or influential. **6.** of real worth, value, or effect. —**sub·stan′tial·ly,** adv.

sub·stan′ti·ate (-shē āt′), v.t., **-at·ed, -at·ing.** to establish by proof or competent evidence. —**sub·stan′ti·a′tion,** n.

sub·stan·tive (sub′stən tiv), adj. **1.** essential. **2.** real or actual. **3.** having practical importance, value, or effect. —n. **4.** a noun. **5.** a word or phrase functioning as a noun.

sub′sta′tion, n. a subordinate station, as a branch of a post office.

sub·sti·tute (sub′sti tōōt′, -tyōōt′), n., v., **-tut·ed, -tut·ing.** —n. **1.** a person or thing acting or serving in place of another. —v.t. **2.** to put in the place of another. —v.i. **3.** to act as a substitute. —**sub′sti·tu′tion,** n.

sub·stra·tum (sub′strā′təm, -strat′əm), n., pl. **-stra·ta** (-strā′tə, -strat′ə), **-stra·tums.** a stratum or layer lying under another.

sub·struc·ture (sub struk′chər, sub′struk′-), n. a structure forming a foundation, as of a building.

sub·sume (səb sōōm′), v.t., **-sumed, -sum·ing.** to consider or include as part of something more comprehensive.

sub·teen (sub′tēn′), n. a young person approaching the teens.

sub·ter·fuge (sub′tər fyōōj′), n. an artifice or expedient used to evade, escape, or conceal.

sub′ter·ra′ne·an (-tə rā′nē ən), adj. **1.** existing, situated, or operating below the earth's surface. **2.** hidden or secret.

sub′ti·tle, n., v., **-tled, -tling.** —n. **1.** a secondary, often explanatory title, as of a literary work. **2.** (in motion pictures and television) a translation of dialogue projected onto the bottom of the screen. —v.t. **3.** to give a subtitle to.

sub·tle (sut′l), adj., **-tler, -tlest. 1.** difficult to perceive; fine or delicate. **2.** characterized by or requiring mental acuteness. **3.** cunning or crafty. **4.** skillful or clever. —**sub′tle·ty,** n., pl. **-ties.** —**sub′tly,** adv.

sub·to·tal (sub′tōt′l, sub tōt′-), n., v., **-taled, -tal·ing** or (esp. Brit.) **-talled, -tal·ling.** —n. **1.** the total of a part of a group or series of figures. —v.t., v.i. **2.** to determine a subtotal (for).

sub•tract (səb trakt′), v.t., v.i. to take (one number or quantity) away from another. —**sub•trac′tion,** n.

sub•tra•hend (sub′trə hend′), n. a number that is subtracted from another.

sub•trop′i•cal, adj. bordering on the tropics.

sub•urb (sub′ûrb), n. **1.** a usu. residential community outside a city or town. **2. the suburbs,** the area composed of such communities. —**sub•ur•ban** (sə-bûr′bən), adj.

sub•ur•ban•ite (sə bûr′bə nīt′), n. a person who lives in a suburb.

sub•ur′bi•a (-bē ə), n. **1.** suburbs or suburbanites collectively. **2.** life in the suburbs.

sub•ven•tion (səb ven′shən), n. a grant of money; subsidy.

sub•ver•sive (səb vûr′siv), adj. **1.** tending or attempting to subvert. —n. **2.** a subversive person. —**sub•ver′sive•ly,** adv.

sub•vert′ (-vûrt′), v.t. **1.** to overthrow (something established). **2.** to undermine the principles of; corrupt. —**sub•ver′sion** (-vûr′zhən, -shən), n.

sub•way (sub′wā′), n. an underground electric railroad, usu. in a large city.

sub•ze′ro, adj. indicating or recording lower than zero on some scale.

suc•ceed (sək sēd′), v.i. **1.** to turn out successfully. **2.** to accomplish what is attempted or intended. **3.** to take over an office, rank, etc. **4.** to come next in order. —v.t. **5.** to come after; follow.

suc•cess′ (-ses′), n. **1.** a favorable outcome, as of endeavors. **2.** the attainment of wealth, position, etc. **3.** someone or something that is successful.

suc•cess′ful, adj. **1.** achieving or having achieved success. **2.** resulting in or attended with success. —**suc•cess′ful•ly,** adv.

suc•ces′sion (-sesh′ən), n. **1.** the coming of one person or thing after another. **2.** a number of persons or things following one another. **3. a.** the act or right by which one person succeeds to the position or rank of another. **b.** the order or line of those entitled to succeed one another.

suc•ces′sive, adj. following in uninterrupted sequence; consecutive. —**suc•ces′sive•ly,** adv.

suc•ces′sor, n. a person who succeeds another, as in an office.

suc•cinct (sək singkt′), adj. characterized by brevity; concise. —**suc•cinct′ly,** adv. —**suc•cinct′ness,** n.

suc•cor (suk′ər), n. **1.** help; aid. —v.t. **2.** to help; aid.

suc•co•tash (suk′ə tash′), n. a cooked dish of lima beans and corn kernels. [< Algonquian]

suc•cu•lent (suk′yə lənt), adj. **1.** full of juice; juicy. **2.** (of a plant) having fleshy and juicy tissues. —n. **3.** a succulent plant, as a cactus. —**suc′cu•lence, suc′cu•len•cy,** n.

suc•cumb (sə kum′), v.i. **1.** to give way; yield. **2.** to die.

such (such), adj. **1.** of the kind indicated or implied. **2.** like or similar: tea, coffee, and such commodities. **3.** of so extreme a kind: never met such a liar. —adv. **4.** to such a degree; so. —pron. **5.** such a person or thing or such persons or things. **6.** someone or something indicated. —**Idiom. 7. such as,** for example.

such′ and such′, adj. **1.** not named or specified. —pron. **2.** something or someone not specified.

such′like′, adj. of such kind; similar.

suck (suk), v.t. **1.** to draw into the mouth by action of the lips and tongue. **2.** to draw (water, air, etc.) by or as if by suction. **3.** to draw liquid from by sucking. **4.** to put into the mouth and draw upon. —v.i. **5.** to draw something in by sucking. —n. **6.** an act or instance of sucking.

suck′er, n. **1.** one that sucks. **2.** Informal. a person easily cheated or deceived. **3.** a part or organ adapted for sucking or for clinging by suction. **4.** a thick-lipped freshwater food fish, mainly of North America. **5.** a lollipop. **6.** a shoot rising from an underground stem or root.

suck•le (suk′əl), v.t., v.i., **-led, -ling. 1.** to nurse or suck at the breast or udder. **2.** to bring up; rear.

suck′ling, n. an unweaned infant or young animal.

Su•cre (sōō′krā), n. the official capital of Bolivia. 86,609.

su•crose (sōō′krōs), n. SUGAR (def. 1).

suc•tion (suk′shən), n. **1.** the act or process of sucking. **2.** the force that owing to a pressure differential attracts a fluid or solid to where the pressure is lowest.

Su•dan (sōō dan′), n. **Republic of the.** a republic in NE Africa. 32,594,128. —**Su•da•nese** (sōōd′n ēz′, -ēs′), n., pl. **-nese,** adj.

sud•den (sud′n), adj. **1.** happening, coming, or done quickly or unexpectedly. **2.** occurring without transition; abrupt. **3.** impetuous; rash. —**Idiom. 4. all of a sudden,** without warning; unexpectedly. —**sud′den•ly,** adv. —**sud′den•ness,** n.

sud′den death′, n. an overtime period in which a tied contest is won after one of the contestants scores.

sud′den in′fant death′ syn′drome, n. death from cessation of breathing in a seemingly healthy infant.

suds (sudz), n. (used with a sing. or pl. v.) **1.** soapy water. **2.** foam; lather. —**suds′y,** adj., **-i•er, -i•est.**

sue (sōō), v.t., v.i., **sued, su•ing. 1.** to bring a civil action (against). **2.** to make petition or appeal (to).

suede or **suède** (swād), n. **1.** leather finished with a soft, napped surface. **2.** a fabric resembling suede.

su•et (sōō′it), n. the hard fatty tissue about the loins and kidneys of cattle and sheep that is the source of tallow.

Su′ez Canal′ (sōō′ez, sōō ez′), n. a canal in NE Egypt connecting the Mediterranean and the Red Sea.

suf-, var. of SUB- before f.

suf•fer (suf′ər), v.i., v.t. **1.** to undergo or feel (pain or distress). **2.** to sustain (injury or loss). **3.** to undergo or experience (an action, process, or condition). **4.** to tolerate or allow. —**suf′fer•er,** n.

suf•fer•ance (suf′ər əns), n. **1.** passive permission resulting from lack of interference; tolerance. **2.** capacity to endure pain or hardship.

suf′fer•ing, n. the state of one that suffers.

suf•fice (sə fīs′), v.i., v.t., **-ficed, -fic•ing.** to be enough or adequate (for).

suf•fi′cient (-fish′ənt), adj. adequate for the purpose; enough. —**suf•fi′cien•cy,** n. —**suf•fi′cient•ly,** adv.

suf•fix (n. suf′iks; v. suf′iks, sə fiks′), n. **1.** an affix that follows the element to which it is added. —v.t. **2.** to add as a suffix. —**suf′fix•a′tion,** n.

suf•fo•cate (suf′ə kāt′), v., **-cat•ed, -cat•ing.** —v.t. **1.** to kill by depriving of oxygen. **2.** to impede the respiration of. **3.** to smother or stifle; suppress. —v.i. **4.** to become suffocated. **5.** to be uncomfortable due to a lack of air. —**suf′fo•ca′tion,** n.

suf•fra•gan (suf′rə gən), n. an assistant or auxiliary bishop.

suf•frage (suf′rij), n. **1.** the right to vote. **2.** a vote.

suf′fra•gette′ (-rə jet′), n. a woman who advocates female suffrage. —**Usage.** See -ETTE.

suf•fra•gist (suf′rə jist), n. an advocate of the grant of political suffrage, esp. to women.

suf•fuse (sə fyōōz′), v.t., **-fused, -fus•ing.** to overspread with or as if with liquid or color; pervade. —**suf•fu′sion** (-zhən), n.

Su•fi (sōō′fē), n., pl. **-fis,** adj. —n. **1.** a member of an ascetic, mystical Muslim sect. —adj. **2.** of or pertaining to Sufis or Sufism. —**Su′fism** (-fiz əm), **Su′fi•ism,** n.

sug•ar (shŏŏg′ər), n. **1.** a sweet crystalline substance obtained esp. from sugarcane and the sugar beet. **2.** a substance of the same class of carbohydrates, as fructose. —v.t. **3.** to sprinkle or mix with sugar. **4.** to make agreeable. —v.i. **5.** to form sugar or sugar crystals. —**sug′ar•less,** adj. —**sug′ar•y,** adj.

Sug′ar Act′, n. a law passed by the British Parliament in 1764 raising duties on foreign refined sugar imported by the colonies.

sug′ar beet′, *n.* a beet with a white root, cultivated for the sugar it yields.

sug′ar•cane′, *n.* a tall grass of warm regions that is the chief source of sugar.

sug′ar•coat′, *v.t.* **1.** to cover with sugar. **2.** to make more pleasant or acceptable.

sug′ar ma′ple, *n.* a maple with a sweet sap that is the chief source of maple syrup and maple sugar.

sug′ar•plum′, *n.* a sweetmeat or bonbon.

sug•gest (səg jest′, sə-), *v.t.* **1.** to mention, introduce, or propose for consideration or possible action. **2.** to indicate indirectly; imply. **3.** to call to mind through association or natural connection of ideas.

sug•gest′i•ble, *adj.* easily influenced by suggestion. —**sug•gest′i•bil′i•ty,** *n.*

sug•ges′tion, *n.* **1.** the act of suggesting. **2.** something suggested. **3.** a slight trace.

sug•ges′tive, *adj.* **1.** tending to suggest. **2.** hinting at something improper or indecent. —**sug•ges′tive•ly,** *adv.* —**sug•ges′tive•ness,** *n.*

su•i•cide (sōō′ə sīd′), *n.* **1.** the intentional taking of one's own life. **2.** a person who intentionally takes his or her own life. —**su′i•cid′al,** *adj.*

su•i ge•ne•ris (sōō′ē jen′ər is, sōō′ī), *adj.* being one of a kind; unique. [< L]

suit (sōōt), *n.* **1.** a set of clothing consisting typically of trousers or a skirt and a matching jacket. **2.** an act or instance of suing in a court of law; lawsuit. **3.** one of the four classes into which playing cards are divided. **4.** the courting of a woman. **5.** a petition, as to a person of rank. —*v.t.* **6.** to be appropriate or becoming to. **7.** to satisfy or please. —*v.i.* **8.** to be appropriate or suitable. —*Idiom.* **9. follow suit,** to follow the example of another.

suit′a•ble, *adj.* appropriate; fitting. —**suit′a•bil′i•ty,** *n.* —**suit′a•bly,** *adv.*

suit′case′, *n.* a usu. rectangular piece of luggage.

suite (swēt; *for 2 often* sōōt), *n.* **1.** a connected series of rooms to be used together. **2.** a set of matching furniture. **3.** a company of attendants; retinue. **4.** a series of instrumental dances in the same or related keys. **5.** a group of computer software programs sold as a unit and designed to work together.

suit•ing (sōō′ting), *n.* fabric for making suits.

suit•or (sōō′tər), *n.* a man who courts a woman.

su•ki•ya•ki (sōō′kē yä′kē, sōōk′ē-, skē yä′kē), *n.* slices of meat and vegetables cooked together in soy sauce.

Suk•koth or **-kot** (sōōk′əs, sōō kôt′, -kōs′), *n.* a Jewish harvest festival commemorating the wandering of the Israelites in the wilderness.

sul′fa drug′ (sul′fə), *n.* any of a group of drugs closely related to sulfanilamide, used in treating various bacterial infections.

sul•fa•nil•a•mide (sul′fə nil′ə mīd′, -mid), *n.* a crystalline sulfur-containing compound formerly used to treat bacterial infections.

sul′fate′ (-fāt), *n.* a salt or ester of sulfuric acid.

sul′fide (-fīd, -fid), *n.* a compound of sulfur with a more electropositive element.

sul′fur (-fər), *n.* a yellow nonmetallic element used in making gunpowder and matches, in medicine, and in vulcanizing rubber. *Symbol:* S; *at. wt.:* 32.064; *at. no.:* 16.

sul•fu′ric (-fyŏŏr′ik), *adj.* of or containing sulfur.

sulfu′ric ac′id, *n.* an oily, corrosive liquid used chiefly in the manufacture of fertilizers, chemicals, explosives, and dyestuffs.

sul•fur•ous (sul′fər əs, sul fyŏŏr′əs), *adj.* of or containing sulfur.

sulk (sulk), *v.i.* **1.** to remain silent or aloof in an ill-humored manner. —*n.* **2.** a state or fit of sulking.

sulk′y, *adj.,* **-i•er, -i•est,** *n., pl.* **-ies.** —*adj.* **1.** marked by or given to sulking; moody. —*n.* **2.** a light, two-wheeled, one-horse carriage for one person. —**sulk′i•ly,** *adv.* —**sulk′i•ness,** *n.*

sul•len (sul′ən), *adj.* **1.** persistently and silently ill-humored or resentful. **2.** gloomy or dismal, as weather. —**sul′len•ly,** *adv.* —**sul′len•ness,** *n.*

Sul•li•van (sul′ə vən), *n.* **1. Annie** (*Anne Mansfield*

Sullivan Macy), 1866–1936, U.S. teacher of Helen Keller. **2. Sir Arthur (Seymour),** 1842–1900, English composer.

sul•ly (sul′ē), *v.t.* **-lied, -ly•ing.** to soil, stain, or tarnish.

sul•phur (sul′fər), *n. Chiefly Brit.* SULFUR.

sul•tan (sul′tn), *n.* a sovereign of an Islamic country. —**sul′tan•ate′** (-āt′), *n.*

sul•tan′a (-tan′ə, -tä′nə), *n., pl.* **-tan•as. 1.** a small seedless raisin. **2.** a wife, concubine, or female relative of a sultan.

sul•try (sul′trē), *adj.,* **-tri•er, -tri•est. 1.** oppressively hot and humid; sweltering. **2.** characterized by or arousing passion.

sum (sum), *n., v.,* **summed, sum•ming.** —*n.* **1.** the result obtained by the mathematical process of addition. **2.** an amount, esp. of money. **3.** an arithmetic problem. **4.** the full amount; total. **5.** a summary. —*v.t.* **6.** to get the sum of, as by addition. **7. sum up,** to summarize.

su•mac or **-mach** (sōō′mak, shōō′-), *n.* a shrub or small tree with compound leaves and clusters of red, fleshy fruit.

Su•ma•tra (sōō mä′trə), *n.* a large island in the W part of Indonesia. —**Su•ma′tran,** *adj., n.*

sum•ma•rize (sum′ə rīz′), *v.t.,* **-rized, -riz•ing.** to make or be a summary of.

sum′ma•ry, *n., pl.* **-ries,** *adj.* —*n.* **1.** a usu. brief restatement of the main points or facts. —*adj.* **2.** brief and comprehensive; concise. **3.** prompt and unceremonious. —**sum•mar•i•ly** (sə mâr′ə lē), *adv.*

sum•ma•tion (sə mā′shən), *n.* **1.** the act, process, or result of summing up. **2.** the final arguments of opposing attorneys before a case goes to the jury.

sum•mer (sum′ər), *n.* **1.** the warm season between spring and autumn. —*v.i.* **2.** to spend or pass the summer. —**sum′mer•y,** *adj.*

sum′mer•house′, *n.* an often rustic structure in a garden to provide shade.

sum′mer sau′sage, *n.* dried or smoked sausage that keeps without refrigeration.

sum′mer•time′, *n.* summer

sum•mit (sum′it), *n.* **1.** the highest point or part, as of a hill. **2.** the highest state or degree.

sum′mit•ry, *n.* the conducting of diplomatic negotiations at the highest level of government.

sum•mon (sum′ən), *v.t.* **1.** to call for the presence of, as by command. **2.** to notify to appear before a court. **3.** to call together; convene. **4.** to call into action; rouse: *summoned up her courage.* —**sum′mon•er,** *n.*

sum′mons, *n., pl.* **-mons•es. 1.** an order to appear before a court or a judicial officer. **2.** an authoritative call to appear at a place for a particular purpose or duty.

su•mo (sōō′mō), *n.* a form of wrestling in Japan in which the contestants are extremely heavy.

sump (sump), *n.* a pit, basin, cesspool, or reservoir in which liquid is collected or into which it drains.

sump•tu•ous (sump′chōō əs), *adj.* **1.** entailing great expense, as from choice materials; costly. **2.** luxurious; lavish.

sun (sun), *n., v.,* **sunned, sun•ning.** —*n.* **1.** (*often cap.*) the star that is the central body of the solar system, around which the planets revolve and from which they receive light and heat. **2.** sunshine. **3.** a self-luminous heavenly body; star. —*v.t., v.i.* **4.** to expose or be exposed to the sun's rays.

Sun., Sunday.

sun′bath′, *n.* exposure of the body to sunlight or a sunlamp. —**sun′bathe′** (-bāth′), *v.i.,* **-bathed, -bath•ing.** —**sun′bath′er** (-bā′thər), *n.*

sun′beam′, *n.* a beam or ray of sunlight.

Sun′belt′ or **Sun′ Belt′,** *n.* the southern and southwestern regions of the U.S.

sun′block′ or **sun′ block′,** *n.* a lotion, cream, etc., containing a substance that provides a high degree of protection against sunburn, often preventing most tanning.

sun′bon′net, *n.* a bonnet with a large brim to protect the face and neck from the sun.

sun′burn′, *n., v.,* **-burned** or **-burnt, -burn•ing.** —*n.* **1.** inflammation of the skin caused by overexposure to sunlight or a sunlamp. —*v.i., v.t.* **2.** to suffer or cause to suffer from sunburn.

sun′burst′, *n.* **1.** a sudden burst of sunlight. **2.** something, as a brooch, that suggests the sun and its radiating beams.

sun•dae (sun′dā, -dē), *n.* a dish of ice cream topped with syrup, nuts, whipped cream, etc.

Sun•day (sun′dā, -dē), *n.* the first day of the week, observed as the Sabbath by most Christians.

sun•der (sun′dər), *v.t., v.i.* to separate; part.

sun′di′al, *n.* an instrument that indicates time by the shadow of a pointer cast by the sun on a dial.

sun′down′, *n.* sunset, esp. the time of sunset.

sun•dries (sun′drēz), *n.pl.* small, miscellaneous items.

sun•dry (sun′drē), *adj.* various or diverse.

sun′fish′, *n., pl.* **-fish, -fish•es.** a North American freshwater fish with a deep, compressed body.

sun′flow′er, *n.* a tall plant with showy, yellow-rayed flower heads and edible seeds that yield an oil.

sung (sung), *v.* a pt. and pp. of SING.

sun′glass′es, *n.pl.* eyeglasses with tinted lenses that protect the eyes from the sun.

sunk (sungk), *v.* a pt. and pp. of SINK.

sunk′en, *adj.* **1.** submerged. **2.** situated on a lower level: *a sunken living room.* **3.** hollow; depressed: *sunken cheeks.*

sun′lamp′, *n.* a lamp that generates ultraviolet rays, used therapeutically or for suntanning.

sun′light′, *n.* the light of the sun.

sun′lit′, *adj.* lighted by the sun.

Sun•na or **Sun•nah** (sŏŏn′ə), *n.* the traditional portion of Muslim law, based on words and acts of Muhammad not recorded in the Koran. [< Ar *sunnah* lit., way, path, rule]

Sun•ni (sŏŏn′ē), *n., pl.* **-ni, -nis.** a member of one of the divisions of Islam, regarding the first four caliphs as legitimate successors of Muhammad. Compare SHI′ITE. —**Sun′nism,** *n.*

sun′ny, *adj.,* **-ni•er, -ni•est. 1.** abounding in sunshine. **2.** cheery, cheerful, or joyous. **3.** of or resembling the sun.

Sun•ny•vale (sun′ē vāl′), *n.* a city in central California. 119,584.

sun′rise′, *n.* **1.** the rise of the sun above the horizon in the morning. **2.** the time of sunrise.

sun′roof′, *n.* a section of an automobile roof that can be slid or lifted open.

sun′screen′, *n.* a substance that protects the skin from excessive exposure to the sun's ultraviolet radiation.

sun′set′, *n.* **1.** the setting of the sun below the horizon in the evening. **2.** the time of sunset.

sun′shine′, *n.* **1.** the direct light of the sun. **2.** cheerfulness or happiness. **3.** a source of cheer or happiness. —**sun′shin′y,** *adj.*

sun′spot′, *n.* one of the dark patches that appear periodically on the surface of the sun.

sun′stroke′, *n.* a sudden and sometimes fatal condition caused by overexposure to the sun's rays.

sun′tan′, *n.* a darkening of the skin caused by exposure to sunlight or a sunlamp.

sun′up′, *n.* sunrise.

Sun Yat-sen (sŏŏn′ yät′sen′), *n.* 1866–1925, Chinese political and revolutionary leader.

sup (sup), *v.i.,* **supped, sup•ping.** to eat supper.

sup-, var. of SUB- before *p.*

su•per (sŏŏ′pər), *n.* **1.** a superintendent, esp. of an apartment house. **2.** a supernumerary. —*adj.* **3.** extreme or excessive. **4.** very good; first-rate.

super-, a prefix meaning: above or over (*superimpose*); exceeding a customary norm (*superconductivity*); larger or more powerful than others of its kind (*superpower*); great or excessive in degree (*superfine*).

su′per•a•bun′dant, *adj.* exceedingly abundant. —**su′per•a•bun′dance,** *n.*

su′per•an′nu•at′ed (-an′yŏŏ ā′tid), *adj.* **1.** retired because of age or infirmity. **2.** too old for use, work, or service.

su•perb (sŏŏ pûrb′, sə-), *adj.* **1.** admirably fine; excellent. **2.** sumptuous; rich. **3.** proudly imposing; majestic. —**su•perb′ly,** *adv.*

su′per•car′go (sŏŏ′pər kär′gō, sŏŏ′pər kär′-), *n., pl.* **-goes, -gos.** a merchant-ship officer in charge of the cargo.

su′per•charge′, *v.t.,* **-charged, -charg•ing.** to supply air to (an internal-combustion engine) at greater than atmospheric pressure.

su•per•cil•i•ous (sŏŏ′pər sil′ē əs), *adj.* haughtily disdainful.

su′per•con′duc•tiv′i•ty, *n.* the disappearance of electrical resistance in certain metals at temperatures near absolute zero. —**su′per•con•duc′tor,** *n.*

su′per•e′go, *n., pl.* **-gos.** *Psychoanalysis.* the part of the personality representing the conscience.

su′per•e•rog′a•to′ry (-ə rog′ə tôr′ē), *adj.* greater than required or needed; superfluous. —**su′per•er′o•ga′tion** (-er′ə gā′shən), *n.*

su′per•fi′cial (-fish′əl), *adj.* **1.** being at, on, or near the surface. **2.** apparent rather than real. **3.** not profound or thorough; shallow. —**su′per•fi′ci•al′i•ty** (-fish′ē al′i tē), *n., pl.* **-ties.** —**su′per•fi′cial•ly,** *adv.*

su′per•fine′, *adj.* extra fine, as in grain or texture.

su•per•flu•ous (sŏŏ pûr′flōō əs), *adj.* being more than is sufficient or required. —**su•per•flu•i•ty** (sŏŏ′pər flōō′i tē), *n.*

su′per•he′ro, *n., pl.* **-roes.** a hero, esp. in comic books and television cartoons, possessing extraordinary, often magical powers.

su•per•high•way (sŏŏ′pər hī′wā, sŏŏ′pər hī′wā′), *n.* a highway designed for travel at high speeds.

su′per•hu′man, *adj.* **1.** above or beyond what is human. **2.** exceeding ordinary human power, achievement, or experience.

su′per•im•pose′, *v.t.,* **-posed, -pos•ing.** to impose or place over, above, or on something else.

su′per•in•tend (sŏŏ′pər in tend′, sŏŏ′prin-), *v.t.* to exercise supervision over (an institution, district, etc.). —**su′per•in•ten′dence, su′per•in•ten′den•cy,** *n.*

su′per•in•tend′ent, *n.* **1.** a person who oversees or directs; supervisor. **2.** a person in charge of the maintenance of an apartment house.

su•pe•ri•or (sə pēr′ē ər, sŏŏ-), *adj.* **1.** higher in station, rank, or degree. **2.** above the average in excellence, merit, or intelligence. **3.** of higher grade or quality. **4.** greater in number or amount. **5.** showing a feeling of being better than others. **6.** not yielding or susceptible. —*n.* **7.** one superior to another. **8.** the head of a monastery or convent. —**su•pe′ri•or′i•ty** (-ôr′i tē, -or′-), *n.*

Su•pe′ri•or, *n.* **Lake,** a lake in the N central U.S. and S Canada: largest of the Great Lakes.

su•per•la•tive (sə pûr′lə tiv, sŏŏ-), *adj.* **1.** of the highest kind or order. **2.** of or being the highest degree of comparison of adjectives and adverbs. —*n.* **3.** the utmost degree. **4. a.** the superlative degree. **b.** the superlative form of an adjective or adverb. —**su•per′la•tive•ly,** *adv.*

su′per•man′, *n., pl.* **-men.** a person of extraordinary or superhuman powers.

su′per•mar′ket, *n.* a large self-service retail store that sells food and household goods.

su•per•nal (sŏŏ pûr′nl), *adj.* celestial or divine.

su′per•nat′u•ral (sŏŏ′pər-), *adj.* **1.** being above or beyond what is natural or explainable by natural law. **2.** of or attributed to God or a deity. **3.** of or attributed to ghosts, goblins, or other unearthly beings.

su′per•no′va, *n., pl.* **-vas, -vae** (-vē). a nova millions of times brighter than the sun.

su′per•nu′mer•ar′y (-nŏŏ′mə rer′ē, -nyŏŏ′-), *adj., n., pl.* **-ar•ies.** —*adj.* **1.** being in excess of the usual or prescribed number; extra. —*n.* **2.** a supernumerary person or thing. **3.** a performer, as in a play or opera, without speaking lines.

su′per•pose′, *v.t.*, **-posed, -pos•ing.** to place above or upon something else. —**su′per•po•si′tion,** *n.*

su′per•pow′er, *n.* a very powerful nation, esp. one with significant interests and influence outside its own region.

su′per•sat′u•rate′ (-rāt′), *v.t.*, **-rat•ed, -rat•ing.** to increase the concentration of (a solution) beyond saturation. —**su′per•sat′u•ra′tion,** *n.*

su•per•scribe (soō′pər skrīb′), *v.t.*, **-scribed, -scrib•ing.** to write at the top or on the outside or surface of. —**su′per•scrip′tion,** *n.*

su′per•script′, *n.* a letter, number, or symbol written or printed high on a line of text.

su′per•sede′ (-sēd′), *v.t.*, **-sed•ed, -sed•ing.** **1.** to replace, as in power or authority. **2.** to set aside as void, useless, or obsolete.

su′per•son′ic, *adj.* **1.** greater than the speed of sound. **2.** capable of achieving supersonic speed: *a supersonic plane.* **3.** ULTRASONIC.

su′per•star′, *n.* a very popular and successful performer or athlete.

su′per•sti′tion (-stish′ən), *n.* **1.** an irrational belief in the ominous significance of a particular thing, circumstance, or occurrence. **2.** a custom or act based on superstition. —**su•per•sti′tious,** *adj.*

su′per•store′, *n.* a very large store that stocks a wide variety of merchandise.

su′per•struc′ture, *n.* **1.** the part of a building above its foundation or basement. **2.** a structure built on something else, as one above the main deck of a ship.

su′per•tank′er, *n.* a tanker with a deadweight capacity of over 75,000 tons.

su′per•vene′ (-vēn′), *v.i.*, **-vened, -ven•ing.** to take place or occur as something additional or extraneous. —**su′per•ven′tion** (-ven′shən), *n.*

su′per•vise′ (-vīz′), *v.t.*, **-vised, -vis•ing.** to watch over and direct (work, workers, etc.); oversee. —**su′per•vi′sion** (-vizh′ən), *n.* —**su′per•vi′sor,** *n.* —**su′per•vi′so•ry,** *adj.*

su′per•wom′an, *n., pl.* **-wom•en. 1.** a woman of extraordinary or superhuman powers. **2.** a woman who copes successfully with the simultaneous demands of a career, marriage, and motherhood.

su•pine (soō pīn′), *adj.* **1.** lying on the back, face upward. **2.** inactive, passive, or inert.

supp., 1. supplement. **2.** supplementary. Also, **suppl.**

sup•per (sup′ər), *n.* the evening meal.

sup′per club′, *n.* a nightclub.

sup•plant (sə plant′, -plänt′), *v.t.* **1.** to take the place of (another), as through force or scheming. **2.** to replace (one thing) by something else.

sup•ple (sup′əl), *adj.*, **-pler, -plest. 1.** bending readily without breaking or splitting; flexible. **2.** limber; lithe. **3.** compliant or yielding. —**sup′ple•ness,** *n.* —**sup•ply** (sup′lē), *adv.*

sup•ple•ment (*n.* sup′lə mənt; *v.* -ment′), *n.* **1.** something added to complete a thing or supply a deficiency. **2.** a part added to a book or an extra part of a newspaper. —*v.t.* **3.** to form or provide a supplement to. —**sup′ple•men′tal, sup′ple•men′ta•ry,** *adj.*

sup•pli•ant (sup′lē ənt), *n.* **1.** a person who supplicates. —*adj.* **2.** supplicating.

sup′pli•cate′ (-li kāt′), *v.*, **-cat•ed, -cat•ing.** —*v.i.* **1.** to make humble entreaty. —*v.t.* **2.** to entreat humbly. **3.** to ask for by humble entreaty. —**sup′pli•ca′tion,** *n.*

sup•ply (sə plī′), *v.*, **-plied, -ply•ing,** *n., pl.* **-plies.** —*v.t.* **1.** to furnish with what is lacking or requisite. **2.** to furnish (something wanting or requisite). **3.** to compensate for (a deficiency or loss). —*n.* **4.** the act of supplying. **5.** a quantity of something on hand or available; stock. **6.** Usu., **-plies.** a stock or store of necessary items, as food. —**sup•pli′er,** *n.*

supply′-side′, *adj.* denoting the hypothesis in economics that reduced taxes will stimulate investment and economic growth. Compare DEMAND-SIDE. —**supply′-sid′er,** *n.*

sup•port (sə pôrt′), *v.t.* **1.** to hold up the weight of

(a load, structure, etc.) without giving way. **2.** to provide with the necessities of existence. **3.** to sustain (a person, the spirits, etc.) under affliction. **4.** to uphold or advocate (a cause, principle, etc.). **5.** to corroborate (a statement, opinion, etc.). **6.** to endure; tolerate. **7.** to perform with (a leading actor) in a secondary role. —*n.* **8.** the act of supporting or state of being supported. **9.** one that supports. —**sup•port′a•ble,** *adj.* —**sup•port′er,** *n.* —**sup•port′ive,** *adj.*

support′ group′, *n.* a group of people who meet regularly to support each other by discussing shared problems.

sup•pose (sə pōz′), *v.*, **-posed, -pos•ing.** —*v.t.* **1.** to assume (something), as for the sake of argument. **2.** to think or hold as an opinion. **3.** to require logically. **4.** to expect or require: *She was supposed to meet me here.* —*v.i.* **5.** to assume something; presume. —**sup•posed′** (-pōzd′, -pō′zid), *adj.* —**sup•pos′ed•ly,** *adv.*

sup•po•si•tion (sup′ə zish′ən), *n.* **1.** the act of supposing. **2.** something supposed.

sup•pos•i•to•ry (sə poz′i tôr′ē), *n., pl.* **-ries.** a solid mass of medicinal substance that melts upon insertion into the rectum or vagina.

sup•press (sə pres′), *v.t.* **1.** to put an end to by or as if by authority; quell. **2.** to hold back or restrain. **3.** to withhold from disclosure or publication. **4.** to keep (a thought, memory, etc.) out of conscious awareness. —**sup•pres′sant,** *n.* —**sup•pres′sion,** *n.*

sup•pu•rate (sup′yə rāt′), *v.i.*, **-rat•ed, -rat•ing.** to produce or discharge pus. —**sup′pu•ra′tion,** *n.*

su•pra (soō′prə), *adv.* above, esp. in a text.

su′pra•na′tion•al, *adj.* above the authority or scope of one national government.

su•prem•a•cist (sə prem′ə sist, soō-), *n.* a person who advocates the supremacy of a particular group, esp. a racial group.

su•prem′a•cy, *n.* **1.** the state of being supreme. **2.** supreme authority or power.

su•preme (sə prēm′, soō-), *adj.* **1.** highest in rank or authority. **2.** of the highest quality, degree, importance, etc. **3.** last or final. —**su•preme′ly,** *adv.*

Supreme′ Be′ing, *n.* God.

Supreme′ Court′, *n.* **1.** the highest court of the U.S. **2.** (*l.c.*) the highest court of most states.

supt., superintendent.

sur-¹, a prefix meaning: over or above (*surcharge*); in addition (*surtax*).

sur-², var. of SUB- before *r.*

Su•ra•ba•ya or **-ba•ja** (soōr′ə bä′yə), *n.* a seaport on NE Java, Indonesia. 2,027,913.

sur•cease (sûr sēs′), *n.* cessation; end.

sur•charge (*n.* sûr′chärj′; *v.* sûr chärj′, sûr′chärj′), *n., v.*, **-charged, -charg•ing.** —*n.* **1.** an additional charge, tax, or cost. **2.** a mark printed over a stamp that alters its face value. —*v.t.* **3.** to subject to a surcharge. **4.** to print a surcharge on (a stamp).

sur•cin•gle (sûr′sing′gəl), *n.* a girth that passes around a horse's belly to hold a blanket, pack, or saddle in place.

sure (shoōr, shûr), *adj.*, **sur•er, sur•est,** *adv.* —*adj.* **1.** free from doubt. **2.** confident, as of something expected. **3.** certain beyond question. **4.** reliable or unfailing. **5.** unerring. **6.** admitting of no doubt; positive. **7.** destined; inevitable. —*adv.* **8.** in a sure manner; certainly. —*Idiom.* **9. For sure,** without a doubt; certainly. **10. sure enough,** *Informal.* as might have been expected. —**sure′ly,** *adv.* —**sure′ness,** *n.*

sure′fire′, *adj. Informal.* sure to work.

sure′foot′ed, *adj.* not likely to stumble, slip, or fall.

sure•e•ty (shoōr′i tē, shoōr′tē, shûr′-), *n., pl.* **-ties. 1.** security against loss or damage. **2.** a person who has assumed legal responsibility for another. **3.** the state or quality of being sure; certainty.

surf (sûrf), *n.* **1.** the swell of the sea that breaks upon a shore. —*v.i.* **2.** to ride a surfboard. **3.** to search haphazardly, as for information on the Internet or for an interesting program on TV. —*v.t.* **4.** to search through (a computer network or TV channels) for information or entertainment. —**surf′er,** n.

sur•face (sûr′fis), n., adj., v., **-faced, -fac•ing.** —n. **1.** the outermost or uppermost layer or area of something. **2.** a face of a body or thing. **3.** outward appearance. —adj. **4.** of or on a surface; external. **5.** apparent rather than real; superficial. —v.t. **6.** to finish the surface of. —v.i. **7.** to rise to or appear on the surface.

surf′board′, n. a long, narrow board on which a person rides in surfing.

sur•feit (sûr′fit), n. **1.** an excessive amount. **2.** overindulgence, esp. in eating or drinking. **3.** disgust caused by excess or satiety. —v.t. **4.** to supply or feed to excess or satiety.

surf′ing, n. the sport of riding the surf.

surge (sûrj), n., v., **surged, surg•ing.** —n. **1.** a strong, wavelike forward movement. **2.** a sudden strong rush or burst: a surge of anger. **3.** a sudden increase of electric current. —v.i. **4.** to move in or as if in a surge. **5.** to increase suddenly.

sur•geon (sûr′jən), n. a physician who specializes in surgery.

surge′ protec′tor, n. a small device to protect a computer, telephone, television set, or the like from damage by high-voltage electrical surges.

sur′ger•y (-jə rē), n., pl. **-ger•ies** for 2, 3. **1.** the art or work of treating diseases, injuries, or deformities by operation on the body, usu. with instruments. **2.** treatment performed by a surgeon. **3.** a room for surgical operations. —**sur′gi•cal,** adj. —**sur′gi•cal•ly,** adv.

sur′gical strike′, n. a bombing raid that is intended to attack a military target and avoid civilian centers.

Su•ri•na•me (sŏŏr′ə nä′mə) also **Su′ri•nam′** (-näm′, -nam′), n. a republic on the NE coast of South America. 443,446. —**Su′ri•na•mese′** (-nəmēz′, -mēs′), n., pl. **-mese,** adj.

sur•ly (sûr′lē), adj., **-li•er, -li•est.** sullenly rude or bad-tempered. —**sur′li•ness,** n.

sur•mise (sər mīz′; n. also sûr′mīz), v., **-mised, -mis•ing,** n. —v.t., v.i. **1.** to conjecture; guess. —n. **2.** a conjecture; guess.

sur•mount (sər mount′), v.t. **1.** to get over or across (barriers, obstacles, etc.). **2.** to prevail over; overcome. **3.** to get to or be on the top of. —**sur•mount′a•ble,** adj.

sur•name (sûr′nām′), n. the name a person has in common with other family members.

sur•pass (sər pas′, -päs′), v.t. **1.** to be greater than; exceed. **2.** to be superior to; excel. **3.** to be beyond the range or capacity of; transcend. —**sur•pass′ing,** adj.

sur•plice (sûr′plis), n. a loose-fitting, broad-sleeved white vestment worn over a cassock.

sur•plus (sûr′plus, -pləs), n. **1.** an amount or quantity greater than needed. —adj. **2.** being a surplus.

sur•prise (sər prīz′, sə-), v., **-prised, -pris•ing,** n. —v.t. **1.** to strike with a sudden feeling of astonishment. **2.** to come upon suddenly and unexpectedly. **3.** to make an unexpected assault on. —n. **4.** a feeling of sudden astonishment. **5.** something that surprises. **6.** the act of surprising. —**sur•pris′ing,** adj. —**sur•pris′ing•ly,** adv.

sur•re•al•ism (sə rē′ə liz′əm), n. a 20th-century style of art and literature stressing the subconscious significance of imagery or the exploitation of unexpected juxtapositions. —**sur•re′al,** adj. —**sur•re′al•ist,** n., adj. —**sur•re′al•is′tic,** adj.

sur•ren•der (sə ren′dər), v.t. **1.** to yield to the possession or power of another on demand or under duress. **2.** to give (oneself) up, as to an emotion. **3.** to abandon or relinquish. —v.i. **4.** to give oneself up. —n. **5.** an act or instance of surrendering.

sur•rep•ti•tious (sûr′əp tish′əs), adj. obtained, done, or made by stealth; clandestine. —**sur′rep•ti′tious•ly,** adv.

sur•rey (sûr′ē, sur′ē), n., pl. **-reys.** a four-wheeled, two-seated, horse-drawn carriage.

sur•ro•gate (sûr′ə gāt′, -git, sur′-), n. **1.** a deputy.

2. a substitute. **3.** a judge in some states having jurisdiction over the probate of wills and the administration of estates.

sur′rogate moth′er, n. a woman who bears a child for another couple, as by being inseminated with the man's sperm.

sur•round (sə round′), v.t. **1.** to enclose on all sides; encircle. **2.** to enclose so as to cut off communication or retreat.

sur•round′ings, n.pl. circumstances or conditions that surround a person; environment.

sur′sum cor′da (sŏŏr′sŏŏm kôr′dä, kōr′-), the words "Lift up your hearts," addressed by the celebrant of the mass to the congregation just before the preface.

sur•tax (sûr′taks′), n. an additional or extra tax on something already taxed.

sur•veil•lance (sər vā′ləns), n. a watch kept over someone or something, as a suspect.

sur•vey (v. sər vā′; n. sûr′vā, sər vā′), v., **-veyed, -vey•ing,** n., pl. **-veys.** —v.t. **1.** to view, consider, or study in a comprehensive way. **2.** to view in detail. **3.** to determine the exact dimensions and position of (a tract of land). —n. **4.** a comprehensive view. **5.** a detailed examination, as to ascertain condition. **6. a.** the act of surveying land. **b.** a plan or description resulting from this.

sur•vey′ing, n. the science of making land surveys. —**sur•vey′or,** n.

sur•vive (sər vīv′), v., **-vived, -viv•ing.** —v.i. **1.** to continue to live or exist. —v.t. **2.** to continue to live or exist after; outlive. **3.** to live through (adversity, misery, etc.). —**sur•viv′al,** n. —**sur•vi′vor,** n.

Su•san•na (sŏŏ zan′ə), n. a book of the Apocrypha, constituting the 13th chapter of Daniel in the Douay Bible.

sus•cep•ti•ble (sə sep′tə bəl), adj. **1.** admitting or permitting: susceptible to various interpretations. **2.** liable or subject to an influence or agency: susceptible to colds. **3.** capable of being affected emotionally. —**sus•cep′ti•bil′i•ty,** n.

sus•pect (v. sə spekt′; n. sus′pekt; adj. sus′pekt, sə-spekt′), v.t. **1.** to believe to be guilty with little or no proof. **2.** to doubt or mistrust. **3.** to think likely or probable; surmise. —n. **4.** a person who is suspected, esp. of a crime. —adj. **5.** open to or under suspicion.

sus•pend (sə spend′), v.t. **1.** to hang from above so as to allow free movement. **2.** to keep from falling or sinking as if by hanging: particles suspended in a liquid. **3.** to defer or postpone. **4.** to make inactive or cause to cease for a time. **5.** to debar temporarily from office, membership, or privilege.

suspend′ed anima′tion, n. a temporary cessation of the vital functions.

sus•pend′ers, n.pl. adjustable straps worn over the shoulders to support trousers or a skirt.

sus•pense (sə spens′), n. **1.** mental uncertainty accompanied by anxiety or excitement. **2.** a state of mental indecision. —**sus•pense′ful,** adj.

sus•pen′sion, n. **1.** the act of suspending or state of being suspended. **2. a.** a state in which the particles of a substance are mixed with a fluid but are undissolved. **b.** a substance in such a state. **3.** something on or by which something else is suspended. **4.** something suspended.

suspen′sion bridge′, n. a bridge with a deck suspended from cables anchored at their extremities.

sus•pi•cion (sə spish′ən), n. **1.** the act of suspecting or state of being suspected. **2.** the state of mind of one who suspects. **3.** a slight trace; hint.

sus•pi′cious, adj. **1.** tending to cause suspicion. **2.** inclined to suspect; distrustful. **3.** feeling or expressing suspicion. —**sus•pi′cious•ly,** adv.

Sus•que•han•na (sus′kwə han′ə), n. a river flowing S from central New York to Chesapeake Bay. 444 mi. (715 km) long.

sus•tain (sə stān′), v.t. **1.** to bear the weight of; support. **2.** to undergo (injury, loss, etc.) without giving way; endure. **3.** to keep (a person, the spirits, etc.) from giving way. **4.** to keep up or keep going;

maintain. **5.** to supply with the necessities of life, as food. **6.** to uphold as valid, just, or correct. **7.** to confirm or corroborate.

sus•te•nance (sus′tə nəns), *n.* **1.** means of sustaining life; nourishment. **2.** means of livelihood. **3.** the process of sustaining. **4.** the state of being sustained.

Sut•ter (sut′ər), *n.* **John Augustus,** 1803–80, U.S. frontiersman.

Sut′ter's Mill′, *n.* the location of John Sutter's mill in California, near which gold was discovered, precipitating the gold rush of 1849.

Sut′ton Hoo′ (hoo͞), *n.* an archaeological site in Suffolk, England: a rowing boat, believed to have been buried A.D. c670 by Anglo-Saxons.

su•ture (soo͞′chər), *n.* **1. a.** a joining of the edges of a wound by stitching. **b.** one of the stitches employed. **2.** a seam where two parts, as two bones of the skull, join.

SUV, *pl.* **SUVs.** sport-utility vehicle.

Su•va (soo͞′vä), *n.* the capital of Fiji, on Viti Levu island. 71,608.

su•ze•rain (soo͞′zə rin, -rān′), *n.* **1.** a state exercising political control over a dependent state. **2.** a feudal overlord. —**su′ze•rain•ty,** *n., pl.* **-ties.**

svelte (svelt, sfelt), *adj.,* **svelt•er, svelt•est.** slender, esp. gracefully slender.

Sverd•lovsk (sverd lôfsk′, -lofsk′, sferd-), *n.* a city in the Russian Federation, in the Ural Mountains. 1,331,000.

SW or **S.W., 1.** southwest. **2.** southwestern.

Sw or **Sw., 1.** Sweden. **2.** Swedish.

swab (swob), *n., v.,* **swabbed, swab•bing.** —*n.* **1.** a mop used esp. on shipboard, as for cleaning decks. **2.** a wad of absorbent material used esp. for cleaning or for applying medicaments. **3.** *Slang.* a sailor. —*v.t.* **4.** to clean, apply, or take up with or as if with a swab.

swad•dle (swod′l), *v.t.,* **-dled, -dling.** to bind (a newborn infant) with strips of cloth to prevent free movement.

swag¹ (swag), *n., v.,* **swagged, swag•ging.** —*n.* **1.** something, as a valance, fastened at each end and hanging down in the middle. —*v.i.* **2.** to hang in or droop with weight.

swag² (swag), *n. Slang.* plunder; booty.

swag′ger, *v.i.* **1.** to strut about with an insolent air. **2.** to boast noisily; bluster. —*n.* **3.** a swaggering manner or walk.

Swa•hi•li (swä hē′lē), *n.* a Bantu language serving as a lingua franca in E and E central Africa.

swain (swān), *n.* **1.** a male admirer or lover. **2.** a country lad.

swal•low¹ (swol′ō), *v.t.* **1.** to take into the stomach through the throat and esophagus. **2.** to take in so as to envelop. **3.** to accept without question. **4.** to put up with; endure. **5.** to suppress (emotion, pride, etc.). **6.** to take back; retract. —*v.i.* **7.** to perform the act of swallowing. —*n.* **8.** the act of swallowing. **9.** a quantity swallowed at one time.

swal•low² (swol′ō), *n.* **1.** a long-winged, fork-tailed songbird noted for its swift, graceful flight. —*Proverb.* **2. One swallow does not make a summer,** a single fact is not enough with which to reach a conclusion.

swal′low•tail′, *n.* **1.** a deeply forked tail like that of a swallow. **2.** any of several butterflies with elongated hind wings.

swam (swam), *v.* pt. of SWIM.

swa•mi (swä′mē), *n., pl.* **-mis.** a Hindu religious teacher. [< Skt, pl. of *svāmin* master]

swamp (swomp), *n.* **1.** a tract of wet, spongy land. —*v.t.* **2.** to flood or drench, esp. with water. **3.** to sink or fill (a boat) with water. **4.** to overwhelm, esp. with an excess of something. —**swamp′y,** *adj.*

swan (swon), *n.* a large aquatic bird with a long, slender neck and usu. pure-white plumage.

swank (swangk), *n., adj.,* **-er, -est.** —*n.* **1.** dashing smartness, as in dress; style. **2.** pretentiousness. —*adj.* **3.** stylish or elegant. **4.** pretentiously stylish.

swank′y, *adj.,* **-i•er, -i•est.** swank. —**swank′i•ly,** *adv.* —**swank′i•ness,** *n.*

swans′down′, *n.* **1.** the down of a swan, used esp. for trimming and powder puffs. **2.** a cotton flannel with a thickly napped face.

swan′ song′, *n.* a final act or farewell appearance.

swap (swop), *v.,* **swapped, swap•ping,** *n.* —*v.t., v.i.* **1.** to trade or barter. —*n.* **2.** a trade or exchange.

sward (swôrd), *n.* the grassy surface of land; turf.

swarm (swôrm), *n.* **1.** a body of honeybees that emigrate, accompanied by a queen, to start a new colony. **2.** a body of bees in a hive. **3.** a great number of things or persons, esp. moving together. —*v.i.* **4.** to fly off in a swarm, as bees. **5.** to move about or congregate in great numbers. **6.** (of a place) to abound or teem.

swarth•y (swôr′thē, -thē), *adj.,* **-i•er, -i•est.** dark or darkish in skin color or complexion.

swash (swosh, swôsh), *v.i.* to splash, as water does.

swash′buck′ler, *n.* a swaggering swordsman, soldier, or adventurer. —**swash′buck′ling,** *adj., n.*

swas•ti•ka (swos′ti kə), *n., pl.* **-kas. 1.** a symbolic or ornamental figure consisting of a cross with arms of equal length, each arm having a continuation at right angles. **2.** a swastika as the emblem of the Nazi Party.

swat (swot), *v.,* **swat•ted, swat•ting,** *n.* —*v.t.* **1.** to hit sharply; slap; smack. —*n.* **2.** a sharp blow; slap; smack. —**swat′ter,** *n.*

SWAT (*as initials or* swot), *n.* a law-enforcement unit trained to deal with esp. dangerous or violent situations.

swatch (swoch), *n.* a sample, as of cloth.

swath (swoth, swôth), *n.* **1. a.** the space covered by the stroke of a scythe or the cut of a mowing machine. **b.** the piece or strip so cut. **2.** a long strip, belt, or line.

swathe¹ (swoth, swāth), *v.,* **swathed, swath•ing,** *n.* —*v.t.* **1.** to wrap, bind, or swaddle with bands of material. **2.** to bandage. —*n.* **3.** a wrapping or bandage.

swathe² (swoth, swāth), *n.* SWATH.

sway (swā), *v.i.* **1.** to move or swing to and fro. **2.** to move or incline to one side or to fluctuate, as in opinion; waver. —*v.t.* **4.** to cause to sway. **5.** to influence (the mind, emotions, etc., or a person). **6.** to rule or govern. —*n.* **7.** a swaying movement. **8.** dominating power or influence. **9.** rule; dominion.

sway′back′, *n.* an excessive downward curvature of the back, esp. of horses. —**sway′backed′,** *adj.*

Swa•zi•land (swä′zē land′), *n.* a kingdom in SE Africa. 1,031,600.

swear (swâr), *v.,* **swore, sworn, swear•ing.** —*v.i.* **1.** to make a solemn declaration by a sacred being or object. **2.** to bind oneself by oath; vow. **3.** to use profane language. —*v.t.* **4.** to declare by swearing by a sacred being or object. **5.** to testify or state on oath. **6.** to bind by an oath. **7. swear by,** to have great confidence in. **8. ~ in,** to admit to office by administering an oath. **9. ~ off,** to promise to give up. —**swear′er,** *n.*

swear′word′, *n.* a profane or obscene word.

sweat (swet), *v.,* **sweat** or **sweat•ed, sweat•ing,** *n.* —*v.i.* **1.** to perspire, esp. freely. **2.** to exude moisture. **3.** to gather moisture from the surrounding air by condensation. **4.** *Informal.* to work hard. —*v.t.* **5.** to excrete (moisture) through the pores of the skin. **6.** to exude in drops. **7.** to cause to perspire. **8.** to force to work too hard. **9. sweat out,** *Informal.* to await anxiously the outcome of. —*n.* **10.** perspiration. **11.** *Informal.* a state of anxiety or impatience. **12.** moisture exuded from something or gathered on a surface. **13. sweats,** clothes, as sweatpants, worn esp. during exercise. —**sweat′y,** *adj.,* **-i•er, -i•est.**

sweat′er, *n.* a knitted jacket or pullover.

sweat′ gland′, *n.* one of the minute, tubular glands of the skin that secrete sweat.

sweat′pants′, *n.* (*used with a pl. v.*) pants of soft, absorbent fabric worn esp. during athletic activity.

sweat′shirt′, *n.* a loose, collarless cotton jersey pullover.

sweat′shop′, *n.* a shop employing workers at low wages, for long hours, and under poor conditions.

Swed., 1. Sweden. **2.** Swedish.

Swede (swēd), *n.* a native or inhabitant of Sweden.

Swe•den (swēd′n), *n.* a kingdom in N Europe. 8,946,193.

Swed′ish, *adj.* **1.** of Sweden, the Swedes, or their language. —*n.* **2.** the Germanic language of the Swedes.

sweep (swēp), *v.,* **swept, sweep•ing,** *n.* —*v.t.* **1.** to remove, clean, or clear with or as if with a broom or brush. **2.** to drive or carry by a steady force, as the wind. **3.** to pass or draw over a surface with a continuous stroke or movement. **4.** to win all of (a series of contests). —*v.i.* **5.** to sweep a floor, room, etc., with or as if with a broom. **6.** to move swiftly and forcefully. **7.** to move or extend in a wide curve or circuit. —*n.* **8.** the act of sweeping. **9.** a sweeping motion. **10.** a swinging or curving movement or stroke. **11.** a continuous extent or stretch. **12.** a winning of all the games or prizes in a contest. —**sweep′er,** *n.*

sweep′ing, *adj.* **1.** of wide range or scope. —*n.* **2.** the act of one that sweeps. **3. sweepings,** matter swept up, as refuse. —**sweep′ing•ly,** *adv.*

sweep′stakes′ also **-stake′,** *n.* (*used with a sing. or pl. v.*) **1.** a contest, as a race, for which the prize consists of the stakes contributed by the competitors. **2.** a lottery in which each participant contributes a stake and the stakes are awarded to one or several winners.

sweet (swēt), *adj.* **1.** having the taste or flavor of sugar, honey, or the like. **2.** not rancid or stale. **3.** not salted: *sweet butter.* **4.** pleasing to the ear. **5.** fragrant; perfumed. **6.** agreeable in disposition. —*n.* **7.** Usu., **sweets.** sweet foods, as candy. **8.** a beloved person. —**sweet′ish,** *adj.* —**sweet′ly,** *adv.* —**sweet′ness,** *n.*

sweet′bread′, *n.* the thymus or pancreas of a young animal, esp. a calf, used as food.

sweet′bri′er or **-bri′ar,** *n.* a Eurasian rose with a tall prickly stem and pink flowers.

sweet′ corn′, *n.* a variety of corn whose grain or kernels are sweet and edible.

sweet′en, *v.t., v.i.* to make or become sweet or sweeter. —**sweet′en•er,** *n.*

sweet′heart′, *n.* a beloved person; lover.

sweet′heart con′tract, *n.* a contract made through collusion between management and labor representatives, having terms detrimental to union workers.

sweet′meat′, *n.* a candy.

sweet′ pea′, *n.* a climbing plant with sweet-scented flowers.

sweet′ pep′per, *n.* **1.** a pepper bearing a mild-flavored, bell-shaped fruit. **2.** its fruit.

sweet′ pota′to, *n.* **1.** a Central American trailing vine widely grown for its sweet, edible, tuberous root. **2.** its root.

sweet′-talk′, *v.t., v.i.* to use cajoling words (on); flatter.

sweet′ tooth′, *n.* a liking or craving for sweets.

swell (swel), *v.,* **swelled, swol•len** or **swelled, swell•ing,** *n., adj.* —*v.i., v.t.* **1.** to grow or cause to grow in bulk, as by absorption of fluid. **2.** to enlarge excessively or abnormally; protrude. **3.** to bulge out, as a sail. **4.** to increase in amount, degree, intensity, or force. **5.** to puff up or become puffed up with pride. —*n.* **6.** inflation or distention. **7.** a protuberant part. **8.** a long and unbroken wave. **9.** an increase in amount, degree, intensity, or force. **10.** a gradual increase in loudness of sound. **11.** *Informal.* a fashionably dressed person. —*adj. Informal.* **12.** stylish; elegant. **13.** first-rate; fine.

swell′head′, *n.* a vain person. —**swell′head′ed,** *adj.*

swell′ing, *n.* **1.** a swollen part. **2.** an abnormal enlargement or protuberance.

swel•ter (swel′tər), *v.i.* to suffer from oppressive heat.

swel′ter•ing, *adj.* suffering from or marked by oppressive heat.

swept (swept), *v.* pt. and pp. of SWEEP.

swept′back′, *adj.* (of the front edge of an airfoil) forming an obtuse angle with the fuselage.

swerve (swûrv), *v.,* **swerved, swerv•ing,** *n.* —*v.i., v.t.* **1.** to turn or cause to turn aside abruptly from a straight or direct course. —*n.* **2.** the act of swerving.

Swift (swift), *n.* **Jonathan,** 1667–1745, English satirist and clergyman, born in Ireland.

swig (swig), *n., v.,* **swigged, swig•ging.** *Informal.* —*n.* **1.** a swallow of liquid, esp. liquor. —*v.t., v.i.* **2.** to drink heartily or greedily.

swill (swil), *n.* **1.** liquid or partly liquid food for animals. **2.** kitchen refuse; garbage. —*v.i., v.t.* **3.** to drink greedily or excessively.

swim (swim), *v.,* **swam, swum, swim•ming,** *n.* —*v.i.* **1.** to move in water by using bodily parts, as limbs or fins. **2.** to float on a liquid. **3.** to move or glide smoothly. **4.** to be flooded: *eyes swimming with tears.* **5.** to be dizzy or giddy. —*v.t.* **6.** to move along in or cross by swimming. —*n.* **7.** an act, instance, or period of swimming. —*Idiom.* **8. in the swim,** alert to or engaged in what is current. —**swim′mer,** *n.*

swim′ming, *n.* **1.** the act of one that swims. **2.** a sport based on the ability to swim.

swim′ming hole′, *n.* a place, as in a stream, with water deep enough for swimming.

swim′suit′, *n.* BATHING SUIT.

swin•dle (swin′dl), *v.,* **-dled, -dling,** *n.* —*v.t., v.i.* **1.** to cheat out of assets, as money; defraud. —*n.* **2.** an act or instance of swindling; fraud. —**swin′dler,** *n.*

swine (swīn), *n., pl.* **swine. 1.** any of a family of hoofed mammals with a disklike snout and a thick hide, esp. the domestic hog. **2.** a coarse, gross, or contemptible person. —**swin′ish,** *adj.*

swing (swing), *v.,* **swung, swing•ing,** *n., adj.* —*v.t.* **1.** to cause to move to and fro. **2.** to cause to move on a fixed point or axis. **3.** to cause to move in a circle or curve. **4.** to suspend so as to hang freely. **5.** *Informal.* to manage as desired: *They swung the deal.* —*v.i.* **6.** to sway to and fro. **7.** to turn on a fixed point or axis. **8.** to move in a circle or curve. **9.** to move with a free, swaying motion. **10.** to hang freely, as a hammock. **11.** to hit at someone or something with or as if with the hand. **12.** *Slang.* to be lively, fashionable, or trendy. —*n.* **13.** the act or manner of swinging. **14.** the amount or extent of a swing. **15.** freedom of action. **16.** active operation; progression: *got into the swing of things.* **17.** a seat suspended from above on which a person may sit and swing for recreation. **18.** a style of jazz often played by a large dance band and marked by a smooth beat and flowing phrasing. —*adj.* **19.** capable of determining an outcome: *the swing vote.*

swing′er, *n.* **1.** one that swings. **2.** *Slang.* a lively, fashionable, or trendy person.

swing′ shift′, *n.* a work shift in industry from mid-afternoon until midnight.

swipe (swīp), *n., v.,* **swiped, swip•ing.** —*n.* **1.** a strong, sweeping blow. —*v.t.* **2.** to strike with a swipe. **3.** to slide (a magnetic card) quickly through an electronic device that reads data. **4.** *Informal.* to steal.

swirl (swûrl), *v.i., v.t.* **1.** to move or cause to move with a whirling motion; spin. —*n.* **2.** a swirling movement. **3.** a twist, as of hair. —**swirl′y,** *adj.,* **-i•er, -i•est.**

swish (swish), *v.i., v.t.* **1.** to move with or make a sibilant sound. **2.** to rustle, as silk. —*n.* **3.** a swishing movement or sound.

Swiss (swis), *n., pl.* **Swiss,** *adj.* —*n.* **1.** a native or inhabitant of Switzerland. **2.** SWISS CHEESE. —*adj.* **3.** of Switzerland or its inhabitants.

Swiss′ chard′, *n.* CHARD.

Swiss′ cheese′, *n.* a firm, pale yellow cheese with many holes.

Swiss′ Fam′ily Rob′inson, a children's novel (1813) by Johann David Wyss.

Swiss′ steak′, *n.* steak that is floured and pounded, then braised.

switch (swich), *n.* **1.** a slender, flexible shoot, rod, or twig. **2.** the act of whipping with or as if with a switch. **3.** a bunch of real or synthetic hair used to supplement one's own hair. **4.** a device for diverting an electric current or for making or breaking a circuit. **5.** a mechanism for diverting moving trains or rolling stock from one track to another. **6.** a shift or change. —*v.t.* **7.** to whip with or as if with a switch. **8.** to move (a cane, tail, etc.) with a swift, lashing stroke. **9.** to change or exchange. **10.** to connect, disconnect, or redirect by operating a switch. **11.** to divert (a train, car, etc.) from one set of tracks to another. —*v.i.* **12.** to change, as direction; shift. **13.** to make an exchange. **14.** to move back and forth briskly; lash. —**switch′er,** *n.*

switch′back′, *n.* a zigzag highway or railroad track arrangement for climbing a steep grade.

switch′blade′, *n.* a pocketknife with a blade held and released by a spring.

switch′board′, *n.* a unit on which are mounted switches and devices for completing telephone circuits manually.

switch′-hit′, *v.i.,* **-hit, -hit·ting.** *Baseball.* to bat both left-handed and right-handed. —**switch′-hit′ter,** *n.*

Switz., Switzerland.

Switz·er·land (swit′sər lənd), *n.* a republic in central Europe. 7,248,984.

swiv·el (swiv′əl), *n., v.,* **-eled, -el·ing** or (*esp. Brit.*) **-elled, -el·ling.** —*n.* **1.** a fastening device that allows the thing fastened to rotate freely on it. —*v.t., v.i.* **2.** to turn or pivot on or as if on a swivel.

swiz′zle stick′ (swiz′əl), *n.* a small wand for stirring mixed drinks.

swob (swob), *n., v.t.,* **swobbed, swob·bing.** SWAB.

swol·len (swō′lən), *v.* a pp. of SWELL.

swoon (swo̅o̅n), *v.i.* **1.** to lose consciousness; faint. —*n.* **2.** a faint.

swoop (swo̅o̅p), *v.i.* **1.** to sweep down through the air, as a bird upon prey. —*n.* **2.** an act or instance of swooping.

swop (swop), *v.t., v.i.,* **swopped, swop·ping** *n.* SWAP.

sword (sôrd), *n.* **1.** a weapon with a long, sharp-edged blade affixed to a hilt. **2.** the sword as a symbol of military power. **3.** military force or aggression. —*Idiom.* **4. at swords′ points,** mutually ready to fight.

sword′fish′, *n., pl.* **-fish, -fish·es.** a large marine food fish with an upper jaw elongated into a blade-like structure.

sword′play′, *n.* the action or technique of wielding a sword.

swords′man, *n., pl.* **-men.** a person skilled in the use of a sword.

swore (swôr), *v.* pt. of SWEAR.

sworn (swôrn), *v.* **1.** pp. of SWEAR. —*adj.* **2.** bound by or as if by an oath.

swum (swum), *v.* pp. of SWIM.

swung (swung), *v.* pt. and pp. of SWING.

swung′ dash′, *n.* a mark of punctuation (~) used in place of a word or part of a word previously spelled out.

syb·a·rite (sib′ə rīt′), *n.* a person devoted to luxury and pleasure. —**syb′a·rit′ic** (-rit′ik), *adj.*

syc·a·more (sik′ə môr′), *n.* **1.** a North American plane tree with lobed leaves and globular seed heads. **2.** a European and Asian maple tree.

Sy·char (sī′kär), *n.* a city in Samaria where Jesus visited Jacob's Well. John 4:5.

syc·o·phant (sik′ə fant, -fant′, sī′kə-), *n.* a self-seeking, servile flatterer. —**syc′o·phan·cy,** *n.* —**syc′o·phan′tic,** *adj.*

Syd·ney (sid′nē), *n.* a seaport in SE Australia. 3,430,600.

syl·lab·i·cate (si lab′i kāt′), *v.t.,* **-cat·ed, -cat·ing.** to form or divide into syllables; syllabify. —**syl·lab′i·ca′tion,** *n.*

syl·lab′i·fy′ (-fī′), *v.t.,* **-fied, -fy·ing.** to form or divide into syllables. —**syl·lab′i·fi·ca′tion,** *n.*

syl·la·ble (sil′ə bəl), *n.* **1.** an uninterrupted segment of speech consisting of a single pulse of breath and forming a word or part of a word. **2.** one or more letters representing a syllable. —**syl·lab′ic,** *adj.*

syl·la·bus (sil′ə bəs), *n., pl.* **-bus·es, -bi** (-bī′). an outline or other brief statement, as of a course of study.

syl·lo·gism (sil′ə jiz′əm), *n.* an argument of a form containing two premises leading to a conclusion. —**syl′lo·gis′tic,** *adj.*

sylph (silf), *n.* **1.** a slender, graceful woman or girl. **2.** an imaginary being supposed to inhabit the air. —**sylph′ic,** *adj.*

syl·van (sil′vən), *adj.* **1.** of or inhabiting the woods. **2.** consisting of or abounding in woods or trees.

sym·bi·o·sis (sim′bē ō′sis, -bī-), *n., pl.* **-ses** (-sēz). the living together of two dissimilar organisms, as in parasitism. —**sym′bi·ot′ic** (-ot′ik), *adj.*

sym·bol (sim′bəl), *n.* **1.** a material object used to represent something, often something immaterial. **2.** a letter, figure, or other conventional mark designating an object, quantity, operation, or function, as in mathematics. —**sym·bol′ic** (-bol′ik), *adj.* —**sym·bol′i·cal·ly,** *adv.*

sym′bol·ism, *n.* **1.** the practice of representing things by symbols. **2.** symbolic meaning or character.

sym′bol·ize′, *v.t.,* **-ized, -iz·ing. 1.** to be a symbol of. **2.** to represent by a symbol. —**sym′bol·i·za′tion,** *n.*

sym·me·try (sim′i trē), *n., pl.* **-tries. 1.** correspondence in size, form, and arrangement of parts on opposite sides of a plane, line, or point. **2. a.** excellence of proportion. **b.** beauty characterized by excellence of proportion. —**sym·met′ri·cal** (si me′tri kəl), **sym·met′ric,** *adj.* —**sym·met′ri·cal·ly,** *adv.*

sym·pa·thet·ic (sim′pə thet′ik), *adj.* **1.** characterized by or proceeding from sympathy. **2.** in harmony with one's tastes, mood, or disposition. **3.** noting that part of the autonomic nervous system that regulates involuntary reactions to stress, as in stimulating the heartbeat and breathing rate. —**sym′pa·thet′i·cal·ly,** *adv.*

sym′pa·thize′, *v.i.,* **-thized, -thiz·ing. 1.** to share in a feeling. **2.** to feel or express a compassionate sympathy. —**sym′pa·thiz′er,** *n.*

sym′pa·thy, *n., pl.* **-thies. 1.** agreement in feeling, as between persons. **2.** harmony of taste, opinion, or disposition. **3.** the ability to share the feelings of another, esp. in sorrow or trouble. **4.** an expression of compassion or commiseration. **5.** favorable or approving accord.

sym·pho·ny (sim′fə nē), *n., pl.* **-nies. 1.** an extended sonatalike musical composition for large orchestra. **2.** Also called **sym′phony or′chestra.** a large orchestra that plays symphonies. **3.** harmony of sounds. —**sym·phon′ic** (-fon′ik), *adj.*

sym·po·si·um (sim pō′zē əm), *n., pl.* **-si·ums, -si·a** (-zē ə). **1.** a meeting or conference at which several speakers discuss a topic. **2.** a collection of opinions or articles on a given topic.

symp·tom (simp′təm), *n.* **1.** a sign or indication. **2.** a phenomenon that arises from and accompanies a disease or disorder and serves as an indication of it. —**symp′to·mat′ic,** *adj.*

syn-, a prefix meaning with or together (*synthesis*).

syn., **1.** synonym. **2.** synonymous. **3.** synonymy.

syn·a·gogue or **-gog** (sin′ə gog′), *n.* **1.** a Jewish house of worship. **2.** a congregation of Jews.

syn·apse (sin′aps, si naps′), *n.* a region where nerve impulses are transmitted from an axon terminal to an adjacent structure, as another axon. —**syn·ap′tic,** *adj.*

sync or **synch** (singk), *n., v.,* **synced** or **synched, sync·ing** or **synch·ing.** —*n.* **1.** synchronization. **2.** harmonious relationship. —*v.t., v.i.* **3.** to synchronize.

syn·chro·nize (sing′krə nīz′), *v.,* **-nized, -niz·ing.** —*v.t.* **1.** to cause to indicate the same time. **2.** to cause to move, operate, or work at the same rate and exactly together. —*v.i.* **3.** to occur at the same time. —**syn′chro•ni•za′tion,** *n.*

syn′chro•nous, *adj.* **1.** occurring at the same time. **2.** going on at the same rate and exactly together. —**syn′chro•nous•ly,** *adv.*

syn•co•pate (sing′kə pāt′, sin′-), *v.t.,* **-pat•ed, -pat•ing.** to shift (a musical accent) to a beat that is normally unaccented. —**syn′co•pa′tion,** *n.*

syn′co•pe′ (-pē′), *n.* the shortening of a word by the omission of one or more sounds from the middle, as in *ne'er* for *never.*

syn•di•cate (*n.* sin′di kit; *v.* -kāt′), *n., v.,* **-cat•ed, -cat•ing.** —*n.* **1.** a group of individuals or organizations combined to undertake a specific transaction. **2.** an agency that sells material for simultaneous publication in a number of newspapers or periodicals. —*v.t.* **3.** to combine into a syndicate. **4.** to publish through a syndicate. —*v.i.* **5.** to combine to form a syndicate. —**syn′di•ca′tion,** *n.*

syn•drome (sin′drōm, -drəm), *n.* a group of symptoms that together are characteristic of a specific disorder or disease.

syn•er•gism (sin′ər jiz′əm), *n.* the joint action of agents, as drugs, that when taken together increase each other's effectiveness. —**syn′er•gis′tic,** *adj.*

syn•fu•el (sin′fyōō′əl), *n.* SYNTHETIC FUEL.

syn•od (sin′əd), *n.* an assembly of church delegates, esp. ecclesiastics.

syn•o•nym (sin′ə nim), *n.* a word having the same or nearly the same meaning as another in the language. —**syn•on•y•mous** (si non′ə məs), *adj.* —**syn•on′y•my,** *n., pl.* **-mies.**

syn•op•sis (si nop′sis), *n., pl.* **-ses** (-sēz). a brief or condensed statement; summary.

syn•op•tic (si nop′tik) also **syn•op′ti•cal,** *adj.* **1.** pertaining to a synopsis; taking a general view of the principal parts of a subject. **2.** (*often cap.*) taking a common view: used chiefly in reference to the first three Gospels.

syn•tax (sin′taks), *n.* the patterns of formation of sentences and phrases from words and the rules for the formation of grammatical sentences in a language. —**syn•tac′tic** (-tak′tik), **syn•tac′ti•cal,** *adj.*

syn•the•sis (sin′thə sis), *n., pl.* **-ses** (-sēz′). the combining of elements into a single or unified entity. —**syn′the•size′** (-sīz′), *v.t.,* **-sized, -siz•ing.**

syn′the•siz′er, *n.* an electronic, usu. computerized device for creating or modifying the sounds of musical instruments.

syn•thet•ic (sin thet′ik), *adj.* **1.** of or involving synthesis. **2.** produced by artificial, esp. chemical, means. **3.** not real or genuine. —*n.* **4.** something made by a synthetic process. —**syn•thet′i•cal•ly,** *adv.*

synthet′ic fu′el, *n.* liquid or gaseous fuel manufactured from coal or in the form of oil extracted from shale.

syph•i•lis (sif′ə lis), *n.* an infectious, usu. venereal disease caused by a spirochete. —**syph′i•lit′ic,** *adj., n.*

Syr•a•cuse (sir′ə kyōōs′, -kyōōz′), *n.* a city in central New York. 159,985.

Syr•i•a (sēr′ē ə), *n.* **1.** a republic in SW Asia at the E end of the Mediterranean. 16,137,899. **2.** an ancient country in W Asia, including modern Syria, Lebanon, Israel, and adjacent areas. —**Syr′i•an,** *n., adj.*

sy•ringe (sə rinj′, sir′inj), *n., v.,* **-ringed, -ring•ing.** —*n.* **1.** a tube with a piston or rubber bulb for drawing in or ejecting fluid. —*v.t.* **2.** to cleanse, wash, or inject by means of a syringe.

syr•up (sir′əp, sûr′-), *n.* a thick, sweet liquid, as of water and sugar or molasses boiled together. —**syr′up•y,** *adj.*

sys•tem (sis′təm), *n.* **1.** an assemblage or combination of things or parts forming a complex or unitary whole. **2.** an ordered assemblage of facts, principles, or doctrines in a particular field. **3.** a method or plan of procedure or classification; scheme. **4. a.** a group of bodily organs or related tissues concerned with the same function. **b.** the body considered as a functioning unit. **5.** a working combination of computer hardware, software, and data communications devices. —*Idiom.* **6. all systems go,** everything is ready for action. —**sys′tem•at′ic** (-tə mat′ik), **sys′tem•at′i•cal,** *adj.* —**sys′tem•at′i•cal•ly,** *adv.*

sys′tem•a•tize′ (-tə mə tīz′), *v.t.,* **-tized, -tiz•ing.** to arrange in or according to a system.

sys•tem•ic (si stem′ik), *adj.* of, affecting, or circulating through the entire body. —**sys•tem′i•cal•ly,** *adv.*

sys′tems anal′ysis, *n.* the methodical study of the data-processing needs of a business or project. —**sys′tems an′alyst,** *n.*

sys•to•le (sis′tə lē′), *n.* the rhythmic contraction of the heart during which the blood in the chambers is forced onward. —**sys•tol•ic** (si stol′ik), *adj.*

Sze•chwan or **-chuan** (sech′wän′, sech′ōō än′), *n.* SICHUAN.

T

T, t (tē), *n., pl.* **Ts** or **T's, ts** or **t's. 1.** the 20th letter of the English alphabet, a consonant. —*Idiom.* **2. to a T,** exactly; perfectly.

't, a shortened form of *it,* as in *'twas.*

T., **1.** tablespoon. **2.** Tuesday.

t., 1. teaspoon. **2.** temperature. **3.** tense. **4.** ton. **5.** transitive.

Ta, *Chem. Symbol.* tantalum.

tab (tab), *n.* **1.** a small flap, loop, etc., used for pulling or hanging. **2.** a small projection from a paper or folder, used as a filing aid. **3.** *Informal.* a bill; check. —*Idiom.* **4. keep tabs on,** to maintain a watch over.

tab•by (tab′ē), *n., pl.* **-bies. 1.** a cat with a striped or brindled coat. **2.** a domestic cat, esp. a female one.

tab•er•nac•le (tab′ər nak′əl), *n.* **1.** a large place of worship. **2.** (*often cap.*) *Bible.* the portable place of worship used by the Israelites during their wandering in the wilderness. Ex. 25-27. **3.** an ornamental receptacle for the reserved Eucharist. [< LL *tabernāculum,* L: tent < *tabern(a)* hut, stall, inn]

ta•ble (tā′bəl), *n., v.,* **-bled, -bling.** —*n.* **1.** an article of furniture consisting of a flat top supported on one or more legs. **2.** such a piece of furniture used for meals. **3.** the food served at a table. **4.** the people at a table. **5.** a flat surface. **6.** a concise list or guide: *a table of contents.* **7.** a compact, orderly arrangement of words, numbers, etc., usu. in columns. —*v.t.* **8.** to lay aside (a bill, motion, etc.) for future discussion. —*Idiom.* **9. turn the tables,** to reverse a situation.

tab•leau (ta blō′, tab′lō), *n., pl.* **tab•leaux** (ta-blōz′, tab′lōz), **tab•leaus.** a representation of a picture, scene, etc., by persons suitably costumed and posed.

ta′ble•cloth′, *n.* a cloth for covering a table, esp. during a meal.

ta•ble d'hôte (tä′bəl dōt′, tab′əl), *n., pl.* **ta•bles d'hôte** (tä′bəlz, tab′əlz). a restaurant meal of preselected courses served at a fixed time and price. [< F: lit., the host's table]

ta′ble-hop′ (tā′bəl-), *v.i.,* **-hopped, -hop•ping.** to move about in a restaurant, nightclub, etc., chatting with people at various tables. —**ta′ble-hop′per,** *n.*

ta′ble•land′, *n.* PLATEAU (def. 1).

ta·ble·spoon', *n.* **1.** a large spoon used in serving food. **2.** a cooking measure equal to ½ fluid ounce (14.8 ml). —**ta'ble·spoon·ful'**, *n.*, *pl.* -**fuls.**

tab·let (tab'lit), *n.* **1.** a small, flattish piece of some solid, as a drug. **2.** a number of sheets of writing paper glued together at the edge. **3.** a flat slab bearing an inscription or carving.

ta'ble ten'nis, *n.* a game resembling tennis, played on a table with paddles and a lightweight hollow ball.

ta'ble·ware', *n.* the dishes, utensils, etc., used at the table.

tab·loid (tab'loid), *n.* a newspaper with small pages, usu. heavily illustrated and concentrating on sensational news.

ta·boo (ta bōō', ta-), *adj.*, *n.*, *pl.* -**boos,** *v.* -**booed,** -**boo·ing.** —*adj.* **1.** proscribed by society as improper or unacceptable. **2.** set apart as sacred; forbidden for general use. —*n.* **3.** a ban based on social convention. **4.** the practice of setting things apart as sacred or forbidden for general use. —*v.t.* **5.** to put under a taboo.

ta·bor or **ta·bour** (tā'bər), *n.* a small drum used to accompany oneself on a pipe or fife. —**ta'bor·er,** *n.*

Ta·bor (tā'bər), *n.* **Mount,** a mountain in N Israel. 1929 ft. (588 m). Judg. 4:6; 8:18.

tab·u·lar (tab'yə lər), *adj.* **1.** of or arranged in a table. **2.** flat like a table.

tab'u·late' (-lāt'), *v.t.*, -**lat·ed,** -**lat·ing.** to put in a tabular form. —**tab/u·la'tion,** *n.* —**tab/u·la'tor,** *n.*

ta·chom·e·ter (ta kom'i tər, tə-), *n.* an instrument for measuring the speed of rotation.

tach·y·car·di·a (tak'i kär'dē ə), *n.* excessively rapid heartbeat.

tac·it (tas'it), *adj.* **1.** understood without being openly expressed. **2.** unspoken. —**tac'it·ly,** *adv.* —**tac'it·ness,** *n.*

tac·i·turn (tas'i tûrn'), *adj.* inclined to silence; uncommunicative. —**tac'i·tur'ni·ty,** *n.* —**tac/i·turn'ly,** *adv.*

tack (tak), *n.* **1.** a short, sharp-pointed nail with a broad, flat head. **2.** a course of action. **3. a.** the direction of a sailing ship with reference to the wind direction. **b.** one movement in the zigzag course of a ship proceeding to windward. **4.** a long, temporary stitch used in fastening seams. —*v.t.* **5.** to fasten with tacks. **6.** to attach as something supplementary. **7.** to change the course of (a sailing ship) to the opposite tack. —*v.i.* **8.** (of a sailing ship) to change course. —*Idiom.* **9. get down to brass tacks,** to concentrate on essentials. —**tack'er,** *n.*

tack·le (tak'əl), *n.*, *v.*, -**led,** -**ling.** —*n.* **1.** equipment, esp. for fishing. **2.** any system of leverage using pulleys to hoist, lower, and shift objects. **3.** *Football.* **a.** the act of tackling. **b.** either of the linemen stationed between a guard and an end. —*v.t.* **4.** to undertake to handle, solve, etc. **5.** *Football.* to seize and throw down (a ballcarrier). —**tack'ler,** *n.*

tack'y¹, *adj.*, -**i·er,** -**i·est.** sticky to the touch. —**tack'i·ness,** *n.*

tack'y², *adj.*, -**i·er,** -**i·est. 1.** in poor taste; vulgar. **2.** of poor quality; shoddy. —**tack'i·ness,** *n.*

ta·co (tä'kō), *n.*, *pl.* -**cos.** a fried tortilla folded over and filled with chopped meat, cheese, lettuce, etc.

Ta·co·ma (tə kō'mə), *n.* a seaport in W Washington. 183,060.

tact (takt), *n.* skill in dealing with difficult or delicate situations. —**tact'ful,** *adj.* —**tact'ful·ly,** *adv.* —**tact'less,** *adj.* —**tact'less·ly,** *adv.*

tac·tic (tak'tik), *n.* a method or maneuver to achieve a goal.

tac'tics, *n.* the science of deploying military forces and maneuvering them in battle. —**tac'ti·cal,** *adj.* —**tac·ti'cian** (-tish'ən), *n.*

tac·tile (tak'til, -tīl), *adj.* of or affecting the sense of touch.

tad (tad), *n. Informal.* **1.** a small child. **2.** a small amount or degree.

tad·pole (tad'pōl), *n.* the aquatic larva of frogs and toads.

Ta·dzhik·i·stan (tə jik'ə stan', -stän', -jē'kə-), *n.* TAJIKISTAN.

Tae·gu (tī'gōō'), *n.* a city in SE South Korea. 2,030,649.

taf·fe·ta (taf'i tə), *n.*, *pl* -**tas.** a smooth, crisp, lustrous fabric, as of silk or rayon.

taff·rail (taf'rāl', -rəl), *n.* a rail above the stern of a ship.

taf·fy (taf'ē), *n.*, *pl.* -**fies.** a chewy candy made of sugar or molasses boiled down.

Taft (taft), *n.* **1. Robert A(l·phon·so)** (al fon'sō), 1889–1953, U.S. lawyer and politician (son of William Howard). **2. William Howard,** 1857–1930, 27th president of the U.S. 1909–13.

Taft'-Hart'ley Act' (härt'lē), *n.* an act of the U.S. Congress (1947) that continues most of the provisions of the National Labor Relations Act and that provides for an 80-day injunction against strikes that endanger public safety and bans certain union practices. [after R.A. *Taft* and Fred Allen *Hartley,* Jr., 1902–69, U.S. politician]

tag¹ (tag), *n.*, *v.*, **tagged, tag·ging.** —*n.* **1.** a piece of paper, plastic, etc., attached to something as a marker or label. **2.** any small hanging part. **3.** a hard tip at the end of a shoelace or cord. **4.** a symbol or other label indicating the beginning or end of a unit of information in an electronic document. **5.** a descriptive epithet. —*v.t.* **6.** to furnish with a tag. **7.** to follow closely. —*v.i.* **8.** to follow closely: *to tag along behind someone.* —**tag'ger,** *n.*

tag² (tag), *n.*, *v.*, **tagged, tag·ging.** —*n.* **1.** a children's game in which one player chases the others in an effort to touch one of them, who then becomes the pursuer. —*v.t.* **2.** to touch in or as if in the game of tag. —**tag'ger,** *n.*

Ta·ga·log (tə gä'ləg, -lôg, tä-), *n.*, *pl.* -**log, -logs** for 1. **1.** a member of a people of the Philippines. **2.** the language of the Tagalogs.

tag' sale', *n.* GARAGE SALE.

Ta·hi·ti (tə hē'tē, tä-), *n.* a French island in the S Pacific. 115,820.

Ta·hoe (tä'hō), *n.* **Lake,** a lake in E California and W Nevada.

t'ai chi ch'uan (tī' jē' chwän', chē'), *n.* a Chinese system of meditative exercises, characterized by slow and stylized movements. Also called **tai' chi'.**

tai·ga (tī'gə, tī gä'), *n.*, *pl.* -**gas.** any of the coniferous evergreen forests of subarctic lands.

tail (tāl), *n.* **1.** the hindmost part of an animal, esp. that forming a distinct, flexible appendage. **2.** something resembling this in shape or position. **3.** the reverse of a coin. **4. tails,** men's full-dress attire. **5.** a person who keeps a close surveillance of another. **6.** the bottom or end part of something. —*adj.* **7.** coming from behind: *a tail breeze.* **8.** being in the rear. —*v.t.* **9.** to follow in order to observe. —*v.i.* **10.** to follow close behind. —**tail'less,** *adj.*

tail'gate', *n.*, *v.*, -**gat·ed,** -**gat·ing.** —*n.* **1.** a board or gate at the back of a vehicle that can be removed or let down, as for unloading. —*v.i.*, *v.t.* **2.** to drive hazardously close to the rear of (another vehicle).

tail'light', *n.* a light, usu. red, at the rear of a vehicle.

tai·lor (tā'lər), *n.* **1.** a person whose occupation is the making, mending, or altering of clothes. —*v.t.* **2.** to make by tailor's work. **3.** to fashion or adapt to a particular taste, need, etc. —*v.i.* **4.** to do the work of a tailor.

tail'pipe', *n.* an exhaust pipe at the rear of a motor vehicle.

tail'spin', *n.* **1.** the descent of an aircraft, nosedown, in a helical path. **2.** a sudden collapse into failure or confusion.

taint (tānt), *n.* **1.** a trace of something bad or offensive. **2.** a trace of infection or contamination. —*v.t.* **3.** to affect with something bad or offensive. **4.** to corrupt or contaminate.

Tai·pei (tī'pā', -bā'), *n.* the capital of Taiwan. 2,640,000.

Tai·wan (tī'wän'), *n.* an island off the SE coast of

China. 20,300,000. Also called **Republic of China.** —**Tai/wan•ese/** (-wä nēz', -nēs'), *adj., n., pl.* -ese.

Ta•jik•i•stan (tə jik/ə stan', -stän', -jē/kə-), *n.* a republic in central Asia, N of Afghanistan: formerly a part of the USSR. 6,031,855.

Taj Ma•hal (täzh/ mə häl', täj/), *n.* a white marble mausoleum built at Agra, India, by Shah Jahan (fl. 1628–58).

take (tāk), *v.,* **took, tak•en, tak•ing,** *n.* —*v.t.* **1.** to get into one's possession. **2.** to hold or grasp. **3.** to seize or capture. **4.** to choose or select. **5.** to receive and accept. **6.** to receive into some relation: *to take a wife.* **7.** to react to: *She took his death hard.* **8.** to derive: *The book takes its title from Dante.* **9.** to receive into the body: *to take a pill.* **10.** to undergo or endure. **11.** to carry off or remove. **12.** to subtract. **13.** to carry with one. **14.** to lead. **15.** to escort. **16.** to affect with or as if with a disease: *taken with a fit of laughter.* **17.** to absorb: *The cloth will not take a dye.* **18.** to require: *That takes courage.* **19.** to employ: *to take measures.* **20.** to use as transportation: *to take a bus to work.* **21.** to occupy: *Take a seat.* **22.** to consume: *It took ten minutes.* **23.** to avail oneself of: *I took the opportunity to leave.* **24.** to do, perform, etc.: *to take a walk.* **25.** to make (a reproduction or photograph). **26.** to write down: *to take notes.* **27.** to study: *to take ballet.* **28.** to deal with. **29.** to assume the obligation of: *to take an oath.* **30.** to experience or feel: *to take pride.* **31.** to understand. **32.** to regard or consider. **33.** *Informal.* to cheat or swindle. **34.** to be used with (a certain grammatical form, case, etc.). —*v.i.* **35.** to catch or engage, as a lock. **36.** to begin to grow, as a plant. **37.** to win favor or acceptance. **38.** to have the intended effect: *The vaccination took.* **39.** to make one's way. **40.** to become: *to take sick.* **41. take after,** to resemble. **42. ~ back, a.** to retract. **b.** to regain. **43. ~ down,** to write down. **44. ~ in, a.** to make (a garment) smaller. **b.** to comprehend. **c.** to deceive; cheat. **45. ~ off, a.** to remove. **b.** to leave the ground, as an airplane. **c.** to depart. **d.** to achieve sudden, marked growth, success, etc. **46. ~ on, a.** to hire. **b.** to undertake; assume. **47. ~ over,** to assume management or possession of. —*n.* **48.** the act of taking. **49.** something taken. **50.** *Informal.* money taken in. **51.** a movie or television scene photographed without interruption. **52.** a recording of a musical performance. —**tak/er,** *n.*

take/-no/-pris/oners, *adj.* wholeheartedly aggressive; zealous; gung-ho.

take/off/, *n.* **1.** the leaving of the ground, as in beginning an airplane flight. **2.** a humorous imitation; parody.

take/out/, *adj.* intended to be taken from a restaurant and consumed elsewhere: *takeout meals.*

take/o/ver, *n.* **1.** the act of seizing authority or control. **2.** the acquisition of a corporation through the purchase or exchange of stock.

tak/ing, *n.* **1.** the act of one that takes. **2. takings,** money earned or gained.

talc (talk), *n.* a soft green-to-gray mineral.

tal/cum pow/der (tal/kəm), *n.* a powder for the skin made of purified talc.

tale (tāl), *n.* **1.** a narrative of some real or imaginary incident. **2.** a falsehood; lie. **3.** a malicious rumor.

tale/bear/er, *n.* a person who spreads gossip.

tal•ent (tal/ənt), *n.* **1.** a special, often creative natural ability. **2.** a person or persons with special ability. **3.** any of various ancient units of weight or money. —**tal/ent•ed,** *adj.*

tal•is•man (tal/is mən, -iz-), *n., pl.* **-mans.** an object engraved with figures supposed to possess occult powers, worn as a charm.

talk (tôk), *v.i.* **1.** to exchange ideas or information by speaking. **2.** to consult or confer. **3.** to chatter. **4.** to deliver a speech or lecture. **5.** to give confidential or incriminating information. **6.** to communicate by means other than speech, as by signs. —*v.t.* **7.** to express in words. **8.** to use in speaking: *to talk French.* **9.** to discuss: *to talk politics.* **10.** to drive or influence by talk: *He talked me into going.* **11. talk back,** to

reply disrespectfully. **12. ~ down,** to speak condescendingly. **13. ~ up,** to promote enthusiastically. —*n.* **14.** the act of talking. **15.** an informal speech or lecture. **16.** a conference: *peace talks.* **17.** rumor; gossip. **18.** dialect or lingo. —**talk/er,** *n.*

talk•a•tive (tô/kə tiv), *adj.* inclined to talk a great deal. —**talk/a•tive•ly,** *adv.* —**talk/a•tive•ness,** *n.*

talk/ing-to/, *n., pl.* **-tos.** a scolding.

talk/ show/, *n.* a radio or television show in which a host interviews or chats with guests.

tall (tôl), *adj.,* **-er, -est,** *adv.* —*adj.* **1.** having a relatively great height. **2.** having height as specified: *a man six feet tall.* **3.** exaggerated: *a tall tale.* —*adv.* **4.** in a proud, erect manner: *to stand tall.* —**tall/ness,** *n.*

Tal•la•has•see (tal/ə has/ē), *n.* the capital of Florida. 133,718.

Tal•linn or **-lin** (tä/lin, tal/in), *n.* the capital of Estonia. 499,800.

tal•lith or **tal•lit** (tä/lis), *n., pl.* **tal•li•thim, tal•li•tim** (tä lä/sim, tä/lə sim/). a shawl with fringes at the four corners, worn over the shoulders or head by Jews during prayer.

tallith

tal•low (tal/ō), *n.* the hard, rendered fat of sheep and cattle, used to make candles and soap. —**tal/low•y,** *adj.*

tal•ly (tal/ē), *n., pl.* **-lies,** *v.,* **-lied, -ly•ing.** —*n.* **1.** an account; reckoning. **2.** a stick with notches cut to indicate the amount of a debt or payment. **3.** anything on which a score or account is kept. —*v.t.* **4.** to mark on a tally; record. **5.** to count; reckon. —*v.i.* **6.** to correspond; agree. **7.** to score a point. —**tal/li•er,** *n.*

tal•ly•ho (tal/ē hō/), *interj.* a hunter's cry on sighting the fox.

Tal•mud (täl/mŏŏd, tal/məd), *n.* a collection of ancient Jewish law and tradition. [< Heb: lit., instruction] —**Tal•mud/ic,** *adj.* —**Tal/mud•ist,** *n.*

tal•on (tal/ən), *n.* a claw, esp. of a bird of prey.

ta•lus (tā/ləs), *n., pl.* **-li** (-lī). ANKLEBONE.

tam (tam), *n.* a tam-o'-shanter.

ta•ma•le (tə mä/lē), *n., pl.* **-les.** minced meat packed in cornmeal dough, wrapped in corn husks, and steamed.

Ta•mar (tā/mər, tä/-), *n.* the daughter of David and half-sister of Absalom. II Sam. 13.

tam•a•rack (tam/ə rak/), *n.* **1.** a North American larch. **2.** its wood.

tam•a•rind (tam/ə rind), *n.* **1.** the pod of a tropical tree, containing seeds in a juicy acid pulp. **2.** the tree itself.

tam•bou•rine (tam/bə rēn/), *n.* a small drum with metal jingles attached, played by striking and shaking.

tame (tām), *adj.,* **tam•er, tam•est,** *v.,* **tamed, tam•ing.** —*adj.* **1.** changed from the wild or savage state; domesticated. **2.** docile or submissive. **3.** spiritless; dull. —*v.t.* **4.** to make tame; domesticate. **5.** to deprive of courage or zest. —**tam/a•ble, tame/a•ble,** *adj.* —**tame/ly,** *adv.* —**tame/ness,** *n.* —**tam/er,** *n.*

Tam•il (tam/əl, tum/-, tä/məl), *n.* **1.** a member of a people living mainly in S India and N and E Sri Lanka. **2.** the language of the Tamils.

Tam′ma•ny Hall′ (tam′ə nē), *n.* a Democratic political organization in New York City, founded in 1789 and associated with corruption and abuse of power.

tam-o′-shan•ter (tam′ə shan′tər), *n.* a cap of Scottish origin, having a round, flat top with a pompom.

tamp (tamp), *v.t.* to pack in tightly by light strokes.

Tam•pa (tam′pə), *n.* a seaport in W central Florida. 285,523. —**Tam′pan,** *n., adj.*

tam•per (tam′pər), *v.i.* **1.** to meddle: *to tamper with a lock.* **2.** to alter improperly: *to tamper with a passport.* **3.** to engage in underhand dealings: *to tamper with a jury.* —**tam′per•er,** *n.*

tam•pon (tam′pon), *n.* a plug of cotton or the like for insertion into a wound or body cavity for absorbing blood.

tan (tan), *v.,* **tanned, tan•ning,** *n., adj.,* **tan•ner, tan•nest.** —*v.t.* **1.** to convert (a hide) into leather. **2.** to brown by exposure to the sun. **3.** to thrash; spank. —*v.i.* **4.** to become tanned. —*n.* **5.** a brown color imparted to the skin by the sun. **6.** a yellowish brown. —*adj.* **7.** yellowish brown.

tan•a•ger (tan′ə jər), *n.* any of numerous New World songbirds, the males of which are usu. brightly colored.

tan′bark′, *n.* the bark of the oak, hemlock, etc., used in tanning hides.

tan•dem (tan′dəm), *adv.* **1.** one following or behind the other. —*n.* **2.** a bicycle for two persons, one behind the other. **3.** a two-wheeled carriage drawn by horses harnessed tandem.

tang (tang), *n.* **1.** a strong taste, flavor, or odor. **2.** a projection from an object, as a knife, serving as attachment for a handle.

Tan•gan•yi•ka (tan′gən yē′kə), *n.* a former country in E Africa: now part of Tanzania.

tan•ge•lo (tan′jə lō′), *n., pl.* **-los.** a fruit that is a cross between a grapefruit and a tangerine.

tan•gent (tan′jənt), *n.* **1.** a line or plane that touches but does not intersect a curve or surface. —*adj.* **2.** in physical contact; touching. **3.** touching at a single point or along a line. —*Idiom.* **4. off on a tangent,** changing suddenly from one course of action or thought to another. —**tan•gen′tial** (-jen′shəl), *adj.*

tan•ge•rine (tan′jə rēn′), *n.* any of several varieties of mandarin, cultivated widely, esp. in the U.S.

tan•gi•ble (tan′jə bəl), *adj.* **1.** capable of being touched. **2.** real or actual. **3.** (of an asset) having physical existence and capable of being appraised. —*n.* **4.** something tangible, esp. a tangible asset. —**tan′gi•bil′i•ty,** *n.* —**tan′gi•bly,** *adv.*

Tan•gier (tan jēr′) also **-giers′,** *n.* a seaport in N Morocco. 266,346.

tan•gle (tang′gəl), *v.,* **-gled, -gling,** *n.* —*v.t.* **1.** to bring together into a confused mass of strands. **2.** to catch in or as if in a snare. —*v.i.* **3.** to become tangled. **4.** to come into conflict. —*n.* **5.** a tangled condition or situation. **6.** a tangled mass.

tan•go (tang′gō), *n., pl.* **-gos,** *v.,* **-goed, -go•ing.** —*n.* **1.** a dramatic ballroom dance of Latin-American origin. **2.** music for this dance. —*v.i.* **3.** to dance the tango. —*Proverb.* **4. It takes two to tango,** some activities require a partner. [< AmSp]

tank (tangk), *n.* **1.** a large container for holding a liquid or gas. **2.** an armored combat vehicle, moving on treads and armed with a cannon. —**tank′ful,** *n., pl.* **-fuls.**

tan•kard (tang′kərd), *n.* a large drinking cup with a handle and hinged cover.

tank′er, *n.* a ship, airplane, or truck designed for bulk shipment of liquids or gases.

tank′ top′, *n.* a sleeveless pullover shirt with shoulder straps.

tan′ner, *n.* a person whose occupation is the tanning of hides.

tan′ner•y, *n., pl.* **-ner•ies.** a place where tanning is carried on.

tan•nin (tan′in), *n.* any of a group of astringent vegetable compounds, as the compound that gives the tanning properties to oak bark. Also called **tan′nic ac′id.**

tan•sy (tan′zē), *n., pl.* **-sies.** a strong-scented, weedy herb with yellow flowers.

tan•ta•lize (tan′tl īz′), *v.t.,* **-lized, -liz•ing.** to torment with the sight or prospect of something desired but out of reach. —**tan′ta•li•za′tion,** *n.* —**tan′ta•liz′er,** *n.*

tan•ta•lum (tan′tl əm), *n.* a hard, rare metallic element that resists corrosion, used for chemical and surgical instruments. *Symbol:* Ta; *at. wt.:* 180.948; *at. no.:* 73.

Tan•ta•lus (tan′tl əs), *n., pl.* **-lus•es.** (in Greek myth) a king who was condemned to remain in Tartarus, chin deep in water, with fruit-laden branches above his head: whenever he tried to drink or eat, the water and fruit receded out of reach.

tan•ta•mount (tan′tə mount′), *adj.* equivalent, as in value or effect.

tan•trum (tan′trəm), *n.* a sudden burst of ill temper.

Tan•za•ni•a (tan′zə nē′ə), *n.* a republic in E Africa. 29,460,753. —**Tan′za•ni′an,** *n., adj.*

Tao•ism (dou′iz əm, tou′-), *n.* a Chinese philosophical tradition advocating a life of simplicity and noninterference with the course of natural events. —**Tao′ist,** *n., adj.*

tap¹ (tap), *v.,* **tapped, tap•ping,** *n.* —*v.t.* **1.** to strike or touch lightly. **2.** to make, put, etc., by tapping: *to tap a nail into a wall.* —*v.i.* **3.** to strike lightly. —*n.* **4.** a light but audible blow. **5.** the sound made by this. **6.** a piece of metal attached to the toe or heel of a shoe. —**tap′per,** *n.*

tap² (tap), *n., v.,* **tapped, tap•ping.** —*n.* **1.** a cylindrical stopper for closing an opening, as in a cask. **2.** a faucet. **3.** a connection made at an intermediate point on an electrical circuit. **4.** an act or instance of wiretapping. **5.** the surgical withdrawal of fluid: *a spinal tap.* **6.** a tool for cutting screw threads inside a hole. —*v.t.* **7.** to draw liquid from (a container). **8.** to draw off (liquid). **9.** to draw upon: *to tap resources.* **10.** to wiretap. **11.** to furnish with a tap. **12.** to cut a screw thread inside (a hole).

tap′ dance′, *n.* a dance in which the rhythm is made audible by taps on the dancer's shoes. —**tap′ dance′,** *v.i.,* **-danced, -danc•ing.** —**tap′-danc′er,** *n.*

tape (tāp), *n., v.,* **taped, tap•ing.** —*n.* **1.** a long, narrow strip of fabric, paper, metal, etc. **2.** a strip of material with an adhesive surface, used for sealing, binding, etc. **3.** a magnetic tape. —*v.t.* **4.** to tie up, bind, or attach with tape. **5.** to record on magnetic tape.

tape′ deck′, *n.* a component of an audio system for playing tapes.

tape′ meas′ure, *n.* a tape marked with subdivisions of the foot or meter and used for measuring.

ta•per (tā′pər), *v.t., v.i.* **1.** to make or become smaller or thinner toward one end. **2. taper off,** to decrease gradually. —*n.* **3.** gradual diminution of width or thickness. **4.** a slender candle.

tape′ record′er, *n.* an electrical device for recording or playing back sound recorded on magnetic tape. —**tape′-record′,** *v.t.* —**tape′ record′ing,** *n.*

tap•es•try (tap′ə strē), *n., pl.* **-tries.** a heavy, decorative, woven fabric used esp. for wall hangings.

tape′worm′, *n.* a long, flat worm that is parasitic in the digestive system of vertebrates.

tap•i•o•ca (tap′ē ō′kə), *n.* a cassava preparation used in puddings and as a thickener.

ta•pir (tā′pər, tə pēr′), *n., pl.* **-pirs, -pir.** a stout, hoofed mammal of tropical America and SE Asia.

tap′room′, *n.* a barroom.

tap′root′, *n.* a main root descending downward and giving off small lateral roots.

taps, *n.* (*used with a sing. or pl. v.*) a bugle signal sounded at night as an order to extinguish lights, and sometimes at a military funeral.

tar (tär), *n., v.,* **tarred, tar•ring.** —*n.* **1.** a dark, sticky product obtained by the destructive distillation of certain organic substances, as coal or wood. **2.** smoke solids or components: *cigarette tar.* —*v.t.* **3.** to smear or cover with tar.

ta·ran·tu·la (tə ran′chə lə), *n.*, *pl.* **-las, -lae** (-lē′). a large, hairy spider with a painful but not highly venomous bite.

tarantula

tar·dy (tär′dē), *adj.*, **-di·er, -di·est. 1.** late; not on time. **2.** moving or acting slowly. —**tar′di·ly,** *adv.* —**tar′di·ness,** *n.*

tare (târ), *n.* **1.** any of various vetches, esp. *Vicia sativa.* **2.** (in the Bible) a noxious weed. Matt. 13:25–30.

tar·get (tär′git), *n.* **1.** an object, usu. marked with concentric circles, to be aimed at in shooting practice or contests. **2.** anything fired at. **3.** a goal or aim. **4.** an object of abuse, scorn, etc. —*v.t.* **5.** to make a target of.

tar·iff (tar′if), *n.* **1.** a schedule of duties imposed by a government on imports or exports. **2.** a duty or rate of duty in such a schedule. **3.** any table of charges or fares.

tar·nish (tär′nish), *v.t.* **1.** to dull the luster of (a metallic surface). **2.** to sully or disgrace. —*v.i.* **3.** to become tarnished. —*n.* **4.** a dull coating caused by tarnishing.

ta·ro (tär′ō, târ′ō, tar′ō), *n.*, *pl.* **-ros.** a stemless tropical plant cultivated for its edible tuber. [< Polynesian]

ta·rot (tar′ō, ta rō′), *n.* any of a set of 22 playing cards used for fortune-telling.

tar·pau·lin (tär pô′lin, tär′pə lin), *n.* a sheet of waterproofed material used as a protective covering.

tar·pon (tär′pən), *n.*, *pl.* **-pons, -pon.** a powerful game fish of warm Atlantic waters.

tar·ra·gon (tar′ə gon′, -gən), *n.* an Old World plant with aromatic leaves used for seasoning.

tar·ry (tar′ē), *v.i.* **-ried, -ry·ing. 1.** to stay in a place. **2.** to delay in acting, starting, etc. —**tar′ri·er,** *n.*

Tar·shish (tär′shish), *n.* an ancient country of uncertain location mentioned in the Bible. I Kings 10:22.

Tar·sus (tär′səs), *n.* a city in S Turkey: birthplace of Saint Paul. 121,074.

tart¹ (tärt), *adj.*, **-er, -est. 1.** sharp to the taste. **2.** sharp in character or expression. —**tart′ly,** *adv.* —**tart′ness,** *n.*

tart² (tärt), *n.* a small pie without a top crust, filled with fruit or custard.

tar·tan (tär′tn), *n.* a woolen cloth woven with stripes crossing at right angles, worn chiefly by the Scottish Highlanders.

tar·tar (tär′tər), *n.* **1.** a hard, yellowish deposit on the teeth. **2.** a sediment that collects in wine casks, consisting chiefly of cream of tartar. —**tar·tar′ic** (-tar′ik, -tär′-), *adj.*

Tar′tar, *n.* **1.** a member of any of various Mongolian and Turkic peoples who ruled parts of W Asia and E Europe until the 18th century. **2.** TATAR (defs. 1, 2).

tar′tar sauce′, *n.* a mayonnaise sauce containing chopped pickles, onions, etc.

Tash·kent (täsh kent′, tash-), *n.* the capital of Uzbekistan. 2,073,000.

task (task, täsk), *n.* **1.** any piece of work. **2.** a matter of considerable difficulty. —*v.t.* **3.** to put a strain on. —*Idiom.* **4. take to task,** to reprimand; censure.

task′ force′, *n.* a group, esp. of military units, for carrying out a specific task or operation.

task′mas·ter, *n.* a person who assigns tasks, esp. burdensome ones, to others.

Tas·ma·ni·a (taz mā′nē ə), *n.* an island S of and belonging to Australia. —**Tas·ma′ni·an,** *adj.*, *n.*

tas·sel (tas′əl), *n.* **1.** a pendent ornament consisting of threads or cords hanging from a roundish knob. **2.**

something resembling this, as at the top of a cornstalk.

taste (tāst), *v.*, **tast·ed, tast·ing,** *n.* —*v.t.* **1.** to test the flavor of by taking some into the mouth. **2.** to eat or drink a little of. **3.** to perceive the flavor of. **4.** to experience slightly. —*v.i.* **5.** to have a particular flavor. —*n.* **6.** the sense by which the flavor of things is perceived when brought into contact with the tongue. **7.** the quality so perceived; flavor. **8.** the act of tasting. **9.** a small quantity tasted. **10.** a partiality for something: *a taste for music.* **11.** a sense of what is proper, harmonious, or beautiful. **12.** a slight experience of something. —**tast′er,** *n.*

taste′ bud′, *n.* one of numerous small bodies, chiefly in the tongue, that are the organs for the sense of taste.

taste′ful, *adj.* having or displaying good taste. —**taste′ful·ly,** *adv.*

taste′less, *adj.* **1.** having no flavor. **2.** having or displaying bad taste. —**taste′less·ly,** *adv.*

tast′y, *adj.*, **-i·er, -i·est.** good-tasting; savory. —**tast′i·ness,** *n.*

tat (tat), *v.i.*, *v.t.*, **tat·ted, tat·ting.** to do or make by tatting. —**tat′ter,** *n.*

ta·ta·mi (tə tä′mē), *n.*, *pl.* **-mi, -mis.** a thick, woven straw mat used in Japanese houses as a floor covering.

Ta·tar (tä′tər), *n.* **1.** a member of a Turkic-speaking people living chiefly in E European Russia. **2.** the language of this people. **3.** TARTAR (def. 1).

tat·ter (tat′ər), *n.* **1.** a torn, loosely hanging piece, as of a garment. **2.** tatters, torn or ragged clothing. —*v.t.*, *v.i.* **3.** to make or become ragged.

tat′ter·de·mal′ion (-di mäl′yən), *n.* a person in tattered clothing.

tat′ting, *n.* **1.** the act or process of making a kind of knotted lace. **2.** such lace.

tat·tle (tat′l), *v.*, **-tled, -tling.** —*v.i.* **1.** to tell something secret about another. **2.** to chatter or gossip. —*v.t.* **3.** to disclose by gossiping. —**tat′tler,** *n.*

tat′tle·tale′, *n.* a person who tattles.

tat·too¹ (ta tōō′), *n.*, *pl.* **-toos. 1.** a bugle call or other signal ordering soldiers to their quarters. **2.** a knocking or strong pulsation.

tat·too² (ta tōō′), *n.*, *pl.* **-toos,** *v.*, **-tooed, -too·ing.** —*n.* **1.** an indelible design made on the skin by puncturing it and inserting pigments. —*v.t.* **2.** to mark with tattoos. **3.** to put (tattoos) on the skin. —**tat·too′er, tat·too′ist,** *n.*

tau (tou, tô), *n.*, *pl.* **taus.** the 19th letter of the Greek alphabet (T, τ).

taught (tôt), *v.* pt. and pp. of TEACH.

taunt (tônt, tänt), *v.t.* **1.** to reproach in a sarcastic or insulting manner. —*n.* **2.** a scornful or sarcastic remark. —**taunt′er,** *n.* —**taunt′ing·ly,** *adv.*

taupe (tōp), *n.* a dark brownish gray.

Tau·rus (tôr′əs), *n.* the second sign of the zodiac. [< L: bull]

taut (tôt), *adj.*, **-er, -est. 1.** tightly drawn, as a rope. **2.** emotionally tense. **3.** tidy or neat, as a ship. —**taut′ly,** *adv.* —**taut′ness,** *n.*

tau·tol·o·gy (tô tol′ə jē), *n.*, *pl.* **-gies. 1.** needless repetition of an idea in different words. **2.** an instance of such repetition. —**tau·to·log′i·cal** (tôt′l-oj′i kəl), *adj.*

tav·ern (tav′ərn), *n.* a place where liquors are sold to be consumed on the premises. [< OF < L *taberna* hut, inn, shop]

taw·dry (tô′drē), *adj.*, **-dri·er, -dri·est.** showy and cheap; gaudy; tasteless. —**taw′dri·ness,** *n.*

taw·ny (tô′nē), *adj.*, **-ni·er, -ni·est.** of a yellowish brown color.

tax (taks), *n.* **1.** a sum of money levied on incomes, property, etc., by a government for its support. **2.** a burdensome charge or demand. —*v.t.* **3.** to impose a tax on. **4.** to burden or strain. **5.** to reprove or accuse. —**tax′a·ble,** *adj.* —**tax·a′tion,** *n.* —**tax′er,** *n.*

taxa′tion without′ representa′tion, a phrase that reflected the resentment of American colonists at being taxed by a British Parliament without elected representatives.

tax•i (tak′sē), *n.*, *pl.* **tax•is**, *v.*, **tax•ied, tax•i•ing** or **tax•y•ing.** —*n.* **1.** a taxicab. —*v.i.* **2.** to ride in a taxicab. **3.** (of an airplane) to move on the ground or water, as in preparing for takeoff.

tax′i•cab′, *n.* a public passenger automobile for hire.

tax•i•der•my (tak′si dûr′mē), *n.* the art of preserving, stuffing, and mounting the skins of animals in lifelike form. —**tax′i•der′mist,** *n.*

tax•on•o•my (tak son′ə mē), *n.* the science or technique of classification, esp. of organisms. —**tax′o•nom′ic** (-sə nom′ik), *adj.* —**tax•on′o•mist,** *n.*

tax′pay′er, *n.* a person who pays a tax. —**tax′pay′ing,** *adj.*

tax′ revolt′, *n.* a movement by taxpayers to rescind increases in property taxes.

tax′ shel′ter, *n.* any financial arrangement, as an investment, that reduces or eliminates the taxes due. —**tax′-shel′tered,** *adj.*

Tay•lor (tā′lər), *n.* **1. Maxwell (Davenport),** 1901–87, U.S. army general. **2. Paul (Belville),** born 1930, U.S. choreographer. **3. Zachary** (*"Old Rough and Ready"*), 1784–1850, 12th president of the U.S. 1849–50.

TB or **T.B.,** tuberculosis.

Tb, *Chem. Symbol.* terbium.

T-ball (tē′bôl′), *n.* a modified form of baseball or softball in which the ball is batted off an adjustable pole or stand.

Tbi•li•si (tə bə lē′sē, -bil′ə-), *n.* the capital of the Georgian Republic. 1,194,000.

T-bone steak (tē′bōn′), *n.* a loin steak with a small piece of tenderloin, characterized by its T-shaped bone.

tbs. or **tbsp., 1.** tablespoon. **2.** tablespoonful.

Tc, *Chem. Symbol.* technetium.

T cell, *n.* any of several closely related lymphocytes that regulate the immune system's response to infected or malignant cells.

Tchai•kov•sky (chī kôf′skē, -kof′-, chi-), *n.* **Peter Ilyich** or **Pëtr Ilich,** 1840–93, Russian composer.

TD, touchdown.

Te, *Chem. Symbol.* tellurium.

tea (tē), *n.* **1.** the dried leaves of an evergreen Asian shrub. **2.** the shrub itself. **3.** a beverage prepared by infusing tea leaves in boiling water. **4.** any similar beverage prepared from other plants. **5.** a light meal or social gathering in the afternoon at which tea is usu. served. [< dialectal Chin]

Tea′ Act′, *n.* an act of the British Parliament (1773) that created a monopoly unfair to American tea merchants: the chief cause of the Boston Tea Party.

teach (tēch), *v.,* **taught, teach•ing.** —*v.t.* **1.** to give instruction in. **2.** to impart knowledge or skill to; give instruction to. **3.** to help to learn, as by example. —*v.i.* **4.** to give instruction. —**teach′a•ble,** *adj.*

teach′er, *n.* a person who teaches, esp. as a profession.

teach′ing, *n.* **1.** the act or profession of a person who teaches. **2.** Often, **-ings.** something taught, esp. a doctrine.

tea′cup′, *n.* **1.** a cup in which tea is served. **2.** a teacupful.

teak (tēk), *n.* **1.** a large East Indian tree yielding a hard, medium brown wood. **2.** its wood.

tea′ket′tle, *n.* a kettle with a cover, spout, and handle, used for boiling water.

teal (tēl), *n.*, *pl.* **teals** or, for 1, **teal. 1.** any of several small freshwater ducks. **2.** a medium to dark greenish blue.

team (tēm), *n.* **1.** a number of persons forming a side in a game or contest. **2.** a number of persons associated in some joint action. **3.** two or more draft animals harnessed together. —*v.i.* **4.** to join in a team. —*adj.* **5.** of or performed by a team.

team′mate′, *n.* a member of the same team.

team′ster (-stər), *n.* a person who drives a team or a truck for hauling.

team′work′, *n.* cooperative effort by a group of persons acting together as a team.

tea′pot′, *n.* a container with a lid, spout, and handle, in which tea is made.

Tea′pot Dome′, *n.* a federal oil reserve in Wyoming: the source of a major scandal in President Warren G. Harding's administration (1921–23).

tear¹ (tēr), *n.* **1.** a drop of the saline, watery fluid lubricating the eye and sometimes flowing from it, as in crying. —*v.i.* **2.** (of the eyes) to fill up with tears. —*Idiom.* **3.** in tears, weeping. —**tear′ful,** *adj.* —**tear′ful•ly,** *adv.* —**tear′y,** *adj.,* **-i•er, -i•est.**

tear² (târ), *v.,* **tore, torn, tear•ing,** *n.* —*v.t.* **1.** to pull apart or in pieces by force. **2.** to divide or disrupt. **3.** to produce by tearing. **4.** to injure by or as if by tearing. **5.** to remove by force or effort. —*v.i.* **6.** to become torn. **7.** to move with force, haste, or energy. **8. tear down,** to pull down; demolish. —*n.* **9.** the act of tearing. **10.** a rip or hole. —**tear′a•ble,** *adj.* —**tear′er,** *n.*

tear′drop′ (tēr′-), *n.* TEAR¹.

tear′ gas′ (tēr), *n.* a gas that makes the eyes smart and water. —**tear′-gas′,** *v.t.,* **-gassed, -gas•sing.**

tear•jerk•er (tēr′jûr′kər), *n. Informal.* a sentimental story, play, etc., designed to elicit tears.

Teas•dale (tēz′dāl′), *n.* **Sara,** 1884–1933, U.S. poet.

tease (tēz), *v.,* **teased, teas•ing,** *n.* —*v.t.* **1.** to irritate with taunts, mockery, pretended offers, etc., often in sport. **2.** to comb or card (wool). **3.** to comb (the hair) toward the scalp so as to give body to a hairdo. —*v.i.* **4.** to tease a person or animal. —*n.* **5.** a person who teases. —**teas′er,** *n.* —**teas′ing•ly,** *adv.*

tea•sel (tē′zəl), *n.* **1.** a plant with prickly leaves and flower heads. **2.** the dried flower head, or a mechanical device, used for raising a nap on cloth.

tea′spoon′, *n.* **1.** a small spoon used to stir tea, eat desserts, etc. **2.** a cooking measure equal to ⅙ fluid ounce (4.9 ml). —**tea′spoon•ful′,** *n., pl.* **-fuls.**

teat (tēt, tit), *n.* the nipple on a breast or udder.

tech., 1. technical. **2.** technology.

tech•ne•ti•um (tek nē′shē əm, -shəm), *n.* a synthetic element obtained in the fission of uranium or by the bombardment of molybdenum. *Symbol:* Tc; *at. wt.:* 99; *at. no.:* 43.

tech•ni•cal (tek′ni kəl), *adj.* **1.** of or characteristic of an art, science, or trade. **2.** of or showing technique. **3.** concerned with the mechanical or industrial arts and the applied sciences. **4.** considered so by a stringent interpretation of the rules. —**tech′ni•cal•ly,** *adv.*

tech′ni•cal′i•ty, *n., pl.* **-ties. 1.** a technical point or detail. **2.** technical character.

tech′nical ser′geant, *n.* a noncommissioned officer in the U.S. Air Force ranking above a staff sergeant.

tech•ni′cian (-nish′ən), *n.* a person skilled in the technique of an art or science.

Tech′ni•col′or, *Trademark.* a system of making color motion pictures.

tech•nique′ (-nēk′), *n.* **1.** the manner in which a person employs technical skills. **2.** technical procedures and methods. **3.** any method used to accomplish something.

tech•noc′ra•cy (-nok′rə sē), *n., pl.* **-cies.** government by technological experts. —**tech′no•crat′** (-nə-krat′), *n.*

tech•nol′o•gy (-nol′ə jē), *n., pl.* **-gies. 1.** the branch of knowledge that deals with applied science, engineering, etc. **2.** the practical application of knowledge. **3.** the materials, techniques, etc., used for a practical end. —**tech′no•log′i•cal** (-nə loj′i-kəl), *adj.* —**tech′no•log′i•cal•ly,** *adv.* —**tech•nol′o•gist,** *n.*

tech•no-thrill•er (tek′nō thril′ər), *n.* a suspense novel in which the manipulation of sophisticated technology plays a prominent part.

tec•ton•ics (tek ton′iks), *n.* the branch of geology that studies the forces that cause the earth's crust to be deformed.

ted′dy bear′, *n.* a stuffed toy bear.

Te De•um (tā dā′ŏŏm, -əm, tē dē′əm), *n.* a Christian hymn of praise to God, composed in Latin c400.

[< LL, the first two words of the hymn (*Tē Deum laudāmus* we praise thee God)]

te·di·ous (tē′dē əs, tē′jəs), *adj.* long and tiresome. —**te′di·ous·ly,** *adv.* —**te′di·ous·ness,** *n.*

te·di·um (tē′dē əm), *n.* the quality or state of being tedious.

tee (tē), *n., v.,* teed, tee·ing. —*n. Golf.* 1. the area from which the first stroke on each hole is played. 2. a small peg from which the ball is driven. —*v.t.* 3. to place (a ball) on a tee. 4. tee off, a. to strike a ball from a tee. b. *Slang.* to make angry.

teem (tēm), *v.i.* to abound or swarm.

teen (tēn), *adj.* 1. teenage. —*n.* 2. a teenager.

teen′age′, *adj.* of, being, or like people in their teens. —**teen′ag′er,** *n.*

teens, *n.pl.* 1. the numbers 13 through 19. 2. the ages of 13 to 19 inclusive.

tee·ny (tē′nē), *adj.,* -ni·er, -ni·est. TINY.

tee·pee (tē′pē), *n., pl.* -pees. TEPEE.

teepee

tee′ shirt′, *n.* T-SHIRT.

tee·ter (tē′tər), *v.i.* 1. to move unsteadily. 2. to waver.

teeth (tēth), *n.* pl. of TOOTH.

teethe (tēth), *v.i.* to grow teeth; cut one's teeth.

tee·to·tal·er (tē tōt′l ər, tē′tōt′-), *n.* a person who abstains totally from intoxicating drink. Also, *esp. Brit.,* **tee·to′tal·ler.**

Tef·lon (tef′lon), 1. *Trademark.* a polymer with nonsticking properties, used for cookware coatings. —*adj.* 2. characterized by imperviousness to blame or criticism: *a Teflon politician.*

Te·gu·ci·gal·pa (tə gōō′si gal′pə, -gäl′pä), *n.* the capital of Honduras. 604,600.

Te·haph·ne·hes (ti haf′ni hēz′) also **Tah·pan·hes** (tä′pən hēz′), *n.* a city in eastern Egypt that was a refuge for the Jews. Jer. 2:16; Ezek. 30:18.

Te·he·ran or **Teh·ran** (te ran′, -rän′, tā′ə-), *n.* the capital of Iran. 6,042,584.

Te·ja·no (tā hä′nō, tə-), *n.* a style of Mexican-American popular music that features the accordion and blends the polka with various forms of traditional Mexican music, often including synthesizers and rock music.

Te·ko·a or **Te·ko·ah** (ti kō′ə), *n.* the home of the prophet Amos. Amos. 1:1.

tek·tite (tek′tīt), *n.* a small glassy body of mysterious origin, found on land and beneath the sea.

tel., 1. telegram. 2. telegraph. 3. telephone.

Tel A·viv (tel′ ə vēv′), *n.* a city in W central Israel. 317,800.

tele-, a combining form meaning: at or over a distance (*telegraph*); of or by television (*telecast*).

tel·e·cast (tel′i kast′, -käst′), *v.,* -cast or -cast·ed, -cast·ing, *n.* —*v.t., v.i.* 1. to broadcast by television. —*n.* 2. a television broadcast. —**tel′e·cast′er,** *n.*

tel′e·com·mu′ni·ca′tions, *n.* the science and technology of transmitting information over great distances in the form of electromagnetic signals.

tel·e·com·mut·ing (tel′i kə myōō′ting), *n.* the act or practice of working at home using a computer terminal electronically linked to one's place of employment. —**tel′e·com·mut′er,** *n.*

tel′e·con′fer·ence, *n.* a conference of participants in different locations via telecommunications equipment.

tel′e·gen′ic (-jen′ik), *adj.* having physical qualities that televise well.

tel′e·gram′, *n.* a message sent by telegraph.

tel′e·graph′, *n.* 1. a system or apparatus for transmitting messages over a distance by coded electrical signals sent by wire or radio. —*v.t., v.i.* 2. to transmit (a message) to (a person) by telegraph. —**te·leg·ra·pher** (tə leg′rə fər), *n.* —**tel′e·graph′ic,** *adj.*

te·leg·ra·phy (tə leg′rə fē), *n.* the construction or operation of telegraphs.

tel·e·ki·ne·sis (tel′i ki nē′sis, -kī-), *n.* the purported ability to move inanimate objects by mental power.

tel′e·mar′ket·ing, *n.* selling or advertising by telephone.

te·lem·e·ter (tə lem′i tər, tel′ə mē′-), *n.* an electronic device used to transmit data from a distant source, esp. from space to a ground station. —**te·lem′e·try,** *n.*

te·lep·a·thy (tə lep′ə thē), *n.* communication between minds by some means other than sensory perception. —**tel·e·path·ic** (tel′ə path′ik), *adj.* —**tel′e·path′i·cal·ly,** *adv.*

tel·e·phone (tel′ə fōn′), *n., v.,* -phoned, -phon·ing. —*n.* 1. an apparatus or system for transmission of sound to a distant point, esp. by an electric device. —*v.t., v.i.* 2. to send (a message) to (a person) by telephone. —**tel′e·phon′er,** *n.*

tel′ephone tag′, *n.* repeated unsuccessful attempts by two persons to connect with one another by telephone.

te·leph·o·ny (tə lef′ə nē), *n.* the construction or operation of telephones.

tel·e·pho·to (tel′ə fō′tō), *adj.* noting a lens that produces a large image of a small or distant object.

tel′e·scope′, *n., v.,* -scoped, -scop·ing. —*n.* 1. an optical instrument for making distant objects appear larger and therefore nearer. —*v.t., v.i.* 2. to force or slide together in the manner of the sliding tubes of a jointed telescope. 3. to condense or become condensed.

tel′e·thon′ (-thon′), *n.* a lengthy television broadcast, usu. to raise money for a charity.

Tel′e·type′, *Trademark.* a brand of teletypewriter.

tel′e·type′writ′er, *n.* a telegraphic apparatus by which a message is typed on a typewriterlike instrument and printed by a distant instrument.

tel·e·van·ge·list (tel′i van′jə list), *n.* an evangelist who regularly conducts religious services on television. —**tel′e·van′ge·lism,** *n.*

tel·e·vise (tel′ə vīz′), *v.t., v.i.,* -vised, -vis·ing. to broadcast by television.

tel′e·vi′sion, *n.* 1. the broadcasting of images via radio waves to receivers that project them on a picture tube or screen. 2. a set for receiving television broadcasts. 3. the television broadcasting industry.

tel·ex (tel′eks), *n.* 1. (*sometimes cap.*) a teletypewriter service channeled through a public telecommunications system. 2. a message transmitted by telex. —*v.t.* 3. to send by telex. [*tel(etypewriter) ex(-change)*]

tell (tel), *v.,* told, tell·ing. —*v.t.* 1. to narrate or relate. 2. to express in words. 3. to reveal or divulge. 4. to discern or recognize: *to tell twins apart.* 5. to inform: *He told me his name.* 6. to order or command. —*v.i.* 7. to give an account. 8. to produce a marked effect. 9. tell off, to rebuke severely. 10. ~ on, to tattle on. —*Idiom.* 11. tell it like it is, *Informal.* to be blunt and forthright. 12. tell tales out of school, to betray a confidence.

Tell (tel), *n.* William, WILLIAM TELL.

tell′er, *n.* 1. a person employed in a bank to receive or pay out money. 2. one that tells; narrator.

tell′ing, *adj.* 1. having force or effect. 2. revealing. —**tell′ing·ly,** *adv.*

tell′tale′, *adj.* revealing what is not intended to be known.

tel·lu·ri·um (te lŏŏr′ē əm), *n.* a rare, crystalline,

silver-white element, used in making alloys. *Symbol:* Te; *at. wt.:* 127.60; *at. no.:* 52.

tel•ly (tel′ē), *n.,* *pl.* **-lies.** *Chiefly Brit.* TELEVISION.

te•mer•i•ty (tə mer′i tē), *n.* reckless boldness.

temp (temp), *n. Informal.* **1.** a temporary. —*v.i.* **2.** to work as a temporary.

temp., **1.** temperature. **2.** temporary.

Tem•pe (tem′pē), *n.* a city in central Arizona. 144,289.

tem•per (tem′pər), *n.* **1.** a state of mind or feelings. **2.** heat of mind or passion, shown in outbursts of anger. **3.** calm disposition: *lost his temper.* **4.** the degree of hardness and strength imparted to a metal. —*v.t.* **5.** to moderate: *to temper justice with mercy.* **6.** to make suitable by or as if by blending. **7.** to impart hardness and strength to (metal) by heating and cooling.

tem•per•a (tem′pər ə), *n.* a technique of painting in which an emulsion of water and egg or of egg and oil is used as a medium.

tem•per•a•ment (tem′pər ə mənt, -prə mənt), *n.* **1.** the combination of mental and emotional traits of a person; nature. **2.** personal nature that is unusually emotional or unpredictable. —**tem′per•a•men′tal** (-men′tl), *adj.*

tem•per•ance (tem′pər əns), *n.* **1.** moderation or self-restraint. **2.** total abstinence from alcoholic liquors.

tem•per•ate (-pər it), *adj.* **1.** showing or characterized by temperance. **2.** moderate in respect to temperature. —**tem′per•ate•ly,** *adv.* —**tem′per•ate•ness,** *n.*

Tem′perate Zone′, *n.* the part of the earth between the tropic of Cancer and the Arctic Circle or between the tropic of Capricorn and the Antarctic Circle.

tem′per•a•ture (-pər ə chər, -prə-), *n.* **1.** a measure of the warmth or coldness of an object or substance. **2. a.** the degree of heat in a living body. **b.** a level of such heat above the normal; fever.

tem′pered, *adj.* **1.** having a specified temper: *eventempered.* **2.** having the desired degree of hardness: *tempered steel.*

tem•pest (tem′pist), *n.* a violent windstorm, esp. one with rain.

tem•pes′tu•ous (-pes′chŏō əs), *adj.* tumultuous; stormy. —**tem•pes′tu•ous•ly,** *adv.* —**tem•pes′tu•ous•ness,** *n.*

tem•plate (tem′plit), *n.* a pattern, mold, or the like, as a thin plate of metal, serving as a gauge or guide in mechanical work.

tem•ple¹ (tem′pəl), *n.* **1.** a building dedicated to the worship of a deity or deities. **2.** (*usu. cap.*) any of the houses of worship in Jerusalem in use by the Jews in Biblical times. **3.** any place or object in which God dwells. I Cor. 6:19. **4.** any large or pretentious public building.

tem•ple² (tem′pəl), *n.* the region of the face that lies on either side of the forehead.

Tem•ple (tem′pəl), *n.* **Shirley** (*Shirley Temple Black*), born 1928, U.S. film actress and diplomat.

tem•po (tem′pō), *n.,* *pl.* **-pos, -pi** (-pē). **1.** the rate of speed of a musical passage or work. **2.** any characteristic rate or rhythm: *the tempo of city life.* [< It < L *tempus* time]

tem•po•ral¹ (tem′pər əl), *adj.* **1.** pertaining to time. **2.** pertaining to the present life; worldly. **3.** temporary or transitory. **4.** secular. —**tem′po•ral•ly,** *adv.*

tem•po•ral² (tem′pər əl), *adj.* of or near the temples of the head.

tem′po•rar′y (-pə rer′ē), *adj., n., pl.* **-rar•ies.** —*adj.* **1.** lasting or serving for a time only; not permanent. —*n.* **2.** a temporary office worker. —**tem′po•rar′i•ly,** *adv.*

tem′po•rize′, *v.i.,* **-rized, -riz•ing.** to be indecisive or evasive to gain time or delay acting. —**tem′po•ri•za′tion,** *n.* —**tem′po•riz′er,** *n.*

tempt (tempt), *v.t.* **1.** to entice to do something unwise or wrong. **2.** to appeal strongly to. **3.** to put to the test in a venturesome way: *to tempt fate.* —**temp•ta′tion,** *n.* —**tempt′er,** *n.*

tempt′ress, *n.* a woman who tempts.

tem•pu•ra (tem poŏr′ə), *n.* a Japanese dish of seafood or vegetables dipped in batter and deep-fried. [< Japn < Pg]

ten (ten), *n.* **1.** a cardinal number, nine plus one. **2.** a symbol for this number, as 10 or X. —*adj.* **3.** amounting to ten in number.

ten•a•ble (ten′ə bəl), *adj.* capable of being held, maintained, or defended. —**ten/a•bil′i•ty,** *n.* —**ten′a•bly,** *adv.*

te•na•cious (tə nā′shəs), *adj.* **1.** holding fast: *a tenacious grip.* **2.** highly retentive: *a tenacious memory.* **3.** persistent or stubborn. **4.** holding together; cohesive. —**te•na′cious•ly,** *adv.* —**te•nac′i•ty** (-nas′i tē), *n.*

ten•ant (ten′ənt), *n.* **1.** a person or group that rents and occupies land, a house, etc., from another. **2.** an occupant or inhabitant. —*v.t.* **3.** to occupy as a tenant. —**ten′an•cy,** *n., pl.* **-cies.**

ten′ant farm′er, *n.* a person who farms the land of another and pays rent with cash or with a portion of the produce.

Ten Bloom (ten blōōm′), *n.* **Carrie,** 1892–1983, Dutch Christian writer who sheltered Jews during the Nazi occupation of The Netherlands.

Ten′ Command′ments, *n.pl.* the precepts given by God to Moses on Mount Sinai; the Decalogue. Ex. 20; 24:12, 34; Deut. 5.

tend¹ (tend), *v.i.* **1.** to be disposed or inclined to do something. **2.** to lead in a particular direction.

tend² (tend), *v.t.* **1.** to attend to by work or services, care, etc. **2.** to watch over and care for.

ten•den•cy (ten′dən sē), *n., pl.* **-cies.** a natural disposition to move or act in some direction or toward some point or result.

ten•den′tious (-den′shəs), *adj.* having a tendency to favor a point of view; biased. —**ten•den′tious•ly,** *adv.* —**ten•den′tious•ness,** *n.*

ten•der¹ (ten′dər), *adj.,* **-der•er, -der•est. 1.** soft or delicate in substance. **2.** weak or delicate in constitution. **3.** young or immature. **4.** light or gentle. **5.** easily moved to compassion. **6.** affectionate or sentimental. **7.** acutely or painfully sensitive. **8.** requiring tactful handling. —**ten′der•ly,** *adv.* —**ten′der•ness,** *n.*

ten•der² (ten′dər), *v.t.* **1.** to present formally for acceptance. —*n.* **2.** an offer of something for acceptance. **3.** something offered, esp. money, as in payment. —**ten′der•er,** *n.*

tend•er³ (ten′dər), *n.* **1.** one who tends someone or something. **2.** a ship that attends other ships, as for supplying provisions. **3.** a railroad car attached to a steam locomotive to carry fuel and water.

ten′der•foot′, *n., pl.* **-foots, -feet. 1.** an inexperienced person. **2.** a newcomer to the ranching and mining regions of the western U.S., unused to hardships.

ten′der-heart′ed, *adj.* soft-hearted; sympathetic. —**ten′der-heart′ed•ness,** *n.*

ten′der•ize′, *v.t.,* **-ized, -iz•ing.** to make (meat) tender, as by pounding. —**ten′der•iz′er,** *n.*

ten′der•loin′, *n.* (in beef or pork) the tenderest portion of the loin.

ten•di•ni•tis (ten′də nī′tis), *n.* inflammation of a tendon.

ten•don (ten′dən), *n.* a cord of dense, tough tissue connecting a muscle with a bone or part.

ten•dril (ten′dril), *n.* a threadlike organ of a climbing plant that winds around something else and supports the plant.

ten•e•ment (ten′ə mənt), *n.* a run-down apartment house in a poor section of a city.

ten•et (ten′it), *n.* any principle, doctrine, etc., held as true by members of a group.

Tenn., Tennessee.

Ten•nes•see (ten′ə sē′), *n.* a state in the SE United States. 5,319,654. *Cap.:* Nashville. *Abbr.:* TN, Tenn. —**Ten′nes•se′an,** *adj., n.*

Ten′nessee Val′ley Author′ity, *n.* a federal corporation created in 1933 to develop the Tennessee

River basin as a source of electric power, irrigation, etc. *Abbr.:* TVA

ten•nis (ten′is), *n.* a game played on a court by players equipped with rackets, in which a ball is driven back and forth over a net.

Ten•ny•son (ten′ə sən), *n.* **Alfred, Lord** (*1st Baron*), 1809–92, English poet: poet laureate 1850–92.

Te•noch•ti•tlán (tā nôch′tē tlän′), *n.* the capital of the Aztec empire: now the site of Mexico City.

ten•on (ten′ən), *n.* a projection on the end of a piece of wood for insertion into a mortise to form a joint.

ten•or (ten′ər), *n.* **1.** general sense; purport; drift. **2.** continuous course or movement. **3. a.** the adult male voice intermediate between the bass and the alto or countertenor. **b.** a part for such a voice. **c.** a singer with such a voice.

ten′pins′, *n.* a form of bowling, played with ten wooden pins.

tense¹ (tens), *adj.,* **tens•er, tens•est,** *v.,* **tensed, tens•ing.** —*adj.* **1.** stretched tight; taut. **2.** in a state of mental or nervous strain. —*v.t., v.i.* **3.** to make or become tense. —**tense′ly,** *adv.* —**tense′ness,** *n.*

tense² (tens), *n.* the inflected form of a verb that indicates the time of its action or state.

ten•sile (ten′səl, -sil, -sīl), *adj.* **1.** of or by tension. **2.** capable of being stretched or drawn out.

ten′sion, *n.* **1.** the act of stretching or state of being stretched. **2.** mental or emotional strain. **3.** a strained relationship between individuals, nations, etc. **4.** the longitudinal deformation of an elastic body that results in its elongation. **5.** electromotive force; potential.

tent (tent), *n.* **1.** a portable shelter of fabric or skins supported by poles. —*v.t.* **2.** to provide with tents. —*v.i.* **3.** to live in a tent.

ten•ta•cle (ten′tə kəl), *n.* a slender, flexible appendage in some invertebrates, used for touching, grasping, etc. —**ten′ta•cled,** *adj.*

ten•ta•tive (ten′tə tiv), *adj.* **1.** made or done as a trial, experiment, or attempt. **2.** unsure; hesitant. —**ten′ta•tive•ly,** *adv.* —**ten′ta•tive•ness,** *n.*

ten•ter•hook (ten′tər hŏŏk′), *n.* **1.** one of the hooks that hold cloth stretched on a drying framework (**ten′ter**). —*Idiom.* **2. on tenterhooks,** in suspense.

tenth (tenth), *adj.* **1.** next after the ninth; being the ordinal number for ten. **2.** being one of ten equal parts. —*n.* **3.** a tenth part, esp. of one (¹/₁₀). **4.** the tenth member of a series.

ten•u•ous (ten′yōō əs), *adj.* **1.** lacking a sound basis; flimsy. **2.** thin or slender in form. **3.** rare or rarefied. —**ten′u•ous•ly,** *adv.* —**ten′u•ous•ness,** *n.*

ten•ure (ten′yər), *n.* **1.** the holding of something, as property or an office. **2.** the period of holding something. **3.** permanent status granted to an employee. —**ten′ured,** *adj.*

te•pee (tē′pē), *n., pl.* **-pees.** a conical tent of animal skins used by Plains Indians.

tep•id (tep′id), *adj.* **1.** moderately warm. **2.** showing little enthusiasm. —**te•pid′i•ty, tep′id•ness,** *n.* —**tep′id•ly,** *adv.*

te•qui•la (tə kē′lə), *n.* a strong liquor from Mexico, distilled from fermented agave mash.

ter•bi•um (tûr′bē əm), *n.* a rare-earth, metallic element present in certain minerals and yielding colorless salts. *Symbol:* Tb; *at. no.:* 65; *at. wt.:* 158.924.

ter•cen•ten•ar•y (tûr′sen ten′ə rē, tûr sen′tn er′ē), *n., pl.* **-ar•ies.** TERCENTENNIAL.

ter′cen•ten′ni•al, *n.* a 300th anniversary or its celebration.

Te•re•sa (tə rē′sə, -zə, -rä′-; *for 2 also Sp.* te RE′sä), *n.* **1. Mother** (*Agnes Gonxha Bojaxhiu*), 1910–97, Albanian nun: Nobel peace prize 1979. **2. Saint.** THE-RESA, SAINT.

term (tûrm), *n.* **1.** a word or group of words designating something, esp. in a particular field. **2.** the time or period through which something lasts. **3.** an appointed time or date, as for payment. **4. terms, a.** conditions or stipulations. **b.** footing or standing: *on friendly terms.* **5.** each of the members of which a mathematical expression, a series of quantities, etc., is composed. —*v.t.* **6.** to apply a term to; designate. —*Idiom.* **7. come to terms,** to reach an agreement.

ter•ma•gant (tûr′mə gənt), *n.* a violent, brawling woman.

ter•mi•nal (tûr′mə nl), *adj.* **1.** situated at or forming the end of something. **2.** closing; concluding. **3.** of or lasting for a term or period. **4.** occurring at or causing the end of life. —*n.* **5.** a terminal part of a structure. **6.** a terminus or a major junction within a transportation system. **7.** a device for entering information into a computer or receiving information from it. **8.** the point where current enters or leaves any conducting component in an electric circuit. —**ter′mi•nal•ly,** *adv.*

ter′mi•nate′ (-nāt′), *v.,* **-nat•ed, -nat•ing.** —*v.t.* **1.** to bring to an end. **2.** to occur at or form the conclusion of. **3.** to dismiss from a job. —*v.i.* **4.** to end. **5.** to issue or result. —**ter′mi•na′tion,** *n.*

ter•mi•nol•o•gy (tûr′mə nol′ə jē), *n., pl.* **-gies.** the terms peculiar to a specialized subject. —**ter′mi•no•log′i•cal** (-nl oj′i kəl), *adj.* —**ter′mi•no•log′i•cal•ly,** *adv.*

ter•mi•nus (tûr′mə nəs), *n., pl.* **-ni** (-nī′), **-nus•es. 1.** the end or extremity of anything. **2.** either end of a transportation line.

ter•mite (tûr′mīt), *n.* any of various social insects that can be destructive to wood.

tern (tûrn), *n.* any of various aquatic birds resembling gulls, though typically smaller.

ter•na•ry (tûr′nə rē), *adj.* consisting of or involving three.

terp•si•cho•re•an (tûrp′si kə rē′ən, -kôr′ē ən), *adj.* of dancing.

ter•race (ter′əs), *n., v.,* **-raced, -rac•ing.** —*n.* **1.** a raised level of earth with vertical or sloping sides. **2.** an open, often paved area connected to a house; patio. **3.** a porch or balcony. **4.** a row of houses on or near the top of a slope. —*v.t.* **5.** to form into a terrace or terraces.

ter•ra cot•ta (ter′ə kot′ə), *n., pl.* **-tas.** a hard, brownish red fired clay used for pottery, building, etc.

ter′ra fir′ma (fûr′mə), *n.* firm or solid earth. [< L]

ter•rain (tə rān′), *n.* a tract of land considered with reference to its natural features.

ter•ra•pin (ter′ə pin), *n.* any of several edible North American turtles inhabiting fresh or brackish waters.

ter•rar•i•um (tə râr′ē əm), *n., pl.* **-i•ums, -i•a** (-ē ə). an enclosed glass container in which plants or land animals are kept.

ter•raz•zo (tə rä′tsō, -raz′ō), *n., pl.* **-zos.** a mosaic flooring composed of stone chips and cement.

ter•res•tri•al (tə res′trē əl), *adj.* **1.** of or representing the earth. **2.** of land as distinct from water. **3.** growing or living on land. **4.** worldly; mundane. —**ter•res′tri•al•ly,** *adv.*

ter•ri•ble (ter′ə bəl), *adj.* **1.** distressing; severe. **2.** extremely bad; horrible. **3.** exciting terror or great fear. **4.** formidably great: *a terrible responsibility.* —**ter′ri•ble•ness,** *n.* —**ter′ri•bly,** *adv.*

ter•ri•er (ter′ē ər), *n.* any of several breeds of usu. small dogs, used orig. to drive game out of its hole.

ter•rif•ic (tə rif′ik), *adj.* **1.** extraordinarily great or intense. **2.** extremely good; wonderful. **3.** causing terror. —**ter•rif′i•cal•ly,** *adv.*

ter•ri•fy (ter′ə fī′), *v.t.,* **-fied, -fy•ing.** to fill with terror or alarm.

ter•ri•to•ry (ter′i tôr′ē), *n., pl.* **-ries. 1.** any large tract of land. **2.** the land and waters under the jurisdiction of a state, sovereign, etc. **3.** a region of a country that does not have the status of a state or province. **4.** a field of action, thought, etc. **5.** an assigned district, as of a sales representative. —*Saying.* **6. It comes with the territory,** certain consequences follow from a situation. —**ter′ri•to′ri•al** (-tôr′ē əl), *adj.*

ter•ror (ter′ər), *n.* **1.** intense fear. **2.** a person or thing that causes such fear. **3.** TERRORISM.

ter′ror•ism, *n.* the use of violence and threats to intimidate or coerce, esp. for political purposes. —ter′ror•ist, *n., adj.*

ter′ror•ize′, *v.t.,* -ized, -iz•ing. **1.** to fill with terror. **2.** to dominate or coerce by intimidation.

ter•ry (ter′ē), *n., pl.* -ries. a pile fabric with uncut loops, used for toweling. Also called **ter′ry cloth′.**

terse (tûrs), *adj.,* ters•er, ters•est. **1.** neatly or effectively concise, as language. **2.** curt; brusque. —terse′ly, *adv.* —terse′ness, *n.*

ter•ti•ar•y (tûr′shē er′ē), *adj.* **1.** of the third order, rank, etc. **2.** (*cap.*) noting or pertaining to the earlier period of the Cenozoic Era, during which mammals gained ascendancy.

tes•sel•late (tes′ə lāt′), *v.t.,* -lat•ed, -lat•ing. to form of small squares in a mosaic pattern.

test (test), *n.* **1.** the means by which the presence, quality, or genuineness of anything is determined. **2.** a set of problems, questions, etc., for evaluating knowledge or skills. **3.** a reaction used to identify or detect the presence of a chemical constituent. —*v.t.* **4.** to subject to a test. —*v.i.* **5.** to undergo or conduct a test. **6.** to perform on a test. —test′er *n.*

tes•ta•ment (tes′tə mənt), *n.* **1.** a will disposing of one's personal property after death. **2.** (*cap.*) either the New Testament or the Old Testament. **3.** a proof; testimony. —**tes′ta•men′ta•ry** (-men′tə rē, -men′-trē), *adj.*

tes•tate (tes′tāt), *adj.* having left a valid will.

tes•ta•tor (tes′tā tər, te stā′tər), *n.* a person who has died leaving a valid will.

tes•ti•cle (tes′ti kəl), *n.* TESTIS.

tes•ti•fy (tes′tə fī′), *v.,* -fied, -fy•ing. —*v.i.* **1.** to serve as evidence. **2.** to give testimony under oath. —*v.t.* **3.** to be evidence of. **4.** to declare under oath. —tes′ti•fi′er, *n.*

tes′ti•mo′ni•al (-mō′nē əl), *n.* **1.** a written declaration recommending a person or thing. **2.** something given or done as an expression of admiration or gratitude.

tes′ti•mo′ny (-nō′nē), *n., pl.* -nies. **1.** the statement of a witness under oath. **2.** evidence in support of a fact or statement. **3.** open declaration, as of faith.

tes•tis (tes′tis), *n., pl.* -tes (-tēz) either of two reproductive glands located in the scrotum.

tes•tos•ter•one (tes tos′tə rōn′), *n.* the sex hormone secreted by the testes.

test′ tube′, a thin glass tube closed at one end, used in laboratory experimentation.

tes•ty (tes′tē), *adj.,* -ti•er, -ti•est. irritably impatient; touchy. —**tes′ti•ly,** *adv.* —**tes′ti•ness,** *n.*

Tet (tet), *n.* the Vietnamese New Year celebration.

tet•a•nus (tet′n əs), *n.* an infectious, sometimes fatal disease characterized by spasms and rigidity of muscles, esp. of the jaw and neck.

tête-à-tête (tāt′ə tāt′, tet′ə tet′), *n., pl.* tête-à-têtes. a private conversation between two people. [< F: lit., head to head]

teth•er (teth′ər), *n.* **1.** a rope, chain, etc., by which an animal is fastened to a fixed object. **2.** the utmost extent of one's ability or resources. —*v.t.* **3.** to fasten with or as if with a tether.

Tet′ Offen′sive, *n.* an offensive by Vietcong and North Vietnamese forces against South Vietnamese and U.S. positions in South Vietnam, beginning on Jan. 31, 1968, the start of Tet.

tet•ra (te′trə), *n., pl.* -ras. a small, brightly colored fish of tropical American waters.

tetra-, a combining form meaning four (*tetrahedron*).

tet•ra•cy•cline (te′trə sī′klēn, -klin), *n.* an antibiotic used to treat infections.

tet′ra•eth′yl•lead′, *n.* a colorless poisonous liquid used as an antiknock agent in gasoline.

Tet•ra•gram•ma•ton (te′trə gram′ə ton′), *n.* the Hebrew word for God.

tet′ra•he′dron (-hē′drən), *n., pl.* -drons, -dra (-drə). a solid contained by four plane faces. —**tet′ra•he′dral,** *adj.*

te•tram•e•ter (te tram′i tər), *n.* a verse of four feet.

Tet•zel or **Te•zel** (tet′səl), *n.* **Johann,** 1465?–1519, German monk: antagonist of Martin Luther.

Teu•ton (tōōt′n, tyōōt′n), *n.* a member of any people speaking a Germanic language, esp. a German.

Teu•ton•ic (tōō ton′ik, tyōō-), *n., adj.* GERMANIC.

Tex., Texas.

Tex•as (tek′səs), *n.* a state in the S United States. 19,128,261. *Cap.:* Austin. *Abbr.:* TX, Tex. —**Tex′an,** *adj., n.*

Tex′as Revolu′tion, *n.* a revolutionary movement, 1832–36, in which U.S. settlers asserted their independence from Mexico.

text (tekst), *n.* **1.** the main body of matter in a written work, as distinguished from notes, appendixes, etc. **2.** the actual words of an author or speaker. **3.** any form in which a writing exists. **4.** any theme or topic. **5.** a textbook. **6.** a passage of Scripture, esp. one chosen as the subject of a sermon. —**text•tu•al** (teks′chōō əl), *adj.*

text•book (tekst′bŏŏk′), *n.* a book used by students as a standard work for a particular branch of study.

tex•tile (teks′tīl, -til), *n.* **1.** any cloth or goods produced by weaving, knitting, or felting. **2.** a material, as a yarn, suitable for weaving. —*adj.* **3.** of textiles or their production.

tex•ture (teks′chər), *n.* **1.** the physical structure given to a material, object, etc., by the arrangement of its parts. **2.** the structure of the threads, fibers, etc., that make up a textile fabric. —**tex′tur•al,** *adj.*

Th, *Chem. Symbol.* thorium.

-th¹, a suffix meaning: act or action (*birth*); quality or condition (*length*).

-th², a suffix used to form ordinal numbers (*fourth*).

Thad•de•us (thad′ē əs), *n.* one of the twelve apostles. Matt. 10:3.

Thai (tī), *n., pl.* Thais. **1.** a native or inhabitant of Thailand. **2.** the language of Thailand.

Thai′land′ (-land′, -lənd), *n.* a kingdom in SE Asia. 59,450,115.

thal•a•mus (thal′ə məs), *n., pl.* -mi (-mī′). the part of the brain that transmits and integrates sensory impulses.

tha•lid•o•mide (thə lid′ə mīd′), *n.* a drug formerly used as a sedative, found to cause severe fetal abnormalities.

thal•li•um (thal′ē əm), *n.* a rare metallic element, used in the manufacture of alloys. *Symbol:* Tl; *at. wt.:* 204.37; *at. no.:* 81.

Thames (temz), *n.* a river in S England, flowing E through London to the North Sea. 209 mi. (336 km) long.

than (than, then; *unstressed* thən, ən), *conj.* **1.** (used after comparative adjectives and adverbs to introduce the second member of a comparison): *She's taller than I am.* **2.** (used after some adverbs and adjectives, as *other,* to denote a difference in kind, place, etc.): *I had no choice other than that.*

Than•a•tos (than′ə tos′, -tōs), *n.* **1.** (among the ancient Greeks) a personification of death. **2.** *Psychoanal.* (*usu. l.c.*) the death instinct, esp. as expressed in violent aggression. —**Than′a•tot′ic** (-tot′ik), *adj.*

thank (thangk), *v.t.* **1.** to express gratitude to. **2.** to hold personally responsible: *We have him to thank for this lawsuit.* —*n.* **3. thanks,** an acknowledgment of a kindness, favor, or the like. —*interj.* **4. thanks,** I thank you. —*Idiom.* **5. thanks to,** because of. **6. thank you,** I thank you.

thank′ful, *adj.* feeling or expressing gratitude. —thank′ful•ly, *adv.* —thank′ful•ness, *n.*

thank′less, *adj.* **1.** not likely to be appreciated or rewarded. **2.** ungrateful. —thank′less•ly, *adv.*

thanks′giv′ing, *n.* **1.** a public celebration in acknowledgment of divine favor. **2.** (*cap.*) a U.S. holiday observed on the fourth Thursday of November.

that (that; *unstressed* thət), *pron.* and *adj., pl.* **those;** *adv.;* *conj.* —*pron.* **1.** the person or thing pointed out or mentioned before: *That is her mother.* **2.** the one more remote in place, time, or thought: *This is my sister and that's my cousin.* **3.** who, whom, or which: *the horse that he bought.* —*adj.* **4.** (used to indicate the person or thing pointed out or mentioned before). **5.** (used to indicate the one more remote in time, place, or thought). **6.** (used to imply contradistinction; opposed to *this*). —*adv.* **7.** to the extent or degree indicated: *Don't take that much.* —*conj.* **8.** (used to introduce a subordinate clause expressing cause, purpose, result, etc.): *I'm sure that you'll like it.* **9.** (used elliptically to introduce an exclamation): *Oh, that I were young again.* —*Idiom.* **10. at that, a.** nevertheless. **b.** in addition. **11. that is,** to be more accurate.

thatch (thach), *n.* **1.** Also, **thatch′ing.** a material, as straw or rushes, used to cover roofs. **2.** a covering of such a material. —*v.t.* **3.** to cover with or as if with thatch.

Thatch•er (thach′ər), *n.* **Margaret (Hilda),** born 1925, British prime minister 1979–90.

thaw (thô), *v.i.* **1.** to pass from a frozen to a liquid state; melt. **2.** to become warm enough to melt ice and snow. **3.** to become less hostile or aloof. —*v.t.* **4.** to cause to thaw. —*n.* **5.** the act of thawing. **6.** weather warm enough to melt ice and snow.

Thay•er (thā′ər, thâr), *n.* **1. Ernest Lawrence,** 1863–1940, U.S. journalist, author of *Casey at the Bat.* **2. Sylvanus,** 1785–1872, U.S. army officer and educator.

THC, the most active chemical ingredient in marijuana. [*t(etra)h(ydro)c(annabinol)*]

Th.D., Doctor of Theology. [< L *Theologicae Doctor*]

the¹ (stressed ᵺē; unstressed before a consonant ᵺə, unstressed before a vowel ᵺē), definite article. **1.** (used to indicate a particular person or thing): *the book you gave me.* **2.** (used to mark a noun as indicating the best-known, most approved, etc.): *the place to ski.* **3.** (used to mark a noun as being used generically): *The dog is a quadruped.* **4.** (used before adjectives that are used substantively): *from the sublime to the ridiculous.*

the² (before a consonant ᵺə; before a vowel ᵺē), adv. **1.** in or by so much: *He looks the better for his nap.* **2.** by how much … by so much: *the more the merrier.*

the•a•ter or **-tre** (thē′ə tər, thēᵃ′-), *n.* **1.** a building or a place for dramatic presentations, motion-picture shows, etc. **2.** a room or hall with tiers of seats. **3. the theater,** dramatic performances as a branch of art. **4.** dramatic works collectively. **5.** a place of action; area of activity.

the•at′ri•cal (-ə′tri kəl), *adj.* **1.** of or suitable for the theater. **2.** artificial and exaggerated; histrionic. —**the•at′ri•cal′i•ty,** *n.* —**the•at′ri•cal•ly,** *adv.*

the•at′rics, *n.* **1.** (used with a sing. v.) the art of staging plays. **2.** (used with a pl. v.) artificial and exaggerated mannerisms or actions.

Thebes (thēbz), *n.* **1.** an ancient city in S Egypt, on the Nile. **2.** a city of ancient Greece. —**The′ban,** *adj., n.*

thee (ᵺē), *pron.* the objective case of THOU.

theft (theft), *n.* an act or instance of stealing.

their (ᵺâr; unstressed ᵺər), *pron.* a form of the possessive case of THEY used attributively: *their home.*

theirs (ᵺârz), *pron.* a form of the possessive case of THEY used as a predicate adjective, after or without a noun: *Are you a friend of theirs? It is theirs.*

the•ism (thē′iz əm), *n.* belief in the existence of a god or gods. —**the′ist,** *n., adj.* —**the•is′tic,** *adj.*

them (ᵺem; unstressed ᵺəm, əm), *pron.* the objective case of THEY.

theme (thēm), *n.* **1.** a topic of discourse, discussion, etc. **2.** the central subject of a work of art. **3.** a short, informal essay. **4.** a principal melodic subject in a musical composition. —**the•mat′ic,** *adj.* —**the•mat′i•cal•ly,** *adv.*

them•selves (ᵺəm selvz′, ᵺem′-), *pron.pl.* **1.** a reflexive form of THEY: *They washed themselves quickly.* **2.** (used as an intensive): *The authors themselves left the theater.* **3.** their normal selves: *After some rest, they were themselves again.*

then (ᵺen), *adv.* **1.** at that time: *Prices were lower then.* **2.** soon afterward: *The rain stopped and then started again.* **3.** next in order of time or place: *We ate, then we slept.* **4.** in addition: *I love my job, and then it pays so well.* **5.** as a consequence. —*adj.* **6.** existing or being at the time indicated: *the then prime minister.* —*n.* **7.** that time: *We haven't been back since then.*

thence (ᵺens), *adv.* **1.** from that place. **2.** from that time; thenceforth. **3.** therefore. —**Usage.** See WHENCE.

thence•forth (ᵺens′fôrth′, ᵺens′fôrth′), *adv.* from that time onward.

the•oc•ra•cy (thē ok′rə sē), *n., pl.* **-cies. 1.** a form of government in which a deity is recognized as the supreme ruler. **2.** a system of government by priests. **3.** a state under a theocracy. —**the′o•crat′ic** (-ə-krat′ik), *adj.*

the•ol•o•gy (-ol′ə jē), *n., pl.* **-gies.** the study of God and of God's relations to the universe; the study of religious truth. —**the′o•lo′gian** (-ə lō′jən, -jē ən), *n.* —**the′o•log′i•cal** (-loj′i kəl), *adj.*

the•o•rem (thē′ər əm, thēr′əm), *n.* **1.** *Math.* a proposition or formula containing something to be proved from other propositions or formulas. **2.** *Logic.* a proposition that can be deduced from the premises of a system.

the•o•ret•i•cal (thē′ə ret′i kəl), *adj.* **1.** of or consisting in theory. **2.** existing only in theory. **3.** forming or dealing with theories. —**the′o•ret′i•cal•ly,** *adv.*

the•o•rize (thē′ə rīz′, thēr′īz), *v.i.,* **-rized, -riz•ing.** to form a theory or theories. —**the•o•re•ti•cian** (thē′ər ə tish′ən, thēr′ə-), **the′o•rist,** *n.*

the•o•ry, *n., pl.* **-ries. 1.** a group of general propositions used as principles of explanation for a class of phenomena. **2.** an explanation whose status is still conjectural. **3.** the branch of a science or art that deals with its principles rather than its practice. **4.** a guess or conjecture.

the•os•o•phy (thē os′ə fē), *n.* any of various forms of philosophical or religious thought based on a mystical insight into the divine nature. —**the′o•soph′i•cal** (-ə sof′i kəl), **the′o•soph′ic,** *adj.* —**the•os′o•phist,** *n.*

ther•a•peu•tic (ther′ə pyōō′tik), *adj.* serving to cure, heal, or maintain health. —**ther′a•peu′ti•cal•ly,** *adv.*

ther′a•peu′tics, *n.* the branch of medicine concerned with the use of remedies to treat disease.

ther′a•py, *n., pl.* **-pies.** the treatment of disease or disorders, as by some remedial, rehabilitative, or curative process. —**ther′a•pist,** *n.*

there (ᵺâr; unstressed ᵺər), *adv.* **1.** in or at that place. **2.** at that point: *He stopped there for applause.* **3.** in that matter: *I agree with you there.* **4.** into or to that place: *We went there last year.* —*pron.* **5.** (used to introduce a sentence or clause in which the verb comes before its subject): *There is no hope.* —*n.* **6.** that place or point: *I come from there, too.* —*interj.* **7.** an exclamation of satisfaction, relief, etc. —**Usage.** It is nonstandard to place THERE or HERE between a demonstrative adjective and the noun it modifies: *that there car; these here nails.* Placed after the noun, both are entirely standard: *that car there; these nails here.*

there′a•bout′ or **-a•bouts′,** *adv.* **1.** near that place or time. **2.** about that number, amount, etc.

there′af′ter, *adv.* after that in time or sequence.

there′at′, *adv.* **1.** at that place or time. **2.** because of that.

there•by (ᵺâr′bī′, ᵺâr′bī′), *adv.* **1.** by means of that. **2.** in that connection or relation: *Thereby hangs a tale.*

there′for′, *adv.* for this, that, or it.

there′fore′, *adv.* as a result.

there′in′, *adv.* **1.** in or into that place. **2.** in that matter, circumstance, etc.

there′of′, *adv.* **1.** of that or it. **2.** from that origin or cause.

there′on′, *adv.* **1.** on that or it. **2.** thereupon.

The•re•sa (tə rē′sə), *n.* **Saint,** 1515–82, Spanish Carmelite nun, mystic, and writer.

there′to′ also **there′un•to′,** *adv.* to that place or thing.

there′to•fore′ (-tə fôr′), *adv.* until that time.

there′up•on′, *adv.* **1.** immediately following that. **2.** in consequence of that. **3.** upon that or it.

there′with′, *adv.* **1.** with that. **2.** following upon that.

ther•mal (thûr′məl), *adj.* **1.** of or caused by heat. **2.** designed to promote the retention of body heat. —**ther′mal•ly**, *adv.*

ther′mal pollu′tion, *n.* the discharge into rivers or lakes of heated industrial waste water, harming water-dwelling life.

thermo-, a combining form meaning heat or hot (*thermoplastic*).

ther•mo•dy•nam•ics (thûr′mō dī nam′iks), *n.* the science concerned with the relations between heat and mechanical energy or work. —**ther′mo•dy•nam′ic**, *adj.*

ther•mom•e•ter (thər mom′i tər), *n.* an instrument for measuring temperature, often a glass tube containing a column of mercury that rises and falls with temperature changes. —**ther•mo•met•ric** (thûr′mə me′trik), *adj.* —**ther•mom′e•try**, *n.*

ther′mo•nu′cle•ar (thûr′mō-), *adj.* **1.** of or involving fusion reactions between nuclei of a light element, as hydrogen, that require temperatures of several million degrees to occur. **2.** of or using energy from such reactions.

ther′mo•plas′tic (thûr′mə-), *adj.* **1.** soft and pliable when heated, as some plastics. —*n.* **2.** a plastic of this type.

Ther•mop•y•lae (thər mop′ə lē′), *n.* a pass in E Greece: Persian defeat of the Spartans 480 B.C.

ther•mos (thûr′məs), *n.* a vacuum bottle used for keeping liquids hot or cold. Also called **ther′mos bot′tle.**

ther′mo•stat′ (-mə stat′), *n.* a device that establishes and maintains a desired temperature automatically. —**ther′mo•stat′ic**, *adj.* —**ther′mo•stat′i•cal•ly**, *adv.*

the•sau•rus (thi sôr′əs), *n.*, *pl.* **-sau•rus•es, -sau•ri** (-sôr′ī). a dictionary of synonyms and antonyms.

these (thēz), *pron.*, *adj.* pl. of THIS.

the•sis (thē′sis), *n.*, *pl.* **-ses** (-sēz). **1.** a proposition proved or maintained against objections. **2.** a formal paper incorporating original research, esp. one presented by a candidate for a degree.

Thes•pi•an (thes′pē ən), *(often l.c.)* —*adj.* **1.** pertaining to the drama. —*n.* **2.** an actor or actress.

Thes•sa•lo•ni•ans (thes′ə lō′nē ənz), *n.* either of two books of the New Testament, I Thessalonians or II Thessalonians, written by Paul.

the•ta (thā′tə, thē′-), *n.*, *pl.* **-tas.** the eighth letter of the Greek alphabet (Θ, θ).

thew (thyoō), *n.* Usu., **thews.** muscle or sinew.

they (thā), *pron.pl.* **1.** nominative plural of HE, SHE, and IT. **2.** people in general.

thi•a•mine (thī′ə min, -mēn′) also **-min** (-min), *n.* a vitamin-B compound, abundant in liver, legumes, and cereal grains.

thick (thik), *adj.*, **-er, -est**, *n.* —*adj.* **1.** having relatively great extent between two surfaces. **2.** measured between opposite surfaces: *a board one inch thick.* **3.** dense: *thick fog.* **4.** not distinctly articulated: *thick speech.* **5.** marked; pronounced: *a thick accent.* **6.** heavy or viscous: *thick syrup.* **7.** close in friendship. **8.** stupid. —*n.* **9.** the thickest part. —**thick′ly**, *adv.* —**thick′ness**, *n.*

thick′en, *v.t.*, *v.i.* **1.** to make or become thick or thicker. **2.** to make or grow more profound or intricate. —**thick′en•er**, *n.* —**thick′en•ing**, *n.*

thick′et, *n.* a dense growth of shrubs or small trees.

thick′set′, *adj.* **1.** heavily or solidly built. **2.** set in close arrangement.

thick′-skinned′, *adj.* **1.** having a thick skin. **2.** insensitive to criticism.

thief (thēf), *n.*, *pl.* **thieves.** a person who steals.

thieve (thēv), *v.t.*, *v.i.*, **thieved, thiev•ing.** to steal. —**thiev′ish**, *adj.*

thiev′er•y, *n.*, *pl.* **-er•ies.** an act or instance of stealing.

thigh (thī), *n.* the part of the lower limb between the hip and the knee.

thigh′bone′, *n.* FEMUR.

thim•ble (thim′bəl), *n.* a small cap worn to protect the fingertip when sewing. —**thim′ble•ful′**, *n.*, *pl.* **-fuls.**

Thim•phu (tim poō′) also **-bu** (-boō′), *n.* the capital of Bhutan. 15,000.

thin (thin), *adj.*, **thin•ner, thin•nest**, *adv.*, *v.*, **thinned, thin•ning.** —*adj.* **1.** having relatively little extent between two surfaces. **2.** having little flesh; lean. **3.** widely separated; sparse: *thin vegetation.* **4.** of slight consistency: *thin soup.* **5.** rarefied, as air. **6.** flimsy: *a thin excuse.* **7.** lacking volume: *a thin voice.* **8.** lacking body or richness: *a thin wine.* —*adv.* **9.** in a thin manner. —*v.t.*, *v.i.* **10.** to make or become thin or thinner. —**thin′ly**, *adv.* —**thin′ness**, *n.*

thine (thīn), *pron.* **1.** the possessive case of THOU used as a predicate adjective. **2.** (used instead of *thy* before a vowel or *h*): *thine eyes.*

thing (thing), *n.* **1.** an inanimate object. **2.** some object that is not or cannot be specifically designated: *Hand me that thing.* **3.** a matter or affair. **4.** an event or circumstance. **5.** an action or deed. **6.** a particular; detail. **7.** an article of clothing. **8. things,** personal possessions. **9.** a living being; creature. **10.** a thought; observation. **11.** a peculiar attitude or feeling: *She has a thing about cats.* **12.** *Informal.* issue; topic. —*Idiom.* **13. do one′s thing,** *Informal.* to pursue a lifestyle that expresses one's self. **14. see** or **hear things,** to hallucinate.

think (thingk), *v.*, **thought, think•ing.** —*v.i.* **1.** to use one's mind rationally. **2.** to have a certain thing as the subject of one's thoughts: *thinking about school.* **3.** to call something to mind: *to think of a number.* **4.** to conceive of something. **5.** to have consideration: *to think of others.* **6.** to have a belief or opinion. —*v.t.* **7.** to have or form in the mind. **8.** to evaluate for possible action upon: *Think the deal over.* **9.** to regard: *He thought me unkind.* —*Idiom.* **10. think twice,** to consider carefully before acting. —**think′er**, *n.*

think′ tank′, *n.* a research organization employed to analyze problems and plan future developments.

thin′ner, *n.* a liquid used to dilute paint to a desired consistency.

thin′-skinned′, *adj.* **1.** having a thin skin. **2.** sensitive to criticism.

third (thûrd), *adj.* **1.** next after the second; being the ordinal number for three. **2.** of or being the third forward gear in an automobile transmission. —*n.* **3.** a third part, esp. of one (¹⁄₃). **4.** the third member of a series. **5.** third gear. —*adv.* **6.** in the third place. —**third′ly**, *adv.*

third′ class′, *n.* **1.** the least costly class of accommodations. **2.** the class of mail consisting of merchandise weighing up to 16 ounces, or unsealed printed material.

third′-class′, *adj.* of the lowest class or quality; inferior.

third′ degree′, *n.* intensive questioning and rough treatment in order to get a confession.

third′ dimen′sion, *n.* **1.** thickness or depth. **2.** an aspect that heightens reality.

third′ per′son, *n.* a pronoun or verb form that refers to the one or ones spoken about.

third′-rate′, *adj.* **1.** of the third rate or quality. **2.** distinctly inferior.

Third′ Reich′, *n.* Germany during the Nazi regime 1933–45.

Third′ World′, *n.* *(sometimes l.c.)* the developing nations of Africa, Asia, and Latin America.

thirst (thûrst), *n.* **1.** a sensation of dryness in the mouth and throat caused by need of liquid. **2.** eager desire; craving. —*v.i.* **3.** to feel thirst. **4.** to have a strong desire. —**thirst′y**, *adj.*, **-i•er, -i•est.** —**thirst′i•ly**, *adv.*

thir•teen (thûr′tēn′), *n.* **1.** a cardinal number, ten plus three. **2.** a symbol for this number, as 13 or XIII. —*adj.* **3.** amounting to 13 in number. —**thir′teenth′**, *adj.*, *n.*

Thir/teen Col/onies, *n.pl.* the American colonies that joined the revolution against British rule in 1776: New Hampshire, Massachusetts, Rhode Island, Connecticut, New York, New Jersey, Pennsylvania, Delaware, Maryland, Virginia, North Carolina, South Carolina, and Georgia.

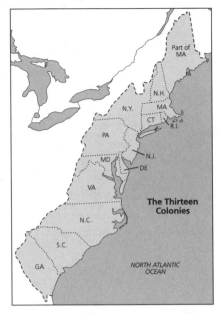

The Thirteen Colonies

thir•ty (thûr/tē), *n.,* *pl.* **-ties,** *adj.* —*n.* **1.** a cardinal number, ten times three. **2.** a symbol for this number, as 30 or XXX. —*adj.* **3.** amounting to 30 in number. —**thir/ti•eth,** *adj., n.*

Thir/ty-Nine/ Ar/ticles, *n.pl.* a set of statements (1563) defining the Church of England's position on matters of doctrine.

Thir/ty Years// War/, *n.* a series of wars (1618–48) that were a struggle for power among most European nations.

this (this), *pron.* and *adj., pl.* **these** (thēz); *adv.* —*pron.* **1.** the person or thing present, near, or just mentioned: *This is my coat.* **2.** the one nearer in place, time, or thought: *This is Liza and that is Amy.* **3.** what is about to follow: *Watch this!* —*adj.* **4.** (used to indicate the person or thing present, near, or just mentioned). **5.** (used to indicate the one nearer in time, place, or thought). **6.** (used to imply contradistinction; opposed to *that*). —*adv.* **7.** to the extent indicated: *this far.*

this•tle (this/əl), *n.* a prickly plant usu. having purple flower heads.

this/tle•down/, *n.* the silky down on the seeds of a thistle.

thith•er (thith/ər, thith/-), *adv.* to or toward that place.

tho or **tho'** (thō), *conj., adv.* a simplified spelling of THOUGH.

thole (thōl), *n.* either of two pins inserted into a gunwale to provide a fulcrum for an oar.

Thom•as (tom/əs), *n.* **1.** an apostle who demanded proof of Christ's Resurrection. John 20:24–29. **2. Dylan (Marlais),** 1914–53, Welsh poet. **3. Isaiah,** 1749–1831, U.S. printer of the first American Bible. **4. Lowell (Jackson),** 1892–1981, U.S. newscaster, traveler, and writer. **5. Martha Carey,** 1857–1935, U.S. educator and women's-rights advocate. **6. Norman (Mattoon),** 1884–1968, U.S. socialist leader. **7. Seth,** 1785–1859, U.S. clock designer.

thong (thông, thong), *n.* **1.** a narrow strip of leather

used for fastening or whipping. **2.** a sandal having a strip of leather or the like that passes between the first two toes.

Thor (thôr), *n.* the Norse god of thunder and the sky.

tho•rax (thôr/aks), *n., pl.* **tho•rax•es, tho•ra•ces** (thôr/ə sēz/). **1.** the part of the trunk between the neck and the abdomen. **2.** the portion of an insect's body between the head and the abdomen. —**tho•rac•ic** (thô ras/ik), *adj.*

Tho•reau (thə rō/, thôr/ō, thōr/ō), *n.* **Henry David,** 1817–62, U.S. naturalist and author. —**Tho•reau/vi•an,** *adj.*

tho•ri•um (thôr/ē əm), *n.* a radioactive metallic element, used as a source of nuclear energy. *Symbol:* Th; *at. wt.:* 232.038; *at. no.:* 90.

thorn (thôrn), *n.* **1.** a hard, sharp outgrowth on a plant. **2.** a thorny tree or shrub. **3.** a source of continual irritation or trouble. —**thorn/y,** *adj.,* **-i•er, -i•est.**

thor•ough (thûr/ō, thur/ō), *adj.* **1.** done without negligence or omissions. **2.** complete; utter: *thorough enjoyment.* **3.** extremely attentive to detail. —**thor/ough•ly,** *adv.* —**thor/ough•ness,** *n.*

thor/ough•bred/ (-ō bred/, -ə bred/), *adj.* **1.** of pure breed or stock. —*n.* **2.** (*cap.*) one of a breed of light racehorses. **3.** a thoroughbred animal.

thor/ough•fare/, *n.* a major road or highway.

thor/ough•go/ing, *adj.* extremely thorough.

Thorpe (thôrp), *n.* **James Francis** ("*Jim*"), 1888–1953, U.S. athlete.

those (thōz), *pron., adj. pl.* of THAT.

thou (thou), *pron. Archaic* (*except in elevated or ecclesiastical prose*). the second person singular in the nominative case.

though (thō), *conj.* **1.** in spite of the fact that. **2.** even if. —*adv.* **3.** however. —**Usage.** There is a traditional objection to the use of THOUGH in place of ALTHOUGH to mean "in spite of the fact that." ALTHOUGH (earlier *all though*) was orig. an emphatic form of THOUGH, but there is nothing in contemporary English to justify such a distinction.

thought[1] (thôt), *n.* **1.** the product of mental activity. **2.** an idea or notion. **3.** the act or process of thinking. **4.** the capacity or faculty of thinking. **5.** consideration or attention. **6.** an opinion or belief.

thought[2] (thôt), *v.* pt. and pp. of THINK.

thought/ful, *adj.* **1.** showing consideration for others. **2.** showing careful thought. **3.** occupied with thought. —**thought/ful•ly,** *adv.* —**thought/ful•ness,** *n.*

thought/less, *adj.* **1.** lacking in consideration for others. **2.** showing lack of thought; heedless. —**thought/less•ly,** *adv.* —**thought/less•ness,** *n.*

thou•sand (thou/zənd), *n., pl.* **-sands, -sand,** *adj.* —*n.* **1.** a cardinal number, 10 times 100. **2.** a symbol for this number, as 1000 or M. —*adj.* **3.** amounting to 1000 in number. —**thou/sandth,** *adj., n.*

thou/sand days/, *n.* (*sometimes caps.*) the presidential administration of John F. Kennedy, which lasted 1037 days (January 20, 1961, to November 22, 1963).

Thou/sand Oaks/, *n.* a town in S California. 110,981.

thrall (thrôl), *n.* **1.** a person in bondage; slave. **2.** slavery; bondage. —**thrall/dom, thral/dom,** *n.*

thrash (thrash), *v.t.* **1.** to beat; flog. **2.** to defeat thoroughly. —*v.i.* **3.** to toss about wildly. **4. thrash out,** to resolve by full discussion.

thrash/er, *n.* **1.** one that thrashes. **2.** a long-tailed, thrushlike bird.

thread (thred), *n.* **1.** a fine cord of a fibrous material spun out to considerable length, used for sewing. **2.** something having the fineness of a thread. **3.** the helical ridge of a screw. **4.** something that runs through the whole course of a thing. —*v.t.* **5.** to pass a thread through the eye of (a needle). **6.** to make (one's way), as around obstacles. **7.** to form a thread on or in (a bolt, hole, etc.). —**thread/er,** *n.*

thread/bare/, *adj.* **1.** having the nap worn off so as to lay bare the threads. **2.** wearing threadbare clothes. **3.** hackneyed; trite.

threat (thret), *n.* **1.** a declaration of an intention to cause harm. **2.** an indication of probable trouble. **3.** one that threatens.

threat′en, *v.t., v.i.* **1.** to utter a threat (against). **2.** to be a threat (to). **3.** to give an ominous indication (of).

three (thrē), *n.* **1.** a cardinal number, 2 plus 1. **2.** a symbol for this number, as 3 or III. —*adj.* **3.** amounting to three in number.

three′-dimen′sional, *adj.* having or seeming to have depth as well as width and height.

three′fold′, *adj.* **1.** having three parts. **2.** three times as great or as much. —*adv.* **3.** in threefold measure.

Three′ Mile′ Is′land, *n.* an island in the Susquehanna River, SE of Harrisburg, Pa: nuclear plant accident in 1979.

three-peat (thrē′pēt, thrē pēt′), **1.** *Trademark.* a third consecutive victory, as in a major sports championship. —*v.i.* **2.** to win a third consecutive victory.

three′ R′s′, *n.pl.* reading, writing, and arithmetic, regarded as the fundamentals of education.

three′score′, *adj.* sixty.

thren•o•dy (thren′ə dē), *n., pl.* **-dies.** a song of lamentation; dirge.

thresh (thresh), *v.t., v.i.* **1.** to separate (grain or seeds) from (a cereal plant or the like), as with a flail or machine. **2.** to beat or thrash. —**thresh′er,** *n.*

thresh•old (thresh′ōld, -hōld), *n.* **1.** the sill of a doorway. **2.** any point of entering or beginning.

threw (thrōō), *v.* pt. of THROW.

thrice (thrīs), *adv.* **1.** three times. **2.** threefold.

thrift (thrift), *n.* economical management; economy; frugality. [< ON] —**thrift′y,** *adj.,* **-i•er, -i•est.** —thrift′i•ly, *adv.* —**thrift′i•ness,** *n.*

thrift′ shop′, *n.* a retail store that sells secondhand goods at reduced prices.

thrill (thril), *v.t.* **1.** to affect with a sudden wave of excitement. —*v.i.* **2.** to experience a wave of excitement. **3.** to move tremulously. —*n.* **4.** a feeling of excitement. **5.** something that produces a thrill. —thrill′er, *n.*

thrive (thrīv), *v.i.* **thrived** or **throve, thrived** or **thriv•en** (thriv′ən), **thriv•ing. 1.** to prosper; be successful. **2.** to develop vigorously; flourish.

throat (thrōt), *n.* **1.** the first part of the passage from the mouth to the stomach and lungs. **2.** any narrowed part or passage. **3.** the front of the neck.

throat′y, *adj.,* **-i•er, -i•est.** (of sound) husky; hoarse. —**throat′i•ness,** *n.*

throb (throb), *v.,* **throbbed, throb•bing.** *n.* —*v.i.* **1.** to beat with increased force or rapidity, as the heart. **2.** to feel emotion. **3.** to vibrate, as a sound. —*n.* **4.** a violent beat or pulsation.

throe (thrō), *n.* **1.** a violent spasm or pang. **2. throes,** any violent convulsion or struggle.

throm•bo•sis (throm bō′sis), *n.* coagulation of blood in the blood vessels or heart.

throm′bus (-bəs), *n., pl.* **-bi (-bī).** a clot formed in thrombosis.

throne (thrōn), *n.* **1.** the seat occupied by a sovereign, bishop, etc., on ceremonial occasions. **2.** the office or dignity of a sovereign. **3.** sovereign power.

throng (thrông, throng), *n.* **1.** a great number of people or things crowded together. —*v.i.* **2.** to assemble in large numbers. —*v.t.* **3.** to fill with a crowd.

throt•tle (throt′l), *n., v.,* **-tled, -tling.** —*n.* **1. a.** the valve that controls the flow of fuel to an engine. **b.** the lever that controls this valve. —*v.t.* **2.** to choke or strangle. **3.** to silence or check. **4.** to control the speed of (an engine) with a throttle. —**throt′tler,** *n.*

through (thrōō), *prep.* **1.** in one side and out the other side of. **2.** past; beyond. **3.** between or among. **4.** throughout. **5.** done with: *What time are you through work?* **6.** to and including. **7.** by the means of. **8.** by reason of: *He ran away through fear.* —*adv.* **9.** in at one side and out at the other. **10.** all

the way: *This train goes through to Boston.* **11.** throughout. **12.** from beginning to end. **13.** to completion: *to see a matter through.* —*adj.* **14.** finished. **15.** extending from one side to the other. **16.** proceeding to a destination, goal, etc., without deviation: *a through flight.* **17.** permitting uninterrupted passage: *a through street.*

through•out′, *prep.* **1.** in, to, or during every part of. —*adv.* **2.** in or during every part.

through′way′, *n.* THRUWAY.

throve (thrōv), *v.* a pt. of THRIVE.

throw (thrō), *v.,* **threw, thrown, throw•ing,** *n.* —*v.t.* **1.** to propel from the hand by a sudden forward motion. **2.** to cast or send forth (words, a glance, etc.). **3.** to put into some place, condition, etc., as if by hurling: *to throw a man into prison.* **4.** to move (a lever or switch) in order to turn on or disconnect. **5.** to lose (a contest) intentionally. **6.** to cause to fall to the ground. **7.** to give or host: *to throw a party.* **8.** to amaze or confuse: *Her dark glasses threw me.* —*v.i.* **9.** to fling or hurl something. **10. throw away, a.** to discard. **b.** to squander. **11. ~ in,** to add as a bonus. **12. ~ off, a.** to free oneself of. **b.** to give off; discharge. **c.** to confuse; fluster. **13. ~ out, a.** to discard or reject. **b.** to eject; expel. **14. ~ together,** to put together hurriedly. **15. ~ up,** to vomit. —*n.* **16.** an act or instance of throwing. **17.** the distance to which something can be thrown. **18.** a lightweight blanket. —**throw′er,** *n.*

throw′a•way′, *adj.* **1.** intended to be discarded after use. —*n.* **2.** a handbill or circular distributed free.

throw′back′, *n.* **1.** a reversion to an earlier type or state. **2.** an example of this.

throw′ rug′, *n.* SCATTER RUG.

thru (thrōō), *prep., adv., adj.* an informal spelling of THROUGH.

thrum (thrum), *v.i., v.t.,* **thrummed, thrum•ming.** to strum (a stringed instrument) idly.

thrush (thrush), *n.* any of various typically dull-plumaged songbirds.

thrust (thrust), *v.,* **thrust, thrust•ing,** *n.* —*v.t.* **1.** to push forcibly; shove. **2.** to put boldly into some position, situation, etc. —*v.i.* **3.** to make a lunge or stab. **4.** to force one's way. —*n.* **5.** an act or instance of thrusting. **6.** a lunge or stab. **7.** a force exerted by a propeller or propulsive gases to propel a missile, ship, or the like. **8.** the main point; essence. **9.** pressure exerted by a thing against a contiguous one. **10.** a military assault.

thru•way (thrōō′wā′), *n.* an expressway providing a direct route between distant areas.

Thu•cyd•i•des (thōō sid′i dēz′), *n.* c460–c400 B.C., Greek historian.

thud (thud), *n., v.,* **thud•ded, thud•ding.** —*n.* **1.** a dull sound, as of a heavy blow. —*v.i.* **2.** to strike or fall with a thud.

thug (thug), *n.* a vicious criminal or ruffian.

thu•li•um (thōō′lē əm), *n.* a rare-earth metallic element. *Symbol:* Tm; *at. wt.:* 168.934; *at. no.:* 69.

thumb (thum), *n.* **1.** the short, thick, inner digit of the hand. —*v.t.* **2.** to soil or wear with the thumbs in handling. **3.** to glance through the pages of. **4.** to solicit (an automobile ride) by pointing the thumb in the desired direction. —*Idiom.* **5. be all thumbs,** to be clumsy.

thumb′nail′, *n.* **1.** the nail of the thumb. —*adj.* **2.** brief and concise.

thumb′screw′, *n.* a screw that may be turned with the thumb and forefinger.

thumb′tack′, *n.* a tack with a broad head, designed to be pressed into a surface with the thumb.

thump (thump), *n.* **1.** a blow with a heavy object. **2.** the dull sound made by such a blow. —*v.t.* **3.** to beat with a thump. —*v.i.* **4.** to strike or fall with a thump.

thump′ing, *adj.* **1.** exceptional or impressive. **2.** of or like a thump.

thun•der (thun′dər), *n.* **1.** a loud noise produced by the expansion of air heated by a lightning discharge. **2.** any loud, resounding noise. —*v.i.* **3.** to give forth thunder. **4.** to make a noise like thunder. **5.** to speak loudly or vehemently. —*v.t.* **6.** to express loudly or vehemently. —**thun′der•er,** *n.* —**thun′der•ous,** *adj.*

Thun′der Bay′, *n.* a port in W Ontario, in S Canada, on Lake Superior. 112,272.

thun′der•bolt′, *n.* a flash of lightning with the accompanying thunder.

thun′der•clap′, *n.* a crash of thunder.

thun′der•cloud′, *n.* a cloud indicative of thunderstorm conditions.

thun′der•head′, *n.* THUNDERCLOUD.

thun′der•show′er, *n.* a shower accompanied by thunder and lightning.

thun′der•storm′, *n.* a storm with lightning and thunder.

thun′der•struck′, *adj.* astonished or dumbfounded.

Thur. or **Thurs.,** Thursday.

Thur•ber (thûr′bər), *n.* **James (Grover),** 1894–1961, U.S. writer, caricaturist, and illustrator.

Thur•mond (thür′mənd), *n.* **Strom,** born 1902, U.S. politician.

Thurs•day (thûrz′dā, -dē), *n.* the fifth day of the week, following Wednesday.

thus (ᴛʜus), *adv.* **1.** in this way. **2.** consequently. **3.** to this extent or degree.

thwack (thwak), *v.t.* **1.** to strike vigorously with something flat. —*n.* **2.** a sharp blow with something flat. —**thwack′er,** *n.*

thwart (thwôrt), *v.t.* **1.** to oppose successfully. **2.** to frustrate or baffle (a plan, purpose, etc.).

thy (ᴛʜī), *pron.* the possessive case of THOU used as an attributive adjective.

Thy•a•ti•ra (thī′ə tī′rə), *n.* ancient name of AKHISAR: site of one of the seven churches of Asia (Rev. 1:11).

thyme (tīm; *spelling pron.* thīm), *n.* an herb with aromatic leaves used for seasoning.

thy•mine (thī′mēn, -min), *n.* a pyrimidine base that is one of the principal components of DNA.

thy•mus (thī′məs), *n.* a gland at the base of the neck that aids in the production of T cells.

thy•roid (thī′roid), *adj.* **1.** of or being an endocrine gland at the base of the neck that secretes hormones to regulate the rates of metabolism and growth. —*n.* **2.** the thyroid gland.

thy•self (ᴛʜī self′), *pron.* a reflexive and intensive form of THOU.

ti (tē), *n.,* *pl.* **tis.** the seventh tone of an ascending diatonic scale.

Ti, *Chem. Symbol.* titanium.

Tian′an•men Square′ (tyän′än men′) also **Tienanmen Square,** *n.* a large plaza in Beijing, China, noted esp. as the site of major student demonstrations in 1989, suppressed by the government.

Tian•jin (tyän′jin′) also **Tientsin,** *n.* a port in NE China. 6,280,000.

ti•ar•a (tē ar′ə, -är′ə, -âr′ə), *n.,* *pl.* **-ar•as. 1.** a jeweled coronet worn by women. **2.** the pope's crown. [< L < Gk *tiára*]

Ti•ber (tī′bər), *n.* a river in central Italy, flowing through Rome into the Mediterranean. 244 mi. (395 km) long.

Ti•bet (ti bet′), *n.* an autonomous region in SW China, on a plateau N of the Himalayas. 2,030,000. —**Ti•bet′an,** *n., adj.*

tib•i•a (tib′ē ə), *n.,* *pl.* **-i•ae** (-ē ē′), **-i•as.** the inner of the two bones of the leg, extending from the knee to the ankle. —**tib′i•al,** *adj.*

tic (tik), *n.* a spasmodic, involuntary muscular contraction.

tick¹ (tik), *n.* **1.** a slight, sharp, recurring click, as of a clock. **2.** a mark used to check off items. —*v.i.* **3.** to emit a tick or ticks. —*v.t.* **4.** to mark with a tick.

tick² (tik), *n.* any of numerous bloodsucking arachnids, some of which transmit disease.

tick³ (tik), *n.* the cloth case of a mattress or pillow.

tick′et (-it), *n.* **1.** a printed slip of paper or cardboard indicating that the holder is entitled to some service: *a train ticket.* **2.** a summons for a traffic or parking violation. **3.** a tag indicating price, content,

etc. **4.** a slate of candidates nominated by a party. —*v.t.* **5.** to attach a ticket to. **6.** to give a ticket to.

tick′ing, *n.* a strong fabric used to cover mattresses and pillows.

tick′le, *v.,* **-led, -ling,** *n.* —*v.t.* **1.** to stroke lightly so as to excite a tingling sensation in. **2.** to excite agreeably; gratify. —*v.i.* **3.** to have or produce a tingling sensation. —*n.* **4.** a tickling sensation.

tick′ler file′, *n.* a file for reminding the user at appropriate times of matters needing attention.

tick′lish, *adj.* **1.** sensitive to tickling. **2.** requiring delicate or tactful handling. —**tick′lish•ness,** *n.*

tick-tack-toe or **tic-tac-toe** (tik′tak tō′), *n.* a game for two players, each trying to make a complete row of three X's or three O's on a nine-square grid.

Ti•con•der•o•ga (tī′kon də rō′gə), *n.* a village in NE New York: site of fort captured by the English 1759 and by Americans under Ethan Allen 1775. 2938.

tid•al (tīd′l), *adj.* of, characterized by, or subject to tides. —**tid′al•ly,** *adv.*

tid′al wave′, *n.* **1.** (not in technical use) a tsunami or other large, destructive ocean wave. **2.** any powerful or widespread movement, opinion, etc.

tid•bit (tid′bit′), *n.* a choice bit, as of food.

tid•dly•winks (tid′lē wingks′), *n.* a game in which small disks are snapped with larger disks into a cup.

tide (tīd), *n., v.,* **tid•ed, tid•ing.** —*n.* **1.** the rise and fall of the waters of the ocean, produced by the attraction of the moon and sun and occurring about every 12 hours. **2.** anything that alternately rises and falls. **3.** tendency or drift. **4.** a season or period: *Eastertide.* —*v.* **5. tide over,** to assist in getting over a period of difficulty. —*Idiom.* **6. turn the tide,** to reverse the course of events, esp. from one extreme to another: *The Battle of Saratoga turned the tide of the American Revolution.*

tide′land′, *n.* **1.** land alternately exposed and covered by the tide. **2.** Often, **-lands.** submerged offshore land within the territorial waters of a nation.

tide′wa′ter, *n.* **1.** water affected by the tide. **2.** the water covering tideland at flood tide.

ti•dings (tī′dingz), *n.pl.* news; information.

ti•dy (tī′dē), *adj.,* **-di•er, -di•est,** *v.,* **-died, -dy•ing.** —*adj.* **1.** neat and orderly. **2.** fairly large; considerable: *a tidy sum.* —*v.t., v.i.* **3.** to make tidy. —**ti′di•ly,** *adv.* —**ti′di•ness,** *n.*

tie (tī), *v.,* **tied, ty•ing,** *n.* —*v.t.* **1.** to fasten with a cord, string, etc. **2.** to fasten by tightening and knotting the strings of. **3.** to fasten together into a knot or bow. **4.** to form (a knot or bow). **5.** to bind or confine. **6.** to make the same score as. —*v.i.* **7.** to make the same score. **8. tie down,** to curtail the activities of. **9. ~ up, a.** to fasten securely by tying. **b.** to stop or impede. **c.** to moor. **d.** to occupy completely. —*n.* **10.** a cord, string, etc., used for tying. **11.** a necktie. **12.** a bond, as of mutual interest. **13.** an equality of scores or votes. **14.** a beam, rod, etc., for keeping two objects from separating. **15.** one of the crossbeams used for supporting and fastening the rails of a railroad track.

tie′ clasp′, *n.* an ornamental clasp for securing a necktie to a shirt. Also called **tie′ clip′.**

tie′-dye′ing, *n.* a method of dyeing fabric in which sections are bound so as not to receive the dye, producing a variegated pattern. —**tie′-dyed′,** *adj.*

tie′-in′, *n.* a link, association, or relationship.

Tien•tsin (tin′tsin′), *n.* TIANJIN.

tier (tēr), *n.* one of a series of rows rising one behind or above another.

tie′-up′, *n.* a temporary stoppage or slowing of traffic, production, etc.

tiff (tif), *n.* a slight quarrel.

Tif•fa•ny (tif′ə nē), *n.* **1. Charles Lewis,** 1812–1902, U.S. jeweler. **2.** his son **Louis Comfort,** 1848–1933, U.S. painter and decorator.

ti•ger (tī′gər), *n.* a large, powerful Asian cat having a tawny coat with black stripes.

tight (tīt), *adj.* and *adv.,* **-er, -est.** —*adj.* **1.** firmly fixed in place. **2.** stretched so as to be tense. **3.** fitting too closely. **4.** difficult to deal with: *a tight situ-*

ation. **5.** of such close texture or fit as to be impervious to water, air, etc. **6.** firm; rigid: *tight control.* **7.** packed closely or full. **8.** nearly even: *a tight race.* **9.** stingy. **10.** characterized by scarcity: *a tight job market.* —*adv.* **11.** securely. **12.** soundly: *to sleep tight.* —**tight′ly,** *adv.* —**tight′ness,** *n.*

tight′en, *v.t., v.i.* to make or become tight or tighter. —**tight′en•er,** *n.*

tight′fist′ed, *adj.* stingy.

tight′-lipped′, *adj.* reluctant to speak.

tight′rope′, *n.* a taut rope or wire cable on which acrobats perform.

tights, *n. (used with a pl. v.)* a skintight garment for the lower part of the body and the legs.

tight′wad′, *n.* a stingy person.

Tig•lath-Pi•le•ser (tig′lath pī lē′zər), *n.* a king of Assyria (745–727 B.C.) who greatly expanded the empire. II Kings 15:29; 16:7–10. Also called **Pul.** II Kings 15:19–20.

ti•gress (tī′gris), *n.* a female tiger.

Ti•gris (tī′gris), *n.* a river in SW Asia, flowing SE from Turkey to join the Euphrates in Iraq. 1150 mi. (1850 km) long.

Ti•jua•na (tē′ə wä′nə, tē hwä′nä), *n.* a city in NW Mexico, on the Mexico–U.S. border. 461,257.

til•de (til′də), *n., pl.* **-des.** a diacritic (~) placed over a letter, as in Spanish, to indicate a nasal sound.

Til•den (til′dən), *n.* **Samuel (Jones),** 1814–86, U.S. statesman.

tile (tīl), *n., v.,* **tiled, til•ing.** —*n.* **1.** a thin slab, as of baked clay or linoleum, used for covering roofs, floors, etc. **2.** a pottery tube or pipe used as a drain. —*v.t.* **3.** to cover with tiles. —**til′ing,** *n.*

till[1] (til), *prep., conj.* UNTIL.

till[2] (til), *v.t., v.i.* to prepare (land) for the raising of crops, as by plowing. —**till′a•ble,** *adj.*

till[3] (til), *n.* a drawer, box, etc., in which money is kept, as in a shop.

till′age (-ij), *n.* **1.** the tilling of land. **2.** tilled land.

til′ler, *n.* a bar or lever for turning the rudder in steering.

tilt (tilt), *v.t.* **1.** to cause to slope. —*v.i.* **2.** to slope or lean. **3.** to charge with a lance or the like. **4.** to engage in a joust or tournament. —*n.* **5.** a slope. **6.** a joust or tournament. —**Idiom. 7. (at) full tilt,** at maximum speed.

tim•ber (tim′bər), *n.* **1.** wood suitable for construction purposes. **2.** growing trees. **3.** a single piece of wood forming part of a structure. —**tim′bered,** *adj.*

tim′ber•line′, *n.* the altitude above sea level at which timber ceases to grow.

tim•bre (tam′bər, tim′-), *n.* the characteristic quality of a sound, independent of pitch and loudness.

time (tīm), *n., adj., v.,* **timed, tim•ing.** —*n.* **1.** the duration of all existence, past, present, or future. **2.** *(sometimes cap.)* a system of measuring the passage of time: *solar time.* **3.** a limited or particular period or interval: *a long time.* **4.** Often, **times. a.** an age or era. **b.** a period with reference to its conditions: *hard times.* **5.** a period experienced in a particular way: *Have a good time.* **6.** a period of work of an employee, or the pay for it. **7.** *Informal.* a term of enforced duty or imprisonment. **8.** leisure or spare time. **9.** a definite point in time: *What time is it?* **10.** the proper moment for something. **11.** each occasion of a recurring action or event: *We saw it five times.* **12. times,** the number of instances a quantity or factor are taken together: *Two goes into six three times.* **13.** *Music.* **a.** tempo. **b.** meter; rhythm. **14.** rate of marching: *double time.* —*adj.* **15.** of or showing the passage of time. **16.** set to detonate at the desired moment: *a time bomb.* —*v.t.* **17.** to measure the speed, duration, or rate of. **18.** to regulate (a train, clock, etc.) as to time. **19.** to choose the proper moment for. —**Idiom. 20. ahead of time,** early. **21. at the same time,** nevertheless. **22. at times,** occasionally. **23. for the time being,** temporarily. **24. from time to time,** occasionally. **25. in time, a.** early enough. **b.** eventually. **26. make time,** to move quickly. **27. on time, a.** punctually. **b.** to be paid for in installments. **28. time after time,** again

and again. —**Proverb. 29. Time heals all wounds,** hurt fades as time passes. **30. Time will tell,** the truth will become known in the future. —**tim′er,** *n.*

time′ clock′, *n.* a clock with an attachment that records the times of arrival and departure of employees.

time′ frame′, *n.* a period of time during which something takes place.

time′-hon′ored, *adj.* respected because of long observance.

time′keep′er, *n.* an official who times, regulates, and records the duration of a sports contest.

time′less, *adj.* **1.** without beginning or end. **2.** restricted to no particular time: *timeless beauty.* —**time′less•ly,** *adv.* —**time′less•ness,** *n.*

time′ly, *adj.,* **-li•er, -li•est.** occurring at a suitable time. —**time′li•ness,** *n.*

time′-out′, *n., pl.* **-outs.** a brief suspension of activity, as in a sports contest.

time′piece′, *n.* a device for measuring and recording time, as a watch.

times, *prep.* multiplied by.

time′-shar′ing, *n.* **1.** a plan in which several persons share the costs of a vacation home, with each using it at separate, specified times. **2.** a system in which users at different terminals simultaneously use a single computer.

time′ta′ble, *n.* a schedule showing arrival and departure times of trains, airplanes, etc.

time′worn′, *adj.* **1.** impaired by time. **2.** trite; hackneyed.

time′ zone′, *n.* one of the 24 divisions of the globe coinciding with meridians at successive hours from the observatory at Greenwich, England.

tim•id (tim′id), *adj.,* **-er, -est.** lacking in self-assurance; shy. —**ti•mid′i•ty, tim′id•ness,** *n.* —**tim′id•ly,** *adv.*

tim•ing (tī′ming), *n.* the adjustment of the time or speed of an action so as to achieve the best effect.

tim•or•ous (tim′ər əs), *adj.* fearful or timid. —**tim′or•ous•ly,** *adv.* —**tim′or•ous•ness,** *n.*

Tim•o•thy (tim′ə thē), *n.* **1.** a disciple and companion of the apostle Paul, to whom Paul is supposed to have addressed two Epistles. **2.** either of these Epistles, I Timothy or II Timothy.

tim•pa•ni (tim′pə nē), *n. (used with a sing. or pl. v.)* a set of kettledrums, esp. as used in an orchestra. —**tim′pa•nist,** *n.*

tin (tin), *n., v.,* **tinned, tin•ning.** —*n.* **1.** a malleable metallic element, used in plating and in making alloys. Symbol: Sn; *at. wt.:* 118.69; *at. no.:* 50. **2.** TIN PLATE. **3.** a container made of tin plate. —*v.t.* **4.** to cover or coat with tin.

tinc•ture (tingk′chər), *n., v.,* **-tured, -tur•ing.** —*n.* **1.** a solution of a drug in alcohol. **2.** a trace; tinge. **3.** a dye or pigment. —*v.t.* **4.** to tinge.

tin•der (tin′dər), *n.* any dry, easily ignitable substance.

tin′der•box′, *n.* **1.** a box for holding tinder. **2.** a potential source of violence.

tine (tīn), *n.* a sharp point or prong, as of a fork.

tin′foil′, *n.* tin, or an alloy of tin and lead, in a thin sheet, used as a wrapping.

tinge (tinj), *v.,* **tinged, tinge•ing** or **ting•ing,** *n.* —*v.t.* **1.** to color slightly. **2.** to add a trace of any quality to. —*n.* **3.** a slight trace, as of color.

tin•gle (ting′gəl), *v.,* **-gled, -gling,** *n.* —*v.i.* **1.** to have a slight prickling or stinging sensation. —*n.* **2.** a tingling sensation. —**tin′gly,** *adj.,* **-gli•er, -gli•est.**

tin•ker (ting′kər), *n.* **1.** a mender of pots and pans. **2.** a clumsy worker. —*v.i.* **3.** to putter or fiddle. **4.** to work clumsily. —**tin′ker•er,** *n.*

tin•kle (ting′kəl), *v.,* **-kled, -kling,** —*v.i., v.t.* **1.** to make or cause to make light ringing sounds. —*n.* **2.** a tinkling sound.

tin′ny, *adj.,* **-ni•er, -ni•est. 1.** of, like, or containing tin. **2.** lacking in resonance: *a tinny piano.* —**tin′ni•ness,** *n.*

tin′ plate′, *n.* thin sheet iron or steel coated with tin.

tin•sel (tin'səl), *n.* **1.** thin strips or threads of glittering metal, paper, or plastic, used for decoration. **2.** anything showy but of little value.

tin'smith', *n.* a person who makes or repairs items of tin plate.

tint (tint), *n.* **1.** a shade of a color. **2.** a delicate or pale color. **3.** a hair dye. —*v.t.* **4.** to give a tint to.

tin•tin•nab•u•la•tion (tin'ti nab'yə lā'shən), *n.* **1.** the ringing of bells. **2.** a sound produced by bells. [< L *tintinnābulum* bell]

tin'type', *n.* an old type of positive photograph made on a sensitized sheet of enameled iron or tin.

ti•ny (tī'nē), *adj.*, **-ni•er, -ni•est.** very small. —**ti'ni•ness,** *n.*

-tion, a suffix meaning: action or process (*convention*); result of action (*reflection*); state or condition (*affliction*).

tip¹ (tip), *n., v.,* **tipped, tip•ping.** —*n.* **1.** the point or end, esp. of something tapered. **2.** a small piece covering the end of something. —*v.t.* **3.** to furnish with a tip. **4.** to form the tip of. **5.** to adorn the tip of.

tip² (tip), *v.,* **tipped, tip•ping.** *n.* —*v.t., v.i.* **1.** to slant or tilt. **2.** to overturn. —*n.* **3.** the act of tipping or state of being tipped.

tip³ (tip), *n., v.,* **tipped, tip•ping.** —*n.* **1.** GRATUITY. **2.** a piece of confidential information. **3.** a useful hint or idea. —*v.t., v.i.* **4.** to give a gratuity (to). **5. tip off,** to supply with confidential information, esp. as a warning. —**tip'per,** *n.*

tip⁴ (tip), *n., v.,* **tipped, tip•ping.** —*n.* **1.** a light blow. —*v.t.* **2.** to strike lightly and smartly.

tip'-off', *n.* a tip; warning.

Tippecanoe and Tyler Too, a political slogan of the 1840 presidential campaign.

tip•ple (tip'əl), *v.i., v.t.,* **-pled, -pling.** to drink (liquor), esp. repeatedly and in small quantities. —**tip'pler,** *n.*

tip'ster (-stər), *n.* a person who sells tips, as for betting.

tip'sy, *adj.,* **-si•er, -si•est. 1.** slightly drunk. **2.** unsteady; shaky.

tip'toe', *n., v.,* **-toed, -toe•ing.** —*n.* **1.** the tip of a toe. —*v.i.* **2.** to go on one's tiptoes, as with stealth. —*Idiom.* **3. on tiptoe, a.** on one's tiptoes. **b.** expectant; eager. **c.** stealthily.

tip'top' (-top', -top'), *n.* **1.** the highest point. —*adj.* **2.** at the very top. **3.** of the highest quality. —*adv.* **4.** very well.

ti•rade (tī'rād, tī rād'), *n.* a prolonged outburst of bitter denunciation.

Ti•ra•në or **-na** (ti rä'nə), *n.* the capital of Albania. 206,000.

tire¹ (tīᵊr), *v.t., v.i.,* **tired, tir•ing. 1.** to make or become exhausted. **2.** to make or become bored.

tire² (tīᵊr), *n.* a ring of rubber or metal placed over the rim of a wheel to provide traction or resistance to wear.

tired (tīᵊrd), *adj.* **1.** exhausted; fatigued. **2.** bored. **3.** hackneyed.

tire'less, *adj.* untiring; indefatigable. —**tire'less•ly,** *adv.* —**tire'less•ness,** *n.*

tire'some, *adj.* causing fatigue or boredom. —**tire'some•ly,** *adv.* —**tire'some•ness,** *n.*

Tir•ol (ti rōl', tī-, tī'rōl), *n.* TYROL.

'tis (tiz), a contraction of *it is.*

Tish•bite (tish'bīt), *n.* **The,** an epithet of Elijah. I Kings 17:1; 21:17; II Kings 9:36.

tis•sue (tish'ōō), *n.* **1.** a mass of cells and cell products forming one of the structural materials of an organism. **2.** TISSUE PAPER. **3.** any of several kinds of soft, gauzy papers: *toilet tissue.* **4.** an interconnected mass: *a tissue of falsehoods.*

tis'sue pa'per, *n.* a very thin, nearly transparent paper used for wrapping or packing.

tit¹ (tit), *n.* a titmouse.

tit² (tit), *n.* a teat.

Ti•tan (tīt'n), *n.* **1.** (in Greek myth) any of a race of giant deities. **2.** (*usu. l.c.*) a person or thing of great size or power.

ti•tan•ic (tī tan'ik), *adj.* of great size or power.

ti•ta•ni•um (tī tā'nē əm), *n.* a corrosion-resistant metallic element, used to toughen steel. *Symbol:* Ti; *at. wt.:* 47.90; *at. no.:* 22.

tit for tat (tit' fər tat'), *n.* an equivalent given in retaliation.

tithe (tīth), *n., v.,* **tithed, tith•ing.** —*n.* **1.** the tenth part of goods or income paid to support a church. —*v.t., v.i.* **2.** to give or pay a tithe (of). —**tith'er,** *n.*

Ti•tian (tish'ən), *n.* (*Tiziano Vecellio*) c1477–1576, Italian painter.

tit•il•late (tit'l āt'), *v.t.,* **-lat•ed, -lat•ing.** to excite agreeably. —**tit'il•lat'ing•ly,** *adv.* —**tit'il•la'tion,** *n.*

ti•tle (tīt'l), *n., v.,* **-tled, -tling.** —*n.* **1.** the name of a work, as a book or poem. **2.** a descriptive appellation of rank or office. **3.** a sports championship. **4. a.** legal right to the possession of property, esp. real estate. **b.** the instrument constituting evidence of such right. —*v.t.* **5.** to furnish with a title.

tit•mouse (tit'mous'), *n., pl.* **-mice.** any of various small, stout-billed songbirds.

tit•ter (tit'ər), *v.i.* **1.** to laugh in a half-restrained, self-conscious way. —*n.* **2.** a tittering laugh.

tit•tle (tit'l), *n.* a very small thing; jot.

tit•u•lar (tich'ə lər, tit'yə-), *adj.* **1.** being such in title only. **2.** of or constituting a title.

Ti•tus (tī'təs), *n.* **1.** a disciple and companion of the apostle Paul, to whom Paul is supposed to have addressed an Epistle. **2.** this New Testament Epistle.

tiz•zy (tiz'ē), *n., pl.* **-zies.** *Slang.* a nervous, excited, or distracted state.

TKO, *pl.* **TKOs, TKO's.** *Boxing.* technical knockout.

Tl, *Chem. Symbol.* thallium.

TLC, tender loving care.

TM, 1. trademark. **2.** transcendental meditation.

Tm, *Chem. Symbol.* thulium.

TN, Tennessee.

TNT, a flammable toluene derivative used as a high explosive. [*t(ri)n(itro)t(oluene)*]

to (tōō; *unstressed* tōō, tə), *prep.* **1.** so as to reach: *Come to the house.* **2.** in the direction of: *from north to south.* **3.** to the extent or limit of: *He grew to six feet.* **4.** before; until: *ten minutes to six.* **5.** (used to express destination or end): *sentenced to jail.* **6.** (used to express a resulting condition): *torn to pieces.* **7.** (used to express the object of inclination or desire): *They drank to her health.* **8.** compared with: *inferior to last year's crop.* **9.** in accordance with: *a room to your liking.* **10.** with respect or relation to: *parallel to the roof.* **11.** contained or included in: *12 to the dozen.* **12.** (used to indicate the indirect object): *Give it to me.* **13.** (used to indicate the infinitive): *To err is human.* —*adv.* **14.** toward a closed position: *Pull the door to.* **15.** toward action or work. **16.** into a state of consciousness: *after he came to.* —*Idiom.* **17. to and fro,** back and forth.

toad (tōd), *n.* any of various mostly terrestrial amphibians related to frogs but having dry, warty skin.

toad'stool', *n.* a mushroom, esp. a poisonous one.

toad'y, *n., pl.* **-ies,** *v.,* **-ied, -y•ing.** —*n.* **1.** a fawning flatterer. —*v.i.* **2.** to be a toady.

toast¹ (tōst), *n.* **1.** sliced bread browned by dry heat. —*v.t.* **2.** to brown (bread, cheese, etc.) by heat. **3.** to warm thoroughly. —*v.i.* **4.** to become toasted.

toast² (tōst), *n.* **1.** a few words of welcome, congratulation, etc., said before drinking to a person or event. **2.** a person or event so honored. —*v.t., v.i.* **3.** to propose or drink a toast (to).

toast'er, *n.* an appliance for toasting bread.

toast'mas'ter, *n.* a person who presides at a dinner, introducing the speakers and proposing toasts.

toast'y, *adj.,* **-i•er, -i•est.** cozily warm.

to•bac•co (tə bak'ō), *n., pl.* **-cos, -coes. 1.** a plant whose leaves are prepared for smoking or chewing or as snuff. **2.** any product made from such leaves.

to•bac'co•nist (-bak'ə nist), *n.* a dealer in tobacco.

To•ba•go (tə bā'gō), *n.* an island in the SE West Indies: part of Trinidad and Tobago. —**To•ba•go•ni•an** (tō'bə gō'nē ən), *n.*

To•bi•as (tə bī'əs), *n.* the son of Tobit.

To•bit (tō′bit), *n.* **1.** a book of the Apocrypha. **2.** a devout Jew whose story is recorded in this book.

to•bog•gan (tə bog′ən), *n.* **1.** a long, narrow, flat-bottomed sled, used in coasting. —*v.i.* **2.** to coast on a toboggan. **3.** to plummet, as prices.

Tocque•ville (tōk′vil, tok′-), *n.* **Alexis Charles Henri Maurice Clérel de,** 1805–59, French statesman and author.

toc•sin (tok′sin), *n.* a signal of alarm sounded on a bell.

to•day (tə dā′), *n.* **1.** this present day. **2.** this present age. —*adv.* **3.** on this present day. **4.** at the present time.

tod•dle (tod′l), *v.i.* **-dled, -dling.** to move with short, unsteady steps, as a young child. —**tod′dler,** *n.*

to-do (tə dŏŏ′), *n., pl.* **-dos.** bustle; fuss.

toe (tō), *n., v.,* **toed, toe•ing.** —*n.* **1.** one of the terminal digits of the foot. **2.** the forepart of a shoe or stocking. **3.** a part resembling a toe in shape or position. —*v.t.* **4.** to touch with the toes. —*v.i.* **5.** to stand or walk with the toes in a specified position: *to toe in.* —*Idiom.* **6.** on one's toes, alert. **7. toe the line** or **mark,** to conform strictly to a rule or command.

toe′hold′, *n.* **1.** a small niche that supports the toes, as in climbing. **2.** any slight advantage or support.

toe′nail′, *n.* the nail of a toe.

tof•fee or **-fy** (tô′fē, tof′ē), *n., pl.* **-fees** or **-fies.** a confection made of brown sugar, butter, and vinegar.

to•fu (tō′fōō), *n., pl.* **-fus.** a soft cheeselike food made from curdled soybean milk. [< Japn]

to•ga (tō′gə), *n., pl.* **-gas, -gae** (-jē, -gē). (in ancient Rome) the traditional formal outer garment of freeborn men. —**to′gaed,** *adj.*

to•geth•er (tə geth′ər), *adv.* **1.** into or in one gathering: *Call the people together.* **2.** into or in union, proximity, etc.: *to sew things together.* **3.** considered collectively: *to cost more than all the others together.* **4.** at the same time. **5.** without interruption: *for days together.* **6.** in cooperation: *to undertake a task together.* —*adj.* **7.** *Informal.* emotionally stable. —**Usage.** See ALTOGETHER.

to•geth′er•ness, *n.* warm fellowship, as among family members.

tog′gle switch′, *n.* an electrical switch controlled by a projecting knob or arm that can be moved through a small arc.

To•go (tō′gō), *n.* a country in W Africa. 4,735,610. —**To′go•lese′** (-gə lēz′, -lēs′), *adj., n., pl.* **-lese.**

toil (toil), *n.* **1.** exhausting labor or effort. —*v.i.* **2.** to work very hard. **3.** to move with great effort. —**toil′er,** *n.* —**toil′some,** *adj.*

toi•let (toi′lit), *n.* **1.** a bathroom fixture consisting of a bowl and a water-flushing device, used for defecation and urination. **2.** a bathroom; lavatory. **3.** the act of dressing or grooming oneself. **4.** a person's dress or costume.

toi•let•ry, *n., pl.* **-ries.** any article or preparation used in grooming oneself, as deodorant.

toi•lette (twä let′), *n.* TOILET (defs. 3, 4).

toi′let wa′ter, *n.* a scented liquid used as a light perfume.

to•ken (tō′kən), *n.* **1.** something serving to represent or indicate a feeling, fact, etc.; sign. **2.** a memento; souvenir. **3.** a piece of metal used in place of money, as for bus fares. —*adj.* **4.** serving as a token. **5.** slight; minimal: *token resistance.* —*Idiom.* **6. by the same token,** for similar reasons.

to′ken•ism, *n.* the practice of making only a minimal effort to offer equal opportunities to minorities.

To•ky•o (tō′kē ō′), *n.* the capital of Japan, in SE Honshu. 11,618,281. —**To′ky•o•lte′,** *n.*

told (tōld), *v.* **1.** pt. and pp. of TELL. —*Idiom.* **2. all told,** in all.

tole (tōl), *n.* enameled or lacquered metal, used for trays, boxes, etc.

To•le•do (tə lē′dō; *for 2 also* -lā′-), *n.* **1.** a port in NW Ohio. 322,550. **2.** a city in central Spain. 57,769.

tol•er•a•ble (tol′ər ə bəl), *adj.* **1.** capable of being tolerated. **2.** fairly good. —**tol′er•a•bly,** *adv.*

tol•er•ance (-əns), *n.* **1.** a fair and permissive attitude toward those whose race, religion, beliefs, etc., differ from one's own. **2.** the capacity to endure something, as pain. **3.** the capacity to resist the action of a drug, poison, etc. **4.** the permissible variation of an object in some characteristic such as hardness or quantity. —**tol′er•ant,** *adj.* —**tol′er•ant•ly,** *adv.*

tol•er•ate′ (-ə rāt′), *v.t.* **-at•ed, -at•ing. 1.** to allow without hindrance; permit. **2.** to put up with; endure. **3.** to resist the action of (a drug, poison, etc.). —**tol′er•a′tion,** *n.*

toll[1] (tōl), *n.* **1.** a fee exacted for some privilege, as for passage over a bridge. **2.** the extent of loss, damage, etc., resulting from a calamity. **3.** a payment for services, as for a long-distance telephone call.

toll[2] (tōl), *v.t.* **1.** to ring (a large bell) with slow, repeated strokes. **2.** to announce, summon, or dismiss by this means. —*v.i.* **3.** (of a bell) to ring slowly. —*n.* **4.** the sound of tolling a bell.

toll′booth′, *n.* a booth, as at a bridge, where a toll is collected.

toll′gate′, *n.* a gate where a toll is collected.

Tol•stoy (tōl′stoi), *n.* **Leo,** Count, 1828–1910, Russian novelist.

tol•u•ene (tol′yōō ēn′), *n.* a flammable liquid used in the manufacture of TNT.

tom (tom), *n.* the male of various animals, as the cat or turkey.

tom•a•hawk (tom′ə hôk′), *n.* a light ax used by American Indians as a weapon or tool.

to•ma•to (tə mā′tō, -mä′-), *n., pl.* **-toes. 1.** a large, pulpy berry, red when ripe, eaten as a vegetable. **2.** the plant bearing this berry.

tomb (tōōm), *n.* a grave or burial chamber for a corpse.

tomb′stone′, *n.* a stone marker on a tomb or grave.

tom′cat′, *n.* a male cat.

tome (tōm), *n.* a very heavy, large, or learned book.

tom•fool•er•y (tom′fōō′lə rē), *n.* foolish or silly behavior.

Tom′my gun′, *n.* a submachine gun.

to•mog•ra•phy (tə mog′rə fē), *n.* a method of making x-ray photographs of a selected plane of the body. —**tom•o•graph•ic** (tom′ə graf′ik), *adj.*

to•mor•row (tə môr′ō, -mor′ō), *n.* **1.** the day following today. **2.** a future period or time. —*adv.* **3.** on the day following today. —*Saying.* **4.** Tomorrow is another day, life may be better tomorrow: popularized by Margaret Mitchell's novel and the motion picture *Gone With the Wind.*

tom′-tom′, *n.* a drum of American Indian or Asian origin, usu. played with the hands.

ton (tun), *n.* a unit of weight, equivalent to 2000 pounds (0.907 metric ton) avoirdupois **(short ton)** in the U.S. and 2240 pounds (1.016 metric tons) avoirdupois **(long ton)** in Great Britain.

to•nal•i•ty (tō nal′i tē), *n., pl.* **-ties.** the sum of relations existing between the tones of a scale or musical system.

tone (tōn), *n., v.,* **toned, ton•ing.** —*n.* **1.** any sound considered with reference to its quality, pitch, etc. **2.** quality of sound. **3.** vocal sound. **4. a.** a musical sound of definite pitch. **b.** a musical interval, as A–B, encompassing two semitones. **5.** a tint or shade of a color. **6.** the normal state of tension or responsiveness of the body's organs or tissues. **7.** a particular style or manner, as of writing. **8.** prevailing character or style: *the liberal tone of the 1960s.* **9.** distinction or elegance. —*v.t.* **10.** to give a certain tone to. **11. tone down,** to soften or moderate. —**ton′al,** *adj.* —**ton′al•ly,** *adv.* —**tone′less,** *adj.*

tone′-deaf′, *adj.* unable to distinguish differences in musical pitch.

Ton•ga (tong′gə), *n.* a kingdom on a group of islands in the SW Pacific, E of Fiji. 100,105. —**Ton′gan,** *n., adj.*

tongs, *n.* (*usu. with a pl. v.*) an implement consisting of two movable arms fastened together, used for picking up an object.

tongue (tung), *n.* **1.** a movable organ in the mouth, functioning in tasting, eating, and, in humans, speaking. **2.** the power of speech. **3.** manner or character of speech: *a flattering tongue.* **4.** a language or dialect. **5. tongues,** incomprehensible speech, typically uttered during religious ecstasy. **6.** anything resembling a tongue in shape or function. —*Idiom.* **7. hold one's tongue,** to refrain from speaking.

tongue′-lash′, *v.t., v.i.* to scold severely. —**tongue′-lash′ing,** *n.*

tongue′-tied′, *adj.* unable to speak, as from shyness.

tongue′ twist′er, *n.* a sequence of words difficult to pronounce rapidly, as "She sells seashells by the seashore."

ton•ic (ton′ik), *n.* **1.** anything that invigorates or strengthens, as a medicine. **2.** carbonated water flavored with quinine, lemon, and lime. **3.** the first degree of a musical scale; keynote. —*adj.* **4.** invigorating physically, mentally, or morally. **5.** pertaining to or based on the keynote.

to•night (tə nīt′), *n.* **1.** this present or coming night. —*adv.* **2.** on this present night.

ton•nage (tun′ij), *n.* **1.** the capacity of a merchant ship, expressed in tons. **2.** ships collectively considered with reference to their carrying capacity.

ton•sil (ton′səl), *n.* a prominent oval mass of lymphoid tissue on each side of the throat.

ton′sil•lec′to•my (-sə lek′tə mē), *n.*, *pl.* **-mies.** the surgical removal of one or both tonsils.

ton′sil•li′tis (-lī′tis), *n.* inflammation of the tonsils.

ton•so•ri•al (ton sôr′ē əl), *adj.* of a barber or barbering.

ton•sure (ton′shər), *n.* **1.** the shaving of the head or of some part of it upon entering the priesthood or a monastic order. **2.** the part of a cleric's head so shaven.

ton•y (tō′nē), *adj.*, **-i•er, -i•est.** stylish; swank.

too (tōō), *adv.* **1.** in addition. **2.** to an excessive degree. **3.** very: *none too pleased with the results.*

took (tŏŏk), *v.* pt. of TAKE.

tool (tōōl), *n.* **1.** a hand implement for performing mechanical operations. **2.** the cutting or working part of a drill or similar machine. **3.** anything used for accomplishing a task or purpose. **4.** a person manipulated by another. —*v.t.* **5.** to work or shape with a tool. **6.** to work decoratively with a hand tool. **7. tool up,** to install machinery and tools for a job.

toot (tōōt), *v.i., v.t.* **1.** to sound (a horn or whistle) in quick, short blasts. —*n.* **2.** an act or sound of tooting.

tooth (tōōth), *n.*, *pl.* **teeth. 1.** one of the hard bodies attached in a row to each jaw, used for biting and chewing. **2.** any projection suggesting a tooth, as on a comb. **3. teeth,** effective power to enforce something. —*Idiom.* **4. in the teeth of,** straight into, against, or in defiance of. —**toothed,** *adj.* —**tooth′less,** *adj.*

tooth′ache′, *n.* a pain in a tooth.

tooth′ and nail′, *adv.* with all one's resources or energy.

tooth′brush′, *n.* a small brush for cleaning the teeth.

tooth′paste′, *n.* a dentifrice in paste form.

tooth′pick′, *n.* a small pointed stick for removing food particles from between the teeth.

tooth′ pow′der, *n.* a dentifrice in powder form.

tooth′some (-səm), *adj.* **1.** pleasing to the taste. **2.** pleasing or desirable.

tooth•y (tōō′thē, -ŧħē), *adj.*, **-i•er, -i•est.** having or displaying conspicuous teeth.

top¹ (top), *n.*, *adj.*, *v.*, **topped, top•ping.** —*n.* **1.** the highest or uppermost point, part, surface, or end of anything. **2.** a lid or covering of a container. **3.** the highest position or rank. **4.** the highest pitch or degree: *at the top of one's voice.* **5. tops,** the part of a plant that grows above ground. **6.** the crown of the head. —*adj.* **7.** of, situated at, or forming the top. **8.** chief or principal. —*v.t.* **9.** to furnish with a top. **10.**

to be at the top of. **11.** to reach the top of. **12.** to exceed in amount, number, etc. **13.** to surpass or outdo. **14.** to remove the top of; prune. —*Idiom.* **15. at the top of one's lungs,** as loudly as possible; with full voice. **16. off the top of one's head,** without thought or preparation; extemporaneously. **17. on top,** successful. **18. on top of, a.** in addition to. **b.** in complete control. **19. on top of the world,** elated; exuberant. **20. over the top, a.** over the top of a trench, as in charging the enemy. **b.** surpassing a goal, quota, or limit. —*Saying.* **21. There's always room at the top,** effort will be rewarded by success.

top² (top), *n.* **1.** a cone-shaped toy with a point on which it is made to spin. —*Idiom.* **2. sleep like a top,** to sleep soundly.

to•paz (tō′paz), *n.* a yellow or brownish mineral used as a gem.

top′ brass′, *n.* high-ranking officers or important officials.

top′coat′, *n.* a lightweight overcoat.

top′-dress′, *v.t.*, **-dressed, -dress•ing.** to fertilize (land) on the surface.

To•pe•ka (tə pē′kə), *n.* the capital of Kansas. 120,646.

top′flight′, *adj.* excellent; superior.

top′ hat′, *n.* a man's tall hat with a stiff brim, worn on formal occasions.

top′-heav′y, *adj.* having the top disproportionately heavy.

To•phel (tō′fel), *n.* the place where Moses addressed the Israelites in the wilderness. Deut. 1:1.

top•ic (top′ik), *n.* a subject of conversation, discussion, discourse, etc.

top′i•cal, *adj.* dealing with matters of current or local interest.

top′knot′, *n.* a tuft of hair or feathers on the top of the head.

top′mast′, *n.* the mast next above a lower mast on a sailing ship.

top′most′, *adj.* highest; uppermost.

top′notch′, *adj.* first-rate.

to•pog•ra•phy (tə pog′rə fē), *n.*, *pl.* **-phies. 1.** the detailed mapping or charting of the physical features of an area. **2.** the relief features or surface configuration of an area. —**to•pog′ra•pher,** *n.* —**top•o• graph•ic** (top′ə graf′ik), **top′o•graph′i•cal,** *adj.* —**top′o•graph′i•cal•ly,** *adv.*

top•ple (top′əl), *v.*, **-pled, -pling.** —*v.i.* **1.** to fall forward, as from being top-heavy. —*v.t.* **2.** to cause to topple. **3.** to overthrow.

top′sail′ (-sāl′; *Naut.* -səl), *n.* a sail next above the lowest sail on a mast of a sailing ship.

top′-se′cret, *adj.* of or designating the highest category of security classification.

top′side′, *adv.* up on the deck.

top′soil′, *n.* the fertile, upper part of the soil.

top•sy-tur•vy (top′sē tûr′vē), *adv.*, *adj.* **1.** upside down. **2.** in confusion or disorder.

toque (tōk), *n.* a soft, brimless, close-fitting hat for women.

torah

To•rah (tōr′ə, tôr′ə), *n.* (*sometimes l.c.*) **1.** the Pentateuch. **2.** a parchment scroll containing the Pentateuch, used in a synagogue. **3.** the body of Jewish religious literature, law, and teaching. [< Heb *tōrāh* instruction, law]

torch (tôrch), *n.* **1.** a light consisting of a stick ignited at the upper end. **2.** a source of illumination or enlightenment. **3.** a lamplike device producing a hot flame, as for soldering. **4.** *Chiefly Brit.* FLASHLIGHT. —*v.t.* **5.** to set fire to, esp. maliciously.

torch′bear′er, *n.* **1.** a person who carries a torch. **2.** a leader in a movement, campaign, etc.

torch′light′, *n.* the light of a torch or torches.

tore (tôr), *v.* pt. of TEAR².

tor•e•a•dor (tôr′ē ə dôr′), *n.* a bullfighter.

tor•ment (*v.* tôr ment′, tôr′ment; *n.* tôr′ment), *v.t.* **1.** to afflict with great bodily or mental suffering. **2.** to worry or annoy excessively. —*n.* **3.** a state of great bodily or mental suffering. **4.** something that causes suffering. —**tor•ment′ing•ly,** *adv.* —**tor•men′tor,** *n.*

torn (tôrn), *v.* pp. of TEAR².

tor•na•do (tôr nā′dō), *n., pl.* **-does, -dos.** a violent windstorm occurring over land, characterized by a funnel-shaped cloud that extends to the ground. [< Sp *tronada* thunderstorm ≪ L *tonāre* to thunder]

To•ron•to (tə ron′tō), *n.* the capital of Ontario, in SE Canada. 612,289. —**To•ron•to•ni•an** (tôr′ən tō′nē ən, tor′-, tə ron-), *adj., n.*

Toron′to bless′ing, *n.* in some charismatic Protestant churches, the manifestation of the Holy Spirit as laughter: named after Toronto, Canada, where the phenomenon occurred.

tor•pe•do (tôr pē′dō), *n., pl.* **-does. 1.** a self-propelled underwater missile containing explosives. **2.** any of various other explosive devices. —*v.t.* **3.** to attack, destroy, etc., with or as if with torpedoes.

tor•pid (tôr′pid), *adj.* **1.** inactive or sluggish. **2.** apathetic; lethargic. —**tor•pid′i•ty,** *n.*

tor′por (-pər), *n.* **1.** sluggish inactivity or inertia. **2.** lethargic indifference; apathy.

torque (tôrk), *n.* something that produces or tends to produce torsion or rotation.

Tor•rance (tôr′əns, tor′-), *n.* a city in SW California. 138,219.

tor•rent (tôr′ənt, tor′-), *n.* **1.** a rushing, violent stream of water. **2.** a violent or abundant stream of anything. —**tor•ren•tial** (tô ren′shəl, tə-), *adj.*

tor•rid (tôr′id, tor′-), *adj.* **1.** subject to parching heat, esp. of the sun. **2.** oppressively hot. **3.** ardent; passionate. —**tor•rid′i•ty, tor′rid•ness,** *n.* —**tor′rid•ly,** *adv.*

Tor′rid Zone′, *n.* the part of the earth between the tropics of Cancer and Capricorn.

tor•sion (tôr′shən), *n.* **1.** the act of twisting or state of being twisted. **2.** the twisting of an object by two equal and opposite torques. —**tor′sion•al,** *adj.*

tor•so (tôr′sō), *n., pl.* **-sos, -si** (-sē). the trunk of the human body.

tort (tôrt), *n. Law.* a wrongful act resulting in injury, for which the injured party is entitled to compensation.

torte (tôrt; *Ger.* tôʀ′tə), *n., pl.* **tortes** (tôrts), *Ger.* **tor•ten** (-tn). a rich cake made with eggs, ground nuts, and usu. no flour.

tor•tel•li•ni (tôr′tl ē′nē), *n.* (*used with a sing. or pl. v.*) small ring-shaped pieces of pasta filled with meat, cheese, etc.

tor•til•la (tôr tē′ə), *n., pl.* **-las.** a thin, round, unleavened bread made from cornmeal or flour.

tor•toise (tôr′təs), *n.* a turtle, esp. a terrestrial one.

tor′toise•shell′, *n.* the horny brown and yellow outer layer of the shell of certain turtles, used for combs and ornaments.

tor•tu•ous (tôr′chŏŏ əs), *adj.* **1.** full of turns or bends; twisting; winding. **2.** deceitfully indirect; devious. —**tor′tu•ous•ly,** *adv.* —**tor′tu•ous•ness,** *n.* —**Usage.** see TORTURE.

tor•ture (tôr′chər), *n., v.,* **-tured, -tur•ing.** —*n.* **1.** the act of inflicting excruciating pain, esp. as a means of punishment or coercion. **2.** extreme anguish of body or mind. —*v.t.* **3.** to subject to torture. **4.** to twist, as in shape. —**tor′tur•er,** *n.* —**tor′tur•**

ous, *adj.* —**Usage.** TORTUROUS refers specifically to what involves or causes pain or suffering: *the torturous heat.* Although some use TORTUROUS to mean TORTUOUS in the sense "twisting, winding," one is generally advised to keep these senses distinct: *a tortuous road.*

To•ry (tôr′ē), *n., pl.* **-ries. 1.** a member of the Conservative Party in Great Britain or Canada. **2.** (*often l.c.*) a conservative. **3.** a person who supported the British in the American Revolution.

toss (tôs, tos), *v.,* **tossed** or **tost** (tôst, tost), **toss•ing,** *n.* —*v.t.* **1.** to throw lightly or carelessly. **2.** to throw or fling about. **3.** to jerk upward suddenly, as the head. —*v.i.* **4.** to move irregularly, as a ship on a rough sea. **5.** to move restlessly about, esp. on a bed. **6.** to throw a coin into the air to decide something by the way it falls (sometimes fol. by *up*). —*n.* **7.** an act or instance of tossing.

toss′up′, *n.* **1.** the tossing of a coin to decide something. **2.** an even chance.

tot¹ (tot), *n.* **1.** a small child. **2.** a small portion, as of liquor.

tot² (tot), *v.t., v.i.,* **tot•ted, tot•ting.** to add; total (often fol. by *up*).

to•tal (tōt′l), *adj., n., v.,* **-taled, -tal•ing** or (*esp. Brit.*) **-talled, -tal•ling.** —*adj.* **1.** comprising a whole; entire. **2.** complete; utter: *a total failure.* —*n.* **3.** the total amount. —*v.t.* **4.** to bring to a total. **5.** to reach a total of. **6.** to demolish beyond repair. —*v.i.* **7.** to amount. —**to′tal•ly,** *adv.*

to•tal•i•tar•i•an (tō tal′i târ′ē ən), *adj.* **1.** noting or pertaining to a government in which one party exercises dictatorial control. —*n.* **2.** an adherent of totalitarian government. —**to•tal′i•tar′i•an•ism,** *n.*

to•tal′i•ty, *n., pl.* **-ties.** the total amount; a whole.

tote (tōt), *v.,* **tot•ed, tot•ing,** *n.* —*v.t.* **1.** to carry or transport. —*n.* **2.** an open handbag or shopping bag.

to•tem (tō′təm), *n.* **1.** a natural object or animate being assumed as the emblem of a clan or family. **2.** a representation of such an object or being. —**to•tem′ic** (-tem′ik), *adj.*

to′tem pole′, *n.* a pole carved and painted with totemic figures by Indians of the NW coast of North America.

tot•ter (tot′ər), *v.i.* **1.** to walk with faltering steps. **2.** to sway on the ground, as if about to fall.

tou•can (tōō′kan, -kän), *n.* a brightly colored bird of the New World tropics, with a very large bill.

toucan

touch (tuch), *v.t.* **1.** to put the hand, finger, etc., into contact with, so as to feel. **2.** to bring into contact with an object or surface. **3.** to come into contact with; be adjacent to. **4.** to attain equality with. **5.** to color slightly. **6.** to affect in some way. **7.** to move to tenderness or sympathy. **8.** to handle, use, or consume. **9.** *Slang.* to seek or get money from. —*v.i.* **10.** to touch someone or something. **11.** to come into or be in contact. **12. touch down,** (of an aircraft or spacecraft) to land. **13. ~ up,** to make minor improvements in the appearance of. —*n.* **14.** the act of touching or state of being touched. **15.** that sense by which an object is perceived by physical contact. **16.** ability; knack. **17.** relationship or communication: *Let's keep in touch.* **18.** a slight attack of illness. **19.** a slight addition or change in completing any piece of work: *finishing touches.* **20.** the manner of fingering a keyboard instrument. **21.** a slight trace. —**touch′a•ble,** *adj.*

touch/ and go/, *n.* a precarious state of affairs. —**touch/-and-go/,** *adj.*

touch/down/, *n.* **1.** the act of scoring six points in football by being in possession of the ball on or behind the opponent's goal line. **2.** the act or moment of landing, as of an aircraft.

tou•ché (tōō shā/), *interj.* (used to acknowledge a touch in fencing or a telling remark or rejoinder.)

touch/ing, *adj.* affecting; moving; pathetic.

touch/screen/ or **touch/ screen/,** *n.* a computer display that can detect and respond to the presence and location of a finger or instrument on or near its surface.

touch/stone/, *n.* a test or criterion for the qualities of a thing.

touch/y, *adj.,* **-i•er, -i•est. 1.** apt to take offense on slight provocation. **2.** requiring tactfulness in handling.

tough (tuf), *adj.,* **-er, -est,** *n.* —*adj.* **1.** strong and durable. **2.** difficult to chew. **3.** sturdy; hardy. **4.** unyielding; stubborn. **5.** hardened; incorrigible. **6.** difficult to perform, accomplish, or deal with. **7.** vicious; unruly, or rough. —*n.* **8.** a ruffian; rowdy. —*Saying.* **9. When the going gets tough, the tough get going,** people who are strong don't give up in a crisis. —**tough/ly,** *adv.* —**tough/ness,** *n.*

tough/en, *v.t., v.i.* to make or become tough or tougher. —**tough/en•er,** *n.*

tou•pee (tōō pā/), *n., pl.* **-pees.** a patch of false hair for covering a bald spot.

tour (tōōr), *n.* **1.** a long journey including the visiting of a number of places. **2.** a journey from town to town, as by a performer. **3.** a period of duty at one place or in one job. —*v.i., v.t.* **4.** to go on a tour (through).

tour de force (tōōr/ də fôrs/), *n., pl.* **tours de force** (tōōrz). an exceptional achievement by an artist, author, or the like. [< F: feat of strength or skill]

tour/ism, *n.* **1.** the occupation of providing various services to tourists. **2.** the promotion of tourist travel.

tour/ist, *n.* a person who makes a tour, esp. for pleasure.

tour•ma•line (tōōr/mə lin, -lēn/), *n.* a mineral occurring in variously colored transparent gem varieties.

tour•na•ment (tōōr/nə mənt, tûr/-), *n.* **1.** a contest in which a number of competitors take part in a series of matches. **2.** a medieval contest in which mounted knights fought with blunted lances for a prize.

tour•ni•quet (tûr/ni kit, tōōr/-), *n.* any device for stopping bleeding by compressing a blood vessel, as a bandage tightened by twisting.

tou•sle (tou/zəl, -səl), *v.t.,* **-sled, -sling.** to disorder or dishevel, as hair.

tout (tout), *Informal.* —*v.i.* **1.** to solicit business, votes, etc., importunately. —*v.t.* **2.** to solicit importunately. **3.** to praise extravagantly. **4.** to sell information on (a racehorse).

tow (tō), *v.t.* **1.** to pull or haul (a car, barge, etc.) by a rope or chain. —*n.* **2.** an act or instance of towing. **3.** something towed. —*Idiom.* **4. in tow, a.** being towed. **b.** in one's charge.

to•ward (tôrd, twôrd) also **-wards/,** *prep.* **1.** in the direction of. **2.** for: *saving money toward a house.* **3.** turned to; facing. **4.** shortly before: *toward midnight.* **5.** with respect to.

tow•el (tou/əl, toul), *n., v.,* **-eled, -el•ing** or (*esp.* Brit.) **-elled, -el•ling.** —*n.* **1.** an absorbent cloth or paper for wiping and drying something wet. —*v.t.* **2.** to wipe or dry with a towel.

tow/el•ing, *n.* a fabric used for hand towels or dishtowels. Also, *esp. Brit.,* **tow/el•ling.**

tow•er (tou/ər), *n.* **1.** a structure higher than it is wide, either isolated or forming part of a building. **2.** such a structure used as a stronghold or fortress. **3.** a vertical case designed to house a computer system standing on the floor. —*v.i.* **4.** to reach or stand high.

tow/er•ing, *adj.* **1.** very high or tall. **2.** surpassing others. **3.** extreme or intense.

tow•head (tō/hed/), *n.* **1.** a head of very light blond hair. **2.** a person with such hair. —**tow/-head/ed,** *adj.*

tow•hee (tou/hē, tō/hē, tō/ē), *n., pl.* **-hees.** any of several long-tailed North American finches.

town (toun), *n.* **1.** a thickly populated area, usu. smaller than a city and larger than a village. **2.** a city or borough. **3.** a township. **4.** the inhabitants of a town. —*Idiom.* **5. go to town,** *Informal.* to do something with speed and efficiency. **6. on the town,** *Informal.* out to have a good time.

town/ house/, *n.* one of a group of similar houses joined by common side walls.

town/ meet/ing, *n.* a meeting of the voters of a town, esp. in New England.

town/ship, *n.* a unit of local government, usu. a subdivision of a county.

towns/man or **-wom/an,** *n., pl.* **-men** or **-wom•en. 1.** a native or inhabitant of a town. **2.** a fellow resident of one's town.

towns/peo/ple, *n.pl.* the inhabitants of a town.

tow•path (tō/path/, -päth/), *n.* a path along the bank of a canal or river, for use in towing boats.

tox•e•mi•a (tok sē/mē ə), *n.* blood poisoning resulting from the presence of toxins in the blood. —**tox•e/mic,** *adj.*

tox•ic (tok/sik), *adj.* **1.** of or caused by a toxin. **2.** poisonous. —**tox•ic•i•ty** (-sis/i tē), *n.*

tox/i•col/o•gy (-si kol/ə jē), *n.* the branch of pharmacology dealing with the effects, antidotes, etc., of poisons. —**tox/i•col/o•gist,** *n.*

tox/ic shock/ syn/drome, *n.* a rapidly developing toxemia, occurring esp. in women using high-absorbency tampons.

tox•in (tok/sin), *n.* a poison produced by an animal, plant, or bacterium.

toy (toi), *n.* **1.** an object for children to play with. **2.** a thing of little importance. —*adj.* **3.** made for use as a toy. **4.** resembling a toy, esp. in size. —*v.i.* **5.** to play or trifle: *to toy with one's food.*

tr., 1. transitive. **2.** translated. **3.** translation. **4.** translator. **5.** transpose. **6.** treasurer.

trace¹ (trās), *n., v.,* **traced, trac•ing.** —*n.* **1.** a surviving mark or sign of the former existence or action of some agent or event. **2.** a barely discernible quantity or quality. —*v.t.* **3.** to follow the track or trail of. **4.** to follow the course or development of. **5.** to ascertain by investigation. **6.** to draw (a line, figure, etc.). **7.** to copy (a drawing) by following its lines on a superimposed transparent sheet. —**trace/a•ble,** *adj.* —**trac/er,** *n.*

trace² (trās), *n.* either of the two straps or chains by which a vehicle is drawn by a harnessed draft animal.

trace/ el/ement, *n.* any chemical element that is required in minute quantities for physiological functioning.

trac/er•y, *n., pl.* **-er•ies.** ornamental work consisting of branching ribs, bars, or the like.

tra•che•a (trā/kē ə), *n., pl.* **-che•ae** (-kē ē/), **-che•as.** a tube extending from the larynx to the bronchi, through which air passes in breathing; windpipe. —**tra/che•al,** *adj.*

tra/che•ot/o•my (-ot/ə mē), *n., pl.* **-mies.** the operation of cutting into the trachea.

trac•ing (trā/sing), *n.* something produced by tracing, as a copy of a drawing.

track (trak), *n.* **1.** a pair of parallel lines of rails on which a train runs. **2.** a mark or series of marks left by an animal, person, or vehicle in passing. **3.** a path; trail. **4.** a course of action or procedure. **5.** a sequence of events or ideas. **6. a.** a course laid out for running or racing. **b.** sports performed on such a course. **c.** track and field events as a whole. **7.** a band of recorded sound, as on a phonograph record. —*v.t.* **8.** to follow the track of. **9.** to make footprints on or with. **10.** to monitor the path of (an aircraft, hurricane, etc.). —*Idiom.* **11. keep** (or **lose**) **track,**

to keep (or fail to keep) informed. —**track′er,** *n.* —**track′less,** *adj.*

track′ball′, *n.* a computer input device for controlling the pointer on a display screen by rotating a ball set inside a case.

track′pad′, *n.* a computer input device for controlling the pointer on a display screen: used chiefly in notebook computers.

tract[1] (trakt), *n.* **1.** an expanse or area of land. **2.** a definite region of the body, esp. a system of organs: *the digestive tract.*

tract[2] (trakt), *n.* a brief pamphlet, usu. on a religious or political topic.

trac•ta•ble (trak′tə bəl), *adj.* **1.** easily managed or controlled. **2.** easily shaped; malleable.

trac•tion (trak′shən), *n.* **1.** the adhesive friction of a body on some surface, as a tire on a road. **2.** the act of drawing or pulling. **3.** the state of being drawn or pulled.

trac•tor (trak′tər), *n.* **1.** a motor-driven vehicle with large, heavy treads, used for pulling machinery. **2.** a truck with a driver's cab but no body, used for hauling a trailer.

trade (trād), *n., v.,* **trad•ed, trad•ing.** —*n.* **1.** the act of buying or selling commodities. **2.** a purchase or sale. **3.** an exchange of items. **4.** an occupation requiring skilled manual or mechanical work. **5.** the customers of a business. —*v.t.* **6.** to buy and sell. **7.** to exchange. —*v.i.* **8.** to carry on trade. **9.** to make an exchange. **10. trade on** or **upon,** to turn to one's advantage. —**trad′er,** *n.*

trade′-in′, *n.* goods given in whole or part payment of a purchase.

trade′mark′, *n.* **1.** any name, symbol, etc., used and usu. officially registered by a manufacturer or merchant to distinguish a product from those of competitors. —*v.t.* **2.** to register the trademark of.

trade′ name′, *n.* **1.** a name used in a trade to designate a commodity, service, etc. **2.** the name under which a firm does business.

trade′-off′ or **trade′off′,** *n.* the exchange of one thing for another, esp. to effect a compromise.

trades′man, *n., pl.* **-men. 1.** a craftsman; artisan. **2.** *Chiefly Brit.* a shopkeeper.

trade′ un′ion, *n.* LABOR UNION.

trade′ wind′ (wind), *n.* any of the winds blowing mainly from the northeast in the Northern Hemisphere and from the southeast in the Southern Hemisphere.

trad′ing post′, *n.* a general store in a remote area where goods are obtained by bartering local products.

tra•di•tion (trə dish′ən), *n.* **1.** the handing down of legends, customs, etc., from generation to generation, esp. by word of mouth. **2.** something that is so handed down. **3.** a long-established way of thinking or acting. —**tra•di′tion•al,** *adj.* —**tra•di′tion•al•ly,** *adv.*

tra•duce (trə dōōs′, -dyōōs′), *v.t.,* **-duced, -duc•ing.** to slander; defame.

traf•fic (traf′ik), *n., v.,* **-ficked, -fick•ing.** —*n.* **1.** the movement of vehicles, persons, etc., in an area or over a route. **2.** the quantity, intensity, or rate of such movement. **3.** trade; commercial dealings. **4.** communication or dealings between persons or groups. —*v.i.* **5.** to carry on traffic, esp. illegally. —**traf′fick•er,** *n.*

traf′fic cir′cle, *n.* a circular roadway at a multiple intersection to facilitate the passage of vehicles from one road to another.

traf′fic light′, *n.* a set of signal lights used to direct traffic at intersections.

tra•ge•di•an (trə jē′dē ən), *n.* an actor who performs tragic roles.

tra•ge′di•enne′ (-en′), *n.* an actress who performs tragic roles.

trag•e•dy (traj′i dē), *n., pl.* **-dies. 1.** an unfortunate or dreadful event or affair. **2.** a drama dealing with a serious or somber theme and ending in disaster. —**trag′ic,** *adj.* —**trag′i•cal•ly,** *adv.*

trail (trāl), *v.t.* **1.** to draw or drag along behind. **2.** to

follow the track or scent of. **3.** to follow along behind, as in a race. —*v.i.* **4.** to drag along the ground or some other surface. **5.** to float after something moving, as smoke does. **6.** to gradually become weaker or smaller: *Her voice trailed off into silence.* **7.** to lag behind. **8.** to grow along the ground rather than taking root. —*n.* **9.** a path in overgrown or rough terrain. **10.** the track, scent, etc., left by an animal, person, or thing. **11.** something that trails behind.

trail′blaz′er, *n.* **1.** a person who blazes a trail. **2.** a pioneer in any field.

trail′er, *n.* **1.** a large vehicle drawn by another vehicle, used esp. in hauling freight. **2.** a vehicle attached to an automobile and used as a mobile home. **3.** one that trails.

train (trān), *n.* **1.** a connected group of railroad cars pulled by a locomotive. **2.** a line of persons, vehicles, etc., traveling together. **3.** something drawn along, as a trailing skirt. **4.** a body of followers; retinue. **5.** a series of events, ideas, etc. —*v.t.* **6.** to form the habits, thoughts, or behavior of by discipline and instruction. **7.** to make proficient by instruction and practice. **8.** to make fit, as for an athletic performance. **9.** to bring (a plant) into a particular shape or position. **10.** to point or direct, as a firearm. —*v.i.* **11.** to be trained. —**train′a•ble,** *adj.* —**train•ee′,** *n., pl.* **-ees.** —**train′er,** *n.* —**train′ing,** *n.*

traipse (trāps), *v.i., v.t.,* **traipsed, traips•ing.** to walk (over) aimlessly or idly.

trait (trāt), *n.* a distinguishing characteristic or quality.

trai•tor (trā′tər), *n.* a person who betrays another, a cause, or any trust. —**trai′tor•ous,** *adj.*

tra•jec•to•ry (trə jek′tə rē), *n., pl.* **-ries.** the curve described by a projectile in its flight.

tram (tram), *n. Brit.* a streetcar.

tram•mel (tram′əl), *n., v.,* **-meled, -mel•ing** or (*esp. Brit.*) **-melled, -mel•ling.** —*n.* **1.** Usu., **-mels.** a hindrance to free action; restraint. —*v.t.* **2.** to hinder or restrain.

tramp (tramp), *v.i.* **1.** to walk with a firm, heavy step. **2.** to travel on foot; hike. —*v.t.* **3.** to step on heavily; trample. **4.** to traverse on foot. —*n.* **5.** a firm, heavy tread. **6.** the sound made by such a tread. **7.** a long, steady walk. **8.** a vagabond; vagrant. **9.** a freight ship that takes a cargo wherever shippers desire. —**tramp′er,** *n.*

tram′ple, *v.,* **-pled, -pling.** —*v.i.* **1.** to tread heavily. —*v.t.* **2.** to tread heavily, roughly, or carelessly on. —**tram′pler,** *n.*

tram•po•line (tram′pə lēn′, -lin), *n.* a canvas sheet attached by springs to a frame, used in tumbling.

trance (trans, träns), *n.* **1.** a half-conscious and sleeplike state, as that produced by hypnosis. **2.** a dazed condition. **3.** a state of complete mental absorption.

tran•quil (trang′kwil), *adj.* peaceful; calm. [< L *tranquillus*] —**tran•quil′li•ty, tran•quil′i•ty,** *n.* —**tran′quil•ly,** *adv.*

tran′quil•ize′ or **-quil•lize′,** *v.t., v.i.,* **-quil•ized** or **-quil•lized, -quil•iz•ing** or **-quil•liz•ing.** to make or become tranquil.

tran′quil•iz′er or **-quil•liz′er,** *n.* a drug that has a calming or muscle-relaxing effect.

trans-, a prefix meaning: across, through, or on the other side (*transatlantic*); changing thoroughly (*transmute*); beyond or surpassing (*transnational*).

trans., 1. transitive. **2.** translated. **3.** translation.

trans•act (tran sakt′, -zakt′), *v.t.* to carry on or conduct (business, negotiations, etc.).

trans•ac′tion, *n.* **1.** the act of transacting or fact of being transacted. **2.** something transacted, esp. a business agreement. **3. transactions,** the published record of the proceedings of a learned society. —**trans•ac′tion•al,** *adj.*

trans•at•lan•tic (trans′ət lan′tik, tranz′-), *adj.* **1.** crossing the Atlantic. **2.** situated beyond the Atlantic.

trans•ceiv•er (tran sē′vər), *n.* a radio transmitter and receiver combined in one unit.

tran•scend (tran send′), *v.t.* **1.** to go beyond the ordinary limits of. **2.** to surpass; excel. —**tran•scend′- ence,** *n.* —**tran•scend′ent,** *adj.*

tran•scen•den•tal (tran′sen den′tl, -sən-), *adj.* **1.** being beyond ordinary experience, thought, or belief; supernatural. **2.** abstract or metaphysical.

tran′scen•den′tal•ism, *n.* a philosophy emphasizing the intuitive and spiritual above the empirical. —**tran′scen•den′tal•ist,** *n., adj.*

transcenden′tal medita′tion, *n.* a technique, based on Hindu practices, for seeking serenity through regular meditation centered upon the repetition of a mantra. *Abbr.:* TM

trans•con•ti•nen•tal (trans′kon tn en′tl), *adj.* **1.** extending across a continent. **2.** on the other side of a continent.

tran•scribe (tran skrīb′), *v.t.,* **-scribed, -scrib•ing. 1.** to make a written or typed copy of (spoken material). **2.** to represent (speech sounds) in written phonetic symbols. **3.** to make a musical transcription of. —**tran•scrib′er,** *n.*

tran′script (-skript), *n.* **1.** a written, typewritten, or printed copy of something transcribed. **2.** an official copy, as of a student's academic record.

tran•scrip′tion, *n.* **1.** the act of transcribing. **2.** a transcript; copy. **3.** the arrangement of a musical composition for a medium other than that for which it was written.

trans•duc•er (trans dōō′sər, -dyōō′-, tranz-), *n.* a device, as a microphone, that converts a signal from one form of energy to another.

tran•sept (tran′sept), *n.* **1.** the part of a church crossing the nave at right angles. **2.** an arm of this.

trans•fer (*v.* trans fûr′, trans′fər; *n.* trans′fər), *v.,* **-ferred, -fer•ring,** *n.* —*v.t.* **1.** to convey or remove from one place or person to another. **2.** *Law.* to make over the possession or control of. **3.** to convey (a drawing) from one surface to another. —*v.i.* **4.** to transfer oneself or be transferred. **5.** to change from one bus, train, etc., to another. —*n.* **6.** the act of transferring or fact of being transferred. **7.** a ticket entitling a passenger to change to another bus, train, etc. **8.** a person who has transferred, as to another college. **9.** *Law.* the conveyance of property to another. —**trans•fer′a•ble,** *adj.* —**trans•fer′al,** *n.* —**trans•fer′ence,** *n.*

trans•fig•u•ra•tion (trans′fig yə rā′shən, transfig′-), *n.* **1.** the state of being transfigured. **2.** (*cap.*) **a.** the supernatural and glorified change in the appearance of Jesus on the mountain. Matt. 17:1–9. **b.** the festival commemorating this.

trans•fig′ure, *v.t.,* **-ured, -ur•ing. 1.** to change in outward appearance. **2.** to change so as to glorify or exalt.

trans•fix′, *v.t.,* **-fixed** or **fixt, -fix•ing. 1.** to make motionless, as with awe. **2.** to pierce through with or as if with a pointed weapon.

trans•form′, *v.t.* **1.** to change in form or appearance. **2.** to change in condition, nature, or character. —**trans′for•ma′tion,** *n.*

trans•form′er, *n.* **1.** one that transforms. **2.** a device that transfers electrical energy from one circuit to another, usu. with a change in voltage.

trans•fuse′ (-fyōōz′), *v.t.,* **-fused, -fus•ing. 1.** to transfer from one to another; instill. **2.** to diffuse into or through. **3.** to transfer (blood) by injection into a vein or artery. —**trans•fu′sion,** *n.*

trans•gen•dered (trans jen′dərd, tranz-) also **trans•gen′der,** *adj.* **1.** appearing or attempting to be a member of the opposite sex, as a transsexual. **2.** pertaining to a transgendered person or transgendered people.

trans•gress (trans gres′, tranz-), *v.i.* **1.** to violate a law, moral code, etc. —*v.t.* **2.** to go beyond (a limit or bound). —**trans•gres′sion** (-gresh′ən), *n.* —**trans•gres′sor,** *n.*

tran•sient (tran′shənt, -zhənt, -zē ənt), *adj.* **1.** not permanent; transitory. **2.** lasting or staying only a short time. —*n.* **3.** a transient person, esp. a temporary boarder. —**tran′sience, tran′sien•cy,** *n.* —**tran′sient•ly,** *adv.*

tran•sis•tor (tran zis′tər), *n.* **1.** a compact solid-state

device that performs the primary functions of an electron tube but uses less power. **2.** a radio that uses transistors. —**tran•sis′tor•ize′,** *v.t.,* **-ized, -iz•ing.**

tran•sit (tran′sit, -zit), *n.* **1.** the act or fact of passing across or through. **2.** transportation of persons or goods from one place to another. **3.** a system of urban public transportation. **4.** a surveyor's instrument for measuring angles.

tran•si•tion (tran zish′ən, -sish′-), *n.* passage from one position, state, etc., to another. —**tran•si′tion•al,** *adj.*

tran•si•tive (tran′si tiv, -zi-), *adj.* of or designating a verb that takes a direct object. —**tran′si•tive•ly,** *adv.* —**tran′si•tive•ness, tran′si•tiv′i•ty,** *n.*

tran•si•to•ry (tran′si tôr′ē, -zi-), *adj.* lasting only a short time; temporary.

transl., 1. translated. **2.** translation. **3.** translator.

trans•late (trans lāt′, tranz-, trans′lāt, tranz′-), *v.t.,* **-lat•ed, -lat•ing. 1.** to turn from one language into another. **2.** to change the form, condition, or nature of. **3.** to explain in simpler terms. —**trans•la′tion,** *n.* —**trans•la′tor,** *n.*

trans•lit•er•ate′ (-lit′ə rāt′), *v.t.,* **-at•ed, -at•ing.** to change (letters or words) into characters of another alphabet. —**trans•lit′er•a′tion,** *n.*

trans•lu′cent (-lōō′sənt), *adj.* permitting light to pass through but diffusing it so that objects are not clearly visible. —**trans•lu′cence, trans•lu′cen•cy,** *n.*

trans•mi′grate, *v.i.,* **-grat•ed, -grat•ing.** (of the soul) to be reborn after death in another body. —**trans′mi•gra′tion,** *n.*

trans•mis′sion (-mish′ən), *n.* **1.** the act or process of transmitting. **2.** something transmitted. **3. a.** the transference of force between machines or mechanisms. **b.** a unit of gears for this purpose, as in an automobile. **4.** the broadcasting of radio waves from one location to another.

trans•mit′ (-mit′), *v.t.,* **-mit•ted, -mit•ting. 1.** to send or convey from one person or place to another. **2.** to pass on by heredity. **3.** to cause (light, sound, etc.) to pass through a medium. **4.** to emit (radio or television signals). —**trans•mis′si•ble** (-mis′ə bəl), **trans•mit′ta•ble,** *adj.* —**trans•mit′tal, trans•mit′- tance,** *n.*

trans•mit′ter, *n.* **1.** one that transmits. **2.** a device for transmitting signals, as in radio.

trans•mute′ (-myōōt′), *v.t., v.i.,* **-mut•ed, -mut• ing.** to change from one nature, substance, etc., into another. —**trans•mut′a•ble,** *adj.* —**trans′mu•ta′- tion,** *n.*

trans•na′tion•al, *adj.* going beyond national boundaries or interests.

trans′o•ce•an′ic, *adj.* crossing the ocean.

tran•som (tran′səm), *n.* **1.** a crosspiece separating a door or window from a window above it. **2.** a window above such a crosspiece.

trans′pa•cif′ic (trans′-), *adj.* **1.** crossing the Pacific. **2.** situated beyond the Pacific.

trans•par′ent (-pâr′ənt), *adj.* **1.** transmitting rays of light through its substance so that objects beyond can be distinctly seen. **2.** so sheer as to permit light to pass through. **3.** easily recognized or detected. **4.** easily understood; obvious. —**trans•par′en•cy,** *n., pl.* **-cies.** —**trans•par′ent•ly,** *adv.*

tran•spire (tran spīr′), *v.i.,* **-spired, -spir•ing. 1.** to occur; happen. **2.** to give off waste matter, watery vapor, etc., through the surface. **3.** to become known. —**tran′spi•ra′tion** (-spə rā′shən), *n.* —**Usage.** The original meaning of TRANSPIRE is "to escape as vapor." Although it has been used to mean "to occur, happen" in all varieties of speech and writing for two centuries, this common meaning is occasionally objected to by some commentators.

trans•plant (*v.* trans plant′, -plänt′; *n.* trans′plant′, -plänt′), *v.t.* **1.** to remove and plant in another place. **2.** to transfer (an organ or tissue) from one part of the body or from one individual to another. **3.** to bring from one region to another for settlement. —*n.* **4.** the act of transplanting. **5.** something transplanted. —**trans′plan•ta′tion,** *n.*

trans•port (*v.* trans pôrt′; *n.* trans′pôrt), *v.t.* **1.** to carry or convey from one place to another. **2.** to carry away by strong emotion. —*n.* **3.** the act of transporting. **4.** a means of transporting, as a ship. **5.** strong emotion, as of joy. —**trans•port′er,** *n.*

trans/por•ta/tion (-pər tā′shən), *n.* **1.** the act of transporting or state of being transported. **2.** the means of transport. **3.** the business of conveying people, goods, etc.

trans•pose′ (-pōz′), *v.t.*, **-posed, -pos•ing. 1.** to reverse the position or order of. **2.** to put (a musical composition) into a different key. —**trans/po•si/tion** (-pə zish′ən), *n.*

trans•ship′, *v.t., v.i.,* **-shipped, -ship•ping.** to transfer from one ship, truck, freight car, or other conveyance to another. —**trans•ship/ment,** *n.*

tran•sub•stan•ti•a•tion (tran′səb stan′shē ā′shən), *n.* (in the Eucharist) the conversion of the whole substance of the bread and wine into the body and blood of Christ.

Trans•vaal (trans väl′, tranz-), *n.* a province in the NE Republic of South Africa. 11,885,000.

trans•verse (trans vûrs′, tranz-; trans/vûrs, tranz/-), *adj.* **1.** lying or extending across. —*n.* **2.** something transverse. —**trans•verse/ly,** *adv.*

trap¹ (trap), *n., v.,* **trapped, trap•ping.** —*n.* **1.** a device for catching game or other animals, as one that springs shut suddenly. **2.** any stratagem for catching a person unawares. **3.** a U-shaped section in a pipe for preventing the escape of air or gases. **4. traps,** the percussion instruments of a band. —*v.t.* **5.** to catch in or as if in a trap. —*v.i.* **6.** to trap animals for their furs. —**trap/per,** *n.*

trap² (trap), *v.t.,* **trapped, trap•ping.** to furnish with trappings.

trap/door′, *n.* a door flush with the surface of a floor or ceiling.

tra•peze (tra pēz′, trə-), *n.* a short horizontal bar attached to the ends of two suspended ropes, used in acrobatics.

trap•e•zoid (trap′ə zoid′), *n.* a quadrilateral plane figure with two parallel sides. —**trap/e•zoi/dal,** *adj.*

trap/pings, *n.pl.* **1.** ornamental articles of equipment or dress. **2.** conventional outward forms or symbols. **3.** an ornamental covering for a horse.

trap/shoot/ing, *n.* the sport of shooting at clay pigeons hurled into the air from a trap.

trash (trash), *n.* **1.** anything worthless or useless. **2.** a disreputable person. **3.** such persons collectively. —*v.t.* **4.** to vandalize. **5.** to criticize as worthless. —**trash/y,** *adj.,* **-i•er, -i•est.**

trau•ma (trou′mə, trô′-), *n., pl.* **-mas, -ma•ta** (-mətə). **1.** a bodily injury, as from an accident. **2.** psychological shock from experiencing a disastrous event. **3.** any distressing experience. —**trau•mat/ic** (trə mat′ik, trô-, trou-), *adj.* —**trau/ma•tize/,** *v.t.,* **-tized, -tiz•ing.**

tra•vail (trə vāl′, trav′āl), *n.* **1.** painfully burdensome work. **2.** pain resulting from mental or physical hardship. **3.** the pain of childbirth. —*v.i.* **4.** to toil. **5.** to suffer the pangs of childbirth.

trav•el (trav′əl), *v.,* **-eled, -el•ing** or (*esp. Brit.*) **-elled, -el•ling,** *n.* —*v.i.* **1.** to go from one place to another. **2.** to pass or be transmitted, as light. —*v.t.* **3.** to journey or pass through or over. —*n.* **4.** the act of traveling, esp. to distant places. —**trav/el•er,** **trav/el•ler,** *n.*

trav/e•logue/ or **-log** (-lôg′, -log′), *n.* a lecture, film, etc., describing or depicting travels.

tra•verse (*v.* trə vûrs′, trav′ərs; *n., adj.* trav′ərs, trəvûrs′), *v.,* **-versed, -vers•ing,** *n., adj.* —*v.t.* **1.** to pass or move over, along, or through. **2.** to extend across or over. **3.** to move laterally. —*n.* **trav•erse 4.** something that crosses or extends across. —*adj.* **trav•erse 5.** lying or extending across. —**tra•vers/al,** *n.*

trav•es•ty (trav′ə stē), *n., pl.* **-ties,** *v.,* **-tied, -ty•ing.** —*n.* **1.** a grotesque or debased imitation. —*v.t.* **2.** to make a travesty of.

trawl (trôl), *n.* **1.** a strong net dragged along the sea bottom to catch fish. **2.** a buoyed line with many short, baited fishing lines attached. —*v.i., v.t.* **3.** to fish or catch with a trawl.

trawl′er, *n.* a boat used in trawling.

tray (trā), *n.* a flat, shallow receptacle with raised edges, for carrying or holding articles.

treach•er•ous (trech′ər əs), *adj.* **1.** likely to betray trust. **2.** deceptive or untrustworthy. **3.** dangerous. —**treach/er•ous•ly,** *adv.* —**treach/er•ous•ness,** *n.*

treach/er•y, *n., pl.* **-er•ies.** betrayal of trust or allegiance.

trea•cle (trē′kəl), *n.* **1.** something excessively sweet or sentimental. **2.** *Brit.* MOLASSES.

tread (tred), *v.,* **trod, trod•den** or **trod, tread•ing,** *n.* —*v.i.* **1.** to step or walk. **2.** to trample. —*v.t.* **3.** to walk on, in, or along. **4.** to trample underfoot. **5.** to perform by walking or dancing: *to tread a measure.* —*n.* **6.** the act, sound, or manner of treading. **7.** something on which a person or thing treads, stands, or moves. **8.** the pattern raised on the face of a rubber tire.

trea•dle (tred′l), *n.* a lever worked by the foot to impart motion to a machine.

tread/mill′, *n.* **1.** a device worked by treading on moving steps or an endless moving belt. **2.** an exercise machine that allows the user to walk or run in place, usu. on an endless belt. **3.** a monotonous routine.

treas., **1.** treasurer. **2.** treasury.

trea•son (trē′zən), *n.* a violation of allegiance to one's country, esp. by acting to overthrow the government. —**trea/son•a•ble, trea/son•ous,** *adj.*

treas•ure (trezh′ər), *n., v.,* **-ured, -ur•ing.** —*n.* **1.** accumulated wealth, as money or jewels. **2.** any person or thing greatly valued. —*v.t.* **3.** to regard as precious. **4.** to put away, as for future use. [< OF < L *thēsaurus* storehouse, hoard]

treas/ur•er, *n.* an officer in charge of the receipt, care, and disbursement of money.

treas/ure-trove′ (-trōv′), *n.* **1.** anything valuable that one finds. **2.** treasure of unknown ownership, found hidden in the earth or elsewhere.

treas/ur•y, *n., pl.* **-ur•ies. 1.** a place where the funds of a government, corporation, etc., are kept. **2.** public or private funds or revenue. **3.** (*cap.*) the department of government that has control over the public revenue.

treat (trēt), *v.t.* **1.** to act or behave toward in some specified way. **2.** to consider or regard in a specified way. **3.** to give medical or surgical care to. **4.** to subject to some agent or action to achieve a particular result. **5.** to provide with food, gifts, etc., at one's own expense. **6.** to deal with in speech, writing, art, etc. —*v.i.* **7.** to deal with a subject. —*n.* **8.** entertainment, food, etc., paid for by another. **9.** anything that affords particular pleasure or enjoyment. —**treat/er,** *n.*

trea•tise (trē′tis), *n.* a formal exposition in writing of some subject.

treat/ment, *n.* **1.** the act, manner, or process of treating. **2.** medicinal, surgical, or therapeutic care.

trea•ty (trē′tē), *n., pl.* **-ties.** a formal agreement between two or more nations.

tre•ble (treb′əl), *adj., n., v.,* **-bled, -bling.** —*adj.* **1.** threefold; triple. **2. a.** of the highest part in harmonized music. **b.** of the highest pitch or range. —*n.* **3. a.** the treble part. **b.** a treble voice or instrument. **4.** a high-pitched voice or sound. —*v.t., v.i.* **5.** to triple.

tree (trē), *n., v.,* **treed, tree•ing.** —*n.* **1.** a plant with a permanently woody trunk and branches. **2.** something resembling a tree in shape: *a clothes tree.* **3.** the cross on which Christ was crucified. —*v.t.* **4.** to drive up a tree. —*Idiom.* **5. up a tree,** in a difficult or embarrassing situation; stumped. —*Proverb.* **6. The tree is known by its fruit,** parents can be judged by their children's character. Matt. 12:33. —**tree/less,** *adj.*

tree′ of knowl′edge of good′ and e′vil, *n.* the tree in the Garden of Eden bearing the forbidden fruit that Adam also tasted by Adam and Eve. Gen. 2:17; 3:6–24. Also called **tree′ of knowl′edge.**

tree′ of life, *n.* **1.** a tree in the Garden of Eden that yielded food giving everlasting life. Gen 2:9; 3:22. **2.** a tree in the heavenly Jerusalem with leaves for the healing of the nations. Rev. 22:2.

tre·foil (trē′foil, tref′oil), *n.* **1.** a plant having leaves with three leaflets, as the clover. **2.** a three-lobed figure or design.

trek (trek), *v.,* **trekked, trek·king,** *n.* —*v.i.* **1.** to travel slowly or with difficulty. —*n.* **2.** a journey involving hardship. —**trek′ker,** *n.*

trel·lis (trel′is), *n.* a lattice used as a support for growing vines.

trem·a·tode (trem′ə tōd′, trē′mə-), *n.* any of various parasitic flatworms with external suckers.

trem·ble (trem′bəl), *v.,* **-bled, -bling,** *n.* —*v.i.* **1.** to shake involuntarily, as from fear or cold. **2.** to be troubled with fear. **3.** to quiver or vibrate: *His voice trembled.* —*n.* **4.** the act or state of trembling.

tre·men·dous (tri men′dəs), *adj.* **1.** extraordinarily great in size, amount, or intensity. **2.** extraordinary in excellence. **3.** terrifying. —**tre·men′dous·ly,** *adv.*

trem·o·lo (trem′ə lō′), *n., pl.* **-los.** a vibrating effect produced on certain instruments and in the human voice.

trem·or (trem′ər, trē′mər), *n.* **1.** involuntary shaking of the body. **2.** any vibratory movement, as of the earth.

trem·u·lous (trem′yə ləs), *adj.* **1.** characterized by trembling or quivering. **2.** timid; fearful. —**trem′u·lous·ly,** *adv.* —**trem′u·lous·ness,** *n.*

trench (trench), *n.* **1.** a long, narrow ditch dug by soldiers as a defense against enemy fire or attack. **2.** a deep furrow or ditch.

trench·ant (tren′chənt), *adj.* **1.** incisive or keen: *trenchant wit.* **2.** vigorous; effective. —**trench′ant·ly,** *adv.*

trench′ coat′, *n.* a belted, double-breasted raincoat with epaulets.

trench′er, *n.* a flat piece of wood on which meat is served or carved.

trench′er·man, *n., pl.* **-men.** a person with a hearty appetite.

trench′ foot′, *n.* a disease of the feet due to prolonged exposure to cold and moisture.

trench′ mouth′, *n.* an acute ulcerating infection of the gums and throat.

trend (trend), *n.* **1.** the general course or prevailing tendency. **2.** style; vogue.

trend′y, *adj.,* **-i·er, -i·est.** of or in the latest trend or style. —**trend′i·ness,** *n.*

Tren·ton (tren′tn), *n.* the capital of New Jersey. 90,790. —**Tren′to/ni·an** (-tō′nē ən), *n.*

trep·i·da·tion (trep′i dā′shən), *n.* fearful anxiety.

tres·pass (tres′pəs, -pas), *n.* **1.** wrongful entry upon the lands of another. **2.** an encroachment or intrusion. **3.** an offense or sin. —*v.i.* **4.** to commit a trespass. —**tres′pass·er,** *n.*

tress (tres), *n.* Usu., **tresses.** long locks of hair, esp. those of a woman.

tres·tle (tres′əl), *n.* **1.** a supporting frame composed of a horizontal bar on two pairs of spreading legs. **2.** one of many transverse frames joined together to support a bridge.

trey (trā), *n.* a playing card or die having three pips.

tri-, a combining form meaning three (*triangle*).

tri·ad (trī′ad, -əd), *n.* a group of three.

tri·age (trē äzh′), *n.* **1.** the process of sorting victims to determine priority of medical treatment. **2.** the determination of priorities for action in an emergency.

tri·al (trī′əl), *n.* **1.** the hearing and deciding of a case in a court of law. **2.** the act of trying, testing, or putting to the proof. **3.** an attempt or effort. **4.** an affliction or trouble. **5.** an annoying thing or person. —*adj.* **6.** of or used in a trial. **7.** done or made by way of trial or test.

tri·an·gle (trī′ang′gəl), *n.* **1.** a plane figure having three sides and three angles. **2.** any three-cornered or three-sided figure or object. **3.** a situation involving three persons. —**tri·an′gu·lar** (-gyə lər), *adj.*

tri·an′gu·late (-gyə lāt′), *v.t.,* **-lat·ed, -lat·ing.** **1.** to survey (an area) by using trigonometric principles. **2.** to divide into triangles. —**tri·an′gu·la′tion,** *n.*

Tri·as·sic (trī as′ik), *adj.* noting or pertaining to a period of the Mesozoic Era, characterized by the advent of dinosaurs.

tri·ath·lon (trī ath′lon), *n.* **1.** an athletic contest comprising three consecutive events, usu. swimming, bicycling, and distance running. **2.** a women's track-and-field competition comprising the 100-meter dash, high jump, and shot put.

tribe (trīb), *n.* **1.** a group of people, esp. an aboriginal people, descended from a common ancestor and sharing customs and traditions. **2.** a group of related plants or animals. —**trib′al,** *adj.*

tribes′man, *n., pl.* **-men.** a member of a tribe.

trib·u·la·tion (trib′yə lā′shən), *n.* **1.** severe trial or suffering. **2.** an instance of this.

tri·bu·nal (trī byōon′l, tri-), *n.* **1.** a court of justice. **2.** a seat of judgment.

trib·une (trib′yōon, tri byōon′), *n.* **1.** a person who defends the rights of the people. **2.** (in ancient Rome) an official elected to protect the rights of the plebeians.

trib·u·tar·y (trib′yə ter′ē), *n., pl.* **-tar·ies,** *adj.* —*n.* **1.** a stream that flows into a larger body of water. **2.** a person or nation that pays tribute. —*adj.* **3.** flowing into a larger body of water. **4.** paying tribute.

trib·ute (trib′yōot), *n.* **1.** a gift, speech, etc., given as an expression of gratitude or esteem. **2.** a sum paid by one state to another in acknowledgment of subjugation or as the price of peace.

trice (trīs), *n.* a very short time: *in a trice.*

tri·cen·ten·ni·al (trī′sen ten′ē əl), *n.* TERCENTENNIAL.

tri·ceps (trī′seps), *n., pl.* **-ceps·es** (-sep siz), **-ceps.** a muscle at the back of the upper arm.

tri·cer·a·tops (trī ser′ə tops′), *n.* a plant-eating dinosaur with three horns.

triceratops

trich·i·no·sis (trik′ə nō′sis), *n.* infestation of the intestines and muscle tissue with parasitic worms, usu. by eating undercooked pork.

trick (trik), *n.* **1.** a device or stratagem intended to deceive or cheat. **2.** a practical joke; prank. **3.** the knack of doing something skillfully. **4.** a clever feat intended to entertain. **5.** a behavioral peculiarity. **6.** a tour of duty. **7.** the set of cards played and won in one round. —*adj.* **8.** inclined to stiffen or weaken suddenly: *a trick shoulder.* —*v.t.* **9.** to deceive or cheat. —**trick′er·y,** *n., pl.* **-er·ies.** —**trick′ster** (-stər), *n.*

trick·le (trik′əl), *v.,* **-led, -ling,** *n.* —*v.i.* **1.** to flow in a small, gentle stream. **2.** to move slowly or irregularly: *The guests trickled out of the room.* —*n.* **3.** a trickling flow or stream.

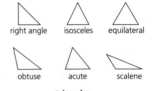

triangles

trick′le-down′ the′ory, *n.* an economic theory that monetary benefits directed by the government to big business will in turn pass down to the general public.

trick′y, *adj.,* **-i·er, -i·est.** **1.** given to deceitful tricks. **2.** unreliable or uncooperative. **3.** involving intricate or clever maneuvers.

tri•col•or (trī′kul′ər), *n.* a flag with three colors, esp. the flag of France.

tri•cy•cle (trī′si kəl, -sik′əl), *n.* a child's three-wheeled vehicle propelled by foot pedals.

tri•dent (trīd′nt), *n.* a three-pronged instrument or weapon.

tried (trīd), *v.* **1.** pt. and pp. of TRY. —*adj.* **2.** tested and proved good or trustworthy. **3.** subjected to hardship.

tri•en•ni•al (trī en′ē əl), *adj.* **1.** occurring every three years. **2.** lasting three years. —**tri•en′ni•al•ly,** *adv.*

tri•fle (trī′fəl), *n., v.,* **-fled, -fling.** —*n.* **1.** something of very little value or importance. **2.** a small amount. —*v.i.* **3.** to deal lightly or without due respect. **4.** to play or toy. —**tri′fler,** *n.*

tri′fling, *adj.* **1.** trivial; insignificant. **2.** frivolous; shallow.

tri•fo•cals (trī fō′kəlz, trī′fō′-), *n.pl.* eyeglasses with a lens in three portions, for near, intermediate, and far vision.

trig•ger (trig′ər), *n.* **1.** a small lever in a firearm that, when pressed by the finger, actuates the mechanism that discharges the weapon. —*v.t.* **2.** to initiate or precipitate (a reaction, process, etc.).

tri•glyc•er•ide (trī glis′ə rīd′, -ər id), *n.* an ester obtained from glycerol, forming much of the fats and oils stored in tissues.

trig•o•nom•e•try (trig′ə nom′i trē), *n.* the branch of mathematics that deals with the relations between the sides and angles of triangles. —**trig′o•no•met′-ric** (-nə me′trik), *adj.*

trill (tril), *n.* **1.** a rapid alternation of two adjacent musical tones. **2.** a similar quavering sound, as that made by a bird. **3.** a speech sound produced with rapid vibration of the tongue or uvula. —*v.t., v.i.* **4.** to sing, utter, or play with a trill.

tril•lion (tril′yən), *n., pl.* **-lions, -lion.** a cardinal number represented in the U.S. by 1 followed by 12 zeros, and in Great Britain by 1 followed by 18 zeros. —**tril′lionth,** *n., adj.*

tril•li•um (tril′ē əm), *n.* a plant of the lily family, having three leaves and a solitary flower.

tril•o•gy (tril′ə jē), *n., pl.* **-gies** a group of three plays, novels, etc., that are closely related.

trim (trim), *v.,* **trimmed, trim•ming,** *n., adj.,* **trim•mer, trim•mest.** —*v.t.* **1.** to make neat or orderly by clipping, paring, etc. **2.** to remove by cutting. **3.** to level off (an airplane) in flight. **4. a.** to balance (a ship), as by rearranging the cargo. **b.** to adjust (the sails) to the direction of the wind. **5.** to decorate with ornaments. —*n.* **6.** the condition or fitness of a person or thing for action or use. **7.** material used for decoration or embellishment. **8.** a trimming by cutting, clipping, or the like. —*adj.* **9.** pleasingly neat or smart. **10.** in good condition or order. **11.** slim; lean. —**trim′ly,** *adv.* —**trim′mer,** *n.* —**trim′ness,** *n.*

tri•ma•ran (trī′mə ran′), *n.* a boat similar to a catamaran but having three hulls.

tri•mes•ter (trī mes′tər, trī′mes-), *n.* **1.** a period of three months. **2.** one of the three terms into which the academic year is sometimes divided.

trim′ming, *n.* **1.** anything used to decorate. **2.** Usu., **trimmings.** an accompaniment to a main dish. **3. trimmings,** pieces cut off in trimming. **4.** a beating or defeat.

Tri•mur•ti (tri mŏor′tē), *n.* (in later Hinduism) a trinity consisting of Brahma the Creator, Vishnu the Preserver, and Shiva the Destroyer. [< Sanskrit *trimūrti = tri* THREE + *mūrti* shape]

Trin•i•dad (trin′i dad′), *n.* an island in the SE West Indies. —**Trin′i•da′di•an** (-dā′dē ən, -dad′ē-), *adj., n.*

Trin′idad and Toba′go, *n.* a republic in the West Indies, comprising the islands of Trinidad and Tobago. 1,273,141.

Trin•i•ty (trin′i tē), *n., pl.* **-ties** for 2. **1.** the union of Father, Son, and Holy Spirit in one Godhead. **2.** (*l.c.*) a group of three.

trin•ket (tring′kit), *n.* **1.** a small ornament of little value. **2.** anything of trivial value.

tri•o (trē′ō), *n., pl.* **tri•os. 1.** a group of three. **2.** a

musical composition for three voices or instruments. **3.** a company of three singers or players.

trip (trip), *n., v.,* **tripped, trip•ping.** —*n.* **1.** a journey or voyage. **2.** a stumble. **3.** an error or blunder. **4.** a light, nimble step. **5.** a device for releasing a spring or lever to stop or reverse a machine. —*v.i., v.t.* **6.** to stumble or cause to stumble. **7.** to make or cause to make an error. **8.** to move or perform with light, nimble steps. **9.** to release or operate suddenly, as a lever. —**trip′per,** *n.*

tri•par•tite (trī pär′tīt), *adj.* **1.** consisting of three parts. **2.** involving three parties.

tripe (trīp), *n.* **1.** a part of the stomach of a ruminant, as an ox, used as food. **2.** *Slang.* something false or worthless.

tri•ple (trip′əl), *adj., n., v.,* **-pled, -pling.** —*adj.* **1.** consisting of three parts. **2.** three times as great. —*n.* **3.** an amount three times as great as another. **4.** a hit in baseball that enables a batter to reach third base. —*v.t., v.i.* **5.** to make or become triple. —**trip′ly,** *adv.*

tri•plet (trip′lit), *n.* one of three offspring born at the same birth.

trip′li•cate (*n., adj.* -li kit, -kāt′; *v.* -kāt′), *n., v.,* **-cat•ed, -cat•ing,** *adj.* —*n.* **1.** one of three identical items, esp. copies of typewritten material. —*v.t.* **2.** to make three copies of. —*adj.* **3.** consisting of three identical parts. **4.** noting the third copy or item. —*Idiom.* **5. in triplicate,** in three copies.

tri•pod (trī′pod), *n.* a three-legged stand or support, as for a camera.

Trip•o•li (trip′ə lē), *n.* the capital of Libya. 858,000. —**Trip•o•li•tan** (tri pol′i tn), *n., adj.*

trip•tych (trip′tik), *n.* a set of three panels side by side, bearing pictures or carvings.

tri•sect (trī sekt′), *v.t.* to divide into three equal parts. —**tri•sec′tion,** *n.*

trite (trīt), *adj.,* **trit•er, trit•est.** lacking in freshness because of constant use; hackneyed. [< L *trītus* worn, common] —**trite′ness,** *n.*

trit•i•um (trit′ē əm), *n.* an isotope of hydrogen having an atomic weight of three.

tri•umph (trī′əmf, -umf), *n.* **1.** victory; success. **2.** exultation over victory or success. **3.** to gain victory or success. **4.** to rejoice over victory or success. —**tri•um′phal, tri•um′phant,** *adj.* —**tri•um′-phant•ly,** *adv.*

tri•um•vir (trī um′vər), *n., pl.* **-virs, -vi•ri** (-və rī′). a member of a triumvirate.

tri•um′vi•rate (-vər it, -və rāt′), *n.* a group of three officials or magistrates jointly exercising authority, as in ancient Rome.

triv•et (triv′it), *n.* **1.** a short-legged plate placed under a hot dish on a table. **2.** a three-legged stand placed over a fire to support cooking vessels.

triv•i•a (triv′ē ə), *n.* (*used with a sing. or pl. v.*) matters or things that are very unimportant.

triv′i•al, *adj.* of very little importance. —**triv′i•al′-i•ty,** *n., pl.* **-ties.**

triv•i•um (triv′ē əm), *n.* (during the Middle Ages) the lower division of the seven liberal arts, comprising grammar, rhetoric, and logic.

-trix, a suffix forming feminine agent nouns. Also, **-trice.** —*Usage.* Most English nouns in -TRIX have dropped from general use and occur rarely or not at all in present-day English. The forms in *-tor* are applied to both men and women. When relevant, sex is specified with the generic term: *Amelia Earhart was a pioneer woman aviator.* Legal documents still use *administratrix, executrix, inheritrix,* etc., but these forms too are giving way to the *-tor* forms. See also ESS.

tro•chee (trō′kē), *n., pl.* **-chees.** a foot of two syllables, the first stressed and the second unstressed. —**tro•cha′ic** (-kā′ik), *adj.*

trod (trod), *v.* pt. and a pp. of TREAD.

trod′den, *v.* a pp. of TREAD.

trog•lo•dyte (trog′lə dīt′), *n.* **1.** a prehistoric cave dweller. **2.** a hermit.

troi•ka (troi′kə), *n., pl.* **-kas. 1.** a Russian vehicle drawn by a team of three horses abreast. **2.** a ruling group of three. [< Russ]

Tro•jan (trō′jən), *adj.* **1.** of ancient Troy or its inhabitants. —*n.* **2.** a native or inhabitant of Troy. **3.** a person who shows pluck or determination.

Tro′jan horse′, *n.* a gigantic wooden horse that the Greeks left at the gates of Troy: soldiers emerging from it allowed the Greek army to enter the city.

Tro′jan War′, *n.* a legendary war between a confederation of Greeks and the city of Troy as a result of the abduction of Helen by Paris.

troll[1] (trōl), *v.t., v.i.* **1.** to sing in a full, rolling voice. **2.** to sing the parts of (a round) in succession. **3.** to fish (in) by trailing a line behind a slow-moving boat.

troll[2] (trōl), *n.* (in Scandinavian folklore) a supernatural being who lives underground or in caves.

trol•ley (trol′ē), *n., pl.* **-leys. 1.** TROLLEY CAR. **2.** a carriage or truck traveling on an overhead track. **3.** a grooved wheel on the end of a pole, used by a streetcar to draw current from an overhead conductor.

trol′ley bus′, *n.* a bus drawing power from overhead wires.

trol′ley car′, *n.* a streetcar propelled electrically by current taken by means of a trolley.

Trol•lope (trol′əp), *n.* **Anthony,** 1815–82, English novelist.

trom•bone (trom bōn′, trom′bōn), *n.* a musical wind instrument with a U-shaped metal tube and a slide for varying the tone.

troop (trōōp), *n.* **1.** an assemblage of persons or things. **2.** a cavalry unit about the size of an infantry company. **3. troops,** a body of soldiers. **4.** a unit of Boy Scouts or Girl Scouts. —*v.i.* **5.** to gather or move in great numbers. **6.** to walk, as if in a march.

troop′er, *n.* **1.** a mounted police officer. **2.** a state police officer. **3.** a cavalry soldier.

trope (trōp), *n.* **1.** the use of words in other than their literal sense. **2.** an instance of this.

tro•phy (trō′fē), *n., pl.* **-phies.** anything taken in war, competition, etc., esp. when preserved as a memento.

trop•ic (trop′ik), *n.* **1.** either of two corresponding parallels of latitude, one **(trop′ic of Can′cer)** about 23½° N, and the other **(trop′ic of Cap′ricorn)** about 23½° S of the equator. **2. the tropics,** the regions lying between these parallels of latitude. —*adj.* **3.** of the tropics.

trop′i•cal, *adj.* **1.** suitable for, characteristic of, or inhabiting the tropics. **2.** very hot and humid.

tro•pism (trō′piz əm), *n.* the orientation of an organism toward or away from a stimulus, as light.

trop•o•sphere (trop′ə sfēr′, trō′pə-), *n.* the lowest layer of the atmosphere, within which nearly all clouds and weather conditions develop.

trot (trot), *v.*, **trot•ted, trot•ting,** *n.* —*v.i.* **1.** (of a horse or other quadruped) to go at a gait in which the legs move in diagonal pairs. **2.** to hurry. —*v.t.* **3.** to cause to trot. —*n.* **4.** the gait of a quadruped when trotting. **5.** the jogging gait of a human being. —**trot′ter,** *n.*

troth (trôth, trōth), *n. Archaic.* **1.** faithfulness; fidelity. **2.** truth or verity. **3.** one's promise, esp. to marry.

Trot•sky (trot′skē), *n.* **Leon,** 1879–1940, Russian Communist revolutionary.

trou•ba•dour (trōō′bə dôr′), *n.* one of a class of lyric poets who lived principally in S France from the 11th to 13th centuries.

trou•ble (trub′əl), *v.*, **-bled, -bling,** *n.* —*v.t.* **1.** to disturb mentally; distress. **2.** to inconvenience. **3.** to cause bodily pain or discomfort to. **4.** to disturb or agitate, as water. —*v.i.* **5.** to put oneself to inconvenience or extra effort. —*n.* **6.** difficulty, annoyance, or disturbance. **7.** a physical disease, ailment, etc. **8.** mental or emotional distress. **9.** inconvenience or extra effort. —**trou′ble•some,** *adj.*

trou′ble•mak′er, *n.* a person who causes trouble.

trou′ble•shoot′er, *n.* an expert in discovering and eliminating the cause of trouble, as in mechanical equipment.

trough (trôf, trof), *n.* **1.** a long, narrow, open receptacle, used chiefly to hold water or food for animals.

2. a gutter under the eaves of a building. **3.** a long depression or hollow, as between waves.

trounce (trouns), *v.t.*, **trounced, trounc•ing. 1.** to beat severely. **2.** to defeat decisively. —**trounc′er,** *n.*

troupe (trōōp), *n., v.*, **trouped, troup•ing.** —*n.* **1.** a company of actors or other performers. —*v.i.* **2.** to travel as a member of a troupe. —**troup′er,** *n.*

trou•sers (trou′zərz), *n.* (*used with a pl. v.*) an outer garment for the lower part of the body, having individual leg portions.

trous•seau (trōō′sō, trōō sō′), *n., pl.* **-seaux** (-sōz, -sōz′), **-seaus.** an outfit of clothing, household linen, etc., for a bride.

trout (trout), *n., pl.* **trouts, trout.** any of various freshwater game fishes of the salmon family.

trow•el (trou′əl), *n.* **1.** a tool with a flat blade, used for working mortar, plaster, etc. **2.** a tool with a scooplike blade, used in gardening.

troy (troi), *adj.* expressed or computed in troy weight.

Troy, *n.* an ancient ruined city in NW Asia Minor.

troy′ weight′, *n.* a system of weights in use for precious metals and gems, in which a pound equals 12 ounces, 240 pennyweights, or 5,760 grains.

tru•ant (trōō′ənt), *n.* **1.** a student who stays away from school without permission. **2.** a person who neglects duty. —*adj.* **3.** absent from school without permission. **4.** neglectful of duty. [< OF: beggar < Celtic] —**tru′an•cy,** *n., pl.* **-cies.**

truce (trōōs), *n.* **1.** a temporary suspension of hostilities by mutual agreement of the warring parties. **2.** a temporary respite, as from trouble.

truck[1] (truk), *n.* **1.** a large motor vehicle for carrying goods and materials. **2.** a wheeled frame or cart for transporting heavy objects. **3.** a frame with two or more pairs of wheels for supporting one end of a railroad car or locomotive. —*v.t.* **4.** to transport by truck. —*v.i.* **5.** to drive a truck. —**truck′er,** *n.*

truck[2] (truk), *n.* **1.** vegetables raised for the market. **2.** *Informal.* rubbish; trash. **3.** dealings. —*v.t., v.i.* **4.** to exchange; barter.

truck′ farm′, *n.* a farm on which vegetables are grown for the market.

truck•le (truk′əl), *v.i.*, **-led, -ling.** to submit or yield obsequiously.

truc•u•lent (truk′yə lənt, trōō′kyə-), *adj.* **1.** aggressively hostile. **2.** savagely brutal. —**truc′u•lence,** *n.* —**truc′u•lent•ly,** *adv.*

trudge (truj), *v.*, **trudged, trudg•ing.** —*v.i.* **1.** to walk, esp. laboriously or wearily. —*n.* **2.** a laborious or tiring walk.

true (trōō), *adj.*, **tru•er, tru•est,** *n., adv., v.*, **trued, tru•ing** or **true•ing.** —*adj.* **1.** conforming to reality or fact. **2.** real; genuine. **3.** loyal; faithful. **4.** conforming to a standard, pattern, etc. **5.** legitimate or rightful. **6.** accurately shaped, fitted, etc. —*n.* **7. the true,** something true; truth. —*adv.* **8.** truly. **9.** in conformity with the ancestral type: *to breed true.* —*v.t.* **10.** to adjust, shape, place, etc., accurately.

True′-blue′, *adj.* unwaveringly loyal.

True′ Vine′, *n.* Jesus. John 15:1.

truf•fle (truf′əl, trōō′fəl), *n.* **1.** any of several subterranean, edible fungi. **2.** a ball-shaped candy of soft chocolate dusted with cocoa.

tru•ism (trōō′iz əm), *n.* a self-evident, obvious truth.

tru•ly (trōō′lē), *adv.* **1.** truthfully or accurately. **2.** really; genuinely. **3.** indeed. **4.** sincerely: *yours truly.*

Tru•man (trōō′mən), *n.* **Harry S.,** 1884–1972, 33rd president of the U.S. 1945–53.

Tru′man Doc′trine, *n.* the policy of President Truman, as advocated in 1947, to provide aid to any country threatened by totalitarian ideology.

trump (trump), *n.* **1. a.** any playing card of a suit that for the time outranks the other suits. **b.** Often, **trumps.** (*used with a sing. v.*) the suit itself. —*v.t., v.i.* **2.** to take (a trick) with a trump. **3. trump up,** to devise deceitfully.

trump′er•y, *n., pl.* **-er•ies. 1.** something without use or value. **2.** nonsense; twaddle.

trum•pet (trum′pit), *n.* **1.** a brass wind instrument consisting of a curved tube and a flaring bell. **2.** something resembling a trumpet, esp. in sound. **3.** a sound like that of a trumpet. —*v.i.* **4.** to emit a loud, trumpetlike sound. —*v.t.* **5.** to proclaim loudly or widely. —**trum′pet•er,** *n.*

trun•cate (trung′kāt), *v.t.,* **-cat•ed, -cat•ing.** to shorten by or as if by cutting off a part; cut short. —**trun•ca′tion,** *n.*

trun•cheon (trun′chən), *n.* the club carried by a police officer.

trun•dle (trun′dl), *v.i., v.t.,* **-dled, -dling.** to roll along. —**trun′dler,** *n.*

trun′dle bed′, *n.* a low bed on casters, usu. pushed under another bed when not in use.

trunk (trungk), *n.* **1.** the main stem of a tree. **2.** a large sturdy box for carrying clothes, personal effects, etc. **3.** a large compartment in an automobile for luggage and storage. **4.** the body of a person or animal excluding the head and appendages. **5.** the long, flexible nasal appendage of the elephant. **6. trunks,** brief shorts worn by men chiefly for athletics.

trunk′ line′, *n.* **1.** a major long-distance transportation line. **2.** a telephone line between two switching devices.

truss (trus), *v.t.* **1.** to tie or bind. **2.** to fasten the legs and wings of (a fowl) before cooking. **3.** to support with a truss. —*n.* **4.** a structural frame designed to support bridges, roofs, etc. **5.** a pad supported by a belt, used for maintaining a hernia in a reduced state.

trust (trust), *n.* **1.** reliance on the integrity, ability, etc., of a person or thing. **2.** confident expectation; hope. **3.** one upon which a person relies. **4.** the responsibility imposed on a person in whom confidence is placed. **5.** charge or custody. **6.** something entrusted to one's care. **7. a.** a fiduciary relationship in which a trustee holds title to property for the beneficiary. **b.** the property so held. **8.** a combination of business firms for the purpose of eliminating competition. —*v.t.* **9.** to have confidence in. **10.** to expect confidently; hope. **11.** to commit with confidence. **12.** to permit to do something without fear. —*v.i.* **13.** to have confidence.

trust•ee′, *n., pl.* **-ees. 1.** a person appointed to administer the affairs of a company, institution, etc. **2.** a person who holds title to property for the benefit of another. —**trust•ee′ship,** *n.*

trust′ful, *adj.* full of trust. —**trust′ful•ly,** *adv.* —**trust′ful•ness,** *n.*

trust′ ter′ritory, *n.* a territory placed under the administrative control of a country by the United Nations.

trust′wor′thy, *adj.* deserving of trust or confidence. —**trust′wor′thi•ness,** *n.*

trust′y, *adj.,* **-i•er, -i•est.** able to be trusted or relied on.

truth (trooth), *n., pl.* **truths** (troothz, trooths). **1.** the true or actual state of a matter. **2.** conformity with fact or reality. **3.** a verified or indisputable fact, proposition, etc. **4.** the state or character of being true. **5.** (*cap.*) Jesus. John. 14:6. —*Idiom.* **6. in truth,** in reality. —*Saying.* **7. The truth shall make you free,** to be truly free, one must know and accept the truth. John 8:32.

Truth (trooth,), *n.* **Sojourner** (*Isabella Van Wagener*), 1797?–1883, U.S. abolitionist and women's-rights advocate, born a slave.

truth′ful, *adj.* **1.** telling the truth, esp. habitually. **2.** corresponding with reality. —**truth′ful•ly,** *adv.* —**truth′ful•ness,** *n.*

try (trī), *v.,* **tried, try•ing,** *n., pl.* **tries.** —*v.t.* **1.** to make an effort to do or accomplish. **2.** to sample, test, or experiment with, as to evaluate. **3.** to examine and determine judicially. **4.** to put to a severe test. **5.** to melt down (fat, blubber, etc.) to obtain the oil. —*v.i.* **6.** to make an effort. **7. try on,** to put on (an article of clothing) to judge its appearance and fit. **8. ~ out, a.** to use experimentally. **b.** to take part in a competitive test, as for a position or role. —*n.* **9.** an attempt or effort. —*Usage.* Although usage

guides generally recommend TRY TO in place of TRY AND, both patterns occur in all types of speech and writing.

try′ing, *adj.* straining one's patience and goodwill. —**try′ing•ly,** *adv.*

try′out′, *n.* a test of fitness, ability, etc.

tryst (trist, trīst), *n.* **1.** a clandestine appointment to meet, esp. one made by lovers. **2.** an appointed meeting or meeting place.

tsar (zär, tsär), *n.* CZAR.

TSE, transmissible spongiform encephalopathy.

tset′se fly′ (tset′sē, tsē′tsē), *n.* any of several bloodsucking African flies, some of which can transmit sleeping sickness.

T-shirt, *n.* a lightweight pullover shirt with short sleeves and a collarless round neckline.

Tsing•tao (*Chin.* ching′dou′), *n.* QINGDAO.

tsp., **1.** teaspoon. **2.** teaspoonful.

T square, *n.* a T-shaped ruler for drawing parallel lines, right angles, etc.

tsu•na•mi (tsoo nä′mē), *n., pl.* **-mis.** an unusually large sea wave produced by an undersea earthquake or volcanic eruption. [< Japn: harbor wave]

tub (tub), *n.* **1.** a bathtub. **2.** a broad, round, open container, orig. one made of wooden staves.

tu•ba (too′bə, tyoo′-), *n., pl.* **-bas.** a valved brass wind instrument having a low range.

tub•by (tub′ē), *adj.,* **-bi•er, -bi•est.** short and fat.

tube (toob, tyoob), *n.* **1.** a hollow, cylindrical body of metal, glass, etc., used for conveying fluids. **2.** a collapsible cylinder from which a paste may be squeezed. **3.** any hollow, cylindrical vessel or organ: *the bronchial tubes.* **4.** ELECTRON TUBE. **5. the tube,** *Informal.* television. **6.** *Brit.* SUBWAY.

tu•ber (too′bər, tyoo′-), *n.* a fleshy outgrowth of an underground stem, as the potato. —**tu′ber•ous,** *adj.*

tu′ber•cle (-kəl), *n.* **1.** a small, rounded projection, as on a bone. **2.** a firm, rounded swelling, esp. the lesion of tuberculosis.

tu•ber•cu•lin (too bûr′kyə lin, tyoo-), *n.* a liquid prepared from the tuberculosis bacillus, used in a test for tuberculosis.

tu•ber•cu•lo•sis (-lō′sis), *n.* an infectious disease characterized by tubercles esp. in the lungs. —**tu•ber′cu•lar, tu•ber′cu•lous,** *adj.*

tub′ing, *n.* **1.** material in the form of a tube. **2.** tubes collectively. **3.** a piece of tube.

Tub•man (tub′mən), *n.* **Harriet** (*Araminta*), 1820?–1913, U.S. abolitionist: escaped slave.

tu′bu•lar (-byə lər), *adj.* **1.** of or shaped like a tube. **2.** consisting of tubes.

tu′bule (-byool), *n.* a small tube.

tuck (tuk), *v.t.* **1.** to put into a small, close, or concealing place. **2.** to thrust in the edge of (a garment, sheet, etc.) so as to hold in place. **3.** to cover or wrap snugly. **4.** to draw or pull up into folds. **5.** to sew tucks in. —*n.* **6.** a fold sewn into cloth, as to make a tighter fit. **7.** *Informal.* a plastic surgery operation: *a tummy tuck.*

tuck′er, *v.t.* *Informal.* to tire; exhaust.

Tuc•son (too′son, too son′), *n.* a city in S Arizona. 434,726.

Tu•dor (too′dər,), *n.* a member of the royal family that ruled in England from 1485 to 1603.

Tues•day (tooz′dā, -dē, tyooz′-), *n.* the third day of the week, following Monday.

tuft (tuft), *n.* **1.** a bunch of hairs, feathers, grass, etc., growing or fastened closely together. **2.** a cluster of cut threads tied together at the base. —*v.t.* **3.** to furnish or decorate with tufts. **4.** to arrange in tufts. —**tuft′ed,** *adj.*

tug (tug), *v.,* **tugged, tug•ging,** *n.* —*v.t.* **1.** to pull at with force or effort. **2.** to move by pulling forcibly. **3.** to tow with a tugboat. —*v.i.* **4.** to pull with force or effort. —*n.* **5.** an act or instance of tugging. **6.** TUGBOAT.

tug′boat′, *n.* a small, powerful boat for towing or pushing ships, barges, etc.

tug′ of war′, *n.* **1.** a contest between two teams

pulling on opposite ends of a rope. **2.** a struggle for supremacy.

tu•i•tion (tōō ish′ən, tyōō-), *n.* the fee for instruction, as at a college.

tu•la•re•mi•a (tōō′lə rē′mē ə), *n.* a plaguelike disease of rabbits, squirrels, etc., transmitted to humans by insects or ticks.

tu•lip (tōō′lip, tyōō′-), *n.* **1.** a plant with large, cup-shaped flowers of various colors. **2.** a flower or bulb of such a plant.

tulle (tōōl), *n.* a thin, fine net of acetate, nylon, rayon, or silk.

Tul•sa (tul′sə), *n.* a city in NE Oklahoma. 374,851. —**Tul′san**, *n., adj.*

tum•ble (tum′bəl), *v.,* -**bled, -bling,** *n.* —*v.i.* **1.** to fall helplessly down, esp. headfirst. **2.** to roll end over end, as in falling. **3.** to decline or collapse suddenly. **4.** to perform gymnastic feats, as somersaults. **5.** to move in a hasty and confused way. —*v.t.* **6.** to cause to tumble. —*n.* **7.** the act of tumbling. **8.** disorder or confusion.

tum′ble-down′, *adj.* dilapidated.

tum′bler, *n.* **1.** a person who performs acrobatic feats. **2.** a part of a lock that, when lifted by a key, allows the bolt to move. **3.** a drinking glass without a stem and handle.

tum′ble•weed′, *n.* a plant whose upper parts become detached from the roots and are driven about by the wind.

tum•brel or **-bril** (tum′brəl), *n.* a farmer's cart that can be tilted to discharge its load.

tu•mes•cent (tōō mes′ənt, tyōō-), *adj.* swelling; tumid. —**tu•mes′cence,** *n.*

tu′mid (-mid), *adj.* **1.** swollen or bulging. **2.** pompous or inflated. —**tu•mid′i•ty,** *n.*

tum•my (tum′ē), *n., pl.* -**mies.** *Informal.* the stomach or abdomen.

tu•mor (tōō′mər, tyōō′-), *n.* an uncontrolled, abnormal, circumscribed growth of cells. Also, *esp. Brit.,* **tu′mour.** —**tu′mor•ous,** *adj.*

tu•mult (tōō′mult, -mált, tyōō′-), *n.* **1.** violent and noisy commotion; uproar. **2.** agitation of mind or feelings.

tu•mul′tu•ous (-mul′chōō əs), *adj.* **1.** full of tumult; disorderly. **2.** highly agitated.

tun (tun), *n.* a large cask.

tu•na (tōō′nə, tyōō′-), *n., pl.* -**nas, -na. 1.** any of several large marine food and game fishes. **2.** Also called **tu′na fish′.** the flesh of the tuna, used as food.

tun•dra (tun′drə, tōōn′-), *n., pl.* -**dras.** a vast, treeless plain of arctic regions.

tune (tōōn, tyōōn), *n., v.,* **tuned, tun•ing.** —*n.* **1.** a succession of musical sounds forming a melody. **2.** the state of being in the proper pitch. **3.** accord; agreement. —*v.t.* **4.** to adjust (a musical instrument) to a correct pitch. **5.** to bring into harmony. **6.** to adjust (a motor, mechanism, etc.) for proper functioning. **7.** to adjust (a radio or television) so as to receive a broadcast. **8. tune in,** to adjust a radio or television so as to receive (signals, a station, etc.). —*Idiom.* **9. to the tune of,** in the amount of. —**tun′er,** *n.*

tune′ful, *adj.* full of melody; melodious.

tune′less, *adj.* unmelodious; unmusical.

tune′-up′, *n.* an adjustment, as of a motor, to improve working condition.

tung•sten (tung′stən), *n.* a rare metallic element, used in electric-lamp filaments. *Symbol:* W; *at. wt.:* 183.85; *at. no.:* 74.

tu•nic (tōō′nik, tyōō′-), *n.* **1.** a gownlike outer garment worn by the ancient Greeks and Romans. **2.** a woman's straight upper garment, usu. extending to the hips.

tun′ing fork′, *n.* a two-pronged steel instrument producing a tone of constant pitch when struck, used for tuning musical instruments.

Tu•nis (tōō′nis, tyōō′-), *n.* the capital of Tunisia. 596,654.

Tu•ni•sia (tōō nē′zhə, -nizh′ə, tyōō-), *n.* a republic in N Africa. 9,183,097. —**Tu•ni′sian,** *adj., n.*

tun•nel (tun′l), *n., v.,* **-neled, -nel•ing** or (*esp. Brit.*) **-nelled, -nel•ling.** —*n.* **1.** an underground passage. **2.** a passageway, as for trains or automobiles, through or under a mountain or other obstruction. —*v.t., v.i.* **3.** to construct a tunnel (through or under). —**tun′nel•er, tun′nel•ler,** *n.*

tur•ban (tûr′bən), *n.* **1.** a man's headdress worn chiefly by Muslims, consisting of a long cloth wound around the head. **2.** any headdress resembling this.

tur•bid (tûr′bid), *adj.* **1.** unclear or murky because of stirred-up sediment. **2.** thick or dense, as clouds. **3.** confused; muddled.

tur•bine (tûr′bin, -bīn), *n.* any of various machines having a rotor with vanes or blades, driven by the pressure of a moving fluid.

tur•bo•fan (tûr′bō fan′), *n.* FANJET (def. 1).

tur′bo•jet′, *n.* **1.** Also called **tur′bojet en′gine.** a jet engine in which air is compressed for combustion by a turbine-driven compressor. **2.** an airplane equipped with such engines.

tur′bo•prop′ (-prop′), *n.* **1.** Also called **tur′bo-propel′ler en′gine.** a turbojet engine with a turbine-driven propeller. **2.** an airplane equipped with such engines.

tur•bot (tûr′bət), *n., pl.* -**bots, -bot.** any of several flatfishes.

tur•bu•lent (tûr′byə lənt), *adj.* **1.** being in a state of agitation. **2.** characterized by disturbance, disorder, etc. —**tur′bu•lence,** *n.* —**tur′bu•lent•ly,** *adv.*

tu•reen (tōō rēn′, tyōō-), *n.* a large, deep, covered dish for serving soup, stew, etc.

turf (tûrf), *n.* **1.** a layer of matted earth formed by grass and plant roots. **2.** a block of peat. **3. the turf, a.** a track for horse racing. **b.** horse racing. **4. a.** the area over which a street gang asserts its authority. **b.** a familiar area, as of expertise.

tur•gid (tûr′jid), *adj.* **1.** swollen; distended. **2.** pompous; bombastic. —**tur•gid′i•ty,** *n.* —**tur′gid•ly,** *adv.*

Tu•rin (tōōr′in, tyōōr′-, tōō rin′, tyōō-), *n.* a city in NW Italy. 1,025,390.

Turk (tûrk), *n.* a native or inhabitant of Turkey.

Turk., Turkey.

Tur•ke•stan (tûr′kə stan′, -stän′), *n.* a vast region in central Asia, from the Caspian Sea to the Gobi Desert.

tur•key (tûr′kē), *n., pl.* -**keys. 1.** a large North American bird with brownish plumage and a bare head and neck. **2.** the edible flesh of this bird.

Tur′key, *n.* a republic in W Asia and SE Europe. 63,528,225.

tur′key vul′ture, *n.* a blackish brown New World vulture.

Tur′kic (-kik), *n.* **1.** a family of closely related languages of Asia and Europe, including Turkish. —*adj.* **2.** of Turkic or Turkic-speaking peoples.

Turk′ish, *adj.* **1.** of Turkey, its inhabitants, or their language. —*n.* **2.** the Turkic language of Turkey.

Turk•me•ni•stan (tûrk′me nə stan′, -stän′), *n.* a republic in central Asia: formerly a part of the USSR. 4,225,351.

tur•mer•ic (tûr′mər ik), *n.* **1.** the aromatic rhizome of an Asian plant. **2.** a powder prepared from it, used as a condiment or a yellow dye.

tur•moil (tûr′moil), *n.* a state of great confusion or disturbance.

turn (tûrn), *v.t.* **1.** to rotate: *to turn a wheel.* **2.** to move around or partly around: *to turn a key.* **3.** to reverse the position of: *to turn a page.* **4.** to change the position or course of. **5.** to change or convert: *to turn water into ice.* **6.** to cause to become sour or spoiled. **7.** to affect (the stomach) with nausea. **8.** to put to some use or purpose. **9.** to go around: *to turn a corner.* **10.** to reach or pass (a certain age, amount, etc.). **11.** to direct or aim. **12.** to shape on a lathe. **13.** to send; drive. **14.** to cause to be antagonistic toward. **15.** to earn or gain: *to turn a profit.* **16.** to wrench: *He turned his ankle.* —*v.i.* **17.** to rotate. **18.** to move around or partly around. **19.** to hinge or depend. **20.** to direct one's interest, effort, etc. **21.** to change or reverse position or course. **22.** to be affected with nausea. **23.** to change one's loyalties, attitude, etc. **24.** to change or alter, as in appearance. **25.** to become sour or spoiled. **26.** to change color. **27.** to become: *to turn pale.* **28.** to have recourse. **29. turn down,** to refuse or reject. **30.** ~ **in, a.** to hand in. **b.** to go to bed. **31.** ~ **off, a.** to stop the flow of (water, gas, etc.). **b.** to extinguish (a light). **c.** *Slang.* to alienate. **32.** ~ **on, a.** to cause to flow. **b.** to switch on (a light). **c.** *Slang.* to arouse the interest of. **d.** to become hostile to. **33.** ~ **out, a.** to extinguish (a light). **b.** to produce. **c.** to result or end. **34.** ~ **over,** to transfer; give. **35.** ~ **up, a.** to uncover; find. **b.** to intensify or increase. **c.** to appear; arrive. —*n.* **36.** a movement of partial or total rotation. **37.** a time for action that comes in due order. **38.** the act of changing course or direction. **39.** the point at which such a change occurs. **40.** a single revolution, as of a wheel. **41.** any change, as in nature or circumstances. **42.** a single twist or coil. **43.** a distinctive form or style of language. **44.** a short walk, ride, etc. **45.** a natural inclination. **46.** a period of work. **47.** an act of service or disservice. **48.** a nervous shock. —*Idiom.* **49. in turn,** in due order. **50. out of turn,** out of proper order. **51. turn one's back on,** to abandon, ignore, or reject. **52. turn the corner,** to pass through a crisis safely. **53. to turn the other cheek,** to refuse to retaliate for an injury. Matt. 5:39; Luke 6:29 —**turn′er,** *n.*

turn′a•bout′, *n.* a change of opinion, loyalty, etc.

turn′coat′, *n.* a person who changes to the opposite party or faction.

turn′ing point′, *n.* a point at which a decisive change takes place.

tur•nip (tûr′nip), *n.* **1.** the thick, fleshy, edible root of either of two plants of the mustard family. **2.** either of these plants.

turn′key′, *n., pl.* **-keys.** a person who has charge of the keys of a prison.

turn′off′, *n.* a small road that branches off from a larger one.

turn′out′, *n.* **1.** the gathering of persons who come to an exhibition, party, etc. **2.** a short side passage that enables trains, automobiles, etc., to pass one another.

turn′o•ver, *n.* **1.** an act or result of turning over. **2.** the rate at which workers are replaced in a given period. **3.** the amount of business done in a given time. **4.** the rate at which items are sold and restocked. **5.** a baked pastry in which half the dough is turned over the filling and sealed.

turn′pike′ (-pīk′), *n.* a high-speed highway, esp. one maintained by tolls.

turn′stile′, *n.* a gate with revolving arms set in a passageway to control the flow of people.

turn′ta•ble, *n.* the rotating disk that spins the record on a phonograph.

tur•pen•tine (tûr′pən tīn′), *n.* a strong-smelling liquid distilled from a substance derived from coniferous trees, used as a paint thinner and solvent.

tur•pi•tude (tûr′pi tōod′, -tyōod′), *n.* vile or base character; depravity.

tur•quoise (tûr′koiz, -kwoiz), *n.* **1.** a sky-blue or greenish blue mineral, used as a gem. **2.** a greenish blue.

tur•ret (tûr′it, tur′-), *n.* **1.** a small tower forming part of a larger structure. **2.** a revolving structure in which a gun is mounted, as on an armored vehicle. **3.** a pivoted attachment on a lathe for holding tools.

tur•tle (tûr′tl), *n., pl.* **-tles, -tle.** any of various aquatic and terrestrial reptiles with the trunk enclosed in a bony shell.

tur′tle•dove′ (-duv′), *n.* any of several doves, esp. a small dove noted for its plaintive coo.

tur′tle•neck′, *n.* **1.** a high, close fitting collar, esp. on pullover sweaters. **2.** a garment with such a collar.

tusk (tusk), *n.* an animal tooth developed to great length, as in the elephant. —**tusked,** *adj.*

tus•sle (tus′əl), *v.,* **-sled, -sling,** *n.* —*v.i.* **1.** to struggle or fight roughly. —*n.* **2.** any vigorous struggle.

tus•sock (tus′ək), *n.* a tuft or clump of growing grass or the like.

Tut•ankh•a•men (tōot′äng kä′mən), *n.* fl. c1350 B.C., king of Egypt.

tu•te•lage (tōot′l ij, tyōot′-), *n.* **1.** the act of teaching or guiding. **2.** instruction or guidance. **3.** the state of being under a guardian or tutor. —**tu′te•lar′y** (-er′ē), *adj.*

tu•tor (tōo′tər, tyōo′-), *n.* **1.** a person employed to instruct another, esp. privately. —*v.t., v.i.* **2.** to act as a tutor (to). —**tu•to′ri•al** (-tôr′ē əl), *adj., n.*

tut•ti-frut•ti (tōo′tē frōo′tē), *n.* a confection, esp. ice cream, flavored with a variety of fruits.

tu•tu (tōo′tōo′), *n., pl.* **-tus.** a short, full skirt worn by ballerinas.

Tu•tu (tōo′tōo), *n.* **Desmond (Mpilo),** born 1931, South African Anglican clergyman and civil-rights activist.

Tu•va•lu (tōo′və lōo′, tōo vä′lōo), *n.* a country on a group of islands in the central Pacific, S of the equator. 8229. —**Tu′va•lu′an,** *adj., n.*

tux (tuks), *n. Informal.* a tuxedo.

tux•e•do (tuk sē′dō), *n., pl.* **-dos.** a man's semiformal suit, traditionally of black or dark blue.

TV, television.

TVA, Tennessee Valley Authority.

twad•dle (twod′l), *n.* silly or tedious talk or writing. —**twad′dler,** *n.*

twain (twān), *adj., n.* two.

Twain (twān), *n.* **Mark,** pen name of Samuel Langhorne CLEMENS.

twang (twang), *v.i., v.t.* **1.** to make or cause to make a sharp, vibrating sound. **2.** to speak or utter with a nasal tone. —*n.* **3.** a sharp, vibrating sound, as one made by plucking the string of a musical instrument. **4.** a sharp, nasal tone. —**twang′y,** *adj.*

'twas (twuz, twoz; *unstressed* twəz), contraction of *it was.*

tweak (twēk), *v.t.* **1.** to pinch and pull with a jerk and twist. **2.** to make a minor adjustment to: *to tweak a computer program.* —*n.* **3.** the act of tweaking.

tweed (twēd), *n.* **1.** a coarse wool cloth in a variety of weaves and colors. **2. tweeds,** garments made of this cloth. —**tweed′y,** *adj.,* **-i•er, -i•est.**

'tween (twēn), *prep.* contraction of *between.*

tweet (twēt), *n.* **1.** a chirping sound, as of a small bird. —*v.i.* **2.** to chirp.

tweet′er, *n.* a small loudspeaker designed for the reproduction of high-frequency sounds.

tweez•ers (twē′zərz), *n.* (*used with a sing. or pl. v.*) small pincers for plucking out hairs, extracting splinters, etc.

twelfth (twelfth), *adj.* **1.** next after the eleventh; being the ordinal number for 12. —*n.* **2.** a twelfth part, esp. of one ($\frac{1}{12}$). **3.** the twelfth member of a series.

Twelfth′ Day′, *n.* Epiphany; formerly observed as the last day of the Christmas festivities.

Twelfth′ Night′, *n.* **1.** the evening before Twelfth Day or the evening of Twelfth Day itself. **2.** (*italics*) a comedy (1602) by William Shakespeare.

twelve (twelv), *n.* **1.** a cardinal number, 10 plus 2. **2.** a symbol for this number, as 12 or XII. **3. the Twelve,** the 12 apostles chosen by Christ. —*adj.* **4.** amounting to 12 in number.

Twelve′ Step′ or **12-step,** *adj.* of or based on a program for recovery from addiction that provides 12 progressive levels toward attainment.

twen•ty (twen′tē), *n., pl.* **-ties,** *adj.* —*n.* **1.** a cardinal number, 10 times 2. **2.** a symbol for this number, as 20 or XX. —*adj.* **3.** amounting to 20 in number. —**twen′ti•eth,** *adj., n.*

twen′ty-one′, *n.* **1.** a cardinal number, 20 plus 1. **2.** a symbol for this number, as 21 or XXI.

twen′ty-twen′ty or **20-20,** *adj.* having normal visual acuity.

twice (twīs), *adv.* **1.** two times. **2.** in twofold quantity or degree.

twid•dle (twid′l), *v.t., v.i.,* **-dled, -dling. 1.** to turn about or play with (something) idly. —*Idiom.* **2. twiddle one's thumbs,** to be idle.

twig (twig), *n.* a small offshoot of a branch or stem.

twi•light (twī′līt′), *n.* **1.** the soft, diffused light from the sky when the sun is below the horizon. **2.** the period during which this light prevails. **3.** a waning period after full development, success, etc. —*adj.* **4.** of or resembling twilight.

twill (twil), *n.* a fabric with a pattern of diagonal, raised lines. —**twilled,** *adj.*

twin (twin), *n.* **1.** either of two offspring brought forth at a birth. **2.** either of two persons or things related to or resembling each other. —*adj.* **3.** born at the same birth. **4.** being one of a pair.

twine (twīn), *n.*, *v.*, **twined, twin•ing.** —*n.* **1.** a strong thread or string composed of two or more strands twisted together. —*v.t.* **2.** to twist together. **3.** to coil or wind. —*v.i.* **4.** to wind around something.

twinge (twinj), *n.*, *v.*, **twinged, twing•ing.** —*n.* **1.** a sudden, sharp pain. **2.** a mental or emotional pang. —*v.t.*, *v.i.* **3.** to affect with or feel a twinge.

twin•kle (twing′kəl), *v.*, **-kled, -kling,** *n.* —*v.i.* **1.** to shine with a flickering gleam of light. **2.** (of the eyes) to be bright with amusement. **3.** to move flutteringly and quickly. —*n.* **4.** a flickering light. **5.** a brightness in the eyes. **6.** an instant; twinkling.

twin′kling, *n.* the time required for a wink; an instant.

twirl (twûrl), *v.i.*, *v.t.* **1.** to rotate rapidly; whirl. —*n.* **2.** the act of twirling. **3.** a spiral or coil. —**twirl′er,** *n.*

twist (twist), *v.t.* **1.** to combine (strands or threads) by winding together. **2.** to wind or coil about something. **3.** to wrench; sprain. **4.** to break off by turning forcibly. **5.** to contort. **6.** to distort the meaning of. **7.** to form into a coil by winding, rolling, etc. **8.** to turn by rotating. —*v.i.* **9.** to become twisted. **10.** to writhe or squirm. **11.** to take a spiral form or course. **12.** to turn so as to face in another direction. —*n.* **13.** a curve; bend; turn. **14.** a rotary motion or spin. **15.** anything formed by twisting. **16.** the act or process of twining strands together. **17.** distortion, as of meaning. **18.** a sudden, unanticipated change, as of events. **19.** a novel treatment, method, etc.

twist′er, *n.* **1.** a person or thing that twists. **2.** *Informal.* a whirlwind or tornado.

twit (twit), *v.*, **twit•ted, twit•ting,** *n.* —*v.t.* **1.** to taunt with reference to anything embarrassing. —*n.* **2.** the act of twitting.

twitch (twich), *v.t.*, *v.i.* **1.** to pull (at) or move with a quick, jerking movement. —*n.* **2.** a quick, jerky movement of the body or a muscle.

twit•ter (twit′ər), *v.i.* **1.** to utter a succession of small, tremulous sounds, as a bird. **2.** to chatter. **3.** to giggle. **4.** to tremble with excitement. —*n.* **5.** the act of twittering. **6.** a twittering sound. **7.** a state of tremulous excitement.

'twixt (twikst), *prep.* contraction of *betwixt.*

two (tōō), *n.*, *pl.* **twos,** *adj.* —*n.* **1.** a cardinal number, 1 plus 1. **2.** a symbol for this number, as 2 or II. —*adj.* **3.** amounting to two in number. —*Idiom.* **4. in two,** into two parts.

two′-bit′, *adj. Informal.* inferior or unimportant.

two′ bits′, *n. Informal.* 25 cents.

two′-faced′, *adj.* **1.** having two faces. **2.** deceitful or hypocritical.

two′-fist′ed, *adj.* strong and vigorous.

two′fold′ (*adj.* -fōld′; *adv.* -fōld′), *adj.* **1.** having two parts. **2.** twice as great or as much. —*adv.* **3.** in twofold measure.

two′-ply′, *adj.* consisting of two layers, strands, etc.

two′some (-səm), *n.* **1.** two people together; a couple. **2.** a golf match between two persons.

two′-way′, *adj.* **1.** allowing movement or communication in two directions. **2.** involving two participants.

twp., township.

TX, Texas.

-ty, a suffix meaning state or condition (*certainty*).

ty•coon (tī kōōn′), *n.* a businessperson of great wealth and power. [< Japn]

ty•ing (tī′ing), *v.* pres. part. of TIE.

tyke (tīk), *n.* a small child.

Ty•ler (tī′lər), *n.* **John,** 1790–1862, 10th president of the U.S. 1841–45.

tym•pa•ni (tim′pə nē), *n.* (*used with a sing. or pl. v.*) TIMPANI. **1.** MIDDLE EAR. **2.** TYMPANIC MEMBRANE.

tym•pan′ic mem′brane (tim pan′ik), *n.* a membrane in the ear canal between the external ear and the middle ear.

tym•pa•num (tim′pə nəm), *n.*, *pl.* **-nums, -na** (-nə). **1.** MIDDLE EAR. **2.** TYMPANIC MEMBRANE.

Tyn•dale (tin′dl), *n.* **William,** c1492–1536, English religious reformer and translator of the Bible.

type (tīp), *n.*, *v.*, **typed, typ•ing.** —*n.* **1.** a group of things or persons sharing certain characteristics. **2.** a thing or person that is representative of a class or group. **3. a.** a metal block with a raised character on its surface, used in printing. **b.** such blocks collectively. **c.** a printed character or characters. —*v.t.* **4.** to write on a typewriter, computer keyboard, or the like. **5.** to classify. —*v.i.* **6.** to write using a typewriter, computer keyboard, or the like.

type′cast′, *v.t.*, **-cast, -cast•ing.** to cast (an actor) repeatedly or exclusively in the same kind of role.

type′script′, *n.* typewritten matter.

type′set′ter, *n.* **1.** a person who sets type. **2.** a machine for setting type. —**type′set′,** *v.t.*, **-set, -set•ting.**

type′write′, *v.t.*, *v.i.*, **-wrote, -writ•ten, -writ•ing.** to write by means of a typewriter; type.

type′writ′er, *n.* a machine for writing in characters similar to printers' types.

ty•phoid (tī′foid), *n.* an infectious disease characterized by fever and intestinal inflammation; spread by food or water contaminated with a bacillus. Also called **ty′phoid fe′ver.**

ty•phoon (tī fōōn′), *n.* a tropical hurricane of the W Pacific and the China seas.

ty•phus (tī′fəs), *n.* an acute infectious disease caused by a microorganism, transmitted by lice and fleas, and characterized by reddish spots on the skin. Also called **ty′phus fe′ver.**

typ•i•cal (tip′i kəl), *adj.* **1.** conforming to or serving as a type. **2.** having the essential characteristics of a particular type. —**typ′i•cal•ly,** *adv.*

typ′i•fy′, *v.t.*, **-fied, -fy•ing. 1.** to serve as a typical example of. **2.** to serve as a symbol of.

typ•ist (tī′pist), *n.* a person who operates a typewriter.

ty•po (tī′pō), *n.*, *pl.* **-pos.** an error in typesetting or typing.

ty•pog•ra•phy (tī pog′rə fē), *n.* **1.** the work of setting and arranging types and of printing from them. **2.** the general appearance of printed matter. —**ty•pog′ra•pher,** *n.* —**ty′po•graph′i•cal** (-pə graf′i-kəl), **ty′po•graph′ic,** *adj.* —**ty′po•graph′i•cal•ly,** *adv.*

ty•ran•ni•cal (ti ran′i kəl, tī-), *adj.* **1.** unjustly cruel or severe. **2.** of or characteristic of a tyrant. —**ty•ran′ni•cal•ly,** *adv.*

tyr•an•nize (tir′ə nīz′), *v.*, **-nized, -niz•ing.** —*v.t.* **1.** to govern tyrannically. —*v.i.* **2.** to exercise absolute power cruelly or oppressively. **3.** to govern as a tyrant.

ty•ran•no•saur (ti ran′ə sôr′, tī-), *n.* a large dinosaur that walked upright on its hind feet.

tyr•an•ny (tir′ə nē), *n.*, *pl.* **-nies. 1.** arbitrary or unrestrained exercise of power. **2.** the government of a tyrant. **3.** oppressive or unjust government. **4.** a tyrannical act.

ty•rant (tī′rənt), *n.* **1.** a ruler or other person in authority who exercises power oppressively or despotically. **2.** an absolute ruler.

ty•ro (tī′rō), *n.*, *pl.* **-ros.** a beginner in learning anything; novice.

Ty•rol (ti rōl′), *n.* an alpine region in W Austria and N Italy. —**Ty•ro′le•an,** *adj.*, *n.*

tzar (zär, tsär), *n.* CZAR.

U

U, u (yōō), *n., pl.* **Us** or **U's, us** or **u's. 1.** the 21st letter of the English alphabet, a vowel. **2.** something shaped like a U.
U (yōō), *adj.* characteristic of the upper classes.
U, *Chem. Symbol.* uranium.
U., 1. union. **2.** unit. **3.** university. **4.** unsatisfactory.
U.A.E. or **UAE,** United Arab Emirates.
UAR, United Arab Republic.
UAW, United Automobile Workers.
u•biq•ui•tous (yōō bik/wi təs), *adj.* existing or being everywhere, esp. at the same time. —**u•biq/ui•tous•ly,** *adv.* —**u•biq/ui•ty,** *n.*
U/-boat/, *n.* a German submarine. [< G; short for *Unterseeboot* lit., undersea boat]
u.c., *Print.* uppercase.
ud•der (ud/ər), *n.* a baggy mammary gland with more than one teat, as in cows.
UFO (yōō/ef/ō/; *sometimes* yōō/fō), *n., pl.* **UFOs, UFO's.** unidentified flying object: any unexplained flying object, esp. one assumed to be from outer space.
U•gan•da (yōō gan/də, ōō gän/-), *n.* a republic in E Africa. 20,604,874. —**U•gan/dan,** *adj., n.*
ugh (ōōкн, uкн, u, ōō; *spelling pron.* ug), *interj.* an exclamation of disgust, aversion, or horror.
ug•li•fy (ug/lə fī/), *v.t.,* **-fied, -fy•ing.** to make ugly. —**ug/li•fi•ca/tion,** *n.*
ug•ly (ug/lē), *adj.,* **-li•er, -li•est. 1.** very unattractive in appearance. **2.** disagreeable; objectionable. **3.** morally revolting. **4.** threatening or ominous. **5.** hostile; quarrelsome. —**ug/li•ness,** *n.*
ug/ly Amer/ican, *n.* an insensitive American in a foreign country. [from a 1965 novel by that name by William J. Lederer and Eugene Burdick]
uh (u, uɴ), *interj.* a sound indicating hesitation or a pause.
UHF, ultrahigh frequency.
UK, United Kingdom.
u•kase (yōō kās/, -kāz/), *n.* an order by an absolute authority.
U•kraine (yōō krān/), *n.* a republic in SE Europe: formerly a part of the USSR. 50,984,635.
U•krain/i•an, *n.* **1.** a native or inhabitant of Ukraine. **2.** a Slavic language spoken in Ukraine. —*adj.* **3.** of Ukraine, Ukrainians, or their language.
u•ku•le•le (yōō/kə lā/lē), *n., pl.* **-les.** a small, guitarlike musical instrument.
UL, Underwriters' Laboratories.
U•lan Ba•tor (ōō/län bä/tôr), *n.* the capital of the Mongolian People's Republic. 500,000.
ul•cer (ul/sər), *n.* **1.** a sore on the skin or a mucous membrane, often containing pus. **2.** any corrupting condition. —**ul/cer•ous,** *adj.*
ul•cer•ate/ (-sə rāt/), *v.i., v.t.,* **-at•ed, -at•ing.** to become or cause to become ulcerous. —**ul/cer•a/tion,** *n.*
ul•na (ul/nə), *n., pl.* **-nae** (-nē) **, -nas.** the bone of the forearm on the side opposite the thumb. —**ul/nar,** *adj.*
ul•ster (ul/stər), *n.* a long, loose, heavy overcoat. [after *Ulster,* former province in Ireland]
ult., 1. ultimate. **2.** ultimately.
ul•te•ri•or (ul tēr/ē ər), *adj.* **1.** intentionally concealed: *an ulterior motive.* **2.** subsequent; future. **3.** lying beyond or outside a specified boundary.
ul•ti•ma (ul/tə mə), *n., pl.* **-mas.** the last syllable of a word.
ul•ti•mate (ul/tə mit), *adj.* **1.** furthest or farthest. **2.** decisive; conclusive. **3.** basic; fundamental. **4.** final; total. **5.** unequaled or unsurpassed. —*n.* **6.** the final point or result. **7.** a fundamental fact. —**ul/ti•mate•ly,** *adv.*

ul/ti•ma/tum (-mā/təm, -mä/-), *n., pl.* **-tums, -ta** (-tə). a final demand or set of terms, as in a dispute.
ul•ti•mo (ul/tə mō/), *adv. Archaic.* in or of the month preceding the current one: *on the 12th ultimo.* [< L *ultimō* (*mēnse*) in the last (month)]
ul•tra (ul/trə), *adj.* going beyond what is usual or ordinary; extreme.
ultra-, a prefix meaning: beyond or on the far side of (*ultraviolet*); extremely (*ultramodern*).
ul•tra•con•serv•a•tive (ul/trə kən sûr/və tiv), *adj.* **1.** extremely conservative, esp. in politics. —*n.* **2.** an ultraconservative person.
ul•tra•fiche (ul/trə fēsh/), *n.* a form of microfiche with the images greatly reduced in size, generally by a factor of 100 or more.
ul/tra•high fre/quency, *n.* a radio frequency between 300 and 3000 megahertz.
ul/tra•light/, *n.* a light airplane that is essentially a motorized hang glider.
ul/tra•ma•rine/, *adj.* **1.** of a deep blue color. —*n.* **2.** a deep blue pigment or color.
ul/tra•son/ic, *adj.* of, being, or utilizing ultrasound.
ul/tra•sound/, *n.* **1.** sound with a frequency greater than 20,000 Hz, approximately the upper limit of human hearing. **2.** the application of ultrasonic waves to medical diagnosis and therapy.
ul/tra•vi/o•let, *adj.* **1.** of, producing, or using electromagnetic radiation with wavelengths shorter than visible light but longer than x-rays. —*n.* **2.** ultraviolet radiation.
ul•u•late (ul/yə lāt/, yōōl/-), *v.i.,* **-lat•ed, -lat•ing.** to howl or wail. —**ul/u•la/tion,** *n.*
U•lys•ses (yōō lis/ēz), *n.* ODYSSEUS.
um•bel (um/bəl), *n.* an inflorescence in which a number of flower stalks spread from a common center.
um•ber (um/bər), *n.* **1.** a brown earth used as a pigment. **2.** a dark dusky or reddish brown.
um•bil•i•cal (um bil/i kəl), *adj.* of, adjacent to, or characteristic of an umbilicus or umbilical cord.
umbil/ical cord/, *n.* a cordlike structure connecting a fetus with the placenta, conveying nourishment and removing wastes.
um•bil/i•cus (-kəs), *n., pl.* **-ci** (-sī/). NAVEL.
um•bra (um/brə), *n., pl.* **-bras, -brae** (-brē). **1.** shade; shadow. **2.** the shadow of a celestial body where the light from the source of illumination is cut off.
um•brage (um/brij), *n.* **1.** offense; displeasure: *took umbrage at his rudeness.* **2.** foliage. **3.** shade or shadows.
um•brel•la (um brel/ə), *n., pl.* **-las. 1.** a fabric cover on a frame mounted on a carrying stick, used for protection against rain or sun. **2.** something that protects. **3.** something that encompasses a number of groups or elements. [< It < L *umbella* sunshade]
u•mi•ak (ōō/mē ak/), *n.* an open Eskimo boat covered with skins.

umiak

um·laut (ŏŏm/lout), *n.* **1.** (in Germanic languages) assimilation in which a vowel is influenced by a following vowel or semivowel. **2.** a diacritical mark (¨) used over a vowel, esp. in German, to indicate umlaut.

ump (ump), *n., v.t., v.i.* UMPIRE.

um·pire (um/pīr), *n., v.,* **-pired, -pir·ing.** —*n.* **1.** a person selected to rule on plays in a sport. **2.** a person selected to settle a dispute. —*v.t., v.i.* **3.** to decide or act as umpire.

ump·teen (ump/tēn/), *adj. Informal.* innumerable; many. —**ump·teenth/,** *adj.*

UN, United Nations.

un-¹, a prefix meaning: not (*unseen*); the opposite of (*unrest*).

un-², a prefix meaning: reversal of an action (*unfasten*); removal or depriving (*unclog*); completely (*unloose*).

un·a·ble (un ā/bəl), *adj.* lacking the necessary power, skill, or resources.

un/ac·com/pa·nied, *adj.* **1.** not accompanied. **2.** without musical accompaniment.

un/ac·count/a·ble, *adj.* **1.** impossible to account for; inexplicable. **2.** not responsible. —**un/ac·count/a·bly,** *adv.*

un/ac·cus/tomed, *adj.* **1.** not accustomed or habituated. **2.** uncommon; unexpected.

un/ad·vised/, *adj.* **1.** without advice or counsel. **2.** imprudent; ill-advised.

un/af·fect/ed¹, *adj.* free from affectation.

un/af·fect/ed², *adj.* not altered or influenced.

un/·A·mer/i·can, *adj.* not typical of or consistent with American standards, values, or goals.

u·nan·i·mous (yōō nan/ə məs), *adj.* being in or showing complete agreement. —**u·na·nim·i·ty** (yōō/nə nim/i tē), *n.* —**u·nan/i·mous·ly,** *adv.*

un·armed/, *adj.* lacking weapons or armor.

un/as·sail/a·ble, *adj.* **1.** not vulnerable to attack. **2.** not subject to denial or dispute.

un/as·sum/ing, *adj.* modest; unpretentious.

un/at·tached/, *adj.* **1.** not attached. **2.** not engaged or married.

un/a·vail/ing, *adj.* not effectual; futile.

un/a·void/a·ble, *adj.* incapable of being avoided. —**un/a·void/a·bly,** *adv.*

un/a·ware/, *adj.* **1.** not aware or conscious. —*adv.* **2.** UNAWARES.

un/a·wares/, *adv.* **1.** unknowingly or inadvertently. **2.** without warning; unexpectedly.

un·bal/anced, *adj.* **1.** lacking balance. **2.** mentally disordered; disturbed.

un·bar/, *v.t.,* **-barred, -bar·ring.** to unbolt; open.

un·bear/a·ble, *adj.* unendurable; intolerable. —**un·bear/a·bly,** *adv.*

un·beat/en, *adj.* **1.** not beaten or pounded. **2.** not defeated. **3.** not trod.

un/be·com/ing, *adj.* not becoming; unattractive or unseemly.

un/be·known/ (-bi nōn/) also **-knownst/** (-nōnst/), *adj.* without one's knowledge.

un/be·lief/, *n.* incredulity or skepticism, esp. in matters of religious faith. —**un/be·liev/er,** *n.*

un/be·liev/a·ble, *adj.* **1.** too improbable to be believed. **2.** extraordinarily impressive. —**un/be·liev/a·bly,** *adv.*

un·bend/, *v.t., v.i.,* **-bent, -bend·ing.** **1.** to straighten from a bent form or position. **2.** to relax.

un·bend/ing, *adj.* not bending; inflexible.

un·bi/ased, *adj.* not biased or prejudiced.

un·bid/den, *adj.* **1.** not commanded. **2.** not asked or invited.

un·bind/, *v.t.,* **-bound, -bind·ing.** **1.** to release, as from restraint; free. **2.** to unfasten or loose.

un·blush/ing, *adj.* **1.** showing no remorse; shameless. **2.** not blushing. —**un·blush/ing·ly,** *adv.*

un·bolt/, *v.t.* to open by or as if by removing a bolt; unlock.

un·born/, *adj.* not yet born.

un·bos/om, *v.t.* **1.** to disclose (a confidence, secret, etc.). —**Idiom.** **2. unbosom oneself,** to reveal one's thoughts and feelings.

un·bound/ed, *adj.* having no limits or bounds.

un·bowed/ (-boud/), *adj.* **1.** not bowed or bent. **2.** not subjugated.

un·bri/dled, *adj.* **1.** not restrained; uninhibited. **2.** not fitted with a bridle.

un·bro/ken, *adj.* **1.** not broken; whole. **2.** not interrupted; undisturbed. **3.** not tamed, as a horse.

un·bur/den, *v.t.* **1.** to free from a burden. **2.** to relieve (one's mind, conscience, etc.) by or as if by confessing.

un·but/ton, *v.t.* to undo the buttons of.

un·called/-for/, *adj.* **1.** not required or wanted. **2.** unwarranted; improper.

un·can/ny, *adj.,* **-ni·er, -ni·est. 1.** seeming to have a supernatural basis. **2.** strange; mysterious.

un·cap/, *v.t.,* **-capped, -cap·ping.** to remove a cap or cover from.

un/cer·e·mo/ni·ous, *adj.* **1.** abrupt; rude. **2.** without formalities; informal. —**un/cer·e·mo/ni·ous·ly,** *adv.*

un·cer/tain, *adj.* **1.** not precisely known or fixed. **2.** not confident. **3.** not clearly determined. **4.** variable; unstable. **5.** not reliable or dependable. —**un·cer/tain·ty,** *n., pl.* **-ties.**

un·char/i·ta·ble, *adj.* not charitable or forgiving, as in judging others.

un·chart/ed, *adj.* not shown on a map; unexplored.

un·chris/tian, *adj.* **1.** not conforming to Christian teaching. **2.** not of the Christian religion.

un·ci·al (un/shē əl, -shəl), *adj.* **1.** of or being a form of writing with a rounded shape used esp. in early Greek and Latin manuscripts. —*n.* **2.** an uncial letter. **3.** uncial writing.

un·cir/cum·cised/, *adj.* **1.** not circumcised. **2.** heathen.

un·clad/, *v.* **1.** a pt. and pp. of UNCLOTHE. —*adj.* **2.** not dressed; naked.

un·clasp/, *v.t.* **1.** to undo the clasp of; unfasten. **2.** to release from the grasp.

un·cle (ung/kəl), *n.* **1.** a brother of one's father or mother. **2.** an aunt's husband.

un·clean/, *adj.* **1.** not clean; dirty. **2.** morally impure. **3.** impure according to Biblical laws, esp. dietary laws.

Un/cle Sam/ (sam), *n.* the government or people of the U.S. personified as a tall man with white whiskers.

Un/cle Tom's/ Cab/in, an antislavery novel (1852) by Harriet Beecher Stowe.

un·cloak/, *v.t.* **1.** to remove the cloak from. **2.** to reveal; expose.

un·clothe/, *v.t.,* **-clothed** or **-clad, -cloth·ing. 1.** to strip of clothes. **2.** to lay bare; uncover.

un·com/fort·a·ble, *adj.* **1.** causing discomfort. **2.** experiencing discomfort. —**un·com/fort·a·bly,** *adv.*

un·com·mit/ted, *adj.* not committed or pledged.

un·com/mon, *adj.,* **-er, -est. 1.** not common; unusual. **2.** exceptional; outstanding. —**un·com/mon·ly,** *adv.*

un/com·mu/ni·ca/tive, *adj.* not inclined to communicate; reticent.

un/com·pro·mis/ing, *adj.* not accepting or making compromises; unyielding.

un/con·cern/, *n.* **1.** absence of concern; indifference. **2.** freedom from anxiety. —**un/con·cerned/,** *adj.*

un/con·di/tion·al, *adj.* not limited by conditions; absolute. —**un/con·di/tion·al·ly,** *adv.*

uncondi/tional surren/der, *n.* a statement by a warring side that warfare will continue until the other side surrenders without conditions: first used by U.S. Grant.

un·con/scion·a·ble, *adj.* **1.** not restrained by conscience; unscrupulous. **2.** excessive or unreasonable. —**un·con/scion·a·bly,** *adv.*

un·con/scious, *adj.* **1.** lacking awareness, sensation, or cognition, esp. temporarily. **2.** not perceived at the level of awareness. **3.** done unintentionally. —*n.* **4. the unconscious,** the part of the psyche that is rarely accessible to awareness but has an influence on behavior. —**un•con'scious•ly,** *adv.* —**un•con'-scious•ness,** *n.*

un'con•sti•tu'tion•al, *adj.* not constitutional; unauthorized by or inconsistent with a constitution. —**un'con•sti•tu'tion•al'i•ty,** *n.*

un'con•ven'tion•al, *adj.* not bound by or conforming to convention. —**un'con•ven'tion•al'i•ty,** *n.* —**un'con•ven'tion•al•ly,** *adv.*

un•cork', *v.t.* **1.** to draw the cork from. **2.** to release or unleash.

un•count'ed, *adj.* **1.** not counted. **2.** innumerable.

un•cou'ple, *v.t.,* -**pled,** -**pling.** to release the coupling between; disconnect.

un•couth (un kōōth'), *adj.* **1.** lacking grace; clumsy. **2.** rude or boorish.

un•cov'er, *v.t.* **1.** to remove the cover, covering, or hat from. **2.** to lay bare; reveal. —*v.i.* **3.** to take off one's hat in respect.

un•cross', *v.t.* to change from a crossed position.

unc•tion (ungk'shən), *n.* **1.** the act of anointing, esp. as a medical treatment or religious rite. **2.** the oil used in anointing. **3.** affected or excessive earnestness.

unc'tu•ous (-chōō əs), *adj.* **1.** characterized by affected earnestness; excessively suave or smug. **2.** oily; greasy. —**unc'tu•ous•ness,** *n.*

un•cut', *adj.* **1.** not cut. **2.** not shortened; unabridged. **3.** not yet given shape, as a diamond.

un•daunt'ed, *adj.* not discouraged or dismayed.

un'de•ceive', *v.t.,* -**ceived,** -**ceiv•ing.** to free from deception.

un'de•cid'ed, *adj.* **1.** not yet decided. **2.** not having one's mind made up.

un'de•mon'stra•tive, *adj.* not given to expression of emotion; reserved.

un'de•ni'a•ble, *adj.* **1.** incapable of being denied; incontestable. **2.** indisputably good. —**un'de•ni'a•bly,** *adv.*

un•der (un'dər), *prep.* **1.** beneath and covered by: *under a tree.* **2.** below the surface of: *under the ground.* **3.** in the position of receiving, sustaining, or enduring: *sank under the heavy load.* **4.** within the heading or category of: *books classified under fiction.* **5.** less than, as in degree or amount: *under $10.* **6.** below in rank. **7.** subject to the authority, effect, or guidance of: *worked under the prime minister.* **8.** in accordance with: *under the provisions of the law.* **9.** in the process of: *under construction.* —*adv.* **10.** below or beneath something. **11.** in or into a lower degree, amount, or limit. **12.** in or into a subordinate position or condition. —*adj.* **13.** lower, as in position, degree, or importance.

under-, a prefix meaning: place or situation below or beneath (*underbrush*); lower in grade or dignity (*understudy*); of lesser degree, extent, or amount (*undersized*).

un'der•a•chieve', *v.i.,* -**a•chieved,** -**a•chiev•ing.** to perform below one's intellectual potential, esp. in school. —**un'der•a•chiev'er,** *n.*

un'der•act', *v.t., v.i.* UNDERPLAY (defs. 1, 3).

un'der•age', *adj.* being below the legal or required age.

un'der•arm', *adj.* **1.** of, situated, or for use under the arm. **2.** UNDERHAND (def. 2). —*n.* **3.** ARMPIT.

un'der•bel'ly, *n., pl.* -**lies. 1.** the lower abdomen. **2.** a vulnerable area.

un'der•bid', *v.t., v.i.,* -**bid,** -**bid•ding. 1.** to bid less than (another). **2.** to bid less than the value of (a contract or hand) at cards.

un'der•brush', *n.* shrubs, saplings, and low vines growing under large trees.

un'der•car'riage, *n.* the supporting framework underneath a vehicle, as an automobile.

un'der•charge (*v.* un'dər chärj'; *n.* un'dər chärj'), *v.,* -**charged,** -**charg•ing,** *n.* —*v.t., v.i* **1.** to charge too little. —*n.* **2.** a less than proper or customary charge.

un'der•class', *n.* a social stratum consisting of persons living in persistent poverty and social isolation.

un'der•class'man, *n., pl.* -**men.** a freshman or sophomore in a secondary school or college.

un'der•clothes' or -**cloth'ing,** *n.* (*used with a pl. v.*) UNDERWEAR.

un'der•coat', *n.* **1.** a coat worn under another. **2.** a growth of short fur or hair beneath a longer growth. **3.** a coat of paint or sealer applied under a finishing coat.

un'der•cov'er, *adj.* **1.** clandestine or secret. **2.** engaged in securing confidential information.

un'der•cur'rent, *n.* **1.** a hidden tendency or feeling. **2.** a current, as of water, that flows below an upper current or surface.

un'der•cut', *v.t.,* -**cut,** -**cut•ting. 1.** to cut under or beneath. **2.** to weaken or destroy the effectiveness of. **3.** to offer goods or services at a lower price or rate than. **4.** to hit (a ball) underhand so as to cause backspin.

un'der•de•vel'oped, *adj.* **1.** improperly or insufficiently developed. **2.** DEVELOPING.

un'der•dog', *n.* **1.** a person expected to lose in a contest or conflict. **2.** a victim of injustice.

un'der•done', *adj.* not cooked enough.

un'der•em•ployed', *adj.* **1.** employed at a job that does not fully use one's abilities. **2.** employed only part-time but available for full-time work.

un'der•es'ti•mate' (-māt'), *v.t.,* -**mat•ed,** -**mat•ing.** to estimate at too low a value.

un'der•ex•pose', *v.t.,* -**posed,** -**pos•ing.** to expose (film) to insufficient light or for too short a period.

un'der•foot', *adv.* **1.** under the feet. **2.** in the way.

un'der•fur', *n.* the soft, thick undercoat of fur animals.

un'der•gar'ment, *n.* an article of underwear.

un'der•go', *v.t.,* -**went,** -**gone,** -**go•ing. 1.** to be subjected to; experience. **2.** to endure or suffer.

un'der•grad'u•ate (-it, -āt'), *n.* a college or university student who has not received a first, esp. a bachelor's, degree.

un'der•ground' (*adv.* -ground'; *adj., n.* -ground'), *adv.* **1.** beneath the surface of the ground. **2.** in secrecy. —*adj.* **3.** existing, situated, or growing underground. **4.** hidden or secret. **5.** published or produced to reflect nonconformist or radical views. —*n.* **6.** the region beneath the surface of the ground. **7.** a secret organization fighting an established government or occupation forces. **8.** *Brit.* a subway.

un'derground rail'road, *n.* (*often caps.*) (before the abolition of slavery in the U.S.) a system for

---

un'a•bashed', *adj.*
un'ab•bre'vi•at'ed, *adj.*
un'a•bridged', *adj.*
un•ac'cent•ed, *adj.*
un'ac•cept'a•ble, *adj.*
un'ac•com'mo•dat'ing, *adj.*
un'ac•com'plished, *adj.*
un•ac'cred'it•ed, *adj.*
un'ac•knowl'edged, *adj.*
un'ac•quaint'ed, *adj.*
un'ad•ven'tur•ous, *adj.*
un'af•fil'i•at'ed, *adj.*
un'a•fraid', *adj.*
un•aid'ed, *adj.*
un'a•ligned', *adj.*

un•al'ter•a•ble, *adj.*
un'am•big'u•ous, *adj.*
un•am•bi'tious, *adj.*
un'an•tic'i•pat'ed, *adj.*
un•ap•par'ent, *adj.*
un'ap•pe•tiz'ing, *adj.*
un'ap•pre'ci•at'ed, *adj.*
un'ap•proach'a•ble, *adj.*
un'ar•tic'u•lat'ed, *adj.*
un'as•cer•tain'a•ble, *adj.*
un'at•tain'a•ble, *adj.*
un'a•vail'a•ble, *adj.*
un'a•venged', *adj.*
un•beat'a•ble, *adj.*
un•bleached', *adj.*

un•blem'ished, *adj.*
un•bound', *adj.*
un•break'a•ble, *adj.*
un•car'ing, *adj.*
un•car'pet•ed, *adj.*
un•cer'ti•fied', *adj.*
un•chal'lenged, *adj.*
un•civ'i•lized', *adj.*
un•claimed', *adj.*
un'com•bined', *adj.*
un•com'pen•sat'ed, *adj.*
un'com•plain'ing, *adj.*
un•com'pli•cat'ed, *adj.*
un•com'pli•men'ta•ry, *adj.*
un'con•firmed', *adj.*

helping fugitive slaves escape into Canada and other places of safety.

un′der•growth′, *n.* UNDERBRUSH.

un′der•hand′, *adj.* **1.** secret and crafty. **2.** executed with the hand below the level of the shoulder. —*adv.* **3.** with an underhand motion. **4.** secretly; stealthily.

un′der•hand′ed, *adj.* UNDERHAND.

un′der•lie′, *v.t.,* **-lay, -lain, -ly•ing. 1.** to lie under. **2.** to form the foundation of.

un′der•line′, *v.t.,* **-lined, -lin•ing. 1.** to draw a line underneath. **2.** to stress or emphasize.

un′der•ling (-ling), *n.* a subordinate.

un′der•ly′ing, *adj.* **1.** lying under. **2.** fundamental; basic.

un•der•mine (un′dər mīn′; *esp. for 1,* un′dər mīn′), *v.t.,* **-mined, -min•ing. 1.** to impair or weaken by imperceptible stages. **2.** to make an excavation under.

un′der•most′, *adj., adv.* lowest, as in position.

un•der•neath (un′dər nēth′, -nēth′), *prep.* **1.** directly beneath; under. **2.** under the control of. —*adv.* **3.** at a lower level or position; below.

un′der•nour′ished, *adj.* not sufficiently nourished to maintain health or normal growth.

un′der•pants′, *n.* (*used with a pl. v.*) drawers or shorts worn under outer clothing.

un′der•pass′, *n.* a passage running underneath, esp. under a railroad.

un′der•pay′, *v.t.,* **-paid, -pay•ing.** to pay less than is customary or deserved.

un′der•pin′ning, *n.* **1.** a system of supports, as beneath a wall. **2.** Often, **-nings.** a foundation or basis.

un′der•play′, *v.t.* **1.** to play (a part or scene) with restraint. **2.** to understate or downplay. —*v.i.* **3.** to underplay a part or scene.

un′der•priv′i•leged, *adj.* denied the normal privileges of a society because of low economic and social status.

un′der•pro•duc′tion, *n.* production that is less than normal or required.

un′der•rate′, *v.t.,* **-rat•ed, -rat•ing.** to rate or evaluate too low.

un′der•score′, *v.t.,* **-scored, -scor•ing.** UNDERLINE.

un′der•sea′, *adj.* **1.** located, carried on, or used under the sea. —*adv.* **2.** UNDERSEAS.

un•der•seas (un′dər sēz′), *adv.* beneath the surface of the sea.

un′der•sec′re•tar′y, *n., pl.* **-tar•ies.** a government official subordinate to a principal secretary.

un′der•sell′, *v.t.,* **-sold, -sell•ing.** to sell more cheaply than (a competitor).

un′der•sexed′, *adj.* having a weak sexual drive.

un′der•shirt′, *n.* a collarless undergarment.

un′der•shorts′, *n.* (*used with a pl. v.*) short underpants for men and boys.

un′der•shot′, *adj.* **1.** having the lower jaw projecting in front of the upper. **2.** driven by water passing beneath: *an undershot water wheel.*

un′der•side′, *n.* an under or lower side.

un′der•signed′, *n.* **the undersigned,** the person or persons signing a letter or document.

un′der•sized′, *adj.* smaller than usual or normal.

un′der•skirt′, *n.* a skirt, as a petticoat, worn under another.

un′der•staffed′, *adj.* having an insufficient number of workers.

un′der•stand′, *v.,* **-stood, -stand•ing.** —*v.t.* **1.** to perceive the meaning of; comprehend. **2.** to have a thorough knowledge of. **3.** to interpret: *She understood his comment to be a criticism.* **4.** to regard as agreed or settled. **5.** to learn or hear. **6.** to infer (something not stated). —*v.i.* **7.** to perceive what is meant. **8.** to accept something tolerantly or sympathetically. —**un′der•stand′a•ble,** *adj.* —**un′der•stand′a•bly,** *adv.*

un′der•stand′ing, *n.* **1.** comprehension. **2.** personal interpretation. **3.** intellectual ability; intelligence. **4.** a mutual agreement, esp. of a private or tacit kind. —*adj.* **5.** characterized by tolerance or sympathy.

un′der•state′, *v.t.,* **-stat•ed, -stat•ing. 1.** to state less strongly than the facts warrant. **2.** to set forth in restrained terms. —**un′der•state′ment,** *n.*

un′der•stood′, *adj.* **1.** agreed upon. **2.** implied but not stated.

un′der•stud′y, *n., pl.* **-ies,** *v.,* **-ied, -y•ing.** —*n.* **1.** a performer who learns another's role in order to serve as a replacement if necessary. —*v.t., v.i.* **2.** to learn (a role) as an understudy (to).

un′der•take′, *v.t.,* **-took, -tak•en, -tak•ing. 1.** to take upon oneself, as a task. **2.** to obligate oneself. **3.** to warrant or guarantee.

un′der•tak′er, *n.* FUNERAL DIRECTOR.

un•der•tak•ing (un′dər tā′king, un′dər tā′-), *n.* **1.** something undertaken. **2.** a pledge or guarantee.

un′der-the-coun′ter, *adj.* illegal; unauthorized.

un′der•tone′, *n.* **1.** a low or subdued tone. **2.** an underlying quality or element. **3.** a subdued color.

un′der•tow′, *n.* a strong subsurface current moving in a direction opposite that of the surface current.

un′der•val′ue, *v.t.,* **-ued, -u•ing. 1.** to put too low a value on. **2.** to have insufficient regard or esteem for.

un′der•wa′ter, *adj.* **1.** existing, occurring, or used under water. —*adv.* **2.** beneath the water.

un′der•wear′, *n.* clothing worn next to the skin under outer clothes.

un′der•weight′, *adj.* weighing less than is usual or proper.

un′der•world′, *n.* **1.** the criminal element of human society. **2.** the place where the spirits of the dead reside.

un•der•write (un′dər rīt′, un′dər rīt′), *v.t.,* **-wrote, -writ•ten, -writ•ing. 1.** to agree to finance (an undertaking). **2.** to guarantee the sale of (a security to be offered for public subscription). **3.** to write one's name at the end of (an insurance policy), becoming liable in case of specified losses. —**un′der•writ′er,** *n.*

un•dies (un′dēz), *n.pl.* women's or children's underwear.

un•do (un doo′), *v.t.,* **-did, -done, -do•ing. 1.** to reverse or annul. **2.** to bring to ruin; destroy. **3.** to unfasten, unlatch, or untie.

un•do′ing, *n.* **1.** a reversing or annulment. **2.** ruin. **3.** a cause of ruin.

---

un•con′quered, *adj.*
un•con′se•crat′ed, *adj.*
un′con•soled′, *adj.*
un′con•sol′i•dat′ed, *adj.*
un′con•strict′ed, *adj.*
un′con•sumed′, *adj.*
un′con•tam′i•nat′ed, *adj.*
un′con•trol′la•ble, *adj.*
un′con•trolled′, *adj.*
un′con•vinc′ing, *adj.;* **-ly,** *adv.*
un′co•op′er•a•tive, *adj.*
un′co•or′di•nat′ed, *adj.*
un′cor•rob′o•rat′ed, *adj.*
un•crit′i•cal, *adj.;* **-ly,** *adv.*
un•crowd′ed, *adj.*

un•cul′ti•vat′ed, *adj.*
un•dam′aged, *adj.*
un′de•ci′pher•a•ble, *adj.*
un′de•clared′, *adj.*
un′de•fin′a•ble, *adj.*
un′de•fined′, *adj.*
un′de•liv′er•a•ble, *adj.*
un′de•mand′ing, *adj.*
un′de•pend′a•ble, *adj.*
un′de•served′, *adj.*
un′de•serv′ing, *adj.*
un′de•sir′a•ble, *adj.*
un′de•tect′ed, *adj.*
un′de•ter′mined, *adj.*
un′de•terred′, *adj.*

un•de′vi•at′ing, *adj.*
un′di•ag•nosed′, *adj.*
un′di•gest′ed, *adj.*
un′dig′ni•fied′, *adj.*
un′di•min′ished, *adj.*
un′dis•cern′ing, *adj.*
un′dis•crim′i•nat′ing, *adj.*
un′dis•guised′, *adj.*
un′dis•mayed′, *adj.*
un′dis•put′ed, *adj.*
un′dis•turbed′, *adj.*
un′di•vid′ed, *adj.*
un•eat′en, *adj.*
un′ed•u•cat′ed, *adj.*
un′e•man′ci•pat′ed, *adj.*

un•doubt′ed, adj. not doubted or disputed; accepted. —**un•doubt′ed•ly,** adv.

un•dress′, v.t., v.i. 1. to remove the clothing (of). —n. 2. informal dress. 3. the state of being unclothed.

un•due′, adj. 1. unwarranted; excessive. 2. inappropriate; improper.

un•du•lant (un′jə lənt, un′dyə-), adj. undulating; wavelike.

un′du•late′ (-lāt′), v.i., v.t., -lat•ed, -lat•ing. 1. to move or cause to move with a wavelike motion. 2. to have or cause to have a wavy form or surface. —un′du•la′tion, n.

un•du′ly, adv. 1. excessively. 2. inappropriately.

un•dy′ing, adj. deathless; eternal.

un•earned′, adj. 1. not earned by work or service. 2. not merited or deserved. 3. (of income) derived from investments.

un•earth′, v.t. 1. to dig out of the earth. 2. to bring to light; uncover.

un•earth′ly, adj. 1. not of this earth or world. 2. supernatural; weird. 3. unreasonable or absurd.

un•eas′y, adj., -i•er, -i•est. 1. lacking ease of mind; restless or perturbed. 2. constrained in manner; awkward. 3. not conducive to ease. —**un•eas′i•ly,** adv. —**un•eas′i•ness,** n.

un′em•ploy′a•ble, adj. unsuitable for employment.

un′em•ployed′, adj. 1. without a job. 2. not in use. —**un′em•ploy′ment,** n.

un•e′qual, adj. 1. not equal, as in rank or ability. 2. not adequate: unequal to the task. 3. uneven or variable. —**un•e′qual•ly,** adv.

un•e′qualed, adj. not equaled or surpassed; matchless. Also, esp. Brit., **un•e′qualled.**

un′e•quiv′o•cal, adj. not ambiguous; clear. —**un′•e•quiv′o•cal•ly,** adv.

un•err′ing, adj. not erring; accurate. —**un•err′•ing•ly,** adv.

UNESCO (yōō nes′kō), n. United Nations Educational, Scientific, and Cultural Organization.

un•e′ven, adj. 1. not level or flat. 2. not uniform; varying. 3. not equitable or fair. 4. not straight, symmetrical, or parallel. 5. (ot a number) odd. —**un•e′ven•ly,** adv.

un′e•vent′ful, adj. lacking in important or interesting occurrences; routine.

un′ex•am′pled, adj. unlike anything previously known; unprecedented.

un′ex•cep′tion•a•ble, adj. not offering any basis for objection; beyond criticism.

un′ex•cep′tion•al, adj. not exceptional; ordinary.

un′ex•pect′ed, adj. not expected; unforeseen. —**un′ex•pect′ed•ly,** adv.

un•fail′ing, adj. 1. completely dependable. 2. inexhaustible; endless.

un•fair′, adj. not conforming to standards of justice, honesty, or impartiality. —**un•fair′ly,** adv. —**un•fair′ness,** n.

un•faith′ful, adj. 1. not faithful to duty, obligation, or promises; disloyal. 2. not accurate or reliable; inexact. —**un•faith′ful•ly,** adv. —**un•faith′ful•ness,** n.

un′fa•mil′iar, adj. 1. not acquainted or conversant:

unfamiliar with the city. 2. different, unusual, or novel. —**un′fa•mil′i•ar′i•ty,** n.

un•feel′ing, adj. 1. lacking feeling or sensation. 2. not sympathetic; hardhearted. —**un•feel′ing•ly,** adv.

un•feigned′, adj. not feigned; genuine.

un•fit′, adj. 1. not suited or suitable. 2. not competent; unqualified. 3. not physically fit.

un•flap•pa•ble (un flap′ə bəl), adj. not easily upset or confused.

un•fledged (un flejd′), adj. 1. lacking sufficient feathers for flight, as a young bird. 2. immature or inexperienced.

un•flinch′ing, adj. not flinching or shrinking.

un•fold′, v.t. 1. to open from a folded state; spread out. 2. to lay open to view; reveal. 3. to disclose in words, esp. gradually. —v.i. 4. to become unfolded. 5. to develop; evolve.

un′for•get′ta•ble, adj. impossible to forget.

un•formed′, adj. 1. not definitely formed; shapeless. 2. not yet developed in character.

un•for′tu•nate, adj. 1. suffering from bad luck. 2. unfavorable or inauspicious. 3. regrettable or deplorable. —n. 4. an unfortunate person. —**un•for′tu•nate•ly,** adv.

un•found′ed, adj. not based on fact or reality; groundless.

un•friend′ly, adj., -li•er, -li•est. 1. not friendly or kind. 2. not favorable; inhospitable. —**un•friend′li•ness,** n.

un•frock′, v.t. to deprive of ecclesiastical rank, authority, and function.

un•furl′, v.t., v.i. to spread out from a furled state, as a flag.

un•gain•ly (un gān′lē), adj., -li•er, -li•est. not graceful; awkward.

un•god′ly, adj., -li•er, -li•est. 1. lacking piety; irreligious. 2. sinful; wicked. 3. outrageous; shocking. —**un•god′li•ness,** n.

un•gov′ern•a•ble, adj. impossible to govern, rule, or restrain.

un•gra′cious, adj. 1. not courteous; ill-mannered. 2. not pleasant; disagreeable.

un•grate′ful, adj. 1. not appreciative. 2. not rewarding; thankless: an ungrateful task. —**un•grate′ful•ly,** adv.

un•guard′ed, adj. 1. not guarded; unprotected. 2. open; guileless. 3. not cautious or discreet.

un•guent (ung′gwənt), n. an ointment or salve.

un•gu•late (ung′gyə lit, -lāt′), adj. 1. having hoofs. —n. 2. a hoofed mammal.

un•hand′, v.t. to release from a grasp.

un•hap′py, adj., -pi•er, -pi•est. 1. sad; wretched. 2. unfortunate; unlucky. 3. inappropriate; unsuitable. —**un•hap′pi•ly,** adv. —**un•hap′pi•ness,** n.

un•health′y, adj., -i•er, -i•est. 1. not in good health. 2. symptomatic of bad health. 3. harmful to good health. 4. morally harmful. —**un•health′i•ness,** n.

un•heard′, adj. 1. not heard. 2. not given a hearing.

unheard′-of′, adj. not previously known; unprecedented.

un•hinge′, v.t., -hinged, -hing•ing. 1. to remove from hinges. 2. to throw into confusion; upset.

---

un′e•mo′tion•al, adj.
un′en•dur′a•ble, adj.
un′en•forced′, adj.
un′en•joy′a•ble, adj.
un′en•light′ened, adj.
un′en•thu′si•as′tic, adj.
un•en′vi•a•ble, adj.
un•es•sen′tial, adj.
un′es•tab′lished, adj.
un•eth′i•cal, adj.
un′ex•ag′ger•at′ed, adj.
un•ex•cit′ing, adj.
un′ex•plored′, adj.
un′ex•posed′, adj.
un•fash′ion•a•ble, adj.

un•fas′ten, v.
un•fath′om•a•ble, adj.
un•fa′vor•a•ble, adj.
un•fer′ti•lized′, adj.
un•fet′tered, adj.
un•flat′ter•ing, adj.
un′fore•see′a•ble, adj.
un′fore•seen′, adj.
un′for•giv′a•ble, adj.
un′for•giv′ing, adj.
un′for•got′ten, adj.
un•for′ti•fied′, adj.
un•fur′nished, adj.
un•grace′ful, adj.; -ly, adv.
un′gram•mat′i•cal, adj.

un•grudg′ing, adj.
un•ham′pered, adj.
un•har′vest•ed, adj.
un•heed′ed, adj.
un•help′ful, adj.
un•hes′i•tat′ing, adj.; -ly, adv.
un•hin′dered, adj.
un′i•den′ti•fi•a•ble, adj.
un′i•den′ti•fied′, adj.
un•im•ag′i•na•ble, adj.
un•im•ag′i•na•tive, adj.; -ly, adv.
un′im•por′tant, adj.
un′im•pos′ing, adj.
un′in•cor′po•rat′ed, adj.
un′in•form′a•tive, adj.

un·ho·ly, adj., -li·er, -li·est. 1. not holy; not sacred. 2. sinful; wicked. 3. dreadful; outrageous.

un·hook', v.t. to detach from or as if from a hook.

un·horse', v.t., -horsed, -hors·ing. to cause to fall from a horse.

uni-, a combining form meaning one (unicycle).

u·ni·cam·er·al (yōō'ni kam'ər əl), adj. (of a legislative body) consisting of a single chamber.

UNICEF (yōō'nə sef'), n. United Nations Children's Fund. [U(nited) N(ations) I(nternational) C(hildren's) E(mergency) F(und), earlier name]

u·ni·cel'lu·lar, adj. of or consisting of a single cell.

u·ni·corn (yōō'ni kôrn'), n. 1. a mythical creature resembling a horse, with a single horn in the center of its forehead: often symbolic of chastity or purity. 2. an animal mentioned in the Bible: now believed to be a wild ox or rhinoceros. Deut. 33:17.

unicorn

u'ni·cy'cle, n. a one-wheeled vehicle driven by pedals.

u·ni·form (yōō'nə fôrm'), adj. 1. identical or consistent with others. 2. not varying; constant. —n. 3. an identifying outfit worn by the members of a given group. —v.t. 4. to clothe in or furnish with a uniform. —u'ni·form'i·ty, n. —u'ni·form'ly, adv.

u·ni·fy (yōō'nə fī'), v.t., v.i., -fied, -fy·ing. to make or become a single unit. —u'ni·fi·ca'tion, n.

u'ni·lat'er·al, adj. 1. of, occurring on, or affecting one side only. 2. undertaken or done by one side or party only; not mutual. —u'ni·lat'er·al·ly, adv.

un·im·peach·a·ble (un'im pē'chə bəl), adj. above suspicion or reproach.

un'in·hib'it·ed, adj. not inhibited, esp. unrestrained by convention. —un'in·hib'it·ed·ly, adv.

un·in'ter·est·ed, adj. not interested; indifferent. —Usage. See DISINTERESTED.

un·ion (yōōn'yən), n. 1. the act of uniting or state of being united. 2. something formed by uniting; combination. 3. a number of persons, states, or nations joined together for a common purpose. 4. the Union, the United States, esp. during the Civil War. 5. LABOR UNION. 6. a device emblematic of union, used in a flag or ensign. 7. the state of being united in marriage. 8. a contrivance for connecting parts, as of machinery.

un'ion·ize', v.t., v.i., -ized, -iz·ing. to organize into or form a labor union.

un'ion jack', n. 1. a national flag consisting of a union. 2. (caps.) the British national flag.

Un'ion of So'viet So'cialist Repub'lics, n. a former federal union of 15 constituent republics, in E Europe and N Asia, comprising the larger part of the former Russian Empire: dissolved in December 1991.

u·nique (yōō nēk'), adj. 1. existing as the only one of a kind. 2. having no equal; unparalleled. 3. not typical; unusual. —u·nique'ly, adv. —u·nique'ness, n. —Usage. Some commentators object to the use of comparative words such as more, very, totally, etc., with UNIQUE, claiming that it represents an absolute state that cannot exist in degrees. However, in the sense "not typical, unusual," such comparison has always been standard: The foliage on late-blooming plants is more unique than that on the earlier varieties.

u·ni·sex (yōō'nə seks'), adj. designed or suitable for both sexes.

u·ni·son (yōō'nə sən, -zən), n. 1. a. identity in pitch. b. the performance of musical parts at the same pitch or at the octave. 2. perfect agreement; accord.

u·nit (yōō'nit), n. 1. a single entity. 2. one of the individuals, parts, or elements into which a whole may be divided. 3. a fixed quantity, as of money, used as a standard of measurement. 4. the least positive integer; one. 5. a machine, part, or system of machines having a specified purpose: a heating unit.

U·ni·tar·i·an (yōō'ni târ'ē ən), n. a member of a Christian denomination founded upon the doctrine that God is one being, and giving each congregation complete control over its affairs. —U'ni·tar'i·an·ism, n.

u·nite (yōō nīt'), v.t., v.i., u·nit·ed, u·nit·ing. 1. to bring or come together in a single whole or unit. 2. to join in mutual sympathy or a common goal.

u·nit·ed (yōō nī'tid), adj. 1. made into or caused to act as a single entity. 2. formed or produced by the uniting of persons or things: a united effort. 3. agreed; in harmony. —Saying. 4. United we stand, divided we fall, cooperation is essential to the success of an endeavor: from The Liberty Song (1768) by John Dickinson. —u·nit'ed·ly, adv.

Unit'ed Ar'ab Em'irates, n. (used with a sing. or pl. v.) an independent federation in E Arabia. 2,262,309.

Unit'ed Ar'ab Repub'lic, n. former name (1961–71) of EGYPT.

Unit'ed Breth'ren, n. a Protestant denomination, of Wesleyan beliefs and practices, founded in 1800.

Unit'ed Church' of Can'ada, n. a Christian denomination founded in 1924–25 by members of the Presbyterian, Methodist, and Congregationalist churches, now the largest Protestant group in Canada.

Unit'ed King'dom, n. a kingdom in NW Europe, consisting of Great Britain and Northern Ireland. 58,610,182.

Unit'ed Na'tions, n. (used with a sing. v.) an international organization formed in 1945 to promote peace, security, and cooperation.

Unit'ed States', n. a republic comprising 48 conterminous states, the District of Columbia, and

---

un'in·formed', adj.
un'in·hab'it·a·ble, adj.
un'in·hab'it·ed, adj.
un'in·i'ti·at'ed, adj.
un'in·spired', adj.
un'in·sured', adj.
un'in·tel'li·gent, adj.
un'in·tel'li·gi·ble, adj.; -bly, adv.
un'in·tend'ed, adj.
un'in·ten'tion·al, adj.; -ly, adv.
un·in'ter·est·ing, adj.
un'in·ter·rupt'ed, adj.
un'in·vest'ed, adj.
un'in·vit'ed, adj.
un'in·vit'ing, adj.

un'in·volved', adj.
un·jus'ti·fi'a·ble, adj.; -bly, adv.
un·jus'ti·fied', adj.
un·leav'ened, adj.
un·li'censed, adj.
un·lik'a·ble, adj.
un·lined', adj.
un·list'ed, adj.
un·liv'a·ble, adj.
un·lov'a·ble, adj.
un·loved', adj.
un·mag'ni·fied', adj.
un·man'age·a·ble, adj.
un·marred', adj.
un·mar'ried, adj.

un·mer'it·ed, adj.
un'mis·tak'en, adj.
un·mo'ti·vat'ed, adj.
un·moved', adj.
un·named', adj.
un·nav'i·ga·ble, adj.
un·need'ed, adj.
un'ob·jec'tion·a·ble, adj.
un'ob·lig'ing, adj.
un'ob·serv'ant, adj.
un'ob·struct'ed, adj.
un'ob·tain'a·ble, adj.
un'ob·tru'sive, adj.; -ly, adv.
un'of·fen'sive, adj.; -ly, adv.
un'op·posed', adj.

Alaska in North America, and Hawaii in the N Pacific. 267,954,767. *Cap.:* Washington, D.C. *Abbr.:* US, U.S.

Unit′ed States′ of Amer′ica, *n.* UNITED STATES. *Abbr.:* USA, U.S.A.

u·ni·ty (yōō′ni tē), *n., pl.* **-ties. 1.** the state of being united; oneness. **2.** the state of being combined with others into a whole. **3.** concord, harmony, or agreement. **4.** *Math.* the number one. **5.** (in literature and art) harmony among the parts or elements of a work. **—Proverb. 6. In unity there is strength,** a group can accomplish more than individuals working separately.

u·ni·va·lent (yōō′nə vā′lənt, yōō niv′ə-), *adj.* having a chemical valence of one.

u′ni·valve′, *n.* a mollusk with a single valve.

u·ni·ver·sal (yōō′nə vûr′səl), *adj.* **1.** of, characteristic of, or affecting all or the whole. **2.** applicable everywhere or in all cases. **3.** used or understood by all. **4.** present or existing everywhere. **—u′ni·ver·sal′i·ty,** *n.* **—u′ni·ver′sal·ly,** *adv.*

u′ni·ver′sal·ize′, *v.t.,* **-ized, -iz·ing.** to make universal.

u′niver′sal joint′, *n.* a coupling between rotating shafts that allows them to move in any direction.

U′niver′sal Prod′uct Code′, *n.* a standardized bar code used esp. in ringing up purchases at the supermarket.

u·ni·verse (yōō′nə vûrs′), *n.* **1.** the totality of objects and phenomena throughout space. **2.** the whole world.

u·ni·ver·si·ty (yōō′nə vûr′si tē), *n., pl.* **-ties.** an institution of higher learning authorized to confer both undergraduate and graduate degrees.

un·just (un just′), *adj.* not just; lacking in justice or fairness. **—un·just′ly,** *adv.*

un·kempt (un kempt′), *adj.* **1.** not combed. **2.** disheveled; messy.

un·kind′, *adj.,* **-er, -est.** lacking in kindness or mercy; harsh. **—un·kind′ness,** *n.*

un·kind′ly, *adj.,* **-li·er, -li·est. 1.** not kindly; unkind. **—adv. 2.** in an unkind manner.

un·know′ing, *adj.* ignorant or unaware.

un·known′, *adj.* **1.** not known; unfamiliar. **2.** not discovered, identified, or ascertained. **—n. 3.** one that is unknown. **4.** a symbol representing an unknown quantity, esp. in algebra.

Un′known Sol′dier, *n.* (*sometimes l.c.*) an unidentified soldier killed in battle and buried with honors, the tomb serving as a memorial to all the unidentified dead of a nation's armed forces.

un·lace′, *v.t.,* **-laced, -lac·ing.** to loosen or undo the lacing of.

un·law′ful, *adj.* **1.** not lawful; illegal. **2.** born out of wedlock; illegitimate. **—un·law′ful·ly,** *adv.*

un·lead′ed, *adj.* (of gasoline) containing no tetraethyllead.

un·learn′, *v.t.* to forget or lose knowledge of.

un·learn′ed (-lûr′nid *for 1;* -lûrnd′ *for 2*), *adj.* **1.** not educated; ignorant. **2.** acquired or known without having been learned: *unlearned behavior.*

un·leash′, *v.t.* to release from or as if from a leash.

un·less (un les′, ən-), *conj.* except under the circumstances that.

un·let′tered, *adj.* **1.** not educated. **2.** illiterate.

un·like′, *adj.* **1.** not alike; different. **—prep. 2.** different from. **3.** not characteristic of.

un·like′ly, *adj.,* **-li·er, -li·est. 1.** not likely; improbable. **2.** holding little prospect of success. **—un·like′li·hood′,** *n.*

un·lim′ber, *v.t.* to make ready for use or action.

un·lim′it·ed, *adj.* **1.** without limitations or restrictions. **2.** boundless; vast.

un·load′, *v.t.* **1.** to take the load, charge, or cargo from. **2.** to discharge (cargo, passengers, etc.). **3.** to relieve of something burdensome or oppressive. **4.** to express (feelings, grievances, etc.) freely. **5.** to get rid of by sale in large quantities. **—v.i. 6.** to unload something.

un·lock′, *v.t.* **1.** to undo the lock of. **2.** to release by or as if by unlocking. **3.** to lay open; disclose.

un·looked′-for′, *adj.* not expected; unforeseen.

un·loose′, *v.t.,* **-loosed, -loos·ing. 1.** to relax (the grasp, hold, etc.). **2.** to let loose from or as if from restraint.

un·luck′y, *adj.,* **-i·er, -i·est. 1.** not lucky; lacking good fortune. **2.** characterized by or bringing misfortune.

un·make′, *v.t.,* **-made, -mak·ing. 1.** to reverse the making of; undo. **2.** to strip of office or authority.

un·man′, *v.t.,* **-manned, -man·ning.** to deprive of manly courage or fortitude.

un·man′ly, *adj.,* **-li·er, -li·est.** not manly; weak or effeminate.

un·manned′, *adj.* lacking a human crew: *an unmanned spacecraft.*

un·man′ner·ly, *adj.* not mannerly; impolite.

un·mask′, *v.t.* **1.** to strip a mask from. **2.** to reveal the true character of. **—v.i. 3.** to take off one's mask.

un·mean′ing, *adj.* devoid of meaning or sense.

un·men′tion·a·ble, *adj.* unfit or improper to be mentioned.

un·mer′ci·ful, *adj.* not merciful; cruel.

un·mind′ful, *adj.* not mindful; unaware.

un′mis·tak′a·ble, *adj.* not mistakable; obvious. **—un′mis·tak′a·bly,** *adv.*

un·mit′i·gat′ed, *adj.* **1.** not softened or lessened. **2.** unqualified or absolute.

un·mor′al, *adj.* lacking or unaffected by a moral sense or moral principles.

un·nat′u·ral, *adj.* **1.** contrary to nature. **2.** at variance with human nature. **3.** at variance with what is normal or to be expected. **4.** not genuine or spontaneous. **—un·nat′u·ral·ly,** *adv.*

un·nec′es·sar′y, *adj.* not necessary; needless. **—un·nec′es·sar′i·ly,** *adv.*

un·nerve′, *v.t.,* **-nerved, -nerv·ing.** to deprive of courage, strength, or determination.

un·num′bered, *adj.* **1.** bearing no number. **2.** countless; innumerable.

un·oc′cu·pied′, *adj.* **1.** without occupants; empty. **2.** not busy or active; idle.

un·or′gan·ized′, *adj.* not organized, esp. not belonging to or represented by a labor union.

un·pack′, *v.t.* **1.** to remove the contents from (a box, trunk, etc.). **2.** to remove from a container, suitcase, or package. **—v.i. 3.** to unpack a container.

---

un·or′tho·dox′, *adj.*
un·paint′ed, *adj.*
un·paired′, *adj.*
un·pal′at·a·ble, *adj.*
un·par′don·a·ble, *adj.*
un·pat′ent·ed, *adj.*
un·paved′, *adj.*
un·planned′, *adj.*
un·pol·lut′ed, *adj.*
un·pop′u·lat′ed, *adj.*
un·prac′ti·cal, *adj.*
un·prac′ticed, *adj.*
un·pre·dict′ed, *adj.*
un·prej′u·diced, *adj.*
un′pre·med′i·tat′ed, *adj.*

un′pre·pared′, *adj.*
un′pre·ten′tious, *adj.*
un′pro·duc′tive, *adj.;* -ly, *adv.*
un′pro·nounce′a·ble, *adj.*
un′pro·tect′ed, *adj.*
un′pro·test′ing, *adj.*
un·proved′, *adj.*
un·prov′en, *adj.*
un′pro·vid′ed, *adj.*
un′pro·voked′, *adj.*
un·pub′lished, *adj.*
un·ques′tion·ing, *adj.*
un·re·al·is′tic, *adj.*
un·re′al·ized′, *adj.*
un′re·cep′tive, *adj.;* -ly, *adv.*

un·rec′og·niz′a·ble, *adj.*
un′rec·on·cil′a·ble, *adj.;* -bly, *adv.*
un′rec′on·ciled′, *adj.*
un·reg′u·lat′ed, *adj.*
un′re·hearsed′, *adj.*
un′re·pent′ant, *adj.*
un′rep·re·sent′a·tive, *adj.*
un′re·quit′ed, *adj.*
un′re·sent′ful, *adj.;* -ly, *adv.*
un′re·sist′ant, *adj.*
un·re·solved′, *adj.*
un′re·spon′sive, *adj.;* -ly, *adv.;* -ness, *n.*
un′re·ward′ing, *adj.*
un·right′eous, *adj.*

un·par'al·leled', *adj.* without parallel; unequaled. Also, *esp. Brit.*, **un·par'al·lelled'**.

un'per'son, *n.* a public figure who for political or ideological reasons is not recognized or mentioned.

un·pin', *v.t.*, **-pinned, -pin·ning. 1.** to remove a pin from. **2.** to unfasten by or as if by removing a pin.

un·pleas'ant, *adj.* not pleasant; disagreeable. **—un·pleas'ant·ly**, *adv.* **—un·pleas'ant·ness**, *n.*

un·plug', *v.t.*, **-plugged, -plug·ging. 1.** to remove a plug, stopper, or obstruction from. **2.** to disconnect (an appliance, a telephone, etc.) by removing a plug.

un·plumbed', *adj.* **1.** not measured with a plumb line. **2.** not understood or explored in depth.

un·pop'u·lar, *adj.* not popular; disliked, disapproved, or ignored. **—un'pop·u·lar'i·ty**, *n.*

un·prec'e·dent'ed, *adj.* without precedent; never before known or experienced.

un·prin'ci·pled, *adj.* lacking or not based on moral principles; unscrupulous.

un·print'a·ble, *adj.* unfit for print, esp. because of obscenity.

un'pro·fes'sion·al, *adj.* **1.** at variance with professional standards or ethics. **2.** lacking professional competence.

un·prof'it·a·ble, *adj.* **1.** not showing a profit. **2.** pointless or futile.

un·qual'i·fied', *adj.* **1.** lacking the necessary qualifications. **2.** not modified or limited. **3.** absolute; complete.

un·ques'tion·a·ble, *adj.* **1.** not open to question; beyond doubt or dispute. **2.** above criticism; unexceptionable: *a person of unquestionable principles.* **—un·ques'tion·a·bly**, *adv.*

un·quote (*contrastively* un'kwōt'), *v.i.*, **-quot·ed, -quot·ing.** (used by a speaker to indicate the end of a quotation.)

un·rav'el, *v.*, **-eled, -el·ing** or (*esp. Brit.*) **-elled, -el·ling. —v.t. 1.** to separate the threads of (a fabric, rope, etc.). **2.** to make plain or clear; solve. **—v.i. 3.** to become unraveled.

un·read' (-red'), *adj.* **1.** not read, as a letter. **2.** lacking in knowledge gained by reading.

un·re'al, *adj.* not real or actual; imaginary, illusory, or false.

un·rea'son·a·ble, *adj.* **1.** not guided by reason or sound judgment. **2.** excessive or immoderate. **—un·rea'son·a·bly**, *adv.*

un·rea'son·ing, *adj.* not reasoning or exercising reason.

un're·con·struct'ed, *adj.* stubbornly maintaining positions or beliefs considered out of date.

un're·gen'er·ate (-it), *adj.* **1.** not regenerate; not repentant. **2.** obstinate; unyielding.

un're·lent'ing, *adj.* **1.** not relenting; relentless. **2.** not easing or slackening, as in intensity. **—un're·lent'ing·ly**, *adv.*

un're·mit'ting, *adj.* not abating; incessant.

un're·served', *adj.* **1.** without reservation; unqualified. **2.** free from reserve; frank. **3.** not set apart for a particular use. **—un're·serv'ed·ly**, *adv.*

un·rest', *n.* disturbance or turmoil; agitation.

un·ripe', *adj.* not ripe; immature.

un·ri'valed, *adj.* having no rival or competitor. Also, *esp. Brit.*, **un·ri'valled.**

un·roll', *v.t.* **1.** to spread out (something rolled). **2.** to display; reveal. **—v.i. 3.** to become unrolled or spread out.

un·ruf'fled, *adj.* **1.** calm; composed. **2.** not ruffled, as a surface.

un·ru·ly (un rōō'lē), *adj.*, **-li·er, -li·est.** difficult to discipline or control; not cooperative.

un·sad'dle, *v.t.*, *v.i.*, **-dled, -dling.** to remove the saddle from (a horse).

un·sat'u·rat'ed, *adj.* **1.** capable of dissolving still more of a substance. **2.** (of an organic compound) having a double or triple bond and capable of forming new compounds by addition.

un·sa'vor·y, *adj.* **1.** tasteless or insipid. **2.** unpleasant in taste or smell. **3.** morally objectionable.

un·scathed', *adj.* not scathed; unharmed.

un·schooled', *adj.* not schooled, taught, or trained.

un'sci·en·tif'ic, *adj.* not scientific, esp. not conforming to the principles or methods of science. **—un'sci·en·tif'i·cal·ly**, *adv.*

un·scram'ble, *v.t.*, **-bled, -bling. 1.** to reduce to order or intelligibility. **2.** to make (a scrambled message) comprehensible.

un·screw', *v.t.* **1.** to loosen a screw from. **2.** to unfasten or withdraw by turning.

un·scru'pu·lous, *adj.* not scrupulous; unprincipled. **—un·scru'pu·lous·ly**, *adv.*

un·seal', *v.t.* to break or remove the seal of; open.

un·sea'son·a·ble, *adj.* **1.** being out of season. **2.** not timely; inopportune.

un·seat', *v.t.* **1.** to dislodge from a seat, esp. from a saddle. **2.** to remove from political office.

un·seem'ly, *adj.*, **-li·er, -li·est. 1.** not in keeping with accepted standards of taste or proper form. **2.** not appropriate. **—un·seem'li·ness**, *n.*

un·self'ish, *adj.* not selfish; generous; altruistic. **—un·self'ish·ly**, *adv.* **—un·self'ish·ness**, *n.*

un·set'tle, *v.*, **-tled, -tling. —v.t. 1.** to cause to be unstable; disturb. **2.** to agitate the mind or emotions of. **—v.i. 3.** to become unsettled.

un·set'tled, *adj.* **1.** not settled; not fixed or stable. **2.** wavering, as in opinion. **3.** not populated. **4.** not determined; undecided. **5.** not adjusted, closed, or paid, as an account. **6.** liable to change; variable.

un·shack'le, *v.t.*, **-led, -ling.** to free from or as if from shackles.

un·sheathe', *v.t.*, **-sheathed, -sheath·ing.** to draw from a sheath.

un·sight'ly, *adj.*, **-li·er, -li·est.** unpleasant to look at; ugly. **—un·sight'li·ness**, *n.*

un·skilled', *adj.* **1.** lacking skill. **2.** not demanding skill. **3.** showing a lack of skill.

un·skill'ful, *adj.* not skillful; inept. **—un·skill'ful·ly**, *adv.*

un·snap', *v.t.*, **-snapped, -snap·ping.** to open or release by or as if by undoing a snap.

un·snarl', *v.t.* to free of snarls; disentangle.

un'so·phis'ti·cat'ed, *adj.* **1.** not sophisticated; naive. **2.** not complex; simple.

un·sound', *adj.*, **-er, -est. 1.** unhealthy, as the body or mind. **2.** not solid or firm, as foundations. **3.** not valid; fallacious. **4.** not strong or secure. **—un·sound'ly**, *adv.*

---

un·safe', *adj.*; **-ly**, *adv.*
un·sal'a·ble, *adj.*
un·sanc'tioned, *adj.*
un'sat·is·fac'to·ry, *adj.*
un·sat'is·fied', *adj.*
un·shared', *adj.*
un·shel'tered, *adj.*
un·shield'ed, *adj.*
un·so'cia·ble, *adj.*
un·so'cial, *adj.*; **-ly**, *adv.*
un·so·lic'it·ed, *adj.*
un·solv'a·ble, *adj.*
un·spec·tac'u·lar, *adj.*
un·spoiled', *adj.*
un·struc'tured, *adj.*

un'sub·stan'ti·at'ed, *adj.*
un'suc·cess'ful, *adj.*; **-ly**, *adv.*
un·suit'a·ble, *adj.*
un·sul'lied, *adj.*
un'su·per·vised', *adj.*
un·sure', *adj.*; **-ly**, *adv.*; **-ness**, *n.*
un'sur·passed', *adj.*
un'sur·prised', *adj.*
un'sus·cep'ti·ble, *adj.*
un'sus·pect'ing, *adj.*; **-ly**, *adv.*
un'sus·tained', *adj.*
un·swerv'ing, *adj.*
un·tapped', *adj.*
un·ti'dy, *adj.*, **-di·er, -di·est.**
un·tir'ing, *adj.*; **-ly**, *adv.*

un·ti'tled, *adj.*
un·trace'a·ble, *adj.*
un·trained', *adj.*
un'trans·fer'a·ble, *adj.*
un'trans·lat'a·ble, *adj.*
un·tried', *adj.*
un·trou'bled, *adj.*
un·trust'wor'thy, *adj.*
un·var'y·ing, *adj.*
un·ver'i·fi'a·ble, *adj.*
un·war'rant·ed, *adj.*
un·work'a·ble, *adj.*
un·world'ly, *adj.*
un·wrin'kled, *adj.*
un·yield'ing, *adj.*

un•spar/ing, *adj.* **1.** liberal or profuse. **2.** unmerciful; harsh.

un•speak/a•ble, *adj.* **1.** exceeding the power of speech; inexpressible. **2.** inexpressibly bad, evil, or objectionable: *unspeakable crimes.* —**un•speak/a•bly,** *adv.*

un•sta/ble, *adj.* **1.** not stable; unsteady. **2.** liable to change or fluctuate. **3.** marked by emotional instability. **4.** not constant; wavering. **5.** of or being a chemical compound that readily decomposes. —**un•sta/bly,** *adv.*

un•stead/y, *adj.* **1.** not steady; unstable. **2.** fluctuating or wavering. **3.** irregular or uneven. —**un•stead/i•ly,** *adv.* —**un•stead/i•ness,** *n.*

un•stop/, *v.t.,* **-stopped, -stop•ping. 1.** to remove the stopper from. **2.** to free from an obstruction.

un•strung/, *adj.* nervously upset; unnerved.

un•stud/ied, *adj.* **1.** not premeditated or labored; natural. **2.** not acquired by study.

un/sub•stan/tial, *adj.* **1.** lacking material substance. **2.** lacking strength or solidity; flimsy.

un•sung/, *adj.* **1.** not sung. **2.** not celebrated in song or verse.

un•tan/gle, *v.t.,* **-gled, -gling. 1.** to disentangle; unsnarl. **2.** to clear up; resolve.

un•taught/, *adj.* **1.** not taught; natural. **2.** not instructed or educated; ignorant.

un•think/a•ble, *adj.* not to be considered; inconceivable.

un•think/ing, *adj.* not thinking; thoughtless or heedless. —**un•think/ing•ly,** *adv.*

un•tie/, *v.,* **-tied, -ty•ing.** —*v.t.* **1.** to loose or unfasten (something tied). **2.** to free from or as if from restraint. —*v.i.* **3.** to become untied.

un•til (un til/), *conj.* **1.** up to the time that or when. **2.** before: *won't go until next year.* —*prep.* **3.** onward to the time or occurrence of: *worked until 6 P.M.* **4.** before: *didn't go until night.*

un•time/ly, *adj.,* **-li•er, -li•est,** *adv.* —*adj.* **1.** not timely; not occurring at a suitable time. **2.** happening too soon or too early. —*adv.* **3.** prematurely. **4.** unseasonably. —**un•time/li•ness,** *n.*

un•to (un/tōō; *unstressed* -tə), *prep.* **1.** to. **2.** until.

un•told/, *adj.* **1.** not told or revealed. **2.** not counted; incalculable.

un•touch/a•ble, *adj.* **1.** not permitted to be touched. —*n.* **2.** a member of the lowest caste in India.

un•to/ward, *adj.* **1.** unfavorable or unfortunate. **2.** not proper; unseemly.

un•true/, *adj.,* **-tru•er, -tru•est. 1.** not true to fact; false. **2.** not faithful; disloyal. **3.** not true to a standard.

un•truth/, *n.* **1.** the state or character of being untrue. **2.** divergence from truth. **3.** something untrue; a falsehood or lie. —**un•truth/ful,** *adj.* —**un•truth/ful•ly,** *adv.* —**un•truth/ful•ness,** *n.*

un•tu/tored, *adj.* not tutored; untaught.

un•used (un yōōzd/ *for 1, 2;* un yōōst/ *for 3*), *adj.* **1.** not put to use. **2.** never having been used. **3.** not accustomed.

un•u/su•al, *adj.* not usual; uncommon. —**un•u/su•al•ly,** *adv.*

un•ut/ter•a•ble, *adj.* not communicable by utterance; inexpressible.

un•var/nished, *adj.* **1.** free of vagueness or subterfuge; frank. **2.** not coated with or as if with varnish.

un•veil/, *v.t.* **1.** to remove a veil or covering from. **2.** to reveal by or as if by unveiling.

un•voiced/, *adj.* not voiced; not uttered.

un•war/y, *adj.,* **-i•er, -i•est.** not cautious or watchful.

un•well/, *adj.* not well; ailing.

un•whole/some, *adj.* **1.** harmful to physical or mental health. **2.** unhealthy, esp. in appearance. **3.** morally harmful. —**un•whole/some•ness,** *n.*

un•wield/y, *adj.,* **-i•er, -i•est.** wielded with difficulty; not easily handled or managed.

un•will/ing, *adj.* not willing; reluctant; averse. —**un•will/ing•ly,** *adv.* —**un•will/ing•ness,** *n.*

un•wind (un wīnd/), *v.,* **-wound, -wind•ing.** —*v.t.* **1.** to undo or loosen from a coiled condition. **2.** to disentangle or disengage. —*v.i.* **3.** to become unwound. **4.** to become relaxed.

un•wise/, *adj.,* **-wis•er, -wis•est.** not wise; foolish. —**un•wise/ly,** *adv.*

un•wit/ting, *adj.* **1.** not intentional; inadvertent. **2.** not knowing; unaware. —**un•wit/ting•ly,** *adv.*

un•wont/ed, *adj.* not customary, habitual, or usual.

un•wor/thy, *adj.,* **-thi•er, -thi•est. 1.** lacking worth or excellence. **2.** not proper; inappropriate. **3.** not deserving. —**un•wor/thi•ness,** *n.*

un•wrap/, *v.t.,* **-wrapped, -wrap•ping.** to remove or open the wrapping of.

un•writ/ten, *adj.* **1.** not actually expressed; customary. **2.** not put in writing; oral.

un•zip/, *v.,* **-zipped, -zip•ping.** —*v.t.* **1.** to open by means of a zipper. —*v.i.* **2.** to become unzipped.

up (up), *adv., prep., adj., n., v.,* **upped, up•ping.** —*adv.* **1.** to, toward, or in a higher position. **2.** to or in an erect position. **3.** out of bed. **4.** above the horizon. **5.** to or at a higher point. **6.** to or at a higher degree, as of intensity. **7.** to or at a point of equal advance or extent: *caught up in the race.* **8.** into or in activity or operation: *to set up shop.* **9.** into existence, view, or consideration: *The lost papers turned up.* **10.** into or in safekeeping or storage: *to put up preserves.* **11.** to an end; entirely: *to be used up.* **12.** to a halt: *The car pulled up.* **13.** (used with a verb for additional emphasis): *Wake him up.* **14.** at bat in baseball. **15.** in the lead. **16.** each; apiece: *The score was seven up.* —*prep.* **17.** to, toward, or at a higher place on or in: *went up the stairs.* **18.** at or to a farther point on or in: *a store up the street.* **19.** toward the source of: *to float up a stream.* **20.** toward the interior of. —*adj.* **21.** moving or facing upward: *the up elevator.* **22.** informed; aware: *up on current events.* **23.** concluded; ended: *Your time is up.* **24.** going on; happening: *What's up?* **25.** in an erect or raised position. **26.** risen above the horizon. **27.** out of bed. **28.** in a state of agitation or excitement. **29.** higher than formerly: *Prices are up.* **30.** ahead of an opponent: *He's two runs up.* **31.** under consideration: *a candidate up for reelection.* —*n.* **32.** a time of good fortune or prosperity: *the ups and downs in a career.* **33.** an upward slope. —*v.t.* **34.** to increase or raise. —*v.i.* **35.** *Informal.* to begin something abruptly: *He upped and ran away.* —*Idiom.* **36. on the up and up,** honest. **37. up against,** faced with. **38. up to, a.** as far as. **b.** as many as. **c.** capable of: *Is he up to the job?* **d.** dependent upon: *It's up to you.* **e.** doing: *What is he up to lately?*

up-, a combining form meaning up (*upland*).

up/-and-com/ing, *adj.* likely to succeed; promising.

up/beat/, *n.* **1.** an unaccented beat in music. —*adj.* **2.** optimistic; happy.

up•braid/ (up brād/), *v.t.* to criticize or reproach severely.

up/bring/ing, *n.* the care and training of children.

UPC, Universal Product Code.

up/chuck/, *v.i., v.t. Informal.* to vomit.

up/com/ing, *adj.* about to take place or appear.

up/coun/try, *adj., adv.* of, toward, or situated in the interior of a region or country.

up•date (up/dāt/; *v. also* up/dāt/), *v.,* **-dat•ed, -dat•ing,** *n.* —*v.t.* **1.** to bring up to date. —*n.* **2.** new or current information used in updating. **3.** an updated version or account.

up/draft/, *n.* an upward movement of air.

up•end/, *v.t., v.i.* to set or stand on end.

up/-front/, *adj.* **1.** invested or paid in advance. **2.** honest; candid.

up•grade (*n.* up/grād/; *v.* up grād/, up/grād/), *n., v.,* **-grad•ed, -grad•ing.** —*n.* **1.** an upward incline. **2.** an increase, rise, advance, or improvement. **3.** an enhanced version, improved model, etc. **4.** something that improves or enhances. —*v.t.* **5.** to raise in rank, quality, value, etc.

up•heav•al (up hē/vəl), *n.* **1.** violent change or disturbance. **2.** a thrusting upward, esp. of a part of the earth's crust.

up•hill′, *adv.* **1.** up the slope of a hill or incline. —*adj.* **2.** going upward on a hill. **3.** laboriously fatiguing or difficult.

up•hold′, *v.t.,* **-held, -hold•ing. 1.** to defend, as against opposition. **2.** to keep from sinking. **3.** to lift upward.

up•hol•ster (up hōl′stər, ə pōl′-), *v.t.* to provide (furniture) with coverings, cushions, stuffing, etc. —**up•hol′ster•er,** *n.*

up•hol′ster•y, *n., pl.* **-ster•ies. 1.** the materials used to upholster furniture. **2.** the business of an upholsterer.

UPI, United Press International.

up′keep′, *n.* **1.** the maintenance necessary for the proper functioning of a machine, building, etc. **2.** the cost of upkeep.

up•land (up′lənd, -land′), *n.* land elevated above other land.

up•lift (*v.* up lift′; *n.* up′lift′), *v.t.* **1.** to lift up; raise. **2.** to improve socially, intellectually, or morally. —*n.* **3.** the act of lifting up. **4.** social, intellectual, or moral improvement.

up′load′, *v.t.* to transfer (software or data) from a smaller to a larger computer.

up′mar′ket, *adj.* UPSCALE.

up•on (ə pon′, ə pôn′), *prep.* on.

up′per, *adj.* **1.** higher, as in place, position, or rank. —*n.* **2.** the part of a shoe or boot above the sole.

up′per•case′, *adj.* **1.** (of an alphabetical character) capital. —*n.* **2.** a capital letter.

up′per class′, *n.* a class of people above the middle class, characterized by social prestige. —**up′-per-class′,** *adj.*

up′per•class′man, *n., pl.* **-men.** a junior or senior in a secondary school or college.

up′per crust′, *n. Informal.* the highest social class.

up′per•cut′, *n.* a swinging blow directed upward, as to an adversary's chin.

up′per hand′, *n.* the controlling position; advantage.

up′per house′, *n.* one of two branches of a legislature, generally smaller and less representative than the lower branch.

up′per•most′, *adj.* **1.** highest in place, order, rank, or power. —*adv.* **2.** in or into the uppermost place or rank.

Up′per Vol′ta, *n.* former name of BURKINA FASO.

up•pi•ty (up′i tē), *adj. Informal.* haughty, snobbish, or arrogant.

up•raise′, *v.t.,* **-raised, -rais•ing.** to raise up; elevate.

up•right (up′rīt′, up rīt′), *adj.* **1.** erect, as in posture. **2.** raised or directed vertically. **3.** righteous, honest, or just. —*n.* **4.** something standing upright. —*adv.* **5.** in an upright position or direction.

up′right pian′o, *n.* a piano with its strings running vertically.

up•ris•ing (up′rī′zing, up rī′-), *n.* an insurrection or revolt.

up′roar′, *n.* a state of violent and noisy disturbance; tumult.

up•roar′i•ous (-ē əs), *adj.* **1.** characterized by uproar. **2.** very funny. —**up•roar′i•ous•ly,** *adv.*

up•root′, *v.t.* **1.** to pull out by or as if by the roots. **2.** to displace from a country or way of life.

up′scale′, *adj.* of or for people at the upper end of an economic scale.

up•set (*v., adj.* up set′; *n.* up′set′), *v.,* **-set, -set•ting,** *n., adj.* —*v.t.* **1.** to knock over; overturn. **2.** to disturb emotionally. **3.** to throw into disorder. **4.** to disturb physically. **5.** to defeat (an opponent favored to win). —*v.i.* **6.** to become overturned. —*n.* **7.** an upsetting or instance of being upset. **8.** an unexpected defeat. **9.** a disturbance or disorder. —*adj.* **10.** overturned. **11.** disturbed or disordered.

up′shot′, *n.* the final outcome; result.

up′side′, *n.* the upper side or part.

up′side down′, *adv.* **1.** with the upper part under-

most. **2.** in or into complete disorder. —**up′side-down′,** *adj.*

up•si•lon (yōōp′sə lon′, up′-), *n.* the 20th letter of the Greek alphabet (ϒ, υ).

up′size′, *v.i., v.t.,* **-sized, -sizing.** to increase in size, as by hiring additional employees; expand: *to upsize a business.*

up′stage′, *adv., adj., v.,* **-staged, -stag•ing.** —*adv.* **1.** at or toward the back of a stage. —*adj.* **2.** of the back of a stage. —*v.t.* **3.** to draw attention away from (another actor), as by moving upstage. **4.** to outdo professionally or socially.

up′stairs′, *adv.* **1.** up the stairs; to or on an upper floor. **2.** to or at a higher level of authority. —*adj.* **3.** of or situated on an upper floor. —*n.* **4.** (*usu. with a sing. v.*) the part of a building above the ground floor.

up•stand′ing, *adj.* **1.** upright; honorable. **2.** standing erect.

up′start′, *n.* **1.** a person who has risen suddenly to wealth, power, or importance, esp. one who is arrogant. —*adj.* **2.** being or like an upstart.

up′state′, *n.* **1.** the northern part of a state. —*adj., adv.* **2.** of, to, or from such an area.

up′stream′, *adv., adj.* toward or in the higher part of a stream.

up′stroke′, *n.* an upward stroke, esp. of a pen.

up′surge′, *n.* a large or rapid increase.

up′swing′, *n.* **1.** an upward swing. **2.** a marked increase or improvement.

up′take′, *n.* **1.** mental grasp; understanding: *quick on the uptake.* **2.** a pipe leading upward, as for conducting smoke.

up•talk (up′tôk′), *n.* a rise in pitch at the end usu. of a declarative sentence, esp. if habitual: often represented in writing by a question mark as in *Hi, I'm here to read the meter?*

up′tight′, *adj. Informal.* **1.** tense or nervous. **2.** stiffly conventional.

up′-to-date′, *adj.* **1.** in keeping with the times; modern. **2.** extending to the present time; current.

up•town (up′toun′, -toun′), *adv., adj.* **1.** to, toward, or in the upper part of a town or city. —*n.* **2.** the uptown section of a town or city.

up•turn (*v.* up tûrn′, up′tûrn′; *n.* up′tûrn′), *v.t., v.i.* **1.** to turn up or over. —*n.* **2.** an upward turn, as in business.

up•ward (up′wərd), *adv.* Also, **up′wards. 1.** toward a higher place, position, or level. —*adj.* **2.** moving or tending upward. —*Idiom.* **3. upward(s) of,** more than. —**up′ward•ly,** *adv.*

up′ward mobil′ity, *n.* movement from one social level to a higher one.

u•ra•cil (yōōr′ə sil), *n.* a pyrimidine base that is one of the fundamental components of RNA.

U′ral Moun′tains (yōōr′əl), *n.pl.* a mountain range in the W Russian Federation, forming a natural boundary between Europe and Asia. Also called **U′-rals.**

u•ra•ni•um (yōō rā′nē əm), *n.* a white, radioactive metallic element used in nuclear weapons and as a nuclear fuel. *Symbol:* U; *at. wt.:* 238.03; *at. no.:* 92.

U•ra•nus (yōōr′ə nəs, yōō rā′-), *n.* the planet seventh in order from the sun.

ur•ban (ûr′bən), *adj.* of, characteristic of, or being a city. [< L *urbānus* < *urbs* city]

ur•bane (ûr bān′), *adj.* suave and polished in manner or style; sophisticated. —**ur•ban′i•ty** (-ban′i tē), *n.*

ur′ban•ize′, *v.t.,* **-ized, -iz•ing.** to make urban in character. —**ur′ban•i•za′tion,** *n.*

ur′ban leg′end, *n.* a modern story of obscure origin and with little supporting evidence that spreads spontaneously in varying forms and often has elements of humor, moralizing, or horror: *Are there alligators living in New York City sewers, or is that just an urban legend?*

ur′ban•ol′o•gy (-nol′ə jē), *n.* the study of urban problems. —**ur′ban•ol′o•gist,** *n.*

ur′ban renew′al, *n.* the rehabilitation of substandard city areas, as by renovating buildings.

ur•chin (ûr′chin), *n.* a mischievous child.

Ur•du (ōōr′dōō, ûr′-), *n.* the official language of Pakistan.

-ure, a suffix meaning: action or result (*pressure*); instrument or means (*legislature*).

u•re•a (yōō rē′ə, yōōr′e ə), *n.* a compound occurring in body fluids, esp. urine.

u•re•mi•a (yōō rē′mē ə), *n.* the presence in the blood of products normally excreted in the urine. —**u•re′mic,** *adj.*

u•re•ter (yōō rē′tər), *n.* a duct that conveys urine from a kidney to the bladder.

u•re•thane (yōōr′ə thān′), *n.* a crystalline, water-soluble powder used esp. as a solvent.

u•re•thra (yōō rē′thrə), *n.*, *pl.* **-thrae** (-thrē), **-thras.** a duct that conveys urine and in most male mammals also conveys semen. —**u•re′thral,** *adj.*

urge (ûrj), *v.*, **urged, urg•ing,** *n.* —*v.t.* **1.** to push along; impel. **2.** to incite, as to speed or effort. **3.** to try to induce or persuade. **4.** to insist on or assert earnestly. **5.** to recommend earnestly. —*n.* **6.** the act of urging. **7.** an impelling action, influence, or force.

ur•gent (ûr′jənt), *adj.* **1.** requiring immediate action or attention. **2.** insistent in urging; importunate. —**ur′gen•cy,** *n.*, *pl.* **-cies.** —**ur′gent•ly,** *adv.*

-urgy, a combining form meaning making or production (*metallurgy*).

U•ri′ah the Hit′tite (yōō rī′ə), *n.* the husband of Bathsheba and an officer in David's army. II Sam. 11.

u•ric (yōōr′ik), *adj.* of, contained in, or derived from urine.

U•ri•el (yōōr′ē əl), *n.* one of the archangels. II Esdras 4.

U•ri•jah (yōō rī′jə), *n.* a priest in Jerusalem who built a heathen altar for King Ahaz. II Kings 16:10–16.

u•ri•nal (yōōr′ə nl), *n.* **1.** a wall fixture used by men for urinating. **2.** a receptacle for urine.

u′ri•nal′y•sis (-nal′ə sis), *n.*, *pl.* **-ses** (-sēz′). a diagnostic analysis of urine

u′ri•nar′y (-ner′ē), *adj.* **1.** of urine. **2.** of the organs that secrete and discharge urine.

u′rinary blad′der, *n.* a distensible, muscular sac in which urine is retained until discharged.

u′ri•nate′ (-nāt′), *v.i.*, **-nat•ed, -nat•ing.** to discharge urine. —**u′ri•na′tion,** *n.*

u•rine (yōōr′in), *n.* the yellowish liquid excreted by the kidneys.

URL, Uniform Resource Locater: a protocol for specifying addresses on the Internet.

urn (ûrn), *n.* **1.** a vase, esp. one with a pedestal. **2.** a vase for holding the ashes of the cremated dead. **3.** a container with a spigot for serving hot tea or coffee.

Ur′ of the Chal•dees′ (kal dēz′, kal′dēz), *n.* the city where Abraham was born. Gen. 11:28, 31; 15:7; Neh. 9:7.

u•ro•gen•i•tal (yōōr′ō jen′i tl), *adj.* GENITOURINARY.

u•rol•o•gy (yōō rol′ə jē), *n.* the medical study of the urinary or genitourinary tract. —**u•rol′o•gist,** *n.*

Ur′sa Ma′jor (ûr′sə), *n.* a constellation containing the stars that form the Big Dipper.

Ur′sa Mi′nor, *n.* a constellation containing the bright star Polaris and the stars that form the Little Dipper.

ur•sine (ûr′sīn, -sin), *adj.* of or resembling a bear.

ur•ti•car•i•a (ûr′ti kâr′ē ə), *n.* HIVES.

U•ru•guay (yōōr′ə gwā′, -gwī′, ōōr′-), *n.* a republic in SE South America. 3,261,707. —**U′ru•guay′an,** *adj.*, *n.*

us (us), *pron.* the objective case of WE.

US or **U.S.,** United States

USA or **U.S.A., 1.** United States of America. **2.** United States Army.

us•a•ble or **use•a•ble** (yōō′zə bəl), *adj.* **1.** available for use. **2.** capable of being used. —**us′a•bil′i•ty,** *n.*

USAF, United States Air Force.

us•age (yōō′sij, -zij), *n.* **1.** a custom, habit, or practice. **2.** the manner in which a language is spoken or written. **3.** a particular expression: *a new usage.* **4.** a way of using; treatment. —**Usage.** The nouns USAGE and USE are related in origin and meaning and overlap to an extent in their use. Perhaps in the belief that it is more impressive, USAGE is sometimes used where USE would be the proper choice: *Has usage of a computer made your work any easier?*

USDA, United States Department of Agriculture.

use (*v.* yōōz *or, for pt. form of 7,* yōōst; *n.* yōōs), *v.*, **used, us•ing,** *n.* —*v.t.* **1.** to put into service; employ. **2.** to consume or expend. **3.** to treat or behave toward. **4.** to take unfair advantage of. **5.** to consume habitually. **6.** to habituate; accustom. —*v.i.* **7.** to be accustomed, wont, or customarily found: *He used to go every day.* —*n.* **8.** the act of using or state of being used. **9.** a way of using. **10.** the purpose for which something is used. **11.** the power or right of using something: *lost the use of an eye.* **12.** utility; usefulness. **13.** occasion or need to use: *Have you any use for a calendar?* —**us′er,** *n.* —**Usage.** See USAGE.

used (yōōzd), *adj.* previously used or owned; secondhand.

use′ful (yōōs′-), *adj.* capable of being used to advantage; serviceable. —**use′ful•ly,** *adv.* —**use′ful•ness,** *n.*

use′less, *adj.* being of no use; not serving a purpose. —**use′less•ly,** *adv.* —**use′less•ness,** *n.*

us′er-friend′ly, *adj.* easy to operate or understand: *a user-friendly computer.*

ush•er (ush′ər), *n.* **1.** a person who escorts people to seats, as in a theater. **2.** a male attendant of a bridegroom. **3.** an officer whose duty it is to walk before a person of rank. —*v.t.* **4.** to act as an usher to. **5.** to precede or herald.

ush′er•ette′ (-ə ret′), *n.* a woman who escorts people to seats, as in a theater.

USMC, United States Marine Corps.

USN, United States Navy.

USO, United Service Organizations.

U.S.P. United States Pharmacopeia.

USS, United States Ship.

Ussh•er (ush′ər), *n.* **James,** 1581–1656, Irish ecclesiastic who calculated a system of Biblical chronology, dating the creation at 4004 B.C.

U.S.S.R. or **USSR,** Union of Soviet Socialist Republics.

usu., usually.

u•su•al (yōō′zhōō əl), *adj.* **1.** predictable on the basis of previous experience: *her usual skill.* **2.** commonly met with or observed in experience. **3.** commonplace; everyday. —**u′su•al•ly,** *adv.*

u•surp (yōō sûrp′, -zûrp′), *v.t.* **1.** to seize and hold (a position, office, power, etc.) by force or without legal right. **2.** to use without authority or right. —**u′sur•pa′tion** (-sər pā′shən, -zər-), *n.* —**u•surp′er,** *n.*

u•su•ry (yōō′zhə rē), *n.*, *pl.* **-ries. 1.** the practice of lending money at an exorbitant interest rate. **2.** an exorbitant rate of interest. —**u′su•rer,** *n.* —**u•su′ri•ous** (-zhōōr′ē əs), *adj.*

UT or **Ut.,** Utah.

U•tah (yōō′tô, -tä), *n.* a state in the W United States. 2,000,494. *Cap.:* Salt Lake City. *Abbr.:* UT, Ut. —**U•tah•an, U•tahn** (yōō′tôn, -tän), *adj.*, *n.*

u•ten•sil (yōō ten′səl), *n.* **1.** an instrument or vessel commonly used esp. in a kitchen. **2.** any useful instrument or tool.

u•ter•us (yōō′tər əs), *n.*, *pl.* **u•ter•i** (yōō′tə rī′), **u•ter•us•es.** a hollow organ of female mammals in which the fertilized egg develops during pregnancy. —**u′ter•ine** (-in), *adj.*

u•til•i•tar•i•an (yōō til′i târ′ē ən), *adj.* **1.** of or characterized by utility. **2.** designed for or concerned with usefulness rather than beauty.

u•til′i•ty, *n.*, *pl.* **-ties. 1.** the state or quality of being useful. **2.** a public service, as the providing of electricity or gas. **3.** PUBLIC UTILITY.

u•ti•lize (yōōt′l īz′), *v.t.*, **-lized, -liz•ing.** to put to profitable or practical use. —**u′ti•li•za′tion,** *n.*

ut•most (ut′mōst′), *adj.* **1.** of the greatest or highest degree or quantity. **2.** being at the farthest point or extremity. —*n.* **3.** the greatest degree or amount.

U•to•pi•a (yōō tō′pē ə), *n., pl.* **-as. 1.** an imaginary island described in Sir Thomas More's *Utopia* (1516) as enjoying perfection in law, politics, etc. **2.** (*usu. l.c.*) **a.** an ideal place. **b.** a visionary system of political or social perfection. [< NL < Gk *ou* not + *tópos* a place] —**U•to′pi•an, u•to′pi•an,** *adj., n.*

ut•ter¹ (ut′ər), *v.t.* **1.** to give audible, esp. verbal, expression to. **2.** to give forth (a sound).

ut•ter² (ut′ər), *adj.* total; absolute. —**ut′ter•ly,** *adv.*

ut′ter•ance, *n.* **1.** the act of uttering. **2.** something uttered. **3.** manner or power of speaking.

ut′ter•most′, *adj., n.* UTMOST.

U′-turn′, *n.* a U-shaped turn made by a vehicle.

UV, ultraviolet.

u•vu•la (yōō′vyə lə), *n., pl.* **-las, -lae** (-lē′). the fleshy, conical body projecting downward from the soft palate. —**u′vu•lar,** *adj.*

ux•o•ri•ous (uk sôr′ē əs, ug zôr′-), *adj.* doting upon or affectionately submissive toward one's wife.

Uz•bek•i•stan (ŏŏz bek′ə stan′, -stän′, uz-), *n.* a republic in S central Asia: formerly a part of the USSR. 23,396,407.

V

V, v (vē), *n., pl.* **Vs** or **V's, vs** or **v's. 1.** the 22nd letter of the English alphabet, a consonant. **2.** something shaped like a V.

V, *Symbol.* **1.** the Roman numeral for five. **2.** *Chem.* vanadium.

v., 1. vector. **2.** verb. **3.** verse. **4.** version. **5.** verso. **6.** versus. **7.** see. [< L *vidē*] **8.** vocative. **9.** voice. **10.** volt. **11.** voltage. **12.** volume.

VA, 1. Veterans Administration. **2.** Virginia.

Va., Virginia.

va•can•cy (vā′kən sē), *n., pl.* **-cies. 1.** the state of being vacant. **2.** a vacant or unoccupied place, esp. one for rent. **3.** an unoccupied position or office.

va′cant (-kənt), *adj.* **1.** having no contents; empty. **2.** having no occupant. **3.** lacking in thought or intelligence. **4.** not filled, as by an incumbent. **5.** free from work, business, or activity.

va•cate (vā′kāt), *v.t.*, **-cat•ed, -cat•ing. 1.** to cause to be vacant. **2.** to deprive of validity; annul.

va•ca•tion (vā kā′shən, və-), *n.* **1.** a period of rest or freedom from regular work, study, etc. —*v.i.* **2.** to take or have a vacation. —**va•ca′tion•er,** *n.*

vac•ci•nate (vak′sə nāt′), *v.t.*, **-nat•ed, -nat•ing.** to inoculate with a vaccine. —**vac′ci•na′tion,** *n.*

vac•cine (vak sēn′), *n.* **1.** a preparation of weakened or killed bacteria or viruses introduced into the body to prevent a disease by stimulating antibodies against it. **2.** a software program that helps to protect against computer viruses.

vac•il•late (vas′ə lāt′), *v.i.*, **-lat•ed, -lat•ing. 1.** to be indecisive or irresolute. **2.** to sway unsteadily. **3.** to oscillate or fluctuate. —**vac′il•la′tion,** *n.*

va•cu•i•ty (va kyōō′i tē, və-), *n., pl.* **-ties. 1.** the state of being vacuous. **2.** absence of thought or intelligence. **3.** something senseless or stupid. **4.** an empty space.

vac•u•ous (vak′yōō əs), *adj.* **1.** lacking contents; empty. **2.** showing a lack of intelligence. —**vac′u•ous•ly,** *adv.*

vac•u•um (vak′yōōm, -yōō əm, -yəm), *n., pl.* **-u•ums** for 1–4, **-u•a** (-yōō ə) for 1–3; *v.* —*n.* **1.** a space entirely devoid of matter. **2.** an enclosed space from which matter, esp. air, has been partially removed. **3.** an emptiness; void. **4.** VACUUM CLEANER. —*v.t., v.i.* **5.** to clean with a vacuum cleaner.

vac′uum bot′tle, *n.* a bottle or flask with a double wall enclosing a vacuum to retard heat transfer.

vac′uum clean′er, *n.* an electrical appliance for cleaning carpets, floors, etc., by suction.

vac′uum-packed′, *adj.* packed, as in a can, with as much air as possible evacuated before sealing.

vac′uum tube′, *n.* an electron tube from which almost all air or gas has been evacuated.

vag•a•bond (vag′ə bond′), *adj.* **1.** wandering without a settled home. **2.** leading an unsettled or carefree life. —*n.* **3.** a usu. homeless person who wanders from place to place. **4.** a tramp; vagrant. —**vag′a•bond′age,** *n.*

va•gar•y (və gâr′ē, vā′gə rē), *n., pl.* **-gar•ies.** a capricious or erratic action, notion, or course. —**va•gar′i•ous,** *adj.*

va•gi•na (və jī′nə), *n., pl.* **-nas, -nae** (-nē). the passage leading from the uterus to the vulva in female mammals. —**vag•i•nal** (vaj′ə nəl), *adj.*

va•grant (vā′grənt), *n.* **1.** a person who wanders about idly with no permanent home or employment. —*adj.* **2.** wandering from place to place. **3.** of or characteristic of a vagrant. **4.** not fixed or settled in course. —**va′gran•cy,** *n., pl.* **-cies.**

vague (vāg), *adj.*, **va•guer, va•guest. 1.** not clearly stated or expressed. **2.** indefinite or indistinct in nature or character. —**vague′ly,** *adv.* —**vague′ness,** *n.*

vain (vān), *adj.*, **-er, -est. 1.** excessively proud of or concerned about one's own appearance or achievements. **2.** unsuccessful; futile. **3.** without significance or value. —*Idiom.* **4. in vain, a.** without effect or avail. **b.** in an irreverent manner. —**vain′ly,** *adv.*

vain′glo′ry, *n.* **1.** excessive and often boastful vanity. **2.** empty pomp or show. —**vain•glo′ri•ous,** *adj.*

val., 1. valuation. **2.** value.

val•ance (val′əns, vā′ləns), *n.* **1.** a short curtain across the top of a window. **2.** a drapery hung from an edge, as of a bed.

vale (vāl), *n.* VALLEY.

val•e•dic•to•ri•an (val′i dik tôr′ē ən), *n.* the student in a graduating class who delivers the valedictory.

val′e•dic′to•ry (-tə rē), *n., pl.* **-ries.** a farewell address, esp. one delivered at commencement exercises.

va•lence (vā′ləns) also **-len•cy** (-lən sē), *n.* the relative combining capacity of an atom or group compared with that of the standard hydrogen atom.

Va•len•ci•a (və len′shē ə, -shə), *n.* a seaport in E Spain. 738,575.

val•en•tine (val′ən tīn′), *n.* **1.** a card or message, usu. amatory or sentimental, sent on Valentine's Day, sometimes anonymously. **2.** a sweetheart greeted on this day.

Val•en•tine (val′ən tīn′), *n.* **Saint,** died A.D. c270, Christian martyr at Rome.

Val′entine's Day′, *n.* February 14, observed in honor of St. Valentine as a day for the exchange of valentines.

val•et (va lā′, val′it, val′ā), *n.* **1.** a male servant who attends to his employer's personal needs, as by taking care of clothing. **2.** an employee who cares for the clothing of hotel patrons.

Val•hal•la (val hal′ə, väl hä′lə), *n.* (in Norse myth) the hall in which Odin received the souls of slain warriors.

val•iant (val′yənt), *adj.* boldly courageous; heroic. —**val′iance,** *n.* —**val′iant•ly,** *adv.*

val•id (val′id), *adj.* **1.** well-founded; sound. **2.** legally effective or binding. —**va·lid·i·ty** (və lid/i tē), val/id·ness, n. —val/id·ly, adv.

val/i·date/ (-i dāt/), v.t. **-dat·ed, -dat·ing. 1.** to make valid; substantiate. **2.** to make legally valid. —val/i·da/tion, n.

va·lise (və lēs/), n. a small piece of hand luggage.

Val·i·um (val/ē əm), Trademark. a brand of tranquilizer.

Val·kyr·ie (val kēr/ē, -kĭ/rē), n. (in Norse myth) one of the female spirits who take the souls of slain warriors to Valhalla.

Val·le·jo (və lā/ō, -yä/hō), n. a city in W California. 111,484.

val·ley (val/ē), n., pl. **-leys. 1.** an elongated depression between uplands, hills, or mountains. **2.** a region drained by a river system.

Val/ley Forge/, n. a village in SE Pennsylvania: winter quarters of Washington's army 1777–78.

val·or (val/ər), n. great courage. Also, esp. Brit., val/our. —val/or·ous, adj.

Val·pa·rai·so (val/pə rĭ/zō, -sō), n. a seaport in central Chile. 278,762.

val·u·a·ble (val/yōō ə bəl, -yə bəl), adj. **1.** having considerable monetary worth. **2.** of considerable use or importance. —n. **3.** Usu., **-bles.** personal articles of great value.

val/u·a/tion (-yōō ā/shən), n. **1.** the act of appraisal. **2.** an estimated value.

val/ue, n., v., **-ued, -u·ing.** —n. **1.** relative or assigned worth or importance. **2.** monetary or material worth. **3.** equivalent worth in money, goods, or services. **4.** a numerical quantity represented by a figure or symbol. **5.** Often, **-ues.** the abstract concepts of what is right or worthwhile. **6.** degree of lightness or darkness in a color. **7.** the relative duration of a musical tone as expressed by a note. —v.t. **8.** to calculate the monetary value of. **9.** to consider with respect to worth or importance. **10.** to regard highly. —val/ue·less, adj.

valve (valv), n. **1.** a device for controlling the flow of a fluid. **2.** a movable part that opens or closes the passage in a valve. **3.** a membranous structure that permits the flow of a body fluid in one direction only. **4.** (in musical wind instruments) a device for changing the length of the air column to alter the pitch of a tone. **5.** one of the separable pieces composing a mollusk shell. —valved, adj.

va·moose (va mōōs/), v.i., **-moosed, -moos·ing.** Slang. to leave hurriedly.

vamp¹ (vamp), n. **1.** the portion of a shoe or boot upper that covers the instep and toes. **2.** an introductory musical passage often consisting of a repeated succession of chords. —v.t. **3.** to repair with a new vamp. —v.i. **4.** to play a musical vamp.

vamp² (vamp), n. **1.** a seductive woman who exploits men. —v.t., v.i. **2.** to seduce (a man) with feminine charms.

vam·pire (vam/pīₑr), n. **1.** (in folklore) a reanimated corpse that is said to suck the blood of sleeping persons at night. **2.** a person who preys on others.

van¹ (van), n. the vanguard.

van² (van), n. **1.** a large covered truck for moving goods or animals. **2.** a boxlike vehicle for passengers, camping, etc.

va·na·di·um (və nā/dē əm), n. a rare silvery metallic element used esp. to toughen steel. Symbol: V; at. wt.: 50.942; at. no.: 23.

Van Al/len belt/ (van al/ən), n. either of two atmospheric regions of high-energy charged particles. [< J. A. Van Allen (b. 1914), U.S. physicist]

Van Bu·ren (van byoŏr/ən), n. **Martin,** 1782–1862, 8th president of the U.S. 1837–41.

Van·cou·ver (van kōō/vər), n. a seaport in SW British Columbia. 431,147; with suburbs 1,226,152.

van·dal (van/dl), n. **1.** (cap.) a member of a Germanic people who sacked Rome in A.D. 455. **2.** a person who willfully destroys or mars property.

van/dal·ize/, v.t., **-ized, -iz·ing.** to destroy or deface willfully. —van/dal·ism, n.

Van Dyck or **Van·dyke** (van dīk/), n. **Sir Anthony,** 1599–1641, Flemish painter.

Van Dyke (van/ dīk/), n. **Henry,** 1852–1933, U.S. clergyman and hymn writer.

Van·dyke/ beard/ (van dīk/), n. a short, pointed beard.

vane (vān), n. **1.** WEATHER VANE. **2.** a blade or plate attached radially to a cylinder or shaft that moves or is moved by a fluid.

van Gogh (van gō/, gôкн/; Du. vän кнôкн/), n. **Vincent,** 1853–90, Dutch painter.

van/guard/, n. **1.** the front part of an advancing army. **2.** the forefront in a movement or field.

va·nil·la (və nil/ə; often -nel/ə), n., pl. **-las. 1.** a climbing orchid bearing podlike fruit. **2.** Also called vanil/la bean/. the fruit of this orchid. **3.** a flavoring extract made from this fruit.

van·ish (van/ish), v.i. **1.** to disappear quickly from sight. **2.** to come to an end.

van·i·ty (van/i tē), n., pl. **-ties. 1.** excessive pride in oneself or one's appearance. **2.** lack of real value; worthlessness. **3.** something worthless or pointless. **4.** a small case for cosmetics. **5.** a table surmounted by a mirror, used while dressing, applying makeup, etc. —**Proverb. 6. Vanity of vanities, all is vanity,** all earthly strivings are ultimately futile. Eccl. 12:8.

van·quish (vang/kwish, van/-), v.t. **1.** to defeat in battle or in a contest. **2.** to overcome: vanquished all doubt.

Van Rens·se·laer (van ren/sə lēr/, ren/sə lər), n. **Stephen,** 1765–1839, U.S. political leader and major general.

van·tage (van/tij, vän/-), n. **1.** a position affording a strategic advantage or commanding view. **2.** an advantage or superiority.

Va·nu·a·tu (vä/nōō ä/tōō), n. a republic consisting of a group of islands in the SW Pacific, W of Fiji. 181,358. —Va/nu·a/tu·an, adj., n.

vap·id (vap/id), adj. lacking spirit or interest; dull. —va·pid/i·ty, vap/id·ness, n.

va·por (vā/pər), n. **1.** visible matter, as fog or smoke, suspended in the air. **2.** a substance in gaseous form that is a liquid or solid under normal conditions. Also, esp. Brit., va/pour.

va/por·ize/, v.t., v.i., **-ized, -iz·ing.** to change into vapor. —va/por·i·za/tion, n.

va/por·ous, adj. **1.** having the form of vapor. **2.** full of, giving off, or obscured by vapor.

va/por trail/, n. CONTRAIL.

var., 1. variable. **2.** variant. **3.** variation. **4.** variety. **5.** various.

var·i·a·ble (vâr/ē ə bəl), adj. **1.** apt to vary. **2.** capable of being varied. **3.** inconstant; fickle. —n. **4.** something variable. **5. a.** a quantity that may assume any given value or set of values. **b.** a symbol that represents this. —var/i·a·bil/i·ty, n.

var/i·ance (-əns), n. **1.** the state of being variable. **2.** degree of difference. **3.** a permit to do something normally regulated by law. —**Idiom. 4. at variance,** in a state of disagreement.

var/i·ant, adj. **1.** exhibiting variety or variation. **2.** differing, esp. from something of the same kind. —n. **3.** one that varies. **4.** a different spelling, pronunciation, or form of the same word.

var/i·a/tion (-ā/shən), n. **1.** an act or instance of varying. **2.** amount or degree of change. **3.** a different form of something. **4.** the transformation of a musical theme with changes in harmony, rhythm, and melody.

var·i·col·ored (vâr/i kul/ərd), adj. having various colors.

var·i·cose (var/i kōs/), adj. abnormally swollen: a varicose vein.

var·ied (vâr/ēd), adj. **1.** characterized by variety; diverse. **2.** changed; altered.

var·i·e·gate (vâr/ē i gāt/, vâr/i-), v.t., **-gat·ed, -gat·ing. 1.** to make varied in appearance, as by adding different colors. **2.** to give variety to. —var/i·e·gat/ed, adj.

va·ri·e·tal (və rī/i tl), adj. **1.** of or being a variety.

2. of or being a wine made chiefly from one variety of grape. —*n.* **3.** a varietal wine.

va•ri′e•ty, *n., pl.* **-ties. 1.** the state of being diversified. **2.** difference; discrepancy. **3.** a number of different things, esp. ones in the same category. **4.** a kind or sort. **5.** a category within a species, based on a hereditary difference. **6.** VAUDEVILLE. —*Proverb.* **7. Variety is the spice of life,** different activities make life more pleasurable.

var•i•ous (vâr′ē əs), *adj.* **1.** of different kinds. **2.** different; dissimilar. **3.** several; many. **4.** individual; separate. **5.** having many different qualities. —**var′i•ous•ly,** *adv.*

var•let (vär′lit), *n. Archaic.* **1.** a knave; rascal. **2.** an attendant or servant.

var•mint (vär′mənt), *n.* **1.** an undesirable, usu. verminous animal. **2.** an obnoxious person.

var•nish (vär′nish), *n.* **1.** a preparation for coating surfaces, as of wood, consisting of resinous matter dissolved, esp. in oil or alcohol. **2.** a coating of varnish. **3.** superficial polish or show. —*v.t.* **4.** to coat with varnish. **5.** to give a superficially pleasing appearance to.

var•si•ty (vär′si tē), *n., pl.* **-ties.** a principal team, esp. in sports, representing a school or college. [Brit. var. of *(uni)versity*]

var•y (vâr′ē), *v.,* **var•ied, var•y•ing.** —*v.t.* **1.** to change, as in form, appearance, or substance. **2.** to give variety to; diversify. —*v.i.* **3.** to show diversity; differ. **4.** to undergo change. **5.** to diverge; deviate.

vas•cu•lar (vas′kyə lər), *adj.* of, composed of, or provided with vessels that convey fluids, as blood or sap.

vase (vās, vāz, väz), *n.* a vessel, as of glass, used to hold flowers or for decoration.

va•sec•to•my (va sek′tə mē, və-), *n., pl.* **-mies.** surgical excision of part or all of the sperm-carrying duct of the testis to effect sterility.

Vas•e•line (vas′ə lēn′), *Trademark.* a brand of petrolatum.

vas•sal (vas′əl), *n.* **1.** (in the feudal system) a person granted the use of land in return for homage and fealty to a lord. **2.** a person subject or subordinate to another. —**vas′sal•age,** *n., adj.*

vast (vast, väst), *adj.,* **-er, -est. 1.** of very great area or extent. **2.** very great in size, quantity, or degree. —**vast′ly,** *adv.* —**vast′ness,** *n.*

vat (vat), *n.* a large container, as a tank, for holding liquids.

VAT, value-added tax: a tax based on the value added to a product at each stage of production.

Vat•i•can (vat′i kən), *n.* **1.** the chief residence of the popes in Vatican City. **2.** the papal government.

Vat′ican Cit′y, *n.* an independent papal state within the city of Rome. 1000.

vaude•ville (vôd′vil, vōd′-, vô′də-), *n.* a form of popular entertainment having a program of separate and varied acts. —**vaude•vil′lian,** *n., adj.*

Vaughan′ Wil′liams (vôn), *n.* **Ralph** (*usu.* rāf), 1872–1958, English composer.

vault¹ (vôlt), *n.* **1.** an arched structure forming a ceiling or roof. **2.** a chamber or passage enclosed by a vault. **3.** a room or compartment for the safekeeping of valuables. **4.** a burial chamber. **5.** something resembling an arched roof. —*v.t., v.i.* **6.** to cover with or curve in the form of a vault. —**vault′ed,** *adj.*

vault² (vôlt), *v.i., v.t.* **1.** to leap (over), esp. with the hands supported by a horizontal pole. —*n.* **2.** the act of vaulting. —**vault′er,** *n.*

vault′ing, *adj.* **1.** leaping. **2.** excessive; overweening: *vaulting ambition.*

vaunt (vônt, vänt), *v.t., v.i.* **1.** to boast (of). —*n.* **2.** a boastful utterance. —**vaunt′ed,** *adj.*

V-chip (vē′chip′), *n.* a computer chip or other electronic device that blocks the reception of violent or sexually explicit television shows. [*v(iolence)* + *chip*]

VCR, videocassette recorder: an electronic device for recording and playing back videocassettes.

VD, venereal disease.

V′-Day′, *n.* a day of military victory.

VDT, video display terminal.

veal (vēl), *n.* the flesh of a calf used for food.

vec•tor (vek′tər), *n.* **1.** a quantity possessing both magnitude and direction. **2.** a person or animal that transmits a disease-causing organism.

Ve•da (vā′də, vē′-), *n., pl.* **-das.** one of the sacred scriptures of Hinduism. —**Ve′dic,** *adj.*

V-E Day, *n.* May 8, 1945, the day of victory in Europe for the Allies in World War II.

veep (vēp), *n. Informal.* a vice president.

veer (vēr), *v.i., v.t.* **1.** to change from one course, position, or direction to another. —*n.* **2.** a change of course, position, or direction.

veg (vej), *n., v.,* **vegged, veg•ging.** *Informal.* —*n.* **1.** *Chiefly Brit.* a vegetable. —*v.i.* **2.** to relax passively, esp. while watching television; vegetate (often fol. by *out*).

veg•e•ta•ble (vej′tə bəl, vej′i tə-), *n.* **1.** a plant whose fruit, seeds, roots, tubers, bulbs, stems, leaves, or flower parts are used as food. **2.** an edible plant part. **3.** a plant. —*adj.* **4.** of or made from edible vegetables. **5.** of or derived from plants.

veg•e•tar•i•an (vej′i târ′ē ən), *n.* **1.** a person who does not eat meat, fish, or fowl. —*adj.* **2.** of vegetarians. **3.** consisting solely of vegetables. —**veg′e•tar′i•an•ism,** *n.*

veg′e•tate′ (-tāt′), *v.i.,* **-tat•ed, -tat•ing. 1.** to grow as or like a plant. **2.** to lead an inactive and lackluster life. —**veg′e•ta′tive,** *adj.*

veg′e•ta′tion, *n.* **1.** all the plants or plant life of a place. **2.** the act or process of vegetating.

veg•gie (vej′ē), *n. Informal.* **1.** a vegetable. **2.** a vegetarian.

ve•he•ment (vē′ə mənt), *adj.* **1.** ardent; impassioned. **2.** marked by great energy or vigor. —**ve′he•mence, ve′he•men•cy,** *n.* —**ve′he•ment•ly,** *adv.*

ve•hi•cle (vē′i kəl), *n.* **1.** a means of carrying or transporting; conveyance. **2.** a means of transmission or communication. **3.** a liquid, as oil, in which a paint pigment is mixed. —**ve•hic•u•lar** (-hik′yə lər), *adj.*

veil (vāl), *n.* **1.** a piece of opaque or transparent material worn over the face, as for concealment. **2.** a part of a headdress, as of a nun or bride. **3.** something that covers or conceals. —*v.t.* **4.** to cover or conceal with or as if with a veil. —*Idiom.* **5. take the veil,** to become a nun. —**veiled,** *adj.*

vein (vān), *n.* **1.** one of the branching vessels conveying blood to the heart. **2.** one of the riblike thickenings that form the framework of an insect's wing. **3.** one of the strands of vascular tissue forming the framework of a leaf. **4.** a mineral deposit occupying a fissure in rock. **5.** a streak, as in marble. **6.** an attitude or mood. **7.** a tendency or quality. —*v.t.* **8.** to furnish with veins. **9.** to mark with or as if with veins. —**veined,** *adj.*

Vel•cro (vel′krō), *Trademark.* a fastening tape consisting of opposing pieces of nylon fabric that interlock when pressed together.

veld or **veldt** (velt, felt), *n.* the open country, with grass, bushes, or shrubs, characteristic of parts of S Africa.

vel•lum (vel′əm), *n.* **1.** calfskin, lambskin, or kidskin treated for use as a writing surface. **2.** writing paper resembling vellum.

ve•loc•i•ty (və los′i tē), *n., pl.* **-ties.** rapidity of motion, action, or operation; speed.

ve•lour (və lŏŏr′) also **-lours′,** *n.* a velvetlike fabric used for clothing and upholstery.

ve•lum (vē′ləm), *n., pl.* **-la** (-lə). **1.** *Biol.* a veillike membranous partition. **2.** the soft palate. —**ve′lar** (-lər), *adj.*

vel•vet (vel′vit), *n.* **1.** a fabric, as of silk or nylon, with a thick, soft pile. **2.** something that resembles velvet, as in softness. **3.** the soft covering of a growing antler. —*adj.* **4.** made of velvet. **5.** resembling velvet. —**vel′vet•y,** *adj.*

vel′vet•een′ (-vi tēn′), *n.* a cotton fabric with a short pile resembling velvet.

ve•nal (vēn′l), *adj.* **1.** open to or associated with bribery. **2.** capable of being purchased, as by a bribe. —ve•nal′i•ty, *n.*

vend (vend), *v.t., v.i.* to sell, esp. by peddling.

ven•det•ta (ven det′ə), *n., pl.* -tas. a prolonged and bitter feud, esp. between families.

vend′ing machine′, *n.* a coin-operated machine for selling small articles, as candy bars.

ven′dor or vend′er, *n.* **1.** one that sells. **2.** VENDING MACHINE.

ve•neer (və nēr′), *n.* **1.** a thin layer of material for facing or inlaying wood. **2.** a superficially good or pleasing appearance. —*v.t.* **3.** to face or inlay with veneer.

ven•er•a•ble (ven′ər ə bəl), *adj.* **1.** worthy of respect or reverence, as because of great age or high office. **2.** hallowed by religious or historic association. —ven′er•a•bil/i•ty, *n.*

ven′er•ate′ (-ə rāt′), *v.t.,* -at•ed, -at•ing. to regard or treat with reverence; revere. —ven′er•a/tion, *n.*

ve•ne•re•al (və nēr′ē əl), *adj.* **1.** transmitted through sexual intercourse. **2.** of sexual intercourse.

vene′real disease′, *n.* SEXUALLY TRANSMITTED DISEASE.

ve•ne′tian blind′ (və nē′shən), *n.* a window blind with horizontal slats that may be opened, closed, or set at an angle.

Ven•e•zue•la (ven′ə zwā′lə, -zwē′-), *n.* a republic in N South America. 22,396,407. —Ven′e•zue/lan, *adj., n.*

venge•ance (ven′jəns), *n.* **1.** infliction of injury, harm, or humiliation in return for an injury or offense. —*Idiom.* **2. with a vengeance, a.** with violent force. **b.** with excessive energy.

venge′ful, *adj.* desiring or seeking vengeance; vindictive. —venge′ful•ly, *adv.*

ve•ni•al (vē′nē əl, vēn′yəl), *adj.* capable of being forgiven.

ve′nial sin′, *n. Rom. Cath. Ch.* a sin that does not deprive the soul of divine grace. Compare MORTAL SIN.

Ven•ice (ven′is), *n.* a seaport in NE Italy. 361,722. —Ve•ne•tian (və nē′shən), *adj., n.*

ve•ni•re•man (vi nī′rē mən, -nēr′ē-), *n., pl.* -men. one summoned to serve as a juror.

ven•i•son (ven′ə sən, -zən), *n.* the flesh of a deer used for food.

Ve•ni•te (vi nī′tē, ve nē′tā), *n.* **1.** the 95th Psalm, used as a canticle at morning prayers. **2.** a musical setting of this psalm. [< L: come ye; so called from the first word of Vulgate text]

ven•om (ven′əm), *n.* **1.** the poisonous fluid secreted by some animals, as snakes, and introduced into the victim by biting or stinging. **2.** malice; spite.

ven′om•ous, *adj.* **1.** capable of secreting venom. **2.** full of venom; poisonous. **3.** spiteful; malicious.

ve•nous (vē′nəs), *adj.* **1.** of, having, or composed of veins. **2.** of or being the oxygen-poor dark red blood carried back to the heart by the veins.

vent¹ (vent), *n.* **1.** an opening serving as an outlet, as for fumes. **2.** a means of exit or escape. **3.** expression; utterance: *giving vent to anger.* —*v.t.* **4.** to give free expression to. **5.** to release or discharge (liquid, smoke, etc.) through a vent. **6.** to provide with a vent.

vent² (vent), *n.* a slit in a garment.

ven•ti•late (ven′tl āt′), *v.t.,* -lat•ed, -lat•ing. **1.** to provide (a room, mine, etc.) with fresh air. **2.** to submit to open examination and discussion. **3.** to give expression to; vent. **4.** to furnish with a vent. —ven′ti•la′tion, *n.* —ven′ti•la′tor, *n.*

ven•tral (ven′trəl), *adj.* **1.** of or near the belly; abdominal. **2.** situated on the lower, abdominal plane of an animal's body.

ven•tri•cle (ven′tri kəl), *n.* either of the two lower chambers of the heart that force blood into the arteries. —ven•tric′u•lar (-trik′yə lər), *adj.*

ven•tril•o•quism (ven tril′ə kwiz′əm), *n.* the art or practice of speaking so that the voice appears not to come from the speaker but from another source. —ven•tril′o•quist, *n.*

ven•ture (ven′chər), *n., v.,* -tured, -tur•ing. —*n.* **1.**

an undertaking, as a business enterprise, involving risk or uncertainty. **2.** something, as money, risked in a venture. —*v.t.* **3.** to expose to hazard; risk. **4.** to take the risk of. **5.** to undertake to express in spite of possible contradiction or opposition: *won't venture a guess.* —*v.i.* **6.** to undertake or embark upon a venture.

ven′ture•some (-səm), *adj.* **1.** disposed to undertake ventures; adventurous. **2.** involving risk; hazardous.

ven′tur•ous, *adj.* VENTURESOME.

ven•ue (ven′yōō), *n.* **1.** the place of a crime or cause of action. **2.** the place where a jury is gathered and a case tried. **3.** the scene or locale of an action or event.

Ve•nus (vē′nəs), *n.* **1.** the Roman goddess of love and beauty. **2.** the most brilliant planet, second in order from the sun.

Ve•nu•sian (və nōō′shən, -shē ən, -nyōō′-), *adj.* **1.** of the planet Venus. —*n.* **2.** a supposed being inhabiting Venus.

Ve′nus's-fly′trap, *n.* a bog plant with hinged leaves that snap shut to trap insects.

Venus's-flytrap

ve•ra•cious (və rā′shəs), *adj.* **1.** truthful. **2.** characterized by truthfulness. —ve•ra′cious•ly, *adv.*

ve•rac•i•ty (-ras′i tē), *n.* **1.** habitual observance of truth; truthfulness. **2.** conformity to fact; accuracy.

Ve•ra•cruz (ver′ə krōōz′, -krōōs′), *n.* a seaport in E México. 327,522.

ve•ran•da or -dah (və ran′də), *n., pl.* -das or -dahs. a usu. roofed porch, often extending across the front and sides of a house.

verb (vûrb), *n.* a word that functions as the main element of a predicate and typically expresses action, state, or a relation.

ver•bal (vûr′bəl), *adj.* **1.** of or consisting of words. **2.** spoken rather than written; oral. **3.** concerned with words rather than with the ideas expressed. **4.** of or derived from a verb. —ver′bal•ly, *adv.* —*Usage.* VERBAL has had the meaning "spoken" for 400 years, and this was even the primary meaning given in some early dictionaries. Despite objections by some commentators, it is entirely standard as a synonym for ORAL: *a verbal agreement.*

ver′bal•ize′, *v.,* -ized, -iz•ing. —*v.t.* **1.** to express in or put into words. —*v.i.* **2.** to express something verbally. —ver′bal•i•za′tion, *n.*

ver′bal noun′, *n.* a noun derived from a verb.

ver•ba•tim (vər bā′tim), *adv., adj.* word for word. [< ML]

ver•be•na (vər bē′nə), *n., pl.* -nas. a plant with showy flower clusters.

ver•bi•age (vûr′bē ij), *n.* **1.** overabundance of words. **2.** manner of expression in words.

ver•bose (vər bōs′), *adj.* expressed in or characterized by the use of many or too many words; wordy. —ver•bos′i•ty (-bos′i tē), *n.*

ver•bo•ten (vər bōt′n, fər-), *adj.* forbidden, as by law. [< G]

ver•dant (vûr′dnt), *adj.* **1.** green with vegetation. **2.** of the color green.

Ver•di (vâr′dē), *n.* **Giuseppe,** 1813–1901, Italian composer.

ver•dict (vûr′dikt), *n.* **1.** the finding of a jury in a matter submitted to their judgment. **2.** a judgment or decision.

ver•di•gris (vûr′di grēs′, -gris), *n.* a green or bluish patina formed on copper, brass, or bronze surfaces.
ver•dure (vûr′jər), *n.* **1.** the greenness of flourishing vegetation. **2.** green vegetation.
verge¹ (vûrj), *n., v.,* **verged, verg•ing.** —*n.* **1.** the point beyond which something begins or occurs; brink. **2.** an edge, rim, or margin. **3.** a staff carried as an emblem of authority or office. —*v.i.* **4.** to be on the verge; border.
verge² (vûrj), *v.i.,* **verged, verg•ing. 1.** to incline; tend. **2.** to slope or sink.
verg•er (vûr′jər), *n. Chiefly Brit.* **1.** a church attendant and caretaker. **2.** an official who carries a verge before a dignitary.
ver•i•fy (ver′ə fī′), *v.t.,* **-fied, -fy•ing. 1.** to prove the truth of. **2.** to ascertain the truth, authenticity, or correctness of. —**ver′i•fi′a•ble,** *adj.* —**ver′i•fi•ca′-tion,** *n.*
ver′i•ly (-lē), *adv. Archaic.* in truth; really.
ver′i•si•mil′i•tude′ (-si mil′i to͞od′, -tyo͞od′), *n.* the appearance or semblance of truth.
ver′i•ta•ble (-tə bəl), *adj.* being truly so; genuine.
ver′i•ty (-tē), *n., pl.* **-ties. 1.** the state or quality of being true. **2.** something, as a statement, that is true.
Ver•meer (vər mēr′), *n.* **Jan** (yän), (*Jan van der Meer van Delft*), 1632–75, Dutch painter.
ver•mi•cel•li (vûr′mi chel′ē, -sel′ē), *n.* (*used with a sing. or pl. v.*) pasta in the form of long threads.
ver•mic•u•lite (vər mik′yə līt′), *n.* any of a group of minerals that expand on being heated, used esp. for insulation.
ver•mi•form (vûr′mə fôrm′), *adj.* resembling a worm in shape.
ver•mil•ion (vər mil′yən), *n.* **1.** a brilliant scarlet red. **2.** a bright red pigment.
ver•min (vûr′min), *n., pl.* **-min. 1.** small objectionable animals, esp. those, as lice or cockroaches, that are difficult to control. **2.** an obnoxious person. —**ver′min•ous,** *adj.*
Ver•mont (vər mont′), *n.* a state of the NE United States. 588,654. *Cap.:* Montpelier. *Abbr.:* VT, Vt. —**Ver•mont′er,** *n.*
ver•mouth (vər mo͞oth′), *n.* a white wine in which herbs have been steeped.
ver•nac•u•lar (vər nak′yə lər, və nak′-), *n.* **1.** the native speech or language of a country or region. **2.** the distinctive language or vocabulary of a class or profession. **3.** the variety of language in everyday use by ordinary people. —*adj.* **4.** of, using, or in the vernacular.
ver•nal (vûr′nl), *adj.* of or occurring in spring.
Verne (vûrn), *n.* **Jules,** 1828–1905, French novelist.
ver•ni•er (vûr′nē ər), *n.* a small graduated scale running parallel to a longer scale, used for measuring a fractional part of a subdivision of the longer scale. [after P. *Vernier* (1580-1637), French mathematician]
ve•ron•i•ca (və ron′i kə), *n., pl.* **-cas.** a plant, as the speedwell, with opposite leaves and clusters of small flowers.
Ver•ra•za•no (ver′ə zä′nō), *n.* **Giovanni da,** c1480–1527?, Italian navigator and explorer.
Ver•sailles (ver sī′, var-), *n.* a city in N France, near Paris: palace of the French kings. 95,240.
ver•sa•tile (vûr′sə tl; *esp. Brit.* -tīl′), *adj.* **1.** capable of turning easily from one thing to another. **2.** having many uses or applications. —**ver′sa•til′i•ty,** *n.*
verse (vûrs), *n.* **1.** one of the lines of a poem. **2.** a particular type of metrical composition. **3.** a poem. **4.** poetry, esp. as involving metrical form. **5.** a stanza. **6.** one of the short divisions of a chapter of the Bible.
versed, *adj.* experienced or practiced; skilled.
ver•si•fy (vûr′sə fī′), *v.,* **-fied, -fy•ing.** —*v.t.* **1.** to put into verse. —*v.i.* **2.** to compose verses. —**ver′si•fi•ca′tion,** *n.* —**ver′si•fi′er,** *n.*
ver•sion (vûr′zhən, -shən), *n.* **1.** an account from a particular standpoint. **2.** a particular form or variant. **3.** a translation, esp. of the Bible.
ver•so (vûr′sō), *n., pl.* **-sos.** a left-hand page of a book.

ver•sus (vûr′səs, -səz), *prep.* **1.** against: *Smith versus Jones.* **2.** as compared to or in contrast with: *democracy versus totalitarianism.* [late ME < L: towards]
ver•te•bra (vûr′tə brə), *n., pl.* **-brae** (-brē′, -brā′), **-bras.** one of the bones or segments of the spinal column. —**ver′te•bral,** *adj.*
ver′te•brate (-brit, -brāt′), *adj.* **1.** having a spinal column. **2.** of or belonging to a subphylum of animals having a spinal column and comprising mammals, birds, reptiles, amphibians, and fishes. —*n.* **3.** a vertebrate animal.
ver•tex (vûr′teks), *n., pl.* **-tex•es, -ti•ces** (-tə sēz′). **1.** the highest point; apex. **2.** *Geom.* **a.** the point farthest from the base. **b.** the intersection of two sides of a plane figure.
ver•ti•cal (vûr′ti kəl), *adj.* **1.** being perpendicular to the plane of the horizon; upright. **2.** of or at the vertex. —*n.* **3.** something vertical, as a line. **4.** a vertical position. —**ver′ti•cal•ly,** *adv.*
ver•tig•i•nous (vər tij′ə nəs), *adj.* **1.** whirling; spinning. **2.** affected with or liable to cause vertigo.
ver•ti•go (vûr′ti gō′), *n., pl.* **ver•ti•goes, ver•tig•i•nes** (vər tij′ə nēz′). a disordered condition in which one feels oneself or one's surroundings whirling about; dizziness.
verve (vûrv), *n.* vivaciousness, energy, or enthusiasm.
ver•y (ver′ē), *adv., adj.,* **-i•er, -i•est.** —*adv.* **1.** to a high degree; extremely. **2.** absolutely; truly: *in the very same place.* —*adj.* **3.** precise; particular: *the very book I wanted.* **4.** mere: *The very thought is distressing.* **5.** sheer; utter: *the very joy of living.* **6.** actual: *caught in the very act.* **7.** (used as an intensive): *the very heart of the matter.*
ver′y high′ fre′quency, *n.* a frequency between 30 and 300 megahertz.
ver′y low′ fre′quency, *n.* a frequency between 3 and 30 kilohertz.
ves•i•cle (ves′i kəl), *n.* **1.** a small sac, cyst, or cavity. **2.** BLISTER (def. 1). —**ve•sic•u•lar** (və sik′yə lər), *adj.*
ves•per (ves′pər), *n.* **1.** vespers, (*often cap.*) a religious service in the late afternoon or evening. **2.** a bell that summons persons to vespers. **3.** *Archaic.* evening.
Ves•puc•ci (ve spo͞o′chē, -spyo͞o′-), *n.* **Amerigo,** 1451–1512, Italian explorer after whom America was named.
ves•sel (ves′əl), *n.* **1.** a craft, esp. a fairly large one, for traveling on water. **2.** a hollow utensil used esp. for holding liquids. **3.** a tube or duct, as a vein, containing or conveying a body fluid. **4.** a water-conducting duct within the xylem of vascular plants.
vest (vest), *n.* **1.** a waist-length sleeveless garment for men, usu. worn under a jacket. **2.** a similar garment for women. **3.** *Brit.* an undershirt. —*v.t.* **4.** to clothe, as in ecclesiastical vestments. **5.** to place in the possession or control of. **6.** to endow with something, as powers or rights. —*v.i.* **7.** to become vested.
ves•tal (ves′tl), *adj.* **1.** chaste; pure. —*n.* **2.** a chaste woman.
vest′ed, *adj.* held completely, permanently, and inalienably.
vest′ed in′terest, *n.* a special interest in a system, arrangement, or institution for personal reasons.
ves•ti•bule (ves′tə byo͞ol′), *n.* **1.** a passage or hall between the outer door and the interior of a building. **2.** a hollow body part serving as an entrance to another hollow part.
ves•tige (ves′tij), *n.* **1.** a trace of something no longer in existence. **2.** a very small amount. **3.** a degenerate or imperfectly developed biological structure that once performed a useful function. —**ves•tig•i•al** (ve stij′ē əl, -stij′əl), *adj.*
vest′ing, *n.* the granting to an employee of the right to pension benefits despite early retirement.
vest′ment, *n.* **1.** an official or ceremonial robe. **2.** a garment worn by the clergy and their assistants, esp. during divine service.

vest'-pock'et, *adj.* very small; compact.

ves•try (ves'trē), *n.*, *pl.* **-tries. 1.** a room in a church in which the vestments are kept. **2.** a room in a church used for meetings and for Sunday school. **3.** a committee that manages the temporal affairs of an Episcopal church.

Ve•su•vi•us (və soo'vē əs), *n.* **Mount,** an active volcano in SW Italy, near Naples.

vet¹ (vet), *n. Informal.* a veterinarian.

vet² (vet), *n.*, *adj. Informal.* veteran.

vetch (vech), *n.* a climbing plant with pealike flowers, cultivated esp. for forage.

vet•er•an (vet'ər ən), *n.* **1.** a person of long service or experience in an occupation or office. **2.** a person who has served in the armed forces. —*adj.* **3.** of or for veterans.

Vet'erans Administra'tion, *n.* a federal agency that administers benefits for veterans of the armed forces. *Abbr.:* VA, V.A.

Vet'erans Day', *n.* November 11, a U.S. holiday in commemoration of the end of World War I and in honor of veterans of the armed forces.

vet•er•i•nar•i•an (vet'ər ə nâr'ē ən), *n.* a person who practices veterinary medicine.

vet'er•i•nar'y (-ner'ē), *n.*, *pl.* **-nar•ies,** *adj.* —*n.* **1.** a veterinarian. —*adj.* **2.** of or being the medical and surgical treatment of animals, esp. domesticated animals.

ve•to (vē'tō), *n.*, *pl.* **-toes,** *v.,* **-toed, -to•ing.** —*n.* **1.** the power of one branch of a government to cancel the decisions or actions of another, esp. the right of a chief executive to reject bills passed by a legislature. **2.** the exercise of this power. **3.** an emphatic prohibition. —*v.t.* **4.** to reject (a proposed bill) by a veto. **5.** to prohibit emphatically.

vex (veks), *v.t.* **1.** to irritate; annoy. **2.** to trouble; distress.

vex•a•tion (vek sā'shən), *n.* **1.** the act of vexing or state of being vexed. **2.** a cause of annoyance. —**vex•a'tious,** *adj.*

VGA, video graphics array: a high-resolution standard for displaying text, graphics, and colors on computer monitors.

VHF or **vhf,** very high frequency.

VI or **V.I.,** Virgin Islands.

v.i., intransitive verb.

vi•a (vī'ə, vē'ə), *prep.* by way of.

vi•a•ble (vī'ə bəl), *adj.* **1.** capable of living or growing. **2.** (of a fetus) sufficiently developed to be capable of living outside the uterus. **3.** practicable; workable. —**vi'a•bil'i•ty,** *n.*

vi'a•duct', *n.* a bridge for carrying a road or railroad, as over a valley.

vi•al (vī'əl, vīl), *n.* a small container, as of glass, for holding liquids.

vi•and (vī'ənd), *n.* an article of food.

vibes¹ (vībz), *n.pl. Slang.* something, esp. an emotional aura, emitted as if by vibration and intuitively perceived; ambiance.

vibes² (vībz), *n.pl.* vibraphone.

vi•brant (vī'brənt), *adj.* **1.** vibrating. **2.** pulsating with vigor and energy. —**vi'bran•cy,** *n.* —**vi'brant•ly,** *adv.*

vi•bra•phone (vī'brə fōn'), *n.* a percussion instrument that resembles a xylophone but has metal bars and electrically powered resonators. —**vi'bra•phon'ist,** *n.*

vi•brate (vī'brāt), *v.,* **-brat•ed, -brat•ing.** —*v.i.* **1.** to move to and fro or up and down quickly and repeatedly; quiver. **2.** (of sounds) to have a pulsating effect; resonate. **3.** to thrill in emotional response. —*v.t.* **4.** to cause to vibrate. —**vi•bra'tion,** *n.* —**vi'bra•tor,** *n.*

vi•bra•to (vi brä'tō, vī-), *n.*, *pl.* **-tos.** a pulsating effect produced by rapid but slight alternations in pitch.

vi•bur•num (vī bûr'nəm), *n.* a shrub of the honeysuckle family bearing white flower clusters.

vic•ar (vik'ər), *n.* **1.** a parish priest in the Anglican Church. **2.** an Episcopal cleric in charge of a chapel.

3. a Roman Catholic ecclesiastic representing a bishop.

vic'ar•age (-ij), *n.* the residence, benefice, or duties of a vicar.

vi•car•i•ous (vī kâr'ē əs, vi-), *adj.* **1.** performed, received, or suffered in place of another. **2.** taking the place of another. **3.** felt or enjoyed through imagined participation in the experience of another. —**vi•car'i•ous•ly,** *adv.*

vice¹ (vīs), *n.* **1.** an immoral habit or practice. **2.** immoral conduct. **3.** a personal shortcoming; foible.

vice² (vīs), *n.* VISE.

vi•ce³ (vī'sē, -sə, vīs), *prep.* instead of.

vice-, a combining form meaning deputy (*vice president*).

vice'-ad'mi•ral (vīs), *n.* a commissioned officer in the U.S. Navy or Coast Guard ranking above a rear admiral.

vice•ge•rent (vīs jēr'ənt), *n.* a deputy to a sovereign or magistrate.

vi•cen•ni•al (vī sen'ē əl), *adj.* occurring every twenty years.

vice' pres'ident or **vice'-pres'ident** (vīs), *n.* **1.** (*often caps.*) an officer next in rank to a president, serving as president if the president dies, is disabled, or resigns. **2.** a deputy to a president, as in a corporation. —**vice' pres'idency,** *n.*

vice•re'gal (vīs-), *adj.* of a viceroy.

vice•roy (vīs'roi), *n.* a person appointed to rule a country or province as the deputy of the sovereign.

vi•ce ver•sa (vī'sə vûr'sə, vīs', vī'sē), *adv.* in reverse order; conversely. [< L]

vi•cin•i•ty (vi sin'i tē), *n.*, *pl.* **-ties. 1.** the area around a place; neighborhood. **2.** the state or fact of being near; proximity.

vi•cious (vish'əs), *adj.* **1.** addicted to or characterized by vice; evil or depraved. **2.** spiteful; malicious. **3.** unpleasantly severe. **4.** savage; ferocious. —**vi'cious•ly,** *adv.* —**vi'cious•ness,** *n.*

vi'cious cir'cle, *n.* a situation in which effort to solve a problem results in aggravation of the problem or the creation of a worse one.

vi•cis•si•tude (vi sis'i tood', -tyood'), *n.* **1.** change or variation. **2.** vicissitudes, changing phases or conditions, as of life.

Vicks•burg (viks'bûrg), *n.* a city in W Mississippi: Civil War siege and Confederate surrender 1863. 25,500.

vic•tim (vik'təm), *n.* **1.** a person who suffers from a destructive or injurious action or agency. **2.** a person who is deceived or cheated. **3.** a living creature sacrificed in religious rites.

vic'tim•ize', *v.t.,* **-ized, -iz•ing.** to make a victim of. —**vic'tim•i•za'tion,** *n.*

vic•tor (vik'tər), *n.* **1.** a winner in a battle, struggle, or contest. —*Proverb.* **2. To the victor belong the spoils,** a winner gains all.

Vic•to•ri•a (vik tôr'ē ə), *n.* **1.** 1819–1901, queen of Great Britain 1837–1901. **2.** the capital of British Columbia, in SW Canada. 66,303.

Vic•to'ri•an, *adj.* **1.** of or pertaining to Queen Victoria or the period of her reign. **2.** having the characteristics, as prudishness, usu. attributed to the Victorians. —*n.* **3.** a person of the Victorian period.

vic'to•ry (-tə rē), *n.*, *pl.* **-ries. 1.** a success or triumph over an enemy, as in war. **2.** success against any opponent, opposition, or difficulty. —**vic•to'ri•ous** (-tôr'ē əs), *adj.*

vict•ual (vit'l), *n.* **1. victuals,** food supplies; provisions. **2.** food for human consumption.

vi•cu•na or **-ña** (vī koo'nə, -kyoo'-, vi-, vi koo'nyə), *n.*, *pl.* **-nas** or **-ñas. 1.** a wild Andean ruminant related to the llama. **2.** a fabric made from its soft wool.

vi•de (vī'dē, vē'dā), *v. Latin.* see (used to refer a reader to parts of a text).

vid•e•o (vid'ē ō'), *n.*, *pl.* **vid•e•os,** *adj.* —*n.* **1.** the visual elements of television. **2.** television. **3.** a videotape. —*adj.* **4.** of television, esp. the visual elements. **5.** of or being the images displayed on a computer screen.

vid•e•o•cas•sette', *n.* a cassette containing a videotape.

vid'eocassette record'er, *n.* See VCR.

vid'e•o•disc', *n.* an optical disc on which a motion picture or television program is recorded for playback on a television set.

vid'eo display' ter'minal, *n.* a computer terminal consisting of a screen on which data or graphics can be displayed.

vid'eo game', *n.* **1.** a game played on a video screen or television set with a microcomputer. **2.** a game played on a microchip-controlled device, as a handheld toy or arcade machine.

vid'e•o•tape', *n., v.*, **-taped, -tap•ing.** —*n.* **1.** magnetic tape on which a television program can be recorded. —*v.t.* **2.** to record on videotape.

vie (vī), *v.i.*, **vied, vy•ing.** to strive in competition or rivalry; contend.

Vi•en•na (vē en'ə), *n.* the capital of Austria. 1,482,800. —**Vi'en•nese'** (-ə nēz', -nēs'), *adj., n., pl.* **-nese.**

Vien•tiane (vyen tyän'), *n.* the capital of Laos. 377,409.

Vi•et•cong or **Vi•et Cong** (vē et'kong', -kông', vyet'-, vē'it-), *n., pl.* **-cong.** a Communist-led army and guerrilla force in South Vietnam during the Vietnam War, supported largely by North Vietnam.

Vi•et•nam or **Vi•et Nam** (vē et'näm', -nam'), *n.* a country in SE Asia, divided into two republics **(North Vietnam** and **South Vietnam)** in 1954 and reunified in 1976. 64,000,000. —**Vi•et'nam•ese'** (-nä mēz', -mēs', -nə-), *adj., n., pl.* **-ese.**

Vietnam' syn'drome, *n.* the belief that foreign military involvement has no enduring chance of success.

Viet'nam War', *n.* a conflict (1954–75) between South Vietnam, aided by the U.S. and other nations, and the Vietcong and North Vietnam, aided by the Soviet Union, Communist China, and other nations, ending in Communist victory.

view (vyōō), *n.* **1.** an act or instance of seeing or looking. **2.** range of sight or vision. **3.** a sight, as of a landscape; scene. **4.** a picture of a scene. **5.** a manner of looking at something: *from a practical view.* **6.** a mental survey. **7.** aim, intention, or purpose. **8.** prospect or expectation. **9.** a personal opinion; judgment. —*v.t.* **10.** to see; watch. **11.** to look at carefully; inspect. **12.** to contemplate mentally; consider. —*Idiom.* **13. on view,** on exhibition. —**view'er**, *n.*

view'find'er, *n.* a camera part for viewing what will appear in the picture.

view'point', *n.* a mental attitude; point of view.

vi•ges•i•mal (vī jes'ə məl), *adj.* **1.** of or based on twenty. **2.** twentieth.

vig•il (vij'əl), *n.* **1.** wakefulness maintained during normal sleeping hours. **2.** a watch or period of watchful attention. **3.** the eve of a church festival.

vig'i•lant (-lənt), *adj.* keenly watchful, esp. to detect danger; wary. —**vig'i•lance**, *n.* —**vig'i•lant•ly**, *adv.*

vig'i•lan'te (-lan'tē), *n., pl.* **-tes.** a member of a group of volunteers organized but not legally authorized to dispense summary justice. —**vig'i•lan'tism**, *n.*

vi•gnette (vin yet'), *n.* **1.** a decorative design used on a page of a book. **2.** a picture shaded off gradually at the edges. **3. a.** a short, graceful literary sketch. **b.** a brief, appealing scene, as in a movie.

vig•or (vig'ər), *n.* **1.** active strength or force; intensity. **2.** healthy physical or mental energy; vitality. Also, *esp. Brit.*, **vig'our.** —**vig'or•ous**, *adj.* —**vig'or•ous•ly**, *adv.*

Vi•king (vī'king), *n.* **1.** one of the Scandinavian pirates of the late 8th to 11th centuries. **2.** one of a series of U.S. space probes in 1975–76 that obtained scientific information about Mars.

vile (vīl), *adj.*, **vil•er, vil•est. 1.** wretchedly bad: *vile weather.* **2.** highly offensive; objectionable. **3.** morally debased; depraved. —**vile'ness**, *n.*

vil•i•fy (vil'ə fī'), *v.t.*, **-fied, -fy•ing.** to speak ill of; defame. —**vil'i•fi•ca'tion**, *n.*

vil•la (vil'ə), *n., pl.* **-las.** a country residence, esp. an imposing estate.

vil•lage (vil'ij), *n.* **1.** a small rural community, usu. smaller than a town. **2.** the inhabitants of a village. —**vil'lag•er**, *n.*

vil•lain (vil'ən), *n.* **1.** a cruelly malicious person; scoundrel. **2.** a character, as in a play, with the role of a villain. —**vil'lain•ous**, *adj.*

vil'lain•y, *n., pl.* **-lain•ies. 1.** the actions or conduct of a villain. **2.** a villainous act.

vil•lein (vil'ən, -ān), *n.* a feudal serf with the rights of a freeman with respect to all persons except his lord. —**vil'lein•age**, *n.*

Vil•ni•us (vil'nē ōōs'), *n.* the capital of Lithuania. 582,000.

vim (vim), *n.* lively or energetic spirit; vitality.

vin•ai•grette (vin'ə gret'), *n.* a dressing, esp. for salad, of oil and vinegar usu. flavored with herbs. [< F]

Vin•cent de Paul (vin'sənt də pôl'), *n.* **Saint,** 1576–1660, French priest noted for his aid to the poor.

Vin•ci (vin'chē), *n.* **Leonardo da,** Leonardo da Vinci.

vin•ci•ble (vin'sə bəl), *adj.* capable of being conquered or overcome.

vin•di•cate (vin'di kāt'), *v.t.*, **-cat•ed, -cat•ing. 1.** to clear, as from an accusation. **2.** to afford justification for. **3.** to maintain or defend against opposition. —**vin'di•ca'tion**, *n.* —**vin'di•ca'tor**, *n.*

vin•dic•tive (vin dik'tiv), *adj.* **1.** disposed to revenge. **2.** proceeding from or showing a revengeful spirit. —**vin•dic'tive•ly**, *adv.* —**vin•dic'tive•ness**, *n.*

vine (vīn), *n.* **1.** a plant with a long stem that grows along the ground or climbs a support. **2.** the stem of a vine. **3.** a grape plant.

vin•e•gar (vin'i gər), *n.* a sour liquid obtained by fermentation, as of wine or cider, used as a condiment or preservative. [< OF: sour wine] —**vin'e•gar•y**, *adj.*

vine•yard (vin'yərd), *n.* a plantation of grapevines.

Vin•land (vin'lənd), *n.* a region in E North America variously identified as a place between Newfoundland and Virginia: visited and described by Norsemen ab. A.D. 1000.

vin•tage (vin'tij), *n.* **1.** the wine or grapes from a particular harvest or crop. **2.** a superior wine from the crop of a good year. **3.** the act or season of gathering grapes or making wine. **4.** the output of a particular time: *a car of 1917 vintage.* —*adj.* **5.** being of a specified vintage. **6.** representing the best of a past time; classic: *vintage movies.* **7.** being the best of a kind: *vintage Shakespeare.*

vint•ner (vint'nər), *n.* a person who makes or sells wine.

vi•nyl (vīn'l), *n.* any of various flexible, tough plastics used esp. in coatings, phonograph records, and flooring.

vi•ol (vī'əl), *n.* a stringed instrument of the 16th and 17th centuries with usu. six strings and a fretted fingerboard.

vi•o•la (vē ō'lə), *n., pl.* **-las.** a stringed instrument of the violin family, slightly larger than the violin and deeper in tone. —**vi•o'list**, *n.*

vi•o•la•ble (vī'ə lə bəl), *adj.* capable of being violated.

vi•o•late' (-lāt'), *v.t.*, **-lat•ed, -lat•ing. 1.** to break (a law, promise, etc.). **2.** to break in upon; disturb rudely. **3.** to rape. **4.** to treat disrespectfully; desecrate.

vi•o•la'tion, *n.* **1.** the act of violating or state of being violated. **2.** a breach, as of a law. **3.** a sexual assault, esp. rape. **4.** desecration or profanation.

vi•o•lence (vī'ə ləns), *n.* **1.** intense force. **2.** abusive or injurious physical force or action. **3.** a violent act. **4.** immoderate vehemence, as of feeling. **5.** damage, as to meaning: *did violence to the translation.*

vi'o•lent, *adj.* **1.** acting with or characterized by uncontrolled physical force. **2.** caused by destructive force: *a violent death.* **3.** intense; severe. **4.** immoderately vehement. —**vi•o•lent•ly,** *adv.*

vi•o•let (vī′ə lit), *n.* **1.** a low plant with purple, blue, yellow, or white flowers. **2.** a reddish blue. —*adj.* **3.** of the color violet.

vi•o•lin (vī′ə lin′), *n.* the treble instrument of the family of modern bowed four-stringed instruments. —**vi′o•lin′ist,** *n.*

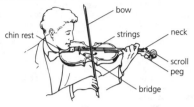

chin rest — bow — strings — neck — scroll — peg — bridge

violin

vi•o•lon•cel•lo (vē′ə lən chel′ō, vī′-), *n., pl.* **-los.** CELLO. —**vi′o•lon•cel′list,** *n.*

VIP, (vē′ī′pē′), *Informal.* very important person.

vi•per (vī′pər), *n.* **1.** any of various venomous snakes. **2.** a malignant or treacherous person. —**vi′per•ous,** *adj.*

vi•ra•go (vi rä′gō, -rā′-), *n., pl.* **-goes, -gos.** a loud-voiced, ill-tempered, scolding woman; shrew.

vi•ral (vī′rəl), *adj.* of or caused by a virus.

vir•e•o (vir′ē ō′), *n., pl.* **vir•e•os.** a small New World songbird with a slightly hooked bill.

Vir•gil (vûr′jəl), *n.* (*Publius Vergilius Maro*) 70–19 B.C., Roman poet: author of *The Aeneid.* —**Vir•gil•i•an** (vər jil′ē ən, -jil′yən), *adj.*

vir•gin (vûr′jin), *n.* **1.** a person who has never had sexual intercourse. **2. the Virgin,** Mary, the mother of Jesus. —*adj.* **3.** of, being, or characteristic of a virgin. **4.** pure; unsullied. **5.** not previously exploited or used: *a virgin forest.* —**vir•gin•i•ty** (vər jin′i tē), *n.*

vir•gin•al (-jə nl), *adj.* **1.** of, characteristic of, or befitting a virgin. **2.** pure; unsullied.

Vir•gin•ia (vər jin′yə), *n.* a state in the E United States. 6,675,451. *Cap.:* Richmond. *Abbr.:* VA, Va. —**Vir•gin′ian,** *n., adj.*

Virgin′ia Beach′, *n.* a city in SE Virginia. 430,295.

Virgin′ia creep′er, *n.* a North American climbing plant with bluish black berries.

Virgin′ia reel′, *n.* an American country dance.

Vir′gin Is′lands, *n.pl.* two groups of islands in the West Indies, E of Puerto Rico, one belonging to the United States and the other to Great Britain. *Abbr.:* VI, V.I.

Vir′gin Mar′y, *n.* Mary, the mother of Jesus.

Vir•go (vûr′gō), *n.* the sixth sign of the zodiac. [< L: virgin]

vir•gule (vûr′gyōōl), *n.* an oblique stroke (/) used as a dividing line in dates or fractions (²/₄) or between words to indicate two alternatives (his/her).

vir•ile (vir′əl), *adj.* **1.** having or showing masculine strength or qualities; manly. **2.** vigorous; energetic. **3.** capable of copulating. —**vi•ril•i•ty** (və ril′i tē), *n.*

vi•rol•o•gy (vī rol′ə jē, vi-), *n.* the study of viruses and viral diseases. —**vi•rol′o•gist,** *n.*

vir•tu•al (vûr′chōō əl), *adj.* **1.** being such in force or effect, though not actually or expressly such. **2. a.** temporarily simulated or extended by computer software. **b.** of, by means of, or existing on computers. —**vir′tu•al•ly,** *adv.*

vir′tual real′ity, *n.* a realistic simulation of an environment, including three-dimensional graphics, by a computer system using interactive software and hardware.

vir•tue (vûr′chōō), *n.* **1.** conformity to moral and ethical principles. **2.** a particular moral excellence. **3.** chastity. **4.** an admirable quality. **5.** effective force; potency. —*Idiom.* **6. by virtue of,** by reason of.

vir•tu•o•so (vûr′chōō ō′sō), *n., pl.* **-sos, -si** (-sē). a person with special knowledge or skill, esp. one who

excels in musical technique or execution. —**vir′tu•os′i•ty** (-os′i tē), *n.*

vir•tu•ous (vûr′chōō əs), *adj.* **1.** conforming to moral and ethical principles. **2.** chaste. —**vir′tu•ous•ly,** *adv.* —**vir′tu•ous•ness,** *n.*

vir•u•lent (vir′yə lənt, vir′ə-), *adj.* **1.** extremely poisonous; noxious. **2.** highly infectious; deadly. **3.** violently hostile. —**vir′u•lence,** *n.* —**vir′u•lent•ly,** *adv.*

vi•rus (vī′rəs), *n., pl.* **-rus•es. 1.** an ultramicroscopic infectious agent that replicates only within the cells of living hosts. **2.** a disease caused by a virus. **3.** a corrupting influence. **4.** a segment of self-replicating code planted illegally in a computer program.

vi•sa (vē′zə), *n., pl.* **-sas.** an official endorsement on a passport that permits the bearer to enter a country.

vis•age (viz′ij), *n.* **1.** the face; countenance. **2.** aspect; appearance.

vis-à-vis (vē′zə vē′), *adv., adj.* **1.** face to face. —*prep.* **2.** in relation to; compared with. **3.** opposite. [< F]

vis•cer•a (vis′ər ə), *n.pl., sing.* **vis•cus** (vis′kəs). the internal organs of the body, esp. those in the abdominal cavity.

vis′cer•al, *adj.* **1.** of or affecting the viscera. **2.** characterized by or proceeding from instinct rather than intellect. —**vis′cer•al•ly,** *adv.*

vis•cid (vis′id), *adj.* glutinous in consistency; sticky.

vis•cose (vis′kōs), *n.* a viscous solution prepared by treating cellulose and used esp. in manufacturing rayon and cellophane.

vis•cos•i•ty (vi skos′i tē), *n., pl.* **-ties. 1.** the state or quality of being viscous. **2.** the property of a fluid that resists the force tending to cause the fluid to flow.

vis•count (vī′kount′), *n.* a nobleman below an earl or count and above a baron.

vis′count′ess (vī′-), *n.* **1.** the wife of a viscount. **2.** a woman holding in her own right a rank equivalent to that of a viscount.

vis•cous (vis′kəs), *adj.* **1.** thick and sticky in consistency; gluey. **2.** having the property of viscosity.

vise (vīs), *n.* a device, usu. having two jaws closed by means of a screw or lever, used to hold firmly an object being worked on.

vise

Vish•nu (vish′nōō), *n.* "the Preserver," the second member of the Hindu trinity, along with Brahma and Shiva.

vis•i•bil•i•ty (viz′ə bil′i tē), *n.* **1.** the quality, state, or fact of being visible. **2.** the greatest distance it is possible to see under given atmospheric conditions.

vis′i•ble, *adj.* **1.** capable of being seen. **2.** apparent; manifest. —**vis′i•bly,** *adv.*

vi•sion (vizh′ən), *n.* **1.** the act or power of seeing. **2.** unusual foresight. **3.** something seen in or as if in a dream or trance. **4.** a vivid imaginative conception. **5.** something of extraordinary beauty. —*Proverb.* **6. Where there is no vision, the people perish,** people must foresee a better life for themselves. Prov. 29:18.

vi′sion•ar′y (-ə ner′ē), *adj., n., pl.* **-ar•ies.** —*adj.* **1.** given to seeing visions. **2.** seen in a vision. **3.** given to or characterized by fanciful or impractical ideas. —*n.* **4.** a person of unusual foresight. **5.** one who sees visions. **6.** a person given to impractical ideas; dreamer.

vis•it (viz′it), *v.t.* **1.** to go or come to see, as for sightseeing. **2.** to stay with as a guest. **3.** to go to for the purpose of official inspection. **4.** to come upon; afflict. **5.** to access (a Web site). —*v.i.* **6.** to make a visit. **7.** to chat casually. —*n.* **8.** an act or instance of visiting.

vis′it•ant (-i tənt), *n.* a visitor.

vis′it•a′tion (-tā′shən), *n.* **1.** a visit, esp. a formal or official one. **2.** an affliction or punishment, as from God.

vis′i•tor, *n.* a person who visits.

vi•sor (vī′zər), *n.* **1.** the projecting front brim of a cap. **2.** a flap mounted on the inside of an automobile to shield the eyes from glare. **3.** the movable front piece on a medieval helmet.

vis•ta (vis′tə), *n.*, *pl.* **-tas. 1.** a view, esp. one seen through a long, narrow passage. **2.** a far-reaching mental view.

VISTA (vis′tə), *n.* Volunteers in Service to America.

vis•u•al (vizh′ōō əl), *adj.* **1.** of or used in seeing or sight. **2.** perceptible by the sense of sight; visible. **3.** performed through the sense of sight: *a visual landing.* **4.** of or involving the use of materials, as pictures, that instruct through the sense of sight. —**vis′u•al•ly,** *adv.*

vis′u•al•ize′, *v.i.*, *v.t.*, **-ized, -iz•ing.** to form a mental image (of). —**vis′u•al•i•za′tion,** *n.* —**vis′u•al•iz′er,** *n.*

vi•tal (vīt′l), *adj.* **1.** of or necessary to life. **2.** energetic, lively, or forceful. **3.** indispensable; essential. **4.** of critical importance. **5.** fatal; deadly. —**vi′tal•ly,** *adv.*

vi•tal′i•ty, *n.* **1.** exuberant physical or mental vigor. **2.** capacity for survival or continuation. **3.** power to live or grow.

vi′tal•ize′, *v.t.*, **-ized, -iz•ing.** to give vitality to; animate.

vi′tal signs′, *n.pl.* essential body functions, comprising pulse rate, body temperature, and respiration.

vi′tal statis′tics, *n.pl.* statistics concerning deaths, births, and marriages.

vi•ta•min (vī′tə min), *n.* any of a group of organic substances found in food and essential in small quantities to normal metabolism.

vitamin A, *n.* a vitamin found esp. in green and yellow vegetables and egg yolk, essential to growth and the prevention of night blindness.

vitamin B₁, *n.* THIAMINE.

vitamin B₂, *n.* RIBOFLAVIN.

vitamin B₃, *n.* NICOTINIC ACID.

vitamin B₁₂, *n.* a vitamin obtained esp. from liver and fish, used to treat anemia.

vitamin B complex, *n.* an important group of water-soluble vitamins containing vitamin B₁, vitamin B₂, etc.

vitamin C, *n.* ASCORBIC ACID.

vitamin D, *n.* any of several related vitamins occurring in milk and fish-liver oils, essential for the formation of normal bones and teeth.

vitamin E, *n.* a vitamin abundant in vegetable oils, cereal grains, butter, and eggs, important as an antioxidant.

vitamin K, *n.* a vitamin occurring esp. in leafy vegetables that promotes blood clotting.

vi•ti•ate (vish′ē āt′), *v.t.*, **-at•ed, -at•ing. 1.** to impair the quality of. **2.** to make less effective. **3.** to debase; corrupt. **4.** to make legally invalid. —**vi′ti•a′tion,** *n.*

vit•i•cul•ture (vit′i kul′chər, vī′ti-), *n.* the cultivation of grapes or grapevines. —**vit′i•cul′tur•ist,** *n.*

vit•re•ous (vi′trē əs), *adj.* **1.** of or resembling glass. **2.** obtained from or containing glass.

vit′reous hu′mor, *n.* the transparent gelatinous substance that fills the eyeball behind the lens.

vit′ri•fy′, *v.t.*, *v.i.*, **-fied, -fy•ing.** to change into glass or a glasslike substance. —**vit′ri•fi•ca′tion,** *n.*

vi•trine (vi trēn′), *n.* a glass cabinet esp. for displaying art objects.

vit•ri•ol (vi′trē əl), *n.* **1.** any of various glassy metallic sulfates. **2.** SULFURIC ACID. **3.** something highly caustic in effect. —**vit′ri•ol′ic** (-ol′ik), *adj.*

vi•tu•per•ate (vī tōō′pə rāt′, -tyōō′-, vi-), *v.t.*, **-at•ed, -at•ing.** to censure harshly; revile. —**vi•tu′per•a′tion,** *n.* —**vi•tu′per•a′tive,** *adj.*

vi•va (vē′və, -vä), *interj.* an exclamation of acclaim or approval.

vi•va•ce (vi vä′chā, vē-), *adv., adj.* in a lively manner (used as a musical direction).

vi•va•cious (vi vā′shəs, vī-), *adj.* lively; animated. —**vi•va′cious•ly,** *adv.* —**vi•vac′i•ty** (-vas′i tē), **vi•va′cious•ness,** *n.*

Vi•val•di (vi väl′dē), *n.* **Antonio,** 1678–1741, Italian composer.

viv•id (viv′id), *adj.* **1.** strikingly bright or intense; brilliant. **2.** having bright or striking colors. **3.** presenting the appearance, freshness, and spirit of life. **4.** clearly perceptible. **5.** forming striking mental images. **6.** full of life; animated. —**viv′id•ly,** *adv.* —**viv′id•ness,** *n.*

viv′i•fy′, *v.t.*, **-fied, -fy•ing. 1.** to give life to; animate. **2.** to enliven; brighten.

vi•vip•a•rous (vī vip′ər əs, vi-), *adj.* bringing forth living young rather than eggs.

viv•i•sec•tion (viv′ə sek′shən), *n.* the cutting into or dissection of a living body, esp. in order to advance scientific knowledge.

vix•en (vik′sən), *n.* **1.** a female fox. **2.** an ill-tempered or quarrelsome woman. —**vix′en•ish,** *adj.*

viz. (viz), that is; namely. [abbr. L *videlicet*]

vi•zier (vi zēr′, viz′yər), *n.* a high governmental official in certain Muslim countries, esp. in the former Ottoman Empire.

vi•zor (vī′zər), *n.* VISOR.

V-J Day (vē′jā′), *n.* August 14, 1945, the day Japan accepted the Allied surrender terms in World War II, or September 2, 1945, the day the surrender was signed.

Vla•di•vos•tok (vlad′ə vos′tok, -və stok′), *n.* a seaport in the SE Russian Federation in Asia. 648,000.

VLF, very low frequency.

V.M.D., Doctor of Veterinary Medicine. [< L *Veterināriae Medicīnae Doctor*]

vo•ca•ble (vō′kə bəl), *n.* a word considered as a combination of sounds or letters without regard to meaning.

vo•cab•u•lar•y (vō kab′yə ler′ē), *n.*, *pl.* **-lar•ies. 1.** the stock of words used by or known to a particular person or group. **2.** a list of words and phrases, usu. arranged in alphabetical order and defined.

vo•cal (vō′kəl), *adj.* **1.** of or uttered with the voice. **2.** rendered by or composed for singing. **3.** having a voice. **4.** giving forth sound or speech. **5.** inclined to express oneself freely; outspoken. —*n.* **6.** a vocal sound. **7.** a musical piece for a singer; song. —**vo′cal•ly,** *adv.*

vo′cal cords′, *n.pl.* either of two pairs of folds of mucous membrane in the larynx that vibrate to produce sound or voice.

vo•cal′ic (-kal′ik), *adj.* of, resembling, or being a vowel.

vo•cal•ist (-kə list), *n.* a singer.

vo′cal•ize′, *v.*, **-ized, -iz•ing.** —*v.t.* **1.** to make vocal; articulate. —*v.i.* **2.** to utter sounds with the vocal cords, esp. to sing. —**vo′cal•i•za′tion,** *n.*

vo•ca•tion (vō kā′shən), *n.* **1.** an occupation, business, or profession. **2.** a strong impulse to follow a particular activity or career. **3.** a divine call to a religious life. —**vo•ca′tion•al,** *adj.*

voc•a•tive (vok′ə tiv), *adj.* of or being a grammatical case, as in Latin, used to indicate the one being addressed.

vo•cif•er•ate (vō sif′ə rāt′), *v.i.*, *v.t.*, **-at•ed, -at•ing.** to cry out loudly, noisily, or vehemently. —**vo•cif′er•a′tion,** *n.*

vo•cif′er•ous, *adj.* characterized by or making a loud, noisy, or vehement outcry. —**vo•cif′er•ous•ly,** *adv.*

vod•ka (vod′kə), *n.*, *pl.* **-kas.** a colorless distilled liquor made esp. from rye or wheat mash.

vogue (vōg), *n.* **1.** the prevailing fashion at a particular time. **2.** popular favor; popularity. —**vogu′ish,** *adj.*

voice (vois), *n.*, *v.*, **voiced, voic•ing.** —*n.* **1. a.** sound uttered through the mouth, esp. of human beings. **b.** the faculty of uttering such sound. **2.** a sound resembling vocal utterance. **3.** expression, esp. in words: *gave voice to her disapproval.* **4.** the right to express desires or opinions: *wants a voice in company policy.* **5.** an expressed will or desire: *the voice of the people.* **6.** an agency or medium of expression. **7.** a melodic part in a musical composition. **8.** the audible result produced by vibration of the vocal cords. **9.** a verb form indicating the relation of the subject to the action of the verb. —*v.t.* **10.** to give utterance or expression to. —**voice/less,** *adj.*

voice/ box/, *n.* the larynx.

voice/ mail/, *n.* an electronic communications system that routes voice messages interactively to appropriate recipients.

voice/-o/ver, *n.* the voice of an offscreen narrator or announcer, as on television.

void (void), *adj.* **1.** having no legal force or effect. **2.** useless; ineffectual. **3.** devoid; destitute. **4.** lacking contents; empty. —*n.* **5.** an empty space; emptiness. **6.** a state or feeling of loss or privation. —*v.t.* **7.** to invalidate; nullify. **8.** to empty; evacuate. —**void/a•ble,** *adj.*

voile (voil), *n.* a lightweight, semisheer fabric.

vol., volume.

vol•a•tile (vol/ə tl), *adj.* **1.** evaporating rapidly. **2.** tending or threatening to erupt in violence; explosive. **3.** changeable; unstable. **4.** (of computer storage) not retaining data when electrical power is turned off. —**vol/a•til/i•ty** (-til/i tē), *n.* —**vol/a•til•ize/,** *v.i., v.t.,* **-ized, -iz•ing.**

vol•can•ic (vol kan/ik), *adj.* **1.** of or produced by a volcano. **2.** potentially explosive; volatile.

vol•ca•no (vol kā/nō), *n., pl.* **-noes, -nos. 1.** a vent in the earth's crust through which lava, steam, and ashes are expelled. **2.** a mountain or hill formed from the ash and lava so expelled.

vole (vōl), *n.* any of several short-tailed, stocky rodents.

Vol•ga (vol/gə, vōl/-), *n.* a river flowing from the Valdai Hills in the W Russian Federation, to the Caspian Sea. 2325 mi. (3745 km) long.

Vol•go•grad (vol/gə grad/, vōl/-), *n.* a city in the SW Russian Federation. 999,000.

vo•li•tion (vō lish/ən, və-), *n.* the act or power of willing, choosing, or resolving. —**vo•li/tion•al,** *adj.*

vol•ley (vol/ē), *n., pl.* **-leys,** *v.,* **-leyed, -ley•ing.** —*n.* **1.** the simultaneous discharge of a number of missiles or firearms. **2.** the missiles so discharged. **3.** a burst of many things at once or in quick succession. **4.** the return of a ball, as in tennis, before it hits the ground. —*v.t., v.i.* **5.** to discharge or be discharged in a volley. **6.** to return (a ball) before it hits the ground.

vol/ley•ball/, *n.* a game in which a large ball is volleyed back and forth over a high net. **2.** the ball used in this game.

volt (vōlt), *n.* the unit of potential difference and electromotive force equal to the difference of electric potential between two points of a conductor carrying a constant current of one ampere when the power dissipated between these points is one watt.

volt•age (vōl/tij), *n.* electromotive force or potential difference expressed in volts.

vol•ta•ic (vol tā/ik, vōl-), *adj.* of or noting electricity produced by chemical action.

Vol•taire (vōl târ/, vol-), *n.* 1694–1778, French writer and philosopher.

volt/me/ter, *n.* an instrument for measuring the voltage between two points.

vol•u•ble (vol/yə bəl), *adj.* characterized by an easy and continuous flow of words; fluent. —**vol/u•bil/i•ty,** *n.* —**vol/u•bly,** *adv.*

vol•ume (vol/yōōm, -yəm), *n.* **1.** the amount of space in cubic units that an object or substance occupies. **2.** a quantity, esp. a large quantity. **3.** amount; total. **4.** mass; bulk. **5.** the degree of sound intensity; loudness. **6.** a book, esp. one of a series. **7.** a set of issues of a periodical.

vo•lu•mi•nous (və lōō/mə nəs), *adj.* **1.** filling or

sufficient to fill a volume. **2.** of great volume, size, or extent. —**vo•lu/mi•nous•ly,** *adv.*

vol•un•tar•y (vol/ən ter/ē), *adj.* **1.** done, made, given, or undertaken of one's own free will. **2.** depending on voluntary action: *voluntary hospitals.* **3.** done by or composed of volunteers. **4.** *Law.* done by intention and not by accident. **5.** controlled by the will. **6.** having the power of willing. —**vol/un•tar/i•ly** (-târ/ə lē), *adv.*

vol•un•teer/, *n.* **1.** a person who voluntarily offers himself or herself for a service or undertaking. —*v.i.* **2.** to offer oneself for a service or undertaking. —*v.t.* **3.** to offer, give, or perform voluntarily.

vo•lup•tu•ar•y (və lup/chōō er/ē), *n., pl.* **-ar•ies.** a person devoted to the pursuit and enjoyment of sensual pleasure.

vo•lup/tu•ous, *adj.* **1.** derived from, affording, or marked by gratification of the senses. **2.** full and shapely. —**vo•lup/tu•ous•ly,** *adv.* —**vo•lup/tu•ous• ness,** *n.*

vo•lute (və lōōt/), *n.* a spiral or twisted object or ornament.

vom•it (vom/it), *v.i., v.t.* **1.** to eject (the contents of the stomach) through the mouth. **2.** to eject or be ejected forcefully. —*n.* **3.** the act of vomiting. **4.** the matter ejected in vomiting.

voo•doo (vōō/dōō), *n., pl.* **-doos. 1.** a polytheistic religion deriving principally from African cult worship. **2.** a person who practices voodoo. **3.** an object of voodoo worship, as a fetish. —**voo/doo•ism,** *n.*

vo•ra•cious (vô rā/shəs, və-), *adj.* **1.** craving or consuming large quantities of food. **2.** exceedingly eager. —**vo•ra/cious•ly,** *adv.* —**vo•rac/i•ty** (-ras/i-tē), *n.*

vor•tex (vôr/teks), *n., pl.* **-tex•es, -ti•ces** (-tə sēz/). **1.** a whirling mass of water; whirlpool. **2.** something like a whirlpool: *the vortex of the controversy.*

vo•ta•ry (vō/tə rē), *n., pl.* **-ries. 1.** a devoted worshiper. **2.** a devout adherent. **3.** a person bound by religious vows.

vote (vōt), *n., v.,* **vot•ed, vot•ing.** —*n.* **1.** a formal expression of opinion or choice, as in an election. **2.** a means, as a ballot, of indicating a vote. **3.** suffrage: *gave women the vote.* **4.** the number of votes cast. **5.** a group of voters. —*v.i.* **6.** to cast a vote. —*v.t.* **7.** to enact, establish, or determine by vote. **8.** to declare by general consent. —*Idiom.* **9. vote with one's feet,** to reject something by leaving it. [< L *vōtum* a vow] —**vot/er,** *n.*

vo•tive (vō/tiv), *adj.* offered, dedicated, or performed in accordance with a vow or as an act of veneration or gratitude.

vouch (vouch), *v.i.* **1.** to provide proof, supporting evidence, or assurance. **2.** to give a guarantee; take personal responsibility.

vouch/er, *n.* **1.** one that vouches. **2.** a document, receipt, etc., that constitutes evidence, as of an expenditure.

vouch/safe/, *v.t.,* **-safed, -saf•ing.** to grant or give, esp. in a condescending manner.

vow (vou), *n.* **1.** a solemn promise, pledge, or commitment. **2.** a solemn or earnest declaration. —*v.t.* **3.** to promise by a vow. **4.** to declare solemnly or earnestly. —*v.i.* **5.** to make a vow. —*Idiom.* **6. take vows,** to enter a religious order.

vow•el (vou/əl), *n.* **1.** a speech sound produced without obstructing the flow of air from the lungs. **2.** a letter representing a vowel.

voy•age (voi/ij), *n., v.,* **-aged, -ag•ing.** —*n.* **1.** a journey, esp. a long journey by water. **2.** a journey through air or space. —*v.i., v.t.* **3.** to make, take, or traverse by a voyage. —**voy/ag•er,** *n.*

vo•ya•geur (vwä/yä zhûr/), *n., pl.* **-geurs** (-zhûrz/, -zhûr/). (in Canada) an expert guide in remote regions, esp. one employed by a fur company.

vo•yeur (vwä yûr/, voi ûr/), *n.* a person who obtains sexual gratification by looking at sexual objects or acts. [< F] —**vo•yeur/ism,** *n.* —**voy/eur•is/tic,** *adj.*

V.P. or **VP,** Vice President.

vs. or **vs,** versus.

V/STOL (vē'stôl'), *n.* an aircraft capable of taking off and landing vertically or on a short runway.

VT or **Vt.,** Vermont.

v.t., transitive verb.

VTOL (vē'tôl'), *n.* an aircraft capable of taking off and landing vertically.

Vul•can (vul'kən), *n.* the Roman god of fire and metalworking.

vul'can•ize', *v.t.,* **-ized, -iz•ing.** to treat (rubber) with sulfur and heat to impart greater strength, elasticity, and durability. —**vul'can•i•za'tion,** *n.*

Vulg., Vulgate.

vul•gar (vul'gər), *adj.* **1.** characterized by lack of good breeding, refinement, or taste. **2.** indecent; obscene. **3.** of or constituting the ordinary people in a society. **4.** spoken by or expressed in the language of ordinary people; vernacular. —**vul'gar•ly,** *adv.*

vul•gar'i•an (-gâr'ē ən), *n.* a vulgar person.

vul'gar•ism, *n.* **1.** vulgarity. **2.** a vulgar word or phrase.

vul•gar'i•ty (-gar'i tē), *n., pl.* **-ties. 1.** the state or quality of being vulgar. **2.** something vulgar, as an act or expression.

vul'gar•ize', *v.t.,* **-ized, -iz•ing. 1.** to make vulgar or coarse. **2.** to popularize. —**vul'gar•i•za'tion,** *n.*

Vul'gar Lat'in, *n.* popular Latin as distinguished from literary or standard Latin.

Vul•gate (vul'gāt, -git), *n.* a Latin version of the Bible prepared chiefly by Saint Jerome at the end of the 4th century A.D. and used as an authorized version of the Roman Catholic Church. [< LL *vulgāta (editiō)* popular (edition); *vulgāta,* der. of *vulgāre* to make common, publish]

vul•ner•a•ble (vul'nər ə bəl), *adj.* **1.** capable of or susceptible to being wounded. **2.** open to or defenseless against criticism or attack. **3.** having won one game of a rubber of bridge. —**vul'ner•a•bil'i•ty,** *n.* —**vul'ner•a•bly,** *adv.*

vul•pine (vul'pīn, -pin), *adj.* of or resembling a fox, esp. in cunning.

vul•ture (vul'chər), *n.* **1.** any of several large birds of prey that feed on carrion. **2.** a greedy or unscrupulous person.

vul•va (vul'və), *n., pl.* **-vae** (-vē), **-vas.** the external female genitalia.

vy•ing (vī'ing), *v.* pres. part. of VIE.

W

W, w (dub'əl yōō', -yōō), *n., pl.* **Ws** or **W's, ws** or **w's.** the 23rd letter of the English alphabet, a semivowel.

W, 1. watt. **2.** west. **3.** western. **4.** wide. **5.** width.

W, *Chem. Symbol.* tungsten. [< G *Wolfram*]

w, 1. watt. **2.** with.

W., 1. Wales. **2.** watt. **3.** Wednesday. **4.** weight. **5.** Welsh. **6.** west. **7.** western. **8.** width.

w., 1. watt. **2.** week. **3.** weight. **4.** west. **5.** western. **6.** wide. **7.** width. **8.** wife. **9.** with. **10.** *Physics.* work.

w/, with.

WA, Washington.

Wac (wak), *n.* a member of the Women's Army Corps.

wack•y (wak'ē), *adj.,* **-i•er, -i•est.** *Slang.* odd or irrational. —**wack'i•ness,** *n.*

Wa•co (wā'kō), *n.* a city in central Texas. 105,892.

wad (wod), *n., v.,* **wad•ded, wad•ding.** —*n.* **1.** a small mass, as of cotton, used esp. for padding and packing. **2.** a roll of bank notes. **3.** a large stock or quantity, as of money. **4.** a plug used to hold the powder or shot in place in a gun or cartridge. —*v.t.* **5.** to form into a wad. **6.** to stuff or hold in place with a wad.

wad'ding, *n.* **1.** a fibrous or soft material for stuffing, padding, or packing. **2.** material used as wads for guns or cartridges.

wad•dle (wod'l), *v.,* **-dled, -dling,** *n.* —*v.i.* **1.** to walk with short steps, swaying from side to side in the manner of a duck. —*n.* **2.** a waddling gait.

wade (wād), *v.i.,* **wad•ed, wad•ing. 1.** to walk through a substance, as water or snow, that impedes motion. **2.** to make one's way laboriously.

wad'er, *n.* **1.** one that wades. **2.** Also called **wad'-ing bird'.** a long-legged bird that wades in water in search of food. **3. waders,** high waterproof boots or pants worn for wading, as while fishing.

wa•di (wä'dē), *n., pl.* **-dis.** (in Arabia, Syria, northern Africa, etc.) a watercourse that is dry except during periods of rainfall.

wa•fer (wā'fər), *n.* **1.** a thin, crisp cake, cookie, biscuit, or candy. **2.** a thin disk of unleavened bread used in the Eucharist.

waf•fle¹ (wof'əl), *n.* a batter cake baked in a hinged appliance (**waf'fle i'ron**) that forms a gridlike pattern on each side.

waf•fle² (wof'əl), *v.i.,* **-fled, -fling.** to speak or write equivocally. —**waf'fler,** *n.*

waft (wäft, waft), *v.t., v.i.* **1.** to carry or float lightly and smoothly through or as if through the air. —*n.* **2.** a faintly perceived sound or odor. **3.** a light current or gust. **4.** the act of wafting.

wag (wag), *v.,* **wagged, wag•ging,** *n.* —*v.t., v.i.* **1.** to move up and down or from side to side. **2.** to move (the tongue) in idle chatter. —*n.* **3.** the act of wagging. **4.** a witty person.

wage (wāj), *n., v.,* **waged, wag•ing.** —*n.* **1.** Often, **wages.** money paid or received for work or services. **2. wages,** recompense; return: *the wages of sin.* —*v.t.* **3.** to carry on (a battle, argument, etc.).

wa•ger (wā'jər), *n.* **1.** something risked or staked on an uncertain event; bet. **2.** the act of betting. —*v.t., v.i.* **3.** to bet. —**wa'ger•er,** *n.*

wag•ger•y (wag'ə rē), *n., pl.* **-ger•ies. 1.** the roguish wit of a wag. **2.** a jest or joke.

wag'gish, *adj.* **1.** full of roguish good humor. **2.** characteristic of or befitting a wag.

wag•gle (wag'əl), *v.,* **-gled, -gling,** *n.* —*v.i., v.t.* **1.** to move up and down or from side to side. —*n.* **2.** a waggling motion.

Wag•ner (väg'nər), *n.* **Richard,** 1813–83, German composer. —**Wag•ner'i•an** (-nēr'ē ən), *adj., n.*

wag•on (wag'ən), *n.* **1.** a four-wheeled vehicle, esp. one for the transport of heavy loads. **2.** STATION WAGON.

wag'on•er, *n.* a person who drives a wagon.

wag'on train', *n.* a train of wagons and horses, as one transporting settlers in the westward migration.

waif (wāf), *n.* **1.** a person, esp. a child, who has no home. **2.** a stray animal.

wail (wāl), *v.i.* **1.** to express sorrow with a prolonged cry. **2.** to make mournful sounds, as the wind. —*n.* **3.** a wailing cry or any similar sound.

wain (wān), *n.* a farm wagon or cart.

wain•scot (wān'skət, -skot, -skōt), *n., v.,* **-scot•ed, -scot•ing** or (*esp. Brit.*) **-scot•ted, -scot•ting.** —*n.* **1.** a paneling of wood on an interior wall, often only the lower portion. —*v.t.* **2.** to panel with wainscot.

wain'scot•ing (-skō ting, -skot ing, -ska ting), *n.* **1.** woodwork for a wainscot. **2.** wainscots collectively. Also, *esp. Brit.,* **wain'scot•ting.**

wain•wright (wān'rīt'), *n.* a wagon maker.

waist (wāst), *n.* **1.** the narrow part of the human body between the ribs and the hips. **2.** the part of a garment covering the waist. **3.** BLOUSE (def. 1). **4.** the narrow central or middle part of something.

waist•band′, *n.* a band, as on a skirt, encircling the waist.

waist•coat (wes′kət, wāst′kōt′), *n. Chiefly Brit.* VEST (def. 1).

waist•line (wāst′līn′), *n.* **1.** the circumference of the body at the waist. **2.** the seam where the skirt and bodice of a dress are joined. **3.** an imaginary line encircling the waist.

wait (wāt), *v.i.* **1.** to remain inactive until something expected happens. **2.** to be available or in readiness. **3.** to be postponed or delayed. **4.** to work or serve as a waiter. —*v.t.* **5.** to await. **6.** to postpone or delay. **7.** to serve as waiter for. **8. wait on, a.** to attend to the needs of (a customer). **b.** to be an attendant or servant for. **9. ~ up,** to postpone going to bed to await a person or event. —*n.* **10.** an act or period of waiting. —*Idiom.* **11. lie in wait,** to wait in ambush. —*Proverb.* **12. Good things come to those who wait,** patience is a key factor in success.

wait′er, *n.* a person, esp. a man, who waits on tables, as in a restaurant.

wait′ing game′, *n.* a stratagem in which action is postponed with a view to gaining an advantage.

wait′ing room′, *n.* a room for the use of persons waiting, as in a railroad station.

wait•ress (wā′tris), *n.* a woman who waits on tables, as in a restaurant.

wait•ron (wā′tron, -trən), *n.* a waiter or waitress.

waive (wāv), *v.t.,* **waived, waiv•ing. 1.** to refrain from claiming or insisting on. **2.** to relinquish (a right) intentionally. **3.** to put off; defer.

waiv′er, *n.* **1.** the intentional relinquishment of a right. **2.** a written statement containing a waiver.

wake¹ (wāk), *v.,* **waked** or **woke, waked** or **wok•en, wak•ing,** *n.* —*v.i.* **1.** to become roused from sleep; awake. **2.** to become aware of something. **3.** to be or continue to be awake. —*v.t.* **4.** to rouse from or as if from sleep; awaken. —*n.* **5.** a vigil by the body of a dead person before burial.

wake² (wāk), *n.* **1.** the track of waves left by a moving ship or boat. **2.** the path or course of something that has passed or preceded. —*Idiom.* **3. in the wake of, a.** as a result of. **b.** close behind.

wake′ful, *adj.* **1.** unable to sleep. **2.** sleepless.

wak′en, *v.t., v.i.* to awake; awaken.

Wal′den Pond′ (wôl′dən), *n.* a pond in NE Massachusetts, near Concord: site of Thoreau's cottage.

wale (wāl), *n., v.,* **waled, wal•ing.** —*n.* **1.** a stripe produced on the skin by a rod or whip. **2.** a vertical rib or cord in woven cloth. **3.** the texture of a fabric. —*v.t.* **4.** to mark with wales.

Wales (wālz), *n.* a division of the United Kingdom, in SW Great Britain. 2,791,851.

Wa•łę•sa (və wen′sə), *n.* **Lech** (lek), born 1943, president of Poland 1990–95.

walk (wôk), *v.i.* **1.** to move on foot at a moderate pace. **2.** (in baseball) to receive a base on balls. **3.** to conduct one's life in a particular manner. —*v.t.* **4.** to proceed along, through, or over on foot. **5.** to cause or help to walk. **6.** to accompany on foot. **7.** (of a baseball pitcher) to give a base on balls to. **8. walk off** or **away with, a.** to steal. **b.** to win (a prize, competition, etc.), esp. with ease. **9. ~ out, a.** to go on strike. **b.** to leave in protest. **10. ~ out on,** to desert; forsake. —*n.* **11.** an act or instance of walking. **12.** a distance walked or to be walked: *a ten-minute walk from here.* **13.** a characteristic manner of walking. **14.** BASE ON BALLS. **15.** a place or path for walking. **16.** a branch of activity, line of work, or position in society: *in every walk of life.* —*Proverb.* **17. You have to learn to crawl before you can walk,** basic skills must be acquired before more advanced ones are possible. —**walk′er,** *n.*

walk′a•way′, *n.* an easy victory or conquest.

walk•ie-talk•ie (wô′kē tô′kē), *n., pl.* **-talk•ies.** a portable combined voice transmitter and receiver.

walk′ing stick′, *n.* **1.** a stick used for support in walking. **2.** any of several insects with a long, slender, twiglike body.

walk′-on′, *n.* a small part in a play, esp. a part without speaking lines.

walk′out′, *n.* a strike by workers.

walk′-up′, *n.* **1.** an apartment above the ground floor in a building with no elevator. **2.** a building, esp. an apartment house, with no elevator.

walk′way′, *n.* a passage for walking.

wall (wôl), *n.* **1.** an upright structure, as of brick, serving to shelter, divide, or protect. **2.** an immaterial or intangible barrier or obstruction. **3.** a wall-like part, thing, or mass. **4.** Usu., **walls.** a defensive rampart. —*v.t.* **5.** to enclose, border, or surround with or as if with a wall. **6.** to seal or fill (an opening) with a wall. —*Idiom.* **7. climb the walls,** *Informal.* to be frantic. **8. drive** or **push to the wall,** to force into a desperate situation. **9. off the wall,** *Slang.* **a.** unreasonable; crazy. **b.** eccentric; bizarre. **10. up the wall,** *Informal.* into a state of frantic frustration. —**walled,** *adj.*

wal•la•by (wol′ə bē), *n., pl.* **-bies, -by.** any of various small to medium-sized marsupials of the kangaroo family. [< Dharuk (Australian Aboriginal language) *wa-la-ba*]

Wal•lace (wol′is, wô′lis), *n.* **1. George (Corley),** 1919–98, U.S. politician: governor of Alabama 1963–67, 1971–79, and 1983–87. **2. Henry (Agard),** 1888–1965, U.S. agriculturalist, author, and statesman: Secretary of Agriculture 1933–40; vice president of the U.S. 1941–45; Secretary of Commerce 1945–46. **3. (William Roy) DeWitt,** 1889–1981, and his wife, **Lila Bell (Acheson),** 1889–1984, U.S. magazine publishers.

wall′board′, *n.* material manufactured in large sheets for use in covering walls and ceilings.

Wal•ler (wol′ər, wô′lər), *n.* **Thomas** ("*Fats*"), 1904–43, U.S. jazz pianist and songwriter.

wal•let (wol′it, wô′lit), *n.* a flat, folding case with compartments, as for paper money and credit cards.

wall′eye′, *n., pl.* **-eyes,** for 1 also **-eye. 1.** Also called **wall′eyed pike′.** a North American game fish with large eyes. **2.** a condition in which the eye or eyes are turned outward. —**wall′eyed′,** *adj.*

wall′flow′er, *n.* **1.** a person who remains at the side at a party or dance, esp. from shyness. **2.** a European plant of the mustard family, bearing sweet-scented yellow or orange flowers.

Wal•loon (wo lōōn′), *n.* **1.** a member of the French-speaking population of S and E Belgium. **2.** their French dialect.

wal•lop (wol′əp), *v.t.* **1.** to beat soundly; thrash. **2.** to strike hard; sock. —*n.* **3.** a hard blow. **4.** the ability to deliver hard blows. **5.** *Informal.* a forceful impression; impact.

wal•lop•ing, *adj. Informal* **1.** very large; whopping. **2.** very fine; impressive.

wal•low (wol′ō), *v.i.* **1.** to roll around, as in mud. **2.** to indulge oneself; luxuriate. —*n.* **3.** an act or instance of wallowing. **4.** a place in which animals wallow.

wall′pa′per, *n.* **1.** paper, usu. with decorative patterns, for covering walls or ceilings. —*v.t.* **2.** to put wallpaper on or in.

Wall′ Street′, *n.* a street in New York City: the major financial center of the U.S.

wall′-to-wall′, *adj.* **1.** covering the entire floor. **2.** *Informal.* **a.** occupying a space completely. **b.** being everywhere.

wal•nut (wôl′nut′, -nət), *n.* **1.** a meaty, edible nut with a hard, wrinkled shell. **2.** a tree bearing walnuts. **3.** the wood of a walnut, used esp. in making furniture.

wal•rus (wôl′rəs, wol′-), *n., pl.* **-rus•es, -rus.** a large mammal of arctic seas, having large tusks and a tough, wrinkled hide. [< D: lit., whale-horse]

waltz (wôlts), *n.* **1.** a ballroom dance in moderately fast triple meter. **2.** music for or in the rhythm of the waltz. —*v.i., v.t.* **3.** to dance a waltz (with). **4.** to move or progress easily.

wam•pum (wom′pəm, wôm′-), *n.* beads made of pierced and strung shells, once used by North American Indians as a medium of exchange.

wan (won), *adj.,* **wan•ner, wan•nest. 1.** unnaturally pale; ashen. **2.** showing ill health or fatigue: *a wan smile.* —**wan′ly,** *adv.*

WAN (wan), *n.* WIDE-AREA NETWORK.

Wan•a•ma•ker (won′ə mā′kər), *n.* **John,** 1838–1922, U.S. merchant.

wand (wond), *n.* **1.** a slender rod, esp. one used by a magician or conjurer. **2.** a staff carried as an emblem of office or authority.

wan•der (won′dər), *v.i.* **1.** to move around without a definite purpose or objective; roam. **2.** to go or extend in an irregular course or direction. **3.** to stray, as from a path or subject. **4.** to deviate in conduct or belief; go astray. —*v.t.* **5.** to travel about, on, or through. —**wan′der•er,** *n.*

Wan′dering Jew′, *n.* any of various trailing or creeping plants with green or variegated leaves.

wan′der•lust′, *n.* a strong desire to travel.

wane (wān), *v.,* **waned, wan•ing,** *n.* —*v.i.* **1.** to decrease, as in strength or intensity. **2.** to decline in power or importance. **3.** to draw to a close. **4.** (of the moon) to decrease periodically in brightness and roundness after the full moon. —*n.* **5.** an act or period of waning.

wan•gle (wang′gəl), *v.t.,* **-gled, -gling. 1.** to bring about or obtain by scheming or underhand methods. **2.** to manipulate for dishonest ends. —**wan′gler,** *n.*

Wan′kel en′gine (wäng′kəl, wang′-), *n.* an internal-combustion rotary engine with a triangular rotor that revolves in a chamber. [after F. *Wankel* (1902–88), German inventor]

wan•na•be (won′ə bē′, wô′nə-), *n., pl.* **-bes.** *Informal.* one who aspires, often vainly, to emulate another's success or attain eminence in some area.

want (wont, wônt), *v.t.* **1.** to feel a need for; wish or desire. **2.** to request the presence of. **3.** to be deficient in. **4.** to require. —*v.i.* **5.** to feel inclined. **6.** to have need. **7.** to be in a state of poverty. —*n.* **8.** something wanted or needed. **9.** deficiency; lack. **10.** a state of destitution; poverty.

want′ ad′, *n.* CLASSIFIED AD.

want′ing, *adj.* **1.** lacking or absent. **2.** deficient. —*prep.* **3.** lacking; without. **4.** less; minus.

wan•ton (won′tn), *adj.* **1.** malicious or unjustifiable; inhumane: *wanton cruelty.* **2.** without motive; unprovoked: *a wanton attack.* **3.** lascivious; lewd. **4.** extravagant or excessive: *wanton luxury.* —*n.* **5.** a wanton person, esp. a lascivious woman. —**wan′ton•ly,** *adv.* —**wan′ton•ness,** *n.*

wap•i•ti (wop′i tē), *n., pl.* **-tis, -ti.** ELK (def. 1).

war (wôr), *n., v.,* **warred, war•ring.** —*n.* **1.** armed conflict between nations or factions. **2.** the science or profession of armed fighting. **3.** any conflict or struggle. —*v.i.* **4.** to make or carry on war.

War′ Between′ the States′, *n.* the American Civil War: used esp. in the South.

war•ble (wôr′bəl), *v.,* **-bled, -bling,** *n.* —*v.i., v.t.* **1.** to sing or whistle with trills or melodic embellishments. —*n.* **2.** a warbled song or trill.

war′bler, *n.* **1.** any of numerous small New World songbirds, often brightly colored. **2.** any of numerous small, chiefly Old World songbirds.

war′bon′net or **war′ bon′net,** *n.* an American Indian headdress consisting of a headband with trailing feathers.

Ward (wôrd), *n.* **(Aaron) Montgomery,** 1843–1913, U.S. mail-order retailer.

war•den (wôr′dn), *n.* **1.** the chief administrative officer of a prison. **2.** an official charged with the enforcement of regulations: *a fire warden.*

ward′er, *n.* a person who guards something; watchman.

ward′ heel′er, *n.* a minor politician who does chores for a political machine.

ward′robe′, *n.* **1.** a collection of clothes or costumes. **2.** a piece of furniture or closet in which to keep clothes.

ward′room′, *n.* (on a warship) the living and dining quarters for all commissioned officers except the commanding officer.

ware (wâr), *n.* **1.** Usu., **wares.** merchandise; goods.

2. a particular kind of merchandise: *glassware.* **3.** pottery: *delft ware.*

ware•house (*n.,* wâr′hous′; *v.* -houz′, -hous′), *n., v.,* **-housed, -hous•ing.** —*n.* **1.** a building for the storage of goods or merchandise. **2.** a large and usu. public custodial institution, as for the mentally ill. —*v.t.* **3.** to place, deposit, or store in a warehouse.

war′fare′, *n.* **1.** armed conflict between enemies. **2.** conflict, esp. when unrelenting, between competitors or rivals.

war′head′, *n.* the section of a missile, as a bomb, containing the explosive or payload.

war′-horse′, *n.* **1.** a horse used in war. **2.** *Informal.* a veteran of many conflicts, as a soldier or politician.

war′like′, *adj.* **1.** fond of war; bellicose. **2.** threatening war. **3.** of or used in war.

war•lock (wär′lok′), *n.* a male witch.

war′lord′, *n.* **1.** a military commander. **2.** (esp. formerly in China) a military commander who has seized control of a region.

warm (wôrm), *adj.,* **-er, -est,** *v.* —*adj.* **1.** having or giving out moderate heat. **2.** having a sensation of bodily heat. **3.** conserving warmth: *warm clothes.* **4.** suggestive of warmth; friendly, affectionate, sympathetic, or hearty: *a warm welcome.* **5.** heated or angry. **6.** strong or fresh: *a warm scent.* **7.** close to something sought, as in a game. **8.** uncomfortable or unpleasant. —*v.t., v.i.* **9.** to make or become warm. **10. warm up, a.** to prepare for strenuous exercise by engaging in moderate exercise. **b.** to increase in excitement, intensity, or violence. —**warm′er,** *n.* —**warm′ish,** *adj.* —**warm′ly,** *adv.*

warm′-blood′ed, *adj.* of or designating an animal, as a mammal, having a relatively constant body temperature that is independent of the environment.

warmed′-o′ver, *adj.* **1.** reheated: *warmed-over stew.* **2.** lacking freshness; stale: *a warmed-over plot.*

warm′ front′, *n.* a transition zone between a mass of warm air and the colder air it is replacing.

warm′heart′ed, *adj.* having or showing emotional warmth.

war′mon′ger, *n.* a person who advocates war. —**war′mon′ger•ing,** *n., adj.*

warmth (wôrmth), *n.* **1.** the quality or state of being warm. **2.** ardor; enthusiasm. **3.** an effect of brightness and cheer achieved esp. by the use of colors such as red and yellow.

warm′-up′, *n.* an act or instance of warming up.

warn (wôrn), *v.t.* **1.** to give advance notice to, esp. of impending danger or possible harm. **2.** to advise to be careful; admonish. **3.** to direct to go or stay away. —*v.i.* **4.** to give a warning.

warn′ing, *n.* **1.** the act of one that warns. **2.** something that serves to warn. —*adj.* **3.** being a warning: *a warning bell.*

War of 1812, *n.* the war between the United States and Great Britain from 1812 to 1815.

warp (wôrp), *v.t.* **1.** to bend or twist out of shape. **2.** to turn away from what is right or proper. —*v.i.* **3.** to become warped. —*n.* **4.** a bend or twist in something formerly straight or flat. **5.** a mental bias or quirk. **6.** the lengthwise threads in a loom or woven fabric.

war′ paint′, *n.* paint applied by American Indians to their faces and bodies before going to war.

war′path′, *n.* **1.** the path or course taken by American Indians on a warlike expedition. —*Idiom.* **2. on the warpath,** ready to fight.

war•rant (wôr′ənt, wor′-), *n.* **1.** authorization, sanction, or justification. **2.** something providing formal assurance; guarantee. **3.** a writ authorizing an officer to make an arrest or search or seize property. —*v.t.* **4.** to authorize. **5.** to be sufficient reason for; justify. **6.** to vouch for. **7.** to give a formal assurance or guarantee of. **8.** to guarantee (something sold) to be as represented.

war′rant of′ficer, *n.* an officer in the armed forces ranking below a commissioned officer.

war•ran•ty (wôr′ən tē, wor′-), *n., pl.* **-ties.** a written guarantee given to a purchaser specifying that the manufacturer will make repairs or replace defective parts free of charge for a stated period of time.

war•ren (wôr'ən, wor'-), *n.* **1.** a place where rabbits breed or abound. **2.** a crowded building or area.

War'ren, *n.* a city in SE Michigan. 142,625.

war•ri•or (wôr'ē ər, wor'-), *n.* a person engaged or experienced in warfare; soldier.

War•saw (wôr'sô), *n.* the capital of Poland. 2,432,000.

war'ship', *n.* a ship armed for combat.

Wars' of the Ros'es, *n.pl.* the conflict (1455–85) between the English royal houses of Lancaster and York, ending with the accession of Henry VII and the union of the two houses.

wart (wôrt), *n.* **1.** a small, often hard growth on the skin, usu. caused by a virus. **2.** a small protuberance, as on the surface of certain plants. —**wart'y,** *adj.,* -i•er, -i•est.

Wart•burg (värt'bŏŏrk'), *n.* a castle in Thuringia, Germany: Luther translated the New Testament here 1521–22.

wart'hog', *n.* a wild African swine with large tusks and warty facial outgrowths.

war' to end' all' wars', *n.* epithet of World War I.

war•y (wâr'ē), *adj.,* -i•er, -i•est. **1.** being on guard; watchful. **2.** characterized by caution. —**war'i•ly,** *adv.* —**war'i•ness,** *n.*

was (wuz, woz; *unstressed* wəz), *v.* 1st and 3rd pers. sing. past indic. of BE.

wash (wosh, wôsh), *v.t.* **1.** to cleanse by dipping, rubbing, or scrubbing in liquid, esp. water. **2.** to remove by or as if by the action of water. **3.** to moisten or wet. **4.** to flow through, over, or against. **5.** to carry or deposit by the action of water. **6.** to overlay with a thin coat, as of metal. —*v.i.* **7.** to wash oneself. **8.** to wash clothes. **9.** to undergo washing without damage. **10.** *Informal.* to prove true when subjected to testing: *His alibi simply won't wash.* **11.** to be carried or driven by water. **12.** to move along in or as if in waves. **13.** to be removed by the action of water. —*n.* **14.** the act or process of washing. **15.** items, as clothes, washed or to be washed at one time. **16. a.** the dash or breaking of water. **b.** the sound made by this. **17.** water moving in waves or with a rushing movement. **18.** the wake of a moving boat. **19.** a disturbance in the air caused by a moving airplane. **20.** a liquid for grooming or medicinal purposes. **21.** Also, **washing.** a thin coat, as of color or metal. **22.** waste liquid matter, as for hogs; swill. —*adj.* **23.** capable of being washed. —**wash'a•ble,** *adj.*

Wash., Washington.

wash'board', *n.* a board with a corrugated metal surface on which clothes are scrubbed.

wash'bowl', *n.* a large bowl for washing the hands and face. Also called **wash'ba'sin.**

wash'cloth', *n.* a cloth for washing the face or body.

washed'-out', *adj.* **1.** faded, esp. from washing. **2.** *Informal.* weary or tired-looking.

washed'-up', *adj. Informal.* done for; having failed.

wash'er, *n.* **1.** one that washes. **2.** WASHING MACHINE. **3.** a flat ring used, as under a bolt, to give tightness to a joint, prevent leakage, etc.

wash'er•wom'an, *n., pl.* -wom•en. a woman whose work is washing clothes.

wash'ing, *n.* **1.** the act of one that washes. **2.** items washed or to be washed.

wash'ing machine', *n.* an apparatus, esp. a household appliance, for washing clothing, linens, etc.

wash'ing so'da, *n.* SODIUM CARBONATE (def. 2).

Wash•ing•ton (wosh'ing tən, wô'shing-), *n.* **1.** George, 1732–99, U.S. general: 1st president of the U.S. 1789–97. **2.** Also called **Washington, D.C.** the capital of the United States: coextensive with the District of Columbia. 567,094. **3.** a state in the NW United States. 5,532,939. *Cap.:* Olympia. *Abbr.:* WA, Wash. —**Wash'ing•to'ni•an** (-tō'nē ən), *n., adj.*

wash'out', *n.* **1.** a washing out of earth by water,

as from an embankment. **2.** *Informal.* a complete failure.

wash'room', *n.* a room with washbowls and toilet facilities.

wash'stand', *n.* a piece of furniture holding a basin and pitcher of water for use in washing the hands and face.

wash'tub', *n.* a tub for use in washing clothes.

wash'y, *adj.,* -i•er, -i•est. **1.** diluted too much; weak. **2.** lacking color; pale. **3.** lacking strength; weak.

was•n't (wuz'ənt, woz'-), contraction of *was not.*

wasp (wosp), *n.* a slender winged insect with a narrowed abdomen, the female inflicting a painful sting.

WASP or **Wasp** (wosp), *n.* a white Anglo-Saxon Protestant.

wasp'ish, *adj.* **1.** like or suggesting a wasp. **2.** snappish or peevish; testy.

was•sail (wos'əl, wo säl'), *n.* **1.** a former English toast to a person's health. **2.** liquor used in such a toast. **3.** a festivity with much drinking. —*v.i., v.t.* **4.** to drink a toast.

Was'ser•mann test' (wä'sər mən), *n.* a diagnostic test for syphilis.

wast•age (wā'stij), *n.* **1.** loss by use, wear, decay, or wastefulness. **2.** something wasted; waste matter.

waste (wāst), *v.,* wast•ed, wast•ing, *n., adj.* —*v.t.* **1.** to consume, spend, or use to no avail or profit; squander. **2.** to fail to use: *Never waste an opportunity.* **3.** to consume gradually; wear away. **4.** to make feeble or thin: *wasted by disease.* **5.** to devastate or ruin. —*v.i.* **6.** to be consumed, spent, or used uselessly or carelessly. **7.** to become gradually used up or worn away. **8.** to become emaciated or enfeebled. —*n.* **9.** an act or instance of wasting. **10.** devastation or ruin. **11.** a devastated area. **12.** desolate country, as desert. **13.** something left over or superfluous: *factory wastes.* **14.** garbage; refuse. **15.** wastes, excrement. —*adj.* **16.** wild; desolate. **17.** left over; superfluous. **18.** rejected as useless or worthless. **19.** unused by or unusable to the organism. **20.** designed to receive or carry away waste. —**wast'er,** *n.*

waste'bas'ket, *n.* an open receptacle for trash, esp. wastepaper. Also called **waste'paper bas'ket.**

waste'ful, *adj.* given to or characterized by waste. —**waste'ful•ly,** *adv.* —**waste'ful•ness,** *n.*

waste'land', *n.* uncultivated or barren land.

waste'pa'per, *n.* paper discarded as useless.

wast•rel (wā'strəl), *n.* a wasteful person; spendthrift.

watch (woch), *v.i.* **1.** to look attentively; observe. **2.** to wait attentively and expectantly: *We watched for the signal.* **3.** to be careful or cautious. **4.** to keep awake; stay vigilant. —*v.t.* **5.** to view attentively or with interest. **6.** to wait attentively and expectantly for. **7.** to guard or tend: *Watch the baby.* **8. watch out,** to be cautious. —*n.* **9.** close, continuous observation. **10.** vigilant guard. **11.** a keeping awake. **12.** a portable timepiece, as a wristwatch. **13. a.** a period of time, usu. four hours, during which a part of a ship's crew is on duty. **b.** the crew on duty during this time. **14.** a lookout, guard, or sentinel. —*Proverb.* **15. A watched pot never boils,** impatient hovering only seems to make something take longer. —**watch'er,** *n.*

watch'band', *n.* a bracelet or strap for holding a wristwatch on the wrist.

watch'dog', *n.* **1.** a dog kept to guard property. **2.** a watchful guardian, as against illegal or unethical conduct.

watch'dog commit'tee, *n.* a legislative committee that investigates government expenditures.

watch'ful, *adj.* vigilant or alert; observant. —**watch'ful•ly,** *adv.* —**watch'ful•ness,** *n.*

watch'man, *n., pl.* -men. a person who keeps watch, esp. at night.

watch'tow'er, *n.* a tower for a sentinel or guard.

watch'word', *n.* **1.** a password. **2.** a slogan.

wa•ter (wô'tər, wot'ər), *n.* **1.** an odorless, tasteless liquid compound of hydrogen and oxygen that constitutes rain, oceans, lakes, and rivers. **2.** Often, **waters.** water obtained from a mineral spring. **3.** a body of water, as an ocean. **4. waters,** the sea bordering on and controlled by a country. **5.** a liquid or aqueous organic secretion, as urine. **6.** a wavy, lustrous pattern, as on silk. —*v.t.* **7.** to sprinkle or drench with water. **8.** to supply (animals) with drinking water. **9.** to dilute or weaken with or as if with water. **10.** to produce a wavy, lustrous pattern on. —*v.i.* **11.** to fill with or secrete water or liquid: *Her eyes watered.* **12.** to drink water. —*Idiom.* **13. hold water,** to be capable of being substantiated or defended.

wa'ter•bed', *n.* a bed with a liquid-filled mattress.

wa'ter buf'falo, *n.* a widely domesticated Asian buffalo with large, curved horns.

Wa•ter•bur•y (wô'tər ber'ē, -bə rē, wot'ər-), *n.* a city in W Connecticut. 103,523.

wa'ter chest'nut, *n.* **1.** an Old World aquatic plant with an edible, nutlike fruit. **2.** the fruit itself.

wa'ter clos'et, *n.* a room or compartment containing a toilet bowl with a mechanism for flushing.

wa'ter•col'or, *n.* **1.** a pigment for which water and not oil is the vehicle. **2.** the art of painting with watercolors. **3.** a picture done with watercolors.

wa'ter•course', *n.* **1.** a stream of water. **2.** the bed of a stream.

wa'ter•craft', *n.* **1.** skill in boating and water sports. **2.** a boat or ship.

wa'ter•cress', *n.* a plant that grows in clear, running streams and bears pungent leaves used esp. in salads.

wa'ter•fall', *n.* a steep fall of water from a height, as over a precipice.

wa'ter•fowl', *n., pl.* **-fowl, -fowls. 1.** an aquatic bird. **2.** aquatic birds collectively.

wa'ter•front', *n.* a part of a city or town on the edge of a body of water, esp. an ocean.

wa'ter gap', *n.* a transverse gap in a mountain ridge, giving passage to a stream or river.

Wa'ter•gate', *n.* **1.** a scandal arising from a break-in at Democratic headquarters at the Watergate building complex in Washington, D.C., in 1972. **2.** any scandal involving corruption, abuses of power, and a cover-up.

wa'ter lil'y, *n.* an aquatic plant with large, disklike floating leaves and showy flowers.

wa'ter line', *n.* one of a series of lines on a ship's hull indicating the level to which it is immersed.

wa'ter•logged', *adj.* so filled with water as to be heavy or unmanageable.

Wa•ter•loo (wô'tər lōō', wot'ər-), *n.* **1.** a village in central Belgium: Napoleon decisively defeated here in 1815. **2.** a crushing defeat.

wa'ter main', *n.* a main pipe for conveying water.

wa'ter•mark', *n.* **1.** a design impressed on paper that is visible when the paper is held to the light. **2.** a line indicating the height to which water has risen. —*v.t.* **3.** to mark with a watermark.

wa'ter•mel'on, *n.* a large melon with a hard, green rind and sweet, juicy, usu. red pulp.

wa'ter moc'casin, *n.* the cottonmouth.

wa'ter pipe', *n.* **1.** a pipe for conveying water. **2.** a tobacco pipe in which the smoke is drawn through water before reaching the mouth.

wa'ter po'lo, *n.* an aquatic game played with an inflated ball by two teams of swimmers.

wa'ter pow'er or **wa'ter•pow'er,** *n.* the power of water used to drive machinery.

wa'ter•proof', *adj.* **1.** impervious to water. —*v.t.* **2.** to make waterproof. —**wa'ter•proof'ing,** *n.*

wa'ter rat', *n.* any of various aquatic rodents, as the muskrat.

wa'ter•repel'lent, *adj.* repelling water but not entirely waterproof.

wa'ter•shed', *n.* **1.** a region or area drained by a river or stream. **2.** a ridge dividing two drainage areas. **3.** an important point of division or transition.

wa'ter•side', *n.* the bank or shore of a river, lake, or ocean.

wa'ter ski', *n.* a short, broad ski on which to glide over water while being towed by a speedboat. —**wa'ter-ski',** *v.i.,* **-skied, -ski•ing.** —**wa'ter-ski'er,** *n.*

wa'ter•spout', *n.* **1.** a spout, duct, or pipe from which water is discharged. **2.** a whirling, funnel-shaped cloud that touches the surface of a body of water, drawing upward spray and mist.

wa'ter ta'ble, *n.* the underground level beneath which soil and rock are saturated with water.

wa'ter•tight', *adj.* **1.** constructed or fitted so tightly as to be impervious to water. **2.** incapable of being nullified or discredited: *a watertight alibi.*

wa'ter tow'er, *n.* a high tower with a tank for storing water.

wa'ter•way', *n.* a body of water serving as a travel or transport route.

wa'ter wheel', *n.* a wheel turned by the weight or momentum of water and used to operate machinery.

wa'ter wings', *n.pl.* an inflatable contrivance worn to keep the body afloat.

wa'ter•works', *n., pl.* **-works.** (*used with a sing. or pl. v.*) a system, as of reservoirs, pipelines, and conduits, by which water is collected, purified, stored, and pumped to urban users.

wa'ter•y, *adj.* **1.** of, consisting of, or full of water. **2.** containing too much water. **3.** resembling water.

WATS (wots), *n.* a service providing unlimited long-distance telephone calls for a fixed monthly charge.

Watt (wot), *n.* **James,** 1736–1819, Scottish engineer and inventor.

watt'age (-ij), *n.* electric power measured in watts.

wat•tle¹ (wot'l), *n.* Often, **-tles.** rods interwoven with twigs or branches and used esp. for making fences and walls. —**wat'tled,** *adj.*

wat•tle² (wot'l), *n.* a fleshy lobe hanging down from the head or neck of certain birds, as the turkey.

Watts (wots), *n.* **Isaac,** 1674–1748, English theologian and hymn writer.

wave (wāv), *n., v.,* **waved, wav•ing.** —*n.* **1.** a moving ridge or swell on the surface of water. **2.** a movement or part resembling a wave: *waves of grain; a wave in her hair.* **3.** a swell, surge, or rush: *a wave of disgust.* **4.** an outward curve, as in a surface. **5.** an act or instance of waving. **6.** a period of unusually hot or cold weather. **7.** *Physics.* a progressive disturbance propagated from point to point in a medium or space, as in the transmission of sound or light. —*v.i.* **8.** to move back and forth or up and down: *flags waving in the wind.* **9.** to curve alternately in opposite directions. **10.** to signal by moving the hand to and fro. —*v.t.* **11.** to cause to wave. **12.** to signal or express by a waving movement: *We all waved good-bye.* —*Idiom.* **13. make waves,** *Informal.* to disturb the status quo.

wave'length', *n.* the distance, measured in the direction of propagation of a wave, between two successive points in the wave.

wave'let (-lit), *n.* a small wave.

wa•ver (wā'vər), *v.i.* **1.** to sway to and fro. **2.** to flicker or quiver, as light. **3.** to be unsteady; falter. **4.** to tremble, as the voice. **5.** to feel or show doubt or indecision. —*n.* **6.** an act of wavering.

wav'y, *adj.,* **-i•er, -i•est.** having, moving in, characterized by, or resembling waves. —**wav'i•ness,** *n.*

wax¹ (waks), *n.* **1.** a solid, yellowish substance secreted by bees in constructing their honeycomb. **2.** any of various similar substances, esp. ones composed of hydrocarbons. **3.** earwax. —*v.t.* **4.** to rub, polish, or treat with wax.

wax² (waks), *v.i.* **1.** to increase, as in extent or intensity. **2.** (of the moon) to increase gradually in brightness and roundness before the full moon. **3.** to become: *waxing resentful.*

wax' bean', *n.* a variety of string bean bearing yellowish, waxy pods.

wax'en, *adj.* **1.** made of or covered with wax. **2.** pallid.

wax' muse'um, *n.* a museum in which wax effigies of famous persons are exhibited.

wax′ myr′tle, *n.* a bayberry of the southeastern U.S. bearing waxy berries used in candlemaking.

wax′ pa′per, *n.* paper made moisture-resistant by a paraffin coating.

wax′wing′, *n.* a crested songbird having wing feathers tipped with a red, waxy substance.

wax′work′, *n.* **1.** a life-size wax effigy of a person. **2.** waxworks, a wax museum.

wax′y, *adj.,* **-i•er, -i•est. 1.** resembling wax. **2.** full of, covered with, or made of wax. —**wax′i•ness,** *n.*

way¹ (wā), *n.* **1.** manner, mode, or fashion. **2.** a characteristic or habitual manner of acting, living, etc. **3.** a method or means for attaining a goal. **4.** a respect or particular: *defective in several ways.* **5.** a direction or vicinity: *He went that way.* **6.** passage or progress on a course: *Lead the way.* **7.** Often, **ways.** distance: *a long way from home.* **8.** a path or course: *the shortest way to town.* **9.** one's preferred manner of acting or doing: *He always gets his own way.* **10.** condition; state: *He's in a bad way.* **11.** space for passing or advancing: *cleared a way through the crowd.* **12. the Way,** Jesus. John 14:6. —*Idiom.* **13. by the way,** incidentally. **14. by way of,** by the route of; through. **15. give way, a.** to withdraw or retreat. **b.** to break down; collapse. **16. under way, a.** in motion; traveling. **b.** in progress; proceeding.

way² (wā), *adv.* to a great degree or at quite a distance: *way too heavy; way down the road.*

way′far′er, *n.* a traveler, esp. on foot. —**way′far′-ing,** *adj., n.*

way•lay (wā′lā′, wā lā′), *v.t.,* **-laid, -lay•ing. 1.** to intercept or attack from ambush. **2.** to await and accost unexpectedly. —**way′lay′er,** *n.*

Wayne (wān), *n.* **1. Anthony** (*"Mad Anthony"*), 1745–96, American Revolutionary War general. **2. John** (*Marion Michael Morrison*) (*"Duke"*), 1907–79, U.S. film actor.

way′-out′, *adj. Informal.* very unconventional.

-ways, a suffix meaning in a specified direction, manner, or position (*sideways*).

ways′ and means′, *n.pl.* methods of raising revenue, esp. for the use of a government.

way′side′, *n.* land adjacent to a road or highway.

way′ sta′tion, *n.* a station intermediate between principal stations, as on a railroad.

way′ward (-wərd), *adj.* **1.** stubbornly willful; disobedient. **2.** capricious or erratic. —**way′ward•ly,** *adv.* —**way′ward•ness,** *n.*

WC, water closet.

we (wē), *pron.pl., poss.* **our** or **ours,** *obj.* **us. 1.** nominative plural of I. **2.** (used to denote oneself and another or others): *We attended a concert.* **3.** (used in place of *I* by a sovereign, an editor, or a writer):

weak (wēk), *adj.,* **-er, -est. 1.** liable to give way under pressure or strain. **2.** lacking in strength or vigor; feeble. **3.** lacking in force, intensity, or efficacy: *a weak president.* **4.** lacking in logical or legal force: *a weak argument.* **5.** deficient in intelligence or judgment: *a weak mind.* **6.** lacking in moral strength or force of character: *too weak to resist temptation.* **7.** deficient in ability or skill: *weak in spelling.* **8.** deficient in the essential or usual properties or ingredients: *weak tea.* —**weak′ly,** *adv.*

weak′en, *v.t., v.i.* to make or become weak or weaker. —**weak′en•er,** *n.*

weak′fish′, *n., pl.* **-fish, -fish•es.** a food fish of U.S. Atlantic and Gulf coasts.

weak′-kneed′, *adj.* yielding readily to opposition, pressure, or intimidation.

weak′ling (-ling), *n.* a person who is physically or morally weak.

weak′ness, *n.* **1.** the state or quality of being weak. **2.** a slight fault or defect. **3.** a special fondness.

weal¹ (wēl), *n.* well-being, prosperity, or happiness.

weal² (wēl), *n.* WHEAL.

wealth (welth), *n.* **1.** abundance of money, property, or possessions. **2.** plentiful amount; abundance: *a wealth of imagery.* **3.** all things with monetary or exchange value. **4.** valuable contents or produce.

wealth′y, *adj.,* **-i•er, -i•est.** having great wealth; rich. —**wealth′i•ness,** *n.*

wean (wēn), *v.t.* **1.** to accustom (a child or young animal) to food other than the mother's milk. **2.** to rid of an undesirable object or practice.

weap•on (wep′ən), *n.* **1.** an instrument or device used for attack or defense. **2.** something used against an opponent or adversary. —**weap′on•less,** *adj.*

weap′on•ry, *n.* weapons collectively.

wear (wâr), *v.,* **wore, worn, wear•ing,** *n.* —*v.t.* **1.** to have on the body as clothing, covering, or ornament. **2.** to bear or have in one's aspect or appearance: *wore a big smile.* **3. a.** to cause to deteriorate by a constant or repetitive action. **b.** to make (a hole, channel, etc.) by such action. **4.** to weary; fatigue: *worn by illness.* —*v.i.* **5.** to deteriorate from or as if from use. **6.** to withstand continued use or strain: *fabric that wears well.* **7.** (of time) to pass slowly or tediously. **8. wear down,** to overcome by persistence. **9. ~ off,** to diminish slowly or gradually. —*n.* **10.** the act of wearing or state of being worn. **11.** clothing of a particular kind: *winter wear.* **12.** gradual deterioration, as from use. **13.** the quality of withstanding use; durability. —**wear′a•ble,** *adj.* —**wear′er,** *n.*

wear′ and tear′ (târ), *n.* damage or deterioration from ordinary use.

wea•ri•some (wēr′ē səm), *adj.* causing weariness; tedious. —**wea′ri•some•ly,** *adv.*

wea′ry, *adj.,* **-ri•er, -ri•est,** *v.,* **-ried, -ry•ing.** —*adj.* **1.** physically or mentally exhausted. **2.** characterized by or causing fatigue. **3.** impatient or dissatisfied: *weary of excuses.* —*v.t., v.i.* **4.** to make or become weary. —**wea′ri•ly,** *adv.* —**wea′ri•ness,** *n.*

wea•sel (wē′zəl), *n., pl.* **-sels, -sel. 1.** a small carnivore, as a ferret or mink, having a long, slender body. —*v.i.* **2.** to evade an obligation or duty. **3.** to be evasive or ambiguous. —**wea′sel•ly,** *adj.*

weath•er (wefh′ər), *n.* **1.** the state of the atmosphere with respect to wind, temperature, moisture, etc. **2.** a strong wind or storm. —*v.t.* **3.** to expose to or affect by exposure to the weather. **4.** to come safely through. —*v.i.* **5.** to endure or resist exposure to the weather.

weath′er-beat′en, *adj.* **1.** worn or damaged by exposure to the weather. **2.** tanned and toughened by exposure to the weather.

weath′er•cock′, *n.* a weather vane in the form of a rooster.

weath′er•ing, *n.* the action of natural agents, as wind and water, on exposed rock.

weath′er•ize′, *v.t.,* **-ized, -iz•ing.** to make (a building) secure against cold weather, as by adding insulation.

weath′er•man′, *n., pl.* **-men.** a meteorologist.

weath′er•proof′ (wefh′ər prōōf′), *adj.* **1.** able to withstand exposure to all kinds of weather. —*v.t.* **2.** to make weatherproof.

weath′er strip′ (or **strip′ping**), *n.* a narrow strip, as of metal, placed between a door or window sash and its frame to exclude rain, wind, and snow. —**weath′er-strip′,** *v.t.,* **-stripped, -strip•ping.**

weath′er vane′, *n.* a rod to which a freely rotating pointer is attached, for indicating the direction of the wind.

weave (wēv), *v.,* **wove** or (*esp. for 6, 8*) **weaved; wo•ven** or **wove; weav•ing;** *n.* —*v.t.* **1.** to interlace (threads, strands, etc.) so as to form a fabric. **2.** to form by weaving: *to weave a basket.* **3.** (of a spider or larva) to spin (a web or cocoon). **4.** to combine into a connected whole. **5.** to introduce as an element. **6.** to make or move by winding or zigzagging. —*v.i.* **7.** to form or construct something by weaving. **8.** to move in a winding or zigzagging course. —*n.* **9.** a pattern of or method for weaving. —**weav′er,** *n.*

web (web), *n., v.,* **webbed, web•bing.** —*n.* **1.** a fabric formed by weaving. **2.** a cobweb. **3.** something that snares or entangles: *a web of lies.* **4.** a membrane connecting the digits of an animal, as an aquatic bird. **5.** an intricate network: *a web of tiny wrinkles.* **6.** (*usu. cap.*) World Wide Web (usu. prec. by *the*). —*v.t.* **7.** to cover with or as if with a web. —**webbed,** *adj.*

web/bing, n. a strong woven material used esp. for belts, straps, and harnesses.

web/foot/, n., pl. **-feet.** a foot with the toes joined by a web. **—web/-foot/ed,** adj.

Web/ page/, n. **1.** a single document on the World Wide Web that can incorporate text, graphics, sounds, etc. **2.** WEB SITE.

Web/ site/ or **web/site/,** n. a group of pages on the World Wide Web regarded as a single entity, devoted to one topic or several closely related topics.

Web•ster (web/stər), n. **1. Daniel,** 1782–1852, U.S. statesman and orator. **2. Noah,** 1758–1843, U.S. lexicographer and essayist.

wed (wed), v.t., v.i., **wed•ded** or **wed, wed•ding. 1.** to marry. **2.** to unite.

we'd (wēd), contraction of *we had, we should,* or *we would.*

Wed., Wednesday.

wed/ding, n. **1.** the act or ceremony of marrying. **2.** the anniversary of a marriage or its celebration.

wedge (wej), n., v., **wedged, wedg•ing. —**n. **1.** a tapered triangular piece of hard material used for raising, holding, or splitting objects. **2.** something shaped like a wedge. **3.** something that serves to part, split, or divide. **—**v.t. **4.** to split with or as if with a wedge. **5.** to insert or fix firmly with a wedge. **6.** to pack tightly into a narrow space. **—**v.i **7.** to force a way like a wedge.

wed/lock/, n. the state of being married; matrimony.

Wednes•day (wenz/dā, -dē), n. the fourth day of the week.

wee (wē), adj., **we•er, we•est. 1.** very small; tiny. **2.** very early: *the wee hours of the morning.*

weed (wēd), n. **1.** an undesirable plant growing wild, esp. to the disadvantage of a crop, lawn, or flower bed. **—**v.t. **2.** to free from weeds. **3.** to remove as being undesirable or superfluous: *weeded out inexperienced players.* **—**v.i. **4.** to remove weeds. **—weed/er,** n.

weeds (wēdz), n.pl. black mourning garments.

weed/y, adj., **-i•er, -i•est. 1.** consisting of or abounding in weeds. **2.** resembling a weed.

week (wēk), n. **1.** a period of seven successive days, usu. beginning with Sunday. **2.** the working portion of a week: *a 35-hour week.*

week/day/, n. any day of the week except Sunday or, often, Saturday and Sunday.

week/end/ (-end/, -end/), n. **1.** the end of a week, esp. the period between Friday evening and Monday morning. **—**v.i. **2.** to pass the weekend.

week/ly, adj., adv., n., pl. **-lies. —**adj. **1.** done, happening, or appearing once a week. **2.** computed or determined by the week: *the weekly rate.* **—**adv. **3.** once a week. **—**n. **4.** a publication appearing weekly.

ween (wēn), v.t., v.i. Archaic. to think; suppose.

weep (wēp), v.i., v.t., **wept, weep•ing. 1.** to shed (tears) from any overwhelming emotion. **2.** to mourn or grieve. **3.** to exude (liquid, as water). **—weep/er,** n.

weep/ing, adj. **1.** shedding tears. **2.** dripping or oozing liquid. **3.** having slender, drooping branches: *a weeping willow.*

weep/y, adj., **-i•er, -i•est.** easily moved to tears.

wee•vil (wē/vəl), n. any of numerous beetles with a long snout that are destructive to nuts, grain, and fruit.

weft (weft), n. WOOF (def. 1).

weigh (wā), v.t. **1.** to determine the heaviness of, esp. by use of a scale. **2.** to evaluate in the mind; consider carefully. **—**v.i. **3.** to have weight or a specified weight. **4.** to have importance or consequence. **5.** to bear down as a burden. **6. weigh down,** to lower the spirits of; depress. **—Idiom. 7. weigh anchor,** to raise up a ship's anchor.

weight (wāt), n. **1.** the amount something weighs. **2.** gravitational force exerted upon a body. **3.** a system of units for expressing heaviness or mass. **4.** a unit of heaviness or mass. **5.** a body of determinate mass for use in weighing on a balance or scale. **6.** a specific quantity determined by weighing. **7.** a heavy load, mass, or object. **8.** a heavy object used to hold

something open or down. **9.** a burden, as of responsibility. **10.** importance, consequence, or influence: *an opinion of great weight.* **11.** a heavy apparatus lifted or held for exercise, body building, or in athletic competition. **—**v.t. **12.** to add weight to. **13.** to burden with or as if with weight.

weight/less, adj. being without apparent weight. **—weight/less•ness,** n.

weight/lift/ing, n. the lifting, pushing, or pulling of weights as a conditioning exercise or in a competitive event. **—weight/lift/er,** n.

weight/ train/ing, n. weightlifting done as a conditioning exercise.

weight/y, adj., **-i•er, -i•est. 1.** having considerable weight. **2.** burdensome or troublesome. **3.** important or momentous. **4.** having or exerting influence or power. **—weight/i•ness,** n.

weir (wēr), n. **1.** a dam in a stream. **2.** a fence, as of brush, set in a stream for catching fish.

weird (wērd), adj., **-er, -est. 1.** suggesting the supernatural; unearthly. **2.** strange; peculiar. **—weird/ly,** adv. **—weird/ness,** n.

wel•come (wel/kəm), n., v., **-comed, -com•ing,** adj. **—**n. **1.** a kindly greeting or reception. **—**v.t. **2.** to greet with pleasure or courtesy. **3.** to receive or accept with pleasure: *to welcome a change.* **—**adj. **4.** gladly received: *a welcome visitor.* **5.** given permission or consent: *She is welcome to try it.* **6.** (used as a conventional response to thanks): *You're welcome.*

weld (weld), v.t. **1.** to unite (metal or plastic pieces) by hammering or compressing, esp. after applying heat. **2.** to bring into complete union or harmony. **—**v.i. **3.** to undergo welding. **—**n. **4.** a welded joint. **5.** the act of welding. **—weld/er,** n.

wel•fare (wel/fâr/), n. **1.** health, happiness, and prosperity; well-being. **2.** organized efforts to improve the living conditions of needy persons. **3.** assistance given to those in need; public relief.

wel•kin (wel/kin), n. Chiefly Literary. the vault of heaven; sky.

well¹ (wel), adv., adj., compar. **bet•ter,** superl. **best. —**adv. **1.** in a good or satisfactory manner: *Our plans are going well.* **2.** thoroughly or carefully: *Shake well before using.* **3.** in a proper manner: *behaves well.* **4.** commendably or excellently: *a difficult task well handled.* **5.** with justice or reason: *I couldn't very well refuse.* **6.** with favor or approval: *thinks well of her.* **7.** comfortably or prosperously: *to live well.* **8.** to a considerable degree: *well below average.* **9.** in a close way; intimately: *knew her well.* **10.** without doubt; certainly: *I cry easily, as you well know.* **—**adj. **11.** in good health: *not a well man.* **12.** satisfactory or good: *All is well.* **13.** proper, fitting, or prudent: *It is well that you didn't go.* **—Idiom. 14. as well,** in addition; also. **15. as well as,** equally as.

well² (wel), n. **1.** a hole drilled or bored into the earth to obtain a natural deposit, as water or petroleum. **2.** a natural source of water, as a spring. **3.** an abundant source: *a well of compassion.* **4.** a container, receptacle, or reservoir, as for ink. **5.** an enclosed space, as for air, stairs, or an elevator, extending vertically through the floors of a building. **—**v.i. **6.** to rise, spring, or gush, as from a well: *Tears welled up in my eyes.*

we'll (wēl; *unstressed* wil), contraction of *we shall* or *we will.*

well/-advised/, adj. **1.** acting with caution, care, or wisdom. **2.** based on or showing wise consideration.

well/-appoint/ed, adj. attractively or properly equipped or furnished.

well/-bal/anced, adj. **1.** correctly balanced, adjusted, or regulated. **2.** sensible; sane.

well/-behaved/, adj. showing good behavior or manners.

well/-be/ing, n. a state characterized by health, happiness, and prosperity; welfare.

well/born/, adj. born of a good, noble, or highly esteemed family.

well/-bred/, adj. showing good breeding, as in behavior.

well′-defined′, *adj.* clearly stated, outlined, or described.

well′-disposed′, *adj.* feeling favorable, sympathetic, or kind.

well′-done′, *adj.* **1.** performed accurately and skillfully. **2.** (of meat) thoroughly cooked.

Welles (welz), *n.* **(George) Orson,** 1915–85, U.S. actor, director, and producer.

well′-fed′, *adj.* fat; plump.

well′-fixed′, *adj.* prosperous; well-to-do.

well′-found′ed, *adj.* having or based on good reasons, sound information, etc.

well′-groomed′, *adj.* **1.** clean, neat, and dressed with care. **2.** carefully cared for: *a well-groomed lawn.*

well′-ground′ed, *adj.* **1.** WELL-FOUNDED. **2.** thoroughly instructed in the basic principles of a subject.

well′head′, *n.* **1.** a fountainhead; source. **2.** a shelter for a well. **3.** the top of a well.

well′-heeled′, *adj.* well-off.

well′-informed′, *adj.* having extensive knowledge, as in a variety of subjects.

Wel•ling•ton (wel′ing tən), *n.* the capital of New Zealand. 325,200.

well′-inten′tioned, *adj.* well-meaning.

well′-knit′, *adj.* having all parts or elements joined closely, carefully, or firmly: *a well-knit plot.*

well′-known′, *adj.* **1.** fully or thoroughly known. **2.** widely known; famous.

well′-made′, *adj.* skillfully built or put together.

well′-man′nered, *adj.* polite; courteous.

well′-mean′ing, *adj.* having or based on good intentions.

well•ness (wel′nis), *n.* **1.** the quality or state of being healthy, esp. as the result of deliberate effort. **2.** an approach to health care that emphasizes preventing illness and prolonging life.

well′-nigh′, *adv.* very nearly; almost.

well′-off′, *adj.* **1.** well-to-do; prosperous. **2.** in a favorable position or condition.

well′-or′dered, *adj.* arranged, planned, or occurring in an orderly way.

well′-preserved′, *adj.* **1.** maintained in good condition. **2.** preserving a good or healthy appearance.

well′-read′, *adj.* having read extensively.

well′-round′ed, *adj.* **1.** having desirably varied abilities or attainments. **2.** desirably varied.

Wells (welz), *n.* **H(erbert) G(eorge),** 1866–1946, English novelist and historian.

well′-spo′ken, *adj.* **1.** speaking well, fittingly, or pleasingly. **2.** spoken in a fitting or pleasing manner.

well′spring′, *n.* **1.** the source of a spring, stream, or river. **2.** a continuous, seemingly inexhaustible supply.

well′-thought′-of′, *adj.* highly esteemed; reputable.

well′-timed′, *adj.* fittingly or appropriately timed; opportune.

well′-to-do′, *adj.* wealthy; prosperous.

well′-turned′, *adj.* **1.** gracefully shaped: *a well-turned ankle.* **2.** gracefully and concisely expressed: *a well-turned phrase.*

well′-wish′er, *n.* a person who wishes well to another.

well′-worn′, *adj.* **1.** showing the effects of extensive use or wear. **2.** trite; hackneyed.

Welsh (welsh, welch), *n.* **1.** (*used with a pl. v.*) the inhabitants of Wales. **2.** the Celtic language of Wales. —*adj.* **3.** of Wales, its inhabitants, or their language.

Welsh′ cor′gi, *n.* either of two Welsh breeds of dogs with short legs and a foxlike head.

Welsh′ rab′bit, *n.* melted cheese, often mixed with ale or beer, served over toast. Also called **Welsh′ rare′bit.**

welt (welt), *n.* **1.** a ridge on the surface of the body, as from a blow. **2.** a strip, esp. of leather, to which the edges of the insole and upper of a shoe are attached. **3.** a strip or cord sewn along a seam for

strength or as decoration. —*v.t.* **4.** to beat soundly. **5.** to furnish with a welt.

wel•ter (wel′tər), *v.i.* **1.** to toss or heave, as ocean waves. **2.** to roll around; wallow. **3.** to lie drenched in something, as blood. —*n.* **4.** a confused mass; jumble. **5.** a state of commotion, turmoil, or upheaval.

wel′ter•weight′, *n.* a boxer weighing up to 147 lb. (67 kg).

Wel•ty (wel′tē), *n.* **Eudora,** born 1909, U.S. writer.

wen (wen), *n.* a cyst containing sebaceous matter.

Wen•ces•laus (wen′sis lôs′), *n.* **Saint** (*"Good King Wenceslaus"*), A.D. 903?–c935, duke of Bohemia 928–935.

wench (wench), *n.* a girl or young woman.

wend (wend), *v.t.,* **wend•ed** or (*Archaic*) **went; wend•ing.** to travel on or direct (one's way).

went (went), *v.* **1.** pt. of GO¹. **2.** *Archaic.* a pt. and pp. of WEND.

wept (wept), *v.* pt. and pp. of WEEP.

were (wûr; *unstressed* wər), *v.* a 2nd pers. sing. past indic., pl. past indic., and past subj. of BE.

we're (wēr), contraction of *we are.*

were•n't (wûrnt, wûr′ənt), contraction of *were not.*

were•wolf (wâr′wŏŏlf′, wēr′-, wûr′-), *n., pl.* **-wolves.** (in folklore) a person who has assumed the form of a wolf.

We′ Shall′ Overcome′, a song of the U.S. civil rights movement of the 1960s.

Wes•ley (wes′lē, wez′-), *n.* **1. Charles,** 1707–88, English evangelist and hymnist. **2.** his brother **John,** 1703–91, English theologian and evangelist: founder of Methodism.

west (west), *n.* **1.** the cardinal point of the compass 90° to the left of north. **2.** the direction in which west lies. **3.** (*usu. cap.*) a region in the west. **4. the West, a.** the western part of the world as distinguished from the East; the Occident. **b.** the western part of the U.S. —*adj.* **5.** lying toward or situated in the west. **6.** coming from the west. —*adv.* **7.** to, toward, or in the west.

West′ Bank′, *n.* a region in the Middle East, between the W bank of the Jordan River and the E frontier of Israel: occupied in 1967 by Israel; formerly held by Jordan.

West′ Berlin′, *n.* See under BERLIN.

west′er•ly, *adj., adv.* toward or from the west.

west′ern, *adj.* **1.** of, toward, or in the west. **2.** coming from the west. **3.** (*usu. cap.*) of the West. —*n.* **4.** (*often cap.*) a story, movie, or radio or television program about the U.S. West of the 19th century. —**west′ern•er,** *n.*

West′ern Hem′isphere, *n.* the half of the globe that includes North and South America.

west•ern•ize (wes′tər nīz′), *v.t.,* **-ized, -iz•ing.** to influence with or convert to western ideas, customs, and practices. —**west′ern•i•za′tion,** *n.*

West′ern Samo′a, *n.* a country on a group of islands in the S Pacific. 219,509.

West′ern Wall′, *n.* a wall in Jerusalem where Jews assemble for prayer and lamentation: traditionally believed to be the remains of the western wall of Herod's Temple. Also called **Wailing Wall.**

West′ Ger′many, *n.* a former republic in central Europe. Compare GERMANY.

West′ In′dies, *n.* (*used with a pl. v.*) an archipelago in the N Atlantic between North and South America. —**West′ In′dian,** *n., adj.*

West•ing•house (wes′ting hous′), *n.* **George,** 1846–1914, U.S. inventor and manufacturer.

West′ Point′, *n.* a military reservation in SE New York: location of the U.S. Military Academy.

West′ Virgin′ia, *n.* a state in the E United States. 1,825,754. *Cap.:* Charleston. *Abbr.:* WV, W.V., W.Va. —**West′ Virgin′ian,** *n., adj.*

west•ward (west′wərd), *adj.* **1.** moving, facing, or situated toward the west. —*adv.* **2.** Also, **west′wards.** toward the west.

wet (wet), *adj.,* **wet•ter, wet•test,** *n., v.,* **wet** or **wet•ted, wet•ting.** —*adj.* **1.** moistened, covered, or soaked with liquid, as water. **2.** in a liquid state: *wet paint.* **3.** rainy or misty. **4.** allowing the sale of alcoholic beverages. —*n.* **5.** something wet, as water. **6.** liquid; moisture. **7.** damp weather; rain. **8.** a person in favor of allowing the sale of alcoholic beverages. —*v.t., v.i.* **9.** to make or become wet. —*Idiom.* **10. all wet,** completely mistaken. —**wet′ness,** *n.*

wet′ blan′ket, *n.* one that dampens or discourages enthusiasm or enjoyment.

wet′land′, *n.* Often, **-lands.** land with wet and spongy soil.

wet′ nurse′, *n.* a woman hired to suckle another's infant.

wet′ suit′, *n.* a close-fitting rubber suit worn for body warmth, as by scuba divers.

we've (wēv), contraction of *we have.*

whack (hwak, wak), *v.t., v.i.* **1.** to strike with a smart, resounding blow. —*n.* **2.** a smart, resounding blow. **3.** an attempt: *took a whack at the job.* —*Idiom.* **4. out of whack,** out of order. —**whack′er,** *n.*

whale[1] (hwāl, wāl), *n., pl.* **whales, whale,** *v.,* **whaled, whal•ing.** —*n.* **1.** one of the larger marine mammals with a fishlike body. **2.** something big, great, or fine of its kind: *I had a whale of a time in Europe.* —*v.i.* **3.** to engage in whaling.

whale[2] (hwāl, wāl), *v.t., v.i.,* **whaled, whal•ing.** to thrash or beat soundly.

whale′bone′, *n.* **1.** a flexible, horny substance hanging from the upper jaws of certain whales. **2.** something, esp. corset stays, made of whalebone.

whal′er, *n.* a person or ship employed in whaling.

whal′ing, *n.* the work or industry of capturing whales.

wham (hwam, wam), *n., v.,* **whammed, wham•ming.** —*n.* **1.** the sound of a sharp impact. **2.** a forcible impact. —*v.t., v.i.* **3.** to hit with or make a forcible impact.

wham′my, *n., pl.* **-mies.** *Slang.* a jinx; hex.

wharf (hwôrf, wôrf), *n., pl.* **wharves** (hwôrvz, wôrvz), **wharfs.** a structure next to which ships moor to load or unload.

Whar•ton (hwôr′tn, wôr′-), *n.* **Edith,** 1862–1937, U.S. novelist.

what (hwut, hwot, wut, wot; *unstressed* hwət, wət), *pron.* **1.** (used interrogatively as a request for information): *What is the matter?* **2.** (used interrogatively to inquire about the character, origin, identity, or worth of a person or thing): *What is wealth without friends? How much?: What does it cost?* **4.** that which: *I will send what was promised.* **5.** whatever: *come what may.* **6.** as much or as many as: *Give what you can.* —*adj.* **7.** (used interrogatively before nouns): *What clothes shall I pack?* **8.** whatever or whichever: *Take what supplies you need.* —*adv.* **9.** to what extent or degree?: *What does it matter?* —*Idiom.* **10. what for,** why.

what•ev′er, *pron.* **1.** anything that: *Do whatever you like.* **2.** no matter what: *Do it, whatever happens.* **3.** what (used interrogatively): *Whatever do you mean?* —*adj.* **4.** no matter what: *whatever problems you might have.* **5.** of any kind: *no friends whatever.* —*interj.* **6.** (used to indicate indifference to a state of affairs, situation, previous statement, etc.)

What′ hath′ God′ wrought!′, a statement sent by Samuel Morse as the first telegraph transmission.

what′not′, *n.* a stand with shelves, esp. for bric-a-brac.

what's (hwuts, hwots, wuts, wots; *unstressed* hwəts, wəts), contraction of *what is, what has,* or *what does.*

what′so•ev′er, *pron., adj.* (an intensive form of WHATEVER).

wheal (hwēl, wēl), *n.* **1.** a burning or itching swelling on the skin. **2.** a wale or welt.

wheat (hwēt, wēt), *n.* **1.** the grain of a cereal grass used esp. in the form of flour. **2.** the plant itself. —**wheat′en,** *adj.*

wheat′ germ′, *n.* the vitamin-rich embryo of the wheat kernel.

whee•dle (hwēd′l, wēd′l), *v.t., v.i.,* **-dled, -dling. 1.**

to influence (a person) by flattering or beguiling. **2.** to obtain by or use artful persuasion. —**whee′dler,** *n.*

wheel (hwēl, wēl), *n.* **1.** a circular frame or disk that can revolve on an axis. **2.** something like a wheel in shape or function. **3.** the steering wheel of a vehicle. **4. wheels, a.** propelling or animating agencies: *the wheels of commerce.* **b.** *Slang.* a car. **5.** someone powerful and influential. —*v.t., v.i.* **6.** to turn, rotate, or revolve. **7.** to move or convey on wheels. **8.** to change direction by or as if by turning around. —**wheeled,** *adj.*

wheel′bar′row, *n.* a small cart for conveying a load that is supported at one end by a wheel and pushed at the other by two handles.

wheel′base′, *n.* the distance from the front-wheel spindle of a motor vehicle to the rear-wheel axle.

wheel′chair′, *n.* a chair mounted on wheels for use by persons who cannot walk.

wheel′er-deal′er, *n.* a clever and crafty person, as in business or politics.

wheel′wright′ (-rīt′), *n.* a person whose trade is making or repairing wheels and wheeled carriages.

wheeze (hwēz, wēz), *v.,* **wheezed, wheez•ing,** *n.* —*v.i.* **1.** to breathe with difficulty and with a whistling sound. —*n.* **2.** a wheezing breath or sound. —**wheez′y,** *adj.,* **-i•er, -i•est.**

whelk (hwelk, welk), *n.* any of various spiral-shelled, often edible marine mollusks.

whelm (hwelm, welm), *v.t.* **1.** to submerge. **2.** to overcome utterly.

whelp (hwelp, welp), *n.* **1.** the young of such mammals as the dog or the wolf. **2.** an impudent youth. —*v.t., v.i.* **3.** to give birth to (whelps).

when (hwen, wen; *unstressed* hwən, wən), *adv.* **1.** at what time or period?: *When are the guests to arrive?* **2.** under what circumstances?: *When is an apology in order?* —*conj.* **3.** at what time: *knows when to be silent.* **4.** at the time that: *when we were young.* **5.** whenever: *The dog barks when the doorbell rings.* **6.** upon or after which: *Stop the car when the light turns red.* **7.** whereas: *Why are you here when you should be in school?* —*pron.* **8.** what or which time: *Since when have you been teaching?* —*n.* **9.** the time of something.

whence (hwens, wens), *adv.* **1.** from what place?: *Whence comest thou?* **2.** from what source, origin, or cause?: *Whence came his wisdom?* —**Usage.** Although sometimes criticized as redundant, the idiom FROM WHENCE is old, well established, and standard: *She arrived in Paris, from whence she bombarded us with postcards.* Among its users are Shakespeare, the King James Bible, and Dickens. The parallel construction FROM THENCE occurs infrequently.

when•ev′er, *adv., conj.* at whatever time; when.

where (hwâr, wâr), *adv.* **1.** in, at, or to what place?: *Where is he? Where are you going?* **2.** in what position, circumstances, respect, or way: *Where do you stand on this question?* **3.** from what source?: *Where did you get such a notion?* —*conj.* **4.** in or at what place, part, or point: *Find where the trouble is.* **5.** in or at the place, part, or point in or at which: *The cup is where you left it.* **6.** in a position or situation in which: *He's useless where tact is needed.* **7.** to what or whatever place: *I will go where you go.* **8.** in or at which place: *They pitched a tent, where they slept.* —*pron.* **9.** what place?: *Where are you from?* **10.** the place in or point at which: *This is where the boat docks.* —*n.* **11.** a place; location. —**Usage.** Constructions with WHERE such as *Where was he at?* and *Where is this leading to?* are generally avoided in formal speech and writing, since the prepositions are redundant.

where′a•bouts′, *adv.* **1.** about where? —*n.* **2.** (*used with a sing. or pl. v.*) the place where a person or thing is.

where•as′, *conj.* **1.** while on the contrary. **2.** it being the case that.

where•at′, *conj.* **1.** at which. **2.** to which; whereupon.

where•by′, *conj.* by what or which; under the terms of which.

where′fore′, *adv.* **1.** for that cause or reason. **2.** *Archaic.* for what reason? why? —*n.* **3.** a cause or reason.

where•in′, *conj.* **1.** in what or in which. —*adv.* **2.** in what way or respect?

where•of′, *adv., conj.* of what, which, or whom.

where•on′, *conj.* on what or which.

where′up•on′, *conj.* **1.** upon what or which. **2.** at or after which.

wher•ev′er, *conj., adv.* in, at, or to whatever place or circumstance.

where•with′, *adv., conj.* with or by means of which.

where′with•al′, *n.* means, esp. money, with which to do something.

wher•ry (hwer′ē, wer′ē), *n., pl.* **-ries.** a light rowboat for one person.

whet (hwet, wet), *v.t.,* **whet•ted, whet•ting. 1.** to sharpen by grinding or friction. **2.** to make keen or eager; stimulate.

wheth•er (hweth′ər, weth′-), *conj.* **1.** (used to introduce the first of two or more alternatives): *I don't care whether we go or stay.* **2.** (used to introduce a single alternative, the other being implied): *See whether she has come.*

whet′stone′, *n.* a stone for sharpening cutlery or tools by friction.

whew (hwyōō), *interj.* an exclamation or sound expressing astonishment, dismay, fatigue, or relief.

whey (hwā, wā), *n.* the liquid that separates from the curd in coagulated milk.

which (hwich, wich), *pron.* **1.** what one or ones?: *Which of these do you want?* **2.** whichever: *Choose which appeals to you.* **3.** (used in relative clauses to represent a specified antecedent): *This book, which I read last night, was exciting.* **4.** (used after a preposition to represent an antecedent): *the house in which I lived.* —*adj.* **5.** what one or ones of a number or group: *Which book do you want?* **6.** whichever: *Go which way you please.*

which•ev′er, *pron.* **1.** any one that: *Take whichever you like.* **2.** no matter which: *Whichever you choose, the others will be offended.* —*adj.* **3.** no matter which.

whiff (hwif, wif), *n.* **1.** a slight gust or puff, as of wind or smoke. **2.** a slight trace, as of an odor; hint: *a whiff of onions; a whiff of scandal.* **3.** a single inhalation, as of tobacco smoke. —*v.i., v.t.* **4.** to blow or drive in whiffs.

whif•fle•tree (hwif′əl trē′, wif′-), *n., pl.* **-trees.** *Northern U.S.* a pivoted crossbar to which the traces of a harness are fastened.

Whig (hwig, wig), *n.* **1.** a member of a former British political party that favored reforms. **2.** a member of a U.S. political party (c1834–55). **3.** an American colonist who supported the American Revolution.

while (hwīl, wīl), *n., conj., v.,* **whiled, whil•ing.** —*n.* **1.** an interval of time: *a long while ago.* —*conj.* **2.** during the time that: *He read the paper while he waited.* **3.** as long as: *While there's quiet I can sleep.* **4.** even though: *While they are related, they don't get along.* —*v.t.* **5.** to cause (time) to pass, esp. pleasantly: *whiling away the hours.*

whi•lom (hwī′ləm, wī′-), *adj.* **1.** former. —*adv.* **2.** formerly.

whilst (hwīlst, wīlst), *conj. Chiefly Brit.* WHILE.

whim (hwim, wim), *n.* a capricious notion; fancy.

whim•per (hwim′pər, wim′-), *v.i., v.t.* **1.** to cry with or utter in low plaintive sounds. —*n.* **2.** a whimpering sound.

whim•si•cal (hwim′zi kəl, wim′-), *adj.* **1.** given to fanciful notions; capricious. **2.** full of or proceeding from whimsy. **3.** erratic; unpredictable. —**whim′si•cal′i•ty,** *n.* —**whim′si•cal•ly,** *adv.*

whim•sy or **-sey** (hwim′zē, wim′-), *n., pl.* **-sies** or **-seys. 1.** playful or fanciful humor. **2.** an odd or fanciful notion.

whine (hwīn, wīn), *v.,* **whined, whin•ing,** *n.* —*v.i.* **1.** to utter a low, usu. nasal complaining sound. **2.** to

complain in a peevish, self-pitying way. —*v.t.* **3.** to utter with a whine. —*n.* **4.** a whining utterance, sound, or complaint. —**whin′er,** *n.* —**whin′y,** *adj.,* **-i•er, -i•est.**

whin•ny (hwin′ē, win′ē), *n., pl.* **-nies,** *v.,* **-nied, -ny•ing.** —*n.* **1.** a subdued gentle neigh of a horse. —*v.i.* **2.** to utter a whinny.

whip (hwip, wip), *v.,* **whipped** or **whipt, whip•ping,** *n.* —*v.t.* **1.** to beat with a flexible implement, as a lash, esp. as punishment. **2.** to spank. **3.** to urge on by or as if by whipping. **4.** to train forcefully: *trying to whip the team into shape.* **5.** to defeat; overcome. **6.** to move, pull, or seize suddenly: *She whipped out her camera.* **7.** to beat to a froth: *whipped cream.* —*v.i.* **8.** to go quickly and suddenly. **9.** to lash about: *flags whipping in the wind.* **10. whip up, a.** to prepare quickly. **b.** to incite; arouse. —*n.* **11.** a flexible implement for whipping. **12.** a whipping stroke or motion. **13.** a dessert of beaten egg whites or cream. **14.** a party manager in a legislative body who secures attendance and directs other members. —**whip′per,** *n.*

whip′cord′, *n.* **1.** a fabric with a diagonally ribbed surface. **2.** a strong, hard-twisted cord, esp. of catgut.

whip′lash′, *n.* **1.** the lash of a whip. **2.** a neck injury caused by a sudden jerking of the head.

whip•per•snap•per (hwip′ər snap′ər, wip′-), *n.* an unimportant but presumptuous person.

whip•pet (hwip′it, wip′-), *n.* a slender swift dog resembling a small greyhound.

whip•ple•tree (hwip′əl trē′, wip′-), *n., pl.* **-trees.** WHIFFLETREE.

whip•poor•will (hwip′ər wil′, wip′-), *n.* a nocturnal North American bird with an insistently repeated call.

whip′saw′, *n.* a saw for two persons, used to cut timbers crosswise.

whir or **whirr** (hwûr, wûr), *v.,* **whirred, whir•ring,** *n.* —*v.i., v.t.* **1.** to move, revolve, or transport quickly with a humming sound. —*n.* **2.** an act or sound of whirring.

whirl (hwûrl, wûrl), *v.,* **1.** to turn around, spin, or rotate rapidly. **2.** to move or be carried rapidly along. **3.** to experience dizziness: *My head is whirling.* —*v.t.* **4.** to cause to whirl. —*n.* **5.** the act of whirling. **6.** a whirling movement. **7.** a rapid round of events: *a whirl of parties.* **8.** a state of dizziness. **9.** an attempt; trial: *gave the diet a whirl.*

whirl•i•gig (hwûr′li gig′, wûr′-), *n.* **1.** something that whirls. **2.** a merry-go-round. **3.** a whirling or spinning toy.

whirl′pool′, *n.* water in swift circular motion producing a downward spiraling action.

whirl•wind (hwûrl′wind′, wûrl′-), *n.* **1.** a small, rapidly rotating mass of air, as a tornado. **2.** something resembling a whirlwind, as in destructive force. —*adj.* **3.** like a whirlwind, as in speed or force. —*Proverb.* **4. They that sow the wind shall reap the whirlwind,** violent deeds bring disastrous results. Hosea 8:7.

whirl•y•bird (hwûr′lē bûrd′, wûr′-), *n.* HELICOPTER.

whisk (hwisk, wisk), *v.t.* **1.** to move with a rapid brushing or sweeping stroke. **2.** to carry or move rapidly. **3.** to whip or blend with a whisk. —*n.* **4.** the act of whisking. **5.** WHISK BROOM. **6.** an implement, usu. of wire, for beating or whipping food.

whisk′ broom′, *n.* a small short-handled broom used chiefly to brush clothes.

whisk′er, *n.* **1.** Usu., **-kers.** the hair growing on the sides of a man's face. **2.** a single hair of the beard. **3.** one of the long bristly hairs growing near the mouth of certain animals, as the cat. —**whisk′ered,** *adj.*

whis•key (hwis′kē, wis′-), *n., pl.* **-keys.** an alcoholic liquor distilled from a fermented mash of grain, as barley.

whis′ky (-kē), *n., pl.* **-kies.** whiskey (used esp. for Scotch or Canadian whiskey).

whis•per (hwis′pər, wis′pər), *v.i., v.t.* **1.** to speak or utter with soft hushed sounds, esp. with no vibration of the vocal cords. **2.** to talk or tell softly and privately. **3.** to make a soft rustling sound. —*n.* **4.** an act or instance of whispering. **5.** a whispered word or remark. **6.** a rumor or insinuation. **7.** a soft rustling sound. —**whis′per•er,** *n.*

whist (hwist, wist), *n.* a card game that is an early form of bridge.

whis•tle (hwis′əl, wis′-), *v.*, **-tled, -tling,** *n.* —*v.i.* **1.** to make a high clear sound by forcing the breath through puckered lips or through the teeth. **2.** to produce a sound or call resembling a whistle. **3.** to move with a whistling sound, as a bullet. —*v.t.* **4.** to produce by whistling. **5.** to call or signal by whistling. —*n.* **6.** an instrument for producing whistling sounds. **7.** a whistling sound. —**whis′tler,** *n.*

whis′tle-blow′er, *n.* a person who informs on another or discloses corruption or wrongdoing. —**whis′tle-blow′ing,** *n.*

whis′tle stop′, *n.* **1.** a small town, esp. one along a railroad line. **2.** a short talk from the rear platform of a train during a political campaign.

whit (hwit, wit), *n.* the smallest amount: *I don't care a whit.*

White (hwīt, wīt), *n.* **1. Edward H(iggins), II,** 1930–67, U.S. astronaut: first American to walk in space 1965. **2. Stanford,** 1853–1906, U.S. architect. **3. Theodore H.,** 1915–86, U.S. journalist and writer.

white′ blood′ cell′, *n.* any of various nearly colorless blood cells of the immune system.

white′cap′, *n.* a wave with a foaming white crest.

white′-col′lar, *adj.* of or designating professional or clerical workers whose jobs do not usu. involve manual labor.

whit′ed sep′ulcher, *n.* an evil person who feigns goodness. Matt. 23:27.

white′ el′ephant, *n.* **1.** a possession unwanted by the owner but of use to another. **2.** a possession entailing expense out of proportion to its value. **3.** an albino Indian elephant.

white′fish′, *n.*, *pl.* **-fish, -fish•es.** any of several freshwater food fishes resembling the trout.

white′ flag′, *n.* an all-white flag used as a symbol of surrender or truce.

white′ gold′, *n.* a gold alloy colored white esp. by the presence of nickel.

white′ goods′, *n.pl.* **1.** household linens, as sheets and towels. **2.** white fabrics, esp. of cotton or linen.

white′ heat′, *n.* **1.** an intense heat at which a substance glows with white light. **2.** a state of intense activity or excitement.

White′horse′, *n.* capital of the Yukon Territory, in NW Canada. 15,199.

White′ House′, *n.* **the, 1.** the official residence of the president of the U.S. **2.** the executive branch of the U.S. government.

white′ lead′ (led), *n.* a white heavy powder of basic lead carbonate used esp. as a pigment and in putty.

white′ lie′, *n.* a harmless lie; fib.

white′ mat′ter, *n.* nerve tissue, esp. of the brain and spinal cord, that is nearly white in color.

whit′en, *v.t.*, *v.i.* to make or become white. —**whit′en•er,** *n.*

white′ sale′, *n.* a sale of household linens.

white′wall′, *n.* an automobile tire with a white sidewall.

white′wash′, *n.* **1.** a composition, as of lime and water, for whitening walls and woodwork. **2.** a concealment of faults or errors or exoneration from blame. —*v.t.* **3.** to whiten with whitewash. **4.** to conceal the faults or errors of; absolve from blame.

white′ wa′ter, *n.* frothy water, as in rapids.

whith•er (hwith′ər, with′-), *adv.* **1.** to what place; where? **2.** to what end, point, or action? —*conj.* **3.** to which place. **4.** to whatever place.

whit•ing[1] (hwī′ting, wī′-), *n.*, *pl.* **-ings, -ing.** any of several marine food fishes.

whit•ing[2] (hwī′ting, wī′-), *n.* pure-white chalk powder used esp. in making putty and whitewash.

Whit•man (hwit′mən, wit′-), *n.* **Walt(er),** 1819–92, U.S. poet.

Whit•ney (hwit′nē, wit′-), *n.* **1. Eli,** 1765–1825, U.S. manufacturer and inventor. **2. John Hay,** 1904–82, U.S. diplomat and newspaper publisher. **3. Mount,** a mountain in E California, in the Sierra Nevada: highest peak in the U.S. outside Alaska. 14,495 ft. (4418 m).

Whit•sun•day (hwit′sun′dā, -dē, -sən dā′, wit′-), *n.* PENTECOST.

Whit•ti•er (hwit′ē ər, wit′-), *n.* **John Greenleaf,** 1807–92, U.S. poet.

whit•tle (hwit′l, wit′l), *v.*, **-tled, -tling.** —*v.t.* **1.** to cut, trim, or shape (wood) by carving off bits with a knife. **2.** to form by whittling. **3.** to reduce gradually. —*v.i.* **4.** to whittle wood. —**whit′tler,** *n.*

whiz or **whizz** (hwiz, wiz), *v.*, **whizzed, whiz•zing,** *n.* —*v.i.* **1.** to make or move with a humming, buzzing, or hissing sound, as of an object flying swiftly through the air. —*n.* **2.** *Informal.* a very skillful person; expert: *a whiz at math.* **3.** a whizzing sound.

who (hōō), *pron.*, *possessive* **whose,** *objective* **whom.** **1.** what person or persons?: *Who is he?* **2.** the person or persons that: *Do you know who called?* **3.** (used in relative clauses to represent an antecedent): *The woman who called this morning is here.*

WHO, World Health Organization.

whoa (hwō, wō), *interj.* a command, esp. to an animal, to stop.

who•dun′it (-dun′it), *n.* a detective story.

who•ev′er, *pron.* whatever person; anyone that: *Whoever did it should be proud.*

whole (hōl), *adj.* **1.** comprising the full quantity, extent, or duration; entire or total. **2.** lacking nothing; complete: *a whole set of china.* **3.** not divided: *a whole cheese.* **4.** *Math.* not fractional. **5.** not broken or damaged; intact. **6.** not injured or hurt; sound. —*n.* **7.** the entire quantity, number, extent, or duration. **8.** a thing complete in itself. —*Idiom.* **9. on the whole, a.** taking everything into consideration. **b.** in general. —**whole′ness,** *n.*

whole′heart′ed, *adj.* completely sincere or enthusiastic. —**whole′heart′ed•ly,** *adv.* —**whole′heart′ed•ness,** *n.*

whole′ note′, *n. Music.* a note equivalent in value to four quarter notes.

whole′ num′ber, *n.* INTEGER.

whole′sale′, *n.*, *adj.*, *adv.*, *v.*, **-saled, -sal•ing.** —*n.* **1.** the sale of goods in quantity, as to retailers. —*adj.* **2.** of or engaged in sale by wholesale. **3.** extensive; broadly indiscriminate: *wholesale firings.* —*adv.* **4.** in a wholesale way. —*v.t.*, *v.i.* **5.** to sell by wholesale. —**whole′sal′er,** *n.*

whole′some (-səm), *adj.* **1.** conducive to well-being; healthful. **2.** suggestive of health, esp. in appearance. **3.** healthy or sound. —**whole′some•ly,** *adv.* —**whole′some•ness,** *n.*

whole′-wheat′, *adj.* prepared with the complete wheat kernel.

who'll (hōōl), contraction of *who will* or *who shall.*

whol•ly (hō′lē, hōl′lē), *adv.* **1.** entirely; totally. **2.** to the exclusion of others; solely.

whom (hōōm), *pron.* the objective case of WHO.

whom•ev′er, *pron.* the objective case of WHOEVER.

whoop (hwōōp, hwŏŏp, wōōp, wŏŏp; *esp. for 2* hōōp, hŏŏp), *n.* **1.** a loud cry or shout, as of excitement. **2.** a deep intake of air with a hollow gasping sound following a fit of coughing. —*v.i.*, *v.t.* **3.** to utter or utter with a loud cry or shout. —**whoop′er,** *n.*

whoop′ing cough′ (hōō′ping, hōōp′ing), *n.* an infectious disease characterized by a series of short, convulsive coughs followed by a whoop.

whoosh (hwōōsh, hwŏŏsh, wōōsh, wŏŏsh), *n.* **1.** a loud, rushing noise, as of air or water. —*v.i.*, *v.t.* **2.** to move or cause to move with a whoosh.

whop•per (hwop′ər, wop′-), *n. Informal.* **1.** something uncommonly large. **2.** a big lie.

whop′ping, *adj. Informal.* uncommonly large.

whorl (hwûrl, hwôrl, wûrl, wôrl), *n.* **1.** a circular arrangement of like parts, as leaves or flowers. **2.** one of the central ridges of a fingerprint. —**whorled,** *adj.*

who's (hōōz), **1.** contraction of *who is.* **2.** contraction of *who has.*

whose (hōōz), *pron.* **1.** the possessive case of WHO or WHICH used as an adjective: *someone whose faith is strong; a word whose meaning escapes me.* **2.** the one or ones belonging to what person or persons: *Whose umbrella is that?*

who'so, *pron.* whoever.

who'so•ev'er, *pron.* whoever.

why (hwī, wī), *adv., conj., n., pl.* **whys,** *interj.* —*adv.* **1.** for what reason or purpose?: *Why do you ask?* —*conj.* **2.** for what cause or reason: *I don't know why he left.* **3.** on account of which: *the reason why she refused.* **4.** the reason for which: *That is why he returned.* —*n.* **5.** the cause or reason. —*interj.* **6.** an exclamation of surprise, hesitation, or impatience. —**Usage.** See REASON.

WI, Wisconsin.

W.I., 1. West Indian. **2.** West Indies.

Wich•i•ta (wich'i tô'), *n.* a city in S Kansas. 310,324.

wick (wik), *n.* a twist of soft threads that in a candle or oil lamp draws up the flammable liquid to be burned.

wick•ed (wik'id), *adj.* **1.** evil or morally bad; sinful. **2.** playfully mischievous. **3.** harmful; dangerous: *wicked roads.* **4.** unpleasant; foul: *a wicked odor.* **5.** *Slang.* wonderful; great; masterful. —**wick'ed•ly,** *adv.* —**wick'ed•ness,** *n.*

wick'er, *n.* **1.** a slender, pliant twig. **2.** wickerwork. —*adj.* **3.** made of wicker.

wick'er•work', *n.* articles, as baskets, made of wicker.

wick•et (wik'it), *n.* **1.** a window or opening, often with a grating, as in a ticket office. **2.** a small door or gate, esp. one beside or forming part of a larger one. **3.** (in croquet) a hoop or arch. **4.** (in cricket) either of the two frameworks at which the bowler aims the ball.

wide (wīd), *adj.* and *adv.,* **wid•er, wid•est.** —*adj.* **1.** of great extent from side to side; broad. **2.** having a specified measurement from side to side: *three feet wide.* **3.** of great range or scope: *wide experience.* **4.** fully opened: *stared with wide eyes.* **5.** far from an objective: *wide of the truth.* —*adv.* **6.** to the utmost; fully; wide open. **7.** away from a target or objective: *The shot went wide.* **8.** over an extensive area: *scattered far and wide.* —**wide'ly,** *adv.* —**wide'ness,** *n.*

wide'-ar'ea net'work, *n.* a computer network that spans a relatively large geographical area. Also called **WAN.**

wide'-awake', *adj.* **1.** fully awake. **2.** alert or observant.

wide'-eyed', *adj.* having the eyes open wide, as in amazement or innocence.

wide'mouthed', *adj.* **1.** having a wide mouth. **2.** having the mouth opened wide, as in astonishment.

wid'en, *v.t., v.i.* to make or become wide. —**wid'en•er,** *n.*

wide'spread', *adj.* **1.** spread over a wide area. **2.** occurring in many places or among many persons.

widg•eon (wij'ən), *n., pl.* **-eons, -eon.** WIGEON.

wid•ow (wid'ō), *n.* **1.** a woman who has lost her husband by death and has not remarried. —*v.t.* **2.** to make (someone) a widow. —**wid'ow•hood',** *n.*

wid'ow•er, *n.* a man who has lost his wife by death and has not remarried.

wid'ow's mite', *n.* a small contribution given by one who can ill afford it. Mark 12:41-44.

width (width, witth), *n.* **1.** extent from side to side; breadth. **2.** something, as a piece of cloth, of a particular width.

wield (wēld), *v.t.* **1.** to exercise (power, influence, etc.). **2.** to use (a weapon, instrument, etc.) effectively; handle. —**wield'er,** *n.*

wie•ner (wē'nər), *n.* FRANKFURTER.

wife (wīf), *n., pl.* **wives** (wīvz). a married woman. —**wife'less,** *adj.* —**wife'ly,** *adj.*

wig (wig), *n., v.,* **wigged, wig•ging.** —*n.* **1.** a covering of natural or artificial hair for the head. **2.** a toupee. —*v.t.* **3.** to furnish with a wig.

wig•eon (wij'ən), *n., pl.* **-eons, -eon.** a freshwater duck with white patches on the forewings.

wig•gle (wig'əl), *v.,* **-gled, -gling,** *n.* —*v.i., v.t.* **1.** to move with quick, irregular side-to-side movements. —*n.* **2.** a wiggling movement or course. —**wig'gler,** *n.* —**wig'gly,** *adj.,* **-gli•er, -gli•est.**

wight (wīt), *n.* **1.** a human being. **2.** *Obs.* a living being; creature.

wig'let (-lit), *n.* a small wig.

wig•wag (wig'wag'), *v.,* **-wagged, -wag•ging,** *n.* —*v.t., v.i.* **1.** to signal by waving a flag or lantern according to a code. —*n.* **2.** the act or process of wigwagging. **3.** a wigwagged message.

wig•wam (wig'wom, -wôm), *n.* a North American Indian dwelling, typically rounded in shape, formed of poles overlaid with bark, mats, or skins.

wild (wīld), *adj.,* **-er, -est,** *adv., n.* —*adj.* **1.** living in a state of nature; not tamed or domesticated. **2.** growing or produced without cultivation, as flowers. **3.** not inhabited; undeveloped: *wild country.* **4.** not civilized; barbarous. **5.** characterized by violence or intensity: *a wild storm.* **6.** characterized by violent feelings: *a wild look.* **7.** frantic; distracted: *drove me wild.* **8.** not disciplined; unruly: *wild children.* **9.** wide of the mark: *a wild pitch.* **10.** (of a card) having its value decided by the wishes of the players. —*adv.* **11.** in a wild manner. —*n.* **12.** Often, **wilds.** an uncultivated region or tract; wilderness or wasteland. —**wild'ly,** *adv.* —**wild'ness,** *n.*

wild'cat', *n., pl.* **-cats,** also **-cat** for 1, *adj., v.,* **-cat•ted, -cat•ting.** —*n.* **1.** any of several medium-sized cats, as the bobcat, related to the domestic cat. **2.** a quick-tempered or savage person. **3.** an exploratory well drilled in an effort to discover deposits of oil or gas. —*adj.* **4.** characterized by or proceeding from unsafe business methods: *wildcat stocks.* —*v.i., v.t.* **5.** to search (an area of unknown productivity) for oil, gas, or ore.

wild'cat strike', *n.* a labor strike that has not been called by union officials.

Wilde (wīld), *n.* **Oscar,** 1854-1900, Irish writer.

wil•de•beest (wil'də bēst', vil'-), *n., pl.* **-beests, -beest.** GNU.

Wil•der (wil'dər), *n.* **1. Laura Ingalls,** 1867-1957, U.S. writer of children's books. **2. Thornton (Niven),** 1897-1975, U.S. novelist and playwright.

wil•der•ness (wil'dər nis), *n.* a wild, uncultivated, uninhabited region.

Wil'derness Road', *n.* a 300-mile (500-km) route from eastern Virginia into Kentucky: a major route for early settlers moving west.

wild'-eyed', *adj.* **1.** having a wild expression in the eyes. **2.** extreme or radical.

wild'fire', *n.* a large fire that spreads rapidly and is hard to extinguish.

wild'flow'er, *n.* the flower of a plant that grows wild.

wild'fowl', *n., pl.* **-fowl, -fowls.** a game bird, as a wild duck.

wild'-goose' chase', *n.* a senseless search for something nonexistent or unobtainable.

wild'life', *n.* undomesticated animals living in the wild.

wild' oat', *n.* **1.** a common weedy grass resembling the cultivated oat. **2. wild oats,** youthful excesses or indiscretions.

wild' rice', *n.* **1.** a tall aquatic grass of N North America. **2.** the edible grain of this plant.

Wild' West', *n.* the western frontier region of the U.S. before the establishment of stable government.

wile (wīl), *n., v.,* **wiled, wil•ing.** —*n.* **1.** a trick or stratagem meant to fool, trap, or entice. **2. wiles,** artful or beguiling behavior. —*v.t.* **3.** to beguile, entice, or lure. **4. wile away,** to pass (time), esp. in a pleasurable fashion.

wil•ful (wil'fəl), *adj.* WILLFUL.

will[1] (wil), *auxiliary v.* and *v., pres.* **will;** *past* **would.** —*auxiliary verb.* **1.** (used to express simple futurity): *I will be there tomorrow.* **2.** (used to express willingness): *Nobody will help us.* **3.** (used to express a command): *You will report to the principal at once.*

4. (used to express probability): *They will be asleep by this time.* **5.** (used to express customary action): *She will write for hours at a time.* **6.** (used to express capability): *This couch will seat four.* —*v.t.*, *v.i.* **7.** to wish; like: *Take what you will.* —**Usage.** See SHALL.

will² (wil), *n.* **1.** the faculty of conscious and deliberate action. **2.** the power of choosing or deciding: *a strong will.* **3.** wish or desire: *went against his will.* **4.** purpose or determination: *the will to succeed.* **5.** disposition toward another: *ill will.* **6.** a legal document specifying the disposition of a person's property after death. —*v.t.* **7.** to decide upon or bring about by an act of the will. **8.** to dispose of by a will; bequeath. **9.** to influence by the power of the will. —*v.i.* **10.** to exercise the will. —**willed,** *adj.*

will′ful, *adj.* **1.** deliberate; intentional. **2.** unreasonably stubborn or headstrong. —**will′ful•ly,** *adv.* —**will′ful•ness,** *n.*

Wil•liam I (wil′yəm), *n.* ("the Conqueror") 1027–87, duke of Normandy 1035–87; king of England 1066–87.

Wil•liams (wil′yəmz), *n.* **1. Ralph Vaughan,** VAUGHAN WILLIAMS, Ralph. **2. Roger,** 1603?–83, English clergyman in America: founder of Rhode Island colony 1636. **3. Tennessee** (*Thomas Lanier Williams*), 1911–83, U.S. dramatist.

Wil′liam Tell′, *n.* a legendary Swiss patriot of c1300 forced by the Austrian governor to shoot an apple off his son's head with a crossbow.

wil•lies (wil′ēz), *n.pl.* nervousness; jitters (usu. prec. by *the*).

will′ing, *adj.* **1.** disposed or consenting; inclined. **2.** cheerfully consenting or ready. **3.** done, given, borne, or used with cheerful readiness. —**will′ing•ly,** *adv.* —**will′ing•ness,** *n.*

will-o′-the-wisp (wil′ə thə wisp′), *n.* **1.** a flickering light seen at night over marshy ground, believed to be due to the burning of marsh gas. **2.** an elusive thing or person.

wil•low (wil′ō), *n.* **1.** a tree or shrub with lance-shaped leaves and tough, pliable twigs used esp. for wickerwork. **2.** the wood of a willow.

wil′low•y, *adj.*, **-i•er, -i•est. 1.** pliant; lithe. **2.** slender and graceful.

will′pow′er, *n.* self-control and determination.

wil•ly-nil•ly (wil′ē nil′ē), *adv.* whether one wishes or not.

Wil•son (wil′sən), *n.* **(Thomas) Woodrow,** 1856–1924, 28th president of the U.S. 1913–21.

wilt¹ (wilt), *v.i.* **1.** to become limp and drooping, as a fading flower. **2.** to lose strength, vigor, or courage. —*v.t.* **3.** to cause to wilt.

wilt² (wilt), *v. Archaic.* second pers. sing. pres. indic. of WILL¹.

wil•y (wī′lē), *adj.*, **-i•er, -i•est.** full of or marked by wiles; cunning. —**wil′i•ness,** *n.*

wimp (wimp), *n. Informal.* a weak, ineffectual person. —**wimp′y,** *adj.*, **-i•er, -i•est.**

wim•ple (wim′pəl), *n.* a woman's headcloth drawn in folds about the chin, worn esp. by nuns.

wimple

win (win), *v.*, **won, win•ning,** *n.* —*v.i.* **1.** to finish first, as in a race. **2.** to succeed by effort. **3.** to overcome an adversary. —*v.t.* **4.** to succeed in reaching, esp. by great effort. **5.** to get by effort, as through labor or competition. **6.** to be victorious in (a game, battle, etc.). **7.** to gain the favor, consent, or support of. **8.** to persuade (someone) to marry oneself. —*n.* **9.** a victory, as in a horse race. —*Saying.* **10. Win this one for the Gipper,** win for the sake of an ad-

mired figure: saying attributed to U.S. football coach Knute Rockne and associated with Ronald Reagan.

wince (wins), *v.*, **winced, winc•ing,** *n.* —*v.i.* **1.** to draw back, as from a blow; flinch. —*n.* **2.** a wincing movement.

winch (winch), *n.* **1.** the crank or handle of a revolving machine. **2.** a windlass for hoisting or hauling.

wind¹ (*n.* wind, *Literary* wīnd; *v.* wind), *n.* **1.** air in natural motion. **2.** a stream of air, as that produced by a bellows. **3. winds, a.** wind instruments collectively. **b.** players of wind instruments. **4.** breath or breathing. **5.** an influential force or trend. **6.** a hint or intimation: *caught wind of a scandal.* **7.** air carrying an animal's scent. **8.** gas generated in the stomach and intestines. —*v.t.* **9.** to follow by scent. **10.** to make short of breath. **11.** to allow to recover breath, as after exertion. —*Idiom.* **12. in the wind,** about to occur.

wind² (wīnd), *v.*, **wound** (wound) or (*Rare*) **wind•ed** (wīn′did); **wind•ing;** *n.* —*v.i.* **1.** to have or take a curving course; meander. **2.** to coil or twine around something. —*v.t.* **3.** to wrap around; encircle or wreathe. **4.** to roll (thread, string, etc.) into a ball or on a spool. **5.** to tighten the spring of: *wound the clock.* **6.** to make (one's way) in a curving course. **7. wind up, a.** to bring or come to a conclusion. **b.** to make tense or nervous; excite. —*n.* **8.** the act of winding. **9.** a single turn, twist, or bend. —**wind′er,** *n.*

wind′break′ (wind′-), *n.* something, as a growth of trees, serving as a shelter from the wind.

wind′chill fac′tor (wind′chil′), *n.* the apparent temperature felt on the exposed human body owing to the combination of temperature and wind speed.

wind•ed (win′did), *adj.* out of breath.

wind′fall′ (wind′-), *n.* **1.** an unexpected gain or piece of good fortune. **2.** something, as fruit, blown down by the wind.

Wind•hoek (vint′hŏŏk′), *n.* the capital of Namibia. 114,500.

wind′ing sheet′ (wīn′ding), *n.* SHROUD (def. 1).

wind′ in′strument (wind), *n.* a musical instrument, as the trumpet or flute, sounded by an air current, esp. the breath.

wind•jam•mer (wind′jam′ər, win′-), *n.* a large sailing ship.

wind•lass (wind′ləs), *n.* a device for hauling or hoisting, commonly having a horizontal drum on which a rope attached to the load is wound.

wind′mill′ (wind′-), *n.* a machine for grinding or pumping that is driven by the wind acting on vanes or sails.

win•dow (win′dō), *n.* **1.** an opening in a building, vehicle, etc., for admitting air or light. **2.** a window with its frame, sashes, and panes of glass. **3.** a windowpane. **4.** something resembling a window in appearance or function. **5.** a period of time available or highly favorable for doing something. **6. a.** a portion of a computer screen on which data can be displayed independently of the rest of the screen. **b.** a view of a portion of a document bounded by the borders of a computer's display screen.

win′dow box′, *n.* a box for growing plants on a windowsill.

win′dow dress′ing, *n.* **1.** the art, act, or technique of trimming the display windows of a store. **2.** something done solely to create a favorable impression. —**win′dow-dress′,** *v.t.*

win′dow•pane′, *n.* a pane of glass for a window.

win′dow-shop′, *v.i.*, **-shopped, -shop•ping.** to look at articles in store windows without making purchases. —**win′dow shop′per,** *n.*

win′dow•sill′, *n.* the sill under a window.

wind′pipe′ (wind′-), *n.* the trachea of an air-breathing vertebrate.

wind•row (wind′rō′, win′-), *n.* **1.** a row of hay left to dry before being raked into heaps. **2.** a row, as of dry leaves, swept together by the wind.

wind′shield′ (wind′-, win′-), *n.* a shield of glass above the dashboard of an automobile.

wind′sock′ (wind′-), *n.* a mounted cloth cone that catches the wind to indicate wind direction.

winds′ of change′, *n.pl.* a decisive shift in political power or policies.

Wind•sor (win′zər), *n.* **1.** (since 1917) a member of the present British royal family. **2.** Official name, **Wind′sor and Maid′enhead.** a city in E Berkshire, in S England, on the Thames: the site of the residence (**Wind′sor Cas′tle**) of English sovereigns since William the Conqueror. 129,900.

wind′storm′ (wind′-), *n.* a storm with heavy wind but little or no precipitation.

wind′surf′ing (wind′-), *n.* the sport of riding on a surfboard mounted with a sail. —**wind′surf′,** *v.i.* —**wind′surf′er,** *n.*

windsurfing

wind′-swept′ (wind), *adj.* exposed to or blown by the wind.

wind′ tun′nel (wind), *n.* a tubular chamber in which an object, as an aircraft, can be studied to determine how it is affected by airflow of controlled velocity.

wind′up′ (wīnd′-), *n.* **1.** the conclusion of an action or activity. **2.** *Baseball.* the movement of a pitcher's arm before throwing the ball.

wind•ward (wind′wərd), *adv.* **1.** toward the wind. —*adj.* **2.** of, situated in, or moving toward the quarter from which the wind blows. —*n.* **3.** the point or quarter from which the wind blows.

Wind′ward Is′lands. *n pl* a group of islands in the SE West Indies.

wind•y (win′dē), *adj.,* **-i•er, -i•est. 1.** accompanied or characterized by wind. **2.** exposed to the wind. **3.** characterized by or given to prolonged empty talk. —**wind′i•ness,** *n.*

wine (wīn), *n., v.,* **wined, win•ing.** —*n.* **1.** the fermented juice of grapes, used esp. as a beverage. **2.** the often fermented juice of another fruit or plant. —*v.t., v.i.* **3.** to supply with or drink wine. —*Idiom.* **4. wine and dine,** to entertain lavishly. [< L *vīnum*]

win′er•y, *n., pl.* **-er•ies.** an establishment where wine is made.

wing (wing), *n.* **1.** either of the two forelimbs or appendages of birds, insects, and bats that are specialized for flight. **2.** a means or instrument of flight, travel, or progress. **3.** the act or manner of flying. **4.** something, as the vane of a windmill, that resembles a wing. **5.** one of a pair of airfoils on the fuselage of an aircraft that provides lift. **6.** a part of a building projecting from a central or main part. **7.** a flank of an army or fleet. **8.** a unit of the U.S. Air Force. **9.** an often extreme faction within an organization: *the liberal wing.* **10.** *Sports.* a position or player on the far side of the center. **11.** Usu., **wings.** the space at the side of a stage, usu. not seen by the audience. —*v.t.* **12.** to equip with wings. **13.** to transport on or as if on wings. **14.** to accomplish by flight. **15.** to traverse in flight. **16.** to wound in the wing or arm. —*v.i.* **17.** to travel on or as if on wings. —*Idiom.* **18. on the wing,** in flight; flying. **19. under one's wing,** under one's protection, care, or patronage. **20. wing it,** to improvise. —**winged,** *adj.* —**wing′less,** *adj.*

wing′span′, *n.* **1.** the distance between the wing tips of an airplane. **2.** WINGSPREAD.

wing′spread′, *n.* the distance between the tips of the outspread wings of a bird.

wink (wingk), *v.i.* **1.** to close and open the eyes quickly. **2.** to close and open one eye quickly as a hint or signal. **3.** to twinkle. —*v.t.* **4.** to make (one or both eyes) wink. **5. wink at,** to ignore (wrongdoing) deliberately. —*n.* **6.** the act of winking. **7.** a hint or signal given by winking. **8.** an instant. **9.** the least bit: *didn't sleep a wink.*

win′ner, *n.* one that wins; victor.

win′ning, *n.* **1.** the act of one that wins. **2.** Usu., **-nings.** something won, esp. money. —*adj.* **3.** successful or victorious. **4.** engaging; pleasing: *a winning personality.* —**win′ning•ly,** *adv.*

Win•ni•peg (win′ə peg′), *n.* the capital of Manitoba, in S Canada. 594,551. —**Win′ni•peg′ger,** *n.*

win•now (win′ō), *v.t.* **1.** to free (grain) of chaff with a forced current of air. **2.** to drive or blow (chaff, dirt, etc.) away by fanning. **3.** to separate, distinguish, or sift. —**win′now•er,** *n.*

win•some (win′səm), *adj.* sweetly or innocently charming; winning. —**win′some•ly,** *adv.* —**win′some•ness,** *n.*

Win′ston-Sa′lem (win′stən), *n.* a city in N North Carolina. 155,128.

win•ter (win′tər), *n.* **1.** the cold season between autumn and spring. **2.** a year: *a man of 60 winters.* **3.** a period of decline or adversity. —*adj.* **4.** of or characteristic of winter. **5.** planted in the autumn to be harvested in the spring or summer: *winter rye.* —*v.i.* **6.** to spend the winter. —*v.t.* **7.** to keep, feed, or manage during winter.

win′ter•green′, *n.* **1.** a creeping evergreen shrub bearing white flowers, red berries, and leaves that yield an aromatic oil. **2.** the oil of the wintergreen.

win′ter•ize, *v.t.,* **-ized, -iz•ing.** to prepare to withstand cold weather.

win′ter•time′, *n.* the season of winter.

Win•throp (win′thrəp), *n.* **John,** 1588–1649, English colonist in America: 1st governor of the Massachusetts Bay colony.

win•try (win′trē), *adj.,* **-tri•er, -tri•est. 1.** of or characteristic of winter. **2.** suggestive of winter, as in lack of cheer.

win′-win′, *adj.* advantageous to both sides, as in a negotiation: *a win-win proposal; a win-win situation.*

wipe (wīp), *v.,* **wiped, wip•ing,** *n.* —*v.t.* **1.** to clean or dry by patting or rubbing: *Wipe your hands.* **2.** to rub or draw (something) over a surface, as in cleaning or drying. **3.** to remove by or as if by rubbing. **4. wipe out, a.** to destroy completely. **b.** to murder. —*n.* **5.** the act of wiping. —**wip′er,** *n.*

wire (wī³r), *n., adj., v.,* **wired, wir•ing.** —*n.* **1.** a slender piece or filament of metal. **2.** a length of wire used as a conductor of current in electrical, cable, telegraph, or telephone systems. **3. a.** a telegram. **b.** a telegraphic system. **4.** the finish line of a racetrack. —*adj.* **5.** made of wire. —*v.t.* **6.** to equip, furnish, or connect with wire. **7.** to send by telegraph. **8.** to send a message to by telegraph. —*v.i.* **9.** to telegraph.

wired, *adj.* **1.** equipped, secured, strengthened, or supported with wires. **2.** *Slang.* tense with excitement or anticipation.

wire′less, *adj.* **1.** having no wire. **2.** operated with or actuated by electromagnetic waves. —*n.* **3.** wireless telegraphy or telephony. **4.** a wireless telegraph or telephone. **5.** *Chiefly Brit.* radio.

Wire′pho′to, *pl.* **-tos.** *Trademark.* a device for transmitting photographs over distances by wire.

wire′ serv′ice, *n.* an agency that sends syndicated news by wire to its subscribers.

wire′tap′, *n., v.,* **-tapped, -tap•ping.** —*n.* **1.** an act or instance of tapping a telephone or telegraph wire for information. —*v.t.* **2.** to listen in on by means of a wiretap. —*v.i.* **3.** to tap a telephone or telegraph wire. —**wire′tap′per,** *n.*

wir′ing, *n.* a system of electric wires, as in a building.

wir′y, *adj.,* **-i•er, -i•est. 1.** resembling wire. **2.** lean and sinewy. —**wir′i•ness,** *n.*

Wis. or **Wisc.,** Wisconsin.

Wis•con•sin (wis kon′sən), *n.* a state in the N central United States. 5,159,795. *Cap.*: Madison. *Abbr.*: WI, Wis., Wisc. —**Wis•con′sin•ite′,** *n.*

wis•dom (wiz′dəm), *n.* **1.** the quality or state of being wise. **2.** scholarly knowledge or learning. **3.** a wise act. —*Idiom.* **4. the wisdom of Solomon,** exceptional wisdom. I Kings 4:34.

wis′dom tooth′, *n.* the third molar on each side of the upper and lower jaws.

wise[1] (wīz), *adj.,* **wis•er, wis•est. 1.** having or showing discernment and good judgment. **2.** having or showing scholarly knowledge or learning; erudite. **3.** knowing; informed. —**wise′ly,** *adv.*

wise[2] (wīz), *n.* way; manner: *in no wise.*

-wise, a suffix meaning: in a particular manner, position, or direction (*clockwise*); with reference to (*timewise*).

wise′a′cre (-ā′kər), *n.* a conceited, often insolent person.

wise′crack′, *n.* **1.** a smart or facetious remark. —*v.i., v.t.* **2.** to make or say as a wisecrack.

Wise′ Men′, *n.pl.* the MAGI.

wish (wish), *v.t.* **1.** to want; desire. **2.** to desire (a person or thing) to be as specified: *We wished the matter settled.* **3.** to express a hope or desire for: *Wish me well.* **4.** to bid, as in greeting: *I wished her a good morning.* **5.** to request or charge: *I wish him to come.* —*v.i.* **6.** to desire; yearn. **7.** to make a wish. —*n.* **8.** an act or instance of wishing. **9.** a request or command. **10.** an expression of a wish. **11.** something wished or desired.

wish′bone′, *n.* a forked bone in front of the breastbone in most birds.

wish′ful, *adj.* having or showing a wish. —**wish′ful•ly,** *adv.*

wish•y-wash•y (wish′ē wosh′ē, -wô′shē), *adj.* **1.** lacking strength or character; ineffectual. **2.** watery, as a liquid; thin and weak.

wisp (wisp), *n.* **1.** a small bundle of straw or hay. **2.** a thin tuft, lock, or mass: *wisps of hair.* **3.** a thin puff or streak, as of smoke. **4.** a person or thing that is small or delicate. —**wisp′y,** *adj.,* -**i•er,** -**i•est.**

wis•te•ri•a (wi stēr′ē ə) also **wis•tar′i•a** (wi stēr′-, -stär′-), *n., pl.* -**as.** a climbing shrub with flower clusters in white, pale purple, blue-violet, or pink.

wist•ful (wist′fəl), *adj.* characterized by pensive longing. —**wist′ful•ly,** *adv.* —**wist′ful•ness,** *n.*

wit[1] (wit), *n.* **1.** the keen perception and clever expression of those connections between ideas that awaken amusement. **2.** a person having or noted for wit. **3.** Usu., **wits. a.** resourcefulness; ingenuity. **b.** mental faculties; senses. —*Idiom.* **4. at one's wit's** or **wits' end,** drained of all ideas or mental resources.

wit[2] (wit), *v.t., v.i.,* **wist** (wist), **wit•ting. 1.** *Archaic.* to know. —*Idiom.* **2. to wit,** that is to say.

witch (wich), *n.* **1.** a person believed to practice magic, esp. black magic. **2.** an ugly or mean old woman; hag. —*v.t.* **3.** to bewitch.

witch′craft′, *n.* the art or practices of a witch; sorcery.

witch′ doc′tor, *n.* a person in some societies who uses magic esp. to cure illness.

witch′er•y, *n., pl.* -**er•ies. 1.** witchcraft; magic. **2.** fascination; charm.

witch ha•zel (wich′ hā′zəl; *for 2 also* wich′ hā′-), *n.* **1.** a shrub that bears small yellow flowers. **2.** an alcoholic solution made from witch hazel leaves or bark and used as an astringent.

witch′ hunt′, *n.* an intensive, often highly publicized effort to discover and expose disloyal or subversive persons.

with (with, with), *prep.* **1.** accompanied by: *I will go with you.* **2.** in relation to: *dealt with the problem.* **3.** characterized by or having: *a person with initiative.* **4.** by means of; using: *cut with a knife.* **5.** in a manner showing: *working with diligence.* **6.** in comparison or proportion to: *How does their plan compare with ours?* **7.** in regard to: *was pleased with the gift.* **8.** owing to: *shaking with rage.* **9.** from: *hated to part*

with the book. **10.** against: *Don't fight with your brother.* **11.** in the keeping of: *left her cat with a friend.* **12.** in the judgment or estimation of: *Her argument carried weight with the trustees.* **13.** at the same time as or immediately after: *With that last remark, she left.* **14.** of the same opinion as: *Are you with me on this issue?* **15.** in the same household as: *He lives with his parents.* —*Proverb.* **16. He that is not with me is against me,** anything less than active support is almost as damaging as direct opposition. Luke 11:23.

with•al (with ôl′, with-), *adv.* **1.** as well; besides. **2.** in spite of all; nevertheless. **3.** *Archaic.* with that; therewith.

with•draw (with drô′, with-), *v.,* -**drew, -drawn, -draw•ing.** —*v.t.* **1.** to draw back, away, or aside. **2.** to remove, retract, or recall. —*v.i.* **3.** to move back, away, or aside. **4.** to remove oneself from participation, as in an activity.

with•draw′al, *n.* **1.** the act of withdrawing or state of being withdrawn. **2.** the act or process of ceasing to use an addictive drug.

with•drawn′, *v.* **1.** pp. of WITHDRAW. —*adj.* **2.** removed, as from circulation. **3.** shy and introverted; retiring.

withe (with, with, wīth), *n.* a tough, flexible twig or stem, as of willow, suitable for binding things together.

with•er (with′ər), *v.i.* **1.** to shrivel; fade. **2.** to lose freshness. —*v.t.* **3.** to cause to shrivel or fade. **4.** to make powerless, as by a scathing glance.

with′ers, *n.* (*used with a pl. v.*) the highest part of the back at the base of the neck of a horse.

with•hold (with hōld′, with-), *v.t.,* -**held, -hold•ing. 1.** to hold back; restrain or check. **2.** to refrain from giving or granting.

withhold′ing tax′, *n.* that part of an employee's tax liability withheld by the employer from wages or salary.

with•in (with in′, with-), *prep.* **1.** in or into the interior of: *within city walls.* **2.** in the compass or limits of; not beyond: *within view.* **3.** in the field, sphere, or scope of: *within the family.* —*adv.* **4.** in or into an interior or inner part. **5.** in the mind, heart, or soul; inwardly. —*n.* **6.** the inside of a place.

with•out (with out′, with-), *prep.* **1.** with no or none of; lacking: *without help; without shoes.* **2.** free from; excluding: *a world without hunger.* **3.** not accompanied by: *Don't go without me.* **4.** at, on, or to the outside of: *both within and without the city.* —*adv.* **5.** outside. **6.** outdoors. **7.** lacking something: *had to go without.*

with•stand (with stand′, with-), *v.t.,* -**stood, -stand•ing.** to resist or oppose; face successfully.

wit′less, *adj.* lacking wit or intelligence; stupid. —**wit′less•ly,** *adv.*

wit•ness (wit′nis), *v.t.* **1.** to see, hear, or know by personal presence and experience. **2.** to be present at as a legal witness. **3.** to give or be evidence of. **4.** to attest by one's signature. —*n.* **5.** one who has witnessed something, esp. one who is able to attest to what took place. **6.** one who gives testimony. **7.** something serving as evidence. **8.** testimony or evidence: *bore witness to her suffering.*

wit′ted, *adj.* having wit or intelligence: *quickwitted.*

Wit•ten•berg (wit′n bûrg′, vit′-), *n.* a city in E central Germany: Luther taught in the university here; beginnings of the Reformation 1517. 54,190.

wit•ti•cism (wit′ə siz′əm), *n.* a witty remark.

wit′ty, *adj.,* -**ti•er, -ti•est.** having or showing wit; amusingly clever. —**wit′ti•ly,** *adv.* —**wit′ti•ness,** *n.*

wives (wīvz), *n.* pl. of WIFE.

wiz•ard (wiz′ərd), *n.* **1.** a magician or sorcerer. **2.** a person of amazing skill or accomplishment. —**wiz′ard•ry,** *n.*

wiz•ened (wiz′ənd, wē′zənd), *adj.* withered; shriveled.

wk., **1.** week. **2.** work.

WNW, west-northwest.

w/o, without.

wob•ble (wob/əl), v., -bled, -bling, n. —v.i. **1.** to move unsteadily with a side-to-side motion. **2.** to be unsteady; tremble. **3.** to vacillate; waver. —v.t. **4.** to cause to wobble. —n. **5.** a wobbling movement. —wob/bly, adj., -bli•er, -bli•est. —wob/bli•ness, n.

woe (wō), n. **1.** grievous distress or trouble. **2.** an affliction.

woe/be•gone/ (-bi gôn/, -gon/), adj. feeling or showing woe; forlorn.

woe/ful, adj. **1.** full of woe; wretched. **2.** affected with, characterized by, or causing woe. **3.** of poor quality; deplorable. —woe/ful•ly, adv. —woe/ful•ness, n.

wok (wok), n. a large bowl-shaped pan used esp. in cooking Chinese food.

wok

woke (wōk), v. a pt. of WAKE¹.

wok/en, v. a pp. of WAKE¹.

wolf (wŏŏlf), n., pl. **wolves** (wŏŏlvz). **1.** any of several carnivorous predatory mammals resembling and related to the dog. **2.** a cruelly rapacious person. **3.** a man who makes amorous advances to women. —v.t. **4.** to devour voraciously. —wolf/ish, adj.

wolf/hound/, n. any of several large dogs once used in hunting wolves.

wolf•ram (wŏŏl/frəm), n. TUNGSTEN.

wol•ver•ine (wŏŏl/və rēn/), n. a strong, stocky Northern Hemisphere carnivore of the weasel family.

wom•an (wŏŏm/ən), n., pl. **wom•en** (wim/in). **1.** an adult female person. **2.** a female servant or attendant. **3.** women collectively; womankind. **4.** feminine nature, characteristics, or feelings. —Usage. Although formerly WOMAN was sometimes regarded as demeaning and LADY was the term of courtesy, WOMAN is the designation preferred by most modern female adults: League of Women Voters; American Association of University Women. WOMAN is the standard parallel to MAN. When modifying a plural noun, WOMAN, like MAN, becomes plural: women athletes; women students. The use of LADY as a term of courtesy has diminished somewhat in recent years, although it still survives in a few set phrases (ladies' room; Ladies' Day). LADY is also used, but decreasingly, as a term of reference for women engaged in occupations considered by some to be menial or routine: cleaning lady; saleslady. See also GIRL, LADY.

-woman, a combining form of WOMAN: chairwoman; forewoman; spokeswoman. —Usage. Compounds ending in -WOMAN commonly correspond to the masculine compounds in -MAN: congressman, congresswoman. The current practice, esp. in edited written English, is to avoid the -MAN form in reference to a woman or the plural -MEN when members of both sexes are involved. Often, a sex-neutral term is used; for example, council member, representatives, or legislators. See also -MAN, -PERSON.

wom/an•hood/, n. **1.** the state or time of being a woman. **2.** traditional womanly qualities. **3.** women collectively.

wom/an•ish, adj. **1.** characteristic or suggestive of a woman. **2.** weakly feminine; effeminate.

wom/an•kind/, n. women as distinguished from men.

wom/an•like/, adj. womanly.

wom/an•ly, adj. having qualities traditionally ascribed to women; feminine.

wom/an suf/frage, n. the right of women to vote.

womb (wŏŏm), n. **1.** UTERUS. **2.** the place in which something is formed or produced.

wom•bat (wom/bat), n. a burrowing, herbivorous Australian marsupial about the size of a badger.

wom/en's libera/tion, n. a movement to combat sexism and to gain rights and opportunities for women equal to those of men.

won¹ (wun), v. pt. and pp. of WIN.

won² (won), n., pl. **won.** the basic monetary unit of North and South Korea.

won•der (wun/dər), v.i. **1.** to think or speculate curiously and sometimes doubtfully. **2.** to be filled with awe; marvel. —v.t. **3.** to be curious about. —n. **4.** a cause of surprise, astonishment, or admiration. **5.** a feeling of amazement, puzzled interest, or reverent admiration.

won/der drug/, n. a new drug with a striking curative effect.

won/der•ful, adj. **1.** excellent; marvelous. **2.** exciting wonder; extraordinary. —won/der•ful•ly, adv.

won/der•land/, n. **1.** an imaginary land of wonders or marvels. **2.** a scene or place of special beauty or delight.

won/der•ment, n. **1.** an expression or state of wonder. **2.** a cause of wonder.

won/drous, adj. wonderful; remarkable. —won/drous•ly, adv.

wonk (wongk), n. Slang. **1.** a student who studies intensively; grind. **2.** a person who studies a subject or issue in an excessively assiduous and thorough manner: a policy wonk.

wont (wônt, wōnt, wunt), adj. **1.** accustomed; used: She is wont to rise at dawn. —n. **2.** custom; habit: It was his wont to meditate daily.

won't (wōnt), contraction of will not.

wont•ed (wôn/tid, wōn/-, wun/-), adj. customary; habitual.

won ton or **won•ton** (won/ ton/), n. a Chinese dumpling filled with minced pork and seasonings boiled and served in soup. [< dial. Chin]

woo (wŏŏ), v.t. **1.** to seek the love of, esp. with a view to marriage. **2.** to seek or invite: to woo fame. —v.i. **3.** to court a woman. —woo/er, n.

wood (wŏŏd), n. **1.** the hard, fibrous substance comprising most of the stem and branches of a tree or shrub beneath the bark. **2.** timber or lumber. **3.** FIREWOOD. **4.** Often, **woods.** a thick growth of trees; forest. **5.** any of a set of four golf clubs that orig. had wooden heads. —adj. **6.** made of wood; wooden. **7.** used to store, work, or carry wood. **8.** dwelling or growing in woods. —v.t. **9.** to plant with trees.

wood/ al/cohol, n. METHYL ALCOHOL.

wood/bine/ (-bīn/), n. any of several climbing vines, as the Virginia creeper.

wood/block/, n. **1.** WOODCUT. **2.** a block of wood.

wood/carv/ing, n. **1.** the art of carving objects by hand from wood. **2.** something made or decorated by woodcarving. —wood/carv/er, n.

wood/chuck/, n. a stocky North American burrowing rodent that hibernates in the winter.

wood/cock/, n., pl. **-cocks, -cock.** either of two plump, short-legged woodland birds of the sandpiper family.

wood/craft/, n. **1.** skill in matters that pertain to the woods. **2.** the art of making or carving wooden objects.

wood/cut/, n. **1.** a block of wood engraved in relief from which prints are made. **2.** a print or impression from a woodcut.

wood/cut/ter, n. a person who cuts down trees, esp. for firewood. —wood/cut/ting, n.

wood/ed, adj. covered with woods or trees.

wood/en, adj. **1.** consisting or made of wood. **2.** stiff, ungainly, or awkward. **3.** lacking animation; spiritless. —wood/en•ly, adv. —wood/en•ness, n.

wood/land/ (-land/, -lənd), n. land covered with woods or trees.

wood/man, n., pl. **-men.** WOODSMAN.

wood/peck/er, n. a climbing bird with a chisellike bill that it hammers repeatedly into wood in search of insects.

wood/pile/, n. a pile or stack of firewood.

wood/ruff (-rəf, -ruf/), *n.* a fragrant plant with small white flowers.

wood/shed/, *n.* a shed for storing firewood.

woods/man, *n., pl.* **-men.** a person accustomed to life in the woods and skilled in the arts of the woods.

woods/y, *adj.,* **-i•er, -i•est.** of or suggestive of woods.

wood/wind/, *n.* a musical wind instrument of the group comprising the flutes, clarinets, oboes, bassoons, and saxophones.

wood/work/, *n.* **1.** objects or parts made of wood. **2.** interior wooden fittings, as doors or moldings. —**wood/work/er,** *n.* —**wood/work/ing,** *n.*

wood/y, *adj.,* **-i•er, -i•est. 1.** abounding with woods; wooded. **2.** consisting of or containing wood. **3.** resembling wood. —**wood/i•ness,** *n.*

woof (woŏf, woōf), *n.* **1.** the threads interlacing at right angles with the warp in a woven fabric. **2.** texture; fabric.

woof•er (woōf/ər), *n.* a loudspeaker to reproduce low-frequency sounds.

wool (woŏl), *n.* **1.** the fine, soft, curly hair that forms the fleece of some animals, esp. sheep. **2.** yarn, a fabric, or a garment of wool. **3.** something resembling the wool of sheep: *steel wool.*

wool/en, *adj.* **1.** of, made of, or consisting of wool. —*n.* **2. woolens,** wool cloth or clothing. Also, *esp. Brit.,* **wool/len.**

Woolf (woŏlf), *n.* **Virginia** (*Adeline Virginia Stephen Woolf*), 1882–1941, English novelist, essayist, and critic.

wool/gath/er•ing, *n.* indulgence in idle fancies and daydreaming.

wool/ly or **wool/y,** *adj.,* **-li•er** or **-i•er, -li•est** or **-i•est,** *n., pl.* **-lies** or **-ies.** —*adj.* **1.** of or resembling wool. **2.** rough, vigorous, and lacking in order: *the wild and woolly West.* **3.** unclear; disorganized: *woolly thinking.* —*n.* **4.** *Western U.S.* a wool-bearing animal; sheep. **5.** a woolen garment, esp. a knitted undergarment.

wool/ly bear/, *n.* any of several caterpillars with woolly hairs.

Wool•worth (woŏl/wûrth/), *n.* **Frank Winfield,** 1852–1919, U.S. merchant.

wooz•y (woō/zē, woŏz/ē), *adj.,* **-i•er, -i•est. 1.** confused; muddled. **2.** dizzy, faint, or nauseated. —**wooz/i•ly,** *adv.* —**wooz/i•ness,** *n.*

Worces•ter (woŏs/tər), *n.* a city in central Massachusetts. 165,387.

word (wûrd), *n.* **1.** a linguistic unit consisting of one or more spoken sounds or their written representation and functioning as a carrier of meaning. **2. words, a.** the text or lyrics of a song. **b.** a quarrel. **3.** a short talk. **4.** something said; expression or utterance. **5.** assurance or promise. **6.** news; information. **7.** a verbal signal, as a password. **8.** an authoritative command. **9.** (*cap.*) Also called **the Word, the Word/ of God/. a.** the Scriptures; Bible. **b.** the Logos. **c.** the message of the gospel of Christ. **d.** Jesus Christ. I John 1:1-14; Rev. 19:13. —*v.t.* **10.** to express in words. —*Idiom.* **11. in a word,** in short. **12. in so many words,** in unequivocal terms; explicitly.

word•age (wûr/dij), *n.* **1.** words collectively. **2.** number of words. **3.** choice of words; wording.

word/book/, *n.* a dictionary.

word/ing, *n.* choice of words to express something.

word/ of mouth/, *n.* oral communication.

word/play/, *n.* witty repartee, esp. a play on words.

word/ proc/essing, *n.* the automated production and storage of documents using computers, electronic printers, and text-editing software. —**word/ proc/essor,** *n.*

Words•worth (wûrdz/wûrth/), *n.* **William,** 1770–1850, English poet: poet laureate 1843–50.

word/y, *adj.,* **-i•er, -i•est.** characterized by or given to the use of too many words; verbose. —**word/i•ness,** *n.*

wore (wôr), *v.* pt. of WEAR.

work (wûrk), *n., adj., v.,* **worked** or (*Archaic except in some senses, esp. 22, 23, 25*) **wrought; work•ing.** —*n.* **1.** exertion or effort to produce or accomplish something; labor. **2.** a task or undertaking. **3.** productive activity, esp. employment: *looking for work.* **4.** a place of employment. **5.** something, as material, on which work is being or is to be done. **6.** the result of exertion, labor, or activity. **7.** an engineering structure, as a bridge. **8.** something, as a wall, constructed as a means of fortification. **9. works, a.** (*used with a sing. or pl. v.*) a place or establishment for manufacturing. **b.** the working parts of a machine. **10.** *Physics.* the transfer of energy measured by the scalar product of a force and the distance through which it acts. **11. the works, a.** everything: *a hamburger with the works.* **b.** unpleasant or abusive treatment: *gave him the works.* —*adj.* **12.** of, for, or concerning work: *work clothes.* —*v.i.* **13.** to do work. **14.** to be employed. **15.** to be functional, as a machine; operate. **16.** to prove effective: *This plan works.* **17.** to come to be, as by repeated movement: *The nails worked loose.* **18.** to have an effect, as on a person's feelings. **19.** to make way with effort or under stress. **20.** to ferment, as a liquid. —*v.t.* **21.** to use or operate (an apparatus, machine, etc.). **22.** to bring about by or as if by work. **23.** to put into or keep in operation. **24.** to carry on operations in (a region). **25.** to make or fashion by work. **26.** to cause to work: *He works his employees hard.* **27.** to solve (a puzzle or problem). **28.** to cause a strong emotion in: *to work a crowd into a frenzy.* **29.** to make or decorate by needlework or embroidery. **30. work off,** to get rid of. **31. ~ on,** to try to influence or persuade. **32. ~ out, a.** to bring about. **b.** to solve, as a problem. **c.** to arrive at by or as if by calculation. **d.** to have a result. **e.** to evolve; elaborate. **f.** to amount. **g.** to prove effective or successful. **h.** to exercise or train, esp. in an athletic sport. **33. ~ through,** to deal with successfully. **34. ~ up, a.** to stir the feelings of; excite. **b.** to prepare; elaborate. **c.** to cause to develop by exertion. —*Idiom.* **35. in the works,** in preparation. **36. out of work,** not employed. —*Proverb.* **37. He who does not work, neither should he eat,** idleness should not be rewarded. II Thess. 3:10

work/a•ble, *adj.* **1.** practicable or feasible. **2.** capable of being worked.

work•a•day (wûr/kə dā/), *adj.* **1.** characteristic of or befitting working days. **2.** ordinary; everyday.

work/a•hol/ic (-hô/lik, -hol/ik), *n.* a person who works compulsively. [*work* + -AHOLIC]

work/bench/, *n.* a sturdy table at which an artisan works.

work/book/, *n.* **1.** a book for students containing questions, exercises, and problems. **2.** a manual of operating instructions. **3.** a book in which a record of work is kept.

work/day/, *n.* **1.** a day on which work is done. **2.** the part of a day during which one works.

work/er, *n.* **1.** one that works. **2.** a laborer or employee. **3.** a sterile bee, ant, wasp, or termite, specialized to collect food and maintain the colony.

work/ eth/ic, *n.* a belief in the moral importance of work.

work/fare/, *n.* a government plan under which employable welfare recipients are required to accept public-service jobs.

work/ farm/, *n.* a farm to which minor offenders are sent.

work/horse/, *n.* **1.** a horse used for heavy labor. **2.** a person who works tirelessly.

work/house/, *n.* **1.** a house of correction in which the prisoners are required to work. **2.** *Brit.* a poorhouse.

work/ing, *n.* **1.** the act of one that works. **2.** operation; action. —*adj.* **3.** engaged in work, esp. manual labor, for a living. **4.** permitting or facilitating continued work: *a working model.* **5.** adequate for usual or customary needs: *a working knowledge of Spanish.*

work/ing•man/, *n., pl.* **-men.** a man who earns his living esp. at some manual or industrial work.

work/load/, *n.* the amount of work that a machine,

employee, or group of employees can be or is expected to perform.

work′man, *n., pl.* **-men.** a man employed or skilled in manual, mechanical, or industrial work.

work′man•like′, *adj.* well executed; skillful.

work′man•ship′, *n.* **1.** the art or skill of a workman. **2.** the quality or mode of execution of work done.

work′out′, *n.* **1.** practice or a test to maintain or determine physical ability or endurance. **2.** a structured regime of physical exercise.

work′place′, *n.* a place of employment.

work′room′, *n.* a room in which work is done.

work′shop′, *n.* **1.** a room or building in which work, esp. mechanical work, is carried on. **2.** a seminar that meets to explore a subject or develop a skill or technique.

work′sta′tion, *n.* **1.** a work area for one person that often accommodates a computer terminal or microcomputer connected to a mainframe, minicomputer, or data-processing network. **2.** a powerful microcomputer used for graphics-intensive processing.

work′ta′ble, *n.* a table for working at.

work′up′, *n.* a thorough medical diagnostic examination.

work′week′, *n.* the total number of working hours or days in a week.

world (wûrld), *n.* **1.** the earth considered as a planet. **2.** (*often cap.*) a particular division of the earth: *the Western world.* **3.** the human race; humanity. **4.** the general public. **5.** a class of people with common interests: *the literary world.* **6.** a sphere, realm, or domain: *the world of dreams.* **7.** everything that exists; the universe. **8.** one of the general groupings of physical nature: *the animal world.* **9.** Often, **worlds.** a great deal: *a world of problems.* **10.** a heavenly body. —*Idiom.* **11. for all the world,** in every respect; precisely. **12. out of this world,** extraordinary; wonderful.

World′ Bank′, *n.* an international bank established in 1944 to help the development of countries that are members of the United Nations. Official name, **International Bank for Reconstruction and Development.**

world′ beat′, *n.* (*sometimes caps.*) any of various styles of popular music combining traditional, indigenous forms with elements of another culture's music.

world′-class′, *adj.* being among the world's best; of the highest caliber.

World′ Commun′ion Sun′day, *n.* the first Sunday in October, on which Christians throughout the world celebrate Holy Communion to affirm their unity in Christ.

World′ Coun′cil of Church′es, *n.* an ecumenical organization formed in 1948, comprising more than 160 Protestant and Eastern churches in over 48 countries, for cooperative theological and secular action.

World′ Cup′, *n.* the trophy for the world championship in soccer, or the quadrennial international competition for this trophy.

world′ly, *adj.,* **-li•er, -li•est. 1.** of this world as contrasted with heaven or spiritual life. **2.** experienced; sophisticated. —**world′li•ness,** *n.*

world′ly-wise′, *adj.* wise as to the affairs of this world.

World War I, *n.* the war (1914–18) in which France, Great Britain, Russia, the U.S., and their allies defeated Germany, Austria-Hungary, Turkey, and Bulgaria.

World War II, *n.* the war (1939–45) in which Great Britain, France, the U.S., the Soviet Union, and their allies defeated Germany, Italy, and Japan.

world′-wea′ry, *adj.* weary of the world; blasé.

world′wide′, *adj., adv.* throughout the world.

World′ Wide′ Web′, *n.* a system of extensively interlinked hypertext documents: a branch of the Internet.

worm (wûrm), *n.* **1.** any of numerous long, soft-bodied, legless invertebrates, as the earthworm. **2.** something resembling a worm in appearance or movement. **3.** a groveling or contemptible person. **4.**

worms, (*used with a sing. v.*) a disorder caused by parasitic worms in the intestines. —*v.i.* **5.** to creep, crawl, or advance slowly, stealthily, or insidiously. —*v.t.* **6.** to cause to move deviously or stealthily. **7.** to get by persistent, insidious efforts: *He wormed the secret out of his sister.* **8.** to insinuate (oneself) into another's favor or confidence. **9.** to free from intestinal worms. —**worm′y,** *adj.*

worm′ gear′, *n.* a mechanism consisting of a rotating shaft engaging with and driving a gearwheel.

worm′wood′, *n.* **1.** a bitter aromatic plant. **2.** a plant mentioned in the Bible, symbolizing the bitterness of sorrow. Jer. 9:15; Lam. 3:15, 19.

worn (wôrn), *v.* **1.** pp. of WEAR. —*adj.* **2.** diminished in value or usefulness through wear or use. **3.** exhausted; spent.

worn′-out′, *adj.* **1.** worn or used beyond repair. **2.** depleted of energy or strength; exhausted.

wor•ri•ment (wûr′ē mənt, wur′-), *n.* **1.** an act or instance of worrying. **2.** a source or cause of worry.

wor′ri•some (-səm), *adj.* **1.** causing worry. **2.** inclined to worry.

wor′ry, *v.,* **-ried, -ry•ing,** *n., pl.* **-ries.** —*v.i.* **1.** to feel uneasy or anxious. —*v.t.* **2.** to make uneasy or anxious. **3.** to disturb with annoyances; plague. **4.** to seize with the teeth and shake or mangle. **5.** to touch or adjust repeatedly. —*n.* **6.** uneasiness or anxiety. **7.** a cause of worry. —**wor′ri•er,** *n.*

wor′ry•wart′, *n.* a person who tends to worry too much.

worse (wûrs), *adj., comparative of* **bad** *and* **ill. 1.** bad or ill to a greater extent; inferior. **2.** more unfavorable or injurious. **3.** in poorer health. —*n.* **4.** something that is worse. —*adv.* **5.** in a worse manner. **6.** to a worse degree.

wors′en, *v.t., v.i.* to make or become worse.

wor•ship (wûr′ship), *n., v.,* **-shiped** *or* **-shipped, -ship•ing** *or* **-ship•ping.** —*n.* **1.** reverence for God, a sacred personage, or a sacred object. **2.** a formal or ceremonious expression of worship. **3.** adoring reverence or regard. **4.** (*cap.*) *Brit.* a title of honor for certain magistrates and others of high rank or station. —*v.t.* **5.** to render religious worship to. **6.** to feel an adoring reverence or regard for. —*v.i.* **7.** to engage in religious worship. —**wor′ship•er,** *n.* —**wor′ship•ful,** *adj.*

worst (wûrst), *adj., superlative of* **bad** *and* **ill. 1.** bad or ill in the most extreme degree. **2.** most faulty or unsatisfactory. **3.** most unfavorable or injurious. **4.** in the poorest condition. **5.** most unpleasant, unattractive, or disagreeable. **6.** least skilled. —*n.* **7.** something that is worst. —*adv.* **8.** in the worst manner. **9.** in the greatest degree. —*v.t.* **10.** to defeat; beat. —*Idiom.* **11. at (the) worst,** under the worst conditions. **12. if worst comes to worst,** if the very worst happens. **13. in the worst way,** very much; extremely.

wor•sted (wŏos′tid, wûr′stid), *n.* **1.** a firmly twisted yarn or thread spun from wool fibers. **2.** wool cloth woven from worsted.

wort (wûrt, wôrt), *n.* an infusion of malt that after fermentation becomes beer.

worth (wûrth), *prep.* **1.** good or important enough to justify: *a place worth visiting.* **2.** having a value of: *a vase worth 20 dollars.* **3.** having property to the value of: *They are worth millions.* —*n.* **4.** excellence, as of character; merit. **5.** value, as in money. **6.** a quantity of something of a specified value: *50 cents' worth of candy.* **7.** property or possessions; wealth.

worth′less, *adj.* without worth; valueless. —**worth′less•ness,** *n.*

worth′while′, *adj.* worthy of the time, work, trouble, or money spent.

wor•thy (wûr′thē), *adj.,* **-thi•er, -thi•est,** *n., pl.* **-thies.** —*adj.* **1.** having merit, character, or value. **2.** deserving; meritorious: *an effort worthy of praise.* —*n.* **3.** a person of worth. —**wor′thi•ness,** *n.*

would (wŏod; *unstressed* wəd), *v.* **1.** pt. of WILL¹. **2.** (used to express the future): *He said he would go tomorrow.* **3.** (used in place of *will* to soften a statement or question): *Would you be so kind?* **4.** (used to express habitual action in the past): *We would take the train every morning.* **5.** (used to express a wish, intention, or inclination): *Nutritionists would have us all eat whole grains.* **6.** (used to express uncertainty): *It would appear that he is guilty.* **7.** (used to express choice or possibility): *They would come if they had the fare.*

would'-be', *adj.* wishing or pretending to be.

would•n't (wood'nt), contraction of *would not.*

wouldst (woodst, wootst) also **would•est** (wood'-ist), *v. Archaic.* 2nd pers. sing. past of WILL[1].

wound[1] (woond), *n.* **1.** an injury, usu. involving the cutting or tearing of tissue. **2.** an injury or hurt to feelings, sensibilities, or reputation. —*v.t.* **3.** to inflict a wound upon; injure.

wound[2] (wound), *v.* a pt. and pp. of WIND[2].

Wound'ed Knee', *n.* a village in SW South Dakota: site of a massacre of about 300 Oglala Sioux Indians on Dec. 29, 1890.

wove (wōv), *v.* a pt. and pp. of WEAVE.

wo•ven (wō'vən), *v.* a pp. of WEAVE.

wow (wou), *interj.* **1.** an exclamation of surprise, wonder, or pleasure. —*v.t.* **2.** to elicit an enthusiastic response from; thrill. —*n.* **3.** an extraordinary success.

WPA, Work Projects Administration: the federal agency (1935–43) charged with administering public works in order to relieve national unemployment.

wpm, words per minute.

wrack (rak), *n.* **1.** damage or destruction: *wrack and ruin.* **2.** a trace of something destroyed.

wraith (rāth), *n.* an apparition; ghost.

wran•gle (rang'gəl), *v.,* **-gled, -gling,** *n.* —*v.i.* **1.** to argue or dispute, esp. noisily or angrily. —*v.t.* **2.** to tend or round up (livestock, as cattle). **3.** to obtain by badgering. —*n.* **4.** a noisy or angry dispute. —**wran'gler,** *n.*

wrap (rap), *v.,* **wrapped** or **wrapt, wrap•ping,** *n.* —*v.t.* **1.** to enclose or cover in something wound or folded about. **2.** to enclose and make fast within a covering, as of paper. **3.** to wind or fold (something) around as a covering. **4.** to surround, envelop, or hide. **5.** to cover (fingernails) with a sheer fabric to repair or strengthen them. —*v.i.* **6.** to become wrapped. **7. a. wrap up,** to finish work on; conclude. **b.** to give a summary of. —*n.* **8.** something, as a shawl, to be wrapped around a person, esp. for warmth. **9.** a wrapper. **10.** a sheer fabric glued to the fingernails to repair or strengthen them. **11.** a beauty treatment in which part of the body is covered with lotion, herbs, or the like and then wrapped snugly with cloth. **12.** a piece of thin, flat bread wrapped around a filling and eaten as a sandwich. —*Idiom.* **13. under wraps,** *Informal.* secret. **14. wrapped up in,** intensely absorbed in.

wrap'a•round', *n.* a garment that wraps around the body and overlaps at a full-length opening.

wrap'per, *n.* **1.** one that wraps. **2.** something in which a thing is wrapped. **3.** a loose garment, esp. a woman's bathrobe or negligee.

wrap'ping, *n.* Often, **-pings.** the covering in which something is wrapped.

wrap'-up', *n.* a final report; summary.

wrath (rath, räth), *n.* **1.** fierce anger; ire. **2.** punishment for sins; retribution. —**wrath'ful,** *adj.*

wreak (rēk), *v.t.* **1.** to inflict (punishment, vengeance, etc.). **2.** to carry out the promptings of (rage, ill humor, etc.), as on a victim.

wreath (rēth), *n., pl.* **wreaths** (rēthz, rēths). **1.** a circular band, as of flowers, used for decorative purposes. **2.** a ringlike, curving, or curling mass or formation.

wreathe (rēth), *v.t.,* **wreathed, wreath•ing. 1.** to encircle or adorn with or as if with a wreath. **2.** to form as a wreath by twisting or twining. **3.** to envelop: *a face wreathed in smiles.*

wreck (rek), *n.* **1.** a building, structure, or object reduced to ruin. **2. a.** wreckage remaining after a shipwreck, esp. when cast ashore. **b.** a shipwreck. **3.** ruin; destruction. **4.** a person of ruined physical or mental health. —*v.t.* **5.** to cause the wreck of. **6.** to tear down; demolish.

wreck'age (-ij), *n.* **1.** the act of wrecking or state of being wrecked. **2.** the remains of something that has been wrecked.

wreck'er, *n.* **1.** one that wrecks. **2.** a vehicle equipped to tow wrecked or disabled automobiles. **3.** a person or business that demolishes and removes buildings. **4.** a person or ship employed in recovering salvage from wrecks.

wren (ren), *n.* any of various small songbirds with streaked or spotted brown-gray plumage.

wrench (rench), *v.t.* **1.** to pull, jerk, or force with a violent twist. **2.** to injure (the ankle, knee, etc.) by a sudden, violent twist. **3.** to affect distressingly as if by a wrench. —*n.* **4.** a sudden, violent twist. **5.** a sharp, distressing strain, as to the feelings. **6.** a tool for gripping and turning or twisting a bolt, nut, etc.

wrest (rest), *v.t.* **1.** to take away by force. **2.** to get by effort. **3.** to twist or turn from the proper course or meaning. —*n.* **4.** a twist or wrench.

wres•tle (res'əl), *v.,* **-tled, -tling,** *n.* —*v.i.* **1.** to engage in wrestling. **2.** to struggle, as for mastery. —*v.t.* **3.** to contend with in wrestling. **4.** to force by or as if by wrestling. —*n.* **5.** an act or bout of wrestling. —**wres'tler,** *n.*

wres'tling, *n.* a sport in which two opponents struggle hand to hand in order to pin or press each other's shoulders to the mat.

wretch (rech), *n.* **1.** a very unfortunate or unhappy person. **2.** a despicable or base person.

wretch'ed, *adj.* **1.** very unfortunate; pitiable. **2.** characterized by or causing misery and sorrow. **3.** contemptible or mean. **4.** worthless; inferior. —**wretch'ed•ly,** *adv.* —**wretch'ed•ness,** *n.*

wrig•gle (rig'əl), *v.,* **-gled, -gling,** *n.* —*v.i.* **1.** to twist and fro; writhe. **2.** to move along by twisting and turning the body, as a worm. **3.** to make one's way by shifts or expedients. —*v.t.* **4.** to cause to wriggle. —*n.* **5.** the act or motion of wriggling. —**wrig'gly,** *adj.,* **-gli•er, -gli•est.**

wrig'gler, *n.* **1.** one that wriggles. **2.** the larva of a mosquito.

Wright (rīt), *n.* **1.** Frank Lloyd, 1867–1959, U.S. architect. **2. Orville,** 1871–1948, and his brother **Wilbur,** 1867–1912, U.S. aeronautical inventors. **3. Richard,** 1908–60, U.S. novelist.

wring (ring), *v.,* **wrung, wring•ing,** *n.* —*v.t.* **1.** to twist forcibly. **2.** to twist or compress to force out a liquid. **3.** to extract by or as if by wringing. **4.** to affect painfully. **5.** to clasp tightly, usu. with twisting: *She wrung her hands in anguish.* —*n.* **6.** the act of wringing.

wring'er, *n.* **1.** one that wrings. **2.** an apparatus for squeezing out liquid, as from wet clothing.

wrin•kle[1] (ring'kəl), *n., v.,* **-kled, -kling.** —*n.* **1.** a small crease in the skin, as from aging. **2.** a slight ridge in a fabric, as from folding. **3.** a problem; fault: *still a few wrinkles to be worked out.* —*v.t., v.i.* **4.** to form wrinkles (in). —**wrin'kly,** *adj.,* **-kli•er, -kli•est.**

wrin•kle[2] (ring'kəl), *n.* a creative innovation.

wrist (rist), *n.* **1.** the part of the forearm where it joins the hand. **2.** the joint between the forearm and the hand.

wrist'band', *n.* **1.** the band of a sleeve that covers the wrist. **2.** a wristwatch strap that encircles the wrist.

wrist'watch', *n.* a watch attached to a strap or band worn about the wrist.

writ (rit), *n.* **1.** a court order directing a person to do or refrain from doing something specified. **2.** something written.

write (rīt), *v.,* **wrote, writ•ten, writ•ing.** —*v.t.* **1.** to form (letters, words, etc.), esp. on paper, with a pen or pencil. **2.** to express or communicate in writing. **3.** to communicate with by letter. **4.** to be the author or composer of. **5.** to transfer (data, text, etc.) from computer memory to an output medium. —*v.i.* **6.** to express ideas in writing. **7.** to write a letter. **8. write in,** to vote for (a candidate not listed) by writing his or her name on the ballot. **9. ~ off, a.** to cancel (an unpaid or uncollectible debt). **b.** to amortize. **10. ~**

out, to write in full. **11.** ~ **up,** to put into writing, esp. in full detail.

write′-in′, *n.* a candidate or vote for a candidate not listed on a ballot but written in by the voter.

write′-off′, *n.* something written off.

writ′er, *n.* a person engaged in writing, esp. as an occupation.

writ′er's cramp′, *n.* a spasmodic, painful contraction of the muscles of the hand and forearm from constant writing.

write′-up′, *n.* a written account, as in a newspaper.

writhe (rīth), *v.,* **writhed, writh•ing,** *n.* —*v.i.* **1.** to twist and turn, as in pain. **2.** to suffer acute embarrassment. —*n.* **3.** a twisting of the body.

writ′ing, *n.* **1.** the act of one that writes. **2.** written matter. **3.** written form: *Put the agreement in writing.* **4.** handwriting. **5.** the style, form, or quality of a composition: *stilted writing.* **6.** the profession of a writer.

writ•ten (rit′n), *v.* pp. of WRITE.

Wroc•ław (vRôts′läf), *n.* a city in SW Poland. 1,119,000.

wrong (rông, rong), *adj.* **1.** not in accordance with what is morally right. **2.** deviating from truth or fact; incorrect. **3.** being in error; mistaken. **4.** not proper; unsuitable. **5.** out of order; amiss. **6.** of or being a surface or side ordinarily kept inward or under. —*n.* **7.** something improper, immoral, unjust, or harmful. —*adv.* **8.** in a wrong manner. —*v.t.* **9.** to do wrong to; harm. **10.** to impute evil to (someone) unjustly; malign. —*Idiom.* **11. in the wrong,** being in error. —*Proverb.* **12. Two wrongs don't make a right,** responding to evil behavior with an equally reprehensible act makes the situation worse, not better. [< Scand] —**wrong′ly,** *adv.* —**wrong′ness,** *n.*

wrong′do′er, *n.* a person who does wrong, esp. a sinner or transgressor. —**wrong′do′ing,** *n.*

wrong′ful, *adj.* **1.** not just; unfair. **2.** not legal; unlawful. —**wrong′ful•ly,** *adv.* —**wrong′ful•ness,** *n.*

wrong′head′ed, *adj.* misguided and stubborn; perverse. —**wrong′head′ed•ly,** *adv.* —**wrong′head′-ed•ness,** *n.*

wrote (rōt), *v.* pt. of WRITE.

wroth (rôth, roth), *adj.* angry; wrathful.

wrought (rôt), *v.* **1.** *Archaic except in some senses.* a pt. and pp. of WORK. —*adj.* **2.** worked; formed. **3.** embellished. **4.** shaped by being beaten with a hammer.

wrought′ i′ron, *n.* a form of iron, almost entirely free of carbon, easily forged and welded. —**wrought′-i′ron,** *adj.*

wrought′-up′, *adj.* stirred up; excited.

wrung (rung), *v.* pt. and pp. of WRING.

wry (rī), *adj.,* **wri•er, wri•est. 1.** contorted; lopsided: *a wry grin.* **2.** abnormally bent or turned to one side; twisted. **3.** bitingly ironic or amusing. —**wry′ly,** *adv.* —**wry′ness,** *n.*

WSW, west-southwest.

Wu•han (wōō′hän′), *n.* a city in E China. 3,400,000.

wuss (wŏŏs), *n. Slang.* a weakling; wimp.

WV or **W.V.,** West Virginia.

W.Va., West Virginia.

WWI, World War I.

WWII, World War II.

WWW, World Wide Web.

WY or **Wy.,** Wyoming.

Wyc•liffe or **Wyc•lif** (wik′lif), *n.* **John,** c1320–84, English religious reformer and Bible translator.

Wy•eth (wī′əth), *n.* **1. Andrew (Newell),** born 1917, U.S. painter. **2.** his father, **Newell Convers,** 1882–1945, U.S. illustrator and painter.

Wyo., Wyoming.

Wy•o•ming (wī ō′ming), *n.* a state in the NW United States. 481,400. *Cap.:* Cheyenne. *Abbr.:* WY, Wy, Wyo. —Wy•o′ming•ite′, *n.*

WYSIWYG (wiz′ē wig′), *adj.* of or being a computer screen display that shows text exactly as it will appear when printed. [*w(hat) y(ou) s(ee) i(s) w(hat) y(ou) g(et)*]

X Y Z

X, x (eks), *n., pl.* **Xs** or **X's, xs** or **x's. 1.** the 24th letter of the English alphabet, a consonant. **2.** something that is shaped like an X.

X, *Symbol.* **1.** the Roman numeral for 10. **2.** Christ. **3.** Christian. **4.** a person or thing of unknown identity.

x, *Symbol.* **1.** an unknown quantity; variable. **2.** times: *8 × 8 = 64.* **3.** a person or thing of unknown identity.

Xa•vi•er (zā′vē ər,), *n.* **Saint Francis** (*Francisco Javier*), 1506–52, Spanish Jesuit missionary.

X′ chro′mosome, *n.* a sex chromosome that determines femaleness when paired with another X chromosome and that occurs singly in males.

Xe, *Chem. Symbol.* xenon.

xe•non (zē′non, zen′on), *n.* a heavy, colorless, chemically inactive gaseous element used for filling radio, television, and luminescent tubes. *Symbol:* Xe; *at. wt.:* 131.30; *at. no.:* 54.

xen•o•pho•bi•a (zen′ə fō′bē ə, zē′nə-), *n.* an unreasonable fear or hatred of foreigners or strangers or of anything foreign or strange. —**xen′o•pho′bic,** *adj.*

Xen•o•phon (zen′ə fən, -fon′), *n.* 434?–355? B.C., Greek historian.

xe•rog•ra•phy (zi rog′rə fē), *n.* a copying process in which areas on a sheet of paper corresponding to those on an original are sensitized by static electricity and sprinkled with resin that is fused to the paper. —**xe•ro•graph•ic** (zēr′ə graf′ik), *adj.*

Xe•rox (zēr′oks), **1.** *Trademark.* a brand name for a copying machine using xerography. —*n.* **2.** (*some*times *l.c.*) a copy made on a Xerox. —*v.t., v.i.* **3.** (*sometimes l.c.*) to print or reproduce by Xerox.

Xerx•es I (zûrk′sēz), *n.* 519?–465 B.C., king of Persia 486?–465.

xi (zī, sī; *Gk.* ksē), *n., pl.* **xis.** the 14th letter of the Greek alphabet (Ξ, ξ).

Xi•an (shē′än′), *n.* a city in central China. 2,330,000.

XL, 1. extra large. **2.** extra long.

Xmas (kris′məs; *often* eks′məs), Christmas.

x-ray or **X-ray,** *n.* Also, **x ray, X ray. 1.** Often, **x-rays.** electromagnetic radiation having very short wavelengths and capable of penetrating solids. **2.** a photograph made by —*v.t.* **3.** to photograph, examine, or treat with x-rays.

XS, extra small.

xy•lem (zī′ləm, -lem), *n.* a woody tissue in vascular plants that helps provide support and conducts water and nutrients.

xylophone

xy•lo•phone (zī′lə fōn′), *n.* a musical instrument consisting of a graduated series of wooden bars struck with small wooden hammers. —**xy′lo•phon′-ist,** *n.*

Y, y (wī), *n., pl.* **Ys** or **Y's, ys** or **y's. 1.** the 25th letter of the English alphabet, a semivowel. **2.** something shaped like a Y.

Y, *Chem. Symbol.* yttrium.

y, *Math. Symbol.* an unknown quantity; variable.

-y¹, an adjective suffix meaning: characterized by or like (*cloudy*); inclined to (*squeaky*).

-y², a noun suffix meaning: dear (*granny*); little (*kitty*).

-y³, a noun suffix meaning: action of (*inquiry*); quality or state (*victory*); goods or business establishment specified (*bakery*).

yacht (yot), *n.* **1.** a boat or ship used for private cruising or racing. —*v.i.* **2.** to cruise, race, or sail in a yacht. —**yachts'man,** *n., pl.* **-men.**

ya•da•ya•da-ya•da or **yad•da-yad•da-yad•da** (yä'də yä'də yä'də), *adv.* and so on; and so forth; et cetera.

ya•hoo (yä'hoo), *n., pl.* **-hoos.** an uncultivated or boorish person; lout.

Yah•weh (yä'we) also **-veh** (-ve), *n.* a name of God, commonly rendered Jehovah.

yak¹ (yak), *n.* a large, shaggy-haired wild ox of the Tibetan highlands.

yak

yak² (yak), *v.,* **yakked** or **yacked, yak•king** or **yack•ing,** *n. Slang.* —*v.i.* **1.** to gab; chatter. —*n.* **2.** incessant idle or gossipy talk.

Yal•ta (yôl'tə, yäl'-), *n.* a seaport in the Crimea: site of wartime conference of Roosevelt, Churchill, and Stalin 1945. 83,000.

yam (yam), *n.* **1.** the starchy, tuberous root of an African climbing vine resembling but unrelated to the sweet potato. **2.** the sweet potato.

yam•mer (yam'ər), *Informal.* —*v.i.* **1.** to whine or complain. **2.** to talk loudly and persistently. —*n.* **3.** the act or noise of yammering. —**yam'mer•er,** *n.*

Ya•mous•sou•kro (yä'mə soo'krō), *n.* the capital of the Ivory Coast. 120,000.

yang (yäng, yang), *n.* See under YIN AND YANG.

Yan•gon (yang gon', -gôn'), *n.* the capital of Myanmar (formerly Burma). 2,459,000. Formerly, **Rangoon.**

Yang•tze (yang'sē', -tsē'), *n.* CHANG JIANG.

yank (yangk), *v.i., v.t.* to pull or tug sharply. —*n.* **2.** an abrupt, sharp pull.

Yank (yangk), *n., adj. Informal.* Yankee.

Yan•kee (yang'kē), *n.* **1.** a native or inhabitant of the United States. **2.** a native or inhabitant of New England. **3.** a native or inhabitant of a Northern state. —*adj.* **4.** of or characteristic of a Yankee.

Yan'kee Clip'per, *n.* epithet of Joe DiMaggio.

Yaoun•dé (youn'dā, youn dā'), *n.* the capital of Cameroon. 436,000.

yap (yap), *v.,* **yapped, yap•ping,** *n.* —*v.i.* **1.** to bark sharply; yelp. **2.** *Slang.* to talk noisily or foolishly. —*n.* **3.** a sharp bark; yelp. **4.** *Slang.* **a.** noisy or foolish talk. **b.** the mouth. —**yap'per,** *n.*

yard¹ (yärd), *n.* **1.** a unit of linear measure equal to 3 feet or 36 inches (0.9144 meter). **2.** a long spar, supported at its center, by which the head of a sail is supported.

yard² (yärd), *n.* **1.** the ground that adjoins or surrounds a building. **2.** an outdoor space surrounded by buildings, as on a college campus. **3.** an enclosure for livestock. **4.** an enclosed area set aside for particular use: *lumberyard.* **5.** a system of railroad

tracks where trains are made up and rolling stock is stored.

yard•age (yär'dij), *n.* measurement or an amount measured in yards.

yard'arm', *n.* either of the yards of a square sail.

yard' goods', *n.pl.* PIECE GOODS.

yard'man, *n., pl.* **-men.** a person who works in a yard, esp. a railroad yard.

yard'stick', *n.* **1.** a measuring stick a yard long. **2.** a standard of measurement or judgment.

yar•mul•ke (yär'məl kə, -mə-, yä'-), *n., pl.* **-kes.** a skullcap worn by Jewish males, esp. during prayer.

yarn (yärn), *n.* **1.** a continuous strand or thread made of fibers and used for knitting and weaving. **2.** a long tale, esp. of adventure or incredible happenings.

yar•row (yar'ō), *n.* a plant with flat-topped clusters of white-to-yellow flowers.

yaw (yô), *v.i.* **1.** to deviate from a straight course, as a ship. **2.** (of an aircraft) to turn around a vertical axis. —*n.* **3.** the movement of yawing.

yawl (yôl), *n.* **1.** a ship's small boat. **2.** a two-masted fore-and-aft-rigged sailing ship with a large mainmast.

yawn (yôn), *v.i.* **1.** to open the mouth wide, usu. involuntarily, as from drowsiness or boredom. **2.** to stretch wide open: *a yawning pit.* —*n.* **3.** an act or instance of yawning. —**yawn'er,** *n.*

yaws (yôz), *n.* an infectious tropical disease characterized by raspberrylike eruptions of the skin.

Yb, *Chem. Symbol.* ytterbium.

Y' chro'mosome, *n.* a sex chromosome present only in males and paired with an X chromosome.

yd., yard.

ye¹ (yē), *pron. Archaic.* YOU (def. 1).

ye² (thē; *spelling pron.* yē), *definite article. Archaic.* THE¹.

yea (yā), *adv., n., pl.* **yeas.** —*adv.* **1.** yes (used in affirmation or assent). **2.** indeed. —*n.* **3.** an affirmative vote. **4.** a person who votes in the affirmative.

yeah (yâ), *adv., n. Informal.* yes.

year (yēr), *n.* **1.** a period in the Gregorian calendar of 365 or 366 days divided into 12 calendar months, reckoned as beginning Jan. 1 and ending Dec. 31. **2.** a division of time equal to the time it takes the earth to complete one revolution around the sun. **3.** a part of the year devoted to a certain pursuit or activity: *the academic year.* **4. years, a.** age: *a person of advanced years.* **b.** a long time: *We haven't spoken in years.*

year'book', *n.* **1.** a book published annually that contains information about the past year. **2.** a commemorative book published by a graduating class.

year'ling (-ling), *n.* **1.** an animal in its second year. **2.** a horse one year old.

year'ly, *adj.* **1.** done, occurring, or appearing once each year. **2.** computed by the year. —*adv.* **3.** once a year; annually.

yearn (yûrn), *v.i.* **1.** to have a strong desire; long. **2.** to feel tenderness.

year'-round', *adj.* continuing, available, or used throughout the year.

yeast (yēst), *n.* **1.** any of various small single-celled fungi capable of fermenting carbohydrates into alcohol and carbon dioxide. **2.** any of several yeasts used in brewing alcoholic beverages and as a leaven in baking breads. **3.** something that causes ferment or agitation.

yeast'y, *adj.,* **-i•er, -i•est. 1.** of, containing, or resembling yeast. **2.** characterized by agitation, excitement, or change. **3.** frothy; foamy. **4.** exuberant; ebullient. **5.** trifling; frivolous.

Yeats (yāts), *n.* **William Butler,** 1865–1939, Irish poet and dramatist.

yell (yel), *v.i.* **1.** to cry out; shout. **2.** to scream, as with pain. —*v.t.* **3.** to say by yelling. —*n.* **4.** a cry uttered by yelling. **5.** a cheer used esp. to encourage a team.

yel•low (yel'ō), *n.* **1.** the color of an egg yolk or a ripe lemon. **2.** something yellow, as the yolk of an egg. —*adj.* **3.** of the color yellow. **4.** having a somewhat yellow complexion. **5.** cowardly. **6.** emphasizing sensational or lurid details: *yellow journalism.* —*v.t., v.i.* **7.** to make or become yellow. —**yel′low•ish,** *adj.*

yel′low fe′ver, *n.* an acute, infectious viral disease of warm climates that is transmitted by a mosquito and characterized by fever and jaundice.

yel′low jack′et, *n.* a small social wasp with black and bright yellow bands.

Yel′low•knife′, *n.* the capital of the Northwest Territories, in N central Canada. 11,753.

Yel′low Riv′er, *n.* Huang He.

Yel′low Sea′, *n.* an arm of the Pacific between China and Korea.

yelp (yelp), *v.i., v.t.* **1.** to give or utter with a sharp, shrill cry or bark. —*n.* **2.** a sharp, shrill cry or bark.

Yem•en (yem′ən, yā′mən), *n.* **Republic of,** a country in S Arabia. 13,972,477.

yen¹ (yen), *n., pl.* **yen.** the basic monetary unit of Japan.

yen² (yen), *n.* a desire or craving. [prob. < dial. Chin]

Ye•ni•sei (yen′ə sā′), *n.* a river in the Russian Federation in Asia. 2566 mi. (4080 km) long.

yeo•man (yō′mən), *n., pl.* **-men.** **1.** an enlisted person in the U.S. Navy whose duties are chiefly clerical. **2.** *Brit.* a farmer who cultivates his own land. **3.** (formerly, in England) **a.** one of a class of lesser freeholders below the gentry. **b.** an attendant in a royal household.

yeo′man•ry (-rē), *n.* yeomen collectively.

Ye•re•van (yer′ə vän′), *n.* the capital of Armenia. 1,199,000.

yes (yes), *adv.* **1.** (used to express affirmation or agreement or to emphasize a previous statement): *Do you want that? Yes, I do.* —*n.* **2.** an affirmative reply or vote.

ye•shi•va or **-vah** (yə shē′və), *n., pl.* **-vas** or **-vahs.** **1.** an Orthodox Jewish school for the religious and secular education of children. **2.** an Orthodox Jewish school of higher instruction in Jewish learning.

yes′-man′, *n., pl.* **-men.** a person who always agrees with superiors.

yes•ter•day (yes′tər dā′, -dē), *adv.* **1.** on the day before this day. **2.** in the recent past. —*n.* **3.** the day before this day. **4.** the recent past.

yes•ter•year (yes′tər yēr′, -yēr′), *n.* **1.** last year. **2.** time not long past.

yet (yet), *adv.* **1.** at the present time; now. **2.** up to a particular time; thus far. **3.** in the time remaining. **4.** as previously; still. **5.** in addition; again. **6.** even: *yet greater power.* **7.** nevertheless. —*conj.* **8.** still; nevertheless.

yew (yōō), *n.* **1.** an evergreen tree or shrub with needlelike foliage. **2.** the fine-grained elastic wood of a yew.

Yid•dish (yid′ish), *n.* a language of esp. central and E European Jews that is based on German and written in the Hebrew alphabet.

yield (yēld), *v.t.* **1.** to give forth by a natural process; bear. **2.** to produce or furnish (profit). **3.** to give up, as to superior power; surrender. **4.** to relinquish or resign. **5.** to give as due or required. —*v.i.* **6.** to give a return; produce or bear. **7.** to surrender. **8.** to give way, as to entreaty. **9.** to give place or precedence. **10.** to give way to force or pressure; collapse. —*n.* **11.** a quantity yielded or produced.

yield′ing, *adj.* **1.** submissive; compliant. **2.** tending to give way, esp. under pressure; flexible.

yin′ and yang′ (yin), *n.* (in Chinese philosophy and religion) two principles, one negative, dark, and feminine **(yin),** and one positive, bright, and masculine **(yang),** whose interaction influences the destinies of creatures and things.

yip (yip), *v.,* **yipped, yip•ping,** *n.* —*v.i.* **1.** to bark sharply. —*n.* **2.** a sharp bark.

YMCA, Young Men's Christian Association.

YMHA, Young Men's Hebrew Association.

yo•del (yōd′l), *v.,* **-deled, -del•ing** or (*esp. Brit.*)

-**delled, -del•ling,** *n.* —*v.t., v.i.* **1.** to sing or call out with frequent changes from the ordinary voice to falsetto and back again. —*n.* **2.** a yodeled song or refrain. —**yo′del•er,** *n.*

yo•ga (yō′gə), *n.* (*sometimes cap.*) **1.** a series of postures and breathing exercises practiced to attain physical and mental control and tranquillity. **2.** a school of Hindu philosophy using yoga to unify the self with the Supreme Being. [< Skt]

yo•gi (yō′gē) also **-gin** (-gin), *n., pl.* **-gis** also **-gins.** a person who practices yoga.

yo•gurt or **-ghurt** (yō′gərt), *n.* a tart, custardlike food made from milk curdled by the action of bacterial cultures.

yoke (yōk), *n., pl.* **yokes** for 1, 3–7, **yoke** for 2; *v.,* **yoked, yok•ing.** —*n.* **1.** a crosspiece or frame for joining together a pair of draft animals, esp. oxen, at the neck. **2.** a pair of draft animals joined by a yoke. **3.** a frame resting on a person's shoulders to carry two loads, as a pair of buckets, one at each end. **4.** an agency or symbol of oppression, subjection, or servitude. **5.** something that binds; bond or tie. **6.** a viselike piece for gripping two parts firmly together. **7.** a shaped and fitted piece in a garment, esp. at the shoulders. —*v.t.* **8.** to put a yoke on. **9.** to attach (a draft animal) to. **10.** to join, couple, link, or unite.

yoke

yo•kel (yō′kəl), *n.* a country bumpkin; rustic.

Yo•ko•ha•ma (yō′kə hä′mə), *n.* a seaport on SE Honshu, in central Japan. 3,072,000.

yolk (yōk), *n.* the yellow and principal substance of an egg. —**yolked,** *adj.*

Yom Kip•pur (yom kip′ər; *Heb.* yôm′ kē pŏŏr′), *n.* the holiest Jewish holiday, observed by fasting and prayers of repentance.

yon (yon), *Archaic.* —*adj., adv.* **1.** yonder. —*pron.* **2.** that or those yonder.

yon•der (yon′dər), *adj.* **1.** being in that place. **2.** being more distant. —*adv.* **3.** at, in, or to that place.

Yon•kers (yong′kərz), *n.* a city in SE New York. 183,490.

yore (yōr), *n. Chiefly Literary.* time past: *knights of yore.*

York (yôrk), *n.* **1.** a member of the royal house of England that ruled from 1461 to 1485. **2.** a city in North Yorkshire, in NE England: the capital of Roman Britain. 102,700.

York•town (yôrk′toun′), *n.* a village in SE Virginia: surrender in 1781 of British General Charles Cornwallis to George Washington in the American Revolution.

you (yōō; *unstressed* yŏō, yə), *pron.* **1.** the person or persons being addressed. **2.** anyone; one: *a tiny mark you can't even see.*

young (yung), *adj.,* **young•er** (yung′gər), **young•est** (yung′gist), *n.* —*adj.* **1.** being in the first or early stage of life or growth. **2.** having the appearance, vigor, or other qualities of youth. **3.** of or pertaining to youth. **4.** not far advanced in years or experience in comparison with others. **5.** junior: *the young Mr. Smith.* **6.** being in an early stage, as of existence, development, or maturity: *a young wine.* **7.** representing or advocating recent or progressive tendencies, policies, or the like. —*n.* **8.** young persons collectively. **9.** young offspring: *a mother hen protecting her young.* —**Idiom.** **10. with young,** (of an animal) pregnant. —**young′ish,** *adj.*

Young (yung), *n.* **Brigham,** 1801–77, U.S. leader of the Church of Jesus Christ of Latter-day Saints.

young′ blood′, *n.* young people.

young′ster (-stər), *n.* **1.** a child. **2.** a young person.

your (yŏor, yôr; *unstressed* yər), *pron.* 1. a form of the possessive case of YOU used as an attributive adjective: *I like your idea.* 2. (used to indicate that one belonging or relevant to oneself or to any person): *The library is on your left.*

you're (yŏor; *unstressed* yər), contraction of *you are.*

yours (yŏorz, yôrz), *pron.* 1. a form of the possessive case of YOU used as a predicate adjective: *Which cup is yours?* 2. the one or ones belonging to you: *Yours was the first face I recognized.*

your•self', *pron.*, *pl.* **-selves.** 1. a reflexive form of YOU: *You can think for yourself.* 2. an intensive form of YOU: *a letter you yourself wrote.* 3. your normal or customary self: *Be yourself at the party.*

youth (yŏoth), *n.*, *pl.* **youths** (yŏoths, yŏoᵗħz). 1. the condition of being young. 2. qualities, as freshness and vigor, characteristic of the young. 3. the time of being young. 4. the period of life from puberty to adulthood. 5. a first or early period of something. 6. young persons collectively. 7. a young person, esp. a young man.

youth'ful, *adj.* 1. characterized by youth; young. 2. of or suggesting youth or its vitality. 3. in an early period, as of existence. —**youth'ful•ly,** *adv.* —**youth'ful•ness,** *n.*

yowl (youl), *v.i.* 1. to utter a long, dismal cry; howl. —*n.* 2. a yowling cry.

yo-yo (yō'yō), *n.*, *pl.* **-yos,** *v.*, **-yoed, -yo•ing.** —*n.* 1. a spoollike toy that is spun out and reeled in by an attached string that loops around the player's finger. —*v.i.* 2. to move up and down or back and forth; fluctuate.

yr., 1. year. 2. your.

yrs., 1. years. 2. yours.

YT or **Y.T.,** Yukon Territory.

yt•ter•bi•um (i tûr'bē əm), *n.* a rare metallic element. *Symbol:* Yb; *at. wt.:* 173.04; *at. no.:* 70.

yt•tri•um (i'trē əm), *n.* a rare metallic element. *Symbol:* Y; at. wt.: 88.905; *at. no.:* 39.

yu•an (yŏo än'), *n.*, *pl.* **-an.** the basic monetary unit of China.

Yu•ca•tan (yŏo'kə tan', -tän'), *n.* a peninsula comprising parts of SE Mexico, N Guatemala, and Belize.

yuc•ca (yuk'ə), *n.*, *pl.* **-cas.** a New World plant with rigid sword-shaped leaves and white flowers.

Yu•go•sla•vi•a (yŏo'gō slä've ə), *n.* a republic in SE Europe: since 1992 comprised of Serbia and Montenegro; formerly (1945–91) included Bosnia and Herzegovina, Croatia, Macedonia, and Slovenia. 10,515,000. —**Yu'go•sla'vi•an,** *adj.*, *n.*

yuk (yuk), *n.*, *v.*, **yukked, yuk•king.** *Slang.* —*n.* 1. a loud, hearty laugh. 2. something evoking a yuk. —*v.i.* 3. to laugh loudly and heartily.

Yu•kon (yŏo'kon), *n.* 1. a river flowing from NW Canada through Alaska to the Bering Sea. ab. 2000 mi. (3220 km) long. 2. Also called **Yu'kon Ter'ritory.** a territory in NW Canada. 23,504. *Cap.:* Whitehorse. *Abbr.* YT, Y.T.

yule (yŏol), *n.* Christmas.

yule'tide', *n.* the Christmas season.

yum•my (yum'ē), *adj.*, **-mi•er, -mi•est.** very pleasing, esp. to the taste.

yup (yup), *adv.*, *n. Informal.* yes.

yup•pie or **-py** (yup'ē), *n.*, *pl.* **-pies.** (*sometimes cap.*) a young, ambitious, and affluent professional who lives in or near a city.

yurt (yŏort), *n.* a tentlike dwelling of nomadic peoples of central Asia.

YWCA, Young Women's Christian Association.

YWHA, Young Women's Hebrew Association.

Z, z (zē; *esp. Brit.* zed), *n.*, *pl.* **Zs** or **Z's, zs** or **z's.** the 26th letter of the English alphabet, a consonant.

Zac•chae•us (za kē'əs), *n.* a tax collector in Jericho whom Jesus invited to dine with him. Luke 19:1–10.

Zach•a•ri•ah (zak'ə rī'ə) also **Zach•a•ri•as** (-rī'əs), *n.* the father of John the Baptist. Luke 1:5.

Za•dok (zā'dok), *n.* a priest at the time of David and Solomon. I Sam. 15:34–37; I Kings 1:7, 8.

Za•greb (zä'greb), *n.* the capital of Croatia. 1,174,512.

Za•ire or **Za•ïre** (zä ēr', zä'ēr), *n.* 1. a former name of the Democratic Republic of the CONGO. 2. official name within the Democratic Republic of the Congo of the CONGO River. —**Za•ir'i•an, Za•ir'e•an,** *adj.*, *n.*

Zam•be•zi (zam bē'zē), *n.* a river in S Africa. 1650 mi. (2657 km) long.

Zam•bi•a (zam'bē ə), *n.* a republic in S Africa. 9,349,975. Formerly, **Northern Rhodesia.** —**Zam'bi•an,** *adj.*, *n.*

Zam•bo•ni (zam bō'nē), *Trademark.* a brand of ice resurfacer. [after Frank J. *Zamboni*, 1901–88, U.S. inventor]

za•ny (zā'nē), *adj.*, **-ni•er, -ni•est,** *n.*, *pl.* **-nies.** —*adj.* 1. absurdly or whimsically comical; clownishly crazy. —*n.* 2. a comically wild or eccentric person. 3. a buffoon; clown. [orig. the name for a character in early Italian comedy; perh. a form of *Gianni* John] —**za'ni•ness,** *n.*

Zan•zi•bar (zan'zə bär'), *n.* an island off the E coast of Africa: part of Tanzania.

zap (zap), *v.*, **zapped, zap•ping,** *n. Informal.* —*v.t.* 1. to attack, destroy, or kill with sudden speed and force. 2. to bombard with or as if with electrical current. —*v.i.* 3. to move quickly, forcefully, or destructively. —*n.* 4. force, energy, or drive.

zeal (zēl), *n.* eager desire or interest; fervor.

zeal•ot (zel'ət), *n.* 1. a person who shows zeal, esp. to an excessive degree. 2. (*cap.*) a member of a radical, warlike group of Jews in Judea during the 1st century A.D.

zeal•ous (zel'əs), *adj.* full of, characterized by, or due to zeal. —**zeal'ous•ly,** *adv.*

Zeb•e•dee (zeb'i dē'), *n.* the father of the apostles James and John. Matt. 4:21.

ze•bra (zē'brə), *n.*, *pl.* **-bras, -bra.** a horselike African mammal with a characteristic pattern of dark stripes on a whitish body.

ze•bu (zē'byŏo, -bŏo), *n.*, *pl.* **-bus.** a domesticated ox of India with a large hump over the shoulders.

Zech•a•ri•ah (zek'ə rī'ə), *n.* 1. a Minor Prophet of the 6th century B.C. 2. a book of the Bible bearing his name.

zed (zed), *n. Chiefly Brit.* the letter Z or z.

Zed•e•ki•ah (zed'i kī'ə), *n.* the last king of Judah. II Kings 24, 25; Jer. 52:1–11.

Zeit•geist (tsīt'gīst'), *n. German.* the general trend of thought or feeling of a particular period of time.

Zen (zen), *n.* a Buddhist movement that emphasizes enlightenment by means of meditation and direct, intuitive insights. [< Japn < Chin < Skt: meditation, thought]

ze•nith (zē'nith), *n.* 1. the point on the celestial sphere that is directly overhead. 2. the highest point or state; acme.

Zeph•a•ni•ah (zef'ə nī'ə), *n.* 1. a Minor Prophet of the 7th century B.C. 2. a book of the Bible bearing his name.

zeph•yr (zef'ər), *n.* 1. a gentle breeze. 2. a fine, light fabric or yarn.

zep•pe•lin (zep'ə lin), *n.* (*often cap.*) a rigid airship consisting of a long cylindrical covered framework supported by gas, esp. helium. [after Count Ferdinand von *Zeppelin* (1838–1917), German designer]

ze•ro (zēr'ō), *n.*, *pl.* **-ros, -roes,** *v.*, *adj.* —*n.* 1. the figure or numerical symbol 0. 2. an origin from which values are calibrated, as on a thermometer. 3. nothing; naught. 4. the lowest point or degree. —*v.t.* 5. to adjust (an instrument or apparatus) to a zero point. 6. zero in, a. to aim at the precise center, as of a target. 7. ~ in on, a. to aim at, focus on, or converge on. b. to direct one's attention to; focus on. —*adj.* 8. amounting to zero. 9. having no measurable quantity or magnitude: *zero economic growth.*

ze'ro hour', *n.* the time set for the beginning of any event or action, esp. a military attack.

ze'ro popula'tion growth', *n.* a condition in which population remains constant because of a balance between the number of births and deaths.

zest (zest), *n.* 1. hearty enjoyment; gusto. 2. something added to impart flavor or relish. 3. piquancy.

4. a strip of citrus peel, esp. lemon, used for flavoring. —zest′ful, adj. —zest′y, adj., -i•er, -i•est.

ze•ta (zā′tə, zē′-), n., pl. -tas. the sixth letter of the Greek alphabet (Z, ζ).

Zeus (zōōs), n. the supreme deity of the ancient Greeks.

Zi•ba (zī′bə), n. a servant of King Saul. II Sam. 9:2–11; 16:1–4; 19:17, 29.

zig•zag (zig′zag′), n., adj., adv., v., -zagged, -zag•ging. —n. **1.** a line, course, or progression characterized by sharp turns first to one side and then to the other. **2.** one of a series of zigzags. —adj. **3.** proceeding or formed in a zigzag. —adv. **4.** in a zigzag manner. —v.t., v.i. **5.** to make into or proceed in a zigzag.

zilch (zilch), n. Slang. zero; nothing.

zil•lion (zil′yən), n., pl. -lions, -lion. Informal. an extremely large, indeterminate number.

Zil•pah (zil′pə), n. the mother of Gad and Asher. Gen. 30:10–13.

Zim•bab•we (zim bäb′wā, -wē), n. a republic in S Africa. 11,423,175. Formerly, **Southern Rhodesia, Rhodesia.** —Zim•bab′we•an, adj., n.

Zim•ri (zim′rē, -rī), n. a king of Israel. I Kings 16:8–20.

zinc (zingk), n., v., zincked or zinced, zinck•ing or zinc•ing. —n. **1.** a ductile, bluish white metallic element used in making galvanized iron and alloys. Symbol: Zn; at. wt.: 65.37; at. no.: 30. —v.t. **2.** to coat or cover with zinc.

zinc′ ox′ide, n. a white powder used as a pigment and in ointments and cosmetics.

zing (zing), n. **1.** a sharp singing or whining sound. **2.** vitality or zest. —v.i., v.t. **3.** to move or cause to move with a zing. —zing′y, adj., -i•er, -i•est.

zin•ni•a (zin′ē ə), n., pl. -ni•as. a New World plant with dense, colorful flower heads.

Zin•zen•dorf (tsin′tsən dôrf′), n. **Count Ni•ko•laus Lud•wig von** (nē′kō lous′ lōōt′viкн fən, lōōd′-), 1700–60, German religious leader: organizer of the Moravian Church.

Zi•on (zī′ən), n. **1.** a hill in Jerusalem, on which Solomon's Temple was built. **2.** the Jewish people. **3.** Palestine as the Jewish homeland and symbol of Judaism. **4.** heaven as the final gathering place of true believers.

Zi•on•ism (zī′ə niz′əm), n. a worldwide Jewish movement for the establishment and development of the state of Israel. —Zi′on•ist, n., adj.

zip¹ (zip), n., v., zipped, zip•ping. —n. **1.** a sudden brief hissing sound. **2.** energy; vigor. —v.i. **3.** to act or move with speed and energy.

zip² (zip), v.t., v.i., zipped, zip•ping. to fasten or unfasten with a zipper.

ZIP′ code′, Trademark. a system to facilitate mail delivery by assigning a numerical code to every postal area in the U.S. [Z(one) I(mprovement) P(rogram)]

zip′per, n. a fastening device consisting of two parallel tracks of teeth or coils that can be interlocked by pulling a sliding piece.

Zip•po•rah (zi pôr′ə, -pōr′ə, zip′ər ə), n. the wife of Moses. Ex. 2:21.

zip′py, adj., -pi•er, -pi•est. full of energy.

zir•con (zûr′kon), n. a mineral that is used as a gem when transparent.

zir•co•ni•um (zûr kō′nē əm), n. a metallic element used esp. in metallurgy and ceramics. Symbol: Zr; at. wt.: 91.22; at. no.: 40.

zit (zit), n. Slang. a pimple.

zith•er (zith′ər, zith′-), n. a musical instrument with numerous strings that is played with a plectrum and the fingertips.

Zn, Chem. Symbol. zinc.

Zo•ar (zō′ər, -âr), n. the city where Lot and his family took refuge. Gen. 19:20–30.

zo•di•ac (zō′dē ak′), n. **1.** an imaginary belt in the heavens that contains the apparent paths of the sun, moon, and principal planets and is divided into 12 divisions or signs, each named after a constellation. **2.** a diagram representing the zodiac. —zo•di′a•cal (-dī′ə kəl), adj.

zom•bie (zom′bē), n., pl. -bies. **1.** (in voodoo) a corpse supernaturally imbued with the semblance of life. **2.** a person whose behavior or responses are wooden, listless, or mechanical.

zone (zōn), n., v., zoned, zon•ing. —n. **1.** an area that differs or is distinguished in some respect from adjoining areas. **2.** any of five divisions of the earth's surface bounded by lines parallel to the equator and named according to the prevailing temperature. **3.** an area or district in which certain circumstances exist or restrictions apply. —v.t. **4.** to divide into, mark with, or surround with zones. [< L < Gk zṓnē] —zon′al, adj. —zoned, adj.

zoo (zōō), n., pl. zoos. a parklike area in which live animals are kept for public exhibition.

zo•ol•o•gy (zō ol′ə jē), n. the scientific study of animals. —zo′o•log′i•cal (-ə loj′i kəl), adj. —zo•ol′o•gist, n.

zoom (zōōm), v.i. **1.** to move with a loud humming or buzzing sound. **2.** to fly a plane suddenly and sharply upward. **3.** to focus a camera with a zoom lens. **4.** to rise suddenly and sharply. —v.t. **5.** to cause to zoom. —n. **6.** the act or process of zooming. **7.** a zooming sound.

zoom′ lens′, n. a camera lens whose focal length can be continuously adjusted to change magnification with no loss of focus.

zo•o•phyte (zō′ə fīt′), n. any of various invertebrate animals resembling a plant, as a coral. —zo′o•phyt′ic (-fit′ik), adj.

Zo•phar (zō′fər), n. a friend of Job. Job 2:11.

Zo•ro•as•ter (zôr′ō as′tər), n. fl. 6th century B.C., Persian religious teacher.

Zo′ro•as′tri•an•ism (-trē ə niz′əm), n. an Iranian religion founded c600 B.C. by Zoroaster.

Zr, Chem Symbol. zirconium.

zuc•chi•ni (zōō kē′nē), n., pl. -nis, -ni, **1.** a cucumber-shaped summer squash with a smooth, dark green skin. **2.** a plant bearing zucchini.

Zu•lu (zōō′lōō), n., pl. -lu, -lus. **1.** a member of a people living mainly in South Africa. **2.** the Bantu language of the Zulu.

Zu•ni (zōō′nē) also Zu•ñi (zōōn′yē), n., pl. -ni, -nis also -ñi, -ñis. **1.** a member of a Pueblo Indian people of W New Mexico. **2.** the language of the Zuni.

Zu•rich (zŏŏr′ik), n. a city in N Switzerland. 840,313.

zwie•back (zwī′bak′, -bäk′, swē′-), n. an egg bread that is baked, sliced and dried, then baked again.

Zwing•li (zwing′glē, swing′-, tsving′-), n. **Ulrich** or **Huldreich,** 1484–1531, Swiss Protestant reformer.

zither

zy•gote (zī′gōt), n. a cell produced by the union of two gametes. —zy•got′ic (-got′ik), adj.

zy•mur•gy (zī′mûr jē), n. the branch of applied chemistry dealing with fermentation, as in brewing.

GUIDE FOR WRITERS

Punctuation

There is a considerable amount of variation in punctuation practices. At one extreme are writers who use as little punctuation as possible. At the other extreme are writers who use too much punctuation in an effort to make their meaning clear. The principles presented here represent a middle road. As in all writing, consistency of style is essential.

The punctuation system is presented in four charts. Since punctuation marks are frequently used in more than one way, some marks appear on more than one chart. Readers who are interested in the various uses of a particular mark can scan the left column of each chart to locate relevant sections.

1. Sentence-Level Punctuation

	Guidelines	Examples
•	Ordinarily an independent clause is made into a sentence by beginning it with a capital letter and ending it with a period.	Some of us still support the mayor. Others think he should retire. There's only one solution. We must reduce next year's budget.
,	Independent clauses may be combined into one sentence by using the words *and, but, yet, or, not, for,* and *so.* The first clause is usually, but not always, followed by a comma.	The forecast promised beautiful weather, but it rained every day. Take six cooking apples and put them into a flameproof dish.
. ,	The writer can indicate that independent clauses are closely connected by joining them with a semicolon.	Some of us still support the mayor; others think he should retire. There was silence in the room; even the children were still.
. .	When one independent clause is followed by another that explains or exemplifies it, they can be separated by a colon. The second clause may or may not begin with a capital letter.	There's only one solution: we must reduce next year's budget. The conference addresses a basic question: How can we take the steps needed to protect the environment?
?	Sentences that ask a question should be followed by a question mark.	Are they still planning to move to Houston? What is the population of Norway?
!	Sentences that express strong feeling may be followed by an exclamation mark.	Watch out! That's a stupid thing to say!
? !	End-of-sentence punctuation is sometimes used after groups of words that are not independent clauses. This is especially common in advertising and other writing that seeks to reflect the rhythms of speech.	Somerset Estates has all the features you've been looking for. Like state-of-the-art facilities. A friendly atmosphere. And a very reasonable price. Sound interesting? Phone today!

2. Separating Elements in Clauses

When one of the elements in a clause is compounded—that is, when there are two or more subjects, predicates, objects, and so forth—punctuation is necessary.

603

Guidelines	**Examples**
When two elements are compounded, they are usually joined together with a word such as *and* or *or* without any punctuation. Occasionally more than two elements are joined in this way.	Haiti and the Dominican Republic share the island of Hispaniola. Tuition may be paid by check or charged to a major credit card. I'm taking history and English and biology this semester.
Compounds that contain more than two elements are called series. Commas are used to separate items in a series, with a word such as *and* or *or* usually occurring between the last two items.	England, Scotland, and Wales share the island of Great Britain. Environmentally conscious businesses use recycled paper, photocopy on both sides of a sheet, and use ceramic cups. We frequently hear references to government of the people, by the people, for the people.
When the items in a series are very long or have internal punctuation, separation by commas can be confusing, and semicolons may be used instead.	Next year, they plan to open stores in Pittsburgh, Pennsylvania; Cincinnati, Ohio; and Baltimore, Maryland. Students were selected on the basis of grades; tests of vocabulary, memory, and reading; and teacher recommendations.

Note: Some writers omit the final comma when punctuating a series, and newspapers and magazines often follow this practice. Book publishers and educators, however, usually follow the practice recommended above.

3. Quotations

Quotations are used for making clear to a reader which words are the writer's and which have been borrowed from someone else.

Guidelines	**Examples**
When writers use the exact words of someone else, they must use quotation marks to set them off from the rest of the text.	In 1841, Ralph Waldo Emerson wrote, "I hate quotations. Tell me what you know."
Indirect quotations—in which writers report what someone else said without using the exact words—should not be set off by quotation marks.	Emerson said that he hated quotations and that writers should instead tell the reader what they themselves know.
When quotations are longer than two or three lines, they are often placed on separate lines. Sometimes shorter line length and/or smaller type is also used. When this is done, quotation marks are not used.	In his essay "Notes on Punctuation," Lewis Thomas gives the following advice to writers using quotations: If something is to be quoted, the exact words must be used. If part of it must be left out because of space limitations, it is good manners to insert three dots to indicate the omission, but it is unethical to do this if it means connecting two thoughts which the original author did not intend to have tied together.

. . .

If part of a quotation is omitted, the omission must be marked with points of ellipsis. When the omission comes in the middle of a sentence, three points are used. When the omission includes the end of one or more sentences, four points are used.

. . . .

Lewis Thomas offers this advice:
If something is to be quoted,
the exact words must be used.
If part of it must be left out...insert
three dots to indicate the omission, but
it is unethical to do this if it means connecting two thoughts which the original
author did not intend to have tied
together.

When writers insert something within a quoted passage, the insertion should be set off with brackets. Insertions are sometimes used to supply words that make a quotation easier to understand.

Lewis Thomas warns that "it is unethical to [omit words in a quotation]...if it means connecting two thoughts which the original author did not intend to have tied together."

[ ]

Writers can make clear that a mistake in the quotation has been carried over from the original by using the word *sic,* meaning "thus."

As Senator Claghorne wrote to his constituents, "My fundamental political principals [*sic*] make it impossible for me to support the bill in its present form."

,

Text that reports the source of quoted material is usually separated from it by a comma.

Mark said, "I've decided not to apply to law school until next year."
"I think we should encourage people to vote," said the mayor.

When quoted words are woven into a text so that they perform a basic grammatical function in the sentence, no introductory punctuation is used.

According to Thoreau, most of us "lead lives of quiet desperation."

' '

Quotations that are included within other quotations are set off by single quotation marks.

The witness made the same damaging statement under cross-examination: "As I entered the room, I heard him say, 'I'm determined to get even.'"

" "

Final quotation marks follow other punctuation marks, except for semicolons and colons.

Ed began reading Williams's "The Glass Menagerie"; then he turned to "A Streetcar Named Desire."

Question marks and exclamation marks precede final quotation marks when they refer to the quoted words. They follow when they refer to the sentence as a whole.

Once more she asked, "What do you think we should do about this?"
What did Carol mean when she said, "I'm going to do something about this"?
"Get out of here!" he yelled.

4. Word-Level Punctuation

The punctuation covered so far is used to clarify the structure of sentences. There are also punctuation marks that are used with words.

Guidelines	Examples
' The apostrophe is used with nouns to show possession:	The company's management resisted the union's demands. She found it impossible to decipher the students' handwriting.
(1) An apostrophe plus *s* is added to all words—singular or plural—that do not end in -*s*.	the boy's hat children's literature a week's vacation
(2) Just an apostrophe is added at the end of plural words that end in -*s*.	the boys' hats two weeks' vacation
(3) An apostrophe plus *s* is usually added at the end of singular words that end in -*s*. Just an apostrophe is added to names of classical or biblical derivation that end in -*s*.	the countess's daughter Dickens's novels Achilles' heel Moses' brother
An apostrophe is used in contractions to show where letters or numerals have been omitted.	he's didn't let's ma'am four o'clock readin', writin', and 'rithmetic the class of '55
An apostrophe is sometimes used when making letters or numbers plural.	45's ABC's *or* 45s ABCs
• A period is used to mark shortened forms like abbreviations and initials.	Prof. M. L. Smith 14 ft. 4:00 p.m. U.S.A. or USA etc.
— A hyphen is used to end a line of text when part of a word must be carried over to the next line.	... insta- bility
Hyphens are sometimes used to form compound words.	twenty-five self-confidence
In certain situations, hyphens are used between prefixes or suffixes and root words.	catlike *but* bull-like preschool *but* pre-Christian recover *vs.* re-cover
Hyphens are often used to indicate that a group of words is to be understood as a unit.	a scholar-athlete hand-to-hand combat
When two modifiers containing hyphens are joined together, common elements are often not repeated.	The study included fourth- and twelfth-grade students.

Note: It is important not to confuse the hyphen (-) with the dash (—), which is more than twice as long. The hyphen is used to group words and parts of words together, while the dash is used to clarify sentence structure. With a typewriter, a dash is formed by typing two successive hyphens(--). Many word-processing programs will create a dash automatically.

AVOIDING INSENSITIVE AND OFFENSIVE LANGUAGE

This essay is intended as a general guide to language that can, intentionally or not, cause offense or perpetuate discriminatory values and practices by emphasizing the differences between people or implying that one group is superior to another.

Several factors complicate the issue. A group may disagree within itself as to what is acceptable and what is not. Many seemingly inoffensive terms develop negative connotations over time and become dated or go out of style as awareness changes. A "within the group" rule often applies, which allows a member of a group to use terms freely that would be considered offensive if used by an outsider.

While it is true that some of the more extreme attempts to avoid offending language have resulted in ludicrous obfuscation, it is also true that heightened sensitivity in language indicates a precision of thought and is a positive move toward rectifying the unequal social status between one group and another.

Suggestions for avoiding insensitive or offensive language are given in the following pages. The recommended terms are given on the right. While these suggestions can reflect trends, they cannot dictate or predict the preferences of each individual.

Sexism

Sexism is the most difficult bias to avoid, in part because of the convention of using *man* or *men* and *he* or *his* to refer to people of either sex. Other, more disrespectful conventions include giving descriptions of women in terms of age and appearance while describing men in terms of accomplishment.

Replacing *man* or *men*

Man traditionally referred to a male or to a human in general. Using *man* to refer to a human is often thought to be slighting of women.

Avoid This		Use This Instead
mankind, man	→	human beings, humans, humankind, humanity, people, society, men and women
man-made	→	synthetic, artificial
man in the street	→	average person, ordinary person

Using gender-neutral terms for occupations, positions, roles, etc.

Terms that specify a particular sex can unnecessarily perpetuate certain stereotypes when used generically.

Avoid This		Use This Instead
anchorman	→	anchor
bellman, bellboy	→	bellhop
businessman	→	businessperson, executive, manager, business owner, retailer, etc.
chairman	→	chair, chairperson
cleaning lady, girl, maid	→	housecleaner, housekeeper, cleaning person, office cleaner
clergyman	→	member of the clergy, rabbi, priest, etc.
clergymen	→	the clergy
congressman	→	representative, member of Congress, legislator
fireman	→	firefighter
forefather	→	ancestor
girl/gal Friday	→	assistant
housewife	→	homemaker
insurance man	→	insurance agent
layman	→	layperson, nonspecialist, nonprofessional
mailman, postman	→	mail or letter carrier
policeman	→	police officer or law enforcement officer
salesman, saleswoman, saleslady, salesgirl	→	salesperson, sales representative, sales associate, clerk

spokesman	→	spokesperson, representative
stewardess, steward	→	flight attendant
weatherman	→	weather reporter, weathercaster, meteorologist
workman	→	worker
actress	→	actor

Replacing the pronoun *he*

The generic use of *he* can also be seen to exclude women.

Avoid This		Use This Instead
When a driver approaches a red light, he must prepare to stop.	→	When drivers approach a red light, they must prepare to stop.
When a driver approaches a red light, he or she must prepare to stop.	→	When approaching a red light, a driver must prepare to stop.

Referring to members of both sexes with parallel names, titles, or descriptions

Don't be inconsistent unless you are trying to make a specific point.

Avoid This		Use This Instead
men and ladies	→	men and women, ladies and gentlemen
Betty Schmidt, an attractive 49-year-old physician, and her husband, Alan Schmidt, a noted editor	→	Betty Schmidt, a physician, and her husband, Alan Schmidt, an editor
Mr. David Kim and Mrs. Betty Harrow	→	Mr. David Kim and Ms. Betty Harrow (unless *Mrs.* is her known preference)
man and wife	→	husband and wife
Dear Sir:	→	Dear Sir/Madam: Dear Madam or Sir: To whom it may concern:
Mrs. Smith and President Jones	→	Governor Smith and President Jones

Race, Ethnicity, and National Origin

Some words and phrases that refer to racial and ethnic groups are clearly offensive. Other words (e.g., Oriental, colored) are outdated or inaccurate. Hispanic is generally accepted as a broad term for Spanish-speaking people of the Western Hemisphere, but more specific terms (Latino, Mexican American) are also acceptable and in some cases preferred.

Avoid This		Use This Instead
Negro, colored, Afro-American	→	black, African-American (generally preferred to Afro-American)
Oriental, Asiatic	→	Asian, or more specific designation such as Pacific Islander, Chinese American, Korean
Indian	→	*Indian* properly refers to people who live in or come from India.
		American Indian, Native American, and more specific designations (*Chinook, Hopi*) are usually preferred when referring to the native peoples of the Western hemisphere.
Eskimo	→	Inuit, Alaska Natives
native (*n.*)	→	native peoples, early inhabitants, aboriginal peoples (but not *aborigines*)

Age

The concept of aging is changing as people are living longer and more active lives. Be aware of word choices that reinforce stereotypes (*decrepit, senile*) and avoid mentioning age unless it is relevant.

Avoid This		Use This Instead
elderly, aged, old, geriatric, the elderly, the aged	→	older person, senior citizen(s), older people, seniors

Avoiding Depersonalization of Persons with Disabilities or Illnesses

Terminology that emphasizes the person rather than the disability is generally preferred. Handicap is used to refer to the environmental barrier that affects the person. (Stairs handicap a person who uses a wheelchair.) While words such as *crazy, demented,* and *insane* are used in facetious or informal contexts, these terms are not used to describe people with clinical diagnoses of mental illness. The euphemisms *challenged, differently abled,* and *special* are preferred by some people, but are often ridiculed and are best avoided.

Avoid This		Use This Instead
Mongoloid	→	person with Down syndrome
wheelchair-bound	→	person who uses a wheelchair
AIDS sufferer, person afflicted with AIDS, AIDS victim	→	person living with AIDS, P.W.A., HIV +, (one who tests positive for HIV but does not show symptoms of AIDS)
polio victim	→	has/had polio
the handicapped, the disabled, cripple	→	persons with disabilities or person who uses crutches *or* more specific description
deaf-mute, deaf and dumb	→	deaf person

Avoiding Patronizing or Demeaning Expressions

Avoid This		Use This Instead
girls (when referring to adult women), the fair sex	→	women
sweetie, dear, dearie, honey	→	(usually not appropriate with strangers or in public situations)
old maid, bachelorette,	→	single woman, woman, divorced
spinster	→	woman (but only if one would specify "divorced man" in the same context)
the little woman, old lady, ball and chain	→	wife
boy (when referring to or addressing an adult man)	→	man, sir

Avoiding Language That Excludes or Unnecessarily Emphasizes Differences

References to age, sex, religion, race, and the like should be included only if they are relevant.

Avoid This		Use This Instead
lawyers and their wives	→	lawyers and their spouses
a secretary and her boss	→	a secretary and boss, a secretary and his or her boss
the male nurse	→	the nurse
Arab man denies assault charge	→	Man denies assault charge
the articulate black student	→	the articulate student
Marie Curie was a great woman scientist	→	Marie Curie was a great scientist (unless the intent is to compare her only with other women in the sciences)
Christian name	→	given name, personal name, first name
Mr. Johnson, the black representative, met with the President today to discuss civil-rights legislation.	→	Mr. Johnson, a member of the Congressional Black Caucus, met with the President today to discuss civil-rights legislation.

MEASUREMENTS

LINEAR MEASURE

U.S. Unit		Metric Unit	Metric Unit		U.S. Unit
1 inch (in.)	=	25.4 millimeters	1 millimeter (mm)	=	0.03937 inch
		2.54 centimeters	1 centimeter	=	0.3937 inch
1 foot (12 in.)	=	304.8 millimeters	1 meter (m)	=	39.37 inch
		30.48 centimeters			3.2808 feet
		0.3048 meter			1.0936 yards
1 yard (36 in.; 3 ft.)	=	0.9144 meter			3280.8 feet
1 mile (5280 ft; 1760 yds.)	=	1609.3 meters	1 kilometer (km)	=	1093.6 yards
		1.6093 kilometers			0.62137 mile

LIQUID MEASURE

U.S. Unit		Metric Unit	Metric Unit		U.S. Unit
1 teaspoon (1/6 fl. oz.)	=	4.9 milliliters	1 milliliter (ml)	=	0.033814 fl. oz.
1 tbps (1/2 fl. oz.)	=	14.8 milliliters	1 deciliter (dl)	=	3.3814 fl. oz.
1 fluid ounce (fl. oz.)	=	29.573 milliliters			33.814 fl. oz.
1 pint (16 fl. oz.)	=	0.473 liter	1 liter (l)	=	1.0567 quarts
1 quart (2 pints; 32 fl. oz.)	=	9.4635 deciliters			0.26417 gallon
		0.94635 liter			
1 gallon (4 quarts)	=	3.7854 liters			

AREA MEASURE

U.S. Unit		Metric Unit	Metric Unit		U.S. Unit
1 square inch (0.007) sq. ft.)	=	6.452 square centimeters	1 square millimeter (mm^2)	=	0.00155 square inch
		645.16 square millimeters	1 square centimeter (cm^2)	=	0.155 square inch
1 square foot (144 sq. in.)	=	929.03 square centimeters	1 square meter (m^2)	=	10.764 square
			1 hectare (10,000 m^2)	=	2471 acres
		0.092903 square meter	1 square kilometer (km^2)	=	0.38608 square mile
1 square yard (9 sq. ft.)	=	0.83613 square meter			
1 acre (43,560 sq. ft.)	=	4047 square meters			
1 square mile (640 acres)	=	2.59 square kilometers			

CAPACITY

U.S. Unit		Metric Unit	Metric Unit		U.S. Unit
1 cubic inch (0.00058 cu. ft.)	=	16.387 cubic centimeters	1 cubic centimeter (cc; cm^3)	=	0.061023 cubic inch
		0.016387 liter	1 cubic meter (m^3)	=	35.135 cubic feet
1 cubic foot (1728 cu. in.)	=	0.028317 cubic meter	1 cubic kilometer (km^3)		(1.3079 cu. yd.)
1 cubic yard (27 cu. ft.)	=	0.76455 cubic meter		=	0.23990 cubic mile
1 cubic mile (cu. mi.)	=	4.16818 cubic kilometers			

MEASUREMENTS

AVOIRDUPOIS WEIGHTS

U.S. Unit		Metric Unit	Metric Unit		U.S. Unit
1 grain	=	0.064799 gram	1 gram (g)	=	15.432 grains
1 ounce (437.5 grains)	=	28.350 grams			0.035274 ounce
1 pound (16 oz.)	=	0.45359 kilograms	1 kilogram (kg)	=	2.2046 pounds
1 short ton (2000 lb.)	=	907.18 kilograms	1 metric ton	=	0.98421 long ton
		0.90718 metric ton			1.1023 short tons
1 long ton (2240 lb.)	=	1016 kilograms			
		1.016 metric tons			

METRIC CONVERSION TABLES

METRIC TO U.S.   **U.S. TO METRIC**

LENGTH

millimeters × 0.04 = inches   inches × 25.4 = millimeters
centimeters × 0.39 = inches   inches × 2.54 = centimeters
meters × 3.28 = feet   feet × 3.04 = meters
meters × 1.09 = yards   yards × 0.91 = meters
kilometers × 0.6 = miles   miles × 1.6 = kilometers

VOLUME

milliliters × 0.03 = fluid ounces   teaspoons × 5 = milliliters
milliliters × 0.06 = cubic inches   tablespoons × 15 = milliliters
deciliters × 3.38 = fluid ounces   cubic inches × 16 = milliliters
liters × 2.1 = pints   fluid ounces × 30 = milliliters
liters × 1.06 = quarts   cups × 0.24 = liters
liters × 0.26 gallons   pints × 0.47 = liters
cubic meters × 35.3 = cubic feet   quarts × 0.95 = liters
cubic meters × 1.3 = cubic yards   gallons × 3.8 = liters
                              cubic feet × 0.03 = cubic meters
                              cubic yards × 0.76 = cubic meters

MASS

grams × 0.035 = ounces   ounces × 28 = grams
kilograms × 2.2 = pounds   pounds × 0.45 = kilograms
short tons × 0.9 = metric tons   metric tons × 1.1 = short tons

AREA

sq. centimeters × 0.16 = sq. inches   sq. inches × 6.5 = sq. centimeters
sq. meters × 1.2 = sq. yards   sq. feet × 0.09 = sq. meters
sq. kilometers × 0.4 = sq. miles   sq. yards × 0.8 = sq. meters
hectares (ha) × 2.5 = acres   sq. miles × 2.6 = sq. kilometers
                              acres × 0.4 = hectares

TEMPERATURE

degrees Fahrenheit − 32 × 5/9 = degrees Celsius
degrees Celsius × 9/5 + 32 = degrees Fahrenheit

CHEMICAL ELEMENTS

Name	Symbol	Atomic No.	Atomic Mass*	Name	Symbol	Atomic No.	Atomic Mass*
Actinium	Ac	89	(227)	Neodymium	Nd	60	144.24
Aluminum	Al	13	26.98154	Neon	Ne	10	20.18
Americium	Am	95	(243)	Neptunium	Np	93	(237)
Antimony	Sb	51	121.75	Nickel	Ni	28	58.71
Argon	Ar	18	39.948	Niobium	Nb	41	92.9064
Arsenic	As	33	74.9216	Nitrogen	N	7	14.0067
Astatine	At	85	(210)	Nobelium	No	102	(256)
Barium	Ba	56	137.34	Osmium	Os	76	190.2
Berkelium	Bk	97	(247)	Oxygen	O	8	15.999
Beryllium	Be	4	9.01218	Palladium	Pd	46	106.4
Bismuth	Bi	83	208.9808	Phosphorus	P	15	30.97376
Boron	B	5	10.81	Platinum	Pt	78	195.09
Bromine	Br	35	79.904	Plutonium	Pu	94	(242)
Cadmium	Cd	48	112.41	Polonium	Po	84	(210)
Calcium	Ca	20	40.08	Potassium	K	19	39.098
Californium	Cf	98	(249)	Praseodymium	Pr	59	140.907
Carbon	C	6	12.011	Promethium	Pm	61	(147)
Cerium	Ce	58	140.12	Protactinium	Pa	91	(231)
Cesium	Cs	55	132.9054	Radium	Ra	88	(226)
Chlorine	Cl	17	35.453	Radon	Rn	86	(222)
Chromium	Cr	24	51.996	Rhenium	Re	75	186.2
Cobalt	Co	27	58.9332	Rhodium	Rh	45	102.9055
Copper	Cu	29	63.546	Rubidium	Rb	37	85.468
Curium	Cm	96	(247)	Ruthenium	Ru	44	101.07
Dysprosium	Dy	66	162.50	Samarium	Sm	62	150.4
Einsteinium	Es	99	(254)	Scandium	Sc	21	44.9559
Erbium	Er	68	167.26	Selenium	Se	34	78.96
Europium	Eu	63	151.96	Silicon	Si	14	28.086
Fermium	Fm	100	(253)	Silver	Ag	47	107.87
Fluorine	F	9	18.99840	Sodium	Na	11	22.9898
Francium	Fr	87	(223)	Strontium	Sr	38	87.62
Gadolinium	Gd	64	157.25	Sulfur	S	16	32.06
Gallium	Ga	31	69.72	Tantalum	Ta	73	180.948
Germanium	Ge	32	72.59	Technetium	Tc	43	(99)
Gold	Au	79	196.967	Tellurium	Te	52	127.60
Hafnium	Hf	72	178.49	Terbium	Tb	65	158.9254
Helium	He	2	4.00260	Thallium	Tl	81	204.37
Holmium	Ho	67	164.9304	Thorium	Th	90	232.0381
Hydrogen	H	1	1.0079	Thulium	Tm	69	168.9342
Indium	In	49	114.82	Tin	Sn	50	118.69
Iodine	I	53	126.9045	Titanium	Ti	22	47.9
Iridium	Ir	77	192.2	Tungsten	W	74	183.85
Iron	Fe	26	55.847	Unnilhexium	Unh	106	(263)
Krypton	Kr	36	83.80	Unnilpentium	Unp	105	(260)
Lanthanum	La	57	138.91	Unnilquadium	Unq	104	(257)
Lawrencium	Lr	103	(257)	Unnilseptium	Uns	107	(262)
Lead	Pb	82	207.2	Uranium	U	92	238.03
Lithium	Li	3	6.94	Vanadium	V	23	50.941
Lutetium	Lu	71	174.97	Xenon	Xe	54	131.30
Magnesium	Mg	12	24.305	Ytterbium	Yb	70	173.04
Manganese	Mn	25	54.9380	Yttrium	Y	39	88.9059
Mendelevium	Md	101	(256)	Zinc	Zn	30	65.38
Mercury	Hg	50	200.59	Zirconium	Zr	40	91.22
Molybdenum	Mo	42	95.94				

*Approx. values for radioactive elements given in parentheses.

612

PERIODIC TABLE OF THE ELEMENTS

Legend:
- Group
- Atomic number
- Symbol
- Atomic mass (approx. values in parentheses)

Example:
1A
1
H
1.00797

1A	2A	3B	4B	5B	6B	7B		8B		1B	2B	3A	4A	5A	6A	7A	8A
1 H 1.00797																	2 He 4.0026
3 Li 6.939	4 Be 9.0122											5 B 10.811	6 C 12.011	7 N 14.0067	8 O 15.9994	9 F 18.9984	10 Ne 20.183
11 Na 22.9898	12 Mg 24.312											13 Al 26.9815	14 Si 28.086	15 P 30.9738	16 S 32.064	17 Cl 35.453	18 Ar 39.948
19 K 39.102	20 Ca 40.08	21 Sc 44.956	22 Ti 47.90	23 V 50.942	24 Cr 51.996	25 Mn 54.938	26 Fe 55.847	27 Co 58.933	28 Ni 58.71	29 Cu 63.54	30 Zn 65.37	31 Ga 69.72	32 Ge 72.59	33 As 74.922	34 Se 78.96	35 Br 79.909	36 Kr 83.80
37 Rb 85.47	38 Sr 87.62	39 Y 88.905	40 Zr 91.22	41 Nb 92.906	42 Mo 95.94	43 Tc (98)	44 Ru 101.07	45 Rh 102.905	46 Pd 106.4	47 Ag 107.870	48 Cd 112.40	49 In 114.82	50 Sn 118.69	51 Sb 121.75	52 Te 127.60	53 I 126.904	54 Xe 131.30
55 Cs 132.905	56 Ba 137.34	57 La 138.91	72 Hf 178.49	73 Ta 180.948	74 W 183.85	75 Re 186.2	76 Os 190.2	77 Ir 192.2	78 Pt 195.09	79 Au 196.967	80 Hg 200.59	81 Tl 204.37	82 Pb 207.19	83 Bi 208.980	84 Po (210)	85 At (210)	86 Rn (222)
87 Fr (223)	88 Ra (226)	89 Ac (227)	104 Unq (257)	105 Unp (260)	106 Unh (263)	107 Uns (262)											

Lanthanide and Actinide series:

58 Ce 140.12	59 Pr 140.907	60 Nd 144.24	61 Pm (147)	62 Sm 150.35	63 Eu 151.96	64 Gd 157.25	65 Tb 158.924	66 Dy 162.50	67 Ho 164.930	68 Er 167.26	69 Tm 168.934	70 Yb 173.04	71 Lu 174.97
90 Th 232.038	91 Pa (231)	92 U 238.03	93 Np (237)	94 Pu (242)	95 Am (243)	96 Cm (247)	97 Bk (247)	98 Cf (249)	99 Es (254)	100 Fm (253)	101 Md (256)	102 No (254)	103 Lw (257)

613

GEOLOGIC TIME DIVISIONS

Era	Years Ago	Period		Epoch	Features and Events
Cenozoic	10,000	Quaternary		Recent	Modern humans
	2 million			Pleistocene	Widespread glacial ice (ice ages)
	10 million	Tertiary		Pliocene	Mountain uplift; cool climate; mammals increase in size and numbers
	25 million			Miocene	Widespread grasslands; grazing mammals; apes; whales
	40 million			Oligocene	Browsing mammals; sabertoothed tigers
	55 million			Eocene	Warm climate; modern birds and mammals; giant birds
	65 million			Paleocene	Mild to cool climate; age of mammals begins; primates
Mesozoic	140 million	Cretaceous			Last dinosaurs; modern insects; flowering plants
	190 million	Jurassic			Age of dinosaurs; first birds and mammals; flying reptiles
	230 million	Triassic			Active volcanoes; age of reptiles begins; first dinosaurs
Paleozoic	280 million	Permian			Conifer forests; extinction of many marine invertebrates
	310 million	Pennsylvanian	Carbon-iferous		Warm climate; swamps and coal forests; first reptiles
	345 million	Mississippian			Shallow seas, low lands; fern forests: age of amphibians begins
	405 million	Devonian			Age of fishes; first amphibians, insects, land animals
	425 million	Silurian			Shellfish abundant; first land plants, modern fungi
	500 million	Ordovician			Primitive fishes; seaweeds; fungi
	570 million	Cambrian			Age of marine invertebrates begins: shellfish, echinoderms, etc.
Precambrian	2.5 billion	Proterozoic			Bacteria; algae; primitive multicellular life
	5 billion	Archeozoic			Earth's crust solidifies; earliest life forms; blue-green algae; free oxygen

614

STATES OF THE UNITED STATES

State	Postal Abbr.	Capital	Population	Total Area Sq. Mi.	Total Area Sq. Km	State Flower	State Nickname
Alabama	AL	Montgomery	4,273,084	51,609	133,670	Camellia	Cotton State
Alaska	AK	Juneau	607,007	586,400	1,519,000	Forget-me-not	Last Frontier
Arizona	AZ	Phoenix	4,428,068	113,909	295,025	Saguaro Cactus Blossom	Grand Canyon State
Arkansas	AR	Little Rock	2,509,793	53,103	137,537	Apple Blossom	Land of Opportunity
California	CA	Sacramento	31,878,234	158,693	411,015	Golden Poppy	Golden State
Colorado	CO	Denver	3,294,394	104,247	270,000	Columbine	Centennial State
Connecticut	CT	Hartford	3,274,238	5009	12,975	Mountain Laurel	Constitution State
Delaware	DE	Dover	724,842	2057	5330	Peach Blossom	First State
Florida	FL	Tallahassee	14,399,985	58,560	151,670	Orange Blossom	Sunshine State
Georgia	GA	Atlanta	7,353,225	58,876	152,489	Cherokee Rose	Empire State of the South
Hawaii	HI	Honolulu	1,183,723	6424	16,638	Hibiscus	Aloha State
Idaho	ID	Boise	1,189,251	83,557	216,415	Mock Orange	Gem State
Illinois	IL	Springfield	11,846,544	56,401	146,075	Native Violet	Land of Lincoln
Indiana	IN	Indianapolis	5,840,528	36,291	93,995	Peony	Hoosier State
Iowa	IA	Des Moines	2,851,792	56,290	145,790	Wild Rose	Hawkeye State
Kansas	KS	Topeka	2,572,150	82,276	213,094	Sunflower	Sunflower State
Kentucky	KY	Frankfort	3,888,723	40,395	104,625	Goldenrod	Bluegrass State
Louisiana	LA	Baton Rouge	4,350,579	48,522	125,672	Magnolia	Pelican State
Maine	ME	Augusta	1,243,316	33,215	86,027	Pine Cone and Tassel	Pine Tree State
Maryland	MD	Annapolis	5,071,604	10,577	27,395	Black-eyed Susan	Old Line State
Massachusetts	MA	Boston	6,092,352	8257	21,385	Trailing Arbutus	Bay State
Michigan	MI	Lansing	9,594,350	58,216	150,780	Apple Blossom	Wolverine State
Minnesota	MN	St. Paul	4,657,758	84,068	217,735	Lady's-slipper	Gopher State
Mississippi	MS	Jackson	2,716,115	47,716	123,585	Magnolia	Magnolia State
Missouri	MO	Jefferson City	5,358,692	69,674	180,455	Hawthorn	Show Me State
Montana	MT	Helena	879,372	147,138	381,085	Bitterroot	Treasure State
Nebraska	NE	Lincoln	1,652,093	77,237	200,044	Goldenrod	Cornhusker State
Nevada	NV	Carson City	1,603,163	110,540	286,300	Sagebrush	Silver State
New Hampshire	NH	Concord	1,162,481	9304	24,100	Purple Lilac	Granite State
New Jersey	NJ	Trenton	7,987,933	7836	20,295	Purple Violet	Garden State
New Mexico	NM	Santa Fe	1,713,407	121,666	315,115	Yucca	Land of Enchantment
New York	NY	Albany	18,184,774	49,576	128,400	Rose	Empire State
North Carolina	NC	Raleigh	7,322,870	52,586	136,198	Dogwood	Tarheel State
North Dakota	ND	Bismarck	643,539	70,665	183,020	Prairie Rose	Flickertail State
Ohio	OH	Columbus	11,172,782	41,222	106,765	Scarlet Carnation	Buckeye State
Oklahoma	OK	Oklahoma City	3,300,902	69,919	181,090	Mistletoe	Sooner State
Oregon	OR	Salem	3,203,735	96,981	251,180	Oregon Grape	Beaver State
Pennsylvania	PA	Harrisburg	12,056,112	45,333	117,410	Mountain Laurel	Keystone State
Rhode Island	RI	Providence	990,225	1214	3145	Violet	Ocean State
South Carolina	SC	Columbia	3,698,746	31,055	80,430	Carolina Jessamine	Palmetto State
South Dakota	SD	Pierre	732,405	77,047	199,550	American Pasqueflower	Sunshine State
Tennessee	TN	Nashville	5,319,654	42,246	109,415	Iris	Volunteer State
Texas	TX	Austin	19,128,261	267,339	692,410	Bluebonnet	Lone Star State
Utah	UT	Salt Lake City	2,000,494	84,916	219,930	Sego Lily	Beehive State
Vermont	VT	Montpelier	588,654	9609	24,885	Red Clover	Green Mountain State
Virginia	VA	Richmond	6,675,451	40,815	105,710	American Dogwood	Old Dominion State
Washington	WA	Olympia	5,532,939	68,192	176,615	Rhododendron	Evergreen State
West Virginia	WV	Charleston	1,825,754	24,181	62,629	Rosebay Rhododendron	Mountain State
Wisconsin	WI	Madison	5,159,795	56,154	145,440	Wood Violet	Badger State
Wyoming	WY	Cheyenne	481,400	97,914	253,595	Indian Paintbrush	Equality State
FEDERAL DISTRICT Dist. of Columbia	DC	Washington	543,213	69	179	American Beauty Rose	

PRESIDENTS AND VICE PRESIDENTS OF THE UNITED STATES

President	Born	Died	Birthplace	Residence	Religious Affiliation	Party	Dates in Office	Vice President	Dates in Office
1. GEORGE WASHINGTON	Feb. 22, 1732	Dec. 14, 1799	Westmoreland Co., Va.	Va.	Episcopalian	Fed.	1789-1797	JOHN ADAMS	1789-1797
2. JOHN ADAMS	Oct. 30, 1735	July 4, 1826	Quincy, Mass	Mass.	Unitarian	Fed.	1797-1801	THOMAS JEFFERSON	1797-1801
3. THOMAS JEFFERSON	Apr. 13, 1743	July 4, 1826	Shadwell, Va.	Va.	Deist	Rep.*	1801-1809	AARON BURR	1801-1805
								GEORGE CLINTON	1805-1809
4. JAMES MADISON	Mar. 16, 1751	June 28, 1836	Port Conway, Va.	Va.	Episcopalian	Rep.*	1809-1817	GEORGE CLINTON**	1809-1812
								ELBRIDGE GERRY	1813-1814
5. JAMES MONROE	Apr. 28, 1758	July 4, 1831	Westmoreland Co., Va.	Va.	Episcopalian	Rep.*	1817-1825	DANIEL D. TOMPKINS	1817-1825
6. JOHN QUINCY ADAMS	July 11, 1767	Feb. 23, 1848	Quincy, Mass.		Unitarian	Rep.*	1825-1829	JOHN C. CALHOUN	1825-1829
7. ANDREW JACKSON	Mar. 15, 1767	June 8, 1845	New Lancaster Co., S.C.	Tenn.	Presbyterian	Dem.	1829-1837	JOHN C. CALHOUN	1829-1832
								MARTIN VAN BUREN (4*)	1833-1837
8. MARTIN VAN BUREN	Dec. 5, 1782	July 24, 1862	Kinderhook, N.Y.	N.Y.	Reformed Church	Dem.	1837-1841	RICHARD M. JOHNSON	1837-1841
9. WILLIAM HENRY HARRISON**	Feb. 9, 1773	Apr. 4, 1841	Berkeley, Va.	Ohio	Episcopalian	Whig	1841	JOHN TYLER (4*)	1841
10. JOHN TYLER	Mar. 29, 1790	Jan. 18, 1862	Greenway, Va.	Va.	Episcopalian	Whig	1841-1845		
11. JAMES KNOX POLK	Nov. 2, 1795	June 15, 1849	Mecklenburg Co., N.C.	Tenn.	Methodist	Dem.	1845-1849	GEORGE M. DALLAS	1845-1849
12. ZACHARY TAYLOR**	Nov. 24, 1784	July 9, 1850	Orange Co., Va.	La.	Episcopalian	Whig	1849-1850	MILLARD FILLMORE (4*)	1849-1850
13. MILLARD FILLMORE	Jan. 7, 1800	Mar. 8, 1874	Cayuga Co., N.Y.	N.Y.	Unitarian	Whig	1850-1853		
14. FRANKLIN PIERCE	Nov. 23, 1804	Oct. 8, 1869	Hillsboro, N.H.	N.H.	Episcopalian	Dem.	1853-1857	WILLIAM R. KING**	1853
15. JAMES BUCHANAN	Apr. 23, 1791	June 1, 1868	Mercersburg, Pa.	Pa.	Presbyterian	Dem.	1857-1861	JOHN C. BRECKINRIDGE	1857-1861
16. ABRAHAM LINCOLN**	Feb. 12, 1809	Apr. 15 1865	Hardin Co., Ky.	Ill.	Nonaffiliated	Rep.***	1861-1865	HANNIBAL HAMLIN	1861-1865
								ANDREW JOHNSON (4*)	1865
17. ANDREW JOHNSON	Dec. 29, 1808	July 31, 1875	Raleigh, N.C.	Tenn.	Nonaffiliated	Dem.***	1865-1869		
18. ULYSSES SIMPSON GRANT	Apr. 27, 1822	July 23, 1885	Point Pleasant, Ohio	Ill.	Methodist	Rep.	1869-1877	SCHUYLER COLFAX	1869-1873
								HENRY WILSON**	1873-1875
19. RUTHERFORD BIRCHARD HAYES	Oct. 4, 1822	Jan. 17, 1893	Delaware, Ohio	Ohio	Methodist	Rep.	1877-1881	WILLIAM A. WHEELER	1877-1881
20. JAMES ABRAM GARFIELD**	Nov. 19, 1831	Sept. 19, 1881	Orange, Ohio	Ohio	Disciples of Christ	Rep.	1881	CHESTER A. ARTHUR (4*)	1881
21. CHESTER ALAN ARTHUR	Oct. 5, 1830	Nov. 18, 1886	Fairfield, Vt.	N.Y.	Episcopalian	Rep.	1881-1885		
22. GROVER CLEVELAND	Mar. 18, 1837	June 24, 1908	Caldwell, N.J.	N.Y.	Presbyterian	Dem.	1885-1889	THOMAS A. HENDRICKS**	1885
23. BENJAMIN HARRISON	Aug. 20, 1833	Mar. 13, 1901	North Bend, Ohio	Ind.	Presbyterian	Rep.	1889-1893	LEVI P. MORTON	1889-1893
24. GROVER CLEVELAND	See number 22						1893-1897	ADLAI E. STEVENSON	1893-1897
25. WILLIAM McKINLEY**	Jan. 29, 1843	Sept. 14, 1901	Niles, Ohio	Ohio	Methodist	Rep.	1897-1901	GARRET A. HOBART**	1897-1899
								THEODORE ROOSEVELT (4*)	1901
26. THEODORE ROOSEVELT	Oct. 27, 1858	Jan. 6, 1919	New York, N.Y.	N.Y.	Reformed Dutch	Rep.	1901-1909	CHARLES W. FAIRBANKS	1905-1909
27. WILLIAM HOWARD TAFT	Sept. 15, 1857	Mar. 8, 1930	Cincinnati, Ohio	Ohio	Unitarian	Rep.	1909-1913	JAMES S. SHERMAN	1909-1912
28. WOODROW WILSON	Dec. 28, 1856	Feb. 3, 1924	Staunton, Va.	N.J.	Presbyterian	Dem.	1913-1921	THOMAS R.	

616

PRESIDENTS AND VICE PRESIDENTS OF THE UNITED STATES, *continued*

29. WARREN GAMALIEL HARDING**	Nov. 2, 1865	Aug. 2, 1923	Bloomington Grove, Ohio	Ohio	Baptist	Rep.	1921-1923 CALVIN COOLIDGE (4*)	1921-1923
30. CALVIN COOLIDGE	July 4, 1872	Jan. 5, 1933	Plymouth, Vt.	Mass.	Congregational	Rep.	1923-1929 CHARLES G. DAWES	1923-1929
31. HERBERT CLARK HOOVER	Aug. 10, 1874	Oct. 20, 1964	West Branch, Iowa	Calif.	Society of Friends	Rep.	1929-1933 CHARLES CURTIS	1929-1933
32. FRANKLIN DELANO ROOSEVELT**	Jan. 30, 1882	Apr. 12, 1945	Hyde Park, N.Y.	N.Y.	Episcopalian	Dem.	1933-1945 JOHN NANCE GARNER	1933-1941
							HENRY AGARD WALLACE	1941-1945
							HARRY S TRUMAN (4*)	1945
33. HARRY S TRUMAN	May 8, 1884	Dec. 26, 1972	Lamar, Mo.	Mo.	Baptist	Dem.	1945-1953 ALBEN W. BARKLEY	1949-1953
34. DWIGHT DAVID EISENHOWER	Oct. 14, 1890	Mar. 28, 1969	Denison, Tex.	N.Y.	Presbyterian	Rep.	1953-1961 RICHARD M. NIXON	1953-1961
35. JOHN FITZGERALD KENNEDY**	May 29, 1917	Nov. 22, 1963	Brookline, Mass.	Mass.	Roman Catholic	Dem.	1961-1963 LYNDON B. JOHNSON (4*)	1961-1963
36. LYDON BAINES JOHNSON	Aug. 27, 1908	Jan. 22, 1973	Johnson City, Tex.	Tex.	Disciples of Christ	Dem.	1963-1969 HUBERT H. HUMPHREY	1965-1969
37. RICHARD MILHOUS NIXON (5*)	Jan. 9, 1913	Apr. 22, 1994	Yorba Linda, Calif.	Calif.	Society of Friends	Rep.	1969-1974 SPIRO T. AGNEW	1969-1973
38. GERALD RUDOLPH FORD	July 14, 1913		Omaha, Nebr.	Mich.	Episcopalian	Rep.	1974-1977 NELSON A. ROCKEFELLER	1973-1974
								1974-1977
39. JAMES EARL CARTER, JR.	Oct. 1, 1924		Plains, Ga.	Ga.	Southern Baptist	Dem.	1977-1981 WALTER F. MONDALE	1977-1981
40. RONALD WILSON REAGAN	Feb. 6, 1911		Tampico, Ill.	Calif.	Disciples of Christ	Rep.	1981-1989 GEORGE H.W. BUSH	1981-1989
41. GEORGE HERBERT WALKER BUSH	June 12, 1924		Milton, Mass.	Tex.	Episcopalian	Rep.	1989-1993 JAMES DANFORTH QUAYLE	1989-1993
42. WILLIAM JEFFERSON CLINTON	Aug. 19, 1946		Hope, Ark.	Ark.	Baptist	Dem.	1993-2000 ALBERT A. GORE, JR.	1993-2000
43. GEORGE WALKER BUSH	July 6, 1946		New Haven, Conn.	Tex.	Methodist	Rep.	2001- RICHARD CHENEY	2001-

*Now the Democratic Party   **Died in office   ***Elected on the Union party ticket   (4*)Succeeded to Presidency   (5*)Resigned

BOOKS OF THE BIBLE

Old Testament

Genesis	Joshua	I Kings	Nehemiah	Ecclesiastes	Ezekiel	Obadiah	Zephaniah
Exodus	Judges	II Kings	Esther	Song of Solomon	Daniel	Jonah	Haggai
Leviticus	Ruth	I Chronicles	Job	Isaiah	Hosea	Micah	Zechariah
Numbers	I Samuel	II Chronicles	Psalms	Jeremiah	Joel	Nahum	Malachi
Deuteronomy	II Samuel	Ezra	Proverbs	Lamentations	Amos	Habakkuk	

Apocrypha

I Esdras	Tobit	(additional parts	Wisdom of	Ecclesiasticus	(additional parts	Prayer of	I Maccabees
II Esdras	Judith	of Esther)	Solomon	Baruch	of Daniel)	Manasseh	II Maccabees

New Testament

Matthew	The Acts	Galatians	I Thessalonians	II Timothy	Hebrews	II Peter	III John
Mark	Romans	Ephesians	II Thessalonians	Titus	James	I John	Jude
Luke	I Corinthians	Philippians	I Timothy	Philemon	I Peter	II John	Revelation
John	II Corinthians	Colossians					

NINE ORDERS OF ANGELS IN THREE HIERARCHIES
(in descending rank of importance)

First hierarchy:
Seraphim (highest angels of love, light, and fire)
Cherubim (angels who pray or intercede)
Thrones (angels who are in charge of justice)

Second hierarchy:
Dominations/Dominions (regulate angel duties)
Principalities (protect religion)
Powers (impose order on heavenly pathways)

Third hierarchy:
Virtues (work miracles on earth)
Archangels (minister and make propitiation for people's sins)
Angels (guard men and nations; act as messengers between God and man)

THE SERMON ON THE MOUNT

5:1–2	The setting
5:3–12	The Beatitudes
5:13–16	The new community
5:17–20	The abiding validity of the law
5:21–48	On practicing righteousness toward others in matters of:
	Murder (5:21–26)
	Adultery (5:27–30)
	Divorce (5:31–32)
	Oaths (5:33–37)
	Retribution (5:38–42)
	Love of enemy (5:43–48)
6:1–7:12	On practicing righteousness toward God:
	Almsgiving (6:1–4)
	Prayer (6:5–15)
	Fasting (6:16–18)
	On not laying up false treasure (6:19–24)
	On not being anxious (6:25–34)
	On not judging (7:1–5)
	On not squandering what is precious (7:6)
	On resting assured that God hears prayer (7:7–12)
7:13–27	Concluding warnings and exhortations

THE TEN COMMANDMENTS

1. I am the Lord thy God, who brought thee out of the land of Egypt, out of the house of bondage. Thou shalt have no other gods before me.
2. Thou shalt not make unto thee any graven image, or any likeness of any thing that is in heaven above, or that is in the earth beneath, or that is in the water under the earth, thou shalt not bow down unto them, nor serve them; for I the Lord thy God am a jealous God, visiting the iniquity of the fathers upon the children unto the third and fourth generation of them that hate Me; and showing mercy unto the thousandth generation of them that love Me and keep my commandments.
3. Thou shalt not take the name of the Lord thy God in vain; for the Lord will not hold him guiltless that taketh His name in vain.
4. Remember the Sabbath day, to keep it holy. Six days shalt thou labor, and do all thy work; but the seventh day is a sabbath unto the Lord thy God, in it thou shall not do any manner of work, thou, nor thy son, nor thy daughter, nor thy man-servant, nor thy maid-servant, nor thy cattle, nor thy stranger that is within thy gates; for in six days the Lord made heaven and earth, the sea, and all that in them is, and rested on the seventh day; wherefore the Lord blessed the Sabbath day, and hallowed it.
5. Honor thy father and thy mother, that thy days may be long upon the land which the Lord thy God giveth thee.
6. Thou shalt not murder.
7. Thou shalt not commit adultery.
8. Thou shalt not steal.
9. Thou shalt not bear false witness against thy neighbor.
10. Thou shalt not covet thy neighbor's house, thou shalt not covet thy neighbor's wife, nor his man-servant, nor his maid-servant, nor his ox, nor his ass, nor any thing that is thy neighbor's.

DECLARATION OF INDEPENDENCE (1776)

When in the course of human events, it becomes necessary for one people to dissolve the political bands which have connected them with another, and to assume among the Powers of the earth, the separate and equal station to which the Laws of Nature and of Nature's God entitle them, a decent respect to the opinions of mankind requires that they should declare the causes which impel them to the separation.

We hold these truths to be self-evident, that all men are created equal, that they are endowed by their Creator with certain unalienable Rights, that among these are Life, Liberty and the pursuit of Happiness. That to secure these rights, Governments are instituted among Men, deriving their just powers from the consent of the governed. That whenever any Form of Government becomes destructive of these ends, it is the Right of the People to alter or to abolish it, and to institute new Government, laying its foundation on such principles and organizing its powers in such form, as to them shall seem most likely to effect their Safety and Happiness. Prudence, indeed, will dictate that Governments long established should not be changed for light and transient causes; and accordingly all experience hath shown, that mankind are more disposed to suffer, while evils are sufferable, than to right themselves by abolishing the forms to which they are accustomed. But when a long train of abuses and usurpations, pursuing invariably the same Object evinces a design to reduce them under absolute Despotism, it is their right, it is their duty, to throw off such Government, and to provide new Guards for their future security.—Such has been the patient sufferance of these Colonies; and such is now the necessity which constrains them to alter their former Systems of Government. The history of the present King of Great Britain is a history of repeated injuries and usurpations, all having in direct object the establishment of an absolute Tyranny over these States. To prove this, let Facts be submitted to a candid world.

He has refused his Assent to Laws, the most wholesome and necessary for the public good.

He has forbidden his Governors to pass Laws of immediate and pressing importance, unless suspended in their operation till his Assent should be obtained; and when so suspended, he has utterly neglected to attend to them.

He has refused to pass other Laws for the accommodation of large districts of people, unless those people would relinquish the right of Representation in the Legislature, a right inestimable to them and formidable to tyrants only.

He has called together legislative bodies at places unusual, uncomfortable, and distant from the depository of their Public Records, for the sole purpose of fatiguing them into compliance with his measures.

He has dissolved Representative Houses repeatedly, for opposing with manly firmness his invasions on the rights of the people.

He has refused for a long time, after such dissolutions, to cause others to be elected; whereby the Legislative Powers, incapable of Annihilation, have returned to the People at large for their exercise; the State remaining in the meantime exposed to all the dangers of invasion from without, and convulsions within.

He has endeavoured to prevent the population of these States; for that purpose obstructing the Laws of Naturalization of Foreigners; refusing to pass others to encourage their migration hither, and raising the conditions of new Appropriations of Lands.

He has obstructed the Administration of Justice, by refusing his Assent to Laws for establishing Judiciary Powers.

He has made Judges dependent on his Will alone, for the tenure of their offices, and the amount and payment of their salaries.

He has erected a multitude of New Offices, and sent hither swarms of Officers to harass our People, and eat out their substance.

He has kept among us, in times of peace, Standing Armies without the Consent of our legislature.

He has affected to render the Military independent of and superior to the Civil Power.

He has combined with others to subject us to a jurisdiction foreign to our constitution, and unacknowledged by our laws; giving his Assent to their acts of pretended legislation:

For quartering large bodies of armed troops among us:

For protecting them, by a mock Trial, from Punishment for any Murders which they should commit on the Inhabitants of these States:

For cutting off our Trade with all parts of the world:

For imposing taxes on us without our Consent:

For depriving us in many cases, of the benefits of Trial by Jury:

For transporting us beyond Seas to be tried for pretended offences:

For abolishing the free System of English Laws in a neighbouring Province, establishing therein an Arbitrary government, and enlarging its Boundaries so as to render it at once an example and fit instrument for introducing the same absolute rule into these Colonies:

For taking away our Charters, abolishing our most valuable Laws, and altering fundamentally the Forms of our Governments:

For suspending our own Legislature, and declaring themselves invested with

Power to legislate for us in all cases whatsoever.

He has abdicated Government here, by declaring us out of his Protection and waging War against us.

He has plundered our seas, ravaged our Coasts, burnt our towns, and destroyed the lives of our people.

He is at this time transporting large armies of foreign mercenaries to complete the works of death, desolation and tyranny, already begun with circumstances of Cruelty & perfidy scarcely paralleled in the most barbarous ages, and totally unworthy the Head of a civilized nation.

He has constrained our fellow Citizens taken Captive on the high Seas to bear Arms against their Country, to become the executioners of their friends and Brethren, or to fall themselves by their Hands.

He has excited domestic insurrections amongst us, and has endeavoured to bring on the inhabitants of our frontiers, the merciless Indian Savages, whose known rule of warfare, is an undistinguished destruction of all ages, sexes and conditions.

In every stage of these Oppressions We have Petitioned for Redress in the most humble terms: Our repeated Petitions have been answered only by repeated injury. A Prince, whose character is thus marked by every act which may define a Tyrant, is unfit to be the ruler of a free People.

Nor have We been wanting in attention to our British brethren. We have warned them from time to time of attempts by their legislature to extend an unwarrantable jurisdiction over us. We have reminded them of the circumstances of our emigration and settlement here. We have appealed to their native justice and magnanimity, and we have conjured them by the ties of our common kindred to disavow these usurpations, which, would inevitably interrupt our connections and correspondence. They too have been deaf to the voice of justice and of consaguinity. We must, therefore, acquiesce in the necessity, which denounces our Separation, and hold them, as we hold the rest of mankind, Enemies in War, in Peace Friends.

We, therefore, the Representatives of the United States of America, in General Congress, Assembled, appealing to the Supreme Judge of the world for the rectitude of our intentions, do, in the Name, and by Authority of the good People of these Colonies, solemnly publish and declare, That these United Colonies are and of right ought to be Free and Independent States; that they are Absolved from all Allegiance to the British Crown, and that all political connection between them and the State of Great Britain, is and ought to be totally dissolved; and that as Free and Independent States, they have full Power to levy War, conclude Peace, contract Alliances, establish Commerce, and to do all other Acts and Things which Independent States may of right do. And for the support of the Declaration, with a firm reliance on the Protection of Divine Providence, we mutually pledge to each other our Lives, our Fortunes and our sacred Honor.

John Hancock

New Hampshire
Josiah Bartlett
Wm. Whipple
Matthew Thornton

Massachusetts-Bay
Saml. Adams
John Adams
Robt. Treat Paine
Elbridge Gerry

Rhode Island
Step. Hopkins
William Ellery

Connecticut
Roger Sherman
Sam'el Huntington
Wm. Williams
Oliver Wolcott

New York
Wm. Floyd
Phil. Livingston
Frans. Lewis
Lewis Morris

Pennsylvania
Rbt. Morris
Benjamin Rush
Benja. Franklin
John Morton
Geo. Clymer
Jas. Smith
Geo. Taylor
James Wilson
Geo. Ross

Delaware
Caesar Rodney
Geo. Read
Tho. M'Kean

North Carolina
Wm. Hooper
Joseph Hewes
John Penn

South Carolina
Edward Rutledge
Thos. Heyward, Junr.
Thomas Lynch, Junr.
Arthur Middleton

New Jersey
Richd. Stockton
Jno. Witherspoon
Fras. Hopkinson
John Hart
Abra. Clark

Georgia
Button Gwinnett
Lyman Hall
Geo. Walton

Maryland
Samuel Chase
Wm. Paca
Thos. Stone
Charles Carroll of
*   Carrollton*

Virginia
George Wythe
Richard Henry Lee
Th. Jefferson
Benja. Harrison
Ths. Nelson, Jr.
Francis Lightfoot Lee
Carter Braxton

AMENDMENTS TO THE CONSTITUTION

The Constitution of the United States of America was written over the summer of 1787, and took effect in 1788 upon ratification by nine of the original thirteen states. The Constitution in its original form established the structure of the national government and enumerated the powers of each of its branches, but said little about the rights of the people. When Americans speak of "constitutional rights," therefore, they are almost invariably referring not to the original text of the Constitution, but to one or another of its amendments.

By one estimate, ten thousand proposed amendments have been introduced in Congress in a little over two centuries; just twenty-seven have been adopted, and they are summarized here. The year that each amendment became part of the Constitution is given in parentheses.

The first ten amendments were adopted almost immediately to address the widespread concern about the Constitution's general lack of explicit protections for individual rights; these are known as the Bill of Rights. Although these amendments were originally intended only as limitations on the power of the federal government, and for most of the nation's history provided no protection against state laws that violated individual rights, most of the provisions of the Bill of Rights have now been made applicable to state governments by virtue of the incorporation doctrine.

The Thirteenth, Fourteenth, and Fifteenth Amendments represent the nation's effort to embody in its fundamental law the principles of equality and human dignity that emerged from the Civil War, and are often referred to as the Civil War amendments.

Amendments to the U.S. Constitution

Amendment I (1791)

Congress shall make no law respecting an establishment of religion, or prohibiting the free exercise thereof; or abridging the freedom of speech, or of the press, or the right of the people to peaceably assemble, and to petition the government for a redress of grievances.

Guarantees freedom of religion, freedom of speech, freedom of the press, freedom of assembly, and the right of petition.

Amendment II (1791)

A well regulated Militia, being necessary to the security of a free State, the right of the people to keep and bear Arms, shall not be infringed.

Concerns the right to bear arms as an aspect of the maintenance of a well regulated militia; interpreted by some as guaranteeing an individual's right to bear arms as well.

Amendment III (1791)

No Soldier shall, in time of peace be quartered in any house, without the consent of the Owner, nor in time of war, but in a manner to be prescribed by law.

Prohibits the housing of soldiers in private homes without the consent of the owner, except in time of war.

Amendment IV (1791)

The right of the people to be secure in their persons, houses, papers, and effects, against unreasonable searches and seizures, shall not be violated, and no Warrants shall issue, but upon probable cause, supported by Oath or affirmation, and particularly describing the place to be searched, and the persons or things to be seized.

Prohibits unreasonable search and seizure and requires a showing of probable cause for the is-suance of any search warrant or arrest warrant.

Amendment V (1791)

No Person shall be held to answer for a capital, or otherwise infamous crime, unless on a presentment or indictment of a Grand Jury, except in cases arising in the land or naval forces, or in the Militia, when in actual service in time of war or public danger; nor shall any person be subject for the same offense to be twice put in jeopardy of life and limb, nor shall be compelled in any criminal case to be a witness against himself, nor be deprived of life, liberty, or property, without due process of law; nor shall private property be taken for public use without just compensation.

Requires indictment by a grand jury before any person can be put on trial for a serious federal crime; bans double jeopardy and compulsory self-incrimination; prohibits the federal government from depriving any person of life, liberty, or property without due process of law; and prohibits the taking of private property for public use without just compensation.

Amendment VI (1791)

In all criminal prosecutions, the accused shall enjoy the right to a speedy and public trial, by an impartial jury of the State and district wherein the crime shall have been committed; which district shall have been previously ascertained by law, and to be informed of the nature and cause of the accusation; to be confronted with the witnesses against him; to have compulsory process for obtaining witnesses in his favor, and to have the assistance of counsel for his defense.

Guarantees criminal defendants the right to a speedy and public trial by jury; also guarantees them the right to be informed of the charges, the right of confrontation of adverse witnesses, the right to use process to compel the attendance of witnesses for the defense, and the right to counsel.

Amendment VII (1791)

In Suits at common law, where the value in controversy shall exceed twenty dollars, the right of trial by jury shall be preserved, and no fact tried by a jury shall be otherwise reexamined in any Court of the United States, than according to the rules of common law.

Preserves for litigants in civil damage actions in the federal courts the common law right of jury trial.

Amendment VIII (1791)

Excessive bail shall not be required, nor excessive fines imposed, nor cruel and unusual punishments inflicted.

Prohibits criminal courts from requiring excessive bail or imposing cruel and unusual punishment.

Amendment IX (1791)

The enumeration in the Constitution of certain rights shall not be construed to deny or disparage others retained by people.

States that the listing of specific rights in the Constitution is not to be interpreted as suggesting that other rights do not exist or are not equally deserving of protection.

Amendment X (1791)

The powers not delegated to the United States by the Constitution, nor prohibited by it to the States, are reserved to the States respectively, or to the people.

Emphasizes that the federal government has only those powers delegated to it by the Constitution.

Summary of Amendments to the Constitution

Amendment XI (1798)

Requires federal courts to respect the sovereign immunity of state governments.

Amendment XII (1804)

Revised the electoral college system to reduce the potential for deadlocks in elections for President and Vice President.

Amendment XIII (1865)

Abolished slavery and involuntary servitude, except for forced labor as punishment for a crime.

Amendment XIV (1868)

Extended American citizenship to people of color by declaring that all persons born or naturalized in the United States and subject to United States jurisdiction are citizens of the United States and of the state where they reside. This amendment also prohibits the states from depriving any person of life, liberty, or property without due process of law, and guarantees all persons equal protection of the laws.

Amendment XV (1870)

Extended the vote to people of color by prohibiting the denial or abridgment of the right of citizens to vote on account of race, color, or previous condition of servitude.

Amendment XVI (1913)

Empowered Congress to institute the federal income tax.

Amendment XVII (1913)

Changed the method of electing United States senators from election by state legislatures to direct election by the people.

Amendment XVIII (1919)

The Prohibition Amendment: prohibited the manufacture, sale, or importation of alcoholic beverages in the United States. Repealed in 1933.

Amendment XIX (1920)

The Woman Suffrage Amendment: extended the vote to women in all states by prohibiting the denial or abridgment of the right to vote on account of sex.

Amendment XX (1933)

Revised the starting dates for terms of office of the President, Vice President, and members of Congress, and made provision for various contingencies in presidential succession such as the death of a President-elect before taking office.

Amendment XXI (1933)
Repealed the Prohibition Amendment and gave the individual states the power to regulate the distribution and use of intoxicating liquors within their borders.

Amendment XXII (1951)
Prohibits any individual from being elected President more than twice, or more than once if the individual has already acted as President for more than two years of a term to which someone else was elected.

Amendment XXIII (1961)
Extended the right to vote in presidential elections to residents of the District of Columbia. The nation's capital still has no voting representation in Congress, even though more Americans live in the District of Columbia than in some states, and even though Congress makes most of the District's laws. A proposed constitutional amendment to allow citizens in the District of Columbia representation and voting rights on an equal footing with citizens of the 50 states was adopted by Congress in 1978 but failed of ratification.

Amendment XXIV (1964)
Abolished the poll tax as a requirement for voting in primary and general elections for national office.

Amendment XXV (1967)
Provides a mechanism for filling vacancies in the office of Vice President, provides that the Vice President will serve as Acting President during periods of presidential disability, and provides procedures for determining whether such a disability exists.

Amendment XXVI (1971)
Lowered the voting age to eighteen.

Amendment XXVII (1992)
Provides that no change voted by Congress in its own compensation may take effect until after the next biennial congressional election.

GETTYSBURG ADDRESS (1863)

Four score and seven years ago our fathers brought forth on this continent a new nation, conceived in liberty and dedicated to the proposition that all men are created equal.

Now we are engaged in a great civil war, testing whether that nation or any nation so conceived and so dedicated can long endure. We are met on a great battlefield of that war. We have come to dedicate a portion of that field as a final resting place for those who here gave their lives that that nation might live. It is altogether fitting and proper that we should do this.

But, in a larger sense, we cannot dedicate—we cannot consecrate—we cannot hallow—this ground. The brave men, living and dead, who struggled here have consecrated it far above our poor power to add or detract. The world will little note nor long remember what we say here, but it can never forget what they did here. It is for us, the living, rather, to be dedicated here to the unfinished work which they who fought here have thus far so nobly advanced.

It is rather for us to be here dedicated to the great task remaining before us—that from these honored dead we take increased devotion to that cause for which they gave the last full measure of devotion; that we here highly resolve that these dead shall not have died in vain; that this nation, under God, shall have a new birth of freedom; and that government of the people, by the people, for the people shall not perish from the earth.

HISTORIC SITES OF THE MIDDLE EAST

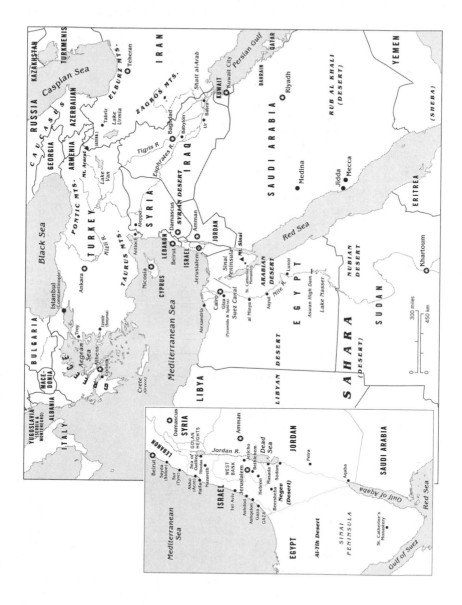

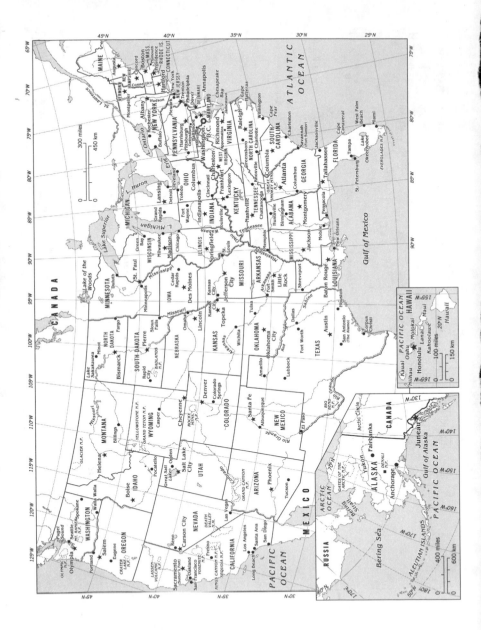